Sixth Edition
Antique Trader
ANTIQUES & COLLECTIBLES
PRICE GUIDE

SIXTH ANNUAL EDITION

The Antique Trader
ANTIQUES & COLLECTIBLES
PRICE GUIDE

Edited by

Kyle Husfloen

A comprehensive price guide to the entire field of antiques and collectibles for the 1990 market.

Illustrated

The Babka Publishing Co.
P.O. Box 1050
Dubuque, Iowa 52001

STAFF

Assistant Editor	Marilyn Dragowick
Assistants	Connie Wagner
	Diane Neumeister
	Carolyn Clark
	Mary Crapp
Subscription Manager	Bonnie Rojemann
Business Manager	Ted Jones
Publisher	Edward A. Babka

ISBN: 0-930625-05-6

Library of Congress Catalog Card No. 85-648650

Additional copies of this book may be ordered from:

THE BABKA PUBLISHING CO.
P.O. Box 1050
Dubuque, Iowa 52001

$12.95 plus $1.00 postage and handling.

A WORD TO THE READER

The Antique Trader has been publishing a Price Guide for nineteen years. *The Antique Trader Price Guide to Antiques and Collectors' Items* has been available by subscription and on newsstands across the country, first as a semi-annual and then as a quarterly publication, and since 1984 it has been published on a bi-monthly basis.

In 1985, in response to numerous requests to combine the material of the bi-monthly issues and provide a large, complete price guide, the first edition of *The Antique Trader Antiques & Collectibles Price Guide* was issued. The book you now hold in your hands is the 1990 guide, our Sixth Annual Edition.

This book is the most current price listing available. We think it is also the most reliable book for dealers and collectors to turn to for realistic values of antiques and collectibles. Prices listed in this guide have not been unrealistically set at the whim of an editor who has no material at hand to substantiate the listed values. The Antique Trader Price Guide staff has always used a very methodical compilation system that is supported by experts from across the country as we select listings for the various categories. Prices are derived from antiques shops, advertisements, auctions, and antiques shows, and on-going records are maintained. Items are fully described and listings are carefully examined by experts who discard unreasonable exceptions to bring you the most reliable, well-illustrated and authoritative Price Guide available.

Our format enables us to maintain a wide range of both antique and collectible items in a running tabulation to which we are continually adding information and prices. Items are diligently researched and clearly described. As new areas of collecting interest develop, new categories are added and if a definite market is established, this material becomes a part of the Price Guide. New categories included in this edition are: Fishing Collectibles, Movie Memorabilia, Wartime Memorabilia and Wiener Werkstatte. Several categories were added to our Ceramics section including Franciscan Ware, Mulberry Wares, Schafer & Vater and Vernon Kilns. In the Glass section we have added listings for New Martinsville and Pillar-Molded glasswares.

Six popular areas of collecting are highlighted in well-illustrated "Special Focus" features which provide background material and tips on collecting. Our 1990 edition includes focuses on Calendar Plates, Carnival Glass, Inkstands & Inkwells, Steiff Animals, Steuben Glass and Wine Glasses.

This book should be used only as a *guide* to prices and is not intended to set prices. Prices do vary from one section of the country to another and auction prices, which are incorporated into this guide, often have an even wider variation. Though prices have been double-checked and every effort has been made to assure accuracy, neither the compilers, editor nor publisher can assume responsibility for any losses that might be incurred as a result of consulting this guide, or of errors, typographical or otherwise.

This guide follows an alphabetical format. All categories are listed in alphabetical order. Under the category of Ceramics, you will find all types of pottery, porcelain, earthenware, parian and stoneware listed in alphabetical order. All types of glass, including Art, Carnival, Custard, Depression, Pattern and so on, will be found listed alphabetically under the category of Glass. A complete Index and cross-references in the text have also been provided.

We wish to express sincere appreciation to the following authorities who help in selecting material to be used in this guide: Sandra Andacht, Little Neck, New York; Marilyn Dipboye, Warren, Michigan; Robert T. Matthews, West Friendship, Maryland; Cecil Munsey, Poway, California and Ruth Schinestuhl, Ocean City, New Jersey.

The authors of our "Special Focus" segments deserve special recognition: "Calendar Plates" by Bettye Street, Littleton, Colorado; "Carnival Glass" by Ruth Schinestuhl, Ocean City, New Jersey; "Inkstands & Inkwells" by James Kolbe, Milford, Connecticut; "Steiff Animals" by Susan Cashman, Fairport, New York; "Steuben Glass" by Bob Rau, Portland, Oregon and "Wine Glasses" by Cecil Munsey, Poway, California.

Photographers who have contributed to

this issue include: Adele Armbruster, Dearborn, Michigan; E.A. Babka, East Dubuque, Illinois; Al Bagdade, Northbrook, Illinois; Stanley L. Baker, Minneapolis, Minnesota; Dorothy Beckwith, Platteville, Wisconsin; Louise Boggess, San Mateo, California; Donna Bruun, Galena, Illinois; David Carter, Stillwater, Oklahoma; Herman Carter, Tulsa, Oklahoma; J.D. Dalessandro, Cincinnati, Ohio; Bill Freeman, Smyrna, Georgia; Vicki Gross, Hillsboro, Oregon; Jeff Grunewald, Chicago, Illinois; Frances Johnson, Gray, Maine; Jim Martin, Monmouth, Illinois; Donald Moore, Alameda, California; Gale Morningstar, Salt Lake City, Utah; Marge Palik, Hinckley, Ohio; Ruth Schinestuhl, Ocean City, New Jersey; Paul Tontini, Connecticut and Bruce Whitehall, Palos Verdes Estates, California.

For other photographs, artwork, data or permission to photograph in their shops, we sincerely express appreciation to the following auctioneers, galleries, museums, individuals and shops: Neal Alford Company, New Orleans, Louisiana; Americana Shop, Chicago, Illinois; Antiques Par Ronay, Snyder, New York; Arman's Auction Service, Woodstock, Connecticut; Susan and Al Bagdade, Northbrook, Illinois; Bell Tower Antique Mall, Covington, Kentucky; Richard A. Bourne Co., Hyannis, Massachusetts; Bruhn's Auction Gallery, Denver, Colorado; Burns Auction Service, Bath, New York; Butterfield & Butterfield, San Francisco, California; Norm and Diana Charles, Hagerstown, Indiana; Christie's, New York, New York; Mrs. J. Ciparcha, Norwood, New Jersey; Cyr Auctions, Bryant Pond, Maine; D. & L. Antiques, North Berwick, Maine; DeFina Auctions, Austinburg, Ohio; Gail DePasquale, Leavenworth, Kansas; Doyle Auctioneers, Fishkill, New York; Edith Dragowick, Dubuque, Iowa; DuMouchelles, Detroit, Michigan; Dunn's Antiques, Buffalo, New York; T. Emert, Cincinnati, Ohio; Frasher's Doll Auction Service, Kansas City, Missouri; Garth's Auctions, Inc., Delaware, Ohio; Glick's Antiques, Galena, Illinois; Morton Goldberg Galleries, New Orleans, Louisiana; Grunewald Antiques, Hillsborough, North Carolina; the late William Heacock; Heather

Higgins, Wilmette, Illinois and House of Seven Fables, Somonauk, Illinois.

Also to the The International Carnival Glass Association, Mentone, Indiana; Jeanne & Keith Antiques, Cassville, Wisconsin; Jean's Antiques, Palos Verdes Estates, California; Jewel Johnson, Tulsa, Oklahoma; Gary Kirsner, Coral Springs, Florida; Sheri Klabo, Seattle, Washington; Rich Kleinhardt, Northbrook, Illinois; Richard Larson, Maple Plain, Minnesota; Joy Luke Gallery, Bloomington, Illinois; Mariann Marks, Honesdale, Pennsylvania; J. Martin, Mt. Orab, Ohio; Sybill McFadden, Lakewood, New York; James Measell, Berkley, Michigan; Terry McGrath, Auctioneer, Auburn, Maine; Hanna Mebane Enterprises, Dunwoody, Georgia; Rosemary Meyer, Dubuque, Iowa; William Miller, Rockford, Illinois; Pettigrew Auction Company, Colorado Springs, Colorado; Phillips, New York, New York; Dave Rago, Trenton, New Jersey; Raven & Dove, Wilmette, Illinois; Jack and Berta Reynolds, Jackson, Michigan; Jane Rosenow, Galva, Illinois; Tammy Roth, East Dubuque, Illinois; Carlton and Rosa Schleede, Spencerport, New York; Robert W. Skinner, Inc., Bolton, Massachusetts; Sotheby's, New York, New York; Doris Spahn, East Dubuque, Illinois; Dave and Carroll Swope, Ohio; Robert B. Taylor, Richmond, Virginia; The Antiquers, Salt Lake City, Utah; Theriault's, Annapolis, Maryland; Time Was Museum, Mendota, Illinois; Town & Country Antiques, Northbrook, Illinois; Travis Auctions, Milwaukee, Wisconsin; Don Treadway Auction Service, Cincinnati, Ohio; Trunzo Auctioneers, Inc., Salt Lake City, Utah; Lee Vines, Hewlett, New York; Doris Virtue, Galena, Illinois; Chris Walker Auctions, Potosi, Wisconsin; Williams Auctions, Harrisonville, Missouri; Wilson House Antiques, Mineral Point, Wisconsin; Wolf's Auctioneers and Appraisers, Cleveland, Ohio and Woody Auction Service, Douglass, Kansas.

The staff of *The Antique Trader Antiques & Collectibles Price Guide* welcomes all letters from readers, especially those of constructive critique, and we make every effort to respond personally.

Kyle Husfloen, Editor

ABC PLATES

These children's plates were popular in the late 19th and early 20th centuries. An alphabet border was incorporated with nursery rhymes, maxims, scenes or figures in an apparent attempt to "spoon feed" a bit of knowledge at mealtime. They were made of ceramics, glass and metal. A boon to collectors is the fine book, A Collector's Guide to ABC Plates, Mugs and Things *by Mildred L. and Joseph P. Chalala.*

CERAMIC

"The Drive"

5" d., humorous scene, two black people w/riddle on front "What fruit does our sketch represent?," answer on back, embossed alphabet border, Staffordshire $225.00

5" d., humorous scene, two black people w/riddle on front "Why is the gentleman in the cap & gown the better logician of the two?," answer on back, embossed alphabet border, Staffordshire 225.00

5½" d., adult activities, "Highland Dance," black transfer scene of people dancing w/green, red & yellow enameling, embossed alphabet border 95.00

5½" d., farm scene, "Gathering Cotton," colorful transfer-printed center scene of black men, women & children picking cotton, embossed alphabet border 195.00

6 1/16" d., religious, "Hush My Dear Lie Still & Slumber - Holy Angels Guard Thy Bed, Heavenly Blessings Without Number Gently Falling on Thy Head," center transfer scene of a mother rocking a child in a cradle w/angels above, embossed alphabet border, Meakin, England, late 19th c. 125.00

6 1/8" d., American political theme, transfer-printed bust portrait of President Garfield in the center, embossed alphabet border, late 19th c. 95.00

6¼" d., "Deaf and Dumb" (so called) series, pink center transfer of Dutch children & goose, sign language printed around center edge, embossed alphabet border on rim, H. Aynsley & Co., Longton, England, ca. 1904 .... 95.00

6¼" d., Franklin Maxim, "Silk and Satins Scarlet and Velvets Put Out the Kitchen Fire," polychromed transfer-printed scene of a vain lady primping in a mirror while ignoring her children & the hearth fire, embossed alphabet border, J. & G. Meakin, England, late 19th c. 175.00

7" d., adult activities, "The Drive," black transfer-printed scene of a couple in a horse-drawn two-wheel cart highlighted w/polychrome enameling, embossed alphabet border, unmarked Staffordshire (ILLUS.) 110.00

7" d., children's activities & games, wine colored transfer-printed scene of a boy playing cricket, embossed alphabet border 55.00

7" d., occupations, "Handling the Ware," Potter's Art Series, two ladies sitting holding pottery w/finished pieces on shelf, embossed alphabet border, unmarked Staffordshire 125.00

7" d., religious, "Sacred History of Joseph and His Brethren," transfer scene in center of Joseph before the Pharaoh, embossed alphabet border, unmarked Staffordshire .. 44.00

7" d., wild animals, center transfer scene of acrobatic monkeys, embossed alphabet border 50.00

7 1/16" d., wild animals, "Stag and Fawn," black transfer center scene w/polychrome enameling, embossed alphabet border (minor stains) 75.00

7 3/16" d., Nations of the World series, "Japanese," polychromed transfer scene of a Japanese man & woman in round reserve to right side, printed alphabet along left side, B.P. Co., England, ca. 1883 .... 95.00

7¼" d., wild animals, "Elephant," transfer of animal in a square at center, printed alphabet border .. 110.00

7 5/16" d., Nations of the World series, "Greek," transfer scene of a Greek man & woman in round reserve to right side, printed al-

phabet border along the left side,
B.P. Co., England, ca. 1883 . . . .   95.00

7 3/8" d., American scenery, Niagara Falls center transfer scene,
blue, red & green polychrome
enameling, embossed alphabet
border 85.00

7½" d., humorous scene, brown
transfer scene of a man sliding
down a hill, embossed alphabet
border, unmarked Staffordshire . .   55.00

"The Candle Fish"

7½" d., Indian series, "The Candle
Fish," brown transfer scene of In-
dians (2) rowing a canoe, em-
bossed alphabet border, Charles
Allerton & Sons, ca. 1890
(ILLUS.) 125.00

8" d., humorous scene, center transfer scene of dancing pigs, embossed alphabet border,
unmarked 34.00

8" d., "Uncle Tom's Cabin, the Vision of Uncle Tom," transfer scene
of Uncle Tom kneeling & looking
up at the vision, embossed al-
phabet border 77.00

8¼" d., Robinson Crusoe series,
"Crusoe on the Raft," transfer
scene in center w/red, blue,
brown & orange enameling, embossed alphabet border, B.P. Co.,
England, 1887-88 . . . .   139.00

GLASS

6" d., Cane patt. center, clear alphabet on stippled ground rim
(small rim chip) 22.00

6" d., President Garfield profile bust
center, clear alphabet border
(ILLUS.). 30.00

6" d., President Garfield profile bust
center, clear w/frosted alphabet
border (tiny rim nick) 30.00

6" d., Starburst center, alphabet

border, scalloped rim, New Mar-
tinsville Glass Mfg. Co. 25.00

President Garfield ABC Plate

7" d., Plain center, embossed alphabet border, beaded rim, milk
white 42.50

ADVERTISING ITEMS

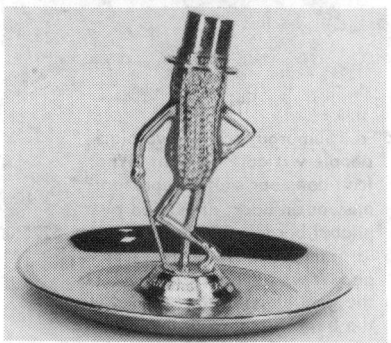

"Planters Peanuts" Ashtray

*Thousands of objects made in various
materials, some intended as gifts with pur-
chases, others used for display or given away
for publicity, are now being collected. They
range from ash and drink trays to toys. Also
see AUTOMOTIVE ACCESSORIES,
BANKS, BASEBALL MEMORABILIA,
BIG LITTLE BOOKS, BOTTLE
OPENERS, BOTTLES & FLASKS,
BUSTER BROWN COLLECTIBLES,
CALENDAR PLATES, CANS & CON-
TAINERS, CARNIVAL GLASS, CHARAC-
TER COLLECTIBLES, COCA-COLA
ITEMS, COOKBOOKS, COOKIE CUT-
TERS, FANS, KITCHENWARES, JEWEL
TEA AUTUMN LEAF WARES, OLD
SLEEPY EYE POTTERY, SALESMAN'S
SAMPLES, SCOUTING ITEMS, STICK-
PINS, TOYS, TRADE CARDS, TRADE
CATALOGS, WATCH FOBS and
WORLD'S FAIR COLLECTIBLES.*

Angel food cake pan, "Swansdown,"
tin, 1923 patent $15.00
Apple butter crock, "Heinz,"
pottery .... 300.00 to 325.00
Ashtray, "Ames Heating Pumps,"
metal, figural heating pump 10.00
Ashtray, "Armstrong Imperial SD
Rhino Flex," model of a rubber
tire w/rhinoceros logo, clear glass
insert, 6" 20.00
Ashtray, "Bengal Gin," ceramic,
large tiger shown 35.00
Ashtray, "Diamond Tires," model of
a rubber tire w/clear glass
insert 15.00
Ashtray, "Goodyear Tires," model of
a rubber tire w/clear glass
insert 14.00
Ashtray, "Planters Peanuts," ceramic, Mr. Peanut standing by shell .. 60.00
Ashtray, "Planters Peanuts," gold
finish metal w/figure of Mr. Peanut center (ILLUS.) 28.00
Ashtray, "Walter E. Schatt Willys
Distributor," Rookwood Pottery ... 90.00
Baby's spoon w/long handle, "Gerber's," silver plate 11.00
Backbar decanter, clear glass, wide
base tapering to slender neck,
round cut crystal stopper, lightly
etched across front "Crystal Bell,"
& monogrammed, 11" h. 32.00
Bag dispenser, hanging-type, "Sun-
beam Bread," lithographed tin ... 45.00
Bank, "Conoco," oil can shape,
"75th Anniversary, 1950" 18.00
Bank, "Eveready Batteries," figural
black cat, plastic, 5½ x 8¼" 12.00
Bank, "John Deere," mailbox
shape 18.00
Bank, "Metz Beer," ceramic, barrel
shape 22.00
Bank, "Rockford National Bank,"
dime-register type, bank
pictured 24.00
Bank, "Sinclair," copper, model of a
dinosaur, 8" (no key) 45.00
Banner, "Creamery Marshmallows,"
canvas, 18½ x 29" 25.00
Banner, "Winchester," horse & rider
center, "Headquarters For Winchester Rifles & Shotguns," fringe
on bottom, on wooden rod,
19½ x 29" 135.00
Beach ball, "Planters Peanuts,"
blow-up ball w/picture of Mr.
Peanut 22.00
Beater jar, "Use This Jar for Beating
& Toma's Groceries for Eating,"
blue lettering on stoneware 69.00
Bell, "Aunt Jemima," figural painted
tin, mint in box, patent date
1941 .... 100.00
Bill clip, "Wingold, Bay State Milling

Co., Winona, Minn.," celluloid,
multicolored 19.50
Bill hook, "Biscay Steel Cut Coffee,"
celluloid, pictures can (edge fox-
ing) 18.50
Bill spindle, "National Cash Register
Co.," brass 25.00
Biscuit cutter, "Cottolene Shorten-
ing," tin w/ring handle 6.00
Biscuit cutter, "Rumford Baking Pow-
der," tin 14.00
Blotter, "Dixon Pencils," Norman
Rockwell illustration, unused 15.00
Blotter, "DuPont Explosives" 12.00
Blotter, "Reid's Ice Cream," pictures
pretty lady, early, unused 35.00
Board game, "Champion Spark
Plug," 1930's, unused 40.00
Book, "Borden's Cartoon Book," fea-
tures Elsie the Cow, colorful
graphics, 1940's 25.00
Book, "Hershey's," entitled "Story of
Chocolate & Cocoa," 1926,
31 pp. 15.00

"Kellogg's Funny Jungleland" Book

Book, "Kellogg's," entitled "Funny
Jungleland Moving-Pictures," 1909
(ILLUS.) .... 25.00 to 30.00
Book, "Quaker Oats," entitled
"Around the World with Hob,"
1931 .... 5.00
Booklet, "Bon Ami," entitled "The
Chick That Never Grew Up" 12.00
Booklet, "Colgate Ribbon Dental
Cream," entitled "The Jungle Pow-
Wow For Nursery Folks," 1911,
12 pp. .... 15.00 to 25.00
Booklet, "Gold Dust Cleanser," enti-
tled "Brite Spots," Gold Dust
Twins shown, 1937 .... 30.00
Booklet, "Jello," entitled "The Jello
Girl Entertains," w/illustrations by
Rose O'Neill 20.00
Booklet, "Teddy Bear Bread," 1908,
colorful early teddies pictured 20.00

Bottle carrier, "Pepsi-Cola," cloth, 1940's 50.00

Bottle carrier, "R.C. Cola," wooden 30.00

Bow tie, clip-on type, "Oscar Mayer," "All Meat Weiner," 1950's. . . . 12.00

Box, "No Rats Seen," cartooned top picturing dog & cat watching rat hole 10.00

Breadboard dough scraper, "Sleepy Eye Flour," wooden handle 408.00

Bung hammer, "Fleischmann's Magnolia Whiskey," wooden, 21" l. . . . 65.00

Bust of Theodore Roosevelt, "Hollywood Roosevelt Hotel," metal, manufactured by Rehberger Co., Chicago, 3 x 4" 125.00

Butter crock, "Domser's Creamery, Utica, N.Y.," grey stoneware w/blue lettering 35.00

Cake carrier, "Pepsi-Cola," tin, 1960's 20.00

Calendar, 1887, "Hood's Sarsaparilla," chromolithograph of little girl in bonnet at top, printed by Major, Knapp & Co., New York 100.00

Calendar, 1889, "E.W. Hoyt & Co.," girl pictured 25.00

Calendar, 1890, "Walter A. Wood Mowing & Reaping Machine Co." 75.00

Calendar, 1893, "Hood's Sarsaparilla," little girl shown 38.00

Calendar, 1897, "Hood's Sarsaparilla," full pad 43.00

Calendar, 1898, "John Hancock Insurance," sports scenes 85.00

Calendar, 1898, "Listers Animal Bone Fertilizers," large full color print w/scene of split-rail fence & road w/loaded hay wagon & large windmill in background, wording above & complete calendar pad below 60.00

Calendar, 1900, "Cream of Wheat," topless girl pictured 550.00

Calendar, 1901, "Grand Union Tea," scenes of women & children surrounded by important 19th century discoveries, "Progress of the Century," 4 pp., 8½ x 12" 45.00

Calendar, 1902, "Quaker Oats," pictures "Queens of Home & Nation" 40.00

Calendar, 1903, "Hood's Sarsaparilla," pictures "Four Friends," complete 40.00

Calendar, 1905, "Westlecher Herald," lithographs of children 40.00

Calendar, 1906, "Deering Harvesters," top section w/large colored lithograph of young woman seated near small fruit tree eating cherries, complete calendar & ad-

vertising at bottom, metal band at top, 13 x 20" 169.00

Calendar, 1914, "Mendenhall's Chill & Fever Tonic," children w/horses, 11 x 14" 28.50

Calendar, 1915, "Walk-Over Shoes," cardboard, large lithograph w/standing young woman in candy-stripe dress holding two chicks, dark green background, titled "A Walk-Over Girl," lower left signed, "C. Ward Traver," small paper calendar in lower right corner, advertising on back, linen-backed for strength, 18½ x 28½" 213.00

Calendar, 1921, "J.R. Watkins," pad complete 18.00

Calendar, 1923, "Wrigley's P.K. Chewing Sweet" 5.00

Calendar, 1926, "Dexter Double Tub," full-color print at top of young Indian maiden standing next to canoe by moonlit lake, advertising & month pages below, 6 x 18" 18.00

Calendar, 1931, "Pepsi-Cola," full pad, from local bottler 65.00

Calendar, 1936, "Mobilgas,"shows "Magnolia Trail South," 11 x 12" . . 32.00

Calendar, 1940, "Virginia Dare Wines," full pad, shows pretty girl, colorful, 21 x 30" 33.00

Carpenter's apron, "Rubberoid Roofing-Shingles," white canvas w/mustached man logo 50.00

Ceiling globe, "We Serve the Cream of Pittsburgh," Pittsburgh Ice Cream Co., red & black lettering on white, 1917 patent, flanged for set screws 325.00

Chair, "Restu Washes White Overnight," wooden frame, porcelain over steel back w/advertising in light & dark blue w/white lettering highlighted in black, 13" w., 35" h. 135.00

Champagne glass, "Compliments of Frederick Bary Co.," trumpet-shaped, 1" engraved letters, cranberry, 22" h. 175.00

Charm, "Swift's Premium," miniature figural glass ham 35.00

Checkerboard, "Banner Lye," folding-type, red outside, yellow w/black & red accents, 12" sq. open 85.00

Cigar crate label, paper, "Wake Up" w/colorful lithograph of large rooster in farm yard, printed by A. Hoen & Co., Richmond, Virginia, dated 1888, 10½" sq. 15.00

Cigar store figure, molded zinc, Indian maiden holds cigars under her right arm & a tomahawk in her hand, shields her eyes w/her left hand, on square base & wooden stand on wheels, polychrome decorated, attributed to William Demuth, New York, ca. 1890, 68¼" h. figure 11,500.00

Cigarette pack, "Black Cat," original stamp, shows cat, unopened 12.50

Clicker gun, "Tip-Top Bread," cardboard, pictures Cisco Kid 20.00

Clock, "Buy St. Joseph Aspirin," electric, shows giant aspirin 85.00

Clock, "Dad's Root Beer," electric, square w/metal frame & plastic face, large colored bottle cap on dial w/"Drink Dad's," 16" sq. 45.00

Clock, "Hudson Terraplane," car on clock face & "No. 1 Car of the Low Price Field" 475.00

Clock, "Nu-Grape," electric, bottle pictured, 15" d. 125.00

Clock, "Red Goose School Shoes," papier-mache, model of a goose, wind clock & head nods, Germany, 23" h. 1,200.00

Clock, "Union Leader," alarm-type, w/black man 245.00

Coffeepot, "Blanke's Drip Coffee Pot" embossed in blue on lid, "Faust Blend" & full figure devil on body & ornate overall design, 9½" 345.00

Cookie cutter, "Robin Hood Flour," plastic, figural Robin Hood 4.75

Cookie jar, "Borden's Dairy," ceramic, figural Elsie the Cow 95.00

Counter display, "Auto-Lite Spark Plugs," rounded glass front & metal back, includes seven old spark plugs 50.00

Counter display, "Elgin Watches," mechanical, man in duster cranking vintage car 185.00

"Hennessy Cognac" Counter Display

Counter display, "Hennessy Cognac," papier-mache model of a St. Bernard dog, ca. 1953, 12" l., 10½" h. (ILLUS.) . . . . 100.00 to 125.00

Counter display, ice cream, compo-

sition, model of a large ice cream cone w/"Eat-It-All" embossed on side of cone, 20½" h. 175.00

Counter display, "Ivory Soap," cardboard, figure of creeping baby, Procter & Gamble, 1884 . . . . 165.00

Counter display case, "Boye Needle Co.," tin, holds needles, bobbins, shuttles for 200 sewing machines, listed, dated 1907, 16" 250.00

Counter display case, "Tootsie Rolls," glass, front reads "Pure Delicious Chocolate Candy" 335.00

Counter display figure, "Beefeater Gin," papier-mache & wood figure of an English yeoman of the royal guard, 16½" h. 80.00

Counter display figure, "Old Crow," composition model of a crow, w/removable cane, 27" h. 250.00

Counter display figure, "Pepsi-Cola," die-cut figure of Santa Claus, 1950's, 11 x 14" 35.00

Counter display jar, "Beich's Candy," 16-sided clear glass jar w/embossed lettering, 10" h. 46.00

Counter display jar, "Curtis Chico's Spanish Peanuts - 5 Cents," clear glass, "by the makers of Baby Ruth Candy Bars," tin lid, 11½" h. . . . . 150.00 to 250.00

Counter display jar, "Planters Peanuts," clear glass barrel-shaped jar & original glass lid w/peanut finial 196.00

Counter display jar, "Planters Peanuts," clear glass fish bowl w/original Planters decal & glass lid w/peanut finial, large size 90.00

Counter display jar, cov., octagonal, "Planters Peanuts," clear glass, peanut finial on lid, "PENNANT SALTED PEANUTS 5 CENTS" on front & back panels, Mr. Peanut figure raised on four panels, 12½" h. 100.00

Cribbage board, "Lash's Bitters," wooden, 4 x 13" 125.00

Crock, "Heinz Preserved Red Raspberries," stoneware w/original label 450.00

Crumb set: tray & scraper; "Steinklein Furniture," brass, early 1900's, 2 pcs. 32.50

Cup & saucer, demitasse, "Kent Cigarettes," porcelain, both picture characters w/cigarette packs, Royal Crown China 35.00

Cup & saucer, "Van Dole's Hot Chocolate," porcelain, wording over reserve w/company logo on cup & saucer, green w/purple iridescent background, made in Japan, cup 3" h., saucer 6" d. 14.00

Cuspidor, "Red Skin Chewing Tobacco," copper & brass, embossed Indian head w/full headdress each side, ca. 1895 . . . . 50.00 to 100.00

Dolls, "C&H Pure Cane Sugar," cloth, Hawaiian boy & girl, pr. . . . 25.00

Doll, "Horsman Little Debbie Snack Cakes," Little Debbie doll, 1972, in original box . . . . 35.00 to 45.00

Doll, "Kellogg's," printed cloth, uncut, front & back design of little dressed bear, marked "Kellogg's Johnny Bear, Copyright 1925," 11½ x 13¼" (minor stains) 125.00

Doorpull, "Camel Cigarettes," tin, pictures dancing cigarette packs w/girl's legs 45.00

Door push plate, "Calderwood Bread," metal 45.00

Door push plate, "Millbrook Bread," metal, bread-shaped 35.00

Egg separator, "Rumford Baking Powder," tin 15.00

Egg separator, "Watkins," tin, "50 Years" 8.00

Envelopes, "Indian Motorcycle," illustrations on both sides, "These Air Mail letters were carried by Indian Cycle, as a souvenir on the last day of the 10 cent ½ oz. Air Mail rate," 1928 . . . . 85.00

Fan, "Coon Chicken Inn," cardboard 20.00

Fan, "Ford Automobile," cardboard, color illustration of very early Model T w/female driver & girlfriend out for a spin by lake, handle of fan shows four more cars & Ford tractor, 8 x 10½" 15.00

Fan, "Moores & Ross Ice Cream," die-cut cardboard Santa & ice cream sundae 40.00

Fan, "Moxie," cardboard, scene of girl & soda jerk 36.50

Flashlight, "Peter's Shoes" 13.50

Flashlight, "Red Goose Shoes" 17.50

Flour bin & sifter, "Superior Flour," 36" h. 300.00

Flour sack, "Bay State" flour, fullcolor front scene of child riding rocking horse w/mother standing in background cutting loaf of bread on table, flour sack in front of table, blue & red lettering, 16" w., 10" h. (small mended tear) 16.00

Flour sifter, "Calumet," tin 15.00

Fork, "Rumford Baking Powder," three-tine, 12" l. 16.00

Frying pan, "Mt. Penn Stoves & Ranges," cast iron, 2½" d. 15.00

Game, "Coon Chicken Inn," paper, optical illusion-type 25.00

Game, "Lion Coffee," lithographed

paper, "Feeding Sambo," pin watermelon in his mouth, 1903, 12 x 20" 150.00

Game, "Lord Calvert Whiskey," dominoes, wooden, w/box 45.00

Gasoline pump top globe, "Crown Extra," glass 150.00

Gasoline pump top globe, "Kendall," glass 165.00

Gasoline pump top globe, "Phillips 66 Flite Fuel," plastic, shieldshaped 75.00

Gasoline pump top globe, "Standard Oil," milk white glass crown w/blue paint 300.00

Gas pump top globe, "White Eagle," milk white glass figural eagle, one-piece 512.00

Gas station map holder, "Texaco," tin 30.00

Gum stand, "Clark's Teaberry," amber pressed glass 50.00

Hat, "Aunt Jemima," paper, chef'stype 15.00

Hat, "Brown Derby Restaurant," in original box picturing restaurant & people dining, "Eat In the Hat," 8" d. 75.00

Jigsaw puzzle, "Campfire Marshmallows," in original mailer 8.00

Jigsaw puzzle, "Heinz," original envelope shows children w/many products 40.00

Jigsaw puzzle, "Singer," full color, man on wagon w/treadle machine, pulled by two buffalo, original envelope, 50 pcs. 25.00

Jug, "Banner Liquor Store, Winona, MN," stoneware, 1 gal. 85.00

Jug, "Jack Daniel Fine Goods Sold & Guaranteed by Tim Motlow, Lynchburg, Tenn.," stoneware, 2 gal. 675.00

Jug, "The Triaca Co. Wholesale Dealers Wines & Liquors, S.W. Cor. Light & Pratt Sts. Baltimore, Md. U.S.A.," pottery w/stenciled lettering, 2 gal. 69.00

Juice reamer, "Sunkist," blue opaque glass 69.00

Key holder, "Gulf Pride Motor Oil," embossed leather, oil can shape. . 12.50

Key ring, "Holiday Cigarettes," plastic 6.00

Lapel pin, "Evinrude Outboard Motors" 25.00

Ledger, pocket-type, "John Deere," 1919 . . . . 10.00

Ledger, pocket-type, "I.W. Harper," 1905 . . . . 8.50

Letter opener, "Dioxogen Chemical Co.," celluloid handle 15.00

Lithograph, printer's proof, "Dixon's American Graphite Pencils," fleshtone picture of lovely young lady standing in peach dress & rust hat looking at printed ad, book under her arm, 1915 (some outside border missing) 400.00

Match holder, wall-type, "Juicy Fruit Gum," tin 75.00

Match safe, pocket-type, engraved "B&B Bluthenthal & Bickart," flattened flask shape, small circle w/stamped design of a hand holding a spread of cards, 1½" w., 2½" l. 36.00

Measuring cup, "Cream Dove Peanut Butter," clear glass 30.00

Measuring cup, "Kellogg's," green transparent glass, w/three spouts 15.50

Mechanical pencil, "Barney Buff Corn Shelling & Welding, Phone 104F13 Piper City, Ill.," red Bakelite 7.00

Mechanical pencil, "Borden's," milk bottle on top 20.00

Mechanical pencil, lady's, "Compliments of Lydia E. Pinkham Medicine Co." 25.00

Mechanical pencil, "Dodge," car floating in oil, pictured giraffe (more head room) & ostrich (more leg room), 1940's 25.00

Menu board, "Hires Root Beer," pictures bottle, colorful, 1940's 35.00

Milk can, miniature, "Huyler's Milk Chocolate" on plaque, tin 65.00

Milk cap extractor, "Made Better Flavoring Extracts, Milwaukee," celluloid 20.00

Mirror, hand-type, "Florsheim Shoes," handle in shape of high-button shoe.................... 30.00

Mirror, pocket-type, "Anderson's Soups," very colorful 30.00

Mirror, pocket-type, "A.T. & T. Nebraska Telephone Co." 30.00

Mirror, pocket-type, "Bells' Mocha & Java Coffee".................. 30.00

Mirror, pocket-type, "Cascarets Laxative," cherub on commode 26.00

Mirror, pocket-type, "Ceresota Flour," little boy trademark, 2" oval 34.00

"Copper Clad" Pocket Mirror

Mirror, pocket-type, "Copper Clad" ranges, oval, 1¾ x 2¾" (ILLUS.).. 30.00

Mirror, pocket-type, "Ghirardelli's Chocolate" 55.00

Mirror, pocket-type, "Good Friends Whiskey," pictures Indian & Pilgrim 185.00

Mirror, pocket-type, "Panama Carbon Paper," 3½" d. 20.00

Mirror, pocket-type, "Red Seal Lye" 28.00

Mirror, pocket-type, "Schaeffer Pianos," oval 48.00

Mirror, pocket-type, "Union Standard Shoes" 22.00

Mirror, pocket-type, "Whirlpool Washer"....................... 11.00

Mirror, pocket-type, "Zoological Gardens, Cincinnati," celluloid ... 15.00

Mirror, wall-type, "Lady Laurel Stoves," beautiful woman & bread, oval 155.00

Mixer, single head, "Horlicks - The Original Malted Milk," white porcelain base, near mint & working 115.00

Mug, "A & W Root Beer," etched glass, small size, early 20.00

Mug, "Flaccus Bros. Wheeling, W. Va.," stoneware 85.00

Napkin holder, "Coon Chicken Inn," chalkware, 5" h. 155.00

Needle threader, "Champion Oil," metal 8.50

Nutcracker, "L.A. Althoff, makers of Headlight Stoves, Ranges, La Porte, Ind.," dog-shaped, ad under base 48.00

Pail, "Worthmore Chocolate Drops," fiberboard, Great Atlantic & Pacific Tea Co., dated 1917, 30 lb., 13" h........................ 45.00

Paint book, "Planter's Famous Men Paint Book," w/envelope, 1935 ... 25.00

Paint brush holder, "Davis Paints," wall-type, tin 45.00

Paper cup, "Heinz," salesman's sample, pictures pickle 15.00

Paperweight, "American Glass & Construction Co., Rochester, N.Y.," glass reinforced w/wire, oblong, 3 x 4½" 15.00

Paperweight, "Aunt Jemima," cast iron, red, 2½" 95.00

Paperweight, "Crane Co., Chicago 75th Anniversary," brass, round, 2 3/8" d. 30.00

Paperweight, "Holt's," model of soap bar, hard black wax w/embossed 1" fancy script letters, 2½ x 3½" oval 10.00

Paperweight, "New York Telephone - Bell System," blue glass, bell-shaped (ILLUS. top next page) 52.00

Paperweight, "North River Insurance

Co.," brass, round, "100th Anniversary, 1822-1922," 3¾" d. 50.00

New York Telephone Paperweight

Paperweight, "Prudential Insurance Co. of America - 50th Anniv. 1875-1925," brass, round, 2 7/8" d. 37.50

Peanut butter maker, "Planters Peanuts," figural Mr. Peanut w/grinder between ears, w/box, 12" h. 28.00

Peg board shopping reminder, hanging-type, "Rumford," w/original pegs..................... 22.00

Pen, "Arm & Hammer Baking Soda," advertising in glass body, in original black celluloid case 25.00

Pencil, "John Deere, Macomb, Ill.," bullet-shaped 15.00

Pencil, mechanical, "Royal Crown Cola," 5½" l. 8.00

Pennant, "McFadden's Electric Brand Coffee," 3' l..................... 135.00

Pennant, "Tellings Ice Cream," felt, pictures children making ice cream........................ 85.00

Photograph, "Kodak," black & white, shows woman taking children's photo, marked "Keep a Kodak Story of the Children," ca. 1920's, 21 x 23"....................... 95.00

Pin, "Schwinn Bicycles," model of a bicycle, 1920's 18.50

Pin, screw-back, "Seven-Up," five-year service type, gold-filled w/gold plate front, enameled green bottle, gold & red labels, oval of leaves, ½ x ¾"......... 75.00

Pinback button, "Borden's," Elsie the Cow, 2" pin on original display card 20.00

Pinback button, "Buster Brown Bread," 1¼" d. 27.50

Pinback button, "High Admiral Cigarettes," pictures Yellow Kid, No. 4, ca. 1896 .... 60.00

Pinback button, "Kellogg's Pep Cereal," Smoky Stover pictured ... 6.50

Pinback button, "Winchester," "The Topperweins Who Always Shoot Winchester Guns & Cartridges" ... 40.00

Pitcher, "Compliments of Paducah Vinegar Co., Paducah, Ky.," pottery, cylindrical w/pinched spout, Albany slip w/sgraffito inscription, 5 7/8" h. (small chip under handle) 65.00

Plaque, "Fairbanks Scales," white porcelain, black world globe center w/"Fairbanks Scales" through globe, 10" d. 45.00

Plates, "Coon Chicken Inn," china, 5½" d., set of 4................ 380.00

Plate, "Palmer's Chocolates," goofus glass, 6½" d. 37.50

Playing cards, "Remington Arms Co.," full deck 22.00

Playing cards, "Royal Crown Cola," war motto, dated 1945........... 10.00

Pocket watch case opener, "Illinois Watch Case Co.," metal, very ornate 35.00

Popcorn sack, "National Theater Supply Central Popcorn Co., Schaller, Iowa," burlap, multicolored theater scene, 100 lb.... 35.00

Postcard, "Kinsey Pure Rye Whiskey," color hunting scene, ca. 1906 .... 15.00

Potato sack, "Parrot Idaho Potatoes," burlap, printed w/wording & central scene of two facing parrots & "Something to Talk About," excellent condition 10.00

Print, "Gerber Baby Products," pictures Gerber Baby, dated 1931, 8 x 10".................... 8.00

Punch-out book, "Kellogg's Singing Lady" premium, 1930's 45.00

Puzzle, dexterity-type, "Nabisco," three beads, shows Rin Tin Tin ... 7.00

Recipe cards, "Towle's Log Cabin Syrup," colorful, set of 24 .... 35.00

Rolling pin, "Columbus Baking Powder, Laurens, N.Y.," aqua glass w/tin cap & original paper label, original contents, 16" l.......... 135.00

Salt & pepper shakers, "Sealtest Dairy," milk bottle shape, pr. 18.00

Sample envelopes, "Monarch Tea," paper w/glassine window, shows the lion tin on each, group of 6 .. 8.00

Sauce pan w/lid, "Quaker Oats Cooker," grey graniteware 78.00

Screen, "Winchester Tools," wood-framed cardboard, three-fold, three tall sections combine to form continuous scene of Toonerville Trolley cartoon characters, top of center panel marked "The Powerful Katrinka Helps the Hammer Demonstration," scene features cartoon characters watching Katrinka's demonstration outside a Winchester tool store, bottom of

center panel has "Winchester
Tools Are Best by Every Test," op-
posite side shows scene entitled
"Winning the West" featuring a
Pony Express rider leaving a station, each panel 18 x 38", overall
48 x 60" (center panel stained) . . 2,200.00
Sheet music, "Aunt Jemima," 1925,
song tells about her pancakes 25.00
Shipping crate, "Arbuckle's
Roasted Coffee," wooden,
15 x 19½ x 32" 75.00
Shopping bag, "CBS - Arthur God-
frey," radio show souvenir, mint,
unused, 1940's 20.00
Smoking stand, "Moxie," flattened
silhouette of a standing man
dressed in a green cap & tails
w/red trousers & holding an ashtray, "Drink Moxie" printed on his
cap & at base, early 20th c.,
35" h. 412.50
Spatula, "Rumford," metal 12.00
Spoon holder, "Bromo Seltzer," co-
balt blue glass 24.00

Luxury Coffee Store Bin

Store bin, "Luxury Coffee," painted
& decorated wood, hinged sloping
rectangualr top opening to a storage area, the front stenciled in
black w/brand name within broken borders on a yellow ground,
late 19th c., wear to paint,
22" w., 32" h. (ILLUS.) 330.00
Store bin, "Spurr's Coffee," wooden
w/vertical slat sides, original
stenciling, Boston, Massachu-
setts 340.00
Store display toy, Unique Art Co.,
Jazzbo Jim toy w/the cabin base
a larger version of the keywind
toy, the dancing figure on the
roof w/composition head, torso &
arms rather than tin, fitted for
electricity, 34" h. 4,180.00
Straining spoon, "Rumford Baking
Powder," slotted bowl 20.00

Tape measure, "Edison Mazda
Lights," Maxfield Parrish artwork,
two medieval boys & light bulb
one side, early electric stove
reverse 135.00
Tea caddy spoon, "Wilson's Pure Tea
Croydon," nickel silver 17.50
Teapot, "Van Dyke Coffee & Tea
Co.," stoneware, miniature 75.00
Teaspoon, "Baker (Walter) Cocoa,"
silver plate, La Belle Chocolatiere
figural handle 35.00
Teaspoon, "Calumet," silver plate,
figural Indian handle 28.00
Teaspoon, "Doe-Wah-Jack (Dowagi-
ac, Michigan) Round Oak Stoves,"
silver plate, figural Indian handle,
stove in bowl . . . . 60.00 to 80.00

Old Sleepy Eye Teaspoon

Teaspoon, "Old Sleepy Eye Flour
Co.," silver plate, Indian head
profile on handle (ILLUS.) 95.00
Thermometer, "Dr. Pepper," tin, ca.
1960's, 20" h. 50.00
Thermometer, "Honey Krust Bread,"
tin, pictures red & blue loaf on
white, 16" l. 85.00
Thimble, "Watkins," aluminum 6.00
Tie bar, "Holsum Bread 50th An-
niversary," mint in box 10.00
Toy automobile, "CBS Radio," tin,
model of a Chevrolet, 1939 . . . . . .   175.00
Toy geography wheel, mechanical,
"Tip Top Bread," map of the
United States, 1944 . . . .   10.00
Toy, pull-type, "Happy Ham Farm
Products," wood, "Happy Ham,"
1920's-30's 55.00
Toy top, "Jenkins One Price Pianos,"
cast iron 52.00
Toy truck, "Barclay Beer," delivery
truck w/original wooden kegs 75.00
Toy vehicle, "Moxie," tinplate Moxie
horse-mobile brightly litho-
graphed, 8½" l. 550.00
Toy whistle, "Aunt Jemima," dated
1919 . . . .   100.00
Tumbler, "Mobilgas," w/Flying Red
Horse logo 25.00
Watch, pocket-type, "Westing-
house," dial w/the letters "W-E-S-
T-I-N-G-H-O-U-S-E" instead of the
numbers 1-12, 17-jewel move-
ment, ca. 1937-38 . . . .   375.00
Whiskey shot glass, "Sanders Sour
Mash & Rolling Fork Whiskies,
Dayton, Ohio," etched 18.50

ALMANACS

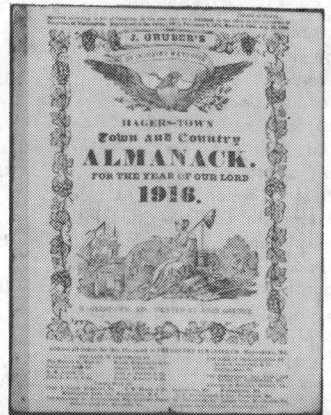

Hagers-Town Town and Country Almanack

Almanacs have been published for decades. Commonplace ones are available at $4 to $12; those representing early printings or scarce ones are higher.

Abe Martin's Almanac for 1909 . . . . . $13.50
Ayer's Almanac, 1879 . . . . 10.00
Capital Almanac, 1893 . . . . 5.00
Dr. Jayne's Medical Almanac,
  1935 . . . . 7.00
Dr. Kilmer's Swamp Root Almanac,
  1932 . . . . 10.00
Dr. Miles' New U.S. Weather Alma-
  nac, 1902 . . . . 7.00
Farm Almanac, Case Threshing Ma-
  chine Co., 1882, color covers,
  32 pp. 40.00
Hagers-Town Town and Country
  Almanack, 1916, printed by John
  Gruber, 31 pp. (ILLUS.) 3.50
Herbalist Almanac (The), 1937 . . . . . . 15.00
Hostetter's U.S. Almanac, 1902 . . . . . 12.50
Hostetter's U.S. Almanac, 1910 . . . . . 12.50
Kickapoo Indian Medicine Almanac,
  1897 . . . . 8.00
Ladies Birthday Almanac, 1902 . . . . . 8.00
Piso's Consumption Remedy Alma-
  nac, 1895, miniature 10.00
Rawleigh's Almanac, 1915 . . . . 10.00
St. John's Family Almanac, 1862 . . . . 21.00
Shaker Almanac, 1884 . . . . 65.00
Standard Oil Almanac, 1931 . . . . 10.00
Studebaker's Farmer's Almanac,
  1912 . . . . 8.00
Watkins Almanac, 1906 . . . . 8.00

ARCHITECTURAL ITEMS

In recent years the growing interest in and support for historic preservation has spawned
a greater appreciation of the fine architectural elements which were an integral part of early buildings, both public and private. Where, in decades past, fine structures might be razed and doors, fireplace mantels, windows, etc., hauled to the dump, today all interior and exterior details from unrestorable buildings are salvaged to be offered to home restorers, museums and even builders who want to include a bit of history in a new construction project.

Building finial, sheet zinc, square
  base tapering up to urn-form supporting tapering spire w/four
  arching wires w/lily-form flowerheads at center, knob finial at
  top, modern green paint, 38" h.
  (flowers a bit battered, one stem
  loose) $55.00
Building finials, cast iron, model of
  a spreadwinged eagle on a block
  base w/molded date "1912,"
  31" wide, pr. 450.0

Mask-form Building Ornament

Building ornament, cast iron, modeled as a classical man's head
  w/flaring feathered headdress &
  long beard, now mounted on black
  stand, America, early 20th c.,
  22" h. (ILLUS.) 6,325.00
Building ornaments, embossed sheet
  zinc, model of classical wreath,
  worn white paint, 20 x 20½", pr.
  (some edge damage) 290.00
Door, oak frame w/leaded glass
  green triangles & diagonals centered by vertical clear beveled
  glass strips in geometric design,
  Prairie School style, Midwest,
  ca. 1910, 34" w., 84" h. 550.00
Doors, walnut, four raised panels,
  original cast-iron & brass lock &
  hinges, old varnish finish,
  1840-1842, 36" w., 83" h., set
  of 6 . . . . .1,590.00
Doorway, Federal-style, carved &

painted pine, triangular pediment &
projecting cornice above a recessed
& arched fanlight above a paneled
door flanked by reeded pilasters,
Trenton, New Jersey, ca. 1800,
120" h. (disassembled, needing
repairs) 1,650.00
Downspouts, solid copper, from
eave troughs, ca. 1880, 8" deep,
10" w., 16" h., pr. 195.00

Federal Fanlight

Fanlight, Federal, lead & glass,
hinged wooden fan-shaped molding set w/mullioned glazed panels
& decorated w/beaded swags,
New England, ca. 1810, 52" w.,
26" h. (ILLUS.) 3,190.00
Fireplace surround, carved marble,
simple, notched mantel above side
panels carved w/stylized fruits &
flowers & a lintel carved w/a bouquet of fruits & tapering scrolls,
France, ca. 1925, 46½" w., 42" h.
(damages & repairs) 1,870.00
Gates, Victorian, wrought iron,
arched w/arrow-form bars, end
supports in the form of a Gothic
niche, Stewart Iron Works,
19th c., 66" l. plus end sections,
4 pcs. 1,045.00
Letter slot escutcheons, cast iron,
rectangular w/ornate scrolled &
stylized floral design, both
w/springed doors one cast "LET-
TERS," designed by Louis H. Sullivan, executed by Yale & Towne
Manufacturing Co. for the Guar-
anty Building, Buffalo, New York,
1894-95, 8¾" l., pr. 770.00
Mantel, Federal-style, pine & composition, very good applied composition decoration w/eagle on shell
w/leafy branches on top center &
rams' heads at top of side columns
above swags of acorns, sheaves
of wheat & grapes, Salem, Massachusetts, early 19th c., 67" w.,
58" h. (stripped of paint) 2,525.00
Mantel, late Classical-style, pine,
overhanging rectangular top
w/rounded edges over carved
classical-style motifs including corbels, anthemions, recessed panels
& moldings, painted blue-green,

America, 19th c., 41¾" w. open-
ing, overall 88" w., 53½" h. 440.00
Mantel, marble, rectangular overhanging shelf w/multiple borders of
leaf-tips & triangles, above a deep
frieze carved in low-relief w/two
frolicking maidens centering a
flame-filled torch raised on scrolling foliage, flanked by geometric
motifs & urns within foliage, the
uprights carved w/elongated slender urns bearing medallions enclosing female allegorical figures,
George III period, England, late
18th c. 8,800.00
Overdoor panel, carved & painted
wood, rectangular, centered w/a
molded arch enclosing a carved
neoclassical urn atop a lappet
swag hung w/floral festoons &
flanked by partially clad cherubs,
grey & cream paint, Louis XVI
era, France, last quarter 18th c.,
65½" l., 42" h. (losses, paint
restoration) 2,750.00
Stairway baluster, copper-plated cast
iron, cast w/designs of a circle
within a diamond within an oval
within a rectangle, designed by
Louis H. Sullivan for the Chicago
Stock Exchange, ca. 1894,
30 1/8" h. 4,180.00

ART DECO

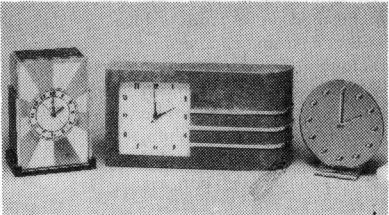

Art Deco Clocks

*Interest in Art Deco, a name given an art
movement stemming from the Paris International Exhibition of 1925, is at an all-time
high and continues to grow. This style flowered in the 1930's and actually continued into
the 1940's. A mood of flippancy is found in
its varied characteristics—zigzag lines resembling the lightning bolt, sometimes steps, often the use of sharply contrasting colors such
as black and white. Look for Art Deco prices
to continue to rise.*

Ashtray, chrome & glass flip-top,
frosted gazelle design in glass
base, "Chase" $30.00
Ashtray, copper-tone metal, figural

nude holding tray overhead, four paw feet, marked "Rembrandt" on base & tray, 10" h. figure, overall 26" h. 185.00

Book ends, cast iron, full figure nude woman kneeling w/leg extended forward & her body arched back, bronze finish, 5 x 7", pr. 65.00

Box, cov., porcelain, figure of an Art Deco lady w/lustre finish forms cover, her skirt forms the bowl, Japan, 2½ x 3½" 40.00

Cigarette lighter, table model, chrome & Bakelite, figure of a knight "Negbaur" 22.00

Clock, alarm-type, mirrored glass & chromed metal, circular blue mirrored glass face w/chromed metal hands & 12 balls for hour marks, raised on a rectangular brushed chromium base, designed by Gilbert Rohde, executed by Herman Miller Clock Co., Zeeland, Michigan, ca. 1932-33, unsigned, 6½" h. (ILLUS. right) 605.00

Clock, mantel-type, enamelled & chromed metal, rectangular face of radiating brush-burnished brass, set in chromed & black enamelled metal housing raised on a black Bakelite base, designed by Paul T. Frankl for Warren Telechron Co., ca. 1929, face painted "Telechron" & w/firm's applied tag, 7¾" h. (ILLUS. left) 170.00

Clock, table model, bird's-eye maple & chromed metal, square face w/black Arabic chapters, in a rectangular bird's-eye maple case w/rounded right side intersected by three chromed metal bands, designed by Gilbert Rohde, executed by Herman Miller Clock Co., Zeeland, Michigan, ca. 1932-33, 13 1/8" l. (ILLUS. center) 1,045.00

Cocktail shaker, chrome, horizontal alternating hammered & smooth panels, decorated black wood handle, "Farber Bros." 15.00

Cocktail shaker w/bar equipment, chrome, cast in the form of an airplane w/tail fins, propeller & removable wheels, two slim flasks w/screw tops as wings, other parts consisting of a cocktail strainer, small circular flask w/removable screw top, small round covered dish for garnishes & four small cordials, all contained within the body, stamped "D.R.G.M. 894884 MADE IN GERMANY," ca. 1930, '' '' l 2,420.00

Dresser set: hair brush, clothes brush, hand mirror, cov. powder box, perfume atomizer, two frames, two cov. rouge boxes & glass tray; celluloid, hot pink & black design on beige, 10 pcs. ... 195.00

Figure of a man playing tennis, wood, chrome & rubber, stylistically modeled as a bald-headed figure wearing a T-shirt & big-legged pants, his arm lifted as he serves the ball, on a flattened circular base, impressed "SK" within a triangle, probably Austrian, ca. 1930, 18 1/8" h. 1,100.00

Fishbowl, pale amber glass, on chalkware base modeled as a lady seated on rocks, original label, overall 4½ x 8¼", 9" h. ... 65.00

Hat rack, aluminum, upright rectangular form w/a rounded rectangular shelf at top continuing to two elongated D-form supports at the sides, each set w/three circular knobs for hats or coats & centering a rectangular mirror plate, the lower section set w/umbrella receptacle, probably America, ca. 1940, 25½" w., 5' 10½" h. 440.00

Lamp, bronze-washed white metal figure of a female nude sitting on pedestal gazing into 5" d. green globe shade 65.00

Lamp, spelter figure of a child artist painting, frosted cylinder shade at side, Paris, France seal, 7" 100.00

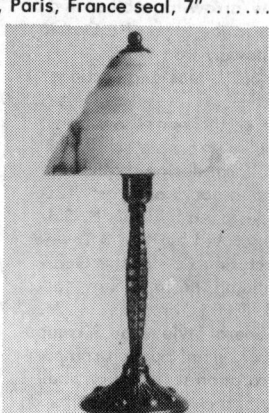

Edgar Brandt Art Deco Lamp

Lamp, wrought iron & alabaster, slender ovoid wrought-iron standard formed of upright horizontally-grooved bands continues to a textured trumpet-form foot molded w/a row of oval cabochons, the flaring circular grey & white alabaster shade carved w/concentric undulations, designed by Edgar

Brandt, stamped "E. BRANDT," ca. 1925, 11 1/8" d. shade, 21 5/8" h. (ILLUS.) 5,775.00

Mirror, wall-type, wrought iron, mirror plate w/a serpentine top & rounded lower edge set within a wide U-form frame applied w/three accordion-form bands, suspended by a thick metallic thread cord, France, ca. 1930, 32¼" w., 20" h................. 660.00

Powder jar, cov., six-sided, pink satin glass, Egyptian head finial on cover 39.00

Tea & coffee service: cov. teapot, cov. coffeepot, cov. sugar bowl & creamer; silver, each of paneled circular form on tiered circular foot, w/mounted wood handles & finials, the latter engraved w/a monogram, Jean E. Puiforcat, Paris, 20th c., 4 pcs. 3,850.00

Tie rack, cast iron, "Hear No Evil, Speak No Evil, See No Evil," women's faces instead of monkeys', enameled trim 110.00

Art Deco Chrome & Glass Tray

Tray, chrome & glass, rectangular glass surface painted w/an abstract design in red, black & ivory, chromed metal edge & gallery, the ends w/hinged metal & wood handles, on four rubber feet, American-made, ca. 1935, 19 5/8" l. w/handles (ILLUS.) 770.00

Vase, sterling silver, oval w/flared sides, lower body applied w/two bands of parcel-gilt scalloping, w/detachable silver plate liner, Jean E. Puiforcat, Paris, ca. 1940, 6¼" h. 7,150.00

ART NOUVEAU

Art Nouveau's primary thrust was between 1890 and 1905 but commercial Art Nouveau productions continued until about World War I. This style was a rebellion against historic tradition in art. Using natural forms as inspiration, it is primarily characterized by un-dulating or wave-like lines. Many objects were made in materials ranging from glass to metals. While interest in Art Nouveau still remains high, especially for jewelry in the Nouveau taste, prices appear to be leveling off.

Candelabra, pewter, five-light, Osiris patt., lobed cylindrical stem bulging at the center & applied w/four organic branches twisting back to the right & joining four curving branches above to become one, terminating in a bud-form knop supporting a scalloped bobeche & cup-form nozzle, the whole resting on a domed circular foot base w/heart-shaped foliate forms, impressed "OSIRIS," Walter Scherf & Co., Nuremberg, Germany, ca. 1900, 16" h., pr. $1,100.00

Card tray, pewter, molded design of a woman w/flowing hair at top, 4½ x 7"........................ 76.00

Claret jug w/original stopper, silver plate & green glass, flaring cylinder w/plated shaped mounts of the narrow spout & flaring base, joined by a whiplash branch-form handle, handle & stopper cast w/grapes, base w/pairs of mermaids w/tendril-like hair forming a continuous border embellished w/leaves, impressed "W.M.F." on base, ca. 1900, 15" h. 550.00

Coffee service: 11¼" h. cov. coffeepot, cov. sugar bowl, creamer & 14" l. oval tray; sterling silver, pear form, repousse & chased w/berried foliage, ear-form handles w/leafy terminals, bud finials, engraved monogram, Tiffany & Co., New York, 1902-07, 4 pcs. 4,070.00

Jardiniere, pottery, square body w/rounded sides tapering toward base, molded spear-shaped vertical bands of Art Nouveau design from base to rim, mottled green glaze, unsigned, early 20th c., 12½" w., 13" h. (chip) 605.00

Lamp, gilt-bronze, figure of Loie Fuller, the dancer clothed in voluminous drapery, her arms upheld & swirling a cloud of drapery above her enclosing a light socket, inscribed "Raoul Larche" & w/circular foundry stamp enclosing "Siot Decauville Paris Fondeur" & numbered T315, ca. 1900, 13" h. 14,300.00

Magnifying glass, sterling silver hollow handle w/ring at end, scrolled leaves decoration,

2 1/8" d. glass, Blackinton mark,
dated 1904, 6¼" l. 110.00
Mirror, hand-type, silver plate, children's faces w/wings in relief,
6 x 11"........................ 90.00
Mirror, table-type, silvered-pewter,
rectangular, the arched crest
pierced w/shaped oval panels
pierced w/berry-laden leafy
branches flanking a whiplash central panel, the lower frame cast
w/a reclining scantily clad sensu-
ous maiden w/flowers in her hair
surrounded by pierced leafage &
whiplash tendrils, Wurttember-
gische Metallwarenfabrik (WMF),
Geislingen, Germany, ca. 1900,
20½" h. 2,475.00
Mirror, table-type, sterling silver,
gently curved & tapered oblong
frame w/elaborate embossed
waves across bottom & up sides
w/nude maiden reclining in waves
across the top, dark oak backing
board, Birmingham, England hallmarks, 1902, 33½" h. 9,350.00
Pitcher, glass w/silver plated
mounts, cylindrical body w/a bulbous base, the neck capped
w/hinged lid & handle in scrolled
silver plate design, body decorated w/green leaves & fuchsia
blossoms in an undulating pattern,
the base mounted w/a band of
iris, resting on four scroll feet,
14½" h. 330.00

Art Nouveau Sterling Silver Tray

Tray, sterling silver, rectangular
w/rounded corners, decorated
w/repousse morning glories on a
matte ground, monogrammed in
center, W. Comyns & Sons, London, England, 1901, 7¾ x 11¼"
(ILLUS.)....................... 357.50
Vase, bronze, cast as cherub faces
in a swirling sea, brown patina
w/gilded faces, artist-signed
"Jules Meliedon 1896" & marked
"Louchet," 6" h. 315.00
Vase, gilt-bronze, figure of Loie Fuller

w/swirling robes forming sides & wide
flaring rim, cast from a model by
Hans Stotenberg Lerche, inscribed
"H.St. Lerche," w/Louchet foundry
seal, Germany, late 19th c.,
5¾" h. 1,430.00
Vases, sterling silver, baluster form
w/elongated flared foot, incurved
neck & wavy scalloped rim, the foot
applied & pierced w/undulating strapwork, the body encircled w/anemones
& foliage, the rim applied & pierced
w/conforming decoration, stamped
"TIFFANY & CO. - 15300 MAKERS
5158 - STERLING SILVER - 925-1000
- T," 1891-92, 15 3/8" h., pr...... 6,325.00

AUDUBON PRINTS

Black Backed Gull

*John James Audubon, American ornithol-
ogist and artist, is considered the finest nature artist in history. About 1820 he
conceived the idea of having a full color book
published portraying every known species of
American bird in its natural habitat. He spent
years in the wilderness capturing their beauty
in vivid color only to have great difficulty
finding a publisher. In 1826 he visited England, received immediate acclaim, and selected Robert Havell as his engraver. "Birds of
America," when completed, consisted of four
volumes of 435 individual plates, double-
elephant folio size, which are a combination
of aquatint, etching and line engraving. W.H.
Lizars of Edinburgh engraved the first ten
plates of this four volume series. These were
later retouched by Havell who produced the
complete set between 1827 and early 1839. In
the early 1840's, another definitive work, "Viviparous Quadrupeds of North America,"
containing 150 plates, was published in
America. Prices for Audubon's original*

double-elephant folio size prints are very high and beyond the means of the average collector. Subsequent editions of "Birds of America," especially the chromolithographs done by Julius Bien in New York (1859-60) and the smaller octavo (7 x 10½") edition of prints done by J.T. Bowen of Philadelphia in the 1840's are less expensive.

American Beaver - Plate XLVI, hand-colored plate from the "Viviparous Quadrupeds of North America," printed & colored by J.T. Bowen, Philadelphia, ca. 1845, 16 1/8 x 23 7/8" $880.00

American Redstart - Plate XL, hand-colored engraving by Robert Havell, Jr., London, 1827-1838, 12¼ x 19¼" 2,310.00

American Sparrow Hawk - Plate CXLII, hand-colored engraving by Robert Havell, Jr., London, 1827-38, 25¼" w., 31½" h. (mounted on board, margins slightly soiled w/short tear in right margin) 2,100.00

Barn Owl - Plate CLXXI, hand-colored engraving by Robert Havell, Jr., London, 1827-38, 26 7/8 x 39½" . .7,150.00

Barn Swallow - Plate CLXXIII, hand-colored engraving by Robert Havell, Jr., London, 1827-38, 12½ x 19½" 2,200.00

Black Backed Gull - Plate CCLI, hand-colored engraving by Robert Havell, Jr., London, 1827-38, 25 5/8 x 38" (ILLUS.) 2,310.00

Bonaparte's Flycatcher - Plate V, hand-colored engraving by W. H. Lizars, colored by Robert Havell, Sr., London, 1827-38, 12½ x 20 3/8" 1,210.00

Brant Goose - Plate CCCXCI, hand-colored engraving by Robert Havell, Jr., London, 1827-38, 25 3/8 x 38 1/8" 2,750.00

Californian Vulture - Plate CCCCXXVI, hand-colored engraving by Robert Havell, Jr., London, 1827-38, 25 3/8 x 38" 1,650.00

Carolina Parrot - Plate XXVI, hand-colored engraving by Robert Havell, Jr., London, 1827-38, 23 7/8 x 33¼" 12,100.00

Canada Lynx (Male) - Plate XVI, hand-colored engraving, printed & colored by J.T. Bowen, Philadelphia, ca. 1845, 17 x 24" . . . . 1,650.00 to 1,800.00

Common American Swan - Plate CCCXI, hand-colored engraving by Robert Havell, Jr., London, 1827-38, 25½ x 38 1/8" 14,300.00

Double-Crested Cormorant - Plate CCLVII, hand-colored engraving by

Robert Havell, Jr., London, 1827-38, 21 7/8 x 30½" 1,100.00

Dusky Duck - Plate CCCII, hand-colored engraving by Robert Havell, Jr., London, 1827-38, 18½ x 23 7/8" 8,800.00

Gadwall Duck - Plate CCCXLVIII, hand-colored engraving by Robert Havell, Jr., London, 1827-38, 16 7/8 x 24 7/8" 3,300.00

Great American Cock Male - Plate I, hand-colored engraving by W.H. Lizars, colored by Robert Havell, Sr., London, 1827, 25 1/8 x 37 7/8" 19,800.00

Great American Hen & Young - Plate VI, hand-colored engraving by W.H. Lizars, colored by Robert Havell, Sr., London, 1827, 25¾ x 38 3/8" 17,600.00

Grey Fox - Plate XXI, hand-colored engraving by J.T. Bowen, Philadelphia, ca. 1845, 17¾ x 23¾" . . . . 2,090.00 to 3,575.00

Ground Dove - Plate CLXXXII, hand-colored engraving by Robert Havell, Jr., London, 1827-38, 25" w., 31½" h. (mounted on board, margins soiled w/tear in right margin) 2,100.00

Hooded Merganser - Plate CCXXXII, hand-colored engraving by Robert Havell, Jr., London, 1827-38, 20 5/8 x 25 7/8" 2,530.00

Hutchin's Barnacle Goose - Plate CCLXXVII, hand-colored engraving by Robert Havell, Jr., London, 1827-38, 21 7/8 x 26" 1,650.00

Louisiana Heron - Plate CCXVII, hand-colored engraving by Robert Havell, Jr., London, 1827-38, 20 5/8 x 26" 17,600.00

Nuttalls Lesser-Marsh Hen - Plate CLXXV, hand-colored engraving by Robert Havell, Jr., London, 1827-38, 12 3/8 x 19 5/8" 770.00

Ocelot, or Leopard-Cat (Male) - Plate LXXXVI, hand-colored lithograph by J.T. Bowen, Philadelphia, ca. 1845, 17¾ x 24 5/8" 2,750.00

Passenger Pigeon - Plate LXII, hand-colored engraving by Robert Havell, Jr., London, 1827-38, 20 7/8' x 26" (ILLUS. top next page) 11,000.00

Pin-Tailed Duck - Plate CCXXVII, hand-colored engraving by Robert Havell, Jr., London, 1827-38, 20¾ x 25¾" 4,400.00

Red Headed Woodpecker - Plate XXVII, hand-colored engraving by Robert Havell, Jr., London, 1827-38, 25 3/8 x 31¾" 2,750.00

Red-Tailed Hawk - Plate LI, hand-

colored engraving by Robert
Havell, Jr., London, 1827-38,
25 3/8 x 38½" 2,200.00

Passenger Pigeon

Snow Goose - Plate CCCLXXXI, hand-
colored engraving by Robert
Havell, Jr., London, 1827-38,
22 x 35 7/8" 2,640.00

Swallow-Tailed Hawk - Plate LXXII,
hand-colored engraving by Robert
Havell, Jr., London, 1827-38,
20¾ x 27¼" 5,500.00

Swift Fox (Male) - Plate LII, hand-
colored lithograph by J.T. Bowen,
Philadelphia, ca. 1845,
18¾ x 23¾" 1,540.00

Tropic Bird - Plate CCLXII, hand-
colored engraving by Robert
Havell, Jr., London, 1827-38,
20 7/8 x 30 3/8"...............3,300.00

Virginia Partridge - Plate 289,
chromolithograph by J. Bien,
New York, New York, 1860,
24 x 36 1/8" 1,540.00

Virginian Partridge - Plate LXXVI,
hand-colored engraving by Robert
Havell, Jr., London, 1827-38,
37¾" w., 25½" h. (mounted on
board, cleaned & margins
trimmed) 5,225.00

Whooping Crane - Plate CCXXVI,
hand-colored engraving by Robert
Havell, Jr., London, 1827-38,
24 x 35 5/8" 11,000.00

AUTOGRAPHS

Values of autographs and autograph letters depend on such factors as content, scarcity and the fame of the writer. Values of good autograph material continue to rise. A.L.S. stands for "autographed letter signed;" L.S.

for "letter signed;" D.S. for "document signed" and S.P. for "signed photograph."

Alexandra Feodorovna, (1872-1918)
last Empress of Russia, wife of
Czar Nicholas II, A.L.S., August 30,
1913, to Countess Anastasia
Gendrikoff, on stationery w/her
gilt Imperial monogram $2,310.00

Arthur, Chester A., (1830-1886) 21st
President of the United States,
A.L.S., New York, Oct. 8, 1861, to
Thomas C. Acton, Commissioner
of Metropolitan Police, 1 p. 875.00

Beatles, S.P., black & white publicity
shot, signed by Paul McCartney,
Ringo Starr & John Lennon 242.00

Coolidge, Calvin, (1872-1933) 30th
President of the United States,
partially printed document signed
as President, Washington, June
30, 1927, appointing Jack Dewey
Hickerson, of Texas, a Foreign
Service Officer, 1 p. 350.00

Gauguin, Paul, (1848-1903) French
artist, A.L.S., Marquesas Islands,
ca. 1903 ....2,200.00

Grant, Ulysses S., (1822-1885) Commander of Union Armies at the
close of the Civil War & 18th
President of the United States,
D.S. as President, August 22, 1870,
1 p............................ 395.00

Hailey, Arthur, (1920-) American
author, A.L.S., quoting from his
best seller "Airport," 1 p 35.00

Harding, Warren G., (1865-1923)
29th President of the United
States, typed L.S. on U.S. Senate
letterhead Marion, Ohio, September 21, 1920, to John A. Stewart
as nominee of the Republican Party for President, 1 p. 350.00

Heidt, Horace, (1901-) American
band leader, S.P., 8 x 10"........ 45.00

Michael Jackson Signed Hat

Jackson, Michael, (1958-) musician,
autographed stage hat, black wool
felt fedora-style, "Michael Jackson"
fedora-style, "Michael Jackson"
printed within inner rim, auto-

graphed on outside brim "Love Michael Jackson," size medium (ILLUS.) 4,125.00

Johnson, Andrew, (1808-1875) 17th President of the United States, D.S. June 1, 1865, appointing Sartell Prentice a Captain in the Army, 1 p. 600.00

Kennedy, John F., (1917-1963) 35th President of the United States, three typed L.S. mentioning appreciation for campaign help & discussing textile industry & U.S. entry into organization for trade cooperation, including two related memoranda, dated from 1954 to 1956, 5 pcs. 1,980.00

Kenny, Bill, (1922?-1978) singer, member of The Ink Spots, S.P., 8 x 10" 65.00

Laughton, Charles, (1899-1962) actor, A.L.S., Hollywood, no date, to playwright Gilbert Miller, 3½ pp. 275.00

Lincoln, Abraham, (1809-1865) 16th President of the United States, D.S., March 19, 1865, appointing Edward R. Farnam Deputy Postmaster at South Bend, Indiana, counter-signed by William Seward, usual folds, in matted frame, 10 x 14" 2,475.00

O'Neill, Rose, (1874-1944) American illustrator & creator of the "Kewpies," & Vance Randolph, American author, autographed book "An Ozark Anthology," w/forward by Vance Randolph 165.00

Powell, Dick, (1904-63) actor, director, producer, S.P., framed, 9½ x 12¼" 10.00

Presley, Elvis, (1935-1977) musician & actor, S.P., color photograph, bust portrait w/printed facsimile signature below & signed in black marker above, 1974, framed, 11½ x 14½" 462.00

Roosevelt, Theodore, (1858-1919) 26th President of the United States, S.P., photograph of Roosevelt as President, dated 1908 .... 400.00

Webster, Daniel, (1782-1852) A.L.S., dated 1848 .... 275.00

AUTOMOBILE LITERATURE

Auto Electrician's Manual, 1928, hardbound, 6½ lb. $20.00

Automobile Blue Book Touring Guide, 1926 .... 15.00

Blumenthal Red Book of Auto-Top &

Body Hardware, Limo Mountings, 1920's, 280 pp. 12.50

Book, "History of Studebaker Corp.," 1924 .... 65.00

Buick owner's manual, 1949 .... 11.00

Chevrolet repair manual, 1931 ...... 26.00

Chevrolet shop manual, 1939 .... 10.00

Chrysler color folder, 1940 .... 15.00

Corvair shop manual, 1961 .... 25.00

DeSoto showroom catalog, 1940 .... 15.00

Dodge Brothers "Book of Information," 1922..................... 24.00

Dodge Luxury Liner showroom catalog, 1940 .... 17.00

Dyke's Automobile Encyclopedia, 1917 .... 22.50

Edsel owner's manual, 1959 .... 35.00

Ford catalog "Enclosed Cars," 1915, 16 pp......................... 24.00

Ford Motor Co. Home Almanac & Facts Book, 1938 .... 8.00

Ford owner's manual, "Care & Operation of Ford Motor Car & Truck & Fordson Tractor," 1927, 293 pp. ... 16.00

Ford owner's manual, 1948 .... 12.50

Ford Thunderbird sales brochure, 1959, eight pages of color, 6¼ x 9" 12.00

Kaiser sales brochure, 1952 .... 12.50

LaFayette showroom catalog, 1920's, full-color 22.00

Lincoln Continental maintenance manual, 1961 .... 30.00

Magazine, "Henney Motor Car 100th Year of Progress," 1939, car made in Freeport, Illinois 45.00

Mississippi Motor News, Iowa & Illinois AAA Club, 1926, December, 1927 models shown, lady on cover 8.50

Motor Age Magazine, 1907, October 31, Auto Club Am. Show issue, ads, new cars, 262 pp. 25.00

Nash Model 41 Series showroom catalog, 1920's 17.00

Nash Special Six Series catalog, 1915, 16 pp. 20.00

Official Handbook of Automobiles, 1929, leather bound, photographs of cars, taxis, buses, trucks & electrics, 6 x 9½", 189 pp. 65.00

Oldsmobile catalog, 1937 .... 29.00

Packard folder, "Clipper," 1956 ..... 8.00

Packard handbook, 1914 .... 20.00

Plymouth brochure, 1937 .... 18.00

Pontiac brochure, 1947............. 10.00

Trade Journal, 1920, February, Chicago Show No., 640 pp........ 32.00

AUTOMOBILES

Bentley, 1958 Model S-1 Saloon, six-

cylinder engine, left-hand drive,
grey & black steel & aluminum
body w/dark green leather
upholstery $17,000.00
Cadillac, 1969 Fleetwood Brougham,
four-door, pale grey exterior
w/grey cloth interior, black vinyl
roof, odometer reading 30,250 ...1,540.00
Chevrolet, 1948 coupe............2,200.00
Chevrolet, 1956 pickup truck.......2,700.00
Ford, 1929 Model A Woody, pie
delivery wagon................9,500.00
Ford, 1946 coupe 3,100.00
Ford, 1950 pickup truck, new tires
& front end, V-8 flat head engine,
original 51,000 miles............1,200.00
Ford, 1971 Thunderbird, one-owner,
60,000 + miles.................6,500.00
Jaguar, 1963 Mark X, black exterior,
beige leather interior, odometer
reading 28,040 ....14,850.00
Lincoln, 1932 sedan 34,000.00
Mercedes Benz, 1968 Model 280SE/C/8
convertible, automatic transmission,
air conditioning, leather interior,
light blue, approximate mileage
62,317 ....24,200.00
Mercedes Benz, 1968 Model 250SL
roadster, automatic transmission,
air conditioning, hard & soft convertible tops, light blue (a
wheel cover missing) 15,400.00
Oakland, 1922 touring car, full-size,
unrestored 600.00
Pontiac, 1962 Catalina Safari station
wagon, pale metallic green exterior, green vinyl interior, odometer reading 26,978............. 715.00

1971 Rolls Royce Silver Shadow

Rolls Royce, 1971 Silver Shadow
Saloon, four-door, 410 cubic inch,
eight cylinder engine, black w/tan
leather interior, odometer reading
54,183 (ILLUS.)................23,100.00
Rolls Royce, 1975 Silver Shadow
sedan, Chassis No. SRD21954,
Engine No. 21954, four-door, left-
hand drive, painted black w/gold
coach lining, trimmed in tan
leather, w/sheepskin rugs, fitted
w/Blaupunkt AM/FM radio & Pio-

neer stereo, air conditioning,
recorded mileage 83,632 ....25,300.00
Studebaker, 1957 President, four-
door, original 46,000 miles 4,000.00

AUTOMOTIVE COLLECTIBLES

Edison Battery Oil Bottle

Bottle, "Edison Battery Oil, Made in
U.S.A., Thomas A. Edison Incorpo-
rated, Bloomfield, N.J., U.S.A.,"
w/original contents, 4½" h.
(ILLUS.)........................ $25.00
Bumpers, rear, "Ford Model A,"
pr............................ 37.50
Carburetor, "Rayfield L2," brass,
1911 .... 50.00
Carburetor, "Stromberg Motor
Devices Co., Chicago, 1909,"
brass 25.00
Chauffeur's badge, 1903, Chicago ... 100.00
Chauffeur's badge, 1926 or 1928,
California, each 36.00
Chauffeur's badge, 1926, Chicago ... 15.00
Chauffeur's badge, 1928, Arizona ... 25.00
Chauffeur's badge, 1931,
California 13.00
Clock, Waltham, 8-day, in tinted,
beveled mirror 55.00
Clock, "Rolls-Royce" 75.00
Distributor, "Ford Model A," Mallory
Twin Point, unused 49.00
Emblem, "Durant".................. 35.00
Gasoline measuring stick, "Ford,"
Atwater Kent, dated 1909 .... 25.00
Gasoline nozzle, "Buckeye," brass,
1926 patent................... 47.50
Gasoline pump, cast iron, large
hand crank, 1915, 5' h. 195.00
Gasoline pump, "194 Butler,"
w/Standard Gold Crown globe,
complete 1,500.00
Gasoline pump globe, "Standard
Gold Crown".................. 225.00
Gearshift knob, marbleized green &
white glass 17.50

Gearshift knob, marbleized grey &
brown plastic 5.00
Gearshift knob, marbleized red &
white glass 42.00
Head lamps, "Ford Model T," pr. ... 50.00
Hood ornament, "Chevrolet," 1935 .. 30.00
Hood ornament, "Pontiac," Indian
head 22.00
Hood ornament, chrome, Art Nou-
veau woman w/flowing hair 47.50
Hood ornament, chrome, flying ea-
gle, 6 x 8½" 26.00
Hood ornament, tin, "Safety First
Traffic Cop," 8" h. 275.00
Horn, "Ford Model T," brass,
complete 200.00
Hubcap, "Ford," 1937 .... 10.00
Hubcap, "Tucker" 20.00
Jack, "Ford Model T," cogwheel-
type 15.00
Lap robe, bearskin 225.00
License plate, 1910, Pennsylvania ... 45.00
License plate, 1913, Massachusetts,
graniteware 22.00
License plates, 1922, Pennsylvania,
pr............................. 20.00
License plates, 1925, California,
pr............................. 35.00
License plate, 1931, Massachusetts.. 6.00
License plates, 1942, Idaho, pr...... 40.00
License plate light, "Ford," 1927 or
1929, each..................... 45.00
Motometer, "Buick," Boyce 40.00
Motometer, "Dodge," Boyce 45.00
Motometer, "Overland" 28.00
Oil can, squirt-type, "Quick Load" .. 18.50
Oiler, "Ford Model T," Everready,
automatic, w/instructions ..75.00 to 85.00
Oil gauge, sight-type, brass &
glass.......................... 25.00
Phonograph record, "Chevrolet," in-
formation on 1932 models, given
to dealers 40.00
Radiator cap, "Ford Model T" 15.00
Radiator cap, "Willys-Knight" 45.00
Radiator flag, "Detinas No. 600,"
silk & lisle flag set & boulevard
holder, enameled front angle
plate......................... 250.00
Spark coils, "Ford Model T," Genuine KW, vibrator-type, unused 20.00
Stop & tail lamp lens, "Ford," plastic, manufactured by Dietz in
original box, 1956, pr. 30.00
Timer, "Ford Model T," crystal, glass
front for visible ignition.......... 25.00
Tire patch kit, "Dutch Girl," Dutch
girl & "Forever Tight," complete
repair kit inside can, 1940's 15.00
Tire pressure gauge, "Economaster,"
original oak box & instructions ... 75.00
Tire pressure gauge, dial-type,
w/leather case................. 18.00
Torch lamp, "Dietz Highway," round

ball-type, used when making
repairs on highway, 1930's 48.00
Vase, clear cut glass, floral
design 47.00
Vase, clear pressed glass, cornucopia shape, 11" h................ 75.00
Vases w/holders, bud, marigold
Carnival glass, pr............... 65.00
Wheel cover spinners, Rambler Clas-
sic or Ambassador, set of 4, each
set........................... 42.00
Whistle, "Aeromore," exhaust-type,
cast iron w/four brass tubes,
1913 .... 30.00
Whistle, "Fulton No. 1 Aeromore,"
exhaust-type.................. 75.00
Wrench, "Ford," 1917, 5¼" l....... 7.50
Wrenches, "Ford Model T," script,
open-end & box-types, 8 pcs..... 25.00
Wrench, "Maxwell".............. 8.00

AVIATION COLLECTIBLES

Recently much interest has been shown in collecting items associated with the early days of the "flying machine." In addition to relics, flying adjuncts and literature relating to the early days of flight, collectors also seek out items that picture the more renowned early pilots, some of whom became folk-heroes in their own lifetimes, as well as the early planes themselves.

Book, "Alphabet of Aviation," 1928,
full-page drawings every other
page $25.00
Book, "Conquest of Air," by Bertron,
1910, engravings & photographs of
balloons, dirigibles & airplanes,
432 pp........................ 35.00
Book, "Lindberghs...Distinguished
Family," by O'Brien, 1935,
illustrated 10.00
Book, "Naval Aviation," by Henry
Woodhouse, 1917, illustrated,
287 pp........................ 75.00
Clock, Art Deco style, model of a
wooden airplane propeller
w/chromed 5" d. Waterbury dial
in center hub, free-standing on
cowled landing gear, 24" l.
overall 145.00
Crocheted piece, Spirit of St. Louis
plane in center, 17½ x 25"....... 62.00
Cup & saucer, demitasse, china,
"Trans-World Airlines," made by
Rosenthal for the Royal Ambassador Flights, white w/red banner
across, center a gold star w/"RA"
in middle..................... 15.00
Flight schedule, 1954, "North Central
Airlines" 6.50

Map, "American Airlines System
Map," folding-type, colorful, 1949,
16 x 20"........................ 9.50
Model of an airplane, painted wood,
stylized top wing monoplane
w/radial engine, rotating propeller & wheels, painted yellow
w/khaki & red detailing, America,
1930's, 26¾" fuselage, 28"
wingspan..................... 385.00
Model of a monoplane, painted
wood & wire fuselage w/var-
nished linen wings, rudder & rear
flaps, wooden propeller turns
when key on clockwork mock
gasoline engine is activated,
painted wheels, weigh lid
w/glass, a German papier-mache
figure of Santa Claus at controls,
made by Charles R. Witteman,
Staten Island, New York, ca. 1912,
62" l., 78" wingspan 2,200.00
Passenger's award certificate,
"TWA," Atlantic crossing, 1957,
colorful, 8½ x 11"............... 8.00
Pencil box, tin, Charles Lindbergh
pictured 40.00
Portrait, Charles Lindbergh, black &
white, by Arlac Ink Co., 1927,
8½ x 11"...................... 8.00
Postcard, Charles Lindbergh & Thomas Edison together in real 1927
photograph 21.00
Propeller, wood, marked "Lang...
Whitestone L.L.," 8½ ft. l.
w/metal tips................... 385.00
Whiskey decanter w/stopper, blue
glass, model of the "Spirit of St.
Louis" w/two glasses hanging
from the wings, U.S. Glass
Company 210.00

BABY MEMENTOES

*Everyone dotes on the new baby and
through many generations some exquisite
and unique gifts have been carefully selected with a special infant in mind. Collectors
now seek items from a varied assortment of
baby mementoes, once tokens of affection to
the newborn babe. Also see CHILDREN'S
BOOKS and CHILDREN'S MUGS.*

Breakfast set: 3¼" h. mug, 7½" d.
plate & bowl; sterling silver,
repousse & chased w/fruit &
vines, engraved "Robin," Black,
Starr & Frost, New York, ca. 1930,
3 pcs..........................$770.00
Carriage (or buggy), painted wood,
large back wheels & smaller front
wheels on metal frame support

narrow shaped wooden body &
arched handle painted white
w/gold, red & blue striping, upholstered seat, slender, lacy metal adjustable frame supports cloth
top, 19th c., 45" l. (worn paint,
worn upholstery & top) 700.00
Cup, silver plate, grape design,
Rogers Quadruple Plate.......... 35.00
Cup, sterling silver, bright-cut design, Reed & Barton 70.00
Feeding dish, china, Dutch children
scene, McNicol Pottery, East Liverpool, Ohio..................... 50.00
Feeding dish, earthenware, Campbell Kids decoration, Buffalo
Pottery 92.00
Feeding dish, earthenware, colorful
scene & verse, "This is the House
that Jack Built," marked "Roma,"
5¼" d., 2" h. 28.00
Feeding dish, glass, three-part, de-
sign on underside, rim has verse
"See Saw Margery Daw" &
"Where Are You Going My Pretty
Maid," scene of children in each
section, two dogs, cat & pig on
rim, green..................... 24.00
Feeding dish, hot water-type, china,
design of chicks around edge, yellow glaze, Goebel Co.,
Germany 90.00
Feeding set: mug, bowl & plate;
porcelain, cobalt trim, scenes of
Little Boy Blue, Old King Cole &
Jack Horner, each w/own verse,
3 pcs.......................... 60.00
Feeding set: mug, bowl & plate;
porcelain, cobalt lettering w/vari-
ous animals between letters, Germany, 3 pcs.................... 70.00
Feeding set: mug & saucer, bowl &
plate; earthenware, lettering &
trim in blue, scene of a dressed
bunny & mouse, marked "Lord
Nelson Pottery, England," 4 pcs... 75.00
Feeding spoon, silver, bear w/ruck-
sack & lunchbox, "830" silver
mark, Denmark, 5½" l.......... 30.00
Feeding spoon, silver plate, "Mary
Had A Little Lamb," Rogers 35.00
Feeding spoon w/curved handle,
sterling silver ABC's on handle,
Watson Company, Attleboro,
Massachusetts 40.00
Food pusher, silver plate, Moselle
patt., monogrammed 95.00
Food pusher, sterling silver, Canter-
bury patt., Whiting Mfg. Co. 35.00
Food pusher, sterling silver, Cupids
patt., Unger Brothers 75.00
Food pusher, sterling silver, Dor-
chester patt., Watson, Newell &
Co., early 20th c. 35.00

Food pusher, sterling silver,
Louis XV patt., Whiting Mfg.
Co. 30.00
Food pusher, sterling silver, Violet
patt., Whiting Mfg. Co. 90.00
Fork, silver plate, "Little Boy Blue,"
Rogers 35.00
Fork, sterling silver, Cordis patt.,
Tiffany & Co. 20.00
Fork & spoon, sterling silver, Lap-
over-Edge patt., Tiffany & Co.,
2 pcs. 125.00
Fork & spoon, sterling silver,
Repousse patt., S. Kirk & Sons,
2 pcs. 55.00
Napkin ring, silver plate, embossed
figure of Bambi, marked "WDP
800," Walt Disney Productions 300.00
Pillow, embroidered child w/wheel-
barrow full of flowers, laced rib-
bon edge, 1920's 18.00
Rattle, miniature, silver, chased
w/foliage, hung w/four balls,
w/coral teether, ca. 1820,
1¾" l. 770.00
Rattle, silver plate, comic standing
figure of policeman, marked
"E.P.N.S.," celluloid ring at top,
3¾" l. overall 65.00
Rattle, sterling silver, model of a
cat's head, English hallmarks,
Victorian 115.00
Rattle, sterling silver, model of a
clown's head, English hallmarks,
Victorian 115.00
Rattle, sterling silver, figure of an
English Bobby, English
hallmarks 125.00
Rattle, sterling silver disc w/bells,
mother-of-pearl ring & handle,
English hallmarks 100.00
Teething ring, mother-of-pearl &
sterling silver, ornate face &
scrollwork 60.00

BAKELITE

Bakelite is the trade-mark for a group of
thermoplastics invented by Leo Hendrik
Baekeland, an American chemist who invented this early form of plastic in 1909, only
twenty years after immigrating to New York
City from his native Belgium where he had
taught at the University of Ghent. Bakelite
opened the door to modern plastics and was
widely used as an electrical insulating material replacing the flammable celluloid. Jewelry
designers of the 1920's considered Bakelite
the perfect medium to create pieces in the Art
Deco style and today Bakelite bracelets, earrings and pins of this period are finding favor with another generation of modish
women.

Barometer, "Taylor," dated 1940,
two-color $20.00
Belt, Bakelite & chrome, four-color. .   50.00
Belt buckle, Egyptian revival design
w/ivory profile on black Bakelite
ground 170.00
Bracelet, bangle-type, red,
5/8" w. 12.00
Brooch, carved red & black cameo . .   18.00
Carving set, ornate mustard-colored
handles, original box & wrappers,
3 pcs. 60.00
Cigarette box, half-cylinder shape,
rotates open, dark brown 30.00
Pin, horse head w/shoes & boots . . .   65.00
Pin, model of a turtle, black & gold,
made in France 19.00
Radio, "Addison," Art Deco style in
swirled green & yellow, plays 550.00
Spoon set, eight teaspoons & eight
soup spoons, red handles, set of
16 . . . .   15.00

BANKS

Original early mechanical and cast-iron still
banks are in great demand with collectors and
their scarcity has caused numerous reproductions of both types and the novice collector
is urged to exercise caution. The early
mechanical banks are especially scarce and
some versions are seldom offered for sale but,
rather, are traded with fellow collectors attempting to upgrade an existing collection.
Numbers before mechanical banks refer to
those in John Meyer's Handbook of Old
Mechanical Banks. In past years, our standard reference for cast-iron still banks was
Hubert B. Whiting's book Old Iron Still
Banks, but because this work is out of print
and a beautiful new book, The Penny Bank
Book - Collecting Still Banks by Andy and
Susan Moore pictures and describes numerous additional banks, we now use the Moore
numbers as a reference preceding each listing and indicate the Whiting reference in
parenthesis at the end. The still banks listed
are old and in good original condition with
good paint and no repair unless otherwise noted. An asterisk (*) indicates this bank has
been reproduced at some time.

MECHANICAL

5   Always Did 'Spise a Mule
    (riding mule). $600.00
23 Boy on Trapeze . .1,500.00 to 2,000.00
33 Cabin . . . . .325.00 to 350.00
39 Cat & Mouse 1,650.00
41 Cat - Jumps for mouse 18,700.00

Clown on Globe

49 Clown on Globe (ILLUS.).....1,980.00
51 Confectionery Store.........5,170.00
53 Creedmore - Soldier aims Ri-
     fle at Target in Tree
     Trunk................... 400.00
56 Darktown Battery...........1,300.00
78 Elephant - Ten O'Clock.....20,350.00

Elephant Bank

79 Elephant - Three Stars
     (ILLUS.).................. 550.00
82 Elephant with Man in
     Howdah.................. 225.00
97 Fowler.........3,500.00 to 4,000.00

Girl Skipping Rope

109 Girl Skipping Rope
      (ILLUS.)................17,600.00
111 Globe on Arc.............. 138.00
126 Horse Race
      (ILLUS.).....12,000.00 to 13,200.00

Horse Race

130 Initiating Bank - First
      Degree.................9,350.00
133 Jolly Nigger, red coat, white
      collar, blue tie
      (aluminum)............. 175.00
154 Magician.................9,050.00
156 Mason and Hod
      Carrier.......5,000.00 to 10,500.00
177 Organ Bank - with Monkey,
      Cat, and Dog......475.00 to 575.00
178 Organ Bank - with Monkey,
      Boy & Girl, patented 1882.. 485.00
186 Panorama Bank..6,500.00 to 9,350.00

Picture Gallery

192 Picture Gallery
      (ILLUS.).......9,000.00 to 10,500.00
222 Stump Speaker....750.00 to 1,000.00
      Rocket bank, metal, 1957
      Houston bank give-away,
      coin shoots into capsule,
      11" h..................... 60.00
      Southern Comfort - Soldier
      Shoots Coin into Bottle.... 62.00

STILL

1621 Apple on Twig & Leaf - with
       Bumblebee on face of
       apple, cast iron, Kyser
       & Rex, Pennsylvania,
       1882, 5¼" w.
       (W. 299).........600.00 to 650.00
20   Baseball Player, cast iron,
       A.C. Williams Coin, Ohio,

ca. 1909, 5¾" h.
(W. 10)..........135.00 to 170.00

1450 Battleship "Oregon" - small,
cast iron, J. & E. Stevens
Co., Connecticut, 1891-
1906, 5 1/16" l.
(W. 144).........200.00 to 225.00

715 Bear - Begging, cast iron,
A.C. Williams, ca. 1910
& Arcade Mfg. Co., Illinios,
1910-25, 5½" h. (W. 330)*.. 65.00

1308 Bear - Bear Stealing Honey
from Beehive, cast iron,
Sydenham & McOustra,
England, ca. 1908, 7" h.
(W. 169)*................. 175.00

701 Bear - Bear Stealing Pig, cast
iron, American-made,
5½" h. (W. 246)*......... 750.00

713 Bear - Mean Bear - standing
w/paws clasped at waist,
cast iron, Hubley Mfg. Co.,
Pennsylvania, ca. 1906,
5½" h. (W. 329)*......... 65.00

80 Billiken variant - "Billiken
Shoes Bring Luck" across
chest, cast iron, A.C.
Williams, ca. 1909, 4¼" h.
(W. 50)................... 65.00

676 Bird - Eagle - Old Abe
w/Shield, cast iron, American-made, ca. 1880,
3 7/8" h.
(W. 255).........725.00 to 750.00

"Save and Smile Money Box"

24 Black Boy - caricature head
w/hat, "Save and Smile
Money Box" on brim of hat,
cast iron, Sydenham &
McOustra or Chamberlain &
Hill, England, 4" w., 4" h.,
W. 46 * (ILLUS.) 350.00

167 Black Man - "Give Me A Penny," cast iron, Wing Mfg.
Co., Illinois, ca. 1894,
5 5/8" h. 250.00

173 Black Man - Darkey (Share-
cropper), toes visible on
one foot, A.C. Williams,
ca. 1900, 5½" h.
(W. 18)..........125.00 to 150.00

45 Boy Scout, cast iron, A.C.
Williams, ca. 1910, 6" h.
(W. 14)*................. 100.00

560 Buffalo - small, cast iron,
Arcade, 1920-25 & A.C. Wil-
liams, 1920-34, 4½" l.
(W. 208)................. 90.00

1210 Building - Boston State House
(Statehouse w/Gold Dome),
cast iron, Smith & Egge, Connecticut, 3½" sq., 5" h.
(W. 271)................1,050.00

980 Building (Church) - Cologne
Cathedral - "Dom-Koln," silvered lead, Germany,
1920's, 4 1/8 x 1½ x 3¾".. 85.00

988 Building (Church) - Old South
Church - replica of Building,
cast iron, American-made,
9¾" h................... 600.00

1077 Building - Columbia, replica
of Columbian Exposition
building, cast iron, Kenton
Hardware Mfg. Co., Ohio,
1893-1904, 5½" sq., 7" h.
(W. 429)................. 225.00

1230 Building - Crown with Tower,
cast iron, J. & E.
Stevens(?), 2 3/8 x
2¾ x 3 3/16"............. 120.00

1145 Building - Cupola Bank -
large, cast iron, Vermont
Novelty Works, 1869 & J. &
E. Stevens, 1872, 5½" h.
(W. 305)................. 135.00

1183 Building - Domed "Bank" -
large, cast iron, A.C. Williams, 1899-1934, 4 x
2 3/8", 4¾" h. (W. 421).... 35.00

1012 Building - 1876 Bank, cast
iron, H.L. Judd Mfg. Co.,
Connecticut, ca. 1895,
2 7/8" h. (W. 389)......... 100.00

1009 Building (Garage) - One Car
Garage, cast iron, A.C. Williams, 1927-31, 2½ x
2 x 1 7/8"............... 69.00

1010 Building (Garage) - Two Car
Garage, cast iron, A.C. Wil-
liams, 1927-31, 2½" h.
(W. 304)................. 135.00

1019 Building - "Home Bank,"
w/fat man on doorstep,
cast iron, H.L. Judd,
3½" sq., 4" h.
(W. 333).........150.00 to 200.00

1201 Building - Home Savings -
"Property of the Peoples
Savings Bank, Grand
Rapids, Mich." over door,
cast iron, American-made,
8 1/8 x 6¼", 10½" h. 425.00

1236 Building - "Home Savings
Bank" w/Finial, cast iron,
J. & E. Stevens, ca. 1891,
2¾ x 2", 3½" h. (W. 345).. 105.00

993 Building (House) - Colonial

House (House w/Porch - small), cast iron, A.C. Williams, 1910-31, 2½ x 2 1/8", 3" h. (W. 404)...........60.00 to 90.00

1029 Building (House) - Gingerbread House, cast iron, key locked trap, France, 3 7/8 x 4¼ x 3 1/8" 1,200.00

1000 Building (House) - One Story House, cast iron, J. & E. Stevens, 1883 & Grey Iron Casting Co., Pennsylvania, 1903, 2¼" w., 3" h. (W. 357)................. 65.00

1002 Building (House) - Two Story House, cast iron, A.C. Williams, 1931-34, 3" h. (W. 355) 35.00

1142 Building (House) - Victorian House, two-storied w/two chimneys & "Bank" on front, cast iron, J. & E. Stevens, 1892, 3¼" w., 4½" h. (W. 352)........... 75.00

1202 Building - Independence Hall Tower, cast iron, Enterprise Mfg. Co., Pennsylvania, ca. 1876, 3 7/8 x 3 7/8", 9½" h................... 260.00

1242 Building - Independence Hall - large, cast iron, Enterprise Mfg., ca. 1876, 9 3/8 x 8", 10" h. (W. 447)* ..400.00 to 450.00

1023 Building - Log Cabin, cast iron, Kyser & Rex, ca. 1882, 3¼ x 2¾", 2½" h. (W. 297)................. 184.00

1116 Building - Palace, ornate building w/tower, double stairway & colonnaded front, cast iron, Ives Mfg. Co., Connecticut, ca. 1885, 8 x 5", 7½" h. (W. 433).... 850.00

1124 Building - Roof Bank, cast iron, Grey Iron, 1903-28, 3¾ x 3¼", 5¼" h. 75.00

1170 Building - Rose Window, building w/towers at front corners, cast iron, England, 2¼ x 1½", 2¼" h. (W. 308)................. 145.00

1241 Building - Skyscraper (six posts), cast iron, A.C. Williams, 1900-31, 4 x 3", 6½" h. (W. 411)*.......... 100.00

1085 Building - "State Bank" - smallest size, cast iron, Kenton, ca. 1890's, 2" w., 3" h. (W. 442)............. 90.00

1053 Building - U.S. Treasury "Bank," replica of Sub-Treasury Building in New York, cast iron w/sheet

metal base, Grey Iron, 1925-28, 3¾" w., 3¼" h. (W. 379)*................. 80.00

1179 Building - Villa, two-story building w/ornamental top & four corner towers, cast iron, Kyser & Rex, ca. 1894, 5 x 3", 5½" h. (W. 376).... 185.00

241 Buster Brown & Tige, cast iron, A.C. Williams, 1910-32, 5½" h. (W. 2)*...... 145.00

242 Buster Brown & Tige (paint variation), cast iron, A.C. Williams, 1920's, 5½" h. (W. 2)*................. 90.00

54 Butler (General), man in form of frog, reads "Bonds & Yachts for Me - For the Masses This is $1,000,000," cast iron, J. & E. Stevens, ca. 1884 (W. 294) ....850.00 to 1,000.00

768 Camel - small, cast iron, Hubley & A.C. Williams, 1920-30's, 4¾" h. 90.00

767 Camel - large, cast iron, A.C. Williams, 1920's, 6¼" l., 7¼" h. (W. 201)........... 234.00

770 Camel Kneeling with Pack, cast iron, Kyser & Rex, 1889, 4 7/8" l., 2½" h., (W. 256).........350.00 to 450.00

163 Campbell Kids, cast iron, A.C. Williams, 1910-20, 3¼" h. (W. 45)*.........135.00 to 185.00

352 Cat with Ball, cast iron, A.C. Williams, 1905-19, 5 5/8" l. (W. 247).........125.00 to 150.00

353 Cat w/Ball, cast iron, American-made, 5 5/8" l., 2½" h. 165.00

Kitty Bank

349 Cat - Kitty Bank, kitten w/ribbon at neck, cast iron, Hubley, 1930-46, 4¾" h., W. 335 (ILLUS.)............ 65.00

1545 Clock - Gold Dollar (Eagle Clock), gold dollar face embossed "Save Your Pennies to Make Dollars," cast iron

& steel, Arcade, 1910-13,
3½" d. (W. 226) ..150.00 to 200.00

1544　Clock - "A Money Saver" - on
face, cast iron & steel, Arcade, 1909-20's, 3½" d.
(W. 224)* 54.00

1546　Clock - "Time is Money" - on
face, cast iron, A.C. Williams, 1909-31, 3½" h.
(W. 225)* 60.00

211　Clown, standing figure
w/pointed hat, cast iron,
A.C. Williams, ca. 1908,
6¼" h. (W. 29)* ...80.00 to 100.00

1315　"Coronation Bank" (George
V), cast iron, Sydenham &
McOustra (?), 1911,
6 5/8 x 4 1/8" * 125.00

544　Cow - Holstein, standing,
small, cast iron, Arcade,
1910-20, 3½" h., 4½" l.
(W. 188) 138.00

553　Cow - standing, cast iron,
A.C. Williams, 1920's,
3¼" h., 5¼" l.
(W. 200)* ....75.00 to 85.00

413　Dog - Boston Bulldog, seated,
cast iron, Hubley, 1930's,
5½" l. (W. 114) 100.00

421　Dog - Boston Bull Terrier -
standing, cast iron, Vindex
Toys, 1931, 5¾ x 5¼"
(W. 112).........100.00 to 125.00

414　Dog - "Cutie," puppy w/rib-
bon at neck, cast iron,
Hubley, ca. 1914,
3 7/8" h. (W. 334) 82.00

417　Dog - "Fido" on collar, cast
iron, Hubley, 1914-46, 5" h.
(W. 337)* 95.00

440　Dog - Newfoundland, standing animal, cast iron, Arcade, 1910- mid-30's,
5½" l., 3½" h. (W. 107) ... 40.00

436　Dog - Retriever with Pack,
cast iron, American-made,
5¼" l., 4 11/16" h. * 30.00

St. Bernard with Pack

439　Dog - St. Bernard with Pack,
small, cast iron, A.C. Wil-

liams, 1905-30, 3¾" h.,
W. 106 * (ILLUS.) 58.00

419　Dog - Scottie, seated, cast
iron, Hubley, 1930-40, 5" h.
(W. 110) 115.00

428　Dog - Tiny Scottie, cast iron,
American-made,
3 1/8" h. 325.00

409　Dog - Spitz, cast iron, Grey
Iron, ca. 1928, 4½" h.,
4¼" l. ....200.00 to 225.00

438　Dog - Water Spaniel w/Pack -
"I Hear a Call," American-
made, 5 3/8 x 7 7/8" 55.00

"Dolphin" Bank

33　"Dolphin," boy in boat
w/"Dolphin" on side, cast
iron, Grey Iron (?), ca.
1900 (?), 4½" h. (ILLUS.) ... 300.00

498　Donkey (hinged saddle), lead,
trick lock, Japan, 3 3/8" l.,
3 5/8" h. 45.00

500　Donkey (large), cast iron,
A.C. Williams, 1920's,
6¼" l. (W. 197) 158.00

615　Duck Bank, cast iron, A.C.
Williams, 1909-35, 4 7/8" h.
(W. 211) 150.00

16　Dutch Girl, cast iron, Grey
Iron (?), 6½" h.
(W. 24)..........400.00 to 625.00

1075　Eiffel Tower, cast iron,
England, 10 3/8" h........ 475.00

445　Elephant - Seated Elephant
w/Turned Trunk, cast iron,
American-made, 4¼" h.
(W. 66) 555.00

450　Elephant - Art Deco Elephant,
w/"G.O.P." on side, cast
iron, American-made,
5½" l., 4" h. (W. 72) 155.00

455　Elephant - Swivel Trunk,
small, cast iron, American-
made, 3½" l. (W. 70) 200.00

457　Elephant w/Howdah (tiny),
cast iron, A.C. Williams,
1934, 3¼" l., 2½" h.
(W. 69) 65.00

447 Elephant - Elephant with Bent
Knee, cast iron, Kenton,
1904, worn olive green,
4 7/8" l., 3½" h. 315.00

483 Elephant on Tub - no blanket,
cast iron, A.C. Williams,
1920's, 5¼" h. (W. 59) 125.00

320 Foxy Grandpa, cast iron,
Wing ca. 1900 & Hubley ca.
1920's, 5½" h.
(W. 23)* . . . . .125.00 to 150.00

692 Frog (Manufacturer's conver-
sion), cast iron, "Iron Art,"
1973, 4 1/8" l. 55.00

781 Globe - Globe Bank, w/eagle
on top, cast iron, Enter-
prise, ca. 1875, 5¾" h. 115.00

789 Globe - Globe on Arc, cast
iron, Grey Iron, 1900-03,
5¼" h. (black
paint) . . . . .75.00 to 85.00

785 Globe - Globe on Wire Arc,
cast iron, Arcade, 1900-13,
4 5/8" h. . . . . .125.00 to 135.00

1381 Hat - Derby Hat ("Pass
'Round the Hat"), cast
iron, American-made,
3 1/8" d., 1 5/8" h.
(W. 260) 200.00

532 Horse - "Beauty," cast iron,
Arcade, 1910-32, 4¾" l.,
4 1/8" h. (W. 82) 57.00

Good Luck Horseshoe Bank

508 Horse - Good Luck Horseshoe, w/Buster Brown &
Tige, cast iron, Arcade,
1908-32, 4¼" h., W. 83
(ILLUS.) 122.00

531 Horse - "My Pet" (slot in
belly), cast iron,
Arcade, 1920's, 5" l., 4" h.
(W. 85) 114.00

517 Horse - Prancing Horse, cast
iron, Arcade, A.C. Williams
Co. & Dent Hardware Co.,
1910-30's, 4¼ x 4 7/8"
(W. 77) 42.00

520 Horse - Prancing Horse
(large), rectangular base,
cast iron, Arcade & A.C.

Williams Co., 1910-34
(W. 78)* 85.00

513 Horse - Prancing Horse on
Oval Base, cast iron,
Hubley Mfg. Co. & A.C.
Williams Co., 1920's,
4¾" l., 5" h. (W. 76) 75.00

521 Horse - Prancing Horse on
Pebbled Base, cast iron,
American-made,
6½ x 7¼"* 85.00

506 Horse - Prancing Horse with
Belly Band, cast iron,
American-made, 4½ x 5" . . 190.00

515 Horse - Rocking Horse
(SBCCA), cast iron, George
C. Knerr, U.S., 1975, 6" l.,
5 5/8" h. 400.00

533 Horse - Work Horse, standing
animal, cast iron, Arcade,
ca. 1910, 5" l., 4" h.
(W. 81)* 50.00

535 Horseshoe - "Tally Ho,"
horsehead framed by
horseshoe w/fox hunt
items, cast iron, Chamberlain & Hill, England,
4 3/16" w., 4½" h.
(W. 168) 150.00

228 Indian - Indian with Tomahawk, cast iron, Hubley
Mfg. Co., 1915-30's,
5 7/8" h. (W. 39)* 190.00

226 Indian - Pocahontas Bust,
lead, key locked trap,
marked "Germany,"
3 1/8" h. 45.00

807 Liberty Bell - "Bailey's Centennial Money Bank," cast
iron, "Proclaim 1776 Liberty
- Centennial Money 1876
Bank," on square marble
base, 4½" w. base, overall
4½" h. (W. 280) 76.00

793 Liberty Bell - Promotional
Bell, steel w/wood yoke,
plaque across front reads
"Banker's Savings & Credit
System Co.," American-
made, 1919, 3¾" w.,
4" h. 7.50

757 Lion - Lion, Ears Up (turnpin),
cast iron, A.C. Williams
Co., 1934, Arcade, 1932,
4½" l., 3 5/8" h. 35.00

747 Lion - Lion on Tub, small, cast
iron, A.C. Williams Co.,
1920-34, 4¼" h. (W. 61) 85.00

746 Lion - Lion on Tub, Decorated,
with cord in mouth, cast
iron, A.C. Williams Co.,
1920-34, 5½" h. (W. 57)* . . . 82.00

760 Lion - Lion on Wheels, cast
iron, A.C. Williams Co.,

Lion on Wheels Bank

1920's, 4 5/8" l., 4½" h.,
W. 95 (ILLUS.) ....185.00 to 200.00

765 Lion - Lion, Tail Left, cast
iron, traces of red paint,
American-made, 4 7/8" l.,
4" h. 48.00

755 Lion - Lion, Tail Right, cast
iron, Arcade, 1910-13, A.C.
Williams Co., 1905-31,
4 7/8" l., 4" h. (W. 90)*.... 38.00

164 Mary & Little Lamb, cast iron,
American-made, 1901,
4½" h. (W. 1)* 400.00

209 McCarthy (Charlie), standing
figure, composition, Crown,
1930's, 9 3/8" h. 110.00

1611 Merry-Go-Round, nickel-
plated cast iron, Grey Iron
Casting Co., 1925-28,
4 3/8" d., 4 5/8" h. * 215.00

36 "Middy Bank" (has clapper),
English Admiralty charac-
ter, cast iron, American-
made, ca. 1887, 5¼" h.
(W. 26)* 135.00

8 Officer (Cadet), cast iron,
Hubley Mfg. Co., 1905-15,
5¾" h. (W. 7)* ...300.00 to 400.00

186 Oriental Boy on Pillow (con-
version), cast iron, Hubley
Mfg. Co., 1920's, 5¼ x
6¼", 5½" h. .....175.00 to 225.00

General Pershing Bank

150 Pershing - Gen. "Pershing,"

bust of the general, bronze
electroplated cast iron,
Grey Iron Casting Co.,
patented 1918, 7¾" h.,
W. 312* (ILLUS.) 100.00

608 Pig - Bismark Pig, cast iron,
American-made, 1880's,
7 3/8" l. (W. 176) 88.00

603 Pig - "Decker's Iowana," gold-
painted cast iron,
American-made, 4 3/8" l.
(W. 182) ....80.00 to 90.00

582 Pig - Seated Pig, cast iron,
A.C. Williams Co., 1910-34,
3" h. (W. 179)* ......55.00 to 65.00

584 Pig - Sleek Pig, nickel-plated
cast iron, American-made,
6¾" l., 3 1/8" h. 65.00

The Wise Pig Bank

609 Pig - "The Wise Pig," seated
on haunches w/plaque
w/writing across stomach,
painted cast iron, Hubley
Mfg. Co., ca. 1930-36,
6 5/8" h., W. 175*
(ILLUS.) 74.00

617 Pig - "The Wise Pig," lead,
Jessie McCutcheon Nelson,
designer, patented 1929,
American-made, 2¾" w.,
6 9/16" h.* 40.00

606 Pig - Pig with Bow, seated
animal, cast iron, Shimer
Toy Co., 1899, 5" l.
(W. 178) 90.00

182 Policeman (Fireman), cast
iron, Arcade, 1920-34,
5½" h. (W. 9) 275.00

1268 Purse - Satchel, bronze-
finished heavy steel,
American-made, 5¾" l.,
3 3/8" h. 175.00

566 Rabbit - Begging Rabbit, cast
iron, A.C. Williams Co.,
1908-20's, 5 1/8" h.
(W. 98)* 94.00

571 Rabbit - Rabbit with Hinged
Back (small), lead, trick

lock, Germany, 4 3/8" l.,
3 3/8" h. 145.00
829 Radio - Radio Bank (3 dials),
cast iron w/sheet iron sides
& back, Kenton Hardware
Mfg. Co., 1927-32, 4½" l.,
3" h. (W. 137) 85.00
830 Radio - Radio Bank (3 dials,
large), cast iron w/sheet
iron sides & back, Kenton
Hardware Mfg. Co.,
1927-31, 6 3/16" l.,
3½" h. 135.00
821 Radio - "Radio Bank," two
dials, painted cast iron,
Hubley Mfg. Co., ca. 1928,
3¼" h. (W. 136) 105.00
721 Rhino, cast iron, Arcade,
1910-25, 5" l.
(W. 252) . . . . 300.00 to 400.00
148 Roosevelt, Franklin D. -
Roosevelt ("New Deal"),
bust, cast iron, Kenton
Hardware Mfg. Co.,
1933-36, 5" h. 205.00
541 Rooster - Polish Rooster,
black w/red topknot, yel-
low legs, cast iron,
American-made, 5½" h.
(W. 186)* . . . . . . 1,000.00 to 1,500.00
548 Rooster, silver w/red comb &
wattles, cast iron, Hubley
Mfg. Co. & A.C. Williams
Co., 1910-34, 4¾" h.
(W. 187)* 85.00
75 Rumplestiltskin, "Do You
Know Me" on feet & base,
cast iron, American-made,
ca. 1910, 2¼" w., 6" h.
(W. 49) . . . . 275.00 to 325.00

"Coin Deposit Bank"

Safe - "Coin Deposit Bank,"
combination lock, cast iron,
4 3/8 x 5½", 6¾" h.
(ILLUS.) 115.00
864 Safe - "Fidelity Safe" medium
(turnpin), cast iron, Kyser &
Rex, ca. 1880, 2 5/8" sq.,
3" h. 95.00
903 Safe - "Fidelity Trust Vault"

(with Lord Fauntleroy), cast
iron, J. Barton Smith Co.,
Chicago, ca. 1890,
5 3/8 x 5 7/8", 6½" h. 425.00
Safe - "Ideal Trust," cast iron
w/worn original bronze
finish, 7" h. 165.00
869 Safe - "Safe," cast iron, key
locked trap, J. & E.
Stevens, ca. 1891,
2¼ x 2½", 3¼" h. 35.00
29 Sailor (large), cast iron,
Hubley Mfg. Co., 1905-15,
5 5/8" h. (W. 16) 175.00
97 Santa Claus - Oriental Santa,
silvered lead, Japan,
4" h. 75.00
50 Sheridan - Gen. Sheridan on
Base, officer astride rearing
horse, cast iron, Arcade,
1910-25, 2 3/8 x 4" base,
6" h. (W. 88) 450.00
1094 Spaceheater (Flowers), cast
iron, England, ca. 1890,
3 7/8 x 4 1/8", 6½" h. 85.00
1345 Stove - Dot Stove, cast iron,
Grey Iron Casting Co.,
ca. 1903, 3 7/8" h. 125.00
1349 Stove - Gas Stove, marked
"Save Your Money & Buy a
Gas Stove" on top & "Pat
App'd For" on base, cast
iron & sheet metal, S. Bern-
stein Co., New York City,
1901, 4" w., 5½" h. 82.50
1344 Stove - Oak Stove, cast iron,
Shimer Toy Co., ca. 1899,
3¼" w., 2 3/8" h.
(W. 134) 175.00
1342 Stove - Roper Stove, cast iron
& sheet metal, Arcade,
3 7/8" l., 4" h. 115.00
1419 Tank, worn brown japanning
w/gold trim, cast iron,
England, ca. 1918, 8¼" l.,
3 5/8" h. (replaced screw
w/washer) 225.00
1414 Tank - "The Tank Bank," embossed "119" on side, cast
iron, John Harper, Ltd.,
England, 7 3/8" l.,
3 5/8" h. 275.00
928 Treasure Chest (small), cast
iron, American-made,
1 7/8 x 2¾", 1 7/8" h. 70.00
1514 Truck - Gas Truck, sheet
metal, painted red w/nickel
grill, Marx, patented 1937,
6 1/8" l., 2¼" h. 60.00
841 U.S. Mailbox - Standing Mailbox, large, cast iron,
Hubley Mfg. Co., 1928-36,
2¼ x 2½", 5½" h.* 90.00
839 U.S. Mailbox - U.S. Mail,

cast iron, Arcade, 1913 &
A.C. Williams, 1908-34,
1 5/8 x 2½", 3½" h. 37.50
837　U.S. Mailbox - U.S. Mail, narrow, hinged coin slot, cast
iron, Kenton Hardware
Mfg. Co. & A.C. Williams
Co., 1912-31, 1 11/16 x
2¾", 4 3/8" h. 44.00

U.S. Mail Bank

838　U.S. Mailbox - U.S. Mail,
small, cast iron, Kenton
Hardware Mfg. Co.,
1904-10 & A.C. Williams Co.,
1912-31, 1 11/16 x 2¾",
3 5/8" h., W. 127 (ILLUS.) .. 34.00
851　U.S. Mailbox - "U.S. Mail
Bank" with Eagle, "Pull
Down" on flap & "Letters"
below, cast iron, Kenton
Hardware Mfg. Co.,
1932-34, 1 3/8 x 3¼",
4 1/8" h. (W. 121) 38.00
855　U.S. Mailbox - "U.S. Mail"
with Eagle, cast iron,
Hubley Mfg. Co., ca. 1906,
1 7/8 x 4", 4" h.* 135.00
152　"Von Hindenburg," bust on
pedestal base, lead, Ger-
many, 1915, 9¼" h. 350.00
138　Washington, George -
Washington (solid base),
standing figure of
Washington, cast iron,
American-made, 6¼" h. 40.00
1428　Zeppelin - "Graf Zeppelin,"
cast iron, A.C. Williams
Co., 1920-34, 6¾" l.
(W. 171) 198.00
1431　Zeppelin - Graf Zeppelin on
Wheels (pulltoy), cast iron,
A.C. Williams, ca. 1934,
7 13/16" l., 2¼" h. 265.00

GLASS

"Buddy Bank," colorful tin figure of young blond boy
standing cross-legged be-

side round glass jar w/tin
lid, marked "Marx," 4" h. ... 190.00

Charlie Chaplin Bank

299　Charlie Chaplin beside barrel,
clear barrel, painted figure,
L.E. Smith Co., 1920's
(ILLUS.) 215.00
Elephant, clear standing fig-
ure, container for
"Grapette" drink 16.00
"Lucky Joe," man's head, con-
tainer for Nash's Mustard,
clear 25.00
Pig, "Ohio Oil Co." 15.00

POTTERY

Tiered-top Bank

1282　Acorn, earthenware pottery,
American-made,
3 1/8 x 3¼" 45.00
Bell-shaped, reddish clay
w/old worn grey paint,
3 5/8" h. (small flakes) 55.00
564　Buffalo - Buffalo Lying Down,
"Expo 1901," earthenware
pottery, American-made,
3 1/8 x 6½" 45.00
Cat's head, white clay
w/overall brown glaze,
3 3/8" h. (edge chips) 55.00
Chest of drawers w/two short
drawers over three long
drawers flanked by turned
columns, redware w/mar-

bleized glaze, 7" w., 5" h.
(edge chips & feet
missing) 145.00

961 Church - Little Brown Church,
earthenware pottery,
2 5/8 x 3½ x 4" 25.00

Eagle head, crudely molded
eagle head w/brown &
green overall sponging &
yellow glaze, 2½" h. (chips
at coin slot) 85.00

1295 Gourd - Round Gourd, earthenware pottery, Mexico,
4 1/8 x 4 5/8" 45.00

1292 Gourd - Teardrop Gourd,
earthenware pottery,
5¾" 45.00

Hen on nest, redware, top
portion w/greenish glaze,
base unglazed, 3 1/8" h.
(chip on beak) 60.00

Jug-form, redware, ovoid,
tooled band & knob finial,
unglazed w/black stenciled
label "Charity," 3 5/8" h.
(small flakes) 150.00

Jug-form w/strap handle,
reddish clay w/old worn
orange paint & gold trim,
3 7/8" h. 30.00

Jug-form w/strap handle,
grey clay w/old worn
reddish brown paint w/gold
trim, 4½" h. 45.00

Jug-form, redware, semi-
ovoid w/angled strap han-
dle, red paint, 4¾" h. (old
repaired flake at coin
slot) 65.00

Jug-form, stoneware, flattened knob at top, dark
brown Albany slip glaze,
4¾" h. (flakes at coin
hole) 40.00

Ovoid, squatty form, grey
clay w/dark brown glaze,
hand-turned, 4" h. (chips on
base) 45.00

Pig, earthenware pottery,
white glaze & brown sponging across back, late,
5¾" l. 65.00

632 Pig - Razor Back Pig, seated,
earthenware pottery,
American-made,
3½ x 5 7/8" 50.00

633 Pig - Two-Tone Pig, standing, earthenware pottery,
American-made, ca. 1880,
2½ x 4" 40.00

Tiered-top on ovoid body,
stoneware w/brushed co-
balt blue bands around top,

incised "Eliza Arkenburgh,"
6¾" h. (ILLUS.) 600.00

TIN

Monkey Tips Hat Bank

Advertising, "Betsy Ross
Tea" 14.00

Advertising, "BIP Orange
Juice" 12.00

Advertising, "Bosco,"
lithographed 45.00

Advertising, "Buick Fireball,"
8" 18.00

Advertising, "Eight O'Clock
(A & P) Coffee," coffee
can replica, red ground,
4" 10.50

Advertising, "Patton Paint
Co.," early lithography 35.00

Advertising, "Peter Pan
Bread" 25.00

Advertising, "Pillsbury
Flour" 14.00

1585 Advertising, "Red Wing
Shoes," model of a shoe,
w/embossed label "Save
with Shoes for the Kid,"
worn black paint,
2 7/8" h. 45.00

Advertising, "Rival Dog
Food," 1940 . . . . 12.50

Advertising, "Sapolin Paints,"
Beehive & "Mr. Speedy,"
the home decorator, pry-
open lid 20.00

Advertising, "Tower Motor
Oil" 35.00

Advertising, "Wolf's Head
Motor Oil" 20.00

Book-shaped, "Tom, Tom the
Piper's Son" rhyme &
picture, colorful 35.00

1405 German Helmet, key locked
trap, Germany, 4 1/8" l.,
2 5/8" h. 175.00

798 Globe - "Globe Bank," key
locked trap, Chein,
ca. 1934-77, 4 3/8" 6.00

Key, model of a key w/(illegible) inscription on handle, tubular support w/slot for coins, brass ring below, "S" curve bit, American-made, 19th c., 26½" l. (some resoldering) 522.50

Mailbox, sidewalk-type, dark green, decal lettering, front coin slot, operable cash door, 4 x 4 x 9" 30.00

Monkey tips hats, semi-mechanical, J. Chein & Co., ca. 1930's, 5" h. (ILLUS.) ... 125.00

BARBERIANA

A wide variety of antiques related to the tonsorial arts have been highly collectible for many years, especially 19th and early 20th century shaving mugs and barber bottles and, more recently, razors. We are now combining these closely related categories under one heading here for easier reference. A selection of other varied pieces relating to barbering will also be found below.

BARBER BOTTLES

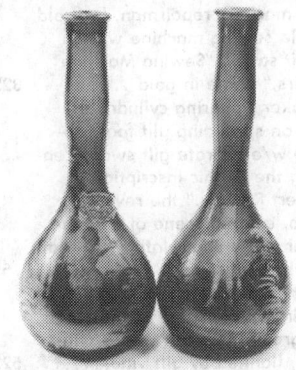

Pair of Mary Gregory-type Bottles

Amethyst glass, bulbous base w/shaped neck, white enamel profile portrait of young woman w/long flowing hair & label "VEGEDERMA," 7 7/8" h. $385.00

Amethyst glass, bulbous base w/tall shaped neck, overall enameled decoration of large Art Nouveau florals w/gilt trim, 8 5/8" h. 150.00

Blue glass, horizontal brown band design highlighted w/applied white enamel floral pattern, same pattern above & below band, 8" h. 112.00

Canary yellow glass, Hobnail patt.,

three-ring neck, 7¼" h. (five hobs damaged, one missing) 40.00

Citron glass, bulbous base tapering to tall straight neck w/sheared lip, h.p. enameled Art Nouveau scrolls design, pontil, 8" h........ 231.00

Clear glass, cylindrical & flared at the base w/cut panels at base & shoulder, copper wheel engraving w/"Skinner & Goodhue Elmira, NY" in a wreath, pewter shaker top, 9¼" h..................... 45.00

Cobalt blue glass, squared cylinder tapering to tall straight neck, enameled w/large white floral design, smooth base 357.50

Cranberry glass, Hobnail patt., three-ring neck w/rolled lip, polished pontil, 7¼" h. 110.00

Cranberry opalescent glass, "Seaweed" patt., squared cylinder w/slender neck & thick rolled lip, 8 3/8" h. 100.00

Emerald green glass, bulbous base w/tall shaped neck, overall enameled gold & white floral decoration, pontil 305.00

Frosted fiery opalescent glass, squatty bulbous base w/tall ring-turned neck, gold & purple enameled leaves, ground mouth, 6 7/8" h. 148.50

"Label-under-glass" types, "Levarn's," one w/"Rose Water Tonic," other w/"Golden Wash Shampoo," 1906, 8" h., pr. (some staining) 121.00

Light blue opalescent glass, "Criss-Cross" patt., cylindrical w/tall, wide neck, thick rolled lip, 9¼" h........................... 75.00

Mary Gregory-type, amethyst glass, bulbous base tapering to tall shaped neck, h.p. white enamel landscape scene w/large two-story house, pontil 687.50

Mary Gregory-types, cobalt blue glass, bulbous base tapering to tall shaped neck, one w/white enameled figure of a girl holding a bird, the other a boy holding a bird, facing pair (ILLUS.) 300.00

Mary Gregory-type, medium pink-amethyst glass, bulbous base tapering to tall shaped neck, white enameled figure of a young woman holding a basket & looking skyward, pontil 275.00

Milk white glass, club-shaped, h.p. oval band w/"Bay Rum" surrounding label-under-glass w/colorful bust portrait of a lovely Victorian lady, pontil 632.50

Purple-blue glass, bulbous base

w/slender straight neck, decorated w/enameled dot & floral bands, sheared mouth, 8" h. 70.00

Spatter glass, white spatters in cranberry, cone-shaped w/flared polished mouth, 8" h. 55.00

Spatter glass, white spatters in light blue, cone-shaped w/flared polished mouth, 8¼" h. 210.00

Teal blue opalescent glass, "Coin Spot" patt., melon-ribbed base ... 167.00

Yellow-green glass, flat-sided bulbous base w/stepped shoulder to tall narrow neck w/flared rim, decorated w/enameled criss-cross bands & flower sprigs at base, 7 5/8" h. 120.00

SHAVING MUGS

(Porcelain unless otherwise noted)

Occupational

Baker, h.p. mustachioed baker placing a loaf of bread in a red brick oven, background shows a stone wall w/a table of bread & a basket, also a flour barrel, water bucket & fire wood, great detail .. 950.00

Barber, h.p. pair of hair clippers, name worn 125.00

Bartender, h.p. scene of bartender pouring a drink, mirrored backbar, bar bottles & glasses, two patrons having drinks & smoking 400.00

Blacksmith, h.p. colored flowers, leaves & blue ribbon surround horseshoe above name, "R.W. Shurtz," bottom marked, "Mew Barber Supply Utica, NY, V&D Austria" 200.00

Brewer, h.p. scene of horse-drawn beer wagon pulled by a team of white horses, wagon loaded w/barrels, driver wearing apron & blue shirt, background w/multi-storied building & board fence, base marked "JPL - France" 800.00

Caboose man, h.p. w/red caboose marked "3982 NYC," blue & green background 325.00

Engineer, h.p. w/finely detailed steam locomotive w/tender marked "LVRR," base marked "T&V - France" 350.00

Glassblower, h.p. scene of man w/blowpipe blowing glass in front of a red brick furnace, flanked by gilt accents, base marked "D&C," finely painted (two large chips in rear, crow's foot in base) 1,000.00

Liveryman, h.p. scene of horse-drawn doctor's buggy driven by a derby-hatted driver in front of a red brick

building w/two large wooden doors & a livery stable sign, reverse painted black 1,100.00

Milkman, h.p. milk wagon drawn by one horse reads "Milk," man stepping down holds can of milk, name in gold, gold on handle & rim (some wear) 525.00

Mineral water employee, h.p. scene of green horse-drawn delivery wagon marked "Mineral Water," blue-coated driver, wagon pulled by one white & one brown horse, reverse w/painted rose 2,300.00

Oyster House proprietor, h.p. w/oysters & clams in foreground, sailing ships & birds in background, flanked by gilt vining & name "FH Gilmore," marked "Royal China International," w/1929 advertisement for owner's oyster house 1,200.00

Plasterer, h.p. mortar board & two trowels, flanked by gilt sprigs, base marked "TECD Co. - Semovit" 140.00

Pugilist, h.p. scene of two men in trunks & boxing gloves facing each other w/gloves up, name painted between them, base marked "T&V - France" 725.00

Sewing machine repairman, h.p. old treadle sewing machine w/sign over it saying "Sewing Machine Repairs," name in gold 325.00

Shoemaker, tapering cylindrical body on spreading gilt foot, obverse w/elaborate gilt swags centering the Gothic inscription "Folkert P. Dow," the reverse w/h.p. colored scene of a shoemaker in his shop, late 19th - early 20th c., 4½" h. 55.00

Tinsmith, h.p. w/man in apron working at bench w/various tools, background is black wall & windows, flanked by gilt vines 525.00

Waiter, h.p. scene of a bespectacled patron sitting at a table set for dinner, a waiter serving a drink, against a red & light yellow background, flanked by floral decoration (gilt worn, small bruise on base) 1,000.00

Miscellaneous

China, h.p. lighted cigar pictured, name in gold 125.00

China, h.p. yellow rose w/red center, base marked "Barber's Supply, St. Louis," incised "Germany" 39.00

China, scuttle-type, figural Chineseman's head, beige color skin,

black mustache & black queue
that forms handle, marked "P.M.
Bavaria," 5¼" d., 3¾" h. 171.00
China, scuttle-type, model of monkey's head, white & pale salmon
pink w/brown hair, marked "P.M.
Bavaria," 5½" d., 3¾" h. 140.00

Masonic Shaving Mug

Fraternal, Masonic emblem in blue,
gilt scroll band below rim, Bavaria
mark on base (ILLUS.) 65.00
Ironstone china, decorated w/man's
name, base marked "Maddock &
Sons, England" 25.00
R.S. Prussia china, blown-out Iris
mold, red roses on blue ground
decoration 195.00

RAZORS

Early Silver Razor Set

Corn razor, "J.A. Henckels Twin
Works, Germany," rounded &
shaped bone handle, plain blade,
original box w/silver embossed
advertising 46.00
Safety razor, "The New Griffon,"
two-part handle w/interchangea-
ble heads, tin container, yellow
w/gold & black lettering & scrolls,
made by American Can Co., last
patent date 1901 . . . . 225.00
Safety razor, "The Star," Kampfe
Bros., New York, cylindrical tin
container, yellow & black, made
by Merstreau Mfg. Co. Boxes,
Brooklyn, N.Y. 273.00
Safety razor, "Valet," ca. 1912, uno-
pened original box 15.00
Safety razor, "Yankee," patent dates
through 1903 on engraved head of
razor, tin container, red w/blue &
white on lid, black advertising on
sides, instructions on interior of
lid, 1¼ x 2½" 182.00

Straight razor, "Asco Cutlery Co.
Magnetised," imitation ivory handle w/Art Nouveau floral
design 31.00
Straight razor, Boker (H.) & Co.,
Solingen, Germany, embossed
celluloid handle w/scene of touring car w/two passengers, trees
in background, blade etched "King
Cutter" 184.00
Straight razor, Crown & Sword, clear
horn handle w/German silver
ends, blade etched w/scene of
Crown & Sword Razor Manufactory, "1873 - 1898" on upper part of
blade 24.00
Straight razor, Fremont (Clauss),
carved bone handle w/fluted &
banded ends & ivory tang scales,
original box 120.00
Straight razor, Holley Mfg. Co.,
plain black celluloid handle 20.00
Straight razor, Keen Kutter, "Junior"
model, in box 16.00
Straight razor, Keen Kutter, em-
bossed horn handle, etched eagle
on blade 75.00
Straight razor, Ontario Cutlery Co.,
Geneva, New York, black & white
celluloid handle, blade etched
w/two crossed American flags
w/a crown about "The Mighty" . . . 26.00
Straight razor, Rodgers (Joseph) &
Sons, Sheffield, stag horn handle
inlaid w/rectangular escutcheon
plate, black wedge 124.00
Straight razor, Simmons Hardware
Co., celluloid handle w/twisted
bamboo design, blade marked
"Barber's Pet" 81.00
Straight razor, Turniss Cutler &
Stacey Sheffield, pressed horn
handle decorated w/two intertwined snakes, rare maker's mark
on blade 615.00
Straight razor, Waterville Cutlery
Co., Waterville, Connecticut, black
celluloid handle w/unique raised
pattern of a large oak leaf in center & scroll containing acorns,
blade etched "Waterville Hand
Forged" 67.00
Straight razor, Wostenholm (Geo.)
Celebrated I XL Razors, Sheffield,
imitation ivory handle w/raised
symbols at both ends, blade
etched w/advertising 31.00
Straight razor set: a pair of razors &
a strop in leather sheath; silver-
gilt razors each chased on both
sides w/husk pendants on matted
ground, engraved w/interlaced
cyphers & crests, steel blades, the
strop w/silver-gilt handle

w/scrolled molded rim, chased
w/husks in a rococo cartouche,
also chased w/same crest, Paul
Storr, London, 1833, razors
5¾" l., the set (ILLUS.) 2,750.00

GENERAL ITEMS

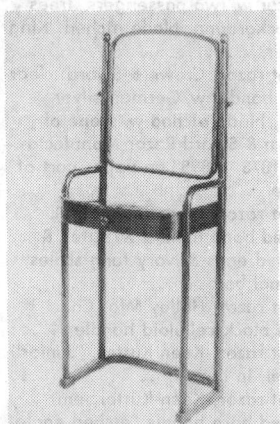

Bentwood Shaving Stand

Barber chair, "Koken & Boppert,"
reclining-type, walnut, patent Oct.
25, 1881, America (restored) 625.00
Barber chair, wood & metal, heavy
round metal base w/round metal
pedestal supports oak-framed
chair decorated w/scrolls &
w/leather-upholstered seat, back,
headrest & arms, footrest marked
"Koken" 210.00
Barber pole, metal, wall-mounted,
red & white stripes, electrified,
(replaced) white globe, 48" h. 175.00
Barber pole, painted wood, wall-
mounted, red & white stripes
w/silver ball top & bottom,
36" l. 495.00
Barber pole, of typical turned
swelling cylindrical form, painted
overall w/spiral red, white & blue
stripes, the ball-form finial
mounted w/a rectangular metal
sign reading "Bath," raised on a
shaped rectangular blue-painted
plinth, Iowa, 19th c., 8' 6" h. 2,475.00
Catalog, "Kochs' Barber Chairs, Furniture & Shop Accessories," 1927,
put out by The Buerger Bros. Sup-
ply Co., Denver, Colorado 40.00
Display case, maple frame, three
glass shelves & sides, front glass
doors w/"Wildroot and Brylcream"
commercial logo emblems, mid-
1950's, 25" deep, 52" wide,
60" h. 650.00
Razor blade bank, porcelain, model

of a barber pole, red & white
striped w/black lettering, 6" h. . . . 22.00
Razor blade sharpener, mechanical,
round steel disc, crank action
moves leather disc against blade,
made by Kriss-Kross Corp., St.
Louis, Missouri, patented
1920-21 . . . . 45.00
Razor hone, "Keen Kutter Kombina-
tion," in fancy embossed advertising tin w/yellow & green w/white
& black lettering, the set 37.00
Razor strop, leather strap stretched
on engine-turned spools joined by
turned & threaded post, underside
of strap bears the inscription
"Ono L. Larpy," probably America,
19th c., 23½" l. (spools
cracked) 110.00
Shaving brush, black & yellow Bake-
lite handle 15.00
Shaving mirror, table-type, Queen
Anne, mahogany, oval mirror
plate in a banded frame tilting
above a circular disked top above
an urn-turned pedestal, on cabriole legs w/shod slipper feet,
18th c., 23½" h. 770.00
Shaving paper waste bowl, cobalt
blue blown glass, h.p. enameled
dot design & gold trim, 5½" d.,
7½" h. 315.00
Shaving stand, Bentwood, the rec-
tangular mirror frame w/rounded
corners set w/a beveled mirror
plate, pivoting between two upright supports w/oval finials &
continuing to a rectangular top
set w/a short drawer w/an oval
pull, raised on an open rectangular
support continuing to flat U-form
stretchers, attributed to Josef
Hoffman, manufactured by J. & J.
Kohn, w/paper labels, ca. 1900,
23¾" w., 4' 5 3/8" h. (ILLUS.) 1,980.00
Sign, "Barber Shop," electric, tin
frame w/red, white & blue paint-
ed plastic insert, 12 x 24" 55.00
Sterilizing cabinet, rectangular upright glass-front cabinet on base
w/two small doors above pierced
apron on four slightly cabriole
legs, on the top on pedestal base
is scroll-decorated round frame
holding round ruby cut to clear
glass sign w/"Sanitary Sterilizer,"
13 x 14", overall 60" h. (glass sign
cracked) 110.00

BASEBALL MEMORABILIA

Baseball was named by Abner Doubleday

as he laid out a diamond-shaped field with four bases at Cooperstown, New York. A popular game from its inception, by 1869 it was able to support its first all-professional team, the Cincinnati Red Stockings. The National League was organized in 1876 and though the American League was first formed in 1900, it was not officially recognized until 1903. Today, the "national pastime" has millions of fans and collecting baseball memorabilia has become a major hobby with enthusiastic collectors seeking out items associated with players such as Babe Ruth, Lou Gehrig, and others, who became legends in their own lifetimes. Though baseball cards, issued as advertising premiums for bubble gum and other products, seem to dominate the field there are numerous other items available.

Ashtray, 1965 World Series, Minnesota Twins	$60.00
Baseball, autographed by Babe Ruth	650.00
Baseball, autographed by 1946 St. Louis Cardinals team	250.00
Bat, Louisville Slugger-type, signed by Joe "Ducky" Medwick, Dizzy Dean trade-mark	60.00
Beverage container, "Yoo Hoo Chocolate - The Drink of Champions," tin, pictures Mickey Mantle, Yogi Berra, Whitey Ford, Tom Tresh & Bobby Richardson	35.00
Book, "Baseball Heroes," cartoon-type, 1952, Babe Ruth on cover	35.00
Book, "Individual Play, Team Strategy," by John W. (Jack) Coombs, 1944, photos	22.00
Book, "1958 Sporting News Baseball Official Guide"	25.00
Book, "Yogi Berra Baseball Guide Book," 1966	9.95
Glasses, "Baltimore Orioles," "Toast the Champs!" American League Champions, 1966, set of 6, in original box	45.00
Magazine, "Baseball," 1928, January, articles on Babe Ruth, 1927 Yankees & 1927 season	30.00
Pamphlet, 1971 New York Yankees roster, cover features Rookie of the Year - Thurman Munson	15.00
Program, 1947, Chicago White Sox	9.50
Radio, shaped like baseball, 1939	475.00
Score card, 1964, Los Angeles Dodgers	9.50
Score keeper, cardboard, mechanical, advertising, "Garland Stoves," early 1900's	7.00
Sun visor, paper, Brooklyn Dodgers Tip Top Bread give-away	18.00
Yearbook, 1947 Unofficial Dodgers, "Baseball's Beloved Bums," w/insert announcing rookie Jackie Robinson	40.00
Yearbook, 1952, St. Louis Cardinals	18.00
Yearbook, 1953, Philadelphia Athletics	18.00

BASKETS

New England Apple Basket

The American Indians were the first basket weavers on this continent and, of necessity, the early Colonial settlers and their descendants pursued this artistic handicraft to provide essential containers for berries, eggs and endless other items to be carried or stored. Rye straw, split willow and reeds are but a few of the wide variety of materials used. The Nantucket baskets, plainly and sturdily constructed, along with those made by other specialized groups, would seem to draw the greatest attention in an area of collecting. Also see FARM COLLECTIBLES, INDIAN ARTIFACTS & JEWELRY and SHAKER ITEMS.

Apple basket, woven splint, circular rim leading to a square base, fixed bentwood handle w/forged iron hanging hook, New England, ca. 1860, 13" d., 11" h. (ILLUS.)	$220.00
Apple basket, woven splint, rounded cylindrical basket w/bound rim, mounted on either side w/bentwood handles, America, 19th c., 25" d., 14½" h.	330.00
Berry basket, woven splint, interlaced oval body w/woven handle, painted overall in milky yellow, New England, mid-19th c., 7½" l., 4½" h.	165.00
Bushel basket, woven splint, wrapped rim w/bentwood handles, 21" d., 15½" h.	150.00

"Buttocks" basket, 16-rib construction, woven splint, 12 x 16", 6½" h. plus bentwood handle 55.00

"Buttocks" basket, 26-rib construction, woven splint, good age & color, 12 x 17", 8" h. plus bentwood handles 400.00

"Buttocks" basket, cov., 20-rib construction, woven natural splint, wide rim & solid board lid flaps, good color, 15½ x 22", 10½" h. plus wide bentwood handle (minor damage) 175.00

Cheese basket, woven splint, 19th c., 16" d. 295.00

Chicken basket, woven willow, waisted ovoid body w/wide everted rim, America, early 20th c., 14" d., 6" h. 55.00

Clam basket, wooden slatted construction, bentwood handle 80.00

Eel basket, woven splint, America, 19th c., 31" h. 192.00

Egg gathering basket, tightly woven splint, melon-ribbed, 7¾ x 8½", 4½" h. plus bentwood handle 70.00

Egg gathering basket, tightly woven splint, melon-ribbed, 9½ x 10½", 9½" h. plus swinging bentwood handle 275.00

Egg gathering basket, woven splint, melon-ribbed, 10 x 11½", 5¾" h. plus arched bentwood handle (minor wear & damage) 155.00

Egg gathering basket, woven splint, circular rim leading to a tapered circular base, painted overall in dark green, America, 19th c., 13" d., 8¾" h. plus bentwood handle 220.00

Field (or gathering) basket, wooden stave construction, old brown paint, ½ bushel size, 15½" d., 9½" h. plus swinging bentwood handle 55.00

Field (or gathering) basket, woven splint, old blue paint, bentwood rim handles, 18½ x 29", 14½" h. 325.00

Hanging wall basket, painted woven splint, back w/two eared hangers above rectangular open basket, split ash rim, painted green, America, 19th c., 11¾" w., 13" h. 1,045.00

Laundry basket, woven splint, oval rim w/two bentwood handles, rectangular base, America, 19th c., 16" l., 7" h. (ILLUS.) 440.00

Laundry basket, woven splint, oval rim leading to a rectangular base, the sides w/pierced handles, Iowa, 19th c., 23½" l., 11" h. (minor loss to center base) 137.50

19th Century Laundry Basket

Lunch basket, woven splint, tapering cylindrical body w/wrapped edge & splint handle, America, 19th c., 12¾" d., 14½" h. 242.00

Market basket w/lift-top, woven splint, oval w/swelled body & two half-moon coil-spring lids & a center wrapped handle w/god's eye supports, America, late 19th - early 20th c., 18" l., 16" h. (slight wear) 55.00

Market basket, woven splint, oval finely woven sides w/dark brown patina, well-shaped bentwood handle attaches outside the rim, 11 x 12½", 6" h. plus handle (minor damage) 225.00

Woven Splint Market Basket

Market basket, woven splint, oval, finely woven rounded sides on rectangular base, fixed bentwood handle, made in Maine, natural finish, 13" l., 12½" h. (ILLUS.) 125.00

Market basket, woven splint w/radiating ribs, rectangular, bentwood handle across top, good age & color, 14 x 17½", 7½" h. (minor damage) 175.00

Market basket, woven splint, rectangular, polychrome bands of various sizes, New England, 19th c., 17" l., 15" h. 88.00

Market basket, woven splint, round, 5½" d., 3" h. plus bentwood handle 425.00

Market basket, woven splint, round w/deep sides & kick-up in bottom, bentwood swing handle, 14" d., 8¼" h. 725.00

"Melon" basket, 16-rib construction, woven splint, 5 x 5½", 3" h. plus bentwood handle................ 210.00

"Melon" basket, 20-rib construction, tightly woven splint, traces of green paint, woven handle, 5½" d., 3½" h. 305.00

"Melon" basket, 24-rib construction, woven splint, oval rim & fixed bentwood handle, some age, 9 x 9½", 5½" h. plus handle..... 75.00

Miniature basket, round, finely woven splint w/block design in rim, 2 3/8" d., 1 3/8" h. 145.00

Nantucket basket, miniature, finely woven splint, deep sides w/circular pine base bearing the initials "J.D.W." & typed verse, shaped swing handle, natural varnish finish, late 19th or early 20th c., 2¾" h. 1,430.00

Nantucket basket, tightly woven rattan sides, bentwood swivel handle, printed label "Light ship Basket made by William D. Appleton, Nantucket, Mass.," some age, 6¼" d., 2 7/8" h. plus handle 850.00

Nantucket basket, tightly woven rattan cylindrical body, turned wooden base w/two concentric rings, bentwood swing handle on brass ears, Massachusetts, 19th c., 10½" d., 5¾" h. 715.00

Storage basket, cov., woven splint, oval w/sloped shoulders tapering to base & two plaited swing handles fastened to the body w/metal rings, w/conforming cover, some original paint, 8" h. 88.00

Storage basket, open, woven splint, oblong, low form w/split ash rim & ear handles at ends, painted dark green, America, 19th c., 16" l., 7½" h. (some breaks) 550.00

Storage basket, open, woven splint, round, bentwood rim handles, good age & color, 6" d., 3¾" h. ... 375.00

Wool basket, woven brown ash splint, round body w/double handles, deep sides, America, early 20th c., 32" d., 24" h. (some breaks) 935.00

BELLS

Animal bells, sheep, brass, three graduated sizes on leather strap, American...................... $39.00

Carriage bell, floor-mounted, nickel-plated brass 135.00

China bell, Nippon, h.p. roses on cobalt blue & gold ground, much gold & beading, original clapper, unmarked 135.00

Choir bells, nickel-plated brass w/leather covered brass handles, set of 30 from small to large, probably turn-of-the-century 1,250.00

Figural bell, brass, Colonial lady, legs are clappers............... 70.00

Figural bell, brass, figural Napoleon handle, scenes around sides of Battle of Waterloo, 3 1/8" d., 6¼" h......................... 75.00

Figural bell, brass, large figural Napoleon handle, 3 3/8" d., 7" h......................... 75.00

Figural bell, brass, figural Neville Chamberlain head handle, 2½" d., 5¼" h. 65.00

Figural bell, brass, two seated spaniel dogs at top, wording below, "Spaniels," 2 7/8" d., 4" h....... 75.00

Glass bell, Bohemian ruby-flashed, etched w/Deer & Castle patt. 95.00

Glass bell, Burmese, glossy finish, clear handle & clapper, 5 3/8" d., 9½" h......................... 450.00

Glass bell, red staining & gold trim, etched w/holly & berries, clear handle & original clapper 75.00

Glass bell, transparent green, squared shape w/rounded shoulders, figural metal walking bear handle, original figural clapper, France 195.00

Locomotive bell, bronze, w/mount & clapper, 12" d.................. 250.00

School teacher's hand bell, brass w/turned wooden handle painted black, 7" h...................... 40.00

School teacher's hand bell, bell metal w/turned wooden handle painted black, 9½" h. 50.00

Sleigh bells, crotal-type, 47 brass bells on red & blue painted leather strap 260.00

BIG LITTLE BOOKS

The original "Big Little Books" series of small format was originated in the mid-30's by Whitman Publishing Co., Racine, Wisconsin, and covered a variety of subjects from adventure stories to tales based on comic strip characters and movie and radio stars. The publisher originally assigned each book a serial number. Most prices are now in the $8.00-$20.00 range with scarce ones bringing more.

Apple Mary and Denny's Lucky Apples, No. 1403, 1939 .... $9.00

Beasts of Tarzan, No. 1410, 1937 ... 25.00

Buck Jones in The Fighting Rangers, No. 1188, 1936 .... 25.00

Buck Jones & the Rough Riders in Forbidden Trails, "movie flip" page corners, No. 1486, 1943 ..... 22.00

Buck Rogers and the Planetoid Plot, No. 1197, 1936 .... 55.00

Buck Rogers and the Super-Dwarf of Space, No. 1490, 1943 .... 55.00

Buck Rogers in the War with the Planet Venus, No. 1437, 1938 ..... 65.00

Buck Rogers on the Moons of Saturn, No. 1143, 1934 .... 55.00

Buck Rogers, 25th Century A.D., No. 742, 1933 .... 35.00

Captain Frank Hawks Air Ace and the League of Twelve, No. 1444, 1938 .... 15.00

Chester Gump Finds the Hidden Treasure, No. 766, 1934 .... 25.00

David Copperfield, No. 1148, 1934 (oversized) 25.00

Dick Tracy and the Boris Arson Gang, No. 1163, 1935 .... 25.00

Dick Tracy & the Hotel Murders, No. 1420, 1937 .... 12.00

Dick Tracy and Yogee Yamma, No. 1412, 1946 .... 15.00

Dick Tracy, From Colorado to Nova Scotia, No. 749, 1933 .... 11.00

Dick Tracy Out West, No. 723, 1933 ....12.00 to 19.00

Dick Tracy Special F.B.I. Operative, No. 1449, 1943 .... 15.00

Draftie of the U.S. Army, No. 1416, 1943 .... 7.00

Flash Gordon and the Tournaments of Mongo, No. 1171, 1935 .... 75.00

Gene Autry and the Land Grab Mystery, No. 1439, 1945 .... 13.95

Gene Autry in Special Ranger Rule, No. 1456, 1941 .... 30.00

G-Man VS the Red X, No. 1147, 1936 .... 17.50

Guns in the Roaring West, No. 1426, 1937 .... 12.00

Houdini's Big Little Book of Magic, No. 715, 1933 .... 21.00

Jackie Cooper in Gangster's Boy, No. 1402, 1938 .... 7.00

Jane Arden, The Vanished Princess, No. 1490, 1938 .... 30.00

Jaragu of the Jungle, No. 1424, 1937 .... 15.00

Joe Louis, The Brown Bomber, No. 1105, 1936 .... 27.50

Joe Palooka, The Heavyweight Boxing Champ, No. 1123, 1934 .... 20.00

King of the Royal Mounted, No. 1103, 1936 .... 25.00

Li'l Abner Among the Millionaires, No. 1401, 1939 .... 25.00

Little Miss Muffet, No. 1120, 1936 ... 10.00

Little Orphan Annie and the Ancient Treasure of Am, No. 1414, 1939 .. 40.00

Little Orphan Annie Big Little Book

Little Orphan Annie and the Ghost Gang, No. 1154, 1935 (ILLUS.) 16.00

Little Orphan Annie with the Circus, No. 1103, 1934 .... 20.00

Little Women, No. 757, 1934 (oversized) 17.50

Mandrake the Magician, No. 1167, 1935 .... 25.00

Mandrake the Magician and the Flame Pearls, No. 1418, 1946 ..... 45.00

Maximo, The Amazing Superman and the Crystals of Doom, No. 1444, 1941 .... 18.00

Mickey Mouse Sails for Treasure Island, No. 750, 1933 .... 30.00

Oswald, The Lucky Rabbit, No. 1109, 1934 (oversized) 30.00

Phantom and the Sign of the Skull, No. 1474, 1939 .... 25.00

Popeye in Quest of His Poopdeck Pappy, No. 1450, 1937 .... 25.00

Radio Patrol, No. 1142, 1935 ...... 15.00

Radio Patrol Trailing the Safe Blowers, No. 1173, 1937 .... 16.00

Roy Rogers at Crossed Feathers Ranch, No. 1492, 1945 .... 25.00

Silver Streak, No. 1155, 1935 (oversized) 15.00

Smilin Jack in Wings Over the Pacific, No. 1416, 1939 .... 25.00

Smitty, Golden Gloves Tournament, No. 745, 1934 .... 20.00

Smitty in Going Native, No. 1477, 1938 .... 15.00

Story of Skippy, No. 761, 1934 ...... 20.00

Tarzan & The Jewels of Opar, No. 1495, 1940 .... 25.00

Tarzan in the Land of the Giant Apes, No. 1467, 1949 .... 20.00

Tarzan of the Apes, No. 744, 1933 .. 58.00

Tarzan's Revenge, No. 1488, 1938 ... 22.50

Tarzan the Fearless, No. 769, 1934 .. 25.00

Tarzan Twins, No. 770, 1934 .... 45.00

Tom Beatty, Ace of the Service, No. 723, 1934 (oversized) 20.00

Tom Beatty, Ace of the Service
Scores Again, No. 1165, 1937 ..... 15.00
Wash Tubbs in Pandemonia,
No. 751, 1934 .... 15.00

RELATED BOOKS

Bonanza, The Bubble Gum Kid,
Whitman, A Big Little Book,
No. 2002, 1967 .... 14.00
Brave Little Tailor (with Mickey
Mouse), 1058 Series, Walt Disney
Hardbound Series, 1938 .... 35.00
Buck Rogers in the City of Floating
Globes, Whitman, Big Little Books
Cocomalt premium, no number,
1935 .... 98.00
Buck Rogers in the 25th Century
A.D., Whitman, Big Little Books
Cocomalt premium, no number,
1933 .... 50.00
It Happened One Night, Saalfield,
Little Big Books, No. 1098, 1935 .. 30.00
Just Kids, Saalfield, Little Big Books,
No. 1052, 1934 .... 30.00

BOOK ENDS

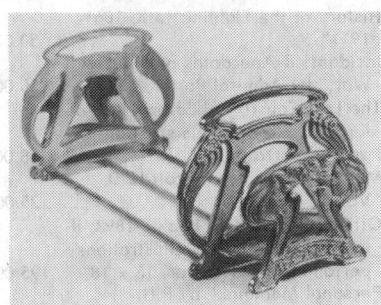

Art Nouveau Book Ends

Art pottery, Halloween cat, signed
"D.A.L." & dated 1925, pr. $55.00
Brass, expanding-type, Art Nouveau
style, 17½" l. (ILLUS.) ....75.00 to 100.00
Brass, model of lady's boot w/high
heel, engraved detail, on oblong
stepped base, 5 3/8" h., pr. 55.00
Bronze, Art Deco style, "The Good
Fairy," girl w/outstretched arms,
signed "J.M.P." 55.00
Bronze, cast as minotaurs, one
w/the torso of a youth w/an animal carcass slung through his
arm, the other w/the torso of a
man w/bear skin draped over his
shoulders, on oblong veined marble plinths, 11½" h., pr. 550.00
Bronze, figural Art Nouveau woman
tending flock of sheep, signed
"Armor Bronze Co.," pr. 145.00
Bronze, figure of seated Buddha,

"dore" finish, signed "Tiffany Studios" & numbered, pr. 295.00
Bronze, model of a lion w/cascading
mane, standing w/one front paw
on a marble ball, on oblong base,
15" h., pr. 935.00
Bronze-finish cast iron, figure of an
Art Nouveau maiden holding the
train of her swirling gown, 7" h.,
pr. 65.00
Bronze-finish cast iron, model of
football player, ca. 1920, pr. 65.00
Bronze-finish pot metal, figural golfer in action, 9½" h., pr. 160.00
Cast iron, figural Art Deco dancing
girls, 1926, pr. 20.00
Cast iron, figural knight slaying
dragon, marked "Hubley, No.
312," pr. 35.00
Cast iron, model of ship, "Old Ironsides," pr. 40.00
China, bust of Queen Nefertiti, jade
green, Lenox, 5 x 8", pr. 95.00
Onyx, figural Art Deco male & female musicians, signed "Green,"
pr. 125.00
Pot metal, model of Scottie dog,
painted black & white, pr. 50.00
Pottery, figural Indian head in relief
on brick-red matte ground, fluted
on three sides, unmarked, 5" sq.,
pr. 65.00
Pressed wood, model of Scottie dog
sitting up, pr. 35.00
Spelterware, model of Scottie dog
on onyx base, pr. 25.00

BOOKS

ANTIQUES RELATED

"A Century of Silver 1847-1947," story of International Silver Co., first
edition $25.00
"American Glass: Volume I - Blown
and Molded," edited by Marvin
Schwartz, & "Volume II - Pressed
and Cut," edited by Robert DiBar-
tolomeo, 1974, articles from *The
Magazine Antiques*, black & white
illustrations, hard cover, worn
dust jackets, 2 vols. 160.00
Bellows, Ina H., "Old Mechanical
Banks," 1940, 6¼ x 9¼" 55.00
Coffin, Margaret, "American Country Tinware," 1968, 7 x 10" 30.00
Downs, Joseph, "American Furniture," 1952, autographed 85.00
Doyle, Robert, "Straight Razor Collecting," 1980, paperback, very
used, 125 pp. 48.00
Drepperd, Carl W., "The ABC's of

Old Glass," 1949, illustrated, hard
cover 30.00

Fales, Dean, "American Painted Furniture, 1660-1880," 1972, E.P. Dutton and Company, New York,
New York, 299 pp. 45.00

Flower, Margaret Cameron Coss,
"Victorian Jewelry," 1951, first
edition, 10 color & 18 b/w plates,
271 pp......................... 36.00

Greaser, Arlene & Paul, "Homespun
Ceramics," 1962, autographed,
6 x 9¼"....................... 105.00

Haeberle, Arminius T., "Old Pewter," 1931, 8 x 10½"............. 55.00

Hornung, Clarence P., "Treasury of
American Design" (two volumes in
one), Abrams, 9½ x 12" 40.00

Knittle, Rhea Mansfield, "Early
American Glass," 1927, black &
white illustrations, 496 pp....... 45.00

Krivine, J., "Jukebox Saturday
Night," 1977, hard cover w/dust
jacket, 160 pp.................. 200.00

Larsen, Ellouise B., "American
Historical Views on Staffordshire
China," 1939, autographed by author, 8¼ x 11".................. 75.00

Lee, Ruth Webb, "Antique Fakes
and Reproductions," 1938, first
edition, illustrated, 224 pp. 235.00

Lindsey, Bessie M., "American
Historical Glass," 1967, black &
white illustrations, 541 pp. 80.00

McClinton, Katharine M., "Antiques
of American Childhood," 1970,
C.N. Potter, 7½ x 10¼",
351 pp........................ 55.00

Meyer, John D., "A Handbook of
Old Mechanical Penny Banks,"
1949, 6¼ x 9¼" 60.00

Parke Bernet Galleries catalogs,
"Early American Glass—The Collection of Alfred B. Maclay," forewords by Sam Laidacker & George
S. McKearin, illustrated, 1935,
2 vols. 60.00

Randall, Richard, "American Furniture in the Museum of Fine Arts,"
Boston, 1962, in slip case 80.00

Rice, A. H. & Stoudt, John B., "The
Shenandoah Pottery," Strasburg,
Virginia, 1929................. 60.00

Ware, William Porter, "Price List of
Occupational and Society Emblems
Shaving Mugs," 1949, Lightner
Publishing, 96 pp. 26.00

Watkins, Lura Woodside, "Cambridge Glass 1818 to 1888," 1930,
black & white illustrations,
199 pp........................ 30.00

CIVIL WAR RELATED

More books have been written about the

Civil War era (1861-65) than any other period in the history of our country. The following listing includes books by and about those directly involved in the fighting, the overall history of the conflict and the years following.

"Abraham Lincoln - The War Years,"
by Carl Sandburg, 1939, Harcourt,
Brace & Co., 426 halftone photos,
244 cuts of cartoons, letters &
documents..................... 75.00

"Butler's Book," by General Benjamin Butler, 1892, autobiography
w/maps & engravings, 1,154 pp... 25.00

"Capture & Escape, Confederate
Prison Life," by Willard Glazier,
1866, Albany (shelf wear) 25.00

"Constitutional View of the Late War
Between the States," by Alexander H. Stephens, 1868 & 1870,
Philadelphia, 2 vols............. 20.00

"Firearms of the Confederacy," by
Fuller & Stewart, 1944, first
edition 50.00

"Grant & Sherman: Their Campaigns
& Generals," by Headley, 1865,
numerous steel engravings
(covers scuffed) 47.00

"History of the Fighting 14th, 1861-
1911" 50.00

"Incidents & Anecdotes of The Civil
War," by Admiral Porter, 1891.... 35.00

"The Lost Cause," by Edward A. Pollard, 1867, numerous steel engraved portraits................ 48.00

"Memoirs of Lt. Gen. Scott LL.D,"
Vol. II, 1864 .... 25.00

"Official War Record Book," 1898, illustrated, over 1,000 illustrations
pertaining to Civil War, 13 x 18".. 195.00

"Personal Memoirs," by P.H.
Sheridan, 1888, 2 vols............ 28.50

"Pinkerton's Report on A. Lincoln's
Passage From Harrisburg to
Washington, D.C.," 1861, full-leather, 20 pp.................. 100.00

"Stories of the Civil War," by Bliasdale, 1890 .... 10.00

"The Union Indian Brigade In the
Civil War," by Wiley Britton,
1922 .... 250.00

"The Uprising of a Great People,"
1861 .... 17.50

"The War With The South," by
Robert Tomes, 3 vols. 100.00

PRESIDENTS & HISTORICAL FIGURES

The following listing includes a wide cross-section of books by and about former Presidents of the United States and other persons of note.

"Abe Lincoln's Yarns & Stories,"
1901, 500 pp. 15.00

"Al Capone's Biography," 1930, published by Ives Washburn 25.00

"The Authentic Life of President McKinley," 1901 . . . . 25.00

"Beethoven - The Man Who Freed Music," by Robert H. Schanffler, 1929, dust jacket over black cloth cover, 659 pp. 40.00

"Biography of Theodore Roosevelt," by William Roscoe Thayer, 1919 . . 15.00

"Buffalo Bill Autobiography," illustrated by N.C. Wyeth, first edition 35.00

"Cartoon History of T. Roosevelt's Career," by Shaw, 1910, New York, first edition, illustrated, 254 pp. 25.00

"Diaries of George Washington," by Fitzpatrick, 1929, Regents edition, Boston, dust jackets, 4 vols 18.50

"Dwight D. Eisenhower at Ease," 1967 . . . . 6.00

"F.D.R., My Boss," by Grace Tully, 1949 . . . . 8.00

"Footprints of Calvin Coolidge," 1938 . . . . 15.00

"From Tannery To the White House - The Life of Ulysses S. Grant," 1885 . . . . 24.50

"The Inner Life of Abraham Lincoln," by F.B. Carpenter, 1877 . . . . 25.00

"Jesse James Was My Neighbor," by Croy, signed, first edition 25.00

"The Last of the Great Scouts, The Life Story of Buffalo Bill," by Helen Cody Witmore, 1918, introduction by Zane Grey, illustrated, w/dust jacket 24.00

"Life and Glorious Deeds of Admiral Dewey," by J. Stickney, 1899, autographed by author 45.00

"Life & Times of Horace Greeley," by Ingersoll, 1874 . . . . 40.00

"Life of Hon. James G. Blaine," 1884, published in Des Moines, Iowa, illustrated 12.00

"Life of Sitting Bull & History of the Indian War," 1891 . . . . 75.00

"Life of William McKinley," by Ingersoll, 1901, first edition 30.00

"Lincoln, Emancipator of Nation," by Hill, 1928, New York, first edition 6.50

"The Marvelous Career of Theo. Roosevelt & the Story of His African Trip," by Charles Morris, 1910, illustrated 17.00

"My Experiences in the World War," autobiography by John J. Pershing, No. 16/2100, dust jackets, 2 vols. 27.50

"The President's War Message," April 2, 1917, by Woodrow Wilson, published by Clode, Grosset & Dunlap, 47 pp. 50.00

"Queen Victoria's Memoirs of the Prince Consort," ca. 1867 . . . . 20.00

"The Story of My Life," by Helen Keller, 1904, Cambridge 55.00

"The Toy Shop Story of Lincoln," 1908 . . . . 10.00

"Up From Slavery," autobiography by Booker T. Washington 25.00

"White House Years, Mandate For Change," by Dwight D. Eisenhower, 1963, illustrated w/photos 10.00

STATE & LOCAL HISTORIES
ALASKA

"Gold Mining in the Yukon & All About Alaska," 1897, good photographs, fair binding 50.00

"Travels in Alaska," 1915, by John Muir 18.50

"Yukon Territory - Its History & Resources," photographs, panoramas & map, Ottawa, first edition 57.00

ILLINOIS

"A Complete History of Illinois from 1673 to 1873," 1874, by Alexander Davidson & Bernard Stuve, 943 pp. 40.00

"Canton, Illinois, Its Pioneers & History," 1871, published by Swan . . . 90.00

"Chicago As It Is & Was," 1872, Chicago fire, by Luzerne, illustrated, 319 pp. 14.00

"Chicago, The Great Central Market," 1921, editorials & illustrations of buildings, theatres, the Field Museum, stockyard & other sites, published by Marshall Field & Co., 12 x 17" 100.00

"History of Round Prairie & Plymouth, Illinois, 1831-75," 1876, first settlers, Mormonism, etc., by Young, Chicago, 302 pp. 60.00

"History of Schuyler & Brown Counties, Illinois," 1882 . . . . 50.00

"History of Stephenson County, Illinois," 1972 . . . . 25.00

"History of Winnebago County, Illinois," 1877, published by H.F. Kett Co. 85.00

"Past & Present of Boone County, Illinois," 1877 . . . . 45.00

"Portrait & Biographical Record of Macon County, Illinois," 1893 . . . . . 55.00

"Reminiscences of Bureau County, Illinois," 1872, by N. Matson 35.00

IOWA

"Census of Iowa," 1905 . . . . 10.00

"Early Days of Rock Island & Davenport," 1942, published by Lakeside Press 15.00

"Fifty Years in Iowa, 1838-1888,"
1888, by J.M.D. Burrows,
Davenport 60.00
"History of Fayette County, Iowa,"
1878, leather bound 45.00
"History of Mt. Pleasant," 1909, over
280 identified homes, churches,
businesses & landmarks 45.00
"Old Stone Capital Remembers
(When Iowa City was Young),"
1929, ex-library 17.50

MASSACHUSETTS
"The City of Chelsea, Mas-
sachusetts," 1898, illustrated 12.50
"History of Worcester County, Massachusetts," 1879, 1,372 pp. 125.00
"Representative Men and Old Fami-
lies of Southeastern Mas-
sachusetts," 1912, published by
J.H. Beers & Co., Chicago, Illinois,
3 vols. 55.00

MISSOURI
"Atlas of Marion County, Missouri,"
1875 . . . . 127.50
"History of Lewis, Clark, Knox &
Scotland Counties, Missouri,"
1887, illustrated, published by
Goodspeed 50.00
"Portrait & Biographical record of
Marion, Ralls & Pike Counties,
Missouri," 1895, 802 pp. 97.50

OHIO
"Centennial History of Columbus and
Franklin Co., O.," 1909, by Wil-
liam A. Taylor, biographical in-
dex, illustrated, Vol. 2, 820 pp.
(rebound) 128.00
"History of Lisbon, Ohio, 1803-1903,"
200 pp. 25.00
"History of the Cincinnati Fire
Department," 1895, first edition . . 215.00
"Steubenville & Jefferson Co.,
Ohio," 1797-1897, 200 pp. 95.00

PENNSYLVANIA
"History & Directory of the Three
Towns - Brownsville, Bridgeport,
West Brownsville," 1904, fold-out
map & bibliography, by J. Perry
Hart, illustrated, flyleaf auto-
graphed, 686 pp. 46.50
"History of Pike & Monroe Coun-
ties," 1886, illustrated (spine
loose) 50.00
"History of Wayne County, Pa.,"
1880, 409 pp., hardbound 65.00
"The Story of Pittsburgh's Sesquicen-
tennial," 1908, by King, many
photographs, large format 25.00

WISCONSIN
"A History of Old Crawford County,
Wisconsin," 1932, 2 vol. 100.00

"Commemorative Biographical Record of Fox River Valley," 1895,
1,295 pp. 90.00
"Illustrated History of the State of
Wisconsin," 1875, 800 pp. (covers
poor) 15.00
"Memoirs of Milwaukee County,"
1909, by Watrous, 2 vol.,
1,640 pp. 90.00
"Pioneer History Milwaukee, 1876-
90," by Buck, 5 vols. 115.00
"Pioneers of Outagamie County,"
1895, 305 pp. 22.00
Plat book, Brown County, 1950, soft
bound 10.00
Plat book, LaCrosse County, 1946,
soft bound 10.00
"Portrait & Biographical Album of
Green Lake, Marquette &
Waushara Counties," 1890,
854 pp. 55.00
"Report on The Transportation Route
Along the Wisconsin & Fox Rivers,
in the State of Wisconsin Between
the Mississippi River & Lake Michigan," by Gouverneur K. Warren &
A.A. Humphreys, 1876, Washington, D.C., complete w/ten fold-out
maps & diagrams & fold-out illustrated title page, brown cloth
covers, ex-library 110.00

BOTTLE OPENERS

Goose Bottle Opener

*Corkscrews were actually the first bottle
openers and these may date back to the mid-
18th century, but bottle openers, as we know
them today, are strictly a 20th century item
and came into use only after Michael J.
Owens invented the automatic bottle machine
in 1903. Avid collectors have spurred this relatively new area of collector interest that requires only a modest investment. Our listing,
by type of metal, encompasses the four basic types sought by collectors: advertising
openers; full figure openers which stand alone
or hang on the wall; flat figural openers such
as the lady's leg shape; and openers with embossed, engraved or chased handles.*

Advertising, "Alpen Brau Beer,"
metal $4.50
Advertising, "Buffalo Beer," metal,
flat figural boot 40.00

Advertising, "Heinz 57," metal 5.00
Advertising, wall-type, "Old Canada
Dry," cast iron 8.00
Advertising, "Pepsi," brass 12.00
Advertising, "Round Oak Stoves,"
metal 20.00
Cast iron, model of a baseball cap,
"New York Mets" 20.00
Cast iron, full figure billy-goat, seat-
ed, John Wright Co. 145.00
Cast iron, figural black face w/wide
grin, red bow tie, exaggerated
features 160.00
Cast iron, full figure cowboy &
cactus 25.00
Cast iron, full figure cowboy, standing w/guitar 155.00
Cast iron, full figure crab 20.00
Cast iron, full figure drunk by
cactus 135.00
Cast iron, full figure drunk at street
sign, "Bourbon Street, New
Orleans," ashtray base, old polychrome paint, 4¾" h. 22.50
Cast iron, full figure elephant
w/trunk down standing on open-
ing device, old polychrome paint,
3 1/8"l. 45.00
Cast iron, full figure goose w/head
down standing on base, black
neck, white body & green base,
worn paint, light rust, 3 5/8" l.
(ILLUS.)..................... 75.00
Cast iron, full figure monkey seated
beside tree stump 195.00
Cast iron, full figure Paddy the
Pledgemaster, young man holding
long paddle................... 235.00
Cast iron, full figure rooster, John
Wright Co.................... 45.00
Cast iron, full figure seagull on
stump, John Wright Co.......... 20.00
Cast iron, full figure squirrel
crouched on branch, John Wright
Co. 75.00
Cast iron, wall-type, figural set of
teeth, original pink & white paint,
hanging holes at sides & top,
marked "Patent pending," 3½" l.
(some paint wear & rust) 10.00
Cast iron, wall-type, four-eyed lady,
Wilton Products 58.00
Cast metal, wall-type w/cap catch-
er, "Sprite," Sprite Boy, 1950's 9.00
Sterling silver, Royal Danish patt.,
International.................. 35.00

BOTTLES & FLASKS

BITTERS
African Stomach Bitters, Spruance,

Stanley & Co., round amber,
9 5/8" h. $65.00
American Life Bitters - P.E. Iler,
Manufacturer, Omaha, Nebraska -
American Life Bitters, cabin-
shaped, amber, pontil,
8 7/8" h............. 1,000.00 to 1,500.00
Angostura Bark Bitters, Eagle Liqueur Distiller, globe-shaped, amber, 7" h. 91.00
Annable's Mandrake & Antibilious
Bitters, True Loverin, Prop.,
Colebrook, N.H., oval, almost complete paper label, aqua, 7½" h. 40.00
Asparagine Bitters, Asparagine Bitters Co. - Patented, round, clear,
embossed asparagus spears at
shoulders, 11" h. 75.00
Atwood's - Vegetable Dyspeptic -
Bitters, rectangular, aqua,
6¾" h....................... 75.00

Augauer Bitters

Augauer Bitters - Augauer Bitters
Co. - Chicago, rectangular, green,
original paper label each side,
8" h. (ILLUS.) .... 75.00 to 125.00
Baxter's (Dr.) - Mandrake Bitters -
Lord Bros - Proprietors - Burlington, Vt., 12-sided, smooth base,
aqua, 6½" h. 15.00
Begg's Dandelion Bitters - Chicago,
Ill., amber, 9½" h. 130.00
Bell's (Dr.) - Blood Purifying - Bitters
- The Great English Remedy, rectangular, amber, 9¾" h. 95.00
Ben-Hur Bitters, square, amber,
9½" h....................... 125.00
Big Bill Best Bitters, square, orange-
amber, w/paper labels,
12 1/8" h. 77.00
Bissell's Tonic, Patented Jany 21,
1868 - O.P. Bissell, Peoria, Ill.,
square, amber, 9" h. 225.00
Botanic Stomach Bitters - Bach
Meese & Co., San Francisco,
square, amber, 9½" h. 125.00
Bourbon Whiskey Bitters, barrel-
shaped, pink-amber,
9¼" h................. 325.00 to 350.00

Brown (F.), Boston, Sarsaparilla &
Tomato Bitters, oval, aqua, pontil,
9½" h. 125.00

Buhrer's Gentian Bitters - S. Buhrer,
Proprietor, square, amber,
8 9/16" h. 100.00

Burdock Blood Bitters - Toronto,
Ont. - The T. Milburn Co. Ltd.,
rectangular, clear, 8½" h. 50.00

Caldwell's (Dr.) Herb Bitters - The
Great Tonic, triangular, amber,
12¾" h. 175.00

Callenders (Dr.) - Liver Bitters,
round, clear, w/paper label,
9¾" h. . . . . .75.00 to 125.00

Campbell's (Dr.) Scotch Bitters,
strap-sided flask, amber, ¼ pt.,
6 1/8" h. . . . . .135.00 to 175.00

Canton (star) Bitters, round w/lady's
leg neck, amber,
12¼" h. . . . . .200.00 to 250.00

Capitol Bitters - U.S.A. - Dr. M.M.
Fenner's, Peoples Remedies -
1872-1900 - Fredonia, NY, rectangular, aqua, w/paper label,
9" h. 47.50

Capuziner Stomach Bitters, Spellman
Distilling Co., Peoria, Illinois,
cabin-shaped, amber, w/paper la-
bel, qt., 8¼" h. 260.00

Clarke's Sherry Wine Bitters,
Sharon, Mass., Only 42 cts., rectangular, aqua, pontil, oversized
qt., 10" h. 325.00

Clarke's Vegetable Sherry Wine Bitters, Sharon, Mass., Only 70 cts.,
rectangular, deep bluish aqua,
pontil, ½ gal., 11 3/5" h. 315.00

Clark's Giant Bitters, Philada., Pa.,
rectangular, aqua, w/paper label,
6¾" h. 45.00

Congress - Bitters, rectangular, am-
ber, 9¼" h. 230.00

Constitution Bitters - A.M.S.2. -
1864, rectangular, amber,
9¼" h. 450.00

Corwitz Stomach Bitters, square,
amber, 7 5/8" h. 72.00

Curtis & Perkins - Wild Cherry - Bitters, round, aqua, pontil, original
label, 6 7/8" h. 82.00

DeWitt's - Stomach Bitters - Chicago,
oval, amber, w/paper label,
7½" h. 50.00

Dods (Dr. J. Bovee) Imperial Wine
Bitters, New York, rectangular,
aqua 100.00

Drake's (S.T.) - 1860 Plantation - Bitters, cabin-shaped, six-log, rare
variant without the "X," golden
amber, 10" h. 80.00

Drake's - Plantation - Bitters -
Patented 1862, cabin-shaped, six-

log, arabesque variant, true yel-
low, 10" h. 200.00

Fish (The) Bitters - W.H. Ware,
Patented 1866, figural fish, am-
ber, 11½" h. 150.00

Gates (C.) & Cos. - Life of Man - Bitters - L....C. Gates Son & Company, Middleton, Annapolis County, Nova Scotia, rectangular,
aqua, w/paper labels, 8" h. 45.00

Goodhue's (Old Dr.) Root & Herb
Bitters - Salem, Mass. - J.H. Russell & Co., rectangular, aqua,
w/paper label, 8 7/8" h. 80.00

Greeley's Bourbon Bitters

Greeley's Bourbon Bitters, barrel-
shaped, ten rings above & below
center band, deep red amber,
w/paper label, 9½" h.
(ILLUS.) . . . . .225.00 to 250.00

Greer's Eclipse - Bitters - Louisville,
Ky., square, amber, 9½" h. 55.00

Griel's Herb Bitters, Griel & Young,
Mftrs., Lancaster, PA. U.S.A.,
round, aqua, 9 3/8" h. 90.00

Hall's Bitters - E.E. Hall, New Haven
- Established 1842, barrel-shaped,
amber, w/paper label, 9 1/8" h. . . . 105.00

Hansard's Trade Mark Genuine Bitters, Swansea and Llanelly, pottery, cream & brown w/black
lettering, 7¾" h. 50.00

Hibbard's (Dr. R.F.) Wild Cherry Bitters, C.N. Crittention - Proprietor,
N.Y., round, aqua, 8¼" h. 365.00

Holtzermans Patent Stomach Bitters,
cabin-shaped, amber, w/paper la-
bel, 9 5/8" h. 145.00

Home Bitters - Jas. A. Jackson &
Co. Proprietors - Saint Louis, Mo.,
square, amber, 9" h. 55.00

Hoofland's (Dr.) German Bitters -
Liver Complaint - C.M. Jackson,
Philadelphia - Dyspepsia & Co.,
rectangular, aqua, w/paper label,
pt. 50.00

Hopkin's (Dr. A.S.) Union Stomach
Bitters, Hartford, Conn., square,
amber, 9¾" h. 55.00
Hostetter's (Dr. J.) Stomach Bitters,
square, amber, w/paper label
reading "Hostetter's Celebrated
Stomach Bitters," 9" h. 35.00
Hostetter's (Dr. J.) Stomach Bitters,
square, amber, w/paper label,
9½" h. 35.00
Iron & Quinine Bitters - Burlington,
Vt. - N.K. Brown, rectangular,
aqua, 7 1/8" h. 70.00
John's (Dr. Herbert) - Indian Bitters -
Great Indian Discoveries, square
w/beveled corners, amber,
8 5/8" h. 190.00
Khoosh Tonic Bitters, Liverpool,
England, ca. 1897 .... 45.00
Kimball's Jaundice - Bitters - Troy,
N.H., rectangular, golden amber,
w/paper label, 7" h. 250.00
Landsberg (M:G.) Chicago (bitters),
square, amber, 11" h. 450.00
Langley's (Dr.) Root & Herb Bitters -
99 (numbers backwards) Union
St., Boston, round, whittled, aqua,
8¼" h. 40.00
Langley's (Dr.) Root & Herb Bitters -
76 Union St., Boston, round,
aqua 35.00
Lash's Bitters Co., New York, Chicago, San Francisco, round, amber,
11" h. 53.00
Lash's Kidney and Liver Bitters - The
Best Cathartic and Blood Purifier,
square, amber, w/paper label, 9"
h. 26.00
Lashs Liver Bitters - Nature's Tonic
Laxative, square, amber,
9 3/8" h. 15.00
Litthauer Stomach Bitters (paper label), Hartwig Kantorowicz, Posen,
Ham - burg, Paris, square case
gin shape, milk white, miniature,
3¾" h. 55.00

Litthauer Stomach Bitters

Litthauer Stomach Bitters (paper la-
bel), Hartwig Kantorowicz, Posen,
Berlin, Hamburg, Germany,
square case gin shape, milk
white, 9½" h. (ILLUS.) 130.00
Malt Bitters Company, Boston,
U.S.A., round, smooth base,
green, pt., 9" h. 34.00
Marks' Kidney and Liver Bitters,
square, amber, 9½" h. 40.00
Marshall's Bitters - The Best Laxa-
tive and Blood Purifier, square,
amber, 8 5/8" h. 40.00
Mishler's Herb Bitters - Table Spoon
Graduation (ruled marker) - Dr.
S.B. Hartman & Co. - 40 Med.
Doses, square, amber, 9" h. 40.00
Moffat (John) - Phoenix Bitters -
Price $1.00 - New York, rectangu-
lar w/wide beveled corners,
aqua, ½ pt., 5½" h. 55.00
Morning (Star) Bitters, triangular,
amber, 12 7/8" h. 185.00

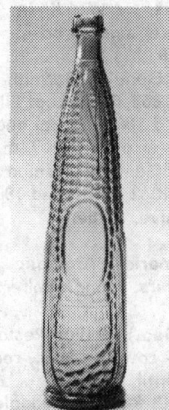

National Bitters Bottle

National Bitters, figural ear of corn,
amber, ¾ qt., 12 5/8" h.
(ILLUS.) 206.00
National Bitters, figural ear of corn,
light yellow-amber, ¾ qt.,
12 5/8" h. 309.00
National Bitters, figural ear of corn,
puce, ¾ qt., 12 5/8" h. 600.00
Old Hickory Celebrated Stomach Bitters - J. Grossman, New Orleans,
square, amber, 8¾" h. 65.00
Old Homestead Wild Cherry Bitters -
Patent, cabin-shaped, amber,
9 7/8" h. 185.00
Old Sachem Bitters and Wigwam
Tonic, ribbed barrel shape,
amber, 9½" (ILLUS. top next
page) 188.00
Original Pocahontas Bitters, Y. Ferguson, round barrel shape w/ten
horizontal ribs above & below em-

bossing, narrow square collar,
aqua, 2¼" d., 9 5/16" h. 1,100.00

Old Sachem Bitters Bottle

Orruro Bitters, round, green, ¾ qt.,
10 5/8" h. 35.00
Pepsin Bitters - R.W. Davis Drug
Co., Chicago, U.S.A., rectangular,
green, 8 1/8" h. 65.00
Peruvian Bitters, w/"W & K" in
shield, square, smooth base,
amber, 9 1/8" h. 40.00
Petzold's (Dr.) Genuine German Bit-
ters, Incpt. 1862, The Great Elixir
of Life - Pat'd 1884, figural beehive, yellow w/olive tint, 7" h. . . . 250.00
Petzold's (Dr.) Genuine German Bitters, Incpt. 1862 - Patented 1884,
figural beehive, amber,
10 5/8" h. 83.00
Peychaud's American Aromatic
Cocktail Bitters, round, amber,
6" h. 40.00
Pierce's (Dr. Geo.) - Indian Restora-
tive Bitters - Lowell, Mass., rectangular, pontil, aqua 45.00
Pineapple - J.C. & Co., pineapple-
shaped, amber, ¾ qt., 8 7/8" h. . . 139.00
Poor Man's Family Bitters, rectangular, aqua, ½ pt., 6 3/8" h. 40.00
Prickley Ash Bitters Co., square,
amber, ¾ qt., 9¾" h. 18.00
Pyramid Bitters, open pontiled
triangle-shaped bottle w/dropped
corners, deep greenish aqua, 4"
base tapering to 1" at top, double
ring lip, 11" h. 150.00
Rainbow Tonic Bitters, rectangular,
three indented panels, full mint
colorful label showing a rainbow,
scene & w/lots of other writing,
honey amber, 8 7/8" h. 35.00
Rattinger's (Dr.) Herb and Root, St.
Louis, Mo., square, amber,
9 1/8" h. 104.00
Renz's (Dr.) Herb Bitters, square,
amber, 9 7/8" h. 125.00
Rex Kidney & Liver Bitters - Rex Bit-
ters, Nothing Else, square, amber,
10" h. 25.00

Rex Kidney and Liver Bitters - The
Best Laxative and Blood Purifier,
square, amber, w/50% of label,
9 5/8" h. 55.00
Richardson's (S.O.) - Bitters - South
Reading - Mass., rectangular
w/wide beveled corners, aqua,
pt., 6 7/8" h 62.00
Richardson's (W.L.) - Bitters - South
Reading - Mass., rectangular,
aqua, 7" h. 65.00
Roback's (Dr. C.W.) Stomach Bitters,
Cincinnati, O., barrel-shaped,
amber, 9 3/8" h. 175.00
Rush's - Bitters - A.H. Flanders M.D.
New York, square, amber,
8 7/8" h. 45.00
Sanborn's Kidney and Liver Vegeta-
ble Laxative Bitters, rectangular,
amber, 10" h. 67.00
Sazerac Aromatic Bitters, w/"PHD &
Co." monogram, lady's leg neck,
milk white, 12½" h. 334.00
Scheetz - Celebrated Bitter Cordial -
Philada., square, aqua, 9½" h. . . . 75.00
Severa (W.F.) - Stomach Bitters,
square, amber, 9 5/8" h. 83.00
Shepard's (Dr.) Compound Wahoo
Bitters, Grand Rapids, Mich., oval,
aqua, 7½" h. 195.00
Simon's Centennial Bitters - Trade
Mark, bust of Washington, aqua,
¾ qt., 9¾" h. 400.00
Skinner's (Dr.) Celebrated 25 Cent
Bitters, So. Reading, Mass., rec-
tangular, aqua, 8½" h. 105.00
Solomon's (Old Dr.) - Indian Wine
Bitters, rectangular, amber,
8 3/8" h. 75.00
Soule (Dr.) - Hop - Bitters - 1872,
scarce variation w/reversed "S" in
Soule, dark black-amber,
9¼" h. 60.00
Soule (Dr.) - Hop - Bitters - 1872,
hop flowers & leaf motif one side
(same side has "1872" on shoul-
der), square, amber, 7¾" h. 225.00
Stewarts (Dr. H.C.) - Tonic Bitters,
Col. O., rectangular, amber,
7½" h. 58.00
Sunny Castle Stomach Bitters, Jos.
Dudenhoefer, Milwaukee, square,
amber, w/label, 9" h. 104.00
Taylor's Trade Mark Perfection Rod-
ney Hop Bitter Brewery, Manchester (England), w/monogram,
round, green 75.00
(Try) Taylors' Hop Bitters - Taylors'
Fermented Ginger Beer, round,
tan pottery, England, 6¾" h. 26.00
Thomas (Dr.) Mayapple Bitters,
square, 90% label w/tax stamp
dated June 21, 1881, yellow am-
ber, 10" h. 50.00

Tippecanoe, H.H. Warner & Co.,
tree bark design w/canoe, golden
amber, ¾ qt., 9" h. 66.00
Toneco Stomach Bitters - Appetizer
& Tonic, square, clear, 9" h. 25.00
Turner Brothers, New York, barrel-
shaped, yellow amber,
9 7/8" h. 180.00
Vermo Stomach Bitters - Tonic and
Appetizer, square, clear,
9½" h. 18.00
Von Hopf's (Dr.) Curaco Bitters -
Chamberlain & Co., Des Moines
Iowa, square, long tapered collar,
amber, 9¼" h. 70.00
Von Hopfs (Dr.) - Curacoa Bitters -
Chamberlain & Co., Des Moines
Iowa, rectangular, amber, w/la-
bel, ½ pt., 7½" h. 58.00
Wait's Kidney and Liver Bitters -
California's Own True Laxative
and Blood Purifier, square,
amber, 8¾" h. 47.00
Wallace's Tonic Stomach Bitters -
Geo. Powell & Co., Chicago, Ill.,
square, amber, 9" h. 65.00
Whitcomb's (Faith) Nerve Bitters (pa-
per label), rectangular, aqua, pt.,
9¼" h. 40.00
Wilsons (Dr.) Herbine Bitters, The
Brayley Drug Co. Limited, St. John
N.B., oval, aqua, 6" h. 30.00
Wonne's (Dr.) Gesundheits Bitters,
square, amber, w/three labels,
9" h. 175.00
Wonser's (Dr.) U.S.A. Indian Root
Bitters, dark amber, ¾ qt.,
11" h. 1,500.00
Woodbury's Bitters - Steinhardt Bros.
& Co. NY, 16-sided, honey amber,
8" h. 38.00
Wood's (Dr.) Sarsaparilla & Wild
Cherry Bitters, rectangular, pontil,
aqua, 9" h. 350.00
Yerba Buena Bitters, S.F. Cal., flask-
shaped, amber, 8½" h. 50.00
Zingari Bitters - F. Rahter, round,
lady's leg neck, amber, 12" h. 180.00

FIGURALS

American silver dollar w/octopus on
top, milk white glass, pocket
size 1,000.00
Bear, applied face, yellow-green
glass......................... 375.00
Bear, Kummel-type, black opaque
glass, 11" h. 70.00
Billy club, amber glass,
10" l. ....60.00 to 90.00
Bust of Garfield (James A.), for
toilette water, ground lip, opening
on base, ca. 1880's 185.00
Bust of Washington (George),
marked "Beecher, Pat. June 9th,

1874," clear glass, 6¾" h. (traces
of sickness)................... 35.00
Cabin, square, "Perrin's Apple Ginger Phila. - Perrin's Ginger (surrounded by apple in relief) -
Depot No. 37 Nth Front St Philada," sloping collar & smooth base,
deep golden amber glass, ca.
1879-89, 10" h................. 75.00
Cigar, embossed "Germany," clear
glass......................... 19.00
Clam, amber glass, large size 69.00
Clock, "Happy Time," embossed
clock face on reverse, 80% front
label, screw lid 6.00
Lady's leg, Boker-type, dark amber
glass, 12" h. (two nicks on lip) ... 32.00
Lady's leg, "Boonekamp Sterndorff"
on base, aqua glass (stain)....... 10.00
Lady's leg, light golden amber glass,
small size 30.00
Mailbox, embossed "U.S. Mail
Patented Dec. 15, 1891," clear
glass......................... 129.00
Moses in Bullrushes, clear glass 85.00
Pig, unglazed pottery, 6¾" l........ 89.00
Pineapple, W. & Co., New York,
amber glass, 8" h. 210.00
Statue of Liberty, milk white glass
(no top) 140.00

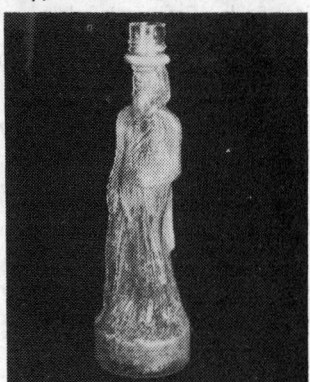

Flaccus Uncle Sam Bottle

Uncle Sam, Flaccus Company,
patented September 13, 1898,
ground lip, clear glass (ILLUS.) ... 55.00

FLASKS

*(Numbers used below refer to those used in
the McKearin's "American Glass.")*

American Eagle obverse & reverse,
head turned left, ribbon & two
semicircular rows of stars above,
edges corrugated horizontally
w/vertical medial rib, plain lip,
pontil, aquamarine, pt. (GII-24) ... 160.00
American Eagle obverse & reverse,
plain lip, horizontally corrugated

edges, pontil, amber, qt.
(GII-26) 950.00

American Eagle obverse & reverse,
plain lip, horizontally corrugated
edges, pontil, yellow-green, qt.
(GII-26) 675.00

American Eagle obverse & reverse,
"X" in oval frame below eagle,
plain lip, pontil, olive-amber,
½ pt. (GII-87) 85.00

American Eagle on oval obverse &
reverse, w/"Stoddard, N.H." in
oval frame on reverse, narrow
vertical rib edges, plain lip, pon-
til, olive-amber, pt. (GII-82) 120.00

American Eagle on oval frame, obverse & reverse, frame 3/8" from
base on obverse & 5/8" from base
on reverse, plain lip, olive-amber,
pt. (GII-83) 95.00

American Eagle w/"W. Ihmsen's"
above & "Glass" below on obverse, Sheaf of Rye w/"Agricul-
ture" above & farm implements
below on reverse, vertically
ribbed edges, plain lip, open pon-
til, pale green, pt. (GII-10) 770.00

American Eagle - Cornucopia, vertically ribbed edges, olive green,
pt. (GII-72) 55.00

American Eagle - Cornucopia, plain
lip, vertically ribbed edges, pontil,
green, pt. (GII-73) 100.00

American Eagle - Cornucopia, plain
lip, vertically ribbed edges, pontil,
olive-amber, pt. (GII-73) 90.00

Anchor w/fork-ended pennants inscribed "Baltimore" & "Glass
Works" on obverse, Phoenix rising
from flames on rectangular panel
inscribed "Resurgam" on reverse,
rounded collar, smooth edges,
aquamarine, pt. (GXIII-53) 75.00

Anchor w/fork-ended pennants inscribed "Baltimore" & "Glass
Works" on obverse, Phoenix rising
from flames on rectangular panel
inscribed "Resurgam" on reverse,
rounded collar, smooth edges,
honey amber, pt. (GXIII-53) 350.00

Chestnut, ten-diamond, long, flared
neck, sheared lip, rare olive-
amber, Zanesville, Ohio,
5¼" h. 2,300.00

Chestnut, 18 swirled ribs, aqua,
Midwestern, 5¼" h. 100.00

Chestnut, 24 vertical ribs, golden
amber, Zanesville, Ohio, 4¾" h.
(some residue) 425.00

Chestnut, 24 vertical ribs, deep amber, Zanesville, Ohio, 5" h. 300.00

Chestnut, 24 vertical ribs, sheared,
slightly flared mouth, green-aqua,
Zanesville, Ohio, 5¼" h. 275.00

Chestnut, deep olive-amber, New
England, 5" h. 120.00

Chestnut, light forest green, un-
usually short neck, New England,
5½" h. 85.00

Chestnut, plain globular body
w/slanted neck w/turned over lip,
sage green, 7 7/8" h. 165.00

Coffin, base embossed "K.H. &
G.Z.O.," aqua 95.00

Cornucopia - Urn, plain lip, vertically ribbed edges, pontil, olive-
amber, pt., GIII-4 (two minor base
chips, heavy wear) 35.00

Cornucopia - Urn, plain lip, vertically ribbed edges, pontil, olive
green, pt. (GIII-4) 50.00

Flora Temple obverse, plain reverse,
narrow rounded collar, smooth
edges, small handle, black cherry
amethyst, pt. (GXIII-21) 275.00

"For Pike's Peak" above prospector
w/staff w/two packs at end, bottle below right arm, & cane in
other hand, walking right on obverse, Hunter at left shooting stag
at right on reverse, aquamarine,
½ pt. (GXI-52) 165.00

"For Pike's Peak" above prospector
w/tools standing on oblong frame
on obverse, American Eagle
w/pennant above oblong frame
on reverse, smooth edges, bright
amber, qt. (GXI-24) 450.00

Hunter facing right wearing flat-top
stovepipe hat, short coat & full
trousers, game bag hanging at
left side, firing gun at two birds
flying upward at left, large puff of
smoke from muzzle, two dogs
running to left toward section of
rail fence - Fisherman standing on
shore near large rock, wearing
round-top stovepipe hat, v-neck
jacket, full trousers, fishing rod
held in left hand w/end resting on
ground, right hand holding large
fish, creel below left arm, mill
w/bushes & tree in left background, calabash, edges w/wide
flutes, minor exterior wear, iron
pontil, shaded reddish amber, qt.
(GXIII-4) 225.00

Jenny Lind bust, obverse & reverse,
wearing broad plain bertha, large
lyre below, scroll-type shape,
edges paneled vertically & forming flaring ten-sided scalloped
base or foot, plain lip, pontil,
aqua, pt. (GI-108) 675.00

"Jeny (sic) Lind" above bust - View
of Glasshouse w/"Glass Factory"
& six-pointed star above, calabash, vertically ribbed edges,

broad sloping collar, pontil,
aqua, qt. (GII-102) 100.00
"Kossuth" above bust - tall tree in
foliage, calabash, smooth edges,
sloping collar w/beveled ring,
pontil, aqua, qt. (GI-113) 50.00
"La Fayette" above bust & "T.S." &
bar below - "De Witt Clinton"
above bust & "Coventry C-T" below, plain lip, horizontally corrugated edges, pontil, olive
amber, pt. (GI-80) 650.00
Masonic Arch, pillars & pavement
w/Masonic emblems - American
Eagle without shield on breast,
plain oval frame below
w/"KCCNC" inside, smooth edges
w/single vertical rib, plain lip,
pontil, dark olive green, pt.
(GIV-18) 160.00
Masonic Arch w/"Farmer's Arms,"
sheaf of rye & farm implements
within arch - American Eagle,
w/shield w/seven bars on breast,
head turned to right, "Zanesville"
above eagle above oval frame
w/"Ohio" inside above "J.
Shepard & Co.," vertically ribbed
edge, open pontil, aqua, pt.
(GIV-32) 275.00
Masonic Arch w/"Farmer's Arms," &
sheaf of rye, pitchfork, shovel,
rake, sickle, axe & scythe within
arch - American Eagle w/shield
w/seven bars on breast, head
turned to right, "Zanesville"
above, eagle stands on oval
frame w/"Ohio" inside & "J.
Shepard & Co." beneath, vertically
ribbed edge, open pontil, olive
yellow, pt. (GIV-32) 1,550.00
Masonic Emblems - American Eagle
w/ribbon reading "E Pluribus
Unum" above & "IP" (old-
fashioned J) below in oval frame,
tooled mouth, plain edges, bright
blue-green, pt. (GIV-1) 275.00
Nailsea-type, pale amber w/pink
loopings (some very light wear on
sides, base pontil chip) 119.00
Pitkin, 30 ribs broken-swirled to the
right, sheared mouth & pontil,
medium green, Midwestern, trace
of exterior wear, 7½" h. 350.00
Pitkin, 36 ribs swirled to left,
sheared mouth & pontil, amber,
6¼" h. 195.00
Scroll w/six-point star above seven-
point star, obverse & reverse, vertical medial rib, plain lip, pontil,
green, pt. (GIX-14) 350.00
Scroll w/two six-point stars, obverse
& reverse, long neck w/plain lip,
aqua, qt., 9" h. (GIX-2) . . . 50.00 to 100.00

Scroll w/two eight-point stars, obverse & reverse, plain lip, aqua,
pt., 7" h. (GIX-11a) 220.00
Spring Tree (leaves & buds) - Sum-
mer Tree, smooth edges, plain
lip, pontil, faint haziness, blue-
green, qt. (GX-18) 80.00
Strap flask, base embossed
"S.S.P.B.," bright green, qt. (small
lip chip) 15.00
Strap flask, embossed anchor,
amber, pt. 12.00
Strap flask, embossed grapes &
leaves, ground screw top, amber,
½ pt. (some outside haze) 19.00
Strap flask, embossed "Winchell &
Davis, Albany, N.Y.," amber 22.00

Success to the Railroad Flask

"Success to the Railroad" around
embossed horse pulling cart -
similar reverse, sheared lip, pontil, deep olive green, pt., GV-3
(ILLUS.) 110.00
"Summer" Tree - "Winter" Tree,
plain lip, smooth edges, pontil,
yellow-green, pt. (GX-15) 500.00
Summer Tree - Winter Tree, plain
lip, smooth edges, pontil, aqua,
qt. (GX-19) 85.00
Sunburst w/sixteen rays, obverse &
reverse, rays converging to a definite point at center & covering
entire side of flask, plain lip,
open pontil, colorless w/faint blue
tinge, pt. (GVIII-26) 253.00
Sunburst w/twenty-one triangular
sectioned rays, obverse & reverse,
sunburst centered by ring w/a dot
in the middle, pontil, blue-green,
½ pt. (GVIII-14) 1,155.00
Sunburst w/twenty-one triangular
sectioned rays, obverse & reverse,
plain lip, open pontil, deep yel-
lowish green, ½ pt. (GVIII-16) 235.00
Sunburst w/twenty-four triangular
sectioned rays, obverse & reverse,

two concentric rings w/dot in center, plain lip, pontil, medium
green, pt. (GVIII-1) 770.00
Taylor bust below "Rough & Ready"
- American Eagle w/shield
w/eight vertical & three horizontal
bars on breast, head turned left,
"Masterson" above 13 five-pointed
stars above eagle, plain lip, open
pontil, pale green, qt. (GI-77) 797.50
U.S. Army officer in full-dress uniform ca. 1851-58, standing at attention w/long rifle w/bayonet
held vertically - large daisy,
edges w/four wide vertical flutes,
calabash, iron pontil, aqua, qt.
(GXIII-15)...................... 140.00
"Washington" above bust - Taylor
bust below "Bridgeton ★ New
Jersey," plain lip, vertically ribbed
edges, pontil, aqua, pt. (GI-24) ... 170.00
"Washington" above bust (facing
right) - "Jackson" above bust,
plain lip, vertically ribbed edges
w/heavy medial rib, pontil, olive
green, ½ pt. (GI-34)............. 145.00
Washington bust - Taylor bust, plain
lip, smooth edges, pontil, cornflower blue, qt. (GI-51) 500.00
Washington bust below "General
Washington" - American Eagle
w/shield w/seven bars on breast,
head turned to right, "E Pluribus
Unum" in semicircle above, vertically ribbed edges, plain lip, open
pontil, emerald green, pt.
(GI-14).......................1,800.00
Washington bust below "The Father
of His Country" - plain reverse,
rolled collar, open pontil, smooth
edges, greenish blue, qt.
(GI-47) 245.00
Washington Monument above "Baltimore" - "Corn For The World" in
semicircle above large ear of
corn, plain lip, smooth edges,
pontil, clear green, ½ pt.
(GVI-7) 750.00

INKS

Umbrella-type Ink Bottle

Boat-shaped, clear mold-blown
glass, applied lip, embossed "Sanford Patent Applied For" on base,
1 15/16 x 2½", 2" h. 35.00
Cathedral, six Gothic arch panels,
cobalt blue glass, embossed
"Carter," ½ pt., 6 1/8" h........ 85.00
Cathedral, six Gothic arch panels,
cobalt blue glass, embossed
"Carter," smooth base, pt.,
7 7/8" h. 74.00
Cone-shaped, amber glass, em-
bossed "Wood's Black Ink" in
shield (pontil crack on base, small
lip chip repair) 100.00
Cone-shaped, round, cobalt blue
glass, 2¼" h. 30.00
Cone-shaped, yellow glass, labeled
"David's Magic Writing Fluid"..... 12.00
Cylindrical, aqua glass, embossed
"Carter's," ½ pt. 9.00
Cylindrical, amber glass, embossed
"S. Fine Blk Ink," open pontil (in-
side stain, lip chip repair)....... 75.00
Cylindrical, cobalt blue glass, em-
bossed "Carter's No. 3," 6" h. 40.00
Cylindrical, cobalt blue glass, em-
bossed "Carter's," 9½" h........ 150.00
Cylindrical, master size, cobalt blue
glass, embossed "Sanford,"
8 oz........................... 20.00
Cylindrical, master size, cobalt blue
glass, embossed "Harrison's
Columbian Ink," open pontil...... 900.00
Cylindrical, master size, dark aqua
glass, pouring lip, embossed
"Hover Phila.," open pontil, 6" h.
(inside stain).................... 95.00
Cylindrical w/pen holder on shoulder, olive green glass, 2" base,
2¼" h. (some lip flakes) 45.00
Domed w/central neck, olive amber
mold-blown glass, embossed "Ber-
tinguiot," open pontil 175.00
Domed w/offset neck, aqua mold-
blown glass, applied lip, embossed "A & F," 1 7/8" h......... 30.00
Domed w/offset neck, very dark
amber, embossed "J & IEM" 140.00
Figural globe, aqua glass, embossed
"J. Raynald, Globe of the World
Ink," embossed continents
w/names, smooth base, 2¼"
tooled lip ....675.00 to 700.00
Figural "Ma" & "Pa" Carter, porcelain, marked "Carter's Inx" on
base, pr. ....150.00 to 175.00
Figural shoe, clear glass, embossed
fancy buckle & flowers, open pontil, tooled & ground lip 89.00
Octagonal, aqua glass, embossed
"Estes N.Y. Ink," open pontil,
2¼" d., 4 1/16" h. 600.00
Octagonal, aqua glass, embossed

"Laughlin and Bushfield, Wheeling, Va.," smooth base 80.00

Octagonal, deep olive yellow glass, embossed "Warrens Congress Ink," open pontil, 1 5/8" d., 2 7/8" h. 925.00

Octagonal, medium cobalt blue glass, embossed "Harrison's Columbian Ink," open pontil, 1 5/8" d., 1 3/8" h. 4,000.00

Paneled cylinder, 12-sided, aqua glass, embossed "Harrison's Columbian Ink," open pontil, 6¼" h. 165.00

Square, cobalt blue glass, 2" h. 15.00

Triangular w/neck at narrow end, blue-green mold-blown glass, applied lip, embossed "Allings Patd Apl 25 1871," 2 3/8" x 2½", 1 7/8" h. 45.00

Umbrella-type (8-panel cone shape), aqua glass, open pontil (ILLUS.) .. 25.00

Umbrella-type (8-panel cone shape), medium green mold-blown glass, folded rim, tubular pontil, 2½" h. 130.00

Umbrella-type (8-panel cone shape), reddish-amber mold-blown glass, probably Stoddard, New Hampshire, early 19th c., 2½" h. 33.00

Umbrella-type (paneled cone shape), green glass, open pontil .. 60.00

MEDICINES

Clemen's Indian Tonic Bottle

Agnew's (Dr.) Cure for the Heart, rectangular, clear, 7¾" h. 12.00

Alexander's Sure Cure For Malaria, Akron, Oh., rectangular, amber .. 24.00

Allen's Lung Balsam, rectangular, aqua, 8" h. 18.00

Allison's Cherry Balsam, Lincoln, rectangular w/beveled corners, light blue, 5 3/8" h. 7.00

American Pulmonary Balsam, round

w/thin flared lip, six-star balsam, ca. 1830, aqua, 5" h. 125.00

Ayer's (Dr. J.C.) Cherry Pectoral, rectangular, aqua, 7" h. 28.00

Baker's Vegetable Blood & Liver Cure, Lookout Mountain Medicine Co. Manufacturers & Proprietors, Greenville, Tenn., oval, amber, 9½" h. 245.00

Balsam of Wild Cherry & Tar, Barnes & Park, New York, rectangular w/indented panels, open pontil, aqua, 8" h. 175.00

Bancroft's (D.W.) Liniment, Instant Relief, Marshfield, Vermont, aqua 12.00

Barclay's American Balsam of Spikenard, Blood Root, Wild Cherry, Comfrey & Elecampane, rectangular, thousands of seed bubbles, crude six-star balsam, aqua, 6" h. 250.00

Barry's Tricopherous for the Skin and Hair, aqua.................. 20.00

Bear Oil, pontil, aqua 15.00

Bell-Ans, Bell & Co., Inc., Orangeburg, N.Y., USA, rectangular, amber, 2¾" h.................... 6.00

Blackman's (Dr.) Genuine Healing Balsam, eight-sided, rolled lip, open pontil, grey flint glass 40.00

Brogas (Dr.) Blood and Liver Syrup, 59 R.R. St., Oneida, N.Y., rectangular, clear, 8¼" h. 35.00

Bromo-Seltzer, Emerson Drug Co., Baltimore, MD, cobalt blue, 2½" h. 5.00

Bromo-Seltzer, round, cobalt blue, 4" h. 6.50

Brown's Household Panacea & Family Liniment, Curtis & Brown Mfg. Co. Ld., New York, rectangular, aqua, 5¾" h. 15.00

Brown's (J.T.) Select Preparation, 292 Washington St., Boston 130.00

Bull's (Dr. W.H.) Herbs and Iron, medium to light amber, 4½" w., 9½" h. 14.00

Caldwell's (Dr. W.B.) Syrup Pepsin, Toronto Ont., clear, 9" h. 10.00

Caldwell's Syrup Pepsin, Mf'd. by Pepsin Syrup Company, Monticello, Illinois, rectangular, aqua, 3" h. 6.00

Carter's (Dr.) Compound Pulmonary Balsam, crude flanged lip, open pontil, aqua 110.00

Cavanaugh Bros. Wonder Colic Cure, rectangular w/flat back & sides & curved front, clear, 4 15/16" h. 15.00

Celro-Kola, Phil Blumauer & Co., Portland, Oregon, square, unusual script embossing, amber, 10" h. .. 56.00

Chamberlain's Cough Remedy, A. N.

Chamberlain, Elkhart, Ind., rectangular, aqua, 6" h. 6.50

Chamberlain's Pain Balm, Chamberlain Med. Co., Des Moines, Ia., U.S.A., rectangular, aqua, in unopened package, 7 1/8" h. (small stain & tear in package) ... 16.00

Cherry Pectoral, Lowell, Mass., open pontil, aqua 35.00

Clarke's (Rev. W.) European Cough Remedy, rectangular w/indented panels, 8" h. 275.00

Clarke's World Famed Blood Mixture, blue 16.00

Clark/Lincoln World Famed Blood Mixture, rectangular, aqua, 7¼" h. 12.00

Clemen's Indian Tonic prepared by Geo. W. House, oval, embossed Indian, pontil, aqua, 95% label, 5½" h. (ILLUS.) 280.00

Conner's Blood Remedy, Chattanooga, Tenn., amber, 7½" h. 30.00

Cox's (Mrs. M.) Indian Vegetable Decoction, Balto., round, unpontiled, aqua, 8" h. (some stain) 75.00

Craigs (Dr.) Kidney Cure, oval, w/embossed kidneys, amber, 9¾" h. 1,100.00

Curlings' Citrate of Magnesia, cobalt blue 10.00

Davis & Miller American Worm Syrup, A Certain Remedy for Worms, six-sided w/thin flared lip, 4½" h. 185.00

Deakin & Hughes Chest Cough & Lung Healer, rectangular, 5½" h. 7.50

D.E.C. Balm, rectangular, pontil, aqua 30.00

Denton's (B.) Vegetable Healing Balsam, eight-sided, open pontil, aqua, 4" h. 42.50

Derma-Balm, Larkin Co., Buffalo, NY, clear, 5" h. 6.00

Duconge's Pectoral Balsam Syrup, New Orleans, aqua 9.00

Elaer's (Dr.) Vegetable Balm, open pontil, aqua, 7½" h. 200.00

Ely's Cream Balm, Ely Bros., New York, Hay Fever, Catarrh, sheared lip, rectangular, amber, 2½" h. .. 6.00

Ely's Nasal Cream Balm, Ely Bros., New York, oblong, amber, 3¼" h. 8.00

Erskine's (Dr.) Cactus Compound, Continental Mfg. Co., St. Louis, Mo., red amber 50.00

Fahnestock's Vermifuge, round, open pontil, aqua, 4" h. 27.00

Fenner's (Dr. M.M.) Kidney & Backache Cure, oval, amber, 95% label, 10" h. 24.00

Flaggs (Prof. H.K.) - (six-point star monogram) - Balm of Excellence, pontil, aqua 80.00

Foley's Indian Botanic Balsam, aqua 12.00

Forestine Kidney Cure, amber, 9¼" h. 75.00

Forsha's Alterative Balm, rectangular, pontil, aqua, 4 1/8" h. 75.00

Fulham's Habits of Drink, labeled stoneware bottle, 1800, 6" h. 65.00

Gallagher's Syrup of Tar, Wild Cherry, Hoarhound etc., Philadelphia, aqua 150.00

Galloway's Celebrated Cough Syrup, The Great London Remedy, aqua, 7" h. 12.50

Garget Cure, C.T. Whipple, Prop., Portland, Me. - W.T. Co. U.S.A., rectangular w/beveled corners, clear, 5 5/8" h. 6.00

Gargling Oil, Lockport, N.Y., teal green, 5½" h. 20.00

Gavins Cough Syrup, partial contents, amber.................... 25.00

Goerss' (Dr.) Chaulmoogra, The East India Cure, amber 18.00

Gordak's (Dr.) Iceland Jelly, rectangular, pontil, aqua, 6¾" h. 120.00

Graefenberg Children's Panacea, open pontil, whittled, aqua 70.00

The Great South American Nervine Tonic Trade (monogram) Mark and Stomach & Liver Cure, oval, clear, 9½" h. 70.00

Green's August Flower, Great Dyspeptic Panacea, front & back labels, w/contents 8.00

Guysotts (Dr.) Compound Extract of Yellow Dock & Sarsaparilla, John D. Park, Cincinnati, O., oval, iron pontil, deep aqua, 10" h. 500.00

Hagee's Cordial Cod Liver Oil Compound, rectangular, full front & back labels, clear, 8" h. 19.00

Hair's (Dr. B.W.) Asthma Cure Cincinnati, Ohio, square, clear variant, 8" h........................ 18.00

Harper's (ToWo) Cough Remedy, open pontil, aqua 45.00

Harter's (Dr.) Fever and Ague Specific, clear (dug) 25.00

Hayman's Balsam of Horehound, rectangular, 4¾" h. 7.50

Hermanus Germany's Infallible Dyspepsia Cure - Prepared for the U.S. by L. and N. Adler Medicine Co., Reading Pa. U.S.A., wording embossed front & back, embossed soldier standing over dead bird on side, square, amber, 8¾" h. 345.00

Hills (embossed H w/arrow) Trade Mark Dys Pep Cu, Cures Chronic Dyspepsia, Indiana Drug Specialty Co., St. Louis & Indianapolis, rec-

tangular w/fluted corners, amber,
8 1/8" h. 14.00

Hunnewell's (John W. & Co.) Universal Cough Remedy, Boston, Mass.,
rectangular w/flared lip, aqua,
6¼" h. 92.00

Ingham's (Dr. H.A.) Nervine Pain Extractor, rectangular, aqua,
4½" h. 27.00

Jackson's (Dr.) Root & Herb Cordial,
Collins Bros. St. Louis, Mo.,
10" h. 40.00

James (Dr. H.) Cannabis Indica,
Crabbock & Co., Proprietors,
No. 1032 Pace St. Phila. Pa.,
mold-blown, applied lip,
aqua, 7 7/8" h. (dug & cleaned) . . 65.00

Jayne's (Dr. D.) Alterative, oval,
very whittled, aqua,
7" h. . . . . .20.00 to 35.00

Jayne's (Dr. D.) Alterative, rectan-
gular, aqua, 7" h. 24.00

Jayne's (Dr. D.) Life Preservative
Philada., open pontil aqua 650.00

Jayne's (Dr. D.) Liniment or Counter
Irritant, Philada., rectangular,
open pontil, aqua, 5 1/8" h. 35.00

Johnson's Anodyne Liniment, open
pontil, aqua 25.00

Johnson's (W.M.) Pure Herb Tonic
Sure Cure For All Malarial Diseases, mold-blown, applied lip,
square w/beveled corners, am-
ber, 8¾" h. 75.00

Jones' (Dr.) Liniment, rectangular,
embossed beaver, aqua, 5" h. 11.00

Joslyn's Kalontericos, open pontil,
aqua, 6" h. 55.00

Keasbey & Mattison Co., Ambler,
PA, cylindrical, cobalt blue,
6" h. 10.00

Keeley's (Dr. L.E.) Gold Cure for
Drunkenness, flat-paneled oval,
clear, 5½" h. . . . . .50.00 to 70.00

Kemp's Balsam, For Throat & Lungs,
LeRoy, N.Y., green, w/label,
5¼" h. 3.00

Kidder's (Mrs. E.) Dysentery Cordial,
Boston, cylindrical, aqua,
7 1/8" h. . . . . .75.00 to 100.00

Kidder's (Mrs. E.) Dysentery Cordial,
Boston, cylindrical, crude, open
pontil, aqua, 3 1/3" d., 7¾" h. 89.00

Kilmer's (Dr.) · Herbal Extract for
Uterine Injection · Binghamton,
N.Y., rectangular, aqua, 4½" h. . . . 25.00

Kilmer's (Dr.) Swamp-Root Kidney
Cure, Binghamton, N.Y., Sample
Bottle, cylindrical, aqua,
3 1/8" h. 27.50

Kilmer's (Dr.) Swamp-Root Kidney,
Liver and Bladder Cure, London,
E.C., rectangular w/beveled cor-
ners, aqua, 7" h. 10.00

Kilmer's (Dr.) Swamp-Root Kidney,
Liver & Bladder Cure, embossed
kidney, full label, rectangular,
aqua, 8¼" h. 35.00

Dr. Kilmer's Swamp-Root Remedy

Kilmer's (Dr.) Swamp-Root Kidney,
Liver & Bladder Remedy, aqua,
8" h. (ILLUS.) 14.00

King's (Dr.) New Discovery For Consumption · H. E. Bucklen & Co. ·
Chicago, Ill., rectangular w/bev-
eled corners, aqua, 6½" h. 10.00

Kodol Dyspepsia Cure, rectangular,
aqua, 6¾" h. 20.00

Lactopeptine For · (embossed Maltese cross) All Digestive Ailments,
heart-shaped, emerald green,
1 7/8" h. 20.00

Lactopeptine · The New York Phar-
macal Association, square
w/rounded shoulders, cobalt blue,
8" h. 40.00

Langenbach's Dysentery Cure, cylindrical, blob top, amber,
5 5/8" h. 32.00

Lewis & Fletcher's New Vegetable
Compound, Franklin, Ind., rectan-
gular, iron pontil, deep aqua 475.00

Licoricine (in script) · Acts Like Magic For Coughs & Colds, rectangu-
lar, aqua, 6 3/8" h. 11.50

Lindsey's · Blood+ Searcher · Hol-
lidaysburg (Pennsylvania), rectan-
gular, light blue, qt. 199.00

Liquid Opodeldoc, cylindrical, thin
flared lip, pontiled, aqua,
4½" h. 20.00

Lyon's Powder · B&P N.Y., cylindri-
cal, amber, 4 1/16" h. 75.00

Lyon's Powder · B&P N.Y., cylindri-
cal, lime green, 4" h. 25.00

MacKenzies (Dr.) Catarrh Cure (on
base), cylindrical, emerald green,
w/ground glass ball stopper,
3 7/8" h. 16.50

Mann's (Dr. S.K.) Celebrated Ague
Balsam, Galion, Ohio, rectangu-

lar, w/indented panels, iron pontil, aqua, 7" h. 250.00

Manning's (Dr.) - German Remedy -
The Great Pain Cure, rectangular,
clear, 4 7/8" h. 16.50

Markley's (Dr.) - Family Medicines -
Lancaster, Pa., open pontil, rich
aqua, 7 1/8" h. 170.00

McMunn's - Elixir of Opium, round,
w/pontil, aqua, 4½" h. 20.00

"M.D. - U.S.A. - One Quart," Medical Department bottle, cylindrical,
clear, qt. 35.00

Mexican Mustang Liniment, round,
aqua, 4½" h. 23.00

Mexican Mustang Liniment, round,
aqua, 5½" h. 22.00

Morris-Morton Drug Co. - Fort
Smith, Ark. - Swamp Chill and Fever Cure, rectangular w/beveled
corners, amethyst, 6¾" h. 20.00

Moxie Nerve Food, Lowell, Mass.,
Patented, round, aqua, 9¾" h. ... 13.50

Murray's (Sir James) Solution of
Magnesia, oval, aqua, 6" h. 9.00

National Kidney & Liver Cure,
square w/beveled corners,
amber, 9" h. 59.00

Newells - Pulmonary Syrup - Reding-
ton & Co., rectangular, applied
lip, aqua (slight haze) 19.00

New York Medical University, back-
ward "S" in embossing, cobalt
blue, 2½" base, 7¼" h. 32.00

Old Indian Liver & Kidney Tonic, The
Cherokee Medicine Co., complete
label on two sides, oval w/pan-
eled shoulder, aqua, 8" h. 40.00

One Minute Cough Cure - E.C.
Dewitt & Co. - Chicago, U.S.A.,
rectangular, aqua, w/label & contents, 5½" h. 10.00

Oregon Blood Purifier, pictures boy,
amber, large size 110.00

Osgood's - India Cholagogue - New
York, rectangular, pontil, aqua,
5 3/8" h. ....30.00 to 45.00

Paine's - Celery Compound, square,
aqua, 10" h. 16.50

Peckham's (Levi) Tincture of Life,
7" h. 20.00

Peruvian Syrup, N.L. Clark & Co.,
Boston, w/detailed paper label,
cylindrical, aqua, 9¼" h. 115.00

Pettits American Cough Cure,
Howard Bros. (all on front panel),
aqua (dug) 10.00

Pierce's (Dr.) Golden Medical Discovery - R. V. Pierce, M.D. -
Buffalo, N.Y., rectangular, aqua,
8 3/8" h. 14.00

Pinkham's (Lydia E.) Vegetable Compound, oval, clear, 8¼" h. 7.50

Porter (R.D.) Oriental Life Liniment,
open pontil, aqua 38.00

Pratt's Distemper & Pink Eye Cure,
"488" on base, rectangular, amber, 6¾" h. 20.00

Primley's Iron & Wahoo Tonic, Milwaukee, amber, 9¼" h. 65.00

Radam's (Wm.) Microbe Killer Cures
All Diseases, embossed man beating skeleton, amber, 10" h. 60.00

Radam's Microbe Killer, The Water
of Life, pictures man beating
skeleton, all the embossing on
base, large, amber 70.00

Radway's Ready Relief (R.R.R.
No. 1), rectangular, aqua,
6½" h. 30.00

Raymond's "Little Doctor," cobalt
blue, in box 15.00

Reakirt's Medicated Breast Julap,
open pontil, aqua 160.00

Redthyme Pain Cure, Waynesboro,
Pa., rectangular, aqua 16.00

Rees' Remedy for Piles, oval, extremely whittled, very large embossing, aqua, 7" h. 325.00

River Swamp (The) - Chill and (embossed alligator) - Fever Cure -
Augusta, Ga., rectangular w/bev-
eled corners, amber, 7" h. 550.00

River Swamp (The) - Chill and (embossed alligator) - Fever Cure -
Augusta, Ga., rectangular w/bev-
eled corners, yellow, 7" h. (small
chip on alligator)............... 550.00

Roger's (Dr. A.) Liverwort, Tar and
Canchalagua - A.L. Scovill - Cincinnati, rectangular, aqua, 8" h. ... 45.00

Rohrer's Wild Cherry Tonic Expectoral

Rohrer's Wild Cherry Tonic Expectoral, Lancaster, Pa., tapered square
w/roped corners, collared mouth,
iron pontil, amber, 10½" h.
(ILLUS.)........................ 170.00

Rush's - Sarsaparilla - and Iron - A.
H. Flanders, M.D., New York, rectangular, aqua, 8 9/16" h. 14.00

Rustins Oil For Rheumatism, cylindri-
cal, 5" h. 95.00
Sallade & Co. Magic Mosquito Bite
Cure & Insect Destroyer, N.Y.,
oval, aqua, 7¾" h. 17.50
Sanford's (Dr.) Invigorator, Sanford
& Co. Proprietors, N.Y., rectangu-
lar, aqua, 6 1/8" h. 62.00
Sanford's - Radical Cure, "Potter
Drug & Chemical Corporation Bos-
ton Mass USA" on base, rectangu-
lar, cobalt blue, 7 5/8" h. 35.00
Schneck's Pulmonic Syrup, eight-
sided, bluish aqua, 7" 52.00
Seelye (A.B.) & Co. Ner-Vena, Abi-
lene, Kansas, amber 12.00
Shiloh's Consumption Cure, S.C.
Wells, LeRoy, N.Y., rectangular,
aqua, 7 7/8" h. 15.00
Shilohs Cure (Sample), rectangular,
w/cork top, aqua, 2 7/8" h. 20.00
Sines (Charles) Dysentery Com-
pound, rectangular, 5" h. (faint in-
side haze) 85.00
Sparks' Kidney & Liver Cure, Cam-
den, N.J., oval w/flat front, am-
ber, 4 1/8" h. 375.00
Steelling's (Dr.) - Pulmonary Syrup -
Bridgeton, N.J., rectangular,
aqua, 6" h. 175.00
Sternberg's (Dr.) Miramedela, eight-
sided (minor flake on base) 125.00
Stewart's Cough Cure, rectangular,
light blue, 4¼" h. 10.50
Swaim's Panacea - Genuine -
Philadelphia, rectangular, open
pontil, aqua, 8" h. 525.00
Swaim's - Panacea - Philada., round
paneled, aqua, 8" h. 45.00
Swaim's - Panacea - Philada., round
paneled, smooth base, dark olive
green, 8" h. . . . . 100.00 to 149.00
Swift's (Dr.) Rheumatic & Gout Cure,
ten-sided, aqua, 4 1/8" h. 57.00
Thorn's Hop & Burdock Tonic, Brat-
tleboro, Vt., square w/beveled
corners, amber, 8¼" h. 30.00
Tobias' (Dr.) Venetian Liniment,
New York, oval, aqua, 4" h. 33.00
Toms - Russian - Liniment, square,
aqua, 4½" h. 85.00
True's (Dr.) Elixir Established 1851
Dr. J.F. True & Co., Auburn,
Maine - Worm Expeller - Family
Laxative, rectangular w/beveled
corners, aqua, 6 5/8" h. 20.00
Turlington's (Robt.) Balsam of Life,
flared lip, open pontil, aqua, Eng-
land, 3" h. 35.00
Uncle Sam's Nerve & Bone Liniment
- Emmert Proprietary Co., Chica-
go, Ill., rectangular, aqua,
7¼" h. 15.00
U.S.A. Hosp. Dept, cylindrical, dou-

ble collar top, crude, whittled,
light yellow amber, qt. 225.00
Vanbaum's (Dr.) - Rheumatic Lotion
- And Magic - Pain Extractor, rectangular, aqua, open pontil,
6" h. 120.00
Van Derheyde's Malt Cough Balsam,
oval, aqua, 5" h. 8.00
Vanderpool's (Dr.) S B Cough & Con-
sumption Cure, rectangular
w/beveled corners, aqua,
6 1/8" h. 25.00
Vaughn's Vegetable Lithontriptic
Mixture, Buffalo, square, aqua,
8" h. 85.00
Vegetable Pulmonary Balsam -
Reed, Cutler & Co., Boston, Mass.
- Proprietors, rectangular w/in-
dented panels, aqua, 7¼" h. 150.00
Veno's Seaweed Tonic, rectangular,
5¼" h. 7.00
Vondersmith's (Doctor E.W.) Indian
Cough Balm, nine-sided, open
pontil, aqua 1,200.00
Wait's White Pine Cough Cure, One
Bottle Cures A Cough, aqua 10.00
Wakelee's Carmelline, rectangular
w/beveled corners, amber,
4¾" h. 6.00
Warner (H.H.) & Co., Ltd., Mel-
bourne, red-amber, 5 5/8" h. 18.00
(Warner's) Log Cabin - Hops and
Buchu - Remedy, "Sept. 6, 1877"
on base, H.H. Warner & Co.,
Rochester, N.Y., three indented
panels on front, flat back, amber,
10" h. 175.00
Warner's Safe Cure (Concentrated),
w/safe, oval, amber, 5½" h 12.00
Warner's Safe Cure, London,
w/safe, oval, emerald green, pt.,
9½" h. 120.00
Warner's Safe Cure, London Eng.,
Toronto Canada, Rochester N.Y.,
w/safe, oval, dark amber,
9½" h. 25.00
Warner's Safe Cure, Melbourne,
Australia, w/safe, amber, pt.,
9½" h. 40.00
Warner's Safe Diabetes Cure, Roch-
ester, N.Y., w/safe, oval, amber,
9¾" h. 50.00
Warners Safe Diabetes Cure, four
cities listed, w/safe, oval, double
ring lip, crude, rare, amber,
9¾" h. 220.00
Warner's Safe Kidney & Liver Cure,
Rochester, N.Y., w/reversed (or
"left-handed") picture of a safe,
oval, amber, 9¾" h. 69.00
Warner's Safe Nervine, Rochester,
N.Y., w/safe, oval, amber, pt.,
9¾" h. 30.00
Warner's Safe Rheumatic Cure,

Rochester, N.Y., U.S.A., w/safe,
oval, amber, w/original paper label, 9¼" h.................... 40.00

Weaver's (Dr. S.A.) Canker & Salt
Rheum Syrup, oval, whittled, iron
pontil, aqua, 9" h. 80.00

Winslow's (Mrs.) Soothing Syrup Curtis & Perkins Proprietors, round,
aqua, 5 1/8" h. 22.00

Wintergreen Great Rheumatic Cure,
J.L. Filkins, aqua, 6" h. 8.00

Wistar's (Dr.) - Balsam of - Wild
Cherry - Philada. - I.B., eight-
sided, aqua, 5" h............... 23.00

Wood's (Dr. J.S.) Elixir, Albany,
N.Y., rectangular w/deeply cut
corners, iron pontil, aqua,
8½" h. (part of original label
remaining) 375.00

World Famed Blood Mixture, light
blue, 7 5/8" h. 17.50

Wright's (Dr. L.B.) - Liquid Cathartic
or - Family Physic, rectangular
w/beveled corners, aqua,
6¾" h...................... 140.00

Yale's (Madame M.) Fruitcura Woman's Tonic, aqua 12.00

MILK

Amber, embossed "V.M.I. Co. Milk-
O," ½ pt. 90.00

Amber, embossed "V.M.I. Co. Milk-
O," qt...................... 65.00

Amber, "Maplewood Dairy,
Fairhaven, Vt. & Hudson Falls,
New York," qt................ 10.00

Clear, "Adams, Rawlins, Wyoming,"
qt.......................... 10.00

Clear, "Adohr," grenade shape,
½ pt....................... 20.00

Clear, "Ayrhill Farms, Adams,
Mass.," qt................... 7.00

Clear, "baby face" top, embossed
"Associated Dairies of Los Angeles," ½ gal., 11" h. 975.00

Clear, "baby face" top, "Brookfield,"
½ pt....................... 75.00

Clear, "baby face" top, Vogel, qt. .. 22.00

Clear, "Blakeney, Poplar Bluff, Mo.,"
qt.......................... 10.00

Clear, "Butler Dairy, Willimantic,
Conn." qt.................... 12.00

Clear, "Chestnut Farms, Chevy
Chase Dairy, Washington, D.C." .. 10.00

Clear, cream-top, "Springdale
Farms, Millington, New Jersey,"
qt.......................... 18.00

Clear, embossed "Borden's," w/Elsie
the Cow, ½ pt. 12.00

Clear, embossed "Borden's," w/Elsie
the Cow, qt.................. 6.00

Clear, embossed "Buy War Bonds,"
in red lettering, "Dublin Co-op".. 35.00

Clear, embossed "Larrimore Dairy,
Seaford, Dela.," pt. 6.00

Clear, embossed "Milk For Health,"
½ pt........................ 6.00

Clear, embossed "Missouri Pacific,"
½ pt........................ 20.00

Clear, embossed "Peoples Milk &
Cream Co., Miami, Florida,"
w/cow's head, qt............... 35.00

Clear, embossed "Waddington Milk
Co., New York," ½ pt. 6.00

Clear, embossed "Whiteman New
York Maker 44 Chambers St. This
Bottle to be Washed and
Returned, Not to be Bought or
Sold," tin top marked "Pat. Jan. 5
1875, issued June 5 77, Pat. April
3 1883" (neck crack) 89.00

Clear, "Grasslands Dairy," qt. 10.00

Clear, "H.L. Hall, Greenfield Center,
New York," pt. 6.00

Clear, "Indian, Greenville, Me.,"
qt.......................... 16.00

Clear, "Potosi, Wisc.," qt. 25.00

Clear, red pyroglaze "Dairylea" &
little girl w/family, qt............ 7.00

Clear, red pyroglaze "Old Pevely" &
pictures, ½ gal................ 25.00

Clear, red pyroglaze "Valley Farms"
& pictures, qt. 25.00

Clear, "Sunlight Dairy, Adams,
Mass.," qt. 6.00

Green, "Stillwater, Okla. City, Enid,
Oklahoma," rectangular, ½ gal... 50.00

Sun-colored amethyst, "Wanzer,
Chicago," qt. 12.00

MINERAL WATERS

Adirondack Spring, Whitehall, N.Y.,
Saratoga-type, emerald green, pt.
(tiny base flake) 124.00

Altenbaugh's (M.) Mineral Water,
slab-sided, cobalt blue 875.00

Ballston Spa Mineral Water, emerald
green, pt. 64.00

Bennett (B.), Williamsport, Pa.,
graphite pontil, aqua 250.00

Bolen Waack & Co., New York,
Mineral Spring Water, Saratoga-
type, green, ½ pt. 100.00

Chase & Co. Mineral Water, San
Francisco, graphite pontil, dark
green 60.00

Clarke & Co., New York, Saratoga-
type, olive green, pt. 62.00

Clarke & White, New York, green,
qt.......................... 35.00

Clarke & White, "C," New York,
Saratoga-type, olive green, pt. ... 27.00

Clarke & White, "C," New York,
Saratoga-type, olive green, qt. ... 28.00

Clinton Dale Elixer Spring Water,
squat, blob top, clear........... 8.50

Congress & Empire Spring Co., "C,"
Saratoga.N.Y. - Congress Water,
rare variant w/raised band
around the "C," emerald green ... 350.00

Congress & Empire Spring Co., "C,"
Saratoga, N.Y. - Congress Water,
deep green, qt. . . . .　45.00
Congress Spring Co., "C," Saratoga,
N.Y. - Congress Water, Saratoga-
type, sloping shoulder, emerald
green, qt. . . . .　34.00
Empire Spring Co., Saratoga.N.Y. -
Empire Water, Saratoga-type,
sloping shoulders, emerald green,
qt. . . . .　36.00
Establissement Thermal de Vichy,
cylindrical, w/complete label, co-
balt blue, 3" d. base, 6½" h. . . . . .　29.00
Felix's (Geo. W.) Mineral Water,
Harrisburg, Pa., squat, iron pontil,
blue-green (dug, base bruise,
treated) . . . .　39.00
Gerdes (J.N.), S.F., Mineral Water,
eight-sided, aqua . . . .　25.00
Gettysburg Katalysine Water,
Saratoga-type, green, qt. . . . .　65.00
Gettysburg Katalysine Water,
Saratoga-type, medium olive
green, qt. . . . .　42.00
Geyser Spring. Saratoga Springs.
State of New York. - "The Sarato-
ga" Spouting Spring, aqua,
7¾" h. . . . .　55.00
Gleason & Cole Mineral Water, slab-
sided, iron pontil, cobalt blue . . . .　450.00
Hathorn Spring, Saratoga, N.Y.,
beer-shaped, label only, amber . .　16.00
Heil (John) Mineral Water, squat,
graphite pontil . . . .　15.00
Hopkins' Chalybeate, Baltimore,
Saratoga-type, iron pontil, crude,
deep yellow-olive . . . .　128.00
Hopkins' Chalybeate, Baltimore,
Saratoga-type, emerald green,
pt. . . . .　88.00
Humboldt Artesian Mineral Water,
blob top, aqua . . . .　14.00
Massena Spring (monogram) Water,
Saratoga-type, deep blue, qt. . . . .　135.00
Middletown Healing Springs, Grays
& Clark, Middletown, VT.,
Saratoga-type, amber, qt. . . . .　40.00
Middletown Healing Springs, Grays
& Clark, Middletown, VT.,
Saratoga-type, yellow-amber,
qt. . . . .　75.00
Missisquoi "A" Spring, embossed
squaw & papoose on reverse,
light yellow-olive, qt. . . . .　345.00
New Almaden Mineral Water,
aqua . . . .　20.00
Oak Orchard Acid Springs - Ala-
bama, Genesee Co., N.Y. (on
shoulders), Saratoga-type, emer-
ald green, qt. . . . .　480.00
Oak Orchard Acid Springs - H.W.
Bostwick Agt. No. 574
Broad.Way.New.York. (on shoul-

der), base embossed "Glass from
F.Hitchins Factory Lockport.N.Y."
in double circle, Saratoga-type,
amber, Oak Orchard-style qt. . . . .　150.00
Ogden, Gibson & Co. Mineral Wa-
ter, Pittsburgh, ten-sided, iron
pontil, light green . . . .　700.00
Pavilion & United States Spring Co.,
"P," Saratoga, N.Y., - Pavilion
Water, Saratoga-type, olive
green, pt. . . . .　185.00
Poland (Moses) Water, w/unique
flared lip, emerald green . . . .　225.00
Queen City Pure Water Co., Buffalo,
New York, blob top, aqua . . . .　20.00
Ryan (John) Excelsior Mineral Wa-
ter, Savannah, GA. - Union Glass
Works Philadelphia, This bottle is
never sold, blob top, graphite
pontil, cobalt blue . . . .　145.00
San Vincente California Mineral Ton-
ic Water, amber, 11½" h. . . . .　30.00
Saratoga Red Spring, Saratoga-type,
pale blue-green, qt. . . . .　125.00
Saratoga (Star) Spring, Saratoga-
type, red-amber, qt. . . . .　95.00
Saratoga Vichy Water, Saratoga,
N.Y. - "V," Saratoga-type, amber,
qt. (cleaned) . . . .　136.00
Stanton & Pierce Proprietors, Mays-
ville, Ky., Upper Blue Lick Water,
blue flask, 10" h. . . . .　400.00
Superior Mineral Water, M.T., Craw-
ford Hartford, Ct., Union Glass
Works, Philada., iron pontil, co-
balt blue . . . .　300.00
Syracuse Springs Excelsior,
Saratoga-type, amber, pt. . . . .　265.00
Vermont Spring, Saxe & Co., Shel-
don, Vt., Saratoga-type, green,
qt. . . . .　54.00
Vichy Water, misspelled "Hambury
Smith," lime green . . . .　49.00
Washington Lithia Well Mineral Wa-
ter, Ballston Spa, NY, Saratoga-
type, aqua, pt. . . . .　265.00
Washington Spring, Saratoga, N.Y.,
whittled, teal green, 8" h. . . . .　100.00
Weston (G.W.), w/arched emboss-
ing, Saratoga-type, olive, qt. . . . . .　70.00
Weston (G.W.), w/horizontal embossing, Saratoga-type, olive,
qt. . . . .　86.00
Whitney's (Dr.) Patent Soda & Miner-
al Water, iron pontil, medium
blue-green . . . .　375.00

NURSING

Clear, pressed glass, embossed
"Comfy" & w/embossed Krazy Kat
figure . . . .　35.00
Clear, pressed glass, embossed
"Comfy" & w/embossed Pluto
figure . . . .　35.00

Clear, pressed glass, "Overlea Pharmacy Ethical Prescriptions" painted label pictures mortar & pestle 20.00

Clear, pressed glass, red pyroglaze label "Temp Guard, Eisele & Co.," inset thermometer, 8 oz., w/paper list 25.00

Clear, pressed glass, embossed elephant, round 25.00

Clear, pressed glass, "Welefine," both ends open & curved up, England 35.00

Clear, turtle-shaped, embossed "Acme Nursing Bottle" & monogram within an 8-point star, 6" oval, pr. 55.00

Deep aqua, mold-blown glass, 15-diamond patt., pontiled, early 19th c. 425.00

Light green, mold-blown glass, 16-diamond patt., open pontil, early 19th c., 6½" h. 149.00

Light olive green, blown glass, ovoid shape w/tapering neck & base & slightly flared lip, late 18th c., 5 3/8" h. 66.00

Pale green, mold-blown glass, sixteen ribs & sixteen diamonds, Midwestern, early 19th c., 6 5/8" h. (some wear) 125.00

PICKLE BOTTLES & JARS

Amber, embossed "Bunker Hill Pickles Skilton Foote & Co." 39.00

Aqua, cylindrical, paper label "Liberty Brand Pickles - Allen Slade & Co., Fall River, Mass.," ½ pt. 12.00

Aqua, embossed "Bunker Hill Pickles," 5" h. 12.50

Aqua, four-sided, cathedral-type w/Gothic arch windows, ornate window designs, ½ gal., 11½" h. 119.00

Aqua, four-sided, cathedral-type w/Gothic arch windows, embossed "Atmore's" on two sides, 11 5/8" h. 185.00

Aqua, four-sided, cathedral-type w/Gothic arch windows, 3⅓" sq. base, 11¾" h. (some inside base haze) 59.00

Aqua, six-sided, cathedral-type w/Gothic arch windows, 1 gal., 13" h. 125.00

Aqua, square, paper label "Star Pickles, Mixed Pickles Phila...," ½ pt. (75% of label) 8.00

Aqua, square w/arched shoulders, neck ring, laid on lip, ½ gal., 3½" sq., 13½" h. (crude) 39.00

Deep aqua, round w/rounded panels, embossed "Wm. Underwood & Co., Boston" around base,

rolled lip, open pontil, 11½" h. .... 275.00 to 375.00

Deep green, four-sided, cathedral-type w/Gothic arch windows, domed base, 13¾" h. 250.00

Emerald green, barrel-shaped, tooled lip, 5 x 10" 35.00

Light emerald green, four-sided, cathedral-type w/Gothic arch windows, 11½" h. 238.00

Olive amber, square base, beveled corners & arched shoulders, 3½" square, 14" h. 150.00

Pale green, arched shoulders, neck ring & laid on lip, ½ gal., 3½" sq., 13½" h., many bubbles 45.00

POISONS

Bright yellow-green, 4 oz. 110.00

Cobalt blue, hexagonal w/four point stars on panels, "16 fl. oz. Poison, Use With Caution," 8½" h. 100.00

Cobalt blue, "Inceto" 10.00

Cobalt blue, octagonal, embossed "Jacob Hulle," w/four labels, all complete, 3¾" h. 42.00

Cobalt blue, oval, vertically ribbed, embossed in medallion "Riker-Hegeman Drug Stores," 3" d. base, 7 3/8" h. 89.00

Cobalt blue, rectangular, ribbed on three sides, embossed "Not to be Taken" on side & "12 oz." on base, 7" h. 22.00

Cobalt blue, rectangular w/rounded edges, vertical ribs, embossed, 32 oz., 9 7/8" h. 55.00

Cobalt blue, round, diamond-quilted body, base embossed "W.T. & Co., U.S.A.," 3½" h. 8.00

Cobalt blue, round, diamond-quilted body, 7" h. 20.00

Cobalt blue, triangular, one panel quilted w/"Poison" vertically, 3" h. 27.50

Cobalt blue, "Triloids," w/full labels 17.00

Olive green, round, ribbed, crude, embossed "Poison," w/original stopper, near 1 gal. capacity, 4 5/8" d., 14½" h. 795.00

SODAS & SARSAPARILLAS

Albuquerque Bottling Works, soda, Hutchinson stopper 35.00

Andrae (G.) Port Huron, Mich., soda, Hutchinson stopper, cobalt blue 80.00

Ayers Sarsaparilla, complete w/box 65.00

Baker's (Dr. Ira) Honduras Sarsaparilla................... 95.00

Beaman (Jos. S.), Central City, Colo., soda, aqua (light stain) 40.00

Black (R.W.) Bottler, Oklahoma
Ter., soda, panel base, Hutchin-
son stopper, aqua 125.00
Black Kow, pictures cows, "Just A
Swell Drink!," soda, amber 20.00
Bodine (J.) & Sons, soda, blob top,
graphite pontil, aqua (case
wear) 25.00
Bristol's Extract of Sarsaparilla,
Buffalo, New York, rectangular,
aqua 55.00
Bristol's Extract of Sarsaparilla,
Buffalo, New York, rectangular,
deep blue-aqua, 5½" h. 95.00
Brown's Sarsaparilla 18.00
Brownell (I.), New Bedford, Mass.,
soda, squat shape, iron pontil,
blue 250.00
Bryce's Soda, paper label, qt. 7.00
Buffum & Co. Pittsburgh Sarsaparilla
and Mineral Water, ten-pin shape,
cobalt blue 1,300.00
Buffum's Sarsaparilla & Lemon
Mineral Water, ten-sided, iron
pontil, cobalt blue 425.00
Bull (A.H.) Extract of Sarsaparilla,
Hartford, Conn., rectangular,
aqua, 7" h. 85.00
Burke Bros., Providence, R.I., soda,
lightning stopper, light purple 10.00
Burns (M.), Dyottville Glass Works,
Phila., soda, squat, smooth base,
green (dug) 15.00
Bussel (Wm.) Balt., soda, round bot-
tom, medium green w/yellow
tone 1,050.00
B.W. & Co. New York Soda Water,
iron pontil, deep cobalt blue (dug,
minor lip roughness) 89.00
Byers (J.G.), 1882, Hoosick, NY,
soda, Hutchinson stopper, clear .. 7.50
Casey (Owen) Eagle Soda Works,
blob top, aqua 25.00
Central Bottling Works, Detroit,
Mich., soda, Hutchinson stopper,
cobalt blue 50.00
Charles Place, Chicago, soda, blob
top, cobalt blue 85.00
Classen & Co. San Francisco, soda,
squat, green 35.00
Cleminshaw (C.) Soda & Mineral
Water, Troy, N.Y., blob top, co-
balt blue 75.00
Clicquot Club Ginger Ale, soda, pa-
per label 4.00
Cloverdale Ginger Ale, soda, w/pa-
per label, 16 oz. 4.00
Coal Creek Bottling Works, Fabrizio
& Son, soda, Hutchinson stopper,
aqua (some light stain) 75.00
Cox (A.R.), Norristown, Pa., soda,
iron pontil, deep blue-green 49.00
Coyle Jr. (T.) Chester Pa., soda,
squat, aqua 25.00

Crosby and Smith, Newark, NJ,
soda, Hutchinson stopper, aqua .. 6.00
Crown Bottling Works, Nacog-
doches, Texas, soda, Hutchinson
stopper, aqua, 7½" h. (dug) 45.00
Crystal Soda Water Co., cobalt blue
(back collar lip chip) 45.00
Darling (W.H.) & Son, Newport, Va.,
soda, Hutchinson stopper, horse-
shoe slug plate, blue-aqua 25.00
Denhalter (H.) & Son, Salt Lake City,
Utah Territory, soda, Hutchinson
stopper, aqua, 6½" h. (dug) 55.00
Dewitt's Sarsaparilla, full label &
contents, w/brochure, aqua 65.00
Dietz (A.F.), Altramont, NY, soda,
Hutchinson stopper, clear 5.00
Dietz (A.F.), Knowersville, N.Y.,
soda, pictures cow, Hutchinson
stopper, 1888, aqua (worn) 5.50
Distilled Soda Water Co. of Alaska,
Hutchinson stopper 350.00
Divine (P.) Bottler Philada., soda,
squat, iron pontil, green 25.00
Dunn & Shanley Keap & Hope Sts.
Brooklyn Aprl 1st 1889, soda,
Hutchinson stopper, light blue (ice
pick chip on lip, cloudy) 12.00
Dyottville Glass Works, soda, blob
top, graphite pontil, green 45.00
Eagle (C & K) Works, Sac City, soda,
squat, cobalt blue 40.00
Edwards Taylor Patent Soda &
Mineral Water, iron pontil, medi-
um emerald green 475.00
El Reno Bottling Works, El Reno,
Okla., soda, slug plate, crown
top, amethyst 8.00
Foley's Sarsaparilla, w/label & con-
tents, amber 45.00
Foley's Sarsaparilla, w/label & con-
tents, aqua 65.00
Fox Snappy Drinks, soda,
embossed 5.00
Gilhuly and Bohen, New Haven,
Conn., soda, Hutchinson stopper,
aqua 5.50
Graf (John), Milwaukee, Wis., soda,
"This Bottle Not To Be Sold," blob
top, panel base, darkest amber .. 25.00
Gray (F.L.), Manchester, New Hamp-
shire, soda, squat, aqua 19.00
Grone (H.), St. Louis, Mo., soda,
blob top, aqua 6.00
Guysott's (Dr.) Yellow Dock Sar-
saparilla, oval, 95% of label,
aqua 85.00
Hallenbeck and Messler, Albany,
N.Y., soda, Hutchinson stopper,
light embossed deer head on
back, aqua (small ding) 8.50
Hamilton Glass Works, N.Y., soda,
squat, pontil, aqua 30.00
Harsch Bottling Works (The), Albu-

querque, N.M., Hutchinson stopper, aqua 165.00

Hausmann, Madison, Wisconsin, 8 oz., 6½" h. 9.50

Hennessy & Nolan, Albany, N.Y., soda, pictures capitol building, Hutchinson stopper, aqua (light stain) 12.00

Hoffman & Joseph, Albany, Oregon, blob-top, embossed griffin (minor lip roughness) 24.00

Holden's (G. A.) Capital Soda Works, Sac., Hutchinson stopper, ice blue aqua (whittled, pinhead burst bubble) 35.00

Hood's Sarsaparilla, London, England, aqua, 7¼" h. 14.00

Horlacher Bottling Co. Allentown, Pennsylvania, soda, Hutchinson stopper, embossing in script at a sharp angle, clear 8.50

Hoxie, Albany, soda, blob top, aqua, ½ pt. 18.00

Johnston & Co., Phila., soda, squat, blob top, green 30.00

Jones (Dr.) & Co. Sarsaparilla, C.O. Jones & Co., Sole Proprietors, Williamsport, Pennsylvania, Hood's-type, aqua (only two known) 225.00

Kimball & Co., soda, squat, pontil, cobalt blue 85.00

Knicker Bocker Soda Bottle

Knicker Bocker (S.S.) Soda Water, ten-sided, potstone star on one panel, blob top, iron pontil, cobalt blue (ILLUS.) 125.00

Koppiseh, Gloversville, N.Y., soda, lightning stopper, aqua 5.00

Krumenaker (Albert), N.Y., soda, light purple vine design.......... 10.00

Lappeus (Wm. W.) Premium Soda or Mineral Waters Albany, ten-sided, iron pontil, cobalt blue 375.00

Lomax (J.A.), Chicago, soda, blob top, cobalt blue (stain) 45.00

Lomax (J.A.), Chicago, soda, Hutchinson stopper, cobalt blue 50.00

Maher (Thos.), soda, squat, crude slug plate, deep green 50.00

Maillard (H.), Lead City, S. F., soda, horseshoe slug plate, Hutchinson stopper 30.00

Mayville Bottling Works, Mayville, Wisconsin, soda, Hutchinson stopper, light green aqua........... 10.00

McFarland (A.) Philada, Registered According to Law, soda, iron pontil, blue-green 45.00

McGoren Brothers, Albany, N.Y., soda, Hutchinson stopper, blue-green 6.50

McLaghlin (J.), soda, squat, blob top, blue-green 40.00

Merkel & Son, Saranac Lake, N.Y., soda, Hutchinson stopper, clear .. 5.50

Murray (P.C.), Monticello, N.Y., soda, star on bottom, Hutchinson stopper, light blue 10.00

Mynderse (John L.), Schenectady, N.Y., soda, pictures eagle, Hutchinson stopper, clear (some wear) 8.50

National Bottling Works, San Francisco, California, 524 Fulton St., soda, embossed eagle w/star 45.00

Nonpareil Soda Water Co., San Francisco, California, tooled blob top, aqua...................... 24.00

Norris (G.) & Co., Detroit, Michigan, soda, Hutchinson stopper, cobalt blue 50.00

Oester (N.), Aurora, Indiana, soda, iron pontil, aqua (only two known)........................ 195.00

Pepper's Iodized Sarsaparilla, aqua (only one known) 150.00

Pepsi-Cola, soda, both complete paper labels, ca. 1930's, amber 45.00

Pepsi-Cola, Greenville, N.C., soda, straight-sided, ca. 1914, aqua 15.00

Pepsi-Cola, Washington, N.C., soda, bimal, amber 40.00

Pioneer Soda Works, Smith & Brian Co., Reno, Nevada, Hutchinson stopper, aqua.................. 185.00

Pocomoke Bottling Works, Pocomoke City, M.O., soda, Hutchinson stopper, aqua 35.00

Primley's Sarsaparilla, The Primley Co., Peoria, Illinois, aqua (base ding)........................ 45.00

Radways Sarsaparilla Resolvent, aqua........................ 17.00

Reed (J.) Bottling Works, Buena Vista, Colorado, soda, Hutchinson stopper, aqua (large chip right rear)........................ 75.00

Rice (J.M.) Norwalk, Ohio, soda, Hutchinson stopper, slug plate, light green (some cloudiness) 14.00

Richardson (M.), Trenton, N.J.,

soda, blob top, iron pontil,
green 32.00
Riker's Compound Sarsaparilla,
aqua 35.00
Robinson, Wilson & Legallee, 102
Sudbury St., Boston, soda, iron
pontil, blue-green, (light outside
wear) 69.00
Rush's Sarsaparilla, golden amber .. 80.00
Ryan (John) 1866 - Excelsior Soda
Works, Savannah, Georgia, squat,
cobalt blue 40.00
Salida Bottling Co., soda, sun-
colored amethyst (some
staining) 40.00
Sande's Sarsaparilla, New York..... 50.00
Schlieper (C.W.), St. Louis, Soda Wa-
ter, iron pontil (light haze) 17.00
Schmidt (F.), Leadville, Colorado,
soda, Hutchinson stopper, aqua .. 25.00
Schmidt (F.), Leadville, Colorado,
soda, tombstone slug plate,
Hutchinson stopper, aqua (light
upper haze) 40.00
Schweinhart (J.), soda, iron pontil .. 75.00
Scutt (Mrs. S.), Verbank Village,
N.Y., soda, blob top, amber (light
staining) 6.50
Seitz & Bros., Easton, Pennsylvania,
soda, squat, cobalt blue (dug) 25.00
Seitz Bros., Easton, Pennsylvania,
soda, squat, blue-green (small lip
bruise) 10.00
Sleigh Bell Soda, cork top, horse-
drawn sleigh, colorful label,
American Stores 30.00
Smile, soda, orange enameled waffle glass, July 11, 1922, 1 gal.,
19" 250.00
Soda & Mineral Water Co., Warren,
Pennsylvania, soda, Hutchinson
stopper, slug plate, sun-colored
amethyst 24.00
"Soda" embossed on one side,
"SA ... A," on reverse, medium
green mold-blown w/bands of hori-
zontal ribbing up sides w/smooth
panel in middle, rough pontil, very
rare, 7¾" h. 1,600.00
Spring Bottling Works, Utica, N.Y.,
soda, Hutchinson stopper, clear .. 6.50
Squeeze Orange Soft Drink, ca.
1920, 10 oz. 12.00
Standard Bottling & Mfg. Co. (The),
Cripple Creek, Colorado, soda,
Hutchinson stopper, aqua 50.00
Standard Bottling Co., Denver,
Colorado, soda, amethyst 20.00
Standard Bottling Co., Silverton,
Colorado, soda, Hutchinson stop-
per, aqua 75.00
Standard Bottling Co., Trinidad,
Colorado, soda, aqua (some wear
& staining)..................... 20.00

Standard Bottling Works, Minneapolis, Minnesota, soda, Hutchinson
stopper, amber 85.00
Standard Bottling Works (The), Peter
Orella, Proprietor, soda, Hutchinson stopper, light amethyst 50.00
Stocker's (Dr.) Sarsaparilla, open
pontil, pale green-aqua 500.00
Townsend's (Dr.) Sarsaparilla, Albany, N.Y., pontil, olive amber (lighter than usual) 135.00
Townsend's (Dr.) Sarsaparilla, Albany, N.Y., square, applied lip, pontil, olive green 160.00
Townsend's (Dr.) Sarsaparilla, Albany, N.Y., square, olive amber
(crude & rare variant) 210.00
Turner's Sarsaparilla, Buffalo, N.Y.,
smooth base, aqua, 12½" h. 412.50
Vess Cola, Madison, Wisconsin,
soda, 8 oz., 6½" h. 9.50
Waco Bottling Works, Waco, Texas,
soda, Hutchinson stopper, slug
plate, blue-aqua (some wear) 12.50
Wallis Bottling Works, Wallis, Texas,
soda, Hutchinson stopper, clear
(dug)......................... 25.00
White (S.N.), Oak Hill, N.Y., soda,
Hutchinson stopper, light blue 7.00
White Rock Ginger Ale, w/paper
labels, ca. 1910, unopened,
amber 20.00
W.T. & Co., 49 Greene St., N.Y.,
soda, blob top, cobalt blue 32.00

WHISKEY & OTHER SPIRITS

Chestnut Grove Whiskey

Beer, "Alois Bube, Mount Joy, Pa.,"
blob top, aqua 48.00
Beer, "Continental Brewg. Co.
Philadelphia," also embossed
w/large scene including Revolutionary War soldier w/rifle,
houses, trees, tents & cannon,
blob top, aqua (some minor lip
flakes) 45.00
Beer, "Dr. Cronks Sarsaparilla
Beer," stoneware, blob top, qt.
(two minor lip chips) 39.00

Beer, "Fauerbach," Madison, Wisconsin, brown, qt. 9.00

Beer, "Goldedge," Vallejo, California, blob top, amber, ½ pt. 25.00

Beer, "Goldedge," Vallejo, California, blob top, aqua, ½ pt. 35.00

Beer, "Golden Gate Bottling Works, San Francisco," embossed bear holding glass, blob top, amber, 8" h. 45.00

Beer, "Kurth," Columbus, Wisconsin, brown, qt. 14.00

Beer, "Michaelis & Loewe, 44 2nd St. Hoboken N.J., Weiss Beer," blob top, aqua. 14.00

Beer, "Phoenix," embossed bird, blob top, amber. 16.00

Beer, "Walter Raupfer Brewing Co. Columbia City, Ind.," embossed eagle on barrel, blob top, amber, qt. 15.00

Beer, "Stettner & Thomas Premium Weiss Bier Brewery, St. Louis Mo.," blob top, amber 7.00

Beer, "Sunshine," smiling boy, green 10.00

Beer, "Trenton Brewing Co., Trenton, N.J.," embossed tiger head, blob top, amber (dug) 12.00

Beer, "United States Brewing Co., Chicago, Ill.," red-amber, qt. 16.00

Beer, "Geo Weber (embossed stars), Weiss Beer Albany N.Y.," blob top, amber 14.00

Case gin, "African," olive green 17.00

Case gin, "Hoytema & Co.," flared lip, olive green 37.00

Case gin, "Meder & Zoon," dark green 75.00

Case gin, hundreds of seed bubbles, open pontil, early 1800's, dark olive green, 10" h. 125.00

Case gin, short neck, flattened top, paddled sides, rough pontil, ca. 1700, olive green................ 195.00

Cider, Green & Clark, Missouri Cider, Rgd. Aug. 27, 1878, blob top, very dark amber (some wear) 25.00

Gin, "Bininger New York," odd color green (small flake off side of base) 550.00

Gin, "Kiderlin's (E.)," olive green, 9½" h. 35.00

Gin, "J. Fred Nagel," tapered, reverse w/fancy medallion & "1873," pale yellow-green, 8" h. 42.00

Schnapps, "J.J. Melchers WZ Aromatic Schnapps Schiedam," "black" glass, 7½"h. 35.00

Schnapps, "M.P. Pollen & Zoon," aromatic, olive green, 10" h. (shoulder flake) 20.00

Schnapps, "Schade & Buysings Aromatic," olive green, qt., 9" h. 30.00

Schnapps, "Daniel Visser en Zonen Aromatic," light green, 7¾" h. 25.00

Schnapps, "Voldners Aromatic," olive green, 10" h. (ping in shoulder)......................... 20.00

Schnapps, "Wolfe's Schnapps," crude "black" glass, 8" h. 35.00

Spirits, "J. Beague," squat cylinder, "black" glass, ca. 1773 .... 750.00

Spirits, "A.M. Binningers & Co., 338 Broadway, N.Y.," pontiled barrel shape 145.00

Spirits, demijohn, "black" mold-blown glass, apple-shaped, extremely crude & heavily whittled, 2 gal. 79.00

Spirits, demijohn, apple-shaped w/long neck, open pontil, golden amber, 2 gal. 149.00

Spirits, demijohn, bulbous shape, very crude & heavily whittled, deep olive amber, 2 gal. 89.00

Spirits, demijohn, crude early dip mold, open pontil, olive-citron, 3 gal. 89.00

Spirits, demijohn, cylindrical, cornflower blue, ½ gal. 79.00

Spirits, demijohn, cylindrical, iron pontil, deep sapphire blue, crude, ¼ gal. (base potstone crack)..... 250.00

Spirits, demijohn, cylindrical, iron pontil, many swirls & bubbles, olive-yellow, ½ gal. 79.00

Spirits, demijohn, cylindrical, whittled, crude, open pontil, blue-green, gal. 69.00

Spirits, demijohn, free-blown, tall cylindrical body w/sloping shoulders to tapered neck w/applied lip, large jagged pontil, dark amber, possibly Keene or Stoddard, New Hampshire, 19th c., 17" h. .. 75.00

Spirits, demijohn, kidney-shaped, open pontil, scarce lime-yellow color, whittled, ¼ gal. 49.00

Spirits, pumpkin seed, marked "City Wine Vaults, 501 Hayes St., S.F., Chas. Martin Prop.," ½ pt........ 20.00

Spirits, squat onion-form, free-blown, Dutch, ca. 1680-1730 ...... 70.00

Spirits, squat onion-form "seal" bottle, seal in form of coat of arms w/shield w/bird, deep olive amber (scarred base, some damage)...........1,000.00

Stout, "M. & J. Duffy Phila. Brown Stout," squat soda bottle shape, blue green (dug) 39.00

Whiskey, miniature, "Mount Vernon Pure Rye Whiskey" 18.00

Whiskey, "Beiser & Fishler, N.Y.," figural pig, golden amber, 9¾" l. ....375.00 to 675.00

Whiskey, "A.M. Bininger & Co., New

York," square, amber, whittled,
qt. 10.00

Whiskey, "Bininger Old Kentucky
1849 Reserve Bourbon," barrel-
shaped, amber 115.00

Whiskey, "G.O. Blake's," w/com-
plete label 12.00

Whiskey,"Chestnut Grove," chestnut
flask-shaped w/applied handle,
open pontil, dark amber (ILLUS.) . . 140.00

Whiskey, "Colonial Pure Old Rye
Whiskey, John C. Horting, Lancaster, Pa.," label only, ½ pt.
(missing 10% of label) 15.00

Whiskey, "S. Crabfelder & Co. Distillers, Louisville, Ky.," rectangu-
lar, amber, ½ pt. 75.00

Whiskey, "Duffy Malt Whiskey Co.,"
amber, 10" h. 15.00

Whiskey, "Durham," w/bull & stop-
light, circular extension pol-
ished 550.00

Whiskey, "Dyottville Glass Works
Phila.," flat applied slanted collar,
two-part mold, olive green,
11¼" h. 40.00

Whiskey, "Eastern Durham," embossed foot on back (stained,
repaired neck) 75.00

Whiskey, "L. Fouchez & Cie Old
Brandy," blown three mold, label
only, also "A Merry Christmas and
Happy New Year Compliments of
Pen-Mar Distilling Co. Norfolk,
Va.," clear (only 90% of label) . . . 16.00

Whiskey, "J.H. Friedenwald & Co.,
Baltimore, MD.," green, qt. 85.00

Whiskey, "J.T. Gayen, Altoona,"
cannon-shaped, collared mouth,
smooth base, amber,
¾ qt. . . . . 650.00 to 700.00

Whiskey, "Good Old Bourbon in a
Hog," figural pig, amber, small . . . 35.00

Whiskey, "Good Old Bourbon in a
Hog," figural pig, clear, 6½" 69.00

Whiskey, "Grandpa's," The Mountain Distilling Co., cork-top, colorful label w/girl pouring whiskey
for grandpa, complete with war
revenue sticker, 1904 St. Louis
Expo award label on reverse,
qt. 100.00

Whiskey, "I.W. Harper, Nelson Co.
Ky.," barrel-shaped, clear,
4¼" h. 35.00

Whiskey, "I.X.L. Valley, E. & B.
Bevan, Pittston, Pa.," urn-shaped,
eight-sided w/embossed star in
each panel, iron pontil, deep red
amber, 8" h. 1,300.00

Whiskey, "Paul Jones," in wicker
holder w/handle, amber blob
seal, 1 gal. 35.00

Whiskey, "Meredith's Diamond Club
Pure Rye Whiskey," china jug,
produced by Knowles, Taylor &
Knowles, East Liverpool, Ohio,
½ pt. 89.00

Whiskey, "Mohawk Whiskey, Pure
Rye Patented Feb. 11th. 1868,"
figural Indian queen, honey-
amber 569.00

Whiskey, "Jesse Moore Hunt,"
w/embossed stag antlers,
orange 20.00

Whiskey, "Old Barbee," colorful label shows women & farmers
drinking at log cabin distillery,
cork top, ca. 1909 . . . . 65.00

Whiskey, "Old Kentucky Home Pure
Copper," w/color label showing
blacks in front of old home, in
wicker holder 85.00

Whiskey, "Pride of Kentucky Whiskey, W.M. & Co. Cleveland, Oh.,"
clear 20.00

Whiskey, "Sample & Co., Successors
to C.B. Lowerre, Wine & Liquors,
84 Front St., NY," amber, qt. 14.00

Whiskey, "Van Beil's Rye and Rock,"
boldly embossed, rectangular,
aqua, 9" h. 16.00

Whiskey, "Webb & Meyer, New
York," cylinder 10.00

Whiskey, mold-blown, beehive-form,
24 ribs, broken swirl to the right,
slight kick-up w/jagged pontil,
aqua, Midwest, 8" h. (trace of in-
terior stain) 120.00

Whiskey, mold-blown, club-shaped,
24 vertical ribs, aqua, Zanesville,
Ohio, early 19th c., 7¼" h. (pin-
point lip flakes) 165.00

Whiskey, mold-blown, club-shaped
w/applied lip, 24 broken-swirl
ribs, aqua, 8¾" h. (minor wear,
traces of sickness) 140.00

Whiskey, mold-blown, globular-
form, 16 ribs, open pontil, blue-
aqua, Midwest, 6¾" h. 129.00

Whiskey, mold-blown, globular-
form, 24 ribs, open pontil, deep
amber, Midwest, 8" h. 325.00

Whiskey, mold-blown, globular-
form, 24 vertical ribs, applied lip
on short neck, pontil w/high kick-
up, bluish aqua, Midwest,
7¾" h. 90.00

Whiskey, mold-blown, lady's-leg
neck, deep kick-up, olive amber,
12" h. (lip roughness) 54.00

Wine, "Golden Gate Wine Co. Baltimore Maryland Fine Old 1874
Port," olive amber, qt. 19.00

(End of Bottle Section)

BOXES

Figural Porcelain Dresser Box

The category of Boxes, formerly included in the Furniture section, has been expanded to include not only wooden boxes but those made of glass, ceramic and various metals.

Band box, oval, bent poplar w/original white & red floral design on grey ground wallpaper covering, mid-19th c., 11¼" l. (some wear) $135.00

Band box, oval, cardboard w/original wallpaper covering w/blue floral design on yellow ground, lined w/1837 Virginia newspaper, 16" l. (wear, edge damage, bottom somewhat loose) 350.00

Band box, wood-constructed w/fitted cover, wallpaper on cover depicts the New York City Hall, sides covered w/wallpaper depicting a coaching party riding through the countryside, interior lined w/1839 newspaper, partial label inside cover of Hannah Davis, Jaffrey, New Hampshire, ca. 1840, 12½ x 16" oval, 13" h. (edges reinforced w/tape, minor paper loss, fading) 990.00

Bible box, carved oak, hinged sloping rising top above plain ends, the front carved w/the initials & date "R.D. 1718," fluted lower border, early Georgian period, England, early 18th c., 26½" l., 11¼" h. 357.50

Bible box, painted pine, rectangular w/dovetailed construction, cotterpin hinges (moved), base w/simple molding, original lock & hasp, deep brown paint, interior w/two tills w/covers & overall light blue paint, Northern Massachusetts, late 18th c., 14 x 19", 7" h. 412.50

Blanket box, miniature, painted finish, rectangular hinged lid opening to well w/till, dovetailed case w/applied brown grain painting over burnt sienna ground, America, 4 5/8 x 9", 4¼" h. (wear & some paint loss) 412.50

Book box, painted pine, rectangular w/domed hinged lid opening to a deep well, the top painted w/flowing red & yellow feathery tulips & leafage, outlined w/cream-yellow striping, the front, sides & back w/more tulip blossoms, all on black ground, w/original tin hinges, Berks or Lancaster County, Pennsylvania, ca. 1800, 6¼" l., 2¾" h. 1,760.00

Bride's box, bentwood oval, pine w/original blue paint & polychrome florals around sides, cover w/standing couple & German verse "Love me, I am yours," good colors, 16¾" l. (minor wear, age cracks & damages) 1,000.00

Bride's box, bentwood oval, painted & decorated, oblong fitted lid w/a picture of a couple in a landscape setting, enclosed by a border w/a sentimental saying in German, conforming case decorated w/floral motifs, Continental, probably Germany, late 19th - early 20th c., 18" l. (wear to paint)..... 440.00

Candle box, pine, w/sliding cover, dry red original paint, early 1800's, 2½ x 7" 175.00

Candle box, hanging-type, pine, shaped & arched backboard above rectangular box w/lift lid, old worn dark finish w/some splashes of white paint, 13½" l. 135.00

Candle box, hanging-type, tin, cylindrical w/hinged lid, 13¼" l....... 99.00

Church collection box, walnut, rectangular open box w/long round handle piercing through one end, old floral carpet lining, old dark finish, overall 24¾" l. 75.00

Cowrie shell box, silver-mounted, mounts & hinged lid pricked w/stylized foliage, George III period, England, ca. 1800, 2¾" l. 467.00

Document box, painted & decorated wood, rectangular hinged domed lid lifting to an open compartment above a conforming case, the whole painted w/red, yellow & green churches & houses enclosed by enlarged tulips issuing from corners, on black ground, attributed to Heinrich Bucher, Reading, Bucks County, Pennsylvania, 1770-80, 9 x 13", 7" h. (handle missing, wear to paint) 6,600.00

Document box, painted wood, rec-

tangular, black ground centering
an oval portrait bust w/gilt stringing & molded edge above a conforming case w/similar painted
decoration on a molded base, in
the manner of Joseph Lehn, late
19th c., 15½" l., 6" h. 220.00
Dresser box, enameled hammered
copper, squat rounded body
w/fitted cover w/round ivory finial tooled to match surround on
cover, enameled interior, base
signed "Cauman," Rebecca Cauman, Boston, Massachusetts, ca.
1925, 5¾" d., 3½" h. 935.00
Dresser box, porcelain, modeled as
the head of actress Louise Brooks,
her stylish cloche hat removable
as cover, realistically painted in
purple, black, brown & red, impressed "12580" & w/painted
number "13," Germany, ca. 1930,
6" h. (ILLUS.) 462.00
Glass box, hinged lid, cobalt blue
w/white enameled dots around
sides, blue violets & green leaves
enameled on lid, 3 5/8" d.,
2 7/8" h. 130.00
Glass box, hinged lid, frosted lime
green w/white enameled flowers
& gold foliage, sprays of same
flowers around sides, 4¼" d.,
3 1/8" h. 140.00
Glass box, hinged lid, cranberry
w/textured 5/8" gold band
w/pink & blue enameled flowers
in circle on lid & in bands around
sides of box, dainty gold trim
w/blue & white enameled dot
trim, 3½" d., 3 5/8" h. 232.00
Jewelry box, gilt-decorated red lacquer, stepped rectangular hinged
lid above the conforming body,
raised on gilt-metal paw feet, the
top decorated w/a stylized St.
George & the Dragon within a
wooded landscape, the sides w/fo-
liate scrolled gilt decoration,
Regence period, France, early
18th c., 9 x 12", 6" h. 3,575.00
Jewelry box, silver, Rococo style,
demilune top w/repousse tavern
scenes surrounded by foliate
scrolls, red velvet interior, Con-
tinental, 19th c., 9" l. 660.00
Knife boxes, inlaid mahogany,
shaped sloping hinged lid opening
to a well pierced for cutlery, the
interior lid centering an inlaid star,
above a conformingly shaped base
w/tiny brass loop handle on lid &
brass keyhole escutcheon on base,
George III period, England, ca.
1795, 8¾ x 11½", 14" h., pr. 3,740.00

Lacquer & mixed-metal box, circular,
decorated w/chrysanthemums in
the Japanese taste, Tiffany &
Company, New York, ca. 1910,
2¼" d., 7/8" h. 1,540.00
Painter's box, painted & decorated
wood, rectangular hinged lid
painted dark green & decorated
w/polychrome scrolls, pinstriping
& flourishes centering the inscription "Wm. E. McMaster - Portrait
Painter," over conforming base,
leather handle center top (replaced), probably New York,
New York, ca. 1850, 9¾ x 16",
5 5/8" h. 2,090.00
Pantry box, bentwood, carved &
painted, round w/fitted lid carved
w/central pinwheel device enclosed by stars & flowerheads
within a sawtooth border, painted
dark green & trimmed w/yellow &
black, inscribed "J.P." on underside of lid, America, early 19th c.,
10¼" d., 5 7/8" h. (minor imper-
fections) 2,090.00
Patch box, hinged lid, black ame-
thyst glass w/white enameled
flowers & leaves, 2 1/8" d.,
1 1/8" h. 78.00
Pill box, sterling silver, tiny en-
graved cross-hatching on cover,
marked "Sterling," 1 x 1½" 30.00
Pill box, sterling silver, oval form
w/chased Art Nouveau design,
England, ca. 1900, 1 7/8" d. (tiny
dents) 165.00
Pipe box, hanging-type, painted pine,
well-scalloped top edges & curved
crest w/two hanging holes, overlapping dovetailed drawer in base,
7" w., 17½" h. (edge damage,
age cracks & repairs) 1,000.00
Pipe box, hanging-type, pine,
scrolled backboard w/mushroom
finial, sides curved w/deep cut
front, small dovetailed drawer
w/brass pull, edges w/deep bead,
America, 18th c., 17 5/8" h. 770.00
Shaving box, chip-carved white
birch, long rectangular body
w/sliding lid carved w/fingerholds
opening to an interior w/two
small compartments, the lid chip-
carved w/diamond, heart, pinwheel & a pot of flowers within
sawtooth borders, one side
w/large compass star, double
heart & pinwheel, the other side
similarly carved w/a thin sliding
lid opening to another compartment, curved handle, attributed to
German settlement of Waldoboro,
Maine, late 18th c., 11½" l. 990.00

Stamp box, Favrile mosaic glass & gilt-bronze, rectangular form, the tapering sides covered w/a fine brickwork pattern of azure, silvery-blue iridescent, sea green & iridescent mustard, sienna & amber mosaic tiles, the hinged cover set w/two amber iridescent scarab beetles on either side of a gilt-bronze orb, set against conforming brickwork mosaic tile ground, opening to reveal an interior cast w/two stamp holders, impressed "TIFFANY STUDIOS - NEW YORK," 1899-1920, 4½" l. 16,500.00

Small Sterling Silver Box

Sterling silver box, the pierced scrollwork lid revealing turquoise enameling, plain body, Worcester, Massachusetts, ca. 1925, 3¾" sq., 2½" h. (ILLUS.) 522.50

Storage box, bentwood, round, single finger lappet construction on base & lid, old worn dark finish, 7¾" d., 3½" h. 95.00

Storage box, domed-top, decorated beech, original h.p. decoration of stylized birds & flowers in blue, white, green & red on deep yellow ochre ground, wrought-iron lock & hasp, wire handle, 19th c., 14½" l. (replaced butt hinges w/original wire staple hinges in place) 450.00

Storage box, embossed leather-covered wood, Arts & Crafts style, rectangular w/embossed floral & line decoration, lid accented by mother-of-pearl cabochons, monogrammed, probably England, ca. 1910, 6 1/8 x 8¾", 3¼" h. ... 192.50

Storage box, painted poplar, rectangular flat top w/central wire bail above conforming sides, decorated w/original red & black graining, black borders & yellow stylized foliage, wire hasp at front, staple hinges, 9¾" l. (hinges worn & loose) 325.00

Tool box w/hinged lid & shallow drawer in base, pine, interior of lid painted w/seascape, flowers,

other decoration & "H.R.N.," exterior w/dark finish, early 20th c., 20" l. 90.00

Tortoiseshell & mother-of-pearl box, rectangular, rounded edge cover w/inlaid mother-of-pearl floral design, metal lion paw & wooden button feet, interior refitted w/velvet compartments, Regency period, England, ca. 1810, 8 5/8 x 11 3/8", 4½" h. 935.00

Trinket box, painted cedar, rectangular plank construction w/bentwood domed top, butt joints w/lap-joined sides, the hinged lid opening to a deep well, the top & sides painted free-hand w/a fluid tulip, leafage & dot design, outlined w/green striping on a red-brown ground, tin hasp & hinges, Lancaster County, Pennsylvania, ca. 1800, 6 x 8½", 4¼" h. 1,320.00

Wall box, painted wood, two-tier, shaped backboard pierced w/hanging hole over sloping sides & rectangular boxes, nailed construction, old light red paint, America, early 19th c., 5¼ x 11¼", 18½" h. (worn paint, water damage to base) 770.00

BREWERIANA

Celluloid Foam Scrapers

Beer is still popular in this country but the number of breweries has greatly diminished. More than 1,900 breweries were in operation in the 1870's but we find fewer than 40 supplying the demands of the country a century later. The small local brewery has either been absorbed by a larger company or forced to close, unable to meet the competition. Advertising items used to promote the various breweries, especially those issued prior to Prohibition, now attract an ever growing number of collectors. The breweriana items listed are a sampling of the many items available. Also see BOTTLES.

Ashtray, "Reisch Beer," glass $20.00
Beer barrel, "Capitol Brewery, Madison, Wisconsin," 5 liter, 6 x 9¾" 10.00

Beer glass, "Bartholomay,"
etched ....15.00 to 20.00
Beer glass, "Beadleston & Woerz,"
etched, brewery scene........... 75.00
Beer glass, "Cumberland Brew,"
etched 18.00
Beer glass, "Edelweiss," etched 47.00
Beer glass, "Fritz Hoppe, Platteville,
Wis.," etched 67.50
Beer glass, "Kuebler," etched, brew-
ery scene 95.00
Beer glass, "Lion," embossed....... 45.00
Beer glass, "Lucky Lager," clear
w/red & yellow lettering........ 14.00
Beer glass, "Pearl Beer," clear
w/green & red lettering, barrel-
shaped 9.00
Beer glass, "Phoenix," embossed ... 195.00
Beer glass, "Tritschler & Tiesse,"
etched 75.00
Beer glass, "Walter Bros.,"
Menasha, Wis., etched 45.00
Beer glass, "Henry Weinhard Brew-
ery," etched 55.00
Beer glass, "Zang Beer," Denver,
etched 110.00
Book, "History of Pabst Brewing
Co.," 1948 .... 50.00
Booklet, "Buckeye Beer," entitled
"The Happenings of Buck & Billy,"
by Lank, 1940 .... 15.00
Calendar, 1904, "Val Blatz
Brewery" 300.00
Calendar, 1906, "Anheuser-Busch,"
beautiful lady w/bottle, 8 x 20" .. 375.00
Calendar, 1932, "Anheuser-Busch" .. 160.00
Clock, electric, "Budweiser," large
revolving pocket watch on chain.. 295.00
Clock, electric, "Duquesne Beer,"
Art Deco style reverse painting,
lighted 350.00
Clock, electric, "Schlitz Beer," "The
Beer That Made Milwaukee Famous," red, yellow & white,
7½ x 10" 125.00
Coaster, "Dick's Beer," cardboard... 18.00
Counter display, "Guinness Stout,"
dwarf figure w/real hair beard &
eyebrows & wearing red cap,
green jacket, red pants & black
boots seated on wooden bench,
holding a large "Guinness Stout"
bottle on one knee & stringed
harp on other knee, 14" w.,
19" h. 100.00
Counter display, "Hampden Ale,"
chalkware, figure of man on keg
w/accordion, 15" 65.00
Counter display, "Heileman Beer,"
metal, figure of a French cavalier,
7½" h. 55.00
Counter display, "Schmidt's Beer,"
pot metal, figure of a bartender,
8" h. 42.00

Cribbage board, "Drink Rhinelander
Beer" 20.00
Foam scrapers, "Budweiser" &
"Anheuser-Busch," celluloid,
1890's, each (ILLUS.) 35.00
Foam scraper, "Feigenspan,"
Bakelite 25.00
Foam scraper, "Grain Belt Beer,"
celluloid 15.00
Foam scraper, "M. Groh's Sons
Breweries" 39.00
Foam scraper, "Schmidt's City Club
Beer" 23.00
Foam scraper, "Standard Brewing,
Scranton"..................... 25.00
Foam scraper, "Stegmaier
Brewery" 17.00
Foam scraper, "Trommer's" 15.00
Knife, pocket-type, "Anheuser-
Busch" 165.00
Light, wall mount, "National Bohe-
mian Beer," pictures cartoon
animals, bright colors 50.00
Mug, "Falstaff," blue & grey stone-
ware, embossed design, marked
"Germany No. 7655" 27.50
Mug, "Otto Huber Brewery," pot-
tery, w/hops on side, marked
pewter lid 85.00
Mug, "Pittsburg Brewing Co.," pot-
tery, red & black lettering on
cream ground, signed 95.00
Mug, "Yuengling," glass 4.00
Necktie, "Edelweiss Beer," silk,
"Cheery-Beery," never worn, in
original box 25.00
Pilsener glasses, "Budweiser
Anheuser-Busch," Christmas-like
decorations, set of 4 .... 20.00
Pin, "Piel's Beer," brass, figural Bert
& Harry Piel, Fan Club, 1950's 25.00
Pinback button, "Miller High Life,"
celluloid, 3" 20.00
Pitcher, "Atlas, Panama," pottery,
bulbous, 2 liter 125.00
Playing cards, "People's Beer, Osh-
kosh, Wisconsin" 20.00
Poker chip, "Chief Oshkosh Beer" .. 10.00
Poker chip, "Lithia Beer" 10.00
Postcard, "Stegmaier Brewing" 5.00

"Gluek's Beer" Salt & Pepper Shakers

Radio, "Premium Grain Belt,"
18" w., 10" h.................. 59.00
Salt & pepper shakers, "Gluek's
Beer," amber glass w/paper
labels & metal caps, 4" h., pr.
(ILLUS. previous page) 13.50
Salt & pepper shakers, "Piel's Beer,"
ceramic, figural Bert & Harry Piel,
pr........................ 50.00
Sign, "Bachmann Brewing, Staten Island," lithographed tin, factory &
hotel pictured, 1890's, 2 x 3' 2,100.00
Sign, "Berghoff Brewing Corp., Ft.
Wayne, Indiana," painted tin, dog
pictured, 13 x 21" 250.00
Sign, "Budweiser," lighted,
revolving-type, Clydesdale horses
w/beer wagon & dogs...900.00 to 995.00
Sign, "Bunker Hill Brewing,"
lithographed tin, girl in low cut
dress pictured, 20 x 30".......... 600.00
Sign, "Cer-ola, Kolb Brewery, Bay
City, Mich.," cardboard, Prohibition era, 12 x 18" 45.00
Sign, "Cook's Goldblume Beer," tin,
scene of dog w/paws on table,
16 x 22" 1,100.00
Sign, "Lemp Beer," Falstaff on
horse, w/maidens, pre-
Prohibition, 24" d.............. 450.00
Sign, "Miller Beer," wooden, girl
standing on box, some color,
13 x 17" oval 175.00
Sign, "Ortlieb Brewery,"
lithographed tin, two clocks for
opening & closing times 38.00
Swizzle stick holder, "Rheingold
Beer," chrome, bar display w/red
logo 20.00
Tap knob, "Busch Bavarian," drum-
shaped 35.00
Tap knob, "Coors"................. 10.00
Tap knob, "Heileman's," wood &
metal 7.50
Tap knob, "Piel's," ball form, double
faced, brass & enamel insert in
plastic frame 15.00
Tap knob, "Schlitz," girl on top 20.00
Thermometer, "Diehl, Defiance,"
tin 85.00
Thermometer, "Rueter & Co. High-
land Spring Brewery, Boston,"
brass, pat. 1885, 9" 175.00
Token, spinner-type, "A. P. Fitzer
Distributers, Luverne, Minnesota,
Hamm's Beer" 17.50
Watch fob, "Blatz Beer," barrel-
shaped 32.00

BROWNIE COLLECTIBLES

The Brownies were creatures of fantasy

*created by Palmer Cox, artist-author, in 1887.
Early in this century numerous articles with
depictions of or in the shape of Brownies appeared.*

Brownie Cloth Dolls

Ball, cloth, Brownies at various
activities $38.00
Book, "The Brownie Clown of
Brownie Town," by Palmer Cox,
color illustrations, published by
Century, hard cover (cover
loose) 85.00
Book, "The Brownies At Home," by
Palmer Cox, 1893 .... 75.00
Book, "The Brownie Yearbook," by
Palmer Cox, 1895, published by
McLoughlin Bros. 175.00
Book, "Busy Brownies," 1897, Vol. 1,
No. 1 .... 25.00
Book, "Queer People," by Palmer
Cox, 1894 (non-Brownie) 30.00
Bottle, enameled Brownies
decoration..................... 18.00
Camera, "Eastman Kodak 2A," pic-
tures Brownie.................. 65.00
Candlestick, majolica, figural Brown-
ie Policeman, 7½" h........... 135.00
Demitasse spoon, sterling silver,
enameled Brownie 25.00
Dolls, printed cloth, uncut sheet of 6
(ILLUS. of part)................. 450.00
Folder, "Brownies Discovery," by
Palmer Cox, Tarrant Co., 1895,
5½" (cover slightly damaged) 40.00
Handkerchief, Brownies at various
activities, pat. 1894, 10" 20.00
Ice cream mold, pewter, figural
Brownie, dated 1894............. 85.00
Paperweight, handled, ornate scroll-
ing on body & square handle
decorated w/gold, four Brownies:
The Chinaman, The Irishman &
two other Brownies; bright colors,
3 x 5¼" 195.00
Patent medicine tin, "Brownie Oint-
ment," Brownies pictured, 1924, in
original box 40.00
Puzzle, "The Christmas Dinner,"
10 x 12"....................... 98.00
Soda bottle, embossed Brownies
decoration, 1926 .... 25.00

Teaspoon, silver plate, Brownie full
figure handle 20.00

BUSTER BROWN

Buster Brown Book

*Buster Brown was a comic strip created by
Richard Outcault in the New York Herald in
1902. It was subsequently syndicated and
numerous objects depicting Buster (and often his dog, Tige) were produced.*

Banks, molded plastic, round base
w/embossed lettering topped by
figural busts of Buster Brown &
Tige, one red & one green,
5½" h., pr. $45.00
Blotter, "Buster Brown Shoes" 25.00
Book, "Buster Brown, His Dog Tige
and Their Troubles," full-color cover (right corner missing), color
comic book-type illustrations inside, dated August, 1904,
11½ x 16" (ILLUS.) 60.00
Camping set, metal, five pieces
w/bowls & cup nested & held in
place w/metal strap across the
top, each piece w/Buster Brown &
Tige logo in bottom, the set 16.00
Club member's set: neckerchief, pinback button & tin whistle; 3 pcs. . . . 25.00
Doll, life-like composition head &
arms, movable legs & arms, cloth
body, original outfit, 28" 266.00
Easter Egg, tin, lithographed 85.00
Game, "Pin the Tie on Buster
Brown," w/12 ties, oil cloth,
signed "Outcault," framed,
27 x 30" 375.00
Growth chart, wall-mounted, full-
color w/advertising for Buster
Brown Shoes, measures from two
feet to five feet, 6' long 28.00
Hatchet, wooden handle, head
marked w/Buster Brown logo,
13" l. 35.00
Knife, hunting-type, black handle,
marked "Buster Brown Health

Shoes" & "Marble's and Brown
Shoe Co.," 8½" l. 55.00
Knife & fork set, silver plate 22.00
Mannequin, plastic, 41" h. 150.00
Mirror, wall-type, painted rectangu-
lar frame (worn) holding mirror
plate w/printing at top "Brown
Bilt Shoes, Buster Brown Shoes,"
18" w., 24" h. (loss of some sil-
vering) 35.00
Mug, porcelain, straight sides slight-
ly tapering to top, color transfer
of Buster Brown making Tige sit
up & beg while balancing a
steaming pot of tea on his nose,
gold trim, 3½" h. 25.00
Plate, china, Buster Brown teaching
Tige tricks, 4¾" d. 15.00
Plate, china, Buster Brown, Tige &
Mary Jane at tea, 6" d. 60.00
Playing cards, complete deck plus
joker, in original box, copyright
1906, 1¾ x 2½" (box worn &
repaired) 54.00
Pocket watch, metal case, white
dial w/Arabic numerals & "Buster
Brown Shoes" around picture of
Buster Brown & Tige in the center,
seconds dial, working, 2" d. 121.00
Postcard, Valentine Greetings, 1903,
signed "Outcault" 17.00
Rocking chair, child's, painted wood,
square slat back & slat seat, flat
arms, Buster Brown advertising
across top of back, 14½" w.,
21" h. (worn paint) 150.00
Roly poly figure, model of Buster
Brown w/original paint, made by
Schoenhut, 6½" h. (some wear) . . 182.00
Rug, round, color bust portraits of
Buster Brown & Tige in center
above "Buster Brown," narrow
blue band w/yellow stars border,
54" d. 213.00
Shoe brush, oval wooden top
w/raised lettering advertising
Buster Brown Shoes, two-tone
brown & cream bristles, 8½" l. . . . 20.00
Waffle iron, embossed scene of
Buster Brown & Tige on flat lid,
coiled-wire handle, raised on iron
base, 10 x 14" 165.00

BUTTER MOLDS & STAMPS

*While they are sometimes found made of
other materials, it is primarily the two-piece
wooden butter mold and one-piece butter
stamp that attracts collectors. The molds are
found in two basic styles, rounded cup form
and rectangular box form. Butter stamps are
usually round with a protruding knob handle*

on the back. Many are factory made items with the print design made by forcing a metal die into the wood under great pressure, while others have the design chiseled out by hand.

Stylized Tulip Stamp

Beaver mold, wooden, two-piece ...$135.00

Cherry sprig mold, cherry, turned & carved, tapering turned cylindrical handle w/domed stamp engraved w/a cherry sprig, painted overall in green, America, 19th c., 1½" d., 2½" h. 99.00

Eagle stamp, wooden, round, carved spread-wing bird, one-piece w/turned handle, 4½" d. 300.00

Floral stamp, wooden, round, stylized tulip-like blossom w/large diamond & two small stars above & two star hex signs below, drilled "air holes," dark finish, one piece w/turned handle, 3 7/8" d. 175.00

Fruit & foliage stamp, wooden, hand-carved stylized specimen surrounded by leaves, 3 3/8" d. ... 165.00

Heart stamp, wood, primitive carving w/incised ridges conforming to outline shape, 2¾" l. 205.00

Hex design butter print scoop, carved walnut, rounded scoop w/stemmed circular handle carved w/a central hex design within a sawtooth border, Pennsylvania, 19th c., 9½" l., 4¾" w. (large chip to scoop) 137.50

House mold, primitive wood, hand-carved five-section mold w/sections secured w/screen door-type latches w/hooks bent together, 5" l. 95.00

Leaf cased mold, round tin case w/two raised bands holds wooden carved plunger, 4 5/8" d. 220.00

Pear stamp, carved wood, large pear hanging from small leafy branch, concentric ring bands at rim, turned handle, 3¼" d. (short age crack) 200.00

Pineapple stamp, carved wood, almond-shaped center fruit flanked by three long leaves on each side, fine notch-carved border band, back carved w/"A.B.L.," & carved-out handle, 3 7/8 x 4 1/8" 140.00

Quail stamp, carved wood, stylized bird w/leaf sprig above, swirled notched band at rim, turned screw in handle, 4" d. (wear, fine age cracks) 500.00

Roses & foliage "lollipop" stamp, primitive carved wood, central rose blossom flanked by leafy branches & surrounded by band of chip-carving near the edge, same design on both sides, dark finish, 9¼" l. (worn edges) 345.00

Shell half-circle stamp, wooden, carved w/wide-ribbed cockle shell, 4 7/8" d. (minor age cracks) 220.00

Stag by tree stamp, wooden, notched band at rim, turned handle, scrubbed finish, 3½" d. 575.00

Starflower "lollipop" stamp, wooden, crudely carved six-petal flower w/grooved petals & small leaflets between each pair of petals, 9¾" l. 200.00

Strawberry stamp, wooden, hand-carved single berry & two leaves, w/brass ring hanger, 4 1/8" d. (minor age crack) 115.00

Swan cased mold, wooden, carved, w/case & plunger, ca. 1830, ½ lb. 220.00

Swan stamp, carved wood, swimming bird w/three-leaf sprig to right side, one-piece turned handle, dark finish, 3¾" d. (some wear) 125.00

Swirled stamp, stoneware, tan Albany slip on stamp & grey salt glaze on back & round handle w/cobalt blue dots & stripes, 4½" d., 3¼" h. (stamp chipped) 1,400.00

Three-leaf clover cased mold, carved wood, rectangular box frame w/four segments each carved w/leaf sprig, scrubbed finish, 4 1/8 x 12¼" 85.00

Tulip stamp, hand-carved stylized blossoms on the obverse, reverse w/the initials "EH" flanking the handle w/star, bird & tulip motif, Pennsylvania, 19th c., 4" d. (ILLUS.)....................... 418.00

"Special Focus"

Calendar Plates

by Bettye Street

Monday's child is fair of face,
Tuesday's child is full of grace,
Wednesday's child is full of woe,
Thursday's child has far to go.
Friday's child is loving and giving,
Saturday's child works hard for its living.
But the child that's born on the Sabbath day,
Is bonny and blithe, and good and gay.

Thirty days hath September,
April, June and November;
February has twenty-eight alone,
All the rest have thirty-one,
Excepting leap-year, that's the time
When February's days are twenty-nine.

Nostalgic verses we learned in childhood and repeated in play were often steeped in superstition with no thought given to the scientific evolution of the calendar. To understand why the calendar plate became a collectible item, it would help to see how the calendar developed.

Man is an orderly creature. Nature was his first timekeeper. The sun, the moon and the stars all played their part in man's awareness of the passing of time. Man became aware of the rising and setting sun-days, basis of the solar calendar. The lunar calendar was developed from the position and phases of the moon. Seasonal changes were noted by weather changes, animals available to hunters, birth of young animals and vegetation changes. The length of year was determined by the cycle of seasons. Time passed and man became more communal as people started to congregate for trading, hunting and the exchanging of ideas. Towns and cities came into existence which brought about the need for a tool for keeping track of time, especially in planning public festivals and celebrations. This tool became the calendar.

Ancient peoples watched the moon, sun and stars and observed their changing positions in the sky. Eventually mankind saw the stars arranged as patterns or "constellations" and gave them names which developed into the signs of the zodiac.

Ancient observations established that the sun traveled through twelve special constellations in a year. The sun was in each constellation about a month. Lunar months gave a shorter year so the twelve month division soon disagreed with the season's cycles. When an extra month was added, to even this out, it caused more problems.

The first recorded calendar was done according to the stars and planets by the Egyptians 5,000 years ago and the Babylonians made observations as early as 4,000 B.C. They determined the year was 365 days long.

The Romans divided months into periods called Nones and Ides. The first day of the month was called Kalends, from which the word "calendar" developed. The Romans borrowed names from the Greeks and also used the names of their emperors and gods to name the months. The Julian calendar of Julius Caesar was based on the lunar calendar and used intercalation of an extra month to keep the calendar from slipping behind the solar calendar. This calendar was set up in 46 B.C. and was still in use in the 16th century, more than 1,500 years later. The Julian calendar used a seven-day week, an Asian concept which was adopted by the Hebrews and later by the Christians.

The Gregorian calendar was designed by Pope Gregory in the 16th century to correct errors in the Julian calendar. The Gregorian calendar is so accurate that the difference between the calendar and the solar year is now only about 26 seconds.

Religious and cultural traditions have created other calendars which are in use today. According to tradition, the Hebrew calendar began with the Creation. The Christian calendar is based on the year Jesus was born. The Islamic calendar begins with Muhammad's flight from Mecca to Medina. The Chinese calendar began in 2,637 B.C. and was invented by Emperor Huang-Ti. The Greek Orthodox calendar is still based on the Julian calendar. There has been a proposal for a world calendar; however, most people in the

West use the Gregorian calendar today.

Knowing about the development of the calendar through the centuries and man's need for an accurate time chart, we can understand why the calendar continues to be an important object in our lives today.

In 1895 in England, someone recognized this importance and combined two functional objects, the calendar and the plate. By doing so, a collectible was created.

Merchants gave the plates to customers each year which almost guaranteed they would be saved and cherished. They were not used for eating but placed on a shelf for decorative purposes. That, perhaps, is the reason many exist in good condition today.

It has been suggested that the calendar plate was introduced in the United States around the turn of the century. I have no proof or documentation, but it is felt that perhaps the plate was introduced at the 1904 World's Fair in St. Louis, Missouri. Since St. Louis is my hometown, I would like to think that this is true. However, in my 22 years of collecting calendar plates, I have never seen one for the year 1904. The earliest one I have in my collection is 1907.

The early plates were of porcelain and semi-porcelain. A variety of designs were used and add to their desirability. I received my first plate as a gift from my mother-in-law in 1966. She purchased it as just a pretty plate and something I would enjoy. I had no idea it would be the beginning of an unusual collection of 109 plates. I began collecting with the idea that it might be interesting to find plates with my parents' and children's birth years. As yet I have not been able to do this for my father and two children.

In the course of collecting, I became aware of how unusual and unique many plates were. They also had their own stories to tell. The early plates used flowers for decorations, usually roses and poppies. Later, designers tried to outdo themselves in unusual ways to present the calendar. This was evident in the placement of the calendar months in the sails of ships, in horseshoes, borders, etc. There were plates that commemorated the end of World War I and the opening of the Panama Canal. Historic locales such as Plymouth Rock and Niagara Falls were shown. Presidential heads were used as the center design of plates and a collection could be built on that topic alone. Styles and clothing of the times may be seen in the pictures of the Gibson-type Girls, which were often used as a center design. A girl in a swimming suit was very daring. Animals, birds, children or anything that would catch the housewife's eye were used as designs.

Advertising on such plates is also very interesting. Some advertising was simple with just a name and address while others were much more detailed, even listing store merchandise. As my grandfather was a traveling salesman or "drummer," I have often wondered if he sold any plates or took orders from merchants. Did they choose the plate that year from a catalog from a china company or was it brought to them by a drummer? The merchant was reached in some such manner as there are identical plates but with different merchants' advertising.

During the 1930's and 1940's few plates, if any, were produced, at least plates from this era have not been seen on the market. This absence might have been due to the economics of the Great Depression and World War II. Perhaps merchants began to give pieces of Depression glass as a substitute for the calendar plate. I recall going to the movies with my parents and a piece of Depression glass would be given to an adult ticket holder. People would return week after week to collect a whole set of dishes.

Later, in the 1950's, the calendar plate returned in the plain white or gold trimmed and decorated ones. In the mid-Sixties, a calendar plate was produced and sold for collectible purposes. The Alfred Meakin and Wedgwood plates were made in England. The Bicentennial Spencer plates and the Artist series plates also fall in this group.

The places where plates are located add to the fun and interest of collecting. Most plates are found in antiques shows and shops but many can be found at garage sales and flea markets. If you are serious in your searching, it may be wise to work with a favorite dealer who always is willing to assist you. I am fortunate to have such a dealer and also many friends who bring me calendar plates from their travels.

Another interesting aspect of collecting calendar plates is to note where a plate originated and where it was found. How did a plate given by a merchant in Mississippi end up in a shop in Colorado? Or how did a plate made in England get all the way to Florida? By what mode did it travel? Was it treasured and loved and handed down from family to family? This is what makes collecting exciting.

The calendar plate that was given by merchants in the past has now been replaced by calendars given by banks, merchants, grocers, real estate offices, dentists and the like. Many of these calendars are beautiful and often saved, but few equal the charm of the calendar plates of yesteryear. Perhaps someday a merchant will have again the brilliant thought of putting a calendar on a china plate and a collectible will be reborn for the future.

I wish to thank Anne Caulkins, Margaret Jackson, Lillian McDermott, Rena Museo,

Madeleine Phelps and Jean Seago, who all have added to my collection.

Special thanks to Alma Street, who started it all, and to my husband, Bob, who did all the photography for me and patiently showed me how to use the word processor.

References:
World Book
First Book of Calendars by Neria H. Apfel.
About the History of the Calendar by A.E. Evenson.
Introductory rhymes from *The Real Mother Goose*, Rand, McNally & Co.

Price Listings:

1907, Christmas holly along edge . . . $79.00

1907, calendar in border w/roses between, purple roses in center. Advertisement: "Compliments - Atkinson Co. - Complete House Furnishers - Tremont, Cor Eliot St. - Boston, Mass." Backstamp: Lebeau Porcelaine, 9¼" d. (ILLUS.)........................ 55.00

1908, semi-porcelain, raised, embossed design on edge of border, gold-trimmed edge, three holly sprays in red & green around center of plate, calendar in center & year "1908" in brown. Advertisement: "Compliments of - A. Arnquist - Bishop Hill, Ill." Backstamp: eagle & "China," 8" d. (ILLUS.)........................ 45.00

1908, semi-porcelain, same plate as above, only not as vivid in coloring & holly sprays slightly different. Advertisement: "Compliments of - Russell Clothing House - Warren, Ill." Backstamp: "N.C. Co." over "E.L.O.," 8" d. (ILLUS.) 18.00

1908, semi-porcelain, calendar months form border in brown, year "1908" at top of plate, in center, in grey, blue & yellow, is picture of the building at Plymouth Rock, Plymouth, Massachusetts. Advertisement: "Bartlett and N. Erkl - Stalle - Fancy Groceries - Pervisions (sic), Etc. - L.N. and N, Esq. - Mt. Vernon, Ohio," 9½" d. (ILLUS.) 55.00

1909, fruit & morning-glories. Advertisement: "Jeweler" 45.00

1909, violets in border & poppies in center........................ 54.00

1909, town shown in center w/group of stores, calendar along edge ... 54.00

1909, bluebird in center, calendar around ruffled edge (ILLUS.)...... 32.50

1909, poppy in center, calendar around edge. Advertisement: "Goldstein, Jeweler" 45.00

1909, St. Bernard dog head in center of plate, calendar along edge 47.00

1909, calendar months form border, each month outlined w/maple & holly leaf design, center of plate is design of peaches & blackberries. Advertisement: "Otto Stelse, - 1894-1909 Broadwell's - Leading Merchant - Broadwell, Ill." Backstamp: "Imperial China," 7¼" d. (ILLUS.)........................ 28.50

1909, calendar months along border, edge of plate pale green & scalloped, colored picture of different season every three months, gold edging motif along inner circle of

plate, robin w/outstretched wings holding rose ribbon w/year "1909" in beak. Advertisement: "Compliments of - Farmer's Supply Co. - Dealers in - General Merchandise - Ste. Genevieve, Mo.," 8½" d. (ILLUS.)........................ 35.00

1909, calendar months in green blocks set in semi-circle over head of Gibson-type Girl, girl has light brown hair w/pale blue scarf over a beige & dark blue trimmed hat, "1909" printed at top of plate. Advertisment: "Moritz Newman - Grocer, - Silver Plume, Colo." (ILLUS.) 25.00

1909, rose in center, calendar along border. Advertisement: "Siegel and Co. - Syracuse, Mo." 35.00

1909, rose in center, calendar along border. Advertisement: "F.J. Dondurand - Aurora, Ks." 42.50

1909, semi-porcelain, calendar months printed in brown squares along border, two squares are outlined w/holly berries & leaves, two w/oak leaves, two w/violets,

two w/roses, two w/poppies &
two w/fruits to depict the seasons, in center are three large
poppies in shades of pink, gold
trim on outer edge of plate. Backstamp: "Carnation/McNicol,"
9½" d. (ILLUS.) 30.00
1910, horseshoe w/sailing ships. Advertisement: "J. Geo. Dieter" 45.00
1910, lighthouse scene in center.
Advertisement: "Cash Store -
General Merchandise - Silver
Lake, Oregon" 45.00

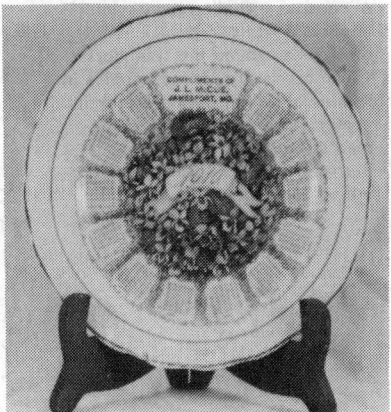

1910, semi-porcelain, narrow embossed edge bordered w/gold on
slightly scalloped edging, center
of plate is mass of violets w/rib-
bon banner in beige & year
"1910," calendar months are
green & circle the violets & are
outlined in reddish brown in scroll
motif. Advertisement: "Compliments of - J.L. McCue -
Jamesport, Mo.," 7" d. (ILLUS.) ... 25.00
1910, rose-colored rose in center,
calendar around border. Advertisement: "D.O. Ooley - The Old

Reliable - One Price Store - Fargo,
Okla.," 8" d.................... 27.50
1910, holly design. Advertisement:
"The Breslin - Broadway and 29th
Street - New York." 46.00
1910, calendar in horseshoe &
fisherman in center of
horseshoe 46.00
1910, minuet dancers in center of
plate, calendar along border 46.00
1910, wishbone in center of plate,
Gibson-type Girl in center of
wishbone 45.00
1910, Niagara Falls scene in
center........................ 25.00
1910, apples in center 24.00

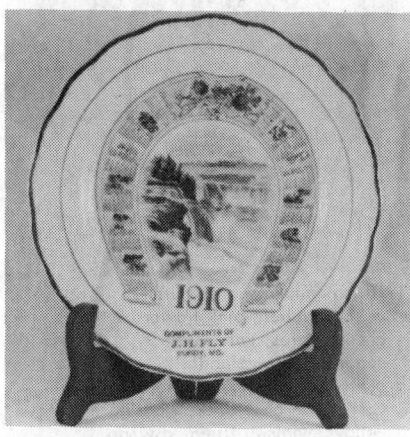

1910, semi-porcelain, Niagara Falls
in center w/horseshoe design in
pale pink over the falls, calendar
months are in the horseshoe &
are separated by sprigs of red
clover, bottom of falls has year
"1910" in green & black. Advertisement: "Compliments of - J.H.
Fly - Purdy, Mo." Backstamp:
"Carnation/McNicol" (ILLUS.) 55.00

1910, semi-porcelain, scalloped, embossed edge trimmed in gold, left side of center has spray of poppies in shades of white, orange & pink & two smaller orange flowers, to the right of the poppies is a large square of brown containing the calendar months w/the year "1910" at the top. Backstamp: "Mellor & Co., Etruria," 8" d. (ILLUS.) 35.00

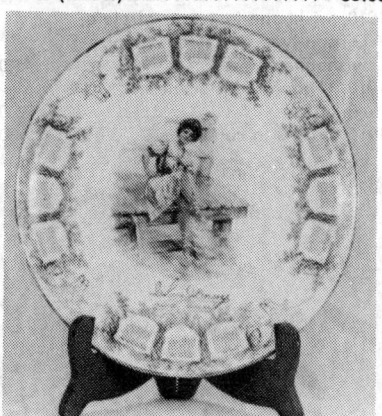

1910, calendar squares outlined w/rose ribbon, pink flowers & green leaves, gold motif separates the calendar months, center of plate is a Gibson-type Girl sitting on a dock, wearing a yellow swimsuit trimmed w/orange, orange stockings & yellow laced shoes, she has dark hair, water is blue-green, gold-trimmed edge. Advertisement: "Isham J. Dorsey - Sells - Furniture, Opelika, Ala." Backstamp: "Dresden China," 8½" d. (ILLUS.) 35.00

1910, semi-porcelain, narrow gold band on outer edge, center of plate is lighthouse on a rock w/"1910" below house &

blue-green water in background, in semi-circle around lighthouse are the calendar months in shape of sails on ships. Advertisement: "John Hands - Jeweller and Optician - 109 E. Washington St. - Iowa City, Iowa." Backstamp: "Pope Gosser China," 8" d. (ILLUS.)........................ 34.00

1910, semi-porcelain, scalloped & embossed gold-trimmed edge, calendar in border in groups of three separated by floral sprays of seasons including holly, violets, poppies & fruits, green ribbon & motif also around the calendars which are brown, three poppies in shades of white, purple & pink in center. Advertisement: "Compliments - Toogood and Webster - Bertrand, Nebr." Backstamp: "Carnation/McNicol," 9" d. (ILLUS.) ... 25.00

1911, semi-porcelain, gold trim on outer edge, frigate ship in center on blue water, calendar months in the sails of ship, "1911" on flag. Advertisement: "Compliments of -

Pittsville State Bank - Pittsville,
Wis. - 1911." Backstamp: "Semi-
porcelain - The E.P.P. Co.," 7" d.
(ILLUS.)............................ 25.00
1911, Lincoln portrait in center (nose
worn). Advertisement: "Brooker
and Mitchell" 24.00
1911, clocks arranged in time
zones 55.00

1911, semi-porcelain, gold edging,
marsh scene in middle w/calendar
months in brown on grey rectangle, mallard ducks in flight & in
water, cattails border the calendar. Advertisement: "Use Oberlin
Best - Best by Test - Oberlin Roller Mills - Oberlin, Kansas," 7" d.
(ILLUS.)........................ 35.00
1911, owl in center 55.00
1911, violets in edge. Advertisement: "Ralph Bros., - Easton,
Pa." 45.00
1911, farm scene in center. Advertisement: "Joseph Labonte - dealer in - Family Meats, Choice and
Fancy" 45.00

1911, semi-porcelain, scalloped,
gold-trimmed edge, calendar

months in border in orange & outlined w/green ribbon & gold,
small violets on corners of ribbon,
center forest scene w/pine trees
& three elk. Advertisement: "Ed.
Fender and Co. - Dealers in - Mil-
linery, Dry Goods, Groceries,
Flour, - Feed and Poultry, Butter
and Eggs. - Holden, Mo.," 8" d.
(ILLUS.)........................ 28.00

1911, semi-porcelain, pale green
edge, center w/grey fence
w/calendar months in brown on
cream, below fence is field
w/three white & four brown rabbits, two small birds on top of
fence, "1911" in center. Advertisement: "Compliments of - J.W.
Mowry - Middletown, Ill.,"
8½" d., some wear (ILLUS.) 30.00

1911, semi-porcelain, gold bands on
border, center w/bunch of purple
violets, around violets, in pale
green & tied together w/pale
blue, are calendar months in
small rectangles, in semi-circle
around calendar months are white
clock faces w/cities around the

world outlined w/orange. Advertisement: "Greetings-1911 - General Furniture Co. - 9139-41 Commercial Ave.," 8½" d. (ILLUS.) 55.00

1911, semi-porcelain, gold-trimmed edge, picture of Teddy Roosevelt in brown suit in center, gold medallions at bottom of plate & calendar months in squares along border, squares outlined w/pink roses & green leaves. Advertisement: "Compliments of - Elmer Shreve - El Paso, Ill." Backstamp: "CROA (crown)-Warranted," 9" d., crazed (ILLUS.) 39.00

1912, flag in center. Advertisement: "The Fair" 39.00

1912, semi-porcelain, pale green border, center w/sundial, two American flags, Liberty Bell & eagle w/spread wings perched on red, white & blue shield, pink wild roses at base of sundial & bottom of plate, calendar in vertical rectangles in circle around scene. Advertisement: "Compli-

ments of - The Fair - Mandel and Bower." Backstamp: "Fine China Co. Virginia," 7¼" d. (ILLUS.) 39.00

1912, same plate as above except there are bands of gold in border, no advertisement, 7¼" d. (ILLUS.) 35.00

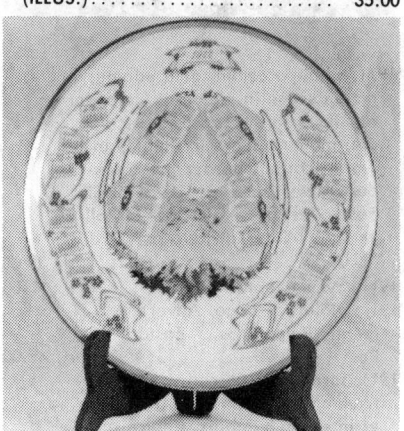

1911-1912, porcelain, two years of calendars. 1911 calendar is in petals of pink poppies in center, 1912 calendar shown in border design in red & green, blue sky in center. Advertisement on back: "Compliments of - Robert Beckman - Dealers in - General Merchandise - Germantown, Nebr.," 8½" d. (ILLUS.) 39.00

1913, robin on top of heart containing calendar 55.00

1913, airplane in center, calendar at rim 54.00

1913, calendar in horseshoe, two horses in center under the horseshoe. Advertisement: "Sloans - Rocker Store - Falfurrias, Texas" . . 27.50

1913, boy & boat in center. Advertisement: "Mort Siemin Company" 57.00

1913, fruit in center. Advertisement: "Rudolph Brunger" 37.00
1914, little boy in center, flow blue trim. Advertisement: "J.H. Tretzen - General Merchandise - Harrison, N.J." 62.00

1915, semi-porcelain, scalloped edge, gold laurel leaf & geometric design along border, center is map of the Panama Canal, top center is "1915" in yellow shield surrounded by two American flags, calendar months along sides of center w/blue background & red, white ribbon crossed at bottom of plate. Backstamp: "D.E. McNicol - Pottery Co., East Liverpool, Ohio," 7" d. (ILLUS.) 35.00

1916, semi-porcelain, scalloped edge, flow blue edging, embossed bow design w/gold motif overlay in border, frontier boatman in canoe in center, gold-orange sky & green-grey water, calendar squares & "1916" in circle around center, 9¼" d. (ILLUS.) 30.00

1916, semi-porcelain, gold motif around edge, center w/large block of calendar months w/advertising in very center, border design top & center of Dutch boys & Dutch sayings, "Dere iss mutch dot I need: but I vant mighty leedle, I tell you." & "It iss mutch better yet to shmile efen if it hurts your face." Advertisement: "Made especially for - Geo. Gisick - Timken, Kansas - From the Store That - Appreciates Your Trade." Backstamp: "Semi-porcelain" over a bow, 9½" d. (ILLUS.) 40.00

1917, semi-porcelain, scalloped edge w/embossed design on four sides, American "Old Glory" flag & "1917" at top of plate, calendar blocks grouped in threes separated by blue U.S. President's flag, Union Jack, Admiral's flag & flag of Secretary of the Navy, center of plate has large bunch of green grapes & leaves. Advertisement: "A Merry Christmas - and - A Happy New Year - J.J. Shutt -

Benld, Ills." Backstamp: "D.E.
McNicol, East Liverpool, O.," 9" d.
(ILLUS.) 25.00

1920, semi-porcelain, scalloped,
gold-trimmed edge, calendar
months in yellow blocks outlined
in blue separated by pale pink
roses on border, top of plate in
border w/blue ribbon banner over
American seal & the word "Victory," bottom of plate has dove &
scale & words "Peace" and "Justice," center of plate has world
w/dove on top surrounded by
flags, dates "1914" on left &
"1919" on right, "Peace" in middle, banner across bottom w/lau-
rel wreath "28 June 1919," below
in black "The Great World War."
Advertisement: "Compliments of -
Amy and Constant - Seaton, Ills."
Backstamp: in a bell, "The Coloni-
al Co.," 7" d. (ILLUS.) 40.00
1920, American flag in center 37.00

1920, semi-porcelain, similar to
earlier plate w/some variations:
center the same w/"Victory" &

"1920" in top of border, on one
side is blue, white & red shield
w/letters "RF" in laurel wreath,
bottom is crest w/lion & unicorn &
Latin motto in red ribbon, another
crest on bottom w/two lions &
crown & motto in French, on left
side is symbol & crest of Switzerland. Advertisement: "Compliments of - J. Karel and Sons -
Oklahoma, Okl." Backstamp:
"D.E. McNicol, East Liverpool, O.,"
9" d., faded, cracked, crazed
(ILLUS.) . . . . .20.00 to 30.00

1921, porcelain, slightly scalloped,
gold-trimmed edge, calendar in
groups of three blocks in border,
separated by bluebirds & dogwood floral sprays, larger bluebird at top of plate & year "1921"
in green & black, gold band outlining center of plate, two whole
apples & cut apple w/nuts & berries in center. Advertisement:
"Compliments of - Dumont Merc.
Co., - Dumont, Minn." Backstamp:
"D.E. McNicol, East Liverpool, O.
XOD," 8½" d. (ILLUS.) 35.00

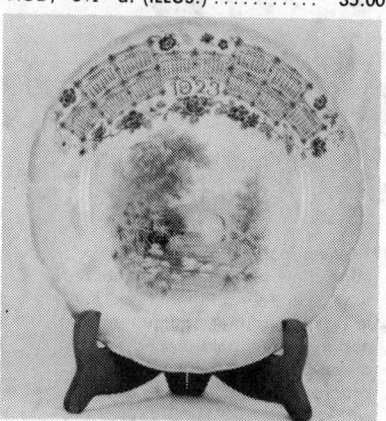

1923, semi-porcelain, gently scalloped edge tinted pale green, calendar months in pink blocks at top of plate, "1923" in green & black, flowers in bright blue & yellow around calendar blocks, center w/pond scene w/arched bridge, trees, water lilies & two swans swimming. Advertisement: "Compliments of - Forrest Seitz." Backstamp: "D.E. McNicol, East Liverpool, O.," 8¼" d., somewhat crazed (ILLUS.) . . . . 20.00 to 30.00

Newer calendar plates:
1950's & after:

There are many plates in the field that are of pottery, semi-porcelain or ironstone. Many were given by merchants and most have advertising on the back. I have them from the mid-Fifties to the Eighties. None are very expensive but they are collectible. Most are decorated with gold and many will show the scenes of the four seasons. Some have colored borders, some may have square corners and fluted borders and some may be in two colors. One group of plates in my own collection is from a merchant jeweler over a long span of years. Many may be found from $1.50 to $6.00. (ILLUS. of one)

1955-1956, tin. Only tin plate in personal collection of 109 calendar plates. I consider it unusual & rare. White enamel over tin w/gold scalloped & floral border, calendar days written in blue in blocks outlined w/gold along outside center of plate, names of months in blue above each block, center of plate w/blue & gold Dutch scene w/windmill, "1956" on rim. What makes this plate doubly interesting is that on the reverse is the same Dutch scene but the calendar year & blocks

are for the year 1955. Some rust marks on the 1956 side. 9" d. (ILLUS.) 25.00

Alfred Meakin Calendar Plates (also known as "Zodiac" plates)
Alfred Meakin is known for ceramic dinnerwares. No longer given by merchants, these plates were made to be sold in gift shops and stores. Features of these plates are that each plate has the signs of the zodiac separating the calendar months on the border with pastoral scenes in the center of each under which are the words "God Bless This House All This Year." Colors are either pink, brown or blue.

1961, cottage scene w/bridge & trees, pink. Backstamp: "Royal Staffordshire - Ceramics - Made in England - Reg. N. APP For." 10.00

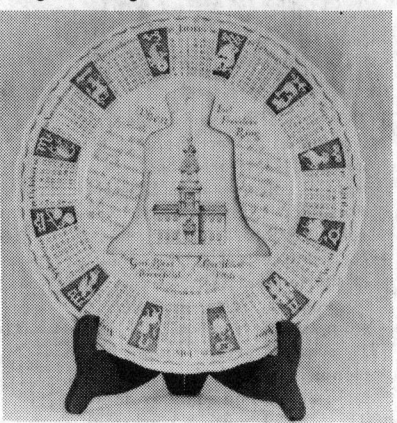

1966, scalloped edge, unusual center design w/the Liberty Bell & Independence Hall, words of the Declaration of Independence fill the remainder of center w/"God Bless Our House Throughout 1966." (All plates thereafter were worded in this manner.) Pink. Backstamp: "Royal Staffordshire -

Ceramics - Made in England - Reg.
N. APP For" (ILLUS.) 25.00
1967, pastoral scene of house
w/long porch & picket fence,
pink. Backstamp: (crown)-"Alfred
Meakin England." 10.00
1970, pastoral scene w/water mill,
stream, fisherman, house, trees &
winding road, brown or pink versions. Backstamp: "Alfred Meakin
Staffordshire England - A hand
engraved pattern - Applied under
the glaze - Detergent and acid -
resistant colors," each ..... 10.00 to 12.00
1971, pastoral scene w/house &
barn & man w/walking stick on
road, brown. Backstamp same as
1970 plate ....10.00 to 12.00
1972, scene of house, barnyard
animals, man w/load of hay on
back, brown. Backstamp same as
above 12.50

1976, scene of house & apple trees
w/children gathering apples &
pumpkins, flag on flagpole in
front of house, pink or blue versions. Backstamp same as above,
each (ILLUS.) 12.00
1978, scene of crossroads w/houses
at sides of road & horse & wagon
w/people on road, blue. Backstamp same as above 10.00
1979, scene of lake w/road & house
alongside & cattle & man on road,
pink. Backstamp same as above .. 10.00
1983, scene of house & blacksmith
in background w/man & woman
in horse & carriage on road. Plate
changed to ironstone w/smooth
edge, pink or blue versions. Backstamp: "English Ironstone - Tableware Ltd.," each 10.00

Wedgwood
Beginning in 1971 the famous Wedgwood
firm of England, established in the 18th centu-

ry by Josiah Wedgwood, introduced a continuing series of calendar plates. Although
collector plate values vary, plates in this series appear to be selling for about their issue
prices on the American market. Early editions
sold for around $14.00 and more recent issues
sell for around $54.00. Some of the early titles
in this series include:
1971 - "A Victorian Almanac"
1972 - "The Carousel"
1973 - "Bountiful Butterfly"
1974 - "Camelot"
1975 - "Children's Games"
1976 - "Robin"

1977 - "Tonotiuh," featuring the Aztec calendar (ILLUS.)

Spencer Gift Calendar Plates
Spencer Gifts is a mail-order company that
came out in 1975 with an American Historical
series beginning with a Bicentennial calendar
plate. Each is a 9¼" white glass plate with all
trim and writing in red, white, blue and gold.
.... $3.50 to $10.00

1976, "200th Anniversary Year - 1776-
1976," eagle over shield & flags &
banner w/"E Pluribus Unum" in
center, calendar in blocks in red &

blue in border, gold edging. Backstamp: "1975 Spencer Gifts, Inc. Made in Japan" (ILLUS.)

1979, "America The Beautiful 1979" around center w/Washington & men in boat crossing the Delaware. Backstamp: "1979 Spencer Gifts, Inc."

1980, "Home of The Free" around center & picture of Lincoln Memorial & "1980" in very center, calendar blocks in border.

1982, Great Seal of U.S.A. w/eagle & "E Pluribus Unum 1982" & red stars. Backstamp: "1981 Spencer Gifts, Inc., Series V11 Calendar Co."

1972: Artist Series. milk white glass, calendar on border, center w/reproduction of a famous artist's painting: 1. "Breezing" by Winslow Homer, 2. "American Gothic" by Grant Wood, 10" d. (ILLUS. of one) ....3.50 to 6.00

1981: One unusual plate in my collection is rectangular & made of ironstone china. It is cream-colored w/gold-brown floral scroll on border. Calendar months are in blocks in center & "1981" in black above. Purchased in England a

number of years ago for about $6.50 at the time. Price today would have to be based on current value of the dollar. Backstamp: "Masons (crown) Patent Ironstone" (ILLUS.)

(End of Special Focus)

CANDLESTICKS & CANDLEHOLDERS

English Brass Candlesticks

Candelabra, ormolu & porcelain, four-light, four open scrolled arms & central spire over bulbous "Sevres" style porcelain body painted w/a courtship scene in gilt reserve, body flanked by long scroll handles continuing down to shaped oblong base w/"drapery" design skirt on fluted legs, late 19th c., 28½" h., pr. $935.00

Candelabra, Sheffield plate, four-light, domed circular base w/acanthus & lobed borders, fluted stem rising from leafage to capital banded w/paterae, the scrolling branches issuing from double shells joined by bunches of grapes, detachable sockets & opening bud finial, England, ca. 1815, pr. (one drilled for electricity, both w/central sockets broken loose) 3,575.00

Candelabrum, bronze, eight-light, cast as branches w/two curved lights attached to each, supported by openwork claws, w/bobeches, central stem concealing a bronze snuffer, green patina, stamped "TIFFANY STUDIOS NEW YORK," 15¼" h. 4,950.00

Candleholder, carved & painted
wood, modeled as a cube
w/chamfered corners in yellow &
green flanked by two carved birds
each perched on geometric
pedestals w/carved flowerhead
around base, all on a rectangular
base w/textured surface, attributed to John Scholl (1827-1916),
Pennsylvania, ca. 1912, 7" l.,
4½" h. (one flowerhead gone) ... 264.00

Candleholder-tinder box, short cylindrical box w/flat fitted cover
w/center candle socket, flat loop
handle at side, fitted inside
w/flint, steel & crimped-edge
damper, 4¼" d., 3½" h. (old soldered repair, small hole in bottom) 325.00

Candlestick, pewter, stepped octagonal base, flaring ring-turned
stem, marked "R. Gleason," Dorchester, Massachusetts, 8¼" h. .. 300.00

Candlestick, opaque violet flint
glass, pressed Petal & Loop patt.,
wafer connector, attributed to
Boston & Sandwich Glass Company, Sandwich, Massachusetts,
ca. 1850 .... 950.00

Candlesticks, brass, urn-form candle
socket on slender stem flaring
slightly toward base w/wide saucer
foot w/slightly upturned rim, The
Jarvie Shop, Chicago, Illinois, 1905,
6 3/8" h., pr. 1,045.00

Candlesticks, brass, Arts & Crafts
style, bulbous candle socket
w/wide, flat bobeche supported
on a cylindrical stem w/turned
discs near top & base, on circular
foot, 20th c., 8½" h., pr. 412.50

Candlesticks, brass, circular foot
w/beaded urn, disc- and trumpet-
turned standard, detachable circular bobeche above spherical candlecup, the whole w/bands,
reeding, palmettes & beading,
Continental, late 18th-early
19th c., 8½" h., pr. 242.00

Candlesticks, brass, Princess of Diamonds patt., England, 1880-90,
10¾" h., pr. (ILLUS.) 250.00

Candlesticks, ebonized w/silver mountings, octagonal base applied
w/radiating strapwork ribbing &
border highlighted w/eight quatrefoils, ribbed columnar shaft interrupted by two silver repoussé
bands, one w/a paneled frieze incorporating two figural scenes
from the passion of Christ & two
alternating panels of narcissus
w/leaves, one w/a lower band
w/narcissus & a symbolic pelican

& rooster, the other w/the Lamb of
God resting on a book, & a lantern
among the narcissus, planished silver nozzle & drip pan resting on a
capital repoussé w/a band of
stylized leaves, Arts & Crafts,
probably English, ca. 1900,
18½" h., pr. 2,475.00

Candlesticks, gilt-bronze, two-light,
on a scalloped oval base w/central
stem as a bud, w/two curving
arms supporting the holders
w/bobeches, held by three openwork claws, stamped "TIFFANY
STUDIOS NEW YORK 1230," 9" h.,
pr. 2,090.00

Candlesticks, canary opalescent
glass, pressed Petticoat Dolphin
patt., Pittsburgh, Pennsylvania,
late 19th c., 6 5/8" h., pr. 135.00

Candlesticks, sterling silver, Tulip
patt., Art Nouveau style, spreading circular foot chased w/an en-
twining design of tulips, undulating
bulbous hourglass form standard,
weighted base, Dominick & Haff,
Newark, New Jersey & New York,
1902, retailed by Shreve & Co.,
9¾" h., pr. 825.00

Candlesticks, sterling silver, George
III style, square molded base,
voluted composite column
w/voluted & acanthus capital,
concave sided bobeche, weighted
base, Reed and Barton, New
York, ca. 1900, 10¼" h., pr. 825.00

Chamberstick, copper, hand-
hammered, removable flared
bobeche & strapwork handle on
cylindrical form in shallow dish
base, stamped mark of Gustav
Stickley, ca. 1913, 9¼" h. 770.00

Chamberstick, ormolu, Empire style,
engine-turned bobeche above
spreading turned stem w/engine-
turned dished base issuing an
acanthus-cast handle ending in an
eagle's head, France, early 19th c.,
3½" h. 2,860.00

Silver-gilt & Rock Crystal Chamberstick

Chamberstick, silver-gilt & rock
crystal, carved rock crystal dish

w/silver-gilt overlay of flowering
twigs, Russia, mid-19th c., 5¾" l.
across handle (ILLUS.) 1,870.00
Girandole set: a pair of single sock-
et candlesticks & a three-arm candelabrum; each w/cast-brass
standing Indian brave w/spear on
rectangular black marble base &
supporting tall standard
w/florette ring w/prisms below
candle socket, mid-19th c., 17½"
& 19" h., 3 pcs. 500.00
Wall sconce, mirrored, convex circu-
lar form, concentric rings of rectangular mirrored tiles, projecting
tin candlearm, 19th c., 9¼" d. . . . 495.00
Wall sconce, tin, three-light, circular
wall plate w/crimped rim, fitted
to hold nine mirrored petals arranged in a fan, above three curving candlearms, each w/a circular
crimped candlecup, America,
19th c., 9¼" d. 352.00
Wall sconce, tin, flaring circular back
set w/numerous star & daisy
molded mirrored reflectors centering large reflector molded w/cir-
cles, above crimped circular drip
pan w/cylindrical candlecup, Amer-
ica, 19th c., 10" h. 4,180.00

CANDY CONTAINERS (Glass)

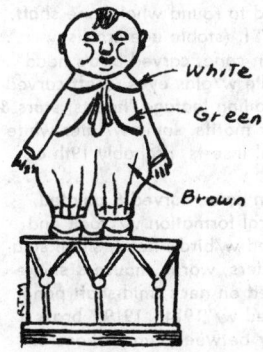

Fat Boy on Drum Candy Container

*Indicates the container might not have
held candy originally. +Indicates this container might also be found as a reproduction.
‡Indicates this container was also made as
a bank. All containers are clear glass unless
otherwise noted. Any candy container that
retains the original paint is very desirable and
readers should follow descriptions carefully
realizing that an identical candy container
that lacks the original paint will be less
valuable.*

Amos & Andy in Open Air Taxi -
painted figures, marked "Victory
Glass Co., etc.," w/tin closure,
1928-30, 4½" l. $350.00
+Automobile - "Station Wagon,"
w/cardboard closure, 4 7/8" l. . . . 43.00
Automobile - streamlined touring
car, w/screw-on cap closure,
3 7/8" l. 25.00
‡Barney Google beside bank, paint-
ed figure, "BARNEY GOOGLE" in
raised letters on bank container,
marked on base under figure
"copyright 1923 - King Features -
syndicate, inc.," 3 1/16" h. 390.00
+Bell - Liberty Bell w/hanger, am-
ber, w/tin closure, 3 3/8" h. 30.00
*Bell - "1776 Liberty," blue, 4" base,
4 1/8" h. 75.00
Boat - Battleship on waves, Cam-
bridge Glass Co., w/tin closure,
ca. 1916, 5¼" l. 95.00
Cannon w/flat tin closure, on two
wheel tin carriage mount - w/tin
wheels, ca. 1930, 3¾" l. 225.00
Chicken on Nest - "Manufactured by
J.H. Millstein Co." on rim of base,
4 5/8" h. (no closure) 20.00
Dirigible - "Los Angeles" marked on
side, painted silver, Victory Glass
Co., aluminum screw-on cap clo-
sure, ca. 1929, 5¾" l. 150.00
Duck on rope top basket, original
paint, marked "V.G. Co.," w/tin
closure, 1920's, 3 1/8" h. 66.00
Elephant - marked "G.O.P." on side,
painted grey, marked "V.G. Co.,"
w/tin closure, ca. 1925, 2 7/8" l.,
2¾" h. 125.00
+Fat Boy on Drum - painted, w/tin
closure on base slotted for use as
a bank, ca. 1915 (Note: *reproduction* does not have the slots in
glass base to hold the tin clo-
sure), 4 3/8" h. (ILLUS.) 215.00
Iron - electric-type w/string as cord,
4½" l. (no closure) 35.00
*Lantern - "Bond Mono Cell," w/bat-
tery in hanger & light bulb that
switches on as handle is raised,
4½" h. 22.50
Lantern - red-stained glass globe
w/flared metal base & metal cap
closure, w/wire bail handle, Vic-
tory Glass Co., 3¾" h. 26.00
Man on Motorcycle w/Sidecar -
painted figure & wheel spokes,
marked "V.G. Co., etc.," w/tin
closure under sidecar, 1918-25,
5 1/8" l. 300.00
Telephone - Millstein's "Tot," desk-
type, w/cardboard closure,
2 3/8" h. 41.00
Telephone - candlestick-type, "Tall,"

w/wooden receiver, marked
"V.G. Co." on base, 7½" h. 95.00
Turkey - gobbler, ca. 1924, w/tin
slide on base, 3½" h. 95.00

CANES & WALKING STICKS

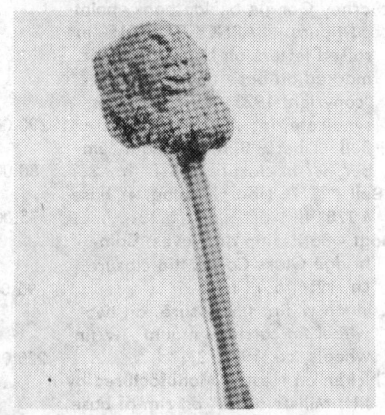

Burlwood Walking Stick

Canes have been used for thousands of years and probably collected for hundreds of years. Seventeenth and eighteenth century court "dandies" often owned numerous canes, coordinating their use to various costumes and occasions. Today's collector looks for canes made of unique materials in a unique form. Gadget canes, such as those that convert into a weapon or conceal a whiskey flask in the handle, are probably the most elusive type for the collector to acquire.

Burlwood walking stick, handle
fashioned from a knot of burl &
carved in the form of a smiling
black man's face, 19th c., 35½" l.
(ILLUS.)........................$880.00
Ebony walking stick, tooled gold-
plated knob handle & presentation
engraving dated "1885," 34½" l... 90.00
Glass cane, clear blown Optic Rib
patt. w/thin ruby swirls inside the
full length of the cane, crook handle, 47" l. 225.00
Glass cane, clear w/inner decorations of three white threads alternating w/three cobalt blue
threads alternating w/three clear
threads, crook handle, 26½" l. ... 95.00
Glass cane, clear w/amber twisted
spiral, 40" l. 145.00
Glass walking stick-baton, clear
glass w/hollow section decorated
w/thin red stripes alternating
w/cobalt blue stripes overlaid

w/another layer of glass decorated w/thin raised ribs alternating
aqua & white, bulbous top, pointed tip, 32¾" l.................. 110.00
Glass walking stick-baton, fiery
opalescent glass decorated w/al-
ternating pastel green, cobalt
blue & red-orange ribbons comprised of single threads laid side
by side & twisted, bulbous knob
top decorated w/a spatter of
white & red enamel, pointed tip
(rough & chipped), 33¼" l........ 110.00
Ivory walking stick, knob finial
w/incised line decoration, hand
grip below octagonal knob w/a
ring, lower section round & tapered, America, early 19th c.,
35" l. (small crack) 302.50
Mahogany walking stick, paneled &
bulbous ivory knob, ivory tip,
33" l. 275.00
Split bamboo cane, natural staghorn
bone handle w/basketweave silver thread collar, the shaft of natural notched bamboo, late 19th c.,
33" l. 77.00
Whalebone & whale ivory walking
stick, bulbous whale ivory knob,
tapering paneled to round whalebone shaft w/slight curve, 34¾" l.
(stable age cracks) 225.00
Whalebone & whale ivory walking
stick, carved whale ivory fist
w/horn segment divider, tapering
fluted to round whalebone shaft,
35½" l. (stable age cracks) 575.00
Wooden cane, carved bird's head
handle w/glas eyes, shaft carved
w/trailing leafage, hearts, stars &
other motifs, some w/later white
metal inserts, probably 19th c.,
32" l. 55.00
Wooden cane, carved & painted,
natural formation w/crook end
carved w/bird's head, small salamanders, worm, mouse & snake
carved on neck, mid-shaft panel
incised w/"1914 - 1919," brass
collar between two sections of
cane, lower section carved w/two
fish, tail to tail, & a green frog
facing the upper fish, ca. 1919,
39" l..........................1,320.00
Wooden walking stick, carved w/a
fat rattlesnake curling around
shaft, head w/open mouth &
fangs resting on top of a red apple, further carved w/a young girl
climbing up shaft, loose rings
above & below a colored ball, a
tobacco pipe held in a claw forming the end, America, ca. 1900,
28" l. (some breaks) 357.50

Wooden walking stick, gnarled
knobby shaft w/relief-carved
vines & "Xmas 1898, Sheridans
Point Va.," old varnish finish,
33½" l. 125.00

Wooden walking stick, weighted
lead cap, shaft carved w/belt &
buckle, jug, diamonds, knotted
tassel, Odd Fellows three-link
symbol, initials, inlaid mirror
pieces & mother-of-pearl oblong
on upper half, lower half carved
w/two entwined snakes, America,
late 19th c., 34" l. 440.00

Walking Stick with "Uncle Sam" Head

Wooden walking stick, carved & animated ivory handle in the shape of
the head of "Uncle Sam" w/button
on hat, pushing button drops his
jaw, scrolled silver ferrule, brass
tip, America, late 19th c., 35" l.
(ILLUS.) 1,540.00

Wooden walking stick, horn handle
carved as horse head w/glass
eyes, wooden shank w/intricate
relief carving of eagle, cannons,
shields, American flags, Maltese
cross, military medals & "U.S.A.,"
embossed brass ferrule, 35" l. 465.00

Wooden walking stick, shaft carved
w/two spiraling snakes, worn
black w/green polka dot & stripe
decoration, 37" l. 155.00

Wooden walking stick, handle
carved as the head of a bulldog
w/glass eyes & silver overlay
trim, marked "Alpacca," 37½" l.
(splits in silver ferrule) 275.00

Wooden walking stick, carved &
painted, grip carved in the form
of a Schimmel-style perched squirrel painted in red, yellow & blue
above a tapering cylindrical shaft,
40" l. (restorations to paint) 88.00

CANS & CONTAINERS

Huntley & Palmers Biscuit Containers

*The collecting of tin containers has become
quite popular within the past several years.
Air-tight tins were at first produced by hand
to keep food fresh and, after the invention of
the tin-printing machine in the 1870's, containers were manufactured in a wide variety
of shapes and sizes with colorful designs.*

Automobile wax, Fiebing Auto Top
Dressing $27.00

Axle grease, Mica sample pail, galvanized tin, red lettering, embossed wagon on wheel on lid,
Standard Oil Co., 2" h. 40.00

Axle grease, Texaco Regal 5 lb.
pail 17.50

Baby powder, McKesson's can, two
babies 45.00

Baby powder, ZBT sample size can . . 10.00

Baking powder, Calumet 1 lb. can,
orange paper label w/Indian 13.00

Baking powder, Calumet 10 lb. can,
Indian 11.00

Baking powder, Davis 1 lb. 8 oz.
can 7.50

Baking powder, Fleischmann's 10 lb.
container 18.00

Baking powder, Health Club sample
can 20.00

Baking powder, McNess Champion
can, plate of biscuits 20.00

Baking powder, Rough Rider can,
Teddy Roosevelt on horseback,
1901, unopened 21.50

Baking powder, Royal can, 1928,
4" h. 9.50

Beverage, Ovaltine 4 lb. can 28.00

Beverage, Postum sample size tin,
1¾" h. 16.00

Bicycle chain, Diamond tin, boy on
bicycle 35.00

Biscuit, Wm. Crawford & Sons
"Globe" tin, England, 1938 . . . . 95.00

Biscuit, Dr. Johnson's Educator
Crackers tin, Boston Company, ca.
1900, 5½ x 5½", 6" h. 50.00

Biscuit, Hamilton Cream Soda pail
w/bail handle................... 45.00
Biscuit, Huntley & Palmers "Egyptian
Vase," embossed scenes of Egyptian people at various pursuits on
sides, shoulder & neck w/colorful
geometric designs, 1924, 8 4/5" h.
(ILLUS. left).................... 145.00
Biscuit, Huntley & Palmers "Globe,"
1907, 7" h. 105.00
Biscuit, Huntley & Palmers "Hamper," simulated wicker w/hinged
lid, 4" d., 6½" h. 115.00
Biscuit, Huntley & Palmers "Marble,"
replica of a marble pillar w/female figure within an arch on
sides, 1909, 7¼" h. (ILLUS.
right) 138.00
Biscuit, Ivin's box, girl & parrot on
black ground, "Say Ivin's," 1910,
5 x 5 x 5" ....35.00 to 45.00
Biscuit, Laurel counter box, 1920's
lady 67.00
Biscuit, Loose-Wiles octagonal box,
Statue of Liberty & panels
w/historical events, 9½" w.,
3½" h..................25.00 to 35.00
Biscuit, Loose-Wiles tin, U.S.S. Idaho
& other World War II ships 25.00
Biscuit, McVitie & Price "Bluebird"
tin, England, 1911 .... 140.00
Biscuit, McVitie & Price "Kiddies"
tin, "Sing A Song of Sixpence"
rhyme & scenes, 1937, 5" h....... 50.00
Biscuit, Montreal Biscuit Co. store
bin, w/glass front 75.00
Biscuit, National Biscuit Co. "Log
Cabin Brownies Box," log cabin
shape, 1920's 100.00
Biscuit, National Biscuit Co. store
bin, glass & brass 75.00
Biscuit, Saltina 10½ oz. round tin,
sailor 27.50
Biscuit, Sunshine tin, colorful White
House scene on cover,
11 x 12½".................... 15.00
Blasting caps, Trojan tin 50.00
Bouillon cubes, Oxo 2¼ oz. tin 12.00
Brake fluid, Indian Brand cone top
can, Indian 15.00
Candy, Bunte Diana "Stuft" Confections square can w/screw-on lid,
arched, colored panels framed
w/Art Nouveau style florals, two
showing a beautiful woman
w/bow & arrows & dog & two
showing scenes of a dish of hard
candy, 10" h. 68.00
Candy, Licorice Lozenges glass front
store display, Sommers Bros.,
1879 .... 175.00
Candy, Lovell & Covel pail, historical
scene 350.00

Candy, Lovell & Covel pail, Jack of
Hearts 85.00
Candy, Lovell & Covel pail, colored
lithographed scenes of Little Red
Riding Hood around body w/story
text below, wire bail handle
w/wooden hand grip, marked,
"Canco" on base, 3" d., 3" h. (no
lid) 50.00
Candy, Lovell & Covel pail, Peter
Rabbit......................... 100.00
Candy, Lovell & Covel pail, Queen
of Hearts 90.00
Candy, Mellow Mints 1 lb. tin 25.00
Candy, Mellow Mints 5 lb. store
bin 80.00
Candy, Nursery Candies 1 lb. can,
Nursery Rhyme figures 100.00
Candy, United Happiness 1 lb. can,
ABC's, Humpty Dumpty on lid 175.00
Candy, Whitman's "Salamagundi"
1 lb. box, Art Nouveau girl 18.00
Candy, Whitman's 2 lb. tin, gold &
black 20.00
Chewing gum, Beech-Nut store
bin 45.00
Chocolate, Yoo Hoo, "The Drink of
Champions" tin, baseball players
Mantle, Berra, Richardson, Tresh
& Ford pictured 35.00
Cigarettes, Lucky Strike flat fifties,
green, red & gold 8.50
Cigarettes, Target box 18.50
Cigars, Advance Agent box,
6 x 8 x 4" 275.00
Cigars, Bagley's Sweet Tips pocket
tin, oval....................... 35.00
Cigars, Camel box, 5½ x 4½ x
2½"........................... 45.00
Cigars, Court Royal container, woman & factory scene ....50.00 to 65.00
Cigars, Popper's Ace box, World
War I biplane, 6 x 3 x 3" 150.00
Cigars, Postmaster canister ..25.00 to 32.00
Cigar, White Ash box, 4 x 3 x 1" ... 30.00
Cleaner, Dustdown tin, shows little
girl cleaning 75.00
Cocoa, Hyler's tall tin............. 75.00
Cocoa, Index 5 lb. tin, Montgomery
Ward & Co., pictures girl......... 110.00
Cocoa, Monarch sample size,
lions ....25.00 to 50.00
Cocoa, Roses Breakfast tin, screw-on lid 40.00
Cocoa, Wessanen's ¼ lb. tin 20.00
Coconut, Plee-zing pail 65.00
Coconut, Schepp's "cake box,"
2-shelf 80.00
Coconut, Schepp's 1 lb. pail, monkeys playing, black & green...... 185.00
Coffee, After Glow 4 lb. pail (ILLUS.
next page) 42.00
Coffee, American Home 1 lb. pail .. 30.00

After Glow Coffee

Coffee, Anza 1 lb. tin, screw-on
lid 22.00
Coffee, Bagdad 5 lb. tin 40.00
Coffee, Beech-Nut Instant 2 oz. tin.. 7.00
Coffee, Blackstone 1 lb. tin, Water-
loo, Iowa 24.00
Coffee, Blanke's Happy Thoughts
pail, trunk-shaped 60.00
Coffee, Blue Flame 5 lb. can 35.00
Coffee, Bokar 1 lb. container,
screw-on lid 15.50
Coffee, Butter-Nut ½ lb. tin 24.00
Coffee, Canova 3 lb. tin 65.00
Coffee, Chase & Sanborn sample
tin 20.00
Coffee, Chief 4 lb. pail, Indian chief
on two sides, New Orleans 55.00
Coffee, Chocolate Cream 1 lb. tin,
key lid 15.00
Coffee, Chocolate Cream 2 lb. tin... 32.00
Coffee, Choisa tin 25.00
Coffee, Dairy Brand pail 85.00
Coffee, Dining Car tin, red & black,
round, 3½" h. 20.00
Coffee, Dwinell-Wright Co. Celebrated Boston Roasted Coffee store
bin, colored medallion design on
lid, red & black w/gold highlights,
19" w., 19½" h................. 525.00

Elephant Brand Coffee

Coffee, Elephant Brand pail, pry-up
lid, 6" d., 7" h. (ILLUS.) 108.00
Coffee, Empress pail 40.00
Coffee, G. Washington 4 oz. tin 25.00
Coffee, Glendora sample size tin ... 17.00
Coffee, Golden West 3 lb. tin 75.00

Gold Medal Coffee

Coffee, Gold Medal 1 lb. can, dark
blue w/gold letters, 6" h.
(ILLUS.)...................... 40.00
Coffee, Griffins 2 lb. tin 20.00
Coffee, Homestead 5 lb. tin 80.00
Coffee, Ivanhoe 1½ lb. can, colorful
castle scene 35.00
Coffee, Jam-Boy 1 lb. can, screw-on
lid 150.00
Coffee, La Touraine 1 lb. can...... 25.00
Coffee, Lincoln Club pail 425.00
Coffee, Luzianne Coffee & Chicory
3 lb. tin, dated 1928 .... 95.00
Coffee, Magnolia Mills 1 lb. tin, red
& gold 50.00
Coffee, Martinson's 1 lb. tin 20.00
Coffee, Matchless 1 lb. can, screw-
on lid 65.00
Coffee, May Day 1 lb. tin 20.00
Coffee, Nash 1 lb. tin, key lid 18.00
Coffee, Nielsen's 3 lb. tin, applied
paper label 45.00
Coffee, Perfect Coffee pail 34.00
Coffee, Red Wolf 1 lb. can 65.00
Coffee, Savory 1 lb. can, full, key
lid 12.00
Coffee, Sears, Roebuck and Co. Spe-
cial Combination 5 lb. tin 85.00
Coffee, Serv-Us 1 lb. can, screw-on
lid 40.00
Coffee, Sundown tin 25.00
Coffee, Testers 1 lb. tin, screw-on
lid ....50.00 to 65.00
Coffee, WGY 1 lb. can, screw-on lid,
blue decoration, 4¼" d.,
6" h...................40.00 to 60.00
Coffee, Wheat Sheaf 5 lb. tin....... 300.00
Coffee, Wish Bone 5 lb. tin........ 85.00
Coffee, Yacht Club 1 lb. tin 20.00
Coffee, Yale 1 lb. tin 65.00
Corned beef, Libby's sample tin 25.00

Crackers, Salerno Finest Cookies &
Crackers lunchbox 45.00
Dental powder, Wernet's sample
tin 3.00
Film, DuPont can, 1920's 29.00
Foot powder, Military tin, colorful
decoration 60.00
Fruitcake, National Biscuit Co. flat
round tin 18.00
Furniture polish, O-Cedar tin, Art
Deco decoration, 1920's 30.00
Gum, Yucatan box, 6 x 6" 275.00
Gun oil, Winchester can, pictures
bull's-eye, reads "Arms & Ammu-
nition Division" 25.00
Gun powder, Bull's Eye Revolver
Smokeless 1 lb. tin, colorful 50.00
Gun powder, DuPont 6¼ lb. barrel,
ship on label 65.00
Gun powder, DuPont Superfine FFF
drum 65.00
Gun powder, Hazard Powder Co.,
Hazardville, Connecticut can,
"Duck Shooting Gunpowder,"
good label on end w/picture of
duck, painted red, 6¼" d.,
7½" h. 95.00
Gun powder, King Quick Shot can,
labels on both ends,
9¼ x 11 3/8" 145.00
Gun powder, Savage tin 205.00
Ice cream, Dairy Brand tin 28.00
Ink, Waterman's tin, original bottle
inside, 1920's 20.00
Insect powder (roach salt), Stern's
Insectago tin, yellow & black 8.00
Lard, Miles 25 lb. tin, Indian
pictured 37.50
Lard, Morrell's Snow Cap 4 lb. pail,
colorful 19.00
Lard, Raco 1 lb. pail 42.50
Lard, Rath Black Hawk pail, Indian
pictured 20.00
Lard, Sugardale 50 lb. tin, blue 22.00
Malted milk, Horlick's trial size tin,
paper label 15.00
Marshmallows, Apollo 4 oz. tin 16.00
Marshmallows, Edwards store bin,
glass lid 225.00
Marshmallows, Sterling 5 lb. tin,
Redel Candy Co., Milwaukee,
Wisconsin 24.00
Marshmallows, Sweet's Snowflake
4 oz. tin 60.00
Meat product, Blue Ridge Pure Pork
Sausage tin, ca. 1927 . . . . 14.00
Mince meat, Veribest 1½ lb. pail . . . 67.50
Motor oil, Capitol Square 2 gal.
can 35.00
Motor oil, Duplex Outboard cone-
top 1 qt. can, men fishing in
motorboat 38.00
Motor oil, Falcon can, pictures
falcon 45.00

Motor oil, Mobilgas Oil 1 pt. can,
pictures flying red horse (full) 20.00
Motor oil, Mobil Oil-Socony-Vac Oil
Co. 5 qt. can 20.00
Motor oil, Pilot 2 gal. can 45.00
Motor oil, Shell Green Crest 2 gal.
can 45.00
Motor oil, Standard Oil of Indiana
5 gal. can, carried on delivery
truck, brass label 85.00
Motor oil, Texaco 2 qt. can,
rectangular 85.00
Motor Oil, Tidex 2 gal. can 45.00
Nuts, Planters Cashews tin 12.50
Nuts, Superior Salted 10 lb. tin, pic-
tures tropical scene 50.00
Paraffin, Standard Oil Co. liquid
1 gal. can, square 48.00
Patent medicine, Allenbury's Throat
Pastilles tin 10.00
Patent medicine, Dr. Kinsman's
Asthma Remedy can, pry-off lid,
full, late 1800's 25.00
Patent medicine, Dr. Morse's Indian
Root Pills tin, oval 12.00
Patent medicine, Grandma's Wonder
Healing Cream container 10.00
Patent medicine, Joy Walk Corn
Plaster container, lady w/dog
scene, 1890's 26.00
Patent medicine, McCormick's
Medicinal Mustard tin 15.00
Patent medicine, Nature's Remedy -
60 Tablets tin 15.00
Patent medicine, Old Bayers Tablets
tin 8.00
Patent medicine, Partola Laxative
Blood Purifier tin, "No Pain or
Griping!" 15.00
Patent medicine, Rawleigh's Cold
Tablets tin 2.00
Patent medicine, Secoral sample
tin 10.00
Patent medicine, 666 Salve tin 5.00
Peanut butter, Clark's 1 lb. can 300.00
Peanut butter, Dixie pail, color
shield-shaped label reads "Origi-
nal Dixie Peanut Butter," black
body, 10" d., 8" h. w/bail handle
(label worn & flaking) 35.00
Peanut butter, King Parrot 3 gal.
tin 20.00
Peanut butter, Larkin pail, 3 7/8" d.,
3¼" h. 48.00
Peanut butter, Merry Christmas can,
dated 1899, "Compliments Of,"
3½" 135.00
Peanut butter, Monarch "Teenie
Weenie" 10 oz. pail 75.00
Peanut butter, Morris Supreme pail,
kids at beach scene (no lid) 70.00
Peanut butter, Ontario 1 lb. can 125.00
Peanut butter, Ox-Heart 1 lb. pail . . 39.00
Peanut butter, Ox-Heart 5 lb. pail . . 45.00

Peanut butter, Peter Pan 10½ oz.
tin (no lid) 23.00
Peanut butter, Pickwick 1 lb.
pail . . . . .60.00 to 90.00
Peanut butter, School Days tin 150.00
Peanut butter, Shedd's 5 lb. pail,
elves 16.50
Peanut butter, Sultana 1 lb. pail,
children, orange 57.00
Peanut butter, Sultana pail, rabbits,
blue 75.00
Peanut butter, Toyland 1 lb. pail 83.00
Peanut butter, Toyland 2 lb. pail 195.00
Peanut butter, Tropical Nut 1 lb.
tin 16.00
Peanuts, Harvard Jumbo 5 lb. tin . . .   75.00
Peanuts, Kibbe's 10 lb. tin 40.00
Peanuts, Mammoth 10 lb.
container 245.00
Peanuts, Old Reliable 10 lb.
container 200.00
Peanuts, Planters 1 lb. tin 45.00
Peanuts, Queen Anne 10 lb. tin (no
lid) 60.00
Peanuts, Star Maid 10 lb. tin 65.00
Peanuts, Teddie Brand Whole Jumbo
1 lb. tin 65.00
Peanuts, Winola 10 lb. can, Indian
maiden pictured 400.00
Popcorn, Jumbo tin, elephant
pictured 27.50
Pretzels, Bachman's Butter tin 15.00
Salmon, Libbey's sample can,
1920's 25.00
Snuff, Pearson's Red Top box, girl
pictured, 1909 . . . .   22.00
Soap, Packers Tar tin, w/original
soap, ca. 1900, 2½ x 3½" 75.00
Spice, A&P Grandmother's, yellow,
1890's 15.00

Arbuckles' Chili Powder Tin

Spice, Arbuckles' Chili Powder tin,
1920-40 (ILLUS.) 8.00
Spice, Durkee's Pure Ground Black
Pepper 6 lb. tin container, red,
6¾ x 7 x 7½" 26.00
Spice, Farmer's Pride Pickling Spices
tin, 4½" d.   15.00

Spice, Jack Sprat Whole Cloves tin . .   9.00
Spice, Polar Bear Nutmeg tin 12.00

Watkins Pepper Tin

Spice, Watkins Pure Ground Pepper,
black & white w/yellow stripes
(ILLUS.) 25.00
Spinach, Libbey's sample can,
1920's 25.00
Stove polish, Union Blacking tin,
early paper label 25.00
Syrup, Towle's Log Cabin 5 lb. tin,
cabin-shaped, "Trading Post" 67.50
Talcum powder, A.D.S. Rose Talc
tin 18.00
Talcum powder, As the Petals tin . . .   80.00
Talcum powder, Avon "To A Wild
Rose" tin 11.00
Talcum powder, Babcock's Corylop-
sis of Japan tin, Geisha girl
pictured 15.50
Talcum powder, Blue Moon tin 40.00
Talcum powder, Borated Talcum tin,
cylindrical, pictures little girl 55.00
Talcum powder, Cadette Baby tin,
shaped like a soldier, colorful 110.00
Talcum powder, Cashmere Bouquet
sample size . . . . .25.00 to 45.00
Talcum powder, Colgate's Baby Talc
sample tin 55.00
Talcum powder, Colgate's Dactylis
tin 35.00
Talcum powder, Devotia tin, colorful
moonlight scene of musician
serenading woman on balcony . . .   45.00
Talcum powder, Dream Girl can, Art
Nouveau lady pictured . . . .25.00 to 35.00
Talcum powder, Elite tin, California
Perfume Co.   55.00
Talcum powder, Gardenia tin 5.00
Talcum powder, Goodyear French
tin 22.50
Talcum powder, Richard Hudnut
Yanky Clover round box, yellow &
green, 5" d.   34.00
Talcum powder, Juliet tin 18.00
Talcum powder, Landers, Lilacs &
Roses tin 17.50
Talcum powder, La Parot tin 17.50
Talcum powder, Mennen Baby Pow-

der, 9 oz. tin, w/powder, pictures
baby 12.50

Talcum powder, Mennen's Violet
sample size tin................. 48.00

Talcum powder, Palmolive After
Shaving tin 9.00

Talcum powder, Palmolive Egyptian
tin, Art Deco style 24.00

Talcum powder, Par Golfer tin 100.00

Talcum powder, Persian Garden tin,
girl & flowers, full.............. 60.00

Talcum powder, Phoenix Violet tin,
1915 .... 25.00

Talcum powder, Rikers Violet sample size tin 25.00

Talcum powder, Robin tin 52.00

Talcum powder, Rose Talcum,
California Perfume Co. 75.00

Talcum powder, Vernafleur tin,
California Perfume Co. 35.00

Talcum powder, White Witch tin 12.50

Talcum powder, Yardley's Old English Lavender Talc, lady &
children 9.50

Tea, Betsy Ross can, tin & cardboard, w/lid, picture of Betsy,
1930's 12.00

Tea, E. Daly & Co., Tea Importers,
London, Canada box, orange,
11½ x 11½ x 13" 90.00

Tea, Mazawatee tin, full color picture of three black children 95.00

Tire patch, Tip Top tin, pictures tire,
shoes, hot water bottles & hose .. 10.00

Tobacco, Abbey upright pocket tin,
blue 110.00

Tobacco, Antonella upright pocket
tin........................... 400.00

Tobacco, Baby's Bottom round tin,
w/paper label, 1930's........... 40.00

Tobacco, Bagdad pocket tin 45.00

Tobacco, Bagdad upright pocket tin,
short 175.00

Tobacco, Bagley's Sweet Tips pocket
tin........................... 45.00

Tobacco, Bagley's Wild Fruit lunch
box 125.00

Tobacco, Beech-Nut store bin, slant
lid, green 195.00

Tobacco, Belmont upright pocket
tin....................200.00 to 245.00

Tobacco, Big John canister 10.00

Tobacco, Big John pocket tin, paper
label, 1930's 10.00

Tobacco, Big Pete pocket tin, w/pa-
per label, 1930's 10.00

Tobacco, Blue Boar Cut Plug canister, hunt scene, paper label...... 25.00

Tobacco, Blue Boar tin, w/litho paper label, fits into silver plated
dispenser etched w/village scene
of carriage in front of Blue Boar
Inn, lid engraved w/a boar,
6½" h......................... 55.00

Tobacco, Blue Sweet Cuba tin,
round 65.00

Tobacco, Bond Street pocket tin 20.00

Tobacco, Buckingham sample size
pocket tin, "Trial Package"....... 93.00

Tobacco, Cadillac cylindrical canister, 2 x 8" 750.00

Tobacco, Central Union lunch box... 48.00

Tobacco, Charm of the West flat
pocket tin 195.00

Tobacco, Checkers pull-top canister,
red & black squares, full w/origi-
nal contents, paper & stamp 595.00

Tobacco, C.H.Y.P. Intercollegiate
Mixture tin, 3 x 5" 150.00

Tobacco, City Club upright pocket
tin, short 375.00

Tobacco, Continental Cubes upright
pocket tin 350.00

Tobacco, Cremo store humidor 195.00

Tobacco, Devoes Sweet Smoke upright pocket tin ....300.00 to 500.00

Tobacco, Dill's Best canister 20.00

Tobacco, Dunnsboro upright pocket
tin........................... 795.00

Tobacco, Edgeworth canister, blue .. 30.00

Tobacco, Edgeworth pocket tin 12.00

Tobacco, Edgeworth Junior vertical
pocket tin 28.00

Tobacco, Eight Brothers Long Cut
12 oz. tin, unopened 20.00

Tobacco, Ensign pocket tin 65.00

Tobacco, Epicure pocket tin 85.00

Tobacco, Eve pocket tin............ 115.00

Fashion Cut Plug Lunch Box

Tobacco, Fashion Cut Plug lunch
box, fashionable couple & early
automobile (ILLUS.)............. 140.00

Tobacco, Forest & Stream pocket tin,
mallard duck 35.00

Tobacco, Fort Mail flat pocket tin ... 90.00

Tobacco, Gail & Ax Navy canister
w/round lift-off lid 275.00

Tobacco, Game Fine Cut store bin .. 465.00

Tobacco, George Washington Cut
Plug lunch pail................. 35.00

Tobacco, Globe sample flat pocket
tin 325.00

Tobacco, Golden Sceptre upright
pocket tin 425.00

Tobacco, Gold Shore pocket
tin....................300.00 to 400.00

Tobacco, Granger Cut Plug
canister 19.00
Tobacco, Granger upright pocket
tin 775.00
Tobacco, Granulated 54 pocket tin . . 65.00
Tobacco, Handbag Cut Plug lunch
box, purse-shaped 125.00
Tobacco, Hand Made pocket tin 145.00
Tobacco, Handsome Dan Mixture
flat box, 2 x 6 x 7" 75.00
Tobacco, Heidsieck pocket tin, em-
bossed picture of champagne bot-
tle, 1930's 10.00
Tobacco, Hickory upright pocket
tin 95.00
Tobacco, Hi-Grade upright pocket
tin, green 795.00
Tobacco, Hindoo pocket tin 675.00
Tobacco, Hi-Plane pocket tin, twin-
engine plane 80.00
Tobacco, Hi-Plane pocket tin, four-
engine plane, full, stamp intact . . . 550.00
Tobacco, Honest Labor box w/round
corners, yellow w/red arm &
hammer 45.00
Tobacco, Honeymoon pocket tin,
man resting on crescent moon,
w/woman's face in clouds 85.00
Tobacco, Honeysuckle 10c Plug 1 lb.
tin 95.00
Tobacco, King Edward upright pock-
et tin 775.00
Tobacco, King George upright pock-
et tin 450.00
Tobacco, Maryland Club pocket tin,
clubhouse 300.00
Tobacco, Matoka upright pocket
tin 1,100.00
Tobacco, Mayo's Cut Plug lunch
box 40.00

Mayo's Roly Poly Tins

Tobacco, Mayo's Roly Poly Mammy
tin (ILLUS. right) . . . . 400.00 to 500.00
Tobacco, Mayo's Roly Poly Satisfied
Customer tin (ILLUS.
left) . . . . 450.00 to 550.00
Tobacco, Mayo's Roly Poly Singing
Waiter . . . . 400.00 to 600.00
Tobacco, Mayo's Roly Poly
Storekeeper . . . . 350.00 to 450.00
Tobacco, Mellow Smoke flat pocket
tin 35.00
Tobacco, Model pocket tin, bust por-

trait of man w/out-sized
moustache 20.00
Tobacco, Mohawk pocket tin, w/pa-
per label, 1930's 15.00

Nigger Hair Pail

Tobacco, Nigger Hair pail (ILLUS.) . . . 150.00
Tobacco, Ojibwa lunch pail 195.00
Tobacco, Old English pocket tin,
curved, 3½ x 4" 24.00
Tobacco, Patterson's Seal lunch box,
basketweave 30.00
Tobacco, Pedro lunch box 145.00
Tobacco, Penny Post lunch box 85.00
Tobacco, Picobac pocket tin 35.00
Tobacco, Pinkussohn's pocket tin . . . 35.00
Tobacco, Pipe Major pocket tin 275.00
Tobacco, Plow Boy store bin 1,100.00
Tobacco, Pride of Virginia flat pock-
et tin, tan, medium size 15.00
Tobacco, Prince Albert "Now King"
pocket tin 250.00
Tobacco, Puritan pocket tin, bust
portrait of Puritan smoking pipe . . 150.00
Tobacco, Rainbow lunch box 195.00
Tobacco, Red Band Scrap store bin,
large, 8" . . . . 400.00 to 450.00
Tobacco, Red Jacket pocket tin 25.00
Tobacco, Revelation pocket tin 24.00
Tobacco, Rip Long Cut tin box,
2 x 3 x 6" 350.00
Tobacco, Rod & Gun pocket tin 20.00
Tobacco, Saratoga Chips flat pocket
tin 30.00
Tobacco, Sensation Christmas lunch
box 60.00
Tobacco, Sensible lunch box 30.00
Tobacco, Shot upright pocket tin 425.00
Tobacco, Sir Walter Raleigh canister
w/knobbed lid 20.00
Tobacco, Snap Shots pocket tin,
paper label, original contents,
1 x 3 1/8 x 4¼" 1,550.00
Tobacco, Snap Shots upright pocket
tin 750.00
Tobacco, Stag pocket tin (ILLUS. top
next page) 50.00
Tobacco, Stanwix upright pocket
tin 1,350.00
Tobacco, Sunset Trail tin, white 175.00

Stag Pocket Tin

Tobacco, Sweet Clover flat upright
  pocket tin 375.00
Tobacco, Sweet Cuba Fine Cut slant
  top store bin, woman's portrait,
  green 250.00
Tobacco, Three Feathers pocket
  tin .200.00 to 275.00
Tobacco, Tiger 5 lb. canister,
  red .125.00 to 175.00
Tobacco, Totem pocket tin 1,500.00
Tobacco, Trout Line pocket tin,
  fisherman w/creel, rod & reel in
  central roundel 725.00
Tobacco, Tuxedo sample size tin,
  1¾ x 2¾" 120.00
Tobacco, Twin Oaks casket,
  4 x 4 x 8" 80.00
Tobacco, Twin Oak pocket tin, roll
  top 52.00
Tobacco, Union Leader 1 lb. canis-
  ter, Uncle Sam 35.00
Tobacco, Union Leader lunch box,
  basketweave w/eagle decor-
  ation 42.00
Tobacco, Union Leader lunch box,
  Christmas poinsettias 155.00
Tobacco, Union Leader sample pock-
  et tin, w/eagle 40.00
Tobacco, Unity upright pocket tin . .1,375.00
Tobacco, U.S. Marine pocket
  tin .175.00 to 225.00
Tobacco, Van Bibber pocket tin 40.00
Tobacco, Wagon Wheel upright
  pocket tin 600.00
Tobacco, Weiserts 54 upright pocket
  tin 700.00
Tobacco, Whip upright pocket tin,
  tall . . . . .300.00 to 500.00
Tobacco, White Manor pocket tin . . .   250.00
Tobacco, Yacht Club flat pocket
  tin 70.00
Tobacco, Yacht Club upright pocket
  tin 275.00
Tobacco, Yosemite store bin 310.00
Tobacco, Yum-Yum lunch pail,
  shows black boy, 8" . . . . .275.00 to 300.00
Toothpowder, Listerine tin, full 25.00
Toothpowder, Merkels tin 8.00

Toothpowder, Sanitol bottle-shaped
  tin, dated 1906 . . . .   20.00
Toothpowder, Sozodent tin, pictures
  man brushing teeth, Ginna Co.,
  before 1900, unusual shape 125.00
Typewriter ribbon, Herald Square
  tin 5.00
Typewriter ribbon, Type-Art tin 8.00
Typewriter ribbon, Underwood tin . .   6.00
Vegetable cubes, Blue Ribbon tin . . .   7.50

CAROUSEL FIGURES

Charles Looff Carousel Deer

The ever-popular amusement park merry-
go-round or carousel has ancient antecedents
but evolved into its most colorful and complex form in the decades from 1880 to 1930.
In America a number of pioneering firms, begun by men such as Gustav Dentzel, Charles
Looff and Allan Herschell, produced these
wonderful rides with beautifully hand-carved
animals, the horse being the most popular.
Some of the noted carvers included M.C. Illions, Charles Carmel, Solomon Stein and
Harry Goldstein.

Today many of the grand old carousels are
gone and remaining ones are often broken up
and the animals sold separately as collectors
search for choice examples. A fine reference
to this field is Painted Ponies, American
Carousel Art, by William Manns, Peggy
Shank and Marianne Stevens (Zon International Publishing Company, Millwood, New
York, 1986.)

Bear, tilted head, open mouth,
  whimsical expression, layered
  trappings, deeply carved fur,
  Gustav Dentzel, ca. 1905 . . . . . .$37,400.00
Bull, muscular figure in running position, strap & bell around neck,
  brass horns, Heyn, Germany, ca.
  1910, 80" l. 5,500.00
Camel w/howdah, child's size, unu-

sual kneeling pose & whimsically
appealing expressive face, the
howdah seats two children,
Matthieu, France, ca. 1920,
42" l., 27" h. 13,200.00
Cat, realistic figure w/elaborately
carved fur detail & folded blanket,
w/fish clamped in jaws, Gustav
Dentzel, ca. 1905 . . . . .35,200.00
Chariot, figure of a woman w/pen-
sive expression & draped in layers
of carved fabric seated on a shell-
like chariot mounted on wheels,
Herschell-Spillman, ca. 1914 . . . . .3,300.00
Chariot, sides carved as dog
pulling a hay cart w/two kittens
as passengers, attributed to The
Sequino Family of Bari, Italy,
42 x 56", 42" h. 2,420.00
Cow, child's size, appealing expres-
sive face, long ears & horns, tasseled blankets & bell hanging from
strap around neck, Matthieu,
France, ca. 1915, 40" l. 4,675.00
Cow w/howdah, expressive face
w/curved horns, howdah ornately
decorated w/drapes of fringed fabric & tassels & brass railings
holds riders on board, Heyn, Ger-
many, ca. 1905, 74" l., 54" h. 5,500.00
Deer, leaping pose, scrolled saddle
pommel, real antlers, deeply
carved hair & double eagle
w/glass eyes at saddle cantle, fine
carvings, Charles Looff, Jr.,
ca. 1895, 62" l. (ILLUS.). 22,000.00
Elephant, child's size, the small
scaled lumbering animal w/trunk
down retains some of its black
paint, wearing a black-trimmed
red blanket on its back, traces of
gilding, fitted w/glass eyes, attributed to Charles W.F. Dare,
New York, 1885-95, 34" l.,
26" h. 3,300.00
Giraffe, outside row figure, large
impressive animal in strolling
pose w/scalloped blanket,
buckled straps & typical
trade-mark rippled ribbons
at bridle straps, Daniel
Muller, ca. 1914, 72" h. 41,800.00
Goat, leaping pose, exquisite Cherni
carving, original body & saddle
paint, fine fur detail, long horns,
Gustav Dentzel, ca. 1903 . . . . . . .25,300.00
Horse, child's size jumper, racing
outstretched pose, fancy layered
trappings, full wind-blown mane,
saddle cantle carvings, C.W. Parker Amusement Co., ca. 1917,
45" l. 3,300.00
Horse, jumper, carved mane & tail
& elaborately painted trappings

& saddle blanket, finished in
mustard yellow, dark green & red,
Orton & Spooner Co., England,
55" l. 2,200.00
Horse, jumper, animated pose, alert
expression, original pin-striping
on layered trappings & flying
parted mane, exquisite factory
paint, Daniel Muller - Gustav
Dentzel, ca. 1927, 55" l. 18,700.00
Horse, jumper, upright pose, large
full protruding mane, suggestion of
bird shape at saddle cantle, wide
breast band, alert expression,
Armitage-Herschell, ca. 1905 . . . .4,400.00
Horse, large jumper, exciting stargazer pose, full protruding mane,
feathers at bridle & panther skin
blanket w/fine claw & head detail,
C.W. Parker Amusement Co., ca.
1917, 67" l. (restored) 12,100.00
Horse, large jumper, tucked head
position, exciting tossed mane, jeweled strap, wolf's head & tassels
at saddle cantle, M.C. Illions &
Sons, ca. 1910, 57" l. 16,500.00
Horse, large jumper, tucked head
position, draped mane, full forelock, layered straps & large
scrolled flaps, Philadelphia
Toboggan Co., ca. 1930 . . . . .16,500.00
Horse, inner row jumper, stargazer
pose, wide straps, fringed blanket
& animated expressive face, Stein
& Goldstein, ca. 1912, 48" l.
(stripped) .17,600.00
Horse, large outside row jumper,
running animated pose, intricately
layered mane, scalloped straps,
jewels, tassels, fringed blanket
w/scroll decoration & fleur-de-lis
embellishments, flower at saddle
cantle, Charles Looff, Jr.,
ca. 1900, 58" l. 14,300.00
Horse, outside row stander, exquisite
carving, cropped mane, large full-
bodied cherub nestled in draped
& folded blanket, double eagle
back saddle, old paint, Gustav
Dentzel, ca. 1905, 62" l. 60,500.00
Horse, outside row stander, long
flowing intricate mane, parted
flipped forelock, checkered blanket, tassels, etched mirror jewels,
applied rosettes, high parrot
cantle, Charles Looff, Jr., ca. 1895
(stripped) .19,800.00
Horse, outside row stander, magnif-
icent carving, thick roached mane,
tucked head position, highly decorative trappings including floral garland at bridle, large eagle's head
at saddle cantle, layered fringed
blankets w/tassels & cropped tail,

Philadelphia Toboggan Co., Muller
Period, ca. 1906 . . . . .56,100.00

Illions Carousel Horse

Horse, outside row stander, outstanding carving, alert expressive
face, intricate peek-a-boo mane,
ornately decorated jeweled trappings w/heart motifs, layer of
armor under blanket, in prime
coat of paint, from Supreme Carousel, M.C. Illions & Sons,
ca. 1921 (ILLUS.) 49,500.00

Horse, second row prancer, sensitive
expressive face, windblown mane,
Indian head, feathers in lariat
decoration, Daniel Muller
(stripped) .24,200.00

Lion, enormous prowling animal w/a
magnificent head framed by massive intricately carved mane, jeweled blanket & straps, flowing tassel at saddle cantle & strong
muscle & sinew, Carmel-Borelli,
ca. 1910, 90" l. 46,750.00

Pig, ridge-carved snout & upturned
ears, wearing saddle, painted
cream pink w/red, white & blue
trappings, attributed to The
Sequino Family of Bari, Italy,
46" l., 22" h. 1,980.00

Pig, running pose, realistic carving
w/high rolled cantle, decorative
mirrored straps & metal curly tail,
Carl Muller, Germany, ca. 1900,
60" l. 7,700.00

Pig, running pose, upturned head
w/open mouth & small tusks,
heavy muscles, creased neckline,
scalloped blanket, leaves & acorn
decoration, curly tail, Gustav
Dentzel, ca. 1905 . . . . .16,500.00

Rooster, bird w/long, slender body
& legs at full-run position, traces
of paint, attributed to Savage
Bros., ca. 1900 (various repairs) . .3,300.00

CASH REGISTERS

National Model No. 311

*James Ritty of Dayton, Ohio, is credited
with inventing the first cash register. In 1882,
he sold the business to a Cincinnati salesman,
Jacob H. Eckert, who subsequently invited
others into the business by selling stock. One
of the purchasers of an early cash register,
John J. Patterson, was so impressed with the
savings his model brought to his company,
he bought 25 shares of stock and became a
director of the company in 1884, eventually
buying a controlling interest in the National
Manufacturing Company. Patterson thor-
oughly organized the company, conducted
sales classes, prepared sales manuals and established salesman's territories. The success
of the National Cash Register Company is
due as much to these well organized origins
as to the efficiency of its machines. Early
"National" cash registers, as well as other
models, are deemed highly collectible today.*

Brass, "Michigan," w/'Amount Pur-
chased' sign $265.00

Brass, "National," Model 47 . . . . 600.00

Brass, "National," Model 311, candy
store model (ILLUS.) . . . . .750.00 to 950.00

Brass, "National," Model 313, candy
store model . . . . .600.00 to 700.00

Brass, "National," Model 317 . . . . 650.00

Brass, "National," Series 500 floor
model on nine-drawer mahogany
base cabinet, brass polished &
lacquered .1,250.00

Oak, "Tucker," under counter-type
cash drawer, original label, wire
combination lock 125.00

Wood, "NCR Woodie," ornate marquetry w/inlaid brass, all wood
handcarved cabinetry, "Barron
Bros." carved into the cabinet,
devils head drawer pull,
24" w. 6,000.00

CASTORS & CASTOR SETS

Austrian Castor Set

Castor bottles were made to hold condiments for table use. Some were produced in sets of several bottles housed in silver plated frames. The word also is sometimes spelled "Caster."

Castor set, 2-bottle, silver-mounted clear glass bottles, mounts engraved w/the same crest, in stand formed as two conjoined cylinders, pierced & engraved w/pales, circles & drapery swags, w/four matching panel feet & beaded borders, scroll handle, marked on base & one bottle mount, Thomas Daniel, London, England, 1775, 6" l. $2,090.00

Castor set, 4-bottle, clear glass King's Crown patt., glass stand ... 85.00

Castor set, 5-bottle, clear glass Daisy & Button patt., original glass stand 95.00

Castor set, 5-bottle, clear etched glass bottles, silver plate stand w/Japanese style decoration including a bird at the bottom of the Gothic-style handle topped by flowers, late 19th c. 145.00

Castor set, 6-bottle, clear etched glass bottles, silver plate stand, marked Rogers.................. 175.00

Castor set, 6-bottle, cranberry glass bottles, silver plate stand 150.00

Castor set, 8-bottle, silver-mounted blue flashed cut glass bottles, shaped rectangular silver stand fitted w/a flower-chased superstructure centered by leaf-chased baluster handle, on four shell & flower feet, Vienna, Austria, ca. 1859, two stoppers missing, 10¾" l. (ILLUS.) 2,420.00

Pickle castor, amber glass Inverted Thumbprint patt. insert, ornate silver plate frame, cover & handshaped tongs, 10" h. 175.00

Pickle castor, blue glass Beaded Dart patt. insert, silver plate frame, cover & tongs, 4 1/8" d., 10" h. 131.00

Pickle castor, blue glass Inverted Thumbprint patt. insert w/floral enameling, silver plate frame, cover & fork, 11" h. 295.00

Pickle castor, clear glass insert w/vertical concave panels alternating w/zipper-like panels, bulbous ribbed base, ornate four-footed silver plate frame & fork.......................... 95.00

Pickle castor, clear glass Strawberry Diamond & Fan patt. insert, ornate silver plate frame, cover & tongs 105.00

Pickle castor, clear & frosted glass Swirl patt. insert, silver plate rib & tree bark frame, cover & tongs, marked Rogers................. 150.00

Pickle castor, cranberry glass insert w/heavy gold scrolling overall & a white enameled cupid w/bow & arrow on front, original silver plate frame w/arched handle, cover & tongs, 8¾" h. 395.00

Pickle castor, cranberry glass insert w/enameled flowers, silver plate frame & tongs, marked Meriden .. 285.00

Pickle castor, cranberry glass insert w/enameled yellow iris & green leaves, silver plate frame, cover & tongs, marked Reed & Barton, 9½" h. 350.00

Cranberry Glass Pickle Castor

Pickle castor, cranberry glass Inverted Thumbprint patt. insert w/enameled flowers & leaves, silver plate frame, cover & tongs, marked Middleton (ILLUS.) ....325.00 to 350.00

Pickle castor, cranberry glass Inverted Thumbprint patt. insert w/satin
finish, enameled w/gold spider
mums, silver plate frame w/or-
nate engraved cover which is part
of the frame & slides up & down
& swings over to fit on insert,
original silver, marked Simpson
Hall 595.00
Pickle castor, cranberry glass Invert-
ed Thumbprint insert w/round ball
shape & a 1" bottom flange that
fits into frame, insert decorated
w/wide silvery opalescent band
w/gold beading outlining the
band, whole piece covered
w/gold enameled netting, ornate
footed silver plate frame & cover,
marked Tufts 495.00
Pickle castor, frosted Rubina glass
insert, etched w/florals & leaves,
resilvered frame 310.00
Pickle castor, golden amber glass
Inverted Thumbprint patt. insert
w/blown-out band in center,
enameled florals & white dotting
on band, original ornate silver
plate frame, cover & tongs,
marked Meriden 325.00
Pickle castor, heavenly blue cased
glass insert w/h.p. gold & floral
leaves decoration & gold bug on
back, lined in white, original silver plate frame & cover, marked
Reed & Barton, 4½" d.,
8 5/8" h. 282.00
Pickle castor, lime green glass Daisy
& Button patt. insert, silver plate
frame, cover & ornate tongs,
marked Rogers 255.00
Pickle castor, lime green glass Daisy
& Button patt. insert, footed silver
plate frame, cover & tongs,
marked Meriden 210.00
Pickle castor, opal peach & light
blue glass insert, decorated
w/heavy free-form gold tracery &
enameled heavy gold ferns &
white forget-me-nots w/gold
centers, ornate high-footed silver
plate frame, cover & tongs 395.00
Pickle castor, vaseline opalescent
blown glass insert, silver plate
frame 425.00

CAT COLLECTIBLES

ORIGINAL ART

"Artist's Model," oil on canvas, by
Ada E. Tucker (British, fl. 1879-
1898), signed, 19 x 23½" $3,800.00
Cat lying down, etching & aquatint,

Cat Lying Down by Foujita
pencil signed & matted, Tsugou-
haru Foujita (Japanese, 1886-
1968), 11 x 14" (ILLUS.) 1,700.00

"Four Cats"
"Four Cats," oil painting, signed
F. Itaya, Paris, 1964. Provenance:
Findlay Galleries Inc., Chicago,
23 x 28" (ILLUS.) 880.00

"Four Kittens and Yarn"
"Four Kittens and Yarn," oil painting,
by Louis Eugene Lambert, signed,
France, 19 x 24" (ILLUS.) 5,500.00
"Friends," oil on board, by Valen-
tine Thomas Garland, signed,
dated 1881, England,
7¼ x 7½" 4,200.00
Painting on porcelain, signed
"B.B./03," attributed to Betsy

Bamber, painting measures 5¼ x
7¼", frame measures 11 x 13" ... 650.00
"White Cat," crayon & bodycolor, by
Charles Culver, signed & dated
1949, 20 x 26½" 675.00

PHOTOGRAPHY
Black & white photograph by B.
Doyle Peterson, dated 1969, pub-
lished by Studio One Poster
Prints, ready to hang, measures
12 x 18" 20.00

PRINTS
"Brother and Sister," etching by
Meta Pluckebaum, signed, ca.
1930, Germany, 12 x 16" in an-
tique frame $50.00
Gallery of Cat Portraits, nine full
color prints w/borders, each a
different breed of cat, by Girard
Goodenow for *Woman's Day*,
1965, 14¼ x 19", each 25.00
"Just Arrived," steel engraving by
Louis Eugene Lambert, France, un-
framed, 12 x 17" 35.00
"Puss in Boots," steel engraving by
Frank Paton (English, 1856-1909),
unframed, 12 x 17" 45.00
"The Segar," chromolithograph by
Louis Eugene Lambert, signed,
France, 12 x 17" in antique
frame 75.00

"Siamese Cat Resting"
"Siamese Cat Resting," lithograph
crayon on paper, by Rosella Hartman (b. 1894), signed, framed,
8 x 10" (ILLUS.) 950.00

MISCELLANEOUS
Andirons, cast iron, seated cat facing out, atop flared pedestal supported on two scrolled flaring
legs, marked "M. Greenwood &
Co.," black repaint over pitted
iron, 12½" h., pr. 125.00
Band, models of six ceramic cats,
each playing a different musical
instrument, marked "Made in Japan," ca. 1950's, each 2¼" h., the
set 35.00
Bank, porcelain, model of cat's
head, 2¼" h. 235.00
Book, "The Cat Scouts," illustrated
by Louis Wain, colorful 45.00
Bottle, cat-shaped, gold-painted
glass, top hat w/cork on head,
7½" h. 25.00
Cardboard cut-out, cat sitting on
box of Meerschaum Tobacco while
her kittens, who are inside, try to
get out 85.00

Cat Cookie Jar
Cookie jar, pottery, blue square-
shaped jar molded w/a grey
striped cat w/pink bow & facial
markings, tail curls up to form
handle on cover, American Bisque
(ILLUS.) 40.00

Cat Creamer & Sugar Bowl
Creamer & sugar bowl, modeled as
black cats, marked "No. 561 -
Shafford - Japan," paper labels,
4½" & 5½" h., pr. (ILLUS.) 40.00
Cordial cups, black ceramic cup
molded w/cat face w/red ears &
tongue, green eyes, "Japan" on
paper label, 2½" h., set of 6 ..... 45.00
Doorstop, Halloween cat, cast iron,
original paint, Hubley, 9¼" h. 175.00
Dressing table bottle, glass
cut w/polished panels, brass lid
embossed w/cat head w/glass
eyes, 1 1/8" w., 3 7/8" h. 28.00

Eyeglasses case, black beaded, front
w/design of a pink cat w/red
bow 25.00

Fan, fold-out type, orange paper
picturing black cat, wooden handle, marked "Made in Germany,"
ca. 1914, 8½" l................. 12.00

Feeding dish, pottery, illustration
of cat & other animals w/nursery
rhyme "Hey diddle, diddle...," alphabet around rim, marked "Er-
phila Germany," ca. 1925,
7¾" d........................ 55.00

Model of a cat, china "fairing," seated black & white animal, worn
rust & white base, 19th c.,
1¼ x 2".................... 75.00

Model of a cat, seated animal,
white w/blue eyes, marked
"Beswick - England," No. 1886,
3¾" h....................... 25.00

Model of a cat, china, Siamese lying
on its back, Lefton paper label,
No. H4032, 4½" l.............. 10.00

Model of a cat, china, white
w/green bow & yellow hat, incised "Cordelia," ca. 1940's,
5" h......................... 28.00

Model of a cat, porcelain, cat w/two
kittens on base, introduced in
1956, discontinued in 1961, Studio
No. 123, marked "Boehm" 595.00

Model of a cat, pottery, reclining
animal, pink w/lavender trim, by
Kay Finch, 5½" l. 30.00

Model of a cat, sewer tile pottery,
reclining feline w/head turned to
side, simple modeling, clear glaze
w/yellow slip details on face,
9" l........................ 225.00

Model of a cat & dog seated on blue
love seat, majolica, 2¼" w. 165.00

Pin, Art Deco style, gold cat face
w/green stone eyes, red, blue &
green stones adorn tips of extended whiskers 38.00

Pin, silver colored cat wearing a
pink suit w/black bow tie, orange
top hat & w/green stone eyes,
moveable tail, marked "©JJ,"
1¾" h........................ 22.00

Postcard, novelty squeaker-type,
black & white glossy picture,
mint 8.00

Press book, from "Cat's Claw Mur-
der Mystery" by Favorite Films,
four-page booklet, cover w/a
mean looking cat showing teeth &
claws, ca. 1940's 25.00

Salt & pepper shakers, pottery,
black cats w/red bows sitting &
scratching their chins, 2½" h. 8.50

Salt & pepper shakers, pottery,
Puss-N-Boots, black w/pink lining,
3¼" h........................ 20.00

Figural Cat Tea Set

Tea set: cov. teapot, cov. sugar
bowl & creamer; pottery, each
modeled as a Siamese cat wearing a red bow, unmarked, the set
(ILLUS.)...................... 85.00

Toothpick holder, ceramic cat & fish
bowl, marked "Japan," 2¾" h. ... 10.00

Toy, pull gong-bell type, nursery
rhyme cat w/fiddle, large rear
wheels & axle are metal, ca.
1930-40...................... 65.00

Toy, rubber "squeak" type, model of
a beige striped cat w/red ribbon,
marked "Ruth Newton, The Sun
Rubber Co., Barberton, Ohio
No. 31," 5" h................. 12.00

Teapot, cov., ceramic, model of a
cream cat w/black spots & orange
ears & mouth, gold eyes, wears
an orange bow, also a jacket outlined w/green ribbon, brown driz-
zled glaze over rust-colored paint
& w/colorful flowers w/gold
centers, marked "Hand painted
TRICO Japan," incised "Patent
141896," 8" h................. 150.00

Teapot, cov., china, white w/the design of a cat holding an orange
fish, marked "Made in China,"
one-cup size 11.00

Cat Wall Pocket

Wall pocket, chalkware, model of a
cat face, incised "1954 Miller
Studio Inc.," 4½" w., 3½" h.
(ILLUS.)...................... 30.00

CERAMICS

ABINGDON

From about 1934 until 1950, Abingdon Pottery Company, Abingdon, Illinois, manufactured decorative pottery, mainly cookie jars, flower pots and vases. Decorated with various glazes, these items are becoming popular with collectors who are especially attracted to Abingdon's novelty cookie jars.

Book ends, model of a horse head,
  w/label, pr. $75.00
Bowl, green glaze, No. 564 .... 10.00
Cookie jar, "Choo Choo," yellow
  glaze w/black trim, No. 651 ...... 85.00
Cookie jar, "Daisy," blue glaze
  w/yellow trim 65.00
Cookie jar, "Hippopotamus," h.p.
  decoration 75.00
Cookie jar, "Miss Muffet," blue
  glaze w/black trim 85.00
Cookie jar, "Little Old Lady" 75.00
Cookie jar, "Pineapple" ......50.00 to 65.00
Cookie jar, "Rocking Horse," brown
  & yellow glaze w/pink trim 95.00
Cookie jar, "Three Bears," relief-
  molded figures on side 125.00
Model of a duck, pink glaze, 4" 25.00
Salt & pepper shakers, figural Elsie
  & Elmer, pr. 45.00
Salt & pepper shakers, Humpty
  Dumpty patt., pr. 45.00
Tiles, Geisha & Coolie, pr. 48.00
Vase, 5" h., pink glaze 14.00
Vase, 8¾" h., two-handled, green
  glaze w/silver overlay decoration
  of deer, trees & grass, silver han-
  dles & rim, No. 152............. 100.00

ADAMS

Members of the Adams family have been potters in England since 1650. Three William Adamses made pottery, all of it collectible. Most Adams pottery easily accessible today was made in the 19th century and is impressed or marked variously ADAMS, W. ADAMS, ADAMS TUNSTALL, W. ADAMS & SONS, and W. ADAMS & CO. with the word "England" or the phrase "made in England" added after 1891. Wm. Adams & Son, Ltd. continues in operation today.

Bowl, 7½" d., Cries of London series, "New Mackerel"............ $27.50
Candlesticks, Cries of London series,
  3½" h., pr. 65.00
Cracker jar, cov., horses & hounds
  decoration, bail handle 275.00

Cup & saucer, handleless, gaudy floral stick spatter decoration,
  marked "Adams Tunstall" (small
  flakes on table rings) 45.00
Cups & saucers, handleless, green
  stick spatter florette bands w/nar-
  row red border bands, impressed
  "W. Adams, Tunstall," set of 6
  (two cups w/slight damage &
  stains) 120.00
Cups & saucers, demitasse size,
  Rose patt., red, green & dark blue
  flowering sprig borders, cup interiors w/simple blue bands, each
  saucer transfer-printed in black
  w/registry mark & "William
  Adams & Co., Tunstall, England,"
  late 19th c., saucers 5" d., set of
  4 .... 110.00
Plate, 8¾" d., flow blue, Chinese
  Chine patt. 120.00
Plate, 9" d., Dr. Syntax series, "Dr.
  Syntax Bound To A Tree by Highwaymen," blue transfer 45.00

AUSTRIAN

Numerous potteries in Austria produced good-quality ceramic wares over many years. Some factories were established by American entrepreneurs, particularly in the Carlsbad area, and other factories made china under special brand names for American importers. Marks on various pieces are indicated in many listings. Also see KAUFFMANN (Angelica) CHINA.

Dresser tray w/attached hatpin
  holder, stickpin holder & ring
  tree, shades of green w/orange
  flowers decoration (M.Z.
  Austria) $275.00
Perfume tray, oval, pansy
  decoration 40.00
Plate, 9" d., portrait of lady holding
  bouquet of roses (Victoria-
  Carlsbad) 65.00
Plates, 10" d., decorated w/baroque
  reserve of multicolor birds, birds
  & butterfly in small reserves in
  gold leaf frames on green ground,
  pr. (Joseph Vater)............. 190.00
Plate, 13" d., pierced to hang,
  cream, green & blue background
  w/dog in black & white, fancy
  gold rococo edge 210.00
Vase, 4¾" h., 4¾" d., bulbous
  base, decal portrait of long-haired
  blonde woman against a blending
  russet brown ground, gold
  trimmed handle, scalloped flared
  top 30.00
Vase, 8½" h., two-handled, portrait

of monk reading newspaper, pink
& gold (Victoria-Carlsbad) 48.00
Vase, 12" h., 5½" d., gold handle,
gold framed portrait of Bohemian
girl, lavender & blue flower
decoration 225.00

BAVARIAN

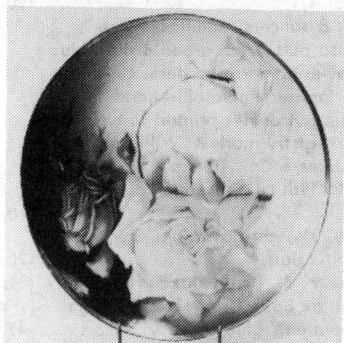

Bavarian Plate with Roses

*Ceramics have been produced by various
potteries in Bavaria for many years. Those
appearing for sale in greatest frequency today were produced in the 19th and early 20th
centuries.*

Cabinet plates, each decorated
w/one of four scenes of elegant
ladies in gardens, centered by an
orange border embellished w/gilt
trellis panels & swags, 11¼" d.,
12 pcs. $770.00
Cake set: master cake plate & six
serving plates; decorated w/red
cherries on dark green ground,
scalloped gold border, artist-
signed, 7 pcs.   200.00
Nut set: master dish, 6" d. & six in-
dividual dishes, 3½" d.; open cut-
out ends, hand-painted in pink,
white & gold, the set 52.00
Pitcher, tankard, 11¼" h., 4 7/8" d.,
bunches of purple & green grapes
on green to cream shaded
ground, gold trim, factory deco-
rated, artist-signed 116.00
Plates, 7½" d., fruit decoration
w/gold tracery, set of 12 . . . .   150.00
Plate, 8½" d., Columbine patt. 15.00
Plate, 10" d., full-blown pink roses
decoration, artist-signed (ILLUS.) . .   50.00

BELLEEK

*Belleek china has been made in Ireland's
County Fermanagh for many years. It is exceedingly thin porcelain. Several marks were
used, including a harp and crown (1863-1880),
and a hound, harp and castle (1863-1891). A
printed hound, harp and castle with the words
"Co. Fermanagh Ireland" constitutes the
mark from 1891. Belleek-type china was also
made in the United States last century by
several firms, including Ceramic Art Company, Columbian Art Pottery, Lenox, Inc.,
Ott & Brewer and Willets Manufacturing Co.*

AMERICAN

Willets Belleek Chalice

Basket, twig handle, ruffled rim, undecorated, 4" w. (Willets) $55.00
Bowl, 3½" d., shell shape, pink lus-
tre interior, white exterior, gold
rim (Ott & Brewer) 110.00
Bowl, 7½" w., two-handled, h.p.
floral swags & inscription dated
1901, ruffled rim, professional
decoration (Willets) 135.00
Bowl, 8" w., silver & black decora-
tions (Willets) 95.00
Chalice, h.p. monk drinking tea,
green ground w/grapes, 11½" h.,
Willets (ILLUS.) 350.00
Chocolate pot, cov., gilded decora-
tion, 8½" h. (Willets) 95.00
Coffee set: cov. coffeepot, creamer
& cov. sugar bowl; pedestal
bases, pink & yellow roses decoration, 1890-1900, 3 pcs. (Ceramic
Art Co.) 175.00
Creamer, overall gilded florals
around handle, top edge & base,
3¾" h. (Ceramic Art Co.) 105.00
Creamer, gold paste florals on
matte ground, gilding, 4½" h.
(Ceramic Art Co.) 110.00
Creamer & open sugar bowl, white
w/embossed & beaded decorations in gold, pink lustre handle &
inside trim, 1890, 2¾" (Ott &
Brewer) 95.00
Cup & saucer, demitasse, embossed
veining traced in gold, eggshell
porcelain (Willets) 50.00

Cup & saucer, demitasse, yellow, green & gold Art Deco decoration (Coxon) 75.00

Cup & saucer, gold paste flowers, eggshell porcelain (Ott & Brewer) 145.00

Cup & saucer, h.p. tiny flowers & fleur de lis, eggshell porcelain, factory decorated (Willets) 80.00

Cup & saucer, tiny yellow & gold paste flowers, factory decorated (Willets) 110.00

Hatpin holder, h.p. grapes & leaves in black & gold, decorated by Pickard, 5" h. (Willets) 130.00

Loving cup, three gold handles, gold Vassar College seal, 3¼" d., 3½" h. (Willets) 65.00

Muffineer, pastel floral band w/gold trim (Willets) 110.00

Mug, gold dragon handle, h.p. corn stalk decorations, artist-signed, 5½" h. (Willets) 150.00

Mug, h.p. brown moose decoration (Willets) 95.00

Mug, monochromatic blue decoration of monk in wine cellar, 6¾" (Ceramic Art Co.) 120.00

Mustard pot, cov., multicolored floral & gold paste decoration (Ott & Brewer) 385.00

Perfume jar w/inner liner, matte Lily of the Valley decoration (Ceramic Art Company) 165.00

Pitcher, 4" h., gold paste embossed & beaded design (Ott & Brewer) .. 375.00

Pitcher, lemonade, 5½" h., h.p. red roses on green ground, artist-signed (Ceramic Art Co.) 135.00

Pitcher, 6" h., 7" w., h.p. colorful pansies, wide body w/beautiful shape (Ceramic Art Company) 200.00

Pitcher, 9½" h., h.p. gold & enameled designs, factory-decorated (Willets) 250.00

Pitcher, tankard, 11½" h., gold dragon handle & mask spout, h.p. leaves & berries decoration (Willets) 250.00

Pitcher, tankard, 12" h., h.p. group of monks surrounded by floral designs (Willets) 300.00

Pitcher, 12¼" h., colorful berries & leaves w/maroon border & handles, gold relief trim 195.00

Pitcher, tankard, 14¼" h., 6½" d., h.p. red cherries & purple blackberries on cream shaded to rust ground, artist initialed (Willets) ... 182.00

Pitcher, tankard, 15" h., applied gold, split-dragon handle, h.p. purple grapes & leaves on cream ground, artist-signed, dated 1910 (Willets) 300.00

Pitcher, cider, h.p. golden storks decoration, artist-signed (Lenox) .. 75.00

Pitcher, lemonade, h.p. peaches decoration, gold handle & rim, artist-signed (Ceramic Art Co.) ... 320.00

Plate, 9" d., h.p. pink & gold paste flowers decoration, ruffled rim (Ott & Brewer) 190.00

Plates, 10½" d., Bouquet patt., set of 12 (Coxon) 600.00

Plates, luncheon, Morning Glory patt., set of 4 (Morgan Belleek China Co.) 350.00

Salt dip, ruffled rim, h.p. floral decoration (Morris & Willmore) ... 35.00

Salt dips, h.p. depicting various flowers, gold ruffled rim, 1890, set of 6 (Willets) 108.00

Soup cup & saucer, two-handled, Tridacna-style body, gold paste florals & butterflies, 6" d. (Ott & Brewer) 195.00

Sugar bowl, cov., gold dragon handles, paste gold & blue enamel flowers (Willets) 75.00

Tray, triangular, rustic handle, undecorated, 5½" w. (Willets) 60.00

Vase, 8" hexagon, h.p. flowers, leaves & geometrics, artist-signed, dated 1919 (Lenox) 85.00

Vase, 8½" h., h.p. mums interior & exterior, dated 1897 (Ceramic Art Company) 250.00

Vase, 10¼" h., 4¼" d., bulbous w/flared opening, lovely array of h.p. variegated spider mums shading from purple to pink w/shaded foliage against a blending colorful ground, ca. 1889 (Ceramic Art Company) 230.00

Vase, 11" h., h.p. peacocks decoration (Lenox) 195.00

Vase, 11½" h., cylindrical, etched gold floral band (Willets) 85.00

Vase, 12½" h., h.p. roses decoration (Willets) 250.00

Vase, 15" h., ovoid shape w/pedestal base, two-handled, h.p. rose & leaf decoration on beige ground, gilt trim (Ceramic Art Co.) 365.00

Vase, 16" h., Art Deco style h.p. swans in black & grey (Willets) ... 450.00

Vase, 19" h., h.p. full portrait of lady on one side, cherubs on other side, artist-signed (Lenox) 1,000.00

IRISH

Basket, narrow w/two pinched-in sides, applied floral decoration, pearl finish, 6" l., 2nd black mark (ILLUS. top next page) 475.00

Basket, Twig patt., three-strand, pearl finish, two pads impressed

w/"Belleek" and "Co. Ferma-
nagh," 8½" oval 2,475.00

Irish Belleek Basket

Basket, Basket Ware, three-strand,
Lily patt., 9½" d. 2,800.00
Bread plate, four handles, Limpet
patt., 3rd black mark 147.00
Bread plate, Tridacna patt., 3rd
black mark 155.00
Bowl, 5" d., 1½" h., Shell patt.,
pink trim, 1st black mark 105.00
Bust of John Wesley, 8¼" h.,
1st black mark 1,950.00
Butter dish, cov., model of a cot-
tage, yellow lustre, 1st green
mark 140.00
Centerpiece, "International," urn on
scrolled base, decorated w/models
of Irish wolfhounds, flowers &
harps, 27" h., 2nd green mark,
(one harp string missing) 12,100.00
Comport, Woven Basket, four-
strand, pearl finish, 3rd
black mark, 6 x 8¼" 935.00
Creamer, Tridacna patt., 2nd black
mark 50.00
Creamer & sugar bowl, Harp Sham-
rock patt., 3rd black mark, pr. . . . 125.00
Creamer & sugar bowl, Ribbon patt.,
cobalt blue trim, 3rd black mark,
pr. 140.00
Cup & saucer, demitasse, Harp
Shamrock patt., 3rd black mark . . 125.00
Cup & saucer, Institute patt., pink
trim, 1st black mark 150.00
Cup & saucer, Limpet patt., cobalt
blue trim, 3rd black mark 125.00
Cup & saucer, Thistle patt., 1st black
mark 155.00
Dejeuner set, Harp Shamrock patt.,
2nd black mark, 8 pcs. 1,320.00
Dessert set: four cups & saucers &
four 6" d. plates; Grass patt., 1st
black mark, 12 pcs. 425.00
Dinner set: cov. coffeepot, creamer,
sugar bowl, bread tray & six each
9 3/8" d. dinner plates, 8¼" d.
luncheon plates & cups & saucers;
Limpet patt., 3rd black mark,
28 pcs. 1,600.00

Dish, Sycamore Leaf patt., 4½", 3rd
black mark 45.00
Ewer, Mask patt., embossed designs
& mask face below handle, green
w/gold trim, 5" d., 8½" h., 2nd
black mark 907.00
Figure of Affection, 14½" h., 2nd
green mark 495.00
Figure of Boy Basket Bearer, 9" h.,
3rd green mark 295.00
Flower pot, Shell patt., footed, pearl
finish, 9", 2nd black mark 1,760.00
Mirror frame, oval, encrusted
w/flowers, grapes, birds, cross &
Belleek symbols of harp, round
tower & Irish wolfhound, made for
Queen Victoria, pearl finish,
22 x 30" 22,000.00
Model of a dog, Boxer reclining on
pillow, 4" w., 3 1/8" h., 6th green
mark 60.00
Model of a dog, Spaniel reclining on
pillow, 4" w., 3" h., 3rd green
mark 95.00

Belleek Model of a Pig

Model of a pig, seated, 3", 3rd
black mark (ILLUS.) 225.00
Model of a round tower, 3rd green
mark 375.00
Mug, w/twig handle, Shamrock-
Basketweave patt., 3rd black
mark 75.00
Pitcher, milk, 4" h., jug-type,
Shamrock-Basketweave patt., 3rd
black mark 135.00
Plates, 6¼" d., Shamrock-
Basketweave patt., 2nd black
mark, pr. 70.00
Plate, 6½" d., Limpet patt., 3rd
black mark 27.50
Plate, 8¼" d., Shamrock-
Basketweave patt., 3rd black
mark 90.00
Plate, 8½" d., Shell patt., 1st black
mark 80.00
Plate, 9¼" d., Greek patt., gilt trim,
1st black mark, impressed
"Belleek" 250.00
Powder bowl, cov., round, Mask
patt., grape finial, 3rd black
mark 225.00
Salt dip, master, Shamrock-

Basketweave patt., 1st green
mark, 3¼" l. 30.00
Salt dip, New Shell patt., 3rd black
mark.......................... 45.00
Snack set: cup, saucer & 6" four-
handled plate; Mask patt., 3rd
black mark, 3 pcs. 138.00
Spill vase, Daisy w/Shamrocks patt.,
3rd black 100.00

Flying Fish Spill Vase

Spill vase, Flying Fish patt., shell
forms vase on fish's back, pink
trim, 2 3/8 x 4 3/8", 4 3/8" h.,
2nd black mark (ILLUS.) 433.00
Sugar bowl, open, Scroll patt.,
green tint & trim, 2nd black
mark.......................... 75.00

Chinese Pattern Teapot

Teapot, cov., Chinese patt., figural
spout, brown w/gilt trim, 1st
black mark w/English registry
mark (ILLUS.) 900.00
Teapot, cov., Erne patt., 1st black
mark.......................... 300.00
Teapot, cov., Harp Shamrock patt.,
3rd black mark 325.00
Teapot, cov., Limpet patt., 3rd black
mark.......................... 350.00
Teapot, cov., Shamrock-
Basketweave patt., 3rd black
mark.......................... 295.00
Tea set: cov. teapot, creamer &
open sugar bowl; New Shell patt.,
1st green mark, 3 pcs........... 295.00
Tea set: 4¼" d., 4" h. cov. teapot,
3¾" d., 3 1/8" h. open sugar

bowl, 3½" d., 3 3/8" h. creamer,
3½" d., 2" h. cup, 5 3/8" d. saucer
& 12¼ x 15" tray; Echinus patt.,
pink trim, 1st black mark,
6 pcs. 1,950.00
Vase, 4½" h., Swirled Shell patt.,
ruffled edge, green mark 65.00
Vase, 6" h., Aberdeen patt., 1st
green mark..................... 125.00
Vase, 6½" h., tree trunk shape,
Shamrock-Basketweave patt., 3rd
black mark 110.00
Vase, 9" h., 4½" d., Princess patt.,
several kinds of applied flowers
in pastel yellow, pink, blue &
white, spray of flowers on back,
2nd black mark 807.00
Whimsey, frog vase, model of frog
w/open mouth & black eyes,
4¾" h., 2nd black mark 850.00

BENNINGTON

Bennington Stoneware Crock

*Bennington wares, which ranged from
stoneware to parian and porcelain, were made
in Bennington, Vt., primarily in two potteries, one in which Captain John Norton and
his descendants were principals, and the other
in which Christopher Webber Fenton (also
once associated with the Nortons) was a prin-
cipal. Various marks are found on the wares
made in the two major potteries, including
J. & E. Norton, E. & L. P. Norton, L. Norton
& Co., Norton & Fenton, Edward Norton, Lyman Fenton & Co., Fenton's Works, United
States Pottery Co., U.S.P. and others.*

*The popular pottery with the mottled
brown on yellowware glaze was also produced
in Bennington, but such wares should be referred to as "Rockingham" or "Bennington-
type" unless they can be specifically attributed to a Bennington, Vermont factory.*

Book flask, binding impressed
w/book title "Bennington Battle,"
mottled Flint Enamel glaze, Ben-

nington Potteries, ca. 1849-58,
5½" h. $990.00

Book flask, binding impressed
w/book title "Buntline's Companion," mottled Flint Enamel
glaze, 7 5/8" h. (some wear,
chips) 325.00

Book flask, binding impressed
w/book title "LADIES - COMPAN-
ION," mottled Flint Enamel glaze,
Bennington Potteries, ca. 1849-58,
7 7/8" h. .1,430.00

Book flask, mottled brown Rockingham glaze, rare large size, impressed mark "53C," 10 5/8" h.
(in-the-making hairlines) 975.00

Cake mold, circular bowl-shaped
w/fluted interior & smooth exteri-
or, raised base, mottled brown
Rockingham glaze, Bennington
Potteries, ca. 1849-67, 6½" d.,
2¾" h. 110.00

Crock, stoneware, straight sides,
eared handles, large slip-quilled
cobalt blue basket of flowers, impressed "J. & E. Norton, Bennington, Vt.," 3 gal., 10½" h. (some
pinpoint blistering on left side of
design) 770.00

Crock, stoneware, slightly ovoid,
eared handles, molded rim, large
slip-quilled cobalt blue scene of
reclining spotted stag in fenced
area w/trees in background, impressed "J. & E. Norton, Bennington, Vt.," 1850-59, 3 gal., rim
chips, base crack, hairline crack
from rim, small spider on reverse,
13½" h. (ILLUS.) 1,650.00

Cuspidor, Scroddled Ware, scalloped rib design, white w/brown
streaking, 9" d. (minor stains &
short hairlines) 625.00

Figural bottle, figure of a Coachman
wearing high hat & long wrap-
around cloak, greyish body
w/light brown sponging, im-
pressed "1849" mark, 10 1/8" h. . . . 600.00

Figural bottle, figure of a Coachman
w/high hat & wrap-around cloak,
brown & yellow enameled mustache, mottled brown Rockingham
glaze, 10¾" h. (in-the-making
separation inside the neck) 900.00

Figure, parian, young boy standing
w/one hand on hip, other arm
supports basket filled w/applied
eggs on his shoulder, round plinth
base, 1847-58, 9¾" h. 85.00

Frame w/mirror, rectangular form
w/shaped edge enhanced
w/molded scrolls & foliage, mottled Flint Enamel glaze, 1849-58,
10½" w., 11½" h. (ILLUS.) 935.00

Bennington Flint Enamel Frame

Inkwell, square form w/molded
pediment & corresponding base,
holes at each corner w/removable
steeple finials, central ink reservoir, the whole raised on cylindrical feet, mottled Flint Enamel
glaze, Bennington Potteries, ca.
1854, 5 1/8 x 5 3/8", 3" h. (one
finial missing) 770.00

Inkwell, graniteware, white model
of a phrenological head w/regions
of the brain printed in black,
scrolled base w/pen hole at front
trimmed in gold, rectangular
plinth base, 1850-59, 5½" h. 175.00

Jar & cover, cylindrical w/vertical
ribbing & small tab handles,
slightly domed cover w/button
finial, mottled brown Rockingham
glaze, impressed "1849" mark,
8" h. (minor glaze flakes) 350.00

Jug, stoneware, semi-ovoid, slip-
quilled cobalt blue long-tailed bird
on branch, impressed "J. Norton
and Co., Bennington, Vt., 2,"
1859-61, 2 gal., 13¾" h. (small
base flake) 600.00

Bennington Decorated Jug

Jug, stoneware, semi-ovoid, slip-
quilled cobalt blue pecking chicken
on a mass of foliage, impressed
"J. & E. Norton. Bennington VT.,"

ca. 1855, 2 gal., minute chip on lip & base, 13¾" h. (ILLUS.) 1,650.00

Jug, stoneware, semi-ovoid, slip-quilled cobalt blue long-tailed bird on stump looking backwards over its shoulder, impressed "J. & E. Norton, Bennington, VT, 2," 1850-59, 2 gal., 14¾" h. (short in-the-making hairline near base) 2,200.00

Jug, stoneware, semi-ovoid, slip-quilled cobalt blue bird on a large flowering branch, impressed "J. Norton & Co. Bennington, Vt. 4," 1859-61, 4 gal., 18" h. 770.00

Paperweight, modeled as a recumbent spaniel dog w/iridescent brown glaze on a rectangular base w/rounded corners, the base trimmed w/cobalt blue, attributed to Bennington Potteries, ca. 1847-60, 2 1/16 x 4", 1¾" h. (firing imperfections) 770.00

Paperweight, octagonal finial centered on stepped rectangular base, mottled Flint Enamel glaze, impressed circular mark on base "Lyman Fenton & Co., - Fenton's ENAMEL - PATENTED - 1849 - BENNINGTON, Vt.," 3¼ x 5¼", 2¼" h. (flake on finial, chip at base) 330.00

Pitcher, 6¼" h., Tulip & Heart patt., paneled baluster form w/heart devices along scalloped rim, mottled Flint Enamel glaze, late 19th c. 467.50

Pitcher, 8¾" h., lobed pear-shaped body on conforming base, scroll handle, mottled Flint Enamel glaze, Lyman Fenton and Company, Bennington, Vermont, 1849-53, impressed mark (flake at spout, hairlines, scratches) 522.50

Pitcher, 9¾" h., hound-handled, baluster-form body w/flaring molded spout, applied handle in the shape of a hound w/front paws resting on rim & muzzle resting on paws, overall molded decoration w/animals & meandering grapevines, mottled brown Rockingham glaze, Bennington Potteries, ca. 1852-67 (star crack in base, small flakes) 1,100.00

Sugar bowl, cov., baluster-form octagonal body w/flaring rim & conforming cover w/steeple finial, applied handles, mottled flame-pattern Flint Enamel glaze, impressed mark, 1849-58, rim chips, 7 5/8" h. (ILLUS. next column) ...1,100.00

Syrup pitcher w/pewter lid, parian, Palm Tree patt., cylindrical body tapering slightly to wide flared spout, molded branch handle, 1853-58, 7 7/8" h. 105.00

Bennington Flint Enamel Sugar Bowl

Toby-barrel bottle, cylindrical body, the neck & shoulders of bottle forming head & shoulders of figure, holding pitcher & glass, sitting astride a barrel, mottled Flint Enamel glaze, ca. 1849, 10¾" h. 2,530.00

General Stark Toby Pitcher

Toby pitcher, modeled as a bust of General Stark, his tricorn hat forming spout, applied grapevine handle, mottled brown Rockingham glaze, Bennington Potteries, ca. 1849-58, restored, 6 1/8" h. (ILLUS.) 715.00

Toby pitcher, model of a stout seated man wearing tricorn hat, grapevine handle, mottled brown Rockingham glaze, J. Norton, Bennington, Vermont, 1849-58, impressed mark, 6½" h. 522.50

Vase, 7½" h. parian, model of an ear of corn w/a figure of a standing child molded on each side of the base, 1847-58 ....45.00

Vase, 8" h., blue & white porcelain, Poppy patt., ovoid footed body molded in relief w/poppy blossoms & leaves on a blue ground & applied at the base of the tall slender ribbed neck w/grape clusters, slender applied S-curve handles, w/leaf scroll ends run from neck to shoulder, 1850-58 ... 85.00

Vase, 9¾" h., parian, ovoid footed
body w/relief-molded oval reserve w/kneeling child, tall
paneled neck flanked on each
side by a seated naked child,
scalloped leaf-molded rim,
1847-58 . . . . 80.00

BERLIN (KPM)

Framed Berlin Plaque

*The mark KPM was used at Meissen from
1723 to 1725, and was later adopted by the
Royal Factory, Konigliche Porzellan
Manufaktur, in Berlin. At various periods it
has been incorporated with the Brandenburg
sceptre, the Prussia eagle or the crowned
globe. The same letters were also adopted by
other factories in Germany in the late 19th
and 20th centuries. With the end of the German monarchy in 1918, the name of the firm
was changed to Staatliche Porzellan
Manufaktur and, though production was halt-
ed during World War II, the factory was
rebuilt and is still in business. The exquisite
paintings on porcelain were produced at the
close of the 19th century and are eagerly
sought by collectors today.*

Bust of woman w/beautiful face,
feathered hat, raised gold & blue
beading on gown, pink accents,
signed $325.00
Cabinet plates, each w/a gilt-
rimmed pink border centering a
Near Eastern scene, the first of a
blackamoor seated w/a parrot,
the second w/a blackamoor w/a
fan attending a young reclining
beauty, 9½" d., pr. 264.00
Cup & saucer, bell-form footed cup
w/everted lip, painted w/scene
depicting the Colonnade in Frein-
zens Bad, w/strolling figures,
buildings & trees, gilt borders,
1849-70 . . . . 412.50

Figure of a gentleman, wearing yellow coat w/gilt buttons, fur cap,
purple breeches, w/bird pecking
his right leg & another seated on
his head biting his right hand,
standing on shaped square tree
stump base, 1755-62, 5½" h. (right
hand & one bird repaired, minor
glaze flaking) 7,040.00
Figure group, man & woman in Em-
pire style clothing, white w/lacy
black & gold decoration, flesh-
toned features, marked "KPM" in
blue under the glaze, 3 3/8" d.,
8½" h. 484.00
Models of Orioles, each perched on
a tree stump, late 19th c., 11" h.,
pr. 467.50
Painting on porcelain, portrait of a
woman of Ancient Greece wearing
a white chiton & standing beside a
pool holding flowers to her ear &
admiring her image in a hand-held
mirror, late 19th c., framed,
4 5/8 x 7¼" 1,540.00
Painting on porcelain, entitled "The
German Bride," portrait of a
maiden of pious expression depicted wearing a white headpiece
continuing to a dark brown velvet
cloak w/a brocade sash, her only
adornment a gold cross, impressed
"KPM" & sceptre marks, late
19th c., 6¼ x 9 3/8" 4,290.00
Painting on porcelain, Ruth wearing
a white scarf over her flowing
brown hair & a flowing grey gown,
holding a bundle of wheat, artist-
signed, late 19th c.,
11 5/8 x 19" 4,675.00
Plaque, rectangular, painted w/an
elderly scholar pointing to an open
science book while a fair young
maiden offers him a painting of
the Nativity, impressed "K.P.M."
& sceptre marks, late 19th c.,
framed, 7 5/8 x 10 1/8" 1,650.00
Plaque, rectangular, Jesus among the
Elders at the Temple, the young
Jesus dressed in a white tunic
standing in the midst of five colorfully robed elders within a col-
umned interior, after Hofmann, impressed "K.P.M." & inscribed
"Jesus als Knabe im Tempel, nach
Hofmann," ca. 1900, framed,
9¾ x 13¼" (ILLUS.) 2,475.00
Stein, applied state shields & eagle,
brown glaze, dated 1866, pewter
lid, 4 liter 467.50
Teacup & saucer, teacup w/interior
ribbing, exterior painted in
magenta w/buildings in a pastoral
setting within a C-scroll half-

cartouche & w/floral sprigs on a white ground, ribbed dished saucer w/similar decoration, both w/gilt foliate swag borders, 19th c. 192.50

Toothpick holder, pair of boots w/clown in center 65.00

K.P.M. Figural Vase

Vase, 23¾" h., modeled w/a large figure of cupid w/curly blonde hair wearing only a quiver of arrows & a flowing pale green drapery, depicted bending under the weight of the large foliate-molded cornucopia vase, the whole set on a square base w/four scrolling feet, printed "K.P.M." & sceptre & crowned orb marks, mid-19th c., minor losses & chips (ILLUS.) 3,190.00

BISQUE

Humorous Bisque Cigarette Stand

Bisque is biscuit china, fired a single time but not glazed. Some bisque is decorated with colors. Most abundant from the Victorian era are figures and groups, but other pieces from busts to vases were made by numerous potteries in the U.S. and abroad.

Basket, twisted vine handle,

modeled w/cover leaning at side, molded w/high-relief bunches of grapes, leaves hang from edge of rim, applied boy climbing ladder on one side, applied girl standing & reaching for grapes on other, molded floral & leaf base, marked "7459" on base, 9" l., 9¼" h. $195.00

Bust of boy, modeled as a screaming child w/metal fly on his nose, blonde hair, molded blue shirt w/quilted bib, old real fabric red & blue plaid collar matches cloth tam w/feathers, paint-trimmed facial features, hat padded for use as a pincushion, unmarked Heubach, w/original cardboard box, 2¼" d., 3½" h. 283.00

Cigarette stand, figural grouping of dressed gentleman pig flanked by shell-shaped container on one side & large top hat on other, stack of books at his feet, scroll-molded base, light blue suit, tan bowl, gold trim, Unger, Schneider & Hutschenreuther mark, 19th c., 5¼" h. (ILLUS.) 155.00

Figure of a baby in a bathtub, blonde baby in beige tub w/one leg up, arms away from body, sweet face, 2¾ x 4", 3½" h. 100.00

Figure of bathing beauty, reclining lady wearing mauve swimsuit & cap, marked Germany, 3½" l. 65.00

Figure of black boy w/phonograph, 4" 215.00

Figure of girl, blonde, holding up ends of her long pleated skirt, pastel pink w/deep pink bodice on dress, green sash, marked Heubach, 4¼" d., 6¼" h. 123.00

Figure of dancing girl, holding edges of tan ruffled dress w/white lace trim, marked Heubach, 3 5/8" d., 6½" h. 93.00

Figure of dancing girl, smiling face, aqua dress w/sanded surface, pink bow, white lace collar, multicolored surface on base, signed Heubach, 11½" h. 505.00

Figure of a veiled infant, child seated on rocks above a river, late 19th c., some later painting, interior restoration, 34" h. (ILLUS. top next page) 935.00

Figures, boy & girl sitting in chairs, each in green & white clothes w/gold dot trim & gold shoes, chairs green, tan & gold, 3" d., 6¼" h., pr. 172.00

Figures, "Rope Jumpers," children in pale green Kate Greenaway-type costumes, sweet faces, Heubach, 9½" h., pr. 300.00

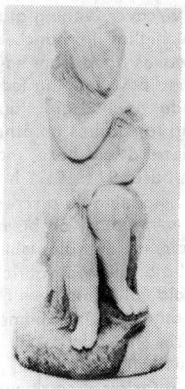

Bisque Figure of a Veiled Infant

Figures, man w/ax in one hand
wipes brow w/other, woman
holds baby in one arm, jug in the
other hand, pastel coloring,
Heubach, 12½" h., pr............ 720.00
Figure group, grandmother w/three
children, grandmother holds bonnet & is dressed in lavender, two
little girls & one boy holding onto
her dressed in pink, blue & green,
marked "Ernst Bohne," 3½ x 4¼",
6¼" h......................... 233.00
Figure group, "Romeo & Juliet,"
standing figures in floral decorated dress & trousers holding
hands, glazed floral highlights,
13" h......................... 275.00
Humidor, cov., figural head of Indian in war bonnet, brightly painted
eyes looking towards right, fine
quality, 6" h. 135.00
Model of a dog, seated white shaggy animal holding large pink &
gold-edged egg between paws,
intaglio eyes, Heubach, 8½" l. ... 400.00
Model of old worn tramp shoe,
pierced eyelets, mother mouse
watches from top rim of shoe
while her baby squeezes out of a
tear, varied shades of charcoal &
greys, touches of pink on feet,
nose & ears, marked Heubach inside of shoe, 5" l., 3¼" highest
point 165.00
Nodding figure, little Irish boy
w/green shamrock on his hat
standing holding a little wire
cane, 4" h. 65.00
Nodding figure, Victorian lady
w/bonnet & long coat stands holding a cat, buff, apricot & brown
trim, 7" h..................... 125.00
Piano baby, seated & dressed in
white gown w/blue trim, brown
dog licking face, curly brown hu-

man hair wig on bald baby head,
2 x 3", 3½" h. 171.00
Piano baby, lying on stomach,
dressed in nightie & bonnet,
green ties on bonnet & bow on
nightie, marked "7122 H," 8" l.,
4½" h......................... 225.00
Piano baby, crawling, wearing white
gown, kicking chubby legs,
Heubach, 8" l., 5½" h. 415.00
Piano baby, reclining, intaglio eyes,
blue scarf on head, holding bunch
of green grapes, Heubach, 8" 300.00

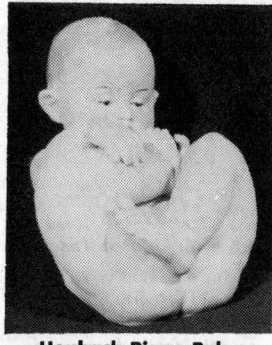

Heubach Piano Baby

Piano baby, lying on back w/legs
curled up & one big toe in his
mouth, Heubach (ILLUS.) 700.00
Planter, figural Colonial boy w/arms
& legs away in front of planter,
beautiful color & detail, marked
Heubach, 3 x 4½ x 4½" 95.00
Planter, figural shepherdess tending
her flock, signed Heubach, 2¾ x
10¾", 4" h..................... 195.00
Plates, pierced to hang, relief-
molded multicolored Indian
Chiefs, signed Heubach, 19th c.,
pr............................ 450.00
Shelf sitter, figural black boy
w/green hat, yellow shirt, orange
breeches, holding fishing pole,
Germany 65.00
Snow Baby seated on polar bear,
2¼" h. 55.00
Snow Babies (2) standing on a large
snowball, 2½" h. 66.00
Snow Baby, girl w/pink pants riding
a sled, 2½" h................. 99.00
Snow Baby sitting in front of large
seashell, on shell-form base
w/souvenir markings for New
Orleans, Louisiana, ca. 1900, 3" .. 145.00
Trinket box, cov., red w/figural colored clown head finial on cover,
signed Heubach, 2½" d.,
3½" h......................... 150.00
Trinket box, cov., figure of a young
girl dressed in blue & pink w/bon-
net & holding a man's watch forms

the cover, shown sitting on white
& gold chamber pot forming base,
2¾" d., 4¼" h. 115.00
Trinket box, model of a gilt-trimmed
white flower w/a character baby
head at center of the lid, the face
w/blue intaglio eyes, open-closed
mouth & brush-stroked molded
hair, base incised "4168," 5" d. . . . 286.00
Vase, 6½" h., 3" d., figural Dutch
boy standing in front of vase, boy
w/blue shirt, tan hat & tan pants,
vase is tan, marked Heubach. 115.00

BOEHM PORCELAINS

*Although not antique, Boehm porcelain
sculptures have attracted much interest as
Edward Marshall Boehm excelled in hard porcelain sculptures. His finest creations, inspired by the beauties of nature, are in the
forms of birds and flowers. Since his death
in 1969, his work has been carried on by his
wife at the Boehm Studios in Trenton, New
Jersey. In 1971, an additional studio was
opened in Malvern, England, where bone porcelain sculptures are produced. We list both
limited and non-limited editions of Boehm.*

ANIMALS
Chipmunk, 1980, 3" w., 3¼" h. $140.00
Deer Mouse, 1980, 2½" w.,
3¾" h. 140.00
Dog, "Pugy," 5" l., 4½" h. 195.00
White Mouse, Preening 80.00

BIRDS
Baby Cedar Waxwing, 3" h. 150.00
Cedar Waxwings on Wild Black-
berry, 1956-61, 12½" h., pr. 3,000.00
Fledgling Blackburnian Warbler, dis-
continued, 2½ x 4". 150.00
Fledgling Blue Jay, 3½" w.,
4½" h. 200.00
Fledgling Robin, 3¾" w., 3½" h. . . . 178.00
Green Jays with Black Persimmon,
1966-74, 18" h., pr. 2,300.00
Indigo Bunting, Male on Wild Rose,
10" h. 495.00
Kingfisher, 3¾" w., 6" h. 160.00
Road Runner with Horned Toad,
introduced in 1968, 14 x 20½" . . .2,500.00

MISCELLANEOUS FIGURALS
Don Quixote 125.00
Firebird, kneeling ballerina, undeco-
rated bisque, 6½" w., 8" h. 125.00
Letter opener, porcelain eagle,
made for 1976 Bicentennial 95.00
Madonna La Pieta, undecorated
bisque, 1952-57, 9½" h. 350.00
The Nutcracker 125.00

BOW

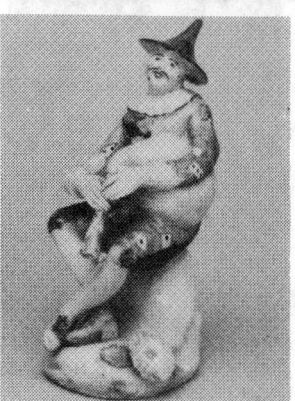

Bow Figure of Harlequin

*The Bow China Works was established in
London about 1747 by Thomas Frye and was
in operation for approximately three decades.
Some fine porcelain was produced but attribution is often difficult.*

Basket, reticulated, Quail patt.,
painted in a Kakiemon palette of
iron-red, blue, turquoise & gold
w/a brace of quail between a
flowering plant & a prunus tree
beneath a gilt-flowering iron-red
vine on the rim, intersections of
interior & exterior w/small iron-
red floral sprigs, 1756-60,
6 5/8" d. (footrim w/grittiness) . . .$990.00
Dish, oval, vine-molded, painted in
the center in shades of rose, yellow, blue, green & brown w/a
cluster of fruit & vegetables &
molded around the gilt-edged
wavy rim w/two clusters of purple
grapes amid rose-veined leaves
edged in rose, yellow & green &
separated by four molded scroll
or leaf devices trimmed in rose,
turquoise & gold, Anchor & Dagger
mark, ca. 1770, 10 11/16" d. 2,200.00
Figure of Harlequin, seated man
wearing a peaked hat & chequered
clothes, holding a bagpipe & sitting
on rockwork & oval base applied
w/flowerheads, ca. 1756, hat,
hands, bagpipes & right arm
restored, 4¾" h. (ILLUS.) 1,045.00
Figure of a lady w/a hurdy gurdy,
wearing a black hat w/green bow,
a green-lined lavender vest w/vari-
colored bows on her sleeves, a floral skirt & lemon-yellow apron,
seated w/the hurdy gurdy on her
left knee, raised on a puce-lined
scroll base applied w/flowers on

Bow Figure of Lady with Hurdy Gurdy

four scroll feet, ca. 1760-65, chips
& repairs to fingers, restoration to
neck of instrument, small chips to
base, 7¼" h. (ILLUS.) 1,650.00
Model of a hen & cockerel, the
rooster w/brown & black striped
tail & iron-red & yellow markings,
the hen w/brown & black speckled
markings, on oval mound base applied w/green leaves & colored
flowers, ca. 1760, 4 3/8" h. (hen's
tail broken, small chip to cockerel's wing, minor chips on
flowers) 6,600.00

BUFFALO POTTERY

Ye Lion Inn Card Tray

*Buffalo Pottery was established in 1902 in
Buffalo, N.Y., to supply pottery for the Larkin Company. Most desirable today is Deldare Ware, introduced in 1908 in two
patterns, "The Fallowfield Hunt" and "Ye
Olden Times," which featured central English scenes and a continuous border. Emerald Deldare, introduced in 1911, was banded
with stylized flowers and geometric designs
and had varied central scenes, the most popular being from "The Tours of Dr. Syntax." Re-*

*organized in 1940, the company now
specializes in hotel china.*

DELDARE
Card tray, Ye Lion Inn, 7¾" d.
(ILLUS.) . . . .$205.00 to 250.00
Creamer & cov. sugar bowl, oc-
tagonal, Scenes of Village Life in
Ye Olden Days, pr. . . . . . .310.00 to 350.00
Cup & saucer, Ye Olden Days 175.00
Dresser tray, Dancing Ye Minuet,
9 x 12" 475.00

Deldare Humidor
Humidor, cov., bulbous, There was
an Old Sailor, etc., 8" h.
(ILLUS.) . . . . .700.00 to 750.00
Humidor, cov., octagonal, Ye Lion
Inn, 7" h. 675.00
Mug, The Fallowfield Hunt,
2½" h. 335.00
Pin tray, Ye Olden Days,
3½ x 6¼" 215.00
Pitcher, 6" h., octagonal, The Fal-
lowfield Hunt, artist-signed,
ca. 1908 . . . . 400.00
Pitcher, 6" h., octagonal, Their Man-
ner of Telling Stories - Which He
Returned with a
Curtsey . . . . .375.00 to 400.00
Plate, 8½" d., The Fallowfield Hunt
- The Death, 1909 . . . . 155.00
Plate, 8½" d., Ye Town
Crier . . . . .135.00 to 150.00
Plate, chop, 14" d., An Evening at
Ye Lion Inn, pierced to hang,
artist-signed . . . . .450.00 to 475.00
Plate, chop, 14" d., The Fallowfield
Hunt - The Start . . . . .500.00 to 525.00
Punch bowl, The Fallowfield Hunt,
14½" d. . . . . .4,000.00 to 4,500.00
Teapot, cov., Scenes of Village Life
in Ye Olden Days,
5¾" h. . . . . .335.00 to 375.00

MISCELLANEOUS
Butter dish, cover & drain insert,
Blue Willow patt., 3 pcs. 110.00

Christmas plate, 1950 . . . .   32.50
Christmas plate, 1951 . . . .   45.00
Christmas plate, 1955 . . . . 25.00 to 35.00
Christmas plate, 1956 . . . . :   35.00
Christmas plate, 1958 . . . .   32.00
Christmas plate, 1959 . . . .   36.00
Christmas plate, 1960 . . . .   36.00
Christmas plate, 1962, designed for
   the exclusive use of Hample
   Equipment Company, Elmira, New
   York . . . . 120.00 to 145.00
Christmas plates, 1950-1960, com-
   plete set 400.00
Gravy boat, Blue Willow patt.,
   1909 . . . .   45.00

Cinderella Jug

Jug, Cinderella, 1906, 6" h.
   (ILLUS.) . . . . 350.00 to 365.00
Jug, Geranium, blue & white,
   6½" h. . . . . 220.00 to 255.00
Jug, Robin Hood, 1906,
   8¼" h. . . . . 345.00 to 375.00
Pitcher, 9¼" h., John Paul Jones
   one side, battle scene reverse,
   blue decoration, 1907 . . . 375.00 to 425.00
Pitcher, 9¼" h., two sailors on one
   side, lighthouse on rocky shore
   reverse, blue decoration, 1906 . . . 550.00
Plate, 9" d., Dr. Syntax disputing his
   Bill with the Landlady, blue &
   white 125.00
Plate, 10" d., historical series, The
   White House, Washington, blue-
   green on white 32.50
Salt & pepper shakers, Abino ware,
   pr. 675.00
Sugar bowl, cov., Blue Willow patt.,
   1911 . . . .   75.00

CANTON

This ware has been decorated for nearly two centuries in factories near Canton, China. Intended for export sale, much of it was originally inexpensive blue-and-white hand decorated ware. Late 18th and early 19th cen-

tury pieces are superior to later ones and fetch higher prices.

Basin, blue & white, painted on
   interior w/Oriental river landscape & on exterior w/floral
   sprays including peony, chrysanthemum & lotus, everted rim
   w/trellis-diaper border &
   pierced for provision of a spigot,
   early 19th c., 25 3/8" d. $8,800.00
Bowl, 10½" d., 5" h., scalloped rim,
   blue & white, h.p. pagoda scene,
   orange peel glaze 525.00
Pitcher, 9" h., model of fish, molded
   base, cobalt blue flows into a
   greyish white glaze, orange peel
   glaze visible around base,
   detailed eyes & fins, scales can be
   seen through the deep cobalt, tail
   curves up towards body forming
   handle 225.00
Platter, 10½ x 13½" oval, blue &
   white, rain cloud border, land-
   scape scene center, 19th c. 220.00
Platter, 13½" l., w/cut corners, dia-
   per border w/rain cloud liner,
   China, 19th c. (hairline repair) 192.50
Platter, 15¼" octagon, w/well-and-
   tree, Blue Willow patt. variant,
   cavetto & rim w/trellis diaper border flanking a dash-and-scallop
   band, all supported by a deep
   well & two bar feet, blue & white,
   19th c. 247.50
Sauce boat, blue and white,
   7½" l. 275.00
Serving dish, deep scalloped rim,
   slightly domed base, rain cloud
   border, blue & white, China,
   19th c., 10" d. 357.50
Shrimp dish, round w/fan-shaped
   handle at top, rain cloud border,
   blue & white, China, 19th c.,
   10 3/8" d. (glaze roughness at
   rim) 302.50
Tureen w/domed cover, octagonal
   w/cut corners, pad finial on cover, boars' head handles on base,
   China, 19th c., 8¼ x 12", 6½" h.
   (staple repair, hairline crack) 495.00
Vegetable dish, cov., oval, deep
   bowl w/shaped rim, cover decorated w/lotus bud finial, rain
   cloud border, China, 19th c.,
   11" l. 247.50

CAPO DI MONTE

Production of porcelain and faience began in 1736 at the Capo-di-Monte factory in Naples. In 1743 King Charles of Naples established a factory there that made wares with relief decoration. In 1759 the factory was moved to Buen Retiro near Madrid, operating until 1808. Another Naples pottery was opened in 1771 and operated until 1806 when its molds were acquired by the Doccia factory of Florence, which has since made reproductions of original Capo-di-Monte pieces with the "N" mark beneath a crown. Some very early pieces are valued in the thousands of dollars but the subsequent productions are considerably lower.

Capo-di-Monte Vases

Box, cov., rectangular w/hinged slightly domed cover molded w/two putti accompanying a ram-pulled chariot w/a bacchic putto, w/molded flowerhead border, conforming body w/further relief & polychrome decoration of frolicking bacchic putti, 19th c., 14" l. $1,430.00

Figure of a "Dandy," standing man wearing a long blue coat, striped trousers & floral vest, holding posies in his right hand, 8" h. 160.00

Figure of a fisherman, seated man wearing a captain's cap, shirt & rolled up blue trousers, holding a bag w/shells & pearls, shell at his foot, signed "Bonalberti," 7½" w., 9½" h. 175.00

Figure of a fisherman, seated man in red tassel cap smoking a pipe & holding net to be mended, seashell at feet, signed "G. Armani," 10½ x 10½" 175.00

Figure group, young girl seated on brick wall w/boy kneeling w/camera in his hand, signed "G. Armani," 8½ x 9½" 150.00

Figure group, boy & girl on teeter-totter, girl in pink dress & hat, boy in tan coat & blue trousers, signed "B. Martino," Crossed Feathers mark, 8 x 11" 125.00

Figure group, old man in wheelbarrow w/wine jug being pushed by

man in tattered clothes, on platform base, signed "G. Armani," 10 x 12" 350.00

Plates, 8¾" d., shaped edge w/gilt rim & brightly painted classical figures in relief above an Ionic scroll framing a centrally painted bunch of summer flowers on a gilt background, one w/central gilt-highlighted white ground, underglaze blue crowned N mark, group of 18 . . . . .2,200.00

Tea set: 9" h. cov. teapot, cov. sugar bowl, creamer, four cake plates & four cups & saucers; molded in relief & colorfully enameled w/continuous scenes of classical figures in landscape settings, crowned N mark, ca. 1900, 15 pcs. 275.00

Vases, 13" h., tall cylindrical bowls tapering to pedestal base w/ring & domed foot, bowl molded in relief w/scantilly clad classical figures decorated w/polychrome, relief-molded putti around foot, late, pr. (ILLUS.) 250.00

CELADON

Celadon Covered Jar

Celadon is the name given a highly-fired Oriental porcelain featuring a glaze that ranges from olive through tones of green, blue-green and grey. These wares have been made for centuries in China, Korea and Japan. Fine early Celadon wares are costly, later pieces are far less expensive.

Bowl, 3½" h., compressed ovoid body w/a wide flared cylindrical neck & everted lip, the glaze of sea-green color revealing the burnt orange body on the foot ring & thinning to silver grey at the lip, Song Dynasty, China $5,775.00

Bowl, 4½" d., molded as a lotus leaf w/the sides rolled up to form the

rounded sides & frilled rim, interior
incised simulating the veins of the
lily pad, centered w/a small tortoise, thick pale green glaze, Song
Dynasty, China (firing crack on
rim) 2,750.00
Charger, molded in the interior w/a
central stylized floral medallion
encircled by a wide band of further blossoms amid scrolling leafy
tendrils, covered overall in a pale
green celadon glaze, 16" d. 440.00
Dishes, leaf-shaped, footed,
enameled w/floral sprays,
6¾" w., 11" l., pr. 357.50
Jar, cov., globular body decorated
w/blue & white slip-trailed Foo
dogs centering a floral boss amid
swirling clouds, 19th c., 8½" h.
(ILLUS.). 275.00
Jardiniere, wide-mouthed cylindrical
vessel w/flaring sides, pierced base
resting on three stump feet, body
molded w/a median band of the
Eight Trigrams between raised horizontal lines & freely carved lotus
sprays, mottled sea-green glaze,
interior center & underfoot w/un-
glazed ring burnt red in the firing,
Longquan, Ming Dynasty, China,
9½" d. 2,200.00
Oil lamp, receptacle set within a
molded lotus bulb, the sides
molded w/overlapping leaves,
raised on a flanged stem molded
w/petal flutes, all beneath a thick,
bubble-suffused glaze of pale
bluish-green, the unglazed base
burnt bright red, Song Dynasty,
China, 3¼" h. 2,200.00
Vase, 11½" h., applied blue & white
prunus decoration 67.50

CERAMIC ARTS STUDIO
OF MADISON

*Founded in Madison, Wisconsin in 1941 by
two young men, Lawrence Rabbitt and Reu-
ben Sand, this company began as a "studio"
pottery. In early 1942 they met an amateur
clay sculptor, Betty Harrington and, recog-
nizing her talent for modeling in clay, they
eventually hired her as their chief designer.
Over the next few years Betty designed over
460 different pieces for their production.
Charming figurines of children and animals
were a main focus of their output in addition
to models of adults in varied costumes and
poses, wall plaques, vases and figural salt and
pepper shakers.*

*Business boomed during the years of World
War II when foreign imports were cut off and,*
*at its peak, the company employed some 100
people to produce the carefully hand-
decorated pieces.*

*After World War II many poor-quality
copies of Ceramic Arts Studio figurines appeared and when, in the early 1950's, foreign
imported figurines began flooding the market, the company found they could no longer
compete. They finally closed their doors in
1955.*

*Since not all Ceramic Arts Studio pieces are
marked, it takes careful study to determine
which items are from their production.*

Bank, figural, Barber Head $20.00
Bank, figural, Mr. Blankety Bank . . . 28.00
Bank, figural, Mrs. Blankety Bank . . 28.00
Bell, figural, Summer Belle 30.00
Figurine, Bass Viol Boy 50.00
Figurine, Bride 35.00
Figurine, Colonial Man 35.00
Figurine, Comedy, grey gown
w/blue mask, 10" h. 25.00
Figurine, Flute Girl 43.00
Figurine, Indian Brave on knee,
5" h. 50.00
Figurine, Mexican Boy 25.00
Figurine, Southern Gentleman 22.00
Figurine, Tragedy, burgundy dress,
10" h. 40.00
Figurines, Cinderella & her Prince,
pr. 72.00
Figurines, Polish Boy & Girl, orange
pants, skirt & caps, unmarked,
5½" h., pr. 45.00
Figurines, Russian Boy & Girl, pr. . . . 15.00
Figurine, shelf-sitter, Farmer Girl,
blue clothes 20.00
Figurines, shelf-sitters, Cowboy &
Cowgirl, pr. 45.00
Figure group, Hansel & Gretel,
7" h. 36.00
Model of Archibald the Dragon 48.50
Model of Daisy Donkey 28.00
Model of Elsie Elephant 30.00
Model of a monkey, Daddy 25.00
Models of dog & doghouse, pr. 15.00
Models of Mother Bear & Baby,
pr. 22.00
Models of Mother Skunk & two
babies, 3 pcs. 20.00
Models of Mr. & Mrs. Penguin, pr. . . 20.00
Pitcher, miniature, Toby 40.00
Pitcher, cow & calf decoration on
green ground 135.00
Salt & pepper shakers, figural horse
heads, pr. 28.00
Salt & pepper shakers, figural Moth-
er Monkey & Baby, pr. 25.00
Salt & pepper shakers, figural Na-
tive Boy & Elephant, pr. 45.00
Salt & pepper shakers, figural Sea-
horse & Coral, pr. 30.00

Salt & pepper shakers, figural Sia-
mese Cats, large & small, pr. 22.00
Salt & pepper shakers, figural Wee
Elephants, pr................... 26.00
Salt & pepper shakers, figural Wee
Pigs, pr....................... 28.00
Wall plaque, pierced to hang, figure
of ballerina, Grace 45.00
Wall plaque, pierced to hang, figure
of ballet dancer, Greg 45.00
Wall plaques, pierced to hang,
figures of ballerinas, Arabesque &
Attitude, pr. 85.00
Vase, bud-type, figural, Chinese girl
Wing Sang.................... 35.00

CHELSEA

Chelsea Model of an Owl

*This ware was made in London from 1754
to 1770 in England's second porcelain factory. From 1770 to 1783 it was operated as
a branch of the Derby Factory. Its equipment
was then moved to Derby. It has been
reproduced and ceramics made elsewhere are
often erroneously called Chelsea.*

Dishes, circular, painted in bright
colors w/a naturalistic flower bouquet surrounded by scattered
flower sprays, the cartouche-
molded rim lined in gilt & puce &
painted w/four groups of exotic
birds amid foliage, Gold Anchor
marks, ca. 1760, 8 5/8" d., pr.
(some wear & rubbing, minor rim
chips) $825.00
Dish, round w/fluted edge, painted
w/a large lettuce leaf surrounded
by a border of shadowed butterflies & two smaller leaves, chocolate brown rim line, Hans Sloane-
type, Red Anchor mark, ca.
1752-58, 10¾" d. (cracked,
restored) 1,320.00
Figure, "Winter," modeled as an old

man in a fur-lined yellow peaked
cap, white overcoat, purple tunic
& black shoes holding a basket of
charcoal, on a circular base applied w/leaves, Red Anchor mark,
ca. 1756, 5 1/8" h. (chips to collar
& leaves) 1,430.00
Figures, Chinese musicians, one
modeled as a boy in puce-flowered
robe, black cuffs & lining, seated
on a flower-encrusted tree stump
playing the piccolo, the other
modeled as a girl in yellow-lined
flowered coat & green trousers,
seated on a flower-encrusted tree
stump playing the drum, one
w/Red Anchor mark, ca. 1755,
5¾" h., pr. (old repairs & chips,
his piccolo gone, one of her drum-
sticks gone) 4,950.00
Figure, "La Nourrice," modeled as a
seated nurse in white cap, grey
bodice, flowered apron & pink
skirt, nursing a baby wrapped in a
blanket banded w/red ribbon, on
rectangular base w/gilt scrolls,
Red Anchor mark, ca. 1752, 7½" h.
(head, left arm, apron & seat
w/surface cracks, some wear) ...5,500.00
Figure group, "Tyrolean Dancers,"
modeled as a dancing couple, she
w/long braids, in puce-flowered
bodice, white apron & purple skirt,
he in a plumed hat & wearing a
mask, a white vest, green sleeves
& yellow breeches, on a gilt-enriched scroll-molded base applied
w/flowers, Red Anchor mark, ca.
1756, 7" h. (chips to her ribbon,
right foot restuck; chips to his
ribbons, plumes & mask, right leg
& hand restuck, some wear to
gilding) 2,200.00
Finger bowl & stand, bowl w/choco-
late-lined scalloped rim, painted
w/a peony & a honeysuckle bouquet w/further scattered sprigs,
the circular stand w/a chocolate-
lined scalloped rim, painted w/a
peony & iris bouquet & scattered
sprigs, Red Anchor mark, ca. 1755,
bowl 2 5/8" h., stand 6" d., 2 pcs.
(minor wear on bowl, fritting &
crazing on stand rim) 1,760.00
Ice pails, slightly lobed & bombe'
bodies molded w/bunches of grapes
& vines & painted w/two flower
bouquets, gilt line & gadrooned
rim, flanked by shell-molded handles, Red Anchor mark, ca. 1755,
8½" h., pr. (both restored, one
w/cracks to handles, painting &
gilding worn on both) 4,950.00
Model of a finch, bird w/brilliant red

& green plumage perched on a tree stump w/applied leaves & painted w/scattered flowers, ca. 1752, 6" h. (chip to base & twig, leaves chipped) 10,120.00

Model of an owl, white bird w/finely molded details, perched on a rock-work base, ca. 1750, small chip to a feather, 8" h. (ILLUS.) 22,000.00

Mug, baluster-shaped, painted w/bou-quet & scattered flowers & choco-late brown rim, Red Anchor mark, ca. 1752, 4 5/8" h. (crack at base of handle) .2,090.00

Plate, 8 5/8" d., botanical decoration w/two pears, each casting a shad-ow, on a leafy branch in tones of brown & green, the border w/scat-tered insects & flower sprays, with-in a shaped chocolate brown line rim, initials "JO" & Red Anchor mark, ca. 1755, rim chip & overall wear 2,530.00

Sauceboat & stand, egg-shaped boat w/green-painted stalk handle ap-plied w/foliage & flowers, the in-terior w/a strawberry leaf spray & two buds, exterior painted w/a flower bouquet & scattered sprays, on four feet painted & molded w/flowers & buds; leaf-shaped stand w/green branch handle painted w/a flower bouquet against a puce-molded vein, choco-late brown rim line, Red Anchor marks, ca. 1752-56, boat 7½" l., stand 9" l., 2 pcs. (restoration to boat handle, stand rim restored) .2,750.00

Vases, 9¾" h., bottle-shaped, long tapering neck gilded w/lappets, scattered foliage & insects, the shoulders applied w/a band of gilt fruiting vine flanked by satyr mask handles w/looped horns & gilt w/trailing vine leaves & butterflies, foliage-molded flaring bases, Gold Anchor marks, ca. 1760, 9¾" h., pr. (chips to leaves) 1,980.00

CHELSEA SPRIG WARE

The name for this ware is somewhat mis-leading since the design is thought to have originated at the Coalport, Shropshire, England porcelain factory during the early 1880's, long after the Chelsea factory closed. In this attractive pattern, small grape clus-ter sprigs are raised in relief in light blue or green or trimmed in copper or purple lustre against a white ground. It was a popular pat-tern from the early Victorian era and con-tinued in production for many years. It is often referred to as "Grandmother's Ware."

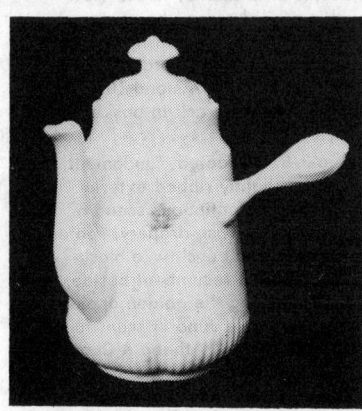

Chelsea Sprig Teapot

Bowl, 6" d.	$28.00
Cake plate, 9" d.	40.00
Cup & saucer	22.50
Plate, 7" d., copper lustre grape sprig decoration.	40.00
Sugar bowl, cov.	50.00
Teapot, cov., individual size, tall cylindrical body w/molded ribs around base & rib-molded side handle, marked "Adderley's, England," ca. 1940, 6 5/8" h. (ILLUS.).	35.00

CHINESE EXPORT

Chinese Export Mug

Large quantities of porcelain have been made in China for export to America from the 1780's, much of it shipped from the ports of Canton and Nanking. A major source of this porcelain was Ching-te-Chen in the Kiangsi province but the wares were also made else-where. The largest quantities were blue and white. Prices fluctuate considerably depend-ing on age, condition, decoration, etc.

Basket & stand, basket w/pierced

sides reserved on the front & reverse w/a solid roundel painted in sepia w/a country house view within a gilt border, the center of the similarly decorated, the rim of each w/a worn gilt border, ca. 1805, basket 10" l., stand 10¾" l., 2 pcs. (hairline crack in basket rim)..........................$550.00

Bowl, 6 3/8" d., footed, "Judgment of Paris," lightly ribbed exterior painted w/a continuous scene of Paris wearing rose drapery, seated on an iron-red bench w/a black-spotted hound recumbent beside him, & offering the golden apple to Venus, while Juno in scant turquoise drapery & Athena & Cupid in yellow-shaded iron-red drapery look on before a strutting peacock, all amid green shrubbery before pale blue hills, interior w/an iron-red delineated gold peony cluster beneath a leaf-scroll & shell border at the scalloped & barbed rim, ridged domed foot w/a slightly worn gilt tracery border, ca. 1755 (foot chip) 1,430.00

Bowl, 10" d., 1 5/8" h., "Nanking" blue & white border, orange peel glaze 275.00

Brush box, cov., blue "Fitzhugh" patt., lid painted in underglaze-blue w/a floral sprig within a medallion of beasts & trellis diaperwork edged in spearheads & dumbbells & surrounded by four clusters of flowers & precious objects, base decorated in polychrome enamels w/butterfly & florals, interior w/two compartments, 19th c., 3¾ x 7¼", 2½" h. (some rubbing)................. 440.00

Charger, center scene of green & blue peacock, rose flowers & green leaves on black ground, blue border w/colored butterflies, scalloped edge, 14½" d 360.00

Cider jug, cov., "Nanking" blue & white border, elaborate intertwined handles, Foo dog finial, 9¼" h. 1,350.00

Models of parrots, green-glazed bird w/coral-red beak & feet, standing on blue-glazed rockwork base, 19th c., 9¼" h., pr.............1,045.00

Mug, barrel-shaped body w/molded strap handle w/heart thumb rest, overall orange fish scale decoration w/floral panels, China, 19th c., pt., 5¾" h. (ILLUS.) 357.50

Mustard pot, cov., barrel-shaped, painted in rose, purple, iron-red & gilt-heightened sepia w/two in-

sects hovering by a central flower spray within three smaller flowering branches, rim w/a floral garland border, entwined strap handle w/gilt-heightened floral terminals, ca. 1785, 3 7/8" h. 550.00

Plates, 8 7/8" d., "Tobacco Leaf" patt., green-centered rose, purple & yellow tobacco blossom superimposed against gilt-heightened underglaze-blue leaf & surrounded by smaller leaves & blossoms in shades of rose, iron-red, purple, yellow, turquoise, pink, green & gold, underside of rim w/three underglaze-blue & iron-red flowering branches, 1770-85, pr............3,575.00

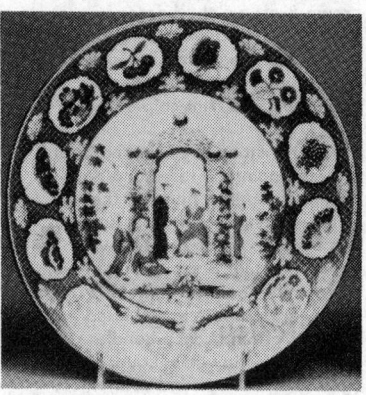

Chinese Export Plate

Plate, 9¼" d., blue & white, painted after Cornelis Pronk in shades of underglaze-blue w/six chinoiserie figures by a pond & an arbor within a wide patterned border reserved w/panels of flowers, fruit & butterflies flanked by shells & plumes, underside of brown-edged rim w/tassel border, center w/traces of gilding, ca. 1740, minor chips (ILLUS.).............2,420.00

Plates, 9 3/8" & 9¼" d., painted in an Imari palette of underglaze-blue, iron-red, light brown & gold w/La Dame au Parasol after Cornelis Pronk, depicting an Oriental lady standing beneath a parasol held by her attendant & watching four waterbirds within a floral border on the cavetto & a diapered border on the rim interrupted by alternating panels of ladies & birds, underside of rim w/seven underglaze-blue insects, 1736-45, pr. (one w/small abrasions, other w/hair crack) 1,210.00

Platter, 11 x 14", shallow oval body w/flared rim, figural, scenic &

symbolic decoration in polychrome
enamels, 19th c. 935.00

Chinese Export Platter

Platter, 12¾" l., oval, decorated
"a la Pompadour," painted in iron-
red, green, blue, yellow, purple,
turquoise, rose & black w/a central
floral spray surrounded on the rim
by four foliate-scroll cartouches
issuing further floral sprays &
containing either crowned eagles
or fish, the rim edge w/an iron-
red, yellow & green diamond &
oval border, the underside w/four
iron-red floral sprays, ca. 1745,
slight rubbing to central enamels
(ILLUS.) 3,300.00
Platter & strainer, 15 7/8" l., orange
"Fitzhugh" patt., floral sprig within a medallion of beasts & trellis
diaperwork edged in spearheads
& dumbbells & surrounded by four
clusters of flowers & precious objects, strainer pierced w/a gilt-
edged central aperture & w/three
rows of smaller holes between the
characteristic central decoration
& the border around the rim, ca.
1810, 2 pcs. 2,750.00
Punch bowl, "famille rose" palette,
exterior painted in full palette
heightened in gilding w/pair of
phoenix birds amidst flowering
branches, peonies, rockwork &
fungi, reverse w/small floral spray,
interior w/a songbird perched
amidst flowering branches beneath
a border of iron-red & gilt tassels
pendent from pink diaper or turquoise rain-cloud lappets centering
blossoms & alternating w/ruyi-
shaped floral panels, ca. 1840,
15¼" d. 3,300.00
Salt dips, blue "Fitzhugh" patt.,
painted in underglaze-blue in the
well w/a pine cone & beast
medallion bordered in spearheads
& dumbbells below a ruffled rim
w/a "Mared" patt. border within
a feathered edge, lightly fluted
sides w/four clusters of flowers &

precious objects, ca. 1820, 4" l.,
pr. 1,430.00
Teapot, cov., ovoid body polychrome
painted w/the arms & crest of Sir
Robert Eden, the last Royal British
Governor of Maryland, surrounded
by tiny insects & flowers, gilt &
green spearhead border, slightly
curved spout & handle w/molded
decoration, ca. 1785 .... 3,520.00
Umbrella stand, "famille rose"
palette, painted w/two dragons &
scrolling flowers, lower lappet &
upper diaper borders, late 19th c.,
24½" h. 1,320.00
Vases, 30½" h., "famille rose" palette, each w/a flared rim, tapering neck & baluster-form body,
painted w/a scrolling peony vine
in tones of pink, green & yellow,
fitted for electricity, pr. 2,530.00
Wall pocket, footed half urn, back
plate pierced for hanging, decorated w/Oriental scene in cobalt
blue, 19th c., 6 5/8 x 9½" 385.00

CLARICE CLIFF DESIGNS

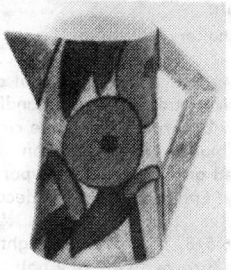

Clarice Cliff Pitcher

*Clarice Cliff was a designer for A.J. Wilkin-
son, Ltd., Royal Staffordshire Pottery, Burslem, England when they acquired the
adjoining Newport Pottery Company whose
warehouses were filled with undecorated
bowls and vases. About 1925 her flair with
the Art Deco style was incorporated into designs appropriately named "Bizarre" and
"Fantasque" and the warehouse stockpile
was decorated in vivid colors. These hand-
painted earthenwares, all bearing the printed signature of designer Clarice Cliff, were
produced until World War II and are now
finding enormous favor with collectors.*

Bowl, 5" d., two-handled, balloon
trees & house decoration $125.00
Bowl, 8¼" d., "Bizarre," blue, black
& orange rings interior, exterior
w/decorative band in similar
colors 242.00

Bowl, fruit, 8¾" d., "Bizarre," Crocus patt. 135.00

Candleholder, Art Deco style, bowl of flowers on post, trees, shrubs, water lily & gold stars on beige ground, 5¼" d., 2¼" h. 69.00

Centerpiece bowl, open water lily shape, oatmeal color, molded lily pads & buds around oval base, 9" l., 5" h. 32.50

Coffeepot, cov., "Bizarre," Crocus patt. 130.00

Cracker jar, cov., "Bizarre," My Garden patt., Art Deco style, green w/deeper green mottling, wicker handles, finial & feet are flowers & leaves in green, blue & rose, 6½" widest d., 7¼" h. 156.00

Creamer, Crocus patt., large 80.00

Cup & saucer w/tea plate, "Bizarre," Art Deco style blue & green flowers, 3 pcs. 115.00

Dish, oblong, "Bizarre," temple scene, Wilkinson Ltd., 6¾" l., 4½" h. 105.00

Gravy boat, "Fantasque," Canterbury Bells patt. 40.00

Marmalade jar, cov., "Bizarre," Gay Day patt. 125.00

Pepper shaker, Bullet patt., 2½" h. 55.00

Pitcher, 4¾" h., triangular spout on cylindrical body w/angled handle, brightly decorated w/orange circles & blue & green petals on sponged green ground, Newport Pottery, England, signed w/decal (ILLUS.) 330.00

Pitcher, 6 5/8" h., 3 5/8" d., eight-sided, "Bizarre," Gay Day patt., cream w/orange & purple florals w/blue, brown & green trim 145.00

Pitcher, 7" h., "Fantasque," Geometric patt. 130.00

Plate, 6½" d., Bullet patt. 20.00

Plate, 8" d., balloon tree decoration 125.00

Plate, 9" oblong, "Bizarre," Viscaria patt. 22.50

Plate, 10" d., "Bizarre," Crocus patt. 45.00

Plate, 10½" d., Tower Bridge patt., "There'll Always Be An England" 30.00

Platter, 12", "Bizarre," Moderne patt. 60.00

Sugar bowl, cov., "Fantasque" 75.00

Sugar shaker, "Bizarre," orange, gold & brown florals on cream & yellow ground, 2¾" d., 5" h. 130.00

Tumbler, "Bizarre," orange, gold & brown florals on yellow ground, 3½" d., 4¼" h. 110.00

Tureen, cov., "Fantasque," Canterbury Bells patt. 90.00

Vase, 6½" h., 3 5/8" d., "Bizarre," Art Deco colorful landscape w/house on hill, flattened oval shape on feet.................. 231.00

Vase, 7¾" h., 5 5/8" d., "Bizarre," Crocus patt., Art Deco bright orange, blue & purple crocus w/yellow top band & rust bottom band 201.00

Vase, 8" h., 5" w., square, "Bizarre," Delicia patt. 175.00

Vase, 9½" h., 5¾" d., "Fantasque," Art Deco bright orange top band & blue base band, exotic designs in orange, blue, green, yellow & rust, Isis shape 587.00

Vase, 12" h., "Bizarre," Trumpet patt., flowers in relief decoration..................... 150.00

CLEWS, J. & R.

Clews "Girl at Well" Pitcher

James and Ralph Clews established this pottery in Cobridge, England in 1814 and operated it until 1836 when it was taken over by Wood & Brownfield. Some of the wares have been reproduced. Also see HISTORICAL & COMMEMORATIVE.

Pitcher, 7 3/8" h., dark blue transfer-printed scene of a girl at a well, impressed "Clews," ca. 1830, hairlines, edge chips (ILLUS.)......................$100.00

Plate, 9¾" d., light blue transfer-printed river scenery design, impressed "Clews" (glaze wear on rim)......................... 40.00

Plate, 9 7/8" d., dark blue transfer-printed w/scene of "Doctor Syntax Mistakes a Gentleman's House for an Inn," from Doctor Syntax se-

ries, impressed "Clews," ca. 1830
(minor pinpoint flakes) 150.00

Plate, 10" d., dark blue transfer-
printed scene of "Doctor Syntax
Taking Possession of his Living,"
from Doctor Syntax series, impressed "Clews," ca. 1830....... 125.00

Plate, 10" d., dark blue transfer-
printed scene of Canterbury Cathedral, impressed "Clews," ca.
1830 .... 125.00

Plate, 10" d., blue transfer-printed
scene of people, cows, a castle &
bridge, ca. 1830 .... 80.00

Platter, 15 x 18½", dark blue
transfer-printed scene of "Sancho
Panza and The Duchess," from the
Don Quixote series, ca. 1820 ..... 650.00

Platter, 18¾" l., oval, medium blue
transfer-printed scene of a still-
life w/bird, impressed "Clews,"
ca. 1840 (stains, minor wear,
small edge chips) 255.00

Platter, 18¾" l., green feather-
edged rim embossed w/swags,
impressed "Clews" (some wear &
scratches) 150.00

Soup plate, dark blue transfer-
printed scene of an English cathedral, impressed "Clews," ca. 1830,
9 7/8" d. (minor wear).......... 100.00

Toddy plate, black transfer-printed
scene of "Rapids above Hadley's
Falls, Hudson River," impressed
"Clews," 6 7/8" d. (wear, minor
glaze flakes).................. 95.00

CLIFTON ART POTTERY

Clifton Indian Ware Vase

William A. Long, an organizer of the Lon-
huda Pottery, and Fred Tschirner, a chemist,
established the Clifton Art Pottery in Newark, New Jersey, in 1905. The first art pottery
produced was designated the Crystal Patina
line and was decorated with a subdued pale
green crystalline glaze which was later also
made in shades of yellow and tan. Indian
Ware, introduced in 1906, was patterned af-

ter the pottery made by the American Indians. These two lines are the most notable in
the pottery's production though Tirrube and
Robin's-egg Blue lines were also produced.
After 1911, production shifted to floor and
wall tiles and by 1914 the pottery's name was
changed to Clifton Porcelain Tile Company
to better reflect this production.

Bowl, 8" d., 5" h., Indian Ware,
small neck & rim on squat bulbous
body, dark brown bands on redware ground, design inspired
by Four Mile Ruin, Arizona,
stamped.....................$137.50

Teapot, cov., Indian Ware, small ... 45.00

Vase, 2½ x 3½", Indian Ware,
squatty, matte red, tan & black
S-curve decoration, bulbous shoulder, base incised "Mississip-
pi/7?09"...................... 50.00

Vase, 8" h., 10" d., Indian Ware,
wide short neck on squat bulbous
body, decorated w/geometric Indian motifs, done in brown &
beige glazes, derived from the
Homolobi tribe as indicated on
underside, signed "Clifton 233,"
ca. 1910 (ILLUS.) 357.50

Vase, 10½" h., 12" d., Indian Ware,
angled rim & short neck on squat
bulbous body, decorated w/dark
brown & beige band designs on
brick red ground, designs based
on Florida Indians as indicated on
the base, impressed "Clifton 241,"
ca. 1910 .... 330.00

COALPORT

Decorative Coalport Covered Urns

Coalport Porcelain Works operated at Coalport, Shropshire, England, from about 1795
to 1926 and has operated at Stoke-on-Trent
as Coalport China, Ltd., making bone china
since then.

Creamer & sugar bowl, Indian Tree
patt., pre-1920, pr. $65.00
Cup & saucer, miniature, overall cobalt blue w/heavy gold & beading, 1" h. cup 95.00
Cup & saucer, miniature, overall
gold decoration on yellow, cup
1" h., saucer 2¼" d. 100.00
Dinner service: 45 dinner plates, 18
soup plates, two deep circular
plates, three circular dishes &
covers, another cover, large two-
handled soup tureen & cover, circular tureen stand, ten graduated
rectangular platters, ten coffee
cups, twelve teacups, 21 saucers,
circular cov. sugar bowl &
creamer; each piece decorated
w/an iron-red bellflower vine intersecting an elaborate gilt scrolling
foliate vine, the rims feather-
molded & gilded, ca. 1820, the
set 17,600.00
Figure, "Stella," swirled green &
lavender gown, 8¼" h. 75.00
Tea service: cov. teapot & stand,
creamer, cov. sugar bowl; Iron-
Red Patt., No. 759, painted
w/shaped cartouches of birds
perched in branches within gilt
scroll, trellis & foliate borders alternating w/similar panels of
flowers reserved on the blue
ground, gilt line rims, ca. 1820,
the set (some wear to gilding,
worn painting on sugar bowl &
stand) 660.00
Tureens, covers & stands, modeled
as a head of cabbage w/over-
lapping green leaves shading from
grass green to chartreuse, the
stand also modeled as six overlapping leaves, ca. 1830, stand
9" d., 4 15/16" h., pr. (hairlines
& repaired chips) 6,325.00
Urns, cov., gilt paneled domed cover
w/gold ball finial above elongated
oviform body w/tripartite partition
panels decorated w/a gilt scrolling
vertical band alternating w/natural-
istically painted flower & bird
reserves on a white ground, pink
ground around panels, raised on
conforming tripod circular base,
late 19th c., 17½" h., pr.
(ILLUS.) 1,650.00

COPELAND & SPODE

W.T. Copeland & Sons, Ltd., have operated the Spode Works at Stoke, England, from
1847 to the present. The name Spode was
used on some of its productions. Its predeces-

sor, Spode, was founded by Josiah Spode
about 1784 and became Copeland & Garrett
in 1843, continuing under that name until
1847. Listings dated prior to 1843 should be
attributed to Spode.

Spode Chestnut Basket

Bowl, 9 3/8" d., 4" h., Spode's Ital-
ian patt., black transfer,
No. 1818, ca. 1876-1915 .... $125.00
Bowl, 10" d., pedestal base,
"gaudy" designs, marked "Spode's
New Stone," ca. 1820 .... 350.00
Bowl, cereal, Spode's Tower patt.,
pink transfer 7.00
Charger, "Aesop's Fables - Lion &
Fox" decoration, brown ground,
Copeland & Garrett, 1840's,
15" d. 100.00
Charger, h.p. decoration of a
Renaissance period woman, ca.
1860, 16½" d. 450.00
Chestnut basket, cov., Caneware,
scalloped rim w/twisted handles,
molded to resemble basket work,
matching cover w/large lobes & a
twisted handle, interior of bowl
section has a high glaze, impressed on bottom in lower case
letters "spode," & letter "G," ca.
1800, 7¾" l., 4" h. (ILLUS.) 110.00
Coffeepot, cov., brown & white
w/gilt trim, ca. 1875-90, 7½" h. .. 75.00
Creamer, Spode's Tower patt., pink
transfer 15.00
Figure group, parian, veiled figure
w/billowing robes above a child,
circular molded base, impressed
"COPELAND- O," 21" h. 1,980.00
Fish platter, pierced, Imari-type pattern, ca. 1847-67,
10 x 14½" oval 150.00
Footrest, pair of arched legs supporting curved rectangular rest,
blue transfer scene, marked
"Copeland Spode-Bridge England,"
10 x 13", 6¾" h. 1,250.00
Gravy boat, Spode's Tower patt.,
pink transfer 35.00
Jam pot, cover & underplate, parian, body molded w/flowers &
leaves, Copeland, 19th c. 70.00
Plate, 9¾" d., Blue Willow patt., ca.
1810 .... 58.00

Plate, 10" d., Spode's Fox & Lion
patt., green transfer............. 75.00
Plate, 10½" d., Spode's Italian patt.,
blue transfer, marked "Spode's
Italian, Copeland, England"...... 25.00
Platter, 11", Spode's Tower patt.,
pink transfer................... 35.00
Platter, 19" l., Spode's Tower patt.,
blue transfer, w/well & tree..... 176.00
Service plates, each w/a narrow gilt
rim enclosing a border of peonies
& roses on a shaded green
ground, the central medallion
similarly decorated, inscribed on
reverse in green "Copeland's
China, England," retailed by
Spaulding & Co., Chicago & Paris,
ca. 1900, 9" d., set of twelve..... 467.50

Spode Blue Willow Soup Plate

Soup plate, Blue Willow patt.,
marked "Spode," 9¼" d.
(ILLUS.)....................... 55.00
Soup plates, central gilt medallion &
apple green border w/gilt wavy
corded edge, underglaze mark
"COPELAND CHINA ENGLAND,"
retailed by A.T. Wiley's & Co.,
Montreal, Canada, 19th c.,
10½" d., set of 12.............. 357.50
Tea cup & saucer, handleless, Persian decoration, Copeland & Garrett, 1840's 85.00
Teapot, cov., hunt scene of men
w/horses on one side, dogs kill-
ing fox on other, blue transfer,
6½" h......................... 115.00
Tea set: cov. teapot, cov. sugar
bowl & creamer; Olympus patt.,
3 pcs. 100.00

CORDEY

*Founded by Boleslaw Cybis in Trenton,
New Jersey, the Cordey China Company was
the forerunner of the Cybis Studio, renowned
for its fine porcelain sculptures. A native of
Poland, Boleslaw Cybis was commissioned
by his government to paint "al fresco" murals
for the 1939 New York World's Fair. Already
a renowned sculptor and painter, he elected
to remain and become a citizen of this country. In 1942, under his guidance, Cordey China Company began producing appealing
busts and figurines, some decorated by ap-
plying real lace dipped in liquid clay prior to
firing in the kiln. Cordey figures were assigned numbers that were printed or pressed
on the base. The Cordey line was eventually
phased out of production during the 1950's
as the porcelain sculptures of the Cybis Studios became widely acclaimed.*

Bust of gentleman, No. 3001 .... $45.00
Bust of girl, No. 5011 .... 55.00
Bust of lady w/ringlets, lace collar,
No. 4013 .... 65.00
Bust of lady, No. 5010 .... 60.00
Bust of lady, picture hat, double
base, No. 5030................. 60.00
Bust of lady, No. 5039 .... 45.00
Bust of Napoleon, No. 5038, green
jacket........................ 90.00
Figure of Neopolitan boy w/basket
of breadsticks, No. 5045,
9½" h........................ 105.00
Figure of an "Old Colony" lady,
holding bouquet in each arm,
No. 5054, 9½" h. 75.00
Figure of woman w/hair in ringlets,
bustle dress, trimmed w/roses,
leaves & lace, standing beside
tree stump, No. 5089, 10¾" h.
(some petal flakes)............. 80.00
Figure of Chinese Goddess, flowing
robe w/medallions, roses & lace,
No. 5073, 12" h. 135.00
Figure of a man, ornately & colorfully dressed in clothing w/lace trim,
flowers & foliage, stump base,
No. 4153, 14" h. 115.00
Figure of boy w/basket, No. 305,
16" h........................ 90.00
Figure of boy w/hat, No. 303,
16" h........................ 95.00
Figure of lady w/basket, No. 302,
16" h........................ 85.00
Figure of lady w/fan, No. 300,
16" h........................ 85.00
Figures, grape harvester (woman)
w/basket of grapes, No. 304 &
grape harvester (man), No. 305,
16" h., pr.............155.00 to 170.00
Model of bird on a stump, black
head & neck, russet breast, grey
& black mottled back, long wings
folded inward, No. 2037,
8½" h........................ 110.00

CYBIS

Though not antique, fine Cybis porcelain

figures are included here because of the great collector interest. They are produced in both limited edition and non-numbered series and thus there can be a wide price range available to the collector.

Windflower

Bear, "Barnaby," No. 686, 1975-77, 7" h.	$125.00
Beatrice, No. 445, 1965-71, 12" h.	985.00
Buffalo, No. 640, 1968-78, 5¾" l., 5" h.	145.00
Calla Lily, No. 515, 1968-74, 16½" h.	1,800.00
Deer Mouse, "In Clover," No. 660, 1970-73, 3½" h.	125.00 to 150.00
Duckling, "Baby Brother," No. 361, 1962-79, 4½" h.	75.00
Goldilocks & Panda Bear, No. 471, 1973-75, 6" h.	355.00
Gretel, No. 476, 1974-76, 7" h.	275.00
Hansel, No. 475, 1974-76, 9" h.	285.00
Head of Boy & Head of Girl, on stands, Nos. 435 & 436, 1963-70, 10" h., pr.	525.00
Heidi, decorated, No. 432, 1966-73, 7½" h.	225.00
Indian Boy Head, "Little Eagle," No. 713, 1975-79, 12½" h.	515.00
Little Bo Peep, No. 498, 1977-82, 10½" h.	375.00
Little Red Riding Hood, No. 473, 1973-75, 6½" h.	265.00
Madonna, "Mystical Rose," decorated, No. 2092, 1950's to early 1960's, 17" h.	145.00
Pandora, No. 454, 1967-83, 5" h.	135.00 to 150.00
Peter Pan, No. 430, 1958-67, 7½" h.	275.00
Pollyanna, No. 465, 1971-75, 7" h.	300.00 to 375.00
Rebecca, No. 443, 1964-72, 6½" h.	335.00
Snail, "Sir Henri Escargot," No. 641, 1968-72, 3" h.	235.00
Squirrel, "Mr. Fluffy Tail," No. 630, 1965-71, 8" h.	275.00
Turtle, "The Baron," w/frog perched on his back, No. 820, 1975-77, 4 x 5", 3" h.	150.00

Wendy, No. 433, 1957-82, 6½" h.	150.00
Windflower with ladybug, No. 506, 1963-83, 8" h. (ILLUS.)	190.00
Wood Wren with Dogwood, No. 336, 1963-81, 5½" h.	260.00

DEDHAM

Dedham "Golden Gate" Plate

This pottery was organized in 1866 by Alexander W. Robertson in Chelsea, Massachusetts, and became A.W. & H. Robertson in 1868. In 1872, the name was changed to Chelsea Keramic Art Works and in 1891 to Chelsea Pottery, U.S.A. About 1895, the pottery was moved to Dedham, Massachusetts, and was renamed Dedham Pottery. Production ceased in 1943. High-fired colored wares and crackle ware were specialties. The rabbit is said to have been the most popular decoration on crackle ware in blue.

Since 1977, the Potting Shed, Concord, Massachusetts, has produced quality reproductions of early Dedham wares. These pieces are carefully marked to avoid confusion with original examples.

Bowl, cov., 6¼ x 9½" oval, Rabbit	$990.00
Bowl, 5½" d., 4½" h., Crackle Ware, plain round shape w/bulbous form & wide mouth, hand-incised "CPUS" in cloverleaf, Chelsea Pottery, late 19th c.	550.00
Bowl, serving, 8" d., cut corners, decorated w/stylized flowers, early 20th c.	1,045.00
Butter pat, Pansy, 3½" d.	302.50
Candlesticks, squat, round cylindrical form, Azalea, 3½" d., 2" h., pr.	330.00
Celery dish, elongated oval, Rabbit, stamped mark, early 20th c., 5" w., 10" l.	357.50
Creamer, cylindrical neck on bulbous form, Elephant, 3¼" h. (imperfection in the making)	550.00

Creamer & sugar bowl, Berry, pr.... 400.00
Cup & saucer, Snowtree, stamped
  mark, early 20th c., 4" d. 247.50
Dish, child's, round & shallow, Rab-
  bit patt. rim & rabbit medallion in
  center, 8" d. 1,100.00
Egg cup, model of a rabbit, 2 3/8".. 200.00
Knife rest, Rabbit, 2½" h........... 467.50
Paperweight, model of a rabbit,
  3" l. 605.00
Paperweight, model of a turtle,
  3½" l. 550.00
Pitcher, 4½" h., No. 12 .... 225.00
Pitcher, 5½" h., Oak Block design,
  tree-trunk form w/raised oak
  leaves & knot holes.............1,430.00
Plate, 6" d., Crab 522.50
Plate, 6" d., Iris.................... 137.50
Plate, 6" d., Polar Bear 605.00
Plate, 7¼" d., Moth 330.00
Plate, 7½" d., Dolphin............ 495.00
Plate, 8½" d., Azalea 195.00
Plate, 8½" d., Turtle 825.00
Plate, 8¾" d., Scottie Dog........1,980.00
Plate, 10" d., "Golden Gate, San
  Francisco," center sunrise scene
  w/poppy flower border, signed
  "HCR" for Hugh Robertson, written
  on reverse "from set by M. Shep-
  hard," early 20th c. (ILLUS.)......2,420.00
Plate, 10" d., Turkey 215.00
Platter, 8½ x 14" oval, Rabbit 770.00
Salt & pepper shakers, model of a
  rabbit, 2¾" h., pr. 290.00

Miniature Dragon's Blood Vase

Vase, miniature, 2 7/8" h., swollen
  cylindrical body tapering towards
  base, wide mouth, Dragon's Blood
  glaze, signed "HCR" for Hugh
  Robertson, late 19th c. (ILLUS.) ... 715.00
Vase, 7½" h., Crackle Ware, ovoid
  body tapering slightly to short,
  wide neck, h.p. white iris on blue
  ground, early 20th c. (small lines
  in neck) 2,420.00
Vase, 15" h., ovoid w/short, straight
  neck, experimental glossy drip
  glaze w/highlights of Dragon's
  Blood, moss green, pale blue &
  rust, incised "HCR" for Hugh
  Robertson, paper label of Burley &

Co., Chicago (old repair to foot,
  possibly mounted on base) 4,675.00
Vegetable dish, cov., Azalea,
  9¼" d.......................... 330.00
Vegetable dish, cov., Rabbit, cover
  w/flared rim, 10¾" d........... 660.00

DELFT

Bristol Delft Punch Bowl

*In the early 17th century Italian potters
settled in Holland and began producing tin-
glazed earthenwares, often decorated with
pseudo-Oriental designs based on Chinese
porcelain wares. The city of Delft became the
center of this pottery production and several firms produced the wares throughout the
17th and early 18th century. A majority of the
pieces featured blue on white designs, but
polychrome wares were also made. The Dutch
Delftwares were also shipped to England and
eventually the English copied them at potteries in such cities as Bristol, Lambeth and
Liverpool. Although still produced today,
Delft peaked in popularity by the mid-18th
century.*

Bowl, 11 5/8" d., 5 1/8" h., overall
  painted polychrome floral decoration, Dutch, 18th c. (short rim
  hairline) $3,800.00
Charger, painted in blue on white
  w/stylized florals around rim &
  stylized bouquet in center, yellow
  rim, signed, Dutch, 18th c.,
  12¼" d. (rim chips) 600.00
Charger, painted w/polychrome
  band of abstract florals around
  brim & w/large star-shaped floral
  reserve in the center, Dutch,
  18th c., 12¾" d. (minor crow's-
  foot in bottom)................. 350.00
Charger, painted in iron-red, blue &
  green w/a central flowerhead &
  overall scattered flowers & foliage, Dutch, early 18th c., 14" d.
  (chips) 495.00
Dish, convex center surrounded by a
  row of flutes & painted in yellow,
  blue & green w/a bird perched

amid flowers on a plateau, fluted
& everted rim painted w/a colorful floral border, Dutch, 1690-
1710, 13½" d. (two hairline
cracks) 825.00
Plate, 9" d., painted in blue on
white w/three stylized floral
reserves on rim & similar wide
band of florals in center surrounding center circle initialed & dated
"MPVD 1786," Dutch (rim chips) .. 450.00
Platter, 20½" l., oblong w/cut
corners, painted blue on white
stylized Oriental floral reserves
around rim, center painted w/styl-
ized Oriental landscape w/fence,
rockwork & florals, Dutch, 18th c.
(rim chips) 1,300.00
Punch bowl, painted around the exterior in iron-red & blue w/two
rows of panels patterned w/floral
sprigs above band & dot borders
around the base, the interior w/a
blue stylized floral sprig beneath
a border of alternating scroll &
husk-and-dot motifs at the rim,
Bristol, England, 1725-40, hairline
crack & some chips, 12" d.
(ILLUS.) 2,530.00
Stein w/domed pewter lid & thumbrest, cylindrical body decorated
w/purple sponging surrounding
blue & white painted scene in
florette-shaped reserve at front
center, Dutch, 18th c., 7¾" h.
(glaze chips, thumbrest resoldered) 700.00
Tile picture, grouping of square blue
& white tiles depicting a large
vase of flowers w/a bird perched
in the branches & flanked by two
rearing horses, on a stepped marble plinth w/an oval reserve of a
man fishing, Dutch, late 18th c.,
21¾ x 26" 825.00

Dutch Delft Vase

Vase, 25" h., double gourd-shaped
body painted in blue on white
w/panels enclosing chinoiseries of
gardens w/flowering plants & trees
within borders of foliate scrolls &
blossoms on a contrasting ground,
Dutch, 19th c. (ILLUS.)...........1,540.00

DERBY & ROYAL CROWN DERBY

Derby Figurines

*William Duesbury, in partnership with
John and Christopher Heath, established the
Derby Porcelain Works in Derby, England,
about 1750. Duesbury soon bought out his
partners and in 1770 purchased the Chelsea
factory and six years later, the Bow works.
Duesbury was succeeded by his son and
grandson. Robert Bloor purchased the business about 1814 and managed successfully
until illness in 1828 left him unable to exercise control. The "Bloor" Period, however, extends from 1814 until 1848, when the factory
closed. Former Derby workmen then resumed
porcelain manufacture in another factory and
this nucleus eventually united with a new and
distinct venture, Derby Crown Porcelain,
Ltd., established in 1878.*

Figurines, a lady & a man gardener,
the lady in a dress w/a pink
bodice & flowered skirt, wearing a
yellow hat & holding flowers, the
man in a yellow hat, green coat &
flowered breeches, both seated on
tree stumps on scrolled-molded
bases applied w/flowerheads,
ca. 1758, 5" h., pr. (restorations
to lady, firing crack in base, some
discoloration) $1,760.00
Figurines, depicting a youth & a
maiden, each seated on a gilt
ladder-back chair, the maiden
w/a dog on her lap, the lad w/a
cat, both on openwork scroll
bases, painted w/imitation Meissen crossed-swords marks, ca.
1815, 5½" h., pr. (ILLUS.) 385.00
Pitcher, 9" h., ovoid bulbous body

on short base ring, body tapering
to short, narrow cone-shaped
neck w/small loop handle, h.p.
multicolored flowers on an ivory
satin ground, gold handle, late
19th c. 395.00

Derby Potpourri

Potpourris, cov., urn-shaped, circular pierced cover w/berry finial
above the pierced edge applied
w/satyr's masks tapering to paw
feet headed by leaf-tips, on
shaped square base w/cut-
corners, decorated overall w/al-
ternating panels of iron-red, blue
& green flowers enriched w/gild-
ing, ca. 1820, one cover repaired,
one base cracked, some wear on
both, 5½" h., pr. (ILLUS. of one). . 715.00
Vase, 3¼" h., 2¾" d., h.p. gold
flowers & leaves on front & reverse on pink ground, embossed
gold roses around top, dated
1893 . . . . 90.00
Vases, 13" h., campana shape,
painted w/figures among ruins in
wooded landscapes, "On The River
Dove, Derbyshire," & "A View of
Scotland," named in red on the
bases, reserved on the blue
ground w/overall gilt fantastic
vegetation, the bulbous lower
parts w/foliage-molded handles,
on square bases gilt w/Vitruvian
scrolls, ca. 1815, pr. (minor wear
to gilding, minute chips to
bases) 11,000.00

DOULTON & ROYAL DOULTON

*Doulton & Co., Ltd., was founded in Lam-
beth, London, about 1858. It was operated
there till 1956 and often incorporated the
words "Doulton" and "Lambeth" in its
marks. Pinder Bourne & Co., Burslem was
purchased by the Doultons in 1878 and in
1882 became Doulton & Co., Ltd. It added
porcelain to its earthenware production in*
*1884. The "Royal Doulton" mark has been
used since 1902 by this factory, which is still
in production. Character jugs and figurines
are commanding great attention from collectors at the present time.*

ANIMALS & BIRDS

Bird, Budgerigar, on stand, green &
yellow, HN 199 . . . .$135.00
Bird, Robin, HN 2549 . . . . 95.00
Cat, Persian, black & white,
HN 999 . . . . 60.00
Cat, Persian, white, HN 2539 . . . . . . 100.00
Dog, Boxer, "Warlord of Mazelaine,"
HN 2643, 6½" 84.00
Dog, Bulldog, brown & white,
HN 1047, small. 150.00
Dog, Bulldog, "Union Jack," British
flag over back, HN 6407, 2 x 4",
2½" h. 185.00
Dog, Bulldog, sitting, K 1, 2¼" h.. . . 60.00
Dog, Bull Terrier, K 14 . . . . 150.00
Dog, Cairn Terrier, begging,
HN 2589, 4" 35.00
Dog, Cocker Spaniel, black & white,
HN 1078, 3½" 85.00
Dog, Cocker Spaniel, liver & white,
HN 1036, 1¾ x 7", 5¼" h. 151.00
Dog, Cocker Spaniel, "Lucky Star of
Ware," HN 1021, 3½" 94.00
Dog, Cocker Spaniel pup in basket,
chewing handle, HN 2586, 2½". . . 35.00
Dog, Cocker Spaniel w/pheasant,
liver & white, HN 1028, 5¼" 112.00
Dog, Cocker Spaniels, sleeping,
HN 2590, 1¾" 35.00
Dog, Collie, "Ashstead Applause,"
HN 1058, 5" 75.00
Dog, Dachshund, "Shrewd Saint,"
HN 1128, 4" 90.00
Dog, Dachshund, "Shrewd Saint,"
HN 1129, 3" 150.00
Dog, Doberman Pinscher, "Rancho
Dobe's Storm," HN 2645, 6¼" 100.00
Dog, English Setter, "Maesydd Mus-
tard," HN 1050, 5¼" 105.00
Dog, Foxhound, sitting, K 7, 2½" . . . 40.00
Dog, French Poodle, HN 2631,
5¼" 100.00
Dog, Gordon Setter, HN 1080,
medium 85.00
Dog, Greyhound, black & white,
HN 1107, medium 425.00
Dog, Irish Setter, HN 1055, 5¼" 90.00
Dog, Pekinese, "Biddee of Ifield,"
HN 1012, 3 1/8" 125.00
Dog, Pekinese, sitting, K 6, minia-
ture, 2" h. 38.00
Dog, Pointer, on grassy base,
HN 2624 . . . . 250.00
Dog, St. Bernard, lying down, K 19,
miniature, 1¾" 40.00
Dog, Scottish Terrier, "Albourne Ar-

thur, Champion," HN 1015,
medium 225.00
Dog, Welsh Corgi, "Spring Robin,"
HN 2559, 3 5/8" 88.00
Dog w/bone in mouth, HN 1159,
3¾" 35.00
Duck, Mallard drake, HN 2555, 6" .. 135.00
Fox, "Huntsman," HN 6448, 1½" 75.00
Horse, Chestnut w/foal, HN 2522 ... 475.00
Horse, Chestnut w/foal, HN 2533 ... 300.00
Horse, "Merely A Minor," brown,
HN 2571, small.................. 385.00
Tiger, crouching, "Flambe' " glaze,
signed "FM," 9½" l............. 395.00

CHARACTER JUGS

'Arry Jug

Anne of Cleves, horse head handle
w/ears up, large 225.00
Apothecary, small 41.00
'Ard of 'Earing, miniature, 2½" h...1,100.00
'Arriet, tiny, 1¼" h. 178.00
'Arriet, miniature, 2¼" h........... 72.00
'Arriet, small, 3½" h. 85.00
'Arriet, "A" mark, small, 3½" h. ... 60.00
'Arry, tiny, 1¼" h. 172.00
'Arry, miniature, 2¼" h. 68.00
'Arry, large, 6¾" h. (ILLUS.)........ 172.00
Auld Mac, tiny, 1¼" h. 200.00
Auld Mac, "A" mark, small,
3½" h. 40.00
Auld Mac, large, 6¾" h. 62.50
Beefeater, miniature, w/GR on han-
dle, 2¼" h...................... 45.00
Beefeater, small, w/GR on handle,
3½" h........................... 50.00
Beefeater, "A" mark, small, w/GR
on handle, 3½" h. 42.00
Beefeater, large, w/GR on handle .. 150.00
Blacksmith, miniature, 2¼" h....... 35.00
Blacksmith, small, 3½" h........... 39.00
Blacksmith, large................. 71.00
Bootmaker, miniature, 2¼" h....... 36.00
Bootmaker, small, 3½" h. 39.00
Bootmaker, large 72.00
(Sergeant) Buz Fuz, small, 3½" h. .. 86.00
(Sergeant) Buz Fuz, intermediate
size............................ 155.00
Cap'n Cuttle, "A" mark, small,
3½" h........................... 88.00

Capt. Henry Morgan, miniature,
2½" h............................. 35.00
Captain Hook, miniature, 2¼" h. ... 385.00
Captain Hook, small, 3½" h....... 292.00
Captain Hook, large, 6" h. 412.00
Cardinal, tiny, 1¼" h. 205.00
Cardinal, miniature, 2¼" h........ 50.00
Cardinal, large, 6½" h. 135.00
Cardinal, "A" mark, large, 6½" h. .. 145.00
Cavalier, small, 3½" h............. 60.00
Cavalier, "A" mark, small, 3½" h. .. 65.00
Cavalier, large.................. 120.00
Cavalier, "A" mark, large 145.00
Cliff Cornell, blue, small, 5½" h. ... 325.00
Clown w/red hair, large 3,800.00
Clown w/white hair, large 1,050.00
Davy Crockett & Santa Anna,
large........................... 85.00
Dick Turpin, mask on face, horse
handle, miniature, 2¼" h. 40.00
Dick Turpin, mask on hat, "A" mark,
miniature, 2¼" h................ 45.00
Dick Turpin, mask on face, horse
handle, miniature, 2¼" h. 30.00
Dick Turpin, mask on hat, gun han-
dle, small, 3½" h. 65.00
Dick Turpin, mask on hat, gun han-
dle, large 145.00
Dick Whittington, large, 6" h. 375.00
Drake, small, 3½" h.............. 68.00
Drake, large, 5 5/8" h. 135.00
Farmer John, small, 3½" h. 65.00
Farmer John, "A" mark, small,
3½" h........................... 75.00
Farmer John, large, 6" h. 135.00
Fat Boy, tiny, 1¼" h.............. 95.00
Fat Boy, "A" mark, miniature,
2¼" h........................... 65.00
Field Marshall Smuts, large........1,885.00
Fortune Teller, miniature, 2¼" h.... 350.00
Gone Away, small, 3½" h......... 42.00
Gone Away, large 75.00
Granny, miniature, 2¼" h......... 28.00
Granny, small, 3½" h. 30.00
Granny, large, 6¼" h............ 68.00
Gulliver, large ....525.00 to 600.00
Gunsmith, miniature, 2¼" h........ 35.00
Gunsmith, large................. 75.00
Izaak Walton, spelled "Izaac" on
base, large 77.00
Jarge, "A" mark, small, 3½" h. 168.00
John Barleycorn, "A" mark, minia-
ture, 2¼" h..................... 55.00
John Barleycorn, small, 3½" h..... 65.00
John Barleycorn, large ....100.00 to 135.00
John Peel, "A" mark, miniature,
2¼" h........................... 58.00
John Peel, "A" mark, large, 6" h.... 175.00
Lumberjack, small, 3½" h. 40.00
Lumberjack, large 80.00
Mad Hatter, small, 3½" h. 50.00
Mad Hatter, large 85.00
Mephistopheles, small,
3½" h. ....900.00 to 1,000.00

Mikado, small, 3½" h.	287.00
Mine Host, miniature, 2¼" h.	30.00
Mine Host, small, 3½" h.	40.00
Mine Host, large	75.00
Mr. Micawber, "A" mark, miniature, 2¼" h.	55.00
Mr. Micawber, intermediate size	180.00
Mr. Pickwick, "A" mark, miniature, 2¼" h.	70.00
Mr. Pickwick, small, 3½" h.	70.00

Mr. Pickwick Jug

Mr. Pickwick, "A" mark, large, 6" h. (ILLUS.)	145.00
Night Watchman, large	73.00
Old Charley, small, 3½" h.	35.00
Old King Cole, small, 3½" h.	102.00
Old King Cole, large, 6" h.	240.00
Pied Piper, large	78.00
Robinson Crusoe, miniature, 2¼" h.	35.00
Robinson Crusoe, small, 3½" h.	45.00
Robinson Crusoe, large	75.00
Ronald Reagan, large	395.00
St. George, large	200.00
Sancho Panza, minature, 2¼" h.	33.00
Sancho Panza, small, 3½" h.	50.00
Sancho Panza, large	73.00
Scaramouche, large	625.00
Simon the Cellarer, small, 3½" h.	68.00
Simon the Cellarer, large	130.00
Simple Simon, large, 6" h.	505.00
Smuggler, small, 3½" h.	42.00
Smuggler, large	70.00
Tam O'Shanter, miniature, 2¼" h.	40.00
Tam O'Shanter, small, 3½" h.	50.00
Tony Weller, miniature, 2¼" h.	40.00
Touchstone, large	275.00
Trapper, small, 3½" h.	45.00
Trapper, large	82.00
Veteran Motorist, miniature, 2¼" h.	35.00
Veteran Motorist, large	100.00
Walrus & Carpenter, miniature, 2¼" h.	45.00
Walrus & Carpenter, large	92.00

DICKENSWARE

Ashtray, Bill Sykes, 3 5/8" d.	48.00
Bowl, 7¾" d., 4" h., Dickens characters (three)	145.00
Bust of Sam Weller, red vest, green coat, yellow & black polka dot	

scarf, black hat, 1½ x 2¼", 2½" h.	54.00
Candlestick, bulbous, The Artful Dodger, 7" h.	98.00
Jug, milk, Cap'n Cuttle, 6½" h.	90.00
Mug, two-handled, Cap'n Cuttle, 4¼" h.	148.00
Pitcher, 8" h., square, Alfred Jingle	85.00
Pitcher, 8¾" h., 4 3/8" d., Barnaby Rudge	141.00
Pitcher, square, Old London	195.00
Plate, 6" d., Old Peggoty	40.00
Plate, rack-type, Dickens portrait center	195.00

Mr. Pickwick Tray

Tray, Mr. Pickwick, signed Noke, 7¼ x 9¼" (ILLUS.)	85.00
Vase, 4¾" h., 2" d., Barnaby Rudge	74.00
Vase, 5" h., square, Artful Dodger	82.00
Vase, 7 5/8" h., two-handled, squared flattened shape, Alfred Jingle	145.00
Vase, 7¾" h., 3½" d., two-handled, Mr. Squeers	156.00
Vase, 7¾" h., 5 3/8" d., two-handled, Alfred Jingle	148.00
Vase, 9" h., 3¾" d., two handles on each side, Sam Weller	151.00
Vase, 9½" h., 3" d., two-handled, Alfred Jingle	157.00
Vase, 9½" h., 7¾" d., Cap'n Cuttle	185.00

FIGURINES

Abdullah, HN 2104, yellow chair, orange turban, 1953-62	480.00
A 'Courting, HN 2004, 1947-53	440.00
Adrienne, HN 2152, rose-red dress, 1964-76	125.00
Afternoon Tea, HN 1748, green dress, 1935-49	295.00
Alexandra, HN 2398, 1970-76	185.00
Alice, HN 2158, 1960-80	115.00
All Aboard, HN 2940, blue shirt, tan pants, black boots & cap, 1982-	138.00
Anna, HN 2802, 1976-82	79.00
Antoinette, HN 2326, white dress, 1967-79	135.00

At Ease, HN 2473,
 1973-79 . . . . .170.00 to 200.00

Autumn Breezes

Autumn Breezes, HN 1911, peach
 dress, green jacket, 1939-76
 (ILLUS.) . . . . .145.00 to 155.00
Autumn Breezes, HN 1913, green
 dress, blue jacket,
 1939-71 . . . . .160.00 to 165.00
Autumn Breezes, HN 1934, red
 dress, 1940- . . . . .110.00 to 130.00
Autumn Breezes, HN 2147, white
 dress, black jacket, 1955-71 . . . . . . 270.00
Baby Bunting, HN 2108, 1953-59 . . . . 248.00
Bachelor (The), HN 2319, 1964-75 . . . 250.00
Ballerina, HN 2116, 1953-73 . . . . 260.00
Barbara, HN 1432, multicolored
 dress, 1930-38 . . . . .700.00 to 750.00
Beachcomber, HN 2487, 1973-76 . . . . 147.00
Bess, HN 2002, red cloak, 1947-69 . . 250.00
Biddy, HN 1513, red dress, blue
 shawl, 1932-51 . . . . 155.00
Blithe Morning, HN 2065, red dress,
 1950-73 . . . . 175.00
Bon Appetit, HN 2444, 1972-76 . . . . . 162.00
Buddies, HN 2546, 1973-76 . . . . 150.00
Captain (The), HN 2260, 1965-82 . . . . 170.00
Carpet Seller (The), HN 1464,
 1931-69 . . . . 234.00
Carrie, HN 2800, 1976-81 . . . . .70.00 to 80.00
Cavalier, HN 2716, 1976-82 . . . . 170.00
Celeste, HN 2237, 1959-71 . . . . 200.00
Cellist (The), HN 2226, 1960-67 . . . . . 377.00
Child from Williamsburg, HN 2154,
 blue dress, 1964-83 . . . . 102.00
Chloe, M 9, 1932-45 . . . . . . .250.00 to 350.00
Chloe, M 29, red & cream ruffled
 gown, 1932-45 . . . . 245.00
Chloe, HN 1765, white-blue dress,
 1936-50 . . . . 232.00
Choir Boy, HN 2141,
 1954-75 . . . . .70.00 to 80.00
Clarinda, HN 2724, 1975-80 . . . . 152.00
Clarissa, HN 2345, 1968-81 . . . . 127.00
Coachman (The), HN 2282, 1963-71 . . 375.00
Cobbler (The), HN 1706, green &
 blue striped shirt & hat w/yellow,
 1935-69 . . . . 203.00

Country Lass, HN 1991, 1975-81 . . . . . 112.00
Cup of Tea (The), HN 2322,
 1964-83 . . . . 106.00
Daffy Down Dilly, HN 1712, green
 dress & hat, 1935-75 . . . . 250.00

Damaris

Damaris, HN 2079, 1951-52
 (ILLUS.) 852.00
Darling, HN 1319, black base,
 1929-59 . . . . 105.00
Delight, HN 1772, red dress,
 1936-67 . . . . 157.00
Delphine, HN 2136, 1954-67 . . . . 266.00
Denise, HN 2273, 1964-71 . .250.00 to 260.00
Dimity, HN 2169, 1956-59 . . . . 344.00
Dreamweaver, HN 2283, 1972-76 . . . . 200.00
Easter Day, HN 1976, white dress,
 blue flowers, 1945-51 . . . .400.00 to 425.00
Easter Day, HN 2039, multicolored
 dress, green hat, 1949-69 . . . . 245.00
Elegance, HN 2264, 1961-85 . . . . 125.00
Eliza, HN 2543, 1974-79 . . . . 162.00
Emma, HN 2834, 1977-81 . . . . 78.00
Enchantment, HN 2178, 1957-82 . . . . . 120.00
Ermine Coat (The), HN 1981,
 1945-67 . . . . 205.00
Esmeralda, HN 2168,
 1956-59 . . . . .300.00 to 400.00
Family Album, HN 2321, 1966-73 . . . . 335.00
Farmer's Boy, HN 2520, farmer on
 horse, 1938-60 . . . . .1,450.00
Farmer's Wife (The), HN 2069,
 1951-55 . . . . .350.00 to 400.00
Fat Boy (The), HN 555, blue jacket,
 white scarf, 1923-52 . . . . . .250.00 to 280.00
Fleurette, HN 1587, 1933-49 . . . . 430.00
Flora, HN 2349, 1966-73 . . . . 257.00
Fortune Teller, HN 2159,
 1955-67 . . . . .380.00 to 400.00
Francine, HN 2422, 1972-80 . . . . 70.00
French Peasant, HN 2075, 1951-55 . . 513.00
Friar Tuck, HN 2143, 1954-65 . . . . 400.00
Gay Morning, HN 2135, 1954-67
 (ILLUS. top next page) 220.00
Genevieve, HN 1962, 1941-75 . . . . . . 196.00
Gentleman from Williamsburg,
 HN 2227, green costume, black

shoes, white stockings, black hat,
seated on wooden bench,
1960-83 . . . . 160.00

Gay Morning

Geraldine, HN 2348, 1972-76 . . . . 134.00
Gollywog, HN 2040, blue overalls,
green hat, 1949-59 . . . . 223.00
Good King Wenceslas, HN 2118,
1953-76 . . . . 260.00
Good Morning, HN 2671, 1974-76 . . . 143.00
Grace, HN 2318, green dress,
1966-80 . . . . 114.00
Grandma, HN 2052, 1950-59 . . . . 310.00
Grand Manner, HN 2723,
1975-81 . . . . 175.00 to 200.00
Griselda, HN 1993, 1947-53 . . . . 452.00
Gypsy Dance (A), HN 2230, purple &
white dress, 1959-71 . . . . 235.00

Her Ladyship

Her Ladyship, HN 1977, 1945-59
(ILLUS.) 264.00
Ibrahim, HN 2095, earthenware,
1952-55 . . . . 550.00 to 650.00
Jacqueline, HN 2000, lilac dress,
1947-51 . . . . 400.00 to 500.00
Jill, HN 2061, 1950-71 . . . . 130.00
Kate Hardcastle, HN 1718, pink
dress, green underskirt,
1935-49 . . . . 600.00 to 700.00

Kate Hardcastle, HN 1719, green
dress, pink underskirt,
1935-49 . . . . 475.00 to 500.00
Lady April, HN 1958, red dress,
1940-59 . . . . 275.00 to 300.00
Lady Betty, HN 1967,
1941-51 . . . . 250.00 to 275.00
Lady Fayre, HN 1557, pink dress,
1933-38 . . . . 550.00 to 650.00
Lady Pamela, HN 2718, 1974-80 . . . . . 152.00
Little Child So Rare and Sweet,
HN 1542, nude child sitting on
blue base, brown hair, 1933-49 . . . 500.00
Lorna, HN 2311, green dress, apricot
shawl, 1965-85 . . . . 80.00 to 100.00
Marguerite, HN 1928, pink dress,
1940-59 . . . . 310.00
Marietta, HN 1341, black costume,
red cape, 1929-49 . . . . 750.00 to 850.00
Masquerade, HN 2251, blue-green
overskirt, 1960-65 . . . . 294.00
Mayor (The), HN 2280,
1963-71 . . . . 350.00 to 400.00
Meditation, HN 2330, peach & white
dress, 1971-83 . . . . 190.00
Melanie, HN 2271,
1965-80 . . . . 110.00 to 120.00
Mendicant (The), HN 1365,
1929-69 . . . . 220.00 to 230.00
Millicent, HN 1714, pink shawl,
1935-49 . . . . 1,000.00
Modena, HN 1846, red dress,
1938-49 . . . . 1,200.00 to 1,700.00
Mrs. Bardell, M 86, grey dress,
white collar, 1949-82 . . . . 55.00
Noelle, HN 2179, 1957-67 . . . . 375.00
Olga, HN 2463, 1972-75 . . . . 206.00
Omar Khayyam, HN 2247, 1965-83 . . 135.00
Paisley Shawl, M 4, green dress,
dark green shawl, black bonnet
w/red feather & ribbons, 4" h.,
1932-45 . . . . 195.00
Paisley Shawl, HN 1392, white
dress, red shawl,
1930-49 . . . . 375.00 to 475.00
Pensive Moments, HN 2704, blue
dress, 1975-81 . . . . 185.00
Perfect Pair (The), HN 581,
1923-38 . . . . 900.00
Pied Piper (The), HN 2102, brown
cloak, grey hat & boots, 1953-76 . . 235.00
Pierrette, HN 644, white & black
dress, 1924-38 . . . . 650.00 to 700.00
Premiere, HN 2343, 1969-79 . . . . 135.00
Professor (The), HN 2281, 1965-80 . . . 135.00
Rendezvous, HN 2212, 1962-71 . . . . . . 342.00
Reverie, HN 2306, peach dress,
1964-81 . . . . 225.00
Romance, HN 2430, apricot dress,
1972-79 . . . . 135.00
Roseanna, HN 1926, red dress,
1940-59 . . . . 275.00
Sabbath Morn, HN 1982, red dress,
green-yellow shawl, 1945-59 . . . . . 225.00

Sailor's Holiday, HN 2442, apricot
jacket, 1972-79 . . . . 170.00
St. George, HN 385, dapple grey
horse, blue-green costume,
1920-38 . . . . 308.00
Sam Weller, M 48, orange vest,
black hat & trousers, 1932-82 . . . . . 55.00
Schoolmarm, HN 2223, 1958-80 . . . . . 145.00
Scotties, HN 1281, red dress,
1928-38 . . . . .1,115.00
Seashore, HN 2263,
1961-65 . . . . .195.00 to 215.00
She Loves Me Not, HN 2045,
1949-62 . . . . 152.00
Shore Leave, HN 2254, dark uni-
form, 1965-79 . . . . 180.00
Simone, HN 2378, olive green dress,
1971-81 . . . . 135.00
Soiree, HN 2312, white dress, green
overskirt, 1967-84 . . . . 135.00
Spook (A), HN 50, blue-green robe,
dark green cap, 1916-1938 . . . . . .2,500.00
Spring, HN 2085, shaded blue & red
gown, 1952-59 . . . . 375.00
Spring Flowers, HN 1807, green
skirt, grey-blue overskirt,
1937-59 . . . . 285.00

Spring Morning

Spring Morning, HN 1922, green
coat, 1940-73 (ILLUS.) 195.00
Stephanie, HN 2807, yellow gown,
1977-82 . . . . 140.00
Stiggins, M 50, black suit, 1932-82 . . 55.00
Suitor (The), HN 2132,
1962-71 . . . . .300.00 to 350.00
Summer's Day, HN 2181, 1957-62
(ILLUS. top right) . . . . .275.00 to 325.00
Sunday Best, HN 2206, yellow gown
w/large white & red floral design
in skirt, yellow bonnet w/red rib-
bons & flowers, 1979-84 . . . . 178.00
Susan, HN 2056, blue skirt,
1950-59 . . . . 325.00
Suzette, HN 2026, 1949-59
(ILLUS. bottom right) . . . .250.00 to 300.00
Sweet & Twenty, HN 1298, red &
pink dress, 1928-69 . . . . 224.00

Summer's Day

Sweet Anne, M 27, cream shaded to
blue skirt, red jacket, 1932-45 . . . . 230.00
Sweet Anne, HN 1496, pink & purple
dress & hat, 1932-67 . . . . .150.00 to 200.00
Sweeting, HN 1935, pink dress,
1940-73 . . . . .125.00 to 150.00
Tall Story, HN 2248, 1968-75 . . . . 172.00
To Bed, HN 1805, green shirt &
shorts, 1937-59 . . . . 150.00
Tony Weller, M 47, red vest, yellow
tie w/spots, dark green coat,
1932-82 . . . . 55.00
Top O' the Hill, HN 1833, green
dress, 1937-71 . . . . 185.00
Town Crier, HN 2119, 1953-76 . . . . . . 235.00
Toymaker (The), HN 2250,
1959-73 . . . . .350.00 to 400.00
Treasure Island, HN 2243, 1962-75 . . 135.00
Twilight, HN 2256, 1971-76 . . . . 175.00
Veneta, HN 2722, white dress,
1974-80 . . . . 120.00
Viking (The), HN 2375,
1973-76 . . . . 250.00
Vivienne, HN 2073,
1951-67 . . . . .225.00 to 250.00
Votes For Women, HN 2816,
1978-81 . . . . 170.00

Suzette

MISCELLANEOUS

Royal Doulton Pitcher with Ships

Ashpot, figural bust, Auld Mac 115.00
Ashpot, figural bust, Old Charley . . . 115.00
Ashtray, figural bust, Dick Turpin . . . 125.00
Ashtray, figural bust, Old Charley . . 125.00
Bowl, 7½" d., 3¾" h., pedestal
   foot, Under the Greenwood Tree
   series, scenes of Robin Hood in
   color 116.00
Bowl, Robin Hood series, "Under the
   Greenwood Tree," D3751 . . . . 325.00
Chamber pot, cov., white w/gold
   pinstriping, 9 x 6" 60.00
Charger, African Series, "Lioness,"
   13½" 60.00
Cigarette lighter, table model, Cap-
   tain Ahab 155.00
Cigarette lighter, table model,
   Falstaff 115.00
Cigarette lighter, table model, Long
   John Silver 120.00
Cigarette lighter, table model,
   Poacher 130.00
Coffeepot, Under the Greenwood
   Tree series - "Robin Hood, the
   King of Archers," 3¼" d.,
   8½" h. 209.00
Cracker (or biscuit) jar, cov., im-
   pressed ferns & other plants,
   brown highlighted plants w/gold
   on blue & beige ground, Silicon
   glaze, 5½" d., 7¼" to top of
   finial 275.00
Cup & saucer, demitasse, h.p. flow-
   ers w/brushed gold, ca. 1888 . . . . . 95.00
Cup & saucer, Under the Green-
   wood Tree series, scenes of Robin
   Hood in color, cup 3 3/8" d.,
   2 7/8" h., saucer 5¾" d. 69.00
Cuspidor, browns w/much gold,
   Burslem 225.00
Dinner service for eight, plus four
   serving pieces, Tiara patt. 1,000.00
Egg cup, blue transfer scene of
   "Glamis Thistle" 18.00
Flask w/stopper, "Dewars," Kings-
   ware, "Ben Jonson" 255.00
Flask w/stopper, "Dewars," Kings-
   ware, "Mr. Micawber" 255.00

Flask w/stopper, "Dewars," Kings-
   ware, "Scotsman" 175.00
Humidor, cov., "After the Hunt" 125.00
Loving cup, Morrisian Ware, Art
   Nouveau style 145.00
Match holder, Dutch series, old
   Dutch man & woman on front
   w/crying child at their feet,
   hallmarked silver band around
   base of striker, 4 3/8" d., 3" h. . . . 150.00
Pitcher, cov., 7" h., 3 1/8" d., hot
   water-type, Shakespeare series,
   colored figure of Orlando against
   forest background 191.00
Pitcher, 2 5/8" h., 1½" d., Dutch se-
   ries, Dutch man on front, woman
   on back 64.00
Pitcher, 2¾" h., 1½" d., Welsh La-
   dies series, two Welsh ladies on
   front, blue shading from top 85.00
Pitcher, 4" h., Babes on Beach
   scene, pre-1930 . . . . 58.00
Pitcher, 4½" h., 3½" d., Welsh La-
   dies series 115.00
Pitcher, 4¾" h., Norfolk patt., blue
   & white 40.00
Pitcher, 5" h., bulbous body taper-
   ing to narrow neck w/high arched
   lip, thick strap handle, floral bouquet across body w/turquoise
   jewelling at neck & gold bands
   around neck & on handle 235.00
Pitcher, tankard, 5" h., h.p. scene of
   sailing ships around body w/dark
   green bands at rim & base, ca.
   1900-10 (ILLUS.) 95.00
Pitcher, 6½" h., Oliver Goldsmith
   House, pre-1930 . . . . 98.00
Pitcher, 7" h., gold rim, relief bust
   of Alfred, Lord Tennyson, both
   sides, vellum ground, Burslem
   mark, date 1892 . . . . 255.00
Pitcher, bulbous, 7" h., 6½" w.,
   Pharaoh in white relief masked
   spout, brown Egyptian people at
   various tasks on tan ground,
   Doulton Lambeth impressed
   mark 118.00
Pitcher, 7" h., pinched spout, pin-
   wheel florals & foliage decoration
   on cobalt blue ground 145.00
Pitcher, 7" h., Under the Green-
   wood Tree series, "Robin Hood,
   King of the Archers" 145.00
Pitcher, jug-type, 7½" h., Authors &
   Inns series, "Chaucer at Tabard
   Inn" 130.00
Pitcher, 8¾" h., Old English Coach-
   ing Scenes series, waisted shape,
   "Old Bob" 125.00
Planter, Jackdaw of Rheims series,
   signed "Noke," 5" d. 225.00
Plate, 9" d., souvenir, blue transfer
   scene of Bethlehem,
   Pennsylvania 26.00

Plate, 9" d., Jackdaw of Rheims series, signed "Noke" 110.00

Plate, 9¼" d., Old Moreton series, "Queen Elizabeth at Old Moreton, 1589" 145.00

Plate, 10" d., Coaching Days series, coach outside inn 55.00

Plate, 10" d., Coaching Days series, coach pursued by highwaymen ... 65.00

Plate, 10" d., Fox-Hunt series, "Across the Moor" 55.00

Plate, 10" d., King of Hearts series, "Knave of Hearts," designed by Augustus Jansson 88.00

Plate, 10" d., rack-type, "The Admiral" 55.00

Plate, 10" d., rack-type, "The Cobbler" 40.00

Plate, 10" d., rack-type, "The Doctor" 60.00

Plate, 10" d., rack-type, "The Huntsman" 50.00

Plate, 10" d., rack-type, "The Jester" 50.00

Plate, 10" d., rack-type, "Robert Burns" 50.00

Plate, 10" d., rack-type, "Shakespeare" 60.00

Plates, 10 3/8" d., gilt central crest w/two winged beasts flanking a shield surmounted by a griffin head, w/inscription "WEDDERBURN AQUILA NON CAPTAT MUSCAS" on ivory ground within pale yellow & green borders w/flower-filled urn medallions surrounded by scrolling floral vines, scalloped rim, early 20th c., set of 12 ...... 825.00

Plate 10½" d., American Views series, "Niagara Falls"............... 40.00

Plate, 10½" d., Fairy Tales series, "The Sleep of Rip Van Winkle" ... 50.00

Plate, 10½" d., flow blue, Shakespeare series, "As You Like It" 90.00

Plate, 10½" d., Zulu Warrior 65.00

Teacup & saucer, h.p. flowers decoration, gold & enameled, Burslem, ca. 1902 .... 80.00

Teapot, cov., Stratmore patt....... 60.00

Teapot, cov., Under the Greenwood Tree series, Robin Hood, Little John & Jovial Friar Tuck scene, 4 1/8" d., 6" h. 204.00

Tea set: cov. tea pitcher, creamer, sugar bowl & two cups & saucers; Jackdaw of Rheims series, signed "Noke," 7 pcs. 625.00

Vase, 2½" h., 2 1/8" d., Welsh Ladies series, four ladies sitting & visiting on front, two walking on reverse 89.00

Vase, 3¼" h., 1¾" d., "Isle of Man," man w/cane & village scene 75.00

Vase, 4 x 5", blue & white enameled daisies on stippled gold ground, Slater's patent 125.00

Vase, 4½" h., china, three gold legs, decorated w/pastel flowers, Burslem 120.00

Vase, 5 3/8" h., 2 5/8" d., two-handled, Welsh Ladies series, Welsh lady by fence, two ladies chatting, in color 105.00

Vase, 5½" h., 4 3/8" d., flow blue, Dutch series, Dutch girl sitting on rock scene, gold trim at top 155.00

Vase, 5 5/8" h., 3 5/8" d., flow blue, Babes in Woods series, young girl carrying basket picking flowers, gold trim 180.00

Vase, 5 7/8" h., 4½" d., ovoid body tapering sharply to base & top, two gold-trimmed loop handles at top, flow blue, Babes in Woods series, little girl holding doll & sitting on log w/frog 172.00

Vase, 6" h., "flambe" glaze, desert scene w/camels, people & palm trees, pre-1930 .... 400.00

Vases, 6" h., matte brown w/blue & white inlays, Silicon Art Pottery, pr. 95.00

Vase, 6 3/8" h, 4 3/8" d., ovoid body tapering sharply to short, narrow neck, flow blue, Babes in Woods series, four children playing Blindman's Buff by tree, gold trim 250.00

Vase, 7" h., "flambe" glaze, country scene, artist-signed............. 300.00

Vase, 7" h., 3¾" d., Welsh Ladies series, Welsh ladies & children walking on path to house 171.00

Vase, 7 1/8" h., 3½" d., cylindrical, flow blue, Babes in Woods series, young girl w/basket picking flowers, gold trim 194.00

Chang Ware Vase

Vase, 9¾" h., Chang Ware, waisted cylindrical shape decorated w/an iridescent deep red & blue glaze, the shoulder w/a yellow-ochre thick drip glaze, overall crackling,

decorated by C.J. Noke, ca. 1925
(ILLUS.) 3,630.00
Vase, 10" h., 3¾" w., stoneware,
simple cylinder, bands decorated
w/stylized leaves in green & blue
on brown ground on either side of
a wide cream band incised
w/grazing horses, modeled by
Hannah Barlow, die-stamped
"Doulton-Lambeth - 1878 - Co.,"
incised on reverse, "BHB - RB -
b49" 500.00
Vase, 10" h., bulbous, h.p. huge
peonies, leaves & buds, artist-
signed & dated 1890 . . . . 300.00
Vases, 11" h., white on cobalt blue
glazed panels w/gold scroll
above, cobalt blue & white glazed
necks, pr. 600.00
Vase, 12 3/8" h., 4½" d., stone-
ware, incised circus horses in
black on tan ground, blue leaves
border, signed by Hannah
Barlow 617.00
Vase, 13¼" h., "flambe" glaze, man
fishing in stream, No. 1617 . . . . 280.00
Vase, 14" h., Rembrandt Ware,
ovoid body surmounted by a short
tapered cylindrical neck decorated
in brown tones w/a portrait of
Francis Bacon on one side opposed by a scene of sailing ships
surmounted w/the inscription
"Knowledge is Power," 19th c. 247.50

DRESDEN

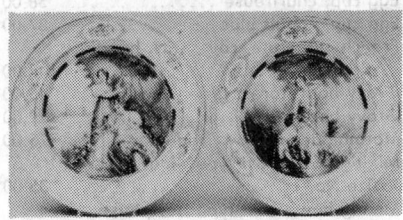

Dresden Cabinet Plates

Dresden-type porcelain evolved from wares made at the nearby Meissen Porcelain Works early in the 18th century. "Dresden" and "Meissen" are often used interchangeably for later wares. "Dresden" has become a generic name for the kind of porcelains produced in Dresden and certain other areas of Germany but perhaps should be confined to the wares made in the city of Dresden.

Cabinet plates, centrally painted
w/diaphanously clad women in a
landscape ruin, enclosed within
gilt banded borders w/floral sprigs
& reserved on a *bleu-celeste*

ground, late 19th c., 13½" d., pr.
(ILLUS.) $1,870.00
Compotes, 4½" h., footed, gilt
beaded banding, floral garlands
entwined within gilt scrolls on
white ground, set of 18 . . . . 467.50
Ewer-vase, flattened oval shape, ornate scrolled openwork handle,
h.p. center scene of two ladies &
cupid in garden, scene continues
on back w/four children playing
blindman's buff, top & bottom maroon w/heavy gold trim, ca.
1890's, 5½" d., 12" h. 807.00
Figure of Colonial girl w/basket of
flowers, 4" h. 75.00
Figure of peasant girl feeding chick-
ens, marked "Carl Thieme, Dres-
den," 4½" 95.00
Figures, Colonial children under
trees encrusted w/flowers,
marked "Kister, Germany," 7" h.,
pr. 225.00
Jardiniere, h.p. continuous panel of
floral swags & clusters in bright
enamels enclosing four large gilt
ram's heads, reserved on a white
ground, late 19th c., 14" d.,
10¼" h. (losses) 247.50
Jardiniere, painted & transfer-
printed w/a central cartouche
scene of a courting couple in a
landscape, within pale yellow
borders, relief floral garlands at
rim highlighted w/gilt, scrolled
feet, late 19th c., 14½" d. 385.00
Loving cup, three-handled, nymph in
woodland scene framed in gold,
5½ x 6½" 450.00
Mirror, easel-type, large porcelain
roses w/leaves & two applied
cupids, ornate, 16" 525.00
Model of a Persian cat, sitting,
white, 8½" h. 275.00
Place card holders, roses, stems &
leaves support card, 5" w., set
of 6 . . . . 125.00
Ramekins, covers & underplates,
h.p. floral decoration, gold trim,
artist-signed, pr. 75.00
Sherbet w/underplate, h.p. scenes
of musicians & lovers, gold
w/green reserves on interior of
each piece, artist-signed, 2 pcs. . . 125.00
Tete-a-tete coffee set: cylindrical
cov. coffeepot, cov. cream jug,
cov. sugar bowl, two cups & saucers & rectangular tray; each piece
painted in colors w/central floral
initials "M.T." within floral garland on a gilt & flowerhead net
pattern ground, blue printed
"Dresden Potschappel" marks,
8 pcs. 770.00

Urn, cov., two panels of lovers in garden scene, red ground w/floral decoration, ca. 1860-1920, 6½ x 12″ 395.00

Urns, baluster-form, coiled double snake handles, octagonal foot, decorated either side w/floral bouquets, molded fluting, reeding & borders accented w/gold, ca. 1900, 17″ h., pr. 550.00

Vase, 9″ h., tapered cylinder, portrait of a dark-haired beauty w/calla lillies in her hair, within gilt-tooled floral spray borders reserved on pale blue ground heightened in gilt w/trellis & foliate scrolls, reverse w/foliate medallion, ca. 1900............. 660.00

FIESTA

Fiesta Carafe

Fiesta dinnerware was made by the Homer Laughlin China Company of Newell, West Virginia, from the 1930's until the early 1970's. The brilliant colors of this inexpensive pottery have attracted numerous collectors. On February 28, 1986, Laughlin reintroduced the popular Fiesta line with minor changes in the shapes of a few pieces and a contemporary color range. The effect of this new production on the Fiesta collecting market is yet to be determined.

Ashtray, cobalt blue $24.00
Ashtray, rose or grey.............. 40.00
Bowl, individual fruit, 4¾″ d., chartreuse...................... 18.00
Bowl, individual fruit, 4¾″ d., ivory......................... 10.00
Bowl, individual fruit, 5½″ d., medium green..................... 29.00
Bowl, 6″ d., chartreuse 30.00
Bowl, 6″ d., grey.................. 34.00
Bowl, individual salad, 7½″ d., medium green 50.00
Bowl, nappy, 8½″ d., chartreuse ... 20.00
Bowl, nappy, 8½″ d., grey 30.00

Bowl, salad, 9½″ d., cobalt blue ... 65.00
Bowl, salad, 9½″ d., turquoise 130.00
Bowl, fruit, 11¾″ d., ivory 97.00
Bowl, fruit, 11¾″ d., red.......... 128.00
Bowl, cream soup, chartreuse 38.00
Bowl, cream soup, cobalt blue...... 18.50
Bowl, cream soup, rose 45.00
Bowl, salad, large, footed, yellow .. 135.00
Candleholders, bulb-type, cobalt blue, pr. 30.00
Candleholders, tripod-type, cobalt blue, pr. 95.00
Carafe, cov., cobalt blue 60.00
Carafe, cov., turquoise 88.00
Carafe, cov., yellow (ILLUS.) 80.00
Casserole, cov., two-handled, ivory, 10″ d....................... 56.00
Casserole, cov., two-handled, rose, 10″ d....................... 138.00
Coffeepot, cov., demitasse, stick handle, ivory 149.00
Coffeepot, cov., demitasse, stick handle, yellow 110.00
Coffeepot, cov., cobalt blue 85.00
Coffeepot, cov., grey 170.00
Compote, 12″ d., low, footed, light green 48.00
Compote, sweetmeat, high stand, cobalt blue 65.00
Creamer, light green 8.00
Creamer, red 16.00
Creamer, individual size, yellow 35.00
Creamer, stick handle, rose 13.00
Cup & saucer, demitasse, stick handle, chartreuse................. 110.00
Cup & saucer, ring handle, cobalt blue 20.00
Egg cup, chartreuse 58.00
Egg cup, cobalt blue.............. 37.00
French casserole, cov., stick handle, chartreuse..................... 142.00
Gravy boat, forest green 45.00
Gravy boat, red.................. 29.00
Marmalade jar, cov., red 75.00
Mixing bowl, nest-type, light green, size No. 1 .... 35.00
Mixing bowl, nest-type, turquoise, size No. 4 .... 30.00
Mixing bowl, nest-type, red, size No. 7 .... 120.00
Mug, forest green 48.00
Mug, medium green 58.00
Mustard jar, cov., light green 65.00
Mustard jar, cov., turquoise 85.00
Onion soup bowl, cov., yellow 160.00
Pie server, light green (Kitchen Kraft) 60.00
Pitcher, jug-type, chartreuse, 2 pt. ... 44.00
Pitcher, jug-type, forest green, 2 pt. 50.00
Pitcher, juice, disc-type, cobalt blue, 30 oz....................... 100.00
Pitcher, juice, disc-type, red, 30 oz....................... 150.00

Pitcher, juice, disc-type, yellow,
  30 oz. 24.00
Pitcher, water, disc-type, grey 125.00
Pitcher, water, disc-type, red 55.00
Pitcher, water, disc-type, yellow 40.00
Pitcher w/ice lip, globular, cobalt
  blue, 2 qt. 63.00
Pitcher w/ice lip, globular, yellow,
  2 qt. 54.00
Plate, 6" d., chartreuse 4.00
Plate, 6" d., grey 4.50
Plate, 7" d., light green or yellow,
  each 4.00
Plate, 7" d., medium green 22.00
Plate, 7" d., rose 14.00
Plate, 9" d., chartreuse 18.00
Plate, 9" d., forest green 15.00
Plate, 9" d., medium green 35.00
Plate, 9" d., red 15.00
Plate, 10" d., grey 38.00
Plate, 10" d., ivory 9.00
Plate, 10" d., yellow 8.00
Plate, grill, 10½" d., cobalt blue ... 15.00
Plate, grill, 11½" d., ivory 32.00
Plate, grill, 11½" d., red 35.00
Plate, chop, 13" d., cobalt blue 20.00
Plate, chop, 13" d., ivory 17.00
Plate, chop, 13" d., red 27.00
Relish tray w/five inserts, ivory 85.00
Salt & pepper shakers, ivory, pr. ... 10.00
Salt & pepper shakers, light green,
  pr. 12.00
Salt & pepper shakers, yellow, pr. ... 10.00
Soup plate w/flange rim, forest
  green, 8" d. 27.00
Soup plate w/flange rim, rose,
  8" d. 35.00
Spoon, red, (Kitchen Kraft w/origi-
  nal label) 50.00
Sugar bowl, cov., individual size,
  yellow 25.00
Sugar bowl, cov., grey 35.00
Sugar bowl, cov., light green 15.00

Fiesta Sugar Bowl

Sugar bowl, cov., turquoise
  (ILLUS.). 25.00
Syrup pitcher w/original lid, cobalt
  blue 147.00
Syrup pitcher w/original lid,
  yellow 138.00
Teapot, cov., cobalt blue, medium
  size (6 cup) 80.00

Teapot, cov., red, medium size
  (6 cup) 75.00
Teapot, cov., cobalt blue, large size
  (8 cup) 90.00
Tray, Figure 8, cobalt blue 27.00
Tray, Figure 8, turquoise 70.00
Tumbler, juice, light green, 5 oz. ... 13.50
Tumbler, juice, rose, 5 oz. 36.00
Tumbler, water, cobalt blue,
  10 oz. 32.00
Tumbler, water, yellow, 10 oz. 25.00
Utility tray, yellow 28.00
Vase, bud, 6½" h., cobalt blue 32.00
Vase, bud, 6½" h., light green 19.00
Vase, 8" h., light green 195.00
Vase, 8" h., yellow 210.00
Vase, 10" h., turquoise 340.00
Vase, 12" h., light green 345.00

FLOW BLUE

Flowing Blue wares, usually shortened to Flow Blue, were made at numerous potteries in Staffordshire, England and elsewhere. They are decorated with a blue that smudged lightly or ran in the firing. The same type of color flow is also found in certain wares decorated in green, purple and sepia. Patterns were given specific names, which accompany the listings here.

ABBEY (George Jones & Sons, ca. 1900)
Bowl, 8" d. $100.00
Cup 27.00
Plate, 7" d. 15.00
Plate, 10" d. 35.00

ALASKA (W. H. Grindley, ca. 1891)
Gravy boat 50.00
Pickle dish 20.00
Pitcher, 6¾" h. 145.00
Platter, 14" l. ....70.00 to 85.00
Platter, 16" l. 100.00
Vegetable bowl, open, 9" 35.00

ALTON (W. H. Grindley, ca. 1891)
Gravy boat 125.00
Plate, 6½" d. 25.00
Platter, 16" l. 172.50

AMOY (Davenport, dated 1844)
Creamer 225.00
Cup & saucer, handleless 85.00
Gravy boat 260.00
Plate, 7¼" d. 45.00
Plate, 8¼" d. 50.00
Plate, 9" d. ....55.00 to 75.00
Platter, 14½" l. 275.00
Platter, 12 x 16" 385.00
Sauce dish, 5" d. 60.00
Saucer 40.00
Vegetable bowl, open,
  6 x 8" ....160.00 to 180.00

ARGYLE (Ford & Sons, ca. 1895)
Gravy boat 57.50
Plate, 9" d. 45.00
Vegetable tureen, cov. 145.00

ARGYLE (W. H. Grindley, ca. 1896)

Argyle Platter

Bone dish 45.00
Butter pat 30.00
Creamer 120.00
Creamer & sugar bowl, pr. (no lid).. 195.00
Platter, 15" l. (ILLUS.) 175.00
Vegetable bowl, cov. (finial reset) .. 120.00

ASHBURTON (W. H. Grindley, ca. 1891)
Butter dish, cover & drain insert,
    3 pcs. 195.00
Gravy boat & underplate........... 125.00
Soup tureen, cov. (professional re-
    pair to finial) 195.00
Vegetable bowl, cov., oval, 9" l 75.00

BENTICK (Cauldon, ca. 1905)

Bentick Dinner Plate

Butter dish, cov. 150.00
Plate, 6" d. 20.00
Plate, 8" d. 35.00
Plate, 10" d. (ILLUS.) 45.00
Platter, 12½" l. 100.00
Platter, 15" l. 130.00
Sauce dish, 6" d. 20.00
Sauce tureen, oval 35.00
Vegetable bowl, cov., oblong 145.00
Vegetable bowl, open, oval ..45.00 to 55.00

BLUE DANUBE, THE (Johnson Bros., ca. 1900)
Bone dish 50.00

Butter pat 25.00
Plate, 6¼" d. 25.00
Platter, 13 x 18" 150.00

BRAMPTON (Ford & Sons, ca. 1900)
Plate, 7" d. 15.00
Plate, 10" d. 20.00
Vegetable bowl, cov. 125.00

BROOKLYN (Johnson Bros., ca. 1900)
Butter pat 16.00
Creamer, large 80.00
Cup & saucer 45.00
Platter, 7 x 10¾" 45.00
Vegetable bowl, open,
    6¾ x 10½" 50.00

CARLTON (Samuel Alcock, 1850)
Plate, 8½" to 9½" d. 60.00
Plate, 10½" d. 85.00
Soup plate w/flange rim, 10½" d. .. 75.00

CASHMERE (Ridgway & Morley, G. L. Ashworth, et al., 1840's on)

Cashmere Soup Plate

Creamer 275.00
Cup & saucer 125.00
Pitcher, 7" h., octagonal, gold band
    at rim 335.00
Soup plate w/flange rim, 9¼" d.
    (ILLUS.)...................... 90.00
Vegetable bowl, cov. 795.00

CHAPOO (John Wedge Wood, ca. 1850)
Cup & saucer 100.00
Plate, 6¼" d. 85.00
Platter, 10½ x 14" 220.00
Sauce dish........................ 32.00

CHEN-SI (John Meir, ca. 1835)
Plate, 8½" d. 80.00
Platter, 14 x 17" 235.00
Waste bowl ....120.00 to 135.00

CHISWICK (Ridgways, ca. 1900)
Cup & saucer 45.00
Platter, 12" l. 55.00
Platter, 16" l. 85.00
Soup plate w/flange rim 30.00

CLAREMONT (Johnson Bros., ca. 1891)
Plate, 8½" d. 40.00
Sugar bowl, cov. 145.00
Waste bowl 70.00

COLONIAL (J. & G. Meakin, ca. 1891)
Butter dish, cover & drain insert 110.00
Pitcher, 6" h. 135.00
Soup tureen 325.00

CONWAY (New Wharf Pottery, ca. 1891)
Bowl, 9" d., shallow 42.00
Butter pat 32.00
Plate, 6" d. 25.00
Vegetable bowl, cov., 9" d. 130.00

DAVENPORT (Wood & Sons, ca. 1907)
Knife rest 135.00
Plate, 8" d. 32.00
Soup plate w/flange rim,
    9" d. . . . . .20.00 to 25.00
Vegetable bowl, cov. 125.00

DUCHESS (W. H. Grindley, ca. 1891)
Bone dish 37.50
Cup & saucer 40.00
Plate, 7" d. 25.00
Plate, 8¾" d. 35.00
Soup plate w/flange rim, 9" d. 45.00
Vegetable dish, individual size, 5¾"
    oval 25.00

FAIRY VILLAS - 3 styles (W. Adams, ca. 1891)
Cup & saucer 50.00
Plate, 7" d. 20.00
Plate, 9" d. 42.50
Soup plate w/flange rim, 9" d. 40.00
Vegetable bowl, cov., rectangular,
    9½ x 12½", 6½" h. 195.00

FLORIDA (W. H. Grindley, ca. 1891)
Butter pat 25.00
Relish dish, 9¼" 80.00
Vegetable tureen 130.00

FLORIDA (Johnson Bros., ca. 1900)
Gravy boat 60.00
Plate, 10" d. 50.00
Vegetable bowl, open, oval, 10" l. . .   40.00

GEISHA (Upper Hanley Potteries Ltd., ca. 1901)
Cake plate 90.00
Cup & saucer 120.00
Plate, 7" d. 40.00

GIRONDE (W. H. Grindley, ca. 1891)
Butter dish, cov. 125.00
Cup & saucer 55.00
Plate, 9" d. 40.00
Plate, dinner, 10" d. 55.00
Soup plate w/flange rim, 9" d. 55.00

GLENWOOD (Johnson Bros., ca. 1900)

Glenwood Dinner Plate

Dinner service for four, 8" & 10" d.
    plates, soup plates, butter pats,
    cups & saucers, 24 pcs. (ILLUS. of
    10" d. plate) 600.00

GOTHIC (Jacob Furnival, ca. 1850)
Plate, 8¼" d. 80.00
Soup plate w/flange rim 65.00
Teapot, cov., bulbous, 7" h. plus
    finial 525.00
Vegetable bowl, open 95.00

HONC (Petrus Regout, ca. 1858)
Creamer 145.00
Plate, 8" d. 75.00
Plate, 9" d. 67.50

IDRIS (W. H. Grindley, ca. 1910)
Bone dish 50.00
Bouillon cup & underplate, two-
    handled 45.00
Vegetable tureen, open 110.00

INDIAN JAR (Jacob & Thos. Furnival, ca. 1843)
Plate, 10½" d.   115.00
Platter, 9¾ x 12 3/8" 285.00
Sauce dish 50.00

JENNY LIND (Arthur Wilkinson Ltd., Royal Staffordshire Pottery, ca. 1895)
Fruit bowl, 7½" d., 3" h. 125.00
Vegetable bowl, 7½" 175.00

KENWORTH (Johnson Bros., ca. 1900)
Butter dish, cov. 150.00
Gravy boat w/attached
    underplate 75.00
Plate, 10" d. 48.00
Platter, 9½ x 12" 75.00

KESWICK (Wood & Sons, ca. 1891)
Bowl, 9½ x 12", shallow 40.00
Platter, 12" l. 75.00
Vegetable bowl, 9 x 12" 65.00

KNOX (New Wharf Potteries, ca. 1891)
Plate, 9" d. 48.00

Soup plate w/flange rim, 9"....... 45.00
Waste bowl, 6" d., 3½" h. 75.00

KYBER (John Meir & Son, ca. 1870; W. Adams & Son, ca. 1891)
Plate, 9" d.................50.00 to 65.00
Plate, 10¼" d. 80.00
Toothbrush holder................ 335.00

LA FRANCAIS (French China Co., ca. 1890)
Bowl, cereal 18.00
Butter pat 6.00
Dinner service, four each 7" & 9" d.
  plates, sauce dishes, butter pats &
  cups & saucers plus a serving
  platter, 25 pcs.................. 375.00
Gravy boat 45.00

LANCASTER (New Wharf Pottery, ca. 1891)
Cup & saucer 56.00
Plate, 9" d. 50.00
Platter, rectangular, 16½" l. 90.00
Saucer 15.00
Soup plate w/flange rim, 9" d. 45.00

LEICESTER (Burgess & Leigh, ca. 1910)
Gravy boat 45.00
Plate, 9" d. 130.00
Vegetable dish, cov., 12½" l.,
  8" w. 130.00

LINDA (John Maddock & Sons, Ltd., ca. 1896)
Butter dish, cov. 75.00
Plate, bread & butter 20.00
Soup tureen, cov. 125.00

LONSDALE (Ridgways, ca. 1910)

Lonsdale Plate

Gravy boat w/underplate 110.00
Plate, 7" d. 30.00
Plate, 10" d. (ILLUS.) 60.00
Platter, 7¼ x 9" 70.00
Platter, 14 x 17" 250.00

LORNE (W. H. Grindley, ca. 1900)
Bone dish 45.00
Butter pat 28.00
Vegetable bowl, oval 65.00

LUGANO (Ridgways, ca. 1910)
Plate, 6" d. 40.00
Plate, 9" d. 55.00
Saucer 16.00

LUSTRE BAND (Elsmore and Forster, ca. 1860, brush-painted)
Cookie plate..................... 90.00
Cup & saucer 50.00
Teapot, cov. 250.00

MADRAS (Doulton & Co., ca. 1900)
Bouillon cup w/underplate 75.00
Plate, dessert.................... 20.00
Plate, dinner.................... 65.00
Plate, luncheon 45.00
Soup plate w/flange rim, 10" d. 48.00
Vegetable bowl, open 55.00

MANHATTAN (Henry Alcock, ca. 1900)

Manhattan Creamer

Creamer (ILLUS.) 110.00
Cup & saucer 55.00
Dinner service, two dinner plates,
  six luncheon plates, six large
  bowls, eight small bowls, six cups
  & saucers, cov. teapot, cov. sugar
  & creamer, 37 pcs. 325.00
Plate, 7½" d. 25.00
Soup plate w/flange rim, 9" d. 48.00
Teapot, cov. 285.00
Vegetable bowl, cov. 185.00

MANILLA (Podmore, Walker & Co., ca. 1845)
Plate, 9" d. 90.00
Plate, 10" d. 100.00
Platter, 16" 395.00
Vegetable bowl, cov., octagonal 450.00

MARECHAL NIEL (W. H. Grindley, ca. 1895)
Bone dish 25.00
Gravy boat 85.00
Platter, 14" 105.00
Platter, 18" 145.00
Toothbrush holder, cov., oval,
  8½" 35.00

MARGUERITE (W. H. Grindley, ca. 1891)
Butter pat 20.00

Sauce tureen, cover & underplate... 175.00
Soup plate w/flange rim 30.00

MARIE (W. H. Grindley, ca. 1891)
Pitcher, 6½" h. 75.00
Platter, 17½" 160.00
Sauce dish....................... 18.00
Soup plate w/flange rim, 7½" d. .. 45.00
Vegetable bowl, open, 9½" oval ... 55.00

NON PAREIL (Burgess & Leigh, ca. 1891)
Butter pat 30.00
Creamer 120.00
Plate, 7½" d...................... 35.00
Plate, 9" d. 55.00
Sauce dish....................... 22.00
Soup plate w/flange rim 75.00
Vegetable bowl, cov., 9½" oval 145.00
Vegetable tureen, cov., 12" l. 345.00

NORMANDY (Johnson Bros., ca. 1900)
Bone dish 45.00
Plate, 10" d...................... 65.00
Platter, 8" 85.00
Sauce dish, 5¼" 30.00
Vegetable dish, cov., oval 225.00

OREGON (T.J. & J. Mayer, ca. 1845)

Oregon Cup Plate

Cup plate, 4" d. (ILLUS.) 120.00
Plate, 10" d. 100.00
Platter, small, octagonal 150.00
Platter, 13½" 250.00
Sauce dish, 5" d.................. 58.00
Soup bowl w/flange rim, 9½" d. ... 100.00
Sugar bowl, cov.................. 225.00

ORIENTAL (Ridgways, ca. 1891)
Butter dish, cov., pattern on insert.. 145.00
Cup & saucer 40.00
Plate, 9" d....................... 42.00
Teapot, cov...................... 265.00
Vegetable bowl, cov.............. 135.00
Vegetable bowl, open, 9½" d. 90.00

OXFORD (Johnson Bros., ca. 1900)
Bowl, berry, 5" d................. 20.00
Bowl, oval 40.00
Creamer & cov. sugar bowl, pr. 145.00
Plate, 6¼" d..................... 24.00

Plate, 7" d. 28.00
Plate, 8¾" d. 45.00
Platter, 14" 100.00
Sauce dish....................... 20.00

PEACH (Johnson Bros., ca. 1891)
Plate, 8" d. 25.00
Plate, 9" d....................... 30.00
Soup plate w/flange rim 35.00
Vegetable bowl, cov., 6 x 8" oval... 50.00

POPPY (W. H. Grindley, ca. 1891)
Gravy boat 85.00
Plate, 10" d. 30.00
Soup plate w/flange rim, 9" d. 35.00

RALEIGH (Burgess & Leigh, ca. 1906)
Bowl, berry...................... 20.00
Butter dish, cover & drain insert 135.00
Cup & saucer, large 40.00
Gravy boat 60.00
Plate, 7" d. 22.00
Plate, 9" d. 35.00
Platter, 14" 125.00
Vegetable bowl, cov.............. 195.00

RICHMOND (Johnson Bros., ca. 1900)
Butter dish, cov. 95.00
Creamer 75.00
Cup & saucer 45.00
Gravy boat w/underplate 85.00
Plate, 7" d....................... 35.00
Plate, 8" d. 38.00
Plate, 9" d. 45.00
Plate, 10" d. 55.00
Platter, 9½ x 13" 75.00
Platter, 10½ x 14½" 95.00
Sauce dish....................... 20.00
Soup plate w/flange rim 40.00
Vegetable bowl, cov............... 225.00

ROSE (Ridgways, ca. 1910)
Creamer, 5¼" h.................. 90.00
Gravy boat w/underplate 120.00
Sauce dish....................... 20.00
Soup plate w/flange rim, 9" d. 20.00

SABRAON (Maker unknown, probably English, ca. 1845)
Gravy boat 150.00
Plate, 9" d. 90.00
Soup plate w/flange rim, 9" d. 95.00

SCINDE (J. & G. Alcock, ca. 1840 and Thomas Walker, ca. 1847)
Cup & saucer 120.00
Cup plate 85.00
Pitcher, 10" h. 750.00
Pitcher, water, 12½" h............ 850.00
Plate, 6½" d. 30.00
Plate, 7" d. 55.00
Plate, 10½" d. 110.00
Platter, 12½ x 16" 465.00
Platter, 15½" 275.00

Sauce dish, 5 1/8" d. 60.00
Soup plate w/flange rim, 10½" d. . . 92.00
Sugar bowl, cov. 345.00

Scinde Vegetable Bowl

Vegetable bowl, open, 6 x 8"
  oblong (ILLUS.) 180.00
Vegetable bowl, cov. w/rose finial
  (repaired) 385.00

STELLA (Bovey, ca. 1905)
Gravy boat 45.00
Platter 45.00
Soup plate w/flange rim 20.00
Vegetable bowl, open, oval 25.00

STERLING (Johnson Bros., ca. 1910)
Plate, 10" d. 25.00
Posset cup. 60.00
Vegetable bowl, cov., 9". 125.00

TEMPLE, THE (Podmore Walker & Co., ca. 1850)
Pitcher, 8" h. 295.00
Plate, 9" d. . . . . .75.00 to 95.00
Plate, 10" d. 110.00
Platter, 12½" l. 295.00
Sauce dish. 40.00
Sugar bowl, cov., 8" h. 250.00
Teapot, cov. 450.00
Vegetable tureen, cov. 450.00
Waste bowl. 175.00

TOGO (F. Winkle, ca. 1900)
Creamer, 5" 85.00
Pitcher, 7" h. 170.00
Platter, 12" l. 60.00
Soup plate w/flange rim 25.00
Sugar bowl, cov. 105.00

TONQUIN (W. Adams & Son, ca. 1845)
Plate, 7½" d. 60.00
Plate, 9½" d. 80.00
Plate, 10¼" d. 95.00
Wash bowl & pitcher 900.00

TOURAINE (Henry Alcock, ca. 1898 and Stanley Pottery, ca. 1898)
Butter dish, cov. 275.00
Butter pat 25.00
Creamer, 4½" h. 140.00
Cup & saucer . . . . .60.00 to 70.00
Pitcher, milk 100.00

Plate, 8" d. 50.00
Plate, 9" d. 55.00
Platter, 7 x 10½" 60.00
Vegetable bowl, cov., 9" oval 200.00
Vegetable bowl, cov., 10". 215.00
Vegetable bowl, open, 9½" oval . . . 90.00

TULIP (Johnson Bros., ca. 1900)
Bone dish 45.00
Creamer 75.00
Pitcher, 6" h. 225.00
Pitcher, 8" h. 235.00
Sauce tureen, cover, underplate &
  ladle, 4 pcs. 185.00

VERMONT (Burgess & Leigh, ca. 1895)
Soup bowl w/flange rim, 9" d. 45.00
Ladle 85.00
Plate, 7" d. 22.00
Plate, 10" d. 48.00
Plate, 10½" d. 65.00
Vegetable bowl, cov. (small chip). . . 150.00

WALDORF (New Wharf Pottery, ca. 1892)

Waldorf Vegetable Bowl

Plate, 9" d. 50.00
Platter, 10¾" 55.00
Platter, 12" 105.00
Platter, 18" 300.00
Sauce dish 20.00
Soup plate w/flange rim, 9" d. 25.00
Vegetable bowl, open, 9" oval
  (ILLUS.). 65.00

WATTEAU (Doulton & Co., ca. 1900)
Bowl, cereal, 6". 20.00
Cup, two-handled 55.00
Dish w/handle, 5½" d. 30.00
Pitcher, 7½" h. 175.00
Pitcher, 9" h. 195.00
Plate, 8" d. 38.00
Plate, 8½" d. 45.00
Platter, 8¼ x 10¼" 95.00
Platter, 14 x 17" . . . . .225.00 to 250.00
Serving dish, two-handled, 7¼" d. . . 40.00
Soup plate w/flange rim, 7½" d. . . . 25.00
Soup plate w/flange rim, 8½" d. . . . 35.00
Soup plate w/flange rim, 9½"d 75.00
Soup tureen w/underplate, large . . . 550.00
Tray, serpentine-shaped,
  5½ x 12½" 275.00
Vase, 10½" h. 595.00

Vegetable bowl, open, 12½" d. 125.00
Wall plaque, 14½" d 250.00
Wash bowl & pitcher 650.00

WILLOW (Doulton & Co., ca. 1891)
Bowl, 7¾" d., 3½" h. 50.00
Cup 20.00
Cup & saucer, mush or "farmer's" . . 75.00
Plate, 7½" d. 20.00
Waste bowl 55.00

(End of Flow Blue Section)

FRANCISCAN WARE

A product of the Gladding, McBean & Company of Glendale and Los Angeles, California, Franciscan Ware was one of a number of lines produced by that firm over its long history. Introduced in 1934 as a pottery dinnerware, Franciscan Ware was produced in many patterns including "Desert Rose," introduced in 1941 and reportedly the most popular dinnerware pattern ever made in this country. Beginning in 1942 some vitrified china patterns were produced under the Franciscan name also.

After a merger in 1963 the company name was changed to Interpace Corporation and in 1979 Josiah Wedgwood & Sons purchased the Gladding, McBean & Co. plant from Interpace. Production ceased in 1984.

Bank, model of a pig, Desert Rose
  patt. $45.00
Bowl, fruit or cereal, October
  patt. 9.00
Butter dish, cov., Ivy patt., ca.
  1948 . . . . 25.00
Chocolate set: cov. chocolate pot &
  6 cups & saucers; Coronado Ware,
  ivory & maroon, ca. 1930's,
  13 pcs. 85.00
Compote, open, Apple patt., ca.
  1940 . . . . 30.00
Creamer & cov. sugar bowl, Apple
  patt., ca. 1940, pr. 35.00
Cup & saucer, Apple patt., ca.
  1940 . . . . 11.00
Cup & saucer, El Patio Ware, ca.
  1930's 11.50
Cup & saucer, California Poppy
  patt., ca. 1950 . . . . 12.50
Dinner service for six, Apple patt.,
  ca. 1940, 36 pcs. 275.00
Dinner service for eight: dinner
  plates, 6" d. plates, nappies,
  cups & saucers, 14" platter &
  10" vegetable bowl; Desert
  Rose patt., 42 pcs. 195.00
Gravy boat, Apple patt., ca. 1940 . . . 25.00
Gravy boat, Ivy patt., ca. 1948 . . . . . 25.00
Pitcher, milk, Ivy patt., ca. 1948 . . . . 22.50

Pitcher, water, Ivy patt., large 43.00
Plate, 6" d., Apple patt., ca. 1940 . . 6.00
Plate, 9½" d., Apple patt., ca.
  1940 . . . . 8.00
Plate, 10" d., Desert Rose patt. 9.50
Plate, 10" d., El Patio Ware, grey . . . 10.00
Plate, 10½" d., Apple patt., ca.
  1940 . . . . 14.00
Platter, 12", Desert Rose patt. 19.50
Platter, 14", Desert Rose patt. 27.50
Platter, 14", Fruit patt. 27.50
Platter, 14", Ivy patt., ca. 1948 . . . . . 27.50
Platter, Apple patt., ca. 1940,
  medium 25.00
Relish dish, leaf-shaped, Coronado
  Ware, coral satin, ca. 1930's 20.00
Teapot, cov., Apple patt., ca. 1940 . . 36.00
Teapot, cov., Coronado Ware, coral
  gloss, ca. 1930's 32.00
Teapot, cov., Coronado Ware, coral
  satin, ca. 1930's 35.00
Tumbler, water, Apple patt., ca.
  1940 . . . . 12.00
Vegetable bowl, Fruit patt., large . . 19.50

FRANKOMA POTTERY

John Frank began producing and selling pottery on a part-time basis during the summer of 1933 while he was still teaching art and pottery classes at the University of Oklahoma. In 1934, Frankoma Pottery became an incorporated business that was successful enough to allow him to leave his teaching position in 1936 to devote full-time to its growth. The pottery was moved to Sapulpa, Oklahoma in 1938 and a full range of art pottery and dinnerwares were eventually offered. Since John Frank's death in 1973, the pottery has been directed by his daughter, Joniece. The early wares and limited editions are becoming increasingly popular with collectors today.

Ashtray, Texas-shaped, green
  glaze $15.00
Book ends, figural seated woman
  w/long hair over face, green &
  brown glaze, pr. 120.00
Bottle-vase, 1973, flame, white in-
  terior, black base, signed "Grace
  Lee Frank," 13" h. 30.00
Bottle-vase, 1977, black & white,
  13" h. 45.00
Breakfast set: barrel shaped pitcher,
  four mugs, creamer, sugar bowl,
  honey jar & tray; bronze & green
  glaze, 9 pcs. 75.00
Casserole, cov., Wagon Wheel patt.,
  tan glaze 15.00
Christmas card, 1952, pitcher-form . . 65.00
Christmas card, 1969, "Moon with
  Moon Capsule," 3" d. 32.00

Dish, four-leaf clover shape, turquoise, 6" d.................... 12.00

Figure, "Fan Dancer," green &
bronze glaze, 13½" l., 8½" h..... 125.00

Figure, "Harlem Hoofer," semi-nude
black dancer, 13" h............. 200.00

Figure of Indian Chief, "Dancing
Warrior," flame glaze, 8" h...... 20.00

Model of a panther, black glaze,
No. 114 .... 45.00

Model of a swan w/open tail, brown
glaze, No. 229, 9" l............. 20.00

Mug, 1969 (Republican) elephant,
"Nixon-Agnew," flame red
glaze 40.00

Planter, Wagon Wheel patt., Prairie
Green glaze, two openings, incised mark, 6½"............... 25.00

Plaque, pierced to hang, portrait of
Will Rogers 125.00

Plate, 7" d., 1972, limited edition,
Teenagers of the Bible series,
"Jesus the Carpenter" 8.00

Plate, 8½" d., 1972, Bicentennial
series, "Provocations," signed
"John Frank" 125.00

Plate, 8½" d., 1973, Bicentennial
series, "Patriots - Leaders"....... 90.00

Plate, 8½" d., Oklahoma Diamond
Jubilee, 1907-82............... 35.00

Vase, 6" h., bulbous, two-handled,
solid slate blue semi-gloss glaze,
No. 27 .... 35.00

Vase, 9" h., bottle-shaped, blended
peacock blue glaze, 1934-42...... 25.00

Wall mask, Indian Chief, Ada clay .. 35.00

Wall masks, "Tragedy" & "Comedy,"
pr........................... 95.00

FULPER

Fulper Centerpiece Bowl

The Fulper Pottery was founded in
Flemington, N.J., in 1805 and operated until
1935, although operations were curtailed in
1929 when its main plant was destroyed by
fire. The name was changed in 1929 to Stangl

Pottery, which continued in operation until
July of 1978, when Pfaltzgraff, a division of
Susquehanna Broadcasting Company of
York, Pennsylvania, purchased the assets of
the Stangl Pottery, including the name.

Bowl, 5" d., green & black streaked
glaze $40.00

Bowl, 9" d., 2" h., rolled rim, blue &
green glossy glaze, vertical
mark......................... 60.00

Bucket w/bail handle, green &
brown glossy glaze, 5" h......... 65.00

Candleholder, turned-up handle, Lily
Pad patt., light & dark brown
glaze 45.00

Candlesticks, flat w/three low handles, turquoise w/crystalline
glaze, 6" d., 1½" h., pr.......... 135.00

Centerpiece bowl on pedestal base,
squat urn shape centered by three
applied scroll feet on platform
base, hammered olive green on
paler green glaze, ca. 1915, minor
bubble bursts, 10½" h.
(ILLUS.) 1,760.00

Cornucopia-vase, mottled blue drip
over speckled brown glaze,
8" h.......................... 70.00

Doorstop, model of a bulldog puppy,
mustard & brown glaze, Vasecraft
label 1,200.00

Jug w/stopper, three-sided, green
crystalline glaze, w/built-in music
box, plays "How Dry I Am,"
10" h......................... 85.00

Fulper Table Lamp

Lamp, table-type, small conical shade
w/vertical pink glass panels, swollen cylindrical standard flaring
towards foot, shaded celery green
& slate grey drip glaze, stamped
"Fulper No. 301," 9½" d. shade,
16" h. (ILLUS.) 2,420.00

Model of a frog ready to leap,
matte green on high gloss glaze,
2¾ x 5½"..................... 45.00

Mug, green crystalline glaze w/embossed "B," unusual shape,
4" h. 85.00

Perfume lamp, figural ballerina, orange dress w/black
hair.....................250.00 to 350.00

Powder jar, cov., figural lady w/purple hat holding a fan in
crossed arms cover, 6½" h. 155.00

Vase, 3¾" h., five graduating concentric rings form body, blue crystalline glaze 60.00

Vase, 6¾" h., ovoid, three strap handles, sky blue "flambe" glaze
w/blue crystalline highlights 385.00

Vase, 7" h., three-handled, slate blue glossy glaze w/green streaks, darker blue cascading
crystals 165.00

Vase, 8" h., 4" d., bottle-shaped, embossed snake wrapped around cylindrical neck, olive green to Chinese blue mirrored flambe'
glaze 1,045.00

Vase, 9 x 8¾", long collared neck, rolled rim, two applied wishbone handles, deep green matte crystalline glaze over "hammered" surface, embossed oval mark 275.00

Vase, 11¼" h., modified trumpet form, body w/raised & indented tapering columns, decorated in green, blue & brownish hues,
stamped "Fulper" 1,045.00

Vase, 12" h., 5" d., buttressed cylindrical form, midnight blue flambe' bleeding through a *cafe au lait* semi-gloss glaze, original factory label, "Panama Exhibition" 1,540.00

Wall pocket, pipes of Pan embossed decoration, matte green glaze.... 185.00

Wash bowl & pitcher, hand-thrown, horizontal ribbing, mottled brown glaze, the set 180.00

GALLE' POTTERY

Fine pottery was made by Emile Galle', the multi-talented French designer and artisan, who is also famous for his glass and furniture. The pottery is relatively scarce.

Bowl, 15" l., 5½" w., 9½" h., crescent-shaped, painted on each side w/a central Heraldic shield & an assortment of bizarre winged & legged creatures w/gilt embellishments, raised on a semicircular row of vertical tall tipped devices, recessed base signed elaborately "Emile Galle fecit/Nancy
depose" $2,970.00

Centerpiece, faience, modeled as a giant molded clam vessel propelled through the turbulent blue waters by two catfish harnessed by a steering frog astride the shell, decorated w/cream engobe, each side illustrated w/a seascape *en grisaille*, the catfish, frog & edges of the shell heightened in sponged gold lustre, ca. 1885,
13½" h. 2,310.00

Model of a cat, dressed in a brocaded waistcoat w/lace cuffs & bonnet laced w/pink ribbons & wearing a locket w/a portrait of her dog friend, signed "E. Galle/Nancy," ca. 1900, 13" h....2,200.00

Galle' Faience Owl

Model of an owl on a raised circular base, faience, thinly glazed & decorated in brown, white, black & earthen tones, signed "Emile Galle'," 12¾" h. (ILLUS.) 4,400.00

Vase, 7½" h., faience, disc-form cast w/leafage & branches & painted on the obverse w/a rabbit reading philosophy in a garden, raised on a stem-form support & circular base cast w/stems, roots & leafage, signed in enamel "E. Galle/Nancy E.G. depose," ca. 1875....1,045.00

Vase, 9¼" h., urn form, three-part handle, thinly glazed, the body enameled w/sailboats & fishermen in shades of brown, light blue & green w/random green, red, white & black shells, rim & base w/enameled frieze of shells in pink, red, black & green, signed "E. Galle Faiencerie Nancy" 1,650.00

Vase, 12" h., composed of three graduated hydrangea balls, all molded in low-relief w/florettes & scrolling leafage in shades of pale blue & aubergine, each ball further decorated w/a landscape panel, signed "E. Galle'/Nancy," ca. 1880 ....1,210.00

GAUDY DUTCH

This name is applied to English earthenware with designs copied from Oriental patterns. Production began in the 18th century. These copies flooded into this country in the early 19th century. The incorporation of the word "Dutch" derives from the fact that it was the Dutch who first brought the Oriental wares into Europe. The ware was not, as often erroneously reported, made specifically for the Pennsylvania Dutch.

Cup & saucer, handleless, Single
   Rose patt. (hairline crack) $352.00
Cup & saucer, handleless, War Bon-
   net patt. 500.00
Creamer, compressed baluster-
   shaped body, Sunflower patt.,
   brown line on base, rim & handle,
   ca. 1820, 4½" h. 550.00
Plate, 5¼" d., War Bonnet patt. 450.00
Plate, 7" d., War Bonnet patt. (mi-
   nor wear & shallow rim flakes) . . . 475.00
Plate, 7½" d., Urn patt. 575.00
Plate, 10" d., Single Rose patt. 550.00
Teapot, cov., Dahlia patt. (hairline
   crack) 521.00
Teapot, cov., War Bonnet patt. 900.00

GAUDY WELSH

Gaudy Welsh Pitcher

This is a name for wares made in England for the American market about 1830 to 1845. Decorated with Imari-style flower patterns, often highlighted with copper lustre, it should not be confused with Gaudy Dutch wares whose colors differ somewhat.

Bowl & pitcher, miniature, Grape IX
   patt., 4 3/8" h., the set (short
   hairline in bowl, under rim chip,
   minor wear) $120.00
Egg cups, Tulip patt., flaring pedes-
   tal base, set of 5 . . . . 120.00
Pitcher, 6½" h., Grape patt.
   (ILLUS.) 140.00
Pitcher, 7½" h., ovoid body w/wide

panels tapering in then flaring out
   to shaped rim w/wide spout, high
   arched scroll handle, Grape patt.,
   ca. 1850 . . . . 175.00
Tea set: cake plate, four bread &
   butter plates, six cups & saucers,
   creamer & waste bowl; Tulip
   patt., the set 175.00
Tea set: cov. teapot (some damage),
   cov. sugar bowl, creamer, waste
   bowl, two serving plates, eight
   cups & saucers (saucers & one cup
   w/hairline) & twelve 6¼" d.
   plates; Tulip patt., teapot, creamer & sugar bowl w/inverted pear-
   shaped bodies on short legs, ca.
   1850, the set (several small
   chips) 650.00

GEISHA GIRL WARES

The beautiful geisha, a Japanese girl specifically trained to entertain with singing or dancing, is the featured decoration on this Japanese china which was cheaply made and mass-produced for export. Now finding favor with collectors across the United States, the ware varies in quality. The geisha pattern is not uniform - Butterfly, Paper Lanterns, Parasol, Sedan Chair and other variations are found in this pattern that is usually colored in shades of red through orange but is also found in blue and green tones. Collectors try to garner the same design in approximately the same color tones.

Bowl, 4" d., footed, red trim $5.00
Bowl, 8" d., multiple patterns of
   decoration, red trim 30.00
Chocolate pot, cov. 65.00
Cup & saucer, demitasse, Boy's
   Processional patt., red trim, Nip-
   pon mark 13.00
Hatpin holder, Garden Bench patt.,
   green trim 35.00
Mug, child's, Geisha in Sampan
   patt., red trim 25.00
Nut set: master bowl & one in-
   dividual nut cup; Gift Processional
   patt., red trim, 2 pcs. 15.00
Pin tray, Garden Bench patt., red
   trim 12.00
Pitcher, 4½" h., green trim 34.00
Plates, luncheon, Parasol patt.,
   shades of orange, set of 14 . . . . . . 70.00
Sauce dish, Oni Dance patt., red
   trim 10.00
Teapot, cov., Flower Arranger patt.,
   red trim 24.00
Tea set: cov. teapot, cov. sugar
   bowl, creamer & four cups & saucers; Parasol patt., shades of
   orange, 11 pcs. 85.00

GOLDSCHEIDER

Goldscheider Figure of a Dancer

The Goldscheider firm manufactured porcelain and faience in Austria between 1885 and 1953. Founded by Friedrich Goldscheider and carried on by his widow, the firm came under the control of his sons, Walter and Marcell, in 1920. Fleeing their native Austria at the time of World War II, the Goldscheiders set up an operation in the United States. They were listed in the Trenton, New Jersey, City Directory from 1943 through 1950 and their main production seems to have been art pottery figurines.

Figure of the Madonna, signed
"Pierre Fumers," 7" h. $110.00
Figure of a lady w/muff, blue & tan
coat & gown, 8" h. 85.00
Figure of a Southern Belle, green
hoop skirt, yellow hat, 9" h. 100.00
Figure of a Southern Belle, blue
hoop skirt, 10½" h. . . . . .65.00 to 75.00
Figure of a girl w/parasol, grey &
pink gown, marked "U.S.A.,"
13" h. 125.00
Figure of a dancer, exotically
dressed w/her arms outstretched
& holding an elaborate cape, in
tones of purple, green, blue, yellow & brown, on a raised circular
base, signed "Laurenzl," w/firm's
stamp "MADE IN AUSTRIA," &
inscribed "5500 36 8," 20½" h.
(ILLUS.) 1,650.00
Models of birds, marked "U.S.A.,"
7½", pr. 80.00
Model of a German Shepherd,
marked "Austria,"
6 x 9" . . . . .150.00 to 165.00
Model of a Spaniel, marked
"U.S.A." 60.00

GOUDA

While tin-enameled earthenware has been made in Gouda, Holland since the early 1600's, the productions of modern factories are attracting increasing collector attention. The art pottery of Gouda is easily recognized by its brightly colored peasant-style decoration with some types having achieved a "cloisonne" effect. Pottery workshops located in, or near, Gouda include Regina, Zenith, Plazuid, Schoonhoven, Arnhem and others. Their wide range of production included utilitarian wares, as well as vases, miniatures and large outdoor garden ornaments.

Basket, twisted handle, black
w/frosted florals & heavy gold,
Regina mark, 7½" $45.00
Bowl, 7¼" d., wide raised ribbon
handle on top, colorful florals,
"Anjar" & house mark 68.00
Candlestick, green, rust, cobalt &
ochre, "Candis - 1137" & house
mark, 3¾" h. 50.00
Candlestick, Damascus patt.,
11½" h. 185.00
Candlesticks, gold, green, white,
yellow, green & rust designs on
black satin finish, "Tokio" & house
mark, 7 1/8" h., pr. 125.00
Chamberstick, Art Deco style, turquoise, royal, orange & yellow
leaf designs, original paper label,
house mark, 5¾" d., 3½" h. 88.00
Inkwell, cov., black, yellow & blue
geometric decoration, house
mark, 7" d., 4" h. 140.00
Pitcher, 5" h., rust, green & tan on
navy blue Art Nouveau design. . . 325.00
Vases, 3¼" h., florals w/crackle
background, glossy glaze, Royal
Zuid mark, pr. 88.00
Vase, 5 3/8" h., 3" d., ewer-shaped,
black, white, orange, green &
gold w/blue florals, satin finish,
house mark. 75.00
Vase, 10" h., bulbous, multicolored
starburst florals, Zuid-Holland
mark. 90.00
Wall pocket, stylized flowers in rust,
light & dark blues, gold & cream
on black ground, marked
"NL #4262," 11½" h. 135.00

GRUEBY

Some fine art pottery was produced by the Grueby Faience and Tile Company, established in Boston in 1891. Choice pieces were created with molded designs on a semiporcelain body. The ware is marked and of-

ten bears the initials of the decorators. The
pottery closed in 1907.

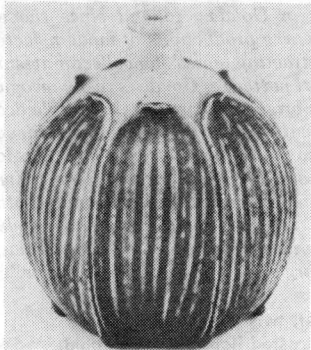

Two-color Grueby Vase

Bowl, 8" d., 1¼" h., swirled glossy
green interior & exterior glaze ...$285.00
Lamp base, wide cylindrical neck on
ribbed bulbous base, mottled
green glaze, signed w/logo, several paper labels including
"World's Fair St. Louis 1904," artist
initialled by Ruth Ericson, undrilled,
lamp fitting probably by Tiffany,
16" h. 5,170.00
Paperweight, model of a scarab,
mottled green glaze, early
20th c., 2¾" l. 125.00
Vase, 4¼" h., 4½" d., bulbous
w/tapered flaring neck, five white
buds alternating w/five short
broad leaves, matte green glaze,
die-stamped mark 1,210.00
Vase, 4¾" h., 5¾" w., squatty, bulbous base tapering to neck, decorated w/tooled pointed leaves
encircling base & part of the
flared neck, die-stamped mark ... 450.00
Vase, 6" h., 4½" d., three-lobed,
three white buds alternating
w/three leaves, textured matte
green glaze.................... 715.00
Vase, 8" h., 4" d., ovoid, gently
flared rim, three applied broad
leaves, green matte glaze 880.00
Vase, 8½" h., 4¾" d., gourd-
shaped, molded leaves, cucumber
green matte glaze 2,640.00
Vase, 9¼" h., elongated bottle neck
on spherical cabbage-form body,
vertical green ribbed leaves over
yellow ground, die-stamped mark,
ca. 1905, drilled & some damage
(ILLUS.) 4,950.00
Vase, 11 7/8" h., cylindrical tapering
body w/angled shoulder to short,
flared rim, embossed buds alternating w/broad leaves around

body, signed w/logo, paper label
& artist initials, ca. 1905........2,860.00

HALL CHINA

Founded in 1903 in East Liverpool, Ohio,
this still-operating company at first produced
mostly utilitarian wares. It was in 1911 that
Robert T. Hall, son of the company founder,
developed a special single-fire, lead-free glaze
which proved to be strong, hard and non-
porous. In the 1920's the firm became well
known for their extensive line of teapots (still
a major product) and in 1932 they introduced
kitchenwares followed by dinnerwares in 1936
and refrigerator wares in 1938.

The imaginative designs and wide range of
glaze colors and decal decorations have led
to the growing appeal of Hall wares with collectors, especially people who like Art Deco
and Art Moderne design. One of the firm's
most famous patterns was the "Autumn
Leaf" line, produced as premiums for the Jewel Tea Company. For listings of this ware see
"Jewel Tea Autumn Leaf."

Bean pot, Orange Poppy patt...... $55.00
Bowl, 8½" d., Wildfire patt......... 15.00
Bowl, flat soup, 8½" d., Orange
Poppy patt..................... 11.00
Bowl, flat soup, 8½" d., Pastel
Morning Glory patt., pink 9.00
Bowls, nested-type, Cactus patt. on
"Five Band" shape, set of 3 ...... 60.00
Cake plate, Blue Bouquet patt. 7.00
Canister set: four cov. canisters &
salt & pepper shakers; Radiance
Mint patt., yellow, 6 pcs. 275.00
Casserole, cov., Blue Bouquet patt.,
"thick rim" 25.00
Casserole, cov., Red Poppy patt..... 25.00
Coffeepot, cov., w/insert, gold dots
on creamy ground 37.50
Coffeepot, cov., Red Poppy patt.,
Daniel shape 20.00
Cookie jar, cov., Blue Blossom patt.,
Sundial shape................. 185.00
Creamer & sugar bowl, Blue Blos-
som patt., pr.................. 65.00
Creamer & sugar bowl, Cameo Rose
patt., pr. 12.00
Cup & saucer, Pastel Morning Glory
patt., pink 7.00
Decanter, figural, standing top-
hatted man holding cane under
one arm & tipping hat w/other,
"I.W. Harper" on stepped base,
white glaze 135.00
Drip jar, cov., Orange Poppy patt.,
Radiance shape 17.00
French baker, Tulip patt............ 10.00

Gravy boat w/attached underplate, Cameo Rose patt. 16.00
Pitcher, cov., Shaggy Tulip patt., Radiance shape 25.00
Pitcher, ball-shaped, Orange Poppy patt. 34.00
Pitcher, water, ball-shaped, Rose Parade patt., blue 24.00
Plate, 9" d., Pastel Morning Glory patt., pink 5.50
Platter, 11½", Red Poppy patt. 8.00
Rolling pin, Silhouette patt. 53.00
Salt & pepper shakers, handled, Orange Poppy patt., pr. 20.00
Teapot, cov., Airflow shape, navy blue & gold 37.50
Teapot, cov., Aladdin shape, Wildfire patt. 48.00
Teapot, cov., Birch shape, blue 20.00
Teapot, cov., Birdcage shape, emerald green.................... 400.00
Teapot, cov., Boston shape, Orange Poppy patt...................... 75.00
Teapot, cov., French shape, blue & gold 27.50
Teapot, cov., Los Angeles shape, brown & gold 35.00
Teapot, cov., Melody shape, cobalt blue 85.00
Teapot, cov., Moderne shape, yellow & gold 20.00
Teapot, cov., Nautilus shape, yellow & gold 66.00
Teapot, cov., New York shape, cobalt blue & gold 35.00
Teapot, cov., Philadelphia shape, cobalt blue & gold, four-cup size.. 30.00
Teapot, cov., Regal shape, green & gold 110.00
Teapot, cov., Streamline shape, Orange Poppy patt. 75.00
Teapot, cov., Surfside shape, emerald & gold 65.00
Teapot, cov., Windshield shape, ivory w/gold dots, Gold Label line .. 25.00

HAMPSHIRE POTTERY

Hampshire Pottery Lamp

Hampshire Pottery was made in Keene, N.H., where several potteries operated as far back as the late 18th century. The pottery now known as Hampshire Pottery was established by J.S. Taft shortly after 1870. Various types of wares, including Art Pottery, were produced through the years. Taft's brother-in-law, Cadmon Robertson, joined the firm in 1904 and was responsible for developing over 900 glaze formulas while in charge of all manufacturing. His death in 1914 created problems for the firm and Taft sold out to George Morton in 1916. Closed during part of World War I, the pottery was later reopened by Morton for a short time and manufactured white hotel china. From 1919 to 1921, mosaic floor tiles became the main production. All production ceased in 1923.

Lamp, squat bulbous base w/incised floral decoration in matte green glaze, impressed "Hampshire," w/etched glass shade, ca. 1910, overall 15" h. (ILLUS.) $330.00
Pitcher, 7½" h., creamy Worcester glaze & transfer scene of Stone House, Guilford, Connecticut 60.00
Pitcher, 7½" h., "Landing of Pilgrims" scene.................... 75.00
Pitcher, 8¼" h., swollen cylindrical form w/molded leaves curling to form spout & intertwined vines to form handle, mottled slate blue glaze w/highlights of pink, signed, early 20th c............. 165.00
Vase, 5½" h., two-handled, pedestal footed, molded leaf design, green matte glaze.............. 95.00
Vase, 7¾" h., 8" d., bulbous form tapering to base, molded overlapping leaf design & blue-green mottled matte glaze, impressed mark......................... 467.50
Vase, 9" h., swollen cylindrical form tapering toward base, wide mouth, repeating molded tulip & running stem decoration, incised "Hampshire Pottery M" within a circle, ca. 1900 (base hairline) 385.00
Vase, 15" h., rolled rim on trumpet-form body w/molded leaves & vines winding to wide circular foot, mottled green glaze, signed, early 20th c. 357.50

HAVILAND

Haviland porcelain was originated by Americans in Limoges, France, shortly before the mid-19th century and continues in production. Some Haviland was made by Theodore Haviland in the United States during the last

World War. Numerous other factories also made china in Limoges, which see.

Princess Pattern Plate

Bouillon cup & saucer, Lucille patt., Theodore Haviland, Limoges, France $35.00

Bowl, fruit, 5" d., Silver Anniversary patt., Blank No. 19 .... 9.00

Bowl, 10½" octagon, Montreaux patt., Theodore Haviland, Limoges, France................ 42.00

Bowl, soup, Apple Blossom patt..... 20.00

Butter dish, cover & drain insert, Ranson blank 15.00

Butter pat, Silver Anniversary patt., Blank No. 19................... 12.00

Chocolate pot, cov., melon-ribbed body, h.p. roses, brown handle, 9" h........................... 275.00

Chocolate pot, cov., melon-ribbed body, upper part & handle in burgundy red & gold, w/pink & yellow floral decoration, 9½" h. 175.00

Cup & saucer, Albany patt.......... 30.00

Cup & saucer, Apple Blossom patt. 35.00

Cup & saucer, Old Blackberry patt. 25.00

Dinner service for eight, Autumn Leaf patt., 60 pcs............... 600.00

Dinner service: eight 8-piece place settings, four platters from 8" to 18" l., two cov. oval serving bowls, open oval vegetable dish & gravy boat w/attached underplate; sprays of delicate roses, gold trim on cups & serving pieces, Schleiger Blank No. 123, 72 pcs. 800.00

Gravy boat w/attached undertray, Silver Anniversary patt., Blank No. 19 .... 85.00

Pitcher, 6½" h., 5½" d., heavy gold flowers, branch & foliage against an off-white ground, unusual double handle, marked "CFH" 172.00

Plate, bread & butter, 6¼" d., Silver Anniversary patt., Blank No. 19 .. 12.50

Plate, salad, 7½" d., Apple Blossom patt. 22.00

Plate, salad, 7½" d., Cloverleaf patt., Blank No. 24, gold edge ... 18.00

Plate, salad, 7½" d., Old Blackberry patt. 12.00

Plate, salad, 7½" d., Silver Anniversary patt., Blank No. 19 .... 15.00

Plate, luncheon, 8½" d., h.p. pansies on pastel background, artist-signed 48.00

Plate, luncheon, 8½" d., Princess patt., Star blank (ILLUS.) 18.00

Plate, dinner, 9¾" d., Albany patt. 20.00

Plate, dinner, 9¾" d., Apple Blossom patt....................... 26.00

Plate, dinner, 9¾" d., Marlborough patt............................ 22.00

Plate, dinner, 9¾" d., Silver Anniversary patt., Blank No. 19 ..... 20.00

Haviland Floral Plate

Plate, 9¾" d., large pink & red roses decoration, gold beaded edge (ILLUS.) 25.00

Platter, 9 x 11", Montreux patt. 37.50

Platter, 13" l., Ranson patt. 30.00

Platter, 14" l., Ganga patt.......... 76.00

Platter, 14" l., Silver Anniversary patt., Blank No. 19 .... 75.00

Platter, 16" l., Apple Blossom patt. 90.00

Platter, 16" l., Spring Bouquet patt., Limoges 27.00

Platter, 11¼ x 16½", small pink & green flowers on white ground, gold & white bows 45.00

Punch bowl, roses in shades of deep pink to white, lavender violets touched w/pink, green stems & green leaves touched w/pink, Haviland & Co. 375.00

Sauce boat, cover & attached undertray, pink roses decoration, France 65.00

Soup tureen, cov., dainty pink roses decoration, gold handles, finial & trim, Haviland & Co., Limoges, 8 x 12", 7" h. 173.00

Tea cup & saucer, Ranson patt. 20.00

Tea set: cov. teapot, creamer & cov. sugar bowl; Old Blackberry patt., Henry II blank, ca. 1895, France, 3 pcs. 190.00

Tureen, pink floral sprays decoration, Charles Field Haviland 75.00

Vegetable dish, cov., Baltimore Rose patt., Ranson blank, Haviland & Co. 95.00

Vegetable dish, cov., oval, rope handle, Moss Rose patt., H & Co. Haviland, Limoges 60.00

Vegetable dish, cov., oval, Silver Anniversary patt., Blank No. 19 .. 110.00

Vegetable dish, open, Silver Anniversary patt., Blank No. 19, 9¼" d. 75.00

Vegetable tureen, small pink roses w/green foliage, gold trim, 8½" d. 85.00

ART POTTERY

Haviland Scenic Vase

Urn, thick-walled baluster-form body, mottled brown glaze, applied w/two budding branches w/large black-shaded white flowerheads w/yellow centers & green leaves & two butterflies in high relief, base inscribed "H & C., N. 4" & "E. LINDENEHER," ca. 1880, 25½" h. (losses to applied decoration) 550.00

Vase, 14½" h., 8" w., pottery, flat rectangular form decorated w/multicolored parrot perched on branch of flowering cherry blossoms, diestamped "Haviland & Co. - Limoges - 56 - 3" (kiln separation on one wall 1,100.00

Vases, 20¼" h., oval body decorated on one side in "Barbotine" style w/a scene inspired by Watteau of a young man w/a lute courting a young woman in a hazy

landscape, in shades of dusty blue, grey-green, olive green, cream, peach, brown & black, the sides, foot & back glazed in mottled blue-black, repairs, decorated by Edmond-Alexandre Dammouse, 1882-86, incised initials, one impressed "HAVILAND & CO./ LIMOGES/52/2," pr. (ILLUS. of one)........................3,300.00

HISTORICAL & COMMEMORATIVE

Baltimore & Ohio Railroad Plate

Numerous potteries, especially in England and the United States, made various porcelain and earthenware pieces to commemorate people, places and events. Scarce English historical wares with American views command highest prices. Objects are listed here alphabetically by title of view.

America and Independence series plate, "States" border w/center scene of mansion w/lake & swans in foreground, dark blue, 10 5/8" d., Clews (minor scratches) $250.00

The Baltimore & Ohio Railroad (Incline) plate, shells border, circular center w/trailing vines around outer edges of center, dark blue, 9" d., Wood (ILLUS.) ..... 500.00 to 550.00

Boston Harbour tea set: two cov. teapots, cov. sugar bowl, creamer, waste bowl, six cups & saucers; dark blue, J. Rogers, 17 pcs. (crazing, some chips & hairline cracks) 7,425.00

Boston State House spit cup, ovoid body w/wide flat rim & floral border, views on exterior & interior, dark blue, 5¼" d., 3¼" h. (Stubbs) 935.00

Cadmus cup plate, dark blue, 3¾" d., Wood (scratches & short hairline)........................ 325.00

City of Albany, State of New York
plate, shell border, dark blue,
10¼" d. (Wood) 350.00

Anti-Slavery Plate

Constitution of the United States
Anti-Slavery plate, center inscribed w/First Amendment,
shield-breasted eagles border,
light blue, 9½" d. (ILLUS.) 357.50
East View of La Grange, the residence of the Marquis Lafayette
plate, floral border, dark blue,
9" d. (Wood & Sons) 185.00
Fall of Montmorenci Near Quebec
plate, shells border, circular center w/trailing vines around outer
edge of center, dark blue, 9" d.
(Wood) 200.00
Fort Edward, Hudson River toddy
plate, brown, 5" d. (Clews) 65.00
Junction of the Sacandaga & Hudson
Rivers plate, black, 7" d.
(Clews) 67.50
Lafayette at Franklin's Tomb handle-
less cup & saucer, dark blue
(Wood) 250.00
Lafayette at the Tomb of Washing-
ton undertray, hexagonal, dark
blue, 7¼" d. (Mayer) 1,980.00
LaGrange, the Residence of the
Marquis Lafayette soup plate
w/flange rim, dark blue, 10¼" d.
(Wood) 250.00
Landing of General Lafayette at
Castle Garden, New York, 16 Au-
gust, 1824 pitcher, floral & vine
border, 7 7/8" h. (Clews) 700.00
Landing of General Lafayette at
Castle Garden, New York, 16 Au-
gust, 1824 plate, floral & vine bor-
der, medium blue, 9" d. (Clews) . . 300.00
Landing of General Lafayette at
Castle Garden, New York, 16 Au-
gust, 1824 platter, floral & vine
border, dark blue, 15" l.
(Clews) 825.00
Landing of General Lafayette at
Castle Garden, New York, 16 Au-

gust, 1824 platter, floral & vine
border, dark blue, 19" l.
(Clews) 1,250.00
Montevideo, Connecticut, U.S. plate,
flowers, shells & scrolls border,
brown, 7" d. (stains & small
flakes) 75.00
Nahant Hotel, Near Boston plate,
spread eagles amid flowers &
scrolls border, dark blue, 9" d.
(Stubbs) 325.00
New York From Heights Near Brook-
lyn platter, flowers & scrolls border, medium blue, 16¼" l.
(Stevenson) 2,250.00
Niagara Falls from the American
Side platter, shells border, dark
blue, 14½" l. (Wood) 1,000.00
The Residence of the Late Richard
Jordan, New Jersey plate, light
blue, 9" d. (J. Heath & Co.) 260.00
Upper Ferry Bridge over the River
Schuylkill platter w/well & tree,
spread eagle amid flowers &
scrolls border, medium blue,
18 7/8" l. (Stubbs) 950.00
View Near Conway, N. Hampshire,
U.S. plate, flowers, shells &
scrolls border, pink, 9" d.
(Adams) . . . . 75.00 to 100.00
Zanesville, Ohio plate, green, black
& gold, rolled rim (Rowland &
Marsellus) 40.00

HULL

Glossy Woodland Basket

*This pottery was made by the Hull Pottery
Company, Crooksville, Ohio, beginning in
1905. Art Pottery was made until 1950 when
the company was converted to utilitarian
wares. All production ceased in 1986.*

Bank, Little Red Riding Hood patt. . . $220.00
Basket, Blossom Flite patt., No. T2,
6" h. 22.00

Basket, Dogwood patt., handle from side to side from base, No. 501-7½", 7½" 100.00

Basket, Ebb Tide patt., heavy gold, No. E11, 16½" l. 82.00

Basket, Woodland patt., glossy glaze, No. W-9-8¾", 8¾" h. (ILLUS.)........................ 32.00

Bowl, 10" d., Calla Lily patt., rose shaded to blue, No. 500/32-10" ... 70.00

Butter dish, cov., Little Red Riding Hood patt...................... 115.00

Candleholders, Magnolia Matte patt., pink shaded to blue, 4", pr.......................... 45.00

Console bowl, Blossom Flite patt.... 37.00

Console bowl, Dogwood patt., No. 511-11½", 11½" d. 65.00

Console bowl, Wildflower patt., No. W-21-12", 12" 38.00

Cookie jar, Little Red Riding Hood patt., all variations, 13" h. 95.00

Cornucopia-vase, Bow Knot patt., No. B-5-7½", 7½" h. 45.00

Cornucopia-vase, Calla Lily patt., No. 570-33-8", 8" h. 30.00

Creamer & cov. sugar bowl, Bow Knot patt., pr. 75.00

Ewer, Bow Knot patt., pink, No. B-1, 5½" h. 28.00

Ewer, Calla Lily patt., No. 506-10", 10" h. 84.00

Ewer, Iris patt., No. 401-8", 8" h. ... 48.00

Ewer, Wildflower patt., yellow matte glaze, No. W-19-13½", 13½" h. 120.00

Figure of accordionist, 6" h. 22.00

Flowerpot w/attached saucer, Water Lily patt., No. L25 .... 45.00

Fruit bowl, footed, turned-up sides, Serenade patt., No. S15 .... 48.00

Jardiniere, Bow Knot patt., pink or turquoise, No. B-18-15½", 15½", each 65.00

Jardiniere, Tulip patt., No. 115-33-7", 7" h. 100.00

Lamp, shape of a teapot, Woodland Gloss patt. 500.00

Mug, barrel-shaped, embossed "Happy Days Are Here Again," green glaze, No. 497, 5" h. 15.00

Mustard jar, cover & original spoon, Little Red Riding Hood patt. 165.00

Pitcher, batter, 7" h., Little Red Riding Hood patt., side spout 125.00

Planter, figure of a dancing girl w/pleated skirt, No. 955, ca. 1940's, 7" h. 25.00

Planter, figure of St. Francis stands on edge of scalloped bowl, Imperial line, No. 89, late 1960's, 11" h. 25.00

Planter, model of a giraffe against

tall grasses, Novelty line, green glaze, No. 115, 8" h. 18.00

Salt & pepper shakers, Little Red Riding Hood patt., small, 3¼" h., pr........................... 28.00

Salt & pepper shakers, Little Red Riding Hood patt., large, 5½" h., pr........................... 45.00

Stein, embossed American Legion emblem, brown glaze on cream body, No. 498, ca. 1920's, 6½" h. 25.00

Sugar bowl, open, crawling figure, Little Red Riding Hood patt. 55.00

Sugar bowl, open, Open Rose patt., No. 112-5", 5" 18.00

Blossom Flite Teapot

Teapot, cov., Blossom Flite patt., No. T14, 8¼" (ILLUS.)........... 45.00

Teapot, cov., Magnolia Matte patt., No. 23-6½", 6½" 42.00

Teapot, cov., Wildflower patt., No. 72-8", 8" 149.50

Teapot, cov., Woodland patt., glossy finish, No. W26, 6½" 42.50

Tea set: cov. teapot, creamer & cov. sugar bowl; Magnolia Gloss patt., pink & blue glaze, gold trim, 3 pcs. 60.00

Tea set: cov. teapot, creamer & cov. sugar bowl; Serenade patt., pink glaze, 3 pcs. 50.00

Vase, 4¼" h., Orchid patt., rose base, No. 308-4¼" 30.00

Vase, 4¾" h., Magnolia Matte patt., No. 13-4¾" 17.00

Vase, 5½" h., Water Lily patt., No. L23-5½" 25.00

Vase, 6" h., Orchid patt., rose base, No. 304-6" 35.00

Vase, bud, 6" h., Tulip patt., No. 104-33-6" 30.00

Vase, 6¼" h., Magnolia Matte patt., pink to blue glaze, No. 11-6¼" ... 30.00

Vase, 6½" h., Bow Knot patt., blue glaze, No. B-4-6½" 62.00

Vase, 6½" h., Dogwood patt., No. 513-6½" 40.00

Vase, 6½" h., Poppy patt.,
No. 612-6½" 45.00
Vase, 6½" h., Thistle patt.,
No. 52-6½" 28.00
Vase, 6½" h., Water Lily patt.,
No. L-6-6½" 30.00
Vase, 8½" h., Bow Knot patt., blue
& pink, No. B-8-8½" 65.00
Vase, 8½" h., Magnolia Matte patt.,
No. 1-8½" 42.50
Vase, 8½" h., Open Rose patt.,
No. 102-8½" 65.00
Vase, 8½" h., Rosella patt.,
No. R-15-8½" 42.00
Vase, 9" h., Butterfly patt., No. B9.. 30.00
Vase, 10½" h., Wildflower patt.,
No. W-15-10½" 55.00
Vase, shell-shaped, 11¾" h., Ebb
Tide patt., No. E9 .... 58.00
Vase, 12½" h., Magnolia Gloss
patt., No. H-17-12½ 65.00
Wall pocket, Bow Knot patt., model
of a cup & saucer, pink & blue
glaze, No. B-24-6," 6" 60.00
Wall pocket, Little Red Riding Hood
patt. ....200.00 to 250.00
Window box, Dogwood patt.,
No. 508-10½", 10½" 55.00

HUMMEL FIGURINES & COLLECTIBLES

"Close Harmony"

The Goebel Company of Oeslau, Germany, first produced these porcelain figurines in 1934 having obtained the rights to adapt the beautiful pastel sketches of children by Sister Maria Innocentia (Berta) Hummel. Every design by the Goebel artisans was approved by the nun until her death in 1946. Though not antique, these figurines with the "M.I. Hummel" signature, especially those bearing the Goebel Company factory mark used from 1934 and into the early 1940's, are being

sought by collectors though interest may have peaked about 1980.

"A Fair Measure," last bee mark
used, 1972-79, 5½" h. $103.00
"Accordion Boy," crown mark,
1934-49, 5" h................ 290.00
"Accordion Boy," stylized bee mark,
1956-68, 5" h................ 85.00
"Adoration," 1934-49, 6¼" h..... 975.00
"Adoration," full bee mark, 1940-57,
6¼" h....................... 275.00
"Adventure Bound," 1972-79,
7½" h............1,000.00 to 1,595.00
"Angel at Prayer" fonts, 1940-57,
4¾" h., pr. 110.00
"Angel at Prayer" font, 1956-68,
4¾" h....................... 100.00
"Angel Duet," 1940-57, 5" h. ... 163.00
"Angel Duet," 1972-79, 5" h..... 78.00
"Angel Duet" candleholder, 1940-57,
5" 225.00
"Angel Duet" font, 1972-79,
4¾" h....................... 22.00
"Angel Serenade," 1972-79,
5½" h....................... 84.00
"Angel with Accordion," 1940-57,
2¼" h....................... 57.00
"Angel (Child) with Flowers" font,
1972-79, 4" h............... 23.00
"Angel with Lute," 1940-57, 2" h. .. 47.00
"Angel with Trumpet" candleholder,
1940-57, 2" h............... 54.00
"Apple Tree Boy," 1956-68,
4" h....................... 68.00
"Apple Tree Boy," 1956-68, 6" h..... 125.00
"Apple Tree Girl," 1940-57,
6" h................200.00 to 250.00
"Apple Tree Girl," 1956-68, 6" h. ... 128.00
"Auf Wiedersehen," 1956-68, 5" h. ... 120.00
"Auf Wiedersehen," 1934-49, 7" h. .. 747.00
"Auf Wiedersehen," 1940-57, 7" h. .. 760.00
"Auf Wiedersehen," w/Tyrolean
cap, 1940-57, 7" h............2,500.00
"Autumn Harvest," 1956-68,
4¾" h....................... 75.00
"Autumn Harvest," 1972-79,
4¾" h....................... 125.00
"Ba-Bee Rings" plaque, 1940-57,
5" d....................... 125.00
"Baker," 1956-68, 4¾" h. 90.00
"Baker," 1972-79, 4¾" h. 75.00
"Band Leader," 1940-57, 5" h. 142.00
"Barnyard Hero," 1940-57, 4" h. 162.00
"Barnyard Hero," 1956-68, 4" h. 86.00
"Barnyard Hero," 1934-49,
5½" h..................650.00 to 700.00
"Barnyard Hero," 1972-79, 5½" h. .. 140.00
"Bashful," 1956-78, 4¾" h. 65.00
"Bashful," 1972-79, 4¾" h. 110.00
"Begging His Share," 1956-68,
5½" h....................... 132.00
"Be Patient," 1956-68, 4¼" h. 126.00
"Be Patient," three line mark,
1963-71, 4¼" h................. 80.00

"Be Patient," 1972-79, 4¼" h. 110.00
"Be Patient," 1963-71, 6¼" h. 119.00
"Big Housecleaning," 1956-68,
   4" h. 95.00
"Big Housecleaning," 1972-79,
   4" h. 128.00
"Bird Duet," 1934-49, 4" h. 292.00
"Bird Duet," 1940-57, 4" h. 130.00
"Bird Duet," 1956-68, 4" h. 82.00
"Bird Watcher," 1972-79, 5" h. 99.00
"Birthday Serenade," 1940-57,
   4¼" h. 286.00
"Birthday Serenade," reverse mold,
   1956-68, 4¼" h. 353.00
"Birthday Serenade," reverse mold,
   1956-68, 5¼" h. 495.00
"Blessed Event," 1972-79, 5½" h. ... 130.00
"Book Worm," 1934-49, 4" h. 275.00
"Book Worm," 1956-68, 4" h. 145.00
"Book Worm," 1972-79, 4" h. 87.00
"Book Worm," 1956-68, 8" h. 650.00
"Book Worm," 1972-79, 8" h. 476.00
"Book Worm" book ends, 1940-57,
   5½" h. 426.00
"Book Worm" book ends, 1956-68,
   5½" h. 242.00
"Boots," 1956-68, 5½" h. 96.00
"Boy with Horse," 1963-71, 3½" h. ... 29.00
"Boy with Toothache," 1956-68,
   5½" h. 125.00
"Boy with Toothache," 1963-71,
   5½" h. 90.00
"Brother," 1940-57, 5½" h. 137.00
"Brother," 1956-68, 5½" h. 89.00
"Brother," 1972-79, 5½" h. 62.00
"Builder," 1963-71, 5½" h. 115.00
"Carnival," 1963-71, 5¾" h. 98.00
"Chef, Hello," 1956-68, 6¼" h. 125.00
"Chef, Hello," 1972-79, 6¼" h. 78.00
"Chick Girl," 1972-79,
   3½" h. ....80.00 to 100.00
"Chick Girl," 1934-49, 4¼" h. 395.00
"Chick Girl," 1956-68, 4¼" h. 128.00
"Chick Girl" candy dish, 1940-57,
   5¼" h. 175.00
"Child Jesus" font, 1956-68, 5" h. ... 35.00
"Chimney Sweep," 1940-57, 4" h. ... 80.00
"Chimney Sweep," 1956-68, 4" h. ... 48.00
"Chimney Sweep," 1972-79, 4" h. ... 42.00
"Chimney Sweep," 1934-49,
   5½" h. 350.00
"Chimney Sweep," 1940-57,
   5½" h. 176.00
"Christ Child," 1940-57, 2 x 6" 106.00
"Cinderella," 1972-79,
   4½" h. ....125.00 to 150.00
"Close Harmony," 1963-71, 5½" h.
   (ILLUS.) ....200.00 to 280.00
"Confidentially," 1972-79, 5½" h. ... 114.00
"Congratulations" (no socks),
   1940-57, 6" h. 151.00
"Congratulations" (no socks),
   1956-68, 6" h. 107.00

"Congratulations" (w/socks),
   1972-79, 6" h. 70.00
"Coquettes," 1940-57,
   5" h. ....200.00 to 225.00
"Coquettes," 1956-68, 5" h. 119.00
"Crossroads," 1972-79, 6¾" h. 175.00
"Culprits," 1934-49, 6¼" h. 395.00
"Culprits," 1956-68, 6¼" h. 124.00
"Culprits" table lamp, 1940-57,
   9½" h. 249.00
"Easter Greetings," 1972-79,
   5¼" h. 76.50
"Eventide," 1940-57, 4¼ x 4¾" 315.00
"Eventide," 1956-68, 4¼ x 4¾" 162.00
"Farewell," 1934-49, 4¾" h. 437.50
"Farewell," 1940-57, 4¾" h. 395.00
"Farm Boy," 1934-49, 5" h. 475.00
"Farm Boy," 1940-57, 5" h. 225.00
"Farm Boy" & "Goose Girl" book
   ends, 1940-57, 4¾" h., pr. 400.00
"Favorite Pet," 1963-71, 4½" h. 170.00
"Feeding Time," 1940-57, 4¼" h. ... 242.00
"Feeding Time," 1956-68, 5½" h. ... 155.00
"Flower Vendor," 1972-79, 5¼" h. .. 105.00
"Flying Angel," 1963-71, 3½" h. 250.00
"Follow the Leader," 1972-79,
   7" h. 475.00

"Forest Shrine"

"Forest Shrine," 1940-57, 9" h.
   (ILLUS.) 1,695.00
"For Father," 1940-57, 5½" h. 198.00
"For Father," 1972-79, 5½" h. 88.00
"Friends," 1972-79, 10¾" h. 538.00
"Girl with Nosegay," 1963-71,
   3½" h. 29.00
"Globe Trotter," 1940-57, 5" h. 225.00
"Globe Trotter," 1956-68, 5" h. 123.00
"Going to Grandma's," 1956-68,
   4¾" h. 164.00
"Good Friends," 1940-57. 4" h. 198.00
"Good Friends," 1956-68, 4" h. 125.00
"Good Shepherd" font, 1934-49,
   2¾ x 5¾" 350.00
"Goose Girl," 1934-49, 4" h. 350.00
"Goose Girl," 1972-79, 4" h. 62.50
"Goose Girl," 1940-57, 4¾" h. 205.00

"Goose Girl," 1934-49, 7½" h...... 750.00
"Goose Girl," 1972-79, 7½" h...... 200.00
"Guardian Angel" font, 1940-57,
  2¼ x 5½".................... 155.00
"Guardian Angel" font, 1963-71,
  2¼ x 5½".................... 30.00
"Happy Days," 1956-68, 4¼" h..... 120.00
"Happy Days," 1940-57, 5¼" h..... 485.00
"Happy Days," 1934-49, 6¼" h..... 575.00
"Happy Pastime," 1934-49, 3½" h. .. 330.00
"Happy Pastime" ashtray, 1940-57,
  3½ x 6¼".................... 275.00
"Happy Traveler," 1940-57, 5" h..... 122.50
"Happy Traveler," 1972-79, 7½" h. .. 278.00
"Hear Ye, Hear Ye," 1972-79,
  5" h......................... 82.00
"Heavenly Angel," 1956-68,
  4¾" h....................... 91.00
"Heavenly Angel," 1956-68,
  6¾" h....................... 120.00
"Heavenly Lullaby," 1963-71,
  3½ x 5"..................... 300.00
"Heavenly Protection," 1956-68,
  6¾" h....................... 255.00
"Holy Family" font, 1972-79, 3 x 4".. 20.00
"Homeward Bound," 1972-79,
  5¼" h....................... 215.00
"Joyful" candy box, 1940-57,
  6¼" h....................... 210.00
"Just Resting," 1956-68, 4" h....... 97.00
"Just Resting," 1972-79, 4" h....... 51.00
"Just Resting," 1972-79, 5" h....... 82.00
"Kiss Me," 1972-79, 6" h........... 110.00
"Latest News," 1934-49, 5" h....... 350.00
"Latest News," 1940-57, 5" h....... 252.00
"Let's Sing," 1934-49, 3" h........ 320.00
"Let's Sing," 1940-57, 3" h........ 126.00
"Let's Sing," 1963-71, 3" h........ 50.00
"Let's Sing," 1972-79, 3" h........ 42.00
"Let's Sing," 1934-49, 4" h........ 390.00
"Little Cellist," 1972-79, 6" h....... 76.00
"Little Cellist," 1972-79, 7½" h..... 177.00
"Little Fiddler," 1934-49, 4¾" h..... 233.00
"Little Fiddler," 1940-57, 4¾" h..... 150.00
"Little Fiddler," 1956-68, 4¾" h..... 81.00
"Little Fiddler," 1972-79, 4¾" h.... 62.00
"Little Fiddler," 1934-49, 6" h..... 360.00
"Little Fiddler," 1934-49, 7½" h..... 630.00
"Little Fiddler" plaque, 1972-79,
  4½ x 5"..................... 104.00
"Little Gabriel," 1940-57, 5" h..... 135.00
"Little Goat Herder," 1963-71,
  5½" h....................... 102.00
"Little Hiker," 1940-57, 6" h........ 191.00
"Little Hiker," 1956-68, 6" h........ 111.00
"Little Hiker," 1972-79, 6" h........ 71.00
"Little Pharmacist," 1972-79, 6" h... 90.00
"Little Scholar," 1940-57, 5½" h..... 156.00
"Little Scholar," 1972-79, 5½" h.... 82.00
"Little Sweeper," 1934-49, 4¼" h.... 190.00
"Little Sweeper," 1940-57, 4¼" h.... 118.00
"Little Tailor,"1972-79, 5½" h....... 83.00
"Little Tooter," 1940-57, 4" h........ 80.00
"Little Tooter," 1963-71, 4" h........ 53.00

"Lost Sheep," 1963-71, 4¼" h....... 58.00
"Lost Sheep," 1972-79, 4¼" h....... 75.00
"Lullaby" candleholder, 1934-49,
  3½ x 5"..................... 490.00
"Lullaby" candleholder, 1940-57,
  3½ x 5"..................... 175.00

"Lullaby" Candleholder

"Lullaby" candleholder, 1934-49,
  6 x 8" (ILLUS.)..................2,500.00
"The Mail is Here," 1940-57,
  4¼ x 6"..................... 600.00
"The Mail is Here," 1956-68,
  4¼ x 6"..................... 397.00
"March Winds," 1940-57, 5½" h.... 128.00
"Max & Moritz," 1940-57, 5" h...... 215.00
"Max & Moritz," 1956-68, 5" h...... 96.00
"Max & Moritz," 1963-71, 5" h...... 90.00
"Meditation," 1972-79, 4¼" h...... 63.00
"Meditation," 1940-57, 5½" h...... 215.00
"Meditation," 1972-79, 5½" h...... 68.00
"Meditation," 1940-57, 6" h....... 172.00
"Merry Wanderer," 1940-57,
  4¼" h....................... 162.00
"Merry Wanderer," 1956-68,
  4¼" h....................... 92.00
"Merry Wanderer," 1934-49,
  4¾" h....................... 430.00
"Merry Wanderer," 1956-68,
  4¾" h....................... 82.50
"Merry Wanderer," 1934-49,
  6¼" h....................... 395.00
"Merry Wanderer," 1956-68,
  7" h......................... 282.00
"Merry Wanderer," 1956-68,
  9½" h....................... 698.00
"Merry Wanderer" plaque, 1940-57,
  4¾ x 5 1/8".................. 110.00
"Merry Wanderer" plaque, 1972-79,
  4¾ x 5 1/8".................. 62.00
"Mischief Maker," 1972-79, 5" h..... 92.00
"Mother's Darling," 1972-79,
  5½" h....................... 72.50
"Mountaineer," 1963-71, 5" h....... 131.00
"Not For You," 1956-68, 6" h........ 265.00
"Not For You," 1963-71, 6" h........ 108.00
"Photographer," 1940-57, 4¾" h. ... 212.00
"Playmates," 1934-49, 4" h........ 276.00
"Playmates," 1940-57, 4" h........ 135.00

"Playmates," 1940-57, 4¼" h. 125.00
"Playmates" candy box, 1940-57,
5¼" h. 300.00
"Quartet" plaque, 1934-49, 6 x 6"... 720.00
"Quartet" plaque, 1972-79, 6 x 6"... 110.00
"Retreat to Safety," 1956-68, 4" h. .. 118.00
"Retreat to Safety," 1963-71, 4" h. .. 80.00
"Retreat to Safety," 1956-68,
5½" h. 182.00
"Retreat to Safety" plaque, 1972-79,
4¾ x 5" 95.00
"Ring Around the Rosie," 1956-68,
6¾" h. 1,425.00
"School Boy," 1940-57, 4" h. 110.00
"School Boy," 1956-68, 4" h. 85.00
"School Boy," 1972-79, 4" h. 65.00
"School Boy," 1956-68, 5" h. 98.00
"Schoolboys," 1963-71, 7½" h. 675.00
"Schoolboys," 1940-57, 10" h. 1,500.00
"School Girl," 1956-68, 4¼" h. 76.50
"School Girl," 1972-79, 4¼" h. 55.00
"School Girl," 1934-49, 5¼" h. 325.00
"Sensitive Hunter," 1934-49,
4¾" h. 280.00
"Sensitive Hunter," 1940-57,
4¾" h. 195.00
"Sensitive Hunter," 1934-49,
5½" h. 550.00
"Sensitive Hunter," 1940-57,
5½" h. 460.00
"Sensitive Hunter," 1956-68,
7½" h. 190.00
"Serenade," 1934-49, 4¾" h. 230.00
"Serenade," 1940-57, 4¾" h. 125.00
"Serenade," 1956-68, 4¾" h. 70.00
"Serenade," 1956-68, 7½" h. 110.00
"She Loves Me," 1940-57, 4¼" h. ... 163.00
"She Loves Me," 1956-68, 4¼" h. ... 100.00
"Shepherd's Boy," 1940-57, 5½" h. .. 225.00
"Signs of Spring," 1940-57, 4" h. 291.00
"Signs of Spring," 1956-68, 4" h. 97.50
"Signs of Spring," 1963-71, 4" h. 80.00
"Signs of Spring," 1972-79, 4" h. 58.00
"Silent Night," 1934-49, 5½" l.,
4¾" h. 465.00

"Sister"

"Silent Night," 1940-57, 5½" l.,
4¾" h. 232.00
"Singing Lesson," 1934-49, 2¾" h. .. 270.00
"Singing Lesson," 1940-57, 2¾" h. .. 123.00
"Singing Lesson" ashtray, 1956-68,
3½ x 6¼" 125.00
"Sister," 1963-71, 4¾" h. 53.50
"Sister," 1972-79, 4¾" h. 65.00
"Sister," 1940-57, 5½" h. 152.00
"Sister," 1956-68, 5½" h. (ILLUS.) ... 112.50
"Skier," 1934-49, wooden poles,
5" h. 407.00
"Skier," 1940-57, 6" h. 225.00
"Soldier Boy," 1956-68, 6" h. 117.00
"Soloist," 1940-57, 4¾" h. 142.50
"Soloist," 1956-68, 4¾" h. 90.00
"Spring Cheer," 1934-49, 5" h. 487.50
"Spring Cheer," 1940-57, 5" h. 165.00
"Spring Cheer," 1972-79, 5" h. 87.00
"Spring Dance," 1972-79, 6½" h. ... 310.00
"Star Gazer," 1940-57, 4¾" h. 197.00
"Stormy Weather," 1934-49,
6¼" h. 607.00

"Stormy Weather"

"Stormy Weather," 1956-68, 6¼" h.
(ILLUS.) 240.00
"Stormy Weather," 1940-57,
6¾" h. 600.00
"Street Singer," 1934-49, 5" h. 247.50
"Street Singer," 1940-57, 5" h. 227.50
"Street Singer," 1956-68, 5" h. 93.00
"Strolling Along," 1956-68, 4¾" h. .. 89.00
"Surprise," 1956-68, 4¼" h. 82.00
"Surprise," 1940-57, 5½" h. 142.50
"Swaying Lullaby" plaque, 1972-79,
4½ x 5¼" 70.00
"Sweet Music," 1956-68, 5¼" h. 92.50
"Telling Her Secret," 1940-57,
5" h. 242.50
"Telling Her Secret," 1956-68,
5" h. 138.50
"To Market," 1956-68, 4" h. 86.00
"To Market," 1972-79, 4" h. 62.00
"To Market," 1934-49, 5½" h. 445.00
"Trumpet Boy," 1940-57, 4¾" h. 120.00
"Trumpet Boy," 1972-79, 4¾" h. 65.00
"Umbrella Boy," 1940-57, 4¾" h. ... 525.00
"Umbrella Boy," 1956-68, 8" h. 810.00
"Umbrella Girl," 1940-57, 4¾" h. ... 625.00

"Umbrella Girl," 1972-79, 4¾" h. ... 265.00
"Umbrella Girl," 1956-68, 8" h. 787.00
"Village Boy," 1956-68, 4" h. 90.00
"Village Boy," 1972-79, 5" h. 47.50
"Village Boy," 1940-57, 6" h. 231.00
"Waiter," 1934-49, 6" h............. 520.00
"Waiter," 1956-68, 6" h............. 115.00
"Waiter," 1972-79, 7" h............. 100.00
"Wash Day," 1972-79, 6" h......... 85.00
"Watchful Angel," 1940-57, 6½" h. .. 350.00
"Wayside Harmony," 1934-49,
    4" h........................... 215.00
"Wayside Harmony," 1940-57,
    4" h........................... 150.00
"Wayside Harmony," 1940-57,
    5" h........................... 176.50
"We Congratulate," 1940-57, 4" h. .. 215.00

HUTSCHENREUTHER

The Hutschenreuther family name is associated with fine German porcelains. Carl Magnus Hutschenreuther established a factory at Hohenberg, Bavaria and was succeeded in this business by his widow and sons, Christian and Lorenz. Lorenz later established a factory in Selb, Bavaria (1857) which was managed by Christian and his son, Albert. The family later purchased factories near Carlsbad (1909), Altwasser, Silesia (1918) and Arzberg, Bavaria and, between 1917 and 1927, acquired at least two additional factories. The firm, noted for the fine quality wares produced, united all these branches in 1969 and continues in production today.

Cake plate, open handles, h.p.
    grapes, orange, pears & pine-
    apple in center, clusters of grapes
    & leaves around rim, heavy gold
    trim, marked Selb, Bavaria,
    11" d......................... $55.00
Dresser set: 12" tray, 6" pin tray,
    six-footed hair receiver, six-
    footed powder jar w/ring finial,
    6" hatpin holder, brown thrush
    decoration, artist-signed, 6 pcs. .. 125.00
Figure group, three frolicking nude
    children, designed by K. Tutter,
    4½ x 9"....................... 90.00
Model of a cat, bisque, sitting tabby
    cat, 6¾" 140.00
Model of an eagle, w/upstretched
    wings about to pounce on its
    prey, supported on a rocky out-
    crop on a circular base, tones of
    brown, grey & green, designed by
    K. Tutter, incised artist's name,
    17½" h....................... 550.00
Paintings on porcelain, each w/a
    beautiful long-haired lady, one in
    a peachy-orange dress, artist-

signed, original gold-leaf frames,
    4 x 5¾", pr................... 425.00
Painting on porcelain, rectangular,
    h.p. w/a portrait of Ruth wearing
    a white veil & a grey dress, a
    sheaf of wheat under her right
    arm & a few stalks in her left
    hand, standing in a field at sun-
    set, artist-signed "V. Creiner," im-
    pressed factory mark, 19th c.,
    framed, 5¾ x 8½" 825.00
Plate, 9½" d., centrally painted w/a
    portrait of Anna R. Kaula depicted
    w/brown hair in a purple dress,
    within a scalloped blue border
    decorated w/gilt foliate arrange-
    ments & flower-filled urns, signed
    "Wagner" (after F. Stieler), factory
    marks, title in red, ca. 1900 .....1,320.00
Plates, 10" d., each painted w/a
    noble beauty of the 18th or 19th
    centuries, named on the reverse,
    centered by a gilt scroll-embel-
    lished cobalt blue ground, set of
    six 5,720.00
Tea set: cov. teapot, creamer &
    sugar bowl; Thistle patt., 3 pcs. .. 60.00
Vase, 9" h., bisque, large parrot on
    branch in relief on each side 150.00

IMARI

Rectangular Imari Tray

This is a multicolor ware that originated in Japan, was copied by the Chinese, and imitated by the English and European potteries. It was decorated in overglaze enamel. Made in the Hizen and Arita areas of Japan, much of it was exported through the port of Imari. Arita Imari often has brocade patterns.

Bottle, tapering squared body
    w/curved shoulders & set w/a
    slender neck flaring at the rim,
    decorated w/*bijin* walking under

blossoming branches, floral medallions & small reserves of *ho-o* & sparrows scattered over the ground w/meandering leafy vines below dragon & *ho-o* roundels on a floral-patterned red enamel ground on the shoulder, stiff-leaf band encircling the neck, late Meiji period, 11¼" h. (surface wear) ...$412.50

Bowls, cov., 9 7/8" d., wide dished rim, tapering sharply to a short ring foot, conformingly shaped fitted top, decorated in gilt, cobalt blue & colored enamels w/a butterfly & large sprigs of blossoming peony of a scrolling *kinrande* (red & gold) ground scattered w/brocade patterned reserves extending to the lower rim, base inscribed *"Zoshuntei tsukuru,"* late 19th c., pr. 770.00

Bowl, 10 1/8" d., the interior w/a gold roundel painted w/a green, blue, iron-red, yellow, aubergine & black exotic bird amid similarly colored blossoms & encircled on the gold-ground sides w/alternating panels of Dutch ships or merchants conversing, the exterior w/similar panels of merchants alternating w/small roundels of Dutch ships reserved on a field of large blossoms & scrolling, for the Dutch market, late 19th c. ...3,850.00

Bowl, 13½" d., foliate-edged, the shallow bowl decorated in the center w/a swirling foliate medallion encircled by goldfish swimming in a meandering stream, the central floral swirl repeated at rim, ca. 1900 (gilt rubbed)........ 412.50

Charger, painted in the center w/a fan & floral medallion encircled by alternating shaped reserves of dragons & roosters, late 19th c., 16¼" d. (gilt rubbed) 412.50

Charger, fluted, decorated in the typical palette w/alternating panels of bamboo & plum blossoms amid rockwork, separated by formal bird & flower medallions, late Meiji period, 18½" d........1,210.00

Charger, delicately enameled in iron-red, pale green, gold & underglaze-blue w/assorted shaped reserves containing romping *shishi*, a group of *karako* (children) playing beside a vat of sake, a dragon confronting a *ho-o* bird & pheasants in a garden, Meiji period, 24½" d. 2,475.00

Jar, cov., high-shouldered ovoid body w/an inverted rolled rim, decorated on the exterior in gilt,

underglaze-blue & colored enamels w/two large shaped reserves of *ho-o* in a flowering landscape alternating w/shaped stylized floral medallions, all on a dense ground of leafy flower sprays above a lappet band at the base, the rounded shoulder w/a diaper pattern band, 19th c., 13¾" d., 10 3/8" h. (rubbed) 880.00

Plate, 12 1/8" d., central floral medallion encircled by three shaped reserves of *ho-o* & paulownia on an underglaze-blue diaper pattern ground overlaid w/red & gilt enamel floral accents, scalloped edge, late Meiji period (rubbed) 385.00

Plate, 13¼" d., slightly fluted body decorated in underglaze-blue, colored enamels & gilt w/a central medallion of a flower vase surrounded by alternating shaped reserves of dragon & floral motifs separated by vertical floral & diaper patterned bands, late 19th c. (gilt rubbed) 550.00

Tray, rectangular w/shaped edges, deep beveled rim w/dragon, bird & floral decoration, central landscape w/three deer near a stream, in shades of orange & green accented w/gold, hole through foot for hanging, 19th c., tiny kiln imperfection on rim, 13½ x 15¾" (ILLUS.) 467.50

Vase, 9 5/8" h., pear-shaped, painted w/shaped reserves of a flowering garden alternating w/reserves featuring *bijin* seated at a low writing desk, all on a red enamel ground scattered w/floral motifs below a stiff-leaf band at the flared rim, base encircled by a lappet-petal band 275.00

IRONSTONE

The first successful ironstone was patented in 1813 by C.J. Mason in England. The body contains iron slag incorporated with the clay. Other potters imitated Mason's ware and today much hard, thick ware is lumped under the term ironstone. Earlier it was called by various names, including graniteware. Both plain white and decorated wares were made throughout the 19th century. We include the Tea Leaf pattern and its variants here.

GENERAL

Baker, open, oval, Hebe shape, all white, Alcock, 7 1/8 x 9 3/8"..... $50.00

Baker, oval, Wheat patt., all
white 58.00

Basin, six hand-colored transfers,
nautical themes, Carr & Sons,
13" d. 125.00

Bowl, 10¼" d., polychrome pattern,
Ashworth..................... 75.00

Bread plate, "Give Us This Day Our
Daily Bread," all white 80.00

Cake plate, handled, Brocade patt.,
Mason, 9" 125.00

Compote, open, Arched Forget-Me-
Not patt., all white............. 110.00

Creamer, miniature, Corn 'N Oats
patt., all white................. 60.00

Creamer, Gothic shape, all white ... 55.00

Creamer, Grenade shape, all
white 60.00

Creamer, Wheat & Clover patt., all
white 55.00

Cup & saucer, handleless, Ceres
patt., all white, Elsmore &
Forster 45.00

Cup & saucer, handleless, Columbia
shape, all white................ 35.00

Cup & saucer, handleless, h.p.
Strawberry patt. 295.00

Cup & saucer, handleless, "gaudy,"
h.p. polychrome floral design
w/purple lustre, impressed registry mark & "E. Walley," Edward
Walley, England, 1845-56 (minor
wear & flakes on cup foot) 115.00

Cup & saucer, Paris shape, all
white, Alcock 30.00

Dish, six-sided, Mandalay Imari
patt., Mason, 6 x 7½".......... 45.00

Gravy boat, Bordered Fuchsia patt.,
all white, Anthony Shaw 38.50

Gravy boat, Ceres patt., all white .. 55.00

Pitcher, 4½" h., Brocade patt.,
Mason 139.50

Pitcher, 5¾" h., multicolored floral
decoration, snake handle,
Mason 125.00

Pitcher, jug-type, 7½" h., Japan
patt., ca. 1815, Mason 275.00

Sydenham Shape Pitcher

Pitcher, milk, 7 7/8" h., Sydenham
shape, all white, T. & R. Boote
(ILLUS.)........................ 185.00

Pitcher, 8" h., "gaudy," embossed
roses & other flowers w/under-
glaze blue & red, blue & green
enameling (wear, glaze flakes) ... 225.00

Pitcher, 8" h., octagonal, flat-base,
high arched spout, angular handle, h.p. morning-glory blossoms
& leaves in underglaze blue 210.00

Pitcher, jug-type, 8½" h., tree-trunk
handle, relief-molded hunting
scene in pale & dark greens, Mason's Patent Ironstone, ca. 1891-
1900, 2 qt......................75.00

Gaudy Ironstone Pitcher

Pitcher, 8¾" h., octagonal tall body
tapering to rim w/arched spout,
angled handle, h.p. "gaudy" floral
pattern w/purple lustre trim, impressed "Ironstone," ca. 1850
(ILLUS.)........................ 325.00

Pitcher, 11¾" h., Wheat & Blackberry patt., all white, Meakin 125.00

Pitcher, hot water, Moss Rose patt.,
Meakin........................ 365.00

Pitcher, water, Berlin Swirl patt., all
white, Mayer & Elliot 115.00

Pitcher, water, Wheat patt., all
white, W.E. Corn 35.00

Plate, 7¾" d., Moss Rose patt.,
Johnson Bros................... 12.00

Plate, 8¾" d., Morning Glory patt.,
all white 22.00

Plate, 9" d., Lily of the Valley patt.,
all white 20.00

Plate, 9½" d., "gaudy" Urn patt.
(stains, pinpoint flakes) 135.00

Plates, 9½" d., 12-sided, Imari-style
pattern, Ashworth Bros., Hanley,
set of 8 .... 480.00

Plates, 10½" d., Imari-type floral
decoration, polychrome enamel
w/gold trim, lion & unicorn mark,
"Stone China," set of 6 .... 465.00

Platter, 12 3/8" l., octagonal, h.p.
"gaudy" Strawberry patt., minor
wear, worn lustre trim, some
scratches, pinpoint flakes & a
shallow rim flake (ILLUS. top next
page) 200.00

Gaudy Ironstone Platter

Platter, 15", two-handled, Moss
Rose patt. 39.00
Platter, 16", Ceres patt., all white,
Elsmore & Forster 55.00
Posset cups, octagonal, all white,
Boote, set of 4 . . . . 110.00
Posset cup, Trent shape, all white,
J. Alcock 25.00
Punch bowl, handled, Berry Cluster
patt., all white 125.00
Relish dish, Wheat patt., all white . . 30.00
Sauce dish, Vintage patt.,
Challinor 12.00
Sauce tureen, cov., Ceres patt., all
white 180.00
Sauce tureen, cover & ladle, Syden-
ham shape, all white, Boote, the
set 225.00
Sauce tureen, cover & undertray,
Fluted Pearl shape, all white,
J. Wedgwood, the set 95.00
Shaving mug, Block Optic patt., all
white 60.00
Shaving mug, Winterberry patt., all
white 60.00
Sugar bowl, cov., miniature, Ceres
patt., all white 75.00
Sugar bowl, cov., Ceres patt., all
white, Elsmore & Forster, small . . . 60.00
Sugar bowl, cov., Moss Rose patt.,
Grindley & Co. 95.00
Sugar bowl, cov., six-sided on tall
six-sided base, flaring, arched
loop handles, domed cover w/ro-
sette finial, "gaudy," Strawberry
patt. (minor stains, small flake in-
side lid) 475.00
Syrup pitcher w/metal lid, Columbia
shape, all white 75.00
Syrup pitcher w/pewter lid, transfer-
printed floral decoration, ca.
1872 . . . . 75.00
Teapot, cov., Ivy patt., impressed
"William Adams," 10" h. 70.00
Teapot, cov., Laurel patt., all white,
Wedgwood 175.00
Teapot, cov., six-sided on high six-
sided base, six-sided "pagoda"
shaped cover w/rosette finial,
flared large loop handle w/"ear"
ridge at top, "gaudy," Strawberry

patt., 9¾" h. (minor stains & pin-
point flakes) 775.00
Teapot, cov., Trent shape, all white,
T. & R. Boote 90.00
Toddy cup, Columbia shape, all
white 25.00
Toddy plate, "gaudy" Urn patt., un-
derglaze blue, polychrome
enamels & lustre trim, 4¾" d. 175.00
Toothbrush holder, cov., Bell Flower
patt., Burgess 45.00
Toothbrush holder w/underplate,
Cable & Ring patt., all white,
Cockson & Seddon 40.00
Toothbrush holder, Moss Rose patt.,
5¼" h. 32.00
Toothbrush holder, cov., octagonal,
Hortz patt., J. Alcock 70.00
Tureen, cov., Mandalay Imari patt.,
Mason, 4½" h. 60.00
Tureens, cov., decorated in the Im-
ari palette in iron-reds, greens,
blues & gilt, the covers w/lotus
bud knobs, on spreading circular
base, impressed kite mark & initials "EL," painted pattern number
11657, possibly Minton, ca. 1870,
5½" h., pr. 330.00

Marmora Pattern Tureen

Tureen, cover & underplate, Marmora patt., blue transfer, w/small
ladle, minor chips, 11" h.
(ILLUS.) 175.00
Tureen, cov., Sharon Arch patt., all
white 185.00
Vegetable bowl, cov., oval, Black-
berry patt., all white 40.00
Vegetable bowl, cov., Ceres patt.,
all white, Elsmore & Forster 125.00
Vegetable bowl, cov., Ivy Wreath
patt., J. Meir & Sons 70.00
Vegetable bowl, cov., Memnon
shape, all white, John Meir & Son,
11¾" l., 6½" h. 115.00
Vegetable bowl, cov., oval, Oak &
Acorn patt., all white, J.W. Park-
hurst, 11¾" l., 7¾" h. 110.00
Vegetable bowl, cov., Savoy patt.,
Boote, 11" 78.00

Vegetable tureen, cov., Cable &
Ring patt., Savoy shape, T. & R.
Boote 40.00

Waste bowl, Fan shape, all white,
Shaw 50.00

Waste bowl, "gaudy," Strawberry
patt., 5 3/8" d., 3 3/8" h. (minor
wear, foot chips) 150.00

Waste bowl, Wheat & Clover patt.,
all white 50.00

TEA LEAF

Tea Leaf Bone Dish

Apple bowl, tall pedestal,
Wilkinson 125.00

Bacon rasher, Grindley & Co....... 35.00

Baker, Square Ridged patt., Mellor,
Taylor & Co. 40.00

Baker, rectangular, Alfred Meakin .. 30.00

Bone dish, scalloped, Alfred Meakin
(ILLUS.)....................... 50.00

Bone dish, crescent-shaped,
Wilkinson 50.00

Butter dish, cover & liner, square,
excellent lustre, Wilkinson 135.00

Cake plate, Wilkinson 60.00

Creamer, Chelsea patt., Alfred
Meakin........................ 195.00

Creamer, Victory (Dolphin) patt.,
John Edwards 195.00

Cups & saucers, handled, Mellor,
Taylor & Co., set of 4 .... 120.00

Cup & saucer, handleless, Chinese
shape, Anthony Shaw, Burslem,
ca. 1850 .... 85.00

Cup & saucer, handleless, Fan patt.,
Anthony Shaw 90.00

Cup & saucer, handleless, Hanging
Leaves patt., Anthony Shaw 95.00

Cup plate, Fish Hook patt., Alfred
Meakin........................ 50.00

Oyster bowl, round, Alfred
Meakin........................ 70.00

Pitcher, 9" h., Square Ridged patt.,
Mellor, Taylor & Co. 180.00

Pitcher, 12½" h., Henry Burgess 175.00

Plate, 7¾" d., Lily-of-the-Valley
patt., Anthony Shaw............ 18.00

Plate, 8¾" d., Henry Burgess 14.00

Plate, 9½" d., Lily-of-the-Valley
patt., Anthony Shaw............ 30.00

Plate, 10" d., Alfred Meakin 15.00

Platter, 8 x 11", Alfred Meakin 40.00

Platter, 14" oval 24.00

Platter, 14 3/8 x 20", Wilkinson 75.00

Relish dish, Fish Hook patt., Alfred
Meakin........................ 25.00

Sauce dishes, scalloped, Alfred
Meakin........................ 22.00

Sauce tureen, cov., Cable patt.,
Anthony Shaw 225.00

Chinese Shape Shaving Mug

Shaving mug, Chinese shape,
Anthony Shaw (ILLUS.) 100.00

Soap dish, cov., Fish Hook patt.,
Alfred Meakin 145.00

Soup plate w/flange rim, Niagara
shape, Anthony Shaw 18.00

Soup plate w/flange rim, Fan patt.,
Anthony Shaw, ca. 1856, 9½" d... 27.00

Soup tureen undertray, Lily-of-the-
Valley patt., Anthony Shaw 140.00

Sugar bowl, Fish Hook patt., Alfred
Meakin, small 55.00

Teapot, cov., Cable & Ring patt.,
Henry Burgess 175.00

Toothbrush holder, Bamboo patt.,
vertical, Alfred Meakin 138.00

Toothbrush holder, Chelsea patt.,
Alfred Meakin 210.00

Vegetable dish, cov., Bamboo
shape, Alfred Meakin, 6½ x 10".. 95.00

Vegetable dish, cov., Fish Hook
patt., Alfred Meakin............ 75.00

Vegetable dish, cov., rectangular,
Henry Burgess 90.00

Vegetable dish, cov., Sunburst patt.,
Wilkinson, 7½ x 12"............ 60.00

Vegetable dish, open, Lily-of-the-
Valley patt., Anthony Shaw,
11½" oval 75.00

Wash bowl, Anthony Shaw,
14½" w., 5½" h................ 95.00

Lily-of-the-Valley Bowl & Pitcher

Wash bowl & pitcher set, Lily-of-the-
Valley patt., Anthony Shaw
(ILLUS.)........................ 445.00

TEA LEAF VARIANTS
Bread plate, Pin Wheel patt.,
Wilkinson 60.00
Cups & saucers, handled, Pepper
Leaf patt., Elsmore & Forster, set
of 3........................... 125.00
Cup & saucer, handleless, Cinquefoil
patt. 50.00
Cups & saucers, handleless, Pepper
Leaf patt., Elsmore & Forster, set
of 5........................... 250.00
Pitcher, milk, Cinquefoil patt. 150.00
Plates, bread & butter, 7½" d., Pep-
per Leaf patt., Elsmore & Forster,
set of 6...................... 85.00
Plate, 10½" d., Pepper Leaf patt.... 25.00
Platter, 12¾ x 16", Morning Glory
patt.......................... 100.00
Platter, 16", Pepper Leaf patt....... 90.00
Platter, Teaberry patt., large oval .. 45.00
Soup plates, Teaberry patt.,
Clementson, 10" d., set of 4...... 70.00
Teapot, cov., Morning Glory patt.,
Elsmore & Forster 265.00
Waste bowl, Pepper Leaf patt.,
Elsmore & Forster 70.00

JEWEL TEA AUTUMN LEAF

Autumn Leaf Soup Bowl

Though not antique, this ware has a devoted following. The Hall China Company of
East Liverpool, Ohio, made the first pieces
of Autumn Leaf pattern ware to be given as
premiums by the Jewel Tea Company in 1933.
The premiums were an immediate success
and thousands of new customers, all eager to
acquire a piece of the durable Autumn Leaf
pattern ware, began purchasing Jewel Tea
products. Though the pattern was eventually used to decorate linens, glasswares and tin-
wares, we include only the Hall China
Company items in our listing.

Bowl, fruit, 5½" d. $3.00

Bowl, soup, 8¼" d. (ILLUS.) 25.00
Bowl, cream soup, two-handled 15.00
Cake plate w/"Goldenray" metal
base 195.00
Candy dish w/"Goldenray" metal
base 300.00
Casserole, cov., round, 1½ qt. 9.00
Coffeepot, cov., eight-cup, 10" h. ... 32.00
Cup & saucer 8.00
Grease jar, cov. 13.00
Marmalade jar, cov., w/spoon,
3 pcs......................... 45.00
Plate, 6" d...................... 3.50
Plate, 9" d...................... 7.00
Plate, 10" d..................... 8.00
Vegetable bowl, cov., oval, 10" 45.00
Vegetable bowl, open, oval, 10½".. 13.00

KAUFFMANN, ANGELICA

Ornate Vase with Kauffmann Scene

Angelica Kauffmann (Marie Angelique
Catherine Kauffmann) was an accomplished
Swiss artist who lived from 1741 until 1807.
Colored decals copied from her original works
often embellish late 19th century porcelain
and pieces carrying her facsimile signature
are quite collectible.

Bowl, 10" sq., maidens & cupid
scene after Kauffmann, cranberry
& gold border, Austrian blank $85.00
Tureen, cov., allegorical panel after
Kauffmann reserved on a forest
green ground, heightened
w/scrolling gilt motifs, w/bands
of anthemia & palmettes, domed
foot, late 19th c., 14¾" h. 412.50
Urn, burgundy w/gold applied design, mythological scene, signed
"Kauffmann," 9½" h. 110.00
Vase, 13½" h., two-handled, alle-

gorical scene of woman dancing,
signed "Kauffmann" 275.00
Vase, 22½" h., two-handled, urn-
shaped w/ovoid body raised on
columnar base, transfer-decorated
w/a cartouche of classically
dressed maidens in a landscape
after Kauffmann, the whole enclosed within gilt borders, mulberry ground, printed mark
"Stoke-on-Trent, England," 20th c.
(ILLUS.)........................ 467.50

KUTANI

*This is a Japanese ware from the area of
Kutani, a name meaning "nine valleys,"
where porcelain was made as early as 1644
by potters returning from the kiln center of
Arita who established a factory in the area.
The early wares, which were a heavy porcelain approaching stoneware, are referred to
as "Ko-Kutani" (old Kutani).*

Bowl, 7½" d., 3" h., scene of a lady
& boy in a garden on the bank of
a river, orange & gold $250.00
Bowl, 10¾" d., interior well painted
w/a stylized red & black floral
medallion encircled by delicately
painted birds in a flowering landscape bracketed by irregular
bands repeated on the exterior,
base inscribed "Dai Nihon Kutani-
tsukuru," 19th c. (wear)......... 192.50
Charger, scene of a beautiful woman & her cat in a garden setting
w/an ornate bridge, Japanese
zodiac border, red, brown & gold,
ca. 1860, 14¾" d. 695.00
Chocolate pot, cov., panels of peony
blossoms & birds alternating
w/panels of people in a garden
w/peony blossoms, orange &
gold, 8½" h 125.00
Nut set: master nut bowl & six individual nut cups; scene of a Geisha dressed in a gold striped
gown & seated in a boat amid
pink blossoms, painted in shades
of grey, green, tan & red w/en-
crusted gold trim against a
Nishikide diapered ground,
signed, 7 pcs................... 75.00
Platter, 21" l. oval, two fan-shaped
reserves w/bird perched on a maple tree branch, alternating
w/reserves of kiku-mon, all on stylized brocade patterned ground,
Meiji period 522.50
Saki cups, slightly flaring cylindrical
form, h.p. gilt & multicolored enamel continous scene of scholars

engaged in various pursuits bracketed by gilt patterned bands, interior w/landscape scene, Meiji
period, 1¾" h., set of 6 .... 220.00
Salt & pepper shakers, Warrior
patt., pr. 50.00
Teapot, cov., Geisha & Bird patt.,
8" h. 65.00
Tea set: cov. 10" teapot & four cups;
Flower & Crab patt., 5 pcs........ 165.00
Vase, 10" h., double gourd form,
birds decoration, gold & orange
ground, 1875................... 125.00
Vase, 14" h., double gourd form,
stylized floral bands & diapered
designs w/three shaped reserves
of landscape scenes w/figures &
horses, orange accented w/gold,
blue & green, 19th c. 660.00

LENOX

Lenox Tea Set

*The Ceramic Art Company was established
at Trenton, New Jersey, in 1889 by Jonathan
Coxon and Walter Scott Lenox. In addition
to true porcelain, it also made a Belleek-type
ware. Re-named Lenox Company in 1906, it
is still in operation today.*

Basket, Thistle patt., beige matte
glaze, relief gold trim, rustic handle, 6" h.......................$850.00
Bouillon cups & saucers, Ming patt.,
black mark, set of 6 .... 225.00
Bowl, footed, Art Deco style sterling
silver overlay on blue glaze 115.00
Bust of young woman, modeled as
woman w/long hair, closed eyes
& long, slender neck resting on
round, columnar base, ivory
glaze, green Wreath mark,
No. 2138, 9" h. 275.00
Candleholders, three-branch, Art
Deco style, 7½" h., pr. 105.00
Cup & saucer, Kingsley patt. 20.00
Dessert server, handled, round,
Ming patt. 50.00
Lamp, ivory handles rising from

mouths of 2½" gargoyle heads,
pale yellow, 19" h. 145.00
Lemonade pitcher, decorated
w/plump lemons w/green leaves
& blossoms against blending
ground, artist-signed, 6½" d. at
base, 10¾" h. 235.00
Model of a penguin, three-color
glaze, green Wreath mark,
No. 1827 . . . . .180.00 to 240.00
Mug, Harvard College decoration,
dated 1910, 5¼" h. 85.00
Nappy, footed shell shape, pink-
tinged beige, 5½ x 7" 35.00
Pitcher, cider, water lily decoration,
artist-signed & dated "1904" 175.00
Plate, 9" d., floral center, blue bor-
der w/white scalloped edge,
green Wreath mark 25.00
Plates, dinner, Ming patt., pr. 40.00
Plate, salad, Kingsley patt. 12.00
Platter, 13¼" l., Ming patt. 40.00
Salt dip, master size, model of
swan, w/24 karat gold trim 40.00
Salt & pepper shakers, four-color
design of hand & cigar, gold
Wreath mark, 5½" h., pr. 45.00
Salt & pepper shakers, figural RCA
"Nipper" dog, pr. 40.00
Soup bowl, double handles, Kingsley
patt. 22.00
Teapot, cov., Ming patt., green
Wreath mark 45.00
Tea set: cov. teapot, creamer &
sugar bowl; cobalt blue w/sterling
silver overlay, 3 pcs. (ILLUS.) 375.00
Toothpick holder, pedestal base, sil-
ver trim, seal of New Jersey Bell
Telephone, American Telephone &
Telegraph Co., 2" across top,
4" h. 55.00
Vases, 6" h., roses decoration,
signed W. Morley, green Wreath
mark, pr. 300.00
Vase, 7½" h., bulbous, medallions
of roses w/gold trim on blue
ground, green Wreath mark 75.00
Vase, 9" h., sawtooth top, melon-
ribbed sides, gold Wreath mark . . 75.00
Vase, 10½" h., pedestal base,
figural swan handles, Empire
style, ivory glaze, green Wreath
mark, ca. 1930 . . . . 70.00
Wall masks, Art Deco style male &
female on square bases, incised
"1933," 8" h. pr. 495.00

LIMOGES

*Numerous factories produced china in
Limoges, France, with major production in
the 19th century. Some pieces listed below are*

*identified by the name of the maker or the
mark of the factory. Although the famed
Haviland Company was located in Limoges,
wares bearing their marks are not included
in this listing. Also see HAVILAND.*

Limoges Tankard Pitcher

Ale set: tankard pitcher & six mugs;
h.p. cluster of grapes decoration,
7 pcs. $385.00
Boudoir set: pin tray, cov. hair re-
ceiver & cov. powder box; Wild
Rose patt., all pieces artist-
signed, 3 pcs. 250.00
Bowl, 9½" d., 4½" h., three colorful
grape clusters interior & exterior
decoration, rococo gold trim, T. &
V., Limoges (Tresseman & Vogt) . . 185.00
Bowl, fruit, 5 x 8½ x 9½", Wildflower patt., butterflies & flowers
in pink, blue, red-orange & yellow, D. & Co., Limoges (R.
Delinieres & Cie.) 65.00
Bowl, 9½" d., h.p. pink roses & vio-
lets, gold trim, L.R.L. under crown
(Lazeyras, Rosenfeld & Lehman) . . 45.00
Bowl, 10" d., 3" h., full-figure portrait of beautiful woman in
draped garment exposing one
breast, seated in a floral swing,
blue ground, framed in scrolling
encrusted gold, heavy gold scalloped rim w/five large blue
stones imbedded, B & H (decorat-
ing firm) 195.00
Box, cov., cobalt blue w/white
cupids in relief, 4¼" sq. 185.00
Cake plate, ovoid w/deeply molded
scroll rim & scroll & button tab
handles at end, all heavily gilded,
center h.p. round reserve of two
cupids bordered by ornate gold lattice & scroll frame on white
ground, 9" w., 11" l., Kittel &
Klingenberg 225.00

Cake platter, h.p. pink, yellow, white & purple mums, artist-signed, 13 x 15" 145.00

Cheese dish, cov., sprays of yellow flowers & leaves, open bud finial on dome cover, irregular edge, 9½" d. 145.00

Chocolate pot, cov., rose decoration w/profuse gilding on handle, top & bottom edge & under spout, factory decorated, 10½" h., T. & V., Limoges 175.00

Chocolate set: 11" h. cov. chocolate pot & four cups & saucers; gold handles, white ground decorated w/border of gold, red & green, 9 pcs. 375.00

Cigarette box, cov., white w/h.p. red & blue flowers, inscribed "The Gift of a Friend," made especially for Tiffany & Co., artist-signed, 3½ x 5¼" 125.00

Compotes, 4¾" d., 3½" h., pedestal base, h.p. orange & green leaves around bowl, wide gold band trim, set of 6 .... 120.00

Creamer & sugar bowl, burgundy & pink roses, gold dotted circles, highlighted w/heavier gold edging, D. & Co., Limoges, pr. 55.00

Cups & saucers, demitasse, white w/gold trim, chain of green leaves around edge, set of 6, J.P.L., France 75.00

Demitasse set: cov. coffeepot & ten cups & saucers; blown-out wreath of tiny roses w/blue ribbons & gold trim, 21 pcs. 375.00

Dessert plates, gilt-edged scalloped border densely decorated in gilt w/flowering leafy stems & scrolling vines & abstract foliate forms & beading on a pale green & cream ground highlighted in pink & white, the inner border w/gilt-edged white floral band on fuchsia ground, late 19th c., 9½" d., set of 11, Charles J. Ahrenfeldt .. 605.00

Dresser tray, irregular shaped rim, leaves, vines & small berries on rose to green shaded ground, 13 x 16", J. Pouyat, Limoges 60.00

Ewer, cream ground w/man & lady portrait panels framed w/gilt beading, artist-signed & dated 1894, 6½" h., J.P.L. 60.00

Fish set: elongated oval platter & 12 scalloped plates; various h.p. fish & floral sprays, salmon & brown on white ground, 13 pcs. 550.00

Game plaque, pierced to hang, h.p. quail in natural woodland setting, gold rococo border, artist-signed, 13½" d. 250.00

Game plates, scalloped rim, encrusted lacy & scrolling gold border, five small sections scroll inward w/pink roses, each plate depicts h.p. birds, each plate different, artist-signed, 9" d., set of 6 .... 465.00

Gravy boat, Wildflower patt., butterflies & flowers in pink, blue, red-orange & yellow 35.00

Hair receiver, h.p. daisies decoration, T. & V. 35.00

Humidor, cov., h.p. pine cones decoration in pale yellow on coral & brown ground, 6½" h. 148.00

Inkwell, cov., yellow w/green forest silhouette decoration, 1½ x 2½" 125.00

Jardiniere, h.p. floral decoration, lion's feet on base, 2 pcs. 600.00

Marmalade jar, cover & underplate, h.p. currants decoration 65.00

Mug, gold handle, h.p. cherries on stems decoration, marked "P.P. Limoges" & "Quality Art Studios," 5¾" h. (Paroutaud Freres) 75.00

Mug, figural arched female handle, h.p. burgundy & green grapes, leaves & vines decoration, 6" h. .. 145.00

Painting on porcelain, country scene w/windmill, stream, peasant woman in purples & greens, artist-signed, 8½ x 11", T & V Limoges (Tressemann & Vogt) 600.00

Pancake server, cov., roses decoration, plate 9¼" d., lid 7½" d. 215.00

Pin box, cov., h.p. scene w/cherub floating among clouds, pastel colors w/rococo swirls trimmed in gold, 2" h. 36.00

Pitcher, cider, 4¾" h., beaded handle, h.p. apples in foliage on dark green ground decoration, artist-signed, J.P. Limoges (Jean Pouyat) 80.00

Pitcher, 5" h., h.p. cherries & branches decoration, J.P. Limoges 65.00

Pitcher, tankard, 12" h., 6" d., h.p. purple & red grapes on deep green shaded to pastel ground (ILLUS.)........................ 151.00

Pitcher, tankard, 12½" h., h.p. scene of fat monk playing a fiddle, light & dark browns 125.00

Pitcher, tankard, 14½" h., h.p. portrait of adorable monk w/eyeglasses on tip of nose gazing fondly at wine bottle, rust ground, gold trim, artist-signed, T. & V.... 395.00

Plaque, pierced to hang, h.p. black & yellow hummingbird w/water lilies in white, fish in water on blue ground, heavy gold rococo border, artist-signed, 10" d. 157.00

Plaque, pierced to hang, h.p. two fish swimming amid purple flowers, gold rococo border, artist-signed, 11½" d. 125.00

Plaque, pierced to hang, h.p. cock & hen pheasant on pastel ground w/pink flowers, dull Roman gold rococo border, artist-signed, 12¼" d. 283.00

Limoges Decorated Plaque

Plaque, pierced to hang, scalloped rim w/gilt trim, h.p. scene of lovely lady w/tambourine sitting on tree branch, pastel background, lady in pink dress, artist-signed, 12½" d. (ILLUS.) 245.00

Plates, 7½" d., scalloped gold edge, h.p. green foliage on white ground, made for Dulin & Martin, Washington, D.C., set of 6, J.P.L. 135.00

Plates, 9" d., one w/lone fisherman on riverbank, the other w/fishing pier, shack & beached boat, natural blues, greens & browns, formal black-framed gold border, artist-initialed, dated 1878, pr. . . . 80.00

Plate, 9 5/8" d., h.p. center of bearded man composing, rich cobalt blue border, scalloped edge, heavy relief-molded gold decoration, panels of dainty florals, one has gold musical notes, artist-signed 185.00

Plate, 13 1/8" d., portrait of lady w/large white ornate collar & rose dress, green ground, cobalt scalloped border w/lacy gold designs overall, artist-signed 284.00

Platters, 13" d., h.p. floral arrangement within a gilt edge, one artist-signed, fitted for wall hanging, 19th c., pr. 302.50

Punch bowl, footed, h.p. purple & coral colored grapes, green leaves & gold rim & scrolls on

shaded blues & greens, interior soft coral w/pale blue & green grapes, signed "Kimmel 1907," 14½" d. 387.00

Relish dish, oval, two-handled, h.p. Art Nouveau style orchid flowers on cream ground, gold handles & rolled rim, T & V Limoges 65.00

Rose bowl, three-footed, h.p. poppies on pastel green ground, gold trim, 5¼" d. 60.00

Sardine set: cov. 4½ x 5½" box & 9 x 10" tray; scalloped deep section at one end of tray, beautiful colors w/swimming fish, starfish & a variety of shells amid seaweed, lovely blending of blue & deep pink, the set, T. & V. Limoges 230.00

Teapot, cov., h.p. yellow & white plaid w/baskets of red flowers decoration, gold handle & spout . . 75.00

Toothpick holder, h.p. pastel flowers decoration on swirled ground 25.00

Tray, scalloped rim, h.p. large pink & white roses on green shaded ground, gilt edging, artist-signed, 15" d., J. Pouyat 145.00

Trivet, h.p. yellow roses, three button feet, artist-signed, 6½" d. 55.00

Tureen, white w/gold trim, narrow leaf border, 8½ x 14", Wm. Guerin & Co. 75.00

Vase, 6" h., 9" d., w/4" opening, h.p. large border of alternating pink & yellow roses on cream ground, heavy gold rim, D & Co., France (R. Delinieres & Cie.) 125.00

Vase, 15" h., h.p. pine cones & needles decoration, artist-signed, dated 1930 . . . . 250.00

Vegetable bowl, cov., Wildflower patt. w/butterflies, flowers in pink, blue, red-orange & yellow, 2 x 6½ x 8", D.C. Limoges 35.00

LIVERPOOL

Liverpool is most often used as a generic term for fine earthenware products, usually of creamware or pearlware, produced at numerous potteries in this English city during the late 18th and early 19th centuries. Many examples, especially pitchers, were decorated with transfer-printed patriotic designs aimed specifically at the American buying public.

Mug, cylindrical, black transfer-printed bust portrait of Oliver Hazard Perry above wreath & inscription "Hero of the Lake," ca. 1814, 5¾" h. (wear, damage, deteriorated repair) $2,150.00

Mug, cylindrical, black transfer-
printed bust portrait of George
Washington in an oval reserve
under a scrolling banner w/printed
inscription, ca. 1800, 6" h. (minor
wear) 1,900.00
Pitcher, jug-type, 4¼" d., 9½" h.,
ovoid body w/black transfer-
printed scene of woman on shore
waving to departing ships, legend
reads "Susan's Farewell" & verse,
verso w/ship under full sail, early
19th c. (minor glaze nubs on
rim) 1,430.00
Pitcher, jug-type, 5½" h., cream-
ware, baluster-form body w/ap-
plied handle & molded spout,
black transfer-printed w/Masonic
emblems, devices, the inscription
"Free Masons Arms" & a sentimental verse on one side, reverse w/sentimental verse
enclosed by border of Masonic
devices, mid-19th c. (chip,
hairlines) 275.00
Pitcher, 8" h., baluster-form, transfer-
printed in black w/an American
eagle & shield flanked on one side
by a scene entitled "Apotheosis"
depicting George Washington
seated on his tomb flanked by
angels & on the other by a scene
of a ship, gilt trellis diaper swag
border at rim, applied strap handle
& pulled spout, early 19th c.
(crack) 1,100.00
Pitcher, jug-type, 9" h., strap han-
dle, black transfer of "Peace -
Plenty" on obverse & "Washington
in Glory" on reverse (putty filled
rim, spout chips, hairline in han-
dle, small base chips) 850.00
Pitcher, jug-type, 9¾" h., ovoid body
w/black transfer-printed legend
"Peace - Plenty - and - Independence" on one side & fifteen states
surrounding Washington reversed
on reverse, wreathed reserve under
spout, inscribed "Phillip and Jane
Gilkey," ca. 1810 (flake at base,
tiny rim chip, discoloration) 2,200.00
Pitcher, jug-type, 10¼" h., cream-
ware, black tranfer-printed Masonic devices & motifs including pillars, compass, keys & trowel over
the inscription "United for the
benefit of Mankind," reverse
w/three-masted ship, under spout
an American eagle enclosed by
"Peace, Commerce and Honest
Friendship with all Nations -
Entangling Alliance with none -
JEFFERSON - Anno Domini 1804,"
trimmed w/red, yellow, green &

blue enamel, vestiges of original
gilt embellishment, ca. 1804 (chips,
hairline, gilt loss) 1,870.00
Pitcher, jug-type, 10 9/16" h., cream-
ware, transfer-printed in black on
one side w/an oval map of the Thir-
teen Colonies flanked on left by
General Washington & a figure of
'Liberty' & on the right by 'Wisdom'
& 'Justice' standing behind the
seated figure of Benjamin Franklin,
all beneath the trumpeting figure
of 'Fame' & an early form of the
American flag; reverse w/a patriotic rhyme amid trophies of liberty
& independence, American eagle
under the handle, 'Hope' leaning
on an anchor beneath a wreath
containing black enamel inscription
"JONATHAN AND MARY ELDRIDGE"
under the spout, floral garland
printed & painted in black at rim,
1800-10 (slight overall discolor-
ation) 1,210.00

LONGWY

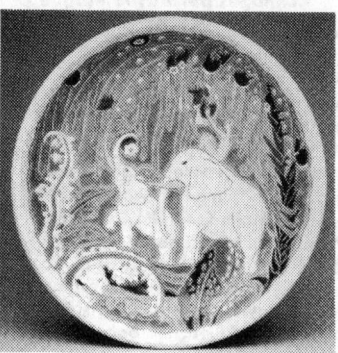

Longwy Charger

*This faience factory was established in 1798
in the town of Longwy, France and is noted
for its enameled pottery which resembles
cloisonne. Utilitarian wares were the first
production here but by the 1870's an Oriental style art pottery that imitated "cloisonne"
was created through the use of heavy enamels
in relief. By 1912, a modern Art Deco style
became part of Longwy's production and
these wares, together with the Oriental style
pieces, have made this art pottery popular
with collectors today. As interest in Art Deco
has soared in recent years, values of
Longwy's modern style wares have risen
sharply.*

Box, cov., enameled multicolored
floral decoration, 2¾ x 3½" $250.00
Charger, shallow circular bowl, in-

cised w/a central scene w/a fawn in an abstract landscape, within a surround incised w/coiling tendrils, in shades of black & crackled ivory, taupe, yellow & tan, ca. 1925, printed "PRIMAVERA/ LONGWY/FRANCE," 14¾" d. 1,430.00

Charger, shallow hemispherical vessel depicting two elephants, a jungle scene w/palms & plants, a nude female astride one elephant, decorated in yellow, lavender, white & earth tones, designed by Charles Catteau, stamped "LONGWY FRANCE ATELIER D'ART BON MARCHE," 15 1/8" d. (ILLUS.) 2,640.00

Plate, 9" d., enameled in white, red & green floral decoration on the turquoise ground to resemble cloisonne, impressed mark 154.00

Vase, 11¾" h., exaggerated pyriform vessel decorated in low-relief w/circles set between undulating waves & dotted borders, glazed in black against a crackled cobalt blue ground, printed "PRIMAVERA - LONGWY - FRANCE" surrounding a crest, ca. 1925 .... 990.00

LUSTRE WARES

Lustred wares in imitation of copper, gold, silver and other colors were produced in England in the early 19th century and onward. Gold, copper or platinum oxides were painted on glazed objects which were then fired, giving them a lustred effect. Various forms of lustre wares include plain lustre — with the entire object coated to obtain a metallic effect, bands of lustre decoration and painted lustre designs. Particularly appealing is the pink or purple "splash lustre" sometimes referred to as "Sunderland" lustre in the mistaken belief it was confined to the production of Sunderland area potteries. Objects decorated in silver lustre by the "resist" process, wherein parts of the objects to be left free from lustre decoration were treated with wax, are referred to as "silver resist."

Wares formerly called "Canary Yellow Lustre" are now referred to as "Yellow-Glazed Earthenwares."

COPPER

Goblet, bands of Sunderland pink over cream on copper lustre body, 4½" $45.00

Inkwell, blue band, Flower & Vine patt. on copper lustre body, center well w/five quill holders on the round shoulder, 3 x 3¾" 295.00

Mug, wide mustard center band, floral decoration on copper lustre body, 3" h. 42.00

Pitcher, 5" h., 1½" lavender band w/orange flowers on copper lustre body 75.00

Pitcher, 6¾" h., rounded base w/embossed basket of colorful enameled flowers on a blue band below sloping shoulder & tall flaring neck decorated in copper lustre, the neck also w/enameled decoration, mask spout & dolphin handle (pinpoint flake at handle) 85.00

Pitcher, 6¾" h., bulbous copper lustre base below tall straight neck w/embossed beaded rim band, base h.p. w/feathery swirling leaves & flowers 50.00

Pitcher, 7½" h., baluster-form footed copper lustre body w/high arched spout & scrolling serpent handle, body embossed w/a scene of a man & woman, green band around rim 60.00

Pitcher, 8 3/8" h., polychrome floral enameling on copper lustre body 55.00

Portrait jug, modeled as the uniformed figure of Wellington wearing a tricorn hat, the light brown exterior highlighted in copper lustre w/bright blue details, early 19th c., 6¾" h. (crack in hat, hairline at brim) 412.50

Teapot, cov., copper lustre body w/figural griffin handle 175.00

Tumbler, flared & fluted sides, pink lustre rim & white interior, blue top band w/flowers & leaves on copper lustre body 175.00

SUNDERLAND PINK & OTHERS

Sunderland Lustre Frog Mug

Bowl, 8" d., deep slightly flaring sides transfer-printed in black w/oval reserve of a landscape w/rim inscription "West View of the Cast Iron Bridge over the River Wear," the scene & rim outlined w/pink lustre bands 175.00

Creamer, transfer-printed in black w/verse "Ladies all I pray make free, and tell me how you like your tea" on pink splash lustre ground, 2¾" h. (pinpoint edge flakes) 95.00

Mug, cylindrical, the side transfer-printed w/a large oval reserve w/a bridge scene highlighted in yellow, green & orange enamels & surrounded by the inscription "West View of the Cast Iron Bridge over the River Wear," pink lustre rim & base bands & pink lustre squiggles around reserve, the interior applied w/the molded model of a small frog, 4¾" h. (ILLUS.) 280.00

Mug, tapering cylindrical form printed & enameled in green, yellow & iron-red, one side depicting a vessel under full sail, the other side inscribed w/a verse within a berried leafy vine, reserved on a splash-pink lustre ground, the rim & applied strap handle highlighted w/a purple-pink lustre line, ca. 1825, 4 7/8" h. 357.50

Pitcher, 6½" h., jug-type, transfer-printed in purple one side w/a ribbon-entwined laurel wreath inscribed w/state names & "Boston" enclosing the inscription "PEACE, PLENTY and INDEPENDENCE" beneath "New York" surmounted by an eagle & sixteen-star American flag & flanked by two female allegorical figures, reverse w/a sixteen-star flag above a scrolling cartouche enclosing a banner inscribed "SUCCESS to UNITED STATES of AMERICA, E. PLURIBUS UNUM" flanked by an eagle & an American Indian girl, highlighted w/pink lustre line borders (rubbed) & a star-form stylized flowerhead beneath the spout, for the American market, early 19th c. 440.00

Pitcher, 6½" h., jug-type, black transfer-printed oval scene of a naval battle under a banner printed w/"Constitution and The Java - 1797, Commodore Bainbridge," black transfer-printed row of stars around rim, pink splash lustre bands around the scene 300.00

Pitcher, 7¼" h., jug-type, the side w/large black transfer-printed armorial w/figures under a banner inscribed "The Shipwright's Arms,"

Sunderland Lustre Pitcher

pink splash lustre surrounding transfer & pink lustre band on handle (ILLUS.) 275.00

Plaque, pierced to hang, rectangular, black transfer at center of "Praise Ye the Lord" surrounded by flower & leaf enameled wreath, molded rim w/relief sprigs at corners & decorated w/pink splash lustre, 6¾ x 7¾" (some wear) 175.00

Plaque, pierced to hang, rectangular, "Prepare to Meet Thy God" in black within a floral & leaf garland in center, molded border w/relief sprigs at corners & decorated w/pink splash lustre, ca. 1850, 6¾ x 7¾" 175.00

Plaque, pierced to hang, center color potrait of Wm. Gladstone, green & gold spatter lustre rim (tiny age line) 90.00

Plate, 9¼" d., pink lustre, House patt., ca. 1850 .... 80.00

Teapot, cov., shouldered cylindrical form w/a short cylindrical neck & recessed cover w/an ovoid knop, applied strap handle, decorated overall w/pink splash lustre, early 19th c., 6" h. 220.00

Tea set, miniature: cov. teapot, cov. sugar bowl, creamer, six cups & saucers & two small cake plates; the globular teapot, sugar bowl & creamer w/a waisted neck & partially ribbed sides, the covers w/tri-foliate finials, each piece enameled in pink lustre w/sprigs & feathered leaves, highlighted w/enameled leaves in green & iron-red & alternating small circles w/leaves on a stained pink ground, the borders in purple-pink lustre, Davenport impressed anchor factory mark, ca. 1852, teapot 4" h., the set 385.00

Watch stand, modeled as a central tall-case clock w/a circular aperture for the watch, molded in shallow relief w/figures in colors within green foliate borders & covered in pink splash lustre, flanked by two allegorical figures wearing pink lustre costumes, on the left a woman in a classical gown (probably Venus), on the right w/Cupid (lacking bow or arrow), each resting against an enameled ribbed plinth standing on a stepped base, the whole raised on a pink splash lustre rectangular base (pierced), ca. 1820, 10¾" h. 770.00

MAJOLICA

Majolica, a tin-enameled-glazed pottery, has been produced for centuries. It originally took its name from the island of Majorca, a source of figuline (potter's clay). Subsequently it was widely produced in England, Europe and the United States. Etruscan majolica, now avidly sought, was made by Griffen, Smith & Hill, Phoenixville, Pa., in the last quarter of the 19th century. Most majolica advertised today is 19th or 20th century. Once scorned by most collectors, interest in this colorful ware so popular during the Victorian era has now revived and prices have continued to rise.

ETRUSCAN

Shell & Seaweed Cup & Saucer

Butter pat, Shell & Seaweed patt.... $75.00
Cake stand, pedestal base, Geranium patt., purple 145.00
Compote, Sunflower patt. 195.00
Creamer, Wild Rose patt., 5" h. 75.00
Cup & saucer, Shell & Seaweed patt. (ILLUS.) 150.00
Fruit tray, oval, Grape patt., brown twined branch border around blue & green leaves & grape cluster, on pink ground 175.00
Fruit tray, Oak patt., green leaves & cream center, 12" l. 275.00
Oyster plate, six oyster shell-shaped wells around center, plain band rim, 9" d. 85.00
Pin tray, Leaf patt. 19.00
Pitcher, 3½" h., Shell & Seaweed patt. 110.00
Pitcher, 4¾" h., Shell & Seaweed patt. (pinhead spout flake) 225.00

Pitcher, 7½" h., Albino, Shell & Seaweed patt. 97.00
Pitcher, 8¼" h., Rustic patt., molded leaves on tree trunk body 195.00
Plate, 6" d., Shell and Seaweed 100.00
Plate, 8" d., Begonia Leaf patt. 85.00
Plate, 8" d., Shell & Seaweed patt. 105.00
Plate, 8½" d., Overlapping Begonia Leaf patt., multicolored glaze 85.00
Plate, 9" d., Bamboo patt. 100.00
Plate, 9" d., molded seated dog in center on green ground, tan floral chain edge decoration 70.00
Plate, 12" d., Leaf patt., w/handle .. 195.00
Plate, Classical series, center scene of two gnomes & girl picking apples 57.00
Plate, Maple Leaf patt. 125.00
Platter, Geranium patt., purple 175.00
Relish, Begonia patt. 65.00
Salad bowl, footed, Daisy patt., pink & green on cobalt blue ground, 9" d., 5" h. 200.00
Sauce dish, Daisy patt., yellow, lavender & green, 8½" l. 285.00
Sauce dish, Wicker & Begonia Leaf patt., 5" l. 35.00
Spooner, Albino, Shell & Seaweed patt. 95.00
Spooner, Albino, Shell & Seaweed patt. in rust 75.00
Spooner, Bamboo patt. 95.00
Spooner, w/seashell handles, Shell & Seaweed patt. 325.00
Sugar bowl, cov., Cauliflower patt. 150.00
Sugar bowl, cov., two-handled, Shell & Seaweed patt. 255.00
Syrup pitcher w/pewter lid, Bamboo patt. 285.00
Teapot, cov., Cauliflower patt. ....175.00 to 225.00
Teapot, cov., Shell & Seaweed patt., straight spout 355.00
Tea set: cov. teapot, open sugar bowl, creamer, three cups & saucers, five plates; Shell & Seaweed patt., the set (sugar bowl repaired at rim) 1,760.00

GENERAL

Bamboo & Basketweave Basket

Basket, model of bird's nest,
9½" l. 180.00
Basket, brown twisted overhead
handle, Bamboo & Basketweave
patt., green & yellow w/lavender
interior, Banks & Thorley, Hanley,
England, 9½" l. (ILLUS.) 300.00
Basket, dark brown twisted handle
w/molded ribbon, blue lined
"pouch" either side, sides further
decorated w/green & lavender
florals & foliage on tan ground,
blue interior, 11" l. 1,050.00
Bowl, 6" d., 2" h., molded green
leaves on green ground, marked
"Wedgwood" 30.00
Bowl, fruit, 9" d., applied yellow &
brown bananas on green ground,
F. Carleton 36.00
Bowl, 10" d., shell-shaped, Joseph
Holdcroft, registration number
1865 .... 125.00
Bowl, 11¼" d., Italian portrait decoration w/copper lustre trim 325.00
Bread box, cov., rectangular, mottled shades of blue, green &
cream, embossed foliage &
"Bread," 9 x 10½" (chips) 400.00
Bread tray, Wheat patt., mottled
brown & yellow center, wheat
border w/yellow wheat against
green, brown edge, 13" l. (damage) 120.00
Cake stand, strawberries & blossoms on pale blue ground, Zell,
Germany 65.00
Candlestick, figure of boy standing
next to large straw-wrapped wine
bottle, probably French, 7" h. 65.00
Charger, Palissy-type decoration,
mother & baby alligators, 7" d. ... 295.00
Cheese keeper & stand, circular
dome surmounted by a figure of a
frog seated amid various seashells,
the circular stand w/a molded
border of lily pads, glazed predominantly in cobalt blue & green,
8¼" d. 8,250.00
Compote, 6 x 9", shell-shaped,
molded shells & seaweed on pedestal base, turquoise exterior,
lilac interior, Morley 140.00
Compote, 9½" d., 6" h., Wild Rose
& Rope patt., cobalt blue w/yel-
low flowers & green leaves, lavender interior 85.00
Creamer, Basketweave & Floral
patt., cream w/pink & green,
brown handle 55.00
Dish, center is variegated olive
green, scene depicts gnomes
amidst leaves, one w/witching
rod, bud & a bird in flight, wide
molded rim w/variegated light

greenish blue design of scrolls &
flowers, 11¼" d., 1¼" h. 115.00
Dishes, dessert, square w/single
shell handle, Water Lily patt.,
white & pink flower on blue
ground, pink handle, 4¼" w.,
overall 5¼" l., set of 9 .... 495.00
Ewer, cobalt blue w/overall relief-
molded fleur de lis design, smiling gargoyle mask at tip,
Minton 550.00

Bison Head Humidor

Humidor & cover, model of a bison
head, brown, Austria, 5" h.
(ILLUS.) 145.00
Humidor & cover, model of large
brindled bulldog sitting on
haunches holding white pipe to
his mouth, pinkish red vest coat,
white collar & tie, 6" w., 8" h. ... 125.00
Humidor & cover, model of a Dachshund, pouch tied at neck w/tas-
seled cord on lid, pipe in mouth,
dog variegated brindle of browns,
black & tan, marked "Austria,"
5" w., 5½" h. 95.00
Ice cream platter, Water Lily patt.,
shell-molded handles, green lily
pads & pink flower on blue
ground, pink handles, 13½" l. 375.00
Jam pot, cov., Corn patt., attributed
to J. S. Taft, Keene, New Hampshire, unsigned, 7" h. 65.00
Jardiniere & underplate, sides embossed w/bird in flight over flowers & foliage, white, brown,
green, black & red on aqua
ground, brown borders w/em-
bossed triangle design, 12" d.,
2 pcs. 700.00
Model of a shoe, rose, brown &
green shades, France, 11¼" l. 125.00
Mug, pink flowers & leaves
w/brown fence in background,
lavender interior 90.00
Pastille burners, model of a toad
supported on three feet w/a
pierced mouth to emit light, the
eyes picked out in ochre-colored
enamel w/black pupils, impressed

"Mintons," late 19th c., 7¼" h.,
pr. 550.00
Pitcher, 4½" h., Pineapple patt. 75.00
Pitcher, 4¾" h., molded fruit, water
lilies & cattails on cobalt & ochre
bands, turquoise interior, incised
"Wedgwood" 195.00
Pitcher, 5½" h., Blackberry patt.,
yellow ground 80.00
Pitcher, 5½" h., Pineapple patt. 125.00
Pitcher, 6" h., brown handle, brown
flowers on aqua ground 95.00
Pitcher, 7" h., bulbous base, Greek
Key patt. decoration around neck,
high-relief lyre & classical instruments on body, mottled cobalt
blue, green, yellow & brown,
probably New Milford Pottery Co.,
New Milford, Connecticut 130.00

Fish Pattern Pitcher

Pitcher, 7" h., 6¼" d., flattened disc
body on foot, tan bamboo handle,
sides molded w/two large swimming fish on a dark blue ground,
foot & neck in turquoise blue,
George Jones, England (ILLUS.) . . . 285.00
Pitcher, 7" h., Pond Lily patt., yel-
low petal rim 160.00
Pitcher, 8¼" h., molded hunting
scene, polychrome, wild pig
spout, dark brown branch handle,
signed "Frie Onnang France" 160.00
Pitcher, 8½" h., figural bulldog
w/open mouth, beige, green &
purple w/fuchsia interior, Frie On-
nang, France 295.00
Pitcher, 9" h., figural rooster, poly-
chrome glaze, cartouche on side
inscribed "Chante/Clair/Pour
/La/France" 200.00
Pitcher, 9¼" h., Bird's Nest patt.,
probably American-made 75.00
Pitcher, 10" h., Bird & Fan patt.,
Wedgwood, England 195.00
Pitcher, 10" h., figural owl, brown,
pink & green, attributed to
George Morley, Wellsville, Ohio . . 225.00
Pitcher, 11" h., figural fish, tail

forms handle, green, white &
brown, attributed to Morley &
Co., Wellsville, Ohio 88.00
Planter, rectangular w/shaped
sides, molded game decoration,
polychrome on white ground,
signed "Frie Onnang," France,
15" l. 400.00
Plaque, royal figure seated on
elaborate decorated horse, green-
blue & mustard yellow coloring,
11" oval, impressed "Elliot" 350.00
Plate, 7" d., Cherry Sprig patt. 40.00
Plate, 8" d., castle scene center,
black on white, George Jones,
England 110.00
Plate, 8" d., double Begonia patt.,
green ground, Wedgwood,
England 65.00
Plate, 8" d., Floral & Three Leaf
patt. 86.00
Plate, 8" d., Strawberry patt. 55.00
Plate, 9" d., Pond Lily patt. 95.00
Plate, 11¼" d., relief-molded center
scene of gnomes w/witching rods
& foliage w/bird in flight above
on blended olive green ground,
wide rim w/molded flowers &
scrolls in variegated light bluish
green 115.00
Platter, 9 x 11", Begonia Leaf shape,
green, brown & pink glaze 115.00
Platter, 10", Pineapple patt. 155.00
Platter, 11" d., Dog & Doghouse
patt., scalloped edge 125.00
Platter, 11½ x 12" oval, Bird & Fan
patt., Wardle & Co., England 200.00
Platter, 12" l., Leaves & Fern patt. . . 115.00
Platter, 24½" l., in the style of Bernard Palissy, molded & applied
salmon pink & blue fish, mottled
blue & green border w/applied
shells, 19th c. 900.00
Relish dish, leaf-shaped, open han-
dle, white, blue, yellow, brown &
green, attributed to Morley & Co.,
Wellsville, Ohio, 7½ x 8" 110.00
Salad bowl, footed, molded in the
form of a conch shell, lemon yellow exterior, pale pink interior,
relief bamboo leaves on base
painted tropical green, attributed
to George Morley, Wellsville,
Ohio, 9" d., 6" h. 130.00
Sardine box, cover w/three silver-
grey fish in relief on a green
grassy ground center, attached
underplate w/band of twined
green blades of grass, blue
w/yellow trim around top rim &
underplate edge, Minton,
England, 9" l. 525.00
Sauce dish, Pineapple patt., 5" 35.00
Spooner, Bamboo patt. 95.00

Spooner, tree trunk shape, blue berries & vines on blue, green &
brown ground, white interior 120.00
Sugar bowl, cov., Basketweave &
Floral patt., cream w/pink &
green 65.00
Sugar bowl, open, Bird & Fan patt.,
Wedgwood, England 125.00
Syrup pitcher w/metal lid, Blackberry patt., Edwin Bennett, Baltimore, Maryland 145.00
Syrup pitcher w/pewter lid, Sunflower patt., Edwin Bennett, Baltimore, Maryland 185.00
Teapot, cov., Basketweave & Floral
patt., cream w/pink & green,
brown handle (chip on spout) 110.00
Teapot, cov., Corn patt. 265.00
Toast rack, four-slice, embossed
basketweave design, mottled
shades of green, brown & blue,
8½" l. 290.00
Umbrella stand, model of a heron
on one leg w/a fish in its beak
standing in front of a tapered umbrella stand modeled as a bunch
of cattails & leaves on a naturalistic rockwork base, in tones of
green, brown, blue, yellow & maroon, marked "J. Holdcroft,"
England, ca. 1885, 32" h. 2,310.00
Vase, 5½" h., double open-work
handles, colorful iris flower, mottled green ground, molded base,
unmarked 40.00
Vase, 10½" h., two panels of molded iris flowers on brown & yellow
ground 150.00
Vase, 21" h., baluster form
w/pierced everted rim, applied
ram's head handles, on shaped
foot, decorated overall w/blue &
gilt-highlighted *rocaille* forms on a
cream ground, impressed "W.S. &
S.," Continental (restorations to
rim)........................... 192.50
Water set: 9½" h. pitcher & four
tumblers; Pineapple patt.,
5 pcs. 250.00

MARBLEHEAD

*This pottery was organized in 1904 by Dr.
Herbert J. Hall as a therapeutic aid to patients in a sanitarium he ran in Marblehead,
Massachusetts. It was later separated from
the sanitarium and directed by Arthur E.
Baggs, a fine artist and designer, who bought
out the factory in 1916 and operated it until
its closing in 1936. Most wares were hand-
thrown and decorated and carry the company mark of a stylized sailing vessel flanked
by the letters "M" and "P."*

Marblehead Pitcher

Book ends, square tile-form side
decorated w/stylized cut-back &
incised panel of a galleon on the
sea, dark blue glaze, incised
mark & paper label, 5½ x 5¾",
pr.............................$150.00
Bowl-vase, bulbous, incised red &
green berries & dark blue leaves
on speckled medium blue ground,
4¼ x 5" 660.00
Pitcher, 6 1/8" h., continuous scenic
frieze within a border of brown
banding, designed by Arthur
Baggs, impressed artist's & firm's
marks, ca. 1915 (ILLUS.) 1,760.00
Tea tile, masted ship cutting
through the waves, blues, greys &
browns, ca. 1905, 6" d. 200.00
Vase, 3¼" h., 3¾" d., bulbous body
tapering to neck, decorated
w/stylized yellow roses, brown
stems & green leaves outlined in
black against a midnight blue
background, incised "M.P." 325.00
Vase, 3½" h., 4¼" d., squat bulbous form, repeating conventionalized panels, each w/ochre sun &
blue rays setting over stylized
brick red mountains on olive
green ground, signed 990.00
Vase, 6" h., ovoid body tapering to
flared rim, decorated w/a wide
band of stylized hanging flowers
in light & darker blue on a matte
grey ground, impressed mark, pa-
per label & artist's initials 935.00
Vase, 7" h., 4¼" w., slender oviform body w/large opening, blue
matte glaze w/tiny black speck-
les, incised mark 120.00
Wall pocket, pinched top, brown
glaze 110.00

MARTIN BROTHERS POTTERY

Martinware, the term used for this pottery,

dates from 1873 and is the product of the Martin brothers - Robert, Wallace, Edwin, Walter and Charles - often considered the first British studio potters. From first to final stages, their hand-thrown pottery was completely the work of the team. The early wares may be simple and conventional, but the Martin brothers built up their reputation by producing ornately engraved, incised or carved designs on their wares. The amusing face-jugs are considered some of their finest work. After 1910, the work of the pottery declined and can be considered finished by 1915, though some attempts were made to fire pottery as late as the 1920's.

Martin Brothers Vase

Jar, cov., modeled as a humorous bird w/head tilted to the left & w/smiling expression, salt-glazed & decorated in colors of brown, mauve, green & blue, head forms cover, mounted on a wooden base, inscribed "R.W. MARTIN & BROS., LONDON & SOUTHALL, 15.4.1903" about neck & base, 10 5/8" h. $8,250.00

Jar, cov., modeled as a comic bird character, salt-glazed & decorated in colors of green, black, grey & mounted on a circular wooden base, head forms cover, inscribed "R.W. MARTIN & BROS. LONDON & SOUTHALL, 5-1884" about the neck & base, 13" h. 7,150.00

Pitcher, 9½" h., "face-jug," realistically modeled on two sides w/faces of a middle-aged man w/buff salt-glazed surface & white & brown glazed eyes, inscribed "MARTIN BROS. LONDON & SOUTHALL," dated "8-1898" 6,050.00

Spoon holder, modeled as a fantastic furry creature on four feet, w/wide mouth to accept spoons, glazed in grey, green & blue, inscribed "27 RW MARTIN LONDON & SOUTHALL, 11-79," 6" l. 7,150.00

Vase, 8¾" h., globular, body w/sgraffito decoration of fish & eels amid seaweed, inscribed "R W Martin & Bros. London & Southall 5-1888" (ILLUS.) 1,210.00

MC COY

Indian Cookie Jar

Collectors are now beginning to seek the art wares of two McCoy potteries. One was founded in Roseville, Ohio, in the late 19th century as the J.W. McCoy Pottery, subsequently becoming Brush-McCoy Pottery Co., later Brush Pottery. The other was founded also in Roseville in 1910 as Nelson McCoy Sanitary Stoneware Co., later becoming Nelson McCoy Pottery. In 1967 the pottery was sold to D.T. Chase of the Mount Clemens Pottery Co., who sold his interest to the Lancaster Colony Corp. in 1974. The pottery shop closed in 1985 and the pottery sold to people in New Jersey in 1986. Reportedly they will reopen the plant.

Ale set: tankard pitcher & four mugs; relief-molded Buccaneer figure on sides, brown glaze, 5 pcs. $195.00

Bank, figural sailor w/large duffle bag over his shoulder, "Seaman's Bank for Savings" 17.50

Centerpiece bowl, shaped rim, finch perched in center, brown & light green glaze, 10" l. 50.00

Cookie jar, Barn, red, 1963 . . . . 200.00

Cookie jar, Barrel w/"Cookie" on finial, black, 1969-72 . . . . 28.00

Cookie jar, Baseball (Boy on Baseball), 1978 . . . . 45.00

Cookie jar, Basket of Potatoes, 1978-80. . . . . 27.50

Cookie jar, Bear (Cookie in Vest), 1943-45 . . . . 40.00

Cookie jar, Betsy Baker, 1975-76 . . . . 52.50

Cookie jar, Bunch of Bananas,
1948-52 . . . . 45.00
Cookie jar, Chef (Bust), w/"Cookies"
on hat band, 1962-64 . . . . 45.00
Cookie jar, Chipmunk, 1959-62 . . . . . 47.50
Cookie jar, Christmas Tree, 1959 . . . 280.00
Cookie jar, Circus Horse with Mon-
key, 1961 . . . . 85.00
Cookie jar, Clown bust, 1945-47 . . . . 30.00
Cookie jar, Clown in Barrel,
1953-56 . . . . 36.00
Cookie jar, Convex Shape, 1942 . . . . 32.00
Cookie jar, Cookie Bank, 1961 . . . . . . 43.00
Cookie jar, Cookie Cabin (log cab-
in), 1956-60 . . . . 38.00
Cookie jar, Cookie Clock, Brush-
McCoy 30.00
Cookie jar, Country Stove (Pot Belly
Stove), white, 1970-72 . . . . 28.00
Cookie jar, Country Stove (Pot Belly
Stove), black, 1963 . . . . 32.00
Cookie jar, Duck, 1964 . . . . 38.00
Cookie jar, Early American (Frontier
Family), plain knob finial,
1964-71 . . . . 32.50
Cookie jar, Elephant, split trunk,
1945 . . . . 100.00
Cookie jar, Engine (Locomotive), yel-
low, 1962-64 . . . . 75.00
Cookie jar, Fruit in Basket (Bushel
Basket), 1961 . . . . 47.50
Cookie jar, Hobby Horse, 1948-53 . . . 60.00
Cookie jar, Hocus Rabbit, 1978-79 . . . 25.00
Cookie jar, Indian, 1954-56
(ILLUS.) 150.00
Cookie jar, Kangaroo w/Joey in
pouch, matte blue finish, late
1960's 175.00
Cookie jar, Mammy, "Dem Cookies,"
1940-47 . . . . 30.00
Cookie jar, Mammy with Cauliflow-
er, 1939 . . . . 365.00
Cookie jar, Owls (Mr. & Mrs. Owl),
1953-55 . . . . 37.50
Cookie jar, Panda Bear, Brush-
McCoy 65.00
Cookie jar, Pepper, yellow,
1972-80 . . . . 25.00 to 35.00
Cookie jar, Puppy (holding cookie
sign) 47.50
Cookie jar, Rag Doll (Raggedy Ann),
1972-75 . . . . 30.00 to 40.00
Cookie jar, Red Riding Hood, Brush-
McCoy 140.00
Cookie jar, Rocking Chair (Dalma-
tians), 1961 . . . . 110.00
Cookie jar, Rooster, 1956-58 . . . . 42.50
Cookie jar, Snoopy, 1970 . . . . 55.00
Cookie jar, Spaceship (Friendship 7),
1962-63 . . . . 45.00
Cookie jar, Teepee, 1956-59 . . . . 112.00
Cookie jar, W.C. Fields, 1972-74 . . . . 78.00
Cookie jar, Wedding Jar, 1961 . . . . . . 37.00
Cookie jar, Windmill (Dutch Wind-
mill), 1961 . . . . 34.00

Cookie jar, Woodsy Owl, 1973-74 . . . 58.00
Cookie jar, Yosemite Sam, cylinder
w/decal, 1971-72 . . . . 40.00
Decanter, Apollo series,
Astronaut 25.00
Pitcher, 7" h., embossed water
lilies, figural fish handle, green
glaze, Shape No. 30 . . . . 35.00
Planter, Banana Boat, Calypso line,
man holding banjo standing by
boat, tan glaze 45.00
Planter, model of an alligator, styl-
ized creature w/bulging eyes,
green glaze 22.00
Planter, model of a frog, green
glaze, 8½" l. 30.00
Planter, model of the Liberty Bell,
dated "8th (sic) July 1776" 50.00
Planter, model of five Scotties lying
in a row, green & brown glaze,
4 x 8 x 3" 25.00
Planter, Village Smithy, blacksmith
standing under tree lettered "Under the spreading chestnut tree,"
horse standing to one side 32.50
Soup tureens, model of a sombrero,
El Rancho patt., 5 qt., pr. 65.00

Pine Cone Tea Set

Tea set: cov. teapot, creamer &
sugar bowl; Pine Cone patt.,
3 pcs. (ILLUS.) 38.50
Vase, 12¾" h., 8" d., underglaze
slip-painted tulips, standard
brown glaze, marked "Loy-Nel-
Art" 295.00
Vase, modeled in the form of hya-
cinth blossoms & leaves 15.00

McCoy Wall Pocket

Wall pocket, model of a bellows,
brown w/red flowers & green
foliage 14.00
Wall pocket, model of a bird bath,
pale green w/bright yellow bird . .   22.00
Wall pocket, model of a blue bird
perched on a large pink & blue
flower (ILLUS.) 15.00
Wall pocket, model of leaf &
berries 15.00
Wall pocket, model of a pear
against green leaves . . . . . .12.00 to 15.00
Wall pocket, model of an umbrella,
yellow glaze 15.00
Watering bottle, model of a turtle . .   15.00

MEISSEN

Meissen Figure of "Tanzerin"

*The secret of true hard-paste porcelain,
known long before to the Chinese, was "dis-
covered" accidentally in Meissen, Germany,
by J.F. Bottger, an alchemist, working with
E.W. Tschirnhausen. The first European true
porcelain was made in the Meissen Porcelain
Works, organized about 1709. Meissen marks
have been widely copied by other factories.
Some pieces listed here are recent.*

Bowl, 8" d., 2½" h., reticulated
sides, four floral medallions, floral center all laced w/gold, artist-
signed, impressed mark $65.00
Bowl, 10¾" d., gold & white design
on cobalt blue ground 295.00
Bowl, 13" l., 11" w., 3¼" h., leaf
shaped, applied branch handle,
coralene w/fine beading covering
exterior & interior, colorful scene
of bird hovering over nest
w/eggs, ferns, leaves, every de-
tail trimmed in gold 675.00
Box w/t..nged lid, shaped sides, lid
w/central scene of youth & maid-
en within magenta borders
heightened w/gilt, sides w/poly-

chrome florals on magenta
ground, gilt brass fittings, crossed
swords mark, 3½" l. 425.00
Box w/hinged lid, rectangular w/in-
dented corners, lid & body decorated w/putti at various pursuits,
interior lid w/a scene of a seated
lady being washed & pampered
by servants, overall gilt trim, late
19th c., 7¼" l. 2,090.00
Bread tray, ovoid cartouche shape
w/molded scroll edge & wide
molded scroll tab handles at ends,
two cobalt blue reserves in center
w/wide white rims trimmed in
heavy gold, 7½ x 12" 250.00
Candelabra, two-light, modeled
w/the figure of Hebe or Jupiter
wearing flower-sprigged draperies
& supported by a large gilt eagle
rising behind them, w/tree-trunk
supports trimmed in gold & pastel
enamels & fitted w/two scrolling
branch arms applied w/fruiting
grapevines, the whole on a circular
base surrounded by a beaded border above swags & florettes, third
quarter 19th c., 14¾" h., pr.
(repairs) 4,070.00
Candlesticks, shaped circular base,
swirl-molded baluster-form standard & bud-form socket, base &
socket molded in relief w/a foliate band highlighted w/white &
gilding on yellow ground, late
19th c., 6½" h., pr. 165.00
Chocolate pot, cov., cylindrical
w/rounded top & conforming cover,
branch-molded spout & handle set
at 90 degree angles, finely painted
w/two large sprays of *deutsche
Blumen* in natural colors & w/smal-
ler sprays, gilt-metal mounts,
turned-wood handle, ca. 1760-70,
6¾" h. 1,650.00
Compote, 8½" d., small colorful
flowers on white ground, reticulated border w/five medallions,
swirled pedestal base, ca. 1890. . .   395.00
Cornucopia-vase, Green Ivy patt.,
4½" 115.00
Creamer, Blue Onion patt.,
mid-20th c.   75.00
Cup & saucer, Blue Onion patt. 65.00
Cup & saucer, applied polychrome
roses w/h.p. foliage, deep saucer,
cup w/scalloped rim, gilt trim
(pinpoint flakes on flowers) 95.00
Cup & saucer, handleless cylindrical
cup tapering at base, painted w/a
fashionable lady seated in a garden within scrolling trellis & floral
borders, the sides w/insects, the
saucer w/her companion within

similar borders, blue crossed
swords mark, ca. 1745 (chips to
footrim) 935.00
Cutting board, Blue Onion patt.,
6 x 10" 75.00
Dish, two-section, handled, Blue Onion patt., 9½ x 11" 225.00
Figural clock & stand, cartouche-
shaped case surmounted by the figure of Jupiter seated on cloud
struck by lightning bolts & at the
base of the case w/the figure of
Prometheus being chained to a
rock by Vulcan, further applied at
the side w/an eagle, the circular
dial surrounded by colorful pastel
flowers applied in relief, the whole
w/gilt details; set on a conformingly shaped stand w/scroll-molded
feet & applied w/flowers & trimmed
in gold, late 19th c., 32¼" h., the
set 4,125.00
Figure of a drummer on horseback,
drummer in black tricorn hat &
steel blue coat seated on a yellow
saddle cloth & a dappled horse
w/two kettle drums, oval base
applied w/flowerheads & foliage,
8" h. (chip to rein) 418.00
Figure of a Harlequin, grotesquely
posed, 19th century, crossed
swords mark, 9" h. 1,250.00
Figure of "Tanzerin," single female
dancer wearing a bonnet, shawl,
flowered ruffled skirt & pantaloons,
modeled by Paul Scheurich,
crossed swords mark, ca. 1913,
hand repaired, 10¾" h. (ILLUS.)..1,650.00
Figure group, "Europa & the Bull,"
Katzhutte mark, ca. 1848, 7" l.,
9" h. 450.00
Figure group, "Love Group," three
couples on rock w/tall tree nearby, designed by Michel Victor
Acier, mid-19th c., 20" h. 925.00
Funnel, Blue Onion patt., 3" 35.00
Ink blotter, rocker-type, w/knob
handle, Blue Onion patt.......... 135.00
Inkwell & cover, lavender ground,
three reserves of orange florals,
elaborate gold, blue crossed
swords mark.................... 135.00
Model of Bolognese Terrier, seated
dog w/black & brown eyes, a
dark brown-spotted curly coat,
grey-tipped paws (repaired chips),
an open mouth revealing a
salmon-colored tongue & white
teeth & wearing a black-edged
pale yellow collar patterned
w/black foliate scrolls & fastened
w/a gilt buckle (chip on top of
right ear), modeled by J.J.
Kaendler, crossed swords mark,
1748-55, 7½" h. 3,575.00

Model of a rooster, the squawking
bird w/well-defined feathers,
standing in a wheat field, all
white, inscribed crossed swords
mark & signature "Weils,"
31" h. 990.00
Models of swans, each bird
w/brown & black eyes, an orange
& blue beak w/salmon tongue,
the plumage delineated in touches
of grey, w/a removable gilt-
bronze coronet around the neck,
black feet partially concealed by
green reeds & yellow-green moss,
inset in gilt-bronze mounts cast as
cattails, foliage & scrolls, late
19th c., 13" h., pr.............13,750.00
Petit four servers, two-tiered, boy &
girl finials, Blue Onion patt.,
crossed swords mark, 19th c.,
16½" h., pr. 3,200.00
Plate, 9" d., cobalt blue w/gold &
white decorations in relief, blue
crossed swords mark, ca. 1860 ... 150.00
Plate, 11" d., three floral medallions
on blue ground 475.00
Platter, 10½" l., Blue Onion patt.,
anchor mark................... 68.00
Platter, 11" l., Daisy & Button pattern border, central floral decoration, blue crossed swords mark... 190.00
Platter, 18" l. oval, sprays of
deutsche Blumen, gilt rim 220.00
Potato masher, Blue Onion patt..... 198.00

Meissen Potpourri Group

Potpourri group, formed as a figure
of a young boy wearing a jacket,
waistcoat & breeches, seated &
holding a bunch of grapes; a
young girl wearing hat, bodice,
white apron & skirt, seated & supporting a basket of flowers on her
lap & a bacchic putto wearing
drapery holding up a bunch of
grapes while he rises from ormolu
tub of grapes beneath a lobed potpourri vase & cover (knob missing),
pierced & applied overall w/color-
ful blossoms supported within an
ormolu grapevine, rococo scrolls

form base, 1755-65, various
damages & repairs, 12½" h.
(ILLUS.) .13,200.00
Rolling pin, Blue Onion patt. 285.00

Meissen Teacup & Saucer

Teacup & saucer, lobed handleless
cup painted in iron-red, blue &
green w/prunus branches & bamboo branches in Kakiemon style,
gilt trim, matching saucer, blue
crossed swords mark, ca. 1735,
hairline in cup, glaze cracks on
saucer, minor rubbing, saucer
5 7/8" d. (ILLUS.) 3,080.00
Urn, ovoid body w/double handles in
the form of entwined snakes,
rising from a gilt-trimmed fluted
circular spreading foot, blue
crossed swords mark, late 19th c.,
15¼" h. 1,540.00
Vase, 6" h., *pate-sur-pate* delicate
celadon green w/gold tracery,
h.p. cartouche featuring angel
playing harp 450.00
Vase, w/pierced cover, 12½" h.,
pate-sur-pate, shield-shaped body
on square base, teal blue ground
w/reserve panel w/gilt borders,
laurel leaf-tips decoration, late
19th c. 1,400.00

METTLACH

Mettlach Plaque No. 2195

*Ceramics with the name Mettlach were
produced by Villeroy & Boch and other potteries in the Mettlach area of Germany. Villeroy and Boch's finest years of production are
thought to be from about 1890 to 1910.*
*For listings of Mettlach steins see the
"Steins" category.*

Bowl, 8¼ x 10½", 7¼" h., Art Nouveau style, squat oval body on
short legs w/scalloped rim,
etched gold & green leaves
w/touch of blue on rich grey
ground, glossy gold trim, dated
1898, No. 2415 . . . .$675.00
Pitcher, cov., 13" h., tall circular
foot supports rounded cylindrical
body tapering at shoulder to tall
neck, pottery inset domed cover,
neck molded w/tall panels each
w/relief molded shield, wide center band of dark blue relief molded w/continuous white band of
merry dancing peasants, molded
panels around base w/scrolling
dividers, 3 liter, No. 2085 . . . . 450.00
Pitcher, cov., footed cylindrical body
flaring to sharply cut-back shoulder below tall neck w/mask
spout, pottery inset domed cover,
tan ground w/oval reserves
around neck decorated w/relief
molded floral sprigs, body divided
into arched panels decorated
w/relief molded floral swags &
coats of arms featuring owls & ea-
gles, 3 liter, No. 2076 . . . . 650.00
Plaque, pierced to hang, etched
scene of four Dragoner lancers on
horseback, signed "Stocke,"
No. 2079, 15" d. 1,500.00
Plaque, pierced to hang, etched
scene of castle above the Rhine
River, gold edge, dated 1895,
No. 1108, 17" d. 870.00

Mettlach Plaque No. 2196

Plaques, pierced to hang, first
etched w/scene of Rheinstein

Castle on cliff above river, second
etched w/scene of Stolzenfels
Castle above river, Nos. 2195 &
2196, 17½" d., pr. (ILLUS.).......2,090.00
Plaque, pierced to hang, blue &
white h.p. Delft-type scene of a
Dutch harbor w/people & boats,
artist-signed, ca. 1897, No. 5080,
17½" d........................ 450.00
Plate, 7½" d., etched, cavalier
smoking pipe & drinking, signed
"Quidenus," No. 2624........... 215.00
Punch bowl, cov., pedestal base,
white cameo relief of classical
women & children on blue
ground, 15½" handle to handle,
16" h., No. 3149 .... 850.00
Trivet, decorated w/stylized blue &
brown flowers, No. 3330........ 25.00
Vase, 10½" h., cylindrical form
tapering outward at the bottom,
incised polychromic decoration
w/swans in landscape, early
20th c., No. 2000................ 605.00
Vase, 10½" h., incised decoration of
turquoise & gold on rust ground,
No. 2856 .... 175.00
Vase, 11" h., arabesques on blue,
No. 1897 .... 345.00
Vases, 12½" h., foliate decoration
in relief w/platinum accents &
children-form handles, ca.
1852-73, No. 327, pr. 275.00

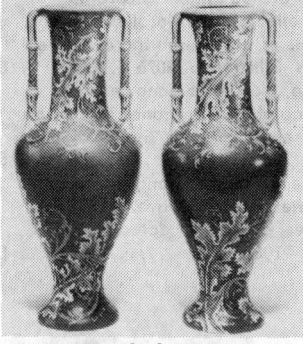

Mettlach Vases

Vases, 16¾" h., classical baluster-
form w/tall neck flanked by slender handles, incised spiral scrolling
leafy vines around neck & base in
green & gold on grey ground, gold
trim, dated 1898, No. 2414, pr.
(ILLUS.) 1,116.00

MINTON

*The Minton factory in England was estab-
lished by Thomas Minton in 1793. The factory made earthenware, especially the
blue-printed variety and Thomas Minton is*
*sometimes credited with invention of the blue
"Willow" pattern. For a time majolica and
tiles were also an important part of production, but bone china soon became the prin-
cipal ware. Mintons, Ltd., continues in
operation today.*

Minton Potpourri Vases

Dinner service: 14 dinner plates,
round footed sauce boat w/cover &
stand, circular footed vegetable
dish w/cover & oblong footed vegetable dish; Japan patt., decorated
in underglaze-blue & over-glaze
polychrome enamels, handles &
pine cone knops highlighted in gilt,
impressed "B.B./New Stone,"
1845-68, 18 pcs. $1,210.00
Marmalade jar, cov., butterfly decoration on blue ground, 1920 ...... 35.00
Model of Guardian Angel, parian,
ca. 1850, 12½" h. 200.00
Oyster plate, Shells & Seaweed
patt., marbleized emerald green
w/aqua background, English
registry mark 130.00
Oyster server, three-tiered, revolving-type, each tier molded in the
form of oyster shells adorned
w/strands of seaweed 3,520.00
Pitcher, jug-type, 6¼" h., applied
hops & vine decoration on deep
blue ground, raised mark (minor
rim repair) 225.00
Plaques, pate-sur-pate, "Morning &
Night," signed "Schenk," each 6",
the pair set in 13 x 23½" frame .. 950.00
Platter, 21", Italian Fruit patt., ca.
1860 .... 150.00
Potpourri vases & covers, ovoid vessel painted w/three classical profile portraits pendent from lilac
ribbons & surrounded by foliate
garlands, joined by floral festoons
of pink roses, all below a wide
bleu celeste border pierced w/styl-
ized foliate openings, the base &
cover similarly decorated & the
cover w/a gilt flower knop (mini-

scule chips), printed "MINTON" &
impressed "MINTON," 1860-66,
10¼" h., pr. (ILLUS.) 2,310.00
Teapot, cov., figural Chinese
Man 1,980.00
Teapot, cov., model of a monkey in
a flower-decorated suit clasping a
nut, his tail forming the handle,
bamboo shoots decorate the body,
ochre body w/naturalistic polychrome coloring, date code for
1875, 7½" h. (finial & spout restored) 638.00
Vases, 10¼" h., baluster-form, two-
handled, reserved w/rustic landscape & flower bouquet within
pale yellow & gilt borders against
gilt-decorated royal blue ground,
ca. 1835, pr. 715.00

MOCHA

Mocha Mustard Pot with Seaweed Band

*Mocha decoration is found on basically
utilitarian creamware or yellowware articles
and is achieved by a simple chemical reaction.
A color pigment of brown, blue, green or black
is given an acid nature by infusion of tobacco or hops. When this acid nature colorant is
applied in blobs to an alkaline ground color,
it reacts by spreading in feathery seaweed designs. This type of decoration is usually ac-
companied by horizontal bands of light color
slip. Produced in numerous Staffordshire potteries from the late 18th until the late 19th
centuries, its name is derived from the similar markings found on mocha quartz. In addition to the Seaweed pattern, mocha wares
are also seen with Earthworm and Cat's Eye
patterns or a marbleized effect.*

Creamer, bulbous body tapering to
top rim, short foot, leaf-embossed
strap handle, brown feathering
seaweed on yellowware,
2 1/8" h. $350.00
Creamer, jug-type, ovoid body
w/strap handle, embossed narrow
white bands divide body decorated w/brown & black marbleized
ground, center band w/applied
flower-like medallions in pale

green, 3 1/8" h. (stains, small
chips, hairline in base) 725.00
Jar, cov., tall flared sides, low
domed cover w/knob finial, wide
white band w/blue seaweed decoration flanked by narrow dark
brown stripes on yellowware,
7" d., 6" h. (minor edge flakes) .. 700.00
Mixing bowl, wide white band
w/blue feathering seaweed on
yellowware, 12¼" d., 5½" h. 235.00
Mug, strap handle, waisted yellowware body w/wide white center
band w/blue seaweed decoration
flanked by brown stripes, East
Liverpool, Ohio, 4" h. 325.00
Mug, leaf-molded handle, narrow
green horizontal striping intersecting w/wide vertical striping between brown, white & black
embossed geometric bands,
4 5/8" h. 525.00
Mustard pot, cov., short cylindrical
body w/flared rim, loop handle,
yellowware w/orange band, black
stripes & black feathering
seaweed, stains, 2 1/8" h.
(ILLUS.)....................... 245.00
Pitcher, 5" h., Cat's Eye patt. w/blue
& teal bands & black striping on
ironstone 335.00
Pitcher, 6 3/8" h., bulbous body
w/embossed bands & wide middle
band w/Earthworm patt., narrower bands in browns, blue, ochre &
white (stains, chips, hairlines) 425.00
Pitcher, 7" h., barrel-shaped, embossed bands & wide center band
w/horizontal free-hand tulip decoration in white, narrower bands of
green, dark brown, blue, white &
deep beige (stains, hairlines, old
repairs) 825.00
Punch bowl, footed, green diaper-
molded rim, wide tan band w/row
of Cat's Eye patt. band, 10" rim d.,
5 5/8" h. (extensive professional
repair) 885.00
Shaker, baluster-shape w/domed
lid, wide middle band w/black
feathering seaweed, narrower
green, orange & white bands,
4 3/8" h. (chips) 375.00
Shaker, pear-shaped w/domed lid,
wide greyish band w/blue Earthworm patt. band flanked by narrow white & black bands, 4½" h.
(minor chips on lid) 525.00
Spill holder, waisted shape w/flared
rim & foot, embossed herringbone
bands & narrow blue & white
stripes surrounding two wide

brown bands w/seaweed decoration, 5 1/8" h. 275.00

Teapot, cov., yellowware w/squat round body, wide white middle band w/green seaweed decoration, blue trim stripes, 5½" h. (minor damage & stains) 950.00

Waste bowl, Earthworm patt., green embossed rim above orange band w/pattern, 5 5/8" d., 3" h. (minor wear & stains) 350.00

MOORCROFT

Moorcroft Silver-Mounted Vase

William Moorcroft became a designer for James Macintyre & Co. in 1897 and was put in charge of their art pottery production. Moorcroft developed a number of popular designs, including Florian Ware, *while with Macintyre and continued with that firm until 1913 when they discontinued the production of art pottery.*

After leaving Macintyre in 1913, Moorcroft set up his own pottery in Burslem and continued producing the art wares he had designed earlier as well as introducing new patterns. After William's death in 1945, the pottery was operated by his son, Walter.

Ashtray, coral hibiscus on green ground $65.00

Bowl, 6" d., pink magnolia on dark blue ground, initialed 125.00

Dish, large white flower on olive green ground, label & impressed mark, 4½" 25.00

Dish, pink magnolia on dark blue ground, initialed, 5 x 9" oval 95.00

Dish, yellow monochrome lustre, 1918-29, 4½" d. 85.00

Lamp base, ovoid body w/wide, short neck, Anemone patt. on deep blue to green ground, ca. 1949, 8" d., 9¾" h. 510.00

Plates, 8½" d., Natural Ware, green & blue glaze, pr. 145.00

Tray, columbine on woodsmoke ground, initialed, 6 x 9" oval 95.00

Vase, 5¾" h., Pansy patt., deep reddish-purple on dark blue, ca. 1913-16....................... 290.00

Vase, 7" h., bulbous, green & peach flowers....................... 135.00

Vase, 10¾" h., baluster-form body painted w/a continuous frieze of stylized trees w/overlapping bushy tops against rolling hills, in rust, translucent dusty rose, olive green & streaked dark blue, w/green slip-decorated outlines, the short cylindrical neck (restored) mounted w/a silver collar w/a turned-over border engraved w/stylized scrolling foliage, first half 20th c. (ILLUS.).............. 330.00

MULBERRY WARES

Jeddo Pattern Plate

Mulberry or Flow Mulberry wares were produced in the Staffordshire district of England in the period between 1835 and 1855 at many of the same factories which produced its close "cousin," Flow Blue china. In fact, some of the early Flow Blue patterns were also decorated with the purplish mulberry coloration and feature the same heavy smearing or "flown" effect. Produced on sturdy ironstone bodies, quite a bit of this ware is still to be found and it is becoming increasingly sought-after by collectors although presently its values lag somewhat behind similar Flow Blue pieces. The standard reference to Mulberry wares is Petra Williams' book, Flow Blue China and Mulberry Ware, Similarity and Value Guide.

Coffeepot, cov., Corean patt., Podmore, Walker & Co. $350.00

Coffeepot, cov., Genoa patt., Davenport, 9 7/8" h. 175.00

Compote, open, tall pedestal, Jeddo patt., W. Adams & Sons 295.00

Creamer, Foliage patt., Edward
Walley 85.00
Creamer, Rhone Scenery patt., T.J.
& J. Mayer, 5¼" h.............. 100.00
Creamer, bulbous, octagon-shaped,
Shapoo patt., T. Hughes,
5 7/8" h. 75.00
Creamer, octagonal, Temple patt.,
Podmore, Walker & Co........... 125.00
Creamer, Vincennes patt., J. Alcock,
5¼" h......................... 82.50
Creamer, Washington Vase patt.,
Podmore, Walker & Co., 5¼" h. .. 75.00
Cup, Jeddo patt., W. Adams &
Sons 45.00
Cup & saucer, handleless, Castle
Scenery patt., Jacob Furnival 50.00
Cup & saucer, handleless, Hyson
patt., J. Clementson 50.00
Cup & saucer, handleless, Jeddo
patt., W. Adams & Sons 75.00
Cup & saucer, handleless, Pelew
patt., Edward Challinor 60.00
Cup & saucer, handleless, Vincennes
patt., Samuel Alcock 55.00
Cup & saucer, handleless, Washing-
ton Vase patt., Podmore, Walker
& Co. 55.00
Cup & saucer, Temple patt., Pod-
more, Walker & Co. 40.00
Cup plate, Allegheny patt., Thomas
Goodfellow 45.00
Cup plate, Corean patt., Podmore,
Walker & Co. 35.00
Cup plate, Ning Po patt., Edward
Challinor 35.00
Gravy boat, Peruvian patt., John
Wedge Wood, 4 5/8" h.......... 65.00
Pitcher, jug-type, milk, 6 3/8" h.,
Corean patt., Podmore, Walker &
Co..................200.00 to 275.00
Pitcher, jug-type, milk, 7½" h.,
Washington Vase patt., Podmore,
Walker & Co. ....185.00 to 225.00
Pitcher, water, 8½" h., Washington
Vase patt., Podmore, Walker &
Co. 250.00
Pitcher, 1½ qt., Jeddo patt., W.
Adams & Sons 195.00
Plate, 7" d., Corean patt., Podmore,
Walker & Co. 40.00
Plate, 7" d., Vincennes patt.,
Samuel Alcock 28.00
Plate, 7¼" d., Castle Scenery patt.,
Jacob Furnival 25.00
Plate, 8" d., Washington Vase patt.,
Podmore, Walker & Co 35.00
Plate, 8½" d., Corean patt., Pod-
more, Walker & Co. 45.00
Plate, luncheon, 8 5/8" d., Rhone
Scenery patt., T.J. & J. Mayer 25.00
Plate, 9" d., Allegheny patt., Thom-
as Goodfellow 40.00
Plate, 9" d., Washington Vase patt.,
Podmore, Walker & Co.......... 40.00

Plate, 9¼" d., Beauties of China
patt., Mellor, Venables & Co. 50.00
Plate, 9½" d., Corea patt., J.
Clementson.................... 50.00
Plate, 9½" d., Jeddo patt., W.
Adams & Sons (ILLUS.) 55.00
Plate, 9½" d., Ning Po patt., Ed-
ward Challinor 70.00
Plate, 9½" d., Rhone Scenery patt.,
T.J. & J. Mayer 45.00
Plate, 9½" d., Temple patt., Pod-
more, Walker & Co. 50.00
Plate, 9¾" d., Cypress patt.,
Davenport 45.00
Plate, 10" d., Calcutta patt., Edward
Challinor 55.00
Plate, 10" d., Corean patt., Pod-
more, Walker & Co. 60.00
Plate, 10" d., Vincennes patt.,
Samuel Alcock 50.00
Plate, 10½" d., Cypress patt.,
Davenport 55.00
Plate, 10½" d., Delhi patt. 75.00
Plate, 10½" d., Peruvian patt., John
Wedge Wood 75.00
Platter, 10 x 13½", Vincennes patt.,
Samuel Alcock 120.00
Platter, 10½ x 14", Temple patt. ... 110.00
Platter, 12 x 15½", Jeddo patt., W.
Adams & Sons 125.00
Platter, 13½", Heath's Flower patt.,
T. Heath...................... 95.00
Platter, 14" l., Bochara patt., John
Edwards...................... 95.00
Platter, 15½", Rose patt., Thomas
Walker 125.00
Platter, 16 x 20", Washington Vase
patt., Podmore, Walker & Co. 160.00
Relish dish, Corean patt., Podmore,
Walker & Co. 70.00
Relish dish, Delhi patt., 5½ x 8½",
MT & Co...................... 65.00
Sauce dish, cov., Beauties of China
patt., Mellor, Venables & Co. 150.00
Sauce dish, Cyprus patt.,
Davenport 25.00
Sauce dish, Peruvian patt., John
Wedge Wood, 5 1/8" d.......... 17.50
Sauce dish, Tivoli patt., Charles
Meigh & Sons 18.00
Sauce dish, Washington Vase patt.,
Podmore, Walker & Co.......... 25.00
Sauce tureen, cover, ladle & under-
tray, Vincennes patt., Samuel Al-
cock, the set.................. 395.00
Soup plate w/flange rim, Foliage
patt., Edward Walley, 9¼" d. 35.00
Soup plate, Peru patt., Peter Hold-
croft, 10¾" d 30.00
Sugar bowl, cov., lion head handles,
Corean patt., Podmore, Walker &
Co. 125.00
Sugar bowl, cov., Vincennes patt.,
Samuel Alcock 135.00

Tea bowl & saucer, handleless, Temple patt., Podmore, Walker & Co., 4" d. 100.00

Teapot, cov., Corean patt., Podmore, Walker & Co., 8" h. 225.00

Teapot, cov., Jeddo patt., W. Adams & Sons 250.00

Teapot, cov., Peruvian patt., John Wedge Wood 200.00

Toothbrush holder w/lid, Marble patt., J. Clementson 40.00

Vegetable dish, cov., Cologne patt., Samuel Alcock, large 185.00

Vegetable dish, cov., Corean patt., Podmore, Walker & Co. 350.00

Vegetable dish, cov., Cyprus patt., Davenport, 10" oval, 8¾" h. 375.00

Vegetable dish, cov., Jeddo patt., W. Adams & Sons 250.00

Vegetable dish, cov., Oriental Flower patt., Davenport, large 180.00

Vegetable dish, cov., hexagonal, Vincennes patt., Samuel Alcock .. 195.00

Vegetable dish, cov., Washington Vase patt., Podmore, Walker & Co. 265.00

Vegetable dish, open, Tivoli patt., Charles Meigh & Sons, 10" d. 75.00

Wash bowl & pitcher, Jeddo patt., W. Adams & Sons, 2 pcs. 525.00

NEWCOMB COLLEGE POTTERY

Newcomb College Tea Set

This pottery was established in the art department of Newcomb College, New Orleans, La., in 1897. Each piece was hand-thrown and bore the potter's mark and decorator's monogram on the base. It was always a studio business and never operated as a factory and its pieces are therefore scarce, with the early wares being eagerly sought. The pottery closed in 1940.

Bowl, 5" d., squat, bulbous shape, crocus decoration around rim, initialed "J.M." (Joseph Meyer) & "HB" (Henrietta Bailey) $500.00

Bowl, 10¼" d., 3½" h., low w/rounded sides, cut-back light blue flowers w/green stems & leaves encircling the rim, die-stamped "NC - F110" & "B," in-

cised in blue "Class of 1911" & "COX" (Paul E. Cox) 750.00

Candlestick, handled, mottled blue, green, cream & pink modified Espanol design, decorated by Sadie Irvine & Jonathan Hunt 995.00

Mug, tapered cylinder, applied curving handle, band of cut-back green-blue oak trees outlined in cobalt blue on cream ground, cobalt blue handle & top rim, medium blue wide bottom band..1,320.00

Tea set: cov. teapot, cov. sugar bowl, creamer & two cups & saucers; each piece w/blue ground decorated w/incised yellow roses, glossy glaze, decorated by Alma Mason, ca. 1911, 7 pcs. (ILLUS.) ..5,610.00

Vase, 4 x 4", squat bulbous form, cut-back blue bellflowers w/yellow centers & green leaves on medium blue ground 467.50

Vase, 4" h., 5½" w., squat, bulbous body, cut-back trees & Spanish moss in blue & green w/a white moon on a pale blue ground, decorated by Sadie Irvine, die-stamped "NC - UB87" 600.00

Vase, 4½" h., 12 beautifully carved daffodils in four colors, initialed "A.M." (Alma Mason)............. 725.00

Vase, 6¼" h., 3¼" w., ovoid body tapering slightly to short neck, scenic decoration of cut-back blue trees w/overhanging Spanish moss against a pale blue sky & white moon, decorated by Sadie Irvine, die-stamped "NC," "78" & "RX63" 650.00

Vase, 6½" h., 4¾" d., bulbous grey-blue bottom gently tapering upward to a conventionalized design of blue & cream incised flowers encircling the top, high glaze, decorated by Leona Nicholson ...2,860.00

Vase, 12" h., round bulbous top tapering toward base, incised & excised frieze of panthers under palm trees in blue, glossy glaze, designed by Sabina Elliot Wells, impressed firm mark & "U89," ca. 1902 ....4,400.00

NILOAK

This pottery was made in Benton, Arkansas, and featured hand-thrown vari-colored swirled clay decoration in objects of classic forms. Designated Mission Ware, this line is the most desirable of Niloak's production which was begun early in this century. Less expensive to produce, the cast Hywood line, finished with either high gloss or semi-matte glazes, was introduced during the economic depression of the 1930's. The pottery ceased operation about 1946.

Mission Ware Vase

Ashtray, Mission Ware, marbleized
swirls $25.00
Bowl, 2½ x 7½", Mission Ware,
marbleized swirls 65.00
Bowl, 5" d., Hywood line, scalloped,
pink glaze 12.00
Candlesticks, Mission Ware, marbleized swirls, w/paper labels,
12" h., pr. 260.00
Jar, cov., Mission Ware, cone shape
w/tab handle, high gloss interior,
marbleized swirls, 4½ x 3" 325.00
Lamp base, Mission Ware, marbleized swirls, drilled by factory,
25" h. 175.00
Model of a deer, yellow glaze 12.00
Model of an elephant on drum, blue
matte glaze, 6" 22.00
Model of a pelican, cream w/orange
beak, 5". 20.00
Model of a swan, blue matte glaze,
miniature size 18.00
Planter, Hywood line, model of a
bear 21.50
Planter, Hywood line, model of a
dog 20.00
Planter, Hywood line, model of a
seal. 20.00
Planter, Hywood line, Wishing Well,
8½" h. 55.00
Powder jar, cov., Mission Ware,
marbleized swirls 225.00
Vase, 2" h., Mission Ware, marbleized swirls 35.00
Vase, 2¼" h., Mission Ware, unusual curved-in lip, marbleized
swirls 35.00
Vase, 3¼ x 4", Mission Ware, marbleized swirls 45.00
Vase, 3¼ x 5½", Mission Ware,
marbleized swirls 52.00

Vase, 6" h., Mission Ware, marbleized swirls 50.00
Vase, 6¾" h., pitcher-shaped
w/handle & small neck, light
green glaze. 15.00
Vase, 7" h., Mission Ware, bulbous
bottom w/slender neck, marbleized swirls 44.00
Vase, 8" h., Mission Ware, marbleized swirls 95.00
Vase, 9" h., Mission Ware, bulbous
base tapered to narrow neck
w/1" d. flange opening, marbleized swirls, signed & labeled .. 135.00
Vase, 10" h., Mission Ware, cylindrical body tapering slightly toward
base, wide, flared rim, marbleized swirls (ILLUS.) 150.00

NIPPON

Nippon Scenic Ferner

This colorful porcelain was produced by numerous factories in Japan late last century and until about 1921. There are numerous marks on this ware, identifying the producers or decorating studios. The hand-painted pieces of good quality have shown a dramatic price increase within the past few years.

Bowl, 5¼" d., 3¼" h., h.p. butterflies on blue lustre ground $195.00
Bowl, 10" across open handles, h.p.
flowers, scrolls & center medallion
decoration (green "M" in Wreath
mark) 85.00
Bowl, 11" d., "gaudy," roses
w/gold, magenta border (Royal
Kinran Crown Nippon mark)...... 170.00
Cake set: 10" d. handled master
cake plate & six 6½" d. individual
serving plates; scene of cottage,
lake & autumn trees, 7 pcs. 95.00
Celery set: 13" l. celery tray & six
individual salt dips; pink roses,
scrollwork & gold beading, 7 pcs.
(green "M" in Wreath mark) 105.00
Chocolate pot, cov., white & caramel marbleized w/heavy overall
gold design..................... 95.00

Chocolate set: cov. chocolate pot & five cups & saucers; h.p. violets decoration, 11 pcs. 230.00

Cider set: pitcher & five tumblers; pastel flowers & gold decoration, 6 pcs. (green "M" in Wreath mark) 280.00

Cracker jar, cov., footed, melon-ribbed, relief-molded dragon decoration 155.00

Cracker jar, cov., fluted body, orange pomegranates & green leaves w/elaborate gold trim, 7" d. (Maple Leaf mark) 165.00

Dresser set: cov. square powder box & hair receiver & rectangular tray; gold filigree & relief-molded floral medallions, 3 pcs. (green "M" in Wreath mark) ..... 95.00 to 110.00

Ferner, footed, castle & water scene on sides, jeweled corners, w/original insert, 5¾ x 7", 4" h. 225.00

Ferner, flat base, scenic panel each side, corners formed as columns rising above sides, 5" h. (green "M" in Wreath mark) 150.00

Ferner, quadrilobed, gold feet & handles, h.p. desert scene w/Arab on camel in an oasis setting, 10¾" w. across handles, 5¾" h. (ILLUS.) 225.00

Hair receiver, overall h.p. pink roses, leaf swags & gold beading (green Maple Leaf mark) 60.00

Humidor, cov., h.p. stylized walking lion on sides, geometric design around rim & on knob finial, moriage trim, 5½" h. (green "M" in Wreath mark) 475.00

Humidor, cov., squared body w/rounded sides, relief-molded horse heads & horseshoes, bisque finish, 7" h. (green "M" in Wreath mark) 675.00

Mug, applied handle w/beaded trim, stylized horseman in medallion on side, relief-molded squiggly design around base & rim, 5½" h. (green "M" in Wreath mark) 195.00

Nut cups, footed, bluebird decoration, set of 4 .... 25.00

Pitcher, 7¾" h., squatty, gold & enameled flowers & geometric decoration 95.00

Pitcher, 8½" h., waisted cylindrical ribbed body, h.p. bouquet of large pink & red roses w/green leaves, cobalt blue base & rim bands & handle trimmed in gold, unmarked 350.00

Pitcher, 9½" h., conical body tapering sharply to narrow neck

w/high arched spout, gold scroll handle down side, h.p. oval reserve of colorful roses surrounded by green brocade background trimmed in heavy gold 125.00

Plaque, pierced to hang, h.p. scene of sailboats in sunset landscape done in oranges & yellows, Moriage border band, 8" d. (blue Maple Leaf mark) 85.00

Plaque, pierced to hang, h.p. scene of Arab on camel at camp site, 10" d. (green "M" in Wreath mark) 275.00

Plaque, pierced to hang, h.p. scene of standing man poling large boat w/high bridge in background, 10" d. (green "M" in Wreath mark) 175.00

Plate, 8" d., ornate h.p. roses decoration.................... 85.00

Plate, 9 7/8" d., h.p. scene of lady & horse's head, profuse gold trim (green "M" in Wreath mark) 195.00

Punch bowl, shallow wide bowl on pedestal foot w/two forked loop gold handles at rim, h.p. scenic interior w/sailboats, trimmed in black & gold, 12" d. including handles (green "M" in Wreath mark) 175.00

Rose bowl, three-legged, floral medallion against green ground w/Moriage trim 295.00

Shaving mug, large blue lotus-like flower & bud outlined in gold w/green leaves, gold stylized band at top, marked 125.00

Smoke set: cylindrical cigarette vase & rectangular matchbox holder on oval tray; each piece h.p. w/stylized Ho-o bird in red & pale green on cream ground, 3 pcs. (green "M" in Wreath mark) 225.00

Stein, tall cylindrical body, h.p. center reserve w/woodland scene against rust & green lattice Moriage background, 5½" h. (green "M" in Wreath mark) 150.00

Nippon Sugar Shaker

Sugar shaker, six-sided w/domed

top, handled, h.p. green bands
around top & base trimmed
w/pink & yellow florals & highlighted w/gold, 3½" d., 5" h.
(ILLUS.)........................ 93.00

Table set: creamer, sugar bowl,
serving bowl & olive dish; each
piece footed w/a melon-ribbed
body, decorated w/jewelled floral
panels trimmed w/gold borders,
4 pcs. (RC Noritake Nippon
mark)........................ 150.00

Teapot, cov., "gaudy," h.p. red
roses & gold decoration.......... 185.00

Tea set: cov. teapot, creamer, cov.
sugar bowl & four cups & saucers;
h.p. pastel scene of a swan, lake,
houses & trees w/elaborate beaded gold border, 11 pcs. (TN
Wreath mark)................. 200.00

Nippon Tea Strainer

Tea strainer & pedestal rest, h.p.
flowers trimmed w/beading &
gold, 2 pcs., Torii Nippon mark
(ILLUS.)........................ 75.00

Tea tile, octagonal, h.p. Egyptian
woman profile bust in center,
wide border band w/alternating
plain & floral blocks in dark blue
& red, 6¼" w. (green "M" in
Wreath mark)................. 125.00

Tea tile, octagonal, h.p. pink florals
on black ground w/gold border
decoration (green "M" in Wreath
mark) 22.00

Trinket box, cov., cylindrical w/low
domed cover, h.p. beaded gold
roses w/pink bands (blue "M" in
Wreath mark)................. 50.00

Urn, footed, "gaudy," ornate gold
shoulder handles, body h.p.
w/red poppies, geometrics & gold
beading, 10" h. (Royal Nishiki
mark) 180.00

Vases, 5½" h., flattened round footed body tapering to short scalloped neck, scrolled gold loop
handles from neck to shoulder,
body h.p. w/pink roses on white
ground w/gold trim, pr. (blue
Maple Leaf mark) 95.00

Vase, 7" h., squat ovoid body tapering to narrow flared neck, relief-
molded overall w/acorns & leaves

design (blue Maple Leaf
mark)..................450.00 to 500.00

Vase, 11½" h., footed ovoid body
tapering to narrow neck w/two
scrolled loop gold handles, body
w/small colorful bust portrait of a
lady in oval center reserve surrounded by delicate & ornate
overall gold scrolls & leaves, unmarked (some gold wear)........ 395.00

Whiskey jug w/bulbous stopper, flat
base on squat bulbous body
w/short flared neck & strap handle, wide h.p. continuous colorful
fox hunt scene around shoulder
framed by narrow Moriage bands
& wider plain green bands, unmarked, 7½" h................. 425.00

Whiskey jug w/stopper, h.p. Dutch
windmill landscape w/city in
background & a strolling lady in
foreground, 9¾" h. (green "M" in
Wreath mark)................. 750.00

NORITAKE

Noritake Azalea Cup & Saucer

*Noritake china, still in production in Japan,
has been exported in large quantities to this
country since early in this century. Though
the Noritake Company first registered in
1904, it did not use "Noritake" as part of its
backstamp until 1918. Interest in Noritake
has escalated as collectors now seek out
pieces made between the "Nippon" era and
World War II (1921-41). The Azalea pattern
is also popular with collectors.*

Ashtray, oval, shallow dish
w/figural clown sitting on edge,
orange lustre ground ("M" in
Wreath - Made in Japan mark) ...$165.00

Ashtray, round, colored playing
cards decoration in center bottom,
5½" d. (green "M" in Wreath -
Made in Japan mark)............ 35.00

Basket, Azalea patt., No. 193,
2½ x 4 3/8", 4" h. 150.00

Basket, low, pearl lustre center,
black border w/orange unicorns,

black handle, 7" l., 5¼" w. (green
"M" in Wreath mark) 38.00
Bonbon, handled, Azalea patt.,
No. 184, 6¼" 20.00
Bowl, 7½" oval, pierced handles,
Tree in Meadow patt. 12.50
Bowl, 8" l., ovoid, figural bird sits
inside bowl edge, floral decora-
tion on orange lustre ground in
bottom (green "M" in Wreath -
Made in Japan mark) 75.00
Bowl, salad, round, Azalea patt.,
No. 12, 10" d. 32.00
Box, cov., figure of a clown, up-
turned head w/wide ruff collar
forms cover, red polka dot suit,
5½" h. (green "M" in Wreath -
Made in Japan mark) 225.00
Box, cov., h.p. desert scene on co-
balt blue ground, gold border,
7¼" d. 175.00
Butter dish, cover & liner, pale
green w/band of daisies & blue
flowers 30.00
Butter pat, Pattern No. 16034, gold
& white 22.00
Cake plate, pierced handles, Azalea
patt., No. 10, 9¾" d. 35.00
Candy dish, cov., round, cover
w/black ground decorated
w/three reserves of abstract orange flowers & gold trim, orange
& gold sprigs on black around
sides of base, 6½" d. (red
Noritake - "M" in Wreath - Japan
mark) 135.00
Casserole, cov., Azalea patt.,
No. 16, 10¼" d. 85.00
Chamberstick, flowers on yellow &
orange ground, black loop handle
& trim, 1¾" h. (red "M" in Wreath
- Made in Japan mark) 18.00
Chocolate set: cov. chocolate pot &
six cups & saucers; Pattern No.
16034, gold & white, 13 pcs. 225.00
Compote, 6½" d., 2¾" h., Azalea
patt., No. 170 . . . . 85.00
Corn set: 7¼ x 11½" platter &
twelve 7½" d. plates; h.p. life-
size corn on mauve ground,
13 pcs. (green "M" in Wreath
mark) 150.00
Cracker jar, cov., ovoid footed body
tapering toward base, cobalt blue
band w/white abstract decorations at top above continuous h.p.
scene of Arab on camel in desert
campfire scene, silver plate cover
& bail handle, 7" h. (Noritake -
blue Tree Crest mark) 175.00
Creamer, model of black cat w/red
neck ribbon, 6½" h. 27.00
Creamer & open sugar bowl, Azalea
patt., No. 449, 2½" h., pr. 265.00

Cup & saucer, demitasse, Howo
patt. 72.00
Cup & saucer, Azalea patt., No. 2
(ILLUS.) 15.50
Dinner service: 12 five-piece place
settings plus platter, oval vegetable dish, creamer, cov. sugar
bowl, salt & pepper shakers & six
rimmed soups; Pasadena patt.,
72 pcs. 295.00
Egg cup, Pattern No. 16034, gold &
white 24.00
Ferner, triangular w/columnar cor-
ner posts topped by red ball finials, sides decorated w/red leaf
sprigs & black berries on white
ground, black bands at top & base
of sides, 6" w. (green "M" in
Wreath - Made in Japan mark) . . . 75.00
Gravy boat w/attached tray, Azalea
patt., No. 40, 8½" l 28.00
Humidor, cov., bulbous body, h.p.
w/house & trees by lake at sunset
landscape, pipe finial on cover,
3¾" h. (green "M" in Wreath -
Made in Japan mark) 105.00

Noritake Figural Inkwell

Inkwell, cov., model of a stylized
owl, head forms cover, decorated
w/blue & orange lustre, white
face w/black & yellow eyes,
3½" h., green Noritake - "M" in
Wreath mark (ILLUS.) 165.00
Lemon dish, handled, Azalea patt. . . . 20.00
Lunch set: tray w/insert & cup; Tree
in Meadow patt., set 25.00
Marmalade jar, cover & ladle, Azal-
ea patt., No. 125, 3 pcs. 110.00
Pickle dish, oval, Pattern No. 16034,
gold & white 22.00
Plate, 7½" d., Azalea patt., No. 4 . . 10.50
Plate, 8½" d., Azalea patt.,
No. 98 . . . . 18.00
Plate, dinner, Baroda patt. 8.00
Platter, 14", Azalea patt., No. 17 . . . 50.00
Platter, 14", Baroda patt. 15.00
Platter, 16", Chaumont patt. 20.00
Powder box, cov., h.p. lady smoker
decoration in center of cover,
pink ground 245.00

Relish dish, Azalea patt., 7¼" l..... 55.00
Salt & pepper shakers, Azalea patt.,
    individual size, No. 126, pr. 25.00
Salt & pepper shakers, Tree in
    Meadow patt., pr................ 10.00
Salt dip, Pattern No. 16034, gold &
    white 10.00
Soup plate, Azalea patt., No. 19 .... 20.00
Spooner, Pattern No. 16034, gold &
    white 55.00
Syrup pitcher, cov., Azalea patt..... 45.00
Teapot, cov., w/gold finial, Azalea
    patt., No. 400 ....400.00 to 500.00
Teapot, cov., Pattern No. 16034,
    gold & white.................... 50.00
Tea set: cov. teapot, creamer, sugar
    bowl & small tray; satiny overall
    gold decoration, 4 pcs. (Nippon
    mark)......................... 65.00
Toothpick holder, Azalea patt.,
    No. 192 .... 88.00
Vase, 4" h., white molded in relief
    figure of a golfer on a blue
    ground, ca. 1920's-30's 125.00
Vase, 11½" h., baluster shape
    w/two gold handles, floral deco-
    ration in light & dark blue, blue &
    yellow phoenix bird (green Nori-
    take - "M" in Wreath mark) 175.00
Vegetable bowl, cov., oval, Pattern
    No. 16034, gold & white 60.00
Vegetable bowl, open, oval, han-
    dled, Azalea patt., No. 172,
    9¼" l. 50.00
Wall pocket, Ho-o bird in relief
    framed by tail feathers, 7" l. 40.00

NORTH DAKOTA SCHOOL
OF MINES POTTERY

All pottery produced at the University of North Dakota School of Mines was made from North Dakota clay. In 1910, the University hired Margaret Kelly Cable to teach pottery making and she remained at the school until her retirement. Julia Mattson and Margaret Pachl were other instructors between 1923 and 1970. Designs and glazes varied through the years ranging from the Art Nouveau to modern styles. Pieces were marked "University of North Dakota - Grand Forks, N.D. - Made at School of Mines, N.D." within a circle and also signed by the students until 1963. Since that time, the pieces bear only the students' signatures. Items signed "Huck" are by the artist Flora Huckfield and were made between 1923 and 1949. We list only those pieces made prior to 1963.

Bowl, 7" d., 3" h., green glaze,
    artist-signed & dated $55.00
Bowl-vase, ox cart decoration, shad-

ed brown glaze, signed "M. Ca-
    ble," 3½" h.................... 525.00
Chamberstick, tan glaze, artist-
    signed 35.00
Finger bowl, brown glaze, signed
    "I.A." 47.50
Paperweight, Rebecca 60.00
Pitcher, 8" h., incised floral design,
    maroon glaze 120.00
Rose bowl, blue glaze, signed "Bec-
    tel," dated 1946..........95.00 to 110.00
Vase, 2½ x 4", green glaze 60.00
Vase, 3" h., yellow glaze 60.00
Vases, 5" h., multicolored bands,
    one signed "Mattson," the other
    "Mix," pr. 225.00
Vase, 7½" h., ringed neck, green
    glaze, signed "Cable"........... 110.00
Vase, 7¾" h., blue marbleized
    glaze, signed "J.I.T." 175.00

OHR (George) POTTERY

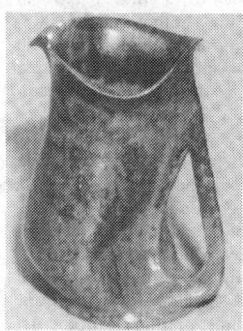

George Ohr Creamer

George Ohr, the eccentric potter of Biloxi, Mississippi, worked from about 1883 to 1906. Some think him to be one of the most expert throwers the craft will ever see. The majority of his works were hand thrown, exceedingly thin-walled items, some of which have a crushed or folded appearance. He considered himself the foremost potter in the world and declined to sell much of his production, instead accumulating a great horde to leave as a legacy to his children. In 1972 this collection was purchased for resale by an antiques dealer.

Bowl, 6½" d., 3½" h., squatty
    w/closed folded rim, pink semi-
    gloss w/green sponging & dappled
    textured dark blue, signed $13,200.00
Creamer, pinched cylindrical form
    w/an open handle, deep violet &
    mottled blue glaze, impressed
    "G.E. OHR Biloxi, Miss.," 5" h.
    (ILLUS.) 4,950.00
Mug, gun-metal grey glaze........ 350.00

Mug, three-handled, green, brown &
grey glaze 700.00
Pitcher, 3 3/8 x 4¾", pleated top,
dimpled mid-section, bright red
glaze w/black speckled mint
green feathering around the
opening, signed 1,210.00
Pitcher, 8" h., bulbous molded body
w/wide mouth & angled handle,
molded w/bust portrait of President Grover Cleveland on one
side & Mrs. Cleveland on the other, mottled navy blue & green
glaze, signed in raised script "G.
E. Ohr Biloxi Miss.," late 19th c.,
(some chips) 770.00
Puzzle mug, slightly tapered cylin-
drical body w/molded rim, heavy
angled handle w/molded flute
pattern, several reticulated holes
around top, high-gloss brown
glaze, incised "G.E. Ohr" in script
& an impressed screw head on
base, 3½" d., 5" h. 330.00
Vase, 2¾" h., bulbous body
w/pinched & crimped gold ovoid
rim, blue mottled exterior glaze,
interior w/mottled green glaze,
impressed "G.E. Ohr, Biloxi,
Miss." 3,300.00
Vase, 4¾" h., 4" d., bulbous w/long
cylindrical neck, in-body twist, one
handle w/double loop & other
w/double kink, gun-metal to mottled brown high glaze, signed . . .3,300.00
Vase, 5" h., 5" d., bulbous, poked,
pinched & squeezed to form an
inner shelf, ending in a piecrust
rim, gun-metal black glaze,
signed 5,500.00
Vase, 6" h., 6" d., bulbous body
tapering to base, pinched in
walls, collared rim, high-gloss
dark brown glaze, die-stamped
mark (underglaze kiln separations
on walls) 605.00

George Ohr Vase

Vase, 6¾" h., footed pear-shape
w/tapered & flaring rim, crystalline
speckled green, brown, blue &

beige glaze, impressed "G.E. Ohr,
Biloxi, Miss.," & "Mobile Clay
10.9.99" 1,045.00
Vase, 7" h., 6¼" d., tall pedestal
base w/an in-body twist at the
bottom flaring to a bulbous top
showing diagonal indentations,
glazed w/cobalt blue exterior
feathered w/gold, green & gun-
metal, top glazed w/raspberry,
green & gold flambe', die-stamped
"GEOHR - Biloxi, Miss." (ILLUS.) . .3,500.00

OLD IVORY

Old Ivory No. 16 Plate

*Old Ivory china was produced in Silesia,
Germany, in the late 1800's and takes its
name from the soft white background coloring. A wide range of table pieces was made
with the various patterns usually identified
by a number rather than a name.*

Berry bowl, 10" d., No. 22 . . . . $75.00
Berry set: master bowl & six sauce
dishes; No. 16, 7 pcs. 223.00
Berry set: master bowl & six sauce
dishes; No. 75, 7 pcs. 166.00
Berry set: master bowl & six sauce
dishes; No. 82, 7 pcs. 285.00
Bowl, 6½" d., No. 15 . . . . 25.00
Bowl, 6½" d., No. 32 . . . . 38.00
Bowl, master berry, 9½" d.,
No. 11 . . . . 65.00
Bowl, 10" d., No. 84 . . . . 80.00
Bowl, nappy, handle inside bowl,
No. 16 . . . . 85.00
Cake plate, pierced handles, No. 15,
10" d. 135.00
Cake plate, pierced handles, No. 22,
10" d. 75.00
Cake plate, pierced handles, No. 84,
10" d. 75.00
Cake set: 12½" master plate & six
7½" serving plates; No. 11,
7 pcs. 150.00
Celery tray, No. 15, 11½" l. 75.00

Celery tray, Thistle patt., gold trim,
12½" l., 5½" w. 45.00
Chocolate cup & saucer, No. 75 . . . . .   50.00
Chocolate pot, cov., No. 15 . . . .   267.00
Chocolate set: cov. chocolate pot &
four cups & saucers; No. 15,
9 pcs. 795.00
Chocolate set: cov. chocolate pot &
five cups & saucers; No. 84,
11 pcs. 526.00
Chocolate set: cov. chocolate pot &
six cups & saucers; No. 73,
13 pcs. 695.00
Creamer, No. 16 . . . .   56.00
Creamer & cov. sugar bowl, No. 11,
pr. 120.00
Cup & saucer, No. 84 . . . .   55.00
Dresser set: cov. powder jar & hair
receiver, No. 16, 2 pcs. (imperfec-
tion inside one rim) 80.00
Plate, 6" d., No. 75. . . . .   15.00
Plate, 6" d., No. 200. . . . .   18.00
Plate, 6¼" d., Thistle patt. 14.00
Plate, 7½" d., No. 11 . . . .   28.00
Plate, 7½" d., No. 16 (ILLUS.) 35.00
Plate, 7½" d., No. 75. . . . .   32.00
Plate, 8½" d., No. 84 . . . .   38.00
Plate, 8½" d., Thistle patt., gold
trim. 45.00
Relish dish, No. 33, 4¾ x 8" 75.00
Relish dish, No. 84 . . . .   38.00
Salt & pepper shakers, No. 84, pr. . . .   140.00
Sugar bowl, cov., No. 84. . . . .   45.00
Sugar shaker, No. 84 . . . .   285.00

OLD SLEEPY EYE

Sleepy Eye Butter Jar

Sleepy Eye, Minnesota, was named after an Indian Chief. The Sleepy Eye Milling Co. had stoneware and pottery premiums made at the turn of the century first by the Weir Pottery Company and subsequently by Western Stoneware Co., Monmouth, Illinois. On these items the trademark Indian head was signed beneath "Old Sleepy Eye." The colors were Flemish blue on grey. Later pieces by Western Stoneware to 1937 were not made for Sleepy Eye Milling Co. but for other business-es. They bear the same Indian head but "Old Sleepy Eye" does not appear below. They have a reverse design of teepees and trees and may or may not be marked Western Stone-

ware on the base. These items are usually found in cobalt blue on cream and are rarer in other colors.

Bowl (salt bowl), 6½" d., 4" h.,
Flemish blue on grey stoneware,
Weir Pottery Co., 1903 . . $400.00 to 450.00
Butter jar, Flemish blue on grey
stoneware, Weir Pottery Co., 1903
(ILLUS.) 400.00
Pitcher, 4" h., cobalt blue on white,
w/small Indian head on handle,
Western Stoneware Co., 1906-37
(half-pint) . . . . .150.00 to 175.00
Pitcher, 5¼" h., cobalt blue on
white, w/small Indian head on
handle, Western Stoneware Co.,
1906-37 (pint) 230.00
Pitcher, 7¾" h., brown on white,
w/small Indian head on handle,
Western Stoneware Co. (half-
gallon) 1,750.00
Pitcher, 8½" h., cobalt blue on
white, w/small Indian head on
handle, Western Stoneware Co.,
1906-37 (gallon) 245.00
Stein, all blue, Western Stoneware
Co., 7¾" h.   580.00
Stein, all green, Western Stoneware
Co., 7¾" h. 1,750.00
Stein, all white, Western Stone-
ware Co., 1906-37, 7¾" h. 453.00
Stein, brown on white, Western
Stoneware Co., 7¾" h. . . .750.00 to 900.00
Stein, Flemish blue on grey stone-
ware, Weir Pottery Co.,
1903 . . . . .500.00 to 550.00
Stein, grey & blue, limited edition,
1979 . . . .   215.00
Sugar bowl, cobalt blue on white,
Western Stoneware Co., 1906-37,
4" h. 325.00
Vase, 9" h., Flemish blue on grey
stoneware, Indian head signed,
dragonfly, frog & bulrushes re-
verse, Weir Pottery Co., 1903 . . . .   310.00
Vase, 9" h., brown on yellow, mold-
ed cattails & dragonflies, Western
Stoneware Co. 425.00

PARIS & OLD PARIS

China known by the generic name of Paris and Old Paris was made by several Parisian factories from the 18th through the 19th cen-tury; some of it is marked and some is not. Much of it was handsomely decorated.

Dessert service: a pair of cov. ice
pails w/liners, a pair of low footed
open compotes, a pair of two-
tiered stands, an open pierced

footed basket & eight plates; all
w/green ground & armorials,
larger pieces painted in the centers
w/cut flowers within gilt foliate
surrounds & a crest, the compotes
& basket w/garlands of flowers,
signed "Feuillet," 19th c., the
set $24,200.00
Tea set: cov. teapot, cov. sugar
bowl, two cups & saucers & a
square tray; teapot & sugar bowl
of small rectangular form w/cant-
ed corners, each piece w/a white
ground decorated w/a gilt foliate
pattern (rubbed) w/small blue
dots, ca. 1880, teapot 5¼" h.,
tray 11" l., the set 192.50
Urns, molded gilt handles, square
gilt foot, obverse w/h.p. scene of
amorous couple, reverse w/h.p.
landscape w/building, late
19th c., 10½" h., pr. (one
w/repaired handles)............. 440.00
Vases, 17" h., tapering baluster
form handled body on a square
spreading foot, decorated w/h.p.
flowers on a white ground
w/gilded borders, mounted as
lamps, 19th c., pr. 1,760.00

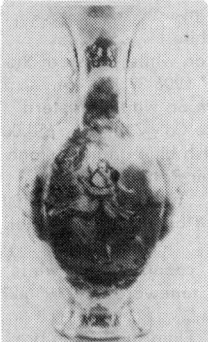

Paris Porcelain Vase

Vase, 22" h., lobed baluster form
w/everted rim, h.p. w/scenes
depicting a young courting couple,
landscape & ribbons w/musical instruments, floral gilt border, base
inscribed w/initial "D," gilding
wear, 19th c. (ILLUS.) 935.00
Vases, cov., baluster-shaped w/later
giltwood scroll-carved domed cover
& stand, base h.p. w/large reserve
scene of Chinese figures w/chil-
dren before buildings & arbors, gilt
foliage surrounds & panels divided
by dragons beneath a band of blue
scrolling foliage on a gilt scale
ground, the neck w/two further
panels on a black ground w/flow-
ers, 19th c., 27½" h. overall,
pr. 3,850.00

PATE-SUR-PATE

*Taking its name from the French phrase
meaning "paste on paste," this type of ware
features designs in relief, obtained by succes-
sive layers of thin pottery paste, painted one
on top of the other. Much of this work was
done in France and England, and perhaps the
best-known wares of this type from England
are those made by Minton.*

Cracker jar, cov., white design on
green ground, Royal Worcester,
ca. 1895-1900 ....$185.00
Moon flask, flattened circular body
carved in white slip w/scene of
winged male holding a maiden,
both nude but for swirling drapes,
sea & setting sun below against
deep green ground within white
leaftip border, reverse w/goddess
in flight supporting winged
nymph, star above & sea below,
shoulders mounted w/seated classical females wearing simple
green tunics, resting on acanthus
molded brackets, flared urn form
neck w/foliate strapwork in pale
green on dark green ground,
raised on scrolled feet centered
by a palmette pendant, George
Jones, ca. 1885, 14¼" h. (restorations) 660.00
Plaques, "Morning" & "Night,"
plaques 6" d. in 13 x 23½" velvet
mounted frame, signed "Schenck,"
pr............................ 910.00
Vase, 8½" h., celadon green ground
w/figure of woman in relief...... 350.00

PAUL REVERE POTTERY

Saturday Evening Girls Breakfast Set

*This pottery was established in Boston,
Massachusetts, in 1906, by a group of philan-
thropists seeking to establish better condi-
tions for underprivileged young girls of the
area. Edith Brown served as supervisor of the
small "Saturday Evening Girls Club" pottery
operation which was moved, in 1912, to a
house close to the Old North Church where
Paul Revere's signal lanterns had been*

placed. *The wares were mostly hand deco-*
rated in mineral colors and both sgraffito and
molded decorations were employed. Although
it became popular, it was never a profitable
operation and always depended on financial
contributions to operate. After the death of
Edith Brown in 1932, the pottery foundered
and finally closed in 1942.

Bowl, 4" d., 2½" h., blue stylized
lotus on white band, early signature & initials, ca. 1910 (some rim
roughness) $110.00
Bowl, cereal, 6" d., green band of
repeating squirrels on white
ground, marked "S.E.G" 300.00
Bowl, 8½" d., 2½" h., open type,
hand-decorated w/stylized dark
green trees & a blue sky against
a dark grey ground, ink mark &
paper label.................... 375.00
Child's breakfast set: 5½" d. cereal
bowl, 7½" d. plate & 4¼" h.
pitcher; bowl w/center scene of a
dancing rabbit & motto around
edge "In the night time at the
right time, so I've understood, it
is the habit of Sir Rabbit to dance
in the woods," plate w/center
scene of mother rabbit knitting &
corresponding motto around rim,
pitcher w/scene of baby rabbit &
corresponding motto at rim, yellow, green & blue figures on blue
ground, signed "SEG 3-17 A.M.,"
ca. 1917, 3 pcs. (ILLUS.) 2,100.00

Paul Revere Pottery Pitcher

Pitcher, 7" h., ovoid form tapering
to foot, wide pinched spout & applied strap handle, indented
decorative band of stylized blossoms around top half in varying
shades of blue, original paper
label (ILLUS.) 715.00
Plate, 8" d., blue & beige tree border on forest green glaze, central
monogram "TMO" for Thomas
Mott Osborne, marked "S.E.G." .. 350.00
Plate, 8½" d., band of eight repeating pigs w/curly tails on green,
brown & yellow border, central

monogram "HOS" for Helen Osborne Storrow, a founder of the
pottery, marked
"S.E.G." ....600.00 to 900.00
Tea tile, incised stand of green
trees on a blue lake, marked
"S.E.G.," ca. 1914, 5¾" d. 325.00
Vase, 7" h., 5¾" d., bulbous, band
of light blue & green stylized water lilies & leaves outlined in
black on light & dark blue ground,
signed "S.E.G." & dated 632.50

PEWABIC POTTERY

Mary Chase Perry (Stratton) and Horace J.
Caulkins were partners in this Detroit, Michi-
gan pottery. Established in 1903, Pewabic
Pottery evolved from their Revelation Pot-
tery, "Pewabic" meaning "clay with copper
color" in the language of Michigan's Chippe-
wa Indians. Caulkins attended to the clay for-
mulas and Mary Perry Stratton was the
artistic creator of forms & glaze formulas,
eventually developing a wide range of colors
for her finely textured glazes. The pottery's
reputation for fine wares and architectural
tiles enabled it to survive the depression
years of the 1930's. After Caulkins died in
1923, Mrs. Stratton continued to be active in
the pottery until her death, at age ninety-four,
in 1961. Her contributions to the art pottery
field are numerous.

Ashtray, turquoise iridescent glaze,
signed "Pewabic, Detroit," 4" l....$120.00
Ashtray, triangular, Art Deco style,
pink & green glossy glaze, 4" 95.00
Plate, 10½" d., tree border decorated in green, blue & brown
glaze on a cream ground, impressed "Pewabic," early 20th c... 522.50
Tile, horse decoration 250.00
Tile, octagonal, Zodiac patt.,
"Aries"........................ 325.00
Tile, octagonal, Zodiac patt.,
"Pisces" 295.00
Vase, 2½" h., folded-in top, lustre
glaze w/thick green overglaze ... 200.00
Vase, 6" h., bulbous w/short neck &
flared rim, raised foot, grey-green
iridescent glaze, impressed signature & paper label, early 20th c.
(some crazing) 275.00

PHOENIX BIRD or FLYING TURKEY

The phoenix bird, a symbol of immortali-
ty and spiritual rebirth, has been handed
down through Egyptian mythology as a bird
that consumed itself by fire after 500 years
and then rose again, renewed, from its ash-

es. This bird has been used to decorate Japanese porcelain designed for export for more than 100 years. The pattern incorporates a blue design of the bird, variously known as the "Flying Phoenix," the "Flying Turkey" or the "Ho-o," stamped on a white ground. It became popular with collectors because there was an abundant supply since the ware was produced for a long period of time. Pieces can be found marked with Japanese characters, with a "Nippon" mark, or a "Made in Japan" or "Occupied Japan" mark. Though there are several variations to the pattern and border, we have lumped them together since values seem to be quite comparable. A word of caution to the collectors, Phoenix Bird pattern is still being produced.

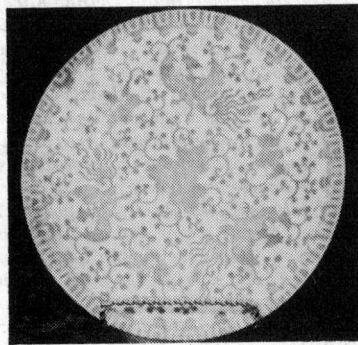

Phoenix Bird Plate

Butter pat, large $12.00
Coffee set, demitasse: cov. coffee-
    pot, creamer, sugar bowl & six
    cups & saucers; Phoenix Bird, Oc-
    cupied Japan, 15 pcs............. 150.00
Cup & saucer, Phoenix Bird 15.00
Plate, 7" d., Phoenix Bird, marked
    "Japan" (ILLUS.)................. 12.00
Platter, 12" oval, Phoenix Bird...... 20.00
Platter, Flying Turkey, marked
    "Noritake - Howo" 40.00
Sauce dish, Phoenix Bird........... 3.50
Tumbler, juice, Phoenix Bird........ 10.00

PICKARD

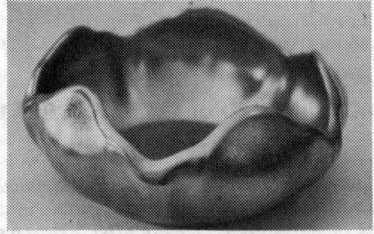

Gold-Etched Pickard Bowl

Pickard, Inc., making fine china today in Antioch, Illinois, was founded as a china decorating company by Wilder A. Pickard in Chicago in 1894. The company now makes its own blanks but once bought them from other potteries, primarily from the Havilands and others in Limoges, France.

Ashtray, overall gold-etched
    decoration..................... $45.00
Bonbon, h.p. scenic & rose decora-
    tion, artist-signed, 9"........... 155.00
Bowl, 5" d., five petal-like lobes
    curving in at rim, overall gold-
    etched decoration outside &
    smooth gold interior (ILLUS.) 35.00
Bowl, 7 1/8" w., 2 7/8" h., square
    w/notched corners, interior heavy
    gold band & lacy gold network
    against cream ground w/bronze
    water lilies & green leaves in
    wide border band, exterior in
    cream w/heavy gold bands at top
    & base & bronze water lilies &
    green leaves decoration, artist-
    signed 170.00
Bowl, Oriental patt., h.p. poppies in
    pink, decorated interior & exteri-
    or, gold & platinum trim, artist-
    signed, 1905-10, large 295.00
Bowl, soup, Cinderella patt......... 14.00
Cake plate, gold handle, Deserted
    Garden patt., artist-signed,
    10½" d. 150.00
Candlestick, Dutch girl decoration,
    6½" h......................... 55.00
Candy dish, two-handled, rich enam-
    el decoration of daisy blossoms
    w/gold trim, 8½" 110.00
Coffeepot, cov., Cinderella patt..... 55.00
Coffee set: 10¾" h. cov. coffeepot,
    creamer & sugar bowl; Aura Ar-
    genta Linear patt., artist-signed,
    3 pcs. 750.00
Compote, 9¼" d., 2½" h., h.p.
    peaches, artist-signed, 1905-10 ... 175.00
Creamer & cov. sugar bowl, Cin-
    derella patt., pr................. 25.00
Creamer & sugar bowl, h.p. violets,
    pr............................. 45.00
Cup & saucer, h.p. mirror-like silver
    & gold florals, artist-signed 80.00
Jardiniere, globular body w/deeply
    fluted gold rim, exterior decorat-
    ed w/overlapping pale pink
    leaves w/green stems & gold
    bands & rims on dark green
    ground, artist-signed, 1895-1910,
    6¾" d., 5½" h. 280.00
Nut dishes, leaf-shaped, h.p. artist-
    signed decoration, 4½" l., set
    of 4........................... 140.00
Pitcher, 6" h., h.p. violets decora-
    tion, artist-signed 185.00

Pitcher, water, 8" h., 5 5/8" d., six-
sided footed body w/wide arched
spout, 1½" w. band of water lilies
in blue, green, white & gold
around middle on gold ground,
artist-signed, 1919-22 .... 272.00
Plate, 8½" d., h.p. landscape of
moon shining through trees, blue
ground, artist-signed 150.00
Plate, 8½" d., h.p. poppies, scalloped border, artist-signed 169.00
Plate, 8 5/8" d., h.p. purple plums
decoration, wide gold border,
Haviland blank, artist-signed 95.00
Plate, 11" d., octagonal, h.p.
Deserted Garden patt., artist-
signed 200.00
Plate, 12½" d., h.p. calla lily decoration, heavy gold trim, artist-
signed 175.00
Plates, h.p. green & violet landscapes, black & gold ground,
Bavarian blanks, artist-signed, set
of 4 different scenes 375.00
Relish, h.p. floral center w/gold
medallion, artist-signed,
6¾ x 11" 195.00
Salt & pepper shakers, overall gold-
etched decoration, pr. 25.00
Tray, h.p. purple flowers & green
leaves decoration, heavy gold
trim, Limoges blank, artist-signed,
ca. 1910, 8 x 11" 65.00
Vase, 6½" h., ovoid body w/short
neck w/arched handles from neck
to shoulder, overall h.p. landscape of palm trees near moonlit
water, artist-signed 305.00
Vase, 10" h., h.p. peacock decoration on half gold, half black
ground, artist-signed 440.00
Wine set: decanter w/stopper, eight
wines & tray; Art Deco decoration
of black ground dripping w/gold
grapes, artist-signed, 10 pcs. 625.00

PICTORIAL SOUVENIRS

*These small ceramic wares, expressly made
to be sold as a souvenir of a town or resort,
are decorated with a pictorial scene which is
usually titled. Made in profusion in Germany, Austria, Bavaria, and England, they were
distributed by several American firms including C.E. Wheelock & Co., John H. Roth (Jonroth), Jones, McDuffee & Co., Stratton Co.,
and others. Because people seldom traveled
in the early years of this century, a small souvenir tray or dish, picturing the resort or a
town scene, afforded an excellent, inexpensive
gift for family or friends when returning from
a vacation trip. Seldom used and carefully
packed away later, there is an abundant sup-*

*ply of these small wares available today at
moderate prices. Their values are likely to
rise.*

Cup, "St. Charles Hotel, New
Orleans" scene, 2¼" d., 2¾" h. .. $12.00
Dish, heart-shaped, "Lincoln School,
Wausau, Wisconsin," green
basketweave ground 20.00
Dish, leaf-shaped, "Niagara Falls,
Canada," Japan, ca. 1930's 7.50
Model of an Isle of Jersey fish bas-
ket, W.H. Goss, 4" l. 25.00
Model of Look-Out House, W.H.
Goss 130.00
Model of St. Nicholas Chapel, W.H.
Goss 190.00
Model of Shakespeare's House,
W.H. Goss.................... 100.00
Mug, one side "Congressional Li-
brary Washington, D.C." w/pic-
ture, other "White House
Washington, D.C." w/picture,
brown ground, gold handle & rim,
1½" d., 2¼" h. 60.00
Mug, "High School, Slatington,
Pennsylvania"................. 15.00
Mug, miniature, "Kentucky State
College," Wheelock 32.00
Pitcher, 3½" h., "Kewanee Post
Office" bright color scene on
white 15.00
Pitcher, tankard, "Masonic Hall,
Chester, Pennsylvania" scene,
blue on white ground........... 225.00
Pitcher, Winnipeg, Canada scene,
W.H. Goss.................... 15.00
Plaque, pierced to hang, "Yel-
lowstone Falls in Yellowstone
Park," h.p., titled on front, artist-
signed, ca. 1891, Limoges,
10 x 13" 165.00
Plate, 5" d., "Temple Square, Salt
Lake," showing Temple &
Tabernacle 7.00
Plate, 6" d., "Post Office & Method-
ist Church, Newton, Kansas,"
made in Germany for The Racket,
Newton 30.00
Plate, 7¼" d., "Boston," Victoria-
Altrohlau, Bohemia mark 32.00
Plate, 8" d., "Garth Memorial Li-
brary, Hannibal, Missouri,"
Germany 22.00
Plate, "Bridge Over Illinois River,
Beardstown" 9.00
Plate, "Newport, Rhode Island,"
blue transfer scene, Jonroth 60.00
Plate, "Philadelphia, Pennsylvania,"
cobalt blue scene, rolled edge,
Rowland & Marsellus 40.00
Sauce dish, "Jennie Wade House,
Gettysburg, Pennsylvania," Aus-
tria mark, 6" d. 12.50

Saucer, views of the Hawaiian Islands, Dresden mark, ca. 1900 ... 75.00

Sugar bowl, open, two-handled, "Pavillion, St. Joseph's, Michigan," made for Drake & Wallace, Germany 20.00

Tumbler, "Souvenir of Buffalo," sepia scenes 13.00

Teapot, cov., "Eisenhower's Boyhood Home, Abilene, Kansas," gold trim 15.00

Vase, 3½" h., "Coat of Arms - Henry of Navarre," W.H. Goss 30.00

Vase, 4¾" h., "Opera House, What Cheer, Iowa," white w/colored scene 12.00

Vase, 5" h., two-handled, "Artesian Well, Woonsocket, South Dakota," made for D.K. Cole & Sons, cobalt w/gold trim, Germany 25.00

PISGAH FOREST

Pisgah Forest Vase

Walter Stephen experimented with making pottery shortly after 1900 with his parents in Tennessee. After their deaths in 1910, he eventually moved to the foot of Mt. Pisgah in North Carolina where he became a partner of C.P. Ryman. Together they built a kiln and a shop but this partnership was dissolved in 1916. During 1920 Stephen again began to experiment with pottery and by 1926 had his own pottery and equipment. Pieces are usually marked and may also be signed "W. Stephen" and dated. Walter Stephen died in 1961 but work at the pottery still continues, although on a part-time basis.

Bowl, cameo-like relief harvest scene, Chinese blue glaze, signed "Stephen" $1,050.00

Creamer, turquoise crackle glaze, pink interior, signed "Stephen - 1941" 32.00

Jug, w/stopper, turquoise high glaze, dated 1935 .... 110.00

Match safe, potter at wheel molded

in relief on front, pre-1928, 2½ x 3" 450.00

Pitcher, 3 7/8" h., light green glaze, signed "Stephen," dated 1949 .... 38.00

Pitcher, 6½" h., green glaze exterior, yellow interior, dated 1951 ... 50.00

Urn, Chinese blue glaze exterior, pink crackle glaze interior, dated 1939 .... 65.00

Vase, 6¼" h., 4" d., bulbous Chinese-shaped body w/long neck flared at the rim, covered w/large blue crystals on a white-to-gold ground, marked "Pisgah" & dated 1939 (ILLUS.) 412.50

Vase, 10" h., cameo-like white relief dancing couples scene on blue ground 700.00

Vase, 12¼" h., 8" d., tall bulbous body tapering to tall wide neck, two handles from neck to shouder, twelve signs of the Zodiac in white cameo-like pate-sur-pate on shoulder along w/a crescent moon & starry sky all against a midnight blue background, the lower half of the piece in turquoise blue, the interior in pink, dated 1931 & w/a note stating it was a special gift order 1,540.00

QUIMPER

Quimper Compote

This French earthenware pottery has been made in France since the end of the 17th century and is still in production today. Because the colorful decoration on this ware, predominantly of Breton peasant figures, is all hand-painted and each piece is unique, it has become increasingly popular with collectors in recent years. Most pieces offered today date from about the mid-19th century to the present. Modern potteries continue to operate today and contemporary examples are available in gift shops.

Book end, bust of Breton infant,

artist-signed by Bertha Savigny,
Grande Maison HB Quimper
(single) $75.00
Bowl, 5" d., peasant woman decora-
tion, Henriot-Quimper 20.00
Cake plate, footed, h.p. blue
dragonflies exterior, Henriot-
Quimper, 7½ x 12" 350.00
Compotes, figural standards of
kneeling Breton man on one &
Breton woman on other, each
supporting shallow round bowl,
Grande Maison HB Quimper, pr.
(ILLUS. of one) 800.00
Creamer & cov. sugar bowl,
peasants decoration on yellow
ground, small, HB Quimper, pr. .. 95.00
Cups & saucers, man & woman, pink
& blue, HB Quimper, France,
6 sets 180.00
Figure, *Joueur de bombarde,* man
playing flute-type instrument,
Henriot-Quimper, 15" h. 425.00
Figures, peasant man & woman,
Henriot-Quimper, 5" h., pr. 450.00
Model of a swan, Henriot-Quimper,
France 295.00
Pitcher, 6" h., male peasant & wide
yellow bands decoration, Henriot-
Quimper 125.00
Pitcher, 7½" h., croiselle design,
matte glaze, Henriot-Quimper 175.00
Plate, 8" d., rooster & floral decora-
tion, HR Quimper 65.00

Late 19th Century Quimper Plate

Plate, 10" d., h.p. Breton fisherman
center, "decor riche" scroll border, Crest of Brittany top center,
HR Quimper, ca. 1890 (ILLUS.) 350.00
Platter, 15" oval, peasant decoration
on yellow ground, HB mark 215.00
Salt dip, double, peasant woman
decoration 250.00
Salt dishes, figural man on one &
woman on other, Henriot-
Quimper, pr. 400.00
Snuff box, model of a book, male
peasant decoration, unsigned 210.00

Soup plate, Rouen patt., Henriot-
Quimper, 9" d. 150.00
Wall pocket, model of a bagpipe,
male peasant decoration, HR
Quimper on front, 5 x 7" 310.00

REDWARE

Decorated Redware Jar

Red earthenware pottery was made in the
American colonies from the late 1600's.
Bowls, crocks and all types of utilitarian
wares were turned out in great abundance to
supplement the pewter and handmade treenware. The ready availability of the clay, the
same used in making bricks and roof tiles, ac-
counted for the vast production. The lead-
glazed redware retained its reddish color,
though a variety of colors could be obtained
by adding various metals to the glaze. Interesting effects occurred accidentally
through unsuspected impurities in the clay
or uneven temperatures in the firing kiln
which sometimes resulted in streaks or mottled splotches.

Apple butter jar, ovoid, applied
strap handle, flared lip w/tooled
line band at neck, mottled greenish glaze, 7½" h. $95.00
Bank, modeled as a seated lion
w/"coleslaw" mane & tail &
molded details, orange glaze
w/highlights of green & brown,
signed "Wagner," probably Pennsylvania, 19th c., 6½" h............1,430.00
Bean pot, cov., cylindrical body
w/rounded shoulders, wide rim
w/lip & pulled spout inset
w/slightly domed cover w/button
finial, applied molded handle,
coggled band at shoulder, glazed
w/brown splashes, probably
Pennsylvania, 19th c., 6½" h.
(minor rim chips)............... 660.00
Bottle, model of a shoe w/incised

laces, clear glaze w/running
brown splotches, 7½" l. 150.00

Bowl, 8½" d., 1¾" h., molded
beaded edge, bold green glaze
w/orange spots & brown
sponging 375.00

Bowl, 13¼" d., 3¼" h., widely flaring sides w/interior undulating
yellow slip band & brown & green
spots (wear, glaze flakes)........ 325.00

Creamer, ovoid body w/flared rim,
pulled spout, applied strap handle, orange glaze w/black manganese drips up from base rim,
Pennsylvania, 19th c., 4¾" h. 341.00

Crock, straight sides, eared handles,
clear glaze w/brown splotches,
9" h. (chips, hairlines) 175.00

Cup, slightly rolled rim, applied
handle, brown spotted glaze,
4" d., 2¼" h. 110.00

Flask, flattened squatty ovoid,
careful script inscription "By John
Flack, Uniontown, July 22nd, 1809,"
4 1/8" h. (broken & reglued).....1,750.00

Flask, ovoid, clear glaze w/brown
splotches, 6" h. (minor lip
flakes) 250.00

Flowerpot w/attached saucer base,
tapering cylindrical body w/band
of coggled decoration around the
rim, above a similar band, incised
on underside "LKT," mottled dark
brown glaze, Lewis K. Tomlinson,
Dryville, Pennsylvania, 19th c.,
6" d., 4¾" h. (chips) 308.00

Flowerpot w/attached saucer base,
finger crimped rims, tooled lines,
amber glaze w/brown splotches,
6 5/8" h. (wear & rim chips)...... 165.00

Grease lamp, wide bulbous font on
short round pedestal set in shallow saucer base, strap handle
from side of font to saucer base,
overall brown glaze, built-in wick
support in font, 4½" h. (chips &
old filled chip on saucer rim)..... 425.00

Hand warmer, modeled in the form
of a duck w/string of daisies
across the breast, detailed molding w/high Albany-type glaze,
loop handle on back w/opening to
fill w/hot water, probably America, 19th c., 8½" l., 6½" h. 143.00

Harvest bottle, doughnut-shaped
w/short spout at top, amber glaze
w/brown flecks, 11¼" h. (lip
chips) 125.00

Jar, cov., high domed cover w/large
acorn finial decorated w/beaded
band fits into base rim w/wide
sloping edge above cylindrical
body decorated w/beaded bands
framing the embossed name "W.

Scrafton," Minerva head handles
at each side of jar, molded base,
clear glaze mottled w/brown &
green splashes, 9¾" h. (short
hairline on rim of cover, small
edge chips) 325.00

Jar, ovoid w/flared rim, tooled lines
at shoulder, clear greenish glaze
w/brown flecks & splotches,
5¾" h. (minor wear) 300.00

Jar, ovoid baluster-shaped, everted
rim, band of double line decoration at the shoulder, slightly
flanged base, glaze w/splashes of
manganese, Pennsylvania, mid-
19th c., 6" h. 154.00

Jar, ovoid, incised bands of straight
& wavy lines w/inscription "Keep
it fore you sake, September the
first 1835, John Dune," worn oran-
gish tan glaze, 6¼" h. (old chips,
old filled hole in bottom, repaired
lip chips) 450.00

Jar, cylindrical w/sloping shoulder &
everted rim, interior covered in
pumpkin glaze, the exterior in
cream glaze w/splashes of brown,
green & russet, hairline cracks &
firing defects, restoration to lip,
Pennsylvania, 19th c., 11¼" h.
(ILLUS.)...................... 286.00

Jug, miniature, barrel-shaped, two
incised bands & a reeded strap
handle, orange glaze, possibly
Scholl Family, Montgomery County, Pennsylvania, first half 19th c.,
4½" h. 242.00

Jug, ovoid w/eared handle, clear
glaze w/black manganese decoration, brass fitting attached to rim
for lamp, Connecticut, ca. 1800,
10" h. (firing imperfections, slight
chips at rim).................. 440.00

Lamp, baluster-form, eared handles,
incised ring decorations at neck &
shoulders, splotches of manganese overall, mounted & fitted
w/pleated shade, probably Pennsylvania, 27" h. (abrasions) 495.00

Milk pan, tapered cylindrical sides
w/molded rim & applied eared
handles above incised line, the interior w/russet glaze & splashes
of black decoration, Montgomery
County, Pennsylvania, 19th c.,
15" d. (chips & wear) 385.00

Model of a dog, seated animal
w/stippled ears, beaded collar &
smooth body, thin oval base,
flecked brown glaze, probably
John Bell, Waynesboro, Pennsylvania, mid-19th c., 4¼" h. (tail
missing, chips)................ 528.00

Model of a dog w/basket, animal

standing on freestanding legs, hand-built w/tooled stylized floral designs on oval base & tooled details in coat, basket, collar & face, clear greenish glaze w/white slip, 4" h. (shallow edge chip, minor glaze flakes) 2,550.00

Redware Model of a Lion

Model of a lion, reclining animal on a rectangular base, overall dark brown glaze, some firing defects, Henry Gast, Lancaster County, Pennsylvania, mid to late 19th c., 10½" l. (ILLUS.) 385.00

Pie plate, coggled edge, random yellow slip sponged decoration, 8¾" d. (rim chip & short hairline)...................... 160.00

Pitcher, miniature, 3¼" h., baluster-shaped ovoid body w/pinched spout, applied strap handle, flaring circular foot, yellow glaze w/splashes of green, possibly Samuel or Solomon Bell, Strasbourg, Virginia, 1833-82 .... 495.00

Pitcher, 6 5/8" h., ovoid body below tall flaring neck w/pinched spout, strap handle, incised spread-winged American eagle & shield across front under spout, clear glaze w/brown flecks & splotches, by Mettinger, 6 5/8" h. 750.00

Porringer, vase-shaped body on circular base, applied strap handle, russet glaze w/mottled manganese decorations, Pennsylvania, 19th c., 3" h. (minor chips to glaze on rim) 198.00

Rattle, modeled in the form of a seated goose w/stippled comb & scored wings, yellow & brown glaze, probably William Maize, New Berlin, Union County, Pennsylvania, 1860-70, 3" h. (base restored)...................... 550.00

Sanding pot, figure of a lady in a long skirt w/apron playing a guitar, wearing a feathered hat (forming cover) & earrings, orange glaze w/splotches of green & brown, also serves as a whistle, possibly John Bell, Pennsylvania, mid-19th c., 5½" h...... 385.00

Shaving mug, tapering cylindrical body w/three lines of beaded decoration, inset w/a shaving cup w/applied molded handle at rim, clear glaze w/splashes of manganese, Pennsylvania, mid-19th c., 4 7/8" h. (chip on rim) ... 330.00

Storage jar, cov., cylindrical body w/applied coggled lug handles & four rows of three bands at regular intervals, the domed cover w/lipped edge & acorn finial, attributed to the Bell Family, late 19th c., 9½" h. (various chips) ...1,100.00

Storage jar, ovoid body w/wide flared rim, applied eared handles, flanged foot, decorated w/a band of incised lines flanked by a row of swags, russet glaze w/manganese, Pennsylvania, 19th c., 8¾" h. (chips, wear to rim) 264.00

Urn, square base w/ovolu corners, square top, classical detail w/acanthus leaves & foliate scrolls, dark brown glaze, 12¾" h. (old chips on rim & foot) 200.00

Dated Redware Wall Pocket

Wall pocket, arched back plate w/pierced holes for mounting above an open pocket decorated w/applied yellow bull's-eyes centering the applied date "1875," America, 10" h. (ILLUS.) 286.00

Water cooler, barrel-shaped, the top w/embossed eagle flanked by the initials "PB," above a protruding hole, the body w/bands of coggle wheel decoration centering a bunghole, the whole covered in manganese glaze, Peter Bell, Hagerstown, Maryland, first quarter 19th c., 10¾" h. (some chips to rim, base & bunghole) 990.00

Whistle, crudely modeled bird w/finger holes for various notes, clear glaze, 2 3/8" h. 165.00

RED WING

Various potteries operated in Red Wing,

Minnesota from 1868, the most successful being the Red Wing Stoneware Co., organized in 1878. Merged with other local potteries through the years, it became known as Red Wing Union Stoneware Co. in 1894, and was one of the largest producers of utilitarian stoneware items in the United States. After a decline in the popularity of stoneware products, an art pottery line was introduced to compensate for the loss and this was reflected in a new name for the company, Red Wing Potteries, Inc., in 1930. Stoneware production ceased entirely in 1947, but vases, planters, cookie jars and dinnerwares of art pottery quality continued in production until 1967 when the pottery ceased operation altogether.

Red Wing Spongeware Bowl

Bean pot, cov., Saffron ware, blue & rust daubing on yellowware $75.00

Beater jar, brown stripes on yellowware 65.00

Beater jar, ribbed, double blue stripe trim 67.50

Bottle, model of yellow ear of corn, 4 x 10" 125.00

Bowl, 7" d., Grey Line, stoneware w/spongeband decoration, w/Cambria, Wisconsin advertising 95.00

Bowl, 7" d., spongeware, blue & rust daubing on grey stoneware (ILLUS.) 65.00

Bowl, 9½" d., Saffron ware, blue & rust daubing on yellowware 69.00

Butter churn, w/lid & dasher, stoneware, large Wing logo, 2 gal. 140.00

Butter dish, cov., Bob White patt.... 22.00

Cookie jar, cov., art pottery line, figural Monk, "Thou Shalt Not Steal" 58.00

Cup & saucer, Bob White patt....... 14.00

Figure of tambourine player, four-color glaze, No. B1416, 10¼" h. ... 55.00

Fruit jar w/screw-on zinc lid, "Stone Mason Fruit Jar, Union Stoneware Co., Red Wing, Minn." printed in black (or blue) on stoneware, half gal. (ILLUS. next column) 175.00

Gravy boat & lid, Bob White patt.... 25.00

Jug, miniature, beehive shape, copy of the "little brown jug," symbol of football rivalry between Min-

nesota & Michigan, brown top half, grey bottom half printed in blue w/"Who Will Win?" 135.00

Red Wing Fruit Jar

Jug, beehive shape, salt-glazed stoneware, large Wing logo, 5 gal. 137.50

Mixing bowl, spongeware, blue & rust daubing on stoneware, 10" d. 75.00

Model of a badger on football, stump base, signed "Red Wing Potteries" & dated 1939 .... 115.00

Mugs, "Hamm's Krug Klub," set of 6 .... 360.00

Pitcher, 8¼" h., Cherry Band patt., blue at borders fading to white... 130.00

Pitcher, 8½" h. (so-called Russian milk pitcher without pouring spout), brown glaze, 1 gal....... 55.00

Planter, model of a Dachshund, green glaze, 7" l. 21.00

Plate, 10½" d., Lexington Rose patt. 6.50

Platter, Capistrano patt., large 10.00

Poultry feeder (or waterer), stoneware, "KoRec Feeder," half gal. ... 85.00

Refrigerator jar, stacking-type, white-glazed stoneware w/blue bands, 4¾" d................... 95.00

Salt & pepper shakers, Blue Shadows patt., pr. 12.00

Teapot, cov., Blue Shadows patt. 16.00

Trivet, "Red Wing, Minn. 1958 Centennial" 25.00

Vase, 10" h., Glazed Ware, waisted cylindrical shape w/embossed stylized lady's head w/scrolling crown on each side, aqua glaze .. 58.00

Vase, 12" h., 6½" d., cylindrical, storks in relief on cream & green ground, Union Stoneware Co., ca. 1890's 81.00

Vase, 15½" h., Glazed Ware, cylindrical w/narrow panels down sides, Egyptian decoration, No. 157, green glaze 43.00

Wall pocket, cornucopia shape, No. 441, yellow glaze, w/original labels, 8", pr................... 22.00

Wall pocket, model of a guitar,
No. M-1484, ivory glaze, 13" 20.00

Red Wing Water Cooler

Water cooler, cov., white-glazed
stoneware w/blue bands, 3 gal.
(ILLUS.). 300.00

ROCKINGHAM

Rockingham-Glazed Flasks

*An earthenware pottery was first estab-
lished on the estate of the Marquis of Rockingham in England's Yorkshire district about
1745 and occupied by a succession of potters.
The famous Rockingham glaze of mottled
brown, somewhat resembling tortoise shell,
was introduced about 1788 by the Brameld
Brothers, and was well received. During the
1820's, porcelain manufacture was added to
the production and fine quality china was
turned out until the pottery closed in 1842.
The popular Rockingham glaze was subsequently produced elsewhere, including Bennington, Vermont, and at numerous other
U.S. potteries. We list herein not only wares
produced at the Rockingham potteries in
England, distinguishing porcelain wares from
the more plentiful earthenware productions,
but also include items from other potteries
with the Rockingham glaze.*

Book ends, figure of seated girl in
long dress leaning on one elbow
w/other arm curved down to her

lap, openings cut under arms,
7½" h., pr. (one w/base chip). . . . $260.00
Bowl, 8¼" d., 3½" h., flared sides
w/molded rim, mottled brown
glaze 55.00
Bowl, 9¼" l., oval, deep sides, mot-
tled brown glaze 85.00
Bowl, 11" d., 5" h., deep sides
w/molded top edge, embossed
double arch pattern, mottled
brown glaze (hairline) 95.00
Butter crock, cov., mottled brown
glaze 110.00
Creamer, bulbous base tapering
slightly to wide rim, scrolled handle, mottled brown glaze,
4½" h. 25.00
Figural bottle, model of a clenched
fist w/upraised thumb, mottled
dark brown glaze on yellowware,
5¼" h. (minor flakes on spout) . . .   225.00
Figural bottle, model of a high-
topped shoe w/embossed laces
down side & marked "Ann Reid
1859," mottled brown glaze,
6" h. 300.00
Flask, flattened ovoid shape, mold-
ed fluting down sides of neck,
embossed scenes of horses & dis-
mounted riders along the sides,
mottled brown glaze, repaired lip
chips, 7" h. (ILLUS. right) 325.00
Flask, flattened ovoid w/wide
panels featuring an embossed
spread-winged American eagle,
one on each side, mottled brown
glaze, chip on one side, chips on
base, 7¼" h. (ILLUS. left) 185.00
Frame, oval, ridged sides & scal-
loped inside edge, mottled brown
glaze, 13¼ x 15¼" (chips on in-
side edge) 700.00
Inkwell, waisted shape w/paneled
sides, each panel embossed
w/acanthus leaves, mottled
brown glaze on yellowware,
3" d., 2¼" h. (small chips) 135.00
Jar, cov., cylindrical w/eared han-
dles & low domed cover w/knob
finial, mottled brown glaze, 8" h.
(small flakes on lid) 185.00
Model of a dog, seated Spaniel-type
animal on thick ovoid base, tooled
detail on paws & tail, overall runny
mottled blue glaze on yellowware,
Ohio, 10¼" h. 1,150.00
Model of a dog, seated Spaniel-type
animal on thick oblong base
w/embossed shells at notched
corners, mottled dark brown glaze
on yellowware, mid-19th c.,
5½ x 8" base, 11" h. 570.00
Model of a lion, recumbent maned
animal on thick rectangular base

w/chamfered edges, covered
overall w/mottled dark blue glaze
on yellowware, Ohio, 9¾" l. 825.00
Mug, slightly waisted shape, strap
handle, mottled brown glaze,
3 7/8" h. (hairline in base) 100.00
Pie plate, shallow flared sides, mottled light brown glaze on yellow-
ware, 9¼" d. 60.00
Pie plate, mottled brown glaze,
9½" d. 45.00
Pitcher w/lid, 9" h., ovoid shape
tapering to top rim, large strap
handle, embossed scene of man
smoking & woman taking snuff,
mottled dark brown glaze (minor
edge flakes, lid chipped) 130.00
Pitcher, 6¼" h., flat bottom below
rounded sides tapering to neck
w/high arched spout, high strap
handle w/thumbrest, embossed
design of cherubs & grape vines,
mottled dark brown glaze (shal-
low flake on bottom rim) 55.00
Pitcher, 8" h., bulbous footed base
tapering to slightly flared rim
w/wide spout, embossed fox
hunting scenes, tree-branch handle, mottled brown glaze (edge
chips, hairlines in bottom) 145.00

Rockingham Shaving Mug

Shaving mug, embossed w/the figure of a seated chubby Toby figure w/a broad-brimmed hat,
mottled brown glaze on yellowware, minor base glaze chips,
4¼" h. (ILLUS.) 300.00
Soap dish, oval, molded running
band of arches under top rim,
mottled brown glaze, 5 1/8" l. . . . 85.00
Toby bottle, rotund man in jacket &
vest wearing top hat (forming
spout) straddles barrel, mottled
brown glaze, 9½" h. 150.00

ROOKWOOD

*Considered America's foremost art pottery,
the Rookwood Pottery Company was established in Cincinnati, Ohio, in 1880, by Mrs.
Maria Longworth Nichols Storer. To ac-
curately record its development, each piece
carried the Rookwood insignia, or mark, was
dated, and, if individually decorated, was*
*usually signed by the artist. The pottery re-
mained in Cincinnati until 1959 when it was
sold to Herschede Hall Clock Company and
moved to Starkville, Mississippi, where it
continued in operation until 1967.*

*A private company is now producing a
limited variety of pieces using original Rookwood molds.*

Monumental Rookwood Vase

Book ends, figural girl on piano,
pink glaze, 1925, pr. $175.00
Book ends, model of an elephant,
celadon glaze, pr. 145.00
Bowl, 9" d., 4¾" h., "closed" type
w/bulbous, squat body, reticulated & raised leaf design encircles
body, Standard glaze, Model
No. 502, 1889, incised "V" 350.00
Bowl, 13" d., 3" h., low open form
decorated w/a highly stylized bird
surrounded by polychromatic flowers, Model No. 2574C, 1929,
Edward Hurley 400.00
Box, cov., circular, cover decorated
w/a seafoam green starburst in
dark blue against a turquoise blue
ground, Model No. 641E, 1923,
William Hentschel, 3¼" d.,
1" h. 110.00
Candleholders, rose floral decora-
tion, Model No. 2473, 1921, pr. . . . 55.00
Candlesticks, mottled blue & green
matte glaze, Model No. 1635,
1921, pr. 160.00
Candlesticks, triangular w/sea-
horses on corners, mustard glaze,
Model No. 1773, 1922, Sallie Too-
hey, 4" h. 200.00
Cracker jar, cov., fruits & flowers in
relief on glossy cream glaze,
1943, 6" h. 175.00
Ewer, squat bulbous base tapering
to thin neck w/ruffled rim, trailing vine w/leaves & berries, Standard glaze, Model No. 715DD,
1896, Amelia Sprague, 6¼" w.,
6½" h. 350.00

Ewer, Standard glaze of brown
shaded to orange, decorated
w/leaves & berries, 1900,
Elizabeth N. Lincoln, 9¼" h...... 350.00
Ewer, squat oval body tapering to
scrolled rim, S-scroll handle, slip-
painted w/a flowering yellow buckeye branch, Standard glaze, Model
No. 550. W., 1890, Kataro Shirayamadani, 12" d., 13" h. 1,000.00
Figure of Spanish woman, four-color
glaze, Model No. 6986, 11" h. 285.00
Jug, moss green ground, carved
ferns & wandering Jew decora-
tion, 2 5/8 x 4½" 250.00
Model of an elephant, Aventurine
glaze of red, brown & gold dust,
Model No. 6490, 1937 .... 220.00
Mug, blue animal designs on pale
yellow ground, French words also
in blue, Model No. 575c, 1946,
Lois Furukawa 165.00
Mug, moon & star decoration, Alpha
Delta Psi special order souvenir,
Vellum glaze, 1905 .... 150.00
Paperweight, model of a dog, ivory
glaze, 1934 .... 120.00
Paperweight, model of an elephant,
white glaze, Model No. 2797,
1930, 4¼" l. 110.00
Pin tray, scene of nude asleep on
side, glossy Sea Green glaze,
1947, 3 x 4½" 105.00
Pitcher, 6" h., trefoil rim & loop
handle on elongated neck & squat
base w/angled shoulder, spider &
marsh grasses in black, white
moon & accents in dark brown
glaze, gilt highlighting, 1882, Maria Longworth Nichols 825.00

Rookwood Scenic Plaque

Plaque, olive & brown trees by a
beige pond & green foliage under
a pink-tinged beige sky, Vellum
glaze, 1917, Lenore Asbury, 5 x 8"
rectangle in original frame
(ILLUS.) 1,045.00
Plaque, entitled "Birches," white &
green birch trees against light blue
& yellow-brown horizon, Lenore
Asbury, original frame & paper
label, 8¼ x 10½" 1,760.00

Tankard, cov., footed ovoid body
w/wide strap handle, domed pottery lid w/pewter band & thumbrest, decorated w/portrait of
President Andrew Jackson on a
yellow-green ground, standard
glaze, inscribed "Andrew
Jackson (Old Hickory) Sturgis
Laurence, Oct. '96," 9¾" h.......1,980.00
Urn, ovoid body w/two loop handles
at rim, porcelain, abstract brown
leaves & dark blue berries against
yellow background, glossy glaze,
Model No. 2640C, 1924, 10½" w.,
14½" h. 500.00
Vase, 3¼" h., bulbous, tapering to
a 1½" d. neck, yellow jonquils on
a shiny ground shading green to
brown, 1901, Leona Van Briggle .. 235.00
Vase, 4¼" h., three-handled, cherries decoration, standard brown
glaze, 1889, E.T. Hurley 350.00
Vase, 5¾" h., 3¾" d., tapering cylinder, blue trees on a snowy
ground against light green to
peach sunset, Vellum glaze, 1919,
Sallie E. Coyne 605.00
Vase, 6" h., 3¼" d., cylindrical
w/stepped-in collared neck, porcelain, swirling stylized red & pink
flowers w/green leaves in a wide
band on light blue to bright peach
ground, 1924, Edward Diers 302.50
Vase, 6¼" h., 3¼" w., slender
ovoid body w/gently flaring rim,
swallow flying over rushes on a
caramel ground, Model No. 143G,
1884, Martin Rettig 300.00
Vase, 6½" h., 4¼" d., bulbous
w/long cylindrical neck, circle of
dark blue leaves on lime green
ground, Sea Green glaze, Artus
Van Briggle 1,210.00

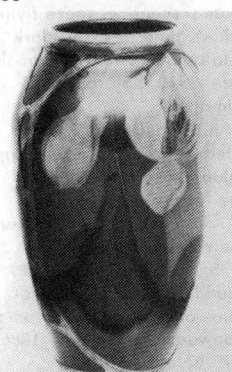

Rookwood Vase with Silver Overlay

Vase, 7¼" h., wide mouth on cylindrical body tapering toward base,
silver rim w/elongated pierced

strapwork in Art Nouveau style,
framing yellow tulips & green
leaves on standard glaze ground,
1906, Clara C. Linderman
(ILLUS.) 1,760.00

Vase, 7½" h., deer & foliage on
cream ground, Model No. 6053,
1929 . . . .   95.00

Vase, 7¾" h., 3¼" d., green w/band
of conventionalized landscape
w/lightly incised & painted houses
& trees, Vellum glaze, 1910, Sara
Sax 1,210.00

Vase, 8" h., cylindrical body
w/short, wide neck, crisp mountainous scene continuing around
body, unusual shading from blue
to white, lavender & purple to
green foreground, Vellum glaze,
1918, Harriet E. Wilcox 935.00

Vase, 8¼" h., 4¼" d., ovoid body
tapering to widely flared neck,
decorated w/a flowering dogwood
branch against a dark blue &
green ground, Sea Green glaze,
Model No. 903C, 1901, Sara
Toohey 800.00

Vase, 8¼" h., 4½" w., bulbous
base tapering to long, cylindrical
neck, white flowers w/grey-green
leaves against a pale grey to
black background, Iris glaze,
Model No. 1278E, 1909, Katherine
Van Horne. 600.00

Vase, 9" h., 6" w., corset-shaped,
slip-decorated w/a branch of pine
cones & needles, Model No. 909C,
1907, Clara Lindeman 200.00

Vase, 9 1/8" h., 4" d., porcelain,
two bluebirds against branches of
pink leaves on grey uncrazed
ground, 1921, Arthur Conant 3,575.00

Vase, 9¼" h., 5" d., tapered cylinder, swamp scene w/geese flying
over lake & pine forest w/dark
brown to gold to yellow dawn sky,
Iris glaze, 1910, Kataro
Shirayamadani 6,875.00

Vase, 10" h., paneled pyriform,
decorated w/green, purple & sapphire blue peacock feathers
w/beige fringes on mauve
ground, chocolate brown interior,
1923, Sarah Sax 660.00

Vase, 10" h., spherical w/gilded
neck, budding branch of white
magnolias among green leaves on
matte powder blue ground, 1886,
Albert R. Valentien 1,100.00

Vase, 11" h., 5¾" d., porcelain,
carved red bleeding hearts &
green leaves on sky-blue to
cream to blue ground, 1946,
Kataro Shirayamadani 660.00

Vase, 11½" h., 4½" d., tall cylindrical body tapering slightly at top &
base, scenic decoration w/green
& blue trees against blue to peach
ground, Vellum glaze, Model
No. 2040C, 1912, Frederick
Rothenbusch 800.00

Vase, 13" h., modified trumpet form,
decorated w/painted slips under
the glaze as a circular frieze of
swimming fish on rainbow hued
ground, Iris glaze, John D.
Wareham (1893-1934) 2,640.00

Vase, 15½" h., 9" d., white cabbage
roses w/golden centers & bushy
green foliage on charcoal grey to
olive green to gold to light pink
ground, Iris glaze, 1903, Sara
Sax 2,750.00

Vase, 21½" h., 10" d., goldenrod on
chocolate to golden-brown ground,
Standard glaze, 1902, Albert R.
Valentien .3,080.00

Vase, 22½" h., baluster-form, encircled by three scenes depicting a
spider in its web, a swimming fish
& a branch w/blossoms & leaves,
each scene divided by a wide gold
band swirling downwards, 1882,
Maria Longworth Nichols
(ILLUS.) 4,180.00

ROSEMEADE

Rosemeade Buffalo

*Laura Taylor was a ceramic artist who su-
pervised Federal Works Projects in her native North Dakota during the Depression era
and later demonstrated at the potter's wheel
during the 1939 New York World's Fair. In
1940, Laura Taylor and Robert J. Hughes
opened the Rosemeade-Wahpeton Pottery,
naming it after the North Dakota county and
town of Wahpeton where it was located.
Rosemeade Pottery was made on a small
scale for only about twelve years with Laura
Taylor designing the items and perfecting
colors. Her animal and bird figures are popu-*

lar among collectors. Hughes and Taylor married in 1943 and the pottery did a thriving business until her death in 1959. The pottery closed in 1961 but stock was sold from the factory salesroom until 1964.

Ashtray, pheasant decoration	$15.00
Flower frog, model of a heron	38.00
Model of a bear	25.00
Model of a boot, blue glaze, 7" h. ...	15.00
Model of a buffalo, brown glaze, 6" l., 6" h. (ILLUS.)	165.00
Model of a horse, blue matte glaze	55.00
Model of mice	15.00
Model of a swan, green & lavender glaze	16.00
Planter, model of a duck, grey glaze, 6" l., 2¼" h.	18.00
Plaque, pierced to hang, "Garden Spot Midwest"	85.00
Salt & pepper shakers, model of a bird, pr......................	15.00
Salt & pepper shakers, model of a black cat sitting cross-legged, large, pr......................	36.00
Salt & pepper shakers, model of a buffalo, pr....................	15.00
Salt & pepper shakers, model of a donkey head, pr................	32.00
Salt & pepper shakers, model of an ear of corn, pr.	22.00
Salt & pepper shakers, model of an ox, brown glaze, pr.	36.00
Salt & pepper shakers, model of a quail, pr.....................	15.00
Salt & pepper shakers, model of a swan, black glaze, pr.	38.00
Table set: creamer, sugar bowl, salt & pepper shakers; Corn patt., 4 pcs......................	25.00
Wall pocket, Indian God of Peace on glossy green ground, 8¼"	110.00
Wall pocket, model of crescent moon, satin blue & rose glaze	28.00

ROSE MEDALLION - ROSE CANTON

Rose Medallion Bough Pots

The lovely Chinese ware known as Rose Medallion was made through the past centu-

ry and into the present one. It features alternating panels of people and flowers or insects with most pieces having four medallions with a central rose or peony medallion. The ware is called Rose Canton if flowers and birds or insects fill all the panels. Unless otherwise noted, our listing is for Rose Medallion ware.

Bough pots, cov., chamfered square body w/a gold ground embellished w/pink-blossoming green vines & applied at the corners w/iron-red tree squirrels clambering over iron-red, yellow & blue berry vines issuing from the gilt rope-twist handles, front & back reserved w/figural panels & sides w/panels of birds perched amid branches above panels of flowers edged in black scrollwork on the flaring foot & repeated on the cover rim, late 19th c., some damage & repair, 9 7/8" h., pr. (ILLUS.)	$3,575.00
Bowl, 6¼" d., 2½" h., marked "Made in China"	45.00
Creamer, marked "Made in China," 4" h.	55.00
Cup & saucer, marked "Made in China"	22.00
Dish, cov., quatrefoil shape, 7 7/8 x 9¾"	300.00
Dish, quatrefoil shape, orange peel glaze, 9½ x 10¼"	350.00
Hot water plate, cov., orange peel glaze, 10" d. (minor rim flakes) ..	375.00
Pitcher, 13" h., slightly ovoid (short glazed-over hairline in handle) ...	600.00
Plate, 8½" d., central mandarin scene, border of floral reserves & butterflies	115.00
Plate, 8½" d., Rose Canton	75.00
Plate, chop, 14½" d.	350.00
Platter, 11½" l., reticulated edge, Rose Canton	185.00
Platter, 18" l., 19th c.............	550.00
Teapot, cov., cylindrical, strap handle, fruit finial, straight spout, 19th c., 5 7/8" h................	440.00
Umbrella stand, cylindrical, decorated w/panels containing genre scenes, alternating floral panels w/birds & butterflies, reserved on a gilt ground heightened w/green scrolling vines, pink blossoms & butterflies, 19th c., 24½" h.......	935.00
Vases, overall 30" h., vase-form body w/flaring neck, decorated overall w/reserves of Chinese figures at daily pursuits alternating w/birds perched among flowering vines, gilt ground w/scrolls & flowers, 19th c., mounted as lamps, pr.	4,400.00

ROSENTHAL

Rosenthal Wall Mask

The Rosenthal porcelain manufactory has been in operation since 1880 when it was established by P. Rosenthal in Selb, Bavaria. Tablewares and figure groups are among its specialties.

Cake plate, open handles, h.p. various colored roses on cobalt blue ground w/gold border, artist-signed, 10¼" d. $48.00
Condiment dish, cov., Moss Rose patt., silver cover & base 38.00
Dish, clover-shaped, scalloped rim, open handle, portrait of a lovely blonde Victorian lady encircled by full-blown roses, RC w/crown & "Malmaison" mark 65.00
Figures of Blackamoors, one standing upright w/hands in front, other walking and carrying plate of food, each in ivory costume & turban, ca. 1930's, 7½" h., pr. .... 350.00 to 400.00
Figure group, semi-nude stylized maiden reclining beside Afghan hound, all-white, on oblong base, stamped "Rosenthal - Germany," 9" h. 770.00
Inkwell, figural satyr listening to singing birds 275.00
Model of a cat, Siamese, reclining, No. 1907, signed "F. Heidenreich," 5½" 110.00
Model of a deer, sitting, 4" l., 3½" h. 185.00
Model of two deer leaping, impressed "H. Meisel," numbered, underglaze green factory mark, 6½" h. 315.00
Model of a dog, Dachshund, signed "Fritz Heidenreich," 4¼ x 8" 280.00
Model of a flamingo, delicate coloring, 5" 85.00
Model of a songbird, polychrome

body on white plinth, No. K610, 7½" 135.00
Plate, 6¾" d., h.p. blue Delft-type windmill scene 30.00
Plate, 7½" d., fruit & butterfly decoration, gold trim 18.00
Wall mask, stylized female face w/cut-out eyes & long arched eyebrows, above angular support, signed "Gerhard Schliepstein," printed factory mark & impressed "402," ca. 1920, 10" l. (ILLUS.) 1,430.00

ROSEVILLE

Roseville Pottery Company operated in Zanesville, Ohio, from 1898 to 1954 after having been in business for six years prior to that in Muskingum County, Ohio. Art wares similar to those of the Owens and Weller Potteries were produced. Items listed here are by patterns or lines.

APPLE BLOSSOM (1948)

White apple blossoms in relief; brown tree branch handles.

Apple Blossom Cornucopia-Vase

Basket w/circular handle, blue or green ground, No. 309-8", 8" h., each .... $80.00 to 105.00
Basket w/asymmetrical overhead handle, green ground, No. 311-12", 12" h. .... 135.00 to 175.00
Basket, hanging-type, blue or pink ground, each .... 90.00 to 125.00
Candleholders, green ground, No. 351, 2" h., pr. 21.50
Cornucopia-vase, green ground, No. 321-6", 6" h. (ILLUS.) 35.00
Ewer, blue or green ground, No. 316-8", 8" h. .... 47.50 to 55.00
Jardiniere, two-handled, blue ground, No. 342-6", 6" h. 75.00
Planter, green ground, No. 368-8", 8" l. 30.00
Tea set: cov. teapot, creamer & sugar bowl; green or pink ground,

No. 371-T,C&S, each
set ....125.00 to 145.00
Vase, 7" h., pink ground,
No. 373-7" 40.00
Vase, 10" h., base handles, blue
ground, No. 388-10" 55.00
Vase, 12" h., pink ground,
No. 369-12" 100.00

BANEDA (1933)

Band of embossed pods, blossoms and leaves.

Bowl, 10" d., 3½" h., two-handled,
green or raspberry pink ground,
each ....100.00 to 120.00
Jardiniere, green ground, 6" h. 85.00
Urn, small rim handles, bulbous,
green ground, 5" h. 135.00
Urn, open rim handles, low foot,
green ground, 7" h. 165.00
Vase, 4" h., tab handles, raspberry
pink ground 40.00
Vase, 4½" h., small rim handles,
sharply canted sides, green
ground 70.00
Vase, 6" h., two-handled, elongated
ovoid, raspberry pink ground..... 75.00
Vase, 9" h., two-handled, bulbous,
green ground 195.00
Vase, 12" h., base handles, green
or raspberry pink ground, each... 225.00

BLACKBERRY (1933)

*Band of relief clusters of blackberries with
vines and ivory leaves accented in green and
terra cotta on a green textured ground.*

Basket w/overhead handle, 9" h. 425.00
Basket, hanging-type, 6½" d.,
4½" h. 145.00
Console bowl, small end handles,
13" l. ....150.00 to 175.00
Jardiniere, two-handled, 4" h. 125.00
Jardiniere, two-handled, 7" h. 250.00
Urn-vase, small rim handles, 6" h. ... 185.00
Vase, 5" h., handles at mid-section,
globular base & wide neck 100.00
Vase, 6" h., two handles at mid-
section ....135.00 to 165.00
Vase, 8" h., handles at mid-section,
slightly globular base & wide
neck, original paper
label..................165.00 to 200.00
Vase, 12½" h., handles rising from
shoulder to rim 345.00
Wall pocket, basket-shaped, narrow
base & flaring rim, original paper
label, 6¾" w. at rim,
8½" h..................245.00 to 285.00

BLEEDING HEART (1938)

*Pink blossoms and green leaves on shaded
ground.*

Basket w/overhead handle, green
ground, No. 359-8", 8" h. 75.00
Basket w/pointed overhead handle,
No. 361-12", w/flower frog,
No. 40, green ground, 12" h.,
2 pcs. 90.00
Console bowl, hexagonal, No. 383-
12", w/flower frog, No. 40, blue
ground, 12" w., 2 pcs. 55.00
Ewer, blue ground, No. 972-10",
10" h. ....85.00 to 95.00
Plate, 10½" w. hexagon, pink
ground, No. 381-10" 55.00
Jardiniere, small pointed shoulder
handles, pink ground, No. 651-3",
3" h. 38.00
Vase, 4" h., two-handled, blue
ground, No. 138-4" 27.50
Vase, bud, 7" h., green ground,
No. 967-7" 40.00
Vase, 8" h., base handles, pink
ground, No. 969-8" ....40.00 to 50.00
Vase, 9" h., pink ground,
No. 970-9" 45.00
Vase, 15" h., two-handled, flaring
hexagonal mouth, blue ground,
No. 976-15" 260.00

BURMESE (1950's)

*Sculptured head of an Oriental-type man or
woman. Also included in the line are some
plain articles.*

Candleholder-book end combination,
man, green glaze, No. 80-B (single) 55.00
Candleholder-book end combination,
man & woman, white glaze,
Nos. 70-B & 80-B, pr. 215.00
Candleholder-book end combination,
woman, green glaze, No. 70-B,
pr. 125.00
Candlesticks, plain, black glaze,
No. 75-B, 4" h., pr. 20.00
Plaque, pierced to hang, man, black
glaze, No. 82-B, 7½" h. 130.00

BUSHBERRY (1948)

*Berries and leaves on bark-textured ground;
brown or green branch handles.*

Bushberry Double Bud Vase

Ashtray, handled, blue ground,
No. 26 ....50.00 to 65.00

Basket w/asymmetrical overhead
handle, green or russet ground,
No. 369-6½", 6½" h.,
each . . . . .45.00 to 65.00
Basket w/asymmetrical overhead
handle, blue ground, No. 370-8",
8" h. 60.00
Basket, hanging-type w/original
chains, blue ground, No. 465-5",
5". 110.00
Bowl, 4" h., two-handled, globular,
blue ground, No. 411-4" 42.00
Console bowl, russet ground,
No. 415-10", 10" 55.00
Ewer, blue or green ground, No. 2-
10", 10" h., each . . . . .65.00 to 90.00
Jardiniere, blue or russet ground,
No. 657-3", 3" h., each . . . .24.00 to 32.00
Mug, russet ground, No. 1-3½",
3½" h. 30.00
Pitcher w/ice lip, green or russet
ground, No. 1325, 8½" h.,
each . . . . .95.00 to 135.00
Planter, handled, green ground,
No. 383-6", 6½" l. 27.00
Tea set: cov. teapot, creamer & sug-
ar bowl; green or russet ground,
No. 2-T,C&S, each set 125.00
Urn, two-handled, blue ground,
No. 411-6", 6" d. 85.00
Vase, double bud, 4½" h., gate-
form, green ground, No. 158-4½"
(ILLUS.). . . . . .35.00 to 45.00
Vase, 7" h., high-low handles, cylin-
drical, low foot, russet ground,
No. 32-7" 35.00
Vase, bud, 7½" h., asymmetrical
handles rising from base, slender
cylindrical body, blue ground,
No. 152-7" 40.00
Wall pocket, high-low handles, blue
or green ground, No. 1291-8",
8" h., each . . . . .85.00 to 95.00

CAPRI (late line)

Basket w/center overhead branch
handle, molded leaf design at terminal, pointed ends, cactus green,
No. C-1012, 10" h. 50.00
Bowl, 9" l., molded fluting at one
end, tapering to pointed opposing
end, cactus green, No. 529-9" 18.00
Bowl, 15" l., slender leaf shape,
metallic red, No. 531-14" 32.00
Vase, 6" h., grotesque free-form
shape, metallic red, No. 580-6" . . . 38.00
Vase, 12" h., footed, deeply cut rim,
sinuous form, metallic red,
No. 586-12" 50.00

CARNELIAN I (1910-15)

*Matte glaze with a combination of two colors
or two shades of the same color with the darker dripping over the lighter tone or heavy*

*and textured glaze with intermingled colors
and some running.*

Candlesticks, green & tan, 1¾" h.,
pr. 23.00
Bowl, 9" d., 3" h., two-handled, low
foot, green & tan 38.00
Vase, 8" h., base handles, fan-
shaped, turquoise blue & aqua . . . 34.00
Vase, 10" h., two-handled, turquoise
blue & aqua 67.00
Wall pocket, long slender handles,
ovoid body w/flaring mouth, turquoise blue & aqua, 9½" h. 120.00

CARNELIAN II

Intermingled colors, some with a drip effect.

Jardiniere, two-handled, intermingled shades of rose, 5" h. 75.00
Urn, two-handled, intermingled
shades of rose, 9" h. 95.00
Vase, 7" h., intermingled shades of
turquoise 35.00
Vase, 12" h., handles rising from
shoulder to rim, ovoid w/short
wide neck, intermingled shades of
blue 150.00
Wall pocket, intermingled shades of
rose, blue & rust glaze, 8" h. 75.00

CHERRY BLOSSOM (1933)

*Sprigs of cherry blossoms, green leaves and
twigs with pink fence against a combed blue-
green ground or creamy ivory fence against
a terra cotta ground shading to dark brown.*

Bowl, 6" d., small handles at shoulder, terra cotta ground 80.00
Candlesticks, ring handles at mid-
section, terra cotta ground, 4" h.,
pr. 95.00
Jardiniere, shoulder handles, terra
cotta ground, 10" h. 300.00
Urn-vase, blue-green ground,
8" h. 225.00
Urn-vase, terra cotta ground,
8" h. 245.00
Vase, 7" h., blue-green ground 120.00
Vase, 7" h., two-handled, jug-
shaped, terra cotta
ground . . . . .135.00 to 165.00
Vase, 8" h., handles at mid-section,
terra cotta ground. 125.00

CLEMATIS (1944)

*Clematis blossoms and heart-shaped green
leaves against a vertically textured ground
— white blossoms on blue, rose-pink blossoms
on green and ivory blossoms on golden
brown.*

Basket w/overhead handle, pedestal
base, brown or green ground,
No. 389-10", 10" h., each . .55.00 to 65.00
Basket, hanging-type, blue, brown

or green ground, No. 470-5", 5",
each ....55.00 to 85.00
Candlesticks, green ground,
No. 1159-4½", 4½" h., pr. 47.50
Console bowl, end handles, blue or
green ground, No. 456-6", 9" l.,
each 28.00
Console bowl, end handles, green
ground, No. 458-10", 14" l........ 45.00
Cookie jar, cov., green ground,
No. 3-8", 8" h................... 110.00
Ewer, green ground, No. 18-15",
15" h......................... 135.00
Flower arranger, blue or brown
ground, No. 50, 4½" h............ 21.00
Flowerpot w/saucer, green ground,
No. 668-5", 5½" h.............. 58.00
Jardiniere, brown ground, No. 667-
4", 4" h...................... 24.00
Jardiniere & pedestal base, green
ground, No. 667-8", 2 pcs. 435.00
Tea set: cov. teapot, creamer & sug-
ar bowl; green ground, No. 5-C,S,
3 pcs. 115.00
Vase, 6" h., two-handled, brown
ground, No. 103-6" 32.00

Clematis Vase

Vase, 7" h., blue ground (ILLUS.) ... 35.00
Vase, 15" h., green ground,
No. 114-15"................... 160.00

COLUMBINE (1940's)

*Columbine blossoms and foliage on shaded
ground — yellow blossoms on blue, pink blossoms on pink shaded to green and blue blossoms on tan shaded to green.*

Basket w/asymmetrical overhead
handle, tan ground, No. 367-10",
10" h. 75.00
Bowl, 12" d., irregular rim forming
handles, pink or tan ground,
No. 405-12", each ....42.00 to 50.00
Console bowl w/small end handles
& flower frog, pink ground,
No. 402-8" & 42, 8" d. bowl,
2 pcs......................... 67.50
Jardiniere, two-handled, blue

ground, No. 655-6", 6" widest d.,
3" h. 30.00
Rose bowl, two-handled, pink
ground, No. 399-4", 4" d. 27.00
Vase, 10" h., tan ground,
No. 23-10".................... 80.00
Vase, 12" h., large pointed handles
at mid-section, blue ground,
No. 25-12".................... 55.00
Vase, 14" h., tan ground,
No. 26-14".................... 265.00
Wall pocket, pink ground,
No. 1290-8", 8" h. 85.00

CORINTHIAN (1923)

*Deeply fluted ivory and green body below a
continuous band of molded grapevine, fruit,
foliage and florals in naturalistic colors, narrow ivory and green molded border at the rim.*

Corinthian Vase

Basket, hanging-type w/chains,
8" d. 87.50
Bowl, 4½" h., low foot 40.00
Bowl, 8" d. 48.00
Candlestick, double cup........... 40.00
Jardiniere, 5" h. 52.00
Vase, double bud, 4½" h. 28.00
Vase, double bud, 7" h., two fluted
columns joined by a reticulated
gate 35.00
Vase, 7" h., bulbous (ILLUS.) 45.00
Vase, 8" h., narrow cylindrical
body 40.00
Vase, 8" h., cylindrical w/flaring
mouth........................ 65.00
Wall pocket, 8" h................ 60.00
Wall pocket, 12" h.........85.00 to 100.00

COSMOS (1940)

*Embossed blossoms against a wavy horizon-
tal ridged band on a textured ground — ivory band with yellow and orchid blossoms on
blue, blue band with white and orchid blossoms on green or tan.*

Basket w/pointed overhead handle,
pedestal base, blue ground,
No. 358-12", 12" h. 125.00
Cornucopia-vase, green ground,
No. 137-8", 8" h. 65.00

Urn, two-handled, green ground,
No. 375-4", 4" h. 45.00
Vase, 5" h., loop handles rising
from footed base, chalice form,
blue or green ground,
No. 945-5" 40.00
Vase, 7" h., handles at base, flaring
rim, tan ground, No. 949-7" 44.00
Vase, 8" h., two-handled, cut-out
top edge, green ground,
No. 905-8" 58.00
Vase, double bud, two slender
cylinders joined by bridge,
No. 133 . . . . 55.00
Wall pocket, circular overhead
handle, tan ground, No. 1285,
6½" h. 70.00

DAHLROSE (1924-28)

*Band of ivory daisy-like blossoms and green
leaves against a mottled tan ground.*

Basket, hanging-type w/original
chains, 7½" h. 125.00
Candlesticks, flaring base w/angular
handles, 3½" h., pr. 70.00
Vase, 5" h., 7" w., pillow-shaped . . . 35.00
Vase, 6" h., angular rim handles . . . 38.00
Vase, 8" h., two handles rising from
mid-section to rim 55.00
Vase, 9" h. 65.00
Vase, 12" h., w/paper label 75.00
Wall pocket, long angular handles,
10" h. 80.00

DOGWOOD (1916-18)

*White dogwood blossoms and brown
branches against a textured green ground.*

Basket, hanging-type, green, 7" d.,
5½" h. 125.00
Bowl, 6½" d., 4½" h. 62.00
Wall pocket, 9½" h. 75.00

DONATELLO (1915)

*Deeply fluted ivory and green body with wide
tan band embossed with cherubs at various
pursuits in pastoral settings.*

Donatello Jardiniere

Basket, hanging-type,
7" h. . . . . 100.00 to 125.00
Basket, 7½" h. 175.00
Basket w/pointed overhead handle,
9" h. . . . . 150.00 to 185.00

Bowl, 8½" d., w/flower frog 55.00
Bowl, 12" d., pedestal base, rolled
edge 175.00
Compote, 4" h. 47.50
Compote, 9½" h., impressed seal . . 110.00
Cuspidor, 5½" h. 250.00
Flower frog 15.00
Jardiniere, 7" h. (ILLUS.) 97.50
Jardiniere & pedestal base, overall
34" h., 2 pcs. 525.00
Plate, 6" d. 260.00
Vase, 6" h., two-handled 125.00
Vase, 8" h., expanding cylinder 85.00
Wall pocket, 9" . . . . 80.00 to 100.00
Wall pocket, 11½" . . . . 105.00 to 125.00

DUTCH (pre-1916)

*Creamware with colorful decal scenes of
Dutch children and adults at various activities.*

Mug, 5" h. . . . . 45.00 to 55.00
Plate, 11" d., rolled rim 75.00
Tumbler, flared sides, 4" h. 45.00

EARLY EMBOSSED PITCHERS (pre-1916)

*Utility pitchers with various embossed
scenes; high gloss glaze.*

"The Cow," green & cream,
7½" h. 125.00
"Landscape," rust & green, 7½" h. . . 65.00
"Tulip," rust & cream, 7½" h. 65.00

EGYPTO (1905)

*Classic shapes resembling those from ancient
Egypt; soft deep green matte glaze.*

Ewer, 5" h. 175.00
Jardiniere, relief-molded scarabs
design, 8" h. 650.00
Planter, 5½" h., in low-footed metal
holder 265.00
Vase, 12½" h., relief-molded geo-
metric design around top and
band of fronds at base 265.00

FALLINE (1933)

Falline Vase

Curving panels topped by a semi-scallop separated by vertical peapod decorations; blended backgrounds of tan shading to green and blue or tan shading to darker brown.

Bowl, 11" d., small end handles, tan
   shading to brown 140.00
Urn-vase, ring handles at shoulder,
   tan shading to brown, 8" h. 200.00
Vase, 6" h., two-handled, swollen
   cylinder, tan shading to
   brown ....135.00 to 150.00
Vase, 7" h., two-handled, tan shading to brown.................... 135.00
Vase, 7½" h., two-handled, slightly
   rounded cylinder, tan shading to
   blue & green 150.00
Vase, 9" h., two-handled, horizontally ribbed lower section, tan
   shading to brown 325.00
Vase, 12½" h., handles rising from
   slightly bulbous base to lower
   part of long cylindrical neck, tan
   shading to green & blue 440.00
Vase, 13½" h., two-handled, tan
   shading to brown (ILLUS.) 460.00

FERRELLA (1930)

Impressed shell design alternating with small cut-outs at top and base; mottled brown or turquoise and red glaze.

Bowl, 12" d., 7" h., low foot, brown
   glaze, No. 212-12 x 7" 250.00
Vase, 4" h., angular handles, short
   narrow neck, brown glaze,
   No. 497-4"..................... 143.00
Vase, 4" h., angular handles, bul-
   bous, turquoise & red glaze,
   No. 498-4"..................... 135.00
Vase, 5" h., two-handled, turquoise
   & red glaze, No. 500-5" 170.00
Vase, 9" h., two-handled, brown
   glaze, No. 507-9"................ 225.00
Wall pocket, brown glaze,
   No. 1266-6½", 6½" h. 275.00

FLORENTINE (1924-28)

Bark-textured panels alternating with embossed garlands of cascading fruit and florals; ivory with tan and green, beige with brown and green or brown with beige and green glaze.

Bowl, 6" d., brown 35.00
Compote, 5" d., brown 40.00
Console bowl, beige, 9" d. 38.00
Jardiniere, beige, 9½" 115.00
Jardiniere & pedestal base, ivory,
   overall 25" h., 2 pcs. .... 550.00 to 625.00
Umbrella stand, ivory, 18½" h. 375.00
Vase, double bud, 6" h., gate form,
   brown 40.00
Vase, 6½" h., ivory 30.00
Vase, 7" h., handles rising from
   mid-section to rim, beige 37.50

Vase, 8" h., handles rising from
   shoulder to above rim, ivory 60.00
Wall pocket, beige, 7" h. ....50.00 to 65.00
Wall pocket, ivory, 8½" h. 70.00
Wall pocket, brown, 9½" h. ...70.00 to 85.00
Wall pocket, brown, 12½" h. 95.00

FOXGLOVE (1940's)

Sprays of pink and white blossoms embossed against a shaded matte finish ground.

Book ends, blue ground, No. 10,
   pr............................. 80.00
Console bowl, blue ground, No. 2,
   10" 70.00
Cornucopia-vase, blue ground,
   No. 163-6", 6" h. 35.00
Ewer, green ground, No. 4-6½",
   6½" h. 78.00
Ewer, blue ground, No. 5-10",
   10" h.......................... 95.00
Ewer, pink ground, No. 6-15",
   15" h. 200.00
Jardiniere, two-handled, green or
   pink ground, No. 659-3", 3" h.,
   each ....25.00 to 35.00
Jardiniere, green ground,
   No. 659-5", 5" h. 48.00
Jardiniere, pink ground, No. 659-6",
   6" h........................... 65.00
Model of a conch shell, blue or
   green ground, No. 426-6", 6" l.,
   each 35.00
Urn-vase, blue ground, No. 161-6",
   6" h.......................... 40.00
Vase, 6" h., pink ground,
   No. 43-6"..................... 40.00
Vase, 9" h., green ground,
   No. 49-9"..................... 52.50
Vase, 16" h., two-handled, blue
   ground, No. 55-16" 325.00
Wall pocket, blue ground,
   No. 1292-8", 8" h. 95.00

FREESIA (1945)

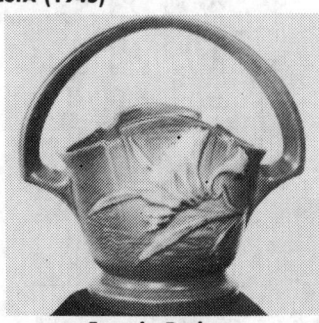

Freesia Basket

Trumpet-shaped blossoms and long slender green leaves against wavy impressed lines - white and lavender blossoms on blended green; white and yellow blossoms on shaded blue or terra cotta and brown.

Basket w/low overhead handle,
blue or terra cotta ground,
No. 390-7", 7" h., each 55.00
Basket w/overhead handle, terra
cotta ground, No. 391-8", 8" h.
(ILLUS.) .... 60.00 to 75.00
Book ends, open book form, green
ground, No. 15, pr. 72.50
Bowl, 10" d., terra cotta ground,
No. 466-10" 70.00
Bowl, 12" d., blue or terra cotta
ground, No. 468-12",
each .... 60.00 to 75.00
Candlesticks, blue ground,
No. 1160-2", 2" h., pr. 35.00
Cookie jar, cov., blue or terra cotta
ground, No. 4-8", 10" h., each 125.00
Cornucopia-vase, terra cotta ground,
No. 198-8", 8" h. 45.00
Ewer, blue, green or terra cotta
ground, No. 20-10", 10" h.,
each .... 55.00 to 70.00
Ewer, terra cotta ground,
No. 21-15", 15" h. 190.00
Flowerpot w/attached saucer, terra
cotta ground, No. 670-5",
5½" h. 60.00
Vase, 6" h., terra cotta ground,
No. 118-6" 42.00
Vase, 8" h., two-handled, terra cot-
ta ground, No. 121-8" 45.00
Vase, 9½" h., handles at mid-
section, green ground,
No. 123-9" 50.00
Vase, 12" h., two-handled, blue or
terra cotta ground, No. 127-12,"
each 95.00
Vase, 18" h., blue ground,
No. 129-18" 245.00
Wall pocket, blue, green or terra
cotta ground, No. 1296-8",
8½" h., each .... 60.00 to 75.00

FUCHSIA (1939)

Fuchsia Vase

*Coral pink fuchsia blossoms and green leaves
against a background of blue shading to yellow, green shading to terra cotta or terra cotta
shading to gold.*

Basket, hanging-type, green ground,
No. 359-5" 95.00

Bowl, 4" d., two-handled, blue
ground, No. 346-4" 50.00
Bowl, 6" d., two-handled, green
ground, No. 347-6" 65.00
Jardiniere, terra cotta ground,
No. 645-10", 10" d. 365.00
Vase, 6" h., two handles rising from
bulbous base to neck, terra cotta
ground, No. 891-6" 45.00
Vase, 8" h., blue ground, No. 898-8"
(ILLUS.) 65.00
Vase, 9" h., two-handled, green
ground, No. 899-9" 95.00
Vase, 12" h., two handles rising
from above base to neck, blue
ground, No. 903-12" 95.00
Vase, 15" h., green ground,
No. 904-15" 295.00
Wall pocket, two-handled, blue or
green ground, No. 1282-8",
8½" h., each 125.00

FUTURA (1928)

Basket, hanging-type, wide sloping
shoulders, sharply canted sides,
terra cotta & brown w/embossed
stylized pastel foliage,
No. 344-5" 235.00
Candleholders, shaped square base
rising to square candle nozzle,
relief-molded stylized green vine
& foliage on sandy beige ground,
No. 1073-4", 4" h., pr. 165.00
Console bowl, stepped rectangular
base, pentagonal w/canted sides,
matte glaze, No. 188-8", 8" w. ... 135.00
Jardiniere, angular handles rising
from wide sloping shoulders to
rim, sharply canted sides, terra
cotta & brown w/embossed sty-
lized pastel foliage, No. 616-6" ... 275.00
Vase, 6" h., stepped shoulders,
square body w/canted sides, ivory
w/grey & green elongated triangles, No. 380-6" 125.00
Vase, 7½" h., square wedge-shaped
base, globular body w/short neck,
relief-molded stylized tapering
blue-green leaf design rising from
base to shoulder against light
blue-green ground, No. 387-7" ... 250.00
Vase, 10" h., four flat vertical handles at flaring collared neck,
cylindrical body, brown & yellow,
No. 432-10" 350.00
Wall pocket, canted sides, angular
rim handles, geometric design in
blue, yellow, green & lavender on
brown ground, 6" w., 8¼" h. 225.00

GARDENIA (1940's)

*Large white gardenia blossoms and green
leaves over a textured impressed band on a
shaded green, grey or tan ground.*

Basket w/circular handle, green
ground, No. 609-10", 10" h. 95.00
Book ends, tan, No. 659, pr. 77.50
Bowl, 6" d., grey ground,
No. 626-6" 50.00
Bowl, 10" d., tan ground,
No. 628-10" 45.00
Bowl, 12" d., grey ground,
No. 630-12" 45.00
Candleholders, grey ground,
No. 651-2", 2" h., pr. 27.00
Cornucopia-vase, double, green
ground, No. 622-8", 8" h. 75.00
Jardiniere & pedestal base, green
ground, No. 645-10", 2 pcs. 590.00
Tray, lobed form, grey ground,
No. 631-14", 15" l. 60.00
Vase, 10½" h., handles rising from
base to shoulder, tan ground,
No. 686-10" 85.00
Vase, 14½" h., two handles rising
from mid-section to below rim,
tan ground, No. 689-14" 160.00
Wall pocket, large handles, grey
ground, No. 666-8", 9½" h. 115.00

IMPERIAL I (1924)

*Brown pretzel-twisted vine, green grape leaf
& cluster of blue grapes in relief on green and
brown bark textured ground.*

Imperial I Basket

Basket w/overhead handle, rounded
sides, 6" h. (ILLUS.) 50.00
Basket w/tall overhead handle,
slanted rim, 13" h. 120.00
Bowl, 7" d., pierced rim handles,
rounded sides, No. 71-7" 35.00
Bowl, 8" d., pierced rim handles,
rounded sides, No. 71-8" 40.00
Vase, 9" h., handles rising from
base to mid-section, cylindrical
body w/slanted rim, No. 31-9" ... 62.50

IMPERIAL II (1924)

Bowl, 8" d., mottled orange & tur-
quoise glaze, No. 204-8" 125.00
Bowl, 9" d., 4" h., horizontal rib-
bing, blue glaze w/yellow spatter,
No. 205-8" 110.00
Vase, 5½" h., horizontal ribbing be-

low middle, mottled turquoise
glaze 75.00
Vase, 7" h., globular w/horizontal
ribbing at neck, mottled rose
glaze 165.00
Vase, 8" h., cylindrical, short neck
w/band of relief-molded florals,
mottled blue & white glaze,
No. 479-8" 170.00
Vase, 11" h., cylindrical w/band of
horizontal ribbing below shoulder,
narrow short neck, mottled blue
glaze, No. 482-11" 345.00
Wall pocket, triple, tapering center
container w/small cylindrical
holder at either side, horizontal
ridges, mottled orange & green
glaze, No. 1264, 6½" h. 235.00

IRIS (1938)

*White or yellow blossoms and green leaves
on rose blending with green, light blue
deepening to a darker blue or tan shading to
green or brown.*

Bowl, 5" d., two-handled, rose
ground, No. 359-5" 40.00
Bowl, 10" d., blue ground,
No. 362-10" 65.00
Jardiniere, two-handled, rose or tan
ground, No. 647-3", 3" h.,
each ....30.00 to 37.50
Vase, 4" h., base handles, blue
ground, No. 914-4" 37.50
Vase, 6½" h., two-handled, rose
ground, No. 917-6" 45.00
Vase, 15" h., two large handles rising from shoulder to rim, blue
ground, No. 929-15" 250.00
Wall pocket, two handles rising
from base to below flaring rim,
blue ground, No. 1284-8", 8" h.... 100.00

IXIA (1930's)

*Embossed spray of tiny bell-shaped flowers
& slender leaves - white blossoms on pink
ground; lavender blossoms on green or yellow ground.*

Bowl, 4" d., pointed closed handles
at rim, pink ground, No. 326-4" .. 38.00
Centerpiece, one-piece console set
w/candleholders attached to cen-
ter bowl, pink ground, 13" l. 145.00
Flower frog, green ground,
No. 34 .... 30.00
Jardiniere, green ground,
No. 640-6", 6" h. 35.00
Jardiniere & pedestal base, pink
ground, No. 640-10", 2 pcs. 800.00
Vase, 6" h., pink ground,
No. 852-6" 27.50
Vase, 8½" h., closed handles at
mid-section, globular w/long wide
neck, green ground, No. 857-8" .. 37.50

Vase, 10½" h., closed pointed handles at shoulder, cylindrical w/short neck, green ground, No. 862-10" 55.00

JONQUIL (1931)

White jonquil blossoms and green leaves in relief against textured tan ground; green lining.

Basket, hanging-type 275.00
Bowl, 5" d., 3" h., two-handled 45.00
Bowl, 12" l. oval, 4" h. 88.00
Jardiniere, 4" h. 55.00
Jardiniere, 6" h. 110.00
Urn, pierced handles, No. 621-4",
  4" h. 40.00
Vase, 4" h., two-handled, globular,
  No. 524-4" 46.00
Vase, 4½" h., globular w/flared
  rim, No. 93-4½" 90.00
Vase, 6½" h., handles rising from
  mid-section to rim, globular
  w/wide mouth, black paper
  label 65.00
Vase, 6½" h., 5¼" d., small handles at shoulder, silver paper
  label 70.00
Wall pocket, side handles rising
  from above pointed base forming
  a pointed overhead handle, flared
  rim, 8½" h. 260.00

JUVENILE (1916 on)

Transfer-printed and painted on creamware with nursery rhyme characters, cute animals and other motifs appealing to children.

Juvenile Feeding Dish

Bowl, 5" d., duck w/hat 45.00
Feeding dish w/rolled edge, chicks,
  "Baby's Plate," 8" d. 50.00
Feeding dish w/rolled edge, nursery
  rhyme "Hickory, Dickory, Dock,"
  8" d. 45.00
Feeding dish w/rolled edge, rabbits
  w/floppy ears, 8" d. 50.00
Feeding dish w/rolled edge, sitting
  rabbits, "Baby's Plate," 8" d.
  (ILLUS.) ....50.00 to 65.00
Mug, ducks, 3½" h. 45.00
Mug, rabbits w/floppy ears, 3" h. .. 45.00

Pitcher, 3½" h., seated dog..60.00 to 70.00
Pitcher, 3½" h., duck w/hat 75.00
Pitcher, 3½" h., sunbonnet girl 48.50
Pitcher, 3" h. & 4½" d. bowl, chicks,
  the set 75.00
Plate, 8" d., duck w/hat 30.00
Plate, 8" d., sunbonnet girl 47.50
Saucer, chicks, 5½" d. 25.00

LAUREL (1934)

Laurel branch and berries in low relief, reeded panels at sides.

Bowl, 13" d., deep yellow 80.00
Console bowl, deep yellow, 9" d.,
  3½" h. 70.00
Vase, 6" h., angular shoulder handles, green or terra cotta,
  No. 668-6", each 65.00
Vase, 9½" h., angular side handles,
  globular base w/wide stepped
  mouth, No. 674-9¼" 75.00

LOMBARDY (1924)

Melon-ribbed sides tapering to a center point at the bottom.

Bowl, 7" d., 3" h., three-footed,
  mottled matte blue glaze,
  No. 175-7 .... 75.00
Vase, 8" h., three-footed, flaring
  rim, light green, No. 350-8 ...... 130.00
Wall pocket, straight rim, light
  green glossy glaze, No. 1257-8,
  8" h. 150.00

LOTUS (1952)

Stylized lotus petals in relief.

Candleholders, footed, blue & white
  high-gloss finish, No. L5, 2½" h.,
  pr. 43.00
Planter, green & yellow high-gloss
  finish, 10½" l. 65.00
Planter, turquoise & tan high-gloss
  finish, 12" l. 75.00
Vase, 10" h., cylindrical, burgundy &
  beige high-gloss finish, No. L3.... 110.00
Wall pocket, blue & white high-gloss
  finish, No. L8-7, 7½" h. 150.00

LUFFA (1934)

Relief-molded ivy leaves and blossoms on shaded brown or green wavy horizontal ridges.

Candlestick, two-handled, bell-
  shaped base, green, 5" h. 40.00
Jardiniere, small angular rim handles, green, 8" 200.00
Vase, 6" h., angular rim handles,
  brown or green, each .....40.00 to 45.00
Vase, 7½" h., two-handled, green .. 70.00
Vase, 8½" h., slightly tapering
  body, two angular handles at

base of short collared neck,
brown.......................... 95.00
Vase, 9½" h., small angular rim
handles, pineapple-shaped body,
green 175.00
Vase, 10" h., two-handled, bulbous,
brown........................ 150.00
Vase, 13" h., flaring base, cone-
shaped body w/angular handles
beneath slightly flared rim,
brown........................ 270.00
Wall pocket, small angular handles
beneath curved rim, green,
8½" h........................ 270.00

LUSTRE (1921)
Bowl, 6" d., canted sides, glossy
blue metallic finish, No. 78...... 45.00
Candlesticks, flaring base rising to
baluster-shaped stem, glossy orange metallic finish, No. 1027,
pr............................. 70.00
Console bowl, footed, glossy silver
grey metallic finish, No. 86,
12" d., 5" h..................... 45.00
Vase, 6" h., cylindrical w/wide
mouth, glossy orange metallic finish, No. 163 .... 25.00

MAGNOLIA (1943)
*Large white blossoms with rose centers and
black stems in relief against a blue, green or
tan textured ground.*

Magnolia Flower Frog

Ashtray, two-handled, low bowl
form, tan, No. 28, 7" d.......... 62.50
Basket w/low overhead handle,
footed, blue or green,
No. 385-10", 13" w., 10" h.,
each ....70.00 to 85.00
Basket, hanging-type, green,
No. 469-5"..................... 77.50
Bowl, 6" d., two-handled, blue,
No. 447-6"..................... 35.00
Bowl, 10" d., two-handled, blue,
No. 450-10".................... 42.50
Candleholders, exaggerated angular
side handles rising from circular
base to rim, blue, No. 1156-2½",
2½" h., pr..................... 55.00

Console bowl, angular end handles,
tan, No. 5-10", 14½" l.......... 60.00
Cookie jar, cov., shoulder handles,
blue, No. 2-8", overall 10" h...... 170.00
Ewer, green, No. 13-6", 6" h. 55.00
Ewer, tan, No. 15-15", 15" h....... 195.00
Flower frog, angular side handle,
green, No. 182-5", 5½" h.
(ILLUS.)...................... 50.00
Jardiniere, two-handled, blue,
No. 665-5", 5" d................ 50.00
Model of a conch shell, green,
No. 454-8", 8½" w. 85.00
Pitcher, cider, 7" h., blue,
No. 132-7"..................... 95.00
Planter, angular end handles, tan,
No. 388-6", 8½" l. 35.00
Tea set: cov. teapot, creamer &
sugar bowl; blue, green or tan,
Nos. 4, 4C & 4S, 3 pcs., each
set ....95.00 to 120.00
Vase, 4" h., ovoid w/angular han-
dles at rim, blue or tan,
No. 86-4", each ....25.00 to 35.00
Vase, double bud, 4½" h., gate-
form, blue, No. 186-4" 35.00
Vase, 7" h., blue or green,
No. 89-7", each................. 40.00
Vase, 9" h., tan, No. 94-9"........ 70.00
Wall pocket, overhead handle
w/pointed ends, blue, green or
tan, No. 1294-8½", 8½" h.,
each ....80.00 to 95.00

MATT COLOR (late 1920's)
Basket, hanging-type, aqua matt finish, No. 364-5", 5" h............ 65.00
Bowl, 5" d., small rim handles, narrow vertical ribbing on lower two-
thirds of body, blue matt finish,
No. 625-5"..................... 35.00
Flowerpot, embossed geometric design, aqua matt finish, No. 549-4",
4" h.......................... 30.00

MATT GREEN (before 1916)
Basket, hanging-type w/original
chains, everted scalloped rim, embossed design, dark green matt
finish, 9" 60.00
Bowl, 8½" d., 3" h., w/flower frog,
dark green matt finish........... 32.50
Jardiniere, rounded handles at
shoulder, bulbous, slightly flared
rim, green matt finish flecked
w/brick red, 6" d., 3½" h........ 55.00
Pot w/pierced flower frog cover,
dark green matt finish, 2½" h.,
2 pcs.......................... 55.00
Pot, embossed geometric design,
dark green matt finish, 4" h...... 30.00
Vase, double bud, 5" h., 8" w., fluted columns joined by a gate, dark
green matt finish................ 37.50

Vase, 6" h., dark green matt
finish 60.00

MEDALLION (pre-1916)

*Creamware decorated with a delicate golden
decal swag of flowers and bows suspending
evenly spaced cameo-like rose or green medallions of the Greek god Mercury.*

Creamer, green medallions, 3" h. . . .   40.00
Dresser set: ring tree, cov. powder
box, cov. hair receiver & 10" d.
tray; rose medallions, 4 pcs. 375.00
Jardinieres, green medallions,
3" d., pr. 65.00

MING TREE (1949)

*Embossed twisted bonsai tree topped with
puffy foliage - pink-topped trees on mint
green, green tops on white ground and white
tops on blue ground; handles in the form of
gnarled branches.*

Ming Tree Vase

Basket w/overhead branch handle,
blue ground, No. 509-12", 13" h. . . 160.00
Basket, hanging-type, blue or green
ground, 6", each 150.00
Ewer, blue, green or white ground,
No. 516-10", 10" h., each . .75.00 to 95.00
Model of a conch shell, blue ground,
No. 563, 8½" w. 35.00
Vase, 6" h., asymmetrical branch
handles, white ground, No. 581-6"
(ILLUS.) 30.00
Vase, 6½" h., single branch handle,
blue or white ground, No. 572-6",
each 60.00
Vase, 8" h., asymmetrical branch
handles, white ground,
No. 582-8" 45.00
Wall pocket, overhead branch han-
dle, blue ground, No. 566-8",
8½" h. 95.00
Window box, blue ground,
No. 569-10", 4 x 11" 85.00

MODERNE (1930's)

*Art Deco style rounded and angular shapes
trimmed with an embossed panel of vertical
lines and modified swirls and circles - white
trimmed with terra cotta, medium blue with
white and turquoise with a burnished antique
gold.*

Bowl, 6" d., footed, white,
No. 296-6" 45.00
Compote, 5" h., open stem, tur-
quoise, No. 295 . . . .   50.00
Vase, 6" h., low foot, cylindrical,
turquoise, No. 789-6" 50.00
Vase, bud, 7" h., two-handled, tur-
quoise, No. 790-7" 75.00
Vase, triple bud, 7" h., medium
blue, No. 792-7" 48.00

MONTACELLO (1931)

*White stylized trumpet flowers with black ac-
cents on a terra cotta band - light terra cotta
mottled in blue or light green mottled and
blended with blue backgrounds.*

Basket w/pointed overhead handle,
flattened globular body w/wide
neck, light green ground,
No. 332-6", 6" h. 275.00
Console bowl, two-handled, light
green ground, No. 225-9", 9" l. . . .   90.00
Vase, 4" h., two-handled, light
green ground, No. 555-4" 60.00
Vase, 5" h., two handles at mid-
section, light terra cotta,
No. 556-5" 95.00
Vase, 5" h., two-handled, terra cot-
ta or green, No. 557-5", each 65.00
Vase, 7" h., two-handled, slightly
ovoid, wide mouth, light terra cot-
ta, No. 561-7" 145.00

MORNING GLORY (1935)

*Stylized pastel morning glory blossoms and
twining vines in low relief against a white or
green ground.*

Basket w/pointed overhead handle,
globular body, green ground,
10½" h. 595.00
Pot, small angular handles at mid-
section, flaring rim, green, No. 5,
5" h. 155.00
Vase, 7" h., pillow-shaped, base
handles, green ground . .175.00 to 200.00
Vase, 10" h., two-handled, white
ground 350.00
Vase, 15" h., shoulder handles,
slightly expanding cylinder, white
ground 500.00

MOSS (1930's)

*Spanish moss draped over a brown branch
with green leaves against a background of
ivory, pink or tan shading to blue.*

Basket, hanging-type, tan ground,
No. 353-5" 100.00
Candleholders, flat disc base, ball-
shaped, ivory ground,
No. 1109-2", 2" h., pr. 55.00
Urn, small angular handles rising
from base to mid-section, globu-
lar, ivory, No. 290-6", 6" h. 80.00

Vase, 6" h., large open angular
handles, pink ground,
No. 774-6" 55.00
Vase, 7" h., angular handles, tan
ground, No. 776-7" 45.00
Vase, 10" h., two-handled, pink
ground, No. 784-10" 185.00

MOSTIQUE (1915)

*Incised Indian-type designs of stylized flow-
ers, arrowhead leaves or geometric shapes
glazed in bright high gloss colors against a
heavy, pebbled ground.*

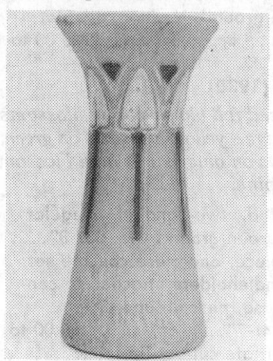

Mostique Vase

Bowl, 5½" d., 2½" h., geometric
design, grey ground 26.00
Bowl, 7½" d., floral design, sandy
beige ground 40.00
Bowl, 9" d., two-handled, floral de-
sign, tan ground 55.00
Jardiniere, floral design, tan
ground, 8" h. 75.00
Jardiniere & pedestal base, floral
design, tan ground, 2 pcs. 315.00
Vase, 6" h., corset-shaped, arrow-
head leaves design, grey
ground 35.00
Vase, 8" h., closed handles at mid-
section, globular base, geometric
design, grey ground 65.00
Vase, 10" h., arrowhead leaves de-
sign, grey ground (ILLUS.) 65.00
Vase, 15" h., corset-shaped, green
& yellow arrowhead leaves design
w/blue triangles on grey
ground 125.00
Wall pocket, floral design, grey
ground, 10½" h. 70.00

NORMANDY (1924)

*Green and ivory vertical fluting with a band
of embossed ivory vines, pink grapes and
green leaves on a brown ground at the rim.*

Jardiniere, 5½" base d., 7" h. 150.00
Jardiniere, 12" d., 9¾" h. 290.00
Jardiniere & pedestal base, overall
28" h., 2 pcs. (ILLUS.) 750.00

Normandy Jardiniere & Pedestal

Umbrella stand, 20" h. 400.00

ORIAN (1935)

Compote, 10½" d., 4½" h., glossy
turquoise w/tan lining 48.00
Vase, 7" h., slender handles rising
from compressed globular base to
middle of long neck w/double
rings, glossy yellow 75.00
Vase, 7" h., slender handles rising
from shoulder of squatty ringed
base to rim of short wide neck,
glossy burgundy w/turquoise
lining 125.00
Vase, 8" h., two-handled, tan
w/blue drip, gold paper label 50.00
Vase, 9" h., slender handles rising
from compressed ringed base to
middle of long wide neck, glossy
blue, small silver label 65.00

PANEL (1920)

*Recessed panels decorated with embossed
naturalistic or stylized florals or female
nudes.*

Bowl, 6½" d., 4" h., slightly canted
sides, stylized florals, dark brown
ground 62.00
Jar, cov., stylized florals, dark
green ground, 10" h. 300.00
Vase, double bud, 5" h., waisted
cylinders joined by panel of
daisies, dark green ground 48.00
Vase, 6" h., fan-shaped, female
nudes, dark brown . . . . . . 175.00 to 250.00
Vase, 6" h., pillow-shaped, small
rim handles, orchid blossoms,
dark green 60.00
Vase, 8" h., fan-shaped, female
nudes, dark green 295.00
Wall pocket, rectangular openwork
handles, scalloped edge, female
nudes, dark brown,
7" h. 195.00 to 255.00

Wall pocket, orchid blossoms, dark
green, 9" h. 95.00

PINE CONE (1931)
*Realistic embossed brown pine cones and
green pine needles on shaded blue, brown or
green ground. (Pink extremely rare.)*

Pine Cone Planter

Ashtray, blue or brown ground,
No. 499, 4½" l., each 67.00
Basket w/overhead branch handle,
cylindrical w/flaring rim & low
foot, blue or brown ground,
No. 338-10", 10" h.,
each . . . . .180.00 to 200.00
Basket, hanging-type, blue, brown
or green ground, No. 352-5", 5",
each . . . . .155.00 to 180.00
Bowl, 6" d., blue or brown ground,
No. 354-6", each . . . . .75.00 to 95.00
Candleholder, triple, brown ground,
No. 1106-5½", 5½" h. 110.00
Cornucopia-vase, brown or green
ground, No. 126-6", 6" h., each. . . 50.00
Console bowl, end handles, brown
ground, silver paper label,
11" l. 120.00
Ewer, blue or brown ground,
No. 909-10", 10" h.,
each . . . . .195.00 to 250.00
Flowerpot & saucer, brown ground,
No. 633-5", 5" h. 115.00
Jardiniere, two-handled, globular,
blue or green ground, No. 632-3",
3" h., each 55.00
Jardiniere, two-handled, blue
ground, No. 632-6", 9" d.,
6½" h. 125.00
Mug, blue or brown ground,
No. 960-4", 4" h., each 100.00
Pitcher w/ice lip, 8" h., branch
handle, blue or brown ground,
each . . . . .135.00 to 200.00
Planter, single side handle rising
from base, green ground,
No. 124-5", 5" h. (ILLUS.). 45.00

Tumbler, brown or green ground,
No. 414, 5" h., each . . . . . .95.00 to 130.00
Vase, 6" h., two-handled, brown or
green ground, No. 839-6",
each .65.00 to 90.00
Vase, 10" h., brown or green
ground, No. 709-10",
each . . . . .95.00 to 110.00
Vase, 12" h., brown ground,
No. 712-12". 235.00
Wall pocket, green ground,
No. 1283-9", 9" h. 150.00
Wall pocket, triple, blue, brown or
green ground, No. 466, 8½" w.,
each . . . . .160.00 to 235.00

POPPY (1930)
*Embossed full-blown poppy blossoms, buds
and foliage – yellow blossoms on green, white
blossoms on blue or soft pink blossoms on a
deeper pink.*

Bowl, 8" d., two-handled, irregular
rim, green ground, No. 337-8". . . . 35.00
Centerpiece, one-piece console set
w/candleholders attached to central vase, pink ground,
No. 341-7". . . . . .85.00 to 100.00
Ewer, ornate cut-out lip, pink
ground, 876-10", 10" h. 85.00
Jardiniere, tiny handles at rim,
globular, green ground,
No. 642-3", 3" h. 25.00
Vase, 6" h., two-handled, pink
ground, No. 867-6" 45.00
Vase, 7½" h., two-handled, green
ground, No. 869-7" 43.00

PRIMROSE (1932)
*Cluster of long-stemmed blossoms and pod-
like leaves in relief on blue, tan or pink
ground.*

Candlesticks, blue ground,
No. 1105-4½", 4½" h., pr. 125.00
Cornucopia-vase, tan ground,
No. 125-6", 6" h. 28.00
Flower frog, pink ground, No. 22 . . . 60.00
Rose bowl, pink ground, No. 284-4",
4" d. 47.50
Umbrella stand, pink ground,
No. 773-21", 21" h. 715.00
Vase, 6½" h., two-handled, tan
ground, No. 762-6" 50.00
Vase, 7" h., two-handled, tan
ground, No. 760-6" 50.00
Vase, 10" h., shoulder handles, tan
ground, No. 770-10" 100.00
Vase, 12" h., pink ground,
No. 771-12". 210.00
Wall pocket, angular side handles,
tan ground, No. 1277-8", 8" h. 170.00

RAYMOR (1952)
Modernistic design oven-proof dinnerware.

Ashtray, souvenir of plant tours,
shell-shaped, yellow glaze, 3½".. 18.00
Butter dish, cov., Avocado green,
No. 181, 7½"................... 30.00
Casserole, cov., individual size,
Autumn brown, No. 199, 7½".... 15.00
Coffee tumbler, handled, Avocado
green, No. 179.................. 40.00
Cup, Autumn brown, No. 150....... 7.00
Cup & saucer, Beach gray......... 15.00
Dinner service: eight each dinner
plates, salad plates, cups & sauc-
ers plus two vegetable dishes,
divided dish, cov. bean pot, cov.
tureen, swinging coffeepot w/cov-
er, cov. creamer, cov. sugar bowl,
large platter w/well, the set 725.00
Pitcher, water, 10" h., Autumn
brown, No. 189................. 85.00
Plate, dinner, Beach gray or Con-
temporary white, No. 152........ 9.00
Plate, salad, Beach gray or Terra
Cotta, No. 154 ....4.00 to 6.00
Platter, Beach gray, No. 163 .... 20.00
Salt & pepper shakers, Beach gray,
Nos. 168 & 169, 3½" h., pr....... 20.00
Sugar bowl, cov., Beach gray,
No. 157 .... 18.00
Vegetable bowl, Beach gray,
No. 160 .... 15.00
Vase, 6" h., globular w/pinched
rim, gold, marked "Raymor Mod-
ern Artware" 60.00

ROSECRAFT (1916)

Untrimmed classic shapes; glossy glazes.

Candleholders, flat base, baluster-
form stem, flaring rim, glossy
black, No. 1029-3¾", 3¾" h.,
pr............................. 75.00
Flowerpot w/attached saucer, flared
rim, glossy blue, No. 598-5",
5" h.......................... 35.00
Vase, 5 x 8", glossy black 65.00
Vase, 8" h., cylindrical w/small
square handles at rim, glossy yellow, No. 249-8" 75.00
Vase, bud, 8½" h., glossy black,
No. 44-8½".................... 57.50
Vase, 12½" h., glossy dark blue.... 125.00

ROZANE (early 1900's)

*Underglaze slip-painted decoration on dark
blended backgrounds.*

Mug, cherries decoration,
4½" h.............130.00 to 165.00
Vase, 4" h., handles rising from
mid-section of bulging base to
neck, floral decoration, No. 862 .. 185.00
Vase, 5½" h., horizontal elongated
body within a circular ring which
forms handles at shoulder & base,
raised on low foot, floral decoration, No. 872.................. 150.00

Vase, bud, 7" h., slender cylinder,
berries decoration.............. 95.00

RUSSCO (1930's)

*Narrow perpendicular panel front and back,
stacked handles and octagonal rim openings;
solid matte glaze or matte glaze with crystalline overglaze.*

Bowl, 7" w., green w/metallic gold
trim.......................... 40.00
Vase, 7" h., two-handled, pillow-
shaped, rust glaze 85.00
Vase, 7" h., blue glaze 75.00
Vase, 8" h., green w/crystalline
overglaze 125.00
Vase, bud, 8" h., aqua glaze 70.00
Vase, 8½" h., two-handled, rust
glaze 55.00
Vase, 9½" h., pear-shaped w/flar-
ing rim, blue glaze 85.00
Vase, 10" h., blue glaze 75.00
Vase, 12½" h., closed handles at
mid-section, low foot, rust glaze.. 110.00

SILHOUETTE (1940's)

*Recessed shaped panels decorated with flo-
ral designs or exotic female nudes against a
combed background.*

Silhouette Fan Vase

Ashtray, florals, tan 20.00
Basket, flaring cylinder w/painted
overhead handle, florals, white,
No. 708-6", 6" h................ 45.00
Basket w/asymmetrical rim & over-
head handle, florals, white w/tur-
quoise blue panel, No. 709-8",
8" h. 65.00
Basket w/curved rim & asymmetrical
handle, florals, tan, No. 710-10",
10" h.......................... 65.00
Basket, hanging-type, florals, rose .. 45.00
Basket, hanging-type, female nudes,
rose 65.00
Bowl, 8" d., florals, rose,
No. 727-8".................... 35.00
Bowl, 10" d., florals, white,
No. 730-10"................... 36.00
Candleholders, sloping base, waist-
ed stem, female nudes, turquoise
blue, No. 751-3", 3" h., pr...... 75.00
Ewer, bulging base, florals, white

w/turquoise blue panel,
No. 716-6", 6" h. 35.00
Ewer, sharply canted sides, florals,
tan, No. 717-10", 10" h. 45.00
Urn, four wing-shaped feet on disc
base, reclining female nudes, turquoise blue or white, No. 763-8",
8" h., each . . . . .195.00 to 225.00
Vase, 5" h., foliage, tan,
No. 779-5" 24.00
Vase, 7" h., fan-shaped, female
nudes, rose, No. 783-7"
(ILLUS.) . . . . .135.00 to 175.00
Vase, 9" h., flat closed handles be-
tween domed base & body,
florals, white w/turquoise blue
panel, No. 758-9" 32.00
Wall pocket, bullet-shaped, florals,
rose, No. 766-8", 8" h. 70.00

SNOWBERRY (1946)

Clusters of white berries on brown stems with green foliage over oblique scalloping.

Snowberry Sugar Bowl

Basket w/low pointed overhead
handle, shaded rose ground,
No. 1BK7", 7" h. 45.00
Basket w/asymmetrical overhead
handle, shaded blue ground,
No. 1BK8", 8" h. 77.50
Basket, hanging-type, shaded blue
or rose ground, No. 1HB5", 5" h.,
each 150.00
Book ends, shaded blue or rose
ground, No. 1BE, each
pr. . . . . .85.00 to 125.00
Bowl, 10" d., shaded rose ground,
No. 1BL1-10" 45.00
Candlesticks, angular side handles,
shaded rose ground, No. 1CS-2",
4½" h., pr. 40.00
Cornucopia-vase, shaded rose
ground, No. 1CC-8", 8" h. 45.00
Creamer & sugar bowl, angular side
handles, shaded rose ground,
Nos. 1C & 1S, pr. (ILLUS. of sugar
bowl) 65.00
Ewer, shaded blue ground,
No. 1TK-10", 10" h. 75.00
Ewer, flaring base, oval body, shad-
ed blue or green ground, No. 1TK-15", 16" h.,
each . . . . .190.00 to 240.00

Teapot, cov., shaded green ground,
No. LTP 85.00
Vase, 12½" h., two-handled, ovoid
w/flaring mouth, shaded rose
ground, No. 1V1-12" 135.00
Vase, 18" h., shaded rose ground,
No. 1V-18" 275.00
Wall pocket, angular handles rising
from base, shaded blue, green or
rose ground, No. 1WP-8", 8" w.,
5½" h., each . . . . .60.00 to 80.00

STEIN SETS (before 1916)

Ale set: tankard pitcher & four
mugs; creamware, Fraternal Order of Eagles (F.O.E.), brown
spread-winged eagle & rock decal
decoration, 5 pcs. 210.00
Ale set: tankard pitcher & four
mugs; creamware, Quaker men
motif, 5 pcs.   950.00
Ale set: tankard pitcher & six mugs;
creamware, Benevolent & Protective Order of Elks (B.P.O.E.),
w/brown elk & clock decal em-
blems, 7 pcs. . . . . .300.00 to 400.00
Ale set: tankard pitcher & six mugs;
creamware, Loyal Order of
Moose, w/brown moose head &
"Howdy Pap" decal decoration,
7 pcs. 275.00
Mug, creamware, B.P.O.E. w/brown
elk & clock emblems . . . . . .75.00 to 85.00
Mug, creamware, F.O.E., brown
spread-winged eagle & rock decal
decoration 85.00
Mug, creamware, Quaker men mo-
tif, 5" h. 125.00
Mug, creamware, Shrine emblem &
"Osman Temple, Feb. 14, 1916" . .   125.00

SUNFLOWER (1930)

Long-stemmed yellow sunflower blossoms framed in green leaves against a mottled green textured ground.

Basket, hanging-type 300.00
Bowl, 4" d., small handles at rim . . .   165.00
Urn-vase, globular w/small mouth,
5½" h. 80.00
Vase, 5" h., two-handled, bulbous . .   95.00
Vase, 5" h., cylindrical w/handles at
mid-section 68.00
Vase, 6" h., angular rim handles,
cylindrical 93.50
Vase, 8" h., bulbous base, wide
neck 195.00
Vase, 8¼" h., two-handled, ovoid
w/flaring rim 235.00
Wall pocket, curved openwork dou-
ble handle, 7½" h. 320.00

TEASEL (1936)

Gracefully curving long stems and delicate pods.

Bowl, 4" h., closed handles at mid-section, beige shading to tan, No. 342-4" 35.00

Vase, 6" h., closed handles at mid-section, cut-out rim, beige shading to tan, No. 881-6" 37.50

Vase, 8" h., closed handles at shoulder, low foot, rose shading to pink, No. 884-8" 40.00

Vase, 9" h., closed handles at base, flaring mouth, beige shading to tan, No. 886-9" 45.00

Vase, 10" h., handles rising from conical foot to mid-section, cylindrical w/rolled rim, shaded blue, No. 887-10" 57.50

Vase, 15" h., ovoid w/double open handles at shoulder, low foot, small mouth, shaded blue, No. 889-15" 325.00

THORN APPLE (1930's)

White trumpet flower and foliage one side, reverse with thorny pod and foliage.

Basket w/pointed overhead handle, conical w/low foot, shaded pink ground, No. 342-10", 10" h. 165.00

Bowl, 6" d., shaded blue or pink ground, No. 307-6", each . .50.00 to 60.00

Cornucopia-vase, shaded pink ground, No. 127-6", 6" h. 40.00

Ewer, shaded blue ground, No. 825-15", 15" h. 275.00

Flower pot, shaded pink ground, No. 639-5", 5" h. 29.00

Vase, 4" h., squatty body w/short narrow neck, angular pierced handles rising from mid-section, shaded pink ground, No. 308-4" . . 45.00

Vase, triple bud, 6" h., three cylindrical tubes of varying heights applied w/foliage & pod decoration, shaded pink ground, No. 1120-6" 65.00

Vase, 6" h., shaded blue ground, No. 810-6" 60.00

Vase, 6" h., angular side handles, low foot, shaded pink ground, No. 812-6" 59.00

Vase, 8" h., shaded blue ground, No. 818-8" 50.00

Vase, 10½" h., angular handles rising from shoulder to middle of wide neck, footed, shaded brown or pink ground, No. 822-10", each .95.00 to 110.00

TOPEO (1934)

Four evenly spaced vertical garlands beginning near the top and tapering gently down the sides.

Bowl, 9" d., 2½" h., sharply canted sides, glossy deep red glaze 125.00

Urn-vase, globular, glossy deep red glaze, 6" h. 90.00

Vase, 6½" h., ovoid w/flaring mouth, glossy deep red glaze 85.00

Vase, 8½" h., glossy deep red glaze 115.00

TOURMALINE (1933)

Bowl-vase, globular base w/two handles rising from mid-section to rim of wide short neck, mottled blue, No. A-517-6", 6" h. 63.50

Cornucopia-vase, semi-gloss medium blue glaze, No. 106-7", 7" h. 25.00

Cornucopia-vase, mottled turquoise blue, 9½" h. 45.00

Ginger jars, cov., mottled terra cotta & yellow, 12" h., pr. 375.00

Vase, 5" h., bulbous, mottled blue . . 65.00

Vase, 6" h., pillow-type, two-handled, horizontally ribbed lower half, tan glaze, No. A-65-6" 40.00

Vase, 7" h., slightly swollen cylinder, mottled turquoise blue, No. A-308-7" 54.00

Vase, 8" h., large base handles, flaring neck, mottled rose shading to grey, No. A-332-8" 60.00

TUSCANY (1927)

Gently curving handles terminating in blue grape clusters and green leaves.

Candleholders, conical base w/open handles rising to mid-section of nozzle, mottled pink, 3" h., pr. . . . 55.00

Console bowl, rectangular w/rounded ends, mottled pink, 11" l. 50.00

Flower arranger, pedestal base, flaring body, open handles, mottled pink, 5" h. 65.00

Flower arranger, open handles rising from base, pierced top, mottled pink, 5½" h. 40.00

Vase, 4" h., ovoid, mottled grey 35.00

Vase, 9¼" h., bulbous, mottled grey 40.00

Wall pocket, long open handles, rounded rim, mottled grey or pink, 8" h., each 85.00

VELMOSS (1935)

Embossed clusters of long slender green leaves extending down from the top and crossing three wavy horizontal lines. Some pieces reverse the design with the leaves rising from the base.

Candleholders, flat disc base, slender cylindrical nozzle, mottled rose, No. 1100-4½", 4½" h., pr. . . . 70.00

Urn-vase, angular pointed side handles, mottled blue, No. 264-5", 8½" d., 5" h. 52.00

Vase, 7" h., angular pointed han-

dles at mid-section, turquoise
blue, No. 716-7" 47.00
Vase, 7" h., angular side handles at
mid-section, cylindrical w/low
foot, mottled raspberry red,
No. 715-7" 60.00
Vase, 9½" h., angular handles,
mottled green, No. 719-9" 75.00
Vase, 14" h., angular pointed handles, expanding cylinder w/low
foot, mottled green, No. 722-14" . . 150.00

VELMOSS SCROLL (1916)

Incised stylized red roses and green leaves on
a creamy ivory matte glaze.

Bowl, 6" d., slightly rounded sides,
No. 116-6" 40.00
Bowl, 7" d., 2" h. 53.00
Candlesticks, flat base, slender
standard w/flaring rim,
No. 1044-8", 8" h., pr. 75.00
Compote, 9" d., 4" h., footed 80.00
Jardiniere, 6½" d., 7½" h. 35.00
Jardiniere, 10" h. 250.00

VISTA (1920's)

Embossed green coconut palm trees and lav-
ender blue pool against grey ground.

Bowl, 7" d., 3½" h., No. 249-7" 60.00
Jardiniere, 8" 300.00
Jardiniere & pedestal base, overall
28" h., 2 pcs. 500.00
Vase, 10" h., cylindrical w/flaring
base 175.00
Vase, 12" h. 137.50
Wall pocket, 9½" h. 195.00

WATER LILY (1940's)

Water lily blossoms and pads against a
horizontally ridged ground. White lilies on
green lily pads against a blended blue ground,
pink lilies on a pink shading to green ground
or yellow lilies against a gold shading to
brown ground.

Water Lily Cookie Jar

Basket w/asymmetrical overhead
handle, curved & sharply scalloped rim, pink shading to green
ground, No. 382-12", 12" h. 82.50

Candleholders, gold shading to
brown ground, No. 1154-2", 2" h.,
pr. 50.00
Console bowl, pointed end handles,
blended blue ground, No. 442-10",
10" l. 45.00
Console bowl, large pointed end
handles, pink shading to green
ground, No. 444-14", 14" l. 70.00
Cookie jar, cov., angular handles,
pink shading to green ground,
No. 1-8", 8" h. (ILLUS.) . .160.00 to 195.00
Cornucopia-vase, large water lily
blossom applied at base, gold
shading to brown ground,
No. 177-6", 6" h. 30.00
Ewer, swollen cylindrical form
on flat base, blended blue or
pink shading to green ground,
No. 12-15", 15" h.,
each . . . . .160.00 to 185.00
Jardiniere, blended blue ground,
9" d., 8" h., No. 663-8" 295.00
Rose bowl, pink shading to green
ground, No. 437-6", 6" d. 47.50
Vase, 4" h., blended blue, gold
shading to brown or pink shading
to green ground, No. 71-4",
each 30.00
Vase, 6" h., waisted form w/large
angular handles at mid-section,
gold shading to brown ground,
No. 73-6" 45.00
Vase, 12" h., angular side handles
rising from globular base to beneath the rim of the long cylindrical neck, gold shading to brown
ground, No. 81-12" . . . . . . .90.00 to 110.00
Vase, 14" h., angular side handles,
pink shading to green ground,
No. 82-14" . . . . .195.00 to 225.00

WHITE ROSE (1940)

White roses and green leaves against a ver-
tically combed ground of blended blue, brown
shading to green or pink shading to green.

Basket w/pointed circular handle,
blended blue ground, No. 363-10",
10" h. 75.00
Candleholders, two-handled, blend-
ed blue or pink shading to green
ground, low, No. 1141, each pr. . . 30.00
Candlesticks, base handles, brown
shading to green ground,
No. 1142-4½", 4½" h., pr. 50.00
Cornucopia-vase, double, pink shading to green ground, No. 145-8",
8" h. 45.00
Creamer & sugar bowl, disc foot,
pink shading to green ground,
No. 1-C & 1-S, pr. 45.00
Ewer, pink shading to green ground,
No. 981-6", 6" h. 50.00

Ewer, pink shading to green ground,
No. 990-10", 10" h. 110.00
Flower frog, basket-shaped w/over-
head handle, pink shading to
green ground, No. 41 . . . . 22.00
Pedestal, brown shading to green
ground, 16¾" h. . . . . .175.00 to 200.00
Rose bowl, two-handled, blended
blue, brown shading to green or
pink shading to green ground,
No. 387-4", 4" d., each . . . .35.00 to 45.00
Urn-vase, handles rising from base
to rim, footed, pink shading to
green ground, No. 146-6", 6" h. . . 35.00
Urn-vase, two-handled, globular
w/wide neck, footed, blended
blue ground, No. 147-8", 8" h. 65.00
Vase, 4" h., cylindrical w/slightly
sloping shoulder, blended blue
ground, No. 978-4" 20.00
Vase, 8" h., base handles, brown
shading to green or pink shading
to green ground, No. 984-8",
each 52.00
Vase, 8½" h., handles rising from
globular base to rim, blended
blue or brown shading to green
ground, No. 985-8", each . .60.00 to 72.00
Vase, 15½" h., two-handled, shaped
rim, blended blue ground,
No. 992-15" 235.00
Vase, 18" h., two-handled, blended
blue ground, No. 994-18" 275.00

WINCRAFT (1948)

Basket w/low overhead handle,
shaped rim, berries & foliage in
relief on glossy yellow ground,
No. 209 12" 60.00
Bowl, 8" d., glossy green,
No. 226-8" 25.00
Coffee set: 9½" h. cov. coffeepot,
creamer & sugar bowl; glossy
blue, Nos. 250P, 271C & 271S,
3 pcs. 95.00
Planter, two-handled, geranium
blossoms & leaves in relief on
glossy shaded blue ground,
No. 268-12", 12" l. 30.00
Vase, 6" h., asymmetrical fan
shape, pine cones & needles in
relief on glossy shaded blue
ground, No. 272-6" 40.00
Vase, 7" h., square, paneled sides
w/swirled Art Deco style design
in relief on glossy shaded blue or
yellow & tan ground, No. 274-7",
each . . . . .50.00 to 60.00
Vase, 8" h., circular w/molded tree
branches in open center, mottled
glossy blue ground, No. 1053 . . . . . 35.00
Vase, 10" h., cylindrical, tab handles, black panther & green palm
trees in relief on glossy shaded

lime green or tan ground,
No. 290-10, each . . . . .150.00 to 225.00
Wall pocket, globular, ivy vine in re-
lief on glossy shaded tan ground,
No. 267-5", 5" h. . . . . .70.00 to 80.00

WINDSOR (1931)

*Stylized florals, foliage, vines and ferns on
some, others with a repetitive band arrangement of small squares and rectangles on mottled blue blending into green or terra cotta
and light orange blending into brown.*

Bowl, 10" d., 3" h., two-handled,
stylized florals against mottled
blue ground, paper
label . . . . .95.00 to 125.00
Candlesticks, base handles, geomet-
ric design against mottled terra
cotta, 4½" h., pr. 165.00
Vase, 5" h., two-handled, stylized
florals against mottled blue
ground 75.00
Vase, 6" h., geometric design
against mottled terra cotta
ground 90.00
· Vase, 7½" h., 10" widest d., two
handles rising from shoulder of
compressed globular base to rim
of short wide mouth, stylized
ferns against mottled terra cotta
ground 175.00
Vase, 9" h., stylized ferns against
mottled blue ground 325.00

WISTERIA (1933)

*Lavender wisteria blossoms and green vines
against a roughly textured brown shading to
deep blue ground; rarely found in only brown.*

Bowl, 9" d., two-handled 115.00
Console bowl, small angular end
handles, No. 243, 12" l. 110.00
Vase, 4" h., squatty, angular han-
dles on sharply canted shoulder,
No. 629-4" 97.50
Vase, 6" h., two-handled, pear-
shaped w/wide mouth,
No. 631-6" . . . . .145.00 to 175.00
Vase, 7" h., angular handles at
shoulder, brown ground,
No. 634-7" . . . . .110.00 to 130.00
Vase, 8½" h., base handles, coni-
cal, No. 635-8" 150.00
Vase, 8½" h., angular handles from
shoulder to rim, globular 138.50
Vase, 9½" h., angular handles,
No. 639-9" 175.00
Vase, 10" h., waisted cylinder w/an-
gular handles at mid-section 250.00
Vase, 15" h., bottle-shaped w/angu-
lar handles at shoulder,
No. 641-15" 425.00
Wall pocket, flaring rim, 8" h. 325.00

ZEPHYR LILY (1946)

Deeply embossed day lilies against a swirl-textured ground. White and yellow lilies on a blended blue ground; rose and yellow lilies on a green ground; yellow lilies on terra cotta shading to olive green ground.

Zephyr Lily Basket

Ashtray, blue or terra cotta ground,
No. 27, each . . . . .40.00 to 45.00
Basket w/overhead handle, low
foot, terra cotta ground,
No. 393-7", 7" h. (ILLUS.) 45.00
Book ends, blue or terra cotta
ground, No. 16, pr. . . . . .65.00 to 75.00
Bowl, 12" l., blue, green or terra
cotta ground, No. 478-12",
each .55.00 to 75.00
Candleholders, two-handled, blue,
green or terra cotta ground,
No. 1162-2", 2" h., each
pr. . . . . .25.00 to 30.00
Console bowl, end handles, green
ground, No. 479-14", 16½" l. 52.50
Cornucopia-vase, blue ground,
No. 204-8", 8½" h. 50.00
Ewer, blue, green or terra cotta
ground, No. 23-10", 10" h., each . .   80.00
Ewer, terra cotta ground,
No. 24-15", 15" h. 165.00
Teapot, cov., blue ground, No. 7T . .   90.00
Vase, 7" h., handles rising from
compressed base to long cylindri-
cal neck, terra cotta ground,
No. 131-7" 35.00
Vase, bud, 7½" h., handles rising
from conical base, green or terra
cotta ground, No. 201-7", each . . .   35.00
Vase, 8½" h., base handles, cylin-
drical, terra cotta ground,
No. 133-8" 38.50
Vase, 10" h., handles at mid-
section, cylindrical w/slightly
bulging base, blue ground,
No. 138-10" 52.50
Wall pocket, two handles at base,
blue, green or terra cotta ground,
No. 1297-8", 8" h., each . . .65.00 to 75.00

(End of Roseville Section)

ROYAL BAYREUTH

Good china in numerous patterns and designs has been made at the Royal Bayreuth factory in Tettau, Germany, since 1794. Listings below are by the company's lines, plus miscellaneous pieces. Interest in this china remains at a peak and prices continue to rise. Pieces listed carry the company's blue mark except where noted otherwise.

CORINTHIAN

Corinthian Pitcher

Chamberstick, classical figures on
green ground, 5" h. $90.00
Chamberstick, classical figures on
red ground, 5" h. 110.00
Creamer, classical figures on black
ground 55.00
Creamer, classical figures on yellow
ground 75.00
Creamer & sugar bowl, classical
figures on red ground, pr. 145.00
Pitcher, 5½" h., classical figures on
black ground, yellow bands
w/leaf decoration around neck &
base (ILLUS.) 54.00
Pitcher, milk, classical figures on
red ground 125.00
Trinket box, cov., square, classical
figures on black ground 75.00
Vase, 5½" h., classical figures on
black ground 75.00

DEVIL & CARDS

Devil & Cards Candy Dish

Box, cov., used for playing cards
storage, full figural devil reclining
on lid, (inner flange of base
damaged) 195.00
Candy dish, 7" d. (ILLUS.) 125.00
Creamer, 4" h..................... 145.00
Cup, figural red devil handle,
2¼" d......................... 145.00
Pitcher, 5½" h., 3 x 5", "Bermuda"
on side....................... 200.00
Salt & pepper shakers, pr. 245.00
Salt dip, master size.............. 135.00

MOTHER-OF-PEARL FINISH
Creamer, Murex Shell patt., spiky
form 85.00
Creamer & cov. sugar bowl, grape
cluster mold, pearlized yellow,
colorful foliage, pr.............. 160.00
Creamer & sugar bowl, Murex Shell
patt., pr. 100.00
Nappy, poppy mold, pearlized
apricot 85.00
Nut dishes, poppy mold, set of 6 .. 120.00
Pitcher, milk, Murex Shell patt...... 145.00
Pitcher, milk, oak leaf mold........ 185.00

ROSE TAPESTRY

Rose Tapestry Hair Receiver

Basket, handled, three-color roses .. 195.00
Bell, w/original wooden clapper,
pink & yellow roses on soft green
ground, row of relief beading
near the base, gold handle 495.00
Creamer, tankard, pinched spout,
red, pink & pale beige roses 295.00
Hair receiver, three-color roses
(ILLUS.)....................... 245.00
Hatpin holder, pink roses, 4½" h. .. 300.00
Match holder, hanging-type 295.00
Plate, 10½" d. 325.00
Wall pocket, three-color roses,
5 x 9"........................ 650.00

SUNBONNET BABIES
Bell w/original wooden clapper,
babies cleaning 595.00
Cake plate, babies cleaning, 6" d. .. 120.00
Candlesticks, one babies fishing,
other babies sewing, tall, unmarked, pr. 475.00
Chamberstick, ring handled, saucer
base, babies cleaning 295.00

Chamberstick, shield back-type,
babies cleaning 495.00
Cup & saucer, babies cleaning...... 120.00
Pitcher, milk, babies fishing........ 295.00
Plate, small, babies fishing 89.00
Plate, large, babies washing 200.00

TOMATO ITEMS

Tomato Sugar Bowl

Tomato covered box, 3¾" d........ 35.00
Tomato covered box, 4½" d........ 45.00
Tomato creamer 42.00
Tomato mustard pot, cov........... 48.00
Tomato sugar bowl, cov. (ILLUS.) ... 48.00
Tomato tea set: cov. teapot, cream-
er & cov. sugar bowl; footed, 3
pcs............................. 180.00

MISCELLANEOUS

Figural Grape Cluster Creamer

Ashtray, figural mountain goat 135.00
Bowl, 10½" d., Art Deco florals
w/pearl lustre finish............. 175.00
Box, cov., donkey boy decoration,
2 x 3¾"....................... 85.00
Box, cov., Little Bo Peep
decoration..................... 85.00
Box, cov., Little Jack Horner
decoration..................... 85.00
Box, cov., Little Miss Muffet
decoration..................... 85.00
Candleholder, figural Basset
hound......................... 335.00
Chamberstick, figural elk,
4½ x 7½"...................... 310.00
Chocolate pot, cov., figural yellow
poppy 525.00
Creamer, figural bear 625.00
Creamer, figural bull's head, brown
& white 160.00

Creamer, figural cow's head, reddish brown w/some grey, 3" d., 4" h. 90.00
Creamer, figural duck 125.00
Creamer, figural fish head 108.00
Creamer, figural frog 145.00
Creamer, figural grape cluster, green (ILLUS.).................. 90.00

Figural Kangaroo Creamer

Creamer, figural kangaroo (ILLUS.)........................ 875.00
Creamer, figural lamplighter 210.00
Creamer, figural lemon 128.00
Creamer, figural lettuce leaf w/lobster handle 63.00
Creamer, figural lobster 45.00
Creamer, figural milkmaid 245.00
Creamer, figural monkey, green 230.00
Creamer, figural pansy 135.00
Creamer, figural pelican 125.00
Creamer, figural perch 235.00
Creamer, figural poppy, white...... 135.00
Creamer, figural robin 175.00
Creamer, cov., figural rose, pink ... 450.00
Creamer, figural strawberry 150.00
Creamer, figural sunflower......... 310.00
Creamer, Little Bo Peep decoration.................... 75.00
Creamer, Little Jack Horner decoration.................... 55.00
Creamer, Little Miss Muffet decoration, 4".................... 75.00
Cup & saucer, demitasse, oyster & pearl decoration 145.00
Dish, "tapestry," clover-shaped, finger handle, Arab & horses decoration.................... 135.00
Dish, handled, figural purple pansy 40.00
Dresser tray, Little Jack Horner decoration, 5 x 7"............... 225.00
Dresser tray & hatpin holder, yellow-orange roses on shaded green ground, 2 pcs. 175.00
Match holder, hanging-type, farmer & horses scene................. 95.00
Match holder, hanging-type, figural elk 135.00

Match holder, hanging-type, figural poppy 210.00
Mug, large yellow roses, satin finish 50.00
Mustard jar, cov., figural grape cluster, pearlized finish 100.00
Nappy, tub-shaped, white oak leaf decoration.................... 49.00
Nut dish, master size, figural poppy, pink 150.00
Pin dish, leaf-shaped, "tapestry," chrysanthemum decoration 195.00
Pitcher, milk, figural apple 90.00
Pitcher, milk, figural butterfly w/open wings 305.00
Pitcher, milk, figural chick 350.00
Pitcher, milk, figural clown, red 225.00
Pitcher, milk, figural clown, yellow 395.00
Pitcher, milk, figural duck 145.00
Pitcher, milk, figural elk 98.00
Pitcher, milk, figural grape cluster 150.00
Pitcher, milk, figural lemon 145.00

Figural Lobster Milk Pitcher

Pitcher, milk, figural lobster (ILLUS.)........................ 95.00
Pitcher, milk, figural monkey, green 324.00
Pitcher, milk, figural oak leaf 160.00
Pitcher, milk, figural parakeet, unmarked 85.00
Pitcher, milk, figural St. Bernard dog 235.00
Pitcher, water, figural coachman ... 430.00
Pitcher, water, figural coral shell ... 235.00
Pitcher, water, figural duck 495.00
Pitcher, water, figural grape cluster, lustre finish.................... 325.00
Pitcher, water, figural lobster, red .. 235.00
Pitcher, water, figural poppy, white satin finish 435.00
Pitcher, water, figural St. Bernard dog 450.00
Plate, 6" d., donkey boy decoration.................... 55.00
Plate, 6" d., Jack & Jill decoration .. 65.00
Plate, 6" d., Jack & the Beanstalk decoration.................... 55.00

Plate, 6" d., Little Jack Horner
decoration 65.00
Plate, 6¼" d., peasant musicians
decoration 60.00
Plate, 7½" d., Little Bo Peep
decoration 85.00
Plate, 7¾" d., Little Jack Horner
decoration 75.00
Plate, 9" d., roses & gold tracery
decoration 42.00
Plate, chop, 13" d., h.p. pink roses
on cream ground 125.00
Salt & pepper shakers, figural elk,
pr. 125.00
Sauce dish & underplate, figural
poppy, satin finish, 2 pcs. 90.00
Sugar bowl, cov., figural head of
lettuce 55.00
Sugar bowl, cov., figural pansy 140.00
Teapot, cov., figural grape cluster,
white 225.00
Teapot, cov., figural pansy 265.00
Teapot, cov., Little Jack Horner
decoration 185.00
Tea set: 4½" h., 3¼" d. cov. tea-
pot, 2½" h., 2¼" d. creamer,
1¾" h., 3" d. sugar bowl, footed
cup & saucer; teapot & cup w/two
horses w/farmer decoration,
creamer & saucer w/farmer holding two horses w/farmhouse on
the back decoration, sugar bowl
w/farmer w/mule decoration,
5 pcs. 273.00
Trinket box, cov., Jack and the
Beanstalk decoration, 2½" sq. . . . 115.00

Figural Rose Tureen

Tureen, cover & underplate, figural
rose (ILLUS. of part) 250.00
Vase, 3½" h., round, portrait of girl
holding candle 60.00
Vase, 4¼" h., five pink & yellow
roses on cobalt blue ground 45.00
Vase, 4¼" h., "tapestry," violets
decoration 325.00
Vase, 4½" h., coach scene around
top, yellow ground 48.00
Vase, 4½" h., portrait busts of two
lovely brown-haired ladies & band
of roses 85.00
Vase, 5" h., "tapestry," cow & bull
scene 225.00

Vase, 6" h., coach scene around
top, green ground 65.00
Vase, 7" h., bulbous, three moun-
tain goats scene 148.00
Wall pocket, "Penny in Pocket is a
Merry Companion," court jester
pictured, shades of green 165.00

ROYAL BONN & BONN

Ornate Royal Bonn Vase

*Bonn and subsequently Royal Bonn china
were produced in Bonn, Germany, in a
manufactory established in 1755. Later wares
made there are often marked Mehlem or bear
the initials FM or a castle mark. Most wares
were of the hand-painted type. Clock cases
were also made in Bonn.*

Cheese dish, cov., multicolored floral decoration on cream ground
w/gold trim $75.00
Cracker jar, cov., pink & blue flow-
ers w/green leaves on beige
ground, brass rim, handle & lid,
5¼" d., 7" h. 116.00
Ewer, encircling gold lizard handle,
h.p. bird, orchids & dragonfly
decoration, 12½" h. 175.00
Urn, cov., two gold handles, h.p.
overall w/flowers on green & yel-
low ground, artist-signed, 13" h. . . . 85.00
Vase, 5½" h., 6" d., green bands
w/ornate gold trim, pink, rose,
yellow & lavender florals on wide
gold band 110.00
Vase, 7" h., globular form, blue
transfer scene, after Boucher, ca.
1850 . . . . 82.00
Vase, 7½" h., deep pastel florals
w/gilt tracery on ivory ground,
gilt collar & side ring handles 225.00
Vase, 8" h., bulbous base, tapering
to small top, overall roses & trees
w/shadows decoration 175.00

Vases, 8" h., colorful iris decoration, pr. 225.00

Vase, 8" h., 5" d., autumn colored florals on brown shaded to yellow ground 95.00

Vase, 9½" h., two-handled, multicolored floral decoration, signed & numbered 125.00

Vase, 11½" h., decorated full-figure Art Nouveau lady, artist-signed .. 645.00

Vase, 12" h., bulbous form, "tapestry,"marsh scene w/flying duck & frogs 245.00

Vase, 13½" h., portrait decoration w/raised gold trim, artist-signed 345.00

Vase, 14½" h., two large handles, pink wild roses on cream ground 70.00

Vase, 18" h., elongated cylindrical form flaring at base, embossed bands of scrolls & branches at rim & base trimmed in gold, decorated w/continuous frieze of scantily clad maidens in a meadow, late 19th c. (ILLUS.) 825.00

Vase, 22" h., elongated ovoid w/swirled neck, applied branch handles, h.p. purple & green grapes & vines, artist-signed 400.00

ROYAL COPENHAGEN

Royal Copenhagen Figure of a Faun

This porcelain has been made in Copenhagen, Denmark, since 1715. The ware is hardpaste.

Bowl, salad, 9½" d., slightly waisted, Flora Danica patt., botanical specimen, gilt dentil rim $880.00

Bust of Art Nouveau maiden, 1885, 8" h. 400.00

Compote, 8¼" d., Flora Danica patt., botanical specimen within pink & gold molded beadwork borders & gilt dentil rim, exterior w/flower & leaf sprig 715.00

Custard cups, covers & square underplates, gilt handles on cup & cover, square underplate w/cut corners, Flora Danica patt., botanical specimen, pink & gold beadwork borders, underplate 4" w., cup w/cover 3" h., set of 12 .... 4,400.00

Figure of a faun on pedestal w/lizard at base, No. 433 (ILLUS.) 275.00

Fish plates, painted in colors depicting various fish species within an aquatic setting, green & gold molded beadwork border & gilt dentil rim, species named in black on reverse, set of 8 .... 4,400.00

Fruit basket, applied twig handles, Flora Danica patt., latticework mid-section applied w/various colored flowerheads, 10" l. 990.00

Model of a stallion, No. 4752, 7½" h. .... 275.00 to 350.00

Plaquette, Theodore Roosevelt center, blue & white, No. 178, 3¼" d. 45.00

Platter, 16 1/8" l. oval, Flora Danica patt., painted w/pink & green floral sprigs within a pink & gold molded beadwork border, gilt dentil rim 1,350.00

Salt dips, Flora Danica patt., botanical specimen within border heightened by pink enamel & gilding, 4½" l., pr. 440.00

Tankard, cylindrical, bouquets & scattered flower sprays between bands of gilt foliage scrolls, front inscribed w/initials "AKS," hinged silver cover w/foliate thumbpiece & embossed in high relief w/warrior on horseback, ca. 1770, 8¼" h. (large chip repair to base) 825.00

Vase, 9" h., White Rose patt., 1895 .... 115.00

Vase, 13½" h., ovoid w/everted rim, painted w/a continuous rural landscape scene 137.50

Wine coolers, Flora Danica patt., applied twig-form handles w/flowerhead & leaf sprig terminals, sides centrally painted w/botanical specimen beneath pink & gold molded beadwork border, 7¼" h., pr. 3,300.00

ROYAL DUX

These wares were made in Bohemia and

many were imported to the United States around the turn of the century. Although numerous pieces were originally inexpensive, collectors have taken a fancy to the wares and the prices of the better pieces continue to rise.

Royal Dux Figures

Bust of a water nymph, bright-eyed young creature w/orchids & animated leaves about her face & among strong waves surging at her breast, glazed in off-white, turquoise, mint green, pale lavender, peach & russet, traces of gilding, applied pink triangle mark, ca. 1900, 21¼" h. $2,310.00

Bust of young woman, smiling face w/a lily bud & blossom in her long hair & further lilies & lilypads about her *decollete* dress, glazed in rose, celery green, tan, ivory & peach, traces of gilding, incised "H. Schuberty," triangular factory mark & numbers, ca. 1900, 16¾" h. 990.00

Centerpiece, molded as two merry young girls, one perched on the edge of a large swirling vortex of water, the other riding the waves below, the waves molded w/abundant sea foliage, glazed in tones of celery green, purple, ivory & pale seafoam green, heightened w/gilt, applied pink triangle mark, ca. 1900, 20½" h. 1,650.00

Figure of a lady Spanish dancer w/a smiling expression, wearing a mantilla & holding a fan in one hand w/her other hand on her hip, cobalt blue & white decoration, pink triangle mark, 9" h. 310.00

Figures, Greek classical woman w/lyre & a man holding an ancient axe, peach & beige decoration, natural skin tones, matte finish, 12" h., pr. 400.00

Figure of a fisherman wearing knee boots & a hat & carrying a net, green & brown decoration, pink triangle mark, 18" h. 635.00

Figure of a young hunter in peasant dress carrying a large dead bird, decorated w/soft earthtones (ILLUS. right) 475.00

Figure of a classically dressed young woman holding a lute seated on one end of an oblong base w/molded leaf & flower detail, the whole backed by a tall shaped & beveled mirror, figure painted w/soft earthtones (ILLUS. left) 900.00

Figure group, young Greek athlete standing on the backs of two horses, one foot on each animal, 14" h. 500.00

Figure group, nude lady w/white tigers, lady holding a cobalt blue glazed drape around her hips, poised standing in the midst of three white-glazed tigers, her back arched & one arm raised gracefully before her, on an oval gilt-rimmed cobalt blue & white base, applied pink factory tag, ca. 1910, 16½" h. 440.00

Model of a bird, No. 2819, pink triangle mark 125.00

Models of cockatoos, pink triangle mark, 16½" h., pr. 500.00

Model of hunting dog w/birds, pink triangle mark, 17½" 195.00

Model of rhinoceros beetle, 3¼ x 5" 125.00

Vase, 5½ x 13", Art Nouveau style, dolphin handles, gold & green trim 195.00

Vases, 36" h., waisted cylinder, painted, molded & applied w/stork & aquatic plants, flanked by well-molded figures of standing herons, spreading base molded w/lily pads, 20th c., pr. 1,045.00

ROYAL RUDOLSTADT

This factory began as a faience pottery established in 1720. E. Bohne made hard paste porcelain wares from 1852 to 1920, when the factory became a branch of Heubach Brothers. The factory, still producing in East Germany, was nationalized in 1960.

Bowl, 9¾" d., h.p. roses decoration $42.00

Bust of Queen Louise, ca. 1880, 8½" h. 140.00

Chocolate pot, cov., decorated w/pink roses, green leaves & white flowers, 10" h. 150.00

Creamer & sugar bowl, pink & white
apple blossoms w/gold trim, pr... 95.00
Dresser tray, roses decoration,
12" l. 50.00
Ewer, h.p. morning glories on cream
ground, gold worn on handle,
12" h. 85.00
Figure, Hunchback, wearing brown
hat w/blue trousers & a red cloak
w/a floral vest, ca. 1880,
5½" h. 125.00
Figure group, 18th c. figures enjoy-
ing a concert modeled w/a woman
seated playing a piano, accom-
panied by a gentleman, w/a dancing couple surrounded by two
other seated couples, each person
elaborately dressed in brocades &
frilly lace, the whole raised on a
rococo-style shaped platform applied w/flowerheads, Rudolstadt-
Volkstedt, early 20th c., 27" l.,
14" h. 1,980.00
Pin dish, Iris patt. 25.00
Pitcher, 15½" h., inlaid gold leaves
w/jeweling 295.00
Plate, 8½" d., cabbage roses in
pink & rose alternate on cream
ground, embossed beading
around the slightly scalloped rim,
decorated in gold 30.00
Plate, 9" d., h.p. poppies 58.00
Plate, chop, 13" d., h.p. poppies.... 95.00
Relish tray, bouquet of three roses
& six single scattered roses, gold
border, 4 1/8" w., 8" l. 12.50
Teapot, cov., pear-shaped body,
domed cover w/rose finial, molded roses & leaves form the handle, pink enameled flowers &
green leaves on beige satin
ground, 5" d., 6½" h. 172.00
Vase, 13" h., decorated w/scene of
a girl feeding birds, copper lustre
glaze 90.00

ROYAL VIENNA

*The second factory in Europe to make hard-
paste porcelain was established in Vienna in
1719 by Claud Innocentius de Paquier. The
factory underwent various changes of administration through the years and finally
closed in 1865. Since then, however, the porcelain has been reproduced by various factories in Austria and Germany, many of which
have reproduced also the early beehive mark.
Early pieces, naturally, bring far higher prices
than the later ones or the reproductions.*

Box, cov., slightly domed lid w/h.p.
scene depicting "The Rape of Europa," the maiden nude but for a
white robe, perched on the back
of a bull draped in pink, figures
gesturing in the distance, within
gilt zigzag, diapered & foliate
scroll borders on a cobalt blue
ground, artist-signed "K.W.," Turn
EW factory mark, late 19th c.,
8½" d., 4½" h. $495.00
Charger, painted w/an opera scene
depicting Tannhauser & Venus
within gilt & pastel-blue borders
reserved on a claret-colored
ground reserving further smaller
pink or yellow panels trimmed in
gold, artist-signed, ca. 1910,
beehive mark & "Austria,"
14 5/8" d.....................1,320.00
Plaque, rectangular, "Heart's Echo,"
painted w/two classical maidens
in a woodland landscape, one
depicted painting a heart on a
column while the other looks on,
the whole within a shaped oval
panel edged by scrolling gilt motifs & reserved on a deep claret
ground, artist-signed, blue beehive mark & "AUSTRIA," ca. 1900,
framed, 7 1/8 x 8 7/8" 880.00
Plates, 8¾" d., portrait-type, each
w/a portrait of a maiden within
similar pastel colored borders reserving claret borders & heightened in gilding, each signed
"Wagner," blue beehive mark &
titles in German, set of 7 (most
w/surface wear)................4,950.00
Plate, 9¼" d., h.p. scene depicting
Hector, Paris & Helen in an architectural setting, within borders
decorated w/gilt foliage &
animals, blue beehive mark & title, late 19th c. 550.00
Plate, 9½" d., "Brunhilde erscheint
Siegmund und Sieglinde," showing
Sieglinde fainting in Siegmund's
arms at their discovery by the
Valkyrie, within borders w/gilt
ovals alternating w/cartouches
painted w/animals & foliage on a
maroon ground w/heavily gilt
scrolling foliage, late 19th c. 440.00
Plate, 9½" d., "Dolce far niente,"
portrait of an innocent young
maiden w/flowing brown hair,
depicted w/hands behind her
head & wearing a flowered rose
kimono over a white slip, artist-
signed, late 19th c............. 880.00
Plate, 9½" d., "Reflexion," portrait
of maiden w/downcast gaze, her
flowing brown curls falling about
her shoulders covered w/a claret-
covered drapery, within a gilt
band, lustrous pink border re-

served w/small shaped claret-colored panels, the whole elaborately gilded, late 19th c. ... 880.00

Urn, cov., elongated ovoid, painted w/a three-quarter portrait of a woman w/curly brown hair, wearing a white dress w/pink sash, within a gilt-tooled border, reserved on a pale green ground enriched w/elaborate gilt foliate scrolls, raised on a socle base, later gilt-metal stand, late 19th c. 1,540.00

Vase, 6¼" h., h.p. scene of a girl w/a bird, burgundy ground w/heavy gold trim, beehive mark 150.00

Vases, 7" h., 5¾" d., ovoid, h.p. portrait of a child, signed "Wahliss," pr. 145.00

Royal Vienna Portrait Vase

Vase, 14" h., "Klea," oval bust portrait of a maiden w/flowing blonde hair & wearing a pink classical dress, contained within a gilt border & reserved on an iridescent purple ground heightened in gilding w/flowers & stylized vines, ca. 1900, blue pseudo shield mark & "AUSTRIA" (ILLUS.) 880.00

Vase, cov., 14 7/8" h., bulbous ovoid shape painted w/a shaped panel of a maiden w/dark hair entwined by laurel leaves, wearing a classical purple garment & holding sprays of chrysanthemums, within gilt borders & reserved on a lustrous pale green shading to tan ground trimmed in gold, ca. 1910, blue beehive mark & "Germany" 2,200.00

ROYAL WORCESTER

This porcelain has been made by the Roy-al Worcester Porcelain Co. at Worcester, England, from 1862 to the present. For earlier porcelain made in Worcester, see WORCESTER. Royal Worcester is distinguished from those wares made at Worcester between 1751 and 1862 that are referred to as only Worcester by collectors.

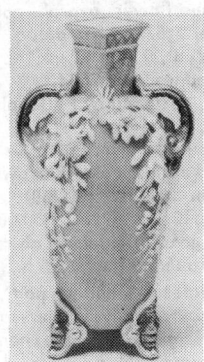

Royal Worcester Vase

Bowl, cov., 10¼" h., footed, circular bowl w/a short reticulated neck, molded in relief & painted on the shoulder & cover w/leafy branches of pink blossoms & berries, raised on three foliate scroll feet on a shaped trefoil base, gilt highlighting, Grainger Worcester shield mark, ca. 1890 . . . . $275.00

Cake plate, round w/silver rim chased w/sprays of leaves centering flowers, the body painted in polychrome w/a basketweave border & baskets of roses, silver marked "Shreve & Co.," San Francisco," 11¾" d. 110.00

Cracker jar, cov., h.p. pink, blue & yellow flowers & green leaves on beige satin finish, silver plate top, rim & handle, 1902, 4¾" d., 6" h. 273.00

Creamer, Lydia patt. 25.00

Dinner service for four, Silver Chantilly patt., 20 pcs. 295.00

Ewer, arched gold handle from tall slender neck w/arched spout to bulbous body, h.p. pink, blue, yellow & coral flowers & green leaves outlined in gold on beige satin finish on body & neck, panel of gold work around shoulder, 1888, 5 3/8" d., 7 7/8" h. 373.00

Figure of a boy holding basket, Kate Greenaway-type, cream & beige w/pink & blue trim, satin finish, 1893, 4" d., 8½" h. 505.00

Figure of a boy w/parakeet, No. 3087, 1950 . . . . 150.00

Figure, "Burma," young girl from Countries of the World series, No. 3068, 1934, signed "F.G. Doughty," 5" h. 155.00

Figures, "Joy" & "Sorrow," standing semi-nude classical ladies on pedestal bases, each soft beige w/pale yellow gowns w/dainty pink & blue flowers overall, gold trim, Nos. 2/57 & 2/58, dated 1894, 3¼" d., 9 7/8" h., pr. 862.00

Figure, "Wednesday's Child," No. 3521, designed by F. Doughty, ca. 1954 . . . . 85.00

Figure, "Yankee," from Countries of the World series, beige & brown decoration, No. 836, ca. 1881, 7 1/8" h. . . . . 350.00 to 400.00

Jardiniere, gold palm leaves on royal blue ground, 9" w., 7½" h. 595.00

Luncheon plates, "Chantilly" patt., classical revival polychrome scroll & floral design on cream & champagne ground, 20th c., 9 1/8" d., set of 11 . . . . 137.50

Model of a Marsh Tit, No. H3336 . . . 25.00

Model of nautilus shell supported by coral branches, pale yellow & peach, ca. 1909, 6¾" h. 375.00

Model of parakeet, blue, on flowered stump, 1940's, 6" h. 83.00

Model of a Percheron horse, designed by Doris Linder, 10 x 11 . . . . 715.00

Pitcher, 3½" h., mask spout, blue, pink & purple flowers outlined in gold, heavy gold on handle, ca. 1895 . . . . 55.00

Pitcher, 7" h., cylindrical w/ornate handle & spout, yellow & rose floral sprays on beige satin ground 300.00

Pitcher, 9" h., tusk-form, floral branch decoration w/green foliage on beige satin ground 300.00

Pitcher, tankard, 10" h., thread-wrapped gold handle joining w/gold ribbing around body creating three sections, upper portion w/high-relief gold branches & florals, middle w/orange & blue florals & lower w/a beautiful spray of purple thistles & pink, gold trim, 1884 . . . . 275.00

Pitcher, 12" h., parian, fish-shaped w/fish handle 130.00

Plates, dinner, 10½" d., Rosemary patt., borders decorated w/flower-filled urns & floral garlands alternating w/floral sprays between bands of cobalt blue, overglaze black factory marks, set of 12 . . . . 385.00

Potpourri jar w/gold pierced cover,

enameled flowers on glossy ground w/heavy gold trim, 5½" h. to top of finial 425.00

Ring tree w/three-prong holder, pink & yellow flowers on beige ground, ca. 1898, 2½ x 4½", 2¾" h. 145.00

Soup plate w/flange rim, Canterbury patt. 15.00

Teapot, cov., Lydia patt. 55.00

Teapot, cov., two joined cylinders form body, decorated w/gold & rust flowers, gold, black & rust butterflies, a green embossed bow, green handle & applied fruit finial, beige satin ground, 1874, 2½ x 4½", 5¼" h. 380.00

Vase, cov., 7½" h., bulbous body w/short cylindrical neck supporting domed reticulated gold cover studded w/gems, body decorated w/castle scene in scrolled reserve against a cobalt blue ground, decorated by Rushton 550.00

Vases, 8½" h., Japanese-style, narrow diamond-shaped neck on squared ovoid cantaloupe-colored body encrusted w/white floral sprays, flanked by leaf-form loop handles, scrolled feet, gold on handles & feet & gold trim on neck, impressed "399," ca. 1874, pr. (ILLUS. of one) 825.00

Vases, 9¼" h., Sabrina Ware, brown w/muted underglaze colors running at bottom, elephant head handles, ca. 1895, pr. 400.00

Wine pot, bulbous body tapering to flared base, over-handle in lustre brown w/gold trim, funnel on one side & long tapered spout on other, five varied colorful floral sprays & green & brown leaves all trimmed in gold, ca. 1884, 10" h. 310.00

R.S. PRUSSIA & RELATED WARES

Ornately decorated china marked "R.S. Germany" and "R.S. Prussia" continues to grow in popularity. According to Clifford J. Schlegelmilch in his book "Handbook of Erdmann and Reinhold Schlegelmilch—Prussia—Germany and Oscar Schlegelmilch—Germany," Erdmann Schlegelmilch established a porcelain factory in the Germanic provinces at Suhl, in 1861. Reinhold, his younger brother, worked with him until 1869 when he established another porcelain factory in Tillowitz, upper Silesia. China bearing the name of this town is credited to Reinhold Schlegelmilch. It customarily bears also the phrase "R.S. Germany." Now collectors seek additional marks including E.S. Germany, R.S. Poland and R.S. Suhl. Prices are high and collectors should beware the forgeries that sometimes find their way to the market. Mold names and numbers are taken from Mary Frank Gaston's books on R.S. Prussia.

R.S. GERMANY

Cabbage Mold Creamer

Basket, oval, rust & green Chinese
  pheasants & trees on dark cream
  ground $245.00
Berry bowls, pink & white roses on
  caramel ground, pr. 30.00
Berry set: master bowl & four in-
  dividual berry bowls; variegated
  orange & yellow roses against a
  brown to light green ground,
  5 pcs. 85.00
Bonbon, side handle, pink carna-
  tions in loops on silvery grey
  ground, lacy gold decorated bor-
  der, 7¾" l., 4½" w. 32.00
Bowls, 5" d., white & green Surreal
  Dogwood patt., pearl lustre finish,
  set of 5 . . . . 100.00
Bowl, 7" d., footed, scalloped edge,
  orange lily decoration 50.00
Bowl, 9" d., cottage scene w/man
  herding sheep 155.00
Bowl, 9" d., single handle, Leaf
  mold, overall white snowballs on
  earth tones, steeple mark 115.00
Bowl, 10", handled, lady w/cows
  near cottage decoration 255.00
Bowl, 10" sq., Cabbage mold, deco-
  rated w/roses 240.00
Bowl, 10½" d., Six-stem Floral
  mold, black ground w/heavy gold
  decoration simulating water on
  which relief-molded water lilies
  rest, 15 h.p. daisies in pastel blue
  & pink w/yellow gold beaded cen-
  ter, steeple mark 600.00
Cake plate, pierced handles, white
  carnations on green ground, 10".. .   75.00
Cake set: cake plate & five serving
  plates; plushy orangy-yellow full
  blown roses on blending ground,
  lacy gold trim on brown border,
  6 pcs. 112.00
Chocolate cups & saucers, pink
  roses w/gold trim, set of 6 . . . .   75.00

Chocolate pot, cov., child's,
  Mold 529, green & white floral
  decoration, 5" h. 120.00
Chocolate set: cov. chocolate pot &
  three cups & saucers; Mold 428,
  cotton boll decoration, 7 pcs. 450.00
Chocolate set: cov. chocolate pot &
  five cups & saucers; ruffled white
  lilies w/gold accented center, lacy
  gold border, silvery grey satin fin-
  ish, 11 pcs. 305.00
Cracker jar, cov., loop handles,
  roses on satin finish, gold knob,
  8 x 6" h. 95.00
Creamer, Cabbage Leaf mold
  (ILLUS.) 30.00
Creamer & cov. sugar bowl, violets
  & pink roses, pr. 75.00
Cup & saucer, white carnations on
  pink ground 32.00
Dresser set: hatpin holder, cov.
  powder jar & hair receiver; pink
  tulips decoration, 3 pcs. 164.00
Gravy boat w/attached underplate,
  cabbage leaf mold, 4½" d.,
  6" l. 30.00
Hair receiver, yellow roses & gold
  banding on white, artist-signed . . .   55.00
Nappy, w/bud-festooned handle,
  flowers in relief w/lush center floral decoration, sapphire blue
  tones 75.00
Plate, 10½" d., Iris mold variant,
  huge lavender & orange burnished
  relief-molded iris 240.00
Relish, open handle, orange poppies
  on grey ground, 11" l. 60.00
Relish, side loop handle, pink &
  white peonies on silvery grey
  ground, gold lacy trim, satin
  finish 45.00
Tidbit, two-tier, white roses on ivory
  ground, satinized borders of floral
  swirls in shades of green interspersed w/gold swatches, spatter
  & banding 55.00
Tray, handled, sheepherder & mill
  scene, 7¼ x 11½" 255.00
Vase, 6" h., two-handled, Night
  Watch patt., heavy gold & red
  trim. 395.00

R.S. PRUSSIA

Berry set: master bowl & six sauce
  dishes; Mold 256, large roses &
  gold tracery on green shaded to
  cream ground, unmarked,
  7 pcs. 295.00
Bowls, berry, Carnation mold, pink
  roses w/gold trim, set of 4 . . . . 175.00
Bowl, 7" d., footed, large white
  roses on shaded grey-green
  ground 150.00
Bowl, 8½" d., Mold 90, relief-

molded petal rim, mauve & lilac
tinged border, red & mauve roses
in center 120.00
Bowl, 8½" d., Mold 182, decorated
w/apples, cherries & grapes 90.00
Bowl, 9" d., Mold 91, pink roses &
white snowballs on shaded pink
ground 235.00
Bowl, 9 3/8" d., Carnation mold,
cinnamon poppies & white & red
roses in relief, glossy finish 185.00
Bowl, 9 3/8" d., Bowl-in-Bowl mold,
Fleur-de-lis mold, fruit
decoration 235.00
Bowl, 9½" d., Mold 347 w/irregular
shape, decorated w/gold leaves &
burrs & white & pale orange
poppies 250.00
Bowl, 10" d., Iris mold, Summer
Season patt., satin finish 900.00
Bowl, 10" d., swan decoration on
satin ground, artist-signed 225.00
Bowl, 10" d., 2½" h., Madame Recamier portrait center scene, red,
gold & black border, unmarked... 575.00
Bowl, 10¼" d., Bowl-in-Bowl mold,
Mold 252, crimson w/white roses
& gold 175.00

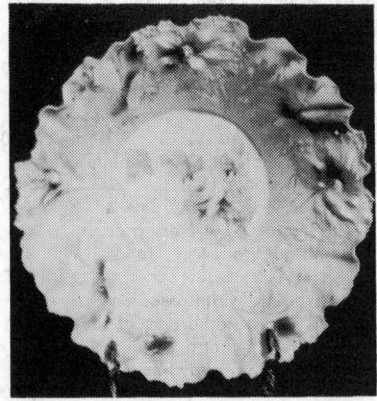

Carnation Mold Bowl with Roses

Bowl, 10¼" d., Carnation mold,
pink & white roses (ILLUS.) 235.00
Bowl, 10½" d., Shell mold, baby
pink roses w/pearlized finish 150.00
Bowl, fruit, 10½" d., 3¼" h., coral,
gold & white floral border in relief, grape clusters & peaches in
center on green ground 195.00
Bowl, 10½" d., Mold 152, roses &
floral decoration 250.00
Bowl, 10½" d., Mold 91, scattered
large flowers decoration, shaded
pink to cream ground 110.00
Bowl, 10¾" d., ripple & quilt-relief
molded rim, roses decoration 170.00
Bowl, 11" d., Mold 14a, Medallion
mold variant, hanging basket of

flowers decoration w/shaded
green spots at rim 250.00
Bowl, 11" d., Bowl-in-Bowl mold,
Mold 632, icicle decoration, molded gold knob feet 450.00
Bowl, 12" d., Carnation mold, pink
roses on green ground 375.00
Bowl, 13" oblong, Icicle mold,
daisies reflected in blue water
decoration, satin finish 185.00
Bowl, 14½" d., Carnation mold,
pink poppies covered w/gold
decoration 1,200.00
Cake plate, pierced handles, Icicle
mold, swan decoration, excellent
gold, 9½" d.................... 750.00
Cake plate, pierced handles,
Mold 78, pink roses decoration,
10" d.......................... 200.00
Cake plate, pierced handles, Jewel
& Ribbon mold, white pearlized
jewels, ribbons & jewels gold outlined, inner rim of draped chain
w/gold stenciled leaves & small
pink & yellow roses, ivory ground,
10½" d. 265.00
Cake plate, pierced handles,
Mold 51, gilt floral tracery at rim,
center w/floral bouquet on shaded cobalt blue ground, some
enameling, 11" d................ 375.00
Cake plate, pierced handles,
Mold 208 w/scalloped border,
decorated w/pansies on green
ground w/heavy gold trim,
11" d.......................... 275.00
Cake plate, pierced handles, Fleur-
de-lis mold, yellow & white rim,
white, pink & yellow roses on
shaded green ground, gold trim,
11" d.......................... 181.00
Cake plate, pierced handles, Pine
Cone mold w/grey-green rim, rich
mauve poppies decoration,
11½" d. 225.00
Celery tray, Stippled Floral mold,
pink & yellow floral bar decoration, 12" l 125.00

Iris Mold Celery

Celery tray, pierced handles, apples, grapes & cherries decora-

tion, heavy gold trim, 13" l.,
6½" w. 295.00
Celery tray, pierced handles, Iris
mold, Autumn Season patt. (ILLUS.
previous page)................. 750.00
Chocolate cup & saucer, Melon Eaters patt., red trim............... 195.00
Chocolate pot, cov., Mold 704, ivy
decoration, applied feet, 10" h.... 295.00
Chocolate pot, cov., pink roses
w/purple & green lustre at base,
relief-molded jewels on handle &
finial, 10½" h. 595.00
Chocolate pot, cov., Mold 644, large
pink roses on light blue ground,
10¾" h. 275.00

Carnation Mold Chocolate Pot with Roses

Chocolate set: 12" h. cov. chocolate
pot & two cups & saucers; Carnation mold, large pink roses on
white ground, 5 pcs. (ILLUS. of
pot)........................... 600.00
Chocolate set: cov. chocolate pot &
five cups & saucers; Mold 704
w/four fleur-de-lis feet & pierced,
beaded handles, autumn leaves
decoration on cream ground,
11 pcs. 1,050.00
Cracker jar, cov., two-handled,
Fleur-de-lis mold, mauve, lavender & crimson florals on pearlized
satin ground 300.00
Cracker jar, cov., Mold 514, peach,
blue & white flowers on pale blue
shaded to white ground 375.00
Creamer & cov. sugar bowl,
Mold 505, red & yellow roses
decoration, pr.................. 135.00
Creamer & cov. sugar bowl,
Mold 607, pedestal base, red &
yellow roses, pink pedestal, pr. ... 195.00
Creamer & cov. sugar bowl,
Mold 648, white lily decoration,
gold trim, pr................... 395.00
Cup & saucer, demitasse, Carnation
mold, cobalt blue 295.00

Cup & saucer, Stippled Floral (525)
mold, colorful floral decoration ... 125.00
Dessert tray, handled, Pie Crust
mold, oval ruffled dish w/tall tapered cylindrical center handle
topped by keyhole-loop handle,
pink roses decoration on pale
green ground, 10¼" w., 8½" h. .. 575.00
Dinner bell, modeled as a long,
nearly closed pink flower blossom
w/green stem, original wooden
clapper, unmarked, 3½" h. 215.00
Dresser tray, open handles, Carnation mold, Fall Season scene,
7 x 11½" 1,500.00
Dresser tray, Medallion mold, Swallows & Shadow Flowers decoration, 11½" l.................... 466.00
Hair receiver, cov., simple lobed
body w/scroll feet, domed lobe
cover w/center hole, pink floral
decoration, 2½" h............... 60.00
Mustache cup & saucer, Mold 637,
four molded feet, poppies decoration w/pearlized finish........... 295.00
Mustard jar, cov., w/spoon, small
roses on satin finish, 3 pcs. 135.00
Pitcher, tankard, 9½" h., Mold 456,
Fall Season scene..............2,250.00
Pitcher, tankard, 9½" h., 8½" d.,
Mold 456, decorated w/large pink
poppies & large green jewels at
rim 500.00

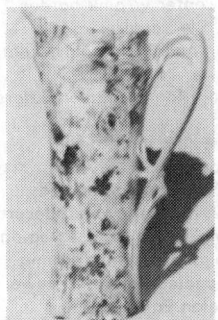

R.S. Prussia Carnation Mold Pitcher

Pitcher, tankard, 13" h., Carnation
mold, pink florals & gold trim on
satin finish (ILLUS.) 825.00
Plaque, pierced to hang, deeply
scalloped rim, wide center decorated w/mill scene on green
ground, lavender & yellow border,
11¼" d. 710.00
Plate, 8" d., Iris mold, Summer Season scene 750.00
Plate, 8½" d., smooth border, decorated w/Gibson Girl (Evelyne)
center portrait 240.00
Plate, 8½" d., Ribbon & Jewel mold,

R.S. Prussia "Melon Eaters" Plate

Melon Eaters "keyhole" scene,
heavy gold trim (ILLUS.) 1,200.00
Plate, 9" d., Iris mold, Fall Season
scene 325.00
Plate, 9" d., Winter Season "keyhole" portrait 1,100.00
Plate, 9½" d., Iris mold, Castle
scene, rare pastel coloring 600.00
Plate, 11" d., Mold 155, Swans &
Pine Trees decoration,
unmarked 225.00
Powder box, cov., Icicle mold, color-
ful flowers on water decoration .. 125.00
Relish dish, Iris mold, Spring Season
scene, 9½" 800.00
Relish dish, Mold 98, golden yellow
roses at center w/pink border
w/roses, 9½" oval 175.00
Relish dish, Medallion mold, Quiet
Cove scene, 14" 375.00
Shaving mug, footed, Melon Eaters
scene 775.00
Teapot, cov., Iris mold, fruit
decoration.................... 600.00
Toothpick holder, two-handled,
Mold 642, ornate jeweled decora-
tion w/pink & white roses on dark
green shaded to white ground.... 250.00
Urn, two-handled, Ribbon & Jewel
mold, Melon Eaters scene 1,500.00
Vase, 7½" h., two-handled, Iris
mold, overall small pink roses &
gold leaves & branches in
relief 325.00
Vase, 8" h., scroll handles,
Mold 901, Melon Eaters scene
w/gold trim & tracery...........1,450.00
Vase, 10" h., two-handled, Spring
Season "keyhole" portrait 825.00
Vase, 14" h., Melon Eaters
scene........................2,000.00

OTHER MARKS
Bowl, 5" d., bird decoration (E.S.
Germany) 48.00
Bowl, 10½" d., overall fox hunt
scene decoration (Prov. Saxe) 48.00

Candlesticks, pink & peach roses
w/brown trim, 6¼" h., pr. (R.S.
Poland) 195.00
Chocolate cup & saucer, woman
w/daisy crown decoration (E.S.
Prov. Saxe).................... 15.00
Chocolate set: cov. chocolate pot &
four cups & saucers; Azalea patt.,
9 pcs. (R.S. Tillowitz-Silesia) 295.00
Creamer & cov. sugar bowl, ornate
gold handles & pedestal base,
purple textured body, gold floral
band around upper rim, signed
"Richards," pr. (E.S. Germany,
Prov. Saxe)................... 45.00
Pitcher & underplate, lilies of the
valley decoration (R.S. Tillowitz
Silesia)...................... 37.50
Plate, 9½" d., center w/exotic bird
in yellow, orange & blue sitting
on heavy gold branch, blue & grey
background, green border
w/heavy gold leaves (Prov. Saxe
Germany) 131.00
Plate, 9½" d., center scene of
"Hamlet & Ophelia," miniature
turquoise jewel beads & heavy
gold on outer rim w/four scenic
diamond-shaped panels, artist-
signed (E.S. Germany) 175.00
Plate, 11¼" d., bust portrait decoration, cobalt blue border (E.S. Germany)....................... 225.00
Relish dish, Iris mold, floral decoration, pearlized finish, 9½"
(Wheelock) 125.00
Salt & pepper shakers, yellow rose
decoration, pr. (E.S. Germany
Prov. Saxe)................... 175.00
Vase, 4" h., Night Watch scene
w/four men & a woman, blue-
green ground (R.S. Poland)....... 300.00
Vase, 4½" h., single rose on shaded
brown ground (R.S. Poland) 105.00
Vase, 4¾" h., ball form, gold handle, medallion w/bust portrait of
lady, gold tracery trim (E.S. Ger-
many Suhl) 175.00
Vase, 7½" h., colored mythological
scene decoration (E.S.
Germany) 100.00
Vases, 8¼" h., cobalt blue w/pale
pink roses decoration, pr. (R.S.
Poland) 225.00
Vase, 14" h., two-handled, roses on
pearlized ground (E.S. Prov.
Saxe) 145.00

RUSSEL WRIGHT DESIGNS

*The innovative dinnerwares designed by
Russel Wright and produced by various companies beginning in the late 1930's were an*

immediate success with a society that was turning to a more casual and informal lifestyle. His designs, with their flowing lines and unconventional shapes, were produced in many different colors which allowed the hostess to arrange a creative table. Although not antique, these designs, which we list below by line and manufacturer, are highly collectible. In addition to dinnerwares, Wright was also known as a trend-setter in the design of furniture, glassware, lamps, fabrics and a multitude of other household goods.

AMERICAN MODERN (Steubenville Pottery Company)

Bowl, nappy, large, single handle, black chutney (deep brown) or chartreuse, each $7.00
Bowl, salad, oval, granite gray 10.00
Bowl, salad, incurved sides, granite gray or seafoam blue, each .28.00 to 38.00
Celery tray, slender w/asymmetrical incurving sides, black chutney, cedar green, granite gray, seafoam blue or white, 13" l., each .15.00 to 18.00
Coffeepot, cov., demitasse, seafoam blue 35.00
Coffeepot, cov., black chutney 50.00
Creamer, chartreuse or granite gray, each . . . . .5.00 to 8.00
Cup & saucer, demitasse, coral or granite gray, each set . . . . .15.00 to 19.00
Cup & saucer, black chutney or chartreuse, each set 10.00
Gravy boat, black chutney or granite gray, each 14.00
Pitcher, water, chartreuse, coral, granite gray or white, each 34.00
Plate, dinner, 10" d., black chutney, chartreuse, coral or granite gray, each .12.00 to 16.00
Plate, chop, 12" sq., granite gray . . . 13.50
Platter, oblong, seafoam blue 15.00
Salt & pepper shakers, chartreuse, pr. 18.00
Sugar bowl, cov., black chutney 9.00
Teapot, cov., black chutney, coral or granite gray, each 40.00
Vegetable bowl, cov., two-handled, cedar green, chartreuse, coral or granite gray, each 30.00
Vegetable bowl, open, two-handled, granite gray 12.00
Vegetable platter, divided, chartreuse or granite gray, each 25.00

CASUAL CHINA (Iroquois China Company)

Butter dish, cov., charcoal, dark green, lettuce green or pink sherbet, ½ lb., each . . . . .35.00 to 40.00
Casserole, cov., lettuce green or white, each . . . . .20.00 to 25.00

Coffeepot, cov., demitasse, nutmeg brown 32.00
Creamer & sugar bowl, stack-type, ice blue, pr. 18.00
Cup & saucer, demitasse, dark green 28.00
Cup & saucer, ice blue or white, each set 12.00
Plate, dinner, 10" d., ice blue, nutmeg brown or pink sherbet, each 6.00
Platter, 14½" l. oval, lettuce green 20.00
Salt & pepper shakers, stacking-type, white, pr. 13.50

SALTGLAZED WARES

Saltglazed Teapot

This whitish ware has a pitted surface texture, which resembles an orange skin as a result of salt being thrown into the hot kiln to produce the glaze. Much of this ware was sold in the undecorated state, but some pieces were decorated. Decorative pieces have been produced in England and Europe since at least the 18th century with later production in the United States. Most pieces are unmarked.

Jug, four embossed wreathed medallions w/people & animals from America, Africa, Asia & Europe, branch handle, also two medallions showing maps of Eastern & Western hemispheres, 5" d., 9 5/8" h. $303.00
Mug, child's, reeded strap handle, cylindrical body painted in shades of rose, blue, green, iron-red & sepia w/an insect crawling on the thorny stem of the stylized rose plant bearing two blossoms & a bud above an iron-red line around the slightly flaring foot (chip), the rim w/an iron-red trellis diaper border reserved w/three panels of demiflowerheads, the interior w/a blue & green foliate sprig, Staffordshire, England, ca. 1760, 2½" h. 2,090.00

Pitcher, 7 3/8" h., straight sides
w/slightly sloping shoulder, cylindrical neck, incised presentation
label "Matilda Dundors from Harry" highlighted in blue, grey
w/green pebbly highlights 260.00
Sauceboat, oval bowl w/wide long
spout & strap handle, molded overall w/cartouches of diaper & basketweave edged w/blue scrollwork, Staffordshire, England, ca.
1765, 5 5/8" l. 1,540.00
Teapot, cov., square body modeled
as a three-story house w/blue
underglazing, the spout w/trailing
vines, Staffordshire, England, ca.
1750, cover crack & restored chips,
two hairline cracks, 4¾" h.
(ILLUS.) 5,280.00
Teapot, cov., spherical, painted on
either side in rose, iron-red, blue,
yellow, green & black w/a floral
bouquet & small sprigs on deep
pink ground, crabstock spout &
handle, Staffordshire, England, ca.
1760, 5¼" h. (spout tip
repaired) 4,675.00

SAN ILDEFONSO (Maria) POTTERY

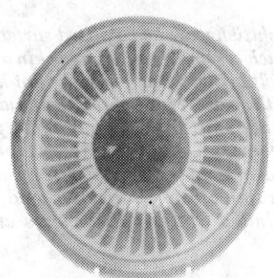

San Ildefonso Feather Motif Plate

A thin-walled and crudely polished blackware has been made at most Rio Grande
Pueblos. Around 1918 a San Ildefonso Pueblo woman, Maria Montoya Martinez and her
husband, Julian, began making a thicker
walled blackware with a finely polished gun-
metal black sheen. It was fired in the traditional manner using manure to smother the
firing process and produce the black coloration. The following is a chronology of Maria's varied signatures: Marie, mid to late
teens-1934; Marie & Julian, 1934-43; Marie &
Santana, 1943-56; Maria and Popovi, 1956-71
and Maria Poveka, used on undecorated
wares after 1956. Maria died in July of 1980.
Rosalia, Tonita, Blue Corn and other signatures might also be found on pottery made
at the San Ildefonso Pueblo. Considered a

true artistic achievement, early items signed
by Maria, or her contemporaries, command
good prices. It should be noted that the
strong pottery tradition is being carried on
by current potters.

Dish, glossy & matte black on black
lizard decoration, signed Reyata
Pena, 7" l. $95.00
Plaque, pierced to hang, glossy &
matte black on black mountain &
feather decoration, signed Blue
Corn, 4 3/8" sq. 250.00
Plate, 5½" d., glossy & matte black
on black feather motif, signed
Marie & Santana (ILLUS.) 600.00
Plate, 5½" d., glossy & matte black
on black, signed Santana &
Adam 325.00
Pot, glossy & matte black on black,
signed Blue Corn, 4" d., 2½" h. .. 350.00
Vase, 2½" h., 3½" d., glossy &
matte black on black feather mo-
tif, signed Blue Corn 350.00
Vase, 3¾" h., 5" d., glossy & matte
black on black, signed Marie &
Julian 950.00
Vase, 6" h., glossy & matte black on
black, signed Tonita & Juan 575.00

SARREGUEMINES

Sarreguemines Vases

This factory was established in Lorraine,
France, about 1770. Subsequently Wedg-
wood-type pieces were produced as was
Mocha ware. In the 19th century, the factory turned to pottery and stoneware.

Character jug, majolica, shaded
beige flesh tones w/ruddy cheeks,
6" d., 6½" h. $85.00
Character jug, majolica, "The Scotsman," 7¾" d., 8" h. 120.00
Character jug, majolica, shaded
flesh tones w/ruddy cheeks &
dark hair, 8½" d., 8½" h. 135.00
Plate, 8½" d., majolica, strawber-

ries & floral trim on aqua
ground 68.00

Plate, opera scene, characters from
"Lohengrin". 55.00

Plate, opera scene, characters from
"Parsifal". 55.00

Plate, opera scene, character from
"Rheingold". 55.00

Vases, 20" h., pearlware, pyriform
shape of Moorish inspiration
painted w/a shaped panel depicting cavaliers in a tavern either
playing a game of dice or having a
drink, the reverse painted w/a for-
tress on the banks of a river, reserved on a rich emerald green
ground enriched by colorful
enamels & gilding w/various
motifs, printed "SARREGUEMINES,"
one w/hairline, the other
w/chipped foot, pr. (ILLUS.) 2,750.00

SATSUMA

Satsuma Censer

*Decorated Satsuma wares have been
produced in Japan since the end of the 18th
century. The early pieces are scarce and high-
priced. Later Satsuma wares are plentiful, affordable and as highly collectible as earlier
pieces.*

Bowl, 5" d., 2" h., interior w/two
women & child having tea outdoors, Mt. Fuji landscape on
exterior $85.00

Censer, cov., ovoid body tapering
sharply at the base & resting on
three animal-mask decorated
splayed supports, the side well
painted in bright enamels & gilt
w/two rectangular figural
reserves on a dense brocade-
patterned ground, further brocade
bands on the squared shoulder &
waisted neck set w/a pair of

raised U-shaped handles flanking
the everted rim & low domed cover w/further brocade patterning &
pierced w/three *mokko*-form cut-
outs encircling a sculptural finial
fashioned as a *karako* seated w/a
fan, late 19th c., gilt rubbed,
8¾" h. (ILLUS.). 605.00

Cracker jar, cov., white & gold flowers on tangerine ground, 8" d.,
7½" h. 125.00

Cup & saucer, Bamboo with Birds
patt., heavy gold 55.00

Dish, shell-shaped, resting on conch
shell feet, center reserve of Seven
Sages, late 19th c., 9½ x 13",
3" h. 1,430.00

Hatpin, head w/dainty overall
florals on cream ground,
ca. 1900 . . . . 40.00

Satsuma Jar

Jar, bulbous baluster form, vertical
panels of Totai decoration alternating w/enameled decoration,
panels separated by raised ribs,
19th c., 7½" h. (ILLUS.) 275.00

Kogo, cov., circular container decorated in gilt & bright enamels
w/shaped figural reserves on a
brocade-patterned ground, the interior w/further figural depiction,
the base w/cartouche reading
"*Hattori-sei*," 3 1/8" d., (slight
wear to gilt) 605.00

Pitcher, cov., 10" h., low-slung
ovoid body surmounted by a long
cylindrical neck encircled by a
high-relief molded three-claw
dragon, its upraised head forming
the spout opposed by its long S-
curved tail serving as the handle,
body painted in gilt & bright enamel w/a continuous view of various blossoming plants & trees
bracketed by patterned bands,
domed cover w/knob finial &
decorated *en suite*, base w/Satsu-
ma mon & inscribed "*Dai Nihon
Satsuma yaki*" & "*Meigyoku*,"
late Meiji period (restorations &
chips) 440.00

Plate, 6¾" d., Bamboo with Birds
patt. 38.00
Saki pot, compressed ovoid shape
w/an angular shoulder supporting
two gilt-painted convoluted dragons forming a pair of vertical
loops, spout also fashioned as an
upraised animal resting on the
body painted w/shaped figural
reserves on a brocade-patterned
ground, base w/Satsuma mon &
inscribed "Satsuma-yaki," late
19th c., 2¼" h. (wear) 440.00
Teapot, cov., miniature, globular
body w/inset cover w/gold knob
finial, enameled Mille Fleur patt.,
Taisho period, ca. 1920, 1½" h. . . 195.00
Vase, 3½" h., double gourd shape,
panels of Geisha in different sur-
roundings, cream ground,
ca. 1880 . . . . 125.00
Vase, 6½" h., miniature elephant
handles, two panels featuring
men, courtesans & children, diapered motif w/heavy gold, ca.
1905 . . . . 395.00
Vases, 8" h., fluted paneled body,
roaring Foo lion handles, Thousand
Face patt., heavy fired gold
ground, early 20th c., pr. 1,925.00
Vase, 9 7/8" h., ovoid, tapering to
slightly flared foot & surmounted
by a small waisted neck w/rolled
rim, sides painted in bright
enamels & gilt w/two rectangular
figural reserves on a deep blue
ground w/elaborate gilt florals,
butterfly & brocade designs on cobalt blue ground, base w/Satsuma
mon & inscribed "Dai Nihon
Satsuma-yaki 'Meigyoku-zan' "
(gilt rubbed) 715.00
Vases, 12 1/8" h., ovoid w/slender
body surmounted by cylindrical
neck w/a rolled rim & decorated
in gilt & colored enamels w/two
large rectangular reserves of
women & children in a spring
landscape on a rich blue ground
w/floral & geometric patterning in
gilt, the base signed "Shuzan,"
pr. 660.00
Vase, 23¾" h., ovoid high-shoul-
dered body w/a waisted neck flaring
to a rolled rim, sides decorated in
gilt & multicolored enamels w/two
large rectangular reserves depicting a group of bijin & children
walking in a pavilion-dotted landscape featuring spring or autumn
foliage, all on a deep blue ground
scattered w/floral & zoomorphic
roundels on a ground of geometric
& floral motifs below a gilt keyfret

band encircling the neck, the base
w/Satsuma mon & four character
cartouche reading "Satsuma
Rinsai," Rinsai, Meiji period (wear
to gilt) 3,025.00

SCHAFER AND VATER

*Founded in Rudolstadt, Thuringia, Ger-
many in 1890, the Schafer and Vater Porcelain
Factory specialized in decorative pieces of
porcelain usually in white or colored bisque.
They produced many novelty figural items
such as creamers, toothpick holders, boxes
and hatpin holders and also produced a line
of jasper ware with white relief decoration in
imitation of the famous Wedgwood jasper
wares. The firm also decorated white ware
blanks.*

*The company ceased production by 1962
and collectors now seek out their charming
pieces which may be marked with a crown
over a starburst containing the script letter
"R."*

Ash pot, figural fat naked cupid,
3½" l., 3" h. $100.00
Box, cov., jasper ware, pink, green
& white busts of Victorian ladies,
man on lid, 3½" d., 2 1/8" h. 58.00
Box, cov., bisque, two round boys'
heads w/googlie eyes form oval
cover on tub-form base, heads
decorated in natural colors, base
in tan, 1 5/8 x 2¾", 3" h. 140.00
Creamer, figural Chinaman w/mon-
key on his back, multicolored,
5½" h. 105.00
Creamer, figural Dutch girl w/bas-
ket on back carrying keys,
3¾" h. 85.00
Creamer, figural Dutch boy's head,
blue & white, 4" h. 108.00
Creamer, figural girl w/jug & black
pocketbook, 5" h. 70.00
Creamer, model of a bear w/mug,
multicolored, 5" h. 95.00
Creamer, model of a seated goat
w/boutonniere, multicolored,
5½" h. 95.00
Creamer, model of a chimpanzee in
dress clothes 80.00
Cup & saucer, relief-molded Art
Nouveau ladies' faces, pink
bisque w/jeweling 98.00
Figure, bisque, girl dressed in pink
& blue holding two large wooden
shoes, 2¾" d., 4½" h. 95.00
Hatpin holder, bisque, "Egyptian"
series, Art Nouveau ladies' heads
w/jewels & brown iridescent glaze
on pink ground, 4½" h. 145.00
Match holder, bisque, model of a

seated cat & kitten on rectangular
base w/holder to one end, black
mother cat w/her back to the
front & wearing a green polka dot
neck bow beside small brown &
white kitten w/yellow polka dot
bow, striker on mother's back,
wording across base reads "Don't
Scratch Me - Scratch Mother,"
3¾" d., 3¾" h. 105.00
Match holder, bisque, mustached
man points to tongue 60.00
Model of a dog, black base w/light
blue dog w/red bow & tongue,
placard on his neck reads "I Am
A Gay Dog," 2½ x 3 1/8",
5¼" h. 105.00
Nodder figure, grinning monkey
holds apple in outstretched paw,
4¼" h. 175.00
Pitcher, milk, figural Oriental lady
w/howling child 115.00
Salt & pepper shakers, smiling apple
& pear, multicolored, pr. 85.00
Teapot, cov., single cup size, smiling apple, multicolored 125.00
Vase, 3" h., 2¾" d., bisque, figural
googlie-eyed boy w/oversized
head w/blue hat & wearing a gold
& white striped outfit sits beside
his brown dog, vase opening at
back 115.00
Vase, 4" h., jasper ware, lavender
w/jeweled cameo-relief of two
ladies 65.00
Vase, 4¾" h., 3" d., white bisque
w/medallion of Grecian lady
against green background, gold
trim & green tassels hanging
down sides 75.00
Vase, 7" h., 1 7/8" d., bisque,
figural girl w/oversized head &
googlie eyes sits on brick stoop
reading a book, wearing a cream-
colored hat, red blouse & green
skirt, vase opening at top of her
head 115.00
Whimsey, figure of Scotsman in kilt,
"Mind your own business" on
base, lift his kilt & it reads, "Of
course I've pants ye fool!,"
5¼" h. 130.00

SEVRES & SEVRES-STYLE

*Some of the most desirable porcelain ever
produced was made at the Sevres factory,
originally established at Vincennes, France,
and transferred, through permission of Madame de Pompadour, to Sevres as the Royal
Manufactory about the middle of the 18th
century. King Louis XV took sole responsibility for the works in 1759 when production*

*of hard paste began. Between 1850 and 1900,
many biscuit and soft-paste porcelains were
again made. Fine early pieces are scarce and
high-priced. Many of those available today
are late productions. The various Sevres
marks have been copied and pieces listed as
"Sevres-Style" are similar to actual Sevres
wares, but not necessarily from that factory.*

Sevres Casket

Casket w/hinged lid, rectangular
cover painted w/a central cartouche depicting two lovers relax-
ing in a landscape, the gentleman
playing a mandolin, within a
scrolling gilt border, reserved on
a *bleu celeste* ground, the interior
painted w/floral clusters, sides
painted w/landscapes, on four
scrolling feet, gilt-bronze mountings, artist-signed, print Louis-
Philippe mark & Chateau des
Tuileries mark in red, mid-19th c.,
8½" l. (ILLUS.) $715.00
Compotes, 6¼" h., Sevres-Style, centered by a figural panel surrounded by a foliate-scrolled gilt
border w/three small rectangular
panels, raised on a circular stem
& socle, pr. 1,430.00
Creamer, helmet-shaped, w/a reserve of fruits on a ledge & two
small heart-shaped reserves of
pansies on the pale green ground,
blue interlaced "L's," date letters
for 1782, painter's & gilder's
marks, 4¼" h. (scratches at base
of handle) 660.00
Creamer, jug-shaped, on three
branch feet headed by flowering
vines & painted w/an urn of flowers on a marble ledge w/a bird &
nest on the *bleu nouveau* ground,
blue interlaced "L's," ca. 1776,
4¾" h. (slight wear to gilding on
feet, small scratch in painting) ...1,045.00
Cup & saucer, demitasse, decorated
w/a gilt trellis & cobalt blue border above a scallop shell band &
manganese fabric swag, artist-

signed, blue interlaced "L's," 1763,
cup 1¾" h. 825.00

Sevres Bisque Figures

Figure, bisque, "La Petit Fille au
Tablier," young girl wearing a
scarf & jacket, holding grapes &
fruit in her outstretched apron,
standing barefoot by a tree
stump, on a shaped oval base,
modeled by Blondeau after
Boucher, ca. 1760, 8" h. (ILLUS.
left)........................... 770.00
Figure, bisque, "Le Jeune Suppli-
ant," young boy depicted standing
barefoot w/clasped hands, wearing a short-sleeved jacket &
breeches, a basket of flowers by
his side, on a rockwork base,
modeled by Blondeau after
Boucher, ca. 1760, incised F, heart
& leaf, 8" h. (ILLUS. right)........ 770.00
Figure group, aristocratic elegantly
dressed couple, lady w/plumed
hat, floral bodice & yellow skirt
holding reticulated basket, gentleman in pink floral waistcoat holding bouquet of flowers, on oval
pedestal, 1795, 8" h 495.00
Gueridon (three-legged stand),
Sevres-Style, circular top inset w/a
painted 'Sevres' plate depicting a
gaming party in 18th century dress
set in an extensive garden within
gilt enriched *bleu de roi* borders,
scale-cast inswept tripod support
joined by a circular floral painted
'Sevres' plaque & ending in scroll
feet, late 19th c. porcelain, artist-
signed, 22" d., 30" h. 1,430.00
Jardinieres, Sevres-Style, painted on
the front w/a figural panel & reverse w/a panel depicting birds
within gilt borders on a *bleu
celeste* ground, flanked by scrolled
handles headed by birds, raised on
a circular base fitted w/putti supporting swags & leaf cast feet, late
19th c., 15" h., pr. 6,050.00
Pedestals, Sevres-Style, bisque,

modeled in relief w/a continuous
frieze depicting a Bacchic cele-
bration including dancing maidens
& musicians, the whole between
bleu du roi borders enriched w/gilt
motifs, artist-signed, ornate gilt-
bronze mountings, late 19th c.,
41" h., pr. 33,000.00
Plates, cabinet-type, 9½" d.,
painted w/lovers wearing 18th century-style clothing at various
leisurely pursuits, the whole within
a scalloped pale apricot border enriched in blue & claret-colored
enamels heightened in gilding
within scrolling devices, artist-
signed, late 19th c., set of 12 ....2,200.00
Plaque, bisque, portrait of a gentleman in profile to the left, his hair
en queue, blue & white, signed
"Collett" & dated "1785," in a
carved giltwood frame, 5 5/8" l.
oval (small cracks) 605.00
Teapot, cov., cylindrical, painted
w/oval cartouches of fruits on a
marble ledge within blue & gilt
line borders reserved in the pale
green ground w/blue, pink *oeil-de-
perdrix* beneath a border of gilt
foliage & pink reserves on a pink-
seeded ground; the lower border
w/gilt & white foliate lozenges on
the pink ground, blue interlaced
"L's," date letters for 1782,
painter's & gilder's marks (spout
w/scratches) 1,100.00
Teapot, cov., oviform, w/scroll
spout & handle, the domed cover
w/flowers finial, painted overall
w/scattered roses between berried laurel borders & gilt dentil
rims, blue interlaced "L's" &
painter's marks, ca. 1775,
5¼" h. 528.00

20th Century Sevres Vase

Urns, cov., Sevres-Style, body decorated w/figural panels one side &
landscape panels reverse, the

whole w/gilt highlights on a *bleu celeste* ground, loop handles, late 19th c., 16½" h., pr. 3,025.00

Vase, 15 3/8" h., globular base tapering to tall slender neck w/flared rim, decorated w/grape clusters, leaves & vines on a white ground in shades of turquoise, purple & green, factory marks & painted "d'apres J. Derrier 10.EX.EX.No.4 MB" & inscribed "JB.20.11.PN," 1921 (ILLUS.) 1,100.00

Vase, cov., 29¼" h., gilt-bronze mounted ovoid vessel painted w/a maiden attended by two cupids leaning against a garden wall, reverse painted w/a cupid soaring above a columnar fragment, the neck, base & cover w/a wide pink border w/gilt details, marked w/interlaced "L's" & "France" ca. 1910 . . . . .1,320.00

SHAWNEE

Tom, Tom Teapot

The Shawnee Pottery operated in Zanesville, Ohio, from 1937 until 1961. Much of the early production was sold to chain stores and mail-order houses including Sears Roebuck, Woolworth and others. Planters, cookie jars and vases, along with the popular "Corn King" oven ware line, are among the collectible items which are plentiful and still reasonably priced. Reference numbers used here are taken from Mark E. Supnick's book, Collecting Shawnee Pottery.

Bank-cookie jar combination, figural Winnie Pig, chocolate colored base $125.00
Butter dish, cov., "Corn Queen" line 24.00
Cookie jar, "Corn Queen" line, No. 66 . . . . 48.00
Cookie jar, Drummer Boy, model of a drum w/boy finial on lid 50.00

Cookie jar, figural Clown w/seal & ball, No. 12 . . . . 62.00
Cookie jar, figural Dutch Boy, blue tie, striped pants 45.00
Cookie jar, figural Elephant, gold decal decoration 95.00
Cookie jar, figural Jug w/heart & tulip decoration 85.00
Cookie jar, figural Owl, gold trim 115.00
Cookie jar, figural Sailor Boy, gold trim & decals 135.00
Creamer, "Corn King" line, 5" h. . . . 13.00
Creamer, Daisy patt. 15.00
Creamer, figural Elephant 13.50
Creamer, figural Elephant, gold trim 67.50
Mixing bowl, "Corn King" line, 5" d., No. 5 . . . . 25.00
Mug, "Corn King" line, 8 oz., No. 69 . . . . 24.00
Pitcher, "Corn King" line, 12 oz., No. 70 . . . . 18.00
Pitcher, Fruit patt., No. 80 . . . . 15.00
Pitcher, figural Chanticleer Rooster, w/flower decals & gold trim 130.00
Pitcher, figural Little Boy Blue, No. 46 . . . . 25.00
Pitcher, figural Smiley Pig, peach, blue & gold flowers 125.00
Planter, figural Dutch Children at Well, No. 710 . . . . 10.00
Planter, model of Dog in Boat, No. 736 . . . . 12.50
Planter, model of an Upright Piano, No. 528 . . . . 14.00
Plate, 10" oval, "Corn King" line, No. 68 . . . . 21.00
Salt & pepper shakers, Daisy patt., large, pr. 15.00
Salt & pepper shakers, figural Chanticleer Rooster, gold decorated, large, pr. 100.00
Salt & pepper shakers, figural Jug w/heart & tulip decoration, large, pr. 15.00
Salt & pepper shakers, figural Mugsey dog, small, pr. 15.00
Salt & pepper shakers, figural Owl, pr. 7.50
Sugar bowl, cov., "Corn King" line, No. 78 . . . . 28.00
Teapot, cov., "Corn Queen" line 25.00
Teapot, cov., Daisy patt. 35.00
Teapot, cov., figural Granny Anne, blue apron 37.50
Teapot, cov., figural Tom, Tom the Piper's Son, No. 44 (ILLUS.) 37.00
Vegetable bowl, open, "Corn King" line, 9" oval, No. 95 . . . . 18.00
Wall pocket, Little Bo Peep, No. 586 . . . . 10.00

SHENANDOAH VALLEY POTTERY

Shenandoah Valley Jar

*The potters of the Shenandoah Valley in
Maryland and Virginia turned out an earthenware pottery of a distinctive type. It was
the first earthenware pottery made in America with a varied, brightly colored glaze. The
most notable of these potters, Peter Bell, Jr.,
operated a pottery at Hagerstown, Maryland
and later at Winchester, Virginia, from about
1800 until 1845. His sons and grandsons carried on the tradition. One son, John Bell, established a pottery at Waynesboro, Pennsylvania in 1833, working until his death in
1880, along with his sons who subsequently
operated the pottery a few years longer. Two
other sons of Peter Bell, Jr., Solomon and
Samuel, operated a pottery in Strasburg, Virginia, a town sometimes referred to as "pot
town" for six potteries were in operation there
in the 1880's. Their work was also continued
by descendants. Shenandoah Valley redware
pottery, with its colorful glazes in green, yellow, brown and other colors, and the stoneware pottery produced in the area, are eagerly
sought by collectors. Some of the more unique
forms can be considered true American folk
art and will fetch fantastic prices.*

Flowerpot w/attached saucer, buff
clay w/brown running glaze, bottom impressed "John Bell,
Waynesboro," 4¼" h. (minor
flakes) $350.00
Flowerpot w/deep attached saucer
base, greenish brown glaze on
redware, impressed "John W.
Bell, Waynesboro, Pa.," 4 7/8" h.
(hairlines, small edge flakes) 275.00
Flowerpot w/attached saucer, slightly canted sides, tooled rim, white
slip w/green & brown running
glaze & clear glaze, 9¼" h. (old
edge chips & short rim hairline
w/professional repair) 250.00
Jar, ovoid, redware w/dark glaze,

impressed "John Bell," 5 5/8" h.
(small flakes & hairline) 200.00
Jar, ovoid, redware w/interior
glaze, impressed, "John Bell,
Waynesboro," 8¾" h. (hairline in
base) 150.00
Jar, ovoid w/eared handles, redware w/unglazed exterior decorated around the shoulder w/a
band of coggled decoration &
manganese flowers, the interior
w/manganese glaze, impressed
"John W. Bell," 1880-95, 12½" h.
(ILLUS.) 528.00
Preserving jar, stoneware, straight
sides, rounded shoulder, grey
shiny glaze w/greenish-yellow
highlights, impressed "John Bell,
Waynesboro, Pa.," 6½" h. 195.00
Preserving jar, stoneware, straight
sides, rounded shoulder, grey salt
glaze, impressed "Solomon Bell,"
8½" h. (irregular lip) 65.00

SLIPWARE

Slipware Bowl

*This term refers to ceramics, primarily red-
ware, decorated by the application of slip, or
semi-liquid paste made of clay. Such wares
were made for decades in England and Germany and elsewhere on the Continent, and in
the Pennsylvania Dutch country and elsewhere in the United States. Today, contemporary copies of early Slipware items are featured in numerous decorator magazines and
offered for sale in gift catalogs.*

Bowl, 9¼" d., 3 1/8" h., bold four-
part "wing" design in yellow slip
& brown glaze in bottom, wavy
yellow slip band & plain brown
band around wide rim on redware
(minor glaze flakes & old rim
chips) $650.00
Bowl, 13½" d., tapering cylindrical

sides w/galleried rim, decorated
in brown w/a central stylized
flowerhead within concentric rings
within wavy line border, on a
mustard yellow ground on redware, Jacob Christ-type, Moravi-
an, probably Salem, North
Carolina, mid-19th c., minor wear
& losses (ILLUS.) 264.00

Charger, coggled edge, alternating
yellow slip four-line wavy &
straight bands across the center
on redware, good, clean condi-
tion, 11 3/8" d. 1,050.00

Dish, round, four alternating rows
of brown slip dots, two straight
yellow slip lines & a center wavy
yellow slip line on redware, Pennsylvania, 19th c., 7" d. 2,200.00

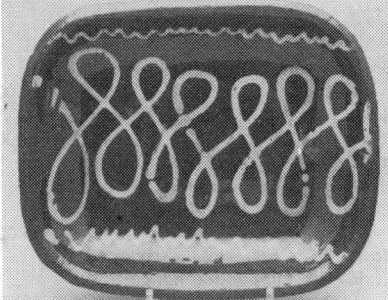

Oblong Slipware Dish

Dish, oblong, decorated in yellow
slip w/interconnected figure-
eights within squiggle borders on
redware, probably New England,
19th c., 11½" l. (ILLUS.).......... 715.00

Flowerpot, tapering cylindrical body
w/molded lip w/coggled edge
above a stippled band over the
yellow slip inscription "William
Dunlap," the whole decorated
w/yellow slip petals on redware,
possibly Simon Singer, Bucks
County, Pennsylvania, late 19th c.,
7½" h. (chips, wear to
inscription) 308.00

Jar, ovoid w/crimped rim, wheel-
incised lines below rim & on
shoulder, natural brown glaze
w/three floral decorations in natural, brown & green slip on redware, probably Pennsylvania,
5½" h........................ 605.00

Jug, ovoid w/ribbed strap handle,
four- and five-line yellow slip
dashes alternating w/squiggles on
redware, 10½" h. (foot chips,
glaze flakes, wear) 2,200.00

Loaf pan, rust glaze, yellow slip
two-line squiggle design
w/"PORK" in center on redware,

Pennsylvania, ca. 1830, 9¼ x
11¾" 350.00

Milk pan, tapering cylindrical sides
w/molded rim & applied eared
handles, interior glazed w/three
bands of concentric cream & black
slip rings alternating w/black slip
scalloped bands on redware, attributed to Henry Weise, Hagers-
town, Maryland, ca. 1870, 18" d.
(repair to base, chips to
handles) 7,700.00

Pie plate, coggled edge, three
bands of triple wavy lines in yellow slip on redware across center, 8" d...................... 175.00

Pie plate, coggled rim, three-line
wavy band of yellow slip across
center & two three-line yellow
slip scrolls at edges on redware,
9 7/8" d. (some wear) 550.00

Plate, 6 1/8" d., coggled edge,
three triple-line yellow slip squiggle bands across redware body
(painted-over rim chips) 220.00

Plate, 9½" d., crimped edge, three
yellow slip wavy lines down center flanked by three yellow slip
straight lines on each side on redware, marked "Odenwalder" on
reverse, Pennsylvania, 19th c. 308.00

Plate, 10" d., crimped edge, alternating wavy bands of yellow &
black slip on redware, Pennsylvania, 19th c. 1,045.00

Platter, 16" l., oval w/slightly sloping
sides & coggled rim, five triple yellow slip wavy lines the length of
the redware body, Pennsylvania,
19th c. (chips & abrasions).......1,760.00

Rare Slipware Tobacco Jar

Tobacco jar, cov., vase-form body
w/flaring scalloped rim & applied
strap handles, flaring foot, decorated w/incised scalloped lines at
the neck above a band of pierced
triangles over a band of five-petal
flowers & leaves, fitted w/conform-
ing knopped cover w/incised five-
petal flowers, the whole covered

in red, cream & green slip glaze
on redware, Pennsylvania, first
half 19th c., missing liner, lip
restored, wear, 6" h. (ILLUS.) 4,950.00

SPATTERWARE

*This ceramic ware takes its name from the
"spattered" decoration, in various colors,
generally used to trim pieces hand-painted
with rustic center designs of flowers, birds,
houses, etc. Popular in the early 19th century, most was imported from England.*

*Related wares, called "stick spatter," had
free-hand designs applied with pieces of cut
sponge attached to sticks, hence the name.
Examples date from the 19th and early 20th
century and were produced in England, Europe and America.*

Cup, miniature, Peafowl patt., free-
hand colored bird on green spatter ground.....................$110.00
Cup & saucer, handleless, Dove
patt., free-hand yellow ochre,
green, blue & black on red spatter
ground (minor stains & wear,
chips on saucer table ring) 750.00
Cup & saucer, handleless, free-hand
cluster of red & green buds on
red & yellow Rainbow spatter
ground (small edge flakes, stain
in saucer) 600.00
Cup plate, free-hand four-part blue
flower on brown spatter ground,
4" d. (glaze flakes, minor
stains) 120.00
Dish, deep round body decorated
w/alternating red & green spatter
stripes around the rim surrounding a similarly decorated roundel,
mid-19th c., 10½" d. 308.00
Plate, 9" d., Peafowl patt., free-
hand colored bird on blue spatter
ground 245.00
Plate, 9 3/8" d., Thistle patt. in red
& green on blue spatter ground
(minor stains & small edge
flakes) 375.00
Plate, 9½" d., free-hand acorns &
leaves in brown, black & two
shades of green on blue spatter
ground (minor stains)........... 400.00
Plate, 9½" d., Peafowl patt., free-
hand colored bird on blue spatter
ground, marked "Adams" 185.00
Plate, 9½" d., Rainbow spatter
bands around surface of plate in
red, blue & green (two rim chips,
minor stains, table ring chip) 300.00

SPONGEWARE

Spongeware's designs were spattered,
*sponged or daubed on in colors, sometimes
with a piece of cloth. Blue on white was the
most common type, but mottled tans, browns
and greens on yellowware were also popular.
Spongeware generally has an overall pattern
with a coarser look than Spatterwares, to
which it is loosely related. These wares were
extensively produced in England and America well into the 20th century.*

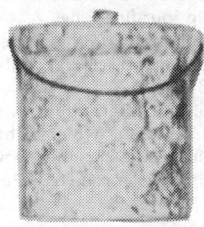

Spongeware Covered Jar

Batter pitcher, black on cream
body $129.00
Bowl, 5" d., blue & rust on cream
body 45.00
Bowl, 8¼" d., 3 5/8" h., embossed
exterior plume-like foliage design, green & brown on
yellowware 55.00
Bowl, 9¼ x 10", slightly scalloped
side & scalloped tab handles at
rim, blue daubing on white 285.00
Bowl, 9¾" d., shallow, molded
swirl-flute edge design, blue on
white 135.00
Bowl, 11" d., blue & rust daubing on
yellowware 85.00
Bowls, nest-type, blue on grey,
plain rim, deep, 5½", 6½" &
10" d., set of 3.................. 225.00
Butter crock, cov., straight-sided,
flat cover w/inset knob, blue on
white, 7½" d., 5" h. (hairline in
lid) 250.00
Chamber pot, cov., blue on white .. 175.00
Cookie jar, cov., lettered "COOKIES"
in black on front, blue, green &
red on cream body, 10" h. 400.00
Creamer, cylindrical, blue & brown
on white ironstone, 3 7/8" h...... 75.00
Cuspidor, blue daubing on white ... 70.00
Custard cup, wide dark blue band at
top, blue & rust on cream body,
4" d., 3½" h. 90.00
Dish, rectangular w/deep sloping
sides, blue daubing on white,
6½ x 8½"...................... 225.00
Feeding bottle, green & rust daubing on cream 350.00
Figural bottle, model of a recumbent pig, brown daubing on yellowware, 8" l. 275.00
Flowerpot w/attached saucer base,

blue on white-glazed yellowware,
8" h. 150.00

Jar, cov., straight sides w/molded
rim, flat inset cover w/knob finial, wire bail handle, blue on
white, 6" h. (ILLUS.) 190.00

Spongeware Mixing Bowl

Mixing bowl, blue daubing on
white, 9" d., 4½" h. (ILLUS.) 260.00

Mixing bowl, brown & green daubing on yellowware, 9½" d.,
5½" h. 35.00

Pitcher, 5¼" h., cylindrical tapering
slightly to short, straight neck,
brown daubing on yellowware
(edge wear, small flakes) 55.00

Pitcher, 6¾" h., bulbous base
w/rounded panels tapering up to
flared spout & scalloped rim,
smeary blue daubing on white . . . 225.00

Pitcher, 8 3/8" h., cylindrical body &
small loop handle, embossed
flower & leaf sprig trimmed in
blue at sides w/blue daubed on
white bands at rim & foot 450.00

Pitcher, 9" h., bulbous waisted
shape w/wide flared spout &
shaped rim, large C-scroll handle,
embossed hunt scene w/hanging
game & "Miss Miria B. Handy,
Marion, Mass.," brown daubing
w/blue, green & ochre highlights
on yellowware, white slip interior
w/frog (hairlines, small rim
chips) 65.00

Pitcher, 9" h., cylindrical w/small
loop handle, embossed flower
sprig w/two blossoms up side
highlighted in cobalt blue, bands
of blue daubing on white at rim &
base 460.00

Plate, 7½" d., scalloped rim, mottled deep blue daubing on white,
Trenton, New Jersey, ca. 1860's . . 65.00

Salt box, hanging-type, embossed
band of peacocks across rounded
front, brown daubing on yellow-
ware, 6" d. (edge chips) 150.00

Sauceboat, rounded oblong bottom
tapering from shoulder to flared
arched spout & high arched handle, blue daubing on white, lion &
unicorn mark, 7¼" l. 300.00

Soap dish, rectangular w/notched
corners, two ribs across the cen-
ter, blue daubing on white, 5" l. . . . 45.00

Syrup jug w/original pewter spring-
lid, tan & white daubing on cobalt
blue, signed on base "Knowles,
Taylor & Knowles," dated in lid
"July 16, 1872" 350.00

Vegetable bowl, open, dark blue
daubing on white, ca. 1820,
6 x 8½" 225.00

Vegetable dish, oval w/slanted
sides, blue on white,
7 3/8 x 9¾" 180.00

Waste jar, cov., blue on white 265.00

STAFFORDSHIRE FIGURES

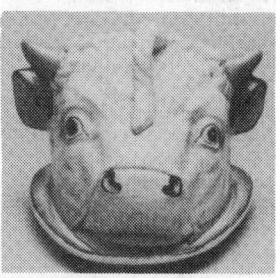

Bull's Head Dish

*Small figures and groups made of pottery
were produced by the majority of the
Staffordshire, England potters in the 19th
century and were used as mantel decorations
or "chimney ornaments," as they were sometimes called. Pairs of dogs were favorites and
were turned out by the carload, and 19th century pieces are still available. Well-painted
reproductions also abound and collectors are
urged to excerise caution before investing.*

Bull's head covered dish, modeled
as a white bull's head w/yellow &
brown highlights, on conforming
dish w/brown border, 19th c.,
9½" l., 7¾" h. (ILLUS.) $385.00

Bust of George Washington, wearing blue coat, on shaped mar-
bleized base, 8" h. 1,100.00

Bust of George Washington, looking
to the left, black coat & polychrome enameling, raised on faux
marble socle, 19th c., 8 3/8" h.
(small flakes) 575.00

Cow, modeled as a standing cow on
a naturalistic base, 25½" h.
(restorations, converted to
lamp) 462.00

Deer, pearlware, Walton-type doe
w/brown topknot & stag w/brown
antlers, white spotted iron-red
coats & brown hooves, each standing before a green & brown mottled tree (branches removed) on a

similarly colored mound base applied w/turquoise moss & molded
at the front w/white & blue scrollwork, ca. 1820, pr. (repairs &
restorations) 1,100.00

Dog, Poodle, white coat, ca. 1840,
2" h. 100.00

Dogs, Poodle, white coat, 5½" h.,
pr............................. 195.00

Dog, miniature, Spaniel in seated
position, red spots & polychrome
features on white, 3½" h. (minor
wear) 85.00

Dog, miniature, Spaniel in seated
position, red spots & polychrome
features on white, 4 3/8" h.
(minor wear) 135.00

Dog, Spaniel in seated position,
white coat w/dark grey ears,
spots & tail, 5¼" h. 165.00

Dogs, Spaniel in seated position,
white coat w/orange ears, spots
& tail, 6¼" h., facing pr. 302.50

Dogs, Spaniel seated on tasseled
pillow, white w/brown spots,
glass eyes, gilt bow at neck, mid-
19th c., 13" h., pr. (minor damage) 412.50

Dogs, Terrier in seated position,
brown w/black markings & curling
tail, 13" h., facing pr. 247.50

Dogs, Whippet in recumbent position, white coat w/dark spots &
trim, on shaped base, 3¼" l.,
pr............................. 247.50

Dogs, Whippet in seated position on
mound base, 4" h., pr. 350.00

Equestrian figures of the Prince &
Princess of Wales, he on horseback w/his arm on his hip & his
cap w/Prince of Wales feathers at
his side, she riding side-saddle &
wearing a feathered hat, both
raised on oval bases w/titles,
13½" h., pr. (cracks & restorations) 550.00

Figure of a farm girl, w/spillholder
vase, standing bodiced figure
holding a dead goose in her left
hand, a dead rabbit in the other,
resting against a green tree-trunk
form vase, 19th c., 11½" h. 165.00

Figures of a Highland lad & lass
w/spaniels, he wearing a feathered cap, striped scarf & plaid
kilt, w/pipe in his right hand,
holding the leash of a large black
& white spaniel behind, she wearing a striped scarf, short-sleeved
blouse & floral printed skirt,
feathered cap in her left hand,
leaning against the large spotted
spaniel behind; each on a
naturalistic grassy mound oval

base, polychrome glaze, 19th c.,
11" l., 9½" h., pr. (glaze
crazed) 825.00

Figure of a man wearing a plumed
hat, cloak, jacket, breeches &
knee boots holding a staff &
standing by a tree trunk w/his
dog by his right foot, 19th c.,
17" h. 385.00

Figure of Saint Paul, bearded figure
seated on a tree stump before
flowering branches, wearing a
yellow shirt & cape, red skirt
trimmed in blue, holding a sword
in one hand & an open book in
the other, on a green oval base
strewn w/floral sprigs & titled in
black, ca. 1800, 9" h. 495.00

Figure of William Shakespeare
standing w/his left arm resting on
a pedestal beside him, a penned
scroll in his left hand, wearing
pink coat over blue vest & yellow
breeches, shaped oval base w/gilt
highlights, mid-19th c., 8¼" h. ... 357.50

Figure group, two figures in a boxing match, entitled "Heenan - Say-
ers," 9¼" h. 357.50

Figure group, woman seated in
high-backed armchair holding a
cat on her lap, 3½" h. 357.50

Figure group, woman wearing a
hooded cloak & holding a basket,
her dog standing beside her on a
mound base, 5½" h. 137.50

Figure group, "The Death of Mon-
row," charcoal-striped grey tiger
w/iron-red-heightened eyes, teeth
& tongue, gnawing the head of the
rigid lieutenant dressed for hunting
in a blue-sashed iron-red jacket
w/yellow epaulets, yellow
breeches & black shoes, brushed
green rectangular base (broken &
riveted) w/grey marbleized apron
molded w/two lozenges inscribed
in black "THE DEATH OF MON-
ROW" above a molded floral garland colored in iron-red, blue &
green & raised on six feet,
Obadiah Sherratt, ca. 1830,
14 1/8" l. (chips & restoration) ...8,800.00

Figure groups of cricket players: the
first group w/two boys, one in a
green coat & holding a bat, the
other in pink pants & holding a
ball, w/a wicket between them;
the second group of two boys
w/one in a blue coat holding a
bat, the other in a yellow coat &
pink pants crouching next to a
wicket, 6½" h., pr.............. 385.00

Hen on nest covered dish, poly-

chromed hen on naturally colored
basketweave base, 12" l. 325.00
Lamb, miniature, recumbent animal
on thick oval base, sanded coat,
black details on white, yellow
stripe around base, 2 5/8" h.
(flake on back edge of base) 75.00

Staffordshire Lion

Lions, standing animal w/one front
paw resting on a ball, glazed in
tones of brown, on shaped rectangular base, cracks & restorations,
19th c., 12" h., facing pr. (ILLUS.
of one) 302.50

STANGL POTTERY BIRDS

Broadbill Hummingbird

*Johann Martin Stangl, who first came to
work for the Fulper Pottery in 1910 as a ceramic chemist and plant superintendent, acquired a financial interest and became
president of the company in 1926. The name
of the firm was changed to Stangl Pottery in
1929 and at that time much of the production
was devoted to a high grade dinnerware to
enable the company to survive the Depression years. Around 1940 a very limited edition of porcelain birds, patterned after the
illustrations in John James Audubon's
"Birds of America," was issued. Stangl subsequently began production of less expensive
ceramic birds and these proved to be popu-*

*lar during the war years, 1940-46. Each bird
was handpainted and each was well marked
with impressed, painted or stamped numerals which indicated the species and the size.
Collectors are now seeking these ceramic
birds which we list below.*

Bird of Paradise, No. 3408,
5½" h. $76.00
Blackpoll Warbler, No. 3810 . . . . 60.00
Blue Bird, No. 3276, 5" h. 65.00
Bluebird, No. 3276-S, 5" h. 60.00
Bluebird (Double), No. 3276-D,
8½" h. . . . . .125.00 to 135.00
Blue-Headed Vireo, No. 3448,
4¼" h. . . . . .35.00 to 45.00
Broadbill Hummingbird, No. 3629,
6½" l., 4½" h. (ILLUS.) 87.50
Broadtail Hummingbird, No. 3626,
6" h. 92.50
Canary facing left - Blue Flower,
No. 3747, 6¼" h. 155.00
Cardinal, No. 3444, 6" h. . . . .60.00 to 80.00
Cerulean Warbler, No. 3456,
4¼" h. 50.00
Chestnut-Backed Chickadee,
No. 3811, 5" h. 70.00
Cockatoo, No. 3405, 6" h. 40.00
Cockatoo, No. 3405-S, 6" h. 40.00
Cockatoo, medium, No. 3580,
8 7/8" h. 85.00
Cockatoo, No. 3584, 15" 190.00
Flying Duck, No. 3443, 9" h. 230.00
Golden Crowned Kinglet, No. 3848,
4" h. 52.00
Grosbeak, No. 3813, 5" h. . . .80.00 to 95.00
Group of Chickadees, No. 3581,
5½ x 8½" 152.00
Group of Goldfinches, No. 3635,
4 x 11½" 165.00
Hen, No. 3446, 7" h. 145.00
Kingfisher, No. 3406, 3½" h. 45.00
Oriole, No. 3402, 3¼" h. 41.00
Oriole, No. 3402-S, 3¼" h. 38.00
Pair of Cockatoos, No. 3405-D,
9½" h. . . . . .70.00 to 80.00
Pair of Lovebirds, No. 3404-D,
4½" h. . . . . .85.00 to 110.00
Pair of Orioles, No. 3402-D,
5½" h. 85.00
Pair of Parakeets, No. 3582, 7" h. . . . 117.00
Pair of Redstarts, No. 3490-D,
9" h. 140.00
Paraquet, No. 3449, 5½" h. 103.00
Rivoli Hummingbird, No. 3627,
6" h. 90.00
Rooster, grey, No. 3445, 9" h. 132.00
Standing Duck, No. 3431,
8" h. . . . . .295.00 to 325.00
Western Blue Bird, No. 3815 . . . . 143.00
White Headed Pigeon (Double),
No. 3518-D, 12½ x
7½" . . . . .450.00 to 525.00
White-Wing Crossbill, No. 3754-D,
8¾" h. 325.00

STONEWARE

Stoneware Batter Jug

Stoneware is essentially a vitreous pottery, impervious to water even in its unglazed state, that has been produced by potteries all over the world for centuries. Utilitarian wares such as crocks, jugs, churns and the like, were the most common productions in the numerous potteries that sprang into existence in the United States during the 19th century. These items were often enhanced by the application of a cobalt blue oxide decoration. In addition to the coarse, primarily salt-glazed stonewares, there are other categories of stoneware known by such special names as basalt, jasper and others.

Batter jug, ovoid w/standing rim fitted w/tin cover, straight spout also w/tin cover, applied handle lugs fitted w/wire handle w/wooden grip, body decorated w/brushed cobalt blue flower sprigs on sides & leaf sprig under spout, impressed mark of Cowen & Wilcox, Harrisburg, Pa. & a "2," 1870-90, 2 gal., 11" h., minor rim chips (ILLUS.) $1,870.00

Bean pot, cov., advertising "Farmer's Grain & Coal," Mitchell, So. Dakota, white bottom, brown top 75.00

Beater jar, grey w/blue stripe, printed advertising, "Montezuma, Iowa" 60.00

Beater jar, w/blue bands, advertising "Ardmore Lumber," Ardmore, So. Dakota 130.00

Butter churn, bail handle, brushed cobalt blue squiggle decoration, blue leaf mark w/size & "Western Stoneware," 2 gal. 135.00

Butter churn, ovoid, molded rim, eared handles, brushed cobalt blue tulip & "4," impressed "I. M. Mead, Magadore, Ohio," 4 gal., 16¾" h. (chips & hairlines) 600.00

Butter churn, slightly ovoid, eared handles, brushed cobalt blue leafy floral sprays sprouting from small double handled container & date "1876," impressed "Whites Utica, N.Y.," 6 gal., 18¼" h. (some damage) 935.00

Butter crock, cov., cylindrical w/eared handles & flat cover w/button finial, brushed cobalt blue band of three-leaf sprigs around center, 12½" d., 7" h. (shallow chip on base, short hairline in lid) 375.00

Cheese crock, straight-sides w/projecting lug handles, banded w/brushed cobalt blue tulip & vine design, possibly New York or Pennsylvania, ca. 1875, 12¼" d., 7" h. (no cover) 687.50

Crock, straight sides w/applied ear handles, cobalt blue slip-quilled bird on branch, impressed label "S.R. Bosworth, Hartford," & "2" highlighted in blue, 2 gal., 9¼" h. (hairline) 175.00

Crock, straight sides, eared handles, two cobalt blue slip-quilled birds w/upturned heads, Samuel Hart & Sons, Fulton, New York, 1832-65, 10¾" d., 10¼" h. (hairline cracks, abraded surface)..... 990.00

Crock, ovoid, cobalt blue slip-quilled bird on branch flanked by stylized florals below blue-washed impressed label "W.H. Farrar & Co., Geddes, N.Y.," mid-19th c., 10½" h. (two cracks through decorated area) 600.00

Crock, ovoid w/straight neck & slightly flaring rim, open loop lug handles, incised bow at shoulder, lug handles & impressed mark highlighted w/cobalt blue brushwork, impressed mark "J. Remmey, Manhattan Wells New York," brown slip interior, John Remmey, New York, New York, 1799-1814, 11¼" h. (chips at base, hairlines).........................1,045.00

Crock, straight sides, eared handles, brushed cobalt blue rose decoration, impressed "Ottman Bros', Fort Edwards, N.Y., 3," 1872-92, 3 gal., 12" h. 352.00

Crock, straight sides, eared handles, brushed cobalt blue stylized flower & leaf spray in criss-cross design basket, impressed "Whites Utica 4," Utica, New York, late 19th c., 4 gal., 11¼" h. (hairline) 485.00

Crock, straight sides, eared handles, slip-quilled cobalt blue floral bou-

quet w/single large blossom &
three large leaves, impressed
"Warren and Wood, Providence,
R.I., 5," 5 gal., 12" h. (chips &
hairlines) 200.00
Crock, straight sides, eared handles,
slip-quilled cobalt blue elaborate
branched flourish across front under impressed label "Kegley
Hyten & Co., Boonsboro, Iowa, 5,"
5 gal., 13" h. (edge chips) 120.00
Crock, straight sides, eared handles,
slip-quilled cobalt blue decoration
of two birds on stylized blossom
bouquet flanking "6" at top center, impressed "W.A. MAC · Pottery Works · N.Y.," Wm. A.
MacQuoid & Co., Manhattan, New
York, 1863-79, 6 gal., 12¾" h.
(hairlines) 450.00
Figural bottle, model of a recumbent pig, crudely molded w/cylin-
drical body, grey salt glaze
w/brushed cobalt blue daubs &
blue trim on face, 6" l. (flakes &
mouth badly chipped)........... 950.00
Flask, ovoid, brushed cobalt blue
three-leaf sprig, 5 7/8" h. (wear,
crazing) 325.00
Flowerpot, cylindrical tapering
slightly toward base, eared handles, cobalt blue slip-quilled flower sprig below impressed label
"A.K. Ballard, Burlington, Vt. 4,"
ca. 1867-72, 4 gal., 11¾" h. 275.00
Harvest jug, miniature, embossed
foliage designs, rich blue sponged
glaze, bottom labeled "Mfg'd by
F. Hawkins, Akron, O.," wire bail
handle w/wooden grip, 5½" h.
(spout chipped) 500.00
Jar, cov., ovoid w/applied ear handles, flaring slightly at top rim,
slightly domed cover w/flat disk
knob, brushed cobalt blue small
bird w/polka dot wings, 8½" d.,
7" h. plus lid (minor edge
flakes) 300.00
Jar, vasiform w/everted rim, slip-
quilled cobalt blue man-in-the-
moon, number "1½" & highlights,
impressed mark of Cowden & Wilcox, Harrisburg, Pennsylvania
(1870-90), 1½ gal., 8¾" h. (two
hairline cracks)................1,540.00
Jar, semi-ovoid w/wide opening
w/molded lip, cobalt blue brushed
& stenciled label "Hamilton &
Jones, Greensboro, Pa. 1½,"
1½ gal., 9" h. 150.00
Jar, cov., slightly ovoid sides, flattened eared handles, slip-quilled
cobalt blue seated, striped dog,
impressed "Edwards & Co., Fort

Stoneware Covered Jar

Edward, New York," 19th c.,
9½" h. (ILLUS.) 2,530.00
Jar, ovoid, eared handles, slip-
quilled cobalt blue "2" flanked by
free-hand laurel wreath, impressed "F. Stetzenmeyer, G.
Goetzman," Rochester, New York,
1857-60, 2 gal., 11¾" h. (minor
flakes) 225.00
Jar, ovoid w/wide mouth & eared
handles, crudely brushed cobalt
blue stylized flower & "3," impressed label "J.F. Brayton & Co.,
Utica," 12½" h. (small chips & minor hairline) 325.00
Jar, baluster form w/everted rim &
two applied handles, impressed
"BOSTON," probably Mas-
sachusetts, 19th c., 13¼" h....... 66.00
Jar, slightly ovoid, eared handles,
cobalt blue brushed roses, stripes,
wavy lines & foliage, cobalt blue
stenciled label "Mallory & Atkinson, Clarington, Ohio, 3," made
for Mallory & Atkinson Hardware
Store, 19th c., 3 gal., 13½" h. 525.00
Jug, ovoid w/strap handle, plain
body, 7½" h. 85.00
Jug, semi-ovoid, slip-quilled cobalt
blue large, bold floral & scrolls
design under impressed label
splashed w/blue "Whites, Utica,"
Utica, New York, 1865-77,
10¾" h. (minor hairlines) 225.00
Jug, semi-ovoid, slip-quilled cobalt
blue bird perched on scrolling
branch, J. & E. Norton, Bennington, Vermont, late 19th c.,
11" h. 330.00
Jug, semi-ovoid, slip-quilled cobalt
blue long-tailed bird on scrolled
branch, impressed label "West
Troy Pottery," West Troy, New
York, ca. 1870-80, 11¼" h. (chip
on lip) 625.00
Jug, ovoid, slip-quilled cobalt blue
large leafy scroll above stenciled
label "Hamilton & Jones, Greensboro," 11½" h. 170.00

Jug, semi-ovoid, slip-quilled cobalt blue long-tailed bird on leafy branch, boldly impressed label "Barnes & Parkman Country Store, 124 Cong St. Troy, N.Y. 2," 2 gal., 13½" h. (handle restored) 300.00

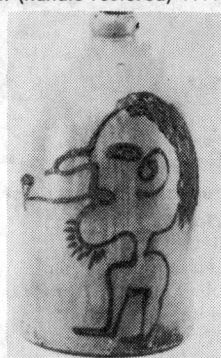

Stoneware Jug with Unique Decoration

Jug, semi-ovoid, applied handle, slip-quilled cobalt blue profile of large man's head w/curly hair, long pointed nose, crude eye & ear, long pipe in mouth & stubble on chin, shortened body, "2" stamped near top, late 19th c., some loss of blue in firing, 2 gal., 14" h. (ILLUS.) 1,650.00

Jug, ovoid, strap handle, brushed cobalt blue stylized flower w/daub of blue on impressed label "H. Purdy, Ohio 2," Henry Purdy, Mogadore, Ohio, 1838 to ca. 1850, 2 gal., 14¼" h. (minor chips & short hairline in base) 500.00

Jug, semi-ovoid, applied loop handles at rim, finely executed slip-quilled cobalt blue script inscription "Viall Ruckel & Co., Middlebury, O.," 19¼" h................2,000.00

Match holder, cone-shaped grey body w/impressed narrow bands around top & base highlighted in cobalt blue wash, serrated striking surface around sides, 2¾" h. 75.00

Meat tenderizer, short cylindrical white stoneware head w/a deep hob overall pattern, simple round wood handle, head marked "Pat'd Dec. 25, 1887," 10" l. 70.00

Milk bowl w/pouring spout, applied handles, brushed cobalt blue "2" w/foliate detail, blue highlights at handles, brown Albany slip interior, impressed label "Lyons," 12¾" d., 6¼" h. (wear, small chips & minor hairline) 475.00

Model of a dog, seated Spaniel-type animal on ovoid base, grey salt glaze w/brown highlights & cobalt

blue detail on paws, collar & eyes, 7½" h. (shallow flake on base) 800.00

Mug, cylindrical tapering slightly toward base, applied strap handle, brushed cobalt blue large leaves at base below incised name "E.E. Hipple" highlighted in cobalt blue, 4" h. (small edge flakes, short hairline in base) 1,100.00

Mug, cylindrical w/applied strap handle, slip-quilled cobalt blue blossoms, attributed to Daniel P. Shenfelder, Marion Township, Berks County, Pennsylvania, 1869-80, 4¾" h................. 440.00

Paperweight, model of an open book incised inscription across center "Holy Bible, Blessed are the Dead which die in the Lord" along w/molded roses, grey salt glaze highlighted in cobalt blue, 4¼ x 5½" (small edge chips) 275.00

Pitcher, beer, cov., 12½" h., baluster form, w/pulled spout & applied handle, incised stylized decoration painted w/cobalt blue slip, flat hinged pewter lid, base incised "W," probably C. Wingender, New Jersey, 19th c. (hairline cracks) 220.00

Pitcher, 7 3/8" h., ovoid body w/tall straight neck w/molded rim & pinched spout, slip-quilled cobalt blue stylized leafy sprig w/blossom across front (hairlines in spout & handle) 275.00

Pitcher, 12½" h., slightly ovoid base below tall slightly waisted neck, brushed cobalt blue lines along spout & on neck, handle & sides above stenciled cobalt blue label "T.F. Reppert, Successor to Jas. Hamilton & Co., Greensboro, Pa. 2," 2 gal. (chips on spout, rim hairline) 1,400.00

Preserving jar, slightly ovoid, stenciled cobalt blue label, blurred but appears to read "J.F. Enrix, New Geneva, Pa.," 6¼" h. (small rim flakes) 65.00

Preserving jar, ovoid, eared handles, flared lip brushed w/cobalt blue, incised initials "S.W.C." on one side brushed w/cobalt blue above brushed cobalt blue squiggle, incised "4" on back side, handles brushed w/cobalt blue, 4 pt., 6½" h. (small edge chips)........ 475.00

Preserving jar, cylindrical w/molded rim, simple brushed cobalt blue three-part leaves at rim, impressed label "S.H. Sonner, Strasburg, Va.," mottled two-tone

greenish-grey & reddish-tan glaze,
9" h. 95.00

Salt box, cov., blue band, relief lettering "Salt" 115.00

Washboard, dark brown Albany slip washboard insert in wooden frame w/scrubbed finish, 13¾ x 24½" (insert chipped) 45.00

Water cooler, keg-shaped, incised lines simulating banding highlighted in cobalt blue, 12" h. 110.00

Water cooler, ovoid w/two strap handles at neck, the front applied w/embossed spread-winged eagle highlighted in cobalt blue, bung hole at base, impressed at top front "Bristols Beer" & on reverse "J. Clark & Co., Troy, New York," ca. 1830, 16" h. 4,400.00

Whimsey, hand-built tree stump w/applied vine & a crude spread-winged bird on top, tan salt glaze, 5¾" h. 275.00

TECO POTTERY

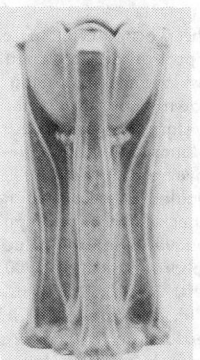

Teco Lotus Flower Vase

Teco Pottery was actually the line of art pottery introduced by the American Terra Cotta and Ceramic Company of Terra Cotta (Crystal Lake), Illinois in 1902. Founded by William D. Gates in 1881, American Terra Cotta originally produced only bricks and drain tile. Because of superior facilities for experimentation, including a chemical laboratory, the company was able to develop an art pottery line, favoring a matte green glaze in the earlier years but eventually achieving a wide range of colors including a metallic lustre glaze and a crystalline glaze. Though some hand-thrown pottery was made, Gates favored a molded ware because it was less expensive to produce. By 1923, Teco Pottery was no longer being made and in 1930 American Terra Cotta and Ceramic Company was sold.

Bowl, 9¾" d., 2" h., low circular form w/an embossed geometric design, green matte glaze, die-stamped "TECO" twice $192.50

Bulb bowl, wide shoulder on round squat body, molded w/stylized leaf decoration, green matte glaze, impressed "TECO," early 20th c., 9" d., 2" h. 220.00

Vase, 5" h., 5½" w., bulbous-bottomed tapering to thin pinched neck & small flared rim, green matte glaze, die-stamped "TECO" four times on base 357.50

Vase, 6½" h., melon-shaped w/open-work & pierced decoration around the rim, designed by Fritz Albert, ca. 1901, impressed "TECO" 2,200.00

Vase, 7¼" h., 4¼" d., double gourd shaped, glazed overall in green & gun metal matte, die-stamped "TECO" twice 121.00

Vase, 8" h., waisted body w/three lug handles running from top to base rims, designed by William D. Gates, impressed "TECO," ca. 1908 . . . . 1,760.00

Vase, 11½" h., organic bulbous lotus flower form w/scalloped edge & elongated stem centered by four vertical serpentine handles, charcoal detail on green matte glaze ground, designed by Ferdinand Moreau, impressed "TECO" twice on base, ca. 1905 (ILLUS.) 3,300.00

Vase, 12" h., oviform body w/fluted vertical bands & concentric rings at the top, green matte glaze, designed by Hugh M.G. Garden, impressed "TECO," ca. 1903 . . . . 11,000.00

Teco Ovoid Vase

Vase, 12¼" h., ovoid body molded w/concentric rings below the lip continuing to outline four panels in the body, green matte glaze, designed by M.G. Garden, stamped "TECO" twice on base, ca. 1903 (ILLUS.) 9,900.00

Wall pocket, circular bottom & rectangular top, embossed w/pinwheel motif, green matte glaze, stamped "TECO" twice on back, 5¼" w., 7" h. 132.00

Wall pocket, shaped like two-handled urn w/tooled leaves decorating its surface & a finial at bottom, overall organic green matte glaze, 9" w., 16" h. 550.00

TEPLITZ

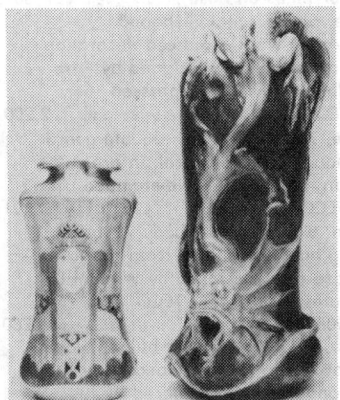

Teplitz - Amphora Vases

These wares were produced in numerous potteries in the vicinity of Teplitz in the Bohemian area of what is now Czechoslovakia during the late 19th and into the 20th century. Vases and figures, of varying quality, were the primary products of such firms as Riessner & Kessel (Amphora), Ernst Wahliss and Alfred Stellmacher. Although originally rather low-priced items, today collectors are searching out the best marked examples and prices are soaring.

Basket, enameled flowers on cobalt blue ground, Amphora, Czechoslovakia mark, 3¾ x 4½" $50.00

Basket, h.p. overall Art Deco style heavy colored roses & green leaves on exterior on mottled beige satin ground, oval Amphora, Czechoslovakia mark, 5 x 9¼", 5¼" h. 151.00

Bowl, 5½" d., decorated w/girl pulling rooster's tail, Stellmacher, Teplitz mark 55.00

Bust of a girl in a bonnet, 9½" h. 125.00

Candlesticks, sinuous form w/yellow decoration, Riessner & Kessel, Amphora mark, 12" h., pr. 100.00

Ewer, model of a frog w/lily pad

decoration, Art Nouveau style, Amphora mark, 7 x 7" 700.00

Ewer, flower-form opening, body w/beige ground decorated w/florals outlined in beading, "RS & K" (Riessner & Kessel), Amphora mark, 9" h. 235.00

Figure of a Greek youth w/mandolin, crown Amphora mark, 15" h. 164.00

Figure of Art Nouveau style seated maiden w/basket, Amphora mark, 16" h. 215.00

Humidor, cov., h.p. boxer dog on front, 4 x 8" 395.00

Vase, 6" h., handled, decorated w/scene of children playing grown-up, Stellmacher, Teplitz mark 95.00

Vase, 7" h., front w/Art Nouveau style head of woman on beige ground w/gold trim, forest scene on back, "RS & K," Amphora mark 550.00

Vase, 8" h., 5½" w., squirrel in bushes decoration in lustrous red, greens & golds, crown Amphora mark 375.00

Vase, 12" h., waisted cylinder, obverse w/portrait of a crowned woman w/long tresses falling over a gown elaborately embroidered w/stars & hearts, in a wooded landscape that continues to the reverse, between gilt thumb-molded sides continuing into the neck & base, blue, pale violet, mauve, rose, navy blue & gilt, Amphora marks, ca. 1900 (ILLUS. left) 1,650.00

Vase, 19½" h., baluster form, dragon w/long neck & tail wrapped around, dragon's eyes bulging from a head surrounded by a webbed mane, shaded gold on mottled blue & green ground w/violet highlights, "RS & K," Amphora mark, ca. 1900 (ILLUS. right) 2,750.00

Vide poche, irregular ovoid form, attenuated female figure w/long flowing hair flanked by flowers & leaves mounted on one side, brown, green, blue & red glaze, Amphora marks, ca. 1900, 16¼" h. 880.00

TIFFANY POTTERY

In 1902 Louis C. Tiffany expanded Tiffany Studios to include ceramics, enamels, gold, silver and gemstones. Tiffany pottery was usually molded rather than wheel-thrown, but it was carefully finished by hand. A limited amount was produced until about 1914. It is scarce.

Tiffany Pottery Vase

Jar, cov., domed circular cover molded w/ivy leaves & openwork branches, straight-sided cylindrical jar w/depressed shoulder molded in medium-relief w/ivy vines supporting small clusters of berries & leafage, the white body w/a light matte celadon glaze, the interior glazed in speckled light & dark blue, base inscribed "LCT," ca. 1914, 6" h. $1,430.00
Vase, 8¼" h., ovoid body w/overall molded bouquet of Queen Anne's lace, the exterior unglazed white, the interior w/a green drip glaze, inscribed w/the monogram "LCT," early 20th c. 1,760.00
Vase, 8¼" h., ovoid body w/overall molded bouquet of Queen Anne's lace, the exterior & interior w/matte green glaze, inscribed w/the monogram "LCT" & "P807," early 20th c. (ILLUS.) 11,000.00
Vase, 12¼" h., cylindrical body molded w/repeating lady-slippers on stems, mottled green glaze, incised "LCT," signed "L.C. Tiffany - Favrile Pottery, Salon 1906" 4,125.00
Vase, 16¾" h., cylindrical body w/flaring squatty base, overall relief-molded hollyhocks in blue, bronze-covered, inscribed "L.C. Tiffany - Favrile Bronze Pottery," & "B. P280," early 20th c. 3,080.00

TILES

Tiles have been made by potteries in the United States and abroad for many years. Apart from small tea tiles used on tables, there are also decorative tiles for fireplaces, floors and walls and this is where present collector interest lies, especially in the late 19th century American-made art pottery tiles.

Grueby Decorated Tile

American Encaustic Tiling Co., Zanesville, Ohio, printed "Rub-A-Dub" nursery rhyme scene, 6 x 6" $70.00
Batchelder Tile Co., California, border type w/grape design, 7 x 12" 95.00
California Faience Company, Berkeley, California, sailing ship decoration, six colors 285.00
California Faience Company, Berkeley, California, viking ship decoration, five colors 450.00
Copeland, Stoke, England, large central square flanked by four smaller squares, each depicting various Shakespearean works, enclosed within light blue glass borders, overall 37½" l. 467.50
Delft faience, sailboat scene, 4½ x 4½" 55.00
Fenton (Lyman) & Company, Bennington, Vermont, patterned w/raised latticework enclosed by molded rim, mottled brown Rockingham glaze, impressed circular mark on base "Lyman Fenton & Co. - Fenton's - ENAMEL - PATENTED - 1849 - BENNINGTON - Vt.," 7" sq. (imperfections) 467.50
Grueby Faience & Tile Company, Boston, Massachusetts, two geese intertwined underneath trees, five colors, decorated by Kiichi Yameda, 4" sq., 5/8" thick 365.00
Grueby Faience & Tile Company, Boston, Massachusetts, color decorated scene of a galleon under full sail on the high seas, w/partial paper label, 9 x 9" (ILLUS.) 2,200.00
Grueby Faience & Tile Company, Boston, Massachusetts, scenic set of six forming a horizontal picture of two groups of pine trees, two small lakes & mountains in the distance in blues & greens, titled "The Pines," each tile 6 x 6", the set . . 4,180.00
Low (J. & G.) Art Tile Works, Chelsea, Massachusetts, female por-

traits, one marked "Industria" & the other "Religieuse," glossy green & amber glazes, original frames, 9" w., 2 pcs. 192.50

Low Art Scenic Tile

Low (J. & G.) Art Tile Works, Chelsea, Massachusetts, village scene in relief w/sheepherder moving his flock down a cobblestone street, glossy brown glaze, signed "A.O." for Arthur Osborne, impressed company mark, framed, late 19th c., 9½" w., 17½" h. (ILLUS.) 1,100.00

Mintons China Works, Stoke-on-Trent, Staffordshire, England, "King Henry," 6 x 6" 65.00

Mintons China Works, Stoke-on-Trent, Staffordshire, England, knight & lady, signed "J. Smith," 6 x 6" 48.00

Mosaic Tile Co., Zanesville, Ohio, General Pershing portrait w/original box 35.00

Owens Pottery, Zanesville, Ohio, stylized floral medallion w/leaves on pale green ground, impressed "Owens" on reverse, early 20th c., 9 x 9" (some chips) 220.00

Pilkington's Tile & Pottery Company, Lancashire, England, modified circus horses & lady trainer, from a painting by Adolph Dehm, "Crack the Whip," ca. 1940, signed 65.00

Rookwood Pottery, Cincinnati, Ohio, two galleons in high-relief, four colors, 8 x 8" 395.00

Rozenberg den Haag, Holland, scene of windmills overlooking sea, artist-signed 250.00

Teco Ware, Terra Cotta, Illinois, full relief crouching gnome that extends 3" from tile face, 9 x 9", 1½" thick 1,850.00

Torquay Terra-Cotta Co., Ltd., Devon, England, motto-type, "O list to me ye ladies fair, And

when ye wish to curl your hair, For the safety of this domicile, Pray place your lamp upon this tile," 5 x 7½" 100.00

TOBY MUGS & JUGS

Bennington Toby Jug

The Toby is a figural jug or mug usually delineating a robust, genial drinking man. The name has been used in England since the mid-18th century. Copies of the English mugs and jugs were made in America.

For listings of related Character Jugs see DOULTON & ROYAL DOULTON.

Bennington Toby, seated gentleman w/tricorn hat, left hand clenched above the right, grapevine handle, mottled brown Rockingham glaze, illegible mark on base, Bennington, Vermont, ca. 1849, 10¾" h. (ILLUS.) $330.00

Evans (Alfred) "Napoleon" Toby, standing figure, pink suit w/polychrome features & gilt trim, marked "Napoleon jug Pat. apl. for, Alfred Evans, Phila., Pa.," 10½" h. (stained) 350.00

Lancaster "Neville Chamberlain" Toby, England, ca. 1950, 3" h. 20.00

Lancaster "Winston Churchill" Toby, England, ca. 1950, 3" h. 20.00

Lenox "William Penn Treaty" Toby, w/Indian head handle, white 120.00

Royal Doulton "Old Charley" Toby, large, 1939-60 . . . . 200.00

Staffordshire Toby, King Charles spaniel seated on his hind legs, wearing an open pink & green glazed tricorn hat, a loop handle attached to his back, copper lustre ears, collar, tail & spots, 19th c., 10" h. 412.50

Staffordshire Toby, pearlware, seated man holding a jug of frothing ale in his right hand, wearing a brown-glazed tricorn hat & shoes & randomly sponged overall, ca. 1780, missing pipe, jug handle broken, drilled & mounted as lamp, 11½" h. 440.00

Staffordshire Toby, standing figure of Admiral Nelson, the English naval hero wearing Admiral's dress, resting on a cannon, base inscribed "Nelson," polychrome glaze, second half 19th c., 12¼" h. 550.00

VAN BRIGGLE

Van Briggle Indian Maiden Ashtray

The Van Briggle Pottery was established by Artus Van Briggle, who formerly worked for Rookwood Pottery, in Colorado Springs, Colorado, at the turn of the century. He died in 1904 but the pottery was carried on by his widow and others. From 1900 until 1920, the pieces were dated. It remains in production today, specializing in Art Pottery.

Ashtray, figure of Hopi Indian maiden kneeling & grinding corn, Turquoise Ming glaze, 8" l., 6" h. (ILLUS.). $85.00

Book ends, model of a bear on tree stump, Turquoise Ming glaze, pr. 225.00

Book ends, model of owls w/spread wings, green matte glaze, pr. 68.00

Book ends, model of a peacock, Persian Rose glaze, pr. 55.00

Book ends, model of a ship, Persian Rose glaze, pr. 55.00

Bowl, 5" d., acorns & leaves patt., Shape No. 670, designed by Emma Kinkead, Persian Rose glaze, pattern introduced in 1907 . . . . 55.00

Bowl, 5½" d., mottled light green w/some maroon glaze, Shape No. 330, ca. 1905 . . . . 450.00

Bowl, 10" d., 5½" h., pine cone patt., Shape No. 762, designed by

Emma Kinkead, medium green to blue matte glaze, ca. 1908-11 . . . . 895.00

Candleholders, double, embossed tulip design, Persian Rose glaze, pr. 68.00

Flower frog, model of a duck, green glaze 38.50

Lamp w/original shade, "Damsel of Damascus," kneeling girl holding urn on shoulder, Persian Rose glaze 205.00

Model of a conch shell, Persian Rose glaze, 17" 90.00

Model of a donkey, black glaze, 3¾" 20.00

Model of a snail, mottled green glaze, signed "Anna Van Briggle, Colo. Spgs.," 4½" l., 2½" w., 4½" h. 40.00

Planter, cylindrical sides embossed w/tulips & stems encircling the body, thin powder blue matte glaze over red-brown clay, incised "Van Briggle - Colorado - 342 - 6 - 7" & "1907," original price tag, 4¼ x 4¼" 302.50

Rose bowl, spade-shaped leaves around top, Turquoise Ming glaze, 5" w., 4" h. 58.00

Teapot, cov., bamboo reeded handle, Turquoise Ming glaze 225.00

Vase, 2¼" h., 4¾" widest d., squat bulbous form, embossed heart-shaped leaves, blue-green matte glaze, ca. 1903 . . . . 660.00

Vase, 3" h., 3¾" d., squat bulbous form tapering to foot & sharply tapering to narrow neck, cocoa brown matte glaze, incised "Van Briggle - III - 107 - OD" & "1902" . . 302.50

Vase, 4" h., 4" d., flaring cylinder w/bulbous rim, embossed stylized poppy buds & stems, blue-green matte glaze, ca. 1902 . . . . 550.00

Vase, 4½" h., large embossed leaves around base & violet blossoms around lip, Shape No. 645, designed by Emma Kinkead, maroon & blue glaze, pattern introduced in 1907 . . . . 65.00

Vase, 4½ x 5", squat bulbous shape, embossed leaves in red clay, flowing spinach green matte glaze, ca. 1907 . . . . 302.50

Vase, 5" h., copper-clad, stylized flowers at rim, Shape No. 696, designed by Martha Patton, ca. 1907-12 . . . . .1,050.00

Vase, 5½" h., flared base tapering to narrow top, sides molded w/spade-shaped leaves, Persian Rose glaze, No. 793, signed by Ned Curtis, dated 1914 . . . . 215.00

Vase, 6¼" h., 3½" d., cylindrical

w/stepped-in rim, embossed bellflowers, lime green matte glaze
blushed w/maroon, ca. 1903 .... 1,100.00
Vase, 9" h., 7¼" d., two swirled
handles at rim & swirling embossed leaf & floral design around
the lower bulbous section of the
body, light green matte glaze, incised "Van Briggle - III - 1903,"
stamped, "10" (two small cracks
at rim) 440.00

VERNON KILNS

*The story of Vernon Kilns Pottery begins
with the purchase by Mr. Faye Bennison of
the Poxon China Company (Vernon Potteries) in July 1931. The Poxon family had run
the pottery for a number of years in Vernon,
California, but with the founding of Vernon
Kilns the product lines were greatly expanded.*

*Many innovative dinnerware lines and pat-
terns were introduced during the 1930's, including designs by such noted American
artists as Rockwell Kent and Don Blanding.
In the early 1940's items were designed to tie
in with Walt Disney's animated features
"Fantasia" and "Dumbo." Various commemorative plates, including the popular
"Bits" series, were also produced over a long
period of time. Vernon Kilns was taken over
by Metlox Potteries in 1958 and completely
ceased production in 1960.*

DINNERWARES

Casserole, cov., Homespun patt.,
green, yellow & rust $20.00
Chowder bowl, Brown Eyed Susan
patt. 7.00
Coffee cup, jumbo, Organdie patt. ... 50.00
Creamer, Gingham patt., yellow &
green 4.00
Creamer & sugar bowl, demitasse
size, Early California line, pr. 12.00
Cup & saucer, Brown Eyed Susan
patt. 8.00
Cup & saucer, Homespun patt.,
green, yellow & rust 8.00
Demitasse set: cov. coffeepot & four
cups & saucers; Ultra California
line, 9 pcs. 110.00
Mug, Gingham patt., yellow &
green 10.00
Plate, bread & butter, 6½" d., Early
California line 2.00
Plate, bread & butter, 6½" d., Or-
gandie patt. 2.00
Plate, bread & butter, 6½" d., Tam
O'Shanter patt. 2.00
Plate, salad, 7½" d., Organdie
patt. 3.00

Plate, dinner, 10¼" d., Brown Eyed
Susan patt. 8.00
Plate, dinner, 10½" d., Early
California line 3.00
Plate, dinner, 10½" d., Native
California line 3.00
Plate, dinner, 10½" d., Tam
O'Shanter patt. 4.00
Plate, chop, 12" d., Brown Eyed Su-
san patt. 10.00
Plate, chop, 12" d., Casa California
line 25.00
Plate, chop, 12" d., May Flower
patt. 15.00
Salt & pepper shakers, Gingham
patt., yellow & green, pr. 7.00
Salt & pepper shakers, Homespun
patt., brown & green, pr. 7.00
Salt & pepper shakers, Organdie
patt., pr. 8.00
Teapot, cov., Homespun patt.,
green, yellow & rust 20.00
Tumbler, tall, Organdie patt. 12.00
Vegetable bowl, round, Tam
O'Shanter patt. 15.00

"BITS" SERIES

Plate, 8½" d., Bits of the Middle
West, "End of the Drought" 35.00
Plate, 8½" d., Bits of the Middle
West, "The Mail Train" 35.00
Plate, 8½" d., Bits of Old New
England, "Tapping for Sugar" 40.00
Plate, 8½" d., Bits of the Old South,
"Tobacco Field" 25.00
Plate, 8½" d., Bits of the Old West,
"The Fleecing" 25.00
Plate, 8½" d., Bits of the Old West,
"The Stage Arrival" 22.00

CITIES SERIES - 10½" d.

Plate, "Atlanta" 10.00
Plate, "Charleston, S.C.," made for
Kerrisons 10.00
Plate, "Denver" 10.00
Plate, "Ft. Worth, Texas" 10.00
Plate, "St. Augustine" 10.00
Plate, "San Francisco" 10.00
Plate, "Yakima, Fruit Bowl of the
Nation" 10.00

DISNEY "FANTASIA" ITEMS

Bowl, 12" d., 2½" h., Fantasia patt.,
pink, relief-molded winged
nymph, No. 122 .... 140.00
Figure of "Satyr," from Disney's
"Fantasia" 250.00
Plate, 9½" d., Flower Ballet patt.... 30.00
Salt & pepper shakers, Fantasia
patt., mushroom-shaped, pr. 125.00
Vase, 10" h., 6½" w., Fantasia
"Goddess" patt., light green
w/white goddess, white interior,
No. 126 .... 225.00

FAMOUS MEN SERIES - 10½" d.
Plate, "Jefferson Davis" 15.00
Plate, "General Douglas
   MacArthur" 15.00
Plate, "Presidential Gallery" 15.00
Plate, "Will Rogers" 20.00
Plate, "Franklin Roosevelt" 20.00

MUSIC MASTERS SERIES - 8½" d.
Plate, portrait of Franz Liszt 15.00
Plate, portrait of Tchaikovsky 18.00

NATIONAL PARKS SERIES
Plate, "Carlsbad Caverns" 10.00
Plate, "Yellowstone" 10.00
Plate, "Yosemite" 12.00

ROCKWELL KENT DESIGNS
Plate, 9½" d., Moby Dick patt., blue
   glaze 30.00
Plate, 10" d., Salamina
   patt. 55.00
Salt & pepper shakers, Salamina
   patt., pr. 65.00

STATES SERIES - 10½" d.
Plate, "Alabama" 10.00
Plate, "Arkansas," 1943 . . . . 20.00
Plate, "Colorado" 10.00
Plate, "Georgia," blue & white 20.00
Plate, "Kansas" 10.00
Plate, "Illinois" 10.00
Plate, "Maine" 10.00
Plate, "Montana" 10.00
Plate, "North Carolina" 10.00
Plate, "Texas" 10.00
Plate, "Utah," 1943 . . . . 20.00
Plate, "Wyoming" 10.00
Plate, "Wyoming," full color 18.00

MISCELLANEOUS COMMEMORATIVES
Plate, "Black Hills Passion Play" 25.00
Plate, "Daughters of the Confedera-
   cy, Texas Division, 1896-1946,"
   blue glaze 20.00
Plate, "Mississippi River Bridge
   Centennial" 65.00
Plate, "U.S. Naval Air Gunners
   School, Purcell, Oklahoma" 13.50
Plate, "Walter Baker & Co., 51st edi-
   tion, 1940" 18.00

WATT POTTERY

Founded in 1922, in Crooksville, Ohio, this pottery continued in operation until the factory was destroyed by fire in 1965. Although stoneware crocks and jugs were the first wares produced, by 1935 sturdy kitchen items in yellowware were the mainstay of production. Attractive lines like Kitch-N-Queen (banded) wares and the hand-painted Red Apple, Cherries and Pennsylvania Dutch (tulip)

patterns were popular throughout the country. Today these hand-painted utilitarian wares are "hot" with collectors.

Watt Star Flower No. 15 Pitcher

Bowl, 4" d., Red Apple patt. $12.00
Bowl, 5" d., Red Apple patt.
   w/advertising 24.00
Bowl, 5¼" d., Red Apple patt.,
   No. 5 . . . . 24.00
Bowl, 6" d., Red Apple patt., adver-
   tising from Pierz, Minnesota 26.00
Bowl, 6" d., Red Apple patt.,
   ribbed 24.00
Bowl, 6¼" d., Red Apple patt.,
   No. 6 . . . . 28.00
Bowl, 7¼" d., Red Apple patt.,
   No. 7 . . . . 35.00
Bowl, cov., 7½" d., 6" h., Autumn
   Foliage patt. 105.00
Bowl, 8" d., Quilted Morning Glory
   patt. 45.00
Bowl, cov., 8" d., 7½" h., Red
   Apple patt. 58.00
Bowl, 8" d., Red Apple patt.,
   w/advertising 26.00
Bowl, 8" d., 5" h., Red Apple
   patt. 42.00
Bowl, 9" d., Red Apple patt.,
   No. 9 . . . . 32.00
Bowl, 9½" d., Red Apple patt.,
   No. 73 . . . . 50.00
Bowl, 12" d., wine w/turquoise
   stripe 22.50
Bowl, Autumn Foliage patt., No. 5 . . 18.00
Bowl, Autumn Foliage patt.,
   No. 65 . . . . 45.00
Bowl, Red Apple patt., ribbed,
   No. 4 . . . . 18.00
Bowl, Red Apple patt., ribbed,
   No. 7 . . . . 34.00
Bowl, cov., Red Apple patt.,
   No. 19 . . . . 36.00
Bowl, Red Apple patt., ribbed,
   No. 601 . . . . 29.00
Bowl, Rooster patt., No. 65 . . . . 50.00
Bowl, cov., Rooster patt., No. 69 . . . 45.00
Bowl, Star Flower patt., No. 7 . . . . . . 28.00

Bowl, Star Flower patt., w/tab handles, No. 18 .... 15.00
Bowl, Tulip patt., No. 65 .... 40.00
Bowl, yellowware, Pink Band patt., No. 6 .... 10.00
Bowls, nest-type, Red Apple patt., No. 4, 5, 6 & 7, set of 4 .... 87.00
Bowls, nest-type, 6¼", 7½" & 9" d., Tulip patt., set of 3 .... 120.00
Canister, cov., Pennsylvania Dutch patt., No. 80 .... 125.00
Casserole, cov., French-type w/stick handle, relief-molded flower design 85.00
Casserole, cov., Red Apple patt., No. 73 .... 80.00
Casserole, cov., Red Apple patt., No. 600 .... 57.00
Casserole, cov., Tulip patt. 95.00
Casserole w/wire stand, Autumn Foliage patt. 50.00
Cookie jar, cov., Red Apple patt. ... 95.00
Creamer & open sugar bowl, Autumn Foliage patt., pr. 95.00
Cup & saucer, Posey patt. 80.00
Pepper shaker, Star Flower patt. ... 68.00
Pie plate, Red Apple patt., 9" d..... 50.00
Pitcher, Cherries patt., No. 15 ...... 26.00
Pitcher, Rooster patt., w/advertising, No. 15 .... 60.00
Pitcher, Star Flower patt., No. 15 (ILLUS.) 32.00
Pitcher, Red Apple patt., No. 16 .... 40.00
Pitcher, Rooster patt., No. 16....... 52.00
Pitcher, Star Flower patt., No. 16 ... 52.00
Pitcher, Red Apple patt., No. 62 .... 30.00
Pitcher, Rooster patt., No. 62....... 30.00
Pitcher, Tulip patt., No. 62 .... 30.00
Plate, salad, 7½" d., Star Flower patt. 45.00
Platter, 12", Cherries patt. 50.00
Platter, 15", Star Flower patt. 75.00
Platter, 15¼" d., Posey patt. 85.00
Salad set: master bowl & eight individual bowls; Red Apple patt., 9 pcs. 150.00
Salad set: master bowl & eight individual bowls; Posey patt., 9 pcs. 140.00
Salt shaker, Cherries patt. 35.00
Spaghetti bowl, Posey patt. 36.00
Spooner, Red Apple patt., No. 98 ... 38.00
Spooner, two-handled, Rooster patt. 35.00
Sugar bowl, cov., Red Apple patt. 125.00

WEDGWOOD

Reference here is to the famous pottery established by Josiah Wedgwood in 1759 in England. Numerous types of wares have been produced through the years to the present.

BASALT

Basalt Plaque

Bust of Aristophanes, marked "Wedgwood" only, 2 1/8" d., 4 3/8" h. $384.00
Bust of Robert Burns, ca. 1860, 8¾" h. 725.00
Bust of Abraham Lincoln, modern limited edition, 8½" h. 95.00
Bust of Sir Walter Scott, ca. 1860, 9¼" h. 690.00
Bust of a vestal virgin, scantily draped w/her hair tied back, on a gilt-metal & marble pedestal, ca. 1880, overall 3½" h. 176.00
Candlesticks, model of dolphin, marked "Wedgwood" only, 3¼ x 5 7/8" base, 8 5/8" h., pr. 705.00
Creamer, jug-type, bulbous body w/straight neck band, strap handle, embossed band of classical figures, marked "Wedgwood" only, 2½" h. 110.00
Figure of Cleopatra, nude figure sitting on rock w/asp curled around her wrist, marked "Wedgwood" only, 5¾" d., 9¼" h. 587.00
Figure of Venus, standing nude beside a tree stump, her head slightly turned to the left, on circular base, ca. 1850, 9½" h. 330.00
Model of a blackbird, glass eyes, 2¼ x 5¼", 4½" h. 395.00
Plaque, scantily draped classical dancer w/trowel & torch in high relief, ca. 1880, in gadrooned wood frame, 11" d. (ILLUS.) 880.00
Portland Vase, of conventional type, the base w/Paris wearing the Phrygian cap, impressed, ca. 1830, 10" h. 1,540.00
Vase, cov., 8 7/8" h., body patterned w/gilt florettes, enriched w/classical borders & decorated in relief w/two bronze & gilt classical medallions flanked by gilt drapery swags suspended from rings, bronze shoulder applied w/two

foliate loop handles, cover w/alternating oak leaves & acorn sprigs surrounding an acorn knop, impressed "WEDGWOOD," pattern No. Z3870, late 19th c. 1,320.00

Vestal oil lamp w/cover, gilt-decorated black, boat-shaped, molded w/acanthus leaves, the rim w/a band of acorns & oak leaves, the top molded w/shallow grooves surmounted by a maiden holding a jug, the cover w/knob finial, on flaring foot & square base w/canted corners, impressed, 8¼" h. (gilt decoration later) 880.00

CALENDAR TILES
1911, U.S. Battleship "Florida" 38.00
1911, U.S. Frigate "Constitution" 30.00
1929, Fairbanks House 1636 . . . . 48.00

CANEWARE

Caneware Tea Set

Game pie dish, cover & liner, oval dish w/exterior molded in relief w/dead game birds suspended from a fruiting grapevine, the glazed interior inset w/a plain glazed liner, the slightly domed cover molded w/groups of rabbits & game birds surrounding a rabbit knop, dish impressed "WEDGWOOD," "S-8" & "AOW" for April, 1868, overall 9 1/8" l. (rim chip on dish, ends chipped on liner, some discoloration) 220.00

Game pie dish w/cov., oval dish w/glazed interior, the exterior decorated in relief w/six groups of pendant game birds & grapevine festoons, the cover w/four groups of various game centering an applied rabbit-form knop, last quarter 19th c., 9¾" l. (crack & interior chip) 220.00

Pastry dish, cov., w/undertray, piecrust rim, relief-molded w/lattice & acanthus leaf decoration, ca. 1800, 9 x 12" 650.00

Teapot, cov., pentagonal body molded as a cluster of bamboo stalks, inset cover w/coiled bamboo sprig knop, impressed "Wedgwood & Bentley," ca. 1779, 3¾" h. 3,080.00

Tea set: cov. teapot, cov. sugar bowl, milk jug (cracked), waste bowl & two cups & saucers; each decorated in relief w/drab-green ferns, daisies & foliate borders, the jug & teapot interiors glazed, each impressed "WEDGWOOD," ca. 1810, tip of teapot repaired w/silver, the set (ILLUS. of part) 1,210.00

CREAMWARE

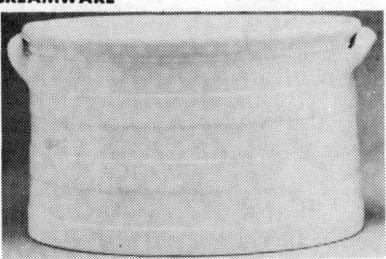

Creamware Footbath

Dish w/drainer & underplate, strawberry-shaped, diamond-shaped foot, ca. 1790, 9 x 12" 650.00

Footbath, deep oval 'leg pan' w/three raised bands & applied w/two loop handles, impressed "WEDGWOOD" & letter "W," ca. 1840, 16" l. (ILLUS.) 990.00

Jelly mold, conical, painted in shades of rose, purple, green, yellow, blue & iron-red w/floral sprays & swags hung from bowknotted ribbons, edges w/brown line borders, base w/four apertures & cone w/two, impressed "Wedgwood" & "D," ca. 1800, 9" h. (tip chipped) 2,750.00

Pitcher, jug-type, 8½" h., transfer-printed in black & enameled in yellow & green one side w/a hunting scene inscribed "STAG CHASE through the THAMES," reverse w/a drinking scene beneath a banner inscribed "SPORTSMANS FESTIVAL" w/a hunting verse below, stag & doe beneath spout & handle, impressed "Wedgwood" & two potter's marks, late 18th c. 1,540.00

Sauce tureen, cover & stand & oval dish, each piece decorated w/an iron-red trimmed silver lustre berried foliage band at the border, the circular tureen w/two bail handles on a spreading circular foot, the cover w/toupie finial,

impressed "Wedgwood," ca. 1800,
tureen 9" d., stand 8" d., dish
12" l., the group 495.00
Soup plate, center colorfully painted
w/the Royal Arms of the Duke of
Clarence above the motto "NEC
TEMERE NEC TIMIDE," rim
transfer-printed in underglaze-
blue w/a border of scallops edged
w/gilded darts, impressed
"WEDGWOOD" & "8" twice, ca.
1821, 9¾" d. 715.00

JASPER WARE

Three-Color Jasper Ware Urns

Bowl, 4½" d., white relief classical
dancing figures & grape leaf swag
& lion's heads at border on blue .. 65.00
Bowl, 9" d., white relief dancing ladies on yellow, marked "Wedgwood" only 320.00
Box, cov., heart-shaped, cover
w/white relief cameo celebrating
"The Anglo-French Treaty of 1786"
on cobalt blue, marked "Wedgwood" only, 4½" across,
1½" h. 155.00
Butter tub, cov., white relief classical ladies on cobalt blue, 5" d. 110.00
Cracker jar, cov., footed ovoid body
w/white relief classical ladies &
cupids on cobalt blue, silver plate
lid, rim & handle, marked "Wedgwood" only, 5" d., 6½" h. 151.00
Cracker jar, cov., tri-color, lavender
bands at top & bottom, green in
center w/white relief classical
figures, silver plate lid, rim &
handle, 9" to top of handle 1,000.00
Custard cup, comma-shaped, serrated rim, white relief trelliswork on
yellow-beige, impressed "WEDG-
WOOD," late 18th c., 2¼" l.
(small repaired chip) 990.00
Jar, cov., cylindrical, tapering slightly toward top, domed cover
w/knob finial, white relief classical figures in panels divided by

white relief columns on cobalt
blue, similar decoration on cover,
marked "Wedgwood, England,"
2" d., 3" h. 99.00
Jardiniere, urn-form w/straight
sides decorated w/white relief
classical maidens between swags
pendent from lions' heads on
blue, impressed "Wedgwood"
only, ca. 1860-91, 9" h. 467.50
Knife handles, white relief designs
on blue, ca. 1800, set of 4 ...... 110.00
Marmalade jar w/silver plate lid,
cylindrical body, white relief classical figures & leaf-sprig rim band
on cobalt blue, marked "Wedgwood" only, 3¼" d., 5¼" h. 124.00
Medallion, oval, modeled in high
relief w/a bust portrait of the
playwright above impressed name
"SHAKESPEARE," yellow-stained,
impressed "Wedgwood & Bentley,"
1776-80, in giltwood frame,
3 3/8" l. 1,430.00
Pitcher, 5½" h., 4" d., bulbous
w/three-petal top, white relief
classical ladies & cherubs on cobalt blue 155.00
Pitcher, 7½" h., 4¼" d., white relief
cameo medallions of Franklin &
Hamilton on olive green, marked
"Wedgwood, England" 350.00
Plaque, pierced to hang, 'The Birth
& Dipping of Achilles,' brown
ground rectangular panel w/white
relief classical figures, green
ground frame separated by a foliate garland, marked "Wedgwood"
only, 18½" l. 770.00
Plaque, 'Achilles in Scyros Among
the Daughters of Lycomedes,'
white relief classical figures on
black, in a black painted & gilt
frame, 19th c., plaque 22" l. (firing flaws) 495.00
Sugar bowl, cov., white relief putti
catching butterflies & figures from
"Domestic Employment" above
band of engine-turned flutes & an
inlaid white footrim on blue, conformingly fluted cover w/a ball
knop surrounded by stiff leaves &
beads, impressed "WEDGWOOD,"
late 18th c., 4" h. 385.00
Syrup pitcher, cov., cylindrical body
w/white relief classical figures &
grapevine rim band on cobalt
blue, hinged pewter cover
w/white porcelain finial, marked
"Wedgwood" only, 3" d.,
5¼" h. 150.00
Tea caddy spoon, solid white w/a
shell-form bowl & slender handle
w/scalloped border, impressed
"Wedgwood," 1780-98, 3 5/8" l. ... 605.00

Teapot, cov., angular handle, square spout, white relief classical figures on dark blue, marked "Wedgwood, England," 5" d., 3 3/8" h. 150.00

Urns, cov., three-color, inverted pear shape w/narrow neck & spreading foot on square plinth, grey ground decorated in green & lavender w/floral motifs, trophies & mythological medallions, 19th c., one extensively restored, other w/restored cover, 14" h., pr. (ILLUS.) 1,430.00

Vase, 5" h., 3½" d., Portland Vase-form, white relief classical ladies on black, marked "Wedgwood" only 333.00

Wedgwood Jasper Ware Vases

Vases, 6 1/16" h., trumpet-form on flared foot, white relief palmette-enclosed vignettes of classical figures including two Muses, Apollo & Hope between fruiting grapevine & laurel & anthemia borders on dark blue, impressed "WEDGWOOD" & letter "Z," early 19th c., pr. (ILLUS.) 770.00

Wall pocket, white relief classical dancing ladies on green, 5¾ x 6½" 115.00

Waste bowl, white relief classical figures in panels around sides on cobalt blue, marked "Wedgwood" only, 4 3/8" d., 2 3/8" h. 74.00

MISCELLANEOUS

Wedgwood Majolica Toilet Box

Bowl, 4½" d., 3" h., octagonal, Fairyland Lustre, "Bai Fuku Waso Byo Ye" interior patt., purple lustre interior, orange lustre exterior 302.50

Bowl, 8¾" d., Fairyland Lustre, "Woodland Elves V - Woodland Bridge" patt. exterior, "Woodland Elves II - Spider & Web" interior patt. on mother-of-pearl ground, initialed three times on body by Daisy Makeig-Jones, ca. 1923 .... 8,250.00

Bowl, 11½" d., octagonal, Fairyland Lustre, "Boxing Match" interior & "Castle on a Road" exterior 4,000.00

Box, cov., Dragon Lustre, mottled deep green lustre outside w/gold dragons designs, inside mother-of-pearl lustre, widow finial, 5 5/8" d., 5¼" h. 432.00

Model of a deer, ivory glaze, designed by John Skeaping, ca. 1920's, 8" 700.00

Model of a polar bear, ivory glaze, designed by John Skeaping, ca. 1920's, 10" l. 700.00

Pitcher, jug-type, 5¼" h., pearl-ware, botanical-type, transfer-printed in black & painted in green, yellow, puce & black w/a spray of lilies on one side & a branch from a flowering berry bush on other, neck, rim & handle enriched w/a brown line border, impressed "WEDGWOOD" & potter's mark, pattern number 493 painted in iron-red, ca. 1810 ..... 825.00

Pitcher, majolica, figural dog handle, hunting scene in relief in emerald green on front & reverse 225.00

Plaque, pierced to hang, Fairyland Lustre, picnic scene by a river, rare color, pattern No. Z5279, 4½ x 10" 4,500.00

Plate, 8" d., Peter Rabbit patt. 27.00

Plate, 8¾" d., h.p. female figures, artist-signed on front, date mark for 1870 .... 500.00

Plate, 8¾" d., commemorative, "Harvard, 1932," rose transfer on white 18.00

Plate, 9¾" d., Moonlight Lustre, deep purplish-pink lustre (like Sunderland lustre), white w/some gold, marked "Wedgwood" only .. 201.00

Plate, 10½" d., commemorative, "Harvard, 1941," rose transfer on white 20.00

Plate, 10½" d., commemorative, "Webb House, Wethersfield, Connecticut," dark blue transfer on white 22.00

Plate, 10¾" d., Fairyland Lustre,
printed in gold & painted w/red-
violet imps crossing a green,
brown & turquoise bridge above a
red-violet imp in a bright green
boat on a royal blue river, brown
goblins at one side & sea flowers
w/green & turquoise boy's-head
centers on the other below a
green roc bird, all within "Rhages
Bead" & "Twyford" borders, the
latter w/an orange lustre ground,
reverse w/a mottled blue, black &
ruby ground, gold over black
printed Portland Vase "WEDG-
WOOD MADE IN ENGLAND" mark,
pattern No. W5(58), ca. 1923.....1,120.00
Plate, dinner, Orient patt. 15.00
Plate, earthenware, decorated
w/black matte glaze enhanced
w/gold decoration, painted in the
Islamic style, decorated by Louise
Powell, marked w/artist's initials
& numbered, 1926 (glaze pits) 137.50
Punch bowl, commemorative, Harvard Tercentenary, red transfers,
1939, 12" d. 195.00
Teapot, cov., Ferra patt., cobalt
blue on white ground, 6¼" d.,
5" h........................ 106.00
Toilet box & cover, lady's, majolica,
glazed in drab grey, blue, brown &
ochre, the cover modeled w/the figure of a medieval lady kneeling on
a pillow, her train, forming a jewel
tray, held by two bowing pages,
rectangular lower section inset w/a
removable tray fitted w/three small
pots, one w/a cover, impressed
"WEDGWOOD" & date cipher for
September, 1872, No. 1263, repairs,
9" l. (ILLUS.) 1,210.00
Tray, bone china, closed handles,
central medallion painted in
shades of lavender, puce, green,
blue, yellow & brown w/bacchic
putti amid grape-filled baskets,
the rim w/fruiting grapevines between gold key-fret borders,
signed "J. P. Thorley," sepia-
printed Portland Vase "WEDG-
WOOD ENGLAND" mark, pattern
No. Z4067, ca. 1910, 16¾" l. 330.00
Umbrella stand, majolica, in the form
of a basket modeled w/rows of alternating yellow & white plaited raffia
decorated w/a green, brown &
blue peacock feather tucked
beneath a pale blue ribbon on
either side, a bowknotted ribbon
at either end, the interior covered
w/a turquoise glaze, Aesthetic
Movement style, impressed "WEDG-
WOOD," pattern number 30073, date

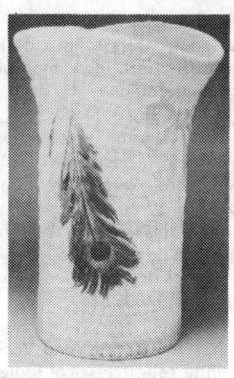

Wedgwood Majolica Umbrella Stand

cipher for April 1883, hairline
crack, 22" h. (ILLUS.)............1,925.00

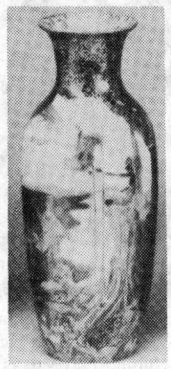

Wedgwood Fairyland Lustre Vase

Vase, 8" h., Fairyland Lustre
"Jeweled Tree," printed in gold
w/'Jeweled Tree' incorporating
panels of "Feng Hwang" and
"Bridge" painted in tones of yellow, purple, blue, green & crimson on a mother-of-pearl ground,
the mother-of-pearl interior w/a
"Floating Fairies" border, Portland
Vase "WEDGWOOD MADE IN
ENGLAND" mark, pattern
No. Z4296, ca. 1920 (ILLUS.) 495.00
Vase, 9½" h., 4½" d., trumpet-
shaped, Fairyland Lustre, fairy lady
in blue amid flowering hawthorne
bushes, birds around top edge,
everything outlined in fine gold,
birds & fairies top interior 1,195.00

WELLER

*This pottery was made from 1872 to 1945
at a pottery established originally by Samuel
A. Weller at Fultonham, Ohio, and moved in
1882 to Zanesville. Numerous lines were*

produced and listings below are by the pattern or lines. Most desirable is the Sicardo line.

BLUE DRAPERY (1915-20)

Clusters of roses pendent from rims against vertical folded blue matte drapery ground.

Bowl, 6" d., 3" h. $30.00
Planter, canted sides, 4" h. 42.00
Vase, 6½" h. 27.00
Wall pocket, 8" h. 75.00

BONITO (1927-33)

Hand-painted florals and foliage in soft tones on cream ground.

Vase, 5" h., flaring cylinder 45.00
Vase, 5" h., open curved handles
　rising from mid-section to above
　rim 48.00
Vase, 6" h., shaped cylinder 60.00
Vase, 6½" h., closed scroll handles
　at mid-section 35.00
Vase, 7" h., open handles from
　shoulder to above rim 35.00
Vase, 7½" h., ornate open
　handles 55.00
Vase, 8" h. 95.00
Vase, 10½" h., ovoid w/closed
　scroll handles at shoulder 200.00

CHASE (late 1920's)

White relief fox hunt scenes on deep blue ground.

Vase, 6" h. 125.00
Vase, 7" h., blue & white 165.00
Vase, 10¾" h., bulbous ...195.00 to 225.00

CLAYWOOD (1910)

Panels of incised designs; tan and dark brown matte finish.

Bowl, 3½" d., 2" h., stylized fish,
　stippled ground 25.00
Mug, star-shaped florals, stippled
　ground, 5" h. 50.00
Vase, 3½" h., star-shaped florals ... 25.00

COPPERTONE (late 1920's)

Blotchy semi-gloss green over brown glaze.

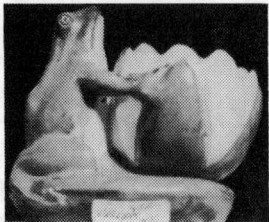

Coppertone Flower Holder

Ashtray, model of a frog seated at
　one end, 6½" w. 87.50

Candleholders, model of a turtle
　w/water lily form candle nozzle
　on his back, 3" h., pr. 150.00
Candleholders, 3½" h., pr. 35.00
Console bowl, model of a frog seat-
　ed at one end, fish on sides,
　10½" l., 7¼" w. 185.00
Console bowl, irregular form, model
　of a frog seated on a lily pad
　w/blossom at one end & lily pad
　& blossom at other, rock form
　flower frog, 10 x 15",
　2 pcs. ....150.00 to 180.00
Flower holder, figural frog w/water
　lily (ILLUS.) 75.00
Model of a frog, 2" h. 50.00
Model of a frog, 4" h. 130.00

DICKENSWARE 1ST LINE (1897-98)

Jardiniere, slip-painted floral sprigs,
　glossy brown glaze, 10" h. 110.00
Jug, relief-molded ear of corn &
　husk, glossy brown glaze, 5" h. .. 125.00
Stein, slip-painted jumping frog,
　glossy brown glaze, 7" h. 435.00

DICKENSWARE 2ND LINE (1900-05)

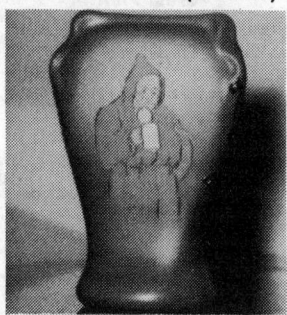

2nd Line Dickensware Vase

Ewer, sgraffito cavalier scene,
　12" h. 385.00
Vase, 6¾" h., 5" w., heart-shaped
　body w/low loop handles at rim,
　sgraffito polychrome portrait of
　Indian in headdress, "Ghose Bull,"
　amber shaded to pale green
　matte ground, die-stamped "DICK-
　ENS WARE," "WELLER," "848," &
　"13" 275.00
Vase, 7½" h., 3½" w., cylindrical
　body tapering to short neck,
　sgraffito bust portrait of American
　Indian, "White Tail," blue & yel-
　low shaded matte background, in-
　cised "E.L.P.," (artist E.L. Pickens)
　on surface & die-stamped "DICK-
　ENSWARE - WELLER," "x" &
　"113" 275.00
Vase, 9½" h., sgraffito portrait of a
　monk (ILLUS.) 420.00
Vase, 10" h., sgraffito portrait of a
　jester 575.00

Vase, 12¼" h., sgraffito scene of
two men on front, verse on back
w/misspelling, "Pickwick Papers,"
high-gloss finish 3,500.00

DICKENSWARE 3RD LINE

Mug, molded & underglaze slip-
painted scene, "Dombey & Son,"
5 5/8" h. 195.00
Vase, 9½" h., molded & underglaze
slip-painted scene, "Dombey &
Son" 385.00
Stein, molded & underglaze slip-
painted scene, verse reverse,
"David Copperfield" 395.00

FOREST (1915)

Realistically molded and painted forest scene.

Forest Planter

Jardiniere, 4¾" h. 80.00
Planter, 22" l., 11" w., 11" h.
(ILLUS.) 650.00
Vase, 8" h., cylindrical . . . . . .55.00 to 65.00
Vase, 10½" h. 90.00

HUDSON (1920-1935)

Underglaze slip-painted decoration.

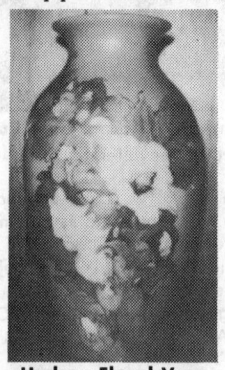

Hudson Floral Vase

Bowl, 12" d., pansies & foliage,
creamy ivory matte glaze 75.00
Vase, 7" h., 6" d., roses & foliage,
white matte glaze 140.00
Vase, 9" h., scene of lake
w/boats against a background
of trees & mountains, signed
by Hester Pillsbury 2,000.00
Vase, 10" h., underglaze slip-
painted white blossoms, blue
matte glaze, artist-signed
(ILLUS.) 300.00

Vase, 11" h., geese in flight, signed
Timberlake .1,500.00
Vase, 13" h., 4" d., tall cylinder
tapering slightly to top, lavender
& blue lilacs, pale pink shaded to
greyish-green ground, signed by
Hester Pillsbury, die-stamped
"WELLER" 225.00
Vase, 15¼" h., 7½" w., tall ovoid
body tapering slightly to wide,
flaring rim, blue & white irises &
light green leaves, pale green
shaded to pink matte ground,
signed by Hester Pillsbury, black
ink mark "WELLER POTTERY" 475.00

JAP BIRDIMAL (1904)

Incised and slip-painted decoration.

Vase, 4" h., standing geese 240.00
Vase, 5" h., 5" d., bulbous, pinched
top, five swimming fish 325.00
Vase, white peacock-type feathers
w/blue centers, glossy grey
ground 145.00
Vase, 7½" h., four flying geese,
heavy beaded trim, glossy green
ground 170.00
Vase, 9" h., flying geese 175.00

KNIFEWOOD (1915-20)

Lamp, peacock molded in low
relief 135.00
Tobacco jar, cov., scene molded in
low-relief of a creamy ivory hunting dog in a brown forest
setting 285.00
Vase, 5" h., scene molded in low-
relief of creamy ivory swans
swimming w/trees on the shore in
foreground 65.00
Vase, 7" h., daisies molded in low-
relief 75.00

L'ART NOUVEAU (1903-04)

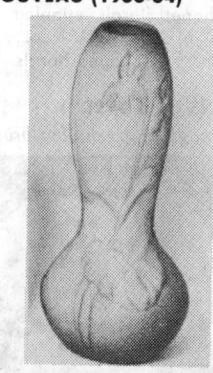

L'Art Nouveau Vase

Vase, 11" h., relief-molded irises at
top 135.00
Vase, 12" h., relief-molded pink

flowers w/trailing stems, green &
rose matte finish
(ILLUS.) ....95.00 to 110.00
Vase, 12" h., square body, relief-
molded blossoms forming rim,
matte finish 220.00
Vase, 14½" h., relief-molded figure
of a lovely blonde woman in flowing gown amid flowers & fruit,
matte finish, unmarked 475.00
Vase, 15½" h., squared form w/bul-
bous base & long neck, relief-
molded figure of a lovely woman
in a flowing gown standing on a
large blossom & holding another
over her shoulder, matte
finish ....500.00 to 600.00

LOUWELSA (1896-1924)

Louwelsa Vase with Indian Portrait

Jug, slip-painted berries, leaves &
thorns decoration 225.00
Lamp, slip-painted floral decoration,
9½" h. plus shade 175.00
Lamp base, slip-painted burnt orange flowers & leaves on green to
dark brown ground, artist-signed,
14" h. 375.00
Pedestal, hourglass shape, slip-
painted mums decoration 400.00
Vase, 5½" h., bulbous, slip-painted
orange flowers on brown ground,
artist-signed 95.00
Vase, 6½" h., cylindrical, slip-
painted flowers decoration, artist-
signed 95.00
Vase, 7" h., pillow-shaped, slip-
painted portrait of St. Bernard
decoration..................... 425.00
Vase, 7½" h., slip-painted blue pansies decoration 500.00
Vase, 10¾" h., tall ovoid body
w/short flared neck, slip-painted
w/bust portrait of American
Indian brave, crazing, ca. 1915
(ILLUS.)....................... 475.00
Vase, 15½" h., slip-painted yellow
jonquils decoration 325.00

MAMMY LINE (1935)

Batter bowl 750.00
Creamer & sugar bowl, figural handles, pr....................... 500.00
Syrup pitcher, cov., figural Mammy,
6" h.......................... 375.00

MARBLEIZED (1914)

Bowl, 7" d., brown & cream swirled
glaze 65.00
Urn, swirled glaze, 9½ x 10½"..... 60.00
Vase, 7" h., jade green swirled
glaze 40.00
Vase, 8" h., octagonal, swirled
glaze 65.00

NOVELTY LINE (1930's)

Ashtray, model of a Dachshund 75.00
Model of a frog w/lotus, 4" 55.00
Planter, model of a Dachshund,
8½" l. 60.00
Planter, model of a duck & rabbit... 45.00
Planter, model of a snail........... 55.00

PANELLA (mid-late 1930's)

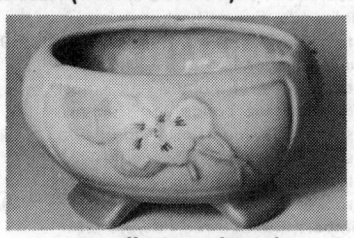

Panella Footed Bowl

Bowl, 3½" h., three-footed, deep
rounded sides, relief-molded
cream blossom & green leaves on
pastel blue ground (ILLUS.)....... 40.00
Cornucopia-vase, relief-molded
cream blossom & green leaves on
pastel ground, 5½" h............ 40.00
Vase, 8" d., flared foot to bulbous
base flanked by arched strap handles, tall flared sides to indented
two-lobe rim, relief-molded cream
blossom & green leaves on shaded tan to brown ground 20.00
Wall pocket, fleur-de-lis form, relief-
molded cream blossom & green
leaves on pastel ground, 8" h. ... 40.00

PEARL (1917-19)

Basket, footed, relief-molded beaded swags joined by pink rose
blossoms on cream ground,
6½" h. 115.00
Vase, 5" h., ovoid body, relief-
molded beaded swags joined by
small florette on cream ground ... 85.00
Vase, 7" h., tall slightly ovoid body,
relief-molded beaded swags
joined by small florettes on cream
ground 85.00

PIERRE (1930's)
Bowl, 5½" d., basketweave mold,
marbleized glazed . . . . 　30.00
Pitcher, 5" h., ovoid body, basket-
weave mold . . . . 　30.00

PUMILA (early 1920's-28)
Bowl, 4" d., w/attached underplate,
molded as large lotus blossom on
lily pad leaf plate . . . . 　30.00
Candleholders, molded as lotus
blossom on lily pad leaf base, yellow blossom interior, shaded
green exterior, 3" d., 4½" h.,
pr. . . . . 　45.00
Vase, 6½" h., flaring cylinder, leaf
stems molded up sides w/broad
lily pad leaves forming scalloped
rim . . . . 　30.00
Vase, 8" h., flaring cylinder, leaf
stems molded up sides w/broad
lily pad leaves forming scalloped
rim . . . . 　55.00

ROMA (1914-late 1920's)
Book ends, flower basket decora-
tion, large, pr. . . . . 　250.00
Candlestick or lamp base, flared
base w/relief-molded egg & dart
& floral vine bands, tall slender
shaft w/molded floral vine down
side, two small loop handles at
top below wide drip ring under
socket, cream ground, 9½" h. . . . . 　40.00
Comport, molded red flowers on
cream ground, 5½" top d.,
7" h. . . . . 　50.00
Vase, 5" h., paneled sides w/incised
pine cone decoration on cream
ground . . . . 　29.00
Vase, triple bud, 8½" h., ribbon &
red rose cluster swag molded
across arched sides . . . . 　48.00
Wall pocket, cone-shaped, molded
pleats below wide rim band
w/relief-molded red roses & purple grape cluster, cream ground . . 　54.00

SABRINIAN (late 1920's)
Bowl, 9" d., 2½" h., scalloped shell
shape w/purple glaze, relief-
molded green seaweed design on
interior . . . . 　95.00
Bowl, 6 x 8" oval, footed, lobed
shells form sides w/relief-molded
sea horse handles, pale purple
w/green dividing bands . . . . 　60.00
Flower frog, molded rock-form base
w/holes supports figural sea
horse at center, 4½" h. . . . . 　40.00

SICARDO (1902-07)
Plaque, low-footed circular form
decorated w/metallic lusters on a

purple iridescent ground depicting
butterflies among thornberries,
inscribed "Weller," & signed "J.
Sicard" on reverse, signed again
by the artist in the design, ca.
1905, 12½" d. 2,860.00

Weller Sicardo Vase

Vase, 7½" h., angled neck twisting
on twisted body swelling towards
base, iridescent purples & greens
w/snails in the design, unsigned,
ca. 1907 (ILLUS.) . . . . 　660.00
Vase, 9" h., flared rim on swollen
cylindrical body, blue iridescent
glaze incorporating thistle design,
unsigned, ca. 1907 (some minor
pitting) . . . . 　440.00
Vase, 10¾" h., cylindrical w/overall
amber leaf & dot design on maroon ground, signed on side
(some crazing) . . . . 　467.50

SILVERTONE (1925-29)
Candleholders, low wide round base
molded w/abstract purple blossoms, green leaves & brown
branches, 3" d., pr. . . . . 　65.00
Vase, 6½" h., two-handled, molded
pink & white blossoms, leaves &
branches on splotched bluish pink
pebbled ground . . . . 　63.50
Vase, 6¾" h., experimental piece,
baluster-shaped body w/twisted
rim handles, relief-molded blossoms on pebbled brown ground . . 　70.00
Vase, 8½" h., bulbous body
w/heavy loop handles at shoulder, short neck w/wide ruffled
rim, molded large purple blossoms, green leaves & brown
stems on pale purple rough peb-
bled ground . . . . 　145.00

SOUEVO (ca. 1910)
Basket, hanging-type, incised geo-
metric American Indian designs . . 　65.00
Mug, incised geometric American
Indian designs . . . . 　75.00

Vase, 4½" h., incised geometric
American Indian designs 65.00
Wall pocket, incised geometric
American Indian designs, 16" h. . . 95.00

TURADA (1897-98)
Bowl, 2¼ x 4½", delicate embossed
white scroll band against dark
glazed ground 85.00
Lamp base, oil-type, delicate em-
bossed scroll band against dark
blue glazed ground 650.00
Potpourri jar, cov., delicate em-
bossed scroll band against dark
glazed ground 350.00

UTILITY WARE
Bowl, 9 x 13½", tan glaze w/brown
stripes 68.00
Casserole, cov., blue glaze 45.00
Pitcher, 7" h., tan glaze w/brown
stripe 48.00

VELVA (ca. 1928-33)
Bowl, 5" h., narrow etched leafy floral band down side against solid
color ground 85.00
Vase, 6" h., ovoid body w/small
scroll tab handles two-thirds distance up sides, narrow etched
leafy floral band down sides
against solid green ground 24.00
Vase, 8" h., fan-shaped, narrow
etched leafy floral band down
side against solid color ground . . . 70.00
Vase, 9" h., tall footed cylindrical
body w/small scroll tab handles
two-thirds distance up sides, narrow etched leafy floral band down
side against solid color ground . . . 38.00

WARWICK (late 1920's)
Basket, interior molded w/brown
tree bark texture w/red fruit &
green leaf sprig, 7" h. 85.00
Basket, interior molded w/brown
tree bark texture w/red fruit &
green leaf sprig, 9" h. 135.00
Console bowl, interior molded
w/brown tree bark texture w/red
fruit & green leaf sprig, embossed
tree branch band at rim & branch
loop handles, 10½" d. 39.00
Vase, 4½" h., exterior molded
w/brown tree bark texture w/red
fruit & green leaf sprig 50.00

WILD ROSE (early-mid-1930's)
Basket, round bulbous footed body
w/sides continuing to form strap
handle across top, this handle
topped by second smaller arched
handle, large white blossom &
green leaf sprig against pale
green ground, 5½" h. 29.00

Bowl, 7½" d., large white blossom
& green leaf sprig against pale
green ground 40.00
Candelabra, three-light, three nar-
row graduated cornucopia-form
arms rise from oblong base,
pr. 55.00
Jardiniere, large white blossom &
green leaf sprig against ivory
ground, 7" d. 65.00
Vase, 6" h., double, two cylinders
angle up from arched feet, joined
at top by arched handle, large
blossoms & leaf sprigs on pale
green ground 25.00
Vase, 7½" h., flaring cylindrical
body on four square tab feet,
large white blossom & green leaf
sprig on pale green ground 70.00

Wild Rose Vase

Vase, 9½" h., two-handled, tall
ovoid body w/tall flaring neck
w/scroll handles from neck to
shoulder, large white blossom &
green leaf sprig on pale green
ground (ILLUS.) 34.00

WOODCRAFT (1920-33)

Woodcraft Planter with Foxes

Bowl, 3½" h., relief-molded purple
plums & brown twig on brown
tree bark ground 45.00
Bowl, 7" d., 5½" h., squatty round
base w/molded branch, leaves &
acorns around rim & figural squir-
rel seated on rim 110.00

Lamp, narrow tree trunk base supports leafy cluster topped by four-sided owl figure, owl-decorated shade, base 12½" h. 350.00

Planter, cylindrical tree trunk form w/three small foxes peeking out at side, 4½" h. (ILLUS.) 125.00

Planter, log-form w/molded leaf & narrow strap handle at top center, 9" l. 55.00

Vase, bud, 9" h., slender tree trunk form w/molded branch & fruit sprigs on side................... 25.00

Vase, 12" h., smooth tree trunk form w/molded leafy branch around rim & down sides w/hanging purple plums 110.00

Wall pocket, conical tree trunk form w/relief-molded branch down front & figural squirrel seated at base, 8" h. ....150.00 to 175.00

Wall pocket, relief-molded apple against tree trunk body, 11½" h. 68.00

WOODROSE (pre-1920)

Bowl, 8½" d., 2½" h., handled, model of a low oaken bucket w/pendent red roses & green leaves at front center, brown matte ground 45.00

Vase, 4" h., model of a tall cylindrical oaken bucket w/pendent red roses & green leaves at front center, brown matte ground........ 19.00

Wall pocket, model of a tall slender oaken bucket w/pendent red roses & green leaves at front center, brown matte ground......... 65.00

(End of Weller Section)

WHIELDON-TYPE WARES

Early Whieldon Plaque

The Staffordshire potter, Thomas Whieldon, first established a pottery at Fenton in

1740. Though he made all types of wares generally in production in the 18th century, he is best known for his attractive, warm-colored green, yellow and brown mottled wares molded in the form of vegetable, fruit and leaves. He employed Josiah Spode as an apprentice and was briefly in partnership with Josiah Wedgwood. The term Whieldon ware is, however, a generic one since his wares were unmarked and are virtually indistinguishable from other similar wares produced by other potters during the same period.

Dish, deep sides, typically mottled in brown, w/shaped hexafoil rim & six "knotted-wood" molded border panels, ca. 1770, 15" d. (surface abrasions) $715.00

Plaques, cartouche-shaped, headed by molded shells & molded in relief w/Mary Squires as a gypsy in a broad-brimmed hat & Sarah Malcolm, washed in ochre, green & manganese, ca. 1765, one w/repaired shell & minor chips to hat, 2 pcs. (ILLUS. of one) 14,300.00

Teapot, cov., rounded hexagonal body molded in relief w/a boy in grapevines & w/a flowerhead finial on the slightly domed cover, overall green glaze, ca. 1760, 4¾" h. (restoration to tip of spout, chips, restorations) 11,000.00

Whieldon Pineapple Teapot

Teapot, cov., globular body molded w/diamond-shaped decoration & leaves to resemble a pineapple, w/reeded spout & handle & a flowerhead cover knop, ca. 1760, spout & cover chipped, 5" h. (ILLUS.) 7,700.00

Tray, rectangular, square handles, gadrooned rim, overall mottled grey-green w/yellow & brown sponging, 1760-70, 6 x 9¼".......2,000.00

WILLOW WARES

This pseudo-Chinese pattern has been used

by numerous firms throughout the years. The original design is attributed to Thomas Minton about 1780 and Thomas Turner is believed to have first produced the ware during his tenure at the Caughley works. The blue underglaze transfer print pattern has never been out of production since that time. An Oriental landscape incorporating a bridge, pagoda, trees, figures and birds, supposedly tells the story of lovers fleeing a cruel father who wished to prevent their marriage. The gods, having pity on them, changed them into birds, enabling them to fly away and seek their happiness together.

BLUE WILLOW

Bone dish, 4½ x 8"	$24.00
Bowl, 4¾" d., Allerton, England	9.00
Bowl, 8½" d., Booth, England	35.00
Bowl, dessert, Occupied Japan	7.50
Bowl, soup, flat, Buffalo Pottery	15.00
Bowl, soup, Royal	10.00
Bread plate, Booth, England	30.00
Butter dish, cover & strainer, Ridgway, England, 3 pcs.	130.00
Butter pat, Allerton, England	16.00
Cake stand, Coalport	145.00
Cheese dish, cov., Coalport	155.00
Chocolate pot, cov., w/warming base, Japan	95.00
Creamer, Booth, England	55.00
Creamer, squat form, advertising "Schweppes," England, turn of the century, 3¾" h.	18.00
Creamer, squat form, Myott, England	20.00
Creamer, Shelton, Stoke-on-Trent, England	7.00
Creamer & cov. sugar bowl, "Booth - Real Old Willow," England, pr.	125.00
Creamer & cov. sugar bowl, John Steventon, England, pr.	45.00
Creamer & open sugar bowl, Sadler, England, pr.	30.00
Creamer & sugar bowl, stacking-type, pr.	12.00
Cup, Buffalo Pottery	12.50
Cup & saucer, Allerton, England	15.00
Cup & saucer, "Booth - Real Old Willow," England	30.00
Cup & saucer, Japan	8.00
Demitasse set, cov. pot, cov. sugar bowl, creamer & six cups & saucers, 15 pcs.	95.00
Egg cup, England	10.00
Ginger jar, cov., Coalport	35.00
Gravy boat, fat-lean type	49.50
Gravy boat, Japan	15.00
Gravy boat w/underplate, Mandarin II center, dagger border, Copeland impressed half-circle mark	55.00
Marmalade jar, cov., Coalport	49.00

Mustard, cov., w/ladle, Japan, 3 pcs.	55.00
Pepper pot, English earthenware, early 19th c.	178.00
Pitcher, 6" h., Meakin	95.00
Plate, 6" d., Allerton, England	8.00
Plate, 6" d., Occupied Japan	3.00
Plates, 7" d., Allertons, set of 5	55.00
Plate, 8" d., "Booth - Real Old Willow"	25.00
Plate, 8¾" d., scalloped edge, unmarked	21.00
Plate, 9" d., scalloped edge, Allertons	16.00
Plate, 9" d., Buffalo Pottery, 1918	15.00
Plate, 9" d., Occupied Japan	7.00
Plate, 9" d., Shenango Pottery	6.50
Plate, 9¾" d., Shelton, Stoke-on-Trent, England	10.00
Plate, 10" d., Olde Alton Ware, England	30.00
Plate, 10" d., Ridgway	25.50
Plate, grill, 10" d., Grimwades, England	30.00
Plate, grill, 10½" d., Japan	20.00
Platter, 8 x 11", Buffalo Pottery	46.00
Platter, 9½", William Adams & Co., Staffordshire, ca. 1900	55.00
Platter, 11½", Homer Laughlin	20.00
Platter, 12½ x 15½", England	55.00
Platter, 15½", Allertons	120.00
Platter, 17¼" l., oval, 19th c. (minor wear, pinpoint flakes)	95.00
Platter, 18¾" l., oval w/slightly angled corners, marked "Spode," 19th c. (minor wear, small glaze flakes on rim)	210.00
Salt & pepper shakers, Japan, pr.	22.00
Sauce dish, Buffalo Pottery	10.00
Sauce dish, scalloped, Allertons	14.00
Sugar bowl, cov., Allertons	40.00
Vegetable bowl, cov., 9 x 11", Allertons	79.00
Vegetable bowl, cov., Grimwades, ca. 1906	95.00
Vegetable bowl, cov., round, Ridgway	75.00
Vegetable bowl, open, deep sides, marked in square "Semi-China, England," 7½ x 9"	22.50
Vegetable bowl, open, Japan, 10¼"	25.00
Vegetable bowl, open, square, William Adams & Co., Staffordshire, ca. 1900	85.00
Waste bowl, Venton Ware, England	28.00

OTHER COLORS

Bowl, 5½" d., pink, Japan	5.00
Bowl, 9" d., mauve	11.00
Bowl, 9" d., red	10.00
Butter pat, pink, Japan	6.50
Cake plate, red, Japan	28.00

Creamer & sugar bowl, pink, Japan,
   pr............................ 17.00
Plate, 6½" d., pink, Japan 3.00
Plate, 9" d., red, Allertons 15.00
Plate, grill, 9" d., mauve........... 15.00
Plate, grill, 10" d., mauve.......... 18.00
Plate, dinner, pink, Japan 7.50
Plate, grill, pink 12.00
Platter, 12", pink, Meakin.......... 18.00
Platter, 13", pink, Japan 17.00

WORCESTER

Worcester Bough Pot

*The famed English Worcester factory was
established in 1751 and produced porcelains.
Earthenwares were made in the 19th century. Its first period is known as the "Dr. Wall"
period; that from 1783 to 1792 as the "Flight"
period; that from 1792 to 1807 as the "Barr
and Flight & Barr" period. The firm became
Barr, Flight & Barr from 1807 to 1813; Flight,
Barr & Barr from 1813 to 1840; Chamberlain
& Co. from 1840 to 1852, and Kerr and Binns
from 1852 to 1862. After 1862, the company
became the Worcester Royal Porcelain Company, Ltd., known familiarly as Royal
Worcester, which see. Also included in the following listing are examples of wares from the
early Chamberlains and early Grainger factories in Worcester.*

Basket, reticulated cover & stand,
   quatrefoil shape, the basket
   molded around the exterior w/a
   flowerhead- and honeycomb-pat-
   terned ground, the interior painted
   cartouches of birds & insects reserved on a blue-scale ground, the
   ends w/branch handles terminating
   in floral clusters, the pierced cover
   similarly decorated w/a branch-
   form handle, on a similar associated stand, First Period, ca. 1775,
   stand 11" w., the set..........$2,090.00
Bough pots & covers, D-shaped body,
   Best Queen's patt., painted in the
   Kakiemon palette of iron-red, blue,
   yellow & gold w/two vertical

panels of chrysanthemums alternating w/cobalt blue panels further
   decorated w/gilt trellis diaper
   work reserved w/iron-red & white
   single flowerheads, the pierced
   conforming covers lined in gilt,
   "Chamberlain's Worcester" in gold
   script, ca. 1800, 8½" w., one pot
   w/hairline, some minor rubbing,
   pr. (ILLUS. of one) 8,250.00
Candlestick, modeled as two alert
   canaries perched in pink apple
   blossom bocage above the scroll-
   molded base enriched w/puce &
   gilt, the back w/a scrolling handle,
   ca. 1770, 6¾" h. (chips, some
   missing pieces, handle cracks) ..18,700.00
Creamer, jug-shaped, fluted, painted
   w/festoons of berried foliage
   divided by vase-shaped panels of
   purple foliage within a lavender &
   gilt herringbone border alternating
   w/panels of purple foliage all
   above a band of turquoise decorated w/grey beads & flowerheads, ca. 1775, 4¼" h..........1,320.00
Dishes, leaf-shaped, each molded as
   two leaves & transfer-printed w/a
   bouquet, scattered flowers & butterflies, ca. 1770, 13¾" w., pr.
   (some pitting, chips) 1,210.00
Dishes, shell-shaped, gadrooned
   edges & painted in the center
   w/an eagle's head crest, w/shell
   handles, impressed crowned
   "FBB" marks, Flight, Barr & Barr,
   ca. 1820, 8¾" w., pr............. 165.00
Figure of a gardener, standing man
   in mauve hat, yellow-lined pink
   coat, white blouse, blue apron &
   flowered breeches, w/a flowering
   plant in a pot in his right hand,
   his left resting on a spade, supported by a tree-trunk on a flower-
   encrusted rocky base, ca. 1770,
   6¾" h. (restorations, small
   chips) 13,200.00

Early Worcester Mug

Inkstand, waisted cylinder, w/a rectangular panel painted w/figures

in a landscape within gilt border
reserves on the grey marbled
ground & w/gilt-line rim, marked,
Barr, Flight & Barr, ca. 1808,
2 7/8" h. (some wear to gilding) ...715.00

Mug, cylindrical w/reeded loop handle, Gardener patt., decorated in
blue on white w/Chinese figures,
one picking a flower by a stream,
the other seated beneath a willow
tree, open crescent mark in underglaze-blue, First Period,
1765-75, 4 7/8" h. (ILLUS. previous
page) 385.00

Pitcher, jug-type, 11¾" h., cabbage-
leaf molded, the spout molded
w/a mask, w/S-scroll handle,
transfer-printed in blue on white
overall w/ribbon-tied bouquets &
butterflies, ca. 1775 .... 605.00

Plate, 8 5/8" d., octagonal, Quail
patt., decorated in typical Kakiemon palette of iron-red, blue,
green & gilt w/quail & flowering
tree within iron-red foliage & gilt
flowerheads, ca. 1765 (crack restored) 220.00

Teabowl & saucer, painted in puce
camaieu w/insects & flower
sprays, some within gilt quatrefoil
cartouches, beneath gilt line rims,
ca. 1770 (some minor rubbing) ... 308.00

Vases, 8 3/8" h., campana-form,
painted in bright colors w/a naturalistic bouquet of flowers within a
gilt scroll border reserved against
the gilt-enriched cobalt blue
ground, a single flower reserve on
the reverse, the lower part gilt
w/trellis panels, flanked by gilt
handles w/mask terminals, on circular base similarly painted, Chamberlain's, ca. 1820, 8 3/8" h., pr.
(minor wear, repaired foot
chips) 1,210.00

YELLOWWARE

*Yellowware is a form of utilitarian pottery
produced in the United States from the 1850's
onward. Its body texture is less dense and
vitreous (impervious to water) than stoneware. Most, but not all, yellowware is unmarked and its color varies from deep yellow
to pale buff. In the late 19th and early 20th
centuries bowls in graduated sizes were widely advertised. Still in production, yellowware
is plentiful and still reasonably priced.*

Bowl, 9" d., 4" h., five brown
bands $55.00
Bowl, 9" d., 4½" h., footed, brown
& white stripes................ 42.00

Cookie jar, cov., rope handles...... 45.00
Figural bottle, figure of a mermaid
w/primitively modeled head &
shoulders on curled under scaly
fish tail, spout at top of head,
clear glaze, 8¼" h. 95.00
Jar w/domed lid, strap handle,
cylindrical body w/slight waisting
& two applied loop handles at
sides, four-part brown slip bands
flank three-part wavy brown slip
band around middle, similar slip
bands on lip, 8¾" h. (small edge
chips & bottom hairline) 525.00
Mug, white band & brown stripes,
3 7/8" h. 95.00
Paperweight, round disk w/high-
relief molded three-quarter portrait of lady in wide-brimmed hat,
clear glaze, 4" d. (small edge
chips) 90.00
Pepper pot, waisted baluster form
w/domed lid, narrow blue &
white stripes around body,
4 1/8" h. (chips on lid).......... 250.00
Pie plate, 8" d. 32.00
Pitcher, 8" h., cylindrical w/heavy
strap handle & pinched spout,
double blue stripes near base &
top rim (crow's-foot in bottom) ... 85.00
Pitcher, 8¾" h., embossed basketweave w/flower decoration 85.00
Toothpick holder 285.00
Tub, cylindrical, brown & white
bands, 6½" d., 5" h. 60.00
Vase, 7¾" h., tall trumpet-shaped
bowl w/embossed sprigs of foliage & horizontal bands all highlighted in blue, domed foot,
overall white glaze, attributed to
Robinson Clay, Akron, Ohio, early
20th c. 125.00

ZSOLNAY

Zsolnay Pottery Centerpiece

This pottery was made in Pecs, Hungary,

in a factory founded in 1855 by Vilmos Zsolnay. Currently Zsolnay pieces are being made in a new factory.

Centerpiece, elongated boat-form, iridescent lustre w/mottled yellow-green, two figural red-glazed & decorated parrots perched on ends, marked "ZSOLNAY - PECS 8850" and "ZSOLNAY-PECS, MADE IN HUNGARY" within monogram, 14½" l. $1,100.00

Centerpiece, elongated boat-form, stylized figure of a fisherwoman in flowing dress at one end shown hauling in her nets molded w/fish & swirling waves, raised on oval base, all glazed in mottled sea green iridescence, impressed "ZSOLNAY - PECS 7037" & over-glaze monogram "ZSOLNAY - PECS MADE IN HUNGARY," ca. 1900, 16" l. (ILLUS.) 3,575.00

Figure group, cubistically modeled as a mother seated w/a child on her knees, glazed in iridescent tones of coppery-brown w/high-lights of turquoise & magenta, ca. 1922, printed factory marks, 8½" h. 2,750.00

Model of a dog, standing, "Puli," Hungarian sheep dog, beige glaze, 4¼ x 5¼" 95.00

Plaque, pierced to hang, oval mythological scene depicting two satyrs w/a maiden in a landscape, within an oval & rectangular blue-green iridescent lustre frame, marked "7895 - ZSOLNAY - PECS," 11" w., 8¼" h. 990.00

Platter, 17" l., figure of a maiden leaning over & filling a jug from the edge of a wave-like pool that forms the shallow tray, the edges curled up in irregular rippling manner, light turquoise iridescent lustre glaze, marked "ZSOLNAY PECS" w/monogram 3,575.00

Vase, 9" h., model of a full-relief cobra snake, lifting his body to form a handle & opening his mouth to form spout, his lozenge-patterned skin glazed in iridescent turquoise, indigo & mustard, marked "ZSOLNAY PECS/M6040," ca. 1920 . . . . 3,575.00

Vase, 10¼" h., shouldered baluster form, iridescent glaze, in gilt-metal mount w/two peacocks in full-relief at the shoulder attached to a decorative band, the long stylized feathered tails continuing down the contour of the sides ending in a flaring circular base set

w/glass jewels in green & blue resembling the "eyes" of the tail feathers, metal impressed "ORION - 272" 3,630.00

Vase, 12¼" h., expanding cylindrical body, glazed in iridescent green, purple, red, gold & blue w/a river scene w/boating, a village in the background, impressed "ZSOLNAY PECS 5282 - 2 - M - 27," ca. 1920 . . . . 6,600.00

Vase, 19¾" h., irregular shape, molded in full-relief w/nearly life-size heads of a king & queen adosse', elaborately modeled w/crowns, bead-decorated hair & jewelry about their necks, iridescent silver-grey, yellow-green, blue-green & ruby red metallic lustres, marked "ZSOLNAY-PECS" within monogram 3,850.00

(End of Ceramics Section)

CHALKWARE

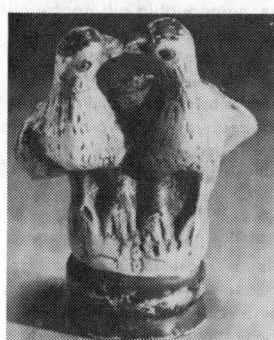

Chalkware Kissing Doves

So-called chalkware available today is actually made of plaster of Paris, much of it decorated in color and primarily in the form of busts, figurines and ornaments. It was produced through most of the 19th century and the majority of pieces were originally quite inexpensive when made. Today even 20th century "carnival" pieces are collectible.

Bank, model of a rooster, white w/red & black details, 8½" h. $150.00

Bust of Hiawatha, turn-of-the-century, 21" h. 100.00

Figure, black boy eating watermelon, "Way Down South," 4" h. 14.00

Mantel garniture, hollow-molded, yellow painted urn overflowing w/a

variety of fruits & foliage in tones
of red, yellow, blue & green, Pennsylvania, mid-19th c., 9¼" h. 1,980.00

Model of a canary, hollow figure
w/head thrust upward, painted in
bright tones of red & yellow, on a
sloping molded base, Pennsylva-
nia, mid-19th c., 6" h. 440.00

Model of a dog, seated, black &
white animal w/wistful face,
wearing a yellow collar, 19th c.,
9½" h. 1,650.00

Model of doves, conjoined, painted
birds perched on a flattened ball
w/'kissing' beaks, red painted
base, Pennsylvania, 19th c.,
4¾" h. (ILLUS.) 880.00

Model of a ewe & lamb, lying side
by side, old gold paint w/green,
yellow & red trim (gold is old addition), 9" l., 6¼" h. 225.00

Model of a German shepherd dog,
animal standing on rocky outcrop
base, carnival prize, ca. 1930's,
4 x 11 x 13" 30.00

Model of a horse standing w/raised
foreleg, on oval shrubbery base,
late 19th c., 10" h. (restorations) 286.00

Model of a lion, early 1900's,
10" plinth...................... 45.00

Model of a poodle, seated, w/mold-
ed stippled body, brown ears, a
red-dotted collar, on a red &
green painted base, Pennsylvania,
mid-19th c., 6½" h. 715.00

Model of a ram in recumbent position, original red & black painted
trim, 3 3/8" h. (repair to one
horn) 225.00

Potholder hook, figural black boy
w/watermelon 18.00

CHARACTER COLLECTIBLES

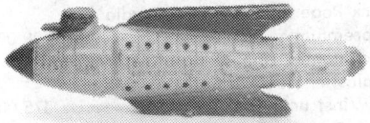

Buck Rogers Battle Cruiser

*Numerous objects were made in the like-
nesses of or named after movie, radio, television, comic strip and comic book personalities
which abounded from the 1920's through the
1960's. Scores of these are now being eagerly collected and prices still vary widely. Also
see ADVERTISING ITEMS, BANKS, BIG
LITTLE BOOKS, BOTTLES, BUSTER*

*BROWN COLLECTIBLES, CANDY CON-
TAINERS, CHILDREN'S DISHES,
CHRISTMAS TREE LIGHTS, CHRIST-
MAS TREE ORNAMENTS, COMIC
BOOKS, DISNEY COLLECTIBLES,
DOLLS, GAMES & GAMEBOARDS and
TOYS.*

Alexander Bumstead figure, wood
composition, marked "K.F.S.,"
1944, 3½" h. $25.00

Amos & Andy candy bar box, pictures characters & Fresh Air Taxi,
orange & black, 1930 (minor
flaws)......................... 85.00

Amos & Andy figures, wood-jointed,
marked "NBC," 1931, 6" h., pr. 350.00

Amos & Andy map of Weber City,
Pepsodent premium, 1935....... 34.00

Amos & Andy radio script, "Amos'
Wedding," 1935 .... 20.00

Amos & Andy stand-up figures, die-
cut cardboard, w/radio story information & radio station timetable, Pepsodent premium,
w/original mailer, ca. 1930,
8½" h......................... 70.00

Andy Gump nodding figure, bisque,
Germany, 4" h. 90.00

Andy Gump pen & ink drawing,
original frame, by Sidney Smith .. 95.00

Andy Gump & Min pencil holder,
copyright by "F.A.S." 185.00

Andy Panda suitcase bank, tin 35.00

Archie & Betty (comics) powder
compact, Archie & Betty jitterbug-
ging, metal, U.S., 2¾" d. 28.00

Barney Google sheet music, "Fox
Trot," 1923 .... 15.00

Batman alarm clock, talking-type ... 25.00

Batman Batbrush, on original card .. 22.00

Batman cape & mask, in package,
1966 .... 15.00

Batman coins, plastic coins on original card, 1966, 20 pcs........... 15.00

Batman fork & spoon, silver plate,
1966, pr. 25.00

Batman hand puppet, Ideal, 1965 ... 50.00

Batman punching bag.............. 25.00

Batman puzzle game, 1966 .... 25.00

Batman toothbrush, battery-
operated 45.00

Batman & Robin pinback button,
"Society Charter Member" 12.50

Batman & Robin thermos bottle 18.00

Batman's Batmobile, battery-
operated, 1972................. 75.00

Beatles album cover, "The Beatles I
Want To Hold Your Hand/I Saw
Her Standing There," addressed to
Jerri & signed by all four mem-
bers of the band, 7 x 7" 770.00

Beatles banner, felt, 1964 .... 75.00

Beatles blanket, wool, Beatles

w/four facsimile signatures, four
drums & two guitars, 57 x 77" 715.00

Beatles book, "The Beatles Biography," Hunter Davies, 1968 ...... 15.00

Beatles book, "The Beatles in Help," Dell, paperback, 1965 .... 20.00

Beatles book, John Lennon, "In His Own Write," hardback, 1964 ..... 30.00

Beatles cake decorations, figures w/instruments 35.00

Beatles coloring book, 1964 .... 27.50

Beatles doll, George Harrison w/guitar, Remco, 4½" h. 53.00

Beatles drawing, pen & ink, John Lennon, "Imagine," depicting the faces of John Lennon & Yoko Ono, w/attached card inscribed "To Jeremy Banks F.A., 'Imagine,' John Lennon," framed, 19½ x 26".....2,640.00

Beatles eyeglasses, John Lennon, gold frames, tinted prescription lenses, dropped at the Troubador in 1974 ....9,350.00

Beatles figures, vinyl, Nems, 1964, set of 4 .... 200.00

Beatles flight bag, TWA, "Beatles To The U.S.A.," red 200.00

Beatles game, "Flip Your Wig," 1964 .... 75.00

Beatles gold record for "Abbey Road," w/plaque inscribed "Presented to George Harrison to Commemorate the sale of more than one million dollars worth of the Capitol Records long playing record album Abbey Road," framed, 15 x 19" 3,080.00

Beatles head scarf, Nems, 1964..... 30.00

Beatles jigsaw puzzle, 1964, near mint 16.00

Beatles key ring, model of a guitar, from Candlestick Park, 1966...... 8.00

Beatles magazines, "Beatles Book," monthly, issue 1 through 77, August 1963 to December 1977 ... 880.00

Beatles medallion on chain, large medallion pictures four Beatles on front, names in filigree on back .. 35.00

Beatles movie cel from "Yellow Submarine," depicting John Lennon running while the bulldogs growl, matted & sealed in original plastic wrapping, w/"One Of A Kind Original Art" seal & Certificate of Authenticity, 11 x 16" 825.00

Beatles pillow, 12" sq. 68.00

Beatles poster, for "Yesterday and Today" album, featuring the rejected "Butcher" version below the title "Incredible," framed, 17½ x 22" 770.00

Beatles self-portrait, John Lennon, black marker on white poster board, depicting John nude, inscribed "I Love Yoko," w/a sun, signed & dated "Y.P. '69 John Lennon 69," 22 x 28" 4,950.00

Ben Casey (T.V.) board game, 1961 .... 25.00

Betty Boop doll, wood & composition jointed body, 12" h. 695.00

Betty Boop playing cards, 1930's, w/box 75.00

Betty Boop wall pocket, Betty twisting Bimbo's ear 135.00

Beverly Hillbillies (T.V.) puzzle, inlaid, Jaymar, 1963............. 12.00

Bewitched (T.V.) Fun & Activity Book, 1965 .... 6.50

Bimbo (Betty Boop's dog) bisque figure, Japan, 3½" h.............. 45.00

Bimbo marble, clear glass w/blue on white bust portrait of dog, name below 40.00

Bing Crosby ice cream container, "Valley Farms Ice Cream," cardboard, colorful, mint, 1950's...... 20.00

Bing Crosby record cleaner........ 15.00

Blondie coloring book 15.00

Blondie paint set, tin box, King Features, 1952, 4½ x 5¾" 15.00

Blondie pinback button, "Pep" cereal premium 6.00

Blondie & Dagwood book, "Blondie & Dagwood's Secret Service," 1942, 248 pages, illustrated 15.00

Bonanza (T.V.) cup, tin, Ponderosa Ranch, Lorne Greene pictured 6.00

Bozo the Clown yo-yo, tin, Japan ... 10.00

Broderick Crawford "Highway Patrol" (T.V.) gun & holster set 90.00

Brutus (Popeye) wind-up toy, "Dippy Dumper," celluloid 350.00

Buck Rogers Atomic Pistol, U-238, w/holster & box, Daisy Mfg. Co., 1948 .... 80.00

Buck Rogers figure, cast lead, Cocomalt premium, 2" h. 11.00

Buck Rogers map, Planet Venus, black & white, 17 x 17½" 75.00

Buck Rogers pinback button, "Satellite Pioneers," 1946.............. 75.00

Buck Rogers Punch-O-Bag, radio premium 29.00

Buck Rogers ring, "Ring of Saturn," plastic, glows in dark, w/instructions 575.00

Buck Rogers toy, Battle Cruiser Rocket Ship, red & yellow, Tootsietoy, Dowst Mfg. Co., 1937, 4¾" l. (ILLUS.) 150.00

Buck Rogers toy, "Strato-Kite," w/envelope, 1946-50 (ILLUS. top next page) 65.00

Buck Rogers toy, Venus Duo-Destroyer Rocket Ship, Tootsietoy, Dowst Mfg. Co., ca. 1937, mint in box, 4" l 150.00

Buck Rogers Strato-Kite

Buffalo Bill cap gun, dated 1923 .... 38.00
Bugs Bunny alarm clock, animated,
square, Ingersoll 100.00
Bugs Bunny record, "Bugs Bunny &
the Tortoise," good condition 25.00
Bugs Bunny vase, bud-type, ceramic,
Los Angeles Potteries, No. 10,
copyright by Warner Bros., 7" h... 44.00
Captain Kangaroo (T.V.) game,
1956 .... 25.00
Captain Kangaroo thermos bottle ... 20.00
Captain Marvel bank, dime
register ....100.00 to 140.00
Captain Marvel wrist watch, yellow
face, picture & logo, blue vinylite
strap, Fawcett, 1948 .... 75.00
Captain Midnight decoder, 1946,
Mirro-Flash Code-O-Graph, Oval-
tine premium 75.00
Captain Midnight decoder, 1947,
Whistling Code-O-Graph, Ovaltine
premium 38.00
Captain Midnight decoder, 1948,
"Miro-Magic Code-O-Graph,"
Ovaltine premium 85.00
Captain Midnight decoder manual,
1947 .... 22.00

Captain Midnight Mug

Captain Midnight mug, Ovaltine
premium, red plastic (ILLUS.) 18.00
Captain Midnight pinback button,
"Flight Patrol," picture of the Captain, advertises Skelly Oil 34.00

Captain Video (T.V.) space ship,
plastic, 1950's, 3" l. 6.00
Casper the Friendly Ghost bank,
ceramic 135.00
Casper the Friendly Ghost Jack-in-
the-Box, w/original box, 1959 .... 32.00
Casper the Friendly Ghost pinback
button, Kellogg's Pep Cereal
premium 6.00
Charlie Chan photograph,
autographed by Warner Oland,
1934 .... 95.00
Charlie Chaplin booklet, "Charlie
Chaplin in Essanay Comedies,"
contains 10 stamps, eight scenes
from his movies, 1915,
2¼ x 3¼" 25.00
Charlie Chaplin decals, Paas Easter
Dye Kit....................... 60.00
Charlie Chaplin doll, Louis Amberg,
1919, original clothes 525.00
Charlie Chaplin film, "Sleepless
Night," 16mm, 100 ft., Dover
Films......................... 35.00
Charlie Chaplin lobby card, "Modern
Times" 95.00
Charlie Chaplin newspaper comic
strip, full-color, 1915, matted 30.00
Charlie Chaplin pencil box, tin,
w/picture 53.00
Charlie McCarthy book, "A Day with
Charlie McCarthy & Edgar Ber-
gen," Whitman, 1938 .... 40.00
Charlie McCarthy comic book,
"Charlie McCarthy's Rocket Ship,"
No. 6, 1950 .... 15.00
Chester Gump figure, bisque, Ja-
pan, 1932-38, 2¾" h. 18.00
Cisco Kid coloring book, unused,
1950 .... 20.00
Cisco Kid gun clicker 25.00
Clarabelle the Clown wallet, plastic,
colorful, insert of Clarabelle,
Flubadub & Dilly Dally 22.00
Daddy Warbucks nodding figure,
bisque, Germany............... 175.00
Daffy Duck figure, ceramic, 5½" h.,
unmarked 55.00
Dale Evans wrist watch, Ingraham,
1951 .... 45.00
Dancing Bear (from Captain Kan-
garoo) hand puppet, Oscar Mayer
premium, 1966 .... 20.00
Dan Dunn Detective Corps badge,
embossed tin, shield-shaped,
reads "Dan Dunn Detective Corps,
Secret Operative 48" 50.00
Daniel Boone rifle, Flintlock
Model 196, Louis Marx & Co., on
original cardboard ....70.00 to 85.00
Death Valley Days (TV) model kit,
20-mule team, in original box 30.00
Dennis the Menace gloves, rawhide
fringe, original tag, 1960 .... 25.00

Denny Dimwit nodding figure,
 composition 165.00
Dick Tracy badge, "Detective
 Club" 16.00
Dick Tracy book, "Ace Detective,"
 by Chester Gould, autographed &
 w/dust jacket 12.00
Dick Tracy book, "Dick Tracy the De-
 tective Feature Book No. 4," color
 cover, black & white comics, 1937,
 8½ x 11¼" 150.00
Dick Tracy camera, Seymore
 Products Co., Chicago, Ill., 5" l.,
 2¾" h. 29.00
Dick Tracy card game, in box, Whit-
 man, 1934 . . . . 20.00
Dick Tracy game, "The Master De-
 tective," 1961 . . . . 55.00
Dick Tracy lunch box, 1967 . . . . 26.00
Dick Tracy movie poster, "Tracy vs.
 Crime," 1930's 75.00
Dick Tracy movie poster, "Tracy vs.
 Phantom Empire" 25.00
Dick Tracy pocket knife, 1940's 40.00

Dick Tracy Friction Squad Car

Dick Tracy toy, "Squad Car No. 1,"
 lithographed tin, friction drive,
 green, Marx, ca. 1949, 6½" l.
 (ILLUS.) 74.00
Dick Tracy wallet, "Crimestoppers,"
 ca. 1950's 7.50
Dick Tracy wrist radio, 1940's 32.00
Dionne Quintuplets blotter, 1935 . . . . 12.00
Dionne Quintuplets book, "Pictorial
 Story of the Dionne Quintuplets,"
 Whitman, 1935 . . . . 22.50
Dionne Quintuplets book, "We're
 Two Years Old," Whitman Publish-
 ing Co., 1936 . . . . 20.00
Dionne Quintuplets calendar, 1936 . . 17.00
Dionne Quintuplets calendar, 1939,
 "This Year They Are Five,"
 11 x 16" 24.00
Dionne Quintuplets calendar, 1941,
 "All Dressed Up," mint, small
 size 22.50
Dionne Quintuplets calendar, 1954,
 "Landing Party," mint, small
 size 22.50
Dionne Quintuplets cereal bowl,
 chrome-plated, 6" d. 25.00
Dionne Quintuplets magazine birth-
 day cover, "Liberty," 1936 . . . . 18.00
Dionne Quintuplets paper dolls, cut
 but mint, Merrill No. 3488, 1935 . . 40.00
Dionne Quintuplets program, thea-

tre owner's promotional for "The
 Country Doctor," 1936 . . . . 20.00
Dragnet (TV) water pistol,
 Knickerbocker 10.00
Dragnet whistle 5.00
Dukes of Hazard (TV) lunch box,
 1980 . . . . 8.00
Ed Wynn (fire chief) figure, wood-
 jointed 65.00
Elvis Presley belt, gold-colored
 metal "Russian Double Eagle" belt
 intricately meshed w/two eagle
 head fasteners 4,776.20
Elvis Presley book, "My Life With El-
 vis," Book Club Edition, Becky
 Yancey 10.00
Elvis Presley clutch purse, 1956 . . . . . 35.00
Elvis Presley necklace, heart on
 chain, dated 1956 . . . . 45.00
Elvis Presley record album, "Moody
 Blue, The Blue Album," in
 jacket 20.00
Elvis Presley stage suit, white, one-
 piece decorated w/'shooting star'
 in gilt studs, complete w/match-
 ing cape, worn at 1972 Madison
 Square Garden concert, w/letter
 of authenticity 47,762.00
Felix the Cat bell, brass, figural
 handle shows Felix pacing
 w/hands behind back, 2½" d.,
 4¾" h. 75.00
Felix the Cat clicker, lithographed
 tin, Germany, 1929 . . . . 25.00
Felix the Cat doll, mohair, w/ear
 button, Chad Valley, 14" (some
 wear) 195.00
Felix the Cat figure, wood-jointed
 w/leather ears, marked "Pat Sullivan Pat. June 23, 1925," Schoen-
 hut, 8½" h. 232.00
Felix the Cat ginger ale bottle 55.00
Felix the Cat toy, pull-type, "Speedy
 Felix," Felix in a roadster, painted
 wood, red car w/black highlights,
 yellow wheels, Geo. Borgfeldt,
 late 1920's, 11¾" l. 650.00
Flash Gordon paint book, Whitman
 Publishing, 1936, 96 pp. 85.00
Flash Gordon space outfit, jacket,
 cap, goggles, boot covers, cuffs &
 belt, manufactured by Esquire
 Novelty Co., 1952, w/original
 box 45.00
Flintstones (TV) glasses, Hanna-
 Barbera, 1962, set of 4 . . . . 25.00
Flintstones "Pebbles" bubble bath,
 boxed 20.00
Gabby Hayes fishing outfit, two
 poles & reels in circular tin con-
 tainer, colorful litho on container,
 complete, set 137.50
Gene Autry book, "Gene Autry &
 The Bad Men of Broken Bow" 22.50

Gene Autry cap pistol, repeating Jr. Model, three-shooter, cast iron, w/jeweled leather holster 60.00

Gene Autry hat band ribbon, red w/Western scene 6.00

Gene Autry lunch box & bullet-shaped thermos bottle, in original box 55.00

Gene Autry punch-outs, "Gene Autry's Melody Ranch," W/990-10, 1950 .... 90.00

Gene Autry song book No. 2, 1934 .... 25.00

Gene Autry writing tablet, unused, 1950's 20.00

George Jetson (TV) cel, George in room w/TV, matted 45.00

G-Men fingerprint set, in box, 1936 .... 25.00

The Goldbergs (TV) puzzle, in envelope 65.00

Happy Hooligan horse-drawn police wagon, cast iron, Kenton, 1911, 17½" l. 3,080.00

Harold Teen figure, bisque, Japan, 1932-38, 3¾" h. 37.50

Henry (cartoon character) cigarette cards, complete set of 50 .... 75.00

Herbie pinback button, Kellogg's Pep premium 6.00

Hopalong Cassidy alarm clock, U.S. Time, 1950 .... 250.00 to 350.00

Hopalong Cassidy book, "Hopalong Cassidy's Private War," 1911, 214 pgs. 15.00

Hopalong Cassidy card tray for canasta, saddle-shaped 125.00

Hopalong Cassidy cereal bowl, white china w/picture of Hoppy .. 31.00

Hopalong Cassidy coloring book, Abbott Publishing, 1950's, 11 x 15" 20.00

Hopalong Cassidy cowboy outfit, original box .... 80.00 to 100.00

Hopalong Cassidy horseshoe, "Good Luck," plastic w/paper display tab 10.00

Hopalong Cassidy lamp, wall-type, gun in holster, Alacite glass, Aladdin .... 130.00 to 150.00

Hopalong Cassidy Lunch Box & Thermos

Hopalong Cassidy lunch box w/ther-

mos bottle, Aladdin Industries, 1950 (ILLUS.) 35.00

Hopalong Cassidy magazine cover, "Life," June 12, 1950 .... 5.00

Hopalong Cassidy napkins in original package 15.00

Hopalong Cassidy pool float, Topper the Horse, inflatable rubber, 1950's 85.00

Hopalong Cassidy postcard, advertising "1942 Chrysler" 10.00

Hopalong Cassidy puzzle, color frame tray, inlay picture puzzle w/sleeve, 1950. .... 25.00

Hopalong Cassidy radio, red or black metal w/silver foil design on front, Arvin, 1948 .... 200.00 to 275.00

Hopalong Cassidy tumbler, milk white glass 20.00

Hopalong Cassidy wrist watch, picture of Hoppy on face, black strap, die-bossed "Good Luck from Hoppy," U.S. Time, 1950-67 ....60.00 to 85.00

Howdy Doody barrettes 7.00

Howdy Doody camera, on original cardboard 35.00

Howdy Doody doll, molded plastic face & hands, cloth body, wearing denim pants, plaid shirt & yellow flowered scarf, marked on back of head, "Eegee Co. - National Broadcasting Co.," 20" l. 110.00

Howdy Doody postcard, photo of Howdy Doody, w/Buffalo Bob's autograph 30.00

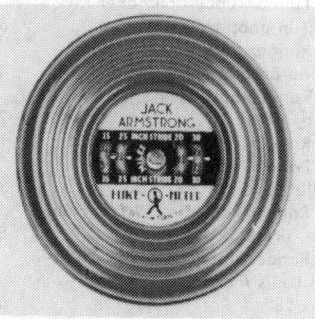

Jack Armstrong Hike-o-Meter

Jack Armstrong pedometer, "Hike-o-Meter," 2¾" d. (ILLUS.) 18.00

Jackie Coogan pencil box, tin, 2 x 7¾" (ILLUS. top next page) 34.00

Jackie Gleason (Honeymooners) pinback button, Bus Driver 25.00

James Bond gun set, w/pistol, holster, silencer, exploding pen & I.D. wallet, boxed 42.00

Jiggs ashtray w/wood cutout, 1930's, 6" h. 120.00

Joe Palooka lunch box, 1948 ....60.00 to 75.00

Jackie Coogan Pencil Box

Krazy Kat film, "Family Affair,"
   boxed, Keystone, 8mm 25.00
Li'l Abner coloring book, 1947 . . . . . .   25.00
Li'l Abner greeting cards, pack of 15
   assorted cards w/envelopes (in-
   cludes Schmoo card), 1950's 25.00
Lillums (of Harold Teen) figure,
   bisque, Japan, ca. 1932-38,
   3¾" h. 20.00
Little Annie Rooney paint book,
   large, ca. 1935 . . . .   55.00
Little King pocket watch & wrist
   watch, pr. 275.00
Little King toy, pull-type, wood, Jar
   Mar Co., 1939, mint in box,
   3½" h. 145.00
Little Lulu & Tubby dollmaker kits,
   mint in unopened boxes, pr. 35.00
Lone Ranger badge, star-shaped,
   "Bond Bread Safety Club," 1938 . . .   40.00
Lone Ranger belt buckle, flasher-
   type, 1976 . . . .   25.00
Lone Ranger coloring book, 1951 . . .   19.00
Lone Ranger compass, silver
   bullet 39.50
Lone Ranger costume, 1940's, child
   size, original box 80.00
Lone Ranger dart board, tin, color-
   ful, Louis Marx & Co., 1938,
   16 x 28" 50.00
Lone Ranger "First Aid" kit, tin,
   manufactured by The American
   White Cross Labs, Inc., dated
   1938, w/contents, 4 x 4" 42.50
Lone Ranger flashlight-ring, com-
   plete in box, w/instruc-
   tions . . . . .150.00 to 175.00
Lone Ranger game, "Ring Toss,"
   Rosebud Art Co., 1946, original
   box 37.50
Lone Ranger game, "Target," tin,
   Louis Marx & Co., 1938, w/stand,
   16 x 27" 85.00
Lone Ranger guitar, 1940's 75.00
Lone Ranger hair brush, wood

w/color decal of the Lone Ranger
   on Silver, original box, 1939 . . . . . .   15.00
Lone Ranger lunch box w/thermos
   bottle 15.00
Lone Ranger movie viewer, w/film,
   1955 . . . .   20.00
Lone Ranger pedometer, 1943, Kix
   Cereal premium 22.50
Lone Ranger pencil pouch, 1959 . . . .   20.00
Lone Ranger phonograph records,
   "Adventures of Lone Ranger Rec-
   ord Series," 78 r.p.m., records
   1-5, set of 5 . . . .   65.00
Lone Ranger photograph, Merita
   Bread premium, in mailer 100.00
Lone Ranger pocket knife, red
   w/picture, slogans & three-
   dimensional silver bullet 42.00
Lone Ranger rocking horse,
   1938 . . . . .375.00 to 425.00
Lone Ranger sheet music, "Hi-Yo Sil-
   ver," Chappell Music Co., 1938
   copyright 35.00
Lone Ranger target, tin, 9½" sq.,
   1938 . . . .   40.00
Lone Ranger tattoos, Philadelphia
   Gum premium, set of 4 . . . .   6.00
Lone Ranger toothbrush holder, dat-
   ed 1938 . . . .   50.00
Lone Ranger toy set, "Action,"
   Hubley 30.00
Lone Ranger wrist watch, New
   Haven, 1939 . . . .   100.00
Lord Plushbottom nodding figure,
   bisque, marked "Germany,"
   3½" h. 100.00
Maggie & Jiggs book, "Bringing Up
   Father, The Big Book," published
   by Cupples & Leon, 1926, w/dust
   jacket 45.00
Man from U.N.C.L.E. board game,
   original box 30.00
Man from U.N.C.L.E. coloring book,
   1967 . . . .   15.00
Man from U.N.C.L.E. license plate,
   metal, Louis Marx, 1967, original
   packet, 2¼ x 4" 8.00
Man from U.N.C.L.E. toy car, blue,
   Corgi, ca. 1966 . . . .   100.00
Margaret O'Brien paint book, 1947 . .   38.00
Midge (Barbie's best friend) jigsaw
   puzzle, 1963, original box,
   100 pcs. 15.00
Mighty Mouse cape, rubber &
   cloth 25.00
Mighty Mouse "Skill Ballgame," mint
   in box 70.00
Monkees doll, Davy Jones, 1970 . . . .   20.00
Monkees playing cards, full deck . . .   25.00
Monkees record album, "Meet the
   Monkees" 25.00
Monkees toy car, Corgi Mobile, cast
   iron, 1968 . . . .   85.00
Moon Mullins cane head, porcelain,
   Japan, 2" h. (ILLUS.) 30.00

Moon Mullins Cane Head

Moon Mullins nodder on ashtray,
bisque, Germany, 3½" 125.00
Moon Mullins "Police Patrol" funny
car, Tootsietoy 225.00
Moon Mullins postcard 12.00
Moon Mullins & Kayo toothbrush
holder, bisque, 4" h. 70.00
Mortimer Snerd puppet, cardboard,
18" h. 55.00
Mr. Magoo jigsaw puzzle, complete
in box 15.00
Muhammad Ali & Howard Cosell
boxing puppets, pr. 30.00
Mutt (Mutt & Jeff) smoking stand,
wooden figure of Mutt holding
tray, bright colors 285.00
Olive Oyl toy, rubber figure
w/squeaker, Rempel, 1950's,
original box 120.00
Orphan Annie decoder, 1935, Ovaltine premium, w/Secret Society
manual 40.00
Orphan Annie decoder, 1936, Ovaltine premium, w/Secret Society
manual & order form for Silver
Star ring, mint in
envelope .... 95.00 to 110.00
Orphan Annie dishes: cup, saucer &
sugar bowl; Lustreware, 1930's,
3 pcs. 80.00
Orphan Annie figure, bisque, Japan,
1932-38, 3¼" h. 38.00
Orphan Annie "hingee," paper assembly toy by King, Larson,
McMahon of Chicago, Illinois,
1944 .... 24.00
Orphan Annie marble, clear glass
w/bust portrait of character
w/"Annie" below, ½" d. 40.00
Orphan Annie mug, creamware pottery, w/decal picture of Annie &
Sandy, Ovaltine premium, signed
Harold Gray 43.50
Orphan Annie "Penny" books, in
original holder, miniature, mint
condition, 1934, set of 6 .... 95.00

Orphan Annie ring, Ovaltine
premium 35.00
Orphan Annie "Secret Ring"
pamphlet 25.00

Orphan Annie Song Book

Orphan Annie's Song Book, Ovaltine
premium, 1931 (ILLUS.) 10.00
Orphan Annie toy electric stove,
green & tan w/good decals,
w/three pots, 8½ x 9½" 65.00
Orphan Annie "Treasure Isle" game
board 45.00
Orphan Annie wrist watch, original
red leather band, New Haven,
ca. 1935, mint in original
box ....225.00 to 250.00
Our Gang brochure, advertising
"Chicago Roller Skates," 1933 .... 50.00
Our Gang coloring book, "photo-
graphic," 1933 .... 40.00
Paul McCartney Yamaha FG-110
acoustic guitar w/nylon strings,
contained in fur-lined carrying
case, ca. late 1960's, w/letter of
authenticity 4,408.80
Perry Winkle nodder, bisque,
Germany 150.00
Perry Winkle pinback button, Pep
Cereal premium 6.00
Pinky Lee puzzles, set of four differ-
ent in box, complete, 1955 ...... 70.00
Popeye bank, ceramic 150.00
Popeye bank, chalkware 65.00
Popeye "Bif-Bat," wood, 1930's 35.00
Popeye book, pop-up type, "Hag of
the Seven Seas," 1935 (pop-ups in-
complete) 50.00
Popeye bowl & plate, Melmac,
1950's, 2 pcs. 22.00
Popeye boxing gloves, child size,
Everlast, 1950's, in original store
package 95.00
Popeye candy holder, Pez 12.00
Popeye doll w/real corncob pipe,
wooden stand, 34" 225.00
Popeye figure, cardboard, full color
lithographed figure jointed for

dancing, marked "Make Your Own," Sweden, 1950's 25.00

Popeye figure, composition, standing figure w/spring-mounted arms, early 1930's, 4½" h. 88.00

Popeye "Foto-Fun Kit," 1958, original box 18.00

Popeye game, "Popeye the Juggler" bead game, glass covered, 1929 copyright, 3½ x 5" 55.00

Popeye game, "Roly Poly Target," lithographed, 1958, original package 70.00

Popeye jigsaw puzzle, 1932 .... 35.00

Popeye lantern, tin & glass, battery-operated, Line Mar Toys, 1950's, original box 175.00

Popeye light bulb, figure within globe, Aerolux, 1930's 195.00

Popeye marbles, Akro Agate, 1930's, in illustrated box 100.00

Popeye modeling clay, 1936, original box 30.00

Popeye movie, "Popeye Seeing Stars," by K.F.S., 1935, in 2 x 2" box w/overall Betty Boop & Popeye decoration in color 38.00

Popeye phonograph record, 45 r.p.m., ca. 1964, in original graphic jacket 5.00

Popeye pocket watch, original box (missing second hand) 475.00

Popeye premium cards, candy product, full color, England, 1930's, each set 85.00

Popeye punching bag, inflatable-type, original box 45.00

Popeye ring, Post Toasties premium 20.00

Popeye soap, "Bath Ball," original box 55.00

Popeye tie clasp, metal, enameled character 37.50

Popeye toy, sand toy seesaw, lithographed tin 225.00

Popeye Wrist Watch

Popeye toy, windup tin, Popeye carrying parrot cages, Marx, 1935 ... 250.00

Popeye tumblers, 1929, set of 4 .... 125.00

Popeye Valentine card, 1929 .... 30.00

Popeye wallpaper roll, 1940, 10 ft. roll 125.00

Popeye wrist watch, New Haven, 1935 (ILLUS.) 350.00

Popeye & Olive Oyl movie cel, both characters on beach 175.00

Popeye & Olive Oyl toy, windup tin roof dancers, Marx, 1936, overall 9½" h. 675.00

Popeye, Olive Oyl & Wimpy soap figures, original lithographed box, 1930's, set of 3 ....110.00 to 140.00

Popeye, Wimpy & Jeep pinback buttons, lithographed tin, 1936, set of 3 .... 30.00

Popeye & Wimpy "Walk-A-Way," Marx, 1964, mint in box 125.00

Popeye Thimble Theatre, original box forms stage, together w/composition figures of Popeye, Olive Oyl & Wimpy, 5" to 6" h. (two short tears in box) 575.00

Punch & Judy cap gun, animated ... 950.00

Raggedy Ann & Andy night light radio 35.00

Red Ranger gun w/holster 25.00

Red Ryder paint book, 1941 .... 25.00

Red Ryder "Penny" book, Whitman Publishing Co., late 1930's, 32 pp., 2½ x 3½" 15.00

Red Ryder Picture Record 22.00

Rin Tin Tin toy, stuffed body, rubber head, Ideal, 20" l. 60.00

Rin Tin Tin & Rusty necktie, child's, colorful 28.50

Robin (Batman series) doll, rubber, Mego, 1973, 5" 22.00

Robin Hood (TV Series) hat, leather 16.00

Rocky Graziano boxing gloves, child size, pr. 19.00

Rocky Jones Space Ranger badge ... 35.00

Roy Rogers belt, leather, w/tag 45.00

Roy Rogers book, "Roy Rogers & Cowboy Toby," Little Golden Book 10.00

Roy Rogers book, "Roy Rogers & the Ghost of Mystery Rancho," inscribed "To My Little Partner Glennie, from Roy," very good condition, Whitman, 1950, w/dust jacket 65.00

Roy Rogers chaps, plastic 30.00

Roy Rogers coloring book, 1951 ..... 7.50

Roy Rogers cowboy boots 75.00

Roy Rogers game, "Horseshoe Set," two tin targets w/sticks & four vinyl horseshoes, Ohio Art Co., 7¼ x 14" box (ILLUS.) 65.00

Roy Rogers Horseshoe Set

Roy Rogers guitar, hard cardboard ..	75.00
Roy Rogers gum card album	75.00
Roy Rogers gun, Derringer, on original card	85.00
Roy Rogers gun, Tuck-A-Way gun, on original card	25.00
Roy Rogers jigsaw puzzle, dated 1950	14.00
Roy Rogers lunch box, "Chow Wagon"	38.00
Roy Rogers magazine cover, "Life," July 12, 1943...................	5.00
Roy Rogers movie poster, "Twilight in the Sierras," autographed, 1950, 27 x 41"..............	65.00
Roy Rogers mug, figural, plastic	14.00
Roy Rogers paint set	90.00
Roy Rogers photograph, premium, early 1940's, in original envelope	75.00
Roy Rogers pinback button, black & white picture on yellow ground, 1¾" d.......................	9.00
Roy Rogers pinback button, "Happy Trails," large	4.00
Roy Rogers record album, "Pecos Bill," 1949	32.50
Roy Rogers record album, "Roy Rogers Rodeo"	32.50
Roy Rogers records, 78 r.p.m., "Make Believe Cowboy," "Yellow Rose of Texas," "Blue Shadows On the Trail," "Along the Navajo Trail," each....................	8.00
Roy Rogers "Riders Lucky Piece," metal	8.00
Roy Rogers ring, sterling silver, w/saddle.....................	57.50
Roy Rogers rodeo program, 1948 ...	36.00
Roy Rogers slippers, children's, felt, pr.............................	45.00
Roy Rogers thermos bottle, "Double R Bar Ranch" ....19.00 to	25.00
Roy Rogers toy, windup tin wagon train, Marx, mint in box	285.00
Roy Rogers toy, windup tin "Zig Zag Stagecoach"	145.00
Roy Rogers toy set, "Magic	

Playaround," original box ....150.00 to	200.00
Roy Rogers & Gabby Hayes record album, "Lore of the West"	30.00
Roy Rogers & Trigger View-Master reel..........................	4.00
Sandy (Orphan Annie's dog) figure, bisque, Japan, 1932-38, 1½" h....	18.00
Sandy figure, wood, jointed, 3½"...	45.00
Schmoo, club buttons, lithographed metal, "Sealtest," two different pictures, each...................	9.00
Schmoo salt & pepper shakers, pr...	65.00
Shadow (The) Bagatelle Game, original package, The Conde Nast Publications, Inc., 1976, 6 x 11¼"......................	32.50
Shadow (The) ring, glow-in-the-dark w/"Blue Coal" jewel on white ring, Blue Coal Company, mid-1930's	275.00
Shirley Temple book, "Shirley Temple in Wee Willie Winkie," story & black & white photos from the 20th Century-Fox movie, Saalfield, 1937, 28 pps., 9½ x 10"	62.50
Shirley Temple mug, cobalt blue glass w/decal portrait of Shirley ..	40.00
Shirley Temple pitcher, cobalt blue glass w/decal portrait of Shirley ..	35.00
Shirley Temple plate, ceramic, "Baby Take A Bow," first edition, mint in box	45.00
Shirley Temple Playhouse, in lithographed box, contents complete, 1935	135.00
Shirley Temple postcard, photograph, black & white	12.00
Shirley Temple sheet music, "The Toy Trumpet" from Rebecca of Sunnybrook Farm	20.00
Shirley Temple theatre sign, stiff cardboard cut-out head & shoulders of Shirley Temple, obverse & reverse, to be hung from theatre lobby ceiling, 1930's, 12 x 16"	150.00
Skeezix figure, nodding, bisque, Germany	70.00
Skeezix & Uncle Walt cartoon book, King Features Syndicate, 1924, hardcover, 7½ x 9½"	40.00
Skippy handkerchief, 1930's	35.00
Skippy toothbrush holder, bisque, movable arms, 5¾" h...........	67.00
Sky King decoder ring, w/magnifier & tiny pen, 1940's	30.00

Sky King's Spy-Detecto Writer

Sky King Spy-Detecto Writer,
w/instructions & mailer (ILLUS.
previous page) 57.00
Smiley Burnett Club membership
card, pledge card & news maga-
zine, 1940, set 65.00
Smitty dinner service, porcelain,
colorful, Germany, 1930's, com-
plete service for 6 . . . . 475.00
Smitty nodder, bisque, marked
"Germany," 4" 55.00
Smitty pinback button, Kellogg's
"Pep" cereal premium 9.00
Smokey the Bear mug, ceramic 15.00
Smokey the Bear pencil sharpener,
figural 25.00
Smokey the Bear salt & pepper
shakers, ceramic, pr. 35.00
Snoopy alarm clock, tennis racket
hands, mint in box, 1958 . . . . 48.00
Snoopy game, "Pound-A-Ball," color-
ful box 20.00
Snoopy lunchbox, dome lid 50.00
Snoopy wrist watch, tennis ball goes
around for second hand, arm
w/racket for minute hand, other
arm for hour hand, 1958 . . . . 25.00
Sonja Henie book, "Wings On My
Feet," 1940 . . . . 55.00
Space Patrol Diplomatic Pouch,
complete 375.00
Space Patrol pistol, dart-type,
w/box 350.00
Space Patrol ring, "Hydrogen Ray
Gun" 145.00
Spider-Man ring, mint on original
"Super Heroes" display card 10.00
Star Trek game, Super Phaser II Tar-
get game, Mego, Paramount Pic-
tures, unused in original box,
1976 . . . . 45.00
Steve Canyon helmet, w/box 75.00
Superman bank, dime register,
1940's 88.00
Superman belt & buckle, embossed
leather, 1940's 60.00
Superman game, "Superman Speed
Game" 95.00
Superman "Krypto Raygun Pocket
Projector," blued steel pistol
featuring a raised flying Super-
man w/outstretched arm pointing,
for showing 16mm films, w/origi-
nal box w/16mm film, Daisy,
6¾" l 528.00
Superman yo-yo, mint in box,
Duncan 10.00
Tarzan, Numa & Akut, the Ape,
masks, colorfully lithographed pa-
per, unused, Northern Paper
Mills, 1933, set of 3 . . . . 150.00
Terry & the Pirates ring, "Gold
Ore" 95.00

Three Stooges ring, flasher type,
shows all three 40.00
Tom Corbett, Space Cadet, machine
gun, Marx 30.00
Tom Corbett, Space Cadet, outfit,
child's size 225.00
Tom Corbett, Space Cadet, wrist
watch, original cardboard rocket-
ship display card, Ingraham,
1951 . . . . 225.00 to 275.00
Tom Mix compass & magnifier,
brass, Ralston radio premium,
1940 . . . . 41.50
Tom Mix cowboy boots, child's size,
unused in original box 225.00

Tom Mix Pocket Watch

Tom Mix pocket watch, dial featur-
ing Tom on his horse swinging a
lariat, the sweep dial featuring a
longhorn steer, back inscribed
"Always find Time for a good deed
- Tom Mix," w/horseshoe fob,
Ingersoll, 1930's, w/original box
(ILLUS.) 1,980.00
Tom Mix wrist watch, dial featuring
Tom, lasso in hand, on his horse,
longhorn steer on subsidiary dial,
band formed of steel "buckle" links
w/a portrait of Tom on top link,
Ingersoll, ca. 1933 . . . . 1,100.00
Tom Sawyer painting set, colorful
lithography on box shows Tom &
Huck in woods, Paramount Pic-
tures, 1931 . . . . 69.00
Tonto photograph, Merita Bread
premium, in mailer w/letter 100.00
Tonto soap figure, dated 1939, near
mint in box 40.00
Trigger (Roy Rogers' horse) bank,
lithographed tin 55.00
Uncle Wiggily book set, eight linen-
like books in original box, 1939 . . 65.00
Uncle Willie & Emma toothbrush
holder, bisque, 1930's, 3¾" h. 115.00
Vitamin Flintheart pinback button,
Kellogg's "Pep" cereal premium . . 8.00
Wild Bill Hickok lunchbox w/ther-
mos, ca. 1955 . . . . 35.00
Wild Bill Hickok money clip badge,
mint on card 25.00
Wild, Wild West lunchbox, 1969 . . . . 40.00
Will Rogers bust paperweight,
bronze finish, metal, 1940's 35.00

Wimpy puppet, hand-type 15.00

Woody Woodpecker book, movie-flip corners, Grape Nuts premium No. 8 .... 6.50

Woody Woodpecker halloween costume, w/cotton gauze face mask, in original box, Collegeville Costumes...................... 35.00

Wyatt Earp cap guns & holsters, cast metal w/plastic grip, each gun marked "Coyote," in box w/picture of Hugh O'Brian, Buntline by Hubley, 1950-60, each 8", the set 60.00

Yogi Bear teaspoon, silver plate 15.00

Yosemite Sam salt & pepper shakers, Warner Bros., pr. 85.00

CHILDREN'S BOOKS

"The Story of Happy Bunny"

The most collectible children's books today tend to be those printed after the 1850's and, while age is not completely irrelevant, illustrations play a far more important role in determining the values. While first editions are highly esteemed, it is the beautifully illustrated books that most collectors seek. The following books, all in good to fine condition, are listed alphabetically.

"ABC Book," Saalfield Publishing Co., No. 2449, 1943 .... $12.00

"ABC of Nursery Rhymes," by Gordon Robinson, 1928, linen 50.00

"A Child's Garden of Verses," by Robert Louis Stevenson, illustrated by Frances Brundage, Saalfield Publishing, 1925............... 25.00

"Alice's Adventures In Wonderland," by Lewis Carroll, illustrated by John Tenniel, published by M.A. Donohue, Chicago 70.00

"Andersen's Fairy Tales," by Hans Christian Andersen, Frances

Brundage cover, Saalfield Publishing, 1922 .... 20.00

"A Visit From St. Nicholas & Other Christmas Stories," 14 full-page unsigned Frances Brundage Santas, toys & dolls, published by McLoughlin Bros., 1901, 7 x 9".... 45.00

"Belinda Blue," by Esther Wood, illustrated by Theresa Kalab, published by Longmons Green & Co., lithographed in USA by Duenewald Printing, 1940, first edition, 7½ x 10¼" 35.00

"Bird Children," illustrated by Ross, 85 full color illustrations, children's faces on birds, 1912 .... 45.00

"Black Beauty," by Anna Sewell, illustrated, Appleton Co., 1935 .... 12.00

"Country Friends," McLoughlin Bros., 1902, animals on cover, paperback, 7 x 9" 10.00

"Digger The Badger Decides to Stay," by Thornton W. Burgess, 1927 .... 50.00

"Don Winslow," Whitman Penny Book, late 1930's, 32 pp., 2½ x 3½" 15.00

"Fairy Tales," by Hans Christian Andersen, nine color plates by Arthur Szyk, New York, 1945 .... 15.00

"Ghost Stories," by Russell Wakefield, London, 1932, w/dust jacket 12.00

"Green Eggs and Ham," by Dr. Seuss, 1960 .... 10.00

"Hans Brinker; or, The Silver Skates," by Mary Mapes Dodge, frontispiece by Frances Brundage, Saalfield Publishing, 1925 .... 55.00

"Heidi," by Johanna Spyri, illustrated by Jessie Willcox Smith, ten pages in full color, 1922 ...... 55.00

"Heidi," by Johanna Spyri, movie edition w/Shirley Temple, Saalfield Publishing, 1940 .... 35.00

"Jack Pumpkinhead and the Sawhorse of Oz," by L. Frank Baum, illustrated by John R. Neill, published by McNally, 1939 .... 30.00

"King of the Royal Mounted," Whitman Penny Book, late 1930's, 32 pp., 2½ x 3½" 15.00

"Little Black Sambo," published by Whitman, 1959 .... 19.50

"Little Black Sambo - Peter Rabbit Paint Book," 1941, large 38.50

"Little Brown Koko," by Hunt, Chicago, 1940, first edition, w/dust jacket 20.00

"Little Child's Home ABC Book," color illustrations, McLoughlin Bros., 1886, linen cover 30.00

"Little Lord Fauntleroy," by Frances Hodgson Burnett, illustrated by

Reginald B. Birch, published by
Scribner's, 1892 .... 20.00
"Little Women," by Louisa May Al-
cott, published by Little, Brown,
1915 .... 15.00
"Mary Poppins & Mary Comes Back,"
by P.L. Travers, illustrated by
Mary Shepard, 17 color illustra-
tions, 1937..................... 25.00
"Now We Are Six," by A.A. Milne,
illustrated by Ernest Shepard,
1955 .... 7.50
"Palette Painting Book," nine excel-
lent color illustrations, McLoughlin
Bros., 1892, some crayoning...... 40.00
"Picture Sounding Rhymes," illustrat-
ed by Winship, published by Whit-
man, 1942, 16 pp., 9½ x 13" 6.50
"Queen Zixi of Ix," by L. Frank
Baum, illustrations by Frederick
Richardson, 1905, hardbound 40.00
"Raggedy Ann & the Laughing
Brook," by Johnny Gruelle, pub-
lished by McLoughin Bros. 12.00
"Robinson Crusoe," by Daniel Defoe,
illustrated by N.C. Wyeth, 1920 ... 35.00
"Rudolph, the Red-Nosed Reindeer,"
by Robert May, 1939, written for
Montgomery Wards.............. 17.50
"The Adventures of Reddy Fox," by
Thornton Burgess, illustrated by
Harrison Cady, 1913 .... 12.00
"The Children of Dickens," illustrat-
ed by Jessie Willcox Smith, 1925,
w/dust jacket 45.00
"The Enchanted Island of Yew," by
L. Frank Baum, illustrated by
Cory, 1903.................... 55.00
"The Road to Oz," by L. Frank
Baum, illustrated by John R. Neill,
published by McNally, 1939 ...... 25.00
"The Story of Happy Bunny and Oth-
er Stories," illustrated, Whitman
Publishing Co., 1923 (ILLUS.) 7.00
"The Tale of Pigling Bland," by
Beatrix Potter, color illustrations,
1941 .... 15.00

"Three Little Pigs"

"The White Cat," color illustrations
by E. MacKinstry, 1928, first
edition 35.00
"Three Little Pigs," illustrated,
Charles E. Graham & Co., New
York (ILLUS.).................. 7.00
"Tom Swift and His Electric Rifle," by
Victor Appleton, published by
Grosset & Dunlap, 1913, tan cover
w/dust jacket.................. 22.00
"Treasure Box of Children's Stories,"
Platt & Munk Co., 1922 .... 15.00
"Uncle Pogo's So-So Stories," by
Walt Kelly, 1953................ 13.00
"Uncle Wiggly & His Friends," by
Howard Garis, color illustrations,
Platt & Munk, 1939 .... 35.00
"When We Were Very Young," by
A.A. Milne, 1961 .... 7.50

CHILDREN'S DISHES

Oval Star Sugar Bowl

*During the reign of Queen Victoria, doll-
houses & accessories became more popular
and as the century progressed, there was
greater demand for toys which would subtly
train a little girl in the art of homemaking.
Also see DEPRESSION and PATTERN
GLASS.*

Bowl, individual berry, pressed
glass, Pattee Cross patt., clear ... $10.00
Bowl, master berry, Inverted Straw-
berry patt., clear............... 25.00
Bowl, cup & divided plate, pressed
glass, Nursery Rhyme patt.,
amber, 3 pcs................... 98.00
Butter dish, cov., pressed glass,
Colonial patt., Cambridge, clear .. 20.00
Butter dish, cov., pressed glass,
Doyle's 500 patt., amber 95.00
Butter dish, cov., pressed glass, Ha-
waiian Lei patt., Higbee mark,
clear......................... 32.50
Butter dish, cov., pressed glass, Lib-
erty Bell patt., clear 200.00

Butter dish, cov., pressed glass,
Nursery Rhyme patt., clear 80.00
Butter dish, cov., Sawtooth Band
No. 1225 (Plain Band) patt.,
Heisey, clear, engraved "Christ-
mas 1898" 165.00
Cake stand, pressed glass, Buttons
& Loops patt., clear 30.00
Cake stand, pressed glass, etched
rose & leaf spray around edge,
clear, 5" d., 3" h. 34.00
Coffee set: cov. coffeepot, pitcher &
two cups & saucers; graniteware,
grey, ca. 1900, 6 pcs. 495.00
Creamer, pressed glass, Alabama
patt., clear 30.00
Creamer, pressed glass, Chimo
patt., clear 22.50
Creamer, pressed glass, Daisy &
Button patt., clear 10.00
Creamer, pressed glass, Fernland
patt., cobalt blue 32.00
Creamer, pressed glass, Grapevine
with Ovals patt., clear 48.00
Creamer, pressed glass, Hobnail
w/Thumbprint Base patt.,
amber 40.00
Creamer, pressed glass, Menagerie
patt., lamb, clear 75.00
Creamer, pressed glass, Ribbed
Forget-Me-Not patt., clear 20.00
Creamer, pressed glass, Stippled
Diamond patt., clear 35.00
Creamer, pressed glass, Tappan
patt., clear 20.00
Creamer, pressed glass, Twin Snow-
shoe patt., clear 20.00
Creamer, pressed glass, Wild Rose
patt., milk white 60.00
Creamer & cov. sugar bowl, china,
square, Blue Willow patt., pr. 25.00
Creamer & open sugar bowl, china,
Lily of the Valley patt., R.S. Prus-
sia, pr. 195.00
Creamer & sugar bowl, pressed
glass, Rexford patt., clear, pr. 25.00
Cruet, pressed glass, Planet patt.,
clear 28.00
Cup & saucer, china, bears writing
on fence decoration 45.00
Cup & saucer, china, full-color scene
of "soldier" boy w/paper hat,
wooden sword, popgun & bugle
challenging Teddy bear,
Germany 25.00
Cup & saucer, pressed glass, Cat &
Dog patt., clear 50.00
Cup & saucer, pressed glass, Lion
patt., clear 55.00
Dinner set: 12 plates (two sizes),
three meat platters, two cov.
vegetable casseroles, gravy boat
& cov. tureen w/separate underplate; china, Teddy bear decora-

tion, Bishop & Stonier, England,
20 pcs. 490.00
Dutch oven, cast iron, Griswold
No. 0 . . . . 79.00
Mug, pressed glass, Bird & Harp
patt., clear 25.00
Mug, pressed glass, Drum patt.,
clear 26.00
Mug, pressed glass, Puritan patt.,
clear 25.00
Mug, pressed glass, Sheep patt.,
Iowa City Glass, clear 50.00
Pitcher, pressed glass, Galloway
patt., clear 25.00
Pitcher, pressed glass, Daisy Medal-
lion patt., clear, 3½" h. 35.00
Pitcher, pressed glass, Pattee Cross
patt., clear 38.00
Plate, china, floral rim, red transfer
"The Happy Children," Wedgwood
& Co., 5¾" d. 125.00
Punch bowl, pressed glass, Flat-
tened Diamond & Sunburst patt.,
clear 27.00
Punch bowl, pressed glass, Thumbe-
lina patt., clear 28.00
Punch cup, pressed glass, Nursery
Rhyme patt., milk white 22.50
Punch set: punch bowl & five cups;
pressed glass, Little Red Riding
Hood patt., milk white, 6 pcs. 145.00
Punch set: punch bowl & six cups;
pressed glass, Tulip & Honeycomb
patt., clear, 7 pcs. 75.00
Spooner, pressed glass, Amazon
patt., clear 25.00
Spooner, pressed glass, Chimo patt.,
clear 22.50
Spooner, pressed glass, Colonial
patt., Cambridge, cobalt blue 35.00
Spooner, pressed glass, Sweetheart
patt., clear 25.00
Spooner, pressed glass, Twist patt.,
opalescent white 100.00
Sugar bowl, cov., pressed glass, Lib-
erty Bell patt., clear 245.00
Sugar bowl, cov., pressed glass,
Menagerie patt., lamb, clear 200.00
Sugar bowl, cov., pressed glass,
Oval Star patt., clear (ILLUS.) 20.00
Sugar bowl, cov., open handle,
pressed glass, Star & Bar patt.,
blue 15.00
Sugar bowl, cov., pressed glass,
Wild Rose patt., milk white 65.00
Table set: cov. butter dish, spooner
& creamer; pressed glass, Oval
Star patt., clear, 3 pcs. 60.00
Table set: cov. butter dish, cov.
sugar bowl, creamer & spooner;
Chocolate glass, Sultan patt.,
4 pcs. 2,400.00
Table set, pressed glass, Aztec
patt., clear, 4 pcs. 65.00

Table set: small plate, mug & brush; sterling silver, acid-etched w/scenes & names of nursery rhymes, Matthews Co., Newark, New Jersey, 1907-30, plate 5½" d., 3 pcs. 247.50

Teapot, cov., china, Blue Willow patt., large 25.00

Tea set: cov. teapot, creamer & sugar bowl; china, figural Chinaman's face, bail handles, Japan, 3 pcs... 20.00

Tea set: cov. teapot, cov. sugar bowl, pitcher & four cups & saucers; pearlware, Peafowl patt., each bird painted in underglaze-blue, yellow & red plumage, perched in a branch w/sponged green foliage, Staffordshire, ca. 1820, 11 pcs. (repairs, minor damage) 825.00

Tea set: cov. teapot, creamer, sugar bowl & six cups & saucers; porcelain, white, France, early 1900's, 15 pcs. in original factory wood box w/old label intact 175.00

Tumbler, pressed glass, Oval Star patt., clear 10.00

Tureen, cov., china, Blue Willow patt. 35.00

Wash basin & pitcher, china, white w/gold trim, marked "K.T.K." (Knowles, Taylor & Knowles), East Liverpool, Ohio, the set 50.00

Water set: pitcher & four tumblers; pressed glass, Pattee Cross patt., clear, 5 pcs. 65.00

CHILDREN'S MUGS

"Humpty Dumpty" Mug

The small sized mugs used by children first attempting to drink from a cup appeal to many collectors. Because they were made of such diverse materials as china, glass, pottery, graniteware, plated silver and sterling silver, the collector can assemble a diversified collection or single out a particular type around which to base a collection. Also see

CHILDREN'S DISHES and PATTERN GLASS.

Blown glass, ruby, handled, w/gilt leaves & bow, says "For A Good Boy," 2¾" h. $45.00

China, "A present for my dear gi--," black transfer of girl & goat, canary ground, 2" h. (rim chip) 300.00

China, "For My Favorite," black transfer of child w/basket & dog, canary ground w/purple lustre trim, 2½" h. (small edge chips) .. 325.00

Coin silver, cylinder w/a die-rolled strap handle & die-rolled base, the sides w/two molded bands, engraved "W.Y.M." in script, Garrett Eoff, New York, New York, ca. 1836, 2¾" h. (minor damage to handle) 308.00

Coin silver, twelve-sided, scroll handle, Josiah Gooding, Boston, Massachusetts, ca. 1830, 3 1/8" h. (small repair to rim) 418.00

Ironstone china, copper Tea Leaf Lustre patt. 165.00

Pressed glass, Anchor patt., clear .. 45.00

Pressed glass, Baby Animals patt., clear 42.00

Pressed glass, Bird On A Branch patt., amber 54.00

Pressed glass, Butterfly patt., clear 35.00

Pressed glass, Fruits patt., amber .. 44.00

Pressed glass, Heron & Peacock patt., opalescent white 69.00

Pressed glass, Humpty Dumpty patt., clear (ILLUS.) 45.00

Pressed glass, Lincoln - Garfield patt., clear 125.00

Pressed glass, Little Miss Muffet patt., clear etched 22.00

Pressed glass, Pointing Dog patt., blue 64.00

Pressed glass, Robin patt., opaque black 54.00

Silver plate, repousse band of flowers, vertical ribbing at base w/row of beading at bottom edge, marked Gorham & Co...... 24.00

Staffordshire pottery, "Dr. Franklin's Poor Richard Illustrated," brown transfer, 2½" h. (base chips) 105.00

Staffordshire pottery, black transfer of animals, "Farm Yard," 2 5/8" h. (wear & minor rim flakes)........ 75.00

Staffordshire pottery, transfer of a boat on the ocean & florals, motto reads "Industry is Fortune's Handmaid" 135.00

Staffordshire pottery, hand-colored transfer w/a political theme shows French & English children in

a tug of war & reads "French &
English" 68.00
Staffordshire pottery, purple transfer of children playing, polychrome enameled trim, 2½" h.
(minor stains) 75.00
Sterling silver, cylindrical w/a
shaped scroll handle, on a flaring
foot rim, the sides decorated w/a
relief frieze of a children's parade, engraved near the rim
"Constance," the base w/inscrip-
tion & dated 1897, Tiffany & Company, New York, New York,
3½" h. 880.00
Sterling silver, flaring cylinder,
scroll handle, molded flaring
cylindrical foot, sides repousse &
chased w/houses & trees centering an inscription "G.F.H. from
Grandma," by George B. Sharp
for Bailey & Co., Philadelphia, ca.
1850, 4½" h. 275.00
Tin, Peter Rabbit scene colorfully
embossed 18.00

CHRISTMAS TREE LIGHTS

*Along with a host of other Christmas-
related items, early Christmas tree lights are
attracting a growing number of collectors.
Comic characters seem to be the most popular form among the wide variety of figural
lights available, most of which were manufactured between 1920 and World War II in Germany, Japan and the United States. Figural
bulbs listed are painted clear glass unless
otherwise noted.*

BULBS

Andy Gump, milk white, painted ... $45.00
Boy w/scarf 35.00
Dick Tracy, milk white, painted 45.00
Donald Duck, painted 35.00
Indian head, pink & orange,
1 7/8" l. 70.00
Japanese lantern, milk glass 18.00
Mickey Mouse, painted 35.00
Orphan Annie, milk white,
painted 45.00
Parrot, painted 10.00
Peacock, painted 20.00
Santa Claus holding bag, 3½" h. ... 18.00
Santa Claus, full figure in long coat,
bright polychrome paint, 4" h. 30.00
Santa Claus full figure, standard
base, 5½" h. 40.00
Santa Claus, full figure, milk white,
double-sided 30.00
Santa Claus atop chimney, milk
white 25.00

Watch, pocket-type, milk white 22.00
Zeppelin, milk white, painted 35.00

SETS
Bubble-type, string of seven lights .. 25.00
Diamond Brite Disney characters,
figural, mint in box 135.00
NOMA Disney characters, set of
fifteen standard series bulbs
w/plastic bell-shaped caps depicting Mickey Mouse, Minnie Mouse
& Donald Duck, the set 75.00
Paramount "Star-Lites," original box,
set of 10 .... 25.00

CHRISTMAS TREE ORNAMENTS

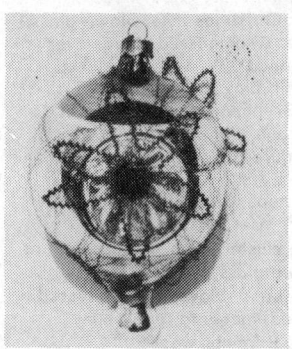

Celluloid Ball Ornament

*The German blown glass Christmas tree or-
naments and other commercially-made ornaments of wax, cardboard and cotton batting
were popular from the time they were first
offered for sale in the United States in the
1870's. Prior to that time, Christmas trees had
been decorated with homemade ornaments
that usually were edible. Now nostalgic collectors who seek out ornaments that sold for
pennies in stores across the country in the early years of this century are willing to pay
some rather hefty prices for unusual or early
ornaments.*

Angel, blown glass, w/gossamer
wings & dress $8.00
Angel, paper scrap on spun glass
half circle 40.00
Angel, tree-top type, die-cut paper
w/spun glass skirt 45.00
Baby Jesus on nest, 2" wax baby on
3" straw nest, France 52.00
Ball-type, celluloid, indented "starburst" & teardrop base, tinsel-
wrapped, Germany, pre-World
War II (ILLUS.) 12.50

Bear, blown glass, w/annealed
legs............................ 295.00
Bell, tinsel-wrapped 24.00
Berry, blown glass, large 15.00
Boxer dog, blown glass........... 58.00
Camel, Dresden-type cardboard 55.00
Clown head, blown glass, double-
faced head atop large ovoid ball,
silvered w/red, blue & black,
5½" h.......................... 95.00
Coffeepot, blown glass 10.00
Dog head, blown glass, gold, two-
faced 150.00
Eagle, Dresden-type cardboard,
spread-winged full-bodied bird,
6" w. 280.00
Elephant, blown glass oblong ball
w/embossed design of standing
circus animal, silver, red & gold,
3" l. 70.00
Father Christmas face, blown glass,
silver w/embossed leaves over
the head 180.00
Football, blown glass 95.00
Foxy Grandpa, blown glass, head
on cone 175.00
Girl figure, pressed cotton w/paper
face 135.00
Girl's head, blown glass, flowers in
hair, inset glass eyes 110.00
Grape cluster w/child's face & arms,
blown glass..................... 230.00
Indian head, blown glass, silvered
w/red, magenta, grey, etc.,
3½" l. (minor wear) 135.00
Jack-o-lantern, blown glass, figural
head w/large round eyes, nose &
toothy grin, deep red w/black &
white, 2½" l. (some wear) 105.00
Kugel, gold mercury-lined glass,
7½" d., ring for hanging 260.00
Kugel, green, 5" d. 55.00
Kugel, silver, 2¾" d. 15.00
Kugel, silver, 4" d. 45.00
Lion's head, blown glass, silvered .. 120.00
Mandolin, blown glass 25.00
Mickey Mouse, papier-mache w/glit-
ter on body 55.00
Mushroom, blown glass, spring
clip 10.00
Owl, blown glass, figural bird
w/long, straight spun glass tail,
silver, gold, red & black, 6" l.
overall 15.00
Parrot, Dresden-type cardboard,
full-bodied w/vibrant colors &
glass eyes, 6" h. 400.00
Policeman, blown glass, wearing
pointed helmet & carrying a billy
club, worn polychrome paint,
4¾" h.......................... 65.00
Rabbit, pressed cotton, blue, 4½" .. 22.00
Reindeer, Dresden-type cardboard,
full-bodied free-standing, glass
eyes, 8" h. 350.00

Sailboat, paper scrap on spun glass
half circle 40.00
Santa Claus, blown glass, figure in
red & pearly white holding gold
tree, 3¼" 30.00
Santa Claus, blown glass, figure
standing on rounded bell w/clap-
per, silvered w/blue, gold &
green, sanded trim & paper angel
head "scrap" on bell, 4½" h.
(minor wear) 55.00
Santa Claus, blown glass, figure
holding Christmas tree, silver,
blue & magenta, 4 5/8" l......... 60.00
Santa Claus in moon, blown glass
ball 55.00
Santa Claus on oak leaf, blown
glass........................... 45.00
Santa Claus on skis, celluloid, 4" ... 35.00
Scottie dog, blown glass, animal
figure in begging pose, silvered
w/red & white, 3¾" h. (minor
wear) 35.00
Sheep, wood, papier-mache &
fleece, Victorian, 4 x 4" 45.00
Shoe on wheels, blown glass....... 65.00
Slipper, lady's, low-heeled, Dresden-
type cardboard, worn platinum
finish, marked "Germany,"
3 5/8" l........................ 65.00
Snowman w/broom, blown glass ... 65.00
Strawberry, blown glass, 2"........ 14.00

Teddy Bear on Swing Ornament

Teddy bear on swing, wool bear
seated on wooden swing w/crin-
kled wire hanger (ILLUS.) 190.00
Truck, blown glass, oblong ball embossed w/side view of a large
truck, gold, silver & red, 2¾" l.
(minor wear) 85.00
Urn w/handles, blown glass, 2½" .. 6.50
Windmill, blown glass, 2½"........ 8.00

HALLMARK KEEPSAKE ORNAMENTS

Antique Toys, "Carrousel" series,
first edition, 1978 .... 300.00
Baby's First Christmas ball, 1979 .... 5.00

Bellswinger, "Bellringer" series, first
edition, 1979 .... 145.00

Birdhouse, "Ready for Christmas -
Handcrafted" ornaments, 1979 .... 45.00

Christmas Angel, "Holiday Highlights," 1979 .... 45.00

Christmas Heart, "Handcrafted" ornaments, 1979 .... 50.00

Dappled, "Rocking Horse" series,
first edition, 1981 .... 214.00

Della Robia Wreath, "Twirl-About"
collection, 1977 .... 90.00

Drummer Boy, "Adorable Adorn-
ments," 1975.................... 90.00

Drummer Boy, "Nostalgia" ornaments, 1975 .... 35.00

Holly & poinsettia "Love" ball,
1978 .... 25.00

Locomotive, "Nostalgia" ornaments,
1975 .... 50.00

Mouse in a thimble, "Thimble" series, first edition, 1978.......... 93.00

Peace on Earth, "Nostalgia" ornaments, 1975 .... 45.00

Praying Angel, "Little Trimmers" ornaments, 1978 .... 20.00

Reindeer Chimes, "Holiday Chimes,"
1978 .... 12.00

Rocking Horse, "Handcrafted" ornaments, 1978 .... 40.00

Santa's Here, "Handcrafted" ornaments, 1979 .... 50.00

Schneeberg bell, "Handcrafted" ornaments, 1978 .... 130.00

Snowman in snowflake, "Twirl-
About" collection, 1977 .... 40.00

Winnie-the-Pooh - Walt Disney ball,
1979 .... 20.00

CIGAR & CIGARETTE CASES, HOLDERS & LIGHTERS

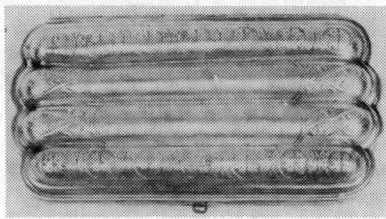

Silver Cigar Case

Cigar case, enameled silver-gilt,
oblong flattened form w/rounded
corners, enameled on both sides
w/multicolored scrolling foliage &
w/dragons, w/geometric borders,
the surround enameled turquoise
blue, the sides w/borders of white

beads, Ivan Saltykov, Moscow,
Russia, 1896, 5" l. $1,980.00

Cigar case, sterling silver, shaped
rectangular form w/four lobed di-
visions, the case engraved w/flo-
ral & scrollwork bands, maker's
mark "J.L.," Birmingham,
England, 1873, 5½" l. (ILLUS.) 357.50

Cigarette case, Bakelite, handshaped closure, France 155.00

Cigarette case, gold & enamel, rectangular, reeded overall & decorated w/blue enamel stripes, the
borders chased w/leaftips on a
matted ground, workmaster Henrik
Wigstrom, Faberge, St. Petersburg,
Russia, ca. 1910, 3½" l. 14,300.00

Cigarette case, sterling silver
w/"niello" decoration, cover decorated in niello w/sprays of leaves
& flowers, gilt interior inscribed
"1912," Tiffany & Co., France,
3 x 3½" 165.00

Cigarette lighter, advertising,
"Dodge Trucks," oil barrel
shape 30.00

Cigarette lighter, advertising, electric company, "Reddy Kilowatt"
logo on side, mint in box, Zippo,
1960 .... 10.00

Cigarette lighter, advertising, "Jack
Daniels," in original box 25.00

Cigarette lighter, advertising,
"Pepsi-Cola," modeled as a bottle
cap, 1960's 25.00

Cigarette lighter, advertising,
"RCA," Zippo 15.00

Cigarette lighter, advertising, "Sinclair Heating Oil," enameled
flame logo..................... 30.00

Cigarette lighter, 14k gold, Florentine finish, Cartier, 9 dwt. 175.00

Cigarette lighter, counter-type, advertising, black desk telephone
shape above tin & glass cabinet-
style base w/original paper label
instructions on back & five different advertisements under glass at
front, marked "Lite-o-phone," ca.
1938, 7¼ x 10 x 11"............. 80.00

CIGAR & TOBACCO CUTTERS

Silver Cigar Cutter

Both counter-type and individual cigar and plug tobacco cutters were in widespread use last century and earlier in this century. Some counter types were made in combination with lighters and vending machines and were used to promote various tobacco packaging companies.

Counter-type, brass, model of ship's wheel, 3" d., 7" base $95.00

Counter-type, cast iron, advertising, ornate nickel-plated side plates embossed "Peter C. Beck Co., Jobbers in Tobacco & Cigars, Racine, Wisc.," 9" h. 100.00

Counter-type, cast-iron, advertising, "Champagne 5c" 185.00

Counter-type, cast iron, advertising, "Five Bros. Tobacco Works, John Finzer & Bros., Louisville, Ky." 48.00

Counter-type, cast iron, advertising, "Que Placer Superior Quality Havana Cigar," shield-shaped plate w/lithographed scene of man smoking cigar & drinking wine above shaped base, made by The Brunhoff Manufacturing Co., Cincinnati, Ohio, ca. 1902 . . . 145.00

Counter-type, cast iron, advertising, "Peter Schuyer" 185.00

Counter-type, cast iron, model of horse head, reads "Black Beauty" 300.00

Counter-type, wood, wire & iron, mechanical, grooved woodblock w/spring operated cutting blade, 4 x 7" 39.00

Desk model, ivory boar's tusk, mounted w/sterling silver, 9" l. . . 175.00

Pocket-type, brass w/mother-of-pearl 35.00

Pocket-type, yellow gold, lion's heads & ruby eyes, fob-type 65.00

Pocket-type, silver, fob-type (ILLUS.) 25.00

CLOCKS

Animated, Lux Clock Company, Waterbury, Connecticut, figural Black Sambo head w/moving eyes & tie, early 20th c. $425.00

Banjo, unknown maker, Empire-style mahogany case, circular face w/black Roman numerals, over a flared throat, the shaped base w/eglomise panel in black & gilt w/the inscription "U.S. LIGHT HOUSE ESTABLISHMENT," w/pendulum & key, used in an American lighthouse, 26¾" h. 550.00

Bracket, Dan Delander, London, England, ebony & gilt-metal-mounted case, silvered dial w/matte center including pendulum & date apertures, adjustment & "Strike Not Strike" in the spandrels, seconds dial in the arch, engraved signed back plate, rectangular molded case pierced w/sound panels, two-train movement strikes four bells, 18th c., 17½" h. 6,600.00

Carriage, gilt-brass, w/silvered platform to cylinder escapement, plain balance, striking the hour & half hour on gong, white enamel dial w/Roman chapters, blued steel hands & subsidiary alarm disk, within a corniche case, 7" h. including handle 3,080.00

Rare Musical Grandfather Clock

Grandfather, Martin Cheney, Windsor, Vermont, Federal inlaid cherry case w/arched hood w/inlaid plinths & gilt urn & eagle finials joined by pierced fretwork above the arched cornice molding & inlaid door flanked by inlaid brass-mounted columns enclosing the floral-painted moonphase dial w/seconds & calendar indicators, inscribed "M. Cheney WINDSOR," & w/the titles of songs as played by the brass eight-day weight-driven movement & ten bells, molded tombstone door w/stringing, quarter fans & panels flanked by inlaid ovals & brass-mounted inlaid quarter columns, conforming inlaid base w/bracket feet, old refinish, ca. 1800, 105" h. (ILLUS.) 40,700.00

Grandfather, Samuel Foster, Amherst, New Hampshire, white-painted iron dial w/second indi-

cator, calendar aperture & moon
dial & signed "S. Foster, Amherst,
1798," inlaid mahogany hooded
Federal case, hood w/three reeded
plinths & brass ball finials joined
by pierced fretwork above arched
cornice molding, glazed door
w/stringing & quarter fan inlay
flanked by brass-mounted reeded
columns, molded tombstone waist
door w/stringing, quarter fan &
branch inlay flanked by brass-
mounted reeded quarter columns,
base w/stringing, quarter fan &
oval patera, ogee bracket feet,
refinished, 86" h. (feet
extended)....................15,400.00
Grandfather, Silas Hoadley, Plymouth, Connecticut, maple case,
arched cornice above glazed door
enclosing a painted wood movement flanked by free-standing
reeded columns above rectangular
door w/stringing flanked by
reeded quarter columns on cut-out
base, 81" h. (refinished, imperfections) 1,980.00
Grandfather, unknown maker, Massachusetts, Federal inlaid mahogany
case, arched hood w/pierced fretwork & three fluted plinths, arched
cornice molding & painted iron
moonphase dial w/seconds & calendar indicators, flanked by brass-
mounted stop-fluted columns, rectangular waist door w/inlaid stringing flanked by brass-mounted stop-
fluted quarter columns on inlaid
base, old finish, ca. 1790, 91" h.
(missing feet) 7,700.00
Lantern, brass, the movement
w/hour strike & anchor escapement, the dial engraved "Thomas
Moore," surmounted at the front &
sides w/pierced filigree panels,
raised on turned feet, England,
19th c., 14" h................1,045.00
Mirror, mahogany case w/flat pilasters at sides, brass rosettes at
corner blocks & scalloped crest,
white painted face w/Roman numerals covered by square reverse-
painted glass w/gilt, red & white
foliage w/brown ground (flaking)
over original rectangular mirror,
brass wheelbarrow movement in
clock w/weight & pendulum, inside
of door has list of persons who
repaired & cleaned the clock & the
date "1826," from New Hampshire,
32½" h. 4,100.00
Shelf, or mantel, Garner Curtis,
Connecticut, Empire style carved
mahogany & mahogany veneer

case, carved spread-winged eagle
crest flanked by square pilasters
above two-panel glass door w/top
panel over painted dial w/Arabic
numerals & floral sprigs in corners, door flanked by quarter-
round acanthus-carved pilasters
above claw-carved front feet,
wooden works, paper label reading "Clocks, made by Garner Curtis and sold by W. Adams,
Wolcottville, Conn.," w/weights &
pendulum, 29" h. (reverse-
painting in bottom door panel
replaced w/clear glass) 700.00

Louis XV Style Mantel Clock

Shelf, or mantel, Louis XV style,
maker unknown, ormolu & patinated bronze, drum case fitted
w/enamel chapters on the ormolu
dial surmounted by a figure of a
seated Chinaman holding a parasol, all supported on the back of
a patinated bronze trumpeting elephant on a foliate-molded *rocaille*
base, late 19th c., 19" h.
(ILLUS.) 3,520.00
Shelf, or mantel, dial inscribed "Ch.
Ludw. Powalky, a Neudienten-
dorff," pierced fretwork cornice
over a circular enameled dial
w/gilt tooled arms, stepped plinth
base, mahogany & ivory, Germa-
ny, ca. 1800, 16½" l., 18½" h. ... 660.00
Shelf, or mantel, maker unknown,
Mission-style (Arts & Crafts movement), oak, three-paneled arched
top above carved leaf & berry details & tooled metal round dial,
three triangular glass inserts at
base revealing berry-designed flat
pendulum, Europe, ca. 1900,
6" w., 12" h................... 550.00

Shelf, or mantel, Eli Terry & Sons,
Plymouth, Connecticut, Pillar &
Scroll mahogany case, glazed door
w/eglomise tablet enclosing
painted wooden dial & weight-

Terry Pillar & Scroll Clock

driven thirty hour wooden movement, ca. 1820, 29" h., some restoration (ILLUS.) 1,650.00

Tiffany "Pine Needle" Clock

Shelf, or mantel, Tiffany Studios,
New York, New York, Favrile
glass & bronze "Pine Needle" pattern case, rectangular body of
white-streaked green glass overlaid w/bronze filigree, raised on
rectangular bronze base, white
circular face w/Roman numerals,
impressed mark on case "TIFFANY
STUDIOS NEW YORK 879," dial
painted "TIFFANY & CO.,"
9 7/8" h. (ILLUS.) 2,420.00
Shelf, or mantel, Aaron Willard, Boston, Massachusetts, Case-on-Case,
mahogany case w/inlay, fretwork
steeple cornice w/three brass
finials above cabinet door
w/rounded arch glass panel over
white painted signed dial, stepped-
out lower case w/square design
formed by inlay, short French feet
at base w/shaped apron, brass
works, pendulum & weight, early
19th c., 36½" h. (replaced feet &
fretwork, added inlay, face
touched up) 4,600.00
Wag-on-wall, white-painted wooden
face w/polychrome floral design

around edge & on arched crest,
brass gears in wooden plates,
w/weights & replaced pendulum,
9½ x 13½"....................400.00
Wall, Marmaduke Storr, London,
England, brass dial engraved
w/Roman & Arabic numerals within
giltwood frame w/pierced & leafy
branches & C-scrolls, ca. 1750,
21" w., 31" h...................3,850.00
Wall regulator, "Grande Sonnerie,"
walnut case w/a shell & foliate
carved arched crest over fluted &
vasiform side columns w/foliated
capitals, the apron carved w/a
scrolling strapwork design, brass
dial & pendulum w/scrolling etched
design, Austria, late 19th c.,
4' 7" h........................1,430.00

CLOISONNE & RELATED WARES

*Cloisonne work features enameled designs
on a metal ground. There are several types
of this work, the best-known utilizing cells of
wire on the body of the object into which the
enamel is placed. In the plique-a-jour form of
cloisonne, the base is removed leaving translucent enamel windows. The champleve technique entails filling in, with enamels, a design
which is cast or carved in the base. "Pigeon
Blood" cloisonne includes a type where foil
is enclosed within colored enamel walls.
Cloisonne is said to have been invented by
the Chinese and brought to perfection by the
Japanese.*

CLOISONNE

Japanese Cloisonne Vase

Bowl, turned in rim, large dragon
on interior, full length dragon on
exterior w/flaming pearl, cloud
scroll ground on black, wave &
scroll borders, 8" d., 2½" h. $215.00
Box w/hinged lid, flowers & variegated green leaves against a dark
blue ground, four ball feet,

marked "China," 3 1/8 x 3 7/8",
1¼" h. 65.00

Box, cov., oval, decorated throughout w/a variety of flowers including peony & chrysanthemum in
predominantly pink, amethyst,
white & green against a light blue
ground, white metal interior, Japan, 3¾" l. 880.00

Incense burner, cov., compressed
globular body decorated w/front-
ed lotus amid multicolored tendrils on a turquoise ground below
a waisted neck & flat gilt metal
rim set w/two upright "U" shaped
handles, the pierced brass cover
w/a coiled dragon finial, China,
early 19th c., 6 1/8" h. (pitting,
losses) 440.00

Mirror, on swivel pedestal base
w/swivel mirror & an etched bird
& flower scene on mirror, China,
18" h. 375.00

Models of horse heads, each slightly
turned & fashioned w/an intense
expression heightened by large
eyes, open mouth & upraised ears
bracketing a stylized mane extending down the gracefully arched
neck, all executed in gilt-bronze
contrasting w/an overall multicolored enamel pattern of stylized
lotus blossoms amid scrolling leafy
tendrils on a turquoise blue ground,
China, 12¾" h., pr. (restorations,
wear) 1,320.00

Ojime (button slide), tubular form,
decorated w/a writhing dragon
contesting a flaming pearl, rendered in brown & red enamels,
Japan, 1 5/8" (some pitting)...... 192.50

Pilgrim flask, decorated in bright
enamels w/two roundels of blossoming peony, prunus & magnolia
set against a dense floral pattern
ground w/large *shou* medallions,
the slender neck w/stiff-leaf band
fronted by *wufu* & flanked by gilt
metal dragon-form handles, China,
14 3/8" h., pr. (damage,
pitting) 1,045.00

Plate, colorful flying bird & water
lily blossom w/two-tone green
fronds on royal blue ground, border of bud squares on black, royal
blue reverse w/spring scroll cloisons, Japan, 10¾" d. 325.00

Teapot, cov., cobalt blue spring coil
cloisons, pink & white florals &
green & orchid foil decoration,
three small feet, 5¾" spout to
handle, 3¾" h. 225.00

Vase, "pigeon blood" cloisonne,

pink & gold roses on *basse-taille*
ground, Japan, 7" h., pr. 695.00

Vase, 'tree-bark' style, ovoid globular body set w/a waisted neck &
tapering towards the foot, decorated in bright enamels w/flower-
ing cherry & peony branches on a
rich translucent red enamel
ground revealing a 'tree-bark' textured surface, metal rims, bottom
rim impressed w/studio mark of
Ando Jubei, Japan, 7¼" h. 302.50

Vase, bulbous baluster form, very
fine cloisons w/polychrome
enamels depicting a pair of
pheasants perched on a rocky formation near a stream, among a
variety of garden flowers & small
finches, geometric borders at rim
& base, silver base rim marked,
Japan, late 19th c., minor enamel
imperfections, 8¼" h. (ILLUS.) 880.00

Vases, variegated florals against a
brick red ground & double "T" fret
cloisons, impressed "China,"
w/teakwood bases, 8¾" h., pr. .. 450.00

Vases, baluster form w/everted rim
above tapering cylindrical body decorated w/overall design of peacocks
perched on blossoming cherry
branches w/irises on light blue
ground, Japan, Meiji period,
14¼" h., pr. 1,430.00

RELATED WARES

Champleve Jardiniere

Champleve gilt-bronze jardiniere,
swelled body fitted at each corner
w/angular handles, raised on a
pierced scrolled base, decorated
overall w/florals & scrolls in tones
of yellow, red & dark blue on a
powder blue ground, signed "F.
BARBEDIENNE," France, third quarter 19th c., 10¼" h. (ILLUS.) 1,980.00

Champleve vase, bulbous form
w/long neck & trumpet-form rim,
squat flared foot, enameled floral

& geometric banded decoration w/a
peacock, dragon & flowers set in
an incised diaper pattern ground
on the neck & foot, China, 19th c.,
35" h. (restorations) 1,100.00
Plique-a-jour pendant, Art Nouveau
style, pale blue Egyptian-
influenced papyrus leaf motif w/a
central freshwater pearl balancing
a pearl drop, original sterling silver chain, signed, ca. 1910,
15" l. 385.00
Plique-a-jour vase, ovoid body
w/angular shoulder & long neck
flaring towards the rim, the sides
w/reticulated shaped floral
reserves on a translucent 'fish
scale' ground scattered w/blos-
soming sprigs, the rim w/jeweled
garland band, 4 7/8" h., pr...... 605.00

CLOTHING

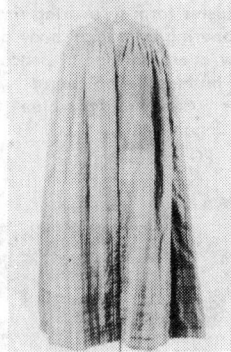

Early 19th Century Cloak

*Recent interest in period clothing, uniforms
and accessories from the 18th, 19th and
through the 20th century has compelled us
to add this category to our compilation. While
style and fabric play an important role in the
values of older garments of previous centuries, designer dresses of the 1920's and 30's,
especially evening gowns, are enhanced by
the original label of a noted couturier such as
Worth or Adrian. Prices vary widely for these
garments which we list by type, with infant's
and children's apparel so designated.*

Baby bonnet, tatted, ribbon
rosettes, lined $12.00
Ball gown, Victorian, black silk
w/lavish crystal & bead trim, lace
sleeves w/crystal beading,
1890's 275.00
Bed jacket, satin, pink w/lavish ecru

lace, B. Altman & Co., New York,
1930's 27.50
Blouse, white cotton, cutwork,
Victorian 20.00
Blouse, ecru lace, evening style,
gathered waist, 1950's, medium
size 18.00
Blouse, cream silk, embroidered
front, 1900's 65.00
Chinese ensemble: jacket, pleated
skirt & pants; silk brocade, heavily embroidered in black and
shades of blue, 1860's, 3 pcs. 750.00
Chinese jacket, lady's, pale silver
silk embroidered w/multicolored
florals, blue & black borders,
hand-sewn, 41" l. 80.00
Christening dress, cutwork embroidery across bodice, sleeve cuff &
ruffle around skirt, tuck pleats
around skirt 65.00
Christening dress, horizontal tuck
pleats from bodice to hem, lace
trim........................... 40.00
Cloak, stiffened linen, Scotch plaid
pattern in red & gold, lined w/a
soft homespun, lining of pockets
sewn w/early fabric scraps,
America, early 19th c., some early repairs (ILLUS.) 825.00
Coat, boy's, linen, hand-stitched,
decorative cuffs, lined 35.00
Coat, lady's, flapper era, black
plush, bat wing sleeves 125.00
Coat, lady's, Irish lace, long fitted
sleeves & cutaway front to nearly
ankle length at back, worked
w/white cotton in a pattern of
flowering foliage & delicate
rosettes, ca. 1910 .... 440.00
Dress, girl's, red silk w/drop waist,
black trim, bowed sash,
ca. 1910....................... 65.00
Dress, black satin, ornate beadwork, w/matching cape, Victorian, 2 pcs. 225.00
Dress, brown silk w/black accents,
ca. 1910....................... 45.00
Dress, flapper era, green chiffon
w/satin underslip, 7" w. black &
silver beaded girdle at hips, silver
beads interspersed w/green &
clear rhinestones around
neckline....................... 75.00
Duster, linen, shawl collar,
1900's......................... 90.00
Ensemble, young girl's, white wool
coat w/red piping, red velvet
dress & straw hat, 3 pcs. 165.00
Evening coat, shrimp velvet w/fox
collar, 1920's................... 65.00
Evening gown, black bugle-beaded
bodice w/narrow straps & fit close
to hipline, full ballerina-length

skirt composed of layers of black
tulle over orange & brown-toned
layers, w/"Samuel Winston by
Charles James" label,
mid-1950's 2,640.00
Evening gown, yellow silk faille,
fitted sleeveless bodice, sculpted
ankle-length skirt & stiffened petticoat hemmed w/dress fabric,
w/Givenchy label, late 1950's 99.00
Evening suit, gentleman's, black
wool tail coat, vest & trousers,
3 pcs........................... 88.00
Hat, lady's, black satin trimmed
w/egret feathers & hand-
embroidered pastel roses 440.00
Hat, lady's, black velour trimmed
w/purple & black ostrich plumes,
Victorian 165.00
Hat, lady's, pillbox style, leopard
skin, together w/matching purse,
2 pcs.......................... 95.00
Hat, man's, straw, dress style 12.00
Jacket, lady's, Irish lace, cream cotton worked in scrolling foliate
motifs against a lattice net
ground, pattern continuing in the
collar and elbow-length sleeves,
irregularly cut hem, ca. 1905 ..... 550.00
Night gown, white, satin stitch butterflies front, back & cuffs, cap
sleeves, Victorian 45.00
Night shirt, child's, ecru linen,
w/monogram & crochet, 1912 .... 20.00
Petticoat, lace, lined, 105" around
hem, 23" l. 39.00
Prom dress, strapless, w/bolero
jacket, light blue, lined full skirt,
1950's 45.00
Robe, apricot velvet, silver-printed
w/the "Bellini" stylized foliate motif & running leaf borders, lined in
grey-green silk faille, w/round &
ribbon labels of "Fortuny" 1,870.00

Fortuny Medieval-Style Robe
Robe, medieval-style, long tapering
sleeves, brown velvet w/front

panel gilt-printed w/interlacing
Islamic-style designs, pleated
silk inserts at the sides, Mariano
Fortuny, Italy (ILLUS.) 6,600.00
Shawl, black lace, tri-cornered,
Spain, 52½ x 66½" 260.00
Shawl, satin, multicolored floral design on a platinum ground, gold
fringe, 68 x 70" plus fringe (some
wear & minor stains) 135.00
Shawl, silk, bright polychrome satin
stitch floral design on ivory
ground w/deep knotted fringe,
China, 19th c., 44" square (some
wear) 385.00
Shift, short petticoat w/crocheted
yoke & lots of tucks, lace trim on
bottom, Victorian 27.50
Shoes, baby's, blue leather, pr...... 45.00
Shoes, child's, black leather, high
button-type, size 2, pr. 35.00

Early Children's Shoes
Shoes, child's, black patent leather,
grosgrain ribbon trim, button
closures, pr. (ILLUS.)............ 15.00
Shoes, child's, leather w/steel buck-
les, wooden soles w/blacksmith
iron rims, rosehead nails, 18th c.,
pr............................. 175.00
Shoes, lady's, high button-style,
black leather, w/12 buttons, pr. ... 35.00
Shoes, lady's, high button-style,
white satin, Victorian........... 75.00
Smoking jacket, black velvet, 1903.. 75.00
Smoking jacket, maroon satin 60.00
Suit, gentleman's, black serge frock
coat, white vest & striped pants,
3 pcs.......................... 220.00
Suit, gentleman's, black serge morning coat, vest & trousers, 3 pcs. .. 66.00
Suit, lady's, wood gabardine, jacket
w/asymmetrical double-breasted
closure, attached self-belt & label
"Adrian Original," straight skirt
w/rear pleat, Adrian blue,
1940's 154.00
Tea gown, "Delphos" style, pleated
rose silk, shaped overblouse &
elbow-length sleeves trimmed
w/terra-cotta & blue Venetian
glass beads, plain floor-length

skirt flaring at the hem, w/gilt-
printed belt, signed on the inseam
"Fortuny De," late 1920's 3,520.00
Tea gown, turquoise silk velvet
printed w/a 17th century-style
design of birds & stylized foliate
motifs, kimono-style sleeves edged
w/patterned glass & carved ivory
beads, floor-length skirt w/train,
designed by Gallenga, ca.
1920-30 ....1,540.00 to 1,870.00
Top hat, light gold brushed beaver,
hand-sewn w/label inside, "W.A.
Andross's Fashionable Hat & Cap,
Warehouse, 104 Broadway, N.Y.,"
w/original wallpaper box w/cover
in predominantly blue paper
w/flower-filled urn on cover,
early 19th c., hat 5¾" h., box
9½" d., 7½" h., the group 412.50
Umbrella, child's, black w/small
scalloped edge.................. 65.00
Uniform, Red Cross Grey Lady,
1930's 35.00
Uniform, United States Naval
Officer's, black wool tunic &
pants, together w/Lt. Commander's shoulder boards & cap
in metal box.................... 165.00
Wedding dress, ivory silk w/lavish
lace trim, World War I era, ca.
1917 (damage) 330.00
Wedding dress, nylon, machine lace
front yoke, overskirt, floor length,
lined, 1940's, size 10 .... 48.00
Wedding dress, white ruffled net
w/voluminous skirt & long train,
World War II era, 1940's 88.00
Wedding dress underdress, all lace
& taffeta, sequin trim at bodice,
size 12, 1950's 75.00

COCA-COLA ITEMS

Coca-Cola Bottle Opener

*Coca-Cola promotion has been achieved
through the issuance of scores of small objects through the years. These, together with
trays, signs, and other articles bearing the
name of this soft drink, are now sought by
many collectors.*

Baseball bat, "Batrite," 32" l........ $54.00
Baseball scorekeeper, "Perpetual
Calendar," for runs, hits & errors,
1906 .... 60.00
Billfold, leather, embossed w/1916
bottle, ca. 1920 .... 85.00
Blotter, 1911, "Western Coca-Cola
Bottling Co."................... 185.00
Blotter, 1912, young man & woman
w/glasses of Coca-Cola, "Pure
and Healthful" 200.00
Bookmark, 1900, celluloid, heart-
shaped, shows Hilda Clark,
2 x 2¼" 1,250.00
Bookmark, 1906, celluloid, owl hold-
ing book, 1 x 3½" ......550.00 to 700.00
Bottle, straight-sided, amber, w/pa-
per label, early 20th c. 75.00
Bottle display rack, for six-bottle
cartons, holds 24, "Take Home
Coca-Cola - 6 for 25c," w/eight
cartons, 1930's 1,400.00
Bottle opener, metal, figural hand,
"Delicious & Refreshing," 1909 .... 25.00
Bottle opener, wall-type, cast iron,
"Star X," 1925, w/box (ILLUS.).... 30.00
Calendar, 1904, picture of Lillian
Nordica standing next to table
w/Coca-Cola glass 2,000.00
Calendar, 1905, picture of Lillian
Nordica standing next to pedestal
holding a large feather fan, all
original ....3,000.00 to 5,000.00
Calendar, 1919, Knitting Girl 450.00
Calendar, 1924, Smiling Girl........ 150.00
Calendar, 1931, farm boy w/dog,
Norman Rockwell illustration 725.00
Calendar, 1947, girl w/skis, matted
& framed 125.00
Calendar, 1963, girl in front of
mirror......................... 27.50
Case rack, wire, tall & narrow
w/slanted sides, round-topped
sign at top w/"Take some Coca-
Cola home today," for holding
wooden bottle cases............ 50.00
Clock, wall-type, electric, square
metal frame, red & white logo in
center, green numerals,
15" square..................... 70.00
Clock, wall-type, electric, square
metal frame, "Drink Coca-Cola" &
bottle in center, ca. 1942,
16 x 16" 950.00
Counter display jar, gum, clear,
square w/cut corners, embossed
near base on front "Franklin -
Caro Co. - Richmond, Va.,"
ca. 1915 .... 150.00
Coupon, "Take Home a Carton,"
shows young woman holding bottle & standing near open refrigerator, 1939 .... 10.00
Doll, figure of Santa Claus standing

holding bottle of Coca-Cola, cloth
stuffed body w/black boots, rub-
ber face, ca. 1940's, 19" h. 60.00
Door pull, plastic, figural Coca-Cola
bottle on die-cast metal fastening
plate painted red w/"Have a
Coke," reverse marked "Milton
Strum & Co. Chicago, Ill.," mint
w/original box, 6" h. 260.00
Fan, cardboard, Sprite Boy & "Have
a Coke," 1950's 25.00
Game, baseball dart board, wood &
cork, 1950's 75.00
Glass, soda fountain-type, 1920's,
"Coca-Cola" in white on clear,
semi-flared 75.00
Glass, soda fountain-type, 1935,
"Coca-Cola" in white on clear,
shaped top . . . . 30.00 to 35.00
Lamp, hanging fixture, round,
Tiffany-type leaded glass,
"Coca-Cola," ca. 1920,
18" d. 3,700.00
Menu board, tin, Art Deco style,
"Drink Coca-Cola" & "Specials to-
day" at top, 1930's 225.00
Menu signboard, wooden, pictures
"December 25, 1923" bottle in
color, 26 x 36" 285.00
Mirror, pocket-type, 1905, Juanita,
"Whitehead & Hoag Co." etc. on
rim, oval 275.00
Mirror, pocket-type, 1917, Elaine,
1¾ x 2¾" oval 285.00
Napkin, rice paper, advertising
Coca-Cola, 1911 . . . .   110.00
Needle case, w/"Party Girl" on
heavy paper cover, 1924-25,
2 x 3" 35.00
Paperweight, glass, solid sphere
w/bubbles & "Coke is Coca-Cola,"
1948 . . . .   295.00
Pencil sharpener, cast iron, figural
miniature bottle, ca. 1935 . . . .   25.00
Pencil sharpener, model of a Coke
can 3.00
Playing cards, 1915, woman seated
at table holding closed parasol . . 1,000.00
Playing cards, 1928, woman
w/bobbed hair 350.00
Postage stamp holder, celluloid,
young lady wearing hat w/large
feather plume, 1901 . . . .   450.00
Postcard, Dick Tracy, 1942 . . . .   15.00
Ruler, wooden, "Delicious & Refresh-
ing," ca. 1930, 7" l. 15.00
Sandwich plate, china, shows bottle
& glass, Knowles China Co., ca.
1930, 7¼" d. 152.00
Seltzer bottle, green glass
w/paneled sides & original metal
top & spout, sides engraved
w/early Coca-Cola advertising,
bottled in Winona, Minnesota,

metal top stamped, "Coca-Cola
Btlg., Fargo, N.D.," 12½" h. 133.00
Sheet music, "Rum & Coca-Cola,"
Andrews Sisters on cover 15.00
Sign, cardboard, picnic scene,
w/two women in foreground &
man in background, 1923,
14 x 24" 2,000.00
Sign, cardboard, waxed w/crimped
black metal edged frame, 16" h.
Coke bottle each end, red, black,
white & brown, "Delicious &
Refreshing," dated 1915,
21 x 60" 750.00
Sign, neon, "Coca-Cola Cigars," red
& green, transformer marked
"Coca-Cola, NYC.," 12 x 23" 2,400.00
Sign, neon, enclosed in chrome
case, "Drug Store, Drink Coca-
Cola," Art Deco style, red & blue,
1930's, 15 x 24" 2,800.00
Sign, reverse-painted glass, "Drink
Coca-Cola," black & silver, 1932,
12" oval 2,500.00
Sign, plywood, triangular, two-
sided, "Ice Cold - Drink Coca-
Cola," 1940's 450.00
Sign, school crossing-type, figure
of a policeman, "Drink Coca-
Cola" 1,000.00
Sign, tin, arrow-shaped, two-sided,
1927, 7¾ x 30" . . . . 325.00 to 375.00
Sign, tin, arrow, two-sided, die-cut,
"Take Home a Carton, 25c,"
11 x 18" 100.00
Sign, trolley-type, "4 Seasons,"
shows four young women w/bot-
tles & glasses of Coca-Cola &
"Drink Coca-Cola, delicious and
refreshing all the year round,"
1923, framed, 11 x 20½" 750.00

Coca-Cola Syrup Dispenser
Syrup dispenser, soda fountain-type,

ceramic, cov. syrup bowl & base
w/brass spigot, embossed scrollwork outlined in gold, Wheeling
Pottery Co., 1896, overall 18" h.
(ILLUS.) ....2,700.00 to 3,000.00

Teaching kit, Transportation series,
contains teacher's manual, 20 pictures, home study book, art panel
& four different posters, in original mailer, 1943................. 350.00

Thermometer, tin, embossed bottle
shape, 1950's, 8½" w., 29" h. 30.00

Thermometer, wood, flat, rectangle
w/rounded top, "Coca-Cola 5c,"
ca. 1905, 5 x 21"............... 267.00

Toy helicopter, mechanical, "Drink
Coca-Cola" 600.00

Toy truck, "Buddy L," yellow metal,
1960, 10½" l................... 55.00

Toy truck, "Metalcraft No. 215,"
w/rubber wheels & working head-
lights, 1930's................... 900.00

Toy, yo-yo, shaped like bottle cap,
red & white plastic, "Drink Coca-
Cola," 1960 .... 10.00

Tray, change, 1912, Hamilton King
Girl......................... 245.00

Tray, change, 1917, Elaine, 4¼ x 6"
oval ....75.00 to 100.00

Tray, 1912, Hamilton King Girl,
10½ x 13¼" oblong 550.00

1917 Elaine Tray

Tray, 1917, Elaine, 8½ x 19" oblong
(ILLUS.) ....175.00 to 200.00

Tray, 1925, Girl at Party,
10½ x 13¼" oblong 160.00

Tray, 1930, Bathing Beauty in
Swim Cap, 10½ x 13¼"
oblong ....130.00 to 150.00

Tray, 1930, Girl with Telephone,
10½ x 13¼" oblong .....130.00 to 180.00

Tray, 1932, Girl in Yellow Swimsuit,
10½ x 13¼" oblong .....225.00 to 275.00

Tray, 1934, Johnny Weismuller &
Maureen O'Sullivan (Tarzan &

Jane), 10½ x 13¼"
oblong ....275.00 to 300.00

Tray, 1935, Madge Evans,
10½ x 13¼" oblong .....125.00 to 175.00

Tray, 1937, Running Girl,
10½ x 13¼" oblong 98.00

Tray, 1938, Girl in the Afternoon,
10½ x 13¼" oblong 97.00

Tray, 1939, Springboard Girl, artwork by Haddon Sundblom,
10½ x 13¼" oblong 66.00

Tray, 1939, Springboard Girl, Spanish version 250.00

Tray, 1940, Sailor Girl, 10½ x 13¼"
oblong ....65.00 to 85.00

Tray, 1942, Two Girls at Car,
10½ x 13¼" oblong ....75.00 to 95.00

Tray, 1948, Girl with Wind in Her
Hair, 10½ x 13¼" oblong........ 46.00

Tray, 1950, Girl w/Menu, French
version, 10½ x 13¼" oblong 100.00

Vending machine, table-top bottle
dispenser, "Icy-O," tin w/wood-
grained finish, 1927.............1,275.00

Vending machine, Vendo model 44,
coin-operated 990.00

Vendor's cap, cardboard, "Drink
Coca-Cola in Bottles" 9.00

Wall sconce, cardboard, green, silver & red, 9" w., 12" h.......... 195.00

Watch fob, brass, "Coca-Cola" in
oval, 1908, w/strap............. 350.00

Watch fob, metal, w/bulldog, ca.
1920's ....200.00 to 225.00

Whistle, metal, bottle cap shape.... 7.50

COFFEE GRINDERS

Inlaid Walnut Coffee Grinder

Most coffee grinders collected are lap or
table and wall types used in many homes in
the late 19th and early 20th centuries. However, large store-sized grinders have recently been traded.

Lap-type, inlaid burl walnut, rectangular top & base inlaid w/a repeating diamond band, America, late 19th c., 7 1/8" w., 10½" h. (ILLUS.) $605.00

Lap-type, turned mahogany, square base w/drawer below cylindrical turned case flaring towards top, screw-off wooden lid w/iron handle, 10" h. (minor edge damage, small glued repair) 175.00

Lap-type, tin, decorative iron mechanism, 5" square 55.00

Lap-type, wooden base, dovetailed construction, pewter hopper, Pennsylvania 95.00

Store counter model, black cast iron crank, "Enterprise No. 1," some old gilded decoration, 12½" h. ... 250.00

Store counter model, two-wheel, cast iron, "Enterprise No. 3," original red paint & decals, 10¾" d. wheels, 15" h. 595.00

Store counter model, two-wheel, cast iron, "J. Wright" 75.00

Table model, clamp-on type, cast iron, "Enterprise Mfg. Co., No. 0," stenciled flags decoration, 11½" h. 160.00

Table model, cast iron, large wheel marked "Peugeot Freres Brevetes," above wooden drawer w/embossed brass label, old worn black paint over green, France, ca. 1900, 20" h. (on new wooden base) 70.00

Wall-type, cast iron & tin, cylindrical tin top in black w/red decal reading "Universal 0012 Coffee Mill," cast-iron base embossed "Landers, Frary & Clark, New Britain, Ct.," 13" h. 55.00

Wall-type, cast iron, "Brighton" 40.00

Wall-type, cast iron & tin, "Parker 50," embossed eagle 40.00

Wall-type, "Royal," cast iron 35.00

COMIC BOOKS

Comic books, especially first, or early issues of a series, are avidly collected today. Prices for some of the scarce ones have reached extremely high levels. Prices listed below are for copies in fine to mint condition.

Action, No. 45 or 47, each $85.00
Batman, No. 47 .... 107.50
Blonde Phantom, No. 16 .... 46.50
Bozo the Clown, 1954 .... 15.00
Buster Brown, No. 41 .... 25.00
Crime Reporter, No. 2 .... 44.00
Detective, No. 69 .... 122.50

Detective, No. 121 .... 70.00
Detective, No. 138, featuring Batman & Robin 55.00
Donald Duck & the Mummy's Ring, No. 29 .... 132.00
Don Winslow of the Navy, No. 61... 8.00

Fantastic Four Comic Book

Fantastic Four, No. 83 (ILLUS.) 5.00
Flash, No. 99 .... 71.50
Gene Autry, No. 12 .... 10.00
Green Lantern, All-American, No. 102 .... 55.00
Human Torch, No. 28 .... 77.00
Incredible Hulk, No. 2, 1962, July 120.00
Invaders, No. 2 or 3, each 9.00
I Spy, No. 3, 1967 .... 12.00
Katy Keene, No. 16 (coupon cut).... 40.00
Katy Keene, No. 18 .... 60.00
Lord Jim, Movie Comics, No. 10156-509, 1965 .... 12.00
March of Comics, No. 46 .... 15.00
Marvel, No. 73 .... 57.50
Marvel, No. 86 .... 60.50
Medal of Honor, No. 1 .... 12.00
Miss Fury, No. 4 .... 46.50
Planet, No. 44 .... 49.50
Rawhide, No. 1160, 1960, April 39.00
Real Fact Comics, No. 1 .... 12.00
Roy Rogers, No. 1 .... 65.00
Seven Seas, No. 1, 1946, April 130.00
Seven Seas, No. 3, 1947 .... 100.00
Shadow, Vol. 6, No. 12, atom bomb panels 65.00
Showcase, No. 16 or 34, each 30.00
Sparkler, No. 3 .... 45.00
Sparkler, No. 19 .... 50.00
Sparkler, No. 25, Hogarth Tarzan cover 40.00
The Spirit, by Will Eisner, March 2 or May 11, 1941, distributed weekly by Buffalo Courier Express, each 30.00
The Spirit, by Will Eisner, June 8, 1941, distributed weekly by Buffalo Courier Express............. 60.00

Strange Tales No. 113 or 115,
each 35.00
Sub-Mariner, No. 20 .... 104.50
Superman, No. 8 .... 225.00
Superman, No. 30 .... 225.00
Superman, No. 32 .... 66.00
Superman, No. 46 .... 55.00
Superman, No. 96 .... 50.00
Tarzan, No. 128, 1962 .... 10.00
Tarzan & The Fires of Tohr, Dell
Four Color, No. 161, 1947 .... 80.00
Tonto, No. 13 .... 10.00
Twilight Zone, No. 1 .... 20.00
Wonder Woman, No. 20 .... 41.00
Wonder Woman, All Star, No. 33 ... 82.50
World's Finest, No. 30, featuring
Batman & Robin 75.90
Wyatt Earp, No. 10 .... 10.00
Young Allies, No. 4 .... 125.00

COMMEMORATIVE PLATES

Limited edition commemorative and collector plates rank high on the list of collectible items. The oldest and best-known of these plates, those of Bing & Grondahl and Royal Copenhagen, retain leadership in the field, but other companies are turning out a variety of designs, some of which have been widely embraced by the growing numbers who have made plate collecting a hobby. Plates listed below are a representative selection of fine porcelain, glass and other plates available to collectors.

ANRI
Christmas
1971, St. Jakob in Groden $71.00
1972, Pipers at Alberobello 83.00
1973, Alpine Horn 372.00
1974, Young Man & Girl 69.00
1975, Christmas in Ireland 65.00
1976, Alpine Christmas 147.00
1977, Legend of Heiligenblut 100.00
1978, The Klockler Singers 73.00
1979, The Moss Gatherers of
Villnoess 85.00
1980, Wintry Church-going in Santa
Christina 85.00
1981, Santa Claus in Tyrol 94.00
1982, Star Singers 117.00
1983, Unto Us a Child Is Born 110.00
1984, Yuletide in the Valley 123.00
1985, Good Morning, Good Cheer .. 127.00

Father's Day
1972, Alpine Father & Children 40.00
1973, Alpine Father & Children 85.00
1974, Cliff Gazing 35.00
1975, Sailing 92.50

Mother's Day
1972, Alpine Mother & Children 43.00

1973, Alpine Mother & Children 40.00
1974, Alpine Mother & Children 50.00
1975, Alpine Stroll 54.00
1976, Knitting 79.00

BAREUTHER
Christmas
1967, Stiftskirche 83.00
1968, Kappl 13.50
1969, Christkindlesmarkt 9.50
1970, Chapel in Oberndorf 9.50
1971, Toys for Sale 10.00
1972, Christmas in Munich 35.00
1973, Christmas Sleigh Ride 22.00
1974, Church in the Black Forest 23.00
1975, Snowman 28.00
1976, Chapel in the Hills 19.00
1977, Story Time 18.00
1978, Mittenwald 16.00
1979, Winter Day 18.00
1980, Miltenberg 18.00
1981, Walk in the Forest 15.00
1982, Bad Wimpfen 18.00
1983, The Night Before Christmas ... 18.50
1984, Zeil on the River Main 21.50
1985, Winter Wonderland 22.00
1986, Market Place in Forchheim ... 25.50

Father's Day

1970 Bareuther Father's Day Plate

1969, Castle Neuschwanstein 36.00
1970, Castle Pfalz (ILLUS.) 13.00
1971, Castle Heidelberg 12.50
1972, Castle Hohenschwangau 14.00
1973, Castle Katz 15.00
1974, Wurzburg Castle 16.00
1975, Castle Lichtenstein 20.00
1976, Castle Hohenzollern 19.00
1977, Castle Eltz 19.00
1978, Castle Falkenstein 25.00
1979, Castle Rheinstein 24.00
1980, Castle Cochem 22.00
1981, Castle Gutenfels 29.00
1982, Castle Zwingenberg 20.00
1983, Castle Lauenstein 20.00
1984, Castle Neuenstein 28.00
1985, Castle Wartburg Near
Eisenach 28.00
1986, Castle Hardegg 25.00

Mother's Day

1969, Dancing		25.00
1970, Mother & Children		12.00
1971, Doing the Laundry		14.00
1972, Baby's First Step		12.00
1973, Mother Kissing Baby		15.00
1974, Musical Children		15.00
1975, Spring Outing		15.00
1976, Rocking Cradle		17.00
1977, Noon Feeding		17.00
1978, Blind Man's Bluff		18.00
1979, Mother's Love		16.00
1980, First Cherries		20.00
1981, Playtime		22.00
1982, Suppertime		20.00
1983, On Farm		20.00
1984, Village Children		26.00
1985, Sunrise		30.00
1986, Playtime		29.50

BELLEEK
Christmas

1970, Castle Caldwell		78.00
1971, Celtic Cross		37.00
1972, Flight of the Earls		48.00
1973, Tribute to W.B. Yeats		53.00
1974, Devenish Island		200.00
1975, The Celtic Cross		55.00
1976, Dove of Peace		45.00
1977, Wren		56.00

Irish Wildlife Christmas

1978, A Leaping Salmon		48.00
1979, Hare At Rest		47.00
1980, Hedgehog		62.00
1981, Red Squirrel		62.00
1982, Irish Seal		62.00
1983, Red Fox		71.50

BING & GRONDAHL
Christmas

1912 Bing & Grondahl Christmas Plate

1895	3,165.00
1896	1,345.00
1897	875.00
1898	450.00
1899	940.00
1900	775.00
1901	260.00

1902	272.00
1903	247.00
1904	111.00
1905	118.00
1906	91.00
1907	95.00
1908	79.00
1909	83.00
1910	69.00
1911	65.00
1912 (ILLUS.)	61.00
1913	70.00
1914	70.00
1915	95.00
1916	68.00
1917	59.00
1918	67.00
1919	70.00
1920	62.00
1921	62.00
1922	60.00
1923	59.00
1924	61.00
1925	62.50
1926	61.50
1927	77.00
1928	52.00
1929	65.00
1930	80.00
1931	61.50
1932	71.00
1933	61.00
1934	60.00
1935	54.00
1936	55.00
1937	75.00
1938	97.00
1939	134.00
1940	110.00
1941	190.00
1942	133.00
1943	122.00
1944	72.00
1945	106.00
1946	65.00
1947	85.00
1948	69.00
1949	56.00
1950	94.00
1951	70.00
1952	66.00
1953	60.00
1954	82.00
1955	73.00
1956	95.00
1957	96.00
1958	72.00
1959	85.00
1960	112.00
1961	74.00
1962	63.00
1963	71.00
1964	40.00
1965	41.00

1966	37.00
1967	35.00
1968	28.00
1969	18.00
1970	17.00
1971	14.00
1972	13.50
1973	16.00
1974	14.50
1975	15.50
1976	15.00
1977	17.00
1978	18.50
1979	21.00
1980	23.00
1981	28.00
1982	29.00
1983	28.00
1984	29.50
1985	30.00

Mother's Day

1969 Bing & Grondahl Mother's Day Plate

1969, Dog & Puppies (ILLUS.)	344.00
1970, Birds & Chicks	22.00
1971, Cat & Kitten	12.00
1972, Mare & Foal	13.00
1973, Duck & Ducklings	13.50
1974, Bear & Cubs	14.00
1975, Doe & Fawns	13.00
1976, Swan Family	16.00
1977, Squirrel & Young	18.50
1978, Heron	14.00
1979, Fox & Cubs	20.50
1980, Woodpecker & Young	24.00
1981, Hare & Young	23.00
1982, Lioness & Cubs	22.50
1983, Raccoon & Young	25.00
1984, Stork & Nestlings	21.00
1985, Bear with Cubs	26.00

FERRANDIZ, JUAN
Christmas - Anri (Wood)

1972, Christ in Manger	139.00
1973, Boy with Lamb	70.00
1974, Nativity	169.00
1975, Flight into Egypt	75.00
1976, Mary & Joseph Pray	127.00
1977, Girl with Tree	51.00

1978, Leading the Way	48.00
1979, Drummer Boy	57.00
1980, Rejoice	59.00
1981, Spreading Word	77.00
1982, Shepherd Family	79.00

Mother & Child - Schmid (Porcelain)

1977, Orchard Mother	76.00
1978, Pastoral Mother	44.00
1979, Floral Mother	48.00
1980, Avian Mother	59.00

Mother's Day - Anri (Wood)

1972, Mother Sewing	84.00
1973, Mother & Child	62.00
1974, Mother & Child	79.00
1975, Mother Holding Dove	79.00
1976, Mother & Child	79.00
1977, Girl with Flowers	59.00
1978, Beginning	71.00
1979, All Hearts	42.00
1980, Spring Arrivals	75.00
1981, Harmony	82.00
1982, With Love	70.00

FRANKLIN MINT (STERLING SILVER)
Norman Rockwell Christmas Series

1970, Bringing Home the Tree	136.00
1971, Under the Mistletoe	106.00
1972, The Carolers	103.00
1973, Trimming the Tree	106.00
1974, Hanging the Wreath	169.00
1975, Home for Christmas	156.00

FRANKOMA
Christmas

1965, Goodwill Toward Men	200.00
1966, Bethlehem Shepherds	113.00
1967, Gifts for the Christ Child	66.50
1968, Flight into Egypt	22.00
1969, Laid in a Manger	18.00
1970, King of Kings	22.00
1971, No Room in the Inn	15.50
1972, Seeking the Christ Child	11.50
1973, The Annunciation	12.00
1974, She Loved & Cared	11.50
1975, Peace on Earth	14.00
1976, Gift of Love	12.00
1977, Birth of Eternal Life	11.50
1978, All Nature Rejoiced	11.50
1979, Star of Hope	10.00
1980, Unto Us a Child Is Born	9.00
1981, O Come Let Us Adore Him	9.50
1982, Wise Men Rejoice	9.00
1983, Wise Men Bring Gifts	13.00
1984, Faith, Hope & Love	10.50
1985, The Angels Watched	12.00

Teenagers of the Bible

1973, Jesus the Carpenter	19.50
1974, David the Musician	14.50
1975, Jonathan the Archer	17.00
1976, Dorcas the Seamstress	18.00
1977, Peter the Fisherman	11.00

1978, Martha the Homemaker 14.50
1979, Daniel the Courageous 14.50
1980, Ruth the Devoted 9.00
1981, Joseph the Dreamer 10.00
1982, Mary the Mother 11.50

GORHAM - NORMAN ROCKWELL
Christmas
1974, Tiny Tim 29.00
1975, Good Deeds 27.50
1976, Christmas Trio 19.00
1978, Planning Christmas Visits 20.00
1979, Santa's Helpers 23.00
1980, Letter to Santa 20.00
1981, Santa Plans His Visit 22.00
1982, The Jolly Coachman 20.00
1983, Christmas Dancers 28.00
1984, Christmas Medley 28.00
1987, The Homecoming 50.00

Four Seasons
1971, A Boy & His Dog, set of 4 .... 216.00
1972, Young Love, set of 4 .... 116.00
1973, The Ages of Love, set of 4 ... 173.00
1974, Grandpa & Me, set of 4 ...... 95.00
1975, Me & My Pal, set of 4 .... 112.00
1976, Grand Pals, set of 4 .... 157.00
1977, Going on Sixteen, set of 4 .... 100.00
1978, The Tender Years, set of 4 .... 82.00
1979, A Helping Hand, set of 4 ..... 67.00
1980, Dad's Boy, set of 4 .... 93.00
1980, Landscape Series, set of 4 .... 95.00
1981, Old Timers, set of 4 .... 62.00
1982, Life with Father, set of 4 ..... 57.00
1983, Old Buddies, set of 4 .... 75.00

HAVILAND & CO.
Christmas
1970, A Partridge in a Pear Tree 75.00
1971, Two Turtle Doves 18.00
1972, Three French Hens 12.00
1973, Four Colly Birds 11.00
1974, Five Golden Rings 18.00
1975, Six Geese A'Laying 18.00
1976, Seven Swans A'Swimming 18.50
1977, Eight Maids A'Milking 27.00
1978, Nine Ladies Dancing 33.00
1979, Ten Lords A'Leaping 25.00
1980, Eleven Pipers Piping 43.00
1981, Twelve Drummers
    Drumming 47.00

Mother's Day
1973, Breakfast 12.00
1974, The Wash 15.00
1975, In the Park 12.50
1976, To Market 9.00
1977, Wash Before Dinner 10.00
1978, An Evening at Home 11.00
1979, Happy Mother's Day 18.00
1980, A Child & His Animals 9.00

HAVILAND & PARLON
Christmas
1972, Madonna & Child (Raphael) ... 83.50

1973, Madonnina (Feruzzi) 74.00
1974, Cowper Madonna & Child
    (Raphael) 39.00
1975, Madonna & Child (Murillo) 30.00
1976, Madonna & Child (Botticelli) .. 31.00
1977, Madonna & Child (Bellini) 24.00
1978, Madonna & Child (Fra Filippo
    Lippi) 51.00
1979, Madonna of the Eucharist (Bot-
    ticelli) 90.00

Tapestry Series
1971, The Unicorn in Captivity 106.00
1972, Star of the Hunt 35.00
1973, Chase of the Unicorn 100.00
1974, End of the Hunt 72.00
1975, The Unicorn Surrounded 37.00
1976, The Unicorn is Brought to the
    Castle 42.00

The Lady & The Unicorn
1977, To My Only Desire 35.00
1978, Sight 25.00
1979, Sound 30.00
1980, Touch 80.00
1981, Scent 33.00
1982, Taste 46.50

HUMMEL (GOEBEL WORKS)
Annual

1971 Goebel Hummel Plate

1971, Heavenly Angel (ILLUS.) 522.00
1972, Hear Ye, Hear Ye 45.00
1973, Globe Trotter 96.00
1974, Goose Girl 46.00
1975, Ride Into Christmas 49.00
1976, Apple Tree Girl 47.50
1977, Apple Tree Boy 60.00
1978, Happy Pastime 36.00
1979, Singing Lesson 26.00
1980, School Girl 40.00
1981, Umbrella Boy 46.00
1982, Umbrella Girl 88.00
1983, The Postman 141.00
1984, Little Helper 46.00
1985, Chick Girl 55.00
1986, Playmates 86.00
1987, Feeding Time 128.00

Anniversary

1975, Stormy Weather	93.00
1980, Spring Dance	56.00
1985, Auf Wiedersehen	138.00

IMPERIAL (GLASS)
Christmas

1970, Partridge in a Pear Tree, crystal	11.50
1970, Partridge in a Pear Tree, carnival	17.00
1971, Two Turtle Doves, crystal	11.00
1971, Two Turtle Doves, carnival	15.00
1972, Three French Hens, crystal	11.50
1972, Three French Hens, carnival	15.00
1973, Four Colly Birds, crystal	12.00
1973, Four Colly Birds, carnival	15.00
1974, Five Golden Rings, crystal	11.50
1974, Five Golden Rings, carnival	15.00
1975, Six Geese A-Laying, crystal	12.00
1975, Six Geese A-Laying, carnival	15.50
1976, Seven Swans A-Swimming, crystal	14.50
1976, Seven Swans A-Swimming, carnival	16.00
1977, Eight Maids A-Milking, crystal	9.00
1977, Eight Maids A-Milking, carnival	16.00
1978, Nine Drummers Drumming, crystal	12.50
1978, Nine Drummers Drumming, carnival	19.00
1979, Ten Pipers Piping, crystal	12.50
1979, Ten Pipers Piping, carnival	17.50
1980, Eleven Ladies Dancing, crystal	14.00
1980, Eleven Ladies Dancing, carnival	17.50
1981, Twelve Lords A-Leaping, crystal	10.00
1981, Twelve Lords A-Leaping, carnival	14.00
1981, Twelve Lords A-Leaping, ruby	22.50

KAISER
Christmas

1970, Waiting for Santa Claus	14.50
1971, Silent Night	14.00
1972, Welcome Home	19.00
1973, Holy Night	32.50
1974, Christmas Carolers	20.50
1975, Bringing Home the Christmas Tree	13.50
1976, Christ the Savior Is Born	15.50
1977, The Three Kings	14.00
1978, Shepherds in the Field	15.00
1979, Christmas Eve	17.00
1980, Joys of Winter	18.00
1981, Most Holy Night	33.00
1982, Bringing Home the Christmas Tree	24.50

Mother's Day

1971, Mare & Foal	12.00
1972, Flowers for Mother	12.50
1973, Cat & Kitten	26.00
1974, Fox & Young	26.50
1975, German Shepherd with Pups	38.50
1976, Swan & Cygnets	13.50
1977, Mother Rabbit & Young	22.00
1978, Hen & Chicks	17.00
1979, A Mother's Devotion	23.00
1980, Raccoon Family	30.00
1981, Safe Near Mother	37.00
1982, Pheasant Family	28.00
1983, Tender Care	40.00

LALIQUE (GLASS)
Annual

1966 Lalique Annual Plate

1965, Deux Oiseaux (Two Birds)	1,170.00
1966, Rose de Songerie, Dream Rose (ILLUS.)	250.00
1967, Ballet de Poisson (Fish Ballet)	164.00
1968, Gazelle Fantaisie (Gazelle Fantasy)	50.00
1969, Papillon (Butterfly)	66.00
1970, Paon (Peacock)	77.00
1971, Hibou (Owl)	60.00
1972, Coquillage (Shell)	60.00
1973, Petit Geai (Jayling)	50.00
1974, Sous d'Argent (Silver Pennies)	35.00
1975, Duo de Poisson (Fish Duet)	51.00
1976, Aigle (Eagle)	107.00

LENOX
Boehm Bird Series

1970, Wood Thrush	131.00
1971, Goldfinch	58.00
1972, Mountain Bluebird	40.00
1973, Meadowlark	37.00
1974, Rufous Hummingbird	56.00
1975, American Redstart	36.00
1976, Cardinals	57.00
1977, Robins	68.00
1978, Mockingbirds	47.50
1979, Golden-Crowned Kinglets	48.00

1980, Black-Throated Blue War-
blers 70.00
1981, Eastern Phoebes 75.00

Boehm Woodland Wildlife Series

1976 Boehm Woodland Wildlife Plate

1973, Raccoons 54.00
1974, Red Foxes 50.00
1975, Cottontail Rabbits 54.00
1976, Eastern Chipmunks (ILLUS.) ... 50.00
1977, Beaver 57.00
1978, Whitetail Deer 59.00
1979, Squirrels 63.00
1980, Bobcats 71.00
1981, Martens 78.00
1982, Otters 89.00

LLADRO
Christmas
1971, Caroling 16.00
1972, Carolers 21.00
1973, Boy & Girl 22.00
1974, Carolers 20.00
1975, Cherubs 50.00
1976, Christ Child 30.00
1977, Nativity Scene 33.00
1978, Caroling Child 33.00
1979, Snow Dance 55.00

Mother's Day
1971, Kiss of the Child 30.00
1972, Bird & Chicks 18.00
1973, Mother & Children 19.00
1974, Mother Nursing 125.00
1975, Mother & Child 27.00
1976, Tender Vigil 34.00
1977, Mother & Daughter 24.50
1978, The New Arrival 39.00
1979, Off to School 56.00

PORSGRUND
Christmas
1968, Church Scene 98.00
1969, Three Kings 8.00
1970, Road to Bethlehem 7.00
1971, A Child is Born 7.00
1972, Hark, the Herald Angels
Sing 10.00
1973, Promise of the Savior 10.50

1974, The Shepherds 20.00
1975, Jesus on the Road to the
Temple 13.50
1976, Jesus & the Elders 14.00
1977, Draught of the Fish 12.00

Traditional Norwegian Christmas
1978, Guests Are Coming 14.50
1979, Home for Christmas 14.50
1980, Preparing for Christmas 15.00
1981, Christmas Skating 14.50
1982, White Christmas 20.50

Father's Day
1971, Fishing 6.00
1972, Cookout 6.00
1973, Sledding 6.00
1974, Father & Son 4.50
1975, Skating 4.50
1976, Skiing 6.00
1977, Soccer 8.50
1978, Canoeing 8.50
1979, Father & Daughter 11.50
1980, Sailing 6.50
1981, Building a Ship 8.50
1982, Father & Daughter 9.00
1983, Father's Day 10.00
1984, Tree Planting 14.00

Mother's Day
1970, Mare & Foal 5.00
1971, Boy & Geese 7.00
1972, Doe & Fawn 6.00
1973, Cat & Kittens 4.00
1974, Boy & Goats 6.00
1975, Dog & Puppies 5.50
1976, Girl & Calf 6.00
1977, Boy & Chickens 7.50
1978, Girl & Pigs 7.50
1979, Boy & Reindeer 5.00
1980, Girl & Lambs 11.50
1981, Boy & Birds 11.50
1982, Girl & Rabbits 9.50
1983, Mother & Kittens 17.00
1984, By the Pond 11.00

RED SKELTON
Freddie the Freeloader Series (Crown Parian)

1979 Red Skelton Plate

1979, Freddie in the Bathtub
(ILLUS.) 162.00
1980, Freddie's Shack 59.00
1981, Freddie on the Green 44.50
1982, Love That Freddie 34.00

Famous Clowns Series (Fairmont)
1976, Freddie the Freeloader 507.50
1977, W. C. Fields 57.00
1978, Happy 43.00
1979, The Pledge 60.00

Freddie's Adventure Series (Crown Parian)
1981, Captain Freddie 29.00
1982, Bronco Freddie 27.00
1983, Sir Freddie 29.00

RORSTRAND
Christmas

1970 Rorstrand Christmas Plate

1968, Bringing Home the Tree 278.00
1969, Fisherman Sailing Home 21.00
1970, Nils with His Geese (ILLUS.) .. 15.00
1971, Nils in Lapland 13.00
1972, Dalecarlian Fiddler 12.00
1973, Farm in Smaland 50.00
1974, Vadstena 47.00
1975, Nils in Vastmanland 10.00
1976, Nils in Uppland 17.00
1977, Nils in Varmland 17.00
1978, Nils in Fjallbacka 15.00
1979, Nils in Vaestergoetland 17.50
1980, Nils in Halland 30.00
1981, Nils in Gotland 30.00
1982, Nils at Skansen in
Stockholm 28.00
1983, Nils in Oland 24.00
1984, Nils in Angermanland 31.00
1985, Nils in Jamtland 42.00
1986, Nils in Karlskrona 33.50

Father's Day
1971, Father & Child 10.50
1972, Meal at Home 9.50
1973, Tilling Fields 9.00
1974, Fishing 11.50
1975, Painting 10.00
1976, Plowing 9.00
1977, Sawing 8.50

1978, Self-Portrait 20.00
1979, Bridge 15.50
1980, My Etch-Nook 15.75
1981, Esbjorn with Playmate 33.00
1982, House Servants 36.00

Mother's Day
1971, Mother & Child 9.00
1972, Shelling Peas 9.00
1973, Old Fashioned Picnic 11.00
1974, Candle Lighting 10.00
1975, Pontius on Floor 8.00
1976, Apple Picking 9.00
1977, Kitchen 9.00
1978, Azalea 14.00
1979, Studio Idyll 14.00
1980, Lisbeth 15.00
1981, Karin with Brita 23.00
1982, Brita 24.00
1983, Little Girl 21.50
1984, Mother & Crafts 23.00

ROSENTHAL
Christmas
1965 .... 54.00
1966 .... 104.00
1967 .... 81.00
1968 .... 76.00
1969 .... 78.00
1970 .... 65.00
1971 .... 49.00
1972 .... 62.00
1973 .... 62.00
1974 .... 42.00
1975 .... 59.00
1976 .... 33.00
1977 .... 63.00
1978 .... 48.00
1979 .... 90.00
1980 .... 99.00
1981 .... 110.00
1982 .... 133.00
1983 .... 147.50
1984 .... 147.50

Wiinblad Christmas
1971, Maria & Child 856.00
1972, King Caspar 377.00
1973, King Melchior 362.00
1974, King Balthazar 286.00
1975, The Annunciation 135.00
1976, Angel with Trumpet 117.00
1977, Adoration of the Shepherds ... 128.00
1978, Angel with Harp 118.00
1979, Exodus from Egypt 114.00
1980, Angel with Glockenspiel 119.00
1981, Christ Child Visits Temple 152.00
1982, Christening of Christ 122.00

Hibel Nobility of Children Series
1976, La Contessa Isabella 101.00
1977, La Marquis Maurice-Pierre 75.00
1978, Baronesse Johanna-Maryke
Van Vollendam Tot Marken 122.00
1979, Chief Red Feather 128.00

ROYAL BAYREUTH
Christmas

1972, Carriage in the Village	52.00
1973, Snow Scene	8.50
1974, Old Mill	9.00
1975, Forest Chalet "Serenity"	14.00
1976, Christmas in the Country	18.00
1977, Peace on Earth	14.00
1978, Peaceful Interlude	25.00
1979, Homeward Bound	25.00

Mother's Day

1973, Consolation	19.50
1974, Young Americans	100.00
1975, Young Americans II	59.00
1976, Young Americans III	41.00
1977, Young Americans IV	34.00
1978, Young Americans V	21.00
1979, Young Americans VI	28.00
1980, Young Americans VII	37.00
1981, Young Americans VIII	28.00
1982, Young Americans IX	30.00

ROYAL COPENHAGEN
Christmas

1917 Royal Copenhagen Christmas Plate

1908	1,848.00
1909	151.00
1910	125.00
1911	128.00
1912	123.00
1913	110.00
1914	108.00
1915	119.00
1916	81.00
1917 (ILLUS.)	73.00
1918	75.00
1919	83.00
1920	77.00
1921	71.00
1922	64.00
1923	72.00
1924	89.00
1925	77.00
1926	71.00
1927	119.00
1928	74.00
1929	77.00
1930	90.00

1931	90.00
1932	83.00
1933	119.00
1934	98.00
1935	141.00
1936	137.00
1937	160.00
1938	215.00
1939	231.00
1940	310.00
1941	269.00
1942	289.00
1943	389.00
1944	165.00
1945	292.00
1946	144.00
1947	184.00
1948	156.00
1949	158.00
1950	169.00
1951	261.00
1952	109.00
1953	106.00
1954	106.00
1955	161.00
1956	134.00
1957	95.00
1958	98.00
1959	96.00
1960	105.00
1961	98.00
1962	157.00
1963	59.00
1964	51.00
1965	45.00
1966	33.00
1967	31.00
1968	22.00
1969	21.00
1970	27.00
1971	15.00
1972	15.00
1973	20.00
1974	20.00
1975	14.00
1976	22.50
1977	18.50
1978	19.00
1979	41.00
1980	24.00
1981	24.00
1982	28.00
1983	27.00
1984	29.00
1985	35.00
1986	31.00

Mother's Day

1971, American Mother	11.00
1972, Oriental Mother	8.50
1973, Danish Mother	8.50
1974, Greenland Mother	8.00
1975, Bird in Nest	8.00
1976, Mermaids	10.00
1977, The Twins	10.00

1978, Mother & Child 9.00
1979, A Loving Mother 10.00
1980, An Outing with Mother....... 12.00
1981, Reunion.................... 11.00
1982, Children's Hour 15.00

Motherhood Series
1982, Mother Robin & Her Young
   Ones........................... 16.00
1983, Mother Cat & Kitten.......... 17.00
1984, Mare with Foal 17.00
1985, Mother Rabbit with Bunny 24.00
1986, Dog & Puppies............... 21.00
1987, Goat & Kid.................. 30.00

SCHMID HUMMEL
Christmas

1973 Schmid Hummel Christmas Plate
1971, Angel...................... 21.00
1972, Angel with Flute............. 15.00
1973, The Nativity (ILLUS.) 74.00
1974, The Guardian Angel 12.00
1975, Christmas Child............. 10.00
1976, Sacred Journey 11.00
1977, Herald Angel 10.00
1978, Heavenly Trio 12.00
1979, Starlight Angel 13.00
1980, Parade into Toyland.......... 20.00
1981, A Time to Remember 14.00
1982, Angelic Procession 20.00
1983, Angelic Messenger........... 22.00
1984, A Gift from Heaven 33.00
1985, Heavenly Light 23.00
1986, Tell the Heavens............. 17.00
1987, Angelic Gifts 38.00

Mother's Day
1972, Playing Hooky 10.00
1973, Little Fisherman 27.00
1974, Bumblebee 14.50
1975, Message of Love............. 13.00
1976, Devotion for Mother 10.00
1977, Moonlight Return 14.50
1978, Afternoon Stroll 15.00
1979, Cherub's Gift 14.00
1980, Mother's Little Helpers 16.00
1981, Playtime 22.50
1982, The Flower Basket 25.00
1983, Spring Bouquet 30.50

1984, A Joy to Share 26.00
1985, A Mother's Journey 23.50
1986, Home from School 27.00

SPODE
Christmas
1970, Partridge in a Pear Tree...... 23.00
1971, In Heaven the Angels
   Singing....................... 14.50
1972, We Saw Three Ships
   A'Sailing 17.00
1973, We Three Kings of Orient
   Are.......................... 32.00
1974, Deck the Halls............... 44.00
1975, Christbaum................. 21.50
1976, Good King Wenceslas 26.00
1977, The Holly & the Ivy 27.50
1978, While Shepherds Watched 21.50
1979, Away in a Manger........... 28.50
1980, Bringing in the Boar's Head... 27.00
1981, Make We Merry 47.00

WEDGWOOD
Christmas

1969 Wedgwood Christmas Plate
1969, Windsor Castle (ILLUS.)....... 151.00
1970, Christmas in Trafalgar
   Square 26.00
1971, Picadilly Circus, London 36.00
1972, St. Paul's Cathedral 34.00
1973, Tower of London............. 40.00
1974, Houses of Parliament 22.50
1975, Tower Bridge 31.00
1976, Hampton Court 24.00
1977, Westminster Abbey 31.00
1978, Horse Guards 18.00
1979, Buckingham Palace 34.00
1980, St. James Palace 20.00
1981, Marble Arch................ 32.50
1982, Lambeth Palace............. 40.00
1983, All Souls, Langham Palace 45.00
1984, Constitution Hill 32.00
1985, The Tate Gallery............. 36.00
1986, Albert Memorial 41.00

Mother's Day
1971, Sportive Love............... 17.00
1972, Sewing Lesson.............. 28.00
1973, Baptism of Achilles 31.00

1974, Domestic Employment 35.00
1975, Mother & Child 19.00
1976, The Spinner 22.00
1977, Leisure Time 24.00
1978, Swan & Cygnets 27.00
1979, Deer & Fawn 32.00
1980, Birds 32.00
1981, Mare & Foal 29.00
1982, Cherubs with Swing 21.00
1983, Cupid & Butterfly 22.50
1984, Cupid & Music 33.00
1985, Cupid & Doves.............. 39.00
1986, Cupids at Play 30.00

COMPACTS & VANITY CASES

Compact by Rene Lalique

Brushed gold compact, w/cloisonne
  medallion, 2½" sq., w/original
  box $40.00
Enameled compact, Art Deco style,
  orange w/bulldog center, chain
  w/lipstick holder, Evans 55.00
Gold & enamel compact, circular
  w/hinged lid, decorated w/a frieze
  of tiny enameled blossoms &
  leaves in green & white, w/a
  larger rose blossom in the center,
  underside enameled w/stylized
  initials, stamped "LALIQUE," by
  Rene Lalique, 2" d. (ILLUS.) 6,600.00
Gold colored metal compact, heart-
  shaped, w/original box 35.00
Leather compact, black w/gold embossed sunburst & deer, 1920's ... 35.00
Mother of pearl compact, large,
  1950's 40.00
Silver compact, brushed finish, Elgin
  American, 1940's, w/original
  box 35.00
Silver compact, overall enameled
  scene, .800 silver 95.00
Silver vanity case, overall chased
  butterflies & flowers, powder, lip-
  stick & compartment for cigarettes, black silk wrist strap,
  .800 silver 85.00
Silver tone metal compact w/green
  gold decoration, brushed finish,

Elgin American, 4", w/flannel
  case & original box.............. 48.00
Sterling silver compact, oval form
  w/engraved floral designs, interi-
  or w/mirror inside lid & gold-
  washed, Birmingham, England,
  ca. 1900, 1¾".................. 55.00
Sterling silver compact, Art Deco
  style, by Richard Hudnut, 2½".... 95.00
Sterling silver compact, circular form
  w/floral border & engine-turned
  field centered by monogram, the
  interior w/inset mirror, America,
  20th c., 6" d. 110.00
Sterling silver compact w/card
  holder, coin holder, cigarette case
  & note pad on a chain w/match-
  ing matchsafe, Whiting-Davis..... 195.00

COOKBOOKS

Jack Benny Jell-O Recipe Book

  *Cookbook collectors are usually good cooks
and will buy important new cookbooks as
well as seek out notable older ones. Many early cookbooks were published and given away
as advertising premiums for various products
used extensively in cooking. While some rare,
scarce first edition cookbooks can be very expensive, most collectible cookbooks are
reasonably priced. We list our advertising
cookbooks alphabetically by the names of the
companies which produced them.*

Advertising, "Best Foods - The Budg-
  et Cookbook," by Ida Allen, hard-
  bound, 1935 .... $15.00
Advertising, "Chicken of the Sea
  Recipe Booklet," pictures
  Hopalong Cassidy, 1951 .... 25.00
Advertising, "Betty Crocker's Picture
  Cookbook," 1950 .... 15.00

Advertising, "Enterprise Mfg. Co. -
Enterprising Housekeeper," 1906 . .   13.50

Advertising, "General Foods - All
About Home Baking," color kitch-
en photos, hardbound, 1933 . . . . . .   8.00

Advertising, "Hershey Chocolate
Recipe Book," 1930 . . . .   7.50

Advertising, "Jell-O - Jack & Mary's
Jell-O Recipe Book," Jack Benny &
Mary Livingstone on cover, 1937
(ILLUS.) 20.00

Advertising, "K.C. Baking Powder -
The Cook's Book," 1931 . . . .   5.00

Advertising, "Log Cabin Syrup,"
1929 . . . .   5.00

Advertising, "Methacol," black
mammy on cover, 1921 . . . .   14.00

Advertising, "Minute Tapioca,"
booklet, 1915 . . . .   4.00

Advertising, "Pillsbury's Best 1,000
Recipes Bake-Off Collection" 20.00

Advertising, "Red Wing Union Stoneware - Home Preserving the Red
Wing Way," w/numerous stone-
ware illustrations 85.00

Advertising, "Shumway's Canning
Recipes," booklet 4.00

"American Woman's Cookbook,"
hardcover, 1939 . . . .   9.00

"Blueberry Hill Menue Cookbook,"
by Masterson, New York, 373 pp.,
1963 . . . .   8.50

"Boston Cooking School Cookbook,"
by Fannie Farmer, 1945 . . . .   8.00

"Buttery Shelf Cookbooks," Tasha
Tudor illustrations 14.50

"Common Sense Cookbook," Whit-
man, wooden cover, 1939 . . . .   15.00

"Cross Creek Cookery," by Rawl-
ings, New York, first edition,
1942 . . . .   22.00

"Davidis Deutches Amerikan Koch-
buch," 1879 . . . .   12.00

"Economy Administration Cook
Book," 696 pp., 1913 . . . .   42.00

"Famous Stars' Favorite Foods," 235
famous stars' photographs & their
recipes, 245 pp., 1938 . . . .   30.00

"The Fanny Farmer Jr. Cookbook,"
by Perkins, first edition, w/dust
jacket 8.50

"Fifty-Two Sunday Dinners by
Elizabeth O. Hiller," 1915 . . . .   15.00

"Happy Eating," by Frances Warfield
Newell, autographed, soft cover,
1952 . . . .   10.00

"Household Searchlight Homemaking
Guide," 1937 . . . .   25.00

"Housekeeping In Old Virginia,"
John Morton & Co., hardbound,
528 pp., 1879 . . . .   98.00

"Imperial Cookbook," Townsend,
527 pp., 1890 . . . .   50.00

"Kate Smith's Favorite Recipes,"
47 pp., 1939 . . . .   7.50

"Pictorial Review Standard Cook-
book," 1934 . . . .   14.00

"Prudence Penny Cookbook," color
plates, 815 pp., 1940 . . . .   8.50

"Science in the Kitchen," 1893 . . . . . .   25.00

"Science of Food & Cookery," by
H.S. Anderson, Pacific Press,
1921 . . . .   17.00

"Singers & Swingers in the Kitchen,"
w/rock stars, Rolling Stones,
Monkees, Supremes, etc., 1967 . . .   30.00

"Stillmeadow Cookbook," by Gladys
Taber, first edition, w/dust
jacket 16.50

"Virginia Housewife Cookbook,"
1838 . . . .   250.00

"White House Cookbook," 1926 . . . . .   32.00

COUNTRY STORE COLLECTIBLES

Diamond Dyes Cabinet

*Country store museums have opened across
the country in an effort to recreate those
slower-paced days of the late 19th and early
20th centuries when the general store served
as the local meeting place for much of rural
America. Here one not only purchased necessary supplies for upcoming weeks, but caught
up on important news events and local gos-
sip. With strong interest in colorful tin cans
during the early 1960's came the realization
that these stores and neighborhood groceries
were fast disappearing, replaced by the so-
called supermarkets, and collectors began
buying all items associated with these early
stores. Also see CANS & CONTAINERS and
CASH REGISTERS.*

Bin, red pepper, "C.E. Crouse-
Syracuse, N.Y.," tin w/lift-lid, ser-

pentine front, lithographed camel
in desert scene, 8½ x 9 x 10" $265.00

Bin, tobacco, "Lorillard's Rose Leaf
Tobacco," round, heavy cardboard
w/wooden top & bottom, pictures
cherubs 125.00

Cabinet, counter-type, creamery
supplies, "DeLaval," tin embossed
front w/separator pictured 450.00

Cabinet, counter-type, drills,
"Mephisto," wooden w/drawers,
nice logo illustrated 45.00

Cabinet, counter-type, dyes, "Diamond Dyes," oak case w/litho-
graphed tin front w/scene of children around hot air
balloon .... 700.00 to 1,000.00

Cabinet, counter-type, dyes, "Diamond Dyes," oak case w/litho-
graphed tin front w/scene known
as "Court Jester" 800.00

Cabinet, counter-type, dyes, "Diamond Dyes," oak case w/litho-
graphed tin front w/scene depicting the "Evolution of Woman"
(ILLUS.) 760.00

Cabinet, counter-type, dyes, "Diamond Dyes," oak case w/litho-
graphed tin front w/scene known
as "The Maypole" w/children
dancing around a ribboned
pole 1,050.00

Cabinet, counter-type, dyes, "Perfection Dyes," oak case
w/lithographed tin front 450.00

Cabinet, counter-type, dyes, "Turkish Dyes," wooden case w/sign
front printed w/"Unequaled for
Richness" above a red shield
w/"Turkish Dyes" & crescent
moon, 14" w., 9" deep, 20" h..... 250.00

Cabinet, counter-type, spool,
"Clark's," walnut six-drawer
model w/ruby glass name
plates 1,200.00

Cabinet, counter-type, spool, "Corti-
celli," 30-drawer oak cabinet,
original finish 1,200.00

Cabinet, counter-type, veterinary
medicines, "Dr. Lesure's Famous
Remedies," oak case w/litho-
graphed tin front showing horse's
head (ILLUS. next column) 2,900.00

Huller, "C.B. Horton's Rice & Buck-
wheat Huller," patent model,
13" 875.00

Price stamper, brass, mechanical
hand-held type w/wooden bulb
handle, marked "The Arvin," 1891
patent date.................... 10.00

Seed counter, oak, ten rows of
drawers w/equal size display
windows on customer side, three

drawers high, manufactured by
Shearer, 12' long, 33" h. 1,500.00

Dr. Lesure's Remedies Cabinet

Store counter, mahogany, w/raised
panels, 120" l., 29" w., 32" h. 275.00

Wrapping counter, oak, w/raised
panel, 72" l., 30" w., 32" h. 225.00

COW CREAMERS

Dutch Silver Cow Creamer

*These silver and earthenware cream jugs
were modeled in the form of that beautiful bo-
vine animal, the original source of their intended contents. The most desirable versions
are the early silver and Dutch Delft faience
creations turned out in the 18th century, as
well as those produced in the Staffordshire
potteries before the mid-19th century. However, traditional style cow creamers, made in
the late 19th or in the 20th centuries, are also
deemed collectible. The following group of
cow creamers were offered for sale, or sold at
auction, within recent months.*

China, brown & white glossy glaze,
marked "Western Germany,"
4 x 6" $15.00

China, rust & white spotted, gold
horns, 4 x 6½" 130.00

Earthenware, standing cow figure
on oval base, blue Willow overall
pattern, horns & nose w/pink

coloring, removable cover on back
of cow, Staffordshire, England,
19th c., 5¼" h. 385.00
Silver, stylized animal w/hinged lid
w/bee on back, Holland, ca. 1900,
repairs (ILLUS.). 605.00
Silver plate, realistically formed
model of a cow w/tail curled over
back to form the handle, cover in
center of the back capped by a
fly, flower-strewn grassy oblong
base, Collis & Co., Regent Street,
London, England, ca. 1850,
6 7/8" l. 825.00
Utilitarian pottery, green & cream
glaze 95.00

CURRIER & IVES

American Country Life

*This lithographic firm was founded in 1835
by Nathaniel Currier with James M. Ives becoming a partner in 1857. Current events of
the day were portrayed in the early days and
the prints were hand-colored. Landscapes,
vessels, sport, and hunting scenes of the West
all became popular subjects. The firm was in
existence until 1906. All prints listed are
hand-colored unless otherwise noted.*

American Country Life, October
Afternoon, after F.F. Palmer, large
folio, N. Currier, 1855
(ILLUS.) . . . .$1,500.00 to 2,000.00
American Farm Scenes - No. 2
(Summer), after F.F. Palmer, large
folio, 1853, framed (soiled & dis-
colored margins, small loss to
sheet edge) 3,025.00
American Farm Scenes - No. 4
(Winter), after F.F. Palmer, large
folio, N. Currier, 1853, framed
(margin tears, some margin &
reverse stains & soiling) 7,700.00
American Steamboats on The Hud-
son, Passing the Highlands, large
folio, 1874 .2,200.00
American Whalers Crushed in the

Ice, "Burning the Wrecks to avoid
danger to other Vessels," small
folio, undated (some center creasing, margin staining, reverse rub-
bing & staining) 1,650.00
Arguing the Point, after A.F. Tait,
large folio, N. Currier, 1855,
framed (stained, margin abrasion,
some discoloration) . .4,500.00 to 5,500.00
Assassination of President Lincoln
(The), small folio, 1865 . . . . 49.50
Beauties of Billiards (The), "A Car-
om off the Dark Red," large folio,
1869 (fair condition, staining,
nicks & tears in margins) 990.00
Brook Trout Fishing - "An Anxious
Moment," after A.F. Tait, large
folio, 1862, framed (slight discoloration in margins, slight rubbed
area in title space, minor defects
in edges) .6,600.00
California Scenery, Seal Rocks —
Point Lobos, small folio, undated,
framed 1,320.00
Camping Out, "Some Of The Right
Sort," after L. Maurer, large folio,
N. Currier, 1856, 19 x 27¼",
framed (uneven margins, repaired
center tear, small scratches in
image, some margin stains, glue
& skinned patches on reverse) . . .3,850.00
Cares of a Family (The), after A.F.
Tait, small folio, 1872-74 (slight
discoloration) 440.00
Celebrated Trotting Team Edward
and Swiveller...(The), after Scott
Leighton, large folio, 1882, framed
(discoloration, losses, pencil marks
in margins) .2,200.00
Clipper Ship "Cosmos," medium folio,
undated (good condition) 1,540.00
Col. Michael Corcoran at the Battle
of Bull Run, small folio, undated . . 38.50
Coming From the Trot. Sports on
Home Stretch, large folio, 1869
(backboard stain) 2,200.00
Darktown Fire Brigade (The) - A
Prize Squirt, small folio, 1885,
framed (lower margin torn) 192.50
Death of Genl. Z. Taylor, 12th President of the United States, small
folio, 1850, matted, unframed
(slightly trimmed, short edge
tears) 75.00
Express Train (The), small folio, 1870,
framed (small repaired margin
tears, slight margin soiling) 3,300.00
Going to the Trot. A Good Day and
Good Track, large folio, 1869
(backboard stain) 2,200.00
Gray's Elegy — In A Country Church-
yard, after F.F. Palmer, large folio,
1864, framed (some staining, es-
pecially in margins) 1,210.00

Great East River Suspension Bridge
(The) - Connecting the Cities of
New York and Brooklyn, View
from Brooklyn, Looking West, large
folio, 1886, framed (tears, creases
& filled losses in margins,
repairs).........................2,640.00

Great Fire at St. John, New Brunswick, June 20th, 1877 (The),
small folio, 1877 .... 220.00

Home of Evangeline (The), "In the
Acadian Land," after F.F. Palmer,
large folio, 1864, framed (pale sky
stains).........................1,210.00

Home Sweet Home, large folio, two
columns, two lines of verse, large
folio, 1869 (some reverse
staining).......................2,420.00

Ice-Boat Race on the Hudson, small
folio, undated, framed (minor
soiling & creases)..............4,400.00

In the Northern Wilds. Trapping
Beaver, small folio, 1872-74 (good
condition) 495.00

Landing of the Pilgrims...(The),
small folio, 1876, framed
(trimmed, water stains).......... 165.00

Life of a Fireman (The) - The Ruins,
large folio, N. Currier, 1854,
framed (minor border staining) ..1,870.00

Life on the Prairie

Life on the Prairie, The Trapper's
Defence "Fire Fight Fire," after
A.F. Tait, large folio, 1862, framed,
some tiny abrasions & stains, some
overall staining, taped to overmat
(ILLUS.) 7,150.00

"Lightning Express" Trains (The).
"Leaving the Junction," large folio,
1863, framed (slight foxing & discoloration, pin hole in
margin).......................19,800.00

Little May Blossom, small folio,
1874 .... 95.00

Lookout Mountain, Tennessee, and
the Chattanooga Rail Road, after
F.F. Palmer, large folio, 1866,
framed (few fox marks, water
stains in margins) 5,225.00

Major Genl. Joseph Hooker, small

folio, undated, framed (fly
specks)........................ 150.00

Mink Trapping - "Prime," after
A.F. Tait, large folio, 1862,
framed (minor discoloration)....13,750.00

Mountain Spring (The), after F.F.
Palmer, medium folio, 1862, in
shadow box frame (minor
stains) 350.00

Mrs. J.K. Polk, from a daguerreotype by Plumbe, small folio, N.
Currier, 1846, framed (stains) 125.00

Old Farm Gate (The), after F.F.
Palmer, 1864 (repaired tear to
margin, slight surface soiling
mostly on reverse).............1,650.00

Prairie Fires of the Great West, small
folio, 1871, 8 3/8 x 12 3/8" (two
pinholes, some surface scrapes,
tiny margin tears & nicks, pale
stains)........................1,540.00

Prairie Hunter (The), "One rubbed
out," after A.F. Tait, large folio,
N. Currier, 1852, 14¼ x 21",
framed (foxmark in margins,
staining) 3,520.00

Return From the Pasture (The), after
F.F. Palmer, large folio, undated,
20 x 28" (margins cut to the image on three sides, some staining, some defects at sheet
edges) 418.00

Road (The) - Winter, large folio,
N. Currier, 1853, framed (slight
discoloration in margins, small
tears in edges, slight glue
stains).......................35,200.00

Rocky Mountains (The), Emigrants
crossing the Plains, after F.F.
Palmer, large folio, 1866,
17½ x 25 5/8", framed (some
staining in margins & on reverse
but generally excellent
condition) 17,600.00

Roses of May, small folio, 1870 ..... 100.00

Snow Storm (The), medium folio, undated, 11 1/8 x 15 3/8" (some
creasing, margin & reverse
stains).......................2,640.00

Stanch Pointer (A), small folio, 1871,
framed (margins slightly
trimmed) 255.00

Summer Flowers, medium folio,
1861, 13 1/8 x 18¼", framed,
water stain in subject at right,
mat staining in margins (ILLUS.
next page) 990.00

Sunny Side, The Residence of the late
Washington Irving, large folio,
undated, 14¾ x 20 3/8", framed
(some pale staining, margin &
reverse surface soiling) 1,210.00

Surprise (The), after L. Maurer, large

folio, 1858, 17¾ x 25½",
framed . . . . .3,400.00 to 3,850.00

Summer Flowers

"Thistle" Cutter Yacht, large folio,
1887, framed (some discoloration
& foxing) 2,200.00
View on the Harlem River, N.Y., The
High Bridge in the distance, after
F.F. Palmer, large folio, 1852 (tear
& pale foxing in margins, some
soiling) 5,500.00
Village Blacksmith (The), after
F.F. Palmer, large folio, 1864,
16 x 23¼", framed (some pale
staining) 11,760.00
Washington at Mount Vernon 1797,
small folio, N. Currier, 1852,
8¼ x 12 3/8", framed (some soil-
ing) 770.00
Whale Fishery (The) - Attacking a
"Right" Whale and "Cutting In,"
large folio, undated, framed (faint
stains) 5,225.00
Winter Morning, after F.F. Palmer,
medium folio, 1861, 11 3/8 x 15 3/8",
framed (small crease & tear in margin, apparently excellent con-
dition) 1,870.00
Zachary Taylor - Millard Fillmore,
small folio, N. Currier, 1848,
framed (minor staining) 275.00

CUSPIDORS

*The cuspidor, or spittoon, is a bowl-shaped
vessel into which tobacco chewers could spit.
These containers were a necessity in an era
when much of the male population chewed
tobacco and even some ladies were known to
"take a chew." Made of metal, earthenware
pottery, china and glass, they ranged in size
from the large barroom floor models to small
glass cuspidors designed for the ladies.*

Cast iron, white enameled finish,
round w/flared top, 8½" d. $50.00
Cast iron & tin, model of a turtle,

step on head raises shell & ex-
poses cuspidor, 1890's, 14" l. 225.00
China, lady's, h.p. flowers on white
ground, Germany, 6¾" d. 105.00
Graniteware, blue 55.00
Pottery, blue & white, Basketweave
patt. 135.00

Early Pottery Cuspidor

Pottery, square-form w/shaped
canted corners above a swelled
body, decorated w/four embossed
spreadwing eagles, on a stepped
base, mottled brown glaze, Pennsylvania, late 19th c., various
chips, 4¼" h. (ILLUS.) 110.00
Stoneware, miniature, two cobalt
blue stripes on white glazed
ground, brown interior, 3¼" d 95.00
Stoneware, brushed cobalt blue foliage decoration, impressed label
"R.C.P. Phila.," 7¼" d., 4" h.
(putty-filled chip on base) 275.00

DECOYS

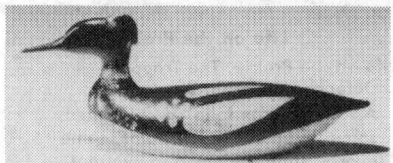

Merganser Drake Decoy

*Decoys have been utilized for years to lure
flying water fowl into target range. They have
been made of carved and turned wood, papier-
mache, canvas and metal, and some are in the
category of outstanding folk art and command high prices.*

Black Duck, by Fred Allen, Monmouth, Illinois (1838-1912), hollow
construction, worn old paint
w/original paint beneath, glass
eyes, 15¼" l. (chipped tail) $140.00

Bluebill Drake, primitive carved wood, old working repaint, glass eyes, Michigan origin, 13" l. 85.00

Bluebill Hen, carved primary feathers, head turned slightly to the left, unknown maker, Quebec, Canada area (minor flaking & wear) 2,200.00

Brant Goose, carved wood, full-bodied stick-up field type, good silhouette w/upturned head, old worn black & white paint w/age cracks, from Prince Edward Island, Canada, 16" l., 26" h. 185.00

Brant Goose, by Wildfowler Co., carved wood, good working repaint, glass eyes, 18½" l. 250.00

Bufflehead Drake sleeper, carved wood, original working paint, glass eyes, mid-20th c., 11" l. 75.00

Canada Goose, balsa body & wooden head, glass eyes, worn old working repaint, 20½" l. 50.00

Canada Goose, galvanized sheet metal, primitive stick-up field decoy, worn paint, iron stake base, 28½" l. 25.00

Canada Goose, carved wood, painted in black, brown & off-white, America, 19th c., 24" l. (restorations) 192.50

Canada Goose, marked "Made by R. Madison Mitchell, Havre de Grace, Md.," carved wood, original paint, 24½" l. (age cracks & puttied hole in head) 400.00

Canvasback Drake, by Roger La Frambois, carved wood, original paint, glass eyes, mid-20th c., 14" l. (minor age cracks) 105.00

Canvasback Drake, Herter's Decoy Co., balsa body w/turned wooden head, original paint, glass eyes, 14½" l. 65.00

Coot, carved wood, original black & white paint w/good wear, branded "Hall," found near Lake Winnebago, Wisconsin, 13¼" l. 75.00

Crows, papier-mache w/straight wire legs, original black paint, glass eyes, 16" l., pr............ 50.00

Crow, primitive carved wood, one-piece stylized body w/black paint, tack eyes, mid-20th c., 11" h. on stand (cracks & some wear) 70.00

Curlew, signed "Roy Conklin," Alexandria Bay, New York (1930-60), solid painted wood, in preening position w/outstretched wings, 11" h. 220.00

Curlew, attributed to Dodge factory, carved wood, original paint, tack eyes, iron nail bill, blurred stamp "Mackey Collection," 11½" l.,

11¼" h. on modern stand (some paint touch-up)................. 600.00

Fish, "Catfish," carved wood, metal fins, glass eyes, leather whiskers, 5¾" l. (age crack, paint wear) ... 65.00

Fish, "Northern," carved wood w/tin fins & tail, glass eyes, painted ... 30.00

Goldeneye Drake, by William E. Pratt Mfg. Co., Illinois (1920-39), old worn paint w/some original paint showing, glass eyes, 13" l. 150.00

Mallard Drake, Mason Standard Grade, good old repaint, glass eyes, 13¼" l.................. 95.00

Mallard Drake w/snaky head, Mason Challenge Grade, worn original paint, glass eyes, 16¼" l. (repaired split in neck) 335.00

Mallard Hen, Hayes Decoy Co., St. Louis, Missouri, carved wood, worn original paint, glass eyes, 16½" l. (old neck repair, one eye damaged) 120.00

Mallard Hen, Mason Standard Grade, glass eyes, old working repaint, 16" l. (wear & damage at neck) 70.00

Merganser Drake, carved wood, original paint, Nantucket, Massachusetts, 19th c. (ILLUS.) 5,225.00

Merganser Drake, attributed to the Carl Woodring Family, Ipswich, Massachusetts, carved wood, brass tack eyes, upright head, old paint (old repair to neck) 1,050.00

Owl, papier-mache, full-bodied, original paint, glass eyes, 16½" h....................... 85.00

Raven, stuffed papier-mache, crudely formed body painted overall in black, raised on a stick standard over a rectangular plinth, America, early 20th c., 14" l., 10½" h...................... 99.00

Red Breasted Merganser Drake, by Chuck Kluka, Mt. Clemens, Michigan, carved wood, turned head, original paint, glass eyes, 16¾" l. (minor separation in head lamination, age crack) 375.00

Redhead Hen, attributed to Chris Smith, Algonac, Michigan (branded C.S.), carved wood, hollow construction, worn old repaint, glass eyes, 15½" l.............. 200.00

Yellowlegs, tin, folding-type, stamped inside "Stratter's Pat. Oct. 27, 1874," set of 4 w/three sticks 350.00

DISNEY COLLECTIBLES

Alice in Wonderland Movie Cel

Scores of objects ranging from watches to dolls have been created showing Walt Disney's copyrighted animated cartoon characters, and an increasing number of collectors are now seeking these, made primarily by licensed manufacturers. Also see BIG LITTLE BOOKS.

Alice in Wonderland movie cel, gouache on celluloid depicting a large portrait of Alice alarmed by flowers in the garden, applied to lithographed background of flowers, 1951, framed, 10¼ x 13¼" (ILLUS.) $1,650.00

Alice in Wonderland paint set, Milton Bradley No. 4725, crayons melted, paints good 12.00

Alice in Wonderland salt & pepper shakers, china, gold trim, Regal China, pr. 95.00

Bambi drawing, pastel on colored paper, depicting Bambi & Faline standing together in a meadow, 1942, framed, 6½ x 7" 715.00

Bambi figure, American Pottery, 7½" h. 68.00

Bambi handkerchief 7.00

Bambi movie cel, depicting Bambi & three rabbits, applied to a gouache background, 1942, 9 x 13" 1,870.00

Captain Hook (from Peter Pan) movie cel, gouache on celluloid depicting Captain Hook placing a ruby ring on his gold dinner hook, applied to a hand-prepared background, 1953, framed, 5½ x 7½" 1,980.00

Cinderella figurine, Ceramic Arts Studio 70.00

Cinderella game, 1950's 35.00

Cinderella handkerchief 7.00

Cinderella jigsaw puzzle, Jaymar . . . 15.00

Cinderella Movie Cel

Cinderella movie cel, multi-sheet celluloid, depicting the stepmother & wicked stepsisters, applied to a hand-prepared background, 1950, matted, 11¼ x 15½" (ILLUS.) 660.00

Cinderella & Prince toy, wind-up plastic, Cinderella & Prince dancing, manufactured by Irwin, copyright Walt Disney Productions, 5" h. 110.00

Davy Crockett ballpoint pen, 12" l. . . 7.50

Davy Crockett bath mat 45.00

Davy Crockett billfold 15.00

Davy Crockett book bag, 1950's 15.00

Davy Crockett clock, animated electric, Davy on horseback, Haddon, 1954 . . . . 125.00

Davy Crockett drawing pad 5.00

Davy Crockett coonskin cap, mint in box, Walt Disney Productions 70.00

Davy Crockett fork, silver plate 12.00

Davy Crockett hobby horse 75.00

Davy Crockett lamp, ceramic base w/figure of Davy & bear by tree, glossy green & brown-toned glaze, Premco Mfg. Co., Chicago, 1955, 8" h. 72.00

Davy Crockett toy chest, wooden, large 75.00

Davy Crockett toy tomahawk 11.00

Disney book, "Living Desert," hardbound 15.00

Disney characters dental certificate, Walt Disney Enterprises, framed . . 30.00

Disney characters quilt, crib size, w/nursery rhymes, ca. 1940's or '50's 225.00

Disney characters sand pail, w/Mickey, Minnie, Donald, Pluto & Goofy, Walt Disney Enterprises, 1938, 8" 95.00

Disney Crossword Puzzle Paint Book, uncolored, 1959, 130 pp. 8.00

Disneyland map, copyright 1964 . . . . 25.00

Disneyland Monorail game, 1960 . . . 25.00

Disneyland spoon, sterling silver . . . 18.00

Disneyland View Master reels, one envelope each for Adventureland, Fantasyland, Frontierland, Main

Street & Tomorrowland, Sawyer,
set of 5 .... 50.00

Donald Duck ball, rubber, Sun Rubber Co. 35.00

Donald Duck bank, Donald sitting on
bricks & waving, colorful, Play Pal
Plastics, 11" h. 25.00

Donald Duck bank, tin, house-
shaped w/color transfer decoration of Mickey & Minnie Mouse on
each side of center slot featuring
Donald's face, his mouth forming
coin slot, stamped, "Chein" on
back, Walt Disney Productions,
3 x 6 x 3" (base rust) 50.00

Donald Duck book, "Donald Duck &
His Friends," 1937 .... 26.00

Donald Duck book, "Donald Duck in
'Bringing Up the Boys'," Story
Hour give-away, 1948 .... 35.00

Donald Duck card game, 1955 ...... 15.00

Donald Duck doll, stuffed cloth,
Character Novelty Co., 12" h. 300.00

Donald Duck doll, cloth, Knickerbocker, 17" h. 45.00

Donald Duck doorstop, Donald
w/stop sign, original paint,
excellent 190.00

Donald Duck drawings, series of pencil drawings of Donald Duck & his
nephews, Huey, Dewey & Louie,
depicting Donald trying to learn
how to play golf, matted, each
approximately 5½ x 6", set of
eight 4,950.00

Donald Duck electric scissors 45.00

Donald Duck feeding dish, three-
compartment, blue, Patriot China,
ca. 1940, 8" d. 52.00

Donald Duck figure, celluloid, movable arms & legs, 1940's, 5" h. ... 65.00

Donald Duck figure, rubber, w/long
beak, Bendey W.D. Toy, 8½" h. ... 25.00

Donald Duck game, skill-type,
"Wrist Twist" 5.00

Donald Duck jigsaw puzzle, Jaymar,
1940's 25.00

Donald Duck lamp, porcelain, figure
of Donald standing next to post,
white w/red & blue trim, 1940's,
12" h. 86.00

Donald Duck paint box, Walt Disney
Enterprises, 1946 .... 25.00

Donald Duck paper mask, 1930's,
10" 75.00

Donald Duck pillow cover, plush,
1940's, 17" sq. 35.00

Donald Duck planter, pottery,
Donald in cowboy suit 38.00

Donald Duck print, "Glow In the
Dark Print," Donald on old bike,
1940's 35.00

Donald Duck pull toy, "Strutter,"
Fisher-Price No. 510, Donald on
wooden cart, 1941 .... 95.00

Donald Duck puzzles, comic pictures, large colorful puzzles in
box, Parker Bros., 1950's, set
of 4 .... 35.00

Donald Duck rattle & teething ring,
rubber, Walt Disney Productions .. 14.00·

Donald Duck toy, wind-up plastic
"Donald Duck the Skier," w/metal
skis, in original lithographed box,
Marx, 1950's, large size 400.00

Donald Duck toy, wind-up plastic
Donald w/umbrella, Louis Marx &
Co. 49.00

Donald Duck toy, wind-up tin,
Donald Duck & Pluto on handcar
in form of doghouse, Lionel,
w/eight sections of track & original box, 10¼" l. (Donald
repaired, Pluto missing ear) 475.00

Donald Duck & Pluto Rubber Car

Donald Duck toy, Donald & Pluto in
car, Sun Rubber Co., 6½" l.
(ILLUS.) 52.00

Donald Duck & Daisy Duck stuffed
figures, Lenci, 8" h., pr. 300.00

Donald Duck & Joe Carioca "turnabout" cookie jar 77.00

Donald Duck & his nephew "turnabout" cookie jar 70.00

Dumbo the Elephant book, "Dumbo:
The Story of the Flying Elephant,"
soft cover, large, 1942 .... 30.00

Dumbo figure, American Pottery 75.00

Dumbo coloring book 15.00

Dumbo jigsaw puzzle, Jaymar,
1940's 25.00

Dumbo movie cel, Timothy Mouse
standing at end of Dumbo's trunk,
applied to water-color & airbrushed background, stamped
lower right, "WDP," & w/Courvoi-
sier Galleries label, matted &
framed, together w/Disney story
sketch of Timothy Mouse standing
in front of peanut, stamped lower
left "WDP" & w/Courvoisier
Galleries label, matted,
8¾ x 10½" & 5¼ x 7", two
pieces 2,750.00

Dwarf Bashful doll, composition
head, cloth body, Knickerbocker
Toy Co. 95.00

Dwarf Bashful doll, felt, 1930's,
12" 150.00
Dwarf Bashful movie cel, applied to
starred airbrushed ground, 1937,
matted & framed, 4½ x 6¾" 880.00
Dwarf Doc figure, composition,
Knickerbocker, 1930's, 9" h. 90.00
Dwarf Dopey doll, composition head
& body, Knickerbocker Toy Co.,
9" 165.00
Dwarf Dopey doll, cloth w/painted
oil-cloth mask face, wearing blue
velveteen tunic & red stockinette
cap, 11½" h. 44.00
Dwarf Dopey doll, cloth, Chad Valley, 1930's 115.00
Dwarf Dopey figure, bisque,
3¼" h. 30.00
Dwarf Dopey figure, rubber, Seiber-
ling, 5½" h. 35.00
Dwarf Dopey movie cel, Dopey
sweeping diamonds into a dustpan,
applied to an airbrushed ground,
1937, matted, 7¼ x 9¼" 2,640.00
Dwarf Dopey planter, Leeds China
Co. 30.00
Dwarf Dopey print, "I'm Dopey,"
original frame 45.00
Dwarf Dopey soap figure, Castile,
Lightfoot Schultz, 1930's, w/box .. 40.00
Dwarf Grumpy figure, composition,
Knickerbocker, 1930's, 9" h. 90.00
Dwarf Grumpy movie cel, depicts
Dwarf Grumpy, applied to a
starred background, Kennedy &
Co. label, 1937, matted & framed,
4½ x 6½" 825.00
Dwarf Happy doll, composition
w/jointed arms, dressed in origi-
nal clothes & hat, marked "Walt
Disney-Knickerbocker Toy Co.," 9"
(small craze on nose) 90.00
Dwarf Happy print, "I'm Happy,"
1938, framed 45.00
Dwarfs Doc & Grumpy brush, metal
& wood 41.00
Dwarfs Bashful, Doc, Dopey,
Grumpy, Sleepy, Sneezy & Happy
figures, hard rubber, Seiberling,
1938, set of 7 .... 325.00 to 375.00
Fantasia Centaurette figure, china,
black, Vernon Kilns, No. 24 ...... 220.00
Fantasia lobby card, "Pastoral Sym-
phony" scene, matted & framed .. 400.00
Fantasyland tie tack, sterling
silver 9.00
Ferdinand the Bull book, "Ferdinand
the Bull," ca. 1938 .... 12.00
Ferdinand the Bull coloring book,
1938 .... 22.00
Ferdinand the Bull figure, composition, jointed, signed Walt Disney
Enterprises & Ideal 125.00
Ferdinand the Bull toy, windup tin

Ferdinand & the matador, Louis
Marx & Co., 1938 .... 290.00
Goofy book, "Dippy the Goof,"
hardbound, Whitman, 1938 ...... 35.00
Goofy flasher pin, red, from Disney-
land, 2½" 40.00

Goofy Movie Cel

Goofy movie cel, full celluloid
depicting Goofy as an Olympic
runner carrying the torch, applied
to a painted cartoon background,
10½ x 12¼" (ILLUS.) 440.00
Goofy toy, windup tin, head & feet
move, tail spins, Line Mar 325.00
Jiminy Cricket bubble gum wrapper,
Dietz, Tomart No. G9116, 1940 ... 40.00
Johnny Appleseed record album,
1949 .... 18.00
Lady and the Tramp movie cel, multi-
sheet celluloid depicting Lady,
Tramp & Tony at the back door of
Tony's restaurant, applied to a
master water-color background,
inscribed "Stand Stop Sc. 42 Pos
for 44 Sc. 42 Start Sto 2079-7-42
SA 44.," 1955, 12½ x 36".....16,500.00
Ludwig Von Drake toy, windup tin,
Ludwig walking, Line Mar, 6" 285.00
Mary Poppins hair dryer, 1964, original box 30.00
Mary Poppins sugar shell, silver
plate, 1964 .... 25.00
Mickey Mouse advertising figure,
composition, semi-round standing
figure of Mickey w/yellow gloved
hands on hips, large moon ears,
pie-cut eyes & swirling tail, figure
tied into a shadowbox frame,
France, ca. 1935, framed, 30 x 44",
38" h. 2,420.00
Mickey Mouse alarm clock, animated, Ingersoll, 1930's 250.00
Mickey Mouse bank, ceramic,
shaped like a television, picture
of Mickey & Pluto on "screen" 55.00
Mickey Mouse bank, composition,
Mickey w/movable head standing
beside chest, Crown Toy Co.,
1940's, 6¼" h. 250.00
Mickey Mouse bank, dime register,

lithographed tin, dated 1939,
2½ x 2½" 75.00

Mickey Mouse book, "Mickey Mouse
in Giantland," 1931-34, color illustrations, hardbound 150.00

Mickey Mouse book, "Mickey Mouse
Presents Walt Disney's 'The Gold-
en Touch,'" hardbound, 1937,
212 pp. (no dust jacket).......... 80.00

Mickey Mouse book, "Mickey
Mouse's Mother Goose," Whitman, 1937 .... 75.00

Mickey Mouse book, "Mickey Never
Fails," hardbound, Heath, 1939 ... 30.00

Mickey Mouse book, "Ye Olden
Days," pop-up type, Blue Ribbon
Books, 1934 (pages brittle) 75.00

Mickey Mouse charm, sterling silver,
¾" 50.00

Mickey Mouse clothes brush, silver
& black metal, Disney Enterprises,
ca. 1930's..................... 60.00

Mickey Mouse coloring book, Walt
Disney No. 887................. 25.00

Mickey Mouse creamer, china, gold
& blue lustre finish 25.00

Mickey Mouse egg cup, china,
1930's........................ 62.00

Mickey Mouse feeding dish, heavy
white china, center w/pie-eyed
Mickey wearing red pants & yellow shoes & playing one-string
guitar, border w/alphabet in
black, marked "Mickey Mouse
China, Authorized by Walter E.
Disney, Made in Bavaria,"
7¾" d........................ 140.00

Mickey Mouse figure, bisque, Mickey playing drum, Japan, 1932-38,
3½" h........................ 55.00

Mickey Mouse figure, hard rubber,
marked "Germany," 2" h........ 75.00

Mickey Mouse game, "Spin-N-Win,"
original box 65.00

Mickey Mouse greeting card, shows
three different sized Mickeys
w/pie-eyes, reads "Feeling Better? Three Cheers," gilt edges,
w/original envelope, "Hall
Brothers, Licence by Walt Disney
Studios," unused 15.00

Mickey Mouse magazine, November
1937, Br'er Wolf Halloween
cover 65.00

Mickey Mouse marionette, papier-
mache & cloth, papier-mache head
w/rat nose, painted pie-eyes, felt
ears & open mouth smile, cloth
body featuring black shirt, grey
shorts, white gloves & boots,
designed by Tony Sarg, ca. 1933,
w/strings 3,080.00

Mickey Mouse movie cel from
"Mickey's Christmas Carol,"
depicts Mickey seated at desk,
shivering & blowing on hands,
museum framed & matted 1,400.00

Mickey Mouse napkin ring, celluloid,
ca. 1938 .... 30.00

Mickey Mouse necklace, enameled
figure of Mickey & two Minnie
figures on silver chain 125.00

Mickey Mouse pencil drawing on paper, from "Steamboat Willie,"
depicting "Steamboat Willie,"
numbered "69" & "379," framed,
1928, 9¾ x 11¾" 770.00

Mickey Mouse pocket watch, Bicentennial edition, Bradley, 1976,
w/box ....100.00 to 125.00

Mickey Mouse porringer, silver
plate, pie-eyed Mickey cut-out
handle, center w/Mickey riding
Horace Horsecollar,
1930's..................75.00 to 110.00

Mickey Mouse rocker, wooden, each
side painted w/an early Mickey
lying in a pool of water, the sides
connected by a seat & play rack,
the Mengel Company, ca. 1935,
w/a photo of the toy & its original
owner, 35" l. (some flaking on
one side) 462.00

Mickey Mouse salt & pepper shakers, Mickey & the Beanstalk,
original box, pr. 12.00

Mickey Mouse slippers, fleece-lined
sheepskin w/Mickey decals on
front & printed Mickey & Minnie
figures on each side, marked
"Size 11," children's, pr. 77.00

Mickey Mouse soap bars, "Soaky,"
24 figural bars w/poster in original box 58.00

Mickey Mouse teapot, cov., Mickey
playing banjo, lustre finish, 5" w.,
4" h........................ 35.00

Mickey Mouse toy, battery-
operated, "Mickey Mouse Krazy
Car," Marx 45.00

Mickey Mouse toy, celluloid & wood
keywind Mickey on a horse wearing chaps & bandana, red wooden
horse mounted on wheels, 1930's,
7"...........................3,520.00

Mickey Mouse toy, Mickey on tractor, rubber w/metal axles, black
& peach Mickey, red tractor
w/white tires, both sides marked
"Mickey's Tractor," bottom
marked "Sun Rubber Co.,"
4½ x 4½"..................... 85.00

Mickey Mouse toy, pull-type, "Mickey Mouse Puddle Jumper," two-
part car w/swaying rear end that
bounces Mickey from side to side,
Fisher-Price No. 310,
ca. 1953.................105.00 to 145.00

Mickey Mouse toy, top, spinning-
type, Walt Disney Enterprises,
1930's 245.00

Mickey Mouse toy set, eight Mickey
soldiers, Walter E. Disney, 1930's,
w/box, 8 pcs. 200.00

Mickey Mouse wrist watch, Mickey
on dial w/conventional subsidiary
dial, metal band w/two figural
Mickey links, Ingersoll, ca. 1939
(band from earlier Mickey
watch) 605.00

Mickey Mouse wrist watch, Inger-
soll, 1947 . . . . 125.00

Mickey Mouse wrist watch, "Elec-
tric" Timex, 1968, original box. . . . 175.00

Mickey & Minnie Mouse cookie jar,
"turnabout". 88.00

Mickey & Minnie Mouse dolls, flannel, each w/flannel bodies, felt
ears, swirling tails & stitched
smiles, Mickey dressed in red
flannel shorts, Minnie wearing a
bubble & dot print green dress,
Mickey 15" h., Minnie 14" h.,
pr. 825.00

Mickey & Minnie Mouse salt & pepper shakers, Leeds China Com-
pany, 1940's, pr. 26.00

Mickey & Minnie Toothbrush Holder

Mickey & Minnie Mouse toothbrush
holder, bisque, names impressed
on back, 1930's, 1¾ x 3½ x 4½"
(ILLUS.) . . . . 150.00 to 250.00

Mickey & Minnie Mouse & Donald
Duck toothbrush holder, bisque,
marked "Walt Disney," original
paint, 1930's 250.00

Mickey Mouse & Pluto toy, celluloid,
featuring Mickey on the back of a
three-wheeled Pluto, tinplate front
wheel houses keywind mechanism,
Japan, 5½" l. 6,600.00

Minnie Mouse cookie cutter, alumi-
num, 4" 55.00

Minnie Mouse doll, pie-cut eyes, sharp
nose & open-mouth smile, velvet
body & orange high heel shoes,
9" h. (tail missing, holes in hat). . 1,760.00

Minnie Mouse toy, windup Minnie on

a trapeze, celluloid figure, Borg-
feldt, 1930's, w/box 1,500.00

Minnie Mouse wrist watch, mint in
box, Bradley, 1973 . . . . 125.00

Peter Pan game, "Peter Pan Adventure Game," Transogram 30.00

Peter Pan Movie Cel

Peter Pan movie cel, full celluloid
depicting a large image of Peter
Pan, applied to a hand-prepared
background, matted, 1953,
7½ x 9" (ILLUS.) 3,300.00

Pinocchio clock, Bayard, France,
1964, original box 350.00

Pinocchio book, "Adventures of
Pinocchio," illustrated, 250 pp. . . . 12.00

Pinocchio book, "Pinocchio," Heath
Publishing Co., 1940, illustrations
by Walt Disney Studio 16.00

Pinocchio charm, plastic, 1" h. 15.00

Pinocchio doll, composition, 11" h. . . 135.00

Pinocchio doll, composition, jointed,
Knickerbocker, 14" h. . . . 275.00 to 290.00

Pinocchio doll, stuffed plush w/mask
face, Gund, 1960's 14.00

Pinocchio figure, composition, jointed body w/Kay Kamen paper label on back, dressed in red &
white clothes, Crown Manufacturing Company, possibly a store display item, ca. 1940, 34" h. (some
crazing, cracks & chips, retouching
to hair). 770.00

Pinocchio figure, rubber, red & yellow outfit w/blue tie, Dakin,
8" h. 22.00

Pinocchio marionette, jointed legs,
colorful, 10½" h. 60.00

Pinocchio mask, rubber, 1950's 20.00

Pinocchio pencil box, w/contents . . . 55.00

Pinocchio pencil sharpener, desk-
type, figural 49.00

Pinocchio tea set, tin, Ohio Art,
w/box 375.00

Pinocchio toy, battery-operated,
"Pinocchio Playing Xylophone,"
Rosko, w/box . . . . 250.00 to 275.00

Pinocchio toy, windup tin, figure of
a walking Pinocchio carrying
buckets, marked "Walt Disney

Ent. C. 1939, Marx," 8½" h. (minor wear) 275.00

Pinocchio transfer decals, apply to skin, Walt Disney Productions, 1961, in colorful 1 x 5¾ x 8¾" box, set of 100 .... 12.00

Pluto bank, wooden, sits on haunches, 11" h. 100.00

Pluto book, "Story of Pluto the Pup," 1938, hardbound 20.00

Pluto child's seat, die-cut & painted wood, steel pipe non-moving legs & handlebars, marked "W.D.P.," 33" l., 18" h. 85.00

Pluto clock, electric, figural, hard plastic, orange w/bone-shaped hands on dial, moving tongue & eyes, ca. 1955, w/original box, 9" h. (eyes cracked) 132.00

Pluto lamp, 1940's 35.00

Pluto toy, friction-type, Pluto driving a four-wheel cart w/lever action handlebars, Marx, Japan, 6" l. 220.00

Pluto toy, Paddle Pop-up Kritter, flexible figure on a paddle, Fisher-Price, No. 440, Walt Disney Enterprises .... 50.00 to 65.00

Pluto toy, squeak-type, rubber w/bells on crib hanger, Walt Disney Productions 35.00

Pluto toy, windup, celluloid Pluto performing on a high bar w/"Gym Toy" pennant, Line Mar, in original box, 13" h. 462.00

Pluto toy, windup tin, "Rollover," plush-covered Pluto runs forward, rolls over & raises up on his feet to beg, "Watch Me Roll Over" on side, Line Mar, in original box, 6½" l. .... 195.00 to 245.00

Sleeping Beauty movie cel, scene of Briar Rose holding a broom, applied to a photographic reproduction background, "Art Corner" label, matted & framed, 1959, 7¾ x 9½" 660.00

Snow White bank, dime register, Walt Disney Enterprises, ca. 1939 .... 160.00

Snow White board game, Parker Bros. 110.00

Snow White book, "Snow White Storybook," 1938 .... 50.00

Snow White figure, bisque, marked, 4¼" h. 58.00

Snow White figure, chalkware, 14" h. 37.50

Snow White figure, china, w/original stand & sticker dated 1960, 5" h. 40.00

Snow White housekeeping set: carpet sweeper, dust pan & brush; tin, w/box, 3 pcs. 65.00

Snow White lamp, chalkware, Walt Disney Enterprises, 1938, 10" h. .. 50.00

Snow White movie cel, multi-sheet celluloid depicting Snow White talking to pigeons sitting on a window sill, applied to a wooden background, matted & framed, 1937, 8¾ x 10" 4,400.00

Snow White planter, ceramic, Leeds China Company 30.00

Snow White postcard, Valentine & Sons 25.00

Snow White refrigerator, tin, Wolverine 30.00

Snow White tumbler, 1938 .... 25.00

Snow White wrist watch, U.S. Time, 1950's ....40.00 to 55.00

Snow White & the Seven Dwarfs art stamp set, 1937, w/box 45.00

Snow White & the Seven Dwarfs blocks, "Put Together Blocks," original box 125.00

Snow White & the Seven Dwarfs charm bracelet................. 65.00

Snow White & the Seven Dwarfs Christmas ornaments, composition, each figure w/painted facial features & sparkle-glitter hollow bodies for candy storage, set of 8 .... 110.00

Snow White & the Seven Dwarfs figures, bisque, each painted, produced by George Borgfeldt Corporation of New York, 1938, 5" h. dwarfs, 7" h. Snow White, set of 8 .... 605.00

Snow White & the Seven Dwarfs handkerchief, Walt Disney Enterprises, 9" sq. 20.00

Snow White & the Seven Dwarfs jigsaw puzzles, two complete picture puzzles w/box, Whitman, 1937 ... 58.00

Snow White & the Seven Dwarfs paper doll set, includes dolls, ten sheets of clothing (some cut) & eight wooden stands, Whitman No. 2185, 1938, original box, set........................... 75.00

Snow White & the Seven Dwarfs sheet music, "Heigh Ho" 15.00

Snow White & the Seven Dwarfs tumbler, Bosco Drink premium ... 35.00

Snow White & the Seven Dwarfs wall rack, child's, wooden, cutout figures along top, three pegs, 12½" l., 7½" h.................. 62.00

Three Caballeros sheet music, "Three Caballeros," 1943 .... 15.00

Three Little Pigs bank, book-type, 1930's 25.00

Three Little Pigs book, Blue Ribbon, 1933 (very nice light coloring on black & white illustrations) 95.00

Three Little Pigs colored pencil set, in sliding box w/colorful graphics 20.00

Three Little Pigs game, "Who's Afraid of the Big Bad Wolf," Walt Disney Enterprises, 1933 .... 125.00

Three Little Pigs movie cel, depicting the three little pigs at their cottage, applied to a water-color background, matted & framed, 1932, 9 x 11½" 6,600.00

Three Little Pigs sheet music, "Who's Afraid of the Big Bad Wolf," 1933 .... 21.50

Three Little Pigs & Big Bad Wolf alarm clock, Ingersoll, 1934 ....465.00 to 595.00

Thumper (from Bambi) planter, ceramic, Leeds China Company ....25.00 to 35.00

Tinkerbell (from Peter Pan) movie cel, multi-sheet celluloid depicting Tinkerbell flying, applied to a photographic background of a house, 1953, 12¾ x 15½" 2,475.00

20,000 Leagues Under the Sea game, Jaymar Games, copyright Walt Disney productions, w/box .. 50.00

Uncle Remus doll, cloth, 1940's, 14" h. 425.00

Walt Disney World map, "Guide To the Magic Kingdom," in wooden frame, used at Disney World, 32 x 36" 150.00

Winnie-the-Pooh cookie jar 62.50

Winnie-the-Pooh movie cel, full celluloid depicting Winnie, Piglet, Owl & Kanga swimming, matted & framed, 1966, 8 x 9½" 880.00

Winnie-the-Pooh wrist watch, Sears, Walt Disney Productions, 1954 .... 48.00

Zorro costume, complete in box 95.00

Zorro Target Game, w/rifle & darts, unopened in box 85.00

DOLL FURNITURE & ACCESSORIES

Walnut Four-Poster Doll Bed

Bed, maple, canopy-style, w/spread & canopy cover, ca. 1910, 7¼ x 11½", 11½" h. $225.00

Bed, painted finish, scrolling headboard flanked by turned & blocked posts w/flattened mushroom finials, shaped footrail w/conforming posts, old red paint 195.00

Bed, walnut, four-poster w/turned posts & cut-out headboard, old finish, 10½ x 16¼" (ILLUS.) 250.00

Bed, wooden, Raggedy Ann, 21" l., 13" w., 16" h. 25.00

Book, Barbie doll, "Here's Barbie," 1962 .... 20.00

Buggy, wicker & wood, corduroy lined interior, wooden handle & wicker hood inset w/smaller round side windows, finished in beige, ca. 1900, 29" l., 34" h. 220.00

Carriage, wire & wire mesh, sleigh-form wire mesh body w/scrolled wire sides, large metal wheels, arched metal handle at back, 23" h. 135.00

Carriage, wood & leatherette, red chassis w/striping, wooden wheels, metal brackets for convertible sun shade, 19th c., 30" long (some wear & damage) 292.50

Chair, ladder-back armchair, splint seat, old worn light green paint over earlier red, 12" h. 95.00

Chest of drawers, walnut, hand-carved bottom & sides, 6 x 9", 9" h. 195.00

Clothes, Barbie doll outfit, "Ballerina 989," complete 15.00

Clothes, Barbie doll outfit, "Dogs'n Duds" 30.00

Coffee grinder, "Little Tot," 3" 85.00

Coffeepot, cov., copper, on legs, marked w/crown & two arrows, 5½" h. 30.00

Coffeepot, cov., graniteware, sky blue 35.00

Coffeepot, cov., toleware, painted flowers on black japanned ground, side spout 225.00

Cooking set: cooking utensils, tea kettle, skillet, open kettle, griddle & waffle iron; marked "Wagner Ware pat. Feb. 22, 1910," boxed set 175.00

Cradle, grain-painted wood, hooded-type on rockers, exterior grain-painted to simulate crotch-grain mahogany, interior painted a putty color, ca. 1840, 19" l., 11" h. (minor damage) 302.50

Cradle, pine, low country-style on rockers, tombstone-type headboard & footboard, shaped canted sides, shaped rockers, square nail construction, nut brown patina, 23½" l. 115.00

Cupboard, painted & decoupaged
pine, step-back style w/flat top
above two glazed doors w/white
porcelain knobs opening to
shelved interior above two long
drawers w/white porcelain knobs
above two doors w/matching
knobs at bottom, original dark
brown finish w/stencilled gold &
silver decoration & decoupage,
late wire nail construction,
17" w., 30¾" h.................. 200.00
Cutlery set, Kiddykook, 28 pcs. in
original cardboard box 18.00
Dollhouse, Barbie's Dream House,
1962 .... 55.00
Dollhouse, Bliss, lithographed paper
on wood, two-story, four pierced
arched windows, hinged door
w/portico supported by two
turned wood columns, hinged
facade revealing two rooms, ca.
1895, 14½" h..................1,100.00

Large Bliss Dollhouse

Dollhouse, Bliss, lithographed paper
on wood in red & multicolored
"brick" facade w/stained glass
curtained windows, railed porch
below double-turret balcony, blue
roof w/two dormer windows,
opens at sides to reveal four
papered rooms, marked on door
"575.B," 12 x 19", 26" h.
(ILLUS.) 6,600.00
Dollhouse, Built-Rite Dollhouse
No. 115, cardboard, furnished
w/27 large furniture pieces, baby
buggy, dog, cat & 12 movable
shrubs, w/attached garage,
1940's, 19" l..................... 73.50
Dollhouse, German cottage-style,
painted wood, yellow sides,
w/steep red roof, trellised porch
& green stenciled shutters, lower
facade opening to reveal two
rooms, one furnished w/painted
blue metal bedroom suite, the
dormer window opens into large

German Cottage Dollhouse

attic, 1920's, 11 x 16", 15" h.
(ILLUS.)...................... 308.00
Dollhouse, Hampton's Cottage
House, white shingles, two rooms,
pillared porch, original curtains,
1920's, 14" deep, 22" h.......... 325.00
Dollhouse, New Jersey shore house,
cream exterior w/green trim &
brown shingled roof, w/architec-
tural details including two-story
bay, dormers, turret & long covered porch w/turned railings, rear
opens to reveal one large room
w/shellwork cabinets, wood pedestal table, upholstered parlor
suite & various ornaments, ca.
1900, 20 x 26 x 17" 1,045.00
Dollhouse bathtub & toilet, wooden,
painted green, 1920's, the set 37.50
Dollhouse bedroom set: bed, vanity,
stool, chest of drawers, boy doll,
table, lamp, two pictures; Petite
Princess, 9 pcs. 95.00
Dollhouse breakfront, Renwal 15.00
Dollhouse candelabra, Petite
Princess 20.00
Dollhouse dining set: 3½" h. oval
dropleaf table, five 2" h. side
chairs & one 2" h. armchair; tin,
7 pcs. 87.00
Dollhouse kitchen, "Cook 'n Serve"
set, complete kitchen w/three
figures, Renwal, ca. 1950 .... 35.00
Dollhouse kitchen stove, Petite
Princess 70.00
Dollhouse refrigerator, Petite
Princess 75.00
Dollhouse sink, Renwal, 4 x 6" 10.00
Dollhouse tea cart, Petite Princess .. 20.00
Doll velocipede, cast iron, wooden
pedals & seat 275.00
Dress, Crissy "Starshine" outfit,
Ideal, 1972, mint in package 15.00
Dress, "Heidi" outfit & pin, fits 36"
Shirley Temple doll 75.00
Dresser w/mirror, wood, three-
drawer, 4 x 9 x 12" 45.00
Egg beater, "Baby Bingo," A & J,
5½" 12.00

Highchair, cast iron, Arcade........ 32.00

Laundry set: wooden folding ironing board, wooden folding drying rack, laundry basket, tin iron, clothespins; the set............. 90.00

Living room set: two armchairs, two side chairs, footstool, center table, drawered lamp table; ormolu trim, French styling, made in Germany, the set.................. 325.00

Quilt, pieced Tumbling Blocks patt., velvet, 16 x 19"................ 65.00

Quilt, pieced Snowball patt., goldenrod & solid blue w/black & white gingham, homespun back, 16½ x 21" (minor stains)........ 300.00

Sad iron, cast iron, 2¼"........... 40.00

Sad iron, "Dover No. 902," hooded........................ 38.00

Stroller, "Sunnie Miss," tin, Ohio Art......................... 35.00

Tea set, "Barbie Silver Anniversary"................... 85.00

Tea set: cov. teapot, creamer, sugar bowl & six cups & saucers; blue graniteware, 15 pcs........... 275.00

Telephone, candlestick-type, metal & wood w/bell, 8" h............. 30.00

Umbrella, ivory handle, gold-decorated black silk, w/original black silk case (for 15½" doll).... 385.00

Waffle iron, cast iron, "Stover Jr.," box w/instructions............. 150.00

Waffle iron, cast iron, "Wagner," dated Feb. 22, 1910............. 75.00

Washboard, scrubbed wood frame w/redware insert, 6¾ x 13½" (minor age cracks)............. 295.00

Washstand, metal, w/cream-colored Kate Greenaway-style decorated divided washbowl, original manufacturer's porcelain label, France....................... 750.00

DOLLS

A.B.G. (Alt, Beck & Gottschalk) bisque socket head baby marked "1361," wobbly tongue, dressed, 16".............................$375.00

A.B.G. bisque head girl marked "1362," blue stationary eyes, pierced ears, blonde mohair wig, (repainted) jointed body, dressed, 21"........................... 242.00

Alexander (Madame) Amish Boy, 1965-69, dressed, 8".....425.00 to 475.00

Alexander (Madame) Brenda Starr, hard plastic body & legs, outside jointed hips, jointed knees, vinyl arms & head, rooted red-orange hair w/long lock on top, 1964, dressed, 12"................... 795.00

Alexander (Madame) "Orphant" Annie, 1965, dressed, 14"...... 150.00

American Character "Betsy McCall," jointed ankles, original dress, 22"........................... 95.00

American Character "Chuckles," original clothing except shoes, 23"...........................125.00

American Character "Toni," dressed in collegiate costume, w/original booklet, 10".................... 69.00

Annalee "Architect," cloth, 1959, 10".................400.00 to 475.00

Annalee "Boy Swimmer," cloth, 1959, 10"..................... 450.00

A.M. (Armand Marseille) bisque socket head baby marked "341," called "My Dream Baby," blue glass sleep eyes, closed mouth, molded hair, jointed composition body, composition hands, dressed, 11"..................350.00 to 395.00

A.M. brown bisque head baby marked "A.M. 351-3K," brown glass sleep eyes, open mouth w/two teeth, pierced ears w/gold earrings, painted hair, brown composition jointed baby body, dressed in yellow pants, black vest, red fez w/long black tassel, 13½"....................... 650.00

A.M. bisque socket head character baby marked "590," blue sleep eyes, open-closed mouth, blonde mohair wig, ball-jointed composition body w/bent limbs, dressed, 17"......................... 880.00

A.M. bisque head "Floradora" marked "370," dark blue eyes, blonde hair, kid body, dressed & w/bonnet, 27".................. 495.00

Arranbee "Nancy Lee," hard plastic, glued on saran wig in ponytail, 1951, dressed, 17".............. 165.00

Bahr & Proschild bisque head toddler marked "604," blue sleep eyes, open-closed mouth w/two teeth, auburn mohair wig, five-piece body, dressed, 14"........ 418.00

Barbie, hollow hard plastic body, hard plastic arms & legs, firmer textured brunette saran hair in a ponytail, No. 850, 1961, dressed .. 90.00

Bergmann (C.M.) bisque head girl, brown glass stationary eyes, blonde h.h. (human hair) wig, dressed, 23".................. 485.00

Bisque toddler marked "P.4," all-bisque, jointed at shoulders, small molded wisps of blonde hair, molded blue socks & brown shoes, Germany, 4½".......... 65.00

Bisque head girl marked "Wimpern,
Gesetzl Geschutzt," brown sleep
eyes, h.h. wig, pink kid body,
fully jointed composition arms &
legs, Germany, late 19th c.,
28½" h. 2,250.00
Borgfeldt (George) bisque head girl
marked "GB," brown sleep eyes,
auburn h.h. wig, jointed composition body, redressed in brown
satin, 25" 242.00
Bru bisque head girl marked "JNE R,"
blue stationary glass eyes, open
mouth, pierced ears, brown h.h.
wig, jointed composition body,
jointed arms, dressed but no shoes,
12" 2,500.00

Bru Bisque Head Bebe

Bru bisque head Bebe marked "BRU
Jne," molded breastplate, blue
paperweight eyes, open-closed
mouth, cork pate, original blonde
wig, pierced ears, dots accenting
eye corners & nostrils, gusseted
kid body w/bisque lower arms
(one finger chipped), wearing
original blue silk dress trimmed
in lace & Bru blue leather shoes,
ca. 1875, 21" (ILLUS.) 20,900.00
Bru bisque head girl marked "JNE R,"
blue glass stationary paperweight
eyes, closed mouth, pierced ears,
dark blonde h.h. wig in long curls,
original ball-jointed composition
body, jointed wrists, dressed,
36" 9,995.00
Buddy Lee, (trademark doll for H.D.
Lee Co.), dressed as an engineer,
13" 250.00
Bye-lo Baby, bisque head marked
"Grace S. Putnam," blue sleep
eyes, original body, dressed, 13"
head circumference, 15" 375.00

Bye-lo Baby, bisque head marked
"Grace S. Putnam," brown sleep
eyes, celluloid hands, dressed,
20" 1,495.00

Carved Walnut and Cloth Dolls

Carved walnut & cloth black man &
woman, each w/embroidered
eyes, mouth & nose, simple
carved jointed arms & legs, losses
to legs & fading to faces, America, ca. 1920, each 17", pr.
(ILLUS.) 412.50
Century Doll Co. (Kestner) bisque
head girl, blue glass eyes, open-
closed mouth w/molded tongue &
two incised upper teeth, jointed
cloth body, composition arms,
dressed, 14" 600.00
Chad Valley Scotsman, all original,
9" 95.00

Chad Valley Princess Elizabeth

Chad Valley "Princess Elizabeth,"
cloth, glass eyes, dressed, 18"
(ILLUS.) 1,850.00
Charlie Chaplin, papier-mache head,
hands & feet w/original polychrome paint, tin ball & socket
body, cloth costume, 7½" h. 235.00

Chase (Martha) stockinette baby, painted blue eyes, blonde hair, dressed, 20" 330.00

China head girl, pink lustre finish, brown eyes, hair in braided bun, cloth body w/molded china bosom & china arms, 14½" 1,600.00

China head girl marked "Germany," blonde molded hair w/center part, china arms & legs, 16" 150.00

China head child, black short molded curls w/bangs & brush-stroked sides, painted blue eyes, cloth body w/china arms & legs, wearing whitework slip under calico dress, 19" 143.00

Clockwork automaton, mother wheeling child in pram, Bru-look bisque head woman w/paperweight eyes, both costumes original, France, ca. 1880, 12" 5,600.00

Cloth doll, man, lithographed in colors, blue eyes, red lips, wavy brown hair, stuffed body, dressed in a red shirt w/yellow lace collar & sleeves, a green band around the waist, blue breeches, red socks, yellow shoes, patented September 16, 1902, 12½" 110.00

Rare "Columbian Doll"

Cloth doll, baby, "Columbian Doll," oil-painted cloth w/original baby dress, created by Emma Adams & entered in the 1892 Chicago Columbian Exposition & won the Gold Medal, pristine condition (ILLUS.) 9,500.00

Dollhouse gentleman, bisqueheaded w/painted eyes & molded beard & mustache, wearing blue wool felt suit over white shirt & waistcoat, 7" 176.00

Dressel (Cuno & Otto) - Simon & Halbig bisque head girl marked "1349 Jutta," brown sleep eyes, pierced ears, auburn h.h. wig, jointed body, dressed, 23" (hands repainted) 385.00

Eden Bebe bisque head girl marked "Eden Bebe" & "Depose" on back of head, blue stationary glass paperweight eyes, open mouth w/upper row of teeth, pierced ears, long curly light brown h.h. wig, ball-jointed body w/jointed wrists, dressed in underclothes, deep pink satin dress w/lace trim, matching shirred pink bonnet w/ostrich plume, socks, no shoes, 26" 1,850.00

Eegee (Eugene Goldberger) "My Fair Lady," vinyl head & body, blonde hair in black net by Mollyes, fancy costume, ca. 1958 .... 55.00

Eegee "Susan Stroller," vinyl head, hard plastic walker body, cries when turned over, 1963, 23" 52.50

Effanbee "Butterball," marked "6569," all vinyl, molded blonde hair, dated 1969, in original box, 12" 60.00

Effanbee baby "Babyette," composition head & hands, moldedpainted brown hair, closed eyes, closed mouth, stuffed pink cloth body, ca. 1945, tagged, mint in box, 11½" 100.00

Effanbee "Dy Dee Baby," caracul wig, original wardrobe including original pin, original labeled trunk, 12" 185.00

Effanbee "Patsy Ruth," composition limbs & head, brown sleep eyes, h.h. wig, cloth body, ca. 1935, dressed, 27" 385.00

Emma Clear "George & Martha Washington," 19" & 18", pr. 700.00

Fleischer Studio "Betty Boop," composition w/wood-jointed arms & legs w/heart sticker on molded dress, 1935 .... 475.00

French Fashion, bisque swivel head, blue threaded glass eyes, pierced ears, outlined closed mouth, auburn wig, gusseted cloth body w/kid lower arms w/individually stitched fingers, dressed, wearing period hat, 13½" 880.00

French Fashion, bisque swivel head incised "ID"(?), blue-grey paperweight eyes, outlined closed mouth, pierced ears, blonde h.h. wig, gusseted kid body, wearing cream silk floral brocade dress, 16" (hands worn) 1,210.00

Frozen Charlie, china, blond hair, tinted face, 10½" 475.00

Fulper Pottery bisque shoulder head girl marked "S10," blue stationary eyes, blonde mohair wig; oil cloth body, bisque arms, dressed, 20" .. 242.00

Gaultier (F.) bisque swivel head girl

marked "F.G.," blue stationary paperweight eyes, closed mouth, pierced ears, black h.h. wig, original kid body, dressed, 18"...1,495.00

Gaultier (F.) bisque swivel head lady marked "F.G.," blue threaded paperweight eyes, pierced ears, closed mouth, replaced blonde h.h. wig, gusseted kid body w/separate toes, wearing later cotton & lace dress, 34" (body repaired) 4,950.00

Handwerck (Heinrich) bisque head girl marked "16 - 99 - DEP - Germany - Handwerck - 17," brown sleep eyes, pierced ears & open mouth w/inset upper teeth, brown h.h. wig, wood & composition ball-jointed body, dressed, 32" ... 880.00

Heubach (Ernst) - Koppelsdorf bisque head baby marked "300.9," brown sleep eyes, brown mohair wig, bent limb body, dressed, 25" 440.00

Heubach (Gebruder) bisque shoulder head character boy marked "2," blue intaglio eyes, closed mouth, molded blond hair, cloth body, composition arms & legs, dressed, 11½" 352.00

Horsman (E.I.) "Baby Dimples," composition, w/clothes, 16" 182.00

Ideal Novelty & Toy Co. "Baby Snooks," composition head & hands, wooden torso, wire limbs, dressed, 12" 200.00

Ideal Novelty & Toy Co. "Bonnie Walker," hard plastic, blue sleep eyes, open mouth w/two upper teeth & molded tongue, cryer in stomach, pin hip walker, dressed, 17" 85.00

Ideal Novelty & Toy Co. "Saucy Walker," vinyl head, flirty eyes, hard plastic body, original dress & wig, ca. 1955, 22" 64.00

Jumeau bisque head portrait girl marked "4," cork pate, blue paperweight eyes, color highlighted eye corners & nostrils, outlined closed mouth, original blonde wig, wood & composition ball-jointed body w/straight wrists, body stamped in blue, "Jumeau, Medaille d'Or, Paris," dressed, 14½" (small chip at earring hole) 4,400.00

Jumeau bisque head girl marked "1907," blue stationary glass eyes, open mouth w/molded upper row of teeth, pierced ears, original brown h.h. wig, original ball-jointed composition body, jointed wrists, dressed, 16¼" 1,150.00

Jumeau bisque-headed bebe, head stamped "Tete Jumeau" w/painted

"HX" & oval sticker on body, blue paperweight eyes, closed mouth, pierced ears, strawberry blonde h.h. wig, jointed composition body, redressed in ivory satin over old undergarments, 21" (body worn) 2,090.00

Jumeau "Two-Faced" Character Girl

Jumeau bisque head "two-faced" character girl, glass paperweight eyes, jointed body, period-style costume (ILLUS.)...............8,500.00

K (star) R (Kammer & Reinhardt) bisque head character toddler marked "101," original blonde wig, ball-jointed toddler body, dressed, 8" 850.00

K (star) R bisque head character baby marked "122," blue sleep eyes, open smiling mouth w/dimples, auburn mohair wig, bent limb body, dressed, 15" 605.00

K (star) R bisque head girl marked "101 46," painted blue eyes, closed "pouty" mouth, original blonde h.h. wig, ball-jointed wood & composition body, dressed, 19" 1,980.00

K (star) R "Moritz"

K (star) R bisque head character
baby marked "K☆R - Simon &
Halbig - 119 - Baby - 69," brown
glass eyes, open-closed mouth,
brown h.h. wig, five-piece composition body, dressed, 24" 5,775.00

K (star) R bisque head character boy
"Moritz" marked "124," flirty eyes,
closed mouth, dressed (ILLUS.
previous page) 18,000.00

Ken (by Mattel), doctor's uniform,
w/stand, 1961 .... 60.00

Kestner (J.D.) bisque head character
baby marked "269," blue sleep
eyes, brown mohair wig, bent
limb body, dressed, 9½"........ 286.00

Kestner (J.D.) bisque head girl
marked "148," brown sleep eyes,
blonde h.h. wig, kid body,
dressed, 14" 250.00

Kestner (J.D.) bisque head baby
marked "211," brown sleep eyes,
open-closed mouth, original h.h.
wig, dressed, 16" 700.00

Kestner (J.D.) bisque head girl
marked "D8 169," brown sleep
eyes, closed mouth, blonde mohair
wig, jointed body, dressed, 19" ..2,090.00

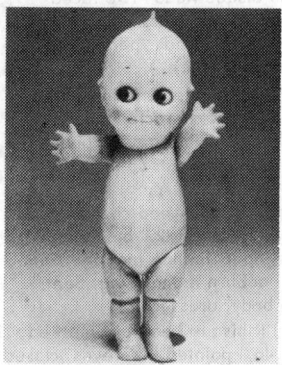

Kewpie Bisque Head Doll

Kewpie bisque head doll by Kestner
marked "ges. gesch. - O'Neill -
J.D.K. - 11," glass "googlie" flirty
eyes, composition toddler body
w/some crazing, 11¾" (ILLUS.) ..4,125.00

Kley & Hahn bisque head girl
marked "Walkure," fixed blue
eyes, pierced ears, blonde mohair
wig, jointed composition body,
wearing a white lawn dress
trimmed w/Irish lace, 28" (ear
chips, body wear) 605.00

Konig & Wernicke bisque head
character baby marked "K & W 9,"
fixed brown eyes, open mouth
w/two teeth, blonde mohair wig,
composition bent-limb baby body,
wearing a sailor shirt & hat &

grey wool pants, 16" (fingers
repaired) 550.00

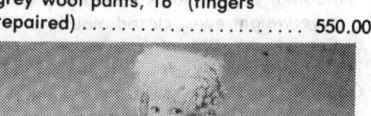

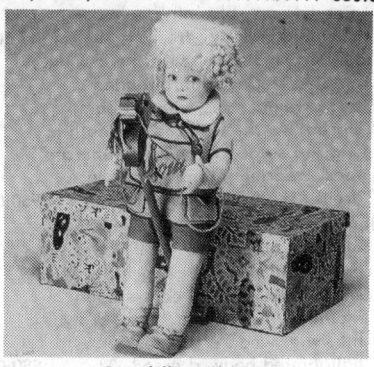

Lenci "Tom" Doll

Lenci boy, "Tom," all-felt body,
painted facial features & blond
curly hair, wearing a two-tone
blue felt shirt, a two-tone brown
smock & grey shorts, riding a hobby horse, Lenci paper label on
shirt, w/original box, ca. 1930,
20½" (ILLUS.) 3,300.00

Lenci Dutchman, felt, painted facial
features, fringe of hair under cap,
wearing a short red jacket &
green pants w/patches, metal
Lenci button in ear, 15" h........ 770.00

Lenci girl, felt, blonde hair, painted
facial features, wearing a pastel
green gauze & felt dress w/a
matching bow in hair, 15" (some
fading in dress) 330.00

Lenci, "Madame Pompadour," felt,
original clothes, 27" 1,200.00

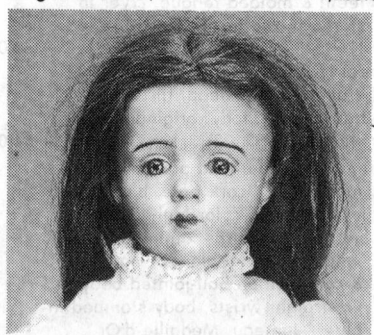

Rare A. Marque Doll

Marque (Albert) bisque head character girl marked "a Marque," wistful blue glass eyes, closed mouth,
composition jointed body, ca. 1916,
one arm replaced, two faint hairline cracks behind head, broken
thumb & baby finger on original
arm, 22" (ILLUS.) 22,000.00

Mechanical doll, papier-mache head
w/black painted hair, pupiless

glass eyes, closed mouth, kid
arms, mounted on a three-wheeled
metal base, when wound the head
moves to side & arms up & down,
wearing worn dress, coat & bonnet, ca. 1840, 11"..............1,045.00
Morimura Brothers bisque head girl
marked "M B" in circle w/"Japan"
& "3" below, sleep eyes, pouty
open mouth, ball-jointed composition body, dressed, ca. 1900,
16".......................... 150.00
Nancy Ann Storybook "Little Joan,"
hard plastic, w/original box...... 40.00
Nancy Ann Storybook "Merry Maid,"
bisque head & bisque body
w/jointed legs, w/original gold
wrist tag...................... 100.00
Papier-mache head lady, black
molded hair w/long ringlets down
the back, exposed ears & painted
facial features, cloth body
w/wood spoon-shaped hands,
cream lace dress, ca. 1820, 7¾".. 220.00
Parian head girl, "Empress"-type,
molded hair w/snood hairdo,
original body w/parian arms &
molded blouse, dressed in two-
piece lavender silk fashion dress,
22".......................... 425.00
Parian head lady, molded blonde
hair w/short tight curls, long
shoulder plate w/molded dress
bodice, dressed, all original,
15½"......................... 485.00
Peddler doll, oil cloth painted face,
fragile original clothing, many
original wares, 21"............. 365.00
R.D. (Rabery & Delphieu) bisque head
girl, blue stationary glass paperweight eyes, closed mouth, pierced
ears, long brown curled h.h. wig,
ball-jointed composition body
w/straight wrists, dressed in
maroon satin dress w/ecru lace
trim & matching bonnet w/ostrich
plume, 28½"..................3,500.00
Rag doll, Amish, hand-sewn, no facial features, faded pink dress &
black bonnet, 8" h. (minor stains
& soiling)...................... 75.00
Rag doll, Creole lady w/cork-stuffed
head, brown silk body & head
w/embroidered features, black
bead eyes, raveled brown silk
hair, original dress w/label, West
Indies, ca. 1839, 16½" (ILLUS.
top next column)............... 440.00
Rag doll, black figure w/embroi-
dered facial features, curly faux
lamb hair, wearing a cotton dress
& underclothes, cotton body
stuffed w/cotton batting, late 19th
or early 20th c., 31" h.......... 220.00

Creole Rag Doll

Rag "topsy-turvy" doll, black figure
on one side, white figure on other, each w/painted faces & colorful red print or yellow calico
dress, 16"..................... 215.00
Raggedy Andy, cloth, printed features, original clothes, Georgene
Novelties, rare size, 30"......... 450.00
Schmidt (Franz) bisque head girl
marked "1272/40 2," blue sleep
eyes, open mouth, brush-stroked
brown hair, jointed composition
body (repainted), wearing later
floral-printed cotton smock, 17".. 715.00
Schoenau & Hoffmeister bisque head
girl, "Pansy," long curly h.h. wig,
composition ball-jointed body by
Seeley, dressed in old-fashioned
drop-waist eyelet dress, 1910-22,
24"........................... 355.00
Schoenau & Hoffmeister bisque head
"Princess Elizabeth," smiling
mouth, five-piece chubby body, original clothes, 1932, 17".........1,900.00
Schoenhut character boy, "pouty"
type, wooden, blue intaglio eyes
& blond mohair wig, wearing a
yellow sweater & short red overalls, incised mark, 16" (crazing on
face).......................... 550.00
Schoenhut character girl, "pouty"
type, wooden, blue intaglio eyes
& replaced red wig, wearing a
silk blouse & dimity jumper, incised mark, 14" (paint retouched
on cheeks & nose)............. 715.00
Schoenhut girl, wooden, original
blonde wig, dressed in original
blue & gold plaid cotton dress
w/lace trim, socks & shoes,
w/original label on body, 14½".. 895.00
S.F.B.J. (Societe Francaise de Fabri-
cation de Bebes et Jouets) bisque
head "googlie" eyed boy marked
"245," blue glass "googlie" eyes
glancing to one side, open mouth

S.F.B.J. "Googlie" Eyed Doll
w/impish smile & molded teeth,
brown wig, wood & composition
jointed body, wearing a blue &
white sailor suit, 9" (ILLUS.) 2,200.00

S.F.B.J. bisque socket head girl
marked "SFBJ 60 Paris 11/0," blue
set eyes, open mouth w/four
molded teeth, composition body,
dressed, 11" 260.00

S.F.B.J. bisque head "pouty" character girl marked "252," stationary
blue glass eyes, closed pouty
mouth, original light brown h.h.
wig, original ball-jointed composition body w/jointed wrists,
dressed in blue suit-dress, straw
bonnet w/ecru lace, shoes, 11½"
(open air bubble on top head rim
under hair, done in making) 4,500.00

S.F.B.J. bisque head character girl
marked "UNIS 251," blue glass
sleep eyes, open mouth w/two
molded upper teeth & red tongue,
brown h.h. wig, ball-jointed composition toddler body w/jointed
wrists, dressed in underclothes,
old pink & white striped cotton
dress & old white bonnet, socks &
no shoes, 19" 1,550.00

S.F.B.J. bisque head character toddler marked "236," dark cobalt
blue sleep eyes, open closed
mouth w/two molded upper teeth,
light brown h.h. wig, original ball-
jointed composition toddler body
w/jointed wrists & w/original
paper label attached, dressed in
original white nursing gown &
jacket w/cap & booties, 20" 1,850.00

S.F.B.J. bisque head character girl
marked "236 Paris," blue sleep
glass eyes w/eyelashes, open-
closed mouth w/two molded upper
teeth, ball-jointed chunky toddler
body w/jointed wrists, dressed in
underclothes, old pink cotton print

dress, old bonnet, socks but no
shoes, 26" 1,950.00

Shirley Temple, vinyl, original
checked dress, hat & purse, 1957,
mint in box, 12" 162.00

Shirley Temple, composition, original wig w/label, dressed in original dress, 1930's, 20" (wig needs
setting) 425.00

Shirley Temple, composition, sleep
eyes, teeth, ringlet hair style,
blue dress w/white daisies, pinback button, 1930's, 22" 700.00

Shirley Temple, vinyl, original
clothing, 1957, 36" 1,200.00

Simon & Halbig bisque Belton-type
head girl marked "949," stationary
brown glass eyes, closed mouth,
pierced ears, long curly light
brown h.h. wig, composition
jointed body w/straight wrists,
dressed in underclothes, light blue
silk dress w/lace trim & straw hat
w/blue trim, socks & shoes,
12" 1,295.00

Simon & Halbig bisque head lady
marked "1469," glass eyes, closed
mouth, pierced ears, blonde mohair wig, jointed composition slim
adult body, wearing an embroidered lawn & lace dress, 14" (ear
chip) 3,080.00

Simon & Halbig bisque head girl
marked "1079," brown sleep eyes,
open mouth, pierced ears, ball-
jointed composition body, dressed
in blue velvet dress, 15" 350.00

Simon & Halbig bisque head girl
marked "949," blue sleep eyes,
closed mouth, pierced ears, blonde
h.h. wig, jointed composition body
w/fixed wrists (repainted), wearing a period ecru silk dress, 16"
(faint firing mark above right
eye) 1,430.00

Simon & Halbig Character Girl
Simon & Halbig bisque head charac-

ter girl marked "S&H 1279 - DEP - Germany - 11½," stationary brown glass eyes, pierced ears, blonde wig, open mouth w/inset upper teeth, wood & composition ball-jointed body, dressed, lower leg off, 24" (ILLUS.)...............1,980.00

Simon & Halbig bisque shoulder head girl marked "1170," brown sleep eyes, heavy brows, large pierced ears, kid body w/bisque arms, 26".................... 550.00

Rare Simon & Halbig Black Child

Simon & Halbig bisque head "pouty" black child marked "1301," brown glass eyes, closed mouth w/"pouty" expression, curly black wig, ball-jointed black composition body, wearing lace-trimmed dress & straw hat (ILLUS.)...........15,000.00

Steiner (Jules) bisque head girl marked "82," known as "Phenix Bebe," blue paperweight stationary eyes, closed mouth, pierced ears, brown h.h. wig, jointed composition body, straight wrists, dressed, 11½".........................1,650.00

Steiner (Jules) bisque head "Bebe Parlant Automatique," threaded blue paperweight eyes, open mouth w/two rows of teeth, pierced ears, blonde skin wig, carton body w/composition arms & legs, when key turned arms wave, legs kick & head turns from side to side, French toy shop sticker on back, wearing a whitework morning coat, 17" 1,760.00

Steiner (Jules) mechanical kicking & crying bebe, bisque dome head, blue stationary paperweight glass eyes, open mouth w/two rows of teeth, composition body, key on side of body, when wound head & legs move & she cries "mama," dressed in underclothes, original

white cotton dress w/bib & matching bonnet, knit shoes, works, 17"...........................2,250.00

Lovely Steiner Girl

Steiner (Jules) bisque head girl marked "Steiner - Paris - Fre. A.17," blue glass paperweight eyes, pierced ears, long curly brown wig, closed mouth, jointed composition body, dressed in long lace-trimmed gown, 24" (ILLUS.) 4,675.00

Stockinette peasant dolls, dressed in Smolensk peasant costume, Russia, ca. 1925, 7", pr............. 165.00

Terri Lee, rubbery composition, auburn hair, tagged print dress, 1950's, 16"..................... 285.00

Tiny Terri Lee, all original, 1950's, 10" 125.00

Unis France bisque head girl marked "Unis France 71 - 149 60," glass sleep eyes, open mouth w/teeth, replaced h.h. wig, papier-mache & wood ball-jointed French body, wearing a pale coral dress, 24" 495.00

Vogue "Ginny," Fairy Godmother, hard plastic, 1951, 7" 250.00

Wagner & Zetske bisque socket head girl marked "Nu 200/6," large sleep brown eyes, open mouth, character-type face, ball-jointed composition body, dressed, 21" 455.00

Wax over papier-mache girl, sleep blue eyes, closed mouth, dressed in beige net fashion dress, 18" ... 350.00

Wax shoulder head girl marked "J" on back of shoulder, blue stationary glass eyes, blonde hair w/artificial flowers in it, cloth body w/wax over composition hands & feet, dressed in underclothes, ivory silk dress & shoes, 15" 495.00

Wellings (Norah) felt gypsy, 21" 110.00

Wellings (Norah) felt old lady, 24" .. 500.00

Wellings (Norah) black girl, glass
eyes, tagged velvet body, 25" 350.00
Wooden lady doll, carved head
w/painted curls on forehead,
painted facial features, carved
tuck comb, pierced ears, jointed
wood body, wearing original
Empire-style dress, ca. 1820-30,
15" 3,300.00
Wooden lady doll, carved head
w/painted hair, tuck comb, painted facial features, pierced ears,
all-wood body w/mortise & tenon
limbs & spoon-shaped hands,
wearing a faded red cotton dress,
ca. 1820, 17" 990.00
Wooden "peddler" doll, carved
wood head gessoed & painted
w/dark hair & facial features, extended ears, carved jointed-wood
body, dressed in peddler garb
w/blue & white dress & red cape,
carrying a woven straw gadget
basket, ca. 1810-20, 8" 550.00

DOOR KNOCKERS

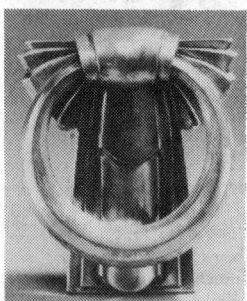

Art Deco Door Knocker

Brass, devil's head, old dark finish.. $59.00
Brass, model of a gargoyle, large .. 28.00
Cast iron, basket of flowers 39.00
Cast iron, figural little girl knocking
on door 80.00
Cast iron, house w/trees & lane 49.00
Cast iron, model of an owl,
Victorian 95.00
Cast iron, model of a parrot on
branch, painted gold, 3 x 4" 35.00
Cast iron & brass, cast w/shell mo-
tifs, second half of 19th century,
7½" l. 302.00
Silvered bronze, Art Deco style, cast
as a stylized bow supporting a
paneled ring, designed by Louis
Sue & Andre Mare, France, ca.
1925, 9½" h. (ILLUS.) 3,850.00

DOORSTOPS

Cat with Arched Back Doorstop

*All doorstops listed are flat-back cast iron
unless otherwise noted. Most names are tak-
en from* Doorstops - Identification & Values, *by
Jeanne Bertoia (Collector Books, 1985).*

Aunt Jemima (Large Mammy), full
figure, old polychrome repaint,
Hubley, 11¼" h. $100.00
Cape Cod, cottage w/picket fence,
original polychrome paint, Eastern
Specialty Mfg. Co., 5¾" h. 115.00
Cat, Halloween, animal standing
w/back arched, AM Greenblatt
Studio No. 19, copyright 1927,
6" w., 9¼" h.................... 200.00
Cat, Modernistic, full figure, angular
seated animal, Hubley, 9¾" h. ... 465.00
Cat, standing animal w/high arched
rounded back & tail curled over
haunches, on tall rectangular
base, cast bronze, 8 5/8" h.
(ILLUS.)....................... 235.00
Chameleon, advertising The Sherwin
Williams Paint Co., 1¼ x 8"...... 200.00
Clown, wide ruffled collar & pointed
hat, bending w/hands on knees,
thin rectangular base, original
polychrome paint w/red suit worn
& faded, 4½" w., 10" h........... 325.00
Cockatoo, full figure, bright polychrome paint, 14" h. 285.00
Colonial Woman, pink & blue gown
& hat, Littco Products & others,
5¾" w., 10¼" h................. 90.00
Cricket, labeled "The Tri State Foundry Co., Cincinnati, Ohio,"
10½" l. 105.00
Daisy Bowl, original paint, Hubley,
5 1/8" w., 7½" h............... 120.00
Deco Girl, standing w/arms outstretched & grasping the hem of
her skirt, old repaint, 7½" w.,
9" h.......................... 260.00
Dog, Beagle Pup, full figure, animal
seated w/front legs spread apart,
white body w/dark ears & area
around eyes, 7½ x 8" 225.00

Dog, Boston Terrier, full figure,
   standing animal w/head turned,
   worn original black & white paint
   w/red trim, 8 x 8¼" 75.00
Dog, Cocker Spaniel, full figure,
   standing black animal, Hubley,
   11" l., 6¾" h. 250.00
Dog, Dachshund, full figure, stand-
   ing on rectangular base, bronze
   finish, 6" h. 65.00
Dog, Fox Terrier, standing on
   rectangular base, worn white
   paint w/polychrome trim,
   10½ x 10¾". 400.00

Gnome & Pup on Pillow Doorstops

Dog, Pup on Pillow, chubby animal
   w/floppy ears seated on pillow
   w/tasseled corners (ILLUS.
   right) 325.00
Dog, St. Bernard, standing animal
   w/brandy keg at his neck, on
   long oval base, original metallic
   brown & black paint, 9¼" l. 135.00
Dutch Girl w/Big Shoes, on low
   base, old polychrome repaint,
   9¾" h. 250.00
Eagle, standing w/wings spread,
   lacy base, gilt paint, 6 x 10" 250.00
Elephant, full figure, walking animal
   w/head slightly turned & trunk
   hanging down, black paint,
   5¾" l. 25.00
Fisherman in Boat, man in yellow
   slicker standing at back of small
   boat, 4" w, 6¾" h. 250.00
Gaucho, full figure, standing man
   w/one hand on hip, old polychrome paint, 7" w., 18½" h. 350.00
Gnome with keys, full figure, carry-
   ing lantern in one hand & keys in
   other, 10" h. (ILLUS. left) 625.00
Horse, "King's Genius," back label
   "Copyrighted 1938, Rife Loth Corp,
   Waynesboro, Va.," unpainted,
   11¾" h. 150.00
Lighthouse, grey w/white windows
   & water base, "A. A. Richardson,
   copyright 1927," 8½" h. 275.00
Lil Red Riding Hood and Wolf, child
   standing beside large animal on

grassy base, marked "NUYDEA
   Little Red Riding Hood," 9½" l.,
   7½" h. 350.00
Lion, full figure, standing animal
   w/head turned to side & tail to
   one side, old gold paint, 9½" l. . . .   160.00
Organ Grinder, man cranking street
   organ w/monkey crouched at his
   feet, 5¾" w., 9 7/8" h. 375.00
Pirate Girl, woman in pirate cos-
   tume w/treasure chest & bags of
   gold, marked "Pirate Girl,"
   7¼" w., 13 7/8" h. 300.00
Rooster, full figure, standing on
   square base, Hubley, 6 1/8" w.,
   15 3/8" h. 385.00
Rose Vase, bouquet of roses in
   cornucopia-shaped vase, old polychrome paint, Hubley No. 441,
   8" w., 10 1/8" h. 125.00
Schooner, brass, 6" w., 9" h. 65.00
Satyr bust w/twisted cornucopia hat,
   rectangular base w/cut corners,
   old crusty black paint, 11¼" h. 230.00
Tulip Vase, Hubley No. 443, 10" w.,
   18" h. 115.00
Violet Bowl, bouquet of violets in
   low footed bowl, Hubley No. 9,
   4¼" w., 6¼" h. 165.00
Warrior, elf holding shield & club
   standing on stepped rectangular
   base, old polychrome paint,
   marked "Bradley & Hubbard No.
   7795," 7¼" w., 13¼" h. 500.00
Windmill, marked "10 Cape Cod,"
   National Foundry, 6¾ x 6 7/8" . . .   110.00
Zinnias, Hubley No. 267, 7 x 7¼". . .   150.00

DRUGSTORE & PHARMACY ITEMS

*The old-time corner drugstore, once a famil-
iar part of every American town, has now giv-
en way to the modern, efficient pharmacy.
With the streamlining and modernization of
this trade many of the early tools and store
adjuncts have become outdated and now fall
into the realm of "collectibles." Listed here
are a variety of tools, bottles, display pieces
and other ephemera once closely associated
with the druggist's trade.*

Bottle, Aurant (S.P.) Co., miniature,
   label under glass, amber,
   4¼" h. $19.00
Bottle, Blose Drug Company (The),
   Cor. 6th & Poplar Sts., Leadville,
   CO, 3½" h.   12.00
Bottle, Gilka (J.A.), Berlin Schutzen
   Str. No. 9, amber 25.00
Bottle, Hopper Struve & Compy.
   Chemists to H.M. the Queen, Roy-
   al German Spa. Brighton & Pall

Mall East London, torpedo shape,
aqua (some haze) 39.00
Bottle, Hordeum, blown glass, w/label under glass & two applied
glass bands, pontil mark, clear,
9½" h. 280.00
Bottle, Levinger Druggist, moldblown glass, clear, 5 1/8" h. 5.00
Bottle, Logan (T.H.) & Co. Druggists
Wheeling, Va., open pontil, aqua
(two small stains) 125.00
Bottle, Merchant (G.W.) Chemist,
Lockport, N.Y., cylindrical,
green 55.00
Bottle, Miller (E.T.), Druggist, York
Pa., blue aqua w/olive green
neck 30.00
Bottle, Owl Drug Co. (The), milk
white glass, 5" h. 45.00
Bottle, Owl Drug Co. (The), embossed, mold-blown glass, clear,
5¼" h. 9.00
Bottle, Owl Pharmacy, Bellingham,
Washington, rectangular, moldblown glass, embossed owl, light
amethyst, 5" h. 35.00
Bottle, Pautanberge (L.) Pharmacien
Paris, dark cobalt blue, 7½" h. 35.00
Bottle, Preston of New Hampshire,
smelling salts, complete w/glass
stopper, deep blue-green (light inside haze) 25.00
Bottle, Sauco (B.), porcelain, banded
w/gilt & trailing blue vines, decorated w/oval gilt medallion
marked "ML" & a stemmed drinking vessel entwined w/a snake,
gilt, green, blue grey & shades of
red decoration, 11" h. to top of
domed cover.................... 140.00
Bottle, "Tinct. of Arnica," rectangular, label only, aqua, 5" h. 12.00
Display jar, amber glass, lid embossed "Ceratum," base embossed w/company name, city &
state, Whitall Tatum Co., Phila. &
NY. (lip chip on lid) 39.00
Display jar, cov., clear glass w/wide
mouth, label under glass
w/"Bucklen's Arnica Salve" in
black & white w/gold trim, fancy
stopper, 6" w., 10" h. (cracks in
label) 300.00
Display jar, clear glass, "teardrop"
shape on pleated base, pleated
cover w/ball finial, frosted flower
& pleat w/amber-stained flowers,
12½" h. 295.00
Display jars, clear glass, gilt &
reverse-painted decoration on
bases & lids, 21" h., pr. (one lid
damaged) 310.00
Dose glass, "Kersten's Pharmacy,"
1920's 11.00

Drug mill, cast iron, hand-crank,
ca. 1910...................... 140.00
Funnel, narrow, tin w/pewter tube
& petcock valve, for filling glass
medicine bottles, 2½ x 5" 26.00
Pharmacist's degree, dated 1889,
framed 20.00
Pill mold, walnut, 1920's 110.00
Pill silverer, globular, turned wood,
double-ended, pedestal base 150.00
Show globe, clear glass, three
graduating ovoid sections on
round domed pedestal base,
designed to hold colored water,
25½" h....................... 100.00

ENAMELS

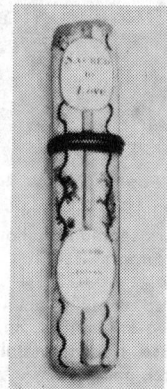

Enameled Bodkin Case

Enamels have been used to decorate a variety of substances, particularly metals. The best-known small enameled wares, such as patch and other small boxes and napkin rings, are the Battersea Enamels made by the Battersea Enamel Works in the last half of the 18th century. However, the term is often loosely applied to other English enamels. Russian enamels, usually on a silver or gold base, are famous and expensive. Early 20th century French enamel or copper wares and those items produced in China at the turn of the century in imitation of the early Russian style are also drawing dealer and collector attention.

Battersea (or Bilston) box, rectangular w/cut corners, polychrome
enameled hunt scene on lid, sides
& bottom decorated w/polychrome floral designs on white
ground, gilt brass fittings, England, 5 5/8" l. (some crazing,

minor chips on back & short edge
crack on lid) $500.00
Battersea (or Bilston) candlesticks,
domed foot, ring- and baluster-
turned stem, white w/deep blue
reserves & polychrome florals,
copper rims at base & lip, England, 9" h., pr. (yellowed
repairs) 900.00
Bodkin case, oblong two-part
cylinder enameled powder pink &
decorated w/pea-green & black
stripes & alternating wavy black
stripes & white dots reserved
w/two oblong panels, one inscribed "Esteem of the Giver," the
other "A Friend's Gift" (one restored), England, late 18th - early
19th c., 3¾" l. (ILLUS.) 330.00
Box w/hinged cover, gold, narrow
oval, cover embossed w/horsemen
in high-relief, sides enameled in
translucent blue & red & engraved
w/scrolls, base similarly engraved,
Continental, mid-19th c.,
3¼" l. 1,320.00
Clock, desk-type, egg-shaped,
supported on the tails of dolphins
forming pedestal above domed
base, the dial enameled w/scroll-
ing foliage, the interior & the back
of the case enameled w/mytholog-
ical scenes, the domed base similarly enameled, Vienna, Austria,
ca. 1880, 7" h. 3,300.00
Crucifix, silver-gilt, the arms of the
cross enameled w/colorful foliate
designs on blue ground, Cyrillic
maker's mark "F.R.," Russia, ca.
1910, 12¼" h. 4,620.00
Demitasse spoons, enamel & silver-
gilt, decorated in multicolored
scrolling & floral design, all
spoons in the same pattern, the
enamels of one spoon in different
colors, five spoons 84 standard,
one spoon 88 standard, w/pseudo
marks in the manner of Moscow,
1908-17, set of 6 . . . . 330.00
Needle case, two-part cylinder,
painted w/gold floral sprays &
pastoral scenes on a pink ground,
South Staffordshire, England, ca.
1770, 4½" l. 440.00
Serving spoon, silver-gilt & *plique-a-
jour*, fig-shaped bowl w/engraved
strapwork design on reverse,
w/sectioned enameled handle,
marked "J.T.," Scandinavia, late
19th c., 8 3/8" l. 247.50
Teapot w/hinged cover, silver-gilt &
shaded enamel, lobed body enameled w/panels of colorfully
plumed birds & foliage on grounds

of sky blue, white, avocado & sea
green, cover similarly lobed, scroll
handle, swan's neck spout, Dmitri
Smirnov, Moscow, ca. 1900,
6½" h. 6,600.00
Teaspoons, silver-gilt & shaded
enamel, backs of the bowls
enameled w/flowering plants on
a cream ground, the plants rising
from pots enameled brick red,
Fyodor Ruckert, Moscow, ca. 1900,
4¼" l., in fitted oak case of retailer, Gratchev Brothers, St.
Petersburg, set of 12 . . . . 3,960.00
Urn, cov., copper, ovoid w/domed
cover, enameled in low- and
medium-relief w/sprays of rhododendron blossoms & leafage in
shades of pink, crimson, lavender,
white, lemon yellow & emerald
green, signed in gilt "C. Faure.
Limoges," ca. 1925, 15¾" h. 3,575.00

EPERGNES

Opalescent Glass Epergne

*Epergnes were popular as centerpieces on
tables of last century. Many have receptacles
of colored glass for holding sweetmeats or
other edible items or for flowers or fruits. Early epergnes were made entirely of metal including silver.*

Aqua opalescent glass, three-lily,
Hobnail patt., ruffled edge,
Fenton $75.00
Blue cased glass, single lily, applied
rigaree, Victorian, 20" h. 350.00
Blue cased glass, four-lily, tall cen-
ter lily surrounded by three short-
er lilies, ruffled cased glass bowl
base, each piece w/white lining,
Victorian, 21" h. 700.00
Clear opalescent glass, single lily,

applied blue rigaree, square base
& lily, Victorian, 20" h. 395.00

Cranberry glass, single lily, clear
ruffled bowl base, 4¾" d., 6" h... 135.00

Cranberry glass, four-lily, large tall
center lily surrounded by three
smaller shorter lilies, each lily
w/applied crystal spiral trim,
large ruffled cranberry bowl base,
11½" d., 20¼" h. 462.00

Frosted glass Caryatid or Madonna
epergne, wide clear bowl
w/etched fern design raised in center to support frosted figure of
standing lady in classical robes
w/wide low bowl w/fern etching
resting on her head & centering a
tall trumpet vase w/further etching,
New England, ca. 1870, 10 3/8" d.,
19½" h. 1,375.00

Green glass, single lily, Victorian,
10" h. 95.00

Milk white glass, single lily, in
10" d. compote w/pedestal foot,
both w/fired-on garland design,
Challinor, Taylor & Co., 12¼" h... 150.00

Orange shaded to clear threaded
glass, four-lily, center cup on tall
clear glass stem surrounded by
three other matching cups on low
clear glass arms above scalloped
bowl base, each cup w/patented
Webb flower petal top, Thomas
Webb & Sons, England, 9½" d.,
15" h. 690.00

Parcel-gilt sterling silver, square
base w/winged square pad feet
supports the stem formed as a classical woman holding in her hands a
hoop fitted w/four shallow circular
bowls w/bud terminals, her head
supporting a larger matching bowl,
all w/frosted surface & gilt borders
of zig-zag ornament, engraved
w/later inscription & dates "1874" &
"1896," Tiffany & Co., New York,
New York, ca. 1865-70, repair to
screw of central bowl, 16" h. 7,700.00

Porcelain, three tiers of triangular
bowls w/applied seashells, coral &
other decoration, further enhanced
w/polychrome florals, attributed to
Tebo the Modeller, England, mid to
late 18th c., 15½" h. (some edge
damage & professional repair) ...1,475.00

Silver plate, oval platform base on
four feet w/mask terminals of an
elderly bearded man, the platform
w/a rolled scrolling foliate design
supporting an inverse trumpet-
shaped shaft suspending a laurel
rope descending from volutes, a
circular gilt-lined bowl on either
side of the shaft w/a conforming

rolled band, the top inserted w/a
blue glass & enamel painted vase
(probably replacement), made by
the Taunton Silver Plate Co., ca.
1886, 15" h. without glass vase ... 550.00

Vaseline opalescent glass, four-lily,
tall ruffled center lily & three
shorter ruffled lilies in square ruffled bowl base, each lily applied
w/vaseline spiral trim around
base, 8" d., 17½" h. 365.00

White opalescent glass w/shaded
blue rims, five-lily, deeply fluted
lilies shading from white opalescent w/blue trim to clear, each
lily applied w/spiral rigaree trim
around the base, scalloped
opalescent glass bowl base
(ILLUS.)........................ 500.00

FABERGE

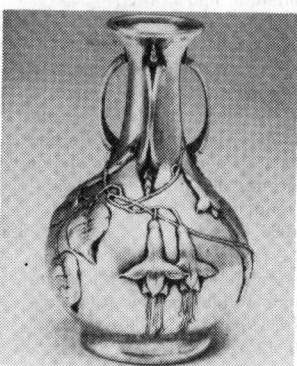

Faberge Silver Vase

*Carl Faberge (1846-1920) was goldsmith and
jeweler to the Russian Imperial Court and his
creations are recognized as the finest of their
kind. He made a number of enamel fantasies,
including Easter eggs, for the Imperial family
and utilized precious metals and jewels in
other work.*

Bowl, silver & palisander, bulbous,
silver lip-mount chased w/anthe-
mion, silver girdle chased
w/acanthus leaves, marked "K.
Faberge" in Cyrillic w/Imperial
warrant & 84 standard, Moscow,
ca. 1900, 3¼" d. $880.00

Box, silver-gilt, triangular form,
enameled translucent pale blue
over a *guilloche* ground, the borders chased w/entwined ribbon,
the cover mounted w/a cabochon
ruby encircled by diamonds,

marked w/the initials of work-master Henrick Wigstrom & "Faberge" in Cyrillic, St. Petersburg, ca. 1900, 1¾" w.........11,000.00

Brooch, gold scroll form set w/three moonstone cabochons w/four gold "pendulums" each set w/a cabochon garnet below a tiny diamond, marked w/Cyrillic initials of workmaster Andrei Gorianov, St. Petersburg, ca. 1900, 1½" l...1,320.00

Cigarette case, flattened silver rectangle w/rounded corners, the cover enameled w/a blue cross & an eagle on a white ground, the back applied w/the Cyrillic inscription "Black Sea Yacht Club, to Vladimir Eduardovich Faltz-Fenn," w/cabochon sapphire thumbpiece, marked "K. Faberge" in Cyrillic, Moscow, ca. 1900, 3 7/8" l......4,675.00

Cuff links, double-sided gold circular form enameled translucent oyster white over a spiralling *guilloche* ground, marked w/the initials of workmaster Erik Kollin, St. Petersburg, ca. 1900, ½" d., pr. (in fitted case).......7,700.00

Easter egg pendant, miniature lobed egg form w/silver ribs dividing the enameled translucent sky blue over *guilloche* ground, the end set w/a cabochon sapphire, marked w/Cyrillic initials of workmaster Michael Perchin, St. Petersburg, ca. 1900, 5/8" l.......5,775.00

Kovsh, silver-gilt globular form enameled w/multicolored foliage & geometric forms in the Old Russian style, marked "K. Faberge" in Cyrillic, Moscow, ca. 1910, 9¼" l.......13,200.00

Model of a boar, pink chalcedony, depicted seated on its hind legs, eyes set w/diamonds, St. Petersburg, ca. 1900, 2½" l.......6,600.00

Model of a crane, standing bird w/the body formed of mother-of-pearl, the gold legs finely chased & set w/diamonds, the head also set w/diamonds, the eyes w/rubies, mounted on an oval rock crystal base, St. Petersburg, ca. 1900, 3¾" h. 37,400.00

Parasol handle, carved bowenite, gold, enamel & jewels, egg-shaped carved bowenite top wrapped w/diamond-set laurel wreaths, the stem enameled translucent rose pink over *guilloche* ground & edged by diamonds, marked w/Cyrillic initials of workmaster Michael Perchin & 56 standard, St. Petersburg, ca. 1886, 3 1/8" l.......8,250.00

Pencil holder pendant, two-color gold & enamel, enameled translucent sky blue over a *guilloche* ground, green gold border chased w/leaftips, marked w/initials of workmaster August Holmstrom, St. Petersburg, ca. 1900, 2½" l.......2,310.00

Salt dip, silver, bulbous circular shape, enameled w/stylized foliage in muted tones of blue & green, marked "K. Faberge" in Cyrillic, ca. 1910, 2" d.......2,860.00

Samovar, silver, urn form, the lower body fluted, engraved w/a monogram below a coronet, the hexagonal base raised on six bun feet, harp-shaped handles, ivory fittings, marked "Faberge" in Cyrillic, Odessa, ca. 1885, 17¾" h. 11,000.00

Stickpin, formed as a cabochon sapphire mounted above three diamonds on a spirally-incised gold stem, marked w/initials of workmaster Alfred Thielemann, St. Petersburg, ca. 1900, w/fitted case, pin 2¾" l.......9,900.00

Tea glass holder, silver, cylindrical w/gilded interior, engraved w/scrollwork & flowers, scroll handle headed by leafage, marked w/Cyrillic initials "K.F." & 84 standard, ca. 1885, 3¾" h. 1,430.00

Vase, silver, three-handled, bulbous body embossed w/flowering vine, marked "K. Faberge" in Cyrillic w/Imperial warrant & 84 standard, Moscow, ca. 1885, 4 5/8" h. (ILLUS.).......3,300.00

Faberge Vodka Cup

Vodka cup, silver, in the form of a helmet of the Imperial Guard, the finial in the form of an eagle w/splayed wings, star enameled yellow, blue & black, marked "Faberge" in Cyrillic w/Imperial warrant, Cyrillic initials of workmaster Julius Rappoport & 88 standard, Moscow, ca. 1900, 3½" h. (ILLUS.).......13,200.00

FANS

19th Century Gold & Jeweled Fan

Advertising, "Hormel Dairy Brand
Ham," die-cut cardboard, farm girl
pictured $30.00
Advertising, "666 Tablets," cardboard, Art Deco style w/girl &
greyhound..................... 6.75
Chantilly lace, black-colored leaf
worked in alternating panels of
foliage & putti, mother-of-pearl
sticks elaborately pierced & gilded
w/arabesques, Continental, ca.
1870, 10½" l. 550.00
Enameled filigree, white metal filigree leaf w/central shield containing a blue & green enameled landscape surrounded by floral sprays,
the guards w/Chinese scenes in
relief, China, mid-19th c.,
7½" l. 1,100.00
Gold mesh over gold sticks, spatu-
late-shaped frontpiece decorated
w/stylized flowerheads set
w/colored stones including emer-
alds, sapphires & rubies & bordered by diamonds, case marked
"Cartier, 1840," Continental, 19th c.
(ILLUS.) 6,050.00
Ivory brise, wide ivory sticks
painted w/a spray of flowers,
signed "Paul de Longpre," France,
third quarter 19th c., 9" l......... 418.00

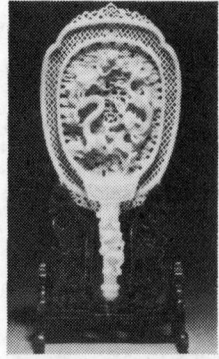

White Jade Fan

Jade, creamy white w/a pierced
trellis outer border, the interior
w/a *shou* medallion within a
field of cloud scrolls & dragons,
reverse matching but w/a high-
relief carved dragon, 13½" l.
(ILLUS.) 2,860.00
Lacquered brise, sticks gilt-
lacquered w/scenes from Chinese
life reserved on an elaborate floral ground, China, mid-19th c., in
gilt pedestal case, 9½" l.,
2 pcs. 660.00
Painted paper, narrow leaf decorated w/scenes of elegant
shepherds & shepherdesses in
pastoral setting, mother-of-pearl
sticks elaborately carved w/court-
ing couples beneath Cupid's gaze,
the gilt sticks backed w/mica,
France, ca. 1850, 10½" l. 495.00
Painted vellum, nymphs & putti floating in a peach & azure sky
w/clouds, pierced ivory sticks decorated w/mother-of-pearl panels &
painted in polychrome w/figures &
foliate forms, France, late 18th c.,
20½" w., within a glazed giltwood
foliate-carved case w/a C-scroll
crest 1,045.00
Pierced horn brise, elaborate gilt &
enameled guard sticks set w/mul-
ticolored 'jewels,' Continental,
19th c., 7" l. 550.00
Rosepoint lace, ivory-colored leaf
worked in a pattern of mixed
blossoms & scrolling foliage,
mother-of-pearl sticks lightly
carved, silvered & gilded, Continental, ca. 1900, 12½" l. 715.00
Sequinned lace, black net leaf overlaid w/cream bobbin lace in the
form of a bird & appliqued w/tiny
sequins, the serpentine tortoiseshell sticks piqued w/steel,
France, ca. 1890, 11" l. 495.00
Tortoiseshell brise, sticks carved
w/scenes from Chinese life, the
guards finely carved w/flowers &
foliage in high-relief, China,
mid-19th c., 9" l. 385.00

FARM COLLECTIBLES

Barn door strap hinges, wrought
iron, 18th c., 24 x 33", pr. $49.00
Bin, painted pine, slant lid opening
to three-part interior, old grey
paint over earlier colors,
37¼" w., 21" deep, 38¼" h. 275.00
Castrating knife, two-blade, cel-

luloid handle, Schrade Cutlery
Co. 120.00
Chicken waterer, round, brown
glazed pottery, marked "W.R. &
Co., Akron, Ohio," ca. 1895 ...... 150.00
Corn dryer, wrought iron 12.00
Corn husker, metal w/leather
strap.......................... 11.00
Corn knife, cast iron, straps to leg,
patented 1874, "I.Z. Merriam,
Whitewater, Wis.," ca. 1892 ...... 66.00
Corn planter, hand-type, hollowed
out of one piece of wood 60.00
Corn sheller, tin, hand-held, scoop
shape w/cutter bar & brace, strap
handle, 2¼ x 3 x 3"............. 85.00
Dehorning clippers 60.00
Egg gathering basket, wirework, circular w/domed hinged lid, circular
foot, stationary handle attached
at shoulder, probably Pennyslva-
nia, 19th c., 18" h. 385.00
Feeding basket, woven splint, made
to fit over the muzzle of feeding
livestock, 19th c. 325.00
Flax break, hard & soft woods, mortised & pinned construction, shoe
feet, refinished, 36" w., 27" h. ... 70.00
Flax hatchel, chestnut board
w/wrought-iron spikes, faded
black & red relief-carved compass
designs, 31" l. 150.00
Grain measures, bentwood w/iron
strap trim, 9", 11½" & 14½" d.,
set of 3 .... 105.00
Hay fork, harpoon-type, cast iron ... 25.00
Hay rake, folding-type, W.C.
Jones 170.00
Hen's nest egg, blown milk white
glass.......................... 40.00
Implement seat, cast iron,
"Champion" 45.00
Implement seat, cast iron, "Deere &
Co." 110.00
Implement seat, cast iron,
"Deering" 40.00
Implement seat, cast iron, "KPCO -
Buckeye"...................... 45.00
Implement seat, cast iron,
"McCormick"................... 40.00
Lightning rod, copper, w/milk glass
ball insulator & cast-iron arrow
directional opposite hollow-bodied
embossed tin running horse,
traces of old paint, tripod mount-
ing bracket, 60" h. (some rust) ... 75.00
Plowshare, iron, single-size, marked
"S. Bateman," made to accept
wooden handle, 12" l. 25.00
Pulley wheel, bird's-eye maple
w/iron fittings, ca. 1898, 5¾" d.,
10" l. overall 39.00
Windmill weight, cast iron, standing
bull realistically cast & painted

Bull Windmill Weight

red & white, on green-painted
base, early 20th c., 15" l., 13" h.
(ILLUS.)..........................550.00
Windmill weight, cast iron, standing
short-tailed horse by Dempster
Manufacturing Co., Beatrice,
Nebraska, old black & white
repaint, 16½" h. ....250.00 to 300.00

FIREARMS

Smith & Wesson First Model Revolver

Musket, Committee of Safety model,
decorative brass butt cap, trigger
guard & other embellishments,
barrel impressed "R.W.," lockplate
impressed "T.F.," Thomas Fancher,
Waterbury, Connecticut, 1770-79,
61" l. $2,090.00
Musket, flintlock, walnut full stock,
lock marked "A.W. Spies warrent-
ed" & barrel marked "London,"
reputedly issued by the New York
State Militia in 1775, from the
Palatine District of Germany,
40" l. barrel, overall 55½" l. 550.00
Pistol, flintlock, walnut stock
w/brass fittings, lock marked "T.
Ketland 1802," barrel pitted at

mark which may read "London,"
8½" l. barrel, overall 14¾" l. 350.00
Pistol, flintlock, wooden handle,
decorative brass butt cap & trigger guard, gunsmith proof mark
on engraved iron barrel, attached
note reads "Pistol carried in The
Revolutionary War by Ensign
David Hopkinson - Loaned by Mrs.
Walter H. Hopkinson," America,
18th c., 19½" l. (some brass embellishments of later addition,
ramrod missing, wood loss) 660.00
Revolver, Smith & Wesson First
Model, second issue, in fitted
velvet-lined case (ILLUS.) 1,200.00
Rifle, Kentucky half-stock, curly maple stock, percussion lock, engraved brass patch box, eight
silver inlays & barrel initials
"C.F.," Charles Flowers, Harmony,
Pennsylvania, 39" l. barrel,
55½" l. overall 650.00
Rifle, Kentucky full stock, carved
maple stock, engraved patch box,
39" l. barrel, overall 55" l. 3,300.00
Rifle, Kentucky full stock, curly
maple stock, percussion lock
marked "Josh Golcher," elaborate
brass patch box, inlaid silver eagle
& octagonal barrel w/engraved
initials, found in Ohio, w/canvas
bag w/powder, bullet mold & shot
flask, 37¾" barrel, 53½" l. overall,
the group 1,400.00
Rifle, Kentucky full stock, curly
maple stock w/percussion lock,
engraved brass patch box, barrel
signed "J. Wallace, Pittsburgh,"
39" l. barrel, 55" l. overall (old
repairs to stock) 1,250.00
Shotgun, Browning Semi-automatic,
engraved design of birds in flight,
carved stock w/hunting dogs,
12 gauge, vented barrel, 33½" l.
barrel 1,540.00
Shotgun, double barrel, carved walnut stock w/percussion locks, bar-
rels w/silver inlaid scroll & inlaid
brass name "Damas Turc,"
32¾" l. barrel, overall 48½" l. 250.00

FIRE EXTINGUISHERS

*Various types of fire extinguishers intend-
ed primarily for use in extinguishing small
fires were made in the 19th and early in the
20th centuries and are now being collected.*

"Firex Grenade," cobalt blue glass,
no embossing, England $60.00

"Harden's Hand Fire Extinguisher
Grenade," amber glass, partial
contents, qt. 742.50
"Harden's Hand Grenade," sapphire
blue glass, embossed star,
w/contents 48.00
"Harden's Hand Grenade," turquoise
blue glass, bulbous w/quilted design, footed, w/contents, pt.
(stained) 65.00
"Harden's Improved Grenade Fire
Extinguisher," clear glass,
segmented 385.00
"Hayward's Hand Fire Grenade,"
deep cobalt blue glass 210.00
"Hayward's Hand Fire Grenade,"
yellow-amber glass w/contents ... 205.00
"H.S. Nutting," amber glass (1" neck
crack) 45.00

Pyrene Fire Extinguisher

"Pyrene," brass cylinder, w/wall
mount back panel & locking catch,
marked "N.P.RY.," 14" l.
(ILLUS.) 50.00
"Red Comet" hand grenade, intact
w/contents, in original box, set
of 6 ....195.00 to 250.00
"Shur-Stop," frosted glass, w/mount-
ing bracket 20.00
"Shur-Stop," purple glass, w/mount-
ing bracket 20.00
"Shur-Stop," glass grenade kit, in
original container, set of 6 .... 75.00
"Unic Grenade Entinctrice," orange-
amber glass....................1,100.00

FIRE FIGHTING COLLECTIBLES

Alarm bell, brass w/cast iron, electric operated box, "Edward's,"
10" $190.00
Badge, "Air Force Fire Chief"....... 40.00

Badge, "Asst. Chief, Rensselaer
FD" 45.00
Badge, "Chicago Fire Dept. - Re-
tired," gold-plated.............. 85.00
Book, "Bucket Brigade To Flying
Squadron," by Herbert Jenness,
1909, hard cover 80.00
Belt, leather, black w/red & white,
marked "Independence 39," 41" l.
(brittle w/age cracks & minor
edge damage) 50.00
Book, "History Hartford, Conn. Fire
Dept.," 1898, pictorial memento,
photos of men & their equipment
as well as various firehouses
where they served, 68 pp.,
9 x 12½" 75.00
Bucket, leather, decorated w/a yellow & brown scrolled banner
bearing the inscription "E.M. &
W.P. Company" enclosing "No. 1"
& the dated "1892," against a red
ground, black rim & base, America, 1892, 11¾" h. (handle de-
tached & broken, some paint
loss) 935.00
Bucket, leather, painted green
ground decorated w/polychrome
American eagle w/shield body
clenching a banner inscribed
"Cambridge Port Fire Society"
surmounting a banner inscribed
"Samuel Sweetser" & the date
"1828," branded "C. M. Domett,
Maker" on underside, America,
12" h. (paint loss, craquelure,
missing handle) 1,210.00
Cap, painted leather, flat white
crown w/arched front crest painted in red, blue & black & marked
"Foreman" w/crossed hook & ladder & "1," inside penciled label
"E.H. Bryant," good color, 9½" l.
(minor wear) 175.00
Certificate, "Wm. T. King appointed
to Engine Co. No. 5," w/a horse-
drawn ladder wagon & hose cart
w/fire ruins in the center, a
steamer in each lower corner,
Cambridge, Massachusetts, 1847,
in painted frame, plus a Fire Service History of Cambridge pamphlet, print 19½ x 23½", 2 pcs.
(minor staining & foxing) 330.00
Chemical fire cart, from Studebaker
factory, original 25 foot hose &
brass nozzle 650.00
Dance invitation, Torrent Engine
Co., No. 3, Dorchester Lower
Mills, March 7, 1856, framed,
6 x 8" 60.50
Engine lamp, brass, red glass 4" d.
front panel finely engraved
w/"FREDERICK MACY 6," White

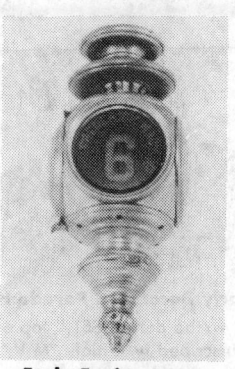

Early Engine Lamp

Mfg. Co., Bridgeport, Connecticut,
minor dents, electrified, 15" h.
(ILLUS.) 1,100.00
Fire alarm call box, "Gamewell,"
"Telegraph Station," 1880's 75.00
Fire mark, cast iron, letters "F.A.,"
correct hollow casting, ca. 1830,
7½ x 11½" oval 550.00
Fire mark, cast iron, "Mutual Assur-
ance Co., Philadelphia," squatty
oval, ca. 1827 .... 700.00
Fire mark, cast iron, "Union Fire Insurance Co., Nashville, Tenn.,"
ca. 1870 (rusty) 850.00
Helmet, leather, an eight-comb High
Eagle type w/white front shield,
red panels & black lettering
"ASST FOREMAN LOWELL VFA
MASS." (rough paint, worn around
brim, early repaint, minor crack
in front brim) 247.50
Hose nozzle, brass, double handle,
removable nozzle, marked "Akron
Brass Mfg. Co., Inc.,"
16" l. 135.00
Lantern, "Dietz King Fire Dept.,"
brass, w/clear "Dietz Fitzall"
globe, 14½" h. (some damage)... 75.00
Lithograph, printed in color, shows
Engine of the Red Jacket Veterans
Firemen's Association, Cambridge,
Massachusetts, Brooks Bank Note
Company, Boston, framed,
18½ x 25½" (minor staining
& foxing) 1,100.00
Paperweight, bronze, "The Charter
Oak Fire Ins. Co., Ltd. Edit.
(No. 301)," produced from Company Firemark Die, w/papers 75.00
Parade hat, pressed felt, top hat
painted black & decorated in polychrome w/vignette of young wo-
man holding a pitcher before a
detailed landscape, the vignette
enclosed by an oval reserve
flanked by banners inscribed
"Spring Garden," the reverse in-

Early Decorated Parade Hat

scribed w/the date "1851," top of crown inscribed w/initials "M.V." within wreathed reserve, the under-brim painted red, some paint loss, 5¾" h. (ILLUS.) 6,600.00

Photograph, shows firefighters in dress uniforms posed in front of their hose wagon & brick fire-house, mounted in oak frame which has three metal medallions depicting hose wagons, two early badges engraved "Storm Hose No. 2" & one small medallion w/helmet, crossed trumpets, lad-der, etc., image 12½ x 16½" 110.00

Rear engine lamps, nickel-plate, tall w/4¼" cut glass panels, the red panel w/a large "1" engraved, blue & clear panels w/geometric floral designs in center, 19½" h., pr. (top of one rusted, one missing wick & reservoir) 2,970.00

Sign, painted tin, fire company sign w/eagle on shield w/ribbon ban-ner reading "Rainbow Fire Com-pany" in oval on background of sea & sky, black edge background w/foliate designs in red & yellow, 10 x 14" (minor flaking).......... 800.00

Trumpet horn, brass, engraved "W. Stachlen, Williamsburg, 1858," 19" 1,200.00

Rare Glass Trumpet

Trumpet horn, presentation-type, coin silver, inscribed "Presented by the City of Lowell to Mazeppa Engine Company No 10 for the third Best Horizontal Playing, July 4, 1856," derby-style bell, 6" d., 16¼" h. 1,430.00

Trumpet horn, presentation-type, cranberry cut to clear glass, fine crossbanding & leaf pattern, 8" d. bell, 16¼" h. (ILLUS. previous column).......................14,300.00

Trumpet horn, toleware, red paint w/black striping & painted initials "A.W.B.," two tassel rings, 6" d., 23" h. (paint chipping, mouthpiece needs repair) 1,320.00

FIREPLACE & HEARTH ITEMS

Brass Fireplace Screen

Andirons, bell metal, Federal style, urn finial topped by swirled flame finial, plain tapered columnar shaft on square plinth, arched legs w/spurs, claw & ball feet, conform-ing log stops, hand-wrought iron shaft w/seamed castings, probably Philadelphia, late 18th c., 32" h., pr. $10,450.00

Andirons, brass, late Federal style, steeple top finial above an octag-onal standard, spurred cabriole legs continuing to conforming log stops, America, mid-19th c., 19" h., pr. 1,870.00

Andirons, cast brass, figural, finial w/detailed portrait head on square columnar support w/styl-ized Gothic window ornamental decoration on inverted U-shaped base, copper-colored acid finish, early 20th c., 27½" l., 25" h., pr............................. 880.00

Andirons, cast iron, gooseneck fini-als, wide set penny feet, good de-tail, 20" h., pr. (pitted) 300.00

Andirons, cast iron, figural, modeled as caricature figures of standing black man & black woman squatting w/hands on knees, America, late 19th - early 20th c., 16½" h., pr. 1,320.00

Andirons, cast iron, figural standing American Indian w/plumed headdress & carrying bow & arrows, 13" h., pr. (pitted w/rust, one rod incomplete) 250.00

Bellows, inlaid wood, walnut sides w/black leaf & geometric inlays, raised turned panel w/a reverse-painted rose insert, carved reeded ivory nozzle, America, 19th c., 9½" w., 22" l. 1,320.00

Bellows, wheel-type, brass & beechwood, shaped platform base supporting a spoked wheel on interlacing bracket standard, the wooden circular casing extending to the brass tapering nozzle, second half of 19th c., 32" l. 165.00

Clock jack (meat roasting rack on clockwork mechanism), brass, embossed label "John Linwood, Warranted," England, 13½" l. (no key, minor dents) 80.00

Fireback, cast iron, square, centering a shell surrounded by a shell & trailing vine border, late 18th or early 19th c., 28½" w., 30" h. 352.00

Fireboard, carved & painted pine, nearly square board painted w/the figure of a large yellow dog chained to a stout post, a tiny man wearing a broad-brimmed straw hat seated under the post, center scene framed in deep shadowbox w/grey & white marbleizing, probably New England, 19th c., 31½" w., 32¼" h. 4,950.00

Fire grate, cast nickel steel, ornate scrolling legs, molded detail w/bust of Minerva at center, early 20th c., 20½" w., 18½" h. 285.00

Fireplace fender, brass & wire, standing frame w/wire screen, top w/brass covering, applied wire decorative scrolls over the standing wires, curved ends, America, early 19th c., 49" l., 10½" h. 660.00

Fireplace hood, Arts & Crafts style, hand-hammered copper, rectangular chimney cover flaring down to hood w/riveted edges, ca. 1910, 12½" w. at top, 36" w. at base, 43" h. 990.00

Fireplace screen, brass, arched form w/embossed floral band border around embossed center scene of

early tavern interior w/three men, 22" w., 31" h. (ILLUS.) 115.00

Fireplace screen, wrought iron & mesh, Arts & Crafts style, triangular loop handles on rectangular frame centering twenty-eight mesh squares, scroll feet (painted), early 20th c., 45" w., 27" h. . . . 715.00

Hearth broiler, rotary-type, wrought iron, alternating wavy & straight bars within circular rim, twisted handle, 31" l. 195.00

Hearth broom, birch, painted blue, New Hampshire, 19th c. 195.00

Hearth brush, decorated wood, slender turned handle & oval end w/original horsehair brush, old green paint w/gilt decoration, brass hanger, 22½" l. (some paint wear) 40.00

Hearth toaster, rotating-type, handforged iron w/four rectangular arches, step-up shaft w/flat shaped handle & big closed ring, 18th c. 260.00

Early Hearth Shovel

Hearth tools: tongs & shovel; each steel w/brass grips w/ribbed & faceted ball finials, the gilt shovel face elaborately decorated w/etched neo-classical ornament centering a spread-wing shield-bearing eagle, made for the American market, England, 1790-1820, 34½" l., pr. (ILLUS. of shovel) . . . 2,420.00

Heat reflector, tin, semi-circular form w/small loop handle for warming food at hearth-side, pierced design of hearts, diamonds, dots & stars, 8" w., 6½" h. (soldered seams w/some added rivets) 505.00

Oven peel, iron, open heart-shaped ram's horn curls at top of handle, 18th c., 48" l. 175.00

Trammel, hand-forged iron, sawtooth-type, movable ring han-

dle top, 23" shortest to 31½"
longest 120.00
Trammel & pot hook, wrought iron,
sawtooth-type, ratchet mechanism
terminating in an incurvate scroll,
twisted pot hook w/tilting device,
Pennsylvania, 1750-1800, 36" l.
trammel 550.00

FISHER (Harrison) GIRLS

The Fisher Girl, that chic American girl whose face and figure illustrated numerous magazine covers and books at the turn of the century, was created by Harrison Fisher. A professional artist who had studied in England and was trained by his artist father, he was able to capture an element of refined, cultured elegance in his drawings of beautiful women. They epitomized all that every American girl longed to be and catapulted their creator into the ranks of success. Harrison Fisher, who was born in 1877, worked as a commercial artist full time until his death in 1934. Today collectors seek out magazine covers, prints, books and postcards illustrated with Fisher Girls.

Book, "A Dream of Fair Women,"
numerous color illustrations by
Harrison Fisher, w/original gift
box w/illustrated cover, Bobbs-
Merrill Co., 1907 ....$165.00
Book, "A Garden of Girls," illustra-
tions by Harrison Fisher, Dodd,
Mead & Co., 1910 .... 125.00
Book, "A Song of Hiawatha," by
Henry Wadsworth Longfellow, il-
lustrated by Harrison Fisher,
Bobbs-Merrill Co., 1906 .... 80.00
Book, "Beverly of Graustark," by
George Barr McCutcheon, novel il-
lustrated by Harrison Fisher,
Dodd, Mead & Co., 1904 .... 15.00
Book, "In The Bishop's Carriage," by
Michelson, novel illustrated by
Harrison Fisher, 1904 .... 35.00
Book, "Jane Cable," by George Barr
McCutcheon, novel illustrated by
Harrison Fisher, Bobbs-Merrill Co.,
1906 .... 35.00
Book, "Lovely Woman," illustrations
by Harrison Fisher, Bobbs-Merrill
Co., 1910 .... 100.00
Book, "Nadra," by George Barr
McCutcheon, novel illustrated by
Harrison Fisher, 1905 .... 35.00
Book, "Splendid Idle Forties," by
Atherton, novel illustrated by Har-
rison Fisher, 1902 .... 35.00
Book, "The Man from Brodney's" by

George Barr McCutcheon, novel illustrated by Harrison Fisher,
Bobbs-Merrill Co., 1908 .... 35.00
Candy tin, "The Yachting Girl," Harrison Fisher illustration 35.00
Postcard, "American Beauties," col-
or, published by Scribners, 1910 .. 5.00
Postcard, "Following the Race," col-
or, published by Scribners, 1910 .. 5.00
Sheet music, "For You A Rose," illustrated by Harrison Fisher,
1917 .... 11.00

FISHING COLLECTIBLES

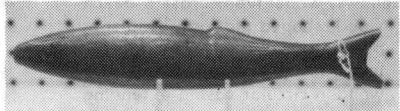

Fish-Shaped Depth Sounder

For centuries sport fishing has been an alluring pastime. The publication of Isaac Walton's classic work "The Compleat Angler" in the 1650's helped establish fishing as a credible and worthwhile pursuit, a worthy activity for men of strength and character. Sport fishing has never diminished in popularity and today the collecting of early and classic fishing-related equipment and memorabilia is a growing hobby and a perfect sideline activity when there's no fishing hole nearby. We list here a selection of recently offered fishing collectibles.

BOOKS & PAPER ITEMS
Book, "Blue Book of Sports," by
Everett Sanders, 1931, au-
tographed copy $55.00
Book, "Dry Fly Fishing," by Emlyn
Gill, 1915, New York 25.00
Book, "Fresh Water Fishing," by
Carhart, 1949 .... 14.50
Book, "Hardy's Anglers Guide,"
1951 .... 20.00
Book, "Professional Fly Tying &
Tackle Making," by Herter, 1941 .. 40.00
Book, "Weber Fly Casting," 11th
Edition 9.00
Catalog, "Gladding, New York,"
1939 .... 3.00
Magazine, "American Angler Fish-
ing," weekly publication, illustrat-
ed, 1882 .... 20.00

LURES
J.T. Buel, Whitehall, New York,
spinner 30.00
Carter's Bestever Bait Co., plug-
type, 3" l. 35.00

Creek Chub Bait Co. "Injured Minnow," No. 1500 series, w/original box, 3¾" l. 18.00

Creek Chub Bait Co. "Jointed Pikie Minnow," No. 2600 series, 4½" l. 25.00

Creek Chub Bait Co. "Pikie Minnow," No. 700 series, mint in box, 4½" l. 28.00

Haskell minnow lure, copper, handmade by Riley Haskell (1827-82), a Painesville, Ohio gunsmith, 1859 patent marking, 3 3/8" l. 22,000.00

Heddon "Baby Crab Wiggler," No. 1900 series, w/original box .. 15.00

Heddon "Basser," No. 8500 series, 4" l. 20.00

Heddon "Crazy Crawler," grey mouse, No. 2100 series, 2½" l. ... 30.00

Heddon "Little Luny Frog," No. 3400 series 40.00

Heddon "Lucky-13," No. 2500 series, w/original box, 4" l. 25.00

Heddon "Vamp Spook," No. 9750, 4½" l. 18.00

Hosmer mechanical "froggie" 3,850.00

Keeling's "Expert Wooden Minnow," 3" l. 50.00

Lane automatic minnow, ca. 1913 .. 3,850.00

Le Boeuf Mfg. Co., Wesleyville, Pennsylvania, "Creeper" 35.00

Model of muskrat w/dark fur on wooden body, bead eyes, string tail, two treble hooks, attributed to "Bud" Stuart, Michigan, 5½" l. 145.00

Moonlight Bait Co. "Pikaroon Muskie," 4" l. 35.00

Charles Orvis flies, in original box .. 50.00

Paw Paw Bait Co. "Popping Lure," No. 2200 series, unused in original box, 3¼" l. 25.00

Pflueger "May Bug" spooner, ca. 1890 .... 4,510.00

Pflueger "Mustang," No. 8600 series, 2½" l. 20.00

Shakespeare "Revolution Bait," 'Mickey Mouse' props, aluminum, 4" l. 50.00

Shakespeare "Slim-Jim Minnow," No. 6541 series, 3¾" l. 30.00

Shakespeare "Swimming Mouse," No. 578 series, 3¼" l. 35.00

South Bend Bait Co. "Bass-Oreno," No. 973 series, 3½" l. 28.00

South Bend Bait Co. "Min-Oreno," No. 927 series, 4" l. 25.00

South Bend Bait Co. "Wounded Minnow," No. 920 Best-O-Luck series, 3 5/8" l. 40.00

Winchester Repeating Arms Co. "June bug" spinner, No. 9716 series 65.00

Winchester Repeating Arms Co.

"Multi-Wobbler," No. 9202, 3½" l. 150.00

Winchester Repeating Arms Co. "Multi-Wobbler," No. 9204, 3½" l. 150.00

Winchester Repeating Arms Co. "Multi-Wobbler," No. 9205, crackle back finish, 3½" l. 175.00

REELS

Brass w/bone handle, Victorian, 2" d. 55.00

Brass, engraved "Kelly & Son, Dublin," 2 3/8" d. 60.00

Brass, "Hendryx," w/seating, ca. 1890 .... 30.00

Hard rubber, Alonzo Fowler "Gem," fly reel, ca. 1872 .... 15,400.00

Mahogany w/brass handles, 4" d. .. 45.00

Mahogany w/brass Starback ratchet, 3½" d. 60.00

Mahogany w/brass Starback ratchet, English, 5" d. 75.00

Metal, J.A. Coxe "Model No. 25c," w/original leather case 75.00

Metal, J.A. Coxe "Model No. 940" .. 125.00

Metal, marked "H.L. Leonard, Maker," fly reel, Philbrook & Payne patents, 19th c. 12,650.00

Metal, Pflueger "Skilkast No. 1953" 10.00

Metal, Shakespeare "Marhoff No. 1964 Model HE, 1940," master reel 35.00

Metal, South Bend Bait Co. "No. 450," w/leather case 15.00

Metal, South Bend Bait Co. "No. 550," casting reel, w/original box 25.00

Metal, Winchester Repeating Arms Co. "No. 1322" 55.00

Metal, Winchester Repeating Arms Co. "Top of Line No. 2450 Take-Down" model 125.00

Nickel plate, Hendryx, patents 1876-88, raised pillar 15.00

Wire metal, William Billinghurst patent "birdcage" model, ca. 1859 .... 12,650.00

RODS

Garrison "Model 209," bamboo 4,950.00

Garrison "Model 212-E," bamboo .. 1,540.00

H.S. Gillum trout-type bamboo rod, 6' 9" l. 13,200.00

H.S. Gillum bamboo rod, 8' l. 3,850.00

Goodwin Granger "Champion," bamboo, ca. 1934, 8½' l. 300.00

Goodwin Granger bamboo fly rod, 9' l. 45.00

George Halstead bamboo fly rod, 6' l. 8,740.00

Horrocks & Ibbotson "Cascade Model," three-section split bamboo fly rod, 4 pcs. 100.00

Jim Payne bamboo fly rod, "banty"
size, 4' 4" l. 6,600.00
"Perfect Model," 'tru-temper' steel,
5' l. 35.00
Phillipson "Pacemaker," bamboo fly
rod, unused w/original tube & ex-
tra tip, 8½' l. 100.00
Shakespeare "A-1363 Ausable," split
bamboo fly rod 40.00
South Bend Bait Co. "No. 359," bam-
boo fly rod, 8½' l. 130.00
Ward's "Hawthorne," tubular glass,
5' 3" l., 5 pcs. & case 30.00
Winchester Repeating Arms Co.
"No. 5650," steel, w/original can-
vas bag 60.00
Winchester Repeating Arms Co.
"No. 6055," fly rod 135.00
Paul Young "Little Giant," bamboo,
7' l. 5,170.00
Paul Young "Perfectionist," bamboo,
7½' l. 4,070.00

MISCELLANEOUS ITEMS
Creel, finely woven splint, leather
trim & straps 35.00
Creel, woven splint, nut brown
patina, ca. 1830 . . . . 220.00
Creel, woven splint, hinged wooden
top, leather straps & hasp, wide . . 75.00
Fly tying kit for bass bugs, w/origi-
nal box 55.00
Fly tying vise, cast iron, boxed 50.00
Depth sounder, cast metal, fish-
shaped, glass eyes (ILLUS.) 225.00
Minnow bottle trap, aqua glass, em-
bossed "McSwain Bait Trap - Min-
nows - Roaches," w/wire handle,
ca. 1890's, 11" l. 50.00
Minnow bottle trap, glass, marked
"Orvis" 45.00
License, Pennsylvania, 1924 . . . . 50.00
Net, wooden, Ed Cummings, Flint,
Michigan 35.00
Net, wooden, South Bend Bait Co.,
"No. 72" 90.00

FOOT & BED WARMERS

Bed warmer, brass pan w/engraved
profile portrait of a man smoking
a pipe surrounded by stylized floral designs, turned walnut handle,
39" l. (old soldered repair
to rim) $525.00
Bed warmer, brass pan w/starflow-
er tooled design on cover, turned
handle w/traces of original red
graining, 41¼" l. 400.00
Bed warmer, brass pan w/circular
lid w/folded rim & punched decoration of a peafowl enclosed by

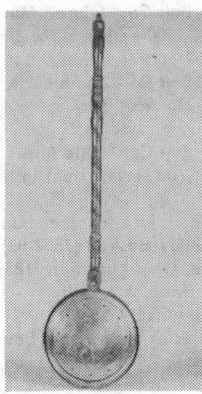

Well Decorated Brass Bed Warmer

scrolls, turned & painted wood
handle w/wear, 43" l. (ILLUS.) 495.00
Bed warmer, deep brass pan
w/etched scroll decoration radiating from center circle, perfora-
tions around rim, original ring
handle, turned wood handle
painted & grained to resemble
walnut, acorn finial, America,
early 19th c., 10½" d. pan, over-
all 44" l. 302.50
Bed warmer, copper pan w/cover
engraved w/florals, long, turned
wood handle, 42½" l. (minor age
cracks) 250.00
Bed warmer, tin pan & cover
w/pierced dot circles, brass
thumbpiece opens cover, turned
wood handle, 34" l. 475.00
Foot warmer, brass, square box-
shaped w/pierced designs on
sides & top & bail handle across
top, door w/punch-engraved inscription & "1723," 8" sq.,
7½" h. 225.00
Foot warmer, pierced tin & wood,
mortised wood frame w/turned
posts holds punched tin panels
w/heart & circle designs, traces of
old red on frame, 8 x 9" (age
cracks in wood, break in one top
slat) 200.00

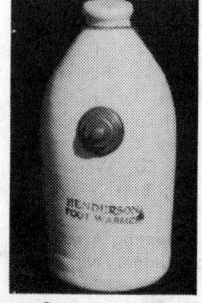

Henderson Stoneware Foot Warmer

Foot warmer, pierced tin & wood, mortised hardwood frame w/turned corner posts holds pierced tin sides & top w/circular designs, old refinishing, 9" l. (some damage) 155.00

Foot warmer, off-white stoneware pottery, "Henderson Foot Warmer," "Dorchester Pottery - Boston, Mass.," 11" l., 6" h. (ILLUS. previous page) 65.00

FOOT & BOOT SCRAPERS

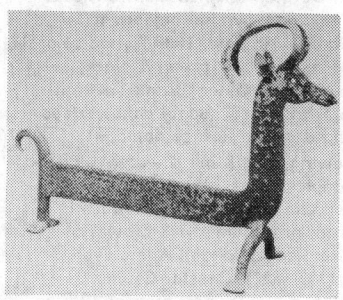

Ram Foot Scraper

Cast iron, model of a cat, cut-out eye, long tail, 10" base $165.00

Cast iron, model of a cow 75.00

Cast iron, model of a fighting cock, resting on a painted wooden block, 20" h. 522.50

Cast iron, model of a Dachshund dog, 21" l. 135.00

Cast iron, model of Scottie dogs (4), 17 lbs. 195.00

Cast iron, scrolled "lyre" shaped scraper mounted in large marble block, 19th c., overall 14" h. 80.00

Wrought iron, "H" form w/two uprights w/faceted knob finials flanking shaped crossbar, mounted in stone block, 13" h. 150.00

Wrought iron, modeled in the form of a ram w/cut & shaped horns & tail, on penny feet, original green paint, probably Pennsylvania, mid-19th c., 13 5/8" l. (ILLUS.) ...4,620.00

FOX (R. Atkinson) PRINTS

Robert Atkinson Fox (1860-1935) was an American artist whose prolific output included romantic landscapes, mountain scenes and portraits of domestic livestock & wildlife. Many of his paintings were reproduced as popular prints early in this century. Today *these prints are increasingly collectible thanks in great part to the well-researched series of articles written by Rita Mortenson for* The Antique Trader Weekly *beginning in 1980. This series then led to her 1985 book,* R. Atkinson Fox, His Life and Work *(Wallace-Homestead). The numbers accompanying our listings are those assigned by Mrs. Mortenson in her works.*

"A Sheltering Bower," No. 96, framed, 16 x 20" $50.00

"Afternoon Call," dated 1914, framed, 17 x 22" 45.00

"An Old-Fashioned Garden," No. 12 .... 45.00

"Autumn Gold," No. 190 .... 50.00

"Blossom Time," No. 83, 10 x 20" ... 60.00

"Blue Lake," No. 5, original blue & gold frame, 15¼ x 19¼" 70.00

"Buffalo Hunt" (The), No. 209, 10 x 12" 48.00

"By A Waterfall," No. 144 .... 80.00

"Clipper Ship," No. 75 .... 58.00

"Country Garden," No. 80, framed, 14 x 18" 52.00

"Dandelion Time," No. 162, 6 x 14" 40.00

"Daydreams," No. 138 .... 48.00

"Dreamland," No. 41, framed, 16 x 24" 60.00

"English Garden," No. 57, 14 x 18" 58.00

"Fallen Monarch," No. 98, 9 x 12" .. 50.00

"Garden of Contentment," No. 78... 56.00

"Garden of Hope," No. 20 .... 56.00

"Garden of Romance," No. 40, 14 x 22" 35.00

"Garden Retreat" & "Garden Realm," Nos. 81 & 82, pr. 75.00

"Glorious Vista," No. 6, 18 x 30" ... 62.00

"Good Shepherd," No. 29, framed .. 70.00

"Haven of Beauty," No. 204, 18 x 30" 85.00

"Heart of the Hills," No. 308, 7 x 9" 22.50

"Heart's Desire," No. 55, original frame, 12 x 22" 42.50

"Indian Summer," No. 35, 17 x 24".. 65.00

"In Flanders Field," No. 76, 8¼ x 16" 55.00

"Inspiration Inlet," No. 58, framed, 10 x 20" 55.00

"Land Where Shamrock Grows," No. 102, 14 x 20" 43.00

"Love's Paradise," No. 13, 10 x 17½" 45.00

"Moonlight & Roses," No. 39, original frame, 14 x 18" 45.00

"Mt. Hood," No. 136, 8½ x 11" 50.00

"Mt. Hood," No. 136, 16 x 20" 125.00

"Mount of Holy Cross" (The), No. 43, 16 x 20" 125.00

"Nature's Grandeur," No. 22, framed, 14 x 22" 58.00

"Nature's Sublime Grandeur,"
No. 64, 16 x 20" 125.00
"Oaks by the Roadside," No. 161,
10 x 16" 59.00
"Old Ironsides," No. 195, 9 x 12" ... 35.00
"Perfect Day," No. 65, 14 x 18" 59.00
"Poppies," No. 45, 15 x 20" 55.00
"Promenade," No. 10, 12 x 20" 58.00
"Romance Canyon," No. 32 .... 48.00
"Spirit of Youth," No. 4 .... 49.00
"Stately Sentinels," No. 25,
14 x 21½" 65.00
"Sunrise," No. 30, framed,
16 x 20" ....100.00 to 115.00
"Sunset Dreams," No. 23, 10 x 18" .. 54.00
"Where Nature Beats in Perfect
Time," No. 155, original frame,
16 x 20" 75.00
No. 52, untitled, poplar trees &
path, 10 x 16" 25.00

FRAKTUR

19th Century Pennsylvania Fraktur

Fraktur paintings are decorative birth and marriage certificates of the 18th and 19th centuries and also include family registers and similar documents. Illuminated family documents, birth and baptismal certificates, religious texts and rewards of merit, in a particular style, are known as "fraktur" because of the similarity to the 16th century type-face of that name. Gay water-color borders, frequently incorporating stylized birds, angels, animals or flowers, surrounded the hand-lettered documents, which were executed by local ministers, school masters or itinerant penmen. Most are of Pennsylvania Dutch origin.

Baptismal record for Johann Frederick
Lupold, water-color & pen & ink,
large central heart containing extensive inscription & flanked by
large flower pots issuing very
large stylized tulips above other
small florals, other small flowers
& tulips above & below the central
heart, attributed to the Lykens

Valley artist, Pennsylvania, dated
1790, framed, 8¼ x 13¼" $2,200.00
Bookplate, pen & ink & water-color
depicting three tulips in red, yellow & green springing from a
feathered heart centering the inscription "Anna Rupp, 1837" &
flanked on top & bottom by yellow & red stripes, Southeastern
Pennsylvania, 3¾ x 6½" 242.00
Bookplate, pen & ink & water-color
on wove paper, stylized fruit tree
in rectangular large reserve w/narrow decorative border above small
rectangular reserve w/inscription
in German script which translates
"This new hymnal belongs to
Samuel Angene, 1830," good colors
of red, yellow, green & black,
mahogany veneer frame, overall
6 5/8 x 9 7/8" (some stains, bleeding & minor surface damage) 1,176.00
Drawing, pen & ink & water-color,
depicting a feathered bird
perched on a budding branch in
red, green, yellow & brown, attributed to Johann Adam Eyer
(1755-1837), Chester County,
Pennsylvania, first quarter 19th c.,
4 x 5" (ILLUS.) 242.00
Drawing, pen & ink & water-color on
wove paper, three large boldly
stylized urns of tulips & vining
foliage w/two large facing birds in
red, blue, green, yellow & black,
signed in two places & dated in
three "Catarina Schmidt, 1824,"
Pennsylvania, framed, 14 x 16"
overall (small holes & slight
damage) 3,900.00
Haus Seegen (house blessing), printed & hand-colored, text in small
hearts arranged around a large
central heart w/two large crowns
at top flanking another heart,
stylized flowers along edges & between hearts, colored in red,
blue, green & brown, marked
"Haus Seegen AD 1785," old
molded pine frame, 15¼ x 19¼"
(repair at center fold line) 400.00
Verse, pen & ink & water-color,
free-hand verse in Pennsylvania
German script within a green oval
wreath surrounded by colorful geometric zigzag border in red,
blue, yellow & black, framed,
4¼ x 5¾" 395.00

FRAMES

Brass, wall-type, beaded edges,
8 x 10" oval, pr. $115.00

Bronze, gilt, Venetian patt., decorated w/blossoms & stems, w/frieze at the bottom of small squirrels among tree branches, stamped "Tiffany Studios New York 1682," 9 x 11¾" 2,200.00

Bronze, rectangular, Zodiac patt., impressed "TIFFANY STUDIOS/NEW YORK 1920," 1892-1920, 14" h. ... 1,430.00

Copper, Art Nouveau style, rectangular w/raised stylized head of a woman above a beveled glass plate, two stylized moths below, early 20th c., 5¾ x 10 3/8" 302.50

Victorian Painted Wood Frame

Painted wood, double-arched top carved w/scrolls, scrolled sides w/carved trim & further carving down the center between the two oval picture openings, black paint, Victorian, 8¼" w., 5¾" h. (ILLUS.) 135.00

Silver Plate, Arts & Crafts style, square outline w/inset square opening in center, marked "DIRK VAN ERP, San Francisco" & windmill mark, 12" sq. 110.00

Stained wood, Shibayama-style, modified rectangular form, carved w/*mokko*-form cut-outs & overlaid w/ivory & stag antler chrysanthemums, iris & butterflies, Japan, ca. 1900, 10" w., 13½" h., pr. 357.50

Sterling silver, 3½ x 4½" oval 25.00

Sterling silver, rectangular w/ribbon & bow crest, easel back, London hallmarks, 1906-07, 4½ x 9" 175.00

Sterling silver & enamel, Art Nouveau style, square outline w/repousse & chased linear & scrolling ornamentation & enameled at the top in blue & green, oak backing board, London, England, 1903, 7¾" h. 2,640.00

Walnut, shadowbox-type, w/ebony & gilt trim, Victorian, 32 x 37".... 200.00

Wooden, carved & gilded, w/Baroque foliate motifs, now set w/a mirror, 55 x 80" 2,530.00

FRATERNAL ORDER COLLECTIBLES

I.O.O.F. Parlor Table

B.P.O.E. (Benevolent & Protective Order of Elks) book, "Elk's Authentic History of Elks," by Charles Ellis, 1910, purple cover, includes history of Chicago Lodge No. 4, over 700 pp. (¼" rip on spine) $35.00

B.P.O.E. pitcher, tankard, china, elk's head & clock emblem & "B.P.O.E.," shaded brown ground, Warwick China, 10½" h. 195.00

B.P.O.E. tip tray, 1909 Convention, Philadelphia 45.00

D.A.R. (Daughters of the American Revolution) membership pin, 14k gold swivel-type, enhanced w/blue enameling & "Daughters of the American Revolution" in gold, engraved w/member's name & number, also w/thirteen gold stars & a draped flag, patent by Caldwell, August 22, 1881, 1 x 1½" 450.00

G.A.R. (Grand Army of the Republic) pokal, pewter, shows military buildings, 12" h. 120.00

G.A.R. spoon, sterling silver, in the shape of a musket, "28th National 1894 Encampment G.A.R., Pittsburgh" on stock 85.00

I.O.O.F. (Independent Order of Odd Fellows) box & clock, carved wood, shaped upper section crested w/carved eagle & decorated w/applied wood symbolic devices including the three links, heart-in-hand, skull-and-crossbones & compass, enclosing a clock, above small flush-fitted drawer front, over squared case fitted w/drawer similarly decorated w/applied symbolic devices & "W.H. MacKenzie," on shaped base, America, early 20th c., 9¾" l., 13½" h. (veneer loss, old breaks) 440.00

I.O.O.F. pitcher, porcelain, bulbous
baluster-shaped ribbed body
w/scrolled handle, Chelsea Sprig
patt. w/black transfer-printed
medallion on side w/emblem of
the organization & "Independent
Order of Odd Fellows M.U.," Eng-
land, mid-19th c., 8¼" h. 75.00

I.O.O.F. table, parlor-type, inlaid
wood, octagonal top w/elaborate
tri-color marquetry & gallery on an
eight-leg inlaid pedestal above a
round base w/Odd Fellow frater-
nity symbols & "Forget me not,
Friendship forever," on eight
shaped legs w/marquetry, America, last quarter 19th c., 35½" d.,
29" h. (ILLUS.) 2,530.00

I.O.O.F. watch charm, enameled
gold, 1920 . . . .   20.00

Masonic anvil, wooden, w/colorful
symbols & letters, "Q.U.A.M.,"
"No. 74," 12" l., 3½" w., 5" h. . . . 150.00

Masonic armchairs, painted & decorated, raised crests continuing to
turned arms on eight turned spindles, plank seats, bulbous turned
legs joined by turned stretchers,
painted black w/free-hand applied
olive green & white striping, crests
centering stenciled Masonic symbols, a compass & square, vinegar
grained seats, Vermont, ca. 1840,
set of 8 (some paint loss, one chair
missing piece of hand-hold) 2,750.00

Masonic ashtray, brass, good de-
tails, dated 1934 . . . .   25.00

Masonic Bible, 22 k gold stamping
on covers, illustrated, 1200+ pp.,
ca. 1931, 2½ x 9½ x 11½" 65.00

Masonic books, "Encyclopedia of
Free Masonry," published by the
Masonic History Co., 1919, black
covers w/gold trim, 2 vols.,
943 pp. 50.00

Masonic box, inlaid & painted wood,
rectangular, decorated overall
w/inlaid & painted Masonic symbols & the inscription "FAITH,
HOPE AND CHARITY 1858," light
inlay on dark ground, lid lifts to
reveal inscription "Oliver King
Lawrence Mass. A.D. 1858,"
4 x 7¼", 2½" h. (some paint &
inlay loss) 880.00

Masonic candlesticks, cast iron,
representing the three Lesser
Lights of the Lodge (the sun,
moon & Worshipful Master),
stepped circular base, baluster-
form shaft w/molded leafage,
molded foliate candlecup, painted
gold, America, 19th c., 28" h., set
of 3 . . . . 770.00

Masonic creamer, pressed glass,
Ruby Thumbprint patt., engraved
"Masonic Temple 1893" 30.00

Masonic match holder, wall-type,
pierce-carved walnut w/Masonic
symbols, 11" 65.00

Early Masonic Toasting Glass

Masonic toasting glass, tapering cylinder form w/flared fluted foot,
wheel-engraved w/leaf border
above a frieze of Masonic symbols
over the inscription "B. Arnold,"
reportedly made for Benedict
Arnold, late 18th - early 19th c.,
4¾" h. (ILLUS.) 1,760.00

O.E.S. (Order of the Eastern Star)
pendant, picture-type, half dollar
size, silver plate w/rhinestones &
tiny real rubies 35.00

Shrine champagne glass, carnival
glass, "New Orleans, Louisiana,"
shows alligators 70.00

Shrine champagne glass, carnival
glass, "Rochester, New York,"
shows photographer 65.00

Shrine champagne glass,
"Pittsburgh-Louisville," 1909 . . . . . .   45.00

Shrine cup & saucer, glass, "Los Angeles, May 1908," mint paint 145.00

Shrine goblet, ruby-stained glass,
pedestal foot, "St. Paul 1908" 50.00

Shrine mug, glass, sword handle,
"Saratoga 1903," w/Indian
Chief . . . . 100.00 to 125.00

Shrine pendant, tiger claw w/Shrine
emblem, Victorian 99.00

FRUIT JARS

American Porcelain Lined, w/mono-
gram, aqua, ½ gal. $27.50

Atlas Strong Shoulder Mason, clear,
½ gal. 8.00

Baker's (J.C.) Patent Aug. 14, 1860,
aqua, qt. . . . . 350.00 to 400.00

Ball Ideal with 1908 Patent

Ball Ideal Patd. July 14, 1908, aqua, pt. (ILLUS.)	3.00
Ball Perfect Mason, aqua, qt.	1.35
Ball Perfect Mason, olive, qt.	80.00
Beaver, amber, qt.	435.00
Beaver, clear, qt.	20.00
Cohansey, aqua, ½ pt.	25.00
Crown, olive, qt.	35.00
Darling (The), w/monogram, aqua, ½ gal.	30.00
Doolittle - The Self Sealer, clear, pt.	90.00
Double Safety, clear, ½ pt.	5.00
Everlasting Jar, aqua, pt.	18.00
Everlasting (Improved) Jar, 14-sided, clear, qt.	18.00
Flaccus (E.C.) Co., w/steer's head, amber, pt.	209.00
Franklin Dexter Fruit Jar, aqua, ½ gal.	38.00
Globe, amber, qt.	56.00
Globe, aqua, qt.	40.00
Globe, clear, qt.	18.00
Green Mountain G.A. Co., aqua, qt.	15.50
Hero, aqua, qt.	15.50
Keystone, clear, qt.	13.50
Knowlton Vacuum Fruit Jar, w/star, aqua, pt.	25.00
Lafayette, aqua, ½ gal.	80.00
Lightning, amber, qt.	55.00
Lightning Trade Mark, amber, ½ gal.	55.00 to 60.00
Lightning Trade Mark, citron, qt.	150.00
"Mason's" Improved (The), amber, ½ gal.	100.00
Mason's Patent Nov. 30th, 1858, w/cross, amber, qt.	125.00
Mason's Patent Nov. 30th, 1858, citron, qt.	95.00
Mason's Patent Nov. 30th, 1858, w/sun, moon & star, aqua, ½ gal.	140.00
Millville Atmospheric Fruit Jar, aqua, qt.	25.00
Moore's Patent Dec. 3d, 1861, aqua, qt.	80.00
Norge, aqua, pt.	10.00
Pet, aqua, qt.	80.00

Pinkerhuff's (A.W.) Patent March 14, 1876, No. 2 Ohio, Made by The Ohio Fruit Jar Co. of Upper Sandusky, O., aqua, 8¾" h. (rough lip ground flat)	400.00
Potter & Bodine Airtight Fruit Jar, Philada., aqua, ½ gal.	575.00
Royal Trade Mark, w/crown emblem, amber, qt.	65.00
Safety, aqua, ½ gal.	35.00
Safety, Kelly green, pt.	65.00
Safety Valve Patd. May 21, 1895, w/Greek Key design circling jar at shoulder & heel, aqua, ½ gal.	30.00
Standard, W. McC & Co., green, qt.	65.00
Stevens Tin Top, Patd. July 27, 1875, aqua, qt.	55.00
Swayzee's Improved Mason, green, ½ gal.	30.00
Winslow (The) Improved Valve Jar, aqua, qt.	400.00
Woodbury, w/monogram, aqua, pt.	37.50

FURNITURE

Furniture made in the United States during the 18th and 19th centuries is coveted by collectors. American antique furniture has a European background, primarily English, since the influence of the Continent usually found its way to America by way of England. If the style did not originate in England, it came to America by way of England. For this reason, some American furniture styles carry the name of an English monarch or an English designer. However, we must realize that, until recently, little research has been conducted and even less published on the Spanish and French influences in the areas of the California missions and New Orleans.

After the American Revolution, cabinetmakers in the United States shunned the prevailing styles in England and chose to bring the French styles of Napoleon's Empire to the United States and we have the uniquely named "American Empire" style of furniture in a country that never had an emperor.

During the Victorian period, quality furniture began to be mass-produced in this country with its rapidly growing population. So much walnut furniture was manufactured, the vast supply of walnut was virtually depleted and it was of necessity that oak furniture became fashionable as the 19th century drew to a close.

For our purposes, the general guidelines for dating furniture will be:
Pilgrim Century - 1620-85
William & Mary - 1685-1720

Queen Anne - 1720-50
Chippendale - 1750-85
Federal - 1785-1820
  Hepplewhite - 1785-1800
  Sheraton - 1800-20
American Empire - 1815-40
Victorian - 1840-1900
  Early Victorian - 1840-50
  Gothic Revival - 1840-90
  Louis XV (rococo) - 1845-70
  Louis XVI - 1865-75
  Eastlake - 1870-95
  Renaissance - 1860-85
  Jacobean & Turkish Revival -
    1870-90
Art Nouveau - 1890-1918
Turn-of-the-Century - 1895-1910
Mission (Arts & Crafts movement) -
  1900-15
Art Deco - 1925-40

All furniture included in this listing is
American unless otherwise noted. Also see
MINIATURES (Replicas.)

BEDS

American Empire Tall Poster Bed

Art Nouveau bed, carved walnut,
gently rounded rectangular headboard carved at the top corners in
full relief w/chrysanthemum blossoms & exotic leaves, w/a central
triangular panel pierce-carved
w/further blossoms & leaves, conforming lower footboard, heavily
carved siderails, designed by
Louis Majorelle, France, ca. 1900,
5' 3" w., 4' 7" h................$9,075.00
Empire, American, low poster bed,
maple, shaped headboard flanked
by baluster- and ring-turned posts
w/ball finials, conforming footposts, baluster- and ring-turned
feet, New England, mid-19th c.,
54" w., 56" h................... 880.00
Empire, American, "sleigh" bed, mahogany, scrolled & paneled head-

and footboards, scrolled feet,
mid-Atlantic states, 1820-30,
43½" w., 85" l., 38" h.......... 770.00
Empire, American, tall poster bed,
painted finish, pillar & scroll
carved paneled headboard flanked
by small turned posts, footboard
joined by turned rail & shaped
board, four block- and baluster-
turned posts w/ball finials, turned
feet, original red & black grained
paint, possibly Mahantango Valley,
Pennsylvania, ca. 1825, 51" w.,
67" h. (ILLUS.)................3,080.00
Federal low poster bed, painted
finish, triangular headboard
flanked by turned posts w/com-
pressed ball finials, footposts
similarly carved centering a shaped
footboard, cylindrical legs, black
over red graining, probably New
Hampshire, 1800-30, 49" w., 74" l.,
35½" h.......................5,060.00
Federal tall poster bed, carved mahogany, head- and footposts reeded
& carved w/flowerheads & acanthus motifs centering a shaped
mahogany headboard on spade
feet, New York, ca. 1795,
56½" w., 6' 7" h...............4,675.00
Federal tester bed, cherry, shaped
headboard flanked by headposts
w/ring-turned capitals above a
reeded double baluster standard &
w/conforming footposts, tapering
feet, w/tester, New England,
1800-20, 64" h.................6,600.00
Federal "trundle" bed, painted
wood, shaped head- and footboards flanking a rectangular
case in two sections, w/extension
trundle w/banded mid-molding
above a shaped skirt, on square
tapering & molded legs, New
England, mid-19th c., 72" l.,
51" w., 36" h................... 550.00

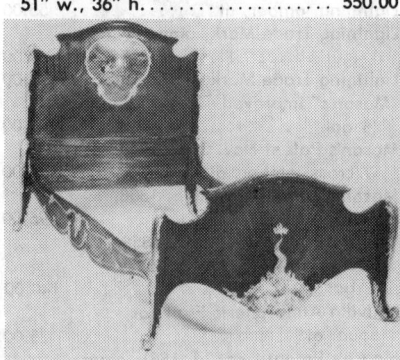

Louis XV Style Bed

Louis XV style beds, mahogany
w/tulipwood marquetry, crested

bombe headboard centered by a
cartouche-shaped marquetry panel
depicting an allegorical scene of a
mother, child & putti floating in a
vessel on water, conforming footboard w/a gilt bronze mount of a
dolphin among waves, the stiles
fitted w/gilt-bronze scrolls, scrolled
siderails further fitted w/gilt-
bronze mounts, 7' l., 45½" h., pr.
(ILLUS. of one) 5,500.00

Mission Style Bed

Mission-style (Arts & Crafts movement) beds, oak, straight crest
above seven straight vertical half
slats over lower panel, uneven
head- and footboards tapering
feet, unsigned, possibly Roycroft,
ca. 1912, single size, 42" w.,
headboard 54" h., pr. (ILLUS. of
one) 715.00
Sheraton tall poster canopy bed,
hardwood & pine, turned hardwood posts w/simple arched
headboard & turned & reeded
footposts w/narrow crossbar, old
dark brown finish, original rope
rails, early 19th c., 47" w., 72" l.,
58" h. (replaced canopy frame
w/modern net tester, minor edge
damage) 2,600.00

Renaissance Revival Bed

Victorian bed, Renaissance Revival
substyle, rosewood, headboard
w/curved top & paneled sides,
w/stenciled label "From A. Roux
French Cabinet Maker 479 & 481

Broadway, New York" w/paper
label used by Roux between 1850
& 1857, 68" l., 48¾" h. (ILLUS.) ..3,080.00

BENCHES

19th Century Bucket Bench

Bucket bench, pine, three rectangular shelves supported by rounded
rectangular sides ending in bootjack feet, inscribed "L.P.
McEathro, Lena, Illinois," 19th c.,
49" w., 31½" h. (ILLUS.) 550.00
Bucket bench, painted pine, wide top
w/rounded front corners & low
splashboard at back overhanging
underslung dovetailed drawer in
center, cut-out ends w/corner
brackets under top joined by wide
medial shelf, old worn brown paint
over earlier blue, 21½ x 57¼",
31" h. 1,400.00
Church pew, pine, rectangular back
above downswept sides & rectangular armrests, plank seat,
Gothic legs, Utah, late 19th c.,
4' 6" w., 33" h................... 220.00
Cobbler's bench, hardwood, primitive w/rectangular top w/seat at
one end & work area w/small
compartments & galleried edge at
opposite end, side drawer under
work area, crude six-sided
straight post legs, 43" w. (repairs
& replacements)................ 225.00
Deacon's bench, painted & decorated, three-chairback style
w/shaped rectangular crestrail
stenciled in brown w/fruit sprays
over horizontal splats above spindles, scrolled arms, plank seat,
cylindrical legs joined by stretchers, painted green, ca. 1820,
6' w. 935.00
Federal country-style bench, painted, tablet crest above 23 ring-
turned spindles flanked by shaped
armrests over similarly turned
arm supports, plank seat on ring-
turned legs joined by a box
stretcher, painted red, early
19th c., 90" w., 32" h. 528.00
Mammy's bench, flat, straight back-

rail above eight simple turned
spindles, shaped arms w/baluster-
turned arm supports joining thick
plank seat w/two-rail lift-off baby
guard at one end, baluster-turned
legs on rockers joined by wide
board box stretchers, undecorated
w/natural finish, 19th c.,
54" w. 600.00
Mission-style (Arts & Crafts move-
ment) piano bench, oak, rectangular seat flanked by plank sides
w/D-shaped handles at top, lower
single stretcher, Model No. 217,
Gustav Stickley paper label, ca.
1907, 36" w., 21" h. 880.00
Oriental bench, carved hardwood,
rectangular paneled top w/round-
ed edges & corners above a
slightly waisted frieze carved w/a
central bracket scroll, supported
by inwardly curving legs resting
on square feet joined by a narrow
stretcher at the base, China,
18th c., 18¾" w., 20½" h. 247.50

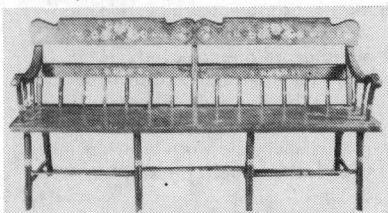

Pennsylvania Settle Bench

Settle bench, painted & decorated,
shaped crestrail painted w/floral
sprigs in beige, rose & green on a
green ground, over rectangular
median horizontal splats over
spindles, scrolled arms, rectangular plank seat, turned cylindrical
legs joined by stretchers, Pennsylvania, ca. 1850, 5' 10" w.
(ILLUS.) 1,430.00
Storage bench, primitive pine, low
back & shaped end arms flank lift-
top seat opening to two-part bin
interior, wide single-board construction w/cut-out feet & scrolled
ends, old dark finish, 62" w.,
32" h. 400.00
Victorian benches, Rococo substyle,
carved walnut, rectangular upholstered top over serpentine shell-
carved skirt on cabriole legs
w/scroll feet & casters, ca. 1860,
36" w., 16" h., pr. 935.00

BOOKCASES

Federal bookcase, carved mahogany,
three-part construction: upper section w/flat top w/molded cornice

above a pair of six-pane glazed
cupboard doors opening to interior
w/adjustable shelves; the middle
section w/pair of paneled cupboard doors opening to shelved
interior; separate molded base (of
later date), Philadelphia, ca. 1800,
55¾" w., 7' h. 6,600.00

L. & J.G. Stickley Bookcase

Mission-style (Arts & Crafts movement) bookcase, oak, flat three-
quarter gallery above rectangular
top over case w/single 16-pane
glazed door opening to shelves,
solid sides w/chamfered, keyed
tenons in each, L. & J.G. Stickley
"Handcraft" label, No. 641, ca.
1906, 36" w., 55" h. (ILLUS.) 2,640.00
Mission-style (Arts & Crafts move-
ment) bookcase, oak, rectangular
top w/three-quarter gallery above
pair of 12-pane glazed doors
w/metal loop latches opening to
shelves, flat base on very short
legs, remnants of Gustav Stickley
paper label, Model No. 719, ca.
1912, 60" w., 56" h. 3,960.00

Renaissance Revival Bookcase

Victorian bookcase, Renaissance Revival substyle, ebonized walnut,
rectangular top w/dentil cornice
above two glazed doors & two
glazed smaller side doors, flanked
on each side by circular columns,

raised on plinth base, overall
incised & w/ebonized stylized foliate decoration, ca. 1870, 7' w.,
5' h. (ILLUS.) 3,025.00

Rococo Bookcase

Victorian bookcase, Rococo substyle,
carved rosewood, pierce-carved
arched crest w/three urn finials on
rectangular top above pair of
arched glazed cupboard doors
w/scroll-carved details opening to
three shelves, outset base
w/scroll-carved chamfered corners
flanking pair of paneled doors on
either side of central scroll-carved
oval medallion, short, round feet,
maple interior, signed "E.W. Hutch-
ings Cabinet Warehouse, 175
Broadway, N.Y.," ca. 1850, original
finish, 58½" w., 9' 2¼" h.
(ILLUS.) 6,600.00

BUREAUS PLAT

Louis XV-Style Bureau Plat

Louis XV bureau plat, ebonized
wood, shaped rectangular top inset
w/brown leather over five drawers
surrounding the kneehole & opposing false drawers, incurved hipped
cabriole legs, later ormolu keyhole
escutcheons & *sabots*, France,
mid-18th c., 5' 5½" l., 31" h. 4,675.00
Louis XV-Style bureau plat, gilt-

bronze mounted tulipwood, shaped
rectangular top inset w/a brown
tooled leather writing surface
within a molded gilt-bronze border,
the angles w/foliate-cast clasps,
the conforming frieze fitted
w/three drawers inlaid w/scrolling
bouquets opposing three conforming simulated drawers, the angled
stiles applied w/cartouche cabochons trailing husks continuing to
conforming *sabots*, 4' 10" l., 31" h.
(ILLUS.) 4,950.00
Louis XVI bureau plat, brass-mounted
mahogany, rectangular brass-
bound top w/tooled inset-leather
writing panel above five paneled
drawers surrounding a kneehole,
the sides fitted w/inset-leather
slides, the back w/five sham
drawers, circular turned tapering
fluted legs headed by fluted
panels, France, last quarter
18th c., 25½ x 51", 29½" h. 20,900.00
Louis XVI-Style bureau plat, ormolu-
mounted kingwood parquetry,
rectangular leather top over a
shaped frieze w/three drawers
raised on square tapered legs,
mounted overall w/leaf, bound
reed, ribbon & wreath-form ormolu
moldings, *chutes*, *sabots* & handles, in the manner of Jean-Henri
Riesener, France, 20th c., 31½ x
60", 30" h. .2,750.00
Neo-Classic bureau plat, tulipwood
& parquetry, rectangular double-
crossbanded top inlaid w/stained
cube-pattern parquetry, the similarly inlaid frieze w/five drawers
surrounding a kneehole, the sides
similarly inlaid & w/parquetry
writing slides, square tapering
legs, North Italy, late 18th c.,
5' 9" l., 31¾" h. (restorations) . . .7,700.00

CABINETS

Art Deco side cabinet, olive, inset
marble top above rectangular parquetry cupboard doors opening to
a shelved interior & centering a
short drawer veneered in blonde-
wood & carved w/stylized overlapping blossoms & geometric devices,
above a single glass shelf & a
lower shelf, the back panels set
w/mirrored glass, w/keys, France,
ca. 1935, 49¼" w., 43 3/8" h. . . .1,760.00
Art Nouveau cabinet, carved walnut
& fruitwood marquetry, rectangular form, upper section w/an open
shelf behind a heart-shaped frame
carved in medium-relief w/blos-
soms & leafage, continuing to a

cupboard door inlaid in various woods w/blossoming branches above other flowers & water lilies in a pond, w/a triangular section carved w/further blossoms continuing into a serpentine apron, outward flaring thumb-molded legs, designed by Louis Majorelle, France, ca. 1900, 21" w., 42½" h. 3,080.00

Arts & Crafts cabinet, oak, rectangular upper portion w/two floral copper-paneled cabinet doors & slide over projecting case w/lower cabinet doors, lower shelf on side stretchers, fitted as a bar, unsigned, England, ca. 1900, 14½ x 31¾", 4' 4" h. (backboard replaced) 1,100.00

China cabinet, Mission-style (Arts & Crafts movement), oak, upright rectangular form, the front w/two doors each w/a glass panel surmounted by twelve glass panes, opening to an interior w/two shelves, one fitted w/cup hooks, the sides w/conforming glass panels & panes, hammered copper escutcheons & handles, Model No. 746, red "Handcraft" decal mark of L. & J.G. Stickley, ca. 1912, 43 5/8" w., 5' 10" h. 3,575.00

Golden Oak China Cabinet

China cabinet, Turn-of-the-Century, golden oak, curved D-shape flat top w/carved cornice over wide gadroon-carved band above wide glazed door opening to four wooden shelves, flanked by fruit & nut-carved columns flanked by curved-glass sides, carved band around base & scroll-carved central apron panel, ca. 1910, 53" w., 5' 10½" h. (ILLUS.) 1,800.00

Federal cabinet, mahogany veneer, scrolled crest above a 9-pane

Federal Mahogany Veneer Cabinet

glazed door w/astragal beading opening to two shelves, short bracket feet, probably New York, 1815-25, 33½" w., 47" h. (ILLUS.) 1,045.00

Jelly cabinet, rectangular top w/three-quarter gallery above a single drawer over two paneled cupboard doors enclosing shelves, raised on turned cylindrical feet, painted overall in pale blue-green, Midwest, second half 19th c., 45½" w., 4' 8" h.............. 880.00

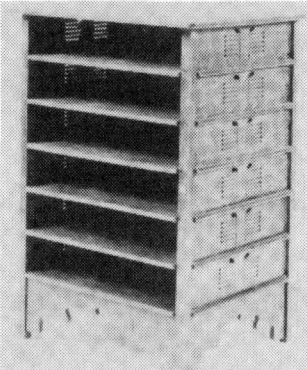

Arts & Crafts Music Cabinet

Music cabinet, Arts & Crafts style, oak, rectangular top above six open shelves, sides pierced w/stylized design, shaped aprons, Roycroft Shops, 1902, 22" w., 30" h. (ILLUS.) 1,870.00

Music cabinet, Victorian, Renaissance Revival substyle, ebonized inlaid wood, single cupboard door w/a central panel elaborately inlaid w/an urn & scrolls, the sides w/canted corners, above a single frieze drawer, raised on turned legs w/a shelf stretcher, ca. 1860, 25" w., 5' 4" h. 2,310.00

Victorian side cabinet, Renaissance

Victorian Side Cabinet

Revival substyle, ebonized wood,
high back crest w/carved & incised
gilded scrolls above stepped rectangular top w/molded edge above
inlaid & gilt line-incised single
drawer above cabinet door w/cen-
tral inlaid floral urn & swag design
& gilt line-incised borders, door
flanked by gilt line-incised pilasters, flat base on thin round feet,
ca. 1870 (ILLUS.)..................506.00
Vitrine cabinet, Art Deco, palissander
& glass, upright cabinet w/canted
front corners & stepped top set
w/a brass-edged glass door within
a molded wood frame, opening to
four glass shelves & a mirrored
back, raised on a short inset plinth
& a faceted domed foot, France,
ca. 1930, w/key, 5' 7" h. 2,200.00
Vitrine cabinet, Louis XV-XVI Style,
giltwood, trefoil top over three
conforming glazed panels, raised
on cabriole legs w/*sabots*, overall
applied floral decoration, ca. 1900,
29" w., 4' 8½" h. (shelves
missing) 3,630.00

CHAIRS

Bentwood Office Desk Chair

Adirondack-style child's rocker, bent
twig construction w/high balloon-
back w/criss-cross woven twigs,
board seat above arched apron
w/looped twig design, 31" h.
(wear, some damage, wired repair) 75.00
American Colonial corner chair,
turned & carved maple, U-shaped
back above two pierced vase-form
splats centering turned uprights,
the slip-seat below on turned legs
joined by turned stretchers on a
frontal Spanish foot, New England,
ca. 1750-80...................3,960.00
American Colonial "ladder-back" side
chair, painted wood, four graduated & arched slats flanked by cylindrical stiles w/ball-turned acorn
finials above a velvet upholstered
seat on cylindrical legs & ball feet
joined by a box stretcher, tripartite
ball-turned front rung, brown
painted finish, Delaware River
Valley, mid-18th c., 43½" h. 1,320.00
Art Nouveau side chairs, arched back
above open-carved fan-shaped
back splat w/four ribs interwoven
w/clematis vines & flowers, upholstered seat above shaped & lightly
carved seatrail continuing to form
gently outcurved front legs, the
firm of Louis Majorelle, France,
early 20th c., pr. 2,640.00
Balloon-back side chairs, painted &
decorated, balloon-back w/shaped
crest above hand-hole, shaped
solid back splat above shaped
plank seat, bobbin- and bamboo-
turned front legs & widely splayed
back legs, original brown graining
on a salmon ground w/yellow striping & polychrome floral decoration,
underside of three signed "A.
Shuyer & Son, Bellefonte, Pa.,"
Pennsylvania, ca. 1850, set of 6..2,700.00
Barber chair, carved oak, original
brass base, "Hercules" 1,400.00
Bentwood armchairs, rectangular
bentwood back frame continuing
to open arms, square seat, four
cylindrical legs conjoined by
arched stretchers, upholstered in
nubby fabric, manufactured by
J.J. Kohn, ca. 1930, pr. 660.00
Bentwood office desk chair, arched
crestrail over tightly woven cane
back, scrolled bentwood arms,
rounded seat w/tightly woven
cane, cross-base w/adjustable
pedestal, ca. 1890 (ILLUS.) 440.00
Bentwood rocking chair, oval back
w/inset oval caned center section
between turned supports, above a

flaring rectangular caned seat &
curved arms continuing to a scrolling support w/integral rockers,
Austria, ca. 1900 . . . . .1,320.00
Biedermeier side chairs, walnut,
curved rectangular crestrail above
an ebonized lotus-shaped splat
flanked by twin swan's neck stiles,
drop-in seat, square tapering out-
curved legs, scroll toes, probably
Austrian, early 19th c., set of 4 . .5,720.00
Child's armchair, "slat-back" style,
maple, arched slats joined to
turned tapered back posts topped
w/shaped finials & joined to
turned arms, (replaced) rush seat,
front turned legs topped w/mush-
room finials, turned stretchers,
old finish, New England, early
19th c., 26" h. (slight height
reduction) 330.00
Child's highchair, "ladder-back" style,
maple & hickory, turned finials
above three slightly arched slats
& rush seat on turned splayed
legs joined by turned box
stretchers, retains much 18th c.
paint, New England,
ca. 1750-70. . . . . .2,200.00

Child's Painted Highchair

Child's highchair, painted wood,
rounded low back painted
w/flowerheads in red & green on
a pale green ground above turned
baluster-form spindles, plank seat
raised on turned cylindrical legs
joined by stretchers, late 19th c.
(ILLUS.). 247.50
Child's highchair-rocker-stroller com-
bination, oak, rounded arched
back w/caned panel, swing-up
arms w/attached tray rest on
shaped supports, caned seat on
shaped legs continuing to convertible arched legs w/wheels which

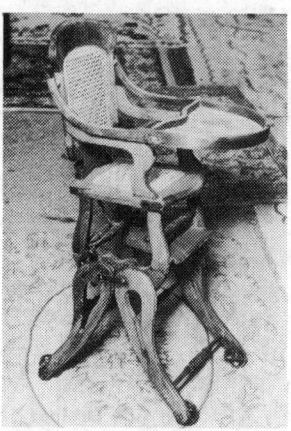

Child's Highchair-Rocker-Stroller

lower to form rocker & stroller,
ca. 1900, 39" h. as highchair
(ILLUS.). 350.00
Child's rocker w/arms, "ladder-
back" style, painted finish, three-
slat back between turned uprights
w/bulbous finials, spindle arms
joined to turned frontal uprights,
(tattered) cane seat, turned legs
w/stretchers on rockers, old red
paint w/black striping 200.00
Child's rocker w/arms, painted
wood, shaped crestrail above slat
back flanked by turned stiles
w/knob finials, wide arms
w/turned supports continuing to
form front legs, box stretchers, on
rockers, slat seat, worn original
brown paint w/red & yellow striping, 25" h. (seat slats partially
replaced) 125.00
Child's bamboo-turned Windsor
highchair, painted wood, simple
bamboo-turned back crest above
six bamboo-turned spindles, simple turned arms join back stiles,
slightly shaped seat on widely
splayed bamboo-turned legs
w/box stretchers & footrest at
front, old red & black repaint
w/yellow striping, 30" h. (one
arm a replacement, repaired
break at side of seat) 475.00
Child's "birdcage" Windsor side
chair, painted wood, bamboo-
turned crest above three similarly
turned spindles over seven spindles, shaped trapezoidal seat,
bamboo-turned legs joined by box
stretchers, later black paint,
stamped "S. Hamlin," New
England, early 19th c., 29" h. 330.00
Child's wing chair, Federal country-
style, mahogany, upholstered back
w/shaped crest flanked by shaped

wings, straight seat, square tapering legs, New England, ca. 1770,
30¼" h. 5,500.00

Chinese Inlaid Armchair

Chinese armchairs, mother-of-pearl
inlaid hardwood, shaped crestrail
suspending a circular medallion
inlaid w/scrolls surrounding a
central marble panel mottled as
an abstract landscape & framed
above a rectangular seat, the
front apron carved in high-relief &
inlaid w/blossoming plum,
straight square legs w/box
stretchers, 38" h., pr. (ILLUS. of
one) 495.00
Chippendale armchair, maple,
shaped crest above a pierced interlaced splat flanked by square
tapering stiles over shaped arms
w/square tapering supports,
trapezoidal rush seat, square
quarter-molded legs joined by a
box stretcher, New England, late
18th c. 605.00
Chippendale side chairs, mahogany,
carved cupid's bow crestrail ending
in foliate scroll-carved ears above
scroll-carved pierced splat flanked
by outward flaring square stiles,
trapezoidal splint seat, square
beaded legs w/stretchers, old
refinish, probably Pennsylvania,
ca. 1780, pr. 5,060.00
Chippendale side chair, walnut,
shaped crest centering a carved
shell above a volute- and acanthus-
carved pierced vase-form splat &
slip seat, cabriole legs w/a shell-
and acanthus-carved motif ending
in claw-and-ball feet, Philadelphia,
ca. 1765 . . . . .8,525.00
Chippendale wing chair, mahogany
base frame, shaped back & wings
above rolled arms, straight seat
frame on square tapering legs

Chippendale Wing Chair

joined by square stretchers, upholstered w/yellow, green & white
plaid cotton, New England,
ca. 1810, 45¾" h. (ILLUS.) 1,980.00
Eames lounge chairs, laminated ply-
wood, rounded backrest above an
S-scroll support, canted rounded
rectangular seat, raised on two inverted U-form legs, designed by
Charles Eames for Herman Miller,
paper label for Evans Product Division of Herman Miller, ca. 1947,
set of 3 . . . . .1,430.00
Early American country-style corner
chair, painted & decorated maple,
U-shaped backrail above two
arched splats centering turned uprights above a rush seat, on turned
legs joined by turned stretchers,
painted & decorated in stylized leaf
motifs in polychrome, the crest
bearing the date "1775," New Eng-
land, 1740-60 . . . . .4,125.00
Early American "ladder-back" arm-
chair, four shaped slats flanked
by ring-turned cylindrical stiles
w/ball-turned finials above
scrolled armrests w/baluster- and
ring-turned stiles over a trapezoidal rush seat, ring-turned legs
joined by a box stretcher,
44½" h. 418.00
Early American "ladder-back" rock-
ing chair, tiger stripe & bird's-eye
maple, four rectangular graduated
slats joined to turned back posts,
arms w/shaped handholds above
turned arm supports, rush seat,
turned stretchers & rockers, New
England, early 19th c., 40" h.
(refinished, restorations) 550.00
Edwardian armchair, painted satin-
wood, shield-shaped open back
painted w/a central floral bouquet
& pendant bellflowers flanked by
shaped arms on molded supports

painted w/trailing vines above an
over-upholstered seat raised on
square tapering legs ending in
spade feet, England, ca. 1905 . . . .1,045.00

Elizabethan Revival Armchair

Elizabethan Revival armchair, over-
stuffed upholstery in oak frame,
rounded upholstered back above
flat oak arms w/upholstered sides
& bulbous turned arm supports
continuing to half-round bun feet,
loose cushion seat, ca. 1925
(ILLUS.) 40.00

American Empire Side Chairs

Empire, American, side chairs, walnut w/mahogany veneer, shaped
back crest w/center roll above
curved stiles flanking vase-form
splat, upholstered slip seat, slightly cabriole front legs & saber-form
back legs, ca. 1825-30, 31¼" h.,
pr. (ILLUS.) 300.00
Federal "arrow-back" side chairs,
maple, tablet crest above five arrow spindles flanked by chamfered stiles over a shaped seat on
bamboo-turned legs joined by
similarly turned box stretchers,
stamped "G. Frote," 19th c.,
32" h., set of 6 . . . . 550.00
Federal dining chairs, carved & inlaid

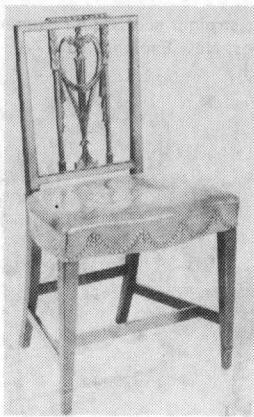

Federal Dining Chair

mahogany, molded square crest
above pierced urn & swag & tassel-
carved splat & serpentine upholstered seat on line-inlaid square
tapering legs ending in crossbanded cuffs, Philadelphia, ca.
1805, some restorations, set of 6
(ILLUS. of one) 12,100.00
Federal "lolling" armchair, mahog-
any, serpentine crestrail above a
tall upholstered back w/shaped &
molded arms on square Marlborough legs joined to square
stretchers, raked rear legs, green
leather upholstery w/brass decorative nail heads, Massachusetts,
1780-1810, 43½" h. (old refinish,
possibly replaced medial
stretcher) 4,950.00
Federal rocking chair, painted &
stenciled wood, stepped crest
above seven spindles, flanked by
shaped arm supports, ring-turned
legs joined by a ring-turned
stretcher, on rockers, 19th c.,
43" h. 330.00

George III Wingchair

George III wingchair, mahogany,

leather-upholstered back & arms
w/serpentine crest continuing to
flared sides w/outscrolled arms,
loose cushioned rectangular seat,
straight tapered legs joined by
stretchers, England, last quarter
of the 18th c. (ILLUS.) 4,950.00

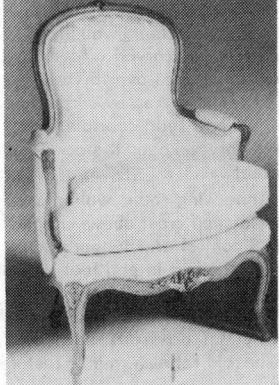

Louis XV "Bergere"

Louis XV "bergeres en cabriolet"
(closed armchairs), beechwood,
shaped molded upholstered backrest, the top rail centered by
flowerheads, padded armrests
raised on voluted supports, the
serpentine-fronted seat raised on
cabriole legs carved at the knees
w/flowerheads, France, mid-
18th c., pr. (ILLUS. of one) 9,900.00
Mission-style (Arts & Crafts move-
ment) armchair, oak, hexagonal
form w/flat crest continuing to
form tops of arms above numerous
narrow, square spindles, short,
square legs w/stepped bases, designed by Frank Lloyd Wright,
probably executed by John W.
Ayers Co., for the Francis W.
Little House, Peoria, Illinois, ca.
1902, 25" w., 23" h. 28,600.00
Mission-style (Arts & Crafts move-
ment) "cube" chair, oak, wide
crestrail over three vertical slats,
drop-arm w/two vertical slats below, spring cushion seat, paper
label for "Life-Time Furniture" line
of Grand Rapids Bookcase and
Chair Company, Grand Rapids,
Michigan, Model No. 688½, ca.
1910, 28 x 30", 32 1/8" h. 880.00
Mission-style (Arts & Crafts move-
ment) dining chairs, oak, wide
center slat w/D-shaped cut-outs
suspended in back rungs, upholstered slip seat, box stretchers,
Gustav Stickley branded mark,
Model No. 308, ca. 1910, 39" h.,
set of 6 (ILLUS. of two) 2,090.00

Stickley Dining Chairs

Mission-style (Arts & Crafts movement) "Morris" armchair, oak, adjustable back w/slightly curved
crestrail above three flat slats
flanked by rectangular stiles, flat
bowed arms above side rails &
skirts w/arched aprons, cane &
web seat, small red decal mark of
Gustav Stickley, No. 336, ca.
1905-06, 37½" h. . . . . .6,000.00 to 8,000.00
Mission-style (Arts & Crafts movement) rocker, armless, oak, flat
crestrail above central grouping of
eight small vertical slats flanked
by stiles, square leather covered
seat, straight flat rungs, one each
front & back, two on each side,
on rockers, remnants of red decal
mark of Gustav Stickley, Model
No. 359, ca. 1907 . . . . 330.00

Stickley Child's Rocker

Mission-style (Arts & Crafts movement) rocker, child's w/arms,
oak, three horizontal slats in
back, flat open arms, original
leather seat, Gustav Stickley red
decal mark & paper label, Model
No. 345, ca. 1904-06, 18" w.,
25½" h. (ILLUS.) 550.00
Queen Anne country-style armchair,

tiger stripe maple, yoked crest above vasiform splat & square tapering & raked backposts, joined to shaped arms on turned supports above block-, vase- and ring-turned legs joined by a bulbous ring-turned front medial stretcher & ending in Spanish feet, New England, mid-18th c., 41¼" h. (old refinish) 4,950.00

Queen Anne country-style transitional armchair, maple, yoked crest above square tapering back posts & a vasiform splat, connected to shaped arms w/vase- and ring-turned arm supports above a replaced rush seat & block- and ring-turned front legs ending in Spanish feet connected to a front medial stretcher, old refinish, New England, 18th c., 41½" h. 2,750.00

Queen Anne country-style side chair, decorated hardwood, tall back w/shaped crest above vase splat flanked by slightly back-curving stiles, rectangular rush seat, vase- and block-turned front legs w/Spanish feet joined by bulbous turned rung, double turned rungs on each side & single plain rung at back, old but not original red & black graining w/gold striping, 18th c. (replaced seat, old repairs) 1,450.00

Queen Anne Side Chair

Queen Anne side chair, mahogany, shaped crestrail above a solid vase-form splat flanked by rounded stiles, balloon seat, cabriole legs ending in pointed pad feet, probably New York, ca. 1760 (ILLUS.) 3,630.00

Queen Anne side chair, maple, yoked crestrail above raking square tapering stiles & vasiform splat, rectangular slip seat on skirt

w/front & side shaping above cabriole front legs ending in pad feet & square tapering chamfered rear legs joined by block-, vase- and ring-turned stretchers, slip seat upholstered in early 20th c. hand-done crewel, New England, ca. 1740.........................3,300.00

Queen Anne side chair, walnut, arched crestrail carved w/a shell flanked by volutes over a vase-shaped splat flanked by serpentine stiles, balloon seat, cabriole legs w/shell-carved knees & stockinged trifid feet 1,870.00

Queen Anne wing chair, walnut & maple, arched crest above shaped wings & conical arm supports, cabriole legs ending in pad feet joined to the rear square raked legs by block- and vase-turned stretchers, probably Massachusetts, ca. 1760, 46¼" h. (old refinish, minor restoration) 46,200.00

Renaissance Style armchair, carved hardwood, tall upholstered back w/arched crest raised above upholstered seat by short turned stiles, shaped & carved open arms w/turned supports go through seat front, straight, turned front legs joined by wide scroll-carved bracket, turned H-stretchers close to floor join front & back legs, stained hardwood frame, ca. 1920's 80.00

Sheraton country-style side chairs, curly maple, flat-topped curved crest above flat curved slat flanked by chamfered stiles, rush seat, bulbous turned front legs w/turned front rung, old worn finish, original seats w/traces of old paint, pr.................... 500.00

Victorian armchair, Aesthetic Movement substyle, carved walnut, leaf-carved galleried crestrail centered by a palmette, the padded arms ending in lionhead terminals on hairy animal paw supports, the flared seat raised on turned cylindrical legs, ca. 1880 .... 467.50

Victorian armchair, Rococo substyle, carved & laminated rosewood, arched & pierce-carved scrolling crest continuing to form sides of shield-shaped tufted back, open padded arms, upholstered seat w/scroll-carved apron continuing into cabriole legs, on casters, attributed to John & Joseph Meeks, New York City, ca. 1860 (ILLUS. top next page) 4,125.00

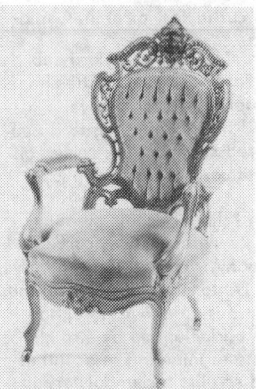

Meeks Rococo Armchair

Victorian "balloon-back" side chair, carved hardwood, arched pierce-carved back w/wildlife & vegetation in tightly carved overall design, needlework round upholstered seat w/conforming seatrails carved w/leafy vines, deeply carved animal-decorated legs joined by an X-form stretcher, Anglo-Burmese school, 19th c., 39½" h. 412.50

Victorian "horn" armchair, arched cow horn crestrail & back above down-turned horn arms, square spring seat on four out-curved horn legs, America, ca. 1880, 36½" h. (unupholstered) 1,100.00

Victorian "horn" side chairs, tufted oval back within a staghorn frame continuing to horn stiles, above a tufted circular seat, raised on in-curved horn legs, Continental, ca. 1890, pr. 1,650.00

Victorian lady's parlor chair, Rococo substyle, pierce-carved laminated rosewood, tall back w/high ornately fruit & flower-carved crest arching above carved scrolls across the top & continuing to form the sides of the back, the scrolls framing pierce-carved grapevines which surround the oval upholstered back, upholstered seat on shaped & carved seatrail & demi-cabriole legs, "Tuthill King" pattern, John Henry Belter, New York, ca. 1850, 38" h. 11,000.00

Victorian parlor armchair, Louis XVI substyle, walnut, arched back crest w/scroll-carved center reserve flanked by raised burl panels w/line-incised decoration, rectangular back w/tufted upholstery, open arms w/padded armrests on curved arm supports,

Victorian Louis XVI Armchair

over-upholstered seat, front seatrail w/line-incised decoration & center carved drop, baluster- and ring-turned front legs on casters, ca. 1875 (ILLUS.) 440.00

Victorian parlor side chairs, Rococo substyle, laminated & inlaid rosewood, tall back w/curved & gently arched crestrail over ornately pierce-carved back w/scrolls centering an oval reserve w/inlaid *trompe l'oeil* design of crossed musical instruments & florals, back stiles carved w/tassels & bell-flowers, round upholstered seat on shaped & carved seatrail, demi-cabriole carved legs w/scroll feet, attributed to Henkels, Philadelphia, ca. 1860, pr. 1,870.00

Belter "Milwaukee" Side Chair

Victorian parlor side chair, Rococo substyle, carved & laminated rosewood, high pierce-carved back crestrail w/flowers, fruit & scrolling leaves continuing to pierce-carved sides framing oblong shaped

upholstered back panel, scrolled
braces at base of back on over-
upholstered seat, carved curved
seatrail continuing to cabriole front
legs w/carved knees on casters,
splayed arched back legs, "Milwaukee" pattern attributed to John
Henry Belter, New York, ca. 1855
(ILLUS.) 5,500.00

Hunzinger "Patent" Armchair

Victorian "Patent" armchair, Renaissance Revival substyle, walnut,
square upholstered back within
a frame of turned stiles, centered
by a female mask, the upholstered
arms supported by female masks,
raised on turned front legs joined
by turned front stretcher, stamped
"Hunzinger - Pat. March 30 - 1869,"
& retailer's label, ca. 1880
(ILLUS.) 3,850.00
Victorian "Patent" rustic side chair,
walnut, rectangular upholstered
back w/ring-turned spindles over
square upholstered seat on ring-
turned legs & stretcher, rear leg
stamped "Pat April 18, 1870 NY
Pat March 30 1869 Hunzinger,"
16" w. seat, 34½" h. 330.00
Victorian "Patent" 'lollipop' rocker,
walnut, rounded back composed of
vertical spindles surmounted by
turned balls & discs, platform base
w/paper label "Hunzinger Patent
Duplex Spring, One drop of Oil on
every joint of spring will prevent
noise," George Hunzinger,
ca. 1885 ....1,980.00
Victorian side chair, Gothic Revival
substyle, walnut, pointed Gothic
arch back w/oval panel upholstered in red plush, spiral-turned
back stiles w/delicate turned finials, red plush upholstered seat,
spiral-turned front legs & front

apron cut in row of arches, mid-
19th c. 450.00
Victorian side chairs, Rococo substyle, rosewood, cartouche-shaped
upholstered & pierce-carved
scrolled back continuing to an upholstered shaped seat, raised on
cabriole carved legs, ca. 1855,
pr. 1,760.00
Victorian "slipper" chair, Renaissance Revival substyle, carved
mahogany, rounded top rail carved
in the center w/a turned acanthus
& bead design above an upholstered back flanked by straight
uprights terminating in acanthus-
carved scrolls, the upholstered
rectangular seat on curved front
w/acanthus, raised on front hairy
paw feet on casters, green & coral cotton paisley upholstery, last
quarter 19th c. 550.00
Wallace Nutting signed Carver side
chair, rush seat, Model 364,
Framingham, Massachusetts, ca.
1920, 47" h. 440.00
Wallace Nutting signed Windsor
"comb-back" armchair, nine-
spindle comb above bowed 14-
spindle back, shaped arms on
turned uprights, shaped seat,
turned splayed legs w/bobbin
stretcher, branded signature &
numbered "415". 850.00
Wallace Nutting signed Windsor "fan-
back" armchair, dark finished
wood, shaped crestrail w/scroll-
carved ears above nine spindles
above medial brace continuing to
form shaped arms w/scrolled hand
rests above 13 bobbin-turned short
spindles in back- & ring- and
bobbin-turned arm supports at
front, shaped seat on splayed
vase- and ring-turned legs joined
by H-stretchers, original dark
finish, original paper label under
seat 1,050.00

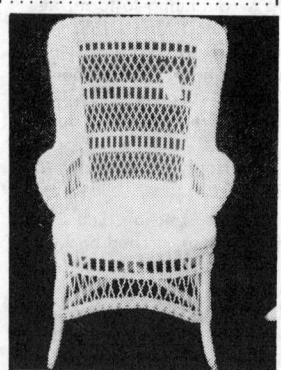

Wicker Armchair

Wicker armchair, flat wide crestrail w/rounded corners continuing to wide curved arms, back w/loosely woven diamond designs & horizontal bands, round seat w/wide loosely woven apron, round slightly flaring front legs, painted white, ca. 1900-10 (ILLUS.)........................ 245.00

Wicker armchair, high flat-topped back w/rectangular piercings w/shallow wings continues to wide, flat arms above skirt w/rectangular piercings, Gustav Stickley, Model No. 88, ca. 1913, 39½" h........................ 800.00

Wicker armchair, tall back w/square cut-outs centered by flat arms continuing over box base w/cut-outs, unsigned Gustav Stickley, ca. 1910, 32" w., 42¾" h................3,850.00

Wicker Armchair & Ottoman

Wicker armchair & ottoman, chair w/rounded back crestrail continuing to form the arms w/woven sides & apron, circular feet, upholstered pad seat; the ottoman decorated en suite, Heywood Brothers & Wakefield, Chicago, Illinois, early 20th c., 2 pcs. (ILLUS.)........................ 825.00

William & Mary armchair, maple, pierced crestrail carved w/C-scrolls & leafage flanked by column-turned stiles w/urn & ball finials centering a padded back, molded arms ending in scrolling grips above ball- and baluster-turned supports, padded seat, baluster-turned front legs centering a pierced frontal stretcher carved w/C-scrolls & leafage, now on casters, Boston or New York, 1710-20, 50" h. (feet slightly reduced)......................7,150.00

William & Mary "bannister back" armchair, shaped crestrail above five split bannister slats flanked

by baluster- and ring-turned stiles w/acorn-shaped finials above shaped arm rests over similarly turned arm supports over a trapezoidal rush seat on ring-turned legs joined by a double box stretcher, 18th c., 44½" h. 440.00

William & Mary corner chair, turned maple, raised shaped crest continuing to flat scrolled arms, supported by three turned, swelled stiles terminating in block- and vase-turned legs joined by bulbous-turned stretchers in front, possibly Connecticut, 18th c., 29½" h. (old refinish) 1,045.00

William & Mary side chair, painted maple, molded crest w/cusped corners above upholstered panel back flanked by molded curving stiles over upholstered seat, baluster-turned legs w/ball feet centering tripartite turned front stretcher (later black paint), Boston area, Massachusetts, 1700-20.........2,640.00

Windsor armchair, painted wood, rectangular crestrail above five-spindle splats flanked by bamboo-turned stiles, the turned arms above similar posts, the plank seat raised on bamboo-turned legs joined by stretchers, painted overall in dark green, New England, early 19th c. 715.00

Windsor "birdcage" side chairs, bamboo-turned, birdcage crest over seven-spindle back & turned uprights, shaped seat, bamboo-turned legs w/stretchers, old black paint, set of 4 (one w/broken spindle)......................1,280.00

Windsor "bow-back" continuous armchair, ash & maple, bowed crestrail above seven-spindle back continuing to form arms, shaped saddle seat, bamboo-turned legs joined by stretchers, old varnished red paint, New England, ca. 1810........................1,650.00

Windsor "comb-back" armchair, turned & painted wood, shaped crest w/volute-carved terminals above nine tapered spindles, elliptical seat once fitted w/chamber pot, baluster- and ring-turned splayed legs joined by H-stretchers, feet reduced, some repainting, Pennsylvania, ca. 1775 (ILLUS. top next page) 3,025.00

Windsor "fan-back" armchair, narrow shaped crest above nine tall, straight spindles joining rounded back cross-band continuing to form shaped flat arms on ball- and ring-

turned arm supports, fifteen short,
straight spindles around back joining wide shaped seat, splayed vase-
and ring-turned legs joined by ball-
and ring-turned H-stretcher, black
repaint w/red showing beneath,
Pennsylvania, 18th c. 3,100.00

Windsor "Comb-Back" Armchair

Windsor "sack-back" armchair,
arched crest centering seven
tapering spindles above shaped
armrests w/baluster- and ring-
turned supports, shaped seat,
baluster- and ring-turned legs
joined by a similarly turned
stretcher, underside of seat
stamped "J. Edling," Philadelphia,
ca. 1797 . . . . 770.00
Windsor "step-down" side chairs,
painted wood, shaped crestrail
above seven turned spindles &
raked back posts, shaped plank
seat, bamboo-turned splayed legs
w/stretchers, old Spanish brown
paint, New England, ca. 1810, set
of 9 (some paint wear). 3,410.00
Windsor "thumb-back" rocker
w/arms, shaped crest w/poly-
chrome fruit & floral devices
above five bamboo-turned spindles, turned arms, plank seat,
bamboo-turned legs joined by
stretchers & rockers, the whole
painted yellow w/black pinstrip-
ing, New England, ca. 1820 . . . . . . 880.00

CHESTS & CHESTS OF DRAWERS

Apothecary chest, painted pine,
rectangular case of thirty square
drawers painted in old blue-green
w/burnt sienna grained drawer
fronts & brass pulls, some drawers
still have printed labels such as
"GUM OPIUM," probably once
built-in, New England, ca. 1830,
44½" w., 41½" h. (ILLUS.) 1,320.00

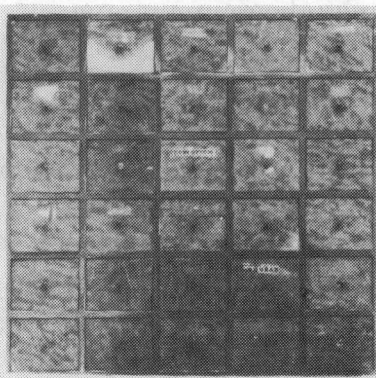

Painted Apothecary Chest

Apothecary chest, poplar, wire nail
construction, molded cornice
above case w/chamfered corners
& molded base, fitted w/twenty
overlapping drawers, original
brass ring pulls, old varnished fin-
ish, 31" w., 34½" h. 600.00
Biedermeier tall chest of drawers,
mahogany, rectangular tablet top
above six flame-veneered drawers,
on slightly shaped bracket feet,
Continental, ca. 1830, 34" w.,
4' 4¼" h. 1,430.00

Decorated Chippendale Blanket Chest

Blanket chest, Chippendale country-
style, painted & decorated, molded
rectangular top w/batten ends lifting above a compartment w/a till
over small drawers, the dovetailed
case w/an applied molding over a
frieze of two drawers above a
base molding, on straight bracket
feet, the surface w/blue paint
w/circular sgraffito patterns, the
moldings painted red, the front
w/three painted panels, each w/an
eagle & foliate decoration & initials
& dates "ELBKS," "1808," "1790,"
Pennsylvania, possibly Hanover
area, York County, ca. 1808,
22¾ x 52", 27 5/8" h. (ILLUS.) . . .8,800.00
Blanket chest, painted & decorated
pine, rectangular top w/molded
rim opening to interior w/till,
dovetailed case on short turned

feet, old yellow & brown "vinegar" painting w/black & green
trim, traces of earlier red show
on top edge, original wrought-iron
strap hinges & bear-trap lock
w/key, Pennsylvania, 50½" w.,
26" h. 475.00
Blanket chest, painted & decorated
pine, rectangular top w/molded
edge opening to a till, the front
painted w/eagle & shield, the
sides painted w/hex signs, on
bracket feet, probably Lehigh
County, Pennsylvania, ca. 1810,
22¾ x 51½", 27½" h. 11,000.00
Blanket chest, tiger maple, six-board
construction, rectangular top
w/molded edge lifting to deep
well w/till, bootjack sides, heavy
base molding & straight front
skirt, New England, early 19th c.,
16½ x 47", 22½" h. 4,510.00

William & Mary Blanket Chest

Blanket chest, William & Mary,
painted pine, rectangular top
w/cleated hinges opening to well
above case w/paneling on front
representing three false small
drawers above one long false
drawer, these above two long
drawers at bottom, black-painted
short turned front legs w/bun feet
& scroll-cut rear bracket feet, bat's
wing brasses, painted red, New
England, early 18th c., 37" w.,
41" h. (ILLUS.) 2,420.00
Chippendale "bow-front" chest of
drawers, carved mahogany,
molded rectangular top above a
case w/four graduated long
drawers within cockbeaded surrounds, molded base on ogee
bracket feet, New England, ca.
1780, 41½" l., 31½" h. 4,070.00
Chippendale chest of drawers, birch,
molded rectangular top above two
short thumb-molded drawers over

three long thumb-molded drawers, bracket feet, 38" w.,
42½" h. 990.00
Chippendale chest of drawers, carved
curly maple, rectangular molded
top above four graduated long
drawers, the upper drawer faced
to simulate two short drawers,
the molded base w/shaped pendant below, on bracket feet, New
England, ca. 1785, 39" w., 39¾" h.
(some restoration to top) 4,675.00

Chippendale Chest of Drawers

Chippendale chest of drawers,
mahogany, rectangular top
w/thumb-molded edge above four
graduated cockbeaded drawers,
fluted quarter-columns flanking
ogee bracket feet, Pennsylvania,
ca. 1770, feet replaced, 39½" w.,
35¼" h. (ILLUS.) 2,640.00
Chippendale chest-on-chest, birch,
two-part construction: the upper
section w/molded cornice above
five graduated long drawers, the
first w/tripartite sham front centering a fan carving; lower section
w/four long drawers over a molded base, ogee bracket feet, late
18th c., 40" w., 76½" h. 3,520.00
Chippendale chest-on-chest, mahog-
any, two-part construction: top section w/flat top w/molded cornice
above two short & four long graduated cockbeaded drawers flanked
by fluted quarter-columns; the
lower section w/three graduated
cockbeaded long drawers flanked
by fluted quarter-columns, ogee
bracket feet, Pennsylvania, ca.
1780, 45¾" w., 6' 5½" h. (restor-
ations to cornice) 8,800.00
Chippendale chest-on-frame, walnut,
three-part construction: removable
cornice w/scroll-carved tympanum;
the middle section w/five short
& four long graduated molded
drawers; the lower section
w/shaped skirt continuing to cab-

riole legs ending in claw-and-ball feet, Pennsylvania, ca. 1770, 41½" w., 73½" h. (restoration to feet) 7,435.00

Chippendale country-style chest of drawers, painted pine, rectangular top above four graduated drawers w/original oval brasses stamped "H.J.," reeded, chamfered corners w/lamb's tongues, shaped apron w/bracket feet, worn yellow graining over original red, 42½" w., 36¾" h. (small repairs & minor replacements) 1,700.00

Chippendale tall chest of drawers, curly maple, rectangular top w/molded cornice above six graduated long drawers, bracket feet, Massachusetts, ca. 1780, 40" w., 56¼" h. 9,900.00

Chippendale Tall Chest of Drawers

Chippendale tall chest of drawers, maple, flat molded cornice above case w/six graduated, thumb-molded drawers on cut-out bracket feet, old worn red paint, earthenware pulls are old replacements, New Hampshire, ca. 1780, minor damage & repairs, 38 1/8" w., 53" h. (ILLUS.) 4,400.00

Empire, American, chest of drawers, cherry & mahogany veneer, rectangular top supporting a two-tiered set of four small handkerchief drawers topped by arched backboard w/scrolled ears, top above deep overhanging top drawer above three long graduated drawers flanked by ornately turned half-round columns, flat apron above tall "hour-glass" shaped turned feet, brass rosette w/round bail pulls on each drawer, mahogany veneering on each

drawer front, Stockton, Massachusetts, early 19th c., 44½" w., 57¾" h. (veneer repair, old refinishing) 1,400.00

Empire, American, chest of drawers, mahogany & mahogany veneer, rectangular top w/pair recessed short drawers & scrolled backboard w/reeded plinths above case w/two cockbeaded short drawers & three long drawers flanked by swelled ring-turned posts continuing to legs, original embossed brass ring drawer pulls, old refinish, Levi Leland, Grafton, Massachusetts, ca. 1830, 43" w., 50" h. 1,650.00

Empire, American, country-style chest of drawers, painted & decorated poplar, rectangular top above overhanging arrangement of two narrow drawers over one deep drawer, all above three graduated drawers flanked by half-round spindle drops at sides of top & base, dramatically grain-painted in two-tone brown to resemble crotch-grain veneer, wooden knobs, short, straight legs, 43" w., 48" h.............. 650.00

Empire, American, country-style chest of drawers, painted & decorated, rectangular top w/pair recessed shallow drawers above case w/deep upper drawer above three slightly recessed long drawers flanked by bold S-scroll stiles w/C-scroll feet, painted w/yellow comb-grained decoration in imitation of curly maple w/burl trim & w/painted varying florals on each drawer front, New York, ca. 1840, all original 3,850.00

Federal "bow-front" chest of drawers, mahogany, rectangular top w/bowed & banded edge above a conforming case w/four long drawers w/cockbeading, banded straight skirt, modified French feet, New England, 1790-1810, 40" w., 35" h. 2,200.00

Federal chest of drawers, curly maple, rectangular top w/outset corners above a case w/four cockbeaded long drawers flanked by outset reeded corners, the deeply valanced apron continuing to turned tapering legs, New York State, ca. 1810, 43" w., 40¾" h. 6,600.00

Federal chest of drawers, figured birch & mahogany, rectangular splashboard flanked by carved pil-

Federal Chest of Drawers

asters above a D-shaped top w/molded edge & outset rounded corners over a conforming case w/four graduated long drawers flanked by spiral-turned columns, baluster- and ring-turned feet, New England, 1810-20, 21½ x 43", 46½" h. (ILLUS.) 2,090.00

Federal sugar chest on stand, inlaid mahogany, rectangular top w/molded edges above conforming case fitted on slightly wider stand w/single long drawer on tapering legs w/fret spandrels, top, front & sides inlaid w/star medallions within line borders, inlaid band around drawer, North Carolina, ca. 1790, 17 x 32", 36½" h. 11,500.00

Federal sugar chest, walnut veneer, rectangular w/hinged banded overhanging top opening to interior w/two compartments over a single drawer on a straight skirt joining four ring-turned tapering legs, wooden pull, refinished, Southern United States, ca. 1820, 15 x 28½", 30¾" h. 880.00

Federal tall chest of drawers, cherry, rectangular top w/coved cornice above a frieze of three short drawers over five long drawers, flanked by chamfered corners, on French feet, Pennsylvania, 1790-1810, 22¾ x 45¾", 5' 4½" h. 4,180.00

Hat chest, hardwood, the upper section fitted w/double doors & removable stile opening to reveal a single shelf all above a lower section of massive double doors fitted w/removable stile & opening to double drawers & lower removable panel for storage, the lower section carved in low relief w/a foliate splat, China, 20 x 49", 5' 1" h. (ILLUS.) 6,600.00

Chinese Hat Chest

Hepplewhite tall chest of drawers, curly walnut, rectangular top w/removable cove-molded cornice above three short drawers over five graduated drawers, each w/oval brass handles & brass keyhole escutcheons, quarter-round pilasters at front corners of case, scalloped apron w/band of curly maple veneer, tall French feet, Pennsylvania, late 18th c., 39¾" w., 5' 7¾" h. (refinished, replaced brasses) 6,500.00

Louis XV Semainier

Louis XV "semainier" (seven-drawer chest), tulipwood, serpentine molded *breche d'alep* marble top above an ogee frieze fitted w/a drawer above six further drawers, on short cabriole legs w/ormolu *sabots*, France, mid-18th c., 14" w., 27½" h. (ILLUS.) 4,180.00

Mission-style (Arts & Crafts movement) chest of drawers w/mirror, oak, rectangular arch-topped frame holds mirror & swivels on two tapering vertical arms, on case w/rectangular top over two short drawers over two long graduated drawers, all w/faceted wood knobs, V-board recessed side panels & exposed tenons, reverse-V apron, short square legs w/through-tenons, red decal mark of Gustav Stickley, Model No. 625, ca. 1902-04, 22 x 41¼", 4' 7¾" h. 5,775.00

Mission-style (Arts & Crafts movement) tall chest of drawers, oak, rectangular top w/low backrail overhanging case w/six small drawers over three graduated long drawers, all w/wooden mushroom knobs, gently bowed sides, curving apron, short square legs, designed by Harvey Ellis, branded signature of Gustav Stickley, Model No. 913, ca. 1912, 20 x 36", 4' 3 1/8" h. . .16,500.00

Mule chest (box chest w/one or more drawers below storage compartment), Federal, painted pine, rectangular lift-top above case w/two cockbeaded false drawers above two working drawers, cutout base, original brown graining on mustard ground, New England, ca. 1800, 19 x 39¼", 40" h. 1,210.00

Pilgrim Century "joined" lift-top & two-drawer chest, carved oak & joined pine, rectangular hinged top opening to well, the front of the case w/three inset panels carved w/stylized scrolled motifs, the center panel w/carved initials "ISM," two long drawers w/small wooden knobs below, the stiles forming feet, the ends w/four panels, Hadley-Hatfield area, Massachusetts, ca. 1710, 20¼ x 46", 41½" h. (one cleat on top restored) 33,000.00

Queen Anne chest-on-chest, maple, two-part construction: upper section w/cove-molded cornice above a long drawer w/three sham short drawer fronts, the center one fan-carved, over four graduated thumb-molded long drawers; lower section w/three sham short drawer fronts, the center one fan-carved, above a scrolled skirt, short cabriole legs w/pad feet, 41¼" w., 6' 4" h. 4,620.00

Queen Anne chest-on-frame, walnut, two-part construction: upper section w/rectangular top w/deep cove-molded cornice over a bolection drawer over three gradu-

ated thumb-molded long drawers; the lower section w/mid-molding above long shallow center drawer flanked by deep drawers all above a shaped & scalloped apron, short cabriole legs w/pad feet, brass butterfly & bail pulls & handles on sides, Pennsylvania or Valley of Virginia, 1740-60, 20 x 38½", 52" h. (one foot pieced, minor repairs to drawer lips, top board loose) 11,000.00

Queen Anne spice chest, walnut, rectangular top w/molded cornice above a pair of hinged doors w/arched panels opening to interior fitted w/small drawers, flat apron, bracket feet, probably Chester County, Pennsylvania, 1750-70, 10 x 18", 18½" h. (lower interior drawer replaced) 19,800.00

Queen Anne tall chest of drawers, tiger maple, rectangular top w/molded edge above two short drawers over four graduated long drawers, each thumb-molded, above a molded base w/carved pendant, short cabriole legs w/pad feet, 35½" w., 43½" h. 3,520.00

Spanish Colonial Chest on Stand

Spanish Colonial chest on stand, painted wood, rectangular lift-top lid w/heavy applied molded edge over a dovetailed box over base, compartmentalized lid, keyholes at front & one side, stand w/heavy turned legs w/turned spindles, old blue over chocolate brown paint, heavy wear, Mexico or New Mexico, 11¾ x 28", 38" h. (ILLUS.) 1,980.00

Tansu chest of drawers, kiri wood, rectangular flat top above row of five drawers fitted w/copper handles & metal lock-plates, copper corner brackets & iron side han-

dles, decorated w/red lacquer,
Japan, 35½" w., 45" h. 495.00
Tool chest, cabinetmaker's, painted
pine, deep rectangular lid edged
in reeded blocks has extra lift top
opening to shallow compartment,
interior fitted w/lift-out dovetailed compartment w/five dovetailed drawers w/bird's-eye maple
fronts & brass pulls & latches,
paneled sides over pair of narrow drawers over single long, narrow drawer across bottom, short
turned legs, rounded wood handles
at ends, worn black over red
w/blue panels paint, 41¼" w.,
27¾" h. (minor edge damage, one
foot chipped) 2,200.00

Turn-of-the-Century Oak Chest

Turn-of-the-Century chest w/mirror,
oak, long narrow oval mirror supported by slender scroll arms
flanked by short scrolls above
bow-front rectangular top over
conforming case w/two short
drawers over single long drawer,
simple wooden drawer knobs,
slightly shaped front legs, on
casters, ca. 1900 (ILLUS.) 245.00
Victorian chest of drawers, country-
style, carved & painted wood,
shaped & carved supports &
carved arched mirror above a
joined chest of three drawers on
stile feet w/pierced front brackets,
mirror supports w/dark red &
black paint, the mirror frame &
drawer fronts bordered by carved
yellow, white, black & red bands,
drawers predominantly yellow
w/white, black-centered daisies
flanked by carved green leaves
& conforming carved & painted
rosettes on which are mounted
Victorian teardrop pulls; recessed
panel ends w/carved green urns &

Victorian Country-Style Chest

three stem branch w/white daisies,
Ohio, ca. 1870 (ILLUS.) 7,150.00

Renaissance Revival Chest of Drawers

Victorian chest of drawers, Renaissance Revival substyle, walnut &
bird's-eye maple, tall back
w/arched pediment w/scroll-
carved crest above tall rectangular mirror w/arched top flanked
by sides w/walnut bandings
around bird's-eye maple veneering & w/candle shelves, white
marble-topped base w/two small
hanky drawers on top above
three long graduated drawers
w/turned walnut pulls & raised
center oblong panels, the whole
case veneered in bird's-eye maple
outlined by walnut bands, ca.
1875 (ILLUS.) 550.00
Victorian chest of drawers, Renais-
sance Revival substyle, walnut &
burl walnut, tall back w/arched
crest above row of bull's-eye
rosettes above tall rectangular

Victorian Drop Well Chest of Drawers

mirror flanked by sides w/raised
burl panels & candleshelves, drop-
well base w/drop-well flanked by
pairs of marble-topped small
drawers, two long drawers across
base w/raised burl panels & central shield-shaped burl panels
w/bull's-eye rosettes, ca. 1870,
replacement pulls (ILLUS.) 550.00

Victorian Rococo Chest of Drawers

Victorian chest of drawers, Rococo
  substyle, carved walnut, wide
  arched pierce-carved crest w/or-
  nate scrolls centering large oval
  cartouche finial w/carved lady's
  head, arch-topped long rectangular
  mirror flanked by additional pierce-
  carved panels over serpentine
  framework resting on conforming
  white marble top over conforming
  case w/three long serpentine
  drawers w/scroll-carved pulls &
  scroll-carved keyhole escutcheons
  flanked by reeded columns flanked
  by rounded side cabinet doors
  w/panels centered by relief-carved

scroll clusters, attributed to
  Mitchell & Rammelsberg, ca.
  1850-60 (ILLUS.) 8,800.00
Victorian tall chest of drawers,
  Renaissance Revival substyle,
  carved & burl walnut, rectangular
  top w/molded edge overhangs two
  shallow drawers over carved narrow band above two deep drawers
  beside tall narrow paneled cupboard locking door w/high-relief
  floral bouquet carving; lower
  section w/three long drawers
  w/banded edging on scallop-
  carved apron on flat round feet,
  paneled sides, wide oval brass
  plates w/square bails on each
  drawer, ca. 1870, 43" w.,
  60" h. 1,320.00

William & Mary Chest of Drawers

William & Mary chest of drawers,
  painted maple, rectangular top
  above two short & three long
  drawers, turned ball feet, painted
  black, New England, ca. 1725, restoration to feet, 37½" w., 36½" h.
  (ILLUS.) 10,175.00
William & Mary chest of drawers,
  walnut, rectangular top w/molded
  edge above case w/two short &
  three graduated long drawers within molded surrounds, molded base,
  ball feet, Philadelphia, ca. 1720,
  40¼" l., 38" h. (restoration to
  feet) 3,300.00
William & Mary chest-on-frame, wal-
  nut, two-part construction: upper
  section w/molded cornice above
  arrangement of two short & three
  graduated long drawers; frame
  w/mid-molding above long drawer
  & arched apron supported on six
  baluster- and trumpet-turned
  tapering legs joined by shaped
  stretcher, ball feet, inscribed in
  ink "Robert Paschall Philad, PA,"
  ca. 1715, 42" w., 61" h. (repairs
  to four legs, two legs & stretchers
  restored) .15,400.00

CRADLES

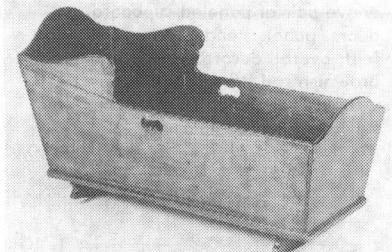

Mahogany Cradle on Rockers

Country-style low cradle on rockers, cherry, dovetail construction, canted & scalloped sides pierced w/hand-holds, old dark finish, 39" l. 125.00

Country-style cradle on rockers, mahogany, shaped head- and footboards, canted & shaped sides pierced w/hand-holds, late 18th c., 42½" l. (ILLUS.) 1,210.00

Country-style low cradle on rockers, painted cherry, dovetail construction, arched head- and footboards w/cut-out heart-shaped handholds, cut-out heart in sides, old red paint, 41½" l. (age cracks, old nailed repair) 400.00

Country-style low cradle on rockers, walnut, square posts w/turned ends, mortise & tenon construction, 18th c., 39" l. 247.50

Hooded cradle on rockers, painted finish, arched hood above a rectangular case w/canted sides, molded base, painted white, early 19th c., 18½ x 39½", 22½" h..... 495.00

Suspended-type cradle, Classical, mahogany, arched & paneled head- and footboards joined by a baluster railing, one side hinged, supported between two columnar standards each on a scrolled trestle base joined by a turned stretcher, 1830-45, 49" w., 37" h. 990.00

Suspended-type cradle, Victorian, walnut, oval w/shaped ends & shaped slat suspended on a trestle base w/a baluster- and ring-turned stretcher & drapery rod carved in the form of a stork's head, 19th c., 46½" w., 4' 5½" h. 385.00

CUPBOARDS

Bucket cupboard, thumb-molded cornice above four double-hinged cupboard doors opening to shelves, over three drawers above shelves, painted yellow &

green, New York, second quarter 19th c. 3,850.00

Chimney cupboard, thick rectangular top above a large cupboard door opening to three shelves, the door w/simple swivel wood block, painted overall in streaked orange paint, first half 19th c., 20" w., 5' 4" h. 2,090.00

Stickley China Closet

China closet, outset rectangular top above pair of glazed doors, each w/twelve small leaded panes above a single glass panel, opening to adjustable shelves, arched toe board, signed "The Work of L. & J.G. Stickley," ca. 1912, 44" w., 16" deep, 58" h. (ILLUS.) 4,290.00

Corner cupboard, Chippendale, carved pine, one-piece construction, molded projecting cornice above a carved frieze & pair of arched glazed doors opening to a red-painted shelved interior, a pair of cupboard doors below opening to shelf & flanked by fluted pilasters, Pennsylvania, ca. 1795, 60" w., 9' h. (some repairs & restoration) 9,900.00

Corner cupboard, Federal, cherry, two-part construction: upper section w/coved cornice above two arched glazed doors opening to three fitted shelves; lower section w/one short drawer flanked by two sham drawers above two paneled cupboard doors opening to a single shelf, flared French feet, New England, 1800-20, 50" w., 84½" h. 8,800.00

Corner cupboard, Federal, inlaid cherry, two-part construction: upper section w/molded swan's-neck cresting above scrollboard inlaid w/stylized eagle & stars above a pair of geometrically glazed & mullioned arched cupboard doors opening to an interior

w/scalloped shelves; the lower section w/a long drawer, paneled to
resemble three drawers, above
two paneled cupboard doors & a
shaped apron w/scroll-cut bracket
feet, probably Pennsylvania, ca.
1800, 48" w., 8' 3" h. 13,200.00

Hanging corner cupboard, pine,
molded cornice above a paneled
cupboard door w/molded edges &
rat-tail hinges opening to a compartment w/a shelf over scalloped
arched compartment w/a projecting molded edge, flanked by
bolection molded sides, 19th c.,
40" w., 49" h. (arch reshaped,
restorations to cornice). 2,090.00

Chippendale Hanging Cupboard

Hanging cupboard, Chippendale,
poplar, coved cornice above a
paneled cupboard door w/incised
edge opening to two shelves,
flanked by chamfered corners
above a thumb-molded short
drawer over a molded base
(molding restored), Pennsylvania,
mid to late 18th c., 27" w.,
36½" h. (ILLUS.) 1,045.00

Hanging cupboard, cherry, narrow
rectangular top above a paneled
door opening to three shelves,
w/later peg handle & swivel lock,
painted red, Pennsylvania,
18th c., 23½" w., 31¼" h. 440.00

Jelly cupboard, painted finish, rectangular top w/low three-quarter
scalloped gallery over two short
drawers above two cupboard doors
opening to shelves, the case continuing to form arched feet, red
painted finish (some flaking),
second quarter 19th c., 50" w.,
51" h. (ILLUS. top next column) . .1,430.00

Jelly cupboard, painted & decorated
poplar, rectangular top on slightly
shaped cornice stepped-in from
edge of case above pair of short

drawers w/turned wooden knobs
above pair of paneled cupboard
doors, paneled ends, turned ball
feet, overall decorated w/bright
brownish red flame graining
w/bold graining on doors, Pennsylvania, 19th c., 43½" w.,
49" h. 2,100.00

Painted Jelly Cupboard

Linen press, Chippendale, cherry,
two-part construction: upper section w/elaborate dentil-carved
projecting cornice above a pair of
hinged arch-topped panel doors
opening to shelves; lower section
w/pair of hinged arch-topped
panel doors opening to shelf, ogee
bracket feet, New York or New
Jersey, ca. 1790, 52½" w.,
6' 5½" h. (lower section of feet
restored) .12,100.00

Pewter cupboard, pine, one-piece
construction, rectangular top above
two open shelves framed by beaded
edged stiles, slightly stepped-out
base w/wide front boards flanking
plain one-board door w/wrought-
iron hook, one-board ends, simple
arched apron w/simple cut-out
feet, worn finish, New York State,
42¼" w., 78" h. (some
renailing) .1,400.00

Pie safe, miniature, hanging-type,
painted & decorated pine & poplar,
rectangular top w/narrow molded
cornice above single door w/four
punched tin panels each w/design
of half-round concentric circles
around edges, door flanked by
wide side boards, decorated w/old
brown combed graining on yellow
ground, late 19th c. wire nail construction, 21½" w., 19" h. (door
latch removed & replaced w/por-
celain knob) 1,250.00

Pie safe, country-style, painted poplar, rectangular top above case

w/a pair of tall cabinet doors w/three punched tin Maltese cross in cartouche shield design panels in each, three conforming panels in each end, iron thumblatch w/brass button at top of one door, tall tapering square legs, old worn blue over earlier painted colors, 19th c., 42" w., 49½" h.........1,100.00

Pie safe, Victorian country-style, painted pine, molded flat cornice above two paneled doors & matching sides, each door mounted w/three rectangular pierced grey-painted tin panels within red-painted wood framework, opening to shelves, raised on splayed feet, Illinois, ca. 1870, 4' ½" w., 6' 10" h. 990.00

Rosemaled Cupboard

Rosemaled cupboard, arched cornice over paneled doors enclosing one shelf on a base w/rectangular chamfered top & conforming sides w/one door enclosing a shelf, painted overall w/floral panels & moldings, inscribed "1811" at top, Sweden, early 19th c., 76" h. (ILLUS.) 2,200.00

Step-back wall cupboard, American Empire, painted poplar, two-part construction: upper part w/molded projecting cornice above pair 6-pane glazed cupboard doors over open pie shelf; lower section w/two short ogee drawers above pair of recessed paneled cupboard doors, shaped skirt, cut-out feet, grain-painted in red-brown to simulate mahogany, Pennsylvania, ca. 1825, 55" w., 87" h.............6,600.00

Step-back wall cupboard, Chippen-

dale, pine, two-part construction: upper section w/projecting molded cornice above two 9-pane glazed cupboard doors opening to a blue-painted interior w/two shelves flanked by fluted pilasters over a sliding bread tray; lower section w/rectangular top above three short drawers flanked by fluted pilasters over two paneled cupboard doors opening to a shelf flanked by pilasters, bracket feet, Pennsylvania, 18th c., 73½" w., 87" h. (minor repairs) 13,200.00

Step-back wall cupboard, painted poplar, two-part construction: upper section w/flat top above molded cornice over pair paneled cupboard doors opening to shelves above open pie shelf; lower section w/pair of drawers w/white porcelain knobs over pair paneled cupboard doors w/cast-iron latches w/white porcelain knobs, simple bracket feet, antique blue repaint, 49" w., 83" h. (one knob replaced) 1,300.00

Step-back wall cupboard, pine, two-part construction: upper section w/rectangular top w/ogee-molded cornice above a pair of long 6-pane glazed cupboard doors opening to two shelves; lower section outset from upper section & composed of two drawers w/turned wooden knobs above a pair of raised-panel cupboard doors, flat apron w/shaped bracket feet, old nut brown finish, 55" w., 85" h. (mullions replaced in top doors, some wear & edge damage).....................2,700.00

Step-back wall cupboard, sponge-decorated, two-part construction: upper section w/projecting molded cornice above two 6-pane glazed green-painted cupboard doors opening to two shelves over an arched opening; lower section w/rectangular top above three short drawers w/pressed glass knobs over two paneled cupboard doors opening to a single shelf, baluster- and ring-turned feet, overall natural wood-grained sponged finish, Berks County, Pennsylvania, early 19th c., 56" w., 89" h. 12,650.00

Wall cupboard, painted, one-piece construction, arched cornice above a large grilled & paneled door opening to six shelves, raised on shoe feet, painted overall in dark brown (minor wear to paint), cen-

Painted Wall Cupboard

tral Wisconsin, ca. 1840, 4' 5" w.,
6' 10" h. (ILLUS.) 1,650.00
Wall cupboard, painted pine, one-
piece construction, molded cornice
above single 6-pane glazed cupboard door opening to shelves
above paneled cupboard door,
framed by moldings, bracket feet,
blue-green painted interior, exterior w/brown paint over original
green, New England, ca. 1810,
13½ x 30½", 71" h. (minor repairs
to front feet) 5,060.00
Wall cupboard, country-style, cherry
& bird's-eye maple, one-piece construction, rectangular top w/pro-
jecting cornice molding above an
applied carved frieze over pair
double-paneled cupboard doors
w/applied matchstick design over
two bird's-eye maple drawers
w/two cupboard doors below,
paneled sides, turned wooden
knobs, possibly New Jersey,
19th c., 42" w., 82¾" h. (old
refinish, replaced cornice molding,
missing feet) 1,320.00
Wall cupboard, Federal, turned &
red-painted pine, two-part construction: upper section w/swan's
neck crest centering a turned
finial above a pair of 6-pane
glazed cupboard doors opening to
a white painted interior w/two
scalloped shelves, flanked by
reeded pilasters; lower section
w/two drawers above two paneled
cupboard doors, turned front legs,
Hackensack, New Jersey, early
19th c., 52¼" w., 7' 9½" h. 9,900.00

DESKS

Art Nouveau lady's fall-front desk,
carved walnut & bird's-eye maple,
rectangular top above a fall-front

door opening to an interior fitted
w/compartments & three drawers,
between sides carved at front
w/scrolling flowering vine continuing to a lower shelf & raised on
a trestle support, carved w/scrolls,
ca. 1900, Louis Majorelle, France,
24½" w., 43 5/8" h. 3,850.00

Arts & Crafts Desk & Chair

Arts & Crafts slant-front desk, inlaid
mahogany, rectangular top w/pro-
jecting ends over slant front
w/inlaid featherhead design over
single drawer centered by two
narrow vertical cabinet doors
w/feather inlay, raised on spindled
sides w/shoe feet & lower shelf,
signed w/paper label reading
"Shop of the Crafters Cincinnati,"
Model No. 285, w/matching side
chair w/bowed sides centering vertical inlaid slat & arched stretchers,
Model No. 285½, ca. 1910, desk
17¼ x 38½", 48½" h., 2 pcs.
(ILLUS.) 8,190.00
Classical (American Empire) butler's
desk, mahogany, rectangular top
above a hinged drawer w/fitted
interior comprising five bird's-eye
maple valanced pigeonholes over
an open slot flanked by six drawers over inset cupboard doors
opening to a shelved interior
flanked by outset Ionic colonettes,
carved hairy paw feet, Mid-
Atlantic States, 1820-40,
24½ x 45½", 41½" h. 528.00
Federal bureau desk, mahogany &
satinwood veneer, rectangular top
above a frieze of two drawers over
a deep bureau drawer opening to
form a writing surface & revealing
a fitted interior w/satinwood
veneered small drawers & valanced
pigeonholes, centered above three
graduated drawers, the case
flanked by reeded pilasters continuing to reeded turned tapering legs

w/brass ball feet, New York,
1800-20, 48½" w., 51" h. 2,640.00

Federal Lady's Writing Desk

Federal lady's writing desk, inlaid &
veneered mahogany, rectangular
top over a pair of veneered cockbeaded doors edged in crossbanded veneer & flanked by panels
of satinwood veneer & stringing
opening to an interior of small
drawers & valanced compartments
over a hinged leather-lined writing
surface above a case of three
cockbeaded graduated drawers
flanked by ring-turned posts
terminating in tapering feet,
facade surfaces outlined in mahogany & satinwood veneer & stringing, pull-out drawer slides, signed
"E. Smith, Boston, 183," replaced
brass pulls, minor old repairs,
ca. 1830, 21 x 42", 51¼" h.
(ILLUS.) 2,200.00
Federal partner's desk, inlaid mahog-
any, rectangular top above two
fitted sides, the first w/a short
central drawer over a kneehole
flanked by two rows of three
graduated drawers w/stringing,
the other side w/a short central
drawer over a kneehole flanked
by two paneled cupboard doors
w/stringing, square tapering legs
w/stringing, brass cuffs w/casters,
Middle Atlantic States, 1790-1810,
34½ x 50¼", 29" h. (feet
reduced) .10,450.00
Federal "tambour" desk, inlaid
mahogany, rectangular overhanging top bordered w/veneer &
stringing above tambour shutters
enclosing an interior fitted
w/drawers & compartments above
a projecting base w/hinged, baize-
lined writing surface over two
short cockbeaded, veneered & inlaid drawers above two tambour
shutters conforming to the serpen-

tine skirt, square tapering legs
inlaid w/stringing & bellflowers,
coastal New England, ca. 1800,
19½ x 41½", 41" h. (old replaced
oval brasses, height loss, minor
restorations) 4,400.00
Louis XV-Style lady's desk, rosewood
marquetry, rectangular galleried
top over a pair of narrow concave
inlaid drawers above a similar
fall-front enclosing a leather writing surface & three drawers & compartments, wide curved apron
w/fine floral band inlay matching
that on upper sections, slender
cabriole legs w/metal *sabots*,
European, 19th c., 28" w., 40½" h.
(restoration) 1,210.00
Mission-style (Arts & Crafts move-
ment) "Chalet" type drop-front
desk, oak, arched gallery top
w/pierced corner cut-outs & keyed
tenon sides over recessed panel
drop-front, interior fitted w/letter
rails, flaring side panels w/keyed
tenons centering lower shelf,
stepped shoe footbase, unsigned
Gustav Stickley, Model No. 505,
ca. 1901-02, 23½" w., 45¾" h. . . .1,760.00
Modern style writing desk, mahogany
veneer, rectangular top w/Greek
Key border overhangs case w/nar-
row center drawer over kneehole
flanked by banks of four graduated
drawers w/cut-out handgrips,
designed by Frank Lloyd Wright
& signed w/red "FLW" logo, produced by Heritage-Henredon Furniture Company, North Carolina,
ca. 1955, 20 x 52", 28" h. 1,210.00
Queen Anne "block-front" slant-front
desk, carved mahogany rectangular hinged slant-lid opening to
an interior fitted w/valanced
pigeonholes over small drawers,
centering prospect drawer opening
to two small drawers, document
drawers flanking, four graduated
long drawers below, each w/cock-
beaded surround, on molded base
w/shaped pendant, continuing to
blocked bracket feet, Boston area,
Massachusetts, ca. 1760, 21 x 42",
43½" h. 27,500.00
Regency "Davenport" desk, rosewood,
leather-lined slant lid & C-scroll
gallery enclosing a maple-veneer-
ed fitted interior supported by
tapering columns on a concave-
fronted plinth base, the side fitted
w/a pen drawer & graduated
drawers w/patent locks, England,
ca. 1825, 19" w., 35½" h. 4,620.00
Schoolmaster's desk on stand, paint-

ed & decorated, two-part construction: upper section w/rectangular top above a slant lid opening to fitted interior w/three open compartments above three short drawers; lower section slightly projecting w/a single drawer over a plain apron on square tapering legs, grain-painted finish, 28" w., 42¾" h. 440.00

Victorian Rococo Lady's Desk

Victorian lady's desk, Rococo substyle, rosewood, pierce-carved scrolling crestrail w/central scroll cartouche above open shelf above narrow horizontal mirror flanked by S-scroll carved shelf supports above rectangular top over serpentine slant-front opening to fitted interior over deep apron w/single long narrow drawer, ornate scroll-carved trestle base, Alexander Roux, New Orleans, ca. 1850 (ILLUS.) 6,050.00

William & Mary Desk

William & Mary desk, painted pine, rectangular top w/slant lid w/applied molded edge enclosing a large open compartment above a case w/astragal bead mid-molding & two short thumb-molded drawers over a molded apron, block-,

baluster- and ring-turned legs joined by a conforming H-stretcher, old red paint, probably Connecticut, 1710-25, 24½ x 34¼", 32" h. (ILLUS.) 6,600.00

DRY SINKS

19th Century Amish Dry Sink

Butternut dry sink, rectangular lid lifting above deep well above case w/a pair of large paneled doors on left side of base & smaller paneled door below small drawer on right side, straight apron, beveled feet, original cast-iron latches (painted gold), refinished, 29 x 54¼", 34" h. 800.00

Grained & painted dry sink, rectangular yellow & green painted recessed top overhanging the base w/single drawer above a cupboard door, front & demilune cut-out ends, overall raw sienna & burnt umber graining, probably Pennsylvania, late 19th c., 16½ x 27¾", 29" h. 715.00

Painted poplar dry sink, rectangular top w/work well above a pair of long drawers w/rounded ends & wooden mushroom knobs above a pair of paneled cupboard doors w/original cast-iron latches w/brass knobs, flat apron w/shaped bracket feet, signed on back "Aufman Smithville Station, Wayne County, Ohio," old red paint, 19th c., 48" w., 36" h. (old metal repair, front edge of well cut down) 2,100.00

Painted wood dry sink, deep welled rectangular top w/applied rounded edge above two paneled cupboard doors, painted in off-white within dark green borders, raised on arched feet, Amish origin, Midwestern, 19th c., 44" l., 38½" h. (ILLUS.) 825.00

Red-painted pine dry sink, rectangular top w/galleried edge, the side boards extending to cut-out feet, joined by a medial shelf, 19th c., 19 x 54½", 30½" h. (paint not original, split in top, losses, over-all wear) 440.00

GARDEN & LAWN FURNITURE

(Cast iron unless otherwise noted)

Fern Design Lawn Furniture

Armchair, wire, arched crestrail w/diamond wire-work back continuing to a trapezoidal seat flanked by similar shaped arms, scrolled legs w/scrolled spandrels, joined by an X-stretcher, painted white, late 19th or early 20th c., 35" h. 176.00

Bench, wood & iron, single slatted wooden back & double slat seat, cast-iron reeded scroll ends w/incurved tops terminating in grotesque masks, armrests ending in capped female masks continuing to animal leg form supports ending in hoof feet, painted, Regency style, England, early 19th c., 4' 10" l. 412.50

Bench, wood & iron, horizontally slatted wooden back & seat, openwork ends cast w/fluted columns, foliage & a central rosette, painted black, Yates Haywood & Co., Rotterdam & London, second half 19th c., 7' 11½" l. 192.50

Settees, composed of intertwined branches & leaves, painted green, late 19th c., 35½" l., pr. 3,575.00

Settee, curved back w/intricate cast floral vines, bird's head arm supports, curved seat, straight front legs, 40" l. (rusted & flaking white paint) 750.00

Settee, triple-back style, each back section w/a stepped crest centering a cast lion's head above three pierced & scrolled splats, the center section w/cast inscription "JOSIE SWEENEY" over a pierced rectangular seat flanked by scrolled arms, molded cylindrical legs w/disc feet, painted green, 44½" l., 36" h. 770.00

Settee, arched back w/rustic woven branch design, rustic branch arched arms continue to form legs, openwork seat, old grey repaint, 49" l. (some joints welded, light rust) 1,050.00

Settee & two armchairs, each w/high curved back continuing to form tall arms, cast overall w/scrolling fern design, slender branch-form legs, old repaint, Victorian, 3 pcs. (ILLUS. of part) 3,850.00

Table, scalloped & reticulated circular top, scrolled legs joined by an X-shaped stretcher, painted white, 39¼" d., 25½" h. 176.00

Table, cast foliage scrolls & vintage grape designs, tripod base w/pedestal supports round top, white repaint, 21" d., 29½" h. 45.00

HALL RACKS & TREES

French Wrought Iron Hall Rack

Hall rack, wrought iron, upright rectangular form w/arched crest, the whole wrought w/highly stylized rose blossoms & concentric rounded arches, set w/six hooks, a central octagonal mirror, two umbrella supports & a marble shelf, France, ca. 1925, 43 1/8" w., 7' 5" h. (ILLUS.) 3,300.00

Hall tree, bentwood, cylindrical standard set at top w/eight scrolling arms conjoined by a circle, raised on four scrolling legs conjoined by a circular stretcher, Thonet, Austria, ca. 1890, 6' 6½" h. 880.00

Hall tree, Victorian, bamboo, peaked top, center section w/fan-shaped beveled mirror set between scrolled bamboo, nine hat pegs frame the outside, base w/sectioned umbrella holder, mid-19th c., 34" w., 38" h. 770.00

Hall tree, carved wood, model of a
female bear stands at the base of
a tree w/a cub sitting in the
upper branches, dished indentation
at front of base, four thick short
tree trunk legs, natural finish,
European, 19th c., 6' 5" h. 3,465.00

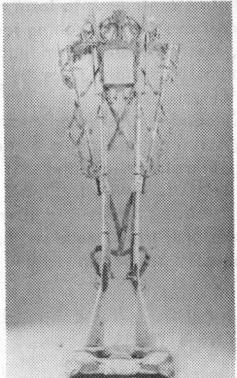

Civil War Cast Iron Hall Tree

Hall tree, painted & gilded cast iron,
cast in the half-round w/uprights
in the form of bayonets criss-
crossed by a pair of eagle-headed
sabres w/two other sabres flanking hung w/rope twists & tassels,
the crossbar in the form of olive
branches centering a small United
States shield above a shield-
shaped mirror plate, the base
w/United States mail pouches,
acorns, tassels & ribbons, ca.
1870, 6' 1" h. (ILLUS.) 4,950.00

Hall tree, Victorian, Renaissance Revival substyle, walnut, triangular
broken cornice over a mirror
plate, marble tablet & umbrella
supports at base, ca. 1870,
42" w., 7' 10" h. 660.00

Hall tree, Victorian, Rococo Revival
substyle, walnut & marble, back
w/brass scroll & gryphon hat
hooks & swivel mirror, marble top
over single drawer flanking umbrella stands, drawer & mirror
back stenciled "Blake & Davenport
12 Cornhill Boston," 7' 6" h. 880.00

Umbrella stand, painted cast iron,
composed of three tiers of scrolling
hat rests above an umbrella well,
painted green, Victorian, late
19th c. 1,210.00

LOVE SEATS, SOFAS & SETTEES

Day bed, American Empire (Classical), bronze-mounted carved mahogany, high out-curved head- and
footboards w/leaf-carved ends
above panels, columns down sides

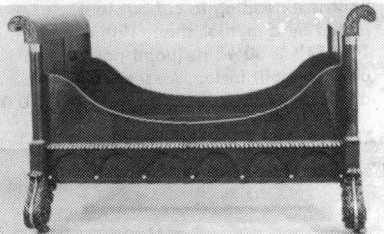

American Empire Day Bed

of endboards, high curved sideboards above gadroon-carved band
& wide band of carved arches,
heavy acanthus-carved outward-
scrolling legs, Philadelphia,
1830-40 (ILLUS.) 5,225.00

Day bed, Mission-style (Arts & Crafts
movement), oak, square canted
end posts joined by straight rails
over four vertical slats, seatrail
over lower long stretcher, signed
w/"Handcraft" decal of L. & J.G.
Stickley, Model No. 292, ca. 1910,
29¾ x 80," 27¾" h. 1,980.00

Recamier, American Empire (Classical), mahogany, shaped padded
backrest w/acanthus-carved top-
rail w/scrolled ends, the supports
carved w/scrolling foliage w/an
over-upholstered seat above a
plain frieze, raised on circular
ring-turned legs, on casters, early
19th c., 80" l. 1,760.00

Settee, American Empire (Classical),
carved mahogany, removable upholstered back surmounted by a
crest w/two wheat-carved panels
centering a panel w/a pair of cornucopias w/wheat, scrolled arm
supports flanking, centering X-form
slats, the sunflower- and acanthus-
carved seatrail flanked by a pair of
stylized baskets on acanthus-
carved tapered feet ending in
brass casters, Boston, Massachusetts, ca. 1815, 84" l. (some
repairs) 8,800.00

Settee, Art Deco, upholstered walnut, rectangular back w/inset upholstered center section continuing
to two partially upholstered scrolling arms & a rectangular seat,
raised on a wide U-form support &
four short legs, upholstered in
white muslin, France, ca. 1930,
5' 1" l. 3,300.00

Settee, Art Nouveau, gilt-bronze-
mounted walnut, high, straight
back & rounded arms set w/a
simple ormolu band in continuous
walnut frame, the back corners
w/ormolu leaves, the straight wal-

nut apron continuing to two massive lug feet applied w/mounts cast in the form of orchids, raised on two back lug feet, upholstered in silk brocade & cotton, Louis Majorelle, France, ca. 1900, 74½" l., 43½" h. 14,300.00

Settee, bentwood, back formed of three arched sections, each set w/round & oval caned sections, continuing to scrolling arms w/padded armrests & a rounded rectangular caned seat, raised on six flaring legs conjoined by a continuous bentwood stretcher, Austria, ca. 1900, 5' 1" l. 495.00

Settee, country-style, painted & decorated wood, shaped crest above three cut-out splats & turned spindles on the rolled plank seat w/scrolled arms on turned supports & turned feet joined by flat stretchers; original ivory paint w/free-hand painted floral & foliate designs in mustard yellow, green & black, Pennsylvania, ca. 1830, 77¼" l., 37" h. (paint wear) 1,320.00

Federal Settee

Settee, Federal, tiger stripe maple, three-section baluster- and ring-turned chair back w/four tall posts, conforming sides, rush seat on baluster- and ring-turned legs, New England, 1800-20, 26 x 71", 37" h. (ILLUS.) 2,200.00

Settee, Victorian Rococo substyle, carved laminated rosewood, gadrooned crestrail centered by a rose-carved foliate spray above pierce-carved foliage, padded armrests w/volute terminals, serpentine seatrail centered by a carved foliate spray, cabriole legs (minor restorations, lacking casters), John & Joseph Meeks, New York City, ca. 1860, 5' 4" l.......................3,575.00

Settee, William & Mary Style, walnut, tall rectangular back & seat upholstered w/a 17th century Flemish tapestry depicting exotic birds among potted plants in primarily

blue, green & red tones, arms, legs & front stretchers carved w/C- and S-scrolls, late 19th c., 74" l., 46½" h. 4,070.00

Settee, Windsor, painted & turned, rectangular crest above twenty-four tapered & turned spindles & plank seat on turned legs joined by turned stretchers; the crest painted w/stylized fruit & leaf motifs in yellow, red & black on a green ground, Pennsylvania, ca. 1825, 84" l. (feet reduced in height) 3,575.00

Settee, Windsor "rod-back," painted wood, circular rod crestrail above twenty-five tapering spindles on a shaped & incised plank seat, end arms w/angled support & two spindles, six tapering bamboo-turned front legs w/five turned H-stretchers joining the raking bamboo-turned rear legs, old worn brown paint on original yellow, New England, ca. 1800, 16¾ x 83", 33" h. (minor height loss) 9,900.00

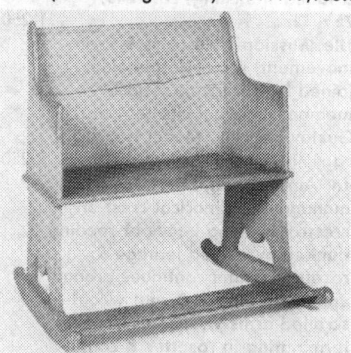

Country Settee on Rockers

Settee on rockers, country-style, painted pine, tall board back flanked by shaped board arms above flat seat on cut-out board legs w/rockers joined by a footrest, green paint, New England, first half 19th c., 28½ x 31", 35" h. (ILLUS.) 1,980.00

Early Child's Settle

Settle, Early American child's,
painted wood, two-board back
connected to the shaped & tenoned
wings which continue to the rectangular raking base w/plank seat,
old black paint, New England, late
18th c., imperfections, 9½ x 25",
22" h. (ILLUS. previous page) 1,650.00

Settle, country-style, pine, straight
board back above a rectangular
seat flanked by shaped board
armrests continuing to shaped
board feet, 19th c., 64" l., 43" h.
(breaks to armrests)............ 495.00

Settle, Federal country-style, rocking-
type, painted & decorated wood,
wide flat crestrail above three-
section back w/medial rails above
twelve arrow-slats, scrolling
arms on turned arm supports,
slightly rolled seat, turned end
legs w/rockers joined by flat
stretcher in front joined by half-
legs, original dark red & black
flame graining w/yellow striping
& faded stenciling, ca. 1840,
75½" l.......................1,250.00

Settle, Mission-style (Arts & Crafts
movement), oak, slatted sides
joined by a horizontal back
member, original cushion seat,
Gustav Stickley, Model No. 225,
ca. 1910, 31 x 77¾", 29¼" h.....8,250.00

Sofa, American Empire (Classical),
mahogany, cylindrical crest on
crestrail w/long bands of reeding
flanked by carved leafage &
rosettes, frame continues around
upholstered back & seat w/out-
scrolled arms w/reeded fronts
terminating in rosettes & continuing to reeded & carved seatrail
on curved legs w/reeding ending
in hairy paw feet, Boston, ca.
1825, 25 x 94", 32" h...........2,090.00

American Empire Sofa

Sofa, American Empire (Classical),
mahogany veneer, wide serpentine crestrail above tufted upholstered back, outswept scroll arms
w/mahogany veneer facing which
joins wide flat seatrail, short
scroll legs, on casters, ca. 1840-50
(ILLUS.)...................... 330.00

Sofa, Chippendale "camel-back,"
mahogany, upholstered arched

back flanked by outscrolled arms
on square molded legs joined by
stretchers, ca. 1780, 81" l. (some
restoration to stretchers, reduced
in height) 3,575.00

Sofa, Federal, carved mahogany,
scrolled crestrail flanked by
carved eagles' heads above
C-scrolled armrests, rectangular
padded seat, the arm supports
w/cornucopia carving continuing
to the straight seatrail, cornucopia
& hairy paw carved feet, 1810-30,
78" l., 33½" h.................. 935.00

Sofa, Federal, carved mahogany,
tablet crestrail centering carved
double swag w/a bowknot above
upholstered back, flanked by
fluted panels continuing to reeded
arms above reeded & leaf-carved
arm supports over carved paterae
flanking a reeded front seatrail,
reeded cylindrical legs, baluster
feet on casters, New York,
1800-20, 77½" l., 35¾" h. (one
front leg restored)............17,600.00

Sofa, Mission-style (Arts & Crafts
movement), oak, wide crestrail
over repeating vertical slats spaced
by single wider slats w/arrow cut-
out, flat drop-arms over single cut-
out slat, single cushion seat, lower
stretchers, paper label for Charles
Limbert Co., Michigan, Model
No. 507, ca. 1906, 25½ x 76¾",
35½" h. (refinished) 1,210.00

Belter Rosewood Sofa

Sofa, Victorian, Rococo substyle,
carved & laminated rosewood, high
back w/undulating crestrail
w/carved gentle scrolls & w/three
fruit- and flower-carved finials,
crestrail continuing down to form
curved arm supports & short cabriole front legs w/floral carved
knees, undulating seatrail w/finely
carved floral & scroll center
reserve, John Henry Belter, New
York, ca. 1850, 65½" l., 37½" h.
(ILLUS.) 3,520.00

"Tete-a-tete," Louis XVI-Style, giltwood, two facing arched uphol-

stered backs raised on circular reeded tapered legs on casters, velvet upholstery, Europe, ca. 1900, 54" l. 1,320.00

LOWBOYS

Queen Anne Lowboy

Chippendale lowboy, carved mahogany, rectangular top above five molded drawers, the center drawer shell-carved, fluted quarter-columns flanking, the shaped skirt below continuing to acanthus-carved cabriole legs ending in claw-and-ball feet, now on casters, Pennsylvania, probably Philadelphia, ca. 1770, 24 x 34", 30½" h. (lacks applied acanthus leaves on shell drawer, restoration to top & some repairs) 27,500.00

Queen Anne lowboy, cherry, rectangular top above case w/single long drawer over central carved drawer flanked by short molded drawers, shaped skirt, cabriole legs w/pad feet, original brass bat's wing handles & keyhole escutcheon, slight repair to left rear leg, Connecticut, ca. 1770, 33" w., 20¾" deep, 30½" h. (ILLUS.) 27,500.00

Queen Anne lowboy, cherry, rectangular top w/boldly scrolled rim above case w/shallow long drawer over central fan-carved drawer flanked by deep short drawers, deeply scalloped skirt, cabriole legs w/slender ankles, duck feet w/pads, original deep reddish brown w/excellent patina, replaced engraved brasses, 20½ x 38" top, 32 1/8" h. (one foot repaired) 145,000.00

Queen Anne lowboy, walnut, rectangular top w/thumb-molded edge above one long & three short molded drawers, shaped skirt continuing to angular cabriole legs

ending in stockinged trifid feet, Pennsylvania, ca. 1770, 34" l., 28½" h. (top reset, some drawer sides & bottoms replaced) 37,400.00

Queen Anne lowboy, walnut, thumb-molded rectangular top above a case fitted w/a frieze drawer, three small drawers below, the central one w/carved fan, all w/cockbeaded surrounds, shaped apron continuing to cabriole legs ending in high pad feet, New England, ca. 1750, 35¼" w., 31½" h. 47,300.00

Queen Anne lowboy, walnut, molded rectangular top w/notched corners above a case fitted w/a thumb-molded frieze drawer & two short drawers flanked by fluted canted corners, the skirt w/central pendant continuing to shell-carved cabriole legs w/stockinged pad feet, Philadelphia, ca. 1760, 33¼" l., 28¾" h. 17,600.00

Queen Anne style "Centennial" lowboy, mahogany, rectangular top w/thumb-molded edge above two long drawers over two short drawers flanking a carved scallop shell centering the undulating apron, raised on molded square cabriole legs ending in circular cupped pad feet, late 19th c., 36½" l., 32¼" h. 5,500.00

MIRRORS

Federal "Courting" Mirror

Art Deco wall mirror, wrought-iron, rectangular frame of hammered, reeded form surmounted by scrolling iron crest featuring a silhouette of a flying crane, stamped "E. BRANDT," 37" h. 11,000.00

Art Nouveau wall mirror, giltwood, undulating pierce-carved frame featuring scrolling, leafy vines in the asymmetrical composition, probably France, ca. 1900, 33" w., 44¾" h. 6,600.00

Chippendale wall mirror, carved
mahogany, elaborately scrolled
crest centering a gilt urn within
a pierced roundel above rectangular mirror plate within a molded
frame above shaped & scrolled
pendant, England or America,
1770-1800, 25¼" w., 53" h. (small
tip restoration on pendant) 5,500.00

Empire, American, overmantel mirror, giltwood, cylindrical baluster-
and ring-turned giltwood frame
flanked by carved rosettes centering two rectangular plates,
1830-40, 58¾" w., 29" h..........275.00

Federal "courting" mirror, carved &
painted, beveled cornice, dentil
carved crest (piece missing) centering a heart, above a scalloped
device, split baluster supports,
rosettes & a carved device surmounting the columns, painted in
old red & black w/yellow ochre
accents, ca. 1820, 12" h.
(ILLUS.) 5,225.00

Federal "girandole" mirror, giltwood,
top surmounted by a spread-
winged American eagle on a rockwork base, the molded frame hung
w/spherules centering the round
convex mirror plate, two projecting
candlearms below w/gilt metal can-
dlecups, early 19th c., 19" w.,
30½" h. 5,225.00

Federal wall mirror, mahogany veneer, circular form w/gilded egg-
and-dart carving surrounding a
mahogany veneered frame enclosing a mirror plate & surmounted by
a gilded eagle & laurel leaves,
early 19th c., 15½" d. 297.00

George II wall mirror, walnut,
molded overhanging cornice surmounted by a triangular pediment
centering a molded tablet w/den-
til-carved borders above a deep
frieze flanked by pierced corbels,
the rectangular mirror plate within
molded borders, England, ca. 1750,
23¾" w., 44½" h. 4,675.00

Louis XV wall mirror, giltwood,
slightly arched rectangular mirror
plate in conforming molded frame
carved w/leaves & C-scrolls on a
lozenge-incised ground surmounted
by a pierced crest w/flower-filled
cartouche, France, mid-18th c.,
29" h. 1,320.00

Mission-style (Arts & Crafts movement) hall mirror, oak, arched top
rectangular frame w/single mirror
plate over four iron hooks along
base, Model No. 66, Gustav Stick-

ley red decal & paper label, ca.
1905-07, 36" w., 28" h. 1,320.00

Neoclassical wall mirror, gilt metal-
mounted fruitwood, rectangular
mirror plate within a molded border surmounted by a cornice decorated w/an egg-and-dart border
w/a gilt-metal & acorn mount,
Continental, first quarter 19th c.,
24¼" w., 45½" h. 1,210.00

Queen Anne "courting" mirror, mahogany veneer, shaped crest
w/reverse-painted hunting scene,
rounded frame w/applied molded
edge, England, mid-18th c.,
19" h. 770.00

Regency Mirror

Regency wall mirror, parcel-gilt &
patinated pine, molded cornice
hung w/sphericals above a deep
frieze w/molding in the form of
diamonds above a rectangular
plate flanked by fluted pilasters
headed by Egyptian hermes & ending in human feet, England, ca.
1810, 25" w., 39½" h. (ILLUS.) ...2,200.00

Victorian "cheval" mirror, brass,
beveled vertical swing mirror in
brass frame supported on turned
column uprights w/clenched fist
terminals, resting on splayed feet,
second half 19th c., 30½" w.,
5' 8" h. 935.00

Victorian novelty folding mirror,
walnut, one drawer base supporting two oval mirrors joined by a
hinged jig-sawn extension, base
11 7/8 x 14 5/8" 550.00

PARLOR SUITES

Art Deco: sofa & two armchairs; each
w/notched, crested back continuing to over-upholstered rounded
arms & a rectangular seat cushion,
the deep apron above two *ebene-
de-macassar* scrolling front feet &
two block-form back feet, upholstered in colorful floral tapestry,

the sofa also w/a figure of a nude
woman, a child & a bird against a
greige ground, Jules Leleu, France,
ca. 1925, 3 pcs.................2,200.00
Art Nouveau: settee, two side chairs
& two armchairs; walnut, each
w/upholstered back w/arched
crestrail carved w/whiplash leaves
continuing into open arms above a
rectangular seat & arched apron,
tapering square front legs ending
in lobed feet, simple outward
flaring back legs, apron, sides
& front legs carved w/further
leaves, upholstered in leopard-
print cotton, designed by Louis
Majorelle, France, ca. 1900,
5 pcs. 6,050.00

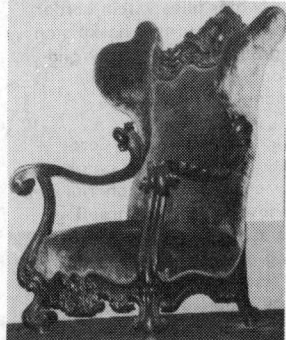

Baroque-Style Armchair
Baroque-Style: settee & a pair of
open armchairs; oak, massive
pieces w/high arched pierce-
carved crest flanked by wide
scrolled upholstered wings above
tall upholstered back joined to
long scrolling arms on tall curved
arm supports, deep upholstered
seat over deep scroll-carved apron
& scrolling legs, ca. 1900, 3 pcs.
(ILLUS. of part) 2,475.00
Victorian, Eastlake substyle: settee,
rocker, armchair & side chair;
maple, turned "faux bamboo"
style, each piece stamped inside
rear leg "Made by Palmer and
Embury NY," ca. 1870, 4 pcs. 1,650.00
Victorian, Renaissance Revival substyle: sofa, lady's armchair & gentleman's closed armchair & four
side chairs; each w/carved walnut
frame, the high pointed crestrail
carved w/central medallion depicting a lady, the arms carved at
front w/a female head & bust,
veneered panels in lower frieze,
wide disc at top of round reeded
legs, gilt-incised trim overall,
attributed to Jelliff, ca. 1870,
7 pcs. 8,250.00

Victorian, Rococo substyle: settee,
armchair & four side chairs; each
carved & laminated rosewood w/cen-
tral rose leaf cresting & C-scroll
& leaf openwork back w/tufted
upholstery oval medallions on
chairs & tufted upholstery back
on settee, covered in purple silk
upholstery, "Hartford" patt. by
J. & J. Meeks, New York, ca. 1850,
6 pcs. 28,600.00

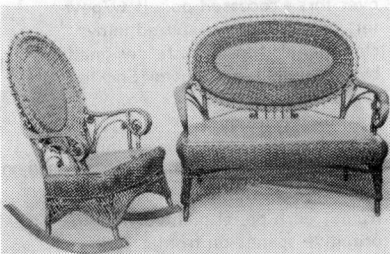

Wicker Parlor Suite
Wicker: settee, open armchair &
rocker; each piece w/long oval
back raised on small spindles
above oblong seat w/fine caned
inset over wide wicker apron
trimmed w/loosely diamond-woven
arched band, signed "Wakefield
Brothers," ca. 1890, 3 pcs. (ILLUS.
of part).......................7,425.00

SCREENS

Louis XVI Style Fire Screen
Fire screen, carved waisted oblong
frame centering needlepoint &
petit point scene of two figures
within a floral border, trestle
base, France, 22½" w., 37" h..... 230.00
Fire screen, Louis XVI Style, giltwood, arched floral & beaded
carved crestrail centered by circular medallions above an oval
Aubusson tapestry panel depicting
putti, flanked by fluted pilasters
& raised on foliate & scroll-carved

legs, France, ca. 1860, 25½" w.,
40" h. (ILLUS.) 1,760.00

Folding screen, two-fold, decorated
w/flock of sparrows feeding by or
perched on leafy bamboo w/moun-
tain peaks in the distance, all on
a gold-foil ground, Japan, 19th c.,
each panel 24½ x 34¼" (wear,
restorations) 2,475.00

Folding screen, three-fold, oak frame
w/arched crest on each segment
over three recessed panels w/pew-
ter, copper & wood stylzed inlay,
cloth panels, dark finish, designed
by Harvey Ellis for Gustav Stickley,
red decal mark in a box, ca.
1903-04, each panel 20" w.,
66¾" h. (minor chips, some inlay
missing, cloth replaced) 19,800.00

Folding screen, three-fold, ash
frame, each panel painted w/two
primitive scenes on front & back
depicting cabins, dogs, horse
head, landscapes, etc., each pan-
el 23½" w., overall 67" h. 475.00

Neoclassical Style Screen

Folding screen, three-fold, Neoclassical style, giltwood, each section
w/a beveled mirror plate surmounted by a pierced ribbon cresting & floral swags over rectangular
red floral striped fabric panels,
the central section w/a mirror
plate over giltwood panels carved
w/ribbon-tied floral wreaths &
swags, the frame in the form of
ribbon-tied reed clusters, probably
French, early 20th c., each panel
17¾" w., 6' 4" h. (ILLUS.) 2,750.00

Folding screen, four-fold, grisaille
painted paper, depicting Chinese
landscapes & garden scenes w/pa-
godas, Charles X period, France,
second quarter 19th c.,
76½" h. .4,160.00

Folding screen, six-fold, painted canvas, painted w/continuous scene
of Chinese figures including a
falconer, an archer & hunters set
in an exotic landscape w/various
animals & beasts within a border
of meandering vines, tones of
cream, red, purple, blue, yellow &
green on black ground, the reverse
w/stylized floral bouquets within
blue foliate borders on a yellow
ground, Continental, early 19th c.,
each panel 21" w., 5' 4" h. (restor-
ations to paint) 4,950.00

Folding screen, six-fold, painted
leather, blue, red, orange & green
exotic birds & waterfowl in a shallow landscape filled w/flowering
trees & water lilies within border
of flower-filled urns & baskets on
black ground highlighted w/gild-
ing, Continental, early 19th c.,
each panel 22" w., overall
9' h. 12,100.00

Folding screen, eight-fold, Coromandel lacquer, carved on one
side w/an elaborate manorial complex showing the host greeting
guests as they enter to enjoy an
evening of festive delights, the
scene flanked at the bottom &
sides by ritual vessels & scholar's
table implements, reversed by an
exotic garden w/tropical birds &
flowers of the four seasons, all
well executed on a mirror black
ground, China, ca. 1900, each
panel 16" w., overall 83" h. (minor
losses, cracking) 1,100.00

Folding screen, ten-fold, Coromandel
lacquer, each panel depicting
figures in landscape w/pavilions
& in interiors within gilt-pierced
upper & lower panels, rectangular
feet, China, 18th c., each panel
19" w., 144" h. 8,800.00

Folding screen, 12-fold, gilt-decorated black lacquer, depicting
various exotic birds, insects &
butterflies in a shallow rocky
landscape w/flowering prunus, in
tones of red & green on a black
ground highlighted w/gilding,
Regency period, England, first
quarter 19th c., each panel
17" w., 8' h. 12,100.00

Pole screen, Chippendale, mahogany,
rectangular screen covered w/old
floral tapestry w/metallic thread
trim slides on pole w/turned detail
at base & turned finial, tripod base
w/cabriole legs w/simple carving
at knees & snake feet, old finish,
18th c., 57¼" h. (one leg
repaired) 1,200.00

Late Federal Pole Screen

Pole screen, late Federal, carved
cherry, rectangular screen made
from water-color theorem painting
hand-drawn & stenciled on a white
velvet ground w/a basket of
brightly colored fruit in a low
bowl, the screen adjustable on a
vertical threaded rod continuing to
a standard w/suppressed ball
turning, tripod cabriole legs
w/chip-carving & molding ending in
snake pad feet, New England,
ca. 1830, 44½" h. (ILLUS.) 4,675.00

SECRETARIES

English Chippendale Secretary

Chippendale secretary-bookcase,
cherry, two-part construction: upper section w/swan's neck pediment w/flower-carved terminals
centering an urn & flame finial
above two arched & paneled doors
opening to an interior w/two
shelves; lower section w/thumb-
molded slant-front lid opening to
a serpentine interior w/eight
pierced & valanced pigeonholes

above four short drawers over two
long drawers centering a prospect
door flanked by fluted document
drawers, all above case w/fluted
quarter-columns & four graduated
long drawers above a molded base
on ogee bracket feet, Connecticut,
1760-80, 20¾ x 36¾", 8' h. (restoration to doors, pediment, feet &
lip of one drawer) 9,350.00

Chippendale secretary-bookcase,
mahogany, two-part construction:
upper section w/rectangular top
w/wide dentil molded cornice
above a pair of geometrically-
glazed doors opening to three
shelves; lower section w/hinged
slant-front lid opening to interior
fitted w/four small drawers flanked by pigeonholes over small
drawers above case w/two short &
two long drawers, bracket feet,
worn old finish, one drawer
w/stenciled label "J. & H. Jewells,
Holborn...," England, 18th c., minor
repairs, replaced feet, one small
interior drawer replaced, replaced
brasses, 24 x 41¾", 7' 5½" h.
(ILLUS.) 5,500.00

American Classical Secretary

Classical (American Empire)
secretary-bookcase, mahogany &
bird's-eye maple, molded overhanging rectangular top over two
glazed & divided cupboard doors
opening to painted & stencil-
decorated drawers & valanced
compartments, on a projecting
base w/a pull-out writing surface
above a convex-shaped & free-
hand decorated drawer & two
drawers w/brass pulls flanked by
carved, turned & brass-decorated
columns terminating in turned
feet on casters, bird's-eye maple

recessed side panels, central Massachusetts, ca. 1830, unrestored, 21 x 38½", 5' 7" h. (ILLUS.) 935.00

Classical (American Empire) secretary-bookcase, cherry, two-part construction: upper section w/flaring cornice w/carved gadrooning & two recessed panel doors opening to a three-shelf interior; lower section w/a slant lid opening to a fitted interior above two long drawers, four turned & carved tapering legs, refinished, probably Wayland, Massachusetts, ca. 1830, 34" w., 6' 4½" h. (replaced wooden pulls) 2,860.00

Country folk art secretary, painted poplar, flat rectangular top w/bobbin-turned front trim above a pair of long double-paneled cupboard doors flanked by narrow bobbin-turned edge bands, desk section w/wide slanted desk top w/bobbin-turned edge above flat apron w/bobbin-turned band along bottom, square tapering legs, doors w/applied bobbin-turned corner ornaments & wooden knobs & thumb latches, old red paint, 26¾ x 40", 5' 6½" h. 1,000.00

Federal secretary-bookcase, carved mahogany, two-part construction: upper section w/molded cornice above a pair of Gothic-arch pointed glazed hinged mullioned doors opening to shelves, w/two drawers below; lower section w/baize-lined writing flap above three pull-out slides & four drawers centering a pair of cupboard doors, on reeded turned short legs, round brass lion-head pulls w/ring bails on lower drawers, probably Salem, Massachusetts, ca. 1815, 24 x 41", 6' 4½" h. (upper section lacks shaped crest) 4,125.00

Federal country-style secretary-bookcase, painted pine, two-part construction: upper section w/rectangular top w/flat molded cornice above a pair of recessed panel cupboard doors opening to three shelves; lower section w/slant-front lid opening to interior fitted w/valanced cubbyholes & drawers, above a case of three graduated thumb-molded drawers, high cut-out base, original red wash, probably Massachusetts, ca. 1800, unrestored, some imperfections, 17 x 39¾", 7' ½" h. (ILLUS. next column) 5,225.00

Queen Anne secretary-bookcase, carved cherry, two-part construction: upper section w/molded dentil-carved swan's neck crest ending in carved pinwheels above a pair of shaped paneled cupboard doors opening to shelves, candleslides below; lower section w/hinged slant-front rectangular lid opening to an interior comprising valanced pigeonholes above blocked small drawers, the open prospect section w/small drawer, document drawers flanking, a hinged lid below opening to a well, all above two short & two long graduated drawers, bracket feet, probably Connecticut, 1740-60, 22 x 38½", 6' 11" h. (some restoration to front left foot facing, other repairs, hood lacks dust bonnet) 22,000.00

Federal Painted Pine Secretary

Victorian secretary-bookcase, Gothic Revival substyle, carved rosewood & satinwood, two-part construction: upper section w/coved cornice above two Gothic arched glazed doors w/quatrefoil tracery opening to a satinwood interior w/three shelves; lower section w/a cylinder roll-top opening to a fitted satinwood interior w/a stack of three short drawers flanked by ten pigeonholes above a sliding writing surface w/three hinged compartments, the center one w/stenciled label "J. & J. W. Meeks, MAKERS, No. 14, Vesey Street, New York," over two paneled cupboard doors w/Gothic cusps opening to a single shelf, bracket feet, 1836-50, 23 x 48½", 7' 5¼" h. (one glass panel cracked) 28,600.00

Victorian secretary-bookcase, Renaissance Revival substyle, walnut & burl walnut, rectangular top

Victorian Cylinder-Front Secretary
w/wide shaped crestboards w/applied machine-cut scrolls above a pair of single-pane glazed doors opening to two shelves above paneled cylinder roll-top w/burl veneer opening to fitted interior, base w/one long drawer over two short deep drawers beside single small paneled cupboard door, stamped brass & bail drawer pulls, ogee bracket feet, ca. 1875, replaced brasses (ILLUS.) 1,210.00

Victorian secretary-bookcase, Rococo substyle, carved rosewood, arched top w/fruit & floral carved cresting over pair arched glazed doors opening to two shelves over three shallow drawers, the lower section w/cylinder roll-top opening to fitted interior of three long drawers over three arched slots flanked by pairs of small drawers, pull-out writing surface at front above narrow panel over two paneled cupboard doors, undulating scroll-carved apron & bracket feet, New York, ca. 1850, 24 x 52", 9' 2" h. 11,550.00

SIDEBOARDS

Federal Revival Sideboard

Art Nouveau sideboard, carved walnut, fruitwood & cameo glass, two-part construction: superstructure w/arched top, scrolling side supports & shallow shelf, well carved w/blossoming wildflowers, the back carved w/further flowers & whiplash motifs, pierced & enclosing two tiers of oxblood red glass panels, the upper tier carved w/fruiting cherry branches; base w/rounded corners above two short drawers continuing to three central short drawers flanked by open shelves & within an open framework carved w/fruiting apple branches, corners further carved w/blossoms & buds, sides set w/highly polished fruitwood panels, on four lug feet, drawers w/stylized bronze pulls & escutcheon, designed by Jacques Gruber, ca. 1900, 4' 11" w., 6' 1" h. 24,200.00

Classical (American Empire) sideboard, mahogany, rectangular grey marble top above a flame-veneered skirt w/three blind drawers over four inset cylindrical columns w/stamped brass capitals & bases centering a hinged concave alcove door flanked by two paneled cupboard doors, each opening to an interior w/a sliding drawer & a short drawer, carved paw front feet, New York, 1810-30, 23¾ x 64", 40½" h. 4,950.00

Federal server, mahogany, bowed rectangular top w/a brass gallery above a conforming case w/a frieze of two drawers over two recessed doors flanked by two bottle drawers, turned reeded legs w/brass ball feet, New York, 49½" w., overall 51" h. 1,540.00

Federal sideboard, inlaid mahogany, rectangular top w/line-incised edge above three short drawers & a pair of convex bottle drawers centering a pair of hinged doors, on reeded tapering round legs ending in tapered feet, Eastern New England, ca. 1815, 67" w., 40¾" h. 9,900.00

Federal sideboard, inlaid mahogany, serpentine-fronted rectangular top above conforming case w/short concave banded end drawers above similar deep cupboard doors centering a bowfront pattern-banded long drawer over double cupboard doors flanked by rectangular panels inlaid w/oval dies w/leaves, square tapering line-inlaid legs headed by elaborate vase & floral inlaid panels, cuffed square tapering feet, probably Maryland, 1790-1810, 71" w., 39¼" h. (minor inlay repairs) . . .18,700.00

Federal Revival Style sideboard, mahogany veneer, demi-lune form w/rounded top w/low backrail above long narrow drawer above two long deep drawers at front center, decorated w/contrasting wide bands of veneer & a central oval inlay w/small compote of flowers at center, turned tapered legs, 1920's (ILLUS.) 220.00

Hepplewhite "Bow-Front" Sideboard

Hepplewhite sideboard, inlaid mahogany, rectangular "bow-front" top above conforming case w/long center drawer flanked by deep bottle drawers, fine flame grained mahogany veneer & band inlays, square tapering legs w/spade feet, England, ca. 1780, 27 x 66", 35½" h. (ILLUS.) 6,160.00

Hepplewhite-Style sideboard, inlaid mahogany, demi-lune bowfront shape top above conforming case w/single long central drawer flanked by two pairs of drawers flanked by single doors w/inlay pattern imitating two drawers, each drawer w/light veneer band around darker veneer center, round cast brass pulls, arched apron under long center drawer w/light fan inlays at corners, square tapering legs ending in spade feet, reproduction by Boker, 26¼ x 72", 36¼" h. 1,100.00

Mission-style (Arts & Crafts movement) server, oak, rectangular top w/backsplash supported by elongated corbels continuing to base, single drawer w/swing pulls & slightly arched skirt, lower stretcher base, signed w/decal of the Lifetime Furniture Company, Michigan, ca. 1912, 18¼ x 40¼", 34½" h. 522.50

Southern huntboard, pine, boldly scalloped crestrail above one-board rectangular top overhanging case w/three rows of two short drawers each, two wooden knobs

on each drawer, tall slender square tapering legs, refinished w/good warm brown color, 19th c., 22 x 71", 48" h. plus crest (one back leg badly warped) 3,000.00

Victorian credenza (flat-based sideboard), Renaissance Revival substyle, rosewood, breakfront-shaped w/molded top w/rectangular platform, the frieze w/ovolo carving above an arched door w/oval panel flanked by columns & similar oval medallions on a plinth base, ca. 1875, 19½ x 70½", 55½" h. (veneer chips) 1,760.00

Victorian Oak Sideboard

Victorian sideboard, Renaissance Style, oak, scrolling crest centering shell carving above acanthus-carved arch supported on columns over recessed mirror-backed shelf enclosed by mullioned doors, base w/rectangular marbled (added) top over two drawers above two cabinet doors w/carved panels over long drawer, carved-paw block feet, late 19th c., 59" w., 6' 10" h. (ILLUS.) 2,090.00

STANDS

Early American Candlestand

Basin stand, Federal, Sheraton-style, mahogany, oblong top pierced for basin & other small vessels w/three-quarter gallery, shaped apron, reeded and ring-turned legs joined by medial shelf w/drawer w/lighter burl veneer front & applied beaded edge below, turned feet, 17¾" w., 16" deep, 30½" h. plus gallery 2,950.00

Candlestand, Chippendale, cherry, circular top on vase- and ring-turned shaft, tripod cabriole leg base terminating in snake feet, New England, ca. 1780, 16" d., 26" h. (refinished) 550.00

Candlestand, Chippendale, tilt-top, walnut, round dished top tilting & revolving above circular birdcage support, urn-turned tapering columnar standard, cabriole tripod legs, elongated pad feet, Philadelphia, 1780-90, 22½" d., 28½" h. 8,250.00

Candlestand, Early American, turned maple, a screw standard supporting a double candlearm & plateau all supported on three bamboo-turned outward flaring legs, probably Pennsylvania, 19th c., 29¾" h. (ILLUS.) 2,640.00

Candlestand, Federal, maple, oval top above a ring- and vase-turned standard continuing to an arched tripod ending in carved feet, New England, late 18th c., 19½" w., 26 3/8" h. 1,320.00

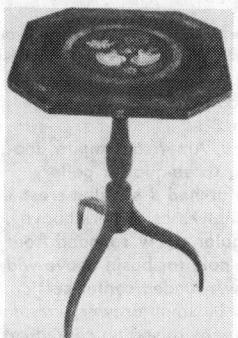

Federal Decorated Candlestand

Candlestand, Federal, painted & decorated, octagonal top on a vase- and ring-turned post & tripod tapering spider leg base, top w/its original freehand decoration incorporating diamond & circle conjoining border centering a circular panel of roses, daisies & lilies, remainder painted flat grey-brown, underside inscribed "2," possibly

Massachusetts, ca. 1820, 18" w., 28½" h. (ILLUS.) 5,225.00

Candlestand, Federal, tilt-top, carved mahogany, octagonal top tilting above an elaborately fluted vase-form standard, on rounded downcurving spider legs w/rounded spade feet, New England, ca. 1805, 15 x 20½", 30½" h. 6,050.00

Candlestand, Federal, tilt-top, tiger stripe maple, circular dished top tilting above a columnar- and urn-turned pedestal on cabriole legs w/pad feet, 19th c., 21¼" d., 27" h. 1,100.00

Candlestand w/drawer, Hepplewhite country-style, inlaid cherry, square top inlaid w/simple four-petal flower & intersecting arcs, single dovetailed drawer mounted under top, vase- and ring-turned standard, downswept cabriole tripod, snake feet, 16¼ x 16¾", 26¾" h. (old refinishing, repaired foot & age crack in top) 2,600.00

Candlestand, Queen Anne, tilt-top, walnut, round dished top tilting & revolving above birdcage support, tapering cylindrical standard w/compressed ball turning, arched cabriole legs, shod slipper feet, Pennsylvania, 1740-60, 21½" d., 25¾" h. 6,600.00

Candlestand, wrought-rion & brass, tripod base, tall tapering support w/spring-operated sliding device, horizontal arm w/candlecups, late 18th c., 5' 4½" h. 1,540.00

Canterbury (music stand), Regency, rosewood, rectangular divided upper section w/pierced lifting handle & circular turned finials, frieze w/single drawer, raised on circular turned legs ending in brass casters, England, first quarter 19th c., 18" w., 21¼" h. 2,860.00

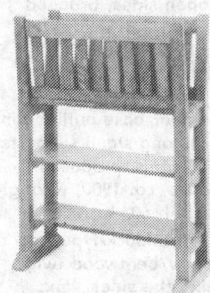

Gustav Stickley Folio Stand

Drink stand, Mission-style (Arts & Crafts movement), oak, square overhanging top above apron, lower shelf on side-stretchers, Model No. 587, L. & J.G. Stickley, signed "Handcraft," ca. 1909, 16" w., 27" h. 495.00

Folio stand, Mission-style (Arts & Crafts movement), vertical slats forming a trough over two lower shelves (some ink stains), trestle base, Model No. 51, red decal mark of Gustav Stickley, 1902-03, 29½" w., 12" deep, 40" h. (ILLUS. previous page) 3,300.00

Chinese Incense Stand

Incense stand, Huanghuali style, wooden, square top above waisted frame & rounded scrolling apron, fitted w/single disguised drawer on slender angular legs ending in trefoil pierced leafy toes, resting on square stretcher base (restorations), China, 17th c., 17½" w., 36½" h. (ILLUS.) 8,525.00

Lectern, wrought iron, Baroque-style, arched reading stand w/central fleur-de-lis, swing candle arms, twist support, tripartite legs, late 19th c., 5' 2" h. 935.00

Magazine stand, Mission-style (Arts & Crafts movement), oak, arched gallery over three open shelves w/arched open sides, branded "The Work of L. & J.G. Stickley," No. 45, ca. 1912, 12 x 21", 44½" h. 1,980.00

Music stand, Art Nouveau, bentwood, triangular base outlined in bentwood, oblong stand supported by bentwood arms, produced by Thonet, France, ca. 1900, w/original paper label, 60" h. 2,420.00

Plant stand, Adirondack-type, rectangular top w/bentwood twig ovals forming the sides, long straight legs joined by stretchers, base further fitted w/corner braces & decorated w/bentwood S-forms & a central horseshoe w/radiating spokes, original

green paint w/daubs of orange & gold, 14 x 51", 39¾" h. (minor damage) 450.00

Plant stand, twisted wire, two-tiered shelves & high arched top, worn white paint, 32" w., 65" h. . . . . 90.00 to 110.00

Renaissance Revival Plant Stand

Plant stand, Victorian, Renaissance Revival substyle, giltwood stick-and-ball construction, several tiers of circular stands supported on turned supports raised on four turned legs, ca. 1880, 20" w. (ILLUS.) 742.50

Umbrella stand, Mission-style (Arts & Crafts movement), oak, four vertical posts joined at base & top w/horizontal members, w/original drip pan, branded mark & paper label of Gustav Stickley, ca. 1912, 33¼" h. 1,100.00

Umbrella stand, sheet metal, cut-out silhouette of seated dog realistically painted in black & white, back has pan & bracket, 24½" h. 650.00

Washstand, American Empire, mahogany, three-quarter gallery w/high arched & scrolled crest & small shelves at corners above rectangular top w/rounded front & cut-out hole for basin above wide apron w/rounded center section flanked by small drawers w/small brass knobs raised on curved-cut sides & solid backboard over lower shelf over single narrow drawer w/two round brass knobs, ring-and baluster-turned legs w/knob feet, ca. 1830, 18 x 19½", 31" h. plus gallery (minor age cracks, old pieced repairs in gallery) 625.00

Washstand, Federal country-style, painted & decorated pine, rectangular top w/three-quarter gallery, very tall splashboard w/two corner shelves above top w/round

opening for wash bowl, turned
legs, lower medial shelf over narrow drawer w/round brass knob,
original yellow w/vinegar graining, stenciled & free-hand floral
decoration on splashboard, gold &
black striping on legs & around
drawer, early 19th c., 29¾" h. ... 385.00
Washstand, Federal, tiger maple,
shaped splashboard above square
top fitted for basin & cups over
medial short drawer, square tapering legs, New England, 1790-1810,
16 x 16", 34" h. 1,320.00
Washstand, Sheraton country-style,
painted & decorated pine & poplar, tall three-quarter gallery
w/shaped ends above rectangular
top w/cut-out for bowl, medial
shelf over single shallow drawer
w/old brass & tin pulls
(damaged), turned legs & posts,
original white paint w/smoked
decoration & black striping, early
19th c., 16½ x 19¾", 33" h. plus
gallery (some paint wear)........ 425.00
Washstand, Rococo, lacquer, circular
basin stand raised on three incurved supports above the balloon-
form body raised on short pierced
cabriole legs decorated in green,
brown & iron-red w/flowers & fantastic birds & an Oriental figure on
yellow ground, Venice, Italy,
mid-18th c., 17" d., 35½" h. 5,500.00

Federal Style Stand

Federal-Style one-drawer stand, inlaid mahogany, rectangular top
w/inlaid edge & canted corners
above a skirt w/drawer & central
rectangular inlaid panel, square
tapering legs w/satinwood bellflower inlay, second half 19th c.,
18¾" w., 28½" h. (ILLUS.).......1,540.00
Federal country-style two-drawer
stand, bird's-eye & tiger stripe
maple, rectangular top w/inset
rounded corners above two draw-

ers w/bird's-eye maple fronts &
wooden mushroom knobs on
baluster- and ring-turned legs,
New England, first quarter
19th c., 18 x 22", 29" h.......... 990.00
Hepplewhite country-style one-
drawer stand, cherry, rectangular
one-board top overhanging apron
w/single dovetailed drawer,
square tapered legs, early 19th c.,
20¼ x 20½", 28" h. (refinished) .. 875.00
Sheraton country-style one-drawer
stand, curly maple, rectangular
top slightly overhanging deep
apron w/single deep drawer
w/clear lacy glass knob, finely
turned legs w/numerous ring
turnings above vase-turned segment above ring-turned & button
feet, early 19th c., 18 x 25½",
28½" h. (refinished) 950.00

STOOLS

Federal Mahogany Footstool

Country-style painted & decorated
footstool, rectangular top painted
brown & decorated w/red & black
vine & flowerhead stenciling,
highlighted w/red striping, over
similarly decorated flaring legs
joined by stretchers, 19th c.,
8 x 13", 5" h. 247.50
Country-style painted & decorated
footstool, rectangular top
w/shaped skirt decorated at center w/polychrome compass & at
sides w/pinstripes, on shaped
splayed legs, painted green, late
19th - early 20th c., 14¾" l.,
7" h. 522.50
Country-style footstool, poplar, rectangular top w/deeply scalloped
aprons, bootjack legs, worn, old
dark finish, 8 x 14¾"............ 110.00
Federal country-style footstool,
painted & stenciled wood, rectangular top w/bowed ends above a
shaped skirt on bracket feet,
decorated w/rosewood graining &
gilt-bronze stenciling, New
England, 1820-30, 21" l., 6" h. 187.00

Federal footstools, mahogany, upholstered rectangular top above
plain skirt on baluster- and ring-
turned legs w/green-painted ball
feet, early 19th c., 9¼ x 12¾",
9" h., pr. (ILLUS. of one) 770.00

George II stool, mahogany, rectangular overupholstered seat, cabriole legs carved at the knees w/a
sunflower & acanthus leaves, pad
feet, England, mid-18th c., 17 x 21"
top, 18" h. 5,500.00

Joint stool, oak, thumb-molded rectangular top over a channel-
molded frame, columnar legs
joined by a box stretcher, 18" w.,
19½" h. 605.00

Milk stool, pine, circular top
w/shaped handle, raised on
flared dipped legs, retains traces
of original pale blue paint, early
19th c., 13¾" l., 12¼" h. 137.50

Mission-style (Arts & Crafts movement) footstool, oak, leather-
covered square top w/flared feet,
red decal mark of Gustav Stickley, No. 302, ca. 1905-06,
11¾" w., 4½" h. 990.00

Russian Neoclassical Stool

Neoclassical "curule" stool, parcel-
gilt fruitwood, upholstered seat
flanked by upper supports &
arched legs joined by turned baluster-shaped stretchers highlighted
w/gilding, applied giltwood flowerheads & paterae & giltwood paw
feet, Russia, early 19th c.
(ILLUS.) 2,200.00

Piano stool, hardwood, scrolling
crest on tall back w/bobbin- and
spiral-turned stiles flanking turned
spindles & large central lyre-
shaped splat, round adjustable
seat on base w/four slightly
arched legs ending in brass &
glass ball-and-claw feet joined by
turned stretchers radiating from

Decorative Piano Stool

turned center post, ca. 1900
(ILLUS.). 297.00

Piano stool, late Classical Revival,
mahogany, rectangular swiveling
adjustable top w/upholstered slip
seat w/elaborately carved leafage
ending in scrolls on two sides,
resting on a turned pedestal
w/four acanthus leaf-carved legs
terminating in carved paw feet,
probably New York, ca. 1835,
14½ x 15½" top, 18" h.
(refinished, casters missing) 440.00

Windsor country-style footstool,
painted & decorated, oval top,
tapering round splayed legs, worn
red & black graining, 8 x 11",
7½" h. 85.00

Windsor country-style stool, painted
finish, round seat on bamboo-
turned legs, green paint, early
19th c., 16½" h. 302.50

TABLES

Chippendale Tea Table

Altar table, rectangular paneled top
above an openwork apron of
keyfret bands above beaded sup-

ports & transverse open panels,
China, 19th c., 17 x 39 x 67" 825.00

Art Nouveau two-tier table, fruitwood, top inlaid in the shape of a
trefoil flower blossom, joined by
carved legs to a triangular tier
w/galleried sides below, branded
"L. Majorelle," France, 20¾" w.
top, 29½" h. 2,860.00

Cafe-type table, wood & cast iron,
round wood top w/wear & stains
& many scorch marks from
cigarettes, octagonal cast-iron
pedestal base w/narrow rings,
base marked "Brunswick, Balke,
Collender Co., Chicago," 46" d.,
29½" h. (underside braced) 400.00

Chippendale card table, carved
mahogany, molded rectangular top
lifting above a conforming skirt
w/a single cockbeaded drawer &
arched molded skirt centering a
carved foliate pendant, cabriole
legs w/acanthus-carved knees &
ball-and-claw feet, 17 x 34",
29½" h. 3,740.00

Chippendale Style drop-leaf table,
mahogany, rectangular top
flanked by 13¼" w. drop leaves,
square molded legs, paper label
of Kittinger Company, 20th century reproduction, 14 x 43¾" plus
leaves, 29¼" h. 265.00

Chippendale tilt-top tea table,
mahogany, round dished top tilting
on birdcage support, ring-turned
column w/suppressed ball above
tripod base w/cabriole legs ending
in snake feet, Pennsylvania,
18th c., 28" d., 29" h. (minor
repairs & restoration) 5,500.00

Chippendale tilt-top tea table, walnut, circular dished top tilting on
birdcage support, baluster- and
ring-turned standard on tripod
base w/cabriole legs ending in
snake feet, Pennsylvania, ca. 1780,
repair to one leg, 28½" d.,
28½" h. (ILLUS.) 4,125.00

Country-style drop-leaf dining table,
curly maple, rectangular two-board
top w/two wide single board drop
leaves, round turned legs, old
worn finish, 21¼ x 46" w/19½" w.
leaves, 29¾" h. 1,650.00

Country-style work table, poplar,
rectangular top w/breadboard
ends widely overhangs deep
nailed apron, square tapering
legs, old scrubbed finish,
33½ x 52½", 28¾" h. 375.00

Empire, American (Classical) card
table, gilt mahogany, rectangular
top w/cut front corners w/hinged

leaf swiveling above a well w/mar-
bleized paper lining, conforming
plain frieze & four pineapple-,
swirl- and ring-turned supports on
acanthus-carved legs w/gilt trim
ending in animal paw feet, on
casters, probably New York, ca.
1825, 18 x 36", 29½" h. (some
minor veneer repair)...........2,420.00

Empire, American drop-leaf "breakfast" table, carved mahogany,
rectangular top w/two drop
leaves above a plain skirt over a
leaf-carved baluster standard,
leaf-carved paw feet, New York,
1830-40, 39½" w., 28½" h........ 418.00

Empire, American (Classical) pier
table, gilt-metal mounted & decorated mahogany, rectangular white
veined marble top above a frieze
centering a stenciled acanthus
motif above columns w/gilt-metal
capitals, carved columns behind
centering a mirror plate all on
shaped lower shelf, acanthus-form
gilded feet, Philadelphia, ca. 1820,
20 x 38¼", 40¼" h. 6,875.00

Federal card table, flamed birch-
inlaid mahogany, oblong top w/ser-
pentine front & hinged leaf above
a conforming shaped frieze centering an oval-inlaid panel, on reeded
tapering round legs ending in
tapered feet, northeastern New
England, ca. 1810, 16¼ x 35",
30" h. (repair to rear swing rail &
two front legs) 4,400.00

Federal card table, mahogany, rectangular top w/inset rounded corners above a conforming mahog-
any-veneered skirt, square tapering legs, New England, first quarter 19th c., 37 x 38¼" (open),
29" h. 1,980.00

Federal dining table, mahogany, two-
part pedestal, comprising two
D-shaped end sections, each
w/hinged leaf above a ring-turned
standard on reeded down-curving
legs ending in brass casters,
w/one extra leaf, attributed to
John Needles, Baltimore, Maryland, ca. 1820, 9' 9" l. extended,
28¾" h. 13,200.00

Federal dressing table, grained &
stenciled pine, rectangular top
w/molded edge w/set-back two-
drawer box w/high scrolled back,
brass mounts & turned ball feet
over single long drawer above
turned, tapering & decorated legs,
overall black & red graining to
simulate rosewood, gold striping
& gilt-bronze stenciling, glass

knobs, New England, ca. 1820,
16 x 33¾", 31¾" h. 1,045.00
Federal drop-leaf dining table,
mahogany, rectangular top w/two
rectangular leaves above a plain
frieze on square tapering legs,
ca. 1800, 48¼" l., 62¼" w. ex-
tended, 29" h. 1,980.00
Federal Pembroke table, maple,
rectangular top w/shaped drop
leaves above a single drawer,
square tapering legs, probably
Pennsylvania, 1790-1810, open
37½" w., 27½" h. 1,760.00
Federal side table, inlaid curly
maple, oblong shaped top w/line-
inlaid edge & outset rounded corners centering five inlaid circles
above a line-inlaid molded drawer
w/cross-banded skirt raised on
molded line-inlaid square tapering
legs, appears to retain original
brass bail handle, New England,
ca. 1800, 17¼ x 20", 26¾" h. . . .38,500.00
Federal work table, bird's-eye maple,
square top centering an ink-drawn
panel depicting a lady sewing on a
porch & young girl seated in garden landscape, sides w/further
ink-drawn decoration, the front &
back w/landscapes & sides w/fruit
baskets, case w/two drawers w/or-
nate brass pulls, on four scrolling
supports centering a turned knop,
reeded sabre legs, brass paw feet
w/casters, supports & legs w/vari-
ous ink-drawn animals against a
black ground, Massachusetts,
1815-25, 16¼" sq. top, 29½" h. . .6,600.00
George III library table, mahogany,
leather-lined drum top above four
drawers & four false drawers
w/lions' mask pulls on a columnar
pedestal & quadripartite base
w/ribbed splayed legs & brass feet
w/casters, England, late 18th c.,
37¼" d. .9,900.00
Hepplewhite sewing table, inlaid
mahogany, hexagonal lift lid
opening to fitted interior w/lidded
compartments & lift-out tray, pull-
out work drawer fitted w/uphol-
stered bag, square tapering legs
w/turned cross stretcher, England,
21¾" w. top, 28¾" h. 750.00
Hepplewhite Style Pembroke table,
inlaid mahogany, rectangular top
flanked by rounded drop leaves,
apron w/curved ends & one end
drawer w/keyhole, square tapering legs w/inlay end in spade
feet, drawer marked "Williamsburg Restoration - Kittinger,"
20th c., 21 x 33" w/13" leaves,

30¼" h. (damaged veneer on
drawer front) 450.00

Early Hutch Table

Hutch (or chair) table, carved pine,
circular top tilting above a base
w/sliding lid opening to a well,
the shaped sides raised on shoe
feet, New England, second half
18th c., lid replaced, 49" d., 28" h.
(ILLUS.) 2,750.00
Hutch table, two-board circular top
tilting above rectangular arms
w/rounded terminals, the rectangular seat raised on chamfered
square legs joined by a stretcher,
painted overall in grey, New
England, late 18th c., 4' d., 26" h.
(flaking to paint) 4,125.00

Ornate Carved Center Table

Indo-Chinese center table, carved
hardwood, circular top inset w/red
marble over a heavily pierce-
carved frieze, cylindrical support
& stepped base ornately carved
w/leaves, birds, pavilions, etc.,
Foo dog feet, 19th c., 44" d.
(ILLUS.) 4,400.00
Louisiana side table, cherry, rec-
tangular top slightly overhanging
deep apron w/scalloped edge &
small drawer, simple cabriole legs,
plantation-made, Alexandria,
Louisiana, late 18th c. 10,450.00
Mission-style (Arts & Crafts move-
ment) drop-leaf table, oak, rectan-

gular top w/drop leaves w/cut
corners supported by gateleg,
branded mark of Gustav Stickley &
remnants of paper label, Model
No. 638, ca. 1912, 42" l., 30" h. . . .3,080.00
Mission-style (Arts & Crafts move-
ment) library table, oak, rectangular top overhanging apron w/two
drawers w/metal pulls, elongated
corbels under apron running down
to lower shelf fitting into side
stretchers, red decal & paper label
of Gustav Stickley, Model No. 614,
ca. 1907, 29½ x 42," 29¾" h.
(refinished) 1,320.00

Mission-Style "Book" Table

Mission-style (Arts & Crafts movement) library "book" table, oak,
nearly square top overhanging
base w/open book shelf & slatted
panel on each side, L. & J.G.
Stickley, ca. 1910 (ILLUS.) 9,900.00
Mission-style (Arts & Crafts move-
ment) side table, oak, rectangular
top w/four flat rails framing
twelve four-inch green Grueby
Pottery tiles over arched skirt
& lower rectangular shelf w/keyed
tenons, slight splay to legs, dark
finish, unsigned but attributed to
Gustav Stickley, ca. 1902-03,
19½ x 23¾", 26" h. (minor rough-
ness) 53,900.00
Modern style game table, blond-
wood, circular top w/inset muslin-
covered surface continuing to an
inward-sloping apron set w/five
drawers w/grooved fronts, each
fitted w/two circular receptacles
& a rectangular cavity, raised on
deeply inset octagonal apron & five
tapering molded legs ending in
pad feet, by Gio Ponti, ca. 1950,
46" d., 31" h. 1,100.00
Pool table, "Manhattan" model,
Brunswick, 1880's, 4' 6" x 9' (com-
pletely restored) 18,000.00
Queen Anne dressing table, oak, rec-
tangular top w/cut corners &

molded edge, apron w/dovetailed
drawer, slender cabriole legs terminating in diamond-shaped feet
w/pads, England, 16¾ x 29" top,
28" h. 2,900.00

Queen Anne Dressing Table

Queen Anne kneehole dressing
table, mahogany, rectangular top
w/notched ends above a single
molded drawer & two tiers of
three drawers centering a hinged
recessed cupboard door & a valanced secret drawer, bracket feet,
original brass & escutcheons,
coastal New England, 1730-60,
16¾ x 31", 31½" h. (ILLUS.) 18,700.00
Queen Anne tea table, cherry & walnut, rectangular breadboard overhanging top w/exposed tenons
above four block-turned tapering
legs ending in pad feet joined by
a molded straight skirt containing
a thumb-molded drawer, fine old
color, probably Rhode Island,
ca. 1760, 23 x 30", 26" h. (one
pad chipped) 33,000.00
"Sawbuck" table, painted wood, rec-
tangular long three-board top
above an X-form base w/medial
stretcher & angled supports, traces
of paint, 19th c., 34¾ x 7' 8",
28" h. 8,250.00

New England "Sawbuck" Table

"Sawbuck" table, pine & ash, rectangular overhanging two-board

top w/breadboard ends over a
partially enclosed X-stretcher
base, stretchers w/beaded edges,
old finish, probably New England,
early 19th c., 26¼ x 43½",
28½" h. (ILLUS.) 495.00

Tavern table, Early American
country-style, maple & pine, oval
pine top above a plain deep apron
on turned slightly swelled legs
ending in button feet, New
England, ca. 1780-1800, 21¾ x 27¾",
28" h. (some repair to tops of legs,
top reset) 2,750.00

Tavern table, painted wood, rectangular top w/batten edges above a
single drawer, baluster- and ring-
turned legs w/turned feet, painted red, 19th c., 33 x 48¾",
29¾" h. (restoration to paint) 990.00

Tavern table, Queen Anne, walnut,
rectangular top widely overhanging
deep apron w/three molded drawers, on circular legs ending in pad
feet, Pennsylvania, second half
18th c., 32½ x 57", 29" h. (top
replaced, some restorations to
feet) 3,025.00

Tavern table, Windsor style, turned
wood, round two-board pine top
w/dark brown patina on underside
& scrubbed top finish, hardwood
base w/four vase- and ring-turned
legs joined by two sets of simple
turned box stretchers, one set near
the top, the other near the base,
worn old red paint on base, late
18th or early 19th c., 29½" d.,
24½" h. 4,700.00

Oak Dining Table

Turn-of-the-Century dining table,
oak, round top opening to accept
leaves above square split pedestal
w/rounded braces resting on
X-base w/rounded feet on
casters, ca. 1900, 45" d. (ILLUS.) .. 401.50

Victorian console table, carved rosewood, D-shaped serpentine &
lobed top over deep scalloped
apron boldly carved w/center

Victorian Console Table

shell & scrolls flanked by leafy
scrolls along edge, four heavy
S-scroll carved legs joined by
boldly carved stretcher w/wide
shell- and leaf-carved pediment
at center, all mounted on shaped
plinth base, attributed to Alexander Roux, ca. 1850 (ILLUS.) 4,675.00

Victorian dining table, mahogany,
extending top w/thumb-molded
edges w/D-ends, on molded cabriole legs ending in claw-and-ball
feet, possibly American-made,
third quarter 19th c., w/two additional later leaves, 7' 5" l. extended, 29¾" h. 825.00

Victorian game table, Renaissance
Revival substyle, ebonized &
parcel-gilt wood, rectangular
round-ended top w/gilt-bronze
beaded molding incised w/check-
erboard & foliate scrolls over single drawer, raised on two turned
fluted supports w/bipartite scroll-
incised legs, ca. 1865, 27½" l.,
30" h........................ 550.00

Victorian Baroque Library Table

Victorian library table, Baroque style,
quartersawn oak, oval top over
wide apron resting on four full-
figure carved seated griffins on
plinth base resting on large bun
feet, ca. 1900 (ILLUS.) 2,750.00

Victorian parlor center table, Renaissance Revival substyle, mother-of-
pearl, walnut & parquetry, molded
circular top variously inlaid w/over-
lapped chequer & cube pattern,
above similarly inlaid frieze, above

Victorian Inlaid Parlor Table
ring-turned stem w/ball finial centering inlaid roundel-carved splayed legs headed by urn finials, on casters, late 19th c., 36" d., 29" h. (ILLUS.) 2,090.00

Belter Parlor Center Table
Victorian parlor center table, Rococo substyle, carved & laminated rosewood, shaped white marble "turtle" top over conforming grape cluster & vine-carved shaped apron on slender cabriole legs boldly carved w/fruit clusters at the knees, legs joined by scrolling X-stretcher w/central urn w/floral bouquet, marble bears script notation "J.H. Belter," John Henry Belter, New York, 1850-60 (ILLUS.) 71,500.00
Victorian side table, Renaissance Revival substyle, walnut, rectangular white marble top w/notched corners above conforming apron w/burl panels, center roundels & carved drops, four angular C-scroll flat legs, each pair joined by large block w/large turned finial & drop, the blocks connected at center by large carved roundel w/mushroom finial, on casters, ca. 1880 (ILLUS. top next column) 550.00
Victorian writing table, Renaissance Revival substyle, walnut, rectan-

gular top w/inset brown leather over a pair of drawers, raised on turned & blocked legs by H-form stretcher, splayed feet, ca. 1880, 30 x 46" 192.50

Victorian Side Table
Wicker table, rectangular mahogany top above deep wicker skirt w/square cut-out accents, open lower shelf, flaring legs terminating in ball feet, early 20th c., 20 x 54¼", 30" h. 825.00
William & Mary stretcher-base table, painted pine, rectangular top w/batten ends over a channel-molded apron, ball-turned legs w/double ball-turned feet, joined by ball-turned box stretchers, later black paint, England, early 18th c., 20¼ x 30½", 23¾" h. 1,760.00
William IV breakfast table, brass-inlaid rosewood, circular top w/crossbanded edge tilting above a gadrooned standard raised on a circular beaded plinth above four leaf-carved & brass-inlaid downward-swept legs ending in brass feet on casters, England, ca. 1830, 4' 3" d., 28" h. 4,950.00

WARDROBES & ARMOIRES
Armoire, Arts & Crafts style, inlaid mahogany, rectangular molded cornice over mirrored arch-topped cabinet doors flanking central section of inlaid cabinet enclosing five sliding shelves over single drawer, molded base w/block feet, mother-of-pearl & fruitwood inlay, labeled on back "GOODALL, LAMB & HEIGHWAY Ld. Cabinet makers & upholsterers, Manchester," England, ca. 1905, 7' 2" h. 660.00
Armoire, Art Nouveau, mahogany & pollard elm, undulating top w/an organically molded cornice above triple-panel sides & a single tapestry-lined door flanked by

shaped end panels over a base
drawer, the molded stiles continuing to "knuckled" swept molded
legs ending in pointed pad feet,
France, ca. 1900-20, 4' 6½" w.,
7' 2" h. 1,100.00

Armoire, Louis XV, carved walnut,
arched molded crestrail above pair
of conforming foliate-carved
paneled doors opening to shelves,
continuing to a scrolling carved
skirt, scrolled feet, mid-18th c.,
5' 3" w., 8' 8" h. (restorations) . . .4,400.00

Victorian Armoire by Meeks

Armoire, Victorian, Rococo substyle,
rosewood, arched molded cornice
w/floral reserve & urn form finials
over conforming mirrored door enclosing shelves & drawers, drawer
w/floral reserve over shaped
apron, bracket feet, drawer stenciled "J. & J.W. Meeks Makers
No. 11 Vesey St. New York," ca.
1850, missing veneer & pieces,
4' 1½" w., 8' 2" h. (ILLUS.) 8,800.00

Armoire, walnut, double thumb-
molded cornice above two
paneled doors w/arched mullions,
raised on bracket feet, Midwest,
second quarter 19th c., 4' 7½" w.,
7' 5" h. 440.00

Schrank (Pennsylvania-German version of a massive wardrobe), William & Mary, walnut, molded
cornice w/Greek key frieze above
two paneled cupboard doors
w/original brass hinges & engraved brass hardware flanked by
molded pilasters over an applied
molding above two sham thumb-
molded short drawers over a
molded base, ball-turned feet,
probably Lancaster County, Penn-

sylvania, 18th c., 6' 2½" w.,
7' 5" h. (restoration to feet) 7,700.00

Wardrobe, American Empire (Classical), stenciled & gilt mahogany,
two-part construction: the upper
section having a removable cornice
w/arched frieze centering stenciled fruit; the lower section comprising a pair of hinged doors
opening to an interior w/two long
drawers below, free-standing columns flanking, on eagle-carved
hairy paw feet, New York, ca.
1825, 5' 6" w., 7' 9" h. (some
restoration to gilding) 7,700.00

Country-style Wardrobe

Wardrobe, country-style, maple,
molded rectangular cornice above
a single cupboard door opening to
shelves, long drawer below,
raised on tapering square legs,
southern Illinois, third quarter
19th c., 2' 10" w., 6' 7½" h.
(ILLUS.). 715.00

Wardrobe, painted & decorated poplar, cove-molded cornice above
two paneled doors over two short
drawers, paneled sides, cut-out
feet, original brown graining,
3' 8" w. 700.00

Wardrobe, Victorian corner country-
style, pine, molded rectangular
top applied w/a scrolled cresting
over a paneled door w/double
tombstone moldings opening to
shelves, a single drawer below,
flanked by canted corners applied
at the top w/stylized scrolled
carving, the sides continuing to
form the simple bracket feet,
Platte, Nebraska, 19th c.,
3' 10" w., 7' h. 467.50

Wardrobe, Victorian Eastlake substyle, walnut & burl walnut,
stepped molded cornice above a

cushion frieze over an arched panel centered by a carved flower-head issuing sprays of leaves over a single glazed door flanked by columns at the sides all above a pair of incised panel drawers w/rectangular brass bail pulls, plinth base, ca. 1870, 46" w., 92" h. 1,100.00

Zoar "kas," walnut, rectangular top w/cut front corners on deep molded cornice above conforming case w/cut corners framing single wide four-paneled cupboard door w/wrought-iron rat-tail hinges, lock w/key & centered brass pull on a large embossed florette, opening to interior w/one shelf & two rows of wooden hooks, flat molded apron on short tapered feet, old dark finish, on casters (one missing), Zoar, Ohio, 19th c., 3' 6" w., 6' 2" h. (minor age cracks, some edge damage) 3,800.00

WHATNOTS & ETAGERES

Rosalie Pattern Etagere

Etagere, George III, walnut, three stepped shelves above two cupboard drawers on bracket feet, w/brass carrying handles, ca. 1800, 23½ x 31", 46" h. 3,700.00

Etagere, painted pine & poplar, turned three-quarter gallery above three rectangular shelves joined by ring-turned slightly swelling stiles, turned feet, painted to resemble rosewood, New England, ca. 1820, 35½" w., 43" h. 495.00

Etagere, Victorian, Rococo substyle, carved & laminated rosewood, high arched crest carved w/roses & other flowers, foliage, grapes & scrolls, central mirror flanked by side mirrors & shelves, white marble top serpentine base, original brass casters, "Rosalie" patt.,

attributed to John Henry Belter, New York City, ca. 1850, 5' 6" w., 7' 1" h. (ILLUS.)...............19,250.00

Whatnot, Regency, rosewood, three rectangular tiers w/baluster-turned supports, the middle tier fitted w/a drawer, on turned feet & casters, England, early 19th c., 39" h. 4,180.00

(End of Furniture Section)

GAMES & GAME BOARDS

19th Century Checkerboard

Addition & Subtraction, Cincinnati Game Co., 1902................. $25.00
Adventures of Tom Sawyer & Huck Finn, Stoll & Edwards, 1925....... 125.00
Auto Race board game, Milton Bradley Co., 1922 .... 45.00
Base-Ball (Game of) board game, McLoughlin Bros., 1886 .... 875.00
Blox-O board game, Lubbers & Bell Mfg. Co., 1923 .... 18.00
Bo Peep board game, McLoughlin Bros., 1895 .... 240.00
Buffalo Bill (Game of) board game, Parker Bros., 1898.............. 85.00
Checkerboard, pine, rectangular panel painted in red & black within yellow borders, against a black ground w/geometric framework, reverse painted in yellow w/a "merels" board within yellow painted geometric borders, flaking to paint, Boonville, Missouri, ca. 1880, 15¼ x 26" (ILLUS.)...... 522.50
Chestnut Burrs, Fireside Game Co., 1896 .... 28.00
Chinese Checkers board game,

Gotham Pressed Steel Co., 1938, board & original Akro Agate marbles in original box (two marbles missing) 23.00

Chiromagica mechanical game, McLoughlin Bros., ca. 1870 .... 400.00

Cities card game, Alderman-Fairchild (All-Fair), 1932 .... 25.00

Dig, Parker Bros., 1940 .... 15.00

Dixie Land (Game of) card game, Fireside Game Co., 1897 .... 95.00

Dominoes, ivory w/inlaid ebony dots, set of 28 in box w/inlaid edging & star on lid, 5 5/8" l. 120.00

Errand Boy or Failure and Successs board game, McLoughlin Bros., 1891 .... 150.00

Fibber McGee and the Wistful Vista Mystery, Milton Bradley Co., 1940 .... 27.00

Fish Pond (The Improved Game of), game of skill, w/fishing poles, numbered fish & playing board resembling pond, McLoughlin Bros., 1890 .... 95.00

Foolish Questions card game, illustrated by Rube Goldberg, Wallie Dorr Co., 1924-26 .... 10.00

Halma board game, E.I. Horsman, May 29, 1888 patent date, complete w/board & instructions 37.50

Hippodrome board game, Tokalon Series, E. O. Clark, ca. 1900 ..... 52.00

Innocence Abroad (The Amusing Game of) board game, Parker Bros., 1888 .... 330.00

Jeu de Course, horse racing game, France, ca. 1895 .... 500.00

Louisa (Game of), McLoughlin Bros., 1888 .... 75.00

Mahjong set, ivorene counters, racks, dice & chips contained in leatherette suitcase, w/rules, 1939, 19¾" l. case 33.00

Monopoly board game, Parker Bros., 1946 edition 25.00

Nancy Drew Mystery board game, Parker Bros., 1957............... 17.00

Office Boy (The) board game, Parker Bros., 1889................ 150.00

Old Glory card game, Parker Bros., 1899 .... 88.00

Old Maid and Batchelor (Game of) card game, Peter G. Thompson, ca. 1880 .... 55.00

Our Bird Friends card game, Sarah D. Dudley, ca. 1910 .... 27.00

Pin the Tail on the Donkey, lithograph on muslin, Saalfield, 1928 .. 15.00

Quien Sabe card game, Parker Bros., 1906 .... 27.00

Ring toss, wooden, hand-made board w/painted numerals on worn black background, turned,

inserted pegs, picture frame edge molding, 25 x 25" (some edge damage) 175.00

Rival Doctors board game, McLoughlin Bros., 1893 .... 60.00

Squadron Insignia, Alderman-Fairchild (All-Fair), 1940's 39.00

Steeple Chase (Game of) board game, Parker Bros., 1895 .... 85.00

Table-top Parlour Croquet Game, rectangular top opening to a divided interior w/color printed label, w/eight mallets, six balls, two cones, metal bracket & arches & two bolts of tape, turned wood, Bliss, late 19th c., 18" l. box 192.05

Telegraph Boy (Game of the) board game, McLoughlin Bros., 1888 .... 230.00

Telegraph Messenger board game, J. H. Singer, ca. 1890 .... 85.00

Trap-Shot (Game of), Parker Bros., ca. 1901 .... 55.00

Wall Street Card Game

Wall Street, The Game of Speculation card game, Milton Bradley, 1933 (ILLUS.) 20.00

War of Nations board game, Milton Bradley, ca. 1915................ 90.00

Wings, The Air Mail Game card game, Parker Bros., 1928 .... 88.00

Yankee Doodle board game, Parker Bros., 1895 .... 410.00

GARDEN
FOUNTAINS & ORNAMENTS

Ornamental garden or yard fountains, urns and figures often enhanced the formal plantings on spacious lawns of mansion-sized dwellings during the late 19th and early 20th century. While fountains were usually reserved for the lawns of estates, even modest homes often had a latticework arbor or cast iron urn in the yard. Today garden enthusiasts look for these ornamental pieces to lend an aura of elegance to their landscaping.

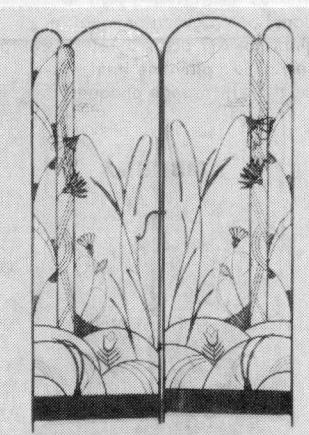

Decorative Wrought Iron Gates

Bird bath, cast iron, two sections: the
upper cast in the form of a putto
w/upraised arms supporting a
large shell, flowering shrubs at his
feet; the lobed octagonal basin
raised on an acanthus & cabo-
chon-cast octagonal baluster standard, painted green, inscribed "Salin
Fondeur," France, 43" d., overall
7' h. $3,300.00

Gates, wrought iron, scalloped top,
body pierced & wrought w/fanciful
flowers on undulating stems growing amid geometric trellises, fluted
rectangular band at bottom, possibly Lansha Studios, America, ca.
1930, each panel 23 1/8" w.,
5' 8½" h., pr. (ILLUS.) 2,200.00

Jardiniere, cast stone, in the form
of a scantily clad putto upholding
a lobed basin, rising from a cast
rockwork base, 43" h. 495.00

Ornament, marble, model of a lamb,
standing animal w/body supported
by clump of lilies, rectangular platform base, American, mid-19th c.,
23" l., 21½" h. (weathered) 1,320.00

Ornament, painted cast iron, model
of a Retriever dog, walking dog
w/raised head, old cream paint,
J. W. Fiske, New York, ca. 1870,
59½" l., 30½" h. 7,700.00

Planters, cast iron, shallow hemispherical form applied w/molded
masks, on a square foot, 19th c.,
31" h., pr. 1,540.00

Urns, cast iron, campana form
w/leaf-molded lip, the bowl w/ivy,
the standard molded w/ivy leaves
& juniper berries & basketweaving,
resting on square base standing on
paneled plinth, painted white,
stamped "J. W. Fiske, No. 21 & 23,

Barclay Street, New York," 19th c.,
21" d., overall 36¼" h., pr. 1,320.00

Urn, cov., composition, Neoclassical
style w/semi-wrythen form molded w/a frieze of acanthus &
w/ram's head handles, domed
cover, on a rising circular foot &
square base w/an impressed Latin
inscription, 28" h. 715.00

GLASS

AGATA

Agata Spooner

*Agata was patented by Joseph Locke of the
New England Glass Co. in 1887. The application of a mineral stain left a mottled effect
on the surface of the article. It was applied
chiefly to the Wild Rose (Peach Blow) line but
sometimes was applied as a border on pale
opaque green. In production for a short time,
it is scarce. Items listed below are of the Wild
Rose line unless otherwise noted.*

Celery vase, scalloped square top
on slightly tapering body, glossy
finish, 6½" h. $715.00

Lemonade tumbler, tapered, applied
curlicue handle, 5 1/8" h. 1,350.00

Spittoon, lady's, squat round body
w/ruffled & scalloped rim,
5 3/8" d., 2¾" h. 550.00

Spooner, round body w/flared & ruffled rim, heavy overall mottling,
4½" h. (ILLUS.) 1,350.00

Spooner, green opaque, 3¾" h. 945.00

Toothpick holder, bulbous
w/pinched-in scalloped rim 795.00

AKRO AGATE

*This marbled ware was made by the Akro
Agate Company in Clarksburg, West Virginia, between 1932 and 1951 and most arti-*

cles bear on the reverse side the likeness of a crow flying through a capital letter A. The majority of these pieces are small.

Colonial Lady Powder Jar

Basket, marbleized orange swirls in white opaque $119.00
Bowl, cereal, marbleized green swirls in white opaque 16.00
Creamer, child's playtime item, Concentric Ring patt., blue 9.00
Cup, child's playtime item, Octagonal patt., blue 10.00
Cup & saucer, child's playtime item, Interior Panel patt., green opaque 14.75
Lamp, marbleized orange swirls in white opaque 175.00
Plate, 4¼" d., child's playtime item, Octagonal patt., blue 2.00
Plate, child's playtime item, Octagonal-O patt., marbleized lemonade & oxblood 10.00
Powder jar, Colonial Lady cover, powder blue opaque (ILLUS.) 67.00
Powder jar, Scottie dog cover, green opaque 90.00
Powder jar, Scottie dog cover, powder blue opaque 75.00
Smoker's set, marbleized green swirls in white opaque, 5 pcs. 28.00
Sugar bowl, cov., child's playtime item, Octagonal patt., white opaque top, yellow opaque base 12.00
Teapot, cov., child's playtime item, Octagonal patt., open handle, blue, large 12.50
Tea set, child's playtime item, Chiquita patt., green opaque, 6 pcs. 35.00
Tea set, child's playtime item, Interior Panel patt., blue, in original box, 8 pcs. 65.00
Tea set, child's playtime item, Octagonal patt., varied opaque colors, in original box, 16 pcs. . . . 90.00
Tea set, child's playtime item, Interi-

or Panel patt., green opaque, in original box, 17 pcs. 155.00
Tumbler, child's playtime item, Octagonal patt., orange opaque 15.00

AMBERINA

Plated Amberina Condiment Set

Amberina was developed in the late 1880's by the New England Glass Company and a pressed version was made by Hobbs, Brockunier & Company (under license from the former). A similar ware, called Rose Amber, was made by the Mt. Washington Glass Works. Amberina-Rose Amber shades from amber to deep red or fuchsia and cut and plated (lined with creamy white) examples were also made. The Libbey Glass Company briefly revived blown Amberina, using modern shapes, in 1917.

Basket, ruffled edge, applied amber handle, Swirl patt., 5 x 6½", 7¾" h. $245.00
Bowl, 4¾" d., 4½" h., rectangular rim w/applied amber rigaree, applied amber handles & feet, Swirl patt., enameled gold flowers & leaves 265.00
Bowl, 5 7/8 x 9½" oval, 5 5/8" h., melon-ribbed, enameled pink, white & yellow flowers, branch w/green leaves & lacy gold foliage, gold top trim, rich cranberry shaded to olive amber 295.00
Bowl, 6¼ x 8½" oval, 7 1/8" h., applied amber feet & ruffled rim, gold & blue florals, gold birds & bug decoration 350.00
Bowl, 10¾" d., 8 1/8" h., fluted rim, amber wafer foot, Swirl patt., heavily enameled gold flowers, berries & tree branch w/leaves . . . 365.00
Celery vase, square scalloped top, polished pontil, Venetian Diamond patt., Mt. Washington Glass Company, 4" d. base, 6¼" h. 335.00
Celery vase, square scalloped top,

Inverted Thumbprint patt., amber
shaded to deep fuchsia, New
England Glass Co., 6½" h. 375.00
Condiment set, two-bottle, Plated
Amberina ribbed salt & pepper
shakers, New England Glass Co.,
original silver plate center-handle
frame marked "Toronto SP Company - 083," shakers 4" h.
(ILLUS.) 1,980.00
Creamer & sugar bowl, square top
w/applied shell handles, Diamond
Quilted patt., pr................ 395.00
Cuspidor, lady's, optic ribbing,
shaded pale amber to violet fuchsia, 5¼" d., 2½" h. 280.00
Dish, cov., two applied amber handles, amber knob on cover, h.p.
heavy gold flowers, leaves &
branches, Swirl patt., 6" d.,
4½" h........................ 365.00
Ewer, w/facet-cut stopper, applied
reeded handle, Inverted Thumbprint patt., New England Glass
Co., 9" h. 145.00
Finger bowl, Swirl patt., New
England Glass Co., 4 3/8" d.,
2¾" h. 145.00
Pitcher, 5¾" h., round body
w/cylindrical neck, applied amber
reeded handle, polished pontil,
Coin Spot patt. (trace of exterior
wear) 192.50
Pitcher, milk, 6½" h., applied
reeded handle, Diamond Quilted
patt.......................... 140.00
Pitcher, water, 7½" h., 5" d., bulbous w/round mouth, applied amber handle, Inverted Thumbprint
patt.......................... 175.00
Pitcher, water, 7½" h., 5½" d., bulbous w/square mouth, applied
amber reeded handle, Inverted
Thumbprint patt., New England
Glass Co...................... 375.00
Pitcher, water, 7¾" h., 5 3/8" d.,
Reverse Amberina, bulbous
w/round mouth, applied clear
reeded handle, enameled lacy
green leaves & pink & blue flowers, the small flowers w/red or
green jewels, ground pontil 245.00
Pitcher, water, 8 1/8" h., 4 5/8" d.,
six-sided top, applied amber
reeded handle, Herringbone
patt.......................... 210.00
Pitcher, 8¼" h., square mouth, applied amber handle, polished pontil, Hobnail patt................ 412.50
Plate, 7" d., Daisy & Button patt. ... 305.00
Punch cup, Plated Amberina, slightly
ribbed bulging sides, applied transparent yellow C-scroll handle, New

Plated Amberina Punch Cup

England Glass Company, ca. 1900,
2¾" h. (ILLUS.) 1,650.00
Punch cup, applied amber reeded
handle, Inverted Thumbprint patt.,
2 5/8" d., 2¾" h. 110.00
Rose bowl, six-crimp top, applied
amber feet, Swirl patt., 9" d.,
6½" h........................ 325.00
Salt shaker, elongated Baby Thumbprint patt., old top 75.00
Sauce dish, Daisy & Button patt.,
5" sq. 115.00
Sugar bowl, cov., tabs on amber
base fit notches on cover, Daisy &
Button patt., 5½" h. (flake on
cover)........................ 535.00
Toothpick holder, Diamond Quilted
patt., deep fuchsia rim 225.00
Toothpick holder, tri-cornered rim,
Venetian Diamond patt. 210.00
Tumbler, Diamond Quilted patt.,
3¾" h........................ 195.00
Tumbler, Plated Amberina, ribbed,
New England Glass Company,
3¾" h........................1,590.00
Vases, 4 5/8" h., 4 1/8" d., applied
ruffled rim, applied amber foot,
Swirl patt., pr.................. 195.00
Vase, 7¾" h., lily-form, flared fold-
ed trefoil rim on thin-walled flute
set upon low pedestal foot 330.00
Vases, 10" h., 5 1/8" d., cylindrical,
Swirl patt., enameled pink &
white flowers w/green leaves,
gold trim around rim, pr. 335.00
Vase, 11" h., ruffled edge, molded
Optic patt., fitted in silver plate
holder w/three handles
w/garlands of flowers draped between them, raised on a flaring
baluster stem set on a domed
foot, base marked "Pairpoint Mfg.
Co.," ca. 1890 (frame replated) ... 220.00
Vase, 13" h., 6" d., cylindrical body
w/wide neck & fluted top, four
applied amber feet w/raised lion's
head at top of each foot, Swirl
patt., enameled blue & white
flowers w/gold leaves &
branches 495.00
Water set: 11½" h., 4¼" d. round
mouthed pitcher & five 5" h.
barrel-shaped tumblers; enameled
pink & white flowers, brown
leaves & lacy gold foliage,
6 pcs......................... 495.00

Amberina Water Set

Water set: 7½" h., 4 3/8" d. pitcher
w/applied amber handle & eight
3 3/8" h. footed tumblers; Swirl
patt., w/a 13" d. amber tray,
10 pcs. (ILLUS.).................. 395.00
Whimsey, hat-shaped, Expanded
Diamond patt., ground pontil,
3¼" d., 2 3/8" h. 145.00
Wine decanter w/original matching
stopper, bulbous body w/long
narrow neck & pedestal foot,
enameled pink & white flowers
w/blue centers & green decoration, 4½" d., 14" h. 235.00

ANIMALS

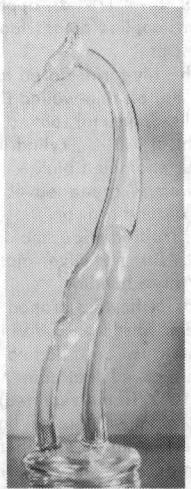

Heisey Giraffe

Americans evidently like to collect glass
animals and, for the past fifty years, American glass manufacturers have turned out a
wide variety of animals to please the buying
public. Some were produced for long periods
and some were later reproduced by other com-

panies, while others were made for only a
short period of time and are rare. We have not
included late productions in our listings and
have attempted to date the productions where
possible. Evelyn Zemel's book American
Glass Animals A to Z will be helpful to the
novice collector.

Angel Fish book end, clear, Ameri-
can Glass Co., 8¼" h. $40.00
Angel Fish book ends, clear, A.H.
Heisey & Co., 2¼ x 3½" wave
base, 7" h., pr. 165.00
Baby Bear, clear, New Martinsville
Glass Mfg. Co., 4¼" l., 3½" h.... 42.00
Bull, clear, A.H. Heisey & Co.,
1948-52, 4" h. 1,100.00
Chinese Pheasant, clear, Paden City
Glass Mfg. Co., 13¾" l., 5¾" h... 50.00
Deer standing, blue, Fostoria Glass
Co., 1 x 2" base, 4½" h. 35.00
Eagle book end, clear, Cambridge
Glass Co., 1964-68, 4½" base d.,
6" h. 70.00
Elephant w/trunk up & extended,
clear, A.H. Heisey & Co., 1944-53,
small, 5¼" l., 4½" h. 135.00
Elephant w/trunk up, clear, A.H.
Heisey & Co., 1944-53, large,
6½" l., 4¼" h. ....275.00 to 300.00
Elephant covered dish, clear, Co-
Operative Flint Glass Co.,
1927-30, 7½" l., 4¾" h. 40.00
Elephant stem bowl, opalescent, Lib-
bey Glass Co., 11" 275.00
Fish match holder, clear, A.H.
Heisey & Co., 3½" h. on wave
base 95.00
Giraffe w/head turned, clear, A.H.
Heisey & Co., 1942-52, 11" h.
(ILLUS.)........................ 160.00
Goose (Mallard) w/wings half up,
clear, A.H. Heisey & Co., 1942-53,
4½" h..................75.00 to 100.00
Horse Head book ends, clear, A.H.
Heisey & Co., 2¾ x 4¾" base,
7¼" h., pr..................... 195.00
Horse Head cigar box, clear, A.H.
Heisey & Co., 4½ x 6¼",
4½" h.................60.00 to 90.00
Horse Head cigarette box, cov.,
clear, A.H. Heisey & Co.,
3¼ x 4", 3½" h. 60.00
Horse rearing book ends, amber,
L.E. Smith, 1940's, 5¾" l., 8" h.,
pr. 42.00
King Fish aquarium, green, L.E.
Smith, 1920's, 15" l., 10" h. 250.00
Mama Bear, clear, New Martinsville
Glass Mfg. Co., 6" l.,
4½" h.................100.00 to 145.00
Penguin decanter w/stopper, clear,
A.H. Heisey & Co.,
8½" h.................175.00 to 200.00

Police Dog (German Shepherd) book
end, clear, New Martinsville Glass
Mfg. Co., 1937-50, 2¼ x 5" base,
5 1/8" h. 45.00
Pony balking, clear, A.H. Heisey &
Co., 1941-45, 1½ x 3 1/8" base,
4" h. 138.00
Pony kicking, clear, A.H. Heisey &
Co., 1941-45, 1½ x 2¼" base,
3" l., 4" h. . . . . 130.00 to 165.00
Pouter Pigeon, clear, A.H. Heisey &
Co., 1947-49, 6½" h. . . . .525.00 to 600.00
Rabbit paperweight, milk white, Im-
perial Glass Co., 1977 limited edi-
tion, 2½" h. 45.00
Ringneck Pheasant, clear, A.H.
Heisey & Co., 1942-53, 11" l.,
4¾" h. . . . . .125.00 to 145.00
Rooster, clear, New Martinsville
Glass Mfg. Co., 8" l., 8" h. 68.00

Fostoria Rooster

Rooster (Chanticleer), clear, Fostoria
Glass Co., 10½" h. at head
(ILLUS.). 150.00
Ruffed Grouse, clear, Duncan & Mil-
ler Glass Co., 7½" l., 6½" h. 200.00
Scottie Dog, frosted, New Martins-
ville Glass Mfg. Co. 40.00
Seal w/ball, frosted, New Martins-
ville Glass Mfg. Co., 7¼" h. 125.00
Squirrel, clear, New Martinsville
Glass Mfg. Co., 5" h. 35.00
Squirrel book end, clear, New Mar-
tinsville Glass Mfg. Co.,
2¼ x 6¼" base, 5¼" h. . . .35.00 to 45.00
Swan, green w/clear neck, Duncan
& Miller Glass Co., 12" 55.00
Wolfhound (Russian) book end,
clear, New Martinsville Glass
Mfg. Co., 1920's, 9" l.,
7¼" h. . . . . .60.00 to 70.00

APPLIQUED

*Simply stated, this is an art glass form with
applied decoration. Sometimes master glass*

*craftsmen applied stems or branches to an art
glass object and then added molded glass
flowers or fruit specimens to these branches
or stems. At other times a button of molten
glass was daubed on the object and a tool
pressed over it to form a prunt in the form
of a raspberry, rosette or other shape. Always
the work of a skilled glassmaker, applied
decoration can be found on both cased (two-
layer) and single layer glass. The English firm
of Stevens and Williams is renowned for the
appliqued glass they produced.*

Basket, applied amber handle,
white opaque w/applied amber
branch & two leaves & two red
cherries w/amber stems, 4¼" d.,
6" h. $175.00
Creamer & open sugar bowl, orange
w/clear applied ruffle around rims
& applied rigaree under ruffle,
applied clear handle w/thumb-
piece on creamer, creamer 3" d.,
4½" h., sugar 5¼" d., 2¾" h.,
pr. 175.00
Ewer, applied clear handle, vaseline
opalescent stripe w/applied pink
flowers, 7¾" 118.00
Rose bowl, six-crimp top, cranberry
w/applied vaseline rigaree
around center, applied vaseline
branches & applied vaseline
matsu-no-ke button-like flowers,
4¾" d., 2½" h. 550.00
Vase, 3¾" h., 3½" d., ovoid body
w/short neck, rich shaded pink
overlay w/applied amber branch
& two applied amber plums, prob-
ably Stevens & Williams 195.00
Vases, 4½" h., 2 3/8" d., cased, tall
ovoid body w/crimped top, applied amber pedestal foot, soft
grey opaque exterior w/applied
amber branches, green leaves &
pink flowers w/amber centers,
pink lining, facing pair 235.00
Vase, 5" h., 5" d., flared fluted top
on squat round body, applied
clear feet, sapphire blue w/ap-
plied clear branch w/large open
flower 165.00
Vase, 6½" h., 3¾" d., cased, ovoid
body tapering to narrow neck
then flaring to rounded eight-
crimp top, cream exterior w/ap-
plied leaf w/cranberry center vein
& green & amber edges spiraling
down the side, pink lining 145.00
Vase, 7¾" h., 3 7/8" d., tall ovoid
body w/flared foot & short neck
w/flared rim, cranberry opalescent Swirl patt., applied w/amber
branches & green leaves w/white
flower & bud w/pink centers 235.00

Water tumbler, amber w/applied
amber pear & apple, green leaves
& amber branch, Stevens & Wil-
liams, 3¼" d., 3¾" h. 225.00

ART GLASS BASKETS

*Popular in the late Victorian era, these or-
nate hand-crafted glass baskets were often
given as gifts. Sometimes made with unusual-
ly tall handles and applied feet, these fragile
ornaments usually command a good price
when they survive intact.*

Aqua opaline, ruffled rim, applied
clear twisted handle, 6 x 6" $108.00
Blue opalescent, melon-ribbed, Swirl
patt., ruffled rim, square thorn
handle, 5" widest d., 7½" h. 260.00
Blue spangled w/silver flakes exterior, white interior, scalloped
top rim & foot, applied clear thorn
handle, 7½" d., 7½" h. 200.00
Caramel & white exterior, Swirl
patt., molded leaves, applied pink
loop thorn handle, 8½ x 9" 235.00
Cased, butterscotch exterior
w/raised Diamond Quilted patt.,
tomato red interior, square shape,
crimped rim w/applied clear ribbon trim, applied pointed thorn
handle, 5" sq., 7½" h. 135.00
Cased, creamy white exterior,
heavenly blue interior, ruffled rim
w/applied amber edging, applied
amber criss-cross handle, 6" d.,
8¼" h. 165.00
Cased, deep yellow w/white spatter
exterior, deep yellow interior,
jack-in-the-pulpit rim, melon-
ribbed body, applied clear twisted
handle, 4¼" d., 5¾" h. 110.00
Cased, gold, pink, maroon & blue
spatter exterior, white interior,
fluted rim, applied clear thorn
handle, 5 x 5¾", 6¾" h. 155.00
Cased, opalescent Coinspot patt. exterior, pastel pink, yellow & blue
spatter in clear interior, applied
clear rim & loop handle, 4¼" d.,
7½" h. 415.00
Cased, opaque white mother-of-pearl
satin Herringbone patt. between
threaded clear exterior & white
middle layer, exterior h.p.
w/shaded gold enameled branch
w/leaves & open blossoms w/white
stamen on obverse & gold butterfly
w/white eyes on reverse, gold rim
& brushed gold highlights, pink
interior, deep oblong four-lobed
shape, applied pointed white thorn

handle, four applied white feet,
signed "972/1B322" 1,250.00
Cased, orange exterior, Swirl patt.,
white interior, eight-crimp top,
dimpled sides, applied clear thorn
handle, applied clear feet,
5¼" d., 8¼" h. 165.00
Creamy white opaque, applied am-
ber handle, applied red cherries
w/applied rose & amber leaves &
applied amber stems & branches,
5¼" h. 195.00
Green opalescent, Swirl patt., ap-
plied deeper green ruffled rim,
applied vaseline twisted handle,
applied vaseline branch w/one
pink & one yellow applied flower,
5" d., 6" h. 145.00
Light blue opalescent, fluted turned-
down rim, applied clear reeded
handle, applied clear thorny nubs
over body, applied clear feet,
3 3/8" d., 7" h. 125.00
Medium blue center w/a band of
clear vaseline, white rim,
enameled orange decoration, applied clear thorn handle, 7½" d.,
7½" h. 350.00
Pink opalescent spangled w/mica
flakes, cranberry applied edging
on scalloped rim, Swirl patt.,
applied clear twisted handle,
4½ x 6", 6" h. 145.00
Rose pink opalescent, Swirl patt.,
ruffled rim, applied vaseline twisted handle, applied vaseline
branch & pink spatter flower on
front, 5 1/8" d., 6" h. 138.00

BACCARAT

*Baccarat glass has been made by Cristaller-
ies de Baccarat, France, since 1765. The firm
has produced various glasswares of excellent
quality and paperweights. Baccarat's Rose
Tiente is often referred to as Baccarat's
Amberina.*

Ashtray, Art Deco style, clear,
heavy, 5 x 5" $95.00
Bowl, 5" d., 2" h., Rose Tiente Swirl
patt., signed 60.00
Candlesticks, ball shape, Rose
Tiente Swirl patt., signed, 1¾" d.,
1¼" h., pr. 95.00
Liqueur bottle, clear bubble stopper
w/gold trim, three-petal top,
enameled w/heavy gold flowers &
leaves on lime green ground,
clear pedestal base, w/original
Baccarat paper label, 3½" d.,
10 1/8" h. 125.00

Perfume atomizer, h.p. scenic,
artist-signed, 8" h. 245.00
Perfume bottle, model of a lady's
hand, clear w/satin finish,
w/original price label "$37.50,"
signed, ca. 1920. . . . . 200.00
Powder jar, cov., round, Rose Tiente
Swirl patt., 3½" d., 4¼" h. 95.00
Salt dip, facet-cut, clear 35.00
Sauce dish, footed, Rose Tiente
Swirl patt., signed, 3" w.,
1½" h. 50.00
Tumbler, footed, Rose Tiente Swirl
patt., signed, 4½" h. 55.00
Water set: 9¼" h., 4¼" d. pitcher,
six 4¾" h., 2½" d. tumblers &
11½" d. round tray; Rose Tiente,
panels of embossed diamond
swirls alternating w/plain swirls,
signed, 8 pcs. 595.00

BLOWN THREE MOLD

Blown Three Mold Decanter

*This type of glass was entirely or partially
blown in a mold from about 1820 in the
United States. The object was formed and the
decoration impressed upon it by blowing the
glass into a metal mold, usually of three but
sometimes more sections, hinged together.
Mold-blown glass actually dates back to ancient times. Recent research reveals that certain geometric patterns were reproduced in
the 1920's and collectors are urged to read all
recent information available. McKearin reference numbers are to George L. and Helen
McKearin's book,* American Glass.

Bowl, 4 7/8" d., 1¾" h., round
w/folded rim above a banded &
ribbed body w/an eight-diamond
base, aquamarine, Mount Vernon
Glass Works, Mount Vernon, New
York, 1820-30 (GI-30). $1,980.00
Bowl, 6¼" d., 1½" h., round
w/folded rim & sloping sides

w/alternating panels of diamond-
sunburst over a band of vertical
ribbing, clear, 1820-40 (GIII-18) . . . 154.00
Celery vase, geometric, baluster-
form w/applied circular foot & a
17 diamond base, clear, 1820-40,
6¾" h. (GII-18) 1,100.00
Creamer, geometric, cylindrical body
tapering to narrow neck & wide,
flared rim & lip, applied strap
handle, sunburst & diamond band
around middle, blue (GIII-26) 2,750.00
Decanter w/original mold-blown
stopper, geometric, diamond point
& starburst band around middle,
three applied rings at neck, clear,
base of stopper chipped, 7" h.
(GIII-5) 175.00
Decanter w/matching stopper,
swirled ribbed design w/lower
band w/"Rum," minor sickness,
8½" h. (GIII-2) 400.00
Decanter w/original mold-blown stop-
per, geometric, semi-barrel shape
w/three double rigaree rings encircling the cylindrical neck, sides
w/inverted ribbing centering a
band of sunburst & diamond point,
rayed base, sapphire blue, ca.
1830, 10" h. (GIII-6) 2,860.00
Decanter w/original pattern-molded
stopper, baroque, barrel-shaped,
tapering cylindrical neck, sides
w/shell & ribbing designs, sapphire
blue, 1820-30, 11¾" h. (GV-8) . . . 2,200.00
Decanter w/original mold-blown
stopper, geometric, barrel-
shaped, flanged lip, rayed base
w/pontil, slight interior stain,
clear, GII-24 (ILLUS.) 385.00
Decanter, no stopper, two-mold,
geometric, square body w/cham-
fered corners, folded flaring lip
above a circular neck over sloping
fan-fluted shoulders, body w/hor-
izontal double banding centering
diamond diapering over a band of
inverted vertical ribbing, plain
base, deep purple amethyst, probably Keene, New Hampshire,
1820-25, pt., 7¼" h. (GII-28) 7,700.00
Decanter, no stopper, geometric,
semi-barrel shape w/tapering
cylindrical neck & sloped shoulders, the sides w/bands of inverted ribbing centering a band
w/alternating panels of bull's-eye-
sunburst & diamond point, olive
amber, probably Keene, New
Hampshire, 1820-40, 7" h.
(GIII-16) 495.00
Flip glass, cylindrical w/diamond
point band around center w/nar-
row ribbed bands above & below,

23 diamond base w/pontil, clear,
4 1/8" d., 5 3/8" h.
(GII-18) 71.50
Flip glass, flaring cylinder w/a
waffle-diamond sunburst decoration between bands of inverted
diagonal ribbing, clear, 1820-40,
6" h. (GIII-22) 440.00
Hat, miniature, model of a tall beaver hat w/cylindrical crown & alternating panels of sunburst & diamond decoration over a band of
vertical ribbing, purple-blue,
1820-40, 2¼" h. (GIII-3) 1,045.00
Inkwell, drum-shaped, band of diamond diapering over a band of
vertical ribbing, brown-amber,
Coventry, Connecticut, 1820-40,
2" h. (GII-18) 110.00
Punch bowl, footed, cylindrical
w/folded rim & two bands of vertical ribbing centering diamond
point decoration, the funnel base
w/19 expanded diamonds on an
applied spreading foot w/folded
rim & similar pattern decoration,
clear, 1820-30, 7½" d., 6 7/8" h.
(GII-18) 3,850.00
Sparking lamp, circular chimney
above a conical font w/Double
Horn of Plenty patt., ring- and
spiral-turned shaft, on sloping
octagonal lacy base w/acanthus
leaf decoration on stippled background, clear, probably Sandwich,
Massachusetts, 1835, chips to base,
7½" h. (GV-18) 1,540.00
Sugar bowl, cov., geometric, domed
lid w/folded rim & button finial
w/scalloped edge in ribbed & diamond point pattern, vase-shaped
bowl w/galleried rim & applied circular foot w/bands of vertical
ribbing centering a band of diamond point, clear, ca. 1830, 6" h.
(GII-18) 1,980.00
Sugar bowl, cov., geometric, domed
lid w/acorn finial & folded rim
molded w/swirled fluting, vase-
shaped bowl w/galleried rim
above bands of vertical ribbing
centering a band of diamond point,
applied circular foot, amethyst,
probably Midwestern, 1820-30,
6½" h. (GII-32) 28,600.00
Tumbler, barrel-shaped w/three diagonal bands centering a band
with diamond-sunburst, clear,
3 5/8" h. (GIII-21) 418.00
Tumbler, tapering cylindrical shape
w/bands of vertical ribbing centering diamond diapering, clear,
1820-40, 3½" h. (GII-18) 110.00
Wine glass, flaring cylindrical bowl

w/band of diamond diapering
above an applied knopped stem &
circular foot, clear, 1820-40,
3¾" h. (small rim chips to
base) 242.00

BOHEMIAN

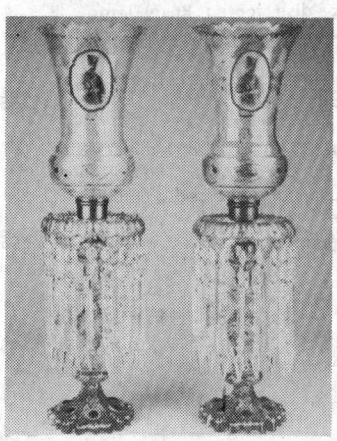

Bohemian "Jewelled" Lustres

*Numerous types of glass were made in the
once-independent country of Bohemia and
fine colored, cut and engraved glass was
turned out. Flashed and other inexpensive
wares also were made and many of these, including amber- and ruby-shaded glass, were
exported to the United States last century
and in the present one. One favorite pattern
in the late 19th and early 20th centuries was
Deer & Castle. Another was Deer and Pine
Tree.*

Beaker, clear engraved cylindrical
shape decorated w/scenes &
quotes from The Lord's Prayer
within arched panels, mid-19th c.,
5½" h. $550.00
Bell, dinner, white cut to blue
w/clear cut handle, 5" d. 55.00
Chalices, cov., shaped body & domed
cover w/frosted engraved deer in
woodland setting, circular base,
circular banded stem, green cut to
clear, 19th c., 21" h., pr. 1,650.00
Compote, 6 x 8½", shield-type cutting at edge, white cut to clear
design overall, interior w/lightly
h.p. gold grapes 90.00
Decanter w/original stopper, Deer &
Castle patt., ruby & clear 95.00
Lustres, clear glass w/sectioned foot,
each section w/applied "ruby,"
supported knopped stem w/gilt
decoration & beading & w/eight-

een clear prism drops, flared
shade w/transfer-printed oval
depicting a Cossack surrounded by
applied "rubies" & etched maple
leaves, 19th c., overall 25" h., pr.
(ILLUS.) 4,180.00
Pokal & cover, amber-flashed faceted bucket-shaped bowl enameled
w/a panel depicting a woman
spinning in the countryside, raised
on a knopped stem, late 19th c.,
12" h. 330.00
Scent bottle, ruby red vines, leaves
& fruit on clear ground 75.00
Tumbler, paneled, h.p. gold continuous stag hunting scene between
a band of gilt dentils & acanthus,
the ruby base gilded w/a hound &
a hare, ca. 1735, 2½" h. 1,650.00
Vase, 8¼" h., white cut to green,
enameled flowers 160.00
Vase, 11¾" h., faceted baluster-
form body w/oval gilt floral decorated ruby-flashed panels on a
gilt vermicule ground, 19th c. 770.00

BRIDE'S BASKETS & BOWLS

Lovely Burmese Bride's Bowl

*These are berry or fruit bowls, once popu-
lar as wedding gifts, hence the name.*

Burmese bowl w/deeply scalloped &
fluted rim & h.p. w/continuous
band of daisy-like floral sprigs,
ornate silver plate stand w/four
slender openwork brackets supporting top & continuing down to
engraved cylinder base supported
by four slender legs w/ball feet &
decorated w/two seated figural
cupids (ILLUS.).................$2,600.00
Cased bowl, butterscotch interior,
iridescent yellow exterior, ruffled
rim, tall ornate silver plate frame
marked "Oneida" 395.00
Cased bowl, lavender-purple w/ap-

plied ruffled rim, raised border of
interlocking lattices, stand w/tall
winged man w/quiver on his back
holding receptacle aloft, 11½" d.
bowl, overall 10½" h. 225.00
Cased bowl, pink to cranberry satin
interior, deeply ruffled applied
clear rim & fold-over top edge,
enameled yellow leaves & scattered blue & white cornflowers,
white exterior, ornate silver plate
frame marked "Barbour"........ 525.00
Cased bowl, pink to pale yellow interior enameled w/lavender &
blue florals, white exterior, silver
plate footed stand w/figural bird
between columns, 12½" d. bowl,
overall 10¼" h. 380.00
Cased bowl, shaded blue satin interior, white exterior w/enameled
lavender, orange & blue flowers &
scrolls, ornate silver plate frame
marked "Adelphi," 11¾" d. bowl,
13" h. holder 600.00
Cranberry w/cream spatter bowl,
closely crimped top, in marked
Tufts silver plate holder w/handle
& applied flowers & leaves decoration, overall 8" d., 11" h. 295.00
Ice blue bowl, Daisy & Button patt.,
silver plate frame marked
"Webster" 320.00
Peach Blow bowl w/ruffled rim,
New Martinsville Glass Mfg. Co.,
in ornamented silver plate stand
marked "Rogers," 11" d. bowl 200.00
Peach Blow bowl w/crimped turned
up & turned down rim, enameled
white flowers w/yellow centers &
golden tan branches, ornate silver
plate stand 550.00
Rose shaded to pink bowl
w/enameled gold scrolls & lacy
foliate decoration, fluted rim,
white exterior, silver plate frame,
13¼" d., 9¼" h. (frame resilvered) 275.00
Rubina verde bowl w/enameled
blue & white forget-me-nots & tiny
heavy gold flowers, leaves & dotting, ruffled rim, in silver plate
frame marked "Meriden," octagonal paneled base w/a row of
heavy beading around edge, two
very ornate galleries around the
body, the lower one scalloped &
beaded & the upper one w/ornate
cut-out flowers & a row of heavy
beading to match base, 12½" d.
bowl.......................... 495.00
Sapphire blue bowl w/applied ruffled rim, w/gold tracery & courting scene decoration, Meriden
ornate footed stand, 11½" d. 285.00

BRISTOL

Bristol Kerosene Lamp

While glass was made in several glass-houses in Bristol, England, the generic name Bristol glass is applied today by collectors to a variety of semi-opaque glasses, frequently decorated by enameling, and made both abroad and in United States glasshouses in the 19th and 20th centuries.

Cologne bottles w/ball stoppers, bulbous, white w/enameled morning glories, pr. $68.00

Cracker jar, cov., light grey w/enameled white, pink & blue flowers w/green leaves & gold stems, silver plate rim, cover & handle, 4 5/8" d., 6" h. 110.00

Cracker jar, cov., apple green opaque w/enameled green & yellow florals & plants, silver plate rim, cover w/strawberry finial, handle & base, 5" d., 7½" h. 145.00

Cracker (biscuit) jar, cov., heavenly blue w/enameled multicolored florals, silver plate rim, cover engraved "Biscuits" & handle 195.00

Dresser tray, turquoise blue w/lacy gold band on bottom, overall gold & yellow florals & leaves w/gold trim, 7¾ x 11" rectangle 118.00

Egg cup, white w/gold band at top & base 15.00

Lamp, kerosene-type, blue w/enameled white egret, colorful flowers & foliage, brass fittings, black base, 13¼" h. (ILLUS.) 295.00

Pitcher, 2¼" h., 3¼" d., squatty, applied turquoise blue handle, turquoise blue w/enameled yel-

low flowers & foliage, gold band trim 60.00

Pitchers, 8½" h., applied clear handles, light green opaque w/enameled bird & flowers decoration, pr. 80.00

Ring box w/domed cover, turquoise blue w/overall enameled gold flowers & leaves, 1¾" d., 1¾" h. 45.00

Rose bowl, four-crimp top, turquoise blue w/gold rope garlands & tassels outlined in white, 3¼" d., 4 1/8" h. 75.00

Vases, 2" h., 1¼" d., turquoise blue w/gold bands, enameled yellow flowers & leaves, pr. 65.00

Vases, 6¾" h., 3½" d., turquoise blue w/gold band around middle w/enameled colored flowers & leaves, pink & white enameled flowers & leaves around base of neck, gold top & bottom bands, pr. 130.00

Vase, 10¼" h., 2½ x 4¼" flattened oval, turquoise blue w/enameled grey, yellow & purple bird on front, white & pink flowers, green leaves & insect reverse, white dots & gold bands on pedestal base 150.00

Vases, 14" h., pink w/enameled floral decoration, pr. 265.00

BURMESE

Burmese Cruet

Burmese is a single-layer glass that shades from pink to pale yellow. It was patented by Frederick S. Shirley and made by the Mt. Washington Glass Co. A license to produce the glass in England was granted to Thomas Webb & Sons, which called its articles Queen's Burmese. Gunderson Burmese was made briefly about the middle of this century.

Basket, Thomas Webb & Sons, 9" ... $450.00

Bell, applied clear handle & clear clapper, rich salmon pink evenly shaded to yellow, glossy finish, Thomas Webb & Sons, 5 3/8" d., 9½" h. 450.00

Bowl, 3¾" d., 2¾" h., flared fluted rim, enameled green ivy leaves & vine, satin finish, unsigned Webb 325.00

Cracker jar, cov., enameled pine cones, silver plate cover & bail in excellent condition, Thomas Webb & Sons, 5" d., overall 6" h. 1,565.00

Creamer, fluted top, applied yellow handle, enameled flowers & green leaves, satin finish, unsigned Webb, 2½" d., 2 5/8" h. 550.00

Creamer & open sugar bowl, collared six-sided top, creamer w/applied vaseline handle, enameled green leaves & red berries, satin finish, original silver plate frame, unsigned Webb, sugar bowl 3¾" d., 3¼" h., creamer 2 5/8" d., 2¾" h., overall 4½ x 7½", 6¾" h., 3 pcs. 950.00

Cruet w/original facet-cut stopper, spout w/second-fired yellow edge, melon-ribbed body, satin finish, Mt. Washington Glass Co., 6½" h. (ILLUS.) 935.00

Finger bowl, upper 1¼" folded into nine scallops, satin finish, Mt. Washington Glass Co., 6" top d., 2¾" h. 285.00

Lamp, parlor-type, two globes on brass tiered base w/onyx shelves, signature on brass oil fonts in Russian "Otto Mhovanish, Siroohd, Russia" & dated 1880, shades signed "Queen's Burmese, Thomas Webb," 10" w. base, 61" h., globes 6½" d., 5½" h. 1,760.00

Marmalade jar, cov., apple-shaped, enameled band of small pink & blue flowers around top, silver plate cover & spoon, 3 3/8" d., 4" h. 195.00

Perfume bottle, ball-shaped, enameled purple flowers, sterling silver screw-on cap, unsigned Webb, 3½" h. 690.00

Pitcher, 4½" h., double pinched spout, slightly bulbous base, two handles rising from midsection of base to middle of straight neck, Mt. Washington Glass Co. 550.00

Pitcher, 6" h., bulbous w/raised & folded rim, h.p. dark green & gold spreading leaves & gilt enameled pods, etched circular mark at side "Thomas Webb & Sons/Queen's Burmese Ware Patented" 990.00

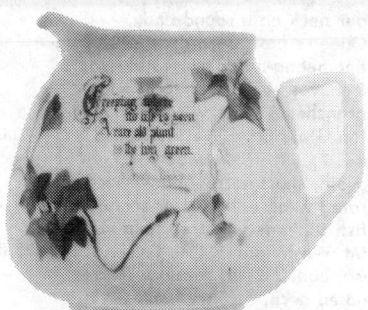

Burmese Pitcher with Quotation

Pitcher, lemonade, bulbous w/applied square handle, quotation "Creeping where no life is seen. A rare old plant is the ivy green." by Charles Dickens & enameled ivy vines on side (ILLUS.) 2,100.00

Rose bowl, eight-crimp top, satin finish, enameled lavender five-petal flower decoration w/green & brown leaves, unsigned Webb, 3" d., 2 7/8" h. 375.00

Salt dip, master size, footed, satin finish, enameled decoration 300.00

Salt & pepper shakers w/original tops, Ribbed Pillar patt., enameled pink & blue forget-me-nots, 4" h., pr. 137.50

Sherbets, deep rounded bowl on low pedestal base, glossy finish, Mt. Washington Glass Co., 3 3/8" d., 2 1/8" h., set of 6 ..... 495.00

Sweetmeat jar, cov., satin finish, green leaves & red berries decoration, silver plate rim, cover & handle, Thos. Webb & Sons, 4½" d., 3½" h. 695.00

Syrup jug w/original ornate silver plate lid & neck band, slightly ovoid, enameled floral decoration, applied angular handle, 6¼" h. ...1,650.00

Toothpick holder, fig mold, w/swirled fingers, enameled pink & yellow spider mums decoration 495.00

Tumbler, cylindrical, satin finish, decorated w/enameled fern fronds, Mt. Washington Glass Co., 3 7/8" h. 770.00

Vase, 3" h., 3¼" d., flower petal top, satin finish, enameled red berries & brown w/green leaves decoration, signed "Thos. Webb Queen's Burmese Ware" 350.00

Vase, 4¾" h., bulbous oval body w/raised rim collar, h.p. clusters of blossoms w/raised enameled petals, Mt. Washington Glass Co. 605.00

Vase, bud, 5¼" h., elongated slen-

der neck on a round body,
Queen's patt. decoration of dotted
enameling on daisy-like blossoms
& leaves w/gilt highlights,
branches & tracery, Mt. Washington Glass Co. 770.00

Vase, 7½" h., 6½" widest d., semi-
ovoid, short narrow neck, decorated w/an underwater scene of
fish & plants w/raised gold net,
Mt. Washington Glass Co. 2,475.00

Vase, bud, 7¾" h., ovoid w/elon-
gated neck, h.p. ivy leaves, vines
& tendrils, circular mark "Thos.
Webb & Sons; Queen's Burmese
Ware/Patented"................. 412.50

Vase, 8" h., 3 7/8" d., satin finish,
green ivy leaves decoration,
signed "Thos. Webb & Sons
Queen's Burmese"............... 695.00

Vase, 10" h., 3½" widest d., bottle-
shaped, satin finish, enameled yellow & rust chrysanthemums, green
leaves & branches, gold trim,
signed "Thos. Webb & Sons
Queen's Burmese Ware" 1,050.00

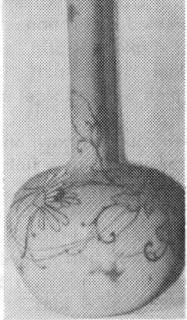

Burmese Vase

Vase, 10¼" h., stick-type, decorated
w/Shasta daisies in the "Queen's
design," Mt. Washington Glass Co.
(ILLUS.) 1,760.00

Vase, 11" h., petticoat-shaped body
w/tall slender neck & flared trefoil top, Mt. Washington Glass
Co. 385.00

Vase, 14" h., 6" widest d., elongated
ovoid w/trefoil lip, decorated obverse w/a large trout swimming
behind a net of raised gold, reverse w/two smaller trout which
appear to be attempting to escape
from the same net, all against a
background depicting a shadowy
seascape, Mt. Washington Glass
Co. 4,500.00

Vase, 18" h., lily-shaped, Mt.
Washington Glass Co. 1,300.00

Whiskey tumbler, Diamond Quilted
patt., glossy finish, Mt. Washington Glass Co., 2¼" d., 2¾" h. ... 195.00

CAMBRIDGE

Crown Tuscan Vase

The Cambridge Glass Company was founded in Ohio in 1901. Numerous pieces are now
sought, especially those designed by Arthur
J. Bennett, including Crown Tuscan. Other
productions included crystal animals, "Black
Amethyst," "blanc opaque," and other types
of colored glass. The firm was finally closed
in 1954. It should not be confused with the
New England Glass Co., Cambridge, Massachusetts.

Ashtray, shell-shaped, footed,
w/card holder, pressed Caprice
patt., blue $10.00

Ashtray, shell-shaped, footed,
pressed Caprice patt., La Rosa
(delicate pastel pink) 10.00

Basket, Ebony (opaque black)
w/coralene decoration, 11½" 85.00

Bonbon, low footed, pressed Caprice
patt., Moonlight (delicate pastel
blue), 6" oval 37.50

Bowl, jelly, 5" d., two-handled,
pressed Caprice patt., blue 27.50

Bowl, 9" d., Tally Ho (No. 1402/69)
line, Royal Blue (dark blue) 17.00

Bowl, 10" d., pressed Honeycomb
patt., Rubina (ruby top blending
to yellowish-green) 100.00

Bowl, 10½" d., crimped, footed,
pressed Caprice patt., blue 65.00

Bowl, 12" d., footed, No. 3400 line,
etched Rose Point patt., No. 4 .... 85.00

Bowl, 12½" d., belled, four-footed,
pressed Caprice patt., blue 70.00

Bowl, 13¼" d., four-footed, pressed
Caprice Alpine patt., crystal 45.00

Bowl, master berry, Near Cut line
(1910-20), crystal 39.00

Brandy, amber bowl, clear Nude
Lady stem 90.00

Brandy, Emerald (light transparent
green) bowl, clear Nude Lady
stem 92.50

Brandy, Mandarin Gold (very light
golden yellow) bowl, clear Nude
Lady stem 90.00

Butter dish, cov., Corinth (No. 3900)

line, etched Rose Point patt.,
No. 52, crystal, ¼ lb............ 275.00

Candlestick, pressed Caprice patt.,
crystal, 2½" h................ 6.00

Candlesticks, pressed Caprice patt.,
blue, 2½" h., pr................ 40.00

Candlesticks, single light, shell
base, curved stem, pressed Caprice patt., blue, w/prism, No. 70,
7" h., pr..................... 75.00

Candlesticks, Doric Column patt.,
Ivory (light cream opaque), pr. ... 150.00

Candy dish, cov., four-footed,
No. 3400 line, etched Wildflower
patt., w/gold trim.............. 68.00

Candy dish, cov., three-part, etched
Chantilly patt., amethyst w/ster-
ling silver finial................ 95.00

Cigarette box, cov., pressed Caprice
patt., blue, 2¼ x 3½".......... 44.00

Cigarette box, cov., dolphin-footed,
Seashell patt., emerald green
w/enameled & gold decoration ... 65.00

Claret, Forest Green (dark green)
bowl, clear Nude Lady stem...... 110.00

Claret, Optic patt., Gold Krystol
(transparent gold) bowl, clear
Nude Lady stem................ 120.00

Coaster, pressed Caprice patt., blue,
3½" d...................... 20.00

Cocktail, Carmen (clear ruby red)
bowl w/etched Rose Point patt.,
clear stem.................... 35.00

Cocktail, crystal bowl, Ebony Nude
Lady stem.................... 75.00

Cocktail, engraved Starlite patt.,
w/original label, crystal......... 9.00

Cocktail, Stradivari/Regency line,
crystal...................... 21.00

Cocktail shaker, cov., etched Rose
Point patt., metal base & cover,
3 pcs....................... 135.00

Compote, open, 5", Corinth
(No. 3900) line, Carmen......... 80.00

Compote, open, 7" d., etched Apple
Blossom patt., Mandarin Gold 55.00

Compote, open, 7" d., 4" h.,
pressed Honeycomb patt.,
Rubina...................... 85.00

Compote, open, 7" d., Carmen
bowl, clear Nude Lady stem...... 160.00

Console bowl, four-footed, etched
Apple Blossom patt., yellow,
12" d....................... 54.90

Cordial, pressed Caprice patt.,
blue........................ 18.00

Creamer, individual size, pressed
Caprice patt., blue............. 20.00

Creamer & sugar bowl, etched Lily
of the Valley patt., frosted crystal, pr...................... 140.00

Crown Tuscan bowl, 7½ x 9", three-
footed, Seashell patt............ 150.00

Crown Tuscan candlesticks, dolphin
stem, 10" h., pr............... 210.00

Crown Tuscan candlesticks
w/bobeches, Nude Lady stem,
pr......................... 450.00

Crown Tuscan candy dish, cov.,
three-part, No. 3500/57......... 65.00

Crown Tuscan compote, open, 7",
Seashell patt., floral decoration .. 125.00

Crown Tuscan compote, open, 8",
Nude Lady stem................ 148.00

Crown Tuscan nut dish, model of a
swan....................... 33.00

Crown Tuscan vase, 5" h., ovoid
body w/flared neck (ILLUS.)...... 44.00

Cruet w/original stopper, pressed
Caprice patt., crystal, 3 oz....... 25.00

Cup & saucer, demitasse, pressed
Decagon patt., amber.......... 12.50

Cup & saucer, No. 3400 line, etched
Rose Point patt................ 45.00

Cup & saucer, Corinth (No. 3900)
line, etched Rose Point patt.,
crystal...................... 42.00

Decanter w/"golf ball" stopper,
pinched sides, Carmen........... 45.00

Decanter w/stopper, No. 3121 line,
etched Wildflower patt. w/gold
trim, 28 oz................... 180.00

Octagonal Dessert Set

Dessert set: octagonal serving plate
& twelve individual octagonal
plates; pink w/sterling silver encrusted rims, 13 pcs. (ILLUS.) 195.00

Figure flower holder, "Bashful Charlotte," crystal, 8½" h........... 56.00

Figure flower holder, "Bashful Charlotte," Moonlight, 11" h......... 550.00

Figure flower holder, "Draped
Lady," green, 8½" h............ 137.00

Figure flower holder, "Draped
Lady," Moonlight, 8½" h......... 290.00

Figure flower holder w/large base,
"Draped Lady," Apple Green (light
green), 13" h................. 400.00

Figure flower holder, "Two-Kid,"
Mocha...................... 220.00

Figure flower holder in bowl, "Bashful Charlotte," etched bowl w/gold rim, pink, 8" h. 140.00
Figure of Buddha, green, 6½" h. . . . 150.00
Flower holder, Heron, crystal, 9" h. 60.00
Flower holder, Heron, crystal, 12" h. 142.00
Flower holder, Sea Gull, crystal, 10½" h. 90.00
Goblet, water, Gadroon (No. 3500) line, etched Rose Point patt., crystal, 10 oz. 22.00
Goblet, luncheon, Tally Ho line, amber, 10 oz. 12.00
Ice bucket w/chrome handle & tongs, Corinth (No. 3900) line, etched Rose Point patt., crystal . . . 135.00
Ivy ball, amethyst bowl, clear Nude Lady stem 165.00
Liqueur set: ball-shaped decanter & six liqueurs; green w/Farberware frames, 7 pcs. 72.00
Mayonnaise dish w/liner, pressed Caprice patt., blue, 8½", 2 pcs. . . 77.50
Model of a swan, milk white, 4½" 135.00
Model of a swan, crystal, w/paper label, 5". 25.00
Model of a swan, Carmen (bright ruby red), 6½". 265.00
Pitcher, water, 8¼" h., Near Cut line, Inverted Thistle patt., ruby-stained 265.00
Pitcher, ball-shaped, pressed Caprice patt., crystal, 32 oz. 58.00
(No. 3500) line, etched Rose Point patt., crystal 18.00
Plate, salad, 8" d., Tally Ho patt., amber 6.00
Plate, salad, 8" d., Corinth (No. 3900) line, etched Rose Point patt., crystal 22.00
Plate, 8½" d., pressed Caprice patt., Mocha (delicate pastel brown) 22.00
Plate, dinner, 9½" d., pressed Caprice patt., Moonlight (delicate pastel blue). 110.00
Plate, 10½" d., etched Chantilly patt., crystal 40.00
Plate, 12" d., Gadroon (No. 3500) line, etched Rose Point patt., crystal 75.00
Plate, 16" d., pressed Everglade patt., crystal 45.00
Relish, rectangular, pressed Caprice patt., blue, 6 x 12" 125.00
Relish, three-part, Gadroon (No. 3500 61-6½") line, etched Rose Point patt., crystal, 6½" 39.00
Relish, five-part, Corinth (No. 3900) line, No. 120/67, crystal, 12" 125.00

Rose bowl, pressed Caprice patt., blue, 6" d. 100.00
Salt & pepper shakers, pressed Caprice patt., blue, pr. 85.00
Salt & pepper shakers, footed, No. 3400/77 line, etched Rose Point patt., crystal, pr. 58.00
Sandwich tray w/center handle, pressed Decagon patt., No. 870, pink 38.00
Sandwich tray w/center handle, No. 3400/10 line, etched Rose Point patt., crystal 110.00
Sherbet, low, Gadroon (No. 3500) line, etched Rose Point patt., crystal, 7 oz. 25.00
Sherbet, low, Stradivari/Regency line, crystal 20.00
Smoking set: cov. cigarette box w/Nude Lady stem & two small flat ashtrays; cobalt blue, 3 pcs. . . . 289.00
Sugar bowl, open, individual, pressed Caprice patt., crystal 10.00
Toothpick holder, Colonial patt., cobalt blue 25.00
Tumbler, barrel-shaped, Corinth (No. 3900) line, etched Rose Point patt., No. 115, crystal, 13 oz. 57.00
Tumbler, flat, pressed Caprice patt., No. 188, cobalt blue, 2 oz. 85.00
Tumbler, footed, pressed Caprice patt., No. 300, crystal, 10 oz. 16.00
Tumbler, footed, Gadroon (No. 3500) line, etched Rose Point patt., crystal, 5 oz. 36.00
Tumbler, footed, Jefferson (No. 1401) line, Mandarin Gold (very light golden yellow), 5 oz. . . . 85.00
Tumbler, iced tea, footed, No. 3625 line, etched Chantilly patt., crystal, 12 oz. 16.00
Vase, 4" h., pressed Caprice patt., Emerald (light transparent green) 30.00
Vase, 5" h., globe-shaped, No. 3400 line, etched Diane patt., crystal . . 48.00
Vase, 7" h., sweet pea-type (tall, slender w/ruffled rim), Rubina (ruby top blending to yellow-green) 135.00
Vase, 9" h., pressed Cascade patt., dark green 75.00
Vase, 10¼" h., etched Chantilly patt., crystal, sterling silver base 89.00
Water set: 80 oz. ball-shaped pitcher & three tumblers; etched Elaine patt., crystal, 4 pcs. 185.00
Wine, Ebony (black) bowl, clear Nude Lady stem. 70.00
Wine, crystal bowl & base, green Nude Lady stem 75.00
Wine, Stradivari/Regency line, crystal 24.00

A Collectors' Update on

CARNIVAL GLASS

by Ruth Schinestuhl

Carnival glass, as a distinguished representative of American glassmaking, has come a long way in the 14 years since the last Special Focus in *The Antique Trader Price Guide* (Winter 1975 issue). It has come a long way because many more local groups have been formed and many specialized Carnival glass auctions have taken place in recent years with prices rising steadily. Also, museums have begun to recognize the importance of exhibiting Carnival, not only as a thing of beauty, but as a historic part of the American glassmaking heritage.

In 1974 the Keystone Carnival Glass Club was formed in Pennsylvania. Today, besides a monthly club meeting, they present an annual show and sale of old Carnival glass in Lititz, Pennsylvania and an annual convention is held in May. This is just one example of a smaller organization founded by those who enjoy Carnival glass. The two oldest national associations, the International and the American Carnival Glass Associations, continue to hold annual conventions in various locations. This past summer Elkhart, Indiana and New Philadelphia, Ohio, respectively, were the sites of these conventions.

Several pages could be written on specialized Carnival glass auctions which have taken place over the past 14 years. Although many auctioneers sell Carnival glass at their sales, two names continue to appear most often in connection with Carnival glass: Tom Burns and John Woody. Most of the major sales have been handled by one of these two gentlemen. Although there have been over 125 specialized Carnival glass auctions during the past 14 years throughout the country, without a doubt the most unusual one was the Wishard Collection sale held by John Woody at Louisville, Kentucky in 1977. The sale lasted three days and offered 6,000 pieces of glass. Some of the rarest items in Carnival were sold at this auction including a green *Farmyard* bowl, $7,500, an amethyst *People's* vase, $5,900, and an amethyst Millersburg *Thistle* punch bowl, $5,800. Another impressive collection was sold in 1982 when the Wil-

son Millersburg Collection was offered by Tom Burns in Strongsville, Ohio. Every piece of glass had been washed and wrapped in plastic wrap to prevent newspaper print from dulling the finish. Among the rare items in this auction were a blue *Rose Columns* vase which sold for $8,000 and five *Wild Rose* lamps ranging in price from $500 to $1,250. Looking to the future, we will see many new auctioneers featuring Carnival glass auctions and we'll also begin to see special pieces of Carnival glass appearing at well-known New York auction houses.

Carnival glass is now being accepted by major museums all across the country. The Fenton Art Glass Company in Williamstown, West Virginia, has exhibited Carnival in their museum, located on the factory premises, for many years. It is probably the only place to go if you want to see glass being hand-made in a 'semi-mass production' process. Many of the same methods and some similar tools used in making old Carnival can still be seen on this unique glass factory tour. Also, in the early 1970's, Rose Presznick had a private museum in Lodi, Ohio.

A new movement to exhibit Carnival in public museums began in England in 1983. Raymond Notley organized and cataloged the exhibit, 'Poor Man's Tiffany,' which had a 600-piece portion of the Notley-Lerpiniere Collection. It toured a dozen museums throughout the United Kingdom.

In 1987 the Corning Glass Museum had an exhibition of about 100 choice pieces of Carnival including a red *Chrysanthemum* bowl, a green *Acorn Burrs* punch set and a *Lattice and Grape* whimsey spittoon in marigold. This exhibit was organized by the American Carnival Glass Association in conjunction with their convention held in upper New York state. The timing was quite appropriate as the theme of the ACGA convention was the 80th birthday of Carnival glass. Mr. Frank Fenton was the keynote speaker and was on hand to help celebrate the occasion. It was his father who 'gave birth' to the pressed patterned glass with iridescence in the fall of

1907. Hundreds of thousands of visitors were able to view the Carnival glass during the four months it was exhibited at Corning. It remained on display for the 27th Seminar on Glass held in October of 1987. "Carnival Glass: Design, Myth, and History," a lecture and slide presentation, was given then by Ray Notley. People attending the seminar, museum curators and glass collectors from all over the world, were given exposure to good Carnival glass in that excellent presentation.

The Museum of American Glass at Wheaton Village in Millville, New Jersey has approximately 60 pieces on display on a long-term basis, again loaned by members of the American Carnival Glass Association. This museum is the second largest glass museum in America. The building was designed to fit in with the Victorian atmosphere of Wheaton Village, where visitors can also visit an operating replica of the 1888 T.C. Wheaton Glass Factory. Other museums, such as the Metropolitan Museum at Fresno, California, have also had special displays of Carnival.

The future of Carnival glass is very exciting when we focus on the club activities, the upcoming auctions and the recognition of our glass by glass museums and art museums around the world.

As the years pass, we learn more about the history of our glass through research. The late Marion T. Hartung and Rose M. Presznick each had a series of pattern identification books written in the early 1960's. These continue to prove very helpful to collectors today. The late William Heacock did a great deal of original research on the correct factory identification of Northwood and Dugan glass.

The rest of this article will focus on the six major companies that produced Carnival glass. We will take a look at each individual glass company history to get a better understanding of Carnival and why this lovely iridescent pressed glass continues to be one of the most desirable collectibles today.

FENTON

The Fenton Art Glass Company in Williamstown, West Virginia was the first to produce what we now call Carnival glass. The glass was first seen at glass shows in early 1908 after being produced in the fall of 1907. The Fenton Art Glass Company had only been in business for ten short months when it began making the iridescent pressed glass. In trade journals of 1907 it was called 'Iridill' and described as glass with 'a metallic lustre much like the Tiffany Favrile glass.' In January of 1908, Frank Fenton was on hand at the Fort Pitt Hotel, the location of many Pittsburgh glass exhibits, to reveal their

most recent creation. He brought a line of vases, compotes and rose bowls. One of the first patterns credited to Fenton was *Water Lily and Cattails* made for Fenton by the Hipkins Mold Company of Martins Ferry, Ohio. After a year, Fenton designed and made many of their own molds in their own mold shop. Two designs they are quite famous for are the *Peacock and Grape* pattern and *Dragon and Lotus* pattern, although no records exist to prove conclusively if they were designed in Fenton's mold shop or at Hipkins'. It is known that Frank L. Fenton had a hand in the designs as he began his career in the glass business in 1898. Carnival glass continued being made at the Fenton Art Glass Company for more than 25 years with a wide range of patterns, shapes and colors produced.

MILLERSBURG

The Carnival glass story continues with John Fenton, Frank's brother, and the Millersburg Glass Company. In 1906, John was president of the Fenton Art Glass Company, with Frank as Secretary, General Manager and Treasurer. Sometime within the next two years, John left Williamstown, West Virginia for Millersburg, Ohio, where he opened his own glass factory. Millersburg was in business for the shortest span of time compared to the other factories that produced Carnival. There is a strong likelihood that the reason Millersburg went out of business so soon was the extravagance and poor business management of John Fenton. He began production in the newly built plant on May 20, 1909. According to a Heacock article titled "The Carnival Glass Connections," the *Indiana Evening Gazette* (Jan. 19, 1910) stated "This factory was considered one of the best equipped glass factories in the country...but it seems that he (John Fenton) was not satisfied, however, and is now adding nearly $20,000 worth more of equipment and is getting ready to operate the plant with two shifts of workmen which virtually means day and night service."

In a short span of 28 months, the Millersburg Company produced some of the finest patterns and shapes found in Carnival today. The *People's* vase and the *Morning Glory* pitcher are two examples of ultimate Carnival rarity. Whimsey items such as the green *Nesting Swan* bowl pinched into a spittoon shape, and the *Cherry* banana boat-shaped compote are examples of the variety of shapes found in Millersburg glass. The Millersburg *Courthouse Bowl*, which was made as a souvenir for the people who helped John Fenton get the gas lines to the factory, shows the great expense invested in mold work for Millersburg glass. In March of 1911, the Hipkins Mold Company took the Millersburg Glass Company to court for non-payment of mold work, ultimately causing the company to declare bankruptcy.

NORTHWOOD

Harry Northwood played a significant part in the history of Carnival glass. He came to this country from England at the age of 20, already well versed in design and glassmaking techniques. He was the son of one of England's most respected and talented glassmakers, John Northwood. Harry began in the United States at Hobbs Brockunier in Pittsburgh as a designer, etcher and engraver in 1881.

He continued in glassmaking and in 1888 opened his own company. Over the next 20 years, he used his glassmaking and business talents at various locations in the Ohio River Valley area. He was successfully operating the Harry Northwood Glass Company at Wheeling, West Virginia in 1907 when Fenton began making iridescent pressed glass. At that time Custard glass, opalescent glass and other varieties of tableware, novelty items and lamps were being made by Northwood.

Fenton's iridescent pressed glass was doing so well Harry added it to his existing line of items, advertising it as 'Parisian Art' in 1909. The chemical formulas for spraying an iridescent finish on glass were well known among glassmakers, as evidenced by the quickness with which other companies introduced their iridescent wares after Fenton introduced it. Northwood soon had an extensive line of iridescent glass because of the quantity of existing molds being used in his other glass lines. For example, *Grape and Cable* can be found in a great variety of shapes in Custard as well as Carnival. Iridescent pressed glass continued to be made at the Northwood plant in Wheeling until the factory closed in 1924, five years after Harry died.

Today Northwood Carnival is highly respected among serious collectors and antiques enthusiasts in general. Northwood is responsible for those very desirable pastel shades of blue and green. Aqua opalescent Carnival glass, an aqua base color with opalescent edge, was primarily made by Northwood. A *Peacock At The Fountain* punch set in this color holds the present record for the highest price paid in Carnival.

DUGAN-DIAMOND

The background of Thomas Dugan is very similar to that of Harry Northwood. They were cousins and came from the same part of England. Dugan came to America only a year after Northwood. He also was employed at Hobbs Brockunier, no doubt due to Northwood's influence. He worked with Northwood

at his various factory locations and in 1899 both Dugan's and Northwood's names appeared on the deed when the Indiana, Pennsylvania Northwood factory joined the National Glass Works. Dugan ran the company for National until 1904 when he himself purchased it from National. It remained the Dugan Glass Company until 1913 when the name was changed to Diamond Glass Company. At this time Thomas Dugan was no longer in the picture.

William Heacock made public in a 1981 article in *The Antique Trader Weekly* the important research he had done on shards of glass found at the Indiana, Pennsylvania factory site. This revolutionary information proved the need to correct old attributions of certain Carnival patterns. It is due to Heacock's labors that the Dugan-Diamond Glass Company is now given credit for *Farmyard*, *Persian Garden* and *Garden Path*, just to name a few patterns. Most peach opalescent Carnival was made at this factory. In fact, almost one-quarter of the Carnival found today was made at the Dugan-Diamond Company sometime between 1910 and 1931, when the factory was destroyed by fire.

IMPERIAL

The Imperial Glass Company began production in 1904. In 1910 it began making iridescent pressed glass. Imperial made many patterns in Carnival in geometric designs. They had their own catalogs to sell their wares and, in addition, sold extensively overseas. They made Carnival until the company fell on hard times in 1931 and had to close its doors temporarily for reorganization. Imperial is known for the NUART trade-mark that they used on some of their goods. It wasn't until 1925 that the *Homestead* plate was seen advertised. This is one of the finest examples of mold work found in any Carnival. It is a piece prized by anyone fortunate enough to own one, especially when it is marked "NUART." Today purple Imperial Carnival is admired for the rich iridescent finish found on such examples as the *Loganberry* vase and *Lustre Rose* water sets.

WESTMORELAND

The Westmoreland Specialty Company of Grapeville, Pennsylvania had been in business since 1889 and they also began producing iridescent glass when it became popular. The first of their advertised iridized glass appeared in a Butler Brothers catalog in 1908. The *Estate* sugar and creamer and the *Miniature Flower Basket* appeared in this ad. They also made the rare *Fruit Salad* punch set in peach opalescent, and the patterns *Carolina Dogwood* and *Daisy Wreath*. It appears that Carnival was only made at Westmoreland until 1912, when advertisements for iridescent glass stopped appearing in Butler Brothers catalogs. The company is now known for its pretty blue opalescent, teal blue and milk glass with a marigold finish. The blues are rich colors that do not resemble cobalt blue or the pastel blue of Northwood, but rather a very deep aqua. Some authors have previously given Millersburg credit for patterns such as *Leaf Swirl*, however, again, Heacock has corrected these attributions. Westmoreland is now known to have made approximately 30 items in Carnival.

CONCLUSIONS

We have not touched on the companies that made a limited amount of Carnival, such as U.S. Glass and Cambridge, nor have we mentioned the foreign glass made since our focus was on the six major producers of Carnival glass.

The values are an everchanging part of Carnival collecting today. Some pieces seem to have made an astonishing jump in price over a short span of time, while other items are worth the same they were ten years ago. This is due to changing trends in popularity. For example, in the 1975 Special Focus in this price guide, an ice blue *Hearts and Flowers* bowl was valued at $68, today its value is $275. A red *Dragon and Lotus* 8" to 9" bowl was listed at $212.50 and today it lists for $775. The marigold *Butterfly and Berry* footed bowl listed for $45.00 in 1975 and has only made a $25 gain in today's listing. This just gives you a sampling of changes in the Carnival market. The following price listings will offer a more in-depth comparison of 1975 vs. 1989 values for various popular patterns.

Enjoy your glass and Happy Hunting!

Source Material:

Heacock, William, *The Antique Trader Weekly,* "Carnival Glass by Dugan and Diamond," February 25, 1981.
Heacock, William, *The Antique Trader Weekly,* "Early Westmoreland Carnival Glass 1908-1912," April 7, 1982.
Heacock, William, *Collecting Glass, Vol. 3,* Antique Publications, Marietta, Ohio, 1984.
Heacock, William, *Fenton Glass, The First 25 Years,* Antique Publications, Marietta, Ohio, 1978.
Notley, Raymond, *Carnival Glass Society Journal,* Vol. 1, 3 and 5.
Welker, John and Elizabeth, *Pressed Glass in America 1825-1925, Encyclopedia of the First 100 Years.*
Wilson, Jack, *Millersburg Research Notes.*

ABOUT THE AUTHOR

Ruth Schinestuhl has been a member of Carnival glass organizations since 1976. She is a collector whose specialized interests are Northwood and pastels. Ruth has worked with the American Carnival Glass Association in conjunction with both the Corning Glass Museum exhibit and the Museum of American Glass at Wheaton Village near her home. While teaching school for the past 12 years, she has also written articles for the Carnival organizations and has been a speaker at some of the annual conventions. She also serves as the in-house Carnival glass authority for The Antique Trader Price Guide.

PRICE LISTINGS:

ACORN BURRS (Northwood)

Acorn Burrs Pitcher

	1975	1989
Berry set: master bowl & 6 sauce dishes; marigold, 7 pcs.	$170.00	$208.00
Berry set: master bowl & 6 sauce dishes; purple, 7 pcs.	227.00	354.00
Bowl, master berry, 10" d., marigold	60.00	80.00
Bowl, master berry, 10" d., purple	90.00	130.00
Butter dish, cov., marigold	127.50	150.00
Butter dish, cov., purple	192.50	225.00
Creamer & sugar bowl, marigold, pr.	210.00	210.00
Pitcher, water, marigold	293.00	315.00
Pitcher, water, purple (ILLUS.)	325.00	450.00
Punch cup, ice blue	65.00	85.00
Punch cup, marigold	16.00	18.00
Punch cup, purple	26.50	27.00
Sauce dish, marigold	45.00	20.00
Table set: cov. butter dish, creamer, spooner & sugar bowl; purple, 4 pcs.	580.00	685.00
Tumbler, green	55.00	57.00

	1975	1989
Tumbler, marigold	45.00	45.00

Acorn Burrs Tumbler

	1975	1989
Tumbler, purple (ILLUS.)	40.00	64.00
Water set: pitcher & 6 tumblers; marigold, 7 pcs.	386.50	542.00
Water set: pitcher & 6 tumblers; purple, 7 pcs.	785.00	833.00

AGE HERALD

	1975	1989
Bowl, 8" to 9" d., collared base, straight edge, purple	699.00	750.00
Plate, 9½" d., purple	750.00	1,275.00

APPLE TREE

	1975	1989
Pitcher, water, marigold	134.00	174.00
Pitcher, water, white	312.50	350.00
Tumbler, blue	35.00	52.00
Tumbler, marigold	19.00	45.00
Water set: pitcher & 5 tumblers; marigold, 6 pcs.	340.00	435.00

BUTTERFLY & BERRY (Fenton)

Butterfly & Berry Pitcher

	1975	1989
Berry set: master bowl & 6 sauce dishes; marigold, 7 pcs.	160.00	200.00
Bowl, 8" to 9" d., footed, blue	66.00	70.00
Bowl, 8" to 9" d., footed, marigold	45.00	70.00

	1975	1989
Butter dish, cov., green	170.00	200.00
Hatpin holder, blue	438.00	700.00
Sauce dish, marigold	17.50	22.50
Sauce dish, purple	22.00	95.00
Table set, marigold, 4 pcs.	195.00	225.00
Tumbler, blue	31.00	36.00
Tumbler, marigold	15.00	22.00
Tumbler, purple	30.00	325.00
Vase, 6" h., blue	28.00	55.00
Vase, 9" h., purple	22.00	50.00
Water set: pitcher & 6 tumblers; marigold, 7 pcs. (ILLUS. of pitcher)	178.00	320.00

COIN DOT (Northwood)

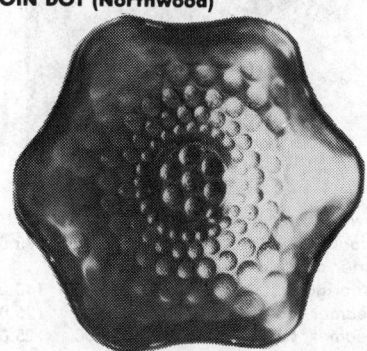

Coin Dot Bowl

	1975	1989
Bowl, 7" d., green (ILLUS.)	28.00	30.00
Bowl, 7" d., marigold	12.00	38.00
Bowl, 7" d., purple	25.00	28.00
Bowl, 8" to 9" d., green	28.00	37.50
Bowl, 8" to 9" d., marigold	16.50	25.00
Bowl, 8" to 9" d., purple	17.50	40.00
Pitcher, water, marigold	87.50	150.00
Rose bowl, green	33.00	52.00
Rose bowl, marigold	39.00	43.00
Tumbler, marigold	32.00	50.00
Water set: pitcher & 6 tumblers; marigold, 7 pcs.	227.00	425.00

CORN VASE

Corn Vase

	1975	1989
Aqua, pastel	450.00	1,150.00
Green	263.00	338.00
Ice blue	170.00	1,200.00
Ice green	138.00	260.00
Purple (ILLUS.)	198.00	454.00
White	151.00	250.00

DAHLIA (Dugan or Diamond Glass Co.)

Dahlia Pitcher

	1975	1989
Bowl, master berry, 10" d., footed, white	175.00	175.00
Butter dish, cov., marigold	260.00	140.00
Creamer, purple	50.00	125.00
Creamer, white	53.00	125.00
Pitcher, water, purple (ILLUS.)	390.00	625.00
Sauce dish, marigold	8.00	40.00
Sauce dish, purple	29.00	45.00

Dahlia Tumbler

	1975	1989
Tumbler, marigold (ILLUS.)	60.00	115.00
Tumbler, purple	95.00	195.00
Tumbler, white	120.00	155.00

DANDELION (Northwood)

	1975	1989
Mug, aqua opalescent	246.00	495.00
Mug, marigold	130.00	285.00
Mug, purple	147.50	280.00
Pitcher, water, tankard, green	250.00	750.00
Pitcher, water, tankard, marigold (ILLUS.)	125.00	365.00
Pitcher, water, tankard, purple	561.00	650.00
Tumbler, green	45.00	90.00
Tumbler, ice blue	51.50	180.00

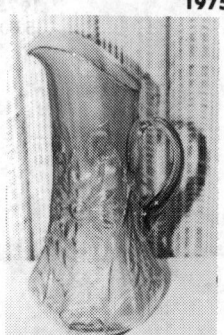

Dandelion Pitcher

	1975	1989
Tumbler, marigold	35.50	36.00
Tumbler, white	75.00	142.00
Water set: pitcher & 6 tumblers; ice blue, 7 pcs.	1,300.00	1,300.00
Water set: pitcher & 6 tumblers; purple, 7 pcs.	850.00	882.00

DRAGON & LOTUS (Fenton)

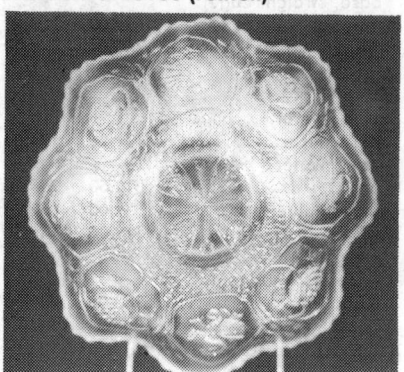

Dragon & Lotus Collared Base Bowl

	1975	1989
Bowl, 7" to 9" d., three-footed, green	34.00	68.00
Bowl, 7" to 9" d., three-footed, marigold	27.00	40.00
Bowl, 7" to 9" d., three-footed, peach opalescent	55.00	500.00
Bowl, 7" to 9" d., three-footed, purple	34.00	90.00
Bowl, 8" to 9" d., collared base, aqua opalescent (ILLUS.)	175.00	700.00
Bowl, 8" to 9" d., collared base, blue	45.00	72.00
Bowl, 8" to 9" d., collared base, green	45.00	95.00
Bowl, 8" to 9" d., red	212.50	763.00
Bowl, 9" d., ice cream shape, collared base, blue (ILLUS.)	40.00	54.00

	1975	1989

Dragon & Lotus Ice Cream Shape Bowl

Bowl, 9" d., ice cream
  shape, collared base,
  marigold 21.00   50.00
Plate, collared base, ruffled,
  marigold 84.00   650.00

FRUITS & FLOWERS (Northwood)

Bonbon, stemmed, two-
  handled, blue 41.00   95.00
Bonbon, stemmed, two-
  handled, green 40.00   68.00
Bonbon, stemmed, two-
  handled, marigold 27.00   42.00
Bonbon, stemmed, two-
  handled, purple 45.00   70.00
Bowl, 9½" d., ruffled,
  Basketweave exterior,
  purple 39.00   61.00
Plate, 7½" d., handgrip,
  pastel marigold 60.00   185.00

GOOD LUCK (Northwood)

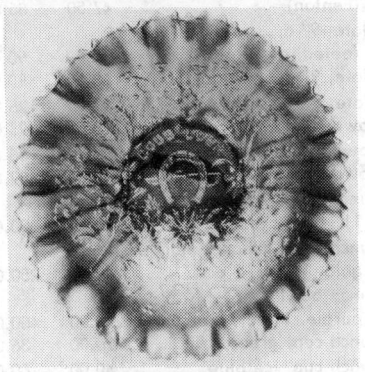

Good Luck Bowl

Bowl, 8" to 9" d., piecrust
  rim, aqua opalescent 223.00 1,250.00
Bowl, 8" to 9" d., piecrust
  rim, blue (ILLUS.) 102.00   248.00
Bowl, 8" to 9" d., piecrust
  rim, green 103.00   260.00
Bowl, 8" to 9" d., piecrust
  rim, marigold 57.00   142.00

	1975	1989

Bowl, 8" to 9" d., piecrust
  rim, purple 97.50   235.00
Plate, 9" d., green 211.50   563.00
Plate, 9" d., marigold 172.00   220.00
Plate, 9" d., purple 188.00   320.00
Plate, 9" d., white 525.00 1,600.00

GRAPE & CABLE

Grape & Cable Butter Dish

Banana boat, blue 217.50   330.00
Banana boat, green 142.50   307.00
Banana boat, ice green 285.00   595.00
Banana boat, marigold 75.00   136.00
Banana boat, purple 161.00   220.00
Berry set: master bowl & 6
  sauce dishes; marigold,
  7 pcs. 140.00   275.00
Berry set: master bowl & 8
  sauce dishes; purple,
  9 pcs. 195.00   400.00
Bonbon, two-handled,
  blue 30.00   60.00
Bonbon, two-handled,
  green 42.50   46.00
Bonbon, two-handled,
  marigold 32.00   40.00
Bowl, 5" d., marigold 12.50   32.00
Bowl, 6" d., red (Fenton) . . .180.00   360.00
Bowl, 7½" d., ball-footed,
  purple (Fenton) 27.50   52.00
Bowl, 7½" d., spatula-
  footed, green (North-
  wood) 27.50   70.00
Bowl, 8" to 9" d., spatula-
  footed, green
  (Northwood) 39.00   70.00
Bowl, 8" to 9" d., spatula-
  footed, marigold
  (Northwood) 26.00   60.00
Bowl, 8" to 9" d., spatula-
  footed, ruffled, purple
  (Northwood) 29.50   63.00
Bowl, berry, 9" d., green 79.00   78.00
Bowl, berry, 9" d.,
  marigold 106.00   75.00
Bowl, berry, 9" d., purple . .115.00   80.00
Bowl, ice cream, 11" d.,
  green 92.50   143.00
Bowl, ice cream, 11" d.,
  purple 129.00   125.00

	1975	1989
Bowl, ice cream, 11" d., white	147.50	275.00
Butter dish, cov., blue	175.00	200.00
Butter dish, cov., green	150.00	175.00
Butter dish, cov., marigold	99.00	175.00
Butter dish, cov., purple (ILLUS.)	225.00	180.00
Candle lamp, green	455.00	530.00
Candle lamp, marigold	400.00	550.00
Candle lamp, purple	550.00	450.00
Candlestick, green	83.00	85.00
Candlesticks, marigold, pr.	125.00	155.00
Candlesticks, purple, pr.	167.50	270.00

Grape & Cable Centerpiece Bowl

	1975	1989
Centerpiece bowl, ice blue (ILLUS.)	355.00	850.00
Centerpiece bowl, marigold	225.00	165.00
Centerpiece bowl, white	140.00	585.00
Cologne bottle w/stopper, green	165.00	223.00
Cologne bottle w/stopper, marigold	129.00	145.00
Cologne bottle w/stopper, purple	284.00	178.00
Compote, cov., large, purple	350.00	400.00
Compote, open, large, green	335.00	425.00
Compote, open, large, marigold	175.00	343.00
Cracker jar, cov., marigold	157.50	246.00
Cracker jar, cov., purple	211.50	300.00
Cracker jar, cov., white	350.00	875.00
Creamer, marigold	46.00	60.00
Creamer, purple	95.00	100.00
Creamer, individual size, marigold	37.50	75.00
Cup & saucer, purple	129.50	450.00
Decanter w/stopper, whiskey, marigold	650.00	488.00
Decanter w/stopper, whiskey, purple (ILLUS. next column)	750.00	825.00
Dresser tray, green	167.00	255.00
Dresser tray, marigold	99.00	110.00
Dresser tray, purple	155.00	175.00
Fernery, marigold	850.00	980.00
Hatpin holder, green	139.00	210.00

Grape & Cable Whiskey Decanter

	1975	1989
Hatpin holder, marigold	119.00	145.00
Hatpin holder, purple	108.00	200.00
Nappy, single handle, green	90.00	75.00
Nappy, single handle, marigold	40.00	45.00
Perfume bottle w/stopper, purple	360.00	575.00
Pin tray, green	165.00	125.00
Pin tray, purple	148.00	155.00
Pitcher, water, 8¼" h., green	160.00	325.00
Pitcher, water, 8¼" h., marigold	121.00	160.00
Pitcher, water, 8¼" h., purple	125.00	175.00
Pitcher, tankard, 9¾" h., green	310.00	1,500.00
Plate, 8" d., footed, green (Fenton)	47.50	85.00
Plate, 9" d., spatula-footed, green	72.00	90.00
Plate, 9" d., marigold	63.00	90.00
Plate, 9" d., purple	72.00	125.00
Powder jar, cov., green	92.50	95.00
Powder jar, cov., marigold	47.50	58.00
Powder jar, cov., purple	71.00	102.00
Punch bowl & base, green, 11" d., 2 pcs.	380.00	600.00
Punch bowl & base, marigold, 11" d., 2 pcs.	240.00	250.00
Punch bowl & base, purple, 11" d., 2 pcs.	275.00	400.00
Punch cup, green	20.00	36.00
Punch cup, ice blue	40.00	60.00
Punch cup, marigold	11.50	21.00
Punch set: 17" bowl, base & 12 cups; purple, 14 pcs.	1,122.50	1,700.00
Sauce dish, marigold	25.00	32.50
Sauce dish, purple	23.00	35.00
Spooner, green	130.00	90.00
Spooner, purple	81.50	85.00
Sugar bowl, cov., green	140.00	110.00

	1975	1989
Sugar bowl, cov., marigold	67.50	75.00
Sugar bowl, cov., purple	140.00	96.00

Grape & Cable Sweetmeat

	1975	1989
Sweetmeat jar, cov., marigold (ILLUS.)	650.00	750.00
Sweetmeat jar, cov., purple	150.00	185.00
Tumbler, green	31.50	45.00
Tumbler, marigold	21.50	32.00
Tumbler, purple	30.00	35.00
Tumbler, tankard, marigold	59.00	65.00
Tumbler, tankard, purple	66.00	40.00
Water set: pitcher & 6 tumblers; green, 7 pcs.	397.50	460.00
Water set: pitcher & 6 tumblers; marigold, 7 pcs.	271.00	330.00
Water set: pitcher & 6 tumblers; purple, 7 pcs.	353.00	434.00
Whiskey shot glass, marigold	182.00	160.00
Whiskey shot glass, purple	197.00	150.00

GREEK KEY (Northwood)

Greek Key Plate

	1975	1989
Bowl, 8" to 9" d., fluted, green	43.00	185.00
Bowl, 8" to 9" d., purple	43.00	167.00

	1975	1989
Pitcher, water, marigold	380.00	700.00
Plate, 9" d., green (ILLUS.)	295.00	500.00
Plate, 9" d., marigold	170.00	450.00
Tumbler, green	92.50	98.00
Tumbler, marigold	90.00	65.00
Water set: pitcher & 6 tumblers; green, 7 pcs.	900.00	1,200.00
Water set: pitcher & 6 tumblers; purple, 7 pcs.	1,275.00	1,400.00

HEARTS & FLOWERS (Northwood)

Hearts & Flowers Compote

	1975	1989
Bowl, 8" to 9" d., ruffled, green	66.00	710.00
Bowl, 8" to 9" d., ruffled, ice blue	69.00	325.00
Bowl, 8" to 9" d., ruffled, marigold	31.00	274.00
Bowl, 8" to 9" d., ruffled, purple	65.00	320.00
Bowl, 8" to 9" d., ruffled, white	72.50	207.00
Compote, 6¾" h., aqua opalescent (ILLUS.)	99.00	445.00
Compote, 6¾" h., electric blue	59.00	270.00
Compote, 6¾" h., green	49.00	950.00
Compote, 6¾" h., marigold	26.50	125.00
Compote, 6¾" h., white	60.00	150.00
Plate, marigold	95.00	330.00

Hearts & Flowers Plate

	1975	1989
Plate, purple (ILLUS.)	150.00	738.00
Plate, white	125.00	2,500.00

IMPERIAL GRAPE (Imperial)

Imperial Grape Wine Set

	1975	1989
Bowl, 7" d., 2½" h., ruffled, purple	22.50	35.00
Bowl, 8" to 9" d., marigold	14.00	26.00
Bowl, 10" d., marigold	28.00	31.00
Bowl, 10" d., purple	100.00	68.00
Cup & saucer, green	59.50	86.00
Cup & saucer, marigold	35.00	62.00
Decanter w/stopper, green	80.00	120.00
Decanter w/stopper, marigold	62.50	86.00
Goblet, marigold	24.00	34.00
Pitcher, water, green	105.00	250.00
Pitcher, water, marigold	60.00	89.00
Pitcher, water, purple	195.00	283.00
Plate, 9" d., ruffled, marigold	25.00	33.00
Sauce dish, ruffled, marigold	14.50	14.00
Tumbler, green	18.00	25.00
Tumbler, marigold	15.00	20.00
Water bottle, green	75.00	100.00
Water bottle, marigold	50.00	75.00
Water set: pitcher & 6 tumblers; marigold, 7 pcs.	109.00	190.00
Water set: pitcher & 6 tumblers; purple, 7 pcs.	335.00	610.00
Wine, green	26.00	28.00
Wine, marigold	16.50	24.00
Wine, purple	50.00	32.00
Wine set: decanter w/stopper & 6 wines; marigold, 7 pcs.	137.00	200.00
Wine set: decanter w/stopper & 6 wines; purple, 7 pcs. (ILLUS. of part)	275.00	325.00

KITTENS (Fenton)

Bowl, cereal, marigold	50.00	105.00

	1975	1989

Kittens Cup & Saucer

	1975	1989
Cup & saucer, marigold (ILLUS.)	107.00	225.00
Dish, turned-up sides, blue	65.00	315.00

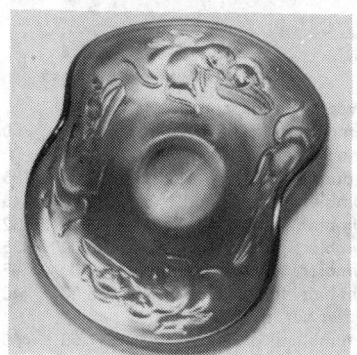

Kittens Dish With Turned-Up Sides

	1975	1989
Dish, turned-up sides, marigold (ILLUS.)	52.00	112.00
Saucer, marigold	39.50	90.00
Spooner, blue	100.00	280.00
Spooner, marigold	75.00	133.00
Toothpick holder, blue	85.00	300.00
Toothpick holder, marigold	60.00	120.00

LION (Fenton)

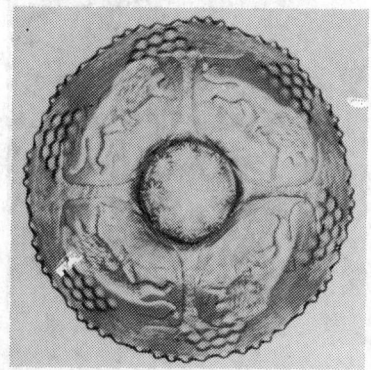

Lion Bowl

	1975	1989
Bowl, 6" d., marigold (ILLUS.)	48.50	100.00
Bowl, 7" d., blue	68.00	305.00
Plate, 7½" d., marigold	185.00	650.00

	1975	1989

LUSTRE ROSE (Imperial)

Lustre Rose Footed Fernery

	1975	1989
Bowl, 8" to 9" d., three-footed, blue	35.00	65.00
Bowl, 8" to 9" d., three-footed, marigold	16.00	40.00
Butter dish, cov., marigold	28.00	75.00
Creamer, marigold	26.50	35.00
Fernery, purple (ILLUS.)	36.00	95.00
Pitcher, water, marigold	30.00	58.00
Plate, 9" d., amber	45.00	85.00

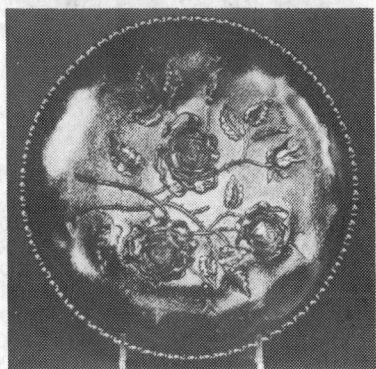

Lustre Rose Plate

	1975	1989
Plate, 9" d., marigold (ILLUS.)	23.00	51.00
Rose bowl, amber	15.00	70.00
Spooner, marigold	11.00	35.00
Sugar bowl, cov., green	80.00	100.00
Sugar bowl, cov., marigold	11.50	45.00
Table set: cov. sugar bowl, creamer, spooner & cov. butter dish; marigold, 4 pcs.	97.50	160.00
Tumbler, purple	48.00	32.50
Water set: pitcher & 6 tumblers; marigold, 7 pcs.	111.00	250.00

MEMPHIS (Northwood)

	1975	1989
Punch bowl & base, marigold, 2 pcs.	143.00	175.00

Memphis Punch Bowl & Base

	1975	1989
Punch bowl & base, purple, 2 pcs. (ILLUS.)	240.00	340.00
Punch cup, green	17.00	35.00
Punch cup, ice blue	45.00	60.00
Punch cup, marigold	12.00	20.00
Punch cup, purple	20.00	26.00
Punch set: bowl, base & 5 cups; marigold, 7 pcs.	285.00	400.00
Punch set: bowl, base & 6 cups; purple, 8 pcs.	360.00	800.00

ORANGE TREE (Fenton)

Orange Tree Loving Cup

	1975	1989
Bowl, 7" d., white	55.00	64.00
Bowl, 8" to 9" d., marigold	20.00	32.00
Bowl, 8" to 9" d., purple	31.50	87.00
Bowl, 10" d., three-footed, blue	107.00	225.00
Bowl, 10" d., three-footed, green	92.50	265.00
Bowl, 10" d., three-footed, marigold	56.00	85.00
Butter dish, cov., blue	160.00	225.00
Compote, 5" d., marigold	13.00	36.00
Creamer, footed, blue	30.00	60.00
Creamer, footed, purple	35.00	50.00
Creamer, individual size, purple	26.00	44.00

	1975	1989
Goblet, marigold	35.00	22.50
Hatpin holder, blue	127.00	200.00
Hatpin holder, green	110.00	335.00
Hatpin holder, marigold	82.00	140.00
Loving cup, blue	95.00	235.00
Loving cup, green	87.50	330.00
Loving cup, marigold	66.50	137.00
Loving cup, purple (ILLUS.)	95.00	200.00
Mug, blue	25.50	48.00
Mug, marigold	17.00	25.00
Mug, purple	28.00	90.00
Mug, red	147.50	380.00
Pitcher, water, blue	286.00	325.00
Pitcher, water, marigold	161.00	275.00
Plate, 9" d., flat, blue	85.00	275.00

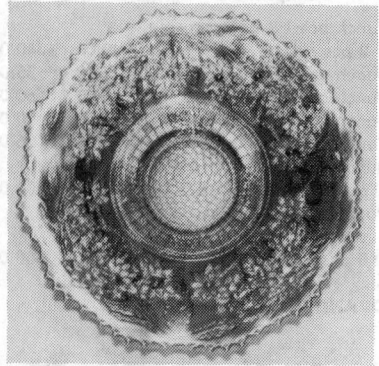

Orange Tree Plate

	1975	1989
Plate, 9" d., flat, marigold (ILLUS.)	47.00	115.00
Plate, 9" d., flat, white	64.00	163.00
Powder jar, cov., blue	58.00	93.00
Powder jar, cov., marigold	32.00	62.00
Punch bowl & base, marigold, 2 pcs.	85.00	154.00
Punch bowl & base, white, 2 pcs.	300.00	325.00
Punch cup, blue	20.00	25.00
Punch cup, marigold	14.00	16.00
Punch cup, purple	13.00	20.00
Punch set: bowl, base & 6 cups; blue, 8 pcs.	307.50	595.00
Punch set: bowl, base & 6 cups; marigold, 8 pcs.	237.00	375.00

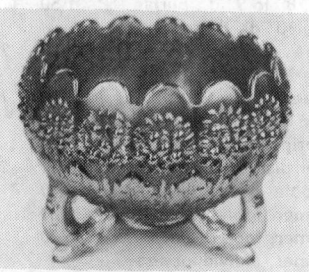

Orange Tree Rose Bowl

	1975	1989
Rose bowl, marigold (ILLUS.)	29.00	54.00
Tumbler, blue	46.00	50.00
Tumbler, marigold	26.50	45.00
Water set: pitcher & 6 tumblers; blue, 7 pcs.	447.00	475.00
Water set: pitcher & 6 tumblers; marigold, 7 pcs.	233.00	430.00
Wine, blue	25.00	50.00
Wine, green	50.00	175.00
Wine, marigold	19.00	28.00

PANTHER (Fenton)

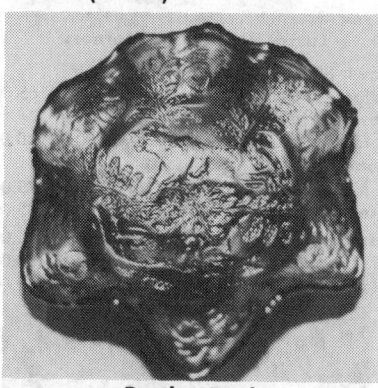

Panther Bowl

	1975	1989
Berry set: master bowl & 6 sauce dishes; marigold, 7 pcs.	200.00	300.00
Bowl, 5" d., footed, marigold	23.00	40.00
Bowl, 5" d., footed, red, (ILLUS.)	230.00	598.00
Bowl, 9" d., claw-footed, blue	138.00	275.00
Bowl, 9" d., claw-footed, green	150.00	600.00

Panther Claw-Footed Bowl

	1975	1989
Bowl, 9" d., claw-footed, marigold (ILLUS.)	77.00	125.00
Bowl, 9" d., claw-footed, purple	147.50	150.00

1975   1989

PEACOCK & URN

Peacock & Urn Ice Cream Bowl

Bowl, 8" to 9" d., blue
(Fenton) 45.00   116.00
Bowl, 8" to 9" d., green
(Fenton) 45.00   165.00
Bowl, 8" to 9" d.,
marigold (Fenton) 35.00   73.00
Bowl, 8" to 9" d., purple
(Fenton) 45.00   130.00
Bowl, ice cream, 10" d.,
marigold (Northwood)....100.00   292.00
Bowl, ice cream, 10" d.,
purple, Northwood
(ILLUS.) 134.00   550.00
Ice cream set: large bowl
& 6 small dishes;
marigold, 7 pcs. 275.00   500.00
Ice cream set: large bowl
& 6 small dishes;
purple, 7 pcs. 324.00   645.00
Ice cream set: large bowl
& 6 small dishes; white,
7 pcs. 420.00   1,250.00
Plate, 9" d., blue 159.00   318.00
Plate, 9" d., marigold 108.00   165.00
Plate, 9" d., white 185.00   335.00
Plate, chop, 11" d., mari-
gold (Millersburg).......300.00   2,800.00
Plate, chop, 11" d., purple
(Millersburg) 433.00   815.00
Sauce dish, blue
(Northwood) 42.00   95.00
Sauce dish, marigold
(Northwood) 20.00   40.00
Sauce dish, purple
(Northwood) 30.00   55.00

PEACOCK AT FOUNTAIN (Northwood)
Berry set: master bowl & 5
sauce dishes; marigold,
6 pcs. 115.00   210.00
Berry set: master bowl & 6
sauce dishes; purple,
7 pcs. 150.00   215.00
Bowl, orange, three-
footed, aqua opal-
escent 2,750.00   2,000.00

1975   1989

Bowl, orange, three-
footed, blue............160.00   280.00
Bowl, orange, three-
footed, purple..........160.00   300.00
Butter dish, cov., green 350.00   500.00
Butter dish, cov., marigold ..99.00   129.00

Peacock at Fountain Butter Dish

Butter dish, cov., purple
(ILLUS.) 147.50   228.00
Butter dish, cov., white 160.00   380.00
Compote, blue 180.00   537.00
Compote, marigold 125.00   408.00
Creamer, marigold 65.00   62.50
Pitcher, water, blue.......281.00   360.00
Pitcher, water, purple.....260.00   305.00
Punch bowl & base, blue,
2 pcs. 350.00   375.00
Punch bowl & base, ice
green, 2 pcs...........550.00   2,500.00
Punch bowl & base, mari-
gold, 2 pcs. 212.00   340.00
Punch bowl & base, white,
2 pcs. 442.00   1,600.00
Punch cup, ice blue 60.00   90.00
Punch cup, marigold 20.00   32.50
Punch cup, white 30.00   60.00
Sauce dish, blue............27.50   35.00
Sauce dish, purple 25.00   28.00
Sugar bowl, cov., blue 70.00   130.00
Sugar bowl, cov.,
marigold................47.50   75.00

Peacock at Fountain Sugar Bowl

Sugar bowl, cov., purple
(ILLUS.) 85.00   85.00

	1975	1989
Table set, marigold,		
4 pcs. 325.00		395.00
Tumbler, blue 26.00		42.00
Tumbler, purple 32.00		47.00
Water set: pitcher & 4		
tumblers; marigold,		
5 pcs. 165.00		380.00
Water set: pitcher & 6		
tumblers; blue, 7 pcs.....317.50		600.00

PEACOCKS ON FENCE (Northwood Peacocks)

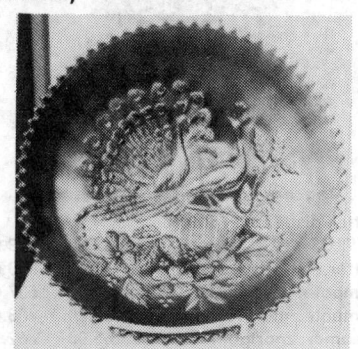

Peacocks on Fence Plate

	1975	1989
Bowl, 8" to 9" d., aqua		
opalescent 196.50		750.00
Bowl, 8" to 9" d., piecrust		
rim, marigold 65.00		205.00
Bowl, 8" to 9" d., piecrust		
rim, purple 95.00		415.00
Bowl, 8" to 9" d., piecrust		
rim, white 145.00		325.00
Bowl, 8" to 9" d., ruffled		
rim, blue 98.00		320.00
Bowl, 8" to 9" d ., ruffled		
rim, marigold 55.00		200.00
Bowl, 8" to 9" d., ruffled		
rim, purple 104.00		330.00
Plate, 9" d., electric blue		
(ILLUS.) 187.50		775.00
Plate, 9" d., green........155.00		1,665.00
Plate, 9" d., ice blue.......195.50		1,875.00
Plate, 9" d., ice green 115.00		425.00
Plate, 9" d., marigold 106.00		345.00
Plate, 9" d., purple 195.00		605.00
Plate, 9" d., white 123.00		390.00

PERSIAN GARDEN (Dugan)

	1975	1989
Bowl, 5" d., blue 20.00		22.50
Bowl, 5" d., white 23.00		73.00
Bowl, ice cream, 11" d.,		
peach opalescent 150.00		900.00
Bowl, ice cream, 11" d.,		
white..................105.00		200.00
Fruit bowl & base, marigold,		
2 pcs. 125.00		150.00
Fruit bowl & base, purple,		
2 pcs. 182.50		300.00
Plate, 6" to 7" d., blue 57.50		80.00

	1975	1989
Plate, 6" to 7" d., purple 50.00		188.00
Plate, 6" to 7" d., white 56.00		114.00
Plate, chop, 11" d., peach		
opalescent 650.00		1,400.00

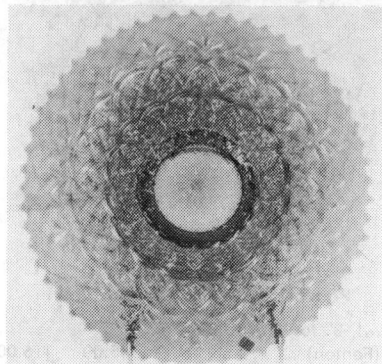

Persian Garden Plate

	1975	1989
Plate, chop, 11" d., purple		
(ILLUS.) 650.00		1,700.00

ROUND UP (Dugan)

Round Up Plate

	1975	1989
Bowl, 9" d., marigold 37.50		50.00
Bowl, 9" d., peach		
opalescent 80.00		300.00
Bowl, 9" d., white 125.00		200.00
Plate, 9" d., blue (ILLUS.)...150.00		244.00
Plate, 9" d., ruffled,		
marigold...............82.50		250.00
Plate, 9" d., flat, peach		
opalescent 113.00		425.00
Plate, 9" d., purple 101.00		292.00
Plate, 9" d., white 125.00		375.00

SINGING BIRDS (Northwood)

	1975	1989
Berry set: master bowl & 6		
sauce dishes; green,		
7 pcs. 250.00		335.00
Butter dish, cov.,		
marigold...............125.00		138.00
Butter dish, cov., purple....165.00		172.00
Creamer, marigold 65.00		52.00
Creamer, purple...........82.50		85.00

	1975	1989
Mug, blue	50.50	110.00
Mug, green	50.50	140.00
Mug, marigold	32.00	52.00

Singing Birds Mug

	1975	1989
Mug, purple (ILLUS.)	50.50	76.00
Pitcher, marigold	195.00	225.00
Pitcher, purple	341.00	275.00
Table set, purple, 4 pcs.	460.00	865.00
Tumbler, green	38.00	45.00
Tumbler, marigold	30.00	25.00
Tumbler, purple	38.00	45.00
Water set: pitcher & 6 tumblers; green, 7 pcs.	533.00	652.00
Water set: pitcher & 6 tumblers; marigold, 7 pcs.	450.00	557.00
Water set: pitcher & 6 tumblers; purple, 7 pcs.	650.00	750.00

STAG & HOLLY (Fenton)

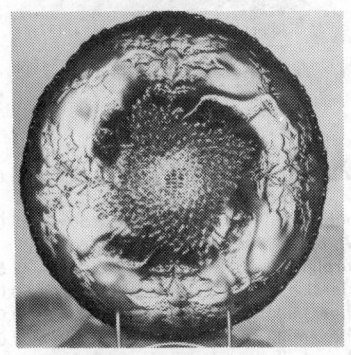

Stag & Holly Bowl

	1975	1989
Bowl, 7" d., spatula-footed, blue	45.00	107.00
Bowl, 8" to 9" d., spatula-footed, blue	82.00	112.00
Bowl, 8" to 9" d., spatula-footed, green	57.50	150.00
Bowl, 8" to 9" d., spatula-footed, marigold	39.00	70.00
Bowl, 8" to 9" d., spatula-footed, purple	64.00	112.00

	1975	1989
Bowl, 10" to 11" d., three-footed, blue (ILLUS.)	109.00	200.00
Bowl, 10" to 11" d., three-footed, green	90.00	425.00
Bowl, 10" to 11" d., three-footed, marigold	63.50	104.00
Bowl, 10" to 11" d., three-footed, purple	185.00	435.00
Plate, chop, 12" d., three-footed, marigold	317.00	525.00
Rose bowl, green, large	150.00	595.00
Rose bowl, marigold, large	102.00	212.00

SWIRL HOBNAIL (Millersburg)

Swirl Hobnail Cuspidor

	1975	1989
Cuspidor, marigold	125.00	495.00
Cuspidor, purple (ILLUS.)	175.00	487.00
Rose bowl, marigold	47.50	225.00
Rose bowl, purple	82.50	288.00

THREE FRUITS (Northwood)

Three Fruits Plate

	1975	1989
Berry set: master bowl & 6 sauce dishes; marigold, 7 pcs.	125.00	175.00
Bowl, 9" d., spatula-footed, aqua opalescent	180.00	435.00
Bowl, 9" d., spatula-footed, ruffled, green	37.50	60.00
Bowl, 9" d., spatula-footed, marigold	30.00	42.00
Bowl, 9" d., spatula-footed, white	65.00	250.00
Bowl, 10" d., green	50.00	65.00

	1975	1989
Plate, 9" d., stippled, aqua opalescent	475.00	3,200.00
Plate, 9" d., blue, non-stippled (ILLUS.)	79.00	152.00
Plate, 9" d., green, non-stippled	63.00	118.00
Plate, 9" d., marigold, non-stippled	44.00	66.00
Plate, 9" d., purple, non-stippled	76.50	97.00

TOWN PUMP NOVELTY (Northwood)

Northwood Town Pump

	1975	1989
Green	257.50	2,000.00
Marigold	481.00	1,335.00
Purple (ILLUS.)	409.00	625.00

TREE TRUNK VASE (Northwood)

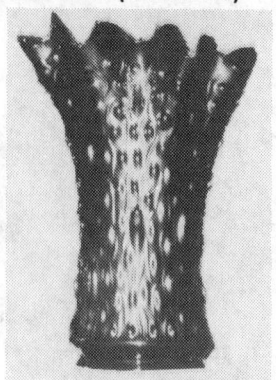

Tree Trunk Vase

	1975	1989
8" h., blue	15.00	45.00
9" h., green	14.00	160.00
10" h., aqua opalescent	40.00	385.00
12" h., blue (ILLUS.)	17.50	80.00
12" h., marigold	17.50	70.00
20" h., blue	32.50	375.00

WATER LILY & CATTAILS

	1975	1989
Banana boat, blue	85.00	168.00
Banana boat, marigold	65.00	140.00
Bowl, 9" d., marigold	19.00	26.00

	1975	1989
Butter dish, cov., marigold	132.50	200.00

Water Lily & Cattails Pitcher

	1975	1989
Pitcher, water, marigold (ILLUS.)	115.00	548.00
Tumbler, blue	18.00	2,700.00
Tumbler, marigold	19.00	30.00
Tumbler, purple	25.00	50.00

WINDMILL or WINDMILL MEDALLION (Imperial)

Windmill Pitcher

	1975	1989
Bowl, 7" d., marigold	12.00	36.00
Bowl, 8" to 9" d., ruffled, marigold	27.50	95.00
Bowl, 8" to 9" d., ruffled, purple	25.00	42.50
Pickle dish, green	25.00	50.00
Pitcher, milk, green	130.00	250.00
Pitcher, milk, marigold	45.00	62.00
Pitcher, milk, purple (ILLUS.)	100.00	315.00
Sauce dish, marigold	10.50	18.00
Tumbler, marigold	13.50	25.00
Tumbler, purple	38.50	90.00
Water set: pitcher & 6 tumblers; marigold, 7 pcs.	75.00 to 150.00	225.00

WISHBONE (Northwood)

	1975	1989
Bowl, 8" to 9" d., footed, purple	53.00	80.00

Bowl, 10" d., piecrust rim,
green 83.00   125.00

	1975	1989

Wishbone Bowl

Bowl, 10" d., piecrust rim,
  marigold (ILLUS.) 36.00   75.00
Bowl, 10" d., piecrust rim,
  purple 56.00   148.00
Epergne, marigold 200.00   495.00
Epergne, purple 195.00   443.00
Plate, 6½" d., purple 85.00   85.00
Plate, 8½" d., footed,
  purple 225.00   240.00
Plate, chop, 11" d.,
  marigold 417.50   550.00
Plate, chop, 11" d.,
  purple 875.00   650.00
Tumbler, green 90.00   130.00

ZIPPERED LOOP LAMP (Imperial)

Zippered Loop Lamp

Lamp, hand, marigold,
  4½" h. 195.00   800.00
Lamp, marigold,
  small ....150.00 to 175.00   325.00
Lamp, marigold, large
  (ILLUS.) 124.00   650.00

(End of Special Focus)

ADDITIONAL LISTINGS

ACANTHUS (Imperial)

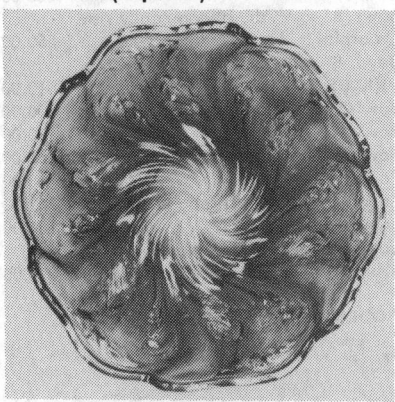

Acanthus Bowl

Bowl, 7" d., green $20.00
Bowl, 8" to 9" d., green 62.50
Bowl, 8" to 9" d., marigold
  (ILLUS.).......................62.00
Bowl, 8" to 9" d., purple 55.00
Bowl, 8" to 9" d., smoky 65.00
Plate, 9" to 10" d., marigold 142.00
Plate, 9" to 10" d., smoky.........182.00

ACORN (Fenton)

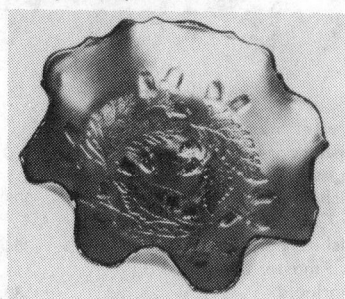

Acorn Bowl

Bowl, 5" d., ribbon candy rim,
  blue 60.00
Bowl, 5" d., marigold over milk
  white 395.00
Bowl, 7" d., ruffled, amber.........110.00
Bowl, 7" d., aqua 75.00
Bowl, 7" d., aqua opalescent 103.00
Bowl, 7" d., blue 45.00
Bowl, 7" d., green 68.00
Bowl, 7" d., ice blue..............150.00
Bowl, 7" d., marigold 32.50
Bowl, 7" d., marigold over milk
  white 155.00
Bowl, 7" d., peach opalescent 140.00
Bowl, 7" d., ruffled, peach
  opalescent....................350.00
Bowl, 7" d., purple 47.50
Bowl, 7" d., red 428.00
Bowl, 7" d., ruffled, vaseline 104.00

Bowl, 8" to 9" d., blue.............   60.00
Bowl, 8" to 9" d., marigold
w/opalescent rim 300.00
Bowl, 8" to 9" d., ribbon candy rim,
purple 50.00
Bowl, 8" to 9" d., ruffled, red
(ILLUS.)......................   510.00
Bowl, ice cream shape, aqua.......   100.00
Bowl, ice cream shape, green......   70.00
Bowl, ice cream shape, red slag....   550.00
Bowl, ruffled, aqua...............   68.00
Bowl, ruffled, peach opalescent 362.00
Bowl, white.....................   180.00
Compote, vaseline (Millers-
burg) ....1,250.00 to 2,000.00

ACORN BURRS (Northwood)

Acorn Burrs Punch Set

Berry set: master bowl & 4 sauce
dishes; green, 5 pcs. 260.00
Berry set: master bowl & 6 sauce
dishes; marigold, 7 pcs. 208.00
Berry set: master bowl & 6 sauce
dishes; purple, 7 pcs.............   354.00
Bowl, master berry, 10" d.,
marigold 80.00
Bowl, master berry, 10" d., purple ..   130.00
Butter dish, cov.,
green ....150.00 to 185.00
Butter dish, cov., marigold 150.00
Butter dish, cov., purple 225.00
Creamer, green...................   90.00
Creamer, marigold 80.00
Creamer, purple 125.00
Pitcher, water, marigold 315.00
Pitcher, water, purple 450.00
Punch bowl, marigold 400.00
Punch bowl base, ice blue 175.00
Punch bowl base, ice green 100.00
Punch bowl & base, ice green,
2 pcs. 1,800.00
Punch bowl & base, purple, 2 pcs. ...   450.00
Punch cup, green 35.00
Punch cup, ice blue 65.00
Punch cup, ice green 65.00
Punch cup, marigold.............   18.00

Punch cup, purple 27.00
Punch cup, white................   58.00
Punch set: bowl, base & 4 cups;
marigold, 6 pcs.................   525.00
Punch set: bowl, base & 6 cups;
green, 8 pcs. (ILLUS.) 1,500.00
Punch set: bowl, base & 6 cups; ice
blue, 8 pcs...................3,750.00
Punch set: bowl, base & 6 cups;
purple, 8 pcs.................1,050.00
Punch set: bowl, base & 6 cups;
white, 8 pcs.................3,200.00
Sauce dish, green 32.00
Sauce dish, marigold 20.00
Sauce dish, purple 58.00
Spooner, green 78.00
Spooner, marigold...............   67.50
Spooner, purple..................   128.00
Sugar bowl, cov., marigold........   95.00
Sugar bowl, open, purple 125.00
Table set: cov. sugar bowl, creamer,
spooner & cov. butter dish; green,
4 pcs.........................   475.00
Table set, marigold, 4 pcs. 450.00
Table set, purple, 4 pcs. 685.00
Tumbler, green 57.00
Tumbler, marigold...............   42.00
Tumbler, purple.................   64.00
Water set: pitcher & 4 tumblers;
green, 5 pcs. 525.00
Water set: pitcher & 4 tumblers;
marigold, 5 pcs.................   458.00
Water set: pitcher & 6 tumblers;
purple, 7 pcs...................   833.00

ADVERTISING & SOUVENIR ITEMS

Elks "Atlantic City, 1911" Bowl

Ashtray, souvenir, "Cleveland
Memorial," purple (Millersburg) ..1,400.00
Basket, "John H. Brand Furniture
Co., Wilmington, Del.,"
marigold 46.50
Basket, "Miller's Furniture,"
marigold 85.00
Bell, souvenir, BPOE Elks, "Atlantic
City, 1911," blue...............1,162.00
Bowl, "Isaac Benesch," 6¼" d., pur-
ple (Millersburg) 172.00
Bowl, "Bernheimer," blue 638.00

Bowl, "Horlacher," Butterfly patt.,
purple 125.00
Bowl, "Horlacher," Peacock Tail
patt., purple 60.00
Bowl, "Horlacher," Thistle patt., pur-
ple ....80.00 to 95.00
Bowl, "Ogden Furniture Co.,"
purple 225.00
Bowl, "Sterling Furniture," purple... 240.00
Bowl, souvenir, BPOE Elks, "Atlantic
City, 1911," blue, one-eyed Elk
(ILLUS.)....................... 292.00
Bowl, souvenir, BPOE Elks, "Detroit,
1910," blue, one-eyed Elk 525.00
Bowl, souvenir, BPOE Elks, "Detroit,
1910," green, one-eyed Elk 560.00
Bowl, souvenir, BPOE Elks, "Detroit,
1910," purple, one-eyed Elk 475.00
Bowl, souvenir, BPOE Elks, "Detroit,
1910," purple, two-eyed Elk
(Millersburg).................... 932.00
Bowl, souvenir, "Brooklyn Bridge,"
marigold 252.00
Bowl, souvenir, "Brooklyn Bridge,"
unlettered, marigold............. 550.00
Bowl, souvenir, "Millersburg Court-
house," purple 426.00
Bowl, souvenir, "Millersburg Court-
house," unlettered, purple 965.00
Card tray, "Fern Brand Chocolates,"
turned-up sides, 6¼" d.,
purple 175.00
Card tray, "Isaac Benesch," Holly
Whirl patt., marigold 65.00
Dish, "Compliments of Pacific Coast
Mail Order House, Los Angeles,
California".................... 700.00
Hat, "John Brand Furniture,"
green 42.00
Hat, "John Brand Furniture," open
edge, marigold 42.00
Hat, "Horlacher," Peacock Tail patt.,
green 85.00
Hat, "Miller's Furniture - Harris-
burg," basketweave, marigold.... 75.00
Plate, "Ballard, California," purple
(Northwood) 375.00
Plate, "Bird of Paradise," purple 220.00
Plate, "Brazier Candies," w/hand-
grip, 6" d., purple............... 250.00
Plate, "Campbell & Beesley Co.,"
w/handgrip, purple.............. 420.00
Plate, "Davidson Chocolate Society,"
6¼" d., purple.................. 230.00
Plate, "Driebus Parfait Sweets,"
6¼" d., purple.................. 175.00
Plate, "Eagle Furniture Co.,"
purple 232.00
Plate, "Fern Brand Chocolates,"
6" d., purple.................. 220.00
Plate, "Gervitz Bros., Furniture &
Clothing," w/handgrip, 6" d.,
purple 350.00

Plate, "Greengard Furniture Co.,"
purple 625.00
Plate, "E.A. Hudson Furniture Co.,"
7" d., purple (Northwood)........ 225.00
Plate, "Jockey Club," w/handgrip,
6" d., purple................... 255.00
Plate, "Old Rose Distillery," Grape &
Cable patt., stippled, 9" d.,
green 233.00
Plate, "Roods Chocolate, Pueblo,"
purple 750.00
Plate, "Season's Greetings - Eat
Paradise Soda Candies," 6" d.,
purple 178.00
Plate, "Morris N. Smith," purple 250.00
Plate, "Spector's Department Store,"
Heart & Vine patt., 9" d.,
marigold 306.00
Plate, "Utah Liquor Co.," w/hand-
grip, 6" d., purple.............. 300.00
Plate, "We Use Brocker's," 7" d.,
purple 495.00
Plate, souvenir, BPOE Elks, "Atlantic
City, 1911," blue 475.00
Plate, souvenir, BPOE Elks, "Par-
kersburg, 1914," 7½" d., blue 785.00

AGE HERALD
Bowl, 8" to 9" d., collared base,
straight edge, purple 750.00
Plate, 9½" d., purple 1,275.00

AMARYLLIS (Northwood)
Compote, marigold............... 143.00
Compote, purple 112.00

APPLE BLOSSOMS

Apple Blossoms Bowl

Bowl, 7" d., collared base, marigold
(ILLUS.)........................ 30.00
Bowl, 7" d., collared base, peach
opalescent ....75.00 to 110.00
Bowl, 7" d., collared base, purple .. 70.00
Bowl, 7" d., ribbon candy rim,
white 125.00
Rose bowl, marigold.............. 35.00

APPLE BLOSSOM TWIGS
Banana boat, ruffled, peach
opalescent.................... 175.00

Bowl, 8" to 9" d., blue	80.00
Bowl, 8" to 9" d., marigold	52.00
Bowl, 8" to 9" d., peach opalescent	125.00
Bowl, 8" to 9" d., purple	97.00
Bowl, 8" to 9" d., white	90.00
Bowl, 10" d., purple	250.00
Plate, 9" d., blue	284.00
Plate, 9" d., ruffled, blue	213.00
Plate, 9" d., marigold	98.00
Plate, 9" d., ruffled, marigold	50.00
Plate, 9" d., peach opalescent	215.00
Plate, 9" d., purple	220.00
Plate, 9" d., ruffled, smoky	350.00
Plate, 9" d., white	208.00
Plate, 9" d., ruffled, white	165.00
Plate, chop, peach opalescent	375.00

APPLE TREE

Pitcher, water, marigold	174.00
Pitcher, water, white	350.00
Tumbler, amber	55.00
Tumbler, blue	52.00
Tumbler, marigold	45.00
Tumbler, white	114.00
Water set: pitcher & 3 tumblers; white, 4 pcs.	750.00
Water set: pitcher & 5 tumblers; marigold, 6 pcs.	435.00
Water set: pitcher & 6 tumblers; blue, 7 pcs.	820.00

AUSTRALIAN

Kangaroo Bowl

Bowl, 9" to 10" d., Emu, marigold	145.00
Bowl, 9" to 10" d., Kangaroo, marigold	100.00
Bowl, 9" to 10" d., Kangaroo, purple (ILLUS.)	170.00
Bowl, 9" to 10" d., Kingfisher, purple	110.00
Bowl, 9" to 10" d., Kiwi, ruffled, marigold	250.00
Bowl, 9" to 10" d., Kiwi, purple	225.00
Bowl, 9" to 10" d., Kookaburra, marigold	98.00
Bowl, 9" to 10" d., Kookaburra, purple	100.00
Bowl, 5½" d., Swan, marigold	50.00

Bowl, 9" to 10" d., Swan, purple	98.00
Bowl, 9" to 10" d., Thunderbird, purple	165.00
Bowl, ice cream shape, 11" d., Kookaburra, marigold	135.00
Bowl, ice cream shape, 11" d., Kookaburra variant, purple	300.00
Bowl, pin-up, purple	65.00
Compote, Butterflies & Waratah, aqua	135.00
Compote, Butterflies & Waratah, purple	210.00
Compote, Butterfly & Bush, purple	110.00
Sauce dish, Emu, marigold	75.00
Sauce dish, Kangaroo, purple	64.00
Sauce dish, Kingfisher, marigold	50.00
Sauce dish, Kingfisher, purple	45.00
Sauce dish, Kookaburra, marigold	30.00
Sauce dish, Kookaburra, purple	45.00
Sauce dish, Thunderbird, purple	73.00

AUTUMN ACORNS (Fenton)

Bowl, 7" d., blue	40.00
Bowl, 8" to 9" d., amber	65.00
Bowl, 8" to 9" d., blue	75.00
Bowl, 8" to 9" d., green	40.00
Bowl, 8" to 9" d., marigold	50.00
Bowl, 8" to 9" d., purple	45.00
Bowl, 8½" d., ice cream shape, Persian blue	750.00
Bowl, ribbon candy rim, green	35.00
Bowl, ribbon candy rim, marigold	30.00
Plate, green	825.00

BASKET (Northwood)

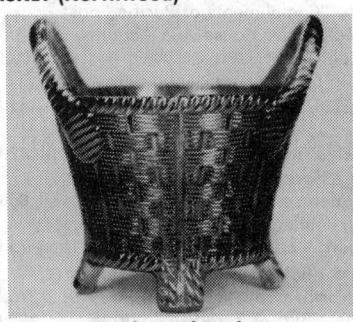

Northwood Basket

Aqua opalescent, 4½" d., 4¾" h.	340.00
Clambroth	400.00
Cobalt blue	110.00
Green	248.00
Ice blue	450.00
Ice green	224.00
Lavender	95.00
Lime green opalescent	900.00
Marigold (ILLUS.)	72.00
Purple	89.00
Smoky	250.00
White	160.00

BASKETWEAVE (Fenton)

Basket, amber	425.00

Basket, aqua 55.00
Basket, blue 38.00
Basket w/clear handle, marigold ... 32.00
Basket, two-handled, green 190.00
Compote, marigold 25.00
Hat shape, jack-in-pulpit style,
 red 225.00
Hat shape, two sides turned up,
 red 200.00
Vase, 5" h., purple 45.00
Vase, 5" h., white................ 85.00
Vase, 8½" h., marigold........... 20.00
Vase, 9" h., white................ 75.00
Vase, 11" h., marigold........... 25.00

BASKETWEAVE CANDY DISH (Fenton's Hat)
Amber 65.00
Aqua 68.00
Blue 30.00
Celeste blue 92.00
Green.......................... 55.00
Ice blue 120.00
Ice green 54.00
Marigold 38.00
Red 224.00
Vaseline 45.00
White 50.00

BEADED BULL'S EYE (Imperial)
Vase, green 35.00
Vase, marigold 30.00
Vase, purple.................... 40.00

BEADED CABLE (Northwood)

Beaded Cable Rose Bowl

Bowl, 7" d., three-footed, ruffled,
 marigold 30.00
Candy dish, green................ 60.00
Candy dish, marigold 32.00
Candy dish, purple 53.00
Loving cup, marigold 125.00
Rose bowl, aqua 345.00
Rose bowl, aqua opalescent 285.00
Rose bowl, blue................. 120.00
Rose bowl, green 89.00
Rose bowl, ice blue.............. 1,025.00
Rose bowl, marigold 75.00
Rose bowl, purple (ILLUS.) 78.00
Rose bowl, white 600.00

BEADED SHELL (Dugan or Diamond Glass Co.)

Beaded Shell Mug

Berry set: master bowl & 3 footed
 sauce dishes; purple, 4 pcs. 185.00
Creamer, marigold 60.00
Creamer, purple ....45.00 to 70.00
Mug, blue 110.00
Mug, marigold 110.00
Mug, purple (ILLUS.).............. 65.00
Mug, white 1,000.00
Pitcher, water, purple 530.00
Rose bowl, green 40.00
Spooner, footed, marigold 42.00
Sugar bowl, cov., marigold........ 65.00
Table set, marigold, 4 pcs......... 245.00
Table set, purple, 4 pcs........... 525.00
Tumbler, blue................... 47.00
Tumbler, lavender............... 95.00
Tumbler, marigold............... 70.00
Tumbler, purple................. 60.00
Water set: pitcher & 1 tumbler; pur-
 ple, 2 pcs..................... 550.00
Water set: pitcher & 6 tumblers;
 marigold, 7 pcs................. 700.00

BEADS & BELLS

Beads & Bells Bowl

Bowl, 7" d., peach opalescent
 (ILLUS.)....................... 60.00
Bowl, 7" d., purple 53.00

BEAUTY BUD VASE
Marigold, 8" h. 30.00
Purple, 8" h..................... 36.00
Marigold, 9½" h. 20.00

BIG FISH BOWL (Millersburg)

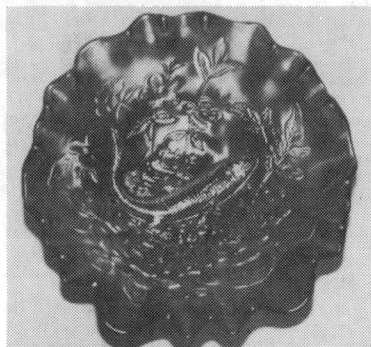

Big Fish Bowl

Green, square 1,000.00
Marigold 400.00
Marigold, ruffled 425.00
Marigold, square 435.00
Purple, ice cream shape 660.00
Purple, ruffled (ILLUS.) 704.00
Purple, square 700.00
Vaseline w/marigold, tricornered ..2,250.00

BIRDS & CHERRIES

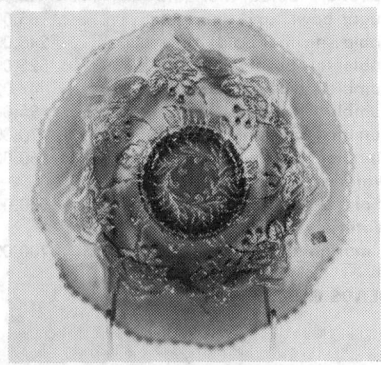

Birds & Cherries Chop Plate

Bonbon, blue 107.00
Bonbon, green 80.00
Bonbon, marigold 49.00
Bonbon, purple 68.00
Bowl, 8" to 9" d., blue 440.00
Bowl, 10" d., blue 450.00
Compote, green 55.00
Compote, marigold 40.00
Compote, purple 58.00
Plate, chop, marigold (ILLUS.) 385.00

BIRD WITH GRAPES
Wall vase, marigold, 8" h.,
  7½" w. 75.00

BLACKBERRY (Fenton)
Basket, blue 40.00
Basket, purple 72.00
Basket, red 240.00
Bowl, 8" to 9" d., ruffled, green 90.00

Bowl, 8" to 9" d., ruffled, purple ... 58.00
Bowl, 10" d., ruffled, blue 650.00
Bowl, nut, open edge, Basketweave
  exterior, purple 60.00
Plate, openwork rim, white 400.00
Vase, whimsey, open edge, blue
  opalescent..................... 900.00

BLACKBERRY BLOCK (Fenton)

Blackberry Block Pitcher

Pitcher, water, green 1,000.00
Pitcher, water, marigold 465.00
Pitcher, water, purple (ILLUS.) 1,000.00
Pitcher, water, vaseline 5,000.00
Tumbler, blue.................... 63.00
Tumbler, green 188.00
Tumbler, marigold................ 38.00
Tumbler, purple 76.00
Tumbler, white................... 500.00
Water set: pitcher & 4 tumblers;
  purple, 5 pcs. 1,300.00

BLACKBERRY BRAMBLE
Compote, ruffled, green 35.00
Compote, ruffled, lavender........ 37.50
Compote, ruffled, marigold 47.50
Compote, ruffled, purple.......... 35.00

BLACKBERRY MINIATURE COMPOTES

Blackberry Miniature Compote

Compote, miniature, blue 73.00
Compote, miniature, green......... 63.00
Compote, miniature, marigold 52.00

Compote, miniature, purple
(ILLUS.). 93.00
Compote, miniature, white 448.00

BLACKBERRY SPRAY
Bonbon, marigold 30.00
Compote, 5½" d., green 42.00
Compote, 5½" d., purple 45.00
Hat shape, amber 45.00
Hat shape, Amberina 200.00
Hat shape, amethyst opalescent 295.00
Hat shape, aqua 62.00
Hat shape, aqua opalescent 350.00
Hat shape, jack-in-pulpit, aqua
opalescent. 300.00
Hat shape, blue 36.00
Hat shape, jack-in-pulpit, crimped
rim, clambroth 27.00
Hat shape, green 48.00
Hat shape, ice green opalescent 300.00
Hat shape, marigold over milk
white 145.00
Hat shape, marigold 40.00
Hat shape, purple 33.00
Hat shape, red. 312.00
Hat shape, red slag 425.00
Hat shape, Reverse Amberina 300.00
Hat shape, vaseline w/marigold
overlay. 54.00

BLACKBERRY WREATH (Millersburg)
Bowl, 5" d., green 48.00
Bowl, 5" d., marigold. 27.50
Bowl, 5" d., ruffled, marigold 35.00
Bowl, 5" d., purple 50.00
Bowl, 7" d., green 45.00
Bowl, 7" d., marigold 32.50
Bowl, 7" d., purple 42.50
Bowl, 7" w., tricornered, purple 80.00
Bowl, 8" to 9" d., green 60.00
Bowl, 8" to 9" d., marigold. 49.00
Bowl, 8" to 9" d., purple 69.00
Bowl, 10" d., green 65.00
Bowl, 10" d., marigold. 84.00
Bowl, 10" d., purple 155.00
Bowl, ice cream, large, marigold . . . 82.00

BLOSSOM TIME COMPOTE
Compote, marigold 150.00
Compote, purple 177.00

BLUEBERRY (Fenton)
Pitcher, water, blue 515.00
Tumbler, blue. 78.00
Tumbler, marigold. 34.00
Tumbler, white. 182.00
Water set: pitcher & 6 tumblers;
blue, 7 pcs.. . . . . 975.00
Water set: pitcher & 6 tumblers;
marigold, 7 pcs.. . . . . 375.00

BO PEEP
Mug, marigold 192.00
Plate, marigold 275.00
Plate, ABC, marigold 300.00

BOUQUET
Pitcher, water, blue 337.00
Pitcher, water, marigold 179.00
Tumbler, blue. 48.00
Tumbler, marigold. 25.00
Water set: pitcher & 1 tumbler;
blue, 2 pcs.. . . . . 400.00
Water set: pitcher & 4 tumblers;
marigold, 5 pcs.. . . . . 375.00

BROKEN ARCHES (Imperial)
Punch bowl, purple, 12" d. 500.00
Punch bowl & base, marigold,
12" d., 2 pcs.. . . . . 198.00
Punch bowl & base, purple, 12" d.,
2 pcs.. . . . . 450.00
Punch cup, marigold. 22.00
Punch cup, purple 33.00
Punch set: bowl, base & 6 cups;
marigold, 8 pcs.. . . . . 335.00
Punch set: bowl, base & 6 cups; pur-
ple, 8 pcs.. 925.00

BUTTERFLIES

Butterflies Bonbon
Bonbon, blue 50.00
Bonbon, threaded exterior, blue
(Northwood) 235.00
Bonbon, green 62.00
Bonbon, marigold 40.00
Bonbon, purple (ILLUS.) 50.00
Bonbon, threaded exterior, purple
(Northwood) 206.00
Bonbon, smoky 85.00

BUTTERFLY & BERRY (Fenton)
Berry set: master bowl & 6 sauce
dishes; blue, 7 pcs. 400.00
Berry set: master bowl & 6 sauce
dishes; marigold, 7 pcs. 200.00
Bowl, 7" d., three-footed,
marigold 65.00
Bowl, 8" to 9" d., footed, blue. 70.00
Bowl, 8" to 9" d., footed,
marigold 70.00
Bowl, 8" to 9" d., footed, purple. . . 175.00
Bowl, master berry or fruit, four-
footed, blue 110.00
Bowl, master berry or fruit, four-
footed, green 115.00
Bowl, master berry or fruit, four-
footed, marigold 52.00

Bowl, master berry or fruit, four-
footed, purple 146.00
Bowl, master berry or fruit, four-
footed, white 200.00
Butter dish, cov., blue 155.00
Butter dish, cov., marigold 105.00
Centerpiece bowl, purple 500.00
Creamer, green 110.00
Creamer, marigold 44.00
Creamer, purple 110.00
Hatpin holder, blue............... 700.00
Nut bowl, blue.................... 725.00
Nut bowl, purple 437.00
Pitcher, water, blue 363.00

Butterfly & Berry Pitcher

Pitcher, water, marigold (ILLUS.).... 195.00
Sauce dish, blue 42.00
Sauce dish, green 45.00
Sauce dish, marigold 22.50
Sauce dish, purple 95.00
Spooner, blue..................... 120.00
Spooner, green 70.00
Spooner, marigold................. 55.00
Sugar bowl, cov., blue............ 140.00
Sugar bowl, cov., green 95.00
Sugar bowl, cov., marigold........ 62.00
Table set: cov. butter dish, cov. sug-
ar bowl & creamer; blue, 3 pcs. .. 450.00
Table set, marigold,
4 pcs................. 200.00 to 250.00
Tumbler, blue..................... 36.00
Tumbler, green 53.00
Tumbler, marigold................. 22.00
Tumbler, purple................... 325.00
Vase, 6" h., blue................. 55.00
Vase, 6" h., marigold............. 38.00
Vase, 8" h., blue................. 65.00
Vase, 8" h., marigold............. 30.00
Vase, 9" h., blue................. 65.00
Vase, 9" h., marigold............. 40.00
Vase, 9" h., purple............... 50.00
Water set: pitcher & 1 tumbler; pur-
ple, 2 pcs....................... 515.00
Water set: pitcher & 6 tumblers;
marigold, 7 pcs.................. 320.00

BUTTERFLY & FERN (Fenton)
Pitcher, water, blue ....300.00 to 450.00
Pitcher, water, green 425.00
Pitcher, water, marigold 250.00

Tumbler, blue..................... 44.00
Tumbler, green 45.00
Tumbler, marigold................. 33.00
Tumbler, purple................... 42.00
Water set: pitcher & 1 tumbler;
blue, 2 pcs. 418.00
Water set: pitcher & 6 tumblers;
green, 7 pcs. 695.00
Water set: pitcher & 6 tumblers;
marigold, 7 pcs................. 630.00
Water set: pitcher & 6 tumblers;
purple, 7 pcs................... 620.00

BUTTERFLY & TULIP
Bowl, 9" w., 5½" h., footed,
marigold 230.00
Bowl, 9" w., footed, purple 700.00
Bowl, 10½" square flat shape,
footed, marigold 384.00
Bowl, 10½" square flat shape,
footed, purple.................1,650.00
Bowl, 12" d., upturned sides,
footed, marigold 332.00
Bowl, vaseline 394.00

BUZZ SAW - See Double Star Pattern

CAPTIVE ROSE

Captive Rose Bowl

Bonbon, two-handled, blue,
7½" d......................... 55.00
Bonbon, two-handled, marigold,
7½" d......................... 45.00
Bonbon, two-handled, purple,
7½" d......................... 55.00
Bowl, 8" to 9" d., amber 65.00
Bowl, 8" to 9" d., blue........... 77.00
Bowl, 8" to 9" d., green 50.00
Bowl, 8" to 9" d., ribbon candy rim,
green 47.00
Bowl, 8" to 9" d., ribbon candy rim,
purple (ILLUS.) 44.00
Bowl, 8" to 9" d., ruffled rim, blue.. 58.00
Bowl, 8" to 9" d., ruffled rim,
marigold 35.00
Compote, blue 82.50
Compote, green................... 50.00
Compote, marigold 45.00
Compote, purple 45.00
Compote, white 98.00
Plate, 9" d., amber 193.00
Plate, 9" d., blue............... 174.00
Plate, 9" d., green 256.00

Plate, 9" d., marigold 150.00
Plate, 9" d., purple 196.00

CARNIVAL HOLLY - See Holly Pattern

CAROLINA DOGWOOD
Bowl, 8½" d., aqua opalescent 350.00
Bowl, 8½" d., blue opalescent 305.00
Bowl, 8½" d., marigold on milk
  white 332.00
Bowl, 8½" d., peach opalescent 110.00
Plate, 8½" d., peach opalescent 475.00

CAROLINE
Basket w/applied handle, peach
  opalescent 343.00
Bowl, 8" to 9" d., peach
  opalescent 53.00
Bowl, 8" to 9" w., tricornered,
  peach opalescent 82.50
Plate, w/handgrip, peach
  opalescent 80.00

CATTAILS & WATERLILY - See Water Lily & Cattails Pattern on Page 434

CHATELAINE
Pitcher, purple 2,000.00
Tumbler, purple 250.00

CHECKERBOARD
Goblet, marigold 310.00
Goblet, purple 162.00
Pitcher, water, purple 1,900.00
Punch cup, marigold 95.00
Tumbler, purple 398.00

CHERRY
Bowl, 6" d., Jeweled Heart exterior,
  purple 32.00
Bowl, 7" d., three-footed, crimped
  rim, peach opalescent 60.00
Bowl, 8" d., ruffled, purple 125.00
Bowl, 8" to 9" d., three-footed,
  marigold 52.00
Bowl, 8" to 9" d., three-footed,
  peach opalescent 75.00
Bowl, 8" to 9" d., three-footed,
  purple 67.00
Bowl, large, peach opalescent 240.00
Dish, ruffled, purple, 6" d. 38.00
Plate, ruffled, purple 114.00
Sauce dish, peach opalescent 64.00
Sauce dish, purple 60.00

CHERRY or CHERRY CIRCLES (Fenton)
Bonbon, two-handled, aqua 280.00
Bonbon, two-handled, blue 60.00
Bonbon, two-handled, marigold 33.00
Bonbon, two-handled, purple 50.00
Bonbon, two-handled, red 1,700.00
Bowl, 5" d., fluted, blue 18.00
Bowl, 7" d., three-footed, peach
  opalescent w/plain interior 90.00

Bowl, 8" to 9" d., marigold 30.00
Bowl, 8" to 9" d., white 70.00
Bowl, 10" d., vaseline w/marigold
  overlay 70.00
Card tray, aqua 125.00
Plate, 6" d., marigold 40.00

CHERRY or HANGING CHERRIES (Millersburg)
Banana compote (whimsey), green .. 715.00
Banana compote (whimsey),
  marigold 735.00
Banana compote (whimsey),
  purple 1,300.00
Bowl, 5" d., ruffled, blue satin 600.00
Bowl, 5" d., ruffled, marigold 50.00
Bowl, 5" d., piecrust rim, purple 49.00
Bowl, 6" d., ruffled, green 95.00
Bowl, 7" d., green 70.00
Bowl, 7" d., marigold 55.00
Bowl, 7" d., purple 82.00
Bowl, 8" to 9" d., dome-footed,
  marigold 65.00
Bowl, 8" to 9" d., purple 60.00
Bowl, ice cream, 10" d., green 122.00
Bowl, ice cream, 10" d., marigold .. 108.00
Bowl, ice cream, 10" d., purple..... 125.00
Bowl, ice cream, 10" d., teal blue .. 850.00
Bowl, ruffled, Hobnail exterior, mar-
  igold, large 468.00
Butter dish, cov., green 227.00
Butter dish, cov., marigold 150.00
Butter dish, cov., purple 175.00
Creamer, green 77.00
Creamer, marigold 55.00
Creamer, purple 80.00
Pitcher, milk, marigold 600.00
Pitcher, milk, purple.............. 418.00
Pitcher, water, green 700.00
Pitcher, water, marigold 200.00
Pitcher, water, purple 600.00
Plate, 6" d., purple 165.00
Plate, 7" d., purple 225.00
Plate, 8" d., green 475.00
Spooner, green 75.00
Spooner, marigold................ 55.00
Spooner, purple 75.00
Sugar bowl, cov., green 85.00
Sugar bowl, cov., marigold 85.00
Sugar bowl, cov., purple 125.00
Table set, marigold, 4 pcs. 375.00
Table set, purple, 4 pcs. ...500.00 to 700.00
Tumbler, green 145.00
Tumbler, marigold................ 274.00
Tumbler, purple 320.00
Water set: pitcher & 5 tumblers;
  marigold, 6 pcs. 1,800.00

CHERRY CHAIN (Fenton)
Bonbon, two-handled, marigold..... 42.50
Bowl, 5" d., blue 35.00
Bowl, 5" d., Orange Tree exterior,
  marigold 26.00
Bowl, 8" to 9" d., blue 47.00
Bowl, 8" to 9" d., white 90.00

Bowl, ice cream, 10" d., vaseline ... 175.00
Bowl, 10" d., Orange Tree exterior,
    blue 68.00
Bowl, 10" d., Orange Tree exterior,
    marigold 43.00
Bowl, 10" d., Orange Tree exterior,
    white 120.00
Plate, 6" to 7" d., blue .....95.00 to 135.00
Plate, 6" to 7" d., marigold 60.00
Plate, chop, white................ 605.00

CHERRY CIRCLES - See Cherry (Fenton) Pattern

CHRISTMAS COMPOTE (Northwood or Dugan)

Christmas Compote

Marigold ....1,500.00 to 2,100.00
Purple (ILLUS.) ....2,100.00 to 2,750.00

CHRYSANTHEMUM or WINDWILL & MUMS
Bowl, 8" to 9" d., three-footed,
    blue 100.00
Bowl, 8" to 9" d., three-footed,
    green 78.00
Bowl, 8" to 9" d., three-footed,
    marigold 46.00
Bowl, 9" d., ruffled, green 275.00
Bowl, 10" d., three-footed, blue 145.00
Bowl, 10" d., three-footed,
    marigold 58.00
Bowl, 10" d., three-footed, purple .. 75.00
Bowl, 10" d., collared base, red 950.00
Bowl, collared base, green......... 238.00
Bowl, collared base, marigold 45.00
Bowl, orange, footed, vaseline 350.00

CIRCLED SCROLL (Dugan or Diamond Glass Co.)
Creamer, marigold 48.00
Creamer, purple 125.00
Pitcher, water, marigold 1,400.00
Spooner, marigold................. 125.00
Tumbler, marigold (ILLUS.) 225.00
Tumbler, purple................... 968.00
Vase, 7½" h., purple............. 52.50
Vase, 9" h., marigold............. 85.00
Vase, hat-shaped, marigold 48.00
Vase, hat-shaped, purple 75.00

Circled Scroll Tumbler

COBBLESTONES BOWL (Imperial)
Green, 9" d...................... 37.50
Purple, 9" d..................... 52.50

COIN DOT

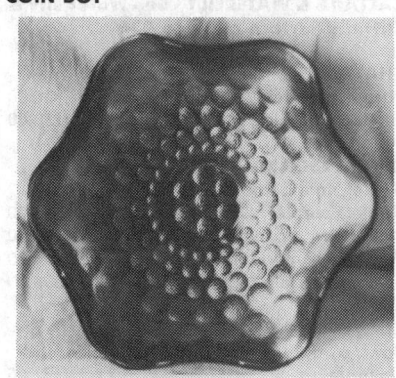

Coin Dot Bowl

Bowl, 6" d., green 20.00
Bowl, 7" d., blue (ILLUS.) 30.00
Bowl, 7" d., marigold............ 38.00
Bowl, 7" d., purple 28.00
Bowl, 7" d., red.........675.00 to 750.00
Bowl, 7" d., ribbon candy rim,
    green 42.50
Bowl, 7" d., ribbon candy rim,
    marigold 40.00
Bowl, 7" d., ribbon candy rim,
    purple 40.00
Bowl, 8" to 9" d., stippled, aqua.... 46.00
Bowl, 8" to 9" d., blue............ 32.00
Bowl, 8" to 9" d., blue opalescent .. 300.00
Bowl, 8" to 9" d., green 37.50
Bowl, 8" to 9" d., marigold........ 25.00
Bowl, 8" to 9" d., purple 40.00
Bowl, 8" to 9" d., ruffled, vaseline .. 55.00
Pitcher, water, marigold 150.00
Plate, purple.................... 58.00
Rose bowl, green 52.00
Rose bowl, marigold.............. 43.00
Tumbler, marigold................ 50.00

Water set: pitcher & 6 tumblers;
marigold, 7 pcs.................. 425.00

COIN SPOT (Dugan)
Compote, 4½" d., peach
opalescent..................... 59.00
Compote, 7" d., blue 125.00
Compote, 7" d., marigold 30.00
Compote, 7" d., fluted, peach
opalescent..................... 55.00
Compote, 7" d., fluted, purple...... 56.00
Plate, 9" d., aqua 295.00
Plate, 9" d., purple............... 35.00
Water set: pitcher & 4 tumblers;
white, 5 pcs..................... 365.00

COMET or RIBBON TIE (Fenton)
Bowl, 8" to 9" d., blue............. 60.00
Bowl, 8" to 9" d., green 45.00
Bowl, 8" to 9" d., marigold......... 40.00
Bowl, 8" to 9" d., purple.......... 50.00
Plate, 9" d., ruffled, blue 173.00
Plate, 9" d., ruffled, marigold 225.00
Plate, 9" d., ruffled, purple 185.00

CONCAVE DIAMOND - See Diamond Concave Pattern

CONCORD (Fenton)
Bowl, blue....................... 118.00
Bowl, marigold................... 125.00
Plate, green 500.00
Plate, marigold 450.00

CONSTELLATION (Dugan)
Compote, marigold 44.00
Compote, white 86.00

CORAL (Fenton)
Bowl, 8" to 9" d., collared base,
green 135.00
Bowl, 8" to 9" d., collared base,
marigold 77.50
Plate, 9" d., marigold 700.00

CORN BOTTLE

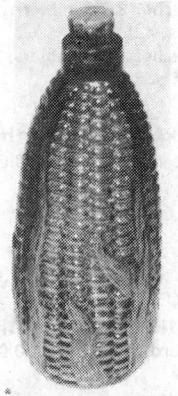

Corn Bottle

Green........................... 275.00
Marigold........................ 232.00
Smoky (ILLUS.) 210.00

CORN VASE (Northwood)

Corn Vase

Aqua, pastel 1,150.00
Blue, pastel..................... 375.00
Green........................... 338.00
Ice blue 1,250.00
Ice green....................... 260.00
Marigold........................ 550.00
Purple (ILLUS.) 454.00
White 250.00

CORNUCOPIA
Candlestick, white................ 85.00
Candlesticks, ice blue, pr. 115.00
Vase, 5" h., marigold............. 30.00

COSMOS

Cosmos Bowl

Bowl, 5" d., green 49.00
Bowl, 9" d., green (ILLUS.) 62.00
Bowl, 9" d., marigold............. 30.00
Bowl, 10" d., marigold............ 45.00
Plate, 6" d., green 90.00
Plate, 9" d., green 65.00
Plate, chop, 10½" d., marigold 245.00

COSMOS & CANE (U.S. Glass Co.)
Bowl, 8" to 9" d., marigold........ 50.00

Bowl, 8" to 9" sq., white 147.00
Bowl, 10" d., white 132.00
Butter dish, cov., amber 235.00
Butter dish, cov., marigold 215.00
Butter dish, cov., purple 100.00
Butter dish, cov., white 275.00
Compote, amber 500.00
Compote, marigold 150.00

Cosmos & Cane Compote

Compote, white (ILLUS.) 850.00
Creamer, honey amber 180.00
Creamer, marigold 110.00
Pitcher, honey amber 1,900.00
Pitcher, white 1,000.00
Rose bowl, Headdress interior,
  marigold 400.00
Sauce dish, green 40.00
Sauce dish, marigold 30.00
Sauce dish, white 60.00
Sugar bowl, cov., honey amber 85.00
Table set, amber, 4 pcs. 595.00
Tumbler, amber 110.00
Tumbler, honey amber 63.00
Tumbler, marigold 75.00
Tumbler, white 210.00

COUNTRY KITCHEN (Millersburg)

Bowl, 5" d., ruffled, marigold 79.00
Bowl, master berry, marigold 110.00
Butter dish, purple 350.00
Spooner, marigold 100.00

CRAB CLAW (Imperial)

Bowl, 8" to 9" d., marigold 35.00
Bowl, 8" to 9" d., fluted, smoky 45.00
Tumbler, marigold 40.00
Water set: pitcher & 6 tumblers;
  marigold, 7 pcs. 300.00

CRACKLE

Automobile vase w/bracket,
  marigold 25.00
Cuspidor, marigold 59.00
Plate, 9½" d., purple 40.00
Tumbler, dome-footed, marigold 15.00
Vase, fan-shaped, marigold 20.00
Water set: cov. pitcher & 5 tum-
  blers; marigold, 6 pcs. 90.00

CRUCIFIX

Candlesticks, marigold,
  pr. . . . . 295.00 to 375.00

CUT ARCS

Bowl, 9" d., marigold 16.50

CUT COSMOS

Tumbler 200.00

DAHLIA (Dugan or Diamond Glass Co.)

Berry set: master bowl & 4 sauce
  dishes; white, 5 pcs. 600.00
Berry set: master bowl & 5 sauce
  dishes; purple, 6 pcs. 275.00
Bowl, master berry, 10" d., footed,
  white 170.00
Butter dish, cov., marigold 140.00
Butter dish, cov., white 350.00
Creamer, marigold 60.00
Creamer, purple 125.00
Creamer, white 125.00
Creamer & cov. sugar bowl, white,
  pr. 275.00
Pitcher, water, marigold 250.00
Pitcher, water, purple . . . . . 600.00 to 650.00
Pitcher, water, white 575.00
Sauce dish, marigold 40.00
Sauce dish, purple 45.00
Sauce dish, white 48.00
Spooner, marigold 60.00
Spooner, purple 75.00
Sugar bowl, cov., purple 100.00
Table set, marigold, 4 pcs. 425.00
Table set, purple, 4 pcs. . . . 825.00 to 850.00
Table set, white, 4 pcs. 900.00
Tumbler, amber 95.00
Tumbler, marigold 115.00
Tumbler, pastel marigold 150.00
Tumbler, purple 195.00
Tumbler, white 155.00
Tumbler, white w/blue flower 275.00
Tumbler, white w/gold flower 195.00
Tumbler, white w/red flower 275.00
Tumbler, white w/silver band 300.00
Water set: pitcher & 1 tumbler;
  white, 2 pcs. 700.00
Water set: pitcher & 6 tumblers;
  marigold, 7 pcs. 1,025.00

DAISIES & DRAPE VASE (Northwood)

Aqua opalescent . . . . 350.00 to 450.00
Blue 370.00
Green 4,500.00
Marigold 270.00
Purple 300.00
White . . . . 150.00 to 170.00

DAISY & LATTICE BAND or LATTICE & DAISY

Pitcher, tankard, marigold . . 90.00 to 125.00
Tumbler, blue 50.00
Tumbler, marigold 25.00
Tumbler, purple 25.00

Water set: pitcher & 4 tumblers;
marigold, 5 pcs.................. 215.00

DAISY & PLUME
Bowl, 8" to 9" d., three-footed,
green 135.00
Candy dish, footed, green 60.00
Candy dish, footed, marigold 50.00
Candy dish, footed, peach opales-
cent (Dugan)................... 60.00
Candy dish, footed, purple 80.00
Compote, green................... 54.00
Compote, marigold 31.00
Compote, purple 53.00
Rose bowl, three-footed, blue 250.00
Rose bowl, three-footed, green 65.00
Rose bowl, three-footed, ice blue ... 900.00
Rose bowl, three-footed, ice
green 900.00
Rose bowl, three-footed, marigold .. 60.00
Rose bowl, three-footed, purple 95.00

DAISY BASKET
Marigold 42.00

DAISY BLOCK ROWBOAT
Marigold, 12" l., 4" w., 3¼" h. 200.00
Purple 300.00

DAISY CUT BELL
Marigold 388.00

DAISY SQUARES
Bowl, 6" d., clear w/marigold 425.00
Compote, amber 265.00
Compote, marigold 425.00
Goblet, green.................... 275.00
Rose bowl, stemmed, green 350.00

DAISY WREATH (Westmoreland)
Bowl, 8" to 9" d., blue opalescent .. 382.00
Bowl, 8" to 9" d., milk white
w/marigold overlay .....150.00 to 200.00
Bowl, 8" to 9" d., peach
opalescent..................... 70.00
Plate, 9" d., ruffled, aqua.......... 350.00

DANDELION (Northwood)

Dandelion Pitcher
Mug, aqua opalescent 495.00

Mug, blue 534.00
Mug, electric blue 558.00
Mug, green 700.00
Mug, ice blue opalescent 895.00
Mug, marigold 285.00
Mug, purple 280.00
Mug, Knight's Templar, ice blue 1,000.00
Mug, Knight's Templar, ice green ... 895.00
Mug, Knight's Templar, marigold ... 495.00
Pitcher, water, tankard, green 750.00
Pitcher, water, tankard, marigold
(ILLUS.) ....350.00 to 375.00
Pitcher, water, tankard,
purple ....450.00 to 590.00
Pitcher, water, tankard,
white........................2,000.00
Tumbler, green 90.00
Tumbler, ice blue 180.00
Tumbler, lavender............... 225.00
Tumbler, marigold............... 36.00
Tumbler, purple................. 45.00
Tumbler, smoky 300.00
Tumbler, white.................. 142.00
Water set: pitcher & 1 tumbler;
white, 2 pcs. 2,500.00
Water set: pitcher & 2 tumblers;
pastel marigold, 3 pcs. 875.00
Water set: pitcher & 6 tumblers;
purple, 7 pcs................... 882.00

DANDELION, PANELED (Fenton)
Pitcher, water, blue 450.00
Pitcher, water, green 325.00
Pitcher, water, marigold 350.00
Pitcher, water, purple 625.00
Tumbler, blue.................... 40.00
Tumbler, green 40.00
Tumbler, marigold................ 32.50
Tumbler, purple................. 44.00
Water set: pitcher & 5 tumblers;
marigold, 6 pcs................. 375.00
Water set: pitcher & 6 tumblers;
blue, 7 pcs..................... 875.00
Water set: pitcher & 6 tumblers;
green, 7 pcs.................... 637.00
Water set: pitcher & 6 tumblers;
purple, 7 pcs................... 650.00

DIAMOND & RIB VASE (Fenton)
Vase, 10" h., blue............... 40.00
Vase, 10" h., green 32.00
Vase, 10" h., marigold............ 20.00
Vase, 10" h., purple............. 30.00
Vase, 11" h., green 38.00
Vase, 11" h., ice green 65.00
Vases, 11" h., purple, pr.......... 80.00
Vase, 12" h., purple 32.50
Vase, 19" h., purple.......500.00 to 600.00
Vase, 20" h., marigold............ 300.00

DIAMOND & SUNBURST
Decanter w/stopper, marigold...... 60.00
Wine, marigold 26.00
Wine, purple.................... 40.00

Wine set: decanter w/stopper & 6
  wines; marigold, 7 pcs. 325.00
Wine set: decanter w/stopper & 6
  wines; purple, 7 pcs. 495.00

DIAMOND CONCAVE or CONCAVE DIAMOND
Pitcher w/cover, vaseline 550.00
Tumbler, ice blue 25.00
Tumbler, vaseline 168.00
Tumble-up (water carafe w/tumbler
  top), ice blue 325.00

DIAMOND LACE (Imperial)

Diamond Lace Pitcher

Berry set: master bowl & 5 sauce
  dishes; marigold, 6 pcs. 80.00
Bowl, 5" d., green 35.00
Bowl, 5" d., marigold 16.00
Bowl, 5" d., purple 30.00
Bowl, 8" to 9" d., marigold 30.00
Bowl, 8" to 9" d., purple 65.00
Bowl, 10" d., purple 76.00
Pitcher, water, purple (ILLUS.) 235.00
Tumbler, marigold. 425.00
Tumbler, purple 45.00
Water set: pitcher & 6 tumblers;
  purple, 7 pcs. 405.00

DIAMOND POINT COLUMNS

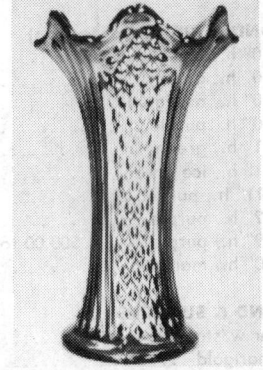

Diamond Point Columns Vase

Bowl, 5" d., 2½" h., marigold 20.00
Creamer, marigold 35.00
Vase, 6" h., green 42.00
Vase, 6" h., marigold. 30.00
Vase, 7" h., purple 40.00
Vase, 8" h., green (ILLUS.) 40.00
Vase, 9" h., purple 42.00
Vase, 10" h., white. 65.00
Vase, 16" h., blue 365.00

DIAMOND RING (Imperial)
Berry set: master bowl & 4 sauce
  dishes; smoky, 5 pcs. 40.00
Bowl, 8" to 9" d., marigold. 75.00
Bowl, 8" to 9" d., purple. 62.50
Bowl, 8" to 9" d., smoky 25.00
Rose bowl, marigold. 300.00

DIAMONDS (Millersburg)
Pitcher, water, aqua 225.00
Pitcher, water, green. 175.00
Pitcher, water, marigold 125.00
Pitcher, water, purple 160.00
Punch bowl & base, marigold,
  2 pcs. 1,600.00
Punch bowl & base, purple, 2 pcs. . . 900.00
Tumbler, amber 42.50
Tumbler, green 60.00
Tumbler, marigold. 45.00
Tumbler, purple 55.00
Water set: pitcher & 1 tumbler; pur-
  ple, 2 pcs. 250.00
Water set: pitcher & 4 tumblers;
  marigold, 5 pcs. 350.00
Water set: pitcher & 5 tumblers;
  green, 6 pcs. 400.00

DIVING DOLPHINS FOOTED BOWL (Sowerby)
Marigold 175.00
Purple 173.00

DOGWOOD SPRAYS
Bowl, 8" to 9" d., dome-footed,
  marigold 40.00
Bowl, 8" to 9" d., dome-footed,
  peach opalescent. 95.00
Bowl, 8" to 9" d., dome-footed,
  purple 65.00

DOLPHINS COMPOTE (Millersburg)
Blue, Rosalind interior 2,500.00
Purple, Rosalind interior . . . 675.00 to 800.00

DOUBLE DUTCH BOWL
Marigold, 7" d. 20.00
Purple, 7" d. 42.00
Green, 8" to 9" d., footed 55.00
Marigold, 8" to 9" d., footed 35.00
Purple, 8" to 9" d., footed 80.00
Clambroth, 10" d., ruffled 69.00

DOUBLE STAR or BUZZ SAW (Cambridge)
Cruet w/stopper, green, small,
  4" 425.00

Cruet w/stopper, green, large,
6" 435.00
Cruet w/stopper, marigold, large,
6" 300.00
Pitcher, water, green 337.50
Pitcher, water, marigold ...425.00 to 500.00
Tumbler, green 50.00
Water set: pitcher & 6 tumblers;
green, 7 pcs. 950.00

DOUBLE STEM ROSE
Bowl, 8" to 9" d., dome-footed,
blue 325.00
Bowl, 8" to 9" d., dome-footed,
celeste blue 420.00
Bowl, 8" to 9" d., dome-footed,
lavender 160.00
Bowl, 8" to 9" d., dome-footed,
marigold 32.00
Bowl, 8" to 9" d., dome-footed,
peach opalescent............... 75.00
Bowl, 8" to 9" d., dome-footed,
purple 45.00
Bowl, 8" to 9" d., dome-footed,
white 117.00
Plate, dome-footed, purple......... 145.00
Plate, dome-footed, white 150.00

DRAGON & LOTUS (Fenton)

Dragon & Lotus Bowl

Bowl, 7" to 9" d., three-footed,
peach opalescent............... 500.00
Bowl, 7" to 9" d., three-footed,
purple 90.00
Bowl, 8" to 9" d., collared base,
amber 155.00
Bowl, 8" to 9" d., collared base,
aqua opalescent 700.00
Bowl, 8" to 9" d., collared base,
blue 72.00
Bowl, 7" to 9" d., three-footed,
blue 52.00
Bowl, 7" to 9" d., three-footed,
green 68.00
Bowl, 7" to 9" d., three-footed, lime
green opalescent............... 300.00
Bowl, 7" to 9" d., three-footed,
marigold 40.00
Bowl, 8" to 9" d., collared base,
green 95.00

Bowl, 8" to 9" d., collared base,
lime green 325.00
Bowl, 8" to 9" d., collared base,
lime green opalescent 684.00
Bowl, 8" to 9" d., collared base,
milk white w/marigold overlay ... 850.00
Bowl, 8" to 9" d., collared base,
peach opalescent ....500.00 to 575.00
Bowl, 8" to 9" d., collared base,
purple 75.00
Bowl, 8" to 9" d., red .....750.00 to 775.00
Bowl, 9" d., ice cream shape, col-
lared base, amber 200.00
Bowl, 9" d., ice cream shape, col-
lared base, blue (ILLUS.) 54.00
Bowl, 9" d., ice cream shape, col-
lared base, marigold 50.00
Bowl, 9" d., ice cream shape, col-
lared base, red................1,400.00
Bowl, 9" d., ice cream shape, col-
lared base, Reverse Amberina ... 650.00
Bowl, blue opalescent 450.00
Bowl, moonstone 1,350.00
Plate, collared base, blue 668.00
Plate, collared base, ruffled,
marigold 650.00
Plate, spatula-footed, marigold 638.00

DRAGON & STRAWBERRY BOWL (Fenton)
Bowl, 9" d., blue 445.00
Bowl, 9" d., green 520.00
Bowl, 9" d., marigold............. 233.00

DRAPERY (Northwood)
Candy dish, tricornered, aqua 115.00
Candy dish, tricornered, aqua
opalescent..................... 150.00
Candy dish, tricornered, ice blue ... 146.00
Candy dish, tricornered, ice green .. 110.00
Candy dish, tricornered, marigold .. 62.50
Candy dish, tricornered, purple..... 110.00
Candy dish, tricornered, white 135.00
Rose bowl, aqua opalescent 280.00
Rose bowl, blue.................. 295.00
Rose bowl, ice blue 550.00
Rose bowl, lavender 110.00
Rose bowl, marigold.............. 325.00
Rose bowl, pastel marigold 385.00
Rose bowl, purple................ 234.00
Rose bowl, white................. 435.00
Vase, 4" h., ice blue 170.00
Vase, 7" h., aqua opalescent 150.00
Vase, 7" h., blue................. 67.50
Vase, 7" h., ice green 65.00
Vase, 7" h., marigold............. 49.00
Vase, 8" h., ice blue 60.00
Vase, 8" h., ice green 100.00
Vase, 8" h., marigold............. 42.00
Vase, 8" h., white................ 95.00
Vase, purple..................... 57.50

EMBROIDERED MUMS (Northwood)
Bowl, 8" to 9" d., ruffled, aqua
opalescent 1,467.00
Bowl, 8" to 9" d., blue............ 296.00

Bowl, 8" to 9" d., ice blue 800.00
Bowl, 8" to 9" d., ice green 800.00
Bowl, 8" to 9" d., ruffled,
   marigold 230.00

Embroidered Mums Bowl

Bowl, 8" to 9" d., purple (ILLUS.) ... 255.00
Plate, ice green 2,000.00

ESTATE (Westmoreland)
Creamer, marigold opalescent 45.00
Creamer, peach opalescent 70.00
Creamer & sugar bowl, aqua, pr. ... 150.00
Mug, marigold 105.00
Sugar bowl, marigold, souvenir 50.00
Sugar bowl, peach opalescent 50.00

FAN (Dugan)
Sauceboat, peach opalescent 85.00
Sauceboat, purple 60.00

FANCIFUL (Dugan)
Bowl, 8" to 9" d., blue 85.00
Bowl, 8" to 9" d., piecrust rim,
   marigold 85.00
Bowl, 8" to 9" d., peach
   opalescent..................... 204.00

Fanciful Ruffled Bowl

Bowl, 8" to 9" d., ruffled, purple
   (ILLUS.)........................ 110.00
Bowl, 8" to 9" d., ruffled, white 105.00
Plate, 9" d., blue................. 170.00

Plate, 9" d., marigold 85.00
Plate, 9" d., peach opalescent 400.00
Plate, 9" d., purple............... 217.00
Plate, 9" d., white 196.00

FANTAIL
Bowl, 9" d., footed, blue........... 128.00
Bowl, 9" d., shallow, footed,
   w/Butterfly & Berry exterior,
   blue 200.00
Bowl, 9" d., footed, green 80.00
Bowl, 9" d., footed, marigold....... 80.00

FARMYARD (Dugan)

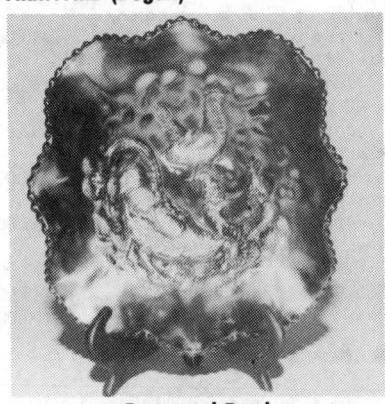

Farmyard Bowl

Bowl, purple 2,600.00
Bowl, fluted, purple............. 2,600.00
Bowl, ribbon candy rim, purple ... 2,350.00
Bowl, square, purple (ILLUS.) 2,800.00
Plate, 10" d., purple 8,125.00

FASHION (Imperial)

Fashion Pitcher

Bowl, 9" d., clambroth............. 30.00
Bowl, 9" d., marigold............. 18.00
Bowl, 9" d., ruffled, smoky........ 46.00
Bowl, 10" d., marigold............ 45.00
Creamer, marigold 22.50
Creamer & sugar bowl, marigold,
   pr............................. 60.00
Pitcher, water, marigold (ILLUS.).... 100.00
Pitcher, water, purple 825.00

Pitcher, water, smoky 335.00
Punch bowl & base, marigold,
  12" d., 2 pcs. 108.00
Punch cup, marigold 14.00
Punch cup, red 300.00
Punch cup, smoky 30.00
Punch set: 12" d. bowl, base & 6
  cups; marigold, 8 pcs. 190.00
Rose bowl, marigold, 7" d. 83.00
Sugar bowl, marigold 20.00
Sugar bowl, smoky 90.00
Tumbler, marigold 22.50
Tumbler, smoky 90.00
Water set: pitcher & 1 tumbler; mar-
  igold, 2 pcs. 148.00
Water set: pitcher & 6 tumblers;
  smoky, 7 pcs. 400.00

FEATHER & HEART

Feather & Heart Tumbler

Pitcher, water, green 450.00
Pitcher, water, marigold 375.00
Pitcher, water, purple 475.00
Tumbler, green 150.00
Tumbler, marigold 85.00
Tumbler, purple (ILLUS.) 92.50
Water set: pitcher & 1 tumbler;
  green, 2 pcs. 500.00
Water set: pitcher & 5 tumblers;
  marigold, 6 pcs. .... 550.00 to 700.00

FEATHERED SERPENT

Berry set: master bowl & 6 sauce
  dishes; marigold, 7 pcs. 195.00
Berry set: master bowl & 6 sauce
  dishes; purple, 7 pcs. 160.00
Bowl, 8" to 9" d., green 65.00
Bowl, 8" to 9" d., marigold 40.00
Bowl, 8" to 9" d., purple 65.00
Bowl, 10" d., amethyst 46.50
Bowl, 10" d., fluted, green 48.00
Bowl, 10" d., marigold 45.00
Bowl, 10" d., flared, purple 69.00
Sauce dish, blue 20.00
Sauce dish, green 26.00
Sauce dish, purple 22.50

FEATHER STITCH BOWL

Aqua 225.00
Blue 88.00
Marigold 40.00
Purple 55.00

FENTONIA

Berry set: master bowl & 4 sauce
  dishes; marigold, 5 pcs. 175.00
Bowl, master berry, blue 95.00
Butter dish, cov., footed, blue 150.00
Butter dish, cov., footed, marigold .. 137.50
Creamer, blue 50.00
Creamer, marigold 65.00
Pitcher, water, blue 700.00
Pitcher, water, marigold 225.00
Spooner, marigold 60.00
Sugar bowl, cov., blue 125.00
Table set: creamer, cov. sugar bowl
  & spooner; blue, 3 pcs. 350.00
Table set, marigold, 4 pcs. 350.00
Tumbler, blue 45.00
Tumbler, marigold 50.00
Water set: pitcher & 6 tumblers;
  blue, 7 pcs. 800.00

FENTON'S (OPEN EDGE) BASKET

Aqua 55.00
Aqua, two sides turned up 80.00
Black amethyst 365.00
Blue 50.00
Green 53.00
Green, low sides 175.00
Ice blue, w/three rows 200.00
Ice green 150.00
Lavender 75.00
Marigold 30.00
Marigold w/advertising 49.00
Marigold, w/two rows 35.00
Purple 110.00
Red 225.00
Red, hat shape 210.00
Red, six-sided, w/two rows 250.00
Vaseline 50.00
White, square 75.00

FENTON'S FLOWERS ROSE BOWL · See Orange Tree Pattern

FERN

Compote, w/Daisy & Plume exterior,
  green (Northwood) 70.00
Compote, w/Daisy & Plume exterior,
  marigold (Northwood) 75.00
Compote, w/Daisy & Plume exterior,
  purple (Northwood) 67.50
Dish, hat-shaped, marigold
  (Fenton) 17.50
Dish, hat-shaped, red (Fenton) 375.00

FIELD FLOWER (Imperial)

Pitcher, water, amber 350.00
Pitcher, water, green 235.00
Pitcher, water, marigold 160.00
Pitcher, water, purple 400.00
Pitcher, water, teal blue 285.00
Tumbler, blue 125.00
Tumbler, green 65.00
Tumbler, marigold 33.00
Tumbler, purple 65.00

Water set: pitcher & 1 tumbler;
green, 2 pcs. 350.00
Water set: pitcher & 6 tumblers;
marigold, 7 pcs. 275.00
Water set: pitcher & 6 tumblers;
purple, 7 pcs. 650.00

FIELD THISTLE (English)
Bowl, 10" d., marigold 50.00
Butter dish, cov., marigold 75.00
Pitcher, water, marigold 250.00
Plate, 6" d., marigold 110.00
Plate, 9" d., marigold 435.00
Spooner, marigold 55.00
Table set: cov. butter dish, creamer
& spooner; marigold, 3 pcs. 175.00
Tumbler, marigold 55.00
Vase, 7" h., marigold 45.00

FILE (Imperial)
Spooner, marigold 50.00
Tumbler, marigold 375.00
Water set: pitcher & 3 tumblers;
marigold, 4 pcs. 950.00

FILE & FAN
Compote, blue opalescent 435.00
Compote, marigold 45.00
Compote, peach opalescent 80.00

FINECUT & ROSES (Northwood)
Candy dish, three-footed, amber . . . 55.00
Candy dish, three-footed, aqua
opalescent 365.00
Candy dish, three-footed, electric
blue 67.50
Candy dish, three-footed, green 68.00
Candy dish, three-footed, ice blue . . 167.50
Candy dish, three-footed, ice
green 175.00
Candy dish, three-footed,
marigold 32.50
Candy dish, three-footed, purple . . . 51.00
Candy dish, three-footed, white 130.00
Rose bowl, aqua opalescent 900.00
Rose bowl, green 128.00
Rose bowl, ice blue 366.00
Rose bowl, marigold 87.00
Rose bowl, purple 75.00
Rose bowl, white 475.00

FINE RIB (Northwood & Fenton)
Bowl, purple 35.00
Vase, 6½" h., 5" d., blue 25.00
Vase, 6½" h., 5" d., green 20.00
Vase, 6½" h., 5" d., marigold 32.00
Vase, 7" h., green 40.00
Vase, 7½" h., white 55.00
Vase, 8" h., aqua 50.00
Vase, 8½" h., blue 40.00
Vase, 9" h., fluted rim, ice
green 40.00
Vase, 9" h., red (Fenton) 215.00
Vase, 9½" h., vaseline (Fenton) 45.00
Vase, 10" h., amber (Fenton) 27.00

Vase, 10" h., aqua
(Northwood) . . . . .70.00 to 80.00
Vase, 10" h., purple 32.00
Vase, 10" h., red (Fenton) 250.00
Vase, 11" h., aqua 50.00
Vase, 11" h., blue 35.00
Vase, 11" h., ice green
(Northwood) 65.00
Vase, 11" h., red
(Fenton) . . . . .150.00 to 200.00
Vase, 12" h., blue 35.00
Vase, 14" h., marigold 38.00
Vase, 15" h., blue 50.00
Vase, 15" h., purple 65.00
Vase, 16" h., red (Fenton) 350.00

FISHERMAN'S MUG

Fisherman's Mug

Marigold opalescent 1,200.00
Marigold 176.00
Peach opalescent 1,250.00
Purple (ILLUS.) 75.00

FISHSCALE & BEADS
Banana boat, peach opalescent,
7" l. 35.00
Bonbon, marigold, 6" 35.00
Bonbon, peach opalescent, 6" 52.00
Card tray, 4 x 7", peach
opalescent 70.00
Plate, 7" d., marigold 48.00
Plate, 7" d., ruffled rim, peach
opalescent 95.00
Plate, 7" d., purple 300.00
Plate, 7" d., white 80.00
Plate, 7½" d., purple 150.00
Plate, flat, pastel marigold 60.00

FLEUR DE LIS (Millersburg)
Bowl, 8" to 9" d., dome-footed,
purple 267.00
Bowl, 10" d., green 198.00
Bowl, 10" d., marigold 150.00
Bowl, 10" d., purple 267.00
Bowl, tricornered, marigold 170.00

**FLORAL & GRAPE (Dugan or Diamond Glass
Co.)**
Pitcher, water, blue 215.00
Pitcher, water, green 275.00
Pitcher, water, marigold 98.00

Pitcher, water, purple 173.00
Pitcher, water, white 280.00
Pitcher, water, variant, white 750.00
Tumbler, blue 35.00
Tumbler, green 60.00
Tumbler, marigold................. 21.00
Tumbler, purple 34.00
Tumbler, white................... 60.00
Water set: pitcher & 1 tumbler;
    blue, 2 pcs. 170.00
Water set: pitcher & 4 tumblers;
    white, 5 pcs.................. 695.00
Water set: pitcher & 5 tumblers;
    purple, 6 pcs................. 325.00
Water set: pitcher & 6 tumblers;
    marigold, 7 pcs................ 200.00

FLOWERS & BEADS
Card tray, tricornered, purple,
    7" w. 62.00
Plate, 7½" w., six-sided, peach
    opalescent.................... 112.00

FLOWERS & FRAMES
Bowl, 7" d., single handle, peach
    opalescent.................... 36.00
Bowl, 7" d., dome-footed, purple ... 80.00
Bowl, 9" d., dome-footed, peach
    opalescent.................... 108.00
Bowl, 9" d., dome-footed, fluted,
    purple 120.00
Bowl, tricornered, peach
    opalescent.................... 135.00

FLOWERS ROSE BOWL - See Little Flowers Pattern

FLUFFY PEACOCK - See Peacock, Fluffy Pattern

FLUTE (Imperial)

Flute Punch Set

Berry set: master bowl & 6 sauce
    dishes; purple, 7 pcs. 175.00
Bowl, 8" to 9" d., marigold......... 18.00
Bowl, 8" to 9" d., purple 70.00
Creamer, breakfast size, marigold .. 29.00
Creamer, breakfast size, purple 60.00
Creamer & open sugar bowl, break-
    fast size, purple, pr............. 130.00

Pitcher, water, clambroth 175.00
Pitcher, water, marigold 300.00
Pitcher, water, purple 293.00
Punch cup, green 12.50
Punch cup, marigold............... 35.00
Punch cup, purple 28.00
Punch set: bowl, base & 6 cups; pur-
    ple, 8 pcs. (ILLUS.) 850.00
Sauce dish, green 34.00
Sauce dish, marigold 18.00
Sugar bowl, open, breakfast size,
    green 60.00
Sugar bowl, open, breakfast size,
    purple 60.00
Toothpick holder, green 58.00
Toothpick holder, marigold........ 53.00
Toothpick holder, purple 64.00
Tumbler, aqua 175.00
Tumbler, cobalt blue 400.00
Tumbler, marigold................ 35.00
Tumbler, purple 80.00
Tumbler, smoky 425.00
Vase, 9" h., purple 82.00
Vase, funeral, 12" h., green....... 32.00
Vase, 17" h., green 65.00
Water set: pitcher & 1 tumbler; pur-
    ple, 2 pcs.................... 175.00

FLUTE (Northwood)
Pitcher, water, clambroth 175.00
Salt dip, master size, blue 45.00
Tumbler, marigold................ 55.00
Tumbler, marigold, variant 85.00
Tumbler, dark marigold........... 95.00

FLUTE & CANE
Goblet, marigold.................. 65.00
Pitcher, milk, marigold 112.00
Pitcher, tankard, marigold 365.00
Tumbler, marigold 1,500.00

FOUR FLOWERS - See Pods & Posies Pattern

FOUR SEVENTY FOUR (Imperial)
Compote, green................... 90.00
Goblet, water, marigold 81.00
Pitcher, milk, green 208.00
Pitcher, milk, marigold 160.00
Pitcher, milk, purple............. 200.00
Pitcher, water, green......225.00 to 400.00
Pitcher, water, marigold 143.00
Pitcher, water, purple .....425.00 to 600.00
Punch cup, green 28.00
Punch cup, marigold.............. 16.00
Punch cup, purple 46.00
Punch set: bowl, base & 4 cups;
    marigold, 6 pcs................ 175.00
Tumbler, green 125.00
Tumbler, marigold................ 22.50
Tumbler, purple 105.00
Vase, 16" h., green 1,925.00
Vase, 16" h., marigold........... 525.00
Water set: pitcher & 4 tumblers;
    marigold, 5 pcs................. 325.00

Water set: pitcher & 6 tumblers;
  purple, 7 pcs. 1,800.00
Wine, marigold 165.00

FROLICKING BEARS (U.S. Glass)

Frolicking Bears Pitcher

Pitcher, green
  (ILLUS.) . . . . .5,000.00 to 7,000.00

FROSTED BLOCK

Bowl, 8" to 9" d., scalloped & fluted,
  clambroth 26.50
Bowl, square, "USA," white 40.00
Bowl, square, clambroth 30.00
Bowl, square, marigold 40.00
Compote, clambroth 65.00
Plate, 7¾" sq., smoky 25.00
Plate, 9" d., clambroth 28.00
Plate, 9" d., marigold 50.00
Rose bowl, clambroth 60.00
Rose bowl, marigold 35.00
Rose bowl, white 45.00
Sugar bowl, clambroth 20.00
Vase, smoky 35.00

FRUIT SALAD

Punch bowl & base, purple, 2 pcs. . . 650.00
Punch cup, marigold 15.00
Punch cup, peach opalescent 100.00
Punch set: bowl, base & 6 cups;
  marigold, 8 pcs. 350.00

FRUITS & FLOWERS (Northwood)

Berry set: master bowl & 6 sauce
  dishes; purple, 7 pcs. 230.00
Bonbon, stemmed, two-handled,
  aqua opalescent 412.00
Bonbon, stemmed, two-handled,
  blue 95.00
Bonbon, stemmed, two-handled,
  electric blue 140.00
Bonbon, stemmed, two-handled,
  green 68.00
Bonbon, stemmed, two-handled, ice
  blue 450.00
Bonbon, stemmed, two-handled, ice
  green 400.00
Bonbon, stemmed, two-handled,
  lavender 195.00

Bonbon, stemmed, two-handled,
  marigold 42.00
Bonbon, stemmed, two-handled,
  purple 70.00
Bonbon, stemmed, two-handled,
  white . . . . .380.00 to 400.00
Bowl, 7" d., purple 60.00
Bowl, 7" d., ruffled, ice green 300.00
Bowl, 7" d., ruffled, marigold 15.00
Bowl, 9½" d., ruffled, Basketweave
  exterior, purple 61.00
Bowl, master berry, 10" d., green . .   82.00
Bowl, master berry, 10" d., ice
  green 750.00
Bowl, master berry, 10" d.,
  marigold 35.00
Bowl, master berry, 10" d., purple . .   66.00
Bowl, 10" d., ruffled, ice green 475.00
Card tray, green 125.00
Plate, 7" d., blue 320.00
Plate, 7" d., green 115.00
Plate, 7" d., purple 135.00
Plate, 7½" d., handgrip, pastel
  marigold 185.00
Plate, 7½" d., handgrip, purple 200.00
Sauce dish, marigold 31.00
Sauce dish, purple 36.00

GARDEN PATH

Berry set: master bowl & 6 sauce
  dishes; white, 7 pcs. 350.00
Bowl, 8" to 9" d., marigold 45.00
Bowl, 10" d., ruffled, marigold 75.00
Bowl, 10" d., ruffled, peach
  opalescent 200.00
Bowl, 10" d., ruffled, white 275.00
Bowl, variant, white 50.00
Plate, 6" d., peach opalescent 625.00
Plate, 6" d., white 260.00
Plate, 6½" d., white 400.00
Plate, chop, 11" d., peach
  opalescent 4,200.00
Plate, chop, 11" d., purple 1,750.00
Sauce dish, peach opalescent 115.00

GOD & HOME

God & Home Pitcher

Pitcher, blue (ILLUS.) 1,130.00
Tumbler, blue 206.00

GODDESS OF HARVEST (Fenton)
Bowl, blue 3,100.00
Bowl, marigold 4,200.00

GOLDEN HARVEST (U.S. Glass)
Decanter w/stopper, marigold 98.00
Decanter w/stopper,
   purple . . . . .150.00 to 175.00
Wine, marigold 20.00
Wine, purple 30.00
Wine set: decanter & 6 wines;
   purple, 7 pcs. 450.00

GOOD LUCK (Northwood)

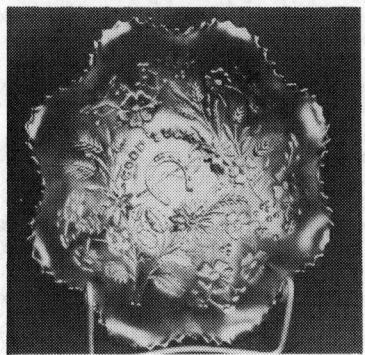

Good Luck Bowl

Bowl, 7" d., ruffled, blue (ILLUS.) . . . 260.00
Bowl, 7" d., ruffled, electric blue . . . 295.00
Bowl, 7" d., ruffled, green 314.00
Bowl, 7" d., ruffled, Basketweave
   exterior, green 285.00
Bowl, 7" d., ruffled, Basketweave
   exterior, marigold 120.00
Bowl, 7" d., ribbed exterior,
   marigold 135.00
Bowl, 7" d., ruffled, stippled, pastel
   marigold 195.00
Bowl, 7" d., ruffled, purple 164.00
Bowl, 7" d., ruffled, Basketweave
   exterior, purple 168.00
Bowl, 8" to 9" d., piecrust rim, aqua
   opalescent .1,250.00
Bowl, 8" to 9" d., piecrust rim,
   blue 248.00
Bowl, 8" to 9" d., piecrust rim,
   green 260.00
Bowl, 8" to 9" d., piecrust rim,
   lavender 700.00
Bowl, 8" to 9" d., piecrust rim,
   marigold 142.00
Bowl, 8" to 9" d., piecrust rim,
   purple 235.00
Bowl, 8" to 9" d., piecrust rim,
   clambroth 450.00
Bowl, 8" to 9" d., ruffled, teal
   blue 700.00
Plate, 9" d., blue 425.00
Plate, 9" d., electric blue 1,400.00
Plate, 9" d., green 563.00
Plate, 9" d., marigold 220.00

Plate, 9" d., purple 320.00
Plate, 9" d., white 1,600.00

GRAPE & CABLE

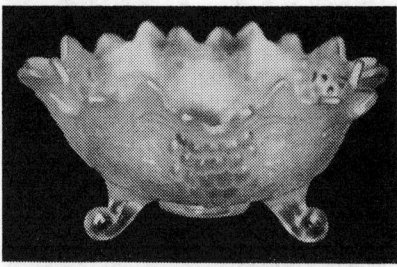

Grape & Cable Orange Bowl

Banana boat, blue 330.00
Banana boat, green 307.00
Banana boat, stippled, green 400.00
Banana boat, ice blue 562.00
Banana boat, ice green 595.00
Banana boat, marigold 136.00
Banana boat, purple 220.00
Banana boat, white 685.00
Berry set: master bowl & 6 sauce
   dishes; green, 7 pcs. 210.00
Berry set: master bowl & 6 sauce
   dishes; marigold, 7 pcs. 275.00
Berry set: master bowl & 8 sauce
   dishes; purple, 9 pcs. 400.00
Bonbon, two-handled, blue 60.00
Bonbon, two-handled, green 46.00
Bonbon, two-handled, marigold 40.00
Bonbon, two-handled, purple 60.00
Bowl, 5" d., blue (Fenton) 25.00
Bowl, 5" d., marigold 32.00
Bowl, 5" d., purple 55.00
Bowl, 6" d., red (Fenton) 360.00
Bowl, 7½" d., ball-footed, amber
   (Fenton) 100.00
Bowl, 7½" d., ball-footed, aqua
   (Fenton) 96.00
Bowl, 7½" d., ball-footed, blue
   (Fenton) 65.00
Bowl, 7½" d., ball-footed, green
   (Fenton) 42.00
Bowl, 7½" d., ball-footed, marigold
   (Fenton) 38.00
Bowl, 7½" d., ball-footed, purple
   (Fenton) 52.00
Bowl, 7½" d., ball-footed, red (Fen-
   ton) 425.00
Bowl, 7½" d., ball-footed, vaseline
   (Fenton) 80.00
Bowl, 7½" d., flat, marigold 50.00
Bowl, 7½" d., ruffled, ice blue 875.00
Bowl, 7½" d., spatula-footed, green
   (Northwood) 70.00
Bowl, 7½" d., spatula-footed, mari-
   gold (Northwood) 26.00
Bowl, 7½" d., spatula-footed, purple
   (Northwood) 60.00
Bowl, 8" d., ice cream shape, foot-
   ed, celeste blue (Fenton) 600.00

Bowl, 8" to 9" d., piecrust rim, aqua
opalescent (Northwood) 2,000.00
Bowl, 8" to 9" d., piecrust rim, elec-
tric blue 338.00
Bowl, 8" to 9" d., ball-footed, blue
(Fenton) 58.00
Bowl, 8" to 9" d., ball-footed,
celeste blue (Fenton) 550.00
Bowl, 8" to 9" d., ball-footed, green
(Fenton) 62.00
Bowl, 8" to 9" d., ball-footed, purple
(Fenton) 45.00
Bowl, 8" to 9" d., ball-footed, red
(Fenton) 1,200.00
Bowl, 8" to 9" d., spatula-footed,
blue (Northwood) 55.00
Bowl, 8" to 9" d., spatula-footed,
green (Northwood) 70.00
Bowl, 8" to 9" d., spatula-footed,
marigold (Northwood) 60.00
Bowl, 8" to 9" d., spatula-footed,
ruffled, purple (Northwood) 63.00
Bowl, 8" to 9" d., stippled, blue 264.00
Bowl, 8" to 9" d., stippled, green ... 95.00
Bowl, 8" to 9" d., stippled, ice
blue 1,000.00
Bowl, berry, 9" d., blue 175.00
Bowl, berry, 9" d., green 78.00
Bowl, berry, 9" d., marigold........ 75.00
Bowl, berry, 9" d., purple 80.00
Bowl, berry, 9" d., teal blue 125.00
Bowl, orange, 10½" d., footed, Per-
sian Medallion interior, blue (Fen-
ton) 252.00
Bowl, orange, 10½" d., footed, Per-
sian Medallion interior, green
(Fenton) 230.00
Bowl, orange, 10½" d., footed, Per-
sian Medallion interior, marigold
(Fenton) 103.00
Bowl, orange, 10½" d., footed, Per-
sian Medallion interior, purple
(Fenton) 208.00
Bowl, orange, 10½" d., footed,
blue 263.00
Bowl, orange, 10½" d., footed,
green 185.00
Bowl, orange, 10½" d., footed, ice
blue (ILLUS.) 875.00
Bowl, orange, 10½" d., footed, ice
green 810.00
Bowl, orange, 10½" d., footed,
marigold 115.00
Bowl, orange, 10½" d., footed,
purple 246.00
Bowl, orange, 10½" d., footed,
white 927.00
Bowl, 10½" d., ruffled, Basket-
weave exterior, green 78.00
Bowl, 10½" d., ruffled, Basket-
weave exterior, purple 135.00
Bowl, ice cream, 11" d., blue....... 600.00
Bowl, ice cream, 11" d., green 143.00

Bowl, ice cream, 11" d., ice
blue 2,050.00
Bowl, ice cream, 11" d., ice
green 625.00
Bowl, ice cream, 11" d., marigold .. 90.00
Bowl, ice cream, 11" d., purple..... 125.00
Bowl, ice cream, 11" d., white 275.00
Bowl, salad, white 600.00
Bowl, footed, cobalt blue opal-
escent (Fenton)................2,100.00
Bowl, footed, Meander exterior,
white 750.00
Breakfast set: individual size
creamer & sugar bowl; green,
pr............................. 123.00
Breakfast set: individual size
creamer & sugar bowl; marigold,
pr............................. 140.00
Breakfast set: individual size
creamer & sugar bowl; purple,
pr............................. 155.00
Butter dish, cov., amber 155.00
Butter dish, cov., green........... 175.00
Butter dish, cov., ice green 250.00
Butter dish, cov., marigold 175.00
Butter dish, cov., purple.......... 180.00
Candle lamp, green 530.00
Candle lamp, marigold 550.00
Candle lamp, purple.............. 450.00
Candle lamp shade, marigold 210.00
Candle lamp shade, purple........ 235.00
Candlestick, green 85.00
Candlestick, marigold............. 60.00
Candlestick, purple.............. 135.00
Candlesticks, marigold, pr......... 155.00
Candlesticks, purple, pr........... 270.00
Card tray, marigold 65.00
Card tray, purple................ 67.00
Centerpiece bowl, blue 625.00
Centerpiece bowl, green...225.00 to 400.00
Centerpiece bowl, ice blue 850.00
Centerpiece bowl, ice green 650.00
Centerpiece bowl, marigold 165.00
Centerpiece bowl, purple 325.00
Centerpiece bowl, white 585.00
Cologne bottle w/stopper, green ... 223.00
Cologne bottle w/stopper,
marigold 145.00
Cologne bottle w/stopper, purple... 178.00

Grape & Cable Large Compote

Cologne bottles w/stoppers, mari-
gold, pr. 450.00
Compote, cov., large, mari-
gold 1,250.00
Compote, cov., small, purple 245.00
Compote, cov., large, purple (ILLUS.
previous page) 400.00
Compote, open, large, green 425.00
Compote, open, large, marigold 343.00
Compote, open, small, purple 300.00
Compote, open, large, purple 388.00
Cracker jar, cov., blue 500.00
Cracker jar, cov., marigold 246.00
Cracker jar, cov., purple 300.00
Cracker jar, cov., white 875.00
Creamer, green 90.00
Creamer, purple 100.00
Creamer, individual size,
green .... 50.00 to 65.00
Creamer, individual size, marigold .. 75.00
Creamer, individual size, purple 65.00
Creamer & cov. sugar bowl, purple,
pr. .... 225.00 to 400.00
Cup & saucer, green 365.00
Cup & saucer, marigold 250.00
Cup & saucer, purple 450.00
Cuspidor, purple .... 4,000.00 to 7,000.00
Decanter w/stopper, whiskey,
marigold 488.00
Decanter w/stopper, whiskey,
purple 825.00
Dresser set, purple, 7 pcs. 2,500.00
Dresser set, marigold, 8 pcs. 1,200.00
Dresser tray, green 255.00
Dresser tray, marigold 110.00
Dresser tray, purple 175.00
Fernery, marigold 980.00
Fernery, white .... 700.00 to 1,000.00
Hatpin holder, green 210.00
Hatpin holder, ice blue 1,450.00
Hatpin holder, marigold 145.00
Hatpin holder, purple 200.00
Hat shape, green 75.00
Hat shape, marigold 37.00
Hat shape, purple 45.00
Humidor (or tobacco jar), cov.,
blue 915.00
Humidor, cov., marigold 260.00
Humidor, cov., purple 375.00
Ice cream set, purple, 7 pcs. 530.00
Nappy, single handle, green 75.00
Nappy, single handle, marigold 45.00
Nappy, single handle, purple 125.00
Nappy, cup whimsey, hairpin,
purple 50.00
Perfume bottle w/stopper,
marigold 425.00
Perfume bottle w/stopper, purple .. 575.00
Pin tray, green 125.00
Pin tray, ice blue 495.00
Pin tray, marigold .... 100.00 to 150.00
Pin tray, purple 155.00
Pitcher, water, 8¼" h., green 325.00
Pitcher, water, 8¼" h., marigold ... 160.00

Pitcher, water, 8¼" h., purple 235.00
Pitcher, tankard, 9¾" h.,
green 1,500.00
Pitcher, tankard, 9¾" h., ice
green 2,400.00
Pitcher, tankard, 9¾" h.,
marigold 468.00
Pitcher, tankard, 9¾" h., purple 585.00
Pitcher, smoky 600.00
Plate, 5" to 6" d., purple (North-
wood) 110.00
Plate, 7½" d., turned-up handgrip,
green 80.00
Plate, 7½" d., turned-up handgrip,
marigold 52.00
Plate, 7½" d., turned-up handgrip,
purple 85.00
Plate, 8" d., footed, green
(Fenton) .... 65.00 to 110.00
Plate, 8" d., green (Northwood) 150.00
Plate, 8" d., footed, purple 99.00
Plate, 9" d., blue 250.00
Plate, 9" d., spatula-footed, green .. 90.00
Plate, 9" d., spatula-footed, ice
green 850.00
Plate, 9" d., marigold 90.00
Plate, 9" d., spatula-footed,
marigold 90.00
Plate, 9" d., purple 125.00
Plate, 9" d., spatula-footed,
purple 125.00
Plate, 9" d., Basketweave exterior,
green 150.00
Plate, 9" d., Basketweave exterior,
marigold 90.00
Plate, 9" d., Basketweave exterior,
purple 125.00
Plate, 9" d., stippled, blue 485.00
Plate, 9" d., stippled, green 235.00
Plate, 9" d., stippled, ice blue 1,700.00
Plate, 9" d., stippled, marigold 150.00
Plate, 9" d., stippled, purple 192.00
Plate, 9" d., stippled, sapphire
blue 2,300.00
Powder jar, cov., green 95.00
Powder jar, cov., marigold 58.00
Powder jar, cov., purple 102.00
Punch bowl & base, blue, 11" d.,
2 pcs. 395.00
Punch bowl & base, green, 11" d.,
2 pcs. 600.00
Punch bowl & base, marigold,
11" d., 2 pcs. 250.00
Punch bowl & base, purple, 11" d.,
2 pcs. 400.00
Punch bowl & base, purple, 14" d.,
2 pcs. 525.00
Punch cup, aqua opalescent 260.00
Punch cup, blue 35.00
Punch cup, stippled, blue 60.00
Punch cup, green 36.00
Punch cup, stippled, green 40.00
Punch cup, ice blue 60.00
Punch cup, ice green .... 55.00 to 75.00

Punch cup, marigold 21.00
Punch cup, purple 27.00
Punch cup, white 58.00
Punch set: bowl, base & 3 cups; purple, 5 pcs 593.00
Punch set: 11" bowl & 6 cups; marigold, 7 pcs 425.00
Punch set: 11" bowl & 6 cups; white, 7 pcs 1,750.00
Punch set: 14" bowl, base & 6 cups; marigold, 8 pcs 595.00
Punch set: 14" bowl, base & 12 cups; purple, 14 pcs 1,400.00
Punch set: 17" bowl, base & 6 cups; marigold, 8 pcs 895.00
Punch set: 17" bowl, base & 10 cups; blue, 12 pcs 4,200.00
Punch set: 17" bowl, base & 12 cups; purple, 14 pcs 1,700.00
Sauce dish, green 26.00
Sauce dish, marigold 32.50
Sauce dish, purple 35.00
Sherbet or individual ice cream dish, green 35.00
Sherbet or individual ice cream dish, marigold 30.00
Sherbet or individual ice cream dish, purple 45.00
Spooner, green 90.00
Spooner, ice green 200.00
Spooner, marigold 52.00
Spooner, purple 85.00
Sugar bowl, cov., green 110.00
Sugar bowl, cov., marigold 75.00
Sugar bowl, cov., purple 96.00
Sugar bowl, individual size, green .. 50.00
Sugar bowl, individual size, marigold 35.00
Sugar bowl, individual size, purple.. 50.00
Sweetmeat jar, cov., marigold 750.00
Sweetmeat jar, cov., purple 185.00
Table set, green, 4 pcs 500.00
Table set, marigold, 4 pcs 450.00
Table set, purple, 4 pcs 490.00
Tumbler, green 45.00
Tumbler, marigold 32.00
Tumbler, purple 35.00
Tumbler, smoky 30.00
Tumbler, stippled, marigold 68.00
Tumbler, stippled, purple 75.00
Tumbler, tankard, blue 72.00
Tumbler, tankard, green 225.00
Tumbler, tankard, marigold 65.00
Tumbler, tankard, purple 40.00
Water set: pitcher & 6 tumblers; green, 7 pcs. 460.00
Water set: pitcher & 6 tumblers; ice green, 7 pcs. 2,400.00
Water set: pitcher & 6 tumblers; marigold, 7 pcs 330.00
Water set: pitcher & 6 tumblers; purple, 7 pcs. 434.00
Water set: tankard pitcher & 6 tumblers; marigold, 7 pcs 825.00

Water set: tankard pitcher & 6 tumblers; purple, 7 pcs. 850.00
Whimsey compote (sweetmeat base), green 175.00
Whimsey compote (sweetmeat base), purple 245.00
Whimsey teacup, purple 115.00
Whiskey set: whiskey decanter w/stopper & 1 shot glass; marigold, 2 pcs. 750.00
Whiskey shot glass, marigold 160.00
Whiskey shot glass, purple 150.00

GRAPE & GOTHIC ARCHES (Northwood)
Berry set: master bowl & 4 sauce dishes; blue, 5 pcs 213.00
Bowl, master berry, blue 60.00
Bowl, master berry, marigold 43.00
Butter dish, cov., green 225.00
Creamer, blue 68.00
Creamer & spooner, blue, 2 pcs..... 90.00
Pitcher, water, blue ......250.00 to 300.00
Pitcher, water, green 235.00
Pitcher, water, marigold 148.00
Sauce dish, aqua 25.00
Sauce dish, marigold 15.00
Spooner, blue 60.00
Spooner, green 225.00
Spooner, marigold 65.00
Sugar bowl, cov., blue 75.00
Sugar bowl, cov., green 67.50
Sugar bowl, cov., marigold 45.00
Table set, blue, 4 pcs. 450.00
Table set, marigold, 4 pcs 250.00
Tumbler, amber 37.00
Tumbler, blue 45.00
Tumbler, green 38.50
Tumbler, marigold 34.00
Tumbler, milk white w/pearl pastel overlay 55.00
Water set: pitcher & 6 tumblers; blue, 7 pcs. 475.00
Water set: pitcher & 6 tumblers; marigold, 7 pcs 375.00

GRAPE & LATTICE
Tumbler, blue 36.00
Tumbler, marigold 29.00
Water set: pitcher & 6 tumblers; marigold, 7 pcs 300.00

GRAPE ARBOR (Northwood)
Bowl, 10" d., footed, blue (Dugan) .. 210.00
Bowl, 10" d., footed, marigold (Dugan) 95.00
Hat shape, blue 80.00
Hat shape, ice green 375.00
Pitcher, water, marigold 350.00
Pitcher, water, purple 540.00
Pitcher, water, white 440.00
Tumbler, blue 175.00
Tumbler, ice blue 185.00
Tumbler, ice green 515.00
Tumbler, lavender 175.00

Tumbler, marigold................. 35.00
Tumbler, pastel marigold 45.00
Tumbler, purple................... 50.00
Tumbler, teal blue 175.00
Tumbler, white.................... 99.00
Water set: pitcher & 4 tumblers;
    white, 5 pcs. 1,250.00
Water set: pitcher & 5 tumblers;
    marigold, 6 pcs. ....475.00 to 525.00

GRAPE DELIGHT

Grape Delight Rose Bowl

Nut bowl, six-footed, blue 95.00
Nut bowl, six-footed, marigold 55.00
Nut bowl, six-footed, purple 57.00
Nut bowl, six-footed, white 95.00
Rose bowl, six-footed, blue 96.00
Rose bowl, six-footed, clambroth ... 60.00
Rose bowl, six-footed, marigold 65.00
Rose bowl, six-footed, purple 75.00
Rose bowl, six-footed, white
    (ILLUS.)........................ 75.00
Wine, purple...................... 23.00

GRAPEVINE LATTICE

Bowl, 7" d., ruffled, marigold 28.00
Bowl, 7" d., ruffled, white 41.00
Bowl, fluted, white 85.00
Hat shape, white................... 65.00
Pitcher, water, blue 287.00
Pitcher, water, marigold ...160.00 to 230.00
Pitcher, water, white 850.00
Plate, 6" to 7" d., blue 80.00
Plate, 6" to 7" d., marigold 60.00
Plate, 6" to 7" d., peach
    opalescent...................... 140.00
Plate, 6" to 7" d., purple.......... 190.00
Plate, 6" to 7" d., white 70.00
Tumbler, marigold................. 38.00
Tumbler, purple................... 42.00
Tumbler, smoky.................... 40.00
Tumbler, white.................... 85.00
Water set: pitcher & 6 tumblers;
    marigold, 7 pcs................. 525.00

GREEK KEY (Northwood)

Bowl, 8" to 9" d., blue.....400.00 to 500.00
Bowl, 8" to 9" d., fluted, green 185.00
Bowl, 8" to 9" d., ruffled,
    marigold 82.00

Bowl, 8" to 9" d., purple........... 167.00
Pitcher, water, green 1,450.00
Pitcher, water, marigold 700.00
Pitcher, water, purple 875.00

Greek Key Plate

Plate, 9" d., green (ILLUS.) 500.00
Plate, 9" d., marigold 450.00
Tumbler, green 98.00
Tumbler, marigold................. 65.00
Tumbler, purple................... 83.00
Water set: pitcher & 6 tumblers;
    purple, 7 pcs. 1,400.00

HAMMERED BELL
Chandelier shade, white 80.00

HANGING CHERRIES - See Cherry (Millersburg) Pattern

HARVEST FLOWER (Dugan or Diamond Glass)

Harvest Flower Tankard Pitcher

Pitcher, tankard, marigold
    (ILLUS.) 1,600.00
Tumbler, amber................... 125.00
Tumbler, marigold................. 84.00

HARVEST TIME - See Golden Harvest Pattern

HATTIE (Imperial)
Bowl, 8" to 9" d., marigold........ 32.00

Bowl, 8" to 9" d., purple 65.00
Bowl, 8" to 9" d., smoky 50.00
Plate, chop, 10½" d., amber 1,000.00
Plate, chop, green 500.00
Plate, chop, marigold 200.00
Rose bowl, marigold 110.00

HEADDRESS BOWL (Imperial)
Blue 55.00
Marigold 37.50

HEART & HORSESHOE (Fenton's Good Luck)
Bowl, marigold 925.00

HEART & VINE (Fenton)

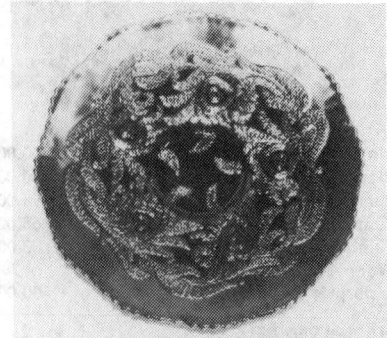

Heart & Vine Plate

Bowl, 8" to 9" d., blue 42.00
Bowl, 8" to 9" d., ribbon candy rim,
  blue 75.00
Bowl, 8" to 9" d., green 67.00
Bowl, 8" to 9" d., ribbon candy rim,
  green 78.00
Bowl, 8" to 9" d., marigold 38.00
Bowl, 8" to 9" d., ribbon candy rim,
  marigold 67.50
Bowl, 8" to 9" d., purple 75.00
Plate, 9" d., blue (ILLUS.) 270.00
Plate, 9" d., marigold 250.00
Plate, 9" d., purple 225.00

HEARTS & FLOWERS (Northwood)

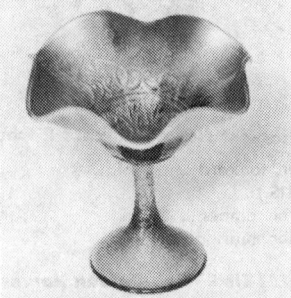

Hearts & Flowers Compote

Bowl, 8" to 9" d., aqua
  opalescent 1,100.00

Bowl, 8" to 9" d., piecrust rim,
  blue 425.00
Bowl, 8" to 9" d., ruffled, blue 450.00
Bowl, 8" to 9" d., electric blue 575.00
Bowl, 8" to 9" d., ruffled, green 710.00
Bowl, 8" to 9" d., piecrust rim, ice
  blue 650.00
Bowl, 8" to 9" d., ruffled, ice blue .. 325.00
Bowl, 8" to 9" d., ruffled, ice
  green 520.00
Bowl, 8" to 9" d., ruffled,
  marigold 274.00
Bowl, 8" to 9" d., piecrust rim,
  purple 355.00
Bowl, 8" to 9" d., ruffled, purple ... 320.00
Bowl, 8" to 9" d., ruffled, white 207.00
Compote, 6¾" h., aqua opalescent
  (ILLUS.) 445.00
Compote, 6¾" h., blue opales-
  cent 1,200.00
Compote, 6¾" h., electric blue 270.00
Compote, 6¾" h., green 950.00
Compote, 6¾" h., ice blue 750.00
Compote, 6¾" h., ice green 809.00
Compote, 6¾" h., marigold 125.00
Compote, 6¾" h., purple 330.00
Compote, 6¾" h., white 150.00
Plate, green 1,600.00
Plate, ice blue 1,750.00
Plate, ice green 1,000.00
Plate, marigold 330.00
Plate, purple 738.00
Plate, white 2,500.00

HEAVY GRAPE (Dugan, Diamond Glass or Millersburg)
Bowl, master berry, 10" d., peach
  opalescent 650.00
Bowl, master berry, 10" d., purple .. 318.00
Bowl, ice cream, purple (Millers-
  burg) 600.00
Compote, purple (Millersburg) 850.00

HEAVY GRAPE (Imperial)
Bowl, 5" d., 2" h., marigold 30.00
Bowl, 5" d., 2" h., purple 32.50
Bowl, 6" d., marigold 30.00
Bowl, 7" d., fluted, green 30.00
Bowl, 7" d., purple 42.50
Bowl, 8" to 9" d., green 58.00
Bowl, 8" to 9" d., marigold 42.00
Bowl, 8" to 9" d., purple 50.00
Bowl, 10" d., purple 125.00
Bowl, square, purple 550.00
Compote, green 850.00
Nappy, handled, green 35.00
Nappy, handled, marigold 28.00
Nappy, handled, purple 35.00
Plate, 7" to 8" d., amber 75.00
Plate, 7" to 8" d., blue 65.00
Plate, 7" to 8" d., green 63.00
Plate, 7" to 8" d., marigold 50.00
Plate, 7" to 8" d., purple 78.00
Plate, chop, 11" d., amber 165.00

Plate, chop, 11" d., green 250.00
Plate, chop, 11" d., marigold 175.00
Plate, chop, 11" d., purple 260.00
Punch bowl, green 225.00
Punch bowl & base, marigold,
  2 pcs. 335.00
Punch bowl & base, purple, 2 pcs. . . 285.00
Punch cup, green 20.00
Punch cup, marigold 20.00
Punch cup, purple 38.00
Punch set: bowl, base & 4 cups; pur-
  ple, 6 pcs. 800.00
Punch set: bowl, base & 5 cups;
  marigold, 7 pcs. 195.00
Punch set: bowl, base & 6 cups;
  green, 8 pcs. 250.00

HEAVY IRIS (Dugan or Diamond Glass)

Heavy Iris Water Set

Pitcher, water, marigold (ILLUS.) 360.00
Pitcher, water, peach
  opalescent .1,000.00
Pitcher, water, white 1,250.00
Tumbler, marigold (ILLUS.) 65.00
Tumbler, purple 62.00
Tumbler, white 250.00
Water set: pitcher & 5 tumblers;
  marigold, 6 pcs. . . . . .650.00 to 685.00
Water set: pitcher & 6 tumblers;
  purple, 7 pcs. 1,800.00

HERON MUG (Dugan)
Marigold 75.00
Purple 225.00

HOBNAIL (Millersburg)
Butter dish, cov., marigold 350.00
Butter dish, cov., purple 625.00
Cuspidor, marigold 465.00
Cuspidor, purple . . . . .460.00 to 600.00
Pitcher, water, blue 1,500.00
Pitcher, water, marigold 1,500.00
Pitcher, water, purple 1,500.00
Rose bowl, marigold 150.00
Rose bowl, purple 325.00
Sugar bowl, cov., marigold 300.00
Tumbler, blue 1,000.00
Tumbler, marigold 750.00
Tumbler, purple 600.00

HOBNAIL, SWIRL - See Swirl Hobnail Pattern on Page 433

HOBSTAR (Imperial)

Hobstar Pickle Castor

Butter dish, cov., marigold 62.50
Celery vase, two-handled,
  marigold 75.00
Compote, green 60.00
Compote, marigold 45.00
Cracker jar, cov., marigold 135.00
Creamer, marigold 35.00
Creamer, purple 50.00
Pickle castor, cov., marigold, com-
  plete w/silver plate frame
  (ILLUS.) 450.00
Punch set: bowl, base & 12 cups,
  marigold, 14 pcs. 300.00
Spooner, marigold 60.00
Spooner, purple 85.00
Sugar bowl, cov., green 50.00
Sugar bowl, cov., marigold 35.00
Table set, marigold, 4 pcs. 110.00

HOBSTAR & FEATHER (Millersburg)

Hobstar & Feather Vase

Punch cup, green 28.50
Punch cup, marigold 26.00
Punch cup, purple 56.00

Punch set: bowl, base & 12 cups;
  marigold, 14 pcs. 1,525.00
Rose bowl, green, 7½" top d.,
  13" h. 1,235.00
Vase, 13" h., purple (ILLUS.) 4,500.00

HOBSTAR BAND
Pitcher, marigold. 167.00
Tumbler, marigold. 45.00
Water set: pitcher & 6 tumblers;
  marigold, 7 pcs. 395.00

HOLLY, HOLLY BERRIES & CARNIVAL HOLLY

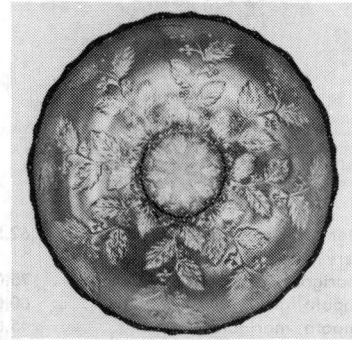

Holly Bowl

Bonbon, two-handled, blue. 65.00
Bonbon, two-handled, green 55.00
Bonbon, two-handled, marigold. 45.00
Bonbon, two-handled, purple 60.00
Bowl, 5" d., marigold 25.00
Bowl, 6" d., blue 35.00
Bowl, 6" d., green (Millersburg) 65.00
Bowl, 7" d., marigold 35.00
Bowl, 7" d., fluted, peach opales-
  cent (Dugan) 45.00
Bowl, 7" d., purple 48.00
Bowl, 8" to 9" d., blue 52.00
Bowl, 8" to 9" d., green 50.00
Bowl, 8" to 9" d., marigold
  (ILLUS.) 46.00
Bowl, 8" to 9" d., purple 50.00
Bowl, 8" to 9" d., red (Fenton) 812.00
Bowl, 8" to 9" d., teal blue 500.00
Bowl, 8" to 9" d., vaseline 80.00
Bowl, 8" to 9" d., white 95.00
Bowl, 10" d., aqua 195.00
Bowl, 10" d., blue 40.00
Bowl, 10" d., fluted, green 78.00
Bowl, 10" d., fluted, marigold 90.00
Bowl, 10" d., purple 75.00
Bowl, 10" d., ribbon candy rim,
  vaseline (Fenton) 193.00
Bowl, amber. 150.00
Bowl, milk white w/marigold
  overlay 1,050.00
Bowl, moonstone 1,100.00
Bowl, ribbon candy rim, amethyst . . 125.00
Bowl, ribbon candy rim, marigold. . . 35.00
Bowl, ribbon candy rim, pastel
  green 65.00

Bowl, ribbon candy rim, purple 42.50
Bowl, ruffled, blue opalescent 1,400.00
Bowl, ruffled, green 125.00
Bowl, ruffled, pastel blue 75.00
Bowl, ruffled, purple 125.00
Bowl, ruffled, white 100.00
Compote, small, aqua w/marigold
  overlay. 45.00
Compote, small, blue 30.00
Compote, small, green 32.00
Compote, ice green opalescent 625.00
Compote, small, marigold 25.00
Compote, small, marigold w/vase-
  line stem 65.00
Compote, small, purple 57.50
Compote, small, red (Fenton) 335.00
Compote, small, vaseline 75.00
Dish, hat-shaped, amber, 5¾" 28.00
Dish, hat-shaped, amethyst
  opalescent. 275.00
Dish, hat-shaped, aqua, 5¾" 70.00
Dish, hat-shaped, blue, 5¾" 28.00
Dish, hat-shaped, green, 5¾" 28.00
Dish, hat-shaped, marigold, 5¾" . . . 22.00
Dish, hat-shaped, milk white
  w/marigold overlay 118.00
Dish, hat-shaped, moonstone 200.00
Dish, hat-shaped, red, 5¾" 250.00
Dish, hat-shaped, vaseline, 5¾" 48.00
Goblet, green. 75.00
Goblet, marigold 30.00
Goblet, red (Fenton) 429.00
Plate, 9" to 10" d., blue 200.00
Plate, 9" to 10" d., celeste blue
  (Fenton) 9,500.00
Plate, 9" to 10" d., clambroth 100.00
Plate, 9" to 10" d., green 413.00
Plate, 9" to 10" d., marigold 85.00
Plate, 9" to 10" d., pastel
  marigold 70.00
Plate, 9" to 10" d., purple. 280.00
Plate, 9" to 10" d., white 150.00
Sauceboat, handled, peach opales-
  cent (Dugan) 70.00
Sauceboat, handled, purple 52.00
Sherbet, red (Fenton) 380.00

HOLLY SPRIG - See Holly Whirl Pattern

HOLLY STAR PANELED or HOLLY STAR (Northwood)
Bonbon, green 50.00
Bonbon, marigold 20.00

HOLLY WHIRL or HOLLY SPRIG (Millersburg, Fenton & Dugan)
Bowl, 7" d., marigold 65.00
Bowl, 8" d., ice cream shape,
  white 110.00
Bowl, 8" to 9" d., ruffled, blue 55.00
Bowl, 8" to 9" d., green 70.00
Bowl, 8" to 9" d., marigold. 42.00
Bowl, 8" to 9" d., purple 50.00
Nappy, single handle, peach opales-
  cent (Dugan) 52.00

Nappy, single handle, purple
(Dugan) 60.00
Nappy, tricornered, green
(Dugan) 73.00
Nappy, tricornered, marigold
(Millersburg).................... 125.00
Nappy, tricornered, purple
(Dugan) 75.00
Nappy, two-handled, amethyst
(Millersburg)................... 65.00
Nappy, two-handled, green 120.00
Nut dish, two-handled, green 69.00
Nut dish, two-handled, marigold.... 48.00
Nut dish, two-handled, purple 67.00
Sauceboat, peach opalescent
(Dugan) 50.00
Sauce dish, purple, 5½" d. (Millers-
burg) 145.00
Sauce dish, marigold, 5¾" d. 125.00
Sauce dish, green, 6½" d. (Millers-
burg) 165.00

HOMESTEAD (Imperial)
Plate, amber...................... 680.00
Plate, blue 1,125.00
Plate, green 890.00
Plate, marigold 325.00
Plate, purple 620.00
Plate, white 700.00

HORSE HEADS or HORSE MEDALLION (Fenton)

Horse Heads Bowl

Bowl, 5" d., footed, marigold....... 57.00
Bowl, 6" d., collared base,
marigold 85.00
Bowl, 7" to 8" d., blue 110.00
Bowl, 7" to 8" d., green (ILLUS.) 132.00
Bowl, 7" to 8" d., marigold......... 60.00
Bowl, 7" to 8" d., purple........... 118.00
Bowl, 7" to 8" d., red............. 800.00
Bowl, ice cream shape, amber 280.00
Bowl, jack-in-the-pulpit shaped,
amber 195.00
Bowl, jack-in-the-pulpit shaped,
blue 135.00
Bowl, jack-in-the-pulpit shaped,
marigold 100.00
Bowl, jack-in-the-pulpit shaped,
purple 265.00

Bowl, jack-in-the-pulpit shaped,
vaseline 130.00
Nut bowl, three-footed, blue 146.00
Nut bowl, three-footed, marigold ... 75.00
Nut bowl, three-footed, red 970.00
Nut bowl, three-footed, vaseline ... 210.00
Plate, 7" to 8" d., blue 500.00
Plate, 7" to 8" d., marigold 143.00
Rose bowl, blue 215.00
Rose bowl, marigold.............. 110.00

ILLINOIS SOLDIER'S & SAILOR'S PLATE
Blue 600.00
Marigold 550.00

ILLUSION (Fenton)
Bonbon, two-handled, blue........ 68.00
Bonbon, two-handled, marigold..... 70.00
Bonbon, two-handled, purple 150.00

IMPERIAL GRAPE (Imperial)

Imperial Grape Wine Set

Basket, marigold 88.00
Basket, smoky 85.00
Berry set: master bowl & 2 sauce
dishes; purple, 3 pcs............ 225.00
Berry set: master bowl & 6 sauce
dishes; green, 7 pcs. 200.00
Berry set: master bowl & 6 sauce
dishes; marigold,
7 pcs..................150.00 to 200.00
Bowl, 7" d., 2½" h., green......... 35.00
Bowl, 7" d., 2½" h., marigold 21.00
Bowl, 7" d., 2½" h., ruffled,
purple 35.00
Bowl, 8" to 9" d., aqua 50.00
Bowl, 8" to 9" d., green 40.00
Bowl, 8" to 9" d., marigold........ 26.00
Bowl, 8" to 9" d., purple......... 44.00
Bowl, 8" to 9" d., white.......... 55.00
Bowl, 10" d., clambroth........... 40.00
Bowl, 10" d., green 50.00
Bowl, 10" d., marigold 31.00
Bowl, 10" d., purple 68.00
Bowl, 10" d., white............... 45.00
Bowl, 11" d., ruffled, purple....... 128.00
Compote, amber 70.00
Compote, green.................. 55.00

Compote, marigold 45.00
Compote, purple 500.00
Compote, smoky 40.00
Cup & saucer, green 86.00
Cup & saucer, marigold 62.00
Decanter w/stopper, green 120.00
Decanter w/stopper, marigold 86.00
Decanter w/stopper, purple 130.00
Goblet, clambroth 45.00
Goblet, green 40.00
Goblet, marigold 34.00
Goblet, purple 55.00
Goblet, smoky 90.00
Pitcher, water, amber 650.00
Pitcher, water, green 250.00
Pitcher, water, marigold 89.00
Pitcher, water, purple 283.00
Pitcher, smoky 275.00
Plate, 6" d., amber 160.00
Plate, 6" d., green 60.00
Plate, 6" d., marigold 40.00
Plate, 6" d., purple 82.00
Plate, 7" d., green 30.00
Plate, 7" d., marigold 28.00
Plate, 8" d., green 75.00
Plate, 8" d., marigold 42.00
Plate, 8" d., purple 85.00
Plate, 9" d., ruffled,
    clambroth . . . . .50.00 to 85.00
Plate, 9" d., ruffled, green 105.00
Plate, 9" d., flat, marigold 100.00
Plate, 9" d., ruffled, marigold 33.00
Plate, 9" d., ruffled, purple 70.00
Plate, 9" d., purple 310.00
Plate, 9" d., ruffled, white 50.00
Rose bowl, amber 175.00
Rose bowl, green 65.00
Sauce dish, amber 20.00
Sauce dish, green 18.00
Sauce dish, ruffled, marigold 14.00
Tray, marigold, center handle 85.00
Tumbler, aqua 130.00
Tumbler, green 25.00
Tumbler, marigold 20.00
Tumbler, purple 38.00
Tumbler, smoky 75.00
Water bottle, green 100.00
Water bottle, marigold 75.00
Water bottle, purple 130.00
Water bottle, smoky 475.00
Water set: pitcher & 1 tumbler;
    amber, 2 pcs. 850.00
Water set: pitcher & 4 tumblers;
    marigold, 5 pcs. 175.00
Water set: pitcher & 6 tumblers;
    green, 7 pcs. 345.00
Water set: pitcher & 6 tumblers;
    purple, 7 pcs. 610.00
Wine, green 28.00
Wine, marigold 24.00
Wine, purple 32.00
Wine, smoky 90.00
Wine, vaseline 40.00

Wine set: decanter w/stopper & 6
    wines; marigold, 7 pcs. 200.00
Wine set: decanter w/stopper & 6
    wines; purple, 7 pcs. (ILLUS. of
    part) 325.00
Wine set: decanter w/stopper & 7
    wines; green, 8 pcs. 250.00

INVERTED COIN DOT
Pitcher, marigold 160.00
Tumbler, marigold 40.00

INVERTED FEATHER (Cambridge)
Compote, jelly, marigold 50.00
Cracker jar, cov., green 180.00
Cracker jar, cov., purple 750.00
Parfait, marigold 65.00
Pitcher, milk, marigold 750.00
Pitcher, water, tankard, marigold . .4,000.00
Tumbler, green . . . . .450.00 to 500.00
Tumbler, marigold . . . . .450.00 to 500.00

INVERTED STRAWBERRY (Cambridge)
Berry set: master bowl & 6 sauce
    dishes; purple, 7 pcs. 320.00
Bowl, 7" d., green 72.00
Bowl, master berry, 10" d., purple . .   155.00
Candlestick, marigold 135.00
Candlesticks, green, 7" h., pr. 225.00
Candlesticks, marigold, 7" h., pr. . .   380.00
Celery, blue 1,200.00
Compote, open, 5" d., 6" h.,
    green 525.00
Compote, open, giant, marigold 250.00
Compote, open, giant, purple 400.00
Cracker jar, cov., green 140.00
Creamer, green 85.00
Creamer, marigold 75.00
Creamer, purple 270.00
Creamer & sugar bowl, purple, pr. . .   325.00
Cuspidor, green 600.00
Cuspidor, marigold 625.00
Decanter, green, marked
    "Near-Cut" .3,550.00
Pitcher, milk, purple 1,300.00
Pitcher, tankard,
    green . . . . .850.00 to 1,200.00
Pitcher, tankard, purple 800.00
Powder jar, cov., green 170.00
Powder jar, cov., marigold 90.00
Spooner, green 225.00
Sugar bowl, cov., green 100.00
Table set: creamer, sugar bowl &
    spooner; marigold, 3 pcs. 550.00
Tumbler, green 100.00
Tumbler, marigold 180.00
Tumbler, purple 186.00
Water set: pitcher & 6 tumblers;
    marigold, 7 pcs. 1,500.00

IRIS
Compote, 6¾" d., blue 155.00
Compote, 6¾" d., green 72.00
Compote, 6¾" d., marigold 48.00
Compote, 6¾" d., purple 60.00

Compote, 6¾" d., white 285.00
Goblet, buttermilk, green 75.00
Goblet, buttermilk, marigold 48.00
Goblet, buttermilk, marigold,
souvenir........................ 80.00
Goblet, buttermilk, purple 75.00

IRIS, HEAVY - See Heavy Iris Pattern

JARDINIERE (THE)
Marigold 325.00
Purple 600.00

JEWELED HEART (Dugan or Diamond Glass)

Jeweled Heart Pitcher

Bowl, master berry, 10½" d., fluted,
peach opalescent................ 145.00
Bowl, purple...................... 80.00
Dish, two turned-up sides, peach
opalescent...................... 25.00
Pitcher, marigold (ILLUS.) ..650.00 to 850.00
Plate, 7" d., ruffled, peach
opalescent...................... 38.00
Sauce dish, peach opalescent 45.00
Sauce dish, purple 41.00
Tumbler, amber................... 115.00
Tumbler, green 35.00
Tumbler, marigold................. 65.00

KITTENS (Fenton)

Kittens Cup & Saucer

Bowl, cereal, blue................. 230.00
Bowl, cereal, marigold............. 105.00
Bowl, ruffled, marigold............ 126.00
Bowl, four-sided, ruffled, aqua 225.00
Bowl, four-sided, blue 240.00
Bowl, four-sided, ruffled, marigold.. 90.00

Bowl, six-sided, ruffled, marigold ... 140.00
Cup, marigold 117.00
Cup & saucer, marigold (ILLUS.) 225.00
Dish, turned-up sides, blue......... 315.00
Dish, turned-up sides, marigold 112.00
Dish, turned-up sides, purple....... 425.00
Plate, 4½" d., marigold 150.00
Saucer, marigold 90.00
Spooner, blue..................... 280.00
Spooner, marigold................. 133.00
Toothpick holder, blue............. 300.00
Toothpick holder, marigold......... 120.00
Vase, blue........................ 215.00
Vase, marigold 125.00

LATTICE & DAISY - See Daisy & Lattice Band Pattern

LATTICE & GRAPE (Fenton)
Pitcher, water, blue 250.00
Pitcher, water, marigold 113.00
Tumbler, blue..................... 35.00
Tumbler, marigold................. 24.00
Tumbler, white.................... 145.00
Water set: pitcher & 1 tumbler;
white, 2 pcs..................... 900.00
Water set: tankard pitcher & 6 tum-
blers; blue, 7 pcs............... 700.00
Water set: tankard pitcher & 6 tum-
blers; marigold, 7 pcs........... 267.00

LATTICE & POINSETTIA (Northwood)

Lattice & Poinsettia Bowl

Bowl, cobalt blue (ILLUS.) 310.00
Bowl, ice blue 1,350.00
Bowl, marigold.................... 175.00
Bowl, purple............. 185.00 to 210.00

LATTICE & POINTS
Bowl, 6" d., low, ruffled, hat-
shaped, clambroth 28.00
Bowl, 6" d., low, ruffled, hat-
shaped, pastel marigold 30.00
Hat shape, marigold............... 28.00
Hat shape, white.................. 30.00
Vase, 5" h., white................. 32.00
Vase, 8½" h., marigold............ 28.00

LEAF & BEADS (Northwood)

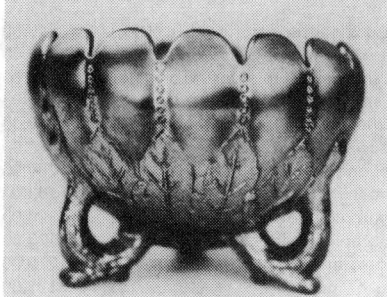

Leaf & Beads Rose Bowl

Candy bowl, footed, aqua
  opalescent...................... 500.00
Candy bowl, footed, green......... 60.00
Candy bowl, footed, marigold 40.00
Nut bowl, aqua opalescent......... 550.00
Nut bowl, handled, green.......... 58.00
Nut bowl, handled, marigold 32.00
Nut bowl, handled, purple 65.00
Rose bowl, aqua 275.00
Rose bowl, aqua opalescent....... 240.00
Rose bowl, blue................... 125.00
Rose bowl, electric blue 175.00
Rose bowl, green 82.00
Rose bowl, interior pattern, green .. 95.00
Rose bowl, ice blue 1,200.00
Rose bowl, ice green opalescent ...1,600.00
Rose bowl, lavender............... 500.00
Rose bowl, marigold............... 68.00
Rose bowl, interior pattern,
  marigold 75.00
Rose bowl, purple (ILLUS.) 85.00
Rose bowl, interior pattern, teal
  blue..........................1,000.00
Rose bowl, white.................. 920.00

LEAF & FLOWERS or LEAF & LITTLE FLOWERS (Millersburg)

Compote, miniature, green........ 333.00
Compote, miniature, marigold...... 265.00
Compote, miniature, purple 318.00

LEAF CHAIN (Fenton)

Bowl, 7" d., aqua 115.00
Bowl, 7" d., blue 54.00
Bowl, 7" d., marigold............. 49.00
Bowl, 7" d., red.................. 500.00
Bowl, 7" d., vaseline w/marigold
  overlay....................... 60.00
Bowl, 7" d., white................ 62.00
Bowl, 8" to 9" d., aqua 165.00
Bowl, 8" to 9" d., blue........... 52.00
Bowl, 8" to 9" d., clambroth........ 50.00
Bowl, 8" to 9" d., green 45.00
Bowl, 8" to 9" d., marigold........ 34.00
Bowl, 8" to 9" d., purple 68.00
Bowl, 8" to 9" d., vaseline 110.00
Bowl, 8" to 9" d., white........... 75.00
Plate, 7" to 8" d., blue 88.00

Plate, 7" to 8" d., marigold 55.00
Plate, 9" d., clambroth 80.00
Plate, 9" d., green 105.00
Plate, 9" d., marigold 140.00
Plate, 9" d., white 170.00

LEAF RAYS NAPPY

Marigold 21.00
Peach opalescent................. 44.00
Purple 34.00
White 40.00

LEAF SWIRL

Compote, purple 45.00
Compote, teal blue............... 75.00
Compote, vaseline 95.00

LEAF TIERS

Berry set: 9" d. master bowl & 4
  sauce dishes; marigold, 5 pcs..... 68.00
Bowl, 5" d., marigold.............. 22.00
Butter dish, cov., marigold 150.00
Creamer, marigold 42.50
Cuspidor, marigold 3,000.00
Pitcher, footed, marigold 300.00
Shade, marigold opalescent 90.00
Tumbler, marigold................. 61.00
Water set: pitcher & 1 tumbler; mar-
  igold, 2 pcs. 500.00
Vase, purple..................... 65.00

LILY OF THE VALLEY (Fenton)

Lily of the Valley Pitcher

Pitcher, water, blue
  (ILLUS.) ....3,900.00 to 4,500.00
Tumbler, blue..................... 300.00
Tumbler, marigold................. 400.00

LINED LATTICE VASE

Marigold 25.00
Peach opalescent, 6" h............ 110.00
Purple 42.00
White 50.00

LION (Fenton)

Bowl, 5" d., marigold............. 110.00

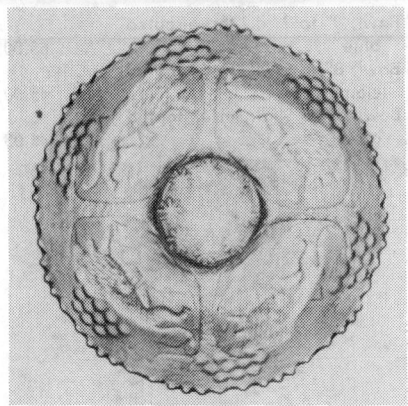

Lion Bowl

Bowl, 6" d., marigold (ILLUS.) 100.00
Bowl, 7" d., blue 305.00
Bowl, 7" d., marigold 120.00
Plate, 6" d., marigold 500.00
Plate, 7½" d., marigold 650.00

LITTLE BARREL PERFUME
Green 70.00
Marigold 68.00
Smoky 97.00

LITTLE FISHES (Fenton)
Bowl, 6" d., three-footed,
  marigold 47.50
Bowl, 6" d., three-footed, purple ... 144.00
Bowl, 8" to 9" d., three-footed,
  blue 185.00
Bowl, 8" to 9" d., three-footed,
  marigold 135.00
Bowl, 10" d., three-footed, blue 162.00
Bowl, 10" d., three-footed,
  marigold 118.00
Sauce, 5" d., footed, aqua 195.00
Sauce, 5" d., footed, marigold 45.00
Sauce, 5" d., footed, vaseline 95.00

LITTLE FLOWERS (Fenton)

Little Flowers Chop Plate
Berry set: master bowl & 3 sauce
  dishes; blue, 4 pcs. ......75.00 to 100.00

Berry set: master bowl & 6 sauce
  dishes; green, 7 pcs. 235.00
Bowl, 5" d., aqua 100.00
Bowl, 5" d., blue 30.00
Bowl, 5" d., green 25.00
Bowl, 5" d., marigold 23.00
Bowl, 8" to 9" d., blue 95.00
Bowl, 8" to 9" d., green 50.00
Bowl, 8" to 9" d., purple 75.00
Bowl, 8" to 9" d., red 1,500.00
Bowl, 10" d., blue 78.00
Bowl, 10" d., ruffled, lavender 116.00
Bowl, 10" d., purple 70.00
Bowl, 10" d., spatula-footed, red ... 850.00
Nut bowl, blue 75.00
Nut bowl, marigold 65.00
Plate, 6" d., marigold 156.00
Plate, chop, marigold (ILLUS.) 400.00

LITTLE STARS BOWL (Millersburg)
Bowl, 7" d., green 118.00
Bowl, 7" d., marigold 75.00
Bowl, 7" d., fluted, marigold 107.00
Bowl, 7" d., purple 82.00
Bowl, 8" d., ruffled, marigold 94.00
Bowl, 8" d., ruffled, purple 125.00
Bowl, ice cream, 8" d., marigold ... 110.00
Bowl, ice cream, 9" d., marigold ... 475.00
Bowl, ice cream, 10" d., blue 300.00

LOGANBERRY VASE (Imperial)
Amber 338.00
Clambroth 225.00
Green 200.00
Marigold 125.00
Purple 360.00
Smoke 225.00

LONG THUMBPRINTS
Creamer, marigold 20.00
Creamer & sugar bowl, marigold,
  pr. 38.00
Sugar bowl, marigold 20.00
Vase, 7" h., green 36.00

LOTUS & GRAPE (Fenton)

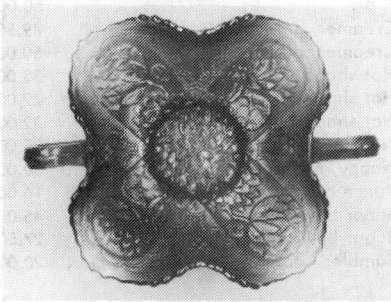

Lotus & Grape Bonbon
Bonbon, two-handled, blue 25.00
Bonbon, two-handled, celeste blue
  (ILLUS.) 185.00
Bonbon, two-handled, green 53.00

Bonbon, two-handled, marigold..... 44.00
Bonbon, two-handled, purple....... 50.00
Bonbon, two-handled, red.........1,100.00
Bowl, 5" d., footed, blue.......... 40.00
Bowl, 5" d., footed, green 67.00
Bowl, 5" d., footed, marigold....... 45.00
Bowl, 7" d., footed, marigold....... 45.00
Bowl, 8" to 9" d., green 105.00
Bowl, 8½" d., ice cream shape,
  Persian blue 400.00
Plate, 9" d., blue................. 750.00
Plate, 9" d., green 675.00

LOUISA (Westmoreland)
Bowl, 8" to 9" d., three-footed,
  green 45.00
Bowl, 8" to 9" d., three-footed,
  marigold 45.00
Bowl, 8" to 9" d., three-footed,
  peach opalescent............... 500.00
Bowl, 8" to 9" d., three-footed,
  purple 42.00
Bowl, 8" to 9" d., three-footed, teal
  blue 40.00
Nut bowl, footed, green 40.00
Nut bowl, footed, marigold 28.00
Nut bowl, footed, purple........... 31.00
Plate, 9½" d., footed, amber....... 137.50
Plate, 9½" d., footed, marigold 146.00
Plate, 9½" d., footed, teal blue 98.00
Rose bowl, footed, amber.......... 125.00
Rose bowl, footed, aqua 84.00
Rose bowl, footed, green 68.00
Rose bowl, footed, lavender 68.00
Rose bowl, footed, marigold 60.00
Rose bowl, footed, purple.......... 60.00
Salt & pepper shakers, marigold,
  pr............................. 22.50

LUSTRE FLUTE (Northwood)
Breakfast set: individual size
  creamer & sugar bowl; green,
  pr............................. 85.00
Breakfast set: individual size
  creamer & sugar bowl; marigold,
  pr............................. 50.00
Creamer, green 49.50
Creamer, purple 50.00
Hat shape, fluted, green, 5" d. 35.00
Hat shape, fluted, marigold, 5" d. .. 22.00
Hat shape, fluted, purple, 5" d. 32.00
Nappy, green 35.00
Nappy, marigold 30.00
Punch cup, green 16.00
Sugar bowl, green 45.00
Sugar bowl, marigold.............. 27.50
Tumbler, marigold 20.00

LUSTRE ROSE (Imperial)
Bowl, 7" d., three-footed,
  marigold 42.00
Bowl, 7" d., three-footed, vaseline.. 100.00
Bowl, 8" to 9" d., three-footed,
  amber 72.00

Bowl, 8" to 9" d., three-footed,
  blue 65.00
Bowl, 8" to 9" d., three-footed,
  clambroth 45.00
Bowl, 8" to 9" d., three-footed,
  green 45.00

Lustre Rose Footed Bowl

Bowl, 8" to 9" d., three-footed, marigold (ILLUS.) 40.00
Bowl, 8" to 9" d., three-footed,
  purple 117.00
Bowl, 10½" d., three-footed,
  marigold 50.00
Bowl, 10½" d., three-footed,
  purple 400.00
Bowl, 10½" d., three-footed,
  smoky 83.00
Bowl, 10½" d., three-footed,
  white 130.00
Bowl, 11" d., ruffled, collared base,
  green 85.00
Bowl, fruit, red 2,300.00
Bowl, whimsey, centerpiece,
  purple 550.00
Butter dish, cov., marigold 75.00
Creamer, marigold ....30.00 to 40.00
Fernery, amber 75.00
Fernery, blue 80.00
Fernery, marigold 38.00
Fernery, purple 95.00
Fernery, red ....,.1,000.00
Fernery, smoky 70.00
Pitcher, water, clambroth 65.00
Pitcher, water, marigold 58.00
Plate, 9" d., amber............... 85.00
Plate, 9" d., marigold 51.00
Plate, 9" d., purple............... 600.00
Rose bowl, amber 70.00
Rose bowl, green 45.00
Sauce dish, green 24.00
Sauce dish, marigold 9.00
Spooner, amber.................. 50.00
Spooner, green 40.00
Spooner, marigold................ 35.00
Spooner, purple 25.00
Sugar bowl, cov., amber 75.00
Sugar bowl, cov., marigold........ 45.00
Table set, marigold, 4 pcs. 160.00
Table set, vaseline, 4 pcs. 375.00
Tumbler, amber.................. 17.00

Tumbler, aqua 395.00
Tumbler, green 35.00
Tumbler, honey amber............. 45.00
Tumbler, marigold................. 18.50
Tumbler, purple.................. 32.50
Water set: pitcher & 4 tumblers;
  purple, 5 pcs.................... 538.00
Water set: pitcher & 6 tumblers;
  clambroth, 7 pcs................ 125.00
Water set: pitcher & 6 tumblers;
  marigold, 7 pcs................. 250.00
Water set: pitcher & 8 tumblers; ice
  green, 9 pcs. 155.00

MANY FRUITS (Dugan)
Punch bowl, 9¾" d., marigold...... 180.00
Punch bowl, 9¾" d., purple 245.00
Punch bowl & base, purple,
  2 pcs..................600.00 to 650.00
Punch cup, blue 50.00
Punch cup, marigold.............. 21.00
Punch cup, purple 38.00
Punch cup, white 65.00
Punch set: bowl, base & 6 cups;
  blue, 8 pcs..................... 500.00
Punch set: bowl, base & 6 cups;
  marigold, 8 pcs................. 375.00
Punch set: bowl, base & 6 cups; pur-
  ple, 8 pcs...................... 730.00
Punch set: bowl, base & 10 cups;
  white, 12 pcs................. 1,600.00

MANY STARS (Millersburg)
Bowl, 8" to 9" d., ruffled, green 400.00
Bowl, 8" to 9" d., ruffled,
  marigold 345.00
Bowl, 10" d., ruffled, blue 650.00
Bowl, 10" d., ruffled,
  purple ....475.00 to 500.00
Bowl, ice cream, 10" d., green 380.00
Bowl, ice cream, 10" d., marigold .. 342.00

MAPLE LEAF (Dugan)
Berry set: master bowl & 5 small
  berry bowls; marigold, 6 pcs. 75.00
Berry set: master bowl & 6 small
  berry bowls; pedestaled, purple,
  7 pcs.......................... 225.00
Bowl, 6" d., small berry, marigold .. 14.00
Bowl, 6" d., small berry, purple 22.50
Bowl, master berry or fruit,
  marigold 100.00
Bowl, master berry or fruit,
  purple 70.00
Butter dish, cov., blue 85.00
Creamer, blue 60.00
Creamer, marigold 42.00
Creamer, purple 58.00
Pitcher, water, purple 165.00
Spooner, marigold................. 46.00
Spooner, purple.................. 60.00
Sugar bowl, cov., marigold......... 40.00
Sugar bowl, cov., purple 95.00
Table set: cov. sugar bowl, creamer
  & spooner; purple, 3 pcs. 235.00

Table set, marigold, 4 pcs. 222.00
Tumbler, amber.................. 75.00
Tumbler, blue.................... 57.00
Tumbler, clambroth............... 75.00
Tumbler, lavender................ 150.00
Tumbler, marigold................ 24.00
Tumbler, pastel marigold 75.00
Tumbler, purple................. 32.00
Water set: pitcher & 6 tumblers;
  marigold, 7 pcs................. 215.00
Water set: pitcher & 6 tumblers;
  purple, 7 pcs................... 375.00

MARILYN (Millersburg)
Pitcher, water, green.............. 675.00
Pitcher, water, purple 750.00
Tumbler, green ....300.00 to 325.00
Tumbler, marigold................ 150.00
Tumbler, purple................. 121.00
Water set: pitcher & 5 tumblers;
  marigold, 6 pcs................. 700.00
Water set: pitcher & 6 tumblers;
  purple, 7 pcs. 1,325.00

MARY ANN VASE (Dugan)
Marigold 55.00
Purple 110.00
Vaseline 350.00

MAYAN (Millersburg)
Bowl, 8" to 9" d., green 68.00
Bowl, 8" to 9" d., purple 125.00

MEMPHIS (Northwood)

Memphis Punch Bowl & Base

Fruit bowl & base, cobalt blue,
  2 pcs. 2,300.00
Fruit bowl & base, marigold,
  2 pcs.......................... 225.00
Punch bowl, 11½" d., marigold..... 62.50
Punch bowl, 11½" d., purple 190.00
Punch bowl & base, green, 2 pcs.... 175.00
Punch bowl & base, ice green,
  2 pcs. 2,950.00
Punch bowl & base, marigold,
  2 pcs. 175.00
Punch bowl & base, purple, 2 pcs.
  (ILLUS.)...................... 600.00

Punch cup, green 35.00
Punch cup, ice blue 60.00
Punch cup, ice green 60.00
Punch cup, marigold 20.00
Punch cup, purple 26.00
Punch cup, white 54.00
Punch set: bowl, base & 4 cups; ice
  blue, 6 pcs. 2,000.00
Punch set: bowl, base & 6 cups;
  marigold, 8 pcs................. 388.00
Punch set: bowl, base & 6 cups; pur-
  ple, 8 pcs...................... 900.00

MIKADO (Fenton)
Compote, 10" d., blue 390.00
Compote, 10" d., marigold 133.00
Compote, 10" d., purple 302.00

MILADY (Fenton)
Pitcher, water, blue 750.00
Pitcher, water, marigold 475.00
Tumbler, blue 85.00
Tumbler, green 675.00
Tumbler, marigold................ 70.00
Tumbler, purple 123.00
Water set: pitcher & 2 tumblers;
  blue, 3 pcs. 1,000.00

**MILLERSBURG HEAVY GRAPE - See Heavy
Grape Pattern**

**MILLERSBURG PIPE HUMIDOR - See Pipe Hu-
midor Pattern**

MIRRORED LOTUS
Bonbon, blue 55.00
Bowl, 7" d., blue 65.00
Bowl, 7" d., ice green 400.00
Bowl, 7" d., marigold............. 55.00
Rose bowl, marigold.............. 450.00
Rose bowl, white................. 500.00

MITERED OVALS (Millersburg)
Vase, green.....................2,200.00
Vase, marigold 2,450.00

MORNING GLORY (Millersburg)

Morning Glory Pitcher

Pitcher, tankard, green 9,000.00
Pitcher, tankard, marigold........5,350.00
Pitcher, tankard, purple
  (ILLUS.) ....6,350.00 to 7,500.00
Tumbler, green 1,200.00
Tumbler, marigold................ 300.00
Tumbler, purple ....950.00 to 1,000.00

MULTIFRUITS & FLOWERS (Millersburg)
Pitcher, water, green...5,250.00 to 7,500.00
Pitcher, water, marigold 4,400.00
Pitcher, water, purple.............4,500.00
Punch bowl & base, marigold,
  2 pcs........................... 600.00
Punch bowl & base, purple, 2 pcs. .. 850.00
Punch cup, green 60.00
Punch cup, purple 40.00
Punch set: bowl, base & 3 cups; pur-
  ple, 5 pcs...................... 950.00
Punch set: bowl, base & 5 cups;
  green, 7 pcs....................1,675.00
Punch set: bowl, base & 6 cups;
  tulip-shaped, marigold,
  8 pcs...............1,000.00 to 1,200.00
Punch set: bowl, base & 8 cups;
  tulip-shaped, marigold, 10 pcs. ..1,425.00
Tumbler, green 1,000.00

MY LADY
Powder jar, cov., marigold 90.00

NAUTILUS (Dugan)
Creamer, peach opalescent 185.00
Creamer, purple 170.00
Creamer & sugar bowl, peach
  opalescent, pr.................. 375.00
Sugar bowl, open, peach
  opalescent..................... 250.00
Sugar bowl, open, purple 235.00

NESTING SWAN (Millersburg)
Bowl, 10" d., amber 225.00
Bowl, 10" d., green 225.00
Bowl, 10" d., marigold............ 165.00
Bowl, 10" d., purple 250.00

NIGHT STARS (Millersburg)
Bonbon, green 308.00
Card tray, purple................. 300.00

NIPPON (Northwood)
Bowl, 8" to 9" d., 3" h., green...... 143.00
Bowl, 8" to 9" d., 2¼" h.,
  ice blue ....200.00 to 225.00
Bowl, 8" to 9" d., ice green 375.00
Bowl, 8" to 9" d., marigold......... 50.00
Bowl, 8" to 9" d., purple 140.00
Bowl, 8" to 9" d., fluted, white 175.00
Plate, 9" d., marigold 392.00
Plate, 9" d., white 600.00

**NU-ART   CHRYSANTHEMUM   PLATE
(Imperial)**
Plate, Chrysanthemum, amber 600.00

Plate, Chrysanthemum, green 350.00
Plate, Chrysanthemum, marigold ... 495.00

Nu-Art Plate

Plate, Chrysanthemum, purple
(ILLUS.)........................ 985.00
Plate, Chrysanthemum, smoky...... 530.00
Plate, Chrysanthemum, white......1,300.00

OCTAGON (Imperial)

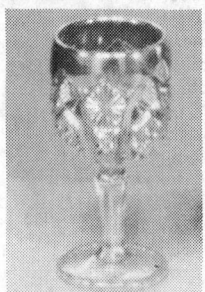

Octagon Goblet

Bowl, 10" sq., green.............. 49.00
Bowl, 11½" d., marigold.......... 45.00
Butter dish, cov., marigold........ 110.00
Compote, jelly, green 75.00
Compote, jelly, marigold.......... 50.00
Creamer, marigold 28.00
Decanter w/stopper, marigold...... 68.00
Goblet, water, marigold (ILLUS.).... 40.00
Pitcher, water, 8" h., marigold...... 70.00
Pitcher, water, 8" h., purple 525.00
Pitcher, water, tankard, 9¾" h.,
marigold 100.00
Pitcher, water, tankard, 9¾" h.,
purple 400.00
Spooner, marigold................ 45.00
Sugar bowl, cov., marigold........ 50.00
Table set, marigold, 4 pcs. 225.00
Toothpick holder, marigold........ 170.00
Tumbler, green 80.00
Tumbler, marigold................ 27.00
Tumbler, purple 175.00
Vase, 8" h., marigold............. 55.00
Water set: pitcher & 1 tumbler; mar-
igold, 2 pcs. 185.00
Water set: pitcher & 1 tumbler; pur-
ple, 2 pcs..................... 425.00
Water set: pitcher & 6 goblets; mari-
gold, 7 pcs.................... 325.00

Water set: pitcher & 6 tumblers;
marigold, 7 pcs................. 250.00
Wine, marigold 32.00
Wine, purple..................... 50.00
Wine set: decanter & 1 wine; mari-
gold, 2 pcs. ....90.00 to 125.00
Wine set: decanter & 1 wine; pur-
ple, 2 pcs..................... 450.00

OHIO STAR (Millersburg)

Compote, jelly, marigold........... 525.00
Vase, green.....................1,100.00
Vase, marigold 300.00
Vase, purple..................... 725.00

OPEN ROSE (Imperial)

Berry set: master bowl & 4 sauce
dishes; amber, 5 pcs............. 60.00
Berry set: master bowl & 6 sauce
dishes; marigold, 7 pcs. 96.00
Bowl, 5" d., amber 28.00
Bowl, 5" d., marigold............. 25.00
Bowl, 7" d., footed, green 65.00
Bowl, 7" d., footed, marigold...... 35.00
Bowl, 7" d., footed, purple........ 58.00
Bowl, 7" d., footed, white........ 65.00
Bowl, 8" to 9" d., amber.......... 50.00
Bowl, 8" to 9" d., aqua 52.00
Bowl, 8" to 9" d., green 42.00
Bowl, 8" to 9" d., marigold........ 35.00
Bowl, 8" to 9" d., purple.......... 95.00
Bowl, 8" to 9" d., smoky.......... 62.50
Bowl, 10" d., marigold............ 85.00
Bowl, 10" d., purple 325.00
Plate, 9" d., amber............... 140.00
Plate, 9" d., clambroth 145.00
Plate, 9" d., green 82.00
Plate, 9" d., marigold............. 78.00
Plate, 9" d., purple............... 168.00
Plate, chop, purple 375.00
Rose bowl, amber 70.00
Rose bowl, green 52.00
Rose bowl, purple 325.00
Spooner, marigold................ 28.00
Tumbler, marigold................ 20.00
Vase, marigold 45.00
Water set: pitcher & 6 tumblers;
marigold, 7 pcs................. 200.00
Water set: pitcher & 6 tumblers;
purple, 7 pcs................... 375.00

ORANGE PEEL

Punch cup, marigold.............. 12.50

ORANGE TREE (Fenton)

Berry set: master bowl & 4 sauce
dishes; white, 5 pcs. 165.00
Berry set: master bowl & 6 sauce
dishes; marigold, 7 pcs. 220.00
Bowl, 7" d., white................ 64.00
Bowl, 8" to 9" d., amber.......... 60.00
Bowl, 8" to 9" d., blue........... 58.00
Bowl, 8" to 9" d., clambroth....... 45.00
Bowl, 8" to 9" d., green 95.00

Bowl, 8" to 9" d., marigold 32.00
Bowl, 8" to 9" d., pastel marigold .. 60.00
Bowl, 8" to 9" d., purple 87.00
Bowl, 8" to 9" d., red 1,750.00
Bowl, 8" to 9" d., white 100.00
Bowl, 10" d., three-footed, blue 225.00
Bowl, 10" d., three-footed, green ... 265.00
Bowl, 10" d., three-footed,
  marigold 85.00
Bowl, 10" d., three-footed, purple .. 175.00
Bowl, 10" d., three-footed, white ... 150.00
Bowl, ice cream, green 175.00
Bowl, ice cream, marigold 25.00
Bowl, ice cream, red 1,200.00
Bowl, ice cream, white 105.00
Bowl, milk white w/marigold
  overlay 1,400.00
Breakfast set: individual size
  creamer & cov. sugar bowl; blue,
  pr............................ 130.00
Breakfast set: individual size
  creamer & cov. sugar bowl; mari-
  gold, pr. 195.00
Breakfast set: individual size
  creamer & cov. sugar bowl; pur-
  ple, pr....................... 125.00
Butter dish, cov., marigold 117.00
Compote, 5" d., blue 60.00
Compote, 5" d., green 85.00
Compote, 5" d., marigold 36.00
Creamer, footed, blue 60.00
Creamer, footed, marigold 35.00
Creamer, footed, purple 50.00
Creamer, footed, white 50.00
Creamer, individual size, blue 52.50
Creamer, individual size, marigold .. 37.50
Creamer, individual size, purple 44.00
Creamer & sugar bowl, footed, blue,
  pr............................ 100.00
Dish, ice cream, footed, blue 45.00
Dish, ice cream, footed, marigold ... 50.00
Goblet, aqua 110.00
Goblet, blue 55.00
Goblet, green................... 138.00
Goblet, marigold 22.50
Goblet, marigold, w/advertising 60.00
Hatpin holder, blue............... 250.00
Hatpin holder, green 335.00
Hatpin holder, marigold 140.00
Hatpin holder, purple............. 300.00
Loving cup, blue 235.00
Loving cup, green 330.00
Loving cup, marigold 137.00
Loving cup, purple 200.00
Loving cup, white 200.00
Mug, amber 135.00
Mug, Amberina 300.00
Mug, aqua 200.00
Mug, blue (ILLUS.)............... 48.00
Mug, green 850.00
Mug, lavender 135.00
Mug, lime green 500.00
Mug, lime green w/vaseline base .. 150.00
Mug, marigold 25.00

Orange Tree Mug

Mug, marigold w/blue base 157.00
Mug, marigold w/green base 120.00
Mug, marigold w/vaseline
  base ....140.00 to 175.00
Mug, purple 90.00
Mug, red 380.00
Mug, teal blue 275.00
Mug, vaseline................... 95.00
Pitcher, water, blue 325.00
Pitcher, water, marigold 275.00
Pitcher, water, white 425.00
Plate, 9" d., flat, blue 275.00
Plate, 9" d., flat, clambroth 150.00
Plate, 9" d., flat, green 650.00
Plate, 9" d., flat, marigold 150.00
Plate, 9" d., flat, white 200.00
Powder jar, cov., blue 93.00
Powder jar, cov., green........... 375.00
Powder jar, cov., marigold 62.00
Powder jar, cov., purple 120.00
Powder jar, open, peach
  opalescent.................... 195.00
Punch bowl & base, blue, 2 pcs. 300.00
Punch bowl & base, marigold,
  2 pcs......................... 154.00
Punch bowl & base, white,
  2 pcs......................... 325.00
Punch cup, blue................. 25.00
Punch cup, marigold............. 16.00
Punch cup, purple 20.00
Punch cup, white................ 45.00
Punch set: bowl, base & 4 cups;
  marigold, 6 pcs................ 365.00
Punch set: bowl, base & 6 cups;
  blue, 8 pcs................... 595.00
Punch set: bowl, base & 7 cups;
  blue, 9 pcs................... 465.00
Rose bowl, blue................. 66.00
Rose bowl, clambroth............. 88.00
Rose bowl, green................ 80.00
Rose bowl, ice green opalescent.... 650.00
Rose bowl, marigold.............. 54.00
Rose bowl, purple............... 110.00
Rose bowl, red................. 575.00
Rose bowl, white................ 250.00
Sauce dish, footed, blue 35.00
Sauce dish, footed, marigold 18.00
Shaving mug, amber 125.00
Shaving mug, Amberina 450.00
Shaving mug, blue 62.50

Shaving mug, green 850.00
Shaving mug, marigold 32.00
Shaving mug, purple ......110.00 to 200.00
Shaving mug, red 435.00
Spooner, blue.................... 75.00
Sugar bowl, blue................. 60.00
Sugar bowl, marigold............. 110.00
Sugar bowl, white................ 50.00
Sugar bowl, open, individual size,
   marigold 20.00
Sugar bowl, open, individual size,
   white 50.00
Tumbler, blue.................... 50.00
Tumbler, marigold................ 45.00
Tumbler, white................... 138.00
Water set: pitcher & 7 tumblers;
   blue, 8 pcs................... 495.00
Wine, aqua 300.00
Wine, blue 50.00
Wine, clambroth 48.00
Wine, green 175.00
Wine, marigold 28.00

ORANGE TREE ORCHARD (Fenton)
Pitcher, blue.................... 500.00
Pitcher, marigold................ 250.00
Pitcher, white................... 515.00
Tumbler, blue.................... 57.00
Tumbler, marigold................ 35.00
Tumbler, white................... 308.00
Water set: pitcher & 3 tumblers;
   marigold, 4 pcs.............. 350.00
Water set: pitcher & 4 tumblers;
   white, 5 pcs................1,025.00
Water set: pitcher & 6 tumblers;
   blue, 7 pcs.................. 750.00

ORANGE TREE SCROLL
Pitcher, marigold................ 130.00
Pitcher, white................... 325.00
Tumbler, blue.................... 72.00
Tumbler, marigold................ 62.00
Water set: pitcher & 1 tumbler; mar-
   igold, 2 pcs. 350.00
Water set: pitcher & 6 tumblers;
   blue, 7 pcs.................. 900.00

ORIENTAL POPPY (Northwood)
Pitcher, water, green...1,000.00 to 1,250.00
Pitcher, water, marigold 290.00
Pitcher, water, purple 550.00
Pitcher, water, white.....895.00 to 1,200.00
Tumbler, blue.................... 200.00
Tumbler, green 55.00
Tumbler, ice blue 165.00
Tumbler, marigold................ 35.00
Tumbler, purple.................. 50.00
Tumbler, white................... 130.00
Water set: pitcher & 1 tumbler; mar-
   igold, 2 pcs. 225.00
Water set: pitcher & 1 tumbler;
   white, 2 pcs................1,900.00
Water set: pitcher & 4 tumblers;
   purple, 5 pcs................ 650.00

Water set: pitcher & 6 tumblers; ice
   green, 7 pcs.................4,000.00
Water set: pitcher & 6 tumblers; ice
   blue, 7 pcs.................1,850.00

PAINTED CHERRIES
Tumbler, blue.................... 15.00
Water set: pitcher & 1 tumbler;
   blue, 2 pcs.................. 175.00

PALM BEACH (United States Glass Co.)
Bowl, 5" d., four turned-in sides,
   marigold 90.00
Butter dish, cov., white 195.00
Creamer, marigold 68.00
Creamer, white 80.00
Pitcher, water, marigold 450.00
Pitcher, water, white 700.00
Rose bowl, amber 125.00
Rose bowl, white................. 75.00
Sauce dish, marigold 30.00
Sauce dish, white 40.00
Spooner, marigold................ 85.00
Spooner, white................... 85.00
Tumbler, amber 80.00
Tumbler, marigold................ 210.00
Tumbler, white................... 152.00
Water set: pitcher & 5 tumblers;
   amber, 6 pcs................. 405.00
Whimsey banana boat, marigold,
   6" ....75.00 to 90.00
Whimsey banana boat, purple, 6"... 115.00
Whimsey vase, white 190.00

PANELED DANDELION - See Dandelion, Paneled Pattern

PANSY and PANSY SPRAY

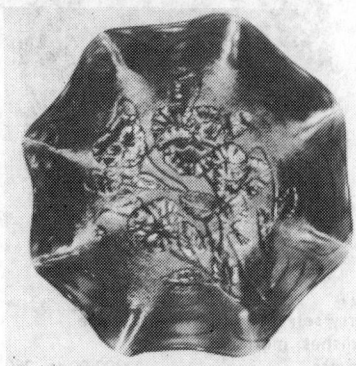

Pansy Bowl

Bowl, 8" to 9" d., amber 20.00
Bowl, 8" to 9" d., green 45.00
Bowl, 8" to 9" d., marigold........ 34.00
Bowl, 9" d., fluted, purple (ILLUS.) .. 63.00
Breakfast set: individual size
   creamer & sugar bowl; purple,
   pr. 35.00
Compote, white 160.00
Creamer, amber 35.00

Creamer, marigold 19.00
Creamer, purple 35.00
Creamer & sugar bowl, amber, pr... 50.00
Creamer & sugar bowl, green, pr. .. 39.00
Creamer & sugar bowl, purple, pr... 130.00
Dresser tray, green 55.00
Dresser tray, marigold 40.00
Nappy, amber 38.00
Nappy, green 28.00
Nappy, lavender 25.00
Nappy, marigold 20.00
Nappy, purple 28.00
Pickle (or relish) dish, amber,
   6 x 9"........................ 49.00
Pickle (or relish) dish, blue, 6 x 9".. 25.00
Pickle (or relish) dish, clambroth,
   6 x 9"........................ 20.00
Pickle (or relish) dish, green,
   6 x 9"........................ 48.00
Pickle (or relish) dish, marigold,
   6 x 9"........................ 20.00
Pickle (or relish) dish, purple,
   6 x 9"........................ 35.00
Pickle (or relish) dish, smoky,
   6 x 9"........................ 55.00
Plate, 9" d., ruffled, smoky 65.00
Sugar bowl, amber 35.00
Sugar bowl, aqua 110.00
Sugar bowl, marigold 22.00
Sugar bowl, smoky 35.00
Sugar bowl, breakfast size, purple .. 54.00

PANTHER (Fenton)

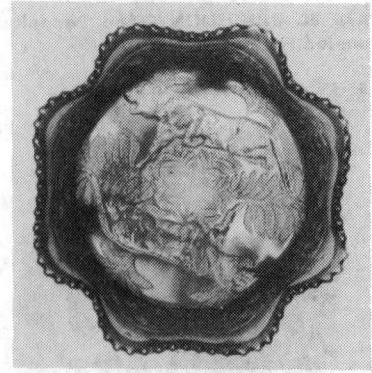

Panther Bowl

Berry set: master bowl & 4 sauce
   dishes; marigold,
   5 pcs...................200.00 to 250.00
Berry set: master bowl & 6 sauce
   dishes; blue, 7 pcs............... 700.00
Bowl, 5" d., footed, aqua 325.00
Bowl, 5" d., footed, blue 76.00
Bowl, 5" d., footed, clambroth...... 35.00
Bowl, 5" d., footed, green 110.00
Bowl, 5" d., footed, marigold....... 40.00
Bowl, 5" d., footed, red 598.00
Bowl, 9" d., claw-footed, blue 275.00
Bowl, 9" d., claw-footed, green..... 600.00

Bowl, 9" d., claw-footed, marigold
   (ILLUS.)....................... 125.00
Bowl, 9" d., claw-footed, purple 150.00
Bowl, 9" d., claw-footed, white..... 625.00
Bowl, low, marigold 300.00
Centerpiece bowl, blue 900.00
Centerpiece bowl, marigold 600.00

PEACH (Northwood)
Berry set: master bowl & 4 sauce
   dishes; white, 5 pcs. 395.00
Bowl, 9" d., white................ 150.00
Butter dish, cov., white 300.00
Pitcher, water, blue...............1,250.00
Pitcher, water, white 450.00
Sauce dish, white 42.50
Spooner, white................... 90.00
Sugar bowl, cov., white ....90.00 to 125.00
Table set, white, 4 pcs............. 575.00
Tumbler, blue.................... 75.00
Tumbler, marigold 2,100.00
Tumbler, white................... 125.00
Water set: pitcher & 6 tumblers;
   blue, 7 pcs. ....900.00 to 1,200.00
Water set: pitcher & 6 tumblers;
   white, 7 pcs. ....550.00 to 850.00

PEACH & PEAR OVAL FRUIT BOWL
Marigold 77.00
Purple 80.00

PEACOCK & DAHLIA (Fenton)
Bowl, 6" d., ice cream, vaseline 65.00
Bowl, 6¼" d., ice cream, green 120.00
Bowl, 7" d., ruffled, aqua
   opalescent...................... 115.00
Bowl, 7" d., ruffled, blue 125.00
Bowl, 7" d., marigold 50.00
Bowl, 7" d., vaseline 185.00
Bowl, 8" d., footed, green 49.00
Bowl, aqua 60.00
Plate, 7½" d., marigold 550.00
Sauce dish, marigold 25.00

PEACOCK & GRAPE (Fenton)
Bowl, 7" d., marigold 25.00
Bowl, 7" d., purple 32.00
Bowl, 7" d., red.................. 975.00
Bowl, 8" to 9" d., flat, ribbon candy
   rim, blue 72.00
Bowl, 8" to 9" d., flat, ribbon candy
   rim, lavender 75.00
Bowl, 8" to 9" d., three-footed,
   amber 100.00
Bowl, 8" to 9" d., three-footed,
   blue 45.00
Bowl, 8" to 9" d., three-footed,
   green 65.00
Bowl, 8" to 9" d., three-footed, ice
   green opalescent................ 515.00
Bowl, 8" to 9" d., three-footed,
   lavender 125.00
Bowl, 8" to 9" d., three-footed,
   marigold 38.00

Bowl, 8" to 9" d., three-footed,
peach opalescent 343.00
Bowl, 8" to 9" d., three-footed,
purple 58.00
Bowl, 8" to 9" d., three-footed,
red 604.00
Bowl, 8" to 9" d., three-footed,
vaseline 125.00
Bowl, 8" to 9" d., three-footed,
vaseline opalescent 400.00
Bowl, 8" to 9" d., collared base,
blue 58.00
Bowl, 8" to 9" d., collared base,
marigold 42.00
Bowl, 8" to 9" d., collared base,
peach opalescent 580.00
Bowl, 8" to 9" d., collared base,
purple 55.00
Bowl, 8" to 9" d., collared base,
ruffled, red 1,100.00
Bowl, 8" to 9" d., collared base,
smoky 588.00
Plate, 9" d., collared base, blue 325.00
Plate, 9" d., collared base,
marigold 260.00
Plate, 9" d., collared base, w/berry
exterior, smoky ice blue 800.00
Plate, 9" d., three-footed, green.... 160.00
Plate, 9" d., three-footed,
marigold 182.00
Plate, 9" d., three-footed, purple ... 260.00

PEACOCK & URN

Peacock & Urn Ice Cream Bowl

Berry set: master bowl & 4 sauce
dishes; marigold, 5 pcs. 225.00
Berry set: master bowl & 5 sauce
dishes; purple, 6 pcs. 750.00
Bowl, 7" d., ruffled, green
(Millersburg) 250.00
Bowl, 7" d., ruffled, marigold
(Millersburg) 375.00
Bowl, 7" d., ruffled, purple (Millers-
burg) 265.00
Bowl, 7½" d., "shotgun," ruffled,
green 425.00
Bowl, 8" to 9" d., blue (Fenton)..... 116.00

Bowl, 8" to 9" d., green (Fenton) ... 165.00
Bowl, 8" to 9" d., green (Millers-
burg) 440.00
Bowl, 8" to 9" d., marigold
(Fenton) 73.00
Bowl, 8" to 9" d., ruffled, marigold
(Millersburg) 106.00
Bowl, 8" to 9" d., marigold (Millers-
burg) 145.00
Bowl, 8" to 9" d., purple (Fenton)... 130.00
Bowl, 8" to 9" d., purple (Millers-
burg) 285.00
Bowl, 8" to 9" d., white (Fenton) ... 150.00
Bowl, 9½" d., berry, purple (Millers-
burg) 425.00
Bowl, 10" d., fluted, green (Millers-
burg) 214.00
Bowl, 10" d., fluted, lavender
(Millersburg) 600.00
Bowl, 10" d., marigold
(Millersburg) 90.00
Bowl, ice cream, 10" d., blue
(Northwood) 575.00
Bowl, ice cream, 10" d., green
(Northwood) ....900.00 to 1,000.00
Bowl, ice cream, 10" d., ice blue
(Northwood) ....850.00 to 1,000.00
Bowl, ice cream, 10" d., ice green
(Northwood) 815.00
Bowl, ice cream, 10" d., marigold
(Millersburg) 366.00
Bowl, ice cream, 10" d., marigold
(Northwood) 292.00
Bowl, ice cream, 10" d., purple
(Millersburg) 250.00
Bowl, ice cream, 10" d., purple,
Northwood (ILLUS.) 550.00
Bowl, ice cream, 10" d., smoky 900.00
Bowl, ice cream, 10" d., white
(Northwood) 542.00
Bowl, 10½" d., ruffled, blue
(Millersburg) 1,325.00
Bowl, 10½" d., ruffled, green
(Millersburg) 280.00
Bowl, 10½" d., ruffled, marigold
(Millersburg) 225.00
Bowl, 10½" d., ruffled, purple...... 245.00
Bowl, 10½" d., ruffled, vaseline
(Millersburg) 1,900.00
Bowl, ice cream shape, blue
(Fenton) 135.00
Bowl, ice cream shape, green
(Fenton) 140.00
Bowl, ice cream shape, marigold
(Fenton) 80.00
Bowl, marigold w/moonstone 1,750.00
Compote, 5½" d., 5" h., aqua
(Fenton) 325.00
Compote, 5½" d., 5" h., blue
(Fenton) 100.00
Compote, 5½" d., 5" h., green
(Fenton) 230.00
Compote, 5½" d., 5" h., ice green
(Fenton) 135.00

Compote, 5½" d., 5" h., marigold
(Fenton) 45.00
Compote, 5½" d., 5" h., purple
(Fenton) 55.00
Compote, 5½" d., 5" h., red
(Fenton) 800.00
Compote, 5½" d., 5" h., vaseline
(Fenton) 150.00
Compote, 5½" d., 5" h., white
(Fenton) 300.00
Compote, blue (Millersburg Giant) .. 475.00
Compote, green (Millersburg
Giant) 1,200.00
Compote, marigold (Millersburg
Giant)......................... 500.00
Compote, purple (Millersburg
Giant)......................... 845.00
Goblet, marigold (Fenton).......... 100.00
Ice cream dish, aqua opalescent,
small (Northwood) .....700.00 to 1,100.00
Ice cream dish, blue, small (North-
wood)......................... 70.00
Ice cream dish, green, small 145.00
Ice cream dish, ice blue, small 240.00
Ice cream dish, ice green, small 475.00
Ice cream dish, marigold, small 50.00
Ice cream dish, purple, small....... 60.00
Ice cream dish, white, small 175.00
Ice cream set: large bowl & 2 small
dishes; blue, 3 pcs.............. 525.00
Ice cream set: large bowl & 4 small
dishes; purple, 5 pcs............ 525.00
Ice cream set: large bowl & 6 small
dishes; marigold, 7 pcs. 500.00
Ice cream set: large bowl & 6 small
dishes; white, 7 pcs.............1,250.00
Plate, 6½" d., marigold 168.00
Plate, 6½" d., purple.............. 235.00
Plate, 9" d., blue................. 318.00
Plate, 9" d., marigold 165.00
Plate, 9" d., white 335.00
Plate, chop, 11" d., marigold
(Millersburg) 2,800.00
Plate, chop, 11" d., marigold
(Northwood) 350.00
Plate, chop, 11" d., purple
(Millersburg)................... 815.00
Plate, chop, 11" d., purple
(Northwood) 350.00
Sauce dish, blue (Millersburg) 123.00
Sauce dish, blue (Northwood) 95.00
Sauce dish, green (Millersburg)..... 75.00
Sauce dish, ice green, 6" d. (North-
wood).................170.00 to 200.00
Sauce dish, lavender (Millersburg) .. 55.00
Sauce dish, marigold (Millersburg) .. 65.00
Sauce dish, marigold (Northwood) .. 40.00
Sauce dish, purple (Millersburg) 165.00
Sauce dish, purple (Northwood) 55.00
Sauce dish, white (Northwood) 185.00
Whimsey sauce dish, 5¼" d.,
purple 185.00

PEACOCK AT FOUNTAIN (Northwood)

Peacock at Fountain Water Set

Berry set: master bowl & 6 sauce
dishes; marigold, 7 pcs. 200.00
Berry set: master bowl & 6 sauce
dishes; purple, 7 pcs............. 215.00
Bowl, master berry, ice blue 290.00
Bowl, master berry, marigold 110.00
Bowl, master berry, purple 145.00
Bowl, master berry, white 275.00
Bowl, orange, three-footed, aqua
opalescent 2,000.00
Bowl, orange, three-footed, blue ... 280.00
Bowl, orange, three-footed,
green 525.00
Bowl, orange, three-footed,
lavender 325.00
Bowl, orange, three-footed,
marigold 165.00
Bowl, orange, three-footed,
purple 300.00
Butter dish, cov., green 500.00
Butter dish, cov., marigold 129.00
Butter dish, cov., purple 228.00
Butter dish, cov., white 380.00
Compote, aqua opalescent 3,100.00
Compote, blue 537.00
Compote, ice blue ....900.00 to 1,200.00
Compote, ice green 1,350.00
Compote, marigold 408.00
Compote, purple 800.00
Compote, white 870.00
Creamer, marigold 62.50
Creamer, purple 90.00
Pitcher, water, blue 360.00
Pitcher, water, green...1,500.00 to 1,750.00
Pitcher, water, ice blue 1,600.00
Pitcher, water, marigold 150.00
Pitcher, water, purple 305.00
Pitcher, water, white 650.00
Punch bowl & base, ice blue,
2 pcs. 2,350.00
Punch bowl & base, marigold,
2 pcs. 340.00
Punch bowl & base, purple, 2 pcs. .. 725.00
Punch cup, blue 50.00
Punch cup, ice blue 90.00
Punch cup, marigold 32.50
Punch cup, purple 40.00
Punch cup, white................. 60.00

Punch set: bowl, base & 1 cup; ice
green, 3 pcs. 2,250.00
Punch set: bowl, base & 1 cup;
purple, 3 pcs. 650.00
Punch set: bowl, base & 4 cups;
marigold, 6 pcs. 500.00
Punch set: bowl, base & 6 cups; ice
blue, 8 pcs. 2,650.00
Punch set: bowl, base & 6 cups;
white, 8 pcs. 2,100.00
Sauce dish, blue 35.00
Sauce dish, ice blue 75.00
Sauce dish, marigold 20.00
Sauce dish, purple 28.00
Sauce dish, teal blue 110.00
Sauce dish, white 65.00
Spooner, blue. 125.00
Spooner, marigold. 58.00
Spooner, purple. 80.00
Spooner, white. 125.00
Sugar bowl, cov., marigold. 75.00
Sugar bowl, cov., purple. 85.00
Sugar bowl, cov., white. 180.00
Table set, marigold, 4 pcs. 395.00
Table set, purple, 4 pcs. 545.00
Tumbler, blue. 42.00
Tumbler, green 350.00
Tumbler, ice blue 200.00
Tumbler, lavender. 125.00
Tumbler, marigold. 32.00
Tumbler, purple. 47.00
Tumbler, white. 185.00
Water set: pitcher & 1 tumbler; ice
blue, 2 pcs. 1,800.00
Water set: pitcher & 4 tumblers;
purple, 5 pcs. 495.00
Water set: pitcher & 5 tumblers;
marigold, 6 pcs. 410.00
Water set: pitcher & 6 tumblers;
blue, 7 pcs. (ILLUS.) 600.00

PEACOCK, FLUFFY (Fenton)
Pitcher, water, blue 650.00
Pitcher, water, green 585.00
Pitcher, water, marigold 325.00
Pitcher, water, purple 490.00
Tumbler, blue. 100.00
Tumbler, green 75.00
Tumbler, marigold. 45.00
Tumbler, purple. 85.00
Tumbler, violet. 75.00
Water set: pitcher & 4 tumblers;
blue, 5 pcs. 900.00
Water set: pitcher & 6 tumblers;
purple, 7 pcs. 925.00

**PEACOCKS ON FENCE (Northwood
Peacocks)**
Bowl, 8" to 9" d., aqua opalescent
(ILLUS.). 900.00
Bowl, 8" to 9" d., electric blue 900.00
Bowl, 8" to 9" d., piecrust rim,
blue 375.00
Bowl, 8" to 9" d., piecrust rim,
green 1,750.00

Peacocks on Fence Bowl

Bowl, 8" to 9" d., piecrust rim, elec-
tric blue. 575.00
Bowl, 8" to 9" d., piecrust rim, ice
blue. 1,500.00
Bowl, 8" to 9" d., piecrust rim, ice
green 1,000.00
Bowl, 8" to 9" d., piecrust rim,
marigold 205.00
Bowl, 8" to 9" d., piecrust rim, pas-
tel marigold 205.00
Bowl, 8" to 9" d., piecrust rim,
purple . . . . .400.00 to 425.00
Bowl, 8" to 9" d., piecrust rim,
white 850.00
Bowl, 8" to 9" d., ruffled rim,
blue . . . . .300.00 to 340.00
Bowl, 8" to 9" d., ruffled rim,
green . . . . .800.00 to 900.00
Bowl, 8" to 9" d., ruffled rim,
marigold 200.00
Bowl, 8" to 9" d., ruffled rim,
purple 330.00
Bowl, ruffled, ribbed back, white . . . 875.00
Plate, 8" d., blue . . . . .550.00 to 600.00
Plate, 9" d., electric blue 775.00
Plate, 9" d., green . . . . .1,650.00 to 1,700.00
Plate, 9" d., ice blue . . .1,800.00 to 1,950.00
Plate, 9" d., ice green 425.00
Plate, 9" d., lavender. 900.00
Plate, 9" d., marigold 345.00
Plate, 9" d., purple. 605.00
Plate, 9" d., white 390.00

PEACOCK STRUTTING (Westmoreland)
Breakfast set: individual size
creamer & open sugar bowl;
purple, pr. 75.00
Creamer, cov., individual size,
purple 40.00
Sugar bowl, cov., individual size,
purple 50.00

PEACOCK TAIL (Fenton)
Bonbon, two-handled, amethyst 47.00
Bonbon, two-handled, blue. . .18.00 to 35.00

Bonbon, two-handled, green 35.00
Bonbon, two-handled, marigold..... 30.00
Bonbon, tricornered, green......... 70.00
Bonbon, tricornered, marigold 25.00
Bonbon, tricornered, purple 35.00
Bowl, 5" d., ruffled, marigold 34.00
Bowl, 5" d., ruffled, purple........ 30.00
Bowl, 7" d., ribbon candy rim,
  amber 40.00
Bowl, 7" d., green 30.00
Bowl, 7" d., purple 35.00
Bowl, 7" d., red................. 575.00
Bowl, 8" d., green 55.00
Bowl, 8" d., purple 32.00
Bowl, 9" d., blue 47.50
Bowl, 9" d., green 50.00
Bowl, 9" d., crimped, green 65.00
Bowl, 9" d., crimped, marigold 34.00
Bowl, 9" d., ribbon candy rim,
  purple 50.00
Bowl, 10" d., green 45.00
Bowl, ice cream, purple 25.00
Bowl, ice cream, red 600.00
Compote, 6" d., 5" h., green 42.00
Compote, 6" d., 5" h., marigold 55.00
Compote, 6" d., 5" h., purple 72.00

Peacock Tail Plate

Plate, 6" d., marigold (ILLUS.) 28.00
Plate, 9" d., marigold 350.00
Whimsey, hat-shaped, green 75.00
Whimsey, hat-shaped, purple....... 25.00

PERFECTION (Millersburg)
Pitcher, water, green 2,630.00
Pitcher, water, marigold 2,700.00
Pitcher, water, purple ..2,000.00 to 3,000.00
Tumbler, green 500.00
Tumbler, purple................. 475.00

PERSIAN GARDEN (Dugan)
Berry set: 11" d. fruit bowl &
  4 sauce dishes; peach opalescent,
  5 pcs. 650.00
Berry set: master bowl & 6 sauce
  dishes; peach opalescent, 7 pcs... 40.00
Bowl, 5" d., blue................ 22.50
Bowl, 5" d., white 73.00
Bowl, 9" d., ruffled, marigold 125.00

Persian Garden Ice Cream Bowl

Bowl, ice cream, 11" d., peach
  opalescent (ILLUS.) 900.00
Bowl, ice cream, 11" d., purple..... 800.00
Bowl, ice cream, 11" d., white 200.00
Fruit bowl (no base), marigold,
  11½" d...................70.00 to 85.00
Fruit bowl (no base), peach opales-
  cent, 11½" d................... 210.00
Fruit bowl (no base), purple,
  11½" d....................... 135.00
Fruit bowl (no base), white,
  11½" d....................... 250.00
Fruit bowl & base, peach opales-
  cent, 2 pcs................... 385.00
Fruit bowl & base, purple, 2 pcs. ... 300.00
Hair receiver, marigold 75.00
Ice cream dish, white, small 65.00
Ice cream set: 11" d. master ice
  cream bowl & 4 small dishes;
  white, 5 pcs.................. 765.00
Plate, 6" to 7" d., blue 80.00
Plate, 6" to 7" d., marigold 90.00
Plate, 6" to 7" d., peach
  opalescent.................... 260.00
Plate, 6" to 7" d., purple ..175.00 to 200.00
Plate, 6" to 7" d., white 114.00
Plate, 9" d., marigold 125.00
Plate, chop, 11" d.,
  purple ....1,400.00 to 2,000.00
Plate, chop, 11" d., white 900.00

PERSIAN MEDALLION (Fenton)
Bonbon, two-handled, amber 60.00
Bonbon, two-handled, Amberina.... 250.00
Bonbon, two-handled, aqua 100.00
Bonbon, two-handled, blue 55.00
Bonbon, two-handled, green 60.00
Bonbon, two-handled, marigold.... 32.50
Bonbon, two-handled, purple 35.00
Bonbon, two-handled, red 450.00
Bonbon, two-handled, vaseline 125.00
Bowl, 5" d., aqua 175.00
Bowl, 5" d., blue 34.00
Bowl, 5" d., green 30.00
Bowl, 5" d., marigold 32.00
Bowl, 5" d., purple 35.00
Bowl, 5" d., red................. 250.00
Bowl, 6" d., ruffled, aqua 65.00

Bowl, 7" d., green 60.00
Bowl, 7" d., marigold 55.00
Bowl, 8" to 9" d., fluted, blue 65.00
Bowl, 8" to 9" d., ribbon candy rim,
   blue 95.00
Bowl, 8" to 9" d., ribbon candy rim,
   green 52.00
Bowl, 8" to 9" d., marigold 40.00
Bowl, 8" to 9" d., ribbon candy rim,
   purple 80.00
Bowl, 8" to 9" d., ruffled rim,
   red .... 900.00 to 1,175.00
Bowl, 9½" d., purple 85.00
Bowl, 10½" d., fluted, blue 90.00
Bowl, orange, blue 130.00
Bowl, orange, purple 185.00
Compote, 6½" d., 6½" h., blue 75.00
Compote, 6½" d., 6½" h., green ... 175.00
Compote, 6½" d., 6½" h.,
   marigold 50.00
Compote, 6½" d., 6½" h., purple .. 100.00
Compote, 6½" d., 6½" h., white ... 400.00
Hair receiver, blue 68.00
Hair receiver, marigold 50.00
Hair receiver, white 97.00
Plate, 6½" d., blue 68.00
Plate, 6½" d., marigold 43.00
Plate, 6½" d., purple 80.00
Plate, 6½" d., white 75.00
Plate, 9" d., blue 118.00
Plate, 9" d., marigold 115.00
Plate, 9" d., white 395.00
Plate, chop, 10½" d., blue 335.00
Plate, chop, 10½" d., white 225.00
Rose bowl, blue 75.00
Rose bowl, marigold 60.00
Rose bowl, white 143.00

PETAL & FAN (Dugan)
Berry set: master bowl & 8 sauce
   dishes; peach opalescent, 9 pcs. ... 450.00
Bowl, 5" d., peach opalescent 35.00
Bowl, 5" d., purple 42.00
Bowl, 5 3/8" d., black amethyst 40.00
Bowl, 11" d., peach opalescent 125.00
Bowl, 11" d., ruffled, purple 375.00
Bowl, 11" d., star-shaped, stippled,
   Jeweled Heart exterior, purple ... 325.00
Bowl, 11" d., fluted, white 350.00
Plate, 6" d., ribbon candy rim,
   purple 225.00

PETALS (Northwood)
Compote, green 60.00
Compote, marigold 45.00
Compote, purple 70.00

PETER RABBIT (Fenton)
Bowl, 8" d., blue 1,100.00
Bowl, 8" d., green .... 850.00 to 900.00
Bowl, 8" d., marigold 1,000.00
Plate, blue 2,000.00
Plate, green (ILLUS. top of next
   column) 3,000.00
Plate, marigold 1,200.00

Peter Rabbit Plate

PILLOW & SUNBURST (Westmoreland)
Bowl, marigold 25.00
Bowl, purple 43.00
Plate, 8" d., aqua 38.00
Wine, marigold 25.00
Wine, purple 50.00

PINEAPPLE (Sowerby, England)
Bowl, 5" d., marigold 30.00
Bowl, 8" d., marigold 38.00
Compote, purple 70.00
Creamer, marigold, 4½" h. 29.00
Creamer & sugar bowl, purple, pr... 50.00
Nut bowl, marigold 15.00
Pitcher, miniature, purple 60.00
Plate, 8" d., purple 135.00
Rose bowl, marigold 50.00
Sugar bowl, aqua 215.00

PINE CONE (Fenton)
Bowl, 5" d., aqua 75.00
Bowl, 5" d., blue 35.00
Bowl, 5" d., marigold 22.50
Bowl, 5" d., purple 35.00
Bowl, 7" d., ruffled, blue 52.00
Bowl, 7" d., ruffled, green 35.00
Bowl, 7" d., marigold 30.00
Bowl, 7" d., ruffled, purple 40.00
Plate, 5" d., aqua 95.00
Plate, 6½" d., amber 400.00
Plate, 6½" d., blue 70.00
Plate, 6½" d., green 105.00
Plate, 6½" d., marigold 45.00
Plate, 6½" d., purple 126.00
Plate, 7½" d., blue 150.00
Plate, 7½" d., marigold 75.00

PIPE HUMIDOR (Millersburg)
Green 3,375.00
Marigold 5,000.00

PLAID (Fenton)
Bowl, 9" d., marigold 62.00
Bowl, ice cream, 10" d., blue 145.00
Bowl, ice cream, 10" d., green 315.00
Bowl, ruffled, green 260.00
Bowl, ruffled, purple 1,500.00

PLUME PANELS VASE (Fenton)
Blue 35.00
Green 45.00
Marigold 30.00
Red ....650.00 to 750.00

PODS & POSIES or FOUR FLOWERS (Dugan)

Pods & Posies Plate

Bowl, 6" d., peach opalescent 36.00
Bowl, 6" d., purple 48.00
Bowl, 8" to 9" d., green 160.00
Bowl, 8" to 9" d., marigold 45.00
Bowl, 8" to 9" d., purple 50.00
Bowl, 10" d., shallow, ruffled,
    lavender 225.00
Bowl, 10" d., peach opalescent 190.00
Bowl, 10" d., purple 145.00
Plate, 6" d., green 250.00
Plate, 6" d., peach opalescent 105.00
Plate, 6" to 7" d., Basketweave ex-
    terior, peach opalescent 102.00
Plate, 9" d., green 575.00
Plate, 9" d., purple 400.00
Plate, chop, 11" d., peach
    opalescent 400.00
Plate, 11" d., purple (ILLUS.) 750.00

POINSETTIA (Imperial)
Pitcher, milk, amber 59.00
Pitcher, milk, green 250.00
Pitcher, milk, marigold 70.00
Pitcher, milk, smoky 152.00

POINSETTIA & LATTICE
Bowl, amethyst 220.00
Bowl, aqua opalescent 3,250.00
Bowl, cobalt blue 250.00
Bowl, ice blue 1,500.00
Bowl, marigold 400.00
Bowl, purple 242.00

POLO
Ashtray, marigold 27.50

POND LILY
Bonbon, blue 70.00
Bonbon, green 72.50

Bonbon, marigold 60.00
Bonbon, white 77.00

PONY

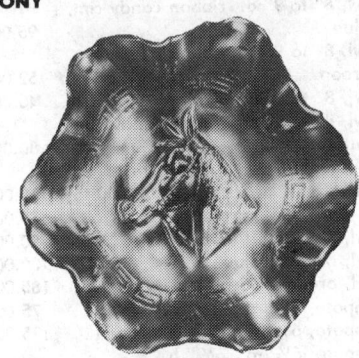

Pony Bowl

Bowl, 8" to 9" d., aqua 400.00
Bowl, 8" to 9" d., lavender 100.00
Bowl, 8" to 9" d., marigold 56.00
Bowl, 8" to 9" d., purple (ILLUS.) ... 122.00
Plate, marigold 475.00

POPPY (Millersburg)
Compote, green 500.00
Compote, marigold 415.00
Compote, purple 1,000.00

POPPY (Northwood)
Pickle dish, aqua opalescent 725.00
Pickle dish, blue 56.00
Pickle dish, electric blue 100.00
Pickle dish, green 62.00
Pickle dish, ice blue 150.00
Pickle dish, marigold 49.00
Pickle dish, purple 245.00
Pickle dish, white 225.00

POPPY SHOW (Northwood)

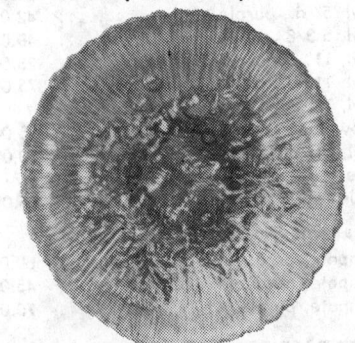

Poppy Show Plate

Bowl, 8" to 9" d., blue 520.00
Bowl, 8" to 9" d., clambroth 190.00
Bowl, 8" to 9" d., electric blue 1,250.00
Bowl, 8" to 9" d., green 1,300.00
Bowl, 8" to 9" d., ice blue 1,200.00
Bowl, 8" to 9" d., ice green 600.00

Bowl, 8" to 9" d., marigold 305.00
Bowl, 8" to 9" d., purple 295.00
Bowl, 8" to 9" d., white 317.00
Plate, blue 638.00
Plate, green (ILLUS.) 2,900.00
Plate, ice blue 1,500.00
Plate, ice green 3,066.00
Plate, marigold 435.00
Plate, purple 1,400.00
Plate, white 492.00

POPPY SHOW VASE (Imperial)
Green 460.00
Marigold 343.00
Pastel marigold 250.00
Purple 1,500.00
Smoky . . . . .275.00 to 500.00

PRIMROSE BOWL (Millersburg)
Green 103.00
Marigold 62.00
Purple 96.00

PRINCESS LAMP
Purple, complete 1,000.00
Purple, base only 225.00

PRISMS
Compote, 7¼" d., 2½" h., two-
  handled, marigold 50.00
Compote, 7¼" d., 2½" h., two-
  handled, purple 55.00

PULLED LOOP
Vase, 5½" h., marigold 28.00
Vase, 9½" h., peach opalescent 64.00
Vase, 10" h., purple 35.00
Vase, 11" h., marigold 17.00

PUZZLE
Bonbon, stemmed, peach
  opalescent 52.00
Bonbon, marigold 25.00
Compote, peach opalescent 36.00
Compote, purple 65.00

QUESTION MARKS
Bonbon, lavender 38.00
Bonbon, footed, marigold, 6" d.,
  3¾" h. 28.00
Bonbon, footed, pastel marigold,
  6" d., 3¾" h. 35.00
Bonbon, footed, peach opalescent,
  6" d., 3¾" h. 58.00
Bonbon, footed, purple, 6" d.,
  3¾" h. 35.00
Bonbon, footed, white, 6" d.,
  3¾" h. 130.00
Bonbon, stemmed, purple 60.00
Plate, dome-footed, Georgia Peach
  exterior, purple 100.00
Plate, stemmed, marigold 80.00

QUILL (Dugan or Diamond Glass Co.)
Pitcher, water, marigold 2,500.00

Tumbler, marigold 275.00
Tumbler, pastel marigold 195.00
Tumbler, purple 400.00

RAINDROPS (Dugan)
Bowl, 9" d., dome-footed, peach
  opalescent 75.00
Bowl, 9" d., dome-footed, purple . . . 125.00

RAMBLER ROSE (Dugan)
Pitcher, water, marigold 115.00
Pitcher, water, purple 325.00
Tumbler, blue 28.00
Tumbler, marigold 29.00
Water set: pitcher & 3 tumblers;
  blue, 4 pcs. 425.00
Water set: pitcher & 6 tumblers;
  marigold, 7 pcs. 295.00
Water set: pitcher & 6 tumblers;
  purple, 7 pcs. 995.00

RANGER
Pitcher, milk, marigold 145.00
Sherbet, marigold 17.50
Tumbler, marigold 105.00
Whiskey shot glass, marigold 95.00

RASPBERRY (Northwood)
Pitcher, milk, green 250.00
Pitcher, milk, marigold 117.00
Pitcher, milk, purple 162.00
Pitcher, water, green . . . . .200.00 to 250.00
Pitcher, water, ice green 2,275.00
Pitcher, water, marigold 129.00
Pitcher, water, purple 222.00
Sauceboat, green 155.00
Sauceboat, marigold 65.00
Sauceboat, purple 85.00
Tumbler, green 45.00
Tumbler, ice blue 162.00
Tumbler, ice green 875.00
Tumbler, marigold 28.00
Tumbler, purple 38.00
Water set: pitcher & 3 tumblers;
  green, 4 pcs. 350.00
Water set: pitcher & 3 tumblers;
  purple, 4 pcs. 375.00
Water set: pitcher & 6 tumblers;
  marigold, 7 pcs. 322.00

RAYS & RIBBONS (Millersburg)
Banana boat, green 850.00
Bowl, 8" to 9" d., green 70.00
Bowl, 8" to 9" d., purple 80.00
Bowl, 10" d., green 60.00
Bowl, 10" sq., green . . . . . .250.00 to 275.00
Bowl, 10", ice cream shape, turned-
  down rim, green 135.00
Bowl, 10" d., marigold 78.00
Bowl, 10" d., purple 65.00

RIBBED FUNERAL VASE
Marigold, 9¼" h. 35.00
Marigold, 18" h. 100.00

Peach opalescent................. 40.00
Sapphire blue, 15½" h. 250.00

RIBBON TIE - See Comet Pattern

RIPPLE
Vase, 7¼" h., marigold........... 85.00
Vase, 9½" h., marigold........... 28.00
Vase, 10" h., purple 50.00
Vase, 11½" h., amber 75.00
Vase, 12" h., marigold........... 21.00
Vase, 15¼" h., amber........... 81.00
Vase, 17" h., marigold........... 65.00
Vase, 18¾" h., green 163.00
Vase, 20" h., marigold........... 200.00
Vase, aqua 160.00

RISING SUN
Pitcher, water, pedestal base,
    marigold 488.00
Tumbler, marigold............... 480.00
Water set: pitcher & 4 tumblers;
    marigold, 5 pcs. 2,950.00

ROBIN (Imperial)

Robin Mug

Mug, marigold (ILLUS.)........... 38.00
Mug, smoky 65.00
Pitcher, water, marigold 155.00
Tumbler, marigold............... 54.00
Water set: pitcher & 1 tumbler; mar-
    igold, 2 pcs. 290.00

ROCOCO VASE
Bowl, 6" d., dome-footed,
    marigold 20.00
Vase, clambroth 40.00
Vase, marigold 74.00
Vase, smoky.................... 90.00

ROSALIND (Millersburg)
Bowl, 8¾" d., ice cream shape,
    green 425.00
Bowl, 10" d., ruffled, green 162.00
Bowl, 10" d., marigold........... 130.00
Bowl, 10" d., purple 175.00
Compote, 6" d., small, ruffled,
    purple 485.00
Compote, 6" d., tall, ruffled,
    marigold 650.00
Compote, 6" d., tall, ruffled,
    purple 1,000.00
Plate, 9" d., green 575.00

ROSE COLUMNS VASE
Amethyst 1,500.00
Amethyst, experimental, factory-
    painted roses decoration 3,250.00
Green 1,235.00
Green w/blue 1,800.00
Marigold..................... 1,200.00

ROSES & FRUIT (Millersburg)
Bonbon, pedestal, light marigold ... 850.00
Compote, purple 1,450.00

ROSE SHOW
Bowl, 9" d., amber 750.00
Bowl, 9" d., aqua opalescent 665.00
Bowl, 9" d., blue 566.00
Bowl, 9" d., green 1,450.00
Bowl, 9" d., ice blue 734.00
Bowl, 9" d., ice green ..1,000.00 to 1,500.00
Bowl, 9" d., ice green opalescent ..2,150.00
Bowl, 9" d., marigold............ 265.00
Bowl, 9" d., purple 421.00
Bowl, 9" d., white 403.00
Plate, 9" d., blue ......1,000.00 to 1,400.00
Plate, 9" d., custard 4,500.00
Plate, 9" d., green 600.00
Plate, 9" d., ice blue ...1,350.00 to 2,000.00
Plate, 9" d., ice green 525.00
Plate, 9" d., marigold 525.00
Plate, 9" d., purple 800.00
Plate, 9" d., white 432.00

ROUND UP (Dugan)
Bowl, 9" d., low, fluted, blue....... 70.00
Bowl, 9" d., marigold............. 50.00
Bowl, 9" d., peach opalescent 300.00
Bowl, 9" d., purple 80.00
Bowl, ice cream shape, peach
    opalescent................... 225.00
Bowl, ice cream shape, purple 225.00
Bowl, ice cream shape, white 163.00
Plate, 9" d., blue............... 244.00
Plate, 9" d., ruffled, marigold 250.00
Plate, 9" d., flat, peach
    opalescent................... 425.00
Plate, 9" d., ruffled, peach
    opalescent................... 350.00
Plate, 9" d., flat, purple 292.00
Plate, 9" d., ruffled, purple 150.00
Plate, 9" d., white 337.00

RUSTIC VASE
Blue, 9" h....................... 40.00
Blue, 12" h...................... 32.00
Blue, 16" h...................... 55.00
Blue, 19" h..................... 165.00
Blue, funeral, 19½" h. 1,300.00
Blue, 21" h..................... 244.00
Blue, 23½" h.................... 270.00
Blue, elephant base 425.00
Green, 11" h.................... 40.00
Green, 14" h.................... 45.00
Green, 16" h.................... 75.00

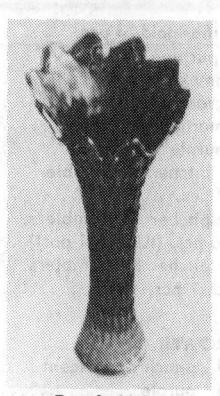

Rustic Vase

Green, 18" h. (ILLUS.) 350.00
Marigold, 11" h. 30.00
Marigold, 16" to 20" h. ....150.00 to 200.00
Purple, 9" h...................... 40.00
Purple, 11" h..................... 28.00
Purple, 15" h..................... 125.00
Purple, 16" h..................... 100.00
Purple, 18½" h.................... 325.00
Purple, elephant base 400.00
White, 6" h. 52.00
White, 18" h. 225.00
White, 20" h. 410.00

SAILBOAT (Fenton)
Bowl, 5" d., amber 250.00
Bowl, 5" d., ruffled, Amberina 400.00
Bowl, 5" d., aqua 109.00
Bowl, 5" d., ruffled, blue 52.00
Bowl, 5" d., clambroth 40.00
Bowl, 5" d., green 57.00
Bowl, 5" d., marigold 25.00
Bowl, 5" d., purple 70.00
Bowl, 5" d., ruffled, red ...500.00 to 550.00
Bowl, 6" d., ruffled, green 105.00
Bowl, 6" d., ruffled, marigold 38.00
Bowl, ruffled, blue 55.00
Bowl, ruffled, green 55.00
Compote, blue 220.00
Compote, marigold 60.00
Goblet, water, green 300.00
Goblet, water, marigold 170.00
Goblet, water, purple 350.00
Plate, 6" d., blue 350.00
Plate, 6" d., marigold 300.00
Wine, blue 100.00
Wine, marigold 30.00
Wine, vaseline 125.00

SCALE BAND
Pitcher, marigold................. 85.00
Plate, 6" d., flat, marigold 22.00
Tumbler, marigold................ 37.00
Water set: pitcher & 6 tumblers;
    marigold, 7 pcs................ 175.00

SCALES
Bowl, 5" d., purple 35.00

Bowl, 7" d., marigold 22.50
Bowl, 7" d., peach opalescent 55.00
Bowl, 7" w., tricornered, peach
    opalescent.................... 155.00
Bowl, 7" d., purple 57.50
Bowl, 8" to 9" d., aqua opalescent .. 308.00
Bowl, 8" to 9" d., milk white
    w/marigold overlay 160.00
Bowl, 8" to 9" d., peach
    opalescent 125.00
Plate, 6½" d., amber.............. 40.00
Plate, 6½" d., marigold 40.00
Plate, 6½" d., peach opalescent 31.00
Plate, 6½" d., purple............. 48.00

SCOTCH THISTLE COMPOTE
Blue 57.00
Green.......................... 50.00
Marigold 48.00
Purple 65.00

SCROLL EMBOSSED
Bowl, 7" d., aqua 85.00
Bowl, 7" d., purple 40.00
Bowl, 8" to 9" d., aqua 60.00
Bowl, 8" to 9" d., green 48.00
Bowl, 8" to 9" d., marigold........ 43.00
Bowl, 8" to 9" d., pastel marigold .. 45.00
Bowl, 8" to 9" d., purple 44.00
Compote, green.................. 45.00
Compote, marigold 30.00
Compote, purple 102.00
Plate, 9" d., green ....75.00 to 100.00
Plate, 9" d., marigold 95.00
Plate, 9" d., purple 200.00
Sauce dish, purple, 5½" d.......... 30.00

SEACOAST PIN TRAY (Millersburg)
Green.......................... 375.00
Marigold 290.00
Purple 330.00

SEAWEED (Millersburg)
Bowl, 8¾" d., low,
    marigold ....350.00 to 450.00
Bowl, 10" d., blue............... 900.00
Bowl, 10" d., ruffled,
    green ....175.00 to 200.00
Bowl, 10" d., ruffled, marigold 220.00
Bowl, 10" d., ruffled,
    purple ....300.00 to 350.00
Plate, 9" d., green 550.00
Plate, 9" d., marigold 500.00

SHELL (Imperial)
Bowl, footed, marigold 18.00
Bowl, footed, purple.............. 35.00
Bowl, ruffled, green 32.50
Plate, smoky.................... 213.00

SHELL & JEWEL
Creamer, cov., marigold 25.00
Creamer & cov. sugar bowl, green,
    pr............................ 60.00

Sugar bowl, cov., green 28.00
Sugar bowl, cov., marigold 20.00

SHELL & SAND
Bowl, 7" d., purple 55.00
Bowl, 8" to 9" d., ruffled, purple ... 57.00
Mug, purple 75.00
Plate, green 80.00
Plate, smoky..................... 325.00
Tumbler, purple 50.00

SINGING BIRDS (Northwood)

Singing Birds Water Set

Berry set: master bowl & 6 sauce
   dishes; green, 7 pcs. ....400.00 to 450.00
Berry set: master bowl & 6 sauce
   dishes; purple, 7 pcs............. 270.00
Bowl, master berry, marigold 75.00
Bowl, master berry, purple......... 90.00
Butter dish, cov., green 230.00
Butter dish, cov., marigold 138.00
Butter dish, cov., purple 172.00
Creamer, green 170.00
Creamer, marigold 52.00
Creamer & sugar bowl, purple, pr... 160.00
Mug, aqua opalescent 957.00
Mug, blue 115.00
Mug, electric blue........150.00 to 200.00
Mug, green....................... 152.00
Mug, ice blue.................... 925.00
Mug, lavender 125.00
Mug, marigold 62.00
Mug, stippled, marigold 150.00
Mug, purple 82.00
Mug, purple, w/advertising, "Hotel
   Verdome" 133.00
Mug, purple, w/advertising, "Ama-
   zon Hotel"..................... 125.00
Mug, white 585.00
Pitcher, green 275.00
Pitcher, marigold................. 225.00
Pitcher, purple 275.00
Sauce dish, green 35.00
Sauce dish, marigold 32.00
Sauce dish, purple 30.00
Spooner, marigold................ 62.00
Spooner, purple.................. 85.00
Sugar bowl, cov., green 185.00
Sugar bowl, cov., marigold........ 75.00

Table set, marigold, 4 pcs......... 375.00
Table set, purple, 4 pcs........... 865.00
Tumbler, amber.................. 60.00
Tumbler, green 45.00
Tumbler, marigold............... 25.00
Tumbler, purple 45.00
Water set: pitcher & 1 tumbler;
   green, 2 pcs. 395.00
Water set: pitcher & 5 tumblers;
   purple, 6 pcs. (ILLUS. of part) 708.00
Water set: pitcher & 6 tumblers;
   marigold, 7 pcs................. 494.00

SINGLE FLOWER
Bowl, 9" d., peach opalescent 50.00
Bowl, 9" d., purple 45.00
Bowl, ribbon candy rim, peach
   opalescent..................... 125.00
Plate, crimped rim, peach
   opalescent..................... 80.00

SIX PETALS (Dugan)
Bowl, 5" d., marigold............. 20.00
Bowl, 7" d., crimped, peach
   opalescent..................... 38.00
Bowl, 7" w., tricornered, peach
   opalescent..................... 80.00
Bowl, 7" w., tricornered, purple 51.00
Bowl, 7" d., white................ 50.00
Bowl, 8" d., peach opalescent 55.00
Bowl, 8" d., purple 66.00
Bowl, 8" d., white................ 80.00

SKI STAR (Dugan)
Banana bowl, peach opalescent 154.00
Banana bowl, purple 92.00
Basket, peach opalescent 520.00
Berry set: master bowl & 4 sauce
   dishes; peach opalescent, 5 pcs... 264.00
Bowl, 5" d., peach opalescent 35.00
Bowl, 5" d., fluted, peach
   opalescent..................... 65.00
Bowl, 5" d., ruffled, peach
   opalescent..................... 55.00
Bowl, 5" d., ruffled, purple......... 50.00
Bowl, 7" d., ruffled, purple 75.00
Bowl, 8" to 9" d., dome-footed,
   peach opalescent............... 80.00
Bowl, 8" to 9" d., dome-footed,
   purple 70.00
Bowl, 10" d., peach
   opalescent...........95.00 to 135.00
Bowl, 10" d., purple 125.00
Bowl, 11" d., peach opalescent 82.00
Bowl, 11" d., purple.............. 185.00
Bowl, tricornered, dome base,
   peach opalescent............... 107.00
Plate, 6" d., crimped rim, peach
   opalescent..................... 125.00
Plate, 8½" d., dome-footed,
   w/handgrip, peach opalescent.... 155.00
Plate, 8½" d., dome-footed,
   w/handgrip, purple............. 240.00

SNOW FANCY
Creamer, marigold 40.00
Sauce dish, marigold 30.00
Sugar bowl, marigold 37.50

SODA GOLD (Imperial)
Basket, marigold, small 22.00
Bowl, 9" d., marigold 48.00
Candlesticks, marigold, 7½" h.,
   pr. 45.00
Candlesticks, smoky, 7½" h., pr. ... 50.00
Console set: bowl & pair candle-
   sticks; marigold, 3 pcs. 45.00
Cuspidor, marigold 50.00
Pitcher, milk, marigold 195.00
Pitcher, water, marigold 128.00
Pitcher, water, smoky 375.00
Tumbler, marigold 27.00
Tumbler, pastel marigold 95.00
Tumbler, smoky 62.00
Water set: pitcher & 6 tumblers;
   marigold, 7 pcs. 250.00
Water set: pitcher & 6 tumblers;
   smoky, 7 pcs. 650.00

SOUTACHE (Dugan)
Bowl, 8" d., dome-footed, ruffled,
   peach opalescent 85.00
Bowl, 8" to 9" d., dome-footed,
   piecrust rim, peach opalescent ... 90.00
Plate, 9½" d., dome-footed, peach
   opalescent 350.00

SPRINGTIME (Northwood)
Berry set: master bowl & 4 sauce
   dishes; green, 5 pcs. 325.00
Bowl, 5" d., green 45.00
Bowl, 5" d., marigold 25.00
Bowl, 5" d., purple 40.00
Bowl, master berry, green 150.00
Bowl, master berry, marigold 75.00
Butter dish, cov., green 400.00
Butter dish, cov., marigold 195.00
Butter dish, cov., purple 300.00
Creamer, marigold 85.00
Creamer, purple 103.00
Pitcher, green .... 950.00 to 1,000.00
Pitcher, marigold .... 300.00 to 400.00
Pitcher, purple 625.00
Spooner, green 150.00
Spooner, marigold 90.00
Spooner, purple 83.00
Sugar bowl, cov., purple 120.00
Table set, green, 4 pcs. 1,600.00
Table set, marigold,
   4 pcs. .... 500.00 to 535.00
Tumbler, green 102.00
Tumbler, marigold 68.00
Tumbler, purple 125.00

"S" REPEAT (Dugan)
Punch cup, purple 110.00
Punch set: bowl, base & 13 cups;
   purple, 15 pcs. 2,900.00
Toothpick holder, blue 100.00

Toothpick holder, marigold 28.00
Tumbler, w/advertising, dated 1910,
   marigold 350.00

STAG & HOLLY (Fenton)

Stag & Holly Rose Bowl

Bowl, 7" d., spatula-footed, blue ... 135.00
Bowl, 7" d., spatula-footed, green .. 125.00
Bowl, 7" d., spatula-footed,
   marigold 55.00
Bowl, 7" d., spatula-footed,
   red 1,050.00
Bowl, 8" d., footed, ice cream
   shape, blue 185.00
Bowl, 8" to 9" d., spatula-footed,
   blue 140.00
Bowl, 8" to 9" d., spatula-footed,
   green 160.00
Bowl, 8" to 9" d., spatula-footed,
   marigold 75.00
Bowl, 8" to 9" d., spatula-footed,
   purple 119.00
Bowl, 10" to 11" d., three-footed,
   amber 536.00
Bowl, 10" to 11" d., three-footed,
   Amberina 838.00
Bowl, 10" to 11" d., three-footed,
   aqua .... 550.00 to 650.00
Bowl, 10" to 11" d., three-footed,
   blue .... 190.00 to 220.00
Bowl, 10" to 11" d., three-footed,
   cobalt blue 125.00
Bowl, 10" to 11" d., three-footed,
   green 425.00
Bowl, 10" to 11" d., three-footed,
   marigold 104.00
Bowl, 10" to 11" d., three-footed,
   purple 435.00
Bowl, 10" to 11" d., three-footed,
   vaseline .... 175.00 to 275.00
Bowl, 11" d., flat, amber 500.00
Bowl, 11" d., flat, marigold 125.00
Bowl, 12" d., ice cream shape,
   marigold 110.00
Bowl, spatula-footed,
   red .... 1,325.00 to 1,375.00
Plate, 9" d., marigold ..... 300.00 to 350.00
Plate, chop, 12" d., three-footed,
   marigold 525.00

Rose bowl, blue, large............ 595.00
Rose bowl, marigold, large
(ILLUS.)........................ 325.00

STAR & FILE (Imperial)
Bowl, 5" d., marigold............. 25.00
Bowl, 7" d., marigold............. 20.00
Bowl, 8" to 9" d., marigold........ 35.00
Card tray, two turned-up sides, mar-
igold, 6¼" d. 22.50
Celery vase, two-handled,
marigold 27.50
Compote, jelly, clambroth.......... 50.00
Compote, jelly, marigold........... 55.00
Compote, large, marigold.......... 32.00
Creamer, marigold................ 30.00
Creamer & sugar bowl, marigold,
pr............................. 48.00
Pitcher, milk, smoky.............. 40.00
Pitcher, water, marigold...100.00 to 120.00
Plate, 6" d., marigold 55.00
Punch cup, marigold.............. 35.00
Relish tray, two-handled, marigold.. 45.00
Rose bowl, marigold.............. 55.00
Sugar bowl, marigold............. 15.00
Tumbler, marigold................ 46.00
Water set: pitcher & 6 tumblers;
marigold, 7 pcs. 255.00
Wine, marigold 34.00
Wine set: decanter w/stopper & 7
wines; marigold, 8 pcs. 350.00

STAR FISH
Compote, peach opalescent 55.00
Compote, purple 45.00

STAR MEDALLION
Bowl, 5" sq., marigold 25.00
Bowl, 7" d., smoky 22.50
Bowl, 8" d., marigold............. 30.00
Bowl, 8" d., smoky 26.00
Celery vase, footed, clambroth 38.00
Compote, marigold 32.00
Goblet, marigold................. 30.00
Pitcher, milk, clambroth 75.00
Pitcher, milk, marigold............ 36.00
Pitcher, milk, smoky.............. 125.00
Plate, 9" to 10" d., clambroth 50.00
Plate, 9" to 10" d., marigold 35.00
Punch cup, marigold.............. 15.00
Rose bowl, marigold.............. 35.00
Sherbet, stemmed, marigold 25.00
Tumbler, marigold................ 30.00
Tumbler, tall, tankard form,
marigold 35.00

STAR OF DAVID (Imperial)
Bowl, 8" to 9" d., collared base,
green 55.00
Bowl, 8" to 9" d., collared base,
marigold 48.00
Bowl, 8" to 9" d., collared base,
purple 65.00
Bowl, 9" d., flat, ruffled, purple 88.00

STAR OF DAVID & BOWS (Northwood)

Star of David & Bows Bowl

Bowl, 7" d., dome-footed, blue 90.00
Bowl, 7" d., dome-footed, green 60.00
Bowl, 7" d., dome-footed, marigold
(ILLUS.)....................... 53.00
Bowl, 7" d., dome-footed, purple ... 50.00
Bowl, 8" to 9" d., dome-footed,
fluted, purple 74.00

STIPPLED FLOWER (Dugan)
Bowl, 8", peach opalescent 24.00
Bowl, 8½" tricornered, peach
opalescent..................... 50.00
Bowl, 8½" d., stippled, fluted,
peach opalescent................ 60.00
Bowl, peach opalescent 40.00

STIPPLED PETALS
Bowl, peach opalescent 80.00
Bowl, purple..................... 67.00
Bowl, white...................... 60.00

STIPPLED RAYS

Stippled Rays Bonbon

Berry set: master bowl & 4 sauce
dishes; green, 5 pcs. 150.00
Bonbon, two-handled, green
(ILLUS.)....................... 39.00
Bonbon, two-handled, ice green 80.00
Bonbon, two-handled, marigold..... 32.00
Bonbon, two-handled, purple 25.00
Bonbon, two-handled, red.......... 260.00

Bowl, 5" d., amber 25.00
Bowl, 5" d., blue 40.00
Bowl, 5" d., green 30.00
Bowl, 5" d., marigold 18.00
Bowl, 5" d., purple ...!.......... 37.50
Bowl, 5" d., red 330.00
Bowl, 6" d., Amberina 100.00
Bowl, 7" d., blue 35.00
Bowl, 7" d., dome-footed, green.... 25.00
Bowl, 7" d., marigold 25.00
Bowl, 7" d., red 240.00
Bowl, 7" d., ruffled rim, red....... 374.00
Bowl, 8" to 9" d., amber 97.50
Bowl, 8" to 9" d., green 57.00
Bowl, 8" to 9" d., marigold 36.00
Bowl, 8" to 9" d., ribbon candy rim,
  marigold 33.00
Bowl, 8" to 9" d., purple 42.00
Bowl, 8" to 9" d., ribbon candy rim,
  purple 42.50
Bowl, 8" to 9" d., red............. 605.00
Bowl, 8" to 9" d., teal blue........ 20.00
Bowl, 10" d., green 60.00
Bowl, 10" d., ruffled, green 110.00
Bowl, 10" d., ruffled, lavender 75.00
Bowl, 10" d., ruffled, marigold 44.00
Bowl, 10" d., purple 55.00
Bowl, 10" d., red slag 450.00
Bowl, 10" d., white............... 242.00
Bowl, dome-footed, Greek Key &
  Scales exterior, purple........... 80.00
Bowl, ruffled, red 330.00
Creamer, blue 25.00
Creamer, green 40.00
Creamer, footed, marigold 12.00
Creamer & sugar bowl, marigold,
  pr............................. 65.00
Plate, 6" to 7" d., blue 40.00
Plate, 6" to 7" d., marigold 28.00
Plate, 6" to 7" d., red 375.00
Sugar bowl, open, blue 27.50
Sugar bowl, open, marigold 22.00
Sugar bowl, open, red 320.00

STIPPLED STRAWBERRY
Bowl, fluted, ice green
  (Northwood)............750.00 to 800.00
Bowl, ruffled, purple 130.00
Plate, 8" d., green 320.00

STORK & RUSHES (Dugan or Diamond Glass Works)
Basket, handled, marigold 90.00
Bowl, master berry or fruit,
  marigold 55.00
Butter dish, cov., marigold 135.00
Creamer, marigold 70.00
Hat shape, marigold............... 25.00
Mug, aqua base w/marigold
  overlay........................ 450.00
Mug, lavender 175.00
Mug, marigold 26.00
Mug, purple 175.00
Pitcher, water, blue 375.00

Pitcher, water, marigold 375.00
Pitcher, water, purple 400.00
Punch bowl & base, marigold,
  2 pcs........................... 200.00
Punch cup, marigold............... 16.00
Punch cup, purple 18.00
Punch set: bowl, base & 7 cups;
  marigold, 9 pcs................. 340.00
Sauce dish, marigold 18.50
Sauce dish, purple 26.00
Spooner, marigold................. 63.00
Table set: cov. butter dish, spooner
  & sugar bowl; marigold, 3 pcs. ... 250.00
Tumbler, aqua 210.00
Tumbler, blue 40.00
Tumbler w/lattice band, blue....... 55.00
Tumbler, marigold................. 24.00
Tumbler, marigold w/pale blue
  base 128.00
Tumbler, purple.................. 32.00
Vase, marigold 22.00
Water set: pitcher & 6 tumblers;
  blue, 7 pcs.....................1,050.00
Water set: pitcher & 6 tumblers;
  marigold, 7 pcs................. 520.00

STRAWBERRY (Fenton)
Bonbon, Amberina 200.00
Bonbon, Reverse Amberina 300.00
Bonbon, two-handled, blue......... 48.00
Bonbon, two-handled, green 59.00
Bonbon, two-handled, ice green
  opalescent..................... 450.00
Bonbon, two-handled, marigold..... 36.00
Bonbon, two-handled, purple....... 29.00
Bonbon, two-handled, red 285.00
Bonbon, two-handled, vaseline
  w/marigold iridescence 150.00
Bonbon, two-handled, vaseline
  opalescent ....600.00 to 650.00

STRAWBERRY (Millersburg)
Bowl, 5" d., green 55.00
Bowl, 5" d., marigold.............. 20.00
Bowl, 5" d., purple 50.00
Bowl, 7" d., green 110.00
Bowl, 8" to 9" d., purple...225.00 to 250.00
Bowl, 8" to 9" d., vaseline 450.00
Compote, amber 45.00
Compote, green................... 250.00
Compote, marigold 104.00
Compote, purple 178.00
Compote, vaseline 640.00

STRAWBERRY (Northwood)
Berry set: master bowl & 4 sauce
  dishes; marigold, 5 pcs. 165.00
Bonbon, blue 55.00
Bonbon, vaseline opalescent 700.00
Bowl, 5" d., fluted, blue 35.00
Bowl, 5" d., marigold............. 27.50
Bowl, 5" d., fluted, purple 40.00
Bowl, 7" d., green 56.00

Bowl, 7" d., marigold 48.50
Bowl, 7" d., purple 33.00
Bowl, 8" to 9" d., stippled, blue 90.00
Bowl, 8" to 9" d., stippled, ribbon
    candy rim, green 150.00
Bowl, 8" to 9" d., stippled, ice
    green 775.00
Bowl, 8" to 9" d., stippled,
    purple 168.00
Bowl, 8" to 9" d., ruffled, Basket-
    weave exterior, green 85.00
Bowl, 8" to 9" d., ruffled, Basket-
    weave exterior, purple 90.00
Bowl, 8" to 9" d., marigold 42.00

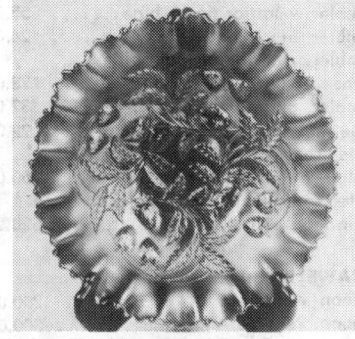

Strawberry Bowl

Bowl, 8" to 9" d., purple (ILLUS.) . . .   63.00
Bowl, 10" d., ice green 700.00
Bowl, 10" d., marigold 71.00
Bowl, 10" d., Basketweave exterior,
    marigold 79.00
Bowl, 10" d., purple 102.00
Bowl, 10" d., Basketweave exterior,
    purple 135.00
Plate, 6" to 7" d., w/handgrip,
    green 140.00
Plate, 6" to 7" d., w/handgrip,
    marigold 83.00
Plate, 6" to 7" d., w/handgrip,
    purple 105.00
Plate, 9" d., green . . . . 140.00 to 160.00
Plate, 9" d., lavender 135.00
Plate, 9" d., marigold 82.00
Plate, 9" d., purple 122.00
Plate, stippled, purple 350.00

STRAWBERRY SCROLL (Fenton)
Pitcher, water, blue 1,990.00
Pitcher, water,
    marigold . . . . 1,250.00 to 1,325.00
Tumbler, blue 200.00
Tumbler, marigold 184.00

SUNFLOWER BOWL (Northwood)
Bowl, 8" d., footed, blue 250.00
Bowl, 8" d., footed, clambroth 350.00
Bowl, 8" d., footed, green 53.00
Bowl, 8" d., footed, marigold 38.00
Bowl, 8" d., footed, purple 60.00

SUNFLOWER PIN TRAY (Millersburg)
Green . . . . 200.00 to 250.00
Purple 210.00

(End of Carnival Glass Section)

CHOCOLATE

Indoor Drinking Scene Mug

This glass is often called Caramel Slag. It was made by the Indiana Tumbler and Goblet Company of Greentown, Ind., and other glasshouses, beginning at the turn of this century. Various patterns were produced, highly popular among them being Cactus and Leaf Bracket.

Animal covered dish, Dolphin,
    smooth rim, Greentown, 9" l.,
    4" h. $350.00
Berry set: master bowl & six sauce
    dishes; Leaf Bracket patt., Green-
    town, 7 pcs. 235.00
Bowl, 8¼" d., Cactus patt.,
    Greentown 125.00
Bowl, Vintage patt., Fenton Glass
    Co. 220.00
Butter dish, cov., Leaf Bracket patt.,
    Greentown 175.00
Cake stand, Cactus patt.,
    Greentown 795.00
Celery tray, Leaf Bracket patt.,
    Greentown, 11" l. 90.00
Compote, jelly, Geneva patt. 110.00
Compote, jelly, 5¼" d., Cactus
    patt., Greentown 145.00
Cracker jar, cov., Cactus patt.,
    Greentown 255.00
Creamer, child size, Sultan patt. 185.00
Creamer, Leaf Bracket patt.,
    Greentown 95.00
Cruet w/original stopper, Cactus
    patt., Greentown 190.00
Cruet w/original stopper, Leaf
    Bracket patt., Greentown 175.00
Mug, Cactus patt., Greentown 83.00

Mug, Indoor Drinking Scene, Green-
town, 5" h. (ILLUS.).............. 163 .00
Mug, Indoor Drinking Scene, Green-
town, 5 5/8" h. 150.00
Mug, Outdoor Drinking Scene,
Greentown 145.00
Mug, Shuttle patt., Greentown 75.00
Nappy, triangular, handled, Leaf
Bracket patt., Greentown 58.00

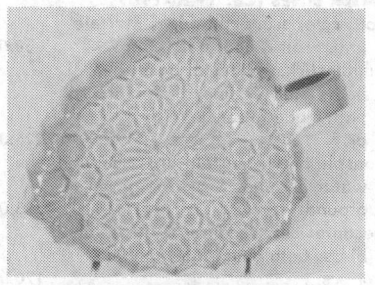

Chocolate Masonic Nappy

Nappy, triangular, Masonic patt.,
McKee (ILLUS.) 135.00
Pitcher, water, Wild Rose with
Bowknot patt., McKee 480.00
Salt shaker w/original top, Cactus
patt., Greentown............... 65.00
Sauce dish, Leaf Bracket patt.,
Greentown 32.00
Sauce dish, Wild Rose with Bowknot
patt., McKee.................. 75.00
Sugar bowl, cov., Leaf Bracket patt.,
Greentown 150.00
Table set: cov. butter dish, cov. sug-
ar bowl, creamer & spooner; Leaf
Bracket patt., Greentown,
4 pcs......................... 425.00
Toothpick holder, Cactus patt.,
Greentown 65.00

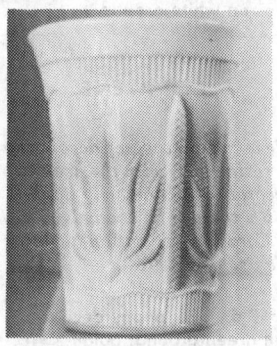

Cactus Tumbler

Tumbler, Cactus patt., Greentown,
4" h. (ILLUS.) 52.00
Tumbler, Fleur-de-lis patt.,
Greentown 100.00
Tumbler, Wild Rose with Bowknot
patt., McKee.................. 110.00

CHRYSANTHEMUM SPRIG, BLUE

Blue Chrysanthemum Sprig Spooner

Some collectors of off-white to near yellow Custard Glass have referred to this blue opaque glass in the Chrysanthemum Sprig pattern as "blue custard." This misnomer is being replaced and this scarce glassware, produced by the Northwood Glass Company at the turn of the century, deserves a classification of its own. Also see CUSTARD GLASS.

Bowl, berry, individual, w/gold
trim ....$125.00 to 145.00
Butter dish, cov. 950.00
Celery vase 1,015.00
Compote, jelly 470.00
Condiment tray 45.00
Cruet w/original stopper........... 625.00
Sauce dish ....95.00 to 115.00
Spooner (ILLUS.).................. 230.00
Sugar bowl, cov. 325.00
Toothpick holder ....295.00 to 310.00
Tumbler................130.00 to 180.00
Water set: pitcher & four tumblers;
signed, 5 pcs. 1,500.00

CONSOLIDATED

The Consolidated Lamp and Glass Company of Coraopolis, Pennsylvania was founded in 1894 and for a number of years was noted for its lighting wares but also produced popular lines of pressed and blown tablewares. Highly collectible glass patterns of this early era include the Cone, Florette and Guttate lines.

Lamps and shades continued to be good sellers but in 1926 a new "art" line of molded decorative wares was introduced. This "Martele" line was developed as a direct imitation of the fine glasswares being produced by Rene Lalique of France and many Consolidated patterns resembled their French counterparts. Other popular lines produced during the 1920's and 1930's were the "Dance of the Nudes" (originally called "Dancing Nymph"), the delightfully Art Deco "Ruba Rombic," introduced in 1928, and the "Catalonian" line, imitating 17th century Spanish glass, which debuted in 1927.

Although the factory closed in 1933, it was reopened under new management in 1936 and prospered through the 1940's. It finally closed in 1967. Collectors should note that many later Consolidated patterns closely resemble wares of other competing firms, especially the Phoenix Glass Company. Careful study is needed to determine the maker of pieces from the 1920-40 era.

Also see COSMOS.

EARLY LINES (Ca. 1894-1920):
Cone
Butter dish, cov., pink satin $85.00
Pitcher, water, cased pink satin 195.00
Sugar shaker w/original top, blue . . 125.00

Consolidated's Criss-Cross (Opalescent)
Bowl, master berry, 8" d.,
   cranberry 155.00
Sauce dish, cranberry 58.00
Spooner, cranberry 132.00

Florette
Condiment set: salt & pepper shakers & mustard jar w/original tops
   in handled stand; cased blue, the
   set . . . . .125.00 to 135.00
Cracker jar w/original silver plate
   rim, lid & bail handle, pink
   satin . . . . .245.00 to 285.00
Lamp, kerosene-type, cased pink
   font, clear base 415.00
Spooner, pink, metal rim &
   handles 70.00
Toothpick, pink 65.00

Guttate

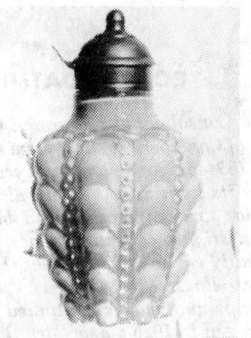

Guttate Syrup Pitcher
Cruet w/original stopper, cased
   pink 295.00
Pitcher, water, 9½" h., 5 7/8" d.,
   applied clear handle, cased
   pink 195.00
Salt shaker w/original lid, pink
   satin 45.00

Sugar bowl, cov., pink satin 110.00
Sugar shaker, cased pink satin 135.00
Syrup pitcher w/original top, cased
   pink (ILLUS.) 180.00
Syrup pitcher w/original top,
   cranberry 425.00
Toothpick holder, cranberry 175.00
Tumbler, pink satin 50.00

LATER LINES (Ca. 1920-1967):
Box, cov., scalloped edge, Martele
   line, Fruit & Leaf patt., 5 x 7" 58.00
Candlesticks, pedestal base, oval
   body, Martele line, Hummingbird
   patt., jade green, 6¾" h.,
   pr. . . . . .195.00 to 225.00
Console bowl, Martele line, sculpted
   water lily pads & fish on green
   ground 195.00
Decanter set: decanter & three tum-
   blers; Catalonian line, amber,
   4 pcs. 120.00
Lamp base, Martele line, Dogwood
   patt., green blossoms on opaque
   ivory ground, partial paper label,
   11" h. 125.00
Plate, 7" d., Ruba Rombic line,
   smoky topaz 35.00
Plate, 10¼" d., Martele line, Bird of
   Paradise patt., deep amethyst
   stain 38.00
Sugar bowl, open, Ruba Rombic
   line, cased honey (golden amber
   blending into yellow) 50.00
Vase, 6" h., sculpted brown cattails
   & green foliage on opaque white
   ground 55.00
Vase, 9½" h., sculpted yellow flow-
   ers w/green leaves & stems on
   opaque white ground 72.50
Vase, 11" h., Dance of the Nudes
   line, pink figures w/flowing blue
   scarves on white ground 395.00

CORALENE

Coralene is a method of decorating glass, usually satin glass, with the use of a beaded-type decoration customarily applied to the glass with the use of enamels, which were melted. Coralene decoration has been faked with the use of glue.

Plate, 7¾" d., pink poppy decoration on green ground, gold
   enamel, beaded rim, patent
   markings $100.00
Tumbler, baby-blue mother-of-pearl
   Diamond Quilted patt. satin glass
   w/orange seaweed pattern cora-
   lene beading 335.00
Vase, 4 3/8" h., 3 3/8" d., ovoid

body w/short, straight neck, shaded pink mother-of-pearl Snowflake patt. satin glass w/yellow beaded coralene stars in the center of each diamond, white lining 450.00
Vase, 4½" h., double handles, green, yellow & purple beading, patent mark 169.00
Vase, 6" h., 4¾" d., ovoid body w/fluted top, ornate applied amber feet, colored coralene leaves & water lilies, gold trim, rich amethyst shaded to clear ground, marked "patent" 325.00
Vase, 6¼" h., 3 1/8" d., yellow wheat pattern coralene on shaded golden yellow mother-of-pearl Snowflake patt. satin glass, gold top rim, white lining 425.00

COSMOS

Cosmos Butter Dish

One of the most popular and widely collected of the glass patterns produced by The Consolidated Lamp and Glass Company of Coraopolis, Pennsylvania, the pieces were produced in milk white glass with molded groupings of Cosmos blossoms. The blossoms and edge bands were then stained with various pastel colors including pink, blue and yellow. For information on other Consolidated patterns see that listing.

Butter dish, cov., pink band decoration (ILLUS.) $210.00
Condiment set, salt & pepper shakers & mustard jar on original glass stand . . . . 300.00 to 450.00
Creamer, pink band decoration 170.00
Cruet w/original stopper 375.00
Pitcher, water, 8½" h., 7" d., pink band decoration 250.00
Spooner, pink band decoration 152.00
Sugar bowl, cov., pink band decoration 170.00

Table set: cov. butter dish, cov. sugar bowl, creamer & spooner; pink band decoration, 4 pcs. 710.00
Tumbler, blue band decoration 52.00
Tumbler, pink band decoration 58.00

CRACKLE

This type of glassware has been made for centuries by submersing hot glass in cold water, reheating it and then blowing it to produce a crackled or fine spider web effect throughout the body of the piece. Another glass sometimes called "Craquelle" is produced by a different technique and is listed in this guide under "Overshot" glass.

Cruet w/original stopper, apple green w/enameled floral decoration, applied handle $250.00
Cruet w/original stopper, pale blue w/enameled decoration, applied handle, 5½" h. . . . . 185.00 to 200.00
Cruet w/original stopper, Parian Swirl patt., clear 110.00
Perfume bottle w/original gold-covered clear ball stopper, cylindrical, cranberry, 2 1/8" d., 4½" h. 95.00
Toothpick holder, cranberry w/applied clear rosettes, enameled decoration 125.00
Vase, 5" h., cranberry, finely enameled w/heron in rushes design 75.00
Vase, 5½" h., bulbous body, electric blue enameled w/seaweed design 65.00
Vase, 10" h., flared rim, flashed cranberry crackle body on clear braided stem & clear base 50.00

CRANBERRY

Cranberry Inverted Thumbprint Pitcher

Gold was added to glass batches to give this glass its color on reheating. It has been made by numerous glasshouses for years and is currently being reproduced. Both blown and molded articles were produced. A less expensive type of cranberry was made with the substitution of copper for gold.

Bell, double gourd handle ending in triple knob, 12½" h. (no clapper) $200.00

Bowl, 5½" d., 3½" h., lobed sides, applied opalescent threading, applid clear rigaree under threaded area, applied clear shell feet. 135.00

Bowl, berry, Hobb's Hobnail patt. . . . 195.00

Box w/hinged lid, lid w/enameled pink rose & blue, yellow & small white flowers, sides w/enameled white & yellow dot flowers, gold trim. 3¾" d., 3 1/8" h. 195.00

Center bowl, permanently mounted in lacy silver plate basket, swans by basket handles, 10½" d., 15¼" h. 195.00

Cheese dish, cov., cover decorated w/white & gold flowers, 9" d. base, overall 8¾" h. 425.00

Cologne bottle w/original clear ball stopper w/decoration, cylindrical body w/gold band at top, overall tiny gold dot flowers & blue dot trim, 2 1/8" d., 5½" h. 130.00

Condiment set: cov. pepper pot, cov. mustard pot w/spoon, oval salt dip & silver plate holder; cut panels, overall 4½" d., 5¼" h., 5 pcs. 185.00

Cracker jar, cov., cylindrical body, h.p. white enamel lacy decoration in a diamond design. 345.00

Cruet w/clear facet-cut stopper, applied clear handle, Inverted Thumbprint patt., 6½" h. 190.00

Cruet w/original stopper, Leaf Sprig patt. 155.00

Dresser set: two cov. jars, perfume bottle, pin holder & tray; gold flowers & leaves decoration, Moser-style, 5 pcs. 725.00

Finger bowl, Inverted Thumbprint patt., enameled flowers 65.00

Finger lamp, applied clear handle, Optic patt., w/burner & chimney, 4¼" d., 5½" h. to top of burner . . 135.00

Jar, cov., round, Inverted Thumbprint patt., knobbed cover, 5" h. 85.00

Liqueur set: 14¼" h. footed decanter w/melon-ribbed bubble stopper & mounted pewter frame & handle at shoulder decorated w/women's head & flowers, five

4¼" h. wines & an 8 x 11½" rectangular tray; 7 pcs. 650.00

Mush set: 3¾" h. cylindrical creamer w/applied handle & 4½" d. deep bowl; each w/sanded gold band design & green flower & white beading, 2 pcs. 170.00

Nappy, heart-shaped, applied clear handle, applied clear shell feet, 5¼" d., 2¾" h. 85.00

Perfume bottle w/original clear facet-cut bubble stopper, squatty bulbous base & tall neck, cut beveled bottle w/scalloped cut base & star cut bottom, 2¾" d., 5½" h. 110.00

Pickle castor, insert w/Inverted Diamond patt., enameled daisy decoration, silver plate frame w/two matching tongs, insert 5" h., overall 11¼" h. 380.00

Pitcher, 4 7/8" h., 3" d., baluster-shaped base w/tall neck w/fluted rim, applied clear handle 65.00

Pitcher, 8" h., 5 1/8" d., bulbous ovoid body w/round mouth, applied clear reeded handle, Inverted Thumbprint patt. (ILLUS.). 135.00

Pitcher, water, 9" h., 6" d., bulbous body w/cylindrical neck w/three-petal rim, applied clear reeded handle, Inverted Thumbprint patt., overall colored enameled lilies of the valley, daisies & blue forget-me-nots 245.00

Pitcher w/ice bladder, 11¼" h., 5 1/8" d., applied clear braided rope-twist handle continuing to form collar around neck, flower prunts at base of handle 375.00

Punch bowl, cov., overall enameled small flowers & gilded leafy design, gilded silver handled footed frame, metal cover w/cherub finial, overall 17" h. 1,360.00

Rhine wines, bell-shaped bowls in ornate cranberry cut to clear design w/clear cut stems & feet, set of 6 . . . . 450.00

Salt & pepper shakers w/original pewter tops, bulbous base, Optic patt., enamel decoration, 2 1/8" d., 3½" h., pr. 135.00

Salt dip, round, in marked sterling silver openwork holder, 2½" d., 1" h. 85.00

Salt dip, round, applied vaseline shell trim around rim, 2 3/8" d., 1¼" h. 48.00

Sugar shaker w/metal top, Venecia patt. 165.00

Syllabub set: 6½" d., 10¼" h. cov. compote on clear pedestal foot, six 4 1/8" h., 2 5/8" d. glasses on

clear feet, clear ladle & 12½" d.
tray; enameled white florals &
lacy gold bands w/gold floral
decoration, bubble knob finial on
compote cover, the set 850.00
Tray, raised rim around swirl-
molded plate raised on conforming swirled pedestal w/folded
base edge, 10¼" d., 2½" h. 247.50
Tumbler, Inverted Thumbprint
patt. 25.00

Ormolu-Mounted Cranberry Tumbler

Tumbler, plain cylindrical body decorated w/ormolu floral swag
mounts, 3¾" h. (ILLUS.) 110.00
Vase, 3 7/8" h., 2¼" d., bulbous
base w/tall cylindrical neck, decorated w/overall sanded gold
scrolls & small blue flowers
w/white leaves 55.00
Vases, 4 3/8" h., 1¾" d., bulbous
base w/tall slender cylindrical
neck decorated w/lacy gold
enameled flowers, pr. 88.00
Vase, 4½" h., 3½" d., bulbous
w/applied clear ruffled rim, Diamond Quilted patt. 89.00
Vase, 5" h., 2" d., baluster-shaped
body w/pedestal base & slender
trumpet neck, two applied clear
handles at shoulder, engraved
parrot & flowers w/gold trim 85.00
Vase, 5¾" h., 2¾" d., footed cylindrical body tapering to narrow
neck w/deep "crown" scalloped
rim, overall dot decoration &
raised side panels w/heavy gold
& white enamel decoration 135.00
Vase, 6¾" h., 3" d., squatty bulbous
base w/tall trumpet-shaped neck,
overall enameled white flowers,
yellow buds & branches 75.00
Vases, 7" h., bulbous base w/tall
neck tapering slightly to folded-up
two-point ruffled rim, applied
clear foot & rigaree bands down
sides, pr. 225.00
Vases, 9½" h., flattened ball shape
w/tapering neck, footed, each
w/a beautifully rendered portrait

of a lady on inset white porcelain
plaque, gold floral trim, pr. 825.00
Vase, 10 1/8" h., 4½" d., white
sanded enamel scalloped rim, h.p.
decorations including grapes &
leaves in white sanded enamel
around center, gold trim, ormolu
feet 245.00
Vase, 12" h., claret shape, Inverted
Panel patt., enameled gold &
white flowers & vines
decoration 150.00
Vase, 14" h., footed, baluster form,
oval porcelain portrait of a dark-
haired Victorian lady, gold
tracery 412.50
Water set: 8¾" h., 5½" d. bulbous
pitcher w/round mouth & applied
clear handle & six tumblers; overall enameled white lattice design
& lacy white leaves & flowers
w/pale yellow centers, 7 pcs. 525.00
Wine decanter, cruet-type, w/origi-
nal clear facet-cut stopper, flattened bulbous shape w/round
mouth, applied clear twisted rope
handle, star cut under base, 5" d.,
8 7/8" h. 145.00
Wine decanter w/clear facet-cut
stopper, bulbous body w/tall slender neck & applied clear handle &
clear wafer foot, engraved flowers & leaves, 3 7/8" d., 9½" h.... 158.00
Wine decanter w/fancy bubble stopper, pewter-mounted neck, ovoid
body w/tall slender neck encased
in embossed pewter frame
w/scroll handle joining neck band
to wide center band w/swags,
domed pewter foot, 4½" d.,
15½" h........................ 395.00

CROWN MILANO

Crown Milano Vase

*This glass, produced by Mt. Washington
Glass Company late last century, is opal glass
decorated by painting and enameling. It ap-*

pears identical to a ware termed Albertine, also made by Mt. Washington.

Bowl, 7 x 9½", enameled flowers outlined in gold decoration, signed $950.00

Condiment set: salt & pepper shakers & mustard pot; ribbed barrel form, h.p. & enameled blueberries & leafy autumn branches on satin white shaded to yellow, original covers & silver plate holder marked "Pairpoint Mf'g. Co 705," 3" h. shakers, the set 385.00

Cracker jar, cov., jeweled flowers & gold leaves on a mottled pink ground, silver plate rim, cover & bail handle, 8" d., 6" h. ....: 975.00

Cracker jar, cov., cylindrical sixteen-panel body, two molded pinkish cream scrolls form top & bottom frames of harbor scene w/six sailboats in blue water w/seagulls flying above in a pale green sky & shoreline in background, base marked "3922/503," cover w/incised "P" in a diamond (Pairpoint logo) & "3932," 5½" d., 9" h. to top of upraised bail 735.00

Cracker jar, cov., enameled leaves & large stylized turquoise blue, coral, yellow, black, white & blue flowers formed from countless tiny dots w/gold dots connecting blossoms & w/raised gold outlines of blossoms & leaves, pastel blue ground, silver plate cover, rim & handle, cover incised "M.W. 4404/a" 485.00

Cup, demitasse, curlicue handle w/tiny gold scrolls, body decorated w/two floral sprays w/each pastel blossom outlined in raised gold, base & rim highlighted w/gold bands, marked, 3" top d., 2" h. 285.00

Perfume w/atomizer, heavy dark florals w/gold veins & dotting, gold leaves & branches, rose shadow scrolling, signed 595.00

Salt & pepper shakers, cylindrical ribbed body, h.p. pink, blue & green pansy blossoms & buds on white satin ground, original covers, 4" h., pr. 110.00

Syrup pitcher, cov., melon-ribbed, alternating panels of white & beige enameled w/pink, yellow & blue floral sprays & raised gold webbing, ornate silver plate domed cover w/attached spout & handle, overall 5½" h...........1,320.00

Tray, ruffled turned up yellow edge w/raised gold scrolls, two flying

"Guba Ducks" decoration, red wreath & crown signature, 9½" .. 325.00

Vase, 6" h., ruffled quatrefoil rim on swirled round body, shaded amber to white satin finish decorated w/h.p. & gilt-defined blossom, stems & leaves, embellished w/aqua, blue & off-white enameling, signed "CM" below crown & above "518" (ILLUS.) 715.00

Vase, 8" h., long slender neck on triangular base, three applied leaf handles, life-like enameled pansies in various colors highlighted w/heavy gold 1,870.00

Vase, 11½" h., neck w/crown-like rolled opening w/gold highlights, two applied thorn handles, enameled gold-shaded large chrysanthemum blossoms, buds & foliage in high-relief on a ground of shadowy chrysanthemum foliage, gold trim, signed 1,250.00

CUP PLATES

Harrison "Cider & Log Cabin" Cup Plate

Produced in numerous patterns beginning some 150 years ago, these little plates were designed to hold a cup while the tea or coffee was allowed to cool in a saucer. Cup plates were also made of ceramics. Where numbers are listed below, they refer to numbers assigned these plates in the book, American Glass Cup Plates, *by Ruth Webb Lee and James H. Rose. Plates are of clear glass unless otherwise noted. A number of cup plates have been reproduced. Also see STAFFORDSHIRE CUP PLATES under Ceramics.*

L & R No. 40-A $45.00
L & R No. 179-A 25.00
L & R No. 197-B 30.00
L & R No. 369 .... 11.00
L & R No. 440-B, blue, scarce, 3½" d...................... 170.00

L & R No. 445, very rare 77.00
L & R No. 477, clear 20.00
L & R No. 477, opalescent 40.00
L & R No. 550, opalescent, set of
  6 .... 104.50
L & R No. 552-A, opalescent, set of
  6 .... 82.50
L & R No. 565-B, blue (scallops
  chipped)...................... 65.00
L & R No. 565-B, electric blue...... 55.00
L & R No. 576 .... 30.00
L & R No. 595, scarce (ILLUS.) 35.00
L & R No. 666-A (minor chips) 23.00
L & R No. 676-C (minor chips) 30.00
L & R No. 677-B (minor flakes)...... 35.00
L & R No. 695, clear (two scallops
  tipped) 95.00
L & R No. 808, blue tint 28.00

CUSTARD GLASS

This ware takes its name from its color and is a variant of milk-white glass. It was produced largely between 1890 and 1915 by the Northwood Glass Co., Heisey Glass Company, Fenton Art Glass Co., Jefferson Glass Co., and a few others. There are 21 major patterns and a number of minor ones. The prime patterns are considered Argonaut Shell, Chrysanthemum Sprig, Inverted Fan and Feather, Louis XV and Winged Scroll. Most custard glass patterns are enhanced with gold and some have additional enameled decoration or stained highlights. Unless otherwise noted, items in this listing are fully decorated.

ARGONAUT SHELL (Northwood)

Argonaut Shell Butter Dish

Berry set, master bowl & 6 sauce
  dishes, 7 pcs. $500.00
Bowl, master berry or fruit, 10½" l.,
  5" h...................125.00 to 150.00
Butter dish, cov. (ILLUS.) 238.00
Compote, jelly, 5" d., 5" h. 110.00
Creamer ....95.00 to 105.00
Cruet w/original stopper........... 445.00
Pitcher, water 302.00
Salt & pepper shakers w/original
  tops, pr....................... 350.00
Sauce dish....................... 48.00
Spooner 110.00
Sugar bowl, cov. 155.00
Table set, cov. butter dish, cov.

sugar bowl, creamer & spooner,
  4 pcs......................... 637.00
Toothpick holder 278.00
Tumbler 71.00
Water set, pitcher & 4 tumblers,
  5 pcs......................... 575.00

BEADED CIRCLE (Northwood)

Beaded Circle Pitcher

Berry set, master bowl & 5 sauce
  dishes, 6 pcs................... 495.00
Bowl, master berry or fruit......... 185.00
Butter dish, cov. 272.00
Creamer ....150.00 to 170.00
Pitcher, water (ILLUS.) 428.00
Salt & pepper shakers w/original
  tops, pr....................... 255.00
Sauce dish....................... 55.00
Spooner 100.00
Sugar bowl, cov. 165.00
Water set, pitcher & 4 tumblers,
  5 pcs......................... 850.00

BEADED SWAG (Heisey)

Goblet 50.00
Goblet, souvenir 80.00
Sauce dish, souvenir.............. 35.00
Wine, w/advertising 75.00
Wine, souvenir................... 60.00

CARNELIAN - See Everglades Pattern

CHERRY & SCALE or FENTONIA (Fenton)

Cherry & Scale Sugar Bowl

Berry set, master bowl & 4 sauce
dishes, 5 pcs. 280.00
Berry set, master bowl & 6 sauce
dishes, 7 pcs. 325.00
Bowl, master berry or fruit......... 115.00
Butter dish, cov. 225.00
Creamer 110.00
Pitcher, water 325.00
Sugar bowl, cov. (ILLUS.)........... 125.00
Tumbler 44.00
Water set, pitcher & 6 tumblers,
7 pcs. 600.00

CHRYSANTHEMUM SPRIG (Northwood)

Chrysanthemum Sprig Tumbler

Berry set, master bowl & 6 sauce
dishes, 7 pcs. 565.00
Bowl, master berry or fruit, 10½"
oval 150.00
Bowl, master berry or fruit, 10½"
oval (undecorated) 135.00
Butter dish, cov. ....200.00 to 225.00
Celery vase...................... 565.00
Compote, jelly 135.00
Compote, jelly (undecorated) 35.00
Condiment set, tray, cruet w/origi-
nal stopper & salt & pepper shak-
ers w/original tops, 4 pcs........1,100.00
Condiment tray 650.00
Creamer ....90.00 to 100.00
Cruet w/original stopper 295.00
Pin tray 20.00
Pitcher, water 368.00
Salt & pepper shakers w/original
tops, pr........................ 200.00
Sauce dish....................... 75.00
Spooner ....85.00 to 90.00
Sugar bowl, cov. 200.00
Sugar bowl, cov. (undecorated) 145.00
Table set, 4 pcs. 585.00
Toothpick holder w/gold trim &
paint, signed 310.00
Toothpick holder (undecorated) 250.00
Tumbler (ILLUS.).................. 60.00
Water set, pitcher & 6 tumblers,
7 pcs. 696.00

DIAMOND WITH PEG (Jefferson)

Berry set, master bowl & 6 sauce
dishes, 7 pcs. 600.00

Bowl, master berry or fruit......... 225.00
Creamer 75.00
Creamer, souvenir 40.00
Mug, souvenir 45.00
Napkin ring, souvenir 145.00
Pitcher, 5½" h. 140.00

Diamond with Peg Tankard Pitcher

Pitcher, tankard, 7½" h. (ILLUS.) ... 250.00
Pitcher, water, tankard 375.00
Punch cup 60.00
Salt & pepper shakers w/original
tops, souvenir, pr. 90.00
Sauce dish....................... 35.00
Sauce dish, souvenir.............. 32.00
Spooner 95.00
Sugar bowl, cov. 165.00
Sugar bowl, cov., souvenir 105.00
Sugar bowl, open 95.00
Toothpick holder 60.00
Tumbler 45.00
Tumbler, souvenir 42.00
Vase, 6" h., souvenir 50.00
Water set, pitcher & 6 tumblers,
7 pcs. 480.00
Whiskey shot glass, souvenir 45.00
Wine 50.00
Wine, souvenir................... 45.00

EVERGLADES or CARNELIAN (Northwood)

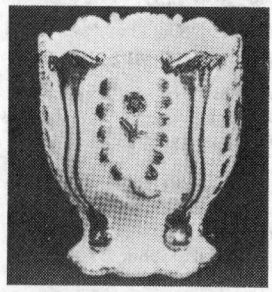

Everglades Spooner

Berry set, master bowl & 6 sauce
dishes, 7 pcs. 725.00
Bowl, master berry or fruit, footed
compote........................ 195.00
Butter dish, cov. 370.00

Compote, jelly 350.00
Pitcher, water 650.00
Salt shaker w/original top 150.00
Salt & pepper shakers w/original
   tops, pr...................... 450.00
Sauce dish....................... 65.00
Spooner (ILLUS.)................... 135.00
Table set, 4 pcs. 850.00
Tumbler 105.00

FAN (Dugan)
Berry set, master bowl & 6 sauce
   dishes, 7 pcs.................... 450.00
Bowl, master berry or fruit......... 180.00
Butter dish, cov. 215.00
Creamer 90.00
Ice cream dish 42.00
Ice cream set, master bowl & 6
   individual ice cream dishes,
   7 pcs......................... 500.00
Pitcher, water 265.00
Sauce dish....................... 55.00
Spooner 72.00
Sugar bowl, cov. 95.00
Table set, cov. butter dish, cov.
   sugar bowl & spooner,
   3 pcs..................350.00 to 450.00
Table set, 4 pcs. ....550.00 to 700.00
Tumbler 50.00
Water set, pitcher & 6 tumblers,
   7 pcs.................550.00 to 650.00

FENTONIA - See Cherry & Scale Pattern

FLUTED SCROLLS
Bowl, master berry or fruit,
   footed 145.00
Creamer 50.00
Pitcher, water, footed 250.00
Salt & pepper shakers w/original
   tops, pr...................... 95.00
Sauce dish....................... 42.50
Spooner 50.00
Sugar bowl, cov. 135.00
Tumbler 38.50
Water set, pitcher & 6 tumblers,
   7 pcs......................... 475.00

**FLUTED SCROLLS WITH FLOWER BAND - See
Jackson Pattern**

GENEVA (Northwood)

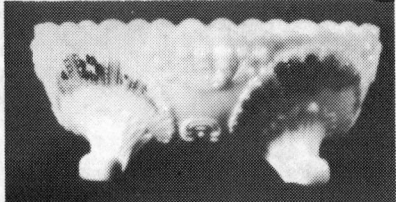

Geneva Sauce Dish

Banana boat, four-footed, 11" oval.. 125.00

Berry set, oval master bowl & 6
   sauce dishes, 7 pcs.............. 335.00
Bowl, master berry or fruit, 8½"
   oval, four-footed 102.00
Bowl, master berry or fruit, 8½" d.,
   three-footed 102.00
Butter dish, cov. 122.50
Compote, jelly 92.50
Creamer 72.00
Cruet w/original stopper........... 250.00
Pitcher, water 200.00
Salt & pepper shakers w/original
   tops, pr...................... 152.50
Sauce dish, oval (ILLUS.) 32.50
Sauce dish, round 35.00
Spooner 104.00
Sugar bowl, cov. 154.00
Syrup pitcher w/original top 250.00
Table set, 4 pcs. 395.00
Toothpick holder 145.00
Toothpick holder (undecorated) 60.00
Tumbler 50.00

GEORGIA GEM or LITTLE GEM (Tarentum)

Georgia Gem Tumbler

Berry set, master bowl & 6 sauce
   dishes, 7 pcs................... 275.00
Bowl, master berry or fruit......... 72.00
Bowl, master berry or fruit (undeco-
   rated) 70.00
Butter dish, cov. 175.00
Butter dish, cov. (undecorated) 98.00
Celery vase...................... 160.00
Creamer 35.00
Creamer (undecorated) 43.00
Creamer, breakfast size 35.00
Creamer & cov. sugar bowl, sou-
   venir, pr...................... 125.00
Cruet w/original stopper........... 250.00
Hair receiver, souvenir 45.00
Pitcher, water 310.00
Pitcher, water (undecorated) 200.00
Powder jar, cov. 45.00
Powder jar, cov., souvenir 54.00
Salt & pepper shakers w/original
   tops, pr...................... 75.00
Sauce dish....................... 29.00
Spooner ....55.00 to 65.00
Spooner, souvenir 60.00
Sugar bowl, cov. 110.00
Sugar bowl, cov. (undecorated) 45.00

Sugar bowl, open, breakfast size,
souvenir 42.50
Table set, 4 pcs. 375.00
Toothpick holder 69.00
Toothpick holder, souvenir 32.00
Tumbler (ILLUS.) 48.00
Water set, pitcher & 4 tumblers,
5 pcs. 435.00

GRAPE & CABLE - See Northwood Grape Pattern

GRAPE & GOTHIC ARCHES (Northwood)
Berry set, master bowl & 6 sauce
dishes, 7 pcs. 475.00
Bowl, master berry or fruit 175.00
Butter dish, cov. 200.00
Creamer 90.00
Goblet 48.00
Pitcher, water 285.00
Sauce dish 37.50
Spooner ....70.00 to 85.00
Sugar bowl, cov. 110.00
Tumbler 59.00
Vase, 10" h. ("favor" vase made
from goblet mold) 60.00
Vase, ruffled hat shape .....60.00 to 85.00
Water set, pitcher & 6 tumblers,
7 pcs. .... 550.00 to 650.00

GRAPE & THUMBPRINT - See Northwood Grape Pattern

INTAGLIO (Northwood)

Intaglio Pitcher

Bowl, fruit, 7½" d. footed
compote 200.00
Bowl, fruit, 9" d. footed
compote .... 300.00 to 375.00
Butter dish, cov. 225.00
Compote, jelly 95.00
Creamer 102.00
Cruet w/original stopper 325.00
Pitcher, water (ILLUS.) 325.00
Salt & pepper shakers w/original
tops, pr. ....150.00 to 175.00
Sauce dish 52.00
Spooner 90.00
Sugar bowl, cov. 115.00
Table set, 4 pcs. 550.00
Tumbler 56.00
Water set: pitcher & 6 tumblers;
green & gold trim, 7 pcs. 575.00

INVERTED FAN & FEATHER (Northwood)

Inverted Fan & Feather Cruet

Berry set, master bowl & 6 sauce
dishes, 7 pcs. 565.00
Bowl, master berry or fruit, 10" d.,
5½" h., four-footed 225.00
Butter dish, cov. ....275.00 to 365.00
Compote, jelly ....300.00 to 350.00
Creamer 135.00
Cruet w/original stopper (ILLUS.) ... 630.00
Pitcher, water 435.00
Punch cup 210.00
Salt & pepper shakers w/original
tops, pr. 468.00
Sauce dish ....45.00 to 65.00
Spooner 115.00
Sugar bowl, cov. 175.00
Table set, 4 pcs. 800.00
Toothpick holder 510.00
Tumbler 75.00
Water set, pitcher & 6 tumblers,
7 pcs. 895.00

IVORINA VERDE - See Winged Scroll Pattern

JACKSON or FLUTED SCROLLS WITH FLOWER BAND (Northwood)
Creamer 56.00
Salt shaker w/original top,
undecorated 40.00
Salt & pepper shakers w/original
tops, pr. 135.00
Tumbler 27.00
Water set, pitcher & 4 tumblers,
5 pcs. ....365.00 to 385.00

LITTLE GEM - See Georgia Gem Pattern

LOUIS XV (Northwood)

Louis XV Master Berry Bowl

Berry set, master bowl & 4 sauce
    dishes, 5 pcs. 410.00
Bowl, master berry or fruit, 7¾ x
    10" oval (ILLUS.) 145.00
Butter dish, cov. 148.00
Creamer 70.00
Cruet w/original stopper 255.00
Pitcher, water 160.00
Salt shaker w/original top 60.00
Salt & pepper shakers w/original
    tops, pr. 215.00
Sauce dish, footed, 5" oval 33.00
Spooner 65.00
Sugar bowl, cov. 88.00
Table set, 4 pcs. 395.00
Tumbler 46.00
Water set, pitcher & 4 tumblers,
    5 pcs. .... 325.00 to 350.00

MAPLE LEAF (Northwood)

Maple Leaf Jelly Compote

Banana bowl 195.00
Berry set, master bowl & 6 sauce
    dishes, 7 pcs. 800.00
Bowl, master berry or fruit 265.00
Butter dish, cov. 228.00
Compote, jelly (ILLUS.) 400.00
Creamer 92.00
Cruet w/original stopper 1,100.00
Pitcher, water 350.00
Salt & pepper shakers w/original
    tops, pr. 500.00
Sauce dish 85.00
Spooner 76.00
Sugar bowl, cov. 185.00
Table set, 4 pcs. 568.00
Toothpick holder 475.00
Tumbler 87.00

NORTHWOOD GRAPE, GRAPE & CABLE or GRAPE & THUMBPRINT (Northwood)

Northwood Grape Ferner

Banana boat 375.00
Bowl, 7½" d., ruffled rim 50.00
Bowl, master berry or fruit, 11" d.,
    flat rim, footed 298.00
Butter dish, cov. 225.00
Cologne bottle w/original
    stopper .... 400.00 to 500.00
Cracker jar, cov., two-handled 615.00
Creamer 100.00
Creamer & open sugar bowl, break-
    fast size, pr. 115.00
Dresser tray .... 195.00 to 275.00
Ferner, footed, 7½" d., 4½" h.
    (ILLUS.) 150.00
Nappy, two-handled 47.50
Pin dish 134.00
Pitcher, water 385.00
Plate, 7" d. 49.00
Plate, 8" w., six-sided 70.00
Plate, 8" d. 42.00
Punch bowl & base, 2 pcs. 800.00
Punch cup 75.00
Sauce dish, flat 38.00
Sauce dish, footed 45.00
Spooner 95.00
Sugar bowl, cov. .... 100.00 to 125.00
Sugar bowl, open, breakfast size ... 55.00
Table set, cov. butter dish, cov.
    sugar bowl & creamer, 3 pcs. 475.00
Tumbler 70.00
Vase, 3½" h. 46.00
Water set, pitcher & 5 tumblers,
    6 pcs. .... 650.00 to 750.00

PRAYER RUG (Imperial)

Nappy, two-handled, ruffled, 6" d. . 55.00
Plate, 7½" d. 12.50
Tumbler 80.00
Vase 50.00

PUNTY BAND (Heisey)

Creamer, individual size, souvenir .. 45.00
Cuspidor, lady's 75.00
Mug, souvenir 55.00
Salt & pepper shakers w/original
    tops, souvenir, pr. 80.00
Toothpick holder, souvenir 65.00
Tumbler, floral decoration,
    souvenir 38.00
Vase, 5½" h., souvenir 75.00
Wine, souvenir 50.00

RIBBED DRAPE (Jefferson)

Butter dish, cov. 265.00
Compote, jelly 180.00
Creamer (ILLUS. top next
    page) 110.00
Cruet w/original stopper 250.00
Pitcher, water 255.00
Salt & pepper shakers w/original
    tops, pr. 175.00
Sauce dish 40.00
Spooner 75.00
Sugar bowl, cov. 145.00
Table set, 4 pcs. (open sugar) 575.00

Ribbed Drápe Creamer

Toothpick holder 95.00
Toothpick holder w/rose
　decoration..................... 195.00
Tumbler 75.00

RING BAND (Heisey)

Ring Band Sauce Dish

Bowl, master berry or fruit......... 115.00
Butter dish, cov. 182.00
Compote, jelly ....155.00 to 200.00
Condiment set, condiment tray, jelly
　compote, toothpick holder & salt
　& pepper shakers, 5 pcs.......... 429.00
Condiment tray ....70.00 to 110.00
Creamer 80.00
Cruet w/original stopper........... 300.00
Mug, souvenir 45.00
Pitcher, water 235.00
Punch cup 60.00
Punch cup, souvenir 26.00
Salt shaker w/original top,
　undecorated 55.00
Salt & pepper shakers w/original
　tops, souvenir, pr. 115.00
Sauce dish (ILLUS.) 40.00
Spooner 89.00
Sugar bowl, cov. 136.00
Syrup pitcher w/original
　top ....200.00 to 300.00
Table set, 4 pcs. 495.00
Toothpick holder, 2½" h. ...85.00 to 110.00
Toothpick holder, souvenir 44.00
Tumbler 55.00
Tumbler, souvenir 35.00
Water set, pitcher & 6 tumblers,
　7 pcs. ....500.00 to 575.00
Whimsey, hat shape (from tumbler
　mold) 295.00

VICTORIA (Tarentum)

Berry set, master bowl & 5 sauce
　dishes, 6 pcs. 575.00
Bowl, master berry or fruit........ 165.00
Butter dish, cov. 285.00
Celery vase...................... 225.00
Creamer 85.00
Pitcher, water 350.00
Sauce dish....................... 50.00
Spooner 85.00
Spooner (undecorated)............ 45.00
Sugar bowl, cov. 165.00
Tumbler 60.00

WINGED SCROLL or IVORINA VERDE (Heisey)

Winged Scroll Table Set

Berry set, master bowl & 4 sauce
　dishes, 5 pcs. (undecorated)...... 200.00
Berry set, master bowl & 6 sauce
　dishes, 7 pcs. 320.00
Bowl, fruit, 8½" d. 170.00
Bowl, master berry, 11" l., boat-
　shaped 100.00
Butter dish, cov. 156.00
Celery vase ....275.00 to 300.00
Cigarette jar..............135.00 to 175.00
Cologne bottle w/original stopper .. 245.00
Compote, 10¾" d., 6¾" h.......... 495.00
Creamer 95.00
Creamer (undecorated) 55.00
Cruet w/original stopper 188.00
Custard cup...................... 45.00
Dresser tray 150.00
Hair receiver 125.00
Match holder ....150.00 to 190.00
Nappy, folded side handle, 6"...... 50.00
Olive dish 42.00
Pin tray, small 195.00
Pitcher, water, 9" h., bulbous 235.00
Pitcher, water, tankard 230.00
Pitcher, water, tankard (undecorat-
　ed) 150.00
Powder jar, cov. 80.00
Powder jar, cov., souvenir 55.00
Salt & pepper shakers w/original
　tops, pr. 165.00
Sauce dish, 4½" d................. 35.00
Spooner 62.00
Sugar bowl, cov. ....155.00 to 175.00
Sugar bowl, cov. (undecorated)..... 95.00
Syrup pitcher w/original top 285.00
Table set, cov. sugar bowl, creamer
　& spooner, 3 pcs. 295.00

Table set, cov. butter dish, creamer
& spooner, 3 pcs. 375.00
Table set, 4 pcs. (ILLUS.)...425.00 to 475.00
Toothpick holder 95.00
Tumbler 65.00
Vase, 9" h. 190.00
Water set, tankard pitcher & 6 tum-
blers, 7 pcs. ....600.00 to 650.00

MISCELLANEOUS PATTERNS
Delaware
Bowl, 5½" (hat-shaped)............ 45.00
Creamer w/rose decoration 62.00
Pin tray w/rose stain, 4½"......... 37.00
Pin tray w/blue decoration......... 58.00
Ring tree, 4" h. 54.00
Sauce dish w/rose stain 65.00
Sauce dish w/blue decoration 45.00
Tumbler, green decoration 50.00

Harvard
Toothpick holder 35.00
Toothpick holder, green
decoration...................... 80.00
Toothpick holder, souvenir 26.00
Vase, 5½" h., w/enameled
decoration...................... 35.00

Heart with Thumbprint
Creamer 40.00
Finger lamp, green decoration 250.00
Sugar bowl, individual, green
decoration...................... 55.00

Peacock and Urn
Berry bowl, master 110.00
Ice cream bowl, master, w/nutmeg
stain, 9¾" d. 235.00
Ice cream dish, individual, w/nut-
meg stain 62.00
Sauce dish...................... 38.00

Vermont
Berry bowl, master.......100.00 to 125.00
Card basket, 7½" d. 95.00
Creamer, green & pink florals 90.00
Pickle tray...................... 30.00
Pitcher, blue trim w/enameled
decoration..................... 250.00
Spooner 78.00
Table set, cov. butter, creamer &
spooner, 3 pcs. 195.00
Toothpick holder, green
decoration..................... 110.00
Toothpick holder, blue trim
w/enameled decoration.......... 88.00
Tumbler, blue decoration 55.00
Vase............................ 25.00
Vase w/enameled decoration 70.00

Wild Bouquet
Butter dish, cov. 325.00
Creamer 135.00
Cruet w/original stopper, enameling
& gold trim 570.00

Cruet w/original stopper (undec-
orated)........................ 300.00
Sauce dish...................... 50.00
Spooner w/gold trim & colored
decoration..................... 138.00
Spooner (undecorated)............ 65.00
Toothpick holder 475.00
Tumbler (undecorated)............ 37.50

(End of Custard Glass Section)

CUT GLASS

*Cut glass most eagerly sought by collectors
is American glass produced during the so-
called "Brilliant Period" from 1880 to about
1915. Pieces listed below are by type of article in alphabetical order.*

BASKETS

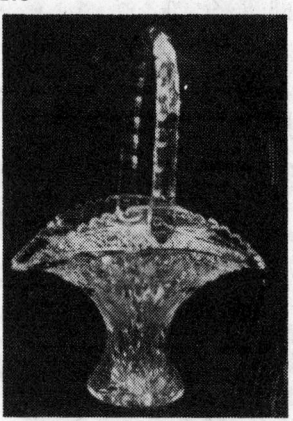

Brilliant Period Basket

Cane border, flowers w/hobnail
centers & leaves, 24-point rayed
base, serrated rim, double
notched handle, 5 x 9½", overall
14" h. (ILLUS.) $385.00
Checkering, small hobnails & three
large hobnails, flat w/slightly
raised sides, strawberry diamond
handle, 6 x 6", overall 5½" h..... 275.00
Cross-cut vesicas of hobstar, hobnail
& fan, scalloped & serrated rim,
applied double-twisted handle,
8" d., overall 5" h. 325.00
Flattened diamond band at curling
elliptical rim, waisted cylindrical
body cut w/flowers & leaf stalks,
notched handle, 12" l. 308.00
Meriden's Diadem patt., flared
edge, 12 x 17½" 750.00

BOWLS
Banana, Hunt's Royal patt., Russian
patt. w/hobstar button, pen-

tagonal strawberry diamond loz-
enge & large hobstars, 12" l. 350.00
Banana, Libbey's Avon patt., sections of Harvard patt. alternating
w/hobstars, hobnail, strawberry
diamond & fan, hobstar base,
scalloped & serrated rim,
7¾ x 11½", 4¼" h. 295.00
Clark signed, Prima Donna (Triple
Square) patt., dentil rim, 8" d. . . . 195.00
Cross-cut diamond, fan & hobstar,
shallow, 8" d. 95.00
Devonshire patt. variant, hobstar,
star, strawberry diamond, fan &
other cutting, serrated rim,
10" d., 5" h. 265.00
Diapered elliptical star & sheaf mo-
tif alternating w/large pinwheel,
petal-cut base, shouldered ovoid
body, 9" d., 7½" h. 220.00
Egginton signed, Brilliant Period cutting, 8" d., 2½" h. 250.00
Elmira Cut Glass Company's Design
No. 100, chain of hobstars, cane,
strawberry diamond & fan, low
sides, 9" d. 275.00
Fruit, Brilliant Period cutting, 15" l.,
7¼" h. 200.00
Harvard patt., 10" d., 3½" h. 125.00
Hawkes signed, Brilliant Period cutting, scalloped rim, 9" d. 335.00
Hawkes' Grecian patt., vesica, fan &
Russian patt., four-sided body,
8¾" d., 2¾" h. 1,445.00
Hawkes' Venetian patt., chain of
hobstars, star, strawberry diamond split vesicas & fan, 8¼" d.,
3½" h. 450.00

Hoare's Wedding Ring Pattern Bowl

Hoare's Wedding Ring patt., 8" d.
(ILLUS.) 2,000.00
Hobstars & strawberry diamond,
hobstar base, 8" d., 3¾" h. 197.00
Hobstars, cane, hobnail & strawber-
ry diamond, 16-point hobstar cen-
ter, 8 7/8" d., 1 7/8" h. 150.00
Hobstars (four large & eight small),

cane, strawberry diamond & fan,
large 24-point hobstar center,
9" d., 2" h. 165.00
Hobstars & swirl cutting, serrated
rim, 9" d. 225.00
Hobstars (four), cane, strawberry
diamond & fan, 5¾ x 9¾" oval,
4" h. 135.00
Hobstars (large & small), strawberry
diamond, fan & deep mitering,
scalloped & serrated rim, 11" d. . . 250.00
Hunt's Royal patt., Russian patt.
w/hobstar button, pentagonal
strawberry diamond lozenge &
large hobstars, 9" d. 250.00
Jubilee patt., tusk motif around
teardrop radiants, large & small
hobstars, strawberry diamond &
fan, 10" d., 4" h. 450.00
Kupfer's Good Luck (Horseshoe)
patt., engraved flowers, cane
horseshoes & other cutting, ca.
1913, 4½ x 9" 295.00
Libbey signed, Glenda (Laurent)
patt., double cross-cut vesicas,
beading, fan, hobnail, star &
strawberry diamond, 9" d. 500.00
Libbey signed, Senora patt., 9" d.,
3¾" h. 475.00
Maple City Glass Company signed,
Fortuna patt., sunburst-type design, scalloped & serrated rim,
9" d. 255.00
Orange, Cane patt. & other cutting,
fan-cut scalloped & serrated rim,
large hobstar base, 9" d.,
3 5/8" h. 160.00
Orange, cut & etched florals & but-
terflies, 11" l. oval, 4½" h. 200.00
Pairpoint's Myrtle patt., 9½" d.,
3½" h. 475.00
Pitkin & Brooks signed, Heart patt.,
notched prism flairs & hobstars,
8" d. 290.00
Ribbon Star patt. variant, six-
pointed star formed by ribbon of
cane, further cut w/sunbursts &
chain of hobstars border, scal-
loped & serrated rim, 8" d. 210.00
Sinclaire signed, Fuchsia patt.,
intaglio-cut fuchsia blossoms &
panels of Russian patt., 8" d. 265.00
Starbursts alternating w/pyramids
enclosing stars, circular petal-cut
foot, flaring serrated rim,
9 3/8" d., 3½" h. 275.00
Star motifs surmounted by fans alternating w/lozenges, large star
center, scalloped & serrated rim,
ca. 1900, 9" d. 500.00
Straus, cross-cut vesicas, hobstars,
strawberry diamond & fan, scalloped & serrated rim, low, 9" d. . . 110.00
Sunburst patt. variant, sunbursts,

hobstars, beading, cane & fan,
9" d., 3¾" h. 175.00
Trellis motif alternating w/stars,
raised on faceted shaft on petal-
cut circular foot, tapering cylindrical body, serrated rim, 8" d.,
6 5/8" h. 302.50
Tuthill signed, intaglio-cut clusters
of grapes & vines w/chain of hob-
stars, 7½" d. 495.00
Tuthill signed, intaglio-cut w/three
varieties of fruit & brilliant vesi-
cas, 8¼" d., 3½" h. 700.00
Tuthill's Rex patt. variant, chain of
hobstars & other cutting,
8½" d. 750.00
Tuthill, intaglio-cut geometric de-
sign, 8" d. 325.00

BOXES

Libbey's Florence Pattern Box

Dresser, Brilliant Period cutting on
hinged lid & base, 2½ x 3" 135.00
Dresser, flower & leaves on hinged
lid, prism cutting around sides,
star-cut base, sterling silver fit-
tings, 6" d. 400.00
Dresser, single large pinwheel
covering entire hinged lid, hobstars & cross-hatched sides, 24-
point star base, silver fittings,
6" d. 275.00
Powder, Brilliant Period cutting on
sides, sterling silver lid w/en-
graved design, 4¼" d., 3" h. 265.00
Powder, Pairpoint's Murillo patt.,
intaglio-cut flowers & butterflies
on hinged lid & sides, 32-point
star-cut base, 5" d. 345.00
Powder, diamond & fan cutting on
sides, sterling silver lid, 5" d.,
3" h. 245.00
Powder, strawberry diamond & fan
on hinged lid, thumbprint & cut
oval sides, star-cut base, silver
plate fittings, 5½" d., 3¼" h. 275.00
Powder, Libbey's Florence patt.,
hinged lid, 6" d. (ILLUS.) 385.00

Powder, Pairpoint's Silsbee patt.,
hinged lid w/intaglio-cut stylized
florals & slender tapering leaves
surrounded by sprays of polished
leaves, almond-cut sides, 6" d. 325.00
Powder, Brilliant Period cutting
overall, 6¼" d. 158.00

BUTTER PATS

Clark Signed Butter Pats

Clark signed, Guernsey patt., 3" d.
(ILLUS. left) 95.00
Clark signed, Jersey patt., 3" d.
(ILLUS. right) 95.00
Comet-type motif w/hobstars 18.00
Laurel Cut Glass Company's Cypress
patt. 32.00

CANDLESTICKS & CANDLEHOLDERS

Star-cut base, baluster form stem,
star & thumbprint cutting at mid-
section w/loop & diamond cutting
above & below, flute cutting at
top, 3¾" d. base, 7" h. 48.00
Star-cut base, hobstars, strawberry
diamond, cane & fan stem,
squared nozzle, 8" h., pr. 450.00
Hawkes signed, rayed foot, overall
Brilliant Period cutting, 9" h.,
pr. 350.00
Hawkes signed, pyramidal star-cut
base, tapering stem w/notched
swirls, fan & single stars, flute-cut
nozzle, 9" h., pr. (chip under
base) 800.00
Hawkes signed, bull's eye cutting on
foot & candle cup, engraved
florals & vertical cutting on stem,
4" base d., 11¾" h., pr. 505.00

CARAFES

Brilliant Period cutting, rayed
base 95.00
Clark signed, hobstars & notched
prism, fluted notched neck,
5¾" d., 7¾" h. 140.00
Cross-cut diamond & fan 135.00
Egginton's Lotus patt., strawberry
diamond, flashed fan, fan & other
cutting 210.00
Harvard patt., step-cut neck,
24-point rayed base, 6" d., 8" h. . . . 225.00
Hobnail & fan, 8½" h. 95.00

Hobstars, fields of diamonds, cross-hatching & fan, notched panel-cut neck, rayed base, 6¾" d., 7¼" h. 132.50

Niland Cut Glass Company's Butter-fly & Flowers patt., design by Thomas Mortensen 180.00

Pineapple & Fan patt., cross-cut diamond & fan, bulbous, notch-cut eight-panel neck, rayed base, 6" d., 8¼" h. 115.00

Straus Signed Carafe

Straus signed, Venetian patt., 8" h. (ILLUS.).......................... 150.00

Straus' Warren patt., 10¼" h. 140.00

Strawberry diamond & fan, rayed base, notch-cut eight-panel neck, 6" d., 8" h. 115.00

CELERY TRAYS & VASES

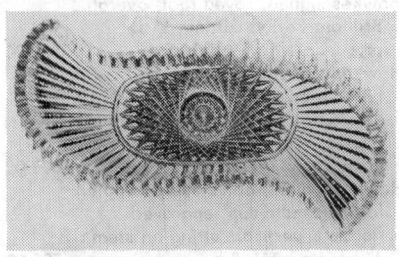

Bergen's Notched Prism Pattern

Tray, Bergen's Notched Prism patt., S-shaped, 12" l. (ILLUS.) 210.00

Tray, Clark signed, Ideal patt. w/pinwheel, 11½" l. 165.00

Tray, Clark's Prima Donna patt., dentil rim, 12" l. 185.00

Tray, Dorflinger's Marlboro patt., chain of hobstars, fan & strawberry diamond, 11" l................ 200.00

Tray, Hawkes signed, comet-type pattern, hobstars & hobstar in diamond field, deeply scalloped & serrated rim, 6 x 11½" 415.00

Tray, Hoare's Newport patt., hobstar motif, 12" l. 145.00

Tray, hobstars, rosettes, cane, fan & cross-cut vesicas of hobstars & strawberry diamond, turned-in scallop & serrated rim, 12" l., 5" w. across center 250.00

Tray, Libbey signed, Imperial patt., cane, fan, hobstar & star, turned over rim, 11½" l. 310.00

Tray, Straus signed, Ducal patt., hobstar motif, 10" l............. 145.00

Vase, hobstars & other Brilliant Period cutting, 7" h............. 275.00

Vase, pinwheels & other Brilliant Period cutting, low foot, 9" h. 350.00

CHAMPAGNES, CORDIALS & WINES

Champagne, Dorflinger's Parisian patt., double knobbed teardrop stem, hobstar base 100.00

Champagne, Libbey's Royal patt., cross-cut diamond, prism, split square & strawberry diamond, double teardrop stem 110.00

Champagne, Russian patt. w/hobstar button (Persian patt.), knobbed stem w/teardrop 125.00

Claret, Hawkes signed, Gladys patt., chain of hobstars, fan & strawberry diamond 40.00

Claret, Libbey's Harvard patt., knobbed stem w/teardrop 60.00

Cordial, Clark signed, San Mateo patt., eight-point star motif 45.00

Cordial, Russian patt. w/clear button (Cleveland patt.), knobbed stem w/teardrop 125.00

Sherry, Hawkes' Venetian patt., chain of hobstars, fan, star & split vesicas of strawberry diamond, knobbed stem w/teardrop 50.00

Sherry, Libbey signed, Jewel patt. .. 40.00

Sherry, Pitkin & Brooks signed, Belmont patt., pinwheel motif 30.00

Wine, Clark signed, King patt., pinwheel motif, flared rim 40.00

Wine, green cut to clear, strawberry diamond & fan 115.00

Wine, Hoare's Monarch patt., cross-cut vesica w/split, hobstars & other cutting...................... 75.00

Wine, ruby cut to clear, Russian patt. 140.00

Wine, Rhine-type, cranberry cut to clear, block pattern 110.00

Wine, Rhine-type, green cut to clear, Hawkes signed, Hobnail patt. 150.00

CHEESE DISHES

Cluster of hobstars, dome lid

w/faceted knob & underplate
w/serrated rim 580.00
Hawkes' Anson patt., dome lid
w/faceted knob & underplate
w/serrated rim 450.00
Hobstar & notched miters, comet
motif, dome lid w/faceted knob &
underplate w/serrated rim 475.00
Hobstar & Russian patt., dome lid &
underplate w/scalloped & serrated rim 595.00

Plymouth Pattern Cheese Dish

Meridan's Plymouth patt., 7" d.,
7" h. dome lid w/faceted knob &
9" d. underplate w/scalloped &
serrated rim (ILLUS.) 400.00
Russian patt., dome lid w/faceted
knob & underplate w/scalloped &
serrated rim 800.00
Strawberry diamond & fan, dome lid
w/faceted knob & underplate
w/serrated rim 375.00

COMPOTES

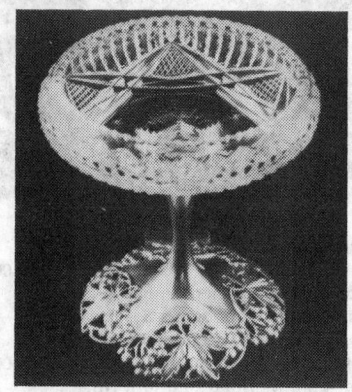

Compote with Sterling Silver Foot

Chain of hobstars border, flowers
w/hobnail centers & foliage center, serrated rim, scalloped
pattern-cut base, flute-cut stem
w/teardrop, 8" d., 9" h. 225.00
Hobstars, strawberry diamond &

fan, petticoat base, two-handled,
5" h. 185.00
Hobstars & other cutting, teardrop
in stem, 12" h. 225.00
Intaglio-cut daisies w/cross-hatching
& cut leaf sprays, notched stem,
6" d., 10" h. 135.00
Parallel miters & cane diamonds,
sterling silver foot, 6" d., 6" h.
(ILLUS.) 230.00
Pitkin & Brooks signed, Corsair
patt., hobstar, fan, hobnail, star &
strawberry diamond, 6" d.,
5" h. 175.00
Strawberry diamond, fan & cross-
hatching, inverted bell-shaped
bowl, stepped circular base,
8¾" h., pr. 412.50
Tuthill's Morning Glory patt.,
intaglio-cut w/flowers & foliage,
5" d., 10" h. 400.00
Unger Bros. signed, hobstars &
cane, 5" d., 11" h. 275.00

CREAMERS & SUGAR BOWLS

Sinclaire Signed Creamer & Sugar Bowl

Flashed Florence star & hobstars,
pedestal base, flute-cut stem,
creamer w/double-notched handle
& flute-cut lip, handleless sugar
bowl, 3½" & 3¼" h., pr. 325.00
Hobstars & other cutting, pedestal
base, pr. 475.00
Libbey signed, pinwheel & other cutting, triple-notched handles,
globular, pr. 175.00
Pitkin & Brooks signed, Heart patt.,
oval, pr. 275.00
Sinclaire signed, Pattern No. 11 &
Engraved, 6" h. creamer & 4½" h.
sugar bowl, pr. (ILLUS.) 450.00
Tuthill signed, Wild Rose patt.,
intaglio-cut florals, pr. 310.00

CRUETS

Brilliant Period cutting overall, including bottom, original faceted
stopper, 6½" h. 125.00
Brilliant Period cutting overall, cone-
shaped, 3½" base d., 7½" h. 70.00
Chain of hobstars, strawberry diamond & fan, hobstar base,

Brilliant Period Cruet

notched handle, tri-pour lip, original faceted stopper, 7" h.
(ILLUS.).......................... 130.00
Fry signed, hobstars, fan, cross-hatching & other cutting, panels of zipper at neck................ 150.00
Pinwheel & other cutting, original stopper 100.00
Sprays of polished leaves & intaglio-cut flowers w/cane centers, rayed base, double bull's eye handle, notched panel neck, tri-pour lip, faceted stopper, 7½" h. 65.00
Strawberry diamond & fan, original stopper 75.00

DECANTERS

Cut Glass Decanter

Alhambra (Greek Key) patt., bulbous........................2,200.00
Cordial, Brilliant Period cutting overall, fan border 1,050.00
Cordial, Egginton signed, Creswick patt., w/matching stopper 2,600.00
Cross-cut vesicas, flashed stars,

strawberry diamond & other cutting, baluster form w/waisted neck, original tall cut stopper, early 20th c., overall 27½" h.
(ILLUS.)........................ 935.00
Harvard patt. w/cut flowers & foliage, bowling pin shape, matching hollow stopper, 5" widest d., 15" h........................... 350.00
Hawkes, Brilliant Period cutting, sterling silver pouring spout marked "Gorham," 14" h. 3,400.00
Hobnail cutting overall, ring neck, matching stopper, applied handle, 4½" d., 10½" h. 550.00
Hobstars, diamond & fan, notched panel neck, star-cut base, cut stopper, 10½" h................. 260.00
Intaglio-cut flowers, berries & foliage, applied handle, 10" h. 550.00
Pinwheel cutting overall, 12" h., pr............................. 350.00
Raised diamonds overall, squat baluster form, original stopper, 10½" h........................ 88.00
Ruby cut to clear, pinwheel & other cutting, 9½" h. 195.00
Strawberry diamond, zipper, fan & four 16-point hobstars 325.00
Wine, Brilliant Period cutting, 13" h........................... 175.00

DISHES, MISCELLANEOUS

Straus Signed Bonbon Dish

Boat-shaped, Clark signed, Brilliant Period cutting, 11½" l. 165.00
Bonbon, Straus signed, Imperial patt., chain of hobstars & strawberry diamond, scalloped & serrated rim, 6 x 7" (ILLUS.) 175.00
Butter ball, Meriden's Pattern No. 26, stick handle, 5¾" d. 175.00
Candy, hobstar within a hobstar cutting, tri-cornered, pedestal base, 4½" w. 175.00
Chalice form, starbursts alternating w/fans, undercut flat circular foot, tapering thread-cut paneled stem, 6¾" h., pr. 154.00

Heart-shaped, shooting stars & fan
around sides, 12-point stars,
strawberry diamond & fan center,
scalloped & serrated rim,
4¾ x 5½" 125.00
Libbey signed, hobstars, flashed
stars & fan, scalloped & serrated
rim, 12" d. 440.00
Nut, Tuthill signed, intaglio-cut
grapes & vines, three-footed,
5¾" d., 3" h. 295.00
Shell-shaped, Tuthill signed, Brilliant
Period cutting, large 5,100.00
Tuthill signed, five-pointed star,
hobstars & intaglio-cut flower,
7" d. 285.00

FERNERS
Brilliant Period cutting, silver plate
rim, original liner 195.00
Brilliant Period cutting, footed,
8" d. 145.00
Hawkes signed, Brilliant Period
cutting 155.00
Hobstars overall, three-footed 90.00
Libbey's Star & Feather patt., three-
footed, 7½" d. 380.00
Monroe (C.F.) Co., large hobstars,
fan & other cutting, ornate silver
rim, original removable metal liner, 8" d., 3" h. 450.00
Pinwheels w/hobstar center, fans &
other cutting, hobstar in base,
three-footed, original chromed
metal liner, 7½" d., 4" h. 135.00

JARS

Libbey Signed Cracker Jar

Cigar, zipper cutting on sides,
4½" d., 5½" h. 100.00
Cigarette, hobstars, strawberry diamond & fan, sterling silver lid
w/gold-washed interior signed
"Tiffany," 3" d., 4¾" h. 275.00
Cracker, Bergen's Golf patt., pin-

wheel & other cutting, barrel-
shaped, 6" d., 11" h. 195.00
Cracker, Libbey signed, chain of
hobstars, panels of notched prism
alternating w/cross-cut diamond,
32-point star base, original cut
bulbous hollow stopper, 13" h.
(ILLUS.) ....600.00 to 650.00
Cracker, star, fan & mitre cutting,
barrel-shaped, star-cut base, silver plate rim, cover & reeded bail
handle, 6½" h. 120.00
Cracker, vesicas of hobstars & fan
alternating w/panels of large hobstars, cylindrical, cover
w/hobstar-cut knob finial,
10" h. 1,760.00
Dresser, notched prism sides, sterling silver cover 100.00
Powder, diamond mitre cutting,
star-cut base, star-cut lid
w/piecrust rim & knob finial,
4¼" d., 3¾" h. 75.00
Tobacco, emerald green cut to
clear, Brilliant Period cutting,
matching cut lid 4,700.00
Tobacco, hobstars overall, large hollow stopper w/hobstar, 4" d.,
6" h. 350.00
Tobacco, star, fan & network design,
elongated cylinder, slightly domed
silver cover applied w/bow-knotted
floral swags & monogrammed "S,"
Shreve & Co., San Francisco,
9½" h. 1,210.00

KNIFE RESTS
Brilliant Period cutting, dumbbell
shape, 4" l. 42.50
Brilliant Period cutting on ends,
plain bar, dumbbell shape,
4½" l. 27.00
Notched prism, star-cut ends, 4" l. ... 35.00
Prism-cut bar, star-cut ends, dumbbell shape, 5½" l. 40.00

LAMPS
Banquet, three-part, St. Louis Diamond patt. overall, 32" h. 4,500.00
Boudoir, mushroom-shaped shade,
pinwheel, fan & strawberry diamond, matching base, flute- and
notch-cut stem, silver rim
w/notch-cut prisms, 7" d. shade,
13" h. 650.00
Boudoir, strawberry-shaped shade,
Sinclaire's Bengal patt., chain of
hobstars, bull's eye & fan, cylindrical stem cut in St. Louis Diamond & flaring to fan-cut base
w/bull's eye cutting at edge, silver
ring w/notch-cut spear prisms ...3,000.00
Table, mushroom-shaped shade,
Strauss signed, La Rabida patt.,

La Rabida Pattern Table Lamp

silver ring w/notch-cut spear
prisms, 12" d., 21" h. (ILLUS.) 4,500.00
Table, strawberry-shaped shade
w/floral & cane cutting, silver rim
w/prisms, one-light, 10" d. shade,
22" h. 900.00
Table, mushroom-shaped shade, Pit-
kin & Brooks signed, Poppy patt.,
intaglio-cut blossoms & chain of
hobstars, conformingly cut baluster-shaped stem & scalloped base,
silver ring w/intaglio-cut prisms,
12" d., 27" h. 3,500.00

MISCELLANEOUS

Brilliant Period Eggnog Bowl

Bell, notched prism cutting, 4" h. . . . 110.00
Canoe, hobstars, fan & diamond,
9" l. 160.00
Centerpiece bowl, squat bulbous
form, hobstars, cross-hatching &
fern below horizontal step-cut

shoulders, flaring scalloped &
serrated rim, 12" d., 8½" h. 1,045.00
Cheese & cracker dish, Double Loz-
enge patt., hobstars, strawberry
diamond & fan, 5½" d. cheese
tray, 10 3/8" d. lower tray 275.00
Door knob, panel-cut 85.00
Eggnog bowl, tulip-shaped, pinwheel,
hobstar & other cutting, large
(ILLUS.) 3,600.00
Eggnog bowl, hobstars, strawberry
diamond & zipper, matching base,
10" d., 10" h., 2 pcs. 600.00
Epergne, Hawkes signed, Brilliant
Period cutting, center bowl
w/numbered metal mount holding
one central & three side trumpet
vases, each fitted w/correspond-
ing numbered mounts, overall
16¾" h. 357.50
Epergne, three tiers of graduating
goblets cut overall w/repeating
panels of thumbprints alternating
w/eight-petal flowers, domed
spreading foot, 17½" h. 385.00
Ewer, Russian patt., sterling silver
Art Nouveau collar & fish-shaped
handle 1,450.00
Ice cream dishes, Brilliant Period
cutting, 6" d., set of 8 . . . . 200.00
Ice cream set: tray & six plates;
Sterling's Arcadia patt., pentagonal strawberry diamond lozenge,
hobstar & star, 7 pcs. 3,000.00
Lemonade set: 10½" h. pitcher & six
3¾" h. tumblers; pinwheel &
other cutting, 7 pcs. 330.00
Loving cup, three-handled, notched
prism, sterling silver collar,
7" h. 750.00
Loving cup, three-handled, Block
patt., pedestal base, 9" w.,
10" h. 750.00
Mayonnaise bowl & underplate,
wide band of strawberry diamond
cutting, prism cut rims, rayed
base, 6½" d. underplate,
the set 165.00
Napkin ring, Brilliant Period
cutting 60.00
Napkin ring, Hawkes signed, three
rings of ovals & darts w/deep triple step cuts between, 2" d.,
1 7/8" h. 85.00
Punch ladle, cranberry cut to clear,
Dorflinger's Montrose patt., bead-
ing, bull's eye & cane, 15" l. 2,500.00
Salad serving fork & spoon, Hawkes'
Hobnail patt., hobnail motif
w/clear vesicas & fan radiants,
the set 145.00
Sherbets, fan & other cutting, scal-
loped foot, set of 8 . . . . 200.00

Cut Glass Sugar Shaker

Sugar shaker, strawberry diamond & fan cutting, 4½" h. (ILLUS.) 125.00

Sugar shaker, bulbous base, hobstar & star cutting w/vertical notched prism, star-pierced sterling silver screw-on top by Peter Krider, ca. 1900, 5" h. 195.00

Sugar shaker, hobstar within pinwheel, fields of diamond point & other cutting, rayed base, original silver plate top w/beaded trim, 3" base d., 6" h. 140.00

Sugar shaker, corset-shaped, notched prism, panels of hobstars & thumbprint, ornate star-pierced sterling silver screw-on top 165.00

Syllabub set: 12" h. cov. ovoid bowl & 12 cups; strawberry diamond & fan, cover notched for ladle, the set 245.00

Talcum powder shaker, tapering four-sided body, bevel-cut diamonds & other cutting, gold-washed sterling silver screw-on top w/blue enamel decoration & engraved rim, marked "sterling 925 S Norway," 2½" sq. base, 5" h. 215.00

Tankard, baluster form, cut w/flowers & undulating foliage, Gorham sterling silver mounts chased w/stylized leafage & cones, the hinged lid engraved w/presentation inscription, early 20th c., 7¾" h. 1,485.00

Tumble-up (water carafe w/tumbler lid), cranberry cut to clear, Brilliant Period cutting, 2 pcs. 4,500.00

Whiskey jug, Dorflinger's Marlboro patt., chain of hobstars, fan & strawberry diamond 425.00

Whiskey jug, chartreuse cut to clear, Libbey's Flute patt. 600.00

Whiskey set: 8½" h. squat cylindrical pitcher-form decanter w/flattened circular stopper & angular handle & six short tumblers; sunbursts alternating w/fans, 7 pcs. 715.00

Wine jug, chain of hobstars, thumbprint, cross-hatching & bands of hobstars & fans, bulbous, cylindrical stopper cut w/hobstar & thumbprints attached to silver collar w/padlock, 12" h. 3,300.00

Wine set: 18¾" h. baluster-form jug w/flat undercut circular foot, notched handle, two ring bands at neck, panel-cut lip & faceted stopper & four 5" h. stemmed wines; continuous starburst & fan band, 5 pcs. 1,650.00

NAPPIES

Expanding star motif, two-handled, 6" d. 110.00

Flowers & leaves center, border of star & fan cutting, serrated rim, loop handle, 6" d. 50.00

Hawkes signed, Centauri patt., chain of hobstars, fan, hobstar & strawberry diamond, 6" d. 85.00

Hoare signed, Steuben patt., single handle, 6" d. 230.00

Hobstars, cross-cut vesicas & cross-hatched ellipticals, 6" d. 40.00

Hunt signed, Royal patt., Russian motif w/hobstar button, pentagonal strawberry diamond lozenge & larger hobstars, single handle, 6" d. 250.00

Russian patt., 6" d. 100.00

Six-petal wheel-cut flower center w/tulip-like florals alternating w/butterflies around sides, serrated rim, applied loop handle, 7¼" w. 58.00

PERFUME & COLOGNE BOTTLES

Cologne, green cut to clear, Dorflinger, Brilliant Period cutting, hobstar base, original clear stopper, 2" w., 4¾" h. 350.00

Cologne, Dorflinger's Colonial patt., cross-cut diamond, fan & strawberry diamond, 3" d., 7" h. 140.00

Cologne, bulbous, hobstar clusters overall, 5" widest d., 7" h. 325.00

Cologne, Russian and Pillar patt., pr. 1,150.00

Cologne, green cut to clear, Brilliant Period cutting, pr. 600.00

Perfume, lay-down type, zipper cutting, brass top w/embossed floral design, 2½" l. 65.00

Perfume, lay-down type, ruby cut to clear, overall Brilliant Period cutting, sterling silver crown-shaped hinged lid, original stopper, 1¾" w., 4" l. 245.00

Perfume, lay-down type, cross-cut
   diamond, sterling silver twist-lock
   hinged cap, 8" l. 155.00
Perfume atomizer, Harvard patt.,
   2½" sq., 8" h. 90.00

PITCHERS

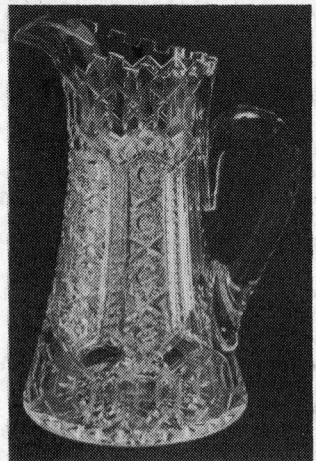

Alhambra Pattern Tankard Pitcher

Champagne, hobstars & other cutting, triple-notched handle,
   13" h. 245.00
Creamer, hobstars & fan 45.00
Creamer, hobstars & mitre cutting,
   notched handle 50.00
Milk, Hawkes signed, Brunswick
   patt., chain of hobstars, zipper &
   flute, 6" h. 450.00
Milk, intaglio-cut large flowers &
   leaves, scalloped rim, 5½" d.,
   6" h. 95.00
Milk, Brilliant Period cutting overall,
   bulbous, 7" h. 285.00
Milk, strawberry diamond, bulbous,
   7" h. 225.00
Milk, Sinclair signed, Brilliant Period
   cutting, bulbous 500.00
Tankard, hobstars & other cutting,
   notched handle, scalloped & ser-
   rated rim, 12" h. 150.00
Tankard, Meriden's Alhambra
   (Greek Key) patt. (ILLUS.) 1,600.00
Water, chain of diamond point
   w/hobstars & notched prism fan,
   bulbous, 8½" h. 275.00
Water, Libbey's Harvard patt.,
   strawberry diamond & checkered
   motif on handle, elongated lip,
   bulbous, 8½" h. 400.00
Water, Cane patt., 9" h. 225.00
Water, intaglio-cut sprays of florals
   & foliage, 9" h. 155.00
Water, hobstars, fields of diamond
   & vesicas, 24-point rayed base,
   double notched handle, 9¼" h. 165.00

Water, Egginton signed, polished
   flowers & leaves, border of
   flashed fan cutting at rim, double
   notched handle, 9½" h. 235.00
Water, hobstars & other cutting, 24-
   point star-cut base, notched handle, paneled facet-cut spout, ser-
   rated rim, 10" h. 165.00
Water, sunburst motif, 10" h. 300.00
Water, zipper cutting, sterling silver
   top, 10½" h. 195.00
Water, large pinwheels w/hobstar
   centers, vesicas & other cutting,
   corset-shaped, rayed base, double
   notched handle, serrated rim,
   11" h. 150.00

PLATES

Brilliant Period Plate

6¾" d., Dorflinger, strawberry diamond, cross-cut diamond & fan
   (ILLUS.). 55.00
7" d., Libbey's Empress patt., cross-
   cut diamond, fan, hobstar &
   strawberry diamond 70.00
7" d., Pairpoint, square motif, cen-
   ter w/Mortenson's engraved But-
   terfly patt. 200.00
8¼" d., Hawkes signed, intaglio-cut
   fruits & foliage 40.00
9" d., Pitkin & Brooks' Roland patt.,
   flashed star, hobstar & prism 275.00
9½" d., Hawkes signed, flowers &
   leaves, 16-point star center 95.00
10" d., center handle, Pairpoint's
   Garland patt., butterfly & flowers
   motif, serrated rim 165.00
10½" d., intaglio-cut roses, leaves,
   buds & stems 40.00

PUNCH BOWLS & SETS

Alhambra (Greek Key) patt., hobstars & cane, Greek Key border,
   dentil rim, conforming base,
   2 pcs. 3,000.00
Cane, hobstars, fan & medallion mo-
   tifs, scalloped & serrated rim,
   matching flared base (top chipped)
   inscribed "Presented to the New
   York Press Club Christmas 1904,"
   18½" d., overall 16½" h., 2 pcs.
   (ILLUS.) 2,200.00

Presentation Punch Bowl

Crosshatching framing stars & fans, marked sterling silver rim ending in a repeating band of repousse scrolls & flowers, monogrammed, 10¾" d., 5¾" h. 522.50

Dorflinger signed, Brilliant Period cutting, matching base & ladle, 3 pcs. 5,000.00

Libbey signed, hobstars, notched prism, fan & other cutting, scalloped & serrated rim, matching flared base, 13" d., overall 19" h., 2 pcs. 1,872.00

Pinwheels, hobstars, fan & diamond fields, matching base, 2 pcs. 1,320.00

Strawberry diamond & fan, scalloped & serrated rim, polished star-cut base, 15" d., 6" h. 605.00

Punch set: 15" h. bowl w/attached base, one cup & ladle; flowers & wheat cutting on cup-shaped bowl & flaring base joined by swirl-cut ring, thumbprint & fringe rims, further decorated w/molded detail, matching ladle w/ornate silver plate bowl by Pairpoint Mfg. Co., 3 pcs. 880.00

ROSE BOWLS

Cross-cut diamond in diamond-shaped fields, fan & other cutting, large hobstar base, 8½" d., 7½" h. 545.00

Egginton signed, chain of hobstars, 4" d., 2" h. 89.00

Hawkes' Brazilian patt., fan, star & strawberry diamond, 6" w., 5" h. 350.00

Hawkes, hobstar panels alternating w/panels of thumbprint, 5½" d., 5" h. 265.00

Hawkes' Venetian patt., chain of hobstars, fan, star & strawberry diamond, 6" w., 5" h. 350.00

Hobstars, diamond point & fan, 4" d. 125.00

Russian patt. overall, three footed, 8½" d., 9" h. 770.00

SALT & PEPPER SHAKERS

Salt & Pepper Shakers by Hawkes

Bull's eye, notched prism, vesicas & fan, original repousse sterling silver tops, 3" h., pr. 30.00

Geometric cutting overall, four-sided, original chrome tops, 4 3/8" h., pr. 25.00

Hawkes, strawberry diamond & notched prism, pewter tops, 1½" d., 3" h., pr. (ILLUS.) 95.00

Zipper patt., glass tops, pr. 85.00

SYRUP PITCHERS

Brilliant Period cutting alternating w/intaglio-cut panels, Gorham sterling silver hinged lid, 2¾" d., 5" h. 285.00

Hawkes signed, Brunswick patt., chain of hobstars, beading & flute, sterling silver hinged lid, spout & collar.................... 265.00

Vertical irregular band of notched prism, pewter hinged lid & handle, 4" h. 55.00

TOOTHPICK HOLDERS

Chain of hobstars, pedestal base ... 135.00

Fluted diamond 42.00

Paneled crosshatching & zipper 25.00

Pinwheel & zipper 25.00

TRAYS

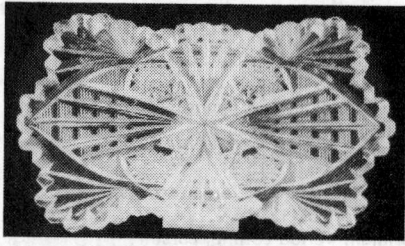

Libbey's New Brilliant Pattern

Bread, diamond point, hobstars & cane, 12" l. 225.00

Clusters of hobstars overall, 8 x 14" 350.00

Dresser, Hawkes signed, Sheraton

patt., bands of triple mitre cutting
w/floral medallions, 7 x 10".......195.00
Hawkes' Festoon patt. variant,
13" d. 3,000.00
Hobstars & fan, 9 x 14"...........350.00
Hobstars, diamond point & fan border, large 16-point hobstar center,
10 x 16" oval 575.00
Hunt's Royal patt., Russian patt.
w/hobstar button & pentagonal
strawberry diamond lozenges,
6 x 9"..........................225.00
Hunt's Royal patt., Russian patt.
w/hobstar button & pentagonal
strawberry diamond lozenges,
12" d. 800.00
Ice cream, hobstars & other cutting,
scalloped & serrated rim, 10 x 17"
oval 440.00
Intaglio-cut peaches, cherries &
leaves, 13" d...................450.00
Libbey signed, Spillane patt., cross-
cut vesicas & notched prism w/a
fan motif between hobstars,
11½" d. 1,250.00
Libbey's Star & Feather patt.,
12" d. 275.00
Pinwheel, leaf sprays & daisies
w/polished star centers,
12½" d. 175.00
Spoon, Libbey's New Brilliant patt.,
beading, fan & hobstar, 4½ x
7½" (ILLUS.) 150.00

TUMBLERS

Hawkes signed, Queens patt., chain
of hobstars & bull's eye..........135.00
Hobstars alternating w/notched
prism, rayed base 19.00
Intaglio-cut sprays of flowers &
foliage 35.00
Libbey signed, Anita patt., hobstar
& deep mitre cutting, set of 4 ....210.00
Pinwheel, diamond & mitre cutting,
star-cut bottom, 9 oz., 3 7/8" h.,
set of 6 ....175.00
Pinwheel, fan & diamond point,
rayed base 20.00
Pinwheel, hobstars, mitre cutting &
fan, flared rim 22.00
Russian patt., star-cut base, 3½" h.,
set of 16 ....495.00
Sinclaire signed, Brilliant Period cutting, 11 oz., set of 6............450.00

VASES

Bands of hobstars, ferns & roses,
cylindrical, 12" h. 225.00
Brilliant Period cutting, corset-
shaped, 10" h. 185.00
Clark signed, Harvard patt.,
10" h. 190.00
Clark signed, vertical notched prism
overall, trumpet-shaped, 32-point
rayed base, 18" h. 375.00

Cranberry cut to clear, cross-
hatching & fan, pyramidal form,
15" h. 425.00
Dorflinger's Parisian patt., beading,
fan, hobstar & strawberry diamond, trumpet-shaped, 14½" h. ...715.00
Egginton's Lotus patt., chain of hobstars, fan, flashed fan, St. Louis
Diamond, star & strawberry diamond, on standard, green,
16" h. 3,200.00

Harvard Pattern Vase

Harvard patt., cylindrical w/a slightly
flaring base, mounted w/an undulating everted Gorham silver rim
chased w/foliate clusters, monogrammed, 25" h. (ILLUS.) 4,400.00
Hawkes' Devonshire patt., fan, hobstar, star & strawberry diamond,
5¾" d., 14¼" h. 675.00
Hawkes' Queens patt., chain of hobstars & bull's eyes, 14" h. 825.00
Hoare, step-cutting from base to 3"
below rim, 10" h. 385.00
Hobstars & fans in lozenge panels
alternating w/waisted panels of
hobnail, flaring scalloped & serrated rim, baluster-form,
14½" h. 825.00
Intaglio-cut floral decorated panels
w/double zipper cut borders,
cylindrical w/flared shaped rim,
21½" h. 302.50
King George patt., square motif
w/notched prism & fan, cylindrical, 4" d., 12" h. 950.00
Libbey signed, overall Brilliant Period cutting w/band of leaves at
mid-section, applied 5" d. foot,
3" d. cylindrical body, 13" h. 245.00
Libbey signed, Corinthian patt.,
cross-cut diamond, hobstar &
strawberry diamond, 7" h. 195.00
Libbey signed, Dianthus patt.,
intaglio-cut w/polished cut medallion border, flared form on teardrop paperweight pedestal,
11½" h. 302.50

Libbey's Wedgemere patt., beading,
flute, hobstar & strawberry diamond, 18" h. 2,400.00
Pairpoint's Silsbee patt., intaglio-cut
stylized flowers & leaves &
polished leaves, 12" h. 350.00
Panels of hobstars, diamond point &
fan, bowling pin shape, 12" h. ... 425.00
Tuthill signed, Wood Lily patt.,
intaglio-cut blossoms & foliage,
sweet pea type form, 5½" w.,
4" h. 325.00

WATER SETS

Pitcher & four tumblers, Hawkes
signed, Navarre patt., 5 pcs. 850.00
Pitcher & four tumblers, Libbey
signed, bull's eye & nailhead diamond, 5 pcs. 250.00
Pitcher & four tumblers, pinwheel
cutting, 5 pcs. 375.00
Pitcher & five tumblers, Harvard-
type patt. & daisy spray, 10½" h.
tankard pitcher, 6 pcs. (one tumbler w/rough rim) 375.00
Pitcher & six tumblers, sunburst motif, 7 pcs...................... 350.00
Pitcher & eight tumblers, Libbey
signed, Poppy patt., 9 pcs. 4,100.00

(End of Cut Glass Section)

CUT VELVET

Cut Velvet Rose Bowl

*Several glasshouses, including Mt.
Washington, produced this two-layered glass
with its velvety or acid finish and raised pattern. The inner casing is frequently white, and
the pattern was developed by blowing into
a mold.*

Bowl, footed, 6½" d., 4½" h., applied clear ruffle at rim, clear applied feet, Diamond Quilted patt.,
deep rose, white lining $195.00
Pitcher, 6", rose coloring 225.00
Rose bowl, four-crimp top, Diamond
Quilted patt., heavenly blue,
white lining, 3½" d., 3 1/8" h. ... 165.00

Rose bowl, four-crimp top, Diamond
Quilted patt., rose, white lining,
3 5/8" d., 3½" h. 175.00
Rose bowl, six-crimp top, Diamond
Quilted patt., blue, white lining
(ILLUS.)........................ 250.00
Vase, 6¼" h., 3¼" d., tall ovoid
body w/squared ruffled rim, Diamond Quilted patt., shaded blue,
white lining.................... 175.00
Vase, 8¾" h., bottle-shaped
w/ovoid body & tall slender
shaped neck w/flat mouth, shaded pink, white lining, glossy
finish 145.00

CZECHOSLOVAKIAN

*At the close of World War I, Czechoslova-
kia was declared an independent republic and
immediately developed a large export industry. Czechoslovakian glass factories produced
a wide variety of colored and hand-painted
glasswares from about 1918 until 1939, when
the country was occupied by Germany at the
outset of World War II. Between the wars,
fine quality blown glasswares were produced
along with a deluge of cheaper, vividly colored spatterwares for the American market.
Subsequent production was primarily limited to cut crystal or Bohemian-type etched
wares for the American market. Although it
was marked, much Czechoslovakian glass is
mistaken for the work of Tiffany, Loetz, or
other glass artisans it imitates. It is often
misrepresented and overpriced.*

Basket, star-shaped, multicolored
spattering, twisted thorn handle,
signed, 5½" w., 7½" h. $125.00
Compote, 10" d., hollow stem,
cased, black exterior, red interior,
signed 68.00
Decanter w/original cut & polished
stopper, applied square ruby handle, opalescent crackle w/ruby
threading....................... 175.00
Ice cream set, topaz w/cut, polished
& sandblasted decoration,
designed by Ludvika Smrchkova,
Ruckl Glassworks, Nizbor, Czechoslovakia, 7 pcs. 695.00
Pitcher, 10" h., topaz streaked
green w/cobalt blue threading,
signed 115.00
Vases, 6¼" h., 2¾" d., triple gourd
form, green w/variegated spatter,
marked "Czechoslovakia," pr. 50.00
Vase, 7 1/8" h., jack-in-the-pulpit
type, brilliant orange w/sponged
designs in black, signed 48.00
Vase, bud, 8" h., ruffled top, cased,
orange exterior, white lining 28.00

Vase, 8½" h., fan-shaped, amber
w/blue threading 85.00
Vase, 9" h., red w/applied cobalt
blue snake & rim, signed 45.00
Vase, 10" h., relief-molded doves,
frosted finish 150.00
Vase, 11" h., cased, yellow
w/enameled bird, signed 45.00
Vases, 12¼" h., vivid orange-red
w/black-edged fluted rim, pr. 150.00
Vase, 13" h., black amethyst w/sil-
ver deposit Egyptian design 55.00
Vase, 13" h., black handles, canary
yellow body 75.00

D'ARGENTAL

D'Argental Cameo Vase

*Glass known by this name is so-called af-
ter its producer, who fashioned fine cameo
pieces in France late last century.*

Cameo bottle, flask-shaped, red &
purple cut to pink w/bell-shaped
florals, wooden collar & cover,
5½" h. $850.00
Cameo bowl, 3½" h., straight sides,
grey splashed w/lemon yellow,
overlaid in raspberry red & carved
w/a river scene w/boating,
signed in cameo "d'Argental"
w/cross of Lorraine, ca. 1920 . . . . . 605.00
Cameo vase, 6" h., ovoid, lemon
yellow overlaid w/Chinese red &
carved w/a Dutch river landscape
w/sailing vessels, signed in cam-
eo "D'Argental," ca. 1920 . . . . 660.00
Cameo vase, 8" h., ovoid, pale pink
overlaid w/lime green & carved
w/undulating unfurling fern
fronds, signed in cameo "d'Argental" w/cross of Lorraine, ca.
1920 . . . . 550.00
Cameo vase, 12½" h., inverted rim

on cylindrical body w/bulbous
base, mottled amber, clear frosted
& yellow body layered w/light &
dark brown, cut w/an expansive
forested landscape w/a turreted
building in the distance, marked
"Chateau de Tournod - Auvergne"
& signed "d'Argental - VStL"
(ILLUS.) 1,650.00

DAUM NANCY

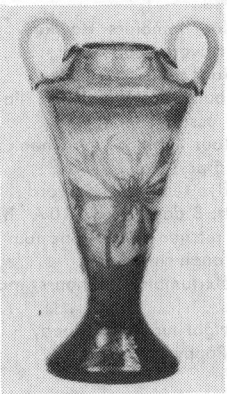

Daum Nancy Cameo Vase

*This fine glass, much of it cameo, was made
by Auguste and Antonin Daum, who founded a factory in 1875 in Nancy, France. Most
of their cameo and enameled glass was made
from the 1890's into the early 20th century.*

Atomizer, medium blue, light blue &
orange-beige w/gold flecks,
signed, 8¼" h. $345.00
Cameo bowl, 10½" d., 5½" h., flar-
ing wide rim, squat round body,
carved deep maroon grasses &
dark red exotic blossoms against
mottled yellow ground, signed &
w/cross of Lorraine 1,760.00
Cameo perfume w/original matching
stopper, miniature, cylindrical
shape, green w/enameled white
dots & cut shiny green leaves,
stopper cut w/same pattern,
signed, 2¾" h. to top of
stopper 400.00
Cameo powder box, cov., green tex-
tured background w/gold & shiny
green cut leaves encircling a
deeply cut scene of a man rowing
a boat, a bridge, houses & trees,
scene repeats on bottom, 5½" w.,
2½" h. 1,950.00
Cameo salt dip, tropical scene
w/black carved trees, mountains

& a lake against a frosted background, 1¾" d., 1" h. 450.00

Cameo spirit bottle, cylindrical, acid-cut in Thistle patt. against shaded deep rubina pink to clear ground, hallmarked silver cap & removable cup chased in matching thistle motif, signed, 5¾" h. (minor silver dents) 715.00

Cameo vase, 3¼" h., ovoid shape, pale melon & mottled chartreuse sides overlaid w/charcoal, brown & white & cut w/a snowy winter scène w/clusters of bare trees, ca. 1910, signed 1,045.00

Cameo vase, 4¾" h., square paneled form, acid-etched, carved & enameled dianthus blossoms & birds against clear ground w/three mottled bands of royal blue, pink w/blue flecks & green w/blue flecks, signed 880.00

Cameo vase, 9¼" h., elongated ovoid body w/pulled-out rim, carved scene w/trees in foreground, water & trees in background, dark brown on red on mottled yellow interior 1,670.00

Cameo vase, 11¼" h., baluster-form, carved & molded w/leafy trees, the lower section w/trees & a village in the distance & finely wheel-carved w/ferns, mosses & fallen leafage in forest & emerald green against a mottled lemon yellow & orange ground, signed in intaglio "Daum Nancy" w/cross of Lorraine, base further signed in intaglio "FRANCE," ca. 1900 . . . . . 2,420.00

Cameo vase, 12¼" h., carved thistle & leaf against emerald green & royal blue hammered ground, early 20th c., signed (ILLUS.) 3,300.00

Cameo vase, 13" h., spherical base on low foot below very tall, very slender neck w/flared rim, green & pink encased in clear glass, crocuses in bloom carved on the base w/carved leaves pendent on the neck, engraved "DAUM NANCY" 12,100.00

Cameo vase, 19¾" h., banjo-form, mottled orange & lemon yellow overlaid w/deep brown & cut w/a river landscape w/boating in background & trees in foreground, ca. 1915, signed 2,640.00

Cameo *veilleuse*, lobed ovoid shape, circular top aperture, mottled aqua & yellow overlaid in inky violet & cut w/a river landscape w/tall trees & low mountains, raised on wrought-iron circular support

w/three scrolling feet, ca. 1910, signed, 5¾" h. 2,310.00

Figure of a classical woman, *pate de verre*, woman w/upswept hair holding her hands to her head, dressed in classical robes, pale lavender shading to deep grape, on a rectangular base, ca. 1910, signed "Daum Nancy" w/cross of Lorraine, 10 1/8" h. (pitted surface) 1,980.00

Table lamp, highly domed shade of shell form overlaid in orange & yellow etched to depict berries, leaves & branches, etched "DAUM NANCY FRANCE," elongated ovoid base tapering to wide circular foot & decorated as the shade, 12¾" h. 15,400.00

Vase, 3 3/8" h., bulbous body w/wide top opening & tapering to narrow base on foot, clear glass encasing blue, pink & green & enameled & etched to depict cornflowers in blossom, engraved "Daum Nancy" 1,430.00

Vase, 7¾" h., tall slightly ovoid form, deep violet, yellow & orange streaked ground etched w/grape clusters, leaves & vines, two applied beige glass handles at sides formed as snails, etched "DAUM NANCY" 9,350.00

Acid-Etched Daum Nancy Vase

Vase, 12¾" h., ovoid body w/sloping shoulder in smokey grey acid-etched in intaglio w/lozenges & zig₂zags, signed in intaglio "Daum Nancy - France" w/cross of Lorraine & remains of original retailer's label, ca. 1925 (ILLUS.) 1,210.00

Vase, 21½" h., inverted trumpet-form on round base, clear ground streaked w/pale yellow, violet & green etched & enameled to depict green leaves, stems, sinuous vines & red pendent berries further enhanced w/randomly applied red glass berries, etched "DAUM NANCY" 4,620.00

DEPRESSION GLASS

The phrase "Depression Glass" is used by collectors to denote a specific kind of transparent glass produced primarily as tablewares, in crystal, amber, blue, green, pink, milky-white, etc., during the late 1920's and 1930's when this country was in the midst of a financial depression. Made to sell inexpensively, it was turned out by such producers as Jeannette, Hocking, Westmoreland, Indiana and other glass companies. We compile prices on all the major Depression Glass patterns. Collectors should consult Depression Glass references for information on those patterns and pieces which have been reproduced.

ADAM (Process-etched)

Adam Pitcher

Ashtray, clear, 4½" sq.	$6.50
Ashtray, green, 4½" sq.	15.50
Ashtray, pink, 4½" sq.	20.00
Bowl, dessert, 4¾" sq., green or pink	9.50
Bowl, cereal, 5¾" sq., green	30.00
Bowl, cereal, 5¾" sq., pink	26.00
Bowl, nappy, 7¾" sq., green	14.50
Bowl, nappy, 7¾" sq., pink	15.50
Bowl, cov., 9" sq., green	57.50
Bowl, cov., 9" sq., pink	38.00
Bowl, 9" sq., green	27.50
Bowl, 9" sq., pink	17.50
Bowl, 10" oval vegetable, green	16.50
Bowl, 10" oval vegetable, pink	15.00
Butter dish, cov., green	215.00
Butter dish, cov., pink	64.00
Butter dish, cov., w/Sierra patt., pink	495.00
Cake plate, footed, green, 10" sq.	15.00
Cake plate, footed, pink, 10" sq.	13.00
Candlesticks, green, 4" h., pr.	70.00
Candlesticks, pink, 4" h., pr.	54.50
Candy jar, cov., green	72.00
Candy jar, cov., pink	56.50
Coaster, clear or pink, 3¼" sq.	14.00
Coaster, green, 3¼" sq.	12.50
Creamer, green	13.50

Creamer, pink	12.00
Cup & saucer, green	19.50
Cup & saucer, pink	20.50
Pitcher, 8" h., 32 oz., cone-shaped, clear	35.00
Pitcher, 8" h., 32 oz., cone-shaped, green (ILLUS.)	31.50
Pitcher, 8" h., 32 oz., cone-shaped, pink	25.00
Pitcher, 32 oz., round base, clear	18.00
Pitcher, 32 oz., round base, pink	36.00
Plate, sherbet, 6" sq., green	4.50
Plate, sherbet, 6" sq., pink	3.50
Plate, salad, 7¾" sq., green or pink	7.50
Plate, salad, round, pink	55.00
Plate, dinner, 9" sq., green or pink	15.50
Plate, grill, 9" sq., green	11.50
Plate, grill, 9" sq., pink	15.00
Platter, 11¾" l., green	13.50
Platter, 11¾" l., pink	11.00
Relish dish, two-part, green or pink, 8" sq.	10.00
Salt & pepper shakers, footed, green, 4" h., pr.	73.50
Salt & pepper shakers, footed, pink, 4" h., pr.	41.00
Sherbet, green	23.00
Sherbet, pink	16.50
Sugar bowl, cov., green	33.50
Sugar bowl, cov., pink	24.50
Sugar bowl, open, green	11.50
Sugar bowl, open, pink	9.50
Tumbler, cone-shaped, green, 4½" h., 7 oz.	14.50
Tumbler, cone-shaped, pink, 4½" h., 7 oz.	16.00
Tumbler, iced tea, green, 5½" h., 9 oz.	28.50
Tumbler, iced tea, pink, 5½" h., 9 oz.	44.00
Vase, 7½" h., green	34.00
Vase, 7½" h., pink	151.00

AMERICAN SWEETHEART (Process-etched)

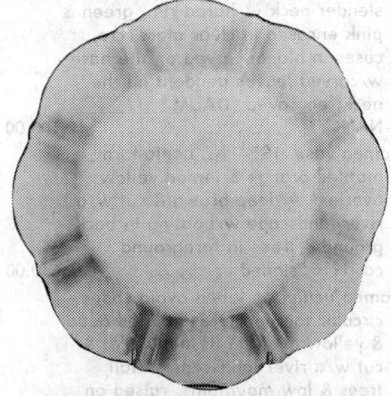

American Sweetheart Salad Plate

Berry set: 9" d. bowl & 6 sauce
dishes; Cremax, 7 pcs. 50.00
Bowl, berry, 3¾" d., pink 23.50
Bowl, cream soup, 4½" d., Monax . . 44.00
Bowl, cream soup, 4½" d., pink . . . 28.50
Bowl, cereal, 6" d., Cremax 6.50
Bowl, cereal, 6" d., Monax or
pink 9.50
Bowl, cereal, 6" d., Monax "Smoke"
w/black edge 25.00
Bowl, berry, 9" d., Cremax 28.00
Bowl, berry, 9" d., Monax 39.50
Bowl, berry, 9" d., pink 22.00
Bowl, soup w/flange rim, 9½" d.,
Monax 38.00
Bowl, soup w/flange rim, 9½" d.,
pink 28.00
Bowl, 11" oval vegetable, Monax . . . 41.50
Bowl, 11" oval vegetable, pink 31.50
Console bowl, blue, 18" d. 850.00
Console bowl, Monax, 18" d. 300.00
Creamer, footed, blue 90.00
Creamer, footed, Monax 6.00
Creamer, footed, pink 8.00
Creamer, footed, ruby red 71.50
Cup & saucer, Monax 8.50
Cup & saucer, pink 11.50
Cup & saucer, ruby red 110.00
Lamp shade, Monax 310.00
Pitcher, 7½" h., 60 oz., jug-type,
pink 357.00
Pitcher, 8" h., 80 oz., pink 325.00
Plate, bread & butter, 6" d.,
Monax 3.00
Plate, bread & butter, 6" d., pink . . . 2.50
Plate, salad, 8" d., Monax (ILLUS.) . . 5.50
Plate, salad, 8" d., pink 6.50
Plate, salad, 8" d., ruby red 55.50
Plate, luncheon, 9" d., Monax 7.50
Plate, dinner, 9¾" d., Monax 12.50
Plate, dinner, 9¾" d., pink 13.50
Plate, chop, 11" d., Monax 9.00
Plate, salver, 12" d., blue 159.00
Plate, salver, 12" d., Monax or
pink 10.00
Plate, 15½" d., w/center handle,
Monax 154.00
Plate, 15½" d., w/center handle,
ruby red 242.00
Platter, 13" oval, Monax 37.50
Platter, 13" oval, pink 20.50
Salt & pepper shakers, footed,
Monax, pr. 202.00
Salt & pepper shakers, footed, pink,
pr. 280.00
Sherbet, footed, Monax, 4¼" h. 12.00
Sherbet, footed, pink, 4¼" h. 10.00
Sherbet, metal holder, clear 3.50
Sugar bowl, cov., Monax 157.50
Sugar bowl, open, blue 90.00
Sugar bowl, open, Monax 5.00
Sugar bowl, open, pink 7.50
Sugar bowl, open, ruby red 64.00
Tidbit server, two-tier, Monax 49.00

Tidbit server, two-tier, pink 59.50
Tidbit server, three-tier, Monax 175.00
Tumbler, pink, 3½" h., 5 oz. 38.00
Tumbler, pink, 4¼" h., 9 oz. 42.00
Tumbler, pink, 4¾" h., 10 oz. 45.00

BLOCK or Block Optic (Press-mold)

Block Creamer & Sugar Bowl

Bowl, berry, 4¼" d., green 5.00
Bowl, cereal, 5¼" d., green 7.50
Bowl, cereal, 5¼" d., pink 6.00
Bowl, salad, 7" d., green 15.50
Bowl, salad, 7" d., pink 11.00
Bowl, large berry, 8½" d., green 15.00
Butter dish, cov., rectangular,
3 x 5", green 34.50
Candlesticks, green, 1¾" h., pr. 47.50
Candlesticks, pink, 1¾" h., pr. 46.00
Candy jar, cov., green or pink,
2¼" h. 27.00
Candy jar, cov., yellow, 2¼" h. 38.00
Candy jar, cov., clear, 6¼" h. 20.00
Candy jar, cov., green, 6¼" h. 39.00
Candy jar, cov., pink, 6¼" h. 48.50
Compote, 4" d., cone-shaped,
green 16.50
Creamer, green (ILLUS. right) 8.50
Creamer, pink or yellow 9.00
Cup & saucer, green 10.50
Cup & saucer, pink or yellow 7.00
Goblet, cocktail, clear, 4" h. 7.50
Goblet, cocktail, green or pink,
4" h. 19.00
Goblet, clear, 5¾" h., 9 oz. 6.50
Goblet, green, 5¾" h., 9 oz. 15.00
Goblet, pink, 5¾" h., 9 oz. 12.50
Goblet, clear, 7¼" h., 9 oz. 5.50
Goblet, green or pink, 7¼" h.,
9 oz. 11.50
Goblet, yellow, 7¼" h., 9 oz. 18.50
Ice bucket, w/handle, clear 20.00
Ice bucket, w/handle, green 27.50
Ice tub, clear 16.00
Ice tub, green 25.50
Ice tub, pink 60.00
Mug, green 25.00
Pitcher, 7 5/8" h., 68 oz., bulbous,
green 51.00
Pitcher, 8" h., 80 oz., clear 24.50
Pitcher, 8" h., 80 oz., green 42.00
Pitcher, 8" h., 80 oz., pink 37.00
Pitcher, 8½" h., 54 oz., clear 13.00

Pitcher, 8½" h., 54 oz., green	25.00
Pitcher, 8½" h., 54 oz., pink	26.00
Plate, sherbet, 6" d., clear, green or pink	1.50
Plate, sherbet, 6" d., yellow	2.00
Plate, luncheon, 8" d., clear or pink	2.50
Plate, luncheon, 8" d., green	3.00
Plate, luncheon, 8" d., yellow	3.50
Plate, dinner, 9" d., clear	4.00
Plate, dinner, 9" d., green	12.00
Plate, dinner, 9" d., pink	18.00
Plate, dinner, 9" d., yellow	20.00
Plate, grill, 9" d., clear	4.50
Plate, grill, 9" d., green	10.00
Plate, sandwich, 10¼" d., clear	13.00
Plate, sandwich, 10¼" d., green	15.00
Plate, sandwich, 10¼" d., pink	12.00
Salt & pepper shakers, squat, green, pr.	25.50
Salt & pepper shakers, footed, clear or green, pr.	23.50
Salt & pepper shakers, footed, pink, pr.	33.00
Sandwich server w/center handle, green or pink	32.00
Sherbet, cone-shaped, footed, green	3.50
Sherbet, stemmed, clear, 3¼" h.	3.00
Sherbet, stemmed, green, 3¼" h.	4.00
Sherbet, stemmed, pink, 3¼" h.	4.50
Sherbet, stemmed, yellow, 3¼" h.	5.50
Sherbet, stemmed, clear, 4¾" h.	4.00
Sherbet, stemmed, green, 4¾" h.	8.00
Sherbet, stemmed, pink, 4¾" h.	7.50
Sherbet, stemmed, yellow, 4¾" h.	9.50
Sugar bowl, clear	6.00
Sugar bowl, green (ILLUS. left)	8.00
Sugar bowl, pink	7.00
Sugar bowl, yellow	8.00
Tumbler, whiskey, green, 2¼" h., 2 oz.	17.00
Tumbler, whiskey, pink, 2¼" h., 2 oz.	25.00
Tumbler, juice, clear, 3" h., 5 oz.	5.50
Tumbler, juice, green, 3" h., 5 oz.	11.50
Tumbler, juice, pink, 3" h., 5 oz.	9.50
Tumbler, juice, footed, clear, 4" h., 5 oz.	9.00
Tumbler, juice, footed, green, 4" h., 5 oz.	12.50
Tumbler, juice, footed, pink, 4" h., 5 oz.	10.00
Tumbler, clear, 9 oz.	4.50
Tumbler, green, 9 oz.	12.00
Tumbler, pink, 9 oz.	9.00
Tumbler, footed, clear, 9 oz.	5.00
Tumbler, footed, green, 9 oz.	12.00
Tumbler, footed, pink, 9 oz.	9.50
Tumbler, green, 10 oz.	13.00
Tumbler, pink, 10 oz.	10.00
Tumbler, iced tea, footed, green or pink, 6" h., 10 oz.	13.50
Tumbler, iced tea, footed, yellow, 6" h., 10 oz.	15.00
Tumbler, green, 14 oz.	20.00
Tumble-up bottle, green	10.50
Tumble-up: bottle & 3" h. tumbler; green, set	45.00
Water set: pitcher & 6 footed tumblers; green, 7 pcs.	125.00

BUBBLE or Bullseye or Provincial (Press-mold)

Bubble Iced Tea Tumbler

Bowl, berry, 4" d., blue	9.50
Bowl, berry, 4" d., clear	2.00
Bowl, fruit, 4½" d., blue	6.50
Bowl, fruit, 4½" d., clear	2.00
Bowl, fruit, 4½" d., green	5.00
Bowl, fruit, 4½" d., milk white	1.50
Bowl, fruit, 4½" d., ruby red	5.50
Bowl, cereal, 5¼" d., blue	7.00
Bowl, cereal, 5¼" d., clear	2.50
Bowl, cereal, 5¼" d., green	6.50
Bowl, soup, 7¾" d., blue	7.50
Bowl, soup, 7¾" d., clear	5.00
Bowl, 8 3/8" d., blue	8.50
Bowl, 8 3/8" d., clear or milk white	3.00
Bowl, 8 3/8" d., green	9.00
Bowl, 8 3/8" d., pink	4.50
Bowl, 9" d., flanged, milk white	30.00
Candlesticks, clear, pr.	9.50
Creamer, blue	20.50
Creamer, clear or green	6.00
Creamer, milk white	2.00
Cup & saucer, blue	3.50
Cup & saucer, clear	2.00
Cup & saucer, green or pink	4.50
Cup & saucer, ruby red	6.00
Lamp, clear	27.50
Lamps, clear (electric), pr.	75.00
Pitcher w/ice lip, 64 oz., clear	39.00
Pitcher w/ice lip, 64 oz., ruby red	37.50
Plate, bread & butter, 6¾" d., blue or green	2.00
Plate, bread & butter, 6¾" d., clear	1.00
Plate, dinner, 9 3/8" d., blue	4.50
Plate, dinner, 9 3/8" d., clear	3.00
Plate, dinner, 9 3/8" d., green	5.50

Plate, dinner, 9 3/8" d., ruby red ... 6.00
Plate, grill, 9 3/8" d., blue 9.00
Platter, 12" oval, blue 9.00
Platter, 12" oval, clear 12.50
Sugar bowl, open, blue 13.50
Sugar bowl, open, clear 3.00
Sugar bowl, open, green 7.00
Tidbit server, two-tier, blue 37.00
Tumbler, juice, clear or ruby red,
   6 oz. 5.50
Tumbler, water, clear, 9 oz. 5.00
Tumbler, water, ruby red,
   9 oz. 6.50
Tumbler, iced tea, ruby red, 12 oz.
   (ILLUS.) 7.50
Tumbler, lemonade, clear,
   16 oz. 11.50
Tumbler, lemonade, ruby red,
   16 oz. 12.00

CAMEO or Ballerina or Dancing Girl (Process-etched)

Cameo Water Tumbler

Bowl, sauce, 4¼" d., clear 5.00
Bowl, cream soup, 4¾" d., green ... 39.00
Bowl, cereal, 5½" d., clear 8.00
Bowl, cereal, 5½" d., green 21.00
Bowl, cereal, 5½" d., yellow 22.50
Bowl, salad, 7¼" d., green 36.50
Bowl, large berry, 8¼" d., green ... 22.00
Bowl, soup w/flange rim,
   9" d., green 27.00
Bowl, 10" oval vegetable, green 17.50
Bowl, 10" oval vegetable, yellow ... 33.50
Butter dish, cov., green 136.50
Cake plate, three-footed, green,
   10" d. 15.00
Cake plate, handled, green,
   10½" d. 55.00
Candlesticks, green, 4" h., pr. 76.50
Candy jar, cov., green, 4" h. 41.00
Candy jar, cov., yellow, 4" h. 62.50
Candy jar, cov., green, 6½" h. 94.50
Compote, mayonnaise, 4" h., cone-
   shaped, green 22.00
Console bowl, three-footed, green,
   11" d. 43.00
Console bowl, three-footed, pink,
   11" d. 25.00

Console bowl, three-footed, yellow,
   11" d. 52.50
Cookie jar, cov., green 38.50
Creamer, green, 3¼" h. 17.00
Creamer, yellow, 3¼" h. 11.50
Creamer, green, 4¼" h. 17.50
Creamer, pink, 4¼" h. 62.50
Cup & saucer, green 12.00
Cup & saucer, yellow 7.50
Decanter, no stopper, green 45.00
Decanter w/stopper, green, 10" h. ... 92.50
Decanter w/stopper, frosted green,
   10" h. 29.00
Domino tray, green, 7" d. 83.50
Domino tray, pink, 7" d. 185.00
Goblet, wine, green, 3½" h. 50.00
Goblet, wine, green, 4" h. 46.00
Goblet, water, green, 6" h. 39.50
Goblet, water, pink, 6" h. 130.00
Ice bowl, green, 3½" h. 114.00
Ice bowl, pink, 3½" h. 425.00
Jam jar, cov., closed handles,
   green, 2" 116.00
Pitcher, syrup or milk, 5¾" h.,
   20 oz., green 150.00
Pitcher, juice, 6" h., 36 oz., green .. 42.00
Pitcher, water, 8½" h., 56 oz., jug-
   type, clear 35.00
Pitcher, water, 8½" h., 56 oz., jug-
   type green 36.50
Plate, sherbet, 6" d., green or
   yellow 2.50
Plate, salad, 7" d., clear 3.00
Plate, luncheon, 8" d., green 7.00
Plate, luncheon, 8" d., yellow 8.00
Plate, 8½" sq., green 27.00
Plate, dinner, 9½" d., green 12.50
Plate, dinner, 9½" d., yellow 6.50
Plate, sandwich, 10" d., green 12.00
Plate, sandwich, 10" d., pink 31.00
Plate, 10½" d., closed handles,
   green 10.00
Plate, grill, 10½" d., green 7.00
Plate, grill, 10½" d., yellow 5.00
Plate, grill, 10½" d., closed han-
   dles, green 46.00
Plate, grill, 10½" d., closed han-
   dles, yellow 6.00
Plate, 11½" d., closed handles,
   green 6.50
Platter, 10½" oval, green 13.50
Platter, 10½" oval, yellow 30.50
Platter, 12", closed handles, green.. 14.00
Platter, 12", closed handles,
   yellow 31.50
Relish, footed, three-part, green,
   7½" 19.50
Salt & pepper shakers, green, pr.... 52.00
Sherbet, green, 3 1/8" h. 9.50
Sherbet, pink, 3 1/8" h. 28.00
Sherbet, yellow, 3 1/8" h. 22.50
Sherbet, thin, high stem, green,
   4 7/8" h. 22.50

Sherbet, thin, high stem, yellow, 4 7/8" h.	28.50
Sugar bowl, open, green or yellow, 3¼" h.	10.00
Sugar bowl, open, green, 4¼" h.	15.50
Sugar bowl, open, pink, 4¼" h.	62.50
Tumbler, juice, footed, green, 3 oz.	41.50
Tumbler, juice, green, 3¾" h., 5 oz.	20.00
Tumbler, water, clear, 4" h., 9 oz.	8.00
Tumbler, water, green, 4" h., 9 oz. (ILLUS.)	17.50
Tumbler, water, pink, 4" h., 9 oz.	55.00
Tumbler, footed, green, 5" h., 9 oz.	20.00
Tumbler, footed, pink, 5" h., 9 oz.	45.00
Tumbler, footed, yellow, 5" h., 9 oz.	12.00
Tumbler, green, 4¾" h., 10 oz.	20.00
Tumbler, green, 5" h., 11 oz.	19.50
Tumbler, yellow, 5" h., 11 oz.	56.00
Tumbler, footed, green, 5¾" h., 11 oz.	45.00
Tumbler, green, 5¼" h., 15 oz.	28.00
Vase, 5¾" h., green	117.00
Vase, 8" h., green	18.00
Water bottle, dark green "White House Vinegar" base, 8½" h.	15.00
Water set: pitcher & 6 tumblers; green, 7 pcs.	200.00

CHERRY BLOSSOM (Process-etched)

Berry set: master bowl & 6 sauce dishes; Delphite, 7 pcs.	84.00
Bowl, berry, 4¾" d., Delphite or pink	9.00
Bowl, berry, 4¾" d., green	11.50
Bowl, cereal, 5¾" d., green	25.50
Bowl, cereal, 5¾" d., pink	19.50
Bowl, soup, 7¾" d., green	37.50
Bowl, soup, 7¾" d., pink	35.50
Bowl, berry, 8½" d., Delphite	28.00
Bowl, berry, 8½" d., green	15.00
Bowl, berry, 8½" d., pink	14.00
Bowl, 9" d., two-handled, Delphite	12.50
Bowl, 9" d., two-handled, green or pink	19.50
Bowl, 9" oval vegetable, Delphite	37.50
Bowl, 9" oval vegetable, green	24.00
Bowl, 9" oval vegetable, pink	20.00
Bowl, fruit, 10½" d., three-footed, green	42.00
Bowl, fruit, 10½" d., three-footed, pink	38.00
Butter dish, cov., green	66.00
Butter dish, cov., pink	57.50
Cake plate, three-footed, green or pink, 10¼" d.	17.50
Coaster, green	8.50
Coaster, pink	11.00

Creamer, Delphite	15.00
Creamer, green or pink	12.50
Cup & saucer, Delphite	16.50
Cup & saucer, green	18.00
Cup & saucer, pink	15.00
Mug, green, 7 oz.	163.00
Mug, pink, 7 oz.	171.00
Pitcher, 6¾" h., 36 oz., overall patt., green	35.50
Pitcher, 6¾" h., 36 oz., overall patt., pink	33.00
Pitcher, 8" h., 36 oz., footed, cone-shaped, patt. top, Delphite	64.50
Pitcher, 8" h., 36 oz., footed, cone-shaped, patt. top, green	37.00
Pitcher, 8" h., 36 oz., footed, cone-shaped, patt. top, pink	35.50
Pitcher, 8" h., 42 oz., patt. top, green	37.50
Pitcher, 8" h., 42 oz., patt. top, pink	29.50
Plate, sherbet, 6" d., Delphite	7.50
Plate, sherbet, 6" d., green or pink	5.00
Plate, salad, 7" d., green	13.00
Plate, salad, 7" d., pink	12.00
Plate, dinner, 9" d., Delphite	10.50
Plate, dinner, 9" d., green	13.50
Plate, dinner, 9" d., pink	11.50
Plate, grill, 9" d., green	17.00
Plate, grill, 9" d., pink	14.00
Platter, 11" oval, Delphite	29.50
Platter, 11" oval, green	24.00
Platter, 11" oval, pink	19.50
Platter, 13" oval, green	32.00
Platter, 13" oval, pink	35.00
Platter, 13" oval, divided, green or pink	31.00
Salt & pepper shakers, green, pr.	950.00
Sandwich tray, handled, Delphite, 10½" d.	13.50
Sandwich tray, handled, green or pink, 10½" d.	12.50
Sherbet, Delphite	11.50
Sherbet, green	12.00
Sherbet, pink	10.00
Sugar bowl, cov., green	20.50
Sugar bowl, cov., pink	19.00
Sugar bowl, open, Delphite	14.50
Sugar bowl, open, green	10.00
Sugar bowl, open, pink	8.50
Tumbler, patt. top, green, 3½" h., 4 oz.	17.00
Tumbler, patt. top, pink, 3½" h., 4 oz.	12.00
Tumbler, juice, footed, overall patt., Delphite or green, 3¾" h., 4 oz.	13.00
Tumbler, juice, footed, overall patt., 3¾" h., 4 oz.	10.50
Tumbler, patt. top, green, 4¼" h., 9 oz.	15.00
Tumbler, patt. top, pink, 4¼" h., 9 oz.	12.50

Tumbler, footed, overall patt., Delphite, 4½" h., 9 oz.	13.50
Tumbler, footed, overall patt., green, 4½" h., 9 oz.	24.50
Tumbler, footed, overall patt., pink, 4½" h., 9 oz.	21.00
Tumbler, patt. top, green, 5" h., 12 oz.	48.00
Tumbler, patt. top, pink, 5" h., 12 oz.	36.00
Water set: pitcher & 6 tumblers; Delphite, 7 pcs.	157.50

JUNIOR SET:

Cherry Blossom Junior Set Pieces

Creamer, Delphite (ILLUS. right)	25.00
Creamer, pink	22.50
Cup & saucer, Delphite (ILLUS. center)	28.50
Cup & saucer, pink	23.50
Plate, 6" d., Delphite	8.00
Plate, 6" d., pink	6.50
Sugar bowl, Delphite (ILLUS. left)	24.50
Sugar bowl, pink	23.00
12 pc. set, Delphite	127.00
14 pc. set, Delphite	168.00
14 pc. set, pink	194.00

CLOVERLEAF (Process-etched)

Cloverleaf Sugar Bowl

Ashtray w/match holder in center, black, 4" d.	46.00
Ashtray w/match holder in center, 5¾" d.	65.50
Bowl, dessert, 4" d., green	11.50
Bowl, dessert, 4" d., pink	7.50
Bowl, dessert, 4" d., yellow	19.00
Bowl, cereal, 5" d., green or yellow	18.00
Bowl, deep salad, 7" d., green	30.00
Bowl, deep salad, 7" d., yellow	35.50
Bowl, 8" d., green	30.00
Candy dish, cov., green	40.50

Candy dish, cov., yellow	82.00
Creamer, footed, black, 3 5/8" h.	12.00
Creamer, footed, green, 3 5/8" h.	7.50
Creamer, footed, yellow, 3 5/8" h.	10.50
Cup & saucer, black or yellow	13.00
Cup & saucer, green	7.00
Cup & saucer, pink	6.50
Plate, sherbet, 6" d., black	23.50
Plate, sherbet, 6" d., green	3.00
Plate, sherbet, 6" d., yellow	4.50
Plate, luncheon, 8" d., black	10.50
Plate, luncheon, 8" d., green or pink	4.50
Plate, luncheon, 8" d., yellow	8.00
Plate, grill, 10¼" d., green	18.00
Plate, grill, 10¼" d., yellow	12.50
Salt & pepper shakers, black, pr.	60.00
Salt & pepper shakers, green, pr.	20.00
Salt & pepper shakers, yellow, pr.	82.50
Sherbet, footed, black, 3" h.	12.50
Sherbet, footed, green or pink, 3" h.	4.50
Sherbet, footed, yellow, 3" h.	8.00
Sugar bowl, open, footed, black, 3 5/8" h.	11.00
Sugar bowl, open, footed, green, 3 5/8" h. (ILLUS.)	7.50
Sugar bowl, open, footed, yellow, 3 5/8" h.	10.00
Tumbler, green, 4" h., 9 oz.	31.00
Tumbler, flared, green, 3¾" h., 10 oz.	25.00
Tumbler, flared, pink, 3¾" h., 10 oz.	17.50
Tumbler, footed, green, 5¾" h., 10 oz.	17.00
Tumbler, footed, yellow, 5¾" h., 10 oz.	20.00

COLONIAL or Knife & Fork (Press-mold)

Colonial Whiskey Tumbler

Bowl, berry, 4½" d., clear	5.50
Bowl, berry, 4½" d., green	8.50
Bowl, berry, 4½" d., pink	6.00
Bowl, cream soup, 4½" d., green	37.00
Bowl, cream soup, 4½" d., pink	31.50
Bowl, cereal, 5½" d., pink	31.00
Bowl, soup, 7" d., clear	13.50
Bowl, soup, 7" d., green	39.50

Bowl, soup, 7" d., pink 32.50
Bowl, 9" d., clear 10.00
Bowl, 9" d., green 18.50
Bowl, 9" d., pink 15.00
Bowl, 10" oval vegetable, clear 12.00
Bowl, 10" oval vegetable, green 22.00
Bowl, 10" oval vegetable, pink 14.00
Butter dish, cov., clear 27.00
Butter dish, cov., green 40.50
Celery or spooner, clear 54.00
Celery or spooner, green 100.00
Celery or spooner, pink 86.50
Creamer or milk pitcher, clear,
    5" h., 8 oz. 7.00
Creamer or milk pitcher, green or
    pink, 5" h., 8 oz. 15.00
Cup & saucer, clear 9.50
Cup & saucer, green, milk white or
    pink 12.00
Goblet, cordial, clear, 3¾" h.,
    1 oz. 14.00
Goblet, cordial, green, 3¾" h.,
    1 oz. 24.00
Goblet, wine, clear, 4½" h.,
    2½ oz. 9.50
Goblet, wine, green, 4½" h.,
    2½ oz. 20.00
Goblet, cocktail, clear, 4" h.,
    3 oz. 9.00
Goblet, cocktail, green, 4" h.,
    3 oz. 17.00
Goblet, claret, clear, 5¼" h.,
    4 oz. 13.00
Goblet, claret, green, 5¼" h.,
    4 oz. 20.00
Goblet, clear, 5¾" h., 8½ oz. 13.50
Goblet, green, 5¾" h., 8½ oz. 21.50
Goblet, pink, 5¾" h., 8½ oz. 16.50
Pitcher, ice lip or plain, 7" h.,
    54 oz., clear 19.50
Pitcher, ice lip or plain, 7" h.,
    54 oz., green 32.50
Pitcher, ice lip or plain, 7" h.,
    54 oz., pink.................... 34.50
Pitcher, ice lip or plain, 7¾" h.,
    68 oz., clear 21.50
Pitcher, ice lip or plain, 7¾" h.,
    68 oz., green 45.00
Pitcher, ice lip or plain, 7¾" h.,
    68 oz., pink 36.00
Plate, sherbet, 6½" d., clear 2.00
Plate, sherbet, 6½" d., green 4.00
Plate, sherbet, 6½" d., pink 2.50
Plate, luncheon, 8½" d., clear 3.00
Plate, luncheon, 8½" d., green or
    pink 5.50
Plate, dinner, 10" d., clear 17.00
Plate, dinner, 10" d., green 45.00
Plate, dinner, 10" d., pink 30.00
Plate, grill, 10" d., clear 15.50
Plate, grill, 10" d., green 18.50
Plate, grill, 10" d., pink 17.50
Platter, 12" oval, clear............ 13.00
Platter, 12" oval, green 14.50

Platter, 12" oval, pink 21.00
Salt & pepper shakers, clear, pr. ... 40.50
Salt & pepper shakers, green, pr.... 115.00
Salt & pepper shakers, pink, pr. 105.00
Sherbet, clear, 3 3/8" h............ 4.50
Sherbet, green, 3 3/8" h. 9.50
Sherbet, pink, 3 3/8" h............. 5.50
Sugar bowl, cov., clear 12.50
Sugar bowl, cov., green 22.50
Sugar bowl, cov., pink 25.00
Sugar bowl, open, clear 6.00
Sugar bowl, open, green or pink ... 10.00
Tumbler, whiskey, clear, 2½" h.,
    1½ oz. 5.50
Tumbler, whiskey, green, 2½" h.,
    1½ oz. 9.50
Tumbler, whiskey, pink, 2½" h,
    1½ oz. (ILLUS.) 7.00
Tumbler, cordial, footed, clear,
    3¼" h., 3 oz. 7.50
Tumbler, cordial, footed, green,
    3¼" h., 3 oz. 16.00
Tumbler, cordial, footed, pink,
    3¼" h., 3 oz. 10.00
Tumbler, juice, green, 3" h.,
    5 oz. 21.00
Tumbler, juice, pink, 3" h.,
    5 oz. 11.00
Tumbler, footed, clear, 4" h.,
    5 oz. 8.00
Tumbler, footed, green, 4" h.,
    5 oz. 23.00
Tumbler, footed, pink, 4" h.,
    5 oz. 11.50
Tumbler, water, clear, 4" h., 9 oz. ... 5.50
Tumbler, water, green, 4" h.,
    9 oz. 19.50
Tumbler, water, pink, 4" h., 9 oz. ... 9.00
Tumbler, footed, clear, 5¼" h.,
    10 oz. 8.50
Tumbler, footed, green, 5¼" h.,
    10 oz. 34.00
Tumbler, footed, pink, 5¼" h.,
    10 oz. 24.50
Tumbler, green, 10 oz. 29.00
Tumbler, pink, 10 oz. 19.00
Tumbler, iced tea, pink, 12 oz. 29.50
Tumbler, lemonade, green, 15 oz. .. 66.00
Tumbler, lemonade, pink, 15 oz..... 40.00

COLUMBIA (Press-mold)
Berry set: master bowl & 6 sauce
    dishes; clear, 7 pcs. 14.00
Bowl, cereal, 5" d., clear 10.00
Bowl, soup, 8" d., clear 11.00
Bowl, salad, 8½" d., clear 11.00
Bowl, 10½" d., ruffled rim, clear ... 14.50
Butter dish, cov., clear 14.00
Cup & saucer, clear 5.00
Plate, bread & butter, 6" d., clear .. 1.50
Plate, luncheon, 9½" d., clear...... 4.00
Plate, luncheon, 9½" d., pink 9.50
Plate, chop, 11" d., clear 6.00
Snack plate, handled, clear 26.50

CUBE or Cubist (Press-mold)

Cube Sugar Bowl

Bowl, dessert, 4½" d., clear	3.50
Bowl, dessert, 4½" d., green or pink	4.00
Bowl, 4½" d., deep, clear	3.00
Bowl, 4½" d., deep, green	4.50
Bowl, 4½" d., deep, pink	4.00
Bowl, salad, 6½" d., clear	5.00
Bowl, salad, 6½" d., green	10.00
Bowl, salad, 6½" d., pink	6.50
Butter dish, cov., green	47.00
Butter dish, cov., pink	42.00
Candy jar, cov., green, 6½" h.	23.50
Candy jar, cov., pink, 6½" h.	20.00
Coaster, green or pink, 3¼" d.	5.00
Creamer, clear or pink, 2" h.	2.00
Creamer, clear, 3" h.	1.00
Creamer, green, 3" h.	5.50
Creamer, pink, 3" h.	5.00
Creamer, open sugar bowl & tray, clear, 3 pcs.	5.50
Cup & saucer, green	8.00
Cup & saucer, pink	5.50
Pitcher, 8¾" h., 45 oz., green	150.00
Pitcher, 8¾" h., 45 oz., pink	125.00
Plate, sherbet, 6" d., clear	1.00
Plate, sherbet, 6" d., green	2.00
Plate, sherbet, 6" d., pink	1.50
Plate, luncheon, 8" d., green	5.00
Plate, luncheon, 8" d., pink	3.00
Powder jar, cov., three-footed, clear	8.50
Powder jar, cov., three-footed, green	15.50
Powder jar, cov., three-footed, pink	12.50
Salt & pepper shakers, green, pr.	25.00
Salt & pepper shakers, pink, pr.	23.00
Sherbet, footed, green	5.50
Sherbet, footed, pink	4.50
Sugar bowl, cov., green, 3" h.	12.00
Sugar bowl, cov., pink, 3" h.	11.00
Sugar bowl, open, clear, 2" h.	1.50
Sugar bowl, open, pink, 2" h.	2.00
Sugar bowl, open, green, 3" h.	6.00
Sugar bowl, open, pink, 3" h. (ILLUS.)	4.50
Tray for 3" h. creamer & sugar bowl, clear, 7½"	3.50
Tumbler, green, 4" h., 9 oz.	36.00
Tumbler, pink, 4" h., 9 oz.	22.50
Water set: pitcher & 4 tumblers; pink, 5 pcs.	200.00

DAISY or Number 620 (Press-mold)

Bowl, berry, 4½" d., amber	6.00
Bowl, berry, 4½" d., clear	3.50
Bowl, cream soup, 4½" d., amber	5.50
Bowl, cream soup, 4½" d., clear	4.00
Bowl, cereal, 6" d., amber	20.50
Bowl, cereal, 6" d., clear	9.00
Bowl, berry, 7 3/8" d., amber	20.50
Bowl, berry, 7 3/8" d., clear	3.50
Bowl, berry, 9 3/8" d., amber	19.50
Bowl, berry, 9 3/8" d., clear	9.00
Bowl, 10" oval vegetable, amber	11.50
Bowl, 10" oval vegetable, clear	5.00
Creamer, footed, amber	6.00
Creamer, footed, clear	3.50
Cup & saucer, amber	5.00
Cup & saucer, clear	3.00
Plate, sherbet, 6" d., amber	1.50
Plate, sherbet, 6" d., clear	1.00
Plate, salad, 7 3/8" d., amber	5.50
Plate, salad, 7 3/8" d., clear	1.50
Plate, luncheon, 8 3/8" d., amber	4.50
Plate, luncheon, 8 3/8" d., clear	3.00
Plate, dinner, 9 3/8" d., amber	5.00
Plate, dinner, 9 3/8" d., clear	3.50
Plate, grill, 10 3/8" d., amber	14.00
Plate, grill, 10 3/8" d., clear	3.50
Plate, 11½" d., amber	9.00
Plate, 11½" d., clear	4.00
Platter, 10¾", amber	9.50
Platter, 10¾", clear	5.50
Relish, three-part, amber, 8 3/8"	16.00
Relish, three-part, clear, 8 3/8"	9.00
Sherbet, amber	5.00
Sherbet, clear	3.00
Sugar bowl, open, footed, amber	5.50
Sugar bowl, open, footed, clear	2.50
Tumbler, footed, amber, 9 oz.	13.50
Tumbler, footed, clear, 9 oz.	6.50
Tumbler, footed, amber, 12 oz.	24.00
Tumbler, footed, clear, 12 oz.	12.00

DIAMOND QUILTED or Flat Diamond (Press-mold)

Bowl, cream soup, 4¾" d., black or blue	14.00
Bowl, cream soup, 4¾" d., green	8.00
Bowl, cream soup, 4¾" d., pink	5.50
Bowl, cereal, 5" d., pink	5.00
Bowl, 5½" d., single handle, black	13.00
Bowl, 5½" d., single handle, green	4.50
Bowl, 5½" d., single handle, pink	6.00
Bowl, 7" d., amber	8.50
Bowl, 7" d., black	18.00
Bowl, 7" d., blue	11.00
Bowl, 7" d., green or pink	6.50
Candlesticks, amber, pr.	10.00
Candlesticks, black or blue, pr.	24.00
Candlesticks, green, pr.	12.00
Candlesticks, pink, pr.	8.50
Candy jar, cov., footed, pink	62.50
Console bowl, rolled edge, pink	28.00

Creamer, amber	5.50
Creamer, black	13.00
Creamer, blue	11.00
Creamer, green or pink	6.50
Cup & saucer, black	12.50
Cup & saucer, green	6.50
Cup & saucer, pink	7.00
Goblet, champagne, pink, 6" h., 9 oz.	11.50
Ice bucket, blue	43.00
Mayonnaise set: three-footed dish, plate & ladle; green, 3 pcs.	27.00
Mayonnaise set: three-footed dish, plate & ladle; pink, 3 pcs.	45.00
Plate, sherbet, 6" d., black	5.00
Plate, sherbet, 6" d., blue	3.50
Plate, sherbet, 6" d., green	2.00
Plate, sherbet, 6" d., pink	3.00
Plate, salad, 7" d., pink	2.00
Plate, luncheon, 8" d., black or blue	10.50
Plate, luncheon, 8" d., green	3.50
Plate, luncheon, 8" d., pink	4.00
Plate, sandwich, 14" d., green	21.00
Punch bowl w/stand, green, 2 pcs.	275.00
Sherbet, amber	3.00
Sherbet, black	8.00
Sherbet, blue	10.00
Sherbet, green	5.50
Sherbet, pink	4.50
Sugar bowl, open, black	10.50
Sugar bowl, open, blue	9.00
Sugar bowl, open, green or pink	5.50
Tumbler, whiskey, green, 1½ oz.	6.00
Tumbler, footed, pink, 6 oz.	6.00
Tumbler, footed, clear, 9 oz.	3.00
Tumbler, iced tea, green, 12 oz.	10.00

DIANA (Press-mold)

Diana Demitasse Cup & Saucer

Bowl, cereal, 5" d., clear	2.50
Bowl, cereal, 5" d., pink	3.50
Bowl, cream soup, 5½" d., amber	6.00
Bowl, cream soup, 5½" d., clear	3.50
Bowl, cream soup, 5½" d., pink	4.00
Bowl, salad, 9" d., amber or pink	6.50
Bowl, salad, 9" d., clear	5.00
Bowl, 12" d., scalloped rim, amber	8.00

Bowl, 12" d., scalloped rim, clear	5.00
Bowl, 12" d., scalloped rim, pink	9.50
Candy jar, cov., round, amber	22.00
Candy jar, cov., round, clear	13.50
Candy jar, cov., round, pink	19.50
Coaster, clear or pink, 3½" d.	3.00
Console bowl, amber, 11" d.	9.50
Console bowl, clear, 11" d.	5.00
Console bowl, pink, 11" d.	7.00
Creamer, oval, amber	4.50
Creamer, oval, clear	3.00
Creamer, oval, pink	5.00
Cup & saucer, demitasse, clear (ILLUS.)	4.50
Cup & saucer, demitasse, pink	16.50
Cup & saucer, amber	7.00
Cup & saucer, clear	4.50
Cup & saucer, pink	10.50
Plate, bread & butter, 6" d., amber	2.50
Plate, bread & butter, 6" d., clear or pink	1.50
Plate, dinner, 9½" d., amber or pink	6.00
Plate, dinner, 9½" d., clear	4.00
Plate, sandwich, 11¾" d., amber or pink	6.50
Plate, sandwich, 11¾" d., clear	4.00
Platter, 12" oval, amber or pink	7.50
Platter, 12" oval, clear	6.00
Salt & pepper shakers, amber, pr.	65.00
Salt & pepper shakers, clear, pr.	19.00
Salt & pepper shakers, pink, pr.	39.00
Sherbet, amber	7.00
Sherbet, pink	9.50
Sugar bowl, open, oval, amber	3.50
Sugar bowl, open, oval, clear	2.50
Sugar bowl, open, oval, pink	4.50
Tumbler, amber or clear, 4 1/8" h., 9 oz.	14.00
Tumbler, pink, 4 1/8" h., 9 oz.	15.00
Junior set: 6 cups, saucers & plates w/round rack; clear, set	39.00
Child's cup, clear	2.50
Child's cup & saucer, clear	3.50

DOGWOOD or Apple Blossom or Wild Rose (Process-etched)

Bowl, cereal, 5½" d., green	16.50
Bowl, cereal, 5½" d., pink	15.00
Bowl, berry, 8½" d., Cremax	32.50
Bowl, berry, 8½" d., green	74.00
Bowl, berry, 8½" d., pink	36.50
Bowl, fruit, 10¼" d., green	117.50
Bowl, fruit, 10¼" d., pink	197.50
Cake plate, heavy solid foot, pink, 11" d.	72.50
Cake plate, heavy solid foot, green, 13" d.	49.50
Cake plate, heavy solid foot, pink, 13" d.	73.50
Creamer, thin, green, 2½" h.	38.00

Creamer, thin, pink, 2½" h.........	10.50
Creamer, thick, pink, 3¼" h........	12.00
Cup & saucer, Cremax..............	34.00
Cup & saucer, green...............	23.50
Cup & saucer, pink	12.50
Dinner service for six, pink, 46 pcs..........................	450.00
Pitcher, 8" h., 80 oz., decorated, green.........................	423.00
Pitcher, 8" h., 80 oz., decorated, pink	124.00
Plate, bread & butter, 6" d., green or pink.........................	4.50
Plate, luncheon, 8" d., clear........	3.00
Plate, luncheon, 8" d., green........	5.00
Plate, luncheon, 8" d., pink	4.50
Plate, dinner, 9¼" d., pink	17.50
Plate, grill, 10½" d., overall patt., green	17.50
Plate, grill, 10½" d., overall patt., pink	14.00
Plate, grill, 10½" d., border design, green	9.50
Plate, grill, 10½" d., border design, pink	11.50
Plate, salver, 12" d., Monax........	19.00
Plate, salver, 12" d., pink	21.50
Platter, 12" oval, pink	245.00
Sherbet, low foot, green	6.00
Sherbet, low foot, pink	18.50
Sugar bowl, open, thin, green, 2½" h..........................	35.50
Sugar bowl, open, thin, pink, 2½" h..........................	10.00
Sugar bowl, open, thick, pink, 3¼" h..........................	9.50
Tumbler, decorated, pink, 3½" h., 5 oz............................	193.00
Tumbler, decorated, green, 4" h., 10 oz............................	70.00
Tumbler, decorated, pink, 4" h., 10 oz............................	22.50
Tumbler, decorated, green, 4¾" h., 11 oz............................	132.00
Tumbler, decorated, pink, 4¾" h., 11 oz............................	31.00
Tumbler, decorated, pink, 5" h., 12 oz............................	34.50
Water set: decorated pitcher & 4 decorated tumblers; pink, 5 pcs...........................	265.00

DORIC (Press-mold)

Bowl, berry, 4½" d., green or pink	5.00
Bowl, cereal, 5½" d., green........	41.00
Bowl, cereal, 5½" d., pink	27.50
Bowl, large berry, 8¼" d., green or pink	13.00
Bowl, 9" d., two-handled, green or pink	12.00
Bowl, 9" oval vegetable, green	12.00
Bowl, 9" oval vegetable, pink	14.00
Butter dish, cov., green...........	68.00

Butter dish, cov., pink	60.00
Cake plate, three-footed, green or pink, 10" d.....................	13.50
Candy dish, three-section, Delphite, 6"	2.50
Candy dish, three-section, green or pink, 6"	5.50
Candy jar, cov., green, 8" h.	30.00
Candy jar, cov., pink, 8" h.	28.00
Coaster, green, 3" d...............	14.00
Coaster, pink, 3" d................	9.50
Creamer, green, 4" h..............	10.50
Creamer, pink, 4" h.	7.50
Cup & saucer, green..............	9.50
Cup & saucer, pink	7.50
Pitcher, 6" h., 36 oz., green or pink	29.50
Pitcher, 7½" h., 48 oz., footed, pink	200.00
Plate, sherbet, 6" d., green	2.50

Doric Sherbet & Plate

Plate, sherbet, 6" d., pink (ILLUS.) ..	3.00
Plate, salad, 7" d., green	12.00
Plate, salad, 7" d., pink	14.00
Plate, dinner, 9" d., green	10.00
Plate, dinner, 9" d., pink	8.00
Plate, grill, 9" d., green	12.00
Plate, grill, 9" d., pink...........	11.00
Platter, 12" oval, green	13.00
Platter, 12" oval, pink	15.00
Relish tray, green or pink, 4 x 4" ...	7.00
Relish tray, green or pink, 4 x 8" ...	9.50
Relish or serving tray, green or pink, 8 x 8"	11.50
Relish, square inserts in metal holder, green	37.00
Relish, square inserts in metal holder, pink	47.00
Salt & pepper shakers, green, pr....	29.00
Salt & pepper shakers, pink, pr.	26.50
Sandwich tray, handled, green, 10" d.........................	10.00
Sandwich tray, handled, pink, 10" d.........................	15.00
Sherbet, footed, Delphite	4.00
Sherbet, footed, green............	8.50
Sherbet, footed, pink (ILLUS.)	9.50
Sugar bowl, cov., green	26.00
Sugar bowl, cov., pink	19.50
Tumbler, green, 4½" h., 9 oz.......	57.00
Tumbler, pink, 4½" h., 9 oz.	28.00

Tumbler, footed, green, 4" h.,
10 oz. 47.00
Tumbler, footed, pink, 4" h.,
10 oz. 25.00
Tumbler, footed, green, 5" h.,
12 oz. 63.50
Tumbler, footed, pink, 5" h.,
12 oz. 45.00

DORIC & PANSY (Press-mold)

Bowl, berry, 4½" d., clear 5.00
Bowl, berry, 4½" d., pink. 6.00
Bowl, berry, 4½" d., ultramarine . . . 9.50
Bowl, large berry, 8" d., pink 17.50
Bowl, large berry, 8" d.,
ultramarine. 60.00
Bowl, 9" d., handled, clear. 16.50
Bowl, 9" d., handled, ultramarine. . . 25.50
Butter dish, cov., ultramarine 490.00
Creamer, ultramarine. 127.00
Cup & saucer, clear 9.50
Cup & saucer, ultramarine 17.00
Plate, sherbet, 6" d., pink 4.50
Plate, sherbet, 6" d., ultramarine . . . 6.50
Plate, salad, 7" d., ultramarine 24.00
Plate, dinner, 9" d., ultramarine 20.50
Salt & pepper shakers, ultramarine,
pr. 337.50
Sugar bowl, open, ultramarine 153.50
Tray, handled, ultramarine, 10" 16.00
Tumbler, ultramarine, 4½" h.,
9 oz. 38.00

PRETTY POLLY PARTY DISHES

Creamer, pink 21.00
Creamer, ultramarine. 29.50
Cup & saucer, pink or ultramarine . . 27.50
Plate, pink 5.50
Plate, ultramarine. 7.00
Sugar bowl, pink 23.50
Sugar bowl, ultramarine 26.50
14 piece set, pink 156.00

ENGLISH HOBNAIL (Hand-finished - not true Depression)

English Hobnail Plate

Bowl, nappy, 4½" d., clear 4.50
Bowl, nappy, 4½" d., green. 8.00
Bowl, nappy, 4½" d., pink 9.00

Bowl, nappy, 4½" sq., clear. 5.50
Bowl, nappy, 4½" sq., pink 12.00
Bowl, cream soup, 4¾" d., clear . . . 8.00
Bowl, 6" d., amber 9.50
Bowl, 6" d., clear 11.00
Bowl, 6" d., green 10.00
Bowl, nappy, 6" sq., green 14.00
Bowl, fruit, 8" d., two-handled, foot-
ed, clear 24.00
Bowl, fruit, 8" d., two-handled, foot-
ed, green 36.50
Bowl, fruit, 8" d., two-handled, foot-
ed, pink 28.00
Bowl, fruit, 8" d., two-handled, foot-
ed, turquoise 44.50
Bowl, nappy, 8" d., clear 10.00
Bowl, nappy, 8" d., green 27.00
Bowl, 12" d., flared, clear. 28.00
Bowl, 12" d., flared, turquoise. 30.00
Candlesticks, amber, 3½" h., pr. . . . 19.50
Candlesticks, blue, 3½" h., pr. 36.50
Candlesticks, clear, 3½" h., pr. 22.00
Candlesticks, green, 3½" h., pr. 27.50
Candlesticks, pink, 3½" h., pr. 23.50
Candlesticks, turquoise, 3½" h.,
pr. 67.50
Candlesticks, clear, 8½" h., pr. 36.50
Candlesticks, pink, 8½" h., pr. 41.00
Candlesticks, turquoise, 8½" h.,
pr. 57.00
Candy dish, cov., cone-shaped,
amber 37.50
Candy dish, cov., cone-shaped,
clear 32.00
Candy dish, cov., cone-shaped,
cobalt blue 252.50
Candy dish, cov., cone-shaped,
green 38.50
Candy dish, cov., cone-shaped,
pink 40.00
Celery tray, clear, 9" l. 12.00
Celery tray, clear, 12" l. 13.50
Cigarette jar, cov., clear 13.00
Cigarette jar, cov., pink 23.50
Cologne bottle, blue or turquoise . . . 37.50
Cologne bottle, clear or pink 24.00
Cologne bottle, green 27.00
Creamer, clear. 6.50
Creamer, green 17.50
Creamer, pink 13.50
Cup & saucer, demitasse, clear 21.50
Cup & saucer, demitasse, pink 38.00
Cup & saucer, clear 6.00
Cup & saucer, pink 21.00
Decanter w/stopper, clear, 20 oz. . . 29.50
Dish, cov., three-footed, blue 14.00
Dish, cov., three-footed, clear 29.00
Dish, cov., three-footed, green 41.00
Dish, cov., three-footed, pink 47.50
Dresser set: cov. puff box & two co-
logne bottles; turquoise, 3 pcs. . . . 120.00
Egg cup, clear 20.00
Goblet, cordial, clear, 1 oz. 10.00
Goblet, wine, clear, 2 oz. 8.50

Goblet, cocktail, clear, 3 oz.	7.50
Goblet, cocktail, green or pink, 3 oz.	15.00
Goblet, claret, blue, 5 oz.	27.00
Goblet, claret, clear, 5 oz.	7.50
Goblet, claret, cobalt blue, 5 oz.	18.00
Goblet, blue, 6¼" h., 8 oz.	34.50
Goblet, clear, 6¼" h., 8 oz.	7.50
Goblet, green, 6¼" h., 8 oz.	17.50
Goblet, turquoise, 6¼" h., 8 oz.	44.00
Lamp, electric, clear, 6¼" h.	29.50
Lamp, electric, green, 6¼" h.	62.00
Lamp, electric, pink, 6¼" h.	42.00
Lamp, electric, amber, 9¼" h.	86.00
Lamp, electric, clear, 9¼" h.	28.00
Lamp, electric, green, 9¼" h.	75.00
Lamp, electric, pink, 9¼" h.	68.50
Lamp, electric, turquoise, 9¼" h.	120.00
Marmalade jar, cov., clear	22.50
Marmalade jar, cov., pink	25.50
Pickle dish, clear, 8" l.	5.00
Pitcher, 39 oz., pink	250.00
Pitcher, ½ gal., straight sides, amber	125.00
Plate, sherbet, 5½" or 6½" d., clear	3.00
Plate, sherbet, 5½" or 6½" d., pink	3.00
Plate, sherbet, 5½" or 6½" d., turquoise	12.00
Plate, 7¼" d., clear (ILLUS.)	4.00
Plate, luncheon, 8" round or square, amber	7.00
Plate, luncheon, 8" round or square, blue	11.00
Plate, luncheon, 8" round or square, clear	6.00
Plate, luncheon, 8" round or square, green	7.50
Plate, luncheon, 8" round or square, turquoise	15.00
Plate, dinner, 10" d., amber or green	18.00
Plate, dinner, 10" d., blue	30.00
Plate, dinner, 10" d., clear	7.00
Puff box, cov., blue	38.00
Puff box, cov., clear	30.00
Puff box, cov., green	27.00
Puff box, cov., turquoise	45.00
Rose bowl, clear, 4"	15.00
Rose bowl, clear, 6"	16.00
Salt & pepper shakers, amber, pr.	54.00
Salt & pepper shakers, clear, pr.	23.50
Salt & pepper shakers, green, pr.	52.00
Salt & pepper shakers, pink, pr.	62.00
Salt & pepper shakers, turquoise, pr.	138.00
Salt dip, footed, amber, 2"	8.50
Salt dip, footed, blue, 2"	13.00
Salt dip, footed, clear, 2"	6.00
Salt dip, footed, cobalt blue, 2"	23.50
Salt dip, footed, green, 2"	16.00
Salt dip, footed, pink, 2"	12.00
Salt dip, footed, turquoise, 2"	23.50

Sherbet, footed, blue	18.00
Sherbet, footed, clear	7.00
Sherbet, footed, green or pink	12.00
Sugar bowl, open, footed or flat, blue	22.50
Sugar bowl, open, footed or flat, clear	7.50
Sugar bowl, open, footed or flat, turquoise	25.00
Tumbler, whiskey, clear, 3 oz.	14.00
Tumbler, clear or green, 3¾" h., 5 oz.	7.50
Tumbler, footed, clear, 7 oz.	10.00
Tumbler, amber, 3¾" h., 9 oz.	6.00
Tumbler, clear, green or pink, 3¾" h., 9 oz.	8.00
Tumbler, footed, clear, 9 oz.	8.00
Tumbler, iced tea, clear, 4" h., 10 oz.	8.00
Tumbler, iced tea, clear, 5" h., 12 oz.	11.00
Tumbler, iced tea, pink, 5" h., 12 oz.	12.00
Tumbler, footed, clear, 12½ oz.	10.00
Tumbler, footed, green, 12½ oz.	15.00
Vase, 5¾" h., clear	22.50
Vase, 7¼" h., clear	45.00
Vase, 7¼" h., green	55.00
Vase, 7¼" h., pink	69.00

FLORAL or Poinsettia (Process-etched)

Floral Pitcher & Tumblers

Bowl, berry, 4" d., green or pink	12.00
Bowl, salad, 7½" d., green	11.50
Bowl, salad, 7½" d., pink	15.00
Bowl, cov. vegetable, 8" d., green or pink	29.00
Bowl, 9" oval vegetable, green	12.50
Bowl, 9" oval vegetable, pink	12.00
Butter dish, cov., green	73.00
Butter dish, cov., pink	70.00
Candlesticks, green, 4" h., pr.	64.50
Candlesticks, pink, 4" h., pr.	55.00
Candy jar, cov., green	31.00
Candy jar, cov., pink	25.50
Canister, cov., Jadite	28.00
Coaster, green or pink, 3¼" d.	7.50
Creamer, green	9.50

Creamer, pink 9.00
Cup, pink...................... 7.00
Cup & saucer, green............. 14.00
Dresser tray, green 250.00
Ice tub, oval, pink, 3½" h......... 495.00
Pitcher, 5½" h., 24 oz., green 420.00
Pitcher, 8" h., 32 oz., cone-shaped,
  green (ILLUS.)................ 24.50
Pitcher, 8" h., 32 oz., cone-shaped,
  pink 21.50
Pitcher, lemonade, 10¼" h., 48 oz.,
  green 225.00
Pitcher, lemonade, 10¼" h., 48 oz.,
  pink 180.00
Plate, sherbet, 6" d., green 4.00
Plate, sherbet, 6" d., pink 3.50
Plate, salad, 8" d., green or pink ... 6.50
Plate, dinner, 9" d., green 12.00
Plate, dinner, 9" d., pink 10.00
Platter, 10¾" oval, green 12.00
Platter, 10¾" oval, pink 10.50
Powder jar, cov., green............ 197.50
Refrigerator dish, cov., green,
  5" sq. 51.50
Refrigerator dish, cov., Jadite,
  5" sq. 15.00
Relish, two-part, oval, green 11.00
Relish, two-part, oval, pink 10.50
Rose bowl, three-legged, green 385.00
Salt & pepper shakers, footed,
  green, 4" h., pr. 36.00
Salt & pepper shakers, footed, pink,
  4" h., pr. 33.00
Salt & pepper shakers, flat, pink,
  6" h., pr. 35.00
Saucer, pink 6.00
Sherbet, green 10.50
Sherbet, pink 10.00
Sugar bowl, cov., green 19.00
Sugar bowl, cov., pink 16.00
Sugar bowl, open, green......... 8.00
Sugar bowl, open, pink 7.50
Tray, closed handles, green or pink,
  6" sq. 13.50
Tumbler, juice, footed, green, 4" h.,
  5 oz. 13.50
Tumbler, juice, footed, pink, 4" h.,
  5 oz. 12.50
Tumbler, water, footed, green,
  4¾" h., 7 oz. (ILLUS.)........... 13.50
Tumbler, water, footed, pink,
  4¾" h., 7 oz. 11.50
Tumbler, green, 4½" h., 9 oz....... 152.50
Tumbler, lemonade, footed, green,
  5¼" h., 9 oz. 36.00
Tumbler, lemonade, footed, pink,
  5¼" h., 9 oz. 29.50
Vase, 6 7/8" h., octagonal, green .. 405.00

(OLD) FLORENTINE or Poppy No. 1 (Process-etched)

Ashtray, green, 5½" 14.50
Ashtray, yellow, 5½"............. 20.00
Bowl, berry, 5" d., clear 6.50

Bowl, berry, 5" d., cobalt blue 13.50
Bowl, berry, 5" d., green or
  yellow 9.50
Bowl, berry, 5" d., pink 11.00
Bowl, cereal, 6" d., green......... 26.00
Bowl, cereal, 6" d., pink 14.00
Bowl, 8½" d., clear or pink 30.00
Bowl, 8½" d., green 22.50
Bowl, 8½" d., yellow 21.50
Bowl, cov. vegetable, 9½" oval,
  green 32.00
Bowl, cov. vegetable, 9½" oval,
  pink 44.50
Bowl, 9½" oval vegetable, green ... 17.00
Bowl, 9½" oval vegetable, pink ... 21.50
Bowl, 9½" oval vegetable, yellow .. 16.00
Butter dish, cov., clear 140.00
Butter dish, cov., green........... 96.00
Butter dish, cov., pink 127.50
Butter dish, cov., yellow 118.00
Candy dish, cov., clear 75.00
Coaster-ashtray, yellow, 3¾" d. 27.50
Creamer, plain rim, clear 5.50
Creamer, plain rim, green or
  yellow 8.50
Creamer, plain rim, pink.......... 9.50
Creamer, ruffled rim, clear 17.00
Creamer, ruffled rim, cobalt blue ... 43.00
Creamer, ruffled rim, green or
  pink 22.50
Cup & saucer, clear 7.00
Cup & saucer, green, pink or
  yellow 9.00
Pitcher, 6½" h., 36 oz., footed,
  clear...................... 29.50
Pitcher, 6½" h., 36 oz., footed,
  green 34.00
Pitcher, 6½" h., 36 oz., footed,
  pink 38.00
Pitcher, 6½" h., 36 oz., footed,
  yellow 42.50

Old Florentine Pitcher & Tumblers

Pitcher, 7½" h., 48 oz., clear
  (ILLUS.)..................... 42.00
Pitcher, 7½" h., 48 oz., green 69.50
Pitcher, 7½" h., 48 oz., yellow 138.00
Plate, sherbet, 6" d., clear 2.50
Plate, sherbet, 6" d., green or
  pink 4.50

Plate, sherbet, 6" d., yellow	3.00
Plate, salad, 8½" d., clear	4.00
Plate, salad, 8½" d., green	5.00
Plate, salad, 8½" d., pink	9.00
Plate, salad, 8½" d., yellow	6.50
Plate, dinner, 10" d., clear	7.00
Plate, dinner, 10" d., green	10.50
Plate, dinner, 10" d., pink	16.00
Plate, dinner, 10" d., yellow	11.00
Plate, grill, 10" d., clear	6.50
Plate, grill, 10" d., green	8.00
Plate, grill, 10" d., pink	11.00
Plate, grill, 10" d., yellow	10.50
Platter, 11½" oval, clear	9.00
Platter, 11½" oval, green	16.00
Platter, 11½" oval, pink or yellow ..	13.50
Salt & pepper shakers, footed, clear, pr.	26.50
Salt & pepper shakers, footed, green, pr.	30.50
Salt & pepper shakers, footed, pink, pr.	45.50
Salt & pepper shakers, footed, yellow, pr.	39.00
Sherbet, footed, clear, 3 oz.	5.00
Sherbet, footed, green, 3 oz.	6.00
Sherbet, footed, pink or yellow, 3 oz.	7.50
Sugar bowl, cov., clear	18.50
Sugar bowl, cov., green	23.00
Sugar bowl, cov., pink or yellow ...	24.50
Sugar bowl, open, clear	6.50
Sugar bowl, open, green	7.00
Sugar bowl, open, pink	7.50
Sugar bowl, open, yellow	9.00
Sugar bowl, open, ruffled rim, clear	20.00
Sugar bowl, open, ruffled rim, pink	23.50
Tumbler, juice, footed, clear, 3¾" h., 5 oz. (ILLUS.)	8.00
Tumbler, juice, footed, green, 3¾" h., 5 oz.	12.50
Tumbler, juice, footed, pink, 3¾" h., 5 oz.	10.50
Tumbler, juice, footed, yellow, 3¾" h., 5 oz.	12.00
Tumbler, water, footed, clear, 4¾" h., 10 oz.	7.50
Tumbler, water, footed, green, 4¾" h., 10 oz.	14.00
Tumbler, water, footed, pink, 4¾" h., 10 oz.	16.00
Tumbler, water, footed, yellow, 4¾" h., 10 oz.	16.50
Tumbler, iced tea, footed, green, 5¼" h., 12 oz.	15.00
Tumbler, iced tea, footed, pink, 5¼" h., 12 oz.	20.50

FLORENTINE or Poppy No. 2 (Process-etched)

Bowl, berry, 4½" d., clear or green	8.50

Bowl, berry, 4½" d., yellow........	12.00
Bowl, cream soup, plain rim, 4¾" d., clear	6.50
Bowl, cream soup, plain rim, 4¾" d., green	9.00
Bowl, cream soup, plain rim, 4¾" d., pink..................	8.50
Bowl, cream soup, plain rim, 4¾" d., yellow................	14.00
Bowl, 5½" d., clear	22.50
Bowl, 5½" d., green	50.00
Bowl, 5½" d., yellow	27.50
Bowl, cereal, 6" d., clear	18.50
Bowl, cereal, 6" d., green..........	25.00
Bowl, cereal, 6" d., yellow	29.00
Bowl, 8" d., clear	5.50
Bowl, 8" d., green	14.50
Bowl, 8" d., yellow	20.00
Bowl, cov. vegetable, 9" oval, clear	26.50
Bowl, cov. vegetable, 9" oval, green	34.00
Bowl, cov. vegetable, 9" oval, yellow	42.00
Bowl, 9" oval vegetable, clear	16.00
Bowl, 9" oval vegetable, green	20.00
Bowl, 9" oval vegetable, yellow	18.50
Butter dish, cov., green	87.50
Butter dish, cov., yellow	115.00
Candlesticks, clear, 2¾" h., pr.	32.50
Candlesticks, green, 2¾" h., pr.....	40.00
Candlesticks, yellow, 2¾" h., pr. ...	36.50
Candy dish, cov., clear	70.00
Candy dish, cov., green...........	85.00
Candy dish, cov., pink	93.50
Candy dish, cov., yellow	131.00
Coaster, green, 3¼" d.	7.50
Coaster, pink or yellow, 3¼" d.	14.50
Coaster-ashtray, clear, 3¾" d.	11.50
Coaster-ashtray, green, 3¾" d......	15.00
Coaster-ashtray, yellow, 3¾" d.	19.50
Coaster-ashtray, clear, 5½" d.	12.00
Coaster-ashtray, green, 5½" d.	19.00
Coaster-ashtray, yellow, 5½" d.	25.00
Compote, 3½", ruffled, clear	12.00
Compote, 3½", ruffled, cobalt blue	42.50
Compote, 3½", ruffled, green	22.00
Compote, 3½", ruffled, pink	8.50

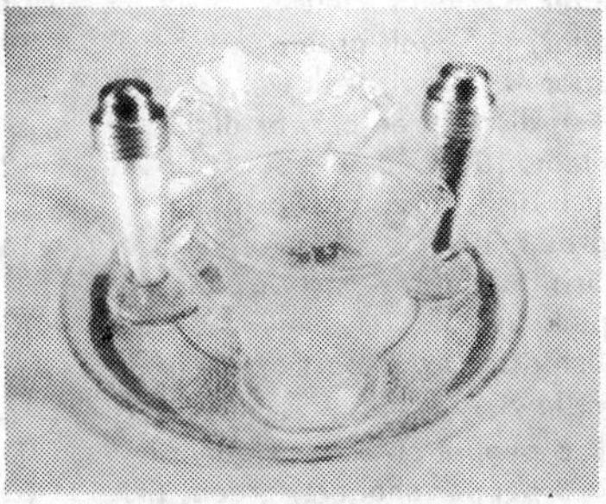

Florentine Condiment Set
Condiment set: creamer, sugar

bowl, salt & pepper shakers &
8½" d. tray; yellow, 5 pcs.
(ILLUS.) 130.00
Creamer, clear 4.50
Creamer, green 6.50
Creamer, yellow 7.00
Cup & saucer, clear 5.50
Cup & saucer, green 8.50
Cup & saucer, yellow 9.00
Custard cup, clear 27.00
Custard cup, green 55.00
Custard cup, yellow 63.50
Gravy boat, yellow 33.00
Gravy boat w/platter, yellow,
11½" oval 67.00
Nut dish, handled, ruffled rim,
cobalt blue 32.00
Nut dish, handled, ruffled rim,
pink 8.50
Pitcher, 6¼" h., 24 oz., cone-
shaped, yellow 90.00
Pitcher, 7½" h., 28 oz., cone-
shaped, clear or green 19.50
Pitcher, 7½" h., 28 oz., cone-
shaped, yellow 21.50
Pitcher, 7½" h., 48 oz., straight
sides, clear 38.00
Pitcher, 7½" h., 48 oz., straight
sides, green 47.00
Pitcher, 7½" h., 48 oz., straight
sides, pink 110.00
Pitcher, 7½" h., 48 oz., straight
sides, yellow 126.00
Pitcher, 8" h., 76 oz., pink 187.50
Pitcher, 8" h., 76 oz., yellow 180.00
Plate, sherbet, 6" d., clear 2.00
Plate, sherbet, 6" d., green 2.50
Plate, sherbet, 6" d., yellow 3.50
Plate, 6¼" d., w/indentation,
yellow 22.50
Plate, salad, 8½" d., clear 4.00
Plate, salad, 8½" d., green 5.00
Plate, salad, 8½" d., yellow 6.00
Plate, dinner, 10" d., clear 7.00
Plate, dinner, 10" d., green 9.00
Plate, dinner, 10" d., yellow 10.00
Plate, grill, 10¼" d., clear 7.00
Plate, grill, 10¼" d., green 12.00
Plate, grill, 10¼" d., yellow 9.50
Platter, 11" oval, clear 8.00
Platter, 11" oval, green 14.00
Platter, 11" oval, yellow 11.00
Relish dish, three-part or plain,
clear, 10" 12.00
Relish dish, three-part or plain,
green, 10" 14.00
Relish dish, three-part or plain,
pink, 10" 13.50
Relish dish, three-part or plain,
yellow, 10" 17.50
Salt & pepper shakers, clear, pr. ... 30.00
Salt & pepper shakers, green, pr. ... 32.50
Salt & pepper shakers, yellow, pr. .. 35.50
Sherbet, clear 4.50

Sherbet, green 6.00
Sherbet, yellow 7.00
Sugar bowl, cov., clear 13.50
Sugar bowl, cov., green 18.00
Sugar bowl, cov., yellow 23.50
Sugar bowl, open, clear or green ... 5.50
Sugar bowl, open, yellow 7.00
Tray, yellow, 8½" d. 60.50
Tumbler, footed, clear, 3¼" h.,
5 oz. 7.50
Tumbler, footed, green, 3¼" h.,
5 oz. 8.50
Tumbler, footed, yellow, 3¼" h.,
5 oz. 10.50
Tumbler, juice, clear or pink,
3½" h., 5 oz. 7.50
Tumbler, juice, green, 3½" h.,
5 oz. 8.00
Tumbler, juice, yellow, 3½" h.,
5 oz. 14.00
Tumbler, green, 3½" h.,
6 oz. 9.00
Tumbler, footed, green, 4" h.,
5 oz. 11.00
Tumbler, water, clear or pink, 4" h.,
9 oz. 8.00
Tumbler, water, cobalt blue, 4" h.,
9 oz. 50.50
Tumbler, water, green, 4" h.,
9 oz. 9.00
Tumbler, water, yellow, 4" h.,
9 oz. 13.50
Tumbler, footed, clear, 4½" h.,
9 oz. 11.50
Tumbler, footed, green, 4½" h.,
9 oz. 17.00
Tumbler, footed, yellow, 4½" h.,
9 oz. 21.00
Tumbler, iced tea, clear, 5" h.,
12 oz. 17.50
Tumbler, iced tea, green, 5" h.,
12 oz. 21.00
Tumbler, iced tea, yellow, 5" h.,
12 oz. 32.00
Vase (or parfait), 6" h., clear 18.00
Vase (or parfait), 6" h., green 33.50
Vase (or parfait), 6" h., yellow 45.00

GEORGIAN or Lovebirds (Process-etched)

(All items in green only.)

Bowl, berry, 4½" d. 4.00
Bowl, cereal, 5¾" d. 14.00
Bowl, 6½" d., deep 49.50
Bowl, berry, 7½" d. 44.00
Bowl, 9" oval vegetable 54.00
Butter dish, cov. 62.00
Creamer, footed, 3" h. 8.00
Creamer, footed, 4" h. 9.50
Cup & saucer 9.00
Hot plate, center design, 5" d. 34.00
Plate, sherbet, 6" d. 3.00
Plate, luncheon, 8" d. 6.00
Plate, dinner, 9¼" d. 17.50

Plate, 9¼" d., center design only . . .   15.00
Platter, 11½" oval, closed handles . .   39.50
Sherbet 8.50
Sugar bowl, cov., footed, 3" h. . . .   30.50
Sugar bowl, open, footed, 3" h. 6.50
Sugar bowl, open, footed, 4" h. 8.00
Tumbler, 4" h., 9 oz. 38.50
Tumbler, 5¼" h., 12 oz. 71.00

HOBNAIL (Press-mold)
Bowl, cereal, 5½" d., clear 5.50
Bowl, salad, 7" d., clear 3.00
Cup & saucer, clear 3.50
Cup & saucer, pink 4.50
Decanter w/stopper, clear, 32 oz. . . .   12.50
Decanter w/stopper, clear w/red
    trim, 32 oz.   15.00
Goblet, water, clear, 10 oz. 4.00
Goblet, iced tea, clear, 13 oz. 5.00
Pitcher, milk, 18 oz., clear 12.50
Pitcher, 67 oz., clear 15.50
Plate, sherbet, 6" d., clear 1.00
Plate, sherbet, 6" d., pink 2.00
Plate, luncheon, 8½" d., clear 2.00
Plate, luncheon, 8½" d., pink 3.50
Sherbet, clear 2.50
Sherbet, pink 3.00
Sugar bowl, footed, clear 3.00
Tumbler, whiskey, clear, 1½ oz. 3.00
Tumbler, wine, footed, clear,
    3 oz. 3.50
Tumbler, juice, clear, 5 oz. 4.00
Tumbler, cordial, footed, clear,
    5 oz. 4.00
Tumbler, water, clear, 9 oz. 4.00
Tumbler, water, clear, 10 oz. 6.00
Tumbler, iced tea, clear, 15 oz. 5.50
Wine set: decanter & 4 footed
    wines; clear w/red trim, 5 pcs. . . .   50.00

HOLIDAY or Buttons and Bows (Press-mold)
(All items in pink unless otherwise indicated.)

Holiday Berry Bowl

Bowl, berry, 5 1/8" d. (ILLUS.) 7.50
Bowl, flat soup, 7¾" d. 30.00
Bowl, berry, 8½" d. 16.50
Bowl, 9½" oval vegetable 14.50
Butter dish, cov. 31.50
Cake plate, three-legged, 10½" d. . . .   55.50
Candlesticks, 3" h., pr. 56.50
Console bowl, 10¾" d. 76.00
Creamer, footed 6.00
Cup & saucer, plain or rayed base . .   7.50

Pitcher, milk, 4¾" h., 16 oz. 45.00
Pitcher, 6¾" h., 52 oz. 24.00
Plate, sherbet, 6" d. 2.50
Plate, dinner, 9" d. 10.00
Plate, chop, 13¾" d. 64.00
Platter, 8 x 11 3/8" oval,
    iridescent 9.50
Platter, 8 x 11 3/8" oval 11.50
Sandwich tray, 10½" d. 9.50
Sherbet 4.50
Sugar bowl, cov. 14.50
Sugar bowl, open 5.50
Tumbler, footed, 4" h., 5 oz. 25.50
Tumbler, footed, 6" h., 9 oz. 64.50
Tumbler, 4" h., 10 oz. 14.50

HOMESPUN or Fine Rib (Press-mold)

(All items in pink only, except child's tea set.)

Bowl, 4½" d., closed handles 4.50
Bowl, cereal, 5" d. 10.00
Bowl, berry, 8¼" d. 14.50
Butter dish, cov. 41.00
Coaster-ashtray 5.00
Creamer, footed 5.50
Cup 5.00
Plate, sherbet, 6" d. 2.00
Plate, dinner, 9¼" d. 9.00
Platter, 13", closed handles 14.00
Saucer 3.00
Sherbet 7.00
Sugar bowl, footed 5.00
Tumbler, footed, 4" h., 5 oz. 5.50
Tumbler, water, 4" h., 9 oz. 11.50
Tumbler, footed, 6¼" h., 9 oz. 8.50
Tumbler, iced tea, 5¼" h., 13 oz. 19.00
Tumbler, footed, 6½" h., 15 oz. 20.00

CHILD'S TEA SET
Cup, pink 25.00
Cup & saucer, clear 17.50
Plate, clear 5.50
Plate, pink 8.50
Saucer, pink 5.00
Teapot, pink 72.00
14 piece set, pink 197.50

IRIS or Iris & Herringbone (Press-mold)
Bowl, berry, 4½" d., beaded rim,
    amber iridescent 6.50
Bowl, berry, 4½" d., beaded rim,
    clear 31.00
Bowl, cereal, 5" d., clear 37.00
Bowl, sauce, 5" d., ruffled rim,
    amber iridescent 6.50
Bowl, sauce, 5" d., ruffled rim,
    clear 5.00
Bowl, soup, 7½" d., amber
    iridescent 26.50
Bowl, soup, 7½" d., clear 86.00
Bowl, berry, 8" d., beaded rim,
    amber iridescent 13.50
Bowl, berry, 8" d., beaded rim,
    clear 63.00

Bowl, salad, 9½" d., amber
  iridescent 7.50
Bowl, salad, 9½" d., clear 8.00
Bowl, fruit, 11" d., ruffled rim,
  amber iridescent 6.50
Bowl, fruit, 11" d., ruffled rim,
  clear 8.00
Bowl, fruit, 11" d., straight rim,
  clear 34.00
Butter dish, cov., amber iridescent .. 29.00
Butter dish, cov., clear 26.50
Candlesticks, two-branch, amber
  iridescent, pr.................. 21.50
Candlesticks, two-branch, clear,
  pr............................ 17.00
Candy jar, cov., clear............. 83.50
Coaster, clear.................... 35.00
Creamer, footed, amber iridescent .. 7.00
Creamer, footed, clear 6.50
Cup & saucer, demitasse, amber
  iridescent 112.50
Cup & saucer, demitasse, clear 91.00
Cup & saucer, demitasse, ruby 92.50
Cup & saucer, amber iridescent..... 11.50
Cup & saucer, clear 14.50
Goblet, wine, amber iridescent,
  4" h., 3 oz. 16.50
Goblet, cocktail, clear, 4¼" h.,
  3 oz.......................... 13.50
Goblet, wine, clear, 4½" h........ 12.00
Goblet, clear, 5¾" h., 4 oz........ 14.00
Goblet, clear, 5¾" h., 8 oz........ 15.50
Lamp shade, blue 31.50
Lamp shade, clear................ 25.00
Lamp shade, pink 28.50
Lamp shade, pink frosted 33.00
Nut set: 11" d. ruffled bowl in metal
  holder, w/cracker & picks; clear,
  set........................... 42.50
Pitcher, 9½" h., footed, amber
  iridescent 26.00
Pitcher, 9½" h., footed, clear 20.00
Plate, sherbet, 5½" d., amber
  iridescent 5.50
Plate, sherbet, 5½" d., clear 7.50
Plate, luncheon, 8" d., amber
  iridescent 7.00
Plate, luncheon, 8" d., clear....... 33.50
Plate, dinner, 9" d., amber
  iridescent 21.00
Plate, dinner, 9" d., clear 31.00
Plate, sandwich, 11¾" d., amber
  iridescent 12.50
Plate, sandwich, 11¾" d., clear 15.00
Sherbet, footed, amber iridescent,
  2½" h........................ 9.00
Sherbet, footed, clear, 2½" h....... 14.00
Sherbet, footed, amber iridescent,
  4" h.......................... 9.00
Sherbet, footed, clear, 4" h....... 11.50
Sugar bowl, cov., footed, amber
  iridescent or clear 13.00
Sugar bowl, open, footed, amber
  iridescent or clear............. 5.50

Tumbler, clear, 4" h. 44.50
Tumbler, footed, amber iridescent
  or clear, 6" h. 11.50
Tumbler, footed, clear, 7" h........ 13.00
Vase, 9" h., amber iridescent 13.00
Vase, 9" h., clear 14.00
Vase, 9" h., pink................. 44.00
Water set: pitcher & 6 tumblers;
  amber iridescent, 7 pcs. 79.00
Water set: pitcher & 6 tumblers;
  clear, 7 pcs.................... 93.00

LACE EDGE or Open Lace (Press-mold)

Lace Edge Butter Dish

Bowl, cereal, 6½" d., clear 5.50
Bowl, cereal, 6½" d., pink 12.00
Bowl, 7¾" d., ribbed, pink 34.00
Bowl, salad or butter dish bottom,
  7¾" d., pink................... 15.00
Bowl, 9½" d., plain or ribbed,
  clear 11.50
Bowl, 9½" d., plain or ribbed,
  pink 13.50
Butter dish or bonbon, cov., pink
  (ILLUS.)...................... 43.00
Candlesticks, pink, pr............. 148.00
Candlesticks, pink frosted, pr....... 44.00
Candy jar, cov., ribbed, clear,
  4" h.......................... 31.00
Candy jar, cov., ribbed, pink,
  4" h.......................... 36.00
Candy jar, cov., ribbed, pink
  frosted, 4" h. 27.50
Compote, cov., 7" d., footed, pink .. 31.00
Compote, open, 7" d., footed,
  pink 17.00
Compote, open, 9" d., footed,
  pink 575.00
Console bowl, three-footed, pink,
  10½" d....................... 125.00
Cookie jar, cov., clear, 5" h. 32.50
Cookie jar, cov., pink, 5" h........ 43.50
Creamer, pink 15.50
Cup & saucer, clear 18.50
Cup & saucer, pink 24.00
Fish bowl, clear, 1 gal., 8 oz. 14.00
Flower bowl w/crystal block, pink .. 20.00
Flower bowl without crystal block,
  pink 14.50
Plate, salad, 7¼" d., pink 13.00
Plate, luncheon, 8¾" d., clear...... 3.50
Plate, luncheon, 8¾" d., pink 12.50
Plate, dinner, 10½" d., clear 17.00
Plate, dinner, 10½" d., pink 18.00

Plate, grill, 10½" d., pink	12.50
Platter, 12¾" oval, pink	17.00
Platter, 12¾" oval, five-part, clear or pink	17.50
Relish dish, pink, deep, 7½" d.	47.00
Relish plate, three-part, clear, 10½" d.	12.50
Relish plate, three-part, pink, 10½" d.	15.00
Relish plate, four-part, solid lace, pink, 13" d.	21.00
Sherbet, footed, pink	57.50
Sugar bowl, open, pink	15.50
Tumbler, pink, 4½" h., 9 oz.	12.00
Tumbler, footed, pink, 5" h., 10½ oz.	46.00
Vase, 7" h., pink	350.00
Vase, 7" h., pink frosted	55.00

LORAIN or Basket or Number 615 (Process-etched)

Lorain Cup & Saucer

Bowl, cereal, 6", green	37.50
Bowl, cereal, 6", yellow	42.50
Bowl, salad, 7¼", green	27.00
Bowl, salad, 7¼", yellow	42.00
Bowl, berry, 8", green	51.50
Bowl, berry, 8", yellow	117.00
Bowl, 9¾" oval vegetable, green	24.00
Bowl, 9¾" oval vegetable, yellow	38.50
Creamer, footed, green	11.00
Creamer, footed, yellow	16.00
Cup & saucer, clear	9.50
Cup & saucer, green	11.50
Cup & saucer, yellow (ILLUS.)	15.50
Plate, sherbet, 5½", green	3.00
Plate, sherbet, 5½", yellow	7.00
Plate, salad, 7¾", clear	5.00
Plate, salad, 7¾", green	6.50
Plate, salad, 7¾", yellow	9.00
Plate, luncheon, 8 3/8", green	12.00
Plate, luncheon, 8 3/8", yellow	18.50
Plate, dinner, 10¼", green	28.50
Plate, dinner, 10¼", yellow	40.50
Platter, 11½", green	19.00
Platter, 11½", yellow	30.50
Relish, four-part, clear, 8"	10.50
Relish, four-part, green, 8"	14.00
Relish, four-part, yellow, 8"	22.50
Sherbet, footed, clear	10.00
Sherbet, footed, green	13.50

Sherbet, footed, yellow	22.00
Sugar bowl, open, footed, clear	9.50
Sugar bowl, open, footed, green	11.00
Sugar bowl, open, footed, yellow	15.50
Tumbler, footed, clear or green, 4¾" h., 9 oz.	14.50
Tumbler, footed, yellow, 4¾" h., 9 oz.	17.50

MADRID (Process-etched)

Madrid Cream Soup Bowls

Ashtray, green, 6" sq.	107.00
Bowl, cream soup, 4¾" d., amber, each (ILLUS.)	9.00
Bowl, sauce, 5" d., amber	4.00
Bowl, sauce, 5" d., blue	6.00
Bowl, sauce, 5" d., clear	3.00
Bowl, sauce, 5" d., green or pink	5.00
Bowl, soup, 7" d., amber or blue	8.00
Bowl, soup, 7" d., clear	7.00
Bowl, soup, 7" d., green	9.50
Bowl, salad, 8" d., amber	11.50
Bowl, salad, 8" d., blue	38.50
Bowl, salad, 8" d., clear	9.00
Bowl, salad, 8" d., green	15.50
Bowl, large berry, 9 3/8" d., amber	14.00
Bowl, large berry, 9 3/8" d., pink	12.50
Bowl, salad, 9½" d., deep, amber	18.50
Bowl, 10" oval vegetable, amber	12.00
Bowl, 10" oval vegetable, blue	26.50
Bowl, 10" oval vegetable, clear	8.00
Bowl, 10" oval vegetable, green	13.00
Butter dish, cov., amber	55.00
Butter dish, cov., clear	135.00
Butter dish, cov., green	63.00
Cake plate, amber, 11¼" d.	12.50
Cake plate, clear, 11¼" d.	14.50
Cake plate, pink, 11¼" d.	10.00
Candlesticks, amber or pink, 2¼" h., pr.	14.00
Candlesticks, clear, 2¼" h., pr.	12.00
Candlesticks, iridescent, 2¼" h., pr.	20.00
Console bowl, flared, amber or iridescent, 11" d.	10.00
Console bowl, flared, clear, 11" d.	13.50
Console bowl, flared, pink, 11" d.	9.00
Console set: bowl & pair of candlesticks; amber, 3 pcs.	33.00
Console set: bowl & pair of candlesticks; iridescent, 3 pcs.	18.00
Console set: bowl & pair of candlesticks; pink, 3 pcs.	23.00
Cookie jar, cov., amber	32.50

Cookie jar, cov., clear	24.00
Cookie jar, cov., pink	29.00
Creamer, amber	5.50
Creamer, blue	13.00
Creamer, clear	4.00
Creamer, green	8.50
Cup & saucer, amber or clear	6.00
Cup & saucer, blue	20.00
Cup & saucer, green	9.00
Cup & saucer, pink	7.00
Gelatin mold, amber, 2 1/8" h.	8.00
Gravy boat & platter, amber . . . . 895.00 to 1,000.00	
Hot dish coaster, amber, 5" d.	31.50
Hot dish coaster, clear, 5" d.	21.00
Hot dish coaster w/indentation, amber	31.50
Hot dish coaster w/indentation, clear	20.00
Hot dish coaster w/indentation, green	29.00
Jam dish, amber, 7" d.	17.00
Jam dish, blue, 7" d.	28.00
Jam dish, clear, 7" d.	7.00
Jam dish, green, 7" d.	15.00
Pitcher, juice, 5½" h., 36 oz., amber	30.00
Pitcher, 8" h., 60 oz., square, amber or pink	34.00
Pitcher, 8" h., 60 oz., square, blue . .	128.00
Pitcher, 8" h., 60 oz., square, green	116.00
Pitcher, 8½" h., 80 oz., jug-type, amber	48.00
Pitcher, 8½" h., 80 oz., jug-type, green	175.00
Pitcher w/ice lip, 8½" h., 80 oz., amber	44.00
Plate, sherbet, 6" d., amber	2.50
Plate, sherbet, 6" d., blue	6.00
Plate, sherbet, 6" d., clear or green	4.50
Plate, sherbet, 6" d., pink	3.00
Plate, salad, 7½" d., amber	7.00
Plate, salad, 7½" d., blue	16.00
Plate, salad, 7½" d., clear	5.00
Plate, salad, 7½" d., green	6.00
Plate, luncheon, 8 7/8" d., amber or clear	5.00
Plate, luncheon, 8 7/8" d., blue	15.00
Plate, luncheon, 8 7/8" d., green . . .	8.50
Plate, dinner, 10½" d., amber or clear	24.50
Plate, dinner, 10½" d., blue	53.00
Plate, dinner, 10½" d., green	28.50
Plate, grill, 10½" d., amber	7.50
Plate, grill, 10½" d., clear	9.00
Plate, grill, 10½" d., green	15.00
Platter, 11½" oval, amber	10.00
Platter, 11½" oval, blue	24.00
Platter, 11½" oval, clear	7.00
Platter, 11½" oval, green	13.00
Relish plate, amber, 10½" d.	12.00
Relish plate, clear, 10½" d.	8.00

Relish plate, pink, 10½" d.	10.00
Salt & pepper shakers, amber, 3½" h., pr.	32.00
Salt & pepper shakers, clear, 3½" h., pr.	40.50
Salt & pepper shakers, green, 3½" h., pr.	57.00
Salt & pepper shakers, footed, amber, 3½" h., pr.	55.00
Salt & pepper shakers, footed, blue, 3½" h., pr.	117.50
Salt & pepper shakers, footed, clear, 3½" h., pr.	36.00

Madrid Salt & Pepper Shakers

Salt & pepper shakers, footed, green, 3½" h., pr. (ILLUS.)	74.00
Sherbet, amber	5.50
Sherbet, blue	9.50
Sherbet, clear	4.00
Sherbet, green	7.00
Sugar bowl, cov., amber	32.00
Sugar bowl, cov., clear	27.00
Sugar bowl, cov., green	43.50
Sugar bowl, open, amber	5.50
Sugar bowl, open, blue	13.00
Sugar bowl, open, clear	3.00
Sugar bowl, open, green	7.00
Tumbler, juice, amber, 3 7/8" h., 5 oz.	11.50
Tumbler, juice, blue, 3 7/8" h., 5 oz.	26.50
Tumbler, juice, green, 3 7/8" h., 5 oz.	48.50
Tumbler, footed, amber, 4" h., 5 oz.	15.50
Tumbler, footed, green, 4" h., 5 oz.	38.50
Tumbler, amber, 4½" h., 9 oz.	11.00
Tumbler, blue, 4½" h., 9 oz.	22.00
Tumbler, clear or pink, 4½" h., 9 oz.	10.00
Tumbler, green, 4½" h., 9 oz.	19.00
Tumbler, footed, amber, 5¼" h., 10 oz.	18.00
Tumbler, footed, green, 5¼" h., 10 oz.	32.00
Tumbler, amber, 5½" h., 12 oz.	15.00

Tumbler, blue, 5½" h., 12 oz. . . . . . .　35.00
Tumbler, green, 5½" h., 12 oz. . . . . .　28.00
Water set: pitcher & 6 tumblers;
　amber, 7 pcs. . . . .　135.00

**MANHATTAN or Horizontal Ribbed
(Press-mold)**
Ashtray, clear, 4" d. . . . .　7.00
Ashtray, clear, 4½" sq. . . . .　25.00
Bowl, sauce, 4½" d., two-handled,
　clear . . . .　5.00
Bowl, berry, 5 3/8" d., two-handled,
　clear . . . .　8.00
Bowl, berry, 5 3/8" d., two-handled,
　pink . . . .　11.00
Bowl, cereal, 5½" d., clear . . . .　5.50
Bowl, large berry, 7½" d., clear . . . .　8.50
Bowl, 8" d., two-handled, clear . . . . .　16.00
Bowl, 8" d., two-handled, pink . . . . .　17.50
Bowl, salad, 9" d., clear . . . .　16.00
Bowl, salad, 9" d., pink . . . .　13.00
Bowl, fruit, 9½" d., clear . . . .　18.50
Bowl, fruit, 9½" d., pink . . . .　22.00
Candleholders, clear, 4½" sq., pr. . . .　10.00
Candlesticks, double, clear, 4¼" h.,
　pr. . . . .　13.50
Candy dish, cov., clear . . . .　21.50
Candy dish, open, three-footed,
　clear . . . .　7.50
Candy dish, open, three-footed,
　pink . . . .　6.00
Coaster, clear, 3½" d. . . . .　8.50
Coaster, pink, 3½" d. . . . .　5.50
Compote, 5¾" h., clear . . . .　17.50
Compote, 5¾" h., pink . . . .　16.50
Creamer, oval, clear or pink . . . .　6.00
Cup & saucer, clear . . . .　15.50
Pitcher, juice, 42 oz., ball tilt-type,
　clear . . . .　15.00
Pitcher, juice, 42 oz., ball tilt-type,
　pink . . . .　28.50
Pitcher, juice, 42 oz., ball tilt-type,
　ruby . . . .　750.00
Pitcher w/ice lip, 80 oz., ball tilt-
　type, clear . . . .　24.50
Pitcher w/ice lip, 80 oz., ball tilt-
　type, pink . . . .　36.00
Plate, sherbet or saucer, 6" d.,
　clear . . . .　3.50
Plate, salad, 8½" d., clear . . . .　7.50
Plate, dinner, 10¼" d., clear . . . . . .　10.50
Plate, sandwich, 14" d., clear . . . . . .　14.50
Relish tray, four-part, clear, 14" d. . .　13.50
Relish tray, five-part, clear w/clear
　inserts, 14" d. . . . .　19.00
Relish tray, five-part, clear w/pink
　inserts, 14" d. . . . .　30.00
Relish tray, five-part, clear w/ruby
　inserts, 14" d. . . . .　36.50
Relish tray, five-part, pink w/pink
　inserts, 14" d. . . . .　33.00
Relish tray insert, clear . . . .　3.50
Relish tray insert, green . . . .　7.50
Relish tray insert, pink . . . .　5.00

Relish tray insert, ruby . . . .　4.50
Salt & pepper shakers, square,
　clear, 2" h., pr. . . . .　13.50
Salt & pepper shakers, square, pink,
　2" h., pr. . . . .　27.50
Sherbet, clear . . . .　5.50
Sherbet, pink . . . .　6.00
Sugar bowl, open, oval, clear or
　pink . . . .　6.00
Tumbler, footed, clear or pink,
　10 oz. . . . .　9.50
Tumbler, footed, green, 10 oz. . . . . .　14.00
Vase, 8" h., clear . . . .　11.50
Water bottle, cov., clear . . . .　16.00
Wine, clear, 3½" h. . . . .　4.50

MAYFAIR or Open Rose (Process-etched)

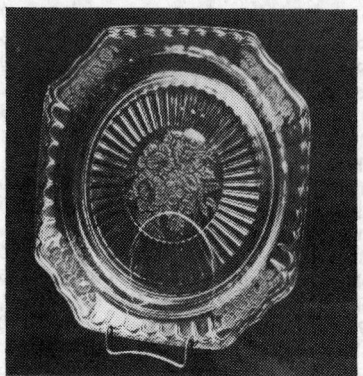

Mayfair Luncheon Plate

Bowl, cream soup, 5", pink . . . .　34.50
Bowl, cream soup, 5", pink
　frosted . . . .　26.00
Bowl, cereal, 5½", blue . . . .　35.00
Bowl, cereal, 5½", pink . . . .　14.00
Bowl, cereal, 5½", pink frosted . . . .　9.00
Bowl, vegetable, 7", blue . . . .　34.50
Bowl, vegetable, 7", pink . . . .　14.50
Bowl, 9½" oval vegetable, blue . . . .　42.50
Bowl, 9½" oval vegetable, pink . . . .　17.00
Bowl, 10" cov. vegetable, blue . . . . .　82.00
Bowl, 10" cov. vegetable, pink . . . . .　66.00
Bowl, 10" open vegetable, blue . . . . .　39.00
Bowl, 10" open vegetable, pink . . . . .　15.00
Bowl, 10" open vegetable, pink
　frosted . . . .　12.00
Bowl, 11¾" d., low, blue . . . .　45.00
Bowl, 11¾" d., low, green . . . .　20.50
Bowl, 11¾" d., low, pink . . . .　33.00
Bowl, fruit, 12" d., deep, scalloped,
　blue . . . .　46.00
Bowl, fruit, 12" d., deep, scalloped,
　green . . . .　21.00
Bowl, fruit, 12" d., deep, scalloped,
　pink . . . .　36.50
Butter dish, cov., blue . . . .　221.00
Butter dish, cov., pink . . . .　49.00
Cake plate, footed, blue, 10" . . . . . .　40.00
Cake plate, footed, pink, 10" . . . . . .　17.50

Cake plate, handled, blue, 12"	43.00
Cake plate, handled, green or pink 12"	31.00
Cake plate, handled, pink frosted, 12"	23.00
Candy jar, cov., blue	142.50
Candy jar, cov., pink	35.00
Candy jar, cov., pink frosted	54.00
Celery dish, blue, 10"	25.00
Celery dish, pink, 10"	22.50
Celery dish, two-part, pink, 10"	118.00
Cookie jar, cov., blue	170.00
Cookie jar, cov., green	587.50
Cookie jar, cov., pink	31.00
Cookie jar, cov., pink frosted	26.50
Creamer, footed, blue	43.50
Creamer, footed, pink	15.50
Creamer, footed, pink frosted	10.00
Cup & saucer, blue	42.50
Cup & saucer, pink	26.00
Decanter w/stopper, pink, 10" h., 32 oz.	108.50
Goblet, pink, 4" h., 2½ oz.	62.50
Goblet, wine, green, 4½" h., 3 oz.	300.00
Goblet, wine, pink, 4½" h., 3 oz. . . .	58.00
Goblet, cocktail, pink, 4" h., 3½ oz.	57.00
Goblet, water, pink, 5¾" h., 9 oz. . . .	41.50
Goblet, water, thin, blue, 7¼" h., 9 oz.	106.00
Goblet, water, thin, pink, 7¼" h., 9 oz.	111.50
Juice set: pitcher & 6 tumblers; pink, 7 pcs.	200.00
Pitcher, juice, 6" h., 37 oz., blue. . . .	92.00
Pitcher, juice, 6" h., 37 oz., clear . . .	15.50
Pitcher, juice, 6" h., 37 oz., pink. . . .	31.00
Pitcher, 8" h., 60 oz., jug-type, blue	108.00
Pitcher, 8" h., 60 oz., jug-type, pink	33.00
Pitcher, 8½" h., 80 oz., jug-type, blue	128.50
Pitcher, 8½" h., 80 oz., jug-type, pink	64.50
Plate (or saucer), 5¾", blue.	13.50
Plate (or saucer), 5¾", pink.	8.00
Plate (or saucer), 5¾", yellow	2.00
Plate, sherbet, 6½" d., pink	8.00
Plate, sherbet, 6½" d., off-center indentation, blue or pink	18.00
Plate, luncheon, 8½", blue	24.50
Plate, luncheon, 8½", green	7.50
Plate, luncheon, 8½", pink (ILLUS.)	16.50
Plate, luncheon, 8½", yellow	72.50
Plate, dinner, 9½", blue	42.00
Plate, dinner, 9½", pink	38.00
Plate, dinner, 9½", yellow	11.00
Plate, grill, 9½", blue or pink	25.00
Platter, 12" oval, open handles, blue	38.00

Platter, 12" oval, open handles, clear	15.50
Platter, 12" oval, open handles, pink	17.00
Relish, four-part, blue, 8 3/8"	37.50
Relish, four-part, pink, 8 3/8"	18.50
Relish, four-part, pink frosted, 8 3/8"	13.50
Salt & pepper shakers, flat, blue, pr.	185.00
Salt & pepper shakers, flat, pink, pr.	44.00
Salt & pepper shakers, flat, pink frosted, pr.	29.50
Sandwich server w/center handle, blue, 12"	44.50
Sandwich server w/center handle, green, 12"	18.00
Sandwich server w/center handle, pink, 12"	27.00
Sandwich server w/center handle, pink frosted, 12"	22.00
Saucer w/cup ring, pink	21.50
Sherbet, flat, blue, 2¼" h.	64.00
Sherbet, flat, pink, 2¼" h.	100.00
Sherbet, footed, pink, 3" h.	12.00
Sherbet, footed, blue, 4¾" h.	58.50
Sherbet, footed, pink, 4¾" h.	45.00
Sugar bowl, open, footed, blue	46.00
Sugar bowl, open, footed, green . . .	98.00
Sugar bowl, open, footed, pink	17.00
Sugar bowl, open, footed, pink frosted	11.00
Tumbler, whiskey, pink, 2¼" h., 1½ oz.	49.00
Tumbler, cocktail, pink, 2 oz.	62.50
Tumbler, juice, footed, pink, 3¼" h., 3 oz.	51.00
Tumbler, juice, blue, 3½" h., 5 oz.	76.00
Tumbler, juice, pink, 3½" h., 5 oz.	34.00
Tumbler, water, blue, 4¼" h., 9 oz.	76.50
Tumbler, water, pink, 4¼" h., 9 oz.	22.00
Tumbler, footed, blue, 5¼" h., 10 oz.	99.00
Tumbler, footed, pink, 5¼" h., 10 oz.	27.50
Tumbler, water, blue, 4¾" h., 11 oz.	85.00
Tumbler, water, pink, 4¾" h., 11 oz.	103.00
Tumbler, iced tea, blue, 5¼" h., 13½ oz.	106.00
Tumbler, iced tea, pink, 5¼" h., 13½ oz.	31.00
Tumbler, iced tea, footed, blue, 6½" h., 15 oz.	109.00
Tumbler, iced tea, footed, pink, 6½" h., 15 oz.	28.50
Vase, 5½ x 8½", sweetpea, hat-shaped, blue.	71.00

Vase, 5½ x 8½", sweetpea, hat-
shaped, pink.................... 112.50
Water set: pitcher & 5 tumblers;
pink, 6 pcs..................... 95.00
Water set: pitcher & 6 tumblers;
pink, 7 pcs..................... 150.00

MISS AMERICA (Press-mold)

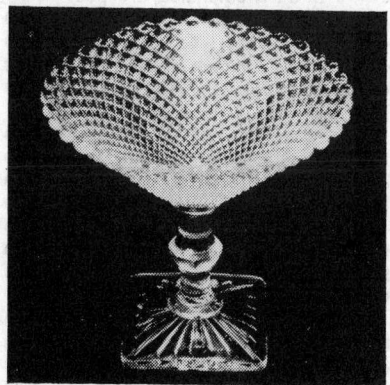

Miss America Compote

Bowl, berry, 4½" d., green 8.00
Bowl, berry, 6¼" d., clear 5.50
Bowl, berry, 6¼" d., green 8.50
Bowl, berry, 6¼" d., pink.......... 12.50
Bowl, fruit, 8" d., curved in at top,
clear..................... 29.00
Bowl, fruit, 8" d., curved in at top,
pink 46.50
Bowl, fruit, 8" d., curved in at top,
red 125.00
Bowl, fruit, 8¾" d., deep, clear 20.50
Bowl, fruit, 8¾" d., deep, pink 40.00
Bowl, 10" oval vegetable, clear.... 11.50
Bowl, 10" oval vegetable, pink 18.00
Butter dish, cov., clear 170.00
Butter dish, cov., pink 347.50
Cake plate, footed, clear, 12" d..... 16.00
Cake plate, footed, pink, 12" d. 28.00
Candy dish, w/metal lid, clear,
6¼" d....................... 17.00
Candy jar, cov., clear, 11½" h...... 47.50
Candy jar, cov., pink, 11½" h. 95.00
Celery tray, clear, 10½" oblong 7.00
Celery tray, pink, 10½" oblong..... 15.50
Coaster, clear, 5¾" d.............. 11.00
Coaster, pink, 5¾" d. 18.50
Compote, 5" d., clear (ILLUS.) 9.00
Compote, 5" d., pink 14.50
Creamer, footed, clear 6.00
Creamer, footed, pink 12.00
Cup, green 7.00
Cup & saucer, clear 9.00
Cup & saucer, pink 18.50
Goblet, wine, clear, 3¾" h., 3 oz. .. 14.50
Goblet, wine, pink, 3¾" h., 3 oz.... 48.50
Goblet, wine, red, 3¾" h., 3 oz. ... 175.00
Goblet, juice, clear, 4¾" h., 5 oz. .. 17.50
Goblet, juice, pink, 4¾" h., 5 oz.... 60.00

Goblet, water, clear, 5½" h.,
10 oz......................... 16.00
Goblet, water, pink, 5½" h.,
10 oz......................... 35.50
Goblet, water, red, 5½" h., 10 oz... 150.00
Pitcher, 8" h., 65 oz., clear........ 45.50
Pitcher, 8" h., 65 oz., pink 84.00
Pitcher w/ice lip, 8½" h., 65 oz.,
clear........................ 47.00
Pitcher w/ice lip, 8½" h., 65 oz.,
pink 94.50
Plate, sherbet, 5¾" d., clear 2.50
Plate, sherbet, 5¾" d., pink 6.00
Plate, 6¾" d., green 5.00
Plate, salad, 8½" d., clear 4.50
Plate, salad, 8½" d., pink 13.50
Plate, dinner, 10¼" d., clear 9.00
Plate, dinner, 10¼" d., pink 18.00
Plate, grill, 10¼" d., clear 6.50
Plate, grill, 10¼" d., pink.......... 13.00
Platter, 12¼" oval, clear........... 9.50
Platter, 12¼" oval, pink........... 16.50
Relish, four-part, clear, 8¾" d 7.00
Relish, four-part, pink, 8¾" d. 13.50
Relish, divided, clear, 11¾" d. 14.50
Relish, divided, pink, 11¾" d. 12.00
Salt & pepper shakers, clear, pr. ... 21.00
Salt & pepper shakers, green, pr... 197.00
Salt & pepper shakers, pink, pr..... 42.50
Sherbet, clear.................... 7.00
Sherbet, pink 11.00
Sugar bowl, open, footed, clear 6.50
Sugar bowl, open, footed, pink..... 13.00
Tumbler, juice, clear, 4" h., 5 oz. ... 11.00
Tumbler, juice, ice blue, 4" h.,
5 oz......................... 15.00
Tumbler, juice, pink, 4" h., 5 oz. ... 32.50
Tumbler, water, clear or green,
4½" h., 10 oz.................. 12.50
Tumbler, water, pink, 4½" h.,
10 oz......................... 24.50
Tumbler, iced tea, clear, 6¾" h.,
14 oz......................... 22.00
Tumbler, iced tea, pink, 6¾" h.,
14 oz......................... 46.00

MODERNTONE (Press-mold)

Ashtray w/match holder, cobalt
blue, 7¾" d..................... 220.00
Ashtray w/match holder, pink,
7¾" d......................... 58.50
Bowl, cream soup, 4¾" d.,
amethyst 10.50
Bowl, cream soup, 4¾" d., cobalt
blue 13.00
Bowl, berry, 5" d., cobalt blue 13.50
Bowl, berry, 5" d., Platonite........ 3.50
Bowl, cream soup w/ruffled rim,
5" d., amethyst 9.00
Bowl, cream soup w/ruffled rim,
5" d., cobalt blue 17.00
Bowl, cereal, 6½" d., cobalt blue ... 44.00
Bowl, large berry, 8¾" d.,
amethyst 13.00

Bowl, large berry, 8¾" d., cobalt
blue 26.00
Bowl, large berry, 8¾" d.,
Platonite 5.00
Butter dish w/metal lid, cobalt
blue 66.00
Cheese dish w/metal lid, cobalt
blue, 7" d...................... 165.00
Creamer, amethyst 7.50
Creamer, cobalt blue 8.50
Creamer, Platonite 3.00
Cup & saucer, amethyst 7.00
Cup & saucer, cobalt blue 10.00
Custard cup, amethyst 9.50
Custard cup, cobalt blue 8.00
Plate, sherbet, 5 7/8" d., amethyst
or cobalt blue................. 3.50
Plate, salad, 6¾" d., amethyst 4.50
Plate, salad, 6¾" d., cobalt blue ... 6.00
Plate, luncheon, 7¾" d., amethyst .. 5.00
Plate, luncheon, 7¾" d., cobalt
blue 6.50
Plate, dinner, 8 7/8" d., amethyst .. 7.00
Plate, dinner, 8 7/8" d., cobalt
blue 10.50
Plate, sandwich, 10½" d.,
amethyst 19.00
Plate, sandwich, 10½" d., cobalt
blue 22.00
Platter, 11" oval, amethyst 17.50
Platter, 11" oval, cobalt blue 24.00
Platter, 11" oval, Platonite 6.00
Platter, 12" oval, amethyst 19.00
Platter, 12" oval, cobalt blue 33.50
Salt & pepper shakers, amethyst,
pr........................... 23.00
Salt & pepper shakers, cobalt blue,
pr........................... 28.00
Salt & pepper shakers, Platonite,
pr........................... 10.00
Sherbet, cobalt blue 8.50
Sherbet, Platonite 2.50
Sugar bowl, open, amethyst or co-
balt blue 8.00
Sugar bowl, open, Platonite 3.00
Sugar bowl w/metal lid, cobalt
blue 28.00
Tea set, "Little Hostess," 16 pcs..... 70.00
Tumbler, whiskey, cobalt blue,
1½ oz.......................... 18.50
Tumbler, juice, amethyst, 5 oz...... 28.00
Tumbler, juice, cobalt blue, 5 oz. ... 25.00
Tumbler, water, amethyst, 4" h.,
9 oz........................... 16.50
Tumbler, water, cobalt blue, 4" h.,
9 oz........................... 17.50
Tumbler, water, Platonite, 4" h.,
9 oz........................... 7.00
Tumbler, iced tea, amethyst,
12 oz.......................... 43.00

MOONSTONE (Press-mold)
Berry set, master bowl & 6 sauce
dishes, 7 pcs.................. 38.00

Bonbon, heart-shaped, w/handle,
6½" w. 7.50
Bowl, berry, 5½" d. 9.00
Bowl, dessert, 5½" d., crimped
rim 6.00
Bowl, 6" w., three-part, cloverleaf-
shaped 7.50
Bowl, 6½" d., two-handled, crimped
rim 7.00
Bowl, 7¾" d., flat................. 8.50
Bowl, 9½" d., crimped 13.50
Candleholders, pr. 13.50
Candy dish, cov., two-handled,
6" d........................... 17.00
Cigarette box, cov., rectangular 15.00
Creamer, footed 5.50
Cup & saucer 8.00
Goblet, 10 oz. 14.00
Plate, sherbet, 6¼" d.............. 2.50
Plate, luncheon, 8" d. 7.00
Plate, sandwich, 10" d., crimped
rim 18.50
Puff box, cov., 4¾" d.............. 15.00
Relish bowl, divided, 7¾" d. 8.50
Sherbet, footed 5.50
Sugar bowl, footed 5.50

Moonstone Bud Vase

Vase, bud, 5½" h. (ILLUS.) 8.50

**MOROCCAN AMETHYST (Early 1960's - not
true Depression)**
Ashtray, 6 7/8" triangle 8.00
Basket 28.00
Bowl, fruit, 4¾" w. 3.50
Bowl, cereal, 5¾" w.............. 4.50
Bowl, 6" d. 7.00
Bowl, 8" oval 10.00
Candy jar, cov. 19.00
Cocktail shaker w/chrome lid,
32 oz.......................... 14.00
Creamer 8.00
Cup.............................. 4.00
Plate, 6" w. 3.00
Plate, salad, 7¼" w. 4.00
Plate, sandwich, w/center handle,
8" oval 8.50

Plate, dinner, 9 3/8" w............. 4.50
Punch cup 4.00
Relish, 8"........................ 6.00
Saucer 2.00
Tidbit server, two-tier 16.50
Tidbit server, three-tier 17.50
Tumbler, juice, 2½" h., 4 oz........ 4.50
Tumbler, old fashioned, 3¼" h.,
  8 oz............................ 6.50
Tumbler, water, 4½" h., 11 oz...... 4.50
Tumbler, iced tea, 16 oz. 8.00

NORMANDIE or Bouquet and Lattice
(Process-etched)

Normandie Cup

Bowl, berry, 5" d., amber or Sun-
  burst iridescent 3.50
Bowl, berry, 5" d., pink............ 4.50
Bowl, cereal, 6½" d., amber 7.00
Bowl, cereal, 6½" d., pink 16.50
Bowl, cereal, 6½" d., Sunburst
  iridescent 6.00
Bowl, large berry, 8½" d., amber .. 13.50
Bowl, large berry, 8½" d., pink 12.50
Bowl, large berry, 8½" d., Sunburst
  iridescent 9.50
Bowl, 10" oval vegetable, amber ... 13.50
Bowl, 10" oval vegetable, pink 21.00
Bowl, 10" oval vegetable, Sunburst
  iridescent 14.50
Creamer, footed, amber or Sunburst
  iridescent 6.00
Creamer, footed, pink 7.00
Cup, Sunburst iridescent (ILLUS.).... 4.50
Cup & saucer, amber 6.00
Cup & saucer, pink 7.00
Pitcher, 8" h., 80 oz., amber 48.00
Pitcher, 8" h., 80 oz., pink 67.50
Plate, sherbet, 6" d., amber or
  pink 2.50
Plate, sherbet, 6" d., Sunburst
  iridescent 2.00
Plate, salad, 8" d., amber or Sun-
  burst iridescent 5.50
Plate, salad, 8" d., pink 6.50
Plate, luncheon, 9¼" d., amber 6.50
Plate, luncheon, 9¼" d., pink 8.00
Plate, luncheon, 9¼" d., Sunburst
  iridescent 9.00
Plate, dinner, 11" d., amber........ 19.50
Plate, dinner, 11" d., pink 41.00
Plate, dinner, 11" d., Sunburst
  iridescent 11.00
Plate, grill, 11" d., amber.......... 8.00

Plate, grill, 11" d., pink............ 16.00
Plate, grill, 11" d., Sunburst
  iridescent 6.50
Platter, 11¾" oval, amber or pink .. 12.50
Platter, 11¾" oval, Sunburst
  iridescent 10.50
Salt & pepper shakers, amber, pr. .. 33.00
Salt & pepper shakers, pink, pr..... 49.00
Sherbet, amber 5.50
Sherbet, clear or pink 5.00
Sherbet, Sunburst iridescent........ 4.50
Sugar bowl, cov., amber 59.00
Sugar bowl, cov., pink 70.00
Sugar bowl, open, amber 4.00
Sugar bowl, open, Sunburst
  iridescent 5.00
Tumbler, juice, amber, 4" h., 5 oz... 13.00
Tumbler, juice, pink, 4" h., 5 oz. ... 28.50
Tumbler, water, amber, 4½" h.,
  9 oz........................... 11.00
Tumbler, water, pink, 4½" h.,
  9 oz........................... 25.00
Tumbler, iced tea, amber, 5" h.,
  12 oz.......................... 17.00
Tumbler, iced tea, pink, 5" h.,
  12 oz. 40.00

NUMBER 612 or Horseshoe (Process-etched)

Bowl, berry, 4½" d., green 17.50
Bowl, berry, 4½" d., yellow........ 16.00
Bowl, cereal, 6½" d., green or
  yellow 17.50
Bowl, salad, 7½" d., green 14.00
Bowl, salad, 7½" d., yellow 17.00
Bowl, large berry, 9½" d., green ... 22.50
Bowl, large berry, 9½" d., yellow .. 27.00
Bowl, 10½" oval vegetable, green .. 16.00
Bowl, 10½" oval vegetable,
  yellow 23.50
Butter dish, cov., green............ 525.00
Candy in metal holder, motif on lid,
  pink 112.00
Creamer, footed, green or yellow .. 12.00
Cup & saucer, green.............. 9.50
Cup & saucer, yellow 10.50
Pitcher, 8½" h., 64 oz., green 165.00
Pitcher, 8½" h., 64 oz., yellow 237.50
Plate, sherbet, 6" d., green 2.50
Plate, sherbet, 6" d., yellow 4.00
Plate, salad, 8 3/8" d., green or
  yellow 6.50
Plate, luncheon, 9 3/8" d., green ... 10.00
Plate, luncheon, 9 3/8" d., yellow .. 7.50
Plate, dinner, 10 3/8" d., green 11.50
Plate, dinner, 10 3/8" d., yellow ... 10.50
Plate, grill, 10 3/8" d., green....... 24.50
Plate, sandwich, 11" d., green...... 10.50
Plate, sandwich, 11" d., yellow 11.50
Platter, 10¾" oval, green 16.00
Platter, 10¾" oval, yellow 14.00
Relish, three-part, footed, green.... 15.50
Relish, three-part, footed, yellow .. 25.00
Sherbet, green 9.00
Sherbet, yellow 12.00

Sugar bowl, open, footed, green ... 10.00
Sugar bowl, open, footed, yellow... 10.00
Tumbler, green, 4¼" h., 9 oz....... 45.00
Tumbler, footed, green or yellow,
  9 oz.......................... 15.50
Tumbler, footed, yellow, 12 oz...... 95.00

OLD CAFE (Press-mold)

Old Cafe Cup & Saucer

Bowl, berry, 3¾" d., clear 2.50
Bowl, berry, 3¾" d., pink.......... 6.00
Bowl, berry, 3¾" d., ruby.......... 3.50
Bowl, nappy, 5" d., handled, clear
  or pink....................... 4.50
Bowl, cereal, 5½" d., pink 5.50
Bowl, cereal, 5½" d., ruby........ 6.00
Bowl, 9" d., handled, clear or
  pink.......................... 7.50
Bowl, 9" d., handled, ruby 8.50
Candy dish, clear, 8" d............ 4.00
Candy dish, pink, 8" d............ 6.50
Candy dish, ruby, 8" d............ 9.50
Cup, pink........................ 3.00
Cup, ruby 5.50
Cup & saucer, pink 12.00
Cup & saucer, ruby cup, clear saucer
  (ILLUS.)...................... 6.50
Olive dish, clear or pink,
  6" oblong...................... 4.50
Pitcher, 8" h., 80 oz., pink 73.00
Plate, sherbet, 6" d., clear 2.50
Plate, sherbet, 6" d., pink 5.50
Plate, dinner, 10" d., pink 15.50
Sherbet, low foot, clear............ 2.00
Sherbet, low foot, pink 7.00
Tumbler, juice, pink, 3" h. 7.00
Tumbler, juice, ruby, 3" h. 5.00
Tumbler, water, pink, 4" h. 7.50
Tumbler, water, ruby, 4" h. 10.00
Vase, 7¼" h., clear 6.50

OYSTER & PEARL (Press-mold)

Bowl, 5¼" heart-shaped, w/handle,
  clear or white w/green 5.00
Bowl, 5¼" heart-shaped, w/handle,
  pink 6.50
Bowl, 5¼" heart-shaped, w/handle,
  white w/pink 10.00

Bowl, 5½" d., w/handle, pink 4.50
Bowl, 5½" d., w/handle, ruby...... 7.50
Bowl, 6½" d., handled, pink 6.00
Bowl, 6½" d., handled, ruby 14.50
Bowl, fruit, 10½" d., clear 14.00
Bowl, fruit, 10½" d., pink.......... 19.50
Bowl, fruit, 10½" d., ruby.......... 32.50
Bowl, fruit, 10½" d., white
  w/green 10.50
Bowl, fruit, 10½" d., white
  w/pink 11.50
Candleholders, ruby, 3½" h., pr. ... 31.50
Candleholders, white w/green,
  3½" h., pr. 11.50
Candleholders, white w/pink,
  3½" h., pr. 15.00
Plate, sandwich, 13½" d., clear 10.50
Plate, sandwich, 13½" d., pink 16.50
Plate, sandwich, 13½" d., ruby 26.00
Relish, divided, clear, 10¼" oval ... 5.00
Relish, divided, pink, 10¼" oval ... 6.00

PARROT or Sylvan (Process-etched)

Bowl, berry, 5" sq., amber 10.00
Bowl, berry, 5" sq., green 17.50
Bowl, soup, 7" sq., amber 25.50
Bowl, soup, 7" sq., green 26.50
Bowl, large berry, 8" sq., green 44.00
Bowl, 10" oval vegetable, amber ... 45.00
Bowl, 10" oval vegetable, green 39.50
Butter dish, cov., green............. 240.00
Creamer, footed, green............. 20.00
Cup, amber...................... 20.00
Cup, green 23.50
Cup & saucer, amber 32.00
Cup & saucer, green 29.50
Plate, sherbet, 5¾" sq., amber..... 9.50
Plate, sherbet, 5¾" sq., green 11.50
Plate, salad, 7½" sq., green 15.50
Plate, dinner, 9" sq., amber........ 25.00
Plate, dinner, 9" sq., green 30.00
Plate, grill, 10½" sq., amber 17.00
Plate, grill, 10½" d., green 19.00
Platter, 11¼" oblong, amber 44.00
Platter, 11¼" oblong, green 27.00
Salt & pepper shakers, green, pr.... 212.00
Sherbet, footed, cone-shaped,
  amber 12.00
Sherbet, footed, cone-shaped,
  green 17.00
Sherbet, green, 4¼" h. 16.50
Sugar bowl, cov., green 106.00
Sugar bowl, open, amber 17.00
Sugar bowl, open, green........... 19.00
Tumbler, green, 4¼" h., 10 oz. 91.00
Tumbler, amber, 5½" h., 10 oz. 109.00
Tumbler, footed, cone-shaped,
  amber, 5¾" h.................. 103.00
Tumbler, footed, cone-shaped,
  green, 5¾" h. 91.00

PATRICIAN or Spoke (Process-etched)

Bowl, cream soup, 4¾" d., amber .. 10.50
Bowl, cream soup, 4¾" d., clear ... 5.50

Bowl, cream soup, 4¾" d., green or
pink 14.50
Bowl, berry, 5" d., amber or
green 7.00
Bowl, berry, 5" d., clear 4.50
Bowl, berry, 5" d., pink 8.50
Bowl, cereal, 6" d., amber 15.50
Bowl, cereal, 6" d., clear 11.50
Bowl, cereal, 6" d., green 18.00
Bowl, cereal, 6" d., pink 16.00
Bowl, large berry, 8½" d., amber .. 29.50
Bowl, large berry, 8½" d., clear.... 16.50
Bowl, large berry, 8½" d., green ... 20.50

Patrician Bowl

Bowl, large berry, 8½" d., pink
(ILLUS.)....................... 16.00
Bowl, 10" oval vegetable, amber or
green 19.00
Bowl, 10" oval vegetable, clear or
pink 13.00
Butter dish, cov., amber 67.50
Butter dish, cov., clear 74.00
Butter dish, cov., green............ 84.50
Butter dish, cov., pink 191.00
Cookie jar, cov., amber 61.00
Cookie jar, cov., clear 68.50
Cookie jar, cov., green 274.00
Creamer, footed, amber 6.50
Creamer, footed, clear 5.50
Creamer, footed, green or pink 8.50
Cup & saucer, amber 13.00
Cup & saucer, clear 8.50
Cup & saucer, green or pink 12.50
Jam dish, amber or green, 6" 21.00
Jam dish, pink, 6"................ 17.00
Pitcher, 8" h., 75 oz., molded han-
dle, amber 83.50
Pitcher, 8" h., 75 oz., molded han-
dle, clear.................... 66.00
Pitcher, 8" h., 75 oz., molded han-
dle, green 73.50
Pitcher, 8" h., 75 oz., molded han-
dle, pink 112.50
Pitcher, 8¼" h., 75 oz., applied han-
dle, amber 81.50
Pitcher, 8¼" h., 75 oz., applied han-
dle, clear.................... 83.00
Pitcher, 8¼" h., 75 oz., applied handle, green 86.00

Pitcher, 8¼" h., 75 oz., applied han-
dle, pink 72.50
Plate, sherbet, 6" d., amber........ 7.00
Plate, sherbet, 6" d., clear 3.00
Plate, sherbet, 6" d., green 5.00
Plate, salad, 7½" d., amber or
green 9.50
Plate, salad, 7½" d., clear 8.50
Plate, salad, 7½" d., pink 10.50
Plate, luncheon, 9" d., amber, green
or pink 7.00
Plate, luncheon, 9" d., clear........ 5.50
Plate, dinner, 10½" d., amber...... 5.50
Plate, dinner, 10½" d., clear 4.50
Plate, dinner, 10½" d., green 32.50
Plate, dinner, 10½" d., pink 17.00
Plate, grill, 10½" d., amber 8.00
Plate, grill, 10½" d., clear 6.50
Plate, grill, 10½" d., green 10.00
Plate, grill, 10½" d., pink 9.00
Platter, 11½" oval, amber 19.00
Platter, 11½" oval, clear........... 12.00
Platter, 11½" oval, green 14.00
Platter, 11½" oval, pink 13.00
Salt & pepper shakers, amber or
clear, pr...................... 40.00
Salt & pepper shakers, green, pr.... 43.50
Salt & pepper shakers, pink, pr. 69.50
Sherbet, amber 7.00
Sherbet, clear.................... 5.00
Sherbet, green or pink 8.50
Sugar bowl, cov., amber 51.50
Sugar bowl, cov., clear 55.00
Sugar bowl, cov., green 45.00
Sugar bowl, cov., pink............ 46.00
Sugar bowl, open, amber or clear .. 6.00
Sugar bowl, open, green 7.00
Sugar bowl, open, pink 8.00
Tumbler, amber, 4" h., 5 oz. 21.00
Tumbler, green, 4" h., 5 oz. 22.00
Tumbler, footed, amber, 5¼" h.,
8 oz.......................... 30.00
Tumbler, footed, clear, 5¼" h.,
8 oz.......................... 32.50
Tumbler, footed, green, 5¼" h.,
8 oz.......................... 37.50
Tumbler, clear or pink, 4½" h.,
9 oz.......................... 17.50
Tumbler, green, 4½" h., 9 oz....... 20.50
Tumbler, iced tea, amber, 5½" h.,
14 oz......................... 28.00
Tumbler, iced tea, clear, 5½" h.,
14 oz......................... 21.50
Tumbler, iced tea, green, 5½" h.,
14 oz......................... 31.50
Tumbler, iced tea, pink, 5½" h.,
14 oz......................... 32.50

PETALWARE (Press-mold)
Bowl, cream soup, 4½" d., plain
Cremax or Monax 7.00
Bowl, cream soup, 4½" d., pink 8.50
Bowl, cereal, 5¾" d., clear or
pink 6.00

Bowl, cereal, 5¾" d., plain or deco-
rated Cremax or Monax 4.50
Bowl, cereal, 5¾" d., Florette 14.50
Bowl, large berry, 9" d., clear 15.00
Bowl, large berry, 9" d., plain
Cremax or Monax 13.00
Bowl, large berry, 9" d., decorated
Cremax or Monax 11.00
Bowl, large berry, 9" d., Florette . . .   26.00
Bowl, large berry, 9" d., pink 12.50
Creamer, footed, clear 2.50
Creamer, footed, plain Cremax or
Monax 4.50
Creamer, footed, decorated Cremax
or Monax 7.00
Creamer, footed, Florette 7.50
Creamer, footed, pink 4.50
Cup, plain Cremax or Monax 4.50
Cup, Florette 4.50
Cup, pink 6.50
Cup & saucer, clear 4.50
Cup & saucer, plain Cremax or
Monax 6.00
Cup & saucer, decorated Cremax or
Monax 4.50
Cup & saucer, Florette 9.50
Cup & saucer, pink 7.00
Lamp shade, Monax, 6" h. 7.50
Lamp shade, pink, 10" h. 8.00
Lamp shade, Monax, 11" h. 13.50
Plate, sherbet, 6" d., clear 1.00
Plate, sherbet, 6" d., plain Cremax
or Monax 2.00
Plate, sherbet, 6" d., decorated
Cremax or Monax 3.00
Plate, sherbet, 6" d., pink 2.50
Plate, salad, 8" d., clear or pink 3.50
Plate, salad, 8" d., plain Cremax or
Monax 4.00
Plate, salad, 8" d., decorated
Cremax or Monax 5.00
Plate, salad, 8" d., Florette 6.50
Plate, dinner, 9" d., clear 3.50
Plate, dinner, 9" d., plain Cremax or
Monax 5.00
Plate, dinner, 9" d., decorated
Cremax or Monax 6.50
Plate, dinner, 9" d., pink 7.00
Plate, salver, 11" d., clear 4.00
Plate, salver, 11" d., plain Cremax
or Monax 6.00
Plate, salver, 11" d., decorated
Cremax or Monax 9.00
Plate, salver, 11" d., Florette 17.00
Plate, salver, 11" d., pink 10.00
Plate, salver, 12" d., plain Cremax
or Monax 7.00
Plate, salver, 12" d., decorated
Cremax or Monax 9.00
Platter, 13" oval, clear 13.00
Platter, 13" oval, plain Cremax or
Monax 13.00
Platter, 13" oval, pink 12.00

Sherbet, low foot, plain Cremax or
Monax, 4½" h. 5.50
Sugar bowl, open, footed, plain
Cremax or Monax 3.50
Sugar bowl, open, footed, decorated
Cremax or Monax 6.00
Sugar bowl, open, footed, Florette . .   7.00
Sugar bowl, open, pink 5.00
Tidbit server, plain Cremax or
Monax 18.00

**PINEAPPLE & FLORAL or Number 618 or
Wildflower (Press-mold)**
Ashtray, clear, 4½" l. 12.00
Bowl, berry, 4¾" d., amber 14.50
Bowl, berry, 4¾" d., clear 31.00
Bowl, cream soup, 4 5/8" d.,
amber 16.50
Bowl, cream soup, 4 5/8" d.,
clear 19.50
Bowl, cereal, 6" d., amber 20.00
Bowl, cereal, 6" d., clear 18.50
Bowl, salad, 7" d., amber or clear . .   5.00
Bowl, 10" oval vegetable, clear 23.00
Compote, diamond-shaped, amber . .   6.00
Compote, diamond-shaped, clear . . .   3.50
Creamer, diamond-shaped, amber . .   8.00
Creamer, diamond-shaped, clear . . .   6.00
Cup & saucer, amber 8.50
Cup & saucer, clear 9.50
Plate, sherbet, 6" d., amber 4.00
Plate, sherbet, 6" d., clear 3.00
Plate, salad, 8 3/8" d., amber or
clear 5.50
Plate, dinner, 9 3/8" d., amber 11.00
Plate, dinner, 9 3/8" d., clear 9.50
Plate, sandwich, 11½" d., amber . . .   10.50
Plate, sandwich, 11½" d., clear 12.00
Plate, 11½" d., w/indentation,
clear 12.00
Platter, 11", closed handles,
amber 11.00
Platter, 11", closed handles, clear . .   10.00
Relish, divided, clear, 11½" 13.00
Sherbet, footed, amber 11.50
Sherbet, footed, clear 15.50
Sugar bowl, open, diamond-shaped,
amber 7.00
Sugar bowl, open, diamond-shaped,
clear 6.00
Tumbler, clear, 4¼" h., 8 oz. 23.00
Tumbler, iced tea, clear, 5" h.,
12 oz. 37.00

PRINCESS (Process-etched)
Ashtray, green, 4½" 48.00
Bowl, berry, 4½", green 16.50
Bowl, berry, 4½", pink 12.00
Bowl, berry, 4½", yellow 35.00
Bowl, cereal, 5", amber or green . . .   20.00
Bowl, cereal, 5", pink 15.50
Bowl, cereal, 5", pink frosted 7.00
Bowl, cereal, 5", yellow 22.00
Bowl, salad, 9" octagon, green 24.00

Bowl, salad, 9" octagon, pink 22.50
Bowl, salad, 9" octagon, yellow 98.00
Bowl, 9½" hat shape, green 27.50
Bowl, 9½" hat shape, green
 frosted 10.00
Bowl, 9½" hat shape, pink 23.00
Bowl, 9½" hat shape, pink frosted.. 12.50
Bowl, 10" oval vegetable, green 17.50
Bowl, 10" oval vegetable, pink 15.50
Bowl, 10" oval vegetable, yellow ... 45.00
Butter dish, cov., green 69.00
Butter dish, cov., pink 66.50
Cake stand, green, 10" 14.00
Cake stand, pink, 10" 15.00
Candy jar, cov., green 36.50
Candy jar, cov., pink 37.50
Coaster, green, 4" 25.00
Coaster, pink, 4" 20.00

Princess Cookie Jar

Cookie jar, cov., green (ILLUS.) 34.00
Cookie jar, cov., green frosted 21.00
Cookie jar, cov., pink 36.00
Creamer, oval, amber 11.00
Creamer, oval, green 12.50
Creamer, oval, pink 9.00
Creamer, oval, yellow 10.00
Cup & saucer, amber 8.50
Cup & saucer, green 12.00
Cup & saucer, pink or yellow 9.50
Pitcher, 6" h., 37 oz., jug-type,
 green 35.00
Pitcher, 6" h., 37 oz., jug-type,
 pink 44.00
Pitcher, 8" h., 60 oz., jug-type,
 amber 49.00
Pitcher, 8" h., 60 oz., jug-type,
 green 36.00
Pitcher, 8" h., 60 oz., jug-type,
 pink 32.00
Pitcher, 8" h., 60 oz., jug-type,
 yellow 60.50
Plate, sherbet, 5½", amber or
 green 5.00
Plate, sherbet, 5½", pink 2.50
Plate, sherbet, 5½", yellow 4.00
Plate, salad, 8", amber or pink 6.00
Plate, salad, 8", green 8.00
Plate, salad, 8", yellow 7.00

Plate, dinner, 9", amber 8.00
Plate, dinner, 9", green 18.50
Plate, dinner, 9", pink 12.50
Plate, dinner, 9", yellow 10.50
Plate, grill, 9", amber or yellow 6.50
Plate, grill, 9", green 11.00
Plate, grill, 9", pink 8.00
Plate, grill, 10½", closed handles,
 amber or yellow 6.00
Plate, grill, 10½", closed handles,
 green 10.00
Plate, grill, 10½", closed handles,
 pink 7.50
Plate, sandwich, 11½", handled,
 green 15.50
Plate, sandwich, 11½", handled,
 pink 11.00
Platter, 12" oval, closed handles,
 green or pink 15.00
Platter, 12" oval, closed handles,
 yellow 48.00
Relish, green, 7½" 60.00
Relish, divided, green, 7½" 18.00
Relish, divided, pink, 7½" 14.00
Salt & pepper shakers, green,
 4½" h., pr. 41.50
Salt & pepper shakers, pink,
 4½" h., pr. 33.50
Salt & pepper shakers, yellow,
 4½" h., pr. 68.00
Salt & pepper (or spice) shakers,
 green, 5½" h., pr. 36.00
Sherbet, footed, green 13.00
Sherbet, footed, pink 10.50
Sherbet, footed, yellow 24.00
Sugar bowl, cov., amber 23.00
Sugar bowl, cov., green 21.50
Sugar bowl, cov., pink 18.50
Sugar bowl, cov., yellow 22.50
Sugar bowl, open, amber or pink ... 7.50
Sugar bowl, open, green or
 yellow 8.50
Sugar bowl, open, pink frosted 4.50
Tumbler, juice, green or yellow,
 3" h., 5 oz. 21.50
Tumbler, juice, pink, 3" h., 5 oz. ... 16.00
Tumbler, water, green, 4" h.,
 9 oz. 20.00
Tumbler, water, pink, 4" h., 9 oz. .. 14.00
Tumbler, water, yellow, 4" h.,
 9 oz. 16.50
Tumbler, footed, green, 5¼" h.,
 10 oz. 22.50
Tumbler, footed, pink or yellow,
 5¼" h., 10 oz. 16.00
Tumbler, footed, green, 6½" h.,
 12½ oz. 68.00
Tumbler, footed, pink, 6½" h.,
 12½ oz. 35.00
Tumbler, footed, yellow, 6½" h.,
 12½ oz. 19.50
Tumbler, iced tea, green, 5¼" h.,
 13 oz. 26.50

Tumbler, iced tea, pink, 5¼" h.,
13 oz. 17.50
Tumbler, iced tea, yellow, 5¼" h.,
13 oz. 18.50
Vase, 8" h., green 21.50
Vase, 8" h., pink 19.50
Vase, 8" h., pink frosted 12.00

QUEEN MARY or Vertical Ribbed (Press-mold)

Queen Mary Cup & Saucer

Ashtray, clear, 2 x 3¾" oval 2.00
Ashtray, clear, 3½" d. 4.00
Ashtray, ruby, 3½" d. 10.00
Bowl, nappy, 4" d., clear 2.00
Bowl, nappy, 4" d., pink 3.50
Bowl, nappy, 4" d., single handle,
clear 2.50
Bowl, nappy, 4" d., single handle,
pink 4.00
Bowl, berry, 5" d., clear or pink 3.50
Bowl, 5½" d., two-handled, clear ... 3.50
Bowl, 5½" d., two-handled, pink ... 4.50
Bowl, cereal, 6" d., clear 4.00
Bowl, cereal, 6" d., pink 8.50
Bowl, nappy, 7" d., clear 5.00
Bowl, nappy, 7" d., pink 9.00
Bowl, large berry, 8¾" d., clear 6.50
Bowl, large berry, 8¾" d., pink 10.50
Butter (or jam) dish, cov., clear 19.00
Butter (or jam) dish, cov., pink 80.00
Candlesticks, two-light, clear,
4½" h., pr. 11.50
Candy dish, cov., clear 15.00
Candy dish, cov., pink 24.50
Celery (or pickle) dish, clear,
5 x 10" oval 6.50
Celery (or pickle) dish, pink,
5 x 10" oval 15.50
Cigarette jar, clear, 2 x 3" oval 3.50
Coaster, clear or pink, 3½" d. 2.50
Coaster-ashtray, clear, 4¼" sq. 3.00
Coaster-ashtray, pink, 4¼" sq. 9.00
Coaster-ashtray, ruby, 4¼" sq. 4.00
Compote, 5¾" d., clear 6.00
Creamer, oval, clear 4.00
Creamer, oval, pink 5.00
Cup & saucer, clear 4.50

Cup & saucer, pink (ILLUS.) 6.50
Plate, sherbet, 6" d., clear 2.00
Plate, sherbet, 6" d., pink 3.00
Plate, 6 5/8" d., clear 2.50
Plate, 6 5/8" d., pink 4.00
Plate, salad, 8½" d., clear 3.50
Plate, salad, 8½" d., pink 4.50
Plate, dinner, 9¾" d., clear 10.50
Plate, dinner, 9¾" d., pink 23.00
Plate, sandwich, 12" d., clear 6.00
Plate, sandwich, 12" d., pink 12.00
Plate, serving, 14" d., clear 7.00
Plate, serving, 14" d., pink 15.00
Relish, three-part, clear, 12" d. 8.00
Relish, three-part, pink, 12" d. 7.00
Relish, four-part, pink, 14" d. 14.00
Salt & pepper shakers, clear, pr. ... 16.00
Sherbet, footed, clear 3.50
Sherbet, footed, pink 5.00
Sugar bowl, open, oval, clear or
pink 4.50
Tumbler, juice, pink, 3½" h.,
5 oz. 6.50
Tumbler, water, clear or pink, 4" h.,
9 oz. 5.00
Tumbler, footed, clear, 5" h.,
10 oz. 12.50
Tumbler, footed, pink, 5" h.,
10 oz. 24.50

RAINDROPS or Optic Design (Press-mold)
(All items listed are green.)

Bowl, cereal, 6" d. 5.00
Creamer 5.50
Cup & saucer 5.00
Plate, sherbet, 6" d. 2.00
Plate, luncheon, 8" d. 3.00
Sherbet 5.00
Sugar bowl, cov. 15.00
Tumbler, whiskey, 1 7/8" h., 1 oz. ... 2.50
Tumbler, 3" h., 4 oz. 3.00
Tumbler, 3 7/8" h., 5 oz. 4.50
Tumbler, 4 1/8" h., 9½ oz. 6.00
Tumbler, 5" h., 10 oz. 7.50

RIBBON (Press-mold)
(While the pattern was also made in black, all items listed are green.)

Bowl, berry, 4" d. 9.00
Bowl, 8" d. 17.00
Candy dish, cov. 23.50
Creamer, footed 6.50
Cup & saucer 6.00
Plate, sherbet, 6¼" d. 2.00
Plate, luncheon, 8" d. 3.50
Salt & pepper shakers, pr. 13.50
Sherbet, footed 4.00
Sugar bowl, open, footed 7.00
Tumbler, 6" h., 10 oz. 15.50

RING or Banded Rings (Press-mold)
Bowl, berry, 5" d., clear 3.00
Bowl, berry, 5" d., clear w/mul-
ticolored bands 3.50

Bowl, berry, 5" d., green	4.50
Bowl, soup, 7" d., clear w/multicolored bands	6.00
Bowl, large berry, 8" d., green	7.50
Butter tub, clear	9.50
Cocktail shaker, clear	10.00
Cocktail shaker, clear w/multicolored bands	17.00
Creamer, footed, clear	3.50
Creamer, footed, green	5.00
Cup & saucer, clear	5.50
Decanter w/stopper, clear	17.00
Decanter w/stopper, clear w/multicolored bands	19.00
Goblet, clear, 7¼" h., 9 oz........	6.00
Goblet, clear w/multicolored bands, 7¼" h., 9 oz.	6.50
Goblet, green, 7¼" h., 9 oz........	8.00
Ice bucket w/tab handles, clear	15.00
Ice bucket w/tab handles, clear w/multicolored bands	17.00
Pitcher, 8" h., 60 oz., clear........	9.00
Pitcher, 8" h., 60 oz., clear w/multicolored bands	12.00
Pitcher, 8½" h., 80 oz., clear.......	12.50
Pitcher, 8½" h., 80 oz., green	23.50
Plate, sherbet, 6¼" d., clear	1.00
Plate, sherbet, 6¼" d., clear w/multicolored bands or green	2.00
Plate, 6½" d., off-center ring, clear	1.50
Plate, 6½" d., off-center ring, clear w/multicolored bands	2.50
Plate, 6½" d., off-center ring, green	3.50
Plate, luncheon, 8" d., green	3.50
Salt & pepper shakers, clear, 3" h., pr...........................	19.00
Sandwich server w/center handle, clear	9.50
Sandwich server w/center handle, green	19.00
Sherbet, low, clear	3.50
Sherbet, low, green	7.50
Sherbet, footed, clear, 4¾" h.......	4.50
Sherbet, footed, clear w/multicolored bands or green, 4¾" h. ...	5.00
Sugar bowl, open, footed, clear	3.50
Sugar bowl, open, footed, clear w/multicolored bands	4.50
Sugar bowl, open, footed, green ...	5.00
Tumbler, whiskey, clear, 2" h., 1½ oz.........................	3.50
Tumbler, whiskey, clear w/multicolored bands, 2" h., 1½ oz.....	6.00
Tumbler, clear, 3½" h., 5 oz.	2.00
Tumbler, clear w/multicolored bands, 3½" h., 5 oz.	4.50
Tumbler, green, 3½" h., 5 oz.......	3.50
Tumbler, clear, 4¼" h., 9 oz.	3.00
Tumbler, green, 4¼" h., 9 oz.......	6.00
Tumbler, clear, 5 1/8" h., 12 oz.....	3.50
Tumbler, clear w/multicolored	

bands or green, 5 1/8" h., 12 oz...........................	4.50
Tumbler, cocktail, footed, clear, 3½" h.........................	4.00
Tumbler, cocktail, footed, clear w/multicolored bands, 3½" h.....	4.50
Tumbler, water, footed, clear, 5½" h.........................	3.50
Tumbler, water, footed, clear w/multicolored bands, 5½" h.....	4.00
Tumbler, water, footed, green, 5½" h.........................	7.00
Tumbler, iced tea, footed, clear, 6½" h.........................	5.00
Tumbler, iced tea, footed, clear w/multicolored bands, 6½" h.....	7.50

ROULETTE or Many Windows (Press-mold)

Bowl, fruit, 9" d., green	10.00
Cup & saucer, green	5.50
Pitcher, 8" h., 64 oz., green or pink	23.00
Plate, sherbet, 6" d., green	2.00
Plate, luncheon, 8½" d., green	5.00
Plate, sandwich, 12" d., green......	8.50
Sherbet, green	4.00
Sherbet, pink	2.50
Tumbler, whiskey, green or pink, 2½" h., 1½ oz.................	6.50
Tumbler, juice, clear, 3¼" h., 5 oz..........................	3.00
Tumbler, juice, green, 3¼" h., 5 oz..........................	12.00
Tumbler, juice, pink, 3¼" h., 5 oz..........................	5.00
Tumbler, water, green, 4 1/8" h., 9 oz..........................	13.50
Tumbler, water, pink, 4 1/8" h., 9 oz..........................	10.50
Tumbler, footed, clear, 5½" h., 10 oz..........................	17.00
Tumbler, footed, green, 5½" h., 10 oz..........................	13.00
Tumbler, iced tea, green, 5 1/8" h., 12 oz..........................	15.50
Tumbler, iced tea, pink, 5 1/8" h., 12 oz..........................	8.50

ROYAL LACE (Process-etched)

Bowl, cream soup, 4¾" d., blue	24.50
Bowl, cream soup, 4¾" d., clear ...	7.50
Bowl, cream soup, 4¾" d., green...	22.50
Bowl, cream soup, 4¾" d., pink ...	12.00
Bowl, berry, 5" d., blue	28.00
Bowl, berry, 5" d., clear	11.00
Bowl, berry, 5" d., green or pink ...	18.50
Bowl, berry, 10" d., blue	42.50
Bowl, berry, 10" d., clear	12.00
Bowl, berry, 10" d., green	24.00
Bowl, berry, 10" d., pink	16.00
Bowl, 10" d., three-footed, rolled edge, blue.....................	225.00
Bowl, 10" d., three-footed, rolled edge, pink.....................	36.50

Bowl, 10" d., three-footed, ruffled edge, blue	185.00
Bowl, 10" d., three-footed, ruffled edge, clear	17.50
Bowl, 10" d., three-footed, ruffled edge, green	41.00
Bowl, 10" d., three-footed, ruffled edge, pink	37.00
Bowl, 10" d., three-footed, straight edge, blue	53.00
Bowl, 10" d., three-footed, straight edge, clear	13.00
Bowl, 10" d., three-footed, straight edge, pink	22.50
Bowl, 11" oval vegetable, blue	41.50
Bowl, 11" oval vegetable, clear	13.50
Bowl, 11" oval vegetable, green or pink	19.00
Butter dish, cov., blue	408.00
Butter dish, cov., clear	58.50
Butter dish, cov., green	234.00
Butter dish, cov., pink	122.00
Candlesticks, rolled edge, blue, pr.	110.00
Candlesticks, rolled edge, clear, pr.	35.50
Candlesticks, rolled edge, green, pr.	56.00
Candlesticks, rolled edge, pink, pr.	37.00
Candlesticks, ruffled edge, blue, pr.	97.50
Candlesticks, ruffled edge, clear, pr.	24.50
Candlesticks, ruffled edge, green, pr.	50.00
Candlesticks, ruffled edge, pink, pr.	38.00
Candlesticks, straight edge, blue, pr.	93.00
Candlesticks, straight edge, clear, pr.	25.00
Candlesticks, straight edge, green, pr.	60.00
Candlesticks, straight edge, pink, pr.	31.00
Cookie jar, cov., blue	227.00
Cookie jar, cov., clear	28.00
Cookie jar, cov., green	55.50
Cookie jar, cov., pink	40.00
Creamer, footed, blue	30.00
Creamer, footed, clear	8.50
Creamer, footed, green	17.50
Creamer, footed, pink	11.00
Cup & saucer, blue	30.50
Cup & saucer, clear	8.00
Cup & saucer, green	18.50
Cup & saucer, pink	12.50
Pitcher, 48 oz., straight sides, blue	104.00
Pitcher, 48 oz., straight sides, clear	35.50
Pitcher, 48 oz., straight sides, green	76.00

Pitcher, 48 oz., straight sides, pink	58.00
Pitcher, 8" h., 68 oz., blue	119.00
Pitcher, 8" h., 68 oz., clear	37.00
Pitcher, 8" h., 68 oz., green	76.50
Pitcher, 8" h., 68 oz., pink	55.00
Pitcher, 8" h., 86 oz., blue	102.50
Pitcher, 8" h., 86 oz., clear	41.00
Pitcher, 8" h., 86 oz., green	76.00
Pitcher, 8½" h., 96 oz., blue	162.00
Pitcher, 8½" h., 96 oz., clear	43.00
Pitcher, 8½" h., 96 oz., green	112.00

Royal Lace Pitcher & Tumblers

Pitcher, 8½" h., 96 oz., pink (ILLUS.)	64.50
Plate, sherbet, 6" d., blue	8.50
Plate, sherbet, 6" d., clear	2.50
Plate, sherbet, 6" d., green	6.00
Plate, sherbet, 6" d., pink	4.50
Plate, luncheon, 8½" d., blue	23.50
Plate, luncheon, 8½" d., clear	5.50
Plate, luncheon, 8½" d., green	11.50
Plate, luncheon, 8½" d., pink	13.50
Plate, dinner, 9 7/8" d., blue	31.00
Plate, dinner, 9 7/8" d., clear	8.50
Plate, dinner, 9 7/8" d., green	20.50
Plate, dinner, 9 7/8" d., pink	13.50
Plate, grill, 9 7/8" d., blue	23.00
Plate, grill, 9 7/8" d., clear	7.00
Plate, grill, 9 7/8" d., green	11.00
Plate, grill, 9 7/8" d., pink	9.00
Platter, 13" oval, blue	37.00
Platter, 13" oval, clear	13.00
Platter, 13" oval, green	28.50
Platter, 13" oval, pink	19.00
Salt & pepper shakers, blue, pr.	191.00
Salt & pepper shakers, clear, pr.	37.50
Salt & pepper shakers, green, pr.	98.00
Salt & pepper shakers, pink, pr.	45.00
Sherbet, footed, blue	28.00
Sherbet, footed, clear	6.50
Sherbet, footed, green	21.00
Sherbet, footed, pink	10.50
Sherbet in metal holder, blue	19.00
Sherbet in metal holder, clear	11.50
Sugar bowl, cov., blue	131.00
Sugar bowl, cov., clear	23.00

Sugar bowl, cov., green	45.50
Sugar bowl, cov., pink	34.50
Sugar bowl, open, blue	22.50
Sugar bowl, open, clear	7.00
Sugar bowl, open, green	13.00
Sugar bowl, open, pink	9.50
Toddy or cider set: cookie jar w/metal lid & 5 roly-poly tumblers; blue, 6 pcs.	150.00
Toddy or cider set: cookie jar w/metal lid, 8 roly-poly tumblers, metal tray & ladle; blue, 11 pcs.	165.00
Tumbler, blue, 3½" h., 5 oz.	30.00
Tumbler, clear, 3½" h., 5 oz.	9.00
Tumbler, green, 3½" h., 5 oz.	20.00
Tumbler, pink, 3½" h., 5 oz.	14.00
Tumbler, blue, 4 1/8" h., 9 oz.	26.50
Tumbler, clear, 4 1/8" h., 9 oz.	8.00
Tumbler, green, 4 1/8" h., 9 oz.	19.50
Tumbler, pink, 4 1/8" h., 9 oz. (ILLUS.)	10.50
Tumbler, blue or green, 4 7/8" h., 10 oz.	56.00
Tumbler, clear, 4 7/8" h., 10 oz.	15.00
Tumbler, pink, 4 7/8" h., 10 oz.	20.00
Tumbler, blue, 5 3/8" h., 12 oz.	47.50
Tumbler, clear, 5 3/8" h., 12 oz.	23.00
Tumbler, green, 5 3/8" h., 12 oz.	43.50
Tumbler, pink, 5 3/8" h., 12 oz.	41.00

ROYAL RUBY (Press-mold)

(All items in ruby red.)

Ashtray, 4½" sq.	4.00
Bowl, berry, 4¼" d.	3.50
Bowl, 5¼" d.	6.00
Bowl, soup, 7½" d.	8.00
Bowl, 8" oval vegetable	23.50
Bowl, berry, 8½" d.	15.00
Bowl, salad, 11½" d.	25.50
Creamer, flat	5.50
Creamer, footed	7.00
Cup & saucer	5.00
Goblet, ball stem	8.00
Lamp	21.00
Pitcher, 22 oz., tilted or upright	24.50
Pitcher, 3 qt., tilted or upright	31.00
Plate, sherbet, 6½" d.	3.50
Plate, salad, 7" d.	3.50
Plate, luncheon, 7¾" d.	4.50
Plate, dinner, 9" d.	7.50
Plate, 13¾" d.	22.00
Playing card box, divided clear base	30.00
Popcorn set, 10" d. serving bowl & eight 5¼" d. bowls, 9 pcs.	150.00
Punch bowl	27.00
Punch cup	2.50
Punch set, punch bowl, base & 12 cups, 14 pcs.	90.00
Sherbet, footed	6.00
Sugar bowl, flat	5.00
Sugar bowl, footed	6.00
Sugar bowl w/slotted lid, footed	14.00
Tumbler, cocktail, 3½ oz.	4.50

Tumbler, juice, 5 oz.	4.00
Tumbler, water, 9 oz.	4.00
Tumbler, water, 10 oz.	5.00
Tumbler, iced tea, 13 oz.	7.50
Vase, 4" h., ball-shaped	3.50
Vase, bud, 5½" h., ruffled top	5.50
Vase, 6½" h., bulbous	6.50
Wine, footed, 2½ oz.	8.00

SANDWICH (Press-mold)

Sandwich Punch Set

Berry set: master bowl & 8 sauce dishes; clear, 9 pcs.	30.00
Bowl, berry, 4 7/8" d., amber or green	3.00
Bowl, berry, 4 7/8" d., clear	5.50
Bowl, berry, 4 7/8" d., pink	4.00
Bowl, 5¼" d., ruby	13.00
Bowl, cereal, 6½" d., amber	9.00
Bowl, cereal, 6½" d., clear	13.00
Bowl, 6½" d., smooth or scalloped, amber	6.50
Bowl, 6½" d., smooth or scalloped, clear	5.00
Bowl, 6½" d., smooth or scalloped, green	26.50
Bowl, 6½" d., smooth or scalloped, ruby	23.00
Bowl, salad, 7" d., clear	6.50
Bowl, salad, 7" d., green	38.50
Bowl, 8" d., smooth or scalloped, clear	7.00
Bowl, 8" d., smooth or scalloped, green	44.00
Bowl, 8" d., smooth or scalloped, pink	7.50
Bowl, 8" d., smooth or scalloped, ruby	28.50
Bowl, 8½" oval vegetable, clear	5.00
Bowl, salad, 9" d., clear	17.00
Butter dish, cov., clear	28.00
Cookie jar, cov., amber	28.00
Cookie jar, cov., clear	26.50
Cookie jar, cov., green	15.00
Creamer, clear	3.50
Creamer, green	15.50
Cup & saucer, amber	5.50
Cup & saucer, clear	3.00
Cup & saucer, green	17.50
Custard cup, clear	4.50
Custard cup, green	2.00

Pitcher, juice, 6" h., 36 oz., clear ... 45.00
Pitcher, juice, 6" h., 36 oz., green .. 87.50
Pitcher w/ice lip, 2 qt., clear 53.00
Pitcher w/ice lip, 2 qt., green 134.00
Plate, 4½" d., clear 6.00
Plate, 4½" d., green 1.50
Plate, dessert, 7" d., amber or
  clear 7.00
Plate, 8" d., clear 3.50
Plate, dinner, 9" d., amber 5.50
Plate, dinner, 9" d., clear 10.00
Plate, dinner, 9" d., green 44.50
Plate, snack, 9" d., clear.......... 4.00
Plate, sandwich, 12" d., amber 9.50
Plate, sandwich, 12" d., clear 16.00
Punch bowl, clear (no base) 13.50
Punch bowl & base, clear 27.00
Punch bowl & base, opaque white .. 15.00
Punch cup, clear or opaque white .. 1.50
Punch set: punch bowl & 9 cups;
  clear, 10 pcs. 30.00
Punch set: punch bowl, base & 12
  cups; clear, 14 pcs. (ILLUS. of
  part) 47.00
Punch set: punch bowl, base & 12
  cups; opaque white, 14 pcs. 25.00
Sherbet, footed, clear 5.00
Sugar bowl, cov., clear 11.50
Sugar bowl, cov., green 16.50
Sugar bowl, open, clear 3.50
Sugar bowl, open, green.......... 14.50
Tumbler, clear, 5 oz. 4.50
Tumbler, green, 5 oz. 3.00
Tumbler, water, clear, 9 oz......... 6.00
Tumbler, water, green, 9 oz. 3.50
Tumbler, footed, amber, 9 oz. 30.00
Tumbler, footed, clear, 9 oz. 15.50
Water set: 36 oz. pitcher & 6 tum-
  blers; green, 7 pcs. 97.00
Water set: 2 qt. ice lip pitcher & 6
  tumblers; green, 7 pcs. 125.00

SHARON or Cabbage Rose (Chip-mold)

Sharon Tumblers

Bowl, berry, 5" d., amber 5.50
Bowl, berry, 5" d., green 8.50
Bowl, berry, 5" d., pink........... 6.50
Bowl, cream soup, 5" d., amber 15.00
Bowl, cream soup, 5" d., green..... 28.50
Bowl, cream soup, 5" d., pink 26.00

Bowl, cereal, 6" d., amber 9.50
Bowl, cereal, 6" d., green......... 16.00
Bowl, cereal, 6" d., pink 15.00
Bowl, soup, 7½" d., amber 25.00
Bowl, soup, 7½" d., pink 27.00
Bowl, berry, 8½" d., amber 4.00
Bowl, berry, 8½" d., green 20.00
Bowl, berry, 8½" d., pink........ 14.50
Bowl, 9½" oval vegetable, amber .. 9.50
Bowl, 9½" oval vegetable, green .. 16.00
Bowl, 9½" oval vegetable, pink 15.00
Bowl, fruit, 10½" d., amber 14.00
Bowl, fruit, 10½" d., green 23.00
Bowl, fruit, 10½" d., pink......... 21.50
Butter dish, cov., amber 37.50
Butter dish, cov., green 66.00
Butter dish, cov., pink 32.00
Cake plate, footed, amber,
  11½" d....................... 17.50
Cake plate, footed, clear, 11½" d... 5.00
Cake plate, footed, green,
  11½" d....................... 45.00
Cake plate, footed, pink, 11½" d. .. 22.00
Candy jar, cov., amber 37.00
Candy jar, cov., green 113.00
Candy jar, cov., pink 33.50
Cheese dish, cov., amber 140.00
Cheese dish, cov., pink 590.00
Creamer, amber 8.50
Creamer, green 13.00
Creamer, pink 10.00
Cup & saucer, amber 8.00
Cup & saucer, green 15.50
Cup & saucer, pink 13.00
Jam dish, amber, 7½" d., 1½" h. .. 24.00
Jam dish, green, 7½" d., 1½" h. ... 23.00
Jam dish, pink, 7½" d., 1½" h. 102.50
Pitcher, 9" h., 80 oz., amber 91.00
Pitcher, 9" h., 80 oz., green 500.00
Pitcher, 9" h., 80 oz., pink 97.50
Pitcher w/ice lip, 9" h., 80 oz.,
  amber 100.00
Pitcher w/ice lip, 9" h., 80 oz.,
  green 325.00
Pitcher w/ice lip, 9" h., 80 oz.,
  pink 91.50
Plate, bread & butter, 6" d.,
  amber 3.00
Plate, bread & butter, 6" d., green .. 4.00
Plate, bread & butter, 6" d., pink ... 3.50
Plate, salad, 7½" d., amber........ 11.00
Plate, salad, 7½" d., green 14.50
Plate, salad, 7½" d., pink 19.00
Plate, dinner, 9¼" d., amber....... 9.00
Plate, dinner, 9¼" d., green 12.00
Plate, dinner, 9¼" d., pink 10.50
Platter, 12¼" oval, amber 10.50
Platter, 12¼" oval, green 14.50
Platter, 12¼" oval, pink 13.50
Salt & pepper shakers, amber, pr. ... 29.00
Salt & pepper shakers, green, pr.... 52.50
Salt & pepper shakers, pink, pr. 30.50
Sherbet, footed, amber 8.50
Sherbet, footed, green............ 23.50

Sherbet, footed, pink	9.50		Sherbet, pink	4.00
Sugar bowl, cov., amber	22.00		Sugar bowl, flat, green	8.50
Sugar bowl, cov., green	38.00		Sugar bowl, footed, green	6.00
Sugar bowl, cov., pink	30.50		Tumbler, water, green, 5" h.,	
Sugar bowl, open, amber	6.00		9 oz.	8.50
Sugar bowl, open, green	9.00			

Sugar bowl, open, pink 8.00
Tumbler, amber, 4" h., 9 oz. (ILLUS.
  left) 19.00
Tumbler, green, 4" h., 9 oz. 52.00
Tumbler, pink, 4" h., 9 oz. 21.00
Tumbler, amber, 5¼" h., 12 oz. 28.00
Tumbler, green, 5¼" h., 12 oz. 66.00
Tumbler, pink, 5¼" h., 12 oz. 32.00
Tumbler, footed, amber, 6½" h.,
  15 oz. (ILLUS. right) 58.00
Tumbler, footed, clear, 6½" h.,
  15 oz. 17.50
Tumbler, footed, pink, 6½" h.,
  15 oz. 38.50
Water set: ice lip pitcher & 8 tum-
  blers; amber, 9 pcs. 245.00

SIERRA or Pinwheel (Press-mold)
Bowl, cereal, 5½" d., green 8.00
Bowl, cereal, 5½" d., pink 6.50
Bowl, berry, 8½" d., green 15.50
Bowl, berry, 8½" d., pink 10.00
Bowl, 9½" oval vegetable, green ... 47.00
Bowl, 9½" oval vegetable, pink 22.50
Butter dish, cov., green 47.00
Butter dish, cov., pink 36.00
Creamer, green 13.00
Creamer, pink 9.00
Cup & saucer, green 12.00
Cup & saucer, pink 11.00
Pitcher, 6½" h., 32 oz., green 80.00
Pitcher, 6½" h., 32 oz., pink 46.00
Plate, dinner, 9" d., green 12.50
Plate, dinner, 9" d., pink 10.50
Platter, 11" oval, green 27.50
Platter, 11" oval, pink 24.00
Salt & pepper shakers, green, pr.... 32.50
Salt & pepper shakers, pink, pr. ... 28.00
Serving tray, two-handled, green .. 13.00
Serving tray, two-handled, pink 9.50
Sugar bowl, cov., green 21.50
Sugar bowl, cov., pink 23.00
Tumbler, footed, green, 4½" h.,
  9 oz. 47.50
Tumbler, footed, pink, 4½" h.,
  9 oz. 30.00

SPIRAL (Press-mold)
Bowl, berry, 4" d., green 7.00
Bowl, berry, 7½" d., green 14.50
Creamer, footed, green 7.00
Cup & saucer, green 6.00
Pitcher, 7 5/8" h., 58 oz., green 26.50
Plate, sherbet, 6" d., green 2.00
Plate, salad, 7½" d., green 3.00
Sandwich server w/center handle,
  green 18.50
Sherbet, green 3.00

SWIRL or Petal Swirl (Press-mold)

Swirl Cup & Saucer

Ashtray, pink, 5 3/8" 6.00
Ashtray, ultramarine, 5 3/8" 10.00
Bowl, cereal, 5¼" d., Delphite 7.50
Bowl, cereal, 5¼" d., pink 4.00
Bowl, cereal, 5¼" d., ultramarine .. 8.00
Bowl, salad, 9" d., Delphite 16.00
Bowl, salad, 9" d., pink 12.50
Bowl, salad, 9" d., ultramarine 15.00
Bowl, fruit, 10" d., closed handles,
  footed, ultramarine 21.00
Butter dish, cov., pink 104.00
Butter dish, cov., ultramarine 161.00
Candlesticks, double, pink, pr. 23.50
Candlesticks, double, ultramarine,
  pr. 27.00
Candy dish, cov., pink 52.50
Candy dish, cov., ultramarine 69.00
Candy dish, open, three-footed,
  pink, 5½" d. 5.50
Candy dish, open, three-footed,
  ultramarine, 5½" d. 13.50
Coaster, pink, 3¼" d., 1" h. 5.50
Coaster, ultramarine, 3¼" d.,
  1" h. 7.50
Console bowl, footed, ultramarine,
  10½" d. 18.50
Creamer, Delphite or pink 6.50
Creamer, ultramarine 9.00
Cup & saucer, Delphite (ILLUS.) 10.50
Cup & saucer, pink 6.50
Cup & saucer, ultramarine 10.00
Plate, sherbet, 6½" d., Delphite 3.00
Plate, sherbet, 6½" d., pink 2.00
Plate, sherbet, 6½" d.,
  ultramarine 4.00
Plate, 7¼" d., ultramarine 7.50
Plate, salad, 8" d., pink 5.00
Plate, salad, 8" d., ultramarine 9.00
Plate, dinner, 9½" d., Delphite 8.00
Plate, dinner, 9½" d., pink 7.00
Plate, dinner, 9½" d., ultramarine .. 9.50
Plate, sandwich, 12½" d., pink 7.50
Plate, sandwich, 12½" d.,
  ultramarine 13.00
Platter, 12" oval, Delphite 19.50

Salt & pepper shakers, ultramarine, pr.	27.50
Sherbet, pink	7.00
Sherbet, ultramarine	9.50
Soup bowl w/lug handles, pink	10.00
Soup bowl w/lug handles, ultramarine	16.00
Sugar bowl, open, Delphite	7.00
Sugar bowl, open, pink	5.00
Sugar bowl, open, ultramarine	9.00
Tumbler, pink, 4" h., 9 oz.	9.50
Tumbler, ultramarine, 4" h., 9 oz.	13.50
Tumbler, footed, pink, 9 oz.	10.00
Tumbler, footed, ultramarine, 9 oz.	19.50
Tumbler, pink, 4¾" h., 12 oz.	13.50
Tumbler, ultramarine, 4¾" h., 12 oz.	26.00
Vase, 6½" h., pink	8.00
Vase, 6½" h., ultramarine	14.50
Vase, 8½" h., ultramarine	17.50

TEA ROOM (Press-mold)

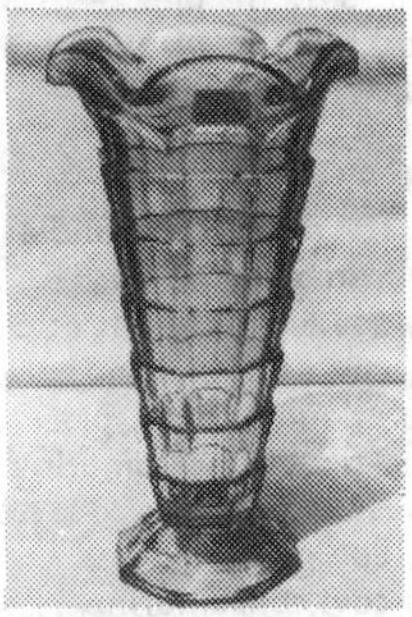

Tea Room Vase

Banana split dish, clear, 7½"	31.00
Banana split dish, green, 7½"	70.50
Banana split dish, pink, 7½"	102.50
Bowl, salad, 8¾" d., green	65.00
Bowl, salad, 8¾" d., pink	48.00
Bowl, 9½" oval vegetable, green	49.00
Bowl, 9½" oval vegetable, pink	39.00
Candlesticks, green, pr.	47.00
Candlesticks, pink, pr.	37.00
Celery or pickle dish, green, 8½"	22.00
Creamer, green, 3¼" h.	15.00
Creamer, clear, 4" h.	9.50
Creamer, green, 4" h.	11.50
Creamer, pink, 4" h.	13.00
Creamer & open sugar bowl on center handled tray, green	55.00
Cup & saucer, green	32.50
Cup & saucer, pink	36.50
Finger bowl, pink	40.00
Goblet, clear, 9 oz.	33.00
Goblet, green, 9 oz.	64.00
Goblet, pink, 9 oz.	52.00
Ice bucket, green	55.50
Ice bucket, pink	47.50
Lamp, electric, green, 9"	46.00
Lamp, electric, pink, 9"	57.50
Marmalade w/notched lid, clear	110.00

Mustard, cov., clear	49.00
Mustard, cov., pink	120.00
Parfait, green	52.00
Parfait, pink	29.00
Pitcher, 64 oz., green	98.00
Pitcher, 64 oz., pink	94.50
Plate, sherbet, 6½" d., green	16.00
Plate, sherbet, 6½" d., pink	16.50
Plate, luncheon, 8¼" d., green	35.00
Plate, luncheon, 8¼" d., pink	31.00
Plate, 10½" d., two-handled, green	45.00
Plate, 10½" d., two-handled, pink	60.00
Plate, sandwich, w/center handle, green	137.00
Plate, sandwich, w/center handle, pink	115.00
Relish, divided, green or pink	15.00
Salt & pepper shakers, green, pr.	52.00
Salt & pepper shakers, pink, pr.	37.50
Sherbet, low footed, green	27.00
Sherbet, low footed, pink	22.00
Sherbet, low, flared edge, clear or pink	17.50
Sherbet, low, flared edge, green	15.50
Sherbet, tall footed, clear	25.50
Sherbet, tall footed, green	31.50
Sherbet, tall footed, pink	28.00
Sugar bowl, open, green, 4" h.	10.00
Sugar bowl, open, pink, 4" h.	8.50
Sugar bowl, cov., footed, clear, 4½" h.	9.00
Sugar bowl, cov., footed, green, 4½" h.	18.50
Sugar bowl, cov., footed, pink, 4½" h.	10.00
Sugar bowl, open, footed, amber, 4½" h.	47.50
Sugar bowl, open, rectangular, green	13.00
Sugar bowl, open, rectangular, pink	11.00
Tray, rectangular, for creamer & sugar bowl, green	29.00
Tray w/center handle, for creamer & sugar bowl, pink	46.00
Tumbler, footed, clear, 6 oz.	28.00
Tumbler, footed, green, 6 oz.	25.00
Tumbler, footed, pink, 6 oz.	23.00
Tumbler, green or pink, 8½ oz.	17.50
Tumbler, footed, green, 9 oz.	24.00
Tumbler, footed, pink, 9 oz.	22.00
Tumbler, footed, green, 11 oz.	38.00
Tumbler, footed, pink, 11 oz.	25.00
Tumbler, footed, clear, 12 oz.	14.50
Tumbler, footed, green or pink, 12 oz.	35.50
Vase, 6" h., ruffled rim, green	69.00
Vase, 6" h., ruffled rim, pink	61.50
Vase, 9" h., ruffled rim, clear	22.00
Vase, 9" h., ruffled rim, green	72.00
Vase, 11" h., ruffled rim, green	121.50
Vase, 11" h., ruffled rim, pink (ILLUS.)	105.00

Vase, 11" h., straight, green 65.00
Vase, 11" h., straight, pink 60.00
Water set: pitcher & 4 tumblers;
green, 5 pcs. 225.00

TWISTED OPTIC (Press-mold)

Bowl, cream soup, 4¾" d., pink 7.00
Bowl, cereal, 5" d., pink 7.00
Bowl, soup or salad, 7" d., green ... 7.00
Candlesticks, amber, 3", pr........ 10.00
Candlesticks, green or pink, 3",
pr................................ 11.50
Candy jar, cov., clear............. 18.00
Candy jar, cov., green 15.50
Candy jar, cov., pink 28.00
Creamer, green 6.00
Creamer, pink 5.00
Creamer, yellow 8.50
Cup & saucer, amber or pink 5.00
Cup & saucer, yellow 9.00
Plate, sherbet, 6" d., amber or
green 1.50
Plate, sherbet, 6" d., pink 2.00
Plate, sherbet, 6" d., yellow 4.00
Plate, salad, 7" d., green 2.50
Plate, 7½ x 9" oval, w/indentation,
yellow 6.50
Plate, luncheon, 8" d., amber or
green 2.50
Plate, luncheon, 8" d., pink 3.00
Plate, luncheon, 8" d., yellow 4.50
Preserve jar w/slotted lid, amber or
pink 12.00
Preserve jar w/slotted lid, clear 18.00
Preserve jar w/slotted lid, green ... 16.50
Sandwich server w/center handle,
amber or green 14.50
Sandwich server w/center handle,
yellow 27.50
Sandwich server, two-handled,
amber 13.00
Sandwich server, two-handled,
yellow 20.00
Sherbet, amber, green or pink 4.00
Sherbet, yellow 5.50
Sugar bowl, open, green........... 4.00
Sugar bowl, open, pink 5.00

WATERFORD or Waffle (Press-mold)

Ashtray, clear, 4" 5.00
Bowl, berry, 4¾" d., clear 3.50
Bowl, berry, 4¾" d., pink......... 8.00
Bowl, cereal, 5¼" d., clear 11.00
Bowl, cereal, 5¼" d., pink 16.50
Bowl, berry, 8¼" d., clear 7.00
Bowl, berry, 8¼" d., pink 11.00
Butter dish, cov., clear 18.50
Butter dish, cov., pink 152.50
Cake plate, handled, clear,
10¼" d........................ 4.00
Cake plate, handled, pink,
10¼" d........................ 8.50
Coaster, clear, 4" d............... 1.50
Creamer, oval, clear 2.50
Cup & saucer, clear 5.50

Cup & saucer, pink 12.00
Dinner service for eight: dinner
plates, cups & saucers & 10 oz.
tumblers; clear, 32 pcs........... 144.00
Goblet, clear, 5¼" h. 11.00
Goblet, clear, 5½" h. 18.00
Goblet, pink, 5½" h. 40.00
Lamp, clear, 4" h................. 30.50
Pitcher, juice, 42 oz., tilt-type,
clear 16.50
Pitcher w/ice lip, 80 oz., clear...... 23.50
Pitcher w/ice lip, 80 oz., pink 100.00
Plate, sherbet, 6" d., clear 1.50
Plate, sherbet, 6" d., pink 5.00

Waterford Plates

Plate, salad, 7½" d., clear
(ILLUS.)........................ 3.00
Plate, salad, 7½" d., pink 6.00
Plate, dinner, 9 5/8" d., clear 5.50
Plate, dinner, 9 5/8" d., pink 11.00
Plate, sandwich, 13¾" d., clear
(ILLUS.)........................ 7.00
Plate, sandwich, 13¾" d., pink 18.50
Relish, five-section, clear, 13¾" d... 15.00
Relish, five-section, clear w/ruby in-
serts, 13¾" d. 26.50
Relish, five-section, green w/ivory
inserts, 13¾" d. 35.00
Salt & pepper shakers, clear, short,
pr.............................. 5.50
Salt & pepper shakers, clear, tall,
pr.............................. 6.50
Sherbet, footed, clear 2.50
Sherbet, footed, pink 7.00
Sugar bowl, cov., oval, clear 4.50
Sugar bowl, open, footed, clear 2.00
Tumbler, footed, pink, 3½" h.,
5 oz............................ 12.00
Tumbler, footed, clear, 5" h.,
10 oz........................... 8.00
Tumbler, footed, pink, 5" h.,
10 oz........................... 12.50
Water set: 80 oz. pitcher & 6 footed
tumblers; pink, 7 pcs. 155.00

**WINDSOR DIAMOND or Windsor
(Press-mold)**

Ashtray, Delphite, 5¾" d. 36.50

Ashtray, green, 5¾" d. 47.50
Ashtray, pink, 5¾" d. 29.50
Bowl, berry, 4¾" d., clear 3.50
Bowl, berry, 4¾" d., green or
pink 6.00
Bowl, 5" d., pointed edge, clear 4.50
Bowl, cream soup, 5" d., green 14.50
Bowl, cream soup, 5" d., pink 19.50
Bowl, cereal, 5 1/8" or 5 3/8" d.,
green 15.50
Bowl, cereal, 5 1/8" or 5 3/8" d.,
pink 12.00
Bowl, 7" d., three-footed, clear 6.00
Bowl, 7" d., three-footed, pink 16.00
Bowl, 8" d., pointed edge, clear 9.00
Bowl, 8" d., pointed edge, pink 24.00
Bowl, 8" d., two-handled, clear 6.00
Bowl, 8" d., two-handled, green 14.50
Bowl, 8" d., two-handled, pink 11.50
Bowl, berry, 8½" d., clear 10.50
Bowl, berry, 8½" d., green 11.50
Bowl, berry, 8½" d., pink 10.00
Bowl, 9½" oval vegetable, clear 10.50
Bowl, 9½" oval vegetable, green . . . 14.50
Bowl, 9½" oval vegetable, pink 13.00
Bowl, 10½" d., pointed edge,
pink 105.00
Bowl, salad, 10½" d., clear 18.50
Bowl, 7 x 11¾" boat shape, clear . . 16.00
Bowl, 7 x 11¾" boat shape, green . . 22.00
Bowl, 7 x 11¾" boat shape, pink . . . 18.50
Bowl, fruit, 12½" d., clear 22.00
Bowl, fruit, 12½" d., pink 75.50
Butter dish, cov., clear 19.00
Butter dish, cov., green 63.50

Windsor Diamond Butter Dish

Butter dish, cov., pink (ILLUS.) 33.00
Cake plate, footed, clear, 10¾" d. . . . 4.50
Cake plate, footed, green,
10¾" d. 13.00
Cake plate, footed, pink, 10¾" d. . . 10.00
Cake plate, green, 13½" d. 14.00
Cake plate, pink, 13½" d. 12.50
Candlesticks, clear, 3" h., pr. 12.50
Candlesticks, pink, 3" h., pr. 67.00
Candy jar, cov., clear 9.50
Coaster, clear, 3¼" d. 6.50
Coaster, green, 3¼" d. 13.50
Coaster, pink, 3¼" d. 8.00
Creamer, flat, clear 3.00
Creamer, flat, green 8.00
Creamer, flat, pink 7.00

Creamer, footed, clear 4.00
Cup & saucer, clear 4.50
Cup & saucer, green 10.00
Cup & saucer, pink 8.50
Pitcher, 4½" h., 16 oz., clear 13.50
Pitcher, 4½" h., 16 oz., pink 107.00
Pitcher, 5" h., 20 oz., clear 5.50
Pitcher, 5" h., 20 oz., pink 18.00
Pitcher, 6¾" h., 52 oz., clear 13.00
Pitcher, 6¾" h., 52 oz., green 35.00
Pitcher, 6¾" h., 52 oz., pink 18.50
Plate, salad, 7" d., clear 3.00
Plate, salad, 7" d., green 12.00
Plate, salad, 7" d., pink 9.50
Plate, dinner, 9" d., clear 3.50
Plate, dinner, 9" d., green or pink . . 10.00
Plate, sandwich, 10¼", handled,
clear 4.00
Plate, sandwich, 10¼", handled,
green 10.00
Plate, sandwich, 10¼", handled,
pink 9.00
Plate, chop, 13 5/8" d., clear 8.50
Plate, chop, 13 5/8" d., green or
pink 18.50
Platter, 11½" oval, clear 5.50
Platter, 11½" oval, green 13.00
Platter, 11½" oval, pink 11.50
Relish, divided, clear, 11½" 6.50
Salt & pepper shakers, clear, pr. . . . 10.50
Salt & pepper shakers, green, pr. . . . 36.00
Salt & pepper shakers, pink, pr. 28.50
Sherbet, footed, clear 3.50
Sherbet, footed, green or pink 6.00
Sugar bowl, cov., flat, clear 7.50
Sugar bowl, cov., flat, green 17.50
Sugar bowl, cov., flat, pink 15.00
Sugar bowl, cov., footed, clear 6.00
Sugar bowl, open, clear 2.50
Sugar bowl, open, green or pink . . . 7.00
Tray, clear, 4" sq. 2.00
Tray, green, 4" sq. 9.00
Tray, pink, 4" sq. 5.00
Tray, clear, 4 1/8 x 9" 7.00
Tray, green, 4 1/8 x 9" 15.50
Tray, pink, 4 1/8 x 9" 6.50
Tray, pink, 8½ x 9¾" 27.00
Tray, handled, green, 8½ x 9¾" . . . 27.50
Tray, handled, pink, 8½ x 9¾" 24.50
Tumbler, clear, 3¼" h., 5 oz. 5.50
Tumbler, green, 3¼" h., 5 oz. 26.00
Tumbler, pink, 3¼" h., 5 oz. 10.50
Tumbler, clear, 4" h., 9 oz. 4.50
Tumbler, green, 4" h., 9 oz. 15.50
Tumbler, pink, 4" h., 9 oz. 11.00
Tumbler, footed, clear, 4" h.,
9 oz. 5.00
Tumbler, clear, 5" h., 12 oz. 6.50
Tumbler, green, 5" h., 12 oz. 26.50
Tumbler, pink, 5" h., 12 oz. 18.50
Tumbler, footed, clear, 7¼" h. 8.50
Water set: pitcher & 6 tumblers;
pink, 7 pcs. 56.00

(End of Depression Glass Section)

DE VEZ & DEGUE

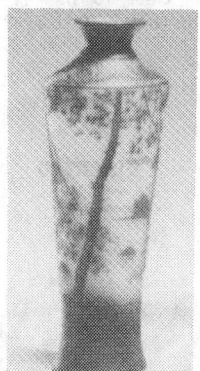

DeVez Cameo Vase

Cameo glass with the name DeVez was made in Pantin, France, by Saint-Hilaire, Touvier De Varreaux and Company. Some pieces made by this firm were signed "Degue," after one of the firm's glassmakers. The official company name was "Cristallerie de Pantin."

Cameo boudoir lamp, carved deep green to coral to soft yellow frosted translucent background in three detailed acid cuttings, green trees in foreground, island w/house, skyline of city at back, clouds in sky, original metal top, signed "DeVez," 3½" d., 6¾" h. (rewired w/switch on cord) $895.00

Cameo bowl-vase, carved dark green to rose poppy-like flowers & leaves in three acid cuttings, soft green translucent satin background w/overall stippling, marked "DeVez," 4 1/8" d., 2¼" h. 275.00

Cameo vase, 4¼" h., 4" d., triple cut w/navy blue cut to rose scene against frosted gold ground, man in boat by shore fishing w/house on island & tree branches at top of scene, marked "DeVez" 575.00

Cameo vase, 6" h., raised rim, baluster form, carved red & blue-black marshy river landscape scene w/mountainous background against opalescent yellow ground, embellished w/finely carved & etched details, signed 825.00

Cameo vase, 8¼" h., shouldered ovoid body in lemon-yellow overlaid in navy blue & orange & cut w/a lakeside scene w/a castle on an island in the background & fir trees in foreground, the neck cut

w/pine cones, signed "De Vez" (ILLUS.)........................ 550.00

Chandelier, eight-sided silvered-bronze frame cast w/birds, blossoms & leafage & set w/four D-form rectangular frosted panels molded w/flowers, the central inverted domical frosted shade molded w/conforming decoration, w/eight-sided ceiling plate cast w/geometric devices, molded "Degue," ca. 1930, 22½" w. 2,310.00

DUNCAN & MILLER

Teardrop Pattern Wine

Duncan & Miller Glass Company, a successor firm to George A. Duncan & Sons Company, was operated by George A. Duncan & Edwin C. Miller in Washington, Pa., from the late 19th century and produced many types of pressed wares and novelty pieces, many of which are now eagerly sought by collectors. George A. Duncan was a pioneer glass manufacturer, associated earlier with several firms.

Baked apple bowl, flanged rim, Spiral Flutes patt. (No. 40), green, 7½" d. $12.00

Bowl, cereal, 6½" d., flanged rim, Spiral Flutes patt. (No. 40), green 8.00

Bowl, 8" d., divided, handled, Canterbury patt. (No. 115), opalescent blue 18.00

Cake plate, footed, Early American Sandwich patt. (No. 41), clear 55.00

Cake set: 13" frosted service plate, eight 6" unfrosted cake plates; Nautical patt., blue, 9 pcs. 195.00

Candleholders, Early American Sandwich patt. (No. 41), one-light, clear w/First Love etched shades & blue prisms, pr. 400.00

Candy dish, cov., Canterbury patt.
(No. 115), blue opalescent 42.00

Champagne, etched Language of
Flowers patt., clear, 6 oz......... 18.00

Cigar box, cov., etched First Love
patt., clear 50.00

Cocktail, Teardrop patt. (No. 301),
clear 18.00

Compote, jelly, Mardi Gras patt.
(No. 42), clear 30.00

Cornucopia-vase, Three Feathers
patt. (No. 117), pink opalescent .. 75.00

Cruet w/original stopper, Bag Ware,
vaseline, large, ca. 1880's........ 59.00

Deviled egg plate, Early American
Sandwich patt. (No. 41), clear 70.00

Flower bowl, handled, Teardrop
patt. (No. 301), clear, 12" oval ... 25.00

Goblet, Early American Sandwich
patt. (No. 41), amber 28.00

Model of a swan, Pall Mall patt.
(No. 30), clear, 7" l............. 97.00

Model of a swan, blue opalescent,
spread wings, 11" w............. 150.00

Pitcher w/ice lip, Radiance patt.,
sapphire blue, ½ gal. 103.00

Pitcher, tankard, Mardi Gras patt.
(No. 42), clear 45.00

Plate, 7½" d., scalloped edge,
Diamond patt. (No. 75), amber,
paper label 4.50

Plate, 16" d., Early American Sandwich patt. (No. 41), clear 35.00

Punch bowl & base, Quarter Block
patt. (No. 55), custard, ca. 1900,
2 pcs. 150.00

Punch cup, Mardi Gras patt.
(No. 42), clear 5.50

Sherbet, Georgian patt. (No. 103),
green 9.00

Sugar bowl, open, Canterbury patt.
(No. 115), vaseline 20.00

Syrup jug w/original lid, Mardi Gras
patt. (No. 42), clear 70.00

Tumbler, Chanticleer patt., cobalt
blue 55.00

Tumbler, Mardi Gras patt. (No. 42),
clear 12.00

Tumblers, highball, Mallard Duck
etching, clear, 16 oz., set of 6 .... 150.00

Vase, 7" h., ruffled rim, Hobnail
patt. (No. 118), pink opalescent .. 75.00

Vase, 10" h., footed, Early American
Sandwich patt. (No. 41), clear 55.00

Water set: tankard pitcher & six
goblets; Diamond Ridge patt.
(No. 48), clear w/gold trim, ca.
1901, the set................... 250.00

Whimsey, model of a hand holding
a Daisy & Square pattern cornucopia w/scalloped rim, on oval
ribbed base, ruby-stained buttons
on cornucopia, late 19th c. 125.00

Whimsey, hat-shaped, Hobnail patt.
(No. 118), clear, 10" h. 65.00

Wine, Mardi Gras patt. (No. 42),
clear 24.00

Wine, Teardrop patt. (No. 301),
clear (ILLUS.) 20.00

DURAND

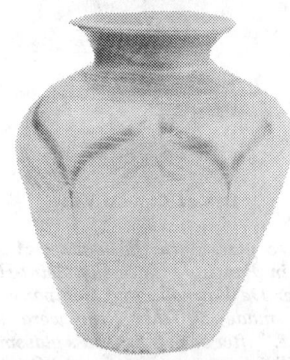

Durand Pulled Feather Vase

Fine decorative glass similar to that made by Tiffany and other outstanding glasshouses of its day was made by the Vineland Flint Glass Works Co. in Vineland, New Jersey, first headed by Victor Durand, Sr., and subsequently by his son Victor Durand, Jr., in the 1920's.

Lamp base, bulbous base tapering
to long neck w/wide flat, flared
rim, yellow-gold iridescent pulled
feather design w/applied iridescent gold random threading
around body, 5¼" d., 9¼" h.
(slight base roughness) $231.00

Sherbet, tall bowl w/flared rim,
round base, green & amber pulled
feather patt., amber base,
3½" d., 6¼" h. 302.50

Tazzas, brilliant ribbed optic crystal
rounds of great clarity on Spanish
yellow twisted stems & ruby
cupped & folded pedestal bases,
7½" d., 4" h., pr. 495.00

Vase, 4½" h., flared & ruffled rim,
overall gold King Tut design on
green ground, gold iridescent interior, signed 875.00

Vase, 7½" h., Hearts & Vine design
in iridescent blue & white, signed
& numbered 450.00

Vase, 8¼" h. baluster-form, everted
rim, Hearts & Vine design on orange iridescent body w/blue foot,
signed 800.00

Vase, 10" h., ovoid body w/broad shoulders tapering to narrow neck w/flaring rim, pulled feather design on iridescent orange ground ornamented overall w/an applied random thread design, signed "Durand - 1710-10" (ILLUS. previous page) 1,870.00

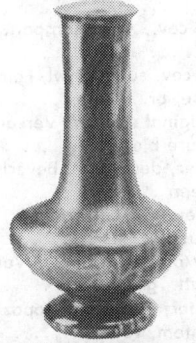

Durand King Tut Design Vase

Vase, 12½" h., flared rim on an elongated neck above a bulbous body on a low pedestal foot, unusual coloring of bright iridescent pink w/pulled & coiled King Tut design, gold iridescent interior, signed "Durand" across the pontil (ILLUS.) 2,530.00

Vase, 17" h., bulbous base tapering to 6½" d. neck opening, green King Tut design, gold iridescent interior 1,200.00

Wine, red & white pulled feather design bowl w/amber stem, 3 3/8" d., 6¼" h. 203.50

FENTON

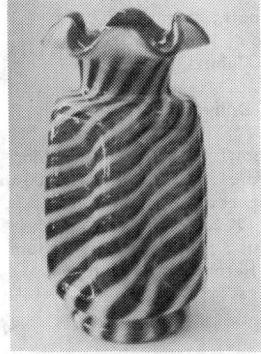

Fenton Spiral Optic Vase

Fenton Art Glass Company began producing glass at Williamstown, West Virginia, in

January 1907. Organized by Frank L. and John W. Fenton, the company began operations in a newly built glass factory with an experienced master glass craftsman, Jacob Rosenthal, as their factory manager. Fenton has produced a wide variety of collectible glassware through the years, including Carnival (which see). Still in production today, their current productions may be found at finer gift shops across the country.

Basket, Hobnail patt., milk white, 6" $15.00
Basket, Coin Dot patt., blue opalescent, 7" 65.00
Basket, Peach Crest, shape No. 203, 7" 40.00
Bowl, 7", ruffled edge, Hobnail patt., cranberry opalescent 50.00
Bowl, 10", Hobnail patt., blue opalescent 65.00
Bowl, 10" d., Silver Crest 18.00
Candlesticks, Aqua Crest, cornucopia-form, shape No. 950, pr. 40.00
Candy dish, cov., shape No. 1780, Colonial blue 42.00
Candy dish, cov., w/dolphin handles, footed, Diamond Optic patt., green 55.00
Candy jar, cov., footed, Stretch glass, Florentine Green, 9" h. 42.00
Cologne bottles w/stoppers, bulbous, Hobnail patt., deep blue opalescent, 4½" h., pr. 45.00
Compote, 7", Aqua Crest 22.00
Cookie jar, cov., w/wicker handle, Big Cookies patt., Ebony 74.00
Cornucopia-vases, Ivory Crest, shape No. 1523, pr. 85.00
Creamer & open sugar bowl, child's, Hobnail patt., vaseline opalescent, pr. 38.00
Cruet w/original stopper, Coin Dot patt., cranberry opalescent, ca. 1951 .... 65.00
Cup & saucer, Georgian patt. (No. 1611), Ruby 17.00
Decanter w/stopper, New World patt., cranberry 75.00
Epergne, three-lily, Hobnail patt., aqua opalescent 95.00
Lamp, Gone-With-The-Wind style, pressed Rose Peach Blow, produced for L.G. Wright, ca. 1960, 16" h. 175.00
Lemonade set: cov. pitcher w/cut Royal Blue handle & six tumblers w/cutting; Celeste Blue Stretch glass, the set 175.00
Pitcher, jug-type, 8" h., applied handle, melon-ribbed base, wide ruffled rim, Rose Overlay, shape No. 192 .... 35.00

Plate, 8" d., Aqua Crest 13.00
Syrup pitcher, Fern & Daisy patt.,
  blue opalescent, made for L.G.
  Wright 53.00
Tumbler, No. 1933 patt., Royal Blue,
  9 oz. 18.00
Tumbler, juice, Plymouth patt.,
  Ruby 12.00
Vase, 5" h., ruffled rim, Coin Dot
  patt., cranberry opalescent, shape
  No. 1450 .... 45.00
Vase, 6½" h., double-crimped rim,
  ribbed body, Peach Crest, deco-
  rated w/roses & violets & gilt
  trim 30.00
Vase, 8" h., ruffled rim, ovoid body,
  Beaded Melon patt., Rose Over-
  lay, shape No. 711, ca. 1940 ..... 55.00
Vase, 8" h., crimped top, Coin Dot
  patt., blue opalescent 95.00
Vase, 8" h., fan-shaped, shape
  No. 847, Lilac, ca. 1932 .... 125.00
Vase, 8" h., pinched sides, ruffled
  rim, Spiral Optic patt., cranberry
  opalescent, shape No. 3252, ca.
  1954 (ILLUS.) 65.00
Water set: pitcher & six tumblers;
  Hobnail patt., aqua opalescent,
  the set 265.00

FOSTORIA

Chintz Pattern Sherbet

Fostoria Glass Company, founded in 1887, is still in operation today in Moundsville, West Virginia. It has produced numerous types of fine wares through the years, many of which are now being collected. Also see ANIMALS under Glass.

Baker, oval, Trojan patt., topaz..... $45.00
Bowl, 12" d., Meadow Rose patt.,
  clear 32.00
Bowl, 12" oval, Versailles patt.,
  rose 55.00
Bowl, fruit, 16" d., footed, American
  patt., clear .... 120.00 to 150.00

Butter dish, cov., round, American
  patt., clear 100.00
Butter dish, cov., round, Pioneer
  patt., green 45.00
Cheese & cracker plate, Chintz
  patt., clear 55.00
Claret, Holly patt., clear 30.00
Cocktail, Romance patt., clear,
  3½ oz. 17.00
Cookie jar, cov., American patt.,
  clear 345.00
Creamer & cov. sugar bowl, Fairfax
  patt., rose, pr. 50.00
Cruet w/original stopper, Versailles
  patt., Azure blue 300.00
Cup & saucer, demitasse, Beverly
  patt., green 29.00
Cup & saucer, Versailles patt.,
  Azure blue 50.00
Decanter w/original stopper, Ver-
  sailles patt., green 500.00
Goblet, water, June patt., topaz
  w/clear stem, 10 oz. 25.00
Hair pin box, cov., American patt.,
  clear 90.00
Hat shape, topper, American patt.,
  clear, 4" h. 47.50
Ice bucket, Fairfax patt., green,
  w/tongs 35.00
Olive tray, Morning Glory patt.,
  clear 12.00
Pitcher, June patt., Azure blue 300.00
Pitcher, Seville patt., amber........ 125.00
Plate, 7" d., Morning Glory patt.,
  clear 12.00
Plate, 7½" d., Mystic patt., green .. 4.50
Plate, 9" d., Chintz patt., clear 20.00
Platter, 15", Fairfax patt., Azure
  blue 48.00
Punch bowl & base, American patt.,
  clear, 14" d., 2 pcs. 125.00
Salt & pepper shakers w/original
  tops, June patt., clear, pr. 100.00
Sandwich server w/center handle,
  Holly patt., clear 50.00
Sauce boat, Trojan patt., topaz 60.00
Sherbet, Chintz patt., clear
  (ILLUS.)...................... 9.50
Sherbet, Dolly Madison patt.,
  clear 10.00
Shrimp bowl, American patt., clear,
  12¼" d. ....225.00 to 265.00
Straw jar, cov., American patt.,
  clear, 12" h. 240.00
Water set: 3 pt. pitcher & eight tum-
  blers; Hermitage patt., topaz,
  9 pcs. 145.00

FRY

Numerous types of glass were made by the H.C. Fry Company, Rochester, Pennsylvania.

One of its art lines was called Foval and was blown in 1926-27. Cheaper was its milky-opalescent ovenware (Pearl Oven Ware) made for utilitarian purposes but also now being collected. The company also made fine cut glass.

Fry Foval Cup & Saucer

Butter dish, cov., Pearl Oven
Ware $65.00
Casserole, cov., Pearl Oven Ware . . 25.00
Coffee set: cov. coffeepot, creamer
& sugar bowl; Foval, opaline
w/applied Jade green handles &
trim, 3 pcs. 450.00
Cup & saucer, Foval, dark blue
stripe on pale blue opaline
ground (ILLUS.). 55.00
Lemonade pitcher, cov., clear
"crackle" w/applied Jade green
handle & finial on lid 100.00
Mugs, clear "crackle," pr. 50.00
Platter, meat, etched rim, Pearl
Oven Ware 19.00
Tea & coffee service: cov. teapot,
cov. coffeepot & two cups & saucers; Foval, opaline w/applied
Jade blue handle, spout & finial
on pots & one cup, w/unadorned
opaline saucer, other cup & saucer w/applied Jade green handle
& embossed silver on cup & sau-
cer rim, 6 pcs. 330.00

GALLE'

Galle' glass was made in Nancy, France, by Emile Galle', a founder of the Nancy School and a leader in the Art Nouveau movement in France. Much of his glass, both enameled and cameo, is decorated with naturalistic motifs. The finest pieces were made in the last two decades of the 19th century and the opening years of the present one. Pieces marked with a star preceding the name were made between 1904, the year of Galle's death, and 1914.

Cameo bowl, 4½" d., round
w/squared rim, carved & enamel

multicolored exotic flowers on
dark green ground, signed $1,300.00
Cameo lamp, sharply conical shade &
trumpet-form base in pale grey
shaded w/dandelion & lemon yellow & sky blue, shade overlaid
in shades of purple & cut w/two
peregrine falcons in flight, base
overlaid in purple, lavender, powder blue & sky blue & cut w/a
winter mountain landscape w/a
bubbling brook in the foreground
shaded by conifers, simple scrolling gilt-bronze mounts, ca. 1900,
shade & base signed in cameo
"Galle'," 13¼" d. shade, overall
26½" h. 26,400.00
Cameo lamp, domical shade & bal-
uster base in brilliant lemon yellow
overlaid in periwinkle blue, purple,
rust & olive green & cut w/Shasta
daisies & leafage, simple scrolling
gilt-bronze mounts, ca. 1920, shade
& base signed in cameo "Galle',"
14 7/8" d. shade, overall
28" h. 24,200.00

Galle' Cameo Tazza

Cameo tazza, carved cherry red to
magenta rose berry-laden wild
strawberry vines against citron yellow ground, translucent grey baluster stem & circular foot washed
in iridescence, ca. 1900, cameo
signature, 14" d. (ILLUS.) 5,775.00

Galle' Cameo Vase

Cameo vase, 5½" h., bulbous body
w/short narrow neck to wide,
flaring rim, pinkish white overlaid
in deep brown etched to depict
ferns, cameo signature (ILLUS.) ..1,650.00
Cameo vase, 6" h., flattened ovoid
form, grey sides shaded w/purple,
overlaid in purple & cut w/pendent
chrysanthemum buds, blossoms &
leafage, the whole fire-polished,
ca. 1900, signed 1,540.00
Cameo vase, 6¾" h., banjo form,
carved shaded brown woodland
scene against yellow-cream
ground 800.00
Cameo vase, 7" h., spherical w/wide
opening at the top, bluish-white
ground overlaid in green & brown
etched to depict a quaint village
seen through the trees, cameo
signature 3,520.00
Cameo vase, 7 1/8" h., ovoid form
w/slender neck, yellow overlaid
w/deep purple & cut w/five-
petalled blossoms, leafage & an
insect, ca. 1900, signed 880.00
Cameo vase, 8 1/8" h., cylindrical
tapering toward flared rim, pink
ground overlaid in purple etched to
depict small blossoms, leaves &
stems, cameo signature 1,100.00
Cameo vase, 8 5/8" h., flattened
spherical form w/elliptical dished
rim, carved twining purple flowers
against amber shaded to white
ground, early 20th c., signed 715.00
Cameo vase, 8¾" h., flattened
ovoid, carved shaded ruby red
blossoming rose branches against
citron yellow ground, ca. 1900,
signed 3,410.00
Cameo vase, 9½" h., cylindrical
w/rolled shoulder, mold-blown &
cameo-carved deep amber & deep
rust clematis blossoms, buds &
leafage against pale amber
ground, ca. 1925, signed 6,600.00
Cameo vase, 10" h., pilgrim flask
form, white ground overlaid in
blue & purple etched to depict a
scene w/mountains, trees & a
lake, cameo signature 6,600.00
Cameo vase, 10¼" h., spherical,
mold-blown & cameo-carved puce
& purple rhododendron sprays
against gold ground, signed 15,400.00

GOOFUS

*This is a name collectors have given a
pressed glass whose colors were sprayed on
and then fired. Most pieces have intaglio or*

*convex designs and were produced by the
Northwood Glass Co.*

Bowl, 8½" d., 3" h., Waffle patt.,
starburst bottom, red scalloped
edge merging into gold, 90%
paint........................... $22.00
Dresser tray, relief-molded flowers
on gold, 6 x 12"................. 15.00
Plate, 8½" d., relief-molded apples
on gold 15.00
Plate, 10½" d., relief-molded red
grapes on gold.................. 20.00
Vase, 12" h., relief-molded daises
on gold 25.00

GREENTOWN

Dewey Mug

*Greentown glass was made in Greentown,
Indiana, by the Indiana Tumbler & Goblet
Co. from 1894 until 1903. In addition to its
famed Chocolate and Holly Amber glass,
which see, it produced other types of clear and
colored glass. Miscellaneous pieces are listed here. Also see PATTERN GLASS -
Dewey.*

Animal covered dish, Bird with
Berry, blue $180.00
Animal covered dish, Rabbit, blue .. 175.00
Butter dish, cov., Dewey patt.,
amber, 4" d..................... 65.00
Butter dish, cov., Dewey patt.,
canary, 4" d. 65.00
Butter dish, cov., Herringbone But-
tress patt., green 195.00
Compote, jelly, 5¼" d., 5" h., Cac-
tus patt., clear................. 110.00
Cracker jar, cov., Cactus patt.,
clear 185.00
Creamer & cov. sugar bowl, Cactus
patt., clear, pr. 250.00
Cruet w/original stopper, Dewey
patt., amber 145.00
Mug, Dewey patt., green (ILLUS.) ... 65.00
Novelty, dustpan, amber........... 55.00
Novelty, hairbrush, clear.......... 55.00

Pickle dish, Cord Drapery patt.,
  clear, 7 3/8" l. $28.00

Cactus Pattern Water Pitcher

Pitcher, water, Cactus patt., clear
  (ILLUS.) 325.00
Pitcher, water, Cord Drapery patt.,
  green 200.00
Salt shaker, Pleat Band patt., clear,
  w/old lid 18.00
Table set: cov. butter dish, creamer,
  sugar bowl & spooner; Austrian
  patt., clear w/gold trim, 4 pcs. . . . 250.00
Table set: cov. butter dish, cov. sug-
  ar bowl, creamer & spooner; Leaf
  Bracket patt., clear, 4 pcs. 350.00
Toothpick holder, Cactus patt.,
  clear 50.00
Toothpick holder, Holly patt.,
  clear 110.00
Tumbler, Austrian patt., canary 125.00
Wine, Herringbone Buttress patt.,
  emerald green 160.00

HANDEL

Handel Ashtray

*Lamps, shades and other types of glass by
Handel & Co., which subsequently became
The Handel Co., Inc., were produced in
Meriden, Connecticut, from 1893 to 1941. Also
see LIGHTING DEVICES.*

Ashtray, squat round bowl of opal
  glass w/"chipped" green finish
  mounted w/bronzed rim, cigar
  holders & a figural pipe, marked
  in shield on base "Handel - Ware
  - #4091 - AE," metal finish worn,
  5¾" d., 3¾" h. (ILLUS.) 302.50

Handel Humidor

Humidor, cov., round flat glass
  cover hinged to a flared base of
  "chipped, sand-finished" glass h.p.
  on exterior w/a lowland Dutch
  landscape in monochromatic greens,
  artist signed "Parlow" below wind-
  mill, 5¼" h. (ILLUS.) 1,100.00
Humidor, cov., "Teroma" glass,
  cylindrical, h.p. tropical seascape
  centering a sailing vessel in shades
  of blue, green, brown & yellow on
  "chipped" finish, conforming
  domed cover, scene artist-signed
  "Bedigie," base stamped "Handel -
  Teroma - 4204," 8½" h. 3,300.00
Humidor, cov., opal glass decorated
  w/scene of playing bear cubs on
  shaded deep green & maroon
  ground, glass cover w/hinged sil-
  ver plate rim 615.00
Humidor, cov., opal glass decorated
  w/a hunting dog on a deep green
  & maroon ground, metal cover,
  signed 525.00
Humidor, cov., opal glass decorated
  w/an owl on a deep green & ma-
  roon ground 650.00
Match holder, opal glass in ovoid
  shape decorated w/bust profile
  portrait of an Indian chief in
  feathered headdress against a
  shaded deep green & maroon
  ground, metal rim band, inscribed
  "MATCHES" on reverse, un-
  marked, 7½" h. 125.00
Plate, 8" d., "Teroma" glass, dog-
  wood branch decoration,
  unmarked 210.00
Vase, 7¾" h., "Teroma" glass, shoul-
  dered cylindrical body w/flared rim,
  "chipped, sand-finished" glass
  h.p. on exterior w/polychrome
  mountainous river scene w/sum-
  mer trees in foreground, signed
  "Handel Co. - 4210" on base 1,870.00
Vase, 10¾" h., Opal Ware,
  elaborate swirled molded baluster
  form w/overall h.p. detailed pink
  & white lilies & green leaves on
  aqua blue & green ground, base
  marked "Handel's Opal Ware" 605.00
Vase, 10¾" h., "Teroma" glass,

Handel "Teroma" Vase
waisted cylindrical form
w/"chipped, sand-finished" glass
painted on the exterior w/birch
trees in a wooded landscape in
shades of green, orange, yellow,
mauve & blue against a frosted
ground, polished interior, artist-
signed scene, base w/Handel mark
(ILLUS.) 2,300.00

HEISEY

Numerous types of fine glass were made by the A.H. Heisey Glass Co., Newark, Ohio, from 1895. The company's trade-mark — an H enclosed within a diamond — has become known to most glass collectors. The company's name and molds were acquired by Imperial Glass Co., Bellaire, Ohio, in 1958, and some pieces have been reissued. The glass listed below consists of miscellaneous pieces and types. Also see ANIMALS under Glass and PATTERN GLASS.

Animal covered dish, hen on nest,
   purple, signed, 6" $425.00
Ashtray, Empress patt., Sahara (yel-
   low) 75.00
Ashtray, Wampum patt., clear 19.00
Basket, helmet-shaped, Flamingo
   (pink), 10" 195.00
Beer mug, Old Sandwich patt.,
   Sahara 130.00
Bowl, 11" d., dolphin footed, Em-
   press patt., Moongleam (green) . .   70.00
Bowl, 11" d., Lariat patt., flower
   etching, clear 45.00
Bowl, 11" oval, footed, Old Sand-
   wich patt., Moongleam 120.00
Bowl, 11½" d., Crystolite patt.,
   clear 30.00
Bowl, 13" d., flat, Waverly patt.,
   original label, clear 36.00
Butter dish, cov., Classic patt.,
   clear 215.00

Cake plate, footed, Plantation patt.,
   clear, 12½" d. 75.00
Candleholders, Twist patt., Flamin-
   go, 2" h., pr. 20.00
Candlesticks, three-light, Cascade
   patt., orchid etching, clear, pr. . . .   95.00
Candlesticks, three-light, Crystolite
   patt., clear, pr. 48.00
Candlesticks, two-light, Fern patt.,
   w/bobeches & prisms, clear, pr. . .   72.50
Candlesticks, three-light, Lariat
   patt., clear, pr. 145.00
Candlesticks, Miss Muffet patt.,
   Flamingo, 3" h., pr. 38.50
Candlesticks, two-light, New Era
   patt., removable bobeches &
   prisms, clear, pr. 110.00
Candlesticks, Petticoat Dolphin,
   Flamingo, 6" h., pr. 300.00
Candlesticks, Sandwich Dolphin,
   cobalt blue, 10" h., pr. 2,250.00
Candlesticks, two-light, Thumbprint
   & Panel patt., cobalt blue, pr. 395.00
Candlesticks, two-light, Whirlpool
   patt., clear, pr. 115.00
Candle-vases, Ipswich patt., clear
   candle insert, cobalt blue vase,
   pr. 425.00
Celery dish, Octagonal patt.,
   Moongleam 35.00
Celery dish, Twist patt., Sahara 35.00
Centerpiece vase, footed, Ipswich
   patt., crystal, 7½" h. 90.00
Champagne, Colonial patt., clear . . .   13.00
Champagne, Jamestown patt., nar-
   cissus etching, clear, 6 oz. 22.50
Champagne, Oceanic patt., clear . . .   20.00
Champagne, Victorian patt., clear . .   32.00
Cheese dish, Fern patt., Zircon
   (blue-green) 25.00
Cigarette set: cov. cigarette box &
   four ashtrays; Wampum patt.,
   clear, 5 pcs. 95.00
Claret, Banded Flute patt., clear 22.50
Coaster, Crystolite patt., Sahara,
   3½" d. 32.50
Coaster, Crystolite patt., Zircon,
   3½" d. 42.50
Coaster, Lariat patt., clear 5.00
Cocktail, Bantam Rooster stem,
   clear 50.00
Cocktail, Duquesne patt., Norman-
   die etching, clear 24.00
Cocktail, Jamestown patt., Barcelo-
   na etching, clear, 3 oz. 25.00
Cocktail, Shasta patt., George IV
   cutting, clear 38.00
Cocktail shaker, etched fisherman,
   clear, 2 qt. 250.00
Cocktail shaker, w/rooster stopper,
   clear 88.00
Compote, 7" oval, Waverly patt.,
   Orchid etching, clear 140.00

Cordial, Crystolite patt., clear 85.00
Creamer & cov. sugar bowl, Fancy
Loop patt., clear, hotel size, pr. ... 95.00
Creamer & sugar bowl, Minuet etch-
ing, clear, pr................... 80.00
Creamer & sugar bowl on tray,
Athena patt., clear, 3 pcs....... 60.00
Cruet, Greek Key patt., clear 65.00
Cup & saucer, Waverly patt., Orchid
etching, clear 60.00
Fruit bowl, Ridgeleigh patt., clear,
12" d......................... 25.00
Goblet, tall, Old Colony etching, Sa-
hara (yellow) 25.00
Goblet, Plantation patt., Ivy etching,
clear 35.00
Ice tub, Twist patt., Moongleam
(green)....................... 77.00
Jug, Cross Lined Flute patt., clear,
½ gal. 40.00
Marmalade jar w/mushroom cover,
Puritan patt., clear, large 40.00
Mustard jar, cov., Twist patt.,
Moongleam................... 68.00
Pitcher, squat shape, Fancy Loop
patt., clear, ½ gal.............. 135.00
Plate, salad, 6" d., Old Colony etch-
ing, Sahara 18.00
Plate, 8" sq., Empress patt., cobalt
blue 72.00
Plate, dinner, 10½" d., Waverly
patt., clear 45.00
Punch bowl & base, Pillows patt.,
clear, 2 pcs. 220.00
Punch cup, Plantation patt., clear ... 20.00
Punch set: 13" d. footed punch
bowl, base & 12 punch cups; Puri-
tan patt., 14 pcs............... 190.00
Relish, three-part, Queen Ann patt.,
Orchid etching, clear, 9" 30.00
Salt & pepper shakers, Fancy Loop
patt., clear, pr. 35.00
Sherbet, Kohinoor patt., Sahara 9.00
Smoking set: cigarette holder & four
ashtrays; Kohinoor patt., Limelight
(green), in original box, 5 pcs. ... 350.00
Spooner, Locket on Chain patt.,
ruby-stained w/gold trim 315.00
Spooner, Prince of Wales - Plumes
patt., clear 65.00
Straw holder, Greek Key patt.,
clear......................... 400.00
Sugar shaker, Yeoman patt., Fla-
mingo (pink)................... 60.00
Table set: cov. butter dish, cov.
sugar bowl & creamer; Winged
Scroll patt., green, 3 pcs. 275.00
Tumbler, Arch patt., cobalt blue 87.50
Tumbler, iced tea, handled, Wabash
patt., Pied Piper etching, clear ... 35.00
Vase, 10" h., Empress patt., Old
Colony etching, Sahara 90.00

HISTORICAL & COMMEMORATIVE

Battleship Maine Plate

*Reference numbers are to Bessie M. Lind-
sey's book,* American Historical Glass. *Also
see* MILK WHITE GLASS.

Admiral Dewey dish, cov., boat-like
base, milk white, 5½" l., 5" h.,
No. 391 .... $75.00
Admiral Dewey dish, cov., ribbed
base, amber, No. 387 .... 230.00
Admiral Dewey plate, bust portrait
of Dewey, clear, 5½" d.,
No. 392 .... 33.00
Admiral Dewey plate, bust portrait
of Dewey & stars transfer center,
openwork club border, milk
white, 7" d., No. 393 .... 28.00
Admiral Dewey water pitcher, bust
portrait of Dewey & flagship
Olympia reverse, w/mounted cannons, crossed rifles, U.S. & Cuban
flags & stacks of cannon balls toward base, clear, No. 400....... 65.00
Admiral Dewey water pitcher, portrait of Dewey within laurel
leaves, "Gridley You May Fire
When Ready," eagle, w/shield,
etc., clear, 9¼" h., No. 401 ..... 108.00
"America" tumbler, etched w/hymn
title & first stanza, clear, 3¾" h.,
No. 458 .... 22.00
Battleship Maine plate, picture of
ship center, pierced club & shell
border, milk white, 7¼" d.,
No. 463 (ILLUS.) 33.00
Battleship Maine plate, battleship
transfer center, 101 border,
green, 5½" d., No. 464 .... 25.00
Battleship Wheeling dish, cov., milk
white, 3 5/8 x 6 5/8", 4" h.,
No. 470 .... 52.00
Bryan plate, bust portrait of William
Jennings Bryan center, flags,
American eagles & stars border,
milk white, 7½" d., No. 359 ..... 52.00

Bunker Hill platter, "Prescott 1776
Stark-Warren 1876 Putnam," clear,
9 x 13½", No. 44 .... 85.00
Carpenter's Hall (Washington Cen-
tennial patt.) bread platter, clear,
No. 28 .... 75.00

Columbus Plate

Columbus plate, bust portrait of
Columbus center w/dates "1492-
1892," pilot wheel border, clear,
9" d., No. 4 (ILLUS.) 50.00
Emblem butter dish, cov., bullet finial, clear, No. 64 .... 280.00
Emblem sugar bowl & cover w/bul-
let finial, eagle w/shield alter-
nates w/ordnance, clear, 4½" d.,
6" h., No. 64 .... 200.00 to 225.00
Faith, Hope & Charity plate,
maidens posed as Three Graces
center, w/1875 patent date, clear,
10" d., No. 230 .... 85.00
Garden of Eden bread plate, log
handles, central fig-like ornament, marked "Give us this day
our daily bread," clear, No. 207
variant 25.00
Garfield "ABC" plate, clear w/frost-
ed bust of Garfield center, 6" d.,
No. 301 .... 68.00
Garfield Memorial plate, Garfield
center, laurel wreath against stip-
pled ground border, clear, 10" d.,
No. 302 .... 45.00 to 60.00
Garfield Star plate, frosted bust of
Garfield center, star border,
clear, 6" d., No. 299 .... 32.50
Gladstone (William Ewart) plate, "In
Memory of England's Statesman,"
clear, 5 1/8" d., No. 442 .... 42.00
Grand Army of the Republic goblet,
insignia one side, inscribed "21
Encampment September 27, 28, St.
Louis, Mo." reverse, clear, 6¾" h.,
No. 506 .... 41.00
Grant "Patriot and Soldier" plate,
bust portrait of Grant center,
decorative border, deep rim,
clear, 9½" sq., No. 291 .... 65.00

Grant Peace plate, bust portrait of
Grand center, maple leaf border,
green, 10½" h., No. 289 .... 35.00
Grant Peace plate, bust portrait of
Grant center, maple leaf border,
green, 10½" d., No. 289 .... 35.00
Independence Hall "ABC" plate,
"1776-1876," clear, 6¾" d.,
No. 33 .... 100.00 to 150.00
Independence Hall platter, "The Na-
tion's Birthplace," w/bear paw
handles, clear, No. 29 ..... 65.00 to 85.00
Jenny Lind match safe, "Pat'd. June
13, 1876," frosted, pierced to
hang, 4½" l., No. 426 .... 52.00
John Paul Jones flask, amber,
No. 48 .... 25.00
Knights of Labor mug, clear, 6" h.,
No. 513 .... 32.00
Liberty Bell plate, closed handles,
scalloped rim w/thirteen original
states & "100 Years Ago," clear,
8" d., No. 37 .... 45.00
Liberty Bell salt dip, clear, 1½ x
2¼" oval, 1" h., No. 36 .... 30.00
Liberty Bell Signer's platter, clear,
9½ x 13", No. 42 ...... 80.00 to 100.00
Liberty Bell w/Shells platter, "Patd
Sept. 28, 1875," no signers, clear,
11¼" l., No. 41 .... 100.00
Lincoln statuette, bust of Lincoln,
opaque white w/acid finish,
marked "Centennial Exhibition,
Gillinder & Sons," 6" h.,
No. 277 .... 300.00 to 375.00
Lincoln's Tribute tumbler, clear,
3¾" h., No. 282 .... 28.00

Martyr's Mug

Martyr's mug, Lincoln & Garfield
bust portraits & inscription, clear,
2 5/8" h., No. 272 (ILLUS.) 76.00
McKinley tumbler, "Our President
1896 to 1900," clear, 3¾" h.,
No. 350 .... 32.00
McKinley Gold Standard tray, full-
length figure of McKinley standing
on plank inscribed "Gold,"
w/Feather Duster patt. border,
clear, 7¾ x 10¼", No. 332 .... 350.00
McKinley Protection & Plenty plate,
portrait of McKinley center, star
border, clear, 7¼" d., No. 333 ... 45.00

Old Abe (eagle) butter dish, cov.,
  clear, No. 478 .... 95.00
Old Abe (eagle) creamer, clear,
  No. 478 .... 55.00
Old Abe (eagle) compote, cov.,
  clear, No. 478 .... 225.00
Old Statehouse Philadelphia tray,
  electric blue, round, No. 32 ...... 88.00
Preparedness toothpick holder,
  clear, 2¼" h., No. 483 .... 225.00
Railroad train platter, Union Pacific
  Engine No. 350, amber, 9 x 12",
  No. 134 .... 135.00
Rock of Ages bread tray, clear
  w/opaque white inlaid center,
  No. 236 .... 168.00
Rock of Ages bread tray, clear
  w/translucent deep blue center,
  No. 236 .... 235.00
Ruth statuette, Ruth shown as
  gleaner resting on one knee
  w/wisps of grain in each hand,
  "Gillinder & Sons Centennial Exhibition" inscribed on base, satin
  finish, clear, 4½" h., No. 216 .... 110.00
Tennessee mug, Cherokee rose &
  clematis blossoms within shield
  one side & American 16-star flag
  reverse, camphor, 3½" h.,
  No. 102 .... 50.00
Washington Bi-Centennial plate,
  bust portrait of Washington center, large star border on stippled
  ground w/reserve at bottom
  w/"G. Washington - 1732-1932,"
  clear, 8" d., No. 258 .... 37.00

HOBBS, BROCKUNIER & CO.

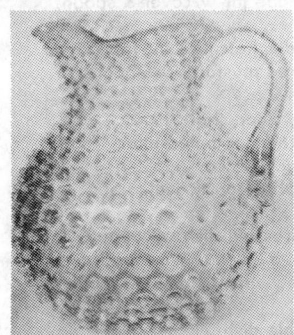

Hobbs' Hobnail Pitcher

About 1845, the Wheeling, West Virginia
glasshouse of Hobbs, Barnes & Co. was
founded by two former employees of the New
England Glass Company, John L. Hobbs and
James B. Barnes. They were soon joined by
their sons, John H. Hobbs and James F.
Barnes. The firm became Hobbs, Brockunier

& Co. in 1863 as John L. and John H. Hobbs
and Charles Brockunier took charge of the
company and hired, in that same year, the
former superintendent of the New England
Glass Company, William Leighton, Sr., to
take charge of production. Leighton revolutionized the glass industry the following year,
1864, when he devised a formula for soda lime
glass, a cheaper method of producing clear
glass. In the 1880's, the firm produced popular Victorian art glass lines including Peach
Blow, Spangled, Amberina and various
opalescent patterns. Hobbs' Hobnail pattern
became one of the most popular of all patterns. Also see OPALESCENT GLASS.

Bowl, 8½" d., flat, Maltese Cross
  patt., clear w/amber stain $50.00
Carafe, water, Hobbs' Block patt.,
  clear frosted w/amber stain 125.00
Cruet w/original stopper, Satina
  Swirl patt., cranberry 395.00
Pitcher, water, Hobbs' Hobnail patt.,
  clear opalescent (ILLUS.) 155.00
Punch cup, Christmas Snowflake
  patt., blue opalescent w/rare
  crackle finish 40.00
Sugar shaker w/original top,
  Coloratura Series, ivory
  w/enameled prunus blossoms 145.00
Sugar shaker, Ring Neck patt., pink
  & white spatter 75.00
Table set, Francesware Swirl patt.,
  frosted clear w/amber stained
  rims, 4 pcs..................... 225.00
Tumbler, Hexagonal Block patt.,
  clear w/amber stained top band
  and engraved banding of flowers
  & leaves...................... 21.00

HOLLY AMBER

Holly Amber Butter Dish

Holly Amber, originally marketed under
the name "Golden Agate," was produced for
only a few months in 1903 by the Indiana
Tumbler and Goblet Company of Greentown,
Indiana. When this factory burned in June

1903 all production of this ware ceased, making it very rare today. The same "Holly" pressed pattern was also produced in clear glass by the Greentown factory. Collectors should note that the St. Clair Glass Company has reproduced some Holly Amber pieces.

Bowl, 7½" d. $600.00
Bowl, oval 425.00
Butter dish, cov. (ILLUS.) 1,000.00
Nappy, handled 550.00
Pickle dish, two-handled 350.00
Plate, square, 7½" 820.00
Vase, 6" h. 800.00

IMPERIAL

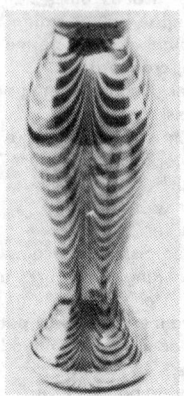

Free Hand Ware Vase

Imperial Glass Company, Bellaire, Ohio, was organized in 1901 and was in continuous production, except for very brief periods, until its closing in June 1984. It had been a major producer of Carnival Glass (which see) earlier in this century and also produced other types of glass, including an Art Glass line called "Free Hand Ware" during the 1920's and its "Jewels" about 1916. The company acquired a number of molds of other earlier factories, including the Cambridge and A.H. Heisey companies, and had reissued numerous items through the years.

CANDLEWICK PATTERN
Ashtray, clear $39.00
Ashtray, w/eagle, clear, 6½" 48.00
Basket, plain handle, clear, 6½" ... 25.00
Bowl, 5" w., 2" h., polished bottom,
  clear 5.00
Bowl, 10" d., clear 18.00
Bowl, float, 13" d., clear 43.00
Buffet set: 14" plate, mayonnaise
  dish, two ladles; clear, 4 pcs. 70.00
Cake plate, ribbed, clear, 10" d. 48.00

Cheese & cracker set, clear 32.00
Cordial, four-bead stem, clear,
  1 oz. 23.00
Creamer & sugar bowl, pedestal
  base, clear, pr. 30.00
Cup & saucer, demitasse, clear 10.00
Deviled egg tray, clear 80.00
Goblet, clear, 7¼" h. 15.00
Ice tub, deep, clear 65.00
Pitcher w/ice lip, clear, 16 oz....... 75.00
Punch set: bowl & 12 cups; clear,
  13 pcs. 149.00
Salt & pepper shakers w/tray, clear,
  the set 30.00
Tray, lemon, handled, 5½" 28.00
Vase, 6" h., No. 400/87C, clear..... 79.00
Vegetable bowl, handled, clear,
  12" d. 28.00

CAPE COD PATTERN
Bitters bottle w/metal tube, beaded
  base, clear, 4 oz. 33.00
Bowl, 8¾" d., clear 13.00
Bowl, fruit, clear 6.00
Butter dish, cov., clear, ¼ lb. 40.00
Cake plate, square, clear 125.00
Cigarette box w/lid, handled,
  clear 33.00
Compote, 6", cov., footed, No. 160-
  140, clear 55.00
Cordial, clear 14.00
Creamer & sugar bowl w/tray,
  square shape, clear, 3 pcs........ 55.00
Cruet, olive green, labels intact,
  4 oz. 25.00
Goblet, dinner, clear 15.00
Horse radish jar, clear 68.00
Hurricane lamp w/shade, clear,
  2 pcs. 90.00
Marmalade jar w/cover & spoon,
  clear 26.00
Mustard & ketchup set: tray & two
  covered mustards w/spoons;
  clear, 3 pcs. 38.00
Pitcher, clear, 2 qt. 55.00
Plate, 16" d., cupped edge, clear ... 32.00
Punch bowl, clear, 12½" d. 43.00
Relish, three-part, oval, clear,
  9½" 35.00
Salad dressing dish w/cupped plate,
  clear, 6 oz. 48.00
Tumbler, water, stemmed, clear,
  9 oz. 13.00
Vegetable dish, clear, 10" d. 23.00
Wine, stemmed, clear 15.00

FREE HAND WARE
Vase, 8½" h., butterscotch
  w/orange lustre throat 95.00
Vase, 8½" h., orange lustre w/dark
  blue pulled loops................ 135.00
Vase, 9" h., slender hourglass
  shape, green hearts & vines on
  pearl lustre ground, marked 135.00

Vase, 9½" h., bright green overall
leaf & vine decoration, orange
lustre interior 300.00
Vase, 10" h., cobalt blue lustre
w/hearts, original paper label 250.00
Vase, 10¾" h., flared rim on classic
baluster form, opal glass w/or-
ange & blue pulled drape decoration & bright lustre finish (ILLUS.
previous page) 247.50
Vase, 11½" h., applied black rim,
white & yellow lustre body w/blue
& grey veined large leaves &
vines 300.00

IMPERIAL JEWELS LINE
Creamer, yellow lustre 35.00
Plate, 9" d., white lustre 65.00

NU-CUT LINE
Bowl, 8½" d., footed, Rose Marie
(pink) 40.00
Creamer & sugar bowl, clear, pr. ... 45.00

JACK-IN-THE-PULPIT VASES

Cranberry Jack-in-the-Pulpit Vase

*Glass vases in varying sizes and resem-
bling in appearance the flower of this name
have been popular with collectors since the
19th century. They were produced in various
solid colors and in shaded wares.*

Cased, white exterior, deep green
interior, slightly scalloped rim, applied clear petal feet, 5" d.,
6 7/8" h. $88.00
Cased, white exterior, shaded maroon interior, ruffled rim, 6" d.,
6" h. 110.00
Cranberry, trumpet-shaped, applied
clear spiral band down sides, applied clear wafer foot, 4¾" d.,
9½" h. (ILLUS.) 110.00
Cranberry & clear, twisted stem,
footed, 13" h. 149.00
Green iridescent, ruffled rim,

pinched-in sides on base, 4½" d.,
6 5/8" h. 125.00
Maroon opalescent ruffled rim
shading to vaseline body, 4" d.,
7" h. 60.00

KELVA

*Kelva was made early in this century by
the C.F. Monroe Co., Meriden, Connecticut,
and was a type of decorated opal glass very
like the same company's Wave Crest and
Nakara wares. This type of glass was
produced until about the time of the first
World War. Also see NAKARA and WAVE
CREST.*

Box w/hinged lid, green w/h.p.
pink & white florals, signed,
4 1/3" w. $150.00
Box w/hinged lid, shaded pink
w/h.p. white & grey florals, ormolu fittings, signed, 4½" d. 275.00
Box w/hinged lid, octagonal, green
w/h.p. pink parrot tulips, silver
plate fittings, signed, 6" w. (no
lining) 495.00
Box w/hinged lid, mottled sage
green w/h.p. pink & burgundy
flowers, blue leaves & brown
enameling, ormolu fittings,
signed, 7¾" d., 3½" h. (no
lining) 425.00
Mirror tray, oval beveled swivel
mirror in ormolu frame above
deep tray w/squared body &
round opening, blue w/h.p. pink
flowers, ormolu rim, 2¼ x 3" mirror plate, overall 6¼" h. 500.00
Pin dish, hexagonal, blue w/h.p.
dogwood blossoms & enameled
dots, ornate ormolu fittings, original lining, 3½" w. 165.00
Vase, 10" h., ormolu handles, footed, green w/h.p. pink flowers 450.00
Vase, 17½" h., green w/h.p. pink
flowers, ormolu fittings 1,150.00

KEW BLAS

*Glass of this name was made by the Un-
ion Glass Works, Somerville, Massachusetts.
These iridescent wares were similar to those
produced by other art glass firms during the
same period in the late 19th and early 20th
centuries.*

Compote, flared ruffled rim on half-
round clear bowl, applied double-
twisted stem on raised pedestal

foot w/folded edge, signed,
6½" d., 7" h. $330.00
Dish & underplate, flared scalloped
bowl on matching scalloped &
ribbed plate, amber glass in
ribbed optic design w/overall gold
iridescence, each signed "Kew-
Blas" across pontil, plate 6¾" d.,
bowl 5" d., 2¼" h., 2 pcs. 137.50
Tumbler, iridescent gold pinched
sides w/flared mouth, polished
pontil w/signature "KEW - BLAS,"
3¼" d., 5 1/8" h. 220.00
Vase, 7½" h., turned over rim
pulled to four points, gold pulled-
feather design, deep orange
iridescent top, signed 775.00

Kew Blas Vase

Vase, 9¼" h., flared raised rim on
narrow amber chalice-form w/un-
usual enclosed hollow pedestal
base, heavy gold iridescence
overall w/mirror-bright pink lustre
within, signed "Kew-Blas" on
polished pontil (ILLUS.) 440.00

LALIQUE

"Anges" Centerpiece

*Fine glass, which includes numerous ex-
traordinary molded articles, has been made
by the glass house established by Rene' Lalique early in this century in France. The firm
was carried on by his son, Marc, until his
death in 1977 and is now headed by Marc's
daughter, Marie-Claude. All Lalique glass is
marked, usually on, or near, the bottom with
either an engraved or molded signature. Unless otherwise noted, we list only those pieces
marked "R. Lalique" produced before the
death of Rene' Lalique in 1945.*

Ashtray, frosted clear intaglio large
curved fish, clear intaglio bubbles,
signed "Lalique France" in script,
6" d. $195.00
Bowl, 2½ x 4½", stylized cherry
tree center medallion, clear &
frosted 75.00
Bowl, 8" d., "Ondines," molded
mermaids, "ouverte" shape,
opalescent, ca. 1932 . . . . 995.00
Bowl, 12" d., "Madagascar," pale
opalescent sides cast in high relief
about the rim w/monkey masks in
a deeper opalescence, ca. 1932,
molded "R. Lalique France" 7,150.00
Box, cov., circular opalescent cover
molded on the interior w/a whorl
of slender fringed flowers
emanating from a curled branch,
silk-covered circular base, ca.
1925, top set w/a silk inner cover
stamped "Houbigant," molded "R.
Lalique," 5½" d. 880.00
Box, cov., "Grande Muguets," cir-
cular shallow body w/slightly
domed cover molded on the interi-
or w/an overall pattern of lilies-
of-the-valley & vines, ca. 1925,
molded "R. Lalique" & inscribed
"France no. 41," 10 1/8" d. 1,650.00
Bracelet, composed of 18 barrel-
shaped sections w/tiered terminals molded w/chevrons, emerald
green, ca. 1932, inscribed "R.
Lalique" 4,950.00
Carafe w/original stopper, expanding
squared neck above gourd-form
body, molded in low- and medium-
relief w/four frogs issuing streams
of water forming panels alternating w/ground of sinuous water
maidens, sharply tapering ribbed
stopper, matte green stain, ca.
1910, inscribed "R. Lalique,
France," 15¼" h. (minor nicks to
stopper) 5,500.00
Centerpiece, "Anges," circular,
molded w/a frieze of kneeling,
praying angels, opalescent, impressed "R. LALIQUE FRANCE,"
14½" d. (ILLUS.) 3,850.00

Clock, round arched frosted & clear
case w/flat base, molded to depict blossoms & stems, intaglio
molded "LALIQUE," ca. 1930,
4½" h. 1,430.00

Dresser set: cov. powder jar & two
cologne bottles; bands of frosted
birds around the body, bottles
w/birds around the stopper,
4¼" w. jar, 5½" h. bottles,
3 pcs. 950.00

Figure of "Sirene," young mermaid
crouching w/her fishscale legs
coiling about her, opalescent,
ca. 1932, 4" h. 2,200.00

Figure of "Moyenne Voilee," frosted
clear figure of a standing female
in diaphanous drapery, inscribed
"R. Lalique France," 11" h. 4,180.00

Unusual Lalique Goblet

Goblet, silver & "cire perdue" (lost
wax), openwork silver vessel w/a
frosted glass lining depicting rose
stems w/an applied decoration of
rose blossoms in "cire perdue"
glass on a similarly decorated stem
& circular openwork foot w/blown
glass inlay, stamped "LALIQUE,"
losses to glass lining, 7¼" h.
(ILLUS.) 4,400.00

Hood ornament, "Coq Nain," rooster, clear, 8" h. 695.00

Hood ornament, "Hirondelle,"
molded as a sparrow, clear &
frosted, molded "R. LALIQUE
FRANCE," 5¾" h. 3,080.00

Hood ornament, "Sanglier," model
of a wild boar, grey frosted,
2¾" h. 990.00

Hood ornament, "Tete D'Aigle,"
eagle head, w/newly made wooden
base 1,100.00

Inkwell, domed circular form w/con-
cave central cavity, molded on the
interior in high relief w/three
semi-opalescent mermaids w/inter-

twined tails & long tresses forming
sprays of beading, dark slightly
opalescent butterscotch, molded
"R. LALIQUE," ca. 1932,
9½" d. 1,320.00

Lamp, "Cariatides," frosted one-piece
mushroom form, shade molded in
low-relief w/radiating leafy willow
branches, the cylindrical standard
molded in low- and medium-relief
w/elongated caryatids, each holding an apple to her breast, on a
flaring circular foot molded w/a
band of florets, signed "R. Lalique"
twice & "France," ca. 1925,
13¼" h. 18,700.00

Lemonade set: 9¾" h. pitcher, 12
tumblers & circular tray; "Hesperides," molded in medium-relief
w/undulating fern fronds, yellow,
acid stamped "R. LALIQUE," ca.
1932........................3,025.00

Model of a bird, "Faucon," clear
w/frosted highlights, on a circular
base, molded "R. LALIQUE," inscribed "France," ca. 1925,
6 1/8" h.....................1,650.00

Model of a rooster, "Coq du Jungle,"
clear & frosted clear, cast in full-
relief as a proud strutting cockerel,
acid-stamped "LALIQUE - FRANCE,"
ca. 1936, 16" h. (base ground) ...1,925.00

Paperweight, "Double Marguerite,"
molded in medium-relief as two
marguerites in full bloom set
back-to-back & bending gently
into the circular foot, amber, acid-
etched "Lalique," ca. 1932,
2 7/8" h. (chip to upper edge).... 660.00

Perfume bottle, "Telline," modeled
in full-relief as a scallop shell
w/conforming finial, green, inscribed "R. Lalique France
No. 508," ca. 1932, 4" h. 3,025.00

Plaque, molded in high-relief w/a
stylized face of a maiden, her face
framed w/open-mouthed scaly
fish, frosted, fitted w/a metal display stand, second half 20th c.,
12½" sq. 1,980.00

Powder box, cov., "Emiliane,"
marked "R. Lalique," 4"........ 262.00

Scent bottle, tinted brown design of
centered profile of woman's head
smelling flower bordered by radiating flowers & leaves, signed
"R. Lalique France," in original
display box for Houbigant,
1 5/8 x 3 7/8 x 5½" 1,800.00

Stemware service: eleven liqueurs,
seven water goblets, seven cham-
pagnes & eleven wines; each
w/clear cup above a cylindrical
frosted stem molded & enameled

in black w/a pattern of grape
clusters & vines, inscribed "R.
Lalique - France," ca. 1932,
36 pcs. 2,640.00
Tumbler, "Hesperides" patt.,
No. 3412, molded design of
swirled frosted leafy fronds aris-
ing from six-sided base, etched
"R. Lalique - France," 5" h........ 330.00
Vase, 4¾" h., "Perles," grey cased
opalescent oviform body w/three
bands of molded pendent glass
pearls, molded "R. LALIQUE" 4,400.00
Vase, 6 5/8" h., ovoid, molded in
medium-relief w/does grazing
amidst fruit-bearing trees, row
of ferns about the base, amber
w/off-white stain, ca. 1930 ......6,380.00
Vase, 7" h., "Druides," bulbous,
molded w/berry-laden leafy
branches, frosted w/traces of a
brown wash, inscribed "R. Lalique
France," ca. 1932................ 880.00
Vase, 9¼" h., "Bacchantes," flaring
trumpet-form body, molded in
medium- and high-relief w/nude
women in various poses, opalescent w/traces of grey wash, acid
stamped "R. LALIQUE FRANCE" (lip
cut down)....................17,600.00

Lalique "Oranges" Vase

Vase, 11¼" h., "Oranges," spherical
body w/short, narrow neck, molded in medium-relief w/bunches of
oranges against a ground of black-
enameled leaves, molded "R.
LALIQUE," ca. 1932 (ILLUS.) 19,800.00
Vase, 13¼" h., "Lezards et Bleuets,"
ovoid, thick black wall molded in
medium- and low-relief w/shaped
panels of thistles enclosed by
serpentine panels of undulating
lizards, molded "R. LALIQUE" ...36,300.00

LATTICINO

Latticino (or Latticinio) glass is character-
ized by threads of colored glass imbedded in
clear glass in simple or intricate, interlacing
patterns. It represents a revival of an ancient
technique that was popular in the 18th cen-
tury and was revived again during the 19th
century and produced by numerous glass-
houses.

Bowls & underplates, 7¼" d., deep
round bowl w/slightly flaring rim
on short round foot & w/clear applied "head" handles at sides, on
wider flattened underplate, each
piece w/alternating wide white
latticino stripes & narrow pink
swirls w/gold flecks, 2 sets $190.00
Ewer, pink w/gold threading,
7½" h........................ 225.00
Finger bowl, footed, swirled deep
blue & white threading in clear,
foot drawn out from body, applied
clear handles impressed w/face of
a cherub, 4½" d., 2¼" h......... 30.00
Finger bowl, footed, swirled white,
gold & emerald green threading
in clear, foot drawn out from
body, applied clear handles impressed w/face of a cherub,
4¼" d., 2½" h................. 60.00
Wine, tall trumpet-shaped w/folded
foot rim, clear w/stripes of gold
alternating w/white latticino
stripes, 5¾" h. 55.00

LEGRAS

Legras Cameo Scenic Vase

Cameo and enameled glass somewhat simi-
lar to that made by Galle', Daum Nancy and
other factories of the period was made at the
Legras works in Saint Denis, France, late last
century and until the outbreak of World
War I.

Cameo bowl, 3¼ x 4¼", carved
scene w/ships, mountains & lakes
against orange ground, signed ...$275.00

Cameo bowl, 8¼" d., carved brown Art Deco style flowers within triangles against a yellow ground, signed 200.00

Cameo vase, 4" h., square body w/quatrefoil pinched rim, acid-cut & enameled overall with a wintery lakeside scene against a mottled green, amber, orange & clear ground, signed 385.00

Cameo vase, 5" h., carved scene w/a figure & cattle amid trees w/mountains in the distance, signed (ILLUS.) 385.00

Cameo vase, 8½" h., bulbous form w/everted rim, acid-etched w/blossoms & leaves, dark amethyst shading from frosted to light peach, signed "Legras" in cameo 440.00

Cameo vase, 9½" h., rectangular w/bulging sides, carved apple green, maize & olive green river landscape w/a profusion of trees in the foreground & background against a grey ground, signed "Legras" in cameo, ca. 1910 ...... 825.00

Cameo vase, 11½" h., swollen cylindrical form, acid-etched w/ivy leaf decoration, pale peach cut to a ground tinged w/mulberry, signed "Legras" in cameo 550.00

LE VERRE FRANCAIS

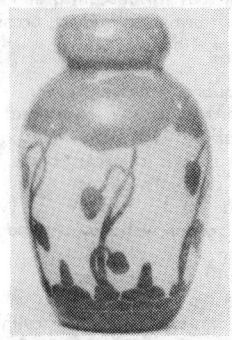

Le Verre Francais Vase

This glass was made in France by Charles Schneider and fairly large quantities of the cameo ware were exported to the United States in the early part of this century. Much of it was sold by Ovingtons, New York City. See SCHNEIDER for further details on this company.

Cameo ewer, baluster body w/elongated spout & angular handle, acid-etched pumpkin walls over-

laid in striated navy blue, purple, grey & white & cut w/stylized flowers & leafage, signed in intaglio, ca. 1925, 13" h. $880.00

Cameo table lamp, domical shade & swollen cylindrical standard, grey mottled w/orange, overlaid in cobalt blue & cut w/stylized blossoms & thorny branches & a tessellated base, wrought-iron three-arm mount, unsigned, ca. 1925, overall 15¼" h. 2,750.00

Cameo vase, 8¾" h., raised sphere on tapering pedestal to flared dome foot, mottled yellow & white overlaid w/shaded red to purple layer cut in three stylized long-stemmed Art Deco style blossoms, etched signature near foot "Le Verre Francais" 412.50

Cameo vase, 11" h., inverted bell form, acid-etched lemon yellow walls overlaid in mottled brown & pumpkin orange & cut w/snails perched on pendent branches, signed in intaglio "Le Verre Francais - France" & w/embedded candy cane, ca. 1920 .... 1,760.00

Cameo vase, 15" h., ovoid body w/acid-etched sides enclosing sunshine yellow, overlaid in deep tomato red shading to burnt umber in the base & cut w/undulating poppy blossoms, buds & leafage above a brickwork ground, signed in intaglio "Le Verre Francais," acid-stamped "France," ca. 1925 (ILLUS.) 3,080.00

Cameo vase, 31¾" h., flaring cylindrical neck & bulbous body in acid-etched grey mottled w/lemon-lime & orange overlaid in orange & chocolate brown & cut w/stylized flowers & leafage, the neck further cut w/brickwork, signed in intaglio "Le Verre Francais," ca. 1925 .... 6,325.00

LIBBEY

Libbey Maize Celery Vase

In 1878, William L. Libbey obtained a lease on the New England Glass Company of Cambridge, Massachusetts, changing the name to the New England Glass Works, W.L. Libbey and Son, Proprietors. After his death in 1883, his son, Edward D. Libbey, continued to operate the company at Cambridge until 1888 when the factory was closed. Edward Libbey moved to Toledo, Ohio, and set up the company subsequently known as Libbey Glass Co. During the 1880's, the firm's master technician, Joseph Locke, developed the now much desired colored art glass lines of Agata, Amberina, Peach Blow and Pomona. Renowned for its Cut Glass of the Brilliant Period (see CUT GLASS), the company continues in operation today as Libbey Glassware, a division of Owens-Illinois, Inc.

Candlesticks, Silhouette patt., clear cup, opalescent figural camel stem, pr.	$245.00
Champagne, Silhouette patt., clear bowl, opalescent figural squirrel stem	80.00
Cocktail, Silhouette patt., clear bowl, opalescent figural kangaroo stem, signed, 6" h.	93.00
Compote, open, 7" h., flaring bowl w/turquoise threading on clear, clear twisted stem, Libbey-Nash series, ca. 1933, signed	145.00
Cordial, Silhouette patt., clear bowl, opalescent figural greyhound stem	175.00
Maize celery vase, clear w/amber iridescent kernels & blue husks (ILLUS. previous page)	165.00
Maize celery vase, creamy opaque w/green husks	160.00
Maize salt & pepper shakers, creamy opaque w/blue husks, pr.	165.00
Maize tumbler, creamy opaque w/yellow husks	125.00
Salt & pepper shakers w/original metal tops, egg-shaped, white w/"Columbian Exposition 1893" in gold, satin finish, signed, pr.	225.00
Vase, 9" h., 5" d., tall slightly flaring cylindrical body w/light vertical ribbing, blue threaded design in opalescent body, Libbey-Nash series, ca. 1933, signed	245.00
Vase, 15" h., Amberina, floriform, hand-blown, ca. 1917	950.00

LOETZ

Iridescent glass, some of it somewhat resembling that of Tiffany and other contemporary glasshouses, was produced by the Bohemian firm of J. Loetz Witwe of Klostermule ard is referred to as Loetz. Some cameo pieces were also made. Not all pieces are marked.

Silver Overlay Loetz Vase

Bowl, 6" d., free-blown organic shape, iridescent gold	$195.00
Cornucopia, gold w/pitted circles, applied swirling leaves, 17" h.	1,950.00
Cracker jar, cov., melon sectioned swirl, bottom half has green splotches, off-white translucent ground, iridescent mother-of-pearl finish, silver plate rim, cover & handle, unsigned, 4¼" d., 6¼" h.	195.00
Cracker jar, cov., iridescent green w/reddish brown threading, brass rim, cover & handle, 5" d., 8¼" h.	165.00
Inkwell, square, iridescent green glass in Art Nouveau style metal framework, 2¾" base, 3" h.	200.00
Inkwell, brass lid, iridescent blues & purples, original well insert, unsigned	239.00
Rose bowl, green w/heavy applied threading, 4" d.	185.00
Rose bowl, iridescent green, 7½" d.	195.00
Tumbler, cameo, cylindrical w/cylindrical expanding shoulder, acid-etched opalescent walls overlaid in cobalt blue & cut about the shoulder w/stylized heart-shaped leafage & coiling tendrils above vertical lines, designed by Hans Bolek, ca. 1910, 4¼" h.	2,200.00
Vase, 4" h., ovoid, iridized transparent navy blue w/spiraled silver overlay in the form of a snake	1,650.00
Vase, 4¼" h., ruffled rim, iridescent green w/three applied snail designs	210.00
Vase, 4½ x 5", round w/square top,	

green w/silvery-blue iridescence, unsigned 145.00

Vase, 4¾" d., squat baluster form, yellow-cased clear w/lower iridescent purple-brown waves, central iridescent gold waves, upper iridescent salmon waves 1,650.00

Vase, 4¾" h., gourd-shaped, opalescent w/lower decoration of thin scarlet waves & upper decoration of iridescent caramel, gold & scarlet waves 1,045.00

Vase, 5½" d., flared cylinder, three iridescent blue ball feet, transparent amber w/heavy gold iridescence, unsigned................ 660.00

Vase, 5 5/8" h., baluster form golden iridescent body applied at the foot & rim w/silver featuring an entwined motif w/French *poincons* & the monogram for the Maison Moderne, designed by Henry Van deVelde for the Maison Moderne, the silver probably executed by Alfonse DeBain in Paris, France, ca. 1898 (ILLUS. previous page) ..9,900.00

LUSTRES

Deep Blue Decorated Lustres

Lustres are glass vase-like decorative vessels with prisms, designed to hold candles and intended as mantel and tabletop decorative adjuncts.

Clear frosted w/cut oval on rim of base, six-scallop rim on rounded bowl on trumpet-form stem w/wide base ring above domed round foot, gilding & h.p. continuous landscape scene on bowl, scene signed "W. Bendt," long clear spear-point cut prisms, 12" h., pr......................$370.00

Deep blue, wide scalloped rim decorated w/enameled heart-scroll

devices & white floral swag band above gilt criss-cross band, baluster-shaped pedestal on domed foot further decorated w/gold bands, double row of facet-cut clear prisms, 14" h., pr. (ILLUS.)......................... 500.00

Ruby, enameled garlands of blue & white flowers, enameled white dots, gold trim, scalloped cut tops, double row of clear spearpoint cut prisms, 14" h., pr...... 850.00

Pink cased w/white polychrome enameled florals & gilt trim, single row of clear prisms, 13" h., pr. (minor chips to prisms) 370.00

Ruby, scalloped flared rim on squat cylindrical bowl decorated w/polychrome enameled floral bands, columnar stem on domed round foot, long clear spear-point cut prisms, 14¼" h., pr. (minor pinpoint flakes) 650.00

White opaque overlay, white panelcutting to cranberry, the panels alternatingly decorated w/florals or crosshatching, scalloped rim, single row of long clear spearpoint cut prisms, 11" h., pr. 1,320.00

MARY GREGORY

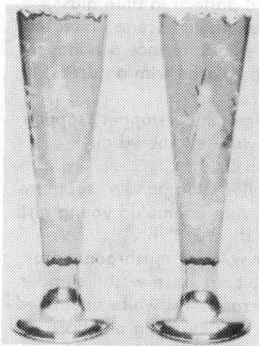

Mary Gregory Vases

Glass enameled in white with silhouette-type figures, primarily children, is now termed "Mary Gregory" and was attributed to the Boston and Sandwich Glass Company. However, recent research has proven conclusively that this ware was not decorated by Mary Gregory nor was it made at the Sandwich factory. Miss Gregory was employed by the Boston and Sandwich Glass Company as a decorator; however, records show her assignment was the painting of naturalistic landscape scenes on larger items such as lamps and shades but never the charming children for which her name has become synonymous. Further, in the inspection of fragments from the factory site, no paintings of children were found. It is now believed that the original "Mary Gregory" glass came from England, Germany and Bohemia by way of an English import wholesale house. For further information see The Glass Industry in Sandwich, Volume 4, by Raymond E. Barlow and Joan E. Kaiser.

Barber bottle, amethyst, white
enameled girl holding flower $185.00
Box w/hinged lid, cranberry, white
enameled running boy on lid &
white enameled flowers around
base, brass rings on side, brass
feet, 2½" d., 3½" h. 275.00
Box w/hinged lid, round, sapphire
blue, white enameled young girl
carrying a basket of flowers & another girl holding some flowers
on lid, white enameled sprays of
flowers around sides, two brass
rings on sides, brass feet,
4 5/8" d., 4½" h. 395.00
Cracker jar, cov., cranberry, white
enameled young girl sitting on a
fence, embossed silver plate rim,
cover & bail handle, 4½" d.,
7½" h. 450.00
Cruet w/original matching bubble
stopper, applied amber handle,
paneled pattern in blue glass,
white enameled scene of seated
girl w/skin-tone face & hands
fishing, colored trim on dress,
7½" h. 375.00
Cruet w/matching stopper, sapphire
blue, white enameled girl
w/hoop 365.00
Cup, applied blue handle, sapphire
blue, white enameled young girl,
3 3/8" d., 2 3/8" h. 70.00
Decanter w/clear mushroom stopper, bulbous base w/tall slender
neck, cranberry, white enameled
young lady standing on shore
looking at swimming swan,
9½" h. 415.00
Goblet, applied clear foot & stem,
cranberry, white enameled boy
w/dish feeding birds, 2 7/8" d.,
5¾" h. 105.00
Mugs, cylindrical, applied amber
handle, amber, white enameled
young boy on one & young girl on
other, both 2¼" d., 4" h., facing
pair 118.00
Perfume atomizer w/original bulb
w/tassel, cranberry, white
enameled young girl, 2½" d.,
5¼" h. 225.00
Perfume bottles w/long tapered

stoppers, necks w/gold trim, cranberry, white enameled boy on
one & girl on other, 10" h., pr. . . . 185.00
Pin dish, oval, chartreuse green,
white enameled young girl on inside bottom, 1 7/8 x 4¾",
1½" h. 79.00
Pitcher, 2" h., medium blue, white
enameled girl holding leaf 225.00
Pitcher, 7½" h., 5" d., round mouth,
applied clear reeded handle, lime
green, white enameled young girl
holding balloon 195.00
Pitcher, water, 8½" h., ruffled rim,
honey amber, white enameled
Victorian boy on tree limb peeking in wooden birdhouse, ground
pontil 325.00
Pitcher, water, 10¾" h., 4¼" d., applied clear reeded handle, light
sapphire blue, white enameled
young girl & foliage w/girl's dress
in gold enamel 275.00
Powder jar, cov., banded design,
green, overall gilded leaves
w/white enameled lady playing
harp in center, large 145.00
Rose bowl, miniature, cranberry
w/gold trim, white enameled
young girl, on short collared base,
2" d., 2" h. 125.00
Salt & pepper shakers w/original
fancy embossed silver plate tops,
amber w/one panel w/white
enameled boy on salt shaker &
girl on pepper shaker, the other
three sides on each w/white
enameled floral decoration, in silver plate holder w/two wells to
hold shakers, bail handle suported by two cupids, holder marked
Meriden Co., holder 6" w., shakers 5¾" h. (tops resilvered) 985.00
Toothpick holder, cranberry w/gold
rim & polished base, white
enameled young girl holding flowers standing in white foliage 225.00
Tumbler, cranberry, white enameled
young boy, 1¾" d., 3" h. 50.00
Tumblers, water, sapphire blue,
white enameled boy on one & girl
on other, gold trim, 2 5/8" d.,
4 1/8" h., facing pr. 110.00
Tumbler, emerald green, white
enameled girl holding flower 67.50
Vase, 4½" h., 1 5/8" d., cranberry
w/clear foot, white enameled
young girl 105.00
Vase, 6" h., 3 5/8" d., square top,
Inverted Thumbprint patt., cranberry, white enameled girl
w/hat 150.00
Vase, 7" h., chalice-shaped, cran-

berry, white enameled boy toot-
ing bugle 135.00
Vases, 7 5/8" h., 3 1/8" d.,
baluster-form, sapphire blue,
white enameled young girl w/hat
on one & young boy w/hat on
other, on ormolu footed base, facing pr. 335.00
Vases, 9½" h., 4 5/8" d., ovoid
footed body w/tall cylindrical
neck, rich opaque pink exterior
w/white lining, white enameled
young girls in long dresses, facing
pr............................. 295.00
Vases, 10" h., 6 1/8" d., cut scalloped rim, two applied reeded
gold trimmed scroll handles, gold-
en honey amber, white enameled
young boy on one & young girl on
other, facing pr. 463.00
Vases, 13¼" h., trumpet-shaped
w/scalloped gilt-trimmed rim,
cranberry, white enameled boy
holding hat on one side & girl
holding skirt on other, set into
sterling silver domed bases, from
W.K. Vanderslice Co., San Francisco, 2nd half 19th c., facing pr.
(ILLUS. page 571) 935.00
Vase, cov., 17¼" h., footed
baluster-form body, domed cover
w/bulbous pointed finial, black
amethyst, white enameled girl
w/basket of flowers & umbrella
standing before a shrine in the
woods 510.00
Water set: 8¾" h. pitcher w/white
enameled boy in tree by nest box
& three 3¾" h. tumblers, two
w/white enameled girl, one
w/white enameled boy; blown
pale cranberry, 4 pcs. 600.00
Whiskey shot glass, barrel-shaped,
cranberry, white enameled young
boy, 2¼" d., 2" h. 85.00
Wine decanter w/original clear bubble stopper, optic rib design,
cranberry, white enameled young
boy, 3 1/8" d., 7 1/8" h. 195.00
Wine decanter w/matching amber
bubble stopper, amber, white
enameled young boy in riding outfit holding riding crop, 4¼" d.,
13½" h. 295.00

MC KEE

The McKee name has been associated with
glass production since 1834, first producing
window glass and later bottles. In the 1850's
a new factory was established in Pittsburgh,
Pennsylvania, for production of flint and
pressed glass. The plant was relocated in
Jeannette, Pennsylvania, in 1888 and operated there as an independent company almost
continuously until 1951 when it sold out to
Thatcher Glass Manufacturing Company.
Many types of collectible glass were produced
by McKee through the years including
Depression, Pattern, Milk White and a variety of utility kitchen wares.

French Ivory Rolling Pin

Animal covered dish, dove on round
base, beaded rim, vaseline,
signed (one bead off rim) $350.00
Beer mug, "Bottoms Up," clear 160.00
Berry set: master berry & eight
sauce dishes; Hobnail with Fan
patt., blue, 9 pcs. 145.00
Bowl, 7" d., Skokie Green 8.00
Bowl, 9" d., Poudre Blue 25.00
Butter dish, cov., Prescut ware,
Wiltec patt., frosted 50.00
Cake stand, Rock Crystal patt.,
amber 35.00
Canister, "Coffee," French Ivory
(custard) 16.00
Cocktail, Rock Crystal patt., green,
3½ oz. 18.00
Compote, open, 7 x 9", Rock Crystal
patt., clear 29.00
Cruet w/original stopper, Wild Rose
w/Bowknot patt., frosted w/some
gilt decoration 115.00
Measuring cup, Skokie Green, two-
spout 100.00
Mug, Serenade (or Troubadour)
patt., amber, 4¾" 75.00
Pitcher, 8" h., Wild Rose w/Bowknot
patt., frosted w/some gilt
decoration 45.00
Rolling pin, French Ivory (ILLUS.) 175.00
Salt & pepper shakers, graduating
side arches, "Salt" & "Pepper" in
black script on French Ivory body,
4" h., pr. 20.00
Sugar bowl, cov., Apollo patt.,
pink 30.00
Tumbler, Gladiator patt., green
w/gold trim 30.00
Water bottle, Prescut ware, Toltec
patt., clear 18.00
Wine, Rock Crystal patt., ruby,
2 oz.......................... 45.00
Wren's Honeymoon Hut, hanging
birdhouse, opaque white textured
glass......................... 65.00

MILK WHITE

Lion Covered Dish

This is opaque white glass that resembles the color of and was used as a substitute for white porcelain. Opacity was obtained by adding oxide of tin to a batch of clear glass. It has been made in numerous forms and shapes in this country and abroad from about the first quarter of last century. It is still being produced, and there are many reproductions of earlier pieces. Also see HISTORICAL and PATTERN GLASS.

Animal covered dish, "The British
 Lion" on base, 6¼" l. $105.00
Animal covered dish, White Cat on
 coarse rib base, 5½" l., 4" h. 40.00
Animal covered dish, Chick in Egg
 on Sleigh 50.00
Animal covered dish, Chicks in
 Square Basket, 2¾ x 4½" base,
 3½" h. 145.00
Animal covered dish, Fox on ribbed
 base, patent dated 150.00
Animal covered dish, Ribbed Fox on
 lacy-edged base. 90.00
Animal covered dish, Hen w/blue
 head on split-rib base 135.00
Animal covered dish, Woolly Lamb
 on Bo-Peep base, 4¼" h. 165.00
Animal covered dish, Lion on scroll
 base, 5¾" l. 50.00
Animal covered dish, Ribbed Lion on
 lacy edge base, patent dated, At-
 terbury (ILLUS.) 145.00
Animal covered dish, Ribbed Lion on
 ribbed base, Atterbury . .130.00 to 150.00
Animal covered dish, Pekingese Dog
 on oblong latticework base,
 3½ x 4¾" 260.00
Animal covered dish, Swan
 w/closed neck on split-ribbed
 base 55.00
Bottle, Bunker Hill, replica of the

monument of Bunker Hill,
 8½" h. 125.00
Bread tray, basketweave, patent
 dated, 9¾ x 12" . . . . .45.00 to 55.00
Butter dish, cov., Blackberry patt. . . .   70.00
Butter dish, cov., Wild Iris patt.,
 decorated 55.00
Charger, Gothic patt., 11¾" d. 39.50
Cologne bottles, w/original hollow
 stoppers, ball-shaped body, overall molded scroll & floral design
 w/traces of gilt & enameled flowers, Victorian, 5¾" d., 9½" h.,
 pr. 65.00
Compote, open, six-sided, Scroll
 patt. 60.00
Corn vase, figural ear of corn
 w/h.p. husks, 4¼" h. 40.00
Covered dish, Crawfish on two-
 handled oblong base, overall
 7½" l. . . . . .115.00 to 135.00
Covered dish, Cruiser ship, 6" l. 57.50
Covered dish, Entwined Fish on lacy
 edge base . . . . .125.00 to 145.00
Covered dish, Snare Drum w/Can-
 non finial, 4½" d., 4" h. 65.00
Creamer, h.p. Apple Blossom patt.,
 yellow band 18.00
Creamer, Marquis & Marchioness
 patt., bust portraits of the Mar-
 quis & Marchioness of Lorne in
 beaded oval reserves, embossed
 roses & swags between portraits,
 beaded rim, tree-bark handle,
 England, dated 1878 . . . . 110.00
Creamer, Paneled Wheat patt. 45.00
Cruet w/original stopper, Netted
 Oak patt. 38.00
Cruet w/original stopper, Tree of
 Life patt. 75.00
Dish, four scroll feet, Wreath patt.,
 8" d. 45.00
Egg cup, Birch Leaf patt., flint 43.00
Match holder, Cornucopia patt. 15.00
Match holder, model of an owl
 w/wings opened 45.00
Match holder, Swan & Cattails
 patt. 45.00
Mug, Bleeding Heart patt., 3½" h. . . .   55.00
Mustard jar, cov., Bull's Head,
 w/ladle 175.00
Pickle dish, model of a fish on base,
 waffle pattern sides & molded
 eyes, 9" l., 4¼" w., 3" h. 68.00
Pitcher, cov., 7¼" l., Dolphin patt.,
 boat-shaped body w/figural dol-
 phin cover 67.00
Pitcher, water, 8½" h., bulbous
 shape, applied handle, Blackberry
 patt. 1,600.00
Pitcher, water, tankard, Scroll
 patt. 58.00
Plate, 6¼" d., Easter Rabbits, old
 paint 42.00

Plate, 7" d., Owl Lovers 48.00
Plate, 7" d., Three Owls 33.00
Plate, 7½" d., Crown border 15.00
Plate, 8" d., Fan & Circle border,
 round 15.00
Plate, 8" w., Triangle S patt. 12.00
Plate, 8¼" d., Three Puppies patt.,
 open leaf border 95.00
Plate, 9" d., Gothic edge 25.00
Plate, 10" d., Lattice Edge border,
 h.p. Apple Blossom patt. 55.00
Relish dish, fish-shaped, marked
 "Patented June 4, '72," Atterbury,
 5¼ x 8" 55.00
Salt & pepper shakers w/original
 tops, h.p. Apple Blossom patt.,
 pr. 60.00
Salt & pepper shakers w/original
 tops, Heron & Lighthouse patt.,
 pr. 95.00
Salt dip, master size, footed, Black-
 berry patt. 28.00
Spooner, Paneled Wheat patt., scal-
 loped rim. 35.00
Spooner, Wild Iris patt., gold trim .. 55.00
Sugar bowl, cov., Basketweave
 patt., dated 1874, 6" h. 40.00
Sugar bowl, cov., melon-ribbed body
 on three leaf-sprig feet, pressed
 Trumpet Vine patt., fired-on origi-
 nal colors, impressed "S.V.,"
 France 65.00
Sugar shaker w/original top, h.p.
 Apple Blossom patt. 100.00

Alba Syrup Pitcher

Syrup pitcher w/original top, Alba
 patt., decorated, Dithridge, 1894
 (ILLUS.). 58.00
Whimsey, hatchet, marked "Souvenir of Hazelton, Pa." in red,
 6" 25.00
Whimsey, model of Uncle Sam's hat,
 color decoration, w/coin bank closure inside brim 45.00
Whimsey, vase, model of a hand,
 2 3/8" d. top, 9" h. 95.00

MILLEFIORI

Millefiori (Italian for "thousand flowers")

glass is decorated or patterned with tiny slices of thin multicolored glass canes and is familiar in paperweights, often filled with closely packed canes. These flower pattern canes have also been used in the production of other objects for many years and the technique is ancient. This type of glass is still being made in Murano, Italy, and elsewhere. Also see PAPERWEIGHTS.

Millefiori Goblet

Dish, octagonal, blue & white canes,
 5" d., ¾" h. $125.00
Goblets, deeply rounded bowl
 w/everted rim, composed of multicolored floral canes, raised on a
 hollow gilt-speckled baluster stem
 on a circular foot w/fold-over rim,
 Venetian, 7½" h., set of 6 (ILLUS.
 of one) 1,045.00
Lamp base, table-type, cylindrical
 standard expanding to a flattened
 globular base, multicolored canes,
 first half 20th c., 10" h. 110.00
Vase, 7" h., hand-blown, multicolored canes. 145.00
Whimsey, slipper, multicolored
 canes, applied camphor glass ruffle & heel, 5" 95.00

MONT JOYE

Cameo and enameled glass bearing this mark was made in Pantin, France, by the same works that produced pieces signed De Vez.

Cameo rose bowl, enameled violets
 on frosted clear ground, 4" d.,
 4½" h. $400.00
Cameo vase, 8¼" h., ovoid body
 w/short rolled foot, lemon-yellow
 w/acid-etched design of stylized
 roses & leafage, signed in cameo
 "MONT JOYE - DS," ca. 1930 ..... 275.00
Cameo vase, 12¼" h., large open
 carved flower, stems, buds &

leaves, gold outlined in dark amber on rough textured gold-brown ground, unsigned 250.00

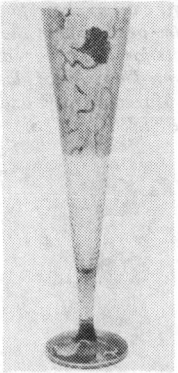

Mont Joye Cameo Vase

Cameo vase, 19¾" h., flared trumpet-form body on flat round foot, amber acid-cut & etched w/foliate designs above & below a broad area of cut honeycomb faceting, signed on base w/"Mont Joye" shield mark (ILLUS.) 715.00

Vase, 6" h., heavily enameled gold design, enameled flowers, green ground, signed................. 350.00

Vase, 8½" h., grotesque type, gold trim & leaves on frosted clear ground, signed................. 225.00

Vase, 20" h., enameled flowers on acid green ground w/heavy gold trim, signed...................1,250.00

MOSER

Ludvig Moser opened his first glass shop in 1857 in Karlsbad, Bohemia (now Karlovy Vary, Czechoslovakia). Here he engraved and decorated fine glasswares especially to appeal to rich visitors to the local health spa. Later other shops were opened in other cities and throughout the 19th and early 20th century lovely colorful glasswares, many beautifully enameled, were produced by Moser's shops and reached a wide market in Europe and America. Ludvig died in 1916 and the firm continued under his sons who were forced to merge with the Meyer's Nephews glass factory after World War I. The glassworks were sold out of the Moser family in 1933.

Bowl, handled, 5" d., 4½" h. to top of handle, enameled multicolored oak leaves & applied black acorns on amber ground, signed $560.00

Box w/lift-off lid, amethyst w/enameled flowers & gold trim, applied amber salamanders on lid & three salamanders form the feet, 4½" d., 4½" h. 605.00

Cameo vase, 12" h., bulbous, amber, carved & enameled elephant in jungle, signed..........1,100.00

Compote, 8¼" d., 4" h., applied clear electric blue rigaree rim & four applied clear electric blue "pigtails" on underside of shallow amber bowl, bowl interior enameled w/brown branches, gold leaves & white cherries woven among twelve enameled white leaves, three white leaves on blue ground, three on yellow, three on red, two on green & one on turquoise, one small enameled branch w/leaves & cherries encircling base, unsigned............. 845.00

Cup & saucer, dolphin handle, cobalt blue w/gold trim, signed 140.00

Decanter w/original stopper, applied handle w/gold trim, cobalt blue w/enameled multicolor grape leaves, gold tendrils & applied green, red & clear grapes, gold bands, unsigned.....................1,295.00

Ewer, pink & white enameled flowers & gold trim on shaded amethyst to clear ground, small applied amethyst jewels, unsigned, 2½" d., 5¾" h........... 225.00

Pitcher, 10¾" h., applied handle, amber w/tableau of two Tyrolian youths seated at a table, one lighting his pipe, other about to drink his glass of beer, a barmaid hurrying to replenish their glasses, in background delineated in gold tracery is the tavern w/its open door & smoking chimney, unsigned 365.00

Plate, 7 3/8" d., Amberina w/lacy gold scrollwork 125.00

Rose bowl, six-crimp rim, inverted vertical ribbing, purple w/enameled scene of maiden pouring drink, gilt scenery surrounds her, polished bottom, numbered but unmarked, 4¾" d. 125.00

Tumbler, juice, four melon-ribbed panels, shaded yellow to clear, 1½" band at top w/colored enamels w/fan ornaments, red & green jewels alternate on panels, signed, 2½" d., 3 5/8" h. 195.00

Vases, 3½" h., 2" d., ovoid base below tall flaring neck, emerald green enameled w/oak leaves & two applied acorns, gold trim, unsigned, pr. 295.00

Vase, 4¾" h., applied amber wishbone feet, pink opalescent shaded to light turquoise ground w/enameled multicolored oak leaves, flying insects & applied acorns decoration 700.00

Vase, 10½" h., ribbed baluster shape, shaded greenish opalescent to clear, enameled red & yellow poppies, gold leaves & branches 325.00

Wine flask, horn-shaped, cranberry w/colorful enameled leaves, brass spigot, fittings & chain, 7½" l. ... 770.00

MOUNT WASHINGTON

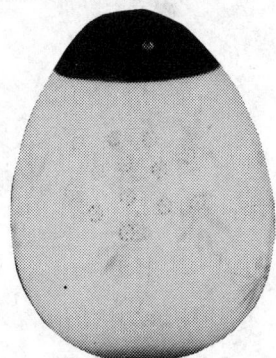

Mount Washington Sugar Shaker

A wide diversity of glass was made by the Mt. Washington Glass Company, of New Bedford, Massachusetts, between 1869 and 1900. It was succeeded in 1900 by the Pairpoint Corporation. Miscellaneous types are listed below, but also see CROWN MILANO, PEACH BLOW and SMITH BROTHERS.

Card tray, fluted rim, turned-in self handles, h.p. clover, daisies & green leaves, lustreless white, 6" d. $110.00

Cracker jar, cov., relief oak leaf at base, enameled pink & brown chrysanthemums, silver plate rim, cover & bail handle, marked "M.W." 650.00

Cracker jar, cov., deeply ribbed, gold daisies on shaded blue ground, ornate silver plate rim, cover & bail handle, 6½" d., overall 9¼" h. 1,190.00

Ewer, elongated pouring lip & applied reeded handle on conical lustreless white body decorated w/h.p. & enameled thistle blossoms & leaves, 7¾" h. 165.00

Rose bowl, lustreless white, enameled pansies, 5" d., 4½" h. 75.00

Salt shaker, original chick-head silver plate top on egg-shaped body, enameled flowers, ca. 1890 ...... 412.50

Salt shaker w/original top, cockle shell mold, enameled florals, ca. 1890 .... 357.50

Salt shaker w/original top, tomato-shaped, enameled florals in blue & white, ca. 1890 .... 236.50

Sugar shaker w/original top, egg-shaped, enameled leafy branch w/pink blossoms on pale blue ground (ILLUS.)................. 215.00

Sugar shaker w/original metal top affixed w/prongs, egg-shaped, enameled sprays of pastel pansies on frosted clear ground, 3¼" widest d., 4" h. 585.00

Sugar shaker w/original domed top, egg-shaped, lustreless shaded blue decoration h.p. w/mauve & amber aster blossoms & buds, green leaves & tracery, 4½" h.... 192.50

Sugar shaker w/original domed top, egg-shaped, lustreless white h.p. overall w/green & brown leaves & enameled bright red berries, w/original label on base "MTW & Co. - PAT. Dec. 31st 1883" 192.50

Sugar shaker w/original top, melon-ribbed, gold tracery & floral decoration on salmon pink shaded to light yellow ground............. 145.00

Vase, 3½" h., "Lava," short bulbous body w/applied reeded black handles, satin finish black body w/inserts of pink, green & grey in a random pattern (small chips at top rim) 550.00

Vase, 10¾" h., tall cylindrical form w/ruffled everted rim, white exterior enameled w/wildflowers & leaves, blue interior, on three gilt-metal animal maskform feet, acid-etched mark, late 19th c. 165.00

MULLER FRERES

The Muller Brothers made acid-etched cameo and other fine glass at Luneville, France, starting in 1910 and until the outbreak of World War II in Europe.

Cameo bowl, 9" top d., 4½" base d., 6½" h., carved red stylized fish on frosted ground w/mica flecks, signed $650.00

Cameo shade, hanging-type, half-round domical form, clear frosted glass mottled amber & bright blue at edge border, layered deep raspberry pink w/blue highlights

carved into poppy blossoms &
darker indigo carved in dramatic
leafy foliage, cameo signature
"Muller Fres - Luneville,"
mounted w/three metal holders for
hanging chains, 15½" d. 4,125.00
Cameo vase, 4½" h., 3¼" d., ovoid
body w/short straight neck, off-
white translucent satin background w/black cut to blue-grey
to peach silhouette scene of a
man w/two cattle by tree,
signed 395.00
Cameo vase, 10" h., flattened spher-
ical body tapering to short, narrow
neck w/flared rim, pale opalescent
lemon yellow streaked w/midnight
blue & lemon yellow at the base,
overlaid in Chinese red & chocolate
brown & cut w/poppy blossoms &
leafage, signed in cameo "Muller
Fres - Luneville," ca. 1920 . . . . 5,500.00
Cameo vase, 12" h., baluster form,
pale grey mottled at base w/lem-
on yellow & purple, overlaid &
enameled w/brown & green &
carved w/a winter landscape
w/leafless trees in foreground,
signed in enamel "Muller Fres
- Luneville," ca. 1920 . . . . 1,650.00
Cameo vase, 13¾" h., globular body
w/narrow short neck, luminous
amber glass overlaid in shades of
teal blue, amber & brown & cut
w/a lake in a mountainous landscape, tall firs & rocky ledges
in the foreground, signed in cameo
"MULLER FRES - LUNEVILLE,"
ca. 1925 . . . . 8,250.00

Monumental Muller Cameo Vase

Cameo vase, 18¼" h., expanding
ovoid body w/flared rim, grey
splashed w/tangerine & aquamarine, overlaid in emerald green
& cut w/a Breton seaport w/a
quaint town in the middle distance
& sailboats & Breton ladies, children & men in the foreground,

cameo signature "Muller Freres -
Luneville," ca. 1920 (ILLUS.) 9,900.00
Vase, 16½" h., ovoid, internally
decorated, deep purple w/silver
foil inclusions encased in outer
layer of clear deeply etched
w/geometric vertical panels, incised "Muller Fres Luneville," ca.
1930 . . . . 1,540.00

NAILSEA

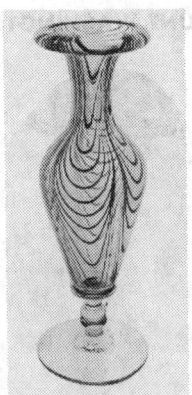

Tall Nailsea Vase

*Glass was made at Nailsea, near Bristol,
England, from 1788 to 1873. Although the
bulk of the products were similar to Bristol
wares, collectors today visualize Nailsea
primarily as a glass characterized by swirls
and loopings, usually white, on a clear or colored ground. Much glass called Nailsea was
made in glasshouses elsewhere, including
America.*

Bowl, 4¼" d., 2¼" h., rim w/six
open loops alternating w/six
turned-in loops, narrow white
loopings on citron background,
ground pontil $95.00
Flask, flattened round body w/short
sheared lip & small rough pontil,
clear w/white loopings, attributed
to South Jersey, some dirt
deposits along inside base,
6¾" h. 140.00
Mug, cylindrical body tapering
slightly to rim, applied clear solid
handle, clear w/white & blue
loopings, rough pontil, 3 5/8" d.,
5¼" h. 357.50
Pipe, deep bulbous bowl, long slen-
der knopped stem, red loopings
on white ground, 18" l. 275.00
Pitcher, 6¼" h., footed, elongated
bulbous body w/swags of white

looping in clear, applied clear strap handle, clear foot w/iron pontil, 19th c. 325.00

Salt dip, clear w/white loopings, wide boldly gauffered rolled rim w/cobalt blue band applied at rim, applied solid foot w/polished pontil, 3¼" d., 1½" h. 425.00

Sugar bowl w/witch ball cover, round footed base w/galleried rim supporting witch ball, both clear w/milk white loopings, probably Pittsburgh area, 19th c., bowl 4½" h., ball 4¾" d., 2 pcs. (heat check in foot) 500.00

Vase, 9 7/8" h., 5¼" d., footed, tall flaring neck above bulbous lower portion w/graceful applied swagging in clear, applied solid white rim, spiraling bands of white in clear body, on heavily applied clear baluster stem w/thick round base, possibly New England, 19th c. 3,200.00

Vase, 13" h., wide partially folded lip tapering to a narrow neck above wide shoulders tapering down to an applied wafered double-knopped solid stem w/thick applied round foot, large rough pontil, clear w/white loopings, Pittsburgh area, minute pinpoint flakes on the wafer (ILLUS. previous page) 425.00

NAKARA

Nakara Hexagonal Box

Like Kelva (which see), Nakara was made early in this century by the C.F. Monroe Company. For details see WAVE CREST.

Box w/hinged lid, hexagonal, lid h.p. w/pink & white florals on green & beige ground highlighted w/white enamel beading, original green satin lining, signed, 3¾" d., 3" h. (ILLUS.) $302.50

Box w/hinged lid, hexagonal, pink to white poppies w/white dot accents, ormolu rim, signed, 6½" d. 475.00

Box w/hinged lid, round shape, lid w/portrait reserve of a standing

Queen Louise in a landscape painted on white edged by pink blossom sprays, all on a light brown ground, base decorated w/pink blossom sprays on a light brown ground, ormolu rims, 8" d. 800.00

Cigar humidor, cov., h.p. Indian portrait, "Cigars" on lid, 5¾" h. .... 1,200.00 to 1,500.00

Hair receiver, Bishop's hat shape, green stain w/enameled pink & white apple blossoms, signed 225.00

Mustard jar, cov., hexagonal, enameled blue & white daisies on pink satin, ornate ormolu cover & handle 395.00

Pin dish, open, hexagonal, blue & white florals on lavender ground, signed, 3" w. 125.00

Ring box w/hinged lid, hexagonal, soft pink ground w/white dotted diamond-shaped medallion on lid decorated w/courting couple, original lining, 2½" d. 395.00

Vase, 8¾" h., pink shaded to steel blue w/enameled white dots outlining scrolls & white flowers, footed ormolu base 405.00

Vase, 14" h., h.p. blue roses & white beading, ormolu dolphin feet 495.00

NEW MARTINSVILLE

Moondrops Pattern Decanter

The New Martinsville Glass Mfg. Co. opened in New Martinsville, West Virginia in 1901 and during its first period of production came out with a number of colored opaque pressed glass patterns and also developed an art glass line they named "Muranese" but which collectors today refer to as "New Martinsville Peach Blow." The factory burned in 1907 but reopened later that year and began focusing on production of var-

ious clear pressed glass patterns many of which were then decorated with gold or ruby staining or enameled decoration. After going through receivership in 1937 the factory again changed the focus of its production to more contemporary glass lines and figural animals. The firm was purchased in 1944 by The Viking Glass Company and some of the long-popular New Martinsville patterns are now produced by this still-active firm. Also see PEACH BLOW.

Basket, footed, Radiance patt.
(No. 4200 Line), amber, 1937-68,
5" d., 8¾" h. $20.00
Book ends, raised sailing ship on
rectangular block background,
clear, ca. 1937-44, 5¾" h., pr. 90.00
Bowl, 5" d., scalloped rim, Peach
Blow (Muranese) art line, "Sun
Glow" color, yellow-caramel shad-
ed to peach-beige 50.00
Butter dish, cov., Moondrops patt.
(No. 37 Line), cobalt blue, early
1930's on 295.00
Butter dish, cov., Radiance patt.,
clear 55.00
Candleholders, ruffled, Moondrops
patt., amber, 3" h., pr. 20.00
Candlesticks, Queen Ann patt.
(No. 18 Line), clear, 1930's, pr. . . . 25.00
Celery dish, Janice patt. (No. 4500
Line), clear, 1926-70, 11" l. 12.00
Console set: console bowl w/match-
ing pair candlesticks, Janice patt.,
silver deposit on clear, 3 pcs. 60.00
Console set: swan-shaped 10½" d.,
bowl & pair 4½" swan candle-
sticks; amber bodies & crystal
necks, 1940-60, 3 pcs. 55.00
Decanter w/original stopper, Moon-
drops patt., amethyst w/clear fan-
shaped stopper, 10½" h.
(ILLUS.) 38.00
Honey jar, cov., Radiance patt.,
ruby red 225.00
Liqueur set: decanter & five 2 oz.
tumblers; Moondrops patt.,
amethyst, 6 pcs. 65.00
Model of a swan, ruby, 12" l. 49.00
Nut dish, two-handled, Radiance
patt., amber, 5" d. 8.00
Plate, 11½" d., Prelude etching,
clear 12.00
Punch cup, Radiance patt., ice
blue 11.00
Relish dish, Radiance patt., three-
handled, three-part, amber,
8" l. 12.00
Shot glass, handled, Moondrops
patt., red 12.00
Water set: tankard pitcher & 2 tum-
blers; Oscar patt., amber, ca.
1930's, 3 pcs. 47.00

OPALESCENT

Presently, this is one of the most popular areas of glass collecting. The opalescent effect was attained by adding bone ash chemicals to areas of an item while still hot and refiring the object at tremendous heat. Both pressed and mold-blown patterns are available to collectors and we distinguish the types in our listing below. Opalescent Glass from A to Z by the late William Heacock is the definitive reference book for collectors. Also see PATTERN GLASS.

MOLD-BLOWN OPALESCENT PATTERNS

BUTTONS & BRAIDS
Pitcher, blue $125.00
Tumbler, cranberry 85.00
Tumbler, white 23.00
Water set: pitcher & 4 tumblers;
blue, 5 pcs. 225.00

COIN SPOT

Coin Spot Water Set

Barber bottle, cranberry 225.00
Celery vase, ribbed, cranberry 110.00
Pitcher, blue 100.00
Pitcher, ruffled rim, blue 120.00
Pitcher, water, cranberry 285.00
Salt & pepper shakers w/original
tops, raised ribs ¾" from base,
cranberry, pr. 165.00
Sugar shaker w/original top,
cranberry 125.00
Water set: pitcher & 6 tumblers;
cranberry, 7 pcs.
(ILLUS.) . . . . 250.00 to 350.00

DAISY & FERN
Barber bottle, cranberry 175.00
Cruet w/clear stopper, blue 95.00
Pitcher, bulbous w/square top,
blue 125.00
Salt shaker w/original top,
cranberry 55.00
Tumbler, cranberry, 3¾" h. 65.00

Water set: pitcher & 6 tumblers;
cranberry, 7 pcs. . . . . .375.00 to 450.00

Daisy & Fern Water Set

Water set: pitcher & 6 tumblers;
white, 7 pcs. (ILLUS. of part) 265.00

FERN

Barber bottle, cranberry 200.00
Finger bowl, ruffled rim,
cranberry 85.00
Salt shaker, cranberry 50.00
Spooner, cranberry 120.00

HOBNAIL, HOBBS

Hobnail Syrup Pitcher

Barber bottle, blue 155.00
Cruet, original stopper, cranberry
(one hobnail chipped) 295.00
Pitcher, lemonade, vaseline 245.00
Syrup pitcher, cranberry (ILLUS.) 225.00

PANELED SPRIG

Cruet w/original stopper, white 110.00
Pitcher, water, cranberry 195.00
Toothpick holder, white 65.00

POINSETTIA

Pitcher, tankard, blue 175.00
Tumbler, cranberry 110.00

Water set: tankard pitcher & 6 tum-
blers; blue, 7 pcs. 450.00

REVERSE SWIRL

Celery vase, cranberry 165.00
Sugar shaker, white 110.00
Syrup pitcher w/original top, blue . . 150.00
Syrup pitcher w/original top,
vaseline 135.00
Tumbler, cranberry 57.00
Tumbler, white 25.00
Water bottle, cranberry, 7" h. 150.00

RIBBED OPAL LATTICE

Cruet w/original stopper,
cranberry 295.00
Salt shaker w/original top, blue 45.00
Salt shaker w/original top, white . . . 43.00
Sugar shaker w/original top,
cranberry 160.00
Toothpick holder, cranberry 75.00

SEAWEED

Barber bottle, cranberry 295.00
Berry set: master bowl & 4 sauce
dishes; blue, 5 pcs. 145.00
Berry set: master bowl & 4 sauce
dishes; cranberry, 5 pcs. 295.00
Cruet w/original stopper, blue 135.00
Rose bowl, vaseline 110.00
Tumbler, cranberry 110.00

SPANISH LACE

Bride's bowl, canary yellow 95.00
Butter dish, cov., cranberry 495.00
Celery vase, ruffled rim, blue 95.00
Cruet w/original stopper, canary
yellow (minute heat check at han-
dle) 125.00
Jam jar, cov., cranberry 450.00
Lamp, miniature, cranberry base,
clear plain chimney 225.00
Pitcher, water, blue 175.00
Rose bowl, blue 49.00
Rose bowl, vaseline, 4" d. 45.00
Sugar bowl, cov., cranberry 295.00
Sugar shaker w/original top, canary
yellow 130.00
Syrup pitcher w/original top, blue . . 225.00
Syrup pitcher w/original top,
vaseline 325.00
Water bottle, bulbous, cranberry,
8½" h. 395.00

SWIRL

Celery vase, ruffled rim,
cranberry 90.00
Pitcher, water, square ruffled top,
applied clear handle, cranberry . . 275.00
Tumbler, blue 22.00
Tumbler, cranberry 45.00
Water set: pitcher & 5 tumblers;
blue, 6 pcs. 190.00

WINDOWS, PLAIN

Cruet w/original stopper,
cranberry 375.00
Pitcher, water, blue 120.00
Syrup pitcher w/original top,
blue 175.00

WINDOWS, SWIRLED

Celery vase, cranberry, tall 95.00
Celery vase, white 39.00
Cruet w/original stopper,
cranberry 325.00
Toothpick holder, cranberry 85.00

PRESSED OPALESCENT PATTERNS

BEATTY RIB

Creamer, white 23.00
Jar, cov., blue 90.00
Jar, cov., white 75.00

BEATTY SWIRL

Pitcher, water, canary 165.00
Tumbler, white 45.00
Water set: pitcher w/applied clear
handle & 2 tumblers; white,
3 pcs. 160.00

CIRCLED SCROLL

Circled Scroll Creamer & Sugar Bowl

Creamer, white 25.00
Creamer & sugar bowl, green
(ILLUS.) 139.00

DIAMOND SPEARHEAD

Bowl, 9" d., blue 30.00
Mug, cobalt blue (ILLUS.) 68.00

Diamond Spearhead Mug

Pitcher, water, tankard-type,
green 225.00
Syrup jug, green 350.00

DRAPERY

Bowl, 4¾" d., individual berry,
vaseline 20.00
Spooner, blue 60.00
Table set: cov. butter dish, cov. sug-
ar bowl, creamer & spooner; blue
w/gold trim, 4 pcs. 425.00
Table set, white w/gold trim,
4 pcs. 395.00
Tumbler, white 18.00

EVERGLADES

Everglades Master Berry Bowl

Bowl, individual berry, blue w/gold
trim 35.00
Bowl, individual berry, canary 23.00
Bowl, master berry, oval, blue
(ILLUS.) 110.00
Bowl, master berry, oval, blue
w/gold trim 175.00
Compote, jelly, blue w/gold trim . . . 85.00
Cruet w/original stopper, vaseline . . 275.00

FLUTED SCROLLS

Fluted Scrolls Spooner

Butter dish, cov., blue, decorated,
7" d., 6½" h. 145.00
Butter dish, cov., vaseline,
decorated 165.00
Butter dish, cov., (puff tray), blue,
small round ¼ lb. size 45.00
Butter dish, cov., (puff tray), vase-
line, small round ¼ lb. size 50.00
Pitcher, water, blue 175.00
Rose bowl, blue 125.00
Spooner, blue (ILLUS.) 40.00

Spooner, blue, decorated 60.00
Sugar bowl, cov., blue............. 95.00
Sugar bowl, cov., blue, decorated .. 125.00
Sugar bowl, cov., vaseline 80.00
Tumbler, blue..................... 25.00
Tumbler, white................... 15.00
Water set: pitcher & 4 tumblers;
    white, 5 pcs................... 225.00

GONTERMAN SWIRL

Gonterman Swirl Pitcher

Pitcher, water, amber, small chip on
    one swirl (ILLUS.) ...'.......... 345.00
Sauce dish, amber top............. 48.00
Sauce dish, blue top............... 40.00
Toothpick holder, amber top 150.00

INTAGLIO

Bowl, master berry, pedestal base,
    blue 195.00
Compote, jelly, blue............... 40.00
Compote, jelly, canary yellow 35.00
Creamer, blue 60.00
Cruet w/original stopper,
    blue ....155.00 to 195.00
Cruet w/original stopper, white 60.00
Pitcher, water, blue 195.00
Spooner, white.................... 35.00
Tumbler, white................... 43.00
Water set: pitcher & 5 tumblers;
    white, 6 pcs. ....195.00 to 225.00

IRIS WITH MEANDER

Bowl, master berry, blue 85.00
Bowl, master berry, green 75.00
Compote, jelly, blue............... 42.50
Pitcher, water, canary yellow 240.00
Spooner, canary yellow 85.00
Toothpick holder, blue............. 125.00
Toothpick holder, green 50.00
Toothpick holder, white........... 39.00
Tumbler, white................... 37.50
Vase, 13" h., green 25.00
Water set: pitcher & 5 tumblers;
    canary yellow, 6 pcs. 475.00

JACKSON

Butter dish, cov., blue 100.00

Candy dish, three-footed, canary
    yellow 40.00
Candy dish, three-footed, vaseline .. 32.00
Cruet w/original stopper, blue 137.50
Epergne, miniature, blue.......... 95.00
Powder jar, cov., blue............. 48.00
Puff box base, vaseline 40.00

JEWEL & FLOWER

Jewel & Flower Sugar Bowl

Creamer, vaseline................. 75.00
Creamer, white 45.00
Sauce dish, white 15.00
Spooner, vaseline 75.00
Spooner, white................... 35.00
Sugar bowl, white (ILLUS.) 60.00
Table set: cov. butter dish, cov. sug-
    ar bowl, creamer & spooner; blue,
    4 pcs.......................... 295.00
Tumbler, vaseline 60.00

JEWELED HEART

Jeweled Heart Berry Set

Berry set: master bowl & 3 sauce
    dishes; white, 4 pcs. (ILLUS. of
    part) 130.00
Berry set: master bowl & 6 sauce
    dishes; green, 7 pcs. 125.00
Bowl, master berry, white 40.00
Pitcher, blue..................... 225.00
Tumbler, water, blue 75.00
Water set: pitcher & 6 tumblers;
    blue, 7 pcs.................... 750.00
Water set: pitcher & 6 tumblers;
    green, 7 pcs. 550.00

Water set: pitcher & 6 tumblers;
  white, 7 pcs..................... 250.00

PALM BEACH
Spooner, vaseline 70.00
Table set, blue, 4 pcs. 515.00
Water set: pitcher & 6 tumblers;
  vaseline, 7 pcs. 750.00
Wine, canary yellow.............. 345.00

PANELED HOLLY

Paneled Holly Creamer

Berry set: master bowl & 5 sauce
  dishes; blue, 6 pcs.............. 310.00
Creamer, blue (ILLUS.) 70.00
Spooner, blue.................... 110.00

REGAL
Bowl, master berry, blue 75.00
Bowl, master berry, green 55.00
Butter dish, cov., white w/gold
  trim........................ 75.00
Compote, jelly, blue 55.00
Compote, jelly, green 50.00
Sauce dish, blue 25.00
Sauce dish, green 20.00
Sauce dish, white 10.00
Table set, blue, 4 pcs. 550.00

SCROLL WITH ACANTHUS
Creamer, green 45.00
Cruet w/original stopper, blue 180.00
Spooner, vaseline 50.00

SHELL
Creamer, blue 75.00
Spooner, blue.................... 95.00
Spooner, green 85.00
Table set, blue, 4 pcs. 895.00

SWAG WITH BRACKETS
Compote, jelly, blue.............. 45.00
Compote, jelly, vaseline 45.00
Cruet w/original stopper, blue 350.00
Cruet w/original stopper, green 285.00
Cruet w/original stopper, vaseline .. 190.00
Pitcher, water, vaseline (minor flat
  chip on bottom of one foot) 185.00
Spooner, blue.................... 58.00
Sugar bowl, cov., blue 95.00
Tumbler, blue.................... 46.50

TOKYO
Bowl, 8" d., blue 28.00
Butter dish, cov., blue 175.00
Spooner, blue.................... 80.00
Sugar bowl, cov., blue w/gold
  trim........................ 100.00
Table set, green, 4 pcs............. 445.00

WATER LILY & CATTAILS
Bowl, fruit, 9¼" d., double scal-
  loped rim, white 35.00
Bowl, 10½" sq., pillow-shaped,
  amethyst 45.00
Pitcher, water, amethyst 375.00
Pitcher, water, blue 395.00
Sauce dish, footed, white 25.00
Spooner, amethyst 65.00

WILD BOUQUET
Bowl, master berry, blue 125.00
Creamer, blue 45.00
Cruet w/original clear stopper,
  blue 250.00
Cruet w/original stopper, green 350.00
Cruet w/original stopper, white 110.00
Sauce dish, blue 35.00
Table set, white, 4 pcs............. 325.00
Tumbler, white................... 22.00

WREATH & SHELL

Wreath & Shell Toothpick Holder

Berry set: master bowl & 5 sauce
  dishes; vaseline w/enameled
  decoration, 6 pcs. 285.00
Celery vase, blue 160.00
Celery vase, vaseline 150.00
Cuspidor, lady's, vaseline ...80.00 to 100.00
Salt dip, blue 95.00
Salt dip, vaseline................. 75.00
Spooner, footed, blue 57.50
Spooner, vaseline w/enameled
  decoration................... 95.00
Sugar bowl, cov., vaseline 120.00
Sugar bowl, cov., vaseline
  w/enameled decor-
  ation...................165.00 to 185.00
Sugar bowl, cov., white............ 55.00
Table set, blue, 4 pcs. ....435.00 to 495.00
Table set, white w/enameled floral
  decoration, 4 pcs........375.00 to 425.00
Toothpick holder, blue (ILLUS.) 265.00
Toothpick holder, vaseline
  w/enameled decor-
  ation...................195.00 to 245.00
Tumbler, blue.................... 51.00

MISCELLANEOUS PRESSED NOVELTIES

Astro Bowl

Astro bowl, 8" d., ruffled, blue
(ILLUS.).......................... 45.00
Astro bowl, ruffled, green 90.00
Aurora Borealis vase, 6" h., white .. 28.00
Beaded Cable bowl, 4¼" d., three-
footed, ruffled, blue 35.00
Beaded Cable rose bowl, ribbon
candy edge, green 35.00
Beaded Cable rose bowl, footed,
white 40.00
Beaded Stars bowl, low base,
green 37.00
Blossoms & Web bowl, footed, white
w/red Goofus decoration 25.00

Cashews Bowl

Cashews bowl, crimped, blue
(ILLUS.)....................... 24.00
Fancy Fantails cruet w/stopper,
blue 375.00
Fancy Fantails rose bowl, vaseline .. 40.00
Greek Key & Ribs bowl, 8" d.,
green 30.00
Jewel & Fan banana boat, green ... 110.00
Jewel & Fan bowl, blue 30.00
Leaf & Beads bowl, 8" d., fluted,
twig feet, blue 37.50
Leaf & Beads bowl, 8½" d., 3" h.,
twig feet, green 40.00
Leaf Chalice jack-in-the-pulpit vase,
5¾" h., 6¼" d., blue 45.00
Many Loops bowl, crimped & fluted,
round, blue................... 44.00

Many Loops bowl, triangular,
green 25.00
Open O's rose bowl, blue 45.00
Palm & Scroll rose bowl, three-
footed, green 67.00
Pearls & Scales rose bowl, footed,
blue 55.00

Piasa Bird Vase

Piasa Bird "swung" vases, blue, pr.
(ILLUS. of one) 110.00
Poinsettia Lattice bowl, 8½" d., ruf-
fled, footed, white 45.00
Pump & Trough, blue, 2 pcs. 115.00
Reflecting Diamonds bowl, 8¾" d.,
blue 30.00
Rose Show bowl, ruffled, blue 125.00
Ruffles & Rings bowl, footed,
green 38.00

(End of Opalescent Glass Section)

ORREFORS

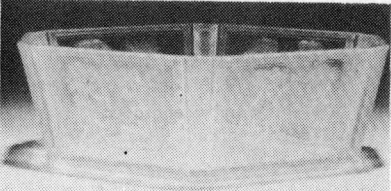

Orrefors Bowl by Simon Gate

*This Swedish glasshouse, founded in 1898
for production of tablewares, has made
decorative wares as well since 1915. By 1925,
Orrefors had achieved an international reputation for its Graal glass, an engraved art
glass developed by master glass blower Knut
Bergqvist and artist-designers, Simon Gate
and Edward Hald. Ariel glass, recognized by
a design of controlled air traps, and the heavy
Ravenna glass, usually tinted, were both developed in the 1930's. While all Orrefors glass
is collectible, pieces signed by early designers and artists are now bringing high prices.*

Bowl, 9 5/8" l., hexagonal w/flaring sides, clear, engraved w/pairs of individual figures of semi-nude women w/wildly flaring long hair between geometric borders, underside engraved w/a starburst, designed by Simon Gate, ca. 1925 (ILLUS.) $2,090.00

Decanter & stopper, rectangular vessel w/a rounded shoulder & short cylindrical neck, shaped rectangular stopper, clear, engraved on the obverse w/the figure of an underwater fisherman, signed, mid-20th c., 11¾" h. 137.50

Vase, 4¼" h., "Ariel," thick-walled bulbous body, interior decorated w/rows of black oblong cells w/clear centers formed by air bubbles, short cylindrical dark grey neck, base inscribed "Orrefors, Sweden, Ariel no 1849E, Edvin Ohrstrom," mid-20th c. 1,210.00

Vase, 5½" h., 3¾" square mouth, Art Deco style, four bulbous sides, clear, thick engraved panel w/full side view of woman holding baby above her head, polished pontil, artist-signed 90.00

Vase, 7" h., "Ariel," "The Gondolier," wide cylindrical body, thick clear walls internally decorated in electric blue w/a musician in his gondola serenading a wavy-haired lady, further decorated w/blossoms, circles, waves & lines, designed by Edvin Ohrstrom, ca. 1962, inscribed "Orrefors Ariel no. 381L Edvin Ohrstrom" 2,200.00

Vase, 7" h., "Graal," bulbous body w/tapered flared neck, decorated w/blue stripes in a free-form pattern, designed by Nils Landberg, inscribed "ORREFORS S. Graal Nr. 285N Nils Landberg," 1940's .. 770.00

Vase, 7½" h., clear w/engraved ship, signed, marked "Expo. n. 3621. d3. A.S." 145.00

PAIRPOINT

Originally organized in New Bedford, Massachusetts, in 1880, as the Pairpoint Manufacturing Company, on land adjacent to the famed Mount Washington Glass Works, this company first manufactured silver and plated wares. In 1894, the two famous factories merged as the Pairpoint Corporation and enjoyed great success for more than forty years. The company was sold in 1939 to a group of local businessmen and eventually bought out by one of the group who turned the management over to Robert M. Gunderson. Subsequently, it operated as the Gunderson Glass Works until 1952 when, after Gunderson's death, the name was changed to Gunderson-Pairpoint. This factory closed in 1956. Subsequently, Robert Bryden took charge of this glassworks, at first producing glass for Pairpoint abroad and eventually, in 1970, beginning glass production in Sagamore, Massachusetts. Bryden's Pairpoint company continues in operation today manufacturing fine quality blown and pressed glass.

Centerpiece bowl, pedestal base, bowl engraved w/Vintage patt., cobalt blue, 12" d. $395.00

Compote, cov., engraved Wilton design, "controlled bubble" ball connector on stem & matching finial on cover, clear.................. 325.00

Compotes, English patt. w/crisscross cuttings, ray cut base, clear, 6½" d., 6" h., pr. 175.00

Compote, 6½ x 6½", light green bowl w/clear "controlled bubble" ball connector 55.00

Compote, 8" d., amber bowl w/clear "controlled bubble" ball connector 65.00

Compote, 9" d., pedestal base, engraved w/Vintage patt. around low, flaring bowl, amethyst 85.00

Cornucopia-vase, light green ribbed horn on clear "controlled bubble" paperweight base, Gunderson-Pairpoint, 8½" h. 125.00

Lamp, helmet-form, clear frosted shade w/molded stylized swags & chevrons, silvered metal three-arm support continuing to a trumpet-form base w/stylized leafage decoration & raised on six ball feet, ca. 1910, marked, 13" h. 440.00

PATE DE VERRE

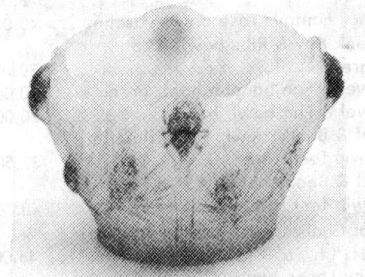

Pate de Verre Bowl

Pate de Verre, or "paste of glass," was molded by very few glass artisans. In the pate de verre technique, powdered glass is mixed with a liquid to make a paste which is then placed in a mold and baked at a high temperature. These articles have a finely-pitted or matte finish and are easily distinguished from blown glass. Duplicate pieces are possible with this technique.

Ashtray, circular shallow dish shape, grey mottled w/emerald green & sapphire blue, the rounded sides molded at intervals w/straps of overlapping leafage in emerald green & sapphire blue, three indentations for cigarettes, signed "G. ARGY - ROUSSEAU," ca. 1925, 4½" d. $1,760.00

Bowl, 3 5/8" h., hemispherical body, sides decorated w/a band of stylized birds in flight above an Aztec border in shades of raspberry, purple & lavender against a grey ground splashed w/lavender & raspberry, signed "G. Argy-Rousseau" & "FRANCE," ca. 1930 . . . . .13,200.00

Bowl, 4¾" h., tapering sides w/two integral flattened handles molded in low- and medium-relief w/berry-laden leafy branches in emerald & olive green, ochre & brown against a lemon yellow ground shaded to mustard, signed "AWalter - Nancy" & "HBerge - Sc.," ca. 1925 . . . . . .3,850.00

Bowl, 6" d., wide-mouthed vessel w/slightly squared corners cast in medium-relief w/panels enclosing pine cones & needles, the corners cast in full-relief w/beetles, in shades of emerald green & rust reserved against a lemon yellow ground, signed "AWALTER - NANCY," modeled by Henri Berge', ca. 1925 (ILLUS. previous page) . .4,950.00

Dish, hexagonal, slightly dished shape, lime green molded in high-relief w/a flying fish in emerald green spotted w/black reserved against a seaweed-strewn ground, signed "AWalter - Nancy" & "Berge - Sc.," 6 3/8" w. 4,400.00

Figure of Pan, seated young god playing his pipes, deep lemon yellow & lime green, modeled by Henri Mercier, signed "AWalter - Nancy," & "h. Mercier," ca. 1925, 3¾" h. 1,650.00

Figure of a woman, "Danuese," the standing figure draped in flowing robes, molded in emerald green shading to white tinged w/green, inspired by Loie Fuller, signed "A.

WALTER/NANCY," ca. 1920, 7 7/8" h. 2,200.00

Lamp, miniature, ovoid grey base splashed w/purple & emerald green, molded in medium-relief w/wildflowers & leafge in purple & emerald green, gilt-metal mounts & miniature hurricane shade, base signed "G. ARGY-ROUSSEAU," ca. 1925, overall 7 7/8" h., 2 pcs. 1,430.00

Paperweight, cast w/a speckled emerald green & black reptile on a circular mustard & grey-streaked ground, signed "A. WALTER - NANCY," ca. 1920, 1¾" d. 2,200.00

Pendant, circular, molded in high-relief w/a stylized bouquet of orange flowers w/black & purple centers on a grey ground, ca. 1925, signed "G.A.R.," G. Argy-Rousseau, 2½" d. (replaced silk cord, original burst air bubble on edge) 1,540.00

Pendant, ovoid, molded in high-relief w/a cicada w/black body & green wings against a mottled rose & lemon yellow ground, signed "A. WALTER/NANCY/H. Berge Sc.," ca. 1925, 3" l. 1,430.00

Vase, 5 5/8" d., "Les Ramiers," deep domical bowl molded w/white wood-pigeons in flight against grey cloud-filled sky, below a faceted border of alternating lappets & rectangles in mottled magenta, rose, violet-black & orange, raised on a faceted foot in conforming colors, signed "G. ARGY-ROUSSEAU," underside marked "FRANCE," ca. 1925 . . . . .20,900.00

Vase, 7¼" h., bulging ovoid, molded in low-relief at the shoulder w/a band of stylized flowers in sapphire blue, emerald green & grey within strapwork grey borders against a grey ground randomly streaked w/sapphire blue & emerald green, signed "G. ARGY-ROUSSEAU," ca. 1925 . . . . .4,950.00

Vase, 10½" h., ovoid, grey streaked w/deepest purple & emerald green, molded in medium-relief w/aquamarine, turquoise & purple fan-form flowers between deep purple scalloped borders, signed "G. ARGY-ROUSSEAU," underside impressed "France," ca. 1925 . . . .7,700.00

Vide poche, shallow irregular oval dish molded in medium-relief w/blossoms & leafage in grey streaked w/emerald green, turquoise, dusty rose & olive green, signed in intaglio "Daum/Nancy," ca. 1910, 8¼" l. 2,200.00

PATTERN GLASS

Though it has never been ascertained whether glass was first pressed in the United States or abroad, the development of the glass pressing machine revolutionized the glass industry in the United States and this country receives the credit for improving the method to make this process feasible. The first wares pressed were probably small flat plates of the type now referred to as "lacy" Sandwich, the intricacy of the design concealing flaws.

In 1827, both the New England Glass Co., Cambridge, Massachusetts and Bakewell & Co., Pittsburgh, took out patents for pressing glass furniture knobs and soon other pieces followed. This early pressed glass contained red lead which made it clear and resonant when tapped (flint). Made primarily in clear, it is rarer in blue, amethyst, olive green and yellow.

By the 1840's, early simple patterns such as Ashburton, Argus and Excelsior appeared. Ribbed Bellflower seems to have been one of the earliest patterns to have had complete sets. By the 1860's, a wide range of patterns were available.

In 1864, William Leighton of Hobbs, Brockunier & Co., Wheeling, West Virginia, developed a formula for "soda lime" glass which did not require the expensive red lead for clarity. Although "soda lime" glass did not have the brilliance of the earlier flint glass, the formula came into widespread use because glass could be produced cheaply.

By 1900, patterns had become ornate in imitation of the expensive brilliant cut glass.

ACTRESS

Actress Celery Vase

Bowl, 6" d., footed	$40.00
Bowl, 8" d., Adelaide Neilson	85.00
Bread tray, Miss Neilson, 12½" l.	72.00
Butter dish, cov., Fanny Davenport & Miss Neilson	75.00 to 80.00

Cake stand, Maude Granger & Annie Pixley, 10" d., 7" h.	120.00 to 140.00
Celery vase, Pinafore scene (ILLUS.)	158.00
Cheese dish, cov., "Lone Fisherman" on cover, "The Two Dromios" on underplate	255.00
Cologne bottle w/original stopper, 11" h.	47.00
Compote, cov., 6" d., 10" h.	100.00
Compote, cov., 8" d., 12" h.	150.00
Compote, cov., 10" d., 14½" h., Fanny Davenport & Maggie Mitchell	150.00
Compote, open, 6" d., 11" h.	130.00
Compote, open, 7" d., 7" h., Miss Neilson	145.00
Compote, open, 10" d., 9" h.	100.00
Creamer, Miss Neilson & Fanny Davenport	80.00
Goblet, Lotta Crabtree & Kate Claxton	62.00
Marmalade jar, cov., Maude Granger & Annie Pixley	107.00
Mug, Pinafore scene	47.50
Pickle dish, Kate Claxton, "Love's Request is Pickles," 5¼ x 9¼"	46.00
Pitcher, water, 9" h., Miss Neilson & Maggie Mitchell	250.00
Platter, 7 x 11½", Pinafore scene	81.00
Relish, Miss Neilson, 5 x 8"	32.50
Relish, Maude Granger, 5 x 9"	67.00
Salt dip, master size	68.00
Salt shaker w/original pewter top	43.00
Sauce dish, Maggie Mitchell & Fanny Davenport, 4½" d., 2½" h.	18.00
Spooner, Mary Anderson & Maude Granger	74.00
Sugar bowl, cov., Lotta Crabtree & Kate Claxton	135.00
Sugar bowl, open	45.00

ALABAMA (Beaded Bull's Eye with Drape)

Butter dish, cov., clear	68.00
Butter dish, cov., ruby-stained	80.00
Castor set, 4-bottle, original silver plate stand	135.00
Celery tray, clear	30.00
Celery tray, ruby-stained	125.00
Compote, cov., 5" d.	65.00
Creamer	42.00
Creamer, individual size	22.00
Cruet w/original stopper	55.00
Mustard pot & cover w/slot for spoon	55.00
Pitcher, water	75.00
Relish, 5 x 8 1/8"	29.00
Sauce dish	17.00
Spooner	35.00
Sugar bowl, cov.	45.00
Syrup pitcher w/original top	85.00 to 95.00
Table set: creamer, cov. sugar bowl,	

spooner & cov. butter dish;
4 pcs. 250.00
Toothpick holder 63.00
Tray, water, 10½" 68.00

ALASKA (Lion's Leg)

Alaska Celery Tray

Banana boat, blue opalescent 215.00
Banana boat, emerald green 85.00
Berry set: master bowl & 4 sauce
dishes; green, 5 pcs. 275.00
Berry set: master bowl & 6 sauce
dishes; blue opalescent, 7 pcs. ... 350.00
Berry set: master bowl & 6 sauce
dishes; vaseline opalescent,
7 pcs. .... 250.00 to 275.00
Bowl, 8" sq., blue
opalescent .... 100.00 to 125.00
Bowl, 8" sq., clear w/enameled
florals 65.00
Bowl, 8" sq., green w/enameled
florals 65.00
Butter dish, cov., blue opalescent ... 350.00
Butter dish, cov., green w/enameled
florals 155.00
Butter dish, cov., white w/enameled
florals 250.00
Butter dish, cov., white w/enameled
florals 85.00
Card tray, blue opalescent 28.50
Card tray, vaseline opalescent 30.00
Celery (or jewel) tray, blue opales-
cent (ILLUS.) 132.00
Celery tray, blue opalescent
w/enameled florals 250.00
Celery tray, green 45.00
Celery tray, vaseline opalescent 140.00
Creamer, blue opalescent 65.00
Creamer, clear to opalescent 45.00
Creamer, green 38.00
Creamer, green w/enameled
florals 70.00
Creamer, vaseline opalescent 57.00
Cruet w/original stopper, blue
opalescent 265.00
Cruet w/original stopper, green 275.00
Cruet w/original stopper, vaseline
opalescent 240.00
Pitcher, water, blue
opalescent .... 340.00 to 380.00
Pitcher, water, blue opalescent
w/enameled florals 550.00
Pitcher, water, clear to opalescent .. 125.00
Pitcher, water, green 88.00
Salt shaker w/original top, blue
opalescent 42.50

Salt shaker w/original top, clear to
opalescent 25.00
Salt & pepper shakers w/original
tops, blue opalescent, pr. 125.00
Salt & pepper shakers w/original
tops, vaseline opalescent, pr. 105.00
Sauce dish, blue opalescent 50.00
Sauce dish, clear to opalescent 22.50
Sauce dish, clear to opalescent
w/enameled florals 24.00
Sauce dish, green 20.00
Sauce dish, green w/enameled
florals & leaves 38.00
Sauce dish, vaseline opalescent 40.00
Spooner, blue opalescent 72.00
Spooner, clear to opalescent 30.00
Spooner, green 36.50
Spooner, green w/enameled
florals 65.00
Spooner, vaseline opalescent 54.00
Sugar bowl, cov., blue opalescent .. 143.00
Sugar bowl, cov., blue opalescent
w/enameled florals 150.00
Sugar bowl, cov., clear to opales-
cent w/enameled florals 65.00
Sugar bowl, cov., green
w/enameled florals 85.00
Sugar bowl, cov., vaseline opales-
cent w/enameled florals 135.00
Table set, blue opalescent,
4 pcs. .... 625.00 to 750.00
Table set, vaseline opalescent,
4 pcs. .... 550.00 to 600.00
Tumbler, green 45.00
Tumbler, vaseline opalescent 63.00
Water set: pitcher & 4 tumblers;
blue opalescent, 5 pcs. 485.00
Water set: pitcher & 6 tumblers;
vaseline opalescent, 7 pcs. 725.00

ALEXIS - See Priscilla Pattern

ALMOND THUMBPRINT (Pointed Thumbprint)

Bowl, 4½" d., 4 7/8" h., footed,
non-flint 20.00
Butter dish, cov., ruby-stained, non-
flint 105.00
Champagne, flint 67.50
Compote, cov., 6½" d., 8" h.,
flint .... 75.00 to 85.00
Egg cup, flint 25.00
Goblet 20.00
Salt dip, master size, flint 20.00
Spooner, fluted, non-flint 20.00
Sugar bowl, cov., non-flint 35.00
Tumbler, footed, flint 30.00
Wine, flint 20.00

AMAZON (Sawtooth Band)

Banana stand 65.00
Bowl, 6" d. 22.00
Bowl, 8" d., scalloped 27.50

Bowl, 9" d. 20.00
Butter dish, cov. 66.00
Cake stand, 8" to 9½" d. 40.00
Celery vase 33.00
Champagne 32.00
Claret 37.50
Compote, open, jelly, 4½" d. 22.50
Compote, open, 6" d., high stand . . .   28.00
Compote, open, 8" d., 5" h. 25.00
Compote, open, 8¾" d., 7¼" h. 42.50
Compote, open, 9½" d., 8" h. 55.00
Cordial 32.50
Creamer 37.00
Creamer, child's miniature 27.50
Creamer & cov. sugar bowl, pr. 65.00
Cruet w/bar in hand stopper,
    amethyst 250.00
Cruet w/bar in hand stopper,
    clear 55.00
Egg cup 14.00
Epergne 37.50
Goblet 25.00
Goblet, etched 30.00
Pitcher, water 53.00
Salt dip, master size . . . . 12.50 to 18.00
Sauce dish, flat or footed . . . . . 4.00 to 11.50
Spooner 20.00
Spooner, child's miniature (ILLUS.
    left) 25.00
Sugar bowl, cov. 40.00
Syrup pitcher w/original top 42.50
Table set: cov. butter dish, creamer,
    cov. sugar bowl & spooner; child's
    miniature, 4 pcs. 150.00
Tumbler 23.00
Wine 21.00

AMBERETTE (English Hobnail Cross or Klondike)

Berry set: master bowl & 4 sauce
    dishes; frosted w/amber cross,
    5 pcs. 385.00
Bowl, master berry or fruit, 8" sq.,
    clear w/amber cross 75.00
Bowl, master berry or fruit, 8" sq.,
    frosted w/amber cross 250.00
Bowl, 11" sq., flared, clear w/amber
    cross 130.00
Butter dish, cov., clear w/amber
    cross . . . . 250.00 to 300.00
Butter dish, cov., frosted w/amber
    cross 370.00
Celery tray, frosted w/amber cross,
    4½ x 10 7/8", 2 7/8" h. 185.00
Celery vase, clear w/amber
    cross 142.50
Celery vase, frosted w/amber
    cross 200.00
Creamer, clear w/amber cross 103.00
Creamer, frosted w/amber cross . . . 160.00
Goblet, clear w/amber cross 95.00
Goblet, frosted w/amber cross 250.00
Lamp, kerosene-type, clear w/am-
    ber cross, 10" h. 155.00

Pitcher, water, clear w/amber
    cross 285.00
Pitcher, water, frosted w/amber
    cross . . . . 600.00 to 900.00
Punch cup, clear w/amber cross 60.00
Punch cup, frosted w/amber cross . . 110.00
Relish, clear w/amber cross, boat-
    shaped, 4 x 9" 115.00
Relish, frosted w/amber cross, boat-
    shaped, 4 x 9" 125.00
Relish, frosted w/amber cross,
    4 x 9" w/silver plate holder, over-
    all 6" h. 145.00
Salt shaker w/original top, clear
    w/amber cross 69.00

Amberette Salt Shaker

Salt shaker w/original top, frosted
    w/amber cross (ILLUS.) 100.00
Salt & pepper shakers w/original
    tops, frosted w/amber cross,
    pr. 200.00 to 250.00
Sauce dish, flat or footed, clear
    w/amber cross 20.00
Sauce dish, flat or footed, frosted
    w/amber cross 80.00
Spooner, clear w/amber cross 95.00
Spooner, frosted w/amber cross 200.00
Sugar bowl, cov., clear w/amber
    cross, 6¾" h. 185.00
Sugar bowl, cov., frosted w/amber
    cross, 4" d., 6¾" h. 250.00
Sugar bowl, open, frosted w/amber
    cross 175.00
Syrup pitcher w/original top, frosted
    w/amber cross 766.00
Table set, frosted w/amber cross,
    4 pcs. 825.00
Toothpick holder, clear w/amber
    cross 200.00
Toothpick holder, frosted w/amber
    cross 415.00
Tumbler, frosted w/amber cross 138.00
Vase, 8" h., trumpet-shaped, clear
    w/amber cross 130.00

ANIMALS & BIRDS ON GOBLETS & PITCHERS
GOBLETS:
Bear climber, acid-etched 95.00
Bird in Swamp 65.00

Deer & Doe w/lily-of-the-valley,
pressed .... 95.00 to 110.00
Dog w/rabbit in mouth, acid-
etched 65.00
Frog & Spider, pressed 126.00
Ibex, etched 62.50
Ostrich Looking at Moon, pressed .. 78.00
Owl-Possum, pressed.............. 80.00
Pigs in Corn, pressed.....250.00 to 350.00
Squirrel, pressed 300.00
Stork & Flowers, etched 55.00

PITCHERS:
Bringing Home Cows 350.00
Fox & Crow...................... 150.00
Heron........................... 143.00
Squirrel, pressed 175.00

APOLLO
Bowl, 8" d. 22.50
Bread tray, square 27.50
Butter dish, cov. 50.00
Cake stand, 9" to 10½" d. 53.00
Celery tray 22.50
Celery vase................ 37.50 to 45.00
Compote, cov., 6" d. 55.00
Compote, cov., 8" d. 65.00
Compote, open, 5" d............. 36.00
Compote, open, 7" d., low stand ... 25.00
Creamer 38.00
Cruet w/original stopper........... 45.00
Goblet 27.50
Lamp, kerosene-type, amber,
9" h. 190.00
Lamp, kerosene-type, blue, 9" h. ... 190.00
Lamp, kerosene-type, canary yel-
low, 9" h. 165.00
Lamp, kerosene-type, clear,
10" h................... 65.00 to 85.00
Lamp, kerosene-type, canary yellow
w/frosted font & stem w/enamel-
ing, 12" h...................... 260.00
Lamp, kerosene-type, frosted,
12" h.......................... 65.00
Pitcher, water, bulbous 65.00
Plate, 9½" sq. 26.50
Salt dip, master size............... 25.00
Sauce dish, flat or footed 8.00
Spooner 32.50
Sugar bowl, cov. 45.00
Sugar shaker w/original top 45.00
Syrup pitcher w/original top 110.00
Tumbler 21.00
Tumbler, frosted 30.00
Water set, pitcher & 6 tumblers,
7 pcs. 200.00

ARGUS (McKee & Brother, Pittsburgh)
Ale glass, footed, flint, 5½" h. 70.00
Butter dish, cov., footed, flint,
8" d........................... 85.00
Celery vase, flint.................. 50.00
Champagne, flint 50.00
Champagne (Hotel Argus), non-
flint........................... 18.50

Compote, open, 6" d., 4½" h.,
flint........................... 55.00
Creamer, applied handle, flint...... 110.00
Egg cup, flint 24.00
Egg cup, handled, flint............. 70.00
Goblet, flint 45.00
Goblet (Barrel Argus), flint......... 42.00
Goblet (Hotel Argus), non-
flint..................... 25.00 to 30.00
Goblet, master size, flint 35.00
Honey dish, flint 20.00
Mug, applied handle, flint 60.00
Pitcher, water, 8¼" h., applied han-
dle, flint....................... 200.00
Punch bowl, pedestal base, scal-
loped rim, 11½" d., 9½" h....... 160.00
Salt dip, master size, flint.......... 35.00
Spillholder, flint 45.00
Spooner, flint 43.00
Sugar bowl, cov., flint 65.00
Tumbler (Barrel Argus), flint 60.00
Tumbler, bar-type, flint 60.00
Tumbler, footed, flint, 4" h. 40.00
Tumbler, footed, flint, 5" h. 60.00
Tumbler, whiskey, handled......... 57.00
Wine, flint, 4" h. 45.00
Wine (Hotel Argus), non-flint 20.00

ART (Job's Tears)

Art Open Compote

Banana stand 98.00
Bowl, 8½" d. 45.00
Bowl, 9¾" d. 37.00
Bowl, triangular................... 45.00
Butter dish, cov., clear 58.00
Butter dish, cov., ruby-stained 65.00
Cake stand, 9" to 10½" d. 73.00
Celery vase....................... 50.00
Compote, cov., 6" d., 10" h........ 55.00
Compote, cov., 8" d., high stand ... 115.00
Compote, open, 8" d., high stand... 35.00
Compote, open, 9" d., 7¼" h....... 45.00
Compote, open, 10" d., 9" h.
(ILLUS.)...................... 55.00
Creamer 43.00
Cruet w/original stopper........... 88.00
Goblet 45.00
Pitcher, milk, ruby-stained ..95.00 to 150.00
Pitcher, water, bulbous 85.00
Plate, 10" d...................... 55.00
Relish, 4¼ x 7¾" 18.50

Relish, ruby-stained 65.00
Sauce dish, flat or footed 18.00
Spooner 27.00
Sugar bowl, cov. 42.00
Tumbler 20.00

ASHBURTON

Ale glass, flint, 5" h. 95.00
Ale glass, flint, 6½" h. 65.00
Bowl, 6½" d., low, footed, flint 72.50
Celery vase, plain rim, flint 64.00
Celery vase, scalloped rim, canary
  yellow, flint 400.00
Celery vase, scalloped rim, clear,
  flint 115.00
Champagne, flint 55.00
Champagne, creased ovals, flint 60.00
Champagne, cut ovals, flint 75.00
Claret, flint, 5¼" h. 50.00
Cordial, flint, 4¼" h. 70.00
Cordial, non-flint 42.50
Creamer, applied handle, flint...... 188.00
Decanter, bar lip, canary yellow,
  flint 550.00
Decanter w/patent pewter stopper,
  canary yellow, flint 1,600.00
Decanter, bar lip & facet-cut neck,
  clear, flint, qt. 50.00
Decanter w/original stopper, clear,
  flint, qt. 62.00
Egg cup, clambroth, flint 125.00
Egg cup, clear, flint 22.00
Egg cup, non-flint 15.00
Egg cup, double, flint 95.00
Flip glass, handled, flint, 7" h. 212.00
Goblet, barrel-shaped, flint 36.00
Goblet, flared, flint 50.00
Goblet, non-flint 25.00
Goblet, "giant," straight stem,
  flint 55.00
Honey dish, 3½" d. 8.50
Mug, applied handle, 4¾" h........ 110.00
Pitcher, water, applied hollow han-
  dle, flint .... 400.00 to 450.00
Plate, 6 5/8" d., flint 60.00
Sauce dish, flint.................. 7.50
Sugar bowl, cov., flint 142.00
Sugar bowl, open, non-flint 32.50
Tumbler, bar, flint................. 60.00
Tumbler, water, footed 85.00
Tumbler, whiskey, applied handle,
  flint.................. 100.00 to 125.00
Vase, 10½" h., flint 80.00
Wine, barrel-shaped, flint 41.50
Wine, clear, flint 40.00
Wine, emerald green, flint 425.00
Wine, peacock green, flint 525.00
Wine, non-flint 20.00

ATLANTA - See Lion Pattern

ATLAS (Crystal Ball or Cannon Ball)

Bowl, cov., large, flat 35.00

Bowl, open, 9" d. 20.00
Butter dish, cov. 45.00
Cake stand, clear, 8" to 10" d. 32.00
Cake stand, ruby-stained, 8" to
  10" d. 95.00
Celery vase....................... 25.00
Champagne, 5½" h. 22.50
Compote, cov., 8" d., 8" h. 55.00
Cordial 35.00
Creamer, flat or pedestal base 25.00
Goblet 30.00
Pitcher, milk, tankard, applied
  handle 38.00
Pitcher, water, tankard, applied
  handle 55.00
Salt dip, individual size 8.00
Salt dip, master size.............. 18.00
Sauce dish, flat or footed ..... 7.50 to 12.50
Spooner 26.00

Atlas Toothpick Holder

Toothpick holder (ILLUS.)........... 20.00
Tumbler 25.00
Wine............................. 21.00

AURORA (Diamond Horseshoe)

Bowl, 7" to 8" d. 23.00
Celery vase....................... 32.50
Creamer, applied handle........... 38.00
Decanter w/original stopper, clear.. 30.00
Decanter w/original stopper, ruby-
  stained......................... 135.00
Goblet 27.50
Pitcher, water, tankard, 9½" h. 40.00
Pitcher, water, tankard, 12" h. 45.00
Salt & pepper shakers w/original
  tops, pr........................ 75.00
Tray, wine, clear, 10" d. 35.00
Tray, wine, ruby-stained, 10" d. 45.00
Wine, clear....................... 35.00
Wine, ruby-stained 40.00
Wine set: decanter w/original ruby
  stopper, 6 wines & tray; ruby-
  stained, 8 pcs. 375.00

AZTEC

Bowl, cov., 8½" d. 75.00
Butter dish, cov. 40.00
Carafe, water..................... 37.50
Champagne....................... 15.00
Cordial 17.00

Creamer 26.50
Creamer, individual size 16.00
Cruet w/original stopper 48.00
Dresser bottle w/original stopper ... 37.50
Goblet 30.00
Pitcher, water 60.00
Punch cup 5.00
Salt shaker w/original top 14.50
Sugar bowl, cov. 35.00
Sugar bowl, open 25.00
Toothpick holder 30.00
Tumbler 20.00
Wine 16.00

BABY FACE

Baby Face Compote

Butter dish, cov., 5¼" d. 150.00
Compote, cov., 8" d., 13" h., scal-
loped rim 395.00
Compote, open, 8" d., 4¾" h.
(ILLUS.) 85.00
Compote, open, 8" d., 8" h. 95.00
Creamer 110.00
Goblet .... 85.00 to 150.00
Pitcher, water 175.00
Spooner 80.00
Sugar bowl, cov. 175.00

BABY THUMBPRINT - See Dakota Pattern

BALDER (Kamoni or Pennsylvania - Late)

Balder Individual Open Sugar Bowl

Bowl, berry or fruit, 8½" d., clear
w/gold trim 24.00
Butter dish, cov. 60.00
Carafe 45.00
Celery tray, 4½ x 11" 28.00
Cheese dish, cov. 62.50

Creamer, clear w/gold trim, small,
3" h. 18.00
Creamer, green w/gold trim, small,
3" h. 58.00
Creamer, large, 4" h. 32.50
Creamer & open sugar bowl, in-
dividual size, clear w/gold trim,
pr. 40.00
Cruet w/original stopper 47.50
Decanter w/original stopper,
10¾" h. 65.00
Goblet 22.00
Pitcher, water 45.00
Plate, 8" d. 29.50
Punch cup 12.50
Relish 10.00
Salt shaker w/original top 35.00
Sauce dish, boat-shaped 22.00
Sauce dish, round or square .. 8.00 to 15.00
Spooner 22.00
Sugar bowl, cov., child's, green
w/gold trim 135.00
Sugar bowl, cov. 45.00
Sugar bowl, open, individual size,
clear w/gold trim (ILLUS.) 18.00
Syrup pitcher w/original top 37.50
Table set, 3 pcs. 125.00
Toothpick holder 28.00
Tumbler, juice 10.50
Tumbler, water, blue, souvenir 42.00
Tumbler, water, clear 23.00
Tumbler, water, clear w/gold trim .. 25.00
Tumbler, water, ruby-stained 49.00
Vase, 5¾" h., clear w/gold trim 17.50
Wine, clear 16.00
Wine, green w/gold trim 40.00

BALTIMORE PEAR

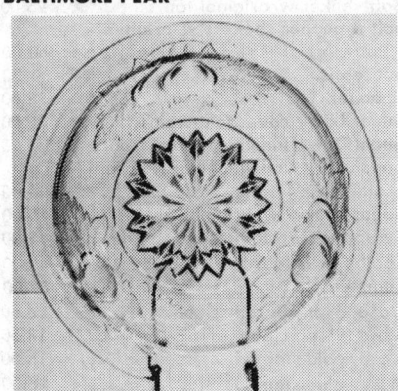

Baltimore Pear Bowl

Bowl, 6" d. (ILLUS.) 29.00
Bowl, berry or fruit, 9" d., footed ... 40.00
Bread plate, 12½" l. 50.00
Butter dish, cov. 50.00
Cake plate, side handles, 10"
octagon 38.00
Cake stand, high pedestal 55.00
Celery vase 50.00

Compote, cov., 7" d., high stand ... 75.00
Creamer 28.00
Creamer & open sugar bowl, pr..... 50.00
Goblet 31.00
Pitcher, water ....75.00 to 95.00
Plate, 9" d........................ 35.00
Relish, 8¼" l..................... 25.00
Sauce dish, flat or footed ....15.00 to 23.00
Spooner 31.00
Sugar bowl, cov................... 42.00
Sugar bowl, open 30.00

BAMBOO - See Broken Column Pattern

BANDED PORTLAND (Portland w/Diamond Point Band)
Butter pat 18.00
Candlesticks, pr.................. 75.00
Carafe, water..................-... 82.50
Celery tray, gold-stained, 5 x 12" ... 25.00
Cologne bottle w/original stopper .. 51.00
Compote, cov., jelly 35.00
Compote, cov., 7" d., high stand ... 95.00
Compote, open, 10" d., high stand .. 50.00
Creamer 35.00
Creamer, individual size 29.00
Dresser jar, cov., 3½" d. 32.00
Dresser set: large tray, pin tray,
   pair cov. pomade jars, pair co-
   logne bottles w/original stoppers
   & ring tree; gold trim, 7 pcs. 195.00
Goblet 50.00
Pickle dish, 4 x 6"............... 15.00
Pitcher, water 65.00
Punch cup, gold trim 18.00
Relish, 4 x 8½" oval............. 14.00
Ring tree, gold-stained 40.00
Salt shaker w/original top 25.00
Salt & pepper shakers w/original
   tops, pr....................... 50.00
Sauce dish...................... 11.50
Spooner 35.00
Sugar bowl, cov., gold-stained 36.00
Sugar bowl, individual size, clear ... 22.50
Sugar bowl, individual size, green-
   stained 25.00
Sugar shaker w/original top 35.00
Syrup jug w/original top 75.00
Toothpick holder 42.00
Tumbler 32.00
Vase, 6" h., flared, clear 16.50
Vase, 9" h., clear 18.50
Vase, gold-stained 15.00
Wine, blue-stained 28.00
Wine, clear 27.00
Wine, gold-stained 35.00
Wine set: tray & 6 wines; clear,
   7 pcs......................... 145.00

BANDED PORTLAND W/COLOR - See Portland Maiden Blush Pattern

BAR & DIAMOND - See Kokomo Pattern

BARBERRY

Barberry Compote

Bowl, 8" oval 20.00
Bread plate..................... 23.00
Butter dish, cov., shell finial 60.00
Cake stand, 9½" d. 35.00
Celery vase.................... 36.00
Compote, cov., 6" d., high stand,
   shell finial................... 45.00
Compote, cov., 8" d., low stand,
   shell finial 72.00
Compote, open, 8½" d., 7" h.
   (ILLUS.).................... 25.00
Creamer 32.50
Egg cup 18.00
Goblet 25.00
Pitcher, water, 9½" h., applied
   handle 85.00
Plate, 6" d. 18.00
Salt dip, master size........... 18.00
Sauce dish, flat or footed .....8.00 to 18.00
Spooner, footed 35.00
Sugar bowl, cov., shell finial 42.00
Sugar bowl, open 27.50
Syrup jug w/original top ....85.00 to 110.00
Tumbler, footed 23.00
Wine......................... 26.00

BARLEY
Bowl, 10" oval 18.50
Bread platter, plain rim,
   9½ x 11½".................. 22.00
Bread platter, scalloped rim,
   9½ x 11½".................. 32.50
Butter dish, cov................ 29.00
Cake stand, 8" to 10½" d. 37.50
Celery vase.................... 32.50
Compote, cov., 7" d., high stand ... 60.00
Compote, open, 6" d., high stand... 30.00
Compote, open, 8½" d., 8" h....... 35.00
Compote, open, 8¾" d., 6½" h.,
   scalloped rim 32.00
Creamer 23.00
Egg cup 17.50
Goblet 25.00
Pickle castor w/frame & tongs...... 82.50
Pitcher, milk 30.00
Pitcher, water 47.00

Plate, 6" d. 25.00
Relish, 6 x 8" 15.00
Relish, handled, 5¼ x 9½" 18.00
Sauce dish, flat or footed 8.00
Spooner 21.50
Sugar bowl, cov. 27.00
Table set, creamer, open sugar
  bowl & cov. butter dish, 3 pcs. ... 110.00
Wheelbarrow sugar cube dish
  w/metal wheels 65.00
Wine, 3¾" h. 30.00

BARRED HOBSTAR - See Checkerboard Pattern

BARRED STAR - See Spartan Pattern

BASKETWEAVE
Bread plate, amber 35.00
Bread plate, blue 35.00
Goblet, amber 22.50
Goblet, blue 35.00
Goblet, clear 20.00
Mug, 3" h. 12.00
Pitcher, water, amber 42.00
Plate, 8¾" d., handled, blue 19.50
Plate, 8¾" d., handled, clear 11.00
Tray, water, scenic center, vaseline,
  12" 47.50
Vase, 8½" h. 12.50

BEADED BULL'S EYE WITH DRAPE - See Alabama Pattern

BEADED DEWDROP - See Wisconsin Pattern

BEADED GRAPE (California)

Beaded Grape Compote

Bowl, 5½" sq., clear 16.50
Bowl, 5½" sq., green 19.50
Bowl, 6½" sq., green 35.00
Bowl, 8" sq., clear 27.00
Bowl, 8" sq., green 35.00
Bowl, 6¼ x 8½" rectangle, green .. 30.00
Bread tray, clear, 7 x 10" 25.00
Bread tray, green, 7 x 10" 40.00
Butter dish, cov., sq., clear 58.00
Butter dish, cov., sq., green 82.00
Cake stand, clear, 9" sq., 6" h. 55.00

Cake stand, green, 9" sq., 6" h. 85.00
Celery tray, clear 33.00
Celery tray, green 42.00
Celery vase 32.00
Compote, cov., 6½" sq., high stand,
  clear 75.00
Compote, open, 7" sq., high stand,
  clear (ILLUS.) 38.00
Compote, open, 8½" sq., high
  stand, clear 72.50
Compote, open, 8½" sq., high
  stand, green 75.00
Cordial 15.00
Creamer, clear 35.00
Creamer, green 45.00
Cruet w/original stopper, clear 65.00
Cruet w/original stopper, green 125.00
Dish, 8¼" sq. 30.00
Egg cup 16.00
Goblet, clear 28.00
Goblet, green 45.00
Pitcher, water, round, green 75.00
Pitcher, water, square, green 100.00
Pitcher, water, tankard, clear 78.00
Plate, 8" sq., clear 25.00
Plate, 8" sq., green 40.00
Relish, 4 x 7" 20.00
Salt shaker w/original top, clear ... 22.50
Salt shaker w/original top, green... 25.00
Salt & pepper shakers w/original
  tops, clear, pr. 42.50
Sauce dish, clear 12.00
Sauce dish, green 15.00
Sauce dish, handled, green 30.00
Spooner, clear 35.00
Spooner, green 40.00
Sugar bowl, cov., clear 47.50
Sugar bowl, cov., green 60.00
Sugar bowl, open, clear 19.00
Sugar bowl, open, green 28.00
Table set, green, 4 pcs. ...300.00 to 350.00
Toothpick holder, clear 27.50
Toothpick holder, green 58.00
Tumbler, clear 27.50
Tumbler, green 40.00
Vase, 7" h., green 32.50
Water set: pitcher & 6 tumblers;
  green, 7 pcs. 255.00
Wine, clear 35.00
Wine, green 65.00

BEADED GRAPE MEDALLION
Bowl, 7" oval 24.50
Butter dish, cov. 38.00
Celery vase 65.00
Compote, cov., 8¼" d., low stand .. 75.00
Compote, open, 8¼" d., low
  stand 19.50
Creamer, applied handle 58.00
Egg cup 29.00
Goblet 28.00
Goblet, buttermilk 40.00
Goblet, lady's 29.00
Honey dish, 3½" d. 8.00

Pitcher, water, applied handle 80.00
Salt dip, master size, footed, oval .. 40.00
Salt dip, flat 15.00
Salt shaker w/original top 35.00
Sauce dish......................... 80.00
Spooner 26.00
Sugar bowl, cov. 45.00
Sugar bowl, open 27.50
Wine............................. 50.00

BEADED LOOP (Oregon)

Berry set, master bowl & 6 sauce
  dishes, 7 pcs. 65.00
Bread platter 27.00
Butter dish, cov. 48.00
Cake stand, 9" to 10½" d. 44.00
Celery vase, 7" h.................. 29.00
Compote, open, jelly 38.00
Compote, open, 7½" d., low
  stand 22.00
Compote, open, 9" d., 7¼" h....... 50.00
Creamer 21.50
Cruet w/faceted stopper 49.00
Goblet 30.00
Mug, footed, clear 38.00
Mug, ruby-stained 25.00
Pickle dish, boat-shaped, 7¼" l..... 12.00
Pickle dish, boat-shaped, 9" l...... 15.00
Pitcher, milk, 8½" h. 39.00
Pitcher, water, tankard 51.00
Relish 12.00
Relish, w/advertising in base for
  "Denver Furniture & Carpet
  Company" 45.00
Salt shaker w/original top 15.00
Salt & pepper shakers w/original
  tops, pr........................ 32.50
Sauce dish, flat or footed 10.00
Spooner, ruby-stained 55.00
Sugar bowl, cov., clear 35.00
Sugar bowl, cov., ruby-stained 46.00
Sugar bowl, open 18.00
Syrup pitcher w/original top 65.00
Table set, 4 pcs. ....150.00 to 200.00
Tumbler 45.00
Vase, small...................... 20.00
Wine............................ 65.00

BEADED MIRROR

Butter dish, cov. 40.00
Castor bottle (mustard) 15.00
Castor bottle w/original stopper,
  "Oil" 25.00
Celery vase...................... 36.50
Egg cup 18.50
Goblet 25.00
Salt dip 18.00
Sauce dish, flat 8.00
Spooner 22.50
Sugar bowl, cov. 45.00
Sugar bowl, open 23.50

BEARDED HEAD - See Viking Pattern

BEARDED MAN (Old Man of the Woods or Neptune)

Berry set, master bowl & 6 sauce
  dishes, 7 pcs.................... 95.00
Butter dish, cov. 52.50
Celery vase...................... 35.00
Compote, cov., 9" h. 60.00
Creamer 40.00
Pitcher, water, 2 qt.............. 58.00
Spooner 40.00
Sugar bowl, open 50.00
Table set, 4 pcs. 250.00

BELLFLOWER

Bellflower Double Vine Creamer

Bowl, 8" d., 4½" h., scalloped rim .. 70.00
Bowl, 6 x 9" oval, rayed base 125.00
Butter dish, cov. 90.00
Castor bottle w/original stopper 28.00
Celery vase, fine rib, single vine ... 80.00
Celery vase, w/cut bellflowers 175.00
Champagne, barrel-shaped, fine rib,
  knob stem, plain base 95.00
Champagne, barrel-shaped, fine rib,
  single vine, knob stem, rayed
  base 95.00
Compote, open, 4½" d., low stand,
  scalloped rim 100.00
Compote, open, 7" d., low stand,
  scalloped rim 35.00
Compote, open, 8" d., 5" h., scal-
  loped rim, single vine 67.50
Compote, open, 8" d., 8" h., single
  vine 245.00
Compote, open, 8¼" d., 7" h., scal-
  loped base, w/cut bellflowers 130.00
Compote, open, 9½" d., 8½" h.,
  scalloped rim, single vine 100.00
Creamer, fine rib, double vine, ap-
  plied handle (ILLUS.)........... 187.00
Creamer, fine rib, single vine 135.00
Decanter w/bar lip, double vine,
  pt............................. 225.00
Decanter w/bar lip, patent stopper,
  double vine, qt.................. 250.00
Egg cup, coarse rib 20.00
Egg cup, fine rib, single vine 38.00

Goblet, barrel-shaped, fine rib, single vine, knob stem 50.00
Goblet, barrel-shaped, fine rib, single vine, plain stem 45.00
Goblet, coarse rib 35.00
Goblet, double vine 65.00
Goblet, single vine, rayed base 42.50
Goblet, fine rib, double vine, w/cut bellflowers 300.00
Lamp, kerosene-type, 7½" h. 275.00
Lamp, kerosene-type, clear font, milk white base, flint, 9½" h. 165.00
Pitcher, water, 8¾" h., coarse rib, double vine.................. 325.00
Pitcher, water, single vine 295.00
Plate, 6" d., fine rib, single vine.... 92.00
Salt dip, cov., master size, footed, beaded rim, fine rib, single vine 75.00
Salt dip, open, master size, footed, scalloped rim, single vine 32.00
Sauce dish, single vine 16.00
Spillholder...................... 42.00
Spooner, low foot, double vine 48.00
Spooner, scalloped rim, single vine 38.00
Sugar bowl, open, double vine 40.00
Syrup pitcher w/original top, applied handle, fine rib, single vine, clear.................. 650.00 to 750.00
Syrup pitcher w/original top, applied handle, fine rib, single vine, fiery opalescent 1,100.00
Table set: cov. butter dish, creamer, open sugar bowl & spooner; fine rib, single vine, 4 pcs. 325.00
Tumbler, bar, fine rib, single vine .. 78.00
Tumbler, coarse rib, double vine ... 95.00
Tumbler, fine rib, single vine, w/cut bellflowers 65.00
Wine, barrel-shaped, knob stem, fine rib, single vine, rayed base .. 75.00
Wine, straight sides, plain stem, rayed base 60.00

BIGLER

Bowl, 9 1/8" d., 2 5/8" h. 50.00
Celery vase..................... 75.00
Champagne...................... 95.00
Decanter w/bar lip, pt. 50.00
Goblet, 6" h. 43.00
Honey dish, canary yellow, 4 1/8" d. 100.00
Lamp, whale oil, clear, 7" h. 125.00
Lamp, whale oil, canary yellow, 10½" h. 650.00
Plate, toddy, 4" d. 11.00
Plate, 6" d., amethyst .... 200.00 to 250.00
Plate, 6" d., canary yellow 135.00
Plate, 6" d., clear 30.00
Sauce dish, canary yellow .... 100.00 to 125.00
Tumbler 90.00
Vase, tulip form, amethyst 935.00

Whiskey, handled, electric blue 95.00
Wine 70.00

BIRD & FERN - See Hummingbird Pattern

BIRD & STRAWBERRY (Bluebird)

Bird & Strawberry Tumbler

Berry set, master bowl & 6 sauce dishes, footed, 7 pcs..... 150.00 to 200.00
Bowl, 5½" d., clear 27.00
Bowl, 5½" d., w/color............ 35.00
Bowl, 7½" d., footed, clear 62.00
Bowl, 7½" d., footed, w/color...... 72.50
Bowl, 9½" l., 6" w. oval, footed, clear...................... 56.00
Bowl, 10" d., flat, clear 45.00
Bowl, 10" d., flat, w/color & gold trim...................... 92.00
Butter dish, cov., clear 90.00
Butter dish, cov., w/color 205.00
Cake stand, 9" to 9½" d. 52.00
Celery tray, 10" l. 35.00
Compote, cov., 6½" d., 9½" h...... 95.00
Compote, cov., 7" d., high stand ... 120.00
Compote, cov., 8" d., low stand ... 65.00
Compote, open, 8" d., 6" h., clear .. 80.00
Compote, open, 8" d., 6" h., scalloped & ruffled rim, w/color 110.00
Creamer, clear.................. 50.00
Creamer, w/color 105.00
Dish, heart-shaped 50.00
Pitcher, water, clear.............. 238.00
Pitcher, water, w/color 265.00
Plate, 12" d. 75.00
Punch cup 17.00
Sauce dish, flat or footed, clear 27.00
Sauce dish, w/color 40.00
Spooner, clear 49.00
Spooner, w/color .... 100.00 to 125.00
Sugar bowl, cov. 64.00
Sugar bowl, open 34.00
Table set: creamer, cov. butter dish & spooner; clear, 3 pcs.......... 350.00
Table set, w/color, 4 pcs... 400.00 to 450.00
Tumbler, clear 47.00
Tumbler, w/color (ILLUS.) 57.00
Wine.......................... 48.00

BIRD IN RING (Butterfly & Fan)

Bread tray 39.00
Spooner 28.50

BLEEDING HEART

Bleeding Heart Spooner

Bowl, cov., 9½" d. 55.00
Bowl, 7¼" oval 27.50
Bowl, 8" 35.00
Bowl, 9¼" oval 30.00
Butter dish, cov. 46.50
Cake stand, 9½" to 11" d. 69.00
Compote, cov., 7" d., w/Bleeding
  Heart finial 65.00
Compote, cov., 8" d., high stand,
  w/Bleeding Heart finial 145.00
Compote, open, 7" d., 6" h. 25.00
Creamer 39.00
Egg cup 36.00
Goblet, buttermilk 22.50
Goblet, knob stem 43.00
Mug, 3" h. 62.50
Pitcher, water 100.00
Relish, 3 5/8 x 5 1/8" oval 27.00
Salt dip, master size, footed 68.00
Sauce dish, flat 13.00
Spooner (ILLUS.) 32.00
Sugar bowl, cov. 52.50
Sugar bowl, open 25.00
Table set, 4 pcs. 325.00
Tumbler, flat 75.00
Wine, plain stem 42.50
Wine, knob stem 175.00

BLOCK (Also see Red Block Pattern)

Celery 15.00
Creamer, large 15.00
Goblet 12.00
Pitcher, water 65.00
Punch cup, applied handle 8.00
Spooner 15.00
Sugar bowl, cov. 15.00
Tumbler 32.00
Wine 14.50

BLOCK & FAN

Bowl, berry, 8" d., footed 22.50

Bowl, 9¾" d. 32.50
Bowl, 10" l., 6" w. rectangle 50.00
Cake stand, 9" to 10" d. 28.00
Carafe, water 47.50
Celery tray 30.00
Celery vase 30.00
Compote, open, 8" d., high stand ... 50.00
Cracker jar, cov. 60.00
Creamer 38.00
Creamer, individual size, ruby-
  stained 32.50
Cruet w/original stopper, small,
  6" h. 22.00
Cruet w/original stopper, medium .. 35.00
Finger bowl 29.50
Goblet, clear 57.50
Goblet, ruby-stained 95.00
Ice bucket 42.50
Pitcher, milk 35.00
Pitcher, water 48.00
Plate, 6" d. 21.50
Plate, 10" d. 19.50

Block & Fan Rose Bowl

Rose bowl (ILLUS.) 25.00
Salt shaker w/original top 14.50
Sauce dish, flat or footed, clear 9.25
Sauce dish, flat or footed, ruby-
  stained 25.00
Spooner, ruby-stained 30.00
Sugar bowl, cov. 40.00
Sugar shaker w/original top 35.00
Syrup pitcher w/original top, 7" h. .. 75.00
Tumbler 30.00
Wine 45.00

BLOCK & STAR - See Valencia Waffle Pattern

BLUEBIRD - See Bird & Strawberry Pattern

BOW TIE

Bowl, 6¾" d., flat 35.00
Bowl, berry, 8" d. 40.00
Bowl, 10" d., 5" h. 60.00
Butter dish, cov. 80.00
Cake stand, 9" d. 55.00
Compote, open, 5½" d., 10½" h. 60.00
Compote, open, 8" d., low stand ... 40.00
Compote, open, 9¼" d., high
  stand 65.00
Compote, open, 10½" d., 10½" h. .. 70.00
Creamer 44.00
Goblet 55.00

Marmalade jar w/cover	60.00
Marmalade jar (no cover)	34.00
Pitcher, milk	55.00
Pitcher, water	75.00
Relish, rectangular	28.00
Salt dip, master size	40.00
Salt shaker w/original top	35.00
Spooner	35.00
Tumbler	55.00

BROKEN COLUMN (Irish Column, Notched Rib or Bamboo)

Broken Column Covered Compote

Banana stand	100.00
Bowl, 7¼" d.	40.00
Bowl, 9" d.	32.00
Butter dish, cov.	60.00
Cake stand, 9" to 10" d.	70.00
Carafe, water	72.50
Celery vase, clear	45.00
Celery vase, w/red notches	155.00
Champagne	65.00
Compote, cov., 5¼" d., 10½" h., clear	60.00
Compote, cov., 5¼" d., 10½" h., w/red notches	225.00
Compote, cov., 7" d., 12" h.	125.00
Compote, cov., 8" d., high stand (ILLUS.)	150.00
Compote, open, jelly, w/red notches	195.00
Compote, open, 6" d., low stand, flared rim	50.00
Compote, open, 8" d., 8¾" h., w/red notches	186.00
Compote, open, 9" d., 7½" h., w/red notches	175.00
Compote, open, 10" d., low stand	110.00
Cracker jar, cov.	80.00
Creamer, clear	40.00
Creamer, w/red notches	108.00
Cruet w/original stopper	61.00
Decanter w/original stopper, 10½" h.	85.00
Goblet	65.00

Marmalade jar w/original cover	85.00
Pickle castor, w/red notches, w/frame & tongs	400.00 to 425.00
Pitcher, water, clear	80.00
Pitcher, water, w/red notches	250.00
Plate, 7" d.	32.50
Plate, 8" d.	35.00
Powder jar, cov.	25.00
Punch cup, blue	75.00
Punch cup, clear	15.00
Relish, clear, 5 x 9"	30.00
Relish, w/red notches, 5 x 9"	110.00
Salt shaker w/original top	45.00
Sauce dish, clear	10.00
Sauce dish, w/red notches	32.00
Spooner, clear	27.00
Spooner, w/red notches	100.00
Sugar bowl, cov., clear	60.00
Sugar bowl, cov., w/red notches	112.00
Syrup pitcher w/metal top	135.00
Tumbler, clear	38.00
Tumbler, w/red notches	52.00
Wine	85.00

BRYCE - See Ribbon Candy Pattern

BUCKLE

Bowl, 10" d., rolled edge	75.00
Butter dish, cov.	52.00
Champagne, flint	60.00
Compote, cov., 6" d., 8½" h.	80.00
Compote, open, 8" d., low stand, flint	35.00
Creamer, applied handle, flint	110.00
Creamer, small size, non-flint	25.00
Egg cup, flint	38.00
Egg cup, non-flint	25.00
Goblet, flint	32.00
Goblet, non-flint	18.00
Goblet, buttermilk, non-flint	24.00
Lamp, kerosene-type, brass & iron base	165.00
Lamp, kerosene-type, clear font, clambroth base	125.00
Pitcher, water, bulbous, applied handle, non-flint	85.00
Salt dip, master size, footed, flint	35.00
Sauce dish, flint	10.00 to 15.00
Sauce dish, non-flint	7.00
Spooner, flint	37.50
Spooner, non-flint	23.00
Sugar bowl, cov., w/acorn finial, flint	65.00
Sugar bowl, cov., w/acorn finial, non-flint	43.00
Sugar bowl, open, non-flint	20.00
Tumbler, non-flint	29.00
Wine, flint	77.50
Wine, non-flint	22.00

BUCKLE WITH STAR

Bowl, 8" oval	15.00
Butter dish, cov.	35.00
Cake stand, 9" d.	35.00

Celery vase........................ 32.00
Compote, cov., 7" d. 60.00
Compote, open, 7" d., 5½" h...... 19.50
Compote, open, 10" d., 7" h....... 30.00
Creamer 35.00
Goblet 25.00
Salt dip 25.00
Sauce dish, flat or footed .....5.00 to 12.00
Spillholder....................... 50.00
Spooner 20.00
Sugar bowl, cov. 42.50

Buckle with Star Open Sugar

Sugar bowl, open (ILLUS.).......... 25.00
Tumbler, bar..................... 65.00
Wine............................ 26.00

BULL'S EYE

Celery vase, flint................. 80.00
Cordial, flint 45.00
Creamer, applied handle, flint...... 110.00
Cruet w/original stopper........... 195.00
Decanter w/bar lip, flint, qt. 120.00
Egg cup, clear, flint 48.00
Egg cup, opaque blue, flint........ 575.00
Goblet, flint 69.00
Salt dip, master size, footed, flint .. 32.50
Spillholder, flint.................. 32.50
Spooner, flint.................... 95.00
Spooner, non-flint 26.00
Sugar bowl, cov., flint 135.00
Tumbler, bar, non-flint............ 30.00
Tumbler, flat, flint................ 75.00
Wine, knob stem, flint 47.00

BULL'S EYE VARIANT - See Texas Bull's Eye Pattern

BULL'S EYE WITH DIAMOND POINT

Celery vase...................... 147.00
Cologne bottle 85.00
Creamer, applied handle........... 175.00
Goblet ....115.00 to 120.00
Honey dish (ILLUS.).............. 30.00
Salt dip, master size.............. 45.00
Salt dip, basket-shaped 85.00
Sauce dish....................... 25.00
Spillholder....................... 75.00

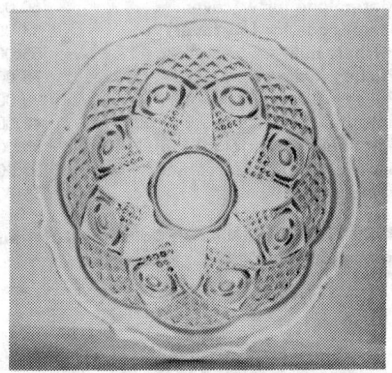

Bull's Eye with Diamond Point Honey Dish

Spooner......................... 135.00
Tumbler, bar..................... 138.00
Wine............................ 120.00

BULL'S EYE WITH FLEUR DE LIS

Bull's Eye with Fleur de Lis Water Pitcher

Bowl, 7½" d. 75.00
Butter dish, cov. 95.00
Creamer 65.00
Goblet 75.00
Lamp, kerosene-type, pear-shaped
    font w/brass standard on marble
    base 150.00
Pitcher, water, 9½" h.
    (ILLUS.)............450.00 to 500.00
Salt dip, master size.............. 52.50
Sugar bowl, cov. 135.00
Sugar bowl, open 55.00

BUTTERFLY & FAN - See Bird in Ring Pattern

BUTTON ARCHES

Basket, ruby-stained handle........ 25.00
Berry set: 8" d. master bowl & 6
    sauce dishes; ruby-stained,
    7 pcs. 158.00
Bowl, 8" d., ruby-stained, souvenir
    (ILLUS. top next page) 45.00
Butter dish, cov., clear 48.00

Button Arches Bowl with Engraving

Butter dish, cov., ruby-stained,
souvenir...................... 65.00
Compote, open, jelly, 4½" h., ruby-
stained........................ 45.00
Creamer, clear................. 18.50
Creamer, ruby-stained............ 48.00
Creamer, individual size, ruby-
stained........................ 25.00
Cruet w/original stopper, ruby-
stained........................ 175.00
Goblet, clambroth............... 26.00
Goblet, clear.................... 24.00
Goblet, ruby-stained............. 37.50
Mug, ruby-stained, souvenir,
3½" h......................... 30.00
Pitcher, 7" h., ruby-stained,
souvenir...................... 60.00
Pitcher, tankard, 8¾" h., clear..... 100.00
Pitcher, water, tankard, 12" h.,
ruby-stained................... 115.00
Punch cup, clear 10.00
Punch cup, ruby-stained 17.50
Salt shaker w/original top, ruby-
stained........................ 26.00
Salt & pepper shakers w/original
tops, ruby-stained, souvenir,
3" h., pr....................... 40.00
Sauce dish, ruby-stained 35.00
Spooner, clear 27.50
Spooner, ruby-stained & engraved .. 44.00
Sugar bowl, cov., clear 30.00
Sugar bowl, cov., ruby-stained & en-
graved ....65.00 to 80.00
Syrup pitcher w/original top, clear.. 40.00
Syrup pitcher w/original top, ruby-
stained........................ 125.00
Table set, ruby-stained, 4 pcs....... 235.00
Toothpick holder, clear 14.50
Toothpick holder, ruby-stained 30.00
Tumbler, clear 17.50
Tumbler, ruby-stained 34.00
Water set: pitcher & 5 tumblers;
clear w/frosted band & gold,
6 pcs......................... 225.00
Water set: pitcher & 6 tumblers;
clear, 7 pcs................... 321.50
Water set: pitcher & 6 tumblers;
ruby-stained, 7 pcs. 256.00
Whiskey shot glass, ruby-stained ... 14.50
Wine, clambroth 25.00
Wine, clear 15.00
Wine, ruby-stained, souvenir 32.50

CABBAGE LEAF

Bowl, cov., 7" d. 275.00
Butter dish, cov., frosted........... 500.00
Celery vase, clear & frosted 85.00
Custard cup, frosted, marked Libbey
Glass Co., "Columbian Expo" on
base 80.00
Pitcher, water, frosted............. 135.00
Rose bowl, amber 175.00
Sauce dish, frosted, w/rabbit
center........................ 45.00

CABBAGE ROSE

Cabbage Rose Goblet

Bitters bottle, 6½" h.............. 100.00
Bowl, master berry, 9" oval 40.00
Butter dish, cov. 62.50
Cake stand, 9½" to 12½" d. 54.00
Celery vase..................... 50.00
Champagne..................... 42.50
Compote, cov., 6" d., low stand 95.00
Compote, cov., 7½" d., high
stand 115.00
Compote, cov., 8½" d., 7" h....... 120.00
Compote, open, 7½" d., high
stand 70.00
Compote, open, 9½" d., low
stand 90.00
Compote, open, 9½" d., high
stand 100.00
Cordial........................ 50.00
Creamer, applied handle.......... 56.00
Dish, 7" d. ....25.00 to 32.50
Egg cup 33.00
Goblet (ILLUS.)................... 35.00
Goblet, buttermilk 46.00
Mug, child's 65.00
Pickle or relish, 7½" to 8½" l. 27.50
Pitcher, water, qt................. 125.00
Pitcher, 3 pint 165.00
Salt dip, master size............. 20.00
Sauce dish...................... 20.00
Spooner 28.00
Sugar bowl, cov. 55.00
Sugar bowl, open 40.00
Tumbler, bar.................... 42.00
Tumbler 40.00
Wine.......................... 42.50

CABLE

Cable Egg Cup

Bowl, 8" d.	45.00
Bowl, 9" d.	70.00
Butter dish, cov.	82.00
Celery vase	68.00
Compote, open, 7" d., 5" h.	55.00
Compote, open, 8" d., 4¾" h.	65.00
Compote, open, 9" d., 4½" h.	55.00
Creamer	365.00 to 500.00
Decanter w/bar lip, qt.	95.00 to 125.00
Decanter w/stopper, qt.	300.00 to 325.00
Egg cup, cov., blue opaque, 5¼" h.	2,200.00
Egg cup, clambroth, flint	550.00
Egg cup, clear (ILLUS.)	45.00
Goblet	62.00
Honey dish, 3½" d., 1" h.	12.00
Lamp, whale oil, 11" h.	122.50
Plate, 6" d.	85.00
Salt dip, master size	35.00
Sauce dish	25.00
Spooner, clambroth	185.00
Spooner, clear	35.00
Spooner, starch blue w/original gilt decoration of grape leaves	1,500.00
Sugar bowl, cov.	95.00
Wine	77.50

CABLE WITH RING

Lamp, kerosene-type, w/ring handle, flint	175.00
Lamp, whale oil, clambroth font, flint, reeded brass stem, marble base	325.00
Sugar bowl, cov., flint	115.00

CALIFORNIA - See Beaded Grape Pattern

CAMEO - See Classic Medallion Pattern

CANADIAN

Bowl, berry, 7" d., 4½" h., footed	63.00
Bread plate, handled, 10" d.	43.00
Butter dish, cov.	85.00
Cake stand, 9¾" d., 5" h.	32.50 to 50.00
Celery vase	55.00
Compote, cov., 6" d., 9" h.	124.00
Compote, cov., 7" d., 11" h.	85.00
Compote, open, 6" d., footed	40.00
Compote, open, 8" d., 5" h.	45.00
Creamer	38.00
Goblet	55.00
Pitcher, milk, 8" h.	140.00
Pitcher, water	94.00
Plate, 8" d., handled	30.00

Canadian Sauce Dish

Sauce dish, flat or footed (ILLUS.)	12.50 to 28.00
Spooner	45.00
Sugar bowl, cov.	75.00
Wine	40.00

CANE

Bread platter, amber	125.00
Candlestick	15.00
Cordial	18.00
Creamer, amber	30.00
Creamer, blue	42.00
Creamer, clear	25.00
Goblet, amber	25.00
Goblet, apple green	35.00
Goblet, blue	35.00
Goblet, clear	15.00
Goblet, vaseline	39.00
Match holder, model of a cauldron, amber	18.00
Match holder, model of a cauldron, blue	16.00
Pickle castor w/tongs, amber	150.00
Pitcher, water, amber	57.00
Pitcher, water, apple green	47.00
Pitcher, water, blue	61.50
Pitcher, water, clear	42.50
Plate, 6" d., amber	12.00
Relish, blue	50.00
Relish, clear, 5¼ x 8" oval	12.50
Sauce dish, footed	10.50
Spooner, amber	42.00
Spooner, apple green	35.00
Sugar bowl, cov., amber	55.00
Toddy plate, amber, 4½" d.	12.00
Toddy plate, apple green, 4½" d.	12.00
Toddy plate, blue, 4½" d.	16.50
Toddy plate, clear, 4½" d.	14.00
Tray, water, blue	60.00
Tumbler, blue	25.00
Waste bowl, amber or apple green, each	30.00

CANNON BALL - See Atlas Pattern

CAPE COD

Bowl, 6" d., handled	20.00

Bowl, 8" d. 32.00
Bread platter 48.00
Compote, cov., 8" d., 12" h......... 130.00
Compote, open, 7" d., 6" h. 37.00
Compote, open, 8" d., 5½" h. 37.50
Cruet w/original stopper 25.00
Goblet 45.00
Pitcher, water 95.00
Plate, 10" d., open handles 30.00
Sauce dish, flat or footed 16.00
Spooner 35.00

CARDINAL BIRD

Cardinal Bird Footed Sauce Dish

Butter dish, cov. 65.00
Butter dish, cov., three unidentified
  birds 100.00
Creamer 36.00
Goblet 33.00
Honey dish, open 18.50
Sauce dish, flat or footed (ILLUS.) ... 16.00
Spooner 35.50
Sugar bowl, cov. 60.00

CATHEDRAL

Bowl, 6" d., clear 20.00
Bowl, 6" d., crimped rim, vaseline .. 35.00
Bowl, berry, 8" d., amber 48.00
Bowl, berry, 8" d., amethyst 60.00
Butter dish, cov. 47.50
Cake stand, blue, 10" d., 4½" h. ... 45.00
Cake stand, vaseline 65.00
Compote, cov., 7¼" d., 10½" h.,
  clear 75.00
Compote, open, 7½" d., high stand,
  fluted rim, amethyst 145.00
Compote, open, 9" d., 5½" h.,
  amber 50.00
Compote, open, 9" d., 5½" h.,
  blue 65.00
Compote, open, 9" d., 7" h.,
  amethyst 75.00
Compote, open, 9" d., 7" h., clear .. 55.00
Compote, open, 10" d., 6" h.,
  amethyst 58.00
Compote, open, 10½" d., 8" h.,
  shaped rim, clear 55.00
Creamer, clear 38.00
Creamer, ruby-stained 50.00
Cruet w/original stopper, amber ... 58.00
Goblet, amber 40.00
Goblet, amethyst 70.00
Goblet, clear 38.00
Goblet, ruby-stained 65.00

Goblet, vaseline 60.00
Pitcher, water, ruby-stained 145.00
Relish, fish-shaped, amber 35.00
Relish, fish-shaped, blue 38.00
Salt dip, master size, amber 25.00
Sauce dish, flat or footed,
  amethyst 35.00
Sauce dish, flat or footed, blue 22.00
Sauce dish, flat or footed, clear 10.00
Sauce dish, flat or footed,
  vaseline ....12.00 to 24.00
Spooner, amber 42.50
Spooner, clear 27.50
Spooner, vaseline 42.50
Sugar bowl, cov., clear 55.00
Sugar bowl, cov., ruby-stained 70.00
Table set: creamer, sugar bowl &
  spooner; vaseline, 3 pcs. 75.00
Tumbler, clear 25.00
Tumbler, ruby-stained 42.50
Wine, amber...................... 35.00
Wine, blue 49.00
Wine, clear 24.00
Wine, ruby-stained 45.00
Wine, vaseline 35.00

CERES (Goddess of Liberty)

Compote, open, 6" d., low stand ... 25.00
Creamer 22.50
Mug, blue 22.50
Mug, clear....................... 17.50
Mug, purple-black 53.00
Spooner, milk white 22.00
Sugar bowl, cov. 45.00

CHAIN

Bread plate...................... 27.00
Butter dish, cov. 35.00
Compote, cov., 7½" d., 8" h....... 36.00
Compote, cov., 7½" d., 12" h....... 45.00
Creamer 18.50
Creamer & cov. sugar bowl, pr. 35.00
Goblet 19.00
Plate, 7" d. 14.50
Relish, 8" oval 11.00
Sauce dish, flat or footed 8.50
Spooner 22.00
Sugar bowl, cov. 35.00
Sugar bowl, open 20.00
Wine............................ 20.00

CHAIN WITH STAR

Bread plate, handled 33.00
Butter dish, cov. 32.50
Cake stand, 8¾" to 10" d. 38.00
Compote, open, jelly 17.00
Compote, open, 8" d., 4" h. 18.50
Compote, open, 8" d., 6½" h....... 20.00
Compote, open, 9½" d. 29.00
Creamer 25.00
Goblet (ILLUS. next page) 19.00
Pickle dish, oval 12.50
Pitcher, water 55.00
Plate, 7" d. 16.50

Chain with Star Goblet

Relish	14.00
Sauce dish	12.50
Spooner	22.50
Sugar bowl, cov.	37.50
Syrup pitcher (no lid)	45.00
Wine	27.50

CHANDELIER (Crown Jewel)

Bowl, 8" d., 3¼" h.	25.00
Butter dish, cov.	60.00
Cake stand, 10" d.	66.00
Celery vase	35.00
Compote, open, 8" d., high stand, etched	95.00
Creamer	45.00
Goblet	52.00
Goblet, etched	60.00
Inkwell	70.00
Salt dip, footed	36.00
Sauce dish, amber	35.00
Sauce dish, flat, clear	12.00
Spooner	30.00
Sugar bowl, cov.	37.50
Sugar shaker w/original top	60.00
Tumbler	35.00
Wine	32.00

CHECKERBOARD (Barred Hobstar)

Bowl, 9" d., flat	20.00
Butter dish, cov.	42.50
Celery tray	30.00
Compote, jelly	25.00
Creamer	12.00 to 20.00
Cruet w/blown stopper	40.00
Goblet	20.00
Honey dish, cov., 5" w.	35.00
Pitcher, milk	35.00
Pitcher, water	30.00
Punch cup	4.50
Sauce dish, flat, clear	14.50
Sauce dish, flat, ruby-stained, gilt trim, 4½" d.	14.50
Spooner	22.50
Sugar bowl, cov.	30.00
Tumbler	15.00
Wine	17.50

CHERRY THUMBPRINT - See Paneled Cherry With Thumbprints Pattern

CLASSIC

Berry set, master bowl & 4 sauce dishes, 5 pcs.	275.00
Bowl, cov., 7" hexagon, open log feet	145.00
Bowl, open, 8" hexagon, open log feet	90.00 to 100.00
Butter dish, cov., open log feet	175.00
Celery vase, collared base	142.00
Celery vase, open log feet	170.00
Compote, cov., 6½" d., collared base	150.00
Compote, cov., 6½" d., open log feet	150.00 to 250.00
Compote, cov., 7½" d., 8" h., open log feet	200.00
Compote, cov., 10" d., open log feet	295.00
Compote, open, 7¾" d., open log feet	160.00
Creamer, collared base	105.00
Creamer, open log feet	150.00
Goblet	195.00 to 225.00
Pitcher, milk, 8½" h., open log feet	450.00 to 600.00
Pitcher, water, collared base	280.00
Pitcher, water, 9½" h., open log feet	300.00 to 325.00
Plate, 10" d., "Blaine" or "Hendricks," signed Jacobus, each	175.00
Plate, 10" d., "Logan"	165.00 to 225.00
Plate, 10" d., "Warrior"	100.00 to 130.00
Plate, 10" d., "Warrior," signed Jacobus	160.00
Sauce dish, collared base	30.00
Sauce dish, open log feet	36.00
Spooner, collared base	90.00
Spooner, open log feet	100.00
Sugar bowl, open, collared base	115.00
Sugar bowl, open, open log feet	150.00

CLASSIC MEDALLION (Cameo)

Classic Medallion Spooner

Bowl, 6¾" d., 3½" h., footed	38.00
Celery vase	22.50
Compote, open, 7" d., 3¾" h.	29.00
Creamer	30.00
Creamer & open sugar bowl, pr.	75.00
Jam jar w/cover	120.00
Pitcher, water	52.50

Sauce dish, footed	9.00
Spooner (ILLUS.)	25.00

COLLINS - See Crystal Wedding Pattern

COLONIAL (Empire Colonial)

Celery vase, flint	75.00
Claret, 5½" h.	47.50
Compote, open, 9" d., 3¾" h., flint	25.00
Goblet, flint	55.00
Plate, 6¼" d., canary yellow, flint	250.00
Salt dip, master size	17.50
Spooner	40.00
Sugar bowl, cov.	95.00
Toothpick holder	22.00
Tumbler, footed, flint	34.00
Tumbler, cobalt blue, flint, 3¾" h.	230.00
Wine, flint	75.00

COLORADO (Lacy Medallion)

Colorado Tumbler

Banana bowl, two turned-up sides, blue	35.00
Berry set: master bowl & 6 sauce dishes; green w/gold, 7 pcs.	175.00
Bowl, 5" d., ruffled rim, blue	35.00
Bowl, 5" d., flared edge, clear	20.00
Bowl, 5" d., green w/gold	45.00
Bowl, 7" d., footed, scalloped rim, blue	25.00
Bowl, 7" d., footed, clear	20.00
Bowl, 7½" d., footed, turned-up sides, blue w/gold	55.00
Bowl, 7½" d., footed, turned-up sides, clear	18.00
Bowl, 7½" d., footed, turned-up sides, green	30.00
Bowl, 8½" d., footed, crimped edge, green	35.00
Bowl, 9" d., footed, three turned-up sides, clear	29.00
Bowl, 9" d., green w/gold	42.00
Bowl, 10" d., footed, fluted, green	39.00
Butter dish, cov., blue w/gold	275.00
Butter dish, cov., clear	65.00
Butter dish, cov., green	115.00
Cake stand	50.00

Card tray, blue	40.00
Card tray, clear	20.00
Card tray, green	32.50
Celery vase, green	48.00
Compote, open, 6" d., 4" h., crimped rim, clear	25.00
Compote, open, 8" d., 7" h., beaded rim, green	77.50
Compote, open, 9½" d., blue	95.00
Compote, open, 10½" d., high stand, blue	215.00
Creamer, blue	85.00
Creamer, clear	34.00
Creamer, ruby-stained	54.00
Creamer, individual size, clear	34.00
Creamer, individual size, green w/gold	42.00
Creamer, green w/gold, large	64.00
Cup, clear	11.00
Cup, green	30.00
Custard cup, green, large	28.00
Mug, clear, souvenir	18.50
Mug, green, souvenir	34.00
Nappy, tricornered, blue w/gold	38.00
Nappy, tricornered, clear	20.00
Nappy, tricornered, green w/gold	32.50
Pitcher, 6" h., green w/gold	42.00
Pitcher, water, green w/gold	176.00
Plate, 7" d., footed	17.50
Punch cup, clear	13.50
Punch cup, green	25.00
Salt dip, master size, footed	30.00
Salt & pepper shakers w/original tops, green, pr.	95.00
Sauce dish, blue w/gold	27.00
Sauce dish, clear	11.00
Sauce dish, green w/gold	22.00
Sauce dish, green, souvenir	35.00
Spooner, blue w/gold	43.00
Spooner, clear	25.00
Spooner, green w/gold	49.00
Sugar bowl, cov., large, clear	30.00
Sugar bowl, cov., individual size, green	32.00
Sugar bowl, cov., large, green	85.00
Sugar bowl, open, individual size, blue or green, each	27.50
Table set: creamer, cov. sugar bowl & cov. butter dish; blue w/gold, 3 pcs.	395.00
Table set, green w/gold, 4 pcs.	330.00
Toothpick holder, blue w/gold	41.00
Toothpick holder, clear w/gold	23.00
Toothpick holder, green w/gold	32.00
Tumbler, green w/gold, souvenir (ILLUS.)	30.00
Vase, 10½" h., blue	80.00
Vase, 12" h., trumpet-shaped, blue w/gold	100.00
Vase, 12" h., trumpet-shaped, green	55.00
Water set: pitcher & 6 tumblers; green w/gold, 7 pcs.	375.00
Wine, clear	20.00

Wine, green w/gold 28.00
Wine, green, souvenir 35.00
Wine, ruby-stained w/gold 40.00

COLUMBIAN COIN
Butter dish, cov., frosted
　coins...................125.00 to 175.00
Butter dish, cov., gilded coins 175.00
Celery vase, frosted coins.......... 85.00
Celery vase, gilded coins 90.00
Claret, gilded coins................ 75.00
Compote, open, 8" d., clear coins .. 68.00
Creamer, gilded coins 150.00
Goblet, gilded coins 66.00
Lamp, kerosene-type, 9½" h. 165.00
Lamp, kerosene-type, frosted coins,
　12" h.......................... 180.00
Pitcher, milk, gilded coins 165.00
Relish, 5 x 8", frosted coins 68.00
Salt & pepper shakers w/original
　tops, frosted coins, pr. 100.00
Sauce dish, flat or footed, gilded
　coins.......................... 32.50
Spooner, frosted coins 42.50
Spooner, gilded coins.............. 46.00
Syrup pitcher w/original top, clear
　coins.......................... 125.00
Syrup pitcher w/original top, frosted
　coins.......................... 180.00
Toothpick holder, frosted coins 95.00
Toothpick holder, gilded coins 135.00
Toothpick holder, red coins 195.00
Tumbler, gilded coins.............. 55.00
Wine, frosted coins.........55.00 to 80.00

COMET (Early Comet)
Goblet 88.00
Spooner 95.00
Sugar bowl, cov. 175.00
Tumbler, bar...................... 95.00
Tumbler, water 110.00
Tumbler, whiskey, handled........ 250.00

COMPACT - See Snail Pattern

CORD & TASSEL

Cord & Tassel Goblet
Bowl, oval....................... 20.00
Butter dish, cov. 48.00
Cake stand, 9½" d. 44.00

Castor bottle...................... 32.00
Compote, open, 8" d., low stand ... 26.50
Creamer 32.00
Goblet (ILLUS.).................... 34.00
Lamp, kerosene-type, applied
　handle 85.00
Pitcher, water 95.00
Salt & pepper shakers w/original
　tops, pr....................... 55.00
Sauce dish, flat 7.50
Spooner 23.00
Sugar bowl, open 26.00
Syrup pitcher w/original top, ap-
　plied handle 110.00
Table set, creamer, open sugar
　bowl & spooner, 3 pcs. 68.00
Wine............................ 38.00

CORD DRAPERY

Cord Drapery Creamer
Berry set, master bowl & 6 sauce
　dishes, 7 pcs................... 58.00
Bowl, 6¼" d., footed, amber....... 175.00
Bowl, 6¼" d., footed, clear 75.00
Bowl, 7" d., flat.................. 28.50
Bowl, 8½" oval 35.00
Bowl, 10" d., 3½" h. 45.00
Butter dish, cov., clear 85.00
Butter dish, cov., green........... 175.00
Cake stand 40.00
Compote, cov., jelly, blue.......... 55.00
Compote, cov., jelly, clear 45.00
Compote, cov., 9" d. 70.00
Compote, open, jelly 30.00
Compote, open, 8½" d., 6¼" h.,
　cobalt blue 180.00
Creamer, blue 125.00
Creamer, clear (ILLUS.) 45.00
Cruet w/original stopper, amber ... 305.00
Cruet w/original stopper,
　clear.................80.00 to 90.00
Goblet 60.00
Mug 40.00
Pickle, 5¼ x 9¼" oval............. 22.50
Pitcher, water, amber 177.00
Pitcher, water, clear.............. 62.00
Pitcher, water, cobalt blue 225.00
Pitcher, water, green............. 245.00
Punch cup 15.00
Relish, 4 x 7"................... 21.00
Salt & pepper shakers w/original
　tops, pr....................... 110.00
Sauce dish, flat or footed,
　blue ....30.00 to 40.00

Sauce dish, flat or footed,
clear 10.00
Spooner 42.50
Sugar bowl, cov., clear 60.00
Sugar bowl, cov., green 165.00
Syrup pitcher w/original top,
amber 265.00
Toothpick holder 95.00
Tumbler, blue 125.00
Tumbler, clear 37.50
Wine, amber 225.00
Wine, clear 90.00

CORDOVA
Banana stand 90.00
Butter dish, cov. 50.00
Celery vase 45.00
Cologne bottle, 5" h. 20.00
Creamer 22.50
Creamer, individual size 35.00
Creamer & cov. sugar bowl, pr. 65.00
Mug 16.50
Pitcher, milk 30.00
Pitcher, water 52.50
Punch cup 7.50
Spooner 27.50
Sugar bowl, cov. ....35.00 to 40.00
Sugar bowl, cov., individual size.... 40.00
Syrup pitcher w/pewter top 98.00
Toothpick holder 20.00
Tumbler 15.00
Vase, bud 15.00
Water set, pitcher & 5 tumblers,
6 pcs. 95.00

CORD ROSETTE
Goblet ....30.00 to 40.00
Lamp, kerosene-type, pedestal
base, original burner 70.00

CORONA - See Sunk Honeycomb Pattern

COTTAGE (Dinner Bell or Finecut Band)

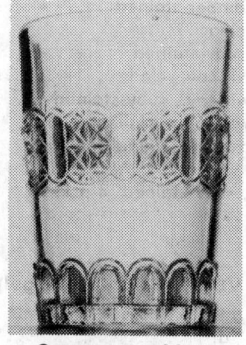

Cottage Tumbler

Bowl, berry, 6½ x 9¼" oval 24.00
Butter dish, cov., clear 42.00
Butter dish, cov., green 78.00
Cake stand, amber 50.00
Cake stand, clear 37.00

Celery vase 31.00
Champagne 52.50
Compote, cov., 7" d., high stand ... 30.00
Compote, open, jelly, 4½" d., 4" h.,
blue 28.50
Compote, open, jelly, 4½" d., 4" h.,
green 39.00
Creamer, amber 76.50
Creamer, clear 23.00
Cruet w/original stopper 35.00
Cup & saucer 35.00
Finger bowl 15.00
Goblet, amber 45.00
Goblet, blue 48.00
Goblet, clear 26.00
Pitcher, milk, amber 60.00
Pitcher, milk, clear 35.00
Pitcher, water, 2 qt. 40.00
Plate, 5" d., clear 11.50
Plate, 5" d., ruby-stained 20.00
Plate, 6" d. 12.00
Plate, 7" d. 18.00
Plate, 9" d. 35.00
Plate, 10" d. 40.00
Salt shaker w/original top 25.00
Sauce dish 7.50
Saucer, clear, 6" d. 10.00
Saucer, green, 6" d. 20.00
Spooner 20.00
Sugar bowl, cov. 47.00
Sugar bowl, open 14.00
Syrup pitcher w/original top 57.50
Tray, water 27.50
Tumbler (ILLUS.) 20.00
Waste bowl 38.00
Wine, blue 45.00
Wine, clear 21.00

CROESUS

Croesus Table Set

Berry set: master bowl & 6 sauce
dishes; green, 7 pcs. 325.00
Berry set: master bowl & 6 sauce
dishes; purple, 7 pcs. 425.00
Bowl, 6¾" d., 4" h., footed, purple
w/gold 173.00
Bowl, 8" d., green 100.00
Bowl, 8" d., purple 175.00
Bowl, berry or fruit, 9" d.,
green ....100.00 to 125.00
Bowl, berry or fruit, 9" d., purple... 155.00
Butter dish, cov., clear 75.00

Butter dish, cov., green 139.00
Butter dish, cov., purple ...175.00 to 200.00
Celery vase, green w/gold 135.00
Compote, open, jelly, purple 260.00
Condiment set: cruet, salt & pepper
  shakers & tray; green w/gold,
  4 pcs. .... 350.00 to 400.00
Condiment set: cruet, salt & pepper
  shakers & tray; purple w/gold,
  4 pcs. .... 400.00 to 550.00
Condiment tray, clear 27.00
Condiment tray, green 60.00
Creamer, green 70.00
Creamer, purple 145.00
Creamer, individual size, green,
  3" h. 193.00
Creamer, individual size, purple,
  3" h. 165.00
Cruet w/original stopper, green 190.00
Cruet w/original stopper, purple ... 350.00
Cruet w/original stopper, miniature,
  green w/gold, 4" h. 85.00
Cruet w/original stopper, miniature,
  purple, 4" h. 189.00
Pickle, purple 78.00
Pitcher, water, green 225.00
Pitcher, water, purple 550.00
Plate, 8" d., scalloped rim, green
  w/gold 153.00
Salt & pepper shakers w/original
  tops, green, pr. .... 120.00 to 135.00
Salt & pepper shakers w/original
  tops, purple, pr. 143.00
Sauce dish, clear 13.50
Sauce dish, green w/gold 35.00
Sauce dish, purple w/gold 45.00
Spooner, green 65.00
Spooner, purple 114.00
Sugar bowl, cov., green 110.00
Sugar bowl, cov., purple 175.00
Table set, green w/gold,
  4 pcs. .... 600.00 to 650.00
Table set, purple, 4 pcs. (ILLUS.) ... 645.00
Toothpick holder, clear 25.00
Toothpick holder, green 86.00
Toothpick holder, purple 95.00
Tumbler, green 44.00
Tumbler, purple 64.00
Water set: pitcher & 6 tumblers;
  green, 7 pcs. 695.00
Water set: pitcher & 6 tumblers;
  purple, 7 pcs. 850.00

CROWFOOT (Turkey Track)
Bowl, 10" d. 30.00
Butter dish, cov. 48.00
Cake stand, 9" d. 48.00
Goblet 30.00
Pitcher, water 55.00
Sauce dish, flat 12.00
Spooner 24.50
Sugar bowl, cov. 35.00
Tumbler 25.00

CROWN JEWEL - See Chandelier Pattern

CRYSTAL BALL - See Atlas Pattern

CRYSTAL WEDDING (Collins)
Banana stand, 10" h. 99.00
Banana stand, low pedestal 85.00
Berry set, 8" sq. bowl & 6 sauce
  dishes, 7 pcs. 125.00
Bowl, cov., 5" sq. 68.00
Bowl, cov., 7" sq. 75.00
Butter dish, cov., clear 65.00
Butter dish, cov., ruby-stained 135.00
Cake stand, 9" sq., 8" h. 58.00
Cake stand, 10" sq. 75.00
Celery vase 45.00
Compote, cov., 4" sq., 6½" h. 35.00
Compote, cov., 5" sq. 46.00
Compote, cov., 6" sq., 9½" h. 52.50
Compote, cov., 7" sq. 75.00
Compote, cov., 7" d., 13" h. 105.00
Compote, open, 4" sq., 6" h. 22.50
Compote, open, 5" sq. 42.50
Compote, open, 6¼" sq., 8" h.,
  scalloped rim 45.00
Compote, open, 7" sq., 8¾" h. 75.00
Compote, open, 8" sq., low stand .. 36.00
Creamer, clear 45.00
Creamer, ruby-stained 52.50
Creamer & cov. sugar bowl, amber-
  stained, pr. .... 180.00 to 195.00
Cruet w/original stopper, amber-
  stained 175.00
Goblet, clear 40.00
Goblet, ruby-stained 62.50
Lamp base, kerosene-type, square
  font, 10" h. 375.00
Pitcher, water 125.00
Salt dip 35.00
Salt shaker w/original top, ruby-
  stained 68.00
Sauce dish 14.00
Spooner, amber-stained 45.00
Spooner, clear 35.00
Spooner, ruby-stained 55.00
Sugar bowl, cov., clear 48.00
Sugar bowl, cov., ruby-stained 100.00
Sugar bowl, open, scalloped rim 30.00
Syrup pitcher w/original top, ruby-
  stained 210.00
Table set, ruby-stained, 4 pcs. 400.00
Tumbler 38.50
Wine 68.00

CUPID & VENUS (Guardian Angel)
Bowl, cov., 8" d., footed 125.00
Bowl, 6½" d. 20.00
Bowl, 9" d., scalloped rim, footed .. 37.50
Bread plate, amber, 10½" d. 125.00
Bread plate, clear, 10½" d. 48.00
Butter dish, cov. 55.00
Cake plate 48.00
Celery vase 42.50

Champagne...................... 62.50
Compote, cov., 7" d., high stand ... 110.00
Compote, cov., 9½" d., low stand .. 87.00
Compote, open, 6" d., low stand ... 35.00
Compote, open, 8½" d., low stand,
    scalloped rim 40.00
Cordial.......................... 85.00
Creamer 34.00
Goblet 65.00
Goblet, buttermilk 50.00
Honey dish, 3½" d. 7.50
Marmalade jar, cov.............. 85.00
Mug, 2½" h..................... 30.00
Mug, 3½" h..................... 34.00
Pickle castor w/resilvered frame,
    cover & tongs 95.00
Pitcher, milk, amber............. 190.00
Pitcher, milk, clear 62.00
Pitcher, water 55.00

Cupid & Venus Sauce Dish

Sauce dish, footed, 3½" to 4½" d.
    (ILLUS.)........................ 11.50
Spooner 35.00
Sugar bowl, cov. 65.00
Wine............................ 103.00

CURRANT

Butter dish, cov. 75.00
Cake stand, 9¼" d., 4¼" h. 75.00
Cake stand, 11" d. 62.00
Celery vase...................... 40.00
Compote, cov., 8" d., high stand ... 195.00
Compote, open, 10½" d............ 50.00
Creamer 45.00
Egg cup 20.00
Goblet 30.00
Goblet, buttermilk 40.00
Honey dish, 3½" d. 16.00
Pitcher, water 70.00
Relish, 5 x 8".................... 12.00
Spooner 26.00
Wine............................ 37.50

CURRIER & IVES

Bitters bottle.................... 38.00
Bowl, master berry or fruit, 10"
    oval, flat w/collared base........ 33.00
Bread plate, Balky Mule on Railroad
    Tracks, blue 85.00
Bread plate, Balky Mule on Railroad
    Tracks, clear (ILLUS.) 50.00

Currier & Ives Bread Plate

Bread plate, children sawing felled
    log, frosted center 75.00
Compote, cov., 7½" d., high
    stand 95.00
Compote, cov., 11½" d., amber ... 145.00
Compote, open, 7½" d., 9" h., scal-
    loped rim...................... 45.00
Creamer 30.00
Cup............................ 15.00
Cup & saucer, blue 85.00
Goblet 22.00
Lamp, kerosene-type, 11" h. 70.00
Pitcher, milk..................... 43.00
Pitcher, water, amber 110.00
Pitcher, water, clear............. 53.00
Relish, 10" oval ....16.00 to 20.00
Salt shaker w/original top, amber .. 45.00
Salt shaker w/original top, blue 55.00
Salt shaker w/original top, clear ... 19.00
Salt shaker w/original top,
    vaseline....................... 52.50
Salt & pepper shakers w/original
    tops, pr....................... 58.00
Sauce dish, flat or footed, amber ... 20.00
Sauce dish, flat or footed, blue 25.00
Sauce dish, flat or footed, clear 10.00
Spooner 21.00
Sugar bowl, cov. ....35.00 to 45.00
Syrup jug w/original top, blue...... 202.00
Syrup jug w/original top, clear 82.50
Tray, wine, 9½" d................ 49.00
Tray, water, Balky Mule on Railroad
    Tracks, blue, 12" d. 110.00
Tray, water, Balky Mule on Railroad
    Tracks, clear, 12" d. 56.00
Tray, water, Balky Mule on Railroad
    Tracks, vaseline, 12" d...100.00 to 125.00
Waste bowl....................... 43.00
Wine............................ 15.00
Wine set, decanter w/original stop-
    per & 6 wines, 7 pcs. 180.00

CURTAIN

Bowl, 7½" d. 20.00
Butter dish, cov. 50.00
Cake stand, 9½" d. 34.00
Celery boat..................... 48.50

Celery vase............................ 29.00
Compote, open, 10" d., 8" h........ 30.00
Condiment set, pair salt & pepper
   shakers & mustard jar, 3 pcs. 65.00
Creamer ....25.00 to 35.00
Goblet 35.00
Mug, amber 65.00
Salt shaker w/original top 15.00
Sauce dish, flat or footed, 4¾" d. .. 8.00
Spooner 25.00
Sugar bowl, cov. 40.00
Tumbler........................ 20.00

CURTAIN TIEBACK

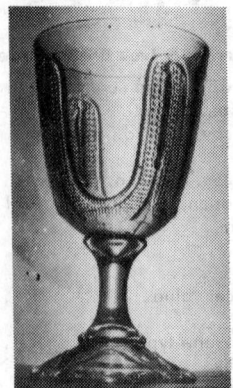

Curtain Tieback Goblet

Bowl, 7½" sq., flat 18.00
Bread tray....................... 37.00
Butter dish, cov. 38.00
Cake stand, 9" d., 6½" h. 23.00
Celery vase..................... 30.00
Creamer 35.00
Goblet (ILLUS.)................... 25.00
Pitcher, water 52.00
Relish 10.00
Sauce dish, flat or footed ....10.00 to 15.00
Spooner 28.00
Sugar bowl, cov. 30.00

CUT LOG

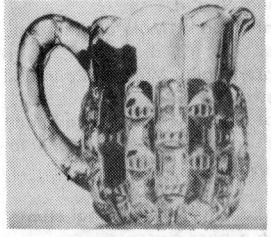

Cut Log Individual Creamer

Bowl, cov., 3" d. 16.00
Bowl, 8½" d., scalloped rim........ 27.50
Bowl, master berry or fruit,
   10½" d., footed................. 40.00
Butter dish, cov. ....65.00 to 75.00

Cake stand, 9" d., 6" h. 55.00
Cake stand, 10" d. 68.00
Celery tray 15.00
Celery vase..................... 32.00
Compote, cov., 5½" d., 7½" h...... 47.50
Compote, cov., 7" d., 10" h........ 60.00
Compote, cov., 8" d., 12½" h....... 75.00
Compote, open, 5" d. 26.00
Compote, open, 6" d., 4¾" h....... 32.00
Compote, open, 8" d., 6½" h....... 28.00
Compote, open, 9" d., 6¼" h 35.00
Compote, open, 10" d., 8½" h.,
   scalloped rim ....75.00 to 85.00
Creamer 38.00
Creamer, individual size (ILLUS.).... 12.50
Cruet w/original stopper, small 34.00
Cruet w/original stopper, large..... 50.00
Goblet 45.00
Jelly, cov. 55.00
Mug 16.50
Mug, large 65.00
Nappy, handled, 5" d. 18.50
Olive dish 18.00
Pitcher, water, tankard 73.00
Relish, boat-shaped, 9¼" l. 30.00
Salt shaker w/original tin top 34.00
Sauce dish, flat or footed ....25.00 to 30.00
Spooner 27.50
Sugar bowl, cov. 49.00
Sugar bowl, cov., individual size.... 32.50
Sugar bowl, open 22.00
Sugar bowl, open, individual size ... 20.00
Tumbler........................ 45.00
Tumbler, juice 22.50
Vase, 16" h. 35.00
Wine.......................... 23.00

DAHLIA

Bowl, 6 x 9" oval................. 16.50
Bread platter, 8 x 12" 36.00
Butter dish, cov., apple green 135.00
Butter dish, cov., clear 55.00
Cake stand, amber, 9" d. 50.00
Cake stand, clear, 9" d. 22.50
Champagne 55.00
Compote, cov., 7" d., high stand ... 50.00
Creamer 15.00
Goblet 32.50
Mug, amber 42.50
Mug, clear..................... 32.00
Mug, yellow 45.00
Mug, child's, blue 40.00
Mug, child's, clear.............. 20.00
Pitcher, milk, clear, applied
   handle 40.00
Pitcher, milk, yellow 58.00
Pitcher, water, amber 67.50
Pitcher, water, blue 95.00
Pitcher, water, clear............. 57.00
Pitcher, water, vaseline........... 77.00
Plate, 7" d. 20.00
Plate, 9" d., w/handles, amber 25.00
Plate, 9" d., w/handles, clear 17.50
Plate, 9" d., w/handles, vaseline ... 38.50

Relish, 5 x 9½"	13.00
Sauce dish, flat, amber	9.00
Sauce dish, flat, blue	15.00
Sauce dish, flat, clear	8.50
Spooner, amber	45.00
Spooner, clear	25.00
Sugar bowl, cov.	28.00
Wine	34.00

DAISY & BUTTON

Daisy & Button Canoe

Basket, silver plate handle, 6" h.	125.00
Berry set: master bowl & 6 sauce dishes; blue, 7 pcs.	85.00
Berry set: octagonal master bowl & 10 sauce dishes; amber, 11 pcs.	140.00
Berry set: master bowl & 12 sauce dishes; vaseline, 13 pcs.	225.00
Boot, high-top, ruby-stained buttons	125.00
Bowl, 8" w., tricornered, vaseline	37.50
Bowl, berry or fruit, 8½" d.	40.00
Bowl, 9" sq., Amberina	200.00
Bowl, 9¼" oblong, amber	32.00
Bowl, 11" l., 8" w. oval, 3" h., amber	65.00
Bowl, 11" l., 10" w. oval, 7¾" h., flared, vaseline	95.00
Bowl, 11" d., amber	38.00
Bowl, 12" l., 9" w., 6" h., clear	100.00
Bowl, fruit, rectangular, ornate silver plate frame	250.00
Bread tray, amber	25.00
Butter chip, fan-shaped	9.50
Butter chip, round, amber	9.00
Butter chip, round, clear	6.00
Butter chip, square, amber	15.00
Butter chip, square, blue	17.50
Butter chip, square, clear	7.50
Butter dish, cov., scalloped base	65.00
Butter dish, cov., square	45.00
Butter dish, cov., triangular, amber	60.00
Butter dish, cov., model of Victorian stove, blue	52.50
Butter tub, cov., 2-handled, vaseline	55.00
Canoe, amber, 8" l. (ILLUS.)	35.00
Canoe, Amberina, 8" l.	495.00
Canoe, apple green, 8" l.	32.50
Canoe, amber, 11" l.	85.00
Castor set, 3-bottle, clear, in glass frame w/toothpick holder at top	50.00
Castor set, 5-bottle, amber, blue & clear bottles, in original frame	100.00 to 145.00

Castor set, 5-bottle, blue, in original frame	225.00
Castor shaker bottle w/original top, amber	16.50
Celery vase, square	65.00
Celery vase, triangular, amber	43.00
Celery vase, triangular, green	35.00
Cheese dish, cov.	65.00
Cologne bottle w/original stopper	22.50
Compote, cov., 8" d., 12" h.	55.00
Compote, cov., 8½" d., 4½" h., amber	60.00
Creamer, amber	32.50
Creamer, clear	29.00
Creamer, ruby-stained buttons	45.00
Cruet w/original stopper, amber	100.00
Dish, amber, deep, 5" sq.	85.00
Dish, fan-shaped, clear, 10" w.	11.50
Goblet, amber	28.00
Goblet, blue	28.00
Goblet, clear	22.50
Hat shape, canary yellow, 1¾" h.	22.50
Hat shape, amber, 2½" h.	30.00
Hat shape, blue, 2½" h.	35.00
Hat shape, clear, 2½" h.	20.00
Hat shape, vaseline, 2½" h.	37.50
Hat shape, from tumbler mold, 4½" widest d.	55.00
Hat shape, blue, from tumbler mold, 4¾" widest d.	47.50
Hat shape, canary yellow, from tumbler mold, 5" widest d., 3¾" h.	48.00
Humidor, cov., amber	185.00
Ice cream dish, scalloped corners, Amberina, 5¾" d.	95.00 to 125.00
Ice cream dish, cut corners, 6" sq.	9.00
Inkwell, amber	145.00
Inkwell w/original insert, cat seated on cover	245.00
Match holder, cauldron w/original bail handle, amber	29.50
Match holder, wall-hanging scuff, amber, 4½" l.	30.00
Match holder, wall-hanging scuff, blue	60.00 to 75.00
Pickle castor, amber insert, w/silver plate frame & tongs	120.00
Pickle castor, sapphire blue insert, w/silver plate frame & tongs	238.00
Pickle castor, vaseline insert, w/silver plate frame & tongs	185.00
Pitcher, 5 1/8" h., applied handle, amber	55.00
Pitcher, water, bulbous, applied handle, clear	55.00
Pitcher, water, bulbous, applied handle, ruby-stained buttons	325.00
Pitcher, water, square	58.00
Plate, 5½" sq., Amberina	85.00
Plate, 7" sq., amber	18.00
Plate, 7" sq., blue	20.00
Plate, 7" sq., clear	15.00
Plate, 10" d., scalloped rim, amber	29.00

Plate, 10" d., blue................. 35.00
Platter, 9 x 13" oval, open handles,
  amber 35.00
Platter, 9 x 13" oval, open handles,
  blue 40.00
Platter, 9 x 13" oval, open handles,
  yellow 40.00
Powder jar, cov., amber, 3¾" d.,
  2" h. 30.00
Relish, "Sitz bathtub," clear 65.00
Salt dip, canoe-shaped, amber,
  2 x 4"...................... 19.50
Salt dip, canoe-shaped, clear,
  2 x 4"...................... 14.50
Salt dip, master size, blue, 3½" d... 12.50
Salt shaker w/original top, corset-
  shaped, blue.................. 25.00
Salt & pepper shakers w/original
  tops, clear, pr................. 20.00
Salt & pepper shakers w/original
  tops, vaseline, pr.............. 30.00
Sauce dish, amber, 4" to 5" sq...... 17.00
Sauce dish, Amberina, 4" to
  5" sq..................85.00 to 100.00
Sauce dish, blue, 4" to 5" sq........ 16.00
Sauce dish, clear, 4" to
  5" sq..................6.00 to 12.00
Sauce dish, cloverleaf-shaped,
  amber 14.50
Sauce dish, tricornered, vaseline ... 15.00
Sauce dish, tricornered,
  yellow ....9.00 to 15.00
Slipper, "1886 patent," clear 52.50
Slipper, ruby-stained buttons 80.00
Smoke bell, amber 65.00
Spooner, amber................. 37.50
Spooner, blue.................... 40.00
Spooner, clear 35.00
Spooner, hat-shaped, amber 32.00
Sugar bowl, cov., amber.....35.00 to 45.00
Sugar bowl, cov., barrel-shaped,
  blue 50.00
Sugar bowl, cov., clear 30.00
Sugar bowl, open, purple 55.00
Syrup pitcher w/original pewter top,
  blue 175.00
Table set: creamer, open sugar
  bowl & spooner; vaseline,
  3 pcs....................... 65.00
Toothpick holder (or salt dip),
  "Bandmaster's cap," blue 35.00
Toothpick holder, square, blue 22.00
Toothpick holder, 3-footed, amber .. 30.00
Toothpick holder, 3-footed,
  Amberina ....145.00 to 185.00
Toothpick holder, 3-footed, electric
  blue 35.00
Toothpick holder, 3-footed,
  vaseline..................... 39.50
Toothpick holder, urn-shaped....... 28.00
Toothpick holder, amber, w/brass
  rim & base 22.00
Tray, ice cream, handled, 9¼ x
  16½", blue 30.00

Tray, water, triangular, green 45.00
Tray, water, triangular, vaseline.... 55.00
Tumbler, water, amber 17.00
Tumbler, water, blue 28.00
Tumbler, water, blue, pattern half
  way up...................... 30.00
Tumbler, water, clear 13.00
Tumbler, water, vaseline 40.00
Tumbler, water, vaseline, pattern
  half way up 30.00
Vase, 6" h., hand holding cornuco-
  pia, blue 50.00
Vase, 6" h., hand holding cornuco-
  pia, ruby-stained buttons 58.50
Waste bowl, blue 28.00
Whimsey, sleigh, amber,
  4½ x 7¾".................... 115.00
Whimsey, "whisk broom" dish,
  amber 28.00

DAISY & BUTTON WITH CROSSBARS (Mikado)

Daisy & Button with Crossbars Bread Tray

Berry set: master bowl & 4 sauce
  dishes; blue, 5 pcs............. 85.00
Bowl, 6 x 9", canary yellow 30.00
Bread tray, apple green 32.50
Bread tray, blue (ILLUS.) 42.00
Bread tray, clear 25.00
Bread tray, vaseline 52.00
Butter dish, cov., blue 58.00
Butter dish, cov., clear 45.00
Cake stand, blue 85.00
Celery vase, amber 39.00
Celery vase, blue 40.00
Celery vase, clear............... 27.00
Celery vase, vaseline 43.00
Compote, open, 6" h., canary
  yellow 38.00
Compote, open, 7" d., 4" h.,
  amber 26.50
Compote, open, 8½" d., 7½" h.,
  amber 45.00
Compote, open, 8½" d., 7½" h.,
  blue 45.00
Compote, open, 8½" d., 7½" h.,
  clear....................... 32.50
Compote, open, 9½" d............ 35.00
Compote, open, 10" d., amber 60.00
Creamer, amber ....30.00 to 40.00
Creamer, blue 45.00

Creamer, clear	30.00
Creamer, individual size, blue	30.00
Creamer, individual size, clear	15.00
Cruet w/original stopper, amber	117.00
Cruet w/original stopper, canary yellow	125.00
Cruet w/original stopper, clear	55.00
Cruet w/original stopper, vaseline	125.00
Goblet, amber	35.00
Goblet, blue	38.00
Goblet, clear	22.50
Goblet, vaseline	38.00
Mug, amber, 3" h.	18.00
Mug, canary yellow, 3" h.	22.50
Mug, clear, 3" h.	12.00
Pitcher, milk, amber	45.00
Pitcher, milk, blue	55.00
Pitcher, milk, clear	46.00
Pitcher, water, amber	83.00
Pitcher, water, blue	90.00
Pitcher, water, clear	52.00
Pitcher, water, vaseline	60.00
Sauce dish, flat or footed, canary yellow	16.50
Spooner, amber	50.00
Spooner, clear	23.50
Spooner, vaseline	30.00
Sugar bowl, cov., blue	55.00
Sugar bowl, cov., clear	25.00
Toothpick holder	28.00
Tumbler, amber	20.00
Tumbler, blue	30.00
Tumbler, clear	15.00
Tumbler, vaseline	25.00
Vase, vaseline	45.00
Waste bowl, canary yellow	22.50
Water set: pitcher & 6 tumblers; canary yellow, 7 pcs.	250.00
Wine	27.00

DAISY & BUTTON WITH NARCISSUS

Bowl, 6 x 9½" oval, footed	45.00
Butter dish, cov.	50.00
Creamer	45.00
Decanter w/original stopper	65.00
Decanter, no stopper	22.50
Goblet	18.00 to 22.50
Nappy, leaf-shaped	65.00
Pitcher, water	70.00
Sauce dish, flat or 3-footed	8.00 to 15.00
Spooner	30.00
Sugar bowl, cov.	42.50
Tray, 10½" d.	30.00
Tumbler	16.50
Wine	19.00
Wine set, decanter w/original stopper & 4 wines, 5 pcs.	75.00

DAISY & BUTTON WITH PANEL

Castor set, 3-bottle, blue, in original blue glass frame	145.00
Compote, open, 9½" d., 11" h.	120.00
Pitcher, water, clear w/gold	40.00
Spooner, amber	29.00

DAISY & BUTTON WITH THUMBPRINT PANELS

Berry set: master bowl & 8 sauce dishes; amber panels, 9 pcs.	300.00
Bowl, 8" sq.	25.00
Bowl, 8½" d., collared base, amber panels	200.00
Bride's basket, in silver plate holder, amber panels	125.00
Butter dish, cov.	150.00 to 200.00
Cake basket, amber panels, 7 x 11", 5½" h.	125.00
Cake stand, 9½" d.	48.00
Cake stand, canary yellow, 10½" d., 7¼" h.	55.00
Celery vase, amber panels	85.00
Celery vase, clear	30.00
Champagne, amber panels	25.00
Compote, cov., 6¾" d., 10½" h.	62.50
Creamer, applied handle, amber panels	68.00
Dish, triangular, 5" w., 2" h.	20.00
Finger bowl	22.50
Goblet, amber panels	49.00
Goblet, blue panels	42.50
Goblet, clear	27.50
Pitcher, water, applied handle, amber panels	135.00
Pitcher, water, applied handle, blue panels	85.00
Sauce dish, flat or footed, amber panels, 5" sq.	15.00 to 30.00
Sauce dish, flat or footed, clear, 5" sq.	9.00 to 12.00
Salt shaker w/original top, amber panels	75.00
Spooner, amber panels	75.00
Syrup jug w/original top, amber panels	125.00
Tumbler, amber panels	38.50
Tumbler, blue panels	25.00
Tumbler, clear	20.00
Water set: pitcher & 5 tumblers; vaseline, 6 pcs.	295.00
Wine, amber panels	35.00
Wine, blue panels	40.00
Wine, clear	15.00

DAISY & BUTTON WITH "V" ORNAMENT

Bowl, 7" d., 2½" h., vaseline	19.00
Bowl, 9" d., blue	34.00
Bowl, 9" d., vaseline	50.00
Butter dish, cov., canary yellow	68.00
Butter dish, cov., clear	45.00
Celery vase, amber	34.00
Celery vase, clear	30.00
Celery vase, vaseline	60.00
Creamer	30.00
Finger bowl, blue	45.00
Mug, blue	22.50
Mug, clear	17.50
Mug, vaseline	25.00
Pitcher, water, amber	90.00
Pitcher, water, blue	90.00

Pitcher, water, clear.............. 40.00
Pitcher, water, vaseline............ 65.00
Sauce dish, amber 15.00
Sauce dish, blue 15.00
Sauce dish, clear 10.00
Spooner, amber 37.50
Spooner, blue..................... 35.00
Spooner, clear 20.00
Sugar bowl, cov., blue............. 49.00
Toothpick holder, amber 30.00
Toothpick holder, blue............ 32.00
Toothpick holder, clear 24.00
Toothpick holder, vaseline 35.00
Tumbler, amber 26.00
Tumbler, clear 15.00
Waste bowl, amber 29.00
Waste bowl, clear............... 22.50
Waste bowl, vaseline............. 28.00

DAISY IN PANEL - See Two Panel Pattern

DAKOTA (Baby Thumbprint)

Dakota Engraved Celery Vase

Butter dish, cov. 50.00
Cake stand, 8" to 10¼" d. 51.00
Cake stand, 9¼" d. 65.00
Celery vase, flat base, engraved
  (ILLUS.)...................... 45.00
Celery vase, flat base, plain 30.00
Celery vase, pedestal base........ 35.00
Compote, cov., jelly, 5" d., 5" h. ... 46.50
Compote, cov., 6" d., high stand ... 65.00
Compote, open, jelly, 5" d., 5" h.... 32.00
Compote, open, 6" d.............. 26.00
Compote, open, 7" d.............. 41.00
Compote, open, 8" d., low stand ... 32.50
Compote, open, 8" d., 9" h........ 60.00
Compote, open, 10" d............. 55.00
Creamer 53.00
Finger bowl 45.00
Goblet, clear, engraved 32.00
Goblet, clear, plain 24.00
Goblet, ruby-stained............. 40.00
Lamp, kerosene-type ......110.00 to 135.00
Mug, ruby-stained, 3½" h. 35.00
Pitcher, milk 80.00
Pitcher, tankard, engraved 112.00
Pitcher, water, 10" to 12" h., clear .. 72.00

Pitcher, water, 10" to 12" h., ruby-
  stained...................... 125.00
Plate, 10" d..................... 63.00
Salt shaker w/original top 42.50
Salt & pepper shakers w/original
  tops, engraved, pr.............. 125.00
Salt & pepper shakers w/original
  tops, plain, pr................. 125.00
Sauce dish, flat or footed,
  engraved..................... 24.50
Sauce dish, flat or footed, plain 14.00
Shaker bottle w/original top,
  5" h.......................... 35.00
Shaker bottle w/original top, hotel
  size, 6½" h. 58.00
Spooner 32.00
Sugar bowl, cov., engraved 58.00
Sugar bowl, cov., plain 50.00
Sugar bowl, open, breakfast size ... 21.00
Table set, 4 pcs. 263.00
Tray, water, piecrust rim, 13" d..... 94.00
Tray, wine..................... 77.50
Tumbler, clear 30.00
Tumbler, ruby-stained 32.00
Waste bowl, engraved 75.00
Waste bowl, plain 58.00
Water set, pitcher & 1 tumbler,
  2 pcs........................ 75.00
Wine, clear 24.00
Wine, ruby-stained 46.00

DARBY - See Pleat & Panel Pattern

DART
Butter dish, cov. 28.00
Compote, cov., 8½" d., high
  stand 38.00
Compote, open, jelly 17.00
Creamer 31.00
Goblet 25.00
Lamp, kerosene-type 45.00
Salt shaker w/original top 28.50
Sauce dish, footed 10.00
Spooner 30.00
Sugar bowl, cov. 32.00

DEER & DOG
Butter dish, cov., pedestal base &
  frosted dog finial............... 130.00
Celery vase, scalloped rim, signed
  "Gillinder".................... 95.00
Compote, cov., 8" oval, 8¾" h.,
  frosted dog finial............... 155.00
Compote, cov., 8" d., 13" h., frosted
  dog finial..................... 250.00
Compote, open, 8" d............. 175.00
Cordial 95.00
Creamer 75.00
Goblet, straight sides............. 52.00
Goblet, U-shaped 76.00
Goblet, V-shaped 50.00
Marmalade jar, cov............... 78.00
Pitcher, milk, 9" h. 165.00
Pitcher, water, applied reeded han-
  dle ....180.00 to 195.00

Sauce dish, footed 18.00
Spooner 52.00
Sugar bowl, cov., frosted dog
    finial 110.00
Wine ....60.00 to 85.00

DEER & PINE TREE

Deer & Pine Tree Butter Dish

Bowl, 5 x 8" 22.00
Bread tray, amber, 8 x 13" 63.00
Bread tray, apple green, 8 x 13".... 78.00
Bread tray, blue, 8 x 13" 80.00
Bread tray, clear, 8 x 13" 40.00
Bread tray, vaseline, 8 x 13" 77.00
Butter dish, cov. (ILLUS.) 92.00
Cake stand 100.00
Celery vase 70.00
Compote, cov., 8" sq., 6" h. 68.00
Compote, cov., 8" sq., 12" h. 168.00
Compote, open, 8" sq., high stand .. 48.00
Creamer 62.50
Finger bowl 57.50
Goblet 42.00
Marmalade jar, cov. 110.00
Mug, child's, amber 45.00
Mug, child's, apple green 45.00
Mug, child's, vaseline 55.00
Mug, large, apple green 65.00
Mug, large, blue 48.00
Mug, large, clear 40.00
Pickle dish 18.00
Pitcher, milk 70.00
Pitcher, water 92.00
Sauce dish, flat or footed ....12.00 to 22.00
Spooner 35.00
Sugar bowl, cov. 62.50
Tray, water, handled, amber,
    9 x 15" 54.00
Tray, water, handled, clear,
    9 x 15" 55.00
Vegetable dish, 5¾ x 9" 50.00

DELAWARE (Four Petal Flower)

Banana boat, amethyst w/gold,
    11¾" l. 125.00
Banana boat, clear w/gold,
    11¾" l. 50.00
Banana boat, green w/gold,
    11¾" l. 68.00
Banana boat, rose w/gold,
    11¾" l. 58.00

Berry set: boat-shaped master bowl
    & 4 boat-shaped sauce dishes;
    clear w/rose flowers & gold,
    5 pcs. 145.00
Berry set: boat-shaped master bowl
    & 5 boat-shaped sauce dishes;
    rose w/gold, 6 pcs. 295.00
Berry set: boat-shaped master bowl
    & 6 boat-shaped sauce dishes;
    green w/gold, 7 pcs. 190.00
Berry set: master bowl & 4 sauce
    dishes; green w/gold, 5 pcs. 125.00
Berry set: master bowl & 6 sauce
    dishes; rose w/gold, 7 pcs. 195.00
Bowl, 8" d., amethyst w/gold 75.00
Bowl, 8" d., clear 50.00
Bowl, 8" d., clear w/gold 55.00
Bowl, 8" d., green w/gold 60.00
Bowl, 8" d., rose w/gold 57.50
Bowl, 9" d., rose w/gold 75.00
Bowl, 9" octagon, clear
    w/gold ....45.00 to 65.00
Bowl, 10" octagon, green
    w/gold ....80.00 to 110.00
Bride's basket, boat-shaped open
    bowl, green w/gold, in silver
    plate frame, 11½" oval 160.00
Bride's basket, boat-shaped open
    bowl, green w/gold, miniature ... 175.00
Butter dish, cov., clear 90.00
Butter dish, cov., green w/gold..... 105.00
Butter dish, cov., rose w/gold 148.00
Celery vase, green w/gold 62.00
Celery vase, rose w/gold 72.50
Claret jug, green w/gold 175.00
Creamer, clear w/gold 43.00
Creamer, green w/gold 52.00
Creamer, rose w/gold 66.00
Creamer, individual size, clear
    w/gold 25.00
Creamer, individual size, rose
    w/gold 60.00
Creamer & open sugar bowl, silver
    plate holder, individual size,
    green w/gold, pr. 75.00
Creamer & open sugar bowl, rose
    w/gold, pr. 95.00
Creamer & sugar bowl, breakfast
    size, rose w/gold, pr. 125.00
Cruet w/original stopper, clear 100.00
Cruet w/original stopper, green
    w/gold 150.00
Dresser tray, clear 30.00
Dresser tray, green w/gold 60.00
Dresser tray, rose w/gold 65.00
Finger bowl, clear w/gold 22.00
Marmalade dish w/silver plate
    holder, amethyst w/gold 45.00
Marmalade dish w/silver plate
    holder, green w/gold 45.00
Marmalade dish w/silver plate
    holder, rose w/gold 95.00
Pin tray, 3½ x 7" 14.50
Pin tray, 4¾ x 9" 17.50

Pitcher, milk, green w/gold ..60.00 to 85.00
Pitcher, tankard, clear w/rose-
    stained & green florals & gold
    trim............................ 125.00
Pitcher, tankard, green w/gold 95.00
Pitcher, tankard, rose w/gold 132.00
Pitcher, water, bulbous, rose
    w/gold 125.00
Pomade jar w/jeweled cover, green
    w/gold................185.00 to 200.00
Pomade jar w/jeweled cover, rose
    w/gold 215.00
Powder jar, cov., green w/gold 135.00
Powder jar, cov., rose w/gold 145.00
Punch cup, clear 14.00
Punch cup, clear w/gold 30.00
Punch cup, green, souvenir 15.00
Punch cup, green w/gold 43.00
Punch cup, rose w/gold........... 40.00
Salt shaker w/original top, rose
    w/gold 45.00
Sauce dish, boat-shaped, clear 30.00
Sauce dish, boat-shaped, green
    w/gold 30.00
Sauce dish, boat-shaped, rose
    w/gold 40.00
Sauce dish, round, green w/gold ... 28.00
Sauce dish, round, rose w/gold..... 21.00
Shade, rose w/gold 105.00
Spooner, clear w/gold 35.00
Spooner, green w/gold 45.00
Spooner, rose.................... 65.00
Sugar bowl, cov., clear 65.00
Sugar bowl, cov., green w/gold 120.00
Sugar bowl, cov., rose w/gold...... 100.00
Sugar bowl, open 34.00
Sugar bowl, individual size,
    green 55.00
Table set, green w/gold, 4 pcs. 400.00
Table set, rose w/gold, 4 pcs....... 450.00
Toothpick holder, clear 30.00
Toothpick holder, clear w/rose-
    stained florals & gold 65.00
Toothpick holder, green w/gold 88.00
Toothpick holder, rose w/gold...... 112.00
Tumbler, clear w/gold 40.00
Tumbler, clear w/rose-stained
    florals......................... 26.50

Delaware Custard Tumbler

Tumbler, custard w/stained florals
    (ILLUS.)......................... 65.00

Tumbler, green w/gold 44.00
Tumbler, rose w/gold 37.00
Vase, 6" h., green w/gold 40.00
Vase, 8" h., green w/gold 115.00
Vase, 9½" h., green w/gold 86.00
Vase, 9½" h., rose w/gold......... 126.00
Water set: pitcher & 6 tumblers;
    clear w/gold, 7 pcs......145.00 to 165.00
Water set: pitcher & 6 tumblers;
    green w/gold, 7 pcs. ....400.00 to 500.00
Water set: pitcher & 6 tumblers;
    rose w/gold, 7 pcs. 325.00

DEW & RAINDROP

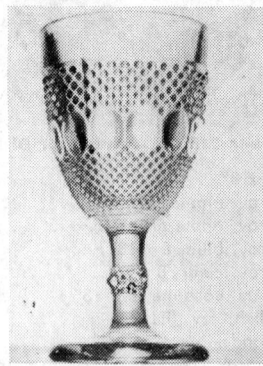

Dew & Raindrop Wine

Bowl, 6½" d. 28.00
Bowl, berry, 8" d................. 38.00
Butter dish, cov. 50.00
Celery 11.00
Compote, cov., jelly 50.00
Compote, open, jelly 35.00
Cordial.......................... 15.00
Creamer 28.50
Goblet 30.00
Pitcher, water 48.00
Punch cup 7.50
Salt & pepper shakers w/original
    tops, pr........................ 40.00
Sauce dish, flat or footed ....10.00 to 12.00
Spooner......................... 35.00
Tumbler 16.50
Vase, bud, 6" h.................. 27.50
Wine (ILLUS.) 21.00

DEWDROP

Bread tray 25.00
Butter dish, cov. 30.00
Cake stand, 8½" d. 20.00
Cordial......................... 40.00
Creamer 25.00
Egg cup, double................. 20.00
Goblet, amber 25.00
Goblet, blue 25.00
Goblet, clear 20.00
Goblet, vaseline 40.00
Mug, applied handle 26.00
Pitcher, water, collared base 50.00
Relish 15.00

Salt shaker w/original top, footed .. 22.00
Sauce dish........................ 8.00
Spooner 25.00
Sugar bowl, open 40.00
Tumbler, blue.................... 27.50
Tumbler, clear 15.00

DEWDROP WITH STAR
Bowl, 7" d. 14.00
Butter dish, cov. 48.00
Cake stand, 9" d. 42.50
Celery vase...................... 40.00
Cheese dish, cov. ....110.00 to 130.00
Compote, cov., 5" d. 60.00
Compote, open, 9" d., 9" h. 45.00
Creamer, applied handle........... 25.00
Pitcher, water, 8" h.............. 95.00
Plate, 5" d. 12.00
Plate, 9" d. 13.50
Plate, 11" d. 15.00
Relish, 9" l...................... 15.00
Sauce dish, flat ....8.00 to 10.00
Sauce dish, footed 7.00
Sugar bowl, cov. 50.00

DEWEY (Flower Flange)

Dewey Spooner

Bowl, 8" d., amber 30.00
Bowl, 8" d., yellow 45.00
Butter dish, cov., amber, 4" d. ... 65.00
Butter dish, cov., clear, 4" d. 55.00
Butter dish, cov., green, 4" d. 82.00
Butter dish, cov., yellow, 5" d. ... 95.00
Creamer, amber 42.00
Creamer, clear.................... 30.00
Creamer, green 42.50
Creamer, yellow 32.00
Creamer & cov. sugar bowl, break-
fast size, vaseline, pr...... 95.00
Cruet w/original stopper, amber ... 145.00
Cruet w/original stopper, clear ... 110.00
Cruet w/original stopper, green 150.00
Cruet w/original stopper, yellow ... 134.00
Mug, amber 60.00
Mug, clear........................ 35.00
Mug, green 65.00
Mug, Nile green 275.00
Parfait, green.................... 35.00
Pitcher, water, amber 110.00
Pitcher, water, clear............. 85.00
Pitcher, water, green 145.00
Pitcher, water, yellow 145.00

Plate, footed, amber 42.00
Plate, footed, clear.............. 15.00
Plate, footed, green 45.00
Plate, footed, yellow 55.00
Relish, serpentine shape, amber,
small 35.00
Relish, serpentine shape, clear,
small 20.00
Relish, serpentine shape, green,
small 38.50
Relish, serpentine shape, Nile
green, small 250.00
Relish, serpentine shape, yellow,
small 42.50
Relish, serpentine shape, amber,
large........................ 62.50
Relish, serpentine shape, Nile
green, large 265.00
Salt shaker w/original top, amber
or green 60.00
Salt shaker w/original top,
yellow 45.00
Sauce dish, amber 20.00
Sauce dish, green 25.00
Sauce dish, yellow 25.00
Spooner, amber.................... 60.00
Spooner, green 35.00
Spooner, yellow (ILLUS.) 35.00
Sugar bowl, cov., clear 35.00
Sugar bowl, cov., green 50.00
Tumbler, amber.................... 50.00
Tumbler, green 45.00
Tumbler, yellow 60.00
Tumbler, vaseline 55.00
Water set: pitcher & 6 tumblers;
clear, 7 pcs.............300.00 to 350.00
Water set: pticher & 6 tumblers; yel-
low, 7 pcs. ....450.00 to 500.00

DIAGONAL BAND
Butter dish, cov. 35.00
Cake stand 30.00
Celery vase....................... 26.00
Compote, cov., 7½" d., 9¼" h...... 45.00
Compote, open, 7½" d., high
stand 18.00
Creamer 30.00
Creamer & open sugar bowl, pr..... 50.00
Goblet 21.00
Marmalade jar w/original lid....... 22.00
Pitcher, milk..................... 32.00
Pitcher, water 35.00
Plate, 8" d. 10.50
Relish, 6 7/8" oval 7.50
Salt dip, footed 25.00
Salt & pepper shakers w/original
tops, pr..................... 30.00
Sauce dish, flat or footed .....7.00 to 10.00
Spooner 20.00
Sugar bowl, open 15.00
Wine............................. 23.00

DIAGONAL BAND & FAN
Butter dish, cov. 40.00

Celery	21.00
Champagne	30.00
Compote, open	25.00
Creamer	35.00
Goblet	20.00
Pitcher, milk	38.00
Plate, 6" d.	11.50
Plate, 8" d.	12.50
Relish, 8" oval	15.00
Sauce dish, footed	13.50
Spooner	25.00
Wine	19.50

DIAMOND & BULL'S EYE BAND - See Reverse Torpedo Pattern

DIAMOND & SUNBURST

Bowl, cov., 8" d.	35.00
Cake stand, 8" d.	28.00
Celery vase	35.00
Compote, cov., 7" d., high stand	48.00
Compote, open, jelly	15.00
Goblet	20.00
Pitcher w/applied handle, milk	40.00
Spooner	15.00
Sugar shaker	22.00
Syrup jug w/original top, applied handle	45.00
Toothpick holder	18.50
Tumbler	25.00
Wine	20.00

DIAMOND BAR - See Lattice Pattern

DIAMOND HORSESHOE - See Aurora Pattern

DIAMOND MEDALLION (Finecut & Diamond or Grand)

Bowl, 6¼ x 9" oval	12.50
Bread plate, 10" d.	21.50
Butter dish, cov.	35.00
Cake stand, 8" d.	20.00
Cake stand, 9" d.	25.00
Cake stand, 10" d.	32.00
Celery vase	25.00
Compote, cov., 7" d., high stand	36.00
Compote, open, 7" d., high stand	22.50
Compote, open, 8" d., 6" h.	19.50
Compote, open, 9" d., high stand	17.50
Creamer, footed	22.00
Goblet	21.00
Pitcher, water	40.00
Relish, 7½" oval	12.00
Salt & pepper shakers w/original tops, pr.	35.00
Sauce dish, flat or footed 6.50 to	9.00
Spooner	20.00
Sugar bowl, cov.	35.00
Wine	35.00

DIAMOND POINT

Bar bottle, flint	55.00
Bowl, 8½" d., flint	95.00

Bread plate	28.00
Butter dish, cov., flint	85.00
Castor set, 4-bottle, flint, in silver plate frame	600.00
Celery vase, pedestal base w/knob stem, flint	65.00
Champagne, flint	75.00
Claret, flint	120.00
Compote, open, 6" d., high stand, flint	65.00 to 100.00
Compote, open, 7½" d., low stand, non-flint	25.00
Compote, open, 10½" d., 8½" h., flared rim, flint	98.00

Diamond Point Creamer

Creamer, applied handle, flint (ILLUS.)	100.00 to 130.00
Decanter w/original stopper, qt.	70.00
Decanter w/bar lip, qt.	65.00 to 85.00
Egg cup, cov., clambroth, flint	550.00
Egg cup, cov., powder blue opaque, flint	750.00
Egg cup, canary yellow, flint	300.00 to 350.00
Egg cup, chartreuse opaque, flint	425.00
Egg cup, clambroth, flint	135.00
Egg cup, clear, flint	37.50
Egg cup, powder blue opaque, flint	300.00
Goblet, clear, flint	52.00
Goblet, amber, non-flint	25.00
Goblet, blue, non-flint	30.00
Goblet, clear, non-flint	20.00
Honey dish, flint	13.50
Honey dish, coarse points, non-flint	7.00
Pitcher, tankard, applied handle, flint, qt.	170.00
Pitcher, water, bulbous, flint	200.00 to 250.00
Plate, 6" d., non-flint	13.50
Salt dip, cov., master size	27.50
Sauce dish, non-flint, 3½" to 5½" d.	6.50 to 12.50
Spillholder, flint	42.00
Spooner, flint	35.00
Spooner, non-flint	22.00
Sugar bowl, cov., flint	95.00
Sugar bowl, cov., non-flint	40.00

Toothpick holder, non-flint 35.00
Tumbler, flint 47.50
Tumbler, bar, flint 65.00
Wine, flint 56.00
Wine, non-flint 10.00

DIAMOND POINT WITH PANELS - See Hino-to Pattern

DIAMOND QUILTED

Diamond Quilted Champagne

Bowl, 6" d. 12.50
Bowl, 7" d., amber 17.50
Bowl, 7" d., vaseline 22.00
Bowl, 8" d., amber 38.00
Bowl, 8" d., vaseline 30.00
Bowl, 9" d., amber 50.00
Butter dish, cov., amber .....42.00 to 50.00
Butter dish, cov., vaseline 75.00
Celery vase, amber 35.00
Celery vase, blue 42.00
Celery vase, vaseline 40.00
Champagne, clear 21.50
Champagne, turquoise blue
 (ILLUS.) 30.00
Compote, cov., 8" d., 13" h.,
 amber 95.00
Compote, cov., 8" d., 13" h., clear .. 75.00
Compote, open, 6" d., 6" h.,
 amber 25.00
Compote, open, 7" d., low stand,
 amber 17.50
Compote, open, 7" d., high stand,
 amber 30.00
Compote, open, 7" d., high stand,
 vaseline 38.00
Compote, open, 8" d., low stand,
 amber 19.50
Compote, open, 9" d., low stand,
 amber 22.00
Creamer, amber 37.50
Creamer & sugar bowl, amber, pr... 85.00
Goblet, amber 50.00
Goblet, amethyst................. 38.00
Goblet, blue 36.00
Goblet, vaseline 36.00
Mug, amber 20.00

Mug, clear........................ 15.00
Pitcher, water, amber 57.50
Pitcher, water, vaseline........... 75.00
Relish, amber, 4½ x 7½" 10.00
Relish, leaf-shaped, amber,
 5½ x 9" 13.50
Relish, leaf-shaped, turquoise blue,
 5½ x 9" 22.00
Relish, leaf-shaped, vaseline,
 5½ x 9" 22.00
Relish, leaf-shaped, vaseline,
 10 x 12" 22.00
Salt dip, vaseline................. 16.00
Sauce dish, flat or footed, amber ... 9.00
Sauce dish, flat or footed,
 amethyst ....12.00 to 18.00
Sauce dish, flat or footed, turquoise
 blue 13.00
Sauce dish, flat or footed,
 vaseline 15.00
Spooner, amber.................. 30.00
Spooner, turquoise blue 38.00
Spooner, vaseline 40.00
Sugar bowl, cov., blue............ 43.50
Sugar bowl, cov., vaseline 60.00
Tray, water, cloverleaf-shaped,
 amber, 10 x 12"..........22.00 to 30.00
Tray, water, cloverleaf-shaped,
 vaseline, 10 x 12" 28.00
Tumbler, juice, amber 20.00
Tumbler, amber 37.00
Tumbler, vaseline 25.00
Wine, amber..................... 22.50
Wine, clear...................... 12.50
Wine, vaseline 26.00

DIAMOND THUMBPRINT

Diamond Thumbprint Compote

Butter dish, cov. ....140.00 to 200.00
Cake stand, 12" d. 195.00
Celery vase...................... 150.00
Champagne...................... 350.00
Compote, open, 7" d., 4½" h., ex-
 tended scalloped rim 68.00
Compote, open, 8" d., 3¼" h. 45.00
Compote, open, 8" d., 6" h. 75.00
Compote, open, 10½" d., 7½" h.
 (ILLUS.)....................... 285.00
Compote, open, 11½" d., 8" h...... 375.00
Cordial, 4" h. 295.00
Creamer, applied handle.......... 200.00
Cup plate....................... 50.00

Decanter w/original stopper, qt..... 195.00
Goblet 325.00
Lamp, whale oil, original burner,
brass stem, marble base........ 265.00
Pitcher, water 575.00
Punch bowl, scalloped rim, pedestal
base, 11½" d., 9 1/8" h......... 425.00
Salt dip, master size.............. 45.00
Sauce dish, flat ....11.00 to 20.00
Sauce dish, footed 45.00
Spillholder, vaseline 875.00
Spooner........................ 86.00
Sugar bowl, cov. 165.00
Tumbler 92.00
Tumbler, bar, 3¾" h.............. 135.00
Tumbler, whiskey, handled........ 300.00
Wine........................... 245.00

DINNER BELL - See Cottage Pattern

DORIC - See Feather Pattern

DOUBLE LEAF & DART - See Leaf & Dart Pattern

DOUBLE LOOP - See Ribbon Candy Pattern

DOUBLE RIBBON
Goblet 27.50
Lamp, kerosene-type, frosted, dated
1872 .... 135.00

DOUBLE WEDDING RING (Wedding Ring)
Champagne...................... 90.00
Goblet 70.00
Lamp, kerosene, hand-type w/flat
base, applied handle 97.00
Sauce dish...................... 25.00
Tumbler, bar.................... 90.00
Tumbler, footed................. 80.00
Wine........................... 75.00

DRAPERY

Drapery Spooner

Butter dish, cov. 40.00
Cake plate, square, footed...40.00 to 45.00
Creamer, applied handle.......... 32.00
Egg cup 21.00
Goblet 28.00
Goblet, buttermilk 30.00

Pitcher, water, applied handle 75.00
Plate, 6" d. 24.50
Spooner (ILLUS.)................. 28.00
Sugar bowl, cov. 40.00
Tumbler 27.00
Water set, pitcher & 6 tumblers,
7 pcs..................275.00 to 325.00

EGG IN SAND

Egg in Sand Milk Pitcher

Bread tray, handled 32.50
Creamer 25.00
Goblet, blue 40.00
Goblet, clear 24.00
Pitcher, milk (ILLUS.) 45.00
Pitcher, water, amber 70.00
Pitcher, water, clear............. 42.00
Relish, 5½ x 9" 18.50
Sauce dish...................... 12.00
Spooner, amber................. 47.50
Spooner, blue................... 35.00
Spooner, clear 25.00
Sugar bowl, cov. 37.50
Tray, water, 12½" oblong........ 42.00
Tumbler 36.00

EGYPTIAN

Egyptian Pickle Dish

Berry set, master bowl & 5 sauce
dishes, 6 pcs................... 150.00
Bowl, 8½" d. 48.00
Bread platter, Cleopatra center,
9 x 12"....................... 53.00
Bread platter, Salt Lake Temple
center........................ 248.00
Butter dish, cov. 73.00
Celery vase..................... 85.00
Compote, cov., 7" d., 12" h., sphinx
base 197.00

Compote, cov., 8" h., high stand,
  sphinx base 200.00
Compote, open, 6" d., low stand ... 50.00
Compote, open, 7½" d., sphinx
  base 82.00
Creamer 39.00
Goblet 41.00
Pickle dish (ILLUS.) 20.00
Pitcher, water ....145.00 to 175.00
Plate, 10" d. 42.00
Plate, 12" d. 85.00
Relish, 5½ x 8½" 20.00
Sauce dish, flat or footed 19.00
Spooner 35.00
Sugar bowl, cov. 67.50
Table set, cov. butter dish, spooner
  & creamer, 3 pcs. 145.00

**EMERALD GREEN HERRINGBONE - See
Paneled Herringbone Pattern**

EMPIRE COLONIAL - See Colonial Pattern

**ENGLISH HOBNAIL CROSS - See Amberette
Pattern**

ESTHER
Berry set: master bowl & 6 sauce
  dishes; green, 7 pcs. 290.00
Butter dish, cov., amber-stained 110.00
Butter dish, cov., clear 70.00
Butter dish, cov., green 120.00
Celery vase, clear 70.00
Celery vase, green 135.00
Compote, cov., high stand 110.00
Compote, open, 5" d., 6½" h.,
  green 59.00
Cracker jar, cov., amber-stained 225.00
Creamer, clear 70.00
Creamer, green 135.00
Creamer & cov. sugar bowl, in-
  dividual size, pr. 95.00
Cruet w/ball-shaped stopper,
  clear 40.00
Cruet w/ball-shaped stopper,
  green ....200.00 to 250.00
Cruet w/original stopper, clear,
  miniature 28.00
Cruet w/original stopper, green,
  miniature 95.00
Goblet, clear 52.00
Goblet, green................... 90.00
Goblet, ruby-stained, souvenir 55.00
Pitcher, water, green 150.00
Plate, 10¼" d. 27.50
Relish, clear, 4½ x 8" 22.50
Relish, green, 4½ x 8½" 24.00
Relish, green, 5½ x 11" 45.00
Salt & pepper shakers w/original
  tops, clear, pr. 95.00
Salt & pepper shakers w/original
  tops, green, pr. 135.00
Sauce dish...................... 17.00
Spooner, clear 38.00

Spooner, green 65.00
Sugar bowl, cov., clear 40.00
Sugar bowl, cov., green 82.00
Table set, green, 4 pcs............ 475.00
Toothpick holder, amber-stained.... 100.00
Toothpick holder, clear 40.00
Toothpick holder, green 76.00
Tray, ice cream, green 145.00
Tumbler, clear 32.00
Tumbler, green 45.00
Water set: pitcher & 5 tumblers;
  green, 6 pcs. 375.00
Wine......................... 32.50

EUREKA
Bowl, 9" oval 30.00
Bread tray..................... 29.00
Butter dish 80.00
Compote, open, jelly, clear 55.00
Compote, open, jelly, ruby-stained.. 75.00
Creamer, clear................. 45.00
Creamer, ruby-stained 65.00
Egg cup 15.00
Goblet 24.00
Salt dip, master size............. 25.00
Salt & pepper shakers w/original
  tops, ruby-stained, pr........... 48.00
Spooner 41.00
Sugar bowl, cov. 55.00
Toothpick holder, clear 25.00
Toothpick holder, ruby-stained 85.00
Tumbler, footed 25.00
Wine......................... 30.00

EXCELSIOR

Excelsior Goblet

Bar bottle, pt. ....35.00 to 50.00
Bar bottle, flint, qt. 70.00
Cake stand, flint, 9¼" h. 150.00
Castor set, 4-bottle, non-flint, pew-
  ter frame 65.00
Celery vase, flint................ 78.00
Claret, non-flint 16.00
Cordial 35.00
Egg cup 28.00
Egg cup, double, clear 35.00
Egg cup, double, fiery opalescent,
  flint 225.00

Flip glass, 8" h. 200.00
Goblet, "barrel". 38.00
Goblet, flint (ILLUS.). 50.00
Mug 25.00
Platter, 9¼" l. 22.00
Salt dip, master size. 18.50
Spillholder, flint 76.00
Sugar bowl, cov. 90.00
Syrup pitcher, applied handle 110.00
Syrup pitcher w/original top,
    green 750.00
Tumbler, bar, flint, 3½" h. 55.00
Tumbler, footed, flint 47.50
Wine, flint 60.00

EYEWINKER
Banana boat, flat, 8½" 85.00
Banana stand 135.00
Bowl, 6½" d. 25.00
Bowl, master berry or fruit, 9" sq.,
    4½" h. . . . . 65.00 to 75.00
Butter dish, cov. 65.00
Cake stand, 8½" to 9½" d. 65.00
Celery vase, 6½" h. 55.00
Compote, cov., 6½" d., 11" h. 49.00
Compote, open, 4" d., 5" h., scal-
    loped rim. 35.00
Compote, open, 6½" sq., 8½" h. . . . 70.00
Compote, open, 7½" d., 4½" h. 37.50
Compote, open, 9½" d., 6½" h. 90.00
Compote, open, 10" d., 8½" h. 75.00
Cracker jar, cov. 125.00
Creamer 45.00
Creamer, miniature 50.00
Creamer & cov. sugar bowl, pr. 100.00
Lamp, kerosene-type, w/original
    burner, 9½" h. 125.00
Pitcher, water 85.00
Plate, 9" sq., 2" h., turned-up
    sides 32.50
Salt shaker w/original top 32.50
Sauce dish, round 38.00
Sauce dish, square 12.00
Spooner 45.00
Sugar bowl, cov. 52.00
Syrup pitcher w/silver plate top 112.00
Tumbler 24.00

FEATHER (Doric, Indiana Swirl or Finecut & Feather)
Banana boat, footed. 75.00
Berry set, master bowl & 6 sauce
    dishes, 7 pcs. 120.00
Bowl, 6½" d. 12.00
Bowl, 7" oval 18.00
Bowl, 7½" d. 20.00
Bowl, 8½" oval, flat 25.00
Butter dish, cov., clear 48.00
Butter dish, cov., green 175.00
Cake stand, 8½" d. 32.00
Cake stand, 9½" d., clear 40.00
Cake stand, 9½" d., green. 158.00
Cake stand, 11" d. 69.00
Celery vase. 34.00

Compote, cov., 8½" d., high
    stand 125.00
Compote, open, jelly, 5" d., 4¾" h.,
    amber-stained 110.00

Feather Jelly Compote

Compote, open, jelly, 5" d., 4¾" h.,
    clear (ILLUS.) 20.00
Cordial . . . . 45.00 to 55.00
Cordials, set of 6. . . . . 300.00
Creamer 32.00
Cruet w/original stopper, clear 42.00
Cruet w/original stopper, green 185.00
Doughnut stand, 8" w., 4½" h. 36.00
Goblet, amber-stained 140.00
Goblet, clear 52.00
Honey dish, 3½" d. . . . . 9.00 to 15.00
Pickle dish. 15.00
Pitcher, milk 48.00
Pitcher, water, clear 53.00
Pitcher, water, green 200.00
Plate, 10" d. 40.00
Relish, 8¼" oval, amber-stained 45.00
Relish, 8¼" oval, clear 15.00
Salt shaker w/original top 25.00
Salt & pepper shakers w/original
    tops, green, pr. 225.00
Sauce dish, flat or footed 12.00
Spooner 28.00
Sugar bowl, cov. 40.00
Sugar bowl, open, large 20.00
Syrup pitcher w/original top, clear . . 100.00
Syrup pitcher w/original top,
    green 315.00
Table set, 4 pcs. 125.00
Toothpick holder, clear 50.00
Toothpick holder, green 185.00
Tumbler 50.00
Wine. 35.00

FESTOON
Berry set, 9¼" d. master bowl & 6
    sauce dishes, 7 pcs. 70.00
Bowl, 4½ x 7" rectangle 22.50
Bowl, berry, 8" rectangle 25.00
Bowl, berry, 5½ x 9" rectangle 31.50
Butter dish, cov. 42.00
Cake stand, high pedestal, 9" d. 42.00
Cake stand, high pedestal, 10" d. . . . 43.00

Compote, open, 9" d., high stand . . . 58.00
Creamer 22.00
Finger bowl, 4½" d., 2" h. 30.00
Goblet 25.00
Marmalade jar, cov. 37.50
Pickle castor, silver plate frame &
   cover w/bird finial 85.00
Pitcher, water 59.00
Plate, 7" d. 35.00
Plate, 8" d. 35.00
Plate, 9" d. 29.00
Relish, 4 x 7" 15.00
Sauce dish 8.00
Spooner 30.00
Sugar bowl, cov. 50.00
Table set, 4 pcs. 185.00
Tray, water, 10" d. 32.50
Tumbler 25.00
Waste bowl 40.00
Water set, pitcher, tray & 4 tum-
   blers, 6 pcs. . . . . 195.00 to 250.00

FINECUT
Bread tray, amber 40.00
Butter dish, cov. 45.00
Cake stand 35.00
Celery vase, vaseline, ornate square
   silver plate holder 115.00
Compote, cov., 9¼" d., 7" h.,
   amber 135.00
Creamer, blue 37.50
Creamer, clear 35.00
Cruet w/matching stopper, amber . . 165.00
Goblet, amber 45.00
Goblet, canary 40.00
Goblet, clear 17.50
Goblet, vaseline 39.00
Pickle dish, 6 x 9" 12.00
Pitcher, water, amber 75.00
Pitcher, water, canary 80.00
Pitcher, water, clear 40.00
Plate, 6" d., blue 20.00
Plate, 6" d., clear 10.00
Plate, 6" d., vaseline 22.50
Plate, 7" d., amber 20.00
Plate, 7" d., vaseline 20.00
Plate, 10" d., amber 20.00
Plate, 10" d., clear 18.00
Salt & pepper shakers w/original
   tops, clear, pr. 25.00
Salt & pepper shakers w/original
   tops, vaseline, pr. 40.00
Sauce dish, vaseline 18.00
Spooner, amber 35.00
Spooner, clear 17.00
Sugar bowl, cov. 35.00
Toothpick holder, hat shape on
   plate, amber 21.00
Toothpick holder, hat shape on
   plate, blue 28.50
Toothpick holder, hat shape on
   plate, vaseline 30.00
Tray, ice cream, lion's head han-
   dles, amber 40.00

Tray, water, clear 45.00
Tray, water, vaseline, 9¼" d. 48.00
Tumbler, clear 15.00
Tumbler, vaseline 28.00
Waste bowl, vaseline 32.50
Whimsey, shoe on skate, amber 30.00
Whimsey, slipper, blue, 4" l. 35.00
Wine 14.00

FINECUT & BLOCK

Finecut & Block Celery Tray

Butter dish, cov., two-handled 75.00
Butter pat, clear w/blue blocks 18.00
Cake stand 35.00
Celery tray, blue, 11" l. 65.00
Celery tray, clear, 11" l. 27.50
Celery tray, clear w/blue blocks,
   11" l. 60.00
Celery tray, clear w/pink blocks,
   11" l. (ILLUS.) 60.00
Celery tray, clear w/yellow blocks . . 65.00
Champagne, amber 70.00
Champagne, clear w/blue blocks . . . 85.00
Compote, open, jelly, blue 50.00
Compote, open, jelly, clear 18.00
Compote, open, jelly, clear w/blue
   blocks 50.00
Compote, open, 8" d., 6½" h.,
   clear 32.50
Compote, open, 8" d., clear w/blue
   blocks 65.00
Compote, open, 8" d., 4¼" h., clear
   w/yellow blocks 45.00
Cordial 70.00
Creamer, clear 30.00
Creamer, clear w/amber blocks 67.00
Creamer, clear w/blue blocks 70.00
Creamer, clear w/pink blocks 75.00
Creamer, clear w/yellow blocks 76.50
Cruet, 5½" h., sapphire blue
   w/clear facet-cut stopper 75.00
Egg cup, single 27.50
Egg cup, double 29.00
Goblet, amber 50.00
Goblet, clear 25.00
Goblet, clear w/blue blocks 65.00
Goblet, clear w/pink blocks 50.00
Goblet, clear w/yellow blocks 52.00
Goblet, buttermilk, clear 25.00
Goblet, buttermilk, clear w/blue
   blocks 50.00
Goblet, buttermilk, clear w/pink
   blocks 80.00
Ice cream tray, clear w/amber
   blocks 85.00
Pitcher, water, amber 85.00

Pitcher, water, clear	42.50
Pitcher, water, clear w/amber blocks	85.00
Pitcher, water, clear w/blue blocks	90.00
Pitcher, water, clear w/pink blocks	125.00
Pitcher, water, clear w/yellow blocks	85.00
Plate, 5¾" d.	23.50
Relish, handled, clear w/yellow blocks, 7½"	140.00
Salt dip, clear w/blue blocks	20.00
Salt dip, clear w/pink blocks	20.00
Sauce dish, blue	14.50
Sauce dish, clear	8.50
Sauce dish, clear w/amber blocks	20.00
Spooner, clear	40.00
Spooner, clear w/amber blocks	45.00
Spooner, clear w/blue blocks	55.00
Sugar bowl, open, clear w/blue blocks	35.00
Table set, clear w/yellow blocks, 4 pcs.	265.00
Tray, corset-shaped, clear w/blue blocks, 12½ x 14½"	75.00
Tumbler, amber	22.50
Tumbler, blue	30.00
Tumbler, clear	17.50
Tumbler, clear w/blue blocks	40.00
Tumbler, clear w/pink blocks	40.00
Waste bowl, amber	45.00
Waste bowl, clear w/yellow blocks	95.00
Wine, clear	23.50
Wine, clear w/blue blocks	45.00

FINECUT & DIAMOND - See Diamond Medallion Pattern

FINECUT & FEATHER - See Feather Pattern

FINECUT & PANEL (Paneled Finecut)

Bowl, 8" oval, amber	18.50
Bowl, 8" oval, clear	18.00
Bread tray, amber, 9 x 13"...35.00 to	50.00
Bread tray, blue, 9 x 13"	45.00
Bread tray, clear, 9 x 13"	28.00
Butter dish, cov., amber	65.00
Cake stand, sq., blue	75.00
Cake stand, vaseline	50.00
Celery vase	35.00
Compote, open, high stand, amber	47.50
Compote, open, high stand, blue	50.00
Compote, open, high stand, clear	32.00
Creamer, amber	35.00
Goblet, amber	38.00
Goblet, clear	18.00
Goblet, clear w/amber bars	35.00
Goblet, vaseline	35.00
Pitcher, water, amber	80.00
Pitcher, water, blue	55.00
Plate, 6" d., amber	25.00
Plate, 6" d., blue	30.00

Plate, 6" d., clear	14.00
Plate, 6" d., vaseline	25.00
Plate, 7" d.	11.00
Relish, 3½ x 7"	22.50
Salt shaker w/original top	35.00
Sauce dish, amber	12.00
Sauce dish, clear	8.00
Sauce dish, vaseline	13.50
Spooner, vaseline	30.00
Sugar bowl, cov., canary	60.00
Tray, water, canary, 12" w.	40.00
Tumbler, clear	18.00
Tumbler, vaseline	38.00
Wine, amber	30.00
Wine, blue	35.00
Wine, canary	35.00
Wine, clear	16.00
Wine, vaseline	30.00
Wine set: decanter & 4 wines; vaseline, 5 pcs.	185.00

FINECUT BAND - See Cottage Pattern

FINE RIB

Butter dish, cov.	75.00
Castor set, complete w/frame	190.00
Celery vase, flint	42.00
Champagne, flint	75.00
Champagne, cut ovals, flint	85.00
Compote, open, 10¼" d., 8¼" h., scalloped foot, flint	185.00
Cordial, flint	130.00
Creamer, flint, 6" h.	325.00
Decanter w/bar lip, qt.	95.00
Egg cup, single, flint	42.00
Egg cup, double, flint	35.00
Goblet, flint	75.00
Goblet, non-flint	35.00
Honey dish, flint, 3½" d.	14.00
Pitcher, water, bulbous, applied handle, flint	425.00
Salt dip, individual size, flint	14.00
Salt dip, master size, footed, scalloped rim, flint	30.00
Sauce dish, non-flint	7.50
Spoonholder, flint	52.50
Sugar bowl, cov., flint	140.00
Tumbler, flint	75.00
Tumbler, whiskey, handled, flint, 3" h.	85.00
Tumbler, whiskey, blue, flint	125.00
Tumbler, whiskey, non-flint	35.00
Wine, flint	44.00
Whiskey taster, flint	55.00

FISHSCALE

Berry set, 8½" d. master bowl & 8 sauce dishes, 9 pcs.	85.00
Bowl, cov., 7" d.	55.00
Bowl, cov., 8½" d.	35.00
Bowl, cov., 9½" d.	40.00
Bowl, 8" d.	18.00
Bowl, 9½" d.	22.00
Bread platter	26.00

Butter dish, cov.	42.00
Cake stand, 10" d.	35.00
Celery vase	26.50
Compote, cov., 7½" d.	45.00
Compote, open, jelly	17.00
Compote, open, 7" d., high stand	31.00
Compote, open, 9" d., high stand	45.00
Condiment tray, rectangular	32.00
Creamer	26.00
Goblet	26.00
Lamp, kerosene, hand-type w/finger grip	65.00
Lamp, miniature, w/nutmeg burner & chimney	55.00
Mug	35.00
Pickle dish	18.50
Pitcher, milk	30.00
Pitcher, water	44.00
Plate, 7" d.	15.00
Plate, 8" d.	21.00

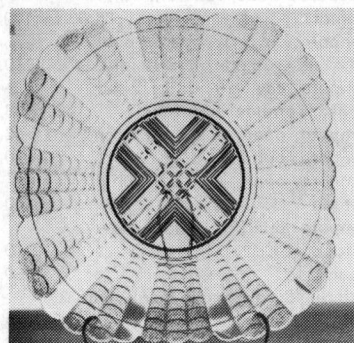

Fishscale Plate

Plate, 9" sq. (ILLUS.)	28.00
Relish, 5 x 8½"	16.00
Salt shaker w/original top	27.50
Sauce dish, flat or footed	12.00
Spooner	21.00
Sugar bowl, cov.	38.00
Tray, water, round	35.00
Tumbler	65.00
Waste bowl	50.00

FLORIDA - See Paneled Herringbone Pattern

FLORIDA PALM

Florida Palm Creamer

Cake stand, 9½" d.	25.00
Celery vase	18.00
Compote, cov., 7" d., high stand	50.00
Compote, open, 9" d.	35.00
Creamer (ILLUS.)	18.50
Goblet	22.50
Plate, 9" d.	15.00
Spooner	20.00
Sugar bowl, cov.	35.00
Tumbler, footed	28.00
Wine	23.50

FLOWER FLANGE - See Dewey Pattern

FLOWER POT (Potted Plant)

Bread tray	60.00
Butter dish, cov.	40.00
Compote, open, 7¼" h.	18.00
Creamer, clear	30.00
Creamer, vaseline	45.00
Goblet	40.00
Pitcher, milk	40.00
Pitcher, water	58.00
Salt shaker w/original top	20.00
Sauce dish	9.00
Spooner, clear	22.00
Spooner, vaseline	45.00
Sugar bowl, cov.	37.50

FLUTE

Ale glass	50.00
Bar bottle, blue, flint, qt.	250.00
Bar bottle, clear, flint, qt.	72.00
Bar bottle, pewter closure w/marble stopper, emerald green, flint, 11" h.	1,700.00
Celery vase	80.00
Claret	25.00
Compote, open, 8¼" d., 3" h.	35.00
Egg cup, single	20.00
Egg cup, single, handled	60.00
Egg cup, double	24.00
Goblet, Bessimer Flute	20.00
Goblet, Brooklyn Flute	35.00
Goblet, Connecticut or New England Flute	17.50
Goblet	28.00
Pitcher, water	75.00
Relish	30.00
Tumbler, six panels, deep purple	120.00
Tumbler, jelly glass shape, 3½" h.	16.00
Tumbler, whiskey, handled	27.50
Whiskey shot glass, footed	25.00
Wine, New England Flute	25.00
Wine, Pittsburgh Flute	45.00
Wine, knob stem	15.00

FLYING ROBIN - See Hummingbird Pattern

FOUR PETAL

Creamer, applied handle	125.00
Sugar bowl, cov., rounded lid	75.00
Sugar bowl, open	45.00

FOUR PETAL FLOWER - See Delaware Pattern

FROSTED CIRCLE

Frosted Circle Open Compote

Bowl, 6" d.	28.00
Bowl, 8" d., 3¼" h.	25.00
Butter dish, cov.	45.00
Cake stand, 9½" d.	47.00
Celery tray	20.00
Champagne	55.00
Claret	45.00
Compote, cov., 5" d., 9" h.	43.50
Compote, open, 7" d., 6" h.	25.00
Compote, open, 9" d., 6" h.	32.50
Compote, open, 9" d., 8½" h.	50.00
Compote, open, 10" d., high stand, scalloped rim (ILLUS.)	57.50
Creamer	35.00
Cruet w/original stopper	42.50
Goblet	32.50
Pitcher, water, tankard	80.00
Plate, 9" d.	65.00
Punch cup	15.00
Relish, 4½ x 8"	20.00
Salt shaker w/original top	35.00
Sauce dish	10.00
Spooner	36.00
Sugar bowl, cov.	49.00
Sugar shaker w/original top	48.00
Syrup pitcher w/original top	110.00
Tumbler	30.00
Wine	32.50

FROSTED LEAF

Celery vase	140.00
Creamer	395.00
Egg cup	88.00
Goblet	102.00
Salt dip	50.00
Sauce dish	22.50
Spooner	65.00
Tumbler, footed	95.00
Wine	110.00

FROSTED LION (Rampant Lion)

Bowl, cov., 3 7/8 x 6 7/8" oblong, collared base	110.00
Bowl, cov., 5½ x 8 7/8" oblong, collared base	125.00
Bowl, open, oval	73.00
Bread plate, rope edge, closed handles, 10½" d.	88.00
Butter dish, cov., frosted lion's head finial	80.00
Butter dish, cov., rampant lion finial	101.00
Celery vase	63.00
Compote, cov., 5" d., 8½" h.	155.00
Compote, cov., 6¾" oval, 7" h., collared base, rampant lion finial	165.00 to 245.00
Compote, cov., 7" d., 11" h., lion head finial	165.00
Compote, cov., 7¾" oval, low collared base, rampant lion finial	100.00 to 125.00
Compote, cov., 8" d., 13" h., rampant lion finial	185.00
Compote, cov., 7¾ x 8½" oval, low collared base, rampant lion finial	85.00 to 120.00
Compote, cov., 5½ x 8¾" oval, 8¼" h., rampant lion finial	110.00
Compote, cov., 10" d., collared base, rampant lion finial	88.00
Compote, open, 5" d., low stand	62.00
Compote, open, 7" d., 6¼" h.	70.00
Compote, open, 7¾" d., high stand	60.00
Compote, open, 8" oblong, low stand	70.00
Creamer	60.00
Creamer & cov. sugar bowl, child's, pr.	175.00
Egg cup	72.00
Goblet	58.00
Marmalade jar, cov., rampant lion finial	88.00

Frosted Lion Paperweight

Paperweight, embossed "Gillinder & Sons, Centennial" (ILLUS.)	115.00
Pickle dish	60.00
Pitcher, water	310.00
Platter, 9 x 10½" oval, lion handles	80.00
Relish	40.00
Salt dip, cov., master size, collared base, rectangular	290.00
Sauce dish, 4" to 5" d.	25.00
Spooner	52.00
Sugar bowl, cov., rampant lion finial	85.00
Syrup pitcher w/original top	300.00
Wine, 4 1/8" h.	125.00 to 150.00

FROSTED RIBBON

Bowl, low	22.00
Bread platter	32.50
Butter dish, cov.	55.00
Celery vase	36.00
Champagne	100.00
Cologne bottle w/stopper	45.00
Compote, cov., 6½" d.	55.00
Compote, cov., 8" d., 11" h.	85.00
Compote, open, 10" d., high stand	40.00
Creamer	50.00
Goblet	30.00
Pitcher, water	65.00
Salt dip, individual size	5.00
Salt dip, master size	8.50
Sauce dish	12.00
Spooner	33.00
Sugar bowl, cov.	54.00
Tray, water	95.00

FROSTED ROMAN KEY (Roman Key With Flutes or Ribs)

Frosted Roman Key Goblet

Bowl, 9¾" d., 3½" h.	42.50
Butter dish, cov.	55.00
Celery vase	75.00
Champagne	77.50
Compote, cov., 7" d.	75.00
Compote, open, 6½" d.	78.00
Compote, open, 8" d., 6" h.	60.00
Cordial	45.00
Creamer, applied handle	56.00
Decanter w/stopper, qt.	85.00
Egg cup	44.00
Goblet (ILLUS.)	43.00
Sauce dish	13.00
Spooner	32.00
Sugar bowl, cov.	82.50
Tumbler, bar	98.00
Tumbler, footed	63.00
Wine	55.00

FROSTED STORK

Bowl, 9" oval, 101 border	45.00
Bread plate, round	58.00
Butter dish, cov.	70.00
Creamer	54.00
Finger bowl	90.00
Goblet	65.00

Pickle castor w/original frame	195.00
Platter, 8 x 11½" oval, 101 border	70.00
Platter, deer & dog border	81.00
Relish, 101 border	55.00
Sauce dish	28.00
Spooner	40.00
Sugar bowl, cov., stork finial	95.00
Tray, water, 11 x 15½"	110.00
Waste bowl	38.00

FROSTED WAFFLE - See Hidalgo Pattern

GALLOWAY (Mirror or Virginia)

Basket, twisted handle, 5 x 8½ x 10"	75.00
Berry set: master bowl & 3 sauce dishes; ruby-stained, 4 pcs.	95.00
Berry set, master bowl & 4 sauce dishes, 5 pcs.	48.50
Berry set: master bowl & 6 sauce dishes; ruby-stained, 7 pcs.	135.00
Bowl, 3½ x 5¼" rectangle	10.00
Bowl, 5½" d.	10.00
Bowl, 6½" d.	17.50
Bowl, 7¼" d., 3½" h.	19.50
Bowl, 8½" oval, flared rim	14.00
Bowl, 9¾" d., flat	35.00
Bowl, ice cream, 11" d., 3½" h.	45.00
Butter dish, cov., clear	50.00
Butter dish, cov., ruby-stained	110.00
Cake stand, 9¼" d., 6" h.	65.00
Carafe	75.00
Celery vase, clear	30.00
Celery vase, ruby-stained	75.00
Compote, open, 4¼" d., 6" h.	30.00
Compote, open, 8½" d., 7" h.	58.00
Compote, open, 10" d., 8" h., scalloped rim	47.00
Creamer	22.00
Creamer, individual size	21.50
Creamer & cov. sugar bowl, engraved, pr.	95.00
Cruet w/stopper	38.00
Finger bowl, 6" d.	22.00
Goblet	72.00
Mug, 4½" d.	37.50
Olive dish, 4 x 6"	16.50 to 25.00
Pickle castor w/silver plate lid & frame	125.00
Pitcher, child's	22.50
Pitcher, lemonade, applied handle	70.00
Pitcher, milk	72.00
Pitcher, water	52.00
Plate, 6½" d.	20.00
Plate, 8" d.	20.00
Punch bowl, 14" d.	145.00
Punch cup	7.50
Relish, 8¼" l.	14.50
Relish, ruby-stained	30.00
Salt shaker w/original top	14.50
Salt & pepper shakers w/original tops, gold trim, 3" h., pr.	30.00
Sauce dish, flat or footed	12.00
Spooner, amber-stained	35.00

Spooner, clear 25.00
Spooner, maiden's blush 80.00
Sugar bowl, cov. 42.50
Sugar bowl, open, individual size ... 12.00
Sugar shaker w/original top 37.50
Syrup pitcher w/metal spring top,
   clear 57.50
Syrup pitcher w/metal spring top,
   ruby-stained 135.00
Toothpick holder, clear 22.00
Toothpick holder, green 55.00
Tumbler 30.00
Vase, 8" h. 25.00
Vase, 9½" h. 30.00
Vase, 11" h. 32.00
Vase, 18" h. 35.00
Waste bowl 25.00
Water set: pitcher & 6 tumblers;
   clear, 7 pcs. ....165.00 to 225.00
Water set: pitcher & 6 tumblers;
   ruby-stained, 7 pcs. 350.00
Water set, child's, pitcher & 4 tum-
   blers, 5 pcs. 50.00
Wine 36.00

GARFIELD DRAPE

Garfield Drape Goblet

Bread plate, "We Mourn Our Na-
   tion's Loss," 11½" d. 50.00
Butter dish, cov. 59.00
Cake stand, 9½" d. 65.00
Celery vase, pedestal base 42.00
Compote, cov., 6" d., low stand 50.00
Compote, cov., 8" d., 12½" h. 135.00
Creamer 36.00
Goblet (ILLUS.) 35.00
Lamp, kerosene-type, cobalt blue,
   9" h. 150.00
Pickle dish, 7¼" oval 20.00
Pitcher, milk 62.00
Pitcher, water 78.00
Plate, 10" d., star center 60.00
Sauce dish, flat or footed 9.00
Spooner 26.00
Sugar bowl, cov. 60.00
Tumbler 30.00

GEORGIA - See Peacock Feather Pattern

GIANT BULL'S EYE
Butter dish, cov. 45.00
Cracker jar, cov. 45.00
Goblet 60.00
Wine 25.00

GODDESS OF LIBERTY - See Ceres Pattern

GOOD LUCK - See Horseshoe Pattern

GOOSEBERRY

Gooseberry Goblet

Butter dish, cov. 50.00
Compote, cov., 7" d. 70.00
Creamer 28.00
Goblet (ILLUS.) 28.00
Mug 26.00
Sauce dish 8.00
Spooner 25.00
Sugar bowl, open 40.00
Tumbler, bar 30.00
Tumbler, water ....22.00 to 30.00

GOTHIC
Bowl, master berry or fruit, flat 70.00
Castor bottle 18.00
Castor set, 5-bottle, w/pewter
   frame 125.00
Celery vase 90.00
Champagne 165.00
Compote, open, 7" d., 3½" h. 53.00
Compote, open, 8" d., 4" h. 62.50
Creamer, applied handle 90.00
Egg cup 42.00
Goblet 58.00
Sauce dish 14.00
Spooner 40.00
Sugar bowl, cov. 80.00
Sugar bowl, open 40.00
Tumbler 95.00
Wine, 3¾" h. ....100.00 to 130.00

GRAND - See Diamond Medallion Pattern

GRAPE & FESTOON
Butter dish, cov., stippled leaf 40.00
Celery vase, stippled leaf ....30.00 to 45.00
Compote, cov., large, high stand,
   w/bird's nest finial 85.00

Creamer, stippled leaf 56.00
Egg cup, stippled leaf 30.00
Goblet, stippled leaf 28.00
Goblet, buttermilk, stippled leaf 29.00
Goblet, veined leaf 25.00

Grape & Festoon Mug

Mug (ILLUS.) 17.00
Pitcher, water, stippled leaf 97.50
Plate, 6" d., stippled leaf 17.50
Relish, stippled leaf 6.00
Salt dip, footed, stippled leaf 24.00
Sauce dish, flat, stippled leaf,
    4" d. 8.50
Sauce dish, flat, veined leaf 13.00
Spooner, stippled leaf 22.00
Spooner, veined leaf 22.50
Sugar bowl, cov., stippled leaf 50.00
Sugar bowl, open, stippled leaf 25.00

GRAPE & FESTOON WITH SHIELD

Compote, cov., 8" d., low stand 39.00
Compote, cov., 10½" h. 65.00
Creamer, applied handle 35.00
Goblet, w/American shield 45.00
Goblet, w/shield & grapes 22.50
Mug, 1 7/8" h. 16.50
Mug, cobalt blue, 2½" h. 27.50
Mug, 3¼" h. 18.50
Pitcher, water, applied
    handle . . . . 65.00 to 70.00
Relish, 4¼ x 7" 16.50
Sauce dish, flat or footed . . . . . 6.00 to 12.00
Spooner 26.50

GRASSHOPPER (Locust)

Berry set, footed master bowl & 11
    sauce dishes, 12 pcs. 127.00
Bowl, cov., 7" d. 27.50
Bowl, cov., 7" d., footed 50.00
Bowl, open, 7" d., footed 20.00
Butter dish, cov. 45.00
Butter dish, cov., w/insect 55.00
Celery vase, w/insect 62.50
Compote, cov., 8¼" d. 65.00
Creamer 32.00
Goblet, w/insect, amber 85.00
Goblet, w/insect, clear 35.00
Pitcher, water 68.00
Plate, 7½" d., footed 15.00
Plate, 8½" d., footed 20.00
Plate, 10" d., footed 25.00
Sauce dish, footed 11.00
Spooner 35.00

Spooner, w/insect 44.00
Sugar bowl, cov. 40.00
Sugar bowl, cov., w/insect 70.00

GREEK KEY (Heisey's Greek Key)

Butter dish, cov. 125.00
Celery tray, 9" l. 38.00
Compote, open, jelly, 5" d., low
    stand 28.00
Creamer & open sugar bowl, pr. 56.00
Goblet . . . . 70.00 to 90.00
Humidor, cov. 285.00
Ice tub, small 95.00
Lamp, kerosene-type, miniature 75.00
Lamp, kerosene-type, large 95.00
Nut dish, individual size 22.00
Pitcher, pt. 125.00
Pitcher, tankard, 1½ qt. 225.00
Punch bowl & pedestal base,
    2 pcs. 250.00
Punch cup 15.00
Punch set, bowl, base & 12 cups,
    14 pcs. 430.00
Salt dip, master size 20.00
Sauce dish 20.00
Sherbet 22.50
Soda fountain (straw-holder) jar 128.00
Spooner 25.00
Tumbler 75.00

**GUARDIAN ANGEL - See Cupid & Venus
Pattern**

HAIRPIN (Sandwich Loop)

Bowl, 5½" hexagon 100.00
Bowl, 6¼" d. 100.00
Bowl, 8¼" d., 1½" h. 300.00
Celery vase 38.00
Champagne 80.00
Compote, open, 8" d., 4¼" h. 85.00
Compote, open, 9½" d., 9" h., milk
    white 225.00
Decanter w/stopper, qt. 90.00
Egg cup, clear 17.50
Egg cup, fiery opalescent 75.00
Goblet 38.00
Pitcher, 8" h. 175.00
Plate, 6¼" d. 100.00
Plate, 7" d. 120.00
Salt dip, master size 20.00
Sauce dish, 4" d. 11.00
Spooner 36.00
Sugar bowl, cov. 95.00
Tumbler 55.00
Wine 50.00

HALLEY'S COMET

Celery vase 30.00
Goblet 35.00
Jar, cov., three-footed 49.00
Pitcher, water 98.00
Relish, 4½ x 7" 15.00
Spooner . . . . 40.00 to 55.00
Tumbler 26.00
Wine 22.50

HAMILTON
Bar bottle, qt. 135.00
Butter dish, cov. 80.00

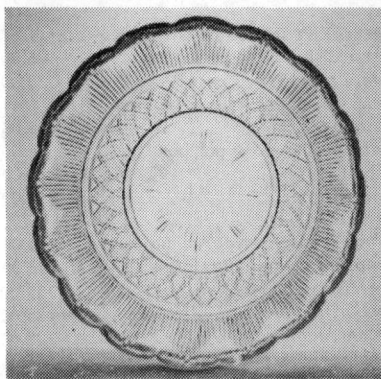

Hamilton Sauce Dish

Cake stand 175.00
Compote, open, 7" d., low stand ... 44.00
Compote, open, 8" d., 5½" h. 45.00
Compote, open, 8" d., 8" h. 70.00
Creamer 65.00
Egg cup 45.00
Goblet 45.00
Pitcher, water ....225.00 to 335.00
Salt dip, footed 30.00
Sauce dish (ILLUS.) 12.00
Spooner 32.00
Sugar bowl, cov. 125.00
Tumbler, bar.................... 65.00
Tumbler, water 80.00
Tumbler, whiskey, applied handle .. 90.00
Wine.......................... 90.00

HAMILTON WITH LEAF
Butter dish, cov., frosted leaf 80.00
Compote, cov., 8" d., 6¼" h........ 60.00
Compote, cov., low stand 78.00
Compote, open, 6" d., 4½" h. 78.00
Compote, open, 8" d., 6½" h., scal-
loped rim..................... 66.00
Compote, open, high stand, large .. 85.00
Creamer, clear leaf 45.00
Creamer, frosted leaf............. 55.00
Creamer & open sugar bowl, frosted
leaf, pr....................... 50.00
Egg cup, clear leaf 55.00
Egg cup, frosted leaf 65.00
Goblet, clear leaf 50.00
Goblet, frosted leaf 55.00
Lamp base, kerosene-type, scal-
loped foot, clear leaf 80.00
Spooner, clear leaf 30.00
Sugar bowl, cov., clear leaf 90.00
Sweetmeat dish, cov., clear leaf 90.00
Tumbler, clear leaf 55.00
Tumbler, frosted leaf 125.00
Tumbler, bar, frosted leaf.......... 125.00
Tumbler, whiskey, handled, clear
leaf.......................... 100.00

Wine.......................... 70.00

HAND (Pennsylvania, Early)
Bowl, 9" d. 37.00
Bread plate, 8 x 10½" oval 28.00
Butter dish, cov. 85.00
Cake stand 55.00
Celery vase..................... 50.00
Compote, cov., 8" d., high stand ... 92.50
Compote, open, 7¾" d., 6¾" h..... 42.00
Compote, open, 9" d., low stand ... 27.50
Compote, open, electric blue 145.00
Cordial........................ 85.00
Creamer 35.00
Creamer, child's................. 45.00
Goblet 40.00
Marmalade jar, cov............... 48.00
Mug 45.00
Pitcher, water 70.00
Sauce dish, 4½" d................ 12.00
Spooner 24.00
Sugar bowl, cov. 65.00
Tumbler, water 135.00
Wine.......................... 55.00

HARP
Bowl, 6½" d., 1½" h., ten-sided,
opaque white.................. 375.00
Goblet, flared sides 650.00
Goblet, straight sides............. 250.00
Lamp, kerosene, hand-type w/ap-
plied finger grip 195.00
Lamp, kerosene, hexagonal font,
shaped base, brass collar, flint,
9½" h........................ 475.00
Spillholder..................... 65.00

HEARTS OF LOCH LAVEN - See Shuttle Pattern

HEART WITH THUMBPRINT

Heart with Thumbprint Bowl

Banana boat, 6½ x 7½" 85.00
Banana boat, 6½ x 11".......... 75.00
Barber bottle w/original pewter
stopper 125.00
Berry set, master bowl & 6 sauce
dishes, 7 pcs.................. 110.00
Bowl, 7" sq., 3½" h. 37.50
Bowl, 8" d., 2" h., flared rim 25.00
Bowl, 9" d. 40.00
Bowl, 10" d., scalloped rim
(ILLUS.)...................... 42.00
Carafe 55.00
Card tray, clear 25.00

Card tray, green 45.00
Celery vase...................... 49.00
Cordial, 3" h. 150.00
Creamer 30.00
Creamer, individual size 20.00
Creamer & open sugar bowl, in-
    dividual size, green w/gold, pr. .. 80.00
Cruet w/original stopper 73.00
Goblet, clear 54.00
Goblet, green w/gold 83.00
Ice bucket 58.00
Lamp, kerosene-type, clear, 8" h.... 112.00
Lamp, kerosene-type, green, 9" h. .. 117.00
Mustard jar w/silver plate cover 95.00
Nappy, heart-shaped 30.00
Olive dish, handled, green 42.50
Pitcher, water 50.00
Plate, 6" d. 22.00
Plate, 10" d. 30.00
Plate, 12" d. 47.50
Powder jar w/silver plate cover 45.00
Punch cup, clear 17.50
Punch cup, green 22.50
Relish, w/gold 17.50
Rose bowl, 3¾" d. 28.00
Rose bowl, 5" d. 35.00
Salt shaker w/original top 50.00
Sauce dish, clear 20.00
Sauce dish, green 32.00
Spooner........................ 40.00
Sugar bowl, cov., large 45.00
Sugar bowl, open 29.00
Sugar bowl, open, individual size,
    clear, pewter rim 21.00
Sugar bowl, open, individual size,
    green w/gold................. 45.00
Sugar bowl, open, individual size,
    green w/gold, pewter rim 40.00
Syrup jug w/original pewter top 108.00
Tray, 4 1/8 x 8 1/8" 25.00
Tumbler, water, clear w/gold 42.00
Tumbler, water, ruby-stained...... 115.00
Vase, 6" h., trumpet-shaped, clear.. 21.00
Vase, 6" h., green 42.00
Vase, 7" h., green 55.00
Vase, 8" h. 35.00
Vase, 10" h., trumpet-shaped 50.00
Waste bowl 65.00
Water set, carafe & 6 tumblers,
    7 pcs. ....300.00 to 325.00
Wine.......................... 40.00

HEAVY PANELED FINECUT (Paneled Diamond Cross)
Cake stand, 9" d. 28.00
Goblet, vaseline 35.00
Spooner........................ 45.00

HERCULES PILLAR (Pillar Variant)
Butter dish, cov. 32.00
Celery vase..................... 47.00
Cordial, 3¾" h. 38.00
Egg cup, double................. 27.50
Goblet 27.50

Syrup jug w/pewter top, amber,
    8" h. 125.00
Syrup jug w/original top, blue...... 140.00
Tumbler 45.00
Whiskey taster.................. 13.50
Wine.......................... 35.00

HERRINGBONE (Herringbone with Star & Shield Motif)
Berry set, master bowl & 6 sauce
    dishes, 7 pcs. 125.00
Celery vase..................... 30.00
Creamer 20.00
Goblet 20.00
Salt dip, master size............. 14.00
Sauce dish..................... 10.50
Spooner 21.50
Sugar bowl, cov. 28.00

HERRINGBONE BAND
Egg cup 18.50
Goblet 13.00
Sauce dish, 4" sq. 9.50
Spooner, pedestal base, scalloped
    rim 22.00
Sugar bowl, open 15.00
Wine.......................... 20.00

HERRINGBONE WITH STAR & SHIELD MOTIF - See Herringbone Pattern

HICKMAN (Le Clede)

Hickman Relish

Banana stand 65.00
Bowl, 5" d., green w/gold 8.00
Bowl, 7" sq. 15.00
Bowl, 6 x 7", green w/gold 25.00
Bowl, 8" d. 16.00
Bowl, 10" d., green 16.00
Butter dish, cov. 37.50
Cake stand, 8½" to 9½" d. 31.00
Celery dish, boat-shaped, green 22.00
Celery tray 18.00
Champagne..................... 21.50
Compote, cov., 5" d. 36.00
Compote, open, jelly, green........ 16.00
Compote, open, 7½" d., 5½" h..... 19.50
Compote, open, 8" d., 6½" h. 32.50
Compote, open, 8½" d., 12" h. 65.00
Compote, open, 9½" d., 8" h. 45.00

Condiment set: salt & pepper shak-
ers & cruet w/original stopper on
cloverleaf-shaped tray; green,
miniature, 4 pcs. 65.00
Creamer, w/gold 25.00
Creamer & open sugar bowl, in-
dividual size, oval, green, pr. 38.00
Cruet w/ball-shaped stopper 45.00
Doughnut stand, scalloped rim,
8" d. 45.00
Goblet, clear 30.00
Goblet, green w/gold 40.00
Ice tub 52.00
Pickle dish, green 15.00
Pitcher, water 60.00
Punch cup, clear 8.00
Punch cup, green 15.00
Punch set, punch bowl & 13 cups,
14 pcs. 125.00
Relish, 4" sq. (ILLUS. previous
page) 14.00
Relish, 5½" l. 15.00
Relish, green 15.00
Relish, green w/gold 24.50
Rose bowl 27.50
Salt shaker w/original top 9.50
Sauce dish, clear 7.00
Sauce dish, green 10.00
Spooner 22.50
Sugar bowl, cov., clear 35.00
Sugar bowl, cov., green 45.00
Sugar shaker w/original top 40.00
Table set, w/gold, 4 pcs. 175.00
Toothpick holder 48.00
Tumbler 25.00
Vase, 10" h. 37.00
Vase, 10½" h., purple 45.00
Vase, 12½" h. 26.00
Water set: pitcher & 6 tumblers;
w/gold, 7 pcs. 225.00
Wine, clear 28.00
Wine, green 30.00

HIDALGO (Frosted Waffle)
Bowl, 9" d., clear & frosted 24.00
Bowl, salad, 11" sq. 22.00
Butter dish, cov. 45.00
Celery dish, boat-shaped, 13" l. 45.00
Celery vase 30.00
Compote, open, 7" d. 20.00
Creamer 37.00
Cruet w/original stopper 60.00
Egg cup 30.00
Goblet 18.00
Pitcher, water 50.00
Relish, shell-shaped ....8.00 to 15.00
Salt & pepper shakers w/original
tops, pr. 20.00
Sauce dish, handled 10.50
Spooner 40.00
Sugar bowl, cov. 35.00
Sugar shaker w/original top 45.00
Syrup pitcher w/original top 70.00
Tray, water 55.00

Tumbler, clear 15.00
Tumbler, ruby-stained 25.00
Waste bowl 25.00

HINOTO (Diamond Point with Panels)

Hinoto Creamer
Butter dish, cov. 90.00
Celery vase 42.50
Champagne 75.00
Creamer, applied handle (ILLUS.) ... 75.00
Egg cup, handled 23.00
Goblet 45.00
Pitcher, tankard, 9" h., applied
handle 110.00
Spooner 38.00
Sugar bowl, cov. 50.00
Tumbler, footed 38.00
Tumbler, whiskey, handled,
footed 45.00
Wine 57.50

HOBNAIL

Hobnail Punch Cup
Barber bottle, applied rigaree at
neck, blue 90.00
Bowl, 7½" d., ruffled rim, blue 35.00
Butter dish, cov., amber 35.00
Cake stand, pedestal base, square .. 85.00
Celery vase, footed,
vaseline ....70.00 to 95.00
Cologne bottle, 6½" h. 22.00
Compote, 6" h., fluted rim, blue 55.00
Creamer, fluted top, applied handle,
amber, 2 x 3" 25.00
Creamer, three-footed, blue 35.00

Creamer, scalloped & ornamented
   top, 6" h......................... 45.00
Creamer, individual size, amber 35.00
Cruet w/original stopper, 4½" h. ... 45.00
Egg cup, single 28.50
Goblet 15.00
Lamp, kerosene, hand-type w/finger
   grip, clear...................... 48.00
Lamp, kerosene, hand-type w/finger
   grip, opaque white w/amber foot
   & handle, 4¼" d., 6" h........... 110.00
Mayonnaise dish, cov.............. 12.00
Mug, amber ....22.50 to 35.00
Mug, clear....................... 15.00
Pitcher, 8" h., flat base, blue....... 195.00
Pitcher, 8" h., square top, amber ... 245.00
Pitcher, 8" h., square top, clear 60.00
Punch cup (ILLUS.)................ 22.50
Rose bowl, 6" d., 5½" h. 85.00
Salt & pepper shakers w/original
   tops, sapphire blue, pr........... 27.50
Sauce dish, square, ruby-stained ... 45.00
Spooner, ruffled rim, amber........ 32.00
Spooner 26.50
Sugar bowl, cov. 20.00
Sugar shaker w/original top 42.50
Syrup pitcher w/original top 72.00
Toothpick holder, amber 30.00
Toothpick holder, blue............. 25.00
Toothpick holder, vaseline 32.50
Tray, water, blue, 11½" d.......... 55.00
Tumbler, amber 28.00
Tumbler, ten-row, amber 60.00
Tumbler, ten-row, blue 28.00
Tumbler, ten-row, clear............ 25.00
Tumbler, ten-row, Rubina Frosted... 95.00
Tumbler, ruby-stained 45.00
Tumbler, vaseline 46.50
Vase, 3¾" h., 4¼" widest d., squat,
   cranberry....................... 79.00
Wine, amber...................... 20.00
Wine, blue 25.00
Wine, clear 20.00

HOBNAIL WITH FAN
Bowl, 6" d. 20.00
Bowl, 7" d., blue................. 47.50
Celery vase....................... 38.00
Creamer, blue 20.00
Goblet 30.00
Sauce dish........................ 8.00
Spooner, blue..................... 45.00

HOBNAIL WITH THUMBPRINT BASE
Butter dish, cov. 55.00
Butter dish, cov., child's, amber 95.00
Butter dish, cov., child's, blue 95.00
Creamer, amber (ILLUS.) 37.50
Creamer, blue 45.00
Creamer, child's, blue 23.00
Pitcher, 7" h., ruby-stained rim 57.50
Pitcher, 8" h., amber 90.00
Pitcher, 8" h., blue 80.00
Spooner, blue..................... 45.00

Hobnail with Thumbprint Creamer

Sugar bowl, cov. 35.00
Sugar bowl, cov., child's, blue 85.00
Table set, vaseline, 4 pcs. 255.00
Waste bowl, amber 40.00

HONEYCOMB

Honeycomb Goblet

Ale glass 42.00
Barber bottle w/pewter top 45.00
Butter dish & cover w/knob finial,
   flint............................ 60.00
Butter dish, cov., non-flint, clear.... 45.00
Butter dish, cov., non-flint, clear
   w/gold 75.00
Cake stand, 10½" d. 35.00
Candlesticks, cobalt blue, flint,
   9½" h., pr..................... 575.00
Celery vase, flint.................. 30.00
Celery vase, Loredo Honeycomb,
   flint............................ 35.00
Celery vase, New York Honeycomb,
   non-flint........................ 20.00
Celery vase, Vernon Honeycomb,
   flint, 9" h....................... 65.00
Champagne, flint.................. 40.00
Champagne, non-flint.............. 8.00
Compote, cov., 6½" d., 8½" h.,
   flint............................ 80.00
Compote, cov., 9¼" d., 11½" h.,
   flint............................ 90.00
Compote, open, 7" d., 7" h., flint ... 48.00
Compote, open, 8¾" d., 7" h., non-
   flint............................ 45.00
Compote, open, 11" d., 8" h.,
   flint...................100.00 to 125.00

Cordial, flint, 3¼" h. 25.00
Creamer, applied handle, flint 30.00
Decanter w/bar lip, flint, 10½" h. . . 75.00
Decanter w/original stopper, flint,
  13" h. 150.00
Egg cup 18.00
Finger bowl, flint 45.00
Goblet, flint 30.00
Goblet, non-flint (ILLUS.) 12.00
Goblet, Banded Vernon
  Honeycomb 18.00
Goblet, Barrel Honeycomb w/knob
  stem 14.50
Goblet, etched 40.00
Goblet, New York Honeycomb 17.00
Mug 30.00
Pitcher, bulbous, 7¼" h., applied
  handle 35.00
Pitcher, water, 8½" h., molded han-
  dle, polished pontil, flint 160.00
Pitcher, water, 9" h., applied han-
  dle, flint 96.00
Pomade jar, cov., flint 48.00
Relish 30.00
Salt dip, pedestal base, flint 35.00
Sauce dish, flint 11.00
Spillholder, flint 22.00
Spooner, flint 33.50
Spooner, non-flint 20.00
Sugar bowl, cov., flint 75.00
Sugar bowl, open, scalloped rim 35.00
Syrup pitcher w/pewter top, flint . . . 128.00
Tumbler, bar 24.00
Tumbler, footed, flint 26.00
Tumbler, Vernon Honeycomb, flint . . 55.00
Tumbler, whiskey, footed, handled,
  flint 45.00
Tumbler, whiskey, Vernon
  Honeycomb 125.00
Vase, 7½" h., 4" d., Vernon Honey-
  comb, flint 45.00
Vases, 10¼" h., Vernon Honey-
  comb, flint, pr 150.00
Wine, flint 45.00
Wine, non-flint 13.00

HORN OF PLENTY
Bar bottle w/pewter pour spout,
  8" 135.00
Bowl, 6¼ x 9" oval 145.00
Butter dish, cov. . . . . .100.00 to 140.00
Butter dish & cover w/Washington's
  head finial .1,100.00
Celery vase 132.00
Champagne 160.00
Compote, cov., 6¼" d., 7½" h. 175.00
Compote, cov., 8¼" oval, 5¾" h. . . . 350.00
Compote, open, 7" d., 3" h. 125.00
Compote, open, 8" d., low stand . . . 110.00
Compote, open, 8" d., 8" h. 118.00
Compote, open, 9" d., 8½" h. 200.00
Creamer, applied handle, 5½" h. 235.00
Creamer, applied handle, 7" h. 158.00
Decanter w/original stopper, pt. 135.00

Decanter w/original stopper, qt. 140.00
Dish, low foot, 7¼" d. 85.00
Dish, low foot, 8" d. 95.00
Egg cup, 3¾" h. 43.00
Goblet 62.00
Honey dish 17.50
Lamp, w/whale oil burner, 11" h. . . . 175.00
Peppersauce bottle w/stopper 168.00
Pitcher, water 575.00
Plate, 6" d. 75.00
Relish, 5 x 7" oval 70.00
Salt dip, master size, oval 108.00
Sauce dish, 3½" to 5" d. 90.00
Spillholder, clambroth 650.00
Spillholder, clear 55.00
Spooner, clear 45.00
Spooner, w/yellow-stained rim 225.00
Sugar bowl, cov. 110.00
Sugar bowl, open 49.00
Tumbler, bar. 70.00
Tumbler, water, 3 5/8" h. 95.00
Tumbler, whiskey, 3" h. 134.00
Tumbler, whiskey, handled 235.00
Wine 120.00

HORSESHOE (Good Luck or Prayer Rug)

Horseshoe Wine

Bowl, cov., 5 x 8" oval, flat, triple
  horseshoe finial 195.00
Bowl, open, 6" d. 12.50
Bowl, open, 7" d., footed 29.00
Bowl, open, 5 x 8" oval, footed 37.50
Bowl, open, 6 x 9" oval 24.00
Bowl, open, 6½ x 10" oval 25.00
Bread tray, single horseshoe
  handles 32.00
Bread tray, double horseshoe
  handles 65.00
Butter dish, cov. 112.00
Cake stand, 8" d., 6½" h. 56.00
Cake stand, 9" d., 6½" h. 65.00
Cake stand, 10¾" d. 85.00
Cake stand, upright horseshoe stem,
  10 x 12" 200.00
Celery vase 50.00
Cheese dish, cov., w/woman churn-
  ing butter in base 225.00
Compote, cov., 8" d., 9" h. 90.00
Compote, cov., 8" d., 11" h. 130.00

Compote, open, 4" h. 24.00
Compote, open, 8" d., 7¾" h. 30.00
Creamer 35.00
Creamer, individual size 38.50
Doughnut stand 57.50
Goblet, knob stem 40.00
Goblet, plain stem 32.00
Marmalade jar, cov. 97.50
Pitcher, milk 105.00
Pitcher, water 75.00
Plate, 7" d. 28.00
Plate, 10" d. 70.00
Relish, 5 x 8" 12.50
Relish, 5½ x 9" 22.50
Salt dip, individual size 19.00
Salt dip, master size, horseshoe
  shape 130.00
Sauce dish, flat or footed 10.50
Spooner 24.00
Sugar bowl, cov. 50.00
Sugar bowl, open 35.00
Sugar shaker w/original top 29.00
Tray, double horseshoe handles,
  10 x 15" 84.00
Wine (ILLUS. previous page) 135.00

HUBER
Celery vase 38.50
Champagne, barrel-shaped 25.00
Champagne, straight sides 40.00
Claret 27.00
Compote, open, 7" d. 55.00
Compote, open, engraved, 8" d. 75.00
Cordial .... 25.00 to 50.00
Creamer 80.00
Egg cup, single 14.00
Egg cup, double 30.00
Goblet 22.50
Goblet, buttermilk 16.50
Salt dip, master size 17.50
Spooner 20.00
Sugar bowl, cov. 56.00
Tumbler, bar 22.50
Tumbler, water 20.00
Vase 18.50
Wine 15.00

HUMMINGBIRD (Flying Robin or Bird & Fern)
Bowl, 6" d., amber 35.00
Butter dish, cov. 49.00
Celery vase, amber 68.00
Celery vase, clear 32.50
Compote, open, 7" d. 48.00
Creamer, amber 52.50
Creamer, blue 50.00
Creamer, clear 32.00
Goblet, amber 60.00
Goblet, blue 65.00
Goblet, clear 32.50
Pitcher, milk, amber 65.00
Pitcher, milk, blue 120.00
Pitcher, milk, clear 47.50
Pitcher, water, amber 105.00

Pitcher, water, blue 122.50
Pitcher, water, clear 80.00
Sauce dish 12.00
Spooner, amber 40.00
Spooner, blue 50.00
Spooner, clear 28.00
Sugar bowl, cov. 55.00
Table set, 4 pcs. 325.00
Tray, water, amber 155.00
Tray, water, blue 125.00
Tumbler, amber 55.00
Tumbler, clear 32.50
Tumbler, bar, amber 45.00
Waste bowl 35.00
Water set: pitcher & 6 tumblers;
  amber, 7 pcs. 350.00

HUNDRED EYE
Compote, open, 5" d., low stand ... 15.00
Creamer 18.50
Goblet 14.50
Mug, blue 25.00
Wine 9.00

ILLINOIS

Illinois Butter Dish

Basket, applied handle, 7 x 7" 95.00
Basket, applied reeded handle,
  7 x 11½" 140.00
Bowl, 5¼" sq. 25.00
Butter dish, cov., 7" sq. (ILLUS.) 60.00
Candlestick 70.00
Celery tray 38.00
Cheese dish, cov., square 60.00
Compote, open 145.00
Creamer, large 30.00
Cruet w/original stopper 40.00
Marmalade jar in silver plate frame
  w/spoon, 3 pcs. 125.00
Pitcher, water, tankard ...... 50.00 to 65.00
Pitcher, water, silver plate rim,
  clear 95.00
Pitcher, water, silver plate rim,
  green 175.00
Plate, 7" sq. 22.50
Relish, 3 x 8½" 15.00
Salt dip, individual size 12.50
Salt & pepper shakers w/original
  tops, pr. 35.00
Sauce dish 16.00
Soda fountain (straw-holder) jar,
  cov., clear, 12½" h. 250.00

Soda fountain (straw-holder) jar,
green, 12½" h. (no lid) 130.00
Spooner 27.50
Sugar bowl, cov. 50.00
Sugar bowl, open 35.00
Sugar bowl, cov., individual size 30.00
Sugar bowl, open, individual size ... 20.00
Sugar shaker w/original pewter
top 65.00
Syrup pitcher w/original pewter
top 95.00
Table set, 4 pcs. 200.00
Toothpick holder 30.00
Vase, 5¾" h. 25.00
Vase, 9" h., 4" d. 40.00

INDIANA
Butter dish, cov. 75.00
Creamer 25.00
Cruet w/original stopper 28.00
Spooner 15.00
Sugar bowl, open 23.00
Toothpick holder 25.00

INDIANA SWIRL - See Feather Pattern

INVERTED FERN

Inverted Fern Sugar Bowl

Bowl, 7" d. 45.00
Butter dish, cov. 57.50
Champagne...................... 115.00
Compote, open, 8" d.............. 55.00
Creamer, applied handle.......... 122.00
Egg cup 28.00
Goblet 38.00
Honey dish, 4" d. 18.00
Pitcher, water 360.00
Salt dip, master size, footed 38.00
Sauce dish, 4" d................. 12.50
Spooner 42.50
Sugar bowl, cov. (ILLUS.).......... 78.00
Tumbler 95.00
Wine........................... 55.00

INVERTED LOOPS & FANS - See Maryland Pattern

INVERTED THISTLE - See Paneled Thistle Pattern

IOWA (Paneled Zipper or Zippered Block)
Bowl, 9" d., 5½" h., ruby-stained ... 135.00
Carafe, water, clear 35.00
Carafe, water, ruby-stained 60.00
Compote, jelly 24.00
Compote, 8½" d., high stand....... 95.00
Creamer, ruby-stained 65.00
Cruet w/original stopper........... 52.50
Finger bowl, ruby-stained 55.00
Lamp, kerosene-type 105.00
Nappy, handled 10.00
Olive dish 16.00
Punch cup 14.00
Salt & pepper shakers w/original
tops, clear, pr. 30.00
Salt & pepper shakers w/original
tops, ruby-stained, pr. 55.00
Sauce dish, flat 7.50
Spooner 16.50
Sugar bowl, cov., ruby-stained 75.00
Sugar bowl, cov., small 20.00
Toothpick holder, clear 18.00
Toothpick holder, ruby-stained 65.00
Tumbler, clear 20.00
Tumbler, ruby-stained 37.50
Vases, gold trim, pr. 18.00
Wine........................... 27.00

IRISH COLUMN - See Broken Column Pattern

IVY IN SNOW

Ivy in Snow Sauce Dish

Bowl, 7" d. 20.00
Butter dish, cov. 50.00
Cake stand, 8" to 10" d. 40.00
Celery vase, 8" h. 27.50
Compote, cov., 8" d., 13" h. 60.00
Compote, open, jelly 25.00
Creamer, clear 18.00
Creamer, ruby-stained ivy sprigs ... 65.00
Goblet 20.00
Honey dish, cov., amber-stained, ivy
sprigs 55.00
Pitcher, water 47.50
Plate, 7" d. 17.50
Plate, 10" d. 22.50
Relish 20.00
Sauce dish, flat or footed
(ILLUS.)...................... 12.00
Spooner 28.00
Syrup jug w/original top, clear 70.00

Syrup jug w/original top, ruby-
stained ivy sprigs 295.00
Tumbler 22.50
Wine, clear 28.00
Wine, ruby-stained, souvenir 70.00

JACOB'S LADDER (Maltese)
Bowl, 6¾" d., 4¾" h., footed 25.00
Bowl, 7¼" d., footed 30.00
Bowl, 5½ x 8½" oval, flat 21.00
Bowl, 8 x 11" oval 25.00
Bowl, 9" d., flat 40.00
Butter dish, cov., Maltese Cross
finial 62.00
Cake stand, 8" to 12" d., each 50.00
Castor set, cruet w/original Maltese
Cross stopper, salt & pepper shak-
ers & mustard jar w/original tops
& pewter frame, 5 pcs. 200.00
Celery vase 38.00
Cologne bottle w/original Maltese
Cross stopper, footed 125.00
Compote, cov., 6½" d., 10¼" h..... 60.00
Compote, cov., 8¼" d., 13" h...... 128.00
Compote, cov., 9½" d., high
stand 165.00
Compote, open, 6" d., 7" h. 22.50
Compote, open, 7" d., low stand ... 32.00
Compote, open, 7" d., high stand ... 41.00
Compote, open, 8" d., low stand ... 19.00
Compote, open, 8" d., high stand ... 34.00
Compote, open, 9" d., low stand ... 52.00
Compote, open, 9½" d., high
stand ....45.00 to 68.00
Compote, open, 10" d., 5" h. 40.00
Compote, open, 13½" d., 9" h. 75.00
Creamer 35.00
Cruet w/original stopper,
footed ....85.00 to 110.00
Dish, 7¾" oval 18.00
Goblet 60.00
Marmalade jar, cov. 85.00
Pickle castor, complete w/stand 132.00
Pickle dish, Maltese Cross handle,
blue 65.00
Pickle dish, Maltese Cross handle,
clear 18.00
Pitcher, water, applied handle 142.00
Plate, 6" d. 26.00
Relish, Maltese Cross handles,
5½ x 10" 20.00
Salt dip, master size, footed 31.00
Sauce dish, flat or footed 9.00
Spooner 32.50
Sugar bowl, open 26.00
Syrup jug w/pewter top 83.00
Tumbler, bar 75.00
Wine 32.00

JEWEL & DEWDROP (Kansas)
Banana bowl 55.00
Bowl, 8½" d. 35.00
Bread tray, "Our Daily Bread,"
10½" oval 45.00

Butter dish, cov. 60.00
Cake stand, 8" to 10" d. 50.00
Cake tray, "Cake Plate,"
10½" oval ....60.00 to 75.00
Celery vase 34.00
Compote, cov., 6" d., high stand ... 67.50
Compote, cov., 7" d., 12" h. 115.00
Compote, open, 6" d. (jelly) 45.00

Jewel & Dewdrop Compote

Compote, open, 7" d., 5" h.
(ILLUS.) 65.00
Compote, open, 7" d., high stand ... 88.00
Creamer 35.00
Dish, cov., 4½" d. 40.00
Doughnut stand 35.00
Goblet 50.00
Mug, child's, 3½" h. 32.00
Mug 14.00
Pitcher, milk 70.00
Pitcher, water 48.00
Plate, 7" sq. 15.00
Relish, 8½" oval 19.00
Salt shaker w/original top 45.00
Sauce dish, 4" d. 12.00
Sugar bowl, cov. 65.00
Syrup jug w/original top 125.00
Toothpick holder 56.00
Tumbler, water, footed 50.00
Whiskey, handled 8.00
Wine, clear 60.00
Wine, ruby-stained w/gilt trim 98.00

JEWEL & FESTOON (Loop & Jewel)
Butter dish, cov. 35.00
Champagne 42.00
Creamer 24.00
Creamer, individual size 35.00
Dish, 5½" sq. 7.50
Goblet 16.50
Pickle dish 17.50
Punch cup 18.00
Relish, 4¼ x 8¼" rectangle 17.00
Sauce dish 12.00
Spooner 29.00
Sugar bowl, cov. 32.50
Sugar bowl, open, individual size ... 25.00
Toothpick holder 30.00
Vase, 8¾" h. 40.00
Wine 30.00

JEWEL BAND (Scalloped Tape)
Bowl, cov., 8" rectangle 35.00

Bowl, open, 6 x 9" oval 19.00
Bread platter . . . . .35.00 to 45.00
Cake stand, 9½" d. 32.50
Celery vase, 8" h. 20.00
Compote, cov., 8¼" d., 12" h. 38.50

Jewel Band Creamer

Creamer (ILLUS.) 30.00
Egg cup 20.00
Goblet 16.00
Pitcher, water, 9¼" h. 58.00
Relish, 7" l. 9.50
Sauce dish, flat or footed . . . . .8.00 to 10.00
Sugar bowl, cov. 35.00
Wine 18.00

JEWELED MOON & STAR (Moon & Star with Waffle)

Bowl, 6¾" d., flat 13.50
Butter dish, cov. 70.00
Cake stand, clear, 8½" d. 29.50
Cake stand, w/amber & blue stain-
    ing, 8½" d. 125.00
Carafe 42.00
Celery, clear 30.00
Celery, frosted w/amber & blue
    staining 92.50
Compote, open, 9" d., 8" h. 40.00
Creamer, w/amber & blue
    staining 47.50
Cruet w/original stopper 19.50
Goblet 28.00
Pitcher, water, bulbous, applied
    handle 175.00
Salt shaker w/original top, clear . . .   20.00
Salt shaker w/original top, w/amber
    & blue staining. 27.00
Sauce dish, clear 8.50
Sauce dish, w/amber & blue
    staining 19.50
Spooner, w/amber & blue staining . .   48.00
Sugar bowl, cov., w/amber & blue
    staining . . . . .78.00 to 100.00
Table set: cov. butter dish, spooner
    & cov. sugar bowl; w/amber &
    blue staining, 3 pcs. 250.00
Tumbler 22.50
Wine. 23.50

JOB'S TEARS - See Art Pattern

JUMBO and JUMBO & BARNUM

Jumbo Spoon Rack

Butter dish & cover w/frosted ele-
    phant finial, oblong 550.00
Butter dish & cover w/frosted ele-
    phant finial, round 450.00
Castor holder (no bottles) 100.00
Compote, cov., 12" h., frosted ele-
    phant finial. . . . . .325.00 to 475.00
Creamer 154.00
Creamer, w/Barnum head at
    handle 250.00
Goblet 700.00
Marmalade jar w/Barnum head han-
    dles & cover w/frosted elephant
    finial 237.50
Pitcher, water, w/elephant in
    base 695.00
Spooner 95.00
Spoon rack (ILLUS.) 800.00
Sugar bowl w/Barnum head handles
    & cover w/frosted elephant
    finial 458.00
Toothpick holder, "Baby Mine" 70.00

KAMONI - See Balder Pattern

KANSAS - See Jewel & Dewdrop Pattern

KENTUCKY

Cake stand, 9½" d. 37.50
Cruet w/original stopper 35.00
Nappy, handled 10.00
Pitcher, water 55.00
Plate, 7" sq.   17.50
Punch cup, green 16.00
Sauce dish, footed, blue w/gold 32.00
Sauce dish, footed, clear 6.50
Sauce dish, footed, green 14.00
Spooner 35.00
Sugar bowl, cov. 30.00
Toothpick holder, clear 26.50
Toothpick holder, green 100.00

Tumbler, green 28.00
Wine, clear 24.00
Wine, green 36.00

KING'S CROWN (Also see Ruby Thumbprint)

King's Crown Mustard Jar

Banana stand 50.00
Bowl, 9¼" oval, scalloped rim,
  round base 40.00
Bowl, berry or fruit, 10½" d.,
  4" h. 22.00
Butter dish, cov. 37.50
Cake stand, 10" d. 78.00
Castor bottle, w/original top 17.50
Celery vase, engraved 60.00
Celery vase, plain 40.00
Compote, cov., 6" d., 6" h. 85.00
Compote, cov., 8" d., 12" h. 145.00
Compote, open, jelly 30.00
Compote, open, 7½" d., high
  stand 45.00
Compote, open, 8½" d., high
  stand 67.50
Compote, open, 9" d., low stand ... 38.50
Cordial 48.00
Creamer, clear 40.00
Creamer, individual size, clear 16.50
Creamer, green 75.00
Creamer, individual size, green 60.00
Cup & saucer 55.00
Goblet, clear 28.50
Goblet, cobalt blue 165.00
Goblet, w/green thumbprints 20.00
Lamp, kerosene-type, stem base,
  10" h. 165.00
Mustard jar, cov. (ILLUS.) 63.00
Pitcher, tankard, 8½" h. 65.00
Pitcher, tankard, 13" h., engraved .. 125.00
Pitcher, tankard, 13" h., plain 95.00
Pitcher, bulbous 115.00
Plate, 7" d. 20.00
Punch bowl, footed 275.00
Relish, 7" oval 10.00
Salt dip, individual size 20.00
Salt dip, master size, footed 22.50
Salt & pepper shakers w/original
  tops, pr. 55.00

Sauce dish, boat-shaped 18.00
Sauce dish, round 7.50
Spooner 43.00
Toothpick holder 26.00
Tumbler, amber 38.00
Tumbler, blue 75.00
Tumbler, clear 25.00
Water set, bulbous pitcher & 6
  goblets, 7 pcs. ....250.00 to 300.00
Wine, clear 20.00
Wine, cobalt blue 200.00

KLONDIKE - See Amberette Pattern

KOKOMO (Bar & Diamond)
Bowl, 8½" d., footed 22.50
Butter dish, cov., pedestal base 30.00
Cake stand 40.00
Celery vase 35.00
Compote, cov., 7½" d., low stand .. 28.00
Compote, open, 8½" d., low
  stand 15.00
Creamer, applied handle 40.00
Cruet w/stopper 26.00
Decanter 65.00
Goblet 27.00
Pitcher, water, bulbous, ruby-
  stained 95.00
Pitcher, water, tankard 40.00
Salt & pepper shakers w/original
  tops, pr. 45.00
Sauce dish, footed 7.50
Spooner, clear 22.50
Spooner, ruby-stained 49.00
Sugar bowl, cov. 45.00
Syrup pitcher w/original top 55.00
Wine 24.00

LACY MEDALLION - See Colorado Pattern

LATTICE (Diamond Bar)
Bread plate, "Waste Not - Want
  Not," 10" d. 40.00
Cake stand, 8" d., 5" h. 38.00
Cake stand, 12½" d. 48.00
Cordial 23.00
Creamer 35.00
Goblet 25.00
Pitcher, water 40.00
Plate, 6" d. 12.50
Plate, 7" d. 15.00
Sauce dish, footed 8.00
Spooner 25.00
Sugar bowl, cov. 30.00
Syrup pitcher w/original tin top 70.00
Wine 20.00

LEAF & DART (Double Leaf & Dart)
Bowl, 8¼" d., low foot 20.00
Butter dish, cov., pedestal base 72.00
Celery vase, pedestal base 38.00
Creamer, applied handle 38.00
Cruet w/original stopper 110.00
Egg cup 22.00
Goblet 31.00

Goblet, buttermilk	35.00
Honey dish, 3½" d.	5.00
Lamp, kerosene-type, applied handle	75.00
Pitcher, milk	125.00
Pitcher, water, applied handle	95.00
Relish	18.00
Salt dip, cov., master size	68.00
Salt dip, open, master size	25.00
Sauce dish	7.50
Spooner	22.00
Sugar bowl, cov.	45.00
Sugar bowl, open	20.00

Leaf & Dart Tumbler

Tumbler, footed (ILLUS.)	28.00
Water set, pitcher & 5 footed tumblers, 6 pcs.	290.00
Wine	35.00

LE CLEDE - See Hickman Pattern

LIBERTY BELL

Bread platter, "John Hancock," shell handles, clear, 7 1/8 x 11½"	150.00
Bread platter, shell handles, without John Hancock signature, clear, 7 1/8 x 11½"	170.00
Bread platter, "John Hancock," shell handles, milk white, 7 1/8 x 11½"	295.00
Bread platter, "John Hancock," twig handles, milk white, 9½ x 13½"	235.00
Bread platter, "Signer's," twig handles	110.00
Butter dish, cov.	140.00
Butter dish, cov., miniature	150.00
Compote, open, 6" d.	95.00
Creamer, applied handle	120.00
Creamer, miniature	82.50
Goblet	45.00
Mug, miniature, 2" h.	110.00
Mug, snake handle	375.00
Pickle dish, closed handles, 1776-1876, w/thirteen original states, 5½ x 9¼" oval	50.00
Pitcher, water	550.00 to 850.00

Plate, 6" d., closed handles, scalloped rim, w/thirteen original states	75.00
Plate, 6" d., no states, dated	58.00
Plate, 8" d., closed handles, scalloped rim, w/thirteen original states	75.00
Plate, 10" d., closed handles, scalloped rim, w/thirteen original states	105.00
Platter, 8¼ x 13", twig handles, w/thirteen original states	85.00
Relish, shell handles, 7 x 11¼"	70.00
Salt dip	35.00
Sauce dish	29.00
Spooner	70.00
Sugar bowl, cov.	110.00
Sugar bowl, open	50.00
Table set, 4 pcs.	400.00 to 450.00

LILY-OF-THE-VALLEY

Lily-of-the-Valley Sauce Dish

Butter dish, cov.	70.00
Celery vase	55.00
Champagne	39.00
Compote, cov., 8" d.	125.00
Compote, cov., 8½" d., high stand	130.00
Compote, open, 8½" d., 5" h.	42.50
Creamer, three-footed, molded handle	71.00
Creamer, plain base, applied handle	60.00
Cruet w/original stopper	80.00
Egg cup	43.00
Goblet	50.00
Goblet, buttermilk	36.00
Honey dish	12.00
Pitcher, milk, applied handle	112.00
Pitcher, water, bulbous, applied handle	85.00 to 125.00
Relish, 5½ x 8"	20.00
Salt dip, cov., master size, three-footed	125.00
Sauce dish (ILLUS.)	10.00
Spooner	37.00
Sugar bowl, cov., three-footed	80.00
Sugar bowl, open, plain base	45.00
Tumbler, flat	9.50
Tumbler, footed	55.00
Wine	130.00

LINCOLN DRAPE & LINCOLN DRAPE WITH TASSEL

Celery vase	90.00
Compote, open, 6¾" d., 5¼" h.	85.00
Compote, open, 7½" d., 3½" h.	50.00
Compote, open, 8" d., medium stand	110.00
Creamer	200.00
Egg cup	49.00
Goblet	85.00
Goblet w/tassel	139.00
Lamp, kerosene-type, miniature	125.00
Salt dip, master size	35.00
Sauce dish, 4" d.	20.00
Spillholder	54.00
Sugar bowl, cov.	92.50
Sugar bowl, open	85.00
Syrup pitcher w/original pewter top	120.00
Syrup pitcher w/original top, opaque white	600.00
Wine	55.00

LION (Square Lion's Head or Atlanta)

Bowl, 5 x 8" oblong, flat	48.00
Butter dish, cov.	100.00
Cake stand	75.00
Celery vase	60.00
Cheese dish, cov.	175.00
Compote, cov., 5" sq., 6" h.	85.00
Compote, cov., 7" sq., high stand	150.00
Compote, cov., 8" sq., 9½" h.	130.00
Compote, open, 4¼" sq., 4" h.	52.00
Compote, open, 6" sq., 7½" h.	57.50
Compote, open, 8" sq., high stand	75.00
Creamer	45.00
Dish, cov., oblong	85.00
Goblet	58.00
Marmalade jar, cov., w/lion's head finial	100.00
Pitcher, water	110.00
Platter, handled	80.00
Relish, boat-shaped	35.00
Sauce dish	22.00
Spooner	52.00
Sugar bowl, cov.	95.00
Syrup pitcher w/original top	240.00
Toothpick holder	45.00
Tumbler	45.00

LION & BABOON

Sauce dish	30.00
Spooner	85.00

LION, FROSTED - See Frosted Lion Pattern

LION'S LEG - See Alaska Pattern

LOCUST - See Grasshopper Pattern

LOG CABIN

Butter dish, cov.	250.00
Compote, cov.	330.00
Creamer, 4¼" h. (ILLUS. right)	116.00

Log Cabin Creamer & Sugar Bowl

Pitcher, water	325.00
Sauce dish, flat, oblong	52.50
Spooner, clear	108.00
Spooner, sapphire blue	395.00
Sugar bowl, cov., 8" h. (ILLUS. left)	250.00
Sugar bowl, cov., vaseline	675.00

LOOP (Seneca Loop)

Bowl, 9" d., flint	80.00
Butter dish, cov., flint	150.00
Celery vase, flint	75.00
Celery vase, non-flint	32.00
Champagne, non-flint	15.00
Compote, open, 8" d., 6" h., non-flint	30.00
Compote, open, 9" d., 7" h., flint	125.00
Compote, open, 10" d., 8" h., flint	80.00
Cordial, non-flint, 2¾" h.	18.50
Creamer, flint	50.00
Creamer, ruby-stained, non-flint	30.00
Decanter, w/original stopper, flint, pt.	130.00
Egg cup, flint	28.50
Egg cup, non-flint	12.00
Goblet, flint	22.00
Goblet, non-flint	15.00
Pitcher, water, applied handle, flint	135.00
Pitcher, water, non-flint	60.00
Salt dip, individual size, flint	18.00
Salt dip, master size, flint	28.00
Sauce dish, non-flint	6.50
Spooner, flint	34.50
Spooner, clear, non-flint	16.00
Spooner, ruby-stained, non-flint	30.00
Sugar bowl, cov., flint	115.00
Sugar bowl, cov., non-flint	29.50
Tumbler, flint	18.00
Tumbler, bar, non-flint	14.00
Tumbler, footed, non-flint	35.00
Wine, flint	30.00
Wine, non-flint	15.00

LOOP & DART

Bowl, 6 x 9" oval, round ornaments	19.50
Butter dish, cov., diamond ornaments, non-flint	38.00
Butter dish, cov., round ornaments, flint	85.00
Butter pat, round ornaments	17.50
Celery vase, round ornaments, flint	47.50

Celery vase, round ornaments, non-flint 44.00

Champagne, round ornaments, flint 65.00

Compote, cov., 6½" d., high stand, round ornaments 95.00

Loop & Dart Covered Compote

Compote, cov., 8" d., 10" h., round ornaments (ILLUS.) 90.00

Compote, cov., 8" d., low stand, round ornaments 75.00

Compote, open, 8" d., 4½" h., round ornaments 42.50

Cordial, 3¾" h. 22.00

Creamer, applied handle, diamond ornaments 32.50

Creamer, applied handle, round ornaments 42.00

Egg cup, diamond ornaments 18.00

Egg cup, round ornaments 25.00

Goblet, diamond ornaments 36.00

Goblet, round ornaments 32.50

Goblet, buttermilk, round ornaments 39.00

Lamp, kerosene-type, round ornaments on font, milk white base ... 85.00

Pitcher, water, round ornaments 90.00

Plate, 6" d., round ornaments 35.00

Relish, diamond ornaments 15.00

Relish, round ornaments 25.00

Salt dip, master size, diamond ornaments 15.00

Salt dip, master size, round ornaments 28.50

Sauce dish, diamond ornaments 5.00

Sauce dish, round ornaments 6.50

Spooner, diamond ornaments 18.00

Spooner, round ornaments 28.00

Sugar bowl, cov., diamond ornaments 30.00

Sugar bowl, cov., round ornaments, flint 57.50

Sugar bowl, open, diamond ornaments 17.50

Sugar bowl, open, round ornaments, flint 35.00

Sugar bowl, open, round ornaments, non-flint 28.00

Tumbler, flat or footed, diamond ornaments 25.00

Tumbler, flat or footed, round ornaments 24.00

Wine, diamond ornaments 32.50

Wine, round ornaments 32.50

LOOP & JEWEL - See Jewel & Festoon Pattern

LOOP & PILLAR - See Michigan Pattern

LOOPS & DROPS - See New Jersey Pattern

LOOPS & FANS - See Maryland Pattern

LOOP WITH DEWDROPS

Bowl, 7" to 8" d. 17.50

Butter dish, cov. 27.50

Creamer 20.00

Goblet 28.00

Pitcher, water 65.00

Sugar bowl, cov. 25.00

Tumbler 17.00

Wine 27.00

LOOP WITH STIPPLED PANELS - See Texas Pattern

MAGNET & GRAPE

Butter dish, cov., frosted leaf, flint 185.00

Celery vase, frosted leaf, flint 150.00

Compote, cov., 4½" d., 9" h., frosted leaf, flint 125.00

Compote, open, 7½" d., high stand, stippled leaf, non-flint 68.00

Cordial, frosted leaf, flint, 4" h. 150.00

Creamer, frosted leaf, flint 160.00

Egg cup, clear leaf, non-flint 20.00

Egg cup, frosted leaf, flint 85.00

Goblet, clear leaf, non-flint 20.00

Goblet, frosted leaf, flint 70.00

Goblet, frosted leaf & American Shield, flint .... 250.00 to 300.00

Goblet, stippled leaf, non-flint 20.00

Goblet, buttermilk, frosted leaf, flint 45.00

Salt dip, frosted leaf, flint.......... 50.00

Sauce dish, frosted leaf, flint 18.00

Sauce dish, stippled leaf, non-flint .. 4.50

Spooner, frosted leaf, flint 77.50

Spooner, stippled leaf, non-flint 30.00

Sugar bowl, cov., frosted leaf, flint 95.00

Sugar bowl, cov., frosted leaf & American Shield, flint 300.00

Sugar bowl, cov., stippled leaf, non-flint 50.00

Tumbler, frosted leaf, flint 85.00

Tumbler, stippled leaf, non-flint 24.00

Wine, frosted leaf, flint 135.00

Wine, stippled leaf, non-flint 40.00

MAINE (Stippled Flower Panels)

Maine Jelly Compote

Bowl, 6" d.	32.00
Bowl, master berry, 8½" d., green	32.50
Bread plate	26.00
Butter dish, cov.	45.00
Cake stand, green, 8½" d.	46.00
Compote, cov., small, green	65.00
Compote, open, jelly, 4¾" d. (ILLUS.)	26.00
Compote, open, 7" d.	32.00
Compote, open, 8" d., clear	38.00
Compote, open, 8" d., green	58.00
Creamer	28.50
Cruet w/original stopper	60.00
Pitcher, water, clear	85.00
Pitcher, water, w/red & green stain	125.00
Platter, oval	38.00
Relish, 7¼" l.	14.00
Salt & pepper shakers, w/original tops, pr.	63.00
Sauce dish	12.50
Spooner	30.00
Sugar bowl, cov., green	60.00
Syrup pitcher w/original top	75.00
Tumbler, w/red & green stain	45.00
Wine, clear	50.00
Wine, green	65.00

MALTESE - See Jacob's Ladder Pattern

MANHATTAN

Basket, large	225.00
Berry set, master bowl & 3 flat sauce dishes, 4 pcs.	35.00
Bowl, 6" d.	27.00
Bowl, 9" d.	22.00
Bowl, master berry, pink-stained	48.00
Bread plate	20.00
Cake stand, clear	44.00
Cake stand, ruby-stained	37.00
Carafe, water, clear	40.00
Carafe, water, pink-stained	65.00
Cracker jar, cov., clear	60.00
Cracker jar, cov., pink-stained	85.00
Creamer	20.00
Creamer, individual size	20.00

Cruet w/original stopper	46.00
Goblet, clear	18.00
Goblet, clear w/gold rim	22.50
Pickle dish, 6 x 8" oval	25.00
Pitcher, water, w/silver rim	100.00
Plate, 5" d., clear	10.00
Plate, 5" d., pink-stained	25.00
Plate, 8" d.	16.00
Plate, 10¾" d.	20.00
Punch bowl, 14" d., 8" h.	110.00
Punch cup	15.00
Relish, 6" l.	10.00
Salt & pepper shakers w/original tops, pr.	30.00
Sauce dish, flat, amber or pink-stained	12.00
Sauce dish, flat	9.00
Sugar bowl, open	20.00
Toothpick holder, blue-stained	55.00
Toothpick holder, clear	22.00
Toothpick holder, clear w/gold trim	18.00
Toothpick holder, purple-stained eyes	30.00
Vase, 7" h.	15.00
Violet bowl	20.00
Wine	25.00

MAPLE LEAF (Leaf)

Grant "Peace" Plate

Berry set: oval master bowl & 10 footed sauce dishes; vaseline, 11 pcs.	145.00
Bowl, 5½" oval, clear	25.00
Bowl, 5½" oval, vaseline	45.00
Bowl, 6 x 10" oval, footed, blue	60.00
Bowl, 6 x 10" oval, footed, clear	35.00
Bowl, 6 x 10" oval, footed, green	55.00
Bowl, 6 x 10" oval, flat, vaseline	50.00
Bowl, 6 x 10" oval, footed, vaseline	57.00
Bowl, 10" sq., crimped rim, blue	85.00
Bowl, 7½ x 12" oval, amber	70.00
Bread plate, Grant, "Let Us Have Peace," amber, 9½" d.	65.00
Bread plate, Grant, "Let Us Have Peace," blue, 9½" d.	85.00

Bread plate, Grant, "Let Us Have
  Peace," clear, 9½" d. (ILLUS.) 75.00
Bread plate, Grant, "Let Us Have
  Peace," vaseline, 9½" d. 52.00
Bread tray, clear, 9¼ x 13¼" 35.00
Bread tray, vaseline, 9¼ x 13¼" . . .   55.00
Butter dish, cov. 80.00
Celery vase 36.00
Compote, cov., 9" d., 10" h.,
  vaseline 163.00
Compote, open, jelly, green 45.00
Creamer, blue 65.00
Creamer, clear 52.50
Creamer, vaseline 65.00
Goblet, amber . . . . 85.00 to 110.00
Goblet, clear 32.00
Goblet, frosted tree trunk stem 150.00
Goblet, vaseline . . . . 90.00 to 110.00
Pitcher, milk, vaseline 74.00
Pitcher, water 67.50
Plate, 9" d., blue 35.00
Plate, 9" d., vaseline 39.00
Platter, 10½" oval, blue 50.00
Platter, 10½" oval, clear 40.00
Platter, 10½" oval, vaseline 48.00
Sauce dish, leaf-shaped, vaseline,
  5½" l. 16.00
Spooner, blue 55.00
Spooner, clear 40.00
Spooner, green 45.00
Spooner, vaseline 65.00
Sugar bowl, cov., blue 95.00
Sugar bowl, cov., vaseline 75.00
Sugar bowl, open 40.00
Table set: creamer, cov. sugar bowl
  & spooner; green w/gold, 3 pcs . . .   195.00
Tumbler 35.00
Waste bowl, vaseline 30.00

**MARYLAND (Inverted Loops & Fans or
Loops & Fans)**
Banana bowl, flat, 5 x 11¼" 25.00
Bread platter 26.00
Butter dish, cov. 57.50
Cake stand, 8" d. 42.00
Celery tray, 12" l. 13.50
Celery vase 27.00
Compote, cov., 7" d., high stand . . .   48.00
Compote, open, jelly 17.50
Compote, open, medium 30.00
Creamer 16.00
Goblet 30.00
Pickle dish 16.50
Pitcher, milk 42.00
Pitcher, water, clear 45.00
Pitcher, water, ruby-stained 105.00
Plate, 7" d. 9.00
Platter 18.00
Relish 13.50
Salt & pepper shakers w/original
  tops, pr. 65.00
Sauce dish 8.50
Spooner 27.50
Sugar bowl, cov. 40.00

Table set, 4 pcs. 150.00
Toothpick holder 35.00
Tumbler 22.00
Wine 36.00

MASCOTTE

Mascotte Creamer

Apothecary jar, cov. 65.00
Butter dish, cov., engraved 52.00
Butter dish, cov., plain 38.00
Butter dish, cov., horseshoe-shaped,
  "Maude S." 100.00
Butter pat 15.00
Cake basket w/handle 55.00
Cake stand 35.00
Celery vase 34.00
Cheese dish, cov. 65.00
Compote, cov., 5" d. 34.00
Compote, cov., 7" d. 45.00
Compote, cov., 9" d., high stand . . .   175.00
Compote, open, jelly 22.00
Creamer (ILLUS.) 32.00
Goblet 32.00
Marmalade jar, cov., 4½" d., 8" h.,
  cranberry-stained, engraved
  date 42.00
Pitcher, water 60.00
Salt shaker w/original top 9.00
Sauce dish, flat or footed, each 12.50
Spooner 31.00
Sugar bowl, cov. 39.00
Table set, 4 pcs. 165.00
Tray, wine 20.00
Tumbler 18.00
Wine 25.00

MASSACHUSETTS
Banana boat, 6½ x 8½" 55.00
Bar bottle, 11" h. 49.00
Basket w/applied handle, 4½ x
  4½", 4¾" h. 55.00
Bowl, 6" sq. 18.00
Bowl, master berry, 8½" sq. 25.00
Butter dish, cov. 45.00
Cologne bottle w/stopper 37.50
Cordial 57.50

Creamer	33.00
Creamer, breakfast size	15.00
Cruet w/original stopper	42.00
Cruet w/original stopper, miniature	55.00
Decanter w/stopper	88.00
Goblet	42.50
Ice cream tray, 8"	16.50
Mug, 3½" h.	18.00
Olive dish, 3½ x 5"	8.50
Pitcher, water	75.00
Plate, 5" sq., serrated rim	19.00
Plate, 6" sq., w/advertising	16.50
Plate, 8" sq.	28.00
Punch cup	12.00
Relish, 8½" l.	12.50
Rum jug, 5" h.	75.00
Spooner	20.00
Sugar bowl, open, two-handled	17.50
Sugar bowl, open, breakfast size	15.00
Table set, 4 pcs.	233.00
Toothpick holder	42.50
Tumbler, juice	17.00
Tumbler, water	35.00
Vase, 6½" h., trumpet-shaped, clear	22.50
Vase, 6½" h., trumpet-shaped, cobalt blue w/gold	40.00 to 60.00
Vase, 6½" h., trumpet-shaped, green	19.00
Vase, 7" h., corset-shaped	13.50
Vase, 9" h., trumpet-shaped, clear	32.50
Vase, 9" h., trumpet-shaped, green	38.00
Vase, 10" h., trumpet-shaped, green	40.00
Whiskey shot glass	12.00
Whiskey set, bar bottle & 6 shot glasses, 7 pcs.	125.00
Wine, blue	110.00
Wine, clear	40.00

MELROSE

Butter dish, cov.	45.00
Cake stand, 8" to 10" d.	27.50
Celery vase, clear	27.50
Celery vase, ruby-stained	65.00
Compote, open, jelly, 5½" d.	14.00
Compote, open, 7" d., 7" h.	25.00
Compote, open, 7½" d., 5¾" h.	23.00
Compote, open, 9" d., high stand	35.00
Creamer	30.00
Goblet	18.00
Pitcher, water	32.00
Plate, 7" d.	16.00
Plate, 8" d.	10.00
Spooner	30.00
Sugar bowl, cov.	38.00
Tray, water, 11½" d.	45.00
Wine	20.00

MICHIGAN (Paneled Jewel or Loop & Pillar)

Berry set: master bowl & 4 sauce dishes; pink-stained, 5 pcs.	75.00

Bowl, cov., master berry or fruit	75.00
Bowl, 8" d., clear	28.50
Bowl, 8" d., pink-stained w/gold trim	75.00
Bowl, 10" d.	35.00
Butter dish, cov., clear	45.00
Butter dish, cov., pink-stained	125.00
Butter dish, cov., yellow-stained, enameled florals	175.00
Carafe, water	150.00
Celery vase	41.00
Compote, open, jelly, 4½" d.	23.00
Compote, open, 8½" d., high stand	50.00
Compote, open, 8½" d., pink-stained	40.00
Compote, open, 9¼" d.	62.50
Compote, open, 10" d.	55.00
Creamer, clear, 5" h.	30.00
Creamer, pink-stained, 4" h.	73.00
Creamer, individual size, clear	14.00
Creamer, individual size, yellow-stained, enameled florals	25.00
Cruet w/original stopper	57.00
Finger bowl	14.50

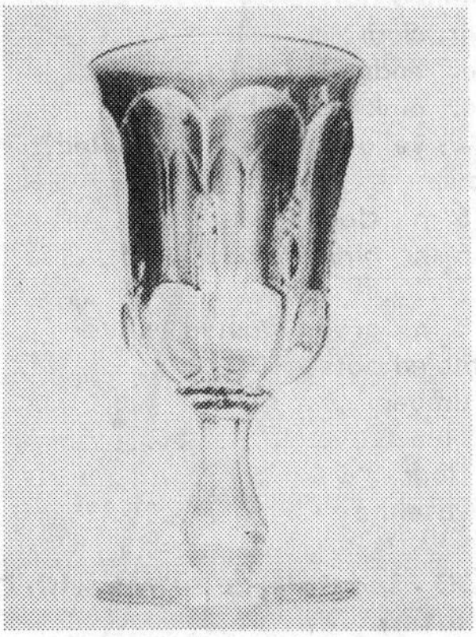

Michigan Goblet

Goblet, clear (ILLUS.)	30.00
Goblet, green-stained, w/enamel	42.00
Honey dish, 3½" d.	8.00
Mug, clear	22.50
Mug, pink-stained, gold trim	38.00
Mug, yellow-stained, enameled florals	33.00
Pickle dish	12.00
Pitcher, water, 8" h.	44.00
Pitcher, water, 12" h., clear	68.00
Pitcher, water, 12" h., pink-stained	155.00
Platter, 8½ x 12½", 7¼ x 10¼" & 6½ x 9½", nested set of 3	125.00
Punch bowl, 8" d., 4½" h.	50.00
Punch cup, enameled decoration	12.00
Relish	20.00
Salt shaker w/original top, clear	27.50
Salt shaker w/original top, enameled decoration	32.00

Salt shaker w/original top, yellow-
stained, enameled florals 45.00
Salt & pepper shakers w/original
tops, individual size, pr. 75.00
Sauce dish, clear 13.00
Sauce dish, pink-stained 20.00
Spooner, clear 25.00
Spooner, miniature 25.00
Spooner, pink-stained 71.00
Sugar bowl, cov., clear 50.00
Sugar bowl, cov., pink-stained, gold
trim . . . . 100.00 to 125.00
Sugar bowl, individual size 26.00
Sugar bowl, individual size, w/pew-
ter holder 70.00
Syrup jug w/pewter top 95.00
Table set, clear, 4 pcs. 165.00
Table set, pink-stained, 4 pcs. 375.00
Toddy mug, tall 45.00
Toothpick holder, blue-stained 75.00
Toothpick holder, clear 36.00
Toothpick holder, clear, enameled
florals 45.00
Toothpick holder, yellow-stained 50.00
Toothpick holder, yellow-stained,
enameled florals 72.00
Tumbler, clear 24.00
Tumbler, enameled decoration 25.00
Tumbler, pink-stained, gold trim 50.00
Tumbler, yellow-stained, enameled
florals 35.00
Vase, 6" h., clear 15.00
Vase, 6" h., pink-stained, gold
trim 18.00
Vase, 8" h., green-stained, white
enameled dots 35.00
Wine, amber 45.00
Wine, blue 30.00
Wine, clear 28.00
Wine, vaseline 55.00

**MIKADO - See Daisy & Button with Cross-
bars Pattern**

MINERVA

Minerva Relish

Bread tray, 13" l. 55.00
Butter dish, cov. 75.00

Cake stand, 9" d. 108.00
Cake stand, 12½" d. 145.00
Compote, cov., 7" d., 10¾" h. 115.00
Compote, cov., 8" d., low stand 95.00
Compote, open, 8" d., 8½" h. 90.00
Creamer 50.00
Goblet 83.00
Honey dish 17.50
Marmalade jar, cov. 150.00
Pickle dish, "Love's Request is Pick-
les," oval 28.00
Pitcher, milk, 7½" h. 72.50
Pitcher, water 200.00
Plate, 8" d., Bates (J.C.) portrait
center, scalloped rim 86.00
Plate, 9" d., handled, plain center . . 56.00
Plate, 10" d., Mars center 49.00
Relish, 5 x 8" oblong (ILLUS.) 30.00
Salt dip, footed, master size 25.00
Sauce dish, flat or footed, each 15.50
Spooner 38.00
Sugar bowl, cov. 65.00
Tumbler 22.50
Waste bowl, 6" d. 55.00

MINNESOTA
Banana bowl, flat 50.00
Basket w/applied reeded handle . . . 50.00
Berry set, 10" d. master bowl & 5
sauce dishes, 6 pcs. 55.00
Bowl, 8½" d., clear 30.00
Bowl, 8½" d., ruby-stained 100.00
Butter dish, cov. 44.00
Carafe 38.00
Celery tray, 13" l. 31.00
Compote, open, 9" sq. 50.00
Creamer, 3½" h. 22.50
Creamer, individual size 15.00
Cruet w/original stopper 32.50
Flower frog, green, 2 pcs. 45.00
Goblet 35.00
Mug 18.00
Mustard jar w/silver plate lid,
handled 40.00
Nappy, 4½" d. 14.00
Olive dish, oval 12.50
Pickle dish 10.00
Pitcher, water, tankard 75.00
Plate, 7 3/8" d., turned-up rim 12.50
Relish, 3 x 5" 9.00
Relish, 6½ x 8¾" oblong 15.00
Salt shaker w/original top, ruby-
stained 50.00
Sauce dish 12.00
Spooner 17.00
Sugar bowl, cov. 30.00
Table set, clear, 4 pcs. 125.00
Toothpick holder, three-handled 24.00
Tumbler 20.00
Wine 26.00

MIRROR, EARLY
Bar bottle 40.00
Bowl, 7" d. 17.50

Celery vase	75.00
Compote, open, 7 1/8" d.,	
5 7/8" h.	40.00
Compote, open, 10" d., 7½" h.	120.00
Goblet	32.00
Goblet, bulb stem	55.00
Pomade jar w/ground stopper,	
3½" h.	35.00
Spillholder	40.00
Sugar bowl, cov.	60.00
Sugar bowl, open	18.50
Tumbler, bar	30.00
Tumbler, footed	45.00
Wine	37.50

MISSOURI (Palm & Scroll)

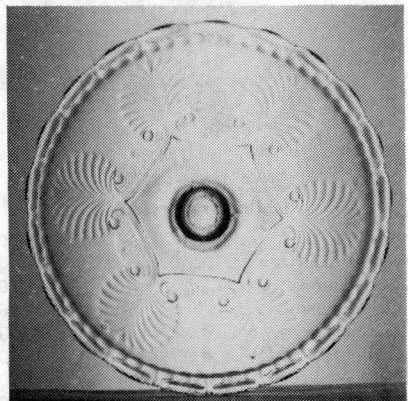

Missouri Doughnut Stand

Bowl, 8¾" d., green	36.00
Butter dish, cov.	55.00
Cake stand, 9" d., 4¾" h., clear	35.00
Cake stand, 9" d., green	48.00
Cake stand, 10" d.	46.00
Celery vase	28.00
Compote, open, 9" d., 7½" h.,	
green	120.00
Compote, jelly	22.50
Creamer, clear	25.00
Creamer, green	30.00
Cruet w/original stopper, clear	45.00
Cruet w/original stopper, green	160.00
Doughnut stand, 6" d. (ILLUS.)	32.50
Goblet	45.00
Mug, clear	30.00
Pitcher, milk	37.00
Pitcher, water, clear	40.00 to 60.00
Pitcher, water, tankard, green	70.00
Relish, clear	10.00
Relish, green	12.50
Salt & pepper shakers w/original	
tops, pr.	50.00
Sauce dish, clear	10.50
Sauce dish, green	12.50
Spooner, clear	24.00
Spooner, green	40.00
Sugar bowl, cov., clear	50.00
Sugar bowl, cov., green	54.00

Syrup pitcher	70.00
Table set, green, 4 pcs.	250.00 to 300.00
Tumbler, green	35.00
Water set: pitcher & 6 tumblers;	
green, 7 pcs.	285.00
Wine, clear	40.00
Wine, green	45.00

MONKEY

Monkey Pickle Jar

Butter dish, cov.	195.00
Dish, cov., milk white	99.00
Mug, amethyst	395.00
Mug, clear	75.00
Pickle jar, cov., 7 3/8" h. (ILLUS.)	100.00
Spooner, clear	50.00
Spooner, white opalescent	175.00

MOON & STARS

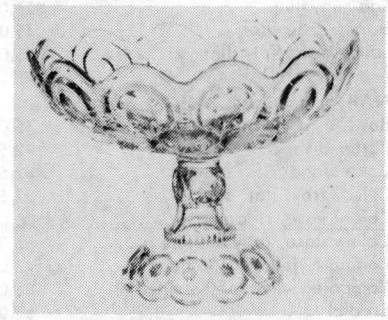

Moon & Stars Compote

Berry set, master bowl & 6 sauce	
dishes, 7 pcs.	95.00
Bowl, cov., 6" d.	30.00
Bowl, cov., 7" d.	28.00
Bowl, 7" d., footed	25.00
Bowl, master berry, 8¼" d., 4" h.	31.00
Bowl, fruit, 9" d., footed	35.00
Bowl, 7 x 10", teardrop-shaped	42.00
Bread tray, scalloped rim,	
6½ x 10¾"	24.50
Butter dish, cov.	46.00

Cake stand, 9" d.	44.00
Cake stand, 10" d.	55.00
Celery vase	40.00
Compote, cov., 6" d., 10" h.	55.00
Compote, cov., 8" d., 12" h.	65.00
Compote, cov., 10½" d., 16¼" h.	185.00
Compote, open, 7" d., 7½" h.	30.00
Compote, open, 8" d., 8" h.	58.00
Compote, open, 9" d., 6½" h. (ILLUS. previous page)	48.00
Compote, open, 10" d., high stand	125.00
Creamer	52.00
Creamer & open sugar bowl, pr.	96.00
Cruet w/original stopper, applied handle	55.00
Egg cup	30.00
Goblet	36.00
Lamp, kerosene-type, table model, amber	190.00
Pickle dish, 8" l.	17.00
Pitcher, water, 9¼" h., applied rope handle	145.00
Relish, oblong	16.00
Salt dip, individual size, footed	15.00
Salt shaker w/original top	20.00
Sauce dish, flat or footed, each	12.00
Spooner	45.00
Sugar bowl, cov.	62.00
Syrup pitcher w/original top	125.00
Toothpick holder	21.00
Tumbler, flat	45.00
Wine	35.00

MOON & STAR WITH WAFFLE - See Jeweled Moon & Star Pattern

MORNING GLORY

Compote, 7¾" d., 5" h., flint	300.00
Egg cup, flint	325.00
Honey dish, flint, 3½"	45.00
Sauce dish, flat, flint	45.00

NAIL

Bowl, 6" d., flat, ruby-stained	45.00
Butter dish, cov.	72.50
Cake stand	42.50
Celery tray, flat, 5 x 11"	22.50
Celery vase, clear	26.00
Celery vase, ruby-stained	65.00
Compote, jelly, 5¼", clear	47.00
Compote, jelly, ruby-stained	86.00
Cordial	55.00
Decanter w/stopper	40.00
Goblet, clear, engraved	60.00
Goblet, clear, plain	46.00
Goblet, ruby-stained	65.00
Pitcher, water, clear	58.00
Pitcher, water, ruby-stained	140.00
Salt shaker w/original top, w/engraving, ruby-stained	28.00
Sauce dish, flat or footed, each	10.00
Spooner, ruby-stained	60.00
Sugar bowl, open	17.00
Syrup jug w/original top	48.00

Tumbler, ruby-stained	62.50
Tumbler, ruby-stained, souvenir	42.50
Water set: pitcher & 5 tumblers; ruby-stained, 6 pcs.	365.00
Wine, clear, engraved	55.00
Wine, clear, plain	52.50
Wine, ruby-stained, souvenir	60.00

NAILHEAD

Nailhead Compote

Bowl, 6" d.	16.00
Butter dish, cov.	46.50
Cake stand, 9" to 12" d.	26.00
Celery vase	52.00
Compote, cov., 6¼" d., 6¼" h.	40.00
Compote, cov., 6¼" d., 9½" h.	45.00
Compote, cov., 7" d., low stand	45.00
Compote, cov., 12" d.	65.00
Compote, open, 6½" d., 6¾" h. (ILLUS.)	25.00
Compote, open, 9" d., 6½" h.	35.00
Compote, open, 10" d., 7" h.	45.00
Creamer	22.00
Goblet	22.00
Pitcher, water	30.00
Plate, 7" sq.	15.00
Plate, 9" d.	16.00
Relish, 5¼ x 8¾"	10.00
Sauce dish, 4"	7.00
Spooner	19.00
Sugar bowl, cov.	35.00
Tumbler	42.50
Wine	20.00

NEPTUNE - See Bearded Man Pattern

NESTOR

Bowl, master berry, green w/gold & enameling	65.00
Butter dish, cov., blue w/gold trim	115.00
Butter dish, cov., clear w/gold trim	65.00
Compote, jelly, purple	37.50
Creamer, blue	40.00
Creamer, green w/gold & enameling	40.00
Cruet w/original stopper, blue w/gold trim	100.00

Cruet w/original stopper, green 70.00
Cruet w/original stopper, purple ... 95.00
Sauce dish, purple w/gold trim 25.00
Spooner, green w/gold &
  enameling 40.00
Spooner, purple w/gold trim 30.00
Sugar bowl, cov., green w/gold &
  enameling 60.00
Table set, blue, 4 pcs. 525.00
Toothpick holder, blue 60.00
Tumbler, blue w/gold trim 75.00
Tumbler, green 30.00
Tumbler, purple w/gold trim 28.00
Water set: pitcher & 6 tumblers;
  green w/gold & enameled decora-
  tion, 7 pcs. 315.00

NEW ENGLAND PINEAPPLE
Bowl, 8" d., footed, scalloped rim,
  flint............................ 80.00
Cake stand, flint 115.00
Champagne, flint 170.00
Compote, cov., 5" d., 8½" h., flint.. 150.00
Compote, open, 8" d., 5" h., flint ... 75.00
Compote, open, 9" d.............. 145.00
Creamer, applied handle, flint...... 160.00
Decanter w/bar lip, flint, qt. 175.00
Decanter w/original stopper, flint,
  qt............................. 200.00
Egg cup, flint 50.00
Goblet, flint 60.00
Honey dish, flint 17.00
Plate, 6" d., flint 85.00
Salt dip, individual size, flint 25.00
Salt dip, master size, flint 40.00
Sauce dish, flint.................. 20.00
Spillholder, flint.................. 58.00
Sugar bowl, cov., flint 140.00
Sugar bowl, open, flint 60.00
Tumbler, bar, flint................ 115.00
Tumbler, water, flint 85.00
Wine, flint....................... 135.00

NEW JERSEY (Loops & Drops)
Bowl, flat........................ 20.00
Bread plate...................... 30.00
Butter dish, cov., w/gold trim 68.00
Celery tray, flat.................. 25.00
Compote, open, jelly 20.00
Compote, open, 7" d., 3½" h....... 12.50
Creamer 32.00
Cruet w/original stopper........... 45.00
Goblet, clear 32.00
Goblet, w/gold trim 36.00
Olive dish 18.00
Pitcher, water 48.00
Plate, 8" d....................... 12.00
Plate, 8¾" d. 13.00
Plate, 11" d. 23.00
Relish 15.00
Salt shaker 35.00
Sauce dish, flat 10.50
Sugar bowl, cov. 40.00
Table set, 4 pcs. 250.00

Toothpick holder, clear 48.00
Toothpick holder, w/gold trim 62.00
Tumbler, clear 26.00
Tumbler, ruby-stained 50.00
Vase, 8" h., green 26.00
Water set, pitcher & 6 tumblers,
  7 pcs..................200.00 to 225.00
Wine........................... 32.00

NORTHWOOD DRAPERY - See Opalescent Glass

NOTCHED RIB - See Broken Column Pattern

OAKEN BUCKET (Wooden Pail)

Oaken Bucket Match Holder

Butter dish, cov., amber 75.00
Butter dish, cov., blue 85.00
Butter dish, cov., clear 65.00
Creamer, amber 40.00
Creamer, amethyst 85.00
Creamer, clear 35.00
Creamer, vaseline................ 40.00
Match holder w/original wire han-
  dle, amber, 2 5/8" d., 2 5/8" h.
  (ILLUS.)...................... 20.00
Pitcher, water, amber 75.00
Pitcher, water, amethyst....80.00 to 120.00
Pitcher, water, blue 100.00
Pitcher, water, clear.............. 50.00
Spooner, amber 40.00
Spooner, blue................... 45.00
Spooner, clear 17.50
Spooner, vaseline 48.00
Sugar bowl, cov., blue............ 48.00
Sugar bowl, cov., clear 35.00
Sugar bowl, cov., vaseline 55.00
Sugar bowl, open, blue 20.00
Sugar bowl, open, miniature,
  amethyst 22.50
Toothpick holder, blue 22.50
Toothpick holder, vaseline 27.50
Tumbler, clear 15.00
Tumbler, bar, amethyst 35.00

OAK LEAF BAND
Bowl, 5½ x 8" oval............... 9.50
Butter dish, cov. 45.00
Compote, cov., 7½" h., acorn
  finial.......................... 75.00

Oak Leaf Band Goblet

Goblet (ILLUS.) 30.00
Mug, applied handle, 3½" h. 37.50
Pitcher, 6" h. 36.00
Relish 10.00

OLD MAN OF THE MOUNTAIN - See Viking Pattern

OLD MAN OF THE WOODS - See Bearded Man Pattern

ONE-HUNDRED-ONE
Bread plate, 10" d. 42.00
Celery 35.00
Compote, open 25.00
Creamer, 4¾" h. 34.00
Goblet 31.00
Pitcher, water 125.00
Plate, 7" d. 18.00
Plate, 8" d. 30.00
Sauce dish 15.00
Sugar bowl, cov. 45.00
Toothpick holder, opaque green 85.00

OPEN ROSE

Open Rose Spooner

Compote, open, 7½" d. 32.50
Creamer 36.00
Egg cup 23.00
Goblet 28.00

Goblet, buttermilk 22.00
Goblet, lady's 28.00
Pitcher, water, applied handle 170.00
Relish, 5½ x 8" 13.50
Sauce dish 10.00
Spooner (ILLUS.) 26.00
Sugar bowl, cov. 52.50
Sugar bowl, open 25.00
Tumbler 40.00
Tumbler, applied handle 65.00
Water set, pitcher & 6 goblets,
  7 pcs. .... 325.00 to 350.00

OREGON NO. 1 - See Beaded Loop Pattern

OREGON NO. 2 (Skilton)
Bowl, 7¾" d., 2½" h. 12.50
Bowl, 8" d., 2½" h., ruby-stained ... 30.00
Butter dish, cov. 40.00
Cake stand, 9" d. 43.00
Celery vase 27.50
Compote, open, 5½" d., 4½" h. 22.50
Compote, open, 8½" d., low stand,
  clear 28.00
Compote, open, 8½" d., low stand,
  ruby-stained 50.00
Creamer, ruby-stained 40.00
Decanter, whiskey 29.00
Goblet 28.00
Pitcher, milk 25.00
Pitcher, water, tankard 40.00
Relish 15.00
Sauce dish 11.00
Spooner, ruby-stained 38.00
Syrup pitcher w/original top 65.00
Tumbler, ruby-stained 39.00
Wine 32.50

OWL IN FAN - See Parrot Pattern

PALM & SCROLL - See Missouri Pattern

PALMETTE
Bowl, 8" d., flat 25.00
Bread tray, handled, 9" 30.00
Butter dish, cov. 49.00
Butter pat 45.00
Cake stand 45.00
Castor set, 3-bottle, complete 75.00
Castor set, 5-bottle, complete 125.00
Celery vase 31.50
Champagne 68.00
Compote, cov., 8" d., high stand ... 85.00
Compote, open, 7" d., low stand ... 30.00
Compote, open, 8" d., low stand ... 27.50
Creamer, applied handle 50.00
Cup plate 45.00
Egg cup 22.00
Goblet 32.00
Lamp, kerosene-type, table model
  w/stem, clear 82.00
Lamp, kerosene-type, table model
  w/stem, milk white 135.00
Pickle dish, scoop-shaped 13.50

Pitcher, water, applied handle	125.00
Relish	17.50
Salt dip, master size, footed	20.00
Salt & pepper shakers w/original tops, 5½" h., pr.................	55.00
Sauce dish.........................	12.00
Spooner	30.00
Sugar bowl, cov.	42.50
Sugar bowl, open	22.50
Syrup pitcher w/original top, applied handle	110.00
Tumbler, water, footed	47.50

PANELED CANE

Creamer & cov. sugar bowl, pr.	32.00
Goblet, amber	25.00
Goblet, blue	30.00
Goblet, clear	20.00
Mug, 2¼" h.......................	9.50
Tray, water	12.00

PANELED CHERRY WITH THUMBPRINTS (Cherry Thumbprints, Paneled Cherry & Cherry & Cable)

Paneled Cherry Table Set

Berry set, master bowl & 6 sauce dishes, 7 pcs...................	135.00
Butter dish, cov.	100.00
Celery dish	45.00
Creamer	45.00
Pitcher, water	110.00
Punch cup, footed	26.00
Sauce dish.........................	12.50
Spooner	45.00
Sugar bowl, cov.	75.00
Table set, 4 pcs. (ILLUS.)...250.00 to	300.00
Tumbler	22.50
Water set, pitcher & 6 tumblers, 7 pcs.................225.00 to	250.00

PANELED DAISY

Berry set, master bowl & 6 sauce dishes, 7 pcs...................	85.00
Bowl, 5 x 7" oval..................	12.50
Bowl, master berry, 5¾ x 8¼" oval	20.00
Butter dish, cov.	40.00
Cake stand, 8" to 11" d., high stand	45.00
Celery vase.......................	29.00
Compote, cov., 5" d., high stand ...	50.00
Compote, cov., large	47.50
Creamer	35.00
Goblet	25.00

Mug	30.00
Pickle dish, handled, 8½" l.........	15.00
Pitcher, water	45.00
Plate, 9" sq.	22.50
Relish, 5 x 7" oval................	12.00
Sauce dish, flat or footed, each	11.00
Spooner	30.00
Sugar shaker w/original top	35.00
Toothpick holder, footed, amber	25.00
Tray, water......................	31.00

PANELED DEWDROP

Bowl, 8½" oval	24.00
Bowl, 11" oval, footed	17.00
Bread platter, 9½ x 12½"	50.00
Butter dish, cov.	65.00
Celery vase.......................	38.00
Cordial, 3¼" h.	28.50
Creamer	22.50
Creamer, individual size	20.00
Creamer & cov. sugar bowl, pr.	60.00
Goblet	24.50
Marmalade jar, cov...............	42.50
Mug, applied handle	35.00
Pitcher, milk	42.50
Plate, 7" to 10" d...........15.00 to	30.00
Sauce dish, flat or footed, each...........5.00 to	10.00
Spooner	35.00
Sugar bowl, cov.	38.00
Wine.............................	20.00

PANELED DIAMOND CROSS - See Heavy Paneled Finecut Pattern

PANELED FINECUT - See Finecut & Panel Pattern

PANELED FORGET-ME-NOT

Paneled Forget-Me-Not Cake Stand

Bread platter, 7 x 11" oval	30.00
Butter dish, cov.	45.00
Cake stand (ILLUS.)...............	45.00
Celery vase.......................	33.00
Compote, cov., 6" d., 9½" h........	45.00
Compote, cov., 7" d., 10" h........	67.50
Compote, cov., 8" d., high stand ...	62.00
Compote, open, 7" d., 5½" h.	28.00
Compote, open, 7¼" d., 7" h.	30.00
Compote, open, 8½" d., 6½" h.	30.00
Compote, open, 8½" d., 12" h.	40.00
Creamer	32.00

Goblet 30.00
Marmalade jar, cov. 54.00
Pitcher, milk 52.00
Pitcher, water 65.00
Relish, handled, 4½ x 7¾" 15.00
Relish, scoop-shaped, 9" l. 19.50
Salt & pepper shakers w/original
   tops, pr. 65.00
Sauce dish, flat or footed, each 12.00
Spooner 32.00
Sugar bowl, cov. 35.00
Wine 38.50

PANELED GRAPE
Butter dish, cov. 57.00
Compote, open, 6½" h. 65.00
Creamer 25.00
Goblet 30.00
Parfait 35.00
Pitcher, water, 8¾" h. 65.00
Sauce dish 15.00
Sugar bowl, cov., small 25.00
Sugar bowl, open 28.00
Tumbler 16.00
Water set, cov. pitcher & 6 goblets,
   7 pcs. .... 200.00 to 250.00
Wine 18.00

PANELED HEATHER
Bowl, 7" d. 12.50
Bowl, 8¼" d., 3¾" h. 27.50
Butter dish, cov., ruby-stained 40.00
Cake stand 30.00
Compote, cov. 40.00
Compote, open, jelly 20.00
Compote, open, 8" d. 27.50
Creamer 19.00
Cruet w/original stopper 30.00
Goblet 22.50
Pitcher, water 38.00
Plate, 12" d. 18.00
Sauce dish, flat or footed, each 7.50
Spooner 20.00
Sugar bowl, cov. 32.50
Table set, h.p. florals, gilt trim,
   4 pcs. 158.00
Tumbler 25.00
Wine 18.50

**PANELED HERRINGBONE (Emerald Green
Herringbone or Florida)**
Berry set: 9" d. master bowl & 6
   sauce dishes; green, 7 pcs. 105.00
Bowl, master berry, 9" sq., green .. 38.00
Bowl, oval vegetable, green,
   medium 17.50
Butter dish, cov., green 85.00
Cake stand, clear 25.00
Cake stand, green 75.00
Celery vase, green 55.00
Compote, open, jelly, 5½" sq.,
   green 45.00
Creamer, clear 20.00
Creamer, green 30.00
Cruet w/original stopper, green 110.00

Goblet, clear 14.50
Goblet, green 35.00
Mustard pot, cov. 22.50
Nappy, green 19.00
Pickle dish, green 22.50
Pitcher, milk, green 75.00
Pitcher, water, clear 42.00
Pitcher, water, green 63.00
Plate, 5" to 7" d., green 22.00
Plate, 9" sq., clear 28.00
Plate, 9", green 37.50
Relish, green, 6" sq. 15.00
Relish, green, 4½ x 8" oval .. 13.50 to 20.00
Sauce dish, green 12.00
Spooner, green 24.00
Sugar bowl, cov., green 50.00
Syrup pitcher w/original top,
   clear 175.00
Syrup pitcher w/original top,
   green 225.00
Table set, green, 4 pcs. ...175.00 to 200.00

Paneled Herringbone Tumbler
Tumbler, green (ILLUS.) 22.50
Water set: pitcher & 6 goblets;
   green, 7 pcs. 275.00
Wine, clear 22.50
Wine, green 48.00

PANELED HOBNAIL
Creamer, blue 65.00
Plate, 7" d., sapphire blue 25.00
Spooner, blue opaque 27.50
Toddy plate, 4½" d., blue.......... 15.00

PANELED JEWEL - See Michigan Pattern

PANELED STAR & BUTTON - See Sedan Pattern

PANELED THISTLE (Inverted Thistle)
Basket w/applied handle, 4¾ x 7",
   2½" h. 35.00
Bowl, cov., 5½" d., 4" h., w/bee in
   base 48.00
Bowl, 6" d., 2½" h., footed 12.50
Bowl, 7" oval, 1¾" h. 15.00
Bowl, 9" d., deep, w/bee 29.00
Bowl, 10" d., flattened rim 27.50

Bread plate 40.00
Butter dish, cov., w/bee 50.00
Cake stand 38.00
Cake stand, w/bee 60.00
Candy dish, cov., footed, 5" sq.,
   6¼" h. 30.00
Celery tray 13.50
Celery vase 45.00
Champagne, flared, w/bee 37.50
Compote, open, 5" d., high stand . . . 25.00
Compote, open, 7½" d., 7" h. 35.00
Compote, open, 9" d., 6½" h. 35.00
Cordial 18.00
Creamer 28.00
Cruet w/stopper 50.00
Goblet 36.00
Honey dish, cov., square 50.00
Pitcher, milk 31.00
Pitcher, water, w/bee 68.00
Plate, 7" sq., w/bee 20.00
Plate, 9½" d. 36.00
Punch cup 16.00
Relish, 4 x 8½" 16.50
Relish, w/bee, 4 x 9½" 24.00
Rose bowl, extra large 50.00
Salt dip, master size 12.50
Sauce dish, flat or footed 16.00
Spooner, handled 18.50
Sugar bowl, cov. 30.00
Toothpick holder 29.00
Tumbler, ruby-stained 45.00
Vase, 8" h., trumpet-shaped 35.00
Vase, 9¼" h., fan-shaped 25.00
Wine 26.50

PANELED ZIPPER - See Iowa Pattern

PARROT (Owl in Fan)
Goblet 31.00
Pitcher, water 75.00
Spooner 25.00
Wine 50.00

PAVONIA (Pineapple Stem)

Pavonia Finger Bowl

Butter dish, cov., clear 78.00
Butter dish, cov., ruby-stained 110.00
Cake stand, 10" d. 44.00
Celery vase, engraved 42.50
Celery vase, plain 38.00
Compote, cov., 6" d., high stand . . . 60.00
Compote, open, 7" d. 48.00

Creamer, engraved 42.00
Creamer, plain 40.00
Creamer, ruby-stained 62.50
Cup plate 28.00
Finger bowl, 7" d. (ILLUS.) 36.00
Goblet 29.00
Mug, applied handle, clear 15.00
Mug, ruby-stained, souvenir 28.00
Pitcher, water, tall tankard, clear . . . 55.00
Pitcher, water, tall tankard, ruby-
   stained 95.00
Salt dip, master size 18.00
Sauce dish, flat or footed, each 10.00
Spooner, clear 32.00
Spooner, ruby-stained 45.00
Sugar bowl, cov., clear 55.00
Sugar bowl, cov., ruby-stained 75.00
Table set, ruby-stained,
   4 pcs. . . . . 250.00 to 300.00
Tray, water 60.00
Tumbler, clear 32.50
Tumbler, ruby-stained 42.50
Water set: tankard pitcher & 4 tum-
   blers; clear, 5 pcs. 185.00
Water set: tankard pitcher & 6 tum-
   blers; ruby-stained, 7 pcs. 350.00
Wine, clear 25.00
Wine, ruby-stained 29.00

PEACOCK FEATHER (Georgia)
Bonbon dish, footed 25.00
Bowl, 8" d. 30.00
Butter dish, cov. 45.00
Cake stand, 8½" d., 5" h. 31.00
Cake stand, 10" d. 50.00
Celery tray, 11¾" l. 35.00
Compote, open, 6½" d., high
   stand 25.00
Compote, open, 6¾" d., low
   stand 18.50
Compote, open, 8" d., high stand . . . 42.50
Compote, open, 10" d., low stand . . 27.00
Creamer 29.00
Cruet w/original stopper 42.00
Decanter w/original stopper 70.00
Dish, tricornered 24.00
Goblet 25.00
Lamp, kerosene-type, low hand-type
   w/handle, blue, 5¼" h. 135.00
Lamp, kerosene-type, low hand-type
   w/handle, clear, 5½" h. 55.00
Lamp, kerosene-type, 7" h. 80.00
Lamp, kerosene-type, table model
   w/handle, blue, 9" h. 220.00
Lamp, kerosene-type, table model
   w/handle, clear, 9" h. 85.00
Lamp, kerosene-type, table model,
   amber, 10" h. 275.00
Lamp, kerosene-type, table model,
   amber, 12" h. 325.00
Mug 20.00
Pitcher, water 54.00
Relish, 8" oval 14.00

Salt & pepper shakers w/original
tops, pr.................... 50.00
Salt & pepper shakers w/glass tray,
set...................... 65.00
Sauce dish................. 8.50
Spooner................... 38.00
Sugar bowl, cov............ 42.00
Table set, creamer, cov. sugar bowl
& cov. butter dish, 3 pcs. 125.00
Tumbler.................. 35.00
Water set, pitcher & 6 tumblers,
7 pcs................. 250.00 to 275.00

PENNSYLVANIA, EARLY - See Hand Pattern

PENNSYLVANIA, LATE - See Balder Pattern

PETAL & LOOP
Compote, open, 9" d., 6" h., flint ... 62.00

PICKET

Picket Sauce Dish

Bread tray, 8 x 13".............. 67.50
Butter dish, cov. 60.00
Celery vase.................... 55.00
Compote, cov., 8" d., low stand 125.00
Compote, open, 7" sq., 7" h........ 30.00
Compote, open, 8" sq., 8" h. 55.00
Creamer 45.00
Goblet 40.00
Lamp, kerosene-type, amber-
stained...................... 195.00
Pitcher, water 75.00
Salt dip, master size.............. 32.50
Sauce dish (ILLUS.) .... 8.00 to 12.50
Spooner..................... 30.00
Sugar bowl, cov. 55.00
Toothpick holder 30.00
Wine....................... 50.00

PILLAR
Ale glass, 6½" h................ 42.50
Champagne, flint, 6" h........... 60.00
Claret...................... 55.00
Compote, open, 8" d............. 55.00
Creamer 70.00
Decanter w/bar lip, pt. 52.50
Goblet .... 40.00 to 50.00
Wine....................... 45.00

PILLAR & BULL'S EYE
Decanter w/bar lip, 10" h. 80.00
Goblet .... 45.00 to 70.00
Pitcher, water, applied handle 325.00
Tumbler 65.00
Wine.................... 50.00 to 65.00

PILLAR VARIANT - See Hercules Pillar Pattern

PILLOW & SUNBURST
Creamer 20.00
Creamer, cov., individual size 15.00
Creamer & sugar bowl, pr......... 32.50
Plate, 10¼" d................... 30.00
Spooner..................... 30.00
Toothpick holder, clear w/gold
trim....................... 25.00

PILLOW ENCIRCLED
(Called Ruby Rosette when ruby-stained)

Berry set: master bowl & 3 sauce
dishes; Ruby Rosette, 4 pcs....... 125.00
Bowl, 7" d., 3" h., Ruby Rosette 27.00
Bowl, 8" d., clear 28.00
Bowl, 8" d., Ruby Rosette 51.00
Butter dish, cov., clear 65.00
Butter dish, cov., Ruby Rosette 65.00
Celery vase, clear 35.00
Celery vase, Ruby Rosette 50.00
Condiment set: 5½ x 9½" tray,
cruet w/original stopper, salt &
pepper shakers w/original tops;
Ruby Rosette, 4 pcs............. 210.00
Creamer, clear.................. 30.00
Creamer, Ruby Rosette 37.50
Creamer & cov. sugar bowl, pr. 75.00
Cruet w/original stopper, enameled
floral decor................... 25.00
Cruet w/original stopper, Ruby
Rosette...................... 135.00
Honey dish, cov., two-handled,
oval........................ 10.00
Lamp, kerosene, w/stem, clear,
10¼" h...................... 36.50
Lamp, kerosene, finger-type, sap-
phire blue.................... 195.00
Pitcher, milk, Ruby Rosette........ 85.00
Pitcher, water, tankard, clear 42.00
Pitcher, water, tankard, Ruby
Rosette...................... 108.00
Salt & pepper shakers w/original
tops, pr..................... 65.00
Sauce dish, footed, clear.......... 13.50
Sauce dish, footed, Ruby Rosette ... 20.00
Spooner, clear .... 25.00 to 30.00
Spooner, Ruby Rosette 62.00
Sugar bowl, cov., clear 32.50
Sugar bowl, cov., Ruby Rosette 41.00
Table set: cov. butter dish, sugar
bowl & spooner; Ruby Rosette,
3 pcs....................... 285.00
Tumbler, clear 25.00
Tumbler, Ruby Rosette 39.00
Water set: pitcher & 5 tumblers;
clear, 6 pcs. 120.00
Water set: tankard pitcher & 6 tum-
blers; Ruby Rosette, 7 pcs. 215.00

PINEAPPLE & FAN
Butter dish, cov. 35.00

Celery tray 38.00
Creamer 30.00
Pickle castor in silver plate holder,
 w/tongs 65.00
Salt & pepper shakers, metal tops,
 pr............................... 40.00
Spooner 15.00
Sugar shaker 43.00
Tumbler, green w/gold 25.00
Wine.............................. 12.50

PINEAPPLE STEM - See Pavonia Pattern

PLEAT & PANEL (Darby)
Bowl, 6" sq., flat 13.50
Bowl, 7" d., 4½" h., footed 21.50
Bowl, 8" rectangle, footed 25.00
Box, cov., 5 x 8" 42.50
Bread tray, closed handles,
 8½ x 13" 48.00
Bread tray, pierced handles 36.00
Butter dish, cov., footed 55.00
Cake stand, 8" sq. 31.00
Cake stand, 9" to 10" sq. 59.00
Celery vase, footed 35.00
Compote, cov., 7" sq., 10½" h...... 50.00
Compote, cov., 8" d., 12" h........ 75.00
Compote, open, 7" d., high stand ... 27.50
Creamer 32.00
Cruet w/stopper 46.00
Finger bowl....................... 37.50
Goblet 27.00
Lamp, kerosene, w/stem 110.00
Marmalade jar, cov................. 54.00
Pickle dish....................... 20.00
Pitcher, water 65.00
Plate, 5" sq...................... 22.00
Plate, 6" sq...................... 20.00
Plate, 7" sq., amber 32.50
Plate, 7" sq., amethyst 95.00
Plate, 7" sq., canary yellow 25.00
Plate, 7" sq., clear 19.00
Plate, 8" sq...................... 32.00
Platter w/open handles 62.00
Relish, cov., oblong, handled, on
 tray........................... 45.00
Relish, open, 4½ x 7" 15.00
Relish, open, handled, on tray,
 5 x 8½"....................... 35.00
Salt dip, master size.............. 18.00
Salt shaker w/original top 35.00
Sauce dish, flat, handled........... 14.00
Sauce dish, footed 14.50
Spooner 35.00
Sugar bowl, cov................... 43.50
Sugar bowl, open 20.00
Tray, oblong, handled, 5 x 9½" 45.00
Tray, water, 9¼ x 14" 62.00
Waste bowl....................... 25.00

PLUME
Berry set, 8½" sq. master bowl &
 five 4½" sq. sauce dishes,
 6 pcs........................... 95.00

Bowl, 6" d. 24.00
Bowl, 8" d., shallow 28.00
Bowl, 8½" sq. master berry 35.00
Bowl, 9¼" d. 20.00
Butter dish, cov. 43.00
Cake stand, 9" d., 5¾" h. 47.00
Cake stand, 9" d., 7" h. 50.00
Cake stand, 10¼" d. 55.00
Celery vase 23.50
Compote, cov., 6½" d., 12" h. 95.00
Compote, open, 5½" d., 6½" h..... 36.00

Plume Open Compote
Compote, open, 7" d., 6¾" h.
 (ILLUS.)......................... 37.00
Compote, open, 8" d., 8" h. 40.00
Compote, open, 9" d., 6½" h. 48.00
Creamer, applied handle, clear 30.00
Creamer, ruby-stained 60.00
Goblet, clear 31.00
Goblet, ruby-stained & etched 55.00
Pitcher, water, clear.............. 82.50
Pitcher, water, ruby-stained 140.00
Relish 26.00
Sauce dish, flat or footed, clear 11.00
Sauce dish, ruby-stained 20.00
Spooner, clear 25.00
Spooner, ruby-stained 55.00
Sugar bowl, cov., clear 30.00
Sugar bowl, cov., ruby-stained 90.00
Sugar bowl, open, clear 20.00
Sugar bowl, open, ruby-stained.... 37.50
Syrup pitcher w/original top, ap-
 plied handle 50.00
Tumbler 35.00
Waste bowl....................... 45.00
Water set, pitcher & 6 tumblers,
 7 pcs........................... 165.00

**POINTED THUMBPRINT - See Almond
Thumbprint Pattern**

POLAR BEAR
Bread tray, frosted 175.00
Claret 120.00
Goblet, clear 110.00
Goblet, clear & frosted 100.00

Pitcher, water, frosted ....250.00 to 350.00

Polar Bear Water Tray

Tray, water, clear, 16" l. (ILLUS.) ... 95.00
Tray, water, frosted, 16" l......... 178.00
Tumbler........................ 95.00
Waste bowl, clear................ 87.50
Waste bowl, frosted.............. 110.00

POPCORN
Butter dish, cov. 49.00
Cake stand, 11" d. 73.00
Celery tray 17.50
Celery vase, 6½" h............... 40.00
Cheese dish, cov., 8 x 11" 185.00
Creamer w/raised ears 47.50
Creamer & cov. sugar bowl, pr. 110.00
Goblet w/raised ears 42.50
Goblet 30.00
Pickle dish, oval 12.50
Pitcher, milk.................... 75.00
Pitcher, water 80.00
Spooner w/raised ears 40.00
Spooner 35.00
Sugar bowl, cov. 47.50
Wine w/raised ears 58.00
Wine........................... 31.00

PORTLAND

Portland Goblet

Basket w/high handle 125.00
Bowl, 9" d. 25.00

Butter dish, cov. 48.00
Cake stand, 10½" 45.00
Candlestick 50.00
Celery tray 18.00
Celery vase 42.50
Compote, cov., 6½" d., high
    stand 115.00
Compote, open, 7½" d., 5½" h..... 48.00
Creamer 20.00
Creamer, individual size 14.00
Creamer & open sugar bowl, oval,
    pr............................ 49.00
Cruet w/original stopper........... 40.00
Dresser jar, cov., 5" d. 22.50
Goblet (ILLUS.)................... 28.00
Lamp, kerosene, 9" h. 65.00
Pitcher, water 52.50
Pitcher, water, miniature 20.00
Punch bowl, 13 5/8" d., 8½" h...... 150.00
Punch cup 21.50
Relish, boat-shaped, 9" l. 12.50
Relish, boat-shaped, 12" l. 18.50
Salt shaker w/original top 16.00
Sauce dish, 4½" d................ 7.50
Spooner 30.00
Sugar bowl, cov. 35.00
Syrup pitcher w/original top 125.00
Toothpick holder 23.00
Tumbler 18.00
Vase, 6" h., scalloped rim 17.00
Vase, 9" h. 30.00
Vase, bud-type................... 25.00
Water set, pitcher & 6 tumblers,
    7 pcs. ....120.00 to 150.00
Wine........................... 26.00

PORTLAND MAIDEN BLUSH (Banded Portland with Color)
Bowl, 3½ x 5½" oval............. 35.00
Butter dish, cov. 165.00
Celery tray, 10" oval 65.00
Celery vase..................... 67.50
Creamer 75.00
Creamer, breakfast size 26.00
Finger bowl, 4½" d., 2" h......... 28.00
Goblet 66.00
Marmalade jar w/silver plate cover,
    frame & spoon 95.00
Perfume bottle w/original stopper .. 85.00
Pin tray, souvenir 12.50
Pitcher, tankard, 11" h........... 167.50
Pitcher, water, child's 32.50
Powder jar, cov. 85.00
Punch cup ....18.00 to 25.00
Relish, 4 x 6½" 25.00
Relish, boat-shaped, 4¼ x 8¾".... 36.00
Salt shaker w/original top 39.00
Sauce dish, boat-shaped, 4¾" l. ... 25.00
Sauce dish, 4½" d................ 30.00
Sugar bowl, cov., large 115.00
Sugar shaker w/original top 120.00
Table set, 4 pcs. 285.00
Toothpick holder 50.00
Tumbler........................ 27.00

Vase, 4" h. 25.00
Vase, 6" h. 27.50
Wine 55.00

**PORTLAND WITH DIAMOND POINT BAND -
See Banded Portland Pattern**

POST (Square Panes)
Bowl, cov., 6¾" d., footed 45.00
Bowl, 8" sq. 25.00
Butter dish, cov. 42.50
Cake stand, 9½" d. 55.00
Celery vase 42.50
Compote, cov., 5" sq., 10" h. 68.00
Creamer 35.00
Goblet 40.00
Lamp, kerosene, 7½" h. 120.00
Lamp, kerosene, 8½" h. 88.00
Lamp, kerosene, 11" h. 95.00
Pitcher, water 75.00
Relish, 4¾ x 7¼" 8.00
Salt dip, master size 7.00
Spooner 26.00
Sugar bowl, cov. 42.00
Table set, cov. sugar bowl, creamer
  & spooner, 3 pcs. 125.00

POTTED PLANT - See Flower Pot Pattern

POWDER & SHOT
Butter dish, cov. 80.00
Compote, open, 7 7/8" d., low
  stand 55.00
Creamer, applied handle, flint 95.00
Egg cup, flint 46.00
Goblet, flint 60.00
Goblet, buttermilk 37.50
Salt dip, master size 42.00
Sauce dish 20.00
Spooner 42.00
Sugar bowl, cov. 85.00
Sugar bowl, open 50.00
Table set, 4 pcs. 350.00

PRAYER RUG - See Horseshoe Pattern

PRESSED LEAF
Bowl, 7" oval 40.00
Butter dish, cov. 60.00
Champagne 21.50
Compote, cov., acorn finial, low
  stand 47.50
Compote, cov., acorn finial, high
  stand 65.00
Cordial 20.00
Creamer, applied handle 35.00
Goblet 25.00
Goblet, buttermilk 25.00
Pitcher, water, applied handle 84.50
Relish, 5 x 7" 12.50
Salt dip, master size 15.00
Sauce dish 9.00
Spooner 22.00
Sugar bowl, cov. 40.00
Wine 33.00

PRIMROSE
Bowl, 8" d., flat 25.00
Bread plate 30.00
Butter dish, cov. 40.00
Cake plate, two-handled, amber,
  9" d. 27.00
Cake plate, two-handled, clear,
  9" d. 15.00
Cake stand, blue, 10" d. 47.00
Card tray, amber w/wire frame,
  4½" d. 32.00
Celery vase 18.50
Compote, cov., 5" d., milk white . . . 28.00
Compote, open, low stand, large . . . 25.00
Creamer 30.00
Goblet 30.00
Pickle dish, amber 17.50
Pickle dish, clear 13.00
Pitcher, milk, amber 65.00
Pitcher, milk, blue 65.00
Pitcher, milk, clear 42.00
Pitcher, water, amber 55.00
Pitcher, water, clear 43.00
Plate, 4½" d., amber or blue 11.00
Plate, 4½" d., clear 13.00
Plate, 6" d., clear 13.00
Plate, 7" d., amber 16.00
Plate, 7" d., blue 18.00
Platter, 8 x 12", amber 22.50
Relish, amber, 5 x 9¼" 18.00
Relish, blue 22.00
Relish, clear 12.50
Sauce dish, flat, blue 9.00
Sauce dish, flat or footed, clear 10.00
Spooner 21.00
Sugar bowl, cov. 42.50
Tray, water, 11" d. 25.00
Wine, amber 37.00
Wine, clear 20.00
Wine, opaque turquoise 60.00

PRINCESS FEATHER (Rochelle)

Princess Feather Compote

Bowl, cov., 7½" d. 35.00
Bowl, 5 x 7¼" oval 25.00
Butter dish, cov. 50.00
Celery vase 41.50
Compote, cov., 8" d., low
  stand . . . . 100.00 to 125.00
Compote, open, 8" d., low stand
  (ILLUS.) 32.50

Creamer 45.00
Egg cup, clear 28.50
Egg cup, opalescent, flint, 3¾" h. .. 180.00
Goblet 32.00
Goblet, buttermilk 25.00
Honey dish 12.50
Lamp, kerosene, 12" h. 75.00
Pitcher, water, bulbous, applied
   handle, flint 112.00
Plate, 6" d., clear, non-flint 32.00
Plate, 7" d., amber, flint 165.00
Plate, 7" d., clear, non-flint 28.00
Plate, 9" d., clear, non-flint 32.50
Relish, 5 x 7" oval 17.50
Salt dip, master size 29.00
Sauce dish, blue, flint 145.00
Sauce dish, clear, non-flint 10.00
Spooner, clear, non-flint 25.00
Spooner, fiery opalescent milk
   white, flint, 5 1/8" h. 120.00
Sugar bowl, cov., clear, non-flint ... 55.00
Sugar bowl, cov., milk white, flint .. 140.00

PRISCILLA (Alexis)

Priscilla Sugar Bowl

Banana stand 75.00
Bowl, 7" d., flat 28.00
Bowl, 8" d., 3½" h., straight sides,
   flat 38.00
Bowl, 8" d., 3½" h., w/pattern on
   base 45.00
Bowl, 8¾" d., 3 3/8" h., flared
   sides 55.00
Bowl, 9" d., shallow 38.00
Bowl, 9¼" d., 5" h. 37.50
Bowl, 9 7/8" d., 2" h. 38.00
Bowl, 10¾" d., shallow 31.00
Butter dish, cov. ....100.00 to 125.00
Cake stand, 9" to 10" d., high
   stand 60.00
Compote, cov., jelly 50.00
Compote, cov., 6" d., 10" h...55.00 to 65.00
Compote, cov., 8" d. 100.00
Compote, cov., 12" d. 145.00
Compote, open, 4¾" d., 4 7/8" h.,
   flared sides 35.00
Compote, open, 6 7/8" d., 7" h. 45.00
Compote, open, 8" d., 8" h. 55.00

Compote, open, 8¾" d., 9¾" h.,
   flared rim 55.00
Compote, open, 9" d., 7" h. 33.00
Cracker jar, cov. 175.00
Creamer 38.00
Creamer, individual size 28.00
Cruet w/original stopper 61.00
Doughnut stand, 4¼ x 5¾" 47.50
Egg cup 17.00
Goblet 40.00
Mug 15.00
Mustard jar, open 25.00
Nappy, handled 28.00
Pitcher, water 135.00
Plate, 10½" d., turned-up rim 26.00
Plate, 10½" d., turned-up rim 26.00
Punch cup 15.00
Relish 23.00
Rose bowl, 3¾" h. 35.00
Salt shaker w/original top 35.00
Sauce dish, flat, 4½" to 5" d. 12.50
Spooner 28.00
Sugar bowl, cov. (ILLUS.) 45.00
Sugar bowl, cov., individual size 32.50
Sugar bowl, open, individual size ... 10.00
Syrup pitcher w/original pewter
   top 135.00
Table set, 4 pcs. ....200.00 to 225.00
Toothpick holder 36.00
Tumbler 25.00
Wine 28.00

PRISM

Bowl, 7" d., flat 8.00
Celery vase 30.00
Champagne 45.00
Claret, 6" h. 22.00
Compote, open, 7" d., 5" h. 65.00
Compote, open, 7½" triangle,
   4½" h. 45.00
Creamer 55.00
Egg cup 25.00
Egg cup, double 27.00
Goblet 32.00
Pitcher, water 100.00
Plate, 7½" d. 25.00
Sauce dish 16.00
Spooner 35.00
Sugar bowl, open 18.00
Tumbler, buttermilk 35.00
Whiskey taster, 2¼" h. 125.00
Wine 38.00

PRISM WITH DIAMOND POINT

Cruet w/original stopper 87.50
Goblet 45.00
Salt dip, master size 17.50
Tumbler, bar 65.00

PSYCHE & CUPID

Bread tray 35.00
Butter dish, cov. 65.00
Celery vase 32.00
Compote, open, 5" d., 6¾" h. 45.00

Creamer	52.00
Goblet	37.50
Pitcher, water	78.00
Plate, 7" d., milk white	18.00
Relish, 6½ x 9½"	32.50
Sauce dish, footed	11.50
Spooner	38.00
Sugar bowl, cov.	42.50
Sugar bowl, open, footed, 6½" h.	40.00
Table set, spooner, cov. sugar bowl & creamer, 3 pcs.	185.00

PYGMY - See Torpedo Pattern

RED BLOCK

Bowl, berry or fruit, 8" d.	65.00
Butter dish, cov.	72.00
Celery vase, 6½" h.	90.00
Creamer, large	58.00
Creamer, small, applied handle	35.00
Creamer & cov. sugar bowl, individual size, pr.	135.00
Cruet w/original stopper	135.00
Decanter, whiskey, w/original stopper, 12" h.	164.00
Dish, rectangular, 5 x 7½"	55.00
Goblet	41.00
Mug	27.00
Pansy bowl, 2¾" h.	65.00
Pitcher, 8" h., bulbous	120.00
Pitcher, tankard, 9 5/8" h.	120.00
Rose bowl	55.00
Salt dip, individual size, two-handled	48.00
Salt shaker w/original top	49.00
Sauce dish, 4½"	24.00
Spooner	40.00
Sugar bowl, cov.	72.50
Table set, 4 pcs.	200.00 to 250.00
Tumbler	30.00
Wine	35.00

REVERSE TORPEDO (Diamond & Bull's Eye Band)

Reverse Torpedo Bowl

Banana stand	115.00
Basket	65.00
Bowl, cov., 9" d.	75.00
Bowl, 5¾" d., piecrust rim	35.00
Bowl, 6¾" d.	35.00
Bowl, 7½" d., piecrust rim (ILLUS.)	70.00
Bowl, 9" d., piecrust rim	65.00
Bowl, 10¼" d., piecrust rim	70.00
Butter dish, cov.	80.00

Cake stand	75.00
Celery vase	70.00
Compote, cov., jelly	39.00
Compote, cov., 6" d., high stand	95.00
Compote, cov., 7" d., low stand	98.00
Compote, open, 5" d., flared rim	50.00
Compote, open, 7" d., 8" h.	55.00
Compote, open, 8" d., piecrust rim	62.50
Compote, open, 9" d., 7" h., turned-over piecrust rim	82.00
Compote, open, 10" d., 6½" h.	70.00
Compote, open, 8½ x 10" oval, 9¼" h., ruffled rim	122.00
Creamer	66.00
Dish, ruffled, 11¼" d., 2¾" h.	85.00
Goblet	85.00
Goblet, w/engraved flower	110.00
Honey dish, cov., square	145.00
Pitcher, water	165.00
Salt shaker w/original top	45.00
Sauce dish	25.00
Spooner	55.00
Sugar bowl, cov.	75.00
Tumbler	75.00

RIBBED FORGET-ME-NOT

Creamer	28.00
Creamer, individual size	25.00
Mug	20.00

RIBBED GRAPE

Compote, open, 7½" d.	42.00
Creamer, applied handle	130.00
Goblet	38.00
Goblet, buttermilk	50.00
Plate, 6" d.	34.00
Sauce dish, 4" d.	20.00
Spooner	37.00
Sugar bowl, cov.	95.00

RIBBED IVY

Berry set, master bowl & 4 sauce dishes, 5 pcs.	105.00
Bitters bottle w/original tulip-shaped stopper	175.00
Bowl, 8" d., 2" h.	67.50
Butter dish, cov.	95.00
Celery	225.00
Champagne	145.00
Compote, cov., 6" d., high stand	250.00
Compote, open, 7½" d., high stand, rope edge rim	100.00
Compote, open, 8" d., 5" h.	80.00
Compote, open, 8½" d., 7½" h., high stand	95.00
Creamer, applied handle	110.00
Decanter w/original tulip-shaped stopper, ½ pt.	120.00
Egg cup	34.00
Goblet	42.00
Salt dip, cov., master size	115.00
Salt dip, open, master size, beaded rim	40.00
Sauce dish	12.00

Spooner 40.00
Sugar bowl, cov. 110.00
Sweetmeat, cov. 325.00
Tumbler, bar ....105.00 to 125.00
Tumbler, water 80.00
Tumbler, whiskey 82.00
Tumbler, whiskey, handled........ 150.00
Wine............................ 96.00

RIBBED PALM

Ribbed Palm Egg Cup

Bowl, 8" d., footed 65.00
Butter dish, cov. 88.00
Celery vase 85.00
Champagne....................... 125.00
Compote, open, 7¼" d., 4¼" h..... 45.00
Creamer ....125.00 to 150.00
Egg cup (ILLUS.) 28.00
Goblet 31.00
Goblet, buttermilk 37.50
Honey dish 12.50
Pitcher, water, 9" h., applied
  handle 295.00
Plate, 6" d. 60.00
Salt dip, master size.............. 35.00
Salt dip, master size, footed 50.00
Sauce dish....................... 14.00
Spillholder....................... 45.00
Spooner 40.00
Sugar bowl, cov. 68.00
Sugar bowl, open 27.50
Tumbler, bar..................... 110.00
Wine............................ 46.00

RIBBON (Early Ribbon)

Bowl, 5 x 9" 60.00
Bread tray 40.00
Butter dish, cov. 69.00
Cake stand, 8½" d. 50.00
Celery vase...................... 42.00
Cheese dish, cov. 145.00
Compote, cov., 8" d. (ILLUS.) 88.00
Compote, open, 7" d., low stand ... 30.00
Compote, open, 8" d., 8" h., frosted
  dolphin stem on dome base 275.00
Compote, open, 5½ x 8" rectangu-
  lar bowl, 7" h., frosted dolphin
  stem on dome base 160.00
Compote, open, 8½" d., 4½" h..... 50.00

Ribbon Covered Compote

Compote, open, 10½" d., frosted
  dolphin stem on dome base 395.00
Creamer 34.00
Goblet 33.00
Marmalade jar, cov............... 45.00
Pitcher, water 90.00
Plate, 7" d....................... 35.00
Platter, 9 x 13" 62.50
Spooner 23.00
Sugar bowl, cov., 4¼" d., 7¾" h. .. 72.00
Sugar bowl, open 40.00
Table set, 4 pcs. 225.00
Tray, water, 15" 115.00
Wine............................ 110.00

RIBBON CANDY (Bryce or Double Loop)

Bowl, cov., 6¼" d., footed 35.00
Bowl, 8" d., flat................. 20.00
Butter dish, cov., flat 48.00
Butter dish, cov., footed 55.00
Cake stand, child's, 6½" d., 3" h.... 35.50
Cake stand, 8" to 10½" d. 35.00
Celery vase...................... 28.00
Compote, cov., 5" d., 8½" h........ 47.50
Compote, open, jelly 22.50
Compote, open, 8" d.............. 30.00
Creamer 20.00
Doughnut stand 32.00
Goblet 30.00
Pitcher, milk..................... 48.50
Pitcher, water 70.00
Plate, 8½" d..................... 25.00
Plate, 9½" d..................... 30.00
Plate, 10½" d.................... 32.00
Plate, 12" d...................... 45.00
Relish, 8½" l..................... 14.00
Salt shaker w/original top 25.00
Sauce dish, 3½" d., flat 10.00
Sauce dish, 4" d., footed.......... 12.00
Spooner 23.00
Sugar bowl, cov. 40.00
Syrup pitcher w/original top 85.00
Table set, 4 pcs. ....125.00 to 150.00
Wine............................ 50.00

RISING SUN

Berry set, master bowl & 6 sauce
  dishes, 7 pcs. 120.00

Bowl, 4½" d., handled, purple
suns 9.00
Bowl, 6½" d., pink suns 8.00
Bowl, master berry, pink suns 30.00
Butter dish, cov., clear 68.00
Butter dish, cov., green suns 85.00
Celery vase, gold suns............. 18.00
Celery vase, pink suns 32.50
Compote, open, jelly, purple suns .. 22.00
Compote, open, 7" d., 6" h. 18.00
Creamer 22.00
Cruet w/stopper 28.00
Goblet, clear 24.00
Goblet, gold suns 17.50
Goblet, green suns 25.00
Goblet, pink suns 20.00
Goblet, purple suns 22.50
Pitcher, water, clear............. 65.00
Pitcher, water, gold suns 38.00
Punch cup, green suns 20.00
Spooner 40.00
Sugar bowl, open, scalloped rim,
green suns 22.00
Toothpick holder, three-handled,
clear 18.00
Toothpick holder, three-handled,
gold suns...................... 25.00
Toothpick holder, three-handled,
green suns 32.50
Toothpick holder, three-handled,
purple suns.................... 25.00
Tumbler, clear 15.00
Tumbler, gold suns 13.50
Tumbler, green suns.............. 25.00
Tumbler, pink suns 22.00
Tumbler, whiskey 8.50
Vase, 6½" h., 4½" d., gold suns ... 25.00
Vase, 6½" h., 4½" d., red suns 18.00
Water set: pitcher & 4 tumblers;
clear, 5 pcs. 120.00
Water set: pitcher & 4 tumblers;
green suns, 5 pcs. ......140.00 to 195.00
Wine, clear 15.00
Wine, green suns 30.00
Wine, pink suns.................. 30.00
Wine, purple suns 20.00

ROCHELLE - See Princess Feather Pattern

ROMAN KEY - See Frosted Roman Key Pattern

ROMAN ROSETTE (Early)
Honey dish, purple, 4 1/8" d., flint.. 200.00
Plate, 6" d., fiery opalescent, flint .. 140.00
Plate, 6" d., deep amethyst, flint ... 400.00
Toddy plate, 5½" d., purple, flint ... 325.00

ROMAN ROSETTE
Berry set, 8" d. master bowl & six
5" d. sauce dishes, 7 pcs. 90.00
Bowl, 6" d. 16.00
Bowl, 7" d. 22.50
Bowl, 8" d. 24.00

Bowl, 6¼ x 9½" oval.............. 22.00
Bread platter, 9 x 11" 35.00
Butter dish, cov., clear 47.00
Butter dish, cov., ruby-stained 105.00
Cake stand, 9" to 10" d. .....45.00 to 55.00
Celery vase, clear 20.00
Celery vase, ruby-stained 95.00
Compote, cov., 5" d. 58.00
Compote, cov., 6" d., 10" h......... 70.00
Compote, open, jelly, 5" d. 26.50
Cordial.......................... 47.50
Creamer 30.00
Goblet 36.00
Honey dish, cov. ....42.50 to 60.00
Marmalade dish, footed, clear.... 38.00
Marmalade dish, footed, ruby-
stained......................... 45.00
Mug, 3" h........................ 14.00
Pitcher, milk 40.00
Pitcher, water 70.00
Plate, 7" d....................... 18.00
Relish, 3½ x 8½" 10.00
Relish, 6 x 9" 20.00
Salt & pepper shakers w/original
tops, clear, pr.................. 32.00
Salt & pepper shakers w/original
tops on original glass stand
w/handle, set................... 42.00
Sauce dish....................... 10.00
Spooner, clear 21.00
Sugar bowl, cov. 40.00
Toddy plate, 5½" d............... 35.00
Tumbler, clear 30.00
Tumbler, ruby-stained 38.50
Tumbler, lemonade................ 16.00
Wine............................ 35.00

ROSE IN SNOW

Rose in Snow Spooner

Berry set, 8¼" sq. footed bowl & 4
footed sauce dishes, 5 pcs........ 75.00
Bitters bottle w/original stopper 135.00
Bowl, 7" d., footed 32.00
Bowl, 7¼ x 10" oval.............. 47.00
Butter dish, cov., round 47.00
Butter dish, cov., square 55.00
Cake plate, handled, amber,
10" d........................... 45.00
Cake plate, handled, clear, 10" d. ... 25.00

Cake stand, 9" d. 70.00
Cologne bottle w/original stopper .. 90.00
Compote, cov., 6" d., 8" h. 70.00
Compote, cov., 7" d., 8" h. 85.00
Compote, cov., 8" d., 10" h. 80.00
Compote, open, 5" d., 5½" h. 55.00
Compote, open, 5¾" d., vaseline ... 55.00
Compote, open, 6" d., 5" h., blue... 70.00
Compote, open, 6" d., low stand ... 30.00
Compote, open, 7" d., low stand ... 40.00
Compote, open, 8¼" d., 7" h. 45.00
Creamer, round, amber 45.00
Creamer, round, blue 55.00
Creamer, round, clear 32.50
Creamer, square, clear 39.00
Creamer, square, vaseline 60.00
Creamer & open sugar bowl, round,
   pr. 90.00
Creamer & open sugar bowl,
   square, pr. 95.00
Goblet, amber 41.50
Goblet, clear 30.00
Goblet, vaseline 65.00
Mug, 3½" h. 45.00
Mug, applied handle, "In Fond
   Remembrance," clear 29.00
Mug, applied handle, "In Fond
   Remembrance," yellow 45.00
Pitcher, water, applied handle,
   amber 112.50
Pitcher, water, applied handle,
   blue 225.00
Pitcher, water, applied handle,
   clear 80.00
Plate, 5" d. 30.00
Plate, 7" d. 30.00
Plate, 8" d., amber 40.00
Plate, 8" d., clear 38.00
Powder jar, cov. 21.00
Relish, 5½ x 8" oval 16.00
Relish, 6¼ x 9¼" 19.00
Relish, double 88.00
Sauce dish, flat or footed 15.00
Spooner, round (ILLUS.) 25.00
Spooner, square 35.00
Sugar bowl, cov., round 37.50
Sugar bowl, cov., square 47.50
Sugar bowl, open, square 20.00
Table set, square, 4 pcs. 178.00
Tumbler 38.00
Wine 20.00

ROSE SPRIG

Bowl, 9" d., footed 23.00
Bowl, 6 x 9" rectangle, vaseline 27.50
Bowl, 8¼ x 9" oval, footed 32.00
Bread tray, two-handled, blue 35.00
Bread tray, two-handled, yellow 40.00
Cake stand, amber, 9" octagon,
   6½" h. 60.00
Cake stand, blue, 9" octagon,
   6½" h. 65.00
Cake stand, clear, 9" octagon,
   6½" h. 62.00

Cake stand, yellow, 9" octagon,
   6½" h. 85.00
Cake stand, amber, 10" square 80.00
Celery vase, amber 45.00
Celery vase, clear 36.50
Compote, cov., high stand, large ... 75.00
Compote, open, 7" oval, amber 36.00
Compote, open, 7" d., 5" h.,
   yellow 37.00
Compote, open, 9" d., low stand ... 19.00
Compote, open, 9" d., high stand,
   amber 37.50
Creamer, yellow 40.00
Goblet, amber 30.00
Goblet, blue 48.00
Goblet, clear 30.00
Pitcher, milk, amber 55.00
Pitcher, milk, clear 45.00
Pitcher, milk, yellow 75.00
Pitcher, water, amber 68.00
Pitcher, water, clear 48.00
Pitcher, water, yellow 70.00
Plate, 6" sq., amber 26.50
Plate, 6" sq., blue 30.00

Rose Sprig Plate

Plate, 6" sq., clear (ILLUS.) 20.00
Relish, handled, 4 x 6" 7.50
Relish, boat-shaped, amber, 8" l. 30.00
Relish, boat-shaped, blue, 8" l. 36.00
Relish, boat-shaped, clear, 8" l. 20.00
Relish, boat-shaped, yellow, 8" l. ... 32.00
Sauce dish, flat, amber 15.00
Sauce dish, flat, clear 12.50
Sauce dish, footed, clear 8.00
Spooner 15.00
Tumbler, amber 30.00
Tumbler, clear 39.00
Tumbler w/applied handle, clear ... 45.00
Wine, blue 50.00
Wine, clear 28.00
Whimsey, sleigh (salt dip), amber,
   4 x 4 x 6" 47.00

ROSETTE

Bowl, 7½" d. 16.00
Bread plate, handled, 11" d. 25.00
Butter dish, cov. 40.00
Cake stand, 8½" to 11" d. 27.00
Celery vase 25.00

Compote, cov., 6" d., 9" h. 70.00
Compote, cov., 11½" h. 50.00
Compote, open, jelly, 4½" d.,
5" h. 16.00
Compote, open, 7¼" d., 6" h. 30.00
Creamer 25.00
Goblet 22.00
Pitcher, milk 42.00
Pitcher, water, tankard 45.00
Plate, 7" d. 20.00
Plate, 9" d., two-handled 21.00
Relish, fish-shaped 12.00
Sauce dish. 8.00
Spooner 32.00
Sugar bowl, cov. 33.00
Tumbler, clear 16.00
Tumbler, ruby-stained 29.00
Wine. 22.50

ROYAL IVY

Royal Ivy Sugar Shaker

Berry set: master bowl & 6 sauce
dishes; clear & frosted, 7 pcs. 200.00
Berry set: master bowl & 8 sauce
dishes; clear & frosted, 9 pcs. 250.00
Bowl, 8" d., craquelle (cranberry &
vaseline spatter) 80.00
Bowl, 8" d., rubina crystal 95.00
Bowl, 8" d., frosted rubina crystal . . 120.00
Bowl, fruit, 9" d., craquelle (cran-
berry & vaseline spatter). 125.00
Bowl, fruit, 9" d., frosted
craquelle 150.00
Bowl, fruit, 9" d., rubina crystal 140.00
Bowl, fruit, 9" d., frosted rubina
crystal 100.00
Butter dish, cov., clear & frosted . . . 175.00
Butter dish, cov., frosted craquelle. . 137.50
Butter dish, cov., frosted rubina
crystal 175.00
Creamer, clear & frosted. 45.00
Creamer, rubina crystal 100.00
Creamer, frosted rubina crystal. 180.00
Cruet w/original stopper, cased
spatter (cranberry & vaseline
w/white lining) 395.00
Cruet w/original stopper, rubina
crystal 285.00
Cruet w/original stopper, frosted ru-
bina crystal. 360.00

Lamp, kerosene, frosted rubina crys-
tal, miniature 85.00
Marmalade jar, w/original silver
plate lid, clear & frosted 100.00
Pickle castor, clear & frosted insert,
complete w/silver plate frame . . . 140.00
Pickle castor, frosted rubina crystal
insert, complete w/silver plate
frame 395.00
Pickle castor, cased spatter (cran-
berry & vaseline w/white lining)
insert, complete w/silver plate
frame & tongs 350.00
Pitcher, water, cased spatter (cran-
berry & vaseline w/white lining). . 285.00
Pitcher, water, clear & frosted. 110.00
Pitcher, water, craquelle (cranberry
& vaseline spatter) 450.00
Pitcher, water, frosted craquelle. . . . 400.00
Pitcher, water, rubina
crystal . . . . 165.00 to 225.00
Pitcher, water, frosted rubina
crystal 275.00
Rose bowl, cased spatter (cranberry
& vaseline w/white lining) 295.00
Rose bowl, rubina crystal . . . . 70.00 to 90.00
Rose bowl, frosted rubina crystal . . . 80.00
Salt shaker w/original top, rubina
crystal 46.00
Salt & pepper shakers w/original
tops, clear & frosted, pr. 69.00
Salt & pepper shakers w/original
tops, rubina crystal, pr. 78.00
Sauce dish, frosted rubina
crystal 32.00
Spooner, cased spatter (cranberry &
vaseline w/white lining) 75.00
Spooner, clear & frosted 38.00
Spooner, frosted rubina crystal 80.00
Sugar bowl, cov., clear & frosted . . . 45.00
Sugar bowl, cov., rubina crystal 128.00
Sugar bowl, cov., frosted rubina
crystal 130.00
Sugar shaker w/original top, cased
spatter (cranberry & vaseline
w/white lining) 185.00
Sugar shaker w/original top, clear &
frosted . . . . 58.00 to 75.00
Sugar shaker w/original top, frosted
craquelle 200.00
Sugar shaker w/original top, rubina
crystal 110.00
Sugar shaker w/original top, frosted
rubina crystal (ILLUS.) 135.00
Syrup pitcher w/original top, cased
spatter (cranberry & vaseline
w/white lining) 490.00
Syrup pitcher w/original top, clear &
frosted 155.00
Syrup pitcher w/original top, rubina
crystal 250.00
Syrup pitcher w/original top, frosted
rubina crystal 450.00
Table set, cased spatter (cranberry

& vaseline w/white lining),
4 pcs. 875.00
Table set, clear & frosted, 4 pcs. ... 265.00
Table set, clear & frosted, 4 pcs. ... 265.00
Table set, craquelle (cranberry &
vaseline spatter), 4 pcs. 850.00
Table set, frosted rubina crystal,
4 pcs. ....625.00 to 650.00
Toothpick holder, craquelle (cran-
berry & vaseline spatter)......... 182.00
Toothpick holder, rubina crystal 85.00
Toothpick holder, frosted rubina
crystal 125.00
Tumbler, whiskey, handled, flint.... 95.00
Tumbler, cased spatter (cranberry &
vaseline w/white lining) 85.00
Tumbler, clear & frosted 25.00
Tumbler, craquelle (cranberry &
vaseline spatter) 76.00
Tumbler, frosted craquelle 125.00
Tumbler, rubina crystal 60.00
Tumbler, frosted rubina crystal 65.00
Water set: pitcher & 4 tumblers;
frosted rubina crystal, 5 pcs. 650.00
Water set: pitcher & 5 tumblers;
cased spatter (cranberry & vase-
line w/white lining), 6 pcs........ 850.00
Water set: pitcher & 6 tumblers; ru-
bina crystal, 7 pcs. ......400.00 to 500.00

ROYAL OAK

Royal Oak Sugar Shaker

Bowl, berry, 7½" d., frosted
crystal 65.00
Butter dish, cov., frosted crystal 55.00
Butter dish, cov., rubina crystal..... 135.00
Butter dish, cov., frosted rubina
crystal 210.00
Creamer, frosted crystal 82.00
Creamer, rubina crystal............ 175.00
Creamer, frosted rubina
crystal ....200.00 to 225.00
Cruet w/original stopper, frosted ru-
bina crystal 310.00
Dresser jar, cov., frosted crystal,
5" w., 5½" h. ....100.00 to 150.00
Pickle castor, frosted rubina crystal
insert, w/silver plate frame &
cover 225.00

Pitcher, 8½" h., frosted crystal 100.00
Pitcher, water, rubina crystal....... 260.00
Pitcher, water, frosted rubina
crystal 312.00
Salt shaker w/original top, rubina
crystal 50.00
Salt shaker w/original top, frosted
rubina crystal 65.00
Salt & pepper shakers w/original
tops, frosted rubina crystal, pr.... 145.00
Sauce dish, frosted crystal 12.50
Sauce dish, rubina crystal 40.00
Spooner, frosted crystal............ 58.00
Spooner, rubina crystal 60.00
Spooner, frosted rubina crystal 95.00
Sugar bowl, cov., frosted crystal 55.00
Sugar bowl, cov., rubina crystal 140.00
Sugar bowl, cov., frosted rubina
crystal 130.00
Sugar bowl, open, frosted rubina
crystal 60.00
Sugar shaker w/original top, frosted
crystal 95.00
Sugar shaker w/original top, rubina
crystal 125.00
Sugar shaker w/original top, frosted
rubina crystal (ILLUS.) 165.00
Table set, frosted rubina crystal,
4 pcs........................... 600.00
Toothpick holder, frosted crystal 52.00
Toothpick holder, rubina crystal 110.00
Toothpick holder, frosted rubina
crystal 125.00
Tumbler, frosted crystal............ 75.00
Tumbler, frosted rubina crystal 80.00
Water set: pitcher & 5 tumblers;
frosted crystal, 6 pcs............. 425.00

RUBY ROSETTE - See Pillow Encircled Pattern

RUBY THUMBPRINT

Ruby Thumbprint Creamer

Berry set, boat-shaped master bowl
& 5 boat-shaped sauce dishes,
6 pcs. 195.00
Berry set, round master bowl & 8
round sauce dishes, 9 pcs. 250.00
Bowl, 8½" d. 45.00

Bowl, master berry or fruit, 10" l.,
  boat-shaped ....100.00 to 125.00
Butter dish, cov. 105.00
Cake stand, 10" d. 125.00
Castor set, 4-bottle, in
  frame.................325.00 to 425.00
Celery vase...................... 75.00
Champagne 35.00
Cheese dish, cov., 7" d. 55.00
Compote, open, jelly, 5¼" h. 58.00
Compote, open, 7" d., plain........ 90.00
Compote, open, 7" d., w/engrav-
  ing 145.00
Compote, open, 8½" d., 7½" h.,
  scalloped rim 230.00
Cordial, plain 28.00
Cordial, w/engraving 40.00
Creamer, plain................... 58.00
Creamer, souvenir, engraved
  w/"Dear Mother" & date (ILLUS.
  previous page)................. 63.00
Creamer, individual size 30.00
Creamer & sugar bowl, individual
  size........................... 85.00
Cup & saucer 53.00
Dish, cov., 8" d., 7" h............. 68.00
Goblet 40.00
Mustard jar, cov.................. 58.00
Mustard jar, cov., engraved "World's
  Fair, 1893"................... 127.50
Olive dish 125.00
Pitcher, milk, 7½" h., bulbous...... 120.00
Pitcher, milk, tankard, 8 3/8" h. 82.00
Pitcher, water, bulbous, large 250.00
Pitcher, water, tankard, 11" h. 132.00
Pitcher, water, tankard, 11" h.,
  w/engraved leaf band 170.00
Plate, 5" d. 22.00
Plate, 7½" d. 22.00
Punch cup 18.00
Salt dip, individual size 145.00
Salt shaker w/original top 28.00
Salt & pepper shakers w/original
  tops, pr....................... 70.00
Salt & pepper shakers w/original
  tops, individual size, pr. 95.00
Sauce dish, boat-shaped 28.00
Sauce dish, round 20.00
Spooner........................ 52.50
Sugar bowl, cov.................. 77.50
Sugar bowl, open 32.50
Table set, 4 pcs. ....250.00 to 350.00
Toothpick holder 30.00
Tumbler........................ 38.00
Water set, bulbous pitcher & 5 tum-
  blers, 6 pcs. 315.00
Water set, tankard pitcher & 7 tum-
  blers, 8 pcs. 395.00
Wine........................... 33.00

SANDWICH LOOP - See Hairpin Pattern

SANDWICH STAR
Butter dish, cov. 195.00

Compote, open, 8½" d., low
  stand 60.00
Compote, open, 12" d., 9½" h.,
  scalloped rim, three dolphin
  base, canary yellow (running
  crack) 3,600.00
Compote, open, 12" d., 9½" h..... 265.00
Decanter w/patented stopper, pt. .. 135.00
Decanter w/bar lip, pt. 70.00
Decanter w/bar lip, qt. 97.00
Decanter w/stopper, qt. 110.00
Lamp, whale oil, six-sided font,
  10½" h. 125.00
Spillholder, clambroth 440.00
Spillholder, clear 50.00
Spillholder, electric blue..........1,200.00

SAWTOOTH

Sawtooth Sugar Bowl

Bitters bottle w/stopper, flint 47.50
Butter dish, cov., flint 78.00
Butter dish, cov., non-flint, clear.... 35.00
Butter dish, cov., non-flint, sapphire
  blue 230.00
Cake stand, non-flint, 7½" d.,
  6" h.......................... 35.00
Cake stand, non-flint, 9½" d.,
  4½" h......................... 75.00
Celery vases, knob stem, flint, pr... 105.00
Celery vase, knob stem, non-flint ... 38.00
Celery vase, stepped pedestal base,
  notched rim, flint 125.00
Champagne, knob stem, flint....... 55.00
Champagne, non-flint............. 32.00
Compote, cov., 7½" d., 11½" h.,
  flint.......................... 85.00
Compote, cov., 8" d., low stand,
  flint.......................... 125.00
Compote, cov., 9¼" d., 4" h., non-
  flint.......................... 48.00
Compote, cov., 9½" d., 14" h.,
  flint.......................... 200.00
Compote, cov., 9½" d., 14" h., non-
  flint.......................... 72.50
Compote, open, 7½" d., 5½" h..... 40.00
Compote, open, 7½" d., 7½" h.,
  flint.......................... 55.00

Compote, open, 8" d., 6" h., non-
flint 36.00
Cordial, non-flint, clear 20.00
Cordial, ruby-stained 35.00
Creamer, applied handle, clear,
flint.......................... 75.00
Creamer, applied handle, cobalt
blue, flint 230.00
Creamer, applied handle, clear,
non-flint...................... 30.00
Creamer, miniature 29.00
Decanter w/acorn stopper, flint,
½ pt. 105.00
Egg cup, flint 43.00
Goblet, knob stem, flint 34.00
Goblet, knob stem, non-flint 20.00
Pitcher, water, applied handle,
clear, flint..................... 115.00
Pitcher, water, applied handle, milk
white, flint 345.00
Salt dip, cov., individual size,
footed, flint................... 35.00
Salt dip, individual size, footed,
flint.......................... 18.00
Salt dip, cov., master size, footed,
flint.......................... 58.00
Salt dip, master size, clear, flint 30.00
Salt dip, master size, clear, non-
flint.......................... 20.00
Salt dip, master size, fiery opales-
cent, flint..................... 150.00
Salt dip, master size, milk white,
non-flint...................... 19.50
Salt shaker w/original top, milk
white, non-flint 19.50
Spillholder, clear, flint 50.00
Spillholder, sapphire blue, jagged
sawtooth rim, 5½" h., flint....... 700.00
Spooner, clear, non-flint 26.00
Spooner, cobalt blue, non-flint 85.00
Spooner, milk white, non-flint 48.00
Sugar bowl, cov., flint (ILLUS.)...... 75.00
Sugar bowl, cov., non-flint 28.50
Sugar bowl, open, flint 39.00
Tumbler, bar, flint, 4½" h......... 58.00
Tumbler, bar, non-flint............ 35.00
Tumbler, flat, flint................ 36.00
Tumbler, footed, flint 65.00
Tumble-up (carafe w/tumbler lid) ... 175.00
Vase, 9 7/8" h. 25.00
Wine, flint 35.00
Wine, non-flint................... 25.00

SAWTOOTH BAND - See Amazon Pattern

SCALLOPED TAPE - See Jewel Band Pattern

SEDAN (Paneled Star & Button)
Butter dish, cov. 38.00
Compote, open, high stand 20.00
Creamer 32.00
Goblet 20.00
Mug, miniature 12.50
Pitcher, water 45.00

Salt dip, master size.............. 12.50
Sauce dish, flat, 4½" d. 5.50
Spooner........................ 25.00
Sugar bowl, cov. 45.00
Wine........................... 16.00

SENECA LOOP - See Loop Pattern

SHELL & JEWEL (Victor)

Shell & Jewel Tumbler

Berry set, 8" d. bowl & 8 sauce dish-
es, 9 pcs....................... 55.00
Bowl, 8" d. 30.00
Bowl, 10" d. 25.00
Butter dish, cov. 60.00
Cake stand, 10" d., 5" h. 40.00
Compote, cov., 8½" d., high
stand 75.00
Compote, open, 7" d., 7½" h. 40.00
Creamer 35.00
Pitcher, milk, blue 75.00
Pitcher, milk, clear 35.00
Pitcher, water, blue or green....... 82.00
Pitcher, water, clear.............. 39.00
Relish, oblong 18.00
Sauce dish, amber 15.00
Sauce dish, clear................. 8.00
Spooner 22.00
Sugar bowl, cov. 42.50
Tumbler, amber.................. 32.00
Tumbler, blue.................... 38.00
Tumbler, clear (ILLUS.)............ 18.00
Tumbler, green 36.00
Water set: pitcher & 6 tumblers; am-
ber, 7 pcs...................... 260.00
Water set: pitcher & 6 tumblers;
blue, 7 pcs..................... 245.00
Water set: pitcher & 6 tumblers;
clear, 7 pcs. ....125.00 to 150.00
Water set: pitcher & 6 tumblers;
green, 7 pcs. 245.00

SHELL & TASSEL
Berry set, 10" oval master bowl & 6
square footed sauce dishes,
7 pcs.......................... 190.00
Bowl, 9" oval 45.00
Bowl, 10" oval 32.00
Bowl, 6½ x 11½" oval, amber 90.00

Bowl, 6½ x 11½" oval, clear 49.00
Bowl, 12" oval 75.00
Bowl, rectangular, amber 75.00
Bread tray, 9 x 13" 50.00
Bride's basket, 8" oval bowl in silver
    plate frame 125.00
Bride's basket, 5 x 10" oval amber
    bowl in silver plate
    frame . . . . 250.00 to 275.00
Bride's basket, 5 x 10" oval clear
    bowl in silver plate frame 87.50
Butter dish, cov., round, dog finial . .   120.00
Cake stand, shell corners, 8" sq. 42.50
Cake stand, shell corners, 9" sq. . . .   62.00
Cake stand, shell corners, 10" sq. . .   65.00
Cake stand, shell corners, 12" sq. . .   82.00
Celery vase, round, handled 51.00
Celery vase, square 48.00
Compote, cov., 5¼" sq. 65.00
Compote, cov., 7½" d., 8" h. 75.00
Compote, open, jelly 50.00
Compote, open, 6½" sq., 6½" h. 48.00
Compote, open, 7½" sq., 7½" h. 45.00
Compote, open, 7½" sq., 9" h. 44.00
Compote, open, 8½" sq., 8" h. 65.00
Compote, open, 9½" d., 9" h. 82.00
Compote, open, 10" sq.,
    8" h. 60.00 to 75.00
Creamer, round 32.00
Creamer, square 55.00
Creamer & cov. sugar bowl, square,
    pr. 120.00
Dish, 7 x 10" 25.00
Goblet, round, knob stem 40.00
Oyster plate, 9½" d. 210.00
Pitcher, water, round 60.00
Pitcher, water, square 75.00
Plate, shell-shaped w/three shell-
    shaped feet, large 67.50
Platter, 8 x 11" oblong 50.00
Platter, 9 x 13" oval 52.00
Relish, 5 x 8" 40.00
Salt dip, shell-shaped 25.00
Sauce dish, flat or footed, 4" to
    5" d. 12.00
Sauce dish, footed, w/shell
    handle 13.50
Spooner, round 35.00
Spooner, square 38.00
Sugar bowl, cov., round, dog
    finial 90.00
Sugar bowl, cov., square, shell
    finial 75.00
Sugar bowl, open, square 25.00
Table set, 4 pcs. . . . . 300.00 to 400.00
Tray, ice cream 44.00
Tumbler 15.50
Vase 100.00

SHERATON

Bowl, 4 7/8 x 6 5/8", amber 23.00
Bowl, 8 x 10", eight-sided 18.50
Bread platter, amber, 8 x 10" 42.50
Bread platter, blue, 8 x 10" 55.00

Bread platter, clear, 8 x 10" 18.00
Butter dish, cov., blue 50.00
Butter dish, cov., clear 40.00
Cake stand, 10½" d. 32.00
Celery vase 24.00
Compote, cov., 8" d. 35.00
Compote, open, 7" d., 5" h.,
    amber 28.00
Compote, open, 7" d., 5" h., clear . .   21.00
Compote, open, 8" d., 7¾" h. 28.00
Compote, open, 10" d. 45.00
Creamer, amber 27.00
Creamer, blue 37.00
Creamer, clear 23.00
Goblet, blue 43.00

Sheraton Goblet

Goblet, clear (ILLUS.) 20.00
Pitcher, milk, amber 40.00
Pitcher, milk, clear 22.00
Pitcher, water, amber 55.00
Pitcher, water, blue 85.00
Pitcher, water, clear 45.00
Plate, 7" sq., amber 20.00
Plate, 8½" sq.   8.50
Relish, handled, amber 16.50
Relish, handled, clear 14.50
Sauce dish, blue, 4" d. 12.00
Sauce dish, clear, 4" d. 9.00
Spooner, amber 30.00
Spooner, blue 32.50
Spooner, clear 22.00
Sugar bowl, cov. 25.00
Tumbler 22.00
Wine 22.00

SHOSHONE

Bowl, 7" flat 11.00
Cake stand, clear 23.50
Cake stand, green 52.50
Carafe 38.00
Celery vase, ruby-stained 85.00
Compote, jelly 17.50
Creamer, amber-stained 47.50
Creamer, clear w/gold trim 40.00
Creamer, green 47.50
Cruet w/original stopper, clear 55.00
Cruet w/original stopper, green 95.00
Cruet w/original stopper, ruby-
    stained 195.00

Plate, 11" d., reticulated rim, milk
white 35.00
Relish, 7½" l...................... 11.00
Salt dip, individual size 20.00
Sauce dish, clear w/gold trim,
5" sq. 12.50
Sauce dish, ruby-stained 23.00
Sauce dish, ruby-stained 23.00
Spooner 35.00
Sugar bowl, cov., clear w/gold
trim........................... 50.00
Toothpick holder, clear w/gold
trim 30.00
Tumbler, ruby-stained 30.00
Wine............................ 45.00

SHRINE

Bowl, 8¼" d. 31.50
Butter dish, cov. 45.00
Champagne...................... 58.50
Compote, cov., high stand 75.00
Compote, open, jelly 22.50
Creamer 32.50
Goblet 37.50
Lamp, kerosene, w/fingergrip, ped-
estal base, 10" h. 145.00
Mug 32.00
Pickle dish....................... 17.50
Pitcher, cider, ½ gal............... 125.00
Pitcher, water 42.00
Salt shaker w/original top 28.50
Sauce dish....................... 13.00
Spooner 26.50
Sugar bowl, cov. 47.50
Toothpick holder 85.00
Tumbler, 4" h. 37.50
Wine............................ 45.00

SHUTTLE (Hearts of Loch Laven)

Shuttle Creamer

Bowl, berry, large................ 30.00
Butter dish, cov. 110.00
Cake stand 125.00
Celery vase...................... 46.00
Champagne...................... 36.00
Cordial, small.................... 32.00
Creamer, tall tankard (ILLUS.) 35.00
Goblet 60.00
Mug, amber 300.00

Mug, clear....................... 28.00
Pitcher, water 140.00
Punch cup 12.00
Salt shaker w/original top 60.00
Spooner, scalloped rim 50.00
Tumbler......................... 50.00
Wine............................ 24.00

SKILTON - See Oregon Pattern

SMOCKING

Bowl, 7" d., footed 38.50
Butter dish, cov. 90.00
Champagne, knob stem............ 85.00
Compote, 6" d., 4" h.............. 45.00
Compote, 7¾" d., low stand 52.00
Creamer, applied handle.......... 150.00
Creamer, individual size 125.00
Goblet 45.00
Spillholder...................... 39.50
Sugar bowl, cov..........150.00 to 200.00
Wine............................ 65.00

SNAIL (Compact)

Snail Goblet

Banana stand, 10" d., 7" h. 190.00
Bowl, 7" d., low 34.00
Bowl, berry, 8" d., 4" h. 32.50
Bowl, 9" d., 2" h. 30.00
Butter dish, cov. 80.00
Cake stand, 10" d. 87.50
Celery vase...................... 50.00
Cheese dish, cov. 80.00
Compote, cov., 7" d.,
11½" h.................100.00 to 125.00
Compote, cov., 8" d., 13" h......... 135.00
Compote, open, 8" d., 9" h......... 58.00
Compote, open, 10" d., 7" h. 145.00
Creamer, clear 60.00
Creamer, ruby-stained 75.00
Cruet w/original stopper, clear 93.00
Cruet w/original stopper, ruby-
stained....................... 225.00
Goblet (ILLUS.) 90.00
Honey dish, cov. 95.00
Pickle dish, 5½ x 8"............... 28.00
Pitcher, cider, bulbous 150.00

Pitcher, water, tankard 98.00
Plate, 7" d. 46.00
Punch cup 27.00
Relish, 7" oval 22.50
Rose bowl, double, miniature 35.00
Rose bowl, large 85.00
Salt dip, individual size 20.00
Salt shaker w/original top, ruby-
stained 65.00
Salt & pepper shakers w/original
tops, pr........................ 110.00
Sauce dish................... 9.00 to 15.00
Spooner, clear 37.00
Spooner, ruby-stained 85.00
Sugar bowl, cov., plain 60.00
Sugar bowl, cov., engraved leaf
band.......................... 85.00
Sugar shaker w/original top, clear.. 100.00
Sugar shaker w/original top, ruby-
stained 193.00
Syrup jug w/original brass top 75.00
Table set, 4 pcs. 275.00
Tumbler, clear 48.00
Tumbler, ruby-stained 54.00
Vase, 12½" h., scalloped rim 55.00
Vase, 17" h. 65.00

SNAKESKIN & DOT
Celery vase...................... 35.00
Compote, cov. 60.00
Creamer 28.00
Goblet 30.00
Plate, 4½" d., amber............. 9.00
Plate, 7" d., milk white 15.00
Plate, 9" d., clear 25.00
Sugar bowl, cov. 45.00

SPARTAN (Barred Star)
Cake stand 25.00
Cordial 15.00
Goblet 22.50
Sauce dish, flat 10.00
Sugar bowl, cov. 60.00
Tumbler 17.50

SPIREA BAND
Bowl, 8" oval, flat, blue 39.00
Butter dish, cov., amber 50.00
Butter dish, cov., blue 57.50
Butter dish, cov., clear 40.00
Cake stand, amber, 8½" d. 45.00
Cake stand, blue, 10½" d. 95.00
Celery vase, blue 35.00
Compote, cov., 7" d., low stand,
amber 55.00
Compote, cov., 7" d., high stand,
blue 65.00
Compote, open, 7" d., low stand,
amber 26.00
Compote, open, 8" d.............. 25.00
Creamer, amber 36.50
Creamer, blue 32.50
Creamer, clear 28.00
Goblet, amber 32.50
Goblet, blue 36.00

Pickle dish....................... 7.00
Pitcher, water, amber 42.50
Pitcher, water, blue 90.00
Pitcher, water, clear.............. 45.00
Platter, 8½ x 10½", amber 25.00
Platter, 8½ x 10½", blue 32.00
Platter, 8½ x 10½", clear......... 20.00
Platter, 8½ x 10½", vaseline....... 28.00
Relish, amber, 4½ x 7"........... 10.00
Relish, amber, 5½ x 9"........... 18.50
Salt shaker w/original top, amber .. 17.00
Salt shaker w/original top, blue 37.50
Salt & pepper shakers w/original
tops, amber, pr. 30.00
Sauce dish, flat or footed,
amber .... 6.00 to 12.00
Sauce dish, flat or footed, blue 12.00
Spooner, amber 25.00
Spooner, blue.................... 33.00
Spooner, clear 18.00
Spooner, vaseline 30.00
Sugar bowl, cov., blue 55.00
Sugar bowl, cov., clear 35.00
Sugar bowl, open, amber 22.00
Tumbler, blue.................... 50.00
Wine, amber..................... 24.00
Wine, blue 28.00
Wine, clear 18.50

SPRIG
Bowl, 8" oval, footed 42.00
Bowl, 9" oval 40.00
Bread platter, 11" oval 35.00
Butter dish, cov. 60.00
Cake stand 44.00
Celery vase 36.50
Compote, cov., 6" d., high stand ... 50.00
Compote, cov., 8" d., low stand 45.00
Compote, open, 6" d. 32.50
Compote, open, 6¾" d., 5½" h..... 17.50
Compote, open, 7" d., low stand ... 24.00
Compote, open, 8" d., high stand... 22.00
Compote, open, 10" d., high stand.. 42.50
Creamer 35.00
Goblet 28.00
Pickle castor, resilvered frame &
tongs 85.00
Pitcher, water 50.00
Relish, 6¾" oval 11.00
Relish, 7¾" oval 18.00
Relish, 8¾" oval 22.00
Salt dip, master size.............. 45.00
Sauce dish, flat or footed 9.50
Spooner......................... 23.50
Sugar bowl, cov. 48.00
Sugar bowl, open 20.00
Wine............................ 37.50

SQUARE LION'S HEAD - See Lion Pattern

SQUARE PANES - See Post Pattern

S-REPEAT
Butter dish, cov., amethyst
w/gold 125.00

Butter dish, cov., apple green 125.00
Condiment tray, amethyst 37.50
Decanter w/stopper, wine,
    amethyst 135.00
Punch cup 16.00
Salt shaker w/original top, sapphire
    blue 42.00
Salt & pepper shakers, pr. 38.00
Toothpick holder, amethyst 62.00
Tumblers, amethyst, set of 5 .... 200.00
Wine, sapphire blue 25.00

STAR ROSETTED

Star Rosetted Goblet

Bowl, 5 x 7¼" oval 6.50
Butter dish, cov. 40.00
Cake (or bread) plate, "A Good
    Mother Makes A Happy Home" ... 60.00
Compote, open, 6½" d 16.00
Compote, open, 7½" d 18.00
Creamer 30.00
Goblet (ILLUS.) 28.00
Plate, 7" d. 10.00
Relish, three-handled, 5 x 9¾" 6.50
Sauce dish, flat or footed 5.00
Spooner 25.00
Sugar bowl, cov. 40.00
Sugar bowl, open 12.00

STATES (THE)

Bowl, 7" d., three-handled 55.00
Bowl, 7½" d. 22.50
Bowl, 9" d. 60.00
Butter dish, cov. 56.00
Card tray, 5 x 7 3/8" 15.00
Celery 30.00
Cocktail, flared 22.00
Compote, open, 5 x 5½" 27.00
Compote, open, 9¼" d., 9" h. 80.00
Creamer 32.00
Creamer, individual size 30.00
Creamer & sugar bowl, individual
    size, pr. 42.50
Goblet 30.00
Nappy, two-handled 22.50
Olive dish 17.50
Pitcher, water 65.00
Punch bowl, 13" d., 5½" h. 70.00

Punch cup 11.00
Salt shaker w/original top 16.50
Salt & pepper shakers w/original
    tops, pr. 54.00
Sauce dish 12.00
Spooner 26.50
Sugar bowl, cov. 46.00
Sugar bowl, open, individual size ... 17.50
Syrup jug 95.00
Toothpick holder 32.00
Tumbler 25.00
Water set, pitcher & 6 tumblers,
    7 pcs. 125.00
Wine 25.00

STEDMAN

Champagne 35.00
Compote, open, 7½" d., 7" h. 45.00
Creamer 40.00
Egg cup 20.00
Goblet 27.50
Goblet, buttermilk 25.00
Sauce dish, flat 14.00
Spooner 40.00
Syrup pitcher, applied handle,
    4¼" d., 8¼" h. 100.00
Wine 50.00

STIPPLED CHAIN

Creamer 30.00
Goblet 19.00
Relish, 6 1/8 x 8¼" 10.00
Salt dip, master size 19.50
Sauce dish 4.50
Spooner 22.50
Sugar bowl, cov. 29.50
Tumbler 20.00

STIPPLED CHERRY

Bowl, master berry, 8" d. 28.00
Bread platter 28.00
Butter dish, cov. 42.00
Celery 35.00
Creamer 22.50
Pitcher, water 52.00
Plate, 6" d. 20.00
Sauce dish, flat 6.50
Spooner 25.00
Tumbler 22.00

STIPPLED DOUBLE LOOP

Butter dish, cov. 40.00
Creamer 30.00
Goblet 47.50
Spooner 20.00
Sugar bowl, cov. 35.00
Tumbler 15.00

STIPPLED FLOWER PANELS - See Maine Pattern

STIPPLED FORGET-ME-NOT

Bread platter 37.00
Butter dish, cov. 48.00

Cake stand, 8" to 9" d. 42.50
Celery vase...................... 31.00
Compote, cov., 8" d., high stand ... 55.00

Stippled Forget-Me-Not Compote

Compote, open, 6" d., 6½" h.
  (ILLUS.)...................... 32.50
Compote, open, 8" d.............. 45.00
Creamer 24.00
Cup & saucer 35.00
Goblet 35.00
Mug 20.00
Pitcher, milk.................. 37.00
Pitcher, water 52.00
Plate, 7" d., w/baby in tub reaching
  for ball on floor center 52.00
Plate, 7" d., w/kitten center 45.00
Plate, 9" d., w/kitten center,
  handled 27.50
Salt dip, master size, oval 35.00
Salt shaker w/original top 25.00
Syrup pitcher w/original top 80.00
Tray, water.................... 75.00
Tumbler 30.00
Wine........................... 42.50

STIPPLED GRAPE & FESTOON
Celery vase.................... 28.00
Compote, 8" d., low stand 38.50
Creamer, w/clear leaf 38.50
Egg cup 25.00
Goblet 30.00
Pitcher, water 98.00
Spooner, w/clear leaf 25.00
Sugar bowl, open 21.00

STIPPLED IVY
Butter dish, cov. 45.00
Creamer, applied handle.......... 35.00
Egg cup 28.00
Goblet 22.00
Salt dip, master size............. 23.00
Sauce dish, flat 8.00
Spooner........................ 27.50
Sugar bowl, cov. 35.00
Sugar bowl, open 27.50

STIPPLED ROMAN KEY
Goblet 36.50
Tumbler 18.00

SUNK HONEYCOMB (Corona)
Celery, ruby-stained 72.50
Cracker jar, cov., ruby-stained 485.00
Creamer, ruby-stained, 4½" h...... 45.00
Cruet w/original stopper, clear 30.00
Cruet w/original stopper, ruby-
  stained, enameled floral
  decoration...................... 135.00
Cup & saucer, ruby-stained........ 35.00
Goblet 43.00
Mug, ruby-stained, 3" h. 16.00
Mug, ruby-stained, souvenir........ 40.00
Punch cup 6.50
Salt dip, master size, ruby-stained .. 65.00
Salt shaker w/original top, clear ... 6.50
Salt shaker w/original top, ruby-
  stained........................ 37.50
Syrup pitcher w/original top, ruby-
  stained....................... 175.00
Toothpick holder, ruby-stained,
  souvenir...................... 52.00
Tumbler, clear, engraved 24.00
Tumbler, ruby-stained 32.00
Wine, clear, engraved 15.00
Wine, ruby-stained 32.50
Wine, ruby-stained, engraved 40.00

SWAN

Swan Creamer

Butter dish, cov., swan finial 90.00
Celery vase.................... 60.00
Compote, cov., w/swan finial,
  8" d....................... 185.00
Compote, open, 8½" h........... 53.00
Creamer, clear (ILLUS.) 46.00
Creamer, milk white 52.00
Goblet, canary yellow 70.00
Goblet, clear 50.00
Marmalade jar, cov.............. 57.50
Mug, footed, clear 27.50
Mug, footed, ring handle, opaque
  blue 68.00
Mug, footed, ring handle, opaque
  purple 68.00
Mustard jar, cov., amber 75.00
Pitcher, water 140.00
Sauce dish, flat or footed 12.00
Spooner....................... 50.00
Sugar bowl, cov. 185.00

Sugar bowl, open, blue 45.00
Sugar bowl, open, clear 40.00

TEARDROP & TASSEL

Teardrop & Tassel Sugar Bowl

Berry set: master bowl & 5 sauce
  dishes; cobalt blue, 6 pcs. 145.00
Bowl, 7½" d., clear 40.00
Bowl, 7½" d., Nile green 35.00
Bowl, master berry or fruit, cobalt
  blue 45.00
Butter dish, cov., clear 59.00
Butter dish, cov., cobalt blue 185.00
Butter dish, cov., emerald green. . . . 200.00
Compote, cov., 5" d., 7½" h. 65.00
Compote, cov., 7" d., 11½" h. 85.00
Compote, cov., 9½" d. 95.00
Compote, open, 5" d. 25.00
Compote, open, 6" d. 35.00
Compote, open, 8½" d. 45.00
Compote, open, Nile green 250.00
Creamer, amber 175.00
Creamer, clear 35.00
Creamer, cobalt blue 125.00
Creamer, Nile green 200.00
Creamer, white opaque 75.00
Creamer & cov. sugar bowl, emer-
  ald green, pr. 325.00
Creamer & cov. sugar bowl, white
  opaque, pr. 150.00
Goblet, clear 150.00
Goblet, emerald green 225.00
Pickle dish, amber 90.00
Pitcher, water, clear. 70.00
Pitcher, water, cobalt blue 175.00
Pitcher, water, emerald green 200.00
Relish, clear 35.00
Relish, emerald green 100.00
Relish, Nile green 175.00
Relish, teal blue 175.00
Salt shaker w/original top 125.00
Salt & pepper shakers w/original
  tops, Nile green, pr. 350.00
Sauce dish, clear 11.00
Sauce dish, cobalt blue 45.00
Sauce dish, emerald green 75.00
Spooner, clear 40.00
Spooner, cobalt blue 90.00
Spooner, Nile green 175.00

Spooner, white opaque 65.00
Sugar bowl, cov., clear 60.00
Sugar bowl, cov., cobalt blue
  (ILLUS.) 135.00
Sugar bowl, cov., Nile green 300.00
Tumbler, clear 35.00
Tumbler, cobalt blue 50.00
Tumbler, emerald green 165.00
Water set: pitcher & 6 tumblers; co-
  balt blue, 7 pcs. 550.00

TEASEL
Celery 20.00
Goblet 22.50
Plate, 7" to 9" d. . . . . .12.00 to 20.00
Sauce dish. 5.50
Sugar bowl, open 30.00
Tumbler 10.00
Wine 12.00

TEXAS (Loop with Stippled Panels)

Texas Individual Size Creamer

Bowl, 8" oval 30.00
Butter dish, cov. 112.50
Cake stand, 9½" to 10¾" d. 65.00
Compote, cov., 6" d., 11" h. 90.00
Creamer 16.00
Creamer, individual size (ILLUS.) 17.00
Cruet w/original stopper, clear 70.00
Cruet w/original stopper, ruby-
  stained 165.00
Goblet, clear 45.00
Goblet, ruby-stained 95.00
Pitcher, water, 8½" h. 120.00
Plate, 8¾" d. 62.50
Relish, handled, 8½" l. 24.00
Salt dip, master size, footed, 3" d.,
  2¾" h. 22.00
Sauce dish, flat or footed 16.00
Spooner 52.50
Sugar bowl, cov. 60.00
Sugar bowl, open, individual size . . . 16.00
Toothpick holder 32.00
Vase, bud, 8" h. 24.00
Vase, 9" h. 36.00
Wine, clear 87.00
Wine, ruby-stained 95.00

TEXAS BULL'S EYE (Bull's Eye Variant)
Celery vase. 50.00

Egg cup 15.00
Goblet 21.00
Lamp, kerosene-type, footed, hand-
 type w/finger grip 37.50
Sugar bowl, open 32.00
Tumbler 30.00
Wine.............................. 21.00

THISTLE - See Paneled Thistle Pattern

THOUSAND EYE

Thousand Eye Egg Cup

Bowl, 8" d., 4½" h., footed,
 amber 35.00
Bowl, 8" d., 4½" h., footed, blue
 opaque......................... 55.00
Bowl, 11" rectangle, shallow,
 amber 32.00
Bowl, 11½" sq., 1¾" h., folded
 corners 45.00
Bread tray, blue 43.00
Bread tray, clear 30.00
Butter dish, cov., amber 70.00
Butter dish, cov., apple green .. 80.00
Butter dish, cov., blue 82.50
Butter dish, cov., clear 42.00
Butter dish, cov., vaseline 70.00
Cake stand, amber, 8½" to
 10" d..................47.50 to 60.00
Cake stand, apple green, 8½" to
 10" d. 67.50
Cake stand, blue, 8½" to 10" d. .. 100.00
Cake stand, clear, 8½" to 10" d. .. 28.00
Celery vase, three-knob stem,
 amber 48.00
Celery vase, three-knob stem, apple
 green 55.00
Celery vase, three-knob stem,
 clear.......................... 36.00
Celery vase, three-knob stem, clear
 to opalescent w/purple tint 50.00
Celery vase, plain stem, amber..... 46.00
Celery vase, plain stem, clear 35.00
Compote, cov., 12" h., clear...... 115.00
Compote, open, 6" d., low stand,
 amber 22.00
Compote, open, 6" d., low stand,
 apple green 31.00
Compote, open, 6" d., low stand,
 blue 34.00

Compote, open, 6½" d., three-knob
 stem, blue.................... 30.00
Compote, open, 7½" d., three-knob
 stem, amber.................. 47.50
Compote, open, 7½" d., three-knob
 stem, blue................... 55.00
Compote, open, 7½" d., 5" h.,
 blue 48.00
Compote, open, 7½" d., 5" h.,
 clear......................... 25.00
Compote, open, 8" d., 3¾" h., ap-
 ple green..................... 37.50
Compote, open, 8" d., 6" h., three-
 knob stem, amber............. 32.50
Compote, open, 8" d., 6" h., three-
 knob stem, apple green 53.00
Compote, open, 8" d., 6" h., three-
 knob stem, blue 38.00
Compote, open, 10" d., 6½" h., ap-
 ple green..................... 45.00
Compote, open, 10" d., 6½" h.,
 three-knob stem, blue 85.00
Creamer, amber 42.00
Creamer, clear................. 21.00
Creamer, clear to opalescent 95.00
Creamer, vaseline.............. 47.50
Creamer & cov. sugar bowl, amber,
 pr............................ 100.00
Cruet w/original three-knob stop-
 per, amber 72.00
Cruet w/original three-knob stop-
 per, apple green 135.00
Cruet w/original three-knob stop-
 per, blue.................... 72.00
Cruet w/original three-knob stop-
 per, clear 32.00
Cruet w/original three-knob stop-
 per, vaseline 90.00
Cruet stand w/pr. cruets w/original
 stoppers, knob stem, amber,
 set.......................... 210.00
Dish, apple green, 5 x 7" 25.00
Egg cup, blue 75.00
Egg cup, clear (ILLUS.) 25.00
Egg cup, vaseline 65.00
Goblet, amber 28.00
Goblet, apple green 33.50
Goblet, blue 46.00
Goblet, clear 27.50
Goblet, vaseline 34.00
Hat shape, clear, small 12.00
Hat shape, vaseline, small 24.00
Honey dish, cov., apple green 125.00
Honey dish, cover w/knob finial,
 rectangular, vaseline 135.00
Inkwell, cov., clear, 2" sq. 30.00
Lamp, kerosene-type, pedestal
 base, amber, 14" h. to collar (22"
 to chimney top) 165.00
Lamp, kerosene-type, pedestal
 base, blue, 12" h. 165.00
Lamp, kerosene-type, flat base, ring
 handle, clear ....105.00 to 120.00
Lemonade set: tankard pitcher, lem-

on dish, 12" tray & 3 goblets; apple green, 6 pcs. 165.00
Mug, amber, 3½" h. 21.00
Mug, blue, 3½" h. 30.00
Mug, clear, 3½" h. 12.50
Mug, vaseline, 3½" h. 27.50
Mug, miniature, amber 19.00
Mug, miniature, apple green 17.50
Mug, miniature, vaseline 25.00
Pitcher, milk, three-knob stem 35.00
Pitcher, water, three-knob stem, amber 210.00
Pitcher, water, three-knob stem, apple green 85.00
Pitcher, water, clear 57.50
Pitcher, water, vaseline 60.00
Plate, 6" d., amber 30.00
Plate, 6" d., apple green 18.00
Plate, 6" d., clear 12.00
Plate, 8" d., amber 25.00
Plate, 8" d., apple green 25.00
Plate, 8" d., clear 18.00
Plate, 8" d., vaseline 26.00
Plate, 10" sq., w/folded corners, apple green 120.00
Plate, 10" sq., w/folded corners, clear 25.00
Plate, 10" sq., w/folded corners, vaseline 35.00
Platter, 8 x 11", blue 42.50
Platter, 8 x 11", clear 30.00
Salt dip, master size 20.00
Salt shaker w/original top, amber . . 21.00
Salt shaker w/original top, apple green 30.00
Salt shaker w/original top, blue 40.00
Salt shaker w/original top, clear . . . 18.50
Salt shaker w/original top, vaseline 30.00
Salt & pepper shakers w/original tops, blue, pr. 88.00
Sauce dish, flat or footed, amber . . . 10.00
Sauce dish, flat or footed, apple green . . . . 10.00 to 14.00
Sauce dish, flat or footed, blue . . . . 12.00 to 25.00
Sauce dish, flat or footed, clear . . . . 7.00 to 9.50
Sauce dish, flat or footed, vaseline . . . . 15.00 to 27.00
Spooner, three-knob stem, amber . . 29.50
Spooner, three-knob stem, apple green 35.00
Spooner, three-knob stem, blue 38.00
Spooner, three-knob stem, clear 30.00
Sugar bowl, cov., three-knob stem, amber 55.00
Sugar bowl, cov., three-knob stem, blue 55.00
Sugar bowl, cov. 37.50
Syrup pitcher w/original top, amber 100.00
Syrup pitcher w/original pewter top, footed, apple green 113.00

Toothpick holder, amber 32.50
Toothpick holder, blue 32.50
Toothpick holder, clear 30.00
Toothpick holder, vaseline 38.00
Tray, water, amber, 12½" d. 90.00
Tray, water, apple green, 12½" d. . . 80.00
Tray, water, clear, 12½" d. 38.00
Tray, amber, 14" oval 60.00
Tray, apple green, 14" oval 85.00
Tray, clear, 14" oval 50.00
Tumbler, amber 24.00
Tumbler, blue 35.00
Tumbler, clear 18.00
Water set: oval tray, pitcher & 5 tumblers; apple green, 7 pcs. 240.00
Whimsey, model of a four-wheeled cart, amber 115.00
Wine, amber 25.00
Wine, blue 40.00
Wine, clear 21.00
Wine, vaseline 40.00

THREE FACE

Three Face Covered Compote

Bread plate 78.00
Butter dish, cov. 145.00
Cake stand, 8" to 10½" d. 145.00
Celery vase 100.00
Champagne 175.00
Claret 152.00
Compote, cov., 4½" d., 6½" h. 85.00
Compote, cov., 6" d. 135.00
Compote, cov., 8" d., 13" h. (ILLUS.) 195.00
Compote, cov., 10" d. 145.00
Compote, open, 6" d., 7½" h. 70.00
Compote, open, 8½" d., 8½" h. 107.00
Compote, open, 9½" d., 9½" h. 160.00
Cracker jar, cov. 1,250.00
Creamer 85.00
Creamer w/mask spout 135.00
Creamer w/mask spout & cov. sugar bowl, pr. 265.00
Goblet 82.00
Lamp, kerosene-type, pedestal base, 8" h. 148.00
Pitcher, water 285.00
Salt dip 50.00

Salt & pepper shakers w/original
    tops, pr. 110.00
Sauce dish. 25.00
Spooner 80.00
Sugar bowl, cov. 115.00
Sugar bowl, open 65.00
Table set, creamer, cov. sugar bowl
    & spooner, 3 pcs. 285.00
Toothpick holder 50.00
Wine. 98.00

THREE PANEL

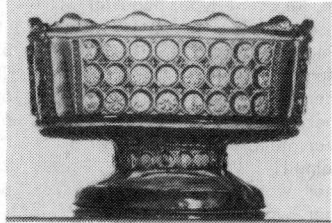

Three Panel Sauce Dish

Berry set: 7" d. footed bowl & 4
    footed sauce dishes; blue,
    5 pcs. 75.00
Berry set: master bowl & 5 sauce
    dishes; clear, 6 pcs. 57.50
Berry set: master bowl & 8 sauce
    dishes; amber, 9 pcs. 150.00
Bowl, 7" d., footed, amber 25.00
Bowl, 7" d., footed, blue. 30.00
Bowl, 7" d., footed, clear 20.00
Bowl, 9" d., footed, amber 33.00
Bowl, 9" d., footed, blue. 25.00
Bowl, 9" d., footed, clear 20.00
Bowl, 9" d., footed, vaseline 45.00
Bowl, 10" d., amber 49.00
Bowl, 10" d., blue 60.00
Bowl, 10" d., clear 20.00
Bowl, 10" d., vaseline 45.00
Butter dish, cov., amber 55.00
Butter dish, cov., clear 55.00
Celery vase, amber 40.00
Celery vase, blue 37.50
Celery vase, clear 35.00
Compote, open, 7" d., low stand,
    amber 25.00
Compote, open, 7" d., low stand,
    blue 32.50
Compote, open, 7" d., low stand,
    clear 20.00
Compote, open, 8½" d., low stand,
    blue 43.00
Compote, open, 8½" d., low stand,
    vaseline 32.50
Creamer, amber . . . . , ... 36.00
Creamer, blue 46.00
Creamer, clear. 22.00
Creamer, vaseline. 50.00
Goblet, amber 30.00
Goblet, blue 39.00
Goblet, clear 23.00
Goblet, vaseline 38.00

Lamp, kerosene-type, amber 145.00
Mug, amber 35.00
Mug, blue 37.50
Mug, clear. 22.00
Mug, vaseline. 35.00
Pitcher, milk, 7" h., clear 44.50
Pitcher, water, amber 85.00
Pitcher, water, vaseline. 110.00
Sauce dish, footed, amber 17.50
Sauce dish, footed, blue 13.00
Sauce dish, footed, clear (ILLUS.) . . . 8.00
Sauce dish, footed, vaseline. 17.00
Spooner, amber 40.00
Spooner, blue. 38.00
Spooner, clear 18.00
Spooner, vaseline 30.00
Sugar bowl, cov., amber 55.00
Sugar bowl, cov., blue 60.00
Sugar bowl, cov., clear 45.00
Sugar bowl, cov., vaseline 65.00
Sugar bowl, open 25.00
Table set, blue, 4 pcs. 245.00
Tumbler, amber 35.00
Tumbler, clear 12.00

THUMBPRINT, EARLY

(Bakewell, Pears & Co.'s "Argus")

Early Thumbprint Covered Compote

Ale glass, footed, 5" h. 31.00
Bowl, 5" d., 5" h., footed 32.00
Butter dish, cov. 115.00
Cake stand, 8" to 9½" d. 85.00
Celery vase, plain base 90.00
Celery vase, scalloped rim, pattern
    in base 135.00
Compote, cov., 6" d., 7½" h.
    (ILLUS.). 225.00
Compote, cov., 7½" d., 11½" h. . . . 85.00
Compote, open, 5" d., 5½" h., scal-
    loped rim. 65.00
Compote, open, 6" d., low stand,
    scalloped rim 35.00
Compote, open, 6" d., high stand . . . 55.00
Compote, open, 7½" d., low
    stand 67.50
Compote, open, 8" d., high stand . . . 90.00
Compote, open, 8½" d., high stand,
    scalloped rim 155.00

Compote, open, 12½" d., 11¼" h. . . 400.00
Creamer 70.00
Decanter, 11" h. 110.00
Egg cup 40.00
Goblet, baluster stem 55.00
Honey dish 16.00
Paperweight, panel-cut top 350.00
Pickle dish 40.00
Pitcher, milk 95.00
Pitcher, water, 8¼" h. 275.00
Salt dip, individual size 15.00
Salt dip, master size, footed 27.50
Sauce dish 9.00
Spillholder 48.00
Sugar bowl, cov. 55.00
Tumbler, bar 30.00
Tumbler, footed 48.50
Tumbler, whiskey, footed 32.50
Tumbler, whiskey, handled,
　footed 150.00
Wine, baluster stem 44.00

TONG
Celery vase 60.00
Spillholder 30.00
Sugar bowl, cov. 50.00

TORPEDO (Pygmy)

Torpedo Goblet

Banana stand 55.00
Bowl, cov., master berry 80.00
Bowl, 7" d., flat, clear 15.00
Bowl, 7" d., flat, ruby-stained 40.00
Bowl, 8" d., clear 17.00
Bowl, 8" d., ruby-stained 35.00
Bowl, 9" d. 31.00
Bowl, 9½" d. 38.00
Butter dish, cov. 53.00
Cake stand, 9" to 11" d. . . . . .55.00 to 82.50
Celery vase 42.00
Compote, cov., jelly 43.00
Compote, cov., 6" d. 78.00
Compote, cov., 7" d., 7¼" h. 65.00
Compote, cov., 8" d., 14" h. 135.00
Compote, open, jelly, 5" d., 5" h. 45.00
Compote, open, 7" d., high stand . . . 52.00
Compote, open, 8" d., high stand,
　flared rim 50.00
Compote, open, 9" d., low stand . . . 55.00

Compote, open, 8 x 10½", 8" h.,
　ruffled rim 145.00
Creamer 40.00
Cruet w/original faceted stopper . . . 49.00
Cup 25.00
Cup & saucer 60.00
Decanter w/original stopper 123.00
Goblet, clear (ILLUS.) 50.00
Goblet, ruby-stained 85.00
Honey dish, cov. 20.00
Lamp, kerosene, hand-type w/finger
　grip, w/burner & chimney 75.00
Lamp, kerosene-type, pedestal
　base, 8½" h. 110.00
Marmalade jar, cov. 55.00
Pickle castor insert 28.00
Pitcher, milk, 7" h. 50.00
Pitcher, milk, 8½" h., clear 62.00
Pitcher, milk, 8½" h., ruby-
　stained 125.00
Pitcher, water, 10" h., clear 84.00
Pitcher, water, 10" h., ruby-
　stained 90.00
Pitcher, water, tankard, 12" h. 70.00
Salt dip, individual size, 1½" d. 30.00
Salt dip, master size 58.00
Salt shaker w/original top 25.00
Sauce dish 16.00
Spooner 32.00
Sugar bowl, cov. 65.00
Sugar bowl, open 25.00
Syrup jug w/original top, clear 74.00
Syrup jug w/original top, ruby-
　stained 186.00
Tray, 9¾" d. 70.00
Tumbler, clear 32.00
Tumbler, ruby-stained 46.00
Waste bowl 60.00
Wine, clear 67.00
Wine, ruby-stained, souvenir 45.00

TREE OF LIFE - PITTSBURGH (Tree of Life with Hand)
Butter dish, cov. 55.00
Cake stand, 8¾" d. 75.00
Celery vase 47.00
Compote, cov., 6" d., 8" h., frosted
　hand & ball stem 65.00
Compote, open, 5½" d., 5½" h.,
　clear hand & ball stem 34.00
Compote, open, 5½" d., 5½" h.,
　frosted hand & ball stem 47.50
Compote, open, 8" d., clear hand &
　ball stem 60.00
Compote, open, 8" d., 8½" h., frost-
　ed hand & ball stem 57.50
Compote, open, 9" d., frosted hand
　& ball stem 85.00
Compote, open, 9½" d., 9½" h. 68.00
Compote, open, 10" d., 10" h., frost-
　ed hand & ball stem 95.00
Creamer, w/hand & ball handle 48.00
Creamer & sugar bowl, pr. 110.00
Pitcher, water, 9" h. 68.00

Relish, oval 29.00
Sauce dish, flat or footed 19.00
Spooner 45.00
Sugar bowl, cov. 52.50
Sugar bowl, open 19.00
Tumbler 23.00
Waste bowl w/underplate 60.00
Wine 28.00

TREE OF LIFE - PORTLAND

Portland Tree of Life Ice Cream Tray

Berry set: master bowl & 4 sauce
   dishes; blue, 5 pcs. 325.00
Bowl, 5½" d., flat 12.00
Bowl, signed "Davis," green, in sil-
   ver plate holder marked "Meriden
   Britannia Co.". 235.00
Bread tray 40.00
Butter dish, cov. 55.00
Butter pat, blue 25.00
Butter pat, clear 13.00
Butter pat, vaseline 25.00
Cake stand, signed "Davis," 9" to
   11½" d. . . . . .45.00 to 60.00
Celery vase, in metal holder 75.00
Compote, open, 6" d., 6" h. 35.00
Compote, open, 7¾" d., signed
   "P.G. Co." 75.00
Compote, open, 7¾" d., 11" h.,
   Infant Samuel stand, signed
   "Davis" 150.00
Compote, open, 8½" d., 5" h.,
   signed "Davis" 60.00
Compote, open, 8¾" d., in two-
   handled Meriden silver plate
   holder, bowl signed "Davis" 185.00
Compote, open, 10" d., 6" h., signed
   "Davis" 125.00
Creamer, signed "Davis" 65.00
Creamer, blue, in silver plate
   holder 225.00
Creamer, clear, in silver plate
   holder 85.00
Cruet w/original stopper, blue 90.00
Dish, leaf handle, blue 40.00

Epergne, single lily, red snake
   around stem, 18" h. 450.00
Epergne, Infant Samuel stand,
   signed "Davis," 2 pcs. 125.00
Goblet 42.00
Goblet, signed "Davis" . . . . . .50.00 to 65.00
Ice cream set, tray & 5 leaf-shaped
   desserts, 6 pcs. 70.00
Ice cream set, tray & 6 leaf-shaped
   desserts, 7 pcs. 105.00
Mug, applied handle, 3½" h. 25.00
Pitcher, water, applied handle 78.00
Pitcher, water, applied handle,
   signed "Davis," amber . . .225.00 to 250.00
Plate, 6½" d. 18.00
Plate, 7¼" d. 50.00
Plate, 10" l., three-footed, shell-
   shaped 85.00
Powder jar, cov., red coiled snake
   finial on cover 350.00
Salt dip, flat, 3" d. 10.00
Salt dip, footed, "Salt" embossed in
   bowl, clear 135.00
Salt dip, footed, opaque green 95.00
Salt shaker w/original top 25.00
Sauce dish, melon-ribbed, 4½" to
   5½" d. 18.00
Sauce dish, leaf-shaped, amber 11.50
Sauce dish, leaf-shaped, clear 20.00
Spooner, handled silver plate holder
   w/two Griffin heads 57.50
Sugar bowl, cov., blue, in silver
   plate holder 225.00
Sugar bowl, cov., clear, in silver
   plate holder 88.00
Sugar bowl, cov., clear 55.00
Toothpick holder, blue 75.00
Tray, ice cream, 14" rectangle
   (ILLUS.) 35.00
Tumbler, 4½" h. 22.50
Tumbler, footed, 6" h. 40.00
Waste bowl, blue, in ornate silver
   plate holder 175.00
Waste bowl, clear 14.00
Waste bowl, cranberry, flint 145.00
Wine 45.00

TULIP WITH SAWTOOTH
Celery vase, flint 65.00
Celery vase, non-flint 42.00
Champagne, non-flint 40.00
Compote, cov., 6" d., high stand,
   flint 120.00
Compote, open, 7" d., low stand,
   non-flint 69.00
Compote, open, 9" d., 7 3/8" h.,
   flint 85.00
Creamer, applied handle, flint 75.00
Cruet w/original stopper, non-flint . . 205.00
Decanter w/tulip-form stopper, flint,
   12" h., pt. 150.00
Decanter w/bar lip, flint, pt. 68.00
Goblet, flint 45.00
Goblet, non-flint 20.00

Pitcher, water, flint 175.00
Salt dip, master size, scalloped rim,
   flint 25.00
Salt dip, open, non-flint 15.00
Sauce dish, flat, non-flint,
   3 7/8" d. 8.00
Spooner, flint 65.00
Spooner, non-flint 28.00
Sugar bowl, open, non-flint 32.50
Tumbler, bar, flint 85.00
Tumbler, bar, non-flint 27.50
Tumbler, flint 30.00
Tumbler, footed, flint 55.00
Wine, flint 60.00
Wine, non-flint 22.50

TWO PANEL (Daisy in Panel)
Bowl, cov., 7" oval, vaseline 55.00
Bowl, 5½ x 7" oval, amber 25.00
Bowl, 7½ x 9" oval, amber 35.00
Bowl, 7½ x 9" oval, apple green ... 37.50
Bowl, 7½ x 9" oval, clear 15.00
Bowl, 8 x 10" oval, blue 65.00
Bowl, 8 x 10" oval, vaseline 50.00
Bread tray, apple green 39.00
Bread tray, blue 45.00
Bread tray, clear 27.00
Butter dish, cov., blue 85.00
Butter dish, cov., vaseline 55.00
Celery vase, amber 30.00
Celery vase, blue 50.00
Compote, cov., 6½ x 8", 11" h.,
   vaseline 85.00
Compote, cov., high stand, apple
   green 130.00
Compote, open, 9" oval, amber 37.00
Compote, open, 9" oval, blue 40.00
Creamer, amber 60.00
Creamer, apple green 40.00
Creamer, blue 35.00
Creamer, clear 22.50
Creamer, vaseline 35.00
Goblet, amber 28.00
Goblet, apple green 30.00
Goblet, blue 40.00
Goblet, clear 22.50
Goblet, vaseline 33.00
Lamp, kerosene-type, pedestal
   base, blue, 7¾" h., No. 1
   burner 145.00
Marmalade jar, cov., clear 36.50
Marmalade jar, cov., vaseline 65.00
Pitcher, water, amber 50.00
Pitcher, water, apple green 55.00
Pitcher, water, clear 36.00
Pitcher, water, vaseline 65.00
Relish, amber 16.00
Relish, blue 22.50
Relish, vaseline 22.50
Salt dip, master size, amber 20.00
Salt dip, master size, apple green .. 18.50
Salt dip, master size, vaseline 22.00
Salt dip, individual size, apple
   green 14.00

Salt dip, individual size, blue 12.00
Sauce dish, flat or footed, amber ... 11.00
Sauce dish, flat or footed, apple
   green ....13.50 to 22.00
Sauce dish, flat or footed,
   blue ....14.00 to 18.00
Sauce dish, flat or footed,
   clear ....7.50 to 15.00
Sauce dish, flat or footed,
   vaseline ....15.00 to 19.00
Spooner, amber 35.00
Spooner, blue 35.00
Spooner, clear 25.00
Spooner, vaseline 35.00
Sugar bowl, cov., amber 50.00
Sugar bowl, cov., clear 30.00
Tray, water, cloverleaf shape, vase-
   line, 8¾ x 10½" oval 55.00
Tray, water, amber, 10 x 15" oval .. 47.50
Tumbler, amber 25.00
Tumbler, vaseline 32.50
Waste bowl, blue 30.00
Water set: pitcher & 6 tumblers;
   blue, 7 pcs. 300.00
Wine, amber 32.00
Wine, apple green 37.00
Wine, blue 35.00
Wine, clear 15.00
Wine, vaseline 35.00

U.S. COIN

U.S. Coin Covered Compote
Bowl, 8" oval, frosted coins 308.00
Bread tray, dollars & half dollars ... 390.00
Butter dish, cov., frosted coins 425.00
Butter dish, cov., dollars & half
   dollars 525.00
Cake plate, frosted coins, 7" d...... 485.00
Cake stand, clear dollars, 10" d..... 265.00
Cake stand, frosted dollars,
   10" d. ....400.00 to 450.00
Candy dish, cov., 6" d. 275.00
Celery vase, clear quarters 245.00
Celery vase, frosted quarters....... 350.00
Champagne, frosted dimes 325.00
Compote, cov., 6 7/8" d., high
   stand, frosted coins 485.00
Compote, cov., 8" d., 11½" h.,
   frosted coins (ILLUS.) ....475.00 to 525.00

Compote, cov., 9" d., frosted
coins 500.00
Compote, open, 6½" d., 8" h., frosted dimes & quarters 215.00
Compote, open, 7" d., 5¾" h., frosted dimes & quarters 400.00
Compote, open, 8" d., 6½" h., frosted coins 475.00
Compote, open, 8½" d., 6½" h.,
frosted quarters on bowl, dimes
on stem 242.00
Compote, open, 9¼" d., 7" h., frost-
ed half dollars on bowl, quarters
on stem 375.00
Epergne, frosted dollars 1,100.00
Goblet, frosted dimes 325.00
Lamp, kerosene-type, round font,
frosted dollars in base 850.00
Lamp, kerosene-type, round font,
handled, clear quarters in base ... 500.00
Mug, frosted coins 345.00
Pickle dish, clear coins, 3¾ x 7½".. 220.00
Pickle dish, frosted coins 210.00
Pitcher, water, frosted dollars 495.00
Relish, frosted coins 185.00
Salt shaker w/original top 125.00
Sauce dish, frosted quarters, 4" d... 110.00
Spooner, clear quarters 225.00
Spooner, frosted quarters 375.00
Sugar bowl, cov., frosted coins 425.00
Syrup jug w/original dated pewter
top, frosted coins 500.00
Toothpick holder, frosted coins 190.00
Tumbler, frosted dollar in base 220.00
Wine, frosted half dimes 450.00

VALENCIA WAFFLE (Block & Star)
Bread platter 25.00
Butter dish, cov., amber 70.00
Butter dish, cov., apple green 60.00
Butter dish, cov., clear 42.50
Butter dish, cov., ruby-stained 110.00
Cake stand, amber 70.00
Cake stand, 10" d., clear 70.00
Celery vase, blue 39.00
Celery vase, clear 32.00
Celery vase, yellow 35.00
Compote, cov., 6" d., 10" h........ 75.00
Compote, cov., 7" sq., low stand,
amber 64.00
Compote, cov., 7" sq., low stand,
apple green 75.00
Compote, cov., 7" sq., low stand,
blue 76.00
Compote, cov., 7" sq., low stand,
clear 50.00
Compote, cov., 8" d. 45.00
Compote, open, 6" d., low stand,
apple green 35.00
Compote, open, 6" sq., low stand,
blue 30.00
Compote, open, 8" d., low stand,
blue 29.50
Creamer 38.00

Goblet, amber 38.00
Goblet, clear 22.00
Pitcher, water, 7½" h., amber 60.00
Pitcher, water, apple green 95.00
Pitcher, water, clear............. 40.00
Relish, amber, 7½ x 10¾" 30.00
Relish, clear, 7½ x 10¾" 10.00
Salt dip, master size, amber 22.50
Salt dip, master size, clear 15.00
Salt dip, master size, yellow 26.00
Salt shaker w/original top 20.00
Salt & pepper shakers w/original
tops, apple green, pr. 50.00
Sauce dish, footed, amber 13.50
Sauce dish, footed, blue 14.00
Sauce dish, footed, clear.......... 12.50
Spooner, amber 40.00
Spooner, clear 18.00
Syrup jug w/original top, amber 100.00
Syrup jug w/original top, blue...... 75.00
Tray, water, amber, 9½ x 13¼",
amber ....37.50 to 45.00
Tray, water, clear 26.00
Tumbler, ruby-stained 30.00

VICTOR - See Shell & Jewel Pattern

VICTORIA
Compote, cov., 8" d., low foot 150.00
Compote, cov., 8" d., high stand ... 200.00
Compote, cov., 10½" d., 15¼" h.... 215.00

VIKING (Bearded Head or Old Man of the Mountain)

Viking Sugar Bowl

Apothecary jar w/original stopper .. 95.00
Bowl, cov., 8" oval 66.00
Bowl, cov., 9" oval 55.00
Bowl, 7" d., 4" h. 25.00
Bread tray, cupid hunt scene
center........................ 68.00
Butter dish, cov. 60.00
Cake stand, 10" d. 67.50
Celery vase 52.00
Compote, cov., 7" d., low stand 82.00
Compote, cov., 8" d., low stand 70.00
Compote, cov., 9" d., low stand 110.00
Compote, cov., 12" h. 150.00

Compote, open, 8" d., high stand . . .   62.50
Creamer 55.00
Egg cup 35.00
Goblet 95.00
Marmalade jar, cov., footed 75.00
Mug, applied handle 62.50
Pickle jar w/cover. 85.00
Pitcher, water, 8¾" h. 82.00
Salt dip, master size 45.00
Sauce dish, footed 13.50
Shaving mug, milk white 62.50
Sugar bowl, cov. (ILLUS.) 58.00

VIRGINIA - See Galloway Pattern

WAFFLE
Celery vase, flint 55.00
Champagne. 145.00
Compote, open, 7" d., 5¼" h. 32.50
Compote, open, 9½" d., 8" h. 75.00
Creamer, applied handle. 125.00
Creamer, footed 45.00
Egg cup 38.00
Goblet 60.00
Salt dip, master size 27.50
Sugar bowl, cov. 55.00
Syrup pitcher, applied handle 85.00
Tumbler, bar. 75.00
Waste bowl, ruffled top. 75.00

WAFFLE AND THUMBPRINT
Bowl, 7¼" d., flint 35.00
Celery vase . . . . 85.00 to 100.00
Compote, open, 8" d., high stand,
    flint. 80.00
Cordial, flint 85.00
Creamer, applied handle, flint 250.00
Decanter w/bar lip, flint, pt. 85.00
Egg cup, flint 31.00
Goblet, flint 64.00
Lamp, w/original two-tube burner,
    hand-type w/applied handle, flint,
    3" h. 135.00
Lamp, w/original whale oil burner,
    flint, 11" h. 153.00
Pitcher, water, flint 300.00
Salt dip, master size, flint. 27.00
Spillholder, flint 115.00
Sugar bowl, cov., flint 175.00
Tumbler, bar, flint. 79.00
Tumbler, footed, flint 110.00
Tumbler, whiskey, flint 79.00
Wine, flint 50.00

WASHINGTON (Early)
Celery vase. 95.00
Claret, flint 135.00
Decanter w/original stopper, qt. 225.00
Egg cup, flint 55.00
Goblet, flint . . . . 60.00 to 80.00
Lamp, kerosene-type, cast iron
    base 125.00
Pitcher, water, flint 225.00

Salt dip, individual size 29.00
Salt dip, master size, flat, round. . . .   27.50

WASHINGTON CENTENNIAL
Bowl, 8½" oval 22.50
Bread platter, Carpenter's Hall 100.00
Bread platter, Carpenter's Hall,
    frosted 125.00
Bread platter, George Washington
    center. 84.00
Bread platter, George Washington
    center, frosted 101.00
Bread platter, Independence Hall
    center. 85.00
Butter dish, cov., footed 87.50
Cake stand, 8½" to 11½" d. 60.00
Celery vase. 50.00
Champagne. 68.00
Compote, cov., 8½" d., 12" h. 105.00
Compote, open, 7" d., low stand . . .   45.00
Compote, open, 8" d., 6½" h. 37.50
Compote, open, 10½" d., high
    stand 70.00
Creamer, applied handle. 80.00
Egg cup 39.00
Goblet 37.00
Pickle dish. 34.00
Pitcher, milk . . , ...   104.00
Pitcher, water 95.00
Relish, bear paw handles, dated
    1876 . . . .   56.00
Salt dip, master size 35.00
Sauce dish, flat or footed 11.00
Spooner 42.00
Sugar bowl, cov. 75.00
Sugar bowl, open 20.00
Syrup pitcher, w/dated pewter top
    w/tiny figural finial 165.00
Toothpick holder 60.00
Tumbler, bar. 65.00
Tumbler 69.00
Wine. 48.00

WEDDING BELLS
Bowl, 8" d., flat, ruby-stained 32.50
Bowl, master berry, gold trim 28.00
Butter dish, cov. 38.00
Celery tray, pink-stained. 27.50
Celery vase. 27.50
Creamer, four-footed 48.00
Goblet 50.00
Pitcher, water, clear. 47.00
Pitcher, water, alternate ruby-
    stained panels 85.00
Punch cup 15.00
Salt shaker w/original top 20.00
Spooner 40.00
Sugar bowl, cov. 55.00
Toothpick holder, clear w/gold
    trim. 55.00
Toothpick holder, pink-stained 80.00
Tumbler 18.00
Water set, pitcher & 4 tumblers,
    5 pcs. 135.00

Wine, clear 22.00
Wine, pink-stained 40.00

WEDDING RING - See Double Wedding Ring Pattern

WESTWARD HO

Westward Ho Creamer

Bread platter 112.00
Butter dish, cov. ....125.00 to 150.00
Celery vase........................ 125.00
Compote, cov., 5" d., 9" h.......... 92.00
Compote, cov., 6" d., low stand 120.00
Compote, cov., 6" d., 12" h......... 183.00
Compote, cov., 4 x 6¾" oval 140.00
Compote, cov., 5 x 7¾" oval,
   10" h.......................... 195.00
Compote, cov., 8" d., low stand 244.00
Compote, cov., 8" d., 11½" h....... 250.00
Compote, cov., 5½ x 8" oval,
   12" h.......................... 290.00
Compote, cov., 8" d., 14" h........ 290.00
Compote, cov., 6½ x 10" oval, low
   stand 292.00
Compote, open, 6" d., low stand 60.00
Compote, open, 6" d., high stand... 127.00
Compote, open, 7" d., low stand ... 175.00
Creamer (ILLUS.) ....100.00 to 120.00
Creamer & cov. sugar bowl, pr. 275.00
Creamer & open sugar bowl, pr..... 175.00
Goblet 70.00
Marmalade jar, cov. 157.00
Mug, child's, 2½" h............... 225.00
Pickle dish, oval 55.00
Pitcher, milk, 8" h. 250.00
Pitcher, water 240.00
Platter, 9 x 13" 170.00
Relish, deer handles.............. 115.00
Sauce dish, footed 40.00
Spooner 82.50
Sugar bowl, cov. 150.00
Water set, pitcher & 6 goblets,
   7 pcs. 595.00
Wine.............................. 200.00

WHEAT & BARLEY
Bowl, cov., 7" d. 42.50
Bowl, cov., 8" d., flat............ 38.00
Bread plate, amber................ 25.00

Butter dish, cov., blue 75.00
Butter dish, cov., clear 35.00
Cake stand, amber, 8" to 10" d. 35.00
Cake stand, clear, 8" to 10" d. 38.00
Cake stand, 11½" d. 40.00
Compote, cov., 8½" d., high
   stand 55.00
Compote, open, jelly, blue 35.00
Compote, open, jelly, clear 18.50
Compote, open, 8¼" d., amber 75.00
Compote, open, 8¾" d., 6¾" h..... 37.00
Creamer, amber 33.00
Creamer, blue 45.00
Creamer, clear................... 22.50
Doughnut stand, blue............. 58.00
Goblet, amber 38.00
Goblet, blue 28.00
Goblet, clear 22.50
Mug, amber 32.50
Mug, clear...................... 20.00
Pitcher, milk, blue 65.00
Pitcher, milk, clear 38.50
Pitcher, water, amber 85.00
Pitcher, water, blue 72.50
Pitcher, water, clear............ 53.00
Plate, 6" d., clear 35.00
Plate, 7" d., blue............... 30.00
Plate, 7" d., clear 18.00

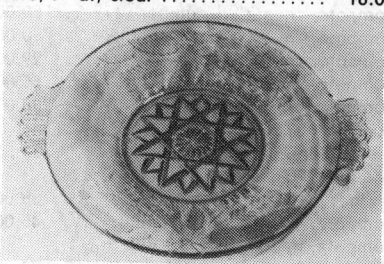

Wheat & Barley Plate

Plate, 9" d., closed handles, amber
   (ILLUS.)....................... 35.00
Plate, 9" d., closed handles, blue ... 27.50
Plate, 9" d., closed handles, clear .. 20.00
Plate, 9" d., closed handles,
   vaseline 35.00
Salt shaker w/original top, blue 44.00
Salt shaker w/original top, clear ... 14.50
Salt & pepper shakers w/original
   tops, clear, pr................. 44.50
Sauce dish, flat, handled, amber ... 13.00
Sauce dish, flat, handled, clear 10.00
Sauce dish, footed, amber 14.50
Spooner, amber 32.50
Spooner, blue................... 30.00
Spooner, clear 19.50
Sugar bowl, cov. 30.00
Table set, creamer, cov. sugar bowl
   & spooner, 3 pcs. 85.00
Tumbler, amber.................. 34.00
Tumbler, blue................... 30.00
Tumbler, clear.................. 20.00
Wine, amber..................... 20.00

WILDFLOWER

Bowl, 5¾" sq.	15.00
Bowl, 6½" sq., blue	22.50
Bowl, 7" sq., footed, amber	29.00
Bowl, 7" sq., clear	14.50
Bowl, 8" sq., 5" h., footed, apple green	35.00
Bowl, 8" sq., 5" h., footed, blue	50.00
Bowl, 8" sq., 5" h., footed, vaseline	20.00
Butter dish, cov., flat, blue	50.00
Butter dish, cov., flat, clear	35.00
Cake stand, amber, 9½" to 11"	48.50 to 65.00
Cake stand, apple green, 9½" to 11"	68.00
Cake stand, blue, 9½" to 11"	50.00 to 85.00
Cake stand, clear, 9½" to 11"	52.00
Cake stand, vaseline, 9½" to 11"	82.00
Celery vase, amber	55.00
Celery vase, blue	60.00
Celery vase, clear	28.00
Champagne, amber	50.00
Champagne, blue	50.00
Champagne, clear	30.00
Compote, cov., 6" d., blue	70.00
Compote, cov., 6" d., clear	42.00
Compote, cov., 7" d., amber	50.00
Compote, cov., 8" d., amber	90.00
Compote, cov., 8" d., clear	29.00
Compote, cov., 10" d.	55.00
Compote, open, jelly	30.00
Compote, open, 7" d., low stand, apple green	23.50
Compote, open, 7" d., low stand, blue	38.00
Compote, open, 9½" d., amber	45.00
Compote, open, 10½" d., 8¼" h., amber	78.00
Creamer, amber	34.00
Creamer, apple green	40.00
Creamer, blue	40.00
Creamer, clear	25.00
Creamer, vaseline	40.00
Creamer & sugar bowl, pr.	62.50
Goblet, amber	32.00
Goblet, apple green	34.00
Goblet, blue	35.00
Goblet, clear	28.00
Goblet, vaseline	38.00
Pitcher, water, amber	52.50
Pitcher, water, apple green	95.00
Pitcher, water, clear	50.00
Pitcher, water, vaseline	62.00
Plate, 7" sq., apple green	24.50
Plate, 7" sq., blue	45.00
Plate, 10" sq., amber	35.00
Plate, 10" sq., apple green	32.50
Plate, 10" sq., blue	35.00
Plate, 10" sq., clear	20.00
Platter, 8 x 11", apple green	45.00 to 69.00
Platter, 8 x 11", clear	35.00

Relish, amber	17.50
Relish, apple green	19.50
Relish, clear	22.50
Salt shaker w/original top, amber	35.00
Salt shaker w/original top, apple green	30.00
Salt shaker w/original top, blue	55.00
Salt shaker w/original top, vaseline	55.00
Salt & pepper shakers w/original tops, pr.	45.00
Sauce dish, flat or footed, amber	13.50
Sauce dish, flat or footed, apple green	13.50
Sauce dish, flat or footed, blue	17.00
Sauce dish, flat or footed, clear	10.00
Sauce dish, flat or footed, vaseline	15.00
Spooner, amber	32.50
Spooner, apple green	35.00
Spooner, clear	28.00
Spooner, vaseline	34.00
Sugar bowl, cov., blue	54.00
Sugar bowl, cov., clear	33.00
Sugar bowl, cov., vaseline	45.00
Sugar bowl, open, amber	20.00
Sugar bowl, open, apple green	35.00
Sugar bowl, open, blue	30.00
Sugar bowl, open, clear	19.00
Syrup pitcher w/original top, amber	140.00 to 160.00
Syrup pitcher w/original top, blue	130.00
Syrup pitcher w/original top, clear	115.00
Table set, 4 pcs.	125.00
Tray, dresser, amber, 4 x 9"	30.00
Tray, dresser, blue, 4 x 9"	45.00
Tray, dresser, vaseline, 4 x 9"	28.50
Tray, water, amber, 11 x 13"	44.00
Tray, water, apple green, 11 x 13"	55.00
Tray, water, blue, 11 x 13"	45.00
Tray, water, clear, 11 x 13"	39.00
Tray, water, vaseline, 11 x 13"	50.00
Tumbler, amber	35.00
Tumbler, apple green	28.00
Tumbler, clear	22.00
Tumbler, vaseline	30.00
Tumbler, yellow	27.50
Vase, 10½" h.	58.00
Water set: pitcher, tray & 6 tumblers; apple green, 8 pcs.	325.00

WILLOW OAK

Bowl, cov., 7" d., flat	39.00
Bowl, 7" d., amber	20.00
Bowl, 7" d., blue	30.00
Bowl, 7" d., clear	14.50
Bowl, 8" d., 2½" h.	19.50
Bread plate, 9" d.	35.00
Bread plate, amber, 11" d.	42.00
Butter dish, cov., amber	65.00
Butter dish, cov., clear	52.50
Cake stand, amber, 8" to 10" d.	55.00
Cake stand, blue, 8" to 10" d.	58.00
Cake stand, clear, 8" to 10" d.	40.00

Celery vase, amber 50.00
Celery vase, clear 40.00
Compote, cov., 6½" d., 9" h....... 47.50
Compote, open, 6" d., scalloped
  top 39.00
Compote, open, 7" d., high stand,
  amber 40.00
Compote, open, 7" d., high stand,
  blue 60.00
Compote, open, 7" d., high stand,
  clear......................... 37.00
Compote, open, 8" d., low stand,
  amber 65.00
Creamer, amber 38.00
Creamer, blue 42.50
Creamer, clear 30.00
Goblet, amber 40.00
Goblet, blue..................... 37.00
Goblet, clear 32.00
Mug, amber 35.00
Mug, blue 42.50
Mug, clear....................... 27.00
Pitcher, milk, amber............. 55.00
Pitcher, milk, clear 40.00
Pitcher, water, amber 90.00
Pitcher, water, clear............ 42.00
Plate, 7" d., amber.............. 35.00
Plate, 7" d., clear 26.00
Plate, 9" d., handled, amber 30.00
Plate, 9" d., handled, blue 45.00
Plate, 9" d., handled, clear 22.50
Salt shaker w/original top, blue 66.00
Salt & pepper shakers w/original
  tops, pr....................... 65.00
Sauce dish, flat or footed 12.00
Spooner, amber.................. 40.00
Spooner, blue................... 38.00
Spooner, clear 22.00
Sugar bowl, cov., amber 62.50
Sugar bowl, cov., clear 39.00
Sugar bowl, open 20.00
Table set, amber, 4 pcs. 375.00
Tray, water, blue, 10½" d......... 58.00
Tray, water, clear, 10½" d. 28.00
Tumbler, amber................. 35.00
Tumbler, blue.................. 37.50
Tumbler, clear 26.00
Waste bowl, amber 48.00
Waste bowl, clear............. 29.00
Water set, pitcher, tray & 2 tum-
  blers, 4 pcs. 170.00

WINDFLOWER
Bowl, 5 x 7" oval................ 27.50
Butter dish, cov. 45.00
Celery vase.................... 40.00
Compote, cov., 8½" d., low stand .. 45.00
Compote, open, 8" d............. 16.50
Creamer 34.00
Egg cup 20.00
Goblet 36.00
Pitcher, water 65.00
Sauce dish..................... 10.00
Spooner 28.00

Sugar bowl, cov.................. 29.00
Sugar bowl, open 18.00
Tumbler, bar................... 35.00
Tumbler, water 40.00
Wine.......................... 29.00

WISCONSIN (Beaded Dewdrop)

Wisconsin Water Pitcher

Banana stand, turned-up sides,
  7½" w., 4" h.................. 75.00
Bonbon, handled, 4".............. 25.00
Bowl, 6½" d. 37.00
Bowl, 8" d. 42.00
Bread tray 45.00
Butter dish, cov. 92.00
Cake stand, 8¼" d., 4¾" h. 35.00
Cake stand, 9¾" d................ 45.00
Celery tray, flat, 5 x 10" 42.50
Celery vase.................... 46.00
Compote, cov., 10½" d. 65.00
Compote, open, 6½" d., 6½" h..... 26.00
Compote, open, 7½" d., 5½" h. 38.00
Compote, open, tricornered, footed,
  7" d., 4" h. 25.00
Creamer, individual size 49.00
Cruet w/original stopper........... 40.00
Dish, cov., oval 26.50
Goblet 49.00
Mug, 3½" h..................... 34.00
Nappy, handled, 4" d. 20.00
Olive dish, two-handled 35.00
Pickle dish.................... 24.00
Pitcher, milk 48.00
Pitcher, water, 8" h. (ILLUS.) 59.00
Plate, 5" sq. 15.00
Plate, 6½" sq. 26.00
Punch cup 18.00
Relish, 4 x 8½" 22.50
Salt & pepper shakers w/original
  tops, pr...................... 45.00
Sauce dish.................... 14.00
Spooner 35.00
Sugar bowl, cov., 5" h. 37.50
Sugar shaker w/original top 63.00
Syrup pitcher w/original top,
  6½" h....................... 75.00
Toothpick holder 41.00
Tumbler 45.00
Wine.......................... 65.00

WOODEN PAIL - See Oaken Bucket Pattern

X-RAY

Berry set: 8" d. master bowl & 1 sauce dish; amethyst, 2 pcs.	35.00
Celery vase, emerald green	48.00
Compote, jelly, emerald green	47.00
Creamer, breakfast size, emerald green w/gold	44.00
Pitcher, water, emerald green, ½ gal., 9½" h.	65.00
Salt shaker w/original top	18.50
Sauce dish, clear, 4½" d.	7.00
Sauce dish, emerald green, 4½" d.	20.00
Sugar bowl, cov., emerald green w/gold	42.00
Sugar bowl, cov., breakfast size, emerald green w/gold	65.00
Syrup pitcher, emerald green w/gold	110.00
Table set, emerald green, 4 pcs.	305.00
Toothpick holder, emerald green	43.00
Tray, condiment	37.50
Tumbler, amethyst	42.50
Tumbler, emerald green	20.00
Water set: pitcher & 4 tumblers; emerald green w/gold, 5 pcs.	230.00

ZIPPER

Bowl, 8" oval	18.00
Butter dish, cov.	39.00
Celery vase	21.00
Cheese dish, cov.	45.00
Compote, cov., low stand	40.00
Creamer	20.00
Cruet w/original stopper, clear	38.00
Cruet w/original stopper, ruby-stained	145.00
Goblet	20.00
Marmalade jar, cov.	35.00
Pitcher, water	35.00
Relish	15.00
Sauce dish, flat or footed ..... 6.00 to	8.00
Spooner	20.00
Sugar bowl, cov.	25.00
Sugar shaker w/silver plate top	28.00
Toothpick holder, clear	15.00
Toothpick holder, ruby-stained	25.00
Wine	30.00

ZIPPERED BLOCK - See Iowa Pattern

(End of Pattern Glass Section)

PEACH BLOW

Several types of glass lumped together by collectors as Peach Blow were produced by half a dozen glasshouses. Hobbs, Brockunier & Co., Wheeling, West Virginia made Peach Blow as a plated ware that shaded from red at the top to yellow at the bottom and is re-ferred to as Wheeling Peach Blow. Mt. Washington Glass Works produced an homogeneous Peach Blow shading from a rose color at the top to pale blue in the lower portion. The New England Glass Works' Peach Blow, called Wild Rose, shaded from rose at the top to white. Gunderson—Pairpoint Co. also reproduced some of the Mt. Washington Peach Blow in the early 1950's and some glass of a somewhat similar type was made by Steuben Glass Works, the Boston & Sandwich Factory and by Thomas Webb & Sons and Stevens & Williams of England. Sandwich Peach Blow is one-layered glass and the English is two-layered. A relative newcomer to the fold is called New Martinsville "Peach Blow." It is a single-layered glass.

GUNDERSON - PAIRPOINT

Butter dish, cov., applied finial, scalloped edge, limited edition ca. 1960's, 9" w., 5" h.	$395.00
Vase, 7½" h., 4" d., crimped rim, polished pontil	160.00
Wine, round foot w/stem drawn to trumpet-shaped flared body, 4 1/8" h.	77.00

MT. WASHINGTON

Mt. Washington Vase

Condiment set: salt & pepper shakers & mustard pot; ribbed barrel form, enameled & h.p. blue & white forget-me-nots w/delicate green leaves & tracery, acid finish, original covers & (replated) silver plate stand marked "Pairpoint Mfg. Co. New Bedford Mass 705," shakers 3" h., the set	3,850.00
Perfume bottle w/original matching facet-cut stopper, enameled sprays of dainty white flowers, 5" h.	600.00
Vase, 12" h., baluster form (ILLUS.)	1,100.00

NEW ENGLAND

Creamer, ribbed 325.00
Punch cup, souvenir, "World's Fair
1893" (Chicago's Columbian Exposition), gold trim ....395.00 to 435.00
Tumbler, glossy finish, thin,
3¾" h. 385.00

NEW MARTINSVILLE

Dish, ruffled & convoluted rim,
5" d., 2¼" h. 110.00
Bowl, 4 7/8" d., ruffled scalloped
rim 53.00
Bride's bowl, frilled rim, "plated" interior, 11" d. 115.00

WEBB

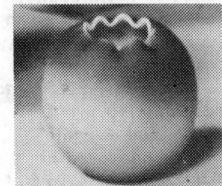

Webb Rose Bowl

Bottle vase, white lining, polished
pontil, 8¼" h. 145.00
Bottle vase, heavy gold leaves &
flowers decoration w/red & black
trim, white lining, 3¾" d.,
9 5/8" h. 395.00
Cracker jar, heavy gold prunus blossoms, pine needles & butterfly
decoration, acid finish, rich
creamy white lining, silver plate
rim, lid & handle, 4½" d., 6" h. .. 895.00
Rose bowl, eight-crimp top, acid finish, creamy white lining, 3¼" d.,
3" h. (ILLUS.) 225.00
Scent bottle w/hallmarked silver
domed screw-on top, gold prunus
blossoms & branches w/gold butterfly reverse, acid finish, creamy
white lining, 3 5/8" d., 4½" h. ... 495.00
Vase, 3" h., ball-shaped, gold
leaves, flower pods & dragonfly,
glossy finish 230.00
Vase, 5" h., 3 3/8" d., overall lacy
gold foliage & silver flowers,
creamy white lining 265.00
Vase, 5¾" h., 4½" d., applied clear
looped branch feet, embossed
swirls, applied clear berries,
leaves & flowers, flower prunt on
base, glossy finish, creamy white
lining 550.00
Vase, 7" h., flattened bulbous base,
slender neck w/flared mouth,
heavy gold daisies & leaves front,
large dragonfly reverse, creamy
white lining.................... 650.00
Vase, 7¾" h., 4¾" d., gold prunus

blossoms & bee, glossy finish,
creamy white lining 650.00
Vases, 10½" h., 5" d., gold
branches, butterfly in flight & prunus blossoms decoration, glossy finish, creamy white lining, facing
pr. 1,250.00

WHEELING

Wheeling Peach Blow

Creamer, bulbous, square mouth,
applied clear reeded handle,
Drape patt., creamy white lining,
4½" d., 4½" h. 795.00
Cruet w/facet-cut stopper, trefoil top,
white lining, 6½" h. 1,285.00
Lemonade glass, cylindrical, glossy
finish, polished pontil, oyster
white lining, 5 1/8" h. (pinpoint
flake at interior of rim) 214.50
Mustard jar w/original pewter rim,
cover & attached handle, ball-
shaped, satin finish, opal lining,
3" h. (ILLUS. left rear) 357.70
Salt & pepper shakers w/original slit
flat tops, ball-shaped, glossy finish, 2¾" h., pr. 660.00
Salt & pepper shakers w/original slit
flat tops, ball-shaped, satin finish,
opal lining, 2¾" h., pr. (ILLUS.
left front)...................... 715.00
Tumbler, cylindrical, satin finish,
oyster lining, 3¾" h. 176.00
Vase, 13¾" h., bulbous body
w/long slender slightly flared
neck, glossy finish, opal lining
(ILLUS. right).................. 605.00

PEKING GLASS

*This is Chinese glass, some of which has
overlay in one to five colors, which has attracted collector interest.*

Bowls, 6" d., bell-form, everted rim
encircled w/a flowering branch &
a lone bird, orange overlay

carved through to creamy white,
pr. $247.50

Peking Glass Bowl

Bowls, 6¼" d., bell-form, raised on
an inset ring foot & deeply carved
w/an elegant chrysanthemum
branch & a long-tailed bird
reversed by a prunus branch
w/two songbirds, opaque yellow,
pr. (ILLUS. of one) 4,125.00
Bowls, 7" l., square body set w/a
wide rim & tapering sharply to a
short, square foot, the exterior
sides carved & incised w/a goldfish, camelia, prunus & blossoming lotus plants, bright opaque
yellow, pr. 880.00
Vases, 5" h., pear-shaped body of
milky-white carved w/blossoming
floral sprigs flanked by wide
green overlay bands, pr. (wear) . . 440.00
Vase, 8 1/8" h., low-slung body surmounted by a tall stick neck flaring towards the wide rim, carved
w/two songbirds amid meandering magnolia branches in bloom,
opaque brownish-mustard 440.00
Vases, 13" h., overlay crimson red
tropical fish & lotus leaves against
white ground, pr. 2,500.00

PELOTON

Peloton Pitcher

Made in Bohemia, Germany and England
in the late 19th century, this glassware is
characterized by threads or filaments of glass

rolled into the glass body of the objects in random patterns. Some of these wares were
decorated.

Bowl, 4" d., 3" h., pinched-in top,
ribbed body, clear w/white, blue,
pink & olive green "coconut"
threading, pastel orchid opales-
cent lining (minor internal flaw) . .$190.00
Cracker jar, cov., ribbed sides,
opaque white w/pink, blue, yellow & white "coconut" threading,
cased in clear, silver plate rim,
cover & handle, 5¾" d.,
5½" h. . . . . .550.00 to 575.00
Pitcher, 5 7/8" h., ribbed tapering
body w/elongated neck, applied
ribbed handle, amber satin finish
w/blue, red & yellow "coconut"
threading, ca. 1880
(ILLUS.) . . . . .165.00 to 190.00
Rose bowl, six-crimp top, white
w/blue, yellow, pink & white
"coconut" threading, cased in
clear, 2½" d., 2¼" h. . . .225.00 to 245.00
Rose bowl, applied clear shell feet,
top pulled up to four points,
ribbed, white opaque w/pink,
blue, yellow & white "coconut"
threading, cased in clear, 3½"
widest d., 3 7/8" h. 275.00
Vase, 3¾" h., applied clear petal
feet & twisted rigaree around
four-point rim, opaque white
w/rose, yellow, blue & white
"coconut" threading, cased in
clear 265.00
Vase, 3 7/8" h., 4¾" d., squat bul-
bous shape, folded-over tricorn
top, ribbed, opaque white w/pink,
blue, yellow & white "coconut"
threading, cased in clear 295.00
Vase, 5 3/8" h., 3¾" d., ball-shaped
w/flared ruffled top, white
w/pink, blue, yellow & white
"coconut" threading, cased in
clear 245.00
Vase, 6¾" h., 3" d., stick-type, yel-
low w/white, rose, blue & yellow
"coconut" threading, white
lining 225.00

PHOENIX

This ware was made by the Phoenix Glass
Co. of Beaver County, Pennsylvania, which
produced various types of glass from the
1880's. One special type that attracts collectors now is a molded ware with a vague
resemblance to cameo in its "sculptured"
decoration. Similar pieces with relief-molded
designs were produced by the Consolidated

Lamp & Glass Co. (which see) and care must be taken to differentiate between the two companies' wares.

Phoenix Wild Geese Vase

Vase, 7" h., Bluebell patt., relief-molded white flowers on grey ground $75.00
Vase, 7" h., 7" d., Star Flower patt., relief-molded white flowers & vertical ribs on green ground 65.00
Vase, 8 x 9", pillow-shaped, white relief-molded flowers on lavender ground 89.00
Vase, 9¼" h., pillow-shaped, Wild Geese patt., relief-molded white birds on brown ground (ILLUS.) . . . 195.00
Vase, 11" h., bulbous shape, relief-molded iridescent white flowers & branches on rose red ground, w/original gold label 175.00
Vase, 11½" h., Philodendron patt., relief-molded white leaves on coral ground 95.00

PILLAR-MOLDED

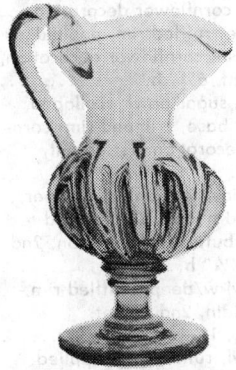

Pillar-Molded Creamer

This heavily ribbed glassware was produced by blowing glass into full-sized ribbed molds and then finishing it by hand. The technique evolved from earlier "pattern

moulding" used on glass since ancient times but in pillar-molded glass the ribs are very heavy and prominent. Most examples found in this country were produced in the Pittsburgh, Pennsylvania area from around 1850 to 1870, but similar English-made wares made before and after this period are also available. Most American pieces were made from clear flint glass and colored examples or pieces with colored strands in the ribs are rare and highly prized. Some collectors refer to this as "steamboat" glass believing that it was made to be used on American riverboats but most likely it was used anywhere that a sturdy, relatively inexpensive glassware was needed, such as taverns and hotels.

Bar bottle, eight-rib, clear waisted cylindrical form w/wide shoulder ring & slightly tapering neck to thick lip, each rib w/applied blue band, Pittsburgh, 19th c., 10 5/8" h. (rough broken bubble on one rib, minute flakes) $450.00
Bowl, footed, 10½" d., 7¾" h., folded rim, clear ribbed sides above a baluster stem on a circular foot, possibly Pittsburgh, first half 19th c. 176.00
Cologne bottle w/matching original stopper, eight-rib, green, 5" h. . . . 450.00
Compote, open, 5¾" d., 4 5/8" h., eight-rib, clear w/thick ribs & flared rim on short, straight pedestal w/wide round base, pontil mark inside bowl, Pittsburgh, 19th c. 550.00
Compote, open, 9" d., 8" h., eight-rib, clear widely flared rim, plain round pedestal & foot, Pittsburgh, mid-19th c. 250.00
Compote, open, 10¾" d., 9" h., eight-rib, clear flaring bowl on applied baluster stem & wide applied foot 405.00
Creamer, footed, clear squat round body w/eight prominent ribs & tall flaring neck w/broad spout, applied strap handle, triple-wafer connecting to pedestal base w/round foot, 6¼" h. (ILLUS.) . . . 1,300.00
Decanter w/applied collar & pewter top, eight-rib, clear wide base tapering to top, applied strap handle w/elaborate trailed & tooled end, mid-19th c., 9½" h. . . 275.00
Lamp, fluid-type, eight-rib, amber ovoid body tapering toward top w/original "rabbit ear" double-spout camphene burner (slightly loose), applied round foot, 5" h. (ILLUS. top next page) 1,900.00
Lamp, hand-type, cone-shaped, eight-rib, clear, w/applied solid

strap handle w/curl end, original
brass collar & camphene burner,
6¼" h. (stress crack at top of
handle) 300.00

Rare Pillar-Molded Lamp

Pitcher, 9¾" h., eight-rib, clear
rounded body w/graceful flared
mouth, wide solid applied handle
w/curled end, polished pontil,
Pittsburgh, 19th c. 300.00
Pitcher, 10¾" h., eight-rib, clear,
w/applied solid strap handle
w/curl end, solid applied heavy
round foot w/polished pontil,
Pittsburgh, 19th c. 185.00
Salt dip, open, footed, eight-rib,
clear rounded body curving in
slightly to rim, solid applied stem
on round foot, 3 3/8" h. 425.00

Pillar-Molded Vase

Vase, 8 3/8" h., eight-rib, clear
body w/flaring rim & ribs twisted
to the right, knob pedestal base
on round foot (ILLUS.) 120.00
Vase, 10" h., eight-rib, sapphire
blue baluster-shaped body
w/sharp right-twist at the neck,
flared mouth, applied solid round
foot w/polished pontil 800.00

Vase, 10½" h., eight-rib, cobalt
blue body w/tooled rim on
pressed hexagonal base & connected w/thick glass wafer, attributed to Boston & Sandwich
Glass Company, Sandwich, Massachusetts, ca. 1850 .... 950.00
Vase, 11 1/8" h., footed, eight-rib,
clear panels alternating
w/opaque, etched panels, bold
flaring mouth, applied baluster
stem & wide round foot, polished
pontil 235.00

POMONA

*First produced by the New England Glass
Company under a patent received by Joseph
Locke in 1885, Pomona has a frosted ground
on clear glass decorated with mineral stains,
most frequently amber-yellow, sometimes
pale blue. Some pieces bore smooth etched floral decorations highlighted with staining.
Two types of Pomona were made. The first
Locke patent covered a technique whereby
the piece was first covered with an acid-
resistant coating which was then needle-
carved with thousands of minute criss-
crossing lines. The piece was then dipped into
acid which cut into the etched lines, giving
the finished piece a notable "brilliance." A
cheaper method, covered by a second Locke
patent on June 15, 1886, was accomplished
by rolling the glass piece in particles of acid-
resistant material which were picked up by
it. The glass was then etched by acid which
attacked areas not protected by the resistant
particles. A favorite design on Pomona was
the cornflower.*

Bowl, 10", cornflower decoration ...$650.00
Celery vase, ruffled rim, applied
glass base, cornflower decoration,
1st patent, 6¼" h. 350.00
Creamer & sugar bowl, scalloped
pedestal base, crimped rim, cornflower decoration, 1st patent,
3" h., pr. 605.00
Cruet w/iridescent amber stopper,
unstained handle & unstained
pansy & butterfly decoration, 2nd
patent, 7¼" h. 465.00
Finger bowl w/deeply ruffled rim,
amber stain, 2nd patent,
5 7/8" d., 1¾" h. 44.00
Finger bowl, ruffled rim, applied
base, cornflower decoration, 2nd
patent, 5½" d., 3" h. 150.00
Finger bowl, trailing vines design,
2nd patent 65.00
Lemonade tumbler, tall cylindrical
body w/applied loop handle near

base, amber-stained rim, silver
rivulet decoration, 2nd patent 185.00
Pitcher, 6¼" h., square top, cornflower decoration, 1st patent..... 395.00
Pitcher, tankard-type, 12" h., tall,
slightly tapering cylindrical body
w/Diamond Quilted patt., amber
stain around mouth & on applied
handle, polished pontil, 2nd
patent 148.50
Punch cup, rivulet design, amber
stain around rim, 2nd patent,
2¾" h....................... 165.00
Punch cup, cornflower decoration,
2nd patent.................... 90.00
Tumbler, cornflower decoration, 2nd
patent 95.00
Tumbler, Oak Leaf Band patt., 2nd
patent 75.00
Vase, 2½" h., 4" w., fan-shaped
w/applied amber scalloped rim,
applied amber scalloped base, 1st
patent 350.00
Vase, 3" h., 6" d., fan-shaped,
amber ruffled rim, amber scalloped feet, cornflower decoration,
1st patent 235.00
Vase, 7" h., cornflower decoration,
2nd patent................... 175.00

QUEZAL

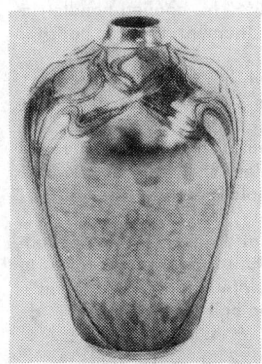

Quezal Silver Overlay Vase

*These wares resemble those of Tiffany and
other glasshouses which produced lustred
glass pieces in the late 19th and early 20th
centuries. They were made by the Quezal Art
Glass and Decorating Co. of Brooklyn, New
York, early in this century and until its closing in the mid-1920's.*

Auto vase, folded rim raised at back
of elongated conical bud vase,
amber glass w/golden iridescence, marked "Quezal" around
base side, 10½" h.............. $137.50

Bowl, 9½" d., stretch rim, pedestal
foot, gold calcite, signed
"Quezal" 795.00
Compote, open, 4¾" h., pedestal
foot, pale pastel blue, signed &
numbered 500.00
Compote, open, 6" h., wide flaring
bowl on slender pedestal w/round
foot, yellow iridescent finish 385.00
Creamer, applied lip, iridescent
gold, 2½" h................... 545.00
Cup & saucer, iridescent gold interi-
or on opal w/hooked feather motif repeated on each piece, both
signed "Quezal" & numbered,
2½" h. 1,045.00
Finger bowl w/underplate, iridescent gold, underplate w/onion-
skin stretched at edges, signed,
2 pcs........................ 550.00
Knife rest, iridescent gold w/two
square ends & a twisted bar between, polished pontil w/signa-
ture "QUEZAL," 3½" w., ¾" h.... 99.00
Plate, 8" d., scalloped edge, iridescent gold 250.00
Vase, 1½" h., ruffled rim, ribbed
body, iridescent gold, signed 400.00
Vase, 3½" h., shouldered ovoid
body w/raised narrow rim, ribbed
opal glass layered w/emerald
green & having gold iridescent
swirled & pulled decoration
around shoulders & onto rim,
signed "Quezal" across pontil....2,310.00
Vase, 6" h., floriform w/ruffled
flared rim, pedestal base, opal
w/gold iridescent interior, green
& gold pulled-feather design exterior, signed "Quezal S/601" 1,045.00
Vase, 6¼" h., ovoid body w/short
narrow neck, iridescent yellow
w/overall ribbon-work, overlaid
w/elaborate scrolling Art Nouveau
silver strapwork, ca. 1900
(ILLUS.) 1,100.00
Vase, 7½" h., bulbous base narrowing toward the top, feathered in
green & gold over opal 762.00
Vase, 11¾" h., jack-in-the-pulpit
type, wide bright amber iridescent
rim, pale yellow body decorated
w/finely striated opalescent feathering edged in amber iridescent,
inscribed "Quezal - N.Y." possibly
at later date, ca. 1901-25........1,430.00
Vase, 12¾" h., short bulbous body,
long waisted neck, wide ruffled
opalescent rim decorated w/amber
iridescent & opalescent green concentric rings, the interior iridescent
bright orange, inscribed "Quezal,"
ca. 1901-25...................1,320.00
Vase, 14¾" h., jack-in-the-pulpit

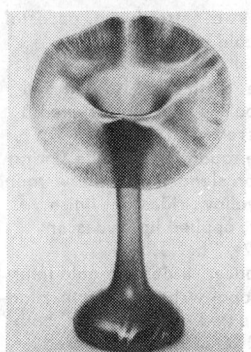

Quezal Jack-in-the-Pulpit Vase
type, widely flaring turn-up rim in
deep amber iridescence tinged
w/green & pink, raised on a cylindrical standard & circular domed
foot, all in amber iridescence
decorated w/silvery-blue & amber
loopings & trailings, 1905-20
(ILLUS.) 2,310.00

ROSE BOWLS

Bristol, turquoise blue, decorated
w/scallops of gold w/gold flowers
& overall lacy gold flowers &
leaves, four-crimp top, 3½" d.,
4¼" h. $110.00
Cased, egg-shaped, shaded heavenly blue satin exterior enameled
w/cream florals, applied clear
lacy trim & applied frosted petal
feet, white interior, eight-crimp
top, 3 5/8" d., 6" h. 135.00
Cased, egg-shaped, rose shaded to
pink satin exterior enameled
w/lavender & yellow pansies
w/green leaves, applied frosted
petal feet, white interior, four-
crimp top, 3¾" d., 5½" h. 135.00
Cased, heavenly blue satin exterior
w/enameled daisies & blue
leaves, rich cream interior, eight-
crimp top, 6" d., 5¾" h. 165.00
Cased, shaded chartreuse green
mother-of-pearl satin Rivulet patt.
exterior, applied frosted ruffled
base, white interior, eight-crimp
top, 3 7/8" d., 3¼" h. 275.00
English cameo, carved overall white
paisley designs on blue-green
ground, 4½" d., 4" h. 1,500.00
Nailsea, frosted cranberry
w/opaque white loopings, three
applied glossy wishbone feet,
nine-crimp top, 6¼" d., 4½" h. .. 325.00
Opalescent pink, Diamond Quilted
patt. w/applied clear threading,

ruffled applied vaseline foot,
eight-crimp top, 4 1/8" d.,
2 7/8" h. 88.00
Rubina crystal, overall enameled
lacy gold flowers & leaves,
smooth rim, 5½" d., 4¾" h. 118.00
Spatter, white, yellow & clear,
cased, round bottom w/squared
crimped top 140.00

RUBINA CRYSTAL

*This glass, sometimes spelled "Rubena,"
is a flashed ware, shading from ruby to clear.
Some pieces are decorated, others are plain.*

Bowl, 4" d., footed, Honeycomb
patt. $88.00
Cologne bottle, clear facet-cut stopper, cylindrical body w/cut
panels, 2½" d., 6¼" h. 95.00
Cracker jar, cov., slightly ribbed
body, decorated w/sanded pink
flowers w/gold & white stems,
white metal cover w/gold trim,
handle & rim, 5" d., 8¼" h. 235.00
Pickle castor insert, Diamond Quilted patt., floral decoration, 3¼" d.
at bottom, 3" d. at top, 4½" h. 165.00
Pitcher, 5½" h., applied clear handle, Optic Rib patt. 75.00
Pitcher, 8¾" h., applied handle, Inverted Thumbprint patt., polished
pontil 225.00
Rose bowl, h.p. overall lacy gold
flowers & leaves, 5½" d.,
4¾" h. 118.00
Sweetmeat dish, ruffled dish w/ap-
plied clear shell trim, in silver
plate holder, overall 6½" d.,
6" h. 115.00
Sweetmeat dish, ruffled w/applied
clear shell trim around center, in
silver plate holder w/scalloped
edge on ball feet, holder 6¾" d.
overall, 6" h. 110.00
Vase, bud, 7" h., decorated
w/enameled flowers 90.00
Vases, 13" h., scalloped top w/gold
trim, enameled mums decoration,
pr. 500.00
Water set: pitcher & 5 tumblers;
Paneled Sprig patt., w/rare factory decoration, the set 300.00

RUBINA VERDE

*This decorative glass, popular in the late
19th and early 20th centuries, shades from
ruby or deep cranberry to green or greenish-
yellow.*

Bowl, 9" d., 5¼" h., footed, rolled
 rim, Honeycomb patt. $100.00
Bowl-vase, pedestal foot, Drape
 patt., 9¼" h. 180.00
Sugar shaker w/metal lid, enameled
 floral decoration, one of Hobb's
 "Coloratura" series 295.00
Tumbler, Inverted Thumbprint
 patt. 95.00
Vases, 9½" h., pinched neck, hollow foot, Straight Optic patt.,
 enameled white flowers, navy
 scrolls & gold jewelling, pr. 250.00
Vases, 12" h., ruffled rim, heavily
 enameled decoration, pr. 350.00

Rubina Verde Vase
Vase, 13" h., tall trumpet-shaped
vase connected by thick glass wafer to flaring domed foot, overall
enameled gold scrolling (ILLUS.) .. 85.00

RUBY-STAINED

*This name derives from the color of the
glass — a deep red. The red staining was thinly painted on clear pressed glass patterns and
refired at a low temperature. Many pieces
were further engraved as souvenir items and
were very popular from the 1890's into the
1920's. This technique should not be confused
with "flashed" glass where a clear glass piece
is actually dipped in molten glass of a contrasting color. Also see PATTERN GLASS.*

Bowl, master berry, Carnation
 patt. $35.00
Bowl, master berry, Sweet Sixty-
 One patt. 50.00
Butter dish, cov., Bordered Ellipse
 patt. 65.00
Butter dish, cov., Box-in-Box
 patt. .... 95.00 to 110.00
Butter dish, cov., Fleur-de-Lis
 patt. 75.00
Celery vase, Pioneer's Victoria
 patt. 85.00

Champagne, O'Hara Diamond patt.,
 4 7/8" h. 55.00
Compote, open, Scalloped Swirl
 patt. 155.00
Creamer, Frost Crystal (Tarentum's
 Peerless) patt. 60.00
Creamer, Naomi patt. 55.00
Creamer, O'Hara Diamond patt.,
 w/etching .... 55.00 to 65.00
Creamer & cov. sugar bowl, in-
 dividual size, Lace Band patt.,
 pr. 65.00
Cruet w/original stopper, Beaded
 Swirl & Lens patt. 85.00
Cruet w/original stopper, teapot
 form w/pouring spout, Pioneer's
 Victoria patt. 395.00
Decanter, water, Tacoma patt. 135.00
Decanter w/original stopper, Tiny
 Finecut patt. 75.00
Goblet, Beaded Dart Band patt. 30.00
Goblet, Henrietta patt. 45.00
Goblet, Loop & Block patt. 40.00
Mugs, Beaded Swag patt., one
 etched "Mother, Mineola Fair,
 1910," the other "Father, Mineola
 Fair, 1910," Heisey, pr. 70.00
Mug, Bordered Ellipse patt. 30.00
Mug, Heart Band patt. 22.00
Nappy, triangular, Prize patt. 25.00
Nappy, triangular, handled, Taren-
 tum's Verona patt. 45.00
Pitcher, water, tankard, Block &
 Double Bar patt. 150.00
Pitcher, water, Block & Lattice
 patt. 110.00
Pitcher, water, tankard, Hexagon
 Block patt. 95.00
Plate, 5" sq., Barred Ovals patt. 35.00
Punch cup, footed, Hexagon Block
 patt. 25.00
Relish, Box-In-Box patt. 28.00
Salt & pepper shakers, Leaf & Star
 patt., pr. 125.00
Salt & pepper shakers, Millard patt.,
 engraved leaf, pr. 66.00
Sauce dish, Harvard patt., 4½" d. .. 20.00
Spooner, Beaded Swag patt. 50.00
Spooner, Henrietta patt. 59.00
Spooner, Prize patt. 52.50
Spooner, Ribbed Thumbprint 52.00
Spooner, Royal Crystal patt. 50.00
Sugar bowl, cov., Champion patt.... 85.00
Sugar bowl, cov., Crescent patt. 130.00
Sugar bowl, cov., Hexagon Block
 patt. 55.00
Sugar bowl, cov., Summit patt. 68.00
Sugar bowl, cov., Zipper Slash
 patt. 85.00
Syrup pitcher w/original top, Zip-
 pered Corner patt. 235.00
Table set: creamer, cov. butter &
 spooner; Frost Crystal patt.,
 3 pcs. 195.00

Table set: cov. butter dish, cov.
sugar bowl, creamer & spooner;
Beaded Swag patt. w/gold trim &
engraving, 4 pcs................. 225.00
Table set, Tacoma patt., 4 pcs...... 245.00
Toothpick holder, Millard patt. 195.00
Toothpick holder, Pleating patt. 28.00
Toothpick holder, Rib & Bead patt... 50.00
Toothpick holder, Swinger patt. 24.00
Tumbler, Blocked Thumbprint Band
patt., engraved 43.00
Tumbler, Box-In-Box patt........... 43.00
Tumbler, Diamond Point Band
patt........................... 18.00
Tumbler, Fleur-de-Lis patt., gold
trim.......................... 35.00
Tumbler, Pioneer's Victoria patt..... 43.00
Tumbler, Truncated Cube patt. 35.00
Water set: squatty pitcher & four
matching tumblers; Block & Lattice
patt., 5 pcs. 165.00
Water set: pitcher & 4 tumblers;
Wellington patt., 5 pcs. 245.00
Wine, Mirror & Fan patt........... 30.00
Wine, Rustic Rose patt. 26.00
Wine, Teardrop & Thumbprint
patt.......................... 48.00

SANDWICH

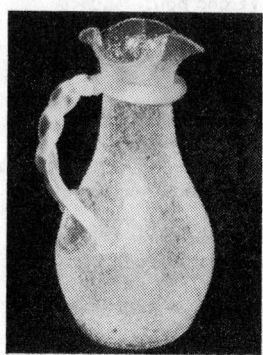

Sandwich Overshot Pitcher

Numerous types of glass were produced at
The Boston & Sandwich Glass Works in
Sandwich, Massachusetts, on Cape Cod, from
1826 to 1888. Those listed here represent a
sampling. Also see PATTERN GLASS.

Bowl, 5 1/16" d., Plume patt., red
amber flint glass, ca. 1860 ....$475.00
Bowl, 6½" d., lacy, Oak Leaf patt... 110.00
Bowl, 9¼" d., 9" h., Loop patt.,
opaque white, flint 110.00
Candlestick, Petal & Loop patt.,
translucent white loop base joined
by wafer to deep electric blue

petal socket, 7" h. (usual mold
roughness) 700.00
Candlesticks, hexagonal candle
socket above a knopped standard
on a sloping hexagonal foot,
clambroth, 1835-40, 7" h., pr. 330.00
Cologne bottle w/original flat mushroom stopper, squatty hexagonal
body, purplish blue, flint......... 395.00
Compote, miniature, footed, Sandwich Ivy patt., clear 85.00
Creamer, cylindrical body w/applied
clear handle, clear w/applied red
threading around base, polished
pontil, 4" h. 132.00
Lamps, Paneled Waffle patt. dome
font, scalloped hexagonal base,
brass ferrule, clear, ca. 1860,
11½" h., pr. (burners missing) ... 275.00
Lamps, Acanthus patt., deep jade
green acanthus pattern font attached w/wafer to columnar milk
white double-stepped base (minor
flaking), 11½" h., pr. 2,700.00
Lamps, Sweetheart patt., clear font
w/burner, chimney & rings for
shade, w/globular waisted frosted
cut to clear shade in a grapevine
design, 19th c., overall 19" h.,
pr............................ 412.50
Lamp, triple-cut overlay, pink to
white to black glass base, frosted
clear glass shade w/engraved
grape & flower design, 19¼" h...2,090.00
Pitcher, 13" h., clear ovoid "overshot" body tapering to ruffled rim,
twisted rope handle wrapping
around neck, ice bladder at back
under handle (ILLUS.) 210.00
Plate, miniature, 2" d., scalloped
rim, lacy center w/concentric circles around border, clear 85.00
Plate, deep, 4 5/8" d., Star & Plume
patt., electric blue, flint 300.00
Salt shaker, "Christmas" salt w/agi-
tator & dated top, amethyst,
3¾" h......................... 125.00
Sugar bowl, cov., lacy, Gothic Arch
patt., hexagonal bowl & domed
hexagonal cover w/knopped finial, circular foot, turquoise blue,
1830-40, 5½" h. 1,540.00
Toilet bottle, w/original Tam
O'Shanter stopper, mold-blown
swirled ribs, bluish purple,
5½" h......................... 525.00
Tumble-up: water carafe w/match-
ing tumbler; "overshot," clear,
2 pcs......................... 135.00

SATIN & MOTHER-OF-PEARL

Satin glass was a very popular decorative

glass in the 1880's and 1890's. It derives its name from the matte or "satin" finish on pieces which was achieved by exposing them to acid fumes after they were formed. This ware is layered, usually with a colored exterior and a white lining and the mother-of-pearl variety is decorated with various patterns, such as Herringbone or Diamond Quilted, formed by air traps between the layers. Satin was extensively produced in both England and America and modern reproductions are widely imported from Europe today.

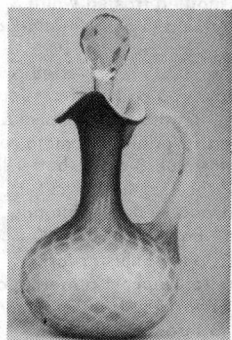

Mother-of-Pearl Diamond Quilted Cruet

Bowl, 6 7/8" d., 2¾" h., tricornered, tightly ruffled rim w/applied clear frosted edge, light blue shaded to rich heavenly blue mother-of-pearl Diamond Quilted patt. interior, white exterior $265.00

Bowl, 9 5/8 x 11¾", 7½" h., fluted rim w/applied frosted edge, shaded teal blue interior w/enameled small red cherries & green leaves, white exterior, ormolu foot 450.00

Cracker jar, cov., rich golden yellow overlay decorated w/gold prunus & heavy gold branches & flowers w/large moth, white lining, silver plate cover, rim & bail handle, 4 5/8" d., 6" h 575.00

Cracker jar, cov., cylindrical, rose mother-of-pearl Diamond Quilted patt., silver plate domed cover w/finial, rim, bail handle & base w/four feet, 5" d., 8¾" h. to top of finial 735.00

Creamer, bulbous w/square mouth, applied frosted clear edge around mouth, applied clear frosted reeded handle, butterscotch mother-of-pearl Raindrop patt., white lining, 4 3/8" d., 4½" h 225.00

Cruet w/clear facet-cut stopper, applied clear frosted reeded handle, shaded blue mother-of-pearl Diamond Quilted patt., white lining, 7" h. (ILLUS.) 630.00

Ewer, bulbous base narrowing to tall, slender neck w/ruffled rim & spout, applied clear frosted thorn handle, shaded deep apricot mother-of-pearl Diamond Quilted patt., white lining, 9½" h 255.00

Pitcher, water, 9" h., ruffled rim, applied clear frosted reeded handle, shaded blue mother-of-pearl Raindrop patt. 425.00

Punch cups, butterscotch shading to white, white interior, applied clear frosted handle, 3" d., 2 1/8" h., pr. 88.00

Rose bowl, eight-crimp top, deep red mother-of-pearl Peacock Eye patt., white lining, 3" d. 900.00

Rose bowl, incurving scalloped rim, applied clear feet, rainbow mother-of-pearl Diamond Quilted patt., alternating deep pink, yellow, blue & other colors w/clear stripes between colors, marked "Patent," 4¼" d., 3½" h. 1,395.00

Sweetmeat jar, cov., squared squatty bulbous body, mother-of-pearl w/h.p. red & gold flower & acorn decoration, silver plate flat cover, rim & bail handle, 4¾" sq., 5" h. to top of handle 755.00

Tumbler, cylindrical, rainbow mother-of-pearl Diamond Quilted patt., pastel red, yellow & light blue, 2½" d., 3 3/8" h. 330.00

Tumbler, square mouth, rainbow mother-of-pearl Diamond Quilted patt., vibrant light blue, yellow & red, white lining, 2½" w., 3 7/8" h. 522.50

Tumble-up set (carafe & tumbler), pastel lavender mother-of-pearl Diamond Quilted patt., 2 pcs. 115.00

Vase, 5" h., 3" d., bulbous body w/wide ruffled rim applied w/frosted clear edge band, five applied frosted clear wishbone feet, shaded orange mother-of-pearl Diamond Quilted patt. 225.00

Vase, 5" h., 8½" d., squat round bowl w/flared ruffled rim in white mother-of-pearl Diamond Quilted patt. layered w/pink, yellow & amber rainbow colors cameo-cut & carved w/apple blossoms & branches, signed "Thomas Webb & Sons - Gem - Cameo" 2,200.00

Vase, 7" h., brown mother-of-pearl Federzeichnung patt. w/gold enameled decoration 1,215.00

Vase, 7" h., 4" d., ruffled rim w/applied frosted clear edge band, shaded lemon yellow to white mother-of-pearl Diamond Quilted patt., enameled blue & pink flow-

ers, yellow branches & buds,
white lining 550.00
Vase, 9" h., 5" d., ribbed oval body
w/ruffled rim, butterscotch shaded to yellow shaded to white
mother-of-pearl Diamond Quilted
patt., white lining 525.00
Vase, 11½" h., bulbous base taper-
ing to tall, slender neck, molded
overall w/26 swirled ribs, bold alternating bands of color each
repeated twice, soft pink, creamy
yellow & robin's egg blue,
enameled gold rim, white lining . .   585.00

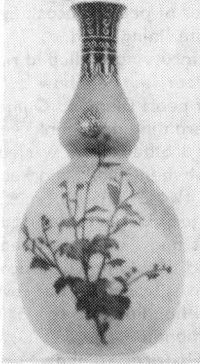

Rare Mother-of-Pearl Satin Glass Vase

Vase, ovoid body w/baluster-form
neck, mother-of-pearl Peacock
Eye patt. decorated w/wide gilt-
trimmed band at rim & large
enameled floral sprig up side
(ILLUS.) 1,100.00

SCHNEIDER

Schneider Enamel Decorated Compote

*This ware is made in France at Cristallerie
Schneider, established in 1913 near Paris by
Ernest and Charles Schneider. Some pieces
of cameo were marked "Le Verre Francais"
and others were signed "Charder."*

Cameo vase, 8½" h., clear ovoid
body invested w/myriad bubbles,
cased about the neck w/a band of
cherry red & wheel-carved overall
w/flowerheads, circular deep red
foot, signed "Schneider" in intaglio,
ca. 1925 . . . . $1,540.00
Cameo vase, 19 1/8" h., tapering
ovoid, circular foot, slightly flaring
lip, deep mahogany shading to
mulberry at the foot carved
w/stylized blossoms & leaves
against mottled frosted white &
apricot ground, signed in intaglio
"Le Verre Francais," ca. 1925 . . . . .   880.00
Cameo vase, 24½" h., inverted pyri-
form body on a cushion-form foot,
grey well mottled w/turquoise &
sea green, overlaid in tomato red
& sapphire blue & cut w/butterflies
in flight, the foot further cut
w/brickwork, signed in intaglio
"Le Verre Francais," ca. 1920 . . . . 3,300.00
Chandelier, open baluster-form
wrought-iron support centering a
basket of wrought-iron roses continuing to three scrolling arms
ending in mottled chocolate & brilliant canary yellow bell-form
shades, centering a wrought-iron
band decorated w/further rose blossoms & centering a conforming
domical shade, shades signed
"Schneider" in enamel, ca. 1925,
32" d. 1,320.00
Compote, 7½" h., opalescent bowl
enameled on the exterior w/scrol-
ling lines & stylized leafage centering four applied clear prunts mottled in blue & enclosing gilt foil,
baluster standard & circular base
in alternating panels of pumpkin
orange & lime green, signed in red
enamel "Schneider" beside a vase,
ca. 1920 (ILLUS.) 1,100.00
Vase, 6¾" h., globular, clear ribbed
sides enclosing controlled air
bubbles, neck overlaid in striated
orange & finely wheel-carved
w/stylized blossoms, signed in intaglio "Schneider/France/B. ALT-
MAN ET Co./PARIS NEW YORK,"
ca. 1920 . . . . 4,125.00
Vases, 8¾" h., ovoid, brilliant ca-
nary yellow molded in medium-
relief w/overlapping angular rays,
acid stamped "SCHNEIDER," ca.
1925, pr. 467.00
Vase, 12¼" h., amphora-shaped
tomato red body, applied narrow
fold-over yellow lip, two applied
yellow handles, on deep amethyst
spreading foot, signed
"Schneider" 440.00

Vase, 17¾" h., on a cushion foot
w/a light blue & green striated
base ascending to a tall, slender
neck, w/red & purple glass inclusions at the base & the neck,
inscribed "V. SCHNEIDER" 7,150.00

SILVER OVERLAY-SILVER DEPOSIT

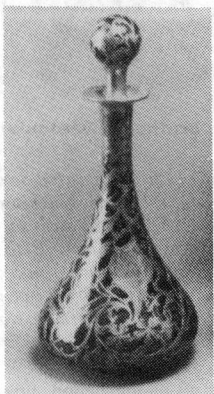

Silver Overlay Decanter

*Silver Deposit and Silver Overlay have
been made commercially since the last quarter of the 19th century. Silver is deposited on
the glass by various means, most commonly
by utilizing an electric current. The glass was
very popular during the first three decades
of this century, and some pieces are still being produced. During the late 1970's, silver
commanded exceptionally high prices and
this was reflected in a surge of interest in silver overlay glass, especially in pieces marked
"sterling" or "925" on the heavy silver
overlay.*

Bowl, fruit, 8½ x 12½", 4" h.,
heavy clear glass w/scalloped
rim, silver overlay inside w/de-
signs of florals & scrolls $70.00
Card tray, ruffled upturned edge,
footed, black w/silver overlay,
9½" d....................... 35.00
Claret jug w/original ball stopper,
clear squat bulbous base tapering
to long slender neck ending in tall
spout, long, graceful handle, silver overlay scrolling vines cover
body, central cartouche unen-
graved, silver by Alvin and Co.,
14" h....................... 990.00
Decanter w/ball stopper, flared rim
on handleless elongated oval
body of emerald green cased on

clear, star-cut on base, overlaid in
silver fully carved w/floral
scrolled designs, monogrammed,
12¼" h. (ILLUS.) 850.00
Lemonade set: tankard pitcher &
eight glasses; emerald green
w/heavy silver overlay depicting a
Colonial couple in a landscape,
the set 750.00
Loving cup, three-handled, cranberry w/silver overlay, marked
"999," 3½" 525.00
Pitcher, 10½" h., applied handle,
clear w/silver overlay on top
half 125.00
Sauce dish w/pedestal foot & underplate, green w/silver overlay,
marked "sterling," underplate
7½" d., 2 pcs. 48.00
Tray, round, clear w/ornately
worked scrolling silver hatched
acanthus leaves within plain border, monogrammed 'R,' 16" d. ...1,210.00
Vase, 5½" h., baluster-form w/flar-
ing lip, grey w/lime green, blue &
purple iridescence against an amber ground w/foliate silver overlay, unsigned Loetz, ca. 1900 ..... 825.00

Silver Overlay Loetz Vase

Vase, 7" h., ovoid body w/tapered
& flared neck, lime green ground
decorated w/green waves & free-
form ovoid lozenges w/gold
iridescence, overlaid w/silver in a
flowing floral design, stamped
"1000 FINE 114," & w/hallmarks,
attributed to Loetz, Austria, ca.
1900 (ILLUS.) 2,860.00
Vase, 10" h., bulbous bottom, light
green w/large silver overlay flowers, buds & vines, ground pontil .. 475.00

SLAG

*Marble and Agate glass are other names ap-
plied to this variegated glass ware made from*

the middle until the close of the last century and now being reproduced. It is characterized by variegated streaks of color. Pink slag was made only in the Inverted Fan & Feather Pattern and is rare.

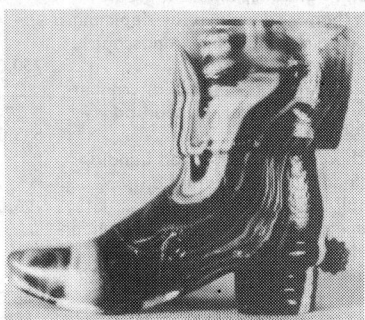

Purple Slag Boot Whimsey

Animal covered dish, squirrel,
  blue $285.00
Bowl, master fruit, 9" d., 5½" h.,
  Inverted Fan & Feather patt.,
  pink 750.00
Butter dish, cov., Block & Star
  Paneled patt., purple 60.00
Celery dish, rowboat-shaped, Daisy
  Block patt., purple, 4 1/8 x 12",
  2½" h........................... 135.00
Celery vase, Jewel patt., purple,
  8¼" h........................... 85.00
Compote, jelly, 5" h., Inverted Fan &
  Feather patt., pink 525.00
Humidor, cov., drum-shaped w/cap-
  shaped finial, blue, 5¼" d.,
  6½" h........................... 245.00
Pitcher, 6¼" h., 3½" d., embossed
  strawberries & leaves, purple 95.00
Punch cup, Inverted Fan & Feather,
  pink .... 200.00 to 250.00
Rose bowl, footed, Beaded Cable
  patt., purple, Fostoria 27.00
Salt dip, master size, urn-shaped,
  footed, two handles, embossed
  ribbing, purple, 3½" d., 2¼" h. ... 55.00
Sauce dish, Inverted Fan & Feather
  patt., pink 200.00
Spooner, Scroll & Acanthus patt.,
  purple, Fostoria 27.00
Tray, Fishscale patt., embossed
  flower border, notched rim, purple, 9½ x 13" oval 80.00
Tumbler, souvenir, marked "A Present from the Bristol Exposition
  1893," purple 45.00
Whimsey, boot w/stirrup & spur,
  purple, 4" l., 3¼" h. (ILLUS.) 48.00
Whimsey, kettle, three-footed, purple, w/wire bail 35.00
Whimsey, model of an obelisk on
  square base, 3½" d., 8" h........ 95.00

SMITH BROTHERS

Smith Brothers Sweetmeat Jar

This company first operated as a decorating department of the Mt. Washington Glass Works in the 1870's and later on as an independent business in New Bedford, Massachusetts. The firm was noted for its outstanding decorating work on glass and also carried on a glass cutting trade.

Creamer & cov. sugar bowl, individual size, melon-ribbed, tiny
  yellow & orange flowers on white
  satin ground, silver plate rim &
  handle on creamer & rim, lid &
  bail handle on sugar bowl, pr. ... $410.00
Powder box, cov.,
  h.p. gold iris blossoms & sword-
  like leaves w/green accents,
  raised borders in contrasting
  shade of gold, 4" d., 3¼" h. 335.00
Salt dip, melon-ribbed, beaded rim,
  h.p. florals on white satin
  ground 90.00
Sweetmeat jar, cov., melon-ribbed,
  h.p. green, brown & pink foliate
  decoration on white satin ground,
  silver plate rim, lid & braided bail
  handle, red Rampant Lion trade-
  mark on base, 5¼" d., 4½" h.
  (ILLUS.)........................ 302.50
Sweetmeat jar, cov., melon-ribbed
  body & lid, h.p. tiny blue flowers
  on white satin ground, silver plate
  collar & braided bail handle,
  5¼" d., 5¼" h. to top of handle.. 635.00
Vase, 4¾" h., round body w/bead-
  ed rim, decorated around shoulder w/dainty h.p. aster blossoms
  w/green & brown leafy tracery on
  white satin ground, red Rampant
  Lion trade-mark on base 192.50
Vase, 6" h., 2¼" d., cylindrical
  w/relief double bands near top &
  base, snow & barren landscape
  scene w/house & pump on
  opaque grey ground, gold trim,
  unsigned 65.00

Vase, 6¾" h., globular w/slender
neck, swirl-molded, blue flowers
& gold flowers on opaque white
ground, signed 425.00
Vase, 7¼" h., 2 x 8", double pilgrim
flask shape, enameled spray of
pink wild roses on butter yellow
ground w/a hint of green, original
paper label 785.00
Vase, 7¾" h., cylindrical, heron &
rushes on soft blue ground, in
original silver plate footed holder
w/ornate curving filigree
handles 85.00

SPANGLED

Spangled glass incorporated particles of
mica or metallic flakes and variegated colored
glass particles imbedded in the transparent
glass. Usually made of two layers, it might
have either an opaque or transparent casing.
The Vasa Murrhina Glass Company of Sandwich, Massachusetts, first patented the process for producing Spangled glass in 1884 and
this factory is known to have produced great
quantities of this ware. It was, however, also
produced by numerous other American and
English glasshouses. This type, along with
Spatter, which see below, is often erroneously called "End of Day."
A related decorative glass, Aventurine, features a fine speckled pattern resembling gold
dust on a solid color ground.

Basket, applied clear thorn handle,
eight-crimp top, blue exterior
w/mica flecks, white lining,
4¾" d., 7½" h. $175.00
Candlesticks, pink & white spatter
w/green Aventurine flecks, white
lining, 3¾" d., 8 5/8" h., pr. 110.00
Ewer, applied clear handle, multicolored spatter w/mica flecks,
white lining, 6¼" h. 70.00
Ewer, squat bulbous base below tall
slender neck to wide tripart rim,
clear applied handle, rose pink
w/numerous mica flecks, white
lining, 5" d., 9 3/8" h. 145.00
Pitcher, 8" h., ruffled rim, applied
clear handle, cream & cranberry
spatter w/gold mica flecks,
ground pontil 145.00
Pitcher, 8½" h., 7½" d., melon-
ribbed body, raspberry shaded to
white w/mica flecks 170.00
Vase, 7 5/8" h., 3¼" d., cylindrical
body w/short neck, two small applied clear loop handles at shoulder, deep rose red shaded to pink
exterior w/mica flecks & enam-

eled garlands of pink & yellow roses & small blue leaves,
white lining 195.00
Vase, 9½" h., 6½" d., ovoid body
tapering to wide neck w/ruffled
rim pulled down on two sides,
melon-ribbed body, autumn colors
in spatter w/mica flecks 75.00

SPATTER

This variegated-color ware is similar to
Spangled glass but does not contain metallic flakes. The various colors are applied on
a clear, opaque white or colored body. Much
of it was made in Europe and England. It is
sometimes called "End of Day."

Candleholders, ruffled petticoat
base w/applied clear twisted
thorn handles, multicolor spatter
in lemon yellow opaque, cased in
clear, 7" h., pr. $75.00
Cruet w/stopper, amber & white
spatter, polished pontil (not origi-
nal stopper) 50.00
Darner, ball-shaped w/handle, dark
blue spatter in blue, cased in
clear, small 48.00
Darner, egg-shaped, multicolor spat-
ter, 3 x 4½" 175.00
Finger lamp, kerosene-type, minia-
ture, applied handle, shaded coral
& tan spatter in white, Nutmeg
burner, 3" h. 95.00
Patch box w/hinged lid, top deco-
rated w/enameled yellow leaves
& dots, yellow spatter in white,
cased in clear, 2½" d., 1½" h. . . . 95.00
Pitcher, 2" h., 1¼" d., bulbous
w/round mouth, applied clear
handle w/gold trim, enameled
lacy gold scrollwork & bands
around middle, yellow spatter in
white, cased in clear 55.00
Pitcher, water, 8" h., 5¼" d., bul-
bous, ruffled rim, applied clear
reeded handle, pink & opaque
white spatter 150.00
Pitcher, water, 8" h., 6" d., bulbous
w/round mouth, applied clear
reeded handle, embossed Swirl
patt., pink & yellow spatter 165.00
Pitcher, water, 8¼" h., 5 7/8" d.,
bulbous w/round mouth, applied
clear handle, deep maroon &
opaque white spatter 110.00
Toothpick holder, embossed Swirl
patt., shaded pink, white & beige
spatter, white lining 95.00
Vase, 9" h., applied clear thorn han-
dles, pastel rainbow spatter 75.00

The Art of
Steuben Glass

by Bob Rau

Steuben — the name is magic. I love to see the wide-eyed expressions on the faces of my guests when they hand me a piece of glass and I look at it carefully and say, "Do you know what you have — you have a piece of Steuben." Talk about name familiarity! And it's all positive. I swear anyone with the name "Steuben" could have run for office last year and made it on name recognition alone. It really ranks in recognition with Tiffany and certainly the iridescence of the glass of Frederick Carder is either equal to or superior to the iridescent lustre glass of Tiffany.

There is a warmth to the gold Aurene that is quite different from that of Tiffany's gold lustre. Side by side you can tell, but apart it is a little difficult until you have held many pieces in your hands and learned the distinction.

It was in 1903 that the Englishman Frederick Carder teamed with Thomas G. Hawkes and formed a new company in Corning, New York, to produce fine art glass. I think there is no question but that they wanted to compete with Louis C. Tiffany but did they possibly believe the name "Steuben" would someday be as widely known as Tiffany's? I doubt it. After all, Steuben was merely the name of the county in which the firm was first incorporated.

The advent of these two men into the art glass field was spurred by a desire to provide spectacular and colorful glass and this they did. Most art glass devotees are aware of this but are also aware of the fine crystal Steuben has produced in limited editions. These finely etched pieces are still being made today.

Almost all of the newer Steuben is signed; however, not all of the older pieces are. We often see the famous fleur-de-lis mark on the lip of art glass shades and other pieces, however, it appears that the silver mark was only stamped on the finished glass and if the owner of the piece was especially diligent and washed it occasionally to show off the color, hue and brilliance, that mark would come off. Look carefully and you still may see traces of it. If that mark came off, imagine what

happened to the small paper labels that were on unsigned pieces. Then, of course, the point comes up — how can you tell it's Steuben if it is not marked?

The answer is: only by careful study. Fortunately, some remarkable books have been published in the past on Steuben and they are a great aid in studying the forms and styles employed by Frederick Carder in the manufacture of his art glass.

Find a great book with line drawings that can show you the hundreds of forms in vases and bowls and more elaborate styles and you, too, can become an expert who can state, "That looks like a piece of Steuben," from fifteen feet away.

Most of the Aurene pieces that I have examined are signed "Aurene." Sometimes the word is quite a scrawl and sometimes you might find "Frederick Carder," also in a scrawl. I understand that one or two of Frederick Carder's close confidantes asked him to sign some of his less recognizable pieces when he was at an advanced age. They would take some of them to him for recognition and upon recognition he would engrave or diamond point scratch his name on the bottom of the piece.

At first I questioned this procedure, but now I believe we owe a vote of thanks to the thoughtful people who accomplished this because, while we might think we recognize the art, they made it possible for us to know that Frederick Carder produced it.

There are so many different types of Steuben art glass, some exceedingly rare and terribly expensive (or perhaps I should say, beautifully expensive). Rarer lines include *Intarsia, Rouge Flambe, Tyrian* and *Diatreta,* and they encompass the whole spectrum of colored transparent glass typical of the 1920's.

Cluthra is another much sought-after glass. It is bubbly in appearance and they say this came about through the use of tapioca during its manufacture. *Cintra,* by comparison, is granular in appearance. It is reported that this was accomplished through the use of

powdered glass in the manufacture.
Frederick Carder's *Jade* glass has almost
the appearance of French opaline and is not
always just in green but comes in blues,
amethyst, rose, alabaster and black.
Some of these lines are very rare while
others show up frequently. I mentioned before that sometimes they are unrecognized,
so it pays to learn their characteristics.

One thing that we can say for certain is
that of all the types of Steuben art glass,
there is none more respected among collectors than *Aurene*, the glass for which Carder
is best known.

"Aurene" and "lustre" probably should not
be mentioned in the same sentence but, in effect, Aurene *is* an iridescent lustre glass made
in shades of gold or blue, as well as green and
red. Generally pieces are signed "Aurene" or
"Steuben."

Blue Aurene seems to be a favorite with collectors who seek the brilliant electric blue and
occasionally bluish silver. The more intense
the color, the higher the price.

Many of Frederick Carder's Aurene pieces
were decorated with "pulled feather" designs
similar to those of Tiffany but when Tiffany
branched out to windows, furniture, bronzes,
lamps and so on, Carder remained true to developing innovations in art glass only.

During World War I, because of the scarcity of materials, reorganization with the
Corning Glass Works became a necessity;
however, Carder himself remained active until his death at the age of 99 in 1963.

Although the wonderful colored glass for
which Carder and Steuben became well
known gradually went out of fashion in the
1920's, Frederick Carder and the Steuben division of the Corning Glass Works survived.
Even during the crises of the 1930's Depression, fine glass continued to be made with the
focus shifting to the fabulous crystal pieces
which today uphold the prestigious reputation of the name "Steuben" and the glass
genius who founded its tradition of excellence, Frederick Carder.

(Editor's Note: *The standard reference on
Steuben glass is "The Glass of Frederick
Carder" by Paul V. Gardner, published by
Crown Publishers, Inc. of New York, in 1971.*)

ABOUT THE AUTHOR

Bob Rau is a well-known antiques authority
and appraiser and a frequent contributor to
The Antique Trader Price Guide. He is currently starring in the popular PBS television series "The Collectors," which he co-hosts with
Dana Garrett. It is presently seen on over 250
public television stations around the country
and is produced by Oregon Public Broadcasting.

Bob has also just authored a new book on
collecting entitled "The Collectors" (Graphic

Arts Center Publishing Company, P.O. Box
10306, Portland, OR 97210. $19.95 ppd.).

PRICE LISTINGS:

*The following presents a current overview
of prices for Steuben glasswares. Listings are
arranged alphabetically by line name. Space
does not permit inclusion of all the varied
Steuben lines which are collected.*

ACID CUT BACK

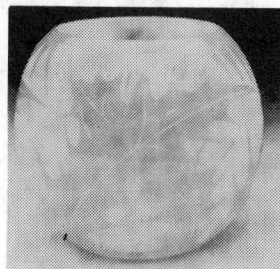

Acid Cut Back Rose Bowl

Lamp, opalescent white Cintra cut to
Spanish green in an Art Deco
design, signed $1,500.00
Lamp, oval flask shape w/flat front &
back, large gold lava drippings
flow from collar, deep rich emerald green w/flowers & stars deeply
cut overall 3,500.00
Rose bowl, spherical body in Rosaline
cut to Alabaster in the Sea Holly
patt., No. 6078, etched fleur-de-lis
mark on side, 6¾" h. (ILLUS.) . . .1,700.00
Vase, 9¼" h., white rim, shiny black
cut to matte background, four very
detailed cut dragons below cut
clouds, signed "S" 2,500.00
Vase, 10" h., deep green Jade
w/stand-up collar, six detailed
large fish flirting in pairs & blowing bubbles, well-defined scales,
waves in white at base 1,450.00

Art Deco Acid Cut Back Vase

Vase, 11" h., cylindrical tapering to

short foot & w/short, straight
neck, cut back scene of seated
nude lady & birds, Art Deco style,
ca. 1930, paper label (ILLUS.) 3,000.00
Vase, 12" h., Rose Quartz cut
w/leaves & dragonflies. 1,900.00
Vase, 12 1/8" h., baluster form
w/Rose Quartz streaked w/rose,
overlaid in white & cut w/stylized
chrysanthemums & leaves, fleur-
de-lis mark, ca. 1920. . . . . .2,200.00

Acid Cut Back Vase with Dragon

Vase, 14½" h., baluster-shaped light
blue body cased in black & acid cut
w/an undulating dragon over a
scrollwork ground, the neck & foot
overlaid w/black & cut w/stylized
leaves, unsigned, some chips to
casing (ILLUS.). 2,400.00

ANIMALS

Steuben Glass Frog Prince

Baby bird. 185.00
Beavers, modeled by Lloyd Atkins
(No. 8306), signed, 9" h., pr. 990.00
Butterfly, molded body supported
within an 18k gold frame, modeled
by Peter Yenawine (No. 1051),
1976, signed, in red leather pre-
sentation box, 2½" h. 1,820.00
Cat, modeled by Donald Pollard
(No. 8274), signed, 4 9/16" h. 605.00

Dinosaur, clear, 1964,
12¾" l. 1,500.00
Dolphin, modeled w/large snout,
eyes & tuft on its head, its tail
curling up in the air, front fins
spread, signed, 11" h. 1,980.00
Dove, signed, 9" w., 5" h. 650.00
Elephant, trumpeting, modeled by
James Houston (No. 8128), signed,
1964, 7½" l. 850.00
Frog Prince, crystal frog wearing
gold crown, modeled by Lloyd
Atkins (No. 1031), 1973, signed,
w/red leather presentation case,
6" h. (ILLUS.) 2,200.00
Koala, modeled by Lloyd Atkins
(No. 8268), signed, 5¾" h. 825.00
Mink, horizontal, modeled by Lloyd
Atkins (No. 8333), signed,
8½" l. 385.00
Mink, vertical, modeled by Lloyd At-
kins (No. 8334), signed,
7 3/16" h., pr. 935.00
Owl, clear, 1955, 5¼" h. 500.00
Partridge in a pear tree, modeled by
Lloyd Atkins (No. 1014), 1968,
signed, in red leather presen-
tation box, 6" l. 2,090.00
Pig, modeled by Lloyd Atkins
(No. 8379), signed, 6" l. 825.00
Sea Horse, clear, 1961, 9¼" h. 750.00
Song bird, clear, (No. 8112), 1963,
4½" l. 350.00
Squirrel, clear, 1963, 5" l. 500.00

ALABASTER

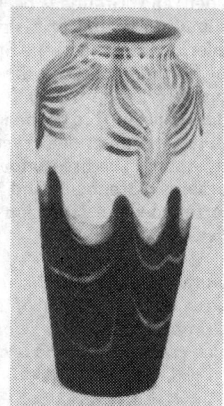

Steuben Alabaster Vase

Vase, 8" h., cylindrical tapering
slightly toward base & w/short,
flared neck, applied undulating
designs in green & gold Aurene,
paper label (ILLUS.) 3,100.00
Vase, 12¾" h., baluster-shaped
w/low flaring rim, Alabaster decorated w/gold & green leaf swirls,

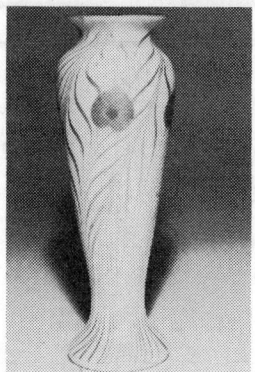

Alabaster Vase with Leaf Design
inscribed "AURENE - 273," 1908-15
(ILLUS.) 2,900.00

AURENE

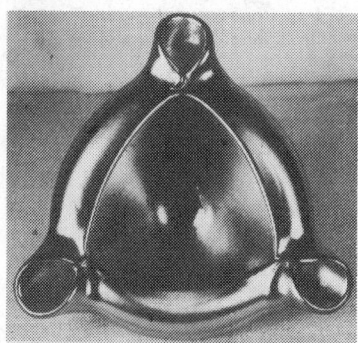

Gold Aurene Ashtray
Ashtray, tricornered w/folded over
edge forming an opening at each
corner, gold Aurene, signed
"Carder" (ILLUS.) 550.00

Gold Aurene Atomizer
Atomizer, tall, slender cylinder
tapering slightly to base w/wide,
flat foot, original gilt metal fittings & mesh-covered bulb, gold
Aurene, 7½" h. (ILLUS.) 600.00

Atomizer, squat bulbous melon-
ribbed body w/short neck, gold
Aurene w/blue highlights,
No. 2183, signed 650.00

Gold Aurene Bowl
Bowl, 6" d., 2" h., round w/faintly
ribbed sides, gold Aurene w/blue
highlights, signed (ILLUS.) 440.00

Gold Aurene Bowl and Candlesticks
Bowl, 8" d., 4" h., deep, rounded
sides w/inverted rim, gold Au-
rene, signed (ILLUS. center) 470.00
Bulb bowl, squat round bowl w/in-
verted rim on three applied prunt
feet, amber Aurene w/gold iridescence, marked "Aurene" on base
w/remnant of triangular label,
8" d., 2¼" h. 192.50
Candlesticks, tall candle socket sup-
ported by twisted tapering stem
on wide, flat foot, gold Aurene,
signed, 8" h., pr. (ILLUS. sides) . . . 865.00

Blue Aurene Compote

Compote, 10" h., shallow bowl
w/wide rim supported on slender
twisted stem w/twisted, ribbed
leaf overlay, round domed foot,
blue Aurene, ca. 1920-28 (ILLUS.
previous page) 900.00

Aurene Console Bowl

Console bowl, widely flared sides,
gold Aurene w/purple highlights,
engraved "aurene 2851," ca. 1900,
14¼" d. (ILLUS.) 600.00
Dish, triangular, gold Aurene,
signed, 5¼" w., 1½" h. 350.00

Gold Aurene Goblet

Goblet, deep flared bowl on slender, twisted stem, flat, round
foot, gold Aurene, signed
(ILLUS.) 400.00

Gold Aurene Perfume Bottle

Perfume bottle w/original stopper,
bulbous melon-ribbed body on
three reeded shell-scroll feet,
melon-ribbed mushroom stopper,
gold Aurene, Haviland & Co.
mark, 3 1/8" d., 3¼" h. (ILLUS.) .. 525.00

Tall Aurene Perfume Bottle

Perfume bottle w/original stopper,
ovoid body tapering to slender
neck w/flat, flared rim, short pedestal base w/round foot, pointed
teardrop stopper, gold Aurene
w/blue highlights & blue stopper,
7" h. (ILLUS.) 520.00
Perfume bottle w/teardrop stopper,
pedestal foot, blue Aurene,
signed, 8" h. 950.00

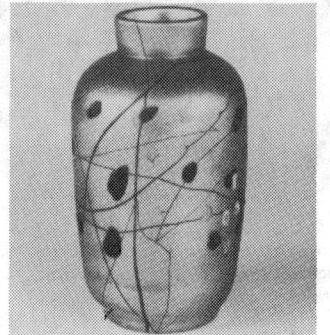

Aurene Vase with Leaves

Vase, 5½" h., cylindrical shape
tapering to short, straight neck,
iridescent amber decorated
w/green leaves & trails & white
millefiori blossoms, unsigned,
1905-30 (ILLUS.) 1,400.00
Vase, 6" h., ribbed body w/bulbous
base below tall flared & ruffled
neck, blue Aurene, No. 7447,
script signature 500.00
Vase, 6" h., three-prong tree stump
shape, blue Aurene, No. 2774,
signed 850.00
Vase, 6" h., 7" d., ovoid shouldered
body w/wide opening & everted
rim, three lobed scrolled handles
at shoulder, circular foot, gold
Aurene, inscribed "Steuben
Aurene - 6627," ca. 1925
(ILLUS.) 750.00

Aurene Handled Vase

Vase, 7½" h., cylindrical body
w/low, flared neck, gold Aurene
w/overall leaf & trailing, No. 506,
signed 400.00
Vase, 8¼" h., bud-type, stick shape
on round base, gold Aurene,
No. 2556, signed "AURENE -
HAVILAND & CO." 325.00

Aurene Fan Vase

Vase, 9" h., inverted conical body
pressed to a flat section, short
knopped stem, circular base, iridescent silvery-blue w/frieze of
stringing & clinging hearts in
amber, green & opalescent, inscribed "STEUBEN AURENE 6287,"
1904-30 (ILLUS.)................1,600.00
Vase, 14½" h., tall urn-form body
w/everted rim & two loop handles
at shoulder, domed foot, blue
Aurene, No. 7104..............2,300.00

BRISTOL YELLOW

Centerpiece bowl, wide, flaring
bowl on knob connector, joined to
high, domed base, free-swinging
ring handles on each side,
No. 2942 .... 450.00
Goblets, Bristol Yellow bowl w/am-
ethyst twist stem, signed, 8½" h.,
each (ILLUS. of pair top next
column) 125.00
Toiletry jar, cov., apothecary-type
w/faceted black cover, 3¼" sq.,
5" h. 450.00

Bristol Yellow Goblets

Vase, 7¾" h., Bristol Yellow body in
diamond pattern w/applied milk
white decoration at top, signed... 300.00
Vase, 12½" h., ovoid w/low flared
neck, Bristol Yellow w/random
black threading, signed by Frederick Carder, No. 2683 .... 775.00

BUBBLY

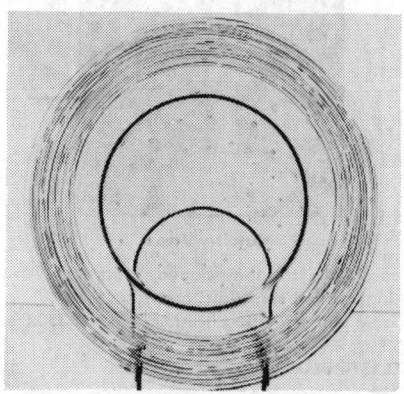

Bubbly Threaded Plate

Plate, 8½" d., Bubbly w/wide band
of applied threading at rim, clear
(ILLUS.)....................... 90.00
Punch cup, antique green w/applied
threading at top & applied handle,
signed, 2¾" h.................. 95.00
Sugar bowl, two applied handles,
pedestal foot, clear Bubbly
w/green threading at top, signed,
3¾" h. 85.00

CALCITE

Bowl, 5 7/8" d., 1 7/8" h., wide ruffled & flared rim, Calcite exterior,
gold Aurene lining 220.00
Bowl, 8" d., 3¼" h., Calcite exteri-
or, blue Aurene lining 500.00
Bowl, 10" d., rolled rim, Calcite exterior, gold Aurene lining 350.00
Centerpiece bowl w/holder, flaring
half-round form, Calcite exterior,
gold Aurene lining, fitting into
purple iridescent open holder

designed to angle the bowl for
display, bowl 12" d., 3½" h. 700.00
Cup & saucer, demitasse, Calcite exterior w/gold Aurene lining on
each, cup in sterling silver holder,
the set 320.00
Salt dip, pedestal foot, Calcite
exterior, gold Aurene lining,
1½" h. 225.00
Vase, 5¾" h., 6" d., flared & scalloped wide rim, slender body flaring to base, Calcite exterior, blue
Aurene lining w/green & purple
highlights 715.00
Vase, 6" h., 5" d., trumpet-shaped,
slightly ruffled rim, Calcite exteri-
or, gold Aurene lining 305.00

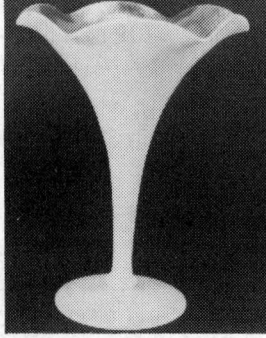

Calcite Vase

Vase, 8" h., trumpet-shaped w/flar-
ing, ruffled rim, Calcite exterior,
gold Aurene lining (ILLUS.) 350.00

CELESTE BLUE

Steuben's Celeste Blue

Compote, 7½" h., Celeste blue &
clear 165.00
Compote, 8" h., deep fluted sides
w/flared rim, Celeste Blue bowl
on Topaz foot (ILLUS. center) 300.00
Goblets, tall flared bowl, twisted
Mandarin Yellow stem, pedestal

foot, fleur-de-lis mark, 8¼" h.,
set of 6 .... 825.00
Punch cups, Celeste Blue w/applied
amber handles, set of 5 (ILLUS.) .. 225.00
Sherbet & underplate, the set 68.00

CINTRA

Cintra Centerpiece Bowl

Bowl, 10" d., 3" h., widely flaring
sides, rose cased in clear,
No. 2035, unsigned 500.00
Centerpiece bowl, deep, ribbed
bowl internally decorated in amethyst, raised on clear ribbed baluster stem & spiral-molded
amethyst base, ca. 1920,
13¼" h. (ILLUS.) 650.00
Plate, trimmed in opal glass,
signed 175.00

Cintra Vases

Vases, 11" & 11¼" h., baluster-
shaped w/tall waisted neck,
speckled dark yellow w/applied
turquoise vine at front, fleur-
de-lis mark, ca. 1920, pr.
(ILLUS.) 3,300.00

CLUTHRA

Bowl, 5" w., 2¼" h., six-sided,
slightly flared rim, shaded pink,
white & clear w/random air-
trapped bubbles 275.00

Pilgrim flask, flattened bulbous body, applied clear glass scrolling stepped handles, sides enclosing irregular air-trapped bubbles, shading from blue at neck to white around shoulder, fleur-de-lis mark, ca. 1925, 10" h. 1,100.00

Vase, 7" h., ovoid body w/low, flared neck, white w/random air-trapped bubbles, No. 2683 . . . . . . 670.00

Vase, 10" h., ovoid body w/low, flared neck, blue w/random air-trapped bubbles, No. 2683. . . . . . .1,650.00

Vase, 10" h., ovoid body w/flaring neck, green body w/two applied opalescent "M" loop handles at shoulders, No. 8508, signed 950.00

Vase, 10" h., 6½" w., three-prong tree stump shape, shaded white to pink, signed "Steuben" in block letters 1,300.00

Cluthra Vase

Vase, 10¼" h., ovoid body w/short, flared neck, mottled light amethyst glass, fleur-de-lis mark, ca. 1925 (ILLUS.) 1,250.00

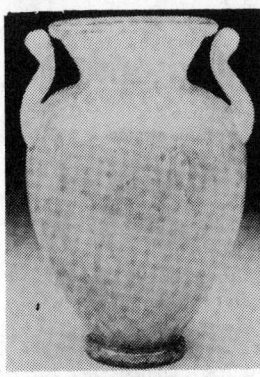

Cluthra Handled Vase

Vase, 10½" h., baluster-shaped body in Pomona Green w/two opal glass loop handles applied at shoulder, No. 2939, unsigned, ca. 1920 (ILLUS.) 1,045.00

Vase, 11" h., 10" d., tall ovoid body w/low, flared neck, green Jade, No. 5133 . . . . .1,100.00

CYPRIAN

Bowl, 6" d., 3½" h. 295.00

Plates, 6" d., circular w/a machine-threaded undersurface molded in a swirled pattern, the wide scalloped border enclosing a dished center, early 20th c., unsigned, set of 4 . . . . 120.00

GOLD RUBY

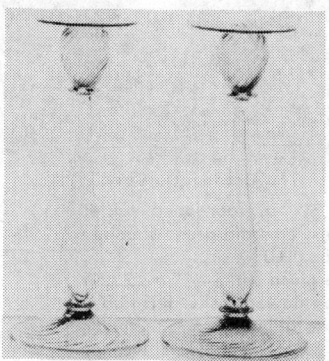

Gold Ruby Candlesticks

Candlesticks, tall baluster-form stem supporting twisted spiral socket w/wide flat rim, wide twisted spiral foot, clear stem & Gold Ruby foot & socket, signed, 10" h., pr. (ILLUS.) 600.00

Champagne, swirled Gold Ruby bowl, clear twisted stem, 6¼" h. 85.00

Gold Ruby Vase

Vase, 10" h., trumpet-shaped w/bell-form top, circular foot, unsigned (ILLUS.) 200.00

GROTESQUE

Bowl, 4¾" h., irregular ruffled

quatrefoil rim on crystal body
w/ribbed corners, subtle purple
rim shades to lavender & blends
to clear at the base, etched
mark......................... 357.50
Bowl, 5½ x 9", 5" h., four-lobed
fluted sides, clear, signed....... 175.00
Bowl, 6" w., 11" l., 7" h., lobed oval
shape w/ruffled sides, clear,
No. 7277 .... 195.00

Grotesque Bowl

Bowl, 7¾" d., four-lobed, ruffled
sides, emerald green shaded to
clear (ILLUS.) 275.00
Centerpiece set: 14¼" d., 7¼" h.
open flower basket form bowl on
pedestal base & pair matching
2¾" h. candleholders; Ivrene,
signed, 3 pcs................... 605.00
Vase, 6½ x 8½", green Bubbly bowl
on pedestal foot, signed 160.00

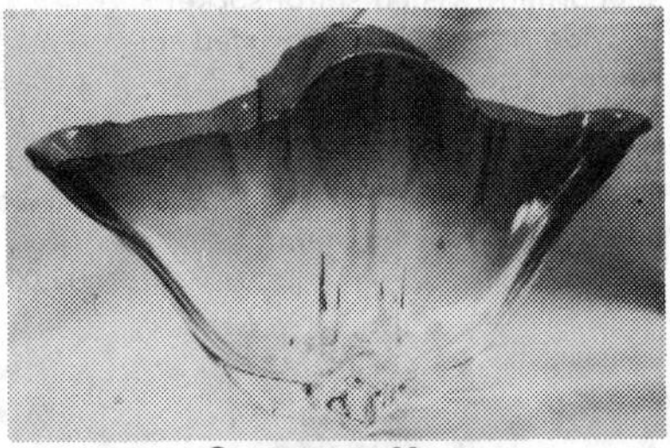

Grotesque Vase

Vase, 7" h., 12" w., flattened, ruffled sides, shading from ruby to
clear (ILLUS.) 275.00

IVRENE

Ivrene Fan Vase

Vase, 5" h., bulbous ribbed body
w/flared neck & top, signed...... 190.00
Vase, 6½" h., jack-in-the-pulpit
form, No. 7560.................. 650.00
Vase, 8½" h., 9½ x 11" oval top,
flaring fan-shaped sides w/rib-
bing, ribbed domed foot, paper
label (ILLUS.) 425.00
Vase, 9¼" h., 6" d., deeply ribbed
body on black Jade pedestal foot,
No. 7331, signed 320.00

JADE

Pair of Jade Vases

Bowl, 8" d., squat bulbous shape
w/inverted rim, green Jade,
No. 2687, signed 150.00
Centerpiece bowl, everted rim, light
green Jade, w/pontil, 11" d.,
unsigned 125.00
Champagne, green Jade bowl w/Al-
abaster twisted stem, signed,
5½" h.......................... 110.00
Goblet, green Jade bowl w/Alabas-
ter funnel-shaped base, outer rim
slightly tooled, rough pontil,
4 1/16" d., 6 3/8" h............. 165.00
Goblet, green Jade bowl w/Alabas-
ter twisted stem, signed, 8" h. ... 125.00
Goblet, green Jade bowl w/Alabas-
ter twisted stem & plain round
foot, copper wheel engraved design of flowers & swags, ground
rim, polished pontil, 8¼" h...... 225.00
Urn, deep rich green Jade body
w/Alabaster handles, 10½" h. ...1,100.00
Vase, 5½" h., square shape
w/overall diagonal ribbing, green
Jade, No. 6339, signed 150.00
Vases, 8" h., oblong ovoid body
w/wide, flared rim, green Jade
body on Alabaster foot, signed,
pr. (ILLUS.) 550.00
Vase, 11" h., 9" w., green Jade fan-
shaped bowl w/faint vertical rib

design on Alabaster stem & slightly domed foot................... 302.50

Wines, straight-sided flared green
Jade bowl on inverted baluster
Alabaster stem, No. 2981, two are
signed, set of 6 .... 395.00

MAT SU NOKE

Candy dish, cov., clear bowl, green
stem, 6½" h. 175.00

Goblets, footed, rounded tapering
body w/flared lip, applied amethyst loop handle, decoration &
rim, 6 1/8" h., set of three....... 155.00

ORIENTAL JADE

Champagne, braided stem,
7¼" h......................... 375.00

Console set, wide center bowl on
pedestal foot & pair 6" h. candlesticks, 3 pcs................... 2,750.00

Goblet, water, braided stem,
8¼" h......................... 475.00

Lamp w/silk shade, all original 800.00

Table service: pair of candlesticks,
circular footed center bowl,
eleven goblets, eleven champagne coupes, eleven sherbet
coupes w/bell-shaped bowls &
twelve plates; all swirl-molded in
green, white & clear glass, the
stems of clear molded glass, each
foot shaded white to clear, center
bowl 12½" d., candlesticks 6" h.,
ca. 1920 (partial table service) ...3,850.00

ROSALINE

Candlesticks, twisted stem, Alabaster
trim, 10" h., pr. 1,200.00

Cornucopia-vase, Rosaline w/Ala-
baster base, 8" h. 425.00

Goblet, Rosaline bowl w/Alabaster
twisted stem & plain round foot,
copper wheel engraved design of
flowers & swags, signed in script
"F. Carder - STEUBEN," ground
rim, polished pontil, 8 3/8" h..... 302.50

Parfait, Rosaline bowl w/Alabaster
pedestal foot, large 225.00

Vase, 7" h., Rosaline w/Alabaster
base, signed.................... 275.00

Vase, 7 3/8" h., baluster shape
w/short, flared neck, Rosaline
w/Alabaster trim, No. 3285 ...... 240.00

Vase, 8¼" h., bud-type, tube-
shaped Rosaline w/Alabaster
foot.......................... 110.00

SILVERINA

Bowl, 11" d., 5" h., graduated
stepped pedestal base, clear & silver, signed 650.00

Console set: bowl & pair candlesticks; air-trapped design,
3 pcs. 595.00

Vase, 10" h., air-trapped diamond
pattern, blue w/mica flecks,
signed 750.00

THREADED

Steuben Threaded Goblets

Goblets, clear bowl w/black thread
rim & black threading around
base of bowl, clear spiral twist
baluster stem & flat, round foot,
6½" h., each (ILLUS. of pair) 90.00

Goblets, pink, w/applied threading,
signed, set of 6 .... 550.00

Vase, 13¾" h., flattened ovoid base
tapering to center & flaring to
trumpet-form top, clear Expanded
Diamond patt., antique green
threaded decoration in random
application around upper third of
vase 192.50

TOPAZ

Candlestick, ribbed socket, twisted
stem, double domed foot, signed,
12" h......................... 95.00

Centerpiece bowl, Topaz bowl
w/Celeste Blue free-swinging ring
handles at side, paper label,
10" d., 5" h. 375.00

Sugar bowl, cov., flattened ovoid
bowl w/flat topped domed lid
w/applied blush pear & green leaf
finial, amethyst baluster-form
swirled rim stem, polished pontil,
4½" d., 6 5/8" h. 357.50

Vase, 6" h., three-prong tree stump
form 250.00

Vase, 8" h., ribbed body w/flared
rim, pedestal foot, signed........ 140.00

Vase, 11" h., Topaz diamond pattern
body w/green applied stem &
foot, signed 250.00

Vase, 12" h., ribbed body w/flared
pedestal foot, signed 175.00

TYRIAN

Vase, 6¾" h., baluster-shaped, iridescent grey-blue, upper section
w/silvery blue-green iridescent

heart-shaped leaves & trailings, ca.
1916, unsigned 3,575.00

Steuben Tyrian Vase

Vase, 7" h., 6½" widest d., ovoid
body w/short, flared neck, purplish
blue w/silver leaves & trailings
(ILLUS.) 4,500.00

VERRE DE SOIE

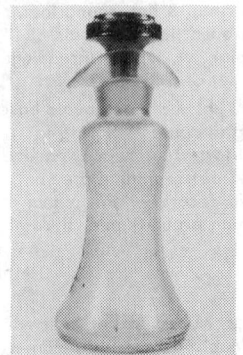

Verre de Soie Cologne Bottle

Bowl, 8" d., 3" h., signed 140.00
Cologne bottle w/sterling silver
stopper, Hawkes engraving of floral design framing word "Co-
logne," 7½" h. (ILLUS.) 200.00

Verre de Soie Compote

Compote, cov., 7" d., 9" h., bowl
w/wide everted rim on knob-
stemmed pedestal w/wide, round

foot, pagoda-shaped cover
w/knob finial (ILLUS.) 550.00
Compote, open, 8" d. 125.00
Console set: 16" d. bowl & pair
4" h. candlesticks; flaring rims,
3 pcs. 675.00
Vase, 5 5/8" h., 6 7/8" d., rounded
body sharply tapering to round
base & to widely flared rim, three
square applied handles from top
of rim to center of body 176.00

MISCELLANEOUS WARES

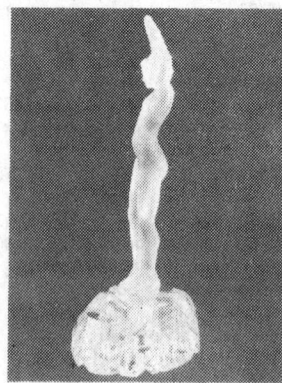

Steuben Figural Flower Frog

Ashtray, clear, No. 8008,
6½" d. 185.00
Bowl, cov., 6½" h., wide flaring
sides tapering to small base, low
cover w/ram's head finial, clear,
signed 350.00
Candlesticks, swirl ribbed top &
foot, hollow stem, amber,
No. 6270, signed, 10" h., pr. 275.00
Candy box, cov., flower finial, rose
amber, signed, 5 x 8½" 850.00
Compote, 6½" d., clear, designed
by J. McNaughton, No. 7807 . . . . . 145.00
Figural flower frog, clear frosted
nude female w/arms raised over
her head standing on clear
faceted block base, 14½" h.
(ILLUS.) 1,700.00
Figure of Quan Yin, green crystal fig-
ure fitted into stepped black glass
base, signed "Steuben," 8½" h.
(tiny chip on corner of base) 1,500.00
Goblet, blue crystal bowl, tall swirl-
ribbed stem, signed, 8½" h. 95.00
Olive dish, clear, designed by J.
McNaughton, No. 7801 . . . . 135.00
Table ornament, engraved & etched
clear glass, Galapagos Island,
in the form of a mountain, etched
w/a tortoise & a lizard near cacti
& the island, designed by Don
Weir, 1966, numbered 2/10,
12" l. 4,125.00

Table ornament, engraved & etched clear glass, Hawaii, in the form of a cloud, engraved w/three natives, hibiscus, pineapple, a tuna & the island, designed by Don Weir, 1966, numbered 2/10, 13½" h....4,675.00

Vase, 12" h., fan-shaped, clear w/engraved ship, on Nile green foot........................... 195.00

Vase, 12" h., campagna urn-form w/handle at each side, knob connector to flaring rectangular pedestal on rectangular foot, clear, No. 7468, designed by Frederick Carder 175.00

Vase, three-prong tree stump form, clear, No. 2744, signed 150.00

(End of Special Focus)

STEVENS & WILLIAMS

This long-established English glasshouse has turned out a wide variety of artistic glasswares through the years. Fine satin glass pieces and items with applied decoration (sometimes referred to as "Matsu-No-Ke") are especially sought-after today. The following represents a cross-section of its wares.

Bowl, 3¾" d., 3½" h., upright box-pleated top, plain panels alternate w/raised embossed beaded panels, white shaded to cranberry, rich, frosted cranberry lining, satin finish $175.00

Bowl, 6" d., 4" h., upright six-crimp top, mother-of-pearl satin Swirl patt., peacock blue lining 850.00

Card tray, applied amber handle & three applied amber feet, rolled edge, translucent opalescent, three applied berries, blossoms & green leaves, 10" l., 4½" h. 730.00

Cracker jar, cov., cranberry cut to vaseline, silver plate rim, cover & bail handle, 4¾" d., 6¾" h. to top of finial..................... 610.00

Cracker jar, cov., creamy opaque w/applied amber & green leaves, deep pink lining, silver plate rim, cover & handle, 5½" h., 7¾" h. ... 275.00

Pitcher, 9" h., clear w/etched Art Nouveau florals & molded teardrops, signed 375.00

Pitcher, tankard, 10" h., 7" d., applied electric blue 6" snakes, applied 2" blue icicles around rim, applied blue handle & spout, topaz body, marked.............. 185.00

Rose bowl, egg-shaped, box-pleated top, rich shaded brown exterior &

cream interior, heavy gold prunus blossoms & branches decoration, satin finish, 3½" d., 5" h......... 475.00

Rose bowl, box-pleated top, embossed Basketweave patt., rich pink satin overlay w/cream satin lining, 4½" d., 6" h.............. 395.00

Sweetmeat jar, cov., squat bulbous body, brick red Peach Blow colored body w/glossy finish decorated w/h.p. gold bamboo stalks, cover, rim & bamboo-form bail handle in gold-finished metal, 5" d., 3" h. 865.00

Tumbler, top w/royal blue cut to pink florals & ovals, lower part paneled, 2½" d., 4" h. 65.00

Vase, 3 7/8" h., 1½" d., square shape, four opalescent applied snail feet, rich pink w/white lining, each side w/intaglio-cut flowers & leaves 195.00

Vase, 8¼" h., 6¼" d., bulbous base w/wide, flared rim, clear w/applied irregular emerald green threading overall, engraved registry numbers in pontil "Rd. No. 36652" 325.00

Vase, 11 7/8" h., 5" d., deep coral w/opalescent top edging, four applied opalescent leaves, cream lining 395.00

Vase, 12" h., baluster-form, "Silveria," green threading on shaded pink & white silver-speckled ground, bright green lining 715.00

STRETCH

Collectors have given this name to a Carnival-type glass that is iridescent and with a surface somewhat resembling the skin of an onion. It was made in various glass factories and some is now being reproduced. Also see FENTON GLASS.

Basket, grey, 10½"................. $70.00
Bonbon, cov., Celeste Blue 25.00
Bonbon, cov., Florentine Green..... 25.00
Bowl, 7" d., purple 25.00
Bowl, 7" d., 3½" h., ruby 55.00
Bowl, 8" d., cupped, ruby 90.00
Bowl, 9¾" d., footed, orange 48.00
Bowl, 10" d., Florentine line, Celeste Blue 45.00
Bowl, 10½" d., Celeste Blue, Fenton 48.00
Candlestick, wide fancy base, vaseline, 9" h. 40.00
Candlesticks, blue, 8" h., pr. 75.00
Candlesticks, blue, 10½" h., pr. 100.00

Console bowl, Celeste Blue, Fenton,
12" d. 35.00
Lemonade pitcher, gracefully curves
out to bulbous base, Diamond Op-
tic patt., vaseline, 9" h. 75.00
Powder jar, cov., footed, vaseline .. 25.00
Vase, 6" h., amber 75.00
Vase, 6" h., fan-shaped, dolphin
handles, pink, Fenton 50.00
Vase, 7" h., flared, scalloped rim,
blue 24.00

TIFFANY

Tiffany Glass Creamer

*This glassware, covering a wide diversity
of types, was produced in glasshouses operated by Louis Comfort Tiffany, America's
outstanding glass designer of the Art Nouveau period, from the last quarter of the 19th
century until the early 1930's. Tiffany revived
early techniques and devised many new ones.*

Basket, iridescent amber bowl
w/flaring lip, fitted into a simple
gilt-metal footed holder w/loop
handle, basket inscribed "L. C.
Tiffany Favrile 1925" & w/original
paper label, stand impressed
"FAVRILE/616" & w/Tiffany Glass
& Decorating monogram, 6" d.
bowl, 2 pcs. $715.00
Bobeche, iridescent gold, stretch
edge, 6" d. 215.00
Bowl, 7" d., flaring curved rim,
ribbed sides, iridescent blue,
signed "L.C.T. Favrile" 825.00
Bowl, 8" d., 2¾" h., stretch interior
of iridescent lavender, opalescent
four-point star in the glass, signed
"L.C.T. Favrile 1855" 760.00
Box w/hinged lid, rectangular,
etched gilt-bronze & Favrile glass
in Pine Needle patt., amber &
opaque white marbleized glass,
impressed "Tiffany Studios, New
York," 1900-28, 6½" l. 110.00
Candleholders, scalloped edge, Optic patt., in fiery opalescent
w/shaded aqua edging, 4" d.,
1" h., pr. 302.50

Candy dish, ruffled rim, iridescent
gold, signed, 5" d., 1¼" h. 175.00
Compote, 6¼" d., 2¼" h., scalloped
rim, pedestal foot, iridescent
gold, signed "L.C.T." 450.00
Compote, 7" d., 3½" h., opalescent
w/internal "paperweight" decoration of red morning glories
w/green centers & leaves inter-
connected w/darker green vines,
exterior enhanced by ten protruding opal hobnails, applied baluster stem & pedestal foot
w/opalescent edge, signed "L.C.
Tiffany-Favrile, 3021P" 1,540.00
Creamer, opal & blue glass w/pulled
& applied decoration of iridescent
blue & gold, iridescent gold handle
w/elaborate scrolled terminal, gold
spout & rim, iridescent blue interior, signed "L.C. Tiffany - Favrile -
8389D," also w/round paper label,
3½" h. (ILLUS.) 1,430.00
Cup & saucer, cup w/applied ribbed
& curled handle, opal rick-rack
pattern on iridescent gold,
signed 525.00
Goblets, turquoise pastel opalescent, matched set of 8 ....5,000.00
Liqueur set: amber decanter w/violet
& pink iridescence & a bulbous iridescent amber stopper & six dimpled liqueur glasses w/amber &
rose iridescence; decanter inscribed "L.C. Tiffany - Favrile 787?,"
glasses "L.C.T. Favrile," or "L.C.T.,"
decanter 9½" h. overall, 7 pcs.
(crack & restoration to one
glass) 1,650.00
Nut bowl, iridescent gold, signed &
numbered, 2½ x 5" 250.00
Peach Melba dish, iridescent gold,
signed "L.C. Tiffany, 638K," over
4½" h. 750.00
Pitcher, 8 7/8" h., straight sides,
applied C-scroll handle, iridescent
amber body decorated w/forest
green leafy vines & trailings,
signed L.C. Tiffany Favrile 12557,
ca. 1892-1928 .... 1,430.00
Plate, 8" w., aqua w/lavender highlights, stretch onionskin edge,
opal Optic patt. reverse, signed
L.C. Tiffany Favrile 485.00
Rose bowl, colloidal, slight Diamond
Quilted patt. in body, gold w/mul-
ticolored iridescent highlights,
signed & numbered, 5½" w.,
5" h. 2,050.00
Salt dip, footed, iridescent gold,
signed "L.C.T. FAVRILE" & numbered "1309" 195.00
Salt dip, round, gold w/blue highlights, signed "L.C.T.," 1 3/8" h. ... 275.00

Sherbets, iridescent amber waisted cup decorated w/opalescent trailings above faceted panels, raised on a faceted slender stem & circular foot w/faceted edge, signed L.C.T. Favrile 197, 1892-1928, 5 1/8" h., set of 12 ....5,500.00

Toothpick holder, bulbous, iridescent blue-gold 425.00

Tumbler, waisted-form, iridescent gold w/applied gold threading around the center, 2½" d., 4" h........................... 231.00

Vase, 2 11/16" h., "Cypriote," ovoid two-handled body w/waisted wide neck, blue-black-green iridescent sides invested w/an irregular Cypriote surface, inscribed "L.C. Tiffany Favrile Q4605" & w/original paper label, ca. 1902 ....2,530.00

Vase, 4" h., bulbous, deep chocolate brown ground decorated about the shoulder w/ochre & amber exaggerated zigzag motifs, inscribed "L.C. Tiffany Favrile V377," ca. 1904 ....3,300.00

Vase, 5 7/8" h., paperweight-type, waisted cylindrical form, internally decorated w/upright white narcissus blossoms w/apricot centers alternating w/rich olive green leaves, against a grey ground washed in amber iridescence, inscribed "L.C. Tiffany - Favrile 2880G," ca. 1912 ....2,310.00

Vase, 6½" h., baluster-form tapering slightly toward base, decorated w/wavy stems & leaves in blue w/an overall blue-grey iridescence, inscribed "0444" & w/paper label 2,860.00

Tiffany Favrile Vase

Vase, 7¼" h., three scrolled applied handles, iridescent gold etched w/green leaves & sinuous stems, signed "L.C. Tiffany Favrile 3127H" (ILLUS.) 2,420.00

Vase, 7¾" h., cylindrical w/bulging

waist, deepest green-black iridescent, decorated w/silvery amber iridescent scrollings & loopings, inscribed "L.C.T. P3321," ca. 1901 ....2,475.00

Vase, bud-type, 8½" h., slender cylindrical neck expanding to a flattened spherical base w/pinched sides in deep amber-blue iridescence, inscribed "L.C. Tiffany Favrile U7969," ca. 1904 ....1,540.00

Vase, 10" h., elongated teardrop shape raised on slightly dished circular foot, brilliant iridescent blue sides intaglio carved w/leafage & vines, inscribed "L.C. Tiffany Favrile 1502-5085L, ca. 1917 .....1,650.00

Vase, 12½" h., ovoid, iridescent amber w/brown band containing yellow chain link design, set on dore bronze holder w/griffin supports on circular foot, signed 4,000.00

Vase, 16" h., tall ovoid body w/tapered neck w/flared rim, on a short rolled foot, overall amber iridescence, inscribed "L.C. Tiffany Favrile 5586G," ca. 1912.........1,980.00

Vase, 17¼" h., trumpet-form body, iridescent amber w/intaglio carved Shasta daisies & leafage up sides, fitted into a pineapple-molded gilt-bronze standard w/circular base, vase inscribed "L.C.T.," base impressed "TIFFANY STUDIOS - NEW YORK - 1043," 1899-1920 ....2,640.00

Vase, 18 1/8" h., tall ovoid body tapering to narrow short neck w/flared rim, rich coffee-colored body decorated w/large feathered lappets superimposed w/vertical bands of "vertebrae," all in iridescence w/highlights of magenta, amber, gold & silvery blue, inscribed "L.C.T. F709," 1899-1920 . .6,050.00

Vase, 20" h., jack-in-the-pulpit form, broad undulating rim w/back side turned up on tall slender stem w/round foot, overall gold iridescence w/crackled effect along edges of the rim, inscribed "L.C. Tiffany - Favrile 32130".........17,600.00

Water set: 8 3/8" h. pitcher w/applied C-scroll handle & 2 tumblers; each a waisted cylindrical form, iridescent amber intaglio-carved about the upper section w/pendent fruiting leafy grapevines, signed "L.C. Tiffany Favrile" & w/original paper label, 1892-1928, 3 pcs. 1,760.00

Wine (or liqueur), stemmed, iridescent gold, signed "L.C.T. Favrile," w/original paper label, 4¾" h. 275.00

TIFFIN

A variety of glasswares were produced by the Tiffin Glass Company of Tiffin, Ohio earlier in this century. One type especially popular with collectors is now called "Black Satin" and is most often found in round vases with a design of molded poppies. Similar vases, as well as candlesticks and other pieces, were also produced in a variety of colors.

Ashtray, clover-shaped, Twilight
  patt., clear, 3" $20.00
Candy dish, cov., cone-shaped,
  Black Satin w/gold sailing ship
  decoration 88.00
Champagne, Fuchsia patt., clear 12.00
Console set: 12" d. bowl & pair
  hollow-stemmed 4½" h. candlesticks; Teardrop patt., amethyst,
  3 pcs. 88.00
Gardenia bowl w/figural fawn insert, shaped oblong low bowl
  w/three candle sockets & socket
  for fawn insert, clear, bowl
  14½" l., fawn 10" h., 2 pcs. 128.00
Pitcher, Byzantine patt., yellow,
  64 oz. 325.00
Punch set: punch bowl, underplate,
  11 cups & ladle; Cascade patt.,
  clear, ca. 1935, 14 pcs. 225.00
Tumbler, footed, June Night patt.,
  clear, 9 oz. 17.00
Vase, bud, 10" h. Cherokee Rose
  patt., clear 25.00

VAL ST. LAMBERT

This Belgian glassworks was founded in 1790. Items listed here represent a sampling of its numerous and varied lines.

Cameo vase, 23" h., slender inverted
  baluster form, brilliant yellow overlaid in deep raspberry red & cut
  w/a continuous river landscape
  w/tall trees in the foreground &
  reflections of the far verdant
  shores in the winding river, ca.
  1925, signed in cameo "Val St.
  Lambert" $3,850.00
Cameo wine set: decanter w/stopper
  & six stemmed goblets; finely cut
  florals in cranberry cut to clear,
  signed, the set 1,795.00
Candlesticks, four feet w/bird on
  each at base, frosted, 11" h.,
  pr. 90.00
Liqueur set: large heavy decanter
  w/12 small liqueurs; overall diamond pattern, emerald green cut

to clear, decanter signed,
  13 pcs. 485.00
Perfume bottle w/stopper, cylindrical body w/short narrow neck
  w/flared rim, cranberry to clear
  acid cut-back designs, clear facet-
  cut stopper, signed, 5¼" h. 190.00

VASELINE

Vaseline Dish

This glass takes its name from its color, which is akin to that of petroleum jelly used for medicinal purposes. Pieces below are miscellaneous. Also see PATTERN GLASS.

Berry bowl, Petticoat patt., 8" d. ... $68.00
Celery tray, ribbed 24.00
Cologne bottle w/original cut stop-
  per, cut decorations, 2½" d.,
  6¾" h. 125.00
Compote, open, Diamond Quilted
  patt. 45.00
Condiment set: cruet w/original
  stopper, salt & pepper shakers
  w/original tops & tray; Pressed
  Optic patt., 4 pcs. 235.00
Condiment tray, Riverside's Ranson
  patt. 87.50
Creamer, Gold Band (or Crown)
  patt., w/gold trim 50.00
Creamer, applied amber handle,
  turned down sides, Inverted
  Thumbprint patt. 45.00
Cruet w/original stopper, Pressed
  Optic patt. 45.00
Cruet w/original stopper, Riverside's
  Ranson patt. 115.00
Cuspidor, lady's, Wreath & Shell
  patt. 85.00
Dish, footed, wide rolled rim,
  pressed Swirl patt., 5 5/8" d.,
  3¾" h. (ILLUS.) 35.00
Goblet, Inverted Thumbprint with
  Star patt. 30.00
Gum stand, "Clark's Teaberry
  Gum" 50.00

Salt dip, figural Santa Claus &
   sleigh 95.00
Salt dip, opalescent w/applied vase-
   line shell trim around center,
   2 3/8" d., 1 3/8" h. 65.00
Salt dip, master size, fluted top,
   cranberry threading around top
   third, 3 1/8" d., 2 1/8" h. 55.00
Spooner, Petticoat patt., gold trim . . 43.00
Spooner, Pressed Diamond patt. 30.00
Sugar bowl, cov., Gold Band (or
   Crown) patt. 65.00
Syrup jug, Pilgrim Bottle patt. 165.00

VENETIAN & VENETIAN-TYPE

*Venetian glass has been made for six cen-
turies on the island of Murano, where it continues to be produced. The skilled glass
artisans developed numerous techniques, subsequently imitated elsewhere.*

Candy dish, cov., high stand, ap-
   plied rigaree, green $45.00
Centerpiece, three-tier, top tier sup-
   ported by swans, gold-flecked
   clear, 13" d. base, 25" h. 325.00
Chalice, elaborate handles & stem,
   quilted aqua bowl & pedestal
   w/clear trim, gold interior,
   19th c., 9" h. 135.00
Compote, 8" d., 7" h., Diamond Op-
   tic patt., clear w/gold flecks & applied w/pink flowers & leaves 120.00
Compote, 8½", blue bowl w/gold-
   flecked ball stem, applied gold
   leaf prunts 75.00
Figure of a lady, black face, white
   clothing, applied clear rigaree,
   8" h. 45.00
Figure of a lady carrying a basket of
   fruit on her head, long full skirt
   w/overall horizontal red swags on
   clear w/gold, 12" h. 72.00
Goblets, trumpet-form latticino cup
   above clear knop set on the interior w/a blown glass figure of a
   cock (2), camel, horse or parrot,
   two in red, two in yellow & one in
   white latticino, ca. 1950, 5" h., set
   of 5 . . . . 550.00
Model of parrots on a stand, each
   stylized parrot shading from red
   to pale purple-blue w/a gold-
   flecked clear glass comb & beak,
   standing on a forked perch embellished w/leaves flecked
   w/gold, on a clear domical base,
   incised "S," paper label printed
   "CAMER GLASS/New York
   Venice/Made in Italy,"
   mid-20th c., 14½" h. 165.00
Models of peacocks, green head &

light blue body, scrolled tail shading from blue to green, w/comb,
   beak & claws & ribbed scrolled
   perch enriched w/gold flecks,
   mid-20th c., 14½" h., pr. 247.50
Model of a rabbit, multicolor body
   w/gold trim, amber ears & tail,
   all cased w/clear, ca. 1950's,
   5" h. 45.00
Pitcher, 6" h., crimped top, applied
   frosted clear handle, cased, amber exterior & blue interior, satin
   finish 75.00

VERLYS

*This glass is a relative newcomer for col-
lectors and is not old enough to be antique,
having been made for less than half a century in France and the United States, but fine
pieces are collected. Blown and molded pieces
have been produced.*

Bowl, 6" d., 1½" h., Pine Cones
   patt., blue $175.00
Bowl, 6" d., 1½" h., Pine Cones
   patt., frosted & clear 60.00
Bowl, 6 x 10", Chrysanthemum
   patt., clear 95.00
Bowl, 8½" d., three-footed, Thistle
   patt. 75.00
Candy dish, two-piece, embossed
   opal flowers, double signed "Ver-
   lys, France," 7" d. 375.00
Centerpiece bowl, oval, handled,
   opalescent sides molded in high-
   relief w/fish swimming amid bubbles, two fishtails forming the integral handles, molded "Verlys,"
   19½" l. 990.00
Console bowl, sculptured bluebirds
   & dragonflies, frosted & clear,
   12" d. 110.00
Console bowl, Water Lilies patt.,
   clear, signed, 13½" d. 165.00
Console bowl, Wild Ducks patt.,
   Directoire blue, 13½" d. 275.00
Console bowl, Wild Ducks patt.,
   dusty rose, 13½" d. 285.00
Dish, scalloped, *Les Anemones*
   patt., blue opalescent, signed,
   5¼" d. 255.00
Model of a fish, opalescent, molded
   signature, 4 x 6" 75.00
Model of a rabbit, clear, 9" 75.00
Plaque, three fantail fish in relief,
   molded signature, 5" d. 55.00
Vase, 4½" h., 6½" w., fan-shaped,
   sculptured lovebirds 110.00
Vase, 7 x 7", polished snowball
   flowers in high-relief, frosted vine
   background, topaz, marked in
   mold, France 98.00

Vase, 8" h., Icicle patt., etched,
clear, signed................... 125.00
Vases, 8½" h., Four Seasons patt.,
Art Deco style, signed "Karl
Schmidt," dated 1940, pr........ 250.00
Vase, 8½" h., maidens w/fruit trees
decoration, clear & frosted....... 180.00

WAVE CREST

Wave Crest Covered Box

*Now much sought after, Wave Crest was
produced by the C.F. Monroe Co., Meriden,
Connecticut, in the late 19th and early 20th
centuries from opaque white glass blown into
molds. It was then hand-decorated in enamels
and metal trim was often added. Boudoir accessories such as jewel boxes, hair receivers,
etc., were predominant.*

Box w/hinged lid, Helmschmied
Swirl mold, pink floral decoration,
3½ x 4"....................... $250.00
Box w/hinged lid, Baroque Shell
mold, blue & white lilac blossoms
on shaded pink ground, signed,
5½" d., 2½" h. (ILLUS.).......... 360.00
Box w/hinged lid, Helmschmied
Swirl mold, decorated w/rust &
orange daisies & purple asters,
6½" w........................ 575.00
Box w/hinged lid, Baroque Shell
mold, Moorish fantasy design in
white & gold on white ground,
signed, 7" w.................. 595.00
Box w/hinged lid, Embossed Rococo
mold, floral decoration on pink
ground, 7¼" w................. 395.00
Box w/hinged lid, deep pink wild
roses & green leaves on a shiny
dark green ground, ormolu mask
feet, pink banner mark, 8½" w.,
5" h......................... 875.00
Cigar container, Baroque Shell mold,
pastel florals & "Cigars," 6" h. 400.00
Collars & cuffs box w/hinged lid,
fuchsia blossoms decoration,
signed, 7½" d., 6" h............ 785.00
Cracker jar, cov., Egg Crate mold,
apple blossoms decoration, silver

plate rim, lid & handle, paper label, 8½" h.................... 225.00
Cracker jar, cov., Helmschmied
Swirl mold, alternating white &
pastel green swirls w/long-
stemmed yellow roses decoration,
silver plate lid w/engraved floral
& leaf design, marked "Quadruple
Plate," 5½" d., 9" h............ 385.00
Cracker jar, cov., Embossed Rococo
mold, yellow florals w/orange &
green leaves decoration, ornate
silver plate rim, lid & bail handle,
overall 10½" h................. 275.00
Creamer & cov. sugar bowl, bird on
a fence, flowers & tree branches
decoration on a shaded pink
ground, ormolu handles & ormolu
cover on sugar bowl, pr.......... 265.00
Ewers, bulbous base, transfer scene
of Buffalo Bill Cody on a horse,
opalescent ground, ormolu rim,
14" h., pr. (damage to one below
attached rim) 395.00
Ferner, Egg Crate mold, blue floral
decoration (no liner)............ 195.00
Finger bowl w/matching underplate,
florals & foliage on yellow shaded
to white ground, the set 295.00
Fork, handle decorated w/blue
forget-me-nots, silver ferrule..... 110.00
Glove box w/hinged lid, lavender
florals on pale pink, signed,
4½ x 8½" oval 440.00
Hair receiver, Embossed Rococo
mold, blue daisies decoration,
original ormolu cover, signed,
6" d...................235.00 to 275.00
Jardiniere, square w/round ormolu
collar, Egg Crate mold, white
w/blue florals, shaded branches &
green leaves, signed, 6¾" sq..... 225.00
Perfume atomizer, square, Egg
Crate mold, apple blossoms
decoration..................... 395.00
Perfume atomizer, bulbous, transfer
scene of cherub w/blue ribbons
amid pink florals obverse, blue
butterfly & pink florals reverse ... 345.00

Wave Crest Photo Receiver

Photo receiver, violet blossoms &
gold enameled decoration, ormolu
rim & footed base, 3½ x 6",
5" h. (ILLUS.) 302.50
Pin tray, Helmschmied Swirl mold,
pastel floral decoration, ormolu
rim, red banner mark,
1½ x 3¼" 90.00
Pomade jar, cov., Embossed Rococo
mold, blue & pink florals & white
enamel dotting decoration, original ornate ormolu lid 375.00
Salt shaker w/original pewter top,
Helmschmied Swirl mold, floral
decoration, unsigned 175.00
Sugar shaker, Helmschmied Swirl
mold, enameled blue forget-me-
nots, satin finish, original ornate
lid 235.00
Syrup pitcher w/original metal top,
collar & handle, Helmschmied
Swirl mold, floral decoration 395.00
Tobacco humidor, cov., Egg Crate
mold, yellow daisies on blue
ground, 5" sq., 4" h. 425.00
Tobacco jar, cov., enameled pink
flowers, marked "Tobacco,"
sponge holder in cover, signed ... 525.00
Toilette set: toothbrush holder,
tooth powder box, small pomade
jar, all w/brass tops & on brass
tray stand; Embossed Rococo mold,
enameled floral decoration on
Burmese ground, 4 pcs. 1,250.00
Tray, open, Baroque Shell mold,
blue floral decoration, ormolu
handles, 6" l. across handles 135.00
Urn, melon-ribbed body, floral decoration on creamy white ground,
ornate ormolu handle, lip &
square foot 150.00
Vase, 3½" h., 3½" base d.,
Baroque Shell mold, blue florals
on creamy white ground, ormolu
handles & collar, black mark 150.00
Vase, 6¼" h., flattened bulbous
base, long slender neck, Embossed Rococo mold, rust & yellow floral decoration on pale
yellow ground, ormolu handles,
collar & footed base 375.00
Vase, 12½" h., semi-ovoid w/raised
rim, h.p. & enameled apple blossoms, leaves & stems on green
background reserved w/lavender
panel borders & embellishments,
ormolu rim, ornate handles &
four-footed base, banner mark ... 605.00

WEBB

*This glass is made by Thomas Webb &
Sons of Stourbridge, one of England's most*
*prolific glasshouses. Numerous types of glass,
including cameo, have been produced by this
firm through the years. The company also
produced various types of novelty and "art"
glass during the late Victorian period.*

Webb Lamp

Bowl, 6" d., turned in ruffled edge,
three applied crystal feet, silver-
spangled white lined w/pink,
signed $125.00
Cameo beverage set: 5¾" h. pitcher
& two 3 3/8" h. tumblers; clear
w/layered & applied clear, red,
green, yellow & opal white decorations carved into freesia blossoms, wildflowers, grasses & stems,
additionally cut w/strawberries,
cherries & a butterfly on the
pitcher, all w/further intaglio-
cut enhancements, signed,
3 pcs. 6,600.00
Cameo perfume bottle, teardrop
form, yellow w/finely detailed
carved white opal floral decoration, fitted w/Birmingham
hallmarked silver hinged rim &
cap chased w/blossom motif, ca.
1893, 4" l., w/conforming teak-
wood stand 825.00
Cameo vase, 2¼" h., 1½" d.,
carved white leaves & branches
against rich blue satin ground,
carved white leaves around neck,
white lining, unsigned 650.00
Cameo vase, 8¾" h., ovoid w/cylin-
drical neck, carved white calla lily
blossoms, various leaves & butterfly obverse, reverse w/climbing
rose branch, against bright opaque
lemon lime ground, neck carved
w/paterae & acanthus within interlocking lozenges, ca. 1900 ....2,200.00
Lamp, kerosene-type, creamy white
mother-of-pearl satin Diamond
Quilted patt. w/overall yellow
coralene design, 20" h. (ILLUS.) ..1,700.00

Potpourri jar, cov., deep aqua border at top w/gold trim, overall multicolored flowers, three-footed brass base, hinged inner lid & ornately pierced outer lid, 5½" h. 610.00

Rose bowl, six-crimp top, shaded blue to cream applied w/garlands of clear rigaree w/clear berry prunts, three applied clear scroll feet, berry pontil, deep cream lining, 4 5/8" d., 3½" h. 275.00

Sugar shaker, pink mother-of-pearl satin Herringbone patt., signed ... 270.00

Vase, 4½" h., 3 1/8" d., shaded green satin w/heavy gold hydrangea blossoms w/gold leaves on front & gold butterfly on back, rich cream lining 335.00

Vase, 5¼" h., 3¼" d., scalloped top, "simulated ivory" w/shaded brown florals, leaves & panel w/three birds on a branch, signed 850.00

Vase, 6" h., 4½" d., enameled blue & white florals outlined in gold & three brown & white birds in flight or on branches against shaded rose satin ground, off-white lining.................... 225.00

Vase, 7 1/8" h., 3¼" d., stick-type, shaded brown satin exterior w/heavy gold prunus & butterfly decoration, cream lining 350.00

Vase, 8¾" h., double gourd form, h.p. blossoms & leaves in shades of pink, blue, brown & yellow highlighted w/raised deeper yellow enameling, lustreless white ground w/repeating monochromatic geometric devices, ca. 1890 .... 770.00

Vases, 9" h., gold seaweed on butterscotch ground, signed, pr........................... 270.00

Water set: pitcher w/scissor-like top & reeded handle & five tumblers; enameled prunus blossoms in white & gold, pink opalescent ground, 6 pcs. 695.00

(End of Glass Section)

GLOBE MAPS

Celestial globe on stand, spherical globe printed by Malby's of London supported by a tripod stand w/spirally fluted urn-turned standard, 17" d., 24½" h. $2,420.00

Celestial & terrestrial globes on stands, celestial model marked

"Made & Sold by L.W. Cary - 8th Strand - London," the terrestrial model marked "London Published by G.J. Cary, St. James, London, Jan 7th 1833," each mounted in four-legged turned mahogany stand, England, 24" h., pr........4,125.00

Terrestrial globe on stand, country-decorated globe w/land masses & impressed lettering painted deep red w/polychrome lettering & floral vine border, on circular frame mounted in a bracketed tripod turned base, New England, ca. 1810, 15" d., 37" h. (minor paint loss, some structural imperfections) 6,050.00

Terrestrial Globe Map on Stand

Terrestrial globe on stand, globe inscribed w/the around-the-world voyage traveled by Lowell Thomas in 1974, engraved brass circumference ring, raised on stained pine & fruitwood stand w/turned baluster-form legs ending in porcelain casters, made by W. & A.K. Johnston, Ltd., Edinburgh & London, 46" h. (ILLUS.) 3,520.00

GRANITEWARE

This is a name given to metal (customarily iron) kitchenwares covered with an enamel coating. Featured at the 1876 Philadelphia Centennial Exposition, it became quite popular for it was lightweight, attractive, and easy to clean. Although it was made in huge quantities and is still produced, it has caught the attention of a younger generation of collectors and prices have steadily risen over the past five years. There continues to be a consistent demand for the wide variety of these utilitarian articles turned out earlier in this

*century and rare forms now command high
prices.*

Graniteware Dinner Bucket

Basting spoon, red	$8.00
Berry bucket, cov., blue speckled	55.00
Berry bucket, cov., blue-green & white marbleized	75.00
Berry bucket, cov., dark green & white marbleized	135.00
Berry bucket, cov., grey mottled, 2 gal.	38.00
Bowl, iris blue & white marbleized, large	50.00
Butter dish w/pewter cover, grey mottled	275.00
Cake pan, tube-type, cobalt blue & white marbleized	185.00
Candlestick, grey mottled	60.00
Chamber pot, cov., child's, blue & white	25.00
Chamber pot, grey mottled, original paper label	20.00
Chamberstick, robin's egg blue w/white insert	26.00
Coffee biggin, cov., two-part, cobalt blue & white marbleized	125.00
Coffee boiler, cov., brown & white marbleized	88.00
Coffee boiler, cov., grey mottled, w/Royal label	30.00
Coffee boiler, cov., w/bail & handle, black & white speckled, 3 qt.	16.00
Coffeepot, cov., grey mottled, 5" h.	24.00
Coffeepot, cov., grey mottled, hinged tin cover, 6" h.	45.00
Coffeepot, cov., white, 11½" h.	38.00
Coffeepot, cov., gooseneck spout, apple green	95.00
Coffeepot, cov., blue & white speckled, large	85.00
Coffeepot, cov., dark green & white marbleized	220.00
Coffeepot, cov., grey mottled, pewter cover, hinged spout & handle	165.00

Colander, pierced for hanging, handled, dark cobalt blue & white speckled	35.00
Colander, grey mottled, 3" deep	14.00
Cooking set, child's, blue, 6 pcs.	150.00
Cuspidor, lady's, blue & white	85.00
Dinner bucket, cov., rectangular, grey mottled (ILLUS.)	75.00
Dipper, blue & white marbleized	52.00
Dipper, hollow handle, grey mottled, 14½" l.	22.00
Double boiler, cov., Thistle Ware	48.00
Egg poacher, three-cup, grey mottled	80.00
Fish boiler, grey mottled, w/label	95.00
Frying pan, blue-green & white marbleized	135.00
Funnel, grey mottled, marked "Extra Agate," small	40.00
Funnel, sky blue	38.00
Grater, azure blue	50.00
Jelly roll pan, round, medium blue & white marbleized	65.00

Graniteware Kettle

Kettle w/bail handle, deep cobalt blue & white marbleized, 10" d. (ILLUS.)	85.00
Ladle, cobalt blue handle w/grey mottled bowl	21.00
Liquid measure, grey mottled, qt.	24.00
Lunch box w/inserts, blue & white marbleized, oval, 3 pcs.	250.00
Milk pan, grey mottled, w/"Royal" paper label, 9" d.	32.00
Mixing bowl, blue & white marbleized, 11" d.	60.00
Muffin pan, 6-cup, grey mottled	22.00
Muffin pan, 8-cup, cobalt blue & white marbleized	170.00
Mug, cobalt blue & white marbleized	40.00
Pan, child's, rolled edge, grey mottled, 5¼" d., 2¼" h.	23.00
Pie pan, blue & white marbleized	25.00
Pitcher, water, w/ice lip, grey mottled, 11" h.	90.00
Plate, green w/colored scene of child picking apples, marked "Germany" & numbered, 7" d.	56.00
Plate, yellow & green marbleized	60.00
Pudding pan, dark brown & white marbleized, 12½" d., 2" h.	36.00

Roaster, cov., w/rack, deep cobalt
blue & white marbleized 90.00
Roaster, cov., emerald green &
white marbleized, large 250.00
Roaster, cov., turkey-size, grey
mottled 44.00
Skillet, grey mottled, 10" d. 20.00
Skimmer, grey mottled 25.00
Slaw cutter, grey mottled, "Ideal" .. 195.00
Soap dish, w/strainer, cobalt blue &
white marbleized............... 60.00
Soup strainer, grey mottled 26.00
Spoon, grey mottled.............. 5.00
Strainer, clips to pan, white w/black
trim & handle, 5" d............. 11.00
Tea kettle, cov., blue speckled 28.00
Tea kettle, cov., cobalt blue........ 250.00
Teapot, cov., brown w/pewter trim,
marked "Manning-Bowman &
Co." 110.00
Teapot, cov., gooseneck spout, blue
& white marbleized, 2 cup 300.00
Teapot, cov., gooseneck spout, grey
mottled 30.00
Teapot, cov., turquoise & white
marbleized 95.00
Tea steeper w/tin lid, blue & white
marbleized 36.00
Wash basin, salesman's sample,
blue & white marbleized 48.00
Wash basin, two-handled, blue &
white marbleized, extra large 48.00

GREENAWAY (Kate) ITEMS

Almanack for 1888

Numerous objects in pottery, porcelain, glass and other materials were made in or with the likenesses of the appealing children created by the famous 19th century English artist, Kate Greenaway. These are now eagerly sought along with the original Greenaway books.

Almanack for 1888, published by
George Routledge & Sons
(ILLUS.)........................ $65.00

Book, "Book of Games," illustrated
by Kate Greenaway, 24 full-page
color plates..................... 29.50
Book, "The Illustrated News of the
World," 1890, Kate Greenaway
cover "The Fairy Ring".......... 40.00
Book, "The Little Folks," illustrated
by Kate Greenaway, painting
book, hardbound............... 50.00
Figurines, bisque, "Rope Jumpers,"
marked "Heubach," 9½" h., pr. .. 600.00
Pin tray, leaf shape, little girl on
blue lustre ground, 6¼" l. 15.00
Salt shaker, silver plate, figural
Greenaway girl w/bonnet &
muff 32.00

HATPIN HOLDERS

China, jasper ware, white relief
Greek figures on blue ground,
Adams $185.00
Limoges china, footed, h.p. pink
roses, gold top & feet, 5" h....... 95.00
Nippon china, h.p. florals w/gold
trim.......................... 55.00
Nippon china, open top, border pat-
tern of pink roses & green leaves,
encrusted gold decoration, green
"M" in Wreath mark............. 35.00
Noritake china, Tree in Meadow
patt. 65.00
Pickard china, h.p. iris w/green
leaves & buds & heavy gold trim.. 110.00
Rosenthal china, green w/silver
overlay........................ 225.00
Royal Bayreuth china, model of an
owl 450.00
Royal Bayreuth china, musicians
decoration, signed "Dixon"....... 285.00
Royal Bayreuth china, pink clover
decoration 225.00
R.S. Germany china, gold Art Deco
straight line design on greens
w/rose panels, artist-signed,
4½" h......................... 95.00
R.S. Germany china, pink flowers
decoration..................... 65.00
R.S. Prussia china, three-footed,
Mold 726, pink & yellow roses &
white daisies on shaded blue to
white ground, 5" h. 250.00
R.S. Prussia china, holly & leaves
decoration..................... 275.00
R.S. Prussia china, Reflecting Water
Lilies patt.................... 225.00
Schafer & Vater china, Babes in Tub
decoration..................... 250.00

HATPINS

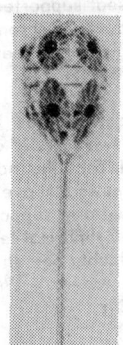

Art Deco Hatpin

Brass, w/escutcheon on top, 9" $27.50
Brass filigree w/19 rhinestones,
  1½" d. head, 12" shank 45.00
Brass, vanity-type, ornate filigree
  head, puff & mirror intact,
  11½" 350.00
Elk's tooth set in gold 125.00
Gold & platinum, Art Deco style,
  pierced platinum ovoid head set
  w/diamonds & onyx, 18k gold
  stem (ILLUS.)................... 990.00
Satsuma china, floral decoration.... 165.00
Sterling silver, Art Nouveau lady on
  head........................ 110.00

HEINTZ ART WARES

*Beginning in 1915 the Heintz Art Metal
Shop of Buffalo, New York began producing
an interesting line of jewelry and decorative
items, especially vases and desk accessories,
in brass, bronze, copper and silver. Their distinctive brass and bronze wares overlaid with
sterling silver Art Nouveau and Art Deco designs are much sought after today. Collectors
eagerly search for pieces bearing their
stamped mark consisting of a diamond surrounding the initials "HAMS." Around 1935
the firm became Heintz Brothers, Manufacturers.*

Ashtray, bronze w/sterling silver
  overlay, original patina, 9"....... $70.00
Ashtray-match holder combination,
  copper w/sterling silver Art Deco
  style overlay.................. 90.00
Box w/hinged lid, bronze w/sterling
  silver Art Deco style overlay,
  green patina, cedar lined,
  3½ x 4½"..................... 100.00
Desk set, bronze w/sterling silver
  overlay, 6 pcs................. 225.00

Vase, bronze w/sterling silver Art
  Nouveau style overlay, 7" h. 75.00
Vase, stick-type, bronze w/sterling
  silver overlay, 10" h. 110.00

HORSE & BUGGY COLLECTIBLES

Hand-Carved Hitching Post Finial

Anatomical chart for a horse, "P.
  Lz's Anatomical Manikan," mounted on folding cardboard, fold-outs
  of skeletal, muscular & circulatory
  systems plus internal organs, used
  at a veterinary college, 37 x 41"..$295.00
Bit, watering-type, U.S. military
  model w/brass rosettes.......... 75.00
Bridle, work-type, brass maker's
  name tag, England 75.00
Bridle rosettes, brass, 2¼" d. on 16"
  leather strap, pr................ 16.00
Conestoga wagon tar bucket, all-
  wood, cylindrical w/wide rim
  band, flat lid w/stick handle,
  replaced leather bail handle,
  10" h. plus handle.............. 65.00
Currycomb, tin & leather, dated
  1909 .... 10.00
Hitching post, cast iron, figural
  horse head on ribbed column post
  w/base decorated w/foliate designs & lions' heads, 69½" h. 475.00
Hitching posts, cast iron, figural
  stylized horse head w/embossed
  mane & ring in mouth, on cylindrical cast post w/square base, old
  white & green paint, 53½" h., pr.
  (some rust, ear chips)..........1,300.00
Hitching post, cast iron, figure of a
  young black boy dressed in green
  breeches & white open-necked
  shirt, advancing w/his right foot
  forward & his right arm raised, on
  scalloped circular platform above
  a flaring faceted base, 48" h. 550.00

Hitching post, cast iron, pineapple finial over shaped capital w/volutes & squared shaft, America, 19th c., 52" h. 440.00

Hitching post finial, painted & carved wood, stylized horse head w/applied ears, copper tack eyes, painted black, mounted on circular base, America, late 19th - early 20th c., 14½" h. (ILLUS.) 770.00

Hoof knife, bone handle, steel blade marked "IXL George Wostenholm," Civil War era 25.00

Horse brush, marked "U.S." 30.00

Horse hames, w/brass balls 15.00

Lap robe, horse hide, 60 x 60" 35.00

Lap robe, wolf fur, Milwaukee furrier's label on back, ca. 1890, very large 425.00

Lap robe, wool, muted red florals & green leaves on tan ground, lattice border, bulldog in center, one glass eye missing, black reverse label "Strook," 8 lbs., 46 x 61" ... 175.00

Lap robe, wool, dog w/bird in mouth, colorful 65.00

Lap robe, wool, red w/cotton crewel embroidery 85.00

Lap robe, wool, three running deer w/glass eyes, colorful 75.00

Sign, "Gickmore's Gall Cure," cardboard, tri-fold, shows horse & man, colorful, 33 x 50" 150.00

Spurs, brass, Civil War era, pr. 48.00

Spurs, brass w/nickel trim & floral tooling, 6" l., pr. 45.00

Spurs, silver, very ornate, Mexico, pr. 125.00

Spurs, child's, silver, Chihuahua, Mexico, pr. 125.00

Vehicle, hearse, draped glass sides w/brass name tag & hubcaps, manufactured by Sayers-Scovill, Cincinnati, Ohio 6,000.00

Vehicle, school bus, open sides, restored 1,800.00

Vehicle, wagon, flatbed-type w/raised seat, excellent shop decoration, restored, 73" l., 40" h. seat 950.00

Wagon jack, painted wood & wrought iron, old red & black paint, engraved date "1793," 17" h. 115.00

Wagon jack, wood & wrought iron, old patina, engraved date "1805," 18" h. 105.00

Wagon seat, maple, double chairback w/two rows of arched slats flanked by shaped armrests above a splint seat, cylindrical legs joined by a double box stretcher, America, 19th c., 17 x 35", 30" h. 605.00

Wagon seat, painted & decorated pine & ash, seat supported by sides painted w/polychrome designs, resting on shoe feet, America, 19th c., 30" w., 26½" h. 275.00

Wagon seat, painted wood, double chairback w/two rows of arched slats & cylindrical stiles flanked by cylindrical armrests above baluster-turned arm supports over a splint seat, cylindrical legs joined by a double box stretcher, painted blue, America, 19th c., 36" w., 29½" h. 550.00

HOUSEHOLD APPLIANCES

Labor saving devices for the housewife as well as appliances to improve the quality of life of the American family began to proliferate in the 19th century. The introduction of electricity helped expand the field even more and today early appliances, especially electric models, are increasingly collectible. Many serious collectors search for early fans and toasters in particular, but old coffee makers, steam irons and vacuum cleaners also have dedicated enthusiasts. All pieces listed are electric unless otherwise noted.

Curling iron, "Duro," green enameled, wooden handle, gold label, celluloid thumb guard, chromed, some metal wear clamp & rod, pre-World War II $12.50

Fan, "Westinghouse," four brass blades, 13" brass cage, name in pierced brass letters, three-speed switch 125.00

Foot massager, "Dr. Scholl's," green enamel metal body on chrome base w/white plastic foot rest, gold label 3½ x 6 x 6" (cord splice) 40.00

Iron, "Steemco Pacemaker," Art Deco style 15.00

Toaster, "Bersted," Model No. 1 .... 17.50

Toaster, "Hotpoint," Model No. 115T17 .... 40.00

Toaster, "Kenmore," Model No. 307-6314 .... 17.00

Toaster, "Speed Master," sides flip open, Son Chief Elec. Co., Winsted, Conn. 30.00

Toaster, "Universal," Model No. E7312A 17.50

Hair dryer, "Handy Hannah," handheld, light green enameled metal, made by Standard Products, Whitman, Massachusetts, pre-World

War II, w/stand, 7" l.,
10" h. 65.00
Television, "Stromberg Carlson," table model, Art Deco style oak cabinet, 9" picture tube, early 1940's 225.00

ICART PRINTS

Basket of Apples

The works of Louis Icart, the successful French artist whose working years spanned the Art Nouveau and Art Deco movements, first became popular in the United States shortly after World War I. His limited edition etchings were much in vogue during those years that the fashion trends were established in Paris. These prints were later relegated to closet shelves and basements but they have now re-entered the art market and are avidly sought by collectors. Listed by their American titles, those appearing below have been sold within the past eighteen months.

Basket of Apples, 1924, 13¼ x 17¾" (ILLUS.) . . . . $990.00 to 1,210.00
Bathers, 1926, 17 x 24½" 2,400.00
Belle Rose, 1933, 17 x 21" 2,200.00
Bluebirds, 1925, 15½ x 19" 990.00
Carmen, 1927, 13½ x 20" 1,100.00
Casanova, 1928,
14 x 21" . . . . 1,100.00 to 1,850.00
Chestnut Vendor, 1928,
14 x 19" . . . . 1,200.00 to 1,900.00
Coursing II, 1929, 15½ x 25" 3,150.00
Fair Dancer, 1939, 19 x 22" 1,470.00
Faust, 1928, 13 x 21" . . . 1,485.00 to 1,540.00
Flower Seller, 1928, 14 x 19" 1,570.00
Girl in Crinoline, 1937,
19½ x 23½" 1,485.00

Hydrangeas, Lilacs, 1929, 17 x 21" oval 850.00
Intimacy, The Green Screen, 1928, 16 x 18" 1,825.00
Japanese Garden, 1925, 15 x 18" . . . 825.00
Lady of the Camelias, 1927,
16½ x 24¼" 855.00
Laziness, 1925, 15 x 19" 1,815.00
Leda, 1934, 21 x 31" 5,115.00
Lilies, 1934, 19½ x 28" 2,220.00
Little Prisoner, 1924, 15 x 19" 1,700.00
Lovers (The), 1930,
14 x 21" . . . . 1,210.00 to 1,430.00
Love's Awakening, 1932,
8½ x 11" 1,320.00
Madame Bovary, 1929,
16 x 20" oval . . . . 895.00 to 1,430.00
Manon, 1927, 13 x 20" . . 1,100.00 to 1,320.00
Masked, 1933, 8½ x 13" 1,025.00
Mealtime, 1927, 13½ x 17½"
oval 1,900.00
Meditation, 1928, 12 x 17" 1,500.00
Mimi, 1927, 13 x 20" . . . . . 990.00 to 1,210.00
Minuet, 1929, 13 x 21" 1,100.00
Mockery, Red Screen, 1928,
16 x 18" 2,200.00
Montmartre I, 1928, 14½ x 21" 1,320.00
Perfect Harmony, 1932,
12½ x 16½" 4,200.00
Spilled Apples, 1928,
12½ x 19½" 1,760.00
Sweet Caress, 1924, 12 x 17½" 935.00
Symphony in Blue, 1936,
19½ x 23½" 1,650.00
Tosca, 1928, 13 x 21" 1,870.00
Venus, 1928, 14 x 19½" oval 3,200.00
Venus in the Waves, 1931,
16 x 19" 4,500.00
Menu cover, etching of woman w/cherub & Bacchus carrying Ayala Champagne, dated 1929 . . . . 150.00

ICE CREAM SCOOPS & SERVERS

During the past decade, the ice cream scoop and ice cream server have become very popular with a growing number of collectors and prices have soared. While the nickel-plated brass scoop with a lever-operated blade that eases the ball-shaped scoop of ice cream from the server seems to be the most popular, there is also interest in the earlier cone-shaped tin scoops and in pewter or aluminum servers. Collectors can select a scoop that served up a small penny-size ice cream cone, a larger nickel-size cone, or a square slice for an ice cream sandwich.

"Benedict Indestructo No. 3," nickel-plated brass, wooden handle, 1920's, 10½" l. $85.00

"Benedict Indestructo No. 6," nickel-plated brass, wooden handle, 1920's, original box 35.00

"Fisher Motor Co., Ltd., Orilla, Ontario, Canada," 'Cold Dog' cylinder-type, German silver, wooden handle, 1920's, 9½" l. . . . 550.00

"Gilchrist No. 31," banana split scoop, nickel-plated brass, wooden handle, 1920's, 11½" l. 300.00

"Gilchrist No. 31," size 8, nickel-plated brass, wooden handle, 11" l. (some wear) 28.00

"Gilchrist No. 31," size 12, nickel-plated brass, wooden handle, 11" l. 25.00

Hamilton Beach, Model 67, three sizes, w/packer, set 43.00

"Keiner-Williams Stamping Co.," conical bowl, steel w/steel wire loop handle, "KW" on ornate wing nut, 1905 patent 29.00

"Kingery Mfg. Co., Cincinnati, Ohio," 'one-handed' conical-style, nickel-plated metal, patented September 1894, 8½" l. 185.00

"Maryland Cream Pie Disher," made by Philadelphia Ice Cream Cone Machinery Co., Philadelphia, Pennsylvania, ice cream slicer for ice cream sandwiches, nickel-plated brass, wooden handle, 1930's, 10½" l. 275.00

"Mayer Mfg. Co., Chicago, Illinois," 'Handy' ice cream disher, ice cream slicer for ice cream sandwiches, German silver, wooden handle, 1920's, 12" l. 225.00

"Shore Craft" container packer, stainless steel, qt., pt. & ½ pt. sizes, set of 3 . . . . 30.00

"Zeroll Co., Toledo, Ohio," aluminum, 1930's, 7" l. 16.00

ICE SKATES

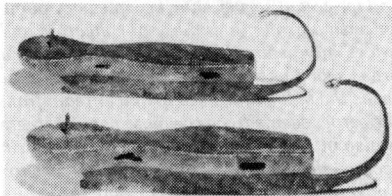

19th Century Ice Skates

Ice skating has long been popular as a sport and a means of transportation. The first skating club was formed in Edinburgh, Scotland in 1642. Ice skating was the major form of transportation in The Netherlands as the canals were frozen for so long each year. Pleasure skating was originally confined to long-distance racing but later became a contest to see who could inscribe the best design on ice. Skates have been made from such diverse materials as animal bone, walrus tusk and even corn stalks - a far cry from today's version.

Iron, hand-forged, figural bird head on front curl, circular & oval open ring pads, 18th c., pr. $260.00

Pine platform, carved & painted green, steel blade w/large curl & brass acorn finial, America, 19th c., 12" l., pr. (ILLUS.) 247.00

Winchester, "B & B," w/original key, pr. 22.00

Winchester, shoe-type, man's, pr. . . 29.50

Wooden platform, racing-type w/long steel blade, snub end, original leather straps, pr. 120.00

Wooden platform, scrolled steel blade, leather toe & heel straps, New England, 19th c., 11" l., pr. . . 88.00

Wooden platform, spade-form red-stained shoe support raised on scrolled black-painted steel blade, one stamped "C.W. Wirt No Oh. O & C," America, late 19th c., 13" l., pr. 192.50

Wooden platform, beautifully curved wrought-steel blade, 12½" l., pr. (replaced leather straps) 85.00

ICONS

Christ Pantocrator

Icon is the Latin word meaning likeness or image and is applied to small pictures meant to be hung on the iconostasis, a screen dividing the sanctuary from the main body of Eastern Orthodox Churches. Examples may be *found all over Europe. The Greek, Russian and other Orthodox churches developed their own styles, but the Russian contribution to this form of art is considered outstanding.*

Christ Pantocrator, silver-gilt & enamel okhlad, Cyrillic maker's mark "S.G.," Moscow, ca. 1900, 10¾ x 12 3/8" $2,200.00

Christ Pantocrator, the Savior holding open Book of Gospels in His left hand & w/His right hand raised in blessing, embossed silver-gilt & shaded enamel okhlad, Ivan Alexaev, Moscow, ca. 1900, 10 5/8 x 12½" (ILLUS.) 3,960.00

Head of John the Baptist, the severed bearded head w/flowing brown hair, resting on an oval platter dripped w/blood, against a dark brown background, a gilt inscription above, Russia, 19th c., 11 5/8" l., 10" h. 440.00

Saints Ulita, Kyrik & Sergei, depicted in an attitude of prayer, Holy Trinity depicted at top of panel, ornate silver border, Russia, 18th c., 10¾ x 12¼" 1,100.00

St. Nicholas the Miracleworker, hagiographical, the saint depicted in the center of the panel surrounded by twelves scenes from his life, engraved silver-gilt okhlad, Moscow, 1848, 10½ x 12½" 2,420.00

Virgin and Child, crowned Virgin behind the Christ Child, the Child standing on a red pedestal, depicted wearing a crown & holding an orb & sceptre, beneath two angels holding an inscribed banner, a ladder & candelabra on either side, on a gilt ground, Russia, 18th c., 7" w., 9" h. (flaking & losses to gilt ground) 357.50

The Visitation & Presentation in the Temple, in two registers, the upper w/the kneeling Virgin w/outstretched arms, an angel in flight above, the lower register w/St. Joseph, Mary, the Christ Child & an Elder, within a temple, Russia, late 19th - early 20th c., 6¼" w., 11 5/8" h. (some flaking, minor warping) 220.00

Vladimirskaya Mother of God, w/pierced silvered & gilt-metal okhlad, giltwood frame & glazed walnut serpentine case, Russia, late 19th c., 11¾" w., overall 16" h. 1,210.00

INDIAN ARTIFACTS & JEWELRY

Tlingit Rattle-Top Basket

Amulet, Northern Plains, umbilical cord, turtle-shaped, fully braided top w/tin cones, wool & hide fringe dangling from each appendage, block & bar beaded design in sky blue, yellow, green, crystal & white-heart red, sinew-sewn, 1880's, 6¾" l. $302.50

Awl case, Plains, beaded leather, fully beaded on both sides w/abstract geometric blue designs on white ground, dentallium shell & brass button closure, tin cone dangles, 1½" w., 11" l. 125.00

Axe head, Plains, inlaid stone, triangular, tan steatite w/pictorial lead inlay of bird track & turtle, late 19th c., 5½" l. 137.50

Bandolier bag, Great Lakes, beaded cloth, beaded foliate design in orange, yellow, violet, shades of blue, red, green, pink & faceted metallic on an opalescent ground, dark brown cotton velvet front bead stitched in floral & linear motifs, brown polished cotton backing, bottom trimmed w/amber & green clear glass tube bead fringes, early 20th c., 42" l. 660.00

Basket, cov., Tlingit, twined spruce root rattle-top type, cylindrical, false embroidered in olive, golden yellow & subdued orange dyed grass w/banded decoration on the closed & open twined body, 5¼" d. (ILLUS.) 550.00

Basket, Hopi, miniature, coiled type w/deep rounded sides, Kachina mask design, 2" d., 1¾" h. 85.00

Basket, Papago, wine brewing "tiswin" type, fine dark patina, fret design in black martynia & in willow, black martynia band, 13¾" d., 7¼" h. 500.00

Basket, Pomo, bowl-shaped, fine de-

sign in redbud, outside varnished
& darkened patina on upper body,
tag on bottom reads " Placer
County, Cal. - 5/14/27," 5" d.,
3" h. 600.00

Basket, Yokuts, deep flaring bowl
shape, rattlesnake design in redbud & black fern, 25½" d., 13" h.
(one rim & one interior stitch
missing) 6,200.00

Blanket, Western, wool, Pendleton-
type, alternating woven light &
dark bands of arrow points & diamonds in red, green, black & grey
on white ground, fine condition,
54 x 61" plus fringe 175.00

Book, "Life & Times of Red Jacket,"
by William L. Stone, 1841, story of
the life of the Great Seneca Chief,
484 pp......................... 97.50

Book, "Memoirs of the American
Folk-Lore Society, Navajo
Legends," collected & translated
by Washington Matthews, Boston,
1897, Number 53 of 500 copies ... 154.00

Boots, Southern Cheyenne-Arapaho,
moccasin-type, hide heavily
beaded w/geometric & butterfly designs in cobalt blue, apple green,
turquoise blue, white-heart red &
yellow on white ground, green pigment on cuffs & feet, sinew-sewn,
1880's, 15" h. (minor separation
of hard soles) 1,980.00

Bottle, Pacific Northwest Coast Attu,
basketry, ovoid body w/tall slender neck fitted w/cap, woven
w/multicolored stylized flowerheads on beige ground, 11" h. 1,870.00

Bowl, Grand Apache, basketry, radiating zig-zag design in martynia &
willow, mint condition w/fine
patina, ca. 1900, 13½" d.,
4½" h. 1,300.00

Bowl, Pomo, coilwork basketry, flaring form w/flat base, finely
woven w/redbud butterfly motif
on a golden ground, remnant red
feathers on outer surface,
2¾" rim d., 1 5/16" h........... 302.50

Bowl, Southwestern, pottery, Bandolier black-on-grey, deep rounded
form w/broad concave interior
base, flaring walls, neck &
straight lip, grey slip over a bisque
body, interior decorated w/black
concentric circles, two bands of enclosed triangles, concentric blocks
& linear devices, one w/a "hand"
termination, angled lines at lip;
the exterior w/three linear bands
at top & bottom enclosing a meandering design of angled triangles,
lines & dots, late 13th-early

14th c., 16½" d. (3" vertical
crack on rim, minor chips & slip
loss)..........................3,630.00

Bracelet, Zuni, silver & turquoise,
3" d. single stone carved in the
form of a leaf, within a leaf-
shaped stamped bezel, supported
on an open-cast cuff (carved in
the style of Leekya Desyee) 412.50

Collar, Plains, woman's, early bone
hairpipe w/brass & blue glass
beads w/dark maroon seeds,
string tassels (two missing),
36" l. 300.00

Concho belt, Navajo, silver & turquoise, seven oval & six butterfly-
shaped conchos, all w/stamped &
repousse decoration & set w/a
single square-cut stone, sandcast
buckle set w/four oval stones ...1,760.00

Cradleboard, Ute, beaded & fringed
hide, basketry hood, bead decorated bow, hood band & chin
strap, yellow pigment-painted
hide, Reservation period, 39" h. ... 715.00

Cribbage board, Eskimo, ivory,
w/applied sidebars, engraved on
underside w/a coastal map depicting the Diomede Islands to Norton Sound, the drilled gameboard
surmounted by various full-figured
carvings, engraved decoration & detailing darkened in black pigment,
inscribed on side "Aloysius Pikon-
ganna," 29½" l. 1,045.00

Doll, Northern Plains, stuffed cotton
muslin body & crochet-edged under-
garment, hide head w/attached
scalp, pigment & beaded facial decoration, wire & glass bead earrings,
strung faceted glass beads on hide
necklace, fringed hide dress, yoke
decorated w/seed attachments,
shanked flat brass button decorated belt, traces of blue & yellow
pigment, plaited dyed porcupine
quill decoration on high-top
leggings, sinew-sewn, 1880's,
18½" h. 1,980.00

Dough bowl, Santo Domingo, pottery, deep rounded sides, double
oval "egg" designs in rectangles
in black on grey slip over red
ochre bottom, signed "Manualita
Lavato, Santo Domingo Pueblo,
New Mexico," 7½" d., 3¼" h. ... 175.00

Dress, Plains, beaded & fringed hide,
"deertail" style, formed of two
skins, stitched in white, sky blue,
black, white-heart red, clear yellow, wine & green wavy pony
beaded panels across bodice,
shoulders & sides, additional
fringed hide at hem, fur covered

hide fringing at end of sleeves,
19th c., 49" w. across sleeves,
51" l. 7,920.00

Sioux Beaded Dress

Dress, Sioux, native tanned leather
hide w/fully beaded yoke in geometric design beadwork on blue
background, fringe from bottom of
arms & dress, sinew-sewn,
50 x 66" (ILLUS.) 2,420.00
Drum, Woodlands, wooden,
"Midewiwin Water Drum," The
Grand Medicine Lodge Society,
encompassed by high-relief
carved serpent, bentwood hoop
securing skin head, 9" h. 605.00
Gauntlets, Plateau Indian, possibly
Blackfoot, leather w/floral beading in pink, green, rose & blue,
fine condition, 14" l., pr. 105.00
Hat, Karok, basketry, domical shape
w/dark zig-zag design on light
ground, finely woven, 6¾" d.,
3¾" h. (small hole at center) 250.00
Headdress, Plains, probably Sioux,
buffalo hide & horn bonnet, the
horns w/incised design colored
w/vermillion, ermine, wrapped hair
dangles & ribbon & hawk bell trim,
beaded forehead band in blue,
dark blue & white w/bead edging,
traditional workmanship & good
age, 14" w. (ribbon worn, splits
in leather in cap) 1,000.00
Jar, Acoma, pottery, small bulbous
bottle shape w/small mouth
raised & supported by hollow
arched handles continuing to bulbous ovoid base container, abstract geometric designs on buff
over red ochre & umber step design on arched handles, early
1900's, 8½" d., 8" h. 475.00
Jar, Zia, pottery, rounded form w/ta-
pering shoulders & cylindrical neck,
indented base, creamy slip over red
clay body, painted w/black & deep
red geometric, foliate & curvilinear
devices, deep red wide band at
base & inner lip, 14" d. 2,310.00

Kachina doll, Hopi, cottonwood,
"Ang-ak-China," standing figure
w/pale blue mask, yellow, white,
orange, light & bright blue
blocked mustache w/cotton fiber
suspensions above long black
beard, pale yellow shoulders &
arms, traditional kilt, first half
20th c., 9" h. (repair to one toe,
minor paint loss) 467.50
Kayak model, Eskimo, detailed
leather & wood construction
w/fine detailing & ivory attach-
ments, 23" l. 225.00
Leggings, Sioux, woman's, beaded
hide, each fully decorated w/con-
centric rectangles, crossed linear
& arrow motifs in blue, green,
yellow & white-heart red beading
on white ground, w/fringe, edge
beaded, cotton muslin tops, sinew
& cotton stitched, Reservation
Period, 9¾" l. 302.50
Moccasins, Arapaho, quilled & bead-
ed leather, fully quilled vamps in
purple, orange & vermillion, tiny
green, dark blue, white, Cheyenne blue & white-heart red
beads around perimeter, ca. 1860,
9" l., pr. (several missing beads,
split to leather, minor wear, rem-
nants of heel fringe) 550.00
Moccasins, Sauk, beaded leather,
long fully beaded cuffs in typical
curvilinear design of white-heart
red, navy, Cheyenne blue, medium blue, pink, white & green
beads, bilaterally symmetrical,
late 19th c., excellent condition,
9½" l., pr. 1,875.00
Necklace, Navajo, "squash blos-
soms," double strand of globular
silver beads supporting twelve
turquoise set blossoms & a turquoise set "Naja" pendant,
24" l 440.00
Pipe, Plains, elbow-shaped carved
catlinite bowl w/high-relief banded decoration & a flattened rectangular light wooden stem,
4½" l. bowl, overall 14¾" l. 302.50
Pipe bag, Sioux-Arapaho, beaded
hide, sinew-sewn, stitched on
both sides, along edges & at
mouth w/bar devices in greasy
yellow, dark & turquoise blue,
lime & white-heart red beading
against turquoise ground, the
openwork parafleche wrapped in
red, blue, purple & yellow dyed
porcupine quillwork, remnant
fringe, bag ornamented w/bead
decorated buffalo hide cuff & a
drop comprised of opaque mandril-

wound black & white glass tube
beads, tin cones, pigment stained
hide & buffalo fur, 1880's, 23½" l.
plus fringe 1,540.00
Rug, Navajo, early Ganado w/bright
red & dark brown in a stepped
diamond design on arbush grey
ground, ca. 1905, 34 x 48" (minor
wear to selvage) 350.00
Rug, Navajo, pictorial w/Yei figures,
birds & cornstalks, red, arbush tan,
brown & natural, 52 x 95" (small
holes, rip at corner, minor
bleeding) 1,600.00
Saddle bags, Blackfoot, leather
w/floral beading in yellow, green,
blue & white on worn red stroud,
19th c., 14" w., 49" l. plus
fringe 850.00
Toy, Plains, beaded & fringed hide,
in the form of a horse saddle,
outfitted w/possible bags, saddle
blanket & crupper, over a stuffed
cotton muslin body, peeled bark
decorated forked stick, decorated
w/greasy yellow, aqua, violet
blue & white-heart red beading,
4½" l. 522.50
Trade token, silver, earwheel design
finely engraved on both sides &
marked "RC" for Robert Cruick-
shank, Montreal, Canada silver-
smith (1779-1806 or 9),
2 3/8" d. 1,000.00
War club, Plains, egg-shaped stone
head mounted on long, slender
wooden shaft w/sinew-sewn blue
& yellow beaded designs & complete w/beaded handle attach-
ments, 36" l. 675.00
Waste basket, Algonquin, Adiron-
dack birchbark-type w/dark cherry bark floral trim, 12½" d.,
10½" h. (few rim stitches
missing) 45.00

INRO

*Originally used by the Japanese to carry
a seal for signing documents, inro eventually were used to carry herbs or medicines in
separate compartments. They are attached by
cord to the sash and held in place by a netsuke. Finest examples are from the Edo and
Meiji periods.*

Ivory & lacquer, three-case, ivory
cases decorated w/a blossoming
plum branch & a gnarled pine tree
set against the background of an
open sea & *matsukawabishi* de-

sign in gold *hiramaki-e, kimpun* &
silver accents, signed "Toyosai,"
w/a carnelian ebony ink stick netsuke ojime & ebony netsuke of an
ink cake, 19th c., 2 5/8" (age
cracks, wear) $880.00

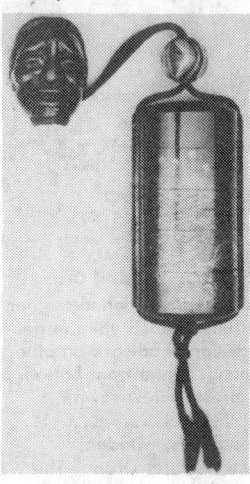

19th Century Inro

Lacquer, four-case, depicting a *torii*
gate sheltered by a grove of pines
looking out onto the sea w/sail-
boats in the distance, rendered in
gold *hiramaki-e, nashiji* & *togi-
dashi* w/red lacquer accents (wear,
minor surface scratches, chips to
case edges), w/glass ojime &
(restored) boxwood mask netsuke,
19th c., 3¾" (ILLUS.) 1,100.00
Lacquer, four-case, depicting a fox
priest procession through the forest
toward a river bank in the moonlight, each animal holding a paper
lantern to guide the way through
the tall, densely grown trees, rendered in gold *takamaki-e, hiramaki-e* & *kirikane on a kinji*
ground, silver accents, *nashiji* interiors, w/coral bead ojime &
ivory netsuke of a basket maker,
inro signed "Koma Kyuhaku Saku,"
19th c., 4¼" (chips to case edge,
wear, minor dents) 2,750.00
Wood, three-case, miniature, carved
in a *mokko* reserve w/a frolicking
shishi reversed by peonies growing from a rocky outcropping,
each set against a *shippo-tsunagi*
ground, silvered metal floral
ojime on cord, signed "Toju,"
19th c., 2" 440.00
Wood, four-case, carved w/a cat
neko posed under a tall pine tree,
its long branches extending to the
reverse over the stylized bamboo

cord runners, unsigned, 19th c.,
4 5/8" (one crack, minor
scratches) 385.00
Wood & pottery, three-case, executed in Ritsuo style w/a series of
pottery & raised lacquer seals on
the brown *ishime* lacquered surface, w/stag antler ojime on cord,
late 18th-early 19th c., 2¾" 3,850.00

IVORY

Ivory Jagging Wheel

Brush rest, carved w/pair of bamboo plants w/a large bamboo
plant behind, two ladybugs crawling up the stalk, reverse carved
as four bamboo segments
w/leaves, China, 18th c.,
9 3/8" l....................... $825.00
Cane handle, long shaft carved &
pierced w/various blossoming
flowers ending above three gold
inlaid initials "VMW" toward bottom, 17 7/8" l. (slight wear)...... 137.50
Chess set, white & green-stained
pieces, kings & queens
w/flowerhead-carved knops,
pierced foliate-carved stems & circular bases, the bishops surmounted by mitres, the knights as
horse's heads, the rooks as towers flying flags (green flags lacking), the pawns of baluster form,
Delhi, India, first half 19th c., 2¼"
to 4" h., 32 pcs. (minor cracks &
chips) 440.00
Figure of Christ at the column,
standing looking over His right
shoulder, His hands tied to the
column at His left (column missing),
School of Francois Duquesnoy,
Franco-Flemish, late 17th - early
18th c., 10 5/8" h. 7,150.00
Figure group of the Three Graces,
the three classical figures clinging
close together w/a length of drapery between them, raised on an
oval waisted ivory base, after

Antonio Canova, late 19th c.,
6¼" h. 1,100.00
Jagging wheel, gracefully carved in
the form of an elongated sea horse
w/small triangular-shaped ears &
trident tail, small silver inlaid eyes,
grasping a pierced fluted crimping
wheel in its forelegs, the head
carved w/a double-tined fork,
America, ca. 1870, repair to tail,
5¾" l. (ILLUS.) 6,050.00
Model of a dog, the seated leonine
animal w/thick curly coat & lolling
tongue, Continental, ca. 1900,
3¾" h. 660.00
Plaque, relief-molded oval panel of
putti, one playing a flute as his
four compatriots dance, in the
manner of Francois Duquesnoy,
Flemish, 18th c., set into a modern
wooden frame, 5¼" w. 2,640.00
Salad servers, silver parcel-gilt collar, w/applied spherules & bright-
cut engraving, Gorham Co., Providence, 1852-65, 11¼" l., pr....... 605.00
Tusks, carved w/the "Seven Gods of
Good Luck," one w/Jurojin & Eibisu
watching a large sea bream below
a figure of Benten playing her *biwa*
to the accompaniment of two children w/a chime, drum & mask; the
second showing Daikoku & Fukuro-
kujin watching a rat beneath the
gaze of Bishamonten, reversed by a
figure of Hotei walking w/a child
playing cymbals, the details incised
& stained for effect, the bases
w/silver rims, Japan, Meiji period,
14 3/8" h., pr. (lacking bottoms,
slight wear, one w/large crack)..4,400.00

JADE

Carved Jade Covered Vases

Bowl, broad circular form on raised

foot ring & w/flaring side slightly
everted at rim, dark green flecked
brown & black w/mottled white
inclusions, China, 8½" d.......$3,080.00
Brush washer, irregularly shaped
oval form, vigorously carved
w/numerous *chilong* amid swirling
clouds, several clambering over
the rim, greyish green suffused
w/veins of lighter green & russet,
Ming Dynasty, 8¾" l. 10,450.00
Censer w/cover, two-handled circular tripod form on scrolled feet
carved at the top w/masks &
joined by mock cords, carved on
the side w/a band of *taotie* masks
reserved on squared spirals, the
octagonal cover formed as a pagoda w/bells suspended from dragons' heads on its roof & pierced
below w/rectangular panels depicting the eight Immortals, spinach
green flecked black & w/occasional
white inclusions (minor chips),
incised Qianlong four-character
mark, China, w/pierced wood
stand, 12½" h................7,150.00
Figure of Guanyin, standing lady
wearing tied long-sleeved gown
over full-length robe, gazing down
& standing before a parrot perched
in pierced fruiting peach branches
issuing from a rocky ridge, holding
to the side a tripod libation vessel,
the stone w/incised details & russet inclusions restricted to the
rear, apple green & mottled white,
China, w/fixed pierced wood
stand, 18" h.................66,000.00
Model of a cicada, the calcified stone
evenly mottled in shades of white
& brown, convex top incised w/cur-
vilinear designs depicting hatched
wings & spiral motifs, angular
ridged bottom incised w/simple linear & V-shaped patterns, Zhou
Dynasty, 2" l. 2,860.00
Table screen, rectangular plaque
depicting a solitary sage gazing at
a waterfall issuing from a cliff &
cascading down to the front & bordered by a large pine tree,
wreathed by scrolling clouds encircling a large phoenix in flight,
spinach green w/dark inclusions,
9 3/8 x 11 1/8" 715.00
Vases, cov., spreading oval foot,
loose rings suspended from monster's head looped handles, flattened baluster-form w/waisted
neck, carved in mirror image
w/scholars & attendants beneath
pine tree & phoenix beside tree
peony, all below foliate lappets,

fluted cover in the form of Bud-
dhistic lion standing four square
w/head turned to the side, dark
green flecked black & w/some
white veining, incised seal marks,
on carved wood stand, 14¾" h.,
pr. (ILLUS. previous page) 7,150.00

JEWELRY

ANTIQUE (1800-1920)

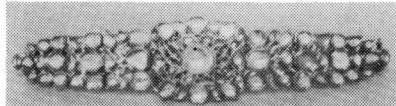

Mogul-Style Victorian Bracelet

In this listing we will focus on early jewel-ry dating roughly from the period of 1800 to 1920. This includes Victorian, Art Nouveau and Edwardian jewelry.

Bar pin, composed of 51 diamonds
in the form of a bow, platinum
mounting & gold pin stick,
Edwardian, England, early
20th c.......................$1,320.00
Bar pin, shaped w/bead & wire
twist decoration surmounted by a
micro-mosaic navette plaque,
Victorian 247.50
Bracelet, Art Nouveau style, composed of nine baroque pearls,
each set within a foliate link, 15k
yellow gold mounting........... 770.00
Bracelet, bangle-type, hinged, of
18k yellow gold surmounted by a
ruby & diamond-set crescent &
star, Victorian 660.00
Bracelet, composed of three gold
pierced plaques set w/a center
cabochon amethyst & seed pearl
florets joined by 21 rows of seed
pearls, marked "Black Star &
Frost" 2,420.00
Bracelet, Mogul-style, composed of
over one hundred table-cut diamonds (some chipped), mounted in
22k gold & cloisonne enamel,
ca. 1875 (ILLUS.)..............3,630.00
Brooch, Art Nouveau style, bird in
flight highlighted by French &
round cut diamonds, hallmarked
18k gold, ca. 1900 ....1,650.00
Brooch, designed as a realistic floral
branch set w/rose-cut diamonds &
centering upon old mine-cut diamond, mounted "en tremblant" in
18k gold & silver, bearing French
hallmarks (forms three pins).....3,410.00

Brooch, 14k gold beaded dome suspending two beads from a foxtail link movable chain, Victorian 385.00

Cameo brooch, mourning-type, black Whitby jet, cameo-carved profile of woman's head, 1 7/8 x 2¼" 350.00

Cameo brooch, oval carved pink coral, high-relief bust of a Bacchic nymph facing left w/bunches of grapes in her hair & wearing a beaded necklace, set in an openwork gold scrolling foliage frame set w/four small diamonds, Victorian, 2¼" h................. 1,760.00

Cameo brooch, oval onyx w/a profile of a lady in white, within a beaded 14k gold frame, Victorian 330.00

Cameo brooch, profile of a lady carved in onyx surrounded by seed pearls set in 14k gold, Victorian 990.00

Cameo necklace, carved shell, formed of gold mesh thread hung w/thirteen oval & teardrop-shaped carved shell cameos depicting Lorenzo de Medici & various classical figures, probably Italian, ca. 1850 .... 2,750.00

Cameo pin, profile of a lady carved in sardonyx, highlighted by seed pearls, 14k gold mounting, Victorian 522.50

Chain, composed of intricate 18k gold links, Victorian, 24" l........ 495.00

Cruciform, Art Nouveau style, scrolling pieced 18k gold arms highlighted by small rose-cut diamonds & a center pearl 495.00

Cuff links, an oval gold disc w/an etched border, marked "Tiffany & Co.," pr. 660.00

Daguerreotype ring, 14k gold engraved mounting w/a center carnelian panel that opens to reveal a daguerreotype portrait of a woman, mid-19th c. 412.50

Earrings, Art Nouveau style, gold, models of ladies' heads, pr....... 150.00

Earrings, black onyx set in sterling silver, oval, 1½" l., pr. 110.00

Earrings, 14k gold pendant terminating in a sphere, highlighted by black enamel, Victorian, pr....... 275.00

Lavalier, Art Nouveau style, a pansy set w/a seed pearl, within a freeform frame, highlighted by turquoise beads, on a fine gold link chain, English hallmarks, ca. 1900 .... 330.00

Locket, Art Nouveau style, profile of a lady w/a diamond set head-

band, 18k gold mounting, ca. 1900 .... 357.50

Mourning pin, marquise-shaped ivory rendered in water-color w/the figure of a young gentleman weeping before a monument inscribed, "S.M. Barker," dated "July 1794," above the legend, "Weep Not For Me But For Yourself," in gold metal case w/fine beaded edge, America, late 18th c. 2,640.00

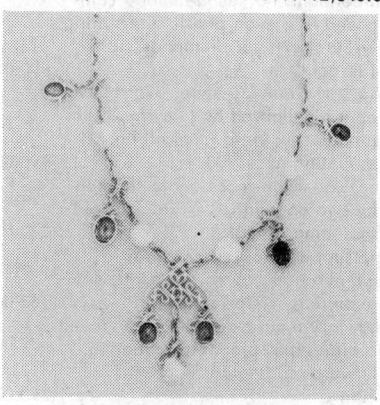

Art Nouveau Necklace

Necklace, Art Nouveau style, composed of a gold chain, spaced by fresh water pearls & six collet-set sapphires & one small diamond, ca. 1900 (ILLUS.) 3,410.00

Necklace, graduated lampwork millefiori beads, each bead ½" to 1" d., 29" l..................... 150.00

Necklace, link-type, gutta percha loops w/2½" rose pendant at end, 20" l..................... 55.00

Pendant, Art Nouveau style, center peridot encircled by eight round sapphires in a 14k mounting, w/fine link chain, ca. 1900 ...... 770.00

Pins, Arts & Crafts style, sterling silver, round orange petaled flowers w/star points between petals, hallmarked & stamped "J.F.," Europe, 20th c., 1¼" d., pr....... 137.50

Edwardian Platinum and Diamond Pin

Pin, composed of full-cut diamonds in a rectangular pierced foliate platinum mounting, Edwardian, England, early 20th c. (ILLUS.) 550.00

Pin, floral spray design w/large central blossom set "en tremblant"

& set w/six pear-shaped & old
mine-cut diamonds, mounted in
gold & silver, mid-19th c. 4,125.00

Pin, heart-shaped, 14k gold mount-
ed w/cultured pearls, 19th c. 75.00

Pin, micro-mosaic, scene of two birds
against a dark blue sky, bordered
by a roped bezel highlighted by a
suspended beetle, 18k yellow gold
mounting 1,650.00

Pin-pendant, horseshoe shape composed of eleven pearls alternating
w/European cut diamonds set in
18k gold 990.00

Ring, Art Nouveau style, oval black
opal highlighted by two small diamonds, 14k yellow gold foliate
mounting, ca. 1900 . . . . 990.00

Ring, cabochon moss agate flanked
by two dogs in a 14k yellow gold
mounting, Victorian 330.00

Ring, intaglio-carved profile of a
woman in sardonyx, in a 14k gold
mounting, Victorian 165.00

Ring, lacy mount set w/diamonds in
a *millegrain* platinum mounting,
Edwardian, England, early
20th c. 1,210.00

Ring, man's, solid pink gold w/gen-
uine citrine, ca. 1900 . . . .   75.00

Ring, shield-shaped agate in a conforming repousse 10k gold ring . . . 302.50

Scarf pin, gold, Etruscan style bead
work w/a center navette in *pietra
dura*, Victorian 165.00

Watch chain w/slide, lady's, 14k
gold w/curb links, slide w/two
pearls & turquoise, America, ca.
1896 . . . . 395.00

Watch chain, round double 14k gold
links w/a slide highlighted by a
diamond & black enamel, Vic-
torian 1,100.00

SETS

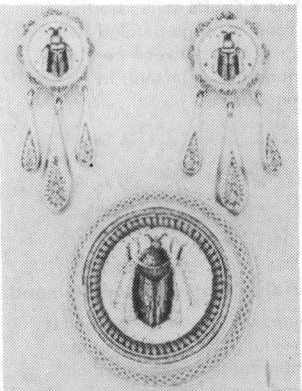

Victorian Micro-Mosaic Set

Brooch-locket & earring set: micro-

mosaic, consisting of a round
brooch-locket w/a center mosaic
of a large beetle within a wire-
twist gold frame, w/matching pair
of earrings, 19th c., minor
damage, the set (ILLUS.) 1,540.00

Necklace & earring set: necklace
composed of 6½ to 8mm pearls &
rose cut diamonds in a silver top
gold mounting & matching earrings, in original leather fitted
box w/tiara frame & screws,
the set 4,290.00

Pin & earring set: pierced foliate
hinged brooch set w/turquoise,
together w/a matching pair of
pendent earrings; 15k yellow gold
mountings, Victorian, 3 pcs. 962.50

MODERN - 1920's - 1960's

Trifari Rhinestone Pin

*The bright sparkling jewelry so popular
from the 1920's through the 1960's has again
come into its own. The baubles of rhinestones
(faceted glass with a foil backing), colored
glass stones and* faux *pearls were affordable
to a large segment of the population with
prices ranging from very low — less than a
dollar for a rhinestone dress clip — to well
over $100 for a well-designed article utilizing
sterling silver mountings set with fine Austrian crystal. Some pieces were in excellent
taste, resembling fine jewelry, while others
were flamboyantly fake with a multitude of
rhinestones interspersed with brilliantly colored glass stones. Also see BAKELITE.*

Bracelet, Art Deco style, sterling silver, heavy, signed "Viking
Crafts" $25.00

Bracelet, bangle-type, baguette
rhinestones, "Hobe" 65.00

Bracelet, 45 brilliant marquise &
round rhinestones, "Eisenberg" . . . 145.00

Clip, seven large topaz stones
w/clear rhinestones, gold-washed
back, "Eisenberg," 2¾" l. 225.00

Earrings, round, cinnabar lacquer, in
silver gilt filigree mountings,
pr. 30.00

Earrings, clip-type, crescent-shaped, set overall w/rhinestones, "Kenneth Lane," 2", pr. 55.00

Necklace, cherry amber faceted oval beads, double strand, 16" l. 145.00

Necklace, multiple strands of tiny amber & brown glass beads, "Miriam Haskell" 65.00

Necklace, faceted aurora borealis stones, single strand, "Lisner," 16" l. 32.00

Necklace, cultured pearls, composed of fifty-one pearls graduating in size from 6¾ to 7¼ mm, marked "Mikimoto," complete w/pearl-set 14k gold clasp, 16" l. 385.00

Pin, American flag, red baguette stones forming stripes, "Weiss," 2" 25.00

Pin, bow form, 14k rose & yellow gold, marked "Tiffany & Co.," ca. 1940 .... 550.00

Pin, rooster, gold-plated metal w/red stone eyes, "Kramer," 2" .. 30.00

Pin, brushed gold-tone metal set w/rhinestones, marked "Trifari," 2½" l. (ILLUS. previous page) 55.00

Pin, boomerang-shaped, mother-of-pearl, "Antonio" 185.00

Pin, w/baroque pearl, "Capricorn," by "KJL" (Kenneth Jay Lane) 98.00

Pin, model of a scarecrow, rhinestones & faux gemstones, "Weiss" 45.00

Pin, bow-shaped, sterling silver, "Eisenberg Original" 185.00

Pin, sterling silver leaves & berries, "Danecraft," 2½" 45.00

Ring, 14k white gold filigree mounting set w/an aquamarine 95.00

Ring, 14k yellow gold domed filigree mounting set w/22 amethyst-type stones 60.00

Ring, sterling silver mounting set w/1" oval turquoise 30.00

Sweater clip, moonstones & enamel, "Trifari" 38.00

SETS

Bracelet & earrings, Peking glass beads & multicolored stones, signed "Miriam Haskell" 75.00

Necklace & clip-type earrings, rhodium mounting pave' set w/round & baguette rhinestones, "Trifari" ... 45.00

Pin & earrings, amethyst stones, "Eisenberg Ice" 120.00

Pin & earrings, gold-tone metal, pinwheel design set w/apple green jade-like stones & pearls, "Weiss" 30.00

Pin & earrings, pearl & coral, "Miriam Haskell" 95.00

JUKE BOXES

Wurlitzer Model 750 Juke Box

AMI (Automated Musical Instrument Co.) Model A, 1946 . . $1,500.00 to 3,000.00

AMI Model E120, 120 selections, 1953 ....1,000.00

AMI Model F120, 45 rpm, 120 selections, early 1950's 400.00

Mills "Throne of Music," 1939 .... 750.00

Rock-Ola Model 1422, 1946 ....3,500.00 to 4,000.00

Rock-Ola Model 1428, 1948 ....2,850.00

Seeburg Model M100A "Select-O-Matic," 1948 .... 950.00

Seeburg Model M100B, 45 rpm, 1950 .... 450.00

Seeburg Model M100C, 1950 ....1,250.00

Seeburg Model P146 (Trashcan), 1946........................1,200.00

Seeburg Model P147, blue mirrored front, woodgrained case, 1947.... 600.00

Wurlitzer Model 24, 24-selection machine w/rotary multi-selector, 1937 ....1,500.00 to 1,800.00

Wurlitzer Model 750, 1941, restored (ILLUS.) 4,500.00

Wurlitzer Model 750E, 1941 ....4,300.00

Wurlitzer Model 850 (Peacock), 1941........................6,600.00

Wurlitzer Model 1015, 1946-47 ....8,925.00 to 9,900.00

Wurlitzer Model 1100, 1948-49 ....3,000.00 to 4,500.00

KEWPIE COLLECTIBLES

Rose O'Neill's Kewpies were so popular in their heyday that numerous objects depicting them were produced and are now collectible. The following represents a sampling.

Rare Kewpie Figure Group

Creamer, jasper ware, seven white
relief-molded Kewpies on blue
ground, signed "Rose O'Neill" $165.00

Drawing, original pen & ink artwork
by Rose O'Neill, shows a group of
Kewpies presenting three little
girls w/bread & jam, museum
framing, 20 x 22" 522.50

Drawing, original pen & ink artwork
by Rose O'Neill, shows a large
group of Kewpies seated on books
& serving tea to a young girl in
the background & a large turkey in
the foreground, museum framing,
21 x 25" 1,650.00

Feeding dish, china, seven action
Kewpies, signed "Rose O'Neill -
Royal Rudolstadt China," 7¾" d... 235.00

Figure, bisque, Kewpie seated
w/mandolin, Germany, 2" h...... 375.00

Figure, bisque, Kewpie w/turkey,
2" h........................... 300.00

Figure, bisque, Kewpie in a wicker-
molded basket, hands holding
edge of basket & head peeking
over the rim, background of blue
& yellow flowers w/green foliage,
3" h........................... 950.00

Figure, bisque, Kewpie Doodle Dog,
white animal w/black markings &
blue wings, 3" h. 1,200.00

Figure, bisque, standing Kewpie
playing large white drum w/red
lacing, drum resting on dark
brown stand, 3½" h. 3,200.00

Figure, bisque, Kewpie "Sweeper,"
4¼" h......................... 495.00

Figure, bisque, Kewpie seated behind wicker basket, looking at
ladybug perched on outstretched
hand, 4¼" 2,500.00

Figures, bisque, "Bride" & "Groom,"
on original stands, w/original
clothes, 4½" h., pr. 295.00

Figure, bisque, Kewpie "Thinker,"
signed "O'Neill," 4½" 130.00

Figure, bisque, Kewpie "Cowboy,"
signed "Rose O'Neill," 5" h...... 200.00

Figure, bisque, standing Kewpie
farmer, holding rake & wearing
large hat, w/original box,
5½" h......................... 950.00

Figures, celluloid, Kewpie twins in
basket, 2" h. 60.00

Figure, celluloid, black Kewpie,
w/original signed & dated 1913 label on back, 2 3/8" h. 110.00

Figures, celluloid, bride, groom &
minister, original stands, original
clothes, Japan, 2½" h., 3 pcs..... 75.00

Figure, composition, Kewpie
"Groom," 8½" h. 200.00

Figure group, bisque, exhibition model
of "The Kewpie Mountain," modeled
as a hillside containing 22 action
Kewpie figures in various poses,
possibly only two in existence,
two figures broken off, 11 x 22"
(ILLUS.) 17,000.00

Pincushion, bisque, Kewpie on
heart-shaped crocheted amber-
ribboned pincushion, 1¼" h.
Kewpie......................... 300.00

Planter, jasper ware, white relief-
molded tumbling Kewpies on blue
ground, signed "Rose O'Neill,"
4½" h......................... 220.00

Plaque, pierced to hang, crescent-
shaped, jasper ware, three white
relief-molded bouncing Kewpies
w/flowers & butterflies on blue
ground, signed "Rose O'Neill" 265.00

Plate, china, three Kewpies sitting
on bench, one larger looking over
shoulder, four smaller around
plate edge, marked "Copyright
Rose O'Neill Wilson, KEWPIE, Germany," 7" d.................... 75.00

Rose O'Neill Kewpie Postcard

Postcard, original design by Rose
O'Neill w/a Kewpie & songbook
in front left corner, written &
mailed by artist Rose O'Neill, dual
side framing (ILLUS.) 550.00

Salt shaker w/original top, china,
Kewpie on both sides, Noritake,
backstamped "No. 15" 25.00

Tea set: tapering cylindrical cov. pot
& similarly shaped cov. sugar
bowl; porcelain, each decorated
w/transfer-printed Kewpies on
each side w/polychrome floral
rims, each marked "copyrighted
Mrs. Rose O'Neill Wilson, Kewpies, Z.S., Bavaria," pot
6½" h., 2 pcs. 242.00
Tray, china, scene of Kewpie playing, marked "Royal Rudolstadt,"
10" d. 130.00
Vase, bud, bisque, slender square
blue shading to tan vase on base
w/a Kewpie w/guitar standing to
one side, 5¼" h. 650.00
Vase, bud, bisque, slender square
tall blue vase on base w/a figure
of a Kewpie holding a Teddy bear
standing next to it, signed 1,100.00

KITCHENWARES

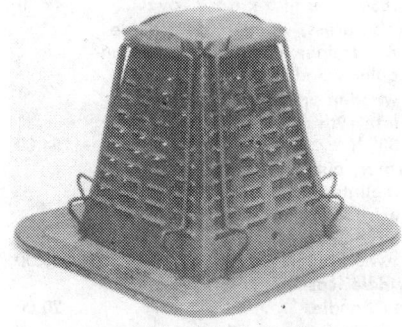

Stove Top Bread Toaster

Apple parer, cast iron, "Bonanza,
Goodell Co., Antrim, New Hamp-
shire," 16" l. $125.00
Apple parer, cast iron, "Gold Medal," open lacy hearts in wheel,
mounted on board 85.00
Apple parer, cherry & iron, hand-
made, shaped board fitted w/iron
handle, fork & clamp, complete
w/table clamp & cutter arm, 14" l.
(crank arm pin missing) 275.00
Apple roaster, tin, half-round cylinder w/hanging loops at top of
ends & strap handle on back,
10" l. (some rust & old repair) 275.00
Biscuit pricker, twisted wire, triangular top, 3" d., 4½" h. overall .. 65.00
Bowl, ash burl w/good figure, simple turned lip, good old worn finish, 13¾" d., 4¾" h. 450.00
Bowl, utilitarian crockery, Apricot

patt., yellow & green, 9½" d. (little rim wear) 75.00
Bread toaster, stove top model, tin,
pyramid style, 6½" sq. base, 5" h.
(ILLUS.) 18.00
Butcher's block table, heavy wooden
block on three stout, turned legs,
32" d., 25½" h. (worn surface) ... 185.00
Butter churn, "Dazey Model B," embossed glass jar, original gears,
red egg-shaped iron finial on lid,
4 qt. 45.00
Butter churn, "Dazey No. 20," February 14, 1922 patent 85.00
Butter churn, "Dazey No. 60" 75.00
Butter churn, dasher-type, wooden
stave construction w/straight tapered sides, one stave extends
above rim as handle, hand-made
rose head nails hold hoops in
place, long-handled dasher
w/fitted cover, America, late
18th c., 36" h. 385.00
Butter ladle, maple, w/hook end ... 25.00
Butter scales, wooden, balance-
type, post w/knob end supporting
pivoting balance arm w/suspend-
ed square wooden trays, well-
carved handle, worn black paint,
27" w. (split in handle, one tray
reglued) 75.00
Butter smoother, curly maple, flat
turned disk w/center handle,
scrubbed finish, 9" d. 40.00
Cabbage cutting board, curly maple,
rectangular board w/arched end &
inset cutting blade, good figure,
color & patina, 6¾ x 20¾" 200.00
Cabbage cutting board, maple,
curved top w/cut-out heart grip,
one-blade, 7 x 15½" 275.00
Canisters, green transparent glass,
large, made by Hocking, three
w/lids, set of 6 .... 130.00
Can opener, cast iron, figural bull's
head & tail, 6¼" l. .... 55.00 to 65.00
Cheese ladder, wooden, mortised &
pinned, beveled & shaped sides,
crossbar handled top, 18th c.,
28 x 44" overall 150.00
Cheese preserver, cov., clear glass,
square 35.00
Cheese sieve, round bentwood
frame w/lappet construction,
holds woven splint mesh, 25" d.
(some mesh damage) 100.00
Cherry pitter, cast iron, "Duke,
Reading Hardware Co.," 11" l.
plus handle 100.00
Cherry pitter, single, cast iron, "Enterprise No. 1," 12" h. 35.00
Cherry pitter, cast iron, "Enterprise
No. 16" 25.00
Chopping bowl, molded line decora-

tion exterior, w/traces of old green paint, early 20th c., 20" d., 6" h. 100.00

Coffee bean roaster, tin, iron & wood, turned wood handle, rectangular, 18th c., 30½" l. overall 395.00

Coffee measure, tin, "Dix Coffee Meter," adjustable sliding disk for 2, 4 or 6 cups, 1908 patent 39.00

Colander, brass w/wrought-iron rim & handles, deep rounded sides w/central punched starflower & swags decoration, 10¼" d. (polished, some dents) 155.00

Cookie board, cast pewter, four-part design: two floral, a woman & a goat; each within an ornamental border, wooden backing, 3 3/8 x 4" 65.00

Cornstick pan, cast iron, seven-ear, "Griswold No. 262," 4¼ x 8½" ... 70.00

Cornstick Pan

Cornstick pan, cast iron, seven-ear, "Griswold Crispy Corn Sticks, No. 273" (ILLUS.) 26.50

Cottage cheese sieve, tin, rectangular w/sliding sides, overall pierced design, Ohio, early 19th c., 6" w., 19" h. 77.00

Cream whip, cov., tin, cast iron & wood, "Fries," ca. 1890, 6" l., 4½" w., 8" h. 70.00

Cutting board, maple, smooth, 1¼" thick, 11 x 13" 65.00

Cutting board, slate, circular form w/pierced rounded extension for hanging, America, early 19th c., 15¾" d. 165.00

Dipper, brass, w/shaped wrought-iron handle, 16¾" l. 135.00

Dipper, copper w/shaped wrought-iron handle w/hook end, ca. 1830, 21" l. 165.00

Dish cover (fly screen), domed wire mesh, 8" d. 45.00

Dough scraper, wrought iron, hoe-form w/tooled brass handle, blade engraved "P.D. 1850,25," made by Peter Derr, 4" l. 425.00

Dutch oven, cast iron, "Griswold No. 10" 95.00

Eggbeater, iron & wire, "A & J" (Ash & Johnson), 1923 patent ....12.00 to 16.00

Eggbeater, "Bonton," patented 9-14-1875 .... 85.00

Egg cooker, cast iron, "Griswold No. 962" 18.00

Egg (or cream) whip, spiraled springy wire, squeeze-type handle, accordion action 10.00

Food chopper, wrought steel, double blades w/horse head blade ends engraved & w/inlaid copper eye & brass bridle button, turned wooden handles w/brass ferrules, 12¼" l. 325.00

Food grinder, cast iron w/tinned finish, "Keen Kutter No. KK22, E. C. Simmons Hardware Co.," 1906 patent 17.00

Food grinder, cast iron w/tinned finish, "Universal, L.F. & C., No. 3".. 18.00

Frying pan, cast iron, "Griswold No. 10" 95.00

Funnel, brass, 2 x 3" oval collar, 1860, overall 5 x 6 x 7" oval 49.00

Grape press, wooden, detachable tin strainer mounted on a rectangular wooden base w/hinged wooden press, on trestle base, late 19th or early 20th c., 40" l., 38" h. 154.00

Grater, punched-tin half-round mounted on walnut board w/rounded end deeply carved w/compass star, hanging hole between points of star, 4¼ x 10" ... 420.00

Griddle, cast iron, "Griswold No. 9," w/handle 20.00

Ice pick, four steel tines, brass ferrule, turned wood handle, marked "Crawford, Newark, New Jersey" 44.00

Kettle shelf, wrought iron & brass, reticulated brass panel w/Masonic design & "Comfort" 150.00

Lemon squeezer, cast iron, hinged, "Landers, Frary & Clark," two-part 25.00

Lifter, tin, slotted, marked "Handee Helper" 6.00

Loaf pan, double, tin, for hearth oven 44.00

Maple syrup thermometer, brass ... 65.00

Measuring cup, green glass, embossed "Measuring & Mixing Cup" on base, "Hazel Atlas," 16 oz..... 25.00

Meat cleaver, wrought iron, 13" l. .. 175.00

Meat press, cast iron, "Columbia" .. 19.00

Muffin pan, cast iron, 11 oval shallow cups, bar handle ends, 1858, 6 x 13" 22.00

Nutmeg grater, wooden, carved acorn coquilla nut, screw top,

opens to expose tin rasp framed
in ivory container below, 2¾".... 220.00
Oven broom, birch splint, hole in
hewn handle for hanging, 1830,
New York State, 10½" l......... 30.00
Oven peel, wrought iron, ram's horn
handle end, 40½" l............. 125.00
Pan, cov., copper w/cast-iron han-
dle, dovetail construction, labeled
"The J. Van Range Co., Manufac-
turers, Cini, O. 8 Qt.," 9" d. 125.00
Pastry wheel, carved bone, in brass
yoke w/turned cherry handle,
2" yoke, 6½" l. 130.00
Pastry wheel, green Catalin handle,
"Vaughn," 1921 .... 20.00
Patty mold, cast iron, heart-shaped,
"Griswold" 15.00
Pie cooling rack, wire, four tiers ... 30.00
Pie lifter, tin w/long wooden han-
dle, round 45.00
Pitcher, utilitarian crockery, Iris
patt., cream & rust shaded 65.00
Pitcher, utilitarian crockery, Rose on
Trellis patt., light green 65.00

Pot Scrubber

Pot scrubber, wire chain links on
handle, 7½" l. (ILLUS.) 18.50
Raisin seeder, hand-held, wire grid,
wooden handle, "Everett" 49.00
Roaster, cast iron, spherical body in
ring-form tripod base w/handle,
wooden crank handle, 7½" h.,
overall 15½" l. (ring w/maker's
label pitted) 175.00
Rolling pin, amber blown glass, pontil, early, 16" l. 98.00
Rolling pin, curly maple, good color,
16¾" l. (age crack in one
handle) 40.00
Sandwich cutters, tin, spade, club,
diamond & heart shapes, boxed
set of 4 .... 14.00
Saucepan, cast iron w/wrought-iron
handle, stamped "Kenrick & Co.,
Improved, half pint," 4" d. 55.00
Sausage grinder, wooden, old red
w/black stenciled label "Coff-
man's Patent 1845, Coshocton
County, Ohio...," mounted on long
board, 42" l. 80.00
Sausage stuffer, cast iron, "Russel &
Irwin, New Britain, Ct., Aug. 17,
86" 35.00
Scrapple pans, sheet iron, nest-type,
movable open wire loop handles

at each end, the largest 14 x 16",
3½" h., set of 5................. 260.00
Sieve, ash, solid shallow sides
w/woven base, remnants of old
dark blue-grey paint, America, ca.
1800, 21½" d. 302.50
Skillet, cast iron, "Erie No. 12" 95.00
Skillet, cast iron, "Griswold
No. 0" 70.00
Skimmer, brass, butterfly-shaped
pierced bowl, openwork handle
formed of diagonal bars, England,
23" l. 65.00
Skimmer, copper, w/pierced oval
spoon-shaped bowl, long handle,
overall 17" l. 130.00
Spatula, brass, w/flat wrought-iron
handle, hook end, marked "F.B.S.,
Canton, Ohio, pat. '86," 14½" l. ... 150.00
Sugar nippers, cast iron, traces of
green paint, 9" l. 85.00
Utensil rack, pine, scrolled arched
top, fitted w/seven wrought-iron
hooks, old dark finish, 29" l. 200.00
Utensil rack, sheet iron, cut-out silhouette crest w/birds & foliate
scrolls, scalloped sides & lower
edge, seven wrought-iron hooks,
old patina w/traces of cream-
colored paint, 27" l. 1,250.00
Vegetable slicer, slanted blade in
rectangular wooden frame, 3½"
handle w/hole for hanging, overall 10" l. 22.00
Wafer iron, cast & wrought iron,
rectangular two-part head w/cast
geometric design w/heart & star,
long wrought handles, 26½" l. ... 115.00
Waffle iron, "Griswold No. 8,"
w/bail-handled holder 60.00

KNIVES

*Knives of all types are collectible today but
especially popular are better quality pocket
types from the late 19th and early 20th century. Even more modern knives by such
makers as Case and Remington are sought-
after. Overall condition of the knife's blade(s)
and handle are very important in pricing with
mint, unsharpened knives bringing premium
prices.*

Advertising, "Cudahy Packing Co.,"
grading & sausage pocket knife,
pearl handle $25.00
Advertising, "Purina," three-blade
pocket knife 15.00
Advertising, "Westinghouse Coolers," embossed handle 29.00
Bowie knife, green-black buffalo

horn handle, unmarked American, w/leather sheath, ca. 1880's, 8" blade, 12" l. overall 75.00

Buck Cutlery pocket knife, figural slim lady's leg light colored bone handle, 2¾" l. closed 57.50

Case "Sod Buster" XX U.S.A. one-blade pocket knife, black composition handle, No. 2138, 1967-70, 5 5/8" l. closed 150.00

Case "Peanut" XX two-blade pocket knife, black composition handle, No. 2229½, 1950-65, 2¾" l. closed (never sharpened)............... 90.00

Case XX two-blade pocket knife, wide red bone handle, silver "Case" nameplate, No. 6250, 1940-65, 4 3/8" l. closed 235.00

Golden Rule Cutlery Co., Chicago, pocket knife, "Our Martyred Presidents" 150.00

Keen Kutter K-32 pocket knife, pearl handle 37.50

Marbles "Woodcraft" hunting knife, leather handle, No. 49, 4½" l. 150.00

Remington "Switchblade w/pull ball" one-blade pocket knife, black composition handle, No. R22, 3 3/8" l. closed 65.00

Remington two-blade pocket knife, candy stripe celluloid handle, No. R555, 3¼" l. closed.......... 130.00

Remington "Whittler" three-blade pocket knife, bone handle, No. R6243, 3¼" l. closed........ 55.00

Remington "Congress" two-blade pocket knife, pearl handle, No. R7034, 3¼" l. closed........ 37.50

Sterling silver pocket knife, two-blade, ornate Victorian handle decoration.................... 49.00

Syracuse Knife Co. two-blade pocket knife, variegated celluloid handle, 3½" l. closed 30.00

Turner Co., "Cutlers to His Majesty" pen knife, bone handle 30.00

Victorinox Swiss army knife, "Champion" model 20.00

Winchester "Pruner" one-blade pocket knife, cocobolo handle, No. 1610, 4 1/8" l. closed 75.00

Winchester "Lockback - Serpentine" one-blade pocket knife, shell celluloid handle, No. 2087, 3" l. closed...................... 80.00

Winchester "Congress" two-blade pocket knife, pearl handle, No. 2363, 3" l. closed........... 100.00

Winchester "Serpentine" two-blade pocket knife, stag handle, No. 2918, 3 3/8" l. closed 95.00

Winchester "Whittler - Lobster" three-blade pocket knife, pearl handle, No. 3371, 3" l. closed 135.00

Winchester "Premium Stockman" three-blade pocket knife, stag handle, No. 3965, 3¼" l. closed .. 75.00

LACQUER

Lacquer Nesting Tables

Most desirable of the lacquer articles available for collectors are those of Japanese and Chinese origin, and the finest of these were produced during the Ming and Ching dynasties, although the Chinese knew the art of fashioning articles of lacquer centuries before. Cinnabar is carved red lacquer.

Altar table, cinnabar, rectangular top w/everted horizontal flanges w/straight beaded apron joined to rectangular legs by wing brackets, legs joined by pierced cut-out panels at both ends in a cloud-scroll design w/a rectangular foot, China, early 18th c., 81" l., 34¾" h. (losses to lacquer surface) $5,255.00

Armchairs, throne-style, pierced fret-carved back w/an arrangement of angular scrolls & w/conforming pierced rectangular arms, decorated w/gilt leafy vines on an inset paneled seat w/an apron carved w/cloud scrolls & rectangular legs ending in block feet, 19th c., pr. 3,300.00

Hibachi, decorated wood, circular, straight sides decorated in colored lacquer w/the 'Six Immortal Poets,' on a textured cinnabar ground, Japan, 12¼" d., 8½" h. (wear) 137.50

Mirror, black lacquer & bamboo, rectangular beveled plate, triangular crest & fitted small flanking

shelves, Japan, late 19th c.,
28" w., 40" h. 880.00
Music stand, black lacquer
w/mother-of-pearl inlay, scroll-cut
rectangular stand w/paper ledge
& painted w/a central flower
spray design within gilt & inlaid
mother-of-pearl borders, on adjustable support raised on three
scrolling cabriole legs,
mid-19th c., 54" h. 605.00
Storage chest, upright rectangular
form, top drawer over two doors
enclosing six drawers w/six drawers beneath, gold *hiramakie* floral
& insect decoration on black
ground, Japan, 19th c., 14¾ x
6 5/8", 21½" h. (some damage) .. 75.00
Tables, nest-type, scarlet lacquer,
each w/shaped supports on a
trestle base ending in scroll toes,
decorated w/gilt scenes of
figures, pavilions, animals & a
palace walkway, China, mid-
19th c., largest 24¼" w., 29¼" h.,
set of 4 (ILLUS. previous page) ...4,400.00
Tray, painted & parcel-gilt black
lacquer papier-mache, dished loz-
enge-shaped tray decorated w/a
horse & two dogs within a gilt
foliate-scrolled border, Victorian,
third quarter 19th c., on a later
stand, 31" l. 7,150.00
Writing brush & cover, cinnabar,
each part decorated w/a sinuous
dragon in pursuit of a flaming
pearl on a ground of clouds,
9½" l. 1,650.00

LIGHTING DEVICES

LAMPS

FAIRY LAMPS

*These are candle burning night lights of the
Victorian era. Best known are the Clarke
Fairy Lamps made in England, but they were
also made by other firms. They were produced
in two sizes, each with a base and a shade.
The Fairy Pyramid Lamps listed below all
have a clear glass base and are approximately 2 7/8" d. and 3¼" h. The Fairy Lamps are
usually at least 4" d. and 5" h. when assembled and these may or may not have an additional saucer or bottom holder to match the
shade in addition to the clear base.*

Fairy Pyramid Lamps
Peach Blow glass shade, decorated
w/green leaves, Thomas Webb &

Sons, on marked "Clarke" clear
glass base, 3¾" h. $405.00
Rose diamond-quilted mother-of-
pearl satin glass shade w/white
lining on marked "Clarke" clear
glass base, 2 7/8" d., 3½" h. 150.00
Verre Moire (Nailsea) glass shade,
frosted red w/opaque white loopings, marked "Clarke" clear glass
base, 5½" d., 4" h. 485.00
Yellow swirl "overshot" cased glass
shade on marked "Clarke" clear
glass base, 2 7/8" d., 3½" h. 100.00

Fairy Lamps

Burmese Fairy Lamp Epergne

Burmese glass shade & matching
squared base w/folded over rims
in rich salmon pink evenly shaded
to yellow, acid finish, marked
"Clarke" clear glass candle cup insert, 6" d., 6 1/8" h. 550.00
Burmese glass epergne, gilt-metal
frame marked "Clarke's Patent
Fairy Lamps" centered by Burmese
waisted pedestal holding aloft
tiered loops w/three cone-shaped
ruffle-rimmed Burmese vases
flanked below by two Burmese
shades set upon marked "Clarke's
Cricklite" clear glass bases,
9½" w., 10" h. (ILLUS.) 770.00
Chartreuse green melon-ribbed
overlay satin glass shade w/white
lining on marked "Clarke" clear
glass base, 3 7/8" d., 4 5/8" h..... 181.00
Coral embossed Raindrop patt. overshot shade on marked "Clarke"
clear glass base, 2 7/8" d.,
4 1/8" h. 115.00
Fuchsia pink shaded to amber satin
glass shade cased w/opal & decorated w/elaborate yellow coralene leafy floral spray, ruffled rim
on matching base, clear candle
holder also w/coralene beading,
6½" h. 300.00
Sapphire blue Diamond Quilted patt.
melon-ribbed glass shade, marked

"Clarke" clear glass base,
3 7/8" d., 4 5/8" h.............. 150.00
Stevens & Williams glass shade
w/matching ruffled base w/turned
down edge, blue, white & crystal
stripes w/satin finish, applied
clear bottom, w/marked "Clarke"
clear glass candle cup insert,
5¼" d., 6" h................... 810.00
Verre Moire (Nailsea) glass shade &
matching ruffled base, frosted
cranberry w/opaque white loopings, marked "Clarke" clear glass
candle cup insert, 5½" d., 5" h. .. 435.00

Figural Fairy Lamps

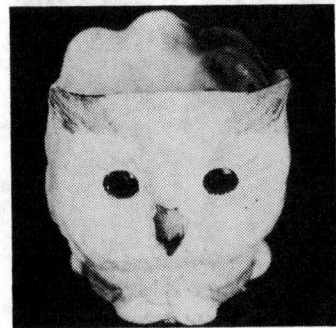

Three-Face Figural Fairy Lamp

Bisque, model of a grey owl head
w/blue bow around neck, amber
& black glass eyes, 3" d.,
4¼" h........................ 200.00
Bisque, three-faced shade, owl, cat
& dog, each w/glass eyes,
marked "Clarke" clear glass candle cup insert, 4 x 4" (ILLUS. of
owl face)..................... 248.00

HANDEL LAMPS (All signed)

Handel "Love Birds" Lamp

Desk lamp, cylindrical textured
green glass shade fitting into a
bronze two-branch harp, base
w/curved adjustable standard on
fluted round foot, shade signed

"MOSSER Handel 6010," base
w/cloth label, 10" w., 12¾" h.
(small nick on shade)........... 825.00
Table lamp, 17½" d. green textured
domical shade w/narrow ivory border band w/dark floral sprig band,
on bronze base w/teakwood-style
pierced plinth & ribbed tapered
shaft, signed twice, 24" h........3,025.00
Table lamp, 17 7/8" d. reverse-painted
"chipped ice" conical shade decorated w/a wooded summer landscape in shades of green, orange,
yellow & black, inscribed "Handel/
5389" & w/ring impressed "HANDEL
PAT'D NO. 979664," raised on a
bronze baluster-form base cast
w/upright leafage ending in a
circular foot w/four lug feet, impressed "HANDEL," early 20th c.,
26" h. 3,850.00
Table lamp, "Love Birds," 18" d. reverse-painted domical shade decorated in a colorful design of
parrots in a jungle w/wisteria
hanging down, signed & numbered
"Handel 6874P," on an octagonal
column base signed "Handel
979664," 23" h. (ILLUS.)........24,750.00
Table lamp, 18" d. reverse-painted
domical shade decorated inside &
out w/autumn leaves edged in a
black motif & orange & brown,
squatty bronze Art Nouveau style
base, 22" h....................3,025.00

MINIATURE LAMPS

Figural Santa Claus Miniature Lamp

*Our listings are arranged numerically ac-
cording to the numbers assigned to the various miniature lamps pictured in Frank R. &
Ruth E. Smith's book,* Miniature Lamps, *now
referred to as Smith's Book I, and Ruth
Smith's sequel,* Miniature Lamps II. *All references are to Smith's Book I unless otherwise
noted.*

"Fire Fly" & six stars embossed on
opaque white font, milk white

glass shade, Olmstead burner,
6½" h. (no chimney), No. 9 ...... 225.00
Milk white glass font embossed
"Nutmeg" w/narrow brass band
forming removable handle, Nutmeg burner, clear glass chimney,
2¾" h. base, No. 29 .... 165.00
"Manilla Pat. Appl.d For" embossed
on clear glass base set in tin
holder, Acorn burner, clear glass
chimney, 2¾" h., No. 30 .... 55.00
"Little Buttercup" embossed on amethyst glass font w/handle, Nutmeg burner, clear glass chimney,
2¾" h. base, No. 36 .... 86.00
Milk white glass base w/applied
handle & enameled red berries,
green leaves & blue bands, Nutmeg burner, clear glass chimney,
3" h., No. 39 .... 117.50
Nickel-plated wall lamp embossed
"Comet," filling spout on wall
reservoir w/slender tubing leading to burner, blue glass beehive
chimney-shade, sometimes called
"Beauty Lamp," 7¼" h., No. 78 ... 54.00
Clear glass stem lamp, plain, Acorn
burner, clear glass chimney,
5½" h. base, No. 104 .... 42.00
Blue glass Block patt. stem lamp,
Nutmeg burner, clear glass chimney, 5¼" h. base, No. 106 .... 67.00
Amber glass Bull's Eye patt. variant
stem lamp, Nutmeg burner, clear
glass chimney, 5" h., No. 111 .... 105.00
Clear glass Bull's Eye patt. stem
lamp, Nutmeg burner, advertised
in Butler Brothers "Our Drummer"
1912 catalogue, 5" h. base (no
chimney), No. 112 .... 63.00
Milk white glass Rib & Panel patt.
footed base, Acorn burner, milk
white glass Rib & Panel patt.
chimney-shade, No. 126 .... 118.00
Milk white glass Ribbed Panel patt.
base & conical shade, Nutmeg
burner, clear glass chimney,
7¼" h., No. 130 .... 125.00
Clear glass ribbed font on pewter
pedestal & matching ball-type
shade w/embossed & painted
florals & leaves, Acorn burner,
clear glass chimney, No. 137 ..... 115.00
Clear glass Lincoln Drape patt. base
& umbrella-type shade, Acorn
burner, clear glass chimney,
5¾" h., No. 143 .... 85.00
Milk white glass footed base & umbrella shade w/embossed iris &
leaves highlighted w/gilt, Acorn
burner, clear glass chimney,
7¼" h., No. 205 .... 162.00
Milk white glass footed base
w/painted blue & white florals &

frosted glass globe-chimney
w/conforming decor, Hornet burner, often called "Nellie Bly" by
collectors, 9" h., No. 219 .... 170.00
Milk white glass w/embossed net
design & flowers highlighted
w/pink, blue & green, Nutmeg
burner, clear glass chimney,
7½" h., No. 229 ....260.00 to 275.00
Milk white glass Drape patt. square
base & globe shade w/shaded
pink wash, original burner, clear
glass chimney, 8½" h., No. 231 .. 222.00
Milk white glass, embossed
w/orange-skin texture & design,
fired-on blue paint, Nutmeg burner, clear glass chimney, 8½" h.,
No. 272 ....265.00 to 290.00
Milk white glass Cosmos patt. base
& umbrella-type shade w/blue
band & painted florals decoration,
Nutmeg burner, 7½" h.,
No. 286 .... 295.00
Milk white glass Sylvan patt. base &
melon-ribbed umbrella-type shade
w/band of yellow flowers, Nutmeg burner, clear glass chimney,
Westmoreland Specialty Co.,
Grapeville, Pa., 7¾" h.,
No. 296 .... 200.00
Cased pink glass melon-ribbed base
& melon-ribbed umbrella-type
shade, Nutmeg burner, clear glass
chimney, by Consolidated Lamp &
Glass Co., Pittsburgh, 7" h.,
No. 390 ....550.00
Pink Satin glass puffy Diamond
Quilted patt. base & umbrella-
type shade, Nutmeg burner, clear
glass chimney, by Consolidated
Lamp & Glass Co., Pittsburgh,
ca. 1894, 8" h., No. 394 .... 415.00
Yellow cased in clear glass puffy
Diamond Quilted patt. base &
umbrella-type shade, Nutmeg
burner, clear glass chimney, by
Consolidated Lamp & Glass Co.,
Pittsburgh, ca. 1894, No. 394 ..... 375.00
Green Satin glass Beaded Drape
patt. base & ball-shaped shade,
Nutmeg burner, clear glass chim-
ney, 9" h., No. 400 .....360.00 to 395.00
Cranberry glass hexagonal base &
paneled globe-chimney, foreign
burner, 9½" h.,
No. 438 ....325.00 to 375.00
Amberina glass paneled base &
globe-chimney shade, Hornet
burner, 8¼" h., No. 439 .... 715.00
Yellow Satin cut velvet Diamond
Quilted patt., applied frosted
ruffle around bottom of base,
Nutmeg burner, 6¾" h., No. 533
(Book II) 1,925.00

Red Satin glass "Artichoke" lamp w/melon-ribbed base & artichoke-molded ball-shaped shade, Nutmeg burner, clear glass chimney, 8" h., Color Plate III . . . . . 500.00 to 550.00

Yellow glass w/green decoration "Artichoke" lamp w/melon-ribbed base & artichoke-molded ball-shaped shade, Nutmeg burner, 8" h., Color Plate III 245.00

Santa Claus, milk white w/painted red suit, facial features, boots & base, Nutmeg burner, by Consolidated Lamp & Glass Co., Pittsburgh, ca. 1894, 9½" h., Color Plate VII (ILLUS. page 738) 4,400.00

TIFFANY LAMPS (All signed)

Tiffany Desk Lamp

Desk lamp, hemispherical shade w/peacock iridescence & wavy decoration, inscribed "L.C.T. Favrile," the green-brown patinated adjustable base w/central tray & two slender columns, stamped "TIFFANY STUDIOS NEW YORK 449," 14½" h. (ILLUS.) 8,800.00

Desk lamp, "Linenfold," paneled shade inset w/linenfold glass in yellow, on a paneled base w/wide dished base, base stamped "TIFFANY STUDIOS NEW YORK 613," 16¼" h. (small crack in one shade panel) 4,950.00

Floor lamp, "Bamboo," 22" d. domed leaded glass shade w/an overall pattern of striated & mottled emerald, olive & mint green & rust bamboo leaves & stalks on a mottled opalescent ground, raised on a cylindrical standard applied w/vertical stringing continuing into the leaf-molded foot, further raised on petal-form feet, shade impressed "TIFFANY STUDIOS NEW YORK 1509-3," base impressed "TIFFANY STUDIOS - NEW YORK - 379," 5' 3½" h. 49,500.00

Floor lamp, "Laburnum," 21½" d. domed leaded glass shade w/irreg-

ular border, yellow, green & mauve flowers among green leaves, on a green & blue ground, the tag stamped "TIFFANY STUDIOS NEW YORK," tall standard w/round, domed leaf-engraved base w/short scrolled feet, stamped "TIFFANY STUDIOS NEW YORK 29443," 5' 1¾" h. 99,000.00

Lily lamp, 12-light, 12 lily-form Favrile glass shades inscribed "L.C.T. Favrile," on bronze base w/an etched design & green patina, stamped "Tiffany Studios New York 312," 21¼" h. 26,400.00

Student lamp, "American Indian," domical bronze shade cast w/Indian motifs about the lower rim pivoting between a harp-shaped support, the square base cast w/Indian motifs & raised on four integral lug feet, 1899-1920, impressed "Tiffany Studios, New York, 655," 12" h. . . . 1,320.00

Table lamp, "Dragonfly," 20¼" d. domed conical leaded glass shade w/a striated deep amber ground shading to green streaked w/rose & set w/amber 'jewels,' the dragonflies w/deep mauve bodies & rose & green wings arranged in a row above three narrow geometric bands along the bottom edge of the shade, shade stamped "TIFFANY STUDIOS NEW YORK 1495," floral form standard on a rounded domed foot w/engraved "scale" design, base stamped "TIFFANY STUDIOS NEW YORK 366," 25" h. 66,000.00

Table lamp, "Geranium," 16¾" d. conical domed leaded glass shade w/blue, pink & greenish yellow blossoms & a circular band of geometric multicolored panels, stamped "TIFFANY STUDIOS NEW YORK," the base enclosing a fuel canister, of baluster-form w/abstract florals inset w/turtle-back tiles as buds, 22" h. 50,600.00

Table lamp, "Peony," 22" d. hemispherical shade w/myriad peonies in deep red, pink & mottled purple w/green leaves & stems on a pastel blue ground, stamped "Tiffany Studios New York 1505," on an adjustable green patinated bronze base cast w/pods & stems & raised on four petal feet, stamped "Tiffany Studios New York 6447," 32" h. 74,800.00

Table lamp, "Poinsettia," 17¾" d. domed leaded glass shade w/radiating bands of mottled yellow & ochre tiles, w/a medial band of deep red blossoms w/mottled green centers & green & grey-blue leafage, stamped "TIFFANY STUDIOS NEW YORK 558," the waisted cylindrical standard w/narrow ribbing raised on domed reeded base w/five ball feet, stamped "TIFFANY STUDIOS NEW YORK 27420," & w/monogram, 22¼" h. 39,600.00

Tiffany "Venetian" Table Lamp

Table lamp, "Venetian," 13" d. domed conical leaded glass shade w/three bands of graduated green ellipses surrounding pink leaves, quatrefoils & fleur-de-lis on a bright blue, purple & red ground, tag stamped "TIFFANY STUDIOS NEW YORK," the gilt-bronze base intricately cast w/foliage & set w/green & red glass 'jewels,' stamped "TIFFANY STUDIOS NEW YORK 5777," 19¾" h. (ILLUS.) ...37,400.00

Table lamp, "Water Lily," 20½" d. conical leaded glass shade w/green-centered pink & textured white blossoms among variegated green lily pads against a background of turquoise blue mottled water, raised on a base cast as twisted vines issuing from a flat circular base, shade stamped "TIFFANY STUDIOS NEW YORK 1490-8," base stamped "TIFFANY STUDIOS - NEW YORK - 443," 26" h. 154,000.00

Table lamp, "Wisteria," 18" d. cylindrical leaded glass shade w/irregular lower rim, decorated w/multi-hued blue, purple & grey flower clusters among green & turquoise leaves pendent from the openwork branches at the shoulder on a bluish-grey fractured glass ground, the tree-form base w/a deep brown patina, stamped "TIFFANY STUDIOS NEW YORK 7806," 27½" h. 143,000.00

MISCELLANEOUS LAMPS

Aladdin, Model No. 3, Bird of Paradise on two sides, 7¼" cased

glass shade, pink interior, white exterior, 14" (electric) 90.00

Aladdin, Model No. 4 boudoir lamp, reverse-painted shade 325.00

Applesauce lamp, Frosted Leaf font......................... 725.00

19th Century Argand Lamps

Argand lamps, cast zinc & tole, green-painted cast zinc female caryatid above a brown-painted square tapering standard w/ochre banding & sunburst decoration over a shaped plinth w/acorn pendant, supporting a cylindrical lamp w/flaring cylindrical shade, glass chimney & bell-shaped glass drip pan, 1820-30, 20½" h., pr. (ILLUS.) 6,050.00

Art Nouveau table lamp, gilt-bronze, two-light, figure of dancer Loie Fuller w/her swirling robes forming the lamp shade above her dancing figure, cast from a model by Raoul-Francais Larche, inscribed "RAOUL LARCHE," Siot-Decauville foundry seal & stamped "1285," France, early 20th c., 18" h. 41,800.00

Astral lamp, ornate cast-brass base w/original fire gilding, three-section foot w/scrolling tapering to slender standard supporting burner, metal shade ring supports conical frosted & cut clear shade w/rolled top rim, cut prisms hanging from shade ring, ring marked "W.F. Shaw, Boston," electrified, 19 3/8" h. (shade flange chipped)......................... 350.00

Astral lamp, shaped circular brass base & elaborate baluster form column, cut frosted shade, single row of 12 clear prisms, Cornelius and Co., Philadelphia, July 14, 1849 patent date, overall 23" h. 1,210.00

Banquet lamp, clear cut glass, domed waffle-cut foot & font,

paneled stem, brass ring at base
& brass collar, 23" h. 400.00
Banquet lamp, triple cut overlay font,
blue to white to clear, fluted metal
stem on stepped marble base, original blown & cut frosted shade
w/grapes & leaves decoration,
Boston & Sandwich Glass Co., ca.
1860, 30" h. (electrified) 2,500.00
Betty lamp, tin, pear-shaped
w/hinged inset lid, twisted shaft
on hook, America, 18th c. 220.00
Betty lamp w/hanger, wrought iron,
swivel lid on font w/engraved design & post marked "No 103,
1834," 5" h. 625.00
Daum Nancy signed table lamp, domed
shade w/matching spherical base
of yellow glass deeply etched
w/radiating columns & random
squares of various sizes, inscribed
"Daum Nancy France," 16" h. . . . 16,500.00
Dirk van Erp signed table lamp, hammered copper, shallow domed
shade w/a short cylindrical border
pierced w/a frieze of stylized
scroll & foliate forms overlaying
eight narrow mica panels, cylindrical base flaring toward the
angled molded foot, top slightly
everted & surmounted by short
flaring cylindrical shaft terminating
in a circular capped finial w/three
light sockets, impressed windmill
mark & "DIRK VAN ERP" w/a
broken box on base, ca. 1915,
16½" d. shade, 16½" h. 3,300.00
Fluid lamp, sapphire blue pressed
glass, tapering font w/Three-
Printie Block patt. above a
knopped & baluster standard on a
square foot, New England Glass
Company, 1847-50, 10" h. 1,045.00
Floor lamp, wrought iron & glass,
half-round inverted dome shade of
mottled yellow, orange & bright
blue glass supported on three
scrolled wrought-iron arms extending into three scrolled wrought-iron
arms extending into open triangular standard fitted w/ivy leaf &
vine panels ending in arched trifid
scrolled feet, shade signed "Muller
Fres - Luneville," 16½" d. shade,
5' 10" h. 3,300.00
Galle' signed table lamp, "Wild Rose"
patt., conical shade & baluster
base w/frosted white ground overlaid in deep red, etched to depict
myriad wild roses, stems & leaves,
cameo signature "Galle',"
21¾" h. 30,800.00
Gone-with-the-Wind lamp, white
Satin glass, Holly Berry & Leaf

patt., w/original chimney,
23" h. 795.00

Gone-with-the-Wind Lamp

Gone-with-the-Wind lamp, ball-
shaped shade decorated w/a bust
profile of a classical maiden on a
maroon ground, inverted pear-
shaped font similarly decorated,
ornate brass fittings & four-footed
base, America, ca. 1880, 29" h.
(ILLUS.) 577.50
Jefferson signed table lamp, 16" d.
domical shade h.p. on interior
w/overall pastoral landscape
w/tall trees, fences & waterfront
pasture in the background, signed
"2366 Jefferson - R," metal rim
fitting on a two-socket baluster-
form octagonal standard, 22" h. . . 1,000.00
Kerosene hand lamp w/finger grip,
footed, pressed glass, Aquarius
patt., amber 165.00
Kerosene hand lamp w/finger grip,
footed, pressed glass, Bull's Eye
patt., green 130.00
Kerosene hand lamp w/finger grip,
pressed glass, Bull's Eye & Fleur-
de-Lis patt., clear, w/old
chimney 55.00
Kerosene hand lamp w/finger grip,
pressed glass, Peacock Feather
patt., clear, w/safety handle 69.00
Kerosene hand lamp w/finger grip,
footed, pressed glass, Prince Ed-
ward patt., emerald green 185.00
Kerosene hand lamp w/finger grip,
footed, pressed Sheldon Swirl
patt., opalescent 495.00
Kerosene hand lamp w/finger grip,
orange & bright cobalt blue Spat-
ter glass, applied clear handle . . . 195.00
Kerosene hand lamp w/finger grip,
pressed model of a Log Cabin,
milk white glass w/brass collar &
burner, Atterbury, dated "1868"
on bottom, 3¾" h. 300.00

Kerosene lamp, hanging-type, h.p. & transfer-printed opal glass shade on floral-decorated brass mounting, central fluid font, possibly Mt. Washington Glass Co., Bedford, Massachusetts, ca. 1880, shade 13½" d. 165.00

Kerosene lamp, hanging-type, domed half-round cranberry Hobnail shade & ruffled Hobnail smoke-bell above, Expanded Diamond cranberry font below, blown swirled cranberry chimney, mounted in fine brass frame w/ornate scrolling bracket arms flanking embossed brass font cup at base, pierced shade rim & chain ring, 14" d., overall 40" h. 1,700.00

Kerosene table lamp, pressed glass, Coin Dot patt., blue opalescent . . . 950.00

Kerosene table lamp, pressed glass, Peanut patt., clear w/original chimney 65.00

Kerosene table lamp, pressed glass, Raindrop patt., Delphinium blue, 12" h. 165.00

Kerosene table lamp, pressed glass, Snowflake patt., cranberry, Hobbs 450.00

Kerosene table lamp, cut-overlay, round font, white cut w/four-petal "blossom" heads & dots to cranberry, brass connector to opaque milk white square base w/rounded corners, brass collar, ca. 1860, 9 3/8" h. (no burner) 600.00

Kerosene table lamp, ruby cut to clear inverted pyriform font w/circles & stars, on turned brass standard & square base, 19th c., 22¾" h. 880.00

Kerosene table lamp w/stem, pressed glass, Prince Edward patt., pink cased w/clear base . . . 645.00

Kerosene table lamp w/stem, pressed glass, Ring Punty Triple Peg and Loop patt., clear w/black base 195.00

Kerosene table lamp w/stem, pressed glass, Riverside's Fern patt., emerald green w/clear base 195.00

Kerosene table lamp w/stem, pressed glass, Swirl & Depressed Daisy patt., milk white 165.00

Lacemaker's lamp, cranberry glass Inverted Thumbprint patt. shade, polished brass base w/handles, w/chimney, 9½" d., 17¼" h. 445.00

Lard lamp, font mounted on shaft w/handle & saucer base, label on front over light green paint "Archer's patent Philad. June, 18, 1842," 7" h. 715.00

Lard lamp, saucer base, green paint w/gilt trim, label on front "Saml Davis Patented May 6th, 1856," w/wick pick on short chain, America, ca. 1856, 7" h. 165.00

Leaded glass table lamp, 22" d. elaborate conical shade w/irregular lower border comprised of shaped segments of fiery opalescent, turquoise & caramel slag glass arranged in repeating geometric & stylized designs, supported by acanthus-decorated gilt metal standard w/stepped levels & decorative turnings below three-bulb fixture & pierced cap, attributed to Duffner & Kimberly Company, New York, overall 27½" h. 2,970.00

Leaded glass table lamp, 23" d. domical shade w/zigzag lower border decorated w/clusters of striated red & opalescent blossoms against a profusion of striated green & opalescent leaves, raised on a cylindrical standard ending in a circular foot, w/finial, America, ca. 1900, 31" h. 4,675.00

Library lamp, hanging-type, cranberry glass Hobnail patt., w/prisms, in polished frame 925.00

Miner's lamp, brass & tin, carbide, labeled "American Safety Lamp & Miners Supply Co., Scranton, Pa.," 11½" h. 65.00

French Moderator Lamp

Moderator table lamp, five-panel lithophane shade decorated w/scenes of family life, stepped cylindrical body w/high-relief scenes of children & Cupid, separate patinated white metal Renaissance Revival pedestal (key missing), a spring-driven piston in the base feeds a viscous fuel to an argand-type burner, invented by Franchot in 1837, France, lamp w/chimney 23", overall 30 7/8" h. (ILLUS.) 770.00

Moe Bridges signed floor lamp,
10 1/8" d. domical shade composed of radiating bands of striated lime-green & opalescent tiles
w/a lower uneven border of
aqua-green tiles, the adjustable
socket on a pivoting C-scroll arm
continuing to a cylindrical standard & tiered circular foot, early
20th c., 4' 8½" h. 880.00
Pairpoint signed candle lamp,
"puffy," wooden candlestick
w/wide top cup fitted w/shade of
blossoms reverse-painted in pink,
blue, yellow & green, unusual
clear glass finish, marked on rim
"Pairpoint Corp. - Patented July 9,
1907," overall 10" h. 715.00

Pairpoint Table Lamp

Pairpoint signed table lamp,
9 7/8" d. reverse-painted "chipped
ice" flaring domical shade decorated
w/a seascape depicting seagulls
flying amid clouds above rolling
waves in lime green, grey, blue,
lavender, black & white, on a
turned wood base decorated *en
suite*, shaded enameled "FRAE" &
gilt "THE PAIRPOINT CORP.," the
base impressed "PAIRPOINT
D8000.," early 20th c., 24¾" h.
(ILLUS.) 6,325.00
Pan lamp, wrought iron, shallow oblong pan w/upright hook handle
attached to sawtooth trammel,
adjusts to 16¾" h. (pitted iron has
been buffed).................... 225.00
Rush light holder, wrought iron,
curved clamp handle w/knob terminal, twisted stem in old turned
tapering wooden base w/dark
patina, 9½" h. (crack in base
makes iron loose) 200.00
Rush light holder, wrought iron,
double-arm type, iron ring w/four
twisted legs, surmounted by a single twisted shaft, candle arms on
right angle arms, one arm lifts
w/scissors action to hold rush,
America, 18th c., 11¾" h. 275.00
Table lamp, "Anywhere," aluminum

"Anywhere" Table Lamp

& enameled metal, 14" d. inverted
dish-shaped shade in off-white enamel resting on bent U-form black
metal base, designed by Greta
von Nessen, ca. 1952, stamped
"NESSEN STUDIO," 15¼" h.
(ILLUS.)....................... 550.00
Table lamp, fluid-burning type,
brass, acorn font w/"rabbit-ear"
double burner, double-knob stem
on flaring round base, 8" h. overall (one burner slightly crooked,
snuffer caps missing) 125.00
Table lamp, kerosene-type, Ripley
"marriage" lamp w/double blue
fonts & clambroth connector
w/match holder on brass connector
above milk white base, marked
"D.C. Ripley & Co. Pat. Pending,"
11 3/8" h. (small bottom edge
flakes).......................1,200.00
Table lamp, kerosene-type, Ripley
"marriage" lamp, clear pressed
glass, double fonts flank match
holder, brass collars & connectors,
base marked "Ripley & Co., Patd
Feb. 1st 1870," match holder
marked "Patented Sept. 20, 1870,"
12¾" h. (chip on rim of match
holder, pinpoint base flakes) 675.00
Table lamp, kerosene-type, Ripley
"marriage" lamp w/double white
fonts & blue match holder on brass
connector above blue base,
marked "Ripley & Co., patd Feb.
1st 1870" (bruise on base) 1,850.00
Table lamp, Art Nouveau style, patinated spelter figure of a young
woman in a diaphanous gown
holding a fan, surrounded by four
electric lights on scrolling leafy
arms ending in beaded crystal
round globes, on circular pedestal
w/plaque inscribed "FONTAINE ET
RUISSEAU par Aug. Moreau (Med.
d'Or)," France, early 20th c.,
38½" h....................... 605.00
Table lamp, Galle cameo glass, conical shade & trumpet-shaped base
in frosted amber glass overlaid in

green & highlighted w/blue, etched
to depict blossoms, stems & leaves,
cameo signature "Galle,"
24½" h. 17,600.00
Table lamps, bronze floriform
scrolling cylindrical standard emanating from a tri-lobed leaf-form
base ending in a floriform mount
holding a bell-shaped shade in
grey cased over mottled pink &
overlaid in mottled lavender, pink
& deep purple & cut w/a stylized
flower pattern within arched reserves, shades inscribed
"FRANCE," 16" h., pr. 2,750.00
"Time" lamp, pewter, long slender
glass tube in a pewter frame,
front of frame calibrated in Roman numerals, small spout lamp
at base of tube, baluster shaft on
saucer base, handle at back, Eu-
rope, late 18th c., 13½" h. 275.00
Whale oil lamps, unusual clear
pressed glass font in the "Star &
Punty" pattern above a wide,
down-turned & scalloped "Diamond Point" bobeche, brass cylindrical stem w/embossed square
foot fitted on square white marble
base, the font & brass stems
w/acid-etched decoration, Sandwich Glass Company, Sandwich,
Massachusetts, ca. 1840, 10½" h.,
pr. 660.00
Whale oil lamps, double burners,
7½" h., pr. 210.00

OTHER LIGHTING ITEMS

CHANDELIERS

Victorian Gilt-Bronze Chandelier

Arts & Crafts style, copper & oak,
five-light, square oak frame supporting four suspended heart cut-

out lanterns & a central lantern on
wrought-iron chains, Gustav Stickley Model No. 205, ca. 1906, 46" l.
(two globes damaged) 61,600.00
Blue-painted wood & wrought iron,
candle-type, urn-turned standard
w/six detachable scrolled arms &
cylindrical candle cups, each set
within a crimped circular pan,
Pennsylvania, 19th c., 13¼" h. . . .1,320.00
Bronze, five-light, the reeded shaft
above a standard headed by a
vase mounted w/three winged
eagle monopodia, raised on a tapering pendant mounted w/leaf-
cast scrolling candlearms alternating w/masks & supporting glass
shades, William IV period, England,
second quarter 19th c., 35" d., over-
all 56" h. 9,900.00
Gilt-bronze, six-light, central baluster
column w/scrolled acanthus leaf
decoration ringed by six scrolled
arms each terminating in a socket
shaded by an etched glass globe,
gas converted to electricity, Victorian, ca. 1860, 60" h. (ILLUS.) 4,700.00
Lalique signed, "Coquilles" patt.,
domical frosted shade molded in
medium-relief w/four radiating
scallop shells, suspended from
simple chrome mounts & four
twisted silk cords ending in a
trumpet-form, frosted ceiling cap
molded w/vertical loopings, ca.
1925, molded "R. Lalique," 12" d.,
26" h. 2,750.00
Lalique signed, "Gaillon" patt., circu-
lar half-section molded to depict
acanthus, w/frosted ceiling mount,
17¾" h. 3,520.00
Le Verre Francais cameo, domical, cut
Art Deco florals in orange & brown
on mottled yellow ground, bronze
tone stylized florals hardware,
14" d. (rewired) 1,645.00
Muller Freres signed, deep domical
central shade in brilliant lemon-
yellow mottled w/pumpkin orange,
medium purple & chocolate brown,
suspended from a wrought-iron
mount pierced w/pendent grape
vines & supporting three scrolling
arms each ending in conforming
bell-form shades, shades acid
stamped "Muller Fres - Luneville,"
ca. 1910, 23½" d. 1,870.00
Ormolu, six-light, central baluster-
shaped shaft cast w/curling lotus
& palmettes above a fluted sphere
& tapering spiral-fluted base issuing six candlebranches cast w/scrol-
ling paterae & acanthus, Charles X
period, France, first quarter

19th c., 15" d., 19½" h. (drilled
for electricity) 9,350.00
Tiffany signed, domical bowl composed of radiating bands of striated medium green glass tiles w/a
lower border of amber-yellow
leaves, the upper edge w/a conforming opalescent "jeweled" band,
lower edge w/beaded border, suspended from four bronze arms &
center post, hemispherical bronze
ceiling cap set at the upper edge
w/a band of square opalescent
"jewels" above a double tier of suspended bronze balls, impressed
"TIFFANY STUDIOS - NEW YORK,"
ca. 1900, 23¾" d., 26½" h.......8,800.00
Tiffany signed leaded glass "Dogwood" patt., sharply conical shade
w/beaded lower border w/an overall pattern of dogwood branches in
white striated w/lime green & fractured in lime green & cherry red &
mottled w/emerald green leafage
reserved against a striated forest
green ground, 1899-1920, w/later
socket standard & hanging
chains, 30" d. 16,500.00
Tin, candle-type, six-light, double
cone center w/six scrolled arms
ending in crimped drip plates &
cylindrical candle cups, hangs from
iron hook & w/loop & hook at center of base, together w/elongated
cone candle snuffer, America,
early 19th c., 20" h., 2 pcs.
(solder break at hook base) 1,430.00

LANTERNS

Stickley Hanging Lantern

Barn lantern, wooden, square
w/four glass sides, slide-out pan
w/tin font & kerosene burner,
iron bail handle & heat deflector,
11¼" h. (mortise joint in door
broken) 145.00
Candle lantern, wide tin bail,

pierced tin cone & base, clear
glass Onion Globe patt., 10½" h.
overall 395.00
Candle lantern, pierced tin, crimped
wafer below flat tin bail, candle
socket inside, ca. 1800, 10½" to
top of cone 195.00
Candle lantern, tin w/clear blown
glass globe, round top cap w/star
& diamond air holes & tapering
top w/large ring handle, round tin
base w/wide, flaring foot, traces
of black paint, probably New England Glass Co., 13½" h. plus ring
handle 250.00
Candle lantern, hanging-type, blown,
tapering cylinder, clear w/etched
design, prunted knop, domed cover,
fitted for suspension, Anglo-
Indian, early 19th c., 8 2/3" d.
cover, lantern 13½" h. 1,760.00
Candle lantern, pierced tin cylinder
w/conical top & ring handle (so-
called Paul Revere lantern),
hinged door w/narrow glass insert, 14½" h. plus ring handle ... 95.00
Candle lantern, pierced tin,
hanging-type, cylindrical body &
domed top pierced w/geometric
motifs, w/hinged door & hanging
ring (so-called Paul Revere lantern), America, 19th c., 18" h..... 275.00
Hall lantern, bronze & glass, Louis
XV-Style, each of the six sides
w/serpentine glazed panel surmounted by a pierced ribbon crest,
suspended by serpentine ribbon-
form members, 19th c., electrified,
26" h. 1,210.00
Hanging lantern, rectangular pine
case w/glazed panels, w/simple
metal swing handle, Connecticut,
19th c., 6" w., 13½" h. 165.00
Kerosene lantern, "Dietz No. 2," red
globe 18.00
Kerosene lantern, "Dietz Monarch,"
blue w/red globe 18.00
Miner's lantern, tin, w/spout,
marked "Eagle," 7" 22.00
Miner's lantern, brass, carbide-type,
large w/bail & hook, "Guy's
Dropper" 25.00
Skater's lantern, tin, clear glass
globe, bail handle, 6¾" h. 60.00
Stickley hanging lanterns, copper
w/cut-out heart motifs, yellow cylindrical glass lining, w/hanging
chain, unsigned Gustav Stickley,
No. 205, 3½" d., 8" h. plus chain,
pr. (ILLUS. of one) 6,930.00
Tiffany signed hanging lantern, hexagonal w/mottled yellow & green
geometric glass as upper & lower
decoration, center set w/five large

yellow turtle-back tiles, w/six green
glass 'jewels' at the top, w/original
ceiling mount & chain, Tiffany Stu-
dios, overall 32" h. 13,200.00

SHADES

Tiffany Stalagmite Shade

Acid cut-back, ovoid w/scalloped
rim, leaves & flowers overall on
frosted ground, orange shaded to
clear, 4" d. fitter, 9¼" d., 7" h.,
pr. 435.00
Cranberry, ruffled rim, Thumbprint
patt., 2" d. fitter, 4" h. 95.00
Cranberry, bulbous bottom & blown-
out double scalloped ridge tapering in then flaring out to eight
deep scallops at the rim, 4" d. fit-
ter, 6¾" d., 7½" h. 225.00
G. Argy-Rousseau "pate-de-verre,"
flaring straight sides w/narrow
panels narrowing to pointed conical top, grey glass splashed
w/deep purple, the top molded
w/Aztec motifs in Chinese red,
signed "G. ARGY-ROUSSEAU -
FRANCE," ca. 1925, 2¾" h., pr. . .4,950.00
Handel, domical form w/thin sides,
lightly "sanded" exterior finish,
interior painted sky blue w/four
trees & landscape border, made
for a boudoir lamp, painted signa-
ture, 8" d., 4½" h. 350.00
Handel, hanging-type, paneled
leaded glass, caramel slag w/skirt
border topped w/red glass,
24" d. 2,350.00
Hobnail patt., ruffled bell-shape,
milky white opalescent, 9" d.,
5" h. 85.00
Hurricane shades, clear blown glass,
baluster-shape w/folded foot rim,
cut w/open & closed star-form
decorations enclosed w/stylized
foliage, 19th c., 21" h., pr. (small
rim chips, minor wear) 1,980.00
Lustre Art, ribbed amber glass

w/fine pink & blue iridescence
overall, trumpet-form, rim signed
"Lustre Art," 5¼" h. 55.00
Lustre Art, gold iridescent interior,
white Calcite-like exterior, 10 spiral ribs, 2 1/8" at collar, 6" d. at
bottom, 5¾" h. 125.00
Lustre Art, green & gold lustre
hearts & gold lustre overall
threading, corset-shaped
w/flared, scalloped rim, signed on
the top "Lustre Art," pr. 253.00
Muller Freres, clear glass ball
w/frosted clear birds & flowers
decoration, signed "Luneville,"
6" d. 195.00
Quezal, iridescent white opal, bul-
bous corset shape w/optic rib pattern, signed, 4¼" d., 4½" h. 77.00
Quezal, white exterior w/gold
iridescent interior, trumpet-form
w/slightly scalloped rim, faint rib
pattern, signed, 5" d., 4¾" h. 104.50
Quezal, gold iridescent, tulip-
shaped, 5" h. 135.00
Quezal, gold at base graduating to
green pulled feathering to white
pulled feathering, scalloped rim,
2 1/8" d. fitter, 3¼" d., 5¼" h.,
set of 4 . . . . .1,250.00
Quezal, iridescent gold, trumpet-
shaped w/"Pebble" patt., scal-
loped rim, signed, 5" d., 5½" h. . . . 77.00
Quezal, gold iridescence w/slight
green tinge, trumpet-shaped
w/flared shoulder near base,
ribbed pattern, signed, 5¼" d.,
5½" h. 104.50
Quezal, green pulled feathering on
white exterior, gold iridescent interior, ribbed, 2¼" d. fitter,
5½" h., pr. 320.00
Quezal, hooked gold feather repeat-
ing design above white creamy
border & iridescent green threaded gridwork overlay exterior, gold
iridescent interior, ovoid shape,
signed, 5¾" h., set of 3 (some
rim roughness) 850.00
Quezal, amber iridescent, lily-form
w/ribbed sides, inscribed "Quezal,"
1905-20, set of 6 . . . . .1,100.00
Satin glass, flower-shaped w/six
long tapering & slightly scrolled
petals, white exterior w/maroon
& blue spatter, pink interior,
2 1/8" d. fitter, 5" d., 4¼" h. 95.00
Steuben, gold Aurene feathers
w/green on Calcite, No. 799,
5" h. 125.00
Striped opalescent vaseline, ruffled
rim, 6½" h., pr. 170.00
Tiffany, leaded glass, opalescent
w/green pulled feathers, bell-

shaped, 2¼" d. fitter, 5½" d.,
4" h., set of 7 . . . . 3,850.00
Tiffany, amber glass w/interior & exterior mirror iridescence w/strong
pink, lavender & blue highlights,
half-round form, signed on top rim
"LCT," 7" d., 4¼" h. 1,430.00
Tiffany, golden green iridescence
shading to pale olive green,
impressionistically decorated
w/blue-green & amber iridescent
morning glories on amber iridescent trailing vines, stalagmite-
shaped, fitted w/bronze collar for
hanging, inscribed "S6929," ca.
1903, 13 3/8" h. (ILLUS.) 2,200.00

(End of Lighting Devices Section)

MAGAZINES

The Etude Magazine

Aero Digest, 1930, July, August or
September, each $15.00
Better Homes & Gardens, 1947,
November, color Coca-Cola ad . . . 5.00
Collier's, 1955, December 23, Grand-
ma Moses on cover 7.50
Delineator, 1913, January w/two
pages of doll cut-outs, Drayton il-
lustrated story 28.00
Ecletic Magazine, 1863, full year
bound 50.00
The Etude, 1931, June (ILLUS.) 5.00
Flair, 1950, February, Vol. 1,
No. 1 . . . . 20.00
Inland Printer New Year's Number,
undated, cover by Will H. Bradley
showing a cloaked figure w/hour-
glass creeping through stylized
forest, bordered by vine scroll,
signed "Bradley" in lower left,
metal process print on grey pa-
per, framed, 7 7/8 x 10¾" 220.00

Life, 1945, August 20, War's End 32.00
Look, 1937, December 21, Shirley
Temple Entertains Santa Claus
cover 25.00
The Magazine of Old Glass, 1939,
full year bound 35.00
Movie Radio Guide, 1943, January,
Lionel Barrymore cover 5.00
New Yorker, 1949, February 3 . . . . . . 8.00
Northwestern Miller, 1897, holiday
issue, Frederic Remington draw-
ings, Flour Mill maps, Sleepy Eye
Mill ad 40.00
Peterson's, 1858, full year bound,
w/12 color fashion plates 50.00
St. Nicholas, 1915, May 5.00
Saturday Evening Post, 1903, Febru-
ary 21, N.C. Wyeth cover 32.00
Scanlons, 1970-71, complete run
from No. 1 to No. 8, radical left
political magazine edited by Sid-
ney Zion (obscure) 35.00
Stage, 1932, October, Ruth Gordon
color cover, Claude Rains, Charles
Laughton 10.00
Television, 1928, July, ed. Gerns-
back, Vol. 1, No. 2, illustrated,
32 pp. 15.00
Time, 1939, June 19, Charles Lind-
bergh cover 30.00
TV Guide, 1960, April 7, Elvis Pres-
ley & Frank Sinatra on cover, New
York Edition 35.00
Vanity Fair, 1919, March, Art Nou-
veau ladies dancing color cover,
portrait of Genthe 25.00
Woman's Day, 1965, August, Car-
nival Glass special issue 10.00
Woman's Home Companion, 1901,
March, Harrison Fisher cover 15.00
Woman's World, 1937, February, two
color full-page ads Dionne Quin-
tuplets for Karo Syrup & Palmolive
Soap 20.00

MATCH SAFES & CONTAINERS

Advertising container, table model,
cast iron, model of an alligator,
"Monon Route Match Dispenser" . . $275.00
Advertising container, wall-type, tin,
"Bode & Larson Good Shoes" 70.00
Advertising container, wall-type, tin,
"DeLaval" 118.00
Advertising container, wall-type, tin,
"Dr. Shoops Health Coffee" 95.00
Advertising container, wall-type,
cast iron, model of a telephone,
"Frisco Line" 250.00
Advertising safe, pocket-type, metal
& celluloid, "1st Natl. of Blairs-
ville" bank, pictures bank 40.00

Advertising safe, pocket-type, brass, "Garlock Packing Co., Palmyra, New York," w/stamps & matches 95.00

Bisque container, table model, figure of a black boy sitting on a log 125.00

Bisque container, table model, figure of a Keystone-type cop, molded striker, 8" h. 75.00

Brass container, table model, model of a kangaroo, pouch holds matches 22.00

Cast iron container, table model, lacy pedestal base, rectangular holder w/rooster finial, old gilt paint, 2 x 3½ x 3½" 130.00

Cast iron container, table model, model of a lady's boot on striker base, Wilton 35.00

Ceramic container, table model, figural French Berber soldier holding flag & bugle, 5¼" h. 95.00

Ceramic container, table model, model of Victorian lady's shoe, tan upper w/large gold buckle, ornate pale blue tongue, black heel & side vents (strikers), red lining, 4" l., 3" h. 65.00

Metal container, wall-type, figural black man w/yellow robe, green jacket & red hat, carrying basket on shoulder 95.00

Pottery safe, table model, model of castle, h.p. floral decoration, gold trim, four-sided striker, signed "MWB to JSB, 6/14/1894," 2½" sq., 3¼" h. 75.00

Silver plate safe, pocket-type, overall embossed playing cards, revolving hands on dials keep score 135.00

Sterling silver safe, pocket-type, design of five cherubs & wishbone, monogrammed 275.00

Tin container, table model, two upright open pockets w/asphaltum scratch surface, molded base, yellow stenciled scroll decor, blue, 2¾ x 3½" 85.00

Wooden container, wall-type, small rectangular wood backboard w/relief-carved starflower at top above pocket container carved w/shell design, old black paint, 2½ x 4½" 300.00

MEDICAL COLLECTIBLES

Baby's "ear tucker," special bonnet $10.00

Book, "Diseases of the Skin," by Crocker, 1905, Vol. II 15.00

Book, "The Endocrines," by Bandler, 1921 . . . . 15.00

Book, "Gunn's New Family Physician," 1884, illustrated, 1,230 pp. 25.00

Book, "Hair, Its Care, Diseases & Treatment," by Leonard, 1879, Detroit, illustrated 8.50

Book, "Medical Advisor," by Foote, 1874, New York, illustrated, 924 pp. 10.00

Book, "Obstetrics & Womanly Beauty," by Conger & Cane, M.D., 1890, Chicago, chart of organs inside back cover 12.00

Book, "People's Medical Advisor," 1888, testimonials & photos of patients, 1,000 pp. 27.00

Book, "Physical Diagnosis," by Loomis, 1893 . . . . 15.00

Book, "Practical Home Physician," 1886, color lithographed flaps of brain, herbs, etc., 1,142 pp. 39.00

Corn razor, bone handle w/German silver ring to secure the blade in lock position, tang marked, "B.B. Fossum," made for Oriental market, original instructions & box marked, "Kane Masu" 65.00

Corn razor, chased aluminum handle decorated on both sides, Hamilton Corn Razor 76.00

Corn razor, rounded & shaped bone handle, plain blade, J.A. Henckels Twin Works, Germany, original box w/silver embossed advertising 46.00

Dentist's tray, cream colored glass, 14" d. 15.00

Disc on chain, round "quack" medical item, "Boyd's Battery," w/matching framed flyer explaining "the miracle," when worn around neck would cure all ills, dated 1878, disc, 1½" d., framed flyer, 8 x 9½", the set 72.00

Doctor's case, leather, folding-type, includes four 6" bottles w/stoppers & screw caps, early 1900's, closed size 6¼ x 7¾" 18.00

Dose kit, traveling-type, clear glass tumbler w/cut panels & small graduated glass vial fit into leatherized cylindrical hinged case, 2 7/8" h. overall, 2 pcs. 35.00

Fleam (blood-letting lancet) knife, brass, 12-blade, spring-loaded, in original case 150.00

Hearing aid, silver plate, engraved "Rhein...London," 19th c. 250.00

Machine, "Cardiotron Model PC2,"

wooden case (no cord or
handle) 150.00
Machine, "Electreat" roller, chrome,
uses flashlight batteries, 1919
patent 35.00
Machine, electric belt-type,
"Thoronoid" 45.00
Machine, "Electric Shock Pulsator,
Medeotronics Model 50,"
chiropractic-type 140.00
Machine, electro-shock type, nickel-
plated metal on walnut case,
George Pilling Co., Philadelphia .. 65.00
Machine, "Farador," chrome-plated,
w/box & instructions 55.00
Medicine spoon, folding-type, sterling silver, teaspoon on one end,
tablespoon on the other, section
between w/six graduating pierced
holes, hallmarked w/a five point
star & a wing, original pigskin
case 95.00
Medicine spoon, sterling silver,
hooded, gold washed, marked "A
Tablespoon," reverse & hood
marked "A Teaspoon When Full,"
ornate openwork handle, original
leather case, Blackinton & Co.
Massachusetts 150.00
Optical lens box, wooden, w/69 various sized concave & convex eye
lenses, also one pair wire-rimmed
glasses, early 20th c.,
10¼ x 11½".................... 75.00
Otoscope, electric, in case, 1920's .. 28.00
Sign, neon, "Cosmos Medical
Healer" 300.00
Surgical kit, pocket-size, holds two
scalpels, two saws & one
hemostat, 5 pcs. w/case 45.00
Vaporizer, steam-type, tin, "Atlas
No. 11," 7" h. 30.00
Verometer (eyeglass tester), elec-
tric, Bausch & Lomb 175.00

METALS

BRASS

Candlewick trimmer & snuffer,
scissors-type, 6¼" l. $48.00
Cauldron, raised on three legs,
spiral-twist handle, Continental,
11" h. 77.00
Dipper, round, shallow bowl, well-
shaped wrought iron handle
w/reshaped hanging hook,
19½" l. 95.00
Incense burner, Foo dog finial on
cover & elephant head each side
of base, Oriental, 5½" h. 75.00
Kettle, cast, cast ears, smooth ta-

pered sides showing lathe marks,
flat bottom, shaped steel bail
handle, probably England, 18th c.,
10¾" d., 5½" h. 82.50

Brass Kettle with Bail Handle

Kettle, spun, iron bail handle attached w/copper rivets, 11½" d.,
6" h. plus handle (ILLUS.) 70.00
Kettle, spun, iron bail handle, labeled "The American Brass Kettle
Manufacturers," 14" d., 9" h. 65.00
Kettle, spun, iron bail handle,
stamped "H.W. Hayden - Waterbury, Conn.," 1851 patent,
15" d. 80.00
Kettle shelf, rectangular top
w/scrolled openwork design
above wide apron w/scroll &
heart openwork design raised on
two cabriole front legs & two
plain back legs, English registry
mark, 11½ x 14¾", 12" h. 245.00
Mug, cylindrical w/rolled copper rim
& copper strap handle, hand-
made, 4" h. 90.00
Seal, "Wells Fargo & Co., Springfield, Ill." 125.00
Stencil, "High Grade Sweepstakes
Ensilage Corn," New York,
8 x 11"....................... 69.00
Taper jack, slender post on round
base w/cross-arm for supporting
wax-covered taper, good detail,
5¼" h. 425.00
Warming pan, domed & pierced circular lid w/chased decoration &
wrought-iron handle, probably
Continental, 18th c., 45" l. 385.00

BRONZE

Ashtray, geometric design border,
signed & numbered "Tiffany Studios - New York - 1855," 7" d.,
2" h. 165.00
Blotter ends, American Indian patt.,
"dore" finish, signed & numbered
"Tiffany Studios - New York -
1181," 19" l., pr. 350.00
Blotter ends, w/blotter & pad,

signed & numbered "Tiffany Studios - New York - 907," the set... 200.00

Cauldron, raised on three legs, scrolled handle, Continental, 12" h. 66.00

Censer, globular body tapering to a two-tier circular base resting on four tall animal-mask supports attached by a tall floriform base, cast w/oval reserves of high-relief bird & flower design flanked by two handles fashioned as hawks bracketing the high reticulated lid surrounded by a sculptural tableau of another hawk perched on rockwork above two smaller birds, Meiji period, Japan, 38" h. (wear, losses) 1,320.00

Bronze Covered Chalice

Chalice, cov., relief-molded & enameled w/alternating bands of acanthus leaf scrolls & friezes depicting hunters before a castle, supported on an inverted baluster standard, raised on a spreading circular base, urn-form finial on domed cover, 20th c., restorations, 19½" h. (ILLUS.) 935.00

Desk set: cov. box, rocker blotter, pair blotter ends, pen tray, calendar holder; Grapevine patt. w/green glass inserts, signed "Tiffany Studios - New York" & numbered, the set 950.00

Jardinieres, deep rectangular well decorated w/berried swags & ribbons, raised on cabriole legs joined by X-stretchers & ending in paw feet, ca. 1900, 37" w., 26" h., pr. 4,950.00

Letter opener, Chinese patt., "dore" finish, signed "Tiffany Studios - New York" & numbered 145.00

Match safe & matching ashtray, Zodiac patt., signed "Tiffany Stu-

dios - New York " & numbered, 2 pcs. 160.00

Paperweight, model of dog, signed "Tiffany Studios - New York," 3".. 195.00

Pen tray, Zodiac patt., brown patina, signed "Tiffany Studios - New York" & numbered 125.00

Tray, short pedestal base, Greek Key patt., "dore" finish, signed "Tiffany Studios - New York" & numbered, 8" d. 170.00

Vase, ovoid w/everted rim & tapering sharply to a flared foot, cast w/an overall *seigaiha* pattern, the base w/cartouche reading "Dai Nihon Houn chu," Meiji period, Japan, 9¼" h. 192.50

COPPER

Arts & Crafts Copper Bowl

Bowl, globular w/crimped rim, applied w/a silver relief plaque of a classical figure, water lilies, fish & bird, Gorham Manufacturing Co., Providence, Rhode Island, 1882, 3½" h. 220.00

Bowl, wide mouth on squat bulbous body, decorated w/tooled scroll feather & loop design around rim, Arts & Crafts style, stamped w/logo of maker Arthur Stone, Gardner, Massachusetts, ca. 1910, 5¼" d., 3" h. (ILLUS.) 3,300.00

Jardiniere, wide mouth on straight-sided body w/flat cut-out handles & three raised feet, unsigned, probably Continental, early 20th c., 13" d., 6½" h. (repatinated) 154.00

Kettle, hand-hammered, rounded circular bowl w/fold-over rim, tied on either side w/wrought-iron handles, possibly America, 19th c., 22½" d. over handles, 8¾" h. 220.00

Kettle, deep rounded container w/heavy rolled rim & wrought-iron loop rim handles, 21½" d., 11" h. (somewhat battered) 80.00

Kettle, tapering cylinder w/rolled
rim, wrought-iron bail handle,
19th c., 28" d., 17" h. 462.00
Sauce pan, cov., cast-iron handle on
pan & cover, both marked "L.E.D.
& H. N.Y.," 9" d. 65.00
Sauce pan, dovetail construction,
cast-iron handle, stamped "E.M.
128, 5 Av, N.Y.," 7¼" d. (slightly
out of round) 55.00
Taster, shallow round copper bowl
w/shaped wrought-iron handle
w/loop end, 8 3/8" l. 185.00
Tea kettle, cov., gooseneck spout,
brass handle, 6" d., 5" h. plus
handle 58.00
Tea kettle, cov., tapering dovetailed
cylinder w/shaped spout, applied
bail handle, 19th c., 11" h. (some
dents) 352.00
Tea kettle, cov., dovetail construc-
tion, large pot w/wide shoulder,
gooseneck spout, unusual scrolled
bail handle across top, brass trim,
11½" h. (dents) 215.00
Umbrella stand, Gustav Stickley,
No. 382, 24" h. 2,500.00

IRON

Case Eagle on Globe

Bill clip, cast, hanging-type, lacy design, strong spring 18.00
Boiler, cast, ovoid vessel w/applied
swelling cylindrical handle,
America, 19th c., 4 qt., 8" d., including handle 18" l. 88.00
Brackets, cast, wall-type, ornate
foliate scrolls w/relief on one
side, flat back, worn black paint
over white, 19th c., 21 x 25", set
of four 520.00
Calling card tray, cast, cupped
hands w/grapes & leaves at
wrists, ca. 1865 . . . . 55.00
Camp stove, hand-wrought, turned

wooden handle at side, good detail & complete, painted black,
9 x 16" (expert metal repair on
edge of bottom pan, pitted) 375.00
Candle mold, cast, hinged in center
w/four candle holes on each half,
partial label w/indistinct writing
"Guillon...," 11" h. 250.00
Candle stand, hand-wrought, tripod
base w/curved feet, tooled rod,
adjustable pan w/candle socket &
spout w/wick support, brass
finial, 44½" h. 3,000.00
Chestnut roaster, hand-wrought,
drum-shaped container w/sliding
lid & slender twisted iron handle
attached to long wooden handle,
39" l. (handle incomplete) 105.00
Derrick torch, cast, cylindrical body
w/two thick, slanted spouts, one
on each side, bail handle, embossed mark on side "Oil Well
Supply Co., Pittsburgh," 8" h. 55.00
Eel spear, hand-wrought, ten-prong
flared spear w/cylindrical mount,
New England, 19th c., 10¾" w.
(lacks wooden handle) 192.50
Fire grate, cast, fleur-de-lis design
on crest, late 19th c., 21½" l. 50.00
Flag base, cast, marked "To the
Grand Army of the Republic Aux-
iliary 1883" 25.00
Fork, hand-wrought, two curved
tines, long handle w/small hook
at end, 26" l. 45.00
Ice tongs, hand-wrought, miniature
scissor-type w/wide, flat blades &
short loop handles, 7" l. 30.00
Kettle, cast, tapering ovoid vessel
w/arched spout, scrolled hanging
hook, swing handle & cover, New
England, 18th c., 9¼" h., 13¼" h.
hook (cover lacks finial) 440.00
Kettle stand, hand-wrought, three
tall, slender legs w/out-curved
feet support sheet-iron ring top
w/three pointed bars & long,
slender side handle, indistinct
maker's mark, 10 x 11", 11" h.
(edges slightly battered) 250.00
Lawn sprinkler, model of an alliga-
tor, 11" (small chip at mouth) 65.00
Meat cooker, hand-wrought, curved
cooker raised on simple legs,
mounted w/turned wood handle,
America, first half 19th c., 23" . . . 165.00
Meat hanging hooks, hand-wrought,
ring w/sharp hooks around edge
& long bail across center w/hang-
ing hook at top, 15" d., 20" h. 190.00
Model of an eagle seated on a world
globe w/"Case" across globe,
original polychrome paint, advertising piece for J.I. Case Supply

Co., on three-legged iron base
(ILLUS.) 3,250.00
Model of a stag, cast, profile relief
w/traces of gilding, continuing to
a cast-iron clamp, on a later
wooden plinth, America, 19th c.,
11" l., overall 13" h. 302.50
Mortar & pestle, cast, worn black
paint, bottom marked "No. 4,"
5" h. 35.00
Pan, hand-wrought, dished circular
bowl w/long rectangular handle
w/hanging hook, America,
19th c., 14¼" d., overall 4' 2" l. . . . 77.00
Pot rack, hand-wrought, hanging-
type, oval band rack mounted
w/eight hooks, suspended on
slanted rectangular bar supports
w/a central hanging ring, America, late 19th - early 20th c.,
28" l., 13½" w., 15" h. 165.00
Shoeshine footrest, cast, long oval
plate on horse base, 6½" h. 30.00
Shooting gallery figure, cast, small
silhouette model of a standing
bear, worn yellow paint, 5¼" l. . . 65.00
Shooting gallery figure, cast, eagle
w/wings spread & head turned
left, worn white paint w/rust,
22" w. (talons damaged, bullet
marks) 175.00
Shooting gallery figure, cast, primi-
tive silhouette model of a squirrel
sitting up, worn orange paint,
7¾" h. (pitted) 25.00
Skewer holder & skewers, hand-
wrought, small bar w/curved up
ends & center flat handle topped
w/hanging hook, holds four
wrought skewers of varying
lengths, 9½" l. overall, the set . . . 375.00
Stove plate, cast, two canopies supported by two outer twisted columns & a central aureole enclosing
a heart tulip on sheep legs, two
stars & two flower pots w/tulips
beneath, bordered inscription in
German, "WASSER DIE FYL LE" &
dated "1768," flanked by tulips
below, Pennsylvania, 17¼" w.,
24" h. 1,100.00
Taper jack, hand-wrought, three
slender L-shaped legs support center twisted shaft w/clip for holding
taper near top, tooled & good
detail, 8" h. 1,025.00
Toaster, swivel-type, hand-wrought,
double arches of twisted iron
w/stylized leaf spray in the middle of each arch, long arched handle w/a twisted ring holder at
end, America, 18th c., 18½" l. . . . 660.00
Umbrella stand, cast, loop handle at
top above eight-hole rack, open-

work pedestal flaring at base &
framing embossed shell & florette
cut-out, rectangular tray base
w/flared rim on knob feet, light
green repaint, 19th c., 26¼" h. . . . 100.00
Wafer iron, cast, two-part, round
end w/pattern of crucifixion & religious symbols, long wrought
handles, marked "Pat. Jul. 26
'81," 34" l. 42.50
Windmill weight, cast, full-bodied
rooster on heavy rectangular
base, traces of old weathered
paint, 19" h. 625.00

PEWTER

Early Pewter Teapot

Basin, Ashbil Griswold, Meriden,
Connecticut, early 19th c., 7¾" d.,
1 7/8" h. 375.00
Basin, Samuel Kilbourn, Baltimore,
Maryland, eagle touchmark,
1814-39, 10" d., 2 5/8" h. 900.00
Bowl, hand-hammered, stylized han-
dles, Tudric, Liberty & Co.,
England, early 20th c., 5" d. 125.00
Bowl, round & shallow w/flanged
rim, William Will, Philadelphia,
Pennsylvania, late 18th c.,
12 1/8" d., 1½" h. (wear & minor
battering) 2,550.00
Cake basket, ovoid body w/chased
decoration, concentric vines &
three berries around rim, high
arched handle attached w/three
stems on either end, six small
feet, stamped "36 KAYSERZINN
4529," Germany, ca. 1900,
17¼" l. 3,520.00
Candlesticks, hand-hammered,
Tudric, Liberty & Co., England,
early 20th c., 7" h., pr 295.00
Chalices, deep conical body attached
to trumpet-form base, three arched
arms rising from top of base to
mid-section of body formed as
branches w/leaf terminals,
stamped "KAYSERZINN 4300," Germany, early 20th c., 14¼" h.,
pr. 1,430.00

Charger, circular, w/thin rim struck
w/English mark & maker's marks
of George Smith, the reverse
struck w/London marks, late
17th c., 15" d. 1,980.00
Clock, upright rectangular form,
front w/shaped rectangular copper face flanked by oval abalone
medallions above a lower inset
shaped rectangular panel also inset w/an oval abalone medallion,
impressed "Tudric/0290," Liberty &
Co., England, ca. 1900,
9 7/8" h. 990.00
Coffeepot, cov., marked "Salem
Pewter," ca. 1920's, 8" h. 75.00
Coffeepot, cov., tapering cylinder
w/flat base & domed lid w/cast
flower finial, engraved floral
decoration, Henry Homan, Cincin-
nati, Ohio, 1847-64 . . . . 95.00
Communion flagon, tapered cylinder
w/wide, flat base, domed lid,
C-scroll handle, Sellew & Co., Cincinnati, Ohio, 1832-60, 10¼" h.
(cast-floral thumbpiece needs to
be reattached) 250.00
Cookie board, flat form divided into
12 rectangles each embossed
w/animals, buildings, etc.,
4 5/8 x 7½" 45.00
Dish, deep, single reed rim, Thomas
Danforth II, Middleton, Connecti-
cut, 1755-82, 9½" d. 412.50
Ewers, each tapering cylindrical
body w/tapering neck, the slightly
domed cover w/sheep-form finial
& berry-form thumbpiece, raised
on a fluted swelling cylindrical
base, the inside cover struck
w/angel & maker's mark "DILL,"
Germany, 19th c., 14¼" h., pr. . . . 522.50
Hot water platter, Thomas Alderson,
London, England, 15½ x 22" (mi-
nor wear & scratches) 275.00
Lamp, petticoat-shaped w/flat base,
cast scroll handle, double-spout
fluid burner w/brass snuffers, bottom w/scratched signature "L.D.
Bartlett," burner marked "J.
Newell's, Patent Oct 4, 1853,"
5 3/8" h. (minor dents) 195.00
Measure, gallon, the flat cover
w/line bands, fleur-de-lis thumbpiece above the plain strap-handle
& undecorated baluster body, probably English, late 18th - early
19th c., 13" h. 4,620.00
Plate, Thomas D. Boardman, Hart-
ford, Connecticut, eagle touch-
marks, early 19th c., 7 5/8" d. . . . 300.00
Plate, single reed brim, Edward
Danforth, Hartford, Connecticut,

1786-95, 7 7/8" d. (minor
pitting) 440.00
Plate, John Danforth, Norwich, Con-
necticut, 1773-93, 9" d. 575.00
Plate, William Will, Philadelphia,
Pennsylvania, 1764-98, back of rim
w/scratched inscription, "1784,
M.S.," 9½" d. (worn & pitted) . . .1,175.00
Porringer, cast handle, Thomas Danforth & Samuel Boardman, Hartford, Connecticut, early 19th c.,
4" d. (small rim dent) 275.00
Porringer, cast crown handle
w/"I.G.," America, 5" d. 400.00
Porringer, Pennsylvania tab handle,
attributed to Samuel Pennock,
East Marlborough Township, Pennsylvania, late 18th or early
19th c., 5 3/8" d. (some wear &
pitting) 475.00
Punch bowl, cov., figural cherub
playing harp finial on cover, ball
& claw feet, ornate decoration,
Kayserzinn, Germany, early
20th c. 550.00
Salt dip, footed, flaring bowl on
wide, round foot, attributed to
William Will, Philadelphia, Pennsylvania, late 18th c., 2¼" h. (bat-
tered) 425.00
Soup plate, George Richardson, Bos-
ton, Massachusetts, early 19th c.,
9½" d. (minor wear) 425.00
Syringe, cylindrical body w/long
narrow nozzle, turned & black-
painted wooden plunger handle,
15" l. 35.00
Tea canisters, lobed cylindrical
form, overall punched floral decoration, Chinese Export, third quar-
ter 19th c., 12" h., pr. 440.00
Teapot, cov., pear-shaped w/domed
cover & S-shaped spout, wood
finial on cover & S-scroll carved
wood handle, marked inside
w/rose & crown touchmark, attributed to Cornelius Bradford, New
York or Philadelphia, 1752-85,
6½" h. (ILLUS. previous page) . . .3,080.00
Teapot, cov., bulbous pigeon-
breasted body on tapered foot,
domed lid w/button finial, black-
painted C-scroll handle, James H.
Putnam, Malden, Massachusetts,
mid-19th c., 7¾" h. 375.00
Teapot, cov., tall "lighthouse"
shape, domed cover, C-scroll
black-painted handle, Rufus Dun-
ham, Westbrook, Maine,
mid-19th c., 10½" h. 350.00
Teapot, cov., tall tapering cylindrical
body on flat base, domed lid, C-
scroll handle, Timothy Sage, St.

Louis, Missouri, 1847-48 (spout expertly resoldered) 750.00
Teaspoons, cast handles, marked "Charles Parker & Co.," Meriden, Connecticut, 1849, 5 7/8" l., pr. ... 110.00
Vase, three projecting handles, three turquoise cabochons on body, Art Nouveau style, Tudric, Liberty & Co., England, early 20th c., 7" h. 325.00

SHEFFIELD PLATE

Sheffield Plate Covered Tureen

Candelabra, single fluted urn-form shaft resting on an oval foot, w/a drop-in branch of three lights, the sides supported by twisted reeded arms, separate drip pans, all rims united by a rope border, unmarked, 18" h. 165.00
Candlesticks, telescopic, cylindrical stem, detachable nozzle, gadroon borders, ca. 1820, 8" h. closed, 9 5/8" h. open, set of 4 ....1,100.00
Candlesticks, domed circular base, vase-shaped stem & campana sconce, detachable nozzle, borders of scrolls, shells & flowers, Walker, Knowles & Co., ca. 1825, 11" h., set of 4 .... 990.00
Entree dishes, cov., gadrooned border w/shells & flowers at corners, cover w/fluted edge & conforming top border, detachable handles w/double bound branch & acanthus leaf terminals, engraved armorial, first half 19th c., 9 x 12½", pr. ...1,320.00
Plates, dinner, straight gadroon rim, ca. 1800, 9¼" d., set of 12 ......2,640.00
Sauce dishes, cov., bowl of simple form w/spiral gadrooned rim resting on base for hot water w/lobed sides, on conforming circular foot w/spiral gadrooned ring, double threaded handles, disc lid w/domed lobed center & gadrooned handle, spoon openings on rim, early 19th c., 5½" d., 6½" h., pr. 715.00

Sauce tureens, cov., circular, partly gadrooned, w/leaf-capped reeded handles, Robert Gainsford, ca. 1815, 7¼" h., pr. 1,045.00
Sauce tureens, cov., bombe oval form, raised on shell & foliate scroll feet, foliate spray handles, rims decorated w/flowers & shells among C-scrolls, maker's mark "C.S.," 7½" l. across handles, pr. 1,760.00
Soup tureen, cov., bombe oval form w/gadroon, shell & foliate borders & paw feet, Matthew Boulton Plate Co., ca. 1820, heraldic silver finial by Richard Sibley, 1823, 15" l. ...2,310.00
Stuffing spoon, Shell patt. 65.00
Teapot, cov., oval straight-sided body, reeded surface w/narrow gadrooned strip at top & bottom, low domed cover w/wooden urn finial & bright-cut design at hinge, straight plain pouring spout, ebony handle, inscribed "John Wardrobe 1780," ca. 1780, 6½" h. 440.00
Tray, two-handled, oval w/beaded bracket handles, applied egg-and-dart border, face w/wide hand-chased foliate design, on four bead feet (one missing), James Dixon & Sons, ca. 1835-80, 28½" l. plus handles 467.50
Tray, two-handled, shaped oval form, reed-and-tie rim & handles w/foliage at intervals, center w/armorial engraving surrounded by scrolling foliage, shells & latticework, on six scroll supports, ca. 1830, overall 28½" l. 1,100.00
Tureen, cov., bombe round urn form bowl raised on four scroll & shell supports, banded reeded bracket handles, applied shell & scroll border bands, domed cover w/engraved crest & attached wreath handle, w/liner, T & J Creswick, early 19th c., 12" d., 11½" h. (ILLUS.) 1,980.00
Tureen, cov., lobed oval body raised on four scrolling feet terminating in acanthus leaves, twisted bracket handles w/similar terminals, rim chased & applied w/scrolls & foliage, domed cover w/conforming handle, side & cover engraved w/armorials, 13" l., 12" h. 1,650.00
Vegetable dishes w/covers on hot water stands, bombe oval form w/gadroon, shell & foliate borders & paw feet, Matthew Boulton Plate Co., ca. 1820, heraldic silver finial by Richard Sibley, 1823, 11¾" d., pr. 1,540.00

SILVER, AMERICAN

Renaissance Revival Hot Water Urn

Asparagus dish & liner, rectangular w/undulating rim applied w/shells, scrolls & flowers, matching pierced & engraved liner, four leafy bracket feet, monogrammed, Tiffany & Co., New York, 1902-07, 14¼" l., 2 pcs. 2,310.00

Beaker, cylindrical form, vertically paneled & engraved at the rim w/a running band of foliage, also engraved w/contemporary monogram "B S R" within sprays of leaves, the back engraved w/later monograms from the same family w/dates "Jan 1845" & "Sept 1879," marked "Revere" in rectangle on base, Paul Revere, Jr., Boston, ca. 1800, 3 3/8" h. 8,800.00

Berry bowl, scalloped rim, Repousse patt., monogram & dates "1863-1888" on base, Whiting Mfg. Co., 8½" d., 3½" h. 550.00

Bonnet brush, Irian patt., R. Wallace & Sons Mfg. Co., Wallingford, Connecticut 115.00

Bowl, parcel-gilt, oval form, the center chased w/a spider in an expanding web below a chased band of blackberry fruits & flowers w/gilt leaves on matted & hammered grounds, interior acid-etched to simulate the intricacies of the web, Whiting Mfg. Co., ca. 1880-90, 10" l. 4,070.00

Box, cov., narrow circular foot ring, cover etched w/foliate medallion applied w/gold borders centering a loose-ring handle of green Peking glass, The Sweetser Company, New York, 1900-15, 5½" d. 1,430.00

Bread & butter plates, Repousse

patt., Samuel Kirk & Sons, Baltimore, Maryland, set of 8 .... 700.00

Bread tray, open handles formed as branches w/applied grapevines, brim repousse & chased w/flowers, leaves & birds, centering script monogram "MMS," Samuel Kirk & Son, Baltimore, Maryland, 1846-61, 14½" l. oval 880.00

Butter dish, reeded domed cover w/cow finial & chased strapwork, ram's head legs w/hoof feet, pierced liner, by John C. Moore for Tiffany & Co., New York, 1854-70, 6" d., 4¾" h. 1,045.00

Butter serving knife, bright-cut design, Julian Fogg, Boston & Salem, Massachusetts, ca. 1880 ..... 25.00

Cake basket, scalloped rim applied w/narrow border of scrolls, brim repousse & chased w/flowers & leaves on punchwork ground, pierced twig-form bail handle, S. Kirk & Son Company, Inc., Baltimore, ca. 1926, 11½" d. 880.00

Cake plate w/handle, pierced sides w/a band of bright-cut floral decoration, the attached pierced stationary strap handle monogrammed, Gorham Mfg. Co., Providence, Rhode Island, 1916, 9½" d. 165.00

Cake platter, Repousse patt., S. Kirk & Sons, 11" d. 640.00

Cane handle, sterling silver & mixed metals, 'Japanese style,' slightly serpentine outline, applied in silver, gold alloy & copper w/an iris, dragonfly, crane in flight & spray of bulrushes on hammered silver ground, initialed & dated "August 27th, 1884," Tiffany & Co., New York, 3 3/8" l. 660.00

Cann, beaded borders, Bailey & Co., Philadelphia, ca. 1850 .... 250.00

Caudle cup, plain pear shape applied w/two S-scroll handles, molded foot rim, the front engraved w/initials "P.C." & the base w/initials "ICP," marked on center of one side below rim "IA," Isaac Anthony, Newport, Rhode Island, ca. 1720, 3½" h. (repaired at handle terminals) 9,130.00

Centerpiece bowl, Martele, oval w/raised shaped edge, chased anemones & bud border w/swag stems, on scrolled raised foot, monogrammed interior, 1881-1906, Gorham Manufacturing Co., Providence, Rhode Island, 12¾" l., 10¾" w., 4¼" h. 3,025.00

Cheese dish, Maintenon patt., Gorham Mfg. Co., Providence,

Rhode Island, retailed by Spaulding & Co., Chicago, 1924, 11¼" d. 467.50

Chocolate pot, cov., Martele, bud finial on domed, fluted hinged cover, elongated lobed neck on squat bulbous melon-shaped base resting on raised scroll foot, slender curved spout & handle, chased w/violets & buds, Gorham Manufacturing Co., Providence, Rhode Island, signed & numbered "9988," ca. 1900, 1½ pt., 11½" h. 3,850.00

Cigarette lighter, sterling silver & mixed metals, 'Japanese style,' pumpkin-shaped w/hammered surface applied in copper w/a seated Chinaman smoking a pipe, a butterfly, a bird & a bee, a spray of bamboo & the initials "M.L.S.T.," fluted domed cover w/attached extinguisher cap, dragon-shaped handle, Gorham Mfg. Co., Providence, Rhode Island, 1882, 2 3/8" h. 1,540.00

Coffeepot, cov., inverted pear shape, gadroon rim & girdle, engraved w/monogram "L.M.B.," leaf-capped scroll handle & domed cover w/foliate finial, spreading base raised on four winged paw feet, Baldwin & Jones, Boston, ca. 1815, 11¾" h. 880.00

Coffee spoon, Medallion patt., Albert Coles, New York, 1836-80 . . . 25.00

Compote, shallow circular bowl w/raised angular handles mounted w/double-sided classical medallions, trumpet-shaped foot w/square knop applied w/four profile medallions, initialed "B," Ball, Black & Co., New York, ca. 1865, 8½" h. 880.00

Compote, shallow scalloped cylinder, serpentine rim chased w/cast applied seafoam border above sides repousse & chased w/dolphins, fountains, cattails, shells & foliage, domed circular foot w/similar decoration, gilt interior centering script monogram, Tiffany & Company, New York, 1883-91, 13½" d. 8,250.00

Creamer, vase-shaped w/curving spout, strap handle, engraved borders, shield enclosing initials "ELL," George Aiken, Baltimore, ca. 1810, 5" h. 330.00

Creamer & sugar bowl, compressed baluster form, scroll handles, crimped rim, etched leaf decoration, gilt interior, Whiting Mfg. Co., 1880-85, 2½" h., pr. 440.00

Cream jug, baluster form, scalloped rim, S-scroll handle, flaring circu-

lar foot ring, engraved on front w/script monogram "TEM," marked "JW" on base, possibly by John Waite, South Kingston, Rhode Island, 1760-80, 2 5/8" h. . . . 770.00

Demitasse pot, cov., sterling silver & mixed metal, 'Japanese style,' tapered cylindrical form w/domed cover, angular handle & straight narrow tapered spout, applied on one side in copper & silver w/two flies above a flowering prunus spray, the other side applied w/a large bug above a bright-cut branch, the cover also applied w/a bug, Whiting Mfg. Co., ca. 1880-90, 7¼" h. 2,090.00

Demitasse service: 7 5/8" h. cov. coffeepot, cream pitcher & open sugar bowl; cylindrical, circular foot, hammer-faceted surface applied w/cast fish, crabs & insects & engraved w/seaweed, traces of gilding, Tiffany & Company, New York, 1878-91, 3 pcs. 15,400.00

Dessert spoon, downturned fiddle handle, S. Brown, New York City, ca. 1820 . . . . 29.00

Dessert spoon, Jenny Lind patt., Albert Coles & Co., New York City, ca. 1850 . . . . 29.00

Dessert spoon, Fiddle Shell patt., J.B. Jones, Boston, ca. 1825 . . . . . . 65.00

Dressing table set: two cov. salve jars, two cov. scent bottles, two cov. powder jars, two cov. puff jars, cov. jewelry box, hatpin tray w/cover & miscellaneous small implements; silver-gilt & ivory, each w/engraved swags & flowers on a matte ground centering a circular reserve w/monogram, in a fitted marquetry case, the top depicting an ancient Greek driving a chariot, the interior fitted w/royal purple velvet lining, w/additional spaces for jewelry & personal items, Gorham Mfg. Co., 1877, retailed by Anderson & Randolph, San Francisco, 20 pcs. 3,575.00

Flask, hammer-faceted surface, front w/a cast applied & gilt fish amid seagrass, back w/raised initials "FTR" & seaweed, threaded cap w/cast applied & gilt crab, Tiffany & Company, New York, 1881-91, 7 5/8" h. 1,870.00

Forks, monogrammed handles, E. Jaccard & Co., St. Louis, ca. 1837-1901, 7 5/8" l., set of 6 . . . . 300.00

Goblets, tulip-shaped bowl on flaring cylindrical foot, hammer-faceted surface, The Randahl Shop, Chi-

cago, ca. 1915, 6 5/8" h., set
of 6 ....1,320.00
Gravy boat, Plymouth patt., Gorham
Mfg. Co., Providence, Rhode
Island 225.00
Hair receiver, Repousse patt., S.
Kirk & Sons, Baltimore.......... 450.00
Hot water kettle on lampstand, oblong body in English Regency taste
w/square base chased w/rococo
ornament, swing handle, ball feet,
detachable triple-spouted lamp,
Tiffany & Co., New York, 1891-
1902, 13¾" h., 2 pcs. 1,980.00
Hot water urn, Renaissance Revival,
trumpet-shaped body ending in a
pressed band of leaves & berries,
surmounted by a lid engraved
w/a scrolling design on a matted
surface, w/a twisted post finial,
handles w/foliate ends & capped
w/a figure of a putto on each, the
child's head forming a thumbrest,
spigot handle topped w/the bust
of a female beauty, legs of the
attached stand of cast openwork
foliage, complete w/burner, Wood
& Hughes, New York, ca. 1870,
20" h. (ILLUS. page 756)......... 935.00
Jewelry box, cov., rectangular, applied design of oak leaves &
acorns on the border & in a band
along the sides, monogrammed,
Shreve & Co., San Francisco,
10" l., 5" w., 2½" h. 412.50
Julep cup, flaring cylinder, molded
rim & foot rim, engraved "Mattie
Carrell," Eli C. Garner, Lexington,
Kentucky, after 1838, 3½" h. 770.00
Julep cup, flaring cylinder, molded
rim & foot rim, engraved "WMB,"
Joseph Werne, Sr., Louisville,
Kentucky, 1838-58, 3 7/8" h. 825.00
Ladle, bright-cut, Isaac Hutton,
Albany, New York, ca. 1795,
14 3/8" l...................... 750.00
Ladle, Olive patt., A. F. Burbank,
Worcester, Massachusetts, ca.
1850, 9 5/6" l. 180.00
Luncheon forks, Fiddle Thread patt.,
Andrew C. Benedict, New York,
1827-40, set of 12 .... 425.00
Monteith bowl, circular w/deeply
scalloped rim, bowl & domed cir-
cular foot repouse & chased
w/flowers & leaves, engraved
monogram in bottom of bowl,
Samuel Kirk & Son, Baltimore,
Maryland, 1880-90, 7½" h. 1,100.00
Mustard ladle, A. F. Burbank,
Worcester, Massachusetts, ca.
1840 .... 28.00
Mustard pot, Repousse patt., S. Kirk
& Son, Baltimore, ca. 1880 .... 650.00

Napkin clip, Repousse patt., Samuel
Kirk & Sons, Baltimore.......... 29.00
Nut bowl, flaring cylinder in the
form of a staved bucket, two cast
moth handles, each w/a pendant
loose ring, engraved w/a stylized
monogram, Gorham Mfg. Co.,
1869, 4¾" w., 2¼" h. 418.00
Nut dish, shell-shaped, footed, Tiffany & Co., New York, 2 x 2¾" .. 48.00
Pastry server, bright-cut, Bigelow
Bros. & Kennard, Boston,
ca. 1850 .... 225.00
Pie fork, applied cow's head, Bailey
& Co., Philadelphia, ca. 1860 ..... 135.00
Pitcher, faceted vase form, octagonal base, scroll handle, Frank
W. Smith Silver Co., Gardner,
Massachusetts, early 20th c.,
8¾" h........................ 715.00
Pitcher, water, baluster form,
chased w/rococo ornaments surrounding a vacant cartouche,
forked handle topped w/a bearded mask, made by William Forbes
for Ball, Black & Co., New York,
ca. 1850, 11" h 990.00
Pitcher, water, vase-shaped, decorated w/deep vertical fluting, harp-
shaped handle, pedestal foot, Tiffany & Co., New York, 1891-1902,
17¼" h. 2,200.00
Plates, bread & butter, Florenz
patt., monogrammed, Gorham
Mfg. Co., Providence, Rhode Island, 1929, 6½" d., set of 10 ..... 935.00
Plates, circular w/scalloped rim,
pierced brim applied w/scrolls &
foliage, centering stylized script
monogram, Redlich & Company,
New York, ca. 1900, 9¾" d., set
of 12 ....5,280.00
Porringer, deep bowl, unornamented,
w/pierced handle, John & Peter
Targee, New York, 1811-25,
7½" l........................1,430.00
Porringer, keyhole handle without
arches, engraved "IBD," Jonathan
Clarke, Newport, Rhode Island,
ca. 1740, 5" d. 1,980.00
Punch bowl, chased & pierced w/a
floral border at the rim & foot,
The Duhme Co., Cincinnati, Ohio,
1898-1907, 14" d. 2,750.00
Punch bowl, circular molded undulating edge & body w/repousse
waterlilies & ripples, base in the
form of three moose heads within
waves, late 19th c., 14¼" d.,
10½" h. 9,075.00
Punch bowl & ladle, Olympian patt.,
circular bowl w/wide band of repousse & chased classical figures
& scrolling foliage, spreading cir-

cular foot w/die-rolled borders, Tiffany & Company, New York, 1891-1902, ladle 14½" l., bowl 11¾" d., 9" h., 2 pcs. 7,150.00

Punch ladle, beaded, W. Tenney, New York, ca. 1850, 11¾" l. 225.00

Salt & pepper shakers, Repousse patt., S. Kirk & Son Co., Inc., 1925-32, pr. 125.00

Salt dips, open, repousse floral design, Wm. Gale & Sons, New York City, ca. 1865, pr. 225.00

Salt spoon, D. Fueter, New York, New York, ca. 1790 .... 95.00

Salt spoon, Lewis & Smith, Philadelphia, ca. 1805 .... 29.00

Salt spoon, J. Musgrave, Philadelphia, ca. 1790 .... 75.00

Salt spoon, R. Swan, Philadelphia, ca. 1790 .... 85.00

Salver, shaped circular rococo form w/an applied border of cartouches & scrolls, resting on three splayed cartouche feet, monogrammed, Gorham Mfg. Co., Providence, Rhode Island, 1897, 13" d. 467.50

Sauceboat, oval, applied stamped rim of leaf-tips on a shaded ground, pedestal foot w/two borders of' palm leaf-tips, leaf-decorated flying scroll handle rising from an anthemion & terminating in a swan's head, Baldwin Gardiner, New York, ca. 1830, 10¾" l. 1,870.00

Sauceboat, Repousse patt., S. Kirk & Sons, Baltimore 450.00

Sauce ladle, Olive patt., S. T. Crosby, Boston, ca. 1850 .... 45.00

Soap dish w/hinged lid, Irian patt., R. Wallace & Sons, Wallingford, Connecticut 255.00

Soup bowls & stands, shaped circular bowl, open handles, serpentine base w/four shaped feet, serpentine rim above border of chased flowers, grapes & leaves, on shaped circular stand w/serpentine brim chased w/flowers, leaves & grapes, Gorham Mfg. Co., Providence, Rhode Island, 1908, 5" d. stand, overall 2 1/8" h., set of 12 .... 9,900.00

Soup ladle, Victorian, Medallion patt., silver-gilt bowl w/scalloped edge, in fitted leather case w/purple velvet lining, unmarked, probably Wood & Hughes, New York, ca. 1860-80, 15" l. 660.00

Strainer, circular, ring handle, bowl pierced w/radiating circular holes, John Brevoort, New York, 1742-75, 3½" d. (ring handle early replacement for scroll hook) 1,540.00

Sugar basket, Repousse patt., S. Kirk & Son Co., Inc., 1925-32 ..... 250.00

Sugar bowl, cov., lobed urn form w/gadroon rim & angular handles, the foot & neck w/a stamped band of scrolling grape & oak sprays, stylized urn finial, marked on base "C.A. Burnett," Alexandria, Virginia, ca. 1815, 8¾" h. 1,980.00

Sugar shell, Currier & Trott, Boston, ca. 1830 .... 35.00

Sugar shell, bright-cut design, twist handle, Hall, Hewson & Brower, Albany, New York, ca. 1860 ...... 45.00

Sugar sifter, Fiddle patt., Bailey & Kitchen, Philadelphia, ca. 1840 ... 110.00

Sugar tongs, Basket of Flowers patt., paw-shaped ends, Abraham Fellows, Troy, New York, 6½" l. 115.00

Sugar tongs, Fiddle patt., H. Lewis, Philadelphia, ca. 1820 .... 75.00

Sugar tongs, bright-cut w/acorn ends, McFee & Reeder, Philadelphia, ca. 1795 .... 195.00

Sugar tongs, scalloped & bright-cut, B. Wenman, New York City, ca. 1805 .... 150.00

Sugar urn, cov., urn-shaped body on square pedestal base, body engraved w/contemporary initials "A.C." on a drapery mantle, reel-shaped cover w/urn finial, beaded borders, marked on base rim "W.G. Forbes," New York, ca. 1790-1800, 10¼" h. 1,760.00

Tablespoon, James Conning, Mobile, Alabama, ca. 1840-73 .... 50.00

Tablespoon, J. David, Jr., Philadelphia, ca. 1785 .... 225.00

Tablespoons, William Kendrick, Louisville, Kentucky, pr. 125.00

Tablespoon, urn of flowers w/monogram & dated "1813," G. W. & N. C. Platt, New York City, 8 5/8" l. 85.00

Tablespoon, S. Richards, Jr., Philadelphia, ca. 1790 .... 150.00

Tablespoon, front midrib, P. Syng, Philadelphia, ca. 1760 (some wear) 350.00

Tea & coffee service: cov. coffeepot, two cov. teapots, cream pitcher, cov. sugar bowl & waste bowl; rounded rectangular form, molded rectangular base w/lion's paw feet, die-rolled borders, covers w/cast finials in the form of recumbent lions, Harvey Lewis, Philadelphia, ca. 1825, 6 pcs. 4,620.00

Teapot, cov., Chrysanthemum patt., Tiffany & Co., New York, 1891-1902, 5" h. 1,430.00

Teapot, cov., Garret Eoff, New York,
1825-35 ....2,400.00
Teapot, cov., Plymouth (New
Plymouth) patt., Gorham Mfg.
Co., Providence, Rhode Island 270.00
Tea service: cov. teapot w/rattan-
wrapped bail handle, cream
pitcher & open sugar bowl; globular, die-rolled leaf rim, matte
finish engraved w/various bright-
cut ornaments in the Japanese
taste, Gorham Mfg. Co., Providence, Rhode Island, 1880-82,
3 pcs. 2,090.00
Teaspoons, monogrammed, T. G.
Calvert, Lexington, Kentucky,
1815-42, 7¼" l., set of 6 .... 180.00
Teaspoons, Coffin Fiddle patt., B.
Cleveland, Newark, New Jersey,
ca. 1805, set of 6 .... 250.00
Teaspoon, front midribs, D. Dupuy,
Philadelphia, ca. 1750 .... 195.00
Teaspoon, D. Hall, Lancaster, Penn-
sylvania, ca. 1780 .... 75.00
Teaspoon, bird-back, W. Haverstick,
Jr., Lancaster, Pennsylvania,
ca. 1795 .... 85.00
Teaspoon, eagle-back, J. Kucher,
Philadelphia, ca. 1790 .... 95.00
Teaspoon, J. Loring, Boston, Mas-
sachusetts, ca. 1790 .... 65.00
Teaspoon, A. Reeder, Trenton, New
Jersey, 1790's 65.00
Teaspoon, G. Terry, Enfield, Mas-
sachusetts, ca. 1790 .... 55.00
Teaspoon, bright-cut, B. Wenman,
New York City, ca. 1790 .... 75.00
Tea strainer, Chrysanthemum patt.,
Tiffany & Co., New York 275.00
Tea tray, handles centered by Roman
emperor medallions, gadroon & ap-
plied bead border, engraved band
of stylized anthemia strapwork,
"Margaret" engraved in center,
Peter L. Krider, Philadelphia,
ca. 1860, 32¾" 2,860.00
Tongs, H. Lewis, Philadelphia,
ca. 1820 .... 75.00
Tray, applied border, Theodore B.
Starr, New York, 1895-1915,
16" l. 800.00
Tureen, cov., two-handled oval supported by flared oval foot w/re-
pousse & chased florals, dragonflies & cattails on hammered
ground, raised domed cover w/cast
loop handle similarly decorated,
Dominick & Haff, Newark & New
York, 1882, 13½" w., 9" h. 12,100.00
Vase, ovoid, four shaped feet, low
cylindrical neck flanked by cast
dragonfly handles, hammer-faceted
surface, Tiffany & Co., New York,
1878-90, 6 5/8" h. 7,150.00

Footed Vase and Stand

Vase & stand, footed champagne
bucket form vase w/foldover lip
pierced & engraved w/scrolling
flowers, the stand similarly
pierced, both w/matching beaded
rims, Shreve & Co., San Francisco,
California, bell mark, overall
13" h., 2 pcs. (ILLUS.) 1,870.00
Vegetable dish, cov., oval w/ser-
pentine rim, domed cover w/foli-
ate ring handle, cover & brim
w/applied foliage & scrolls, Redlich & Company, New York, ca.
1900, 12¼" l. 715.00
Waste bowl, globular body w/lobed
sides on concave paw-and-ball
feet terminating in acanthus
leaves, ring handles attached over
lion mask roundels, William
Thomson, New York, 1811-25,
7½" d. 330.00
Wine bottle holder, caster-form,
hinged domed top w/floral & foliate pierced design, sides pierced
w/an overall shell design, front
w/shield engraved w/initial "M,"
circular foot rim, Lebolt & Company, Chicago, ca. 1920, 8¾" h. .. 880.00

SILVER, ENGLISH & OTHERS

17th Century Caudle Cup

Basket, George III, oval, scalloped

rim, pierced inner border, center bright-cut w/an armorial & monogram, oval pierced foot, threaded swing handle, Peter & Ann Bateman, London, 1795, 14½" l., 3½" h. plus handle 1,820.00

Beaker, tapered cylindrical form w/molded rim & broad granulated band, Johann Hoffler, Nuremberg, Germany, ca. 1680-90, 3 5/8" h. 1,430.00

Beaker, tapered cylinder form, lightly engraved w/birds perched on swags of fruit pendant from a collar of interlaced straps enclosing scrolling foliage, later engraved w/English crest & motto, the Netherlands, probably Harlingen, mid-17th c., 4½" h. 1,760.00

Bowls, dessert, threaded bands at rim, circular footed base, monogrammed, gilt interior, G. Keller, Paris, France, post-1879, 950 standard, 4¼" d., 2¾" h., set of 12 . . . . 1,650.00

Bowl, Chinese Export, deep rounded sides chased overall w/flowering prunus trees w/birds & two crescent moons on a matte ground, plain molded rim band, Luenwo, late 19th c., w/a carved wood base, 9" d. 990.00

Bowl, shell-shaped w/fluted sides, rim applied w/an alternating ball & bead pattern within a meander, four scroll feet w/fluted palmette terminals, A. Aucol, France, 950 standard, 17½" l., 4 3/8" h. 1,430.00

Cake basket, chased to simulate basketweave w/an overlaid napkin, wirework handles, Moscow, 1882, 10½" l. 1,540.00

Cake basket, George III, circular body divided into twelve fluted panels, peaked rim applied w/a border of running leaves on reeded ground, conforming reeded swing handle & pedestal foot, Solomon Hougham, London, 1803, 11 5/8" d. 2,310.00

Cake basket, George III, gadroon rim, fluted sides, gadrooned collet foot, matching swing handle rising from shells, center engraved w/contemporary armorials below a duke's coronet, London, 1785, 14¾" l. 5,225.00

Castor, Victorian, in the form of a Jester in appropriate medieval attire holding a staff w/a finial in form of Punch, R. Hennell, London, 1875, 5¼" h. 1,870.00

Castors, vase form w/applied festoons & borders of beading & en-

graved collars of scrolling foliage, reel-shaped covers w/bud finials, engraved w/later crests & mottoes, Rudolph Sondag, Rotterdam, The Netherlands, 1794, 9¼" h., pr. . . . 7,150.00

Caudle cup & cover, Charles II, pearshaped body embossed & chased w/a ram & a wyvern among fullblown large flowers & foliage, lobate scroll handles topped by female heads, low domed cover embossed w/a hound chasing a rabbit surrounded by large flowers, finial formed as four addorsed grotesque heads, maker's mark "TA," fully marked on base & cover, London, 1663, 7 5/8" h. (ILLUS. previous page) 10,450.00

Caudle cup, Queen Anne, chased w/sloping gadroons & w/cable collar, stamped w/acorns & quatrefoils, one side embossed w/baroque cartouche headed by a winged cherub head & engraved w/late 18th c. arms, scroll handles, base w/initials, John East, London, 1707, 5½" h. 2,640.00

Chalice, base chased w/borders of leaves, bowl & base applied w/enamel plaques, bowl w/an overlay of filigree silver, plaques bordered by simulated diamonds, silver-gilt decoration, Andrei Grigoriev, Moscow, 1809, 13¾" h. 4,125.00

Chamber pot, bombe circular form lightly engraved w/scrolling flowers & oval cartouches, shellcapped foliate scroll handle, France, ca. 1850, 8½" d. (dents, one repair) 1,650.00

Chocolate pot, cov., cylindrical barrel form w/engraved staves & applied reeded hoops, engraved w/contemporary arms, short fluted spout, straight turned wood handle, domed cover engraved w/crest & w/sliding baluster finial, maker's mark "W.S.," London, England, 1793, 8½" h. 2,640.00

Claret jug, Victorian, bell-shaped, spirally fluted & chased w/scrolling foliage & flowers, pedestal foot, scroll handle, Martin & Hall, London, 1890, 12" h. 990.00

Coffeepot, cov., pear-shaped w/short spout & domed foot, side-hinged domed cover w/baluster finial, scrolling wooden handle, Johannes Szakall, Klausenburg, Hungary, ca. 1780, 7½" h. (repairs to handle terminals) 1,320.00

Coffeepot, cov., Victorian, pearshaped, chased w/flower & scroll

cartouches, flat cover w/melon
finial, James Dixon & Sons,
Sheffield, 1857, 9 1/8" h. 770.00
Coffeepot, cov., Queen Anne,
tapered cylindrical form, engraved
w/contemporary armorials below a
scrolling foliate mantel & w/later
crest above, slender swan's neck
spout applied w/a rat-tail at right
angles to the wood scroll handle &
w/hinged flap, high domed cover
w/molded banding & bell-shaped
finial on molded disc, upper handle
mount on a cut-card motif, Joseph
Walker, Dublin, Ireland, 1706-07,
10¼" h. (old repairs above molded
base) 8,800.00
Coffeepot, cov., George III, baluster
form on pedestal foot, swan's neck
spout, domed cover w/urn finial,
Hester Bateman, London, 1788,
12½" h. 1,760.00
Coffee service: cov. coffeepot
w/ivory handle, creamer w/ivory
handle & cov. sugar bowl; Blossom
patt., Georg Jensen, Denmark,
coffeepot 7" h. 2,750.00
Coffee tray, George III, reeded rim,
matching handles rising from
leaves, engraved w/contemporary
armorials, maker's mark "W.B.,"
London, 1801, 20¾" l. 5,500.00

Compote by Georg Jensen

Compotes, lightly hammered circular
bowl w/applied lower band of
grape clusters & vines, supported
by spiraled column w/repousse
grape clusters & raised on a
domed foot, Georg Jensen, Denmark, post-1945, 12 1/8" h., pr.
(ILLUS. of one) 14,300.00
Cream ladles, stems formed as
forked twigs sprouting ruffled
leaves & berries, the bowls
w/fluted rims, Paul Storr,
London, England, 1826,
6 3/8" l., pr. 2,310.00
Cup, William IV, urn form w/multi-
scroll handle, pedestal base,
blank cartouche, gilt interior,

Charles Gordon, London, 1830,
4½" h. 385.00
Cups, George III, campana form, cast
collar of scrolling foliage on
matted ground, inscribed "A
Pledge of Affection from a Father,"
pedestal base w/projecting foliate
knop & w/chased lobed band,
Joseph Angel, London, 1819,
5½" h., pr. 1,870.00
Cup, George I, bell-shaped bowl en-
graved above molded girdle w/con-
temporary armorials in a scrolling
foliate cartouche, leaf-capped
harp-shaped handle, pedestal foot,
William Archdale, Dublin, Ireland,
1723, 7" h. 1,870.00
Dessert spoons, Shell & Thread
patt., G. Adams, London, 1845-46,
set of 6 . . . . 290.00
Dressing spoon, Victorian, Fiddle
Thread & Shell patt., Samuel
Hayne & Dudley Cater, London,
1844 . . . . 330.00
Egg cruet, four-cup, George IV,
quatrefoil form platform stand
w/shell & scroll rim, raised on four
shell supports, four-ring superstructure centered w/a wreath
form handle on tall stem, fitted
w/four gilt lined pedestal cups
w/gadroon rims, Benjamin Smith II,
London, 1823, 7¼" h. 1,320.00
Egg spoons, Chinese Export, Fiddle
Thread & Shell patt., four by
Wongshing, Canton, 1830-55, two
by Khecheong, Canton, 1840-70,
set of 6 . . . . 220.00
Marrow scoop, George III, Thomas
Northcote, London, 1779, 8¾" l. . . . 274.50
Marrow scoop, George III, Richard
Crossley, London, 1800, 9" l. (later
crest) 110.00
Models of fighting cocks, the birds in
fighting positions w/outspread
wings, apparently unmarked, possibly Nurnberg, Germany, 7" &
9½" h., pr. 1,430.00
Model of a dog, recumbent animal
w/raised head, the tail outstretched on a rectangular plinth,
maker's mark "PED" or "LED" in
Cyrillic, 84 standard, St. Petersburg, Russia, late 19th c.,
15¾" l. 1,430.00
Mustard pot, George III, bombe oval
pot w/harp handle, domed hinged
lid w/urn finial, crested, later
monogram, Elizabeth Morley, Lon-
don, 1809, 3" h. 220.00
Mustard pot, cov., Louis XVI, classi-
cal tripod form w/cast & applied
swagging, a pendent laurel wreath
opposite the scrolled handle, lid

chased w/a fluted & coffered design topped w/a bud-shaped finial, engraved monogram on lid, blue glass liner, Jacques-Antoine Levasseur, Paris, 1775, 3¾" h. . . .1,100.00

Mustard pot, repousse florals, Edw. Power, Dublin, Ireland, 1825 . . . . . 375.00

Nut dishes, rim decorated w/garlands & medallions on a pricked ground, sides embossed & chased w/a baby cupid embracing Psyche w/a putto watching, gilt interior, marked "B & Z," Germany, 800 standard, 3¾" d., set of 6 . . . . 412.50

Pepper shaker, Queen Anne, cylindrical, scroll handle, pierced domed cover w/bayonet fixing, engraved underneath w/contemporary initials, John East, London, 1710, 3¼" h. (repair to base of handle) 2,640.00

Porringer, octafoil form w/pierced handles, base w/Tudor rose design, J. Parkes & Co., London, 1901, 4¼" d. 99.00

Porringer, George III, reeded rim, bombe sides, w/initial "H," initial repeated on the grid handle, Peter, Ann & William Bateman, London, 1805, 5½" d. 1,870.00

Punch bowl, plain circular form w/incurved neck & molded rim, raised on round molded pedestal base, Richard Gurney & Thomas Cook, London, England, 1746, 9 7/8" d. 19,800.00

Salt dips, trencher-type, Queen Anne, plain oval form engraved w/interlaced cyphers, base engraved w/scratch weights, David Willaume I, London, 1712, 3¼" l., pr. 3,740.00

Salt dips, Victorian, in the form of knobbly shells raised on sprays of coral & conch shells, gilt interiors, John S. Hunt, London, 1849, 4" l., pr. 3,300.00

Salver, George III, shaped piecrust rim w/beaded border, surface chased w/later armorial, three claw & ball feet, Hester Bateman, London, 1781, 10" d. 1,540.00

Sauceboats, George II, boat form, gadrooned rim, sides w/repousse & chased flowers w/an armorial under spout, tripod shell feet w/shell terminals, flying double C-scroll leaf-capped handle, William Grundy, London, 1759, 6½" l., 4¾" h., pr. 2,750.00

Snuff mull, top mounted w/silver plate engraved "JCK," Scotland, 19th c., 5½" l. 450.00

Soup ladle, George IV, Fiddle patt., George Piercy, London, 1822 . . . . . 247.50

Soup tureen, cov., oval boat shape w/leaf-tied reeded borders, applied armorials, foliate scroll handles spreading from flowers, coronet on tasseled cushion finial, pedestal foot, C. Aucoc, Paris, France, 1840-50, 15½" l. 6,875.00

Soup tureen, cov., Victorian, lobed oval bombe shape, rim applied w/cast band of waterlily buds & pads, matching handles & finials, domed cover w/chased border to match, four scroll supports headed by foliage & shells, engraved w/later arms & crests, liner w/scroll grips, John S. Hunt, London, 1855, 17¼" l. (restorations) 8,250.00

Spoon, Apostle-type, gold-washed bowl, Hutton & Sons, England, ca. 1896, 7" l. 125.00

Spoons, Apostle-type, parcel-gilt, deep fig-shaped bowls, bases of the stems formed as a vacant cartouche on the reverse & chased on front w/armorials & initials "R.S.G.E.," hexagonal stems & well-modeled apostle terminals, Christoph Stimmel, Breslau, Germany, ca. 1600, 9" l., set of 12 . . . . .63,800.00

Spoon, fig-shaped bowl engraved w/heart pierced by arrow, sword & saw below a sun & crescent moon within strapwork border engraved "Far*Mat*I* Gus * Nan," back of bowl engraved w/ribbonwork monogram & w/further inscription in foliated strapwork band, tapered flat handle engraved w/scalework, banded ball finial, Michel Plumeion, Bergen, Norway, ca. 1600, 5 7/8" l. 1,980.00

Table ornament, model of an owl w/chased plumage & glass eyes, Germany, retailed by I.F. and Son Ltd., marked "sterling," 9¼" h. . . .1,045.00

Table ornaments, models of a male & female pheasant, chased plumage, Germany, marked "sterling," male 16½" l., female 14" l., pr. 1,980.00

Tankard, Charles II, tapered cylinder, later chased w/baroque fluting & stamped w/flowerheads & leaves on matted ground, scroll handle pricked w/contemporary initials, lobate cartouche thumbpiece, maker's mark only "SR," a cinquefoil & pellets below, London, ca. 1680, 7¼" h. 2,310.00

Tankard, barrel form, chased w/a continuous hunting scene depicting

Diana & Actaeon, domed base applied in relief w/four stag's heads, finial in the form of Diana w/raised bow & leaping hound, thumbpiece formed as a lion rampant holding a shield, gilt interior, Neresheimer, Hanau, Germany, late 19th c., 19½" h.............5,500.00

Tea & coffee service: cov. teapot, cov. coffeepot, cov. hot water jug, creamer, sugar bowl, waste bowl, kettle on lampstand & footed tray; Victorian, baluster form chased w/rococo ornament & panels of diaper, flower finials, tray engraved w/armorials, remainder w/matching crests, silver-gilt, R. Hennell & Hunt & Roskell, London, 1842-67-69, assembled set of 8 pcs......................11,000.00

Tea caddy spoon, engraved handle & bowl, w/monogram & "1836," Birmingham hallmarks for 1834 ... 110.00

Teapot, cov., George IV, bombe circular body engraved w/contemporary armorials & embossed w/four demi-Chinamen surrounded by scrolls & flowers on a matted ground, four paw feet headed by bearded masks, duck's head spout, finial in the form of a reclining youth, Paul Storr, London, 1820, 6½" h. 1,760.00

Tea service: cov. teapot, cov. two-handled sugar bowl & creamer; bombe circular form w/engraved key pattern collars, applied w/shields flanked by winged putti, one finial formed as a child seated on a lily pad, the other as Cupid, Mce. Mayer, Orfevre de l'Empereur, Paris, ca. 1870, teapot 7 3/8" h., 3 pcs. 880.00

Tea tray, two-handled, oval w/pierced border, cut-out handles surrounded by grapevine, Cyrillic maker's mark "I.Ye.," assay-master Michael Karpinski, Moscow, 1821, 20½" l.......................3,410.00

Tray, round w/faux bamboo rim, bas relief dragon border, engraved dragon on stippled ground in center, button feet, marked w/Chinese characters for "Nanking store" & "silver," China, late 19th c., 14¾" d. 715.00

Vase, in the form of a swimming swan w/arched neck & outstretched webbed feet, open back w/frosted glass feather-molded bowl, Germany, marked "sterling," 10" l., 9½" h. 2,200.00

Wine coasters, George IV, large circular shaped form, bases of

turned mahogany w/crested silver bosses, fluted & ribbed spreading rims decorated w/bunches of grapes, M. R. Boulton, Birmingham, 1827, set of 4 ....7,700.00

SILVER PLATE (Hollowware)

Silver Plate Tureen

Biscuit barrel, cov., Victorian, horizontal barrel form w/a swivelling handle w/cover attached w/a lift-off catch mechanism, the surface flat-chased w/scrolls, the ends embossed w/leafage & flowers, angled claw-and-ball feet attached to lion mask terminals, marked "JD & S," 8½" l., 9" h.......................... 275.00

Bowl, oval, neoclassical style, body w/band of spiral gadrooning terminating at each end in lion's mask w/loose ring handles, four paw feet w/acanthus terminals, 17¾" l., 6¾" h................. 605.00

Butter dish, cover & drain insert, two ornate handles & knife rest, engraved florals, ornate border w/medallions of various bird species, Meriden Silver Plate Co., Meriden, Connecticut 40.00

Card tray, Victorian, model of owls at top w/butterfly on branches below, embossed "Should Owl's Acquaintance Be Forgot" at top, Derby Silver Plate Co., Birmingham, Connecticut................ 225.00

Castor set, five-bottle, etched, dated Nov. 26, 1878, Wilcox Silver Plate Co., Meriden, Connecticut........ 125.00

Centerpiece, circular, centering a fully-molded female figure w/wings standing on a dolphin, above three putti over three small circular fruit dishes, base w/die-rolled border w/three applied masks, three stylized foliate feet, Meriden Britannia Co., Meriden, Connecticut, ca. 1875, 15½" d., 25¼" h. 2,420.00

Compotes, boat form, plain rectangular bowl w/sloping sides, on spreading conforming rectangular pedestal stand on four scrolling

foliate feet, 13 1/8" l., 8" h.,
pr. 825.00
Creamer & sugar bowl, Argosy
patt., 1847 Rogers Bros., ca. 1926,
pr. 75.00
Egg caddy set: four egg cups on
footed center-handled tray that
holds four egg spoons; Rogers
mark, 9 pcs. 50.00
Hot water urn, globular body on
footed conforming circular stand,
containing inner heating chamber,
cover w/knop finial, unmarked,
17½" h. (copper showing) 220.00
Lemonade set: pitcher w/porcelain
liner, spooner & two stemmed
cups; Victorian, repousse parrots,
fern & overall florals, pitcher
w/Old Man of the Sea mask
spout, Reed & Barton, Taunton,
Massachusetts, 4 pcs. 675.00
Pitcher, water, Victorian, the sides
w/bright-cut foliate sprays, double wall interior lined w/enamel,
monogrammed, Wm. A. Rogers,
Ltd., New York, second half
19th c., 12" h. (re-plated) 220.00
Plate, bread & butter, Argosy patt.,
1847 Rogers Bros., ca. 1926 ...... 24.00
Plates, service, plain design, molded
rim, Gorham, 11" d., set of 12 ... 385.00
Plateau mirror, high foot, double
fleur-de-lis relief molded sides
w/cut-out design, double beveled
mirror plate, 11" w. 115.00
Salt & pepper shakers, Argosy patt.,
1847 Rogers Bros., ca. 1926, pr. .. 33.00
Sauceboat w/underplate, Vintage
patt., the rococo form sauceboat
w/a scalloped border of applied
grape clusters & leaves, chased
below w/a parallel band of grape
clusters on the vine, the border of
the undertray similarly decorated
Barbour Silver Plate Co., International Silver Co., Hartford, Connecticut, late 19th c., tray 8¾" l.,
sauceboat 4 3/8" h., 2 pcs. 99.00
Spoonholder-sugar bowl combination, 12 spoon slots, bird finial on
cover, marked "Columbia Silver
Co., quadruple 59," 9" across handles, overall 9" h. 125.00
Syrup pitcher, figural child blowing
horn finial on hinged lid, mask
spout, relief heads on sides &
handle, pedestal foot 45.00
Tea & coffee service: cov. teapot,
cov. coffeepot, cov. sugar bowl,
creamer, waste bowl & 18 x 30"
tray; King Francis patt., Reed &
Barton, ca. 1938, 6 pcs. 795.00
Tray, Argosy patt., 1847 Rogers
Bros., ca. 1926, 12½ x 18¼" 115.00

Tray, footed, well-and-tree center,
vegetable wells at each end, Heritage patt., 1847 Rogers Bros.,
ca. 1953, 16 x 25" 100.00
Tureen, for serving turtle soup,
model of a turtle w/detachable
hinged lid, realistic markings on
body & shell, Sheffield style,
unmarked, 14" w., 20" l.
(ILLUS. previous page) 1,760.00
Water set: 12" h. cov. pitcher on
stand w/cup; Victorian, double
walled pitcher w/hinged lid, engraved scrollwork on sides, rolled
floral bands at base, neck & lid,
resting in a stand fitted for pouring into goblet also resting in the
fitted ring base, removable pan
under pitcher, The Cromwell Plate
Co., Cromwell, Connecticut,
1881-85, the set (one end of carrying handle loose) 330.00
Wine coasters, sides embossed
w/repeating repousse frieze
depicting a female mask crowned
w/grapes amid scrolling grape
vines & leaves on pricked ground,
wooden base w/central insert engraved w/an armorial, England,
5¾" d., pr. 550.00

FLATWARE (Silver Plate)

AMERICAN BEAUTY ROSE (Holmes & Edwards)

Butter serving knife	16.00
Dinner fork	12.00
Dinner knife, hollow handle	18.00
Meat fork, gold-washed tines	29.00
Salad fork	16.50
Sugar shell	16.00
Tablespoon	13.00
Teaspoon	9.00

ARBUTUS (Wm. Rogers Mfg. Co.)

Berry fork	17.00
Butter pick	22.00
Cocktail fork	11.50
Cold meat fork	20.00
Dinner fork	8.00
Dinner knife	30.00
Gravy ladle	19.00
Teaspoon	5.00

BIRD OF PARADISE (Oneida Community)

Berry spoon	25.00
Butter spreader	6.50
Demitasse spoon	7.50
Gravy ladle	17.50
Luncheon fork	8.50
Luncheon knife	8.50
Pickle fork	12.00
Pie server	17.00
Sugar tongs	24.00
Tomato server	24.00

COLUMBIA (1847 Rogers Bros.)

Cake lifter	50.00
Dinner fork, hollow handle	20.00
Dinner knife, hollow handle	19.00
Fish serving fork, large	75.00
Fruit spoon	17.00
Gravy ladle	32.00
Sugar tongs	45.00
Tomato server	71.00

CREST (1847 Rogers Bros.)

Bouillon spoon	10.00
Gravy ladle	20.00
Meat fork	20.00
Salad fork	13.00

DEAUVILLE (Oneida Community)

Bouillon spoon	10.00
Dinner fork	7.00
Dinner knife	6.00
Luncheon knife	8.00
Pickle fork	7.50
Salad fork	7.50
Tablespoon	8.00
Teaspoon	4.00

FLORAL (1835 R. Wallace)

Bouillon spoon	12.00
Butter spreader	12.00
Carving set, 2 pcs.	90.00
Cream soup spoon	17.00
Fish serving fork	40.00
Fruit knife	17.00
Jelly trowel	50.00
Pickle fork, long handle	28.00
Sugar shell	12.50
Youth set, 3 pcs.	50.00

ISABELLA (Wm. Rogers Mfg. Co.)

Butter serving knife, twist handle	10.00
Demitasse spoon	5.00
Dessert spoon, oval	7.00
Fork, 7" l.	6.50
Pickle fork	11.00

OLD COLONY (1847 Rogers Bros.)

Berry spoon	45.00
Cocktail fork	9.00
Dessert knife, flat handle	12.00
Ice cream spoon	22.00
Olive fork	22.00
Oyster ladle	25.00
Pastry fork	20.00
Salad fork	9.00
Sandwich fork	75.00
Seafood fork	5.00

PAUL REVERE (Oneida Community)

Butter serving knife	8.00
Dinner fork	7.00
Dinner knife	6.00
Tablespoon	8.00

VANITY FAIR (Gorham)

Bouillon spoon	7.00
Dinner knife	8.00
Jelly server	8.00
Meat fork, small	15.00
Salad fork	7.50

FLATWARE (Sterling Silver)

ALHAMBRA (Whiting Mfg. Co.)

Asparagus server	150.00
Berry spoon	80.00
Fish serving fork	275.00
Luncheon fork	29.00
Pie server, flat handle	85.00
Salad serving set, 13½" l. handles	525.00
Tablespoon	45.00
Teaspoon	13.00

AMERICAN BEAUTY (George W. Shiebler)

Bonbon scoop, pierced bowl	120.00
Butter spreader	22.00
Cheese scoop	65.00
Cold meat fork	85.00
Ice tongs	210.00
Meat fork	85.00
Sugar spoon	45.00
Tomato server	85.00

ARLINGTON (Towle Mfg. Co.)

Butter serving knife	45.00
Demitasse spoon	11.00
Dinner fork	39.00
Ice cream fork	45.00
Meat fork	110.00
Preserve spoon	88.00
Soup spoon, oval bowl	23.00
Sugar shell	48.00

BEADED (Georg Jensen, Denmark)

Dinner fork	75.00
Dinner knife, 9¼" l.	75.00
Lemon fork	35.00
Luncheon fork	42.00
Luncheon knife	40.00
Pie server, silver blade	195.00
Sugar tongs	75.00
Tomato server	120.00

CARNATION (R. Wallace & Sons)

Bouillon spoon	27.00
Cream ladle	45.00
Cream soup spoon	16.00
Dinner fork	20.00
Dinner knife	15.00
Ice cream slice, hollow handle	75.00
Olive spoon, pierced bowl	50.00
Serving spoon	38.00

EMPIRE (Whiting Mfg. Co.)

Cracker scoop	255.00
Cucumber server	75.00
Gravy ladle	75.00
Macaroni server	295.00
Olive fork, gold-washed tines	20.00
Sardine tongs	85.00

Soup ladle, large 350.00
Tea caddy spoon 65.00

HYPERION (Whiting Mfg. Co.)
Dessert spoon 45.00
Fish slice 95.00
Gravy ladle 87.00
Ice cream spoon 20.00
Luncheon fork 22.00
Luncheon knife 26.00
Sauce ladle, 6" l. 30.00
Teaspoon 11.00

JAPANESE or Audubon (Tiffany & Co.)

Tiffany's Japanese Pattern

Berry spoon 550.00
Carving set, roast, 2 pcs. 195.00
Dinner fork 95.00
Fish slice & fork 975.00
Gravy ladle 125.00
Luncheon fork 50.00
Soup ladle, rectangular bowl 750.00
Youth set, knife, fork & spoon,
   3 pcs. 300.00

KING (Samuel Kirk & Son)
Cocktail fork 10.00
Demitasse spoon 35.00
Luncheon fork 34.00
Pea server 275.00
Salad fork 25.00
Sugar shell 25.00
Stuffing spoon, 12" l. 425.00
Teaspoon 15.00

LILY OF THE VALLEY (Gorham Mfg. Co.)
Cake breaker 59.00
Carving set, 2 pcs. 175.00
Cocktail fork 23.00
Gravy ladle 48.00
Luncheon fork 26.00
Luncheon knife 23.00
Meat fork 59.00
Serving spoon, pierced bowl 45.00

NO. 10 (Dominick & Haff)
Bouillon ladle 195.00
Chocolate spoon, gold-washed
   bowl 24.00
Dessert spoon 30.00
Fruit knife 20.00
Gravy ladle 48.00
Ice spoon 225.00
Jelly knife 98.00
Mustard ladle 65.00
Soup ladle, large 360.00
Sugar sifter 75.00
Teaspoon 12.00

1776 (Dominick & Haff)
Cold meat fork 42.00
Demitasse spoon 13.00
Gravy ladle 45.00
Iced tea spoon 19.00
Mustard ladle 17.00
Pickle fork 14.00
Salad fork 24.00
Teaspoon 13.00

WAVE EDGE (Tiffany & Co.)
Asparagus fork, large 550.00
Cold meat fork 225.00
Crumb knife 295.00
Fish serving set, 12¼" l. knife &
   9¼" l. fork, 2 pcs. 595.00
Grapefruit spoon, gold-washed
   bowl 35.00
Gravy ladle, scalloped bowl 120.00
Ice tongs 360.00
Jelly spoon 125.00
Pie server, serrated silver blade 400.00
Soup ladle, fluted bowl 550.00
Sugar tongs 95.00
Waffle server 395.00

TIN & TOLE

Tin Model of a Pocket Watch

Apple dish, tole, square w/everted
   rim & sloping sides stenciled in
   gold w/bunches of grapes &
   leaves, probably Connecticut, late
   19th c., 11" d., 3" h. 154.00
Basket, tin, 10th Anniversary wed-
   ding gift 195.00
Bread tray, tole, rectangular tray

w/wide everted rim, decorated
overall in tones of red, green,
blue, brown, silver & gilt
w/Oriental figures at various pursuits in garden settings, on a
black ground, Victorian, third
quarter 19th c., 13¾" l. 247.50

Candle mold, tin, three widely
spaced tubes in a line, deep rectangular tray top, brown japanned
finish, 3 x 5 x 6½" 195.00

Candle mold, tin, twelve-tube, two
rows of six each, rectangular tray
top w/handle & rectangular base,
11" h. 65.00

Candle sconce, tin, tapering half
cylinder w/three candle arms at
base, crimped drip pans, oval
crimped reflectors, 10½" h. (old
resoldering) 1,600.00

Candle sconce, tin, decoratively
scalloped crest w/embossed sunburst design, 14" h. (removable
reflector old match) 425.00

Canister, tole, worn original green
paint w/gold striping & large
painted "33," embossed label
"Bartlett & Sons, Bristol," 17" h.
(minor dents) 85.00

Canteen, tin, flat ovoid shape
w/punched star & circle designs,
5 5/8" l. 95.00

Coal hod, tole, hinged lid painted
w/birds in garden landscape w/a
gilt leaf vine border, the body
w/two side handles & similarly
decorated, England, 17 x 18" 3,850.00

Coffeepot w/slightly domed lid,
tole, old but not original decoration of colorful floral & foliage designs on black ground, alligatored
surface, 10¼" h. (some flaking) . . 500.00

Coffeepot, cov., tole, tapering cylinder, flaring foot, applied strap
handle, serpentine spout, free-
hand red, yellow & green floral
decoration on black ground,
11" h. 1,760.00

Colander, pierced tin, square shape
w/canted sides w/strap handles
at rim, pierced overall w/geomet-
ric designs, on small loop feet,
New England, first half 19th c.,
10" w., 7" h. 495.00

Cream whipper, tin, w/crank handle
& wire rotating beaters, box-like
foot 85.00

Document box, cov., tole, rectangular w/domed cover, original dark
japanning w/band of flowers & foliage in red, green & white,
8¾" l. 100.00

Document box, cov., tole, rectangular w/low domed cover, free-hand

yellow brush stroke leaves on
cover, single line panels on sides,
floral spray on front w/red flowers, green leaves & yellow tendrils, wire ring handle, 19th c.,
5 x 8¾", 5¾" h. 330.00

Document box, cov., tole, rectangular w/domed cover, original
pumpkin colored paint w/black
striping & band of black & gold
stenciled pineapples, 9¼" l. (mi-
nor wear, hasp incomplete) 200.00

Lamp bases, tole, columnar form
w/gilt Corinthian capital & raised
on square pedestal base, decorated overall w/polychrome flowers,
England, 19" h., pr. 880.00

Mirror, hired man's, tin, impressed
pattern frame w/decorated comb
pocket in front, 9½ x 12" 75.00

Model of a pocket watch, tin, round
watch w/lined ruled paper face
inscribed w/Roman numerals,
hinged case, stem suspended
from a ring hanger, 10th Anniversary wedding gift, America,
19th c., 5½" l. (ILLUS. previous
page) 660.00

Mug, tole, tall cylinder w/flat strap
handle, original dark brown
japanning w/red & yellow floral
decoration, 4¼" h. (minor
wear) 275.00

Picture frame, tin, 10th Anniversary
wedding gift, holds anniversary
couple's photograph w/history on
back of photo 490.00

Sugar bowl, cov., tole, cylindrical
w/slightly flaring sides, low
domed cover w/small loop finial,
red tole ground w/original yellow,
blue, black, white & brown stylized fruit & leaves design, good
color, 4" h. (some wear) 500.00

Teapot w/hinged lid, tole, oval
body, applied strap handle,
straight spout, free-hand red &
green florals on original dark
brown japanned ground, 5½" h.
(some wear) 185.00

Victorian Tole Tray

Trays, scalloped edge, h.p. w/exotic birds & floral motifs in polychrome on a lacquered ground, America, mid-19th c., 14" l., pr. (ILLUS. of one) 715.00

Tray, tole, oval, pierced gallery centering painted reserve depicting a castle, on oval stand w/square tapering legs, 20" h. 385.00

Wall clock, tole, octagonal watchform case contains striking movement stamped "Japy Freres," France, 19th c., 15½" d. (bell missing) 385.00

(End of Metals Section)

MINIATURES (Paintings)

Miniature Painting by Jacob Maentel

Bust portrait of Chandler Price, Esquire, on ivory, w/powdered hair, brown jacket, white vest & cravat, w/greyish-blue ground, ca. 1827, octagonal, mounted in gold frame w/brooch back, engraved on reverse "Chandler Price, Esq., Merchant of Philadephia, Died Dec. 27, 1827 Aged 62 years," later engraved "(Ellen M. Price), Adelaide S. Eakin Jones 1894, E. Russell Jones 1915," American School, 1 3/8" h.................$1,540.00

Bust portraits of two children on ivory, brown & blond hair, wearing white dresses w/blue, red & white ribbons, sky blue ground, ca. 1830, in gold frame, American School, 2" h. oval 1,650.00

Bust portrait of Mrs. John Cadwalader, three-quarter view facing right, w/powdered hair *en bouffant* & set w/a feather & budded branch-form hair brooch, mauve dress & white ruffled bodice & fichu white lace choker, attributed

to Charles Wilson Peale, ca. 1775, in oval moulded wood frame, 2 1/8" oval.....................7,150.00

Bust portrait of a man in uniform on ivory, possibly Spanish, wearing a gold-embroidered uniform & a medal, brown hair, grey ground, ca. 1815, in gilt metal mounted frame, 3¾" h. 495.00

Bust portrait of a lady, depicted in profile wearing a sheer white cap tied under the chin & a brown dress trimmed in white, executed in water-color & pen & ink on paper, American School, probably Pennsylvania, ca. 1815, 2 7/8 x 4¼" oval, in period frame 330.00

Half-figure of a little girl, watercolor on ivory mounted on cardboard, blonde haired child in a pink dress w/drop-shoulders holding a pink rosebud w/a potted rose at her side, unsigned, American School, 19th c., 2¼ x 2¾" (discoloration) 1,210.00

Half-figure of a lady depicted in profile wearing a starched white organdy cap & brown print dress w/white bertha collar, executed in water-color & pen & ink, by Jacob Maentel, 1763-1863, 3½ x 5½" (ILLUS.) 3,410.00

Memorial scene, water-color on paper, well detailed scene of church, trees & tomb w/urn inscribed "Sacred to the Memory of Samuel A. Merrill," old gilt frame, 4¾ x 5½".................. 425.00

Portrait of a lady, hair piled high upon her head, wearing blue dress, white transparent collar, attributed to Henry Benbridge, ca. 1775, set in gold oval frame w/engine-turned reverse, 1 7/8" h. 385.00

Portrait of a young girl on ivory, w/short brown hair, wearing a white Empire-style dress, coral necklace, standing beside a birdcage enclosing a yellow bird, w/landscape background, ca. 1810, in gilt metal mounted wood frame, 4 1/8" h.....................2,090.00

MINIATURES (Replicas)

Andirons, cast iron, three-legged w/tall front post w/top loop & button finial, worn black paint, 3½" h., pr.................. $75.00

Banquet lamp, three-tier, swirled

Miniature Hot Water Kettle
deep rose red shading to pink &
cased in white lampshade
w/flared ruffled rim, set upon gilt
metal fittings above conforming
pink swirled font on peg inserted
in reeded columnar standard,
overall 18" h.................... 412.50
Bed, late Federal style, figured maple, arched headboard flanked by
arrow- and ring-turned headposts
& ring-turned legs, footposts similarly turned, 19th c., 8¼" w.,
9½" h. 220.00
Blanket chest, figured maple, rectangular top w/molded edge slightly
overhangs base w/dovetailed corners, bracket feet, highly figured
maple w/walnut back & lid molding & pine bottom, interior till,
10¾" l. 2,150.00
Bucket, wooden, stave construction,
pine staves secured w/iron bands,
shaped swing handle attached
w/wooden pegs, inscribed in ink
on underside "George H. Thompson - Bartlett - N.Y. - 1854," 4" d.,
3½" h. (loose staves)........... 385.00
Candle box, painted pine, rectangular w/sliding lid & three batwing
fingerholds, painted a reddish
brown w/a single yellow tulip
blossom on each side, Jacob Weber, Lancaster County, Pennsylvania, 1840-50, 2¼ x 4 1/8",
2¼" h. 770.00
Chest of drawers, Classical (American Empire) style, wood, top
w/square backboard & two
recessed glove drawers over
projecting drawer & two long
drawers flanked by scrolled supports terminating in scrolled feet,
marked "Manufactured by Wa-
truns Andurex," Connecticut, ca.
1840, 5¾ x 9", 9" h............. 412.50
Coach, wooden, early style coach
w/body raised on curved spring
suspension & high driver's seat
above front axle, back wheels

slightly larger than front wheels,
hand-made, original polychrome
paint, 15" l. 55.00
Coffeepot w/slightly domed lid,
tole, tapering cylindrical body
w/straight spout & strap handle at
back, old worn red paint,
2 3/8" h. (lid hinge loose)........ 150.00
Cookstove, tin, patent model, cylindrical model of stove w/worn
black paint, complete w/papers,
"Magazine Cooking and Heating
Stove, 1877" 225.00
Desk, slant-front type, penwork &
ivory, molded rectangular cornice
above a long drawer & four short
drawers flanked by two cupboard
doors, the base w/slant-front
enclosing three pigeonholes &
seven drawers, all above a long
drawer fitted w/compartments, on
bracket feet, variously engraved
w/panels of architectural landscapes within trailing floral borders, on a later black-painted
stand, Anglo-Indian, early 19th c.,
25" w., 61" h. 12,100.00
Fire grate, cast iron, square fireplace opening flanked by wide
embossed foliage designs &
topped by embossed lion & unicorn crest, old black paint w/light
rust, wooden base, 13¼" h....... 105.00
Hand mirror, carved maple, simple
hand-carved frame holding mirror
plate, short cylindrical shaft &
ring handle shaped from single
piece of maple, natural varnish
finish, early 19th c., 3¾" l. 137.50
Hot water kettle, cov., silver, inverted pear shape w/shell rims,
raffia-wrapped swing handle, stand
on three scroll supports & w/scroll-
work apron, burner cover missing,
George III period, ca. 1760, 5½" h.
to handle (ILLUS.)..............1,100.00
Keg, baleen, stave construction, engraved w/a series of motifs, including a heart pierced by arrows,
a large handled pot w/flowers, a
Phrygian cap, the barrel top w/ka-
leidoscopic compass star, on a
paneled black wood base, probably
New England, mid-19th c., 3" d.,
6½" h. 1,210.00
Model of an eagle, carved, painted &
gesso pine, diminutive bird w/out-
stretched wings, the smooth body
& crosshatched wings painted a
dark reddish brown w/yellow &
black markings, the crown & feet
painted yellow, now mounted on a
turned wood base, Wilhelm
Schimmel, Cumberland Valley,

Pennsylvania, ca. 1880, 4¾" wingspan, 3½" h. plus base 2,750.00
Pier table, Classical (American
Empire) style, mahogany & giltwood, rectangular white veined
marble top above a figured frieze
& columnar supports w/gilt capitals, a mirror plate behind flanked
by tapered pilasters, on ribbed gilt
feet, New York, ca. 1820, 6¾ x
14¼", 12¾" h. 13,200.00
Pitcher, redware, baluster-shaped
w/pulled spout & applied strap
handle, mottled glaze, Pennsylvania, 19th c., 3" h. 264.00
Rolling pin, blown aqua glass,
6" l. 135.00
Shower bath, tin, patent model,
spherical object w/low, round foot
& a cap at top, worn polychrome
paint, complete w/papers, "Portable Shower Bath - 1880," 7½" h... 165.00
Sugar bucket, cov., stave construction, finger lappet bentwood
bands, pegged swing handle,
fitted lid impressed "E.L.H.,"
natural finish, New England, late
19th c., 2¼" h. (break at handle
end) 522.50

MOLDS - CANDY, FOOD & MISC.

Lily Ice Cream Mold

Cake, graniteware, blue
marbleized $78.00
Cake, lamb, cast iron, two-part,
14" 60.00
Candy, Santa Claus, metal, four-
section, 1930's 35.00
Candy, three carved hearts w/ini-
tials "J.H.," primitive wood, for
maple sugar candy, 6¼ x 28½"
(minor age cracks) 85.00
Chocolate, basket, tin, clamp-type,
4½ x 10" 65.00
Chocolate, cherub on rocking horse,
tin, two-part, marked "Ringers,"
3½" h. 65.00
Chocolate, duck, pewter, hinged,
2¾ x 3" 48.00
Chocolate, fat boy playing soccer,

tin, hinged, 4 5/8" h. (hinged
base closure missing) 55.00
Chocolate, football, pewter, hinged,
3 x 4" 55.00
Chocolate, girl & rabbit, pewter,
7" h. 70.00
Chocolate, hatchet head, pewter,
letters in relief, "G.W.," 3½" 38.00
Chocolate, heart, pewter, hinged,
2½ x 3" 48.00
Chocolate, hen on nest, pewter,
15" w., 10" h. 200.00
Chocolate, Kewpies, cast iron,
6 x 10" 150.00
Chocolate, peanut, pewter, hinged,
2½ x 3½" 24.00
Chocolate, pig, tin, two-part,
large 66.00
Chocolate, rabbit, pewter, 10" w.,
22" h. 200.00
Chocolate, rabbit in cabbage, tin,
two-part 55.00
Chocolate, rabbit mother w/baby,
tin, two-part 50.00
Chocolate, rabbits (two), metal,
hinged, marked "T.C. Gandt Co.,
New York," 6¾" h. 55.00
Chocolate, rabbit w/basket,
hinged 49.00
Chocolate, schoolhouses (six),
wooden, rectangular board carved
in deep relief, 19th c.,
1 7/8 x 11¾" 137.50
Chocolate, turkey, pewter, hinged,
marked "Eppelsheimer," 4 x 5" ... 65.00
Chocolate, walnut, pewter, hinged,
2½ x 3¼" 24.00
Cigar, wooden, 22" l., 6" w.,
1914 .... 35.00
Food, ear of corn, cast iron, Wagner
Ware, 7" 95.00
Food, fish jumping, copper, 10" l.... 115.00
Food, fish, graniteware, cobalt
blue 85.00
Food, fish, redware, green glaze,
Shenandoah Valley, 10 3/8" l.
(minor edge chips) 145.00
Food, fish, tin, oval body w/ruffled
sides & embossed fish & leaves
across top, 9" l. (light rust) 55.00
Food, fruit, brown-glazed ironstone,
6½ x 8" 40.00
Food, grapes & leaves, ironstone ... 32.50
Food, hen on nest, copper w/worn
tin plating, two-part, 7¾" 135.00
Food, lion lying down, tin & copper,
oval w/deep ruffled sides, 5¼" l.
(light rust) 120.00
Food, melon, graniteware, grey,
6 x 8" 60.00
Food, rose blossom & leaves, tin &
copper, oval w/deep ruffled sides,
7" l. 85.00

Food, round, graniteware, grey mar-
bleized, 6½" d. 45.00
Food, Turk's turban, mottled brown
Rockingham glaze w/some green
flint enamel, 8½" d. 75.00
Ice cream, airplane, pewter,
5¼" l. $55.00
Ice cream, baked potato, pewter ... 25.00
Ice cream, Brownies, pewter 85.00
Ice cream, bunch of asparagus,
pewter, 3 5/8" h. 20.00
Ice cream, bunch of grapes, pewter,
5" l. 27.50
Ice cream, cabbage w/bunny, pew-
ter, 3 5/8" l. 22.50
Ice cream, cherub riding Easter bun-
ny, pewter, 4" h. 20.00
Ice cream, cornucopia, pewter,
4 3/8" h. 15.00
Ice cream, envelope w/heart
pierced by an arrow & "VALEN-
TINE," pewter, 4¼" l. 15.00
Ice cream, flag, 13-star, pewter 52.00
Ice cream, flower, No. 548 .... 40.00
Ice cream, hearts (2) joined by a
banner inscribed "LOVE," pewter,
4½" l. 10.00
Ice cream, Kewpie, pewter, dated
1913 .... 135.00
Ice cream, lily, pewter, three-part,
E. & Co. (ILLUS.) .... 38.00 to 48.00
Ice cream, locomotive, tender & two
Pullman cars, pewter 495.00
Ice cream, Maltese cross w/Roman
cross in center, pewter, 4¼" h. .. 20.00
Ice cream, man in the moon, pew-
ter, "E & Co, N.Y. copyright 1888,"
5½" h. 70.00
Ice cream, mushroom, pewter,
"CC814BIS," 2½" to 3" 20.00
Ice cream, peach, pewter, "CC811
Brevete" 20.00
Ice cream, pear, pewter, "CC849
Brevete" 20.00
Ice cream, pineapple, pewter,
"CC815 Brevete," 2½" to 3" 20.00
Ice cream, Santa Claus, pewter,
4½" .... 45.00 to 65.00
Ice cream, steamboat, pewter 85.00
Ice cream, tulip, pewter, "E & Co,
N.Y.," 4 1/8" h. 30.00
Ice cream, designed to make a two-
color square w/cherub center, tin,
6¼" l. 30.00
Ice cream, Uncle Sam, tin, 5¾" 90.00
Maple sugar, crowing rooster,
carved wood, worn patina,
6¼ x 15" 325.00
Maple sugar, round crimped cups (6)
on rectangular rolled edge tin
plate, 6 x 9" overall 55.00
Pudding, bunch of grapes & leaf,
collar footed, Wedgwood Creamware, 3 x 5 x 7" oval 110.00

Pudding, pineapple, tin & copper,
5 x 5 x 6½" oval 65.00
Pudding, round w/flared fluted
sides, tin, 3 x 6" 10.00

MOVIE MEMORABILIA

Costume from "Flash Gordon"

*Also see CHARACTER COLLECTIBLES
and DISNEY COLLECTIBLES.*

BOOKS

"Mary Astor, My Story," autobio-
graphy, 1959, 1st edition $19.00
"Blue Book," from silent screen
days, 1924, 375 pp. 65.00
"Masters & Masterpieces of the
Screen," 1927, published by Collier, 16¼" l., 112 pp., hardbound 40.00
"The Misfits," Arthur Miller, Marilyn
Monroe on cover 10.00
"Poor Little Rich Girl," by Elnor
Gates, illustration of Mary Pick-
ford, from Photoplay 15.00
"The Sea Beast," Moby Dick, starring John Barrymore, 1925,
w/photographs 15.00
"Steps in Time," Fred Astaire autobiography, New York, 1959,
illustrated 20.00
"Wings," movie photoplay, first Oscar winner in 1927, autographed
by star of film, Buddy Rogers 125.00
"Jane Withers: Her Life Story," 1936,
w/photos from 20th Century Fox,
published by Whitman, soft
cover 20.00
Booklet, "A Day with 'Our Gang',"
by Packer, 1929, full-color pictures
of original cast, 21 pp. 35.00

Booklet, "Pictorial Boards," Charlie Chaplin, 1916, illustrated, 10 pp., 6½ x 12¼" 20.00

Press book, "The Broken Wing," by B. Schulberg, 1923, 20 pp......... 20.00

Press book, "The Flying Aces," all black cast, silent movie, 14 x 22", 4 pp........................... 25.00

Press book, "Jailhouse Rock," Metro-Goldwyn-Mayer, starring Elvis Presley, 1957.............. 19.00

Press book, "The Love Bug," "Crimson Skull," "Green Eyed Monster" & "The Bull Dogger with Bill Pickett," 9 x 12", 4 pp.............. 20.00

Press book, "White Eagle," w/Buck Jones, 1932.................... 60.00

Press book, "Zircon," 15 chapter, colored serial, 9 x 12", 4 pp...... 15.00

COSTUMES

Julie Andrews, blue-green printed linen dress, "Sound of Music," Twentieth Century Fox, 1965, floral-printed dress w/fitted bodice & straight skirt, the three-quarter length sleeves & Peter Pan collar trimmed w/blue-green leather, w/matching leather belt, designed by Dorothy Jeakins, labeled, w/movie still 440.00

Fred Astaire, man's casual three-piece suit, "Belle of New York," Metro-Goldwyn-Mayer, 1952, tan corduroy jacket w/gold braid trim & initials "CH" embroidered on breast pocket, tan wool pants & cream wool vest, designed by Giles Steele, studio label, w/movie still, 3 pcs. 770.00

John Barrymore, jacket, "Don Juan," Warner Bros., 1926, black velvet & satin w/white collar & slit full sleeves w/white silk inserts, United Costumer's label 825.00

Clara Bow, beaded Flapper costume, probably from "Red Hair," Paramount, 1928, short silver lamé & pink georgette dress embroidered w/pink, blue, silver & brown beads & sequins in a stylized floral pattern & trimmed in turquoise ostrich feathers, studio label "Clara Bow, Ball of Fire"......... 308.00

James Cagney, suit, "Yankee Doodle Dandy," Warner Bros., 1942, turquoise blue wool jacket, vest & pants, w/shirt, tie & yellow brocade vest, studio label.......... 880.00

Gary Cooper, suit, "Saratoga Trunk," Warner Bros., 1943, ivory wool, tailcoat, vest & pants, w/studio label 880.00

Joan Crawford, cocktail dress, "This

Woman is Dangerous," Warner Bros., 1952, strapless dress w/black & gold lace over pink satin, w/studio label 660.00

Bette Davis, dress, "All This and Heaven Too," Warner Bros., 1940, grey wool w/lace neckline, floral motif in silver cording 302.00

Bette Davis, gown, "The Private Lives of Elizabeth and Essex," 1939, two-piece off-white brocade, square neckline, full sleeves & very full skirt, w/studio label 990.00

Olivia DeHavilland, gown, "The Private Lives of Elizabeth and Essex," Warner Bros., 1939, bodice w/squared V-shaped neckline, plunging V-shaped waistline ending in a full skirt, whole w/ivory floral lace over blue satin, w/studio label 715.00

Marlene Dietrich, gown & cape, "Shanghai Express," Paramount, 1932, dress w/scoop neckline, gold geometric embroidery down the front & sleeves in gold lamé, w/matching cape & cap, label w/star's name, costume designed by Travis Banton, 3 pcs..........1,430.00

Clark Gable, jacket, "escape from Atlanta" scene in "Gone With the Wind," Metro-Goldwyn-Mayer, 1939, off-white wool, w/pair of pants supposedly worn w/this suit, label w/star's name, costume designer Walter Plunkett, the set w/movie still of actor in costume 3,850.00

Greta Garbo, camislip, "Camille," Metro-Goldwyn-Mayer, 1936, full-length peach silk taffeta garment w/lace-trimmed georgette upper bodice & lace-edged hem, designed by Adrian 462.00

Judy Garland, dress, "A Star is Born," Warner Bros., 1954, red wool crepe, three-quarter length sleeves, four self-covered buttons, w/studio label 1,650.00

Charlton Heston, rag loincloth & tunic, "Planet of the Apes," Twentieth Century Fox, 1968, both garments of brown cotton flannel w/artfully placed rips & holes, designed by Morton Haack, w/movie still, 2 pcs............. 165.00

Rex Harrison, suit, "My Fair Lady," Warner Bros., 1964, three-piece taupish brown wool herringbone jacket w/leather buttons, together w/matching vest & pants, 3 pcs. ... 880.00

Katharine Hepburn, nightdress, "Mary of Scotland," RKO, 1936, peach satin w/high accordion-ruffled collar & matching cuffs, trimmed w/hand-made lace, designed by Walter Plunkett 220.00

Danny Kaye, dressing gown, "The Inspector General," Warner Bros., 1949, full-length maroon brocade w/maroon velvet collar & cuffs, brocade w/foliate motif, studio label 440.00

Burt Lancaster, suit, "The Crimson Pirate," Warner Bros., 1952, beige wool gabardine suit w/a tailcoat trimmed in gold lamé bands & eight gold buttons down the front, w/matching pants, w/studio label 330.00

Jeanette MacDonald, beaded ivory satin gown, "The Firefly," Metro-Goldwyn-Mayer, 1937, empire-style gown w/short puffed sleeves, décolleté neckline & high rhinestone-studded waistband, trained skirt gathered at the rear, the whole embroidered in delicate patterns of silver beads, designed by Adrian, w/movie still 1,980.00

Charles Middleton, robe, in the role of 'Ming, the Merciless,' "Flash Gordon," Universal, 1936, rust velvet w/white trim decorated w/black lightning streaks, high collar, label w/star's name, w/movie still of actor in costume (ILLUS. page 772) 14,300.00

Marilyn Monroe, blue velvet & green jersey jumpsuit, "Gentlemen Prefer Blondes," Twentieth Century Fox, 1953, plunging V-neck bodice of Kelly green wool w/long fitted sleeves, attached straight-legged pants of sapphire blue velvet, designed by William Travilla, labeled, w/movie still...........1,980.00

Marilyn Monroe, dress, "Let's Make Love," Twentieth Century Fox, 1960, beige silk w/a V-neck & gathered at the front, w/matching belt, costume designed by Dorothy Jeakins, three pieces w/two movie stills of actress in costume 1,650.00

Barbara Stanwyck, gold lamé gown, "The Great Man's Lady," Paramount, 1942, Victorian-style two-piece gown w/sleeveless V-neck bodice, the full skirt hung w/self drapes caught w/salmon pink roses repeated at the shoulders, designed by Edith Head, studio label, w/movie still 176.00

Elizabeth Taylor, dress, "Who's Afraid of Virginia Woolf?" Warner Bros., 1966, two-piece grey wool outfit w/Poodle wool trim at neckline, sleeve & hemline, w/matching belt 440.00

Rudolph Valentino, matador suit, "Blood & Sand," Paramount, 1922, bolero jacket heavily embroidered w/gold bullion, sequins & "jewels," matching gold-embroidered pants & vest, studio label w/star's name, 3 pcs. 2,090.00

John Wayne, Naval officer's uniform, "The Sea Chase," Warner Bros., 1955, blue wool flannel double-breasted overcoat w/gold buttons down the front & four gold stripes on each sleeve, w/matching pants & two-cornered hat, studio label 550.00

Adam West, suit, "Batman," 20th Century Fox, 1966, leotard tights, trunks, pair of blue suede boots, blue bat cape & leather bat mask, studio label w/star's name, the set w/movie still of actor in costume 8,525.00

Mae West, dress, "Belle of the Nineties," Paramount, 1934, two-piece, tan w/fitted jacket w/decorative cording on the fur-trimmed full sleeves, matching skirt, designed by Travis Banton, 2 pcs. (tear in jacket) 495.00

Natalie Wood, tunic jacket, "The Great Race," Warner Bros., 1965, red wool flannel w/yellow braid trim on sleeves, collar & down the front, w/studio label, together w/movie still of star wearing the costume..................... 605.00

LOBBY CARDS (11 x 14")

"The Burning Hills," starring Natalie Wood & Tab Hunter, 1956 .... 10.00

"Double Indemnity," starring Barbara Stanwyck, Fred MacMurray & Edward G. Robinson, 1944 .... 50.00

"Loaded Pistols," starring Gene Autry, 1948 .... 40.00

"Love Me Tender," starring Elvis Presley, 1956 .... 75.00

"The Primal Lure," starring William S. Hart, 1921................... 35.00

"Suspicion," directed by Alfred Hitchcock, starring Cary Grant & Joan Fontaine, 1941 .... 65.00

"Wizard of Oz," 1955, re-release.... 75.00

"Yellow Fingers," silent movie, starring Olive Borden, 1926.......... 12.50

POSTERS

"The Beast of Budapest," Nazi soldier beating girl, battle scene, 1958, one-sheet, 27 x 41" 25.00

"The Brain from the Planet Arous," science fiction movie, 1957, 40 x 60" 15.00

"Casablanca," 1942, six-sheet.....17,600.00

"Fishy Tales," starring The Little
Rascals, 1951, 26 x 42" 35.00
"Kid Galahad," starring Elvis Pres-
ley, 40 x 60" 75.00
"Public Enemy," starring James Cag-
ney, 40 x 60" 35.00
"The Ten Commandments," 1956,
full-color, 40 x 60" 150.00
"Yankee Doodle Dandy," starring
James Cagney, 1942, six-sheet ...3,300.00

MISCELLANEOUS

Marilyn Monroe by Cecil Beaton

Blotter, advertising, "Gone With the
Wind - Third Anniversary
Showing"..................... 7.00
Blotter, advertising, "Philadelphia
Story," 1941 .... 7.00
Magazine, "The Modern Screen,"
1931, June, Dorothy Jordan
cover 25.00
Magazine, "The New Movie Maga-
zine," 1930, September, Gloria
Swanson cover 35.00
Magazine, "The New Movie Maga-
zine," 1931, June, Constance Ben-
nett cover by Rolf Armstrong 35.00
Magazine, "Photoplay," 1931, July,
Claudette Colbert cover by Earl
Christy 25.00
Medallion, cast metal, "Paramount
Silver Jubilee for Adolf Zukor,
Commemorating 25 Years of Dis-
tinguished Service to Motion Pic-
tures, 1912-37," 3" 200.00
Photograph, Hedda Hopper, signed
w/personal inscription to friend,
together w/press release, 1947,
8 x 10"...................... 20.00
Photographic study of Marilyn
Monroe, mounted on cardboard,
signed "1/1 Cecil Beaton,"
ca. 1956 , 9¾ x 9 7/8" photo-
graph plus (worn) mount
(ILLUS.) 4,180.00
Playing cards, each card w/different

movie star, Charlie Chaplin on the
joker, 1916, complete deck....... 72.50
Postcards, actresses from the silent
film era, photographs one side &
biographical information reverse,
includes Chatterton, Ellis, Frederick & others, lot of 17 .... 55.00
Postcards, cowboys from the silent
film era, photographs one side &
coupon reverse, includes Gibson,
Canutt, Holt & others, lot of 16 ... 55.00
Program, "Ben Hur," ca. 1926, colorful cover, illustrated, 16 pp....... 25.00
Program, "The Big Parade," 1925 ... 30.00
Program, "The Four Horsemen of
the Apocalypse," 1921, Rudolph
Valentino on cover 30.00
Program, "The Ten Command-
ments," by Cecil B. DeMille,
1923 .... 29.95
Thermometer, promotional item for
movie "Some Like It Hot," featuring Marilyn Monroe.............8,450.00

MUCHA (Alphonse) ARTWORK

Mucha Print "Reverie"

A leader in the Art Nouveau movement,
Alphonse Maria Mucha was born in Moravia
(now part of Czechoslovakia) in 1860. Displaying considerable artistic talent as a child, he
began formal studies locally, later continuing
his work in Munich and then Paris, where it
became necessary for him to undertake commercial artwork. In 1894, the renowned actress Sarah Bernhardt commissioned Mucha
to create a poster for her play "Gismonda"
and this opportunity proved to be the turning point in his career. While continuing his
association with Bernhardt, he began creating numerous advertising posters, packaging

*designs, book and magazine illustrations and
"panneaux decoratifs" (decorative pictures).*

Magazine cover, "La Plume," 1897,
beautiful woman holding a plume,
Pegasus in background **$65.00**

Magazine cover, "Literary Digest,"
October 29, 1910, color cover of
two women 35.00

Poster, "Gismonda - Bernhardt -
Theatre de la Renaissance,"
design of actress Sarah Bernhardt
in the costume of Gismonda, on
two joined sheets, printed by
Imprimeries Lemercier, Paris, 1894,
29 1/8 x 85 5/8" (some discoloration, few tears & small losses,
margins reinforced) 5,775.00

Poster, "Job" at top above figure of
seated Art Nouveau woman holding a lit cigarette, printed in colors
by F. Champenois, 1898, w/mar-
gins, framed, 36 x 54¾" 5,500.00

Poster, "La Dame aux Camelias,"
Sarah Bernhardt, printed in colors
on two joined sheets, by Imprimerie F. Champenois, Paris, 1896,
w/margins, framed, 29 1/8" w.,
81¼" h. (light staining) 3,575.00

Poster, "La Trappistine," design of a
young standing Art Nouveau style
maiden holding bouquet of flowers
in one arm w/her other hand on a
bottle of La Trappistine liqueur, on
two joined sheets, printed by Imp.
F. Champenois, Paris, 1897,
30 5/8 x 80 7/8" (some discoloration & soiling, tear in the right
margin, few small tears & other
defects, margins reinforced) 6,600.00

Poster, "Lorenzaccio - Theatre de la
Renaissance," design of a standing
young man in 17th century costume
holding a book, on two joined
sheets, printed by Imp. F. Champenois, Paris, 1896, 28 1/8 x
79 1/8" (trimmed to image at top
& bottom, some restorations) 5,775.00

Poster, "Moet & Chandon - Champagne - White Star," design of Art
Nouveau lady in swirling gown holding a tray of grapes, printed by
F. Champenois, Paris, 1899,
framed, 7 5/8 x 22 5/8" (colors
somewhat faded) 3,300.00

Poster, "Tragique Histoire d'Hamlet -
Prince de Danmark - Sarah Bernhardt - Theatre Sarah Bernhardt,"
design of actress Sarah Bernhardt
as the character Hamlet, on two
joined sheets, printed by Imp. F.
Champenois, Paris, 1899,
30 1/8 x 81¾" (few small tears,

slight creasing, soiling in the mar-
gins, linen-backed) 11,000.00

Print, "Lierre," printed in colors, by
F. Champenois, Paris, 1901,
framed, 14½ x 14¾" 3,850.00

Prints: "Oeillet," "Iris" & "Lys;"
printed in colors on silk, by
F. Champenois, Paris, 1898, fine
impressions, w/margins, framed,
each 16 3/8" w., 40" h., set
of 3 . . . . .13,200.00

Print, "Reverie," dreamy-looking Art
Nouveau style young woman
seated against a large circle of
floral wreaths, F. Champenois,
Paris, 1898, framed, 18¾ x 24½"
(ILLUS. previous page) 3,080.00

MUSICAL INSTRUMENTS

American Classical Piano Forte

Accordion, "Lakeside," w/case $135.00

Banjo, "Gibson Tenor," w/hard-shell
case 250.00

Banjo, "Remo Weather King," Chica-
go, w/case 50.00

Banjo-guitar, "The Gibson Master-
tone," six-string, ca. 1926 . . . . . . 950.00

Banjo-mandolin, "Bacon," w/hard-
shell case 225.00

Bass fiddle, poplar back & sides,
pine top, beech neck, labeled
"Seth C. Elias, Feb. 1838, Orange,
Massachusetts," w/pine case finished in yellow ochre, 30 7/8" l. . . 165.00

Clarinet, "McClellan Universal
34N-81-426OL," w/case 149.00

Cornet, "F. Jaubert, Paris," B-flat,
silver plate, bell engraved "Lyon
& Healy Sole Agents, Chicago,"
ca. 1890, original green velvet
lined hard-shell case 165.00

Fife, rosewood w/nickel-plated trim,
marked "Geo. Cloos, Crosby,"
15 3/8" l.   45.00

Flute, "Gemeinhardt," student mod-
el, w/case 145.00

Flute, greyish-green jade, pierced w/gilt-metal mounts to receive a tassel, 20½" l. 1,980.00

Flute, "Holton Collegiate," w/case .. 25.00

French horn, "King Marine Corps," 1890's 150.00

Guitar, "Marca Aquila," tenor, pearl inlaid buttons on wood tailpiece, pearl on fingerboard, ca. 1920, 23" l. 60.00

Guitar, "Martin," tenor, four-string, ca. 1930 .... 450.00

Harmonica, "The Handicap," Germany 20.00

Harmonica, "Hohner - Marine Band," w/original box, 4" l. 18.00

Harmonica, "Jolly Jack," made in Germany, w/original box 20.00

Harp, neoclassical style, Sebastian Erard, London, ca. 1830 ....3,300.00

Mandolin, "Oliver Ditson," gourd-shaped, original cloth case 90.00

Organ, "Bruder," 50 keys, 158 pipes 7,000.00

Organ, church model, oak case, Seybold patent, reed pipes, 20 stops, 440 reeds, ca. 1914 ....1,100.00

Organ, pump-type, "Story & Clark," china pull-outs, w/metal claw leg stool & original bill of lading, 1889-1900 ....1,195.00

Piano, baby grand, "Baldwin," ebonized case on square tapering legs, Serial No. R116910, 5' 7" l........................5,225.00

Piano, baby grand, "Estey," Louis XV-style, carved walnut case resting on molded cabriole legs carved w/wreaths & acanthus, together w/needlepoint upholstered bench, 5' ½" l., 2 pcs. 1,650.00

Piano, baby grand, "Hamilton," wal-nut, molded cabriole legs, Serial No. 85619, 60½" l., w/matching bench, 2 pcs....................3,300.00

Piano, baby grand, "Mehlin and Sons," "Louis XV" style mahogany case resting on cabriole legs, together w/bench, Serial No. 41850, 5' 5" l., 2 pcs........2,475.00

Piano, baby grand, "Sohmer and Co.," ebonized case, square taper-ing legs ending in spade feet, Serial No. 112378, 4' 11¼" l., w/matching bench, 2 pcs. 1,210.00

Piano, baby grand, "Steinway & Sons," parcel-gilt walnut, the shaped rectangular case raised on cabriole legs carved w/gilt-leafage & ending in parcel-gilt scrolled toes, Serial No. P2807, first quar-ter 20th c., 6' l...............18,700.00

Piano, concert grand, "Decker Bros.," refinished rosewood case, original

ivory keys, ca. 1875, restored, w/matching bench, 9' l., 2 pcs. ..9,500.00

Piano, grand, "Mason and Hamlin," stained mahogany case w/applied carved decorations of elongated C-scrolls & foliated flowers, resting on cabriole legs, Serial No. A22802, 5' 10" l......................3,300.00

Piano, grand, "Matushek," refinished rosewood case, ca. 1875, 5½' l., 3' h..........................3,000.00

Piano, grand, "Young Chang, Model G-185," ebonized case on square tapering legs ending in spade feet, 5' 11½" l., w/matching bench, 2 pcs..................3,300.00

Piano on stand, grand, "Erard," Paris, gilt-bronze mounted thuyawood case decorated in the Louis XVI taste w/paneled sides enriched w/beaded borders & gilt-bronze rosettes in the corners, the lower frieze embellished w/a continuous border of berried laurel, the trestle stand w/paneled pair of square tapering supports joined by con-forming geometric stretchers out-lined in cable molding & ending in cappings & casters, the pedal leg of lyre form w/applied rosettes & laurel, Serial No. 85587, 7' 1" l.......................12,100.00

Piano, square grand, "Knabe," met-al damper frame, 88-note, good original condition 950.00

Piano, square grand, "Steinway," rosewood, rectangular case on massive scrolling legs, 19th c., 6' 8" l., 36½" h. 605.00

Piano, upright, "Celebrity Starr," rosewood case, A-440 tuning action, new strings, ca. 1885.....3,650.00

Piano forte, Classical style case, mahogany w/gilt-metal mounts, crossbanded top w/hinged cover opening to the keyboard, on spi-rally-turned legs ending in brass casters, labeled inside by J.A. & W. Geib, New York, ca. 1835, together w/Classical style mahog-any stool, piano 57½" l., 33½" h., 2 pcs. (ILLUS. previous page) 1,760.00

Piano forte, inlaid mahogany, rec-tangular case w/five octave com-pass w/three handstops, separate trestle base, signed "Hoan Berzer Londini Fecit 1784 Compton Street Soho," George III era, England, 5' ½" l., 32½" h...............1,980.00

Psaltery, elongated wooden case w/strings, hand-made, America (ILLUS. top next page) 470.00

Saxophone, "Buescher," nickel, Elk-hart, Indiana, True-Tone No. 213133, pat. 1914, w/case........ 245.00

Early Hand-made Psaltery

Trumpet, "Barclay," brass, Czecho-
slovakia, w/case 195.00
Trumpet, "Ludwig," No. 543, nickel,
Chicago, Illinois, w/wood case ... 195.00
Ukulele, Jonah Kumalae, Honolulu,
original case 55.00
Violin, "Januarius Gagliano Silius
Alexandri, Fecit neop. 1770, made
in Germany," w/case 150.00
Violin & bow, maple & tiger stripe
maple, made by Michele De Lucca,
1952, 2 pcs. 2,000.00
Xylophone, "J.C. Deagan," dated
1916 .... 650.00

MUSICAL INSTRUMENTS, MECHANICAL

Nelson-Wiggen Orchestrion

Band organ, "Wurlitzer Model 103,"
ca. 1923 (restored) $11,000.00
Band organ, "Wurlitzer
Model 150" .... 25,000.00 to 35,000.00
Coin-operated piano, "Cremona
Style G" (restored) 11,500.00

Coin-operated piano, "Peerless
Style D," art glass case, w/three
"A" rolls (restored) 6,500.00
Coin-operated piano, "Seeburg
Style A," w/mandolin & orchestrion
bells 7,000.00
Coin-operated piano, "Western Electric Selectra Model B," w/mandolin
& xylophone attachments,
1920's 7,000.00
Coin-operated piano, "Wurlitzer A,"
w/pipes, quarter-sawn oak case
(restored) 18,000.00
Orchestrion, "Nelson-Wiggen
Style 5X," mahogany cabinet
w/glazed triple panel front over a
pair of glazed doors flanked by
free-standing columns, ca. 1925,
5' 8" h. (ILLUS.) 8,250.00
Orchestrion, "Seeburg Style G,"
w/piano, flute pipes, snare drum,
bass drum, timpani & cymbals, in
golden oak case, the front w/four
art glass panels, the outer panels
w/projecting flaming torches, central arched panels w/upper roundels containing cottages & windmills in landscapes, serial number
162413, w/three rolls,
6' 7½" h. 24,750.00
Orchestrion, "Wurlitzer CX," two
ranks of pipes, orchestra bells,
drums, piano, etc., w/automatic
roll changer & wonder light (mostly
restored & playing) 25,000.00
Organ, "Aeolian Duo-Art Pipe,"
15-rank w/harp, w/80
recordings 4,500.00
Player organ, "Aeolian-Hammond,"
w/speaker cabinet, bench & 50
rolls, ca. 1938 .... 3,000.00
Player organ, "Aeolian Style 1500,"
rosewood case, 46-note, ca.
1900 .... 3,200.00
Player piano, grand, Knabe Duo-Art,
contained in a green painted case
decorated in the neoclassical taste
in gilt w/medallions & musical
trophies amid foliate mantling over
a lower repeating border of oval
wreaths enclosing rhomboid medallions, resting on paired square
tapering legs painted w/pendent
husks, together w/upholstered
bench, piano 5' 4" l., 2 pcs. 1,430.00
Player piano, grand, "M. Schulz
Recordo," burled walnut Bardini/Ital-
ianate cabinet, 5' h. (fully restored
& refinished) 15,000.00
Player piano, grand, "Steinway Duo-
Art Model XR," walnut case, ca.
1928, w/bench, piano 6' 2", 2 pcs.
(unrestored) 9,050.00
Player piano, grand, "Weber Duo Art

Artcase," William & Mary style case w/inlaid panels (unrestored)..................5,500.00

Player piano, upright, "Poppers Konzertist," w/real violin, ca. 1930, w/39 rolls 2,500.00

Reproducing piano, grand, "Chickering Ampico A," refinished, restrung, pneumatically rebuilt, w/50 rolls, 6' 5" 6,900.00

Reproducing piano, grand, "Fisher Ampico," unusual nine-legged artcase 5,200.00

Reproducing piano, grand, "Mason & Hamlin Ampico," burl walnut case w/matching bench & 60 rolls, piano 5' 4", the group (completely restored) 13,500.00

Violano (violin player), Mills Grand Model Violano-Virtuoso, w/single violin, golden oak case enclosed by two pairs of folding glazed doors over a pair of stepped panel doors flanked by shallow projecting pilasters w/carved foliate capitals, ca. 1925, 5' 4" h. 7,700.00

MUSIC BOXES

Regina Disc Music Box

Criterion disc music box, walnut carved case w/the original lithograph trade-mark on lid, peripheral-driven movement w/a double comb, start - stop & fast - slow levers, crank wound at side, America, ca. 1890, w/twenty-one 15 2/3" d. discs, 21" l. $2,750.00

Jacot (Swiss) cylinder music box, table model, ten-tune, hand crank, ebony case w/inlaid rosewood veneer, inner glass lid, 11" cylinder, 24" l., 8" h. 2,750.00

Mermod Freres (Swiss) "Empress Concert Grand" disc music box, floor model, mahogany case w/satin-

wood inlay, crank-type, last patent date of 1905, w/twenty-four 19" discs, 23 x 30", 39" h...........4,675.00

Mojon Manger (Swiss) cylinder music box, ten-tune, stop - start & change - repeat levers, lever wound to side, original tune sheet inside lid, rosewood case w/fruitwood banding & a musical & floral inlay on lid, late 19th c., 13" cylinder, 25" l....................1,210.00

Music box & clock combination, sterling silver & enamel, four columns rising from rectangular base & supporting a diamond-shaped clock beneath a sharply canted roof w/owl perched at peak, France, 7" h. 2,640.00

Paillard (Swiss) cylinder music box, twelve-tune, rosewood case w/fruitwood banding, original tune sheet & tune pointer, double spring barrel, two combs, zither attachment, stop - start & change - repeat levers, ca. 1880, 16" cylinder, 33½" l....................2,200.00

Polyphon (Polyphon Musikwerke, Leipzig, Germany) coin-operated disc music box, central driven movement w/a double comb, crank wound at side, contained in a mahogany two-part cabinet w/hinged glass door flanked by half-round pilasters on top portion & a paneled door opening to storage cabinet in lower section, ca. 1900, w/twenty-seven discs, 79" h. 9,900.00

Regina (American subsidiary of Polyphon Musikwerke, Rahway, New Jersey) automatic changer coin-operated disc music box, peripheral-driven movement w/double comb, spring barrel, rack for twelve discs, disc selector & crank wound at side, contained in mahogany case topped by spooled railing w/urn finials above arched pierce-carved spandrels in the form of dragons over glass panel, glass-fronted lower case over the disc, on casters, ca. 1898, w/30 discs, 76" h. 17,600.00

Regina disc music box, in floor-standing bow front mahogany case enclosed by an arched glazed door w/flanking barleytwist columns, base fitted w/a drawer raised on square cabriole legs joined by an undertier, retailed by Sherman Clay and Co., San Francisco, ca. 1900, w/seventeen 15½" discs, 26½" w., 5' 8" h. (ILLUS.) 12,100.00

"Singing Bird Box," enamel over sterling silver, rectangular, brightly colored bird rises from filigree grille beneath a hinged oval panel set in the center of the lid, panel depicts game birds & a monkey in a garden setting, sides in translucent royal blue within silver & white enamel geometric frame, front panel flanked by enamel columns, center reserve depicts fighting cocks, mechanism button in the form of a bird in flight, Swiss, late 19th c., 3 x 4", 2" h. 3,850.00

Swiss 'bells-in-sight' cylinder music box, ten-tune, ebonized case decorated w/Japanese motifs, nine saucer bells w/wasps strikers applicable at will, zither attachment, stop - start & change - repeat levers, two combs, ca. 1880, 15" cylinder, 27" l. 1,870.00

NAPKIN RINGS

Engraved Tiffany Napkin Ring

All napkin rings listed are silver plate unless otherwise noted.

Baby in cradle, James W. Tufts, Boston $295.00
Barrel-shaped ring w/two cherubs holding dolls, Meriden Britannia Co. 135.00
Birds (2) & tulips, beaded base & ring, Rockford Silver Plate Co. 80.00
Boy w/cookie, begging dog, engraved "Awarded for Tied Leg Racing, 1885," Meriden 185.00
Brownie figure climbing up side of ring, after Palmer Cox 165.00
Butterfly on leaf, Tufts 78.00
Cherub atop ring w/leash holding swan, Wilcox Silver Plate Co. 240.00
Cherub riding a swan, Middletown Plate Co. 195.00
Children playing musical instruments deeply engraved around ring, w/engraved "John Parading," Tiffany & Co., sterling silver (ILLUS.) 125.00
Dog pulling sled, embossed on the

sides of the sled are greyhounds, engraved "Sara," Meriden 165.00
Double rolled band of palmettes, unmarked but numbered one to six, Victorian, in fitted leather case w/purple velvet interior, each 1¾" d., set of six 77.00
Eagles (2), w/spread wings on either side of ring, Rogers 95.00
Floral, bright-cut, beaded rim, sterling silver, 1½" w. 28.00
Fox pulling cart w/movable wheels 295.00
Girl on sleigh pulling ring 249.00
Greenaway boy w/hat & ruffled collar, Meriden 225.00
Greenaway boy sitting holding stick w/begging dog beside him, Meriden 255.00
Greenaway boy pulling rope holding ring on his back, Rogers & Bros., No. 155 . . . . 87.50
Greenaway girl w/stick in hand on one side, w/Greenaway child on tree branch on other side, round petal base on feet 185.00
Male nude runner holding torch, square base 150.00
Oriental fans crossed to form ring, repousse flowers & hummingbirds decoration 75.00
Parrot on wheels, Simpson, Hall, Miller & Co. 175.00
Sailor holding tall oar standing by ring 350.00
Windham patt., Tiffany & Co., sterling silver 68.00

NAUTICAL ITEMS

Brass Ship's Lantern

The romantic lure of the sea, and of ships

in general, has opened up a new area of collector interest. Nautical gear, especially items made of brass or with brass trim, is sought out for its decorative appeal. Virtually all items that can be associated with older ships, along with items used or made by sailors, are now considered collectible for technological advances have rendered them obsolete. Listed below are but a few of the numerous nautical items sold in recent months.

Barograph, brass, rectangular hinged mahogany case w/brass handle & glazed sides encloses the cylindrical brass barrel w/paper graph, metal arm & coil, w/key, marked "Naudet 7306," France, case 9" l. $330.00

Bell, bronze, from the MS Hoegh Mistral, usual form w/iron clapper w/ring terminal for rope, pierced finial for hanging, inscribed in relief "M/S HOEGH MISTRAL 1909," 9" h. 302.50

Binnacle, brass, sestral yacht-type, domed lid w/sliding cover opening to reveal the floating compass, on a swinging gimbal mount on a circular wood base, marked "Henry Browne & Son, Essex, No. 17918/D/V," England, 8¾" h. 220.00

Cabin light, brass & metal, hexagonal glazed body w/circular tube guards, surmounted by a domed cylindrical chimney w/suspension loop, the interior fitted w/a kerosene lamp w/glass chimney, mounted w/a plaque inscribed "CLIPPER SHIP LAMP No. 1266, DUMBARTON, SCOTLAND, 1869," 24½" h. 192.50

Chest, sailor's, painted wood, hinged rectangular lid opening to a till & well, base molding, green paint, retains partial steamship line label, 19th c., 29" l., 14" h. . . . 192.50

Chronometer, brass, eight-day model, silver dial w/black Roman numerals, subsidiary seconds & up/down dials, contained within a gimbaled mount, brass-mounted rosewood box (lacking lid & base), marked "Poole, London," Number 908, first or second quarter 19th c., 4½" d. bezel 1,760.00

Compass, brass, fitted in box w/lid lifting to reveal the gimbaled floating compass, dial inscribed "Dirigo, Seattle, Washington," 4½" d. (some discoloration to dial) 137.50

Depth gauge, brass & wood, the hinged rectangular wood case

opening to a black-painted tin tube, brass gauge & calibrated ruler marked in fathoms, the lid interior w/typed instructions in French, marked "Wigzell's Patent (Atmospheric Type) Sea-Sounding Instrument," Scotland, 27" l. 165.00

Inclinometer, brass, circular brass case enclosing a card calibrated from Port to Heel to Starboard, 50 to 50 degrees, mounted on a coved circular wood wall plaque, marked "Kelvin Hughes Division, S. Smith & Sons, Ltd.," England, ca. 1910, overall 13" d. 192.50

Jetty light, brass & painted cast iron, domed brass cap above a ribbed molded clear glass shade enclosing red-tinted panels w/slanted brass tubular guards, raised on a red & white-painted columnar base, declared surplus by the Coast Guard from Bodega Bay, America, 24½" h. 440.00

Lantern, brass, battle-type, rectangular case w/circular 'porthole' lamp, surmounted by a simple bracket handle, marked "Benjamin Electric Mfg. Co., Des Plaines, Illinois," 9-X-5293-L Type JR-2S, pre-World War II, 8" w., 9½" h. . . 220.00

Octant, ivory & brass-mounted ebony, ebony frame w/later ivory blank panel, the rim w/calibrated ivory panel, the brass index arm engraved 'Dolland, London,' w/adjustable horizon mirror, set of interchangeable colored filters, fore & back sighting vanes, w/hinged pine case, England, late 18th - early 19th c., 11¼" w., 13½" l. . . 605.00

Pulley, double, whale bone w/copper eyelet, worn original canvas & ropework, 4¾" l. 350.00

Sextant, black-painted & brass, black-painted index arm, vernier, two sets of colored filters, telescope lens & ebonized grip, marked "Leopold & Stevens Instruments, Portland, Oregon," U.S. Maritime Commission model, w/wood case, 9½" l. 330.00

Ship model, the Clipper 'M Argo' of San Francisco, painted wood, green & black painted hull, the lined deck fitted w/cabin, lifeboats, anchor, skylight, capstan, windlass, steps & coiled rope, the three masts fully rigged w/rope ladders, pulleys & linen sails, the stern inscribed "M ARGO, SAN FRANCISCO," w/wood trestle stand, second half 19th c., 4' l., 39" h. 990.00

Ship portrait, oil on canvas, two-
masted fore & aft schooner in open
seas, ship "Tempest," signed "W.P.
Stubbs," & dated, "83," framed,
22 x 36" (some damages)........4,400.00
Ship's gangway boards, mahogany,
relief-carved, brass fittings, America, third quarter 19th c., overall
44" h., pr. 1,700.00
Ship's lantern, brass & glass, rectangular w/glass sides & plaque inscribed "Samuel Hall, Ship
Chandler, East Boston," mounted
as a lamp, 15" h. (ILLUS.
page 780) 440.00
Ship's wheel, mahogany, maple &
brass, brass center w/eight radiating baluster-turned maple
spokes, mahogany outer rim,
America, 43" d. (refinished) 302.50
Whistle, boatswain's, silver, typical
form w/ball terminal, probably
America, ca. 1900, 5½" l.
(dents) 88.00

NEEDLEWORK PICTURES

Silk-on-Silk Needlework Picture

*The art of embroidering scenes on backings
of canvas, linen or silk dates back at least to
the 17th century but became especially popular in England and America in the late 18th
and early 19th centuries. Many young ladies
were trained in this art at "schools" operated to train them in lady-like pursuits. Sam-
plers are closely related to these but we compile on them separately (see TEXTILES).*

Needlework embroidered on silk, center oval reserve w/two standing
children framed by floral wreath,
embroidered in faded colors &
w/drawn faces & hands, pen & ink
labels on front reading "The Children in the Wood - Abigail Mendenhall, 1817," framed & w/old
exercise book w/drawings marked
"Abigail Mendenhall," framed,
8 x 10", 2 pcs. (worn, stains, color
bleeding) $1,400.00
Needlework embroidered & painted
on silk, scene depicting country
girl w/dog, staff & basket, face,
arms & sky rendered in water-
color, ornate giltwood frame
w/oval opening, 9¼ x 11½" 275.00
Needlework embroidered on silk,
scene of a girl seated on an over-
turned basket knitting, at her left
a stone cottage w/a cat perched
on a ledge, an Alpine scene in
the distance w/goats, probably
England, 19th c., framed,
10 x 11"........................ 302.00
Needlework embroidered on linen,
depicting a verse surrounded by
figures of trees, birds & baskets
of flowers w/a geometric outer
border, worked in polychrome
threads, signed "Anne Oram" &
dated "1824," England, 10 x 12"
(browning) 440.00
Needlework embroidered on silk,
religious scene of the figures of
three clerics standing by the in-
terred figure of Christ, worked in
yellow, white & blue silk threads
& heightened w/gilt threads, the
whole within a rose blossom &
bud border, probably England,
late 17th - early 18th c., framed,
10½ x 14½"................... 550.00
Needlework embroidered on silk,
oval scene depicting a memorial
setting w/an urn inscribed "sacred
to the memory of Thomas Williams, who was born June 5 1761
ob. Feb 21st 1797," original
eglomise mat inscribed "wrought
by Anna Williams," worked in silk
threads, America or England, dated 1797," 12 x 14¼"............ 550.00
Needlework embroidered on silk,
scene of a young mother & her
infant seated beneath a leafy tree,
a thatched-roof cottage in background, worked in green, gold,
brown, beige & yellow chenille
& silk thread on painted silk
ground, eglomise mat inscribed
w/the gilt initials "A.H.," probably
by Samuel Folwell, Philadelphia,
early 19th c., framed,
12¼ x 15" 2,970.00
Needlework embroidered on flannel, scene of a young woman
w/shepherd's pipe & a goat in a
stylized landscape, w/appliqued

felt & hand-colored paper detail, 13 x 14¾" oval (minor moth damage) 350.00

Needlework embroidered on silk, mourning scene w/a monument inscribed w/the initials "E.C.," having a footed urn w/flowers resting on its top, a large shield at the left stitched w/a pious verse, 19th c., framed, 13½ x 15½".................... 522.00

Needlework embroidered on silk, scene of a young maiden embracing a little lamb in the foreground, behind her a frame house & a silo, a ruined castle at extreme left, all within an oval reserve w/black eglomise mat inscribed in gilt "A.C.I.," worked in green, blue, beige, gold & yellow silk & chenille threads on a painted silk ground, signed "A.C. Ives," probably Pennsylvania, early 19th c., framed, 14 x 15½" 3,080.00

Needlework embroidered on linen, scene of a Georgian house in a landscape w/young ladies in Empire gowns, animals, chairs & trees on a lawn, within an elaborate flower, meandering vine & bird border, silk yarns worked in a variety of stitches in shades of green, blue, yellow & cream, signed "Mary E. Strickler Work," mid-Atlantic States, ca. 1820, 16 x 19" (soiled, yarn loss & fading) 990.00

Needlework embroidered & painted on silk, depicting a classical scene of a young seated woman teaching two children under a heavily draped portico w/an elaborately patterned floor, a water & hill-filled landscape beyond, executed in silk & chenille yarns, metallic braid & water-color, original eglomise mat inscribed "Aspasia instructing Two Young Athenians," & "D. Cone," worked by Dorothy Cone, Bacon Academy, Colchester, Connecticut, ca. 1805, original gilt frame, 17½ x 22½" 8,800.00

Needlework embroidered on canvas, scene of an elegant colonial mansion in an ornate floral landscape depicting a boy & girl in elaborate dress accented w/beadwork detail, two dogs & a large bird, silk yarns finely worked in a variety of stitches in shades of blue, peach, gold, tan & ivory, signed "Mary Ann Rowe's Work, Reading, 1834," Reading, Pennsylvania, in the original frame & glass, 22½" w., 18" h. (excellent condition) 16,500.00

Needlework embroidered on silk, depicting a young maiden seated on a rock beneath a leafy clump of trees, her flock at right, a man driving a flock of sheep in the background, inscribed at the bottom "Shepherdess of the Alps," worked in a variety of green, gold, beige, yellow & pale pink silk threads on a painted silk ground, possibly Samuel Folwell, Philadelphia, late 18th c., framed, 19 x 24" 1,540.00

Needlework embroidered on linen, sampler-type, entitled "The Beggar's Petition," two panels of verse surmounted by a scene depicting a Pennsylvania stone farmhouse flanked by trees, w/dog, sheep, birds & playing children, meandering floral surround, worked in polychrome silk & wool threads, Sarah Hadley, probably Pennsylvania, 1841, 24 x 24" (tears & some discoloration) 3,080.00

Needlework embroidered on silk, landscape w/three figures & a dog w/cottage & monument in background, worked in polychrome silk threads, signed on the mat "MW, The little Slumberer, 1801," mat replaced, America, 1800-15, 24 x 28¾" (ILLUS. previous page).........................6,050.00

NETSUKE

These decorative toggles were used by the Japanese to secure an inro, tobacco pouch or other small personal article by means of a cord slipped through a Kimono sash. They are carved of ivory and other materials. There are many reproductions.

Figure of household god, Jurojin, holding a fan, bone, 19th c., 2½" h. (fine age lines) $137.50

Model of a deer, ivory, recumbent animal looking over its shoulder, unsigned, early 19th c. 275.00

Model of a Kirin, fierce animal seated on its haunches, the head turned to its back, 19th c.........................1,320.00

Model of a puppy, ivory, animal w/well-carved fur & inlaid eyes, recumbent on a fan, unsigned, 19th c. 825.00

Model of a Shishi, ivory, recumbent animal scratching its nose, unsigned, 18th c. 1,320.00

Model of a skull, detailed w/rat on top, ivory, artist-signed 325.00

Model of a turtle, wood, realistically carved w/legs & tail tucked in, unsigned, 19th c. 330.00

NUTCRACKERS

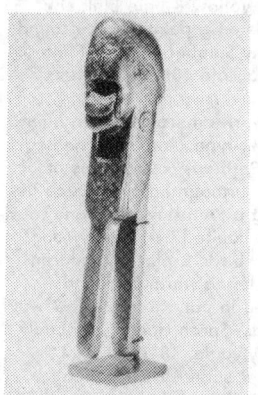

Early Carved Wood Nutcracker

Brass, figural Bill Sykes & Fagin, 5" $33.00
Brass, figural Punch & Judy 65.00
Brass, figure of a long-necked sailor straddling a barrel 250.00
Brass, figure of a sailor & lady, they kiss when handles are squeezed together, 6¼" 65.00
Cast iron, model of a dog, silver plate, 13" l., 6" h. 75.00
Sterling silver, Acorn patt., Georg Jensen 225.00
Wooden, carved ram w/glass eyes, 8½" l. 65.00
Wooden, carved walnut w/abstractly rendered head of a man wearing low-rolled queue w/hinged jaw, incised initials "TW" & the date "1799," probably Pennsylvania, 8½" l. (ILLUS.) 715.00

NUTTING (Wallace) COLLECTIBLES

In 1898, Wallace Nutting published his first hand-tinted pictures and these were popular for more than 20 years. An "assembly line" subsequently colored and placed a signature and (sometimes) a title on the mat of these copyrighted photographs. Interior scenes featuring Early American furniture are considered the most desirable of these photographs.

Nutting's photographically illustrated travel books and early editions of his antiques reference books are also highly collectible.

BOOKS
"American Windsors," w/pages 192a-d insert, 1917, first edition . . $77.00
"Connecticut Beautiful," first edition 35.00
"England Beautiful," in original box 154.00
"Furniture Treasury," Vols. I, II & III, first edition 121.00
"Maine Beautiful," first edition 35.00
"New Hampshire Beautiful," first edition 35.00
"Pathway of the Puritans," contains many rare Nutting pictures, 1930, first edition 71.50
"States Beautiful" series, second edition, set of 10 . . . . 209.00
"Virginia Beautiful," 1930, first edition 35.00
"Wallace Nutting's Biography," 1936, first edition, w/dust jacket 66.00

PRINTS
Canopied Mirror (The), interior scene, framed, 7 x 9" 210.00
Children of the Sea, exterior scene, six little girls, barefoot, in dresses romping at water's edge, framed, 9 x 11" 550.00
Critical Examination (A), framed, 6½ x 6½" 60.50
Dahlia Jar (The), dark red & yellow flowers in a brown jug, framed, 8 x 10" 330.00
Dainty China, interior scene, framed, 10 x 16" 65.00
Dog-On-It, eight little puppies sitting on a garden bench, framed, 7 x 11" 1,292.50
Dutch Sails, exterior scene, framed, 7 x 11" 105.00
Four O'Clock, exterior scene, cows by a stream at the foot of a hill, framed, 14 x 17" 1,430.00
Garden of Larkspur (The), exterior scene, path leading through garden to thatched cottage, copyright 1914, framed, 17½ x 21½" 74.00
Great Wayside Oak (The), exterior scene, framed, 7½ x 9½" 165.00
Heifers by the Stream, cows grazing in a pasture by a stream, framed, 8 x 12" 275.00
His Move, interior scene, bearded man & woman playing checkers, framed, 15 x 16" 495.00
Holland Express, exterior scene, framed, 4 x 9" 115.00
Hollyhock Cottage, framed, 18 x 22" 185.00

Honeymoon Cottage, framed,
11½ x 21"...................... 70.00
Indian Maidens, two Indian girls at
lakeside, rare, framed, 12 x 15".. 825.00
Into the Birchwood, original gift
frame, 22 x 26" 125.00
Jersey Banks, exterior scene,
framed, 14 x 17" 145.00
Life of the Golden Age (The),
framed, 13 x 17" 143.00
Little River with Mount Washington
(The), exterior scene, framed,
17 x 21"...................... 77.00
Maine Coast Sky, seascape w/pink
cloudy sky, framed, 11 x 14" 352.00
May in the Berkshires, framed,
7 x 9"....................... 135.00
Mills at the Turn (The), windmills at
the bend of a river, framed,
11 x 14"...................... 187.00
News in Brief (The), interior scene,
three ladies at table w/ironstone
tea service, fireplace in background, framed, 14½ x 17" 165.00
Old Settee (The), interior scene,
teenaged boy & girl on settee in
the parlor, framed, 11 x 17" 522.50
Pine Landing, framed, 7 x 11" 33.00
Pride of the Lane (The), exterior
scene, framed, 14 x 16" 42.50
Returning from a Walk, interior
scene of young lady in purple
dress on stairs, framed,
14 x 17"...................... 242.00
Sea Ledges, seascape w/waves on a
rocky shoreline, framed,
16 x 20"...................... 187.00
Southern Puritan (A), girl in purple
dress standing on a brick porch,
framed, 13 x 16" 550.00
Three Chums, interior scene of two
girls & a cat by a fireplace
w/pewter display on mantle,
framed, 14 x 17" 220.00
Unbroken Flow (The), framed,
12 x 21"...................... 55.00
Under the Blossoms, exterior scene,
sheep & lambs grazing, framed,
14 x 17"...................... 264.00
Way It Begins (The), interior scene,
man in red jacket watching young
lady playing piano, framed,
12 x 14"...................... 715.00
White Waves, sepia seascape, rare,
framed, 11 x 17" 143.00

MISCELLANEOUS ITEMS
Calendar, 1931, birches & country
lane pictured, gold metal frame,
3 x 4"....................... 77.00
Calendar, 1931, illustrated w/print
entitled "A Rug Pattern," in gold
metal frame, 3 x 4" 121.00
Colorist's instructions, model picture

w/instructions beneath, framed,
14 x 17" 242.00
Greeting card, Easter, exterior
scene & verse, rare, 4 x 10"...... 176.00
Greeting card, Mother's Day, silhouette on front, verse to mother
inside, 4 x 6" opening to
4 x 12"....................... 71.50
Greeting card, exterior scene above
a verse to a friend, 4 x 6" 77.00
Photograph, 19 Wallace Nutting studio employees including E.J. Don-
nelly, 1928.................... 110.00
Salt dish, turned walnut, footed, incised block signature 275.00

OCCUPIED JAPAN

*American troops occupied the country of
Japan from September 2, 1945, until April 28,
1952, following World War II. All wares made
for export during this period were required
to be marked "Made in Occupied Japan."
Now these items, mostly small ceramic and
metal trifles of varying quality, are sought
out by a growing number of collectors.*

Bank, bisque, model of an owl $60.00
Bust of the Madonna, bisque,
7" h.......................... 45.00
Candlesticks, bisque, figures stand-
ing on scrolls, petaled socket cups
& bobeches, 12" h., pr. 120.00
Clock, wooden, pop-eyed dog, 12".. 225.00
Creamer & sugar bowl, china, model
of red peppers, pr............... 15.00
Cup & saucer, demitasse, petal-
form, yellow, white & gold,
marked "Kipp Ceramics" 16.00
Figure of cupid w/horn, 3¼" h. 12.50
Figure of a girl, bisque, barefoot
lass w/basket at feet, 5¼" h. 18.00
Figure of a gondolier w/gondola,
bisque, 8 x 10" 90.00
Figures of ornately costumed man &
woman holding doves, bisque,
Victorian-style, 11" h., pr. 85.00
Figure group, men shoeing horses,
china, gold decoration, Ardalt,
13" h......................... 450.00
Lamp, china, figural Colonial couple,
w/original shade, 14" h. 40.00
Model of a black cat w/arched back
& tail raised, plaster-filled
celluloid...................... 9.00
Mugs, china, model of an elephant
w/trunk handle, 5½" w., 5" h.,
set of 4 .... 60.00
Parasols, paper & wood, in original
package, small size, set of 6 ..... 7.50

Planter, ceramic, model of donkey &
cart, large 6.00
Plaques, pierced to hang, full figure
Colonial woman & man in high relief w/upper portion of each away
from the background, 4¼ x 7¼",
pr. 40.00
Salt & pepper shakers, china, model
of a pelican, pr. 12.00
Salt & pepper shakers, china, model
of strawberries, 3¾" h., pr. 16.00
Tape measure, celluloid, model of a
bear 45.00
Tape measure, celluloid, model of a
pig 28.00
Toby jug, china, full-figure street
peddler w/tray of goodies,
7 3/8" h. 60.00
Toy, windup, celluloid, alligator
swallowing pencil w/negro
head 45.00
Toy, windup, celluloid, baby
crawling 25.00
Toy, windup, celluloid cat, chases
ball, 3½" 45.00
Toy, windup, celluloid, New York
Yankees baseball catcher 55.00
Toy, windup, "Circus Tricycle," celluloid boy rides tin trick cycle in
circles, mint in box 45.00
Toy, windup, tin, bear, brown fur . . .   65.00
Toy, windup, tin seal w/ball
on nose 15.00

OPERA GLASSES, LORGNETTES & EYEGLASSES

Art Nouveau Gold Jewelled Lorgnette

Eyeglasses, lady's, gold rimless style
w/hairpin $35.00
Eyeglasses, sliding brass frame 25.00
Lorgnette, Art Deco style, 14k white
gold w/onyx & diamond, the handle channel-set w/onyx & a round
diamond in 14k white gold mount-
ing, w/black cord 275.00
Lorgnette, Art Nouveau style, highly
chased & pierced 14k gold frame
& handle 550.00

Lorgnette, Art Nouveau style, highly
chased 14k gold frame & handle,
completed by a fine link chain,
set w/oval shaped amethysts,
ca. 1900 . . . . .1,430.00
Lorgnette, Art Nouveau style, highly
chased 14k gold frame & handle,
highlighted by an oval amethyst
& two small full-cut diamonds
(ILLUS.) 1,540.00
Lorgnette, gold-filled, on ornate
neck chain . . . . ,   95.00
Lorgnette, ivory w/carved handle,
France, 2¾" 150.00
Lorgnette, sterling silver
w/enameling 145.00
Opera glasses, mother-of-pearl &
brass w/long handle, made in
London, England 75.00

PAPER COLLECTIBLES

*Also see CHARACTER COLLECTI-
BLES, FIRE FIGHTING COLLECTI-
BLES, FRATERNAL ORDER ITEMS,
MAGAZINES, MUCHA ARTWORK, PA-
PER DOLLS, POLITICAL ITEMS, RA-
DIOS, ROYCROFT ITEMS, SIGNS &
SIGNBOARDS, STEAMSHIP COLLECT-
IBLES and WORLD'S FAIR COL-
LECTIBLES.*

Admission ticket, "Riverview
Amusement Park," dated 1942 . . . $18.00
Calendar, 1913, "Busy Man's,"
comic-style, colorfully illustrated
cardboard pages 15.00
Calendar, 1931, "Sacred Art Calen-
dar," N.C. Wyeth print of "Child
Samuel" on cover, 9¼ x 15½" . . .   40.00
City directory, "Polk's," St. Paul,
Minnesota, 1938 . . . .   25.00
City directory, Sioux City, Iowa,
1926 . . . .   10.00
Newspaper, "Boston Globe,"
November 23, 1963, "President
Kennedy Assassinated" 18.00
Newspaper, "Boston Record Ameri-
can," November 25, 1963, Oswald
shooting 18.00
Newspaper, "Chicago Herald,"
November 11, 1918, "Kaiser A
Prisoner - Krupps Arrested"
headline 17.00
Newspaper, "Lynchburg Republican,"
June 23, 1845, Lynchburg, Vir-
ginia, "Funeral honors to Gen.
Jackson, Ex-President of the Unit-
ed States...the announcement of
whose death just reached us..."
heavy black borders for mourning,
4 pp., 18 x 24" 400.00

Newspaper, "Manchester Union Leader," November 23, 1963, "President Kennedy Assassinated" 18.00

Newspaper, "New York Daily News," November 23, 1963, "President Kennedy Assassinated" 20.00

Newspaper, "Pittsburgh Post Gazette," May 7, 1937, "Hindenburg Explodes," front page only 25.00

Pamphlet, "Tidal Wave Sweeps Hawaii," 1946, report on worst one in modern history w/running story of the great disaster 7.50

Prints on cardboard, used to teach children how to tell time, shows all 12 hours of the day, illustrated by Mary LeFetra Russell, 9 x 12" prints, set of 12 .... 100.00

Program, "Ice Follies," 1954, Fitzwillis cover w/gorgeous Petty-type girl, Helen Rose costumes, 9½ x 12" 15.00

Program, "Indianapolis 500," May 1953 .... 8.50

Program, theatre, "Anna Pavlova Farewell Tour," book & program, 1924-25 .... 35.00

Program, theatre, "Judy Garland, Palace Theatre, New York, 1951," Judy on cover 18.50

Program & review stand ticket, "Tournament of Roses Parade," 1950, 2 pcs 12.00

Timetable, Greyhound Bus, 1943 .... 20.00

PAPER DOLLS

Advertising, "Clark's Spool Cotton," Bride, Bridesmaid & Bridegroom, set of 3 .... $30.00

Ann Sothern, uncut book, Saalfield No. 4415, 1959 .... 40.00

Barbie, Goin' Camping, uncut book, Whitman No. 1951, 1974 .... 15.00

Betty Grable, uncut book, Merrill No. 2552, 1953 .... 125.00

Blondie, uncut book, Whitman No. 993, 1945 .... 85.00

Claudette Colbert, uncut book, Saalfield No. 322 .... 65.00

Debbie Reynolds, uncut book, Whitman No. 1955, 1957 .... 35.00

Diahann Carroll as "Julia," uncut book, Saalfield No. 6055, 1968.... 18.00

Dolly Dingle, uncut sheets from Pictorial Review, 1930-31, by Grace Drayton, 13 different sheets 130.00

Dresses Worn by First Ladies of White House, uncut book, Saalfield No. 2164, 1937 .... 60.00

Fairy Tale Figures album, Luana Patten on cover, Hallmark, 1948 ..... 25.00

Grace Kelly, uncut book, Whitman No. 2609, 1956 (2 small cuts) 75.00

Jeanette MacDonald Costume Parade, uncut doll & paint book, Merrill No. 3641, 1941 .... 185.00

Lennon Sisters, uncut folder, Whitman No. 1979, 1958 .... 30.00

"Little Women," five dolls, uncut book, Saalfield No. 1377 .... 20.00

"Make Mary's Clothes," real cloth & patterns, Mary is heavy cardboard, Whitman No. 5338, 1940's, Mary 8" h 28.50

Malibu Skipper (Barbie's little sister), uncut book, Whitman No. 1952, 1973 .... 15.00

Mary Martin, uncut book, Saalfield No. 2601, 1952 .... 95.00

Minnie Warren, McLoughlin, complete in envelope 110.00

"Mouseketeer" Annette, uncut book, Whitman No. 1958, Walt Disney Productions, 1956 .... 28.00

Munsters, uncut book, Whitman No. 1959, 1966 .... 65.00

"My Little Margie," uncut book, Saalfield No. 1598, 1954 .... 75.00

Navy Scouts, uncut book, Merrill No. 3428, 1942 .... 35.00

Our Gang, uncut book, Whitman No. 900, 1931 .... 55.00

Our Soldier Jim, uncut book, Whitman No. 3980, 1943 .... 45.00

Pat Crowley, uncut book, Whitman No. 2055, 1954 .... 45.00

Piper Laurie, uncut book, Merrill No. 2551, 1953 .... 75.00

Polly's Playmates, "Phyllis In a Spanish Dance," uncut sheet, Boston Post, 1911 .... 25.00

Raggedy Ann, uncut book, Milton Bradley No. 4106, four dolls, eight pages of clothes, 1941 .... 43.00

Rhonda Fleming, uncut book, Saalfield No. 5191, 1954, w/coloring book 45.00

Rosemary Clooney, uncut book, Artcraft No. 1806, 1959 .... 65.00

Shirley Temple, "Now I Am 8," Saalfield, 1937 .... 20.00

Sonja Henie, uncut book, Merrill No. 3475, 1939 .... 200.00

The Tale of Peter Rabbit, uncut book, Saalfield No. 963, 1934, stand-ups 35.00

Twiggy, uncut book, Whitman No. 1999, 1967 .... 15.00

Vera Miles, uncut book, Whitman No. 2086, 1957 .... 100.00

White House Party Dresses, uncut book, Merrill No. 1550, 1961 ..... 25.00

PAPERWEIGHTS

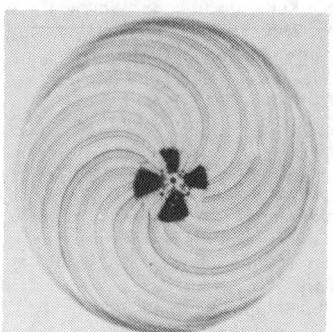

Clichy Swirl Weight

Advertising, brass, "PAX Granulated Skin Cleaners," model of a crowing rooster on a base, 6" l., 5" h. $40.00

Advertising, glass, "Best Pig Forceps - Compliments of J. Reimers, Davenport, Iowa," model of a pig, 6" 95.00

Advertising, glass, "Macbeth-Evans Glass Company, Pittsburgh, USA," w/picture of glass blower, 2½ x 4" 40.00

Advertising, nickel-plated metal, "Kerran Shell Bar Grate Patd June 8, 1908," model of stove grate, 4½" l. 15.00

Baccarat, faceted "Ducks on a Pond" weight, hollow interior w/three ducks, one colored & two white, swimming on a pond within a translucent green & white flecked border in imitation of water weeds, cut w/a window & six printies, on an extended star-cut base, 3 1/8" d. 5,500.00

Baccarat, faceted patterned millefiori weight, seven circlets in shades of blue, white & green-centered white, each enclosing a large arrow's head cane, the exterior flashed in ruby & cut w/a window & six printies above thumb flutes, 2 7/8" d. 3,300.00

Baccarat, dated close millefiori weight, tightly packed canes revealing in places short lengths of latticinio thread & including silhouettes of a monkey, a goat, a cockerel, a dog, a horse & w/a cane inscribed "B 1848," 3" d. 1,870.00

Baccarat, concentric millefiori weight, central pink & white star cane enclosed within three circles of canes in shades of pale green, white & blue within an outer cir-

cle of alternate red & turquoise & white canes, 2½" d. 605.00

Baccarat, "Pansy" weight, classic purple & yellow pansy w/central millefiori cane, green leaves & stem, pansy bud at side, clear ground w/star-cut base, 2¾" d. . . . 330.00

Baccarat, "Snake" weight, dark red reptile w/black spine markings lying coiled on a buff rockwork ground enriched in green & silver, 3" d. 9,350.00

Bronze, model of a crouching panther poised to pounce, dark patina, impressed on base "Tiffany Studios - New York - 887," 3¾" l., 1¼" h. 440.00

Cast iron, hotel-type, pyramidal base w/model of a silver eagle on ball at top, 7" h. 45.00

Cast iron, model of an eagle w/head turned to one side, its spread wings supporting the letters "N R A," on rectangular base, old blue & red paint, 3 5/8" h. . . . 75.00

Clichy, faceted double-overlay concentric millefiori mushroom weight, the tuft within six circles of canes in shades of green, purple, pink & white & w/pink roses alternating w/pale blue canes about a central turquoise cane contained in a basket of white staves, the sides overlaid in dark pink on opaque white & cut w/a window & five printies, on a strawberry-cut base, 3 1/8" d. (minor chipping to edge of printies) 5,500.00

Clichy, "Rose" weight, clear glass set w/a large rose cane w/numerous shaded pink petals about a yellow stamen w/a central red & green pastrymold cane, growing from a curved shaded green stem w/four serrated leaves & a pink & green bud w/three further leaves about the flower, 2 9/16" d. 4,400.00

Clichy, scattered millefiori weight, spaced colored canes in predominant shades of blue, pink & white set on a translucent emerald green ground, 3" d. 1,045.00

Clichy, "swirl" weight, alternate pale pink & white staves, radiating from a central large cobalt blue & white cane, 3 1/8" d. (ILLUS.) 1,540.00

Feldspar & gemstone weight, green chunk of feldspar mounted w/seventeen rubies and six diamonds in 14k gold settings incorporating two carved ivory snails, 14k gold conforming holder & central base w/monogram "CV" conjoined, 3¼" d. 1,375.00

Gillinder, flower weight, bright red flower w/two rows of petals about a swirl center growing from a green stalk & w/a red bud on a secondary stalk, w/two green leaves at the base, on a cushion of double-spiral latticinio thread, 2 7/8" d. 935.00

Lotton (David) weight, frosted clear weight w/iridescent green & gold heart-shaped leaves & pink flowers decoration, signed, 1977 ..... 55.00

Millville, "Rose" pedestal weight, the flower w/numerous dark red petals rising from three turquoise leaves, set in a clear glass sphere, on a circular foot, 3½" h. 880.00

Millville "Rose" Weight

Millville, "Rose" pedestal weight, the flower w/numerous bright yellow petals rising from three green leaves, set in a clear glass sphere, on a circular foot, 3¾" h. (ILLUS.) 1,320.00

Mt. Washington, magnum "Rose" weight, fully blown salmon-pink flower w/numerous petals about a central white & green cane, w/five greenish turquoise leaves showing behind & w/a green stalk, 4" d. 3,850.00

New England, "Apple" weight, naturally modeled fruit in shades of pink merging to yellow lying on a circular pad base, 3½" d. 1,100.00

New England, floral weight, three central millefiori cane "blossoms" upon a four-leaf stem, clear ground, 2¼" d. 110.00

New England, "Pear" weight, naturally modeled fruit of pink tint merging to pale yellow lying on a circular pad base, 2¾" d. 990.00

St. Louis, "crown" weight, dark red & green twisted ribbon alternating w/latticinio thread radiating from a central cluster in shades of pale yellow, blue & pink, 2¾" d. 2,090.00

St. Louis, faceted "Fruiting Vine" weight, bunch of ripe grapes pendent from an ochre stalk w/three green leaves, cut w/a window & a row of circular facets above six printies, 2¾" d. 3,850.00

St. Louis, close concentric millefiori weight, central claret & lime-green setup surrounded by five circles of canes in shades of green, blue, white, salmon-pink & pink & w/a circle of lime-green canes at the periphery, 2¾" d. 2,420.00

St. Louis, "Fuchsia" weight, clear glass set w/a flower composed of three bright pink petals about a cobalt blue stamen center w/long pink pistils & stem entwined w/an ochre branch w/four green leaves & three pink buds, set on a white latticinio ground, 2 1/8" d. 1,650.00

St. Louis, garlanded sulphide weight, portrait of a young Queen Victoria in profile to the left, set within a garland of alternate green & pink & white canes, the base flashed in amber, 2½" d. 1,430.00

Sandwich, "Pansy" weight, flower composed of two cobalt blue upper petals & three lower pale blue petals about a green & white "Clichy-type" rose cane stamen w/a red center, growing from a curved green stalk w/two serrated leaves, 2 13/16" d. 880.00

Sandwich, "Poinsettia" weight, pink flower w/ten petals about a white central cane, the stalk w/three green leaves, on a cushion of white double-spiral latticinio thread, 3" d. 495.00

Snow-type weight, boy & girl under an umbrella, bisque figures 20.00

Souvenir weight, round glass dome over lake scene of "Brainerd, Minnesota," 3" d. 30.00

Stankard (Paul), "Lady Slipper" weight, clear glass set w/two mottled pink blossoms partially exposing pale green stamen centers w/yellow-orange pistils, each w/four twisted brown & green leaves, other blossoms above & green stalks & tan roots below, dated 1983, 3" d. 1,650.00

Steuben, "crown" weight, clear, signed, 2¾" d., 4" h. 440.00

Terra cotta weight, model of setter dog lying down on rectangular base, signed "New York Architectural Terra Cotta Co., 1886," 3½ x 5" 75.00

PAPIER-MACHE

Papier-Mache Jewelry Cask

Various objects including decorative adjuncts were made of papier-mache, which is a substance made of pulped paper mixed with glue and other materials or layers of paper glued and pressed and then molded.

Cake plate, painted & gilded, molded border centering a highland hunting scene, mounted w/metal handle, Victorian, mid-19th c., 11½" oval (damage) $440.00

Candy container, figural Chinaman sitting on log, 4" 245.00

Candy container, model of black cat lying on box 125.00

Candy container, model of a black cat on pumpkin 120.00

Candy container, model of a Dalmatian puppy, 11" 27.50

Candy container, model of a donkey w/glass eyes, blanket on back, Germany, 5" 208.00

Candy container, model of a duck, wing lifts for candy, Germany 30.00

Candy container, model of an elephant, head comes off, turn tail & it's a music box 350.00

Candy container, model of rabbit, glass eyes, Germany, 6 x 7" 50.00

Jewelry cask, rectangular box w/domed lid w/angled sides, red ground decorated on sides & lid panels w/cream-colored reserves featuring colored transfer prints of 18th c. pastoral scenes w/figures, h.p. scroll trim, France, ca. 1880, 8 x 10½", 5" h. (ILLUS.) 250.00

Models of chickens, crudely molded white birds w/red & yellow trim, small rectangular wood base marked "Germany," 4¼" h., set of 3 .... 150.00

Model of a horse, life-sized, complete w/harness & tack, on wooden plank base (ILLUS. top next column) 1,430.00

Model of a horse, 16-hands high, dapple grey, real mane & tail....1,250.00

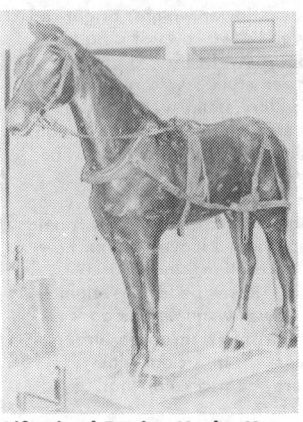

Life-sized Papier-Mache Horse

Model of a lion & a tiger, realistically painted, 4¾" & 6¾" l., pr. 130.00

Plate, decorated w/primitive painting of a cat, back marked "Patented August 8, 1880," small drilled hole for hanging, 12" d. (some wear & edge damage) 37.50

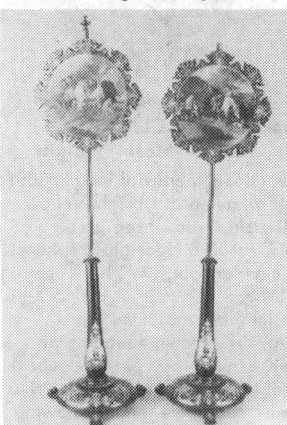

Victorian Papier-Mache Pole Screens

Pole screens, each adjustable circular screen w/scrolled & gilt-decorated borders centering a painted scene of hunters & their game, raised on a gilt-decorated pole w/a circular base & ending in scrolled toes, Victorian, mid-19th c., 4' 8½" h., pr. (ILLUS.) 1,650.00

Tea caddy, serpentine rectangular form, hinged lid w/mother-of-pearl inlaid leaves within a scroll border w/spandrels opening to a divided interior, conforming body w/gilt scrolls & medallion, Victorian, England, mid-19th c., 12¼" l. 385.00

Tray, cartouche-shaped, center finely painted w/an extensive bay scene

Fine Papier-Mache Tray

w/a sandy shoreline & a single figure in the foreground seated on a
cliff overlooking a city w/a central
church spire, tones of blue, brown
& green w/a red highlight, within
a gilt cavetto & border highlighted
w/scrolling foliate forms, artist-
signed, Victorian, second quarter
19th c., 26½ x 31¼" (ILLUS.) 1,870.00
Tray, octagonal, central polychrome
panel depicting tropical scene
w/two gentlemen making an exchange for a slave maiden on
black ground, Regency era,
England, early 19th c., 21¾" w. .. 412.50
Tray, oval, gilt-decorated gallery enclosing an inlaid mother-of-pearl
leafy central medallion, Victorian,
29½" l. (on faux bamboo stand of
later date)..................... 880.00
Tray, serpentine molded edge, center
w/painted hunt scene, England,
19th c., 23 x 31" (on modern stand
w/serpentine apron on tapering
cylindrical legs w/a cross stretcher,
20" h.)........................3,080.00

PARRISH (Maxfield) ARTWORK

During the 1920's and 1930's, Maxfield Par-
rish (1870-1966) was considered the most
popular artist-illustrator in the United States.
His illustrations graced the covers of the
most noted magazines of the day-Scribner's,
Century, Life, Harper's, Ladies' Home Journal *and others. High quality art prints, cop-*
ies of his original paintings usually in a range
of sizes, graced the walls of homes and offices
across the country. Today all Maxfield Par-
rish artwork, including magazine covers, ad-
vertisements and calendar art, is considered
collectible but it is the fine art prints that
command the most attention.

Advertisement, magazine, "Fisk Tire
- The Magic Circle".............. $45.00

Advertisement, magazine, "Jell-O,"
small 'King & Queen' 40.00
Advertisement, "Jell-O," small 'Polly
Put the Kettle On'..............   42.00
Book, "The Arabian Nights," illus-
trated by Maxfield Parrish,
1909 ....100.00 to 125.00
Book,"The Arabian Nights," illustrat-
ed by Maxfield Parrish, 1935
Scribner's reprint..............   38.50
Book, "The Golden Age," by Ken-
neth Grahame, illustrated by
Maxfield Parrish, 1899 ....   165.00
Book, "Mother Goose in Prose," by
L. Frank Baum, illustrated by
Maxfield Parrish, 1905 ....   650.00
Book illustration, from "Knave of
Hearts," Cooks & Tarts 25.00
Book illustration, from "Knave of
Hearts," King & Pomdibile 25.00
Book illustration, from "Knave of
Hearts," List of Characters 50.00
Calendar, 1927, for Edison-Mazda,
entitled "Reveries," large,
framed.......................   400.00
Calendar, 1928, for Edison-Mazda,
entitled "Contentment," small 195.00
Calendar, 1928, for Edison-Mazda,
entitled "Contentment," large,
framed.......................   400.00
Calendar, 1930, for Edison-Mazda,
entitled "Ecstasy," small 235.00
Calendar, 1942, for Brown & Bigelow
Publishing Co., entitled "Silent
Night," medium 165.00
Calendar, 1944, for Brown & Bigelow
Publishing Co., entitled "Thy
Rocks & Rills," large,
13½ x 18½".................   150.00
Calendar, 1945, for Brown & Bigelow
Publishing Co., entitled "Lights of
Home," medium................   175.00
Calendar, 1951, for Brown & Bigelow
Publishing Co., entitled "Day-
break," extra large, unframed ...   195.00
Calendar, 1962, for Brown & Bigelow
Publishing Co., entitled "Quiet
Solitude," full margins, 11 x 14" ..   30.00
Greeting card, "Afterglow," Brown
& Bigelow Publishing Co. 12.00
Greeting card, "Christmas Morning,"
Brown & Bigelow Publishing Co. ..   12.00
Greeting card, "Thy Rocks & Rills,"
Brown & Bigelow Publishing Co. ..   35.00
Menu, for the Broadmoor Hotel.....   250.00
Playing cards, for Edison-Mazda,
"Contentment," full deck.........   125.00
Poster, "Scribner's Fiction Number.
August," shows a profile of a nude
seated in a landscape, signed &
dated "Maxfield Parrish, 1897,"
metal process print on grey paper,
13 7/8 x 19 3/8"...............1,100.00

Print, "Air Castles," for Ladies'
Home Journal, 1904, 11 x 16" 160.00
Print, "The Canyon," House of Art -
Reinthal Newman, 1924, large,
original frame, 12 x 15" 138.00
Print, "Cleopatra," House of Art -
Reinthal Newman, 1917, small,
matted & framed, 6½ x 7½" 215.00
Print, "Cleopatra," House of Art -
Reinthal Newman, 1917, medium,
framed, 15 x 16" 450.00
Print, "Daybreak," House of Art -
Reinthal Newman, 1922, small,
6 x 10" 80.00
Print, "Daybreak," House of Art -
Reinthal Newman, 1922, medium,
10 x 18" 175.00
Print, "Daybreak," House of Art -
Reinthal Newman, 1922, large,
18 x 30" 252.00
Print, "Dream Garden," 1915,
7½ x 19½" 125.00
Print, "Dreaming," House of Art -
Reinthal Newman, 1928, small,
framed, 6 x 10" 65.00
Print, "Evening," House of Art -
Reinthal Newman, 1922, large,
12 x 15" 245.00
Print, "Garden of Allah," House of
Art - Reinthal Newman, 1918,
small, w/mirror, 4½ x 8½" 175.00
Print, "Garden of Allah," House of
Art - Reinthal Newman, 1918,
medium, original frame, 9 x 18" .. 89.00
Print, "Hilltop," House of Art -
Reinthal Newman, 1927, small,
6 x 10" 162.50
Print, "The King of the Black Isles,"
Dodge Publishing Co. & Colliers,
1907, 9 x 11" 50.00
Print, "The Lute Players," House of
Art - Reinthal Newman, 1924,
small, 6 x 10" 135.00
Print, "Reveries," House of Art -
Reinthal Newman, 1928, small,
framed, 6 x 10" 95.00
Print, "Reveries," House of Art -
Reinthal Newman, 1928, large,
14½ x 22" 350.00
Print, "Stars," House of Art - Rein-
thal Newman, 1927, small,
6 x 10" ....140.00 to 190.00
Print, "White Birch," 1931, trimmed,
9 x 11" 55.00
Print, "Wild Geese," House of Art -
Reinthal Newman, 1924,
12 x 15" ....145.00 to 195.00
Puzzle, jigsaw-type, "The Prince,"
1926, w/box 115.00
Thermometer, "Sunrise" print w/ad-
vertising, Thomas Murphy Co.,
1930's, 5 x 7" 200.00

PERFUME, SCENT & COLOGNE BOTTLES

Decorative accessories from milady's boudoir have always been highly collectible and in recent years there has been an especially strong surge of interest in perfume bottles. Our listings also include related containers such as pocket bottles and vials, tabletop containers and atomizers. Most readily available are examples from the 19th through the mid-20th century, but earlier examples do surface occasionally. The myriad varieties have now been documented in several recent reference books which should further popularize this collecting specialty.

ATOMIZERS
Amber glass, cylindrical body w/em-
bossed facing pairs of nude
maidens joined by leafy swags,
tall waisted cylindrical gilt-metal
top w/engraved floral swags, R.
Lalique $315.00
Amethyst glass, paperweight-style,
Marcel Franc, 1940's 135.00
Apple green glass, footed, w/origi-
nal bulb, DeVilbiss, 1920's 75.00
Cameo glass, baluster-form, carved
w/day lilies, leafage & grasses in
purple against a lemon yellow
ground, gilt-metal fittings, signed
in cameo "Galle," ca. 1900, overall 11" h. 990.00
Cranberry glass, etched Vintage pattern, DeVilbiss 60.00
Frosted clear glass, shouldered cylinder, "Enfants," frosted body
molded in relief w/a continuous
frieze of putti carrying a rose garland above their heads, stepped
shoulder molded w/three
recessed bands of flowerheads,
shaded w/traces of blue enamel,
acid-stamped block letters "R.
LALIQUE/FRANCE," ca. 1920,
overall 4" h. 935.00
Fuchsia glass, glowing color,
w/mesh bulb & cord, DeVilbiss,
6½" h. 107.00
Green opalescent glass, Coin Spot
patt., original bulb, 3" d. 40.00
Pink enameled copper, vase-shaped,
elaborately scrolled spout & handle, domed threaded cap,
w/plunger, beaded shoulder,
body, neck & foot covered in pink
enamel, marked "Sigmund Ster-
nau & Company, Brooklyn, New
York," ca. 1896, 7 3/8" h. 330.00
Rubina enameled glass, ormolu footed base w/red jewel in each foot
& one on top 110.00
Silver crackle glass, w/plunger,
DeVilbiss 45.00

Tomato red cut to clear glass, new
bulb 85.00
White opalescent glass, Coin Dot
patt., DeVilbiss 45.00
White Satin glass, decorated
w/heavy gold leaves & pink rhinestones, original label "Germany
US Zone," 3½ x 4½" 75.00

BOTTLES

Etched Glass Perfume Bottle

Acid-etched glass, clear w/heavily
etched criss-cross pattern,
small spherical stopper, inscribed "Marinot," France,
4¼" h. (ILLUS.) 2,640.00
Amber blown glass flask, simple
outline cutting w/circular
enameled painting on front of a
hunter w/gun slung over his
shoulder & smoking a porcelain
pipe, reverse w/a circle of small
blue & white enameled flowers,
1850's, 3¼" w., 4" h. (some wear
on enameling & small chips on top
near opening).................. 225.00
Amber cut glass, fan-shaped stopper, heavy, 7½" h.............. 450.00
Amethyst frosted glass, Cabbage
Rose patt., butterfly stopper,
3 3/8" h. 135.00
Apple green glass, cylindrical body
w/wide ring base & ring at shoulder, matching green cut pointed
stopper, decorated overall w/sat-
in cream scrolls & gold trim,
3¼" d., 6¾" h. 100.00
Aquamarine mold-blown glass, elliptical w/sloping shoulders, long
neck w/plain lip, obverse
w/scrolls, leaves & star inside Roman arch w/three rows of beads,
reverse w/large sunflower above
oval panel all within Roman arch
w/three rows of beads, open pontil, early 19th c., 4¼" h. 119.00
Aquamarine mold-blown glass,
Gothic shape w/deep paneled
base & sloping shoulders, long

neck w/flange lip, obverse w/two
columns framing Madonna &
Child, reverse w/latticed panels
between pillars, sides the same
except each diamond w/dot in
center, base panels w/dotted lattice, Victorian, 5" h............ 75.00
Black glass encased in ornate ormolu metal, engraved screw-on
top w/ruby stone, connecting
chain & bar pin, all gold-tone,
marked on base "Made in
France," bottle ¾ x 1", overall
length 2" 55.00
China, Art Deco fan shape w/ap-
plied flowers & rhinestones,
5 x 5½"....................... 75.00
Clear glass w/cranberry threading,
inverted cone shape on clear pedestal foot, clear bubble stopper
w/white lace spiral in center of
stopper, 2¾" d., 7½" h......... 140.00
Cobalt blue cut to crystal glass, bulbous body on tall slender facet-
cut pedestal base, pointed facet-
cut teardrop stopper, 7½" h...... 175.00
Cranberry glass, cylindrical body
w/rounded shoulders to slender
cut neck, decorated w/a garland
of blue & white flowers, green &
gold leaves, clear cut bulbous
stopper, 2½" d., 7½" h......... 140.00
Cranberry cased bluish-green glass,
paperweight-type, ball-shaped,
ball stopper, polished base,
2¾" d., 4½" h., pr. 195.00
Crystal glass, beaded gold trim &
lattice design around middle
w/colorful enamel flower in relief, rayed base, stopper w/thick
long dauber, 3" d. at base,
4¾" h......................... 30.00
Cut glass, clear, Art Deco abstract
faceted cuttings, paperweight-type
w/tall angled stopper, 6" h....... 38.00
Cut glass, clear, diamond & small
abstract cutting, block cutting under base, 1" sq. hollow cube stopper, square 1¾" base 28.00
Cut & enameled glass, baluster-form
body w/faceted pointed stopper,
body cut w/large roundels alternating w/vesicas, all h.p. w/poly-
chrome scroll & floral decoration
& ruby flashed outlines, 7" h.,
pr............................ 302.50
Cut overlay glass, bell-form body
cut from pastel blue to white to
clear w/a band of Gothic arches
around the body & small thumbprints around the base, hollow
trumpet-form stopper, gilt enamel
decoration in & around the arches
& on the stopper, 5½" h., pr. 330.00

Czechoslovakian glass, clear base
w/intaglio flower decoration, blue
double stopper w/dauber,
6½" h. 155.00
Czechoslovakian glass, clear w/mi-
ter cut decoration, w/stopper,
4 x 7½", overall 5½" h. 140.00
Czechoslovakian glass, clear w/gold
panels, applied h.p. enameled
flowers, original label 155.00
Czechoslovakian glass, transparent
topaz w/2¼" clinging topaz satin
bird on each side, heads resting
on shoulders of bottle, crystal
stopper, signed "Ingrid," 5" h. 85.00
English cameo glass, bulbous ovoid
body w/short foot, carved white
thorny raspberry brambles, leaves
& blossoms against red ground,
original cut glass stopper within
hallmarked silver hinged rim &
ornate chased cover, Thomas
Webb & Sons, 5¼" h. 1,650.00
English cameo glass vial, long teardrop form, carved white blossoming branch one side, reverse w/a
leafy vine, against a teal ground,
Gorham screw-on silver cap
w/applied monogram, probably
Thomas Webb & Sons, ca. 1900,
6¾" l. 770.00
Figural ballerina, porcelain w/blue
trim, stopper w/dauber, Germa-
ny, 7" h. 55.00
Figural clown, painted blown glass,
Germany 22.00
Figural Golliwog, round glass body
w/sealskin & glass head, "Le Golliwog" by Vigny, ca. 1922,
3½" h. 195.00
Figural monster, green blown glass,
Germany, w/paper label, 4" h. . . . 95.00
Figural sailor, frosted glass w/blue
tie & black hat & shoes, 3" h. 25.00
Figural "Scarlett O'Hara," glass &
plastic, Pinaud, ca. 1940, full,
6½" h. 55.00
Figural wicker-covered demijohn,
aqua mold-blown glass, rolled lip,
open pontil, 3" h. 45.00
Galle' glass, flared bulbous base
tapering up to silver rim, translucent green ground etched to depict blossoms, leaves & stems,
enameled in gold, lavender & yellow, w/matching flat glass enameled stopper, marked "Galle'
depose GG," 5¼" h. 2,090.00
Green cut to clear glass, cone-
shaped w/vertical bands of prism
& mirror cutting, clear facet-cut
stopper, 3" d., 6" h. 130.00
Ivory satin glass, w/silver top, flattened bulbous shape, green bam-

boo branches, maroon & green
flowers, gold bamboo shoots &
leaves, silver pull-off lid, Webb,
2½ x 3¾", 5½" h. 282.00
Lalique glass, "Ambre D'Orsay,"
square section, molded w/classical
maidens at the four corners, stopper molded w/blossoms, frosted
black, molded "Ambre D'Orsay
Lalique," 5¼" h. 1,980.00
Lalique glass, "Amphytrite, " model
of a snail w/a nude female figural
stopper, green, inscribed "R.
Lalique France," 3 7/8" h. 4,950.00
Lalique glass, made for "Worth,"
flattened spherical contour, butterscotch, amber & lemon yellow
sides molded in low-relief w/tiers
of chevrons, supporting a conforming stopper, molded "R.
LALIQUE/FRANCE" & "WORTH,"
ca. 1932, 5¼" h. 3,025.00
Lalique glass, "Marquita," trian-
gular, molded w/pearls, frosted
blue, inscribed "R. Lalique
France," 3½" h. 7,150.00
Malachite "lithyalin" glass, mar-
bleized green w/molded roses &
cut & polished sides, 5½" h. 250.00
Model of a Dutch shoe, clear glass,
5 7/8" l. 68.00
Pale blue shading to pink glass over
a middle layer of transparent yellow & white interior layer, exterior
w/heavy gold flowers & butterfly
decoration, round bulbous shape
w/sterling silver screw-on cap,
3½" d., 5" h. 1,215.00
Pink overlay satin glass, bulbous
body w/silver cap, enameled teal
green branches, blue flowers,
green leaves, 3¼" d., 4¼" h. 232.00
Porcelain, octagonal w/concave
sides, eight-pointed stopper,
decorated w/colorful flowers
against white on four panels, gilt
at corners coming across shoulders w/green & gold decoration,
florals on stopper, 2" w., 2½" h.,
pr. 58.00
Porcelain, square body w/blue
mushroom stopper, royal blue
ground w/white panels front &
back, gold decoration & flowers
on blue & pink, yellow & white
flowers w/green leaves on white
panels, 3 x 3¾", 5½" h. 130.00
Pressed glass, red-stained clear,
model of a scroll-embossed footed
inkwell, ornate scrolling feather
stopper, 6" h. 95.00
Rainbow satin mercury glass, ornate
blown-out shape w/enameled
florals, ornate silver plate neck &

figural floral screw-on top,
2¾" base d., 3½" h. 225.00
Ruby red glass, ovoid body w/cut
panels, panel-cut pointed mushroom stopper, gold trim on bottle
& stopper, 3½" d., 6½" h. 150.00
Satin glass, ivory ground decorated
w/ferns & bamboo leaves in
green, gold & maroon, sterling sil-
ver top, 3¾" h. 350.00
Silver plate, overall repousse deco-
ration, w/chained cap, Victorian,
ca. 1875-1900 . . . . 95.00
Spatter glass cased w/clear, gold
lettering across the body reads
"Ricksecker's Sweet Clover Cologne, N.Y.," brass ring-handled
stopper w/"Ricksecker's," 1¾" d.,
8½" h. 245.00
Sterling silver, bright-cut designs on
beveled sides, ribbed base &
shoulders, eight-sided screw-on
cap w/dauber, 1 3/8" w.,
1¾" h. 115.00
Sterling silver, cylindrical form
w/hinged cap, overall chased foliate decoration, attached swing
handle, the interior fitted w/glass
bottle & stopper, fitted leather
case, maker "S.M.," London, 1882,
2½" h. 192.50

Sterling Silver Perfume Bottle

Sterling silver, bottle-shaped w/long
cylindrical neck w/pair of lug handles w/attached chain, circular
screw-on cap, the ovoid lower
section unscrewing to reveal a
vinaigrette, the exterior w/en-
graved foliate spiraling bands & a
circular reserve w/monogram,
marked "Tiffany & Co. - Sterling -
Union Square," & "#2261" &
"#1354" w/an impressed oval
w/Gothic letter "M," ca 1870-75,
4" l. (ILLUS.) 880.00
Yellow enamel, oval lay-down type,
overlaid w/silver in the form of

flowers, screw-on closure
w/dauber, 2¼" d., 2" l. 245.00

PHONOGRAPHS

Victor Model D Phonograph

Columbia Type AA Cylinder, oak
case, w/horn $300.00
Columbia Type AO, w/large horn . . . 700.00
Edison Amberola 30 . . . . 350.00
Edison Fireside, Model A, oak case,
metal cygnet horn, ca. 1909 . . . . . 875.00
Edison Gem, Model A, metal case . . 375.00
Edison Opera, cylinder-type,
mahogany case, wooden horn, ca.
1912 . . . . 3,000.00
Edison "Red Gem," Model D, red
metal cabinet & red metal morn-
ing glory horn, ca. 1910 . . . . 750.00
Edison Standard, oak case, w/nice
horn, ca. 1899 . . . . 475.00
Edison Triumph, oak case, morning
glory horn, ca. 1901 . . . . 1,250.00
General Phonograph, child's, crank-
type, dovetailed wood case, original paint & decals, ca. 1920 . . . . . 650.00
Klingsor Gramophone, sound box,
horn aperture w/covering of lyre
& strings, crank at side, 11" d.
turntable, Germany, ca. 1910,
17" w., 35" h. 550.00
"Peter Pan" miniature gramophone,
black leatherette covered camera-
form case, 1920's, 4½" w. 275.00
Vanitrola Mini-Phone, portable
Victrola 165.00
Vanophone, Garford Mfg. Co. 50.00
Victor Model D, oak case, wood
morning glory horn (ILLUS.) 1,700.00
Victor Model O 875.00
Victor Model 6, mahogany case

w/fluted columns at the corners supporting gilt capitals, w/fluted mahogany horn 3,025.00

Victor Model VV-IV, table model, oak case 150.00

Victor Model VVXX, table model, oak cabinet, hand-cranked, brake & speed regulator, 12" turntable, plays 78 RPM, ca. 1915, 15 x 20".. 300.00

PHOTOGRAPHIC ITEMS

No. 1A Gift Kodak Camera

Almanac, "British Journal Photographic Almanac," 1917, hardbound, 780 pp.................. $75.00

Ambrotype, Civil War Union soldier, 2¾ x 3½" 65.00

Book, "History & Handbook of Photography," by J. Thomson, 1877, New York 85.00

Cabinet photograph, Annie Oakley holding rifle, 1870's-80's, 4 x 6½" 95.00

Cabinet photograph, Black minstrels, 1870's-80's, 4 x 6½" 25.00

Cabinet photograph, gymnast, 1870's-80's, 4 x 6½" 30.00

Cabinet photograph, Horace Greeley, 1870's-80's, 4 x 6½" 40.00

Cabinet photograph, man & his bike, early 1900's 12.00

Cabinet photograph, Sarah Bernhardt, Nadar (Paris), 1870's-80's, 4 x 6½" 65.00

Camera, B&J Press Camera, Burke & James, Inc., w/Graflex strobe 85.00

Camera, Bolsey B2, Bolsey-Delmonico Corp. of America, ca. 1948-49, w/case & flash.......... 22.50

Camera, Cycle Poco No. 2, Rochester Camera & Supply Co., ca. 1900, w/leather case 200.00

Camera, Eastman Kodak No. 1-A Autographic Jr., folding-type, original case, 1914-26............ 48.00

Camera, Eastman Kodak No. 2 Autographic Brownie, folding-type, ca. 1921.................. 23.00

Camera, Eastman Kodak No. 3 Autographic, 1914-26, w/original box & booklet 35.00

Camera, Eastman Kodak Bantam Flash, w/48mm F4.5 Anastar lens, 1947-53........................ 20.00

Camera, Eastman Kodak No. 2 Brownie, in original decorated Brownie box, 1901-24............ 65.00

Camera, Eastman Kodak No. 2 Beau Brownie, brown vinyl case w/metal lid set w/chromed metal geometric design of squares & rectangles, in brown hues, w/Kodak paper label inside, designed by Walter Dorwin Teague, 1930, 5" l., 5¼" h......1,320.00

Camera, Eastman Kodak No. 3A Folding Pocket Kodak, Model C, 1903-15........................ 25.00

Camera, Eastman Kodak No. 1A Gift Kodak, leather case w/hinged cover enameled w/geometric devices in medium & dark brown & orange edged in chrome, w/rectangular cedar box w/applied cover w/conforming decoration, designed by Walter Dorwin Teague, ca. 1930, w/original cardboard gift box & manual, 4 pcs. (ILLUS.) 2,860.00

Camera, Eastman Kodak Six-16, folding-type, 1932-36, w/case 21.00

Camera, Eastman Kodak Stereo Camera, 35 mm, complete w/"Kodaslide Stereo Viewer II," 1954-59........................ 135.00

Camera, Expo (EX100) miniature watch-style, Expo Camera Co., 1905-39...................... 150.00

Camera, Graphlex 3A, 1907-26, w/original carrying case 95.00

Camera, Polaroid Model 95, first model...................... 16.00

Camera, Seneca Scout No. 3, folding-type, ca. 1916, w/box & instructions 45.00

Camera, Voightlander "Stereofleckstoskop," stereo plate model, w/film holder, ca. 1914, 2 x 5¼"...................... 385.00

Carte de visite, John Wilkes Booth.. 55.00

Carte de visite, cats in human poses, "Chess," 1860's-70's, 2½ x 4"...................... 35.00

Carte de visite, Sgt. Boston Corbett, 16th N.Y. Cavalry, "Who Shot J.W. Booth," by Brady, 1865, Boston Corbett in uniform sitting in a chair alongside a table with the clock on it, Corbett appears to be reading a book w/his eyes cast down towards the book, 2 3/8 x 4" 850.00

Carte de visite, deep sea diver in

full gear, 1860's-70's, 2½ x 4" 40.00
Cartes de visite, Southwestern
American Indians, seven different
photographs of women, children,
warriors, etc., unknown photographer, 1860's, 2½ x 4 1/8", set
of 7 .... 1,500.00
Catalog, Eastman Kodak, 1923,
cameras & accessories 35.00
Daguerreotype, mother & children,
quarter plate 45.00
Daguerreotype in soft case, a Quaker couple, identified as Johnathan
Peabody & his intended bride, together w/a document certifying
his membership in the Quaker
community, 2 pcs. 82.50
Daguerreotype case, thermoplastic,
"Union Forever" 55.00
Photograph, Civil War, battlefield
view of Resaca Station, Georgia,
by George Bernard, ca. 1865,
11¾ x 14" 75.00
Photograph, Civil War, view of
Nashville from Courthouse, by
George Bernard, ca. 1865,
11¾ x 14" 95.00
Photograph, "Hawaii, Diamond
Head," w/buildings, ca. 1900,
framed, 8 x 18" 25.00
Photograph, Indian mother at grave,
by Barry, 7½ x 9½" 375.00
Projector, Kodascope, 16mm silent
film-type, first Kodak school model, ca. 1925 .... 450.00
Tintype, Civil War Confederate soldier, sixth plate 150.00
Tintype, full figure portrait of a lady
wearing an ankle-length black
gown, whole plate 25.00

PINCUSHION DOLLS

*These china half figures were never intend-
ed for use as dolls, but rather to serve as ornamental tops to their functional pincushion
bases which were discreetly covered with silk
and lace skirts. They were produced in a wide
variety of forms and quality, all of which are
now deemed collectible, and were especially
popular during the first quarter of this
century.*

Bisque half figure of a lady, molded
curls, arms away from body, torso
attached to stuffed body on china
legs forming base, Schneider,
"14275 - Germany," 3" h. $150.00
Bisque half figure of a little girl,
both arms away from body, wearing a yellow bonnet, Germany ... 100.00

China half figure of an Art Deco
lady, cloche hat, narrow jacket,
original pin-striped pincushion
skirt, "7190 - Germany" 98.00
China half figure of a Colonial lady,
right arm extends & returns to
hair, grey hair, yellow flower in
bodice, Germany, 3½" h. 40.00
China half figure of a Colonial lady
w/ribbon in hair, one hand on
hip, other holding blossom at bosom, "6347 - Germany," 3½" h. ... 65.00
China half figure of a Colonial lady
w/both hands at bodice, head tilted up, molded bouffant hairdo
w/molded decoration at top &
curls down the back, high-necked
bodice w/molded blossoms at
waist, "15503 - Germany,"
3¾" h. 40.00
China half figure of a Colonial lady,
long curls to shoulders, one arm
back to shoulder, other across
waist, low-cut bodice w/rose at
center, "5033 - Germany" 38.00
China half figure of a Dutch girl,
holds pink object in crook of arm,
arm slightly extends & returns to
object, Germany, unmarked,
2¾" h. 50.00
China half figure of a Dutch girl,
marked "Nippon," 5" h. 35.00
China half figure of a "flapper,"
nude lady, arms slightly extend &
return to breast, thin waist, black
flapper hair, Germany, 3" h. 60.00
China half figure of a "flapper," one
arm returns to waist, wearing
pastel orange cloche hat, blue &
yellow outfit, Germany, 4" h. 60.00
China half figure of a "flapper,"
nude w/right arm holding a small
fan & extended completely free of
body, other arm behind back at
hip, head tilted up, black bobbed
hair, molded earrings & necklace,
large expressive eyes, "8669,"
5½" h. 150.00
China half figure of a lady, head
tilted & wearing a domed cap
w/flowers molded at sides, one
arm behind back, other at front
holding a neck ribbon at bodice,
"5160 - Germany," 3¼" h. 30.00
China half figure of a lady, long
bunches of curls at each side of
slightly tilted head, one hand at
shoulder, other holding fan at
shoulder, row of bows down front
of bodice, "7942 - Germany,"
3½" h. 45.00
China half figure of a lady w/arms
out in front, mohair wig, lace
shawl, "4367½ - Germany,"
3½" h. 85.00

China half figure of a lady w/arms
away from body, head w/molded
curls at sides over ears & molded
flowers at one side, Schneider,
"14366 - Germany," 4" h. 65.00
China half figure of a lady, long
grey hair, one hand on head,
"16347 - Germany" 30.00
China half figure of a lady looking
down at hand, Goebel 375.00
China half figure of a lady w/arms
away from body, "6545 - Ger-
many," 1920's 250.00
China half figure of a lady clown,
pink hat & collar, both arms
slightly extended, one returns to
head, other to breast, Japan,
3½" h. 25.00
China half figure of Pierrette, head
tilted up wearing a black skull
cap, light brown hair curling toward right, arms extended & free
from body w/hands clasped close
to left side, "5768," 2½" h. 110.00
China half figure of Pierrette
w/arms extended free of body &
hands clasped near right shoulder, tilted head w/short brown
hair, black skull cap, grey eye
shadow, Dressel & Kister, Germany, 2½" h. 135.00
China half figure of Pierrette lying
on stomach, separate puff holds
the china legs 250.00
China figure of 1920's bathing
beauty, seated, h.p. bathing suit
& cap, 2" 45.00

design, gold trim, English Registry
No. 408444, the set 550.00
Flow Blue china, Oxford patt., the
set 495.00
Flow Blue china, Romantic patt.,
rectangular shapes, the set 750.00
"Gaudy" Ironstone, rose decoration
in underglaze-blue & red w/green
enamel, 10½" h. pitcher, 12¾" d.
bowl (minor crow's foot in bowl),
the set 275.00
"Gaudy" Ironstone, green, blue, red
& black florals, w/band of red
stick-spatter around neck of pitcher, marked "Malkin & Co.,"
12¼" h. pitcher, 13¾" d. bowl
(hairlines in bowl), the set 100.00
Ironstone, "Columbia" patt., octagonal pitcher & twelve-sided
bowl, blue transfer on white, W.
Adams, England, ca. 1850, bowl
13" d., pitcher 11¾" h., the set .. 200.00
Ironstone, white w/embossed design, ruffled rim, Homer Laughlin,
the set 90.00
Staffordshire earthenware, Blue Willow patt., small size, early
19th c., bowl 10½" d., the set
(ILLUS.) 192.50
Tole, old red repaint w/white trim &
painted scenes, heavily alligatored finish, 12¾" d., 13" h., the
set (worn) 175.00

PITCHER & BOWL SETS

Early Blue Willow Pitcher & Bowl Set

China, child's size, pink rose buds
on white ground, marked "Min-
ton," the set $350.00
China, flowing blue Art Nouveau

POLITICAL, CAMPAIGN & PRESIDENTIAL ITEMS

CAMPAIGN ITEMS

Cleveland & Harrison Figures

Bandanna, 1892 campaign, Cleveland (Grover) & Stevenson (Adlai
E.), pictures both men in draped
flags w/large eagle & shield,

reads "A Public Office is a Public Trust," framed, 22¾ x 23¼" $195.00

Banner, 1928 campaign, Smith (Alfred E.), cloth, large 495.00

Book, "Democratic Convention 1936," soft cover, 396 pp., 11 x 14" 95.00

Convention ticket, 1928, Republican Delegate 15.00

Figures, 1888 campaign, Cleveland (Grover) vs. Harrison (Benjamin), bisque figures wrapped in American flags suspended at each end of a wooden balance scale, 5½" l. (ILLUS.) 550.00

Handkerchief, 1888 campaign, Harrison (Benjamin) & Morton (Levi P.), printed cotton in red, white, blue & brown, outer edge border of bold stars around short bold stripes surrounding central design of spread-winged American eagle & stars above large crossed American flags overprinted w/oval portrait reserves of the candidates w/their names below, all above dated "1888" over "PROTECT HOME INDUSTRY," 22 x 24¾" (some penciled numbers) . . . 300.00

Hat, 1952 campaign, Eisenhower (Dwight D.), paper, "I Like Ike" . . . 12.00

Lithograph, 1856 campaign, Fremont (John C.), hand-colored print, "John C. Fremont, Republican candidate for 15th president...," N. Currier, small folio, matted & unframed, 10 x 14" (margin slightly trimmed, minor water stains, embossed stamp in one corner) 100.00

Lithograph, 1860 campaign, Lincoln (Abraham) & Hamlin (Hannibal), printed in color, "National Republican Chart - Presidential Campaign - 1860," shows presidential & vice-presidential candidates at Chicago, Illinois, May 8, 1860, published by H.H. Lloyd & Company, unframed, 28½ x 36" 660.00

Medal, 1960 Democratic Convention, John F. Kennedy on obverse 12.00

Pillow sham, 1904 campaign, Roosevelt (Theodore) & Fairbanks (Charles), cotton, double portraits, "Roosevelt/Fairbanks" & "1904 - Protection to American Industries," red, white & blue w/eagle flags, 24 x 24" 125.00

Pipe, 1848 campaign, Taylor (Zachary), red clay, the bowl modeled as the head of Taylor wearing a laurel wreath & w/"Old Rough and Ready" (no stem, some chips) 55.00

Pitcher, 1888 campaign, Harrison

(Benjamin) & Morton (Levi P.), ironstone, "For President/Benjamin Harrison," reverse "For Vice President/Levi P. Morton," w/portraits, sepia, 8" h. 385.00

Spoon, 1908 campaign, Taft (William H.), sterling silver, "Billy Possum" 175.00

Torch, copper, embossed spread-winged eagle w/double spout burners, old patina, ca. 1840-60, 9½" w., 23" h. (one eye holding wire bracket is missing; ferrule, post & bracket are replaced) 675.00

Walking stick, 1896 campaign, McKinley (William), tin shaft w/horn at top, stamped w/political slogan "Patriotism, Protection, Prosperity," 33" l. (mouthpiece on horn slightly battered) 85.00

NON-CAMPAIGN ITEMS

Advertisement, full page, "Chesterfield Cigarettes," Ronald Reagan, then actor, pictured, 1948 . . . . 25.00

Book, "Cartoon History of Teddy Roosevelt," by Shaw, 1910 . . . . . . 60.00

Booklet, "Roosevelt for King," satire on Franklin D. Roosevelt, 1937, 9 x 12" 35.00

Bookmark, Dwight D. Eisenhower, woven silk 22.50

Bust of President John Kennedy, chalkware, marked "Orland Statuary," Chicago, 1966, 12" h. 18.00

Game, "Who Can Beat Nixon," board game, 1971 . . . . 35.00

Inaugural pin & ribbon, Jimmy Carter, 1976 . . . . 5.00

Jigsaw puzzle, Spiro Agnew, 1970, never used 15.00

Letter, on U.S. Senate stationery, typed by John F. Kennedy, November 21, 1960, Palm Beach postmark 340.00

Lithograph, hand-colored, "George Washington at Mt. Vernon," group portrait of Washington & his family, by Kurtz & Allison, published 1889, gilt frame, 20 x 24" print, 26 x 30" frame (minor stains, small holes, margins trimmed, some frame damage) 70.00

Magazine, "Youth in Politics," 1946, cover features 29-year-old John Kennedy 45.00

Newspaper, "Chicago Tribune," 1948, November 3, "Dewey Defeats Truman" headline 550.00

Phonograph record, "President Wilson's War Message," spoken by Erwin Goodfellow, 1917, 78 r.p.m., 7" double disc, Emerson 25.00

Pincushion, "Teddy Roosevelt," on
the left a full figure Teddy
Roosevelt holding his hat, on the
right a full-figure bear holding on
to a stump pincushion lettered
"Teddy & the Bear," 3½" w.,
3¾" h. 150.00
Plate, china, Eisenhower & Nixon,
Vernon Kilns, signed "Davidson".. 30.00
Postcard, President Wilson in Court
of Honor, 1917 .... 8.00
Teaspoons, silver plate, Presidents
Washington through Johnson, set
of 34 .... 150.00

POSTCARDS

Advertising, "American Pipe Works,
Phoenix, Arizona," 1912 .... $5.00
Advertising, "Bull Durham's Trip
Around The World," South Ameri-
ca & Switzerland scenes, pr. 50.00
Advertising, "Cook's Cigarette
Case," picture of "Camels,"
1920's 9.00
Advertising, "Lemp Brewing Co.,"
1909 .... 10.00
Advertising, "Remington Guns,"
1950's, set of 4 .... 12.50
Advertising, "Rockford Watches,"
1910, unused 12.50
Advertising, "SA Horse Blankets,"
shows farmer, two children &
blanketed horse................ 10.00
Airplane, "Keep 'Em Flying," linen,
Series E, set of 7 .... 18.00
Atlantic City, New Jersey, 1908..... 2.00
Basketball, "State Champions -
1918-19," identified photograph
postcards of Edison College play-
ers, set of 10 ...., ... 34.00
Boston, Massachusetts, "Scollay
Square," 1900 .... 3.00
Brooklyn Bridge, 1906 .... 3.00
Brooksville, Florida, blacks in tur-
pentine works, set of 7 .... 65.00
Chinesé torture, atrocities, decapita-
tion, etc., photographic, set
of 20...................... 125.00
Christmas Greetings, Ellen H. Clap-
saddle artwork.................. 8.00
Christmas Greetings, Raphael Tuck,
"Father Christmas" 5.00
Comic, "Private Breger" series, art-
work by Sgt. Dave Breger, 1945,
set of 19 .... 35.00
Death Valley Scotty & his ranch, real
photographs, set of 12 .... 20.00
Fisher (Harrison), "American Girls
Abroad," the set 185.00
Hold-to-light, Christmas winter
scene 25.00

Long Point, Chautauqua Lake,
1912 .... 2.00
New York City, "The Flatiron Build-
ing," postmarked 1910 .... 5.00
New York City, "Metropolitan Opera
House," Raphael Tuck, 1906 ...... 6.00
New York City, "The Obelisk - Cen-
tral Park," Raphael Tuck 6.00
New York, "Niagara Falls," 1908.... 2.00
Oberammergau, Germany, 1910, set
of 50.......................... 50.00
Pasadena, California, Tournament of
Roses Parade, 1950, souvenir
packet 9.00
President, "Roosevelt & Family,"
pre-1910 (corner bump) 6.00
President, "President Wilson,"
France, 1918, set of 3 .... 15.00
Steamboat, real photographs, men
righting capsized passenger
steamboat, Series 7, 1900's, the
set............................ 21.00
Telephone, candlestick-type, real
photograph, 1913............... 6.50
Women, "Here Is To Women,"
signed by Ryan 5.00
World War I, "Negro Troops," real
photograph, France, 1919 .... 8.00

POSTERS

French Bicycle Poster

Almanac, "Paris - Almanach - Edite
par Sagot," lithograph printed in
colors showing turn-of-the-century
lady holding almanac, printed by
Imprimerie Bourgerie, Paris, 1894,
designed by Georges DeFeure,
framed, 23 7/8 x 31¼"........$2,200.00
Amusement park, "Cannstatter
Park," overall view of the park &
smaller view of a monument, Baltimore, Maryland, ca. 1915,
24 x 36"...................... 125.00
Animal show, Christy Bros. Wild An-

imal Show, depicting various wild
animals in cages amusing a crowd
of people, Riverside Print Compa-
ny, Chicago and Milwaukee, 3370,
framed, 28 x 42" 495.00
Bicycles, "Cycles Medinger," Art
Nouveau style scene of ladies w/a
bicycle, by George Bottini, printed
in color by G. Bataille, Paris,
France, 1897, framed, 34¼ x 49"
(ILLUS. previous page) 1,760.00
Boxing, pictures 35 boxers including
Joe Louis, Rocky Graziano, Sugar
Ray Robinson, Willie Pep, Billy
Conn, etc., 22½ x 28" 30.00
Cartridges, "Austin Cartridge Co.,"
titled 'Comrades,' ca. 1901 . . . . 465.00
Concert, "Woodstock," depicting a
white dove perched on a blue &
green guitar neck w/orange,
black & white lettering, signed in
pencil by the artist, 24 x 35½" . . . 418.00
Liqueur, "La Raphaelle Liqueur
Bonal," color lithograph scene of
waiter racing to catch a tray of
drinks falling from an early bi-
plane, France, dated 1907,
36 x 48" 300.00
Magic, "George the Supreme Master
of Magic," graphic & colorful
w/devils, pyramids, Geishas,
sphinx, witch & more, ca. 1930's,
27 x 41" 75.00
Movie, "The Lady and The Monster,"
car wreck scene, featuring Erich
von Stroheim, Richard Arlen &
Vera Hruba Ralston, ca. 1940's,
22 x 28" 110.00
Patent medicine, "Baldwin's Bilious
and Liver Pills," 1905, 20 x 26" . . .   40.00
Poultry feed, "International Poultry
Food," lithographed scene of a
lady & hen, No. 8 in a series 175.00
Printers, "Meeting of Printer's Association of New York," lithographed & mounted on cardboard,
oval inset bust of Albert B. Kriet-
ler, president of the Printer's
Union, ca. 1883, 26 x 32" 210.00
Red Cross, "Disaster Relief, " color
lithograph on board, Art Deco geometric design, 1929, 12 x 17" 25.00
Red Cross, "Have YOU a Red Cross
Service Flag?," scene of young
boy seated at window holding up
service flag, artwork by Jessie
Willcox Smith, World War I era,
dated 1918, framed, 21½ x 30" . . .   70.00
Syrup, "Alaga Syrup," Willie Mays
pictured, 1960's, 15 x 22" 20.00
Theatre, "To Die at Dawn," marked
"Goes Litho. Co. Chicago," three-
sheet size, 43 x 78" (minor resto-
ration) 150.00

World War I, "Be A U.S. Marine!,"
standing Marine w/gun drawn in
front of American flag background, James Montgomery
Flagg, ca. 1918, 28 x 42" 185.00
World War I, "Gee, I wish I were a
Man - I'd Join The Navy, Naval
Reserve or Coast Guard," pretty
young woman dressed in sailor
suit, Howard Chandler Christy,
ca. 1918, 27 x 41" 99.00
World War I, "His Home Over There
- YMCA - YWCA," snowy landscape w/welcoming home in
background, Albert Herter,
ca. 1918, 23 x 41½" 100.00
World War I, "Keep Him Free - Buy
War Savings Stamps," features
large American eagle, Charles
Livingston Bull, 20 x 30" 66.00
World War I, "Sure! We'll Finish the
Job," smiling farmer digging into
his pocket, Gerritt A. Beneker,
ca. 1918, 26 x 28" 71.50
World War I, "The Hun - his Mark -
Blot it Out - with Liberty Bonds,"
large red hand-mark above word-
ing, J. Allen St. John, 20 x 30" . . . 125.00
World War I, "U.S. Marines - Active
Service on Land and Sea - Enlist
at...," Marine in dress uniform
marching w/ship & city port in
background, Sydney Reizenberg,
ca. 1917, 28 x 42" 93.50
World War II, "Buy War Bonds," Un-
cle Sam shown, cardboard stand-
up type, 22 x 28" (never used) . . . 300.00
World War II, "Let's Finish the Job,"
Merchant Marine recruiting post-
er, Marth Sawyers, 20 x 38" 44.00
World War II, pictures Hitler as a
monkey & Uncle Sam as organ
grinder, dated 1943, 15 x 20" 20.00
World War II, "When the Lights
come on again - Buy Bonds Today," General Electric advertising,
large photographs of Lockheed
bombers & Sherman M. tank at-
tached, 24 x 32" 65.00

POWDER HORNS & FLASKS

Brass flask, "Colt," Navy-type,
6¾" $150.00
Brass flask, w/"E Pluribus Unum" &
13 stars, Civil War era, 4" 80.00
Pewter & brass flask, relief-molded
floral motif, mechanism complete
& working (flask seam needs mi-
nor re-soldering) 50.00
Horn, engraved w/stylized hearts,
stars, birds & spirit w/fish body,

initialed & dated "1883," wooden
ends (one missing) secured
w/brass tacks, bung hole w/old
cork, 6¾" l. (some insect damage
& old holes) 400.00

Horn, mottled w/carved nozzle end
& wooden plug w/metal hook
ring, 7¼" l. 60.00

Horn, engraved flowerheads within
petal borders joined by circle
chain swag, America, late 19th c.,
8" l. 55.00

Horn, engraved w/geometric designs & "James, Feb 1774, Amasa
Newton," 9¼" l. 170.00

Horn, wooden plug w/relief-carved
stylized tulips & stamped name "J.
Munro," center hole in plug restored to original condition,
9½" l. 85.00

Decorated Powder Horn

Horn, engraved designs of a spread-
wing eagle holding a ribbon
w/"E. PLURIBUS UNUM" beside a
cartouche w/date "1843," also a
figure in Indian dress wearing a
tricorn hat, holding a bow &
arrow, several dogs chasing a deer
& the words "Black Hawk," together w/original cord attached to
antler tip powder measure carved
w/a grotesque face & an eagle's
head at the tip, Midwestern, horn
10" l., the set (ILLUS.) 1,320.00

Horn, decorative ring carving at
end, 13¼" l. 105.00

Horn, pouring end faceted in two
tiers, wooden base plug w/incised
six-point star, painted green &
brown, late 18th c., 16½" l. 150.00

PURSES & BAGS

Beaded, Art Deco flowered designs
in dark reds, blues & golds, 2"
fringe, silver plate handle &
frame, marked "Germany,"
7 x 8" $50.00

Beaded, black, green, gold, chartreuse & silver Art Nouveau zig-

zag, diamond & floral designs, ornate silver frame, Germany,
7 x 10½" 100.00

Beaded, copper iridescent glass
beading, box-type, frame
w/braided, beaded handle, 5" w.,
5½" l. 65.00

Beaded, midnight blue bugle beaded
drawstring miser's purse 20.00

Early Embroidered Purse

Embroidered overall floral patterns
at intervals within a narrow floral
border, worked in Queens stitch
in orange, blue, pink, green & off-
white silk on a dark brown
ground, brown silk binding, pine
green silk lining, embroidered initials "H R M" & dated "1818,"
some yarn wear & damage to en-
closure tape, Pennsylvania, ca.
1818, 4 x 6" (ILLUS.) 495.00

Embroidered silk, square white silk
embroidered on the obverse w/a
spread-winged American eagle
beneath rose & pink stars & a stylized cloud-like banderole, the
whole within a delicate meandering floral border, the reverse w/a
basket of blossoms & leafage
w/two butterflies hovering above,
both sides initialed "CL," in gilt
metallic threads, Catherine Lee,
Massachusetts, drawstring closure, ca. 1790, 7 x 7½" (some
fabric loss) 4,400.00

Enameled mesh, aqua & pink diamond design, Whiting-Davis 60.00

Enameled mesh, gold, peach & rust
in ornate gold frame,
Mandalian 120.00

German silver mesh, flower embossed frame & ball trim 53.00

Gold finish mesh, pouch-type,
w/compact & mirror, gold mesh
strap & amethyst-set clasp 65.00

Sterling silver mesh, blue stone
clasp, 1920's 135.00

PYROGRAPHY

Pyrography is the process of producing designs on wood, leather or other materials by using heated tools or a fine flame. Commonly referred to as "burnt-wood" wares, creating these articles became a popular home craft earlier in this century after the invention of the platinum-pointed needle which could be safely heated. Prior to this a hot poker was used to scorch a design in the wood. But because of the accuracy the needle allowed, burning a design into wood became a hobby with many and companies issued kits with all the tools necessary to create the design on a pre-stamped softwood box or article. A wide variety of designs were available including flowers, animals and scrolls. Women were popular subjects and the rights to Charles Dana Gibson's famous "Gibson Girl" were obtained by Thayer and Chandler Co. of Chicago who also sold items pre-stamped with the Sunbonnet Babies. Modest prices are still associated with burnt-wood wares unless the overall workmanship or design is exceptional.

Box, cov., burnt design of Art Nouveau style girl & "Frank" on cover, 4 x 10" $14.00
Frame, holds six photographs of Gibson Girls, burnt design of "Old Sweet Hearts of Mine," signed "Gibson Girl" & also marked "Harper's," 16 x 19" 85.00
Glove box, cov., burnt scene of lady w/golf clubs 15.00
Glove box, cov., burnt design of red poinsettias 18.50
Handkerchief box, cov., burnt design of oak leaves & acorns 15.00
Plaque, burnt design of "Their First Quarrel," ca. 1905.............. 22.50
Woodburning set, "Magic Stylus," w/nine wooden illustrated plaques, in original box 22.00

RADIOS & ACCESSORIES

Book, "Experimental Radio," by Ramsey, 1929, Bloomington, Illinois, illustrated $10.00
Book, "Principles & Practical Radio Servicing," by Hicks, 1939, New York, illustrated................ 10.00
Book, "Radio Trouble-Shooting," by E.R. Haan, 1929, Chicago, illustrated, 361 plus pp.............. 12.00
Catalog, "Franklin Radio," 1932, receivers, parts, servicing, equipment, 16 pp.................... 8.50

Catalog, "Paramount Salesman Radio Electric Catalog," September 1927 .... 10.00
Instruction book, Atwater Kent Radio, 1929 .... 7.50
Magazine, "Radio Merchandising," August 1926 .... 6.00
Manual, "Vacuum Tubes in Wireless Communication," 1918, New York, illustrations, 174 pp............. 12.50
Radio, Addison, oblong molded maroon Bakelite case & knobs w/banded amber trim, Toronto, Canada, ca. 1935, 4 5/8 x 9¼", 6" h.......................... 660.00
Radio, Atwater Kent Model 30 ...... 100.00
Radio, Bendix Aviation Corp. Model 526MC, black & green marbleized plastic case............600.00 to 800.00
Radio, Coast-to-Coast, "Musicaire," brown Bakelite Art Deco style case 35.00
Radio, Concertone, coin-operated motel nightstand model, 25¢ play, original finish, working (back door missing) 295.00
Radio, Crosley Model 124, Playtime grandfather clock radio, 1931 .... 375.00
Radio, Crosley Model XJ 185.00
Radio, Emerson model CF255, brown Bakelite case, 3½ x 5 x 6½"..... 80.00
Radio, Emerson model CF255, brown Bakelite case, 3½ x 5 x 6½"..... 80.00
Radio, Emerson Model No. 508, portable model, white Bakelite case w/hinged top 50.00
Radio, Emerson Model 520, Art Deco style Catalin case 265.00
Radio, FADA, streamlined Bakelite case w/flat top & flaring rounded sides, narrow oval dial at top above speaker opening, caramel-yellow w/red accents, Long Island City, New York, ca. 1938, 5 3/8 x 11", 7" h. 605.00
Radio, FADA Model 209, brown plastic case.................... 120.00
Radio, FADA Model 711, Art Deco style green & white Catalin case.. 795.00
Radio, Firestone "Airchief," table model, red plastic case w/white dial 40.00
Radio, Freed-Eisemann FE 15, 5-tube model........................ 200.00
Radio, General Electric Model 415, ivory plastic case, working 20.00
Radio, Jetco, pay-type, Art Deco style oak case, 10¢ play, working 295.00
Radio, Kennedy Model 42 .... 275.00
Radio, Meck Trail Blazer, 1940's 100.00
Radio, Musicaire Model MD-16, red Catalin case 300.00
Radio, National Model SW-35, short-

wave model, metal case, 1946,
working 35.00
Radio, Philco Model 42.350, table
model, wood case w/dial & push-
button tuning, AM/FM &
shortwave 175.00
Radio, Philco Model 60, cathedral-
type, ca. 1933, working 185.00
Radio, Philmore, crystal set, original
box 30.00
Radio, RCA "Radiola Model 17,"
w/headphones, 1920's 75.00
Radio, RCA "Radiola Model 18,"
w/speaker, 1927 . . . . 240.00
Radio, Sentinel Model No. 1U352-2,
bright red plastic case w/orange
knobs, 1950's, working 85.00
Radio, Sonora Model No. RCU208,
table model, wooden case 25.00
Radio, Spartan "Blue Mirror"
Model 517, three-knob,
1936 . . . . 1,250.00
Radio, Willcox/Gay Model A33,
"Teledial," 1937 . . . . 100.00
Radio, Zenith "Long Distance," table
top model, brown Bakelite case,
top handle, 7 x 14¼", 8¼" h. 35.00
Radio, Zenith Model 6D015, brown
Bakelite case 40.00
Rado horn, wooden, morning glory
shape, "Amplion" 295.00
Radio speaker, Radiola 103 . . . . 125.00

RAILROADIANA

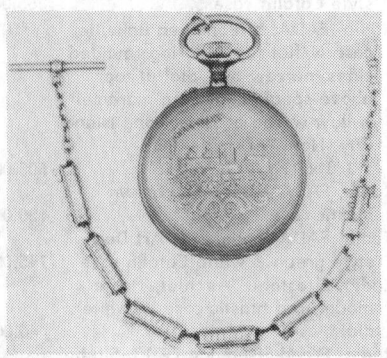

Silver Railroad Watch & Chain

Agent's hat, Burlington Route $95.00
Annual report, "Great Northern
Railroad," first annual, 1890 . . . . . . 10.00
Annual report, "Northern Pacific
Railroad," 17th edition, dated
1913, w/large map 20.00
Ashtray, "Santa Fe RR," Super Chief,
glass 10.00
Badge, "Frisco Lines" (St. Louis - San

Francisco Railway), nickel, mail
handler's 50.00
Badge, "Milwaukee Railroad," met-
al, waiter's 8.50
Badge, "Southern Railroad," metal,
baggage master's, cap-type 18.50
Baggage tag, "Northern Pacific,"
brass, monad logo, 2¼ x 2½" . . . 20.00
Blanket, Pullman, tan w/logo,
48 x 72" 115.00
Bond, "Pacific & Idaho Northern
Railroad," printed by the Ameri-
can Bank Note Co., 1899 . . . . 130.00
Book, "Historic Adventure Land of
the Northwest, Great Northern
Railway," 1927, softbound 14.00
Book, "Poor's Manual of Railroads,"
23rd annual, 1,423 pp. 125.00
Book, "Utah," published by the pas-
senger department of the Denver
& Rio Grande & the Rio Grande
Western Railroad, "The Scenic
Line of the World," pictures early
Utah, 1902, 80 pp. 20.00
Booklet, "California," by Union Pa-
cific Railroad, 48 pp., 1931,
softbound 25.00
Booklet, "Northern Pacific Railroad
Rocky Mountain Division Seniori-
ty," 1919 . . . . 10.00
Booklet, "The Railway Study Club
Series on Thermit Welding," by
Railway Educational Press, 1925,
illustrated 10.00
Bouillon cup, "Chicago, Indianapolis
& Louisville," china, mono-
grammed 125.00
Bouillon cup, "Wabash," china, ban-
ner logo decoration 65.00
Bowl, cream soup, "Soo Line," chi-
na, Only at Grandpa's patt. 100.00
Boxcar seal, "Danville & Western
Railway Company," copper 15.00
Bracket lamps, "N.Y.C.S." (New
York Central), brass, w/spring-
loaded candles, 6¾" h., pr. (no
chimneys) 95.00
Brakeman's uniform, "Santa Fe,"
w/cap & badge 195.00
Brochure, "Panoramic Views Along
the Denver & Rio Grande," color
illustrations, 1920's 10.00
Brochure, Santa Fe Railroad, "Winter
Excursion to Summerland," 1928 . . 5.00
Bucket, cov., w/bail handle, "D&H
RR" (Delaware & Hudson Rail-
road), metal, half of cover hinged
to open 40.00
Butter pat, "Baltimore & Ohio R.R.,"
china, blue, marked "Scammell's,"
3½" d. 38.00
Calendar, 1954, "Union Pacific" 20.00
Catalog, "Adlake Lamps," 1911, col-
or illustrations 75.00

Charter document, "Brotherhood of
Locomotive Engineers 1903," large
& beautiful, framed 295.00

Coffee cup, "Illinois Central," china,
Coral patt., unmarked 12.50

Coffeepot, cov., "Pennsylania Railroad," silver plate, International
Silver Co., individual size,
10 oz. 85.00

Conductor's hat, "N.Y., N.H. & H.
R.R." (New York, New Haven &
Hartford Railroad) 50.00

Cup & saucer, "AT & SF RR" (Atchi-
son, Topeka & Santa Fe Railroad),
china, California Poppy patt.,
Syracuse China 35.00

Cup & saucer, "Santa Fe," china,
Mimbreno patt. 165.00

Cuspidor, "S.A.L. RY" (Seaboard Air
Line Railroad), white enamel
w/blue lettering on side rim,
8½" d., 5" h. (minor rust spot) ... 50.00

Dessert spoon, "Illinois Central Railroad," silver plate, handle marked
"Illinois Central" 12.50

Fire extinguisher, embossed "Chicago Northwestern," glass,
3 x 18" 95.00

Fireman's shovel, "CMStP & P"
(Chicago, Milwaukee, St.
Paul & Pacific) 45.00

Flagman's kit, "Erie," can w/flag &
three flares, marked "Erie RR" ... 85.00

Hammer, ball-peen-type, "MKTRR"
(Missouri, Kansas, Texas Railroad), head marked 15.00

Hand towel, "UPRR" (Union Pacific
Railroad), white w/interwoven
white initials across white stripe,
16 x 17" 10.00

Kerosene can, "D&RG RR" (Denver &
Rio Grande Railroad) 20.00

Lantern, "CCC&StL Ry" (Cleveland,
Cincinnati, Chicago & St. Louis
Railway), Adams & Westlake bell-
bottom type, clear cast glass
globe, cleaned & lacquered frame,
marked on lid, 5 3/8" h. globe ... 92.00

Lantern, "C&NW" (Chicago & Northwestern), red cast glass globe,
tall 100.00

Lantern, "Colorado Midland,"
w/original globe 250.00

Lantern, "DM&N Ry" (Duluth, Mis-
sabe & Northern Railway), etched
amber glass globe, 1913 .... 425.00

Lantern, "Erie Railroad," whale oil,
tin, round tin carrying handle,
pierced tin conical cap, heavy
free-blown glass globe marked
"E.R.R." (Erie Railroad), removable
lamp (burner missing), base
marked "---J. SANGSTER PATENT
JUNE...," ca. 1840, 17" h. 550.00

Lantern, "Frisco," Handlan wire
frame w/twist-off bottom, red
cast glass globe, cleaned & lacquered frame, marked on lid,
5 3/8" h. globe 55.00

Lantern, "Missouri Pacific," Handlan
Buck bell-form twist-off bottom,
double wire horizontal bands, red
cast glass embossed globe
marked "M P" 190.00

Lantern, tin & glass, round carrying
handle, perforated conical cap,
ovoid red glass globe, perforated
star design tin base, removable
lamp w/early kerosene burner,
ca. 1840, 18" h. (some rust) 247.50

Ledger, "Atlantic Coast Line Railroad," freight way bill ledger, onionskin paper, covering 1924 to
1926, all handwritten, 1" thick x
15½ x 19½" (fair condition) 175.00

Locomotive ornament, painted sheet-
iron, silhouetted figure of a
running Indian chief w/full feathered headdress, drawn bow & arrow, painted yellow & red, America, last quarter 19th c.,
16" w., 23" h. 1,540.00

Map, "Burlington Route," United
States, 1900 .... 8.00

Medallion, "Illinois Central," centennial year logo, bronze 45.00

Menu holder, "Illinois Central Railroad," silver plate, w/pencil
holder, bottom marked 50.00

Milk bottle, "Missouri Pacific,"
½ pint 20.00

Mustard, cov., "New York Central
System," china 35.00

Napkin, "Burlington Route," white,
interwoven square center logo,
20 x 20" 12.50

Oil can, "CB&Q RR" (Chicago,
Burlington & Quincy Railroad) 15.00

Oil can, "Missouri Pacific Railroad" 40.00

Padlock, "Buffalo, Rochester & Pittsburgh RR," brass, w/key 40.00

Padlock, "C&O RR" (Chesapeake &
Ohio Railroad), brass, w/key 25.00

Padlock, "Union Pacific," brass,
heart-shaped, embossed on back
"Union Pacific Roadway & Bridge
Dept.," w/original key 53.00

Paperweight, "Chicago, Milwaukee
& St. Paul Railroad," model of a
bear 65.00

Photograph, 23 "Railroad Maintenance Employees," all holding
tools, pre-1900, 7x 9" 25.00

Pillowcases, inkstamped "Property
of Pullman Co.," white, 14 x 30",
pr. 12.50

Plate, "Burlington," Violets & Daisies
patt., 5½" d. 14.00

Plate, "MKT" (Missouri Kansas Texas
RR), china, Old Abbey patt., beige
w/blue band, Alamo in center,
back-stamped, 10½" d. 360.00

Plate, "Santa Fe," china, Adobe
patt., 9" d. 40.00

Platter, "Penn. RR," china, Mountain
Laurel patt., Syracuse China,
7½" l. 42.00

Platter, "Southern Pacific," china,
Wildflower patt., 9" l. 35.00

Playing cards, "Cotton Belt Route,"
each card has great color, black
girl eating watermelon, ace of
spades reads "Pullman Sleepers,
Parlor Cafe, fine reclining chair
cars," full deck w/original box
w/graphics & tax stamp, dated
1903 .... 250.00

Playing cards, "New York Central,"
pictures locomotive "Highlands of
the Hudson," extra picture of NYC
Station, boxed deck 25.00

Postcard folio, "CM&StP" (Chicago,
Milwaukee & St. Paul), 15 color
pictures, seven double-sided
cards, early 1900's, 5½ x 7" 15.00

Relish dish, "Union Pacific R.R.," china, Historical patt. 110.00

Salad plate, "Union Pacific," china,
Winged Streamliner patt., top side
depicts winged Art Deco train,
backstamped "Sterling China,"
6½" d. 30.00

Saucer, "Chicago, Indianapolis &
Louisville," china, 7¼" d. 100.00

Soup bowl, "Southern Pacific," china, Desert Flower patt., back-
stamped, 9" d. 37.50

Stock certificate, "Cape Cod Railroad
Company," 1854 .... 75.00

Stock certificate, "Chicago, Burlington & Quincy RR Co.," locomotive
pictured, 1900................... 8.00

Switch key, "Pennsylvania Railroad,"
brass 17.00

Swizzle stick, "Union Pacific," Gold-
en Spike Centennial 7.00

Tablecloth, "Burlington Route,"
white, interwoven square center
logo, 40 x 50" 20.00

Timetable, "Boston & Maine," 1925.. 20.00

Timetable, "New York Central R.R.,"
w/sale prices of 1907 World's Fair
(Jamestown) 22.00

Timetable, "Niagara Falls Short
Line," 1894 .... 38.00

Watch & chain, coin silver open face
case, Breguet jewelled gilt movement, white dial w/Roman numerals, subsidiary seconds dial, back
cover engine-turned & decorated

w/steam locomotive, together
w/plated figural chain consisting
of locomotive & various cars,
minor damage, 2 pcs. (ILLUS.
page 804) 1,100.00

REVERSE PAINTINGS ON GLASS

A Scene From "Sorrows of Werter"

Church & trees landscape, good
bright colors, early beveled
frame, 9 3/8 x 11 3/8" $300.00

Classically draped ladies in landscapes depicting the personifica-
tion of "Spring" & "Summer,"
good color, framed, 11¾ x 15¾"
(minor flaking) 375.00

Country landscape w/stone bridge &
half-timber cottage, old label on
back reads "Jane & Thomas Dun-
stan brought this picture from
England in 1872," ogee bird's-eye
maple veneer frame, overall
18½ x 26½" 125.00

Landscape primitively painted
w/scene of buildings, trees, lawn
& sky in red, white, yellow, black,
blue & green, beveled walnut
frame, 13½ x 15½" 255.00

"Napoleon," three-quarter length portrait of man in white uniform
w/gold & red on a green oval in a
black rectangle w/gilt flowers in
the spandrels, beveled frame
w/worn black paint, 12½ x 14½"
(upper right corner area of
flaking) 1,000.00

Profile portrait of a gentleman in
gilt against a black background,
in an elaborate rosewood frame
w/wide edges w/carved & gilded
corner fans, 6¼ x 7" 235.00

Portrait bust of George Washington
in oval reserve, shown wearing a
blue coat w/gold trim & white col-

lar, "Washington" below reserve,
10¼ x 12¼" (reframed) 450.00
Portrait bust of a young dark-haired
girl in circular reserve above
name "Rachel," good detail &
bright colors on orange ground,
paper edging painted blue (worn),
cloth tape hanger, 4 x 5 1/8". 135.00
Scenes from the life of Don Quixote
within Empire style giltwood
frames, Spain, 19th c., 21½ x
31½" frames, set of 5 . . . . .19,800.00
Scenes from "Sorrows of Werter," one
depicting Charlotte at the piano
singing to Werter, the other of
Charlotte & Werter expressing
their grief at her betrothal to
another, circular panels within
star-studded border & carved giltwood frames, Chinese Export,
early 19th c., 21½" w., 22" h.,
pr. (ILLUS. of one) 3,575.00

ROGERS (John) GROUPS

"Taking the Oath"

*Cast plaster and terra cotta figure groups
made by John Rogers in New York City in
the mid to late 19th century were highly popular in their day, originally selling for $10 to
$25. Many offer charming vignettes of Vic-
torian domestic life or events of historic or
literary importance and those in good condition are prized today.*

"Charity Patient" $650.00
"The Picket Guard," 1861 . . . . 750.00
"Taking the Oath and Drawing
Rations" (ILLUS.) 425.00
"Weighing the Baby" 450.00

ROYALTY COMMEMORATIVES

Queen Victoria Jubilee Plate

QUEEN VICTORIA (1837-1901)
Bracelet, sterling silver, commemorating 50 Year Jubilee,
dated 1887, 6½" l. $100.00
Bust, parian on wood base, base
painted black, back reads "Original in possession of the Queen,"
1897, 1¾" d., 6½" h. 90.00
Pitchers, 7" h., earthenware, bul-
bous body w/cylindrical neck,
brown handle, oval green portraits of the Queen in 1837 & 1897
on a blue ground, impressed
Doulton mark, artist-signed, ca.
1897, pr. 440.00
Plate, earthenware, brown & blue
transfer of Queen Victoria below
banner reading "County Borough
of St. Helens," & flanked by the
dates "1837" & "1897," com-
memorates 60th year of her reign,
6¾" d. (ILLUS.) 90.00
Program, memorial service held at
Trinity Church, 1901, lists those invited, limited to 200 copies,
40 pp. 6.00

GEORGE V (1910-1936)
Beaker, earthenware, commemora-
tive of 1911 coronation, shows
The Crystal Palace, Royal
Doulton 145.00
Box, cov., tin, George V & Queen
Mary Silver Jubilee, 1935,
3½ x 4¾ x 6¾" 35.00
Medal, metal, 1911 . . . . 12.00
Mug, china, Silver Jubilee, 1935 . . . . 40.00
Photograph, King George V &
Queen Mary, crown & scepter be-
tween w/"1911 June 22nd," poly-
chrome, 4" 60.00
Pitcher, china, 1911 coronation com-
memorative, Doulton, 5" h. 115.00
Plate, pressed glass, Silver Jubilee,
1935, scalloped edge, 10" d. 65.00

Plate, "Coronation of King George V
in 1911," blue & white, Wedgwood, 10½" d................... 125.00
Tray, brass, profiles of King George
& Queen Mary, 1935 Jubilee,
11" l. 28.00

George V & Queen Mary Wine Jug

Wine bottle, green & tan stoneware,
Andrew Usher Distillers, Cope-
land-Spode, 1911 coronation commemorative, 9½" h. (ILLUS.) 125.00

EDWARD VIII (1936, Abdicated)
Beaker, china, portrait of Edward,
4½" h........................ 40.00
Candy tin, rectangular, Edward
w/Windsor Castle in back-
ground 25.00
Creamer, china, for the planned
coronation in May 1937,
Wedgwood 25.00
Dish, china, square, prepared for
planned coronation of King Edward VIII, May 13, 1937,
Shelley 40.00
Scarf, "A King's Farewell," red on
white w/blue border, silk, 1936,
19" sq. 20.00

GEORGE VI (1936-1952)

George VI Coronation Plate

Ashtray, glass, amber, triangular,
portrait of George VI & Queen
Elizabeth 20.00
Basket, pressed glass, 7" h........ 30.00
Beaker, china, Wedgwood, 5" h..... 20.00
Beaker, china, scene of George VI &
family, Spode 50.00
Book, "Story of Coronation, George
VI," 1937, London, color illustra-
tions, 384 pp. 15.00
Creamer & sugar bowl, china, coro-
nation commemorative, Paragon,
pr............................ 49.00
Doll, cloth, wearing coronation
robe, ca. 1937, made by Farnells
Alpha Toys, London 500.00
Doll, cloth, full dress uniform of the
R.A.F., made by Farnells Alpha
Toys, London, ca. 1937.......... 450.00
Handkerchief, silk, pictures King
George VI & Queen Elizabeth 20.00
Mug, pottery, 1937 coronation com-
memorative, Moorcroft 165.00
Pitcher, 1937 coronation com-
memorative, jasperware, blue,
Wedgwood 75.00
Plate, china, King George & Queen
Elizabeth visit Canada & U.S.A.,
1939, Colclough, England, 9" d... 30.00
Plate, pressed glass, clear, "Corona-
tion of King George VI, May 12,
1937," w/crown in center, scal-
loped rim, 10½" d. (ILLUS.) 25.00
Spoons, figural, sterling silver,
"Monarchs of the Century, 1837-
1937," shows English kings &
queens, w/presentation box, set
of 8......................... 225.00
Toy, coronation coach w/eight
mounted horses, cast iron, 1937 .. 395.00

QUEEN ELIZABETH II (1952-)

Queen Elizabeth Coronation Cup & Saucer

Bowl, china, Queen, flags, etc., in
center, coronation commemorative, marked "Mid-Winter,
Staffordshire, Eng., semi-
porcelain," June 2, 1953,
4½ x 6"...................... 20.00
Box, cov., "Queensware," coronation portrait, 1953, Wedgwood,
5" d......................... 75.00
Candy dish, bone china, coronation

commemorative, 1953, portrait of
Queen Elizabeth II, dated "June
2nd, 1953" 75.00
Coloring book, 1953, coronation
commemorative, Saalfield. .12.00 to 15.00
Cookie jar, cov., china, Queen
Elizabeth & Prince Philip on cover,
Carr & Co. 26.00
Cup & saucer, china, coronation por-
trait, 1953, Aynsley, England 45.00
Cup & saucer, china, profile portrait
of Elizabeth, 1953 coronation com-
memorative, Royal Harvey,
Staffordshire, England (ILLUS.) 22.00
Cup & saucer, china, commemorat-
ing Queen's 60th Birthday 45.00
Goblets, glass, beautifully decorat-
ed, Silver Jubilee, 1977, by Raven-
head, pr. 75.00
Loving cup, china, "Coronation,"
1953, Royal Doulton, 10" h. 875.00
Mush cup, china, 25th Wedding Anniversary of Queen Elizabeth &
Prince Philip, 1947-72 . . . . 25.00
Pincushion, crown-shaped, corona-
tion commemorative, red velvet
w/gold wording, "Elizabeth II
1953" 48.00
Pitcher, pottery, relief bust portrait
of Queen Elizabeth, banner & royal coat of arms in gold on brown
glazed ground, coronation commemorative, 1953, Devon,
England, 4" h. 42.00
Pitcher, pottery, coronation portrait
in relief, 1953, Royal Doulton,
6½" w., 6" h. 135.00
Plate, china, Silver Jubilee, 1977,
sepia portrait in center, turquoise
border, 9" d. 35.00
Stamp box, cov., ceramic,
w/Queen's portrait, 25th Jubilee
commemorative, 1977,
Staffordshire 40.00
Trinket box, cov., china, Silver Jubi-
lee, 1977, Coalport 65.00

ROYCROFT ITEMS

*Elbert Hubbard, eccentric entrepreneur of
the late 19th century, founded Roycroft Shops
and established a craft community in East
Aurora, New York in 1895. Individuals were
trained in the trades of bookbinding, leather
tooling and printing. Craft-style furniture in
the manner of Gustav Stickley and known as
"Aurora Colonial" furniture was produced.
A copper workshop, begun in 1908, turned out
numerous items. All of these, along with the
Buffalo Pottery china which was produced exclusively for use at the Roycroft Inn and carries the Roycroft symbol, constitute a special
category associated with the Arts and Crafts
movement.*

Roycroft Copper Basket

Basket, hand-hammered copper,
twisted wire handle on cylindrical
body w/flared ruffled rim, decorated w/vertical blade & splotch
design, brass wash, signed
w/Roycroft logo, ca. 1920, 9" d.,
11½" h. (ILLUS.) $110.00
Book, "Justina & Theodora," by
Elbert & Alice Hubbard, published
by the Roycrofters, title page
designed by Dard Hunter in black
& orange, suede cover, hand-
illuminated, ca. 1906 . . . . 220.00
Bookcase, oak, rectangular top
w/stepped molded cornice over
panel incised w/"Roycroft" above
single beveled glass door & fluted
detail opening to shelves, long
drawer at base w/two incised orb
logos centered by applied molding,
marked "No. E 084," ca. 1904,
31¼" w., 60½" h. (minor
nicks) 5,500.00
Book ends, hand-hammered copper
w/leather owl inserts, pr. 75.00
Booklet, "A Message to Garcia," by
Elbert Hubbard, published by the
Roycrofters, signed by Elbert Hubbard, suede cover, hand-
illuminated, No. 348 of 980,
1899 . . . . 192.50
Bowl, hand-hammered copper w/sil-
ver patina, 6" d., 2¼" h. 40.00
Bridal chest, oak, extended serpentine sides w/keyed tenons centering a lift-top lid w/copper strap-
ware, box incised below latch
"Roycroft," Model No. 097, ca.
1912, 31 x 36½", 26" h. 7,425.00
Candleholders, hand-hammered
brass, dual bobeche w/flared rim
on cylindrical U-shaped stem
mounted to rectangular platform
base, stamped mark, early
20th c., 6¾" d., 6" h., pr. 330.00
Catalog, "Roycrofter's Catalog of

Epigrams, The Motto Book," 1909,
56 pp. 92.50

Desk, lady's dropfront-style, oak,
wide rectangular top above slant
front w/incised orb logo & two
wood knobs opening to fitted interior, above single long drawer
w/angular metal pulls, square
tapering legs w/club feet,
Model No. 091, ca. 1910,
18¾ x 39½", 44¼" h. 1,980.00

Dish, hand-hammered copper, shallow round form w/three pinched-
in notches spaced around wide
rim, central floral medallion,
signed w/Roycroft logo, early
20th c., 8¼" d. 165.00

Footstool, oak, rectangular w/ex-
tended tapering corner posts, side
stretchers, upholstered top, unsigned, ca. 1912, 12 x 17¾",
15" h. 357.50

Goblets & tray, hand-hammered
silver-washed metal, set of six
conical goblets on circular feet &
rectangular tray w/cut corners,
signed, early 20th c., goblets
3½" h., tray 7 1/8 x 19½", the
set. 247.50

Magazine, "Roycroft Magazine,"
October 1917 . . . . 12.00

Stand, oak, square top over wide
skirt w/incised "Roycroft," tapering splayed legs & lower stretchers, Model No. 050½, 12" w.,
20" h. (some roughness) 605.00

Vase, hand-hammered copper,
rolled rim on swollen form tapering towards base, signed w/orb
trade-mark, early 20th c.,
4½" h. 137.50

Vase, copper & silver, four buttress
handles w/applied silver squares
at their juncture to the rim,
stamped w/the firm's logo, ca.
1910, 7¾" h. 2,090.00

Walking stick, oak, square tapering
form incised w/orb logo & dated
"July 4, 1903," ca. 1903, 35" l.
(minor roughness) 495.00

RUGS — HOOKED & OTHER

HOOKED

Bird on branch in center, surrounded by stylized foliage scrolls &
straight bands at edge, woven initials at one end "F.E.B." & woven
date at other end "1920," shades
of dark red, orange, olive, black,
brown & tan on beige ground,

good color, 26 x 52" (minor
wear) $150.00

Canoes (2) on water being paddled,
each holding several figures, fir
trees on distant shore, good detail & color, initial "P" in bottom
corner, probably Grenfell but
unmarked 325.00

Checkerboard patt. of four patch
stripes w/alternating beige
squares w/three-part green & red
flower buds, soft colors, 23 x 38"
(some wear) 250.00

Collie dog, standing animal in black
& white on grey ground w/red &
tan border, 23 x 38" (minor
wear) 150.00

Conestoga wagon & team, yellow
houses, trees, girl fishing & other
details against colorful stylized
landscape, Amish, 27 x 49" 140.00

Cows (3) in a landscape setting
within an oval reserve, mottled
navy blue border, America, early
20th c., 26 x 47" 220.00

Dog, moss green animal w/variegat-
ed pink stripes surrounded by various geometric shapes against
textured brown ground, variegated striped border, America,
19th c., 31 x 60" 660.00

Dogs by fence, two Cocker Spaniel-
type dogs in front of flower bed-
lined white picket fence, wide
dark border, 23 x 44" (minor
wear) 165.00

Dog, Scottie, standing black dog
on red ground w/blue border &
polychrome floral decorations,
25½ x 40" (wear, edge
fraying) 155.00

Dog sled team w/three dogs & driver w/whip, shades of brown,
green, pink, grey & black on
white snowy ground, cloth label
"Grenfell, Labrador Industries,"
20½ x 32½" (minor wear & fad-
ing) 550.00

Eagle, bird w/wings spread standing
on a rocky ground, diamond patterned side borders, worked in
shades of red, grey, brown
w/purple accents on beige
ground, 20 x 38½" 425.00

Farm scene in a rectangular panel
depicting a red barn, purple
house & green trees, pond in
foreground w/ducks & chicks,
birds in flight in distance, Pennsylvania, early 20th c., 11 x 39" . . 275.00

Floral, stylized tulips center, oak
leaf corners, predominantly red
w/blue, olive green, white &
black, 25 x 48". 175.00

Floral & geometric design, stylized
flower & leaves on a cross-
hatched ground center within an
oval band w/further stylized
florals & foliage, floral corners,
rope-twist border, worked in
shades of olive green, grey, pink,
maroon, slate blue & black,
Amish, 25 x 40" 225.00

Floral Bouquet Hooked Rug

Floral bouquet, various flowers in a
bordered rectangular panel,
shades of red, yellow, blue &
green on a beige ground, America, 19th c., some wear, 31 x 55"
(ILLUS.) 605.00
Floral vines, floral vines looping
over & around rectangular center
band, ribbon bows at corners,
shades of blue w/yellow-green
leaves, Amish, made by M. Stoltz-
fos, Lane County, Pennsylvania,
ca. 1920, 27½ x 44" 85.00
Geometric design in shades of red,
blue, grey, white & black, Amish,
26 x 37½" 350.00

Geometric Hooked Rug

Geometric designs in a rectangular
panel w/a central large diamond
radiating four small diamonds
against a horizontal striped
ground, shades of black, white,
brown, blue & green, America,
19th c., 35 x 37" (ILLUS.) 302.50

Hooked Rug with Lambs

Lambs (2) worked in white in oval
reserve w/leafy sprigs on green
ground, bands of red & green floral sprigs near ends, all framed
by rectangular border, made by
Bernie Lami, Herman, Missouri,
ca. 1930, 23½ x 44" (ILLUS.) 247.50
Lion, recumbent animal in center of
rectangular panel within rope
borders surrounded by leafage,
pale tones of brown, green & red,
America, late 19th - early 20th c.,
29 x 55" 302.50
Melons & flowers center in shades of
red, green, yellow & purple on a
subtle tile-designed brick-red
ground, within a grape cluster &
vine border, America, initialed &
dated "1950," 65 x 93" 1,320.00
Parlor scene w/fire burning in large
stone hearth, tall case clock,
ladder-back chair, pictures on the
wall, curtains at the windows,
black & white dog & yellow cat,
made by Mrs. Yoder, Big Valley
area, Pennsylvania, ca. 1930,
26½ x 58" 4,290.00
Polo player on horseback in center
w/wide edge border, black,
green, red & other colors,
19 x 37" 175.00
"Purina Broiler Chow" repeated
twice in center, geometric checkerboard design top & bottom,
dark colors, 27½ x 36½" (some
wear) 265.00
Rooster & hen in barnyard, egg &
dart scallop pattern border in
brown, lavender & pale grey
frames multicolored center scene,
framed, 22½ x 36¾" 300.00
Sailboat worked in shades of brown,
beige, black & purple against blue
sky w/white clouds & two-tone
green sea, black border w/yellow
stripe, 20th c., 30 x 42" 500.00
Stagecoach w/passengers & driver,
pulled by team of four horses
driving along country road, background w/church, houses & multicolored trees, floral border at
bottom, America, 20th c.,
46 x 66" 880.00

Steam locomotive pulling train
across prairie w/raging fire in
background distance, done in
greys, browns, red, black, purple
& white, 30 x 34" (some edge
damage) 300.00
Triangles in a variety of colors,
joined by brilliant stripes, tape
bound edges, early 20th c.,
108 x 120" 825.00
Village scene in rectangular panel,
worked in shades of brown,
green, pale red & white, horse-
drawn cart in foreground, hills in
the distance, within striated black
& brown borders, America, early
20th c., 31 x 37" 137.50

OTHER

Needlework rug, rectangular
w/deeply zig-zag edges, black
wool twill ground w/embroidered
pattern of running squares each
containing an appliqued felt flower in red, yellow, green & blue,
some felt applique puffed out,
good colors, 27½ x 41" (some
overall wear & edge damage) 100.00
Needlework rug, rose-colored bows
& garlands w/naturalistic flowering vines rendered in petit point
within a needlepoint border of
pearl grey flowering vines on a
lemon yellow field, silk & wool,
England, late 18th c., 4' 1" x 5' 4"
(restorations)................. 1,760.00
Penny rug, embroidered felt, composed of overlapping tan & brown
petals w/embroidered blue & red
edges, the center applied w/a
brown oval panel embroidered
w/a vase filled w/three floral
sprigs in red & green on a brown
ground, America, early 20th c.,
28 x 34½" 467.50
Penny rug, appliqued & embroidered, elongated hexagonal field
appliqued w/purple, brown, green
& black circular patches decorated
w/floral sprigs in green, yellow,
ochre, white & brown, all on a
white field, the border w/dark
brown petals decorated w/multi-
colored stitching & white borders,
Iowa, early 20th c., 32 x 63" 275.00
Penny rug, appliqued felt, octagonal
rug composed of hexagonal & circular felt patches in shades of
blue, brown, green & off-white,
arranged in a star pattern w/cen-
tral floral medallion, America, ca.
1900, 35" d. 165.00
Shirred wool, rectangular field w/two
vases holding floral bouquets enclosed by a border of flowerheads

& clover, wool yarn fringe, worked
in wool fabric in shades of beige,
khaki, rose, burgundy, blue &
green on homespun ground, possibly Maine, mid-19th c., 28 x 53"
(some fabric & fringe loss)....... 2,640.00
Woven ingrain runner, floral design
in two shades of red w/border
down each side, 19th c.,
22½" w. x approximately 20' l.
(some wear) 115.00

SALESMAN'S SAMPLES

South Bend Chilled Plow Co. Replica

*The traveling salesman or "drummer" has
all but disappeared from the American scene.
In the latter part of the 19th century and up
to the late 1930's, they traveled the country
calling on potential customers to show them
small replicas of their products. Today these
small versions of kitchenwares, farm equipment, and even bath tubs, are of interest to
collectors and are available in a wide price
range.*

Axe, hatchet & hammer handles,
wooden, Kelley & Arrowhead,
16 pcs. in rollup kit............ $300.00
Baseball bat, wooden, oval embossed logo "Louisville Slugger,"
Hillerich & Bradsbury Co., Louisville, Kentucky," 7½" 20.00
Bed, cast iron, "Englander," spring
construction, painted blue........ 400.00
Brick, "Acme Brick," give-away to
be used as a paperweight 25.00
Cabinetmaker's chest, cherry, three-
drawer, America, 1830's, 25" h. .. 950.00
Cooking range, cast iron, "Early
Bird" 950.00
Display case, store-type, brass,
glass & wood, "General Case Co."
on brass tab, slant-front,
5½ x 13"....................... 245.00
Doorstop, cast iron, flower basket .. 35.00
Dust pan, metal, embossed letter-
ing, early 1900's 20.00
Fabric carrying case, "Redwood
Fabrics," three-section wooden
carrying case w/leather handle,

fine graphics inside lid,
7 x 10 x 22" 32.00
Furnace, metal, wood burning &
electric combination, in carrying
case 600.00
Hat, "Stetson," in original box 15.00
Horse collar, leather, 6½ x 7½" 85.00
Milk bowl, crockery, w/bail handle,
brown lining, 2½" 45.00
Parking meter, metal 95.00
Parlor stove, cast iron, "Round
Oak" 795.00
Piano stool, wooden, late 19th c.,
9" h. 145.00
Plow, pine & steel, splayed handles &
projecting plow support, the blade
below, painted & decorated in gilt
on a red ground, inscribed "South
Bend Chilled Plow Co. Pat. May 25,
1886 No. 15 trademark," ca. 1886,
23½" l. (ILLUS. previous page) ...1,980.00
Saddle, tooled leather, 1940-50's,
9" l. 125.00
Shoe, "Dr. Scholl's" 15.00
Tea kettle, cast iron, "Wagner," porcelain knob, spring handle,
3" h. 100.00
Washtub, wooden, yellow paint
w/stenciled label "Made by Jacob
Kirby, Middletown, Ind." & free-
hand trim, w/wooden interior agi-
tator & metal clamp-on wringer
w/rubber rollers 595.00
Window, wooden, double-hung style
w/automatic spring-operated
sashes, 14½ x 24½" 95.00

SCALES

Early Brass Scale

Baby weighing scale, tin, full-sized,
decorated w/dressed bunnies,
ducks & mice doing various human activities $45.00

Baker's scale, cast iron, w/brass
slide weight, painted red 125.00
Balance scale, countertop, brass, columnar standard supported on a
flared circular base w/projecting
arms supporting two circular trays,
stamped on one arm "H. Troemner,
Philadelphia," first half 19th c.,
27" h. (ILLUS.) 2,640.00
Balance scale, countertop, brass,
tapering cylindrical & knopped
standard supporting a balance
arm w/beaten brass circular
weighing pans, square base applied w/floral ornament, probably
England, 19th c., 4' h. 165.00
Balance scale, countertop, brass
w/original brass pan & large
brass dial, made by Wrigley's
Gum of Chicago, late 1800's patent date 125.00
Balance scale, countertop, painted
iron base & brass weight, beam &
pan, Empire Hardware Co., New
York, 1867 patent date 250.00
Balance scale, hanging-type,
wrought steel, w/double hooks on
each end, good detail, polished,
19½" l. 65.00
Butcher's scale, enameled metal,
"Standard Computing" 75.00
Butter scale, hanging-type, two
wooden round bowl-shaped pans,
carved center clothespin hanger,
hewn bar, 8" d. pans, 14" l.,
10" h. w/ropes................. 570.00
Coffee scale, brass-faced, "Ariosa
Coffee for 30 years, The Standard," 20 lb. size 75.00
Coin-operated sidewalk scale,
lollipop-type, "Peerless," blue
porcelain 850.00
Coin scale, balance-type, brass,
signed "W. & T. Avery," Birmingham, England, w/label in Spanish, made for Spanish market,
19th c., w/oblong mahogany box,
6¾" l. 242.00
Countertop scale, cast iron & brass,
"Perfection Scale," 5 lb. size
(professionally restored in deep
red paint) 95.00
Countertop scale, fan-type, green
metallic paint w/brass hardware
& pan, manufacturer's plaque
reads "Toledo Scale Company,
Toledo, Oh.," latest patent date
1917, gold, black & red lettered
decals on front, 14" l., 14½" h.... 155.00
Countertop scale, "The Micrometer,"
cast iron w/brass trim, Dodge
Sales Co., 5 lb. size (professionally restored in dark green) 150.00
Egg grading scale, brass, graduated-

type, mounted on rectangular
board, label & instructions
intact 130.00
Market scale, brass, hanging-type,
"Fairbanks," bushel size 275.00
Pharmacy scale, on oak base, cased
in glass, "Torsion Balance" 95.00
Postal scale, brass & steel, "Pelouze
Victor," dated 1898, 4½ x 4½" ... 27.00
Postal scale, nickel-plated metal
w/scroll panels, "Pelouze," 1895
patent, 5½" h................. 35.00
Steelyard scale, wrought iron,
"Chatillon, New York," 90" l.
(some rust) 25.00

SCIENTIFIC INSTRUMENTS

Astrolabe, brass, comprising plain
alidade w/shaped fiducial edge,
pin, horse, mater w/solid shaped
throne, the edge of the mater
engraved w/360 degree scale, &
rete for 26 stars, the reverse engraved w/altitude scales in the
upper half enclosing concentric
zodiacal calendar giving the vernal
equinox as 9 March, the central
portion w/shadow below signature
in arc & unequal hour lines, also
w/three plates, each w/locking tab
& each engraved w/various scales,
inscribed & signed by Muhammad
B. Ahmad Al-Battuti, North Africa,
1706-07, 20 cm d.............$11,550.00
Binoculars, by Ross of London, 1938,
in case 495.00
Kaleidoscope, "Bush," ca. 1875,
walnut stand (refinished) 1,000.00
Megalothoscope, wood, mounted on
paneled cabinet w/two long
drawers over doors, the instrument
w/tapered body tube w/paneled
shutters to admit light, series of
light stops & incorporating rotating
mount for photographic views, the
large viewing lens, focusing by
sliding handles, w/25 slides,
signed "Ponti, Venezia, Magaleto-
scopio, Privlegiato," Italy,
mid-19th c., 35½" l., 52" h.......1,100.00
Microscope, compound-type, lacquered brass, tripod foot, compass
joint to pillar of triangular section,
focusing by means of rack & pinion
to stage, England, second quarter
19th c., w/fitted mahogany case
w/numerous accessories, 7¼" l.
tube body, the set 1,210.00
Sun dial, tablet-type, wood, cover
w/printed & colored gazeteer, the
interior w/vertical & horizontal

string gnomon dials & glazed compass, Nuremberg, Germany,
19th c., 67 mm l................ 264.00
Surveyor's compass, brass, silvered
dial, blued steel needle, tangent
screw & vernier read-out for mag-
netic offset, two spirit levels &
detachable 7½" sight vanes, ball
& socket staff mount, Meneely &
Oothout, West Troy, New York,
1836-38, in fitted mahogany case,
15½" l. 770.00
Surveyor's transit, brass, mounted
on movable base w/telescopic
sight, marked "Buff & Berger, Boston," late 19th c., w/carrying case
& tripod stand, 15" h............ 440.00
Telescope, brass, two-draw, brass
cylinders w/canvas cover, braided
bindings at each end, marked
"Day or Night, Proctor Beilly &
Co., London," England, early 19th
c., w/cover w/hinged cover, case
painted deep green, case 22" l. ... 220.00

SCOUTING ITEMS

*Scout rules and regulations, handbooks and
accouterments have changed with the times.
Early items associated with the Scouting
movements are now being collected. A sampling follows.*

BOY SCOUT
Book, "The Boy Scouts in the Cana-
dian Rockies," by Ralph Victor,
1911 (fiction)................... $30.00
Book, "Golden Anniversary Book of
Scouting," 1959, Norman Rockwell
cover illustration, Golden Press,
New York 30.00
Bugle, brass, "Rexcraft" 32.00
Calendar, "A Scout is Reverent,"
Norman Rockwell artwork, 1940 .. 40.00
Diary, 1931, 3 x 4¾", 255 pp. 15.00
Figure of a Boy Scout, bronze-finish
metal, marble base, 1930's,
15" h......................... 60.00
Handbook, 1921, 3rd edition, 23rd
printing, Leyendecker cover 26.00
Hat, Scoutmaster's, 1930's, in origi-
nal box 95.00
Jamboree patch, first National Jam-
boree, to have been held in
Washington, D.C., but cancelled
due to a polio outbreak, 1935 .... 100.00
Medallion, "Get Out the Vote" cam-
paign, embossed scene of George
Washington praying, gold-colored
metal, 1952................... 15.00
Paperweight, cast iron, model of
Boy Scout's hat, painted 27.00

Shaving mug, earthenware, h.p. color scene of Scouts working around campfire, base marked "T.P.C.D. Co., Semi-Vit." 55.00

Sheet music, "March of the Boy Scouts," 1912, colorful cover 12.00

Signaler, "Fleron," official double set in original box w/Morse code instruction booklet, 1922 .... 24.00

Trade card, Boy Scout & dog, advertising "C.D. Kenney Co." 8.00

Watch, brass, "The Sunwatch," combination compass & sundial, instructions on inside of brass case, w/original green, black & orange box, 1921, 2 x 3" 40.00

Cub Scout cap & neckerchief w/slide, 1954 .... 15.00

Cub Scout membership card, 1936 .. 3.00

Cub Scout ring, sterling silver 17.50

GIRL SCOUT

Diary, 1937, used, 192 pp. 12.00

Handbook, 1940 .... 15.00

Lunch box, tin, rectangular box w/flat lid & swing bail handle, printed overall w/full color scenes of Girl Scouts camping, 6" l., 3" h. (some lid wear) 24.00

Ring, 10k gold-filled ....8.00 to 10.00

Uniform, complete w/hat, belt, pins & merit badges, ca. 1929 ...... 125.00

Postcards, "Camp Fire Girls," real photographs on cards, 1920's, set of 10 .... 10.00

SCRAPBOOKS & ALBUMS

Album, autograph, celluloid & velvet cover, dated 1896, 5 x 7½" $25.00

Album, calling cards & diecuts, cover w/three Santas w/feather tree & old toys, dated 1876 (spine broken) 95.00

Album, photograph, musical, celluloid cover, tintypes & old photographs, 1890's 125.00

Album, postcard, Art Deco cover, 76 unused cards of Florida, blacks, trains, etc., 1930's 50.00

Album, postcard, brown leather covers, great variety of cards including Halloween, Christmas, florals, leathers, souvenir & many series, America & Europe, 19th & 20th c. 440.00

Album, postcard, "Old Chicago," turn-of-the-century, historical Iroquois Theatre fire & White Amusement Park, all postcards prior to 1920, set of 400 .... 400.00

Album, postcard, w/75 European postcards 30.00

Album, trade cards, American Cigarettes, "Fish from American Waters," 1889 .... 50.00

Album, trade cards, American Cigarettes, "Terrors of America," 1889 .... 50.00

Scrapbook, w/newspaper & magazine clippings, programs & over 400 pictures pertaining to Nelson Eddy 80.00

Scrapbook, "Victory," cover w/flags, Saalfield, 1942, 35 pp. 29.50

SCRIMSHAW

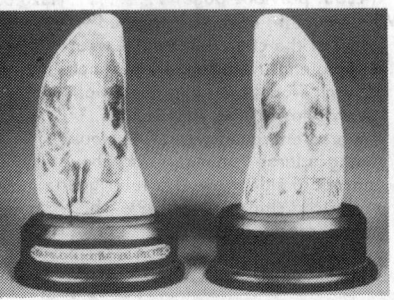

Engraved Whale's Teeth

In recent years a flood of fine grade hard plastic scrimshaw reproductions have appeared on the market and the novice collector is urged to learn to distinguish these new items from the 19th century pieces.

Cane, ivory Turk's head knob on metal inlaid, rope-carved & banded ivory upper shaft over incised whale bone lower shaft, America, 19th c., 35" l. (age cracks) $770.00

Corset busk, whale bone, shaped top, sketch of Washington at the top, three-masted schooner, front of the Capitol of Rhode Island at Newport & a sketch of Hancock at the bottom, late 18th c., 13½" l. 900.00

Cribbage board, walrus tusk, top w/cribbage game flanked by two eagles, a bear, walrus & branch w/a butterfly, reverse w/moose, factory building, an elk & the American flag, cap at one end to hold pegs, America, late 19th c., 23" l. 1,210.00

Letter opener, thin piece of whale bone, overall engraved decoration of anchor above a deserted whale boat, an eagle in flight, sun &

moon w/detailed faces; reverse
w/Masonic symbols of all-seeing
eye, heart above two olive
branches, large whale w/smiling
face, two-masted ship at anchor &
birds in flight above the ship &
whale, America, 19th c., 12" l. . . . 165.00
Whale's teeth, one engraved w/a
bust-length portrait of Paul Jones
above a banner inscribed "PAUL
JONES" over a rectangular reserve
depicting two ships flanked by an
anchor, the other depicting a full-
length portrait of Major General
La Fayette, each mounted on a
wooden base (each w/cracks &
filled w/zinc), signed "C. W. De
Montigny," New York, late 19th c.,
the first 9" h. overall, pr.
(ILLUS. previous page) 1,320.00
Whale's tooth, obverse engraved w/a
view of the church at Bethel w/a
stipple-engraved banner "Mariners
Church," above an engraved starboard view of the ship BETHEL,
reverse engraved w/a State House
flying a large American flag above
starboard side view of a full-rigged
American ship, ca. 1840, 9½" h.
(small crack on base) 7,150.00

SEWING ADJUNCTS

Miniature Sewing Box

Bodkin, turned & pierced whalebone, turned tapering shaft terminating w/a large flat finial
pierced w/a heart & scrolling
devices outlined w/pinpricking,
third quarter 19th c., 8½" l. $220.00
Books, "Singer Sewing Library,"
1929, colored advertising on
covers, set of 4 . . . . 15.00
Cloth clamp, clamp-on type,
wrought steel, table clamp base
w/thumbscrew supports cloth

clamp w/arched finger piece below small cloth pincushion at top,
5¼" l. 115.00
Darner, blown white cased in clear
glass w/apple green loopings,
bulbous head w/loopings extend-
ing to end of pulled-out handle . . . 605.00
Darner, tiger stripe maple w/turned
handle, tapered ball end, overall
6½" l. 95.00
Emery cushion, model of a rabbit,
velvet body w/glass eyes,
1½ x 2" 57.00
Eyelet punch w/sliding gauge, ebo-
ny handle, dated "Oct. 26, 1909,"
extended length 5¾" 20.00
Needle case, carved dark wood &
bone, model of an umbrella,
4" l. 102.00
Pincushion, needlework, heart-
shaped, the front worked in cross-
stitch in a geometric design, the
bottom flap worked in Irish stitch,
in pink, orange, blue & green
wool, probably New England, mid-
18th c., 2¾" l. (wear to
stitching) 176.00
Pincushion, painted silk, oblong
cream pillow edged in silk ruching
decorated w/a water-color portrait of a large Georgian house
w/attached barn surrounded by
trees & fences on one side & a
pin work & water-color wreath of
roses on the reverse, Massachusetts, ca. 1820, 7¼" l.,
5½" h. 357.50
Pincushion, velvet, red & black
dimensional ball-form w/four
stuffed, petaled flowers, attached
long red ribbon for hanging,
ca. 1860 . . . . 110.00
Scissors, buttonhole-type, marked
"Henry Sears & Son," 1865 patent
date 37.00
Sewing basket, child's, wicker, Pe-
king glass beaded tassels, 6" d. . . . 35.00
Sewing bird, clamp-on type, brass
bird & angular screw-clamp, embossed, blue velvet covered pincushion at top of clamp under bird
& smaller one on bird's back,
5" l. 175.00
Sewing bird, nickel-plated brass,
double velvet-covered cushions,
4¾" h. 105.00
Sewing box, miniature, stenciled
wood, rectangular top w/gold
stenciled fruit basket & inscribed
"Mrs. Susan Mathews" above conforming case w/four graduated
long drawers, each w/stenciled
decoration, America, 19th c., feet
missing, 9¼ x 14", 10" h.
(ILLUS.). 286.00

Tape measure, brass, model of a
royal coach w/red windows, Ger-
many, 3" 75.00
Tape measure, celluloid, model of a
fish, marked "Belfast, Mass.,"
4½" l. 28.00
Tape measure, celluloid, model of a
pig 37.50
Tape measure, metal, model of a
shoe, inscribed "Three feet in one
shoe" 95.00
Tape measure, porcelain, figural Art
Deco lady's head, tape inside
mouth 110.00
Tape measure, sterling silver, model
of a turtle 95.00
Thimble, brass, advertising, "Hud-
son's Soap" 39.00
Thimble, 14k gold, engraved,
Victorian 90.00
Thimble, gold, three-color, banded
w/green, gold leaves & gold
roses 350.00
Thimble, sterling silver, etched stars
on band decoration 30.00
Thread caddy, turned walnut,
domed foot w/narrow turned
short pedestal supporting wide
bowl-shaped container w/over-
hanging slightly domed cover
w/turned finial, interior w/wire
spindles for spools & a pincushion, original varnish finish
w/"102" painted on both base &
cover, bottom stamped "Pat'd
Nov. 12, 1887," 9" d., 8½" h. (mi-
nor edge damage) 65.00

SHAKER COLLECTIBLES

Early Shaker Cupboard

The Shakers, a religious sect founded by

*Ann Lee, first settled in this country at
Watervliet, New York, near Albany, in 1774
and by 1880 there were nine settlements in
America. Workmanship in Shaker crafts is an
extension of their religious beliefs and features plain and simple designs reflecting a
chaste elegance that is now much in demand
though relatively few early items are
available.*

Basket, cov., woven split poplar,
rectangular w/slightly rounded
sides, inside of flat cover inscribed in pencil "Lucy Bandby,"
4 x 7½", 3¾" h. $185.00
Booklet, "The Manifests," published
by the United Societies, Shaker
Village, New Hampshire, April
1884, 6 x 9" 35.00
Box, cov., bentwood gift-type, orig-
inal chrome yellow paint, inscribed
"From Abraham Perkins, Canterbury, N.H., Nov. 22, 1859," small
size 12,100.00
Brush, slender baluster-turned cher-
ry handle w/pointed button terminal attached to wooden bar
holding white horsehair bristles,
8¼" l. 75.00
Bucket, cov., laminated bentwood,
turned cover, bentwood swivel
bail handle w/knob fasteners,
printed paper label "Shaker's Apple Sauce, N.F. Mount Lebanon
N.Y.," original varnish finish,
7" d. (label stained) 300.00
Candle box, yellow pine, rectangu-
lar hinged lid opens to well of
conforming case fitted w/single
drawer, 19th c., 4 5/8 x 12 7/8",
5" h. 495.00
Carrier, bentwood oval, two finger
lappets w/copper tacks, bentwood
handle, original varnish finish in
rich alligatored brown, 8½" l.
(repaired break in one side &
rim) 350.00
Chest of drawers, tall, painted wood,
rectangular top over six small
drawers over six long drawers
each w/original turned cherry
knobs, rectangular cutout ends
& square canted feet, original
mustard yellow wash, signed in
drawer "Minnie Mortens," New
Lebanon, New York, 1840-50 . . . . 99,000.00
Cupboard, painted pine & poplar,
one-piece construction, flat molded
cornice above a rectangular recessed molded panel door opening
to shelved interior w/six tombstone compartments & recessed
drawer, a shorter door below
flanked by rounded corners, on a

flat base, old ivory-green paint
over old red stain, possibly Watervliet, New York, ca. 1830,
15 x 28", 7' 2¾" h. (ILLUS.) 1,540.00
Flour scoop, wood w/copper
fasteners, three-piece construction, half-round w/turned handle,
patent date of 1877, 7 x 14"...... 130.00
Mittens, woman's, woven, black,
pr............................. 45.00
Pantry boxes, cov., bentwood oval,
single-lappet construction, 19th c.,
graduated set of 6, 2 1/8" l. to
4¾" l., the set 4,950.00
Rocking chair w/arms, child's,
turned shaped finials above (replaced) woven red & green twill
tape back & matching seat,
shaped arms w/mushroom finials,
dark varnished finish, labeled
"Shaker's No. O, Mt. Lebanon,
N.Y.," ca. 1880-1920, 23" h.......1,650.00
Rocking chair w/arms, maple, four
arched slats joining turned stiles
w/elongated finials, woven tape
seat, turned tapering legs w/cuffs
where rockers are attached, possibly North Union or Union Village,
Ohio, ca. 1850.................3,630.00
Seed box, wooden w/original red
paint, labeled "Shakers Seeds, Mt.
Lebanon, N.Y." 1,430.00
Side chair, maple, three arched
slats joining turned stiles w/finials,
rush seat, turned legs joined
by double stretchers, old stain,
Canterbury, New Hampshire,
19th c........................1,870.00
Spice box, cov., bentwood oval
w/finger lappet construction, copper tacks, worn green paint, possibly Harvard Society, early
19th c., 4¾ x 6¼", 2½" h....... 220.00
Straw press, cherry, mortised &
pegged, w/threaded knobs,
Alfred, Maine.................. 880.00
Yarn swift, clamp-on type, all wood
w/original yellow varnish finish,
22" h. (end of one stave damaged
& w/overlapped repair).......... 125.00

SHEET MUSIC

"America Here's My Boy," 1917..... $15.00
"Adoring You," 1924, Ziegfeld Fol-
lies Vargas cover 42.00
"And They Called It Dixieland,"
1916, black Mammy on cover..... 12.00
"As Time Goes By," from "Casablan-
ca," Humphrey Bogart on cover... 12.00
"Barney Google Fox Trot," 1923,

"Barney Google Fox Trot"

cartoon cover, Jerome H. Remick
& Co., publisher (ILLUS.) 25.00
"Cat-Tails," 1927, cover by Grace
Drayton 35.00
"Charlie My Darling," ca. 1927,
Charles Lindbergh on cover 15.00
"Der Fuehrer's Face," 1942, Walt
Disney cartoon cover 25.00
"Feelin' Weary," 1929, cover by
G.G. Drayton 15.00
"Follow Thru," 1928, golf motif
cover 7.00
"Good-Bye Broadway, Hello France,"
1917, blacks on cover........... 9.00
"Harvey Girls," Judy Garland on
cover 12.00
"Like An Angel You Flew Into Every-
one's Heart," 1927, Charles Lind-
bergh on cover 15.00
"Lindy's Triumphant March, 1920's .. 12.00
"The Little Ford Rambled Right
Along," 1914, comedy cover, cars
causing chaos in road 25.00
"Little Nemo," cartoon cover 20.00
"Mammy's Chocolate Soldier," 1918,
Mitchell & Gottler, publisher 15.00
"March To Victory," 1942, Winston
Churchill on cover 17.50
"The Merry Old Land of Oz," 1939,
from the movie "The Wizard of
Oz," Leo Feist, Inc., publisher 30.00
"The Midnight Flyer," 1903, cover by
E.T. Paull, spectacular train
cover 35.00
"Mr. Ford, You've Got The Right
Idea," 1916, pictures Henry Ford
sailing on Ship of Peace 25.00
"My Mammy Knows," 1921, train on
cover 12.00
"Mystic Shrine March," John Philip
Sousa cover 12.00
"Napoleon's Last Charge," 1928, cov-
er by E.T. Paull 15.00
"Oh! Min," 1928, Andy Gump on
cover 35.00
"Ol' Man River," from the movie
"Showboat," special motion pic-
ture edition................... 15.00

"On the Good Ship Lollipop," Shirley
Temple on cover 10.00
"Over Yonder Where the Lilies
Grow," 1918, Norman Rockwell
cover 25.00
"Poor Little Rich Girl," 1936, Shirley
Temple on cover 14.00
"Prisoners Hope" & "Let the Rebels
Put That in Their Pipes," Civil War
era, 2 pcs.................... 48.00
"So Dear To My Heart," 1948, Walt
Disney tune.................. 10.00
"Something," lithograph of Beatles
crossing Abbey Road on back
cover 18.00
"Tara," theme of "Gone With the
Wind," Clark Gable on cover 20.00
"Three Little Words," 1930, Amos 'n
Andy color cover, Harms, Inc.,
publisher 30.00
"When the Ship Went Down,"
ca. 1912, Titanic on cover 25.00
"Yours For A Song," 1939 New York
World's Fair cover 15.00

SIGNS & SIGNBOARDS

Welch's Grape Juice Sign

Ale, "Carlings Red Cap Ale," tin
over cardboard, w/"Nine Pints of
the Law" policeman scene,
12 x 21".....................$100.00
Apothecary, painted wood, model of
a mortar & pestle, white w/gilt
highlights, 22½" h............. 247.50
Automobile oil, "Gargoyle Mobiloil -
Vacuum Oil Company," porcelain,
double-sided, red gargoyle
w/black letter on a white ground,
16 x 20".................... 120.00
Beer, "Ballantine's Brews - Newark,
NJ," self-framed tin, lettering
across bottom of frame, colored

scene of a seated 17th century
man smoking a long pipe & holding a stein of beer, marked "The
Meek Co - Mastercraft Metals,
Copyright 1909," 23 x 31" 725.00
Beer, "Lone Star," neon, star above
lettering surrounded by red outline of Texas, 19 x 19"........... 215.00
Beverage, "Bomba," embossed tin,
"You'll go for Bomba papaya
beverage," 1930's, 16 x 20" 40.00
Beverage, "Welch's - The National
Drink," lithographed tin, depicting
a bottle of grape juice on a simulated leather ground w/a band of
grapevines running horizontally in
the background, 8½ x 12"
(ILLUS.)...................... 220.00
Beverage, "Welch's Grape Juice,"
carved & painted wood, model of
a large bottle w/painted label,
America, 20th c., 30" h.... 880.00
Biscuits, "McVities," mother & children in living room, Mickey &
Minnie Mouse dolls on floor,
1930's, 15 x 19" 245.00
Bootmaker, painted metal, model of
a boot w/an exaggerated instep.. 522.50
Bread, "Merita Bread," embossed
tin, pictures Lone Ranger on Silver
above loaf of bread & wording,
24 x 36"...................... 675.00
Brewery, "American Brewing Co. -
Pittsburgh, Pa. - Brewery at Ben-
net, Opp 33rd St.," self-framed
tin, lettering above & below oval
center reserve w/colored scene of
ladies & gentlemen in ornate restaurant being served by a black
waiter, 24½ x 29" (substantial
wear, nail holes) 120.00
Car wheel chains, "Weed Chains,"
lithographed tin, name in large
letters across top above adjustable gas cost number w/"Gasoline
Today 16 Cents," to lower left "As
Necessary As Gasoline," & to lower right the rear end of an early
auto w/chains on the rear tire,
the sign is cut out to reveal the
various prices & amounts of gas
on a disc mounted on the reverse,
red & black lettering on a yellow
background w/shades of blue &
green, 17 x 23½"...............1,100.00
Cereal, "Grape-Nuts," self-framed
tin, scene of young girl walking
w/large St. Bernard dog above
wording "To school well fed on
Grape-Nuts - 'There's a Reason',"
20 x 31"...............500.00 to 800.00
Chocolates, "Fulton," die-cut litho of
two beautiful women & a nattily
dressed gent offering them choco-

lates from a box of the product, easel back, 20 x 23".............. 195.00

Cigarettes, "Camel," cloth-like banner, "I'd Walk A Mile For A Camel," 96" l., 44" h................ 125.00

Cigarettes, "Lucky Strike," tin, embossed cigarette pack, 1940's, round.......................... 40.00

Cigars, "John Ruskin Cigars," lithographed metal, Pony Express Rider pictured.................1,275.00

Cigars, "Marcosa Cigars," pine, model of a "rolled" brown painted cigar w/gilded band w/circular portrait medallions at either end, inscribed in relief-carved yellow painted letters, late 19th c., 59½" l........................3,575.00

Cigars, "Purity Cigars," lithographed paper, printed black on white w/"Purity Cigars - Now 5 Cents," framed & matted, 10 x 14¾"..... 12.50

Cloth, "Quaker Lace Cloth," lithographed cardboard, bust portrait of Quaker man above wording at bottom, framed, 13 x 23".. 50.00

Clothing, "Duxbak Hunting Clothes," self-framed tin, hunter & dogs in field, 1910, 16 x 19"............. 450.00

Coffee, "Arbuckles," tin, embossed girl & daddy, "It smells good," multicolor, 11 x 27" (some nail holes)...................... 195.00

Condensed milk, "Red Cross Condensed Milk," tin, red & yellow, pictures can, 4 x 19"........... 55.00

Crackers, "Grubbs-Kemker Candy & Cracker Co.," Nashville, Tn., printer's proof paper, pictures quail & crackers, 14 x 17"........ 65.00

Crystal Springs Dairy Farm

Dairy farm, "Crystal Springs Dairy Farm," painted canvas on wood, painted on both sides w/comical center scene of boys milking a cow, 40 x 60½" (ILLUS.)......... 500.00

Farming, "Farmer's Union Member," tin, blue w/white lettering, depicts walking plow, hoe & rake...................... 85.00

Fish seller, patinated copper, model of a full-bodied cod fish, 38" l. ... 715.00

General merchant, painted wood, lettered "Albert - Carter - dealer in - General Merchandise," black lettering on a white ground, 17¼ x 95"..................... 165.00

Gum, "Chew Carnation Gum and Taste the Smell," self-framed tin, pictures "Carnation Girl" w/bouquet, 1908, 13½ x 13½"......... 650.00

Gum, "Wrigley's," cardboard, "Extra Protection - Wrigley's - Kept Right in Cellophane," w/stylized running man, 1930's, 11 x 21"....... 50.00

Hatter, red-painted tin model of a top hat mounted above a projecting scrolled wrought-iron standard over a detachable red-painted glove, gilt trim, United States, mid-19th c., 39" w., 42½" h......4,180.00

Hotel, "Center Hotel," carved & painted pine, oval panel consisting of two cut & sized planks w/molded black-painted frame & wrought-iron straps, painted on both sides w/a standing chestnut horse w/lettering above & below, America, 19th c., 47" l., 37" h..........7,975.00

Ice cream, "Peter Pan," embossed tin, "Demand Peter Pan Ice Cream," "Take Home a Pint," w/figure of Peter playing pipes, 1930's, 16 x 20"................. 65.00

Inn, wooden, scrolled crest & base, centered by framed panel painted one side w/figure holding glass & reverse w/punch bowl on yellow ochre ground, above lettering "J. Read Inn," America, late 18th c., 35" w., 49½" h. (some damage to base) 1,210.00

Insurance, "The Concordia Fire Ins. Co. of Milwaukee," porcelain, 14 x 20"...................... 150.00

Insurance, "Continental," self-framed tin, Revolutionary War soldier w/musket, 1900, 20 x 31" 1,100.00

Jeweler's, wood & metal, model of a large pocket watch w/a gilt-painted frame & painted white dial w/Roman numerals, center inscribed "E.D. FREY, jeweler, engraver, optician," America, late 19th c., 14" w., 20" h. (some paint loss) 605.00

Locksmith, carved & painted wood, model of a skeleton key, painted brown, 76" l. 385.00

Milk, "Borden's," metal, Elsie the Cow in the middle of daisy-shaped sign, 24" d.............. 150.00

Motor oil, "Shell," tin, shell-shaped,

side-mount type, "Shell Motor Oil" 185.00

Paint, "Lincoln Paints," porcelain, flange-type, red, white & black graphics picturing Lincoln's head, 15 x 20" 200.00

Boschee's German Syrup Sign

Patent medicine, "Boschee's German Syrup for Coughs & Colds.," "Green's August Flower for Dyspepsia & Liver Complaint.," lithographed tin, seascape w/wording printed on rocky bluffs in background & fully-rigged ship w/people in right foreground, wood frame, abraded paint varnished, 12 x 18" (ILLUS.) 200.00

Pens, "Waterman's Ideal Fountain Pen," lithographed & embossed tin, Waterman advertising on dark ground beside another reserve w/"High Class Jewelry and Watch Repairing," both above white reserve w/"Caspar Ritzi, Brookville," colored in red, white & blue, 10 x 27½" 80.00

Rat poison, "Common Sense Exterminator Kills Rats," tin, rat wearing top hat & reading news of the dread killer, 7 x 8" 165.00

Roofs, "Mule-Hide Roofs," enameled metal, four-color w/picture of mule, flange-type, 21" d. 435.00

Saws, "Simonds Saw Blade Co.," enameled metal, worker holding axe, 1920, 14 x 20" 350.00

Skin cream, "Satin Skin," lithographed paper, color portrait of lovely lady holding fan & product containers w/advertising for skin cream & powder above & below, 1903, 26 x 42" 85.00

Soap, "20 Mule Team Borax," lithograph on cardboard, woman pouring soap on hands pictured, 14 x 27" 375.00

Soft drink, "Dub-L-Valu Root Beer," embossed tin, 1930's, 11 x 18".... 30.00

Soft drink, "Sun Crest," tin, bottle-shaped, 7 x 20" 65.00

Sporting goods, "Winchester,"

lithographed paper on cardboard, folding-type, center section w/colored scene of two hunters in a canoe, trap shooters & rifle range scenes on folding side panels, across the bottom in foreground are various types of ammunition manufactured, 38 x 56" 700.00

Tea, "Salada," porcelain, double-sided, model of a teapot, "Salada Tea Served Here" 150.00

Telephone, "Public Telephone / Independent," porcelain, double-sided, telephone in a circle, 11" sq. (very minor chips) 55.00

Telescope maker, copper, model of a single-draw spy glass, 62" l. (some dents).................... 412.50

Tobacco, "Bull Durham," lithographed paper under glass, colorful bull fight scene w/bull & toreador in the center of the bull ring w/royalty seated in box seats, "A Royal Victory," w/original frame, ca. 1909, 26½ x 44½" 907.50

Tobacco, "Mayo's Plug," canvas, rooster standing on tobacco plugs, ca. 1910, 24 x 60" 75.00

Toilet seats, "Never-Split Seats," self-framed tin, two toilet seats pictured, 13 x 19" 325.00

Undertaker, "Whitis & Lawhorn, Undertakers," painted wood, grey, olive, gold & black paint, 47½ x 69½" 300.00

Watches, "Elgin," wood, farm boy holding watch, 1900, 15 x 22" 350.00

Whiskey, "Cork," tin, "Cork Distilleries Co. Ltd.," bottle of whiskey & box pictured, 14 x 22" 75.00

Whiskey, "Paul Jones," self-framed tin, shows old man in straw hat pouring a shot 375.00

Whiskey, "Red Raven," metal, giant bird being hugged by Victorian girl, 1900, 24" d. 1,500.00

SILHOUETTES

These cut-out paper portraits in profile were named after Etienne de Silhouette, Louis XV's unpopular minister of finance and an amateur profile cutter. As originally applied, the term was synonymous with cheapness, or anything reduced to its simplest state. These substitutes for the more expensive oil paintings or miniatures were popular from about 1770 until 1860 when daguerreotype images replaced the vogue. Silhouettes may be either hollow-cut, with the head cut away leaving the white paper frame for mounting against a dark background, or the profile it-

self may be cut from black paper and pasted to a light background.

Edouart Silhouette of a Gentleman

Boy standing, full-length, black paper w/gilt detail on ink-wash background, back of frame labeled "D.W.R. Buchanan 1847," gold frame, 12½ x 15" $205.00

Bust portrait of a gentleman, hollow-cut & mounted on black cloth, ink inscription "Joshua Reed Giddings, U.S. Congress, 1838 - Thos. Edwards 1838," framed, 6¼" w., 7½" h. 300.00

Bust portrait of a woman, black paper w/brushed detail in black, white & gold on white background, framed, ca. 1840, 5¼ x 6½" 105.00

Cleric in a pulpit, full-length, cut & pasted on paper against an ink-wash church interior scene, probably Edouart, bird's-eye maple veneer ogee frame, 10¾ x 13½" ... 235.00

Family group, free-cut full-length gentleman smoking a pipe, gazing at his seated wife & child, flanked by two trees within a water-color landscape, 19th c., framed, 9¾ x 13¾" 308.00

Gentleman standing facing left holding cigar, hollow-cut & mounted on black background, top-hatted figure w/sketched background scene of a busy waterfront, signed in lower right "N. Orleans Feb 6, 184__," Auguste Edouart, framed, 6 7/8 x 10¾" (ILLUS.) 1,045.00

Young child in long dress, full-length, hollow-cut & mounted on black cloth, molded pine frame, 5¼ x 7¼" 195.00

SNUFF BOTTLES & BOXES

The habit of taking snuff (powdered tobacco meant for inhaling) began in 17th century France and reached its peak during the 18th century, spreading to England, elsewhere on the Continent, and even to China, probably introduced there by Spanish or Portuguese traders. In Europe, tightly hinged porcelain or metal boxes were considered desirable containers to house the aromatic snuff. Orientals favored bottles of porcelain or glass, or carved of agate, ivory or jade, often modeled in the form of a human figure or fruit. By mid-19th century the popularity of snuff declined and consequently production of these exquisite containers diminished.

BOTTLES

Aquamarine, small flattened baluster-form carved w/a man balancing a heavy yoke laden w/bundles of rice, reversed by a flute player riding on the back of an ox, carved w/butterflies at the shoulders, the lid in the form of a bird, China........................$1,100.00

Jade, cylindrical contour w/a slightly rounded shoulder & a long tapering neck, dark spinach green w/white & black inclusions, amethyst stopper, cabinet-type, 4 3/8" h. 165.00

Peking glass, flattened ovoid carved to one side w/bats above a sea & a rock outcropping issuing smoke & a flaming jewel, reversed by a small duck below a fruiting vine, red overlay, China 660.00

Silver-mounted agate, carved mottled brown agate of flattened ovoid form set on a high pedestal opposed by two silver dragon handles & enclosed by openwork set w/turquoise & coral stones & a collar of florettes, Mongolia (wear) 220.00

BOXES

Agate & silver, rectangular top inset w/agate stone, overall engine-turned design on silver, silver gilt interior, Nathaniel Mills, Birmingham, England, 1836-37, 2¾" l., 1½" h. 302.50

Brass, model of a heart, w/hinged top, engraved w/paddlewheel riverboat, New Orleans Packet, the name "The Eclipse" at top, 3½ x 3½" 395.00

Coin silver, rectangular w/hinged lid, flat chased on all sides w/ripple borders, palmette leaves at each corner centering a cartouche

medallion at center, unmarked,
America, mid-19th c., 2 x 3 1/8".. 137.50
Gold & enamel, rectangular w/cut
corners, the cover enameled w/a
putto in a garden on a blue
ground, the sides enameled black
& engraved w/leafage, maker's
mark "G.W.," Switzerland, ca.
1815, 3 1/8" l.................4,950.00
Ivory & antler, rectangular ivory
cover w/bas-relief carved scene
of pack of dogs attacking a wild
boar, slim rectangular box fashioned of split antler sections, 19th
c., 2¾ x 4 7/8", 7/8" h. (hinges
damaged, traces of silver foil on
interior) 220.00
Lacquer, round black lacquer w/flat
lid h.p. w/bust portraits of three
ladies in early 19th c. costume, inscription & signature on inside of
lid, 4" d. (painting alligatored,
edge chips) 105.00
Maple, w/hinged lid, speckled burl,
body carved from one piece, ca.
1810, 2 x 3" 130.00
Porcelain, rectangular w/the hinged
cover & sides painted w/a scene of
figures in a garden landscape, the
interior of the cover w/a similar
scene, Meissen, ca. 1765,
3½" w.......................2,420.00
Silver, cartouche shape w/molded
rims, cover engraved w/cypher,
w/interior hinged lid, Amsterdam,
Holland, ca. 1740, 1 7/8" l. 1,045.00

SOUVENIR SPOONS

Albuquerque skyline cut-out handle,
"Albuquerque" in bowl $54.00
Atlantic City cut-out skyline
w/named buildings on handle 45.00
Bear & California figural handle,
Long Beach, California Auditorium
in bowl........................ 18.00
Bear atop decorative handle, San
Francisco "Mission Dolores 1776"
& gold pan in bowl 38.00
Black jockey riding alligator figural
handle, "Old Gate - St. Au-
gustine" embossed in bowl....... 75.00
Blind Justice figural handle, "Court-
house, Hammond, Ind." in bowl .. 34.00
Chief Oshkosh on handle, "Oshkosh,
Wisconsin" in bowl 22.00
Eddy (Mary Baker) figural handle ... 130.00
Indian bust handle, reverse of han-
dle w/bow & quiver, unusual
shaped bowl w/scene of Niagara
Falls w/canoe, 1891 patent....... 55.00
Indian full figure profile handle

w/seated dog, bow & other
devices, "Hyannis, Massachusetts"
in bowl........................ 55.00
"Indiana" on handle, "State Capitol,
Indianapolis" in bowl 65.00
Kachina doll & Hopi snake dancer
on front handle, seated Indians
reverse, Arizona, Grand Canyon
embossed in bowl 45.00
Kansas City, Missouri handle, Con-
vention Hall in bowl (demitasse).. 35.00
McDermott Falls on handle, "Glacier
National Park" in bowl 22.00
Mormon Temple on handle, "Salt
Lake City, Utah" in bowl (demi-
tasse) 22.00
Presidents of the United States
figural handles, silver plate,
Rogers, set of 35 in fitted case ... 95.00
Skyline handle, Seattle in bowl 54.00
"Texas" w/steer & star in wreath on
handle, bowl w/head of longhorn
steer & "Pride of Texas, Houston,
10-14-02" 45.00
Texas State, Alamo Bldg., cotton
bale, longhorn steer & Confederate Monument on front of handle,
Lone Star, Texas reverse, plain
bowl.......................... 28.00
Wisconsin State emblem & motto
handle, "Dells - Kilbourn" written
in bowl........................ 23.00
"Yellowstone Park," full-figure bear,
stag's head & buffalo head on
handle, falls & other scenes on reverse lower, falls etched in
bowl 30.00

SPINNING WHEELS

Early American Flax Wheel

Flax wheel, turned wood, round

wheel w/turned spokes, raised on bobbin turned legs joined by a trestle stretcher, retains traces of original green paint, America, 19th c., 16" w., 28¼" h. $357.50

Flax wheel, blue-painted wood, round wheel w/baluster-turned spokes, flared rectangular support w/turned cylindrical arm supporting cylindrical winders, raised on turned cylindrical legs joined by a trestle movable stretcher, probably New England, ca. 1860, 38" l., 35" h. 440.00

Flax wheel, green-painted hardwood, wheel w/twelve turned spokes on base w/turned raking legs, complete 275.00

Flax wheel, turned wood, round wheel w/simply turned spokes, canted base w/turned legs joined by trestle stretcher, marked "B. Sanford," Connecticut, ca. 1820 (ILLUS. previous page) 200.00

Wool wheel, wheel w/eleven spokes on turned upright, base w/splayed turned legs, old brown patina, 48" d. wheel, overall 61" h. 275.00

STATUARY

Bronzes, and other statuary, are increasingly popular with today's collectors. Particularly appealing are works by "Les Animaliers," the 19th century French school of sculptors who turned to animals for their subject-matter. These, together with figures in the Art Deco and Art Nouveau taste, are available in a wide price range.

BRONZES

Bronze Figure of a Young Hunter

Aitken, Robert Ingersoll, figure of

Diana, dark greenish brown patina, signed "Aitken" & stamped "Roman Bronze Works N-Y-Foundry," 32" h. $14,000.00

Barye, Antoine-Louis, group of Theseus slaying the Centaur, the muscular hero astride the centaur, preparing to strike his antagonist with a mallet held overhead, dark green patina w/red highlights, mid-19th c., 13½" h. 6,600.00

Bonheur, Isidore-Jules, figure of a stag standing on a rough rectangular base, dark brown rubbed patina, third quarter 19th c., 31 5/8" l. 5,500.00

Bouret, Eutrope, figure of a farmgirl w/kerchief on her head & holding a musical instrument, on a leaf-cast circular ground, light brown patina, late 19th-early 20th c., 27¼" h. 1,430.00

Bouval, Maurice, figure of a young hunter, the striding figure wearing only a loincloth carries his kill tied to his waist, a slingshot in his right arm, on an oval leaf-molded base, dark green patina, inscribed "M Bouval," ca. 1900, 27½" h. (ILLUS.) 825.00

Carvin, L., model of German Shepherd dog, enameled metal, dog running over green foliage, solid green onyx base, Paris seal, retailed by Ovington's, New York City, 14½ x 18" 650.00

Chiparus, Demetre, "Tanara," figure of a seated dancer in form-fitting "beaded" top, helmet-form cap & flaring pleated skirt, seated as she ties her slippers, parcel-gilt & silvered bronze w/carved ivory face & hands, on stepped onyx base, figure inscribed "Chiparus," ca. 1925, overall 12 3/8" l. (minor restorations to base; one lace lacking) 4,950.00

Contenot, D.H., figure of a seated shepherd, the young Roman shepherd seated on a rocky base wearing a short tunic & long flowing cape, a straw hat over his back & holding a shepherd's crook in his left hand, golden brown patina, France, late 19th c., 26" h. 770.00

Descomps, Joe, figure of a young woman dressed in an elaborate jeweled cloche hat, halter & harem pants, w/a length of drapery about her arms, polychromed & gilt-bronze w/carved ivory face, arms, torso & feet, elaborate green onyx base inscribed "Joe Descomps," ca. 1925, overall 19¾" h. 5,500.00

Bronze Figure of Sophocles

Donoghue, John T., figure of Sophocles, monumental standing nude wearing only sandals & holding a tortoiseshell & horn lyre in one outstretched arm, the other arm poised above, raised on a rectangular plinth inscribed in Greek 'Sophocles - Salamis,' inscribed "J. Donoghue, F. BARBEDIENNE FONDEUR, PARIS," brown patina, 44½" h. (ILLUS.) 44,000.00

Dubois, Paul, figure of a seated philosopher, the draped man holding a tablet & a pen in his right hand, inscribed "P. DuBois, F. Barbedienne Fondeur Paris 337" & stamped w/the *Reduction Mecanique* seal, rich brown patina, France, late 19th - early 20th c., 25" h. 8,250.00

Foyatier, Denis, figure of an allegorical male, the nude figure holds tools in each hand crossed over his muscular chest, standing in front of a pedestal draped w/a cloth, inscribed "Foyatier," & dated "1830," raised on a rectangular base, green patina 3,080.00

Garnier, Jean, figure of boy holding violin marked "J. Garnier," boy dressed in pants, vest, jacket & hat w/violin tucked under one arm & both hands in pockets, brown patina, wood socle, 15½" h. 495.00

Gratchev, Vasili, "The Kiss," equestrian figure depicting a soldier kissing his sweetheart goodbye, signed & w/Woerffel foundry mark, St. Petersburg, Russia, late 19th c., 9¼" h. excluding marble base . . . 1,650.00

Kauba, Carl, silvered-bronze group of Saint George & the Dragon, the armor-clad saint on his rearing steed attacking the wounded dragon below, inscribed "C. Kauba," on green marble base, late 19th c., 10" h. 1,375.00

MARBLE

Marble Group of Two Putti

Barranti, P., figural group of young female garbed in Roman costume balancing an urn on her head & holding her small child, Florence, Italy, late 19th or early 20th c., on round base, 14" h. 2,200.00

Falconet, Etienne-Maurice, figure group of two putti, the putto on the left trying to keep the putto on the right from crushing a heart w/his raised right foot, inscribed "D'apres FALCONET" (after Falconet), France, 19th c., base chipped, 19¾" h. (ILLUS.) 5,500.00

Figure of a partly draped classical maiden, standing gazing to the right clutching drapery in an animated stance, on a circular socle base, white, late 19th c., 35½" h. 522.50

Figure group of five infant musicians, the lively naked & semi-naked children w/tousled hair gleefully playing various instruments or singing, on an irregular rectangular base carved w/Bacchanalian motifs, Italy, late 19th c., 40" l. (minor losses) 4,125.00

Figures, Minerva w/arm raised & Mars reaching for his bow, on circular socle bases, 22" & 23" h., the two 495.00

Romanelli, Prof. R., figure group, Rebecca at the Well, maiden standing, wearing cloth headdress, earrings, necklace, dress & sandals, he seated on the well, w/cloth headdress, necklace & tunic, w/bare feet, sheep drinking from a pool below, raised on naturalistic

base, Italy, last quarter 19th c.,
40" h. 4,950.00
Rougelet, Benoit, Bacchanalian
group, possibly representing the
young Bacchus & two child com-
panions, all three drunken infants
staggering on an oval base carved
w/goatskins & grape clusters, inscribed "B. Rougelet," late 19th c.,
25½" h. (weathered, losses). 2,750.00
Vichi, E., bust of a young girl
w/lacy collar & sleeves, 18" h. . . . 150.00
Weigele, Henri, figure of a woman,
the nude figure looking up to her
extended left arm, clutching a
length of cloth in her right hand,
standing on base of clouds, inscribed "H. Weigele," ca. 1900,
46" h. (weathered, losses). 1,925.00

OTHER MATERIALS

Cast lead, spread-winged eagles,
facing pair of fierce looking birds
perched on rock-style oblong
bases, 19th c., 27" h., pr. 29,700.00
Soapstone, group of Cupid & a sleep-
ing putto, Cupid seated on a rock-
ery base leaning against his
quiver, a putto lying sleeping on
his lap, inscribed "U. Biagini," late
19th c., w/marble pedestal, 31" h.
group, 2 pcs. (losses &
damages) .2,860.00
Terra cotta, bust of La Comtesse de
Sabran, classically draped lady
looking left, bust truncated below
the shoulders, after Jean-Antoine
Houdon, France, 19th c., w/sep-
arate terra cotta socle, 24 5/8" h.
bust, 2 pcs. (restored). 6,050.00

STEAMSHIP MEMORABILIA

*The dawning of the age of world-wide air-
line travel brought about the decline of the
luxury steamship liner for long-distance travel. Few large liners are still operating, but
mementoes and souvenirs from their glamor-
ous heyday are much sought-after today.*

Advertising display, "SS United
States - World's Fastest Liner,"
lighted travel agency type,
42" w., 7" deep, 43" h. $175.00
Ashtrays, "Cunard Steamship Com-
pany," clamshell-shaped, white
bone china w/gold pinstriping,
4½", pr. 20.00
Baggage tag, "Pacific Coast Steam-
ship Co.," celluloid 25.00
Book, "The Steamship Island Wan-

derer," 1884, 1,000 Islands, St.
Lawrence River, w/advertising &
steamship illustrations, 64 pp.
(cover loose). 35.00
Bouillon cup, "American Mail Line,"
china 37.50
Butter pat, "Northwest - Duluth,"
sterling silver, embossed ship in
center (slight dent on edge). 30.00
Catalog, "Savannah Line Steam-
ship," die-cut in shape of an orange, color w/black & white
illustrations, 16 pp. 35.00
Deck plan, "SS Hamburg," fold-out
type, 1930 . . . . 35.00
Document, surviving crew members
of the Titanic, 27 signatures,
w/letter from Titanic Historical
Society authenticating & appraising
the document, 1912 . . . . .7,500.00
Lithograph, view of steamer "Amos-
keag" & men in background, by
Mayer & Stetfield's Litho, 97 State
Street, Boston, Massachusetts,
w/walnut frame, 19½ x 27½"
(minor foxing & staining) 1,430.00
Model of the liner "America," paint-
ed wood, maroon, black & white
w/solid hull construction & finely
detailed superstructure, 1/16 in.
= 1 ft., 45½" l. 935.00
Passenger list, "City of Berlin,"
1888 . . . . 20.00
Passenger's diary, "Lanconia," 1913,
"My Trip Abroad," ornate leather
book 20.00
Pencil case w/note pad & pencil,
"Steamship Blucher," Hamburg-
American Lines, silver plate, gilt
edge on note pad, heavily em-
bossed steamship on cover, ca.
1890, the set. 120.00
Plate, "S.S. Carmania," milk white
glass, forget-me-not gilt rim,
transfer picture of steamship 35.00
Playing cards, "Cunard Lines," ca.
1900, complete deck 24.00
Pocket mirror, "American Line -
Philadelphia, Liverpool,
Queenstown" 15.00
Postcard, "S.S. Baltic Steamship" . . . 5.00
Sign, "Anchor Line - Transatlantic,
Oriental, Mediterranean, and
West Indian Steamships," litho-
graphed paper, two-masted, one-
stack ship moving through the
water scene, litho by Joseph A.
Knapp - Lith., New York,
20 x 29" 180.00
Timetable & map, "Pacific Coast
Steamship Co.," 1890 . . . . 12.50
Toothpick holder, liner "R.M.S. Sax-
onia," sterling & gold 85.00

Collecting
Steiff Animals

by Susan Cashman

The Steiff Company began, quite by accident, in the little German town of Giengenon-the-Brenz. Margarete Steiff, stricken by polio as a child, was confined to a wheelchair and deprived of the use of her right arm. An extremely creative woman determined to be self-sufficient, Margarete earned her living as a seamstress. In 1877, at the age of 30, she opened her own dressmaking shop. This enterprising woman had a fanciful side as well — in 1880 Margarete created small elephant-shaped pincushions as gifts for her nieces and nephews. So delighted were the children that soon the "pincushion" became the world's first soft stuffed toy.

Six felt elephants were produced in 1880. By 1886, 5,066 elephants had been produced by Margarete and a small group of seamstresses. Donkeys, horses, pigs and camels were then added to the line.

Come 1900 and Margarete had enlisted the aid of four nephews to help with various business aspects including the creation of new toy designs. The famous Teddy Bear can be greatly attributed to the efforts of Margarete's nephew, Richard Steiff, an art student who had made sketches of bear cubs while visiting an animal show at Stuttgart. His concept of producing a bear made of the newly introduced mohair fabric in the form of a doll (that is, fully jointed) was not embraced by Margarete at first. Through his insistence, the bear was indeed produced and introduced at the Leipzig Trade Fair in 1903. An American buyer was the first to pay heed and ordered 3,000 of the creatures. By year's end, 12,000 of the bears had been sold. Although bear sales continued to rise steadily, it wasn't until 1907, "The Year of the Bear" according to Steiff, that the small fellows actually hit their tremendous stride.*

The story is that a caterer for Alice Roosevelt's (President Theodore Roosevelt's daughter) wedding was befuddled for a theme for the table decorations. In desperation, he purchased a number of bears, outfitted them in various hunting togs and posed them to represent the President's favorite sport. A guest asked President Roosevelt exactly what sort of bears these were, when another guest declared that they were "Teddy's bears!" Thus, the little bears had a name, skyrocketing sales in 1907 to 974,000 from approximately 95,000 in 1906. Such power in a name!

This power has continued, not only in the name of Teddy, but in the name of Steiff. Because of Margarete's strenuous personalized training, supervision, and stringent quality control over her business, the toys made with the Steiff name have endured, as all fine art will.

It was this pride in craftsmanship that prompted the want of identification for Steiff toys. Evolving from paper tags attached to the animal's bow or collar in 1897, the metal button in ear ("Knopf im Ohr") trade-mark first appeared circa 1903. Space does not permit the in-depth study of Steiff ID, but books are currently available which offer much information on the ID and chronology of Steiff, including: *Teddy Bears and Steiff Animals* by Margaret Fox Mandel (both Volumes One and Two) and *Teddy Bears Past and Present* by Linda Mullins. Each contains extensive research and information for both the novice and experienced collector.

One of the best methods of learning is from the Steiff dealers. It is from them one learns what pieces are in demand, rare and costly. It is important to develop a relationship with a dealer who is knowledgeable and in whom you can trust. The reference books impart vast information, but the key is to incorporate the information from the books with what is happening in the Steiff world TODAY.

By far Teddies are the most popular. The most sought bears are those produced prior to 1910 in mint condition, but there are as many preferences with Steiff collectors as there are collectors. No one individual has exactly the same tastes or desires, consequently there seems to be that one special piece for everyone.

The majority of antique bear (1920's and

earlier) collectors insist on specific qualities which constitute the term "mint." The mohair (fur fabric) should be in perfect or near perfect condition, showing no obvious signs of wear. Large bald spots, particularly about the head and facial area, are unacceptable. The nose area is the exception: the fur on the nose was clipped at the factory and was originally sparse. As it is also the most "well-loved" portion, children adore nuzzling Teddy noses, minimal hair loss in this area should be expected.

Eyes should be original black shoe/boot buttons on very early bears. Amber glass eyes appeared around 1915. Some say the glass eyes were used as early as 1908, but since changes in toys were accomplished over an extended period of time, no one really knows for sure.

The nose and claw embroidery should be original and match in color — black noses and black claws on most bears; rose for white bears. The nose stitches on bears 14" and under are horizontal; over 14" they are vertical. Four claws should be in evidence on each foot.

Felt paw pads should be original and perfect. If mended, as much of the original felt should remain as possible, with repairs done *under* the original felt. Completely replaced paw pads do not significantly alter the value of the Teddy, but he is not then considered truly mint.

Some collectors will buy a less than perfect bear if the overall "look" is appealing and/or if it is especially desirable, i.e.: a center seam bear (circa 1903-1905. Considered rare, these have a seam running from center back of head to center nose); or an unusual color such as white. White bears were made in an approximate ratio of 1 white to every 25 gold.

Bears 18" and over command the highest prices. As with diamonds, there is that crucial point at which prices soar. Premiums are especially paid for those 24" and larger.

Newer mohair bears (1930's to late 1960's) are expected to be mint and having at least one form of ID.

Condition is also the most prevalent demand concerning the other animals, followed by rarity and ID. A mint pre-1920 piece with ID is a collector's treasure. The newer pieces should be mint with ID, particularly 1950-1968 pieces which are usually expected to be "store new." Lack of ID on this latter group can lower price by 10 to 25 percent, depending upon the desirability of the piece. The more rare the piece, the less lack of ID will affect value.

Reference books and old catalogs from Steiff and F.A.O. Schwarz prove invaluable. A dog, for example, may appear mint, but would you know if it was originally made with a keg and leather collar around its neck? Various animals were produced with collars, leashes, ribbons, bells, etc., that should be present to be considered truly mint.

Size also plays a significant role. Most animal pieces were produced in at least three sizes (miniature, junior and large) in an approximate ratio of 2:3:1 respectively. (Bears, though, were made 3½" and up in approximately 2" increments.) Miniatures are eagerly sought. The large pieces are desirable, not only because there are fewer of them, but because they usually have the most well-articulated details: the small kangaroo was made with a plastic joey, but the larger sizes have a velvet joey — minis unto themselves!

As stated previously, rare pieces attract much attention in the Steiff world. Some pieces were soon discontinued because they were considered to be threatening to children and are now sought with vigor. A perfect example is a circa 1967 life-sized red fox sitting up on its rear legs as if begging. This piece was offered exclusively by F.A.O. Schwarz, limiting its availability even as it was introduced. (A number of Steiff pieces and sets were offered exclusively through Schwarz and are highly prized today). This piece, because of its "frightening" posture, was rapidly discontinued. His price has soared from the original $28.50 to over $700 today. Though not considered old in terms of Steiff, the short production period makes him extremely collectible. Similar examples are dinosaurs, spiders, bats and lobsters.

At the other extreme, some exceptionally popular pieces are equally difficult to find in mint condition as they were so well loved by the children. These include Teddies, fully jointed animals and some farm animals.

In essence, what was considered threatening to children, unpopular, or became too expensive to produce (such as fully jointed and mohair animals which virtually disappeared from the retail market around 1968) is now the delight of collectors.

Steiff has always been very much concerned with the child market, as their motto "Only the best is just good enough for our children" implies, but the past nine years have seen a shift to the adult market as Steiff is creating a vast array of Limited Editions, Collector's Editions, and museum copies annually.

The first Limited Edition (now referred to as "Papa Bear" or "Papa Steiff") was issued in 1980 to commemorate Steiff's 100th anniversary. This bear was limited to 11,000 pieces worldwide and offered at $150. The big surprise to many collectors came in 1981, when a matching Limited Edition Mama Bear and Baby were produced. Suddenly it seemed everyone was in search of "Papa" to join "Mama," and within one year he was in such great demand that his price rose to $350+ on the secondary market. His value finally peaked at $600-$700, as newer pieces attracted attention and interest in this particular bear dwindled. By 1983 it became clear Steiff had unleashed a whole new market that had been either practically nonexistent or previously ignored: the adults.

Limited Editions, Collector's Editions (special mohair animals manufactured with no production limit) and Museum Series pieces began to appear in ever increasing numbers — up to 18 or more annually.

The largest scale Limited Edition is Steiff's Circus Series: an animal train, clown bears, various circus animals and accessories, are being introduced at an alarming rate, causing not only tremendous confusion on the part of the collector, but also serious financial strain. At this writing prices range from $400-$500 on the secondary market for the now discontinued Elephant and Calliope to a minimum of $100 each for smaller new pieces, the average price hovering around $135. Considering there are presently over 20 pieces to the set, plus additional pieces planned for coming years, substantial investment is required to keep pace.

All this causes consternation among collectors as most people cannot afford to purchase each new piece as it first becomes available. The question arises: "What should I buy?" The only legitimate answer is to purchase pieces you truly admire — it's anyone's guess as to which will someday be the most valuable. If investment is closest to your heart, select those pieces with the lowest production number, i.e.: a Limited Edition of 3,000 pieces as opposed to 10,000. Be prepared to keep the item or wait a year or more for demand and values to escalate. Some simply never do.

As for pre-1968 vintage Steiff — the perennial favorite among collectors — consult a well-respected Steiff dealer and the Steiff reference books. The best way to avoid an expensive mistake is to acquire a good education. As with any collectible, it takes time and experience for pieces to become self recognizable. Many dealers have their own specialties and will happily share their experience with you. Purchase the very best pieces you can afford: mint condition, with ID, and the earlier the piece (or the more rare), the better. When the time comes to upgrade your collection, it will be much easier to sell at the highest market value. Equally as essential: purchase pieces that please YOU, and you will enjoy them for many years to come.

Editor's Note: For the record we will note that there is another contrasting view on the origins of the famous "Teddy Bear." The American version involves Brooklyn merchant Morris Michtom who, after seeing a political cartoon of Theodore Roosevelt refusing to shoot a baby bear, designed a stuffed toy bear and placed it in his shop window. The toy became an immediate success and eventually led to the founding of the Ideal Toy Corporation.

TERMS: (Courtesy Barbara Baldwin, Old Friends Antiques, Sparks, Maryland)

Supermint: Store new condition, all ID usually present.

Mint: Outstanding unhandled condition. ID may or may not be present.

Near Mint: Mohair and overall condition fine, however, there may be some signs of natural aging.

Excellent: Mohair and overall condition reflect some signs of handling.

Very Good: Signs of wear readily evident although not extreme.

Photos by Debbie Pugliani and the author.

ABOUT THE AUTHOR

Susan Cashman is a collector and dealer specializing in Steiff toys. Her shop, Sheep's-in-the-Meadow Antiques & Collectibles, is located in Fairport, New York.

PRICE LISTINGS:

NOTE: Animals listed are from the 1950's and 1960's unless otherwise stated. They are assumed to be in mint condition.

Alligator: "Gaty," green variegated mohair, open felt mouth, 14" l.... $95.00

Bat: "Eric," tan-cream mohair, mohair-covered wire limbs, plastic wings, bead eyes & nose, rare, 8" h........................... 325.00

Early Bear on Wheels

Bear on cast-iron wheels: wool nap bear, shoe button eyes, felt foot pads, button in ear, original cast-iron wheels & chain, very good condition, 1913, 9" h. including wheels (ILLUS.)................. 595.00

"Nagy" Beaver

Beaver: "Nagy," brown frosted mohair, black glass eyes, ruled felt
tail, felt teeth, swivel head,
1960's, super mint, 9½" h.
(ILLUS.)........................ 175.00
Bird: "Bluebonnet," mohair, blue &
yellow markings, heavy metal
legs & feet, 5" h................. 195.00

Bison

Bison: brown-rust mohair, ruled felt
horns, glass eyes, squeaker, rare,
1960's, super mint, largest size
made, 11" h. (ILLUS.)............ 550.00
Cat: "Fiffy," lying position, cream
mohair w/black stripes, swivel
head, green glass eyes, ribbon &
bell, 7" l....................... 175.00
Cat: "Gussy," standing, white mohair w/black ears, tail, feet &
spots on body, green glass eyes,
swivel head, rare, 4" h. 100.00
Cat: "Kitty Cat," cream w/grey
stripes, original ribbon, jointed,
6" h. 125.00

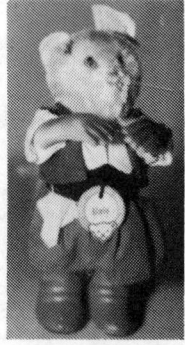

"Lixie" Cat

Cat: "Lixie," tabby coloring, mohair
head, rubber arms & legs &
shoes, felt clothing, rare, 3½" h.
(ILLUS.)........................ 350.00

"Mama" Cat & Kittens

Cats: "Mama" & three kittens on pillow, grey striped cream mohair,
green glass eyes, F.A.O. Schwarz
exclusive, 1950's, Mama 15" l.,
kittens 4" l., pillow 12 x 15", the
set (ILLUS.).....................1,000.00

"Puss in Boots"

Cat: "Puss in Boots," tabby coloring,
green glass eyes, jointed head &
arms, red felt paw pads, red felt
boots, red sash w/sword, tag
w/"U.S. Zone Germany," 1945-52,
10" h. (ILLUS.) 600.00

"Susi" Cat

Cats: "Susi," sitting position, cream
mohair w/grey stripes, green
glass eyes, swivel head, tag
w/"U.S. Zone Germany" sewn in
leg seam, ca. 1946, 2½" h. 150.00
6½" h. (ILLUS. of both sizes) 350.00

"Bessy" Cow

Cow: "Bessy," rust & white mohair, felt udder & horns, w/collar & bell, 1960's, super mint, 6" l. (ILLUS.)........................ 155.00

Dinosaur: "Brosus," standing on all fours, multicolor mohair, glass eyes, felt spine, rare, 12" l. 1,000.00

Dinosaur: "Tysus," standing on hind legs, tan, brown & green mohair, open felt-lined mouth, felt spines along back, swivel arms, rare, 17" h. 1,200.00

Dog: "Arco," German Shepherd, standing position, brown, black & cream mohair, open felt-lined mouth, glass eyes, 7" h. 115.00

Dog: "Bully," Bulldog, white mohair w/black markings, horsehair ruff, velvet muzzle, underscored "ff" button, ca. 1925, rare, 6½" h..... 475.00

"Musical Cockie" Dog

Dog: "Musical Cockie," black & white mohair, open felt-lined mouth, brown glass eyes, 6½" h. (ILLUS.) 600.00

St. Bernard on Wheels

Dog: St. Bernard on cast-iron wheels, cream mohair, rust markings, felt-lined ears, glass eyes, button in ear, ca. 1912, super mint, 9" h. (ILLUS.) 1,200.00

Dog: St. Bernard, standing position, cream mohair, rust markings, glass eyes, underscored "ff" button, ca. 1915, 11" h.............. 200.00

Dog: "Waldili," dressed hunter Dachshund, standing, rust mohair head, hands & feet, cream felt body under green felt hunting clothes, w/wooden rifle, F.A.O. Schwarz exclusive, ca. 1965, scarce, 9" h.................... 200.00

"Dormy" Dormouse

Dormouse: "Dormy," brown mohair, black glass eyes, super mint, rare, overall 7" l. (ILLUS.) 95.00

Fox: "Xorry," standing on all fours, orange & cream mohair, black markings, 4" h. 85.00

"Froggy" Frog

Frog: "Froggy," green & yellow velvet, black air-brushed markings, glass eyes, 1960's, super mint, 3½" h. (ILLUS.) 55.00

Gazelle: "Yuku," tan & gold mohair, rare, 8½" h. excluding rubber antlers 160.00

Horse: brown & white mohair, leather bridle, 6½" h.............. 95.00

Kangaroo: "Linda," grey & beige mohair, jointed head & arms, velvet joey in pouch, 18" h......... 425.00

Lamb: "Lamby," white mohair, green glass eyes, w/ribbon & bell, 11" h. 175.00

Lamb: "Swapl," black curly mohair w/white spot on head, w/ribbon & bell, 5½" h. 125.00

Lesser Panda: "Pandy," standing, orange, black & cream mohair, swivel head, 8" h................. 525.00

Lion: "Lea," sitting, tan & cream mohair, glass eyes, 3½" h. 80.00

Lion: "Leo," gold & brown mohair, glass eyes, all jointed, 6½" h. ... 150.00

Lion: "Leo," brown & beige mohair, pink floss nose, glass eyes, 1960's, super mint, 16" l. excluding tail (ILLUS.) 175.00

"Leo" Lion

Llama: long cream mohair, black & brown markings, glass eyes,

Llama

scarce, 1960's, super mint, 11" h. (ILLUS.) 155.00

Lobster: "Crabby," orange & red mohair, chenille-covered wire legs, red cord feelers, rare, 12" l. 525.00

"Moosy" Moose

Moose: "Moosy," brown, tan & cream mohair, felt antlers, all ID, rare, largest size made, 8½" h. excluding antlers (ILLUS.) 495.00

"Rocky" Mountain Ram

Mountain ram: "Rocky," tan mohair, orange underbelly, ruled felt horns, no ID, ca. 1960's, mint, 9" h. excluding horns (ILLUS.) 75.00

Ocelot: lying position, gold & cream mohair w/brown spots, orange glass eyes, 9" l. 155.00

"Wittie" Owl

Owl: "Wittie," tan & cream mohair, felt beak, tail, feet & wing tips, tufts on swivel head, yellow glass eyes, 1960's, super mint, 4" h. (ILLUS.) 40.00

Ox: "Oxy," tan shaded mohair, "googlie" eyes, rope tail, 5" h. ... 150.00

Panda: white & black mohair, open felt-lined mouth, glass eyes, suedene pads, all jointed, rare, 8" h. 650.00

Pig: "Jolanthe," pink mohair, blue glass eyes, felt nose, tail & mouth lining, original braided silk cord around neck, 8½" l. 155.00

Polar bear: standing on all fours, white mohair, sheared snout, blue glass eyes, felt paw pads, w/collar & bell, 6" h. 150.00

Easter Bunny

Rabbit: Easter Bunny, tan mohair, jointed head & arms, basket damaged, hard to find, body near mint, 1960's, 9" h. excluding ears (ILLUS.) 145.00

Running Rabbit

Rabbit: "Manni," begging position,
gold & cream mohair, swivel head
& arms, 20" h. including ears..... 475.00
Rabbit: running, gold & brown mohair, felt inner ears, w/ribbon,
bell & chest tag, ca. 1950's, mint,
9" l. (ILLUS. previous page)....... 95.00

"Renny" Reindeer

Reindeer: "Renny," tan & cream mohair, felt antlers, chest tag, ca.
1960's, hard to find, 5½" h. excluding antlers (ILLUS.) 125.00
Sea horse: "Cosy Sigi," multicolor
dralon, 8" h.................... 475.00
Snail: "Nelly," brown velvet, cream
plastic underside, iridescent rubber shell & antennae, 6½" l...... 200.00
Spider: "Spidy," multicolored mohair, mohair-covered wire legs,
seven black bead eyes, rare,
9" l. 750.00
Spider: "Spidy, as above but w/pipe
cleaner legs, 5" l. 325.00

"Perri" Squirrel

Squirrel: "Perri," brown & cream
mohair, black glass eyes, felt
feet, 1960's, super mint, 3½" h.
(ILLUS.)....................... 45.00
Tiger: "Bengal," sitting, orange &
cream mohair w/black stripes,
open felt-lined mouth w/teeth,
18" h......................... 750.00
Turkey: "Tucky," brown mohair, red
velvet head, felt tail & wings,
metal legs & feet, scarce, 5" h.... 165.00

"Slo" Turtle

Turtle: "Slo," tan & yellow mohair,
rubber shell, black glass eyes, felt
claws, 1960's, super mint, 4½" l.
(ILLUS.)....................... 40.00
Weasel: "Minky," champagne dralon
w/brown airbrushed highlights,

1970's, 17" l. including tail,
8" h.......................... 150.00

New Wolf Figure

Wolf: grey mohair, glass eyes, new
issue from limited edition "Red
Riding Hood" set, 3½" h.
(ILLUS.)....................... 60.00
Zebra: cream mohair w/black
stripes shading to brown, felt
hooves, glass eyes, 10" h. 130.00

Group of Steiff Animals

Group photo (left to right): Skunk,
black velvet body, white & black
mohair back, glass eyes, 1960's,
rare, super mint, overall 7" l. 95.00
Giraffe, cream mohair, rust spots,
black glass eyes, closed mouth,
brushed mane, 1960's, super mint,
11" h. 65.00
Cocker Spaniel, "Revue Susi," gold
mohair, "googlie" eyes, swivel
head, red leather collar, 1960's,
super mint, 4" h..................60.00
Cocker Spaniel, "Cockie," gold mohair, swivel head, "googlie" eyes,
leather collar, super mint, 1960's,
6" h...........................85.00
Elephant, grey mohair, red felt bib,
"googlie" eyes, plastic tusks, rope
tail, 1960's, super mint, 3½" h......55.00

TEDDY BEARS: (Listed by size)
Caramel mohair, black bead eyes,
hard to find, mint, 1950's,
3½" h. 275.00
Gold mohair, glass eyes, w/original
ribbon, 1950's, 5½" h............ 235.00
"Zotty" bear, long brown frosted
mohair, orange hair upper chest,
open felt-lined mouth, glass eyes,
felt pads, sheared snout, all jointed, 8" h. 250.00
Teddy Baby, apricot shaggy mohair,
open felt-lined mouth, shaved

Teddy Baby Bear

muzzle, fully jointed, missing
leather collar & bell, rare,
8½" h. (ILLUS.) 1,200.00

White Mohair Teddy Bear

White mohair, glass eyes, rose nose
& claw floss, underscored "ff" button, ca. 1920, super mint, 12" h.
(ILLUS.) 2,100.00

Ca. 1907 White Teddy Bear

White mohair, shoe button eyes,
rose nose & claw floss, ca. 1907,
some wear, very good condition,
no ID, 12" h. (ILLUS.) 1,100.00

Beige Bear, Ca. 1905

Beige mohair, shoe button eyes,
minor nose & pad wear, no ID,
near mint, ca. 1905, 14" h.
(ILLUS.) 1,900.00

1950's Teddy Bear

Caramel mohair, felt paw pads,
growler, no ID but signed by Mr.
Steiff, ca. 1950's, mint, 14" h.
(ILLUS.) 350.00
Teddy Baby, dark brown mohair,
sheared tan mohair snout & top of
feet, felt-lined open mouth & pads,
glass eyes, all jointed, w/collar
& bell, 1950's, rare, 15¾" h. 1,500.00

Ca. 1904 Teddy Bear

Apricot mohair, shoe button eyes,
blank button, signed by Mr. Steiff,
super mint, extremely rare,
ca. 1904, 16" h. (ILLUS.) 3,200.00

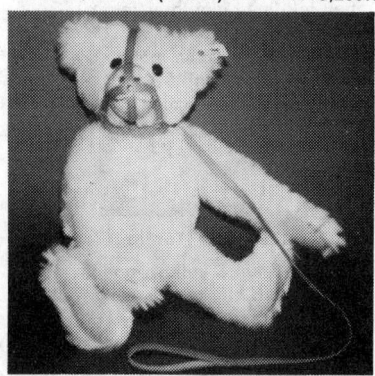

1988 Limited Edition Bear

White mohair, black eyes, growler,
w/leather muzzle & leash, 1988
Limited Edition, 18" h. (ILLUS.).... 375.00

Early Center-Seam Bear

Gold mohair, center-seam type, boot
button eyes, some wear on nose &
paw pads, excellent condition,
no ID, ca. 1903, rare, 24" h.
(ILLUS.) 5,500.00

Curly Mohair Bear

Tan curly mohair, glass eyes, growler,
signed by Mr. Steiff, 1950's, super
mint, 24" h. (ILLUS.) 1,800.00

THE COVER: *A grouping of cuddly Steiff
animals, including several Teddy bears, all
decked out for Christmas. See the listings for
values.*

(End of Special Focus)

STEINS

Character, "Balloon," pottery, tan,
green & brown, marked "TW,"
1 liter $770.00
Character, Figural colored man
smoking long pipe, dressed in tan
jacket, blue, yellow & red trim,

big red, white & blue bow, yellow
hoop earrings, holding cane in
other hand, black hair, yellow
handle, majolica, 4" d., 7½" h.... 325.00
Character, "Gentleman Rabbit," porcelain, painted tan, browns &
green, porcelain lid, marked
"Musterschutz," ½ liter 2,530.00
Character, "Happy Radish," pottery,
painted full color, pottery lid,
marked "757-8 Germany,"
½ liter 495.00
Character, "Kaiser Wilhelm I,"
stoneware, blue & purple glaze,
inlaid stoneware lid, marked
"809," ½ liter 660.00

Character Steins

Character, "Military Bear," porcelain, ½ liter (ILLUS. right) 2,750.00
Character, "Monkey," brown animal
in seated position w/hangover expression on face, tail forming
handle, black top hat on head,
one arm rests on a blue scroll
w/German verse that translates
"If you don't want the results,
avoid the cause," 9¼" h. 275.00
Character, "Munich Child," stoneware, painted black, yellow &
red, inlaid stoneware lid, marked
"J. Reinemann, Munchen,"
¼ liter 286.00
Character, "Owl," nutmeg staining
accents the fine feathered detail,
hinged pewter collar, circular
base, cobalt enamel leaves
around his feet, numbered on
base, Germany, 8¼" h. 135.00
Character, "Perkeo," porcelain,
painted full color, bisque glaze,
inlaid lid, ½ liter ...... 800.00 to 850.00
Character, "Sad Radish," porcelain,
inset lid w/leaves finial, cream &
beige w/green leaves, marked
"Musterchutz," 3 3/8" d., 6¾" h.,
½ liter 307.00
Character, "Singing Pig," porcelain,
painted white & pinks, inlaid lid,
marked "Musterschutz,"
½ liter .... 400.00 to 470.00
Character, "Uncle Sam," porcelain,

beige, brown & white, marked "Musterschutz," ½ liter (ILLUS. left) 1,320.00

Commemorative, "Huckleberry Indians, N.Y.A.C." (New York Athletic Club), dated March 26, 1904, pewter, figural bust of Indian w/full feather headdress on hinged lid, marked "Ricerzinn" on base, 7" h. 185.00

Glass, clear, blown, silver plate lid w/man on high wheel bicycle finial, ½ liter 308.00

Glass, clear, blown, engraved cherub, pewter lid, ca. 1850, ½ liter .. 357.50

Glass, clear, blown, engraved florist w/house & plants, pewter lid & base, ca. 1820, ½ liter 1,210.00

Glass, blown, Russian cut, brass lid forms a castle, top brass rim w/postman's horn, an eagle & a stein in relief, dated 1899, 2 liter 1,895.00

Ornate Carved Ivory Stein

Ivory & silver, hinged silver cover w/an ivory finial in the form of a fruit-bearing putto above a silver repousse & chased silver section w/bunches of fruit & scrolling leaves & set w/stone cabochons, the oval body of ivory carved w/a procession of Neptune & a woman enthroned on a barque pulled by sea horses & attended by various putti & nymphs, on a silver repousse foot w/conforming decoration & set w/further stones, C-scroll ivory handle carved w/a young bacchante, Continental, late 19th c., 14½" h. (ILLUS.) 5,225.00

Majolica, molded child's head front, relief-molded serpentine scrollwork ground, yellow, pink, blue & green, 10" h. 235.00

Mettlach, No. 171, grey & tan w/blue band w/relief-molded

white figures, pottery inset lid, 3¼" d., 5¾" h., ¼ liter 181.00

Mettlach, No. 979(1909), PUG (printed-under-the-glaze), School in East Africa, pewter lid, ½ liter 495.00

Mettlach, No. 1054(2262), PUG, Gambrinus & his followers, pewter lid, 4.2 liter 1,100.00

Mettlach, No. 1163, incised w/four musicians, signed "C. Warth," pewter-mounted lid, ½ liter 165.00

Mettlach, No. 1394, etched, German card stein, inlaid lid, ½ liter 412.50

Mettlach, No. 1396, central band incised w/a putti in a tree drinking from an urn, flanked by two shields, signed "C. Warth," replaced embossed & engraved lid, ½ liter 357.50

Mettlach, No. 1526, scenes of Berlin, ½ liter 125.00

Mettlach, No. 1646, incised scene of a man sitting at a table smoking & drinking, w/a German verse, pewter lid, ½ liter 137.50

Mettlach, No. 1654, incised mosaic decoration of stylized vines, w/pewter-mounted lid, ½ liter ... 275.00

Mettlach, No. 1796, incised w/a drinking Renaissance figure flanked by a cat & a monkey, signed "C. Warth," pewter-mounted lid, ½ liter 330.00

Mettlach, No. 1932, etched, Cavaliers drinking scene around body, signed "Warth," inlaid lid, ½ liter 375.00

Mettlach, No. 2001C, modeled as a shelf of books for scholar philosophers, hand-painted, inlaid lid, ½ liter .... 450.00 to 475.00

Mettlach Stein No. 2002

Mettlach, No. 2002, etched, Munich stein w/Munich Child & banner on upper half & lengthy inscription on lower half, inlaid lid, ½ liter (ILLUS.) .... 350.00 to 400.00

Mettlach, No. 2035, etched, scene of Bacchus carousing, inlaid lid, ½ liter 425.00

Mettlach, No. 2083, etched, scene of boar hunt, inlaid lid, 1 liter, 10½" h. 1,650.00

Mettlach, No. 2211, white relief figures of bowlers on sides on blue, pewter bowling pin thumblift, turnips & pipe on inlaid lid, ca. 1898, green stamp mark, 3/10 liter 225.00

Mettlach, No. 2481, etched, scene of wounded & resting warriors in body armor receiving aid from the maiden Hildegund, resting horses, swords & helmets in foreground, artist-signed, jeweled inlaid lid, 1.4 liters, 14½" h. overall 1,250.00

Mettlach, No. 2580, etched, "Die Kannenburg" stein, knight in castle scene, signed "Schlitt," conical pottery lid, 1 liter 725.00

Mettlach, No. 2582, etched, jester performing on table in front of tavern, signed "Quidenus," inlaid lid, 1 liter . . . . 500.00 to 700.00

Mettlach, No. 2872, etched, Cornell University scenes around the body, inlaid lid, ½ liter 650.00

Porcelain, h.p. profile of lovely Art Nouveau lady & iris florals, shaded sepia tones, pewter hinged lid w/inlaid porcelain decorated w/a four-line verse surrounded by yellow jonquils, ornate scrolled thumblift, marked "Issued by the O'Hara Dial Co., Waltham, Mass., Paris, France," inside a fleur-de-lis stamp on base, 4" d., 5½" h. to thumblift 185.00

Pottery, decorated w/the figures of four ladies representing the Four Seasons, all on an olive green ground, incised triangle & castle mark & "Germany," ½ liter 250.00

Pottery, multicolor relief of New York City scenes in three panels, Singer Building, Metropolitan Life Building & Statue of Liberty, pewter lid, Germany, ½ liter, 8 3/8" h. 85.00

Regimental, porcelain, "Bav. Inft. Nr. 13, Neu Ulm, 1814-1914," commemorative, two side scenes, roster, lion thumblift, screw-off lid w/pewter scene, ½ liter 660.00

Regimental, porcelain, "Garde Gren. Regt. Nr. 3, Charlottenburg, 1908-1910," two side scenes, roster, gargoyle thumblift, ½ liter . . . 495.00

Regimental, porcelain, "Train Batl. Nr. 2, Alt Damm, 1901-1903," two

side scenes, roster, shako helmet figural lid, ½ liter 2,200.00

Pottery Regimental Stein

Regimental, pottery, "Res. Dietz. 1 Eskadron Ulam...1901-1904," central reserve of h.p. soldier on horseback w/molded scrolls above & colored ribbon banner below, embossed domed pewter lid w/mounted knight finial, eagle figural thumbrest, ½ liter, 11" h. (ILLUS.) . . . . 700.00 to 800.00

Silver, repousse & chased exotic sea creatures, shells & strapwork, gilded, Pavel Ovchinnikov, Moscow, ca. 1885, 11" h. 3,410.00

Silver-gilt, barrel chased w/classical busts above lambrequins pricked w/embroidery, within strapwork, shells & foliage on matte ground, double-domed cover & domed base chased w/strapwork to match, double-scroll handle capped by a leaf & chased w/matted reserves, quatrefoils & husks, forked scroll thumbpiece w/shell & openwork husk, large bud finial, Michael May II, Brasso, Hungary, ca. 1740, 10 5/8" h. 13,750.00

Stoneware, pewter-mounted, saltglazed, cylindrical, incised w/a goose between foliate branches in blue on the grey ground, probably Grenzhausen, Germany, 16th c., 7½" h. 880.00

Stoneware, Westerwald, etched birds & flower, pewter lid inscribed "1745," 1 liter 467.50

STRING HOLDERS

Before the widespread use of paper bags, grocers and merchants wrapped their goods in paper, securing it with string. A string holder, usually of cast iron, was, therefore, a necessity in the store. Homemakers also found many uses for string and the ceramic or chalkware wall-type holder became a common kitchen item.

Young Girl with Hat String Holder

Advertising, "Pepsi Cola," metal,
two-sided, 1930's, 15 x 20" $375.00
Advertising, "7-Up," tin 300.00
Advertising, "Top Snuff," cast iron,
model of toy top, red, white &
blue 875.00
Bentwood, cylindrical body & circular cover painted blue & red
w/Norwegian inscription & stylized flowerheads, Norway, late
19th c., 3 3/8" d., 3¼" h. 137.50
Cast iron, beehive-shaped,
5½ x 6" 65.00
Cast iron, table model, solid round
sphere w/domed solid foot, comical woman's head on top
w/mouth as string opening, old
red paint, 8¼" h. (rust under
foot) 190.00
Chalkware, apple w/worm 27.50
Chalkware, bust of American
Indian 68.50
Chalkware, bust of young girl wearing hat, original paint, 6½ x 8½"
(ILLUS.) 46.50
Chalkware, full-figural chef, ca.
1941 .... 65.00
Chalkware, model of cat w/ball of
yarn 25.00
Pottery, figural black bellhop,
Fredericksburg Art Pottery, 6½".. 135.00
Redware, bust of lady w/curly
hair 95.00
Tin, model of an apple,
"Wyandotte" 28.00

TEDDY BEAR COLLECTIBLES

Theodore (Teddy) Roosevelt had become a

national hero during the Spanish-American War by leading his "Rough Riders" to victory at San Juan Hill in 1898. He became the 26th President of the United States in 1901 when President McKinley was assassinated. The gregarious Roosevelt was fond of the outdoors and hunting. Legend has it that while on a hunting trip, soon after becoming President, he refused to shoot a bear cub because it was so small and helpless. The story was picked up by a political cartoonist who depicted President Roosevelt, attired in hunting garb, turning away and refusing to shoot a small bear cub. Shortly thereafter, toy plush bears began appearing in department stores labeled "Teddy's Bears" and they became an immediate success. Books on the adventures of "The Roosevelt Bears" were written and illustrated by Paul Piper under the pseudonym of Seymour Eaton and this version of the Teddy bear became a popular decoration on children's dishes.

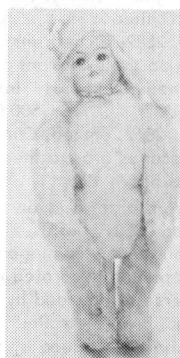

Teddy Bear with Bisque Head

Book, "Roosevelt Bears," by Seymour Eaton, ca. 1907 .... $125.00
Book, "The Teddy Bears," by Adah
Louis Sutton, 1907, black & white
Teddy bear sketches, some full
page colored prints, hardbound,
155 pp., 7 x 9" 55.00
Cup & saucer, china, transfer scene
of Teddy bear playing volleyball .. 80.00
Feeding dish, "Teddy & the Bear,"
pottery, bears on a seesaw 95.00
Hot water bottle, red rubber, figural
Teddy bear, w/Cub Scout
uniform 65.00
Mug, china, transfer scene of Teddy
bear roller skating & playing
baseball 85.00
Plate, china, Roosevelt Bears, "Up
San Juan Hill," bears w/rifles &
swords & poem, pierced edge,
7" d. 145.00
Postcards, leather, "Days of the
Week," dated 1907, set of 7 ...... 125.00

Postcard, Roosevelt Bears, "Days of
the Week" series, by Wm. S.
Heal, 1907, set of 7 .... 65.00
Teddy bear, two-faced, ca. 1940,
probably Schuco, 3½" 750.00
Teddy bear, stiff yellow mohair, pin
jointed, glass eyes, 4½" 70.00
Teddy bear, two-tone beige & gold
wooly plush straw-stuffed body,
jointed limbs, 1940's, 9½" 75.00
Teddy bear, dark brown mohair
straw-stuffed body, jointed limbs,
1930's, 11½" 125.00
Teddy bear, mohair clown bear,
blown glass eyes, red & blue felt
clothes, gauze collar, 1920, 12" ... 250.00
Teddy bear, bisque child's face
w/inset glass eyes, open mouth
w/teeth, mohair wig, straw-filled
body, all jointed, shoulder plate
incised "370 AM 5/0 DEP Made in
Germany," 13" (ILLUS.) 137.50
Teddy bear, dark gold plush hair-
cloth w/grey felt paw pads, embroidered features & button eyes,
articulated limbs, 15" (minor
wear) 250.00
Teddy bear, brown mohair straw-
stuffed body, shoe button eyes,
hump, new pads, original red
suit, ca. 1920, Germany, 17½" ... 275.00
Teddy bear, blonde mohair, button
eyes, swivel neck, jointed at
shoulders & hips, dressed in a
pink suit & white tucked cotton
blouse, average wear, ca. 1930,
20" 198.00
Teddy bear, plush, wide apart ears,
glass eyes, long snout, hump at
the back, hinged arms & legs
w/cloth pads, wearing a button at
his neck inscribed "(?) ROLL,"
Continental, early 1900's, 30"
(one pad repaired) 550.00

TELEPHONES

Candlestick-type, black metal,
"American Telephone & Tele-
graph," patent dates from 1913
through 1920, 12" h $55.00
Candlestick-type, "Kellog Switch-
board & Supply Co." 145.00
Candlestick-type, "Stromberg Carl-
son," 'oil can' shaft (renickeled) .. 363.00
Candlestick-type, "Western Electric,"
patent dated 1915 .... 75.00
Candlestick-type, "Western Electric,"
dial model, patent dated 1919 .... 75.00
Desk-type, cradle hand-ring,
"Jydsk," black enamel base bear-

ing colored coat of arms, early
20th c., European 250.00
Lineman's, in leather case, complete 25.00
Wall-type, "American Electric," oak
case, original maker's plaque on
front marked "American Electric
Telephone Co. Makers, Chicago,"
7½" w., 20" h 170.00
Wall-type, "Simplex Int. Tel., Cincinnati, " oak case, intercom
model 225.00
Wall-type, "Western Electric," oak
case, pair of top mounted nickel-
plated bells, front mounted
mouthpiece, side mounted receiver hook, side marked, patent
dates from 1890 through 1903,
4½ x 6 x 9" 90.00

TEXTILES

COVERLETS

Two-piece Double Woven Coverlet

Jacquard, single weave, one-piece,
large starflower in center surrounded by floral bands, inner
corner brackets w/cornucopias &
leaf scrolls, outer border bands of
large leaf sprigs & double classical columns flanked by oak leaf
sprigs, natural white, red & olive
green, end borders signed
"Manufactured by A. & T. Fehr in
Emaus, Lehigh County, Pennsylva-
nia," 76 x 88" (overall wear) $165.00
Jacquard, single weave, one-piece,
star medallion center w/border
bands of small diamonds & floral
bands, natural white, navy blue,
red & light green, signed in corners "North Lima, Ohio, 1850,"

76 x 88" (red fringe added, top
edge worn) 160.00

Jacquard, single weave, two-piece,
abstract floral medallions in center, borders of two birds & two
roses & large rose blossoms, eagles in corners, natural white, red
& blue, corners signed "Knox
County, Ohio 1849, U.S.A.,"
70 x 77" (overall wear, no
fringe) 325.00

Jacquard, single weave, two-piece,
floral medallions in center & double row of buildings border, rich
colors of red, blue, gold & natural
white, signed in corners "Jacob
Saylor, Saltcreek Township Pica-
way Co., Ohio, 1856," 78 x 82"
(worn & holes) 200.00

Jacquard, single weave, two-piece,
floral medallions surrounded by
feather wreaths in center, grape
vine & roses in baskets borders,
cornucopias in corners w/"Ohio,"
blue & white, 78 x 82" 310.00

Jacquard, single weave, two-piece,
floral medallions in center w/vin-
tage grape border, natural white,
red, navy blue & olive brown,
signed in corners "W. in Mount
Vernon, Knox County, Ohio,"
78 x 84" (minor wear) 375.00

Jacquard, single weave, two-piece,
small floral medallions in center
w/border consisting of two rows
of stars & a meandering foliage
vine, two shades of blue, red & a
narrow stripe of green, corners
signed "Rebecca Funk 1896,"
76 x 88" (overall wear, some
fringe missing) 200.00

Jacquard, single weave, two-piece,
large floral medallions in center
w/meandering feather borders,
abstract tulips in corners w/"Mag-
dalene Harham 1867," blue &
white, 72 x 90" 300.00

Jacquard, double woven, one-piece,
central floral urn flanked by two
pheasants, floral borders, natural
white, tomato red, olive & greyish
green, 86 x 90" (some wear &
stains) 250.00

Jacquard, double woven, two-piece,
alternating bands of Bird of Paradise & Penelope's Flowerpot patterns w/bands of elaborate fruiting
urns & exotic birds perched in
branches feeding chicks, within alternating Western & Oriental house
borders, blue & white, edge dated
"PIQUA 1849," 74 x 88" (minor
wear & discoloration) 1,210.00

Jacquard, double woven, two-piece,

center panel w/ornate star motif
alternating w/star & blossom motif within vine, leaf & lattice borders, blue & white, signed "Jacob
Impson, Cortland Village, New
York, 1842 - 'Lady's Fancy,' "
80 x 88" (wear, soiled) 412.50

Jacquard, double woven, two-piece,
four-rose medallions in center
w/eagle & tree borders & corners
labeled "The Property of S.M.S.
Orleans County, N.Y. 1839," natural & navy blue, minor wear &
stains, 80 x 90" (ILLUS.) 610.00

Linsey-woolsey, scarlet top composed of three panels lavishly
quilted in an overall geometric &
floral pattern, the ground filled
w/parallel line stitching, backed
w/natural homespun, America,
late 18th - early 19th c., 71 x 76"
(patched, some holes) 660.00

Overshot, dark blue w/white
repeating design of stylized floral
medallions interspersed w/geo-
metric medallions enclosing
flowerheads, within a repeating
border of sprays & flowers, two
corners dated "1848," 71½ x 85"
(one border missing) 385.00

Overshot, two-piece, four-block &
optical plaid design, dark blue &
white, Shelburne Falls, Massachusetts, early 19th c.,
71 x 86" 650.00

Overshot, two-piece, blue & white
optical pattern, 77 x 90" (minor
wear & stains) 275.00

Overshot, two-piece, red & blue-
green geometric pattern w/self-
fringe on one side, 74 x 92" 88.00

Overshot, two-piece, bold plaid patterns in blue, green & natural
white w/red, good fringe,
66 x 95" 400.00

Overshot, three-piece, reversible,
interrupted horizontal stylized
flowerhead & rectangular panels
alternating w/square panels,
probably Missouri, 19th c.,
70 x 90" (some wear & hole) 137.50

LACES
Battenburg
Doily, all lace, 10" sq. 14.50
Handkerchief, all lace 18.00
Table centerpiece, 8" triangle of
lace at each corner, drawn-work
center, 15½" sq. 42.00
Table runner, lace border,
16 x 48" 105.00

Other
Burano needle lace border, worked
in mid-18th c. design of daisy

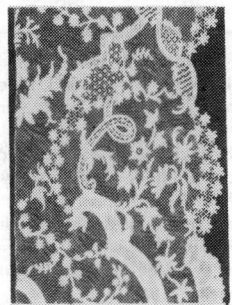

Burano Needle Lace Border

chains, serpentine ribbon, scattered flowers & C-scrolls, Italy, late 18th c., 12 x 186" (ILLUS.) 825.00
Cluny lace tablecloth, linen center, 84 x 118" 145.00
Gros point needle lace panel, worked in a complex baroque scrolling foliate pattern, mounted on green satin, probably Italian, late 17th c., 9¼ x 34½" 242.00
Hardanger tablecloth, 50" sq. 45.00
Point d'Angleterre bobbin lace panel, worked in a pattern of large flowerheads, scattered blossoms & foliage within scrolling borders, probably French, early 19th c., 36 x 108" 1,210.00
Point de Sedan needle lace flounce, worked in a pattern of full-blown flowers & fruits, France, late 17th - early 18th c., 15 x 126" 440.00
Point de Venise banquet cloth, the white lace against a blue linen ground embroidered w/flowers, w/twelve matching napkins, the set 418.00

LINENS & NEEDLEWORK

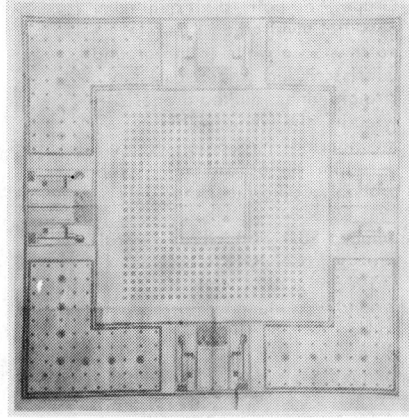

Cotton Damask Tablecloth

Bed set, sheet w/hemstitching &

fagoting, matching pair pillowcases, 3 pcs. 75.00
Blanket, homespun wool, two-piece, natural white & pale pink w/pinstripes of yellow & brown, handsewn hems, 56 x 78" 155.00
Blanket, homespun wool, two-piece, hand-embroidered candlewicking in designs of abstract overall floral & leaf branches & houses in red, blue-green & dark brown on light background, signed "R.A. P.Nov. 1886," found in North Carolina, 60 x 87" (minor wear & stains) 400.00
Blanket, homespun linen & wool, rectangular panel woven in overall blue & white plaid pattern, Indiana, second quarter 19th c., 72 x 84" 330.00
Doily, crocheted w/a rooster in center, white, 10 x 13" 23.00
Dresser scarf, drawn-work border w/ducks, eight-pointed star in corners, 17 x 33" 40.00
Handkerchief, homespun cotton, tricornered, muted plaid design, ca. 1830, 24 x 35" 39.00
Pillow sham, red embroidery of morning glories w/"Rise Bright," 25 x 26½" 36.00
Sheet, homespun linen, two-piece, hand-sewn central seam & hem, 74 x 76" 45.00
Sheet, homespun linen, two-piece, hand-hemmed, Ephrata, Pennsylvania, 76 x 100" 40.00
Tablecloth, Irish linen w/hand-crocheted & lace inserts, monogrammed "M," 52 x 64" 95.00
Tablecloth, crewel, stylized trees, flowers & natives stitched in wool yarn in shades of orange, lavender, brown, green & pink on natural white cotton twill, two seams, cut & tied border, 66 x 96" (some wear, stains & fading) 350.00
Tablecloth, homespun linen, wide stripes w/narrow bands, wide border entirely made up of narrow stripes, America, early 19th c., 60 x 104" 165.00
Tablecloth & napkins, cotton damask, in Jugendstil style, the square cloth woven in a deep border of blue stars & flowerheads within a blue & white checked border, each side w/a central panel depicting two women w/long thick hair each w/a tray holding four objects & centering a stylized fruiting tree, all woven in blue & gold, w/six square luncheon napkins woven w/a matching

design, monogrammed "CL,"
tablecloth 60" sq., napkins
15" sq., the set (ILLUS. of tablecloth, previous page) 2,310.00
Tablecloth & napkins, hemstitched
w/lavish blue Madeira embroidery, tablecloth 68 x 100",
w/twelve matching napkins,
13 pcs. 225.00
Tablecloth & napkins, linen w/cut-
work & filet lace inserts, tablecloth 76 x 116", w/twelve extra
large napkins, 13 pcs. 310.00
Towel, homespun linen, coarsely
woven fabric w/tied fringe at one
end, 18½ x 25" plus fringe 45.00
Towel, homespun linen, hand-
hemmed, tape loop hanger, red
embroidered initials "A.N." &
"N.J.," 18 x 42" 35.00

QUILTS

Fine Amish Crib Quilt

Crazy Quilt, embroidered & hand-
painted satin & velvet patches arranged in vertical bands w/velvet
ribbon borders, variety of stitches,
initialed "LRL," 19th c., 64" square
(unbacked) 660.00
Crazy Quilt, colorful prints, painted
& embroidered flowers, animals &
people, dated "1887," striped border, 56 x 70" (minor wear) 550.00
Crib-size, pieced cross designs, four
geometric crosses in pale grey on
a black ground within a pale grey
primary border & subsidiary large
border, pale grey edge, highlighted w/chain, foliate vine & vertical
bar quilting, Amish, probably
Ohio, ca. 1930, 37 x 45" (ILLUS.) .. 330.00
Crib-size, pieced Double Irish Chain
patt., blue & white 465.00
Crib-size, pieced Irish Chain patt.,
blue blocks on white field, very

good quilting & feather quilted
border, 34 x 54" (minor wear) 275.00
Crib-size, pieced Wild Goose Chase
patt., blue on white ground, blue
edge band, 31 x 43" (minor wear
& stains) 625.00
Appliqued Album patt., 16 white cotton blocks appliqued w/a variety
of motifs including floral sprays,
wreaths & grapevines, "Miss Lydia
Emeline Keller, 1867" cross-stitched
in corner, field heightened w/quilt-
ing, America, 1867, 84 x 86"
(minor fabric wear & staining) ...2,310.00

Oak Leaf Appliqued Quilt

Appliqued Oak Leaf patt., composed
of three rows of three four-point
feathered circles in green on a
white ground, within pink & green
band borders, background highlighted w/diamond quilting,
signed "Josephine Cope," America, third quarter 19th c., minor
staining, 81 x 83" (ILLUS.) 330.00
Appliqued, pieced & embroidered
Grape Vine patt., a kit quilt composed of vivid green & purple
patches on a white cotton ground
w/crisscrossed grape clusters on
straight vines, quilted grapes &
wreaths, the whole within a
meandering vine border, embroidered inscription, Lillian V. Myers,
probably California, dated July 6,
1935, 76 x 84" 1,430.00
Appliqued Rose patt., three central
vines w/rosebuds & blossoms in
red & green on a white background w/a meandering rose vine
border, 80 x 82" (minor
staining) 825.00
Appliqued & pieced Starburst &
Mariner's Compass patt. variant,
red, green, blue, pink & yellow
patches, the starbursts separated
by groups of counterposed green

oak leaves, the whole within red & green swag & tassel borders, on white cotton field w/half-inch diagonal line quilting, America, ca. 1850, 73 x 93" 4,400.00

Pieced Cross & Crown patt., composed of four rows of three cross & square motifs in printed black, white, brown, grey, blue & green patches on various printed grounds within blue printed band borders, calico, America, late 19th c., approximately 60 x 84"... 275.00

Crown of Thorns Pattern Quilt

Pieced Crown of Thorns patt., composed of six rows of blue triangular patches alternating w/white patches embroidered w/stylized foliate motifs within blue & white band borders & blue & white scalloped edges, probably Midwestern, ca. 1920, 69 x 80" (ILLUS.)......................... 522.50

Pieced Diamond in the Square patt., teal blue, purple, magenta & hunter green patches, stitched w/central star, flowerhead, flower on stem & featherwreath, edged w/lavender binding, backed w/green cotton, Amish, possibly Pennsylvania, early 20th c., 78 x 79" (binding wear, minor repair & discoloration) 660.00

Pieced Dutchman's Puzzle patt., black, bright blue & purple patches, diagonal diamond & running chain quilting, embroidered initials "E.J.S." & date "1940," Amish, Pennsylvania, 70 x 89".... 605.00

Pieced Geese in Flight patt., jade green, red, beige & brown printed calico & glazed chintz patches, the 'geese' separated by vertical panels of beige & rose chintz, the whole within triangular borders of

red & brown chintz featuring diamond quilting, probably Maryland, ca. 1840, 112 x 120" 5,775.00

Monkey Wrench Pattern Quilt

Pieced Monkey Wrench patt., composed of yellow stylized pinwheel designs on a white ground, quilted w/center squares w/stylized floral sprig & berry alternating w/sections of diamond quilting, yellow edge, Missouri, 1930, 69 x 78" (ILLUS.) 660.00

Pieced Octuple Irish Chain patt., composed of thousands of small squares of light blue, navy, red & white cotton, the field w/diagonal line quilting, maroon & blue borders, America, ca. 1915, 71 x 72" 1,760.00

Pieced Sawtooth Diamond in the Square patt., dark green patches on light green ground w/lavender highlights, Amish, probably Ohio or Indiana, late 19th - early 20th c., 77 x 80" 440.00

Pieced Snail Trail patt., red patches on white ground, pencil pattern intact, 76 x 92" (some age stains) 225.00

Pieced Star patt., central large six-point star in lavender & pale lavender on a black ground within lavender & black borders, heightened w/concentric feathered wreath, leaf, potted plant & chain quilting, Amish, Lancaster County, Pennsylvania, late 19th c., 77 x 84" (minor soiling) 3,850.00

Pieced Sunshine and Shadow patt., composed of pink, grey, blue, black, green, red, maroon & purple wool squares arranged in a radiating diamond pattern within a wide purple border quilted w/ribbon-tied floral sprigs & trelliswork, grey edge, Amish, Pennsyl-

vania, initialed "K.S.," early
20th c., 79" sq. 3,575.00
Pieced Tumbling Blocks patt., all silk
patches in lavender, blue, pink,
maroon, gold, yellow, green,
bronze, orange & black silk repp &
taffeta, diamond-sawtooth outer
border w/scalloped black edging,
America, ca. 1880-90, 52 x 67"
(back replaced). 3,750.00
Trapunto "bride's" quilt, all-white
cotton, central area worked w/an
elegant urn mounted on a pedestal
topped w/a pineapple, surrounded
by feathered tassels pendant from
floral chains, the outer borders
w/undulating grapevines w/daisy
sprigs & clover leaves, the outer
borders w/sprigs & buds, probably
Baltimore, Maryland, early 19th c.,
100 x 104" (some wear, repair &
minor stain) 1,100.00
Trapunto, white cotton, diamond
quilted panel w/rounded rectangular feathered borders enclosing
an elaborate floral vine trapunto
border, America, mid-19th c.,
74 x 81" 1,540.00

SAMPLERS

Early 19th Century Sampler

Alphabets & inscription in rows
above panel w/basket of flowers
flanked by four-point stars, all
surrounded by strawberry & twining vines border, stitched in
shades of red, green, yellow,
grey & pale blue on homespun
linen, signed "Ann Spencer,
Steubenville, July 18, 1828," from
Ohio, modern wooden frame, overall 20 x 21" (small hole, slightly
faded) 2,750.00
Alphabets & numerals above
"Rachel Hartley her sampler made
in the year 1787" stitched in a variety of colors on a homespun lin-

en fabric, matted & framed,
18½ x 22½" 500.00
Alphabets, short verse & inscription
"Rhoda Roger's Sampler wrought
in the 11 year of her age 1804"
within an octagonal medallion,
enclosed by a border of vibrant
sienna & ivory flowers & two-color
sawtooth outer band, undulating
grass at base, executed in silk
yarns on linen, Newbury, Massachusetts, framed (no size
given) 6,600.00
Basket of flowers, corner floral
sprigs & geometric strawberry border enclosing alphabet & scene
depicting house, undulating grass,
trees, flowers & birds, worked in
multicolored silk yarn on linen
ground, signed "Polly Church,
Watterford," Vermont, 1831
(ILLUS.) 1,980.00
Landscape w/a three-story house &
fenced garden containing birds &
a small dog, a large rooster perched on the fence, central register
w/a flower basket flanked by two
deer below two brief pious verses
framed w/flowers, all within a carnation border, executed in multicolored silk & cotton stitches on
linen, signed & dated "Catherine
Sickels, age 10 1826," framed,
17 x 18" 1,210.00
Landscape scene of a large red brick
house surrounded by flowers, trees
w/perched birds & pine trees, executed in green, red, blue, yellow &
white wool stitches on canvas
ground, lower register w/an apple
tree, pine trees, reindeer, carnations & baskets of fruit, signed
"Ann Jones's Work," late 19th c.,
22½ x 23½" 1,045.00
Pious verse "A Request to the Divine
Being...Ann Browne her work done
in the 13 year of her age" within
flowering borders w/birds centering a cherub's head w/wings &
crown, stitched in several shades
of green & blue w/pink, red,
white, black & brown on homespun
linen fabric, framed, 11½" sq.
(some wear & small holes) 1,000.00
Pious verse "The Diety and Humani-
ty of Christ...." & "Mary Ann
Redear finished this sampler June
the 30, 1787 in the fourteenth
year of her age," all within a floral border, multicolored stitches
on homespun linen fabric, gilt
frame, 15 x 18" (small holes) 550.00
Pious verse centering Academy building above rows of animals & land-

scapes over inscription "Nancy
Vredenburghs work wrought at
Mount Tabor Academy East Chester
(New York) in 14 days August 29th
1838," all within meandering floral
border, 17¾ x 22¾" 1,045.00
Poem "On Education..." & "Sarah
Younge work September 1797"
within a vining floral border above
pastoral scene w/house, trees,
birds, green hills, dog & shepherd
boy & girl worked in a variety of
colors on homespun linen fabric,
framed, 13½ x 15¾" (minor wear
& small holes)................2,600.00
Scenic sampler w/wide border band
framing undulating tulip & rose
vines surrounding ornately stitched
center w/a small top center blue
sawtooth reserve w/the names of
members of the Larzelere family
just above the inscription "Elizabeth Larzelere, her sampler
Wrought in the 13th Year of her
age 1812," large central area
filled w/sprays of pink carnations,
birds perched on flowering vines,
lilies of the valley, baskets of fruit
all above a tall two-story brick
house w/yellow windows & door at
bottom on a stepped green lawn
w/a pair of pine trees at each
side, Pennsylvania, framed,
17¼ x 21" 3,300.00

STEVENGRAPHS

Bookmark, "A Birthday Gift" ....　50.00
Bookmark, "Declaration of Inde-
pendence," framed, 7¼"........ 160.00
Bookmark, George Washington,
1876 Centennial ....　90.00
Bookmark, "Happy Christmas" verse
& flowers on black silk ....　75.00
Bookmark, "Happy May Thy Birthday
Be" ....　45.00
Bookmark, "Home Sweet Home," no
tassel ....　40.00
Bookmark, "Norwich, Conn. 250th
Anniversary" ....　50.00
Bookmark, "Garibaldi"............　90.00
Bookmark, "To My Father" ....　40.00
Picture, "The Crystal Palace," origi-
nal mat ....　95.00
Picture, "The Death".............. 450.00
Picture, "For Life or Death - Heroism
on Land," fire engine rushing to
burning house, matted & original
frame 305.00
Picture, "Full Cry" 350.00
Picture, "The Good Old Days,"
bright colors, original mount &
original label 145.00
Picture, "The Present Time," in two-
way frame w/title on back 425.00

Picture, "Robert Burns," in two-way
frame w/title on back 185.00

TAPESTRIES

Flemish Verdure Tapestry

Austrian, scene of an 18th century
courting couple in an Italian landscape, enclosed within a floral
framed border, worked in shades
of grey, green, ochre & pink,
signed "Elas Ackerman, Wein
1930," 4' 2" l., 3' 4" h. 165.00
Austrian, Athena & Aphrodite surrounded by amorini in a classical
architectural setting, woven in
shades of ochre, green, purple &
peach, 20th c., 5' 4" l., 4' 6" h. ... 825.00
Continental, forest scene w/animals
& woodcutters, tones of brown,
red & green, ca. 1900,
6' 11" x 8' 6".................. 990.00
Flemish, Baroque, historical scene of
warriors in armor & mail, carrying
shields, w/turreted structures in
the background, woven in tones of
blue, rust, green, grey, olive &
indigo, mid-17th c., 9' 4" x 11' 6"
(restorations)................9,350.00
Flemish, "verdure," mythological
scene depicting Hercules slaying
the Nemean lion in a wooded landscape w/two figures & a horse to
the side, within foliate cartouche
borders, worked in yellow &
brown, mid-17th c., 9' 8" x 10' 3"
(ILLUS.) 16,500.00
French, Aubusson, Blind Man's Buff,
depicting a group of five players,
one wearing a blindfold, in a
forest setting, picture frame border, tones of rust, green, ivory,
red & ochre, inscribed lower right
corner *Manufacture Royale
Aubusson 1747*, second half
19th c., 8' 10" x 9' 10"
(restorations).................3,850.00

French, Aubusson, hunting scene
woven in tones of green, rust, red,
ivory & indigo, later selvedge border, last quarter 18th c.,
5' 8" x 6' 10" 7,700.00
French, Gobelins, needlepoint copy
of a Cluny tapestry showing ladies
playing a portable organ flanked
by unicorns bearing banners on a
flowered coral ground, 5' 6" l.,
4' 5" h. 770.00

(End of Textiles Section)

THEOREMS

Fruits & Basket Theorem

*During the 19th century, a popular pastime
for some ladies was theorem painting, or stencil painting. Paint was allowed to penetrate
through hollow-cut patterns placed on paper
or cotton velvet. Still-life compositions, such
as bowls of fruit or vases of flowers, were the
favorite themes, but landscapes and religious
scenes found some favor among amateur
artists who were limited in their ability and
unable to do freehand painting. Today these
colorful pictures, with their charming ar-
rangements, are highly regarded by collectors. The following theorems are by unknown
American artists.*

Basket beside large group of fruits
on velvet, yellow basket & grapes,
melons & peaches, found in Connecticut, ca. 1825, w/early gilt
frame, 13½ x 17" (ILLUS.) $2,860.00
Basket full of fruit on velvet, open
lattice flat-bottomed basket
w/large loop handles piled high
w/varied fruits, old gilt frame,
19th c., 9¾ x 12" 12,100.00
Basket full of fruit on velvet, handled
basket w/loop handles & criss-

cross diamond pattern piled high
w/varied fruits & leaves, ca. 1830,
narrow gilt frame, 17½ x 20" 6,325.00
Bouquet of flowers on paper, bright
green & yellow w/faded blue &
red, old gilt frame, 12½ x 15¼"
(minor stains) 125.00
Bowl of fruit on velvet, melons,
plums & berries in a striped bowl
w/butterfly hovering at side, in
vivid shades of yellow, green, blue
& red, ogee frame, New England,
19th c., 9¾ x 13½" (some discolor-
ation & fabric loss) 1,540.00
Bowl of fruit, water-color & mica on
paper, large ribbed bowl filled to
overflowing w/grapes, peaches,
pears, cherries & a pineapple,
wheat & strawberries scattered
around foot of bowl, paper label
w/maker's name & place of origin
on reverse, Massachusetts, early
19th c., w/early gilt frame,
15 x 16½" 11,550.00
Bowl w/watermelon, strawberries &
grapes on velvet, yellow bowl
holds green & red watermelon,
red berries & purple grapes,
signed along bottom edge, "Cyn-
thia L. Sears, Sharon," ca. 1830,
original veneered frame,
16½ x 18½" 33,000.00
Compote of fruit & leaves on linen,
striped compote w/pears, grapes,
strawberries & leaves in red,
greens, yellow & blue, unframed,
7½ x 9½" (stains, fabric loss) 275.00
Compote of fruit & leaves, oil on
linen, striped compote w/fruit &
leaves in green, blue, red &
brown, unframed, early 19th c.,
8¾ x 13½" (stains, tiny holes) . . .3,300.00
Pattern glass bowl filled w/fruit on
velvet, ca. 1830, original frame,
9¾ x 13" .1,980.00
Plate of fruit on paper, applied
printed paper border, gilt frame,
10½ x 12½" (surface damage,
glue stains, wrinkles & fold
line) 400.00
Rose floral wreath on beige silk
faille, original gilt frame, ca.
1835, 9 x 9" (minor staining) 165.00
Scene depicting a man fishing be-
fore a house in a tree-filled landscape on velvet, America, 19th c.,
framed, 9¼ x 14" 770.00
Spray of moss roses, oil on linen,
rich red & green, unframed, early
19th c., 9" w., 7" h. (stains) 302.50

TOBACCO JARS

Elephant Tusk Tobacco Jar

Advertising, embossed "Mild LaPalina Senators Made Good," Chase brass, 6¼" h. . . . . $15.00 to 20.00

Earthenware, model of a pig in a barrel, 6¼" h. 110.00

Elephant tusk, the body formed by an oval-shaped section of an elephant's tusk, mounted w/heavy silver moldings at rim & base, on four feet, conical oval cover w/a ball finial, opening to a silver cylindrical removable liner, rim & base moldings repousse & chased in stylized floral motifs in the Indian taste, feet similarly decorated, ca. 1884-91, marked on base, Tiffany & Company, New York, 10½" h. (ILLUS.) 10,450.00

Limoges china, gold top decorated w/clumps of poppies, artist-signed 85.00

Majolica, bust of a bearded Turk . . . 120.00

Majolica, model of a frog 225.00

Majolica-type, model of a hen, putty glaze w/red comb & wattles, 10" h. 80.00

Nippon china, playing cards decoration, 7½" h. 395.00

Nippon china, swans on a placid lake scene. 95.00

Pottery, burlap bag form, "$100,000" in white label on front 85.00

Silver plate, hinged box w/sponge container, 2" h. model of a pug dog w/glass eyes on lid, 4 x 5 x 6" 200.00

Stoneware, body w/embossed half-figure of a man holding a clay pipe w/curling wisps of smoke & arch w/flowers & foliage overhead, mottled tan glaze, silver lid, Scotland, 10¼" h. 275.00

Wooden, African mahogany w/copper lining, plaque engraved "Ivory Dunhill," 1936, Alfred Dunhill Co., 10¼ x 12¼", 5½" h. 495.00

TOOLS

Inlaid Wood Planes

Adz, "Rochester No. 7" $35.00

Bow saw, wrought-iron fittings in well-shaped wooden frame w/dark patina, stamped "W.S. Thomas," 22" l. 55.00

Brace, piano maker's, "Bagshaw & Field, Philadelphia". 175.00

Brace, "Winchester No. 3602," 8" . . . 50.00

Broad axe, "Zenith," handle original hickory, 7 lbs., right or left handed, large Zenith star & Zenith name below in ½" letters & below in curve, Marshall Wells, 12" 200.00

Caliper rule, "Stanley No. 38," ivory w/German silver trim, 6" l. 160.00

Caliper rule, "Stanley No. 78½," four-fold, 24" l. 65.00

Calipers, steel, ends terminate in small feet, stamped "W.T.I. 1863," 18" l. 85.00

Draw shave, tiger maple, striped, hand carved, two-handled, w/hand forged blade, hole for hanging, 12" l. 55.00

Drill, hand-type, "Winchester No. 3533" 50.00

Drill press, post-type, "Ganedy Mfg. Co., Chicago Heights, Illinois," automatic, 6' 450.00

Hacksaw, wrought-iron frame w/simple rounded wooden handle w/brass ferrule, end of frame where handle attaches w/parrot-head shaped end, 14" l. 65.00

Hatchet, "Marbles No. 2½," w/nail puller 425.00

Inclinometer level, "Melich," iron, pat. 1889, 12" 550.00

Knife, paper hanger's, "Winchester" 32.00

Level, "Davis & Cook," wooden, 28" 30.00

Level, "Keen Kutter No. 2," brass ends 35.00

Level, "Stanley No. 3," brass ends, 1891 . . . . 25.00

Level, "Starrett No. 96," 12" 95.00

Level & grade finder combination, marked "Edward Helb, Railroad, Pa.," in original wooden box 350.00

Mallet, carpenter's, small burl wood
head w/turned rings, hickory handle, 10½" l. 35.00

Plane, "Auburn Tool Co.," block-
type, stock, wedge & thumb rest
inlaid w/contrasting woods, bone
& horn in Masonic symbols & geometric devices, the double iron
stamped "Auburn Tool Co., Thistlebrand Auburn N.Y.," 19th c.,
10¼" l., 5½" h. (ILLUS. left) 880.00

Plane, "Auburn Tool Co.," trying-
type, stock & wedge inlaid w/con-
trasting woods & bone in a variety
of Masonic symbols & geometric
devices (some losses), the double
iron stamped "Auburn Tool Co.
Thistlebrand Auburn, N.Y.,"
19th c., 23" l., 6¾" h. (ILLUS.
right) 990.00

Plane, "Keen Kutter No. KK10" 110.00

Plane, "Ohio No. 09314," block-
type 200.00

Plane, "Sandusky No. 119," plow-
type, mahogany w/brass......... 79.00

Plane, "Stanley No. 4½" 47.00

Plane, "Stanley No. 45," w/18
blades 85.00

Plane, "Winchester No. 3005" 120.00

Router, "Stanley No. 71½," hand-
type 85.00

Rule, folding-type, "Keen Kutter
K680" 15.00

Rule, folding-type, "Lufkin
No. 1206," aluminum, brass-
jointed, six-fold 25.00

Rule, "Stanley No. 62" 12.50

Saw, hand-type, well-shaped wood-
en handle w/brass trim & two
spirit levels, top straight edge of
blade has 24" ruler, pull-out
scribe in handle, handle marked
"Diston, Patented May 21 - Diston
& Son, Phila.," 31" l. 175.00

Saw, stair-type, "Keen Kutter"...... 65.00

Saw, "Winchester No. 9".......... 65.00

Screwdriver, "Winchester No. 117,"
10" l. 30.00

Screwdriver, "Winchester No. 7160,"
1½" l. 45.00

Slate hammer, wrought iron, round
wooden handle, marked "Auld &
Conger, Cleveland, O.," 11½" l.... 30.00

Spoke shave, "Stanley No. 80" 20.00

Square, carpenter's, steel blade,
rosewood handle inlaid w/brass,
handle stamped "H.D. Aupke,"
20" l. 45.00

Windmill wrench, "International
Harvester"..................... 30.00

Wire rope measure, "A. Roellings &
Sons," w/all specifications for
wire rope 175.00

Wrench, alligator-type, "Shapleigh-
DE," pat. May 26, 1903 .... 125.00

Wrench, open end, "Winchester
No. 1801," 1/8 x 3/16".......... 30.00

TOOTHPICK HOLDERS

Cat-on-a-Pillow Toothpick Holder

*Reference numbers listed after the holders
refer to the late William Heacock's book, 1000
Toothpick Holders.*

Amber glass, pressed Cat-on-a-
Pillow patt. (ILLUS.) $67.50

Amber glass, pressed Darwin patt.,
model of a monkey's head,
No. 335 .... 50.00

Amber glass, pressed Hobb's Hobnail patt., No. 109.............. 20.00

Amberina glass, three-cornered,
Venetian Diamond patt. 210.00

Amethyst glass, pressed Swag
w/Brackets patt., No. 300....... 66.00

Bavarian china, two-handled, rose
decoration.................... 20.00

Bisque, model of an owl, feathers
outlined w/brown 50.00

Bisque, model of a skull w/a nodding jaw sitting atop book, 4" 250.00

Bisque, nodder, figural standing
Teddy Roosevelt w/blue frock coat
w/red lining & lapels, white vest,
gold buttons, white trousers
w/brown stripes, black top hat,
3½" h......................... 275.00

Blue glass, pressed Nestor patt.,
w/enameled decoration,
No. 184 .... 110.00

China, three-handled, Gaudy Welsh
Oyster patt., Allerton........... 75.00

Clear glass, pressed Alexis patt.,
No. 661 .... 18.00

Clear glass, pressed Czarina patt.,
No. 599 .... 22.00

Clear glass, pressed Duncan & Miller No. 42 patt. 32.50

Clear glass, pressed New Hampshire patt. 30.00

Clear glass, pressed Priscilla patt. . . 40.00

Clear glass, pressed Rock Crystal patt., McKee Glass Co. 28.00

Cranberry opalescent glass, Windows patt. 145.00

Custard glass, Diamond & Peg patt., w/rose decoration 92.50

Emerald green glass, pressed Georgia Gem patt., No. 180 . . . . 95.00

Green opalescent glass, pressed Iris w/Meander patt. 58.00

Green opaque glass, pressed Pansy patt. 30.00

Majolica, figure of little old lady sitting by hollow tree stump 155.00

Milk white glass, pressed Four Rabbits patt., four relief-molded rabbit heads in foliage around sides, No. 398 . . . . 110.00

Royal Bayreuth china, four-handled, old woman & house scene 85.00

Royal Bayreuth china, model of a round, handled coal scuttle, "tapestry" finish. 395.00

R.S. Germany china, two-handled, floral decoration w/satin finish . . . 65.00

R.S. Prussia china, three-handled, scalloped base, white satin finish w/white rose on front, tiny gold flowers, pink blush & gold trim . . . 195.00

Rubina glass, Optic patt. 45.00

Ruby-stained glass, pressed Bead Swag patt., souvenir 29.00

Ruby-stained glass, pressed Columbian Coin patt. 225.00

Ruby-stained glass, pressed Eureka patt. 79.00

Sapphire blue glass, pressed Idyll patt., No. 171 . . . . 95.00

Sapphire blue glass, turned out scalloped rim, pressed Daisy & Button patt., w/scrolled metal overlay . . . 85.00

Schafer-Vater china, model of a smiling pig 75.00

Silver plate, model of a dog by basket, paw on bone, glass eyes 75.00

Silver plate, model of a mouse, Rogers Bros. 125.00

Silver plate, model of a porcupine, marked "Meriden" 42.00

Vaseline glass, pressed Gold Band patt. 55.00

Vaseline glass, pressed Petticoat patt., No. 231 . . . . 110.00

TOYS

Also see CHARACTER COLLECTI-

BLES, CHILDREN'S DISHES, DISNEY COLLECTIBLES and DOLLS.

Schoenhut Circus Giraffe

Acrobat slide toy, carved & painted wood, modeled as a monkey in a red & blue costume w/articulated arms & legs mounted on a pole w/later pine stand, 19½" h. (losses to paint) $220.00

African Safari animal, Alligator, wooden, painted eyes, Schoenhut (Philadelphia), regular size 285.00

Airplane, 1910 Bleriot, die-cast metal, Tootsietoy (Dowst Brothers, Chicago, Illinois, 1922-61), mint condition 105.00

Airplane, "Spirit of St. Louis," sheet metal, Line Mar (Japan) 100.00

Airplane, "Flying Bomb," metal, Wyandotte (All Metal Products Co., Wyandotte, Michigan), 18" . . . 100.00

Airplane, "Mono Coupe," cast iron, Arcade (Freeport, Illinois), No. 353 . . . . 50.00

Airplane, "Pan American," metal, Louis Marx & Co. (New York City), 27" wingspan 145.00

Air rifle, Daisy 102, Daisy Manufacturing Co. 20.00

Air rifle, Markham Air Rifle Co., 1888 . . . . 175.00

American Logs, wood, Halsam Co. (Chicago, Illinois), complete set in round can 50.00

Army truck w/trailer, pressed steel, original olive paint, large, Buddy L (Moline Pressed Steel Company, East Moline, Illinois), 1930's-40's . . 250.00

Automobile, closed coupe, cast iron, original green paint, A. C. Williams Co. (Ravenna, Ohio), 4" l. . . . 50.00

Automobile, 1964 Ford Fairlane 500 Sports Coupe, metal, promo car . . 50.00

Automobile, Ford Model T, cast

iron, w/"Anthony Company, Inc., Streator, Illinois" on side, black & grey w/white rubber tires, Arcade 1,650.00

Automobile, Ford Thunderbird, die-cast metal, Tootsietoy, 1950's 15.00

Automobile, Ford Thunderbird, 1958 model, sheet metal, flywheel mechanism, painted turquoise & white, AMT (Japan), mint in box 75.00

Automobile, Harris Roadster, 1903 model, cast iron, 2 x 3 3/8 x 2 7/8".......................... 600.00

Automobile, Micro Racer, Schuco (Germany), 3½", w/box 18.00

Automobile, w/3" sq. steel sign reading "Sophie Tucker-Roi-Tan Radio Show," pressed steel, red, streamlined shape, 4" l. 95.00

Battery-operated, "Bubble Blowing Elephant"...................... 50.00

Battery-operated, "Bunny the Magician" 83.00

Battery-operated, "Busy Housekeeper Rabbit," lady rabbit w/vacuum moves head while vacuuming, vacuum lights, 10" h.....125.00 to 175.00

Battery-operated, "Cap Firing Tank," Louis Marx & Co................ 50.00

Battery-operated, "Charlie Weaver Bartender" ....60.00 to 80.00

Battery-operated, "Cycling Daddy," man pedals tricycle while waving & smoking a lighted pipe 50.00

Battery-operated, "Fred Flintstone's Bedrock Band," mint condition.... 175.00

Battery-operated, "High Jinx at the Circus Clown," w/cymbal-playing monkey 220.00

Battery-operated "James Bond 007 Car," A.C. Gilbert Co. (New Haven, Connecticut), mint in box, 11½" l. 450.00

Battery-operated, "Lunar Patrol," Cragston (Japan) 285.00

Battery-operated, "Milk Drinking Cat," no box................. 75.00

Battery-operated, "Overland Stage-coach," Cragston, 15" l 95.00

Battery-operated, "Picnic Bunny," mint in box 75.00

Battery-operated, "Sleepy Baby Bear," no box.................. 125.00

Battery-operated, "Smoky Bill & His Crazy Car"...................... 95.00

Battery-operated, "Super Rotate-O-Matic Astronaut" 125.00

Battery-operated, "Teddy the Artist" ....150.00 to 175.00

Battery-operated, "Western Special Locomotive," Japan, mint in box.. 55.00

Battleship, "Oregon," wood & cardboard, covered by chromolitho-graphs in orange, green, yellow & black, red wooden wheels, wooden cannon on deck, Spanish-American War era, ca. 1900, 24" l. 260.00

BB gun, Daisy Buzz Barton 90.00

Bell ringer toy, jockey on horse on platform w/wheels, gears & bells below, nickel-plated 450.00

Bell ringer toy, "The Landing of Columbus," cast iron, gilt finish ....250.00 to 350.00

Blocks, alphabet-type, wooden, red & white w/embossed designs in blue & black, w/original box, 7¾ x 9¾" box, set of 20 (minor wear) 125.00

Blocks, lithographs on wood, animals dressed as people w/bears, rabbits, monkeys, dogs, etc., Victorian, graduated set of 6...................... 650.00

Blocks, building-type, "Richters Anchor Blocks," stone blocks in varied sizes & shapes in three-tier wooden box, many colored pictures & diagrams, Germany, 1911 .... 225.00

Blocks, puzzle-type, lithographed paper on wood, blocks form pictures of a cow, camel, donkey, horse, zebra & elephant, marked "Germany," set of 12, overall 4¼ x 5¼"...................... 60.00

Blocks, "Safety Blocks," Halsam Co., 1926, set of 25 in box w/cover depicting airship 87.50

Boat, "Big Caesar," Roman-style warship, plastic, motorized, Remco, 1950's, 30" l., 7" h..........1,000.00

Boat, sailboat, wooden hull & mast, cloth sail, tin rudder & fins, "Toy Tinkers, Evanston, Ill.," 4 x 10 x 11" 50.00

Britains (soldiers), "Heavy Howitzer," Set No. 1266, mint in box, 18" 165.00

Britains (soldiers), Herald Series, Set No. 7809 Horse Guards, includes two sentry boxes, 18 soldiers & four horses, mint in box 60.00

Britains (soldiers), U.S. Marine Corps Band, marching in winter dress uniforms w/instruments, Set No. 2014, set................3,080.00

Bus, "Greyhound," die-cast metal, Tootsietoy, 6" l................. 60.00

Bus, "Greyhound Lines," tin w/lithographed tin passengers, shades of green, Marusan (Japan), 12½" l. 475.00

Cannon, "Big Bang," cast iron, olive drab green w/red wheels, w/original box, 8¾" l. 53.00

Cap pistol, "Big Horn," disc-type,
cast iron, Kilgore Manufacturing
Co. (Westerville, Ohio), 1940's 38.00
Cap pistol, "Buc-A-Roo," cast iron,
Kilgore, 7½" l., in original box ...   52.00
Cap pistol, "Buffalo Bill," cast iron,
long barrel, Kenton Hardware Co.
(Kenton, Ohio) 125.00
Cap pistol, "Lawmaker," cast iron,
Kenton, 1939, w/box 65.00
Cap pistol, "Long Tom," cast iron,
Kilgore, 10" l., w/original box....   110.00
Cap pistol, "U.S. Secret Service,"
cast metal w/plastic grips, Kil-
gore, 1950-60, w/shoulder holster
in original box, 6½" l...........   23.00
Carpet sweeper, Bissell's "Little
Gem" 55.00
Circus animal, Donkey, wooden,
painted eyes, Schoenhut, reduced
size 60.00
Circus animal, Giraffe, wooden,
glass eyes, Schoenhut, regular
size, 11" h. (ILLUS. page 849) 250.00
Circus animal, Horse w/saddle
(brown), wooden, painted eyes,
Schoenhut, reduced size 130.00
Circus animal, Tiger, wooden, glass
eyes, Schoenhut, regular
size....................200.00 to 235.00
Circus performer, Crackerjack
Clown, wooden, Schoenhut, 8" ...   98.00

Schoenhut Circus Ringmaster

Circus performer, "Ringmaster,"
wooden w/wooden head, painted
eyes, Schoenhut, regular size,
8½" h. (ILLUS.) 155.00
Circus truck w/matching circus wagon, pressed steel, Wyandotte, No.
503, w/original composition lions,
ca. 1936, 19" l., the set 195.00
Clockwork mechanism, autobus,
painted tin, finished in brown,
yellow & white, EPL No. 590, Lehmann (Germany), ca. 1920,
8" l............................1,870.00

Clockwork mechanism, battleship,
tin, hull painted deep brown &
grey, the deck w/four lifeboats on
davits, eight single & four double
revolving gun turrets, two cranes,
probably Fleischmann, Germany,
ca. 1930, 21" l.................2,860.00
Clockwork mechanism, cat, white
rabbit fur w/green glass eyes,
moves forward & opens mouth to
emit squeak, France, early
20th c., 20" long w/tail,
10½" h.......................   192.50
Clockwork mechanism, carrousel,
painted tin, central standard supporting three white painted horses
w/wheels mounted on the hind
legs below a blue & red cotton
canopy trimmed w/fringe, Germany, late 19th c., 12" h.
(inoperative) 1,540.00
Clockwork mechanism, "Li-La" han-
som cab, painted tin, shows two
ladies & a dog w/driver, EPL No.
520, Lehmann, early 1900's, 5¾" h.
(inoperative)..................   715.00

Clockwork Ocean Liner

Clockwork mechanism, ocean liner,
painted tin, three-level deck
w/four funnels, ten lifeboats on
davits, twelve ventilators & two
flagpoles w/red & white flags, hull
painted red & white, probably Germany, ca. 1930, 28" l. (ILLUS.) ...7,700.00
Clockwork mechanism, violin player,
painted tin, musician playing violin while his hat moves back &
forth & cymbals play on the drum
attached to his back, possibly
Gunthermann (Germany), ca.
1900, 10" h. 825.00
Clockwork mechanism, "Walking
Turk," molded cloth head & cap,
painted facial features & kid
hands, the clockwork mechanism
concealed within a cardboard
underskirt supported by moving
legs & feet, wearing a blue &
brick-red cotton outfit, trimmed
w/brocade, w/original box, Enoch
Rich Morrison (United States),
ca. 1862, 10" h. (tear in sleeve &
bottom of skirt, no key) 1,320.00
Clown, tin, penny-type, figure suspended on a rod, mechanical
w/good action 225.00

Coaster wagon, wooden, removable slat sides w/worn original varnish finish & "Delivery Truck" in red paint, rubber-rimmed metal wheels, 20th c., 20" l. (worn & weathered) 135.00

Early Wooden Coaster Wagon

Coaster wagon, wooden, red paint w/h.p. lettering "Express" on sides & "C.V. Jackson" on end board (ILLUS.) 412.50

Combine, "Massey Ferguson," Ertl Toy Co. (Dyersville, Iowa), No. 169, w/box 95.00

Concrete mixing truck, pressed steel, Structo Manufacturing Co. (Freeport, Illinois), 21" l. 155.00

Conestoga wagon, horse-drawn, metal & wood wagon w/fabric top & pair of lithographed paper on wood & metal articulated horses, Canton, Ohio, 1910, 19" long overall 247.50

Crane, painted metal, "Ride-Em" construction crane w/magnetic "hook" at end of boom cable, Keystone Manufacturing Co. (Boston, Massachusetts), red body w/black wheels & crane boom, 28" l., 11" h. 120.00

Dump truck, "Mack," cast iron, Arcade, 1930, 13" l. 750.00

Dump truck, metal, John C. Turner Co. (Wapakoneta, Ohio), red & blue, 20" l. 295.00

Dump truck, pressed steel, Sturditoy (The Sturdy Corp., Providence, Rhode Island), bed cranks from side to side, 1920's, 25" l. 1,375.00

Erector set, A.C. Gilbert No. 4½, "The Motorized Set," metal box, manual, original price tag, copyright 1954 (box w/slight rust inside & out, manual w/two corners slightly worn) 10.00

Erector set, Gilbert, No. 10053, rocket launcher, w/original case & manual 70.00

Erector set, Marklin (Germany), No. 102, w/manual, 1930's, mint in box 245.00

Fire engine, cast iron, model of ear-

ly motorized pumper-type engine, red & gold paint w/nickel wheels, 6¼" l. (slight wear & light rust on wheels) 100.00

Fire engine, tin, red-painted body w/gilt borders w/detachable borders retaining portions of original paint, America, early 20th c., 20" l. (flaking to paint & some minor corrosion to metal)... 330.00

Fire hook & ladder wagon w/three horses & two drivers, cast iron, four wooden ladders (two damaged), worn original red & white paint w/blue, gold & black, 33" l. overall 725.00

Fire truck, pressed steel, Buddy L, No. 321, late 1940's, mint in box.. 125.00

Friction-type, Cord Coupe Model 810, pressed steel body, rubber tires, Wyandotte, 1936-37, 13" l. (old repaint) 175.00

Friction-type, race car, "Silver Bullet," pressed steel, Buffalo Toys & Tool Works (Buffalo, New York), 26" l. 345.00

Friction-type, train engine, metal, painted black, rounded barrel w/two stacks, the underside w/red undercoat, America, early 20th c., 14¼" l. 275.00

Frog, "Croaker the Frog," rubber, Rempel Manufacturing (Akron, Ohio), mint in box, 10½" h....... 45.00

Garbage truck, pressed steel, Structo, 21" l. 165.00

Gasoline tank truck, "American Oil Co.," cast iron, green & silver w/gold trim, nickel wheels, 10½" l. 375.00

Gasoline tank truck, "Shell Oil," die-cast metal, 1949 Ford F-6, Tootsietoy, 6" l. 25.00

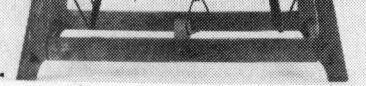

American Hobby Horse on Frame

Hobby horse on frame, wooden, white-painted galloping horse depicted w/leather pricked ears, horsehair mane & tail, open mouth, black saddle & red saddle blanket, black hooves, w/leather & metal stirrups, swings on red-painted wooden trestle base, America, 19th c., 34" l., 28½" h. (ILLUS.)........................ 770.00

Hobby horse on frame, wooden, laminated construction w/good carved detail, well-shaped legs & hooves & slightly turned head w/flared nostrils, worn white painted surface w/traces of dapple grey, one glass eye, mane, leather ear (one missing), old replacements, original harness, saddle & worn tail, wooden frame w/original red paint w/stenciled decoration of yellow, black & green, 39" l., 33" h. (iron brace added to bentwood support under horse)........................ 600.00

Hobby horse on rockers, pine, logform cylindrical body, simple post neck & stylized head, raised on branch-form legs on a rocker base, retains traces of original blue-green paint, Midwestern America, late 19th - early 20th c., 23½" l., 18½" h................ 192.50

Hobby horse on rockers, burlapcovered wood, horse depicted w/leather ears & partial harness, wood nose & open mouth, leather partial saddle & strap, yarn tail, wood hoofs, raised on pine rocker base, Pennsylvania, 19th c., 29" l., 25½" h. (leather distressed & repair to rocker base) 715.00

Hobby horse on rockers, wood & burlap, prancing horse depicted w/shaggy mane & tail, brown body w/orange saddle & blue saddle blanket, raised on a shaped rectangular red-painted wood plank on four metal wheels, now attached to a curved red-painted wood rocker, America, ca. 1900, 4' l., 36" h. 2,475.00

Hobby horse, stick-type, wooden, figural horse head, bottom w/wheel, red, white & black paint, 22" l. 40.00

Horse-drawn two-wheeled cart, tin, George W. Brown & Co. (Forestville, Connecticut), 1870's, 9" horse...................... 295.00

Ice cream freezer, wooden stave construction w/wire bands, metal mechanism in top w/crank handle w/wooden handhold, marked "White Mountain Junior," traces of paper label, 7¼" h. (one pin holding gear box broken) 150.00

Iron, electric-type, "Little Lady," Kokomo Toys (Kingston Products Corp., Kokomo, Indiana), in original box 29.00

Iron, electric-type, tin w/red Bakelite handle, Wolverine Co. (Pittsburgh, Pennsylvania), 3½ x 7" ... 12.50

Ironing board, lithographed tin, Wolverine Co...................... 15.00

18th Century Jack-in-the-Box

Jack-in-the-box, painted wood, composition, fabric & papier-mache, spring-mounted figure of a Chinaman w/painted composition head & hands contained within a wood box covered w/marbleized paper printed w/the legend "What wonder Miss, May be in this, Make me Free, And you'll see!," probably England, 18th c., overall 8" h. (ILLUS.)........................ 440.00

Jack-in-the-box, "Jolly-Tune the Clown," Mattel, late 1940's 15.00

Jigsaw puzzle, "Steamer & Hose," shows three fire engines drawn by horses passing village stores, Milton Bradley & Co. (Springfield, Massachusetts), ca. 1900, 40" w... 115.00

Jigsaw puzzle set, "Peep at the Circus," four circus puzzles in wooden box w/colorful cover, McLoughlin Bros., set 250.00

Kiddy car, painted wood, rectangular seat raised on narrow frame w/upright handle, hard rubber tires w/wire spokes, original black, orange & red paint w/"The Irish Mail, Hill Standard & Co., Anderson, Ind.," 40" l. (worn & damaged tires)................... 160.00

Kitchen cabinet, lithographed tin, buff & green, Wolverine Co....... 55.00

Lawn mower, "Rotor Mower," lithographed tin, colorful, J. Chein & Co. (New York City), 10 x 10" .. 20.00

Lincoln Logs, Set No. 2C, includes original directions, all parts & box, ca. 1952 .... 38.00

Lincoln Logs, Set No. 3 w/directions, mint in box, 1934 .... 75.00

Merry-go-round, lithographed tin,
lever operated, J. Chein & Co.,
ca. 1930 .... 175.00
Microscope, Rexina Beginner's Model F-5400, in box 22.00
Milk bucket, lithographed tin, pictures girl milking cow, Louis Marx
& Co. (New York City) 15.00
Motorcycle, "Indian" four-cylinder,
cast iron, Hubley (Lancaster,
Pennsylvania), 9¾" l............ 675.00
Motorcycle, "Police Squad," in original box, Louis Marx & Co.,
1940's 325.00
Movie projector, "Keystone Junior,"
original box, Keystone Mfg. Co. .. 125.00
Noah's Ark, painted wood, w/four-
teen carved & painted animals,
original blue, red & black paint,
8 5/8" l. (cloth hinges broken).... 350.00
Noah's Ark animal, lion, Schuco 80.00
Noah's Ark animal, panda, Schuco,
2½" h........................ 150.00

Pedal Car

Pedal car, two-passenger vehicle
w/twin side lights, a front lamp &
a horn, overall 80" l. (ILLUS.) 3,850.00
Pedal car, 1936 Chevrolet,
Gendron......................1,750.00
Pedal car, 1936 Ford.............. 800.00
Pedal car, 1940 Lincoln
Zephyr 450.00
Penny toy, train w/four cars, tin,
"C.K.O.," Germany 165.00
Piano, "Baby Grand Piano," floor
model, variation w/18 keys, origi-
nal stained rosewood finish in ex-
cellent condition, Schoenhut
(Philadelphia) 295.00
Pistol, Fanner 50 w/holster & 18"
Bad Guy who draws against you,
w/instructions 100.00
Pistol, flintlock-type, Hubley, origi-
nal box 50.00
Play set, "Battle of the Blue &
Gray," No. 4745, Louis Marx &
Co., mint in box 300.00
Pull toy, camel on wheels, wooly
flannel-covered body & nodding
head, glass eyes, cloth trim, cast
iron wheel on each foot, 11" h.
(worn) 120.00

Gibbs Pioneer Wagon

Pull toy, covered wagon w/two
horses, wood, metal & canvas,
Gibbs Manufacturing Company
(Canton, Ohio), Model No. 57
"Gypsy Wagon," patented 1910,
overall 19" l., 9" h. (ILLUS.) 85.00
Pull toy, cow on wheels, "Moo-oo
Cow," black & white w/vinyl
horns & spring tail, Model 155,
Fisher-Price, Inc. (East Aurora,
New York), 1958-62 .... 20.00
Pull toy, frog on wheels, "Jolly Jumper," green acetate feet that flip
around rear wheels & move body
up & down, googlie eyes that roll
back & forth, Model 450, Fisher-
Price, Inc., 1954-56 .... 15.00
Pull toy, horse, burlap-covered
standing figure w/papier-mache
nose & open mouth, tack-studded
eyes & horsehair tail, black-
painted wood hooves, raised on a
shaped rectangular platform
mounted w/metal wheels, Ameri-
ca, late 19th c., 15½" l., 16" h.... 330.00
Pull toy, Polar bear on wheels,
wooden body w/wooly flannel
white coat, glass eyes, worn harness, legs rest on spokes of small
tin wheels, 6½" l................ 200.00
Pull toy, rabbit pulling cart, "Bunny
Cart," bunny pulls fiberboard can
w/metal bottom, Model 10,
Fisher-Price, Inc. (East Aurora,
New York), Easter 1940 .... 55.00
Pull toy, rabbit pulling cart, "Bunny
Cart," Model 401, Fisher-Price,
Inc., 1954, 10½" l. 40.00
Pull toy, train engine, "Looky Chug-
Chug," Model 161, Fisher-Price,
Inc., 1949...................... 30.00
Pull toy, turtle, "Tip-Toe Turtle,"
Model 773, Fisher-Price, Inc.,
1962-81, 8½" l. 20.00
Punching bag, "Everlast Jack Demp-
sey Sock-O-Bag," complete
w/metal foot stand & Dempsey-
portrait leather punching bag,
1930's 150.00
Puzzle, two-sided, advertising
"Hood's Sarsaparilla," one side a
gentleman in horse-drawn buggy,
other side a family watching an
air balloon, both colorful &

w/much detail, in original box,
ca. 1900 . . . . 195.00
Remote control "Tin Lizzy" automo-
bile, lithographed tin, yellow
w/printed graffiti such as "Dig
This Crazy Car" & " '23 Skiddo!,"
the composition driver & three
passengers in painted swanky
1930's attire, hand-crank remote
control box, in partial original box,
Arnold, ca. 1948, 10" l. 1,045.00
Robot, electric, red plastic & metal,
Morse code on back of head,
Louis Marx & Co. (New York, New
York), 14½" h. 300.00
Sand pail, lithographed tin, "Funny
Face," pictures clown face,
3" h. 45.00
Sand pail, lithographed tin, colorful
rodeo horses & cowboys, J. Chein
& Co. (New York, New York),
w/original shovel, 4" h., 2 pcs. . . . 22.00
Schoolroom toy model, comprising
twenty painted composition children seated at ten wooden desks
or on wooden stools, a schoolmaster w/podium & two lesson
cards, contained in a painted &
papered wooden schoolhouse
w/hinged opening, probably
Germany, late 19th c.,
6½ x 8 x 11" 660.00

"Sew Master" Sewing Machine

Sewing machine, "Sew Master,"
blue metal, working model
w/needle & thread, KAYanEE,
Germany, w/original box,
4½ x 8", 4½" h. (ILLUS.) 55.00
Sewing machine, metal, "Singer,"
leather case w/Bakelite handle,
w/hem gauge & needles, 1930's . . 95.00
Sled, painted & decorated wood, the
round ended deck painted red &
decorated w/black & yellow pinstriping centering "FAIRY," enhanced w/black & red flourishes,
natural varnished metal-braced
runners, America, late 19th c.,
33" l., 7" h. (some paint loss) 605.00
Sled, wooden w/metal-tipped run-
ners & cast-iron swan's head fini-

als, worn original varnish finish
w/red & black striping, padded
leatherized cloth top, 33½" l. (top
damaged) 325.00
Sleigh, push-type, wooden w/metal-
tipped runners & braces, original
red paint w/yellow striping & natural varnish finish, labeled on
bottom "Made by Paris Mfg. Co.
South Paris, Me. U.S.A.," 48" l.
(some wear) 450.00
Squirt gun, metal, "Daisy No. 72,"
mint in box 45.00
Stable & animals, miniature, carved
wood, tiny building w/fifteen tiny
carved farm animals w/poly-
chrome paint, Germany, building
4 5/8" l. (cloth hinges on roof are
broken) 165.00
Steam roller, pressed steel, red &
black paint, w/decals, Keystone,
20" l. (some rust & paint loss) 288.00
Stove, "Jewel Range Jr.," cast iron,
highly detailed w/working doors,
flues, dampers & ash pans,
Detroit Stove Works, includes cast
iron cooking pots & pans, 18" l.,
18" h. (one trivet missing from
stove) 495.00
Stove, kitchen range, tin-plated
w/orange lithographed sides &
painted top w/embossed doors,
w/pots & pans, ca. 1900's, 5" h. . . 145.00

Early Stuffed Monkey

Stuffed animal, monkey, brown mo-
hair, glass eyes, 24" h. (ILLUS.) . . . 192.50
Stuffed animal, monkey, jointed,
mohair w/character velvet face &
hands, original scarf, Merry-
thought, 17" h. 80.00
Taxi cab, cast iron, "Yellow Cab,"
Hubley Mfg. Co. (Lancaster, Penn-
sylvania), 8" l. 675.00
Telephone, wall-type, lithographed
tin w/wooden handle, cowboy
motif, Gong Bell Mfg. Co. (East
Hampton, Connecticut) 42.00
Theater, "Fold-A-Way Theatre,"
cardboard, contains backdrops,

wings, costumes, characters & dialogues for three plays: Little Red Riding Hood, Cinderella, & Little Black Sambo; Will Pente (Chicago, Illinois), ca. 1932 .... 75.00

Tool chest, "Big Boy," A.C. Gilbert Co. (New Haven, Connecticut), No. 3 .... 75.00

Top, wooden, original polychrome paint, impressed "Patented July 1, 1899," w/pull string, 4¼" h. (some paint wear)............... 70.00

Tractor, "Fordson," cast iron, red paint w/black trim, nickel wheels, Arcade Mfg. Co. (Freeport, Illinois), 6" l..................... 185.00

Tractor, "Oliver 70," row crop-type, cast iron, w/implements, Arcade Mfg. Co. 500.00

Tractor w/cattle box trailer, heavy tin, green tractor & silver trailer, trailer decal reads "Structo Cattle Farms, Inc., Load Limit 45,000 Lbs.," rubber tires marked "Structo Toys," Structo Mfg. Co. (Freeport, Illinois), 5 x 7 x 21", 2 pcs......................... 75.00

Train accessory, bridge, Lionel Mfg. Co. (New York, New York) No. 280, original box 225.00

Train car, boxcar, Lionel No. 6464 425, New Haven Boxcar 30.00

Train car, "Jail Car," painted tin, motorized car finished in maroon & black inscribed in gold "Metropolitan Express," Lionel, Gauge 2 7/8, No. 800, ca. 1903, 14½" l. (some wear & paint chips)....... 2,750.00

Train engine, Lionel, No. 42, eight-wheel electric, standard gauge ... 475.00

Train set: cast-iron electric 0-4-0 engine, four-wheel tender marked "N.Y.C. & H.R.," one passenger & one mail car; Gebruder Bing (Nuremberg, Germany), 1906-12, the set 250.00

Train station, tinplate, comprised of green base, four small buildings, hinged gates, two stairways, adjustable destination board & V-sloped corrugated roof, O gauge, Marklin (Germany), 14" l., 6½" h., the set 550.00

Tricycle, wrought iron, two large rear wheels & a small front wheel, a central steering handle & an upholstered seat, Victorian, 61" l. 605.00

Truck, "Bell Telephone," cast iron, Hubley, 5¼" l.................. 400.00

Truck, cargo-type, pressed steel, Structo, No. 702, mint in box 125.00

Truck, delivery-type, rare pressed steel Model T Ford truck, Buddy L

(Moline Pressed Steel Company, East Moline, Illinois), Model 210, original paint (tiny rust spot on box) 925.00

Truck, Mack, cast metal, Tootsietoy (Samuel Dowst Co., Chicago, Illinois), 1930's, 3" l............... 25.00

Typewriter, metal, "Dependable," Unique Art Mfg. Co. (New York, New York), w/box 75.00

Washing machine, hand-crank type, glass tub, metal lid, base & wringer, Wolverine Co. (Pittsburgh, Pennsylvania), 5½".............. 135.00

Wheelbarrow, child size, painted poplar, original green paint w/yellow striping, red flower & red handles, bottom dated "March 15, 1896," 28" l. (some damage & repair) 175.00

Windup celluloid dancing couple, Occupied Japan, 5" h........... 75.00

Windup tin "African Native Drummer," TPS, Japan............... 115.00

Windup tin airplane, "Air Mail," three-engine biplane, Girard Model Works (Girard, Pennsylvania), 1920's 750.00

Windup tin "Amos & Andy Fresh Air Taxi," Louis Marx & Co., early 1930's .... 700.00 to 850.00

Windup tin "Balky Mule," Louis Marx & Co., 1930's .... 90.00 to 110.00

Windup tin "Blue Bird," lithographed bird w/movable top stands on its own circular base, McVitie & Price, ca. 1911-12, 9" h.......... 660.00

Windup tin "Charleston Trio," featuring a fiddler, a dancer & a dancing dog w/cane in mouth, on lithographed base, Louis Marx & Co., 1921, w/original box 1,320.00

Windup tin "G.I. Joe & His Jouncing Jeep," Unique Art, ca. 1940, 6½" l. 198.00

Windup tin "Hobo Train," boxcar featuring a dog grabbing a hobo by the coattails, the figures rock back & forth as the car rolls forward, sides of toy lithographed w/various other riders of the rail, Unique Art, 8" l. 1,430.00

Windup tin "Jazzbo Jim on Roof," Ferdinand Strauss, 1921, w/original box, 10" h. .... 450.00 to 650.00

Windup tin Louis Armstrong playing trumpet, cloth costume, plastic head, hands & horn, marked "T.N.," Japan, 9½" h. 220.00

Windup tin "Mammy's Boy" walker, lithographed black man w/cane & face which moves up & down, Louis Marx & Co., 11" h................... 500.00 to 700.00

Windup tin "Merry Makers Mouse
Band," Louis Marx & Co., 1930's,
9" h. 725.00

Windup tin "Oh My" dancer,
lithographed blue coat, red
striped pants & yellow hat,
No. 685, Lehmann (Germany),
9" h. 588.00

Windup tin "Skidoodle Jalopy," lithographed yellow, red & blue
w/graffiti such as "Don't rush me,"
the seat containing a man backed
by a woman balancing a child on
her knees, as auto lurches forward
the family see-saws back & forth
activating a bellows-operated
horn, Nifty, ca. 1925, 9½" l. 2,640.00

Windup tin "Sweeping Mammy,"
No. 1750, Lindstrom, 1930's,
8" h. 185.00

"Tidy Tim" Toy

Windup tin "Tidy Tim," old man
pushing trash barrel, Louis Marx
& Co., ca. 1938 (ILLUS.) 350.00

Windup tin "Uncle Wiggily Car,"
Louis Marx & Co., 1935 . . 450.00 to 550.00

TRADE CARDS

*The Victorian trade card evolved from in-
formal calling cards and hand-decorated
notes. From the 1850's through the 1890's, the
American home was saturated with these
black-and-white and chromolithographed advertising cards given away with various
products.*

Automobiles, "Edsel," various
models & colors w/specifications
reverse, 3½ x 7", set of 5 . . . . $29.00

Baking powder, "Royal,"
mechanical 35.00

Baking soda, "Arm & Hammer," 242

assorted cards in plastic pages in
leather booklet 75.00

Cigarettes, "Turkey Red," Fable se-
ries, set of 10 . . . . 7.50

Clothing, "Todtman Clothier," die-
cut, black youngster in wash
tub 10.00

Coffee, "A & P," die-cut, easel-back,
girl feeding pug dog at table,
1885 . . . . 15.00

Coffee, "Lion," Nursery Rhymes,
black & white, set of 22 . . . . 55.00

"Hoyt's German Cologne"

Cologne, "Hoyt's German Cologne,"
chromolithograph of a girl &
doves, 1894 calendar reverse
(ILLUS.) 10.00

Fire engine, "Comb. Ladder Co.,
Providence, Rhode Island," color
photo of 1907 Auto Chemical En-
gine, 4 x 7" 17.50

Grocery store, "A & P Tea Co.,"
"United We Stand, Divided We
Fall" 20.00

Insurance, "Pacific Mutual Life Insurance Company of California,"
folding-type, court plaster inside,
1 x 2" 3.00

Soap, "Larkin," President series, set
of 5 . . . . 17.00

Soap, "Soapine," whale-shaped,
sailor washing whale 10.00

Stoves, "Garland Stoves & Ranges,"
black entering untidy room 8.00

Tea, "Union Pacific Tea Co.," black
boy on front 20.00

Telephone company, "Missouri &
Kansas Telephone Co.," bell-
shaped, dark blue cardboard, "We
Reach the People," 3 x 3½" 15.00

Thread, "Clark's Mile End," little
girls on front 7.00

Tobacco, "Newsboy Plug Tobacco,"

chromolithographs of people in
Victorian costumes, fisherman,
puppies & other scenes, 1892, set
of 6 . . . .   35.00

TRADE CATALOGS

Abbey & Imbrie Fishing Catalog,
1911, w/mailing envelope $68.00
Abbott's Magic Novelty Co. Sup-
plementary Catalog, No. 10,
1940's, 90 pp. 30.00
Abrams & Cox, 1898, stove items,
172 pp. 65.00
Ansco, 1915-16, cameras, 64 pp.,
6 x 8" 30.00
Bannerman Military Goods, 1931 . . . 140.00
Beardslee Chandelier Co., 1915,
Catalog No. 27, lighting accesso-
ries, 12½ x 15" 100.00
Buckwalter, 1899, stove items,
178 pp. 45.00
Butler Bros., 1929, Fall, 556 pp. 40.00
California Perfume Co. Catalog,
1916, color, tabs 150.00
Carson Pirie Scott & Co., Chicago,
1929, jewelry, 286 pp. 24.00
Chicago Mail Order, 1929, Spring &
Summer 40.00
Cleveland Bicycle, 1896, history of
company w/bike illustrations,
31 pp. 75.00
Dailey Co., Chicago, 1939, municipal
supplies, badges, firearms, fire
engines, 34 pp., 9 x 11" 17.50
Delta Power Tools, 1957, 87 pp. 6.00
Dennison, 1905, tags & stationers'
specialties, 149 pp. 15.00
Doyle (M.L.) Fashion Catalog, 1882 . .   55.00
Duncan Miller Glass, 1939, No. 77,
w/extra literature & letter 85.00
Enterprise Mfg. Co., 1899, coffee
mills, meat grinders, fruit presses,
109 pp., 3½ x 6" 35.00
Estey Organs, 1901, 24 pp.,
8 x 11½" 30.00
Falker-Stern, 1891, crockery, china,
glassware, lamps, fancy goods,
64 pp. 20.00
Farley Loetscher, Dubuque, Iowa,
1901, Design Book No. 9, mill-
work, large, hardbound 20.00
Garrison-Wagner, 1941, store dis-
plays, 90 pp.   12.00
Gibson (George), Belfast, Ireland,
1930, Irish linens, 22 pp. 20.00
Gilchrest, 1916, fountain equipment,
dippers, etc.   45.00
Gold Coin, 1890, stove items,
96 pp. 75.00
Gump's Feed Mill & Flower Equip-
ment Machinery Co., 1928-29 . . . . .   35.00

Hamilton Garment Co., 1923-24,
80 pp. 30.00
Hart Bros., Chicago, 1905, Spring,
men's wear 17.50
Hotpoint Electric Ranges, 1926,
32 pp. 30.00
International Sterling Minuet Serv-
ice, 1926, 32 pp. 22.00
Ivanhoe Division of the Miller Co.,
Cleveland, Ohio, 1925, lighting
glassware & fixtures, 63 pp.,
8 x 11" 48.00
Kalamazoo Stoves, 1920's, 84 pp. . . .   25.00
Keith Bros., Chicago, 1915, hats for
men & children 15.00
Kodak, 1917, cameras, 6 x 8½" 25.00
Laurel Gas Ranges, 1917 . . . .   8.00
Liege Double Gun Catalog, 1905 . . . .   31.00
Low (Daniel), Salem, Massachusetts,
1912, jewelry 35.00
McCray Refrigerators for Grocers,
early 1900's, color pictures 45.00
Montgomery Ward & Co., 1905,
1,124 pp. 55.00
Morris Stationery, 1938, office sup-
plies, pens, etc., 275 pp. 30.00
National Brass Co., 1925, brass
household hardware, 183 pp. 75.00
Nokes & Nicolai, 1910, drums & ac-
cessories, 96 pp. 50.00
Paramount Gas Ranges, 1920,
15 pp. 25.00
Perry, Dame Co., 1917-18, Fall &
Winter, 149 pp. 50.00
Pflueger Fishing Tackle, 1940,
128 pp. 38.00
Premier Bicycle, 1920, bicycles, sup-
plies, 54 pp.   38.50
Rexall Drug Store Premium Catalog,
1915, toys, perfumes, phono-
graphs, etc., 68 pp., 8 x 11" 20.00
Richardson Dry Goods, St. Joseph,
Missouri, 1907, Spring 25.00
Schoenhut Toy Catalog, 1907,
50 pp. 50.00
Sears, Roebuck and Co., 1899, or-
gans, pianos & musical instru-
ments, 50 pp. 75.00
Sears, Roebuck and Co., 1910-11,
Fall & Winter, Style Book for La-
dies, Misses & Girls, 96 pp. 78.00
Sears, Roebuck and Co., 1920, Fall . .   55.00
Sears, Roebuck and Co., 1947,
Christmas 40.00
Sioux City Iron Co., Sioux City,
Iowa, 1939-40, special catalog
No. 84 . . . .   45.00
Steinfeld, 1927, w/price list, chil-
dren's chairs, dining sets, scoot-
ers, teddy cars & doll carriages,
40 pp., 7¾ x 10¾" 45.00
Trebing Co. Gift Catalog, 1929, fish-
ing tackle, 586 pp. 35.00
Ulman Children's Automobiles &
Carriages, 1927 . . . .   75.00

Vick's Floral Guide, 1887, seeds 22.00
Warner Hardware Co., 1910, No. 4,
  tools & locks, 829 pp............ 45.00
Winchester, 1907 .... 165.00

TRAMP ART

Tramp Art Mirror

Tramp art flourished in the United States from about 1875 into the 1930's. These chip-carved woodenwares, mostly in the form of boxes or other useful items, were made mainly from old cigar boxes although fruit and vegetable crates were also used. The wood is predominantly edge-carved and subsequently layered to create a unique effect. Completed items were given an overall stained finish which was sometimes further enhanced with painted highlights. Though there seems to be no written record of the artists, many of whom were itinerants, there is a growing interest in collecting this ware.

Box, cov., oblong, pedestal base,
  two step-carved points on cover &
  three on each side w/one at each
  end, hinged cover w/original paper advertising label for cigars inside, old finish, 8 7/8" l. (minor
  edge damage) $65.00
Chest of drawers, miniature, high
  backboard crest w/arched center
  & pointed corner "ears," band of
  carved diamonds across top of
  crest, rectangular top over two
  drawers w/stepped panels of
  chip-carving & stepped panels at
  sides, old silver paint, 10" w.,
  15 3/8" h. 85.00
Clock case, wide arched pediment
  w/ornate scroll & button chip-
  carving above rectangular case
  w/ornate chip-carved pilasters

flanking center clock face opening
  surrounded by further carving,
  thick base w/sloping edges, natural finish w/good brown color,
  14" w., 14½" h. 200.00
Comb case, hanging-type, applied
  horseshoe crest enclosing the
  words "GOOD LUCK" above a
  notch-carved & scalloped backboard w/a center glass within a
  double heart frame, over a
  projecting case w/a pocket above
  two drawers w/applied notched
  molding & bow-knot knobs, the
  whole decorated w/chip-carved &
  applied rosettes & swiveling
  wings, probably Pennsylvania, ca.
  1930, 23½" h. (small breaks &
  wear) 770.00
Desk, miniature, slant-front type,
  upright rectangular form
  w/hinged lid opening to a com-
  partmented interior lined w/bright
  blue paper, the case w/four small
  drawers & two long drawers, all
  surfaces w/multi-layered chip-
  carved stars, compasses & circles
  along w/other geometric shapes,
  America, ca. 1930, 7½ x 15",
  21" h. 990.00
Frame, unusual scalloped borders
  on inside & outside edges, well-
  detailed chip-carved hearts & other designs highlighted in gold
  paint, 19½ x 23½" (top edge
  damage) 200.00
Frames, border composed of two
  chip-carved bands w/a carved
  heart at the center of each side,
  old dark brown paint w/gold
  paint on hearts, pr., 20 x 25¾"
  (some edge damage) 650.00
Jewelry box w/hinged lid, lift-out
  interior tray & hidden drawer in
  lid, chip-carved layers, brass trim
  & panels w/worn paper inserts on
  sides, top w/red velvet insert, incomplete applied paper letter inscription & date "1903," 10½" sq.,
  9" h. (some edge damage) 55.00
Magazine rack, hanging-type, simple chip-carved design, applied
  diamond-shaped ornamentation &
  brass tack trim, original dark finish, 15" w. (glued repair to
  crest) 40.00
Mirror, shaped rectangular frame
  w/multi-layered crescent moons,
  circles, hearts & geometric shapes
  centering a rectangular mirror
  plate, America, ca. 1930,
  12¼" w., 20½" h. (ILLUS.) 935.00
Wall pocket, pointed crest w/shaped
  sides, pierced design & chip-

carved edges, applied decorative
strips of carved wood on pocket
front, simple scrollwork at base,
11" w., 16½" h.................. 50.00

TRAYS, SERVING & CHANGE

Champagne Velvet Tray

*Both serving & change trays once used in
taverns, cafes and the like and usually bearing advertising for a beverage maker are now
being widely collected. All trays listed are
heavy tin serving trays, unless otherwise noted. Also see COCA-COLA ITEMS.*

Anheuser-Busch "Bevo" (non-
  alcoholic beverage of Prohibition
  era), Anheuser-Busch delivery
  wagon & team of horses
  (change) $82.00
Arnold's Top-N-Och Bread, round
  (change) 48.00
Bartel's Porter & Ale, Kingston, New
  York, winged wheel, pre-
  Prohibition 55.00
Bettendorf Axle Co., Davenport,
  Iowa, The Bettendorf Steel Gear
  Wagon shown.................. 195.00
Biff 3c Cigar, cigar pictured
  (change) 65.00
Blatz - Old Heidelberg Brew, colored
  scene of glass of beer, bottle &
  sandwich on plate, rectangular,
  10½ x 13".................... 85.00
Butts (Art) Sporting Goods, Oneon-
  ta, New York, hunting dog in
  field, scalloped crimped border,
  3 x 5" (change) 35.00
Century Beer, Schneider Brewing
  Co., Trinidad, Colorado, old cou-
  ple having "A Social Drink," pre-
  Prohibition (change) 135.00
Champagne Velvet Beer, Terre
  Haute Brewing Co., Terre Haute,
  Indiana, colorful scene of Colonial
  couples standing & raising toast
  around dinner table w/cherubs

overhead, ca. 1910, 12 x 15" oval
  (ILLUS.)....................... 165.00
Chicago Brewery, San Francisco,
  California, lady offering glass of
  beer to man 495.00
Chief Oshkosh Beer, Oshkosh Brewing Co., Oshkosh, Wisconsin, Indian chief wearing top hat in
  center........................ 45.00
Cleveland & Buffalo Steamship Co.,
  center scene of large steamship
  on lake, "The Great Seeand-
  bee..." along bottom edge,
  4½ x 6¼" oval (change)........ 250.00
Cottolene Shortening, black woman
  & child picking cotton (change) ... 75.00
Crescent Brewing Co., Nampa, Ida-
  ho, picture of pretty girl 110.00
Doelger (Peter) Beer, eagle holding
  First Prize ribbon standing on First
  Prize awards (change) 125.00
Edelweiss Beer, bust of pretty girl in
  center, floral border, 13" d....... 145.00
Ehrenpreis-Bucyrus Brewing Co.,
  lady holding glass (change) 60.00
Ehret's Hell Gate Brewery, New
  York, entwined "G.E." within star,
  pre-Prohibition, large oval 195.00
Esslinger's Beer, George Esslinger &
  Son, Philadelphia, Pennsylvania,
  cartoon man carrying a tray of
  beer w/wording "Good Old Es-
  slinger's Beer," red, yellow &
  blue 40.00
Evansville Brewing Co., Evansville,
  Indiana, old judge shown 115.00
Falls City Brewing Co., waitress car-
  rying tray w/glasses of beer, ca.
  1915, 12" d. 285.00
Falstaff Beer, St. Louis, Missouri,
  man seated being served by bar-
  maid, 24" d. 145.00
Franklin Life Insurance, picture of
  Benjamin Franklin (change) 30.00
Garrett & Co. Wines, scene of Paul
  & Virginia running, 13" d. 215.00
Gettleman's Beer, Milwaukee, Wis-
  consin, hand holding green mug .. 53.00
Goebel Beer, Detroit, Michigan,
  Dutch girl in center scene........ 125.00
Green River Whiskey, black man &
  horse, 12" d. 225.00
Grossvater beer, scene of elderly
  men sitting around table & drink-
  ing, 10½ x 13¼" rectangle 200.00
Hanley's "Peerless Ale," Providence,
  Rhode Island, "The Connoisseur,"
  gentleman closely examining
  clear glass beer schooner, 1930's,
  12" d. 115.00
Havana Superfina Cigars, Indian
  scene, 3" d. (change) 125.00
Highland Evaporated Cream, picture
  of can, 4½" d. (change) 40.00

Hyroler Whiskey, man in evening
clothes holding glass, 4¼" d.
(change) 40.00

International Harvester, horse
shown (change) 35.00

Kenney Co. (C.D.), Thanksgiving
scene (change)................. 150.00

Leemhuis (John H.), Fine Boots &
Shoes, Blue Earth, Minnesota, picture of dead game, oval, large ... 125.00

Miller High Life Beer Tray

Miller "High Life Beer," Milwaukee,
Wisconsin, girl on crescent moon,
13" d. (ILLUS.) ....50.00 to 60.00

Moxie, girl w/violets decoration
(change) 150.00

Narragansett Brewing Co., "Lager &
Ale," Arlington, Rhode Island,
Chief Pansett, round............. 65.00

National Brewery Co., St. Louis,
Missouri, factory scene w/logo &
bottle, rectangular 285.00

Ogden's St. Julien Tobacco, "Cool &
Fragrant," wood-grained
lithographed background, ornate
lettering, 13" d................. 35.00

Old Export Beer, black & gold, pictures logo 60.00

Old Export Beer, black & gold, pictures logo (change)............. 50.00

Old Heidelberg, bottle, glass & food
shown 45.00

Old Reliable Coffee, w/pretty lady,
ca. 1907, approximately 5" d.
(change) 42.00

Our Brands, National Cigar Co.,
lovely lady (change)............ 60.00

Pabst Blue Ribbon Beer, elderly man
pouring a glass of beer,
10½ x 13¼"................... 60.00

Pacific Beer, Tacoma, Washington,
center w/round scene of "Mt. Tacoma" on wood-grained ground,
1930's, 12" d. 100.00

Pepsi-Cola, girl at soda fountain,
ca. 1908, 4½ x 6" oval ..600.00 to 700.00

Pepsi-Cola, three cartoon-style children singing, red, white & blue,
ca. 1930's, 11 x 14"............. 25.00

Rainier Beer, Seattle Brewing &
Malting Co., sexy Victorian girl

resting on bearskin rug,
1900 ....175.00 to 275.00

Rockford Watches Change Tray

Rockford High-Grade Watches, lady
center "For Sale by Engels & Dris-
sen, Green Bay, Wis.," 3½ x 5",
change (ILLUS.) 60.00

Rockford Watches, South Fork,
Pennsylvania, Victorian lady
w/bare shoulders (change)....... 70.00

Ruhstaller's Beer, pretty girl dropping flowers (change) 95.00

Smith Typewriters, horses pictured
(change) 150.00

Stegmaier Brewing Co., Wilkes-
Barre, Pa., color bust portrait of a
lovely dark haired girl wearing a
low-cut gown, printed around rim
"Compliments Stegmaier Brewing
Co, Wilkes-Barre, Pa.," 13¼" d. .. 75.00

Stocker (H.P.) Brewery, heads of
three charging white horses
(change) 85.00

Storz Brewing Co., Omaha, Nebraska, picture of glass, bottle & can,
round 75.00

Stroh's Brewery, Detroit, Michigan,
waiter w/striped vest carrying
tray of bottles & beer glasses,
pre-Prohibition 245.00

Teacher's Highland Cream Whiskey,
Scotland, copper, pub scene,
12" d......................... 45.00

Utica Club Beer, Utica, New York,
factory scene in center, ca. 1915,
13" d......................... 40.00

White Rock Table Water, semi-nude
lady on rock (change) 95.00

Wilson's Invalid's Port Wine, tin,
woman dressed in gown wearing
her hair down & shown taking a
sip.......................... 165.00

TRIVETS

When numbers are noted following trivets

*listed below they refer to numbers in the long
out-of-print books,* Trivets, *Book I and*
Trivets, Old and Re-Pro, *Book II, both by*
Dick Hankenson. *All are cast iron except
where otherwise noted.*

Bellows-shaped, brass & copper,
  pierced w/two heart-shaped
  voids, raised on wrought-iron feet
  fastened w/copper pins, Pennsylvania, 18th c., 10" l.............$440.00
"C" letter, Book I, No. 138 .... 20.00
Circular, inlaid in a Gothic pattern
  w/pieces of gold, white, purple &
  green iridescent Favrile glass,
  bronze base stamped "TIFFANY
  STUDIOS NEW YORK 28292,"
  7" d. 2,200.00
Circular, the molded edge enclosing
  pierced pinwheel & leaf decorations, centering a pinwheel & sunburst design, on three tapering
  feet, the handle w/notched designs extending to a pierced pinwheel, marked "M. Westley,"
  Pennsylvania, 19th c., 12" d. 264.00
"J.R. Clark Co., Minneapolis" in
  open lettering, long rail open at
  each point, Book I, No. 106 ...... 30.00
"C.S.A." in cut-out letters, Richmond, Va., 1922 reunion 90.00
Engraved pot of flowers, heart cut-
  out at base of handle, triangular
  cut-out at pointed end, beaded
  edge, 9½" l. (brass)............. 25.00
Enterprise "E," spiderweb 15.00
Enterprise "E," waffle.............. 15.00
"Favorite Stoves & Ranges,"
  w/hanging bar 20.00
Fox standing beneath tree, 8 1/8" l.
  (brass) 165.00
George Washington bust portrait in
  relief center, Book I, No. 17...... 70.00
Griswold No. 1728 .... 25.00
Griswold No. 1900 .... 25.00
Heart design, six cut-out hearts of
  varying sizes forming center design, 8½" l. (brass) 55.00
Heart-shaped w/loop between two
  halves, black paint over gold
  paint, hand-wrought, 6½" l. 65.00
Heart-shaped, wrought iron, w/'serpent' handle, raised on three
  feet, Pennsylvania, late 18th c.,
  8" l., 1¾" h.................1,980.00
Heart-shaped w/whippet-type dog
  center against a geometric
  ground, 9¼" l. (brass) 85.00
Heart-shaped w/heart cut-out in
  center, baluster-turned wooden
  handle w/brass ferrule, bulbous
  cast feet, 12¾" l. 200.00
"Howell H." "The W.H. Howell Co.,
  Geneva, Ill." embossed in

recessed panels, wavy railing,
  Book I, No. 125 .... 19.00
Iwantu Spade, "Iwantu Comfort Iron,
  Strause Gas Iron Co., Phila., Pa.,
  U.S.A.," Book I, No. 148 .... 40.00
Lady's head, cast brass, Bradley &
  Hubbard...................... 60.00
Lyre form w/curving bars, wrought-
  iron legs, turned wood handle,
  12½" l. (brass)................. 105.00
Pinwheel w/border of half-circles,
  revolving-type, two-piece,
  9½" d......................... 105.00
Ram's horn type scrolling design,
  two graduated pairs of scrolling
  devices w/center strip, beveled
  handle w/ring end, hand-wrought,
  8½" l....................... 135.00
Rectangular top above a scalloped
  apron, the sides w/turned handles, raised on front cabriole legs
  ending in pad feet, the rear
  w/cylindrical legs, brass Victorian, 10½" h.................. 220.00
Reticulated circular brass plate
  w/scalloped edge sliding on an
  arched iron rod, w/a pierced iron
  base plate, hanging-type, Continental, late 18th c., 7" d. plate 88.00
Rope twist triangle w/in-curving
  sides, long handle, hand-wrought,
  overall 10" l. 45.00
"Sensible" pierced in wavy edge oblong w/three holes each side,
  Book I, No. 129 ....35.00 to 45.00
Spade-form, hand-wrought, slender
  outside frame w/center brace running from handle to tip & decorated w/two wrought loops, flat
  handle continues from center
  brace & end w/scrolled tip, on
  scrolled feet, 6" l................ 325.00
Spanish wavy band, turned wood
  handle, 8½" l., Book II, No. 156
  (handle damaged)............... 35.00
Starflower in center surrounded by
  compass circle & arch designs,
  round, 6¼" d. 45.00
Star & sunburst, embossed "The
  Cleveland Foundry Co." in
  recessed panels, Book I,
  No. 122 .... 23.50
Tree of Life variant or Family Tree,
  Book II, No. 261................. 10.00
Triangular, one piece, hand-
  wrought, 18th c., 5½" sides 75.00
Trident-form, wrought iron, two long
  side arms joined by cross bar &
  w/short legs at ends, shorter
  pointed center tine joined to outer
  tines by four scrolling loops, third
  leg at base of tines, turned &
  shaped wood handle, 14" l. 75.00
U-form w/reticulated design, brass
  & iron, w/turned wood handle, on

an iron tripod stand w/disc feet, joined by a medial stretcher, 14" l., 14" h., 2 pcs. 242.00

TRUNKS

Unusual Leather-Covered Trunk

These box-like portable containers are used for transporting or storing personal possessions. There are many styles to choose from since they have been made from the 16th century onward. Thousands arrived in this country with the immigrants and more were turned out to accommodate the westward movement of the population. The popular dome-top trunk was designed to prevent water from accumulating on the top. Hinges, locks and construction, along with condition and age, greatly determine the values of older trunks.

Dome-top, alligator skin-covered, hinged lid opening to a fitted interior, leather handles, 19th c., 16" l. $220.00
Dome-top, leather-covered pine, hinged lid opening to an interior lined w/blue & white glazed wallpaper, the top w/the intitials "FMP" in brass tacks, along w/diamonds & lines & stylized trees also rendered in brass tacks, the front & sides similarly decorated, the back inscribed w/tacks "March the 29, 18 & 26," leather carrying handle, America, 17" l., 9½" h. (ILLUS.) 385.00
Dome-top, painted wood, overall sponge decoration in dark brown on yellow-ochre ground, narrow dark brown border, America, early 19th c., 9½ x 18", 9¼" h. 467.50
Dome-top, painted wood, top decorated w/standing rose, swag & tassel borders on front & sides framing floral array, brass furniture handles at ends, interior lined w/1799 map of Eastern Seaboard, America, early 19th c.,

11 x 18¾", 11" h. (paint loss, heavily crackled) 990.00
Flat-top, painted leather, rectangular top & sides decorated w/red florals on a black ground, Chinese Export, ca. 1800, 36" l. 412.50
Immigrant-type, dome-top, grain-painted pine, dovetail construction, wrought-iron end handles & strap hinges, old brown graining, 34" l. 110.00
Immigrant-type, dome-top, oak, dovetail construction, truncated base w/bracket feet, wrought-iron hinges, lock & side handles, old refinishing, European, 46" l. 450.00
Immigrant-type, dome-top, painted oak, dovetail construction, rectangular top opening to interior fitted w/till, old red paint over black w/salmon painted label "Maria Kruger...," embossed brass escutcheon, wrought-iron end handles & hinges, 23½ x 46¾", 26½" h. (lock removed, minor edge damage) 300.00
Steamer, wood & metal banding, brown & yellow striped, manufactured by Louis Vuitton, ca. 1900, 39" l. 385.00

VENDING & GAMBLING MACHINES

Caille's "Superior" Slot Machine

Arcade, "Chicago Digger," Buckley Mfg., 1934 . . . . $600.00
Arcade, "Coon Hunt," Seeburg, w/manuals (working w/rebuilt amp) 1,800.00
Arcade, "Happy Home," Caille, shutter on front of house raises to show three-dimensional view of lady preparing for bed, large cast-iron legs, ca. 1910 . . . . 750.00

Arcade, "Iron Claw," Exhibit Supply
Co., 1926 ....1,250.00

Arcade, "Love Analyst," Mutoscope,
fancy cabinet 650.00

Arcade, "Love Tester," Exhibit Supply Co., w/vertical row of light
bulbs, ca. 1925.................. 750.00

Arcade, "Shoot the Bear," Seeburg,
w/manuals (original condition)...1,500.00

Arcade, "Spear the Dragon," Exhibit
Supply Co., ca. 1927 (restored)...5,500.00

Arcade, "Test Your Strength," contained in oak case, 5-cent play,
Spain, ca. 1905, 81" h........... 440.00

Arcade, "The Wizard Fortune Teller,"
Mills Novelty Co., 1-cent play,
ca. 1920 ....3,000.00

Candy vendor, "Belvend," four-
column, Belvend Mfg. Co., Inc. ... 50.00

Chocolate vendor, "Wilbur's Chocolate," National Vending Machine
Co., glass dome, metal base,
ca. 1904 ....2,500.00

Chocolate vendor, "Wilbur-Suchard
Chocolate," L. Miles 300.00

Cigarette vendor, "Silver Comet,"
Redco Products, La Crosse, Wisconsin, counter-top, 1-cent operation, ca. 1930's, 6 x 6½ x 8" 160.00

Cup dispenser, "Dixie Cups," die-
cast metal mechanism mounts on
22" l. glass cylinder to hold cups,
1-cent operation 120.00

Gambling, Baker's "Pacers" console
slot machine, 5-cent play, "long
cabinet" version, 1939-42 ......8,500.00

Gambling, Bally's "High Hand" console slot machine, five-reel poker
w/free plays instead of cash payouts, 5-cent play, ca. 1940-42 ....2,000.00

Gambling, Caille's "Bull Frog"
slot machine, 1904..12,000.00 to15,000.00

Gambling, Caille's "Commander"
slot machine, side vendor,
ca. 1930 .... 625.00

Gambling, Caille's "Musical Puck"
floor model slot machine, six-
way, ca. 1903 ....8,500.00

Gambling, Caille's "Nude Front"
counter-top slot machine, 5-cent
play, ca. 1929 ....2,500.00

Gambling, Caille's "Silent Sphinx"
counter-top slot machine, 5-cent
play, ca. 1932 ....2,000.00

Gambling, Caille's "Superior" counter-
top slot machine, 5-cent play,
ca. 1926 (ILLUS.) 1,500.00

Gambling, Jennings' "Improved Century Vender" counter-top slot
machine, 5-cent play (restored
cabinet) 1,500.00

Gambling, Jennings' "Little Duke"
counter-top slot machine, 1-cent
play...........................1,950.00

Gambling, Jennings' "New Victoria
Vender" (Model B) counter-top
slot machine w/front vender,
5-cent play (restored) 1,700.00

Gambling, Jennings' "Standard Chief"
counter-top slot machine, 25-cent
play (restored) 1,350.00

Gambling, Jennings' "Victoria Silent"
counter-top slot machine, 5-cent
play 1,700.00

Gambling, Jennings' machine w/Rock-
ola Jackpot front, ca. 1928 ......1,400.00

Gambling, Mills' "Black Cherry"
counter-top slot machine, 5-cent
play (repainted) 1,400.00

Gambling, Mills' "Bonus Bell"
counter-top slot machine, 25-cent
play, 1937 ....1,600.00

Gambling, Mills' "Extraordinary"
counter-top slot machine, 10-cent
play, ca. 1933 ....1,500.00

Gambling, Mills' "Four Bells" console slot machine, 5-cent play,
1939-48 .... 700.00

Gambling, Mills' "Futurity" counter-
top slot machine, 25-cent play,
1936-41 ....2,100.00

Gambling, Mills' "Golden Falls"
counter-top slot machine, 5-cent
play 1,200.00

Gambling, Mills' "Jack Pot" (Torch
front) counter-top slot machine,
25-cent play, ca. 1928-29 ....1,650.00

Gambling, Mills' "Owl" upright
slot machine, oak cabinet,
ca. 1897 ....5,500.00 to 7,500.00

Gambling, Mills' "Silent Golden Bell"
(Roman Head front) counter-top
slot machine, 25-cent play,
ca. 1930's ....1,500.00 to 1,600.00

Gambling, Mills' "Silent Gooseneck"
(Lion front) counter-top slot
machine, 5-cent play 1,750.00

Gambling, Mills' "Twentieth Century"
upright slot machine, single wheel,
25-cent play, ca. 1902 ....10,500.00

Gambling, Mills' "Vest Pocket" slot
machine, 5-cent play, 1938,
8" h........................... 385.00

Gambling, Mills' "War Chief," 25-cent
play 1,500.00

Gambling, Mills' "War Eagle"
counter-top slot machine, 10-cent
play, post-1937 (restored) 2,000.00

Gambling, Pace's "Bantam Bell"
counter-top slot machine, 1-cent
play, 1928-36 ....1,200.00

Gambling, Pace's "Comet" counter-
top slot machine, 25-cent play,
ca. 1932 ....1,300.00

Gambling, Watling's "Lincoln De Lux"
counter-top slot machine, 5-cent
play, 1926-29 ....2,000.00

Gambling, Watling's "Rol-A-Top Vendor" counter-top slot machine, 5-cent play, 1935 ....3,000.00

Gambling, Watling's "Treasury" counter-top slot machine, 5-cent play, ca. 1936 ....2,750.00

Gambling, Watling's "Treasury" counter-top slot machine, 25-cent play, ca. 1936 ....2,900.00

Gumball vendor, "Advance Model D," 1-cent operation, ca. 1923 (restored) 200.00

Gumball (or nut) vendor, "Bantam," Atlas Mfg. & Sales Corp., 5-cent operation ....125.00 to 150.00

Gumball vendor, "Burnham & Mills," 1-cent operation (restored) 1,250.00

Gum vendor, "Columbus Model 14," profit sharing type w/1-2-1-2-3 mechanism 310.00

Gum vendor, "Cop Directing Traffic (Stop & Go)," policeman holding a stop & go sign, Pulver Mfg. Co., 1-cent operation 365.00

Gum vendor, "Master," Atlas Mfg. & Sales Corp., 1-cent/5-cent operation, glass top, 1954 ....50.00

Gum vendor, "Master," Norris Mfg. Co., 1-cent operation, ca. 1923, 16" h......................185.00

Gum vendor, "Trucky," metal truck drives in a circle picking up gumball from hopper & dropping it down hole leading to outside, A M Co., 1-cent operation, w/stand 1,850.00

Gum vendor, "Woody Woodpecker," Pulver Mfg. Co., 1-cent operation...........................750.00

Gum vendor, "Yellow Kid," wooden case, Pulver Mfg. Co., patented May 30, 1899 ....2,800.00

Gum vendor, "Zeno Gum," Zeno Mfg. Co., Chicago, Illinois, oak case, embossed tin front panel lists flavors, 1-cent operation, ca. 1890's 595.00

Match vendor, "Northwestern Vending Corp.," cast iron w/dolphins design, 1-cent operation, w/attached cigar cutter 475.00

Peanut vendor, "Columbus Model M," cast iron, "bell-bottom," red or green enamel, green porcelain or all chromium plate ...100.00 to 175.00

Peanut vendor, "Mabey Electric Eat 'Em Hot," ca. 1934, w/original cup dispenser......................350.00

Pinball machine, "Chicago World's Fair Rockola," 1-cent play, 1933 ..1,500.00

Pinball machine, "Contact Junior," floor model, earliest battery electronics, wooden case, Pacific Amusement Mfg. Co., 1933 ......750.00

Pinball machine, "Cyclone," Williams Mfg. Co., 1947 ....325.00

Pinball machine, "Liberty Bell," Gottlieb, 1933...................450.00

Pinball machine, "Little Manhattan," cast-iron case, Caille (restored) ..1,400.00

Trade stimulator, "Chicago Club House," counter-top, 1-cent gumball vendor w/poker wheels, Daval 360.00

Trade stimulator, "Draw Poker," cast-iron counter-top model, Mills, ca. 1900 ....5,750.00

Trade stimulator, "Fairest Wheel," 5-cent cigar machine, oak counter-top model, Decatur, ca. 1895 ....900.00

Trade stimulator, "Imp," Groetchen, 1940-51........................295.00

Trade stimulator, "Jumbo," upright wooden model, Mills...........2,900.00

Trade stimulator, "Mayflower," cast-iron counter-top model, Caille ...5,500.00

WARTIME MEMORABILIA

Since the early 19th century, every war that America has fought has been commemorated with a variety of war-related memorabilia. Often in the form of propaganda items produced during the conflict or as memorial pieces made after the war ended, these materials are today quite collectible and increasingly important for the historic insights they provide. Most commonly available are items dating from World War I and II and since the fall of 1989 marks the fiftieth anniversary of the beginning of World War II, there should be added interest in this collecting field.

SPANISH-AMERICAN WAR (1898)

Badge, souvenir, "Camp Alger," 1898 ....$11.00

Book, "Record of Indiana Volunteers in the Spanish-American War, 1898-99"......................35.00

Book, "The Story of the War of 1898 (illustrated) for the Army," by W. Nephew King, published by Peter Fenelon Collier, copyright 1898 ...45.00

Table lamp, cast iron, copper & brass, kerosene-type, copper & tin bullet-shaped body embossed w/"Remember The Maine," advertises Bill Anthony Cigars, brass fixtures, cast-iron base, glass chimney, end embossed "Jacob Stahl Jr. & Co., Makers, NY," ca. 1900 ....275.00

Pinback button, "Remember the Maine," w/flag 40.00

Tankard, stoneware, Battleship Maine pictured, "Destroyed Havana Harbor 1898," ½ liter 88.00

WORLD WAR I (The Great War, 1914-1918)

Book, "Germany's Fighting Machine," by Henderson, 1914, Bobbs-Merrill publishers (cover stains) 22.00

Book, "History of the World War," by Francis A. March, 1918........ 5.00

Book, "The United States in the Great War" by Willis Abbot, one or more photographs on each page, 325 pp.................... 60.00

Books, "U.S. Official Pictures of the World War," ca. 1921, photographs from the official files of the War Department, written documentary including names & photos of recipients of Congressional Medal of Honor, plus General Pershing's final report, hardbound, 1,009 pp., 4 vols...... 250.00

Books, "YMCA History, World War I," illustrations of fighting men & many maps, 2 vols........ 30.00

Handkerchief, silk, pictures world leaders of the era............... 9.00

Phonograph, portable-type, sent to soliders in the trenches in France, small album of 20 records included, 1917...................... 400.00

Print, "Soldier's Record," colorful w/11 Allied Generals & other action pictures, signed & dated 1917, tramp art frame, 16 x 21" .. 125.00

WORLD WAR II (1939-1945)

Maastricht, Holland Liberation Plate

Arcade machine, "Poison This Rat," illustrates Hitler, one-cent play, 1942 .... 475.00

Ashtray, figural soldier, gold-colored metal, 5" h.............. 20.00

Atlas, "Kaltenborn's War Atlas," 1943 .... 12.00

Bank, ceramic, model of Hitler as a

pig, "Make Him Squeal, Save For Victory," original paint 90.00

Bank, tin, model of a drum, "Remember Pearl Harbor" 30.00

Banner, cloth, "General MacArthur - Our Hero," five colors, 1945, 12 x 18"....................... 35.00

Book, "Colliers Photographic History of World War II," over 800 pictures w/20 pages in full color, hardbound, 10¼ x 15½"........ 20.00

Book, "Submarine Operations W.W. II," published by Naval Institute, many photographs & statistics, hardbound..................... 30.00

Book, "Victory Through Air Power," by Major DeServersky, 1942 ...... 8.00

Book, "World War II in Headlines & Pictures," Evening Bulletin newspaper headlines book, 100 pp., 1946 .... 45.00

Bottle stopper, bisque, figural Hitler 25.00

Carnival game, Hitler w/breakable noses 395.00

Clock, aviation-type, made for military plane, rim wind & rim set, eight-day movement, made by Keyless Auto Clock Co., fits into airplane dashboard.............. 495.00

Coin savings book, Brownies promoting Savings Bonds, colorful 10.00

Decals, including zeppelins, airplanes, tanks, cowboy, flags, etc., 144 on card, the group 15.00

Ditty bag, American Red Cross model....................... 10.00

Lunchbox & thermos, "V" for victory markings, the set 45.00

Manual, "Recognition Pictorial Manual War & Navy Dept. 1943, Restricted" 40.00

Medal, Purple Heart, w/case 100.00

Model kit, paper, model of a battleship, unassembled, in original sleeve, 7 x 10"................. 12.50

Photograph, Battleship Ballou, along w/a 1948 souvenir edition of the ship's newspaper including servicemen's names, maps & information about the ship, 11 x 14" photo, 2 pcs. 20.00

Pin, "V for Victory," sterling silver w/mother-of-pearl heart 20.00

Pinback button, "Uncle Sam & Hitler," Sam dunks Hitler in well 55.00

Pinback button, mechanical, "Let's Pull Together," Hitler pictured ... 25.00

Pinback button, mechanical, Uncle Sam hanging Hitler.............. 34.00

Pincushion, chalkware, figure of Hitler bending over w/pincushion forming his posterior 85.00

Plaque, wall-type, curved glass,
"Remember Pearl Harbor," color-
ful scene 40.00

Plate, earthenware, Dutch inscription around edge translates to
"Liberation of Maastricht by the
Americans, 14 Sept. 1944," made
by Petrus Regout & Co., Maastricht, Holland, 8" d., (ILLUS.
previous page) . . . . 15.00 to 25.00

Postcards, made for soldiers to mail
home, in original container for
mailing, 1942, book of 32 . . . . 17.50

Punch board, "Take A Punch At
Hitler," one-cent play, Hitler pic-
tured, unpunched 10.00

Puzzles, mechanical, hand-held,
featuring "Atomic Bomb" & "Trap-
A-Jap," by A.C. Gilbert, set of 6 . . 50.00

Sign, "America Gives Him Opportunity...He Must Not Lose It.," die-
cut hanging cardboard, multicolored w/eagle, torch, stars &
red, white & blue shield that says
"Buy War Bonds," bedroom scene
of young boy daydreaming while
building model plane, made by
7-Up, 1943, 15 x 21" 125.00

Sign, tin, shows "ruptured duck,"
says "Welcome back — wearer of
this badge of honor. You have
served your country well — we
thank you," 6¼ x 16½" 15.00

V-Mail kit, Sheaffer Voyager, never
opened. 8.00

WATCHES

Man's Hunting Case Watch

Hunting case, lady's, American
Waltham Watch Co., Waltham,
Massachusetts, Model 1890, 16-
jewel damascened nickel move-
ment, 0 size (1 5/30"), signed
"Lady Waltham," signed white en-

amel dial w/Arabic numerals,
blued-steel hands, subsidiary sec-
conds, engraved 14k gold case
cast & chased w/flutes &
beading $770.00

Hunting case, lady's, American
Waltham Watch Co., 15-jewel
Swiss movement, round white dial
w/Roman numerals, subsidiary seconds dial, foliate decorated bi-
color 14k gold case highlighted by
a diamond. 302.50

Hunting case, lady's, Elgin Watch
Co., Elgin, Illinois, 15-jewel movement, 0 size, yellow gold-filled
case w/multicolor gold decoration, w/chain w/large hammered
links 185.00

Hunting case, man's, American Watch
Co., Waltham, Massachusetts,
Model 1857, 15-jewel movement,
18 size (1 23/30"), key wound &
set, signed white enamel dial
w/Roman numerals, blued-steel
hands, subsidiary seconds, engine-
turned 18k gold case enhanced
w/scrolls, monogrammed cartouche & fluted pendant,
ca. 1868 . . . . 1,100.00

Hunting case, man's, Charpentier
Oudin, Palais Royal, Paris, France,
white enamel dial w/Roman numerals & subsidiary seconds dial,
gold case w/nielloed cover
w/Russian Imperial eagle, presentation piece, complete w/gold fob
chain, ca. 1900, watch
1 7/8" d. 2,860.00

Hunting case, man's, Elgin National
Watch Co., 17-jewel damascened
movement, 16 size (1 21/30"),
gold cuvette, signed white enamel
dial w/Roman numerals, blued-
steel hands, subsidiary seconds,
14k multicolored gold case w/box
hinge w/engraved band enclosing
three racehorses w/diamond eyes,
reverse w/vacant cartouche &
wreath (ILLUS.) 3,300.00

Hunting case, man's, Hamilton Watch
Co., Lancaster, Pennsylvania,
Model 947, 23-jewel nickel movement, 18 size, full plate, signed
double sunk white enamel dial
w/Arabic numerals, blued-steel
hands, 14k gold case engraved
w/a border of leafy scrolls 4,950.00

Open face, man's, American
Waltham Watch Co., 15-jewel
nickel movement, round white
fancy dial w/Arabic numerals & a
subsidiary seconds dial, highlighted w/Louis IV openwork hands,
14k gold case, ca. 1885 . . . . 385.00

Open face, man's, American Watch
Co., P.S. Bartlett Model, 18 size,
key wound & set, coin silver case,
ca. 1866 .... 225.00
Pocket travel watch, man's, Rolex,
15-jewel lever movement, signed
silvered dial w/Arabic numerals,
blued-steel hands, Art Deco style
reeded silver case opening to
form stand 715.00
Railroad, Ball Watch Co., Cleveland,
Ohio, 21-jewel nickel movement
No. 999B by Hamilton Watch Co.,
16 size, white enamel dial w/Ara-
bic numerals, blued-steel hands &
subsidiary seconds, gold-filled
case 308.00

WATCH FOBS

Advertising, "Allis-Chalmers
H019" $42.50
Advertising, "Alpha Portland
Cement" 35.00
Advertising, "Armour Co.," cow
head 50.00
Advertising, "Baltimore, Maryland
Yacht Club," brass, 1927 .... 29.00
Advertising, "Blue Brute Cement
Mixers" 37.50
Advertising, "Bull Durham,"
w/bull 35.00
Advertising, "Case Threshing
Machine" 65.00
Advertising, "Caterpillar Crawler" .. 45.00
Advertising, "Delta Files," enamel .. 32.00
Advertising, "Dr. Pepper," w/Bil-
liken & factory scene 70.00
Advertising, "Elgin," combination
fob & pry tool, ornate stem &
loop 45.00
Advertising, "Gardner Denver,"
jackhammer 20.00
Advertising, "W.D. Howard - Hoard's
Dairyman," white metal 35.00
Advertising, "International Har-
vester," two world globes 70.00
Advertising, "Jap Rose Soap" 35.00
Advertising, "Kellogg's Toasted
Cornflakes" 70.00
Advertising, "Leisy Brewing," por-
celain & brass 100.00
Advertising, "Marquette Cement
Co." 25.00
Advertising, "Massey-Harris
Tractors" 72.00
Advertising, "Oliver Chilled Plow" .. 32.50
Advertising, "Sanico Stove," brass .. 65.00
Advertising, "Silver Saws" 18.00
Advertising, "Washburn-Crosby Co.
Foods - Gold Medal," celluloid in
shield 60.00

Brass, double locket, dated 1916.... 25.00
Carnelian & moonstone, 14k gold
mounting, England, ca. 1850 ..... 215.00
Elk's tooth, initials "E.B." 45.00
Fraternal, "I.B. of Blacksmiths," 10k
gold-filled 35.00
Fraternal, "Order of Railroad
Telegraphers" 35.00
Souvenir, "Kitty Hawk," Orville
Wright, bi-plane on fob 125.00
Souvenir, "U.S.S. California,"
launched November 20, 1919,
Mare Island, California 30.00

WEATHERVANES

Running Horse Weathervane

Arrow, sheet copper & zinc, flattened
scroll bands flank arrow shaft &
scrolling diamond forms tail, fine
verdigris w/small traces of original
gilding, cast zinc arrowhead, probably F.W. Fiske, New York, late
19th c., 54" l. $2,530.00
Arrow & lyre, sheet iron & zinc,
pierced cast zinc arrow followed by
a sheet iron lyre-shaped body &
stylized peacock feather tail, attributed to J. Howard Co., West Bridgewater, Massachusetts, early 19th c.,
70" l., 18½" h. (gilt loss) 2,750.00
Banneret, copper & zinc, cast acorn &
scroll openwork at one end & diamond openwork w/stylized blossom at the other, surmounted by
cast lightning bolt & ball finial,
America, 19th c., 66" w., overall
72" h. (regilded) 1,760.00
Cannon, sheet copper, silhouette of
a cannon on a wheeled mount
w/pile of cannon balls beyond,
traces of gold leaf, verdigris surface, America, late 19th c.,
24" l. 825.00
Dove, molded copper, full-bodied
bird w/sheet copper wings & tail
perched on a ball over an arrow
directional, America, late 19th -
early 20th c., 31" w. arrow,
14" h. 1,650.00

Dove, molded zinc, full-bodied standing bird w/raised wings, mounted on a copper rod continuing to a copper ball, now mounted on a black metal stand, America, 19th c., 14¾" l., 14½" h. (repair to left wing) 1,320.00

Eagle, molded copper, full-bodied figure of eagle w/raised braced sheet copper wings, cast head & open talons mounted on ball & iron bracket, attributed to A.L. Jewell & Co., Waltham, Massachusetts, late 19th c., 25" l., 18" h. (breaks & dents) 1,870.00

Fish, painted sheet metal, on carved wooden base w/directionals, 14" l., 20½" h. 242.00

Fox, cast zinc, full-bodied, painted silver, mounted on a rod in a stepped black painted wood base, 25" l., 28" h. 990.00

Goddess of Liberty, molded copper, swell-bodied standing figure of Liberty wearing a Phrygian cap w/sawtooth crown & a sash impressed w/five-point stars, over a full-skirted gown, holding a ball-topped standard on a shaped base, attributed to Cushing & White, Waltham, Massachusetts, ca. 1870, 35" h. 29,700.00

Horse jumping through hoop, copper, flattened full-bodied animal fitted w/sheet copper mane, ears & tail, the solid copper hoop w/stamped design, America, possibly A.L. Jewell & Co., late 19th c., 28" l., 18" h. (repaired, breaks) 3,025.00

Horse prancing, cast iron, full-bodied figure of a prancing horse w/sheet iron tail, mounted on metal rod & base, weathered surface, Rochester Iron Works, Rochester, New Hampshire, late 19th c., 36" l., 26" h. (crack at withers) 12,100.00

Horse running, molded copper & zinc, flattened full-bodied animal w/zinc head & ears, applied mane, America, 19th c., dents, hole, gilt loss, 27½" l., 16" h. (ILLUS. previous page) 990.00

Horse running, molded copper & zinc, full-bodied figure of the famous 19th century trotter "Black Hawk," good verdigris surface, America, 19th c., 34" l., 23¼" h. (filled bullet holes) 3,740.00

Horse running, molded copper, full-bodied animal w/mane & tail flying, good finish w/traces of old gilding, green patina & yellow paint, cast iron rod & directionals, 40" l.

figure, overall 74" h. (some old soldered repairs) 3,000.00

Horse standing, cast iron, full-bodied horse w/left foreleg raised, molded mane, wavy sheet metal tail, mounted on a rod in a black metal base, retaining traces of yellow & grey paint, third quarter 19th c., Rochester Iron Works, 23½" l., 19¼" h. 6,050.00

Horse standing, sheet iron, shaped & pierced silhouette of animal w/supporting iron rod braces mounted on a base w/directional arrow, 8½" l. 550.00

Horse & rider, molded & gilded copper, fashioned from heavy gauge copper soldered in two sheets, the upright figure of a rider wearing a cap, the stylized horse w/prancing legs & sheet copper reins, retains much gilding & some polychrome, attributed to A.L. Jewell & Co., ca. 1870, 24" l., 19¼" h. 8,525.00

Lion, molded copper, full-bodied recumbent animal w/cast zinc head, now on a tree trunk stand, 22½" l., 12" h. 990.00

Pigeon, sheet metal, silhouette in the form of a bird mounted on an arrow, supporting vertical bar surmounted by ball finial, gilt surface, w/directionals, America, mid-19th c., 27" w., 45" h. (some gilt loss) 467.50

Plow, sheet copper & cast zinc, the flat silhouette form w/abstract positive & negative space formed by the details of the plow, w/cast zinc front end & gilded sheet copper back end, mounted on a rod in a black metal base, J. Howard & Co., West Bridgewater, Massachusetts, ca. 1860, 52" l., 23" h. 5,500.00

Quill, molded copper & zinc, well-defined veining in the feather, traces of gold leaf, New England, late 19th c., 24½" l., 25½" h. (no directionals) 1,980.00

Rooster, molded copper, full-bodied rooster w/puffy swell-body & curved tail, mounted on a wrought-iron rod in a black metal base, 19th - 20th c., Canada, 20" w., 24" h. 4,675.00

Rooster, molded & gilded copper, upright, swell-bodied rooster w/molded comb, neck, tail & body feathers, standing on cast zinc feet, the whole covered in a variegated gilded patina w/underpaint of yellow and verdigris, mounted in a black metal stand,

19th c., America, 28½" w.,
25" h. 4,400.00
Rooster, molded, gilded & poly-
chromed zinc & copper, full-
length swell-bodied standing bird,
the neck feathers & body in
molded zinc, w/applied & repousse
sheet copper tail & legs, retains
much of its yellow polychrome &
gilding along w/verdigris, mounted
on a black wood base, J. Howard
& Co., Bridgewater, Massachusetts,
third quarter 19th c., 25" w.,
29" h. 7,425.00
Rooster, sheet iron, silhouette of
bird w/high comb & tail, mounted
on a rod, traces of paint, America, late 19th c., 12½" w., 16½" h.
(bullet hole in tail) 330.00
Sheep, molded copper & zinc, swell-
bodied standing animal w/cast zinc
head & sheet copper ears, molded
folds & scoring on copper body,
standing on a rod, now mounted
on a black metal base, probably
Harris & Co., Boston, Massachusetts, third quarter 19th c.,
26½" w., 21¼" h. 11,000.00
Simple Simon, iron, flat silhouetted
figure of the pieman, Simple Simon & his dog near a street lamp,
mounted on an arrow, painted
black & silver, America, ca.
1940's, 54" w., 48" h. 770.00
Train, molded sheet copper, sil-
houette of locomotive & second car,
engine streaming steam & w/engi-
neer in the cab, rolling on sheet
copper tracks, large faceted rod &
pinnacle, in a black metal & white
wood stand, late 19th c., America,
63" l., 95" h. 22,000.00
Train, sheet iron, silhouette of
locomotive & tender on railroad
track w/smoke billowing from engine stack, America, late 19th or
early 20th c., 22" l. (weathered
surface) 715.00

WIENER WERKSTATTE

*The Wiener Werkstatte (Vienna Workshop)
was co-founded in 1903 in Vienna, Austria by
Josef Hoffmann and Kolomon Moser. An off-
shoot of the Vienna Secession movement,
closely related to the Art Nouveau and Arts
& Crafts movements elsewhere, this studio
was established to design and produce unique
and high-quality pieces covering all aspects
of the fine arts. Hoffmann and Moser were
the first artistic directors and oversaw the
work of up to 100 workers, including thirty-*

*seven masters who signed their work. Book-
binding, leatherwork, gold, silver and lacquer
pieces as well as enamels and furniture all
originated from this shop over a period of
nearly thirty years. The finest pieces from the
Wiener Werkstatte are now bringing tremendous prices.*

Wiener Werkstatte Brass Centerpiece

Book, "The Wiener Werkstatte 1903-
1928: The Evolution of the Modern
Applied Arts," color & black &
white illustrations, orange & black
embossed papier-mache binding,
published by Krystall-Verlag,
Vienna, 1929, 8¾ x 8¾" $800.00
Bust of a woman, pottery, long neck
& face, slight smile & exotic green
eyes, her neck applied w/abstract
bows & ribbons, painted in watery
blue, deep ochre, mottled mustard,
purple & white, designed by
Gudrun Baudische, ca. 1920, impressed "WW" within a square &
"Made in Austria/345/GB/2,"
9 5/8" h. (repair to edge of
base) 3,190.00
Candelabrum, silver, eight-light,
spreading circular foot supporting
eight upward-curving tapering tubular branches terminating in
trumpet-form sconces, hammered
surface, designed by Josef Hoffmann, ca. 1925, base w/Hoffmann
monogram, "Wiener Werkstatte,
Made in Austria," Austrian punch
mark & "900," 11 5/8" d.,
8 1/8" h. .22,000.00
Centerpiece, brass, ribbed, half-
melon form cup applied w/two
looping & coiling handles, raised
on a ribbed inverted trumpet-form
foot, designed by Josef Hoffmann,
ca. 1920, stamped "WIENER/WERK/
STATTE, JH (in monogram) MADE/
IN/AUSTRIA," 12" l. across handles
(ILLUS.) .15,400.00
Centerpiece, silver, elongated octag-
onal form, bombe' sides & incurved
neck divided into checkerboard
pattern of panels of vertical lobes

& berried foliage, raised on eight angular claw supports, each grasping a melon-fluted ball, the base w/domed center all w/hammered finish, ca. 1920, designed by Dagobert Peche, base stamped "WIENER WERKSTATTE/(monogram) DP/MADE IN AUSTRIA/900/(state stamp for second standard)," w/beveled glass liner, 10 5/8" l. 26,400.00

Figure, earthenware, kneeling male carrying baskets w/two baskets before him on a square base in shades of yellow, blue, orange, black & earthtones, impressed "WW MADE IN AUSTRIA 367," & w/designer's mark "GB," designed by Gudrun Baudische, 10¼" h....3,520.00

Figure, pottery, young woman seated on an oval base w/a length of drapery about her hips & legs, glazed in sky blue, orange, turquoise & deep green blue, ca. 1920, impressed "WW/ MADE IN/AUSTRIA/96214," 6½" h. 880.00

Wiener Werkstatte Brass Lamp

Lamp, brass, cylindrical standard w/beaded top & bottom edge, decorated w/an overall pattern of blossoming rose branches; on a slightly waisted simple domed base, w/a modern cream silk shade w/black & white braided details, designed by Otto Prutscher, stamped "WIENER - WERK - STATTE," w/artist's monogram & rose mark, ca. 1915, 17½" h. (ILLUS.) 5,500.00

Lamp, silvered metal, tapering paneled standard w/beaded top edge raised on a horizontally-fluted square base, w/a modern white silk flaring domed shade w/black & white braid detail, designed by Josef Hoffmann,

stamped "WIENER - WERK - STATTE," designer's monogram & third illegible mark, ca. 1920, 19" h. 5,500.00

Mask, enamel on copper, oval w/cutout eyes, enameled in brilliant ruby, powder blue, magenta & white w/chevrons & other abstract devices, further decorated w/small gold foil stars, applied w/randomly curving & angled sections & pendent silver-colored coils resembling hair, & earrings in the form of triangular pendants decorated w/blossoms, all in bright forest & pea green, blue & pink enamel, designed by Fritzi Low, ca. 1920, silvered hanging hook stamped "WW," obverse enameled "A/S," reverse w/remains of Wiener Werkstatte paper label, 13" l. ...11,000.00

Piano lamp, silver plate, the square domed base supporting an attenuated S-scroll arm w/circular ring hung w/black & white checked pattern cloth shade, together w/a copy of the original Wiener Werkstatte worksheet, No. 1412, designed by Josef Hoffmann, ca. 1908, 18½" d., 7 7/8" h., 2 pcs. 10,450.00

Purse, brown moroccan leather, rectangular w/flap opening & two interior compartments, tooled in gilt w/vertical bands enclosing squares & rectangles tooled w/chevrons & straight lines, probably designed by Josef Hoffmann, ca. 1910, stamped "Wiener Werkstatte," 5 11/16" l. (silk lining torn & partially missing) 770.00

Side chair, stained beech, upholstered tapered back, bowed seat raised on square tapered legs, aluminum feet, w/partial Kohn label, ca. 1905, 35" h. 385.00

Tea service: 6½" h. teapot w/hinged cover, cov. sugar bowl, creamer & 16" l. oval tray w/scalloped gallery; brass, lobed cylindrical sides, teapot & creamer w/mounted C-scroll wooden handles, teapot & sugar bowl covers w/pineapple finials, designed by Josef Hoffmann, ca. 1920, each piece stamped "Wiener Werkstatte" & w/Hoffmann monogram, 4 pcs., (handle of teapot cracked) 11,000.00

Vase, glass, conical w/scalloped paneling, deep blue, designed by Josef Hoffmann, ca. 1918, 7¾" h. 1,540.00

Decorated Wine Glasses

Colorful & Collectible

by
Cecil Munsey

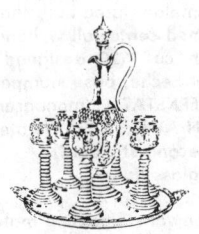

Twenty years ago I gave my wife a beautifully decorated wine glass for *my* birthday — a tradition that has continued for all the years since. In fact, the wine glass giving has not only endured but has expanded and we give each other wine glasses on any occasion. That may sound quaint and an easy enough thing to start and continue. Not so! The glasses we both like more than any others are those of the late 1890's through the 1920's designed by the Art Nouveau stylists. The glasses are hard to find and getting more expensive all the time. A twenty- dollar bill used to get a fine example for the collection; the same kind of glasses today are over eighty dollars when they can be found.

Not only are the glasses hard to find but so is specific information about them. The knowledge we have acquired over the years has come almost exclusively in bits and pieces from books and articles on the larger subject of *"glass."* Much information, of value to us as we try to learn about our collection, not only comes from readings about glass but about the more specific subcategory of *"stemware."* Indeed, we learned quickly that all wine glasses are stemware but not all stemwares are wine glasses. While stemware can be broadly defined as drinking glasses with bowls, stems, and feet, some pieces were designed to hold jelly, sherbet, and other solid foods.

Further, not only are our favorite glasses hard to find and information about them even harder to acquire, but fellow collectors just don't seem to abound. For the two decades we have collected we have only come across a handful of people who specialize in collecting wine glasses. We have met many glass collectors who include wine glasses in their collections but they tend not to limit their glasses to any one period. While that is all true, it is interesting that antiques dealers (the primary source of our favored Art Nouveau glasses) indicate they have a constant market in general glass collectors and that prices consistently are on the increase as a result.

Just as with the umbrella subject of glass, the history of wine glasses (stemware) is a long, extensive, and complicated one. Certainly more than can be covered here. To give a proper foundation, however, a brief discussion of stemware of the 19th century seems appropriate. During those times only a few stemware shapes were made in free-blown and mold-blown glass. Specific-purpose glasses were not of much concern in those early years in America. The same glass shape was advertised for sale as "egg or wine glasses" circa 1850. Large goblets of the same shape were used interchangeably as wine, beer, or cider glasses. Today such a size and shape would be for water but water was not served with meals in those days. Medium-size glasses were sold as wine glasses and were used for any type of wine. Today, each kind of wine can have its own type of glass. The flute-shaped glass was the exception in early 19th century America — the flute was used exclusively for champagne.

The development of the pressing machine in the 1820's caused a revolution of sorts. Glassware could be made on a mass-produced basis in many shapes and patterns. That brought about matching tableware at affordable prices. By the last decades of the 19th century distinct functions were assigned to different stemware — sizes and shapes steadily increased. The price of the mass-produced pressed glassware was reasonable. Many glasshouses catered to the more affluent by designing, blowing, and decorating glassware — it is mostly this latter type that comprises our collection.

The 1890's through the 1920's Art Nouveau-influenced wine glasses were often related by shape and decoration to brightly colored Venetian glassware of the 19th century. For Americans it was the first time it was thought to be proper, or at least acceptable, to drink wine from colored glasses.

Colored glass, one is reminded, comes about as a result of adding metallic oxides to the basic ingredients of glass — sand, soda ash & lime. Manganese or nickel added will produce purple. Blues of various shades are achieved by adding cobalt or copper. Yellows and/or greens can be had by the inclusion of chromium or copper in varying amounts. Red can be made by the addition of gold oxide or copper or, in modern times, selenium. Browns are accomplished with the addition of carbon or nickel. Tin or zinc produces milk glass. These latter two colors and some others, such as black glass, are not of much significance in the study of wine glasses because they were seldom used.

Perhaps even more important than the color of wine glasses is decoration. Color is something that is part of the basic glass ingredients when a wine glass is originally produced. Decoration is almost exclusively achieved through the use of a second art or craft after the glass has been annealed and is cold. Actually some of the decorative arts and techniques are quite divorced from the glasshouse and are accomplished in separate locations by independent businesses.

Two of the oldest decorating processes are cutting and engraving. CUTTING is a three-step process. The first step is *roughing out,* which is accomplished with an iron wheel with sand and water as the abrasive agent. *Smoothing* is the second step and is done with a stone wheel and pumice powder. The third step is *polishing* with a willow wheel and putty made up of tin or lead.

ENGRAVING is most often accomplished by the scratching of the surface by a rotating diamond-pointed object. Some engraving used to be achieved by the use of a series of copper wheels and a mixture of water and oil, and pumice.

Similar to engraving is the decorative technique of ETCHING. Etching produces a frosted appearance like that of engraving. It is accomplished through the use of hydrofluoric acid which attacks the glass. Before the acid is applied, the parts that are not to be etched must be covered with acid-resisting substances such as beeswax, paraffin, or rosin, through which the design is cut, or by a copper plate into which the design has been cut.

OVERLAY is a decorative technique which involves the use of different colored glass and glass cutting. Layers of different colored glass are blown over each other; the resulting object has a series of colors sandwiched together. The decorating is accomplished by cutting away those parts of the layers of glass that are not part of the design. The first layer of glass is usually the predominant color of the wine glass.

GILDING is a method of decorating achieved by fixing gold to the outside of a wine glass. It is done by mixing an oxide of gold with a flux (potash) and oil of turpentine; the mixture is painted on the glass and fired in a small furnace. The firing burns away the turpentine and leaves the gold fused to the glass. The gold is then polished with a burnishing stone. Gilding will wear or scratch off. In collecting wine glasses the condition of gilding is a big indicator of value.

Another decorating technique is FLASHING. This technique involves coloring only a small amount of molten glass, then dipping a hot wine glass into the colored batch. The outside layer of glass provides the desired color at a greatly reduced cost. Flashing will wear or scratch off.

STAINING is like flashing and is used with economy in mind. Unlike flashing, staining is used to decorate only a particular portion of a wine glass. The staining compound, which varies with color, is applied with a brush; the glass is then fired in a small furnace. Like flashing and gilding, stain will wear or scratch off.

ENAMELING employs a composition of lead (the flux), tin (for opaqueness), and a metallic oxide (for coloring). The mixture is ground to a powder and mixed with oil. The resulting paint-like substance is brushed on the glass, which is then fired in a small furnace which fuses the enamel to the glass.

In the 1880's, glassmakers created new heat-sensitive glass that could be partially shaded by reheating certain portions. Some of the most popular of these art glass shades include Peach Blow, Amberina, Burmese, Agata, and Wild Rose. These new trends, which required decoration of the entire surface, also fostered more elaborate glass cutting patterns. "Brilliant cut glass," as it was called, was popular from about 1880 until 1915. Production was centered at the Libbey Company in Toledo, Ohio, and at C. Dorflinger & Sons in Pennsylvania, and at several cutting firms in Corning, New York.

At the turn of the century, Art Nouveau glass, originally a French style, became fashionable in the United States. The most prominent American Art Nouveau glassmakers were Louis C. Tiffany (Tiffany Glass & Decorating Co.) and Frederick Carder (Steuben Glass Works). Tiffany, the son of the owner of the famous New York jewelry store, imitated the iridescence found on ancient glass. Frederick Carder made all types of colored and fancy glassware.

To capitalize on the demand for colored glass, the pressed glass factories added gilding or red and amber staining to some of their patterns. They sprayed other patterns with chemicals to make them iridescent, a technique that proved especially popular. The resulting purple, orange, and green iridescent glass manufactured between 1905 and 1920 is collected today as "Carnival Glass."

Still, of all wine glasses of that period, those by Tiffany and Steuben are the most sought and valuable. Fine examples of their wine glasses can fetch as much as $500.

Before featuring some of the beautiful decorated wine glasses from our collection, it may be helpful to share several important points about dating wine glasses we have learned over two decades: (1) The more colorful a glass, the more likely it was produced in the latter part of the 19th or early 20th century. (2) The longer the stem is in relation to the size of the bowl, the later the glass. (3) Heavy cut glasses were popular from about 1880 to 1915. (4) Lighter-weight, thinner glasses with delicate cutting and engraving were most popular from about 1915 to 1940.

ABOUT THE AUTHOR

Teacher-author Cecil Munsey follows various aspects of the collectors' market closely. An educator with a Ph. D., he serves as a Curriculum Coordinator for the San Diego County Office of Education, San Diego, California. Through the years, Dr. Munsey has researched and written several books for collectors, including: The Illustrated Guide to the Collectibles of Coca-Cola *(1972);* Disneyana - Walt Disney Collectibles *(1974); and* The Illustrated Guide to Collecting Bottles *(1970), all published by Hawthorn Books, Inc., New York City. He has authored books related to the education field and contributed numerous articles to a wide variety of magazines and journals.*

Price Listings:

Modified trumpet-shaped bowl, clear w/white opaque-twist (inside) stem & circular foot, bowl base w/air bubble. Free blown w/unpolished pontil scar on foot, possibly England, 18th c., 2 3/8" d. rim, 6¼" h. $300.00

Trumpet-shaped bowl attached to hollow stem & applied circular foot, unpolished pontil scars in-

side bowl base & on foot; brilliant ruby red throughout. Lightweight thin glass w/crudely blown bowl & gadrooning near base achieved by the use of a dip mold, ca. 1870, 3" d. rim, 7 3/8" h. 250.00

Cranberry glass w/enameled lacy leaves, foliage & scrolls, gold trim on foot, ca. 1890, 5¼" h. 48.00

Rose Amber (Amberina), fuchsia shading to amber, Mt. Washington Glass Co., ca. 1890 . . . . 175.00

Large trumpet-shaped bowl attached to hollow (open at bottom) stem/foot, clear glass w/gilded & enameled design over almost entire goblet, enameling features floral designs in pink, blue, green, purple & white, gilt designs symmetrically executed throughout, bowl & stem/foot blown in separate molds, ca. 1890, 3 3/8" d. rim, 8 1/8" h. 225.00

Round-bottomed bowl w/long knopped (near base) stem & modified circular foot, red-stained bowl over thick (1/8") clear glass w/gilding, bowl & stem blown

from separate molds; bowl is cut
both w/vertical ridges & horizonal
grooves, stem & foot also cut;
bowl, stem & foot gilded in mostly
random designs, rim of bowl &
knop near foot w/solid gilding,
ca. 1890, 2 5/8" d. rim, 7½" h. 100.00

Elongated modified trumpet-shaped
bowl attached to a tooled stand &

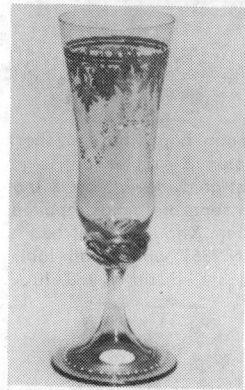

Bell-shaped bowl w/short stem &
circular foot, magenta glass overlaid w/clear glass, design of bowl
& stem achieved by cutting, 1/8"
thick glass throughout except
near rim of bowl where it was cut
down for effect, unpolished pontil
scar on foot, applied, tooled stem
& foot, ca. 1900, 2 7/8" d. rim,
9½" h. 175.00

Bell-shaped bowl connected to short
stem and circular foot, clear glass
w/enameled design on bowl &
foot in pink, blue, orange, green
& white, also a figure of a Colonial man walking w/a cane under
his arm & his other arm around a
woman, gilding around rim of
bowl & foot, bowl & stem blown
in separate molds, ca. 1900,
2¾" d. rim, 6" h. (ILLUS. top of
next column) 225.00

short hollow stem & round foot,
slightly purple w/enameled &
gilded decoration on both bowl &
foot, enameled design consists of
white dots near rim & on foot,
w/green garland w/red roses
ending in white daisies on bowl,
bowl & stem blown from separate
molds, ca. 1900, 2 3/8" d. rim,
7½" h. 175.00

Round-bottomed bowl w/long stem

& circular foot, white overlay on
ruby glass bowl w/enameled floral design & gilding around rim,
stem & foot blown separately of
clear glass, gilding around rim of
foot, glass of bowl & applied foot
1/16" thick, ca. 1900, 2 3/8" d.
rim, 6¾" h. 140.00

Large trumpet-shaped bowl w/short
twisted stem & circular foot,
iridescent gold, bowl, stem & foot
blown in separate molds, applied,
tooled stem & foot, acid-etched
"STEUBEN 2361" underneath foot,
ca. 1910, 3¾" d. rim, 6 1/8" h. . . . 400.00

Round-bottom bowl w/cut hollow
stem & circular foot, clear glass
stem & foot, magenta glass bowl,
gilded design around foot, on
stem & bowl, bowl, stem & foot
blown in separate molds, ca.
1910, 2 5/8" d. rim, 6¾" h. 135.00
Round-bottomed bowl attached to a
knopped stem & circular foot, red
glass bowl w/gilding, stem
ground w/bubble in the knop,
foot gilded as well as the bowl,
gilding on bowl features garlands
of several designs & four lion
heads in circular frames, bowl &

stem formed together, foot ap-
plied, ca. 1910 . . . . 135.00

Round-bottomed bowl w/cut hollow
stem & circular foot, clear glass
stem & foot, jade green glass
bowl, gilded design on bowl &
around foot, bowl, stem & foot
blown in separate molds, ca.
1910, 2¼" d. rim, 6¾" h. 125.00

Round-bottomed bowl w/cut hollow
stem & circular foot, clear glass
stem & foot, lime green glass

bowl, gilded design on bowl & on foot, bowl & stem blown in separate molds, ca. 1910, 2 5/8" d. rim, 6 5/8" h.................. 130.00

rim of bowl, ca. 1920, 2½" d. rim, 7½" h......................... 75.00

Bell-shaped round bowl w/long stem & circular foot, opalescent purple bowl w/transparent stem & opalescent white foot, bowl & stem blown in separate molds, applied, tooled stem & foot, acid-etched "L.C.T. Favrile" underneath foot, ca. 1915, 3¼" d. rim, 7 3/8" h....................... 400.00

Bell-shaped round bowl w/long stem & circular foot, opalescent "Peach Jade" bowl w/milky opalescent stem & foot, bowl & stem blown in separate molds, applied, tooled stem & foot, acid-etched "STEUBEN" underneath foot, ca. 1920, 3" d. rim, 6 3/8" h. 325.00

Modified cup-shaped bowl & hollow (open at bottom) stem/foot, bowl & stem/foot blown in separate molds, pink glass bowl & clear glass stem/foot, gilded-topped-by-enamel design on bowl & foot, ca. 1915, 2 3/8" d. rim, 6 7/8" h. 250.00
Bell-shaped bowl connected to long stem & circular foot, green-stained glass bowl & clear glass stem & foot, bowl, stem & foot blown in same mold, floral design embossed on bowl & gilded, gilded circles on foot, stem, near base of bowl, has a cut appearance, green color strongest near

Cup-shaped bowl w/hollow stem/foot, bowl & stem/foot

blown in separate molds, pale
grass-green glass w/enameled &
gilded crest applied to one side of
bowl, gilding around rim of bowl,
three beads of solid glass attached to knop supporting bowl,
ca. 1920, 2 3/8" d. rim,
7 3/8" h. 90.00

Cup-shaped bowl w/hollow stem &
circular foot, bowl, stem & foot
blown in separate molds, clear
glass bowl & smokey green stem
& foot, enameled design & gilding
on bowl, stem & foot, enameled &
gilded crest on obverse of bowl,
ca. 1920, 2½" d. rim, 7 3/8" h. 100.00

Large bell-shaped bowl w/short
stem & circular foot, white overlay on ruby glass bowl
w/enameled floral designs & gilding around rim & base of bowl,
stem & foot blown separately,
simulated polished pontil scar on
foot, gilding around knop & rim of
foot, glass in bowl & applied foot
is 1/8" thick, ca. 1920, 3½" d.
rim, 6¾" h. 120.00
Round-bottomed bowl connected to
a long stem & circular foot, clear

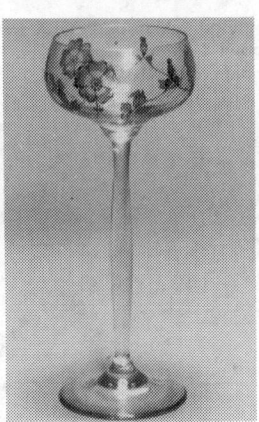

glass decorated (by staining)
w/hand-painted pink flowers &
green leaves outlined in black,
gilding added around the bowl
rim & base of foot, bowl, stem &
foot blown in separate molds,
foot displays an unpolished sand
pontil scar, ca. 1925, 2 7/8" d.
rim, 8" h. 70.00

Round-bottomed bowl connected to
long, hollow (open at bottom)
stem/foot, clear glass decorated
(by staining) w/hand-painted
green leaves, vine & yellow
grapes w/vine, leaves & grapes
outlined in black, bowl &
stem/foot blown in separate
molds, ca. 1925, 2¼" d. rim,
7 3/8" h. 70.00
Trumpet-shaped bowl connected to
long stem & circular foot, clear
glass decorated (by staining)
w/hand-painted blue/yellow/pur-
ple flowers & green leaves, outlined in black, gilding added
around the bowl rim & base of
foot, bowl, stem & foot blown in
separate molds, foot displays an

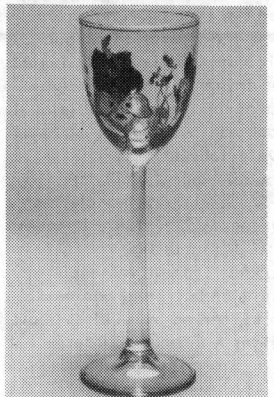

unpolished sand pontil scar, ca.
1925, 2 7/8" d. rim, 9" h. . . . .　70.00

Round-bottomed bowl connected to
hollow (open at bottom)
stem/foot, stained pink bowl &
clear glass stem/foot, bowl &
stem/foot blown in separate
molds, etched floral design on
bowl gilded for a three-
dimensional effect, also gilding
around rim of bowl & on
stem/foot, four drops of glass applied near base of stem/foot, ca.
1930, 2 3/8" d. rim, 7 5/8" h. . . . .　50.00

(End of Special Focus)

━━━━━━━━━━━━

WOODENWARES

　*The patina and mellow coloring, along with
the lightness and smoothness that come only
with age and wear, attract collectors to old
woodenwares. The earliest forms were the
simplest and the shapes of items whittled out
in the late 19th century varied little in form
from those turned out in the American colo-*

*nies two centuries earlier. Burl is a growth,
or wart, on some trees in which the grain of
the wood is twisted and turned in a manner
which strengthens the fibers and causes a
beautiful pattern to be formed. Treenware is
simply a term for utilitarian items made from
"treen," another word for wood. While maple was the primary wood used for these
items, they are also abundant in pine, ash,
oak, walnut, and other woods. "Lignum Vi-
tae" is a species of wood from the West Indies that can always be identified by the contrasting colors of the dark heartwood and
light sapwood and by its heavy weight, which
causes it to sink in water.*

Small Burl Bowl

Apple bowl, deep rounded rectangular vessel w/rounded rectangular
flat ends, the underside notched,
America, 19th c., 38" l., 18" w.
(some cracks) $220.00
Ashtray, mahogany, carved figure of
a standing hunter w/his sitting
dog at one side of oval base,
other end of base w/indentation
for ashes carved along side
w/raccoons, varnished finish,
signed "Charles Williams 10-2-52,"
8½" h. . . . .　105.00
Bed wrench, carved & painted,
faceted polychromed top pierced
w/handle on cylindrical neck above
a four-sided mid-section, each
section carved w/a compass star
motif, on a divided, shaped base,
probably Pennsylvania, 19th c.,
13¾" h. (paint worn) 1,210.00
Bowl, ash, turned from single piece
of wood, worn surface w/traces
of old red, 20¾ x 21½", 7" h. 225.00
Bowl, burl, deeply rounded tapering
body raised on a slight circular
foot, America, 19th c., 5½" d.,
3" h. (ILLUS.) 192.50
Bowl, burl, deep slightly sloped
sides, good figuring, worn patina,
13" d., 4¾" h. (minor age
cracks) 900.00
Bowl, curly maple, shallow w/wide
slightly slanted rim, good wear &
patina, 12¼ x 12¾", 1 7/8" h.
(old age crack) 800.00
Bowl, walnut, tapering cylindrical

form w/coved rim, the exterior engraved w/stylized floral sprigs, America, late 19th c., 13½" d., 5¼" h. 220.00

Bowl, oval w/flaring sloped sides, chip-carved on outside w/decoration of flutes, sunbursts & other motifs, old worn red repaint, 8¼ x 12", 3" h. (rim chips, short hairlines) 700.00

Bread board, pine, three-panel circular board w/shaped handle pierced for hanging, America, late 19th - early 20th c., 23" d. 88.00

Bread box, cov., bentwood circular body w/bentwood band base, the circular top inscribed "BREAD," stenciled underneath "J.T. Hoobry, Boydsville, Mo. to Carrington," painted overall in pale green, Missouri, late 19th c., 15" d., 5 1/8" h. (paint flaking) ... 330.00

Bucket, cov., circular lid w/single lappet, planked body w/two bentwood lappets, mounted w/simple metal handle w/turned wood attachment, painted overall in blue-grey, New England, 19th c., 8" d., 7½" h. 357.50

Bucket, cov., circular lid w/bentwood rim, planked body w/three bentwood lappets, applied on either side w/a simple bentwood swing handle, painted overall in blue-grey, New England, 19th c., 9 3/8" d., 9 3/8" h. 247.50

Bucket, cov., circular lid w/bentwood rim, planked swelling cylindrical body w/two single bentwood lappets, mounted w/a simple bentwood swing handle, painted overall in blue-grey, stamped "C. Alleder & Son, SO. HINGHAM, Massachusetts," 19th c., 9" d., 10" h. (minor losses to paint on lid) 385.00

Busk, good chip-carved hex signs, hearts, diamonds & other designs, nut-brown patina, 13½" l. 250.00

Butter churn, child size, cylindrical vessel w/three metal bands & raised hanging handle, painted in red, white & green w/two rose sprig borders, old replaced circular cover & mixer, Pennsylvania, mid-19th c., 15½" h. 467.50

Butter churn, dasher-type, stave construction w/bentwood banding, tapering cylinder, worn old red paint, 19½" h. 165.00

Butter churn, floor model, painted & decorated poplar, tall square body supported on raised base w/cut-out apron & bracket feet, long,

angled flat brace extends from base of one side up to support long round pivoting handle joined to flat dasher inserted through center of top, original red graining w/black trim w/white brushed decorative detail, 35" h. 290.00

Butter paddle, burl, well-shaped bowl & angled hook handle, excellent dense burl figure throughout, 10" l. (minor age crack) 550.00

Butter paddle, curved rectangle w/long slender round handle at one end, carved in relief w/heart, hex signs & intricate border, 12½" l. (worm holes & insect damage) 375.00

Cake board, rectangular, central shaped oval reserve carved w/fan motifs flanked by four stars & surrounded by crenellated inner border, 13¾ x 20" 132.00

Candle box, carved walnut, rectangular top w/stippled border opening to a plain interior, the front relief-carved w/a panel depicting opposing birds within circular foliate wreath borders against a punched ground, flanked by black-painted arrow motifs, probably Pennsylvania, early 19th c., 15 1/8" l., 6¼" h. 275.00

Candle dipping & drying rack, mortised & pinned ladder w/six-bar grid, hewn rods through grid, 18th c. 275.00

Canteen, stave construction w/metal bands, simple scratch-carved compass designs & indistinct inscription, good patina, 7¼" d. 150.00

Charger, birch, carved, 18th c., 20" d. 495.00

Cheese box, cov., painted bentwood, interlocking lappets, dark green paint, cover carved "S. Taylor," New England, 19th c., 16" d., 7¼" h. (minor paint wear) 302.50

Cookie board, pine & pewter, rectangular board w/pewter insert w/high-relief foliate & scroll design, 6 x 7½" 185.00

Cookie board, pine & pewter, rectangular board w/notched corners holding almond-shaped pewter insert w/relief songbird in fruit tree & initials "F.B.," good patina, found in Albany, New York area, 4½ x 9" (age crack in wood) 575.00

Cranberry scoop, painted finish, rectangular scoop w/rod handle & sharpened spikes, old blue paint, America, 19th c., 15" w., 18" l. (ILLUS. top next page) 192.50

Cranberry scoop, painted, curved

stick handle at back & large bentwood handle across scoop section,
wooden tines w/tin reinforcing,
original red paint, branded "Cranberry Co.," 12¾ x 20" plus handles, 32" l. overall (some wear &
age cracks) 225.00

19th Century Cranberry Scoop

Cutlery tray, cherry, dovetail construction, high arched divider
w/cut-out grip, 8½ x 11½" 100.00
Cutlery tray, curly maple, rectangular w/canted sides, center divider
w/pierced handle, 19th c., 13" w.,
7" h. 462.00
Cutlery tray, painted & decorated,
center divider w/copper handle,
one side w/two birds & leafy
sprig, initialed "S" "S" & "JULY
The, 30" continuing to front
w/"1833," other side centering a
female figure in colorful dress
flanked by two turkeys on a semi-
circle, another bird & leafy sprigs
within, back w/initials "J.L." within an oval leafy vine, painted in
green & accented w/other colors
on red ground, America, ca. 1833
(some paint wear).............. 880.00
Cutlery tray, pine, typical flared rectangular form, arched central
divider w/pierced oval hand grip,
traces of original grey paint,
America, early 19th c., 17½" l.... 137.50
Cutting board, cut in the outline of
a pig w/simple carved details for
face & ears, ring tail forms hanging hole, dark patina, good wear,
13¼" l. 302.50
Dipper, burl maple, simple dished
oval form w/rectangular handle,
New England, mid-19th c., 6½" l.,
5¼" w. 88.00
Dipper, maple, dished circular bowl
w/slightly arched flattened cylindrical handle, America, 19th c. ... 192.50
Dipper, long, straight handle w/oval
burl bowl, 18¾" l. 350.00
Dough trough, cov., painted poplar,
canted sides, tight fitting cover
w/breadboard ends, dark grey
repaint, 23¾" l................ 105.00

Dough trough on stand, cov., pine,
thick rectangular breadboard lift-
top above conforming straight-
sided case on heavy square,
slightly tapered legs, cleaned
down to old bluish green paint,
22½ x 37", 27¾" h. 350.00
Dough trough on stand, cov., pine,
rectangular top lifting above rectangular dough trough w/canted
sides, on raking baluster-turned
legs joined by a turned H-
stretcher, 49½" w., 29½" h......1,210.00
Drying rack, pine, two square crossbars mortised & pinned in square
uprights on shoe feet, good
brown patina, 22¼ x 23" (worm
holes) 325.00
Drying rack, pine, of simple form,
rectangular uprights w/three
bars, raised on shoe feet, painted
white, America, 19th c., 37¼" w.,
5' h. 137.50
Dry measure, bentwood, cylindrical
body, stamped "made by Ebirye
Wilton, New Hampshire," late
19th - early 20th c., 5 7/8" d.,
3½" h. 55.00
Dry measures, bentwood, graduated
cylinders, painted red, green or
blue, America, 19th c., set of 3... 220.00
Flax break, hand-made framework
w/mortised construction & shoe-
foot base, worn greyish color,
36" l., 27½" h................. 65.00
Flax hatchel, oblong board w/gently
arched sides & flat ends w/round
finger holes, center round pad of
iron spikes, carved initials & date
"M.W.F. 1833," 27" l 55.00
Flax hatchel, wood w/wrought-iron
braces in the shapes of birds,
tulips, arrows, rams' horns, etc.,
iron is dated "1819," old dark patina, 32" l. (age crack in wood
w/iron brace) 500.00
Funnel, stave construction w/metal
bands, tubular spout, old red
paint, used for sugar maple sap,
14 x 14½", 20" h. 65.00
Funnel, walnut, turned in bell form
w/tapering hexagonal spout,
America, 19th c., spout chipped,
4¼" d., 6" h. (ILLUS. top next
page, right)................... 110.00
Game rack, pine & wrought iron,
scrolled backboard w/pendant
apron, pierced for hanging,
mounted w/eight wrought-iron
hooks, America, 19th c., 31¼" l.,
8" h. 302.50
Grain measure, bentwood round,
old natural patina, 15¼" d.,
8¼" h. 55.00

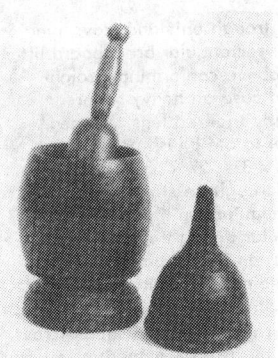

Wooden Funnel and Mortar & Pestle

Jar & cover w/bail handle & wooden grip, turned, attributed to Pease of Ohio, worn varnish finish, 4¼" d., 4¼" h. (short hairline in cover).......................... 240.00

Jar & cover, turned, squatty bulbous body tapering to neck, slightly domed lid w/small knob, scrubbed white finish, attributed to Pease of Ohio, 5¾" h. (short age cracks)..................... 140.00

Jar & cover, turned, bulbous sides, collared base, domed lid w/small button finial, wire bail w/wood grip handle, attributed to Pease of Ohio, 6¾" h. (minor cracks & chips)......................... 425.00

Keg, cov., stave-constructed cylinder, old red paint, cover w/porcelain knob, 23" h. (bands damaged)..................... 50.00

Magazine rack, hanging-type, pine, scalloped back, hinged chained movable front w/carved saddle horse on front, dark green paint, Victorian, 12 x 21".............. 250.00

Match box, hanging-type, painted pine, shaped back pierced for hanging, painted w/a large blossom above the figure of a peacock in profile, the well painted w/ringed circles each centering a small smiling face, executed in shades of red & black on a yellow ground, inscribed reverse "Newsom(?), Yates of Vermont, 1806," 7½" h. (repairs).......................1,870.00

Measuring cup, maple, hourglass shape, double ended, finely turned, one piece, 3¾" h. 49.00

Mortar & pestle, turned pine, ovoid mortar raised on a turned circular foot, pestle w/cylindrical pounder & shaped turned handle, America, first half 19th c., pestle 10" l., mortar 5" d., 7" h., 2 pcs. (ILLUS. left).......................... 247.50

Pantry box, cov., bentwood, circular cover w/bentwood edge, bentwood body w/plank base, inscribed "Mrs. C.E. Lindsley, Maria Lint Earle, Matilda Earle Lindsley and Emily Earle Lindsley," New England, 19th c., 9" d., 4½" h. (large chip to top).............. 110.00

Pantry box, cov., bentwood, circular plank top w/bentwood rim, the circular bentwood body w/bentwood band, applied w/simple metal & wood swing handle, painted overall in dark green, America, 19th c., 9 7/8" d., 5¼" h......................... 192.50

Pantry box, cov., bentwood, circular top w/bentwood rim, bentwood circular body w/planked bottom, applied w/simple metal & wood handles, painted overall in blue-grey, America, 19th c., 9½" d., 5½" h. (wear to paint, top scrubbed) 247.50

Peat bucket, mahogany, circular reeded body w/engraved brass binding at base & below rim, brass loop handle, Victorian, 19th c., 17¼" h................2,750.00

Pepper can, circular wooden top above the red painted cylindrical body w/bentwood bands, retaining partial paper label "PEPPER," decorated w/a scene depicting a Spanish bullfight, America, early 20th c., 14" d., 19½" h........... 55.00

Pipe box, hanging-type, maple, shaped backplate pierced to hang, scrolled sides above single molded drawer, New England, early 19th c., 5¼" w., 4¾" deep, 19½" h. 2,200.00

Pitcher, "noggin" type, 5 5/8" h. (minor chips & hairlines) 60.00

Plate, burl, well detailed rim, good figure throughout, good patina, 7¼" d. (worn surface) 350.00

Plate, hand-turned w/beaded rim, good wear & patina, 7 x 7½" 200.00

Porringer, child's, walnut, carved & turned, two-handled, early 18th c., 3 x 4½" 175.00

Rolling pin, bird's-eye maple, two elongated knob handles, 19" l. ... 55.00

Salt dip, cov., egg-shaped turned body on round foot w/turned dome lid w/finial, original dark alligatored finish, 4½" h. (age crack in bowl) 155.00

Salt dip, burl, turned w/round foot, good detail, 2 7/8" h. 170.00

Scoop, burl, shallow bowl w/raised handle at one side, small hole in handle for hanging, America, late

18th c., 8" l. (minor cracks, old
lead-filled knot hole repair) 605.00
Shoe rack, pine, rectangular up-
rights joined by five shaped vertical shelves, raised on splayed
metal wheels, Vermont, early
20th c., 42½" w., 4' 7" h. 165.00
Smoothing (or mangling) board,
carved stylized horse handle, old
dark brown paint w/polychrome
design & "Ann 1832," 22½" l.
(paint not as old as date
indicates) 135.00
Smoothing (or mangling) board, sim-
ple primitive chip-carved design &
"M.F. 1886," old natural finish,
29" l. 95.00
Spoon, maple w/curl in bowl, thick
oval bowl, long round straight
handle, 14½" l. 125.00
Spoon, curly maple, flat round bowl
& long, slender handle w/drilled
hole for hanging cord, 18½" l. . . . 105.00
Spoon rack, box-type, painted
wood, high backboard w/shaped
crest, two slotted racks attached
to the board, deep open box at
base, sides flared back to front,
front of box w/fan decoration, incised ribs in face of box, red
paint w/black border, America,
early 19th c., 13¾" w., 22¾" h.
(old repair to lower rack) 715.00

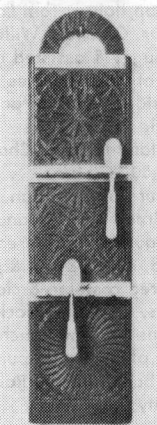

Carved Spoon Rack

Spoon rack, hanging-type, whalebone
& carved walnut, rectangular panel
w/pierced semi-circular handle at
top, carved w/three registers of
hex, spiral & geometric designs,
mounted w/three whalebone
panels supporting two spoon racks,
signed "Tho. Lehigh," & dated
"1827," w/two carved whalebone
small spoons, America, 5½" w.,
20½" h., the group (ILLUS.) 2,200.00

Early Burl Sugar Bowl

Sugar bowl, cov., hand-turned burl,
turned flattened dome cover w/flat-
tened ball finial & decorated
w/double incised banding, round
bowl w/banded & incised border,
America, early 19th c., 5¼" d.,
5" h. (ILLUS.) 1,980.00
Sugar bucket w/cover, stave con-
struction w/copper tacks, wire
bail w/wooden handle, old worn
brown finish, 7½" h. (edge chips
on cover) 65.00
Sugar bucket w/cover, circular cover
w/single lappet bentwood edge,
planked swelling cylindrical body
w/three single lappet bentwood
bands, painted overall in grey,
fixed on either side w/a simple
bentwood swing handle, New
England, 19th c., 9½" d.,
9¾" h. 137.50
Tankard w/hinged lid, stave con-
struction, old blue repaint w/gold
bands & green & brown floral
decoration, inscribed "H.H. 1858,"
11¾" h. 75.00
Tape loom, hand-carved board
w/rounded end carved w/sun-
burst, open-carved tape slats to
other end w/sides curved in &
w/open-cut heart, scratch-carved
date "1823," brown patina,
7 x 20½" (minor age cracks) 575.00
Toby mug, carved & painted, bust
portrait of man w/tri-cornered
hat, long hair, dark coat & ruffled
cravat, original polychrome paint
w/alligatored finish, 6 1/8" h.
(minor wear) 500.00
Trencher, dished flared oval bowl
w/simple lip, America, 19th c.,
21¼" l. 165.00
Urn, cov., turned bowl-shaped body
painted w/white, blue, red &
green circles on yellow pedestal
base, low domed cover w/yellow &
red circles, tall spire finial, possibly Pennsylvania, 19th c.,
7¾" h. 2,090.00
Utensil rack, pine, long board

w/scalloped crest & chip-carved
vertical bands, nine wrought-iron
hooks along base, old worn fin-
ish, 31" l. (some crest damage)...   65.00

Painted Pine Wall Box

Wall box, painted pine, flared &
curved rectangular box painted in
red, yellow, & white w/concentric
hearts centered by foliate sprigs,
the serpentine edge w/wriggle-
work & curving line borders, the
shaped & arched superstructure
painted w/hearts & foliate sprigs,
a foliate sprig-painted pendant
below, decorated overall on a
black ground, the reverse w/in-
distinct pencil inscription, New
England, 19th c., 10" w., 19" h.
(ILLUS.)........................ 440.00
Watch hutch, pine, rectangular case
w/identical top & base, glass panel in door w/rounded top, glass
fragment fitted into wooden door,
hand-made nails & twisted wire
hinges, America, late
18th c., 4¼" w., 8½" h. (nail for
watch hanger missing)........... 825.00
Wheelbarrow, flared body w/stick
handles & green painted framework, w/single central wire-
spoked wheel w/rubberized rim,
wood body painted overall in red,
Fort Wayne, Indiana, early
20th c., 4' l. 192.50
Winnnower, bentwood, curved gallery mounted w/two bentwood
handles, the three-board base
slightly arched, America, 19th c.,
4' 8" w. 165.00

WOOD SCULPTURES

*American folk sculpture is an important
part of the American art scene today. Skilled*

*wood carvers turned out ship's figureheads,
cigar store figures, plaques and carousel
animals of stylized beauty and great appeal.
The wooden shipbuilding industry, which had
originally nourished this folk art, declined after the Civil War and the talented carvers
then turned to producing figures for tobac-
conist's shops, carousel animals and show
figures for the circuses. These figures and other early ornamental carvings that have survived the elements and years are eagerly
sought. Carousel animals are listed
separately.*

Wood Figure of a Baseball Player

Apothecary shop figure, Tom Long,
who drove Dr. Crawford William-
son Long's buggy & assisted in the
preparation of his medicines,
standing beside large mortar &
holding pestle in his hands,
painted & gilded hickory, Charles
Oliver, 1942-50, 57" h. $33,000.00
Cigar store figure of an Indian,
carved & painted wood, standing
full-length figure w/feathered headdress of gold, green & red & wearing a feathered costume & cloak of
similar colors, holding a block of
tobacco in one hand w/bunch of
cigars in the other, green-painted
composition base, Samuel Robb,
New York City, ca. 1880,
67" h. 19,800.00
Cigar store figure of an Indian Chief,
standing figure wearing a peace
medal around neck & buckskin outfit w/feathers at waist & on headdress, right hand is brandishing a
tomahawk & left hand holds a
bowie knife, ca. 1860, 72" h., plus
12" h. base (some wear & previous
restoration) 3,300.00
Cigar store figure of Punch, standing
figure w/pointed hat & hump back,
holding a bunch of cigars, on rec-

tangular base on casters, painted
in polychrome w/gilt highlights,
American-made, second half
19th c., 82" h. 25,300.00
Figure of a baseball player, carved
& painted wood, silhouette figure
in white w/black hair & hands, on
white ground, applied w/red &
white striped leather cap, eyes,
leggings & shoes, raised on plinth
base, Missouri, second quarter
20th c., 26½" h. (ILLUS.) 467.50
Figure of a woman, carved pine,
standing stylized figure w/hair in
chignon & wearing a full-skirted
dress w/arm akimbo, America,
ca. 1840, 7" h. 440.00
Model of an American eagle
w/spread wings above shield &
crossed flags, carved from single
piece of pine, natural varnish
finish on eagle, slightly worn red,
white & blue paint on shield &
flags, 24" l. 2,050.00
Model of a parrot, carved pine,
perched on wire ring, painted red
body, green, yellow, blue, gilt &
white accents & features, ca.
1910, 7½ x 22" 440.00
Model of a sea gull, lifesize stand-
ing bird w/natural coloration, on
painted stepped rectangular
stand, early 20th c., 14½" w.,
20½" h. (bill chipped) 605.00
Whirligig, green stained pine sol-
dier, roughly carved standing figure depicted wearing a cap,
carved w/simple features, his
hinged arms holding large flared
paddles, raised on a modern
ebonized block stand, America,
ca. 1900, 16¼" h. overall 440.00
Whirligig, wood & pipe, small wood-
en figure of black man w/wire &
spring-jointed articulated limbs
mounted atop home-made galvanized pipe frame w/tin propeller at front & tin fan-shaped tail
w/worn paint reading "Tango
Shoes 1915-1929," on modern
stand, 50" l., 28" h. 300.00

WORLD'S FAIR COLLECTIBLES

*There has been great interest in collecting
items produced for the great fairs and expo-
sitions held through the years. During the
1970's, there was particular interest in items
produced for the 1876 Centennial Exhibition
and now interest is focusing on those items
associated with the 1893 Columbian Exposition. Listed below is a random sampling of*

*prices asked for items produced for the vari-
ous fairs.*

1876 PHILADELPHIA CENTENNIAL

Model of Independence Hall

Ale glass, paneled body w/protrud-
ing star, "1876" on one side &
"1776" on other, clear,
7" h. . . . .$40.00 to 50.00
Book, "Visitors' Guide," w/maps,
hardbound 85.00
Bust of Shakespeare, frosted glass,
Gillender & Sons, 5" h. 195.00
Lamp, hand-type, American Shield
patt., eight shields in relief alternating around body w/two stars
between each, heavy applied
glass handle, brass collar, no
chimney, clear 125.00
Model of Independence Hall in
Philadelphia, made to scale, executed in "German silver" plated
in copper for the brickwork &
roof, silver for the ornamental details & gilt on the doors, some
shutters, clock & dome, interior
fitted throughout & w/silvered gilt
details including figures & furnish-
ings, made for display at the Centennial Exhibition by John Dean
Benton, ca. 1875, 41¾" l., 62" h.
(ILLUS.) 38,500.00
Sugar bucket w/lid, stave construc-
tion w/bentwood bandings &
bentwood handle, lid embossed
"Our Centennial Best 1776-1876,"
old finish, 10" h. (old damage to
lid rim) 95.00

1893 COLUMBIAN EXPOSITION

Admission ticket, paper, engraved
on left side of front w/Indian
chief wearing war bonnet, dated
October 1893 . . . .   8.50

Advertising booklet, "Singer Sewing Machine Co.," black & white & color illustrations, 31 pp. 25.00

Bell, glass, engraved "World's Fair 1893" 150.00

Bone dish, china, transfer of fair scene, Bridgewood & Co. 35.00

Book, "New York At the World's Columbian Exposition," 1894 ..... 35.00

Change purse, leather & metal 22.00

Creamer & sugar bowl, china, shell design w/creamy ground edged in gold, gold handle on creamer, bottom marked "Chicago 1893 Exposition - Coalport - England," pr............................ 150.00

Cup & saucer, demitasse, china, scene of the Electrical Building, crossed swords mark 35.00

Magic lantern slides, glass, each slide w/four views of the fair, set of 6 .... 35.00

Pincushion, model of a lady's slipper, pewter, signed, 4" l. 30.00

Postcards, Official Souvenir, Goldsmith series, set of 10 .... 195.00

Prints, photographic, different fair building on each, folio form w/tissue separators, 14 x 18", set of 28 .... 75.00

Railroad pass, for early engine "John Bull," oldest steam locomotive in America, reverse describes history of the engine in continuous use from 1831 to 1870 .... 20.00

Salt shaker w/original top, Nail patt., ruby-stained & etched "World's Fair 1893" 45.00

Special Tiffany Snuff Box

Snuff box, gold & jewel-mounted agate, oblong box w/chamfered corners, agate sides w/gold-mounted rims chased w/scroll & applied w/emerald & diamond floral motifs, agate ranges in color from pink to grey to ochre, made for the 1893 World's Columbian Exposition, Tiffany & Co., New York, 3¼" l. (ILLUS.) 3,960.00

Straight razor, plain black celluloid handle, blade etched "World's Fair Razor 1893," w/globe in center ... 46.00

Sugar bowl, open, glass, Peach Blow, two loop handles, enameled w/"World's Fair, 1893," signed ... 425.00

Teaspoon, sterling silver, bust of Columbus on handle, Woman's Building engraved in bowl, 4" l. ... 50.00

Teaspoon, sterling silver, figure of Columbus at end of twisted handle, "World's Fair 1893" engraved in bowl, 4" l. 17.00

Teaspoon, sterling silver, handle engraved w/a woman & "Chicago," bowl engraved w/Manufacturers & Liberal Arts Building, 6" l. 65.00

Towel, linen, bust of Columbus in red 18.00

Trade catalogue, Singer Sewing Machines, nine full color pages, 32 pp........................ 30.00

1901 PAN-AMERICAN EXPOSITION

Demitasse spoon, silver plate, frying pan handle, Temple of Music in bowl 14.00

Plate, glass, Temple of Music 20.00

Teaspoon, sterling silver, President McKinley & eagle engraved on handle, Temple of Music engraved in bowl, 4½" l. 50.00

Trinket box, cov., round, glass, Winged Scroll patt., green w/gold trim, engraved w/souvenir notation 38.00

Tumbler, glass, Manufacturing & Liberal Arts Building transfer, 3½" h....................... 25.00

1904 ST. LOUIS WORLD'S FAIR

Bell, aluminum, w/Indian Head penny 20.00

Book, "Ainu Group At St. Louis Expo," by Starr, well illustrated, hard cover, 118 pp. 44.00

Book, "World's Work Guide Book," special edition w/photos, stories & contributing advertisers, 218 pp..................... 35.00

Letter, to traveling men of U.S., dated 11-15-03, noting that recommendations are available, signed by D.R. Francis, President of the Louisiana Purchase Exposition 35.00

Mug, glass, ruby-stained, Button Arches patt., w/souvenir marking...................... 50.00

Pinback button & ribbon, celluloid, "Celebrating the LPE," 7½" l. ribbon 60.00

Plate, china, U.S. Government Building scene, 9½" d. 42.50

Pocket mirror, Missouri State Building illustrated 35.00

view cards, T.W. Ingersoll, set of 100 in original box 150.00

Tumbler, glass, ruby-stained, Button

Arches patt., w/souvenir
marking 50.00
Vase, pottery, girl holding banner
that reads "St. Louis 1904," un-
marked Weller, 3" h. 150.00
Watch fob, "Walter Wood Harvesting
Machines" on front, "St. Louis
Fair, 1904" on reverse . . . . . 50.00 to 75.00

**1915 PANAMA-PACIFIC INTERNATIONAL
EXPOSITION**
Book, "Official Colortypes of the
Panama-Pacific Exposition, San
Francisco" 20.00
Book, guide-type, w/maps & photos,
published by Remington Type-
writer Co., 30 pp. 30.00
Dish towels, embroidered, set
of 4 . . . .   30.00
Letter opener, silver plate handle,
scenes of Ferry Building, Mission
Dolores & Cliff House 35.00
Pipe, china, transfer of the Palace
of Horticulture, 11½" l. 125.00
Postcards, three exposition views,
unmailed, set of 3 . . . .   20.00

1933-34 CHICAGO WORLD'S FAIR
Ashtray, model of tire, gold finish,
"Century of Progress, Firestone
1934" 28.00
Book, "Horticultural Exhibition Sou-
venir Book," 96 pp. 18.00
Book, "Official Century of Progress
Scenic Book" 25.00
Cigarette case, metal, 6½" 20.00
Doll crib, label says "Selected for
1933 Century of Progress," 9 x 20"
plus rockers 89.00
Playing cards, views of World's Fair,
in box 30.00
Photograph album, "Century of Pro-
gress in a Nutshell" 28.00
Postcard, Otis Elevator Exhibit 3.00
Salt & pepper shakers, silver plate,
engraved "Century of Progress" . .   35.00
Tapestry, "Century of Progress,"
50 x 84" 100.00
Tapestry, "Science Hall," 20" sq. 45.00
Toothpick holder, cast iron, model
of a woodpecker on log, picks up
toothpick w/pointed beak,
marked "Century of Progress,
1934" 40.00

1939-40 NEW YORK WORLD'S FAIR
Ashtray, brass, Trylon & Perisphere
logo in center, 3¼" d. 20.00
Ashtray, silvered metal, embossed
Trylon & Perisphere in center 22.00
Bank, metal, model of a typewriter,
"Underwood" 25.00
Book, "Official Paint Book" 8.00
Bottle, clear glass, bulbous base &
tall cylindrical neck, embossed

New York World's Fair Bottle

map of the world, "World's Fair -
1939 - 1940," 9" h. (ILLUS.) 15.00
Bowl, pottery, colorful World's Fair
Trylon & Perisphere logo in cen-
ter, bowl made at fair in a work-
ing kiln by Paden City Pottery,
Paden City, West Virginia,
10" d. 50.00
Bracelet, brass, w/seven embossed
views of fair, 7/8" w. 20.00
Cane, wooden, "Kan-O-Seat," cane
opens to form spectator chair, pic-
tures Trylon & Perisphere on seat,
Greyhound bus label on back 27.00
Coffeepot, cov., drip-type, china,
"Porcelier China" 120.00
Map, official pictorial map, created
by Tony Sarg, color 32.00
Nut set: large bowl & four individual
nut bowls; metal, advertising
"Planters Peanuts," printed nuts
w/Mr. Peanut beside Trylon &
Perisphere in center, marked
"New York World's Fair 1940,"
5 pcs. . . . . 25.00 to 50.00
Place mats, silk, Brooklyn Bridge,
Waldorf Astoria Hotel, Times
Square & other famous New York
scenes, all dated, set of 10 . . . . . .   75.00
Plate, Fiesta pottery, "Capitol & La-
bor Exhibit - The American Pot-
ter," aqua blue, 7" d. 38.00
Pocket knife, Statue of Liberty one
side, "World's Fair" other side 30.00
Postcards, official fair scenes, set
of 11 . . . .   15.00
Poster stamps, licensed, 54 uncut
stamps in color & in original enve-
lope, 1940 . . . .   20.00
Toy, ferris wheel, U.S. Royal Giant
Tire, souvenir of U.S. Royal Ex-
hibit, in box 75.00
Vase, china, Art Deco styling, cream
colored glaze, embossed fair logo,
made for Ovington's, New York,
Lenox China, 7½" h. 225.00

Collecting

Inkstands & Inkwells

by Jim Kolbe

"What an odd thing to collect," probably is the most frequent thought which passes through most minds when someone learns there are people who actually collect inkwells. But people collect all sorts of unusual objects for a variety of personal reasons. Certainly inkwells are no odder to collect than paperweights, walking sticks, or Royal Bayreuth creamers. In fact, inkwells can be uniquely beautiful and hold a tangible value as well as a decorative appeal. In addition to their utilitarian function in years past, inkwells were, and continue to be, used for pure adornment of a desk top. They are historically significant in that much of what man has "recorded" through the years would be lost forever without the use of ink and its containers. But today, it is the inkwell's extraordinary beauty which most collectors cite as their motivation to collect.

Who collects inkwells? Collectors are plentiful and represent a varied cross section of the population, slightly tilted toward the professional and, surprisingly, split equally between men and women. The single common characteristic of collectors appears to be a tendency to be uncommunicative. Collectors are very reluctant to discuss inkwells, even with other collectors! Take, for example, Ralph Lauren, the designer, who won't verify he is a collector despite a *Time* magazine article citing a ruby inkwell as inspiration for the Lauren perfume bottle. The value of "museum quality" collections may be the reason for secrecy, in addition to the basic desire for privacy.

Inkwells have been in existence nearly as long as instruments used for writing and recording events. Undoubtedly man first used his finger for this purpose followed in succession by sharpened stones and twigs, reeds, styluses of metal and bone, and quill pens. Quill pens reigned as *the* writing tool for centuries. Most frequently these quill pens were made from the tail feathers of geese and were quite fragile. The development of separate nibs or points, especially those made of metal that slipped over the end of a quill,

extended its durability. Experimenting with the shape and length of pen nibs and the size and shape of the opening or slit in the nib, which regulates the flow of ink to paper, eventually produced the fountain pen. The fountain pen's ability to store ink, followed by the acceptance and popularity of the ball-point pen in the 1960's, are probably the two major reasons for the demise of the inkwell.

Though the exact origin and history of the development of ink is still disputed, it's generally agreed that the first inks were human and animal blood, and plant secretions. Later inks were made by combining soot and/or charcoal, oil, and gum resin. Colored inks were derived from dyes and natural pigments or plants.

The heaviness of early inks led to the creation of both the quill cleaner and the penwipe. Some elaborate inkstands have "wipes" as separate components of the stand, with brushes built into the tops of their containers. Quill cleaners were either separate containers or matching components in a stand and were produced in as many materials as inkwells. Felt and stiff bristles of horsehair were commonly used for penwipes.

During the 19th century the bottles in which ink was sold were quite varied in size and shape, and often very attractive. Blown colored glass bottles in umbrella and conical shapes often served as inkwells. It was convenient to do so. However, these were meant to be disposable, having cork stoppers, and are of interest primarily to bottle collectors today. Larger quantities of ink were held in "master" ink bottles, usually of pottery or glass, and most popularly in the pint size. Again, these are historically significant but have been erroneously referred to as inkwells.

It wasn't until the year 1836 that "modern" fluid writing ink was developed with its long-awaited ability to render the written word durable on paper; most earlier inks faded over time. Ink at that time was primarily made by chemists and sold in bottles of varying sizes and shapes at apothecaries and in bookstores. Prior to the introduction of modern ink it's of interest to note that ink was stored in powder form and, even earlier, in small sticks or cakes. It was then mixed with water in an inkwell as needed. An "inkhorn" was sometimes used to store the powdered form, and in the mid-1700's the inkhorn was an early travelling inkwell, designed to be lightweight and easy to carry. Similar to the larger gunpowder horn, the early vessel was cylindrical and tapering (or horn-shaped) and generally made of horn or leather. The inkhorn was later made of stone and glass, the term more generically defined as any small desk top ink holder.

Obviously the precautions used indicate that ink was relatively valuable then. In order to prevent spillage inkwells were fitted with saucer-type bottoms and, later, hinged and locking lids were standard features. Sturdy construction and material allowed the inkwell to serve also as a paperweight, again inhibiting spills. To prevent evaporation, stoppers and pouring spouts became part of the ink container's design. Separate "ink pourers" (small pitchers with spouts) were used to prevent spills when transferring ink from a master ink bottle to an individual well.

The basic shape and form of the inkwell was dictated by necessity: a solid, heavy base provided stability; a somewhat shallow well deep enough for only the length of the quill point for inking; a narrow or tapered neck inhibited evaporation and served to keep out dust, etc. The earliest inkwells were generally made of stone, wood or pottery and date to the first century. Redware inkwells are a good example of early and highly collectible wells. Pewter inkwells, in the familiar capstan style (also known as countinghouse type), were introduced in the 17th century, their wide saucer-type bases prevented spillage as they were first designed for use aboard a ship. The capstan design was patented and its popularity extended through the early 20th century at which time these inkwells were highly visible in banks, post offices and municipal offices.

The dawn of the 19th century saw an increase in general literacy, particularly with respect to the public's desire to engage in written correspondence. Inkwells took on new forms with new and ever varied materials; bear in mind they have always been a "status" item, indicating the office or wealth of an individual. Commoners tended to dip their ink directly from the disposable ink bottles much the same as the old school desk ink. Wealthier citizens enhanced the demand for inkwells tremendously and the variety kept pace with demand. The most elaborate and costly were the inkstands, or *standishes,* generally fashioned of sterling silver and equipped with a container for ink and a matching container for *pounce* or sand, called a pounce pot/box or sand caster. The pounce pot had a perforated lid from which to distribute the fine powder onto unsized paper or to prevent ink from spreading over an erasure. The later more elaborate inkstands featured, in addition to two inkpots, one for black and one for red ink generally, one or more of the following choice accoutrements: a taperstick or candleholder for a small candle to melt the sealing wax; a fancy "seal" or stamping device to emboss the sealing wax and personalize it as well as seal important correspondence; a penknife, used to sharpen quills; a matching pounce pot; a wafer box which held thin hard paste disks used to seal less important letters.

An important characteristic of Victorians, in general, was their fascination with gadgets, novelties and inventions of all kinds. The inkwell market readily responded with a barrage of "patented" and ingeniously designed inkwells displaying a wide range of specialty features. The "teakettle" type with its neck (or font) angled upward from the base is an early example; it is quite collectible and precious today, especially in the rarer brilliant colored glass with original screw cap on the font. Fountain-type or "snail" inkstands were variations with revolving containers and generally set in alloy or cast metal bases. The "self-closing" patented inks concentrated on preventing evaporation of ink. More sophisticated styles were equipped with internal plungers to force ink up to a font, while others relied on gravity feed for ink. Hotel-type stands are similar, incorporating a pen rest and, again, are very plentiful. Several patented inkwells were outstanding in color and design, the Jacobus and Draper styles most notably. Generally inexpensive and available, this group would make a good choice for a beginning collector.

The very earliest glass wells were blown by hand, starting with a gather or glob of molten glass and worked into a variety of shapes. The "pontil" or rough scar at the bottom side of a well is that area from which the molten glass was broken away from the pipe used to form it. Whether or not the pontil is left rough or ground and polished can help determine the approximate age. For example, circa 1850-1860 a device called a "snap case" replaced the pontil rod as a means of finishing the piece and eliminated the pontil mark generally left on the bottom. Wells finished in this method are termed "bimal," another clue to age and possibly attribution. Blown glass was also frequently forced into a mold to give the glass shape and/or pattern. These blown mold wells would then assume the pattern or design within the mold. Blown three mold inkwells were predominant during the 1815-1840 period. Again, to achieve shape and pattern, molten glass was hand-blown into a full size piece mold customarily made in three pieces. These are easily recognizable by their seams. Most inks in this category were 2" to 4" in diameter and height. Some are also square. Blown mold inkwells are highly collectible and prized because of their age, and also some are attributed to The Boston and Sandwich Glass Company, which produced them primarily from colored bottle glass. Many were available in gorgeous shades of olive, olive amber, light green, aqua, and clear (very rare today).

The Pitkin well is an example of blown mold glass, although made somewhat earlier. The dominant shapes were slightly flared conical and cube with almost all displaying diagonal swirls or vertical ribbing. Note that the direction of the swirls (left to right or vice versa) is not evidence of attribution, as commonly believed. The other common denominator for these early inks was a center depression and inking hole, generally closed by a cork. Blown mold inkwells, ink bottles and novelty inks (e.g., patented variety, etc.) are given in-depth treatment and excellent coverage including photos and numbering system for identification purposes in the Covill book (see bibliography).

Mechanical pressing of glass into a mold rather than blowing proved less expensive and more expedient, and resulted in "pressed" glass proliferating through much of the 19th century. Circa 1825, The Boston and Sandwich Glass Company revolutionized glassmaking by perfecting the glass press, and by 1850 the technique was refined and very clear pressed glass became extremely popular. Cut glass, on the other hand, involved quite an expensive procedure using a finer quality glass with a much higher lead content. During the so-called "Brilliant Period" (1880-1915) cut glass inkwells were ornately engraved and cut in a variety of patterns both all over the well and at the bottom. Elaborate lids of sterling silver or matching cut glass made them gems then and very collectible now.

Glass and pottery were the most popular materials for inkwells since their non-porous surfaces were not subject to stains and they resisted the corrosive effects of the ink. Porcelain, brass, silver (both sterling and plated) and bronze all became popular materials for inkwells. The period from 1870 through the 1920's is considered the "golden age" when the finest inkwells, inkstands and standishes were made. Most inkwells available on the market today, as well as those most collectors want, were made either in the United States or Europe and date from the 1800's to the 1930's.

By far the most popular material for an inkwell, both then and now, is glass. The basic cut crystal inkwell with silver top, especially those with intricate cutwork, holds a certain fascination for most collectors. The many varieties of glass available and the numerous ways in which glass is made requires a good deal of study and perseverance. Glass can be blown, molded, pressed, cut, etched, cased, flashed (as with color), or engraved and an exact determination is sometimes difficult. (For an excellent, concise discussion of glass decorating techniques, see June 1989 *Special Focus* on "Decorative Wine Glasses.") Since an inkwell can't easily be tapped lightly to hear its crystal "ring," the best way to determine if it is fine cut glass is by its clarity, sparkle, and the sharpness of the cut pattern. As mentioned, cut glass is generally very high quality and, therefore, with its high lead content is heavy compared to inferior glasses.

Some cut glass from the late 19th century was actually signed with a pressed or acid-etched trade-mark or with a paper label. Heisey and Baccarat used pressed signatures; paper labeling was inconsistent at best. The cutwork of the inkwell's lid can be a very good clue to age generally, but not always. Covers came separate or hinged (almost always with brass or silver collars) and were often faceted. Sterling silver lids are more easily dated through marks or catalogs (Gorham, International Silver, etc.).

Colored cut glass inks are available today in a vast array of colors. The most collectible examples feature matching cut glass lids generally secured with brass collars. Again the details of the brass collar or facets and cutwork can help determine age and, possibly, country of origin. A personal favorite of the author, as well as most collectors, colored glass wells are difficult to find, especially in outstandingly brilliant colors. In general order of rarity, the most sought after are: ruby, amethyst (translucent, not black), emerald or deep green, cobalt or deep cobalt blue, deep aqua green, deep amber and vaseline. Sapphire or medium blue is probably the most common color found.

Art glass was popularized during the late Victorian period and recently art glass inkwells have become exceptionally popular. Unfortunately, very few art glass pieces are signed. Many, however, are attributed to Loetz, Legras, Durand, etc. Characterized by colorful iridescence, the bulbous all-glass wells are usually seen with semi-embossed brass hinged lids. The most common colors are varied shades of blue or purple, cranberry, caramel or green-brown. A clear glass insert, usually blown if original, rests inside the well just under the lid.

Tiffany & Co. executed a variety of inkwells and desk sets in what can also be classified as art glass. Favrile glass in amber and green tones was used and some resembles slag glass in its mottling. The familiar Tiffany "etched metal and glass" designs are handsome and generally the glass is overlaid with patinated bronze in brown or green, or in a gold-plated wash. There were many patterns made (Grapevine, Zodiac, etc.), and signed pieces are available. Complete matching desk sets had as many as 10 to 20 items including an inkstand, blotter, calendar, memo pad, stamp box, tray, letter rack, reading glass, book ends, etc. Full sets are very scarce today. Perhaps the most sought after examples are the bronze with blown glass forced into the mold thus appearing "bubbled," and then encrusted with "jewels" of semi-precious stones or cut glass.

Two other types of "museum quality" inkwells deserve mention. The Boston and Sandwich Glass Company, though frequently known for its brilliant colored pressed glass items, produced a magnificent swirled blown glass well, usually in blue or pink swirls alternating between clear and white, topped with a hinged pewter lid. The shape is somewhat common, but the glass and color are outstanding.

Cameo glass inkwells were produced here and in Europe and though infrequently found on the market today, those made by Thomas Webb, Daum Nancy, Galle' and Legras are available to the serious collector. These are extraordinary pieces of art and well worth the hunt, but priced in the $1,000.00 and up range.

The variety of ceramic inkwells on the market today is endless. Most frequently seen are pottery, porcelain and, occasionally, the very early redware and soapstone inkwells. French faience pottery inkwells are extremely colorful and, for the most part, affordable. Quimper, Rouen, Limoges and the famed American art potteries all produced inkwells. Gouda, Moorcroft, Rookwood, Weller and Bennington pottery inkwells have all been recently available on the market. Majolica is quite rare but worth the hunt for its color. Fine porcelain inkstands were crafted by Dresden, Staffordshire, et al. and they tended to imitate their sterling silver counterparts with similar designs and components.

Silver, sterling and plated, was the favored material for most inkstands and became very popular for the "presentation" inkwells. These are so-called since they were awarded for merit, years of service, retirement, promotions, etc. Other metals which are found on the market today include pewter, copper, brass, bronze, nickel, white metal, lead and various alloy metals. These are covered under other categories including figural, novelty, capstan-type, etc. Sterling silver was predominantly used in the earlier standishes, both European and American. Even trim or border work in sterling silver sets an ink-

well apart and adds elegance. These are primarily for the advanced collector due to prices today, however, good values are out there if you're patient. The sterling silver topped inks frequently had crystal or swirled cut glass ink vessels. Baccarat produced many of the cut glass bases for these inks, but few were signed.

Travelling inkwells are a specialty category whose number and variety are beyond the scope of this article. In general, though, as the demand for inks grew, people were anxious to correspond at all times. Most travelling inks are equipped with a locking top mechanism and small self-contained ink bottle which is held securely by a top. Leather-covered boxes (1"-1½" sq.) and wooden screw-top type (Silliman) are seen often in the market.

Figural inkwells are very popular today as well. Usually metal or porcelain and most often displaying an animal form, these are highly collectible and further illustrate the fascination most Victorians had with novelty items. Staffordshire, Dresden and Doulton all made gorgeous figural inkwells and inkstands including reclining greyhounds and picnic scenes. Highly decorated floral motifs are also available and quite pricey. Again, the "figurals" are another speciality deserving in-depth attention. The Rivera book (see bibliography) is an excellent source for further information on these and all inkwells.

Other miscellaneous materials found today include ivory, horn and, more rarely, tortoise shell. Interestingly, a noted authority once explained that, even though they were certainly made, he had never seen a Carnival glass ink. Can anyone help with this?

Condition is very important when collecting inkwells. Remember, they were used, and it is perfectly acceptable for cut glass inks to have small scratches or nicks but large cracks are not acceptable and will detract from value. Try to get the original lid or cover; mismatched lids can be unsightly and obvious. The inserts are another story. Of course, get the original if possible but many times this is not the case, and "marriages" for inserts are certainly much more acceptable than for lids. For pottery wells and stands, small "flakes" from the glaze or surface are totally acceptable; major breaks, or hairlines, should be avoided if at all possible. Porcelain, on the other hand, because of its highly fired body should not exhibit any chips or cracks. Again, "perfect" is in the eye of the beholder. Avoid inks with completely missing lids or covers. Broken collars or hinges are difficult to repair or replace; be careful and consult an expert for any repair work on metal. Broken pieces in cast metals (bronze, brass, etc.) can be fixed and new cast molded pieces inserted. Again, this is a specialty and should only be done by an expert if the piece warrants it. If it's sterling silver, it should be hallmarked or identified in some way. Of course, if available, always get the provenance and attribution. Slight dents or creases in sterling silver are totally acceptable; they can usually be buffed, hammered, or polished out. The single most important determinant should always be you and how much you like the piece. If you love it, buy it and try to get compensated for the flaw or problem with a price reduction.

Inkwells are a fascinating and rewarding collectible. They're a testament to man's intellect and ability to pen his innermost thoughts indelibly in time. Obviously, the Baccarat folks agree: the Compagnie des Cristalleries de Baccarat has announced their limited editions (300 each) of four exquisite classic crystal inkwells, all gorgeously faceted. Known as their "Museum Collection," the original designs dated from 1864 to 1900. Further information is available through the Society.

For further information:
Collectors' Club: The Society of Inkwell Collectors, 5136 Thomas Avenue South, Minneapolis, MN. 55410. Vincent D. McGraw, Editor. (612) 922-2792

References and Further Reading:
Rivera, Betty & Ted, *Inkstands & Inkwells: A Collector's Guide*, Crown Publishers, New York City, N.Y., 1973, 2nd edition
Covill, William E., Jr., *Ink Bottles and Inkwells*, William S. Sullwold Publishing, Taunton, Mass., 1971
McGraw, Vincent D., *McGraw's Book of Antique Inkwells*, Vol. 1, Minneapolis, MN, 1972 (through the Society of Inkwell Collectors)

Dealers and Auction Houses Specializing:
Kaplar Antiques, 9730 Gas House Pike, Frederick, MD 27101 (301) 662-7834
Mast Swamp Antiques, Box 163, Torrington, CT 06790
Graymoor Antiques, Baltimore, MD
Douglas Auctioneers, Route 5, So. Deerfield, MA 01373

PRICE LISTINGS:
All prices shown are to be used as a guide only. Condition and circumstances will affect value; prices shown were paid at auction, antiques shops at retail and wholesale, and by mail-order. Auction prices, especially if paid by collectors, may represent "top dollar" retail for the item. All inkwells are mint unless specified. Major attributes to value are shown, e.g., signature, exceptional color or cutwork,

extreme rarity, etc. Values of lesser examples must be adjusted accordingly.

GLASS INKWELLS:

Clear cut glass, swirl base, probably Baccarat, w/sterling silver twist-lock lid, fully hallmarked, 2¾" sq., 3" h. $275.00

Blown glass, clear, funnel-type w/center depression, ten-sided cut at bottom, flat bottom, polished pontil, 2¼" d. . . . .20.00 to 25.00

Cut glass, clear, pyramid shape, brass hinged collar, matching pyramid-shaped faceted lid, 1 7/8" d., 3¼" h. 95.00

Cut crystal, clear, eight-sided melon-shaped base, sterling silver neck extended to conform into all

eight ribs, mushroom-shaped
hinged lid, w/Gorham hallmark,
ca. 1910, 2½" d.,
3¾" h. . . . . 275.00 to 325.00

Cut crystal & sterling silver
paperweight-type inkwell
w/matching sterling silver tray,
silver beading around lid & tray
perimeter, solid block well
w/rounded corners, flat base,
twist-lock lid (a.k.a. traveler's
lid), signed "Tiffany & Co.," sterling hallmark, 1908, 3 3/8" sq.
well, 5½" sq. tray, 3¾" h. over-
all . . . . 800.00 to 900.00

Cut crystal w/sterling silver overlay
in Art Nouveau floral design, cut
Harvard pattern, 12-diamond cut
bottom, sterling silver hinged lid,
marked "sterling," 2" sq., 2¾" h.
(rare) . . . . 375.00 to 425.00

Blown three-mold inkwell, deep
olive green-amber, funnel opening, 14-diamond base, Keene
Glass Works, Keene, New Hampshire 1815-1840, 2½" d., 2" h.
(GII-18F) . . . . 100.00 to 125.00
Cameo glass, ivory overall color,
dome-shaped gently flaring to the
base, tri-medallion cameo design
in sepia, each centered amidst
flowering branches, original clear

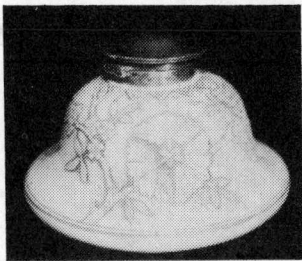

blown glass insert, hallmarked
sterling silver hinged lid, very rare
form in cameo, signed at base
"Thomas Webb & Sons," England,
ca. 1900 . . . . 975.00 to 1,150.00

Cranberry glass, Legras-type, etched
opalescent glass w/cranberry floral overlay, silver plate hinged
bulbous top, 6½" sq. base, 5" h.
(rare color) . . . . 800.00 to 850.00

Striped blown glass, clear w/pink &
white alternating swirls, polished
pontil, original pewter neck ring &
cap, Boston & Sandwich Glass
Co., ca. 1865-1875, perfect and
rare, 3¼" d., 2 3/8" h. 1,500.00

Art glass, Loetz-type, opalescent
overall color w/deep amethyst
threading, bulbous shape w/three
protrusions from base, hinged

brass lid, clear blown glass insert,
ca. 1900-1920, 4¼" d. . . .275.00 to 350.00

Teakettle ink, rare barrel shape,
deep cobalt blue, bimal, original
neck band & cap on font, perfect,
extremely rare color & shape,
2" d., 2 1/8" h. . . . . . .1,000.00 to 1,350.00

Teakettle ink, aqua, eight cut side
panels, rounded top w/double
pen rest grooves, smooth base,
tooled lip, "Pat. July 13th 1880"
on base, original cap missing,
2" h., 2½" d. (Not illus.) 175.00

COLORED CUT GLASS INKWELLS:

Cut glass, sapphire blue, double
well, block base, matching brass-
hinged cut & faceted lids, ca.
1890, 3¾" l., 2¾" h. . . . .190.00 to 220.00

Cut glass, opaque black, brass-
hinged collar w/matching faceted
lid, ca. 1890-95, 1 5/8" sq.,
2¼" h. (Not illus.) . . . . . .125.00 to 150.00

Cut glass, brilliant sapphire blue,
pyramid-shaped w/matching
peaked & faceted hinged lid,
brass collar, excellent color, very

unusual shape, ca. 1890-1900,
3" sq. base, 3 1/8" h. . . .250.00 to 275.00

Cut glass, deep amber, double well,
single pen rest at front of block
base, outstanding color, matching
brass-hinged faceted lids,
3 3/8" l., 2 5/8" h. . . . . . .295.00 to 350.00

Cut glass, very deep amber, octagon cut sides at base w/extraor-
dinary faceted & rounded cutwork
on body of well, highly polished,
matching eight-faceted peaked
solid glass lid, fancy brass-hinged
collar, 2¼" d., 3¼" h. . .300.00 to 350.00

Cut glass, very deep cobalt blue,
elongated diamond shape
w/matching faceted hinged lid,
16-diamond cut pattern on sides,
excellent cutwork, extraordinary
color, 2 5/8" l., 2 1/8" w.,
2¾" h. 350.00

Cut glass, medium sapphire blue,
double well w/matching brass-

hinged lids & three stair-step pen rests at front base, 4 7/8" l., 3½" h. 240.00

Cut glass, vaseline, brilliant yellow, fluted octagon-shaped base, brass-hinged collar, matching cut faceted lid, extraordinary color, 3 1/3" d., 2 7/8" h. . . . . .350.00 to 400.00

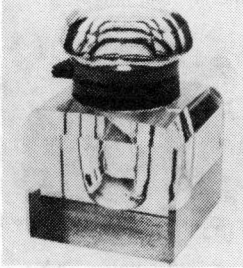

Cut glass, vaseline, matching brass-hinged faceted lid, excellent color, 2" sq. . . . . .175.00 to 225.00

Cut glass, deep emerald green, slightly flared block base ending

in single curved pen rest, matching brass-hinged faceted lid, excellent rare color, 2½" w., 3" l., 3" h. . . . . .410.00 to 450.00
Cut glass, deep translucent amethyst, square block base w/brass-hinged matching lid w/cut facets, extremely rare color (Not illus.) . . . . .450.00 to 500.00

Cut glass, very deep emerald green, octagon cut sides on base, matching pyramid-shaped cut lid, brass-hinged collar, rare color, 2¼" d., 2½" h. 400.00

SILVER, PEWTER, BRASS, BRONZE INKWELLS & INKSTANDS:

Brass inkwell, tri-floral in circle design on four sides & top, matching hinged brass lid, clear glass insert, ca. 1920, 2½" sq., 3" h. .80.00 to 95.00

Silver plate over brass inkwell, Art

Nouveau floral design, undulating swirls ending in footed front which is concealed pen rest, clear glass insert, stamped "D.W. Read," 1906, 2¾" d., 3" h. (also available in brass) ....85.00 to 95.00

Pewter, "capstan" well w/attached saucer bottom, hinged pewter lid, w/ceramic insert, four quill holes, England, ca. 1800-1850, 4¾" d., 1¾" h...................... 150.00

Sterling silver, double wells set into flared saucer base, overall round, base slightly weighted, hinged lids, blown clear glass inserts, fully hallmarked, England, 1838, 4¼" d., 2¼" h. (unusual, nice shape) 275.00

Bronze inkwell, burnished & green patination, "Pine Needle" pattern over variegated green opalescent glass, matching hinged lid, clear glass insert, signed on bottom "Tiffany Studios, New York, 846," 3¾" d., 2¼" h.........350.00 to 400.00

Sterling silver & shell inkstand, fluted crystal well w/sterling silver

hinged cover set into center of shell, cone-shaped silver stand as base, silver taperstick, ringed fingerholder for carrying, chain-secured candle extinguisher, pen rest, fully hallmarked, England, 1832, 2½" d. base, 4½" h. overall (Not illus.) ....750.00 to 950.00

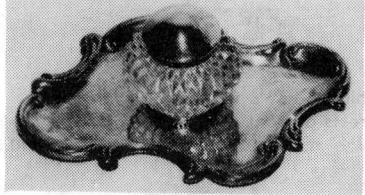

Sterling silver tray, cut crystal well set into rim on tray, Art Nouveau-style scrolling on tray, overall deep cut diamond-shaped facets on well, separate loose silver cover, hallmarked, ca. 1900-1910, 6½" l., 2¼" d., 2½" h...175.00 to 200.00

Sterling silver inkwell, Art Nouveau pierced & scrolled design overall, hinged silver lid w/undulating swirls, two quill holders at sides, pierced disk under lid holds cobalt blue glass well w/star-cut base, fully hallmarked, Chas. T. Fox & George Fox, England, 1838-1846, museum quality, 5" d., 4½" h. approximately (Not illus.) 1,100.00

Sterling silver "Presentation" inkwell, Art Deco style, octagonal ribbed flaring base tapers to flattened hinged lid, original clear blown glass insert, fully hallmarked & inscribed on front panel "J.H. from D.W.I.W., 26th Sept. 1898 to 7th Oct. 1926," 5 5/8" d., 2 5/8" h. .....225.00 to 275.00

Sterling silver standish (inkstand), George II, oval tray scalloped at ends, rope design on borders, four scrolled feet, holds inkwell w/loose cover & center quill hole, pounce pot w/intricately pierced lid, matching taperstick in center, complete & fully hallmarked, London, 1752, 9" l., 6½" w., 3½" h. (Not illus.) ...2,500.00 to 3,500.00

CERAMIC, POTTERY, PORCELAIN INKWELLS:

Pottery, French faience or Rouen ware, melon hexagonal shape, blue & yellow swirl & floral design, separate loose lid & insert, signed, ca. 1900, 3½" d., 2¾" h. . . . . 150.00 to 200.00

Ceramic, apple-shaped, grey & blue spatter overall, silver plate lid, 2¼" d., 2½" h. . . . . 75.00 to 95.00

Ceramic, deep blue & white overall florals, inkpot w/separate loose lid & matching dish, marked "T" on bottom of dish, 5" l., 3" h. (minor chips under lid & rim) . . 80.00 to 90.00

Porcelain, white & pale green floral & "fishscale" design, matching

hinged lid, probably France, ca. 1890-1910, 2" d., 3" h. . . . . . 75.00 to 95.00

Porcelain, blue & white Oriental motif overall, matched hinged lid, brass collar, "pagoda" shape to lid, France, ca. 1900, 2" d., 3¼" h. 100.00

Pottery inkwell, square body, one side w/multicolor florals, another depicting a butterfly, spider & web, the third w/a bouquet of flowers inscribed "beaucoup," & the fourth w/a single flower & unopened buds inscribed "un peu," all on a white ground, footed base, separate pottery insert, lip & matching coiled snake cover, signed "St. Clement, Galle' Nancy" at bottom, 3¾" h., 2¾" sq. (very minor flakes), museum quality & very rare, possibly unique, ca. 1860 . . 1,000.00 to 1,500.00

Pottery, deep blue ground w/multicolor florals, built-in insert, loose matching cover, glossy glaze, Moorcroft, ca. 1920, signed, 2¼" sq. overall (Not illus.) 250.00

FIGURAL, NOVELTY, MISCELLANEOUS INKWELLS & INKSTANDS:

Figural, "Gondola" w/oarsman, excellent detail throughout, center cabin lifts to reveal small well, bronze-like patina, ca. 1900-1920, 9" l., 2 7/8" h . . . . 175.00 to 200.00

Cloisonne inkwell, predominantly deep forest green, sunburst & floral multicolor, matching loose cover, white porcelain insert, footed curved pen rest at front, ca. 1900-1920, unmarked, 4 3/8" l., 2 5/8" h. (nice, unusual form) . . . . 250.00 to 275.00

Tortoise shell inkwell, Art Deco style pyramid shape set in sterling silver w/matching tortoise & sterling silver hinged lid, porcelain insert, fully hallmarked, England, ca. 1930 (rare in tortoise) 350.00

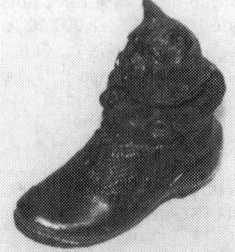

Figural, "cat in boot," novelty-type, cast metal, cat's head is hinged lid of well, clear glass insert, ca. 1920-1930 . . . . 95.00
Ivory, horn & brass inkstand, very Art Nouveau w/curved ivory base supported by carved brass feet holding ivory tube well at top

fitted w/hinged brass lid, clear glass insert, brass scrolled pen rest at front, probably French Canadian, ca. 1900-1910, 5½" l., 3½" h. 250.00

(End of Special Focus)

ADDITIONAL LISTINGS

Early writing accessories are popular collectibles and offer a wide variety to select from. A collection may be formed around any one segment—pens, letter openers, lap desks or inkwells—or the collection may revolve around choice specimens of all types. Material, design and age usually determine the value. Pen collectors like the large fountain pens developed in the 1920's but also look for pens and mechanical pencils that are solid gold or gold-plated.

LAP DESKS

Early Painted Lap Desk

Bird's-eye maple & mahogany w/brass inlay, lid centered by a cut-brass cartouche within a brass-inlaid border (small cracks, losses to brass), the interior w/stamped purple velvet lining, Napoleon III era, France, third quarter 19th c., 17½" l $385.00
Carved wood, William & Mary style, rectangular top above hinged slant lid w/molded edge lifting to an open compartment w/three short drawers over a rectangular case w/carved base molding, ball feet,

Pennsylvania, early 18th c.,
34" w., 17¾" h. (restorations to
base & feet, two drawers gone)..1,320.00
Cherry, rectangular top opening to
dovetailed fitted interior, old
refinishing w/some wear, 20" l. . . 225.00
Grain-painted wood, imitation of
exotic wood, fitted interior,
13" l. 45.00
Painted maple, rectangular w/a
hinged lid enclosing a fitted interior w/a writing surface & inscribed "Mrs. Mary H. Cross,
1843, Mrs. M.C. Babcock," the top
decorated w/a country village
scene, the sides decorated
w/stenciled shell still lifes & the
front w/fruit baskets, New York
state, ca. 1840, 10 x 19", 7" h.
(ILLUS.) 2,200.00
Primitive poplar, square-nail con-
struction, rectangular slant lift-top
opening to divided shallow compartment, single nailed drawer,
old dark worn finish, 16¾" l.
(damage along hinge rail,
replaced leather hinges) 155.00
Rosewood w/brass inlay, letter slot
interior, Victorian, 7 x 10" 240.00
Rosewood w/brass binding, rectan-
gular top opening to fitted interior, 13¾" l. (minor damage) 105.00
Wooden, top inlaid w/exotic wood,
silver, ivory & abalone shell,
14¾" l. 95.00

LETTER OPENERS
Advertising, "Hotel Showboat, Las
Vegas," plastic w/working rou-
lette wheel in center 35.00
Advertising, "Remington," w/knife
blade 15.00
Advertising, "Yale Locks" 27.00
Brass, figural Shakespeare bust han-
dle, sword-shaped blade inscribed
"Shakespeare," 6" l. 15.00
Celluloid, figural Egyptian mummy
handle 30.00
Chrome, cast-iron model of a seated
Scottie dog at end, blade marked
in inches for use as a ruler,
8" l. 30.00
Copper, cut-out design on handle,
tapered blade, Dirk Van Erp open-
box mark. 50.00
Ivory, helmeted warrior at end of
handle, 13" l. 60.00
Sterling silver handle, Acanthus
patt., Georg Jensen, Denmark . . . 65.00
Sterling silver handle, Acorn patt.,
Georg Jensen, Denmark 70.00
Sterling silver handle, Calvert patt.,
S. Kirk & Son 22.00
Sterling silver handle, florals &

scrollwork in high relief, Jacobi &
Jenkins 125.00
Sterling silver handle, Rose patt.,
Stieff. 25.00
Sterling silver & jade, Arts & Crafts
style, flat jade blade w/rounded
end attached to molded & raised
hand-hammered sterling handle,
early 20th c., 8½" l. 302.50
Wooden, hand-carved w/black
man's head on handle 25.00

PENS & PENCILS
Conklin "Crescent Fill No. 30" foun-
tain pen 39.00
Conklin "Endura" fountain pen,
lady's 10.00
Dip pen, mother-of-pearl & gold
handle, no nib, original silk-lined
case 55.00
Dip pen, ornate chased sterling sil-
ver handle, gold nib, original
plush case 65.00
Eclipse fountain pen, Canada, 1925,
large 35.00
Henber mechanical pencil, silver,
5" l. 45.00
Parker "Duofold Jr., Lucky Curve"
fountain pen, green mottled 40.00
Parker "Duofold Sr., Lucky Curve"
fountain pen, green mottled 59.00
Ronson "Penciliter," combination
mechanical pencil & cigarette
lighter 50.00
Sheaffer "Admiral Snorkel" fountain
pen & mechanical pencil, boxed
set 29.00
Sheaffer "Feather Touch" fountain
pen, burgundy 30.00
Sheaffer "Lifetime" mechanical pen-
cil, gold-filled trim 30.00
Tiffany & Co. fountain pen &
mechanical pencil set, 14k gold
pen 345.00
Wahl fountain pen & mechanical
pencil set, gold-filled, 1940's 39.00
Wahl-Eversharp mechanical pencil,
yellow gold-filled. 18.00
Wahl-Eversharp sterling silver
mechanical pencil, w/floral
design 30.00
Waterman "No. 52½" fountain pen,
black, w/box 22.50
Wearever fountain pen, bar filler,
rubber sack, black & chrome 15.00

YARD LONG PRINTS

*These out of proportion colorful prints were
fashionable wall decorations in the waning
years of the 19th century and early in the 20th
century. They are all 36" wide and between*

8" and 10" high. A wide variety of subjects, ranging from florals and fruits to chicks and puppies, is available to collectors. Prices for these yard-long prints have shown a dramatic increase within the past years. All included in this list are framed unless otherwise noted.

A Carnation Symphony, violin, birds
  & carnations $45.00
Chickens 157.50
Chrysanthemums 100.00
Dahlias.......................... 95.00
Kittens, signed Guy Bedford........ 110.00
Kittens, signed Vandenburg 85.00
Puppies, bulldog in center, signed
  Guy Bedford 120.00
Puppies w/bowl................... 165.00
Swallows, ca. 1897 .... 145.00
Tug of War, kittens & puppies pull-
  ing on piece of rope............. 195.00

YARN WINDERS

Trestle-Base Yarn Winder

Floor model, carved & turned wood, five cylindrical rods supported on rectangular drilled panels, raised on a split log-form base, late 19th - early 20th c., 20" w., 32¼" h...................... $88.00
Floor model, various hardwoods, six-arm reel on upright mortised through square base w/splayed legs, chip-carved edges, old varnish finish, 30½" d. reel, 33" h. .. 95.00
Floor model, red-painted wood, large circular wheel w/turned baluster spokes, metal crank, mounted in red-painted trestle base, America, 19th c., 26" d., 34½" h. (ILLUS.)...................... 165.00
Niddy noddy hand reel, turned wood, serpentine perpendicular ends joined by a bamboo-turned

cylindrical rod, America, 19th c., 18¼" l., 12" w, ... 44.00
Niddy noddy hand reel, turned walnut, serpentine perpendicular ends engraved "L.H.D." & "M.Z.," joined by a turned lock & cylindrical rod, America, 19th c., 18¼" l., 12½" w. 77.00
Niddy noddy hand reel, wooden, well-shaped w/chip-carved detail, good dark patina, 18½" l. (short crack in one arm) 195.00
Table model yarn "swift," wooden, clamp-on type, expandable reel on turned standard, worn original yellow varnished finish, Shaker, 22" h. (four members replaced)... 200.00
Table model yarn "swift," wooden, clamp-on type, adjustable arms, old yellow stain, 24" h. (two slats replaced)..................... 125.00
Table model yarn "swift," walnut, brass, ebony, ivory & marble, probably English, ca. 1830 .... 595.00
Table model yarn winder, revolving X-form winder w/crank handle, raised on trestle support on a molded rectangular base, turned wood, possibly Shaker, 19th c., 24" w., 32" h.................. 110.00

ZEPPELIN COLLECTIBLES

Book, "The Zeppelins," by Ernst Lehmann, 1927, New York, 15 plates $40.00
Book, "Weltfahrten," Volumes 1 & 2, the set 500.00
Cocktail shaker, chromium-plated, Art Deco style replica of a zeppelin, the nose fitted w/a cover & pierced straining lid, the tail housing a corkscrew, jigger & small cover, stamped "D.R.G.M./GERMANY," ca. 1930, 12½" h. 550.00
Newspaper, "Kenosha Evening News," 1937, May 7, report on Hindenburg crash 25.00
Pin, enameled, "Graf Zeppelin LZ-127 Weltfahrt 1929" 50.00
Timetable, three-fold paper, "Hindenburg," in French, 3 7/8 x 8 3/8" folded 20.00
Toy, pull-type, cast iron, model of zeppelin marked "Navy," 4 5/8" l. 85.00
Toy, windup tin, model of "Graf Zeppelin" on wheels, worn original paint, some damage, 9" l. 175.00

INDEX

*Denotes "Special Focus" section

THE ANTIQUE TRADER WEEKLY

The leading publication of the antiques hobby for over thirty-two years. This tabloid sized newspaper has approximately 100 pages each week and is filled with advertisements for antiques and collectibles both for sale and wanted from around the nation. It also lists auction and show information plus news, feature stories and informative question and answer columns for the antiques collector.

$24.00 per year (52 issues)
Sample copy $1.00

Your money back if not satisfied!

Send to:
THE ANTIQUE TRADER WEEKLY
P.O. Box 1050
Dubuque, Iowa 52001

Name _____

Address _____

City _____

State_____ Zip_____

Enclosed is $24.00. Please enter my subscription to **THE ANTIQUE TRADER WEEKLY** for one year.

Or charge my ( ) MasterCard, or ( ) Visa Card.

Card No. _____

Expiration Date _____

You can enter your order **FREE** by phone and charge one of the above credit cards. Have card handy.

Call **TOLL FREE 1-800-334-7165** except in Iowa, Alaska or Hawaii 1 (319) 588-2073.